CONTEMPORARY
ARTISTS

OTHER ART TITLES FROM ST. JAMES PRESS

Contemporary Architects

Contemporary Artists

Contemporary Designers

Contemporary Fashion

Contemporary Hispanic Artists

Contemporary Masterworks

Contemporary Photographers

Contemporary Women Artists

International Dictionary of Architects and Architecture

International Dictionary of Art and Artists

St. James Guide to Black Artists

St. James Guide to Hispanic Artists

St. James Guide to Native North American Artists

CONTEMPORARY
ARTISTS

FIFTH EDITION

VOLUME 1: A-K

Editor:
Sara Pendergast and Tom Pendergast

Advisers:
Jean-Christophe Ammann, Robert Atkins,
Szymon Bojko, Jorge Glusberg,
Carin Kuoni, Hans Ulrich Obrist,
Frank Popper, Robert Rindler,
Jose Lebrero Stals, Atsuo Yasuda

ST. JAMES PRESS

Detroit • New York • San Diego • San Francisco
Boston • New Haven, Conn. • Waterville, Maine
London • Munich

Sara Pendergast and Tom Pendergast, *Editors*

Christa Brelin, Joann Cerrito, Stephen Cusack, Kris Hart, Margaret Mazurkiewicz, Carol A. Schwartz, Michael J. Tyrkus, *Contributing Editors*

Peter M. Gareffa, *Managing Editor, St. James Press*

Mary Beth Trimper, *Manager, Composition and Electronic Prepress*
Evi Seoud, *Assistant Manager, Composition Purchasing and Electronic Prepress*
Dorothy Maki, *Manufacturing Manager*
Rhonda Williams, *Buyer*

Barb Yarrow, *Manager, Imaging and Multimedia*
Dean Dauphinais, *Senior Editor, Imaging and Multimedia*
Kelly A. Quin, *Editor, Imaging and Multimedia*

Maria Franklin, *Manager, Permissions*
Kim Davis, *Permissions Associate*

Cover photo: Larry Bell, *Stickman #24*, 1994. Photo by Paul O'Connor. ©Larry Bell.

Library of Congress Catalog Cataloging-in-Publication Data
Contemporary artists / editors, Sara Pendergast and Tom Pendergast; advisers, Jean-Christopher Ammann . . . [et al.].—5th ed.
p. cm. — (Contemporary arts series)
Includes bibliographical references and index.
Contents: v. 1. A-K — v. 2. L-Z.
ISBN 1-55862-407-4 (alk. paper)
1. Artists—Biography. 2. Art, Modern—20th century. I. Pendergast, Sara. II. Pendergast, Tom. III. Series.

N6490 .C6567 2001
709'.2'2—dc21
[B]

2001048443

British Library Cataloguing-in-Publication Data
A catalogue record for this book is available from the British Library

ISBN 1-55862-407-4 (set)
ISBN 1-55862-488-0 (volume 1)
ISBN 1-55862-489-9 (volume 2)

Printed in the United States of America

St. James Press is an imprint of Gale Group
Gale Group and Design is a trademark used herein under license
10 9 8 7 6 5 4 3 2 1

CONTENTS

EDITOR'S NOTE

Contemporary Artists provides comprehensive profiles of nearly 850 of the most significant artists working in the contemporary era. The vast majority of these artists have done their most significant work in the years after 1960.

Artists were nominated for inclusion by an advisory board of international art scholars and curators. The artists selected for inclusion have exhibited in major galleries or museums and have attracted significant critical attention. All areas of the fine arts are represented, including painting, graphics, sculpture, mixed media, and performance; this edition, like the one before it, also contains a number of artists active in the fields of computer and Internet art. *Contemporary Artists* includes some deceased artists, but in order to provide coverage of a greater number of living artists we have removed any artist who has died before 1990 (with several exceptions). Several of these artists are among the best known artists of this century; however, the editors feel certain that researchers will be able to gather adequate information on these artists from previous editions of this work and from other published sources.

Each artist entry includes biographical data, a selected list of both individual and group exhibitions, a list of public collections that include work by the artist, and primary and secondary bibliographies. Many entries also include mention of permanent public installations, performances, or other categories of artistic production. Many artists have contributed a statement about their work or about art in general, as well as a photograph of a representative work. Finally, critical essays have been contributed by specialists in the field.

In order to provide accurate and up-to-date profiles, the editors have made every attempt to gather information directly from the artists themselves. In many cases, however, the information has been provided by galleries or gathered through research in secondary sources.

Acknowledgments

This work could not have been completed without the efforts of hundreds of people, from artists and gallery owners who provided us with up-to-date information, to writers who contributed their specialized knowledge, to the researchers and copyeditors who tried their best to be sure that the information provided was recent and accurate, to those at the publisher who will turn all this information into the book you hold today.

We wish to extend a special thanks to the following people: Christa Brelin, our contact at the St. James Press, for her consistent support and professionalism throughout the project; Michael Najjar, for his dogged research; Amy Moeller, Joyce Youmans, and Marcia Welsh, for taming the chaos of artist CVs into the entries you see in this book; and translators Stanley Anderson, Joerg Fiegler, Claudia Hoffmann, and Dan Newland. Finally, we would like to thank our advisers, whose thorough knowledge of contemporary art helped bring to this collection a wide variety of fascinating artists.

ADVISERS

Jean-Christophe Ammann
Museum für Moderne Kunst, Frankfurt am Main

Robert Atkins
Editor, AIDS-Art Forum, and Media Arts Editor, The Media Channel, New York

Szymon Bojko
Art Critic, Warsaw

Jorge Glusberg
Museo Nacional de Bellas Artes, Buenos Aires

Carin Kuoni
Independent Curators International, New York

Hans Ulrich Obrist
Musee d'Art Moderne de la Ville, Paris

Frank Popper
University of Paris VIII

Robert Rindler
School of Art, Cooper Union, New York

Jose Lebrero Stals
Museu d'Art Contemporani de Barcelona (MACBA)

Atsuo Yasuda
Hara Museum of Contemporary Art, Tokyo

CONTRIBUTORS

Daniel Abadie
Dietrich Albrecht (Albrecht D.)
Lawrence Alloway
Jean-Christophe Ammann
Sharon Matt Atkins

Marius Babias
Bradley Bailey
Carrie Baker
D. C. Barrett
Peter Barton
Konstantin Bazarov
Andreas Bee
László Beke
Jane Bell
Maurice Berger
Florent Bex
Eugen Blume
Willard Bohn
Szymon Bojko
Achille Bonito Oliva
Jean-Luc Bordeaux
David Bourdon
Betty Ann Brown
David Brown
Glen R. Brown
Maria Elena Buszek
Carly Butler

James D. Campbell
Massimo Carboni
Valerie Cassel
Gary Catalano
Barbara Cavaliere
Martin Clark
Robin Clark
Ronny Cohen
Michael Compton
Lynne Cooke
Barbara Cortright
Fenella Crichton

Aline Dallier-Popper
Natalie de Ligt
Janneke de Vries
Giorgio Di Genova
Deirdre Donohue
Gillo Dorfles
Merridawn Duckler
Mari Dumett
Beth Duncan

Mary Ellis
Muriel Emanuel
Thomas Epstein
Britta Erickson

Zdenek Felix
Michael Alistair Findlay
Uwe Fleckner
Marnie Fleming
Michael Florescu
Andrew Forge
Claude Fournet
Marietta Franke
Alison Fraser
B. H. Friedman
Kenneth Friedman

Edda Gazzerro
Sabine Gebhardt
Marcin Giżycki
Ron Glowen
Jorge Glusberg
Janet Goleas
Petra Gördüren
Klaus Görner
Olle Granath
Andy Grundberg

Jaimey Hamilton
James Harithas
Herbert R. Hartel, Jr.
Dean Higgins
Vanessa Hirsch
Roman Hollenstein
Ihor Holubizky
Klaus Honnef
Rosemarie Martha Huhn

Aaron Jacobs
Demetra James
Heather Belnap Jensen
Jill Johnston
Dorothy Joiner

Paul J. Karlstrom
Fiona Kearney
Victoria Keller
Jane Kelly
Alicja Kepinska
Joshua Kind
Elaine A. King
April Kingsley
Tammy A. Kinsey
Mason Klein
Daniel Kletke
Helena Kontova
Richard Kostelanetz
Mario Kramer
Rachel E. Kuhn
Udo Kultermann

Roberto G. Lambarelli
Sharon Lancer
Elise LaRose
Lavinia Learmont
Dominique Liquois
Marco Livingstone
Peter Lunenfeld

Alfred Mac Adam
Alastair Mackintosh
Audrey Mandelbaum
Elizabeth Mangini
Andrée Maréchal-Workman
Henry Martin
Carine Maurice
Marguerite K. Mayhall
Cecile N. McCann
Paul McGillick
Arthur McIntyre
Marco Meneguzzo
Thomas Messer
Günter Metken
Tamon Miki
Yusuke Minami
Christine Miner Minderović
Alan Moore
Joan Murray
Italo Mussa

Yusuke Nakahara
Fumio Nanjo
Roald Nasgaard
Percy North
Anna Novakov

Joan Oleck
Harold Osborne

Demetrio Paparoni
Loredana Parmesani
Keith Patrick
Ralph Pomeroy
Frank Popper

Cay Sophie Rabinowitz
Hans Rudolf Reust
John Roberts
John Robinson
Marlee Robinson
Ken Rogers

Richard Salkeld
Britt Salvesen
Merle Schipper
Eva Schmidt
Werner Schulze-Reimpell

Barry Schwabsky
Dieter Schwarz
Peter Selz
Michael Shepherd
Tazmi Shinoda
Dagmar Sinz
Jennifer A. Smith
Katherine Smith
Lucy Soutter
Charles Spencer
Heinz Spielmann
José Lebrero Stals
Ryszard Stanislawski
Shepherd Steiner
Mary Stofflet
Anne Swartz
Mark Swartz
Marie Luise Syring

Agnieszka Taborska
Daniel Thomas
Miang Tiampo
Yoshiaki Tono
Alan Trachtenberg

Dorothy Valakos
H. J. A. M. van Haaren
Radu Varia
Luca Venturi
Giorgio Verzotti
Alicia Volk
Monika von Zitzewitz
A. F. Wagemans
Sarah Wagner
Sarah Webb
Kathleen Wentrack
G. S. Whittet
Karen Wilkin
Sheldon Williams
Adina Wingate
Paula Wisotzki
Mara Witzling
Lisa Wolford
Aida-Yuen Wong

Joyce Youmans
Tara Reddy Young

Jennifer S. Zarro
Annalisa Zox-Weaver

CONTEMPORARY

ARTISTS

LIST OF ENTRANTS

Magdalena Abakanowicz
Marina Abramovic
Vito Acconci
Valerio (Romani) Adami
Dennis Adams
Nicholas Africano
Yaacov Agam
Vincenzo Agnetti
Doug Aitken
Pierre Alechinsky
Rene Pierre Allain
Terry Allen
Laurie Anderson
Carl Andre
Giovanni Anselmo
Horst Antes
Eleanor Antin
Stephen Antonakos
Richard (Joseph) Anuszkiewicz
Siegfried Anzinger
Karel Appel
Shusaku Arakawa
Nobuyoshi Araki
Siah Armajani
Arman
Kenneth Armitage
John M(ichael) Armleder
Robert Arneson
Eduardo Arroyo
Richard (Ernst) Artschwager
Roy Ascott
Michael Asher
David Askevold
Nora Aslan
Conrad Atkinson
Bernard Aubertin
Frank Auerbach
Ay-O
Alice Aycock
(Anthony) Aziz and
(Sammy) Cucher

Silvia Bächli
Francis Bacon
Enrico Baj
John Baldessari
Miroslaw Balka
Stephan Balkenhol
Balthus
Walter Darby Bannard
Clive Barker
Matthew Barney
Stéphan Barron
Robert Barry
Jennifer (Losch) Bartlett
Gianfranco Baruchello
Georg Baselitz
Leonard Baskin
Carlo Battaglia
Herbert Bayer
Thomas Bayrle
Jack Beal
Romare (Howard) Bearden
Bernhard and Hilla Becher
Bill Beckley
Jacques Bedel
Krzysztof M(aria) Bednarski
Vanessa Beecroft
Larry Bell
Claude Bellegarde
Maurice Benayoun
Lynda Benglis
Billy Al Bengston
Lucie Beppler
Jake Berthot
Jean-Pierre Bertrand
Joseph Beuys
Mike Bidlo
Sanford Biggers
Max Bill
Dara Birnbaum
James Bishop
Peter (Thomas) Blake
Peter Blume
Mel Bochner
Alighiero E. Boetti
Marinus Boezem
Christian Boltanski
Peter Booth
Jacobo Borges
Jon(athan) Borofsky
Derek Boshier
Fernando Botero
Martha Boto
Louise Bourgeois
Arthur (Merrick
Bloomfield) Boyd
Mark Boyle
Monika Brandmeier
Erich (or Arik) Brauer
Claudio Bravo
George Brecht
Robert C. Breer
K. P. Brehmer
Stuart Brisley
Stanley Brouwn
Larry Brown
Tania Bruguera
Günter Brus
Stephen Buckley
Chris Burden
Daniel Buren
Victor Burgin
Alberto Burri
Nancy Burson
Pol Bury
Michael Buthe

Paul Cadmus
John Cage
Miriam Cahn
Cai Guo-Qiang
Sophie Calle
Pier Paolo Calzolari
Peter Campus
Louis Cane
Rafael (Gomez) Canogar
Janet Cardiff
Anthony (Alfred) Caro
Ian Carr-Harris
Leonora Carrington
Pietro Cascella
Enrico Castellani
Luciano Castelli
Maurizio Cattelan
Patrick Caulfield
Alik Cavaliere
Vija Celmins
Mario Ceroli
(Baldaccini) Cesar
Lynn (Russell) Chadwick
John (Angus) Chamberlain
Alan Charlton
Grégory Chatonsky
Sandro Chia
Judy Chicago
Eduardo Chillida
Marek Chlanda
Christo and Jeanne-Claude
Chryssa
Roman Cieslewicz
Jürgen Claus
Francesco Clemente
Chuck Close
Susanna Coffey
Bernard Cohen
James Coleman
Robert Colescott
James Collins
Gianni Colombo
Alex Colville
Bruce Conner
Pietro Consagra
William Nelson (CPLY) Copley
Corneille
Claudio Costa
Robert Cottingham
Tony Cragg

Michael Craig-Martin
Jordan Crandall
Leonardo Cremonini
Carlos Cruz-Diez
Enzo Cucchi
José Luis Cuevas
Greg Curnoe
Roger Cutforth

Dado
Walter Dahn
Salvador Dali
Ken Danby
Nassos Daphnis
Hanne Darboven
Alan Davie
John Davies
Douglas (Matthew) Davis
Gene Davis
John Davis
Richard Deacon
John (Louis) De Andrea
Gino De Dominicis
George Deem
Raoul De Keyser
Ger(rit Hendrik) Dekkers
Willem de Kooning
Paul Delvaux
Thomas Demand
Nicola De Maria
Walter (Joseph) De Maria
Agnes (Cecilia) Denes
Herman De Vries
Jean Dewasne
Daniel Dezeuze
Antonio Dias
Jan Dibbets
Richard (Clifford Jr.) Diebenkorn
Hans-Jurgen Diehl
Erik Dietmann
Braco Dimitrijević
Jim Dine
Juan Carlos Distefano
Mark Di Suvero
Jiri Georg Dokoupil
César Domela
Hernán Dompé
Heri Dono
Stan Douglas
Jimmie Durham
David Dye
Friedel Dzubas

Don Eddy
Olafur Eliasson
Thomas Eller
Stephen Ellis
Toshikatsu Endo
Pieter Engels
(Gudmundur Gudmundsson) Erró
Richard Estes

Luciano Fabro
Murray Favro
Jackie Ferrara
Rafael Ferrer
Rainer Fetting
Robert Filliou
Ian Hamilton Finlay
Eric Fischl
Peter Fischli and David Weiss
Ebon Fisher
Joel Fisher
Barry Flanagan
Dan Flavin
Jochen Flinzer
Fred Forest
Terry (Alan) Fox
Sam Francis
Helen Frankenthaler
Donald Hamilton Fraser
Lucian Freud
Tom Friedman
Elisabeth Frink
Katharina Fritsch
Terry Frost
Ernst Fuchs
Hamish Fulton
John Furnival
Klaus Fussmann

Charles Gagnon
Daniel García
Marco Gastini
Yves Gaucher
Winfred Gaul
Johannes Geccelli
Juan Genovés
Isa Genzken
Karl Gerstner
Franz Gertsch
Jochen Gerz
Ralph Gibson
Piero Gilardi
Gilbert and George
Sam Gilliam
Liam Gillick
Jean-Pierre Giovanelli
Bruno Gironcoli
Milton Glaser
Robert Gober
Mathias Goeritz
Ralph (Ladell) Goings
Ken Goldberg
Leon (Albert) Golub
Guillermo Gómez-Peña
Tony Gonzalez
Douglas Gordon
Ludwig Gosewitz
Dan Graham
K. M. Graham
Robert Graham
Rodney Graham
Josep Grau-Garriga
Gotthard Graubner
Morris (Cole) Graves
Nancy Graves
Alan Green
Gloria Greenberg
Joseph Grigely
Gronk
Red Grooms
Nancy Grossman
Robert (Strawbridge) Grosvenor
Johannes Grützke
Andreas Gursky

Hans Haacke
Raymond Hains
Etienne Hajdu
Nigel Hall
Richard Hamilton
Gabi Hamm
David Hammons
Duane Hanson
David Hare
Helen (Mayer) Harrison
Newton Harrison
Grace Hartigan
Kay Hassan
Mona Hatoum
Erich Hauser
Stanley William Hayter
Tim Head
Erwin Heerich
Bernhard Heiliger
Michael Heizer
Al Held
Jean Hélion
Geoffrey Hendricks
Anton Henning
John Heward
Sheila Hicks
Dick Higgins
Anthony Hill
Gary Hill
John Hilliard
Thomas Hirschhorn
Damien Hirst
Perry Hoberman
David Hockney
Howard Hodgkin
Rudolf Hoflehner
Tom Holland
Carsten Höller
Nancy Holt
Jenny Holzer
Gottfried Honegger

Martin Honert
Rebecca Horn
Roni Horn
John Hoyland
Alfred Hrdlicka
Douglas Huebler
Friedensreich Hundertwasser
Bryan Hunt
Richard (Howard) Hunt
Pierre Huyghe

Dorothy Iannone
Taka(hiko) Iimura
Jörg Immendorff
Robert Indiana
Francisco Infante
Will Insley
Jean (Robert) Ipoustéguy
David Ireland
Robert Irwin

Alfredo Jaar
Christian Jaccard
Alain (Georges Frank) Jacquet
Horst Janssen
Valerie Jaudon
Paul Jenkins
Neil Jenney
Luis (Alfonso, Jr.) Jimenez
Jasper Johns
Lester Johnson
Ray Johnson
Joan Jonas
Allen Jones
Michel Journiac
Donald Judd
Isaac Julien
Dieter Jung

Ilya Kabakov
Eduardo Kac
Horst Egon Kalinowski
Michael Kalmbach
Howard Kanovitz
Tadeusz Kantor
Anish Kapoor
Allan Kaprow
Dani Karavan
Emiko Kasahara
Axel Kassebõhmer
Alex Katz
(Robert) Craig Kauffman
Tatsuo Kawaguchi
Takashi Kawamata
On Kawara
Hachiya Kazuhiko
Mike Kelley
Ellsworth Kelly
Michael Kenny
William Kentridge

Anselm Kiefer
Edward Kienholz
Phillip King
William (Dickey) King
Alain Kirili
Per Kirkeby
R(onald) B(rooks) Kitaj
Konrad Klapheck
Harold Klunder
Milan Knížák
Alison Knowles
J(iři) H(ynek) Kocman
Peter Kogler
Jiří Kolář
Komar and Melamid
Jeff Koons
Igor and Svetlana Kopystiansky
Gyula Kosice
Leon Kossoff
Joseph Kosuth
Jannis Kounellis
Piotr Kowalski
Joyce Kozloff
Dieter Krieg
Richard Kriesche
Barbara Kruger
Nicholas Krushenick
Tetsumi Kudo
Gary Kuehn
Ewa Kuryluk
Yayoi Kusama
Robert Kushner
Tadaaki Kuwayama

Gerald (Ogilvie) Laing
László Lakner
Colin Lanceley
Lois Lane
Nikolaus Lang
John Latham
Bob Law
Louis Le Brocquy
Jean Le Gac
Jan Lenica
Thomas Lenk
Julio (Alcides) Le Parc
Barry Le Va
David Leverett
Les Levine
Marilyn (Anne) Levine
Sol Lewitt
Micah Lexier
Alexander Liberman
Roy Lichtenstein
Martin Liebscher
Glenn Ligon
Liliane Lijn
Maya Lin
Pam Lins
Richard Lippold

Frank Lobdell
Richard (J.) Long
Robert Longo
Gustavo López Armentia
Antonio Lopez Garcia
Sarah Lucas
Reinier Lucassen
Ken Lum
Evert Lundquist
Ana Lupas
Markus Lüpertz
Urs Lüthi

Heinz Mack
Leopoldo (Mario) Maler
Alfred Manessier
Robert (Peter) Mangold
Giacomo Manzù
Conrad Marca-Relli
Christian Marclay
Brice Marden
Tom Marioni
Chris Marker
Agnes Martin
Ron Martin
John Mason
André (Aimé René) Masson
Georges Mathieu
Yutaka Matsuzawa
Roberto (Sebastian Antonio Echaurren) Matta
Bruce Mau
Fabio Mauri
Ann McCoy
John McCracken
James McGarrell
Bruce McLean
F(rederick) E(dward) McWilliam
Christian Megert
Cildo Meireles
Fausto Melotti
Stephan Melzl
John Meredith
Richard (Marshall) Merkin
Mario Merz
Annette Messager
Gustav Metzger
Keith (Arnold) Milow
Joan Mitchell
Tatsuo Miyajima
Ryuji Miyamoto
Guido Molinari
Jacques Monory
Henry Moore
François Morellet
Yasumasa Morimura
Malcolm Morley
Robert Morris
Margaret Morton

A

ABAKANOWICZ, Magdalena

Nationality: Polish. **Born:** Falenty, 20 June 1930. **Education:** School of Fine Arts, Sopot, 1949; Academy of Fine Arts, Warsaw, 1950–54, M.A. 1955. **Family:** Married Jan Kosmowski in 1956. **Career:** Independent artist, Warsaw, since 1954; has concentrated on woven constructions and sculptures since 1961. Instructor, 1965–74, associate professor, 1974–79, and professor, 1979–90, Academy of Fine Arts, Poznan. Member, Z.A.I.K.S. Union of Polish Artists, Writers and Composers, Warsaw, 1965. **Awards:** State Travel Fellowship to France, Warsaw, 1962; 1st Prize, Ministry of Culture, 1965; Gold Medal, Polish Artists' Union, 1965; Gold Medal, *Bienal,* Sao Paulo, 1965; Grand Prize of the Ministry for Foreign Affairs, 1970; State Prize of the Polish Folk Republic, Warsaw, 1972; Grand Prize, World Crafts' Council, New York, 1974; Golden Cross of Merit, Polish Folk Republic, Poznan, 1974; Special Professor's Prize, State College of Art, Poznan, 1975; Gottfried-von-Herder Prize, Vienna, 1979; Cross of Polonia Restituta, Warsaw, 1980; Jurzykowski Foundation Award, New York, 1983; Chevalier, Ordre des Arts et Lettres, France, 1985; Award for Distinction in Sculpture, Sculpture Center, New York, 1993; elected honorary member of American Academy of Arts and Letters, 1996; Commander Cross with Star of the Order of Polonia Restituta, 1998; Oficier dans L'Ordre des Arts and the Lettres, Paris, 1999; Orden pour le Merite für Wissenshaften und Kunste, Bonn, Germany, 1999. Honorary doctorate: Royal College of Art, London, 1974; Rhode Island School of Design, 1992; Academy of Fine Arts Lodz, Poland, 1997; Pratt Institute, New York, 2000. **Agent:** Marlborough Gallery Inc., 40 West 57th Street, New York, New York 10019, U.S.A. **Address:** ul. Bzowa 01, 02–708 Warsaw, Poland. **Web site:** www.abakanowicz.art.pl.

Individual Exhibitions:

1960 Kordegarda, Warsaw
1962 Galerie Dautzenberg, Paris
1965 Galerie Zacheta, Warsaw
Biuro Wystaw Artystycznych, Zakopane, Poland
1967 Galerie Alice Pauli, Lausanne
Kunstindustrimuseet, Oslo (travelled to Vestlandske Kunstindustrimuseum, Bergen; the Stavanger Kunstforening; and the Trondheim Kunstforening)
1968 Van Abbemuseum, Eindhoven, Netherlands (travelled to the Frans Halsmuseum, Haarlem; Groninger Museum, Groningen; and the Stedelijk Museum, Schiedam)
Helmhaus, Zurich
1969 *Tapisserien und Raumliche Texturen,* Kunsthalle, Mannheim
Stedelijk Museum, Arnhem, Netherlands
1970 Nationalmuseum, Stockholm
Textil Skulptur/Textile Environment, Konsthall, Sodertalje, Sweden
1971 Galeria Wspolczesna, Warsaw
Pasadena Art Museum, California
1972 Aberdeen Art Gallery, Scotland
Textile Strukturen und Konstruktionen, Environments, Kunstverein für die Rheinlande und Westfalen, Dusseldorf
1973 Arnolfini Gallery, Bristol
Galerie Alice Pauli, Lausanne (with Jagoda Buic)
Galerie des Beaux-Arts, Bordeaux
1974 Museum Sztuki, Lodz, Poland
1975 Galerie Zacheta, Warsaw
Whitechapel Art Gallery, London
1976 Art Gallery of New South Wales, Sydney (travelled to the National Gallery of Victoria, Melbourne)
1977 Konsthall, Malmo, Sweden
Sonja Henie-Niel Onstadt Kunstsenter, Oslo
1979 Galerie Alice Pauli Lausanne (retrospective)
1980 Polish Pavilion, at the *Biennale,* Venice
1982 ARC/Musée d'Art Moderne de la Ville, Paris
Galerie Jeanne Bucher, Paris
Walter Phillips Gallery, The Banff Centre, Alberta, Canada
Museum of Contemporary Art, Chicago (toured the United States and Canada)
1983 De Cordova Museum, Lincoln, Massachusetts (retrospective)
National Academy of Sciences, Washington, D.C.
Musée d'Art Contemporain, Montreal
Visual Arts Centre of Alaska, Anchorage
1984 Dallas Museum of Arts, Texas
University of California, Los Angeles
Portland Art Museum, Oregon
1985 Virginia Museum of Fine Arts, Richmond
Xavier Fourcade Inc., New York
1986 Catholic University Art Gallery, Lublin, Poland
McIntosh-Drysdale Gallery, Washington, D.C.
1988 Mucsarnok Palace of Exhibitions, Budapest, Hungary
Turske and Turske, Zurich, Switzerland
Laumeier Sculpture Park, St. Louis, Missouri
1989 Stadtische Galerie im Stadelschen Kunstinstitut, Frankfurt, Germany
Marlborough Gallery, New York
1990 Galerie Pels-Leusden, West Berlin, Germany
Gemeentemuseum Arnhem, Holland
Richard Gray Gallery, Chicago
Marlborough Fine Art, London
1991 Sezon Museum of Art, Tokyo, Japan (travelled to the Museum of Modern Art, Shiga, Japan; Art Tower, Mito, Japan; and Hiroshima City Museum of Contemporary Art, Hiroshima, Japan)
Marlborough Fine Art, Tokyo, Japan
Muzeum Narodowe, Wroclaw, Poland
Muzeum Sztuki, Lódz, Poland
1992 The Nelson-Atkins Museum of Art, Kansas City, Missouri
Arboreal Architecture: Bois de Nanterre—Vertical Green, Marlborough Gallery, New York
Walker Art Center-Sculpture Garden, Minneapolis, Minnesota
1993 Biuro Wystaw Artystycznych, Kraków, Poland

The Institute for Contemporary Art P.S. 1 Museum, New York
Marlborough Gallery, New York
Reynolds Gallery, Richmond
Museum of Art, Rhode Island School of Design
Palmer Museum of Art, Pennsylvania State University
1994 Galerie Des Polnischen Instituts, Dusseldorf, Germany
Mandeville Gallery, University of California, San Diego, California
Weatherspoon Art Gallery, University of North Carolina, Greensboro, North Carolina
Galeria Kordegarda, Warsaw, Poland
McIntosh/Drysdale Gallery, Washington, D.C.
Museum Sztuki, Lódz, Poland
Galeria Marlborough, Madrid, Spain
Fundacio Pilar i Joan Miro a Mallorca, Palmas
1995 Els Jardins de Can Altamira, Barcelona, Spain
Centre of Polish Sculpture, Oronsko, Poland
Ujazdowski Castle, The Centre for Contemporary Art, Warsaw
Yorkshire Sculpture Park, England
1996 Galerie Marwan Hoss, Paris
Oriel Mostyn Gallery, North Wales
Charlottenborg Exhibition Hall, Copenhagen (travelled to Kulturhuset Stockholm)
1996–97 Doris Freedman Plaza, New York
1997 *MUTANTS,* Marlborough Gallery, New York
Miami Art Museum, Miami, Florida
1997–98 Marwan Hoss Gallery, Paris
1998 Starmach Gallery, Kraków, Poland
1999 *Abakanowicz on the Roof,* Metropolitan Museum of Art, New York
Les Jardins du Palais Royal, Paris
CAMMINANDO, 30 Basel Art Fair, Basel, Switzerland
Wild Flowers (drawing exhibition), Marlborough Gallery, New York
2000 *Working Process,* Giuliano Gori Collection, Italy
Ninety Five Figures from the Crowd of One Thousand Ninety Five Figures, Marlborough Gallery, New York

Selected Group Exhibitions:

1984 *An International Survey of Recent Painting and Sculpture,* Museum of Modern Art, New York
1986 *Biennale,* Sydney, Australia
Eva und die Zukunft, Kunsthalle, Hamburg
1987 *The Avant-Garde in the Eighties,* Los Angeles County Museum of Art
1988 *Orwell und die Zukunft,* Museum Moderner Kunst, Vienna
1990 *New Works for New Spaces,* Wexner Center for the Visual Arts, Columbus, Ohio
1992 *. . . Reperti. . . : Environment Through the Eyes of 18 of the World's Major Artists,* Museu Nacional de Belas Artes Rio de Janeiro, Brazil
1993 *Art in Politics,* 3rd Minos beach Art Symposium, Crete
1994 *Europa, Auropa das Jahrhundert der Avantgarde in Mittel-und Osteuropa,* Kunst-und Ausstellungshalle der Bundesrepublic Deutschland, Bonn
1995 *After Auschwitz: Responses to the Holocaust in Contemporary Art,* Royal Festival Hall, London
1996 *Les Champs de la Sculpture,* Paris
1997 *A Century of Sculpture—The Nasher Collection,* Guggenheim Museum, New York
1999 *To the Rescue, Eight Artists in an Archive,* American Jewish Joint Distribution Committee, New York
2000 *Verteidigung der Moderne Positionen der Polnischen Kunst nach 1945,* Museum Wurth, Kunzelsau, Germany

Collections:

Muzeum Narodow, Warsaw; Muzeum Sztuki, Lodz, Poland; Stedelijk Museum, Amsterdam; Nationalmuseum, Stockholm; Henie-Onstad Kunstsenter, Oslo; Centre Georges Pompidou, Paris; Museu de Arte Moderna, Sao Paulo; National Museum of Modern Art, Kyoto; Australian Gallery of Art, Canberra; Museum of Modern Art, New York; Caracas Museum of Modern Art, Caracas, Venezuela; Hiroshima City Museum of Contemporary Art, Japan; Israel Museum, Jerusalem; Jardin des Tuleries, Paris; Ludwig Museum, Cologne, Germany; Museo Nacional Centro de Arte Reina Sofia, Madrid; Museum of Modern Art, Shiga, Japan; National Museum of Modern Art, Pusan, South Korea; National Gallery of Art, Washington, D.C.; National Museum of Contemporary Art, Seoul, South Korea.

Permanent Public Installations:

Sarcophagi in Glass Houses, Storm King Art Center, Mountainville, New York; *Katarsis* and *Magnus,* Giuliano Gori Spazi d'Arte, Santomato di Pistoia, Italy; *Negev,* Billy Rose Sculpture Garden, Israel Museum, Jerusalem; *Space of Dragon,* Seoul Olympic Park, Korea; *Two Sagacious Heads,* Walker Art Center, Minneapolis; *Sagacious Head and Black Standing Figure,* Nagoya City Art Museum, Japan; *Space of Nine Figures,* Wilhelm Lembruck Museum, Diusburg, Germany; *Becalmed Beings,* Hiroshima City Museum of Contemporary Art, Japan; *One of the Crowd,* Hakone Open Air Museum, Japan; *Hand-Like Trees,* Runnymede Sculpture Farm, California; *Manus,* Western Washington University; *Hand-Like Trees,* Venice; *Standing Shape,* Elblag City, Poland; *Negev,* Israel Museum, Jerusalem; *Neun Figuren Raum,* Wilhelm Lehmbrusk Museum, Duisburg, Germany; *Cecyna,* Grounds For Sculpture, New Jersey; *Space of Unknown Growth,* collection of Europos Parkas, Lithuania; *Fish,* Metropolitano Orient Station, Lisboa, Portugal; *Manus Ultimus,* Jardin des Tuileries, Paris; *Figure on Trunk,* Metropolitan Museum, New York.

Publications:

By ABAKANOWICZ: Books—*Katarsis* (with Pierre Restany), Firenze, Italy 1987, 1991; *Abakanowicz* (with Ryszard Stanislawski, Michael Brenson and Jasia Reichardt), Warsaw 1995; *Magdalena Abakanowicz—Bronze Sculpture* (with Jasia Reichardt and Judith Collins, with an introduction by Peter Murray), 1996; *Magdalena Abakanowicz—Mutants,* exhibition catalog (with text by Michael Brenson), New York 1997.

On ABAKANOWICZ: Books—*Abakanowicz,* exhibition catalog, with text by André Kuenzi, Lausanne 1967; *Magdalena Abakanowicz: Tapisserien und Raumliche Texturen,* exhibition catalog, with text by Heinz Fuchs, Mannheim 1969; *Magdalena Abakanowicz: Textil Skulptur/Textil Environment,* exhibition catalog with text by Eje Hogestatt and Danuta Wroblewska, Sodertalje, Sweden 1970; *Beyond Craft: The Art Fabric* by Mildred Constantine and Jack Lenor

Larsen, New York 1972; *La Nouvelle Tapisserei* by André Kuenzi, Geneva 1974; *Biennale di Venezia '80: Magdalena Abakanowicz,* exhibition catalog, with text by Aleksander Wojciechowski, Warsaw 1980; *Magdalena Abankanowicz,* with texts by John Hallmark Neff, Mary Jane Jacob, Jasia Reichardt, and Magdalena Abakanowicz, Chicago and New York 1982; *Magdalena Abakonowicz: About Men,* exhibition catalog, New York 1985; *Magdalena Abakanowicz: Recent Works,* exhibition catalog, New York 1989; *Magdalena Abakanowicz,* exhibition catalog, London 1990; *Magdalena Abakanowicz: Arboreal Architecture,* exhibition catalog, New York 1992; *Magdalena Abakanowicz: Sculpture,* exhibiton catalog with text by Michael Brenson, New York 1993; *Magdalena Abakanowicz* by Barbara Rose, New York 1994; *Voicing Today's Visions: Writings By Contemporary Women Artists* by Mara Witzling, New York and London 1994, 1995.*Magdalena Abakanowicz,* exhibition catalog, with text by Michael Brenson, 1996; *Ninety Five Figures from the Crowd of One Thousand Ninety five Figures,* exhibition catalog, with text by Eleanor Heartney, 2000. **Films**—*Abakany,* 1969; *Abakanowicz in Australia,* 1976; *Division of Space,* 1976; *Abakanowicz,* 1976; *Division of Space,* 1976; *War Games,* 1993; *Magdalena Abakanowicz. Inside Outside,* 1999.

*

I was destined to live during times which were extraordinary for their various forms of collective hate and collective adulation. As a small girl I even envied those youngsters in brown shirts from the neighboring country who so worshipped their leader and so firmly believed in his ideals. When they marched in to kill us, everything turned to hate, until the killers themselves where defeated and killed.

Then enthusiastic marchers worshipped new ideals that would last forever and another leader, great and good.

When the beloved leader became a mass murderer, new successors of lesser stature sprang up to replace him. Parades continued marching to celebrate visions that would bring happiness to all.

The reality that followed was unreal. Thoughts and words diverged. Actions followed an alien liturgy and an alien ritual. One hated by orders and loved by orders. Finally, the common abhorrence and a craving for truth prevailed. Old leaders were forced to yield to new leaders. Totalitarian oppression gave way to Liberty.

Within it, new grasping ambitions have already started to hatch. Hand-to-hand fighting has begun, each against each, zealously trying to drag everything toward a private nest. (1990)

I wanted to tell you that art is the most harmless activity of mankind, but I suddenly recalled that art was often used for propaganda purposes by totalitarian systems.

I wanted to tell you also about the extraordinary sensitivity of an artist, but I recalled that Hitler was a painter and Stalin used to write sonnets.

Art will remain the most astonishing activity of mankind born out of struggle between wisdom and madness, between dream and reality in our mind.

Each scientific discovery opens doors behind which we are confronted with new closed doors.

Art does not solve problems but makes us aware of their existence. It opens our eyes to see and our brain to imagine. To have imagination and to be aware of it means to benefit from possessing an inner richness and a spontaneous and endless flood of images. It means to see the world in its entirety, since the point of the images is to show all that which escapes conceptualization. (1993)

Grain of Sand

I immerse in the crowd like a grain of sand in the friable sands.

I am fading among the anonymity of glances, movements, smells, in the common absorption of air, in the common pulsation of juices under the skin.

I become a cell of this boundless organism of the crowd, like others already integrated and deprived of expression.

Destroying each other, we regenerate. Through hate and love, we stimulate each other.

—Magdalena Abakanowicz

* * *

The manipulation of fiber into thread and the weaving of those threads into intricately constructed forms and surfaces are skills that can be counted among humankind's earliest and most enduring accomplishments. Those same techniques, and the casting and carving of stone and metal, which for thousands of years have produced shelters, utilitarian artifacts, and garments to warm, feed and protect human bodies, are the means by which Magdalena Abakanowicz shapes hauntingly eloquent and powerful sculptures. Many take possession of the spaces in which they are placed, sometimes seeming to become architectural elements of the structures that enclose them; other groups of works assume more specific referential form.

Abakanowicz was born in 1930 to an aristocratic Polish family who traced their lineage to Abaka (Ghengis) Khan, and whose isolated, tranquil way of life on a wooded country estate outside Warsaw was irrevocably shattered by WWII. Witness and survivor to the brutal regimes of first Nazism and then Stalinism, Abakanowicz has chosen to remain living and working in her native country, pursuing her art despite great difficulties of circumstance, including the harsh economic and environmental realities of post-Solidarity Poland.

In her first exhibitions Abakanowicz presented highly abstract environments called "Abakans," binding fibers together into long, attenuated hawsers, shaping large organic forms and weaving stiff, heavy hangings or huge dark cocoons of rough jute. The alleyways and mazes created by these installations simultaneously functioned as enclosures and as impediments to free movement; their dark rough textures were pleasant to see but harsh to touch. A viewer walking among the forms could experience their impressive strength as both comforting and intimidating, much like the experience of individuals who find themselves both cared for and oppressed by the omnipotent apparatus of the socialist state.

The political and existential implications of Abakanowicz's work became more explicit in the mid-1970s. Working with burlap sacking impregnated with glue and molded into the plaster cast of the human form, Abakanowicz produced the well-known cycles *Seated Figures* (1974–79) and *Backs* (1976–81). Shell-like and fragmentary, these multiple broken, emptied husks of human bodies were installed in mute throngs or lined up in poignant queues. "As indicators of both presence and absence... poised on the threshold between permanence and impermanence" (Tina Wasserman), these works evinced a haunted, archeological quality, bespeaking the erosion of individual identity through the cyclical, mutable processes of human history and natural decay, but transmitting at the same time a stark and stubborn power to endure. A series of very large wrapped heads succeeded the figures, followed later by the *Embryology* series, groups of hollow, burlap-covered ovoid forms, some intact and some fractured, in a wide range of sizes.

Since the late 1980s Abakanowicz has experimented with new materials, scale and form, creating monolithic animal heads in bronze (the *Sagacious Heads* cycle, 1988–90), or housing burlap figures and wooden sarcophagi inside steel scaffolding or frames. The artist returned to the spiritual sanctuary of the ancient Polish woodlands of her childhood in the huge bronze *Hand-Like Trees* series (1992–93), hiding in the folds of these primitive, cumbersome metal forms secret inner cavities. In the abstract *War Games* cycle (1987–93), Abakanowicz wrapped sections of the stripped trunks of large trees with cuffs of iron, then projected them horizontally on low metal stands, so that the solid, natural forms, thus truncated and bound, appeared to be simultaneously menacing and victimized.

This lack of an easy reading, this conflation of what is archetypal, distant, or past with what is physically present in all its rich tactility and associative complexity, gives Abakanowicz's sculpture the rare power to raise profound and troubling questions about the fragile nature of human identity without becoming despairing or didactic. The sheer expressive force and dark beauty of her work attest to the resilience of the human spirit in the face of natural and social forces of destruction, degradation, and negation.

—Essay by Cecile N. McCann; updated by Dorothy Valakos

In the decade since her retirement from her position as professor at the Poznan Academy of Fine Arts (1990), Magdalena Abakanowicz has remained an active creator, and her works have been widely exhibited. She has continued to explore many of the themes she had worked with in earlier years, in works such as ''Figura Prima'' (1995) or ''Handlike Tree'' (1994), a twelve foot bronze exhibited in New York's Central Park. These bronze ''trees'' seem a logical transposition of the ''War Games'' series that immediately preceded them, in which she recycled huge, irregular tree trunks, found deep in the Polish forest. Like the pieces in ''War Games,'' those of the ''Handlike Tree'' series insinuate a sense of the fragmented, contorted body, one of her major artistic concerns in all media.

Abakanowicz continues to explore the theme of the individual lost within a crowd, of individuality and variety within sameness, in several later works. ''Bambini'' (1998–99) an ensemble of forty bronze, headless, late adolescent figures, is part of a monumental display of five of Abakanowicz's more recent sculptures that were installed on the roof garden of the Iris B. and Gerald Cantor Roof Garden at New York's Metropolitan Museum of Art in May 1999. Two other pieces were made especially for this installation: ''Skulls'' (1998–99)—two monumental bronze heads—and ''Birds'' (1998–99, aluminum), bespeaking forms in flight. Abakanowicz has used aluminum as a medium in other recent works.

In her art and writing, Abakanowicz feels a visceral identification with nature's continuous cycle of renewal, and although her forms bespeak loss and fragmentation they also contain the potential for growth.

—Mara Witzling

ABRAMOVIC, Marina

Nationality: Serbian. **Born:** Belgrade, 1946. **Education:** Academy of Fine Arts, Belgrade. **Career:** Independent performance artist, Belgrade, from 1972; currently lives and works in Amsterdam. **Address:** Brouwersgracht 196, Amsterdam, Netherlands.

Individual Exhibitions:

1974 Galerija Suvremene umjetnosti, Zagreb
Galleria Diagramma, Milan
1975 Studio Morra, Naples
1987 Centre d'Art Contemporain, Paris
1991 Musée d'Art Contemporain, Montreal
1992 Ecole Nationale Superieure des Beaux-Arts, Paris
1993 Neue Nationalgalerie, Berlin
1994 *Departure,* Laura Carpenter Gallery, Santa Fe
1995 *Marina Abramovic: Objects, Performances, Video, Sound,* Museum of Modern Art, Oxford
1996 Sean Kelly Gallery, New York
1999 *Spirit Cooking,* Galerie Cent 8, Paris
Expiring Body, Fabric Workshop and Museum, Philadelphia
2000 *Public Body—Artist Body,* Kunstverein Hannover

Selected Group Exhibitions:

1970 *April Meeting,* Student Cultural Centre, Belgrade (and 1971, 1972)
1972 *Young Artists and Young Critics,* Museum of Modern Art, Belgrade
1973 *Post-Object Trends in Yugoslav Art,* Museum of Modern Art, Belgrade
8 Yugoslav Artists, Richard Demarco Gallery, Edinburgh
1974 *Contemporanea,* Parcheggio Villa Borghese, Rome
1975 *Contemporary Yugoslav Art,* Richard Demarco Gallery/ Fruit Market Gallery, Edinburgh (toured the U.K.)
1979 *Expansion: International Biennale für Graphik und Visuelle Kunst,* Stadtpark, Vienna
1980 *ROSC '80,* University College, Dublin
1987 *Avant-Garde in the Eighties,* Los Angeles County Museum of Art
1991 *Of Flesh & Blood,* Stedelijk Museum Schiedam, Netherlands
1994 *Dialogue with the Other,* Museet for Fotokunst, Odense, Denmark
1997 *Balkan Baroque,* 47th Venice Biennale, Italy
BODY, Art Gallery of New South Wales, Sydney
1999 *Missing Link: Menschen-Bilder in der Fotografie,* Kunstmuseum, Bern
Unfinished Business: Marina Abramovic and Students, Haus am Lützowplatz, Berlin
Abramovic & Ulay: Vidéo-Performances 1976–1988. Nightsea Crossing 1981–1986, Musée d'Art Contemporain, Lyon, France
Rest/Energy: Marina Abramovic and Ana Mendieta, Sean Kelly Gallery and Galerie Lelong, New York

Dream Machines, Dundee Contemporary Arts, Dundee, Scotland (traveled to Mappin Art Gallery, Sheffield and Camden Arts Centre, London)

Publications:

By ABRAMOVIC: Books—*Relation Work and Detour: First Complete Works,* Nijmegen, Netherlands 1980. **Articles**—Interview with Bernard Goy in *Journal of Contemporary Art,* vol. 3, no. 2, Fall-Winter 1990; ''Art is About Energy'' in *Art & Design,* vol. 8, no. 7–8, July-August 1993; ''Places of Power: Monograph Taken from Marina Abramovic: Cleaning the House'' in *Art & Design,* vol. 10, May/June 1995; Interview with Kevin Hnderson and Alan Woods in *Transcript* (London), vol. 1, no. 3, February-March 1996; ''Cleaning the House: A Workshop'' in *Art Journal,* vol. 58, no. 2, Summer 1999; Interview with Bernard Goy in *Journal of Contemporary Art,* fall/winter 1990; Interview with Janet A. Kaplan in *Art Journal,* vol. 58, no. 2, Summer 1999. **Videotapes**—*Television is a Machine,* 1972; *Rhythm 4,* 1974; *Smaile,* 1975; *I Won't. . . ,* 1975.

On ABRAMOVIC: Books—*Marina Abramovic,* exhibition catalog with text by Davor Maticevic, Zagreb 1974; *Contemporary Yugoslav Art,* exhibition catalog with text by Richard Demarco and others, Edinburgh 1975; *Expansion: Internationale Biennale für Graphik und Visuelle Kunst,* exhibition catalog with text by Horst Gerhard Haberl, Georg F. Schwarzbauer and others, Vienna 1979; *The Lovers,* with Ulay, exhibiton catalog, 1989; *Marina Abramovic,* exhibition catalog, Paris 1992; *Marina Abramovic,* exhibition catalog with text by Bojana Pejic and Doris von Drathen, Berlin 1993; *Marina Abramovic: Objects, Performances, Video, Sound,* exhibition catalog, Oxford 1995; *Ulay/Abramovic,* exhibition catalog with text by Jan Debbaut, Chrissie Iles and Paul Kokke, Eindhoven 1997. **Articles**—''Marina Abramovic: Reflections on the Mental and Physical Conditioning of the Artist'' by Johan Pijnappel in *Art & Design,* vol. 9, September/October 1994; ''Marina Abramovic'' by Sotiris Kyriacou in *Art Monthly,* no. 186, May 1995; ''Marina Abramovic'' by Tim Martin in *Third Text* (London), no. 33, Winter 1995–1996; ''Marina Abramovic: Double Bind'' by Aline Brandauer in *Sculpture* (Washington, D.C.), vol. 14, July/August 1995; ''Interperformance: The Live Tableaux of Suzanne Lacy, Janine Antoni, and Marina Abramovic'' by Jennifer Fisher in *Art Journal,* vol. 56, Winter 1997; ''Marina Abramovic'' by Katie Clifford in *Art News,* vol. 97, March 1998; ''Marina Abramovic'' by Megan Ratner in *Art/Text,* no. 61, May/July 1998; ''Marina Abramovic: Fabric Workshop and Museum'' by Robert Ayers in *Art Monthly,* no. 223, February 1999; ''Performing Life, Living Art: Abramovic/Ulay and Kwiekulik'' by Katarzyna Michalak in *Afterimage,* vol. 27, no. 3, November/December 1999; ''Doppelgangers and the Third Force: The Artistic Collaborations of Gilbert & George and Marina Abramovic/Ulay'' by Charles Green in *Art Journal,* vol. 59, no. 2, Summer 2000.

* * *

Prior to meeting in 1975, Marina Abramovic and her collaborator of 12 years, Ulay, were both engaged in a kind of radical body art that brought them to the limits of danger and physical resistance. In their first collaborative performance, *Relation in Movement,* at the 1976 Venice Biennale, the couple expressed ideas about relationships, symbolic and physical, through their interactions. As the collaboration grew, their work developed into a sort of ascetic practice, involving forms of physical suffering such as self-starvation and self-mutilation. ''You have to nearly break your body before you can free your mind,'' declared Ulay after one of their more grueling rituals, during which both of them went without food for several days.

In *Nightsea Crossing,* performed at various locations between 1982 and 1984, the couple sat motionless in chairs, facing each other, for hours at a time. The piece represented not only the symbolic challenge of a relationship, but the view of relationship as a metaphysical act of evolving consciousness. In another ongoing piece, *Anima Mundi,* the couple adopted various poses (embracing, lying side by side, a Pieta, with Abramovic cradling Ulay in her arms) in which they suggested archetypal phases in relationships. In these works and others, the artists utilized photography and other electronic media to present the static gestures as a photographic tableau vivant. The atemporal quality of still photography helped emphasize the universality of their themes.

Exploring universality and difference through contact with people of other cultures became an important element in the work of the 1980s, during which the pair travelled to Thailand, India, Australia, Tibet, and China. Driven by similar desires to expand their consciousness through intense experience, the couple enacted performances abroad and invited Tibetan monks and aboriginal Australian tribespeople to perform with them in Amsterdam. Crossing cultural boundaries between East and West represented a radical act politically in some sense, whereas culturally it challenged a fine line between colonialism and aesthetic exploration.

The video piece *City of Angels* perhaps best represents these explorations in a way that is both effective and problematic. For this work, the artists staged five stunning tableaux arrangements of costumed people (Bangkok citizens) and props against the backdrop of the ruins of the Ayuthaya temple in Thailand. The scenes are static, like photographic stills, with the exception of certain small but detectable traces of movement. The combination of a time-suspending anti-narrative and what appears to be culture-specific gestures and costumes entices the viewer's sense of the exotic without providing explanatory information. In this sense, the images are beautiful, but elusive, drawing a vague if powerful connection between contemporary people and the ancient religious site.

Another such internationally focused work was also the grand finale of Abramovic and Ulay's collaboration. In 1988, they walked the length of the Great Wall of China, each one starting at one end, and eventually, meeting in the middle. Culminating in a series of gallery installations, Abramovic made creative use of a minimalist aesthetic to convey the spiritual experience of having traversed this politically significant monument. The work moves between the physical and the metaphysical, expressing once again the idea that physically challenging ordeals help empty the mind in ways that release the spirit.

Marina Abramovic's life and art are so deeply intertwined that to explore the themes of her work is to trace the progression of her life, which she herself did in the piece *Biography* (1992–93). *Biography* involved live performance and projected images of her previous work, and encompassed childhood memories, her relationship with Ulay, and the personal motivations behind her work. Abramovic's emotional directness, like that of contemporary performance artist Karen Finley, is a refreshing contrast to the cynical climate of the late twentieth century.

—Essay by Helena Kontova; updated by Audrey Mandelbaum

ACCONCI, Vito

Nationality: American. **Born:** New York City, 25 January 1940. **Education:** Holy Cross College, Worcester, Massachusetts, B.A. 1962; University of Iowa, M.F.A. 1964. **Career:** Independent poet and writer, New York, 1965–69. Independent visual artist, concentrating on performance and environment works, New York, beginning in 1969; concentrating on projects for public spaces since 1988. Lecturer in Art Theory, School of Visual Arts, New York 1968–71; instructor in post-studio art, California Institute of Art, Valencia, 1976; guest instructor, Yale University, New Haven, Connecticut, 1988–94. Formerly, co-editor, *0 to 9* magazine, New York. **Agent:** Barbara Gladstone Gallery, 515 West 24th Street, New York, New York 10011, U.S.A. **Address:** 39 Pearl Street, Brooklyn, New York 11201, U.S.A.

Individual Exhibitions:

1969 Rhode Island School of Design, Providence
Emmanu-eul Midtown Y.M./Y.W.H.A., New York
Architectural League of New York
Far Broadway, New York
1970 Gain Ground Gallery, New York
Art Institute of Chicago
Nova Scotia College of Art and Design, Halifax
1971 74 Grand Street, New York
A Space, Toronto, Ontario (2 shows)
93 Grant Street, New York
Trappings, Kunstmuseum, Mönchengladbach, Germany
Protetch-Rivkin Gallery, Washington, D.C.
Rhode Island School of Design, Providence
Museum of Conceptual Art, San Francisco
John Gibson Gallery, New York
Wisconsin State University at Whitewater
Sonnabend Gallery, New York
1972 California Institute of the Arts, Valencia
Sonnabend Gallery, New York
Galerie Sonnabend, Paris
Galleria L'Attico, Rome
1973 Modern Art Agency, Naples, Italy
Galerie D. Brussels
Galleria Schema, Florence
1974 Galleria Forma, Genoa
Galleria Alessandra Castelli, Milan
1975 Sonnabend Gallery, New York
Portland Center for the Visual Arts, Oregon
And/Or Gallery, Seattle
Carp Gallery, Los Angeles
Museum of Conceptual Art, San Francisco
Hallwalls Gallery, Buffalo, New York
Fine Arts Building, New York
Whitney Museum, New York
1976 The Kitchen, New York
Lerner-Heller Gallery, New York
Anthology Film Archives, New York
Sonnabend Gallery, New York
1977 Ohio State University, Columbus
School of Visual Arts, New York
University of Massachusetts, Amherst
Anthology Film Archives, New York
Sonnabend Gallery, New York
Modern Art Agency, Naples
Galerie D, Brussels
Institute of Art and Urban Resources, New York
Centre d'Art Contemporain, Geneva
Galeria Stampa, Basel
1978 Studio Ala, Milan
San Francisco Museum of Modern Art
Galerie Nachst St. Stephan, Vienna
International Cultureel Centrum, Antwerp, Belgium
The Kitchen, New York
Kunstmusuem, Lucerne
Stedelijk Museum, Amsterdam (retrospective)
Galleria Mario Diacono, Bologna
Tampa Bay Art Center, Florida
1979 Young-Hoffman Gallery, Chicago
Sonnabend Gallery, New York
Galerie De Appel, Amsterdam (toured the Netherlands)
University of Rhode Island, Kingston
Galerie Sonnabend, Paris
1980 Muhlenberg College, Allentown, Pennsylvania
Vito Acconci: A Retrospective 1969 to 1980, Museum of Contemporary Art, Chicago (retrospective)
1981 *Machineworks: Vito Acconci, Alice Aycock, Dennis Oppenheim,* Institute of Contemporary Art, Philadelphia
Museum of Fine Arts, Montreal
Indianapolis Museum of Art, Indiana
Young-Hoffman Gallery, Chicago
Institute of Contemporary Art, Philadelphia (with Alice Aycock and Dennis Oppenheim)
1982 Virginia Museum of Fine Arts, Richmond
Portland Center for the Visual Arts, Oregon
San Diego State University, California
University of Massachusetts, Amherst
1983 Miami-Dade Community College, Florida
Whitney Museum, New York
Williams College, Williamstown, Massachusetts
1984 Gallery Nature Morte, New York
University of Nebraska, Omaha
Zone Center for the Arts, Springfield, Massachusetts
1985 University of North Carolina, Chapel Hill
Carpenter and Hochmann Gallery, New York
City Hall Park, New York
Rhona Hoffman Gallery, Chicago
Brooklyn Museum, New York
Wadsworth Atheneum, Hartford, Connecticut
1986 Kent State University, Ohio
The Palladium, New York
University of South Florida, Tampa
Zone Gallery, New York
1987 International Center of Photography, New York
International with Monument, New York
La Jolla Museum of Contemporary Art, California
1988 Museum of Modern Art, New York
Rhona Hoffman Gallery, New York
Brooke Alexander Gallery, New York
1989 Barbara Gladstone Gallery, New York
Mai 36, Luzern, Switzerland
1990 James Corcoran Gallery, Los Angeles

Landfall Press, New York
1991 Barbara Gladstone Gallery, New York
Centre d'Art Contemporain, Grenoble, France
Galerie Anne de Villepoix, Paris
1992 Museuo Luigi Pecci, Prato, Italy
1993 Osterreichisches Museum für Angewandte Kunst, Vienna
Monika Spruth Gallery, Cologne
Stroom, The Hague, Netherlands
Barbara Gladstone Gallery, New York
1998 *Vito Acconci: Public Spaces,* Museum of Modern Art, New York (catalog)
Spoken Rooms, Barbara Gladstone Gallery, New York (catalog)
2001 *Vito Acconci and Ana Mendieta: A Relationship Study, 1969–1976,* Galerie Lelong, New York (catalog)

Selected Group Exhibitions:

1971 *Biennale,* Musée d'Art Moderne, Paris
1972 *Documenta 5,* Kassel, West Germany (and *Documenta 7,* 1982)
1974 *Art and Image in Recent Art,* Art Institute of Chicago
1976 *Biennale,* Venice
1978 *Performance Art Festival,* Vienna
1982 *Metaphor: New Projects by Contemporary Sculptors,* Hirshhorn Museum, Washington D.C.
1987 *Concrete Crisis: Urban Images of the 80s,* Exit Art, New York
1989 *The Experience of Landscape,* Whitney Museum, New York
1991 Taormina Video Festival, Sicily
1993 *Different Natures,* La Defense, Paris
1995 *Temporarily Possessed: The Semi-Permanent Collection,* New Museum of Contemporary Art, New York (catalog)
1996 *a/drift: Scenes from the Penetrable Culture,* Center for Curatorial Studies Museum, Bard College, Annondale-on-Hudson, New York (catalog)
1997 *Rooms with a View: Environments for Video,* Guggenheim Museum Soho, New York (catalog)
2000 *The End: An Independent Vision of Contemporary Culture, 1982–2000,* Exit Art/The First World, New York (catalog)

Collections:

Museum of Modern Art, New York; Los Angeles County Museum of Art, California; Musée National d'Art Moderne/Centre Georges Pompidou, Paris; Whitney Museum, New York.

Permanent Public Installations:

Coca Cola USA, Atlanta, Georgia; The Palladium, New York; Chicago Dock and Canal; C.W. Post College, New York; City of Zolle, Netherlands; Arvada Center, Arvada, Colorado; Metrotech Center, Brooklyn, New York; P.S.3., Bronx, New York; Plaza Design, University of Illinois at Chicago, 1991; *Land of Boats,* St. Aubin Park, Detroit, Michigan, 1991; Indoor Park, Departures Terminal, Philadelphia Airport, 1998; billboard, Breda Garbage Dump, Breda, The Netherlands, 1999; Entrance for Shibuya Subway Station, Tokyo, Japan, 2000.

Publications:

By ACCONCI: Books—*Four Books,* New York 1968; *Transference: Roget's Thesaurus,* New York 1969; *Notes Toward the Development of a Show,* Hamburg 1972; *Leap/Think/Rethink/Fall,* Dayton, Ohio 1977. **Essays—**"Television, Furniture, and Sculpture: The Room with an American View," in *Illuminating Video,* edited by Doug Hall and Sally Jo Fifer, New York 1991; "Public Space in a Private Time," in *Art and the Public Sphere,* edited by W. J. T. Michell, Boulder, Colorado 1992. **Films—***3 Frame Studies,* 1970; *2 Inceptions, 3 Adaption Studies,* 1970; *2 Clearance Studies,* 1970; *Openings,* 1970; *Hand and Mouth,* 1970; *Twin Cover Studies,* 1970; *4 Studies for a Meditation Chamber,* 1970; *Three Relationship Studies,* 1970; *See-Through Rubbings,* 1970; *Applications,* 1970; *Watch,* 1971; *Second Hand,* 1971; *Control Room,* 1971; *Zone,* 1971; *Combination,* 1971; *Pickup,* 1971; *Waterways,* 1971; *Conversions 1, 2, 3,* 1971; *Training Ground,* 1971; *Trappings,* 1971; *Dress Up,* 1971; *Directions,* 1971; *Seedbed Transference Zone,* 1972; *Supply Room,* 1972; *Cross Fronts,* 1972; *Anchors,* 1972; *Reception Room,* 1972; *Air Time,* 1972; *My Word,* 1974; **Video—***Corrections,* 1970; *Pryings,* 1971; *Centers,* 1971; *Feelers,* 1971; *Claim,* 1971; *Passes,* 1971; *Association Area,* 1971; *Trials,* 1971; *Contacts,* 1971; *Pull,* 1971; *Sound Barrier,* 1971; *Waiting Room,* 1971; *Filles,* 1971; *Focal Points,* 1971; *2 Track,* 1971; *Eyespots,* 1971; *Sounding Board,* 1971; *Remote Control,* 1971; *Projections,* 1972; *Supply Room,* 1972; *Undertone,* 1973; *Face Off,* 1973; *Home Movies,* 1973; *Walk-Over,* 1973; *Theme Song,* 1973; *Full Circle,* 1973, *Stages,* 1973.

On ACCONCI: Books—*Conceptual Art* by Ursula Meyer, New York 1972; *Pop Art et Cie* by Francois Pluchart, Paris 1972; *6 Years: The Dematerialization of the Art Object from 1966 to 1972* by Lucky R. Lippard, London and New York 1973; *Senza Titolo* by Germano Celant, Milan 1974; *Il Corpo come Linguaggio* by Lea Vergine, Milan 1974; *Vito Acconci* by Mario Diacono, New York 1976; *Vito Acconci* by Kate Linker, New York 1994. **Exhibition Catalogs—** *Software* (with introduction by Jack Burnham), New York 1970; *Documenta 5,* edited by Harald Szeemann and others, Kassel, West Germany 1972; *Art and Image in Recent Art* (with text by Anne Rorimer), Chicago 1974; *Vito Acconci* (with text and interview by Martin Kunz), Lucerne 1978; *Vito Acconci: A Retrospective 1969 to 1980* (with texts by John Hallmark Neff and Judith Russi Kirshner), Chicago 1980; *Machineworks: Vito Acconci, Alice Aycock, Dennis Oppenheim* (with texts by Janet Kardon and Kay Larson), Philadelphia 1981; *Italians and American Italians: Etchings by Francisco Clemente, Janis Kounellis, Italo Scanga, Tom Marioni, Vito Acconci* (with an introduction by Kathan Brown), Oakland, California 1981; *Metaphor: New Projects by Contemporary Sculptors* (with text by Howard N. Fox), Washington, D.C. 1982; *Vito Acconci: Domestic Trappings* (with essay by Ronald J. Onorato), La Jolla 1987; *Public Places* (with essay by Linda Shearer), New York 1988; *Vito Acconci* (with essays by Jeffrey Kipnis and Jeff Rian), Prato, Italy 1993; *Vito Acconci: The City Inside Us* (with essays by Anthony Vidler and Peter Noever), Vienna, 1993. **Articles—**"The Outsider Moves Indoors" by Allan Schwartzman in *INC.,* February 1988; "Vito Acconci" by Kim Levin in *Village Voice,* 2 April 1988; "Vito Acconci, A-Cup Architecture" by Joshua Decter in *Flash Art,* May-June 1991;

''Skeptics in Utopia'' by Eleanor Heartney in *Art in America,* July 1992; ''Artists Are the Directors, and a Stage Is Their Canvas'' by Kay Larson in *New York Times,* 8 October 1995; ''The Carnivalized Sublime, Vito Acconci's Architectural Projects'' by Gregory Volk in *Daidalos,* no. 73, 1999; ''Curriculum Vito'' by Tim Griffin in *Time Out,* 1 February 2001.

*

My work started as poetry. The page was considered a field for movement—my activity of writing the page, the readers' activity of reading the page. The words referred to the page they were on; the words functioned as acts of language (idioms, puns) that would self-dissolve.

Since I had reached a dead end, there had to be a leap; and that leap was off the page and on to actual space—the floor, the street. The first work in an art context, in the late 1960s and early 1970s, used my own presence and was in the form of film and video performance. The work focused on the act of art doing. The mode was the presentation of myself to others, to viewers; the work constructed and deconstructed my ''self'' and placed that self in relation to viewers. The art occasion was an exchange—a system by means of which artist met (came face-to-face with) viewer.

By the mid-1970s, ''me'' shifted to ''you,'' or to viewers and the space of which they were a part. Work was in the form of installations, with furniture-like sets and audiotaped texts. An exhibition space was treated as a community meeting place; a piece functioned as an instrument that pushed the viewer up against the wall—to a point where a viewer revels and analyzes. A piece was designed for one particular place, one cultural situation, and could not be repeated elsewhere.

In the early 1980s, viewers *made* the pieces, activated the pieces. A piece consisted of a vehicle that, once used by a viewer, erected a shelter that, in turn, carried a sign. The building of a shelter equalled the building of meaning. Viewers were complicit in the image/sign/propaganda they raised. Art was the occasion for a viewer's decision making—the viewer took sides and the viewer made or broke the piece.

The mid-1980s work shifted from the *act* of building to the buildings themselves—in small form (furniture) and in large (houses and parks). The work functioned as a grounding of people's activity—a grounding in space and in conventions and culture. Conventions were turned upside down and collided one with the other, so that the powers behind those conventions could be questioned and reconsidered and potentially changed.

By this time, the work wasn't art anymore; it was architecture and landscape architecture, and it has continued that way.

The impetus of a project—almost the designer of a project—is the site and the situation. The projects shouldn't have stylistic quirks that connect one to the other (as in a family). The project comes from the site and hence fits into the site. But it doesn't have to quite fit in all the way; it could be having a dialogue with the site, an argument with the site—the project can subvert and/or reinvent a site.

The mode is to go under a site, so that the site isn't as stable as it used to be; to attach something onto the site, like a leech, so that the site isn't so closed anymore; to replicate elements of the site, so that the site isn't so unique—so sure of itself—anymore.

The recent works, while concentrating on public places, attempt to ''move'' those places away from the piazza and the town square and the town commons and onto vehicles, circulation systems, and media. The hope is to put space into conflict with hyperspace.

—Vito Acconci

* * *

For many artists in the 1960s who sought to evade the cul de sac of formalism and its concomitant obsession with the art object, the continued aesthetization of art became untenable. The institutions of painting and sculpture were surpassed by other forms of advanced art and especially by photography, which offered new possibilities for a generation who grew up surrounded by the imagery of television. Vito Acconci both identified and defined the very terms of his art of the 1970s—his investigations of the self within the broad scope of conceptual art—in the photographic and cinematic medium of video.

The video projects Acconci produced in the late 1960s and early 1970s sought to transpose the aesthetic and philosophical terms of Minimalism and Process Art, both explorations of self-referential, temporal, and phenomenological conditions. Similar to the temporal/physical passage from one state to another experienced in Process Art, video permitted the artist to further intensify a dismantling of the myth of the subject as something given and preconstructed.

Minimalism's disavowal of structural closure and the myths of universal meaning became for Acconci a positive, liberating force. In his full-length video *The Red Tapes,* 1976–77—a trilogy reflecting the full range of his social, political and semiotic concerns—the artist, in fact, perpetuates the 1960s revolutionary spirit with just such a message: ''Let's make the symbols our own.'' Challenging the origin of the work of art in memory and *a priori* assumptions, the temporal experience of Minimalism tended to decenter our perception of the object. Attempting to exceed that movement's primary interest in formal concerns, Acconci began to exploit the dominant Minimalist aesthetic—temporal manipulations and the concomitant loss of self—as analogous to the fractured nature of consciousness as it is reproduced in video. Despite the proliferation of cultural types immediately accessible during the media-oriented 1960s, a period fascinated by social change, Acconci was aware that the co-option of the self by the political economy of late capitalism would render hopeless any search for a ''new'' or fixed identity.

Mirroring the reflexive nature of consciousness, video's electronic feedback allowed both the artist and viewer to dialectically explore the self as object and subject. Such a process suggested the distinction experienced by the patient in psychoanalysis between a subjectivity experienced and the conceptual projection of the self as object. Acconci contrasted one's identity as felt with one's own seen/heard projection, for example, in *Air Time,* 1973, in which the artist faces a mirror and for minutes engages his own reflection in a monologue. In *Centers,* in which the artist filmed himself pointing at the center of a television monitor for 20 minutes, Acconci moved toward a condition of self-enclosure in an effort to constitute or encapsulate a self—a particularly ironic exercise, during a cultural period of sexual and psychological openness, of disillusioning futility.

It was, however, this fundamental conjunction (and consequent diffusion) of the personal by a subsuming public ''other'' that connects Acconci's earlier video and performance work with his later furniture-like sculpture. For nearly two decades, he transgressed convention, continually challenging our standards of normalcy by relentlessly blurring the categories (landscape, architecture, site) that define the spaces in which we live. Acconci's strategy of representation, based on the pragmatics of language, hinges on the latter's arbitrariness. In order to combat the rigidity of our lives, Acconci's recent work increasingly has assumed the status of ''play.'' The notion of play—with its irreverent collapse of convention and constant assertion of new rules—is manifest in many of the artist's recent fantasy-rooted works. Pieces such as *Garden Chair* [1986], *Bad Dream House* [1984] or *Sleeping Dog Couch* [1984] have permitted Acconci to create a deceptively simple fusion of form and content, one which is *engaging* rather than alienating.

—Mason Klein

Vito Acconci's reputation as a primary interdisciplinary, conceptual artist rose to prominence in the 1970s for such provocative performances as *Seed Bed* (1971), *Pornography in the Classroom,* 1975, and *Where Are We Now...* (1976), along with a spectrum of other irascible works. Acconci remains today a resilient, inventive artist who perseveres in reformulating the definition of art and art making beyond something to look at. His work cannot be conveniently typed because of its metamorphosed nature, spanning fantasy to political statement. Throughout Acconci's oeuvre his ideas emanate in many media—performance, installation, architectural collaboration, and public art. While his art has taken many turns over the past twenty years, from what he refers to as a ''me aesthetic,'' to a public concern, Acconci continues to make demands on his viewer. Never can his audience be a passive viewer; instead they must always engage in the work presented in order to complete the experience. What remains a constant in his artistic production is his persistence in manipulating visitor's psychological senses and their physical sensations of space, or of the specific site itself. Moreover, Acconci predicates that visual form and mental formulation are inextricably linked.

Acconci in the 1980s produced clever constructions incorporating text and some elements of theatrical performance, as well as designed outdoor public site works and designed proposals for public gardens and parks. During this period he introduced his furniture/design/sculpture forms, as well as turned his attention to architectural fabrication. In some work he transformed simple, ordinary objects into something other than what is implied through the employment of linguistic systems. The obvious meaning of a particular form became infused with non-conventional meanings that relate to elements in his personal vocabulary.

The ''Name Calling Chairs,'' produced from 1984–1990, were never intended to be read as mere props—they function as a type of alphabet to build basic language that conveys basic insults. In ''People's Wall'' (1985), the viewer confronts a multiplicity of body forms and shadows that activate a wall's surface—Acconci blurs the sense of self-importance and stresses a shared commonality among humankind.

Since the mid-1980s Acconci's work evinces his development of a theory for public art and space that transcends convention and rebels against acceptable norms about public art. His interest in getting art into real space can be traced back to his 1969 performances ''Street Works I, II, and III.'' The mid-career survey exhibition *Vito Acconci: Public Spaces,* at the Museum of Modern Art, 1998, attended to a series of dramatic public site project proposals, including *Face of the Earth, House of Cars, and Bad Dream House.*

His shift away from producing a self-absorbed art toward public space and human relationships is pronounced. Since the late 1980s he has moved away from working as a solo artist—today he represents himself as Vito Acconci & Studio, collaborating with others on proposals for buildings and parks that aspire to assert their artistic authority and to celebrate a sense of individualism toward structure and space. He is fond of the concept of designing new public art environments—of creating energized environments that aim to provoke thought in order to destabilize cultural norms. Most of his proposals for communal projects entail peripheral spaces—facades of buildings, secluded sections of university campuses—or attempt to transcend a fictionalized reality of the day-to-day into something else by undoing the existing physical reality. His constructions are intended to surprise, invite discovery, and to interrupt society's visual habits of not seeing. An important theme throughout his work has been the specific cultural preconditions of the exhibition space.

Several key permanent commissions include the Entrance for Shibuya Subway Station, Tokyo, Japan, 2000, a billboard for Breda Garbage Dump, Breda, The Netherlands, 1999, an Indoor Park for the Departures Terminal, Philadelphia Airport, 1998, a Plaza Design for the University of Illinois at Chicago, and *Land of Boats,* St. Aubin Park, Detroit, Michigan, 1991. He also has designed the seating and lighting for a transit corridor at the San Francisco Airport. Despite the humor, wit, and poetry evident in Vito Acconci's sculptural installations, a sense of pathos abounds—perhaps it is Acconci's dissatisfaction with norms and a need to subvert it that provokes his ideas about art and architecture and drives him to ever peel away at entrenched perceptions.

—Elaine A. King

ADAMI, Valerio (Romani)

Nationality: Italian. **Born:** Bologna, 17 March 1935. **Education:** Studied painting, under A. Funi, at the Accademia de Brera, Milan, 1951–54. **Family:** Married Camilla Adami in 1962. **Career:** Independent painter and graphic artist since 1955, working in Milan, 1955–61, in London, 1957, 1961–62, and in Arona, Italy, since 1961, and in Paris 1962, 1963, 1964. **Agent:** Galerie Lelong, 13 rue de Teheran, 75008 Paris, France. **Address:** Villa Cantoni, via San Carlos 56, 28041 Arona, Italy.

Individual Exhibitions:

1958 Galleria San Fedele, Milan
1959 Galleria del Naviglio, Milan
1960 Galerie Art Bremen, Bremen, Germany
1961 Galleria L'Attico, Rome
Salone Annunciata, Milan
1962 Institute of Contemporary Arts, London
1963 *Disegni e Parole,* Galleria del Naviglio, Milan
1964 Galleria del Cavallino, Venice
1965 Galeria Ad Libitum, Antwerp
Galleria Schwarz/Studio Marconi, Milan
Galleria L'Attico, Rome
1966 Galleria Il Punto, Turin
Galerie Aujourd'hui, Brussels
Galleria Schwarz/Studio Marconi, Milan
1967 Studio Marconi, Milan
Galleria L'Attico, Rome

Gallerie Aujourd'hui, Brussels
Galleria Schwarz/Studio Marconi, Milan
1968 Institute of Contemporary Art, Boston
Deson Gallery, Chicago
Fondacion Mendoza, Caracas
Privacy, Galerie B. Mommaton, Paris
Galerie Withofs, Brussels
Institute of Contemporary Arts, London
1969 Museo de Bellas Artes, Caracas
Galleria Schwarz, Milan
Studio Marconi, Milan
Galerie Withofs, Brussels
1970 Hansen Gallery, San Francisco
Musée d'Art Moderne de la Ville, Paris
Kunstverein, Ulm, Germany
Galerie Maeght, Paris
62 Elsworthy Road, London
Galerie Wunsche, Bonn
Studio Marconi, Milan
1971 Museo de Bellas Artes, Caracas
1972 Galerie Schmela, Dusseldorf
Galerie Maeght, Zurich
Galleri Lowenadler, Stockholm
Galerie Maeght, Paris
Galerie Wunsche, Bonn
1973 Galerie Jacqueline Storme, Lille, France
Kunstverein, Hamburg
Galerie Maeght, Paris
Galerie Wunsche, Hamburg
1974 University of Wisconsin, Madison
1975 Bijou Galerie, Grenoble, France
Galerie Karl Flinker, Paris
Galerie Maeght, Paris
1976 Galerie Jacqueline Storme, Lille, France
Centre d'Arts Plastiques Contemporains, Bordeaux
Pinturas, Dibuixos, Aquarelles 1970–1975, Galeria Maeght, Barcelona
Galerie Maeght, Paris
Galerie Maeght, Zurich
1977 Musée Cantini, Marseilles
1978 Palais des Beaux-Arts, Charleroi, Belgium
Abbaye de Fontevraud, France
Galerie Maeght, Zurich
1980 Musée de Grenoble, France
1981 Galerie Maeght, Zurich
Judith Posner Gallery, Milwaukee, Wisconsin
1982 Lens Fine Art, Antwerp
Centre d'Animation Culturelle, Mulhouse, France
Galleria Stamparte, Bologna, Italy
1983 Galleria Giulia, Rome
Galerie Maeght, Paris
Fuji Television Gallery, Tokyo
Goldman Kraft Gallery, Chicago
1984 Marisa del Re Gallery, New York
Galeria Alencon, Madrid
Museo de Bellas Artes de Asturias, Oviedo, Spain
1985 Musée de la Ville, Vitry, France
Galerie Il Punto, Monte Carlo
Centre Georges Pompidou, Paris
Palazzo Reale, Milan
Galerie Les Cordeliers, Chateauroux, France
Galerie A.C.A.P., Le Touquet, France
1988 Galerie Lelong, Paris
1990 Marisa del Re Gallery, New York
1991 Galerie Man, Paris
Galerie Lelond, Paris
IVAM Centre Julio Gonzalez, Valencia
1992 Marisa del Re Gallery, New York

Selected Group Exhibitions:

1956 *Premio Marzotto,* Milan
1959 *Possibilita di Relazione,* Galleria L'Attico, Rome
1960 *Young Italian Painters,* Museum of Kamakura, Japan
1962 *Italian New Figurative Painters,* Piccadilly Gallery, London
1969 *Maler und Modell,* Staatliche Kunsthalle, Baden-Baden, Germany
1971 *Radical Realists,* D. M. Gallery, London
1977 *La Traccia del Racconto,* Villa Comunale Ormond, Sanremo, Italy
1982 *Arte Italiana 1960–82,* Hayward Gallery, London
1983 *Bonjour Monsieur Manet,* Centre Georges Pompidou, Paris
1985 *Il Cinema,* Galleria Gastaldelli, Milan
1992 *The Neopolitan Grimace: 30 Italian Artists from Paris,* Musee-Galerie de la Seita, Paris
1996 *Black is a Color,* Galerie Maeght, Barcelona

Collections:

Galleria d'Arte Moderna, Milan; Musée National d'Art Moderne, Paris; Kunstverein, Ulm, Germany; Museo de Bellas Artes, Caracas; Rhode Island School of Design, Providence.

Publications:

By ADAMI: Book—*Dix Lecons sur le Reich,* with Helmut Heissenbuttel, Munich and Paris 1974. **Film—***Vacances dans le Desert,* with Giancarlo Adami, 1970. **Record—***Concerto per un quadro di Adami,* with Henry Martin, 1970.

On ADAMI: Books—*Valerio Adami: Disegni e parole,* exhibition catalog with text by Enrico Crispolti, Milan 1963; *Le Pop Art* by Enrico Crispolti, Milan 1966; *Painting in the 20th Century* by Werner Haftmann, New York 1967; *Art of Our Time* by Will Grohmann, London 1967; *Pop Art* by Lucy R. Lippard, London 1967; *Righe per Adami* by Carlos Fuentes, Venice 1968; *Adami: Privacy,* exhibition catalog with text by Gerald Gassiot-Talabot and Henry Martin, Paris 1968; *Adami,* exhibition catalog with text by Carlos Franqui, Milan 1969; *Adami,* exhibition catalog with texts by Pierre Gaudibert, Henry Martin, Carlos Fuentes and others, Paris 1970; *Art Without Boundaries 1950–1970,* edited by Gerald Wood, Philip Thompson and John Williams, London 1972; *Valerio Adami,* exhibition catalog with texts by Hans Gerd Tuchel, Castor Seibel and Jacques Dupin, Hamburg 1973; *Adami* by Hubert Damisch and Henry Martin, Paris 1974; *Adami: Pinturas, dibuixos, aquarelles 1970–1975,* exhibition catalog with text by Xavier Rubert de Ventos, Barcelona 1976; *Valerio Adami,* exhibition catalog with text by Nicolas and Elena Calas, Charleroi, Belgium 1978; *Valerio Adami,* exhibition catalog with text by Italo Calvino, Zurich 1981; *Valerio Adami,* exhibition catalog with text by Pietro Bonfiglioli, Bologna 1982; *Adami, presence contemporaine,* exhibition catalog with texts by Nicolas and Elena Calas, Marc Le Bot and others, Aix-en-Provence, France 1984; *Adami,* exhibition catalog, Valencia 1990; *Valerio Adami,* exhibition catalog, New York 1990; *Valerio Adami: Aquatinta-Radierungen* by Octavio Paz and Hanns Theodor Flemming, Offenbach am Main 1992.

* * *

Arturo Schwarz of Milan lists Valerio Adami as one of the top international avant-garde. He is certainly crisp in the Pop Art sense of the world, but he is also blessed with a tight ingredient of irony which slots comfortably into his unusual dislocated imagery. His flat colours vary between primaries and interesting tints, and generally every colour has a black edge to it.

Adami, armed with his personal style, is able to make wry comments upon sex and eroticism, intellectualism, psychology, social conditions, and art itself (as for instance in the ''Surrealist Map of the World,'' 1972). What change there has been in his works has been a gradual drift from curious abstractions to a more formal figuration which began to take place in the late 1960s. Yet although the figuration may become steadily more and more recognizable to the unsophisticated eye, the colours continue their wayward direction; the woodwork or metal of a chair can be white, but the upholstery is straight green, the cushion red. It all sounds normal enough, but the talent of Adami transforms the three into the abstract colours of a flag or a trademark. These colours are bright, never gaudy; their message is immediate, magnetic.

In very different moods this painter has things in common with two such disparate artists as Jean-Pierre Raynaud and Tom Wesselmann. In his jigsaw-styled interiors he sometimes introduces bourgeois fixtures that Raynaud might employ as adjuncts for his ''objects'' (one thinks of the lavatory—impersonalised by Raynaud, but sharply ludicrous in an Adami painting) or that Wesselmann interpolates into his visions of ''the American way-of-life.'' Of course the climates in the works of all three artists are entirely different but, just because their imagery can overlap at times, they can, however disconnected, be seen to belong to their own special era.

—Sheldon Williams

ADAMS, Dennis

Nationality: American. **Born:** Des Moines, Iowa, 15 November 1948. **Education:** Drake University, Des Moines, Iowa, B.F.A., 1969; Tyler School of Art, Philadelphia, Pennsylvania, M.F.A., 1971. **Family:** Sons: Todd and Jack. **Career:** Visiting artist, Copper Union, New York, 1988, 1991, 1995–96; visiting professor, Ecole Nationale Supérieure des Beaux-Arts, Paris, 1992, and Akademie der Bilden Künste, Munich, 1993–94; graduate advisor, Parsons School of Design, New York, 1990–2000; project advisor, Rijksakademie van Beddende Kunsten, Amsterdam, 1992—; director, visual arts program, Massachusetts Institute of Technology, Cambridge, Massachusetts, 1997—. **Awards:** Individual Artist Fellowship Grant, National Endowment for the Arts, 1984, 1988, 1995; Manhattan Borough President's Award for Excellence in the Arts, New York, 1986; DAAD Fellowship, Berliner Künstlerprogramm, 1989. **Agents:** Kent Gallery, 67 Prince Street, New York, New York 10012; Galerie Gabrielle Maubrie, 24 Rue Sainte Croix de la Bretonnerie, 75004 Paris; Lumen Travo, Lijnbaansgracht 314 1017 W2 Amsterdam. **Address:** 42 Walker Street, New York, New York 10013.

Individual Exhibitions:

1971 Philadelphia Art Alliance, Philadelphia, Pennsylvania
1972 Akron Art Institute, Akron, Ohio
1974 Carl Solway Gallery, Cincinnati
1979 Artists Space, New York
1980 California State University, Long Beach
Miami University, Oxford, Ohio
1984 The Kitchen, New York
1987 Alternative Museum, New York (catalog)
1988 The Clocktower, New York
1990 Hirshhorn Museum and Sculpture Garden, Smithsonian Institution, Washington, D.C. (catalog)
1991 Museum of Modern Art, New York
1993 Portikus, Frankfurt
1994 Museum van Hedendaagse Antwerpen, Antwerp (catalog)
Contemporary Arts Museum, Houston, Texas (catalog)
1995 Stroom, The Hague, Amsterdam (catalog)
1996 Queens Museum of Art, New York
1999 Museum of Contemporary Art, Zagreb, Yugoslavia (catalog)
2000 13 Quai Voltaire, Caisse des Depots et Consignations, Paris

Group Exhibitions:

1974 *American Painting and Sculpture Today,* Contemporary Arts Center, Cincinnati
1978 *Artwords and Bookworks,* Los Angeles Institute of Contemporary Art, Los Angeles
1979 *Reality of Illusion,* Denver Art Museum, Colorado (toured)
1981 *Libres d'Artista/Artists' Books,* Metronom, Barcelona
1984 *Metamanhattan,* Whitney Museum of American Art Downtown, New York
1987 *Dennis Adams, Tony Brown, Dan Graham, Rodney Graham,* De Appel Foundation, Amsterdam
1989 *The Photography of Invention: American Pictures of the 1980s,* National Museum of American Art, Smithsonian Institution, Washington, D.C. (traveled to Museum of Contemporary Art, Chicago; Walker Art Center, Minneapolis) (catalog)
Magiciens de la Terre, Musée National d'Art Moderne, Centre Georges Pompidou (traveled to La Grande Halle, Parc La Villette, Paris) (catalog)
1990 *Passages de l'Image,* Musée National d'Art Moderne, Centre Georges Pompidou, Paris (traveled to Fundació Caixa de Pensions, Barcelona; Wexner Art Center, Columbus, Ohio; San Francisco Museum of Modern Art, San Francisco, California) (catalog)
1992 *The Power of the City/The City of Power,* Whitney Museum of American Art Downtown, New York (catalog)
1993 *Images Pour la Lutte Contre le Sida,* Musée National d'Art Moderne, Centre Georges Pompidou, Paris (catalog)
1995 *Semblances,* Museum of Modern Art, New York

Dennis Adams: *Outtake* (video still) 1998. ©Dennis Adams.

1998 *Do All Oceans Have Walls?,* Gesselschaft fur Aktuelle Kunst, Bremen, Germany
1999 *Stimuli,* Witte de With, Rotterdam, The Netherlands
2000 *Open Ends/One Thing After Another,* Museum of Modern Art, New York
Whitney Biennial, Whitney Museum of American Art, New York

Collections:

Centre National d'Art Contemporain, Paris; Fonds National d'Art Contemporain, Paris; Gemäldegalerie, Staatliche Museen Preussischer Kulturbesitz, Berlin; Israel Museum, Jerusalem; Musée d'Art Moderne et Contemporain, Geneva; Museum of Modern Art, New York; Muzej Suvremene Umjetnosti, Zagreb; Walker Art Center, Minneapolis, Minnesota; Whitney Museum of American Art, New York.

Public Installations:

Patricia Hearst—A Second Reading, 10 windows on Eighth Avenue, New York 1978; *Bus Shelter IV,* Domplatz, Münster, Germany 1987; *Public Commands/Other Voices,* Martin Luther King Jr. Metrorail Station, Miami, Florida 1988; *Reworking,* multiple urban sites, Geneva 1988; *The Procession,* La Grande Arche, La Défense, Paris 1989; *Ticket Booth,* Lobby, Whitney Museum of American Art, New York 1989; *Una Vez,* Plaza del Generalisimo, Úbeda, Spain 1992; *Coda,* Schiphol Airport, Amsterdam 1995; *Outtake,* Berlin 1998; *Tribüne,* Neue Messe München, Munich 2000.

Publications:

By ADAMS: Books—*Behind Social Studies,* New York 1977. **Articles**—''An Interview with Dennis Adams'' by Larry Rindner in *Artpaper,* May 1988; ''The Critical Frame'' in *Art in America,* April 1990; ''Interview with Dennis Adams,'' interview with Peter Doroshenko in *Journal of Contemporary Art,* Spring/Summer 1991; ''Public Discourse, Private Interests, and the Public Street'' with Eleanor Heartney in *Art Papers,* March/April 1992; ''Masquerade and Ambivalence'' in *Place-Position-Presentation-Public,* The Netherlands 1992; ''La Foundation Anon. . .'' in *L'observatoire,* no. 2, 1992; ''Markers: The Gender of Urban Space'' with Anna Novakov in *Nonspectacle and the Limitations of Popular Opinion,* symposium catalog, Northbrook, Illinois, 1993; ''Temporary Connections: A Conversation with Dennis Adams'' by Anna Novakov in *Public Art Review,* Spring-Summer 1994; ''Street Ventriloquist'' with Nada Beros in *Art Press,* December 1999.

On ADAMS: Books—*Special Effects: The Photographic Experience in Contemporary Art* by Gregorio Magnani, Daniela Salvioni, and Giorgio Verzotti, Milan 1989; *The Architecture of Amnesia,* New York 1990; *Port of View,* Marseille 1992; *Contemporary Public Sculpture: Tradition, Transformation, and Controversy* by Harriet F. Senie, New York 1992; *Dennis Adams/Selling History,* Houston 1994; *Dennis Adams: Transactions,* Antwerp 1994; Dennis Adams: 10 thru 20, The Hague 1995; *Art Goes Public/Von der Gruppenausstellung im Freien zum Projekt im Nichtinstitutionellen Raum* by Claudia Büttner, Munich 1997; *Dennis Adams: Takedown,* Zagreb 1999; *Light Boxes: Leuchtkastenkunst* by Stephan Trescher, Nürnberg, Germany 1999. **Articles—**''Second Generation Post-Photography'' by Gregorio Magnani in *Flash Art,* March/April 1988; ''Politiques de l'Image'' by Régis Durand in *Beaux Arts,* January 1989; ''When Worlds Collide'' by David Deitcher in *Art in America,* February 1990; ''Von der Dunklen Höhle zur Hellen Kammer/From the Dark Cave to the Camera Lucida'' by Werner Fenz in *Camera Austria,* no. 41, 1992; ''Dennis Adams: Trans/Actions'' by Jochen Becker in *Kunstforum,* October-December 1994; ''Light Construction'' by Sandy Heck in *Architectural Review,* 1995; ''Sculpture's in the Public Sphere'' by Maureen Sherlock in *Sculpture Magazine,* April 1998.

* * *

Dennis Adams caught the attention of the New York art world almost twenty years ago with several bus shelters he constructed and situated throughout the city. ''Bus Shelter I'' (1983), located at Broadway and 66th Street, was equipped with a light-box that displayed a photograph of Auschwitz survivors coupled with the text ''Your invisibility is obscene.'' Subsequently, this same shelter contained an image of the McCarthy HUAC hearings paired with the words ''Invisibility is your revenge.'' Since the early 1980s, Adams' work has been concerned with the intersection between public space and historical memory. His installations, which often utilize street furniture, are tactical interventions intended to provoke a reinterpretation of social and political history.

Adams' work fits into a broader public art movement—including artists Vito Acconci, Hans Haacke, Alfredo Jaar, Antoni Muntadas, and Krzysztof Wodiczko—which is ideologically descended from the Situationist International group active in Europe during the late 1950s and 1960s. Although Dennis Adams is an American artist living in New York, his public projects, in addition to his more than fifty gallery and museum exhibitions, have been executed predominantly in the urban centers of Europe, such as Munich, Geneva, Paris, and Frankfurt. It is perhaps this position as a perpetual visitor or outsider that has fed some of his best work. He is an artist who, upon coming to a new city, methodically researches the history of its sites as a way of excavating the layers of memory embedded in the built environment. He unmasks public places by laying bare their historical references hidden within the spectacle of the present day.

The construction of architectural armatures that hold and re-present historical photographs dominates Adams' installations. The photographs are often appropriated historical documents which are enlarged and inserted into the architectural armatures built to house them. By isolating these images, he is able to locate them as cultural triggers intended for the eyes of the passersby. His appropriation of photographic images has emerged from an interest in mass-media as the dominant cultural language. Working within the space of the city, he uses urban discourse as a strategy for undermining the dominant, ubiquitous voice of commerce.

Recently, Adams has branched out into more performance-oriented work. In 1998, he completed ''Outtake'' a video/performance in which the artist distributed 416 stills from Ulrike Meinhof's film titled *Bambule* on the streets of Berlin. The distribution of the stills, which took two hours and sixteen minutes, was filmed by the artist with the use of a prosthetic device that secured the video camera to his arm.

In both recent and earlier works, Dennis Adams is most often concerned with issues of memory as a hidden or lost component of collective history. The subtleties of historical amnesia preoccupy his public installations as well as his gallery and museum production. This illusive mining of collective memory is the binder and strongest component of his diverse forms of production.

—Anna Novakov

AFRICANO, Nicholas

Nationality: American. **Born:** Kankakee, Illinois, in 1948. **Education:** Illinois State University, B.A. (English literature) 1970, M.A. (painting), 1974, M.F.A. (painting), 1975. **Address:** 601 Oglesby, Normal, Illinois 61761

Individual Exhibitions:

1976 University of Illinois, Urbana
Nancy Lurie Gallery, Chicago
1977 Sheldon Memorial Art Gallery, University of Nebraska, Lincoln
Daddy's Old, Holly Solomon Gallery, New York
New Concepts Gallery, University of Iowa, Iowa City
Insulin, Holly Solomon Gallery, New York
University of Rhode Island, Kingston
Personal Information, Nancy Lurie Gallery, Chicago
1978 *The Man Who Lived in a Hat,* Walker Art Center, Minneapolis
1979 *The Battered Woman,* Holly Solomon Gallery, New York
Battered Woman Series, Mayor Gallery, London
Asher/Faure Gallery, Los Angeles
Galerie Farideh Cadot, Paris
1980 Holly Solomon Gallery, New York
Galerie 't Venster, Rotterdam
1981 *The Girl of the Golden West,* Holly Solomon Gallery, New York
Middendorf/Lane Gallery, Washington, D.C.
Asher/Faure Gallery, Los Angeles
1982 Dart Gallery, Chicago
Greenberg Gallery, St. Louis
1983 Asher/Faure Gallery, Los Angeles
1984 North Carolina Museum of Art, Raleigh
1985 Fuller/Goldeen Gallery, San Francisco
Dart Gallery, Chicago
1986 Holly Solomon Gallery, New York
1987 Cleveland Center for Contemporary Art, Ohio
Dart Gallery, Chicago
Fahey/Klein Gallery, Los Angeles
1988 Marilyn Butler Gallery, Scottsdale, Arizona

Nicolas C. Africano: *Untitled,* 2000. ©Nicolas C. Africano.

1989 East Carolina University, Greenville, North Carolina
Dart Gallery, Chicago
Linda Farris Gallery, Seattle
1990 Michael Lord Gallery, Milwaukee, Wisconsin
St. Olaf College, Northfield, Minnesota
Macalester College, St. Paul, Minnesota
Tweed Museum of Art, University of Minnesota, Duluth
Plains Art Museum, Moorhead, Minnesota
Jan Weiner Gallery, Kansas City, Missouri
Galerie Susan Wyss, Zurich
1991 The Lannan Foundation, Los Angeles
The Contemporary Museum, Honolulu
Madison Arts Center, Madison, Wisconsin
Galerie Langer Fain, Paris
Holly Solomon Gallery, New York
Thomas Solomon's Garage, Los Angeles
Espace Art et Culture EBEL, Villa Hardoff, Basel, Switzerland
Michael Lord Gallery, Milwaukee, Wisconsin
1992 Holly Solomon Gallery, New York
1993 *New Paintings and Sculpture,* Holly Solomon Gallery, New York
*Lost Boy, Laughing Man: Paintings and Figurines from 1985–1986,*The Center for Visual Art, Illinois State University
1994 *Nicolas Africano: New Paintings and Drawings,* Galerie Blancpain/Stepczynski, Geneva
1995 *Portraits of Rebecca,* Michael H. Lord Gallery, Art Chicago 1995 at Navy Pier, Chicago
Portraits of Rebecca, Linda Farris Gallery, Seattle, Washington
Works on Paper 1988–1994, Jon Oulman Gallery, Minneapolis, Minnesota
1996 *Nicolas Africano: Recent Works,* Weinstein Gallery, Minneapolis
Two Sisters, A Work in Progress, Meyerson and Nowinski Art Associates, Seattle
Nicolas Africano: New Paintings and Sculpture, Irving Galleries, Palm Beach, Florida
1997 *Nicolas Africano: New Sculpture and Works on Paper,* Maya Polsky Gallery, Chicago
1998 *Nicolas Africano: New Paintings and Drawings,* Maya Polsky Gallery, Chicago
Nicolas Africano: New Paintings, Sculpture and Drawings, Meyerson and Nowinski Art Associates, Seattle
1999 *Nicolas Africano,* Weinstein Gallery, Minneapolis
Nicolas Africano, Allene LaPides Gallery, Santa Fe, New Mexico
2000 *Nicolas Africano, New Paintings, Sculpture and Drawings,* Winston-Wachter Fine Art, Seattle

Selected Group Exhibitions:

1977 *American Painting '75, '76, '77,* Sarah Lawrence College, Bronxville, New York (travelled to the Museum of the American Foundation for the Arts, Miami, and the Contemporary Arts Center, Cincinnati, Ohio)
1978 *Narration,* Institute of Contemporary Art, Boston
1979 *New Image Painting,* Whitney Museum, New York
1980 *The Pluralist Decade,* at the *Biennale,* Venice (toured Europe, 1980–81)
Chicago/Chicago, Contemporary Arts Center, Cincinnati, Ohio
1981 *Contemporary Drawings in Search of an Image,* University of California Art Museum, Santa Barbara
1982 *New York Now,* Kestner-Gesellschaft, Hannover
1984 *The Human Condition,* San Francisco Museum of Modern Art
1990 *Seoul International Arts Festival: Works on Mulberry Paper,* The National Museum of Contemporary Art, Seoul, South Korea
1991 *Pleasures and Terrors of Domestic Comfort,* The Museum of Modern Art, New York
1992 *American Figuration,* Henie-Onstad Art Centre, Hovikodden, Norway
1993 *8 American Artists: Africano, Byron, Katz, Longo, Mullican, Sherman, Salle, Warhol,* Galerie Bernd Kluser, Munich
1994 *Of the Human Condition: Hope and Despair at the End of the Century,* Spiral/Wacoal art Center, Japan

1995 *Altered and Irrational: Selections from the Permanent Collection,* Whitney Museum of American Art, New York
1996 *Art at the End of the 20th Century: Selections from the Whitney Museum of American Art,* Whitney Museum of American Art, New York
1997 *Selections from the Collection,* The Museum of Contemporary Art, New York
1998 *Drawings. . . ,* Meyerson and Nowinski Art Associates, Seattle
1999 *The Art of Craft: Works from the Saxe Collection,* M. H. deYoung Memorial Museum, San Francisco, California
2000 *Glass: A Celebration,* Nancy Hoffman Gallery, New York

Collections:

The Metropolitan Museum of Art, New York; Milwaukee Art Museum, Wisconsin; Museum of Contemporary Art, Chicago; Neuegalerie-Sammlung Ludwig, Aachen, Germany; Whitney Museum of Modern Art, New York; American Academy of Arts and Sciences, New York; Fine Arts Museum of San Francisco, California; Espace Art Et Culture EBEL, Basel, Switzerland.

Publications:

On AFRICANO: Exhibition catalogs—*Nicholas Africano: Paintings 1976–1983,* exhibition catalog with essay by Mitchell D. Kahan, Raleigh 1983; *Nicolas Africano: Two Sisters,* exhibition catalog by Lisa Lyons, Seattle 1997. **Articles—**''Nicholas Africano'' by Peter Frank in *The Village Voice* (New York), 7 November 1977; ''Nicholas Africano's Primitivism'' by Howard Singerman in *Artweek,* 29 September 1979; ''New York, New York: Nicholas Africano'' by Valentin Tatransky in *Flash Art,* March/April 1979; ''Rodney Ripps and Nicholas Africano'' by John Russell in the *New York Times,* 16 May 1980; ''Nicholas Parables'' by Joan Hugo in *Artweek,* 16 May 1981; ''Nicholas Africano'' by Alan G. Artner in the *Chicago Tribune,* 12 February 1982; ''Africano's Ballet on Canvas'' by Benjamin Forger in the *Washington Post,* 10 November 1983; ''Nicolas Africano'' by Susan A. Harris in *Art in America,* November 1984; ''Nicolas Africano'' by Michael Brenson in the *New York Times,* 14 November 1986; ''Nicolas Africano at Holly Solomon'' by Holland Cotter in *Art in America,* March 1987; ''Nicolas Africano, Dart Gallery'' by James Yood in *Artforum,* September 1989; ''Nicolas Africano Explores the Melding of Innocence and Experience'' by Michael Brenson in the *New York Times,* 3 May 1991; ''Africano's Strength Is Uncertainty'' by Lynn Andreoli Woods in *The Los Angeles Reader,* 8 February 1991; ''Sentiment Meant'' by Peter Schjeldahl in *The Village Voice,* 17 March 1992; ''Africano Stirs in Diverse Sources'' by Alan Artner in *Chicago Tribune,* 5 June 1992; ''Some of the Best in Recent Glass'' by Susanne K. Frantz in *New Glass,* February 1998; ''Art: Nicolas Africano'' by Mary Abbe in *Star Tribune,* 14 May 1999.

* * *

Nicholas Africano places one or two tiny figures, molded in lumpy bas-relief, close to center in large monochrome fields or sometimes directly on the wall. His pictorial methodology makes us draw closer to focus in on the mini-people who are unattractively lumpy and primitivizing and marked by a cartoony flavor relating them with the Chicago-based group ''The Hairy Who,'' particularly with Jim Nutt's bizarre and theatrical figures.

Africano's kind of ''knowing'' naivete and true grit encourages an attitude of uncomfortable empathy toward his intimately scaled object of attention, who is characteristically poised during a moment of tension, facing some basic psychological state with tentative indecision. The ambiguously portrayed drama borders on the narrative but is never quite elaborated on in specific terms. Trained as a writer, Africano wants to evade the formal element and concentrate on evoking meaning. The pictorial elements, however, are used quite effectively to lead to underlying content. Africano's uses of proportion and location place the figure at an introspective removal from the world at large, and his use of densely modeled form lends his figures a sense of physicality in their vulnerability. The primitivizing quality lies somewhere in between Africano's regard for the Italian primitives and for the cartoonist's satire. He starts, in fact, with a series of sketches like the frames of the cartoon format.

During the late 1970s, Africano produced a number of works in the autobiographical vein, such as *Nicholas Waiting* (1976, oil, acrylic, wax, linoleum shelf), which concentrated on the bearded figure of the artist himself. His 1978 series, *Battered Woman,* moves away from the autobiographical, coming closer to a narrative of social implications. In a series of ten canvases, Africano portrays the dilemmas faced by the battered woman in question, who is going through a set of psycho-sociological situations with an aura of dread understandable to any sympathetic viewer. The fifth in the series, *The Door,* exemplifies Africano at his more effective moments. The miniaturized victim stands facing a simply rendered door, leading to the unknown, whether within or without. The moment of poignant vulnerability is captured with a rugged sensitivity which avoids sentimental melodrama successfully, though precariously.

Africano creates humane stage settings of a contemporary tragicomic order, locating himself on the borderline between the real and the surreal and on the fragile tightrope which aims at avoiding the literally illusionistic while realistically evoking the basic alienation felt by the young in today's society, whether they be artists or not. His is a youthful, quirky expression, and it remains to be seen how well it will serve in his future development.

—Barbara Cavaliere

AGAM, Yaacov

Nationality: Israeli. **Born:** Jacob (Yaacov) Gipstein in Rishon Letzion, Palestine, now Israel, 11 May 1928; adopted pseudonym ''Agam'' Paris, 1953. **Education:** Studied art at the Bezalel School, Jerusalem, 1947–48; at the Kunstgewerbeschule and the Eidgenossische Technische Hochschule, Zurich, 1949; and art at the Atelier d'Art Abstrait, Paris, 1951. **Family:** Married Clila Agam in 1956 (deceased); children: Ron, Orram and Orit. **Career:** Independent artist, in Paris, since 1951; first transformable paintings, 1951; first polyphonic paintings, 1953; first sound paintings, 1961; stainless steel sculptures, from 1968. Guest instructor, Illinois Institute of Technology, Chicago, 1961; visiting lecturer, Harvard University, Cambridge, Massachusetts 1968. **Awards:** Painting Prize, *International Festival of Painting,* Cagnes-sur-Mer, France 1971; Emunah Man of Vision award, 1985; Grand Prize, Artech International Biennial, Nagoya, Japan, 1989. Chevalier, 1974, and Commandeur, 1985,

Ordre des Arts et Lettres, France. **Address:** 26 rue Boulard, 75014 Paris, France.

Individual Exhibitions:

1953 Galerie Craven, Paris
1954 Galerie Fyrstenberg, Paris
1955 Doris Meltzer Gallery, New York
Galerie Denise René, Paris (with Soto)
1956 Galerie Denise René, Paris
1958 Galerie Aujourd'hui, Brussels
Tel-Aviv Museum
Galerie Denise René, Paris
1959 *Transformable Painting/Painting in Movement,* Drian Gallery, London
Galerie Suzanne Bollag, Zurich
Städtisches Museum, Leverkusen, Germany
1962 *Peinture Transformable, Peinture Polyphonique, Peinture et Mouvement,* Galerie Suzanne Bollag, Zurich
1966 Marlborough-Gerson Gallery, New York
1969 Whitechapel Art Gallery, London (with Lifshitz and Zaritzky)
1971 *Transformables,* Galerie Denise René, New York
1972 Musée d'Art Moderne, Paris (travelled to the Stedelijk Museum, Amsterdam, Städtisches Museum, Dusseldorf; and the Tel-Aviv Museum)
1975 *Selected Suites,* Jewish Museum, New York
1980 Guggenheim Museum, New York
Palm Springs Desert Museum
Liatowitsch Gallery, Basel
Queen Victoria Museum, Launceston, Tasmania
Burnie Art Gallery, Burnie, Tasmania
Ararat Art Gallery, Ararat, Australia
Undercroft Art Gallery, Perth, Australia
Caulfield Arts Centre, Caulfield, Australia
Ivan Dougherty Gallery, Sidney
Rockhampton Art Gallery, Rockhampton, Australia
1981 Circle Gallery, Chicago (travelled to San Diego, Denver, Seattle, and St. Louis)
1982 Circle Galleries, Pittsburgh and San Francisco
1983 Circle Galleries, New Orleans, Chicago, and Denver
1984 Circle Gallery, Miami Beach
Laurence Ross Galleries, Beverly Hills
Park West Galleries, Southfield, Michigan (retrospective)
1985 Queen's Quay Terminal, Toronto
Kansas City Gallery of Art
Circle Gallery, San Diego
1986 Los Angeles Art Fair
Image a memoire dynamique, FIAC and Galerie Denise Rene, Paris
1987 Kahala Fine Art Gallery, Honolulu
1988 Galerie Denise Rene, Paris
1989 Isetan Museum of Art, Tokyo (retrospective; travelled to Osaka and Kawasaki)
Gallery Art Point, Tokyo
1990 Gallery West, Los Angeles
Park West Gallery, Las Vegas
1991 Circle Galleries, Denver and San Diego
1992 Circle Fine Art Gallery
Tampa Museum of Art
Gallery Buschlen Mowatt, Vancouver
Galerie Denise Rene, Paris
1993 Jewish Community Center of Greater Palm Beach, Florida
Nogizaka Art Gallery, Tokyo
Jewish Community Center, Colombus, Ohio
Circle Gallery, Chicago
Jewish Community Center of Greater Kansas City
1994 South Florida Art Center, Miami Beach
Deutser Gallery, Houston
1995 Jewish Community Center Association, St. Louis
Kisa Gallery, Tokyo

Selected Group Exhibitions:

1954 *Salon des Réalités Nouvelles,* Musée d'Art Moderne, Paris
1958 *Carnegie International,* Carnegie Institute, Pittsburgh
1961 *Bewogen Beweging,* Stedelijk Museum, Amsterdam
1963 *7th Bienal,* Sao Paulo
1965 *The Responsive Eye,* Museum of Modern Art, New York
1967 *Art and Movement,* National Gallery of Canada, Ottawa (toured Canada)
1970 *International Festival of Painting,* Cagnes-sur-Mer, France
1972 *12 Ans d'Art Contemporain en France,* Grand Palais, Paris
1973 *The Non-Objective World 1914–1955,* Annely Juda Fine Art, London (travelled to the University of Texas, Austin)
1988 *LightsOROT,* Yeshiva University Museum, New York
1993 *Manifeste: Une Histoire Parallele,* Centre Georges Pompidou, Paris

Collections:

Centre Georges Pompidou, Paris; Kaiser-Wilhelm-Museum, Krefeld, Germany; Kunstmuseum, Dusseldorf; Julliard School, Lincoln Center, New York; Museum of Modern Art, New York; Metropolitan Museum, New York; Hirshhorn Museum, Washington, D.C.; Israel Museum, Jerusalem; Tel Aviv Museum.

Permanent Public Installations:

Sculptures: Cities of Paris, Jerusalem, Tel Aviv; New York, Frankfurt; Julliard School of Music, New York; University of Dijon; Mayo Clinic, Rochester, Minnesota; Hadassah Hospital, Jerusalem; Kennedy Airport, New York; Haidrah Rabahh Study Center, Jerusalem; Mondrian Hotel, Los Angeles; Tampa Museum of Fine Art. **Murals:** Harris Bank, Chicago; Tel Aviv Museum; Forum Leverkusen, Germany; Port Authority, New York; Mount Sinai Hospital, Los Angeles. **Fountains:** Dizengorf Square, Tel Aviv; Tampa Convention Center.

Publications:

By AGAM: Films—*Recherches et Inventions,* with I. Mambush, 1956; *Le Desert Chante, Microsalon,* with I. Mambush, 1957.

On AGAM: Books—*Agam: Transformable Painting/Painting in Movement,* exhibition catalog with texts by Michel Ragon and Eugene Kolb, London 1959; *Yaacov Agam: Peinture Transformable,*

Peinture Polyphonique, Peinture et Mouvement, exhibition folder with text by Siegfried Giedion, Zurich 1962; *Yaacov Agam* by Jasia Reichardt, London 1966; *Yaacov Agam,* exhibition catalog with texts by Haim Gamzu and Jasia Reichardt, New York 1966; *Neue Dimensionen der Plastik* by Udo Kultermann, Tübingen 1967; *New Tendencies in Art* by Aldo Pellegrini, London 1967; *Beyond Modern Sculpture* by Jack Burnham, New York 1968; *Origins and Development of Kinetic Art* by Frank Popper, London and New York 1968; *Movements in Art since 1945* by Edward Lucie Smith, London 1969; *Op Art* by Cyril Barrett, London 1969; *Yaacov Agam: Transformables,* exhibition catalog with texts by Haim Gamzu and Jean-Jacques Leveque, New York 1971; *Agam,* exhibition catalog with texts by Jean Leymarie, Blaise Gautier, Germain Viatte and others, Paris 1972; *Yaacov Agam: Peintures, Sculptures,* exhibition catalog with text by Haim Gamzu, Tel-Aviv 1973; *Yaacov Agam: Selected Suites,* exhibition catalog with text by Paul Kaniel, New York 1975; *Agam* by Frank Popper, New York 1976, 1980; *Yaacov Agam* by Günter Metken, London 1977; *Agam: Father of Kinetic Art,* exhibition catalog with texts by Michel Ragon and Frank Popper, Tokyo 1989; *Agam and Jewish Art* by Sayako Aragaki, Tokyo 1993. **Articles—** ''Agam'' by Luc Vezin in *Beaux Arts Magazine,* no. 64, January 1989; ''Agam Reconsidered'' by Avraham Ronen in *Ariel,* no. 103, 1996.

* * *

Agam is one of the pioneers of Kinetic Art and in particular of the trend which is concerned with the participation of the spectator. Having begun with paintings, reliefs, play objects and sculptures, he then experimented with the forces of light, air, water and fire before reaching a stage where his works are developed on the environmental scale, sometimes with the aid of the newest technological means.

But it is impossible to dissociate Agam's plastic achievements from the metaphysical implications of his research, his religious and his cosmological beliefs. Agam's search for the perceptible absence of the image, his demonstration of the irreversibility of time, and the simultaneity of significant happenings which can be found in most of his works have a biblical and epistemological origin.

All of Agam's works are ''transformable,'' since a time sequence is implicit in their structure. But this term is reserved by the artist himself for works in which the basis of transformation lies in the possibility of modifying the pictorial structure, a research begun back in the early 1950s which has given rise to a great number of statements ranging from ''polyphonic'' pictures destined for the interior or the exterior of private dwellings to environmental installations like the ''Salon de l'Elysée'' in Paris, ''Agam Space'' at the Forum in Leverkusen or the ''Aenaitral Tower'' and the ''Panoramagam'' created for the artist's one-man show at the Guggenheim Museum in New York in 1980. A series of multidimensional works, generally on the environmental scale, produced since 1985 consist in a superimposition of cylinders turning simultaneously backwards and forwards at different speeds in an attempt to go even beyond the fourth, the time, dimension. In these works, Agam is trying to create another reality made visible by their multiple metamorphoses. All these transformable pictorial statements imply the spectator's participation since their chromatic structures are revealed only through his movements.

However, the movable structures and play objects of the early 50s which preceded the Tactile works and which were followed by a great variety of small- and large-scale metal sculptures provoked a still more complete participation of the spectator who was induced to freely exercise his creative powers.

The multiplicity of the pursuits of Agam and the great diversity of his works can only be measured if one also mentions his graphics works and inventions, ranging from the single print to the holograph by way of multigraphs, polymorph graphics, interspaceographs, environmental graphics, prismographics, and video graphics. Agam's other achievements include constructions with artificial light, waterfire sculptures, monumental mixed media works such as the Fountain at the Défense complex near Paris and the one at the Dizengoff Square in Tel-Aviv, and incursions into other domains like the theatre as well as many pedagogical projects and technological experiments. Among the latter is a series of ''Visual Music Orchestrations,'' mobile, graphic and chromatic compositions permuted by computer and simultaneously broadcast on some fifteen video monitors. In these works the artist tries to test the spectator's visual capacities and to have him discover the entire recent past of optical and kinetic art by citations from other artists' plastic statements.

All these endeavours show clearly the tendency of Agam's thought: his entirely optimistic and dynamic interpretation and celebration of the force of life in art and his total faith in the participation of the public in the creative process.

—Frank Popper

AGNETTI, Vincenzo

Nationality: Italian. **Born:** Milan, 14 September 1926. **Education:** Academy of Dramatic Art, Milan; Liceo Artistico, Accademia di Brera, Milan. **Family:** Married Bruna Soletti in 1949 (divorced); daughter: Germana. **Career:** Worked as actor, Piccolo Teatro, Milan, 1949–51. Concentrated on ''informal painting,'' Milan, 1953–61; settled in Buenos Aires, 1961–67; returned to Milan, 1967–81; spent year in Rome, 1969–70; visited New York frequently, 1977–81. Lecturer in art, Accademia di Brera, Milan; guest lecturer, in art and architecture, universities of Rome, Milan and New York, 1974–81. **Award:** Premio Pascali, Rome, 1972. **Agent:** Bruna Soletti, Piazza S. Alesandro, 6 Milan. **Died:** Milan, 1 September 1981.

Individual Exhibitions:

1967	Pallazzo dei Diamanti, Ferrara, Italy
1968	Galleria Visualità, Milan
1971	Galleria La Tartaruga, Rome
1972	Galleria Lambert, Milan
	Galleria Martano, Turin
	Galleria Schema, Florence
	Galleria Toselli, Milan
1973	Galerie Annemarie Verna, Zurich
	Galleria Rumma, Naples
	San Fedele Teatro, Milan
	Galleria Marilena Bonomo, Bari, Italy
	Galleria Nazionale d'Arte Moderna, Rome
	Galleria Forma, Genoa
1974	Galleria Seconda Scala, Rome
	Bolaffi Arte, Turin

Galleria Alessandra Castelli, Bergamo, Italy
Museum am Ostwall, Dortmund, West Germany
Galleria Allesandra Castelli, Milan
1975 Ronald Feldman Fine Arts, New York
Studio Canaviello, Rome
Sonnabend Galerie, Paris
Art in Progress, Munich
1976 Galleria La Tartaruga, Rome
Mercato del Sale, Milan
1977 Israel Museum, Jerusalem
Studio Guiliana de Crescenzo, Rome
Galleria Civica d'Arte Moderna, Castello di Portofino, Italy
1978 Ronald Feldman Fine Arts, New York
Galerie Wintersberg, Cologne
Arta Studio, Milan
1979 Ronald Feldman Fine Arts, New York
Palazzo Grassi, Venice
1980 Ronald Feldman Fine Arts, New York
Galleria Toselli, Milan
Padiglione d'Arte Contemporanea, Milan
1981 Galleria Bruna Soletti, Milan
1982 Galleria d'Arte Moderna, Bologna
Galleria Il Luogo di Gauss, Milan

Selected Group Exhibitions:

1969 *Principia,* Historical Archives, Biennale, Venice
1970 *Vitality of the Negative,* Palazzo delle Esposizione, Rome
1972 *Documenta 5,* Kassel, Germany
1973 *Bienal,* Sao Paulo
1976 *Artists and Photograph,* Israel Museum, Jerusalem
1986 *Aspects of Italian Art 1960–85,* Kunstverein, Frankfurt

Collections:

Galleria Nazionale d'Arte Moderna, Rome; Galleria d'Arte Moderna, Parma, Italy; Raccolte Civiche d'Arte, Milan; Galleria d'Arte Moderna, Livorno, Italy; Galleria d'Arte Moderna, Cagliari, Italy.

Publications:

By AGNETTI: Books—*Intorno alla,* Milan 1967; *Obsoleto,* Milan 1967; *Rigoree Utopia,* Milan 1968; *Ciclostile,* Milan 1968; *Tesi,* Milan 1969; *Spazio perduto e Spazio Costruito,* Marcerata, Italy 1972; *Progetto per un Amieto Politico,* Genoa 1973; *Tradotto azzerato presentato,* Milan 1974; *Image of an Exhibition,* Milan and New York 1974; *Machiavelli 30,* Milan 1978; *Lettre dal Deserto,* Milan 1981. **Articles—**''Intervento'' in *Tavole di Accertamento* by Piero Manzoni, Milan 1958; ''Intervento'' in *Linea* by Piero Manzoni, Milan 1959; ''Non commettere atti Impuri'' in *Azimuth* (Milan), 1959; ''Indulgentia'' in *Nuova Corrente* (Milan), March 1968; ''Copia dal Vero Numero Primo'' in *Domus* (Milan), nos. 495–498, 1971; ''Utopia'' in *Ricerca Contemporanea* (Milan), nos. 1–3, 1971; ''High Fidelity'' in *Documenta 5,* exhibition catalog, Kassel, Germany 1972; interview with Mario Peruzzi in *Corriere della Sera* (Milan), February 1972; **Video—***Vobulazione e Bioloquenza: NEG,* with G. Colombo, 1970; *Documentario No. 2,* Centro Diffusione Grafica, Florence 1973; *Machiavelli 30,* with Licitra, Roselli and Pagano, 1978.

On AGNETTI: Books—*Manzoni* by Germano Celant, Rome 1971; *Territorio Magico* by Achille Bonita Oliva, Florence 1972. **Articles—** Tommasso Trini and Pierre Restany in *Domus* (Milan), February 1973; ''The Why of Things and Gestures'' by Jane Bell in *Arts Magazine* (New York), October 1974; ''Arte e Critica dopo l'Avanguardia'' by Maurizio Calvesi in *Corriere della Sera* (Milan), February 1975; ''Torniami alle Armi'' by Pierre Restany in *Vincenzo Agnetti,* exhibition catalog, Bologna 1982.

* * *

Milanese conceptual artist Vincenzo Agnetti emerged from a thoroughly European tradition, that which finds its roots in the image of the ''Renaissance Man.'' Agnetti's studies in film, theater, philosophy, and applied engineering not only weave in and out of his work as esoteric references, but also serve as a solid foundation for his complex *oeuvre,* both visual and linguistic. This ''intervention'' (i.e., conscious interdisciplinary approach to an entire system) was from the beginning crucial to his work, although in no way can he be dismissed as another ''multimedia'' artist. Only by understanding this precept can the work be at all accessible.

There are certain obvious parallels to other artists using the conceptual mode; like *Art-Language,* Agnetti used verbal structures; like Hanna Darboven, he based a good deal of his work on numerical anti-systems; and, like Beuys, whom he most closely resembles, he used the tape-recorded dialogue format. But he attempted to carry the conceptual premise further still, away from tautologies and freedom from (or negation of) content. In his 1975 New York exhibition he demonstrated post-Duchampian irony combined with a serious investigation of perceptual distortions, primarily of time and space. His work is as complex, although less formal and more free-wheeling, as that of his conceptual colleagues. What concerns him, in such works as ''Herewith I Transmit a 30-Minute Tape Recording,'' ''Architectural Translated for all the Peoples of the World,'' and ''1870–1974,'' is a quest for anti-meaning, a meaning which transcends that of pure gesture, into a fundamentally eccentric world of paradox and imaginative constructs. The disciplines that he chose (whether electronic, photographic, or apparently mathematical) became catalytic tools, replacing, as he said himself, ''the how it is done'' by ''the why it is done.'' Apparently analytic in method, Agnetti's work is not, in fact, analytical in intent. It differs also from other conceptual work in the fact that it is not hermetic; it is not only unselfconscious, but rarely self-absorbed. What concerned him is the *behavior* of phenomena and mental processes themselves.

Much of the value in Agnetti's investigations, perhaps best exemplified by ''A's Median Age,'' a ''translation'' of a woman's face taken from photographs from different stages of her life culminating in a composite, very nearly ideational construct, lies in his critical and even admittedly prejudiced approach to his subjects. The work is in the nature of speculation, as a search for conclusions, even if he would occasionally perform an entirely unexpected about-face and negate those same conclusions; this method is used to great effect in his ''Architecture Translated for all the Peoples in the World,'' in which his final conclusion (after an impeccably, apparently inevitably reached solution) negates his initial premise.

Agnetti's *oeuvre* is thus a combination of rigorous but potentially pliable thought and an intuitively formal elegance, concerned with the whole culture, and not simply with the strictly visual arts. As he wrote in 1974, ''I am only an intuitive creator of signs who makes paintings out of philosophy by searching out shape and design in the dialogue, by looking for forms in the culture that has crystallized our common experience.'' It is this common experience, or what Henry Martin has termed the ''universalization of culture and experience,'' that underscores the importance of Agnetti's ironic speculations.

—Jane Bell

AITKEN, Doug

Nationality: American. **Born:** Redondo Beach, California. **Education:** Studied at Marymount College, Palos Verdes, California, 1986–87; Art Center College of Design, Pasadena, California, B.F.A., 1991. **Career:** Independent photographer, filmmaker, and video and installation artist; has directed numerous music videos featured on MTV; lives and works in New York and Los Angeles. **Awards:** Premio Internazionale, 48th Venice Biennale, 1999 (for the installation *Electric Earth*). **Agent:** 303 Gallery, 525 West 22nd Street, New York, New York 10011.

Selected Individual Exhibitions:

1993 *Dawn,* AC Project Room, New York
1994 *Fury Eyes,* 303 Gallery, New York
Autumn, 303 Gallery, New York
I'd Die For You, Pasco Art Center, Holiday, Florida
1996 Taka Ishii Gallery, Tokyo
1997 *Diamond Sea,* 303 Gallery, New York
Cathouse, 303 Gallery, New York
1998 *Metallic Sleep,* Taka Ishii Gallery, Tokyo
2001 *Metallic Sleep,* Kunstmuseum Wolfsburg, Germany
I Am In You, Kunst-Werke, Berlin

Selected Group Exhibitions:

1991 *Artworks/Artworkers,* AC Project Room, New York
1992 *Multiplicity,* Christopher Middendorf Gallery, Washington, D.C.
The Art Mall: A Social Space, New Museum of Contemporary Art, New York
Invitational 92, Stux Gallery, New York
1993 *Okay Behavior,* 303 Gallery, New York (catalog)
Outside Possibilities, Rushmore Estate, Rushmore, New York
Underlay, 15 Renwick St, New York
Doug Aitken and Robin Lowe, AC Project Room, New York
1994 *Life Size,* Centro per l'Arte Contemporanea Luigi Pecci, Museo d'Arte Contemporanea, Prato, Italy (catalog)
Audience 0.01, Flash Art Museum, Trevi, Italy (catalog)
New York, New York, Prague, Czech Republic
Out West and Back East, Santa Monica Museum of Art, California
1995 *La Belle et la Bête,* Musée d'art de la Ville de Paris (catalog)
The Image and The Object, Museo Laboratorio di arte Contemporanea, Rome; Universita Degli Studi di Roma, Rome
Telluride Film Festival, Colorado
1996 *Campo 6: The Spiral Village,* Galleria Civica D'Arte Moderne e Contemporanea, Turin, Italy; Bonnefanten Museum, Maastricht (catalog)
29'—0"/East, Kunstraum Vienna, Austria; Kunsthalle New York (catalog)
A/drift: Scenes from a Penetrable Culture, Bard Center for Curatorial Studies, Annandale-on-Hudson, New York
Intermission, Basilico Fine Arts, New York
1997 *1997 Whitney Biennial,* Whitney Museum of American Art, New York (catalog)
2000 *2000 Whitney Biennial,* Whitney Museum of American Art, New York (catalog)
Speed of Vision: On the Construction and Perception of Time in Video Art, Aldrich Museum of Contemporary Art, Ridgefield, Connecticut; Pittsburgh Center for the Arts (catalog)

Publications:

By AITKEN: Books—*Metallic Sleep,* Tokyo 1998. **Articles—**''A Thousand Words: Doug Aitken Talks About Electric Earth'' in *Artforum International,* May 2000.

On AITKEN: Articles—''10 Artists for the 90s'' by Jerry Saltz in *Art & Auction,* May 1993; ''Making Work Without Boundaries'' by Francesco Bonami in *Flash Art,* May-June 1998; ''Doug Aitken at 303'' by Nicole Krauss in *Art In America,* March 1999; ''Hollywood Installed in Cork Street'' by Louisa Buck in *The Art Newspaper* (London), October 1999; ''Doug Aitken: Immoral Video'' by David Hunt in *Art/Text,* November 1999-January 2000; ''Man in Motion'' by Amy Gerstler in *Los Angeles Magazine,* November 2000.

* * *

Doug Aitken is a film-maker, installation artist, photographer and sometime maker of music videos whose work concerns itself with the human interaction in the world of nature, both man-made and otherwise. His short films are reminiscent in form of the music videos that constitute his professional background. Similarly their emphasis is on enigmatic images and a disconnection from the narrative traditionally associated with film. Although these films have been shown at cinematic venues, his work is increasingly sited at museums as installation art and even as framed series of stills. The *New Yorker* has stated Aitken's work adds ''several new wrinkles to the already complicated relationship between fine art and entertainment.''

Much of Aitken's work surveys disenfranchised lands and places, a kind of moral nature documentary. Aitken sets a 1995 video piece *Monsoon* in Guyana at the previous site of a mass suicide. *Eraser* from 1998 is set in Montserrat a year after it has been leveled by a volcano eruption. Often these films are shown in a multi channel video installation to soundtracks which range from human speech to footsteps, wind, and electronic pulse. In *Diamond Sea* (1997), machines seek diamonds in the Namibian desert but otherwise man is absent. Such videos link landscape and human habitation without seeming to implicate the camera itself as the work of human artistry. The relationship of man to nature is an outward theme of Aitken's where the selectivity of the artist's eye is an unexamined component. In this way Aitken does follow, with however seemingly different technology, in the footsteps of traditional landscape painting presenting views purportedly through a disinterested, naive, or non-represented outlook.

Soundtracks are one tool that distinguishes Aitken's landscape from, say, Turner's. Although Aitken avoids using rock and pop music as a video format in his artwork, his content does make direct references to his former professional interests. For example *Hysteria* (1998) utilizes rock music audiences to underscore the title topic being addressed. In the *These restless minds* (1998) auctioneers provide the soundtrack to further visions of increasingly urbanized (though no less desolate) landscapes. Their sing-song cadence and the fact that that they are almost unintelligible unless understood in cultural context could make them almost a precursor of rap. *Electric Earth* (1999), shown at the Venice Biennial 1999, actually uses a rare narrator who informs the viewers, "A lot of times I dance so fast that I become what surrounds me." This may also be a comment on the relationship between camera, cinematographer, audience, and culture.

Aitken has recently authored a book *I am a Bullet: Scenes from an Accelerating Culture,* with Dean Kuipers. A collection of photographs and essays on acceleration in modern culture, the volume suggests less a new direction for Aitken than a continuation of his video and audio explorations. His interest in moral comment and the nature of disconnection holds greater sway than the dimensional, compositional or other formal aspects of the video experience.

—Merridawn Duckler

ALECHINSKY, Pierre

Nationality: Belgian. **Born:** Brussels, 19 October 1927. **Education:** Brussels, also studied clarinet there; studied book illustration and typography, at the Ecole Nationale Supérieure d'Architecture et des Arts Décoratifs, La Cambre, Brussels, 1944–48, and engraving, under S. W. Hayter, at Atelier 17, Paris 1952. **Family:** Married Michele (Micky) Dendal in 1949; sons: Ivan and Nicolas. **Career:** Painter, designer and illustrator, in Brussels, 1947–51, in Paris, since 1951; Teacher at École nationale de Beaux-Arts, Paris, 1983–87. **Awards:** Prix Helene Jacquet, La Louvière, 1950; Prix Jeune Peinture Belge, Brussels, 1950; Special Award, *Festival du Film d'Art,* Bergamo, Italy, 1957; Hallmark prize, New York, 1960; Diploma of Honour, *Festival of Cultural Film,* Tokyo, 1961; First prize, *Triennale de la Gravure en Belgique,* Brussels 1966; First prize, *Biennale Internationale de la Gravure,* Cracow 1966; Premio Marzotto, Valdagno, Italy, 1968; Andrew W. Mellon prize, Carnegie Institute, Pittsburgh, 1976; Herbert-Boeckl Prize, Salzburg, 1988. Honorary doctorate from Université libre de Bruxelles, 1996. **Member:** Jeune Peinture Belge group, Brussels, 1947–51; founder-member, Les Ateliers du Marais community studios, Brussels, 1949–51; founder-member, with Karel Appel, Corneille, Asger Jorn, Constant, Pedersen, etc., COBRA (Copenhagen-Brussels-Amsterdam) group, 1949–51. Committee member, *October Salon,* Paris 1953; organizer, *Autour de S. W. Hayter,* touring exhibition, Amsterdam, Brussels, Copenhagen and Florence, 1953; member, management committee, *Salon du Mai,* Paris, 1958–70; contributor, *Daily Bul,* La Louvière, Belgium, 1957, and *The Situationist Times* and *La Breche,* Paris 1963; Associate member, Académie royale de Belgique. **Agent:** Galerie LELONG, 13 rue de Téhéran, F-75008 Paris, France. **Address:** 6–8 rue Henri Barbusse, F-78380 Bougival, France.

Selected Individual Exhibitions:

1947 Galerie Lou Cosyn, Brussels
1948 Galerie Apollo, Brussels
1953 Kunsthandel Martinet, Amsterdam (with Shinkichi Tajiri)
1954 Galleria Schwarz, Milan
Galerie Nina Dausset, Paris
1955 Palais des Beaux-Arts, Brussels
Nabis Gallery, Tokyo
1956 Galerie du Dragon, Paris
1957 Galerie Espace, Haarlem, Netherlands
Galerie Aujourd'hui, Brussels
Galerie Michael Warren, Paris
1958 Institute of Contemporary Arts, London
1960 Galerie Benador, Geneva
1961 Carnegie Institute, Pittsburgh
Stedelijk Museum, Amsterdam (with Reinhoud; travelled to the Kunstkring, Rotterdam)
Galerie Van de Loo, Munich
1962 Galerie de France, Paris
Lefebre Gallery, New York
1963 Stedelijk Van Abbemuseum, Eindhoven, Netherlands
Librairie-Galerie La Hune, Paris
Stedelijk Museum, Amsterdam
Lefebre Gallery, New York
1964 Galerie Birch, Copenhagen
Galerie Espace, Amsterdam
Galleria Il Punto, Turin
Instituto Torcuato di Tella, Buenos Aires (with Reinhoud)
1965 Lefebre Gallery, New York
Arts Club of Chicago (travelled to University of Minnesota, Minneapolis; and the Jewish Museum, New York)
1966 Galerie de France, Paris
Stedelijk Museum, Amsterdam
Galleria La Medusa, Rome
1967 Museum of Fine Arts, Houston
Lefebre Gallery, New York
Librairie-Galerie La Hune, Paris
Galerie La Balance, Brussels
20 Jahre Impressionen, Galerie Van de Loo, Munich
1968 Galerie de France, Paris
Museum voor Schone Kunsten, Ghent
Staatliche Kunstgalerie, Bochum, West Germany (travelled to the Kunstverein, Freiburg)
Galerie Birch, Copenhagen
Lefebre Gallery, New York
Galleri Moderne, Silkeborg, Denmark
APIAW, Liège, Belgium
Kaleidoscoop Galerie, Ghent
1969 Palais des Beaux-Arts, Brussels
Louisiana Museum, Humlebaek, Denmark
Kunstverein, Desseldorf
Kunsthalle, Bremen, Germany
Galerie La Taille Douce, Brussels
International School, Brussels
Dom Galerie, Cologne
Nielsen Gallery, Boston
Galerie de Montreal
J. L. Hudson Gallery, Detroit

Pierre Alechinsky: *Central Park* 1964. Photo by Adam Rzepka. ©2001 Artists Rights Society (ARS), NY/ ADAGP, Paris.

1970 London Arts Gallery, London
Librairie-Galerie La Hune, Paris
Israel Museum, Jerusalem
Galleria Rotta, Milan
Lefebre Gallery, New York
Galerie Birch, Copenhagen
Chez Stephane Janssen, Brussels
1971 Galerie de France, Paris
Galleri Haaken, Oslo
Galerie Espace, Amsterdam
Galerie du Fleuve, Bordeaux
Lens Fine Art, Antwerp
Grand Rapids Art Museum, Michigan (with Reinhoud)
1972 Maison des Jeunes et de la Culture, Annecy, France (toured France)
Lefebre Gallery, New York
Galerie de l'Auditorium, Brussels
Galerie Benador, Geneva
Galerie in der Blutgasse, Vienna
Galleria San Sebastianello, Rome
1973 Lefebre Gallery, New York
Galerie de France, Paris
Galerie Birch, Copenhagen
Galleria del Milione, Milan
Palazzo Municipale, Asolo, Italy
Galerie Vega, Liège, Belgium
Galerie Stephane Janssen, Brussels
Librairie-Galerie La Hune, Paris
Lens Fine Art, Antwerp
Musée d'Art Moderne, Brussels
1974 Le Miroir d'Encre, Brussels
Galerie Espace, Amsterdam
Mathildenhoehe, Darmstadt (toured Europe)
1975 Galerie Birch, Copenhagen
Galeria Turner, Madrid
Galeria 42, Barcelona
Musée Cantini, Marseilles
Galerie Van de Loo, Munich
Galerie Stephane Janssen, Basel
Librairie-Galerie La Hune, Paris
Graphica Club, Milan
1976 Lefebre Gallery, New York
Maison de la Culture, Chalon-sur-Saône, France (toured Europe)
Galeria Aele, Madrid
Galerie Birch, Copenhagen
La Maison Bleue, Strasbourg
1977 Galerie Fleuve Trois, Bordeaux
Galeria Aele, Madrid
Herzog Galerie, Orleans, France
Galeria Ponce, Madrid
Halifax University, Nova Scotia
Le Miroir d'Encre, Brussels
Galerie de France, Paris (with Reinhoud)
Paintings and Writings, Carnegie Institute, Pittsburgh (retrospective; travelled to the Art Gallery of Ontario, Toronto)
Lens Fine Art, Antwerp
Lefebre Gallery, New York
Riis Gallery, Trondheim, Norway
Librairie-Galerie La Hune, Paris
1978 *Les Dessins d'Alechinsky,* Centre Georges Pompidou, Paris
Galerie de France, Paris (with Karel Appel; toured Europe)
Galerie Van de Loo, Munich (travelled to Galerie Rolf Ohse, Bremen)

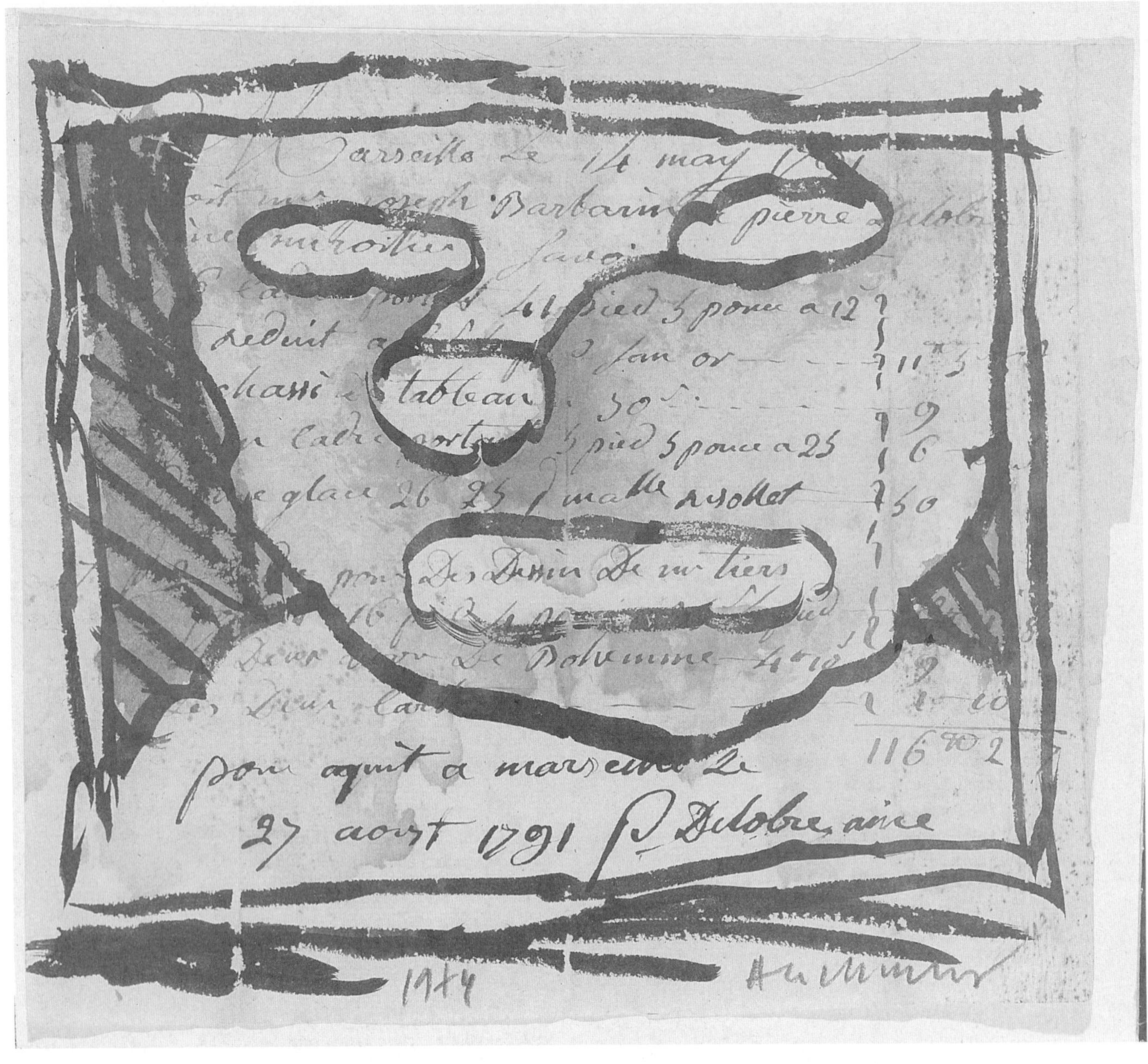

Pierre Alechinsky: *Facture honoree,* 1974. Photo by Jacqueline Hyde. ©2001 Artists Rights Society (ARS), NY/ADAGP, Paris.

1979 Lefebre Gallery, New York
Le Miroir d'Encre, Brussels
1980 Museo de Arte Moderno, Mexico City
Galerie Maeght, Paris
Galerie Maeght, Zurich
Kaneko Gallery, Tokyo
Kestner-Gesellschaft, Hannover (retrospective)
Museum of Modern Art, New York (print retrospective)
1981 Lefebre Gallery, New York
1982 Galerie Moderne, Silkeborg, Denmark
Galerie Birch, Copenhagen
1983 Galerie M, Hannover
1984 Kaneko Art Gallery, Tokyo
Lefebre Gallery, New York
Galerie Maeght Lelong, Paris
1985 Galerie Le Mejan, Arles, France
Galerie Birch, Copenhagen
Gand Gallery, Seoul, Korea
Musée d'Art et d'Histoire, Metz, France
Galerie Van de Loo, Munich
1986 Lefebre Gallery, New York
Artcurial, Paris
Galerie La Hune, Paris
Galerie Maeght Lelong, Paris
1987 Lefebre Gallery, New York
Isselbacher Gallery, New York
Guggenheim Museum, New York
1988 Musées Royaux des Beaux-Arts de Belgique, Art Moderne, Brussels
The Open Museum, Industrial Park, Tefen, Israel

Ecole des Beaux-Arts, Peking
2 RC Edizioni d'Arte, Milan
1989 Museo de Bellas Artes, Caracas
Galleri Gummesons, Stockholm
1990 Galerie André Emmerich, New York
Galerie La Hune, Paris
Galerij BBL, Antwerp
Musée Réattu, Arles, France
Galleri Faurschou, Copenhagen
1991 Rupertinum, Salzburg
Galerie Calligrammes, Ottawa, Canada
2 RC Edizioni d'Arte, Rome
1992 Galleria Stamparte, Bologne
Exposition Universelle, Seville
1993 Fine Art Museum, Taipei
Saarland Museum, Saarbrücken, Germany
1994 Silkeborg Kunstmuseum, Denmark
Galerie Lelong, Paris
1995 Shinsegae Hyundai Art, Seoul
Galerie Marika Marghescu, Hannover
1996 Instituto de Artes Graficas, Oaxaca, Mexico
Hayakawa Gallery, Osaka
1998 Galerie nationale du Jeu de Paume, Paris
Cabinet des Estampes du musée d'Art et d'Histoire, Geneva
1999 Museo de Arte Contemporaneo, Monterrey, Mexico
Bawag Foundation, Vienna
2000 IVAM, Centre Julio Gonzales, Valence, Spain

Selected Group Exhibitions:

1948 *Les Mains Eblouies,* Galerie Maeght, Paris
1949 *Cobra: 1st Exhibition of Experimental Art,* Stedelijk Museum, Amsterdam
1959 *European Art Today,* Minneapolis Institute of Art
1968 *Painting in France 1900–1967,* National Gallery of Art, Washington, D.C. (toured the United States)
1976 *Daily Bul & Co.,* Fondation Maeght, St. Paul de Vence, France (travelled to Studio du Passage 44, Brussels)
1978 *Cobra 1948–78,* Statens Museum for Konst, Copenhagen
1980 *L'Affiche en Belgique,* Musée d'Affiche, Paris
1983 *Informele Kunst 1945–60,* Rijksmuseum Twenthe, Enschede, Netherlands
1985 *Painterly Visions 1945–85,* Guggenheim Museum, New York
1987 *Galerie Espace 1956–86,* Galerie Espace, Amsterdam
30 Jahre Galerie van de Loo 30 Bildwerke, Galerie van de Loo, Munich
1989 *Epokha otkritij-iskousstvo XX viéka va Frantsii,* Musée Pouchkine, Moscow
1990 *Octavio Paz: los privilegios de la vista,* Centro cultural, Arte contemporaneo, Mexico
1993 *An Aspect of the Contemporary Art in Belgium,* Himeji City Museum of Art, Himeji, Japan
1995 *A Century of Artists Books,* Museum of Modern Art, New York
1997 *Flemish and Dutch Painting from Van Gogh, Ensor, Magritte, Mondrian to Contemporary Artists,* Palazzo Grassi, Venice
1998 *Schenkung Otto van de Loo Auf der Spur von Cobra,* Neue Nationalgalerie, Staatliche Museen, Berlin
2000 *Art-Worlds in Dialogue—From Gauguin to the Global Present,* Museum Ludwig, Cologne
Cobra: un art expérimental, Art Media, Hôtel Wielemans, Brussels

Collections:

Musées Royaux des Beaux-Arts de Belgique, Brussels; Centre Georges Pompidou, Paris; Stedelijk Museum, Amsterdam; Museum der Stadt, Darmstadt; Galleria Nazionale d'Arte Moderna, Rome; Guggenheim Museum, New York; Museum of Modern Art, New York; Carnegie Institute, Pittsburgh; Musée d'Art Contemporain, Montreal, Quebec; Israel Museum, Jerusalem.

Publications:

By ALECHINSKY: Books (and portfolios)—*Trades,* 9 etchings with text by Luc de Heusch, Brussels 1948; *Les Poupées de Dixmunde,* Brussels 1950; *Bites,* etchings portfolio, Milan 1962; *Titres et Pains Perdus,* Paris 1965; *Ideotraces,* Paris 1966; *Le Test du Titre,* Paris 1967; *Minutes,* Venice 1967; *Indivisible Prints,* with Arman, text by Joyce Mansour, London 1969; *Vulcanologies,* lithos portfolio, Paris 1970; *Roue Libre,* Geneva 1971; *L'Avenir de la Propriété,* Paris and Geneva 1972; *Les Estampes: Pierre Alechinsky 1946–1972,* Paris 1972; *Krach,* engravings portfolio, Paris 1973; *Au Fil du Bois,* woodcuts portfolio, Paris 1973; *Blindly,* etchings portfolio, Rome 1974; *Serpent,* engravings portfolio, Paris 1977; *Far Rockaway,* Montpellier 1977; *Monument Tobacco,* with text by Marcel and Gabriel Piqueray, Paris 1978; *Encres à Deux Pinceaux,* with Karel Appel, text by Hugo Claus, Paris 1978; *Papiers Traites,* 6 lithographs, Paris 1978; *La Vie comme Elle Tourne,* drawings portfolio with text by André Frenaud, Paris 1979; *Réponse à un questionnaire,* Caen 1987; *L'autre main,* Saint-Clément 1988; *Notes sur Orsay,* Caen 1987; *Dotremont et Cobra Forêt,* with excerpts from *La Cobraïde* by Christian Dotremont, Paris 1988; *À la maison de Balzac,* Saint-Clément 1989; *Plan sur la comète,* Paris 1992; *Baluchon et ricochets,* Paris; *La danse des petits pains,* Saint-Clément 1994; *Vadrouille lithographique,* Paris 1995; *Le jardin fragile,* with Jean Tardieu, Paris 1995; *Cobra et le Bassin parisien,* Paris, 1997; *La gamme d'Ensor,* Saint-Clément 1997. **Books illustrated**—*Le Sens des Tarots* by Marcel Lecomte, Brussels 1948; *Zonder Vorm van Proces* by Hugo Claus, Brussels 1950; *La Reine des Murs* by Christian Dotremont, Paris 1960; *Les Tireurs de Lange* by Amos Kenan, Turin 1961; *Moi Qui J'Avais* by Christian Dotremont, Paris 1961; *A la Gare* by Amos Kenan, Milan 1962; *One Cent Life* by Walasse Ting, Zurich 1964; *Carre Blanc* by Joyce Mansour, Paris 1965; *De la Mort* by Francois Nourisier, Brussels 1967; *Le Bleu des Fonds* by Joyce Mansour, Paris 1968; *Tourmente* by Michel Butor, with Bernard Dufour and Jacques Herold, Montpellier 1968; *Au Demeurant* by Achille Chavee, La Louvière, Belgium 1969; *Hoire-Voire* by Michel Butor, Milan 1970; *Pointes* by Louis Scutenaire, Paris 1972; *Laborinthe* by Jean-Clarence Lambert, Paris 1973; *Un Mannequin sur le Trottoir* by Roger Caillois, Paris 1974; *Reve de l'Ammonite* by Michel Butor, Montpellier 1975; *Par Experience* by Yves Bonnefoy, Paris 1976; *Vacillations* by A. M. Cloran, Montpellier 1980; *Carta Canta* by Jean Tardieu, Paris 1987; *Plier boutique* by Pierre-André Benoît, Alès 1979–87; *Chaque matin* by Eugène Ionesco, Paris 1988; *Traité des excitants modernes* by Honoré Balzac, Paris 1989; *Le Volturno* by Blaise Cendrars, Paris

1989; *Eclipses* by Jean Frémon, Paris 1990; *Flore Danoise* by Michel Sicard, Paris 1991; *Traversées* by Yves Bonnefoy, Paris 1991; *L'Innocence utile* by Jean Paulhan, Paris 1994; *Les trains psychiques* by Pierre Bettencourt, Paris 1994; *Plume* by Jean-Yves Bosseur, Arles 1995; *Zoek de zeven* by Hugo Claus, Antwerp 1995; *La Plenète Aréthuse* by Pierre Bettencourt, Paris 1996; *La légende de Novgorode* by Blaise Cendrars, Saint-Clément 1997; *Flores* by Michel Sicard, Paris 1998; *Odessa Mama* by Amos Kenan, Paris 1999. **Film—** *Japanese Calligraphy* with Francis Haar, Roger Blin and others, 1956.

On ALECHINSKY: Books—*The COBRA Library: Alechinsky* by Luc de Heusch, Copenhagen 1950; *Pierre Alechinsky: 20 Jahre Impressionen,* exhibition catalog, Munich 1967; *Alechinsky* by Jacques Putman, Milan and Paris 1967; *Alechinsky* by Alain Bosquet, Paris 1971; *Pierre Alechinsky,* exhibition catalog with text by Bernd Krimmel, Darmstadt 1974; *Kunstpocket no. 3: Alechinsky* by Freddy de Vree, Schelderode 1976; *Pierre Alechinsky: Paintings and Writings,* exhibition catalog with texts by Leon A. Arkus and Eugene Ionesco, Pittsburgh 1977; *Les Dessins d'Alechinsky,* exhibition catalog with text by Pierre Georgel, Paris 1978; *Pierre Alechinsky eine retrospektive,* exhibition catalog with text by Carl Haenlein, Hannover 1980; *Pierre Alechinsky: Bouches et Grilles,* exhibition catalog with essay by Pierre Descargues, Paris 1986; *Pierre Alechinsky: Margin and Centre,* exhibition catalog with texts by Michael Gibson and Octavio Paz, New York 1987; *Alechinsky, L'encrier volcan* by Jacques Dupin, Paris 1988; *Alechinsky sur Rhône* by Michel Sicard, Arles 1990; *Alechinsky, travaux d'impression* by Michel Butor and Michel Sicard, with preface by d'Antoine Coron, Paris 1992; *Alechinsky, Livres de Pierre* by Daniel Abadie, Paris 1994; *Alechinsky, Séquence, 1980–1992* by Michel Sicard, Paris 1994; *Alechinsky, entre les lignes* by Peter Handke, Jean Tadieu, Dr. E.-G. Güse and Marcelin Pleynet, P. A., Paris 1996; *Pierre Alechinsky, Labor de imprenta de 5 décadas* by Ivan Alechine, Robert Valerio, Octavio Paz and Patricia Sloane, P. A., Mexico 1997; *Le Grand Jeu de Pierre* by Paul Cox, Brussels 1997; *Alechinsky* by Alain Robbe-Grillet, Pierre Daix, John Yau and Daniel Abadie, Paris 1998; *Pierre Alechinsky, noir sur blanc, 1948–1997* by Rainer Michael Mason, Pierre-André Benoît and Yvon Taillandier, P. A., Geneva 1998; *Alechinsky* by Pierre Daix, Neuchâtel 1999; *Alechinsky, La brûlure de l'encre* by Jean Clair, Paris 1999. **Film—***Encre* by Jean Cleinge, with Pierre Alechinsky and Karel Appel, 1963; *Alechinsky d'après nature* by Luc de Heusch, 1970; *Dotremont-les-logogrammes* by Luc de Heusch, 1972; *Peter and Pierre* by Ole Henning Hansen, 1985; *Divertissement à la Maison de Balzac* by Pierre Coulibeuf, with Pierre Alechinsky and Michel Butor, 1989; *Alechinsky sur Rhône* by Pierre Coulibeuf, 1990; *Alechinsky, l'oeil du peintre* by Pierre Dumayet and Robert Bober, 1997.

* * *

A great debate has raged for years about what values training at an art school can bestow upon an artist in embryo. Sometimes the experience provides full knowledge of useful techniques, sometimes the bonus amounts to little more than the chance to take advantage of important contacts that will reduce the teething pains of starting an art career.

Pierre Alechinsky belongs to the first category. At the Ecole Nationale Supérieure d'Architecture et des Arts Décoratifs in Brussels he mastered "book illustration" which involves wide knowledge and experience of all kinds of graphic printing, including typography.

Today he is recognized as one of the prime graphic artists. As early as 1948 he was able to design a set of tarot cards for the Belgian surrealist Marcel Lecomte and he also made the pictures for "Les Metiers" by Luc de Heusch.

In Paris Alechinsky made contact with the surrealist movement through Max Ernst. He was also recognized by Dubuffet who saw in his works a flavour of *Art Brut.*

In 1949 he joined the COBRA group with Appel, Corneille, Constant, Dotremont, Jorn and Pedersen, and a few years later he went to work at S. W. Hayter's Atelier 17 in order to still further improve his graphic techniques. But perhaps the greatest influence he received came when he visited Japan (1955) and made a careful and professional study of the art of that country, particularly as it applied to the printed image and to calligraphy (about which he made a prize-winning film).

It is tempting to concentrate upon his graphic works because of his confident expertise in this wide field, but it should not be overlooked that Alechinsky is a good painter and an attractive collagist.

In all his works he retains his own version of COBRA imagery. Strange beasts, strange people, strange flowers; but he is also adept in the storytelling which inspires his own fantasy comicstrips—a genre he exploits both in his painting and in his prints. Good examples of this narrative painting are found in large canvases like "The Voyeur Seen," "Stars and Disasters" and "Central Park."

Whilst his colours are not those of Jorn or Appel, and certainly not those of Pedersen, they are rich with COBRA tints and toning. The rusts and cerulean blues are particularly appealing. But, as with every painting, there is always more than just the colour scheme. Alechinsky's imagery, whether solid or in line, has a rangy-ness that makes the eye restless, makes it search for inner meanings. The composition also arouses this tatters-in-the-wind sensation (when it is not volcanic). Even so, his early experience as an illustrator has given him a well-defined sense of balance.

—Sheldon Williams

ALLAIN, Rene Pierre

Nationality: Canadian. **Born:** Montreal in 1951. **Education:** Studied at Loyola University of Montreal, 1969–72; University of Ottawa, B.A., 1982; Hunter College, New York, M.F.A., 1986. **Career:** Painter; lives and works in Brooklyn, New York. **Awards:** National Endowment for the Arts fellowship; New York Foundation for the Arts fellowship; Canada Council grants; Ontario Arts Council grants.

Individual Exhibitions:

1981 *Depot Central,* Saw Gallery, Ottawa
1983 *Transformer Site,* Gallery 101, Ottawa
Works in Progress, Galerie De-La-Salle, Ottawa
1984 *The Core Island Complex,* London Regional Art Gallery, London, Ontario
1986 Hunter Gallery, New York
1989 Roger Ramsay Gallery, Chicago
Julian Pretto Gallery, New York
The Knitting Factory, New York

1990 Roger Ramsay Gallery, Chicago
Julian Pretto Gallery, New York
1991 Julian Pretto Gallery, New York
1992 Julian Pretto Gallery, New York
Samuel Lallonz Gallery, Montreal
1993 Genereux Grunwald Gallery, Toronto
Roger Ramsay Gallery, Toronto

Selected Group Exhibitions:

1984 *Present anterieur,* Museum of Contemporary Art, Montreal (travelled to nine cities)
1989 *War, Peace and Victory,* Memorial Arch, Grand Army Plaza, Brooklyn
1991 *Open Mind: The Le Witt Collection,* Wadsworth Atheneum, Hartford, Connecticut
Allain, Beall, Dean, Gallery Moos, Toronto
Abstract Painting: Process and Materials, Ben Shahan Gallery, William Patterson College, New Jersey Invitational, Berland/Hall, New York
1992 *Geometric Strategies,* Marilyn Pearl Gallery, New York
Painterly Object, S. Bitter-Larkin Gallery, New York
Slow Art: Painting in New York Now, P.S. 1 Museum, New York
1993 *Abstraction: Which Way From Here?,* University of Lethbridge, Canada Trust Tower, Calgary
Presence, Les cent jours d'art contemporarin, Centre International D'art Contemporain, Montreal

Collections:

National Gallery of Canada; Brooklyn Museum; Art Gallery of Hamilton; Canada Council Art Bank; London Regional Art and Historical Museum; Le Witt Collection; AT&T; Champion Papers; London Life Insurance; Royal Bank of Canada; Sun Life Assurance; The Prudential.

Publications:

On ALLAIN: Books—*The Core Island Complex,* exhibition catalog, London Regional Art Gallery, 1984; *Present anterieur,* exhibition catalog, Montreal 1984; *Postmarked New York,* exhibition catalog, Lethbridge, Alberta, 1987; *War, Peace and Victory,* exhibition brochure, Brooklyn 1989; *Presence,* exhibition catalog with text by David Clarkson, Montreal 1993. **Articles**—"Preliminary Findings" in *Arts Canada,* November 1982; "A & B Associes, Public Sculpture" in *Vanguard,* April 1984; "Core Island" in *C Magazine,* Summer 1984; "Present anterieur" *Vanguard,* Summer 1984; "A & B Associes" in *Vie des Arts,* Summer 1985; review in *Art in America,* September 1990; review in *C Magazine,* Fall 1991; review in *Artforum,* October 1991; "The Necessity of Impassioned Arguments" in *ETC,* February 1992.

* * *

Rene Pierre Allain's compelling paintings occupy a post-Modernist realm in which the old vocabulary of abstraction is at once undermined and renewed.

His work is metaphorical in the best sense of that word. For several years now, Allain pursued an abstract practice that functions as a commentary upon and a critique of late Modernist painting. He has chosen to eschew the conventional trappings of painting—paintbrush, oil paint, canvas—in favour of implements traditionally used by sculptors, carpenters and other tradespeople: taping knife, wood substructure and pigment-added plaster compound.

Some mention should be made of his methodology. He constructs each work himself, laboriously and from A to Z hands-on. Allain applies plaster compound on burlap-wrapped wood supports with a taping (spackle) knife. The plaster is mixed with pigments and/or acrylics. As each application of the plaster dries, the artist sands down the surface, applying alternate colours by taping off the preceding ones. He builds up an anecdotally rich internal history in the painted surface, through some ten (often even more) individual coats. Finally, the plaster surface is sealed with an acrylic varnish.

The "painting" is then encased in a heavy steel structure which resembles a "frame" but which is in fact integral to the work itself. He has a welding studio in which he fabricates the structures. No arbitrary addition, the steel structure must not only enhance but extend the metaphorical reach of the work itself. Indeed, it is this steel structure that allows the work to lift off of the wall plane, impinging on our own space like a truly environmental artefact.

The paintings themselves resemble classic Modernist abstract paintings: stripes and other geometric structures yield haunting echoes of Barnett Newman and Ad Reinhardt. But Allain does not actually "paint"—he never lifts brush to stretched canvas sheet. Of further interest, and distancing him even further from the Modernist tradition per se, is the source for his abstract language. He draws upon a daunting inventory of forms and symbols taken directly from the realm of military insignia and military architecture. The geometric painted element in a given work is the representation of a military symbol—a ribbon, badge or crest, for instance—perhaps even one reproduced line for line, or colour for colour. Naturally, he takes esthetic liberties with the source material as he sees fit, but the military sources themselves lend his work a dark and coruscating ironic edge.

Allain's work is important because the military sign and the Modernist signifier seem almost interchangeable here. Neither wins out, but the wild promiscuity between these two sets of seemingly incompatible signs always holds sway. Herein, a "stripe" abstract painting undergoes a sea change.

Allain usually keeps a very low-key colour structure in his painting, evoking camouflage and a wilful neutrality. He imbues his work with a very suggestive patina, and one that works with a surface itself suggestive of the attrition of time. There is an archeological aspect to his work. In terms of the steel encasements, Allain uses a gun-blueing solution that at once darkens and lends them a sleek, functional ethos we associate with military hardware and architecture (as in bunkers, for instance).

Most recently, Allain has extended his series of Steel Painting—paintings in which there is no painted element, and the work is entirely made of treated steel plate—into several fruitful new directions. These works are constructed out of various panels of hot and cold rolled steel both with and without treatment of the gun-blueing solution (which as noted darkens them appreciably) and which are presented in the same steel encasements as the plaster paintings. The recent Shields are particularly compelling objects, subtly shaped, they harbour alternately a sense of quiet menace and maximal protection from harm.

Allain's paintings are important and subversive because what seem at first heroic exemplars of late Modernist art are in fact based upon and evoke military insignia and architecture that undermine the putative purity of the Modernist endeavour. Allain's is a critical abstraction because it displaces the purist ideal of more traditional Modernist practice, recontextualizes its signs, and displaces the spectator, who must reconcile what is seen and what is known (or suspected).

If Allain avoids closure by problematizing abstraction itself, referencing a military/industrial complex with all its attendant menace, he also points towards what abstraction might as a practice become, proving once and for all that there is life after formalism.

—James D. Campbell

ALLEN, Terry

Nationality: American. **Born:** Wichita, Kansas, 7 May 1943; raised in Lubbock, Texas. **Education:** Studied at Chouinard Art Institute, Los Angeles, B.F.A. 1966. **Career:** Independent artist since 1966, working in a wide variety of modes including musical and theatrical performance, sculpture, painting and video. Taught drawing classes at Chouinard Art Institute, Los Angeles, 1968–69; guest artist, University of California at Berkeley, 1971; on faculty of California State University at Fresno, 1971–79. **Awards:** National Endowment for the Arts Fellowship, 1972, 1979; Guggenheim Fellowship, New York, 1986; Bessie Award, New York, 1986; Isadora Duncan Award, San Francisco, 1986; Adaline Kent Award, San Francisco, 1989; Wexner Center for the Arts, Artist's Residency Fellowship, Columbus, Ohio, 1992; Dallas Dance Club Award, Best Club Interior, *RED JACKET,* 1996; Inducted into The Buddy Holly "Walk of Fame," 1997, Lubbock, Texas. **Address:** c/o Lawrence Markey, 55 Vandam Street, New York, New York 10013, U.S.A.

Individual Exhibitions:

1966 Gallery 66, Los Angeles
1968 Michael Walls Gallery, San Francisco
Pasadena Art Museum, California
1970 Michael Walls Gallery, San Francisco
1971 Mizuno Gallery, Los Angeles
Museum of Contemporary Art, Chicago
1973 Michael Walls Gallery, Los Angeles
1974 Michael Walls Gallery, New York
1975 *Juarez Series,* Contemporary Art Museum, Houston
1976 Claire S. Copley Gallery, Los Angeles
Morgan Art Gallery, Kansas City, Kansas
1978 Hansen-Fuller Gallery, San Francisco
Nancy Lurie Gallery, Chicago
Landfall Press Gallery, Chicago
1979 Lubbock Lights Gallery, Texas
Morgan Art Gallery, Kansas City, Kansas
Miami-Dade Community College, Florida
1980 Baxter Art Gallery, California Institute of Technology, Pasadena
1981 Portland Center for the Visual Arts, Oregon
Ring, Nelson Gallery/Atkins Museum, Kansas City, Missouri
The Southern Voice: Terry Allen, Vernon Fisher, McGowin, Fort Worth Art Museum, Texas
1983 *Rooms and Stories,* La Jolla Museum of Contemporary Art, California
University of California, San Diego
Morgan Art Gallery, Kansas City, Missouri
1984 *Sprawl/Prowl/Growl,* Espace Lyonnais d'Art Contemporain, Lyon, France
Barbara Gladstone Gallery, New York
1985 Betty Moody Gallery, Houston
China Night, Fresno Art Center, California
1986 *Revelations,* Southwest Center for Arts and Crafts, San Antonio, Texas
Ohio, Wright State University, Dayton, Ohio
John Weber Gallery, New York
Gallery Paule Anglim, San Francisco
1988 L.A. Louver Gallery, Venice, California
Santa Barbara Contemporary Arts Forum, California
Pittsburgh Center for the Arts, Pennsylvania
Moore College of Art, Philadelphia
Institute of Contemporary Arts, Boston
Madison Art Center, Wisconsin
Gallery Paule Anglim, San Francisco
John Weber Gallery, New York, New York
Terry Allen: Youth in Asia Series, Pittsburgh Center for the Arts, Pittsburgh, Pennsylvania
1989 *Big Witness* (living in wishes), San Francisco Art Institute, San Francisco, California
Them Ol' Love Songs, Cranbrook Art Museum, Bloomfield Hills, MI; Betty Moody Gallery, Houston, Texas; John Weber Gallery, New York, New York; Installation and Concert, Laumiere Sculpture Park, St. Louis, Montana
1991 *Terry Allen: New Work,* L.A. Louver, Venice, California
The Artist's Eye: Terry Allen, Kimbell Art Museum, Fort Worth, Texas
1992 *A Simple Story* (Juarez), Wexner Center for the Visual Arts, Columbus, Ohio
Gallery Paule Anglim, San Francisco, California
Betty Moody Gallery, Houston, Texas
1992–1993 *Youth in Asia,* Southeastern Center for Contemporary Art, Winston-Salem, North Carolina (travelled to Modern Art Museum of Fort Worth, Texas; Newport Harbor Art Museum, Newport Beach, California; The Contemporary Museum, Honolulu, Hawaii)
1993 *Voices in the Wilderness,* L.A. Louver Gallery, Venice, California
1994 *Poison Amor* (Collaboration with James Drake), Blue Star Art Space, San Antonio, Texas (travelled to Blaffer Museum, University of Houston, Houston, Texas)
1994 *Bronzes,* Schneider Art Museum, Ashland, Oregon
1995 *Bronzes & Drawings,* UMKC Gallery of Art, Kansas City, Montana
1996 *Liquid Assets,* L.A. Louver Gallery, Venice, California
Terry Allen, Faith and Charity, Hope Gallery, Hope, Idaho
New Prints, Betty Moody Gallery, Houston, Texas
1997 Michael Solway Gallery, Cincinnati, Ohio
Barry Whistler Gallery, Dallas, Texas

Selected Music and Theatre Performances: Since 1964, Allen has made numerous appearances as a solo performer in both country and western music venues and in galleries and museums; since 1978 he has frequently appeared with the Panhandle Mystery Band. *Dialogues in Drag. . . a Satire,* Lucille Street Theatre, Los Angeles, 1968; *The 20th Century Pronto, Arrived,* Lucille Street Theatre, Los Angeles, 1968; *The Levels* (performance for Robert Irwin), University of California at Berkeley, 1970; *The Embrace. . . Advanced to Fury,* Spinoza Arena/Theatre, Houston, 1978; *Anterabbit Bleeder (a biography),* La Jolla Museum of Contemporary Art, 1983; *Face to Face/Back to Back,* California State University, Fullerton, 1984; *Pedal Steel,* Brooklyn Academy of Music, New York, 1985; *Leonce and Lena,* Walker Art Center, Minneapolis, 1987; *Rollback* with Margaret Jenkins Dance Company and Bruce Nauman, Kimo Theater, City of Albuquerque, New Mexico, 1988; *Out of Time* with Mike Henderson and William T. Wiley, Cuesta College Art Gallery, San Luis Obispo, California, 1988; *Juarez: A Work in Progress* with Jo Harvey Allen and the Panhandle Mystery Band, Brattle Theater, Cambridge, Massachusetts, 1990; *Pioneer* (as Paul Dresher Ensemble), with Jo Harvey Allen, Rende Eckert and John Duykers, directed by Robert Woodruff, Spoleto Festival, Garden Theatre, Charleston, South Carolina, 1990; *Pioneer* with Paul Dresher Company, (written by Terry Allen, Jo Harvey Allen, Rende Eckert), directed by Robert Woodruff, UCLA Center for the Performing Arts, Los Angeles, California, 1991; *Chippy (Diaries of a West Texas Hooker),* Cross Currents work-in-progress, American Music Theater Festival, Play and Players Theater, Philadelphia, Pennsylvania, 1993; *Amarillo Highway (and other roads)* with Butch Hancock, Michael Ventura, Jesse Taylor, Charlene Hancock, Lubbock or Leave It, Austin, Texas; Jazz Club, Santa Cruz, California; St. Anne's Cathedral, Brooklyn, New York; Paramount Theater, Austin, Texas, 1994.

Selected Group Exhibitions:

1973 *Extraordinary Realities,* Whitney Museum, New York
1976 *The Great American Rodeo Show,* Fort Worth Art Museum, Texas
Painting and Sculpture in California: The Modern Era, San Francisco Museum of Modern Art (travelled to the National Collection of Fine Arts, Smithsonian Institution, Washington, D.C.)
1977 *10th Biennale de Paris*
The Record as Artwork, Fort Worth Art Museum, Texas (toured the United States and Canada)
1979 *Image & Object in Contemporary Sculpture,* Detroit Institute of Arts (travelled to P.S. 1, New York)
1982 *Sydney Biennale,* Art Gallery of New South Wales, Australia
1984 *Content: A Contemporary Focus 1978–84,* Hirshhorn Museum, Washington, D.C.
1986 *The Texas Landscape 1900–86,* Museum of Fine Arts, Houston
1987 *Avant Garde in the Eighties,* Los Angeles County Museum of Art
1988 *Lost and Found in California: Four Decades of Assemblage Art,* James Corcoran Gallery, Pence Gallery, Shoshona Wayne Gallery, Santa Monica, California; G. Ray Hawkins Gallery, Los Angeles, California
Out of Time, Cuesta College Art Gallery, San Luis Obispo, California
1989 *Heroics Recast,* School of the Museum of Fine Arts, Boston, Massachusetts
Forty Years of California Assemblage, Wright Art Gallery, University of California, Los Angeles, California
A Different War, Whatcom Museum of History and Art, Bellingham, Washington (traveled to De Cordova Museum and Sculpture Park, Lincoln, Massachusetts; Northwestern University, Evanston, Illinois; Akron Art Museum, Ohio; Madison Art Center, Madison, Wisconsin; Wright Art Gallery, UCLA, Los Angeles, California; CU Art Galleries, University of Colorado, Boulder, Colorado; and Washington State University Museum of Art, Pullman, Washington)
1990 *Northwest x Southwest-Painted Fiction,* Palm Springs Desert Museum, California; Yellowstone Art Center, Montana; Bellingham Museum, Washington; University of Houston, Texas
1992 *Profiles II: On Paper,* Adair Margo Gallery, El Paso, Texas (traveled to Weber State University, Ogden, Utah; and Arlington Museum, Arlington, Texas)
1991 *Positions on the Desert,* Gallery Paule Anglim, San Francisco, California
Critical Reactions, Rena Bransten Gallery, San Francisco, California
Singular Visions, Museum of Fine Arts, Museum of New Mexico, Santa Fe, New Mexico
Drawings: An Exhibition of Artists of the John Weber Gallery, John Weber Gallery, New York, New York
1993–1994 *La Frontera-The Border,* Museum of Contemporary Art, San Diego, California (traveled to Centrok Cultural, Tijuana; Tocama Art Museum, Tacoma, Washington; Scottsdale Center for the Arts, Scottsdale, Arizona; Neuberger Museum, State University of New York; San Jose Museum of Art, San Jose, California)
1994 *Insite 94, Bi-National Exhibition,* San Diego, California/ Tijuana, Mexico
1996 *Landfall Press; Twenty-Five Years of Printmaking,* Milwaukee Art Museum, Milwaukee, Wisconsin
American Kaleidoscope: Art at the Close of this Century, National Museum of American Art, Smithsonian Institute, Washington, D.C.
Les Arts Du Vin, Les Musees Royaux D'Art, Brussels, Belgium
1997 *Contemporary Sculpture, The Figurative Tradition,* Leigh Yawkey Woodson Art Museum, Wausau, Wisconsin
Scene of the Crime, Armand Hammer Museum, UCLA, Los Angeles, California
Still Life (The Object in American Art 1915–1995), Selections from The Metropolitan Museum of Art, New York, New York

Collections:

Museum of Modern Art, New York; Fort Worth Art Museum, Texas; Detroit Institute of Arts; University Art Museum, Berkeley, California; Nelson Gallery/Atkins Museum, Kansas City, Missouri; La Jolla Museum of Contemporary Art, California; The Stuart Collection, La

Jolla California; Los Angeles County Museum of Art; Metropolitan Museum of Art, New York.

Publications:

By ALLEN: Books—*China Night,* with Roxy Gordon, Fresno, California 1985; Terry Allen's ''Ohio,'' with essay by Dave Hickey, Dayton, Ohio 1986. **Selected Recordings**—''Gonna California'' and ''Color Book'' (single), Bale Creek Records, Los Angeles 1968; *Juarez* (album), Landfall Press, Chicago 1975 (re-released by Fate Records, Chicago 1980); *Lubbock (on everything)* (album), Fate Records, Chicago 1978; ''Cajun Roll'' and ''Whatever Happened to Jesus (and Maybe-line)?'' (single), Fate Records, Chicago 1979; *Smokin the Dummy* (album), Fate Records, Chicago 1980; ''The Arizona Spiritual'' (single), 1983; *Bloodlines* (album), 1984; ''Cocktail Desperado'' (single), 1986; *In Concert: Terry Allen,* Cranbrook Art Museum, Bloomfield Hills, MI, 1989; *The Event: Terry Allen and Jo Harvey Allen,* Des Moines Art Center, Des Moines, IA, 1989; *Terry Allen: Concert,* Laumeler Sculpture Part, St. Louis, MO, 1989.

On ALLEN: Books—*Juarez Series: Terry Allen,* exhibition catalog by Paul Shimmel, Michael Walls and Dave Hickey, Houston 1975; *Performance Anthology,* edited by Carl Loeffler and Darlene Tong, San Francisco 1980; *Ring: Terry Allen,* exhibition catalog by Marcia Tucker and Sherry Cromwell-Lacy, Kansas City, Missouri 1981; *Rooms and Stories by Terry Allen,* exhibition catalog by Dave Hickey, Robert McDonald and Lynda Forsha, La Jolla, California 1983; *Sprawl/Prowl/Growl: A Geographic Survey of Works by Terry Allen* by Thierry Raspail, Marcia Tucker and others, Lyon, France 1984; *Terry Allen: Visual and Aural Mythologies* by Ron Gleason and Val Greenfield, Calgary, Alberta 1985; *KaChina Night* by Craig Adcock, Tallahassee, Florida 1986; *Ohio* with text by Dave Hickey, Wright State University, Dayton, Ohio, 1986; *A Simple Story,* Wexner Center for the Arts, Columbus, Ohio, 1992. **Articles**—''Earthscapes, Landworks and Oz'' by Dave Hickey in *Art in America* (New York), September/October 1971; ''The Ironic L.A. Artist'' by Sandy Ballatore in *Artweek* (Oakland, California), 2 November 1974; ''Terry Allen's C & W Imagery at CAM'' by Charlotte Moser in the *Houston Chronicle,* 16 November 1975; ''The Art of Terry Allen: A Personal Evaluation'' by Claire Copley in *Journal* (Los Angeles), October/November 1976; ''Terry Allen's Narratives'' by Robert McDonald in *Artweek* (Oakland, California), 22 April 1978; ''Wrestling with Human Relationships'' by Janice Ross in *Artweek* (Oakland, California) 4 November 1978; ''Objecting to Image'' by Kay Larson in the *Village Voice* (New York), 14 January 1980; ''Dallas/Ft. Worth You Can Go Home Again'' by Janet Kutner in *Artnews* (New York), December 1981; ''West Texas Dada'' by Jonathan Crary in *Art in America* (New York), September 1983; ''Terry Allen: The Return of Vietnam'' By Gregory Galligan in *Arts Magazine* (New York), April 1987.

* * *

Terry Allen is a musician and songwriter, storyteller and visual artist hailing from none other than Lubbock, Texas. Though he's spent most of his adult life in southern California, he retains his ''southernness'' most obviously in his compositions (a little rock 'n roll, a little country western) which tell the tale of waitresses, truckers, mobile home life, card playing and drinking whiskey on their own down home surface. It is underneath the surface, however, that Allen's writing as well as his visuals become more dense, more circuitous. In his visual art of every conceivable medium, all of the above ambitions fuse to create cryptic narratives which meander somewhat autobiographically around the conflicts and passages of his heroes and heroines.The Installations themselves combine such dramas as murder, denial, anger, love, alcoholism and confusion (to name very few) which are represented by an odd assortment of everyday objects doubling as loaded symbols which address his perplexing soap operas. Crows, playing cards, male and female silhouettes, high heels, books and rocks combine with an infinite array of materials ranging from live birds to typewritten notes to videotape and much, much more. The viewer, inevitably disoriented by these intricate tales must tug at and dig through each revolving metaphor to cull out whatever drama may reside in these abstruse worlds of passion and intrigue.Like a scavenger, the viewer picks and pulls at details both visual and ''verbal'' which, though they are certainly no exercise in futility, lead to no plot and no resolution. But Allen is more than merely a perpetrator of tricky labyrinths. His circular stories catapult the viewer into a world which defines the very stuff they're made of. Each phrase, while leading into another, also confirms or denies its own identity within the context of the myth as a whole and the separate components which reveal it. There is so much happening in Allen's work at any given moment that it is difficult to assign any specific or literal ''meaning'' to it. Perhaps his most renowned piece, ''Ring'' is a four-section, four-year work of individual but ideologically connected installations, a videotape (theatre occurrence, as Allen would say) written by Allen (he does not perform in these) and several smaller pieces. The installations (''The Evening Gorgeous George Died'' and ''Messages from Wrestlers in Hell'') include both two and three dimensional elements as well as varying typewritten narratives which partially illuminate an obscure relationship between the stars, HE and SHE. Intricate details of these participants' lives are revealed through their discussions of marriage, drinking, affairs and fantasies. Though these characters lead and acknowledge their complex existences as more than simple fictions, they remain only shadows on the wall—emblems of Allen's ruminations and not their own. Their identity is that of mythical situations rather than actual folks. Clearly, in his work, Allen develops a mysterious dialogue in which the skeletons of a private saga are uncloaked for us all. But still, we must excavate the obscure threads with which these tales are woven to reveal the humour, intensity and reality of their games.

—Janet Goleas

ANDERSON, Laurie

Nationality: American. **Born:** Wayne, Illinois, in 1947. **Education:** Barnard College, New York, B.A. 1969 (magna cum laude with honors in art history; Phi Beta Kappa); studied sculpture at Columbia University, New York, M.F.A. 1972. **Career:** Performance artist, New York, since 1972. Instructor in art history, City College, New York, 1973–75; formed ''etc'' (Electronic Theater Company) in association with Interval Research Corporation, 1998. **Awards:** New York State Council on the Arts grant, 1974, 1977; National Endowment for the Arts grant, 1974, 1977, 1979; Villager award, 1981; Guggenheim fellowship, New York, 1983. Honorary doctorate: San

Laurie Anderson, 1995. ©Lynn Goldsmith/Corbis.

Francisco Art Institute, 1980; Distinguished Alumna Award, Columbia School of the Arts, 1994; ''Marlene'' Award for the Performing Arts, Munich, 1996. **Agent:** (for visual works) Monterey Peninsula Artists, 509 Hartnell St., Monterey, California 93940; (for press contact) Annie Ohayon Media Relations, 525 Broadway 6th Floor, New York, New York 10012. **Address:** 530 Canal Street, New York New York 10013, U.S.A. **Website:** http://www.laurieanderson.com.

Individual Exhibitions:

1970 Barnard College, New York
1973 Harold Rivkin Gallery, Washington, D.C.
1974 Artists Space, New York
1977 Holly Solomon Gallery, New York
Hopkins Center, Dartmouth College, Hanover, New Hampshire
1978 And/Or Gallery, Seattle
Projects Gallery, Museum of Modern Art, New York
Matrix Gallery, Hartford Atheneum, Connecticut
1979 University of California Art Museum, Berkeley
1980 *Dark Dogs, American Dreams,* Holly Solomon Gallery, New York
1981 *Scenes from ''United States,''* Holly Solomon Gallery, New York
1982 *Retrospective,* Institute of Contemporary Arts, London
1983 Institute of Contemporary Art, Philadelphia (travelled to Los Angeles; Houston; Flushing, New York)
1984 Laforet Museum, Akasaka, Tokyo
Nihon Seinehkau, Tokyo
Sankei Hall, Osaka, Japan
Kyoto Kaikan, Tokyo
1996 *Whirlwind,* New York Artists Space Gallery (retrospective)

Performances: *Automotive,* Town Green, Rochester, Vermont, 1972; *O-Range,* Lewisohn Stadium, City College of New York, 1973; Artists Space, New York, 1974; The Clocktower, Institute for Urban Resources, New York, 1974; Projects Gallery, Boston, 1974; *Duets on Ice,* 5 New York City locations, 1974; *How to Yodel,* The Kitchen, New York, 1974; music, Whitney Museum Downtown Branch, New York, 1975; *Songs and Stories for the Insomniac,* Artists Space, New York, 1975; *Songs and Stories for the Insomniac . . . Continued,* Oberlin College, Ohio, 1975; *Out of the Blue,* University of Massachusetts, Amherst, 1975; *Dearreader,* Holly Solomon Gallery, New York, 1975; *Dearreader-2,* Sarah Lawrence College, Bronxville, New York, 1975; *Dearreader-3,* Rhode Island School of Design, Providence, Rhode Island, 1975; From ''For Instants,'' Whitney Museum, New York, 1976; From ''For Instants,'' Brockport College, New York, 1976; *Fast Food,* Artist Space, New York, 1976; From ''For Instants,'' Skidmore College, Saratoga, New York, 1976; From ''For Instants-3,'' Philadelphia College of Art, 1976; From ''For Instants,'' California Institute of the Arts, Valencia, 1976; From ''For Instants-4,'' University of California at San Diego, 1976; From ''For Instants-4,'' Museum of Contemporary Art, La Jolla, California, 1976; *Stereo Stories,* M. L. D'Arc Gallery, New York, 1976; *Engli-SH,* Akademie der Kunst, Berlin, 1976; *Engli-SH,* Louisiana Museum, Humlebaek, Denmark, 1976; *Road Songs,* St. Mark's Poetry Center, New York, 1976; *Songs,* New School, New York, 1976; *For Instants-5: Songs for Lines, Songs for Waves,* The Kitchen, New York, 1977; *Audio Talk,* School of Visual Arts, New York, 1977; De Appel, Amsterdam, 1977; From ''For Instants,'' at *Arte Fiera,* Bologna, 1977; *Some Songs,* International Cultural Center, Brussels, 1977; *That's Not the Way I Heard It,* at *Documenta,* Kassel, West Germany, 1977; *On Dit,* at the *Biennale,* Paris, 1977; *That's Not the Way I Heard It-2,* Galleria Salvatore Ala, Milan, 1977; *For Instants-Continued,* Otis Art Gallery, Los Angeles, 1978; *Some Songs,* And/Or Gallery Seattle, 1978; *Like a Stream,* The Kitchen, New York, 1978; reading, The Ear Inn, New York; *Like a Stream-3,* with St. Paul Chamber Orchestra, at Walker Art Center, Minneapolis, 1978; *Down Here,* Texas Opry House, Houston (sponsored by Contemporary Art Museum, Houston), 1978; *Some Songs,* Mills College, Oakland, California, 1978; *Some Songs-2,* Portland Center for the Visual Arts, Oregon, 1978; *For Instants-6,* DC Space, Washington, D.C., 1978; *A Few Are . . . ,* Art Gallery of Ontario, Toronto, 1978; *Songs for Self-Playing Violin,* Contemporary Art Center, Cincinnati, Ohio, 1978; *Songs for Self-Playing Violin,* Real Art Ways Hartford, Connecticut, 1978; *Some Are . . . ,* benefit for Hallwalls, Buffalo, New York, 1978; *Americans on the Move—Preview,* Carnegie Recital Hall, New York, 1979; *Americans on the Move,* The Kitchen, New York, 1979; at *Theatre of Nations Festival,* Hamburg, 1979; Groningen Museum, Netherlands, 1979; International Cultural Center, Brussels, 1979; Dany Keller Gallery, Munich Cultural Center, Bonn, 1979; CAPC, Bordeaux, 1979, Stadtparkforum, Graz, Austria, 1979; Modern Art

Gallery, Vienna, 1979; Aspen Center for the Visual Arts, Colorado, 1979; *Blue Horn File,* with David van Tieghem and Peter Gordon, Mudd Club, New York, 1979; *Commerce,* with Peter Gordon, U.S. Customs House, New York, 1979; at *Cabrillo Festival,* California, 1979; at *Autumn Festival,* Paris, 1979; at *OGGImusica Festival,* Lugano, Switzerland, 1979; Real Art Ways, Hartford, Connecticut, 1979; San Francisco Art Institute, 1979; Mills College, Oakland, California, 1979; Thorne Hall, Northwestern University, Chicago, 1979; University of Virginia, Richmond, 1979; Glenbow Museum, Calgary, Alberta, 1979; *Für Augen und Ohren,* Akademie der Kunst, Berlin, 1980; Santa Barbara Museum of Art, California, 1980; a *Performance Festival,* Florence, 1980; Harvard University, Cambridge, Massachusetts, 1980; at *Rome Performance Festival,* 1980; *New Music America,* Walker Art Center, Minneapolis, 1980; Parachute Magazine Performance Series, Montreal, 1980; University of Northern Iowa, Cedar Falls, 1980; Levande, Gothenburg, Sweden, 1980; Paul Klee Kunstmuseum, Berne, 1980; Kunstmuseum, Zurich, 1980; Mixage International, Rotterdam, 1980; Rust/Roost, Middleburg, Netherlands, 1980; at *ROSC,* Dublin, 1980; Benefit for Volume Magazine, Irving Plaza, New York, 1980; Lenbachhaus, Munich, 1980; Paramount Theatre, with Oakland Youth Symphony, California, 1980; Orpheum Theatre, New York (sponsored by the Kitchen), 1980; Glenbow Museum, Calgary, Alberta, 1981; Western Front, Vancouver, 1981; York University, Toronto, 1981; Kunstmuseum, Basel, 1981; Cirque Divers, Liège, Belgium, 1981; Pension Building, Washington, D.C. (sponsored by DC Space and WPA), 1981; Detroit Institute of Arts, 1981; Institute of Contemporary Art, Philadelphia, 1981; University of California at San Diego, 1981; University of California at Davis, 1981; *Privates,* New York (sponsored by Franklin Furnace), 1981; *Bonds* (sponsored by The Kitchen), New York, 1981; Riverside Studios, London 1981; Pension Building, Washington, D.C., 1981; *It's Cold Outside,* Alice Tully Hall, New York (commissioned by American Composers Concerts), 1981; *United States,* Moore Theatre, Seattle, 1982; *United States I-IV,* Park West, Chicago (sponsored by the Museum of Contemporary Art, Chicago), 1982; *Mister Heartbreak,* toured the United States, Canada and Japan, 1984–85; *Empty Places,* 1990; *Voices from Beyond,* 1992; *Stories from the Nerve Bible,* 1993; *The Speed of Darkness,* 1997; *Dal Vivo,* The Fondazione Prada and San Vittore Prison, 1998; *Songs and Stories from Moby Dick* (traveling performance), 1999; *the Meltdown Festival,* Royal Festival Hall, London, 2001.

Selected Group Exhibitions:

1973 *Thought Structure,* Pace University, New York
1976 *New Work, New York,* Fine Arts Gallery, California State University at Los Angeles
1977 *Surrogates/Self-Portraits,* Holly Solomon Gallery, New York
Words at Liberty, Museum of Contemporary Art, Chicago
1978 *American Narrative Story Art,* Contemporary Art Museum, Houston (travelled to the University of California Art Museum, Berkeley)
1979 *10 Artists: Artists' Space,* Neuberger Museum, State University of New York at Purchase (travelled to the New Museum, New York)
1980 *Drawings: The Pluralist Decade,* at the *Biennale,* Venice (toured Europe; American version shown at Institute for Contemporary Art, Philadelphia)
1987 *Avant-Grade in the Eighties,* Los Angeles County Museum of Art
1988 *Identity: Representations of the Self,* Whitney Museum of American Art, New York (catalog)
On Track: An Exhibition of Art in Technology, NOVA Building, Calgary, Alberta (catalog)
Art and Language: The 1980s—Selected Work, Centre d'Histoire de l'Art Contemporain, Rennes, France (catalog)
1990 *Culture and Commentary: An Eighties Perspective,* Hirshhorn Museum and Sculpture Garden, Washington, D.C. (catalog)
1991 *High and Low: Popular Culture—Six Evenings of Performance,* Museum of Modern Art, New York (catalog)
1992 *10th World Wide Video Festival,* Kijkhuis, Hague (catalog)
1995 *13th World Wide Video Festival,* World Wide Video Centre, Hague (catalog)
1996 *Under Capricorn: The World Over—Art in the Age of Globalisation* (traveling exhibition) (catalog)
2001 Musée Art Contemporain Lyon, France

Publications:

By ANDERSON: Books—*The Package,* New York 1971; *October,* New York 1972; *Transportation Transportation,* New York 1973; *The Rose and the Stone,* New York 1974; *Notebook,* 1976; *Typisch Frau,* Regensburg, West Germany 1981; *Artifacts at the End of a Decade,* with an essay by John Perreault, 1981; *Laurie Anderson's Postcard Book,* 1990; *Empty Places: A Performance,* New York 1991; *Stories from the Nerve Bible: A Retrospective, 1972–1992,* New York 1993. **Articles—**''From 'For Instants''' in *Individuals,* edited by Alan Sondheim, New York 1977; ''From 'Americas on the Move''' in *October* (New York), Spring 1979; interview, with Robin White, in *View* (Oakland, California), vol. II, no. 8, 1980; ''Dark Dogs American Dreams'' in *Hotel,* New York 1980; ''Laurie Anderson: Interview,'' with David Sparkman, in *Washington Review,* October/November 1981; ''Artists, Audiences and Censorship'' in *Dialogue,* vol. 16, no. 5, September-October 1993; ''Laurie Anderson and Pipilotti Rist: Conversation in the Lobby of a Hotel in Berlin'' in *Parkett,* no. 48, 1996; ''Control Rooms and Other Stories: Confessions of a Content Provider'' in *Parkett,* no. 49, 1997; ''Program Notes for *Songs and Stories from Moby Dick,*'' in *UCLA Performing Arts Magazine,* vol. 33, no. 10, October 1999; interview with Clifford Ross in *Bomb,* no. 69, Fall 1999. **Films—***14 Americans,* 1979; *Film du Silence,* 1981; *Home of the Brave,* 1986; *Laurie Anderson: Collected Videos,* 1990. **Records—***It's Not the Bullet That Kills You, It's the Hole,* 1977; *Airwaves,* 1977; *New Music for Electronic and Recorded Media,* 1978; *Big Ego,* 1979; *Walk the Dog, O Superman,* 1981; *Big Science,* 1982; *Mister Heartbreak,* 1984; *Bright Red,* 1995; *The Ugly One with the Jewels and Other Stories,* 1995; *The Speed of Darkness,* 1997; *Laurie Anderson,* 2001. **CD-ROMs—***Puppet Motel,* 1995.

On ANDERSON: Books—*Variants: Drawings by Contemporary Sculptors,* exhibition catalog, Houston 1981; *Laurie Anderson* by John Howell, 1992; *Laurie Anderson* by Roselee Goldberg, New York 2000. **Articles—**''Laurie Anderson'' by Robert Pincus-Witten in *Art Rite* (New York), April 1974; 5–11 November 1980; ''Laurie Anderson Grows as a Performance Artist'' by John Rockwell in the

New York Times, 27 October 1980; ''Laurie Anderson: American on the Move: Touching, Funny, Vivid, Assured'' by Gregory Sandow in the *Village Voice* (New York) 5–11 November 1980; ''The United States of Laurie Anderson'' in *Soho News* (New York, 5–11 November 1980; ''Amplifications: Laurie Anderson'' by Craig Owens in *Art in America* (New York), March 1981; ''Laurie Anderson: Ephemeral turns Permanent'' by Robert Palmer in the *New York Times,* 21 April 1982; ''Laurie Anderson: 3 Article Special Section'' in *Parkett,* no. 49, 1997; ''Laurie Anderson: Real and Virtual'' by Scott Stroot in *Art New England,* vol. 19, no. 3, April/May 1998; ''Performance, Video, and the Rhetoric of Presence'' by Anne M. Wagner in *October,* no. 91, Winter 2000; ''Unnecessary Duplicates: Identity and Technology in the Performances of Laurie Anderson'' by Philip Auslander in *Art Papers,* vol. 24, no. 1, January/February 2000; ''Laurie Anderson's Rhythmic Eye'' by RoseLee Goldberg in *Aperture,* no. 160, Summer 2000.

* * *

During her art historical training at Barnard College in New York, performance artist Laurie Anderson explored the proliferating critical discourse of the 1970s—the semiological and structuralist theories that formed the basis of Minimal and Conceptual Art. Anderson's early Minimalist sculpture was influenced by Process Art (especially the work of Eve Hesse), an art that questioned the non-objectivity of materials whose intrinsic qualities could elicit a range of psycho-sexual responses and whose installations often created a theatrical effect. The static modernist art object, with its authoritative ideologies that sustained belief in the universality of meaning vested in form, was no longer tenable. Moreover, a Minimalism rooted in phenomenalogical rather than cultural conditions precluded textual, postmodern and, most importantly, feminist discourse, ideas important to Anderson.

After a number of one-person performances, invariably accompanied by a mechanically enhanced violin, Anderson, beginning with *Americans on the Move* in 1979, enlarged her production. At first, she increased her musical accompaniment to five musicians playing electronic instruments, eventually introducing film and photographic imagery into her performances. In her seven-hour, four-part opus, *United States* (''Transportation,'' ''Politics,'' ''Money'' and ''Love,'' 1979–83), the artist transcended the personal and autobiographical tone of her earlier work in favor of a multi-media examination of the social codes and mythologies that pervade popular culture. With *United States,* she arrived at a basic theme in her oeuvre—a questioning of the linguistic and semiological systems by which information is transmitted and received and their concomitant ideologies. In whole or in part based on songs from *United States,* her two albums *Big Science* [1982] and *Mister Heartbreak* [1984]—the latter resulting in an international tour that formed the basis for Anderson's first movie *Home of the Brave* [1986]—allowed Anderson to reach an even larger audience.

Anderson's imagery—generalized depictions of cityscapes, highways and newscasts culled from advertising and the media—is a veritable field of semiotic signs in the form of maps, clocks, airplanes, roads and hands. Such a panoply of urban images is, of course, foreboding, and is aggressively compounded by the use of a cold, corporate voice speaking the demands of ''big brother,'' by a radical plurality of altered voices and characters, and by a constant sense of temporal and geographic dislocation. Further denuding herself of a stable identity through the use of parody and quotation, Anderson acts as an electronic magician who both controls and receives the messages of a technocratic society.

Despite the multitude of technological and theatrical effects, which both augment her performance works and diffuse her personality, the focus rarely shifts from Anderson's finely honed persona. Exchanging the rarified aesthetics of the modernist art object for the temporal and confrontational medium of performance (in an age when the music video was first being launched), Anderson's complex media-driven persona reveals the relative purity of the Minimalist performances of Yvonne Rainer, Robert Morris and Simone Forti. In an age of cultural icons inflated by the media, Anderson presents herself in order to wryly comment on the cultural and textual nature of postmodernism.

—Mason Klein

After holing up in the studio for five years, Anderson emerged in 1995 with a barrage of projects, including a U.S. tour, a spoken word collection, an album of original music, and her first CD-ROM, *Puppet Motel,* which culled bits from all of her current work. Through the world wide web, she interacts with fans and has also discussed her hopes for a postmodern theme park in the heart of Barcelona, to be realized in conjunction with former collaborator Peter Gabriel and Brian Eno, who produced her 1995 album, *Bright Red.* While Anderson's projects and concerns increasingly encompass an internationalist world-view, she retains her place as a preeminent figure in the insular art scene of downtown New York.

—Mark Swartz

After the enormous technological undertaking of 1995's *Puppet Motel* and *Stories from the Nerve Bible* tour (in which the artist hauled thirty-three tons of equipment from performance to performance), it is not surprising that Anderson would choose to spend the next several years in comparatively low-tech endeavors. In 1996 she premiered her stripped-down performance *Speed of Darkness*, in which the artist performed on a bare stage with little more than a keyboard, violin, and a few voice filters to tell this intimate story of art, self, and technology. Over the next several years Anderson performanced the piece widely, and also contributed to and curated various exhibitions and festivals (including the 1996 *Hugo Boss Awards Exhibition*, for which she was nominated), kept up an impressive international lecture schedule, and mounted a new multimedia installation, *Dal Vivo (Life)* at the Fondazione Prada in Milan.

In the midst of this flurry of activity, Anderson found time to produce perhaps her most ambitious performance to date, *Songs and Stories from Moby Dick*, which she debuted in 1999. The work, based on Herman Melville's novel, both marked a return to the monumental performance style of her *United States* cycle and a departure from previous work for its reliance upon professional actors' performances as well as her own, not to mention its foundation in the popular and historical work of another author. Unsatisfied with her attempts to capture the music and performances from this show in an audio recording, she has recently chosen to instead release only a few choice selections from *Moby Dick* alongside all new compositions on a forthcoming, self-titled album, which will be her first for the Nonesuch label.

—Maria Elena Buszek

ANDRE, Carl

Nationality: American. **Born:** Quincy, Massachusetts, 16 September 1935. **Education:** Quincy Public Schools, 1941–50; Phillips Academy, Andover, Massachusetts, with Patrick and Maude Morgan, Hollis Frampton, Michael Chapman, Frank Stella and Harry Curtis, 1951–53. **Military Service:** Served in the United States Army, in North Carolina, 1955–56. **Family:** Married Rosemarie Castoro (divorced). **Career:** Freelance artist. Worked for the Boston Gear Works, Quincy, and travelled in England and France, 1954; moved to New York, 1957; worked as an editorial assistant, New York, 1957–58; freight brakeman and conductor, Pennsylvania Railroad, 1960–64. Member, Art Workers Coalition, New York, 1967–72. **Agents:** Paula Cooper Inc., 155 Wooster Street, New York, New York 10012; Konrad Fischer, Platanestrasse 7, 4 Dusseldorf, Germany. **Address:** P.O. Box 1001, Cooper Station, New York, New York 10003, U.S.A.

Individual Exhibitions:

1965 Tibor de Nagy Gallery, New York
1966 Tibor de Nagy Gallery, New York
1967 Dwan Gallery, New York
Dwan Gallery, Los Angeles
Konrad Fischer Gallery, Dusseldorf
1968 Stadtisches Museum, Monchengladbach, Germany
Heiner Friedrich Gallery, Munich
Wide White Space, Antwerp
Irving Blum Gallery, Los Angeles
1969 Dwan Gallery, New York
Konrad White Space, Antwerp
Haagsgemeentemuseum, The Hague
Galleria Gian Enzo Sperone, Turin
1970 Guggenheim Museum, New York
Ace Gallery, Los Angeles
1971 St. Louis Art Museum
Dwan Gallery, New York
Konrad Fischer Gallery, Dusseldorf
Locksley-Shea Gallery, Minneapolis
Galerie Yvon Lambert, Paris
Wide White Space, Antwerp
Heiner Friedrich Gallery, Munich
1972 John Weber Gallery, New York
Konrad Fischer Gallery, Dusseldorf
Friends of Contemporary Art, Denver
Janie C. Lee Gallery, Dallas
Lisson Gallery, London
1973 John Weber Gallery, New York
Thayer Academy, Braintree, Massachusetts
Galleria Gian Enzo Sperone, Turin
Portland Center for the Visual Arts, Oregon
Addison Gallery, Phillips Academy, Andover, Massachusetts
Institute for Contemporary Art, Boston
Museum of Modern Art, New York
Konrad Fisher Gallery, Dusseldorf
Max Protetch Gallery, Washington, D.C.
1974 Wide White Space, Antwerp
Konrad Fischer Gallery, Dusseldorf
Ace Gallery, Vancouver
1975 Barbara Cusak Gallery, Houston
Ace Gallery, Vancouver
Lisson Gallery, London
Galleria Sperone, Rome
Sperone Westwater Fischer Gallery, New York
Dan Weinberg Gallery, San Francisco
Museum of Modern Art, Oxford
Sculpture 1958–1974, Kunsthalle, Berne
John Weber Gallery, New York
1976 Barbara Cusak Gallery, Houston
John Weber Gallery, New York
Ace Gallery, Venice, California
Ace Gallery, Los Angeles
Konrad Fischer Gallery, Dusseldorf
Galerie Yvon Lambert, Paris
Carl Andre/Richard Long/Barry LeVa, Corcoran Gallery, Washington, D.C.
Davidson Art Center, Wesleyan University, Middletown, Connecticut
The Clocktower, New York
Detroit Institute of Arts
Kabinet für Aktuele Kunst, Bremerhaven, Germany
Minneapolis College of Art and Design
1977 Sperone Westwater Fischer Gallery, New York
Joseloff Gallery, Hartford Art School, Connecticut
Otis Art Institute, Los Angeles
1978 *Sculpture 1959–1977,* Sperone Westwater Fischer Gallery, New York
Sculpture 1959–78, Whitechapel Art Gallery, London
Laguna Gloria Art Museum, Austin, Texas
Contemporary Arts Center, Cincinnati
Albright-Knox Art Gallery, Buffalo, New York
Art Institute of Chicago
1979 La Jolla Museum of Contemporary Art, California
University of California Art Museum, Berkeley
Museum of Fine Arts, Dallas
Musée d'Art Contemporaine, Montreal
Musée d'Art Moderne de la Ville, Paris
1980 Institute of Contemporary Arts, Boston
Paula Cooper Gallery, New York
Lopoukhine Nayduch Gallery, Boston
David Bellman Gallery, Toronto
National Gallery of Canada, Ottawa
Portland State University, Oregon
Galerie Konrad Fischer, Dusseldorf
1981 Susan Caldwell Gallery, New York
Seagram Plaza, New York
Wurttembergischer Kunstverein, Stuttgart
Anthony D'Offay Gallery, New York
Museum Haus Lange, Krefeld, Germany
Graeme Murray Gallery, Edinburgh
1982 Susan Caldwell Gallery, New York
Galerie Konrad Fischer, Dusseldorf
Alberta College of Art, Calgary
University of New Mexico, Albuquerque
Colorado State University, Fort Collins
University of Wyoming, Laramie
Galerie Hans Mayer, Basel
University of Miami, Coral Gables

1983 Galerie Konrad Fischer, Zurich
Paula Cooper Gallery, New York
Health Gallery, Atlanta, Georgia
Galerie Daniel Templon, Paris
Nouveau Musee, Lyon, France
Le Coin du Miroir, Dijon, France
The Clocktower, New York
Flow Ace Gallery, Venice, California
Galerie Plus-Kerns, Brussels
1984 Broward Community College, Fort Lauderdale, Florida
Richland College, Dallas
Westfalischer Kunstverein, Munster, Germany
Galerie Konrad Fischer, Dusseldorf
Galleria Primo Piano, Rome
Galerie im Kornerpark, Berlin-Neukolln
State University of New York at Stony Brook
Galerie Plus-kern, Brussels
Galerie Andre, Berlin
1985 Paula Cooper Gallery, New York
Galerie Daniel Templon, Paris
Kunstraum Munchen, Munich
Galerie Konrad Fischer, Dusseldorf
Galleria Gian Enzo Sperone, Rome
1986 Galerie Plus-Kern, Brussels
Galerie Konrad Fischer, Dusseldorf
1987 Van Abbemuseum, Eindhoven, Netherlands
Haags Gemeentemuseum, The Hague
Museo d'Arte Contemporanea, Castello di Rivoli, Italy
1992 Julian Pretto Gallery, New York
1995 Gagosian Gallery, New York

Selected Group Exhibitions:

1964 *Eight Young Artists,* Hudson River Museum, Yonkers, New York (and Bennington College, Vermont)
1968 *Minimal Art,* Gemeentemuseum, The Hague (travelled to Dusseldorf and Berlin)
1970 *Unitary Forms: Minimal Sculpture,* San Francisco Museum of Art
1974 *Andre / Broodthaers / Buren / Burgin / Gilbert and George / On Kawara / Long / Richter,* Palais des Beaux-Arts, Brussels
1975 *The Condition of Sculpture: A Selection of Recent Sculpture by Younger British and Foreign Artists,* Hayward Gallery, London
1976 *Drawing Now,* Museum of Modern Art, New York (toured Germany, Israel and Norway)
1977 *Paris—New York,* Musée d'Art Moderne, Centre Georges Pompidou, Paris
1980 *Andre/Judd/Morris: Sculpture Minimal,* Galleria Nazionale d'Arte Moderna, Rome
1985 *Transformations in Sculpture,* Guggenheim Museum, New York
1987 *A Century of Modern Sculpture,* Dallas Museum of Art, Texas (and National Gallery of Art, Washington, D.C.)

Collections:

Museum of Modern Art, New York; Albright-Knox Art Gallery, Buffalo, New York; Walker Art Center, Minneapolis; National Gallery of Canada, Ottawa; Tate Gallery, London; Stedlijk Museum, Amsterdam; Kunstmuseum, Basel; Hessisches Landesmuseum, Darmstadt; Wallraf-Richartz Museum, Cologne.

Publications:

By ANDRE: Books—*First 5 Poems,* New York 1961; *The Xerox Book,* with others, New York 1968; *7 Books of Poetry: Passport, Shape and Structure, A Theory of Poetry, 100 Sonnets, American Drill, 3 Operas, Lyrics and Odes,* New York 1969: *Attica Book,* with others, edited by Benny Andrews and Rudolf Barabik, New York 1972; *Quincy Book,* Andover, Massachusetts 1973; *144 Blocks and Stones,* Portland, Oregon 1973; *11 Poems,* Turin 1974; *Wood/Carl Andre,* with additional text by R. H. Fuchs, Eindhoven, Netherlands 1978; *12 Dialogues: 1962–1963,* with Hollis Frampton, New York and Halifax, Nova Scotia 1980. **Articles—**''Frank Stella'' in *Allen Memorial Art Museum Bulletin* (Oberlin, Ohio) Fall 1959; ''Preface to Stripe Painting (Frank Stella)'' in *16 Americans,* exhibition catalog, New York 1959; ''beam. . . room'' in *Primary Structures: Younger American and British Sculptors,* exhibition catalog, New York 1966; ''Art Is What We Do/Culture Is What Is Done to Us'' in ''Sensibility of the 60's'' in *Art in America* (New York), January/February 1967; ''New in New York: Line Work'' in *Arts Magazine* (New York), May 1967; ''Artist Interviews Himself'' in *Carl Andre,* exhibition catalog, Monchengladbach, Germany 1968; ''Flags: An Opera for 3 Voices'' in *Studio International* (London), April 1969; ''Carl Andre: Form, Structures, Place: in *Arts Magazine* (New York), May 1969; ''A Reasonable and Practical Proposal for Artists Who Wish to Remain Free Men in These Terrible Times'' in *Open Hearing: Art Workers Coalition,* New York 1969; ''Questions et Responses'' in *VH101* (Paris), Spring 1970; ''An Interview with Carl Andre,'' with Phyllis Tuchman in *Artforum* (New York), June 1970; statement in ''The Artist and Politics: A Symposium'' in *Artforum* (New York), September 1970; ''Carl Andre,'' interview with Jeanne Siegel, in *Studio International* (London), November 1970; ''Carl Andre,'' interview with Willoughby Sharp, in *Avalanche* (New York), Fall 1970; ''A Juror's Statement'' in *Centennial Exhibition,* exhibition catalog, San Francisco 1971; ''Letters'' in *Artforum* (New York), March 1972; ''Interview with Carl Andre,'' with Achille Bonito Oliva, in *Domus* (Milan), October 1972; ''A Note on Bernhard and Hilla Becher'' in *Artforum* (New York), December 1972; statement in *Deurle 11/7/73,* exhibition catalog, Brussels 1973; ''Dialogues with Carl Andre,'' with Andrea Gould, in *Arts Magazine* (New York), May 1974; ''Carl Andre,'' interview with Irmeline Lebeer in *L'Art Vivant* (Paris), June 1974; ''Against Duchamp'' in *Praxis* (Chicago), Spring 1975; ''The Role of the Artist in Today's Society'' in *Art Journal* (New York), Summer 1975; ''8 Statements (on Matisse)'' in *Art in America* (New York), July/August 1975; ''Versions of Witness: A Note on Sculpture and Scholarship'' in *Art Journal* (New York), Winter 1975–76; ''An Interview with Carl Andre,'' with Michael Ballou and George Morgenstern, in *Minneapolis College of Art and Design* newspaper, 1976; ''Billy Builder; or, The Painful Machine,'' chapters I-IV, in *Tracks* (New York), Spring 1976; ''Public Notice'' in *Artforum* (New York), April 1976; statement in ''Views from the Studio'' by Henry Gerrit in *Art News* (New York), May 1976; ''Correspondence'' in *Studio International* (London), May/June 1976; ''Commodity and Contradiction; or, Contradiction as Commodity,'' with Jeremy Gilbert-Rolfe, in *October* (New York), Summer 1976; ''Billy Builder; or, The Painful Machine,'' chapters V-XI, in *Tracks* (New York), Fall 1976; notes in

Bienal, exhibition catalog, Sao Paulo 1977; ''Questions, Public? Sculpture? For Münster?'' in *Skulptur Ausstellung in Münster,* exhibition catalog, Münster, Germany 1977; ''Billy Builder; or, The Painful Machine,'' chapters XII-XVI, in *Tracks* (New York), Spring 1977; statement in ''The 20th-Century Artists Most Admired by Other Artists'' in *Art News* (New York), November 1977; interview in *Artists in Their Own Words* by Paul Cummings, New York 1979; ''Interview with Carl Andre,'' with Ida Panicelli, in *Neue Kunst in Europa* (Munich), January/February 1985; interview with David Batchelor in *Artscribe International,* summer 1989; ''The Bricks Abstract'' in *Art Monthly,* March 1993.

On ANDRE: Books—8 *Young Artists,* exhibition catalog, by C. E. Goossen, Yonkers, New York 1964; *Carl Andre,* exhibition catalog, Monchengladbach, Germany 1968; *Carl Andre,* exhibition catalog, by Enno Develing, The Hague 1969; *Unitary Forms: Minimal Sculpture by Carl Andre, Don Judd, John McCracken, Tony Smith,* exhibition catalog, by Suzanne Foley, San Francisco 1970; *Carl Andre,* exhibition catalog, by Diane Waldman, New York 1970; *The New Avant-Garde* by Gregoire Müller, New York 1972; *Carl Andre: Sculpture 1958–1974,* exhibition catalog, by Angela Westwater, Berne 1975; *Carl Andre; Sculpture 1959–78,* exhibition catalog, with an essay by Nicholas Serota, London 1978; *Carl Andre: Sculpture 1959–1977,* exhibition catalog, by David Bourdon, with a foreword by Barbara Rose, New York 1978; *Carl Andre: Sculpture 1983,* exhibition catalog, with essay by John Howett, Atlanta, Georgia 1983; *Carl Andre* (catalog raisonne), The Hague 1987. **Articles—** ''Carl Andre: Poems 1958–74'' by Lynda Morris in *Studio International* (London), September/October 1975; ''An Andre Is What It Is, Not Another Thing'' by John Russell in the *New York Times,* 20 February 1976; editorial in *Studio International* (London), March/April 1976; ''Carl Andre: Art Versus Talk'' by Jeff Perrone in *Artforum* (New York), May 1976; ''Carl Andre Has the Floor'' by Thomas Hess in *New York,* 7 June 1976; ''Carl Andre on Work and Politics'' by Sandy Ballatore in *Artweek* (Oakland, California), 3 July 1976; ''Trivialization of Art by the Press'' by Pat Gilmour in *Arts Review Yearbook,* London 1977; ''Minimalism and Critical Response'' by Phyllis Tuchman in *Artforum* (New York), May 1977; ''Carl Andre'' by David Bourdon in *Arts Magazine* (New York), December 1977; ''Background of a Minimalist: Carl Andre'' by Phyllis Tuchman in *Artforum* (New York), March 1978; ''Andre in Retrospect'' by Kenneth Baker in *Art in America* (New York), April 1980; ''Bricklaying with Andre'' by Waldemar Januszczak in *The Guardian* (London), 12 December 1985.

*

My works are not the embodiments of ideas or conceptions. My works are, in the phrase of William Blake, ''Lineaments of gratified desire.''

—Carl Andre

* * *

Carl Andre's Minimalist work of the 1960s was part of a radical disruption of the reverential condition of traditional sculpture. His early work—wooded columns influenced by Brancusi's totemic figures—eventually yielded to austere, floorbound arrangements of ordinary, prefabricated materials such as brick, metal plates or ribbon, and wood. The promotion of a minimal aesthetic, exemplified by Andre's work of the late 60s, represented a prolonged reaction against Abstract Expressionism specifically, and the spiritual and utopian agenda of modernism in general. Andre's disenchantment with the antigravitational illusionism of 20th century sculpture led him to explore the possibilities of earthworks, stating that the ''ideal piece of sculpture is a road.'' The artist's interests in the idea of passage, perhaps related to his employment in the 1960s as a freight brakeman and conductor for the Pennsylvania Railroad, resulted in a rejection of the conventional model of sculpture as an elevated and sanctioned object. *Spill* (1968), a ''scatterpiece'' in which 800 identical plastic blocks were flung to the gallery floor, further emphasized this rejection. While *Spill* has been tenuously compared to Jackson Pollack's overall compositions, it is, on the contrary, antithetical to Pollack's painting in its tacit repudiation of the modernist preoccupation with internal paradox, structural balance, and artistic control. Instead, Andre's floorbound arrangements of magnesium, lead, copper, and steel plates aim for a continuity with their ambient space: ''FORM = STRUCTURE = PLACE'' Andre has written, in a kind of theoretical formula for his work. Rather than possessing internal or metaphorical content, these minimalist pieces function at the level of externality; it is the temporal experience, and the specificity of the ''real,'' which lies at the core of his work.

Engaged in a continuing dialogue with modernism, Andre's minimalist pieces, therefore, cannot be seen as entirely ahistorical. *Lever* (1966), an early and generative work composed of a single row of unattached firebricks, marked an auspicious beginning for the artist's offensive against sculptural convention. Andre's position toward modernism is suggested in a remark made in relation to *Lever:* ''All I am doing is putting Brancusi's *Endless Column* on the ground instead of in the air. . .'' Toppled from its ''pedestal,'' *Lever* is representative of the postmodernist attack against the rarefaction of the art object. The underlying principles of modernism, as Andre's statement indicates, were not entirely rejected; rather, they were brought to the threshold of something radical and new.

Though Andre has continued to emphasize material and spatial specificity in his work to date, contemporary critical frameworks have cast the minimalist debate into a new light, raising some provocative questions: Is the reductivism of minimalist works more closely related to modernism than was implied in the 60s? Does the persistence of Andre's strategy result from philosophical conviction or market success? Does the reconstruction of old works like *Sand-Lime Instar* (1966, 1994) signify a re-treading of old ground, or an interest in a historical recontextualization (a somewhat radical concept, considering minimalism's roots)? Certainly, the unique elegance of Andre's work remains one of its most salient aspects, leading one to speculate on how aesthetics may outlive concept in the career of this artist.

—Essay by Maurice Berger; updated by Audrey Mandelbaum

ANSELMO, Giovanni

Nationality: Italian. **Born:** Borgofranco d'Ivrea, 5 August 1934. Lives and works in Turin. **Agent:** Galleria Christian Stein, 206 Piazza

San Carlo, 10121 Turin. **Address:** Corso Galileo Ferraris 57, 10128 Turin, Italy.

Individual Exhibitions:

1968 Galleria Sperone, Turin
1969 Galleria Sperone, Turin
Galerie Sonnabend, Paris
1970 Galleria Sperone, Turin
Galleria Toselli, Milan
1971 Galleria Sperone, Turin
Galleria Multipli, Turin
1972 Galleria Sperone, Turin
John Weber Gallery, New York
1973 Galerie MTL, Brussels
Kunstmuseum, Lucerne
1974 Galleria Marilena Bonomo, Bari, Italy
Galleria Sperone-Fischer, Rome
Studio d'Arte L. Rumma, Naples
Galleria Sperone, Turin
Galerie Foksal, Warsaw
1975 Galleria Sperone, Turin
Galleria Sperone, Rome
Galleria Area, Florence
Saman Galleria, Genoa
Kabinett für Aktuelle Kunst, Bremerhaven, Germany
1976 Galleria Ghiringelli-Sperone, Milan
Sam Galleria, Genoa
Nuovi Strumenti, Brescia, Italy
1977 Galleria Sperone, Rome
Kabinett für Aktuelle Kunst, Bremerhaven, Germany
Galleria Il Tritone, Biella, Italy
Galleria G. de Crescenzo, Rome
1978 Galleria Salvatore Ala, Milan
Studio Tucci Russo, Turin
Galerie Paul Maenz, Cologne
Galerie Durand-Dessert, Paris
Sperone-Westwater-Fischer Gallery, New York
1979 Kunsthalle, Basel
Galerie, Rudiger Schöttle, Munich
Galleria Emilio Mazzoli, Modena
1980 Stedelijk van Abbemuseum, Eindhoven
Galerie Helen van der Meij, Amsterdam
Forum Kunst, Rottweil, Germany
Musée de Grenoble, France
Galleria Sperone, Turin
1981 Salvatore Ala Gallery, New York
1982 Galleria Christian Stein, Turin
Galerie Durand-Dessert, Paris
Galerie Helen van der Meij, Amsterdam
1983 Galleria Christian Stein, Turin
1984 Marian Goodman Gallery, New York
Galerie Michele Szwacjer, Antwerp
Castello di Rivoli, Turin
1985 Musee d'Art Moderne de la Ville, Paris
1986 Kunstnernes Hus, Oslo
Galleria Christian Stein, Milan
1987 Galerie Tanit Kunigk und Mollier, Munich
1988 Galleria Christian Stein, Turin
Galleria Micheline Szwajcer, Antwerp
Spazio Pitti Uomo, Firenze
1989 Galleria Civica d'Arte Moderna, Modena
Marian Goodman Gallery, New York
Musée d'Art Contemporain, Lione
Lloyds Bank Chambers, Wales
1990 Galleria Christian Stein, Turin
XLIV Biennale di Venezia, Padiglione Italia, Venice
Affinités Sélectives I, Palais des Beaux-Arts, Brussels
Galerie Tanit, Monaco
Galerie Buchmann, Basel
Jean Bernier Gallery, Atene
Then and Now: Giovanni Anselmo, Sol Lewitt, Stein Gladstone Gallery, New York
1991 Galleria Alfonso Artiaco, Pozzuoli
Galleria Marga Paz, Madrid
1992 Marian Goodman Gallery, New York
Early Multiples, Baron-Boisanté Gallery, New York
1993 Centre d'Art Contemporain, Geneva
1994 Galleria Micheline Szwajcer, Antwerp
Galerie de l'Ancienne Poste, Calais
XXII Bienal Internacional, San Paolo
1995 Centro Galego de Art Contemporanea, Santiago de Compostela
1996 Musée d'Art Moderne et Contemporain, Nice
Marian Goodman Gallery, New York
Galerie Konrad Fischer, Düsseldorf
Inviter 3, Forum d'Art Contemporain, Casino du Luxembourg
1997 The Renaissance Society, University of Chicago
1998 Haus of Prints Multiple Drawings, Antwerp
2001 Marian Goodman Gallery, New York

Selected Group Exhibitions:

1967 *Group Exhibition,* Galleria Sperone, Turin
1968 *9 at Castelli,* Leo Castelli Warehouse, New York
1969 *When Attitude Becomes Form,* Kunsthalle, Berne (travelled to the Museum Haus Lange, Krefeld, Germany, and the Institute of Contemporary Arts, London)
1970 *Vitalita del Negativo nell'Arte Italiana 1960–1970,* Palazzo delle Esposizioni, Rome
1972 *Documenta 5,* Kassel, Germany
1974 *Art and Image in Recent Art,* Art Institute of Chicago
1978 *Words,* Kunstmuseum, Bochum, Germany (travelled to the Palazzo Ducale, Genoa)
1981 *Identite Italienne: L'Ari en Italie depuis 1959,* Centre Georges, Pompidou, Paris
1983 *Presence Discrete,* Musee des Beaux-Arts, Dijon, France
1985 *The European Iceberg,* Art Gallery of Ontario, Toronto
1986 *Qu'est-ce-que la sculpture moderne?,* Museo National de l'Art Moderne, Centres Georges Pompidou, Paris
1987 *Skulptur Projekte in Münster 1987,* Westfäliches Landesmuseum, Münster
1989 *Italian Art in the Twentieth Century,* Royal Academy of the Arts, London
1990 *Die Endlichkeit der Freiheit,* Berlin
1991 *Toward a New Museum,* Museum of Modern Art, San Francisco, California

1993 *Gravity and Grace: The Changing Condition of Sculpture,* Hayward Gallery, London
1994 *The Italian Metamorphosis 1943–1968,* Solomon Guggenheim Museum, New York
1995 *Revolution: Art of the Sixties,* Museum of Contemporary Art, Tokyo
Reconsidering the Object of Art, 1965–1975, Museum of Contemporary Art, Los Angeles
1996 *Cast-Cut, Assemble: Contemporary Sculpture from the Permanent Collection,* Museum of Modern Art, San Francisco
1997 *Arte Povera, Arbeiten und Dokumente aus der Sammlung Goetz 1958 bes heute,* Neues Museum Weserburg, Bremen
1998 *Arte Italiana 1945–1995: Il visibile e l'invisibile,* Museum of Contemporary Art, Tokyo
1999 *A Homage to Granite—The Island of Sculptures,* Pontevedra
2000 *Le temps-vite,* Centre Georges Pompidou, Paris
Minimalism and After, Museum of Modern Art, New York

Collections:

Stedelijk van Abbemuseum, Einhoven; Stedelijk Museum, Amsterdam; Rijksmuseum, Kroller-Muller, Otterlo, Netherlands; Groninger Museum, Groningen, Netherlands; Australian National Gallery, Canberra; Museum of Modern Art, New York; Centre Georges Pompidou, Paris; San Francisco Museum of Modern Art; Museo d'Arte Contemporanea, Castello di Rivoli, Rivoli; Galleria Civica d'Arte Moderna, Turin; Musée d'Art Contemporain, Lyon; Isla de Esculturas, Pontevedra, Spain; Stedelijk Museum voor Actuele Kunst, Gent.

Publications:

By ANSELMO: Books—*Leggere,* Turin 1972; *116 Particolari Visibili e Misurabili di Infinito,* Turin 1975.

On ANSELMO: Books—*Anselmo,* exhibition catalog, by Maurizio Fagiolo, Turin 1968; *Giovane Scultura Italiana* by Germano Celant, Casabella, Italy 1968; *Arte Povera* by Germano Celant, Salerno/Milan/Tübingen/New York 1969; *Giovanni Anselmo,* exhibition catalog, by Jean-Christophe Ammann, Lucerne 1973; *Giovanni Anselmo,* exhibition catalog, by Jean-Christophe Ammann and Rudi Fuchs, Basel 1979; *Giovanni Anselmo,* exhibition catalog, by Thierry Raspail, Grenoble, France 1980; *Anselmo,* exhibition catalog with text by Suzanne Page, Paris 1985; *Giovanni Anselmo,* exhibition catalog, Lyon 1989; *Giovanni Anselmo,* exhibition catalog, Turin 1994; *Giovanni Anselmo,* exhibition catalog, Santiago de Compostela 1995; *Giovanni Anselmo,* exhibition catalog, Nice 1996; *Giovanni Anselmo,* Lugano, Switzerland 1998.

* * *

By the time Giovanni Anselmo had held his first one-man show at the Galleria Sperone in Milan in 1968, the group known as Arte Povera, of which he was a member, had already been formed. In this exhibition of his work, with its balanced cubes, floating bubbles, suspended sheets of plexiglass and hanging chains, Anselmo had abandoned the traditional picture plane in an attempt to create a more direct representation of the themes of gravity and movement. He was striving for an immediate relation to the real world, both visible and invisible.

In 1966 he had made a work consisting of a small cube above which was fixed a slender baton. The work was labeled *Untitled,* but the materials employed were precisely noted: iron, wood and the force of gravity. A work of 1967–68, *Direzione,* is made of a heavy triangular granite block containing a small compass. The stone is oriented to the north as indicated by the compass needle. Anselmo thus commented on the magnetic forces residing in all natural objects.

Torsione of 1968 is made of cowhides partially embedded in a block of concrete. The lengths of hide emerging from the cement block are stretched out and secured by a sturdy piece of wood piercing and keeping the hides in tension from its position leaning against the wall.

Anselmo's work makes play with the themes of infinity and energy, and the notion that the artist intervenes in a natural order, impressing his own definition of reality on the materials at his disposal.

From 1970 onwards he began using projected slides together with parallelopiped prism shapes made of lead onto which words were engraved. *Infinito* is a work of 1971 in which Anselmo uses a projection, focused to infinity of the word ''Infinito.'' In other works he projects the word ''particolare'' (detail) onto a wall to distinguish it from the remainder of the unlit surface. In *Invisibile,* the projection focuses the word ''visibile'' into an empty space so that the word *is* genuinely invisible. He uses the same idea when he engraves a parallelopiped of lead with the word ''visibile'': the space in which we would expect to find the prefix ''in-'' is missing, and all that remains is ''visibile.''

The different ways in which Anselmo pursues these ideas are all aimed at establishing an appropriate expressive rapport between the energies of the invisible and the infinite. His work is thus intended to be a part, or fragment, which indicates an invisible totality.

—Roberto Lambarelli

ANTES, Horst

Nationality: German. **Born:** Heppenheim, 28 October 1936. **Education:** Primary school in Heppenheim, 1942–47, Heppenheim College, 1948–57; studied at the Staatliche Akademie der Bildenden Künste, under H. A. P. Grieshaber, Karlsruhe, 1957–59. **Family:** Married Dorothea Grossman in 1961; children: Aaron and Salomea. **Career:** Lived in Florence, 1962; in Rome, 1963. Professor of art, Staatliche Akademie der Bildenden Künste, Karlsruhe, 1965–73; guest professor of Art, Academy of Fine Arts, Berlin, 1967–68. **Awards:** Kunstpreis, Hannover, 1959; Pankofer prize, 1959; Stipendium des Kulturkreises im Bundesverband der Deutschen Industrie, 1960; Junger Western fellowship, Recklinghausen, 1961; André Malraux prize, *Biennale,* Paris, 1961; Villa Romana prize, Florence, 1962; Villa Massimo fellowship, Rome, 1963; Guggenheim Award, 1964; Aldegrever-Gesellschaft fellowship, Münster, 1966; Unesco prize, *Biennale,* Venice, 1966; Premio Marzotto-Europa, Valdango, 1968. **Agents:** Galerie Brusberg, Kurfürstendamm 213,

1000 Berlin 15, Germany; Galerie Gunzenhauser, Maximilianstrasse 10, 8000 Munich 22, Germany; Nishimura Gallery, 4–3-13 Ginza, Chuo-ku, Tokyo 104, Japan. **Address:** 11 Hohenbergstrasse, 75000 Karlsruhe 41, Germany.

Individual Exhibitions:

1960 Galerie der Spiegel, Cologne
Galerie Richentor, Basel
Galerie Boukes, Wiesbaden, Germany
Galerie 61, Freiburg, Germany
1961 Kellergalerie im Schloss, Darmstadt
Galerie Baier, Mainz, Germany
Studio for Neue Kunst, Wuppertal, Germany
1962 Stadtheater, Remscheid, Germany
1963 Galerie der Spiegel, Cologne
Galerie N., Bremen, Germany
Musée d'Art Moderne, Paris
Städtisches Museum, Ulm, Germany
1964 Städtisches Galerie, Munich
Freie Galerie, Berlin
Kurbuchhandlung and Galerie Krohn, Badenweiler, Germany
Galerie d'Eendt, Amsterdam
Galerie Schmucking, Braunschweig, Germany
Kleiner Raum Clasing, Münster, Germany
1965 Deutsche Bibliothek, Brussels
Galerie der Spiegel, Cologne
Galerie Stangl, Munich
1966 Galerie Altes Theater, Ravensburg, Germany
Kunstverein, Ulm, Germany
Galerie Valentien, Stuttgart
Galerie Maercklin, Stuttgart
Galerie Schmucking, Braunschweig, Germany
Städtische Kunsthalle, Mannheim
Galerie Defet, Nuremberg, Germany
1967 Lefebre Gallery, New York
Studentenhaus, Universität Tübingen, Germany
Kunstkabinett am Institut für Lehrerweiterbildung, Berlin-Pankow
Bundesgartenschau, Karlsruhe (travelled to the Badischer Kunstverein, Karlsruhe)
Kurbuchhandlung and Galerie Krohn, Badenweiler, Germany
Städtischer Kunstpavillon, Soest, Germany
Kleiner Raum Clasing, Münster, Germany
Kunstmuseum, Basel
Galerie d'Eendt, Amsterdam (with Hans Andreus)
Galerie Gimpel and Hanover, Zurich
Staatliche Kunsthalle, Baden-Baden, Germany
Freunde Mainfränkischer Kunst und Geschicht, Wurzburg, Germany
1968 Gimpel Fils, London
Kunstverein, Braunschweig, Germany
Galleria d'Art del Naviglio, Milan
Galerie Lochte, Hamburg
Galerie Junge Generation, Innsbruck
Arts Studeo, Aarhus, Denmark
Galerie Junge Generation, Vienna
Worpsweder Kunsthalle, Bremen, Germany
Galerie Stangl, Munich
Galerie Forum 67, Linz, Austria
Theater Stadt Nordhorn, Germany
1969 Lefebre Gallery, New York
Galerie Prisma, Copenhagen
Tatkreis Kunst der Ruhr, Essen
Galerie Trost, Lippstadt, Germany
Galerie Regio, Lorrach, Switzerland
Goethe Institut, Marseilles
Galleria d'Arte del Cavallino, Venice
1970 Galerie Valentien, Stuttgart
Sitzende Figur mit Scheibe und Ei, Gimpel and Hanover Galerie, Zurich
Gimpel Fils, London
Galerie Jesse, Bielefeld, Germany
1971 Galerie Muchow, Freiburg, Germany
Galerie Walther, Dusseldorf
Kunsthalle, Kiel, Germany
Städtische Verkehrsamt, Offenburg, Germany
Galerie Schmucking, Braunschwieg, Germany
Bilder und Skulpturen 1965–1971, Kunsthalle, Baden-Baden, Germany (travelled to the Gesellschaft der Kunstfreunde, Lindau; Kunsthalle, Berne; Kunsthalle, Bremen; and the Frankfurter Kunstverein)
Antes in der Sammlung Wolf und Ursula Hermann, Kabinett 2 Graphisches Kabinett, Bremen, Germany
1972 Galerie Hoeppner, Hamburg
Kunsthalle, Wilhelmshaven, Germany
Lefebre Gallery, New York
Kunstverein Gentofte, Copenhagen
Nordjutland Museum, Aalborg, Denmark
Galerie Stangl, Munich
Galerie Pudelko, Bonn
Galerie Defet, Nuremberg, Germany
1973 Goethe Institut, Rome
Theater der Stadt, Schweinfurt, Germany
Gimpel Fils, London
Gimpel and Hanover Galerie, Zurich
Kunstkreis Hameln, Germany
1974 Ulmer Museum, Germany
Städtisches Galerie, Rosenheim, Germany
Lefebre Gallery, New York
Galerie Orek, Constance, Germany
Librairie et Galerie La Hume, Paris
P and P Galerie, Zug, Switzerland
1975 Galerie Stangl, Munich
Lippische Gesellschaft für Kunst, Detmold, Germany
1976 Gimpel Fils Gallery, London
Lefebre Gallery, New York
Arts Club of Chicago
1978 Gimpel-Hanover-André Emmerich Galleries, Zurich
Lefebre Gallery, New York
1980 Lefebre Gallery, New York
1981 Galerie Valentien, Stuttgart
Nishimura Gallery, Tokyo
1982 Galerie Brusberg, Hannover
Galerie Schloss Hardenberg, Velbert-Neviges, Germany
Galerie Rehklau, Augsburg, Germany
Kreissparkasse, Reutlingen, Germany
Galerie Der Spiegel, Cologne

Galerie Schaefer, Giessen, Germany
Galerie Bernd Lutze, Friedrichshafen, Germany
Lefebre Gallery, New York
1983 Galerie von Loe, Konigstein, Germany
Galerie Brusberg, West Berlin
Kuhnsthalle, Bremen, Germany
Stadtische Galerie, Frankfurt
Kunstmuseum, Hannover
Galerie Gunzenhauser, Munich
Stadthalle, Weiden, Germany
Goethe-Institut, Athens
Dada Art Gallery, Athens
Wilhelm-Hack-Museum, Ludwigshafen, Germany
Kunstverein, Ludwigshafen, Germany
1984 Goethe-Institut, Cairo
Goethe-Institut, Nicosia, Cyprus
Freilichtgalerie, Ludwigsburg, Germany
Villa Franck, Ludwigsburg, Germany
Galerie Der Spiegel, Cologne
Galerie Ilverich, Meerbusch-Ilverich, Germany
Galerie Albrecht, Kaltern/Bozen, Germany
Lefebre Gallery, New York
Guggenheim Museum, New York
Galerie Hor, Nuremberg, Germany
Nishimura Gallery, Tokyo
Galerie Defet, Nuremberg, Germany
1985 Lefebre Gallery, New York
Galerie Krohn, Badenweiler, Germany
Kupferstichkabinett, Dresden, Germany
Galerie Michael Neumann, Dusseldorf
Kunstverein, Bayreuth, Germany
1986 Lefebre Gallery, New York
Kunstbuchhandlung Art Service, Karlsruhe-Durlach, Germany
Stadtsparkasse, Gladbeck, Germany
Galerie Reichard, Frankfurt
Galerie Funck, Mannheim, Germany
Taimei Gallery, Tokyo
Galerie Schmucking, Archsum/Sylt, Germany
Galerie Gunzenhauser, Munich
1987 Galerie Holbein, Lindau, Germany
Galerie Wilbrand, Cologne
Stadtische Galerie, Villingen-Schwenningen, Germany (and Kunstverein Hochrhein, Bad Sackingen)
Galerie K. G. Schafer, Frankfurt
Galerie Ilverich, Meerbusch-Ilverich, Germany
Galerie Gunzenhauser, Munich
2000 Galerie Schlictenmaier, Gafenau, Germany

Selected Group Exhibitions:

1959 *1st Biennale des Jeunes Artistes,* Musée d'Art Moderne, Paris
1961 *Carnegie International,* Pittsburgh
1964 *Documenta 3,* Kassel, Germany
1966 *Biennale,* Venice
1968 *European Painters Today,* Musée des Arts Decoratifs, Paris (toured the United States)
1971 *2nd Triennale of India,* New Delhi
1974 *From Picasso to Lichtenstein,* Tate Gallery, London
1982 *Torso als Prinzip,* Kunstverein, Kassel, Germany
1985 *Kunst in der Bundesrepublik 1984–85,* Nationalgalerie, West Berlin
1987 *Fifty Years of Collecting,* Guggenheim Museum, New York

Collections:

Kunstmuseum, Basel; Neue Nationalgalerie, Berlin; Städtische Kunstsammlungen, Bonn; Wallraf-Richartz, Cologne; Musée Royaux des Beaux-Arts, Brussels; Centre Georges Pompidou, Paris; Gemeentemuseum, The Hague; Museum Boymans-van Beuningen, Rotterdam; Museum des 20. Jahrhunderts, Vienna; Guggenheim Museum, New York.

Publications:

By ANTES: Articles—''Interview mit Horst Antes,'' with Otmar Engel in *Civis* (Bonn), no. 9–10, 1963; *Deutsche Kunst: Eine Neue Generation* by Rolf-Gunter Dienst, Cologne 1970; *Noch Kunst—Neestes aus deutschen Ateliers* by Rolf-Günter Dienst, Dusseldorf 1970; *Horst Antes: Sitzende Figur mit Scheibe und Ei,* exhibition catalog by Willy Rotzler and Mark Rothko, Zurich 1970; *Antes in der Sammlung Wolf und Ursula Hermann,* exhibition catalog, Bremen, Germany 1971; *Horst Antes,* exhibition catalog by Willy Rotzler, Zurich and London 1973.

On ANTES: Books—*Horst Antes,* exhibition catalog with text by Herbert Pee, Ulm, Germany 1963; *Vortrag zur Eroffnung der Ausstellung Horst Antes-Das graphische Werk 1959–1967* by Gunther Gercken, Baden-Baden, Germany 1967; *Kunst unserer Zeit* by Will Grohmann, Cologne 1970; *Bis Heute* by Karin Thomas, Cologne 1971; *Horst Antes: Bilder and Skulpturen 1965–1971,* exhibition catalog by Carlo Huber, Berne 1971; *Contemporary Prints* by Riva Castleman, New York 1973; *Antes,* exhibition catalog by Wolf Hermann, Rosenheim, Germany 1974; *Horst Antes Poggibonsi 1979–1980* by Klaus Gallwitz, Frankfurt 1980; *Horst Antes Votives,* exhibition catalog with texts by Werner Haftmann and Thomas Messer, New York 1984; *Horst Antes—Dreiundfunfzig Bilder, Dreiunddreisig Sammler aus Suddeutschland,* edited by Volker Huber, Offenbach am Main 1987; *Horst Antes. Arbeiten, Sammlungen 1959–1995,* Karlsruhe Stadt Galerie, 1995; exhibition catalog, Galerie Schlictenmaier, Germany, 2000.

* * *

Though he studied at Karlsruhe and returned there to teach at the Academy of Fine Arts from 1965 to 1973, Horst Antes could be described as the explorer of a territory known only to himself, as anthropologist specialising in creatures discovered in his own imaginative experience.

His early paintings in the late 1950s were strong, highly coloured works deriving partly from the Expressionism of the previous generations of German painters and partly from the example of his professor H. A. P. Grieshaber. They were a variant of the New Figuration that was popular among German artists at the time. Antes then developed his own figuration in his ''Gnome'' people, massive beings who presented their profiles impassively on the canvas. Bright synthetic colours heightened the surrealist effect of these strange personages, often crippled or distorted so that a head would surmount two legs without a trunk, one arm waving in futility. Large in scale, these brooding heads sometimes with eyes set vertically one above the other recall such visual twists by Picasso while a landscape of a deserted classic temple beneath floating white clouds takes on the atmosphere of a naive Chirico.

Within a year of leaving the Karlsruhe Academy Antes had his first one-man show at the Spiegel Gallery, Cologne, and since then he has shown continuously in Europe and the U.S.A. In 1962 and 1963 he lived in Italy and now spends much of his time in Tuscany. His interest in the paintings of the Italian Primitives had its effect on his work which became more pure and simplified in colour.

Antes's ''family'' of art figures possess formidable sculptural elements often truncated and disjointed and painted in monochrome. On two facing figures prehensile toes of equal length and stylised hands assume schematic patterns akin to the hieratic reliefs of Assyrian wall sculpture.

The severe iconography of the pictures, their economy of colour and simplicity of motives demand a concentration upon meaning that is never clarified. Deliberate malformation of humanity carries with it some of the ominious messages transmitted by Bacon but in more mechanistic effigy and at the same time carrying something of the haunting masks of primitive societies.

Man as mask is likewise suggested in other connotations such as ''Portrait with Slide'' where a man looks out from the apertures in his helmet of skin. Affinities with Leger seem superficial; in the projected puzzle there is more of the early surreal drama of Max Ernst and the prehistoric imagery of Easter Island gods.

Iconic and personal, the paintings and prints of Horst Antes illustrate not a phase of art history but the concrete externalisation of community dreams. He has created the identifiable hero of contemporary myth, conveying in each successive work satisfaction of a curiosity aroused in all sagas: what happens next? He maintains the strength of his figurative concepts by involving the spectator in the funambulist contest of his rudimentary compositions.

—G. S. Whittet

ANTIN, Eleanor

Nationality: American. **Born:** Eleanor Fineman in New York City, 27 February 1935. **Education:** Attended the Tamara Daykarhanova School for the Stage, New York; studied creative writing at the College of the City of New York. **Family:** Married the poet David Antin in 1961; child: Blaise. **Career:** Worked as a professional actress, 1955–58; now a full-time artist, living and working in California. Visiting lecturer, University of California at Irvine, 1974–75. Assistant professor, 1975–78, associate professor, 1978–79, and since 1979 professor of visual arts, University of California at San Diego. **Awards:** National Endowment for the Arts grant, 1979; Pushcart Prize, 1982; Vesta Award for Performance, 1984; Dorothy Arzner Special Recognition Crystal Award, 1992. **Agent:** Ronald Feldman Fine Arts, 31 Mercer Street, New York, New York 10013. **Address:** Post Office Box 1147, Del Mar, California 92014, U.S.A.

Individual Exhibitions:

1968 Long Island University, Brooklyn, New York
1970 *California Lives,* Gain Ground Gallery, New York
1971 *Library Science,* Brand Library Art Center, Los Angeles
Portraits of 8 New York Women, Chelsea Hotel, New York
1972 *Traditional Art,* Henri Gallery, Washington, D.C.
Library Science, California Institute of the Arts, Valencia, California
Library Science, University of California at San Diego
Library Science, Austin Peay State University, Clarksville, Tennessee
Traditional Art, Orlando Gallery, Los Angeles
1973 *100 BOOTS,* Museum of Modern Art, New York
Part of an Autobiography, Portland Center for the Visual Arts, Oregon
More Traditional Art, Northwood Experimental Art Institute, Dallas
I Dreamed I Was a Ballerina, Orlando Gallery, Los Angeles
1974 *Several Selves,* Everson Museum, Syracuse, New York
The Ballerina and the King, Galleria Forma, Genoa
Black Is Beautiful, University of California at Irvine
1975 The Kitchen, New York (video exhibition)
2 Transformations, Stefanotty Gallery, New York
1976 *Eleanor Antin, R.N.,* The Clocktower, New York
1977 *The Angel of Mercy,* D'Arc Gallery, New York
The Angel of Mercy, La Jolla Museum of Contemporary Art, California
The Nurse and the Hijackers, Ronald Feldmand Fine Arts Gallery, New York
100 BOOTS Once Again and Choreographies, Wadsworth Atheneum, Hartford, Connecticut
1978 *The Ballerina,* Whitney Museum, New York
The Nurse and the Hijackers, Long Beach Museum of Art, California
Ballerina, Los Angeles Institute of Contemporary Art
1979 *Before the Revolution,* Ronald Feldmand Fine Arts Gallery, New York
100 BOOTS: Transmission and Reception, Franklin Furnace, New York
The Black Ballerina, Marianne Deson Gallery, Chicago
1980 *Recollections of My Life with Diaghilev,* Ronald Feldman Fine Arts Gallery, New York
1981 *Angel of Mercy,* Los Angeles Institute of Contemporary Art
Nova Gallery, Vancouver
Early Works, Palomar College, California
1982 *Recollections of My Life with Diaghilev,* Minneapolis College of Art and Design, Minnesota
La Mamelle, San Francisco
Rutgers University, New Brunswick, New Jersey
1983 *El Desdichado,* Ronald Feldman Fine Arts, New York
Recollections of My Life with Diaghilev, Tortue Gallery, Los Angeles
1986 *Loves of a Ballerina,* Ronald Feldmand Gallery, New York
1988 *Loves of a Ballerina,* MAG Galleries, Los Angeles, and Installation Gallery, San Diego
1989 Artemisia, Chicago (retrospective)
1991 *The Man without a World,* San Diego Museum of Contemporary Art, La Jolla, California (travelled to film festivals throughout the world)

1995 *Minetta Lane: A Ghost Story,* Ronald Feldman Fine Arts, New York, and Santa Monica Museum of Art, California

Performances: *The Ballerina Goes to the Big Apple,* Woman's Building, Los Angeles, 1974; *Eleanor 1954,* Woman's Building, Los Angeles, 1974; *The King's Meditations,* Center for Music Experiment, University of California at San Diego, 1975; *The Ballerina Goes to the Big Apple,* Stefanotty Gallery, New York, 1975; *The Battle of the Bluffs,* Fine Arts Gallery, San Diego, 1975; *The Battle of the Bluffs,* Palace of Fine Arts, San Francisco, 1975; Escape, Palace of the Legion of Honor, San Francisco, 1975; *The Battle of the Bluffs,* The Clocktower, New York, 1976; *The Battle of the Bluffs,* Los Angeles Institute of Contemporary Art, 1976; *The Battle of the Bluffs,* at the *Biennale,* Venice, 1976; *The Battle of the Bluffs,* at the *American Theatre Association Convention,* Los Angeles, 1976; *Escape from the Tower,* The Clocktower, New York, 1976; *It's Still the Same Old Story,* The Clocktower, New York, 1976; *The Angel of Mercy,* D'Arc Gallery, New York, 1977; *The Angel of Mercy,* La Jolla Museum of Contemporary Art, California, 1977; *The Battle of the Bluffs,* Museum of Contemporary Art, Chicago, 1978; *The Battle of the Bluffs,* Contemporary Arts Museum, Houston, 1978; *The Battle of the Bluffs,* Center for Music Experiment, University of California at San Diego, 1978; *Before the Revolution,* Kitchen Center for Music, Video and Dance, New York, 1979; *Before the Revolution,* Santa Barbara Museum of Art, California, 1979; *Recollections of My Life with Diaghilev,* Ronald Feldman Fine Arts Gallery, New York, 1980; Recollections of My Life with Diaghilev, 80 Langton Street, San Francisco, 1980; *The Battle of the Bluffs,* at the *National Women's Caucus for Art,* New Orleans, 1980; *The Battle of the Bluffs,* performed at the Ford Theatre, at the *11th Annual International Sculpture Conference,* Washington, D.C., 1980; *The Battle of the Bluffs,* College of Art, Calgary, Alberta, 1980; *The Battle of the Bluffs,* Western Front, Vancouver, 1981; *The Battle of the Bluffs,* Concordia University, Montreal, 1981; *The Battle of the Bluffs,* Newport Harbor Art Museum, California, 1981; *Angel of Mercy,* Los Angeles Institute of Contemporary Art, 1981; *Recollections of My Life with Diaghilev,* Contemporary Arts Museum, Houston, 1981; *Recollections of My Life with Diaghilev,* School of the Art Institute of Chicago, 1981; *Recollections of My Life with Diaghilev,* University of Regina, Saskatchewan, 1981; *The Battle of the Bluffs,* La Mamelle, San Francisco, 1982; *Recollections of My Life with Diaghilev,* Oklahoma City Museum of Fine Arts, 1982; *The Battle of the Bluffs,* Hofstra University, Hempstead, New York, 1982; *Recollections of My Life with Diaghilev,* California State University, Chico, 1983; *Recollections of My Life with Diaghilev,* Institute of Contemporary Art, Boston, 1984; *Student Days in Paris,* Radio Station WGBH, Boston, 1984; *Recollections of My Life with Diaghilev,* Laguna Beach Museum of Art, California, 1985; *Help! I'm in Seattle,* L.A.C.E., Los Angeles, 1986; *Help! I'm in Seattle,* Franklin Furnace, New York, 1987; *Who Cares About a Ballerina,* Bowery Theatre, San Diego, California, 1987.

Selected Group Exhibitions:

1969 *Language 3,* Dwan Gallery, New York
1975 *Video Art U.S.,* at the *Bienal,* Sao Paulo
1976 *Autobiographical Fantasies,* Los Angeles Institute of Contemporary Art
1977 *American Narrative/Story Art 1967–1977,* Contemporary Arts Museum, Houston (travelled to the Fine Arts Museum, New Orleans; Fine Arts Museum, Vancouver; University of California Museum of Art, Berkeley; and the University of California at Santa Barbara)
1979 *Directions,* Hirshhorn Museum and Sculpture Garden, Smithsonian Institution, Washington, D.C.
1984 *Content: A Contemporary Focus,* Hirshhorn Museum, Washington, D.C.
Revising Romance: New Feminist Video, Institute of Contemporary Art, Boston (toured the United States, 1984–86)
1985 *From the Collection of Sol LeWitt,* California State University, Long Beach (toured the United States)
1989 *Biennale Exhibition,* Whitney Museum of American Art, New York
1990 *Myths,* Museum of Modern Art, New York

Collections:

Museum of Modern Art, New York; Wadsworth Atheneum, Hartford; Connecticut, San Francisco Museum of Modern Art; Long Beach Museum of Art, California; Walker Art Center, Minneapolis; The Jewish Museum, New York; Los Angeles County Museum of Art.

Publications:

By ANTIN: Books—*Before the Revolution,* Santa Barbara, California 1979; *Being Antinova,* Los Angeles 1983; *The Antinova Plays,* Los Angeles 1987. **Articles—**''Women without Pathos'' in *Artnews* (New York), January 1971, reprinted in *Art and Sexual Politics,* edited by Elizabeth Baker and Thomas Hess, New York 1973; ''Out of the Box'' in *Art Gallery,* June 1972; ''Reading Ruscha'' in *Art in America,* September/October 1973; ''Recollections of My Life with Diaghilev'' in *Artweek,* 27 October 1973; ''Letter to a Young Woman Artist'' in *Anonymous Was A Woman,* Valencia, California 1974; ''Video as a Medium'' in *Art-Rite,* October 1974; photo-texts of ''Ballerina and the Bum'' and ''Little Match Girl Ballet'' in *Video Art,* edited by Ira Schneider and Beryl Korot, New York 1976; interview, with Leo Rubenfein, in *Art in America,* September/October 1978; ''Interview with Eleanor Antin,'' with Dinah Portner, in *Journal: Southern California Art Magazine,* February/March 1980; interview, with Nancy Bowen, in *Profile: Eleanor Antin,* publication of the Video Data Bank, School of the Art Institute of Chicago, 1981; ''Pocahontas'' in *Skew,* no. 1, 1981; ''Revolutions Per Minute,'' interview with Carter Ratcliff, in *Inter-View* (New York), September 1982; ''Before the Revolution'' in *Women and Performance: A Journal of Feminist Theory,* no. 1, 1990. **Films—***It Ain't the Ballet Russe,* 1986; *The Last Night of Rasputin,* 1989; *The Man without a World,* 1991.

On ANTIN: Books— *Art Talk* by Cindy Nemser, New York 1975; *Video Art* edited by Ira Schneider and Beryl Korot, New York 1976; *Angel of Mercy,* exhibition catalog with essays by Jonathan Crary and Kim Levin, La Jolla, California 1977; *Originals: American Women Artists* by Eleanor Munro, New York 1979; *Directions,* exhibition catalog with an essay by Howard Fox, Washington, D.C. 1979; *Performance Anthology: Source Book for a Decade of California Performance Art* edited by Carl Loefler and Darlene Tong, San Francisco 1980; *The Amazing Decade: Women and Performance Art in America 1970–1980* edited by Moira Roth, Los Angeles 1983; *Women Artists* by Nancy Heller, New York 1987; *The Object of*

Performance by Henry M. Sayre, Chicago 1989; *Making Their Mark* by Catherine Brawer and Randy Rosen, New York 1989; *The Pink Glass Swan* by Lucy Lippard, New York 1995; *Eleanor Antin* by Howard N. Fox, Los Angeles 1999. **Articles**—review by Lawrence Alloway in *The Nation* (New York), 23 February 1970; ''Los Angeles 1971'' by Elizabeth Baker in *Artnews* (New York), September 1971; ''The Post Perceptual Portrait'' by Amy Goldin in *Art in America* (New York), January/February 1975; ''4 Artists of Sensuality'' by Cindy Nemser in *Arts Magazine* (New York), March 1975; ''When Greatness Is a Box of Wheaties'' by Carol Duncan in *Artforum* (New York), October 1975; ''Eleanor Antin: Wishes, Lies and Dreams'' by Peter Frank in *Soho Evening News* (New York), 19 February 1976; ''Eleanor Antin's Historical Daydream'' by John Russell in the *New York Times,* 23 January 1977; ''Life/Art/Life; Quentin Crisp and Eleanor Antin: Notes on Performance in the 70's'' by John R. Clarke in *Arts Magazine* (New York), February 1979; ''Entries; Maximalism'' by Robert Pincus-Witten in *Arts Magazine* (New York), February 1981; ''Antin/Antinova: The Self as Art Medium'' by Sanda Agalidi in *Michigan Quarterly Review* (Ann Arbor), Winter 1984; ''Antinova Dances Again'' by Henry Sayre in *Artweek* (Oakland, California), 31 May 1986; ''Ethnic Notions and Feminist Strategies of the 1970s: Some Work by Judy Chicago and Eleanor Antin'' by Lisa Bloom in *Jewish Identity in Modern Art History*, edited by Catherine M. Soussloff, University of California Press 1999.

*

For some time I have been considering my art as an exploration of the self, which means that I have been attempting to define my self by moving out to its frontiers, where knowledge of what I cannot and will not be gradually helps shape what I am.

Apparently I have an action or acting theory of the self, because I tend to think of the self as a collection of possible characteristic roles that wait in the wings for their chance to play. No actor can play all roles. A good one can play at most three or four fundamental ones, which he or she can, with effort and talent, bend, stretch and transform to satisfy the casting demands life makes on him or her. The inferior actor—the impoverished self—can play only one role over and over again, no matter what demands life makes on him. This boring and impoverished performance is considered sincerity by an equally boring and impoverished criticism, which supposes one life, one truth. I have never accepted such a trivial truth, and I have determined by empirical investigation of my soul that I am by nature typecast as a King, a Ballerina, a Nurse, and a color—Black. A King must rule or try to rule, a Ballerina must star, a Nurse must help, and as all of my selves turn Black, I transform my eccentric Blackness in a white culture into a virtue and a power. My work has taken the course through drawing, painting, writing, photography, video and performance—of allowing these figures of my soul to play out their roles, and answer to all the demands that life makes on me—an artist, a woman, an American in the last quarter of the 20th century.

—Eleanor Antin

* * *

Eleanor Antin is a small woman who looks remarkably kingly in the cape and beard she wears during performances as the King of Solana Beach. The King visits the people of Solana Beach (where Antin happens to live) and discusses politics while participating in daily activities. The real life encounters are documented in black and white slides which become part of performances such as *The Battle of the Bluffs.* The King feels that Solana Beach is a small but natural kingdom ''for no kingdom should extend further than a King can walk on any given day.'' Although Antin is not interested in having Solana Beach revert to the 17th century, a time more familiar to a King dressed like a Van Dyke portrait, the emphasis on naturalness is significant. The ''battle'' refers to a confrontation between real estate developers and a band of young skateboarders and elderly citizens with shuffle board sticks who are organized by the King to stop excessive construction in the small California beach town. There are arrests, and the King escapes down a cliff to travel around the country and alert others. ''The world restored will have trees and homegrown food,'' says the King. Antin's performance work is autobiographical, yet it has historical and art historical roots. As the King, Antin is pleased with her resemblance to Charles I as painted by Van Dyke, finding him to be ''a very small man, like me, a stubborn romantic, and all in all, an impossible person. . . . I recognized all these things in myself. So I knew what sort of man I was, and that he was my political self because a king rules a country.'' As Eleanora Antinova, she presents herself as a black dancer with Diaghilev's troupe, reminiscing over her triumphs and failures. As a nurse, she occasionally uses material from the life of Florence Nightingale. At all times Antin is completely immersed, not only in her part but in many parts. *The Battle of the Bluffs* is done as a narrative, and although Antin wears the King's costume and performs in front of slides of the King's activities in Solana Beach, she provides the voices for all the characters, lending a ''charming story hour at the library'' ambiance to the work. Autobiography blends with historical allusions and the real history of Antin's characters, documented for performance in slides, or, for Eleanora Antinova, photographs of the ballerina in her greatest roles. Antin's self, therefore, manifests itself in several characters and across several centuries. She is in a position of power as the King, and in a position of powerlessness as the black dancer whose career is thwarted. She controls the performance, yet she is always a vulnerable character. As King, she travels on foot, unprotected, through her kingdom in a manner no one expects of leaders or royalty. By mingling her own vision and experiences with the past, she gives clues to the self of Eleanor Antin in a context which redefines not only the artist but some concepts about power and traditional roles for women. While she has not abandoned any of her characters, Antin has focused on Eleanora Antinova, the black ballerina, in the 1980s. In 1983 she published *Being Antinova,* a detailed account of the twenty-day build up and let down of transforming herself from a performance artist living in California to Antinova, dancer in New York. The milieu is the contemporary New York art world, with an astonishing quantity of frank comments and gossip, but the artist's familiarity as a native New Yorker enables her to provide a wide-ranging commentary on class and race consciousness in the Big Apple past and present. Antinova resurfaced in 1986 in *Help! I'm in Seattle,* a performance wherein she hits the skids as a performer in vaudeville houses in the 1930s, and mourns her past with Diaghilev. Once again Antin poses seemingly unsolveable questions about the relation between theater and performance art, couching them in Antinova's own dilemma.

—Mary Stofflet

While the work of Eleanor Antin has frequently been understood within a feminist context, her performances acknowledge both ethnic and gendered difference, as she exposes otherness within patriarchal, white culture. This intersection of the historical with the personal is expressed in her filmic installation *Vilna Nights* (1993). Within the gallery space, the viewer is confronted first by the bombed-out ruins of a Jewish ghetto before being beckoned to peer through the windows, witnessing the demise of Jewish culture and, according to Antin, ''the ghosts of the vanished inhabitants.'' Antin invokes a narrative of loss. She mourns both the lives lost during the Holocaust, but also the loss of Jewish tradition through acculturation and assimilation. Eleanor Antin's art of the 1990s continues to incorporate personal identity, but it has expanded beyond the self and invented autobiography to confront (historical) collective experience—both seen and silenced.

—Sarah Webb

ANTONAKOS, Stephen

Nationality: American. **Born:** St. Nicholas, Gythion, Greece, 1 November 1926; settled with his family in the United States, 1930. **Education:** Studied at Brooklyn Community College, New York. **Career:** Independent artist, New York, since 1950. Instructor in Painting, Brooklyn Museum Art School, 1965–67; instructor, University of North Carolina, Greensboro, 1967 and 1969; artist-in-residence, Viterbo College, LaCrosse, Wisconsin, 1968; instructor, Yale University, New Haven, Connecticut, 1968; instructor in sculpture, Brooklyn College, 1970; artist-in-residence, University of Wisconsin, Madison, and Fresno State College, California, 1971. **Awards:** Creative Artists Public Service Program Grant, New York, 1972; National Endowment for the Arts grant, 1973. **Address:** 435 West Broadway, New York, New York 10012, U.S.A.

Individual Exhibitions:

1958 Avant-Garde Gallery, New York
University of Maine Art Gallery, Orono
1964 Byron Gallery, New York
Schram Galleries, Fort Lauderdale, Florida
Miami Museum of Modern Art
1967 Fischbach Gallery, New York
1968 Fischbach Gallery, New York
1970 Fort Worth Art Center Museum, Texas
Fischbach Gallery, New York
1971 Madison Art Center, Wisconsin
Fischbach Gallery, New York
Allen Priebe Art Gallery, Wisconsin State University, Oshkosh
Contemporary Arts Museum, Houston
1972 Fishbach Gallery, New York
Fresno State College Art Gallery, California
1973 State University of New York Galleries, Albany (toured the United States)
1974 Rosa Esman Gallery, New York
John Weber Gallery, New York
Albright-Knox Art Gallery, Buffalo, New York
Discussions: Works/Words, The Clocktower, New York
Cusack Gallery, Houston
Fort Worth Art Museum, Texas
1975 *Incomplete Blue Neon Circles,* Galleria Marilena Bonomo, Bari, Italy
Galerie 26, Paris
Galleriaforma, Genoa
Wright State University Art Gallery, Dayton, Ohio
John Weber Gallery, New York
1976 *Incomplete Neon Circles,* Galerie December, Duseldorf
John Weber Gallery, New York
Art and Project, Amsterdam
Galerie Bonnier, Geneva
Nancy Lurie Gallery, Chicago
1977 *Neons—Stockholm—1977,* Galerie Aronowitsch, Stockholm
John Weber Gallery, New York
Jean and Karen Bermier, Athens
1978 University of Massachusetts Art Gallery, Amherst
Drawings, Galerie Tanit, Munich
Young Hoffman Gallery, Chicago
1979 *Neons/Paris/1979,* Galerie Nancy Gillespie/Elisabeth de Laage, Paris
1980 *Neons, Drawings, Collages, München, 1980,* Galerie Tanit, Munich
Lowe Art Museum, Miami
1982 Nassau Country Museum of Art, Roslyn, New York
1983 Maison de Culture, Nevers, France
Three Neons, Le Coin du Miroir, Dijon, France
Bonnier Gallery, New York
Neons, Jean Bernier Gallery, Athens
1984 *Neons and Works on Paper,* La Jolla Museum of Contemporary Art, California
1985 Sandpiper Gallery, Tacoma, Washington
Neons, Davenport Art Gallery, Iowa
1986 *Neons and Drawings,* Brandeis University, Waltham, Massachusetts
University of Wisconsin, Madison (installation)
1987 *Neons and Drawings,* Burnett Miller Gallery, Los Angeles
Dalsheimer Gallery, Baltimore, Maryland
1988 Ileana Tounta Contemporary Art Center, Athens, Greece
1989 Kouros Gallery, New York
1990 *Neons and Drawings,* Galerie d'Art Contemporain, Geneva
1992 Ileana Tounta Contemporary Art Center, Athens, Greece
1993 Macedonian Museum of Modern Art, Salonika, Greece
Chapel of the Saints, The Fortress of St. George, The Old City, Rhodes, Greece
1995 *Drawings,* Werner Kramarsky, New York
1996 *The Room,* The Art Institute of Boston, Massachusetts
1997 *Praise,* Ileana Tounta Contemporary Art Center, Athens
The Chapel of the Heavenly Ladder, Representing Greece at the XLVII Venice Biennale, Venice
Inner Light, Smith College Museum of Art, Northampton, Massachusetts
Meditation Room, Samuel P. Harn Museum, Gainseville, Florida
Recent Aspects, Stux Gallery, New York
1998 *Chapel Models,* Lucas Gallery, Visual Arts Program, Princeton University, New Jersey
Plastivellum Drawings, Center for Hellenic Studies, Princeton University, New Jersey
Selected Drawings, Jan Abrams Fine Art, New York

Early Assemblages and ''Blue Box,'' Mitchell Algus Gallery, New York
1999 *''Welcome'' and ''Chapel for P.S. 1,''* P.S. 1 Center for contemporary Art, Long Island City, New York
Blue Cross Meditation Chapel, The Arts Center, Portsmouth, Virginia
''The Chapel of the Heavenly Ladder'' and Other Works, St. Peter's Church, New York
Color and Light, Gallery Camino Real, Boca Raton, Florida
Greek Travel Collages, Foundation for Hellenic Culture, New York
2000 *Time Boxes 2000,* Rose Art Museum, Brandeis University, Waltham, Massachusetts
Public Work 1973–2000, State Museum of Contemporary Art, Salonika, Greece
Praise, State Museum of Contemporary Art, Salonika, Greece
Proscenium, Neuberger Museum of Art, State University of New York, Purchase, New York

Selected Group Exhibitions:

1977 *Documenta 6,* Kassel, West Germany
1978 *A Shade of Light,* San Francisco Museum of Modern Art
1979 *Minimal Tradition,* Aldrich Museum of Contemporary Art, Ridgefield, Connecticut
1980 *Aspects of the 70's: Site Work,* Jewett Arts Center, Wellesley College Museum, Massachusetts
1981 *Summer Light,* Museum of Modern Art Penthouse, New York
1983 *Elektra,* Musée d'Art Moderne de la Ville, Paris
1984 *Intermedia Space,* Aldrich Museum of Contemporary Art, Ridgefield, Connecticut
1987 *XIX Bienal de Sao Paulo,* Brazil
1989 *Artec,* International Biennale, Nagoya, Japan
1992 *Greek Artists from Greece and the Diaspora,* installation on the Pinakotiki, National Gallery of Art, Athens, Greece
1994 *Antonakos and Takis,* European Union Hall, Zapion, Athens
1995 *Time is a Child Playing and Throwing Dice; to the Child Belongs the Power,* Municipal Gallery of Athens (travelled to Patras, Volos, Santorini, Rhodes and Larcana)
1997 *Raum Aeichen Licht,* Kartner Landesgalerie, Museum for Moderne Kunst, Bozen, Germany
1998 *25th Anniversary Exhibition,* Carl Schlosberg Fine Arts, Sherman Oaks, California
1999 *Modern Odysseys,* Queens Museum, Queens, New York (travelled to the State Museum of Contemporary Art, Salonika, Greece)
2000 *Belsios Collection,* Trikala, Greece

Permanent Public Installations:

Red Neon Circle Fragments on a Blue Wall, Federal Building, Dayton, Ohio 1978; *Incomplete Circles and Squares,* Crown Center, Hampshire College, Amherst, Massachusetts 1978; *Incomplete Red Neon Square on Exterior Corner,* University of Massachusetts, Amherst 1979; *Four Walls for the Hartsfield International Airport,* Hartsfield International Airport, Atlanta 1980; *Neon for 42nd Street,* 42nd Street, between Ninth and Tenth Avenues, New York 1981; *Neon for Charles Street Station,* Charles Center Mass Transit Station, Baltimore 1983; Center Resident Theatre; *Neon for the Bagley Wright Theater,* Seattle, Washington 1983; *Neon for York College,* York College, New York 1986; *Neons for Southwestern Bell,* Southwestern Bell Texas Headquarters, Dallas 1984; *Neons for Tacoma Dome,* Tacoma Dome, Washington 1984; *Neon for the Columbus Museum of Art,* Columbus Museum of Art, Ohio 1986; *Neon for Greektown Station,* Detroit, Michigan 1988; *Neon for the 59th Street Marine Transfer Station,* New York 1990; *Neons for Momoci,* Fukuoka, Japan 1992; *Neons for the Stadtsparkasse,* Cologne, Germany 1993; *The Blue Room,* San Antonio Public Library, Texas 1995; *Neons for the Reading Power Plant,* Tel Aviv, Israel 1999; *Procession,* Ambelokipi Station, Attiko Metro, Athens 2000.

Collections:

Whitney Museum, New York; Museum of Modern Art, New York; Milwaukee Art Center; Miami Museum of Modern Art; La Jolla Museum of Contemporary Art, California; Phoenix Art Museum, Arizona; Newark Museum, New Jersey.

Publications:

On ANTONAKOS: Books—*Minimal Art: A Critical Anthology,* edited by Gregory Battock, New York 1968; *The Magic Theatre* by Ralph T. Coe, Kansas City, Missouri 1970. **Exhibition catalogs—** *New Forms/New Media* by Lawrence Alloway and Allan Kaprow, New York 1960; *Stephen Antonakos: Six Corner Neons* (with essay by Naomi Spector), New York 1973; *Stephen Antonakos* (with texts by Xavier Dourous, Franck Gautherot and Naomi Spector), Dijon 1983; *Neons and Works on Paper* (with essay by Sally Yard), La Jolla 1984. **Articles—**''New Talent'' by Larry Aldrich in *Art in America* (New York), July/August 1966; ''Stephen Antonakos: 5 Neons for the San Francisco Show'' by Naomi Spector in *Data* (Milan), autumn 1973; ''Stephen Antonakos'' by Lawrence Campbell in *Artnews* (New York), April 1974; ''Stephen Antonakos'' by Ellen Lubell in *Arts Magazine* (New York), April 1974; ''Stephen Antonakos at the Fort Worth Art Museum'' by Janet Kutner in *Art in America* (New York), September/October 1975; ''Stephen Antonakos' Neons'' by Hugh Davies in *Arts Magazine* (New York), January 1979; ''Lights of the Night'' by Michael Webb in *Sky* (New York), February 1984; ''Creations in Neon'' by William Zimmer in the *New York Times,* 15 March 1987.

*

My work concerns light, color and space: neon used in relation to architectural sites, painted canvases, and painted wood panels. My drawings, prints, books, and other projects are also very important to me in working out my ideas about placing elements in relation to each other. Neon is endless. Its ability to change and be changed by various elements—alone, or in combination—is a continuing source of inspiration to me. I am interested in a direct visual experience which will allow the viewer to participate fully, which will provide a feeling of heightened consciousness, or excitement.

—Stephen Antonakos

* * *

Stephen Antonakos's work has never been a search for new technical possibilities. His concern for light as a means of expression is the sole impetus for his perseverance with a potentially dated art form, neon. Yet he is no ''light artist,'' but a sculptor and a painter. His search is rather for new ways of commanding ever more intense and refined statements from his formal vocabulary.

Born in southern Greece, Antonakos immigrated to the United States in 1930. He graduated from the New York Institute of Applied Arts and Sciences in 1947, then worked two years as a commercial artist until becoming frustrated by the restrictions of drawing in black and white. After assisting Umberto Romanoin 1951, Antonakos spent nine months in Europe visiting galleries and museums. During that period he formulated an individual approach to painting in colour.

Nearly all of Antonakos's work contains the leitmotif of incompletion. In the late 1940s and early 1950s he developed a complicated vocabulary of forms and a penchant for natural and found materials and colours. The result was a composition of found objects and fragments glued, pinned, or sewn to the canvas called ''sewlages.'' He devoted his energies in the late 1950s to free-standing, wooden assemblages. Beginning in September 1962, Antonakos conceived all of the renowned ''Pillow'' series in one intense 14-month period. The pillows communicate in words, in forms, in materials, in symbols, and with real objects. They deliver themes of interruption, chaos, loss and pain, offering riddles, promising revelations, and ultimately define the struggle of an identity unable to reconcile what it wants to be with what it really is. The pillows tell a story of how they must overcome being ripped open, sewn up, and nailed down to achieve understanding and to reach wholeness.

The focus of his work shifted again in 1962 as he developed a regime of light as environment. The first neons were fully three-dimensional sculpture forms, traditional pedestal objects whose constituent tubes emitted intense coloured light and were programmed to turn on and off in series. With the advent of environmental art during the decade following, Antonakos persistently exploited the full potential of a medium which projects colour and creates volume without sculptural mass.

The three-dimensional forms gradually evolved into neons which conspicuously hugged the plane of the wall. In this sense his work has progressed from assertively sculptural to architectural and finally to environmental painting. The latter is characterised by a dramatic increase in scale, as many neon elements are arranged across the entire two-dimensional surface in mural fashion. The painting's actual dimensions are obfuscated by deliberate perspectival distortions: the bright neon elements establish a flat plane, although the neon itself appears to float, making the depth of the rear supporting wall ambiguous.

Antonakos discovered that painting the supporting walls in colours compliments the neons they entertain. Background colour defines the boundaries of the work and alters the ambient light. He reiterates his original leitmotif by painting the walls in fragments of squares or circles, incomplete shapes that suggest the language of minimalism.

Yet his work seems to adhere to no single identifiable group. Being conspicuously versatile it satisfies dogmatists of most spheres: technological utopianism, geometric reduction, grammatical vision. Because neon is so direct it seems uncomplicated at first, but even in the same piece it can be completely different in meaning: it is quiet and inconspicuous in the daylight, more alert and assertive at dusk, progressively more dominating and abstract at night. From different points of view it is a series of illusions which succeeds as an architectural statement both indoors and out.

The power of these neons rests undeniably in their ability to excite and evoke. Antonakos is particularly sensitive to the warmth and ambiance of colour—mostly reds, blues and greens—and rhythm. When the light goes off, the tubes often seem to become immaterial, and when they burst back on, the shock is extremely effective, especially in rhythmic repetition. This rhythmic quality is one his most crucial elements. From the beginning the forms—especially the linear ones—appear in repetitive patterns hinting at rhythms of various sorts.

While the emanation of ambient light and the resulting environmental command it bears resemble artists like Flavin, the colour and composition of his neon paintings echo the works of Matisse. Indeed his work bears comparison to a range of artists and dogmas, although the constant evolution in Antonakos's work continues to avoid type-casting.

—Carrie Barker

ANUSZKIEWICZ, Richard (Joseph)

Nationality: American. **Born:** Erie, Pennsylvania, 23 May 1930. **Education:** Cleveland Institute of Art, Ohio, B.F.A., 1953; School of Art and Architecture, Yale University, New Haven, Connecticut (studied with Joseph Albers), M.F.A., 1955; Kent State University, Akron, Ohio, B.S. (in education), 1956. **Career:** Independent artist known for hard-edge, nonobjective paintings and prints. Instructor, Cooper Union, New York, 1963–65; artist-in-residence, Dartmouth College, Hanover, New Hampshire, 1967; visiting artist, University of Wisconsin, Madison, Cornell University, Ithaca, New York, and Kent State University, Ohio, 1968; instructor in painting, School of Visual Arts, New York, 1983–86. **Awards:** Pulitzer Travelling Fellowship, National Academy of Design, 1953; Charles of the Ritz Oil Painting Award, Silvermine Guild of Artists, Silvermine, Connecticut, 1963; Silvermine Guild Award for Oil Painting, Silvermine Guild of Artists, Silvermine, Connecticut, 1964; Purchase prize, Flint Institute of Arts, Michigan, 1966, 1980 and 1988; Cleveland Arts Prize, Cleveland Women's City Club Foundation, Ohio, 1977; New York State Art Teacher's Association Award, New York, 1994; Emil and Dines Carlsen Award, National Academy of Design, New York, 1995; New Jersey Pride Award, New Jersey Monthly Magazine, 1996; Richard Florsheim Fund Grant, 1997; Lee Krasner Award, Pollack-Krasner Foundation, 2000. **Address:** 76 Chestnut Street, Englewood, New Jersey 07631, U.S.A.

Individual Exhibitions:

1955 Butler Art Institute, Youngstown, Ohio
1960 The Contemporaries, New York

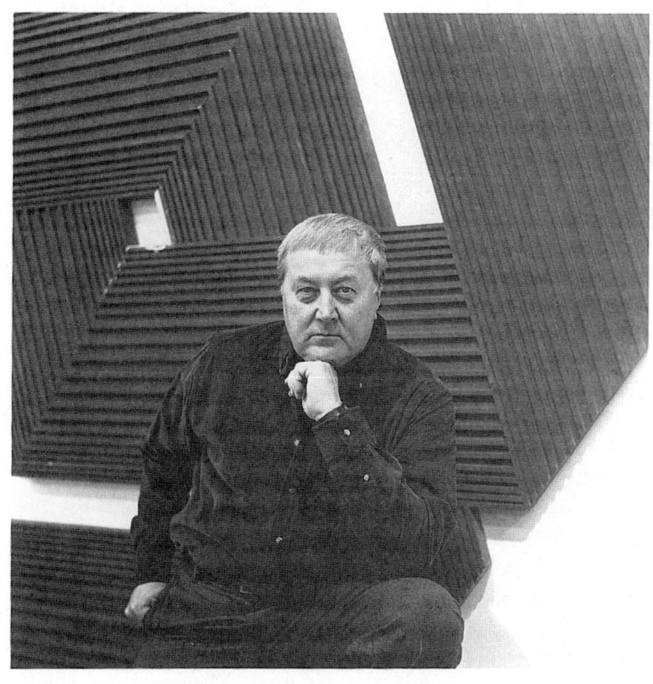

Richard Anuszkiewicz. ©Richard Anuszkiewicz/Licensed by VAGA, New York.

1961 The Contemporaries, New York
1963 The Contemporaries, New York
1965 Sidney Janis Gallery, New York
1966 Cleveland Museum of Art
1967 Sidney Janis Gallery, New York
Hopkins Art Center, Dartmouth College, New Hampshire
Galerie der Spiegel, Cologne, Germany
1968 Kent State University, Akron, Ohio
1969 Sidney Janis Gallery, New York
1971 Sidney Janis Gallery, New York
1972 DeCordova Museum, Lincoln, Massachusetts
Jacksonville Art Museum, Florida
Loch Haven Art Center, Orlando, Florida
1973 Sidney Janis Gallery, New York
Summit Art Center, Summit, New Jersey
1975 Andrew Crispo Gallery, New York
Ulrich Museum of Art, Wichita, Kansas
1976 Ulrich Museum of Art, Wichita, Kansas
La Jolla Museum of Contemporary Art, California
1977 University of California Art Museum, Berkeley
Columbus Gallery of Fine Arts, Ohio
1978 Ringling Museum, Sarasota, Florida
Allentown Art Museum, Pennsylvania
1979 Alex Rosenberg Gallery, New York
Clark Art Institute, Williamstown, Massachusetts
1980 Brooklyn Museum, New York
Carnegie Institute, Pittsburgh
1981 University Fine Arts Galleries, Tallahassee, Florida
Museum of Fine Arts, St. Petersburg, Florida
Lowe Art Museum, Coral Gables, Florida
Hokin Gallery, Bay Harbor Islands, Florida
1982 Museum of Art, Fort Lauderdale, Florida
Charles Foley Gallery, Columbus, Ohio
Museo Rayo, Roldanillo, Valle, Columbia
1983 Atlantic Center for the Arts, New Smyrna Beach, Florida
1984 Butler Art Institute, Youngstown, Ohio
Hecksher Museum, Huntington, New York
Pembroke Gallery, Houston, Texas
Graham Modern, New York
Canton Art Institute, Canton, Ohio
1985 Hokin/Kaufman Gallery, Chicago
Schweyer-Galdo Galleries, Pontiac, Michigan
Charles Foley Gallery, Columbus, Ohio
1986 Tampa Museum, Florida
Brevard Art Center and Museum, Melbourne, Florida
Pelham Art Center, Pelham, New York
1987 Stetson University, Deland, Florida
Daytona Museum of Arts and Sciences, Daytona Beach, Florida
Richard Green Gallery, New York
Polk Museum of Art, Lakeland, Florida
1988 Hokin Gallery, Palm Beach, Florida
Edison Community College Gallery of Fine Art, Fort Meyers, Florida
Harmon-Meek Gallery, Naples, Florida
Anuszkiewicz, Four Decades, Richard Green Gallery, New York
Art and Culture Center, Hollywood, Florida
Galleria Sagittaris, Centro Iniziative Culturali, Pordenone, Italy
Cleveland Institute of Art, Ohio
Charles Foley Gallery, Columbus, Ohio
1989 Hokin Gallery, Bay Harbor Islands, Florida
Gallerie Civiche D'Arte Moderna, Ferrara, Italy
1990 Newark Museum, Newark, New Jersey
Maruzen Company, Ltd., Tokyo
1991 Harmon-Meek Gallery, Naples, Florida
ACA Galleries, New York
Maruzen Company, Ltd., Tokyo
Charles Foley Gallery, Columbus, Ohio
1992 *Anuszkiewicz, Works Produced at Graphicstudio,* Graphicstudio, University of South Florida, Tampa
Abante Fine Art, Portland, Oregon
Nations Bank Plaza, Tampa, Florida
1993 Camino Real Gallery, Boca Raton, Florida
Center for the Arts, Vero Beach, Florida
Intermission Gallery, John Harms Center for the Arts, Englewood, New Jersey
1994 *Richard Anuszkiewicz Paintings and Sculpture, 1941–1994,* Williams Center for the Arts, Lafayette College, Easton, Pennsylvania
1995 Harmon Meek Gallery, Naples, Florida
1996 Camino Real Gallery, Boca Raton, Florida
1997 *Richard Anuszkiewicz: Paintings and Painted Constructions—A Retrospective Survey from 1954 to 1995,* Josef Albers Museum, Quadrat im Stadtgarten, Bottrop, Germany (travelled to Landesmuseum für Kunst und Kulturgeschichte, Oldenburg, Germany and Städtische Kunstsammlungen, Chemnitz, Germany)
Richard Anuszkiewicz: Graphic Works, Catherine J. Smith Gallery, Appalachian State University, Boone, North Carolina

1998 *Richard Anuszkiewicz: Paintings and Painted Constructions—A Retrospective Survey from 1954 to 1995,* Haus für konkrete und konstruktive Kunst, Zürich, Switzerland (travelled to Wilhelm Hack Museum, Ludwigshaven, Germany)
ProArta Galerie, Zürich, Switzerland
Richard Anuszkiewicz Retrospective, Boca Museum, Boca Raton, Florida
Camino Real Gallery, Boca Raton, Florida
2000 *Richard Anuszkiewicz at the Millenium,* Harmon-Meek Gallery, Naples, Florida
OK Harris Gallery, New York

Selected Group Exhibitions:

1962 *Geometric Abstraction in America,* Whitney Museum, New York (travelled to Boston, Columbus, St. Louis, and Utica)
1965 *The Responsive Eye,* Museum of Modern Art, New York
1968 *Dokumenta IV,* Kassel, Germany
1970 *The 1970 Pittsburgh International Exhibition of Contemporary Painting and Sculpture,* Carnegie Institute, Pittsburgh, Pennsylvania
1971 *The Structure of Color,* Whitney Museum, New York
1975 *34th Biennial of Contemporary American Painting,* Corcoran Gallery, Washington, D.C.
1982 *Curator's Choices,* Metropolitan Museum of Art, New York
1986 *The 42nd Venice Biennale,* Italy
1988 *Olympiad of Art of the Seoul Olympics,* Seoul, South Korea
1991 *Jestesmy Zacheta,* Warsaw, Poland
1992 *Works on Paper,* ACA Galleries, New York
1993 *168th Annual Exhibition,* National Academy of Design, New York
1994 *Black and White (Crno & Belo), World Known Constructivist Artists,* Cultural and Congress Centre, Ljubljana, Slovenia
1995 *Printmaking in America, Collaborative Prints and Presses 1960–1990,* Zimmerli Art Museum, Rutgers University, New Brunswick, New Jersey (travelled to Block Gallery, Northwestern University, Evanston, Illinois; Museum of Fine Arts, Houston, Texas and National Museum of American Art, Smithsonian Institution, Washington, D.C.)
1996 *Gli Anni Sessanta—Le Immaginial Poteree,* Fondazione Mazzotta, Milano, Italy
1997 *Exposition Gráfica en Taller de Arts Plásticas Rufino Tamayo,* Oaxaca, Mexico
1998 *Kunst im Aufbruch: Abstraaktion Zwischen 1945 une 1959,* Wilhelm Hack Museum, Ludwigshafen am Rhein, Germany
1999 *Sign and Gesture: Contemporary Abstract Art from the Haskell Collection,* North Carolina Museum of Art, Raleigh, North Carolina (travelled to The Cummer Museum of Art, Jacksonville, Florida; Knoxville Museum of Art, Knoxville, Tennessee and Birmingham Museum of Art, Birmingham, Alabama)
2000 *Six Abstract Artists at the Millenium,* Dorsky Gallery, New York

Collections:

Metropolitan Museum of Art, New York; Museum of Modern Art, New York; Whitney Museum, New York; Albright-Knox Art Gallery, Buffalo, New York; Yale University Art Gallery, New Haven, Connecticut; Corcoran Gallery of Art, Washington, D.C.; Smithsonian Institution, Washington, D.C.; Art Institute of Chicago; Detroit Institute of Arts, Michigan; Philadelphia Museum of Art, Pennsylvania; Chicago Museum of Contemporary Art, Illinois; Guggenheim Museum, New York; Hirschhorn Museum and Sculpture Garden, Washington D.C.; Hokkaido Museum of Modern Art, Sapporo, Japan; Louisiana Museum, Humlebaek, Denmark; Museo de Arte Moderno, Ciudad Bolivar, Venezuela; Museum Morsbroich, Leverkusen, Germany; National Museum of Contemporary Art, Seoul, Korea; Tel Aviv Museum, Israel; Wilhelm-Hack-Museum, Ludwigshafen am Rhein, Germany.

Permanent Public Installations:

Volumes, First National Bank of Chicago, 1970; Exterior Wall Mural, YWCA Building (50th St. and 8th Ave.), New York City, 1972; *Cay Pyramid,* Orlando International Airport, Florida, 1981; *Complimentary Gothic I -Complimentary Gothic II,* Port Authority Bus Terminal (8th Ave. and 41st St.) New York City, 1984; *Oranges and Reds with Blues,* Research Tower Addition, University of Medicine and Dentistry of New Jersey, Piscataway, 1985; *Astral Squares,* New International Airport Terminal C, Newark, 1988; *Chroma Avenue,* New Jersey State Department of Transportation Building, Trenton, 1989; *Complementary Reversal—Yellows, Oranges and Reds,* The Aidekman Center for Molecular and Behavioral Neuroscience, Rutgers University, Newark, New Jersey, 1992; *Astral,* Washington National Airport, Washington, D.C., 1997.

Publications:

On ANUSZKIEWICZ: Books—*The New Art: A Critical Anthology* edited by Gregory Battcock, New York 1966; *Purposes of Art* by Albert Elsen, New York 1967; *Constructivism: Origins and Evolution* by George Rickey, New York 1967; *Optical Art: Theory and Practice* by Rene Parola, New York 1969; *Op Art* by Cyril Barrett, New York 1970; *Richard Anuszkiewicz: Constructions and Paintings, 1986–1991,* by Martin H. Bush, New York 1991; *Anuszkiewicz: Op Art,* exhibition catalog, with text by Thomas Buchsteiner and Ingrid Mössinger, Ostfildern, Hatje 1997. **Articles—**''A Theology of Hard Edge'' by Edouard Roditi in *Arts Magazine* (New York), December 1963; ''Art That Pulses, Quivers and Fascinates'' by John Canaday in the *New York Times,* February 1965; ''Anuszkiewicz Sets Legs in Motion'' by Bernadine Morris in the *New York Times,* May 1965; ''Richard Anuszkiewicz: It's Baffling'' by John Canaday in the *New York Times,* April 1969; ''Graphics '70: Richard Anuszkiewicz'' by Donald Karshan in *Art in America* (New York), March 1970; ''Trays by 10 Artists'' by Mario Amaya in *Art in America* (New York), January 1971; ''Portrait of the Artist: Richard Anuszkiewicz'' by Jay Jacobs in *Art Gallery* (Ivoryton, Connecticut), March 1971; ''At Lincoln: Anuszkiewicz Acrylics'' by Susan Drysdale in the *Christian Science Monitor* (Boston), March 1972; ''Lines of Luminosity'' by Barry Schwabsky in *Art in America,* January 2001.

*

Space and color have always been primary elements in my work. My earliest abstract works from the mid-fifties are best described as organic abstractions consisting of complementary colors juxtaposed in ambiguous spatial relationships such as figure and ground reversal.

Line began to appear in my paintings during the sixties. This development resulted from my interest in ''optical mixture''—using the eye to mix color as opposed to mixing the paint physically on a palette (a method associated with both impressionism and pointillism). The shapes or ''figures'' that had previously been organic, became more geometric and regular. This freed me to fully explore color as a variable, with the use of line.

Over the next twenty-five years, I used ''optical mixture'' in a variety of ''series.'' These series implemented a consistent geometric format within which the color(s) would vary; among these were: ''geometric abstractions,'' ''portals,'' ''pairs,'' ''spectral complementaries,'' ''centered squares'' and finally the ''temple series.'' This last series evolved after a trip I made in 1981 to view the ancient art of Egypt. The line in the ''temple series'' became so bold that the paintings had an almost architectural dimension. I began to pursue this ''architectural'' quality, creating a series of constructions built with lines in three-dimensional relief. These constructions were no longer bound by the constraint of a square or rectangular format.

In the early nineties I freed, or removed line from the background and began to create fully dimensional linear sculptures. I think of them as linear color drawings in space. The current exhibition (*Linear Sculptures,* OK Harris Gallery, 2000) consists of these new works of painted steel which explore the creation of transparent and opaque space. The five newest works introduce the idea of the ''Broken Square.''

—Richard Anuszkiewicz

* * *

Born in 1930 of Polish emigrant parents, Richard Anuszkiewicz is one of the most outstanding exponents of colorism, the movement which developed from abstract expressionism and pop art. At first, Anuszkiewicz leaned toward realism. The change took place as a result of meeting Josef Albers at Yale while he was studying there. Albers opened his eyes to the way colours behave and to their mutual influence on each other which causes ''everything to depend on everything else.''

Despite his respect for the master, Anuszkiewicz rejects total acceptance of Albers's theory. Other theories of colour also interest him—those of Paul Klee, in particular. He has found Klee less pedantic and more poetic in his perception of the world of colour.

Anuszkiewicz was one of the first American painters to be interested in creating space in a picture, introducing the effect of vibrations on a flat surface. He was a pioneer in applying the technique of mixing colours optically—i.e., instead of physically mixing colours on a palette, he achieves the same impression on the retina. This, of course, was nothing new; the process had been in use since divisionism. Developed now, in terms of non-representational art, based on geometric form—it brought a new element to painting. Anuszkiewicz's painting, while exploiting 19th century colour physics and Chevreul's and Helmholtz's theories of colour, also makes use of new technology. This kind of painting distinguishes itself by a specific atmosphere. Created as it is under warm light conditions, it ideally needs to be viewed in a similar light. The intensity of colour, the precision of its optical limits, the technical elegance of coloured surfaces, by rays or a regular network, the juxtaposition of complementary colours which causes after-images—all form a tight, logical system.

This system, recalling Albers's theoretical assumptions, is inherent in the structure of the square. The square forms an unlimited collection of alternatives; divisions into quadrilateral compartments are filled with ever greater or ever smaller fields of squares. These, in turn, yield not only diagonal rhombuses, networks, screens, modules, cuboid spatial variants covered by a network of lines giving the impression of being concave or convex, but also deformations of perspective. Optical illusions also arise on a flat, square surface. If a geometric shape is given by the grouping or separation of lines, the space between them is formed by a subtle gradation of chromatic shades of equal intensity.

The construction of complicated linear and interlinear structures (both inside and outside the modulated squares) has become possible from a technological point of view, thanks to industrial innovations. The fact is that, at the beginning of the 1960s, fast-drying paints (acrylics) appeared as did masking tapes—adhesive and varying in width from 0.2 cm—used hitherto in technical projects. When stuck on the surface of a painting, the tapes cover the parts already painted, thus protecting them from being covered by the next layer of paint. When the tapes are removed, the outline of the resulting image appears. Thanks to the tapes the business of masking can be carried out with ideal precision, impossible with any other technique. Even the thinnest lines have sharp, well-defined edges. But that is not the artist's goal. ''What I am trying to do,'' Anuszkiewicz has said, ''is to achieve a soft effect by means of so-called hard media.'' That is why his paintings, in spite of his emphasis on geometry, differ from classical geometrical abstraction by a softness, blurred forms and a chromatic subduing, despite a simultaneously bright palette. They also differ from op-art—although articles about him usually refer to Anuszkiewicz as an op-artist. This kind of classification is not wholly wrong. Artists interested in optics, optical illusion and kinetics are also called perpetuators of the Bauhaus and Constructivist traditions. Thus Anuszkiewicz, Vasarely, Riley and others all share a common antecedent.

Anuszkiewicz proclaimed his particular view of painting in the United States, but maintained a certain independence from other American artists, retaining his own vision during two decades, the 1960s and 1970s. Nothing augurs a change in his artistic attitude.

—Szymon Bojko

In the mid-1980s, Anuszkiewicz departed from his distinctive focus on coloristic effects and began working in relief and on shaped supports. By reducing the number of colors and painting on alternately raised and lowered surfaces, paintings such as ''Grand Midnight Palace'' (1989) appear to swell and flatten in different parts of the composition, creating an illusion of volume reminiscent of fluted columns. Beginning in 1990, Anuszkiewicz developed his use of relief into spare, painted, three-dimensional works that have been called ''a form of colored drawing in three dimensions.'' The works of the 1990s are composed of thin, rectangular lengths of wood or metal that follow a geometric structure similar to that of his paintings from the early 1970s. For his ''Translumina'' series (1990), he used real rather than illusionistic volumes, with the same geometric regularity of sculptures by Sol Lewitt, albeit more open and colorful. In the mid-1990s, he began experimenting with painted constructions, which, unlike the ''Translumina'' series, occupy a single plane, but create the illusion of receding planes and open, three-dimensional volumes through the arrangement of intersecting lines. Color is used less for optical or sensual effects than as a means to distinguish between different geometric forms. Unlike the brilliant coloristic intensity of his most popular paintings, the later works reveal an growing interest in perspectival recession, volumes and modeling, or, in his own words, ''to create from an empty space, or void, a form that can be seen as either solid or transparent.'' Anuszkiewicz was honored with a retrospective of his works from the 1950s to the 1990s that traveled through Europe in 1997.

—Bradley Bailey

ANZINGER, Siegfried

Nationality: Austrian. **Born**: Weyer, in 1953. **Education:** Steyr, until 1971; studied art, under Professor Melcher, Akademie der bildenden Kunste, Vienna, 1971–77. **Family:** Married to the painter Marie-Luise Lebschik. **Career:** Independent painter, Vienna, since 1977, and in Cologne, since 1981. **Address:** Neusser Strasse 27/29, 5000 Cologne 1, Germany.

Individual Exhibitions:

1976 Galerie Herzog, Vienna
1978 Galerie Ariadne, Vienna
1979 Osterreichische Hochschulerschaft, Vienna
1980 Galerie und Edition Sigrid Friedrich/Sabine Knust, Munich
Galerie Krinzinger, Innsbruck
Galerie Ariadne, Vienna
1981 Galerie und Edition Sigrid Friedrich/Sabine Knust, Munich
Perspektive, at *Art 12, '81,* Basel
1982 Galerie Buchmann, St. Gallen, Switzerland
Galerie t'Venster, Rotterdam (with Hubert Schmalix)
Galerie Bitterlin, Basel (with Hubert Schmalix)
Galerie Krinzinger, Innsbruck
Galerie Nachst St. Stephan, Vienna
Galerie Thaddaus J. Ropac, Lienz, Austria
1983 Galerie Sigrid Friedrich, Munich
Galeria Heinrich Ehrhardt, Madrid (with Hubert Schmalix)
Galerie Vera Munro, Hamburg
Galerie Albert Baronian, Brussels
Galerie Gugu Ernesto, Cologne
1984 Galerie Farideh Cadot, Paris (with Hubert Schmalix and Alois Mosbacher)
Holly Solomon Gallery, New York (with Hubert Schmalix)
Studio Cannaviello, Milan
Galerie Bleich-Rossi, Graz, Austria
1985 Kunstmuseum, Basel
Galerie Buchmann, Basel
ORF, Graz, Austria
Galerie Gugu Ernesto, Cologne
Burnette Mille Gallery, Los Angeles (with Hubert Schmalix)
Galerie Six Friedrich, Munich
Museum für Gegenwartskunst, Basel (travelled to Bonn and Linz 1985–86)
1986 Neue Galerie Graz, Austria
Kunsthalle, Hamburg
Galerie Krinzinger, Vienna
Kunstverein, Frankfurt
Galerie Sigma, Bregenz, Austria
1990 De Vleeshal, Middelburg, Netherlands
1992 Tanit Gallery, Munich
1997 Deweer Art Gallery, Otegem, Belgium
1998 Museum Moderner Kunst Stiftung Ludwig Wien, Vienna

Selected Group Exhibitions:

1977 *Interkunst,* Palais Liechtenstein, Vienna
1980 *Malerei 80,* Galerie Annasaule, Innsbruck
1981 *Neue Malerei in Ostereich,* Landesgalerie Joanneum, Graz, Austria
1982 *Documenta 7,* Museum Fridericianum, Kassel, West Germany
1983 *Einfach gute Malerei,* Museum des 20. Jahrhunderts, Vienna
1987 *Arco 87,* Madrid

Collections:

Kupferstichkabinett, Basel; Neue Galerie der Stadt Linz, Austria.

Publications:

By ANZINGER: Books—*Laokoon Ubt,* with introduction by Peter Weiermair, Innsbruck and Vienna 1986; *Siegfried Anzinger,* Klagenfurt 1988; *Siegfried Anzinger im Gespräch mit Wilfried Dickhoff,* Köln 1996.

On ANZINGER: Books—*Siegfried Anzinger: Malerei, Gouachen, Zeichnungen,* exhibition catalog with introduction by Dieter Ronte, Vienna and Munich 1982; *Siegfried Anzinger: Werke auf Papier 1977–1985,* exhibition catalog with text by Dieter Koepplin, Basel 1985; *Siegfried Anzinger: Zeichnung, Malerie, Skulpture,* exhibition catalog by Dieter Koepplin, Innsbruck 1986; *Siegfried Anzinger,* exhibition catalog, Middelburg 1990; *Siegfried Anzinger,* exhibition catalog with introduction by Jo Coucke, Otegem 1997; *Siegfried Anzinger,* exhibition catalog with text by Lorand Hegyi, Wolfgang Drechsler and Marcus Steinweg, Vienna 1998. **Articles—**''Venice Biennial: A Report on the Major Pavillions'' in *Flash Art (International Edition),* no. 142, October 1988; ''Out of Human Suffering: Siegfried Anzinger'' by Demetrio Paparoni in *Tema Celeste,* no. 26, July-October 1990; ''Tanit Gallery, Munich'' in *Arts Magazine,* vol. 66, March 1992; ''Siegfried Anzinger: Museum Moderner Kunst: Exhibit'' in *Artforum International,* vol. 37, no. 2, October 1998.

APPEL, Karel

Nationality: Dutch. **Born:** Amsterdam, 25 April 1921. **Education:** Royal Academy of Fine Arts, Amsterdam, 1940–43. Met Corneille, Louis Van Lint, and Marc Mendeksin, 1946. **Career:** Co-Founder of the Dutch experimental artists group ''Reflex'' (known as ''CO-BRA'' in Paris), Amsterdam, 1948; moved to Paris, 1950, and officially ended ''COBRA''; met the avant-garde art critic Michel Tapie, Paris, 1951; first travelled to America and Mexico, 1957;

established studios at the Chateau de Molesmes, Auxerre, France, 1964–72. **Awards:** Unesco Prize, *Biennale,* Venice, 1954; Prize at the *Premio Lissone,* Italy, 1957; Graphics Prize, *Biennale,* Ljubljana, 1957; International Prize for Painting, *Sao Paolo Bienal,* 1959; First Prize from the Netherlands Committee, and First Prize for Painting, *Guggenheim International Exhibition,* New York, 1960. Honorary Citizen, Hamilton, Ontario, 1977. Knight of Orange Nassau, Netherlands, 1968.

Individual Exhibitions:

1946 Beerenhuis, Groningen, Netherlands
1947 Guildhall, Amsterdam
1948 Santee Landweer, Amsterdam
1951 Van Lier Gallery, Amsterdam
1952 Het Venster Gallery, Rotterdam
1953 Palais des Beux-Arts, Brussels
Bennewitz Gallery, The Hague
1954 Martha Jackson Gallery, New York
Studio Fachetti, Paris
1955 Bennewitz Gallery, The Hague
Galerie Rive Droite, Paris
Cultural Center, Schiedam, Netherlands
Stedelijk Museum, Amsterdam
1956 Galleria dell'Ariete, Milan
1957 Institute of Contemporary Arts, London
Galerie Espace, Haarlem, Netherlands
Galleria Tartaruga, Rome
Martha Jackson Gallery, New York
1958 Galerie Claude Bernard, Paris
Galerie Anna Abels, Cologne
Palais des Beaux-Arts, Brussels
1959 Galerie Espace, Haarlem, Netherlands
Gimpel Fils, London
Charles Lienhard Gallery, Zurich
Gendai Gallery, Tokyo
Musée d'Art, Neuchatel, Switzerland
1960 Martha Jackson Gallery, New York
Gimpel Fils, London
Galleria Lorenzelli, Bergamo, Italy
Nova Gallery, Boston
Fairweather-Hardin Gallery, Chicago
Rudolf Zwirner, Essen
Esther Robles Gallery, Los Angeles
David Anderson Gallery, New York
Galerie Rive Droite, Paris
1961 Esther Robles Gallery, Los Angeles
David Anderson Gallery, New York
Gallery Espace, Amsterdam
Galerie d'Art Moderne, Basel
Stedelijk Van Abbe Museum, Eindhoven
Haags Gemeentemuseum, The Hague
Irving Gallery, Milwaukee
Tirca Karlis Gallery, Provinceton, Massachusetts
Galleria Le Medusa, Rome
Gallery Moos, Toronto
Gres Gallery, Washington, D.C.
Galleria Blu, Milan
Museum of Art, San Francisco (retrospective)
Pasadena Art Musuem, California (retrospective)
Phoenix Art Museum, Arizona (retrospective)
Santa Barbara Art Museum, California (retrospective)
1962 Galerie Rive Droite, Paris
Gallery Moos, Toronto
La Jolla Art Museum, California
Gimpel Fils, London
Galleria dell'Ariete, Milan
Gallery Charles Lienhard, Zurich
Galerie Agnes Lefort, Montreal
Stephen Hahn Gallery, New York
Martha Jackson Gallery, New York
James Goodman Gallery, New York
Park Gallery, Detroit
Anderson-Mayer Galerie, Paris
Esther Robles Gallery, Los Angeles
1964 Gimpel Fils, London
Martha Jackson Gallery, New York
Stephen Hahn Gallery, New York
American Art Gallery, Copenhagen
Gallery Krikhaar, Amsterdam
1965 Kunsthallen, Göteborg, Sweden
Palais des Beaux-Arts, Brussels
Donald Morris Gallery, Detroit
Gallery Leger, Malmo, Sweden
Stedelijk Museum, Amsterdam (retrospective)
City Museum, Copenhagen (retrospective)
Moderna Museet, Stockholm (retrospective)
Museum of Bochum, Germany (retrospective)
1966 Stedelijk Museum, Breda, Netherlands (retrospective)
1967 Martha Jackson Gallery, New York
Redfern Gallery, London
Galerie Agnes Lefort, Montreal
1968 Centre National d'Art Contemporain, Paris
Stedelijk Museum, Amsterdam
1969 Martha Jackson Gallery, New York
Galerie Gimpel und Hanover, Zurich
Gallery Gimpel, London
Galerie Krikhaar, Amsterdam
Kunsthalle, Basel
Palais des Beaux-Arts, Brussels
1970 Centraal Museum, Utrecht (retrospective)
Galleria La Medusa, Rome
Winterthur, Lucerne
Richard Gray Gallery, Chicago
Gallery Moos, Toronto
Galerie Nova, Spectra, The Hague
1971 Galerie Nova, Spectra, The Hague
Galerie Ariel, Paris
Martha Jackson Gallery, New York (thrice)
Galerie Teatre, Brussels
Nantensi Gallery, Tokyo (twice)
Kunstgalleri, Aarhus, Denmark
London Arts Gallery, Detroit
London Arts Gallery, London
Academy of Fine Arts, Philadelphia
Galleria d'Arte Rinaldo Rotta, Milan
1972 London Arts Gallery, Detroit
S. A. Freedman Gallery, Jamaica, New York
Rothman's of Pall Mall, Toronto (retrospective)
Rothman's Art Gallery, Stratford, Ontario (retrospective)

Musée d'Art Contemporain, Montreal (retrospective)
Art Gallery of Greater Victoria, British Columbia (retrospective)
Edmonton Art Gallery, Alberta (retrospective)
Winnipeg Art Gallery, Manitoba (retrospective)
1973 Art Gallery of Ontario, Toronto (retrospective)
Martha Jackson Gallery, New York
Dalhousie University Art Gallery, Halifax, Nova Scotia (retrospective)
London Public Library and Art Museum, London, Ontario (retrospective)
Art Gallery of Hamilton, Ontario (retrospective)
New York Cultural Center, New York (retrospective)
Miami Art Center (retrospective)
Gallery Moos, Toronto
1974 Oklahoma Art Center, Oklahoma City (retrospective)
Ft. Lauderdale Museum, Florida (retrospective)
Phoenix Art Museum, Arizona (retrospective)
Galleria La Medusa, Rome
Galerie Ariel, Paris
Gimpel Fils, London
Gimpel and Weitzenhoffer, New York
Court Gallery, Copenhagen
Gloria Lauria Gallery, Miami
1975 Gimpel and Weitzenhoffer, New York
Galerie Nova Spectra, The Hague
David Gallery, Pittsford, New York
Aberbach Fine Arts, New York
Wildenstein Gallery, London
1976 Galerie Nova Spectra, The Hague
Gallery Moos, Toronto
Modern Master Tapestries Inc., New York
1977 Galerie Ariel, Paris
Galerie Krikhaar, Amsterdam
Museo de Arte Moderno, Mexico City (retrospective)
Hamilton Museum, Ontario
Museum Terneuzen, The Netherlands
Museum 'Slot Zeist, The Netherlands
Palm Springs Desert Museum, California
Gallery Collection d'Art, Amsterdam
Lillian Heidenberg Gallery, New York
1978 Galerie Nova Spectra, The Hague
Galerie Krikhaar, Amsterdam
Museo de Bellas Artes, Caracas (retrospective)
Museo de Arte Moderno, Bogota (retrospective)
Moderne Galerie Saarlandmuseum, Saarbrucken, Germany
Museum Van Bommel, Van Dam, Venlo, The Netherlands
Cultureel Centrum Hasselt, Belgium
Brewster Gallery, New York
1979 Vienna Museum, Austria (retrospective)
Bonn Museum, Germany (retrospective)
Janus Gallery, Washington, D.C.
6 Scandinavian Museums (retrospective; tour)
1980 Galerie Daniel Templon, Paris
Janus Gallery, Washington, D.C.
State University of New York, Binghamton
Bede Gallery, Jarrow, England
Museum Wilhelmshafen, Germany
1981 Galerie Ariel, Paris
Gimpel Fils, London
Kunstforum Schelderode, Belgium
Stedelijk Museum, Amsterdam
Fame Gallery, Houston, Texas
London Arts Gallery, Detroit
Fundacao Gulbenkian, Lisbon
Museu de Arte Moderna, Rio de Janeiro
Museu de Arte Moderna, Sao Paulo
1982 Biblioteca Nacional, Madrid
Gemeentemuseum, The Hague
Museum Boymans-van beuningen, Rotterdam
Galerie Collection d'Art, Amsterdam
Staatliche Kunsthalle, Baden-Baden, Germany
1984 Kunstforening, Copenhagen
National Gallery of Iceland, Reykjavik
Palais des Beaux-Arts, Brussels
Galerie Collection d'Art, Amsterdam
1985 Palazzo di Medici, Florence
1986 Arnolfini Gallery, Bristol, Avon
Marisa del Re Gallery, New York
Fort Lauderdale Museum of Art, Florida
Virginia Miller Gallery, Coral Gables, Florida
1987 Galerie d'Art Contemporain, Nice, France
Douglas Hyde Gallery, Dublin
Marisa del Re Gallery, New York
1988 Galerie Beyeler, Basle

Selected Group Exhibitions:

1946 *Salon de Mai,* Paris (regularly until 1971)
1951 *2nd COBRA International,* Palais des Beaux-Arts, Liege, Belgium
1953 *2nd Biennial,* Museum of Modern Art, Sao Paolo
1955 *Expressionism* 1900–1955, Walker Art Center, Minneapolis (toured the United States)
1959 *50 Years of Research,* Stedelijk Museum, Amsterdam
1964 *Documenta 3,* Kassel, Germany
1969 *Portraits in Contemporary Art,* Museum of Modern Art, New York
1972 *Humor, Satire, Irony,* New School for Social Research, New York
1973 *25th Anniversary Exhibition of COBRA,* Court Gallery, Copenhagen
1982 *On The Road: The Jack Kerouac Exhibit,* Boulder Center for the Visual Arts, Colorado

Collections:

Stedelijk Museum, Amsterdam; Stedelijk Van Abbe Museum, Eindhoven, Netherlands; Musée Royal des Beaux-Arts, Brussels; Centre National d'Art Contemporain, Paris; Tate Gallery, London; National Museet, Copenhagen; Museum of Modern Art, New York; Guggenheim Museum, New York; Museum of Fine Arts, Boston; Los Angeles County Museum; Hamilton Museum, Ontario; Art Gallery of Ontario, Toronto; Montreal Museum of Fine Arts.

Publications:

By APPEL: Books—*A Beast-Drawn Man,* portfolio, with Bert Schierbeek, Paris 1962; *Karel Appel over Karel Appel,* with a foreword by Albert Rikmans, Amsterdam 1971; *Encres à Deux*

Pinceaux et Leurs Poemes par Hugo Claus, with Pierre Alechinsky, Paris 1978; *Forty Years of Paintings, Sculptures and Drawings,* Paris 1987; *Nocturne de San Ildefonso,* with poems by Octavio Paz, Paris 1987.

On APPEL: Books—*Art since 1945* by Marcel Brion and Samuel Hunter, New York 1958; *Karel Appel: Painter* by Hugo Claus, New York 1962; *Karel Appel: Nudes,* exhibition catalog by Bert Schiebeek, New York 1964; *Karel Appel: Reliefs 1964–1968,* exhibition catalog by Julien Alvard, Paris 1968; *Appel* by Peter Bellew, Milan 1968; *Het Tidschrift Cobra* by Anne Choisez, Brussels 1970; *Appel's Oogappels,* exhibition catalog by Simon Vinkenoog, Utrecht 1970; *Appel's Appels,* exhibition catalog by Luke Rombout, Toronto 1972; *Karel Appel: The Early 50's,* exhibition catalog, New York 1973; *Opere di Karel Appel* by Armondo Nocentini, Florence 1973; *Karel Appel: Recent Works,* exhibition catalog, New York 1973; *Cobra + Contrasts,* exhibition catalog by Willem Sandberg, Detroit 1974; *Appel,* exhibition catalog by Herbert Read, London 1975; *Karel Appel: Pintor de Insolita Expresividad,* exhibition catalog by Antonio Rodriguez, Mexico City 1977; *Visages-Payages,* exhibition catalog, Paris 1977; *Karel Appel* by Peter Berger, Venlo, Netherlands 1977; *Het Gezicht van Appel* by Nico Koster and Edward Wingen, Venlo, Netherlands 1977; *Eloge de la Folie* by Jean-Clarence Lambert, Paris 1977; *30 Years of Painting by Appel* by Edward Wingen, Venlo, Netherlands 1977; *Karel Appel,* exhibition catalog, Bogota 1978; *Karel Appel: Works on Paper* by Jean-Clarence Lambert, with a foreword by Marshall McLuhan, New York 1980; *Karel Appel* by Alfred Frankenstein, New York 1980; *Karel Appel: Paintings 1980–85,* exhibition catalog with introduction by Rupert Martin, Dublin and Bristol 1986; *Karel Appel: Recent Paintings,* exhibition catalog with text by Sam Hunter, New York 1986; *Karel Appel: Recent Paintings and Sculpture,* exhibition catalog with text by Donald Kuspit, New York 1987; *Karl Appel: De Biographie* by Catherine van Houts, Amsterdam, 2000.

*

Over the years my work has changed, and the philosophy behind my thinking about my work has changed too, and still is changing today. I mean by this, that painting is always a fight with yourself and the material. The most difficult thing is the concentration and tension to be ''one'' with myself, my painting and my materials. It's an inner fight, and inner fight means the inner evolution that the artist can see in his work—in his paint, in his image, in his expression, in his color—that means his *inner* evolution is going on.

Take television, for instance. Television is something like the artist—a reality of our planet. The only difference is that television shows only reality and I show the future. I work on the future, and that is the most important thing for me, and thus the reason why my work started changing after the war.

When we started to paint seriously, we formed the *Cobra* group and we met people, other artists, who were busy with the same phenomena, problems and concerns. We made good comrades. *Cobra* was the only real new movement after the War in Europe. A real movement like Dada, Surrealism, Tachism and so on. All these movements existed before the War and there was nothing new about them. But the *Cobra* group started new, and first of all we threw away all these things we had known and started afresh, like a child—fresh and new. Sometimes my works look very childish, or child-like, schizophrenic or stupid, you know. But that was the good thing for me. Because, for me, the material is the paint itself. The paint expresses itself. In the mass of paint, I find my imagination and go on to paint it. I paint the imagination I find in the material I paint.

—Karel Appel

* * *

During his COBRA period Karel Appel stood out together with the Dane Asger Jorn and the Belgian Corneille as the most extreme representatives of a wild and uncontrolled Expressionism which had more in common with the vehement impetuosity of the traditional Dutch and Flemish Expressionism than with the more sober classicism of the French. Working in very thick impasto, Appel produced swirling abstract masses of vigorously contrasting colours and clusters of contorted linear scribbling stamped with the imprint of sweeping brush-strokes. The effect was one of apparently unrestrained spontaneity which, as H. H. Arnason has said, was at first sight reminiscent of Ruskin's remark about Whistler—a pot of paint thrown in the face of the public. Or, to quote Herbert Read, when looking at Appel's pictures one has the impression of ''a spiritual tornado that has left the images of its passage.'' Relying heavily on the evocative power of the materials when moulded into abstract shapes, his work anticipated ''art informel'' and represented a violent reaction from the principles of order and harmony which dominated de Stijl. In its largely automatic procedures, spontaneous brush-strokes and excited linear gestures it represented an early European parallel to American Action Painting. The aim was direct expression unguided by the intellect. Associations were aroused and the mechanism of the unconscious was set in motion by the act of painting itself. Like his fellow-countryman De Kooning in America, Appel did not eschew figuration, but his aim was to stimulate associations and set in motion the unconscious phantasy by the dramatic power and evocative force of his waves of speaking colour—as is evidenced, for example, by ''Red Nude'' (1960) and ''Angry Landscape'' (1967). His later, post-COBRA, work displayed no radical change although the pigment became somewhat more fluid and the facture smoother, while the images often emerged more explicitly as the strange faces in ''Two Times'' (1974) which in the words of Arnason possess ''a wonderful quality of childlike madness.'' Appel's images are in the tradition of Bosch and Ensor: distorted vestiges of human or animal bodies, grimacing masks, strange demonic figures reminiscent of Nordic mythology and folklore. His portraits were often composed of contorted clusters of spiky lines and masses of spontaneous colour without apparent figuration, as in his ''Portrait of Willem Sandberg'' (1956).

In 1968 Appel began to do relief paintings, and from this he progressed to sculpture in painted wood and polychrome polyester. Of this work he said: ''These materials open for me more possibilities to work in space—which is the feeling I want to achieve in my paintings.'' He then worked in aluminum sheet and made sculptures with movable parts, of which he said: ''I hinge the ears so that you can play with them, and they move in the wind as well, which changes the whole shape of the sculpture. The toy principle, you know.''

In an exhibition catalog Herbert Read summed up the painting of Appel:

> Violent as they are, I do not find terror in his images; as Christian Dotrement has said, he captures the beast but does not kill it. He then identifies himself with

> its animal vitality. One must always distinguish between vitality and violence. Though Appel's paintings may be said to stream with the blood of animals, they are not patches on the floor of an abattoir: they represent the physical substance of life itself. Their colors are living, moving, never coagulated or faded. They stream through the field of vision as natural forces, conveying life to hearts that are invisible only because they are hidden within our own breasts.

In a less poetic vein Appel himself said of the change that took place in his work:

> Around 1967–58 my painting was a fight. I did not paint—I hit! . . . My red, for instance, was blood. Now my red is space. . . . My work was a war, was a fight . . . little by little I have gone over more to a magic space feeling. . . . I set my frame of mind in a child-like feeling or toy feeling. My work is like a toy for adults. I believe that through the coming atomic age there will be more time for people to express themselves and to express their own desires as a play element in life. This being the same feeling of inner joy as a child gets with its toys. This is one of the feelings I project as a sound of the future in my work.

—Harold Osborne

ARAKAWA, Shusaku

Nationality: Japanese. **Born:** Nagoya, 6 July 1936; has lived in New York since 1961. **Education:** Studied medicine and mathematics, in Tokyo, 1954–58, Musashino College of Art, Tokyo. **Awards:** DAAD Fellowship, West Berlin, 1972; Chevalier des Arts et des Lettres from French government, 1986; Guggenheim fellowship, 1987–88; Belgian Critics' prize, 1988–89; inauguration of Arakawa room in Nordrhein-Westfalen Museum, Düsseldorf, 1994. **Agent:** Ronald Feldman Fine Arts, 31 Mercer Street, New York, New York 10013, U.S.A. **Address:** 124 West Houston Street, New York, New York 10012, U.S.A.

Individual Exhibitions:

1958 Museum of Modern Art, Tokyo
1961 Mudo Gallery, Tokyo
1963 Galerie Schmela, Düsseldorf
1964 Dwan Gallery, Los Angeles
Palais des Beaux-Arts, Brussels
1965 Galerie Schmela, Düsseldorf
Minami Gallery, Tokyo
Galleria dell'Ariete, Milan
1966 Dwan Gallery, New York
Dwan Gallery, Los Angeles
Minami Gallery, Tokyo
Galerie Schmela, Düsseldorf
Wide White Space, Antwep, Belgium
Wurttembergischer Kunstverein, Stuttgart
Stedelijk van Abbemuseum, Eindhoven, Netherlands
1967 Von der Heydt Museum, Wuppertal, Germany
Dwan Gallery, New York
Dwan Gallery, Los Angeles
Galleria Schwarz, Milan
Galerie Seyfried, Monaco
1968 Dwan Gallery, New York
Galerie Lauter, Mannheim, Germany
1969 Galerie Yvon Lambert, Paris
Galleria Schwarz, Milan
Dwan Gallery, New York
Minami Gallery, Tokyo
Whitney Museum, New York (film)
1970 Musée d'Art Moderne de la Ville, Paris
Kunstverein, Hannover, Germany
Badischer Kunstverein, Karlsruhe, Germany
Biennale, Venice
1971 Fendrick Gallery, Washington, D.C.
Harcus-Krakow Gallery, Boston
Galerie Yvon Lambert, Paris
Galleria Schwarz, Milan
Angela Flowers Gallery, London
ROSC, Dublin
CAYC, Buenos Aires
Whitney Museum, New York (films)
1972 Kunsthalle, Hamburg National Galerie, Berlin
Lenbachhaus, Munich
Kunstverein, Frankfurt
Kunsthalle, Bern, Switzerland
Art in Progress, Zurich
Galleria Bertesca, Genoa, Italy
Ronald Feldman Fine Arts, New York
1973 Daytons Gallery 12, Minneapolis
Margo Leavin Gallery, Los Angeles
1974 Alessandra Castelli Gallery, Milan
Museum of Modern Art, New York
University of Wisconsin at Eau Claire
Ronald Feldman Fine Arts, New York
University of Missouri at Rolla
University of Oklahoma, Norman
Moorhead State College, Minnesota
Multiples Gallery, New York
Louisiana Museum, Humleback Denmark
1975 Galerie Art in Progress, Düsseldorf
Galerie Aronowitsch, Stockholm
Galerie Yvon Lambert, Paris
Isy Brachot, Brussels
Pasquale Trisorio, Naples
Henie Onstad Museum, Oslo
Michael Berger Gallery, Pittsburgh
Carl Solway Gallery, Cincinnati
1976 Ronald Feldman Fine Arts, New York
Multiples, New York
Galeria 42, Barcelona
Art Gallery of Ontario, Toronto
Rubicon Gallery, Los Altos, California
Margo Leavin Gallery, Los Angeles
Delahunty Gallery, Dallas
Grupo Quince, Madrid
Galerie Art in Progress, Munich

Dorothy Rosenthal Gallery, Chicago
ICC, Antwerp
University of Wisconsin Art History Gallery, Milwaukee
Stadtische Kunsthalle, Düsseldorf
Galerie Maeght, Paris
Galerie Art in Progress, Düsseldorf
Museo de Arte Moderno, Bogota
1978 Gallery Takagi, Nagoya, Japan
Stedelijk Museum, Amsterdam
Margo Leavin Gallery, Los Angeles
Galerie Maeght, Paris
Neue Galerie am Landesmuseum Johanneum, Graz, Austria
1979 Stadtische Kunstsammlungen, Ludwigshafen, Germany
Seibu Museum of Art, Tokyo
Austrian Landesmuseum, Graz
National Museum, Osaka, Japan
Ronald Feldman Fine Arts, New York
Minneapolis Institute of Arts
Gallery Takagi, Nagoya, Japan
Dorothy Rosenthal Gallery, Chicago
1980 John Stoller and Company, Minneapolis
Gallery Luria, Palm Beach, Florida
Gallery Takagi, Nagoya
Galerie Maeght, Zurich
1981 Ronald Feldman Fine Arts, New York
Lenbachhaus, Munich
Kestner Gesellschaft, Hannover
The Arts Club of Chicago
1982 Galerie Yvon Lambert, Paris
Galerie Maeght, Paris
1983 Matrix Gallery, Wadsworth Atheneum, Hartford, Connecticut
Ronald Feldman Gallery, New York
Kitakyushu Museum, Kyushu, Japan
1984 Padiglione d'Arte Contemporanea, Milan
Aldrich Museum of Contemporary Art, Ridgefield, Connecticut
1985 Ronald Feldman Gallery, New York
Arnold Herstand Gallery, New York
1986 Gallery Blu, Milan
Satani Gallery, Tokyo
1987 Ronald Feldman Gallery, New York
Von Straaten Gallery, Chicago
Galerie Yvon Lambert, Paris
Seibu Museum, Tokyo
Satani Gallery, Tokyo
1988 Seibu Museum, Karuizawa
Ronald Feldman Gallery, New York
Isy Brachot, Brussels
1989 Touko Museum, Tokyo
1990 Joseloff Gallery, Hartford
DAAD Gallery, Berlin
Ronald Feldman Gallery, New York
Busche Galerie, Cologne
1991 National Museum of Modern Art, Tokyo
1992 National Museum of Kyoto
1993 Busche Galerie, Berlin
1994 Nagi Museum of Contemporary Art, Nagi
Hara Museum of Contemporary Art, Tokyo

Selected Group Exhibitions:

1975 *View of Japanese Contemporary Art,* Seibu Museum of Art, Tokyo
1976 *Artist-Immigrants of America 1876–1976,* Hirshhorn Museum, Washington, D.C.
1977 *Documenta 6,* Kassel, Germany
Words: A Look at the Use of Language in Art, Whitney Museum Downtown, New York
1978 *Art about Art,* Whitney Museum, New York
Drawings of the 70's, Art Institute of Chicago
1980 *Lettres et Chiffres,* Galerie Beyeler, Basel
1981 *American Prints and Printmaking 1956–1981,* Pratt Graphics Center, New York
1988 *Modes of Address: Language in Art Since 1960,* Whitney Museum, New York
1990 *Contemporary Art and Urbanism in France,* Musee des Arts de Tsukuba, Ibaraki, and Musee National d'Art, Osaka, Japan
1994 *Japanese Art after 1945: Scream against the Sky,* Guggenheim Museum, New York

Collections:

Museum of Modern Art, New York; Metropolitan Museum of Art, New York; Walker Art Center, Minneapolis; Kunsthalle, Bern; Kunstmuseum, Basel; National Galerie, Berlin; Musée d'Art Modern, Paris; Stedelijk Museum, Amsterdam; National Museum of Modern Art, Tokyo; Australian National Gallery, Canberra; Guggenheim Museum, New York.

Publications:

By ARAKAWA: Books—*The Mechanism of Meaning,* with Madeline H. Gins, Munich 1971; *For Example (A Critique of Never),* with Madeline H. Gins, Milan 1974; *To Not To Die,* with Madeline H. Gins, Paris 1987. **Articles**—"Forgettance (Exhaustion Exhumed)" in *Arts Magazine* (New York), 1975; "Some Words" in *Arakawa,* exhibition catalog, Düsseldorf 1977; "The Tentative Constructed Plan as Intervening Device (for a Reversible Destiny)," with Madeline H. Gins, in *A+U: Architecture and Urbanism,* December 1991; "Person as Site in Respect to a Tentative Constructed Plan," with Madeline H. Gins, in *ANYWHERE,* 1992; "Landing Site/The End of Spacetime," with Madeline H. Gins, in *Art and Design,* May/June 1993.

On ARAKAWA: Books—*Icons and Images* by Nicolas Calas, New York 1971; *Prints of the 10th Century: A History* by Riva Castleman, New York 1976; *Constructive Concepts: A History of Constructive Art from Cubism to the Present* by Wily Rotzler, Zurich 1977; *The Transfiguration of the Commonplace* by Arthur Danto, Boston 1983; *Helen Keller or Arakawa* by Madeline Gins, Santa Fe 1994. **Exhibition catalogs**—*Arakawa,* Düsseldorf 1977; *Arakawa,* Tokyo 1979; *Arakawa* (essay by Danielle Rice) The Arts Club of Chicago, 1981; *Arakawa: Builder und Zeichnungen, 1962–1981* (essay by Armin Zweite), Munich 1981–82; *Arakawa* (essay "Longitude 180 W or E" by Jean-François Lyotard), Milan 1984; *The Exhibition of Shusaku Arakawa,* Tokyo 1990; *Constructing the Perceiver—ARAKAWA: Experimental Works,* Tokyo 1991; *Impossible Texts* (essay by Akira Tatehata), Tokyo 1994; *Reversible Destinies* with Madeleine Gins,

Guggenheim Museum, 1997. **Articles—**''Arakawa's Paintings: A Reading'' by Lawrence Alloway in *Arts Magazine* (New York), November 1969; ''Arakawa: The Mechanism of Meaning'' by Lawrence Alloway in *Art International* (Lugano), November 1972; ''Art: The Universe of Arakawa'' by John Russell in the *New York Times,* 7 September 1974; ''Playing in the Surd'' by John Loring in *Arts Magazine* (New York), February 1975; special issue of *Derriere le Miroir* (Paris), no. 223, 1977; ''Traces of the Unimaginable: On Arakawa's Recent Work'' by Rolf Dieter Hermann in *Arts Magazine* (New York), April 1978; ''Arakawa'' by Brian Wallis in *Arts Magazine* (New York), September 1979; ''Arakawa: 'I Am Looking for a New Definition of Perfection''' by Paul Gardner in *Art News* (New York), May 1980, '''Some Place Enormously Movable': The Collaboration of Arakawa and Madeline H. Gins'' by Robert Creeley in *Artforum* (New York), summer 1980; ''Arakawa's Work Lets Energy Flow'' by Helen Cullinan in *Plain Dealer* (Cleveland), 14 August 1983; ''Gins and Arakawa: Building Sensoriums'' by Arthur Danto in *The Nation,* 15 October 1990; ''Arakawa'' by Stephen Eisenman and Brian Lukacher in *Art Magazine,* June 1983; ''Forum: Arakawa's The Sharing of Nameless, 1982–83'' by Madeline H. Gins in *Flash Art,* April 1987; ''Arakawa'' by Donald Kuspit in *Flash Art,* April 1987; ''Simply Everywhere'' by Stephen-Paul Martin in *American Book Review,* July/August 1990.

* * *

Born in Nagoya in 1936, Shusaku Arakawa left Tokyo's Musashino College of Art before completing his studies. In 1958 he began submitting paintings to the Yomiuri Independent exhibitions and in 1960 joined the Neo-Dada Organizers group. In a happening, by placing himself in a pitch-black room in a ''feigned state of death,'' he experimented with the physical bounds of man. In his ''Box'' series, which in one instance consisted of a glob of cement and cotton placed on a blanket and called ''Foetus,'' he gave expression to fear and madness. This work attracted attention as being an original expression of the contemporary spirit of the times. In 1962 he went to the United States, and abandoned work in the ''Boxes'' series in favor of a new series, ''Diagram.'' In this series of paintings on canvas he juxtaposed silhouettes of such things as tennis rackets, combs, footprints, arrows, circles and other symbols, to depict structurally the ''relationship'' of man to the material world.

After participating in a group show at the Sidney Janis Gallery in New York in 1963, Arakawa had a number of one-man shows at the Dwan Gallery in Los Angeles, at the Alfred Schmela Gallery in Düsseldorf, and elsewhere. He won the grand prize at the *Contemporary Art Exhibition of Japan* in 1968, and also showed his work at the Venice *Biennale* in 1970. From about this time, even the ''silhouettes'' disappeared from his paintings, and almost all his paintings were given simple names such as ''Window Place'' and ''Room,'' and Arakawa painted words on the canvas. By this means, words, which are symbols of images and things, themselves became the objects painted, and the image evoked by the words was assigned a secondary place.

His new development is a series called ''Mechanisms of Meaning.'' In 1969 he made a full-length film, *Why Not: A Serenade of Eschatological Ecology,* which became a sensation because of the way he depicted the relationship between man and object within a lifeless domain of sex. A sequel, *For Instance,* was completed in 1971. Although Arakawa's concept remains unchanged throughout the 1970s up to the present, his large paintings in the 1980s reveal more and more intricate diagrammatic vertigo with multi-directional arrow signs, indicating a conceptual relationship between the physical presence and the metaphysical contemplations.

—Yoshiaki Tono

ARAKI, Nobuyoshi

Nationality: Japanese. **Born:** Tokyo, 25 May 1940. **Education:** Studied photography and film-making, Department of Engineering, Chiba University, B.A., 1960. **Family:** Married Yoko Aoki, 1971 (died 1990). **Agent:** Yoshiko Isshiki, 2–17-13, Kayabacho Nihonbashi, Chuo-ku, Tokyo 103–0025, Japan; Luhring Augustine Gallery, 531 West 24th St., New York, New York 10011, U.S.A.

Selected Individual Exhibitions:

1965 *Satchin and his Brother Mabo,* Shinjuku Station Building, Tokyo
1966 *Subway,* Mitsubishi Denki Gallery, Tokyo
Middle-Aged Women, Mitsubishi Denki Gallery, Tokyo
1967 *Ginza,* Mitsubishi Denki Gallery, Tokyo
Zoo, Mitsubishi Denki Gallery, Tokyo
1970 *Sur-sentimalist Manifesto No. 2: The Truth about Carmen Marie,* Kunugi Gallery, Tokyo
Kitchen Ramen Ero-realism, Kitchen Ramen Restaurant, Tokyo
1973 *Flowers in Ruins,* Shimizu Gallery, Tokyo
Pseudo-documentary: Chirring Cicadas in Chorus, Kinokuniya Gallery, Tokyo
1974 *Actresses,* Gallery Matto Grosso, Tokyo
1975 *Actress, Kisaki Sekimura,* Minolta Photo Space, Tokyo
1976 *Wandering in Tokyo,* various public spaces throughout the city of Tokyo
Yoko, My Love, Ginza Nikon Salon, Tokyo; Osaka Nikon Salon, Osaka
1977 *Tokyo Blues,* Ginza Nikon Salon, Tokyo; Osaka Nikon Salon, Osaka
Last Year's Photos, Shirakaba Gallery, Tokyo
This Year's Photos, Shirakaba Gallery, Tokyo
1978 *My Scenes: 1940–1977,* Ginza Canon Salon, Tokyo
Actresses: A Senti-roman, Horindo Art Space, Tokyo
Eizo, Camp Gallery, Tokyo
1979 *First Visit to New York,* Minolta Photo Space, Tokyo; Obihiro Budding Gallery, Obihiro
1980 *Pseudo-Photos* and *Recent Photos,* Room 301, Harada Building, Tokyo
Zigeunerweisen: Fictitious truth, Kinokuniya Photo Space, Tokyo
100% of Nairon, Bar Nylon 100%, Tokyo
Wet Dreams on a Summer Night and the End of the War, Kinokuniya Gallery, Tokyo
1981 *Rika: Pseudo High-school Girl,* Shinjuku Yamiichi Shop, Tokyo
Theory of Photography, Tojusha
1982 *I Am Photography,* Doi Photo Plaza, Tokyo
Storm of Love, Doi Photo Plaza, Tokyo

1984 *A World of GIrs,* Zeit-Foto Salon, Tokyo
A Balthus Summer, Photo Space, Osaka
1985 *An Immoral Woman,* K's Bar, Tokyo
A Pseudo-story About Girls, Bar New Dug, Tokyo
1986 *Araki's Tokyo Erotomania Diary,* Zeit-Foto Salon, Tokyo
Araki Shoots Shibuya Like Atget, K's Bar, Tokyo
Shibuya Streets, Doi Photo Plaza, Tokyo; Inax Showroom, Fukuoka
1987 *Puppet Prince,* Spiral Hall, Tokyo
Arakism: 1967–1987, Zeit-Foto Salon, Tokyo
A Part of Love, Art Space Mirage, Tokyo
1989 *11 Photographers: 1967–1975,* Yamaguchi Prefectural Museum of Art, Yamaguchi
Nobuyoshi Araki '89: Selected Photographs, Gallery Kosai, Tokyo
1990 *Chiro My Love,* Book Center Libro, Ikebukuro, Tokyo
Skyscapes, Gallery Verita, Tokyo
Towards Winter: Tokyo, A City Heading for Death, Egg Gallery, Tokyo
1991 *Winter Journey,* Egg Gallery, Tokyo
A's Nude Exhibition: Lovers, Apt Gallery, Tokyo
On the Move, Egg Gallery, Tokyo
From Close Range, Hosomi Gallery, Tokyo
Japanese Photography in the 1970's, Tokyo Metropolitan Museum of Photography
1992 *Photo Maniac Diary,* Egg Gallery, Tokyo
Akt-Tokyo: Nobuyoshi Araki 1971–1991, Forum Stadtpark, Graz Austria (toured Europe)
Angel's Festival, Pacro Gallery, Tokyo; Sapporo Parco, Hokkaido; Shinsaibashi Parco, Osaka
1993 *Nobuyoshi Araki,* Setagaya Art Museum, Tokyo
1994 Luhring Augustine, New York
Jay Jopling/White Cube, London
Arakinema: Obscenities, Studio Ebisu, Tokyo
1995 *Erotos,* Camera Austria, Graz
Nobuyoshi Araki, Torch, Amsterdam
The First Year of Heisei, Le Garage, Reims, France
Tokyo Novelle, Kunstmuseum Wolfsburg, Germany (catalog)
1996 *Face vs. Bodies,* Spiral Garden, Tokyo
The Face, the Dead, Pace Wildenstein, Los Angeles
1997 *A's Life,* Kachimai Hall, Obihiro; La Foret Harajuku, Tokyo
Galerie Bob van Orsouw, Zürich
Araki Retrographs, Hara Museum of Contemporary Art, Tokyo
Wiener Secession, Vienna
Gallery Starmach, Krakow, Poland
Studio Guenzani, Milan
1998 *Tokyo Shijyo,* Deichtorhalleh, Hamburg
The Past, Stadtisches Museum Leverkusen Schloss Morsbroich, Germany
Portraits and Flowers, Photographers Gallery, London
A's Life, traveld to Toyama, Yokohama, Sapporo, and Fukuoka
1999 *Sentimental Journey, Sentimental Life,* Museum of Contemporary Art, Tokyo
Scalo Art Space, New York
1973–1999, Galerie Bob van Orsouw, Köln
Contemporary Art Gallery, Vancouver, British Columbia
2000 *Araki: Viaggio Sentimental,* Museo d'Arte Contemporanea, Prato
Voyage sentimental, Centre national de la photographie, Paris
Rebecca M. Camhi Gallery, Athens, Greece
Narcisse Blesse: Autoportraits contemporains 1970–2000, Passage de Retz, Paris
Araki: Tokyomani, Gallerie Kamel Mennour, Paris, France
2001 *Nobuyoshi Araki,* IKON Gallery, London
Kaei, Gallery Art Graph, Tokyo
Shikijyo kyo, Taka Ishii Gallery, Tokyo

Selected Group Exhibitions:

1971 *The Tenth Modern Japanese Art Exhibition,* Tokyo Metropolitan Art Museum, Tokyo
1972 *The Eleventh Modern Japanese Art Exhibition,* Tokyo Metropolitan Art Museum, Tokyo
1974 *Photographs on Photography,* Shimizu Gallery, Tokyo
15 Photographers, National Museum of Modern Art, Tokyo
1975 *Towards an I-Reality,* Shimizu Gallery, Tokyo
1977 *Neue Fotografie aus Japan,* Graz City Museum, Graz
1979 *Japan: A Self-Portrait,* International Center of Photography, New York; Venice Biennale, Venice
1983 *Modern Japanese Art II: Encounters with Sites,* Miyagi Prefectural Museum of Art, Tokyo
A 6 x7 Woman, Zeit-Foto Salon, Tokyo
1985 *Paris, Tokyo, New York,* Tsukuba Museum of Photography, Tokyo
1986 *Fotografia Japonesa Contemporanea,* Casa Elizalde, Barcelona (toured Spain)
1989 *11 Photographers: 1967–1975,* Yamaguchi Prefectural Museum of Art, Yamaguchi
1990 *Tokyo: A City Perspective,* Tokyo Metropolitan Museum of Photography, Tokyo
Photos de famille, Grand Halle, La Villette, Paris
1991 *Japanese Photography in the 1970s,* Tokyo Metropolitan Museum of Photography
1993 *Nobuyoshi Araki, Sophie Calle, Larry Clark, Jack Pierson,* Luhring Augustine Gallery, New York
The Image of the Body, Frankfurter Kunstverein, Frankfurt
1994 Luhring Augustine, New York
Of the Human Condition: Hope and Despair at the End of the Century, Spiral Garden, Tokyo; Ashiya City Museum of Art and History, Hyogo
Liquid Crystal Futures, Fruitmarket Gallery, Edinburgh, Scotland (traveled through Europe and to Tokyo)
Photography and Beyond in Japan, Hara Museum of Contemporary Art, Tokyo (toured in Mexico and the United States)
1995 *Art in Japan Today, 1985–1995,* Museum of Contemporary Art, Tokyo
Texture and Touch: Contemporary Photography from Japan, The Art Gallery of New South Wales, Sydney, Australia
The Dead, National Museum of Photography, Film, & Television, Bradford, United Kingdom
Sites of Being, Institute of Contemporary Art, Boston
26th Arles International Photo Festival, Arles, France

1996 *Private Tokyo,* Museum für Moderne Kunst, Frankfurt, Germany
Images of Woman in Japanese Contemporary Photography 1930–1990, Shoutou Museum, Tokyo
1997 *Lust und Leere: Japanische Photographie der Gegenwart,* Kunsthale Wien (catalog)
10th International Biennial of the Image, Nancy Center Culturel, Nancy, France
Shashin, Kobe Fashion Museum, Kobe; Shinjuku Mitsukoshi Museum, Tokyo; Fukuoka Prefectural Museum of Art, Fukuoka
1998 *Recycling Art History,* Pittsburgh Center for the Arts, Pittsburgh, Pennsylvania
Life Is A Bitch, De Appel, Amsterdam
Nuit Blanche, Musée d'art Modern de la Ville de Paris, France (traveled to Norway, Finland, and Sweden)
Cho nichijo (Sur-eeryday-life), Shanghai Art Museum, Shanghai
1998 Taipei Biennial: Site of Desire, Taipei Fine Arts Museum, Taipei
The Promise of Photography, Hara Museum of Contemporary Art, Tokyo
1999 *Change of Scene XV,* Museum für Moderne Kunst, Frankfurt, Germany
Collected Works I: Contemporary Art since 1968, Kunstmuseum Wolfsburg, Wolfsburg
Love and Desire, Galleria Photology, Milan
2000 *The Arsfutura Show,* arsFutura Galerie, Zurich
Bourgeois Hero, Galleria Civica Modena, Modena, Italy
Copenhagen Festival, Denmark

Publications:

By ARAKI: Books—*Sentimental Journey,* 1971; *Landscapes: 1981–1984,* 1985; *Tokyo Diary: 1981–1989,* 1989; *The Works of Nobuyoshi Araki 1–20,* Heibonsha 1996–1997; *The Novel Works of Nobuyoshi Araki 1–8,* Heibonsha 1997–99; dozens of other books of photographs and exhibition catalogs.

On ARAKI: Books—*Travelling Eye,* edited by Hans-Ulrich Obrist and Stella Rollig, Oktagon Press 1997; *Veronica's Revenge; Contemporary Perspectives on Photography: LAC Switzerland,* edited by Elizabeth Janus and Marion Lambert, Zürich, Berlin, and New York 1998.. **Articles—**''Indecent Exposure'' by David Brittain in *Dazed & Confused,* no. 33, August 1997; ''Nobuyoshi Araki at Blum and Poe'' by Virginia Rutledge in *Art in America,* September 1997; essay by Simona Lodi in *TemaCeleste,* no. 66, January-March 1998; essay by Joshua Decter in *Artforum,* February 1998; ''Children and Sexuality'' by Anna Burns in *Contemporary Visual Arts,* no. 18, 1998; ''Nobuyoshi Araki, Across the Great Divide'' by Michael Cohen in *Flash Art,* October 1998.

* * *

Araki, the most controversial Japanese photographer of the last two decades, is known for his images of nude women and genitalia, sado-masochistic bondage pictures, and documentary photographs that bring out the hidden side of male-female relations.

What was scandalous about these photographs was not just the full nudity, but also the fact that the models seemed to enjoy exposing themselves in front of the camera. Araki's work suggested that there are many women who are happy to show off their nude bodies of their own free will and even find a kind of self-fulfillment in this act. This was shocking in Japanese society, especially to men, because of the preconceived idea that Japanese women are naturally modest and shy.

Araki's subject matter was not limited to unclad women. He was initially recognized for the documentary series *Satchin,* focusing on a young boy and his neighborhood. These photographs were originally stills from a documentary film on children in a poor section of Tokyo, influenced by Italian neo-realism. Thus, Araki took a documentary approach from the beginning of his career, attempting to shoot reality as straightforwardly as possible.

Araki went on to carry out impressive experiments in photographic expression. The studies that remain from his early career show traces of minimalist and conceptualist approaches reminiscent of artists like Andy Warhol and David Hockney.

The spirit of *Satchin* reappears in *Sentimental Journey,* a highly acclaimed photographic book that documents Araki's honeymoon with his wife Yoko in nostalgic black and white prints. In spite of his emotional involvement with his new wife, he observes her with the cool eye of the documentary photographer. This voyeuristic revelation of personal life became a characteristic of his work.

Later works focused on his relations with different women and the nightlife of clubs in Shinjuku and Ginza, but his energetic documentary approach also extended to flowers, food, city streets, and travel. All of Araki's photographs reflect his child-like curiosity. He sees everything in a fresh way, like an infant looking at the reality around him for the first time, and this has led him to use anything and everything as subjects for his photography. This fresh outlook reminds adult viewers of the significance of looking at things intently.

Araki's wife, Yoko, died in 1990, and this marked the beginning of a new stage in his career. He began working even more furiously, showing his determination to go on with life and perhaps instinctively protecting himself from his loss.

In recent years, Araki has traveled extensively and taken photographs in many Asian countries and has held numerous exhibitions in Western museums. He has added even more subjects to his oeuvre and continues to work with a larger vocabulary. The Araki retrospective held at the Museum of Contemporary Art, Tokyo, in 1999 brought together a huge number of photographs under one roof, reconfirming the diversity and abundance of Araki's work, his boundlessness curiosity, and versatile talent.

Araki's achievement was to demonstrate the possibilities of casual photography, the drama that can be captured in snapshots of everyday life, and the truths that appear from its mix of fact and falsehood, making a seemingly carefree approach into a dramaturgy of art. By deliberately revealing things that people do not want to have seen or talked about even though they exist in reality, Araki depicts the deepest human desires and the basic realities of society.

—Fumio Nanjo

ARMAJANI, Siah

Nationality: American. **Born:** Tehren, Iran, 1939. **Education:** Studied anthropology, philosophy, pure mathematics, Macalester College, St. Paul, Minnesota, B.A., 1963. **Career:** Pioneer of ''Public Art;'' created the Dictionary for Building, containing more than 1000 small

Siah Armajani: *Glass Room,* 2000. ©Siah Armajani, courtesy of Senior & Shopmaker Gallery, New York.

models, 1974–75; designed reading rooms and reading gardens, beginning in 1978; creates other public squares and structures for use. **Agent:** Senior & Shopmaker Gallery, 21 East 26th Street, Madison Square Park, New York, New York 10010.

Selected Individual Exhibitions:

1978 *Red School House for Thomas Paine,* Philadelphia College of Art (catalog)
1979 *First Reading Room,* Max Protech Gallery, New York (traveled to Cleveland and Kansas City)
1982 *Picnic Garden,* Grand Rapids Art Museum, Michigan
1985 *Siah Armajani: Houses, Communal Spaces,* Dictionary for Building, Institute of Contemporary Art, University of Pennsylvania (catalog)
1987 *Siah Armajani,* Westfalisches Landesmuseum, Munster (traveled to Portikus, Frankfurt; catalog)
1988 *Siah Armajani, Sacco and Vanzetti Reading Room #2,* List Visual Arts Center, Massachusetts Institute of Technology, Cambridge
1991 *Siah Armajani,* Max Protech Gallery, New York (catalog)
1993 *Recent Works,* Wright Museum, Beloit College, Wisconsin
1994 *Siah Armajani Anarchistic Contributions 1992–1994,* Villa Arson, Nice (catalog)
1995 Musee d'Art Moderne et Contemporain, Geneva, Switzerland
1996 *Siah Armajani,* The Customs House, Newcastle, England
Siah Armajani: Reading Spaces, Museu d'Art Contemporani, Barcelona (catalog)
1998 *Siah Armajani: Dictionary for Building,* Matthew Architecture Gallery, University of Edinburgh, Scotland (catalog)
1999 *Siah Armajani,* Museo Nacional Centro de Arte Reina Sofia, Madrid, Spain (traveled to Disputaction de Huesca, Spain, and Fundacion Cesar Manrique, Canary Islands)
2000 *Siah Armajani: Glass Room,* Senior & Shopmaker Gallery, New York
Siah Armajani, Museo Nacional Centro de Arte Reina, Sofia (catalog)

Selected Group Exhibitions:

1969 *Art by Telephone,* Museum of Contemporary Art, Chicago
1970 *Information,* Museum of Modern Art, New York
1978 *Architectural Analogues,* Whitney Museum of American Art, New York
1980 *Drawings: The Pluralist Decade,* 39th Venice Biennale, Venice (toured)
1981 *Biennial,* Whitney Museum of American Art, New York
1983 *New Art,* Tate Gallery, London
1984 *An International Survey of Recent Paintings and Sculpture,* Museum of Modern Art, New York
Furniture, Furnishings: Subject and Object, Museum of Art, Rhode Island School of Design (toured)
1986 *The Artist as Social Designer: Aspects of Public Urban Life Today,* Los Angeles County Museum of Art, California
1987 *Documenta 8,* Kassel, Germany
Avant-Garde in the Eighties, Los Angeles County Museum of Art
1988 *View Points: Post-War Painting and Sculpture,* Solomon R. Guggenheim Museum, New York
1991 *20th Century Art,* Museum fur Moderne Kunst, Frankfurt, Germany
1996 *Monument et modernite: Etat des lieux: commandes publiques en France, 1990–1996,* Au musee du Luxembourg, Paris
1997 *Views from Abroad: European Perspectives on American Art,* Museum fur Moderne Kunst, Frankfurt, Germany
National Airport Artists on Paper, Numark Gallery, Washington, D.C.
1999 *Comfort Zone: Furniture by Artists,* Paine Webber Art Gallery, New York

Selected Permanent Public Works:

1979 *Reading House,* Lake Placid, New York
1980 *Reading Garden No. 1,* Roanoke College, Virginia
1982 *Louis Kahn Lecture Room,* Samuel S. Fleisher Art Memorial, Philadelphia
1983 *NOAA Bridges,* National Oceanic and Atmospheric Administration, Seattle
1985 *Garden,* University of Maryland, College Park
1987 *Munster Garden,* Munster, Germany
1988 *Humphrey Garden,* Hubert H. Humphrey Institute of Public Affairs, University of Minnesota, Minneapolis

Sky Bridge #1 (with Cesar Pelli), Minneapolis
1989 *Sky Bridge #2,* Minneapolis
Battery Park City (with Scott Burton, Cesar Pelli, and Paul Friedberg), New York
1990 *Covered Walkway,* General Mills, Inc., Minneapolis
1991 *Sacco and Vanzetti Reading Room No. 3,* Museum fur Moderne Kunst, Frankfurt, Germany (catalog)
1992 *Poetry Garden,* Lannan Foundation, Los Angeles
1993 *Gazebo for Two Anarchists: Gabriella Antolini and Arberto Antolini,* Storm King Art Park, Mountainville, New York
1994–95 *Garden* and *Garden Part II,* Villa Arson Museum, Nice, France
1996 *The Lighthouse and Bridge,* Staten Island, New York
Bridge, Tower, Cauldron, 1996 Centennial Olympics, Atlanta, Georgia
1997 *Garden Part III,* Villa Arson Museum, Nice
Bow-Front Balustrade for Washington, D.C. National Airport, Arlington, Virginia
Three Skyway Bridges for City of Leipzig, Germany
1999 *Lannan Poetry Garden #2,* Beloit College, Wisconsin
2000 *Bridge for Iowa City,* Iowa
Gazebo with Picnic Table and *George Simmel Bridge,* Strasbourg, France

Publications:

By ARMAJANI: Articles—Article in *Project for PCA: Red School House for Thomas Paine,* Philadelphia 1978; ''Perspecta 18'' in *Yale Architecture Journal,* 1981; ''Site: The Meaning of Place in Art and Architecture'' in *Design Quarterly,* no. 111, 1983; ''Manifesto: Public Sculpture in the Context of American Democracy'' in *Arte Suisse* (Geneva), February 1996; ''The University of Iowa Bridge'' in *Iowa Architect,* Des Moines 1998; articles in *El Pais,* 1 October 1999 and 9 October 1999.

On ARMAJANI: Books—*Five Artists at NOAA: A Case Book on Art in Public Places* by Patricia Fuller, Seattle 1985; *Not Style, Construction: Siah Armajani's Appropriation of Modernism* by Hans Alrich Reck, Frankfurt, Germany 1991; *Contemporary Public Sculptures* by Harriet F. Senie, New York 1992; *Siah Armajani: The Poetry of Public Art* by Thomas H. Wilson, Beloit, Wisconsin 1997. **Articles—**''Process and Imagination'' by Christopher Finch in *Design Quarterly,* no. 74/75, 1969; ''Siah Armajani: Populist Mechanics'' by Robert Pincus-Witten in *Arts Magazine,* October 1978; ''Armajani's Open-Ended Structures'' by Robert Berlind in *Art in America,* October 1979; ''The Expulsion from the Garden: Environmental Sculpture at the Winter Olympics'' by Kay Larson in *Artforum,* April 1980; ''Metaphor: The Mechanical Obssession'' by Jane Allen in *New Art Examiner,* February 1982; ''A Plea for New Art in Public Places'' by Jean-Christophe Ammann in *Parkett,* July 1984; ''Siah Armajani's Constitution'' by Patricia C. Phillips in *Artforum,* December 1985; ''Master Builder'' by Nancy Princenthal in *Art in America,* March 1986; ''Sculpture Goes Public'' by Douglas C. McGill in *New York Times Magazine,* 27 April 1986; ''The Act of Engagement'' by Victoria Geibel in *Metropolis,* July/August 1986; ''Sighted in Munster'' by Eleanor Heartney in *Art in America,* September 1987; ''Siah Armajani'' by Paola di Antonelli in *DOMUS,* February 1990; ''Report from Germany: A Tale of Two Cities'' by David Galloway in *Art in America,* January 1992; ''American Art of the Twenties and Thirties in Siah Armajani's 'Sacco and Vanzetti Reading Room'' by Rolf Lauter in *Views from Abroad: European Perspectives on American Art,* Frankfurt, Germany 1997; ''Siah Armajani: Poetry in the City'' by Pierre Restany in *DOMUS,* April 1998.

* * *

''The Kantian philosophers believe that art is good because it is useless; I believe that art is good because it is useful, functional,'' Siah Armajani noted in an exhibition catalog by the Museo Nacional Centro de Arte Reina Sofia in 2000.

The defining aspect of Siah Armajani's work is his manifesto: ''Public Art in the Context of American Democracy.'' Compiled between 1968 and 1978 and revised in 1993, Armajani's 26-point manifesto outlines his commitment to public art—the reason he creates public artworks almost exclusively, and his belief in the fundamental purpose of art-making: to improve people's lives.

Beginning by questioning the nature of American culture itself, ''Public Art in the Context of American Democracy'' first asks ''What is American art?'' Thus primarily concerned with the social relevance of art, the manifesto asserts that public art must first engage the culture it comes from. This engagement is, for Armajani, a political consideration, rooted in the belief that there should be no distinction between the practical and fine arts.

In answer to the question, ''What is public art?'' Siah Armajani writes in an exhibition catalog by the Museo Nacional Centro de Arte Reina Sofia in 2000 that ''Public Art is not about self but others. It is not about personal taste but the needs of others.'' To this end Armajani creates public structures—such as bridges, reading rooms, gazebos, offices and school rooms—that are functional artworks, meant to be used and enjoyed by everyone—not only a gallery-going public.

Working within a particular and uniquely specific aesthetic of construction, Armajani's structures all relate to the philosophies that sustain and inspire them: a combination of utopian fantasy, Shaker austerity, and Russian Constructivist formalism. Assembled like children's building toys, Armajani's seemingly simple forms create a sense of unreality through the introduction of seemingly misplaced elements—slightly skewed proportions or unnecessary forms that juxtapose function with metaphor, interior and exterior spaces, and thus hint at deeper meaning by making us question their fundamental purpose.

Precise and geometric, yet also bright and inviting, Armajani's public environments are perfect and sanitized reconstructions of the models that inspired them. These architectural models were an early and integral part of Armajani's work, unrealized until later in his career, and often meant as purely hypothetical environments. Beginning in the mid-1970s, Armajani's on-going ''Dictionary for Building'' consisted of a series of whimsical architectural models of single elements of building construction—ranging from the banal ''Front Door/Back Door,'' ''Dinner Table,'' or ''First Floor and Attic Window'' to the more fanciful, such as ''Chair Over Table'' or ''House Over Bridge.'' Made from cardboard, these doll-house scale models were investigations of space and form, experiments with everyday design, as well as engagements with conceptualism.

The first of these structures to be realized as public art projects were his *Reading Rooms*—communal spaces for reading, learning, and dialogue. With benches, tables, and structures designed to hold a replenished supply of paper, pencils, magazines, and newspapers,

Armajani's *Reading Rooms* exemplify his concerns with both language and community. It was here also that text began to be incorporated as part of his architecture and was to become an ongoing consideration in his work. As early as 1981, Armajani used philosophical quotations and poetry, text that often referred directly to the political intent of his work. His *Meeting Garden,* from 1981, for example, includes this quote from philospher John Dewey: ''As long as art is the beauty parlor of civilisation, neither art nor civilisation is secure.''

The importance of poetry is also crucial to an understanding of Armajani's work as primarily dedicated to communication. As an Iranian, this poetic consciousness can be seen as directly linked to Persian culture, a culture that prides poetry as the highest of all art forms. Armajani writes in his manifesto: ''the essential language of being is poetry.'' In 1994, he created a project in Los Angeles specifically for poetry, *Poetry Garden,* dedicated to the poet Federico Garcia Lorca. As an integral part of language, and of life, using poetry is part of Armajani's on-going commitment to the social, a rejection of reason and logic that enables optimism and the questioning of art's purpose.

Armajani's attempt to create fully functional structures led to his construction of a series of footbridges, beginning in the late 1980s and continuing today. Here, the symbolic metaphor inherent in ''bridging'' and linking (often two separate neighborhoods for example) is realized literally in a useful structure. Again, these projects were the culmination of early conceptual ideas and models such as ''Bridge Over a Tree'' realized in 1970.

The harmony between conceptualism, whimsy, and the practicality of his structures, be they parks, gazebos, bridges, or other public structures, is what makes Armajani a pioneer of public sculpture. Forcing us to ask how we, the public, benefit from art, Armajani offers the artist as part of the community. It is with this generosity and commitment that he forces the public to consider the possibility that art is for everyone; that art has an important social and political function that can benefit the society it comes from.

—Carly Butler

ARMAN

Nationality: American. **Born:** Armand Fernandez in Nice, France, 17 November 1928; relinquished surname in 1947; adopted name Arman, as a result of printing error, 1958; emigrated to the United States; naturalized citizen, 1972. **Education:** Cours Poisat School, 1934–40; studied at the Ecole du Louvre and Ecole Nationale des Arts Décoratifs, Paris. **Military Service:** Served in the French Army, 1952. **Career:** Hitch-hiked with Yves Klein and Claude Pascall in Europe, 1947; concentrated on Zen Buddhism and astrology, 1947–53; lived in New York, 1963; worked on series of assemblages in colaboration with Renault Car Company, Paris, 1967; artist-in-residence, University of California at Los Angeles, 1967–68. **Awards:** Prize, *International Biennale, Exhibition of Prints,* Tokyo, 1964; second prize, Premio Marzotto, 1966; Commander, Order of Arts and Letter, France, 1984. **Agent:** Marisa del Re Gallery, 41 East 57th Street, New York, New York 10022. **Address:** 430 Washington Street, New York, New York 10013, U.S.A.

Individual Exhibitions:

1956 Galerie du Haut Pave, Paris
1957 Galerie La Roue, Paris
1958 Galerie Iris Clert, Paris
1959 Galleria Apollinaire, Milan
Galerie St. Germain, Paris
1960 Galerie Iris Clert, Paris
Galerie Schmela, Düsseldorf
1961 Galleria Schwarz, Milan
Cordier and Warren Gallery, New York
1962 Galerie Saggarah, Gstaad, Switzerland
Dwan Gallery, Los Angeles
Galerie Aujourd'hui, Brussels
Galerie Lawrence, Paris
1963 Galleria Schwarz, Milan
Galerie Lawrence, Paris
Sidney Janis Gallery, New York
Galerie ad Libitum, Antwerp
Galerie Schmela, Düsseldorf
1964 Walker Art Center, Minneapolis
Stedelijk Museum, Amsterdam
Museum Haus Lange, Krefeld, Germany
Sidney Janis Gallery, New York
1965 Richard Feigen Gallery, Chicago
Galerie Bonnier, Lausanne, Switzerland
Galerie Lawrence, Paris
Galleria del Leone, Venice
1966 Galerie Saggarah, Gstaad, Switzerland
Svensk-Franska Konstgalleriet, Stockholm
Palais des Beaux-Arts, Brussels
Galerie La Vielle Echoppe, Saint-Paul-de-Vence, France
Musée de la Ville, Saint-Paul-de-Vence
1967 Galerie Ileana Sonnabend, Paris
Galleria Il Punto, Turin
Galerie Francoise Meyer, Brussels
Galeriedes Ponchettes, Nice
Galleria La Bussola, Turin
Galleria Sperone, Turin
Palazzo Grassi, Venice
1968 Galleria Schwarz, Milan
Sidney Janis Gallery, New York
Biennale, Venice
1969 Galerie Bonnier, Lausanne
Arman: Verk frân 1964–1969, Svensk-Franska Konstgalleriet, Stockholm
Accumulations Renault, Musée des Arts Décoratifs, Paris (toured Europe)
Galerie Ileana Sonnabend, Paris
Galerie Mathias Fels, Paris
1970 Galerie Ileana Sonnabend, Paris
Städitsche Kunstsammlungen, Ludwigshafen, Germany
Ace Gallery, Los Angeles (travelled to the Ace Gallery, Vancouver)
Galerie der Spiegel, Cologne
Galleria dell'Ariete, Milan
Studio Sant'Andrea, Milan
Galerie Lambert-Monet, Geneva
Galerie Bonnier, Geneva
Galerie Jacqueline Soisson, Nice

Lawrence Rubin Gallery, New York
1971 Galerie Bonnier, Geneva
Galerie de la Salle, Saint-Paul-de-Vence
Lawrence Rubin Gallery, New York
Galerie Bischofberger, Zurich
Galerie Semiha Huber, Zurich
Galleria Arte Borgogna, Milan
Galerie Venise, Casablanca
1972 Galleria del Leone, Venice
Galleria Arte Borgogna, Basel
Galleria Sanluca, Bologna
Galerie Guillaume Campo, Antwerp
Galerie de l'Oeil, Paris
1973 Galerie Kriwin, Brussels
Le Tas de Echanges, Galerie Entre, Paris
Arman: Selected Activities, John Gibson Gallery, New York
Galerie Aronovich, Stockholm
White Gallery, Lausanne
Galleria Arte Bologna, Milan
Rosa Esman Gallery, New York
Concrete Lyrics, Andrew Crispo Gallery, New York
1974 Andrew Crispo Gallery, New York
Musée d'Arles, France
Galerie Daniel Templon, Paris
Arman: Selected Works 1958–1974, La Jolla Museum of Contemporary Art, California (travelled to Henry Art Gallery, University of Washington, Seattle; Fort Worth Art Museum, Texas; Des Moines Art Center, Iowa; and Albright-Knox Art Musuem, Buffalo, New York, 1974–75)
Dartmouth College, Hanover, New Hampshire
1975 Musée d'Art Moderne de la Ville, Paris
Galerie Bonnier, Geneva
Galerie Tchou, Paris
John Gibson Gallery, New York
Lyrical Surfaces, Andrew Crispo Gallery, New York
1976 Andrew Crispo Gallery, New York
Musée d'Art Moderne de la Ville, Paris
Galerie Sapone, Nice
Artcurial, Paris
1977 Galerie Valeur, Nagoya, Japan
Ulrich Museum of Art, Wichita State University, Kansas
1978 Gallerie Jollenbeck, Cologne
Andrew Crispo Gallery, New York
Galerie Beaubourg, Paris
Galerie Valeur, Nagoya, Japan
Galerie Charles Kriwin, Brussels
Galerie Verbeck, Paris
1979 André Emmerich Gallery, New York
Galleria Cavellini, Brescia, Italy
Gallerie Bonnier, Geneva
Foundation de Jau, Perpignan, France
1980 Amano Gallery, Osaka
Satani Gallery, Tokyo
1981 Galerie Beaubourg, Paris
Grand Palais, Paris
1982 Galerie Sapone, Nice
Galerie Beaubourg, Paris
Solomon Gallery, Dublin
1983 Goldman's Gallery, Haifa, Israel
Galerie Beaubourg, Paris
1984 Gloria Luria Gallery, Bay Harbor Islands, Florida
Galerie Reckermann, Cologne
Galerie Rene Ziegler, Zurich
Marisa del Re Gallery, New York
1985 Seibu Museum of Art, Tokyo
1986 Marisa del Re Gallery, New York
1988 Galerie de Poche, Paris
Galerie Beaubourg, Paris
Marisa del Re Gallery, New York
Reflex Modern Art Gallery, Amsterdam
1989 Gana Gallery, Seoul
James Mayor Gallery, London
Gallery Guy Pieters, Knokke-Zoute, Belgium
1990 Marisa del Re Gallery, New York
Riva Yares Gallery, Scottsdale, Arizona
Artcurial, Paris
Gallerie GKM Siwert Bergström, Malmö, Sweden
Fiorella Urbinati Gallery, Los Angeles
Vrej Baghoomian Gallery, New York
1991 Galerie Freites, Caracas
Fondazione Mudima, Milan
Galerie Holtmann, Cologne
Fuji Television Gallery, Tokyo
Museum of Fine Arts, Houston, Texas (retrospective; travelled to Brooklyn and Detroit)
1992 Reflex Modern Art Gallery, Amsterdam
Galerie Beaubourg, Paris
Sonnabend Gallery, New York
Remba Gallery, California
1993 Haut de Cagnes, Cagnes sur Mer, France
Elleni Galleria d'arte, Bergamo, Italy
Galerie Beaubourg, Paris
1995 Reflex Modern Art Gallery, Amsterdam
Gallery George Philippe Vallois, Paris
Ace Contemporary Exhibitions, Los Angeles
L'espace Fortant de France, Sète, France
Galerie 3, Athens
Musée Royal de Mariemont, Mariemont-Chapelle, Belgium
Avanti Galeries Inc., New York
1996 Sidney Janis Gallery, New York
Museo Jose Luis Cuevas, Mexico City
Modern Art Gallery, Taiwan
Galerie Daniel Blaise Thorens, Basel
1997 Cascades Ileana Sonnabend Gallery, New York
Galerie RL Beaubourg, Paris
Galerie Enrico Navarra, Paris
James Mayor Gallery, London
2000 Daniel Templon Gallery, Paris
Georges-Philippe et Nathalie Vallois Gallery, Paris
Ludwig Museeum, Coblens
Couvent des Cordeliers, Paris

Selected Group Exhibitions:

1967 *Expo '67,* Montreal
1968 *Documenta 4,* Kassel, Germany
1970 *Expo '70,* Osaka, Japan

1984 *Salvaged: Altered Everyday Objects,* Project Studio One, Long Island City, New York
1985 *Art in Boxes,* Museo Rufino Tamayo, Mexico City
1986 *World Exposition,* Vancouver
1988 *The World Expo 88 Collection,* Philip Bacon Galleries, Brisbane, Australia
1990 *The 20th Anniversary Fuji Television Gallery,* Fuji Television Gallery, Tokyo
1991 *La Sculpture Contemporaine après 1970,* Foundation Daniel Templon, Musée Temporaire, Fréjus, France
1993 Contemporary Self-Portrait—''Here's Looking at Me,'' ELAC, Lyons, France
1994 *Arman/Karel Appel,* Galerie Wild, Frankfurt
Objets d'Artistes, Galerie Beaubourg, Vence, France
The Art of Assemblage: Early Works, Locks Gallery, Philadelphia, Pennsylvania
Worlds in a Box, The South Bank Centre, City Arts Center, Edinburgh, England
Neo-Dada: Redefining Art, 1958–1962, The American Federation of the Arts, Equitable Gallery, New York
Portraits de Femmes, Galerie Beaubourg, Vence, France.
The Pop Image: Prints and Multiples, Marlborough Graphics, New York
1995 *Dessins et Oeuvres sur Papier de la collection Ahrenberg,* Maison de la Culture d'Amiens, Amiens, France
1996 *Les Champs de la Sculpture (Captain Nemo),* Paris
Arte Contemporeneo: Antiguo Antiguedades, La Galeria Santiago de Chile
The Gun: Icon of Twentieth Century Art, Ubu Gallery, New York
2000 Museo de Monterrey, Monterrey, Mexico
2001 Biennale de Venice

Collections:

Museum of Modern Art, New York; Albright-Knox Art Museum, Buffalo, New York; Walker Art Center, Minneapolis; Stedelijk Museum, Amsterdam; Musée Royal des Beaux-Arts, Brussels; Musée d'Art Moderne, Ghent; Louisiana Museum of Art, Humlebaek, Denmark; Museum Haus Lange, Krefeld, Germany, Centre Georges Pompidou, Paris; Musée des Arts Décoratifs, Paris; Hirshhorn Museum and Sculpture Garden, Washington, D.C.; Metropolitan Museum of Art, New York; National Gallery, Berlin.

Publications:

By ARMAN: Articles—''Interview d'Arman,'' with Michel Ragon, in *Chorus,* nos. 5/6, 1970; ''Arman Qualité Quantité,'' interview with Catherine Millet, in *Art Press* (Paris) December/January 1974.

On ARMAN: Books—*Arman: Ateliers d'Aujourd'hui* by Otto Hahn, Paris 1972; *Arman* by Henry Martin, New York 1973; *Arman* by Jan van der Marck, New York 1984; *Arman* by Bernard Lamarche-Vadel, Paris 1987; *Arman Catalog Raisonné II* by Denyse Durand-Ruel, Paris 1991; *A World of Art* by Henry M. Sayre, Englewood Cliffs, New Jersey, 1994. **Exhibition catalogs—***Arman* (with text by Pierre Restany), Los Angeles 1962; *Arman* (with text by Alain Jouffroy), Milan 1963; *Arman* (with text by Pierre Restany and Claude Pascal; and statement by Arman), Amsterdam 1964; *Arman,* Stockholm 1966; *Arman* (with texts by Otto Hahn, Pierre Restany, and Michael Sonnabend), Paris 1967; *Arman* (with text by John Ashbery), New York 1968; *Arman* (with text by Pierre Restany), Milan 1968; *Arman: Accumulations Renault* (with text by Francois Mathey and interview by Claude Renard), Paris 1969; *Arman: Verk from 1964–1969,* Stockholm 1969; *Arman,* Milan 1970; *Arman* (with introduction by Pierre Restany), Antwerp 1972; *Arman: Selected Activities* (with texts by Peter Schjeldahl and Jan van der Marck), New York 1973; *Arman: Concrete Lyrics* (with text by Andrew Crispo), New York 1974; *Arman: Selected Works 1958–1974* (with an introduction by Jan van der Marck), La Jolla, California 1974; *Arman: Lyrical Surfaces,* New York 1975; *Arman: Objets Armés 1971–74* (with text by Jacques Lasaigne), Paris 1975; *From Reinhardt to Christo,* Oberlin, Ohio 1980; *Arman* (with text by Masashi Miura), Tokyo 1985; *Arman: Gods and Goddesses* (with essay by Henry Geldzahler), New York 1986; *Arman: Monochrome Accumulations* by Donald Kuspit, New York 1990; *Arman 1955–1991* (with text by Alison di Lima Greene and Pierre Restany), Houston 1991.

* * *

Of all the ''New Realists'' who appeared at various places in Europe at the beginning of the 1960s, Arman ranks surely as the purest poet of the object. He's also the artist of the group with the clearest commitment to a concept of significant form, and the power of his work depends on an almost relentless classicism. He is never sentimental. Even though he seems to allow the objects he deals with to speak entirely by themselves, he also allows his procedures a very similar sort of privilege, and it's the procedures of the artist rather than the objects of reality that finally hold the upper hand. The object is almost always reduced to a statuesque icon or an element of an all-over pattern, and the excitement of these configurations lies in the way we are invited to deal both with what the objects that go into them used to be and as well as with what they have since become. Arman keeps us spell-bound by creating an almost palpable tension between things we know with our intellect and things we see with our eyes.

Arman first came into his own around 1955 when he ceased to be what Pierre Restany has called a ''Sunday painter'' dedicated to '''nice' painting in the taste of the period, a post-Cubism at first figurative and later on abstract.'' That was the moment at which he invented the first of a whole series of new and entirely personal genres. He began to make works that consisted of repeated stampings of the same rubber stamp (his *cachets*); he then went on to making tracings (*allures*) of objects other than rubber stamps by inking them and sending them scudding across sheets of paper or canvas; he then decided that the object itself can be a trace of itself and put a definitive end to his work with rubber stamps by sealing them all into a box and this was the beginning of the *accumulations,* which were also later to become accumulations of trash called *pubelles* (trash cans). Later still he began to work with the possibility of smashing, burning, and sectioning objects (often musical instruments, and especially violins) and these became his *colères* (rages). He has made accumulations of everything from dollar bills to crucifixes, machine-gun bullets, dolls, Kodak brownie cameras, sewing machines, cigarette butts, trombones, chess men, tea pots, gas burners from old kitchen stoves, guns, parts of automobiles, cogs and wheels for watches, tennis shoes, pencils and squeezed tubes of artist's oil paint; his way of dealing with these accumulated objects is sometimes to weld them together, at other times to nail them to a board or simply to heap them into a glass-covered box; still other accumulations, like many of the destroyed violins, are drowned in polyester or embedded in cement. With his *colères,* he has been known to take an axe to quarry as large as a grand piano and to dynamite a sports car. He once went before an audience and destroyed the entirety of the contents of a fully furnished three-room middle-class apartment that had been set up for him in a New York art gallery.

Arman's work, finally, simply isn't understood at all unless it's understood to be an always on-going ritual. He is always bending the object to his entirely personal and purely arbitrary will as though to tell us that will is what we are most truly made of; the utilitarian objects in which will is codified and limited are destroyed or accumulated into almost purely visual pattern as though to tell us that we must know how to look beyond them if we're to see the essence of the human capacity that went into pulling them into existence in the first place.

—Henry Martin

The 1990s find the artist Arman still into... well, garbage. Included in a 1992 Brooklyn Museum exhibition of his works—spanning his prodigious output since the 1950s—was a recently created lifesize wreck of an aging car cast in bronze, with a green patina, and a demolished bicycle given the same treatment. "A direct heir of Yves Klein and Marcel Duchamp, Arman made his own world of twentieth-century art one that will probably outlast many a high-art garbage heap, Gerritt Henry wrote.

Journalist Patrick Pacheco agrees. In *Art & Antiques,* he wrote that "in both [Arman's] work and his extraordinary private collections, the accumulator par excellence celebrates the allure of objects—from the lowliest castoff to the most exalted rarity." Pacheco reported that his visit to the artist's Manhattan home yielded visions of objects ranging from Japanese arms and armor to African sculpture to jukeboxes. In fact Arman has written that "the power of objects lies in their ultimate ability to chronicle and withstand the pressure of time."

Showing Pacheco around his home, Arman observed that people frequently collect what they perceive as exotic. "It enhances your vision when the experience is translated through another culture. Oddly, alien customs and traditions give you reassurance about what you are." As an example, he noted two helmets, one Ionian, the other from the Basongye tribe in Zaire, which he displayed together because he found the disparate representations "quite fierce and interesting."

This "interesting" disparity has showed itself in Arman's recent art. In July 1995, the *New York Times* reported that the sculptor had found just the right spot for his new creation, *Hope for Peace,* after searching for 19 years. The spot? The Yarze district of Beirut near the presidential palace and Defense Ministry. "It is a lot of tanks embedded in concrete and is a 106-foot-tall pyramid that weighs 6,000 tons," Arman told the *Times.* "I made the first model of it in 1976 and tried to have it in the United States, in Europe and in Israel, but it cost too much." He added that he finally settled on Lebanon because that country is now at peace after years of war.

Arman said he hoped to do more versions of the buried-weapons-as-warning theme. "It's a good way to use weaponry," he noted, but added, "I am not sure that it will bring peace."

—Joan Oleck

ARMITAGE, Kenneth

Nationality: British. **Born:** Leeds, Yorkshire, 18 July 1916. **Education:** Studied at the Leeds College of Art, 1934–37; Slade School of Fine Art, London, 1937–39. **Military Service:** Served in the British Army, 1939–46. **Career:** Independent sculptor, since 1946. Visited Caracas; formed workshop, together with other Venezuelan sculptors, 1964; lived in Berlin, 1967–69; chairman, sculpture department, Bath Academy of Art, Crosham, 1946–56; visiting professor, Boston University, 1970. Visiting tutor, Royal College of Art, London, since 1974. **Awards:** Gregory Fellowship in Sculpture, Leeds University, Yorkshire, 1953–55; First Prize International War Memorial Competition, Krefeld, West Germany, 1956; David E. Bright Foundation Award, *Biennale,* Venice 1958; Prize, International Drawing and Engraving Exhibition, Lugano, Switzerland, 1958; Berlin Arts Programme Fellowship, 1967–69. C.B.E. (Commander of the Order of the British Empire), 1969. **Address:** 22a Avonmore Road, London W14 8RR, England.

Individual Exhibitions:

1952 Gimpel Fils, London
1954 Bertha Schaefer Gallery, New York
1956 Bertha Schaefer Gallery, New York
1957 Gimpel Fils, London
1958 Paul Rosenberg Gallery, New York
Musée Nationale d'Art Moderne, Paris
Biennale, Venice (with Stanley William Hayter and William Scott; toured Europe)
1959 Whitechapel Art Gallery, London
British Council World Tour (until 1976)
1960 Kestner Gesellschaft, Hannover (with Lynn Chadwick; toured Europe and Japan, 1960–61)
1962 Paul Rosenberg Gallery, New York
Marlborough Fine Art, London
Galerie Suvremene Umjetnosti, Zagreb
1963 Galerie Charles Linehard, Zurich
Galerie Wilhelm Groshennig, Dusseldorf
Galerie Blu, Milan
1965 Marlborough Fine Art, London
Arnolfini Gallery, Bristol
1972 Castle Museum, Norwich (toured the U.K., 1972–73)
1974 Hester van Royen Gallery, London
Gallery Kasahara, Osaka
1975 New Art Centre, London
1978 Fuji Television Gallery, Tokyo (travelled to the Galerie Humanite, Nagoya, and the Gallery Kasahara, Osaka)
1980 Gimpel Fils, London
1981 City Museum and Art Gallery, Stoke-on-Trent, Staffordshire
1982 Sala Mendoza, Caracas Taranman Gallery, London
1985 Artcurial, Paris (retrospective)

Selected Group Exhibitions:

1952 *Biennale,* Venice
1953 *Open Air Sculpture Exhibition,* Middleheim Park, Antwerp
1955 *The New Decade,* Museum of Modern Art, New York
1957 *Bienal,* Sao Paulo

1959 *New Images of Man,* Museum of Modern Art, New York
1962 *British Sculpture Today,* San Francisco Museum of Art (toured the United States)
1967 *Guggenheim International Sculpture Exhibition,* Guggenheim Museum, New York
1972 *British Sculptors 72,* Royal Academy of Art, London
1982 *British Sculpture of the 20th Century, Parts I and II,* Whitechapel Art Gallery, London
1987 *British Art of the 20th Century,* Royal Academy of Arts, London (travelled to Staatsgalerie, Stuttgart)

Collections:

Tate Gallery, London; Arts Council, London; Victoria and Albert Museum, London; Midleheim Museum, Antwerp; Musée Royale des Beaux-Arts, Brussels; Centre Georges Pompidou, Paris; Kunsthalle, Hamburg; Galleria Nazionale d'Arte Moderna, Rome; Albright-Knox Art Gallery, Buffalo, New York; Museum of Modern Art, New York.

Publications:

On ARMITAGE: Books—*Artists of Our Time, No. 7: Kenneth Armitage* by Sir Roland Penrose, Amriswil, Switzerland 1960; *Arts in Progress: Kenneth Armitage* by Norbert Lynton, London 1962; *Kenneth Armitage* by Charles Spencer, London 1973; *Kenneth Armitage: Sculptures and Drawings,* exhibition catalog, with foreword by Roland Penrose, Tokyo 1978; *Kenneth Armitage: Richmond Oaks and Other Works,* exhibition catalog, with introduction by John McEwen, London 1980; *Kenneth Armitage: New Sculptures and Collages,* exhibition catalog, with introduction by John McEwen, London 1982; *Kenneth Armitage: Life and Work,* exhibition catalog, 1997. **Articles—**''Kenneth Armitage'' by John Glaves-Smith in *Artscribe* (London), no. 16, 1979; ''Artists' Dialogue'' by Connie Glenn in *Architectural Digest* (Los Angeles) February 1982. **Films—** *Kenneth Armitage,* directed by John Read, BBC Television, London 1960; *5 British Sculptors Work and Talk,* directed by Warren Forma, 1964; *Armitage in Berlin,* Berlin 1969.

*

The character of my work divides into periods, some short, others long-lasting, in the way we tend to wear different clothes at different times. For example, the Oak Tree love affair in Richmond Park lasted non-stop from 1975 to 1986 with one or two large versions yet to be made. Others, like the attempts to combine drawing and sculpture, went no further than five or six pieces although a ten-foot relief combining both has now started, and a residual of black pubic and head hair still occurs. The series called *Chair* (based on my bedroom chair) lasted only through four versions. Demonstrating a time-lag *can* exist between forming an idea and testing it in one or several maquettes—and the full-scale realization may be delayed for several years. Conversely, I can finish something started long ago, like the big *Arm* made in Berlin in 1968 (cast temporarily in white resin and shown like that in Japan and London), is now receiving attention with a sprayed camouflage design based on drawings made in 1968 but never used until now. I regard it all as a body of work without much care for what was done when and where nothing is final. A lifetime is so very short anyway, and the time-scale of art enormous. I sometimes look at a small engraving on a reindeer antler fragment in the British Museum with an age estimated at 11,000 BC—which might have been made by a good artist last week. We often hear people on television say, ''way back in (say) 1985,'' when an Irish sense of time can range over centuries as though it was only recent. This easy communication across race, language and vast spans of time is comforting in an age when indifference to art seems general.

—Kenneth Armitage

* * *

Although he gained his international laurels as one of that group of young British sculptors that included Butler, Chadwick and Paolozzi, which showed at the Venice *Biennale* in 1952, Kenneth Armitage has generally stood aside from the prevailing ethos. Herbert Read rhetorically dubbed artists of this self-consciously angst-ridden post-war era the ''geometry of fear'' sculptors, but unlike many of the others Armitage stuck to the human figure rather than employing bestial or insect hybrids to serve as metaphors for the human condition. Moreover, Armitage's figures were not loaded with a tragic import; they were depicted in low-key casual situations, as seen in ''People in a Wind.'' Their scale was usually small, the observations modest and delivered sotto voce. In these respects his work owed more to artists like Giacometti and Picasso than to Surrealism and Moore.

When he adopted a larger scale and a more public manner in such works of the later 1950s as ''Diarchy,'' Armitage invested his figures with a hieratic monumentality: the torsos are flattened into plaques or tablets from which protrude the architectonic limbs. They are static and silent images, with a rare grandeur that is free from bombast and posturing.

During the 60s he experimented with various new figurative subjects and new materials, including resins and aluminum, but recently he has retured to bronze, long his favorite material. A new richness of color and material is evident in his series of Richmond Oaks from the late 70s. Armitage has always made drawings, both sketches and presentation works; they act as aids to observation but not as blue-prints for sculptures. Once again numerous studies, this time of trees in Richmond Park, accompany this group of new works. Characteristically, these sculptures are modest in scale and statement, but no less powerful for that. Armitage has abandoned the figure almost for the first time in his career, yet he never anthropomorphizes his oaks, and that elusive sense of poetic metaphor which inhabits his best works is found here too.

—Lynne Cooke

ARMLEDER, John M(ichael)

Nationality: Swiss. **Born**: Geneva, 24 June 1948. **Education:** Studied at the Ecole des Beaux-Arts, Geneva, 1966–67; with John Epstein, Glamorgan Summer School, Wales, 1969. Associated with the Groupe Luc Bois artists' group, Geneva, 1963; **Career:** Independent artist, from 1969; founder, with Patrick Lucchini and Claude Rychner, Groupe Ecart, Geneva, 1969; Galerie Ecart, Geneva, from 1973; Ecart Publications, Geneva, 1972; Ecart Performance Group,

Geneva, 1974; Ecart/Books, Geneva, 1975; International Institutions Register, Geneva, 1976; Leathern Wing Scribble Press, 1977; Laboratorio artists' co-operative, Milan, 1977. **Awards:** Graphics Prize, *Xylon VI* exhibition, Geneva, 1972; Kiefer-Hablitzel-Stipendium, Geneva, 1972, 1974, 1976; Eidgenossiche Kunststipendium, Geneva, 1977, 1978, 1979; Prize of the Banque Hypothecaire du Canton de Geneve, 1986. **Agents:** Ecart Books, rue Philippe, Plantamour 6,1211 Geneva, Switzerland; Galerie Marika Malacorda, rue de l'Eveche 1, 1204 Geneva; Galerie Toni Gerber, Gerechtigkeitsgasse 74, 3011 Berne, Switzerland. **Address:** 3 rue des Paquis, P.O.B. 253, 1211 Geneva, Switzerland.

Individual Exhibitions:

1973 Galerie Ecart, Geneva
Palais de l'Athenee, Geneva
Galerie Ecart, Geneva (with Patrick Lucchini)
1975 Galerie Gaetan, Carouge, Switzerland
1976 Palais de l'Athenee, Geneva
1977 Galerie Marika Malacorda, Geneva
1980 Rue Vignier, Geneva
Kunstmuseum, Basle
C Space, New York (with Helmut Federle and Christoph Gossweiler)
1981 Centre d'Art Contemporain, Geneva (with Martin Disler and Helmut Federle)
1982 Musee d'Art et d'Histoire, Fribourg, Switzerland
Gangurinn/The Corridor, Reykjavik
Galerie Toni Gerber, Berne
Galerie Marika Malacorda, Geneva
Vitrine Fri-Art, Fribourg, Switzerland
Nylistasafnid/The Living Arts Museum, Reykjavik
1983 Kunstmuseum, Solothurn, Switzerland
Gymnase Cantonal du Bugnon, Lausanne
Galerie Grita Insam, Vienna
Galerie Rivolta, Lausanne
Galerie Susanna Kulli, St. Gallen, Switzerland
Le Consortium, Dijon, France
1984 Galerie Marika Malacorda, Geneva
John Gibson Gallery, New York
Galerie Claudia Knapp, Chur, Switzerland
Galerie Filiale, Basle (with Christian Floquet)
1985 Galerie Marika Malacorda, Geneva
John Gibson Gallery, New York
Galerie Media, Neuchatel, Switzerland
Galerie und Lager Rudolf Zwirner, Cologne
1986 Galerie Susanna Kulli, St. Gallen, Switzerland
Ecole Nationale d'Art Decoratif, Limoges, France
Galerie Rivolta, Lausanne
John Gibson Gallery, New York
Galerie Tanit, Munich
Swiss Pavilion, *Biennale,* Venice
Galerie Catherine Issert, St. Paul-de-Vence, France
Galarie Toni Gerber, Berner
Galerie Bama, Paris
Lisson Gallery, London
Musée d'Art et d'Histoire, Geneva
Verein Kunsthalle, Zurich (with Helmut Federle and Olivier Mosset)
Stadtische Galerie, Regensburg, West Germany (with Olivier Mosset)
1987 Galleria Piero Cavellini, Milan
Galerie Munro, Hamburg
Galerie Daniel Buchholz, Cologne
Galerie Nachst St. Stephan, Vienna
Galerie Susanna Kulli, St. Gallen, Switzerland
Galerie Jean-Francois Dumont, Bordeaux, France
Kunstmuseum, Winterthur, Switzerland (travelled to Paris, Dusseldorf, and West Berlin)
John Gibson Gallery, New York
Pat Hearn Gallery, New York
Daniel Newburg Gallery, New York
Musee de Peinture et de Scuplture, Grenoble, France
Galerie Marika Malacorda, Geneva
Galerie Tanit, Munich
Hoffman Borman Gallery, Santa Monica, California
Galerie Joost Declercq, Ghent, Belgium
Kunstverein, Aachen, West Germany
Maison de la Culture, St. Etienne, France (with Olivier Mosset; travelled to Nevers)
1988 Galerie Tanit Kunigk und Moller, Munich
1991 John Gibson Gallery, New York
1993 Galerie Marika Malacorda, Geneva
Villa Arson, Nice
1994 Le Capitou, Centre d'Art Contemporain, Fréjus Factory, Geneva
Galerie Sollertis,Toulouse
1995 Cabinet des Estampes du musée d'Art et d'Histoire, Geneva
Galerie Jean-François Dumont and Galerie Air de Paris, Paris
Galerie Jean-François Dumont, Bordeaux
1996 Villa Carlotta, Fondation Ratti, Tremezzo
Galerie Art & Public, Geneva
Galerie Tanit, Münich
Galerie Sollertis, Toulouse
Galleria 1991 Joào Graça, Lisbon
Galerie Art & Public, Geneva
Galerie Susanne Kulli, Saint-Gallen
ECAL, Lausanne
Territorio Italiano, Piacenza
Galerie 360 Degrés, Tokyo
Galerie Tanit, Münich
Galerie Art & Public, Geneva
Fondation Mamco, Geneva.
1997 *Peintures murales 1967–1997,* Le Parvis, Ibos
1998 *Wall Paintings 1967–98,* Casino Luxembourg
Galerie Erna Hécey, Luxembourg

Selected Group Exhibitions:

1972 *Xylon VI,* Musee d'Art et d'Histoire, Geneva
1974 *Ambiente 74: 28 Schweizer Kunstler,* Kunstmuseum, Winterthur, Switzerland (travelled to Geneva and Lugano)
1976 *Rubber Stamp Exhibition,* La Mamelle Arts Center, San Francisco
1978 *Artwords and Bookworks,* Los Angeles Institute of Contemporary Art

1981 *CH '70-'80,* Kunstmuseum, Lucerne (travelled to Bologna, Genoa, Bonn and Graz)
1982 *Zwitserse Avant-Garde,* Galerie Nouvelles Images, The Hague
1984 *Peinture Abstraite,* Galerie Ecart, Geneva
1986 *Tableaux Abstraits,* Villa Arson, Nice France
1987 *Documenta 8,* Museum Fridericianum, Kassel, West Germany

Collections:

Kunstmuseum, Basle; Kunstmuseum, Lucerne; Musee d'Art et d'Histoire, Geneva; Cabinet des Estampes, Geneva; Kunsthaus, Zurich; Kunstmuseum, Winterthur; Staatsgalerie, Stuttgart; Musee Saint-Pierre, Lyon; Musee d'Art et d'Industrie, Saint-Etienne; Musee de Grenoble.

Publications:

By ARMLEDER: Books—*Lezards Sauvages,* Geneva 1973; *Ayacotl,* with Patrick Lucchini, Geneva 1973; *Ayacotl-Excerpts,* Geneva 1973; *12 Portes + 1,* with Patrick Lucchini, Geneva 1973; *Correspondances avec John Armleder,* with Endre Tot, Geneva 1974; *Niente Purtroppo,* Geneva 1975; *John Armleder,* with texts by Heinz Breloh, Jochen Gerz and others, Geneva 1975; *The John Armleder Is a Vegetarian Book,* Geneva 1975; *Une Pluie d'Etoiles Filantes,* Geneva 1975; *Dictionnaire Moderne Francais-Arabe,* Geneva 1975; *Dieu Expulse du Paradis,* with Claude Rychner, Geneva 1976; *3 x (2 x 1): A Chhjlnoruxy Production,* with Patrick Lucchini and Claude Rychner, Lucerne and Geneva 1977; *Hall,* with Dougal, Geneva 1977; *Sketches to Higgins' Intermedia Object No. 1,* with Patrick Lucchini, Geneva 1977; *Lezards Sauvages IIA: Egouttes,* Geneva 1979; *Titles Untitled,* Geneva 1979; *The D. S. Lick Nets,* with Helgi Thorgils Fridjonsson, Reykjavik 1982; *The Geneva Pond Bubbles,* with Arni Ingolfsson and others, Reykjavik 1982; *The Rex-Headed Master,* with Dadi Gudbjornsson and others, Reykjavik 1982; *One Year Lick,* with Dadi Gudbjornsson and Helgi Thorgils Fridjonsson, Reykjavik and Geneva 1983; *One Year Net,* with Thorgils Fridjonsson and Thor Vigfusson, Reykjavik and Geneva 1983; *Ecrits et Etretiens,* with Helmut Federle and Olivier Mosset, St. Etienne and Grenoble 1987; *Furniture Sculpture 1979–1986,* with texts by Nena Dimitrijevic and Christoph Schenker, Dudweiler 1987. **Articles**—"The Peripatetic Artist" in *Art in America,* July 1989; interview with Helena Kontova and Giancarlo Politi in *Flash Art,* October 1992.

On ARMLEDER: Books—*AMAM: Premieres Acquisitions et Donations,* exhibition catalog with text by Rainer Michael Mason, Geneva 1976; *John M. Armleder: 891 und weitere Stucke,* exhibition catalog with text by Dieter Koepplin, Basle 1980; *John M. Armleder/Martin Disler/Helmut M. Federle,* exhibition catalog with text by Christoph Schenker, Dieter Schwarz and others, Geneva 1982; *John M. Armleder: Arbeiten auf Papier 1962–83,* exhibition catalog with texts by André Jamber and Ben Vautier, Solothurn 1983; *John Armleder,* exhibition catalog with text by Jean-Hubert Martin, Dijon 1983; *John Armleder: Paintings and Furniture Sculpture,* exhibition catalog with text by Stuart Morgan, London 1986; *John M. Armleder,* exhibition catalog with text by Maurice Besset and Dieter Schwarz, Winterhur 1987.

* * *

For about seven years now the public has been seeing pictures and articles of furniture by John Armleder, an artist who had previously made a name for himself via graphics and performance art. If his first pictures still owed something to graphics, Armleder was soon elaborating a working style which, although it could not have been described as 'painterly,' was nevertheless clearly distinct from the poetic refinements of work on paper. These next works, rather than embodying a specifically subjective style, offered a neutral stage for the representation of various techniques; the drawings might incorporate traces of 'happening-activities' or they might equally follow paraconstructive lines (to use Armleder's terminology); simple designs might appear alongside designs based on complex random methods. Armleder was already playing with a variety of referents which would be evident to the acute observer; references to compositions by Cage, to graffiti, but also to Balla, Picabia and the Russian Constructivists. If there seemed to be a connection between these works and the Swiss graphic mentality of the seventies this was as a result of the intimacy of the medium rather than of a deliberate strategy. In contrast to his colleagues, Armleder was concerned with deconstructing a closed poetic universe rather than with a steady materialisation of the same; his pictures and furniture now confirm that beyond doubt.

In 1984 Armleder exhibited a large number of pictures for the first time, putting on a one-man exhibition in Geneva and contributing a selection of his work to a group exhibition which he himself had organised under the title *Peinture abstraite.* This exhibition, whose title, in a period when figurative art was in retreat, almost took on the quality of a manifesto, contained a mixture of abstract pictures of a geometric type in which Armleder's own works were completely at home. The choice of works by foreign artists was determined by circumstances and by the pressure towards improvisation; it demonstrated, not historical continuity, but abstraction as the icon of modernity. That in this exhibition concrete artists of the Zurich School (Loewensberg) hung beside Americans of the most diverse provenance (Held, Motherwell and Ryman on the one hand, minimal artists such as Lewitt and Mangold on the other), in combination with younger artists like Merz, Mosset and Armleder himself, was a clear indication that Armleder was concerned, not with a precise stylistic definition of his work, but with a practical blurring of the boundaries which the various schools of abstract art have erected. From the various processes of abstraction Armleder takes up for his own use only certain elements which point to the modernistic tradition without representing it in all its consequences.

Armleder's pictures are not painterly in the first instance, because it is not his aim to carry on working through the problems of an art radicalized by the modern approach. He avoids the formalistic tradition, which continues to preoccupy artists such as Toroni or Mosset, and concerns himself with the concept of 'modernism' as hypostatised by the avant-garde in the first half of the century. Consequently, he is not caught up in an exclusively geometric approach but takes as his theme the historical representation of this method: A rhetoric which establishes itself in an idealised sphere beyond mediation, seduction and expropriation. By distancing himself, however, from the geometric approach, Armleder has not shifted to a new form of representation. In this, he differs from artists like Schuyff or Taaffe who produce pictures which either verbally cite models from the '60s or use the geometric approach as a means to the production of a, yet again, illusionistic field of vision. In contrast too to Halley, for whom the geometric elements serve as pretext for a symbolical scenery, Armleder extracts from his simple polka dots the possibility for a dissolution of content. In denying the significance of an isolated picture and concentrating instead on its contextualisation, he abandons the sphere of pure painting. An example of this is to be found in the group exhibition Armleder organized, and also in his one-man exhibitions: Each of his dot pictures relates first to the other dot pictures present, which differ from one another according to their physical composition, the materials used and variations in the organization of the ground plan, and secondly to the whole range of dot and scanning patterns in modernist art. The dots are especially relevant to Armleder's purpose, since on the one hand they mark out a simple latticework distribution of the picture's surface, but on the other, in contrast to a quadratic arrangement, they disturb any uninterrupted perception of that surface.

In his combination of pictures and objects Armleder finds further possibilities for contextualisation. The objects, be they old pieces of furniture or newly produced consumer articles, are set, as anonymously produced decorative elements, over and against painting itself. It is not by chance that Armleder began with old drawing room furniture, sofas and dressing tables, more recently replaced by musical instruments. If the furniture devalues the picture (which furnishes the background to conversation) as part of the furnishings, the canvases on the other hand, often hung in place of mirrors, reflect the narcissistic position of the subjectively determined abstract painting, which was suppressed in the modernistic tradition by the concept of the autonomy of the painting. The musical instruments for their part repeat a popular still-life motif (compare, for example, the guitar employed by the Cubists), at the same time shifting the pictures out of the painterly tradition and into association with the contemporary entertainment industry.

Pictures and objects are not parts of a continuum. Picture and object react one upon the other: The pictorial composition turns to account formal qualities of the neighbouring object and the object defines the picture's real location. They do not interreact like parts of a surrealistic montage in which the alienating co-existence of objects very different to one another provides the key note. In contrast to Rauschenberg with his *Combine Paintings,* Armleder is not interested in the graduation of planes between painting, reproduction and real object. His so-called *Furniture Sculptures* intervene in painting, treating the picture no longer as an autonomous object but as a commodity and presenting commodities as possible extensions of painting.

—Dieter Schwarz

ARNESON, Robert

Nationality: American. **Born:** Benicia, California, 4 September 1930. **Education:** Benicia High School, 1945–49; Marin College, Kenfield, California, 1949–51; California College of Arts and Crafts, Oakland, B.A. (art education) 1954; Mills College, Oakland, M.F.A. (art; studied under Antonio Prieto), 1958. **Family:** Married 1) Jeanette Jensen in 1955 (divorced 1972); sons: Leif, Derek, and Kirk; 2) Sandra Shannonhouse in 1973; daughter: Tenaya. **Career:** Sports cartoonist, *Benicia Herald,* 1949–52. Independent artist since 1958; established studio with Richard McLean, East Oakland, 1961–62; established studio in old saloon, Benicia, 1975; art teacher, Menlo-Atherton High School, Atherton, California, 1954–57, Santa Rosa Junior College, 1958–59, and Fremont High School, Oakland, 1959–60; instructor in design and crafts, Mills College, Oakland, 1960–62; University of California at Davis, assistant professor of art and design, 1962–68, associate professor of art, 1968–73, professor of art, 1973–1992, professor emeritus, 1991–92. **Awards:** Creative Arts Grant, University of California, 1967; Artists' Fellowship Grant, 1971, and Apprentice Fellowship Grant, 1978, National Endowment for the Arts; National Council on Education for the Ceramic Arts Award, 1979; D.F.A.: Rhode Island School of Design, Providence, 1985; American Academy and Institute of Arts and Letters award, 1991. **Agents:** Fuller-Goldeen Gallery, 228 Grant Avenue, San Francisco, California 94108, U.S.A.; Allen Frumkin Gallery, 50 West 57th Street, New York, New York 10022, U.S.A. **Died:** 2 November 1992.

Individual Exhibitions:

1960 Oakland Art Museum, California (with Tony De-Lap)
1962 M. H. de Young Memorial Museum, San Francisco
Barrios Gallery, Sacramento, California
1963 Richmond Art Center, California
1964 Cellini Gallery, San Francisco
Home Economics Building, University of California at Davis
Allan Stone Gallery, New York
1967 San Francisco Museum of Art
1968 Hansen-Fuller Gallery, San Francisco
1969 Hansen-Fuller Gallery, San Francisco
Bob and Roy Ceramics, Esther Robles Gallery, Los Angeles (with Roy De Forest)
Candy Store Gallery, Folsom, California
1970 *Recent Art Works in Porcelain,* Hansen-Fuller Gallery, San Francisco
Bob and Roy Ware, Candy Store Gallery, Folsom, California (with Roy De Forest)
Fresno State College of Art Gallery, California
1971 Hansen-Fuller Gallery, San Francisco
Candy Store Gallery, Folsom, California
Manolides Gallery, Seattle (with William T. Wiley)
University of Calgary, Alberta
1972 Hansen-Fuller Gallery, San Francisco
Miami-Dade Junior College, Florida
1973 Hansen-Fuller Gallery, San Francisco
Church Fine Arts Gallery, University of Nevada, Reno
1974 Hansen-Fuller Gallery, San Francisco
Deson-Zaks Gallery, Chicago
Museum of Contemporary Art, Chicago (retrospective; travelled to the San Francisco Museum of Art)
Candy Store Gallery, Folsom, California
1975 Allan Frumkin Gallery, New York
Hansen-Fuller Gallery, San Francisco
Ruth Schaffner Gallery, Los Angeles
Dootson/Calderhead Gallery, Seattle
1976 Hansen-Fuller Gallery, San Francisco
Fendrick Gallery, Washington, D.C.
Memorial Union Art Gallery, University of California at Davis
Allan Frumkin Gallery, Chicago
National Collection of Fine Arts, Smithsonian Institution,Washington, D.C.
1977 Hansen-Fuller Gallery, San Francisco

Allan Frumkin Gallery, New York
1978 *Works on Paper,* Allan Frumkin Gallery, New York
Allan Frumkin Gallery, Chicago
1979 *Heroes and Clowns,* Allan Frumkin Gallery, New York
Self-Portraits 1965–1978, Moore College of Art, Philadelphia
Allan Frumkin Gallery, New York
1980 Hansen-Fuller-Goldeen Gallery, San Francisco
Frumkin and Struve Gallery, Chicago
1981 Allan Frumkin Gallery, New York
1982 Foster Goldstrom Gallery, San Francisco
University of California, Davis
Fuller-Goldeen Gallery, San Francisco
1983 Allan Frumkin Gallery, New York
Landfall Press Inc., Chicago (travelled to Beloit, Wisconsin; Saginaw, Michigan; Springfield, Missouri; Tulsa, Oklahoma; Shawnee Mission, Kansas; Muncie, Indiana)
Yares Gallery, Scottsdale, Arizona
Crocker Art Museum, Sacramento, California
Triton Museum of Art, Santa Clara, California (travelled to Sacramento, California; Fresno, California; Portland, Oregon)
1984 Allan Frumkin Gallery, New York
Fuller-Goldeen Gallery, San Francisco
Frumkin and Struve Gallery, Chicago
1985 Fuller-Goldeen Gallery, San Francisco
1986 Pittsburgh Center for the Arts
1987 Frumkin/Adams Gallery, New York
1988 Fuller-Gross Gallery, San Francisco
Dorothy Goldeen Gallery, Santa Monica
1990 The Wadsworth Atheneum, Hartford
1991 Massachusetts Institute of Technology, Cambridge
Museum of Fine Arts, Springfield
1992 Dorothy Goldeen Gallery, Santa Monica
Institute of Contemporary Art, University of Pennsylvania, Philadelphia
1993 Fine Arts Museums, San Francisco
John Berggruen Gallery, San Francisco
1997 San Francisco Museum of Modern Art, San Francisco

Selected Group Exhibitions:

1964 *Ceramic National,* Everson Museum of Art, Syracuse, New York (toured the United States, 1964–66)
1967 *Funk Art,* University of California Art Museum, Berkeley
1968 *Dada-Surrealism and Their Heritage,* Museum of Modern Art, New York
1970 *Teacups, Teapots and Gorillas,* Moore College of Art, Philadelphia (with Ron Nagle, David Gilhooly, and Michael Frimkess)
1972 *A Decade of Ceramic Art 1962–1972,* San Francisco Museum of Art
1976 *Painting and Sculpture in California: The Modern Era,* San Francisco Museum of Modern Art (travelled to the National Gallery, Smithsonian Institution, Washington, D.C., 1977)
1978 *American Art since 1950,* Whitney Museum, New York
1981 *Ceramic Sculpture: Six Artists,* Whitney Museum, New York (travelled to San Francisco Museum of Modern Art, 1982)
1982 *100 Years of California Sculpture,* Oakland Art Museum, California
1984 *California Sculpture Show,* University of Southern California, Los Angeles (travelled to Bordeaux, France; Mannheim, West Germany; West Bretton, Yorkshire; Hovikodden, Norway)
1988 *Life Stories, Myth, Fiction & History in Contemporary Art*, University of Washington, Seattle
1990 *Figuring the Body,* Museum of Fine Arts, Boston
1991 *Experiencing Sculpture*, Hudson River Museum, Yonkers
1992 *Split Personalities: Portraiture and the Imagination*, Norman Mackenzie Art Gallery, Regina, Saskatchewan

Collections:

Whitney Museum, New York; Museum of Contemporary Crafts, New York; Hirshhorn Museum and Sculpture Garden, Smithsonian Institution, Washington, D.C.; Philadelphia Museum of Art; University of California at Berkeley; San Francisco Museum of Modern Art; Oakland Museum, California; E. B. Crocker Art Gallery, Sacramento, California; Stedelijk Museum, Amsterdam; Australian National Gallery, Canberra; Museum of Fine Arts, Boston; University of Chicago, Chicago; Los Angeles County Museum of Art, Los Angeles; University of California, Davis; Emily Carr College of Art; The Wadsworth Atheneum, Hartford; Museum of Modern Art, New York; Santa Barbara Museum of Art, Santa Barbara; Triton Museum, Santa Clara; Seattle Art Museum, Seattle; Virginia Museum of Fine Arts; Richmond.

Publications:

By ARNESON: Exhibition catalog—*My Head in Ceramics,* San Francisco, 1972. **Articles**—''About Arneson, Art and Ceramics,'' interview, with Cecile N. McCann, in *Artweek* (Oakland, California), 26 October 1974; ''Robert Arneson in Conversation with Gwen Stone'' in *Visual Dialog* (Los Altos, California), vol. 2, no. 1, 1977; ''Guardians: the Spirit of the Work'' in *Ceramics Monthly*, vol. 39, pt. 4, April 1991.

On ARNESON: Books—*American Sculpture in Process 1930–1976* by Wayne Anderson, New York 1975; *Tradition and Change: The American Craftsman* by Julie Hall, New York 1977; *History of American Ceramics: The Studio Potter* by Paul S. Donhauser, Dubuque, Iowa 1978. **Exhibition catalogs**—*A Decade of Ceramic Art 1962–1972* (with text by Suzanne Foley), San Francisco 1972; *Robert Arneson* (with texts by Suzanne Foley and Stephen Prokopoff), Chicago 1974; *Painting and Sculpture in California: The Modern Era,* San Francisco 1977; *Heroes and Clowns* (with text by Michael McTwigan), New York 1979; *Robert Arneson: Self-Portraits 1965–1978* (with text by Beth Coffelt), Philadelphia, 1979; *A Century of Ceramics in the United States 1878–1978* (with texts by Garth Clark and Margie Hughto), New York 1979; *Robert Arneson: the Last Works,* San Francisco, 1993; *Arneson and Politics: Commemorative Exhibition,* San Francisco, 1993; *Robert Arneson: Self-Reflection,* (with text by Gary Garrels, Janet C. Bishop and Jonathan Fineberg), San Francisco, 1997. **Articles**—''Sweet Land of Funk'' by Harald Paris in *Art in America* (New York), March/April 1967; ''Arneson, Richardson'' by Cecile N. McCann in *Artweek* (Oakland, California), 23 May 1970; ''Sacramento!'' by John FitzGibbon in *Art in America,* November/December 1971; ''Crock Art'' by Douglas Davis in *Newsweek* (New

York), 5 July 1971; ''Arneson, Moses—Study in Contrasts'' by Cecile N. McCann in *Artweek,* 14 October 1972; ''Arneson and Towbridge'' by Cecile N. McCann in *Artweek,* 20 October 1973; ''Robert Arneson's Feats of Clay'' by Dennis Adrian in *Art in America,* September/October 1974; ''Bob Arneson: Take Notice'' by David Van Houten in *Artweek,* 25 January 1975; ''Arneson's Landscape'' by R. F. Stepan in *Artweek,* 24 January 1976; ''The Ceramic Sculpture of Robert Arneson, Transformation of Craft into Art'' by Alfred Frankenstein in *Artnews* (New York), January 1976; ''Sculpture—From Boring to Brilliant'' by Hilton Kramer in the *New York Times,* 15 May 1977; ''Robert Arneson at Frumkin'' by Sarah McFadden in *Art in America,* July 1977; ''A Modern Way with Clay'' by Bill Marvel in *Horizon* (New York), September 1978; ''57,500 Ceramics Commission'' in *Ceramics Monthly* (Athens, Ohio), May 1981; ''Arneson's Bust'' by Robert Sommer in *Arts and Architecture* (Los Angeles), 1 August 1982; ''A Monumental Side to Arneson'' by Dennis Adrian in *San Francisco Chronicle,* 22 February 1984; ''Arneson's Outrage'' by Donald Kuspit in *Art in America,* May 1985; ''Robert Areneson: Critical Clay'' by Robert Hobbs in *Sculpture* (Washington, D.C.), vol. 12, pt. 6, November-December 1993; ''Black: Late Drawings of Robert Arneson'' by Beth Coffelt in *American Ceramics,* vol. 12, pt. 1, 1995.

*

I think I've always been a social political artist. My art is accessible. Recently, I've done a body of work on the nuclear issue. *Ground Zero* (1984) is a typical example. It visualizes the effects of a nuclear holocaust on mankind. It's not fun to look at, but I wanted to bring my concern of the dangers of nuclear proliferation to an expanded art audience—the museum and gallery visitor—to let them know that art and life were inseparable.

—Robert Arneson

* * *

Robert Arneson's explicitly autobiographical sculptures confront his pleasures and embarrassments with a wry, self-deprecating humor that touches a responsive chord for most viewers. It is easy to identify with the blissful face that surveys a table loaded with festive foods or the ceramic head which shows the sculptor on the receiving end of a gob of clay—mud in his eye, or perhaps a metaphor for critical barbs occasionally flung at his work.

Beyond the clearly personal comments, the work contains wide-ranging art-historical references. Arneson has so thoroughly studied the history of ceramics that he has made both the concepts and techniques of the past accessible for his own uses. At one time he created a series of irreverent small sculptures that used imagery resembling fruit stand souvenirs, and made them of exquisitely finished, celadon-glazed porcelain as seductive as a Sung bowl. One homage to ancient Rome took the form of a self-portrait bust set head-high on an accurately reproduced classical column, the calm austerity of the piece punctured by male genitals protruding from the smooth cylinder at the appropriate position and bare toes lifting the column's base as if it were the hem of a toga. Pomposity and self-importance are not permitted to linger in this artist's work.

More recently Arneson preferred low-fire white ware as a medium, indulging his painter's eye in the pleasures of skillfully handled color only possible with the brilliance of low-temperature glazes. The self-portraits continued, their good-natured jocularity reflecting the more pleasant aspects of Arneson's daily life. If the cheerfulness at times seems over-insistent, perhaps this has some connection with the long, sustained effort necessary to produce a sculpture. In the immediacy of watercolors and drawings, Arneson occasionally recorded darker thoughts and grim self-images, as if to purge them from his mind and let happier moods return. Happy or sad, it is himself and the small concerns that define a personality which Arneson records with detailed accuracy.

—Cecile N. McCann

ARROYO, Eduardo

Nationality: Spanish. **Born:** Madrid, 26 February 1937. **Education:** Lycée Francais, Madrid, 1949–53; studied journalism at the Ecole Supérieure de Journalisme, Madrid, 1956–57; mainly self-taught in painting, from 1949. **Military Service:** Served in the Spanish Infantry, 1956–57. **Career:** Worked as freelance journalist, Madrid, 1957; as independent painter, Paris, 1958–68; in Milan, 1968–72; in West Berlin, 1975–76; permanently in Paris, since 1973. Instructor, Atelier Populaire, Ecole des Beaux-Arts, Paris, 1968. Worked as freelance theatre, set and costumer designer, in Milan, Bremen, Dusseldorf, Frankfurt, Berlin, and Paris, 1969–76. **Awards:** Deutscher Akademischer Austauschdienst (D.A.A.D.) Grant, Berlin, 1975–76. **Agent:** Galerie Karl Flinker, 25 rue de Tournon, 75006 Paris, France. **Address:** 2 Passage Dantzig, 75015 Paris, France.

Individual Exhibitions:

1961 Galerie Claude Levin, Paris
1962 Crane Kalman Gallery, London
1963 Galleria Biosca, Madrid
1964 Galerie 20, Amsterdam
Galerie 20, Arnhem, Netherlands
Galerie Bernheim Jeune, Paris
1965 Galerie André Schoeller Jr., Paris
Galerie 20, Amsterdam
1967 Galleria de'Foscherari, Bologna
Galleria Mendoza, Caracas
Galleria Il Fante di Spade, Rome
1968 Studio Marconi, Milan
Studio Bellini, Milan
Galleria Il Canale, Venice
Galleria La Chiocciola, Padua
1969 Galleria La Bussola, Turin
Galleria La Robinia, Palermo
Galerie André Weill, Paris
1970 Galerie Withofs, Brussels
Galleria Il Fante di Spade, Rome
Galleria Aldina, Rome
Galleria Arte Borgogna, Milan
Galleria San Michele, Brescia
1971 *30 Jahre Danach,* Kunstverein, Frankfurt (travelled to the Musée d'Art Moderne de la Ville, Paris)
Museum Hedendaagse Kunst, Utrecht
Kunstverein, Munich
Kunstverein, Berlin

Palazzo del Gobernatore, Parma
Galleria People, Turin
1972 Galerie 9, Paris
Stadtische Kunsthalle, Dusseldorf
Galerie d'Eendt, Amsterdam
1973 Galleria d'Arte Borgogna, Milan
Gastaldelli Arte Contemporanea, Milan
Galleria Nuove Muse, Bologna
1974 *Portraits,* Galerie Karl Flinker, Paris
Studio P. L., Milan
1975 Galerie Fred Lanzenberg, Brussels
Galleria L'Aprodo, Turin
1976 D.A.A.D. Akademie der Künste, Berlin (with Grazia Eminente)
Galerie Leger, Malmo, Sweden
1977 Galeria Maeght, Barcelona
Galeria Juana Mordo, Madrid
Galeria Val y 30, Valencia
1978 Fondation Nationale des Artes Graphiques et Plastiques, Paris
Galerie Karl Flinker, Paris
1979 Galerie Karl Flinker, Basle
Gallery Art Package, Highland Park, Illinois
1980 Galerie Maeght, Zurich
Städtische Galerie in Lenbachhaus, Munich
Galerie Michael Hasenclever, Munich
1981 Galerie Karl Flinker, Paris
1982 Modern Art Museum, Madrid
Centre Georges Pompidou, Paris
Eva Cohen Gallery, Highland Park, Illinois
1983 Leonard Hutton Galleries, New York
1984 Galerie Levy, Hamburg
Guggenheim Museum, New York (retrospective)
1985 *FIAC,* Galería Gamarra y Garrigues, Paris
Galería Temple, Valencia
Galerie Isy Brachot, Brussels
Galerie La Hune, Paris
Art Cologne, Galerie Levy, Colonia
Nouvelle Biennale de París, Grande Halle de La Vilette, Paris
1986 Fundación Santillana, Madrid
Art Basel, Galerie Levy, Basilea
Galerie Orangerie-Reinz, Colonia
Galerie Stemmle-Adler, Heidelberg
Institut Alfons el Magnanim, Valencia
1987 Galería Carles Taché, Barcelona
Galería Gamarra y Garrigues, Madrid
Galería Temple, Valencia
SAGA-Paris, Galerie Berggruen, Paris
Galerie BUK, Dortmund
Galerie Levy (with Bruno Bruni), Hamburg
Festival d'Avignon, Grande Chapelle du Palais Des Papes Aillaud (with Gilles), Avignon
Museum für Kunst und Kulturgeschichte der Stadt Dormund, Dormund
1988 *ARCO'88,* Galería Gamarra y Garrigues, Madrid
Galerie de France, Paris
Galerie Hasenclever, Munich
Gallery Levy of Hamburg, and Galería Gamarra y Garrigues of Madrid, Paris
Musée Cantini, Marsella
Musée d'Art et d'Histoire, Belfort
1989 Galería Carles Taché, Barcelona
SAGA-París, Galerie Bergrueen, Paris
Feria de Milán, Galerie Levy, Hamburgo/París/Madrid
Multiples au singulier, Galerie Levy Dahan, Paris
Galerie Redmann, Berlin
Bilder Zeichnungen Graphik, Manuspresse, Stuttgart
1990 Bilder Skulpturen Zeichnungen Collagen Graphik, Bilder, Alemania
Art Cologne, Galería Carles Taché, Colonia
ARCO'90, Collages 89, Galerie Bergrueen Paris, Madrid
Galerie Stemme-Adler, Heidelberg
Nising, Frankfurt
Remberti Galerie, Bremen
1991 Espace Fortant de France, Sere
Galerie Hasenclever, Munich
Galerie Thomas Levy, Hamburg
1992 Galería Gamarra y Garrigues, Madrid.
Galería Trece, Ventalló, Girona
Art Cologne'92, Galerie Thomas Levy, Colonia
1993 *Cyprus Art,* Sant Feliu de Boada, Girona
Galería Barcena y Cia, Madrid
Galería Francesc Machado, Girona
Galería Gamarra y Garrigues, Madrid
Sombreros para Alicia, Galería Tiempos Modernos, Madrid
Galerie Anton Meier, Ginebra
Galerie Beeckman, Brussels
Galerie Dionne, Paris
Galerie Françoise Courtiade, Toulouse
Palacio de Sástago, Diputación de Zaragoza
Sala Pelaires, Palma de Mallorca
1994 Galería Cromo, Alicante
SAGA-París, Galerie $, Paris
FIAC 94, Gallerie San Carlo, Paris.
Gallery Levy, Hamburg
Museo Casa de la Moneda, Madrid
Tamaño natural (1963–1993), Museo de Bellas Artes de Bilbao, Bilbao
Palacio de la Audiencia, Soria
Chimeneas y Deshollinadores, Sala de Exposiciones, Bilbao
1995 Box-Schule Charly Bühler, Berne
Galería Carles Taché, Barcelona
Galería Charpa, Valencia
Lithographies pour contes de Perrault, Galería Maeght, Paris
Galerie Dionne, Paris
De Gutenberg a Madonna, Galleria San Carlo, Milán
Bienal de Venecia, Pabellón de España, Venecia
1996 Eduardo Arroyo, Works 1973–1993, Cynthia Bourne Gallery, London
Die Galerie, Frankfurt
Galería Cadaqués, Cadaqués
Suite Senefelder and Co., Galería Gamarra, Madrid
Arroyo Arbeiten auf Papier, Galerie Kühn, Lilienthal
Suite Senefelder and Co., Museo de Bellas Artes de Bilbao, Bilbao
1997 Suite Senefelder and Co., Galería Carles Taché, Barcelona

Knock-out, Musée Olympique, Lausana
Suite Senefelder and Co., Musée Olympique, Lausana
1998 Galería Rosalía Sender, Valencia
Retrospectiva, Museo Nacional de Arte Reina Sofía, Madrid
1999 Galería Durero, Gijón
Galeria Louis Carré, Paris
Galeria Carles Taché, Barcelona

Selected Group Exhibitions:

1960 *Salon de la Jeune Peinture,* Paris
1964 *Neue Realisten und Pop Art,* Akademie der Künste, Berlin
1965 *Pop Art: Nouveaux Réalistes,* Palais des Beaux-Arts, Brussels
1970 *Kunst und Politik,* Kunstmuseum, Karlsruhe, West Germany
1971 *Peintures et Objets,* Musée Galliera, Paris
1972 *Immagini per la Città,* Palazzo Reale, Genoa
1974 *L'Arte contre il Fascismo,* Palazzo della Loggia, Brescia
1976 *Realidada Social 1936–76,* at the *Biennale,* Venice
1979 *1968–79: Tendances de l'Art en France II,* Musée d'Art Moderne de la Ville, Paris
1980 *L'Art et le Sport,* Centre Culturel, Boulogne-Billancourt, France
1995 Biennale de Venice
1997 *Hommages. Hommes illustres, heros et hommes du commun,* Musée de Picardie, Amiens; Espace culturel François Mitterand

Collections:

Musée d'Art Moderne de la Ville, Paris; Centre Georges Pompidou, Paris; Ministère de la Culture et de la Communication, Paris; Fondation Maeght, St. Paul de Vence, France; Musée des Beaux-Arts, Lausanne; National Galerie, Berlin; Hirshhorn Museum, Washington, D.C.

Publications:

By ARROYO: Book—*''Panama'' Al Brown 1902–1951,* Paris 1982.

On ARROYO: Books—*Kunst und Politik,* exhibition catalog, Karlsruhe 1970; *Eduardo Arroyo: 30 Jahre Danach,* exhibition catalog, with text by Gerard Gassiot-Talabot, Frankfurt 1971; *Arroyo: Portraits,* exhibition catalog, with text by Michel Tournier, Paris 1974; *Eduardo Arroyo,* exhibition catalog, with text by Gilbert Lascault, Paris 1978; *Eduardo Arroyo: Blinde Maler und Exit,* exhibition catalog, with text by Armin Zweite, Munich 1980; *Arroyo* by Pierre Astier, Paris 1982; *Eduardo Arroyo,* exhibition catalog with texts by Dominique Bozo and Werner Spies, New York 1983; *Eduardo Arroyo* by F. Calvo Serraller, Madrid 1991; *Eduardo Arroyo,* exhibition catalog, Bienal de Venecia 1995; *Eduardo Arroyo,* exhibition catalog, Madrid 1998.

* * *

There has always been an element of nakedness about Eduardo Arroyo's imagery. Even in early times, when the paint of his pictures was a little thicker, it was present. This is the surface effect, but below it lies an active conscience that dictates imagery. Not the sort of artist who can live comfortably in the cloying atmosphere of a dictatorship. This Spaniard with his direct approach tinted with character is a fine example of *engagierte kunst.* The Buonaparte paintings he showed in Paris made this very plain. But even politics as an inspiration for artists has not necessarily got eternal appeal.

Some of his later work has been concerned with the boxing ring, especially with black fighters. In these new works he is able to give a fresh and wholly unexpected dimension to the promotional side of ''commercial art,'' although in Arroyo's case it is fine art, not the product of advertising nor some hybrid hyperrealist artist that is under consideration.

Arroyo's paint is flat. The subject (at one time he even divided his canvases into sections like a comic strip, although hardly in the same vein as those of CPLY's) is painted sparingly with the minimum of chiaroscuro. Colours tend to be block, and there is virtually no tinting. All of his pictures have a careful, even traditional, sense of composition. Carried out by another artist, they might even have been associated with the pop image.

—Sheldon Williams

''Retromatón,'' Arroyo's 1994 retrospective, showcased the wide range of his artistic interests: drawings and relief and free-standing sculpture, as well as the better-known paintings and theater designs. His unusual selection of persons to memorialize in portraits included friends, historical figures, and celebrities. Upon exiting the retrospective, visitors were allowed to pose in a photo booth, which was rigged to produce strips of silhouettes complete with stamps of Arroyo's signature. As with Felix-Gonzalez-Torres's piles of candy and multiple prints, the technique enabled ordinary people to own and enjoy an original work of art.

—Mark Swartz

ARTSCHWAGER, Richard (Ernst)

Nationality: American. **Born:** Washington, D.C., 26 December 1923. **Education:** Studied chemistry and mathematics at Cornell University, Ithaca, New York, 1943–44, 1946–48, B.A. 1948; studied art with Amedee Ozenfant, New York, 1950. **Military Service:** Served in the United States Army, 1944–46. **Family:** Married Elfriede Wejmelka in 1947 (divorced, 1971); daughter: Eva; married Catherine Kord in 1972 (divorced, 1989); married Molly O'Gorman (divorced 1993); children: Clara, Augustus; married Ann Sebring, 1995. **Career:** Worked as a baby photographer for Stork Diaper Service, New York; lathe operator for Efrem Natkin Flexible Couplings, New York; and in export/import department, Colonial Trust Company, New York, 1950–55; operated a furniture factory, New York, 1955–65. Full-time artist, New York, since 1970. **Awards:** Cassandra Award, New York, 1969; National Endowment for the Arts grant, 1973. **Agent:** Mary Boone Gallery, 417 W. Broadway, New York, New York, 10012, U.S.A. **Address:** P.O. Box 12, Hudson, NY, 12534–0012.

Individual Exhibitions:

1965 Leo Castelli Gallery, New York
1967 Leo Castelli Gallery, New York

1968 Galerie Konrad Fischer, Dusseldorf
1969 Galerie Ricke, Cologne
1970 Lo Guidice, Chicago
Eugenia Butler Gallery, Los Angeles
Onnasch Galerie, Berlin
1972 Leo Castelli Gallery, New York
Galerie Ricke, Cologne
1973 Leo Castelli Gallery, New York
Dunkelman Gallery, Toronto
Museum of Contemporary Art, Chicago
1974 Daniel Weinberg Gallery, San Francisco
Galerie Ileana Sonnabend, Geneva
1975 Leo Castelli Gallery, New York
Daniel Weinberg Gallery, San Francisco
Jared Sable Gallery, Toronto
Galerie Neuendorf, Hamburg
Galerie Sonnabend, Paris
1976 Walter Kelly Gallery, Chicago
Castelli Graphics, New York
1977 Sable-Castelli Gallery, Toronto
1978 Texas Gallery, Houston
Clocktower, New York
Institute for Art and Urban Resources, New York
Morgan Gallery, Shawnee Mission, Kansas
Kunstverein, Hamburg
1979 Leo Castelli Gallery, New York
Albright-Knox Art Gallery, Buffalo, New York
Institute of Contemporary Art, University of Pennsylvania, Philadelphia
1980 La Jolla Museum of Contemporary Art, California
Young-Hoffman Gallery, Chicago
1982 Leo Castelli Gallery, New York
1985 Kunstverein, Basel
Leo Castelli Gallery, New York
1986 CAPC Musée d'Art Contemporain, Bordeaux, France
1988 Whitney Museum, New York (retrospective; travelled throughout the U.S. and Europe)
1989 School of Fine Arts, Boston (with John Baldessari)
1990 Daniel Weinberg Gallery, Santa Monica, California
1991 Rhona Hoffman Gallery, Chicago
1992 Museum of Fine Arts, Boston
1993 Mary Boone Gallery, New York
1995 Kent Gallery, New York
1997 Mary Boone Gallery, New York
Nolan/Eckman Gallery, New York
1999 Lehmann Maupin Gallery, New York

Selected Group Exhibitions:

1964 *Boxes,* Dwan Gallery, Los Angeles
1966 *Primary Structures,* Jewish Museum, New York
1967 *The 1960s,* Museum of Modern Art, New York
1968 *Documenta 4,* Kassel, West Germany (and *Documenta 5,* 1972; *Documenta 8,* 1987; *Documenta 9,* 1992)
1969 *When Attitudes Become Form,* Kunsthalle, Berne (toured Germany and Great Britain)
1974 *American Pop Art,* Whitney Museum, New York
1976 *200 Years of American Sculpture,* Whitney Museum, New York
1977 *Improbable Furniture,* Institute of Contemporary Art, University of Pennsylvania, Philadelphia
1995 *Recaptured Nature,* Marian Goodman Gallery, New York
1996 *Landscape: The Pastoral to the Urban,* Center for Curatorial Studies Museum, Annondale-on-Hudson, New York
1997 *City Scapes: A Survey of Urban Landscapes,* Marlborough Gallery, New York
Forty Years of Exploration and Innovation: The Artists of the Castelli Gallery 1957–1997, Leo Castelli Gallery, New York
On the Edge, Museum of Modern Art, New York
Wood not Wood/Work not Work, A/D Gallery, New York
1998 *View: Two,* Mary Boone Gallery, New York
The Imagined World, Nolan/Eckman Gallery, New York
Travel and Leisure, Paula Cooper Gallery, New York
1999 *Dream Architecture,* Kent Gallery, New York
2001 *VOX2001,* Kent Gallery, New York

Collections:

Museum of Modern Art, New York; Whitney Museum, New York; Wadsworth Atheneum, Hartford, Connecticut; Kansas City Museum, Missouri; Detroit Institute of Arts; La Jolla Museum of Contemporary Art, California; Art Institute of Chicago; Rotterdam Museum; Wallraf-Richartz Museum, Cologne; Kunstmuseum, Basel; Centre Georges Pompidou, Paris; Emily Fisher Landau Foundation, New York; Museum Ludwig, Cologne; Walker Art Center, Minneapolis.

Publications:

By ARTSCHWAGER: Books—*Leo Castelli: 20 Years,* pamphlet, New York 1977. **Articles**—"The Hydraulic Door Check" in *Arts Magazine,* November 1967; "Statements on Art" in *N.A.M.E Gallery, Book I,* edited by Donald Sultan and Nancy Davidson, Chicago 1977; "Actual Art" in *Skira Annual 79,* Geneva 1979; "Parade in the Face of Death: Robert Stanley" in *Galleries Magazine,* September 1987.

On ARTSCHWAGER: Books—*Direction I: Options,* exhibition catalog, with introduction by Lawrence Alloway, Milwaukee 1968; *Documenta 5,* exhibition catalog, Kassel, West Germany 1972; *Richard Artschwager* by Richard Armstrong, New York and London 1988; exhibition catalog, Centre Georges Pompidou, Paris 1989. **Articles**—"The Object: Still Life" by Jan McDevitt in *Craft Horizons,* September/ October 1965; "Artschwager's Mental Furniture" by Elizabeth C. Baker in *Art News,* January 1968; "Richard Artschwager" by William Zimmer in *Arts Magazine,* June 1975; "Richard Artschwager" by Noel Frackman in *Arts Magazine,* January 1977; "The Elastic Vision of Richard Artschwager" in *Art in America,* May/June 1978; article by John Russell in the *New York Times,* 8 July 1979; "The Artschwager Enigma" by Roberta Smith in *Art in America,* October 1979; "Richard Artschwager's Sleight of Mind" by Steven Henry Madoff in *ARTnews,* January 1988; "Richard Artschwager" by Jack Bankowsky in *Flash Art,* March/April 1988.

*

It has been known since the Renaissance that art is produced by artists, and the notion has been available for more than a century that art is internal to the recipient; in a sense, ''made'' by the recipient. The first notion has tended to block off the availability of the second, and I think my contribution has been to make it not only available but Necessary, i.e., to force the issue of the context or, to put it in more old-fashioned terms, to make art that has no boundaries. At the beginning (around 1962) this was worked out in two steps: first make something which is ''art,'' then insert in into a demanding, absorbent context, like inserting a garlic sliver into a joint of mutton. I have done some other things, but this certainly got the ball rolling!

—Richard Artschwager

* * *

Artschwager studied cell biology at Cornell University, with an interruption for military service, between 1941 and 1948. In 1949 and 1950 he studied in New York with Amadee Ozenfant. In 1953 he took up cabinet-making and by 1956 he was mass-producing simple furniture.

With the encouragement of his first wife he turned his energies towards actively being an artist by the early 1960s. He began to produce his ''infactory'' works which were Constructivist in tone with identical sheets of plywood cut-offs joined into stacks, fans and baffles. By the mid 1960s (when he began to exhibit with Leo Castelli Gallery), his work had become more like highly simplified furniture shapes frequently with formica or laminated surfaces. This neo-Dada type work came to be classified as ''Minimalist.'' Barbara Rose wrote in 1965 on Minimalist Art: ''It is part of the irony of the works—and irony plays a large part in them—that they blatantly assert their unsaleability and functionlessness. Some, like Artschwager's pseudofurniture or Warhols's Brillo boxes, are not too unwieldly to be sold, but since they approximate real objects with actual uses, they begin to raise questions about the utility of art, and its ambiguous role in our culture.''

At the same time as he was producing the ''pseudo-furniture,'' Artschwager was making grisaille pictures, frequently of high-rise apartment blocks, by grid-enlarging photos and reproducing them with acrylic on celotex, a paperlike substance used in building construction. In 1967 he developed an object which he termed a Blp and which he used as a kind of installation piece that could be installed anywhere, (a gallery wall, or on the sidewalk). The Blp was a long flat oval of any size, painted black. The name Blp came from a military expression Artschwager had learned during the war; it is an object connected with a sound as it moves on a radar screen. In the late 1960s there came a lapse into pure Surrealism when Artschwager produced hair boxes and wall reliefs.

By the early 1980s, Artschwager had become one of the sculptors involved in the U.S. government's General Services Administration's Art in Architecture programme. This partnership had a high profile with the Battery Park City development in southwestern Manhattan, where Artschwager's work was sited.

—Victoria Keller

In the 1990s, as furniture designers have begun to follow Artschwager into experimental and nonutilitarian directions, he has continued to investigate the conceptual art issues to be found in furniture. For instance, his *Splatter Chair,* shown at Documenta 9 (1992) envisions an elastic chair hurled into the corner and adhering, cartoon-like, to the walls. Using formica, wood, celotex, and other materials associated with home furnishings, Artschwager plays games with the forms and conventions of furniture, often to illustrate how relationships between a person and a work of art can be physical as well as visual.

—Mark Swartz

ASCOTT, Roy

Nationality: British. **Born:** Bath, 26 October 1934. **Education:** City of Bath Boys' School; studied under Victor Pasmore and Richard Hamilton at Kings College, University of Durham, BA in Fine Art with honors, 1959. **Military Service:** Fighter Control, RAF, 1955–59. **Career:** Artist and educator. Studio demonstrator in fine arts, King's College, Durham University, 1959–61; head of foundation studies, Ealing School of Art, and head of department of fine art, Ipswich Civic College, 1961–64; head of department of painting, Wolverhampton Polytechnic, 1967–71; visiting lecturer in painting, Slade School of Fine Art, University of London, 1968–71; president, Ontario College of Art, Toronto, 1971–72; visiting tutor in sculpture, St. Martin's School of Art and Central School of Art and Design, London 1973–77; professor of fine art, Minneapolis College of Art and Design, 1974–75; vice-president and academic dean, San Francisco Art Institute, 1975–78; founding head of the department of communications theory, University of Applied Arts, Vienna, 1985–92; head of fine art, 1980–91, head of the field of interactive arts, 1991–94, and reader in interactive arts and director of the Centre for Advanced Inquiry in the Interactive Arts, 1994–, University of Wales College, Newport. **Awards:** Fellow, Royal Society of Arts, 1972. **Address:** 64 Upper Cheltenham Place, Bristol BS6 5HR, England.

Individual Exhibitions:

1960 Univision Gallery, Newcastle upon Tyne
1961 Artists International Association Gallery, London
St. John's Gallery, York
1963 Molton Gallery, London
1964 Galerie Suzanne de Connick, Paris
1965 Hamilton Galleries, London
Queen's University, Belfast
1968 Ikon Gallery, Birmingham, England
Laing Art Gallery and Museum, Newcastle upon Tyne
1969 Exe Gallery, Exeter
1970 Angela Flowers Gallery, London
1972 University of Guelph, Ontario
1978 Anna Gardner Gallery, Stinson Beach, California
1980 Dartington Hall, Totnes, England

Selected Group Exhibitions:

1993 *The Sixties Art Scene in Britain,* Barbican Art Gallery, London

Computer Networking Projects:

Terminal Art, 1980; *Four Wings,* 1982; *La Plissure du Texte,* 1983; *Organe et Fonction d'Alice au Pays des Merveilles,* 1985; *Sonart,*

1985; *Planetary Network,* 1986; *Digital Body Exchange,* 1987; *Making the Invisible Visible,* 1988; *Aspects of Gaia,* 1989; *Texts, Bombs, and Videotape,* 1991; *Virtuelle Werelden,* 1991; *The Geometry of Silence,* 1991; *Telenoia,* 1992; *Gasflow,* 1994.

Publications:

By ASCOTT: Books—*Theories and Documents of Contemporary Art,* edited by K. Stiles and P. Selz, Berkeley, California 1995; *Consciousness Reframed: Art and Consciousness in the Post-biological Era,* University of Wales, Newport, 1997; *Reframing Consciousness: Art, Mind and Technology,* Exeter, 1999; *Consciousness, Mind @ Large,* Bristol and Portland, Oregon, 2000. **Articles—**''Art and Telematics: Towards a Network Consciousness'' in *Art + Telecommunication,* edited by Heidi Grundmann, Vienna, 1984; ''Is There Love in the Telematic Embrace?'' in *Art Journal,* vol. 49, no. 3, Fall 1990; ''Behaviourables and Futuribles'' in *Theories of Modern Art,* edited by Kristine Stiles and Peter Selz, Berkeley, California, 1996.

On ASCOTT: Books—*Telematic Embrace: Visionary Theories of Art, Technology and Consciousness by Roy Ascott,* edited by Edward A. Shanken, Berkeley, California, 2001.

* * *

Roy Ascott was among the first artists to launch an appeal to total participation of the spectator; for him the strict antinomy between action and contemplation was to be abolished. Ascott aimed to achieve a wider 'cybernetic' awareness through acting on the psychology of the observer who was invited to regroup the elements of the technological universe and exploit certain of its meanings. Although the concept of participation in Roy Ascott's demarche is primarily didactic in character, it may in fact best be described as 'cybernetic'. Ascott was in the first place concerned with creating 'triggers', and thereby initiating creative behaviour in the observer. His justification in adopting a 'cybernetic stance' is founded in the following considerations. Modern art, he claims, is characterized by a behaviourist tendency in which system and process are cardinal factors. As distinctions between music, painting, poetry etc. become blurred and media are mixed, a behaviourist synthesis is seen to evolve, in which dialogue and feedback within a social structure indicate the emergence of a Cybernetic vision in art as in science.The different artefacts produced by Roy Ascott at the time, although far from neutral in visual terms, have had from the outset a 'cybernetic' purpose, which may be defined as inculcating creativity or eliciting creative behaviour from the spectator. But Ascott wanted to go beyond the incorporation of 'behavioural triggers' with feedback in his work by putting the spectator into a position where he could himself handle ideas. The spectator both was to make decisions and to react physically to the work.

For Ascott cybernetics was also a psychological phenomenon which could be utilized directly in educational projects. He exploited the effects of familiar objects in an unusual context, inviting the spectator or pupil to alter the relationship of the various elements. It was up to the spectator to find out the latent possibilities contained in each work. Ascott has also worked on the development of an elementary course in art education. It might in fact be said that the primary concern of all his artistic enterprises in the 1960s, whether they went under the name of 'chance-paintings' or 'kinetic constructions,' was with the education and bearing of the spectator. This ties in with the way in which he defined his works as structures which were subject to the same human pressures and the same likelihood of transformation as our purely intellectual notions. Ascott went on from this point to consider the future of art as a 'cybernetic' activity or discipline.

At present, Ascott can be considered as being the outstanding artist and theoretician in the field of telematics. It was Simon Nora and Alain Minc who coined the term 'telematics' in 1987 to describe the new electronic technology derived from the convergence of computers and telecommunication systems, incorporating the telephone, the telex and the fax. The process of 'telematization' is most clearly seen in the ubiquitous and rapid growth in France of Minitel, the public video-text system that enables widespread interaction between users and databases across an enormous range of services.

Ascott has put to good use the central feature of the video system, its ability to facilitate interaction via the electronic space of computer memory and beyond the normal constraints of time and space that apply to face-to-face communication. His projects employing telematic media and interactive participation have included *The Pleating of the Text: A Planetary Fairy Tale* (in homage to Barthes' *The Pleating of the Text*), devised for the 'Electra' exhibition at the Musée d'Art Moderne de la ville de Paris in 1983. It involved the creation of a text by the 'dispersed authorship' of groups of artists located in eleven cities around the world, each group participating through an electronic network.The story developed gradually as each day a piece of text was logged in from each terminal. Most of the terminals were linked to data projectors so that the text being generated could be publicly accessible.

For Ascott, the art of our time is one of system, process, participation and interaction. As our values are relativistic, our culture pluralistic, our images and forms evanescent, it is the processes of interaction between human beings which create meaning and consequently cultures. Hence, those systems and processes which facilitate and amplify interaction are the ones that will be used by artists in order to encompass a world audience, with the aid of telematic systems based on computer-mediated cable and satellite links.

In accordance with this philosophy, an elaborate and complex multi-media interface was created by Ascott as part of the 'Electronic Arts Festival of Art and Technology' (*Ars Electronica*) in Linz, Austria, in 1989. *Aspects of Gaia: Digital Pathways Across the Whole Earth* was a computer-networking project and interactive installation conceived in collaboration with Peter Appleton, Mathias Fuchs, Robert Pepperell, and Miles Visman. It involved interaction in electronic dataspace between artists, musicians, scientists and other creative individuals from a number of different countries, and produced representations of the Earth (Gaia) from a multplicity of perspectives: scientific, cultural, spiritual and mythological. Conceived of within the tradition of the *Gesamtkunstwerk,* or more appropriately *Gesamtdatenwerk,* these connecting pathways constituted a kind of conceptual umbrella or digitized noosphere aspiring to planetary harmonization via the creative and energizing transformation and reconstitution of digital images, texts and sounds, which could be accessed and interacted with at many locations around the world.

Virtual space, virtual image and virtual reality are also categories of experience that can be shared through telematic networks conceived by Ascott. They too allow for movement through 'cyberspace' and engagement in a 'hyperreality' with the virtual presence of others who are physically removed. By the use of a headset, dataglove or other data-wear, these interactions and the feelings and perceptions created in this way are experienced as 'real.' According to Ascott, the passage from real to virtual should be seamless, just as the changes to social behaviour deriving from the omnipresent human/computer symbiosis are flowing unnoticed into our individual psyches.

Nowadays, the five defining features of his art and indeed of the art of our time which so conspicuously differentiate it from the art of earlier areas, are 'connectivity,' of part to part, person to person, mind to mind; 'immersion,' into the whole, and the dissolution thereby of subject and ground; 'interaction,' as the very form of art, such as that art as behaviour of forms has become art as a form of behaviour; 'transformation,' perpetual flux of image, surface and identity; and 'emergence,' the perpetual coming into being of meaning, matter and mind.

—Frank Popper

ASHER, Michael

Nationality: American. **Born:** Los Angeles, California, 15 July 1943. **Education:** Liberal arts and sciences at Orange Coast College, Costa Mesa, California, 1961–63; anthropology and art, University of New Mexico, Albuquerque, 1963–64; New York Studio School, 1964–65; fine arts, University of California at Irvine, 1965–67, B.A. 1966. **Career:** Worked as advertising sales representative for West Coast Industries, New York, 1964; worked as research assistant for use of cardboard materials in furniture, Los Angeles. Independent sculptor and environmental artist, Los Angeles, since 1966. Assistant instructor in sculpture, 1966–67, and painting instructor, 1967–68, University of California at Irvine; instructor in art, California Institute of Arts, Valencia, 1976. Artist-in-residence, University of California at Irvine, 1973, California Institute of the Arts, Valencia, 1973, Nova Scotia College of Art and Design, 1974, and Otis Art Institute, Los Angeles, 1975. **Awards:** Purchase Award, Contemporary Art Council, Los Angeles County Museum of Art, 1967; Short-Term Activities Fellowship Grant, National Endowment for the Arts, 1973; Guggenheim Fellowship, 1974; Artists Fellowship Grant, National Endowment for the Arts, 1975. **Address:** 262 Carmelina Avenue South, Apt. 6, Los Angeles, California 90291, U.S.A.

Individual Exhibitions:

1969 La Jolla Museum of Art, California
1970 Gladys K. Montgomery Art Center, Pomona College, Claremont, California
1972 Market Street Program, Venice, California
1973 Gallery A 402, California Institute of the Arts, Valencia
Cambridge School, Weston, Massachusetts
Lisson Gallery, London
Galerie Heiner Friedrich, Cologne
Galleria Toselli, Milan
1974 Claire S. Copley Gallery, Los Angeles
Anna Leonowens Gallery, Nova Scotia College of Art and Design, Halifax
1975 Otis Art Institute, Los Angeles
1976 The Clocktower, New York
The Floating Museum, San Francisco
1977 Van Abbemuseum, Eindhoven, Netherlands
1980 *Exhibitions in Europa 1972–1977,* Van Abbemuseum, Eindhoven, Netherlands
1984 Hofhour Gallery, Albuquerque, New Mexico
1986 Hofhour Gallery, Albuquerque, New Mexico
1991 Centre Georges Pompidou, Paris

Selected Group Exhibitions:

1967 *I Am Alive,* Los Angeles County Museum of Art
1969 *Anti-Illusion: Procedures: Materials,* Whitney Museum, New York
Plane und Projekte als Kunst, Kunsthalle, Berne (travelled to Aktionsraum I, Munich, and the Kunsthaus, Hamburg)
1970 *Art in the Mind,* Allen Art Museum, Oberlin College, Ohio
1971 *24 Young Los Angeles Artists,* Los Angeles County Museum of Art
1972 *Documenta 5,* Kassel, West Germany
1973 *3D into 2D: Drawings for Sculpture,* New York Cultural Center
1975 *University of California, Irvine, 1965–75,* La Jolla Museum of Contemporary Art, California
1976 *Ambiente,* at *Biennale,* Venice
1977 *Skulptur,* Westfälische Landesmuseum, Münster, West Germany
1997 *Sunshine and Noir: L.A. Art 1960–1997,* Museum of Modern Art, Humlebaeck, Louisiana
1999 *The Museum as Muse: Artists Reflect,* Museum of Modern Art, New York

Collections:

Museum of Contemporary Art, Chicago; Stuart Collection, University of California, San Diego.

Publications:

By ASHER: Book—Commentary in *Michael Asher: Exhibitions in Europa 1972–1977,* exhibition catalog, Eindhoven, Netherlands 1980; *Writings 1973–1983 on Works 1969–1979,* Nova Scotia College of Art and Design Press, 1983.

On ASHER: Books—*Anti-Illusion: Procedures: Materials,* exhibition catalog, with texts by James Monte and Marcia Tucker, New York 1969; *8e Biennale de Paris,* exhibition catalog, with texts by J. Cahen-Salvador and others, Paris 1973; *Michael Asher: Exhibitions in Europa 1972–1977,* exhibition catalog, with essays by R. H. Fuchs and B. H. D. Buchloh, Eindhoven, Netherlands 1980; *The Museum as Muse: Artists Reflect,* edited by Kynaston McShine, New York 1999. **Articles—**''Michael Asher: La Jolla Art Museum'' by T. H. Garver in *Artforum* (New York), January 1970; ''Michael Asher: An Environmental Project'' by B. Munger in *Studio International* (London), October 1970; ''The Art of Existence: 3 Extravisual Artists, Works in Progress'' by Robert Morris in *Artforum* (New York), January 1971;

''Michael Asher: The Thing of It Is . . .'' by Peter Plagens in *Artforum* (New York), April 1972.

*

I feel it is implicit, yet perhaps not immediately recognized through background information, that those activities which pertain to my art and those activities which pertain to me in general, are determined by one another.

—Michael Asher

* * *

Having emerged as an artist in the early 1970s, at the high water mark for pared-down, austere Conceptual Art, Michael Asher has continued to work with a remarkable intellectual rigor and economy of means. His works, which might be described best as interventions, rather than installations or sculptures, are always specific to their location, and draw attention to the conditions in which art is exhibited, interpreted, and consumed. A Los Angeles artist and influential teacher at The California Institute of the Arts, Asher has been particularly well recognized in Europe.

In many of Asher's earliest works, the intervention was so subtle as to be almost imperceptible, often involving a removal of sound, light, or architectural elements in order to display their function. His contribution to the 1970 exhibition ''Spaces'' at the Museum of Modern Art in New York involved the construction of a rectangular container of sound-absorbing material. This piece emphasized the absence of perception; the walls of the space muffled and deadened the experience of sound, while the unlit container provided very little in the way of visual stimulation. By isolating a particular aspect of the museum exhibition, Asher invited visitors to a new awareness. For an exhibition at Claire Copley Gallery in Los Angeles in 1974, Asher isolated and removed an architectural element in order to underline the economic and social dynamic of the commercial art gallery. Removing the partition between the office and exhibition area, the artist put the business of the gallery on display. In doing so, he refrained from producing any object that might be bought or sold as art within the gallery system.

In many works, Asher causes the viewer to question the way that institutions construct and present history. In 1979, for the 73rd Annual American Exhibition at the Art Institute of Chicago, Asher reframed a work from the museum's collection, creating a domino effect of altered meaning. Asher took a sculpture of George Washington, a bronze replica of the work by French sculptor Jean-Antoine Houdon, and moved it from its usual position outside the museum's main entrance into the 18th century European period gallery. This simple gesture reframes an American icon as a product of French aesthetics and political experience. As Asher's contribution to a contemporary art exhibition, the piece also drew attention to the separation between different curatorial departments and the narratives they present. In order to see Asher's contribution, viewers had to leave the contemporary American exhibition and take a mini-tour of the European period rooms. With its foregrounding of historical style and iconography, this piece may be understood as Asher's particularly understated exploration of postmodernism. Asher's unusual practice also meshes with the postmodern idea that authorship is itself a construction. By reframing an old object, rather than creating a new one, Asher produces a work that stands apart from the usual myths about artistic creation. As he writes of the Chicago piece, ''In this work I was the author of the situation not of the elements. The given elements remained a part of their specific context and the dynamic of the situation was a function of the integration of the predetermined elements within the institution.''

While his later works often introduce more variables and more constructed elements, they retain a subtlety and restraint. Asher's work at the Bern Kusthalle in 1992 involved structural transformation on an unprecedented scale. For the piece, Asher stipulated that all the museum's enormous cast iron radiators be moved into the entrance hall. All the piping for the heating system, usually hidden, was brought to the surface of the walls, making manifest an element of the building's original structure. This work juxtaposed the logic of the heating system, a grid of striking parallel lines, with the beaux-arts grandeur of the museum architecture. While the impact of the work was monumental, the impressive effect was a function of the supports and structures already existing beneath the façade of an arts institution.

Created for a specific location at a specific moment in time, Asher's works usually cease to exist at the end of the exhibition, and remain only in the form of written and photographic documentation. As well as giving the work a kind of extended life, this documentation is also key to understanding Asher's projects, as it allows the viewer to trace the artist's research and thought process in ways that may not be available from the experience of the work itself. A 1983 book, *Michael Asher: Writings 1973–83 on Works 1969–1979*, produced in collaboration with art historian Benjamin Buchloh, is an essential resource for understanding Asher's early work.

For the 1999 exhibition ''The Museum as Muse: Artists Reflect,'' curated by Kynaston McShine at the Museum of Modern Art in New York, Asher produced a piece that served as its own document. In counterpoint to the Museum's well-known publications documenting their permanent collection and recent acquisitions, Asher organized an inventory of pieces deaccessioned, i.e. sold or traded away, over the museum's history. A slim volume, matched in style to MoMA's standards for graphic design, Asher's contribution points out the difference between the history of objects selected by the museum, and the version of the history of art that the museum presents to the public. This piece typifies Asher's work in its specificity and graceful simplicity. Using the least possible means, ordered with the same kind of elegance as well-solved mathematical equations, Asher gives viewers unexpected opportunities for critical analysis within the framework of art.

—Lucy Soutter

ASKEVOLD, David

Nationality: American. **Born:** Conrad, Montana, 30 March 1940. **Education:** Attended University of Montana, Missoula, 1956–63; attended Brooklyn Museum School of Art (on Max Beckman Painting Scholarship), New York, 1963–64; Art Institute of Kansas City, Missouri, B.F.A. (painting and sculpture), 1968. **Career:** Taught at Nova Scotia College of Art and Design, Halifax, 1968–74, 1985–87, and 1991; taught at University of California at Irvine, 1976–78, and California Institute of the Arts, Valencia, 1977–78; instructor, Art Center College of Design, Pasadena, California, 1979–80; lecturer,

York University, Downsview, Ontario, 1981–83; visiting artist in media arts, Minneapolis College of Art and Design, 1984–85. **Agents:** Studio Cannaviello, Piazza Beccaria 10, 20122 Milan, Italy; Galerie Paul Maenz, Bismarckstrasse 50, 5000 Cologne 1, Germany.

Individual Exhibitions:

1970 Nova Scotia College of Art and Design, Halifax
1971 Anna Leonowens Gallery, Nova Scotia College of Art and Design, Halifax
1972 Anna Leonowens Gallery, Nova Scotia College of Art and Design, Halifax
Galerie Paul Maenz, Cologne
Galleria Francoise Lambert, Milan
Jack Wendler Gallery, London
Art and Project Gallery, Amsterdam
1973 John Gibson Gallery, New York
Galerie Yvon Lambert, Paris
1974 Anna Leonowens Gallery, Nova Scotia College of Art and Design, Halifax
Galerie Paul Maenz, Cologne
Galleria Francoise Lambert, Milan
1975 Galerie Yvon Lambert, Paris
John Gibson Gallery, New York
Art Metropole, Toronto
1976 Fine Arts Gallery, University of California at Irvine
1977 John Gibson Gallery, New York
1978 Thomas Lewallen Gallery, Los Angeles
Foundation for Art Resources, Los Angeles (with Michael Kelley)
1980 Van Abbemuseum, Eindhoven, Netherlands
Cannaviello Studio d'Arte, Milan
1981 Jancar Kuhlenschmidt Gallery, Los Angeles
1984 Coburg Gallery, Vancouver, British Columbia
1988 Anna Leonowens Gallery, Nova Scotia College of Art and Design, Halifax
1990 The Centre for Art Tapes, Halifax
The Clock Tower Gallery, New York
Willoughby Sharp Gallery, New York
1992 Articule Gallery, Montreal, Quebec
1993 Mount St. Vincent University Art Gallery, Halifax
1995 Confederation Centre of the Arts, Charlottetown

Selected Group Exhibitions:

1970 *Information,* Museum of Modern Art, New York
1971 *Pier 18,* Museum of Modern Art, New York
1976 *The Artist and the Photograph,* Israel Museum, Jerusalem
1977 *Documenta,* Kassel, West Germany
1978 *Story/ Narrative Art,* Contemporary Art Museum, Houston (travelling exhibition)
1980 *Artist and Camera,* Arts Council of Great Britain (travelling exhibition)
1981 *5 Wiener International Biennale,* Vienna
1986 *Vintage Video,* Art Resource Centre, Toronto, Ontario
1988 *Image Forum,* Hara Museum, Tokyo
1993 *Terra Firma,* Mount St. Vincent University Art Gallery, Halifax
1997 *Time Capturing Art,* National Art Gallery, Reykjavik, Iceland
1999 *Fixations,* Mount Saint Vincent University Art Gallery, Halifax

Collections:

Van AbbeMuseum, Eindhoven, Netherlands; Museum of Contemporary Art, Houston, Texas; National Gallery of Canada, Ottawa; Vancouver Art Gallery, British Columbia; Art Metropole, Toronto; Art Gallery of Nova Scotia.

Publications:

By ASKEVOLD: Book—*Extra,* Cologne, April 1975. **Articles—**''Liberal Art University Experiences: David Askevold in Conversations with Paul McMahon'' in *Studio International* (London), April 1972; article in *Video by Artists,* edited by Peggy Gale, Toronto 1976. **Films—***Pull,* 1969; *Knife Throw,* 1969; *Nova Scotia Fires,* 1970; *Catapult,* 1970; *It's No Use Crying,* 1971; *Rubber Band,* 1971; *Physical Fork Pairs,* 1971; *Concert C with Door,* 1971; *Inflations,* 1971; *Twin Hills,* 1971; *Two Plant Perspectives Reacting to a Walking Dog,* 1971; *Three Cameras Over a Double-Sided Mirror and Back Again,* 1971; *Accelerations,* 1972; *The Dream of Descartes,* 1973; *Four Notes Through a Wall and into the Grass,* 1974; *Green Willow for Delaware,* 1974. **Videos—***Fill,* 1970; *Concert Cover,* 1972; *Audience Empathy,* 1972; *Learning about Cars and Chocolate,* 1972; *The Murdered Rancher and the 15 Million Dollar Insurance Policy,* 1972; *George,* 1973; *Recall Sequences,* 1973; *My Recall of an Imprint from a Hypothetical Jungle,* 1973; *Synapses,* 1975; *Visits,* 1976; *Very Soon You Will,* 1977; *John Todd and His Songs,* 1977; *Rhea,* 1982; *Jumped Out,* 1985; *Makes No Sense At All & Love Is All Around,* 1985; *Honky Tonkin,* 1986; *1/4 Moon,* 1986–87; *How Long Have You Known Barbara?* 1987; *Six Fifty,* 1987–89; *Two Rotating Candle Chandeliers,* 1990.

On ASKEVOLD: Books—*6 Years: The Dematerialization of the Art Object* by Lucy Lippard, New York 1973. *Individuals: Post Movement Art in America,* edited by Alan Sondheim, New York 1977. **Exhibition Catalogs—***The Artist and the Photograph #2,* Jerusalem 1977; *Narrative Art,* Groningen, Netherlands 1979; *From Sea to Shining Sea,* Toronto 1987; *Fixations,* with text by Robert Zingone, Canada 1999. **Articles—**''Artist as Film-Maker'' by Annabel Nicholson in *Art and Artists* (London), December 1972; review in *Arts* (New York), February 1974; article in *Kunst Magazine* (Munich), March 1974; article in *Artforum* (New York), September 1974; article by Ronald Shuebrook in *Artscanada* (Toronto), December 1974; article in *Data* (Milan), nos. 16/17, 1975; articles in *Artweek* (Oakland, California), 4 February 1977, and 14 July 1979; article in *Kunstforum* (Cologne), Fall 1979; article in *Artweek* (Oakland, California), 13 February 1979; article in *Artforum,* May 1981; article in *Vanguard* (Vancouver), February 1988.

* * *

David Askevold is perhaps one of the most prolific and experimental of all the artists associated with the school of Narrative Art. In many ways he differs from them wildly. Unlike Bill Beckley, he has never remained with one primary medium (the large glossy color photograph and short, pithy text); and unlike French artist Jean Le Gac, he is not concerned with the gentler aspect of a series of banal incidents and certainly does not invest his narrative with mild or startling humor. Rather, Askevold steers his work through a variety of medias and even concerns, depending upon their appropriateness at a given time. He has, of course, made many still works (the conventional Narrative device of visual sign and quasi-expository text), but he has also made discrete films and videotapes, and ambitious film, video, and slide installations. Furthermore, these are frequently and deliberately obscure, and therefore do not share with other work in the genre an immediate and engaging

This is not to say that there is not an active and linking sensibility throughout Askevold's oeuvre. This takes the form of a complex approach and an occasionally sinister iconography. First of all, Askevold rarely if ever follows the structural pattern of several of his colleagues, in which image and text deliberately diverge (i.e., the texts meandering while the images form a logical dramatic sequence). Instead, the combination of word and sign create, as Filiberto Menna has pointed out in a catalog essay, ''a perfect parallelism between the two terms, so that the text accompanies and comments upon the horizontal, concatenation of the images . . .'' (This, of course, applies specifically to Askevold's more conventionally Narrative pieces, such as ''Elektra,'' a series of eleven photos and text, completed in 1974.) Secondly, Askevold has never felt restricted by the convention of his chosen genre, and on several occasions has used an extraordinary ambitious formal structure, as in his installation ''Four Notes Through a Wall and Into the Grass'' (1972–73) which used a series of 80 color slides, audiotape, drawing and super-8 film. And, as far as Askevold's iconography is concerned, it involves a frequent use of snakes, as in the previously mentioned ''Four Notes'' and ''Kepler's Music of the Spheres to Be Played by Six Snakes,'' (1971–73), as well as paradigms from algebra and physics, and quasi-psychological experiments.

In one of his most major sequences, ''Dream of Descartes,'' Askevold takes a theme through several media: In his still version, he uses four photographs and a number of versions of a nearly identical text (with phrases added or deleted), as well as 16 millimeter color film, and later, a fairly ambitious installation using two super-8 film, projections and scored music, combined with Kepler's ''Music of the Spheres.'' Askevold's is, in a sense, an art of retrieval, both physical and conceptual, never linear or progressive, but continually evolving both backwards and forwards, borrowing from and expanding upon itself.

—Jane Bell

ASLAN, Nora

Nationality: Argentine. **Born:** Buenos Aires, December 19, 1937. **Education:** Studied architecture, University of Buenos Aires, 1956–60; workshops with Marta Viñals, Víctor Chab, María Luisa Manassero, Héctor Giuffré, Ana Eckell, and Carlos Boccardo. **Family:** Married Jorge Aslan; four children. **Address:** Ayacucho 284, (1643) Beccar, Buenos Aires Province, Argentina.

Individual Exhibitions:

1977 Praxis Gallery, Buenos Aires
1978 Praxis Gallery, Buenos Aires
1982 *Trabajos sobre papel* (Works on Paper), Atica Gallery, Buenos Aires
1984 *Textos Téxtiles* (Textile Texts), Atica Gallery, Buenos Aires
1991 Sculptures, Harrods Space, Buenos Aires, Argentina.
1993 *Canceled Flights,* Madison Art Gallery, Buenos Aires
1997 *Alfombras* (Rugs), National Museum of Fine Arts, Buenos Aires, Argentina (catalog)
2001 *Ventanas Chinas* (Chinese Windows), Recoleta Cultural Center, Buenos Aires
Punto de Vista (Viewpoint), Patricia Ready Gallery, Santiago, Chile.

Selected Group Exhibitions

1981 International Biennial, Laussane, Switzerland (catalog)
1986 Havana Biennial, Havana, Cuba (catalog)
International Biennial, Laussane, Switzerland
1989 Textile Event, Porto Alegre, Brazil
Havana Biennial, Havana, Cuba (catalog)
International Biennial, Laussane, Switzerland
1990 International Textile Design, Van Bommel-Van Dam Museum, Venlo, The Netherlands
1991 *Contemporary Latin America Art II,* Best Maugard Gallery, Mexico
''A Mata,'' Museum of Contemporary Art, Sao Paulo, Brazil
1992 *Eleven Critics Present Eleven Artists,* Harrods in Art, Buenos Aires Critics Conference
1993 Reading Public Museum, Reading, Pennsylvania
1994 *The World's Women On Line* (Internet event), National Museum of Women in the Arts, Washington, D.C.
Installation, 13th Critics Conference, Buenos Aires
1995 Palermo University Prizes, National Museum of Fine Arts, Buenos Aires
Chandon Prize, National Museum of Fine Arts, Buenos Aires
1996 *70–80-90,* Borges Cultural Center, Buenos Aires (catalog)
Pasion Por Frida (A Passion for Frida), Recoleta Cultural Center, Buenos Aires
Austria '96 Prize, National Museum of Fine Arts, Buenos Aires
Costantini Prizes, National Museum of Fine Arts, Buenos Aires (catalog)
Mayorazgo Foundation Prize, National Museum of Fine Arts, Buenos Aires
1997 Novartis Prizes, National Museum of Fine Arts, Buenos Aires
1998 Costantini Prizes, National Museum of Fine Arts, Buenos Aires (catalog)
Identidad (Identity), Recoleta Cultural Center, Buenos Aires
1999 Costantini Prizes, National Museum of Fine Arts, Buenos Aires (catalog)
2nd Mercosur Biennial, Porto Alegre, Brazil (catalog)
2000 7th Havana Biennial, Havana, Cuba (catalog)
Costantini Prizes, National Museum of Fine Arts, Buenos Aires
Museo de la Ciudad, Valencia, Spain

Collections:

Museum of Modern Arts, Vienna, Austria; Museum of Modern Arts, Sarajevo; Sívori Museum, Argentina; Michoacano Textile Museum, Mexico; Latin American Collection, University of Essex, United Kingdom.

Publications:

On ASLAN: Books—*Arte Argentino Hoy* (Argentine Art Today), Buenos Aires 1986; *Das Vanguardas ao fim do Milenio,* Lisbon 1999; *Sarajevo 2000,* exhibition catalog, Vienna 2000. **Articles—**Essay by Rita Caurio in *Artextil no Brasil,* Rio de Janeiro, 1985.

* * *

In the decade from 1975 to 1984, Nora Aslan worked and excelled in textile art until she ended up feeling limited and restricted in that field. She then went on to the creation of objects, veritable organisms that were as unprecedented as they were disturbing. She executed them using discarded and common everyday elements. Through them, she alluded with humor and natural self-assurance to contemporary society and its myths. Along these same lines, and now in a third stage, she later forged her own versions of popular adages, twisting the significance of the materials used in order to insist on the dismemberment of their appearance and an exploratory approach to the realities portrayed.

Along this road, in 1995, she reached her *Mediciones* (Measurements) series—collages that portrayed the paradox of the authority of formal languages as a means to encompass and control human life, by abstracting themselves from it, no longer functioning as instrumental media at the service of Man, but rather, becoming absolute ends in themselves.

And the alternatives or dichotomies between regular and virtual, natural and artificial, accepted and discordant, established and unusual, occult and manifest, exclusive and intrusive, dominant and relative, certain and dubious, return once more in the series of works that inaugurate the latest stage of Aslan's work. These are rugs, tablecloths, or quilts that the artist exhibits like tapestries. But at the same time, they encompass both verisimilar and simulated objects. Or better said, perhaps, the verisimilitude generates the simulation, or vice versa. In short, they *are* rugs, tablecloths, and quilts, and yet, they *are not.* They have not been made for traditional use—to cover a floor, a table or a bed—but they are, indeed, in accordance with the forms and standards of these uses. Made to be *seen,* these rugs, tablecloths and quilts only make sense when they are *looked at,* when the visitor to the exhibition goes from far to near, becoming a *spectator,* or in other words, becoming someone who contemplates, who observes. The old saying, ''seeing is believing,'' here becomes ''looking is learning.''

On drawing near the works we have been seeing from afar, we discover their meaning. It is when appearance (viewpoint) gives way to reality (being), and in this case, to thought, since in these works, reality is always ideological. What is it that we look at in these spans of cloth? Repressed multitudes, a show of weaponry, seas of skulls, weeping women, starving children, scenes of war and violence, helplessness and misery, racial persecution, waste, insects, rats, all in contrast with flowers, gold ingots, scenes of religious piety. The allusions and references are direct: They speak to us of marginality, of people without homes or rights, of famine and pestilence, of abandonment and despotism, of flagrant inequality.

All of these images—in which, in many cases, we are moved by the (symbolized) presence of death—are part of the finery of these rugs, tablecloths, and quilts, a finery whose traditional arabesques and figurations Aslan has respected in accurately and inventively minute detail. So it is that she changes those real images—taken from photos and engravings and reworked by means of collage, multiplication, inversion, and other technical effects—into a new visual message for the spectator. These images that we look at, look back at us. The faces we examine, examine us. The scenes we observe, observe us. The situations we glimpse, glimpse us. This silent dialog sought by the artist opens and closes her work.

Walter Benjamin, expounding on his theory of ''aura,'' quoted this passage from Marcel Proust's *A la recherche du temps perdu* (1919): ''Some mystery-lovers flatter themselves by thinking that something of the looks that once fell on them remains. . .This chimera might be true if only it referred to the sole present reality for the individual—namely, the world of his sentiments.'' And Aslan's works do nothing but translate the world of her sentiments—a world that, as in all artists, is the driving force behind her poetic reason—and transmit it to the spectator, whose gaze remains, in turn, on the works, because the gazes of the works also remain on the spectator. This coming and going, this give and take, were also pointed out by Gaston Bachelard in his *La poétique de l'espace* (1957), when he referred to the spaces man inhabits: ''The images of a house are within us as much as we are within them.''

By using common everyday objects as the vehicle for her art, Aslan seeks not just to get into our awareness, but also into our lives. The reference to the domestic is undeniable: the floor, the table, the bed, all represent the major axes on which our lives rotate, the unfolding of our ordinary existence: land, food, love, dreams, hope, everything the human beings that people Aslan's works are lacking. But beyond this, the artist also approaches other notions, emptying them of their traditional content so as to fill them with new, challenging proposals: finery as a disguise, decoration as demand, ''good taste'' as a sign of superiority, comfort in its facet as death-defying regime, the yearning to *have more* as a contemporary antidote for *being more,* the obsession with the emblematic as a means of dividing social classes, conservative talent as a unique attitude (materialized by Aslan in the preservation of floors with rugs, tables with tablecloths, beds with quilts), and last but not least, the isolation of lack of solidarity, and mental and moral blindness.

—Jorge Glusberg

ATKINSON, Conrad

Nationality: British. **Born:** Cleator Moor, Cumbria, 15 June 1940. **Education:** Cumbria primary schools; studied painting at the Carlisle College of Art, 1957–61, Liverpool College of Art, 1961–62, and the Royal Academy of Art Schools, London, under William Townsend, 1962–65. **Family:** Married Margaret Harrison in 1967; daughter: Sophie. **Career:** Printmaking adviser, the Royal Academy of Art Schools, London, 1963–65; exhibition organizer, Northern Arts Gallery, Newcastle upon Tyne, 1975–76. Since 1978, lecturer, Slade School of Fine Art, London. **Awards:** National Book League Prize, 1955; Second Prize, Northern Young Artists, Middlesborough, 1965;

Leverhulme Award, 1965; Abbey Travelling Scholarship, 1965; Granada Fellowship, 1967; Churchill Fellowship, 1972. Associate, School of Advanced Studies, Manchester, 1968; Fellow in Fine Arts, Northern Arts Association, Newcastle upon Tyne, 1974–76; Henry Moore Foundation Residency, 1991. **Member:** Art Science Working Party, University of London, 1971; National Committee, British Society for Social Responsibility on Science, 1972; Chairman, Artists' Union, London, 1974; Visual Arts Panel, Northern Arts, Newcastle upon Tyne, 1975–76; Tyneside Trade Unionists for Socialist Arts, Newcastle upon Tyne, 1975–76. **Agent:** Ronald Feldman Fine Arts, 31 Mercer Street, New York, New York 10013, U.S.A. **Address:** 172 Erlanger Road, London SE14, England. **Address:** 96 Lyndhurst Grove, London SE15, England.

Individual Exhibitions:

1967 *2 Painters,* City Art Gallery, Manchester (with Gerald Park)
1972 *Strike at Brannans,* Institute of Contemporary Arts, London
1974 *Work, Wages, and Prices,* Institute of Contemporary Arts, London (toured the U.K.)
1975 *A Shade of Green, an Orange Edge,* Northern Ireland's Arts Council Gallery, Belfast
1976 *Northern Ireland 1968: Mayday,* Art Net Gallery, Nottingham
1977 *Approaching Reality,* Northern Arts Gallery, Newcastle upon Tyne
1978 Serpentine Gallery, London
1979 *Material: Six Works,* Ronald Feldman Fine Arts, New York
The Craft of Art, Walker Fine Art Gallery, Liverpool
1980 *1975–1980: Work about the North,* Pentonville Gallery, London
Project Arts Centre, Dublin
Carlisle Museum and Art Gallery
1981 *At the Heart of the Matter,* Institute of Contemporary Arts, London
1983 Touring exhibition, Sydney, Melbourne, Hobart, Brisbane, Adelaide, Perth, Newcastle
1985 Anna Lowens Gallery, Halifax, Nova Scotia
Mercer Union, Toronto
Goldfish, Ronald Feldman Fine Arts, New York
1987 Talbot Rice Art Centre, Edinburgh
Known Billboards, London and Sheffield
1988 Interim Art, London
1989 *Newspaper Works,* Victoria and Albert Museum, London
Front Pages, Ronald Feldman Fine Arts, New York
1990 *Good Sports: Tales of New York,* Solo Gallery, New York
Exhibition Hall at Avtozavodskaya, Moscow (with Andrej Monastyrskij)
Anne Berthoud Gallery, London
1992 *For Emily,* Henry Moore Sculpture Trust Studio, Halifax, England
Zones of Gold, Brandford City Art Gallery
1993 Ruth Bloom Gallery, Los Angeles
Mandeville Gallery, San Diego
Newsfiles, Institute of Contemporary Art, Moscow
Richard L. Nelson Gallery, University of California, Davis
1995 Gallery Paule Anglim, San Francisco
1996 *Transient,* Tullie House Museum and Art Gallery, Carlisle, England
1997 Ronald Feldman Fine Arts, New York
1998 *Mining Culture in Technicolor,* Atlanta College of Art Gallery, Atlanta

Selected Group Exhibitions:

1965 *Northern Young Artists,* City Art Gallery, Middlesborough
1968 *Royal Academy Bicentenary,* Royal Academy of Art, London
1975 *Bienale de Paris*
1979 *Un Certain Art Anglais,* Musée National d'Art Moderne, Paris
1980 *Photography into Print,* Victoria and Albert Museum, London
1981 *Landscapes,* Tate Gallery, London
1983 Art Institute of Chicago
1984 *Content,* Hirshorn Museum and Sculpture Garden, Washington, DC
1987 Victoria and Albert Museum, London
1994 *Elvis + Marilyn: 2x Immortal,* Institute of Contemporary Art, Boston (travelled throughout the United States)
1995 *The Art of Justice, Part II,* Lehman College Art Gallery, Bronx
1996 *Withdrawing,* Ronald Feldman Fine Arts, New York
Face a l'Histoire, Centre Georges Pompidou, Paris
1997 *U.S. Campaign to Ban Land Mines,* Very Special Art Gallery, Washington, D.C.

Collections:

Arts Council of Great Britain, London; British Museum, London; Victoria and Albert Museum, London; Brooklyn Museum; Museum of Modern Art, New York; The Power Gallery, Sydney; Tate Gallery, London; Australian National Gallery, Canberra.

Permanent Public Installations:

Miners' Monument, Cumbria, England

Publications:

By ATKINSON: Books—*A Shade of Green: An Orange Edge,* exhibition catalog, with John Hewitt and Caroline Tisdall, Belfast 1975; *Newcastle Writings,* Newcastle upon Tyne 1977; *Art for Whom,* exhibition catalog, London 1978; statement in *The Craft of Art,* exhibition catalog, by Edward Lucie Smith, Liverpool 1979; *Shamrock's Truth: The 1st Casualty: The British Media and Northern Ireland,* 1979; *State of the Art: The Art of the State,* Sydney 1991. **Articles**—''Lost Horizons'' in *Art and Artists,* January 1973; ''Conrad Atkinson: An Interview,'' with Richard Cork in *Studio International,* March/April 1976; ''Capitalist Realism or Socialism in One Person'' in *Skira Annual,* Geneva 1977; ''Art and Ideology'' in *Audio Arts,* 1977; ''Polemic'' in *Art Monthly,* 1978; introduction to *Conrad Atkinson 1975–1980: Work about the North,* exhibition catalog, London 1980; ''John Lennon'' in *Art Monthly,* April 1980; ''Passive Action/Active Passion'' in *Artforum,* September 1980; ''The Only Man Who Ever Brought Work to Cleator Moor Was Adolf Hitler'' in *Radio Times,* October 1981; ''Desires of Permanence: Dreams of

Transience'' in *Wave/Another Country: Irish Exile and Dispossesion,* Huddersfield, Ireland 1991; Interview with Rebecca Cochran in *Sculpture,* September 1998.

On ATKINSON: Books—*The Craft of Art,* exhibition catalog, by Edward Lucie Smith, Liverpool 1979; *Art in the 70's* by Edward Lucie Smith, Oxford 1980; *Conrad Atkinson: Picturing the System,* edited by Caroline Tisdall and Sandy Nairne, London 1981; *For Emily,* exhibition catalog, 1992; *Conrad Atkinson: Selected Works,* exhibition catalog with essay by Miranda McClintic, Davis, California 1993; *Mapping the Terrain* edited by Suzanne Lacy, Seattle 1995; *Transient,* exhibition catalog, 1997. **Articles**—''Art Politic'' in *Art and Artists,* 7 September 1972; ''The Art of Work'' by Caroline Tisdall in *The Guardian* (London), April 1974; ''A Struggling Artist'' by Bobby Campbell in *The Morning Star* (London), April 1974; ''Atkinson in Northern Ireland'' by Caroline Tisdall in *The Guardian* (London), 1976; ''Conrad Atkinson: The Dilemma of Political Art'' by Allan Wallach in *Arts Magazine,* December 1979; ''Conrad Atkinson'' by John Loughery in *New Art Examiner,* April 1989; ''Tart Wit, Wise Humor'' by Donald Kuspit in *Artforum,* January 1991; ''Conrad Atkinson's Tactical Art'' in *Art Papers,* January-February 1995. **Film**—*Conrad Atkinson: Art Worker,* BBC Television, 1980; *Conrad Atkinson,* BBC Television, 1981.

*

To deal with living situations and forces is obviously a difficult undertaking for an artist. Fraught with pitfalls, it is an era unexplored by artists since the 1920s, and it is one in which attitudes to both form and content have a vast and unexplored potential.

One of the main problems for any artist is the necessity to isolate sections of our perceptions in order to examine and express them. Yet we have to maintain a sense of total relationships. The uneasy tug of war between these two conflicting necessities is the battleground on which the specialist and the generalist fight. In this difficult question of isolating an area of research without alienating oneself from overall problems, there is a tension which creates new solutions.

Most of my works have a potency and an impact on the social dynamic of their communities which artists trained as academic easel painters might well enjoy in its immediacy, its utilization within its community and its context. This is where art touches base. The relevance of this art is central to the philosophies and ideologies which it supports and in some cases advances. All societies lay down rules the main function of which is naturally to preserve those societies and hopefully to develop their aims and ideas. These rules tend to operate as mechanisms for preserving the status quo. Most of the citizens of societies understandably go along with these rules and laws, and artists, contrary to popular opinion, are in general no exception. Nevertheless, no matter what sort of society is involved, the values and aspirations of that society need to be constantly either affirmed, probed, developed or denied; to analyse and create a picture for these purposes is one of the important functions of art.

Artists, I think, have had a dialogue with themselves and with other artists for far too long during the course of the 20th century. I believe one must start from a belief that art is not about art, but that art is about anything which is not art, and my work should be seen as an attempt to relate to the aims and aspirations of the mass of the people, the opposite in fact to the popular view of the artist as an isolated individual committed to the exploration of his own psyche. It then follows that a whole range of subjects become open to investigation for artists from regional development to the EEC, from wage differentials to strikes, from minority rights to profit, from property to politics, from education to pensions, housing, factories, leisure—any human activity becomes a possible subject and open to the artist in a different way than hitherto. In this way, the artist can move towards a more central position in society, a position from which real issues, real analyses, real dialogue, and real gains can be made.

It may be that art has a problem for all solutions. If that is the case, then artists in their relationship to society may reconsider another famous slogan in the attempt to break art from the magic hedonism of current art forms: ''If you are not part of the solution, you must be part of the problem.''

—Conrad Atkinson

* * *

Conrad Atkinson is an artist who works in a radical tradition of politics and social reality. This is, in large measure, due to his background and the formative influences of his birth and upbringing in Cleator Moor, a small mining village in a depressed industrial area which lies in a narrow strip on the western coast of Cumbria. Previously a place of heavy industry, as the coal and iron ore were exhausted a pall of unemployment and poverty enveloped the community and the men were driven away to find work. Thus the young Conrad was faced with the basic problems of life from his earliest years. During the 1950s there was a brief period of boom during the building of the nuclear power station known as Calder Hall, later to bear the ominous name of Windscale and now known as Sellafield. Atkinson himself worked for a short time for British Nuclear Fuels. The mining industry had always taken its toll annually in injuries and deaths from its workers but after the opening of the nuclear power station the local population had to learn to live with persistent and disquieting anxieties about radioactive fallout.

Conrad Atkinson studied art first at the nearby School of Art at Carlisle and then at the Royal Academy Schools in London but he has never distanced himself from the place where he was born and its people. In his art he shows his deep involvement by creating telling images of the bitter contrast between the depressed west coast industrial wasteland and the Lakeland National Park. The latter he has described as a ''middle class, high income bracket, outdoor museum and playground. 'The English Lake District' in which the workers are 'invisible' or 'hidden' as were the workers in Engel's Manchester . . .''

In a major work entitled ''For Wordsworth, For West Cumbria'' (1980), which has since been acquired by the Tate Gallery, London, he shows these concerns in an imaginative assemblage of sixteen panels displayed in two rows of eight. They are in a mixed media of photography, acrylic, iron ore and coal. The images reveal how passionately he feels but the treatment in this cool, documentary mode creates a tension between subject matter and manner which reinforces their impact.

The upper row of eight panels which is mainly photographic are all of an outstretched hand and a daffodil flower. This row is bright and inviting with its pale yellow and pale green lettering superimposed which invites the viewer to draw nearer and read the quotation from Wordsworth, the Lake Poet. The outstretched hand represents 'man' and the yellow daffodil stands for 'nature' and changes in scale tell of a changing imbalance between the two. The lower row is bleaker to look at; a photograph of a picket line in a long drawn out strike has a superimposed picture postcard 'scenic' view of the Lakes; a contour map of the Lake District has a tracery of the dangers and perils to which workers in the area have been and are exposed; one panel shows a lump of iron ore between two excerpts from a poem by an immigrant worker forced to leave Cleator when the iron ore and the work ran out; the record of the first acknowledged death from exposure to radioactive waste which caused a young worker to contract leukemia; disused mining machinery with nature encroaching; and under words from Wordsworth after the loss of his brother at sea in 1805 a panel commemorates the drowning of six local men in the wreck of an oil rig onto which unemployment had driven them to work.

Wordsworth is important to Atkinson who said he only really discovered him after he had grown up and realised the relevance of Wordsworth and the Romantic poets, through their commitment politically and economically, to social issues and the crucial relationship between man and the landscape—a landscape which man both helps to create and preserve and also to destroy and which may, in its turn, destroy him. Atkinson points up vividly the harsh choice that so many West Cumbrian workers have had to make between 'life and livelihood' both from the perils of mining and the unseen, insidious dangers of nuclear power. In his work Atkinson skillfully avoids the dangers inherent in strongly polemical and controversial issues of becoming either shrill or hectoring and presents his arguments with thoughtful sensitivity.

—Mary Ellis

AUBERTIN, Bernard

Nationality: French. **Born:** Fontenay-aux-Roses, 29 July 1934. **Education:** Initially self-taught in painting, studying cubist and futurist works, until 1951; at the Ecole des Metiers d'Art, and the Ecole du Professorat de Dessin, Paris, 1952–54. **Military Service:** Served in the French Army, 1957–58. **Family:** Married the artist Denise Demaldent in 1955; sons: Vincent and Frederic; lived with Joelle Fontaine, 1975–86; children: Julien and Solene. **Career:** Painter, influenced initially by Yves Klein, Paris, since 1957; first monochrome red paintings, 1958; rednail-paintings, 1960–71; fire-paintings, 1961; burned-book works, 1962. Lived in Brest, Finistere, 1975–86. **Agents:** Stiftung für Konkrete Kunst, Eberhardstrasse 14, D-72764 Reutlingen, Germany; Galerie Schoeller, Poststrasse 2, D-40213 Düsseldorf, Germany; Galerie Wack, Morlautererstrasse 80, D-67657 Kaiserslautern, Germany; Galerie Patrick Seguin, 32–34 Rue De Charonne, F-75011 Paris, France; Francesco Conz, Vicolo Quadrelli 7, I-37129 Verona, Italy. **Address:** c/o Stiftung Für Konkrete Kunst, Eberhardstrasse 14, D-72764 Reutlingen, Germany.

Individual Exhibitions:

1962 Galerie Wulfengasse 14, Klagenfurt, Austria
1967 Galerie Weiller, Paris
Galerie M. E. Thelen, Essen
1968 Galerie des Quatre Vents, Paris
Galerie Riquelme, Paris
Kleine Galerie, Frankfurt
1969 Galerie Senatore, Stuttgart
1971 Galerie Ursula Lichter, Frankfurt
1972 Centre National d'Art Contemporain, Paris (retrospective; with Fred Deux and Otto Schauer)
1973 Galerie Toni Brechbuhl, Grenchen, Switzerland
Musee de l'Abbaye Sainte-Croix, Les Sables-d'Olonne, France
Galerie Seebacher, Vorarlberg, Austria
1974 Galerie 2, Stuttgart
Studio Brescia, Brescia, Italy
Galleria Banco, Brescia, Italy
Studio Firenze, Florence
Galleria dei Mille, Bergamo, Italy
Galleria Delta, Salerno, Italy
Studio F. 22, Palazzolo, Italy
Galleria Il Canale, Venice
1975 Studio Brescia, Brescia, Italy
Galleria Il Canale, Venice
Galleria Il Punto, Turin
1977 Galleria Rebus, Florence
1978 Palazzeto dello Sport, Abano Terme, Italy
Galerie 44, Kaarst bei Dusseldorf, West Germany
1979 Galerie Weiller, Paris
1983 Galerie J. et J. Donguy, Paris
Galerie Toni Brechbuhl, Grenchen, Switzerland
1986 Galerie Charley Chevalier, Paris
1987 Galerie Beatrix Wilhelm, Stuttgart
1988 Galerie Gilbert Brownstone & Cie, Paris
Stiftung für Konkrete Kunst, Archiv, Reutlingen, Germany
1989 Galerie Schoeller, Düsseldorf
Galeria Oscar Ascanio, Caracas, Venezuela
1990 Galerie Gilbert Brownstone & Cie, Paris
Galleria Vinciano, Milan
Galerie Jousse Seguin, Paris
1991 Kunsthaus Schaller, Stuttgart
Galerie Wack, Kaiserslautern, Germany
1991–92 Galerie von Braunbehrens, Munich
1993 Galerie Jousse Seguin, Paris
Bernard Aubertin, Le Rouge Retrospective, Stiftung für Konkrete Kunst, Reutlingen, Germany
1994 Galerie Gudrun Spielvogel, Munich
Le Feu de la Couleur Hommage à Bernard Aubertin Accompagné de Ses Amis du Mouvement Zéro, Espace de L'Art Concret, Mouans-Sartoux, France
1995 Stiftung für Konkrete Kunst, Reutlingen, Germany
1996 Institut Français de Cologne
Galerie Schoeller, Düsseldorf
1997 *Bernard Aubertin Dokumentarisch,* Stiftung für Konkrete Kunst, Reutlingen, Germany
Bernard Aubertin le Feu et le Rouge, Ludwig Museum im Deutschherrenhaus, Koblenz, Germany
1998 *L'Ancien et le Nouveau Rouge Bernard Aubertin,* Stiftung für Konkrete Kunst, Reutlingen, Germany
Galerie Durhammer, Frankfurt am Main
1999 *Tout Rouge Bernard Aubertin zum 65 Geburtstag,* Stiftung für Konkrete Kunst, Reutlingen
2000 Galerie Wack, Kaiserslautern, Germany

Selected Group Exhibitions:

1961 *Zero,* Galerie Dato, Frankfurt
1965 *Zero Avant-Garde,* Atelier de Fontana, Milan
1967 *Luminism,* George Washington Hotel, New York
1968 *Cinetisme,* Maison de la Culture, Grenoble, France
1969 *Dynamozero 1959–1969,* Galerie Ursula Lichter, Frankfurt
1971 *Sammlung Cremer: Kunst der 60er Jahre,* Kunstverein, Heidelberg
1972 *Douze Ans d'Art Contemporain en France,* Grand Palais, Paris
1976 *Kunst der 60er und 70er Jahre,* Kunstmuseum, Bonn
1985 *Eine Europaische Bewegung,* Museum Carolino Augusteum, Salzburg
1987 *Ephemerite,* Chapelle St. Louis de la Salpetriere, Paris
1988 *Zero, Vision und Bewegung, Werke aus der Sammlung Lenz Schönberg,* Städtische Galerie im Lenbachhaus, Munich
1989 *Das Ende der Komposition,* Stiftung für Konkrete Kunst, Reutlingen, Germany
1990 *3rd Internationale Biennale der Papierkunst,* Leopold-Hoesch-Museum Düren, Germany
1991 *Diversité Contemporaine en Europe: Non Peinture et Sculpture,* Galerie 1900–2000, Paris
1992 *Le Regard Libéré,* Espace de L'Art Concret, Château de Mouans-Sartoux, France
1993 *De Rechte Lijn-Die Gerade Linie,* Stiftung für Konkrete Kunst, Reutlingen, Germany
1994 L'Hôtel Bouhier de Savigny Accueille le Frac, Dijon, France
1995–96 *L'Art Concret Aujourd'hui,* Espace de L'Art Concret, Château de Mouans-Sartoux, France
1996 *5 Jahre Jubiläumsausstellung der Galerie,* Galerie Gudrun Spielvogel, Munich
1997 *Only Paper?,* Kunstmuseum Heidenheim, Germany
1998 *Zero et Paris—1960,* Musée d'Art Moderne et Contemporain de Nice, France
1999 *Le Feu Aux Poudres,* Galerie de la Marine, Nice, France
2000 *Ausstellung Einfach Weiß: Ausstellung Einfach Schwarz,* Stiftung für Konkrete Kunst, Reutlingen, Germany
2000–01 *Bricolage?,* Musée des Beaux-Arts, Dijon, France

Collections:

Centre National d'Art Contemporain, Paris; Mobilier National, Paris; Musee de l'Abbaye Sainte-Croix, Les Sables-d'Olonne, France; Musee de Grenoble, France; Kunstmuseum, Dusseldorf; Kunsthalle, Tubingen, West Germany; Landesmuseum Joanneum, Graz, Austria; Leopold-Hoesch-Museum, Düren, Germany; Museo de Arte Moderno Fundacion Jesus Soto, Cuidad Bolivar, Venezuela.

Publications:

By AUBERTIN: Books—*Bernard Aubertin: 6 Textes,* Paris 1962; *Bernard Aubertin: 9 Textes,* Paris 1968; *Aubertin Pyromane,* Paris 1969; *Aubertin par Aubertin pour Aubertin,* Brest, France 1985; *30 Ans de Réflexions ou le Journal de la Théorie du Réalisme en Art,* Paris 1991; *Textes Rédigés à Paris et à Reutlingen,* Paris 1991; *Mitglied der Gruppe 'Zero,'* Paris 1991; *Le Cahier de Bernard Aubertin 2,* 1993; Le Feu de la Couleur Bernard Aubertin, exhibition catalog with text by Bernard Aubertin, Odile Biec, and Gottfried Honneger, Mouans-Sartoux 1994; *Bernard Aubertin das Feuer und das Rot le Feu er le Rouge,* exhibition catalog with text by Bernard Aubertin, Beate Reifenscheid, Gottfried Honegger, Gabriele Kübler, Udo Kultermann and Otto Piene, Bielfeld 1997. **Articles—**''Esquisse de la situation picturale du rouge dans un concept spatial'' in *Zero* (Dusseldorf), no. 3, 1961; ''La Monochromie'' in *Nul=0* (Arnhem, Netherlands), no. 1, 1962; ''La Couleur'' in *Nul=0* (Arnhem, Netherlands), no. 2, 1963; ''Je suis un realiste'' in *Integration* (Arnhem, Netherlands), no. 4, 1965; ''L'Art dans la Societe Capitaliste d'Aujourd'hui'' in *Integration* (Arnhem, Netherlands), no. 7–8, 1967; ''Sur Pierre Manzoni'' in *Robho* (Paris), no. 3, 1968; ''Yves le bleu vu par Bernard le rouge'' in *La Galerie des Arts* (Paris), no. 64, 1969; ''La Cage Rouge de Fumee . . .'' in *Robho* (Paris), no. 5–6, 1971; ''A Propos de mes Nouvelles Sculptures'' in *Integration* (Eschenau, Netherlands), no. 13–14, 1972; ''Rouge'' in *Kunstkonkret 3,* 1996.

On AUBERTIN: Books—*Bernard Aubertin,* exhibition catalog, with text by Udo Kultermann, Essen, West Germany 1967; *Douze Ans d'Art Contemporain en France,* exhibition catalog, with texts by F. Mathey, V. Huchard, D. Cordier and others, Paris 1972; *Aubertin/Deux/Schauer,* exhibition catalog, with texts by Hans Haacke, Bernard Rancillac, Udo Kultermann and others, Paris 1972; *Factotum Book 5: Bernard Aubertin,* with text by Egidio Mucci, Padua 1978; *Bernard Aubertin: Le Point Zero de la Peinture,* exhibition catalog, edited by Charley Chevalier, Paris 1986; *Bernard Aubertin,* exhibition catalog, with essay by Gabriele Kübler, Stuttgart 1987; *Bernard Aubertin Monochrome Rouge et Feu 1958–1990,* exhibition catalog, Paris 1990; *3éme Biennale Internationale der Papierkunst,* exhibition catalog with text by Gabriele Kübler, Düren 1990; *Eikon=Das Bild,* exhibition catalog, Reutlingen 1991; *Mise à Feu,* exhibition catalog by Giovanni Joppolo, Paris 1992; *L'Hôtel Bouhier de Savigny Accuelille le Frac,* exhibition catalog, Dijon 1994; *Tout Rouge Bernard Aubertin zum 65 Geburtstag,* exhibition catalog, Reutlingen 1999; *Augenblicke Begegnungen mit Künstlern aus der Sammlung Lenz Schönberg 1968–1996* by Anna Lenz, 1999; *Aubertin Rouge,* Paris 2000.

*

I started painting in my 21st year after having studied two years in an artist's studio preparing to enter the State schools of decoration. On receiving admission I disdained returning there: I wanted to dedicate myself to painting, my vocation. Until the age of 23 I painted portraits, landscapes, still-lifes, and above all did plenty of drawing. The figurative or abstract painting I saw in the galleries did not satisfy me. In 1957 I met Yves Klein and this meeting was for me, of major importance. Under his influence I completed about 15 canvases, which were monochrome, red and very structured. I used to do this with every type of painter's knife, even the prongs of a fork, the round back of a spoon, etc. The whole painted surface was a unity composed of repeated structures. These structures didn't give me entire satisfaction: They weren't specific enough for my taste. One day I threw a handful of nails into the red colour spread on the canvas. Accidentally, I had just discovered in the nail the structure which corresponded to that precision which I was looking for. From here the idea of planting the nails one by one in the support, rather than scattering them at random on it, followed naturally. I was recreating the unity of the surface by filling it with nails. My work on nail-pictures divides into two periods: 1) the picture presents the nail head-outwards; 2) the picture presents the point of the nail, the head of the nail being the picture.

I soon had the idea of using elements other than nails in series: Screws, pitons, matches. With matches, I invented fire-painting. All my researches are inspired by one ideal: To humanize. From my own observation of what is going on in the culture of our present-day world, I have acquired the opinion that our present art expresses, for the most part, the impossibility, for man, of communicating harmoniously with his fellows. Our present art is founded on a therapy on the level of the individual, without any message for other men concerning the transformation of human nature demanded of humanity. It is the statement of the misery of a humanity in conflict with itself, dehumanized. It is journalism, news in brief; it offers itself up to the caprices of fashion, creates it, and finally reveals itself as completely incapable of exerting a vaguely spiritual influence.

The truth is that it is incumbent upon the artist, aware of the always dehumanized state of society, to base art first of all on man.

Art, in my sense, can not be envisaged except as a therapy on the collective level, which brings about the fraternization of men and ennobles the dose of therapy inherent in all art. Our role as artists is to lead to the TOTALITY, shorn of all contradictions, of human nature. In this way, man will always be in a position to foresee the needs of humanity and to reply to them. In acting for collectivity, we liberate ourselves from nature and from our own natures.

That is why, in the field of the realisation of a plastic work, I find it necessary to reduce the role of manual execution to its dominant function: The hand is nothing else than a manufacturing tool; to entrust it with the responsibility of fixing the various tensions—emotive, instinctive, animal even—accumulated in the soul, is an error.

We must strive to take distance in comparison with nature, if we want to realise ourselves as a specific human species. The creation of a distance in the execution is the means that one finds to take distance in comparison with nature and with our own natures.

Thus, to fill the surface regularly with the help of nails, screws, pitons, matches etc. signifies, in my case, the creation of this distance in the execution. If form in art is limitation, if it corresponds, in the plastic arts, to the natural and social order in which we live (we all know that man is determined), it must not be unchanging. On the contrary, it must be constructed by means of the relief which catches the light and modifies it naturally. (Form can be rendered mobile by many other means; I'm talking here of what I do myself.) The distribution of the light on the reliefs of my pictures changes according to the times of day. In this way, the picture is never completely the same.

I am seeking to obtain greater precision in the definition of human nature. In this sense, I think I have the right to say: I am a realist.

—Bernard Aubertin

* * *

Where does Bernard Aubertin begin? One would like to reply: At the stake stripped of all his witches. To ignite things like this, by vocation, at least with a ''flash in the pan'' of the metaphors, would not easily resolve that linguistic impression that the world is an artifice—hence this determination to strike things which, from the blow, take fire with a made hope: To illuminate the art of ashes.

The technique is simple: Fire. The proposition ''water propagates, fire reduces'' is thus articulated in this way: The machinery of fire, as play of flames, starting from propositions reduced to homothetic multiplications (matches) forms a system. Hence the difficulty of any extraneous propositions: Water does not extinguish fire. For the pyromaniac who Aubertin demands of himself is substituted a flamboyant fireman.

The Aubertin rises again from his ashes and explains himself historically. Use of the time where the history of art stores away its recipes. It's practically everything (the question at least) since there must be a ''reader'' or a ''spectator'' which is *the question itself,* posed to Aubertin.

Therefore an obstinate question situated at *his* origin, towards a first glance, in a gesture which does not lack antecedents: Heraclitus the hydropic marking the rhythm of the first (philosophical) cadence, Empedocles and Etna—but this time with matches: Another Ulysses, of the time of Mr. Bloom, whom one meets in the tobacconist, carrying out his provision of combustibles.

This symbol is clear (he is lighting things up); in it one forgets that ''reality'' does not invent itself. That it suffices to ''trap'' it with the means at hand: Means which are objective, existing, taken as given—the setting fire as ''act'' not justifying an investment, but the operation which results from an excessive confrontation. Burning as radicalization. Setting ablaze as opening out. In such a way that escaping from subjectivism comes back to risking any gesture (any breath) in a given matter. Aubertin excels at explaining it, and there is no reason not to read it. What he is showing passes beyond the fabrication of what he is applying. One can see in it what one wills: Broaching the subject, as sufficient reason. When all is allowed it suffices to know where.

In the titles first of all—for once explicit: Fire-pictures, monochromes dedicated, as he writes, to the dynamism of colour. More exactly a trajectory of flame, from red to black, from burning to burnt. A brief, momentary act from which there is no reconversion. What has been used once has been used for good in the sense that the work with fire measures its adequacy in igniting as much as possible to consume as surely as possible. Nevertheless the object resists. There are thus unexpected versions: The remains stick to the ash, support it. A new limit is shown, a new route can be hazarded. When Aubertin partially burns telephone books (which are difficult to burn, he acknowledges), ''using'' the debris (of the phone books) to construct his ''avalanches,'' to constitute ''series'' where he arranges other fragments, the reference he is making is to the geography of an act begun more than 10 years ago. In the same way the red monochromes and the nail-pictures *imagine* the flame and the work in fire: I mean that they determine the place of an act which symbolically unites all these acts. The symbolic place, for the artist (in this case Aubertin, as will have been guessed . . .), reducing itself to a machinery where chance (including Aubertin) tests the states; the works only correspond to stratificatory moments which never add up to the entirety of the researches. In this sense, no ''master works,'' no over-meaningful points, but a series of connotations, ''object-arts,'' ''fabrication-routes,'' in the very judgement which presents them as works.

One understands that Aubertin asserts himself (with obstinacy) as a realist. He is so to the scandal of all dogmatism. Because ''reality'' does not stop, it does not copy itself, it does not depict itself. Either it does work or it doesn't work. And it always works differently in the sense that the principal of identity, so dear to a certain rationalism, in art, designates its imposture. It is therefore to a ''lesson in reality'' that we invite Aubertin with all the ardour which is wasting away there.

—Claude Fournet

AUERBACH, Frank

Nationality: British. **Born:** Berlin, 29 April 1931; emigrated to England in 1939; naturalized, 1947. **Education:** Attended Kent primary schools; attended art classes at Hampstead Garden Suburb Institute, London, 1947; attended Borough Polytechnic, London (studied under David Bomberg), 1947–48; attended St. Martin's School of Art, London, 1948–52; attended Royal College of Art, London, 1952–55 (Silver Medal, 1955). **Family:** Married Julia Wolstenholme in 1958; one son. **Career:** Independent painter, London, since 1955. Lecturer, art schools in Sidcup, Kent, and London boroughs: Ealing, Bromley and Camberwell; and Slade School of Fine Art, London, 1956–58. **Awards:** Golden Lion Award, *42nd Biennale,* Venice, 1986. **Agent:** Marlborough Fine Art, London. **Address:** c/o Marlborough Fine Art, 6 Albemarle Street, London W1S 4BY, England.

Individual Exhibitions:

1956 Beaux Arts Gallery, London
1959 Beaux Arts Gallery, London
1961 Beaux Arts Gallery, London
1962 Beaux Arts Gallery, London
1963 Beaux Arts Gallery, London
1965 Marlborough Fine Art, London
1967 Marlborough Fine Art, London
1969 Marlborough Gerson Gallery, New York
1971 Marlborough Fine Art, London
1972 Villiers Art Gallery, Sydney
1972 Toorak Gallery, Melbourne
1973 University of Essex, Colchester
Galleria Bergamini, Milan
1974 Marlborough Fine Art, London
1975 Municipal Gallery of Modern Art, Dublin
1976 Marlborough Galerie, Zurich
1978 Hayward Gallery, London (travelled to the Fruit Market Gallery, Edinburgh)
1979 Bernard Jacobson, New York
1982 Marlborough Gallery, New York
1983 Marlborough Fine Art, London
Anne Berthoud Gallery, London
1986 British Pavilion, XLII Venice Biennale (travelled to Kunstverein, Hamburg, Museum Folkwang, Essen, West Germany, and Centro de Arte Reina Sofia, Madrid)
1987 Marlborough Fine Art, London
1989 Rijksmuseum Vincent Van Gogh, Amsterdam
1990 Marlborough Fine Art, London
1990–91 Yale Center for British Art, New Haven, Connecticut
1991 Rex Irwin, Woollahra
1994 Marlborough Gallery, New York
1995 National Gallery, London
Campbell-Thiebaud Gallery, San Francisco
1996 Rex Irwin, Woolahra
1997 Marlborough Fine Art, London
1998 Marlborough Gallery, New York
2000 Charloltenborg, Copenhagen
Rex Irwin, Woollahra

Selected Group Exhibitions:

1958 *Critics' Choice,* Arthur Tooth and Sons, London
1961 *Pittsburgh International,* Carnegie Institute, Pittsburgh
1967 *Stuyvesant Foundation Exhibition,* London and Zurich
1970 *Painting and Perception,* MacRobert Centre Art Gallery, University of Stirling, Scotland
1972 *Immagine per la Citta,* Palazzo dell'Accademia and Palazzo Reale, Genoa
1977 *British Painting 1952–1977,* Royal Academy of Art, London
1979 *This Knot of Life: Paintings and Drawings of British Artists,* Louver Gallery, Venice, California
1981 *A New Spirit in Painting,* Royal Academy of Art, London
1984 *The British Art Show,* City Art Gallery and Ikon Gallery, Birmingham (travelled to Edinburgh, Sheffield and Southampton)
1987 *A School of London,* Kunstnernes Hus, Oslo (travelled to Venice and Düsseldorf)
1990 *The Pursuit of the Real: British Figurative Painting from Sickert to Bacon,* Manchester City Art Gallery (travelled to London and Glasgow)
1995 *From London,* Scottish National Gallery of Modern Art, Edinburgh (travelled to Luxembourg, Lausanne, and Barcelona)
1998–99 *L'Ecole de Londres: De Bacon à Bevan,* Fondation Dina-Vierny-Musée Maillol, Paris (travelled to Santiago de Compostela and Vienna)

Collections:

British Museum, London; Tate Gallery, London; Scottish National Gallery of Modern Art, Edinburgh; National Gallery of Australia, Canberra; National Gallery of Victoria, Melbourne; Metropolitan Museum of Art, New York; Museum of Modern Art, New York; Los Angeles County Museum of Art; Tamayo Museum, Mexico City; Museo de Art Moderna da Bahia, Salvador, Brazil; St. Louis Art Museum, Missouri; Cleveland Museum of Art, Ohio.

Publications:

By AUERBACH: Articles—''7 Portraits'' in *Ark 23* (London), 1958; ''Fragments from a Conversation'' in *X Quarterly* (London), November 1959; ''Reply to a Letter from Michael Peppiatt'' in *Cambridge Opinion,* January 1964; ''Frank Auerbach Talks to Christopher Battye'' in *Art and Artists* (London), January 1971; ''Frank Auerbach'' interview with Judith Bumpus in *Art and Artists,* June 1986; ''Frank Auerbach, An Interview by Richard Cork'' in *Art e Design,* vol. 4, no. 9/10, 1988; ''Paint or Die: Meeting Frank Auerbach'' interview by Geordie Greig in *Modern Painters,* Autumn

1988; ''Hidden Talent'' interview by Geordie Greig in *Times Magazine,* 12 December 1998.

On AUERBACH: Books and Exhibition Catalogs—*Frank Auerbach* by William Feaver, Zurich 1976; *Frank Auerbach* by Leon Kossoff and Catherine Lampert, London 1978; *Frank Auerbach: Recent Paintings and Drawings* by Stephen Spender, New York 1982; *Frank Auerbach: XLII Venice Biennale* by Catherine Lampert, London 1986; *Frank Auerbach* by Robert Hughes, London 1990. **Articles—** ''A Stick in the Dark'' by John Berger in *New Statesman* (London), April 1961; ''Titian and Auerbach'' by Richard Wollheim in *The Listener* (London), October 1973; ''A Fierce Independence'' by Siri Huntoon in *Artnews,* April 1992; ''Urban Gestures'' by David Ebony in *Art in America,* December 1994.

* * *

Frank Auerbach came to England from Berlin at the age of eight. In retrospect it is difficult to believe that he had been anywhere else than in the London in which he works and whose portrait he has painted so many times. Even harder to understand is how he somehow absorbed and subsequently recorded in his painting an Englishness that has been a kind of national art accent right through the Bloomsbury period of British culture. The scenes are right. Even the friendly contact with the subjects of the portraits is right. And so is the ungainly sprawl of nudes who seem to have come out of an age when central heating never functioned properly. The penny-in-the-slot gas fire epoch.

None of these remarks relates to the way in which Auerbach paints. They have been made because the mood or moods which invade his paintings must be accepted as ''English'' in a very strong way—especially English. This anglicization is almost unique (unless one counts David Bomberg as British).

Auerbach is famous for his thick pigment. No one past maturity should attempt to lift any but the smallest canvases. If this heavy paint has not been of quite the same density in recent years, that is not to suggest that it is still not laid onto the picture like paste. The result is a dour sort of late expressionism whose temperament is occasionally lightened by swathes of bright colour.

Where Auerbach succeeds is in his extraordinarily effective control of so much viscous material. How successful he may seem to have been with each picture may depend upon the character of the viewer. Some may reject some of the paintings as being too lumbering or opaque, while others will recognize in them the uncanny skill with which he makes the paint not only do his bidding but also turn *itself* into whatever figuration he seeks.

—Sheldon Williams

In 1994 Auerbach exhibited sixty-four new paintings and sketches, most completed between 1990 and 1994. The subjects of these works are Auerbach's usual ones: portraits, cityscapes near the artist's London studio, and studies of old-master paintings from the National Gallery. Although painstakingly rendered, these paintings and sketches still evince a sense of immediacy and sudden realization. Several layers of paint cover most canvases; in places, layers of somber-hued paint have been scraped away from canvas, as the artist worked and reworked toward a true and immediate image. Likewise, many sketches reveal the marks of repeated erasures and redrawings. Ironically, through this process of overpainting and reworking, Auerbach manages to capture the elusive moment of a single sitting or sketch.

While these recent works reveal Auerbach's devotion to formal painting, they possess the emotional intensity registered in most of Auerbach's previous work. In *From the Studios* (1992), the small figures of an adult and child move cautiously, almost anxiously, through a barely controlled urban scene, depicted in swirls and strong, definitive lines of purple, brown, and green. The unpeopled cityscape of *The Chimney—Mornington Crescent* (1991—92), with its muted hues of black, green, and brown, emanates a sense of loss held just below the surface.

—Beth Duncan

AY-O

Nationality: Japanese. **Born:** Takao Iijima in Ibaraki Prefecture, Japan, 19 May 1931. **Education:** Kyoiku University, Tokyo, B.A. 1954. **Family:** Married Ikuko Yoshida in 1955; child: Hanako. **Career:** Independent artist: began as engraver and lithographer, then expanded work to include painting, sculpture, environments, and happenings; joined ''Demokrato'' avant-garde artist group, 1954, lived in New York, 1958–66; joined ''Flux'' avant-garde artist group, 1962; travelled in Europe and India before returning to Japan, 1966; has concentraded on producing rainbow-hued silk-screens, since mid-1960s; again lived in New York, 1968–71; returned to Japan, 1971; travelled in Britain, Europe, and Nepal, 1973. Visiting professor of painting, University of Kentucky, Lexington, 1968–69. **Awards:** Special Prize, *Vancouver International Prints Biennial,* 1967; Grant Prize, 1969, and Minister of Foreign Affairs Award, 1971, *Japan Art Festival;* Award, *Mainichi Modern Art Exhibition,* National Museum of Modern Art, Kyoto; Brazil Bank Prize, *Bienal,* Sao Paulo, 1969; Prize, *Tokyo International Print Biennial,* National Museum of Modern Art, Tokyo, 1970; Bridgestone Museum Prize, *Mainichi modern Art Exhibition,* Japan, 1971; Prize, *Exposition International de Dessins Originaux,* Originaux, Rijeka, Yugoslavia, 1973; Grand Prize, Listowele Print Biennial, 1980; Zagreb Contemporary Art Gallery Prize, Original Drawings Exhibition, Rijeka, Yugoslavia, 1982; Warsaw National Museum Prize, International Drawing Triennale, Wroclaw, 1982; Grand Prix, *Japan Art,* 1990. **Agent:** Suzuki Graphics Inc., 797 Madison Avenue, New York, New York 10021, U.S.A. **Address:** 2-6-38 Matsuyama, Kiyoseshi, Tokyo 100–31, Japan.

Individual Exhibitions:

1955 Takemiya Gallery, Tokyo
1956 Forme Gallery, Tokyo
1962 Gordon's Fifth Avenue Gallery, New York
1963 Gordon's Fifth Avenue Gallery, New York
1964 Smolin Gallery, New York
1965 Smolin Gallery, New York
1966 Gordon's Fifth Avenue Gallery, New York
Minami Gallery, Tokyo
1967 Gallery 669, Los Angeles
1969 Melida Gallery, Louisville, Kentucky
Hank Baum Gallery, San Francisco
1971 Minami Gallery, Tokyo

1972 Nantenshi Gallery, Tokyo
Suzuki Graphics Gallery, New York
Hank Baum Gallery, San Francisco
1973 Suzuki Graphics Gallery, New York
Museum of Modern Art, New York
1974 Suzuki Graphics Gallery, New York
1975 Suzuki Graphics Gallery, New York
1976 Suzuki Graphics Gallery, New York
Nantenshi Gallery, Tokyo
Hank Baum Gallery, San Francisco
Bonino Gallery, New York
1977 Minami Gallery, Tokyo
1978 Hank Baum Gallery, San Francisco
1979 Ikeda Museum of Contemporary Art, Japan
1980 Graphics Gallery, San Francisco
Wako Hall, Tokyo
Hank Baum Gallery, San Francisco
Suzuki Graphics Gallery, New York
1982 Fuji Television Gallery, New York
1985 Fuji Television Gallery, Tokyo
1986 Eiheiji Zen Temple, Japan
1987 Eiffel Tower Project, Paris
1990 Fiji TV Gallery, Japan
Venice, Italy
1991 Permanent Environment, New York
Emily Harvey Gallery, New York
1993 Emily Harvey Gallery, New York and Galerie J & J Donguy, Paris
1996 Emily Harvey Gallery, New York
1997 Kitakyushu Municipal Museum of Art, Japan

Selected Group Exhibitions:

1964 *Rainbow Happening: Flux-Orchestra Concert,* Carnegie Recital Hall, New York
1965 *Rainbow Happening: Flux Concert,* Carnegie Recital Hall, New York
1966 *Rainbow Tactile Room,* at the *Biennale,* Venice
1967 *Annual Avant-Garde Festival,* New York (and 1968, 1972, 1977, 1980)
1969 *Tactile Rainbow Room,* at *Expo 70,* Tokyo (travelled to the Cincinnati Art Museum, Ohio, and the University of Kentucky, Lexington)
Modern Japanese Art, National Museum of Art, Kyoto
1971 *Bienal,* Sao Paulo
1973 *Japanese Artists in the Americas,* National Museum of Modern Art, Kyoto
1987 *FIAC '87,* Grand Palais, Paris
1992 *Fluxus Show,* Walker Art Center, Whitney Museum, and various countries in Europe
1994 *Contemporary Japanese Prints: 1950–1990,* Telefonica Museum, Madrid (catalog)

Collections:

National Museum of Modern Art, Tokyo; National Museum of Modern Art, Kyoto; Museum of Modern Art, New York; Metropolitan Art Museum, Tokyo; National Museum, Warsaw; Cincinnati Art Museum, Ohio; Stedelijk Museum, Amsterdam; British Museum, London.

Publications:

By AY-O: Book—*Rainbow Prints: Catalog Raisonne 1954–1979,* compiled by Sadajiro Kubo, Tokyo 1979.

On AY-O: Books—*FLUXshoe,* exhibition catalog, edited by David Mayor and Felipe Ehrenberg, Cullompton, England 1972; *Japanese Artists in the Americas,* exhibition catalog, by T. Ogura, Kyoto 1973; *Ay-O: Arc-en-ciel,* exhibition catalog, with introduction by Akira Asahi, Paris 1987. **Article**—''Tokyo Letter'' by J. P. Love in *Art International* (Lugano, Switzerland), March 1971.

* * *

Ay-O has nearly magical power by which he metamorphoses objects which are a part of everyday life into metaphysical tactile objects which demand to be sensually experienced. His 1961 ''Ay-O's Box,'' exemplifies this. It consists of a series of cubical wooden boxes snugly fitting into an attache case; each box has a hole through which an unexpected sensory experience is obtained by inserting a forefinger into the holes. The rainbow series on which he has been working since 1964 is nothing less than the creation of versicolored environments, of walls, furniture, utensils and other ordinary articles used in daily life. One work in this series, ''Rainbow Tactile Room,'' was exhibited at the 1966 Venice *Biennale.*

Born Takao Iijima in Ibaraki Prefecture in 1931, the artist graduated from the art department of Tokyo's University of Arts and Science in 1954. He started as an engraver and lithographer and gradually expanded his scope of activity to include painting, sculpture, environments and happenings. In 1966 he returened to Japan after nine years overseas, and had a show at Minami Gallery, Tokyo. Since 1962 he has often been among the Japanese artists exhibiting in the Tokyo *International Biennale Exhibition of Prints.* Ay-O was awarded the JAFA Prize in the 1969 Japan Art Festival. The same year, he won the Kyoto National Museum of Modern Art Prize at the Ninth Modern Japanese Art Exhibition.

Ay-O was a member of the Fluxus movement in New York in the early 1960s, making a lot of performance events with George Maciunas and other Fluxus artists. His recent manifestation was on the Eiffel Tower in Paris. A truly astonishing effect was created in 1987 by a 300-meter long banner in rainbow colour flowing down to the ground from the tower's observation platform.

—Yoshiaki Tono

AYCOCK, Alice

Nationality: American. **Born:** Harrisburg, Pennsylvania, 20 November 1946. **Education:** Douglass College, New Brunswick, New Jersey, 1964–68, B.A. 1968; Hunter College, New York (studied under Robert Morris), 1968–71, M.A. 1971. **Family:** Married Mark Segal in 1968. **Career:** Independent sculptor and installation artist, since 1972, known for large-scale semi-architectural and machine-like projects. Adjunct lecturer in Art, Hunter College, 1972–73; visiting sculptor and teacher, Rhode Island School of Design, Providence, 1977; taught foundation and advanced sculpture courses at the School of Visual Arts, New York, 1977–78; visiting sculptor and teacher, Princeton University, New Jersey, 1979; visiting sculptor and teacher, San Francisco Art Institute, 1979. Since 1979, teacher at the School of Visual Arts, New York; director of graduate sculpture studies, Yale University, 1988–1992. Artist-in-residence, Williams College, Williamstown, Massachusetts, 1974. **Awards:** National Endowment for the Arts Fellowship, 1975, 1980, 1986, New York State Creative Artists Public Service Grant, 1976. **Agent:** John Weber Gallery. **Address:** c/o John Weber Gallery, 142 Greene St., New York, New York 10012–3236, U.S.A.

Individual Exhibitions:

1972 Nova Scotia College of Art and Design, Halifax
1974 112 Greene Street Gallery, New York
Project inc., Cambridge, Massachusetts
Williams College Museum of Art, Williamstown, Massachusetts
1976 Wheaton College, Norton, Massachusetts
1977 Projects Room, Museum of Modern Art, New York
1978 Portland Center for the Visual Arts, Oregon
John Weber Gallery, New York
University of Rhode Island, Kingston
Salvatore Ala, Milan
Projects for PCA, Philadelphia College of Art
Cranbook Academy of Art, Bloomfield Hills, Michigan
Projects and Proposals, Muhlenberg College, Allentown, Pennsylvania
1979 *Flights of Fancy,* San Francisco Art Institute
The Contemporary Art Center, Cincinnati, Ohio
Machinations, Protect-McIntosh Gallery, Washington, D.C.
The Large Scale Disintegration of Microelectronic Memories, Art on the Beach, Battery Park Landfill, New York
Collected Ghost Stories from the Workhouse from the series *How to Catch and Manufacture Ghosts,* University of South Florida, Tampa
1980 *The Miraculating Machine in the Garden,* Douglass College, New Brunswick, New Jersey
1981 *The Savage Sparkler,* New York State University at Plattsburgh
Machineworks: Vito Acconci/Alice Aycock/Dennis Oppenheim, Institute of Contemporary Art, Philadelphia
John Weber Gallery, New York
1982 *Drawings,* Locus Solus, Genoa
Lawrence Oliver Gallery, Philadelphia
New Work, John Weber Gallery, New York
1983 Museum of Contemporary Art, Chicago
Protetch McNeil Gallery, New York
Wurttembergischer Kunstverein, Stuttgart (retrospective; travelled to Cologne, Marl, The Hague and Lucerne)
1984 *New Work,* John Weber Gallery, New York
1985 Humanic Corporation Gallery, Graz, Austria
Serpentine Gallery, London
New Drawings, Insam Gallery, Vienna
1986 Sculpture Park, St. Louis, Missouri
John Weber Gallery, New York
Tel Aviv Museum, Israel
1987 Central Park, New York
Galerie Walter Storms, Munich
1990 Storm King Art Center, New York
Yoshiaki Inove Gallery, Osaka, Japan
1991 Galerie Grita Insam, Vienna
1993 John Weber Gallery, New York
1997 School of Visual Arts, New York
1998 John Weber Gallery, New York
1999 Dieu Donné Papermill, New York

Selected Group Exhibitions:

1972 *Untitled V,* Museum of Modern Art, New York
1974 *Interventions in Landscape,* Massachusetts Institute of Technology, Cambridge
1977 *Documenta 6,* Kassel, West Germany
1978 *Biennale,* Venice
1979 *Whitney Biennial,* Whitney Museum, New York
1980 *International Sculpture Conference,* Washington, D.C.
1981 *Mythos & Ritual in der Kunst der 70er Jahre,* Kunsthaus, Zurich
1984 *Land Marks,* Bard College, Annandale-on-Hudson, New York
1985 *Modern Machines: Recent Kinetic Sculpture,* Whitney Museum, New York
1987 *Avant-Garde in the Eighties,* Los Angeles County Museum of Art

Collections:

Museum of Modern Art, New York; Guggenheim Museum, New York; Hirshhorn Museum, Washington, D.C.; Whitney Museum, New York.

Publications:

By AYCOCK: Books—Project entitled "The Beginnings of a Complex . . .," New York 1977; *After Years of Ruminating on the Events That Led Up to This Misfortune, Alice Aycock—Projects and Proposals,* with essays by Stuart Morgan and Edward Fry, Allentown, Pennsylvania 1978; *Alice Aycock Projects 1979–1981,* with an introduction by Edward Fry, Tampa 1981; *Alice Aycock: Retrospective of Projects and Ideas 1972–1983,* exhibition catalog, Stuttgart 1983. **Articles**—"Four 36–38 Exposures" in *Avalanche* (New York), Spring 1972; "5 Semi-Architectural Projects" in *c. 7500,* Valencia, California 1973; "New York City Orientations" in *Triquarterly* (Evanston, Illinois), Winter 1975; "Notes on Project for a Simple Network of Underground Wells and Tunnels" in *Projects in Nature,* Far Hills, New Jersey 1975; "Interviews with Some Modern Mazemakers—Interview with Alice Aycock" by Janet Kardon in *Art International* (Lugano, Switzerland), April/May 1976; "Work 1972–1974" in *Individuals: Post-Movement Art in America,* edited by Alan Sondheim, New York 1977; "Projects for My Body" in *17 Lotus International* (New York), December 1977; "An Interview with Alice Aycock" in *D.A.A. Journal* (Cincinnati, Ohio), no. 1, 1980; "2 Fantasies of a Mythical Waterworks," with James Freed, in *Artists and Architects Collaboration,* edited by Barbara Lee Diamonstein, New York 1981; "A Conversation with Alice Aycock," interview with Aimee Price Brown, in *Architectural Digest* (Los Angeles), April 1983; *Woman's Art Journal,* vol. 6, no. 1, Spring/Summer 1985; *ArtNews,* vol. 85, October 1986; *Artforum,* vol. 29, October 1990; *Artforum,* vol. 34, Summer 1996; *ArtNews,* vol. 96, May 1997; *Sculpture,* vol. 18, no. 1, January-February 1999. **Video**—*Alice Aycock,* interview with Kate Horsfield, Video Data Bank, School of the Art Institute of Chicago, 1977.

ON AYCOCK: Books—*6 Years: The Dematerialization of the Art Object* by Lucy R. Lippard, New York 1972; *From the Center* by Lucy R. Lippard, New York 1976; *Unbuilt America,* by Alison Sky and Michelle Stone, New York 1976; *Metaphor: New Projects by Contemporary Sculptors,* by Howard N. Fox, Washington, D.C. 1982; *Avant-Garde in the Eighties,* exhibition catalog, with introduction by Howard Fox, Los Angeles 1987; *Making Their Mark,* New York 1989; *Complex Visions,* exhibition catalog, New York 1990. **Articles**—''Aligned with the Nazca'' by Robert Morris in *Artforum* (New York), October 1975; ''Projects in Nature'' by Jonathan Crary in *Arts Magazine* (New York), December 1975; ''Labyrinths, Philadelphia College of Art'' by April Kingsley in *Artforum* (New York), February 1976; ''The Modern Maze'' by Ronald Onorato in *Art International* (Lugano, Switzerland), April/May 1976; '''Sculpture Sited' at the Nassau County Museum'' by Lucy Lippard in *Arts in America* (New York), March/April 1977; ''American Women Architects'' by John Lobell in *Artforum* (New York), summer 1977; ''Mystery Under Construction'' by Margaret Sheffield in *Artforum* (New York), September 1977; ''6 Women at Work in the Landscape'' by April Kingsley in *Arts Magazine* (New York), April 1978; ''Alice Aycock: A Certain Image of Something I Like Very Much'' by Stuart Morgan in *Arts Magazine* (New York), March 1978; ''The Present Tense of Space'' by Robert Morris in *Art in America* (New York), January/February 1978; ''Women of the Fourth Wave; Humboldt's Daughters'' by Eleanor Munro in *Originals: American Women Artists,* New York 1979; ''Discovery of the Sources: Model of History'' by Jean-Luc Daval in *Art Actuel: Skira Annual '79,* Geneva 1979; ''Complexes: Sculpture in Nature'' by Lucy Lippard in *Art in America* (New York), January/February 1979; ''Ancient Places and Personal Spaces: Homage to Alice Aycock'' by Elter, McCormick, McKeon and Reynolds, ''Alice Aycock's Explanation, An, of Spring and the Weight of Air'' by Jonathan Kamholtz, and ''The Work of Alice Aycock: A Pictorial Section'' in *D.A.A. Journal* (Cincinnati, Ohio), no. 1, 1980; ''Aycock's Dream Houses'' by Donald Kuspit in *Art in America* (New York), September 1980; ''Beyond Revivalism and the Bauhaus: A New Partnership in the Arts'' by Jonathan Barnett in *Artists and Architects Collaboration,* New York 1981; ''Alice in Duchamp-Land'' by Kay Larson in *New York,* 25 May 1981; ''The Poetic Machines of Alice Aycock'' by Edward Fry in *Portfolio* (Boulder, Colorado), November-December 1981; ''Alice Aycock'' by Antje von Graevenitz in *Museumjournaal* (Amsterdam), no. 27, 1982; ''Reading Alice Aycock'' by Monroe Denton in *Sculpture,* July/August 1990.

* * *

For over 30 years, the sculptor Alice Aycock has produced a body of work that is distinguished by its ambitious scale and its physical and conceptual complexity. Her elaborate architectural and mechanical fantasies exist in the realm where logic meets imagination, and where science and faith intermingle. Based on an almost encyclopedic array of historical, scientific, occult, and literary sources, Aycock's astounding confabulations of intellect and curiosity push at the limits of human understanding to border on the irrational, the perverse, and the dangerous.

Aycock's early work was generally associated with environmental sculpture and installation art due to its site-specificity and use of organic materials. Often built into or onto the land, the work addressed issues of privacy and interior space, of physical enclosure, and of the body's relationship to vernacular architecture and the built environment. While sharing affinities with the work of artists such as Vito Acconci and Mary Miss, a distinguishing feature of Aycock's work was its strong physical and emotional impact on the viewer. Her structures served to privatize our response to built spaces by compelling the participant into precarious, cramped, or dislocating dwellings or passageways. *Maze,* 1972, consisted of five six-foot high concentric rings of wood, with three random openings through which the view could enter. Once inside, the viewer had to negotiate a labyrinth of narrow passageways to reach the piece's center, becoming disoriented and temporarily entrapped in the process. To exit meant repeating the same uncomfortable experience.

Another early piece, *Low Building with Dirt Roof (for Mary),* 1973, was designed as a memorial for the unexpected death of Aycock's 12-year-old niece. Only thirty inches in height , with a low, wood-framed roof covered with dirt and supported by stone walls, the tomb-like structure recalled both cellar and attic. The viewer could enter the building's dank, dark interior only by crawling. The resulting sense of claustrophobia and discomfort was heightened by awareness of the roof's potential collapse.

After 1977, these recurrent themes of danger and unease were augmented by Aycock's growing interest in metaphysical issues, giving her work an aura of increased theatricality and eccentricity. The sculptures now excluded viewer participation and looked more like fantastical stage sets, accompanied by elaborate titles and lengthy appending notes. These elements reflected Aycock's fascination with levitation, magic, and schizophrenia—phenomena involving transformation or the fluidity of boundaries between physical and psychological realities. *How to Catch and Manufacture Ghosts,* from 1979, demonstrates Aycock's increasing use of such materials as steel, aluminum, glass, motors, batteries, and other mechanical and scientific paraphernalia. The artist described the piece as ''an attempt to mix science and magic,'' pointing to the invisible nature of both forces. A live dove in a glass jar provided power for the piece—the jar was wound with wires connected to a primitive battery made out of a lemon. With its theatrical assemblage of props, cranks, and pulleys, the piece hearkened back to the early days of scientific experimentation, when some inventors attempted to capture supernatural presences with electrical and magnetic apparatuses.

Equally important to Aycock as a source for *How to Catch and Manufacture Ghosts* were the hallucinations of ''N.N.,'' a schizophrenic who, by mental association, could project himself through boundaries of space, time, and causality. Kay Larson has written, ''Aycock's machines are the physical corollaries of free thought. . . Doctrines of transmutation, whether rational or not, supply her with parts. . . Aycock's machines are her private version of the philosopher's stone, a device that allows anything to be converted into anything else, through the action of self on matter.'' (Kay Larson, ''Machineworks,'' in the catalog for the exhibition *Machineworks,* Institute of Contemporary Art, University of Pennsylvania, 1981). Not to be overlooked is a humorous aspect which relieves even Aycock's most abstruse or ominous pieces. Her sculptures rely for their effect upon playful juxtapositions of materials, the clever contrivance of many discreet parts into a working whole.

After 1982, Aycock began designing ''blade machines,'' sculptures made out of revolving, motorized metal blades. Sleekly menacing, these sculptures extended the notion of danger in Aycock's work to address competing urges of attraction and fear. Like the Cuisinart food processors that partially inspired the artist, the blade machines manifested both creation and destruction. The interdependence of these awesome, primitive forces may be seen as two aspects of one reality, an idea that Aycock explored in *The Solar Wind,* 1983, a non-kinetic blade sculpture based on the cosmic diagrams of the Renaissance mystic Robert Fludd. Other blade machines were overtly frightening or bizarre, like devices out of science fiction. *A Salutation to the Wonderful Pig of Knowledge,* 1984, seduces and terrifies us simultaneously, with its shining steel, copper, and brass components, and whirling blades. The terror here refers not just to the threat of physical violence, of being literally sliced, but to emotional vulnerability as well, since positive processes of growth and change necessarily involve relinquishing or destroying the familiar and risking the unknown.

The dynamics of chance have played an enlarged role in Aycock's work of the last decade. An almost Duchampian fascination with the design and construction of games, the schematics of the solar system, of astrology, of war strategy, and of choreography and dance have fueled Aycock's continued invention of fantastical three-dimensional models of cosmic designs. *The Islands of the Rose Apple Tree Surrounded by the Oceans of the World, For You, Oh My Darling,* 1987, renders an ancient hieroglyph in the form of a long, low concrete maze filled with water. *Some Night Action,* 1993, consists of an undulating brushed aluminum slide that empties onto a low, rotating circular platform, mapped with constellations and white lines and pocked with holes. Every thirty seconds, blue marbles resurface from the disk's central opening, to be drawn up through a tube running parallel to the slide. Emptied into an aluminum bowl, the marbles descend the slide again, forming random clusters of ''stars'' on the rotating disk. Like a miniature version of the heavens, the constellations in *Some Night Action* are governed by measurable laws of physics and the unruly laws of chance. They temporarily coalesce into discernible patterns when they fall upon the schematized white lines that rule the disc, only to be thrown once more into chaos, subsumed by its endless process of reconfiguration.

With its obsessive erudition, intuition, and awe, Aycock's art testifies to the human need to grasp the mysteries of the universe, even while celebrating its vast and totalizing grandeur. Many commentators have compared Aycock's cosmic machines to the stories of Jorge Luis Borges, with their private metaphysics of mind, dreams, space, and time. Like Borges, Aycock provokes us with the underlying sense of terror that the prevailing higher order is ultimately incomprehensible. Our endless attempts at understanding may result in mere illusions or elaborate fabrications, but paradoxically, it is the very magic and strange beauty of these constructs that allows us to glimpse our true nature.

— Dorothy Valakos

AZIZ (Anthony) and CUCHER (Sammy)

Nationality: American. **Born:** Anthony Aziz: United States. Sammy Cucher: Venezuela. **Education:** Aziz: San Francisco Art Institute, M.F.A., 1990; Cucher: San Francisco Art Institute, M.F.A., 1992. **Career:** Aziz: Professor, Maryland Institute, College of Art, Baltimore; Cucher: Professor, Maryland Institute, College of Art, Baltimore; New York University; Parsons School of Design, New York. Have collaborated on and exhibited digital photography projects and sculpture since 1991; live and work in Brooklyn, New York. **Address:** Aziz + Cucher, 230 Jay Street #17a, Brooklyn, New York 11201. **Web site:** http://www.azizcucher.net.

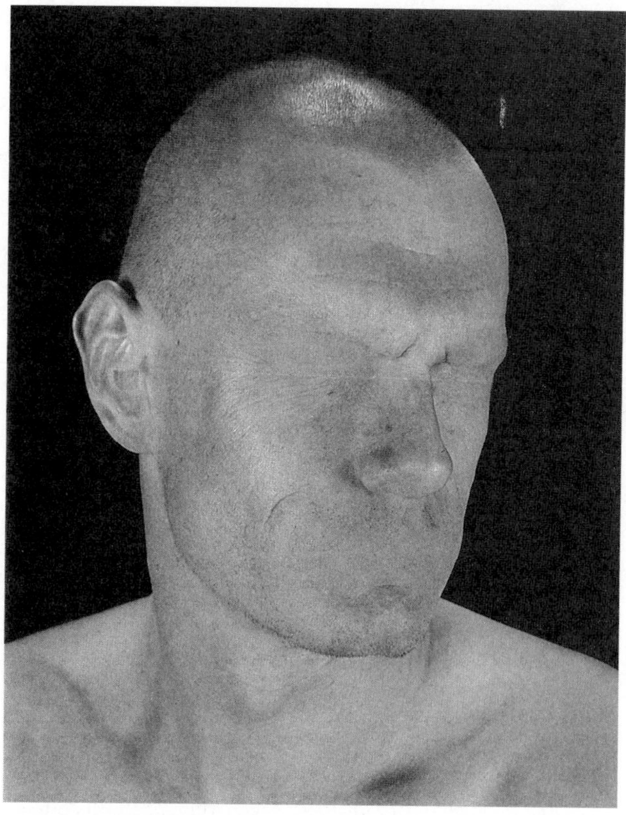

Aziz + Cucher: *Chris,* 1994. ©Aziz + Cucher. Courtesy Henry Urbach Gallery, New York.

Selected Individual Exhibitions:

1992 *Faith, Honor and Beauty,* New Langton Arts, San Francisco; Jack Shainman Gallery, New York
1995 Venice Biennale, Venezuelan Pavilion, Venice (catalog)
Dystopia, Jack Shainman Gallery, New York
1996 *Unnatural Selection,* Galleria Photology, Milan; Photographer's Gallery, London (catalog)
New Work, Espace d'Art, Yvonamor Palix, Paris (catalog)
Unnatural Selection, Galleria Photology, Milan (catalog)
Aziz + Cucher, Kemper Museum of Contemporary Art, Kansas City, Missouri
1997 *Plasmorphica,* Jack Shainman Gallery, New York
Les Rencontres d'Arles, France
1998 *Aziz + Cucher,* Reali Arte Contemporanea, Brescia, Italy
1999 *Aziz + Cucher,* Museo Nacional Centro de Arte Reina Sofia, Madrid (catalog)
2000 *Series 96:00,* Museo Alejandro Otero, Caracas, Venezuela
2001 *Recent Work,* Henry Urbach Gallery, New York

Selected Group Exhibitions:

1993 *The Final Frontier,* New Museum of Contemporary Art, New York

1994 *The Ghost in the Machine,* List Visual Arts Center, MIT, Cambridge, Massachusetts (catalog)
1995 *Photography Nacht Photography,* Siemens Kulturprogramm, Munich (catalog)
Obsessions: Fram WunderKammer to Cyberspace, Rijksmuseum Twenthe, Amsterdam (catalog)
1996 *Family, Nation, Tribe, Community, Shift,* Haus der Kulturen der Welt/NGBK, Berlin (catalog)
Prospect '96: An International Survey of Contemporary Art, Frankfurter Kunstverein, Frankfurt (catalog)
1998 *Magritte and Contemporary Art,* Oostende Museum of Modern Art, Belgium
Interface—Art and Technology in the Bay Area, Duke University, Durham, North Carolina
1999 *One Hundred Years of Art in Germany,* Nationalgalerie, Berlin
Hamburg Triennale, Deichtorhällen, Hamburg
Ghost in the Shell: Photography and the Human Soul, 1850–2000, Los Angeles County Museum of Art (catalog)
The Anagrammatical Body, Kusthaus Mürzzuschlag, Graz, Austria
2000 *Sharing Exoticism,* Biennale de Lyon
Made in California: Art, Image, and Identity, 1900–2000, Los Angeles County Museum of Art (catalog)
100 Years of the Body, Musée de l'Eysee, Lausanne, Switzerland
The Body in Art: 1950–2000, Arken Museum of Modern Art, Copenhagen

Publications:

By AZIZ + CUCHER: Articles—''Nachrichten aus Dystopia'' in *Kunstforum International,* November 1995-January 1996; ''Aziz + Cucher'' in *European Photography,* Fall-Winter 1997.

On AZIZ + CUCHER: Books—*Un homme et son image* by André Martin and Thérèse Saint-Gelais, Montreal 1994; *Aziz + Cucher, Unnatural Selection,* exhibition catalog with essays by Patrick Roegiers and Fabrizio Caleffi, Paris 1996; *Aziz + Cucher, Recent Work 1998–99,* exhibition catalog with essay by Thyrza Nichols Goodeve, Bielefeld, Germany 1999. **Articles—**''Here's Looking at You, Cyberface'' by Carole Boulbes in *Art Press,* November 1998; ''The Technology We Deserve'' by Frazer Ward in *Parkett,* 2000.

* * *

Since the early 1990s, the collaborative team of Sammy Cucher and Anthony Aziz has been producing images at the forefront of investigations of new technologies, including digital imaging. Their work is distinguished from that of many other artists who combine traditional photographic and new digital techniques in that their methodology is a direct consequence of their subject. Simply put, they use new technology in the production of photographic images that are about the implications new technologies hold for human life.

Aziz + Cucher address the brave new world of technology in terms that relate it to the human body. They foresee a time in which computer digitization, medical research, and genetic engineering come together in an unsettling, ominous future. In a picture from their first digital series, ''Faith, Honor and Beauty'' (1992), for example, a nude man carrying a laptop computer points an extended arm upward, as if striding into a bright future. But the man's heroic stance reveals a sobering limitation: he lacks any genitals and therefore is unable to reproduce.

This removal of a vital human function, carried out by the artists through the digital manipulation of their own studio-quality photographs, signals Aziz + Cucher's ambivalence about technological progress. It is also the precursor to a subsequent series of work, ''Dystopia'' (1994), which consists of individual head-and-shoulders portraits done in a conventional, commercial style. But the subjects' expressions in these pictures are limited by their lack of mouths and eyes. In addition, their nostrils and ears are covered over by skin, so that any sensations except touch are no longer available to them. These subjects are in effect prisoners inside their own bodies, and thus are emotionally distanced from the world, and from us as viewers of their pictures.

In 1996 Aziz + Cucher shifted their focus from portraiture to product photography, producing two series of pictures called ''Discontinued . . . Now!'' and ''Plasmorphica.'' Both bodies of work depict imagined, computer-related devices that the artists fabricated. For the former, they used sophisticated CAD-CAM technologies to create objects that look like computer accessories, complete with serial ports. For the latter, they simply bought consumer products at stores like Radio Shack and Office Depot and shrouded them in a plastic ''skin.''

Two more recent bodies of work, ''Chimera'' and ''Interior Series'' (both 1998–99), take the idea of skin more literally, using digitally ''sampled'' human skin to cover the surface of the depicted objects. The objects in the ''Chimera'' pictures are totem-like towers that reference themselves to tribal fetishes and the phallus; the interiors are architectural spaces representing entryways and stairways. The fact that the walls, floors, and ceilings of these interiors are actually made of human skin, complete with moles, blemishes, and hair, reverses the normal experience of skin being an exterior attribute. It also suggests what the ''Dystopia'' pictures also tell us: that our skin, as a surface poised between the outside world and our biological interiors, is a barrier that has positive and negative attributes.

As their work has progressed in the last 10 years, Aziz + Cucher have managed to find poetic analogs for many of the issues facing us today and in the future: the relationship of the body to science, ethical concerns about bio-engineering and cloning, and questions about the consequences of knowledge in a digital age. At the same time, their personal interest in the AIDS crisis (Cucher is HIV positive) has given their work a specificity that grounds these larger issues in a concrete, compelling sense of present-day reality.

—Andy Grundberg

B

BÄCHLI, Silvia

Nationality: Swiss. **Born:** Wettingen, Aargau, Switzerland, 16 March 1956. **Education:** Schule für Gestaltung, Basel, 1976–80; Ecole Superieur d'Art Visuel, Geneva, 1977–78. **Family:** Married Eric Hattan in 1993. **Career:** Co-organized, with Eric Hattan, ''Filiale,'' a non-profit artist-space, 1981–85; professor, Staatliche Akademie der Bildenden Künste Karlsruhe, 1993 to present. **Awards:** Kuratorium Aargau, Switzerland, 1980, 1982; Eidgenössisches Kunststipendium, 1982, 1984; Kiefer-Hablitzel-Stipendium, 1982; Manor Preis, 1990; Prix Breguet d'Art Contemporain, 1991; Prix BCG, Geneva, 1998. **Agents:** Galerie Philip Nelson, 40 rue Quincampoix, Paris, France; Galerie Vera Munro, Heilwigstrasse 64, Hamburg, Germany; Galerie Friedrich, Lorrainestrasse 19, Bern, Switzerland; Galerie Barbara Gross, Thierschstrasse 51, Munich, Germany; Galerie Karlheinz Meyer, Ernststrasse 88, Karlsruhe, Germany. **Addresses:** Mörsbergerstrasse 52, 4057 Basel, Switzerland; 15, rue Deveria, 75020 Paris, France.

Selected Individual Exhibitions:

1987 Kunsthalle Basel, Switzerland (catalog)
1989 Museum für Gegenwartskunst, Basel
1991 Aargauer Kunsthaus, Aarau, Switzerland (catalog)
1994 Centre d'Art Contemporain, Geneva (catalog)
1996 Kunsthalle Bern, Switzerland (catalog)
1997 Kunstmuseum Bonn, Germany (catalog)
1998 A/D, New York
1999 Städtische Galerie, Wolfsburg, Germany (catalog)
2000 Kasseler Kunstverein, Kassel, Germany

Selected Group Exhibitions:

1989 *1. Triennal de Dibuix Joan Mirò,* Fundacio Joan Mirò, Barcelona
1994 *Szenenwechsel VI,* Museum für Moderne Kunst, Frankfurt am Main, Germany
1995 *Selections Winter '95,* The Drawing Center, New York
1996 *Views from Abroad,* Museum für Moderne Kunst, Frankfurt am Main at Whitney Museum, New York
1998 *Im Reich der Zeichnung,* Kunsthaus Aarau, Switzerland (catalog)
Freie Sicht auts Mittelmeer, Kunsthaus Zürich, Switzerland
2000 *Szenenwechsel XIX,* Museum für Moderne Kunst, Frankfurt am Main, Germany

Collections:

Kunstmuseum Basel, Switzerland; Museum für Moderne Kunst, Frankfurt am Main, Germany; Centre Georges Pompidou, Paris; Aargauer Kunsthaus, Aarau, Switzerland; Hamburger Kunsthalle, Hamburg, Germany; Fogg Museum, Harvard University, Cambridge, Massachusetts.

Publications:

On BÄCHLI: Articles—''Vom objekt zur Situation'' by Roman Kurzmeyer in *Nike,* no. 26, 1988; ''Über Silvia Bächli'' by Ulrich Loock in *Artist Kunstmagazin,* no. 16, 1993; ''L'Ecriture de Soi: Entretiens avec Silvia Bächli et Jean Thibaudeau'' by Jean-Christophe Royoux in *Galeries Magazines,* Spring 1994; ''Suchen als Synonymm für Zeichnen, zum Werk von Silvia Bächli'' by Elisabeth Gerber in *Kunst-Bulletin,* November 1996; ''Von der Bescheidenheit des Erfindens'' by Bernhard Balkenhol in *das fridericianum magazin,* no. 5, 2000.

*

To draw, for me, is to be looking for the right sound, for the right phrasing of which I have, beforehand, no idea how it looks.

My drawings are rarely about symbolic meanings. They are just about what's being shown. Brief moments of sensation, a couple of minutes, a lingering a little longer with something we all know, but to which we don't pay all that much attention. An example: how do the legs feel right now? Or: a face flashing through my mind which I've noticed while shopping, without being able to remember it in detail. What kind of clothing is there in the winter wardrobe, what's missing? Where have I run through, yesterday? Or: the reason for a drawing also might simply be the playing with a line, like a melody played on a saxophone.

I'm organizing my drawings into multilayered relational nets. Breaks and gaps are just as important. White wall/space is part of the work. The sheets discolour each other, reach into each other, imperceptibly undergo changes, borrow moods, make contact.

I'm not looking for finished stories, but for an exchange, a conversation about experiences, perceptions, and observations as regards content, between the drawings and the viewer. The installations of drawings represent an experimental order of fields of reference, a kind of cluster.

—Silvia Bächli; translated by Udo Breger

* * *

Not with spectacular breaks, but with a high continuity in its openness, Silvia Bächli expands the spectrum of drawing and develops new forms of presentation. Starting out from small observations of daily life or from experiences during the work process itself, she produces many small sheets that appear to be of great immediacy. Every single sheet—for the time being a singular picture—has in itself a high implicitness, as if it had been there even before it started to exist. No construction or gesture reveals the artist's proceedings. One sheet seems to formulate a picture-thought so precisely—condensed and at the same time so enfolding—that there is no room left for discursive additions. Its wordless thoughts have neither been sought for nor found, but are simply occurring in the moment.

But Silvia Bächli has also repeatedly been concerned with a conscious design of contexts. In the beginning of the 1980s, the singular drawings were collected in books and thus provided a linear reading. After 1984, the single sheets were compiled into groups to

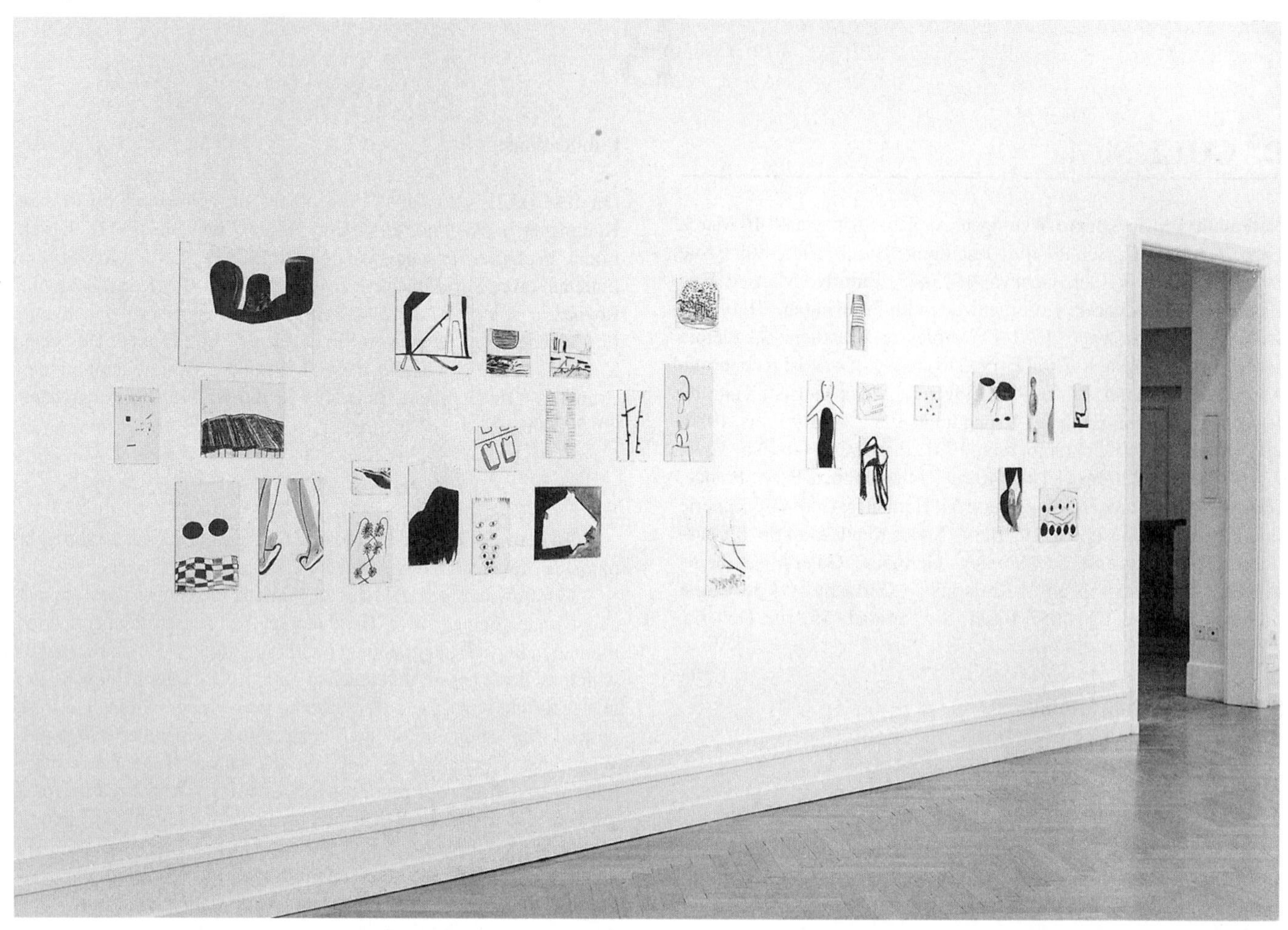

Silvia Bächli: *Ammassalik,* 15 parts, 1995–96, *O.T,* 9 parts, 1995, *hüte,* 1991, displayed in Kunsthalle, Bern, 1996. ©Silvia Bächli, courtesy of Galerie Vera Munro, Hamburg.

form picture installations. The defined constellation seems to rid the drawings of some of their own fleetingness. Through the precise specification of arrangement and the distances between the single sheets, specific associations were suggested without formulating them in an exclusive way. The combination of different formats and techniques (water color, coal, chalk, gouache) open the constellations further and make them more complex in their inner relations, their confrontations. The precision with which Silvia Bächli includes the empty spaces between the sheets opens up infinite cognitive horizons. The winding gaze can create a variety of associative connections in the open topography of the installation. The gaze moves between the sheets with floating attention, which, almost film-like, can change from focusing on a detail to the whole and further to zoom on to a small group of motifs. The wandering gaze is shown a sequence of stills in changing settings without a linear narration. Single picture conceptions, however, can be named: the blatant focusing, laconic omissions, recesses, slight displacements, overexpansions, or hybrid doublings.

Since 1994, photographs occasionally appear in the picture constellations, on equal footing with the drawings. The imagination of precise picture-thoughts tempts the viewer to compare single forms, lines, or motifs in the flow of the association in an attempt to create an order out of the artistic repertoire. At the exhibition in the Kunsthalle Bern in 1996, single families of drawings were placed on tables, for the first time following criteria of contextual and formal relationships: body parts, clothes, vast empty landscapes, net-like entangled plants, a lengthily stretched line, vibrating spots, microorganisms—the list of themes is open-ended. All order remains precarious, however, because each motif initiates an uncontrollable series of inner pictures, which rid these motifs of fixed attributions. But tables also allow alternative groupings. The mobility between the chosen orders differentiates meanings; the validity of each order is at the same time put into perspective by the next. A self-evident continuation of this work are tables presenting relations of drawings, her own or found photographs, or copies

The large-sized pictures of floral forms, appearing since 1998, connect single efflorescences in a netting, which are both self-evident and imaginary and thus play around linear perceptions. Attempting to describe one of these sheets reveals a surprising discontinuity of motifs, when just a second ago an order appeared to be unmistakably present. Although the presentation omits vague hints and rather with only a few lines creates a distinct form, rhythmic and contrasting, our memory is not granted a constant picture. Even a motif that has long been apparent can abruptly become fleeting. Its sensuality appears bodyless and the differentiated inner structure takes away our memory's focus point. Because of this late blurriness, and not because of their lack of color, the pictures resemble shadows of familiar things. Besides the fixed picture works, Silvia Bächli has created seven temporary shadow installations in different rooms. Models placed on the floor throw their shadows in the light of precisely installed light sources and thus create an enfolding picture on the walls.

The core of this constantly expanding work is still the single drawings, which in scattered moments appear like events in order to take on and generate further, deepened, and more complex meanings. The white piece of paper is more an element than a carrier of the drawing, working in, with, and against it. The greater number of drawings have been drawn in black on white and the variations are concentrated on lines, structures, and different surface designs. In the meantime, the first polychrome sheets have been created, where the clash of contrasting color fields reaches a similarly unstable clarity.

The drawing, one of the oldest media, reaches its current potential under Silvia Bächli: it becomes a form to read the world. The immediacy of the realization, which shapes this medium like no other, corresponds to an accelerated way of living that leans towards a simultaneous expression. Bächli's drawings confront a culture which is frantically collecting data so as to be up-to-date. But data—the given—at the same time always stands in contrast to the possible. By being allowed to forget themselves, the drawings are withdrawn from the world of available information as well as withdrawn from the state of being informed. With each sheet, there is a growth of potential of what cannot be remembered, through which the cognition between one blink and the next becomes an event. Each drawing offers the possibility of a just now already missing picture.

—Hans Rudolf Reust

BACON, Francis

Nationality: British. **Born:** Dublin, Ireland, 28 October 1909 of English parents. **Education:** Mainly self-taught in art, from 1927. **Military Service:** Served in Civil Defence Corps, London 1942–45. **Career:** Worked in an office, London 1925; visited Berlin and Paris, 1926- 27; worked as an interior decorator, London 1928–31. Independent painter, London 1929–46, Monte Carlo, 1946–50 and again in London since 1950; study-travels in South Africa 1950, in Italy 1954, with Peter Lacey in Tangier, 1956–59; visited New York and Rome, 1968; death of friend and model George Dyer, in Paris, 1971. **Awards:** Painting Prize, *Carnegie International,* Pittsburgh, 1966; Rubenspreis, Siegen, West Germany 1967. **Agent:** Marlborough Fine Art, London. **Died:** Of heart failure caused by asthma, in Madrid, Spain, 28 April 1992.

Individual Exhibitions:

1930 Bacon Studio, London (with Roy Le Maistre)
1934 Transition Gallery, London
1949 Hanover Gallery, London
1950 Hanover Gallery, London
1951 Hanover Gallery, London
1952 Hanover Gallery, London
1953 Durlacher Gallery, New York
Beaux-Arts Gallery, London
1954 Hanover Gallery, London
1955 Institute of Contemporary Arts, London
Hanover Gallery, London (with William Scott and Graham Sutherland)
1957 Galerie Rive Droite, Paris
Hanover Gallery, London
1958 Galleria Galatea, Turin, Italy (travelled to the Galleria dell'Ariete, Milan and the Galleria dell'Obelisco, Rome)
Victoria Art Gallery, Bath, Avon (with Matthew Smith and Victor Pasmore; toured Britain)
1959 Richard Feigen Gallery, Chicago
British section, at the *5th Bienal,* Sao Paulo
Hanover Gallery, London
1960 Marlborough Fine Art, London
University of California at Los Angeles (with Hyman Bloom)
1961 University of Nottingham
1962 Galleria Galatea, Milan
Tate Gallery, London (travelled to Mannheim, Turin and Zurich)
1963 Galleria Il Centro, Naples (with Graham Sutherland)
Galleria La Loggia, Bologna (with Graham Sutherland)
Granville Gallery, New York
Marlborough Fine Art, London
Guggenheim Museum, New York (travelled to Art Institute of Chicago, and the Houston Contemporary Arts Association)
1965 Kunsthalle, Hamburg (travelled to the Moderna Museet, Stockholm, and the Museum of Modern Art, Dublin)
Marlborough Fine Art, London
1966 Galleria Toninelli, Milan
Galerie Maeght, Paris (travelled to Marlborough Fine Art, London)
1967 Oberes Schloss, Siegen, West Germany
1968 Marlborough-Gerson Gallery, New York
1970 Galleria Galatea, Turin
1971 Grand Palais, Paris (travelled to the Kunsthalle, Dusseldorf)
1972 Galleria del Milione, Milan
1975 Metropolitan Museum of Art, New York
Marlborough Galerie, Zurich
1976 Musée Cantini, Marseilles
1977 Galerie Claude Bernard, Paris
Museo de Arte Moderna, Mexico City (travelled to the Museo de Arte Contemporaneo, Caracas)
1978 Fundación Juan March, Madrid (travelled to the Fundación Joan Miró, Barcelona)
1980 Marlborough Gallery, New York
Stadtische Kunsthalle, Mannheim
1983 National Museum of Modern Art, Tokyo (travelled to Kyoto and Nagoya)
Marlborough Fine Art, London
1984 Galerie Maeght/Lelong, Paris
Marlborough Gallery, New York
1985 Marlborough Fine Art, London
Tate Gallery, London (travelled to Stuttgart and West Berlin)
1987 Marlborough Gallery, New York
Galerie Beyeler, Basel
Galerie Lelong, Paris
1988 Central House of the Union of Artists, Moscow

Francis Bacon with his painting *Triptych 1976* at the Galerie Georges Bernard, Paris, 1975. Hulton-Deutsch Collection/Corbis ©2001 Estate of Francis Bacon/ Artists Rights Society (ARS), New York.

1990 *Francis Bacon,* Tate Gallery Liverpool (catalog)
Francis Bacon, Hirshhorn Museum and Sculpture Garden, Washington, D.C. (traveling exhibition) (catalog)
Francis Bacon: Paintings Since 1944, Tate Gallery Liverpool (catalog)

1993 *Francis Bacon 1909–1992: Small Portrait Studies,* Marloborough Fine Art, London (catalog)
Francis Bacon, Museo d'Arte Moderna, Lugano (catalog)
Francis Bacon: Imaginable, Museo Correr, Venice (catalog)

1996 Centre Georges Pompidou, Paris (retrospective)
Francis Bacon, Haus der Kunst, Munich, Germany

1997 *Bacon: Triptych '71,* Kunst-Station Sankt Peter Koln, Cologne (catalog)

1998 *Francis Bacon: The Human Body,* Hayward Gallery, South Bank, London (catalog)
Francis Bacon, Louisiana Museum of Modern Art, Humlebaek, Denmark

1999 *Francis Bacon: Working on Paper,* Tate Gallery, London (catalog)
Francis Bacon: A Retrospective, Yale Center for British Art, New Haven

2000 *The Barry Joule Archive: Works Attributed to Francis Bacon,* Irish Museum of Modern Art, Dublin
Francis Bacon: The Posthumous Canvases, Galerie Lelong, Paris
Francis Bacon: Ten Years On—Popes and Others, Galerie Lelong, Paris
Hugh Lane Gallery, Dublin

Selected Group Exhibitions:

1937 *Young British Painters,* Agnew Gallery, London

1945 *Recent Paintings: Bacon/Hodgkins/Moore/Smith/ Sutherland,* Lefevre Gallery, London

1973 *Cuatro Maestros Contemporaneos: Giacometti, Dubuffet, De Kooning, Bacon,* Museo de Bellas Artes, Caracas (travelled to Sao Paulo and Rio de Janeiro)

1977 *Englische Kunst der Gegenwart,* Kunstlerhaus, Bregenz, Austria

Francis Bacon: *Portrait of George Dyer,* 1967–68. ©2001 Estate of Francis Bacon/Artists Rights Society (ARS), NY.

1981 *A New Spirit in Painting,* Royal Academy of Art, London
1983 *Modern Art in the West,* Metropolitan Museum, Tokyo
1985 *Painterly Visions 1940–85,* Guggenheim Museum, New York
1987 *A School of London,* Kunstnernes Hus, Oslo (travelled to Copenhagen, Venice and Dusseldorf)
1990 *Selections from the Beatrice and Philip Gersh Collection,* Museum of Modern Art, Los Angeles (catalog)
1991 *From Bacon to Now: The Outsider in British Figuration,* Palazzo Vecchio, Florence (catalog)
The Transformation of Appearance: Andrews, Auerbach, Bacon, Freud, Kossoff, Sainsbury Centre for the Visual Arts, University of East Anglia, Norwich (catalog)
1992 *British Figurative Painting of the 20th Century,* Israel Museum, Jerusalem (catalog)
1993 *1993 Venice Biennale,* Italy
Seven British Painters: Selected Masters of Post-War British Art, Marlborough Fine Art, London (catalog)
Directions in Modernism: The Beyeler Collection, Nationalgalerie, Staatliche Museen Preussischer Kulturbesitz, Berlin (catalog)
1995 Fondation Maeght, St. Paul de Vence, France
Surrealism: Dream of Centuries, Galerie Beyeler, Basle (catalog)
From London, Scottish National Gallery, Edinburgh (catalog)
1996 *Velázquez and Bacon: Paintings of Popes,* National Gallery, London
Negotiation Rapture: The Power of Art to Transform Lives, Museum of Contemporary Art, Chicago
Trapping Appearance: Portraits by Francis Bacon and Alberto Giacometti from the Robert and Lisa Sainsbury Collection, Sainsbury Centre for Visual Arts, University of East Anglia, Norwich, England
1998 *Francis Bacon, Louise Bourgeois, and Franz Xaver Messerschmidt,* Cheim & Read, New York
The Jacqueline Delubac Collection: From Manet to Bacon, Musee des Beaux-Arts, Lyons, France
Art Treasures from England: The Regional Collections, Royal Academy of Arts, London (catalog)
1999 *The School of London from Bacon to Bevan,* Fondation Dina Vierny-Musee Maillol, Paris (catalog)
2000 *Art in the Labyrinths of the Intimate: From Munch to Boltanski,* Galleria d'Arte Moderna, Bologna, Italy

Collections:

Tate Gallery, London; Ulster Museum, Belfast; Centre Georges Pompidou, Paris; Nationalgalerie, West Berlin; Musée des Beaux-Arts, Brussels; Museum of Modern Art, New York; Guggenheim Museum, New York; Art Institute of Chicago; National Gallery of Canada, Ottawa; National Gallery of Australia, Canberra.

Publications:

By BACON: Books—*The Artist Observed: 28 Interviews with Contemporary Artists* by John Gruen, Chicago 1991; *Francis Bacon: In Conversation with Michael Archimbaud,* London 1993; *Bacon: Portraits and Self-Portraits,* with introduction by Milan Kundera and essay by France Borel, London 1996. **Articles**—interview with David Sylvester in *Modern Painters* (London), vol. 5, no. 2, Summer 1992; interview with Jacques Saraben in *Art Press,* no. 215, July-August 1996.

On BACON: Books—*Art Now* by Herbert Read, London 1933; *Francis Bacon,* exhibition catalog, with text by M. Clarac Serou, London 1955; *Francis Bacon,* exhibition catalog, with text by Helen Lessore, Nottingham 1961; *Francis Bacon,* exhibition catalog, with text by John Rothenstein, London 1962; *Francis Bacon,* exhibition catalog, with texts by Thomas Messer and Lawrence Alloway, New York 1963; *The Masters: Francis Bacon* by John Rothenstein, London and Milan 1963, Paris 1967; *Francis Bacon* (catalog raisonne) by John Rothenstein and Ronald Alley, London 1964; *Francis Bacon* by John Russell, London, Paris and Berlin 1971; *Francis Bacon,* exhibition catalog, with text by Michel Leiris, Paris 1971; *The Age of the Avant-Garde: An Art Chronicle of 1956–1972* by Hilton Kramer, New York and London 1974; *Interviews with Francis Bacon* by David Sylvester, London and New York 1975; *Francis Bacon* by Lorenza Trucchi, Milan and New York 1975, London 1976, rev. ed. Milan 1984; *Francis Bacon: Logique de la Sensation* by Gilles Deleuze, Paris 1981, 1984; *Francis Bacon: Full Face and in Profile* by Michel Leiris, London, New York, Paris and Munich 1983;

Francis Bacon by Dawn Ades and Andrew Forge, London and Berlin 1985; *Francis Bacon: Vier Studien zu einem Portrait* by Wieland Schmied, Berlin 1985; *Francis Bacon: Kreuzigung* by Jorg Zimmermann, Frankfurt 1986; *Francis Bacon* by Hugh Davies and Sally Yard, New York 1986; *Francis Bacon and the Loss of Self* by Ernst Van Alphen, London 1993; *Francis Bacon* by John Russell, London 1993; *Francis Bacon: Study for Portrait of van Gogh* by Bruce Bernard, London 1994; *Bacon,* edited by Jose Maria Faerna, Dresden 1995; *Francis Bacon: ''Taking Reality by Surprise''* by Christophe Domino, London 1997. **Articles—**''Francis Bacon at 80'' by Peter Jenkins in *Modern Painters* (London), vol. 2, no. 4, Winter 1989–1990; ''In Francis Bacon's Studio'' by Michael Peppiatt in *Art International,* no. 8, Autumn 1989; ''Francis Bacon with Interview: 5 Article Special Section'' in *Art International,* no. 8, Autumn 1989; ''The Body Unbound: The Postmodern Aesthetics of Francis Bacon'' by Ernst Van Alphen in *Word and Image,* vol. 7, no. 1, January-March 1991; ''Hommage à Francis Bacon'' by Eddy Batache in *Connaissance des Arts,* no. 484, June 1992; ''Bacon's Course'' by David Sylvester in *Modern Painters* (London), vol. 6, no. 2, Summer 1993; ''Francis Bacon in 1930: An Early Exhibition Rediscovered'' by Richard Shone in *Burlington Magazine* (London), vol. 138, no. 1117, April 1996; ''A Nuisance Named Bacon: Book Excerpt'' in *Cimaise,* vol. 43, July/August 1996; ''Francis Bacon: Introduction'' by Steingrim Laursen in *Louisiana Revy,* vol. 38, no. 2, January 1998; ''Fatum as Theme and Method in the Work of Francis Bacon'' by John G. Hatch in *Artibus et Historiae,* vol. 19, no. 37, 1998; ''Bacon: A Personal Memoir: Interview with Barry Joule'' in *Art Review* (London), vol. 51, December 1998/January 1999; ''Francis Bacon: The King of Pain'' by John W. Whitehead in *Gadfly* (Charlottesville, Virginia), June 1999. **Films—***Love Is the Devil* by John Maybury, 1999.

* * *

The two biggest names Britain has bestowed upon the contemporary art world are Moore and Bacon. Moore has moved steadily and unhesitatingly forward in world esteem, but Francis Bacon, ever since Herbert Read reproduced his ''Crucifixion'' (1933) in the first issue of *Art Now,* has shot up and, in recent years, with meteoric velocity.

Bacon, from being a one-time designer of ''modern furniture'' (actually reviewed in the *Studio* magazine, 1930), proved himself in 1966 one of the only British artists able in those days to beat Parisian chauvinism. Against all forecasts by experienced pundits his exhibition at the Galerie Maeght was a sell-out. But by then he had already made his reputation in Italy, the U.S., Brazil, Germany, Sweden, Switzerland and Ireland. The following year brought him the coveted Rubens International Prize.

Contemporary Bacon began 30 years ago. It was at that point that his style became identifiably his own. Since then he has passed through a number of specific phases and enthusiasms. Once he had overcome his fascination for the umbrella (although it certainly reoccurred), he turned to other categories like the series of near-monochrome business men (in expensive if shadowy suits), his portraits of the popes at peace or screaming, the oil collection of pictures he made based upon studies by the photographic pioneer Muybridge, the Van Gogh self-portraits, animals and sphynxes—especially the lonely dog caught in some kind of proto-Chirico piazza, and so on to the nudes like butchers' cadavers splayed or jumbled up after they have been defrozen and have been taken off the hook. Hypodermics, narcotics, addicts, all the sublife of the seedy 60s.

How is Bacon now, compared with then?

During all this time when he has been establishing a world reputation, his style became steady and consistent, but he also acquired a kind of personal painterly finesse which is particularly evident in the portraits (especially the portrait studies). The brushstrokes in these display a kind of skilful instantaneous ease remote from the tortured and heavy impasto that clad many of his earlier paintings. It is as if the food has been cooked with greater expertise and experience, but has the strange exoticism of the meal lived up to the mysterious quality of those in the past? The world seems to think so. There will be many more Bacon Crucifixions (although nowadays they seem to spread into enormous triptychs), but will they ever revive the visual shriek of the one that Herbert Read picked to illustrate in *Art Now* more than 45 years ago?

—Sheldon Williams

Francis Bacon's work continued to explore the arenas of horror and the complexities of the human psyche until his death in 1992. His paintings became larger in the late 1960s, and this notion of working on a grand scale gave increased potency to the images he created in the 1980s. The triptych form which he embraced in the late 1960s and early 1970s became an almost exclusive theme for Bacon in the last decade of his life. Huge panels displayed side by side further emphasized the religious motifs in his work. The visceral style of Bacon's pieces continued to evolve as he created work which was at once confrontational and disturbing.

Bacon's paintings became ever more personal as he aged. His 1984 triptych *Three Studies for a Portrait of John Edwards* paid homage to his model and companion of the previous decade. In the early 1970s, Bacon had created a similar work upon the death of George Dyer, his model and partner of several years. The obsession with self-exploration and the human body continued throughout Bacon's career. In 1985, he painted a massive triptych which illustrated his continuing quest to depict the self, *Study for Self-Portrait.* London's Tate Gallery honored Bacon with a retrospective that year. In 1988, Bacon returned to his famous 1944 triptych, *Three Studies for Figures at the Base of the Crucifixion,* and painted a second version of the work. A comparison of the two shows the aging artist working in a less grotesque, but still quite hallucinatory, manner. In both works, the figures are elongated, their faces featureless save the mouths and teeth, but in the later work, these creatures occupy less space on the canvas. This is particularly interesting in that the later work is also nearly twice the size of the original study. The background field is far more moody in the 1988 version as well, the reds now the color of blood and dappled with areas of black. Bacon's final years found him reexamining the themes of his earlier work from the perspective acquired from a long life.

—Tammy A. Kinsey

BAJ, Enrico

Nationality: Italian. **Born:** Milan, 31 October 1924. **Education:** Attended schools in Milan and Geneva; studied medicine and law, 1942–48; painting, at the Accademia di Brera, 1945–48. **Family:** Married Gigliola Olivieri in 1954; daughter; Lucilla; married Roberta

Enrico Baj, *The Volcan,* 1990. ©Enrico Baj.

Cerini de Castegnate in 1966; children: Angelo, Andrea, Pietro and Marianna. **Career:** Independent painter, writer and graphic artist, since 1948. Founder-member, with Sergio Dangelo, Nuclear Art Movement, Milan, 1951; founder, with Asger Jorn, International Movement for an Imaginary Bauhaus, Albissola, Italy, 1953; founder-editor, with Sergio Dangelo, *Il Gesto* magazine, Milan, 1955–1959; produced first collages and assemblages, Milan, 1956; associated with the Nouveau Realiste group, Paris, 1959; founder, with Raymond Queneau, Institute of Pataphysics, Milan, 1963; friendly with Max Ernst, Marcel Duchamp and André Breton, Paris, 1963–66. **Agent:** Studio Marconi, Milan. **Address:** Via delle Ville 18, 21029 Vergiate, Italy.

Individual Exhibitions:

1951 Galleria San Fedele, Milan (with Sergio Dangelo)
1956 Kunstkredsen, Copenhagen
1957 Gallery One, London
1958 Galleria Gruppo, Bergamo (with Lucio Fontana and Piero Manzoni)
Galerie Daniel Cordier, Paris
1959 Gallery One, London
Galerie Rive Gauche, Paris
1960 Galleria del Naviglio, Milan
1961 Galerie Raymond Cordier, Paris
Galleria Schwarz, Milan
1962 Sevenarts Gallery, London
Galerie Berggruen, Paris
1963 Cordier and Ekstrom Gallery, New York
1964 Galerie Alice Pauli, Lausanne
Palazzo Reale, Milan
1965 Galerie Pierre, Stockholm
Costello Spagnolo, L'Aquila, Italy
Galerie Berggruen, Paris
1966 Galleria Odyssia, Rome
Arts Club of Chicago
1967 Studio Marconi, Milan
Gemeentemuseum, The Hague
Museum voor Schone Kunsten, Ghent
1969 Studio Marconi, Milan
Galerie Creuzevault, Paris
1970 Studio Condotti, Rome
Galerie Georges Moos, Geneva
1971 Musee de l'Athenée, Geneva
Palazzo Grassi, Venice
Museum of Contemporary Art, Chicago
1973 Museum Boymans-van-Beuningen, Rotterdam
Moderna Museet, Stockholm
Kunsthalle, Dusseldorf
1974 Koninklijk Museum voor Schone Kunsten, Antwerp
Palazzo Reale, Milan (travelled to the Kunsthalle, Dusseldorf, and the Palais des Beaux-Arts, Brussels)
Musée d'Art et d'Histoire, Cabinet des Estampes, Geneva
Galerie Spectrum, Vienna
1975 Studio Marconi, Milan
Centre Design, Lugano, Switzerland
Galerie Christel, Helsinki
1976 Arras Gallery, New York
Arte Contacto, Caracas
Castello Sforzesco, Milan
1977 Galerie Actu-Art, Helsingor, Denmark
Palazzo dei Diamanti, Ferrara, Italy
1978 Arras Gallery, New York
Indianapolis Museum of Art
Palais de l'Europe, Menton, France
1979 Studio Marconi, Milan
Dartmouth College, Hanover, New Hampshire
1980 Galerie l'Ile de France, Paris
1981 Studio Marconi, Milan
1982 Palazzo della Regione, Mantua, Italy
1983 Studio Marconi, Milan
1985 Center of Fine Art, Miami, Florida
Castello di Bard, Val d'Aosta, Italy
1987 Palazzo Bellini, Comacchio, Italy
1988 Villa Borbone, Viareggio
1990 Musei Civici, Varese
Rattner Gallery, Chicago
Galerie Beaubourg, Paris
1991 Studio Marconi, Milan
Mairsa del Re, New York
1992 Museum voor Moderne Kunst, Ostende, Belgium
1993 Musei di Locarno, Italy
1994 Castello di Lerici
Castello di Portovenere
Fondation Coprim, Paris
1995 Banca Commerciale Italiana, Milan
1997 Galleria Marconi, Milan
1998 Galerie Ronny van de Velde, Antwerpen
MAMAC (Musée), Nice

1999 Galerie Beauborg, Paris
2000 Musée des Beaux Arts, Chartres

Selected Group Exhibitions:

1961 *The Art of Assemblage,* Museum of Modern Art, New York
1962 *Art Since 1950,* World's Fair, Seattle
1964 *Nieuwe Realisten,* Gemeentemuseum, The Hague
1965 *Exposition internationale du surréalism,* Paris
1970 *Surrealism?* Moderna Museet, Stockholm
1982 *Italian Art,* Hayward Gallery, London
1984 *Primitivism in 20th Century Art,* Museum of Modern Art, New York
1989 *Baj, Fontana, Manzoni,* Marisa del Re Gallery, New York
1991 *André Breton: La beauté sera convulsive,* Centre Pompidou, Paris
1992 *Automatismos Parallelos,* Sala de la Communitad, Madrid
1996 *Face á l'histoire,* Centre Georges Pompidou, Paris
1997 *Materiali Anomali,* Galleria d'Arte Moderna, Bologna
Pataphysics, Observatory Museum, Grahamstown, and Gertrude Posel Gallery, Johannesburg
The Pop '60: Transatlantic Crossing, Centro Cultural de Belém, Lisbon
Ecce Ubu, Maison du Spectacle La Bellone, Brussels
1998 *Il Movimento Nucleare,* Palasso Sertoli, Palasso Pretorio, and Palazzo Martinengo, Sondrio
1999 *Surrealism: Two Private Eyes,* Guggenheim Museum, New York
World Artists at the Millennium, United Nations, New York

Collections:

Centre Georges Pompidou, Paris; National Gallery of Australia, Sydney; Stedelijk Museum, Amsterdam; Moderna Museet, Stockholm; Museum des 20. Jahrhunderts, Vienna; Tate Gallery, London; Lodz Museum, Poland; Galleria d'Arte Moderná, Milan; Museum of Contemporary Art, Chicago; National Gallery, Washington, D.C.; Museum of Modern Art, New York; Musée d'Art et d'Histoire, Geneva; Skopie Museum, Skopie; Galleria Nazionale d'Arte Moderna, Bologna.

Publications:

By BAJ: Books—*Manifeste de la peinture nucleaire,* with Sergio Dangelo, Brussels 1952; *Contro lo stile,* with others, Milan 1957; *Arte interplanetaria,* with others, Planeta Terra, Italy 1959; *Manifeste de Naples,* with others, Naples 1959; *A Proposito de coesistenza e modificazione,* Naples 1959; *Pittura e realtà,* Milan 1959; *Alternativi attuali,* exhibition catalog, L'Aquila, Italy 1962; *Autodame,* Bologna 1980; *Patafisica,* Milan 1982; *Automitobiografia,* Milan 1983; *Impariamo la pittura,* Milan 1985; *Cose, fatti, persone,* Milan 1988; *Baj-Jorn lettres,* Musée de Saint Etienne 1989; *Cose dell'altro mondo,* Milan 1990; *Ecologia dell'arte,* Milan 1990; *Realtà e fantasia* (with Renato Guttuso), Milan 1986; *Che cosa è la patafisica,* Salorino, 1994; *Kiss Me, I'm Italian,* Hamburg, 1997; *Scritti sull'arte,* Bertiolo (Italy), 1997. **Articles**—''Pop Napoli'' in *Marcatre* (Milan), June 1965; ''Milano Caves'' in *Marcatre* (Milan), December 1965; ''La Vita e l'Uomo'' in *Del Pezzo,* exhibition catalog, Milan 1966; ''Parigi: FON 2104'' in *Marcatre* (Milan), April 1966; ''Ho visto Dio'' in *Marcatre* (Milan), June 1966; ''L'affaire des Generaux'' in *L'Ultimo dei Generali,* Italy 1968; ''Deflorando'' in *Guido Biasi,* exhibition catalog, Turin 1969; ''L'Australia ha sete'' in *Corriere della Sera* (Milan), May 1969; ''Da Breton alla Luna'' in *Corriere della Sera* (Milan), August 1969; ''Baj da San Francisco'' in *Flash Art* (Milan), no. 13, 1969; ''Lattuga a Porno'' in *Corriere della Sera* (Milan), October 1970; ''Buzzati sexpittore'' in *Dino Buzzati: Un Caso a Porte,* Rome, 1971; ''Milano Cinquanta'' in *Milano 70 / 70 Un Secolo d'Arte,* Milan 1972; ''Sonnenstern'' in *Multiplicata Internationale,* Stockholm and Zurich 1972; ''Venne la Crisi e fu la Catastrofe'' in *Corriere della Sera* (Milan), 25 May 1975; ''Signorno all Autoritarismo'' in *Doppiovu* (Milan), December 1976; ''Pompidou chez Baj: Baj chez Pompidou'' in *La Nuova Rivista Europea* (Trento, Italy), September / October 1977; ''Baj on Baj,'' interview with Ellen Wardwell Lee in *Baj,* exhibition catalog, by Joanne Muller Kuebler, Indianapolis 1978; ''Baudrillard, il gioco dell'incertezza,'' in *Corriere della Sera* (Milan), August 2000.

On BAJ: Books—*Los mueblos de Enrico Baj* by Octavio Paz, Mexico City 1961; *Le meubles de Baj* by Raymond Queneau, Paris 1962; *Baj* by Jan van der Marck, 1962; *Baj: Catalog de l'Oeuver et des Multiples,* 2 vols., by Jean Petit, Geneva 1970, 1974; *Baj* by Alain Jouffroy, Paris 1972; *Catalogo Generale Bolaffi Opere di Baj* by Enrico Crispolti, Turin 1973; *Enrico Baj, Dada Impressionist* by Herbert Lust, Turin 1973; *Enrico Baj, Apocalisse,* edited by Umberto Eco, Milan 1979; *Enrico Baj* by Jean Baudrillard, Paris 1980; *Testa a Testa* by Umberto Eco, Padua 1980; *Baj, dal generale al particolare* by Italo Calvino, Gerard G. Lemaire and Jan van der Marck, Milan 1985; *Baj: Graphic works—catalog raisonné,* edited by Roberto Sanesi and Jan van der Marck, Milan 1986; *Baj, nostalgia del futuro* by J. Baudrillard, P. Bellasi and others, Milan 1987; *Baj: Disegni* by Dan Cameron, Milan 1989; *Transparence du kitsch* by Jean Baudrillard, Paris 1990; *The Garden of Delights,* with texts by Baudrillard, Eco, and Donald Kuspit, New York 1992; *Baj and Kostabi,* with texts by Pierre Restany and Roberto Sanesi, Milan 1992; *Baj chez Proust* by Alain Jouffroy and Silvia Pegoraro, Paris, 2000; *Enrico Baj: Frammento & Frammento,* with text by Silvia Pegoraro, Luciano Caprile, Alan Jones, and Michel Mafesoli, Castelbasso, 2000.

*

On other occasions, I have put forward a distinction between art-as-invention, i.e. art capable of affecting the current vision of things, and art-as-representation—which is to say, art which simply records and is more or less descriptive or analytical. At the ultimate level of ignominy is to be found commemorative art, seen without question in the art so dear to Stalin and Hitler, and at the Museum of Modern Art when engaged in the defence of Campbell's Soup or Coca-Cola. Celebrative art is art that does not content itself with merely representing power or is extreme in homogenising degenerations, but even glorifies with marble monuments and kitsch imagery the commandant-bosses and / or the flavour of the month—be it neon lights, cartoons and plastic packages or any of the variety of junk with which we identify our finer feelings.

Today, more than ever, in our landscape made of conditioned and computerised responses, art as invention anticipates the new systems of communication in new visual languages capable of confronting an all-embracing robotization.

The spaces of the gallery Studio Marconi in Milan lend themselves to this type of research. There, space, which is everything for the painter, allows the exhibition of large canvases and the organization of the exhibit as the manifestation of different states of mind. I do have a system for filling such spaces—in fact, for some time I returned wholeheartedly to the technique of the 'fifties: action painting, dripping, gesture and sign. These methods of mine between 1951 and 1959 were constrained within the walls of small (not to say minimal) studio spaces in Milan; the constraints of the place inhibited my gesture and my dance around the canvas placed on the floor.

Living now in the countryside and the open air, I have recovered a completely different dimension. Onto a fine green meadow—a green I've always loved—I lay out a fresh canvas (which looks like an airport runway) and there my action begins, my own way of making pictures, which is the ultimate in the exultation, continuation and mega-inflation of painting *au plein air.* Man must return to nature. Never again should he fight it, if he is to survive! This is the message of Georgescu Roegen and the message of the hope of a solar civilization. A new message and a new hope—new because they are given to us in highly philosophical and scientific terms, and not just to satisfy a naturalistic urge. At times, I work only with black on a white canvas, and I retrieve signs, symbols and scribbles reminiscent of the famous Rorschach test. At other times, I have abandoned black to give myself over to the manic and overwhelming joy of colour, I grind it, splash it, dilute it with turpentine and various solvents, or allow it to coagulate in the sun until concentrated, stringy and viscous to the touch before using it to create contrasts with other chromatic dilutions. Sometimes, I work with a kind of abstract drawing or pointillism, attracting me into a vacuum made up of a thousand colours. On other occasions, mindful of the cultural revolution of May 1968, when everybody spraypainted on walls the slogan of his own political failures, I try to produce ancestral languages and figures precisely in spraypaint, a sign language similar to the man of Altamira. The feelings we experience, the messages we intercept, the materials at our disposal are by now extremely varied, manifold and often contradictory, so that my exhibition will include a dual series of watercolours and drawings. The watercolours are reminiscent of a kind of cubo-futurism I practised at the time of my Manifesto for Static Futurism. Pastel drawings, on the other hand, emerged together with my use of the big spray green canvases. Finally, other canvases incorporate the symbolic transposition of bits and pieces of wood collected off the ground during the construction of my new studio.

Such wooden fragments, due to their humble, ephemeral and weathered look, have a charge which I would define as archaeological. They imply an ancient discourse redolent of the gesture of the carpenter's or bricklayer's art. Effectively, our houses are already archaeological. We live in archaeology as is demonstrated by the continual restoration of old farmhouses and decaying city centres. Today, the streets where brothels operated, the Fossati cinema building and the industrial premises are precious relics that we should clean up and restore.

Some of the canvases with wooden fragments are used to represent my family, whereas another is freely inspired by Pythaogras' theorem. One is a study for Voltaire's Micromegas. The famous conversation between the inhabitants of Sirio and Saturno reverberates in my latest works, as in the Citta del Sole for which I am indebted to another great Utopianist (T. Campanella).

"Megalizzazione" and "miniaturizzazione" face one another in everyday life. It should not be difficult to understand that, faced with grand general projects (and their frequent failure), we opt for the cure of the particular.

—Enrico Baj

* * *

What we might regard as a new iconology, combining the influence of popular and of cultured iconology and reviving the mytho-poetical qualities of present-day man, has always been present in Enrico Baj's work. Ever since 1951—the time of the *Movimento Nucleare,* of which he was a member—Baj has understood the importance of those mocking creatures that fill the popular horizon and in the end can be heard breathing within the "cultured" painting, and he has press-ganged them into his paintings and assemblages. Thus we have seen the first clumsy sketches of the "ultrabodies" or of the flying saucers, and after them those of the Generals and the Dames: a whole gallery teeming with people and events which are beginning to be organized and which the artist has used as a background against which to compose his pictures.

In Baj's case, in addition to the readymade material constituted by the *objet trouve,* used just as it is as an emotional and fanciful starting point, there is always the desire to give life to the shapeless, to find the right relationship between forms and colours. Even since his first grotesque drawings, the artist has been able to combine his sense of humour with his feeling for experiment, his narrative ability with his eagerness for research into materials; thus he has worked with stained cloth from mattresses or tapestries, for use as background to his "monsters"; he has borrowed our grandfathers' looking-glasses, but in order to create an ambiguous medium that would reflect the image of the past and that of the future together.

While almost all American and British pop art used "found objects" as symbols of everyday life, Baj took a completely opposite line. The wide use he made of old, out-of-date materials, of old 19th-century trimmings, of ancient medals, of our great-grandparents' ribbons and lace, tells us how the artist has pointed out the importance of creating a "kingdom of memory," haunted by the ghosts of an age already far away from us but in which we can still recognize our origins. When Baj invented his "Dames" and "Generals," the Pop adventure was still a long way off; it was too easy, later, to lump his pictures together with those of other masters of United States pop.

If, then, we want to analyse the signs and symbols in some of Baj's figures and collages, we must notice the subtle metaphorical game that he plays with the heteroclitic materials he uses; we must notice that it is no accident that the discs he uses for eyes are buttons, the nipples are skittles, the sex organs are rough brushes.

There are too many examples to quote here, but they show us how there nearly always exists in these works a Concept side by side with an Object; a linguistic search (for a visual-verbal metaphor) side by side with a plastic search. And it is this that, in the last years, has enabled Baj to tackle the great socio-political themes, depicted in some of his gigantic works like "Watergate," "The Anarchic Pinelli" and "The Apocalypse," in which the same humorous elements from the past have been used for a more exacting, more austere purpose: to put in relief the sins of our civilization and draw attention to the threats that supreme political power can exert on present and future society.

—Gillo Dorfles

BALDESSARI, John

Nationality: American. **Born:** National City, California, 17 June 1931. **Education:** Sweetwater High School, National City, 1945–49; studied painting at San Diego State College, California, 1949–57, B.A. 1953, M.A. 1957. **Family:** Married Carol Wixom in 1962 (divorced 1986); children: Annamarie and Antonio. **Career:** Professional artist since 1957. Instructor, Fine Arts Gallery, San Diego, 1953–54, San Diego city schools, 1956–57, San Diego State College, 1956, 1959–61, and Southwestern College, Chula Vista, California, 1962–68; assistant professor of art, University of California at San Diego, 1968–70; instructor, La Jolla Museum of Art, California, 1966–70; professor, California Institute of Arts, Los Angeles, since 1970. Visiting instructor, Hunter College, New York, 1971. **Awards:** National Endowment for the Arts Grant, 1973, 1974–75. **Agents:** Sonnabend Gallery, New York; and James Corcoran Gallery, 8223 Santa Monica Boulevard, Los Angeles, California 90046. Lives and works in Santa Monica, California. **Address:** c/o Sonnabend Gallery, 420 West Broadway, New York, New York 10012, U.S.A.; c/o Margo Leavin Gallery, 812 N. Robertson Blvd., Los Angeles, California 90069–4997.

Individual Exhibitions:

1960 La Jolla Museum of Art, California
1962 Southwestern College, Chula Vista, California
1964 Southwestern College, Chula Vista, California
1966 La Jolla Museum of Art, California
1968 Molly Barnes Gallery, Los Angeles
1970 Richard Feigen Gallery, New York
Eugenia Butler Gallery, Los Angeles
1971 Galerie Konrad Fischer, Dusseldorf
Art and Project, Amsterdam
Nova Scotia College of Art and Design, Halifax
1972 Galerie MTL, Brussels
Art and Project, Amsterdam
Galleria Franco Toselli, Milan
Jack Wendler Gallery, London
1973 Sonnabend Galleries, New York and Paris
Galleria Schema, Florence
Galerie Konrad Fischer, Dusseldorf
1974 Galerie Folker Skulima, Berlin
Jack Wendler Gallery, London
Galleria Franco Toselli, Milan
Art and Project/Galerie MTL, Antwerp
1975 Galerie Felix Handschin, Basle
Galerie MTL, Brussels
Saman Gallery, New York
Sonnabend Galleries, New York and Paris
Stedelijk Museum, Amsterdam
Modern Art Agency, Naples
Southwestern College, Chula Vista, California
The Kitchen, New York
University of California at Irvine
1976 Ewing Gallery, University of Melbourne, Australia
Auckland Art Gallery, New Zealand
University of Akron, Ohio
Ohio State University, Columbus
Cirrus Editions Gallery, Los Angeles
James Corcoran Gallery, Los Angeles
Experimental Art Foundation, Adelaide
Undercroft Gallery, University of Western Australia, Perth
Institute of Modern Art, Brisbane
Institute of Contemporary Art, Sydney
1977 Galleria Massimo Valsecchi, Milan
Matrix, Hartford Atheneum, Connecticut
John Baldessari: Films, Fox Venice Theatre, Venice, California
Robert Self Gallery, London
Julian Pretto Gallery, New York
1978 Portland Center for the Visual Arts, Oregon
Sonnabend Gallery, New York
Recent Films, Theatre Vanguard, Los Angeles
Films by Baldessari, Artists' Space, New York
Three Films, Pacific Film Archives, Berkeley California
Baldessari: New Films, Whitney Museum, New York
Institute of Contemporary Art, Boston
1979 Halle für Internationale Neue Kunst, Zurich
1980 *Fugitive Essays,* Sonnabend Gallery, New York
1981 *Werken 1966–1981,* Stedelijk Van Abbemuseum, Eindhoven, Netherlands
John Baldessari/Deborah Tuberville, Sonnabend Gallery, New York
The New Museum, New York
Museum Folkwang, Essen, Germany
CEPA Gallery, Buffalo, New York
Albright-Knox Art Gallery, Buffalo, New York
Galerie Rudiger Schottle, Munich
Samangallery, Genoa, Italy
1982 Contemporary Art Center, Cincinnati
Wright State University, Dayton, Ohio
Contemporary Arts Museum, Houston, Texas
1983 Galerie Stampa, Basle
Marian Deson Gallery, Chicago
Galerie Arte Viva, Basle
1984 Sonnabend Gallery, New York
Margo Leavin Gallery, Los Angeles
Galerie Gillespie-Laage-Salomon, Paris
Douglas Drake Gallery, Kansas City, Missouri
1985 Le Consortium Center d'Art Contemporain, Dijon, France
1986 University Art Museum, University of California, Berkeley
California Viewpoints, Santa Barbara Museum of Art, California
Margo Leavin Gallery, Los Angeles
Galerie Peter Pakesch, Vienna
Hegel's Cellar, Multiples, Inc, New York
1987 Centre National d'Art Contemporain de Grenoble, France
Dart Gallery, Chicago
Sonnabend Gallery, New York
1988 Margo Leavin Gallery, Los Angeles
Galerie Laage Salomon, Paris
Lisson Gallery, London
Galleria Primo Piano, Rome
Kestner-Gesellschaft, Hannover, Germany

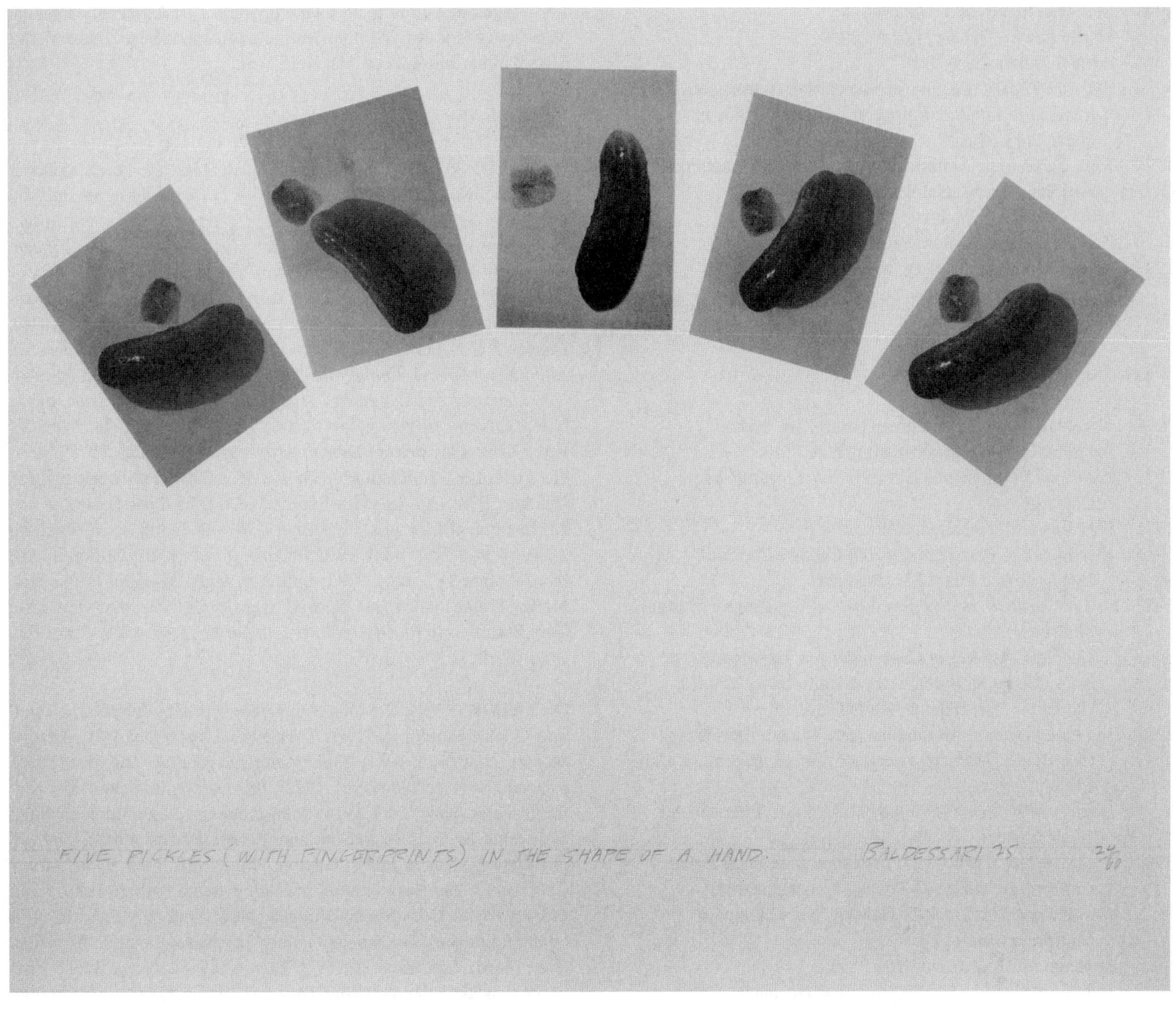

John Antony Baldessari: *Five Pickles (with Fingerprints) In the Shape of a Hand,* 1975. ©Geoffrey Clements/Corbis.

1989 Stephen Wirtz Gallery, San Francisco
Laurence Olivier Gallery, Philadelphia
Ni Por Esas—Not Even So, Centro de Arte Reina Sofia, Madrid (traveled to Bordeaux and Valencia)
School of the Museum of Fine Arts, Boston

1990 Museum of Contemporary Art, Los Angeles (exhibiton traveled to San Francisco, Washington, DC, Minneapolis, New York, and Montreal)
Brooke Alexander Editions, New York
Christopher Grimes, Santa Monica
Sonnabend Gallery, New York
C. Grimaldis Gallery, Baltimore

1991 Donald Young Gallery, Chicago
Walker Art Center, Minneapolis
Mai 36 Galerie, Lucerne
Galerie Crousel-Robelin Bama, Paris
Galeria Weber, Alexander, y Cobo, Madrid

1992 Galerie Meert Rihoux, Brussels
Mai 36 Galerie, Lucerne
Margo Leavin Gallery, Los Angeles
Casa de Parra, Santiago de Compostela, Spain
Sonnabend Gallery, New York
Texas Gallery, Houston
Chinati Foundation, Marfa, Texas

1993 Mai 36 Galerie, Zurich
Brooke Alexander Editions, New York
Galleria Primo Piano, Rome
Galleria Klemens Gasser, Bolzano, Italy

1994 *Artist's Choice: John Baldessari,* Museum of Modern Art, New York (catalog)
Municipal Center for Contemporary Art, Breda, The Netherlands
Newark Museum, New Jersey
Gemini G.E.L. at Joni Moisant Weyl, New York
Remba Gallery, West Hollywood
Sonnabend Gallery, New York

1995 Blancpan Stepcynski, Geneva
Margo Leavin Gallery, Los Angeles
Printed Matter, New York
This Not That, Cornerhouse, Manchester (retrospective; traveled to London; Stuttgart; Tomsiceva, Slovenia; Oslo; and Lisbon)
1996 *John Baldessari: National City,* Museum of Contemporary Art, San Diego (catalog)
1997 Galerie Marian Goodman, Paris
Galerie Laage Salomon, Paris
1999 Marion Goodman Gallery, New York
Sonnabend Gallery, New York
2000 Sprengel Museum, Hanover, Germany (catalog)

Selected Group Exhibitions:

1978 *Narration,* Institute of Contemporary Art, Boston
Art about Art, Whitney Museum, New York
1979 *American Photography in the 70's,* Art Institute of Chicago
1981 *Westkunst,* Messehallen, Cologne
1985 *Extending the Perimeters of 20th Century Art,* San Francisco Museum of Modern Art
1987 *Avant-Garde in the Eighties,* Los Angeles County Museum of Art
1992 *Knowledge: Aspects of Conceptual Art,* University Art Museum, Santa Barbara (travelled to Santa Monica, California, and Raleigh, North Carolina)
1993 *Photoplay,* Center for the Fine Arts, Miami, Florida (travelled to Mexico, Venezuela, Brazil, Argentina, and Chile)
Spheres of Influence, Whitney Museum of American Art, New York
1994 *American Art, 1960–1992: In French Provincial Public Collections,* Musee de Toulon, France (catalog)
Fool's Paradise, Track 16 Gallery, Santa Monica, California (catalog)
Museum of Modern Art, New York
1995 *Public Informaion: Desire, Disaster, Document,* San Francisco Museum of Modern Art (catalog)
Critiques of Pure Abstraction, Sarah Campbell Blaffer Gallery, University of Houston (catalog)
Made in L.A.: The Prints of the Cirrus Editions, Los Angeles County Museum of Art (catalog)
1997 *Sunshine & Noir: Art in L.A. 1960–1997,* Louisiana Museum, Humlebaek, Denmark
Silent and Violent, MAK Center, Los Angeles
1998 *Conceptual Photography from the '60s and '70s,* David Zwirner Gallery, New York
1999 *8th Biennial of Moving Images,* Centre pour l'Art Contemporain Saint-Gervais, Geneva
Bad-Bad: That is a Good Excuse, Staatliche Kunsthalle Baden-Baden, Germany (catalog)

Collections:

Museum of Modern Art, New York; Los Angeles County Museum of Art; La Jolla Museum of Art, California; Wallraf-Richartz Museum, Cologne; Stedelijk Museum, Amsterdam; Kunstmuseum, Basle; Australian National Gallery, Canberra. Museum of Contemporary Art, Los Angeles; Museum of Contemporary Art, Chicago; Houston Museum of Fine Art; Whitney Museum of American Art, New York; Metropolitan Museum of Art, New York.

Publications:

By BALDESSARI: Books—*Ingres and Other Parables,* London 1972; *Choosing: Green Beans,* Milan 1972; *Throwing Three Balls in the Air to Get a Straight Line (Best of Thirty-Six Attempts),* Milan 1973; *Throwing a Ball Once to Get Three Melodies and Fifteen Chords,* Irvine, California 1975; *Four Events and Reactions,* Amsterdam 1975; *Artists and Photographers,* portfolio, with others, New York 1975; *Raw Prints,* portfolio, Los Angeles 1976; *Brutus Killed Caesar,* Akron, Ohio 1976; *A Sentence of Thirteen Parts (with Twelve Alternative Verbs) Ending in Fable,* Hamburg 1977. **Articles**—''Photography and Language,'' interview, in *John Baldessari,* exhibition catalog, Los Angeles 1976; ''John Baldessari: Interview,'' with Diane Spodarek, in *Detroit Artists' Monthly,* June 1976; interview with Leo Rubinfein in *Art in America* (New York), September/October 1978; also, interview for the Video Data Bank, School of the Art Institute of Chicago, 1973; interview with Judith A. Hoffberg in *Artweek,* vol. 22, 6 June 1991; interview with Liam Gillick in *Art Monthly,* no. 187, June 1995; interview with Roswitha Fricke and Marion Fricke in *Art Press,* Special Issue no. 17, 1996; interview with Gary Simmons in *Flash Art (International Edition),* vol. 31, no. 202, October 1998.

On BALDESSARI: Books—*Pop Art Redefined* by John Russell and Suzi Gablik, London and New York 1969; *Conceptual Art* by Ursula Meyers, New York 1971; *Video Visions: A Medium Discovers Itself* by Jonathan Price, New York 1972; *Video Art* by Ira Schnneider and Beryl Korot, New York 1976; *John Baldessari,* exhibition catalog, with texts by Marcia Tucker and Robert Pincus-Witten, and an interview by Nancy Drew, Dayton, Ohio 1981; *John Baldessaari: California Viewpoints,* exhibition catalog, Santa Barbara 1986; *John Baldessari* by Coosje van Bruggen, New York 1990. **Articles**—''John Baldessari, Sonnabend Gallery'' by Nancy Foote in *Artforum* (New York), September 1976; ''When is a Book Not a Book?'' by Grace Glueck in the *New York Times,* 18 March 1977; ''Pictures and Picture Books'' by April Kingsley, in the *Soho Weekly News* (New York), 21 April 1977; ''John Baldessari and Daniel Buren'' by Jeff Perrone in *Artforum* (New York), September 1977; ''Making Light of Heavy Art'' by Kenneth Baker in the *Boston Phoenix,* 10 January 1978; review by Paul Stimson in *Art in America* (New York), March/April 1979; ''John Baldessari's Blasted Allegories'' by Hal Foster in *Artforum* (New York), October 1979; ''Well Hung'' by Ben Lifson in the *Village Voice* (New York), 5 November 1980; review by Joan Casademont in *Artforum* (New York), January 1981; ''John Baldessari: Recalling Ideas'' by Jeanne Spiegel in *Artforum,* March 1988; ''John Baldessari: Gentleman'' by Gerrit Henry in *The Print Collector's Newsletter,* vol. 20, May/June 1989; ''John Baldessari'' by Jerry Saltz in *Forum International,* September/October 1992; ''John Baldessari'' by Nicolas Saada in *Cahiers du Cinema,* no. 516, September 1997; ''John Baldessari'' by Victoria Sancho in *JAB: The Journal of Artists' Books,* no. 9, Spring 1998.

*

WHAT THINKS ME NOW.
I want to re-enchant and remythologize.

I want to drill a hole deep-down in art to discover the mythic infrastructure.

(I am less interested in the form art takes than the meaning an image evokes.)

(I am interested in myth as a way of knowing.)

I want to express myself in archetypal imagery.

I want to stand at the edge rather than the center.

I want to recall what I always knew. (I am interested in what thinks me.)

(I would rather discover the memory of the soul than to be correct in thought.)

I want to move away from racial amnesia.

I want to produce images that startle one into recollection.

I want to think of history so that it is not a record of events but is a method of release.

I want to see the world as something else than serial progression.

I want to know the matrix of events in history.

(What appears to be trivial in a fairy tale, etc. could be the lingering remnant of the memory of the soul.)

I want to engage in the spiritualization of matter and the materialization of the spirit.

I want to think of time as synchronic.

I want to see all variants of a myth in a single imaginary space w/o regard to historical context.

I want to sift information from noise.

I want to avoid the tedium of sectarianism and dogma.

I want to consider language as an articulartion of the limited to express the unlimited.

I want to be at home with the paradoxical, the ambiguous, and the random.

I want to eroticize time, consciousness, and human culture.

I want to blur the boundaries between truth and fiction.

—John Baldessari

* * *

Baldessari is a Californian who—like his long-time friend William Wegman—rejected a '60s modernism become too self-important and aloofly formalist. He will for long be known for his declaration *I will not make any more boring art,* and the burning in 1970 of his earlier work, the ashes ending up in a book-shaped urn marked with his name and the dates 1953–1967. Although Baldessari is more broadly classed a conceptual artist and has worked with photography, video, film and texts, through his use of media imagery, he can be held a pioneer ''image appropriator.'' (Salle and Brauntuch number among his students.) His work harbors ambiguity, yet its mystery is not that of modernist symbolism and ego-centered stream-of-consciousness. Instead Baldessari can be said to be a post-modernist in his casual and good-natured didacticism; and thus a post-structuralist in his dissection of signs and their information bearing dimensions. His pervasive flavor has then been an enigmatic conjunction of imagery, often with text to influence the nature of the viewer's perception, and most often pointing to some semantic issue: the cliches of perception a constant focus. Such an overriding philosophical reflection in his work be-speaks his long-time absorption with spiritual relationships in the world, perhaps evinced by his church membership into early adulthood. While in his earliest such work, in the later 1960s and on into the following decade, the construct was achieved through his own photography, he then became a collector of literature and images. When he turned to the popular media, and for instance came to use television imagery as a major source, he positioned three cameras to face three soundless TV screens; within the past decade, his most important source came to be still photographic scenes from the history of film, thus tacitly acknowledging their ready availability and his residence in Los Angeles. Through his wit and intelligence, Baldessari has not permitted himself to become a mere illustrator of theoretical premises—he retains his position as major representative of a cerebral-founded visual art.

The Duchampian underpinnings of Baldessari's art, and his turn to idea-based work, were made clear in a late 1990s exhibition called *The Commissioned Paintings.* In 1969, the artist commissioned these 12 paintings to be produced from photographs supplied to 12 county fair artists. The photographs, all made by Baldessari, all showed a hand pointing at an ordinary object or area. The image was perhaps intended as a specific reference to the pointing hand in Duchamp's well known painting ''Tu m''' (1918). Then Baldessari had a professional sign painter caption every work with the artist's name—''A painting by. . .'' By no coincidence the artist's well-known *Cremation* project was also seen in New York at this time—as if there were a nostaglic yearning for the vitality inherent in the earliest appearances of Conceptual Art at the onset of the 1970s.

A critic remarked that a mid-1990s New York exhibit which featured 25 years of Baldessari's ''Books and Ephemera'' revealed an on-going fault of the artist's often quite large work: through their small scale, these works appear precise and focused and thus avoid the ''diffuse and thin'' look often felt in the large scale photographic images. And as well these hand-held works presented a tension and fun equally missing in the larger works.

But the large scale ''allegories''—in his long-time photo-text idiom—have continued. And the works continue to present the long-time teasing sense of the simultaneously random and/or ''higher meaning.'' The *Goya Series,* new works of the late 1990s, return to Baldessari's 1960s format of text and image on canvas; and as well to a work of that time in which he had paired an an art world image wih a Goya-derived caption from the *Disasters of War* etching series. The images in this series are printed digitally, but nonetheless Baldessari returned to the Duchampian conceit and again used hand lettering for the Goya phrase.

—Joshua B. Kind

BALKA, Miroslaw

Nationality: Polish. **Born:** Warsaw, Poland, 1958. **Education:** Academy of Fine Arts, Warsaw, 1985.

Selected Individual Exhibitions:

1985 *Remembrance of the First Holy Communion,* Zukow
Wolves, Nowolves, TPSP, Warsaw
A series of exhibitions with Neue Bieriemiennost (including Miroslaw Filonik and Marek Kijewski)

1986 *Percepta Patris Mei Servivi Semper,* Galeria Pokaz, Warsaw
One Night Flower, Galeria Dziekanka, Warsaw
After Holiday Presentation, Galeria Wieza, Warsaw
For Peace, Galeria Wieza and Galeria Dziekanka, Warsaw

For All Saints, Galeria Wielka, Poznan
1987 *For Jean Bedel Bokassa,* Galeria Stodola and Galerie Rzezby, Warsaw
1989 *Keine Neue Bieriemiennost,* Galeria BWA, Bialystok
Installation Abel, Galeria PO, Zielona Gora
River, Galeria Labirynt 2, Lublin
1990 *xxx,* Galerie Nordenhake, Stockholm
Good God, Galeria Dziekanka, Warsaw
1991 Stichting De Appel, Amsterdam, (catalogue)
April/Mv body cannot do everything I ask for, Galeria Foksal, Warsaw
IV/IX My body cannot do everything I ask for, Galerie Isabella Kacprzak, Cologne
XI/My body cannot do everything I ask for, Burnett Miller Gallery, Los Angeles
1992 *No body,* Galerie Peter Pakesch, Vienna
bitte, Museum Haus Lange, Krefeld
36,6, The Renaissance Society at the University of Chicago, Chicago
1993 *37,1,* Galeria Foksal, Warsaw
36,6, List Visual Arts Center, M.I.T., Cambridge
37,1 (cont.), Polish Pavilion, 45th Venice Biennial, Venice
Die Rampe, Galerie Marc Jancou, Zürich
1994 *Laadplatform,* Van Abbemuseum, Eindhoven
Rampa, Museum Sztuki, Lodz
Buenas Noches, Galeria Juana de Aizpuru, Madrid
37,1 (cont.), Lannan Foundation, Los Angeles
Rampen, Galerie Nordenhake, Stockholm
Winterhilfsverein, Moderna Galerija, Ljubljana
1995 *J'ai en ma possession un certificat de vaccination contre: le cholera, Ia fievre jaune, le typhus, la variole. Le Creux de L'Enfer,* Centre d'art contemporain, Thiers
Un Dia, Galeria Juana de Aizpuru, Sevilla
When you wet the bed, /1987/, Galeria Miejsce, Cieszyn
Dawn, Tate Gallery, London
1996 *Pause,* Galeria Foksal, Warsaw
Pax, Studio per l'Arte Contemporanea Tucci Russo, Torre Pellice (with Alfredo Pirri)
1997 *Selection,* Museet for Samtidskunst, Oslo
a, e, i. o. u, Galeria Foksal, Warsaw, and Kunsthalle Bielefeld, Bielefeld
Revision 1986–1997, IVAM, Centre Del Carme, Valencia (catalog)
Ordnunq, Galeria Nordenhake, Stockholm
Out, London Project, London
1998 *Hygiene,* Galeria Labirynt 2, Lublin
Fundacao de Serralves, Porto, Portugal, (with Luc Tuymans)
1999 *be good,* Barbara Gladstone Gallery
Mañana, Galeria Juana de Aizpuru, Madrid
2001 *Quit,* White Cube, London
Between Meals, National Museum of Art, Osaka, Japan

Selected Group Exhibitions:

1986 *Expression of the Eighties,* Galeria BWA, Sopot
Figures and Objects, Galeria BWA, Pulawy
1987 *11th Biennial of the New Art,* Zielona Gora
1988 *Sculpture in the Garden,* SARP, Warsaw
B.K.K., Haags Centrum voor Aktuele Kunst, The Hague
Polish Realities, Third Eye Centre, Glasgow
1989 *Middle Europe,* Artist's Space, New York
Dialog, Kunstmuseum Düsseldorf and Centrum Sztuki Wspolczesnej, Warsaw
Feelings, Galeria Dziekanka, Warsaw
1990 *Aperto '90,* 44th Venice Biennial, Venice
Galerie Peter Pakesch, Vienna
Possible Worlds, ICA/Serpentine Gallery, London
1991 *Sculpture,* Burnett Miller Gallery, Los Angeles
Metropolis, Martin-Gropius-Bau, Berlin
Miller-Nordenhake, Cologne,
Kunst, Europa, Bonner Kunstverein, Bonn
Le Monde Critique, Kunstverein Hamburg
Europe Unknown, Palac Sztuki, Krakow
Kolekcja Sztuki XX w. w Muzeum Sztuki w Lodz, Galeria Zacheta, Warsaw
Borealis V, Kunstmuseum Pori, Pori
Körper und Körper, Grazer Kunstverein, Graz
Rosa e Giallo, Galeria Pieroni, Rome
Von Angesicht zu Angesicht, Stadtgalerie, Kiel
1992 *Von Angesicht zu Angesicht,* Galerie Isabella Kacprzak, Cologne
Documenta IX, Kassel
Muzeum Sztuki w Lodz 1931–1992, Musee d'art Contemporain & ELAC, Lyon
Galeria Foksal, Warsaw
Polnische Avantgarde 1930–1990, Neuer Berliner Kunstvereins, Berlin
The Boundary Rider, 9th Biennial of Sydney, Sydney
1993 *Zeichnungen Setzen Zeichen. 44 Künstler der Documenta IX: Arbeiten auf Papier,* Galerie Raymond Bollag, Zürich
Rosa e Giallo, Le Creux de l'enfer, Centre d'art Contemporain, Thiers
Rosa e Giallo, La Criee, Halle d'art Contemporain, Rennes
Baltic Sculpture, Gotland 93, Visby
Artificial Paradises, Burnett Miller Gallery, Los Angeles
Restaurant, Restaurant La Bocca, Paris
1994 *Till Brancusi,* Malmö Konsthall, Malmö
Europa, Europa, Kunst- und Ausstellungshalle der BRD, Bonn
The Little House On The Prairie, Marc Jancou Gallery, London
Tuning Up #2, Kunstmuseum Wolfsburg, Wolfsburg
1995 *ARS 95,* The Museum of Contemporary Art, Helsinki
Incidentes. Seis visiones desde Europa, Casa da Parra, Santiago de Compostela
Where Is Abel, Thy brother?, Galeria Zacheta, Warsaw
Rites of Passage: Art for the End of the Century, Tate Gallery, London
Ripple Across the Water, Watari Museum, Tokyo
Carnegie International, Carnegie Museum of Art, Pittsburgh
1996 *City Space,* Kopenhagen
Distemper, Hirshhorn Museum and Sculpture Garden, Washington D.C.
Horizons, Sonje Museum of Contemporary Art, Kyongju

For the Museum of Contemporary Art Sarajevo 2000, Moderna Galerija, Ljubljana
Betong, Malmö Konsthall, Malmö (catalogue)
Styki/Contact Prints, Galeria Foksal, Warsaw
1997 *Sztuka z Polski / Art from Poland 1945–1996,* Mucsarnok, Budapest
Niemandsland, Museum Haus Lange, Krefeld
Art from Poland 1945–96, Konsthall, Tallin
1998 *Wounds Between Democracy and Redemption in Contemporary Art,* Moderna Museet Stockholm (catalogue)
Displacements, Art Gallery of Ontario, Toronto (catalogue)
Sao Paulo Biennial, Sao Paulo, Brasil
National Museum of Art, Osaka, Japan
Minimal Maximal, Neues Museum Weserburg, Bremen (catalogue)
1999 *I'm Not Here: Constructing Identity at the Turn of the Century,* Susquehanna Art Museum, Pennsylvania
Lost Paradise, Zhang Huan, Miroslaw Balka, Presença Galeria, Porto, Portugal
The Liverpool Biennial of Contemporary Art, Liverpool
Negotiators of Art: In the Face of Reality, Laznia Centre of Contemporary Art, Gdansk, Poland
As Above, So Below, The Fabric Workshop and Museum, Philadelphia
Three Stanzas: Miroslaw Balka, Robert Gober, and Seamus Heaney, Institute of Contemporary Art, Philadelphia,
Triennale der kleinplastik 1998. Europa Afrika, SüdwestLB, Stuttgart
2000 *Still,* Alexander and Bonin, New York
Between Cinema and the Hard Place, Tate Modern, London
Ombra della Ragione, Galleria d'Arte Moderna, Bologna, Italy
The Oldest Possible Memory, Sammlung Hauser & Wirth, St. Gallen, Switzerland
Absolut Ego, The Musee des Arts Decoratifs, Palais du Louvre, Paris (catalog)
Wanas 2000, Wanas, Sweden
The Vincent, Bonnefanten Museum, Masstricht
A Celebration of Contemporary Art, The Virginia Museum of Fine Arts, Richmond, Virginia
L'autre moitié de l'Europe, Jeu de Paume, Paris, France
Negotiators of Art: Facing Reality, The Balthouse Centre of Contemporary Art, Poland
Jeu de Paume, Paris, France

Publications:

On BALKA: Books—*Bitte* (exhibition catalog), with text by Julian Heynen, Krefeld, Poland 1992; *36,6* (exhibition catalog), with text by Julian Heynen, Peter Schjeldhal, Chicago and Cambridge, Massachussetts 1992; *Die Rampe* (exhibition catalog), with text by Selma Klein Essink, Jaromir Jedliñski, Maria Morzuch, and Anda Rottenberg, Eidenhoven 1994; *Dawn* (exhibition catalog), with text by Frances Morris, London 1995; *The 20th Century Art Book,* London 1996; *Selection* (exhibition catalog), with text by Andrzej Przywara, Adam Szymczyk, and Karin Hellandjo, Oslo 1997; *Revision 1986–1997* (exhibition catalog), with text by Juan Vincente Aliaga, Valencia 1997; *Hygiene* (exhibition catalog), with text by Marek Goydziewski, 1998; *Art at the Turn of the Millenium* by B. Riemschneider and U. Grosenick, Berlin 1999; *Between Meals* (exhibition catalog), with text by Miroslaw Balka and Akiko Kasuya, Osaka 2000; *Around 21015'00''E 52006'17''N + Go-Go (1985–2001)* (exhibition catalog), with text by Bart De Baere, Magdalena Kardasz, Anda Rottenberg, and Rafal Jakubowicz, Warsaw 2001.

* * *

Like many young artists in Poland in the early 1980s, Miroslaw Balka ventured beyond the art establishment and state-run institutions in search of his artistic identity. Significantly, his thesis project, *First Communion Memory* (1985), was presented not as part of a regular graduate show at the Academy of Fine Arts in Warsaw but in an abandoned house in the remote village of Lukóv. This piece already manifested all the major elements which would characterize his later work: autobiographical references, interest in memories and traces of the past preserved in ordinary objects, sensitivity for the spirit of a place. Soon after, he joined forces with two other young artists, Miroslaw Filonik and Marek Kijewski, and created a group called Neue Bieremiennost, with which he exhibited for the next four years while simultaneously continuing to work independently.

Until 1989 Balka mostly focused on the human figure or, more precisely, the space occupied by the body—his figures usually hollow, often truncated, deprived of individual features (*St. Adalbert,* 1987; *Salt Seller,* 1988/89). In the following year the artist abandoned figurative representations in favor of simple constructed or ready-made objects. They were not given conventional titles and named according to their dimensions, e.g. *164x64x94* (1990). He arranged them in groups of two or three, somewhat like pieces of furniture and basic utensils in a monk's cell, thus creating contemplative spaces.

In the 1990s Balka gradually started to apply the dimensions of his own body to his arrangements of space, as in his installation in the Polish pavilion at the Venice Biennial in 1993, where he covered the walls with a layer of soap up to the height of his own body (6'3''). Soap, which has since then become the artist's favorite material, engages our sense of smell and brings out memories of childhood, a feeling of warmth; it is also associated with notions of birth and death. We are washed with soap when we come into this world and when we leave it. Balka also began to use other substances and properties associated with human body: salt, ashes, temperature (utilizing space heaters in some of his pieces).

Balka has always claimed that his works derive from his own experience and are deeply rooted in the place of his upbringing, his family's home in Otwock near Warsaw (where he has now his studio). The geographical co-ordinates of this place are reflected in the title of one part of his show held in 2001 at the Zacheta Gallery in Warsaw (*Around 21015'00''E 52006'17''N,* 2001). The second part of this exhibition (*Go-Go [1985–2001]*) was an attempt to visualize symbolically the body of work which the artist had created up to that point in his life. Along the gallery walls the artist placed tombstones (carved by his father, a stone-mason) engraved with the titles and dates of his past shows. This ''cemetery'' of Balka's artistic past showed that although he touches upon the ultimate issues of life and death in his work, he has not entirely forgotten about self-irony.

On the surface, Balka's sculptures often possess minimalist qualities. Some critics compare them with the works of Arte Povera artists. However, these visual similarities are misleading. Despite the absence of a human figure, the artist's works pose profound existential questions.

—Marcin Gilycki

BALKENHOL, Stephan

Nationality: German. **Born:** Fritzlar/Hessen, Germany, 1957. **Education:** Hochschule für Bildende Künste, Hamburg, M. A. (Art Education), 1982 (studied under Sigmar Polke and Nam June Paik; studio assistant for Ulrich Rueckriem). **Career:** Taught at Hocschule für Bildende Künste, Hamburg, 1988–89, and Hochschule für Bildende Künste, Frankfurt, 1990–91; professor at the Academy for Fine Arts, Karlsruhe, Germany, since 1992; lives and works in Karlsruhe, Germany, and Meisenthal, France. **Awards:** Karl-Schmidt-Rottluff-Stipendium, 1983; Arbeitsstipendium der Freien und Hansestadt Hamburg, 1986; Förderpreis zum Internationalen Preis des Landes Baden-Würtemberg, 1989; Bremer Kunstpreis, 1990; Lehrauftrag an der Hochschule für Bildende Künste in Frankfurt/M Städelschule, 1990. **Agent:** Barbara Gladstone Gallery, 515 West 24th Street, New York, New York, 10011.

Selected Individual Exhibitions:

1984 Galerie Löhrl, Mönchengladbach, Germany
1985 A.O. Kunstraum, Hamburg
1987 Kunstverein Braunschweig, Braunschweig, Germany
Deweer Art Gallery, Otegem, Belgium
1988 Galerie Löhrl, Mönchengladbach, Germany
Kunsthalle Basel, Basel (traveled to Portikus, Frankfurt; Kunsthalle Nürnberg, Nuremburg)
Galerie Johnen & Schöttle, Cologne
1989 Galerie Rüdiger Schöttle, Munich
Mai 36 Galerie, Lucerne, Switzerland
Staatliche Kunsthalle Baden-Baden, Germany
1990 Deweer Art Gallery, Otegem, Belgium
Westwerk, Hamburg
1991 Galerie Rüdiger Schöttle, Paris
Städtische Galerie im Städel, Frankfurt
Galerie Löhrl, Mönchengladbach, Germany (traveled to Mai 36 Galerie, Lucerne, Switzerland; Hamburger Kunsthalle, Hamburg; Mannheimer Kunstverein, Mannheim, Germany)
The Irish Museum of Modern Art, Dublin (catalog)
1992 Witte de With, Center for Contemporary Art, Rotterdam
Galerie Roger Pailhas, Marseille and Paris
1993 Deweer Art Gallery, Otegem, Belgium
Kabinett für aktuelle Kunst, Bremerhaven, Germany
Galerie Johnen & Schöttle, Cologne
Regen Projects, Los Angeles
1994 Galerie Akinci, Amsterdam
Neue Nationalgalerie, Berlin
Musée Départemental d'Art Contemporain de Rochechouart, France (traveled to Musée des Beaux-Arts, Dole, France; Musée des Beaux-Arts, Haute-Normandie, France)
Mai 36 Galerie, Zurich
1995 Hirshhorn Museum and Sculpture Garden, Smithsonian Institution, Washington, D.C. (traveled to The Montreal Museum of Fine Arts) (catalog)
Barbara Gladstone Gallery, New York
Stephen Friedman Gallery, London
Carnegie International, Pittsburgh
1996 *Stephan Balkenhol, Sculptures and Drawings,* The Montreal Museum of Fine Arts
Stephan Balkenhol at the Saatchi Collection, London (catalog)
Myths and Magical Fantasies, California Center for the Arts Museum
A travers l'arbre, Centre Europeen d'Actions Artistiques Contemporaines, Strasbourg France; Galerie Rüdiger Schöttle; Munich Galerie Bernd Klüser
1997 Galerie Dörrie & Priess, Hamburg
Barbara Gladstone Gallery, New York
Galerie Johnen & Schöttle, Cologne
Galleri Lars Bohman, Stockholm, Sweden
1998 Arts Club of Chicago (catalog)
Museum Kurhaus Kleve—Ewald Mataré-Sammlung, Kleve, Germany (catalog)
Von der Heydt-Museum-Wuppertal/Kunsthalle im Haus der Jugend, Wuppertal, Germany (traveled to Gerhard Marcks-Haus, Bremen, Germany) (catalog)
Stephen Friedman Gallery, London
1999 *Stephan Balkenhol: Skulpturen und Zeichnungen,* Bawag Foundation, Wien, Austria
Galerie Thaddaeus Ropac, Paris (catalog)
Galleria Civica di Arte Contemporanea, Trento, Italy
Parc Régional Tournay-Solvay, Brussels
2000 *Stephan Balkenhol. Neue Arbeiten,* Galerie Löhrl, Mönchengladbach, Germany
Stephan Balkenhol, New Works, Forum for Contemporary Art, St. Louis, Missouri
The Contemporary Arts Center, Cincinnati, Ohio (catalog)
Stephen Friedman Gallery, London
2001 Centro Galego de Arte Contemporanea de Santiago de Compostela, Spain

Selected Group Exhibitions:

1983 Galerie Löhrl, Mönchengladbach, Germany
1984 *Die Stipendianten der Karl-Schmidt-Rottluff-Stiftung,* Brücke-Museum, Berlin (traveled to Ausstellungshallen Mathildenhöhe, Darmstadt, Germany)
Es ist wie es ist, Kunstverein für die Rheinlande und Westfalen, Dusseldorf
Skulptur in Hamburg, Landesvertretung der Freien und Hansestadt Hamburg, Bonn
1986 Skulpturenausstellung Jenisch-Park, Hamburg
Kunstverein Braunschweig, Braunschweig, Germany
Kasseler Kunstverein, Kassel, Germany
Neue Deutsche Skulptur, Deweer Art Gallery, Otegem, Belgium (traveled to International Cultureel Centrum, Antwerp)
1987 *Neue Kunst in Hamburg,* Kampnagelfabrik, Hamburg
Eté de la Sculpture, Parc de la Pepiniere, Nancy, France
Westfälische Landesmuseum für Kunst und Kulturgeschichte, Munster Kunstrai 1987, Amsterdam

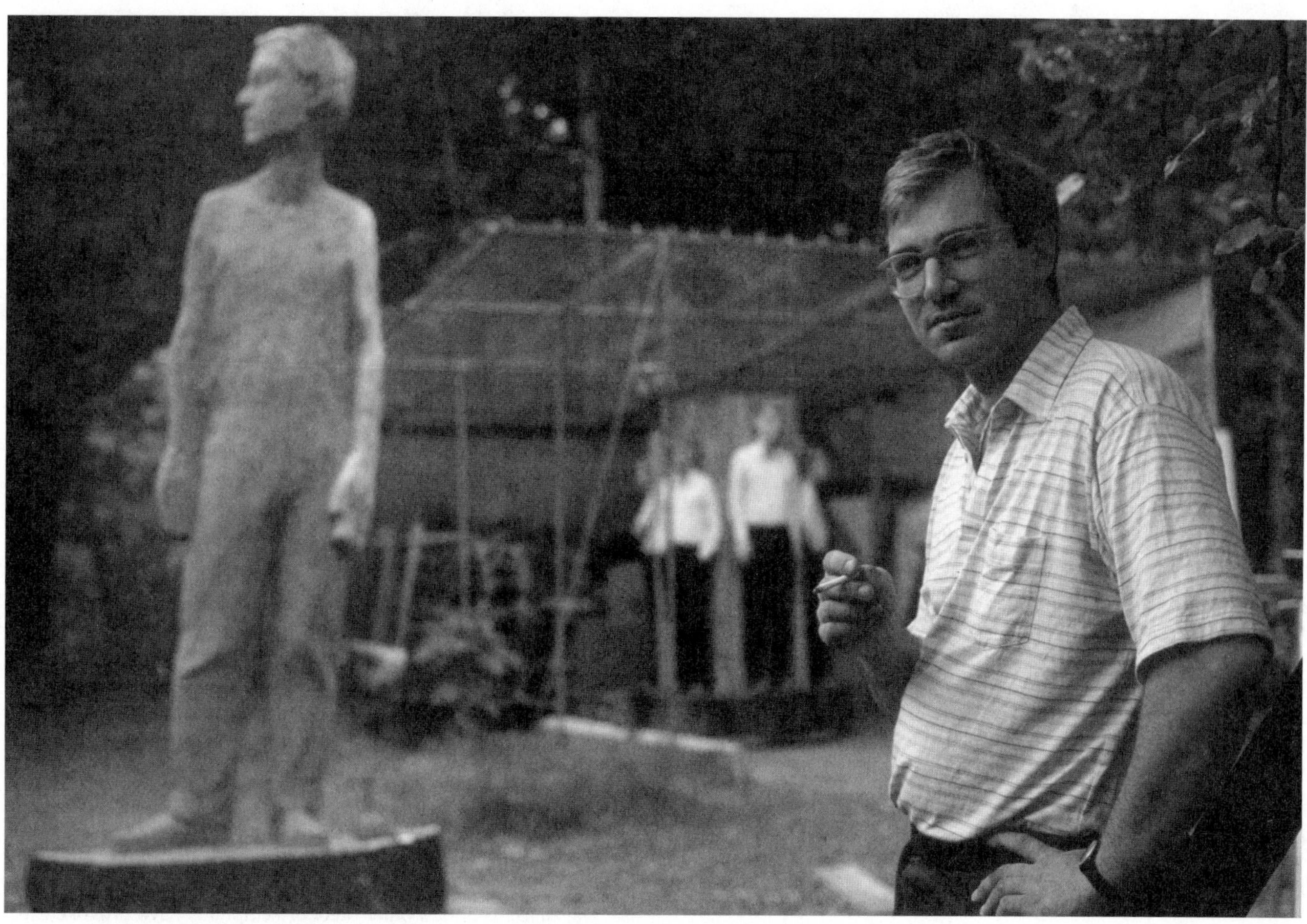

Stephan Balkenhol with a statue in Hamburg, Germany, ca. 1988. ©2001 Artists Rights Society (ARS), NY/VG Bild-Kunst, Bonn.

1988 *Binationale: German Art of the Late 80s/American Art of the Late 80s,* Städtische Kunsthalle/Kunstsammlung Nordrhein-Westfalen/ Kunstverein für die Rheinlande und Westfalen, Dusseldorf (traveled to Museum of Fine Arts, Boston)
Dorothea von Stetten-Kunstpreis 88, Städtische Kunstmuseum Bonn, Bonn
1989 *Prospect '89,* Frankfurter Kunstverein und Schirn Kunsthalle, Frankfurt
Bremer Kunstpreis '89, Kunsthalle Bremen in Zusammenarbeit mit dem Stifterkreis
Sei Artisti Tedeschi, Castello di Rivara, Turin
Das goldene Zimmer, Nymphenburger Schlosspark, Munich
1990 *Possible Worlds,* Serpentine Gallery, London
A New Necessity, First Tyne International, Newcastle
1991 Andrea Rosen Gallery, New York
Kunstmuseum Basel
Erholungshaus der Bayer AG, Leverkusen, Germany (traveled to Museum für Moderne Kunst, Bozen, Germany; Galerie Jahrhunderthalle, Hoechst, Germany)
Hamburg Abroad, European Visual Arts Centre, Ipswich, Germany
1992 *Doubletake: Collective Memory and Current Art,* Hayward Gallery, London (traveled to Kunsthalle Wien, Vienna)
Qui, Quoi, Où?: Un regard sur l'art en Allemagne en 1992, Musée d'Art Moderne de la Ville de Paris
Post Human, FAE Musée d'Art Contemporain, Lausanne (traveled to Castello di Rivoli, Turin; Italy; Deste Foundation for Contemporary Art, Athens; Deichtorhallen, Hamburg)
Current Art in Public Spaces, EXPO '92, Seville
1993 *Ludwig's Lust: die Sammlung Irene und Peter Ludwig,* Germanisches Nationalmuseum, Nuremberg
51 Grad 48'-0 Grad 40', Kalkhaven, Centrum Beeldende Kunst Dordrecht
Karl-Schmidt-Rotluff Stipendium Städtische Kunsthalle Düsseldorf
1994 *Summer Group Show,* Baumgartner Galleries, Washington D. C.
The Day After Tomorrow: Lisbon, Cultural Capital of Europe '94, Centro Cultural de Belém, Lisbon
Still Life, Barbara Gladstone Gallery, New York
Zenenwechsel VI, Museum für Moderne Kunst, Frankfurt
1995 *1995 Carnegie International,* Carnegie Museum of Art, Pittsburgh
Zeichen & Wunder, Kunsthaus Zürich (traveled to Centro Galego de Arte Contemporánea, Santiago de Compostela)
Africus: Johannesburg Biennale '95, Johannesburg

People, Galerie Monica de Cardenas, Milan
1996 *From Figure to Object,* Frith Street Gallery, London
A Collection: Sculptures, Caldic Collection, Rotterdam
Ars Aevi 2000, Museo Pecci, Prato
1997 *Selected Work from 1996–97 Gallery Exhibitions,* The Aldrich Museum of Contemporary Art, Ridgefield, Connecticut
Kunsthaus Bregenz, Kunst in der Stadt, Bregenz, Austria
Kunst-Arbeit: From the Collection Südwest LB, Südwest LB forum, Stuttgart
1998 *Extensions-Aspects of the Figure,* Joseloff Gallery, Hartford Art School, Connecticut
1999 *Collected Rooms—Collected Dreams: German Art from 1960 to 2000, The Hans Grothe Collection,* Martin Gropius Building, Berlin
2000 *Stephan Balkenhol, Christian Hahn,* Galerie Rüdiger Schöttle, Munich

Public Installations:

Man on Horse, Heide, Germany, 1988; *Man with White Shirt and Black Trousers,* Expo-Parc, Seville, Spain, 1991; *Tower Sculpture,* Giessen University, Germany, 1992; *Big Head-Column,* Konstanz University, Germany, 1993; *Four Buoy-Figures,* Hamburg, various sites in the harbor, 1993; *Buoy-Figure and Wall Relief,* Amiens, France, 1993; *Pair of Acrobats,* Rapperswil, Switzerland, 1993; *Three Figures for an Altar,* Inzell, Germany, 1995; *Global Couple,* Johannesburg, 1995; *Man with Green Shirt and Grey Trousers,* Krefeld, Germany, 1995; *Group of Musicians,* Karlsruhe, Germany, 1996; *Man with Bird on Shoulder,* Bremen, Germany, 1996; *Twenty Dancing Couples,* Copenhagen, Denmark, 1996.

Publications:

On BALKENHOL: Book—*Stephan Balkenhol: Sculptures and Drawings* by Neal Benezra, Washington, D.C. 1995; *Stephen Balkenhol* by Jeff Wall, Ludger Gerdes, and Hervé Vanel, Paris 1997. **Articles**—''The Figure in the Block'' by Nancy Princenthal in Art in America (New York), vol. 84, no. 6, June 1996; ''Stephan Balkenhol: Sculptures of Narcissism'' by Wolf-Günter Thiel in *Flash Art,* November-December 1996; ''Stephan Balkenhol: über totgeliebte Teddybären und andere Skulpturprobleme'' by Heinz-Norbert Jocks in *Kunstforum International,* March-April 1999; ''Steven Balkenhol: Contemporary Arts Center, Cincinnati'' by Joan Seeman Robinson in *Artforum* (New York), vol. XXXIX, no. 5, January 2001.

* * *

Stephen Balkenhol was born in 1957 in Fritzlar, West Germany. After a few relocations, the family settled in Kassel in 1968. This location proved fortuitous for Balkenhol, since it was the venue for the important international exhibition held every five years, *Documenta.* In 1972, Balkenhol attended *Documenta 5,* where he saw works by Pop artists and photo realist painters. He was enthralled with what he saw, especially the figurative work. In 1976, Balkenhol enrolled in art school in Hamburg, where he studied under the abstract sculptor Ulrich Rückriem.

Balkenhol made his first carved wooden figures, the work that would become his signature, in the early 1980s. By working figuratively at a time when most people in the art world found the figure hopelessly unfashionable, Balkenhol established himself as an independent voice. His work, unlike many of his contemporaries, is not ironic or conceptual. Instead, the straightforward sculptures are approachable and subtly humorous. Balkenhol began with full-length nude sculptures, but quickly became uncomfortable with the inevitable reading of the figures as Adam and Eve. Determined to avoid narrative, Balkenhol began to carve clothed figures, correctly assuming that with clothing, the sculptures seem more familiar to the viewer, more like someone we might see in a crowd.

Balkenhol carves each sculpture from a single piece of wood, leaving the chisel marks that attest to the artist's presence. He then roughly paints the clothing, the hair, and some facial features, leaving the untreated wood to stand for skin. While he is, in a sense, continuing the long-standing tradition of German woodcarving, Balkenhol takes a different approach from his predecessors. Whereas traditional German wood sculptures are highly detailed and fully painted, with marked expressions, Balkenhol's are pared-down, selectively painted, and expressionless.

Balkenhol's sculptures hover between the realistic and the fantastic. On one hand, they are approachable and comfortably ordinary. On the other hand, they are often quite disconcerting. Their scale is disquieting, either tiny, just shy of life-size, or gargantuan. Their pointed anonymity makes them both familiar and elusive.

Balkenhol's public sculpture magnifies these characteristics that we see in his studio work. In 1987, Balkenhol installed his first major public sculpture, *Man with Green Shirt and White Pants,* in a citywide outdoor sculpture exhibition in Münster, Germany. Made in concrete to withstand the elements, this relief sculpture was installed in an uncharacteristically inconspicuous place for a public sculpture—a ledge above a storefront. The work fit so perfectly into its architectural setting that many viewers mistook the figure for a real person; several of Balkenhol's other outdoor sculptures have provoked the same reaction.

Balkenhol has used animal figures as frequently as, and often in combination with, human figures. One of his best-known works is *57 Penguins* (1991), in which each penguin seems to have its own distinct personality. Each figure sits on a separate perch; both the penguin and the stand are carved from the same log. Balkenhol's use of pedestals evokes public monuments in which respected leaders are raised above the level of the common man. Balkenhol subverts that intent, instead raising his Everyman to the exalted level usually reserved for a hero.

Since his days as a student, Balkenhol's art has been about the object. Coming of age professionally at a time when other artists rooted themselves firmly in Postmodernism, Balkenhol pursued a different modus operandi, one in which the obviously handmade object was paramount. While his work often lacks narrative or political content, work of the last decade suggests that this may be changing. In 1991, Balkenhol installed three wooden figures in a garden at the Stadtische Galerie in Frankfurt. Two of these figures each stood inside a small stone structure, while a third figure perched in a niche in the wall of the museum. The placement of these three figures facing each other suggests some kind of a narrative, and marks the first time that Balkenhol placed multiple figures in a setting that might evoke such a reading.

In 1995, Balkenhol injected a political note into his work. Chosen as Germany's representative in the Johannesburg Bienniale, he referenced apartheid in South Africa by installing two figures, a black male and a white female, on top of the pavilion in which the exhibition was held.

In 1995–1996, Balkenhol had his first museum retrospective, organized by the Hirshhorn Museum and Sculpture Garden, Washington, D.C. This exhibition included not only his signature human and animal sculptures in the round, but also several of his relief sculptures and a number of his often funny line drawings.

—Tara Reddy Young

BALTHUS

Nationality: French. **Born:** Comte Balthazar Klowssowski de Rola, of Polish parents, in Paris, 29 February 1908. **Education:** Studied in Paris in 1924, but mainly self-taught in art. **Military Service:** Served in the French Army in Morocco, 1929–33; recalled, Paris, 1939, but demobilized shortly thereafter because of ill health. **Family:** Married 1) Antoinette de Watteville (1937); sons: Stanislas and Thadee 2) Setsuko Ideta; daugher: Harumi. **Career:** First book of drawings published, Geneva, 1920; worked on frescoes, Church of Beatenburg, Bernese Oberland, 1928; designed sets and costumes for *The Cenci* by Antonin Artaud, Paris, 1935; during Occupation, lived in Switzerland; returned to Paris, 1945; designed sets and costumes for *Cosi fan tutti,* Aix-en-Provence, 1950; settled in Morvan, France, 1954. Director, French Academy, Rome, since 1961. **Awards:** Premio Via Condotti, Rome, 1983. **Died:** 18 February 2001 in Rossinère, Switzerland.

Individual Exhibitions:

1934 Galerie Pierre, Paris
1938 Pierre Matisse Gallery, New York
1943 Galerie Moos, Geneva
1946 Wildenstein Galerie, Paris
1949 Pierre Matisse Gallery, New York
1952 Lefevre Gallery, London
1956 Wildenstein Galerie, Paris
Museum of Modern Art, New York
1961 Galleria Civica d'Arte Moderna, Turin
1962 Pierre Matisse Gallery, New York
1963 E. V. Thaw and Company, New York
1964 Arts Club of Chicago
Massachusetts Institute of Technology, Cambridge
1966 Casino Municipal, Knokke-le-Zoute, Belgium
Pierre Matisse Gallery, New York
Musée des Arts Decoratifs, Paris
Galerie Henriette Gomes, Paris
1967 Pierre Matisse Gallery, New York
1968 Tate Gallery, London
1969 Donald Morris Gallery, Detroit
1971 *Dessins et Aquarelles,* Galerie Claude Bernard, Paris
1973 Musée Cantini, Marseilles
1977 Pierre Matisse Gallery, New York
1978 Pierre Matisse Gallery, New York
1980 Scuola Grande di Giovanni Evangelista, Venice
1982 Museo d'Arte, Spoleto, Italy
1983 Musée d'Art Moderne, Paris
1993 Musée des Beaux-Arts, Lausanne (retrospective)
1999 Shoshana Wayne Gallery, Santa Monica

Selected Group Exhibitions:

1976 *Group Exhibition,* Galerie Jacques Benador, Geneva
1980 *Biennale,* Venice
1981 *The New Spirit in Painting,* Royal Academy of Arts, London
1982 *A Century of Modern Drawing,* British Museum, London

Collections:

Centre Natiional d'Art Contemporain, Paris; Tate Gallery, London; Museum of Modern Art, New York; Hirshhorn Museum and Sculpture Garden, Smithsonian Institution, Washington, D.C.; Wadsworth Atheneum, Hartford, Connecticut; Institute of Art, Minneapolis; Art Institute of Chicago; National Gallery of Victoria, Melbourne.

Publications:

On BALTHUS: Books—*Balthus,* exhibition catalog, by James Thrall Soby, New York 1938; *Balthus,* exhibition catalog, by Albert Camus, New York 1949; *Balthus and a Selection of French Paintings* by Cyril Connolly, London 1952; *Balthus,* exhibition catalog, by James Thrall Soby, New York 1956; *Balthus,* exhibition catalog, by John Russell, London 1968; *Balthus: Dessins et Aquarelles,* exhibition catalog, by Jean Leymarie, Paris 1971; *Balthus: Paintings and Drawings, 1934–1977,* exhibition catalog, with essay by Federico Fellini, New York 1977; *Balthus, peintures, aquarelles, dessins,* exhibition catalog, with text by Jean Clair and others, Rome 1990; *Balthus* by Claude Roy, Paris 1996; *Balthus: A Biography* by Nicholas Fox Weber, New York 1999; *Das Haus des Malers: Balthus im Grand Chalet,* with photographs by Kishin Shinoyama and text by Gero von Boehm, Munich 2000. **Articles**—''Balthus Presents Balthus'' by Jed Perl in *New Criterion,* October 1993; ''Balthus' Lessons'' by Sabine Rewald in *Art in America,* vol. 85, no. 9, September 1997; ''Balthus'' by Merlin James in *The New Criterion,* vol. 18, no. 5, January 2000; ''Summer Madness: On Art and Tradition'' by Jed Perl in *Modern Painters,* vol. 13, no. 3, Autumn 2000; ''Balthus, 1908–2001'' by Sabine Rewald in *Art in America,* vol. 89, no. 4, April 2001. **Video**—*Balthus the Painter*, BBC and RM Arts, directed by Mark Kidel, 1996.

* * *

Nearly unique in this century in his allegiance to the traditions of figurative art, Balthus has worked aloof from the torrents of abstraction. He has contributed at least three great portraits to those traditions—of the painters Derain and Miro and of the art patron Marie Laure, Vicomtesse de Noilly. He has added luminous, direct landscapes as well, and, perhaps most importantly of all, a series of narrative compositions centering on young girls.

If the portraits contain a little of the doll-like quality sometimes produced by Goya, the large compositions of Paris streets recall the arrested drama that charges the frozen figures of Seurat—also, in another way, doll-like. And of course these unexplained, ''plotless'' dramas raise many questions, chiefly: who are these people? and what are they doing? We are made uneasy in the presence of gesturing orientals, misshapen children, streets without traffic, forms smoothed down as though carved from wood. The isolation of each figure—though caught forever in reaction to others—reminds us of Piero della Francesca. Like that painter, Balthus stops time, "correcting reality" to use the marvellous phrase Camus once wrote in an essay about him.

Again and again it is evident how much Balthus learned from the painters of the past. Even the "awkwardly" posed adolescents—forever at their games, or reading, sprawled on couch or floor for which he is most famous—can be seen echoed, say, in the posture of Noah, passed-out, in "The Drunkenness of Noah" by Giovani Bellini. And yet the formal power of these paintings, with their close-value browns, greys and reds, their light-struck whites, and their elaborate design, cannot displace the force of their subject matter: young nudes with heads thrown back in Mannerist transport; girls with legs raised in invitation, arms behind their heads provocatively; girls kneeling uncomfortably over books; girls arched over chairs—all, usually, occupying rooms of stifling respectability and often accompanied by disturbing, unclear—in the sense of who or what they are—dwarf-like figures busy pulling back curtains or lighting fires. Many compositions feature a cipher cat sometimes sitting sphinx-like, sometimes actively involved wearing a cunning, even satanic expression.

It is all a bit like the world of Lewis Carroll taken several extreme steps further. No wonder Balthus had been able to create a superbly apt set of illustrations for *Wuthering Heights* and that Picasso, a master of erotic games, kept one of Balthus' paintings nearby until his death.

—Ralph Pomeroy

Like Picasso, Balthus maintained a strong interest in sexuality into old age, capturing in paint endless variations of nude young girls with such symbolic props as guitars and cats while continuing, in the words of Jed Perl, to "raise nearly unanswerable questions about the tangled relations of art, eroticism, and pornography." In addition, Balthus represents the last gasp of the community that formed European modernism, one that includes, in addition to Picasso, some of Balthus's closest associates: the writers Rainer Marie Rilke and André Gide and the artists Alberto Giacometti and Pierre Bonnard.

—Mark Swartz

Regardless of extensive art historical attempts to lend biographical narratives to Balthus' elusive canvases, the artist maintained until his death in 2001 contempt for such interpretation of his work. Reminiscing upon Balthus' detached approach to his own oeuvre, Federico Fellini recalled: "we stood looking at those paintings as if they were finds, as if we were confronted with something which he, Balthus, had not executed but rather found, excavated, and brought to light." However, his explicitly sexual, symbolic, and disturbing work will inevitably continue to inspire psychoanalytical interpretations despite his protestations. Whatever the approach to or intention behind Balthus' work, the artist's response to the controversy surrounding the work from his first exhibition in 1934 could surely apply to the entirety of his long and enigmatic career: "I had only planned to strike the gong violently in order to somehow shake people up and make them more aware. I think I succeeded."

—Maria Elena Buszek

BANNARD, Walter Darby

Nationality: American. **Born:** New Haven, Connecticut, 23 September 1934. **Education:** Attended Phillips Exeter Academy, Exeter, New Hampshire, 1950–52; Princeton University, New Jersey, B.A. 1956. **Relations:** Married Mya Hay in 1977; son: William. **Career:** Independent artist, Princeton, since 1956. Visiting critic, Columbia University Art School, New York, 1968; visiting professor, Princeton University Creative Arts Program, 1974; visiting artist, Kent State University, Ohio, 1974; visiting artist and lecturer, University of Texas at Austin, 1975; visiting critic, Brooklyn Museum Art School, New York, 1975; instructor in painting, San Francisco Art Institute, 1979; chair of art department, University of Miami, Florida, since 1989. Contributing editor, *Artforum,* New York, 1973–74; juror, Davidson National Print and Drawing Competition, North Carolina, 1974; adviser, *The Flowering of American Folk Art,* exhibition at the Whitney Museum, New York, 1974; curator, *Hans Hofmann* exhibition, Hirshhorn Museum, Washington, D.C., 1976. **Member:** Art Advisory Committee, Phillips Exeter Academy, since 1977; cochairman, International Panel on the Visual Arts, National Endowment for the Arts, Washington, D.C., since 1979. **Awards:** Guggenheim Fellowship, 1968; National Endowment for the Arts Award, 1968; Purchase Award, New Jersey State Museum, 1971; Francis J. Greenburger Foundation Award, 1986; Richard A. Florsheim Art Fund Grant, 1991. **Agent:** Knoedler Contemporary Art, 19 East 70th Street, New York, New York 10021, U.S.A. **Address:** Department of Art and Art History, P.O. Box 248106, Coral Gables, Florida 33124–4410, U.S.A.

Individual Exhibitions:

1965 Tibor de Nagy Gallery, New York
Kasmin Gallery, London
1966 Tibor de Nagy Gallery, New York
Richard Feigen Gallery, Chicago
1967 Nicholas Wilder Gallery, Los Angeles
Tibor de Nagy Gallery, New York
1968 Kasmin Gallery, London
Tibor de Nagy Gallery, New York
1969 Kasmin Gallery, London
Tibor de Nagy Gallery, New York
New Gallery, Bennington College, Vermont
David Mirvish Gallery, Toronto
1970 David Mirvish Gallery, Toronto
Lawrence Rubin Gallery, New York
Joseph Helman Gallery, St. Louis
1971 Neuendorf Gallery, Cologne
1972 Lawrence Rubin Gallery, New York
Newport Harbor Art Museum, Newport Beach, California
Kasmin Gallery, London
David Mirvish Gallery, Toronto
1973 Lawrence Rubin Gallery, New York
Pasadena Art Museum
Walter Darby Bannard, 1957–1973, Baltimore Art Museum (retrospective; toured the United States)
Tibor de Nagy Gallery, Houston
1974 Knoedler Contemporary Art, New York
1975 Tibor de Nagy Gallery, Houston
Douglas Drake Gallery, Kansas City, Kansas

David Mirvish Gallery, Toronto
Olympia Gallery, Philadelphia
Knoedler Contemporary Art, New York
1976 Knoedler Contemporary Art, New York
1977 Knoedler Contemporary Art, New York
Watson/de Nagy Gallery, Houston
Lamont Gallery, Phillips Exeter Academy, New Hampshire
Greenberg Gallery, St. Louis
1978 Knoedler Contemporary Art, New York
David Mirvish Gallery, Toronto
1979 Knoedler Contemporary Art, New York
Watson/de Nagy Gallery, Houston
Miami University, Oxford, Ohio
1980 Knoedler Contemporary Art, New York
Douglas Drake Gallery, Kansas City, Kansas
Ulrich Art Museum, Wichita
State University of Kansas, Wichita
Gallery 700, Milwaukee, Wisconsin
Knoedler Gallery, New York
Wichita State University, Kansas
Douglas Drake Gallery, Kansas City
Gallery 700, Milwaukee
1981 Watson/de Nagy Gallery, New York
Knoedler Gallery, New York
1982 Martin Gerard Gallery, Edmonton, Alberta
Knoedler Gallery, New York
Watson/de Nagy Gallery, New York
James Madison University, Harrisonburg, Virginia
Clayworks Studio Workshop, New York
Virginia Technical University, Blacksburg
1983 Mint Museum of Art, Charlotte, North Carolina
Martin Gerard Gallery, Edmonton
Edmonton Art Gallery, Alberta
1984 Knoedler Gallery, New York
Watson/de Nagy Gallery, New York
1986 Salander-O'Reilly Gallery, New York
1987 St. Lawrence University, Canton, New York
1990 Miami Dade Community College, Florida
1991 Montclair Museum of Art, Montclair, New Jersey, (retrospective; catalog)
Knoedler Gallery, London, England
1992 Jaffe Baker Gallery, Boca Raton, Florida
1993 Farah Damji Gallery, New York City, New York
1996 Dorsch Gallery, Miami Florida
1997 *Walter Darby Bannard* (retrospective) Lee Scarfone Gallery, University of Tampa, Florida (catalog)
1999 *Darby Bannard: Paintings 1987–1999* (retrospective), Lowe Art Museum, Coral Gables, Florida (catalog)

Selected Group Exhibitions:

1965 *The Responsive Eye,* Museum of Modern Art, New York (toured the United States)
1968 *Art of the Real,* Museum of Modern Art, New York (toured the United States and Europe)
1970 *Color and Field 1890–1970,* Albright Knox Art Gallery, Buffalo, New York (toured the United States)
1974 *The Great Decade of American Abstraction: Modernist Art 1960 to 1970,* Museum of Fine Arts, Houston
1977 *Private Images: Photographs by Painters,* Los Angeles County Museum of Art
1979 *Art in America after World War II,* Guggenheim Museum, New York
1980 *Aspects of the 70's: Painterly Abstracolor,* Brockton Art Museum, Massachusetts
1983 *Touch,* Laguna Gloria Art Museum, Austin, Texas
1985 *PrePostmodern,* St. Lawrence University, Canton, New York
1987 *Luminous Impressions,* Mint Museum of Art, Charlotte, North Carolina
1988 *Color Field,* Currier Art Gallery, Manchester, New Hampshire
1989 *American Rainbow,* Galerie de Poche
1991 *Eight Young Artists—Then and Now, 1964–1991,* City University of New York, 1991
1992 *Stars of Florida,* Fort Lauderdale Museum of Art
1993 *The Denver Art Museum, 1883–1993,* The Denver Art Museum
1994 *Vitreographs,* Gallery 323, Madison Wisconsin; Tate Gallery, University of Georgia
1995 *Passion for Art,* Glenbow Museum, Calgary, Alberta
1997 *Florida Invitational,* Sarasota Visual Art Center, Sarasota, Florida
1998 *Masters of the Masters,* Butler Institute of American Art, Youngstown, Ohio (catalog)
1999 *Sixth Annual Exhibition of Painting and Sculpture,* Edmonton Contemporary Artists Society, Alberta, Canada
2000 *Tibor de Nagy: The First 50 Years, 1950–2000,* Tibor de Nagy Gallery, New York

Collections:

Guggenheim Museum, New York; Metropolitan Museum of Art, New York; Whitney Museum, New York; Museum of Modern Art, New York; Albright-Knox Art Gallery, Buffalo, New York; Princeton University, New Jersey; Newark Museum, New Jersey; Fogg Art Museum, Cambridge, Massachusetts; Baltimore Museum of Art; Museum of Fine Arts, Houston; University of Texas at Austin.

Publications:

By BANNARD: Books—*Chihuly: Form from Fire,* Daytona Beach, Florida, and Seattle 1993. **Exhibition Catalogs—***The Structure of Color,* New York 1971; *Hans Hofmann,* Washington D.C. 1976. **Articles—**"Notes on American Painting of the 60's" in *Artforum* (New York), January 1970; review of Michael Fried's *Morris Lewis* in *The Print Collector's Newsletter* (New York), July/August 1971; "The War Against the Good in Art" in the *New York Times,* 6 August 1972; "He Comes to Praise the Net" in the *New York Times,* 1 July 1973; "Morris Louis and the Restructured Picture" in *Studio International* (London), July/August 1974; "The Museum and the Living Artist," essay in *On Understanding Art Museums,* New York 1974; "On Postmodernism" in *Arts* (New York), February 1984; "The Art Glut" in *Arts* (New York), December 1986; "The Unvarnished Truth about Art and Money, *USA Today,* July 1992.

On BANNARD: exhibition catalogs—*The Development of Modern Painting: Jackson Pollock to the Present* (with text by R. T. Buck Jr.),

St. Louis 1969; *The Structure of Color* (with an essay by Marcia Tucker), New York 1971; *6 Painters* by G. Smith, New York 1971; *Walter Darby Bannard* (with an essay and interview by J. H. Cone), Baltimore 1973; *Walter Darby Bannard* (with text by Terry Fenton), Edmonton, Alberta 1983; *Walter Darby Bannard: Paintings from the 70's and 80's* by R. Sindelir, 1990; *Walter Darby Bannard, Recent Works, 1987–1990* by R. Koenig, 1991. **Articles—**''Darby Bannard: The Possibilities of Color'' by David Bourdon in *Art International* (New York), May 1967; ''London Commentary: Bannard at Kasmin'' by J. Mashek in *Studio International* (London), November 1969; ''Walter Bannard at Kasmin Gallery'' by John Eiderfeld in *Studio International,* November 1972; ''Walter Darby Bannard at the Baltimore Museum'' by David Bourdon in *Art in America* (New York), March/April 1974; ''Third Generation Abstraction'' by K. Carpenter in *Arts Magazine* (New York), February 1975; ''The Impasto World of Walter Darby Bannard'' by V. Raynor in the *New York Times,* 29 May 1981; Walter Darby Bannard's New Pictures'' by J. Walsh in *Arts* (New York), September 1982; ''Walter Darby Bannard'' by J. Link in *Arts,* York), October 1986; ''Walter Darby Bannard'' by Robert C. Morgan in *Arts Magazine,* April 1989.

*

Like everybody else, I just keep working and try to do the best I can.

—Walter Darby Bannard

* * *

Walter Darby Bannard is probably as well known for his perceptive writings about art as he is for his economical abstract paintings. A frequent contributor to art journals, he is also the author of, among other essays, an important critical study of the work of Hans Hofmann. Bannard, however, considers himself first and foremost a painter and feels that being a practitioner gives him special insight as a critic.

His reputation was first established as a painter, soon after he turned 30, when he began to exhibit spare color abstractions that marked him as one of the most thoughtful and original young artists of the mid-1960s. By then, Bannard had been painting seriously for about a decade, since his student days at Princeton. Frank Stella had been a fellow student and a friend, but the two young painters worked in quite different ways. Unlike Stella, Bannard was unaffected by the seductions of minimalism. His earliest paintings often seemed to allude, albeit distantly, to landscape motifs or floating figures, and while he soon radically simplified these pictures, it was to clarify what they were about, not to conform to theory.

During his first years of concentrated paintings, Bannard realized that his primary concern was color and stripped his imagery down to allow himself to focus on how colors affected one another when set side by side. Like many of the best young painters of the period, he arrived at simplified, clear formats that resolved, for the moment, issues of where to put color. Bannard's paintings from about 1959 through 1961 were usually symmetrical, often square, with narrow framing borders and centralized disc shapes. Thinly painted, with no sense of anything having been concealed, they demonstrated Bannard's opposition to the layered, gestural de Kooning-inspired version of Abstract Expressionism of the time. Yet even the most severe of his ''band'' and ''framed circle'' pictures of these years was conspicuously handmade and intuitive. Bannard may have dissected painting into what he saw as essential components of field, figure and edge, but he did so in the service of making color as eloquent as possible, not as a demonstration of a system.

In the 1960s and 1970s, Bannard seemed primarily a colorist. His distinctive palette of odd, chalky pastels was unmistakable and criticism of the time frequently praised him for having managed to detach cosmetic, candy hues from their conventional associations. Bannard, on the other hand, claims simply to have liked the colors and to have had no particular associations with them. His primary concern remained the unexpected juxtaposition of the disparate. The extreme close-valuing of his palette brought even the most unlikely pairings into tonal unity and at the same time, made the smallest nuances of differences in hue or surface of overmastering importance. Bannard's sensibility was so subtle that, on occasion, the chief distinction between areas of identical color could be the difference between mat and gloss.

Bannard has never hesitated to change the look of his pictures quite dramatically, in order to explore his changing ideas of what a painting could be. During the 1960s and 1970s, his compositions remained essentially geometric, but became increasingly complex, as though he had expanded his reach. The pared-down, centered band and framed circle layouts gave way to arrangements of hard-edged intersecting arcs and later to ''checkerboards'' and floating rectangles. He seemed to rely less on predetermined placement of colors or, at least, on predetermined *areas* in which to set colors, and by the late 1960s, he seemed more willing to let the making of the picture dictate its structure rather than to rely on a simplified and preconceived format. His profound understanding of Hofmann's ability to construct with color is apparent in these paintings, particularly in a series that juxtaposed relatively solidly painted rectangles against multicolored grounds. They could be described as ''Hofmann disembodied,'' a translation of Hofmannesque attitudes into then current notions about color as pure optical experience, richly evocative and expressive, but as detached from any material presence as possible.

Bannard's pictures of the late 1960s and early 1970s are remarkable for their complex structure: overlapping layers of color, repeated passes of a spreading tool, create intricate intersecting color shapes. Only Bannard's meticulous orchestration of pale values keeps these canvases unified and makes one's experience of them that of all-over painting rather than of violent polychromy. The tension between their deadpan surfaces—an overwhelming sense of a flat, uninterrupted expanse—and their notably broad color range—which breaks that expanse into smaller units—constitutes part of these pictures' strength and part of Bannard's originality.

Bannard's next series, made in the early 1970s, appears, in retrospect, like a deliberate effort to explore completely opposite notions to those examined in the pale, flat color paintings of the previous few years. Each of the series has a single, dominant, startling hue—off-white, poison green, or funky lavender, for example—distributed in thick, aggressively scraped strokes. Paint is piled and trowelled in broad bands that fold around one another; underlying colors are glimpsed between strokes. The act of moving the paint across the surface of the canvas is what *makes* the image, literally and metaphorically. It is a logical extension of the attitude that led to Bannard's checkerboards of the preceding years, but all vestiges of preconception have been banished. The checkerboards and their fellows were made very directly, but still depended upon a tacit acknowledgement of the given vertical and horizontal dimensions of the canvas. In Bannard's best paintings of the series that followed, there is no sense of a preexisting rectangle's having been divided. Instead, the expanse and dimension of the painting seem to have been created by the momentary coalescence of the broad, juicy strokes of paint.

Bannard relaxed his innate sense of the geometric in his subsequent series, while giving free rein to his growing taste for materiality. Like many of his colleagues, he was fascinated with the expanded properties of the acrylic paints and gels beginning to be commonly available in the late 1970s and early 1980s: thickeners and additives that allowed greater surface advantage of these possibilities, exploiting gel-thickened acrylic's ability to retain the mark of a tool or the rhythm of a gesture. A group of pictures from the early 1980s depended upon his typically surprising color sensibility, but presented in new ways; underlying layers of color were revealed by the pulling back of a superimposed layer of thicker, shinier paint in a contrasting hue. For the first time, drawing and surface inflection—here a playful scalloping—seemed as important as color itself. The danger was that Bannard's method could be a little insistent, but in the most successful of the series, inventive color and exuberant drawing made considerations of how the pictures were made seem irrelevant.

The next series was still more complex, as Bannard layered a variety of paint applications, masking and reexcavating buried courses of color. As surfaces grew more elaborate, however, color became more restrained, so that the series is characterized by a range of greys, silvers and unnameable neutrals. As if in reaction to the density and complexity of these pictures, Bannard's most recent paintings are as direct and pared down as those of 20 years ago. They are once again transparent and made, apparently, by a single campaign of overscaled sweeps and passes. The best seem to happen as we look, drawing, painting and structure having magically and instantaneously fused. Bannard has, for the moment, abandoned the high chroma that preoccupied him until a few years ago, but paradoxically, the subtle metallic greys, greens, sepias and the like of his 1987 pictures seem closer, in their clarity, to the pastels of his earlier palette than to the "off" shades of the thick, worked pictures that preceded them. In the earlier, thickly painted canvases, neutral hues appeared to have been the result of many different colors cancelling each other out; by contrast, Bannard's newer pictures have a limpid, monochrome transparency.

Of course, the monochrome, textured, all-over picture is not unique to Bannard, any more than paintings based on thinly applied and various colors were unique to him in the 1960s. He shares common attitudes with, for example, his older colleagues, Kenneth Noland and Jules Olitski, and his contemporary, Lawrence Poons. All take as their point of departure the assumption that a painting is a flat surface whose raw materials can be both expressive and communicative in themselves and the carriers of the painter's deepest feelings. In a period riddled with trend, dictated by fashion, Bannard takes his place among the uncompromising American artists who have remained faithful to these notions. In his more than 25 years of painting, Bannard's work has provided intense pleasure and, at the same time, it has been a rigorous examination of the implications of postwar abstraction. He has been described as a lyrical painter, but his lyricism depends on considerable toughness. The intelligence manifest in Bannard's writing is equally present in his art.

—Karen Wilkin

BARKER, Clive

Nationality: British. **Born:** Luton, Bedfordshire, 29 August 1940. **Education:** Luton primary schools; studied at the Luton College of Technology and Art, 1957–56. **Relations:** Married artist Rose Bruen in 1961 (separated 1985); sons: Tad and Erasmus. **Career:** Worked at Vauxhall Motors, Luton, 1960–61; as a pawnbroker, in London, 1962–64; began creating art objects, 1962; worked on series of 12 bronze studies of Francis Bacon, 1978; lecturer, Maidstone School of Art, Kent, 1965, and Croydon School of Art, 1971. **Awards:** Arts Council Purchase Prize, London, 1978; Elephant Trust Award, London, 1983. **Agent:** Whitford Fine Art, 6 Duke Street St. James's, London SWIY 6BN, England. **Address:** 6 The Clock Tower, Heath Street, London NW3 6UD, England.

Individual Exhibitions:

1968 Robert Fraser Gallery, London
1969 Hanover Gallery, London
1974 Anthony d'Offay Gallery, London
1978 Felicity Samuel Gallery, London (in collaboration with Robert Fraser)
1981 *Sculpture, Drawings and Prints,* Mappin Art Gallery, Sheffield (toured to Stoke, Eastbourne and Cheltenham, 1981–82)
1983 *War Heads,* Imperial War Museum, London
1985 *Boxes,* Wolverhampton Art Gallery, Staffordshire
1987 National Portrait Gallery, London
1994 Independent Gallery, London

Selected Group Exhibitions:

1962 *Young Contemporaries,* FBA Galleries, London
1964 *118 Show,* Kasmin Gallery, London
1966 *New Idioms,* Robert Fraser Gallery, London
1967 *Salon de la Jeune Peinture,* Musee d'Art Moderne, Paris
1968 *Young British Artists,* Museum of Modern Art, New York
1969 *Pop Art,* Hayward Gallery, London
1970 *New Multiple Art,* Whitechapel Art Gallery, London
1971 *Metamorphose de l'Objet,* Palais de Beaux-Arts, Brussels (toured Europe)
1972 *XI Premi Internacional Dibuix Joan Miró,* Barcelona
1973 *Kunstler aus England,* Baukunst-Galerie, Cologne, West Germany
1974 *Zen Jahre Baukunst,* Baukunst-Galerie, Cologne
1975 *Desenhos Britanicos Contemporaneos,* XIII Bienal de São Paulo, Brazil

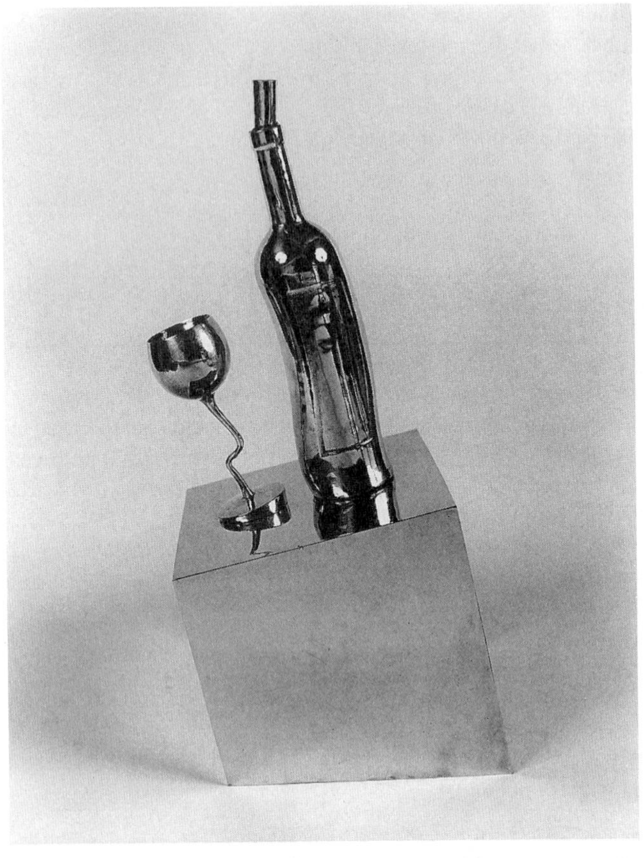

Clive Barker: *Drunken Still Life,* 2000. ©Clive Barker.

1976 *Summer Exhibition,* Royal Academy of Arts, London
1977 *British Artists of the '60s,* Tate Gallery, London
1979 *Furniture Sculpture,* Ikon Gallery, Birmingham, England
1981 *13th Biennale Internazionale,* Padua, Italy
1982 *Milestone in Modern British Sculpture,* Mappin Art Gallery, Sheffield
1983 *BlackWhite,* Robert Fraser Gallery, London
1984 *British Pop Art,* Robert Fraser Gallery, London
1986 *Faces for the Future,* National Portrait Gallery, London
1987 *Pop Art USA-UK,* Odakyu Grand Gallery, Tokyo (travelled to Osaka and Yokohama)
1988 *Contemporary Portraits,* Angela Flowers Gallery, London
1991 *Objects for the Ideal Home—The Legacy of Pop Art,* Serpentine Gallery, London
1992 *Pop Art,* Galerie Michael, Darmstadt, Germany
1993 *Declarations of War,* Kettle's Yard, Cambridge
1994 *Worlds in a Box,* City Art Centre, Endinburgh (travelled to Sheffield, Norwich, and London)
1995 *Works on Paper,* Duncan R. Miller Fine Arts, London
1996 *The Berardo Collection,* Sintra Museum of Modern Art, Lisbon
1997 *Les Sixties: Great Britain and France 1962–1973, The Utopian Years,* Brighton Museum and Art Gallery, Brighton
1998–99 *Modern British Art,* Tate Gallery, Liverpool
1999 *A Cabinet of Curiosities from the Collections of Peter Blake,* Morley Gallery, London
1999–2000 *Portrait Collection of Mr. Chow,* Galerie Enrico Navarra, Paris
2000 *Things: Assamblage, Collage and Photography since 1935,* Norwich Gallery, Norwich (travelled to Edinburgh and Sheffield)

Collections:

Arts Council of Great Britain, London; Imperial War Museum, London; Victoria and Albert Museum, London; Tate Gallery, London; Kunsthalle, Mannheim; Smithsonian Institution, Washington, D.C.; National Portrait Gallery, London; Wolverhampton Art Gallery, Staffordshire; Ferens Art Gallery, Hull, Yorkshire.

Publications:

On BARKER: Books—*Pop Art* by Christopher Finch, London 1968; *Pop Art Redefined* by John Russell, London 1969; *Image as Language* by Christopher Finch, London 1969; *Art in Britain 1969–1970* by Edward Lucie-Smith, London 1971; *Pop Art, A Continuing History* by Marco Livingstone, London, 1990. **Exhibition Catalogs—***Heads and Chariots* by Sir Roland Penrose, London 1974; *Clive Barker: Sculpture, Drawings and Prints* by George Melly, Sheffield, Yorkshire 1981; *Clive Barker: Portraits* (with introduction by Norbert Lynton), London 1987; *Cliver Barker: Recent Work,* Whitford Fine Art, London, 2000.

* * *

Clive Barker initially made his name in the late 1960s with chrome-plated sculptures of steel, bronze and brass both of objects from everyday life—including buckets, Coca Cola bottles, cowboy boots, a newspaper and even a set of false teeth—and of artefacts conceived as materializations from the work of famous painters such as Magritte, Picasso and Soutine. Of all these homages the most Pop in flavour were undoubtedly *Van Gogh's Chair* (chrome-plated bronze, 1966) and *Van Gogh's Sunflowers* (bronze, 1969), both of them devoted to images which had entered the public domain through an incessant reproduction by which the aura of the originals had been replaced by their status as icons of modern art. Baker's habit of coating his objects in a uniform shiny surface had the effect both of distancing them from reality and of creating for them a new identity as symbols of another level of experience. As Christopher Finch remarked in the catalog to Barker's 1968 exhibition at the Robert Fraser Gallery. 'The banal is metamorphosed into the perfect . . . Their perfection is not an end in itself but acts as a foil for . . . an irony of affirmation. The perfection of an *objet d'art* is intrinsically prosaic since it contains no ambiguities . . . Barker's objects, by contrast, are lyrical in themselves—charged by the ambiguities that exist between banality and perfection.' The two *Art Boxes* that Barker produced in 1967—one in chrome-plated steel, the second in gold-plated brass—are quintessential Pop sculptures that bring together Barker's favoured theme of art about art with his innate feeling for objects. The irony of a sculptor producing a three-dimensional replica of the tools of a painter —rendering them passive and useless—is compounded by means of the simple tactic of casting actual brushes and tubes of paint.

Although the human head has occupied Barker's attention at intervals since the early 1970s—notably in the threatening group of gas masks shown in 1974 and in a series of portraits of Francis Bacon, beginning with a life mask in 1969 and elaborated in a group of studies in 1978—it is from other art that he has continued to draw the most sustenance. *Venus Escargot* is his latest mutation of the Venus de Milo, that fragment of classical perfection which has exerted such a powerful hold over the collective imagination.

—Marco Livingstone

BARNEY, Matthew

Nationality: American. **Born:** San Francisco, California, 1967. **Education:** Yale University, New Haven, Connecticut, B.A., 1989. **Career:** Independent artist; lives and works in New York. **Awards:** Europa 2000 Prize, Aperto 93, XLV Venice Biennale, Italy, 1993; Hugo Boss Award, Guggenheim Museum, New York, 1996. **Agent:** Barbara Gladstone Gallery, 515 West 24th Street, New York, New York, 10011.

Selected Individual Exhibitions:

1988 *Scab Action,* Rainforest Alliance, Open Center
1989 *Field Dressing,* Payne Whitney Athletic Complex, Yale University, NewHaven, Connecticut
1991 Barbara Gladstone Gallery, Los Angeles
Matthew Barney: New Work, San Francisco Museum of Modern Art (catalog)
1994 *Portraits from Cremaster 4,* Regan Projects, Los Angeles
1995 Barbara Gladstone Gallery, New York
Tate Gallery, London
Fondation Cartier, Paris
Pace Car for the Hubris Pill, Museum Boymans-van Beuningen, Rotterdam; Musée d'artContemporain, Bordeaux, France; Kunsthalle Bern, Switzerland
1996 *Transexualis and Repressia, Cremaster 1,* and *Cremaster 4,* San Francisco Museum ofModern Art
1997 *Portikus, Cremaster 5,* Frankfurt
Cremaster 5, Barbara Gladstone Gallery, New York
Cremaster 1, Kunsthalle Wien, Vienna
1998 *March with the Anal Sadistic Warrior,* KunstKanaal, Amsterdam
Cremaster 5, Fundació La Caixa, Barcelona; Regen Projects, Los Angeles
Cremaster 1, Öffentliche Kunstsammlung Basel, Kunstmuseum, Switzerland
1999 *Cremaster 2: The Drones' Exposition,* Walker Art Center, Minneapolis (catalog)
2000 *Matthew Barney, Cremaster 2,* Centre Georges Pompidou, Paris; San Francisco Museum ofArt; Artangel/Metro Cinema, London

Selected Group Exhibitions:

1990 *Viral Infection: The Body and its Discontent,* Hallwells Contemporary Arts Center, Buffalo, New York
Althea Viafora Gallery, New York
Drawings, Althea Viafora Gallery, New York
Video Library, Andrea Rosen Gallery, New York
1991 Barbara Gladstone Gallery, New York
Regen Projects, Los Angeles
ACT-UP Benefit Art Sale, Paula Cooper Gallery, New York
1992 *Documenta IX,* Kassel
Post Human, FAE Musée d'Art Contemporain, Pully/Lausanne, Switzerland; Castello diRivoli, Turin, Italy; Dete Foundation, Athens; Deichtorhallen, Hamburg
Périls et Colères, Musée Bordeaux, France
Spielhölle, U-Bahn Station, Frankfurt am Main, Germany
1993 *Aperto 93,* 45th Venice Biennale
Biennial Exhibition, Whitney Museum of American Art, New York
Action/Performance and the Photograph, Turner-Krull Galleries, LosAngeles
Works on Paper, Paula Cooper Gallery, New York
1994 *Hors Limites,* Centre Georges Pompidou, Paris
Of the Human Condition: Hope and Despair at the End of the Century, Spiral Gallery,Tokyo
Acting Out—The Body in Video: Then and Now, Royal College of Art, London
Drawing on Sculpture, Cohen Gallery, New York
1995 *Drawing on Chance: Selections from the Collection,* The Museum of Modern Art, NewYork
Ripple Across the Water 95, WATARI-UM Museum of Tokyo
Biennial Exhibition, Whitney Museum of American Art, New York
ARS 95, Museum of Contemporary Art, Helsinki, Finland
The Masculine Masquerade, MIT List Visual Center, Cambridge (catalog)
1996 *Hugo Boss Prize Exhibition,* Guggenheim Museum—SoHo Branch, New York
Defining the Nineties: Consensus-making in New York, Miami and Los Angeles, Museum of Contemporary Art, Miami
Passions Privées, Musée d'Art Moderne, Paris
Foreign Body, Museum fur Gegenwartskunst, Basel
1997 *De-Genderism,* Setagaya Art Museum, Tokyo
Rrose is a Rrose is a Rrose: Gender Performance in Photography, Solomon R. Guggenheim Museum, New York; Andy Warhol Museum, Pittsburgh
Loco-Motion, Cinema Academia Dorsoduro, Venice
Biennale de Lyon, France
1998 *Wounds Between Democracy and redemption in Contemporary Art,* Moderna MuseetStockholm, Sweden, 1998
Scratches on the Surface of Things, Museum Boymans van Beuningen, Rotterdam, The Netherlands
Emotion: Young British and American art from the Goetz collection, Deichtorhallen, Hamburg
Global Vision: New Art from the 90s, with new acquisitions from the Dakis Joannou Collection, Deste Foundation, Athens
1999 *Regarding Beauty,* Hirshhorn Museum and Sculpture Garden, Washington D.C.
The Promise of Photography: Selected Works from the DGBank Collection, PS1, NewYork

2000 *Seeing Time: From the Kramlich Collection,* San Francisco Museum of Modern Art
Voilà: Le mode dans la tête, Musée d'Art Moderne de la Ville de Paris

Publications:

By BARNEY: Books—*Matthew Barney: New Work,* San Francisco 1991; *Cremaster 5,* Frankfurt and New York 1997; *Cremaster 1,* Basel and Wien 1997.

On BARNEY: Articles—''Travels in Hypertrophia'' by Thyrza Nichols Goodebe in *Artforum International,* May 1995; ''Hungarian Rhapsody'' by David Frankel in *Artforum International,* October 1997; ''Unspeakably Beautiful'' by Mark Sladen in *Art Monthly,* June 1998; ''Nurture Boy'' by Katy Siegel in *Artforum International,* Summer 1999; ''Onan the Magnificent'' by Roger D. Hodge in *Harper's,* March 2000.

* * *

In the early 1990s, Matthew Barney began a series of investigations into the limits and possibilities of the human body. In actions and films, most notably his *Cremaster* series, Barney has developed an intensely personal iconography that explores the essence of human life, limits, and desires. An attempt to decipher Barney's esoteric symbolism is a hazardous endeavor that can lead to facile readings of his work. His complex sign-system has developed over a long engagement with the subject and in the context of his entire body of work, the signs transcend their literal or clichéd meanings.

In early performance works like *Field Dressing* (1989), *Mile High Threshold: The Flight of the Anal Sadistic Warrior* (1992) and *Ottoshaft* (1992), Barney begins to explore the possibilities of the human body and form with direct athletic references. Whether harnessed to the ceiling of the gallery or shimming up an elevator shaft, the artist tests the adaptability of his own body by imposing physical challenges and restraints on his movement. The sports metaphors in such early works, seen in the characters (ex-Oakland Raider Jim Otto and the anti-heroic ''Anal Sadistic Warrior'') and the props (dumbbells, weight machines, pulleys), recall the most prevalent cultural instances of self-imposed resistance to mutate the human form: athleticism and bodybuilding. While the manipulation of the physical body will continue to be a part of Barney's later work, he also began in these early works to develop a complex iconography of ambiguous, symmetrical, malleable, and dialectically opposed forms and substances, such as wax, petroleum jelly, silicon, and symbols relating to the shapes of the human body.

In a series of actions titled *Drawing Restraint* (1991–1993), which are documented in film like all of his performances, Barney brings the same physical restrictions into an artistic practice, limiting his physical ability to draw by such means as suspending himself from the gallery ceiling. In one short, two satyrs wrestle in the back of a limousine to draw with their horns in the condensation gathering on the sunroof. The satyr character will appear again in Barney's work as well. Half-man, half-beast, he is an impossible, frightening, forbidden, and strangely desired mutation made flesh. Mythologically, he is a humanoid creature without the social restraint, from which we derive the term *satyriasis* or uncontrollable lust.

In *Cremaster,* a series of five feature-length films begun in 1995 and developed out of numerical sequence, Barney continues a series of experiments in controlled mutation that often feature anti-heroes like the satyr and androgynous characters, suspended in a state of constant transition. The title ''Cremaster'' comes from the muscle used to control the ascension and descention of the male testes. In grown males, this basically regulates temperature, while in embryonic development, the movement of this muscle determines an individual's sex. Barney goes back to this earliest and most basic stage of differentiation among humans, and develops a series of films about such transitions, states of in-between, and ambiguous determinations.

The mesmerizing scenography of the Cremaster films draws us into the strange world of veiled desires and hybrid mythologies. In some ways, the characters and plot lines are excruciatingly ambivalent. In the first film, *Cremaster 4* (1995), two teams of side car racers, one dressed in yellow (female) the other in blue (male) take off in opposite directions. (The conventional color designations of yellow and blue for female and male trace back to the middle ages and were expounded upon in the 20th century by German painter Franz Marc.) They race along the winding roads circling the Isle of Man. As they get farther apart from each other, they also come closer to their eventual crossing point. A parallel narrative is occurring at the meeting point with a character, half-man, half-ram, played by Barney: the Loughton Candidate, named after the sheep found only on the Isle of Man that have one horn pointing up and the other pointing down. Similar ambiguities and symmetries infuse Barney's other *Cremaster* films: good/evil, incarceration/freedom (in the characters Gary Gilmore and Harry Houdini of *Cremaster 2* 2000), synchronized cheerleaders forming ovaries patterns on the football field at mile-high stadium in *Cremaster 1,* escape/capture in *Cremaster 5.*

—Elizabeth Mangini

BARRON, Stéphan

Nationality: French. **Born:** Caen, Normandy, France, 23 February 1961. **Education:** University of Paris VIII, Doctorate in Aesthetics and New Technologies, 1997. **Career:** First person to develop the concept of Technoromantisme (Technoromanticism); participated in many conferences, including Colloque Artcom at Ecole des Beaux-Arts de Paris in January 1986, Colloque Vers une culture de l'interactivité at Cité des Sciences et de l'Industrie (Paris) in May 1988, Ecole d'Art de Sarrebrücke in November 1992, Colloque sur Vilèm Flüsser (Anvers) in October 1993, Université européenne de la Recherche (Paris) in November 1993, Séminaire de Fred Forest Université de Nice in 1996, Akademie der Bildenden Künste (Munich) in November 1997, Colloque Musiques, arts, nouvelles technologies (Barcelona) in December 2000. **Awards:** Grant from Villa Médicis, 1996; grant from the Ministry of Culture FIACRE, 1999. **Address:** 235 Avenue du puech de Massane, F 34 080 Montpellier, France. **Web site:** http://www.technoromanticism.com.

Selected Individual Exhibitions:

1987 Galerie Fashion Moda, New York
1989 Galerie Schüppenhauer, Cologne
Musée de Bochum, RFA
Ars electronica

Stéphan Barron: *Autoportrait,* 1994. ©Stéphan Barron.

1990 Galerie Art et Essai, Université de Rennes 2, Rennes, France
Hôtel de ville d'Hérouville
1991 Galerie Spala, Prague
Galerie Donguy, Paris
Galerie Galea, Caen, France
Galerie Sakschewski, Berlin
1993 Médiathèque, Faches-Thumesnil, France
1994 School of Fine Arts, Tourcoing, France
1995 Arte no Seculo, São Paulo, Brazil
1996 Adelaïde International Festival, Australia

Publications:

By BARRON: Doctoral Thesis—''Art Planétaire et Romantisme techno-écologique,'' Université Paris VIII, January 1997. **Articles—** ''Artiste de la communication'' in *L'estetica de la comunicazione,* Salerne 1987; essay in *Vers une culture de l'interactivité, actes du Colloque,* Paris 1989; essay in the catalog from the Wortlaut exhibition, Cologne 1989; ''Lines: A Project by Stéphan Barron and Sylvia Hansmann, Connectivity: Art and interactive Telecommunications'' in *Leonardo,* vol. 24. no. 2, 1991. **CD-ROM—***Art Planétaire,* includes 18 projects from Stéphan Barron and texts by Derrick de Kerkhove, Pierre Restany, Frank Popper, and others, Editions Rien de Spécial 2000.

On BARRON: Books—*Art in the Electronic Age* by Frank Popper, London 1993; *Le sublime Technologique* by Mario Costa, Lausanne 1994; *Elektrographie, Analoge und digitale Bilder* by Klaus Urbons, Cologne; *La technologie dans l'art* by Edmond Couchot, 1998; *L'art à l'heure d'internet* by Fred Forest, 1998; *Cyberart, un essai sur l'art du dialogue* by Olga Kisseleva, 1998; *Technoromanticism: Digital Narrative, Holism, and the Romance of the Real* by Richard Coyne, Cambridge, Massachusetts 1999. **Articles—**''L'estestetica della communicazione, cronologia et documenti'' by Mario Costa, 1988; ''Mirror, mirror off the wall. . .'' by Derrick de Kerkhove in the catalog from Les transinteractifs, Paris/Toronto 1988; ''El projecte Linies'' by Anna Capella in *Espais Papers d'Art,* no. 23, October 1989; ''Installacio del projecte Linies'' by Anna Capella in *Catalogue Espais Activitats 1989,* Girona 1990; ''Le voyage de Stéphan et Sylvia'' by Mario Costa in *Dépliant de Traits,* Secqueville-en-Bessin 1990; essay by Mario Costa in the Artmedia catalog, Salerno, November 1990; ''Le méridien ou le trait fractalisé'' by Pierre Restany, Secqueville-en-Bessin 1990; ''Traits-Linien'' by Markus Müller in *Dépliant de Traits,* Secqueville-en-Bessin 1990; ''Stéphan Barron, artiste hypermédia'' by Jacques Donguy in *Dépliant de l'exposition à Faches Thumesnil,* April 1993; ''Stéphan Barron at the Old Treasury Building'' by Paul Brown in the catalog from the International Festival of Adelaïde, 1996.

* * *

Stephan Barron studied engineering before becoming a communications and new media artist. In the early 1980s he utilized transatlantic communication facilities such as telefax and radio in a number of his performances before making use of advanced technologies such as the computer and the Internet in an attempt to provoke planetary consciousness and an ecological sensibility in his audience, an undertaking that could be described as artistic techno-ecology or technoromanticism.

Among Barron's early projects, *Orient-Express* (1987), a reflection on space and on how to travel in an era of instantaneous communication, was followed by *Traits* (1989), a straight line drawn by Stephan Barron and his partner Sylvia Hausmann which pursued the Greenwich Meridian. The purpose was to establish a new representation of the line, one of the first symbols of humanity, a mental representation that integrated space, time, and the human imagination.

In 1994, Stephan Barron created *Le Bleu du Ciel,* where two computers, one located in Tourcoing, in northern France, the other in Toulon, on the Mediterranean sea, were connected by telephone. They calculated, in real time, the average of the colours in the northern and southern skies. A similar planetary interactive installation was shown in 1995 as operating between Paris and Munich and this device now forms part of a project in which two monochromes calculated in real time by two computers, one in France and the other in Japan, are to be made visible by a video-projector.

In *Ozone* (1996), measurements taken of ozone produced by motor car pollution in the city of Lille, in northern France, and measurements taken of ultraviolet radiation coming through the ozone layer were transformed by Barron into sounds via the Internet and were projected into the streets of nearby Roubaix and also into the garden of the Old Treasury Building in Adelaide, Australia.

This installation was conceived as a metaphor for an ''ozone pump'' between the ozone produced by pollution and the naturally produced ozone, between Europe and Australia, between man and nature. In a poetic way, *Ozone* illustrates what is considered as a major ecological problem for Australians—the hole in the ozone layer. A paradox is apparent in the dissemination of ozone: it is produced in too large quantities by cars in the city, but is now depleted in the stratosphere. The hole in the ozone layer has caused an alarming increase of skin cancer cases in far-off Australia. The ozone project expresses a mixture of unease and astonishment in the face of terrestrial phenomena. It expresses also the immateriality and complexity of phenomena that contemporary man must face.

An entirely interactive online artwork was launched by Stephan Barron under the name *Com_post* in December 2000, in which web surfers are invited to send in their texts by e-mail. All forms of writing—poetry, texts expressing love, hate, or utopian views—are accepted in this project and all are then composted. Composting on the Internet is a celebration of slowness during a time of instantaneousness, a jubilant look at the microcosmic and microscopic in an interrelated and interdependent world. It praises everyday individual gestures related to a collective whole.

Another project, *Contact* (2001), is a planetary installation that consists only of two copper plates, placed in two different countries, which relay their temperatures by telephone and so make one feel the temperature variation between two distant locations.

These very varied multi-sensorial, multi-oriented, and multipurpose projects and realisations by Stephan Barron form a whole through the theoretical positioning of the artist as a technoromanticist. In his opinion, technological progress must be accompanied by a parallel development of the human spirit. This new anthropological stage consists in man's adaptation to his new power over nature and over other persons. This increase in the powers of technology should be accompanied by an increase in the powers of consciousness. This new phase in human consciousness and activity is theorized and formulated by an ecological option taking different spiritual, corporeal, economic, and social forms. If ecology is defined as the study of the interactions between different living beings and their environment, then any attempt to disrupt the equilibrium of the biosphere should be interpreted as a menace to mankind.

Techno-ecological romanticism is therefore a wide concept which encompasses art but also other human activities. Technological art must be based on ethical principles in order to give it a meaning and a soul. For Stephan Barron, technoromanticism is a spiritual quest in the area of technological art.

—Frank Popper

BARRY, Robert

Nationality: American. **Born:** Bronx, New York, 9 March 1936. **Education:** Hunter College, New York, B.F.A., 1957, M.A. 1963. **Agent:** Holly Solomon Gallery, 172 Mercer Street, New York, New York 10012, U.S.A.

Individual Exhibitions:

1964 Westerly Gallery, New York
1969 Seth Siegelaub Gallery, Los Angeles
Galleria Sperone, Turin
Art and Project, Amsterdam
1970 Eugenia Butler Gallery, Los Angeles
Galleria Sperone, Turin
1971 Galerie Yvon Lambert, Paris
Galerie Paul Maenz, Cologne
Leo Castelli Gallery, New York
Art and Project, Amsterdam
Eugenia Butler Gallery, Los Angeles
1972 Galleria Toselli, Milan
Jack Wendler Gallery, London
Galerie MTL, Brussels
Tate Gallery, London
Leo Castelli Gallery, New York
Art and Project, Amsterdam
1973 Galleria Sperone, Turin
Galleria Toselli, Milan
Gian Enzo Sperone and Fischer Konrad, Rome
Galerie Paul Maenz, Cologne
Galerie Yvon Lambert, Paris
Galeria Foksal, Warsaw
Im Kabinett fur Actuelle Kunst, Bremerhaven, West Germany
Jack Wendler Gallery, London
1974 Galerie Yvon Lambert, Paris
Leo Castelli Gallery, New York
Jack Wendler Gallery, London
Galerie Paul Maenz, Cologne
Galerie MTL, Brussels
Art and Project, Amsterdam
Kunstmuseum, Lucerne, Switzerland
Galerie Rolf Freisig, Basel
Galleria Gain Enzo Sperone, Turin
Stedelijk Museum, Amsterdam
Rhode Island School of Design, Providence
1975 Gian Enzo Sperone Gallery, New York
Cusack Gallery, Houston
Galerie Paul Maenz, Cologne
1976 Leo Castelli Gallery, New York
Galerie Rolf Preisig, Basel
Galerie Paul Maenz, Cologne
Galleria Enzo Sperone, Rome
Julian Pretto Gallery, New York
P.S.1 Gallery, Long Island City, New York
1977 Stedelijk Van Abbemuseum, Eindhoven, Netherlands
Robert Self Ltd., London
Galerie Yvon Lambert, Paris
Galerie Rudiger Schottle, Munich
Galerie Paul Maenz, Cologne
1978 Museum Folkwang, Essen, West Germany
Galerie MTL, Brussels
Leo Castelli Gallery, New York
Museum of Conceptual Art, San Francisco
University of Colorado Museum, Boulder
1979 Leo Castelli Gallery, New York
Galleria Francois Lambert, Milan
Galerie Rolf Preisig, Basle
Galerie Paul Maenz, Cologne
1980 Joslyn Art Museum, Omaha, Nebraska
Galerie Paul Maenz, Cologne

Leo Castelli Gallery, New York
Banco/Massimo Minini, Brescia, Italy
Saint-Baume, France
1981 Galerie Yvon Lambert, Paris
Leo Castelli Gallery, New York
Art and Project, Amsterdam
Centre d'Arts Plastique Contemporains de Bordeaux, France
1982 Ulmer Museum, Germany
Museum Folkwang, Essen
Museum of Conceptual Art, San Francisco
1983 Leo Castelli Gallery, New York
Art and Project, Amsterdam
Galleria Francoise Lambert, Milan
Galleria Locus Solus, Genoa
Galerie l'Hermitte, Coutances, France
1984 Galerie Yvon Lambert, Paris
David Bellman Gallery, Toronto, Ontario
1985 The Renaissance Society, University of Chicago
1986 Delfryd Celf Gallery, Lloyds Bank, Wales
Le Consortium, Dijon, France
1987 Galerie Chislain Mollet-Vieville, Paris
Galerie Paul Maenz, Cologne
Galleria Christian Stein, Turin (with Lawrence Weiner)
Galleria Primo Piano, Rome
Julian Pretto Gallery, New York
Delfryd Celf Gallery, Lloyds Bank, Wales
1988 Wasserman and Edition E Gallery, Munich
Delfryd Celf Gallery, Lloyds Bank, Wales
Gallerie Meert Rihoux, Brussels
Galerie Paul Maenz, Cologne
Galerie Yvon Lambert, Paris
Sperone Westwater, New York
1989 Holly Solomon Gallery, New York
Leo Castelli Gallery, New York
Julian Pretto Gallery, New York
Delfryd Celf Gallery, Lloyds Bank, Wales
Thomas Solomon Gallery, Los Angeles
Galleria Ugo Ferranti, Rome
Centre National d'Art Contemporain, Grenoble
Musée St. Pierre, Art Contemporain, Lyons
Roy Boyd Gallery, Los Angeles
1990 Rena Bransten Gallery, San Francisco
Haags Gemeentemuseum, The Hague
Holly Solomon Gallery, New York
Salama-Caoro Gallery, London
Galerie Yvon Lambert, Paris
Galerie Meert Rihoux, Brussels
1991 Galeria 57, Madrid
Galerie Pierre Huber, Geneva
Wasserman Galerie, Cologne
Galeria Foksal, Warsaw
Galleria Ugo Ferranti, Rome
Le Consortium, Dijon, France
Holly Solomon Gallery, New York
1992 Galleria Ugo Ferranti, Rome
Galerie Bugdahn und Kaimer, Düsseldorf
Galerie Klemens Gasser, Bolzano
2000 Holly Solomon Gallery, New York

Selected Group Exhibitions:

1966 *Systematic Painting,* Guggenheim Museum, New York
1970 *Nirvana,* Kyoto Municipal Museum of Fine Arts, Japan
1971 *Artist, Theory and Work,* Kunsthalle, Nuremberg
1972 *Documenta 5,* Kassel, West Germany
1974 *Concept Art,* Kunstverein, Braunschweig, West Germany
1979 *73rd American Exhibition,* Art Institute of Chicago
1980 *Music, Sound, Language, Theater: John Cage, Tom Marioni, Robert Barry, Joan Jonas,* Cowell College Gallery, University of California at Santa Cruz (toured the United States)
1986 *Individuals: A Selection of Contemporary Art,* Museum of Contemporary Art, Los Angeles
1988 *Modes of Address: Language in Art Since 1960,* Whitney Museum of American Art, New York
1990 *Language in Art,* Art Gallery of Ontario, Toronto
1991 *Histoire d'Il,* Le Nouveau Museé, Villeurbanne, France
1998 Musée d'art moderne, Villeneuve, France
1999 *Scripta Manent,* Esso Gallery, New York
Infrform, Lance Fung Gallery, New York

Collections:

Stedelijk Museum, Amsterdam; Museum of Modern Art, New York; Kunstmuseum Basel; Australian National Gallery, Canberra; Musée Saint Pierre, Lyons; Musée des Beaux Arts, Toronto, Ontario; National Gallery of Art, Washington, D.C.; Sprengel Museum Hannover, Germany.

Publications:

By BARRY: Books—*An Untitled Book,* Turin, Editions Sperone, 1970; *One Billion Dots,* Turin, Editions Sperone, 1971; *30 Pieces as of 14 June 1971,* Cologne: Gerd de Vries, 1971; *Two Pieces,* Turin, Editions Sperone, 1972; *It is . . . It Isn't . . . ,* Paris, Yvon Lambert Editions, 1972; *There It Is,* Aachen, West Germany, Ottenhausen Verlag, 1982; *Imschoot,* Gent, Belgium, 1992.

On BARRY: Books—*Arte Povera* by Germano Celant, Milan, 1969; *Conceptual Art* by Ursula Meyes, New York 1972; *6 Years: The De-Materialization of the Art Object from 1966 to 1972* by Lucy R. Lippard, New York 1973; *Idea Art* by Gregory Battcock, New York 1973; *Robert Barry* by Robert C. Morgan, Germany 1986; **Exhibition Catalogs**—*Systematic Painting,* with text by Lawrence Alloway, New York 1966; *Robert Barry* (with text by Jean-Christophe Ammann), Lucerne 1974; *Robert Barry* Eindhoven, Netherlands 1977; *Robert Barry* (with text by Holliday T. Day), Omaha, Nebraska 1980; *Music, Sound, Language, Theater: John Cage, Tom Marioni, Robert Barry, Joan Jonas,* edited by Robin White (with essays by Kathan Browne and others), Oakland, California 1980. **Articles**—''Systematic Painting'' by Robert Pincus-Witten in *Artforum* (New York), November 1966; ''Painting Is Obsolete'' by Gregory Battcock in *New York Free Press,* January 1969; ''Impossible Art'' by David Shirey in *Art in America* (New York), May/June 1969; ''Art after Philosophy'' by Joseph Kosuth in *Studio International* (London), November/December 1969; ''Concept Art'' by Klaus Honnef in *Kunst* (Mainz, West Germany), 1970; ''Book as Artwork'' by Germano Celant in *Data 1,* Milan 1971.

BARTLETT, Jennifer (Losch)

Nationality: American. **Born**: Long Beach, California, 14 March 1941. **Education:** Mills College, Oakland, California, 1961–63, B.A. 1963; Yale School of Art and Architecture, New Haven, Connecticut, with Jack Tworkov, James Rosenquist, Al Held and Jim Dine, 1963–65, B.F.S. 1964, M.F.A. 1965. **Career:** Instructor, University of Connecticut, Storrs, 1968–72; visiting artist, Art Institute of Chicago, 1962. instructor in Painting, School of Visual Arts, New York, 1972–77. **Awards:** Creative Artist Public Services Fellowship, 1974; Harris Prize, Art Institute of Chicago, 1976; Lucas Visiting Lecture Award, Carleton College, Northfield, Minneapolis, 1979; Creative Arts Award, Brandeis University, Waltham, Massachusetts, 1983; American Institute of Arts and Letters Award, New York, 1983; Harris Prize and M.V. Kostamm Award, Art Institute of Chicago, 1986; American Institute of Architects Award, New York, 1986. **Address:** Charles Street Artists Studio, 134 Charles Street, New York, NY 10014, U.S.A.

Selected Individual Exhibitions:

1963 Mills College, Oakland, California
1970 119 Spring Street Gallery, New York
1972 Reese Palley Gallery, New York
1973 Jacob's Ladder, Washington D.C. (with Jack Tworkov)
1974 Paula Cooper Gallery, New York
Saman Galleria, Genoa
1975 John Doyle Gallery, Chicago
Garage, London (with Joel Shapiro)
1976 Paula Cooper Gallery, New York
Dartmouth College, Hanover, New Hampshire
Contemporary Art Center, Cincinnati, Ohio
1977 Wadsworth Atheneum, Hartford, Connecticut
Paula Cooper Gallery, New York
1978 Saman Galleria, Genoa
University of California at Irvine
San Francisco Museum of Modern Art
Hansen-Fuller Gallery, San Francisco
Art Museum of South Texas, Corpus Christi
Baltimore Art Museum
1979 Margo Leavin Gallery, Los Angeles
The Clocktower, New York
University of Akron, Ohio
Carleton College, Northfield, Minnesota
Heath Gallery, Atlanta
Paula Cooper Gallery, New York
1980 Galerie Mukai, Tokyo
Akron Art Institute, Ohio
Hallwall, Buffalo, New York
Albright-Knox Art Gallery, Buffalo, New York
1981 Paula Cooper Gallery, New York
Margo Leavin Gallery, Los Angeles
1982 Joslyn Art Museum, Omaha
Paula Cooper Gallery, New York
Tate Gallery, London
McIntosh/Drysdale Gallery, Houston
1983 Margo Leavin Gallery, Los Angeles
Gloria Luria Gallery, Harbor Islands, Florida
Heath Gallery, Atlanta, Georgia
Paula Cooper Gallery, New York
1984 Brandeis University, Waltham, Massachusetts
Long Beach Museum of Art, California
University of California, Berkeley
1985 Paula Cooper Gallery, New York
Lowe Art Museum, Coral Gables, Florida
Knight Gallery, Charlotte, North Carolina
Carpenter + Hochman Gallery, Dallas
Hodges Taylor Gallery, Charlotte, North Carolina
Walker Art Center, Minneapolis (travelled to Kansas City, Missouri; Brooklyn, New York; La Jolla, California; Pittsburgh)
1986 Cleveland Museum of Art, Ohio
Greg Kucera Gallery, Seattle, Washington
1987 Harvard Graduate School of Design, Cambridge, Massachusetts
Paula Cooper Gallery, New York
1988 Paula Cooper Gallery, New York
1989 John Berggruen Gallery, San Francisco
1990 Paula Cooper Gallery, New York
John Berggruen Gallery, San Francisco
1992 Paula Cooper Gallery, New York
John Berggruen Gallery, San Francisco
Orlando Museum of Art, Floridia (traveled)
1994 Paula Cooper Gallery, New York
Baldwin Gallery, Aspen
1995 Baldwin Gallery, Aspen
Numark Gallery, Washington D.C.
1997 Berggruen Gallery, San Francisco
Gagosian Gallery, Los Angeles
Jim Kempner Fine Art, New York
1998 Numark Gallery, Washington D.C.
Berggruen Gallery, San Francisco
1999 Richard Gray Gallery, New York
Baldwin Gallery, Aspen
2000 Julie Sylyester Fine Art, Bermuda
Greenberg-VanDoren Gallery, New York
Museum of Fine Arts, Houston
Baldwin Gallery, Aspen

Selected Group Exhibitions:

1975 *37th Corcoran Biennial,* Corcoran Gallery, Washington, D.C.
1976 *The Liberation: 14 American Artists,* Aarhus Museum of Art, Denmark (toured Europe)
1977 *Documenta 6,* Kassel, West Germany
1978 *New Image Painting,* Whitney Museum, New York
1979 *Corner,* Hayden Gallery, Massachusetts Institute of Technology, Cambridge
1980 *Urban Encounters,* Institute of Contemporary Art, University of Pennsylvania, Philadelphia
Printed Art: A View of 2 Decades, Museum of Modern Art, New York
1981 *Biennial Exhibition,* Whitney Museum, New York
1983 *Back to the U.S.A.,* Rheinisches Landesmuseum, Bonn (travelled to Lucerne and Stuttgart)
1987 *The Monumental Image,* Sonoma State University, Rohnert Park, California (toured the United States)

1988 *Three Decades: The Oliver Hoffman Collection,* Museum of Contemporary Art, Chicago
1989 *Making Their Mark,* Cincinnati Art Museum (traveled)
First Impressions: Early Prints by Forty-Six Contemporary Artists, Walker Art Center, Minneapolis (traveled)
1990 *Terra Incognita: New Directions in Contemporary Landscape,* Museum of Art, Rhode Island School of Design
1991 *Whiteney Biennial,* Whitney Museum of American Art, New York
Among Friends: Contemporary Works on Paper from a Collection formed by Ingeborg and Jan van der Marck, Muskegon Museum of Art, Michigan (traveled)
1995 *Printmaking in America: Collaborative Prints and Presses, 1960–1990,* Mary and Leigh Block Gallery, Northwestern University, Chicago (traveled)
1996 *Thinking Print: Books to Billboards, 1980–95,* Museum of Modern Art, New York
1997 *Still Life: The Object in American Art, 1915–1995,* Marsh Art Gallery, Richmond, Virginia (traveled)
2000 *Modernism and Abstraction: Treasures from the Smithsonian American Art Museum,* Art Museum at Florida International University, Miami, Florida

Selected Collections:

Museum of Modern Art, New York; Metropolitan Museum of Art, New York; Whitney Museum, New York; Albright-Knox Gallery, Buffalo, New York; Yale University Art Gallery New Haven, Connecticut; Philadelphia Museum of Art; Allen Memorial Art Museum, Oberlin, Ohio; Walker Art Center, Minneapolis; Museum of Fine Arts, Dallas; Metropolitan Museum of Art, Tokyo; Denver Art Museum, Denver; Museum of Contemporary Art, Chicago; Rhode Island School of Design Museum of Art, Providence; Yale University Art Gallery, New Haven, Connecticut.

Publications:

By BARTLETT: Books—*Cleopatra I-IV,* poems, New York 1971; *Autobiography,* New York 1973; *History of the Universe* New York 1973; texts in *The World: Autobiography Issue,* edited by Lewis Warsh, New York 1973.

On BARTLETT: Books—*Painting and Sculpture Today,* exhibition catalog, Indianapolis 1972; *Arts Without Limits,* exhibition catalog, by Ira Licht, New York 1972; *Painting: New Options,* exhibition catalog, Minneapolis 1972; *Art in Evolution*, exhibition catalog, by Anthony Sorce, New York 1973; *Jennifer Bartlett and Jack Tworkov,* exhibition catalog, Washington D.C. 1973; *34th Biennial of Contemporary American Painting,* exhibition catalog, Paris 1975; *72nd American Exhibition,* exhibition catalog, by Anne Rorimer, Chicago 1976; *New Work/New York,* exhibition catalog, Los Angeles 1976; *Matrix* by Andrea Miller Keller, Hartford, Connecticut 1977; *Painting '75, '76, '77,* exhibition catalog, New York 1977; *Documenta 6,* exhibition catalog, Kassel, West Germany 1977; *Critics' Choice,* exhibition catalog, New York 1977; *New Image Painting,* exhibition catalog, New York 1978; *New York Now,* exhibition catalog, Phoenix, Arizona 1979; *Corners,* exhibition catalog, Cambridge, Massachusetts 1979; *Printed Art: A View of Decades,* exhibition catalog by Riva Castleman, New York 1980; *Extensions: Jennifer Bartlett/Lynda Benglis/Robert Longo/Judy Pfaff,* exhibition catalog, Houston 1980; *Aspects of the 70's: Painterly Abstractions,* exhibition catalog, by Marilyn Friedman Hoffman, Brockton, Massachusetts 1980; *Drawings: The Pluralist Decade,* exhibition catalog, with an introduction by Janet Kardon, Philadelphia 1980; *Jennifer Bartlett; Selected Works,* exhibition catalog, Buffalo, New York 1980; *20 Artists; Yale School of Art 1950–1970,* exhibition catalog, New York 1981; *American Art Since 1970: Painting, Sculpture and Drawings from the Collection of the Whitney Museum of American Art,* by Richard Marshall, New York 1984; *Jennifer Bartlett,* with text by Marge Goldwater, Roberta Smith, and Calvin Tompkins, New York 1990; *Jennifer Bartlett: A Print Retrospective* Orlando, Florida, 1994; *The American Century: Art and Culture 1950–2000* by Lisa Phillips, Whitney Museum of American Art, 1999; *Artists' Gardens* by Bill Laws, Orion Publishing Group 1999. **Articles**—''Jennifer Bartlett'' by Sally Webster in the *Feminist Art Journal* (Brooklyn, New York), Vol. 5, no. 3, 1976; ''Jennifer Bartlett: Artist Who Keeps Pushing'' by Caroline Drewes in the *San Francisco Examiner,* 24 May 1978; ''The Abstract Image'' by Roberta Smith in *Art in America* (New York), March/April 1979; ''Les nouvelle images de la peinture Americaine'' by Thomas B. Hess in *Art Press International* (Paris), May 1979; ''Jennifer Bartlett'' by Barbara Schreiber in *Atlanta Art Workers' Coalition,* January/February 1980; ''Young Artists New Yorkers Are Talking About'' by Lee Wohlfett in *Town and Country* (London), September 1980; ''Adding Up Jennifer Bartlett'' by Daine Bertolo in the *Buffalo Evening News,* 30 November 1980; ''Bartlett's Pairs'' by Kim Levin in the *Village Voice* (New York), 4 February 1981; ''She's Got Style'' by Jeff Perone in *Arts Magazine* (New York), April 1981; ''Profiles: Getting Everything In: by Calvin Tomkins in *The New Yorker* (New York), 15 April 1985; ''The Bartlett Variations'' by Holland Cotter in *Art in America,* May 1986; ''Pastel Paradise: New Yorker Jennifer Bartlett finds Bermuda the perfect inspiration for a change of art'' in *The Bermudian,* October 1998.

* * *

''The series,'' Jennifer Bartlett has said, ''permits a range of possibilities; it reminds us that things can change.'' Since 1968, the series has constituted the central theme of Barlett's work. ''Rhapsody'' (1975–76), a series of 987 gridded, one-foot square enameled plates, represents a monumental exploration of serial structure. Like most of the artist's work, ''Rhapsody'' juxtaposes the raw and the cooked, examining the way the world is filtered through the human mind and is encoded into cultural conventions or sign systems. The work offers a succinct discourse on the strategies of representation: a sophisticated ''botanical'' drawing of a tree is matched with a naive rendering of the same subject, or a simple geometric form (a square of a triangle) is contrasted by a signifying one (a house). On another level, Bartlett locates the work historically, advancing a subtle commentary on the paradoxical situation of modernism (e.g. the integrity of abstraction over decoration). In the end, ''Rhapsody'' is about transition and stasis, continuity and discontinuity suspended in a matrix of resonant formal and intellectual values.

Mapped onto a field of facts, images, and associations, Bartlett's serial structure is often analogous to conventional systems for organizing the world. A ''pointillist'' map of the United States (from ''Series XIV,'' 1971–72) is further subdivided into 15 parts, establishing a parallel relationship between the formal conditions of Bartlett's serial projection and cartographic apportionment based on real political boundaries. The artist's recurrent use of points, dot, or dashes to compose her imagery creates a situation in which each unit serves as a node within a network of scale systems. Bartlett's fascination with the series extends even to her large-scale public work ''Swimmers Atlanta'' (1979), a 9-painting series commissioned by the General Services Administration for the lobby of a federal court building in Georgia's capital city. While the obsessive interest in serial form has subsided in Bartlett's most recent work, the seemingly arbitrary scale relationships of ''Up the Creek'' and ''To the Island'' (1981–82), two 10-part multi-media works, appear to be governed by a personal, internal logic. Concentrating on problems of condition and place (the syntax of the present work hinges on locative prepositions), these paintings are neither fully autonomous nor serial; in their indecisiveness, they fail to obtain a convincing balance. The historian Michel Foucault, in his brilliant *The Archaeology of Knowledge,* has explored the shift in historical methodologies from a continuous to a discontinuous view of events and monuments. As attention has turned away from ''vast unities like 'periods' or 'centuries' to the phenomena . . . of discontinuity,'' Foucault argues that an internal organizing structure must come into play to make ''relevant'' an otherwise ungrouped mass of elements: ''The problem now is to constitute series,'' he writes, ''to define elements proper to each series, to fix its boundaries, to reveal its own specific type of relations, to formulate its laws, and beyond this, to describe the relations between different series.'' Postmodernism has produced a similar challenge for the artist at a time when the continuities of modernist thought have yielded to a more pluralistic attitude. In her most resolute exploration of the series, Jennifer Bartlett has clearly understood the dynamics of this challenge.

—Maurice Berger

BARUCHELLO, Gianfranco

Nationality: Italian. **Born:** Livorno, 29 August 1924. **Education:** Studied in Rome. **Family:** Married to Agnese Naldoni; daughter: Paolina. **Career:** Lives and works in Rome. **Agent**: Galleria Schwarz, Via Gesu 17, 20121 Milan. **Agent:** Gallerie Milano, Via Manin 3, Milan 20121, Italy. **Address:** Via di Santa Cornelia, m. 695 (Prima Porta), Rome, Italy.

Individual Exhibitions:

1963 Galleria La Tartaruga, Rome
1964 Cordier and Ekstrom Gallery, New York
1965 Galleria Schwarz, Milan
1966 Galleria Il Punto, Turin
Cordier and Ekstrom Gallery, New York
IOIOMISS, Galleria Schwarz, Milan
1967 Palais des Beaux-Arts, Brussels
Galerie Yvon Lambert, Paris
1968 Galleria Schwarz, Milan
Galleria Roma, Chicago
1969 Studio Condotti 85, Rome
Galerie Schmela, Dusseldorf
Galerie Lauter, Mannheim
1970 Galleria Schwarz, Milan
1971 Galeria Buchholz, Munich
1972 Studio Condotti 85, Rome
Centro d'Arte Europa, Naples
Galleria La Bertesca, Genoa
1973 Galleria L'Uomo e L'Arte, Milan
Galerie Der Spiegel, Cologne
Galerie Craven, Paris
1975 Galleria Schwarx, Milan
Galleria L'Arcipelago, Turin
Galleria Etrusculudens, Rome
1976 Italian Pavilion, at the *Biennale,* Venice
Galleria Valsecchi, Milan
Galerie Fred Lansenberg, Brussels
Galerie Gilbert Delorme, Paris
1977 Galleria Il Mercato del Sale, Milan
Galleria Margherita, Rome
Galerie Arta, Geneva
Galerie Bama, Paris
1981 Galleria Milano, Milan
1983 Galerie Reckermann, Cologne
1987 Galleria Milano, Milan
1992 Tour Fromage, Aosta (travelled to Mirella Bandini, Milan)

Selected Group Exhibitions:

1962 *Collage et Objet,* Galerie du Cercle, Paris
1963 *4th Biennale,* San Marino (and *6th Biennale,* 1967)
1966 *European Drawings,* Guggenheim Museum, New York
1967 *Pictures to Be Read, Poetry to Be Seen,* Museum of Contemporary Art, Chicago
1968 *Le Collage,* Kunstverein, Frankfurt (travelled to the Kunstgewerbemuseum, Zurich)
1969 *Al di la della Pittura,* Galleria Pilota, Modena, Italy
1970 *Il Cocodrillo,* Teatro dell'Opera, Rome (deoors for V. Bucchi opera)
1975 *Baruchello/Erro/Fahlstrom/Liebig,* Musée d'Art Moderne de la Ville, Paris
Let's Mix All Feelings Together, Städtische Galerie im Lenbachhaus, Munich (travelled to Frankfurt and Paris)
1978 *La Traccia del Racconto,* Villa Comunal Ormond, Sanremo, Italy
1997 *Artisti contemporanei a Villa Mimbelli,* Museo Civico, Livorno

Collections:

Museum of Modern Art, New York; Guggenheim Museum, New York.

Publications:

By BARUCHELLO: Books—*Mi Vione in Mente,* Milan 1966; *Enonce Impossible,* Milan 1967; *In Cold Fact,* Milan 1968; *La Quindices,* Rome 1968; *Avventure nell'Armadio di Plexiglass,* Milan 1968; *Fragments of a Possible Apocalypse,* with Henry Martin, Milan 1978; *Agricola Cornelia S.P.A. 1973–81,* Milan 1981; *Faraone dei Sentimenti,* Milan 1987; *Baruchello, fuoricampo* with Carla Subrizi, Livorno 1997. **Films and videos**—*La Verifica Incerta,* with Alberto Grifi, 1964; *Costretto a Scomparire,* 1968; *Perforce,* 1968; *Complete di Colpa,* 1968; *Norme per gli Olocausti,* 1969; *Per una Giornata de Malumore Nazionale,* 1969; *Non Accaduto,* 1969; *Limbosigne,* 1969; *A Little More Paranoid,* 1969; *I Giorni di Lun,* 1969; *In Quarantasette Secondi,* 1969; *La de'Gringolade,* 1970; *Pietro Bessone en Renato*

Ghittoni, due gemme della Lotta di Liberazione, 1970; *LAP,* 1971; *Deep Sea Show,* 1971; *Beaufort no.* 2, 1971.

On BARUCHELLO: Books—*Gianfranco Baruchello,* exhibition catalog, with text by Giorgio Manganelli, Milan 1965; *Gianfranco Baruchello: IOIOMISS,* exhibition catalog, Milan 1966; *Gian Franco Baruchello,* exhibition catalog, with text by Italo Calvino, New York 1966; *Baruchello,* exhibition catalog, with interview by Arturo Schwarz, Milan 1968; *Introduzione a Baruchello* by Tomasso Trini, Milan 1975; *Let's Mix All Feelings Together,* exhibition catalog, Munich 1975; *La Traccia del Racconto,* exhibition catalog, Sanremo, Italy 1978; *Gianfranco Baruchello: The Plateau of Uncertainty,* exhibition catalog, Milan 1992. **Articles—**"'Subject X': Notes on Performance Art—Part 1" by Barry Schwabsky in *Art/Text,* no. 60, February-April 1998.

* * *

Between 1959 and 1963 Gianfranco Baruchello's investigations into art moved through a series of widely differing but interconnected problems and experiences. His first works were a kind of super-cold abstract expressionism; these works were abandoned in favor of found objects that seem a little reminiscent of Dada; the found objects turned into assemblages or constructions and also furnished images for drawings that have the flavor of a harsh and expressive surrealism. These assemblages then simplified themselves and entered into a kind of New Realism while the drawings turned into paintings full of an internal debate about the relative weight and importance of paint quality and personally significant imagery. The decision went clearly, after not too long, to personally significant imagery, and Baruchello began to work on large squares of aluminum sheet metal, first primed white and then sprinkled with minuscule drawings of schematic trees, imaginary monsters, non-existent machines, arrows, words, sentences and paragraphs written in various languages, tiny representations of the various organs of the body, patches of hair, diagrams, articles of clothing, splotches of numbers, a veritable convention of erudite references to a host of personal mysteries at the point where they encounter public and political confusions.

And just as Baruchello's paintings have not always been what they are today, they are also a part of a vast series of aesthetic activities that include objects, films, theater pieces, books, video tapes, stage sets, postal happenings, sound tracks, sculptures, narrative series of drawings, assemblages of odds and ends and cardboard cut-outs in plexiglass cases and wooden boxes, and he has also reported on the experience of running a farm as though it were a work of art. The relationship between the paintings and these other activities is a fairly curious relationship: the themes of these other activities frequently find their source in the paintings and the "results" of these activities are usually reintroduced into the paintings.

Painting for Baruchello is the Queen of the Sciences just as theology was the Queen of the Sciences for the Scholastics of the Middle Ages: his paintings always seem to want to do more than what any rigorously materialistic definition of the act of painting would allow him to do, and his excursions into other media help him to define more clearly the impossible tasks to which his paintings must be put. His paintings are what all of reality must be reduced to; they're the crucible in which reality, as Phoenix, is to be experimentally incinerated and then resurrected as myth. The intention is to deal with all of reality in a way that will make all of reality coherent, self-reflexive, and emotionally meaningful.

Baruchello's technique is to work by themes, each of which, as it exhausts itself, is responsible for spawning another. It's as though he were trying to discover the myth that's the source of all myth, and he is always interrogating the facts of his daily experience to see what sort of a place they can have within it.

—Henry Martin

BASELITZ, Georg

Nationality: German. **Born:** Georg Dern in Deutschbaselitz, Saxony, now Germany, 23 January 1938; adopted name "Baselitz" in 1961. **Education:** Attended Volksschule and Gymnasium, Kamenz, until 1955; studied art at the Kunstakademie, East Berlin, 1956–57; under Hann Trier, Akademie der Künste, West Berlin, 1957–64. **Family:** Married Elke Kretzschmar in 1962; sons: Daniel and Anton. **Career:** Painter, in West Berlin, 1961–66, in Osthofen bei Worms, 1966–70, in Forst, 1970–73, in Mussbach, 1973–75, in Derneburg, Lower Saxony, since 1975; published "Pandemonium" manifestos, with Eugen Schönebeck, West Berlin, 1961, 1962. Instructor, 1977–78, and professor, 1978–83, Staatliche Akademie der bildenden Kunste, Karlsruhe; Professor, Hochschule der Kunste, West Berlin, since 1983. **Awards:** Villa Romana Scholarship, Florence 1965; Kulturpreis der Deutsche Industrie, 1968; Kaiserring-Prize, City of Goslar, 1986; Kunstpreis der Nord/LB, Hannover, 1986; Rhenus Art Award, Geneva, 1999. **Agents:** Galerie Michael Werner, Friesenstrasse 50, Cologne; Michael Werner Gallery, 4 East 77 Street, New York; PaceWildenstein, 32 East 57 Street, New York; Anthony d'Offay Gallery, Dering Street, London; Sabine Knust-Maximilian Verlag, Maximilianstraße 14, Munich; Catherine Putman/Editions, 4 rue de Talleyrand, Paris. **Address:** Schloss Derneburg, 31188 Holle (bei Hildesheim), Germany.

Selected Individual Exhibitions:

1961 *Pandemomnium,* Schaperstrasse 22/Fasanenplatz, West Berlin (with Eugene Schönebeck)
1963 Galerie Werner und Katz, West Berlin
1964 Freie Galerie, West Berlin
Galerie Werner, West Berlin
1965 Galerie Friedrich + Dahlem, Munich
Galerie Krohn, Badenweiler, West Germany
Galerie Werner, West Berlin
1966 Galerie Springer, West Berlin
1967 Galerie Obere Zaune, Zurich
Galerie Beck, Erlangen, West Germany
1969 Galerie Beck, Erlangen, West Germany
1970 *Zeichnungen,* Kunstmuseum, Basel
Galerie Berner, Stuttgart
Franz Dahlem Galeriehaus, Cologne
Tekeningen en Schilderijen, Wide White Space Gallery, Antwerp
1971 Galerie Rothe, Heidelberg
Galerie Borgmann, Cologne
Galerie Tobies & Silex, Cologne
1972 Galerie Grafikmeyer, Karlsruhe
Gemalde und Zeichnungen, Kunsthalle, Mannheim
Kunstverein, Hamburg
Staatliche Graphische Sammlung, Munich

Georg Baselitz: *Orangenesser I,* 1981. ©Georg Baselitz, 2001.

Galerie Loehr, Frankfurt
Galerie im Goethe-Institut, Amsterdam
Galerie Rudolf Zwirner, Cologne
1973 *Bilder, Objekte, Filme, Konzepte,* Galerie Heiner Freidrich, Munich
Galerie Loehr, Frankfurt
Galerie Grunangergasse, Vienna
Ein neuer Typ, Galerie Neuendorf, Hamburg
1974 Galerie Heiner Friedrich, Cologne
Radierungen 1963–1974/Holzschnitte 1966–1967, Städtisches Museum Schloss Morsbroich, Leverkusen, West Germany
Städtisches Galerie Altes Theater, Ravensburg, West Germany
1975 Galerie Heiner Friedrich, Munich
Galerie Michael Werner, Cologne
Galerie Loehr, Frankfurt
1976 Staatsgalerie Moderner Kunst, Munich
Malerei, Handzeichnungen, Druckgraphik, Kunsthalle, Berne
Galerie Heiner Friedrich, Cologne
Kunsthalle, Cologne
1977 Galerie Heiner Friedrich, Cologne
Galerie Heiner Friedrich, Munich
1978 Galerie Helen van der Meij, Amsterdam
Galerie Heiner Friedrich, Cologne
1979 Galerie Gillespie/De Laage, Paris
Bilder 1977–78, Stedelijk van Abbenuseum, Eindhoven, Netherlands
32 Linolschnitte aus den Jahren 1976 bis 1979, Josef-Haubrich-Kunsthalle, Cologne
Tekeningen/Zeichnungen, Groninger Museum, Groningen, Netherlands
1980 Galerie Heiner Friedrich, Cologne
Galerie Gillespie/De Laage, Paris,
Galerie Rudolf Springer, West Berlin
Whitechapel Art Gallery, London (with Max Beckmann)
Centre d'Arts Plastiques Contemporains, Bordeaux (with A.R. Penck and Joseph Beuys)
1981 kastrupgardsamlingen, Kastrup, Denmark
Galerie Michael Werner, Cologne
Stedelijk van Abbemuseum, Eindhoven, Netherlands
Kunsthalle, Dusseldorf (with Gerhard Richter)
Kunstverein, Braunschweig, West Germany
Das Strassenbild, Stedelijk Museum, Amsterdam
Galerie Annemarie Verna, Zurich
Galerie Fred Jahn, Munich
Xavier Fourcade Inc, New York
1982 *Zeichnungen,* Galerie Michael Werner, Cologne
Sonnabend Gallery, New York
Waddington Galleries, London
Galerie Fred Jahn, Munich
Galerie Rudolf Zwirner, Cologne
Anthony D'Offay, London
Galerie Helen van der Meij, Amsterdam
Galerie Springer, West Berlin
Xavier Fourcade Inc., New York
Young Hoffman Gallery, Chicago
Galerie Nachst St. Stephan, Vienna
Kunstverein, Gottingen, West Germany
1983 Galerie Michael Werner, Cologne
CAPC Musée d'Art Contemporain, Bordeaux, France
Galerie Albert Baronian, Brussels
Galerie Springer, West Berlin
Galerie am Markt, Schwabisch Hall, West Germany
Galerie Gillespie-Laage-Salomon, Paris
Xavier Fourcade Inc., New York
Sonnabend Gallery, New York
Galerie Neuendorf, Hamburg (twice)
Akron Art Museum, Ohio (with Julian Schnabel)
Whitechapel Art Gallery, London
Galerie Folker Skulima, West Berlin
Galerie Fred Jahn, Munich
Los Angeles County Museum of Art
1984 Van Abbemuseum, Eindhoven, Netherlands (drawings retrospective)
University of California, Berkeley
Kunstmuseum, Basel
Kunsthalle, Basel
Mary Boone/Michael Werner Gallery, New York
Neue Pinakothek, Munich (graphics retrospective)
Galerie Borgmann, Cologne
Stadtische Kunstmuseum, Bonn
Musée d'Art et d'Histoire, Geneva
Kunstverein, Freiburg, West Germany
Galerie Meyer-Ellinger, Frankfurt
Kunsthalle, Nuremberg, West Germany

Artotheque, Lyon, France
Waddington Galleries, London
Vancouver Art Gallery, British Columbia
Deweer Art Gallery, Zwevegem-Otegem, Belgium
Galerie Michael Werner, Cologne

1985 Galerie Fred Jahn, Munich
Stadtisches Museum Simeonstift, Trier, West Germany
DAAD-Galerie, West Berlin
Kunstverein, Hannover
Galerie Gillespie-Laage-Salomon, Paris
Bibliothèque Nationale, Paris (print and sculpture retrospective)
Galerie Collection d'Art Amsterdam
Galerie-Lager Rudolf Zwirner, Cologne
Galerie Joachim Becker, Cannes, France
Anthony d'Offay, London
Haus am Waldsee, West Berlin
Kunsthalle, Bielefeld, West Germany
Galerie Thomas Borgmann, Cologne
Ernst Barlach Haus, Hamburg
Alpha Gallery, Boston
Kunstverein, Oldenburg, West Germany

1986 Kunstmuseum, Winterthur, Switzerland
Mary Boone/Michael Werner Gallery, New York
Galerie Beyeler, Basel
Muzej Savremene Umetnosti, Belgrade
Obalne Galerije, Piran, Yugoslavia
Galerija Loza, Koper, Yugoslavia
Cankarjev Dom, Liubliana, Yugoslavia
Galerija Grada, Zagreb, Yugoslavia
Galerija Suvremene Umjetnosti, Zagreb, Yugoslavia
Galerie Beuamont, Luxembourg
Galerie Thaddaeus Ropac, Salzburg, Austria
Galerie Chobot, Vienna
Sonja Henie/Nils Onstads Stifelser, Oslo
Monchehaus Museum fur moderne Kunst, Goslar, West Germany
Wiener Secession, Vienna
Galerie Heike Curtze, Vienna
Galerie Springer, West Berlin

1987 Maximilian Verlag/Sabine Knust, Munich
Meine Kleine Galerie, Hildesheim, West Germany
Gallerie Christian Stein, Milan
Galerie Collection d'Art, Amsterdam
Kestner-Gesellschaft, Hannover
Galerie Buchmann, Basel
Museum Ludwig, Cologne
Galerie Neuendorf, Frankfurt
Anthony D'Offay Gallery, London

1990 Pace Gallery, New York
Michael Werner Gallery, New York
Anthony d'Offay Gallery, London
Musée de l'Abbaye Sainte-Croix, Sables d'Olonne, France

1991 Mary Boone Gallery, New York
Anthony d'Offay Gallery, London
Galerie Michael Werner, Cologne

1992 Michael Werner Gallery, New York
Busch-Reisinger Museum, Harvard University, Cambridge, Massachusetts
Pace Gallery, New York

1993 Galerie Fred Jahn, Munich
Kunstmuseum Basel, Basel, Switzerland
Musée National d'Art Moderne, Centre Georges Pompidou, Paris
The Pace Gallery, New York
Gana Art Gallery, Seoul, South Korea

1994 Saarland Museum, Saarbrücken
Galerie Beaumont, Luxembourg
Anthony d'Offay Gallery, London
Georg Baselitz—Druckgraphik 1965–1992, Institut für Auslandsbeziehungen, Stuttgart
Stedelijk Museum, Amsterdam
Edicions T Galeria d'Art, Barcelona

1995 Galerie Hübner und Thiel, Dresden
Galerie Jamileh Weber, Zürich
Departamento de Artes Plásticas de la Facultad de Artes, Universidad de Chile, Santiago
Guggenheim Museum, New York
PaceWildenstein, Los Angeles, California

1996 Michael Werner Gallery, New York
Galerie Kornfeld, Zürich
Galerie Borkowski, Hannover
Galerie Springer, Berlin
Musée d'Art Moderne de la Ville de Paris, Paris

1997 PaceWildenstein, New York
Dresdner Kunstverein im Residenzschloß, Dresden
Galleria d'Arte Moderna di Bologna, Bologna
Galerie Lempertz, Bruxelles

1998 Museo Rufino Tamayo, Mexico City
L.A. Louver, Venice
Galerie Michael Werner, Köln, Germany
PaceWildenstein, New York
Galeria Arnés und Röpke, Madrid

1999 Stedelijk Museum, Amsterdam
Galeria Joan Prats, Barcelona
Musée Rath, Musée d'Art et d'Histoire, Geneva
Galerie Laage-Salomon, Paris
Galerie Marlies Hanstein, Saarbrücken
Maximilian Verlag-Sabine Knust, Munich

2000 Galleri Bo Bjerggaard, Copenhagen
Galería Estiarte, Madrid
Die Galerie, Frankfurt
Gagosian Gallery, London

Selected Group Exhibitions:

1968 *14 x 14,* Kunsthalle, Baden-Baden, West Germany
1969 *Kunst und Kritik,* Städtisches Museum, Wiesbaden, West Germany
1971 *Zeichen und Farbe,* Staatsgalerie, Stuttgart
1972 *Documenta 5,* Kassel, West Germany (and *Documenta 7,* 1982)
1973 *Prospekt '73,* Städtische Kunsthalle, Dusseldorf
1975 *Bienal,* Sao Paulo
1980 *Biennale,* Venice
1981 *A New Spirit in Painting,* Royal Academy of Art, London
1985 *The European Iceberg,* Art Gallery of Ontario, Toronto
1987 *Berlinart 1961–87,* Museum of Modern Art, New York (travelled to San Francisco Museum of Modern Art)

1989 *Refigured Painting: The German Image 1960–88,* Toledo Museum of Art, Ohio (travelled to Guggenheim Museum, New York)

1989–90 *Art in Berlin: 1815–1989,* High Museum of Art, Atlanta, Georgia

1991 *Metropolis: Internationale Kunstausstellung Berlin 1991,* Martin-Gropius-Bau, Berlin

1992 *Korrespondenzen,* Galerie Michael Werner, Köln, Germany

1992–93 *Parallel Visions: Modern Artists and Outsider Art,* Los Angeles County Museum of Art, Los Angeles, California (travelled to Museo Nacional Reina Sofía, Madrid; Kunsthalle Basel, Basel, Switzerland; Setagaya Art Museum, Tokyo)

1994 *The Romantic Spirit in German Art 1790–1990,* Royal Scottish Academy and FruitMarket Gallery, Edinburgh (travelled to Hayward Gallery, London; Haus der Kunst, Munich)

1995 *Identità e Alterità: Figure del Corpo 1895/1995,* Bienniale de Venezia, Palazzo Grassi, Venedig

1995 *Carnegie International,* Carnegie Museum of Art, Pittsburgh, Pennsylvania

Collections:

Kunsthalle, Hamburg; Städtisches Museum, Braunschweig, West Germany; Hessisches Landesmuseum, Darmstadt; Sammlung Ludwig, Cologne; Stedelijk Museum, Amsterdam; Museum Boymans-van Beuningen, Rotterdam; Centre Georges Pompidou, Paris; Louisiana Museum of Modern Art, Humlebaek, Denmark; Museum of Contemporary Art, Sydney, Australia; Nationalgalerie, Staatliche Museen zu Berlin; Der Reichstag, Berlin; Ludwig Museum, Budapest; Museum of Art, Kochi, Japan; National Museum of Contemporary Art, Seoul, South Korea; Ludwig Museum im Russischen Museum, Staatliches Russisches Museum, Saint Petersburg; Museo Nacional Centro de Arte Reina Sofia, Madrid; Kunsthaus, Zürich; Scottish National Galley of Modern Art, Edinburgh; Tate Gallery of Modern Art, London; Chicago Art Institute, Illinois; Guggenheim Museum, New York; Metropolitan Museum of Art, New York; Museum of Modern Art, New York; Hirshhorn Museum and Sculpture Garden, Washington D.C.; National Gallery of Art, Washington D.C.

Publications:

By BASELITZ: Books and Pamphlets—*Pandemonium: First Manifesto,* with Eugen Schönebeck, West Berlin 1961; *Pandemonium: Second Manifesto,* with Eugen Schönebeck, West Berlin 1962; *Warum das Bild 'Die grossen Freunde' ein gutes Bild ist,* manifesto and poster, West Berlin 1966; *Comte de Lautreamont: Die Gesange des Maldoror,* gouache illustrations, Munich 1976. **Articles**—''Liber Herr W.'' in *Die Schastrommel* (Berlin/Bolzano), March 1972; ''Vier Wande und Oberlicht'' in *Kunstforum International* (Mainz), no. 4, 1979; ''George Baselitz,'' special monograph issue of *Lo Spazio Umano* (Milan), January/March 1983; ''Painter's Equipment'' in *Burlington Magazine,* April 1988; interview with Siegfried Gohr in *Flash Art,* summer 1993; ''Was du Nicht Bist, ist ein Selbstportrait?'' in *Das Magazin,* June 1994; ''Wrubel'' in *Michail Wrubel—Der Russische Symbolist,* exhibition catalog, Düsseldorf 1996; ''Beim Gerede über die Multikulturelle Gesellschaft. . .'' in *Lufthansa Magazin,* January 1998; ''Es War Einmal'' in *Frankfurter Rundschau,* May 1999; ''Gruß aus Oslo'' in *Kunsthaus Zürich, 57 Meisterwerke—Liber Amicorum Für Felix Baumann,* exhibition catalog, Zürich 2000; ''Russenbilder'' in *Georg Baselitz,* exhibition catalog, New York 2000.

On BASELITZ: Books—*Baselitz,* exhibition catalog, with text by Martin G. Butler, Herbert Read and Edouard Roditi, West Berlin 1963; *Baselitz: Zeichnungen,* exhibition catalog, with text by Dieter Koeppplin, Antwerp 1970; *Georg Baselitz: Zeichnungen und Radierungen,* exhibition catalog, with text by Herbert Poe, Munich 1972; *George Baselitz: Gemalde und Zeichnungen,* exhibition catalog, with text by Heinz Fuchs, Mannheim 1972; *George Baselitz: Ein neuer Typ,* exhibition catalog, with text by Günther Gercken, Hamburg 1973; *Bilder, Objekte, Filme, Konzepte,* exhibition catalog, Munich 1973, *Georg Baselitz: Radierungen 1963–1974/Holzschnitte 1966–1967,* exhibition catalog, with text by Rolf Wedewer, Fred Jahn and Mircea Eliade, Leverkusen, West Germany 1974, 13. *Bienal de Sao Paulo:* George Baselitz, exhibition catalog with text by Evelyn Weiss, Cologne 1975; *Baselitz: Malerei, Handzeichnungen, Druckgraphik,* exhibition catalog, with text by Theo Kneubuhler, Berne 1976; *Georg Baselitz* exhibition catalog, with text by Carla Schulz-Hoffman, Günther Gercken and Johannes Gachnang, Munich 1976; *Georg Baselitz: Bilder 1977–78,* exhibition catalog, with text by Rudi Ruchs, Eindhoven, Netherlands 1979; *Georg Baselitz: 32 Linolschnitte aus den Jahren 1976 bis 1979,* exhibition catalog, with texts by Siegfried Gohr and Fred Jahn, Cologne 1979; *Georg Baselitz: Tekeningen/Zeichnungen,* exhibition catalog with texts by Frans Haks and Johannes Gachnang, Groningen, Netherlands 1979; *Georg Baselitz: Biennale de Venezia 1980,* exhibition catalog, with texts by Johannes Gachnang, Theo Kneubuhler and Klaus Gallwitz, Stuttgart 1980; *Georg Baselitz: Das Strassenbild,* exhibition catalog, with text by A. van Grevenstein, Amsterdam 1981; *George Baselitz: Zeichnungen,* exhibition catalog, with text by H. Heere, Cologne 1982; *Georg Baselitz: Holzplastiken,* exhibition catalog, with texts by A. Franzke, R. H. Fuchs and S. Gohr, Cologne 1983; *Baselitz: Paintings 1960–83,* exhibition catalog with texts by N. Serota and R. Calvocoressi, London 1983; *Georg Baselitz: Das malerische Werk 1960–83, Linolschnitte 1976–79,* exhibition catalog, with texts by J.C. Ammann and R. Calvocoressi, Basel 1984; *Georg Baselitz: Selected Prints 1963–85,* exhibition catalog, with text by J.E. Fink, Boston 1985; *Georg Baselitz: Baume,* exhibition catalog, with texts by E. Kob, O. Rychlik and H. Hrachovec, Vienna 1986; *Georg Baselitz: Skulpturen und Zeichnungen 1979–1987,* exhibition catalog, with texts by C. Haenlein, A. M. Hammacher and others, Hannover 1987; *Georg Baselitz* by Andreas Franzke, Munich 1989; *Georg Baselitz* by Barry Barker, London 1990; *Georg Baselitz—Eine Fotographische Studie von Edward Quinn* by Edward Quinn, Bern 1993; *Georg Baselitz—Skulpturen,* exhibition catalog with text by Uwe M. Schneede and Günther Gercken, Hamburg 1994; *Georg Baselitz bei Jamileh Weber,* exhibition catalog with text by Franz Meyer, Zürich 1995; *Georg Baselitz—Holzschnitte,* exhibition catalog with text by Siegfried Gohr, Wien 1996; *Über Baselitz—Aufsätze und Gespräche, 1976–1996* by Siegfried Gohr, Köln 1996; *Georg Baselitz—Charabia et Basta, Entretiens avec Éric Darragon* by Éric Darragon, Paris 1996; *Georg Baselitz—Fracture Paintings,* exhibition catalog with text by Richard Shiff, New York 1997; *Georg Baselitz—Neue Bilder,* exhibition catalog with text by Werner Schade, Köln 1998; *Wie Ungewöhnlich Modern* by Norman Rosenthal, Düsseldorf 1999; *Georg Baselitz—Schlafende Hunde,* exhibition catalog with text by Heinrich Heil and Georg Baselitz, Munich 1999; *Maleri og Tegning/Paintings and Drawings—Georg Baselitz,* exhibition catalog with text by Peter Laugesen, Copenhagen 2000.

* * *

From the end of the 1960s, in a search for a new equilibrium—new, but still within the dimension of painting, clarifying the control of the actual picture through well-thought analytical premises—Georg Baselitz has continually explored the modalities of a procedure which, while making use of recognizable images, refutes the classical conceptions—the sense of space, composition, perspective, the idea of style, etc. What we see is thus the continuous and constant presentation of the negation of exposition, of meaning, of the subject-object relationship that makes reality manifest as if reflected in a mirror.

Since 1969, Baselitz has produced images of upside-down human figures, painted and drawn with loose, choppy gestures in bright, raw colors. By inverting the subject, Baselitz's paintings tend to confuse the viewer, distorting the organized mechanisms of visual perception. They repudiate sensuousness, the quality of traditionally accepted painting, the subject, and all those other elements that show painting to be a reference *to* something. The picture, the work, thus becomes just a picture, a work—an enquiry into painting filtered through a complex pre-established mental process and a play of arbitrary elaborations. ''The reality is the picture, it is most certainly not in the picture.'' (GB)

Baselitz's figures since the mid-eighties have become further fragmented or dissolved against crudely gridded, splotched, or dense backgrounds. The artist has also created a number of sculptural figures from limewood, carved and painted with a primitivist force and directness.

What is exceptional in Georg Baselitz's methods lies in the fact that his works repudiate ''painting with images'' by actually using recognizable images which are presented directly as themselves, with no suggestion of story or description. The picture thus has to be looked at, not as a mirror on the world, but as a world in itself, self-sufficient.

It is as if these works had been executed with a technique such as might be used to build a boat actually in the sea during a shipwreck. Painting that does not have to flirt with structuralism, but is rather looked at casually, establishes an equilibrium of its own; the boat will not sink provided there are eyes to be sure of being present at the shipwreck—that of the modern age. The artist is building rafts with his pictures, fragments at a time of the recent past which, despite everything, are still in our present time and fragments of the present projected into the next moment, fragments which together (deliberately or not, it matters little) build a bridge towards ''that which has been.''

—Essay by Demetrio Paparoni; updated by Dorothy Valakos

BASKIN, Leonard

Nationality: American. **Born:** New Brunswick, New Jersey, 15 August 1922. **Education:** At a yeshiva, Brooklyn, New York, 1929–38; studied at New York University of School of Architecture and Allied Arts, 1939–40; Yale University School of Fine Arts, 1941–42; Académie de la Grande Chaumiére, Paris, 1950; Accademia di Belle Arte, Florence, 1951. **Military Service:** Served in the United States Navy, 1943–46. **Career:** Independent artist active in sculpture, painting and printmaking as well as calligraphy, design and illustration. Instructor in Printmaking, Worcester Art Museum, Massachusetts, 1952. Has taught at Smith College, Northampton, Massachusetts, since 1953. **Awards:** Honorable Mention for Sculpture, Prix de Rome, 1940; Tiffany Foundation Fellowship for Sculpture, 1947; Guggenheim Fellowship, 1953; Ohara Prize, National Museum of Tokyo, 1954; National Institute of Arts and Letters Grant, 1961; Mather Prize, Art Institute of Chicago, 1961; Widener Medal, Pennsylvania Academy of Fine Arts, 1965; Special Medal of Merit, American Institute of Graphic Arts, 1965; Medal, National Institute of Arts and Letters, 1969; Cultural Achievement in the Arts Award, National Foundation for Jewish Culture, 1995; Honorary Degree, Springfield College, Springfield, Massachusetts, 1997. **Agent:** R. Michelson Galleries, 132 Main St., Northampton, Massachusetts 01060, U.S.A. **Died:** 3 June 2000.

Individual Exhibitions:

1952 Mount Holyoke College, South Hadley, Massachusetts
1957 Worcester Art Museum, Massachusetts
1961 Museum Boymans-van Beuningen, Rotterdam
Le Centre Culturel Americain, Paris
University of Minnesota, Minneapolis
1962 Royal Watercolor Society Galleries, London
Bowdoin College Museum of Art, Brunswick, Maine
1963 Maxwell Galleries, San Francisco
1966 Peale House, Pennsylvania Academy of the Fine Arts, Philadelphia
1968 Stockholm National Museum (travelled to Oslo, Norway and Gothenburg, Sweden)
1970 *Leonard Baskin: The Graphic Work 1950–1970,* FAR Gallery, New York
Smithsonian Institution, Washington, D.C.
Illustrations for the Divine Comedy of Dante by Leonard Baskin, Yale University, New Haven, Connecticut
1971 Kennedy Galleries, New York
1972 *Indian Drawings,* Amon Carter Museum, Fort Worth, Texas
Brookhaven National Laboratory, Associated Universities, Upton, New York
1973 Kennedy Galleries, New York
1974 Kennedy Galleries, New York
Summit Art Center, New Jersey
Museum of Fine Arts, Springfield, Massachusetts
1975 Kennedy Galleries, New York
Watercolors for a Passover Haggadah, Fine Arts Museums of San Francisco
1976 Kennedy Galleries, New York
Indianapolis Museum of Art
Townson State College Art Gallery, Baltimore, Maryland
1977 Prince Arthur Galleries, Toronto
Port Washington Public Library, New York
Lockhaven Art Center, Orlando, Florida
1978 *Images of Man,* Washington University Gallery of Art, St. Louis
Recent Works, Kennedy Galleries, New York

1980 Kennedy Galleries, New York
1981 Cottage Gallery, London
Leonard Baskin's West, Amon Carter Museum, Forth Worth, Texas (toured the Western United States)
1982 *Sculpture and Watercolors,* Kennedy Galleries, New York
1991 *Leonard Baskin: Images in Diverse Media,* Gallery 68, Belfast, Maine
1992 *Angels to the Jews,* Midtown Payson Gallery, New York (travelled to Portland Museum of Art, Portland, Maine)
44 Years of Printmaking, Art Institute of Boston, Massachusetts
The Gehenna Press Fifty Years, Bridwell Library, Southern Methodist University, Dallas, Texas (toured the United States)
1993 *Recent Prints and Drawings,* Dorothy McRae Gallery, Atlanta, Georgia
1994 *Caprices, Grotesques and Homages: Leonard Baskin and The Gehenna Press,* Library of Congress, Washington, D.C.
Monotypes, Susan Conway Gallery, Georgetown, Washington, D.C.
Prints of Leonard Baskin, Ann Arbor Art Association, Ann Arbor, Michigan
R. Michelson Galleries, Northampton, Massachusetts
1995 *Recent Work,* Midtown Payson Gallery, New York
Recent Works on Paper, Callahan Gallery, Boston, Massachusetts
Leonard Baskin: Retrospective, Instituto de Artes Graficas, Oaxaca, Mexico
Angels and Ancestors, Wilshire Boulevard Temple, Beverly Hills, California
1996 *Native Americans: Second Series,* Corporate Center, Cleveland, Ohio
Leonard Baskin: Prints, Sculpture, Drawings and Books, Bradley University, Peoria, Illinois
The Human Condition, Selected Works by Leonard Baskin, S.F.A. Gallery, Stephen F. Austin State University, Nacogdoches, Texas
1997 *Leonard Baskin: Bronze Reliefs and Drawings for the FDR Memorial,* Serge Sorokko Galleries, San Francisco, California
Leonard Baskin Monotypes, Etchings and Sculpture, Susan Conway Gallery, Washington, D.C.
Leonard Baskin FDR Memorial, R. Michelson Galleries, Northampton, Massachusetts
Leonard Baskin Sculpture, Salander-O'Reilly Gallery, New York
1998 Hunter Museum of American Art, Chatanooga, Tennessee
Leonard Baskin, The Monumental Woodcuts, 1952–1997, Aschenbach Foundation, San Francisco Palace of the Legion of Honor, California
1999 *Works from Children's Books,* R. Michelson Galleries, Northampton, Massachusetts
2000 *Monumental Woodcuts,* DeYoung Museum, San Franicsco, California
Final Works, R. Michelson Galleries, Northampton, Massachusetts
Leonard Baskin: Memorial Exhibition, R. Michelson Galleries, Northampton, Massachusetts

Selected Group Exhibitions:

1961 *Bienal,* San Paulo
1962 *American Paintings and Drawings from Michigan Collections,* Detroit Institute of Arts
1969 *The Figurative Tradition in Recent American Art,* at the Biennale, Venice (travelled to National Collection of Fine Arts, Washington, D.C. and Sheldon Gallery, University of Nebraska, Lincoln)
1979 *The American View,* Mac Nider Museum, Mason City, Iowa
1980 *Sculpture in the 70s: The Figure,* Pratt Manhattan Center Gallery, New York
A Penthouse Aviary, Museum of Modern Art, New York
1992 *William Morris and His Heirs: A Kelmscott Centennial: Baskin, Van Vliet, and Hammer,* Minnesota Center for the Book Arts, Minneapolis
1995 *Celebrating the New Gallery: Inaugural Exhibition,* R. Michelson Gallery, Northampton, Massachusetts
Sculpture and Drawings, Islington Design Center, London
1996 *Poets At Gehenna 1959–1995,* University of California, San Diego, California (toured the United States)

Collections:

Museum of Modern Art, New York; Whitney Museum, New York; Hirshhorn Collection, Smithsonian Institution, Washington, D.C.; National Gallery of Art, Washington, D.C.; Museum of Fine Arts, Boston; Art Institute of Chicago; Detroit Institute of Arts; Amon Carter Museum of Art, Fort Worth, Texas; Vatican Museum, Rome; Albright-Knox Gallery, Buffalo, New York; Bezelel National Museum, Jerusalem, Israel; British Museum, London, England; Kunst Pa Arbeidsplassen, Oslo, Norway; Library of Congress, Washington, D.C.; National Museum of American Art, Smithsonian Institution, Washington, D.C.; Victoria and Albert Museum, London.

Public Installations:

Woodrow Wilson Memorial, Washington, D.C.; *Holocaust Memorial,* University of Michigan, Ann Arbor 1994; *Franklin Delano Roosevelt Memorial,* Washington, D.C. 1997.

Publications:

By BASKIN: Books—*To Color Thought,* New Haven, Connecticut 1967; *Figures of Dead Men,* Amherst, Massachusetts 1968; *5 Addled Etchers,* Hanover, New Hampshire 1969; *Baskin: Sculpture, Drawings, Prints,* New York 1970; **Books Illustrated—***Creatures of Darkness by Esther Baskin, Boston 1962; The Iliad of Homer,* translated by Richmond Lattimore, Chicago 1962; *The Poppy and Other Deadly Plants* by Esther Baskin, New York 1967; *The Divine Comedy* by Dante Alighieri, translated by Thomas Bergin, New York 1969; *Hosie's Alphabet* by Hosea, Tobias and Lisa Baskin, New York 1972; *Selected Poems 1957–1967* by Ted Hughes, New York 1973; *A Passover Haggadah,* New York 1974; *Season Songs* by Ted Hughes, New York 1975; *Hosie's Aviar* by Tobias, Hosea, Lucretia and Lisa Baskin, New York 1979; *Chosen Days* by David Rosenberg, New York 1980; *Hosie's Zoo* by Tobias, Hosea, Lucretia and Lisa Baskin, New York 1981; *Under the North Star* by Ted Hughes, New York

1981; *Did You Say Ghosts* by Richard Michelson, 1993; *Animals That Ought to Be* by Richard Michelson, 1996; *A Book of Flies* by Richard Michelson, 1999; *Ten Times Better* by Richard Michelson, 2000. **Articles**—''New Talent in the USA: with Note by the Artist'' in *Art in America* (New York), February 1956; ''The Necessity for the Image'' in *Atlantic Monthly* (Boston), April 1961; ''To Wear Blood Stain with Honor'' in *Judaism* (New York), vol. 10, 1961; ''On the Nature of Originality'' in *Show* (New York), August 1963; ''Of Roots and Veins: A Testament'' in *Atlantic Monthly* (Boston), September 1964; ''Studio Talk . . . Industrial Sand Casting in Bronze: An Interview with Leonard Baskin'' in *Arts* (New York), February 1967.

On BASKIN: Books—*Conversations with Artists* by Selden Rodman, New York 1961; *The Sculpture of Leonard Baskin* by Irma Jaffe, New York 1980; *Profiles of American Artists Represented by Kennedy Galleries* by Gloria-Gilda Deak, New York 1981; *Leonard Baskin,* exhibition catalog, San Francisco, California 1990; *Leonard Baskin: Angels to the Jews,* exhibition catalog, New York 1991; *The Gehenna Press: The Work of Fifty Years, 1942–1992,* exhibition catalog by Lisa Unger Baskin and Hosea Baskin, Dallas 1992. **Articles**—''Art: Baskin's Foreboding Reflections'' by Dore Ashton in the *New York Times,* 2 April 1958; ''Nouvelles Images de L'Homme'' by Peter Selz in *L'Oeil* (Paris), February 1960; ''Leonard Baskin'' by Brian O'Doherty in *Art in America* (New York), Summer 1962; ''Leonard Baskin'' by Brian O'Doherty in *Art in America* (New York), August 1963; ''Baskin and the Sooty God'' by John Canaday in the *New York Times,* 9 February 1964; ''Leonard Baskin: Printer, Teacher, Affluent Artist—The Pleasant Pariah'' by Jane Howard in *Life* (New York), 24 January 1964; ''Leonard Baskin's Gehenna Press'' by D. R. Roylance in *Art in America* (New York), November 1966; ''Baskin—His Graphic Work'' by J. T. Butler in *Connoisseur* (London), May 1970; ''Art's Poet Laureate'' by Douglas Davis in *Newsweek* (New York), 29 June 1970; ''Images of Man'' by Alfred Werner in *Art and Artists* (London), October 1976; ''FDR Memorial: A Monument to Politics, Bureaucracy and the Art of Accommodation'' by M. N. Carter in *Artnews* (New York), October 1978; ''History and Fate in Leonard Baskin's Sculpture'' by J. Deckert in *Arts* (New York), June 1980. **Films**—*Unseemly Passions: A Visit with Leonard Baskin* by Christopher Lydon, 1993.

* * *

Leonard Baskin is one of those anomalies of contemporary art, though more complex than most. He belongs to the 20th century, to a certain extent is of it, yet repudiates it. He has not received the recognition he deserves, simply because he is not and did not want to be in the so-called mainstream of modern art. It is hard to say whether the neglect of this major artist is due to his own intransigence or to the myopia of art critics and art historians. There is another element: for me, at least, his output is uneven; that is, one could defend the neglect with reference to certain works. This makes an assessment of Baskin's achievement difficult.

Although his reputation rests on his sculpture, to my mind his chief title to fame is as a draughtsman and watercolourist and, secondly, as a printer, engraver, maker of wood-cuts and lithographs, in that order. His illustrations for Ted Hughes's poem *Crow* are masterly, the equal of any studies of birds by Picasso.

Even in his sculpture he was unfailingly successful in his treatment of birds, some pathetic, some menacing. His treatment of the human form is not quite so successful. Some works have the simplicity, if not the charm, of Barlach, whom Baskin much admired—he even did a head of Barlach in 1959; most impressive. His ''Seated Woman'' and ''Seated Man with Owl'' have the simple eloquence of the best of 20th century sculpture, well worthy of Barlach. Like Barlach, Baskin has been in search of humanistic, spiritual and religious values in sculpture which reach back beyond the Renaissance, to the late Middle Ages, to the simple expression of Tino de Camaino, particularly the sinister Counsellors of Pisa.

Baskin's themes are mostly drawn from the Bible and classical mythology, with some symbolic representations of abstract ideas—expulsion, thought, silence. The human figure, usually cast in bronze, sometimes nude, sometimes elaborately swathed in garments, is central to his work, as it was to the sculptors of the Renaissance and to Rodin, whom, in his more elaborate works, he closely resembles—there is the same malleability of material, the sensuousness of moulding of garments, etc.

At his best Baskin could produce powerful and impressive sculptural images. But he had a tendency to over dramatize and to be highly emotional, when restraint would have been more effective, as in his ''Prodigal Son'' (compare it with Barlach's version of the same subject). And, at times, his fantastical works made very little impact and seem to belong to a private, eccentric vision, rather than to one which can be shared.

But his versatility, not only in the variety of media in which he is supremely competent, but also in the variety of visual ideas, is remarkable. I have mentioned his studies of birds (and other animals studies must be added); add his treatment of the human form, of legendary and symbolic subjects (to which one must add subjects from European and American literature, Dante, Shakespeare, etc), and his fantasies. There are also his portraits of artists (Gericault, Corot, Velasquez) and of literary figures (Melville, Blake, John Skelton). And there are excellent pastiches, such as his ''Homage to August Saint-Gaudens.''

Baskin will probably not be seen for what he is—an artist in the European tradition, who continued that tradition, while being open, in part, to new developments in the visual arts, artist of individual, original, if sometimes eccentric, vision—until the dust of 'modernism' settles.

—D. C. Barrett

BATTAGLIA, Carlo

Nationality: Italian. **Born:** La Maddalena, Sardinia, 28 January 1933. **Education:** Studied at the Accademia delle Belle Arti, Rome, 1952–57. **Military Service:** Served in the Italian Air Force, 1958–59. **Family:** Married 1) Anna Paparetti in 1959 (divorced, 1962); 2) Carla Panicali in 1972. **Career:** Designed scenery for *La Merce Esclusa* by Elio Pagliarani, at the Teatro Parioli, Rome, 1965; assistant professor of scenography, Accademia delle Belle Arti, Rome, 1970–72. **Agent:** Galleria L'Isola, Via Gregoriana 5, 00187 Rome. **Address:** Via di Monserrato 111, 00186 Rome, Italy.

Individual Exhibitions:

1964 Galleria La Salita, Rome
1965 Galleria La Metopa, Bari, Italy

1966 Galleria Salone Annunciata, Milan
1968 Galleria Editalia, Rome (with Nicola Carrino)
Galleria Salone Annunciata, Milan
Galleria Arco d'Alibert Rome
Galleria Qui Arte Contemporanea, Rome
1969 Galleria Flori, Florence
Galleria Qui Arte Contemporanea, Rome
Galleria Editalia, Rome
1970 Galleria Salone Annunciata, Milan
Biennale, Venice
1971 Deson-Zaks Gallery, Chicago
Galleria Salone Annunciata, Milan
1972 Galleria Editalia, Rome
Galleria Peccolo, Livorno
Galleria Qui Arte Contemporanea, Rome
Westend Galerie, Frankfurt
Studio 3Bi, Bolzano, Italy
1973 Galleria Godel, Rome
Galleria Nova Arte Moderna, Prato, Italy
1974 Galleria Salone Annunciata, Milan
Carlo Battaglia, Palazzo Grassi, Venice
Studio Soldano, Milan
1975 Studio 3Bi, Bolzano, Italy
Galleria Il Sole, Bolzano, Italy
Galleria Il Segnapassi, Pesaro, Italy
Galerie Daniel Templon, Paris
Galleria La Bertesca, Genoa
1976 Galeria Arnessen, Copenhagen
Galleria Salone Annunciata, Milan
Galeria La Bertesca, Düsseldorf
Palazzo dei Diamante, Ferrara
1977 Studio 2Bi, Bolzano, Italy
Galleria Il Sole, Bolzano, Italy
Galleria La Bertesca, Rome
Studio Ennesse, Milan
1978 Galleria E Tre, Rome
Kunsthalle, Düsseldorf
1980 Studio 3Bi, Bolzano
Sergio Tosi, New York
Galleria Civica, Alessandria, Italy
Galleria E Tre, Rome
Studio Grossetti, Milan
Ann Jacob Gallery, Atlanta, Georgia
Biennale, Venice
Galleria Il Sole, Bolzano, Italy
1981 Lo Spazio, Naples
1983 Galleria Il Sole, Bolzano
Galeria Albrecht, Caldaro, Bolzano
Galleria L'Isola, Rome
Studio Carlo Grossetti, Milan
1984 Ann Jacob Gallery, Atlanta
1985 Galleria Arte Duchamp, Cagliari, Italy
Galleria L'Isola, Rome
1986 Galleria Forzani, Terni, Italy
Museo Civico d'Arte Contemporanea, Gibellina, Italy
Studio Marconi, Milan
1987 Galleria Ellequadro, Genoa
1988 Galleria L'Isola, Rome
Galleria L'Iride, Nuoro
1989 Deson Saunders Gallery, Chicago
Galleria Trimarchi, Bologna
1991 Galleria Paola Steltzer, Trento, Italy
Galleria L'Isola, Rome
1992 Studio Ghiglione, Genoa
1994 Galleria L'Isola, Rome
1996 Galleria L'Isola, Trento, Italy
1998 Studio, La Maddalena, Italy

Selected Group Exhibitions:

1964 *Arte Nuova,* Konsthall, Lund, Sweden
1966 *Peintures Italiennes d'Aujourd'hui,* Teheran
1968 *6th Biennale Romana,* Palazzo Esposizioni, Rome
1972 *Proposta a Quattro,* Galleria del Milione, Milan
1975 *Tendensen Moderne Kunst,* Nordjylands Kunstmuseum, Aalborg, Denmark (travelled to Stifts Museum, Odense, Denmark)
1978 *Biennale,* Venice
1980 *Arte e Critice,* Museo Nazionale d'Arte Moderna, Rome
1982 *Arte Italiana 1960–82,* Hayward Gallery, London
1984 *Art from Italy,* Hirshhorn Museum, Washington, D.C.
1986 *Arte e Scienza-Colore,* at the *Biennale,* Venice
1987 *Mélanos,* Galleria Anna D'Ascanio, Rome
1988 *Kunstzaken,* Beurs van Berlage, Amsterdam
1989 *Progetto Firenze per l'Arte Moderna,* Fortezza da Basso, Firenze
1990 Arte Fiera, Bologna
1994 Art Fair, Basel, Switzerland
1999 *Lavori in corso,* Stabilimento ex Birreria Peroni, Rome

Collections:

Museo Nazionale d'Arte Moderna, Rome; Boymans-van Beuningen Museum, Rotterdam; Louisiana Museum, Humlebaek, Denmark; Museo Soto, Ciudad Bolivar, Venezuela; Hirshhorn Museum and Sculpture Garden, Smithsonian Institution, Washington, D.C.

Publications:

By BATTAGLIA: Articles—''3 Artists: Ryman, Marden and Bell'' in *Qui Arte Contemporanea* (Rome), June 1973; ''Come Dipingono,'' interview with Griffa Verna, in *Data* (Milan), summer 1973; ''La Pittura come Disciplina,'' with Maurizio Fagiolo, in *Bolaffi Arte* (Turin), April 1975; ''L'Immagine parallela'' in *L'Immagine parallela ed altre congetture,* Genoa 1976; ''Arshile Gorky al Guggenheim'' in *Flash Art* (Milan), no. 105, 1981; ''Fontana, de l'image à l'objet,'' in *Lucio Fontana* (exhibition catalog), Paris, Centre Georges Pompidou, 1987; ''Oltre lo specchio,'' in *David Klamen* (exhibition catalog), Rome, Galleria L'Isola, 1995; *Arte e Critica,* vol. 5, no. 11/12, Spring 1997.

On BATTAGLIA: Books—*Carlo Battaglia* by Tommaso Trini, Milan 1974; *Lo Studio dell'Arcipelago,* Amministrazione Comunale La Maddalena, 1998. **Exhibition Catalogs**—*Elementi per Carlo Battaglia* by Roberto Sanesi, Venice 1974; *Carlo Battaglia* by Filiberto Menna, Düsseldorf 1978; *Carlo Battaglia* by Dore Ashton, New York 1980; *Il corpo della pittura: critici e nuovi pittori in Italia 1972- 76* by Claudio Caritelli, Turin 1986; *Carlo Battaglia* by L'Isola Galleria D'Arte, Trento, 2000. **Articles**—''La Pittura come Paesaggio'' by Gabriella Otudi in *Data* (Milan), May 1972; ''Carlo Battaglia: Ambiguita Visionaria'' by Guido Ballo in *Arte Milano* (Milan), March 1973; ''Carlo Battaglia'' by Filiberto Menna in *Opus International* (Paris), September 1974; ''Carlo Battaglia a Palazzo Grassi, Venezia'' by Gianni in *Nac* (Milan), December 1974; ''Il quadro di Carlo Battaglia'' by Vittorio Fagone in *Data* (Milan), July/September 1976; ''Incontro col pittore Carlo Battaglia'' by Maurizio Fagiolo in *Il Messaggero* (Rome), 18 April 1977; ''Carlo Battaglia, La metrica del mare'' by Vito Apuleo in *Il Messaggero* (Rome), 7 June 1983; ''I paesaggi di Carlo Battaglia'' by Enzo Bilardello in *Corriere della Sera* (Milan), 16 December 1985.

*

''My aspiration is to catch everyone's attention, even those people who know nothing about painting. The idea of landscapes, which obsesses me at the moment, could also be this: The vague discernment of a common need for contemplation. Contemplating is a fundamentally irrational act. I want to pursue this gratuitous impulse until I attain the mutable visionariness of landscapes which escapes the control of logic, but is conveyable by virtue of its obviousness. I see the risks I am running: The idolatry of the mists of emotions or the unconditional surrender to popular banality. Two blind alleys for anyone who is tempted to nullify the enigma of expression. Except I have already made my choice, beyond the point of no return. I say so without hesitation.''

This is an excerpt from an article by Gabriella Drudi about my work in 1972, entitled ''Painting as Landscape,'' an article which, miming a series of conversations we had, put words into my mouth that are much more specific than I was able to formulate at that time. The result of that remote and still vague motive are these pictures. I don't know if I have surmounted those risks, doubt is always the only certainty, but I am relieved to know that I have carried out what I felt obliged to do: This is the only conceit I allow myself. Observation and love lie at the root of these paintings. Identification between painting and landscape, landscape as a place of memory, dreamy distance, timeless portrayal. The reflections in perpetual motion in the clear pure light of the archipelago, the shadows, mysterious abstract clippings, summon up memories, fragments, pictures loved to the point of becoming a part of me, presences, awareness. The ''Madonna Enthroned with Child and Saints'' at S. Zaccaria, the giddy interplay of countless sources of light, sublime challenge of the ''Martyrdom of St. Lawrence'' at the Jesuits, the gold ground no longer a flat emblematic surface but a glowing atmosphere of light-space in the polyptych of the Misericordia in Sansepolcro, the appearance of the city of Delft in Den Haag as the sudden, unexpected materialization of those islands suspended between cobalt blue and ultramarine, murky with green, haloed with pink and violet. An ancient landscape, the presence of the sacred in the absence of man, a landscape that already in itself is structure, archetype.

So I haven't painted rocks and shrubs as such. They are tokens, essential traits shaped by the age-old erosion of wind and sea, precious traces for re-inventing a pictorial structure free of imitation of representation, a ''parallel code.'' I have sought to paint the air between object and object, island and island, foreground and distances inside a spherical space. The sea, crazed anamorphosis of a checkerboard. To pinpoint the eternal in the prime elements, earth, water, air. Not a specific landscape but the place of universal landscapes. I don't feel like, nor up to, giving theoretical explanations of my work. I am also aware of its probable unactuality as well as its ineluctability. What I can say is that I have attempted to do something that exists once and for all.

As to feelings, passions, expectations and dramas I choose not to speak of them. If I have been capable of expressing them they are contained in the pictures, hence visible to all.

—Carlo Battaglia

* * *

Carlo Battaglia's first one-man show was in 1964 at the La Salita Gallery in Rome. At that time, his work was based on the rapport between space and colour. The show heralded a significant change in his work which, as noted by Milton Gendel in 1966, signified ''the end of his research between the School of Paris and of New York.'' In *Spazio Ambiguo* of 1966, a large rectangle occupies the central part of the canvas in the manner of a window across which an orthogonal takes on the character of a road moving to infinity until interrupted by a horizontal line.

From 1967 his painting changed, in accordance with that particular tendency characterised by Argan as the transition of Cubism from Mondrian to Constructivism. In this year, after a brief stay in Paris, Battaglia moved to New York for some time. The works of this period convey a strong geometric character. Between 1967 and 1968, he produced a series of works forming the cycle Misterioso in which he organized the picture plane in different perspectival planes to create an advancing and receding space. Our attention is directed around an ordered geometrical space of outlines and blocks of form to create a perspectival illusion.

The year 1969 was marked by a new departure. *Light Visionario* and *Solitario* both make their impact as large monochrome canvases with soft and hazy mood. Liberated from any geometric reference these works have become like large windows open to a sky of visionary light. In 1970, the year he took part in the Venice Biennale, Battaglia produced the first works based on two opposing characters, one geometric, and the other evocative and visionary. By now, he had arrived at his personal poetic style. The structure of the surface is abbreviated to horizontal marks or isolated strokes of geometric form overlaying the visionary field of colour and light. Out of this period come *Cadmus, Calypso, Renir, Spargi, Diaspro*—all works of 1970—that confirm the artist's declaration: ''What I have sought to do is to imbue the picture with as much significance as possible, including signifiers whose origin seems quite obscure, to give force to this garden of images.'' Gradually, the geometric shapes give way to the colour-light field which has now assumed a dominant role. Having abandoned geometric rigour, Battaglia releases the picture, free to evoke a natural world.

Grande immagine parallela (1976), a large work of ten metres length, constitutes a poetic introduction to the work which will follow. In this parallel image of the natural world, Battaglia attempts to overcome the anachronistic dichotomy between figuration and abstraction, a position that is to become clearer in later work. Emblematic of this intention is *Grande Oceana Blu* of 1980/81. An area of sea (as evinced by the title) is painted as an arrangement of wavy marks in chiaroscuro. This work recalls those made ten years earlier which evoked a luminescent blue sky, while the most recent works, such as the series *Oltremare* (1982–83), the reference is to the ocean depths.

In this most recent work, references to the natural world are more pronounced. By means of a highly refined technique, Battaglia continually inserts an element of ambivalence, making the meaning difficult to grasp—as in *Gli dei a Gibellina* of 1985, where the landscape continually moves between land and sea. In this way Battaglia stresses his need to put in every significance possible.

—Roberto Lambarelli

BAYER, Herbert

Nationality: American. **Born**: Haag, Austria, 5 April 1900; emigrated to the United States, 1938; naturalized, 1944. **Education:** Gymnasium, Linz, Austria, 1911–17; apprentice in architecture and decorative arts, under architect George Schmidthammer, Linz, 1919; graphic design and typography assistant to architect Emanuel Margold, Darmstadt, Germany, 1920; studied mural painting and design, with Vasily Kandinsky, at the Staatliche Bauhaus, in Weimar, 1921–23, and in Dessau, 1925–28. **Military Service:** Served in Infantry Regiment 14, Austrian Army, 1917–19. **Family:** Married Irene Hecht in 1925 (divorced); daughter: Julia; married Joella Haweis Levy in 1944. **Career:** Young Master of Typography and Graphic Design, Staatliche Bauhaus, Dessau, 1925–28; director, Dorland Studio of Design, and active as painter, photographer, graphic designer and exhibition architect, Berlin 1928–30; painter, photographer, graphic designer, and exhibition architect, New York, 1938–45; director, Dorland International design company, New York, 1945; consultant designer, 1945–56, and chairman of department of design, 1956–65, Container Corporation of America, Chicago. Consultant and architect, Aspen Institute of Humanistic Studies, Colorado, 1946–85; art and design consultant, Atlantic Richfield Company, Los Angeles, 1966–85. Visiting artist, Jerusalem Foundation, 1977; artist-in-residence, American Academy, Rome, 1978. **Awards:** First Prize, *Foreign Advertising Photography* exhibition, New York, 1931; Medal, City of Salzburg, Austria, 1936; Gold Medal, Art Directors Club of Philadelphia, 1961; Trustees Award, Aspen Institute for Humanistic Studies, Colorado, 1965; Ambassador's Award for Excellence, London, 1968; Kulturpreis for Photography, Cologne, 1969; Gold Medal, Amercian Institute of Graphic Arts, 1970; Adalbert Stifter Preis für Bildende Kunst Verliehen, Linz, Austria, 1971; Austrian Cross of Honor for Art and Science, 1978. Honorary Doctorate: Technische Hoschschule, Graz, Austria, 1973; D.F.A.: Philadelphia College of Art, 1974. **Member:** Honorary Member, Alliance Graphique Internationale, 1975; Honorary Fellow, Royal Academy of Fine Art, The Hague, Netherlands, 1975. Fellow, American Academy of Arts and Sciences, 1979. **Agent:** Marlborough Gallery, 40 West 57th Street, New York, New York 10019. **Died:** Montecito, California; 30 September 1985.

Individual Exhibitions:

1929 Kunstverein Marz, Linz, Austria
Galerie Povolotsky, Paris
1931 Staatcliche Bauhaus, Dessau, Germany
1936 Kunstverein, Salzburg, Austria
1937 London Gallery
1939 Black Mountain College, North Carolina
P.M. Gallery, New York
1940 Yale University, New Haven, Connecticut
1943 Willard Gallery, New York
North Texas State Teachers College, Denton
1944 Outline Gallery, Pittsburgh
1947 *The Way Beyond Art,* Brown University, Providence, Rhode Island (retrospective; toured the United States, 1947–49)
1952 Cleveland Institute of Art
1953 Hans Schaeffer Galleries, New York
1954 Kunstkabinett Klihm, Munich
Galleria del Milione, Milan
1955 Aspen Institute for Humanistic Studies, Colorado
1956 *33 Years of Herbert Bayer's Work,* Germanisches Nationalmuseum, Nuremberg, West Germany (retrospective; travelled to Munich, Zurich, Berlin, Braunschweig and Vienna, 1956–57)
1957 Kunstkabinett Klihm, Munich
1958 *Recent Works,* Fort Worth Art Center, Texas (travelled to the Walker Art Center, Minneapolis)
1959 Kunstkabinett Klihm, Munich
1960 Städtische Kunsthalle, Dusseldorf
Museum am Ostwall, Dortmund, West Germany
1961 Bauhaus Archiv, Darmstadt, West Germany
1962 Stadtisches Kunstmuseum, Duisberg, West Germany (retrospective; toured the United States, Germany and Italy)
1963 Andrew Morris Gallery, New York
Neue Galerie, Linz, Austria
1964 Aspen Institute for Humanistic Studies, Colorado 5207 Galleries, Oklahoma City
1965 Byron Gallery, New York
Esther Robles Gallery, Los Angeles
Boise Art Association, Idaho
1966 University of New Hampshire, Durham
1967 Galerie Klihm, Munich
Galerie Conzen, Dusseldorf
Philadelphia Art Alliance
1968 Marlborough New London Gallery
1969 University of California at Santa Barbara
Two Visions of Space: Herbert Bayer and Ingerborg ten Haeff, Hudson River Museum, Yonkers, New York
1970 Dunkelman Gallery, Toronto
Germanisches Nationalmuseum, Nuremberg
Galerie Conzen, Dusseldorf
1971 Marlborough Gallery, New York
Centre Culturel Allemand, Paris
Goethe-Institut, Paris
Die Neue Sammlung, Munich
Österreichisches Museum für Angewandte Kunst, Vienna
1972 Marlborough Gallery, Montreal
Mer-Kup Galerias, Mexico City
1973 Landesbildstelle, Hamburg (travelled to Krefeld and Leverkusen)
Saarland Museum, Saarbrücken
Herbert Bayer: A Total Concept, Denver Art Museum (retrospective)
1974 Marlborough Galerie, Zurich
Galerie Klihm, Munich
Galerie Nächst St. Stephan, Vienna (travelled to Innsbruck and Graz)
Marlborough Graphics, New York (toured the United States, 1974–75)

Das Druckgrafische Werk bis 1971, Haus Deutscher Ring, Hamburg pretrospective; (toured Germany, Switzerland, Portugal and Spain, 1974–76)

1975 Marlborough Gallery, Toronto
Arte Contacto Galeria, Caracas

1976 *Beispiele aus dem Gesamtwerk 1919–1974,* Neue Galerie, Linz, Austria
Graphics and Small Sculptures, Marlborough Gallery, New York
Photomontages, Marlborough Gallery, New York

1977 Marian Locks Gallery, Philadelphia
From Type to Landscape, Hopkins Center, Dartmouth College, Hannover, New Hampshire (Amercian Federation of Art show; toured the United States)
Photographic Works, Arco Center for Visual Art, Los Angeles (toured the United States)

1978 *Tapestries and Environmental Designs,* Galerie Klihm, Munich Museum Bochum, West Germany (retrospective)

1979 *Recent Works,* Marlborough Gallery, New York
Photographic Exhibition, Galerie Breiting, West Berlin

1980 *Inaugural Exhibition of the Herbert Bayer Archive,* Denver Art Museum
Neue Gallery, Linz, Austria
Galerias Mer-Kup, Mexico City

1981 *A Selected Survey,* Grapestake Gallery, San Francisco
Centre Georges Pompidou, Paris (with Umbo)
University of California, Santa Barbara

1982 Bauhaus Archiv, West Berlin (travelled to Basle)

1983 Galerie Thomas, Munich

1984 Galerie Lopes, Zurich
Saidenberg Gallery, New York

1986 Museum fur Gestaltung, West Berlin

1987 Quadrat Moderne Galerie, Bottrop, West Germany
Kunsthaus, Zug, Switzerland
Oberosterreichisches Landesmuseum, Linz, Austria

Selected Group Exhibitions:

1923 *Kunst and Technik: Eine neue Einheit,* Bauhaus und Staatliches
Landesmuseum, Weimar

1929 *Film und Foto,* Stuttgart

1936 *Entartete Kunst,* Haus der Deutschen Kunst, Munich

1959 *V Bienal,* São Paulo

1964 *Documenta,* Kassel, West Germany

1966 *Les Années 25,* Musée des Art Décoratifs, Paris

1967 *50 Jahre Bauhaus,* Württembergische Kunstverein,
Stuttgart (toured Europe, the United States, Canada, Argentina and Japan)

1978 *Paris-Berlin 1900–1933,* Centre Georges Prompidou,Paris

1980 *Avant-Garde Photography in Germany 1919–1939,* San Francisco Museum of Modern Art (toured the United States)

1985 *Das Aktfoto,* Fotomuseum im Stadtmuseum, Munich

1989 *Inside Vision: Surrealist Photography of the 1930s and 1940s,* Museum des 20, Vienna

1992 *Prints and Multiples by Contemporary Masters,* Museo de Arte Moderno, Mexico City

1995 *Paste-up, Past and Present,* Kent Gallery, New York

1997 *The Quick and the Dead: Artists and Anatomy,* Royal College of Art, London (travelled to Mead Gallery, Coventry; Leeds City Art Gallery, Leeds)

1998 *Exodus from Austria: Emigration of Austrian Photographers 1920–40,* Kunsthalle Wien, Vienna

Collections:

Museum of Modern Art, New York; Fogg Art Museum, Cambridge, Massachusetts; Denver Art Museum, Colorado (Archives); Santa Barbara Museum of Art, California; San Francisco Museum of Modern Art; Neue Galerie der Stadt Linz, Austria; Museum Folkwang, Essen; Bauhaus Archiv, Berlin; Nationalgalerie, Berlin; Nazionale d'Arte Moderna, Rome; Brandeis University; Busch-Reisinger Museum, Cambridge, Massachusetts; Wallfraf-Richartz Museum, Cologne, Germany; Wilhelm-Lehmbruck Museum, Germany; Kunstmuseum der Stadt, Düsseldorf, Germany; Hudson River Museum, Yonkers; Vassar College, Poughkeepsie, New York; Oklahoma Art Center, Oklahoma City, Oklahoma.

Publications:

By BAYER: Books—*Fotomontagen,* portfolio of 11 photomontages, Berlin 1932; *Fotoplastiken,* portfolio of 10 photos, Berlin 1937; *Bauhaus 1919–1928,* with Ise and Walter Gropius, New York 1938, 1959, 1975; *Seven Convolutions,* portfolio of lithographs, Colorado Springs 1948; *World Geo-Graphic Atlas,* Aspen, Colorado 1953; *Book of Drawings,* Chicago 1961; *Eight Monochrome Suite,* portfolio of lithographs, Los Angeles 1965; *Herbert Bayer: Paintings,* portfolio of reproductions, Chicago 1965; *Herbert Bayer: Painter/Designer/Architect,* New York, Ravensburg, London and Tokyo 1967; *Herbert Bayer,* portfolio of 6 silkscreens, with introduction by Dieter Honisch, Stuttgart 1968. **Articles—**''Reflections from One of the Sculptors Who Contributed to the 'Route of Friendship''' in *Architecture Formes et Fonctions* (Lausanne), 1969; ''Typography and Design'' in *Concepts of the Bauhaus: Busch-Reisinger Museum Collection,* exhibition catalog, Cambridge, Massachusetts 1971; foreward to *The Graphic Design of Yusaka Kamekura* by Masuro Katsumi, New York 1973; ''Herbert Bayer,'' interview in *Dialogue with Photography,* edited by Paul Hill and Thomas Cooper, London 1979; ''Many Paths from the Bauhaus,'' interview, in *Darkroom Photography (San Francisco),* January/February 1981.

On BAYER: Books—*The Way Beyond Art: The Work of Herbert Bayer* by Alexander Dorner, New York 1947; *Fotoauge Herbert Bayer,* exhibition catalog, edited by Jan Tschichold, Munich 1967; *Herbert Bayer,* exhibition catalog, with text by Ludwig Grote, London 1968; *50 Jahre Bauhaus,* exhibition catalog, by Wulf Herzongenrath, Stuttgart and London 1968; *Two Visions of Space: Herbert Bayer and Ingeborg ten Haeff,* exhibition catalog, with introduction by Carl Black, Jr., New York 1969; *The Bauhaus* by Hans M. Wingler, Cambridge, Massachusetts 1969; *Painters of the Bauhaus* by Eberhard Roters, New York 1969; *Bauhaus and Bauhaus People,* edited by Eckhard Neumann, New York 1970; *Herbert Bayer: A Total Concept,* exhibition catalog, with introduction by Karl Otto Bach, Denver 1973; *Herbert Bayer: Das Druckgraftsche Werk bis 1971,* with text by Hans M. Wingler and Peter Hahn, Berlin 1974;

Herbert Bayer, exhibition catalog, with introductions by Ida Rodriguez Prampolini, Zurich 1974; *Photographie als Kunstlerisches Experiment* by Willi Rotzler, Lucerne and Frankfurt 1974; *Herbert Bayer: Un Concepta Total* by Ida Rodriguez Prampolini, Mexico City 1975; *Beispiele aus dem Gesamtwerk 1919–1974,* exhibition catalog, with introduction by Peter Baum, Linz 1976; *Photomontage* by Dawn Ades, London and New York 1976; *Herbert Bayer: From Type to Landscape,* exhibition catalog, with text by Jan van der Marck, New York 1977; with text by Leland Rice and Beaumont Newhall, Los Angeles, 1977; *Kunstlerphotographie im XX. Jahrhundert,* exhibition catalog, edited by Carl-Albrecht Haenlein, Hannover 1977; *Neue Sachlichkeit and German Realism of the Twenties,* exhibition catalog, by Wieland Schmied and Ute Eskildsen, London 1978; *Das Experimentelle Photo in Deutschland 1918–1940* by Emilio Bertonati, Munich 1978; *Paris-Berlin 1900–1933,* exhibition catalog, by Herbert Molderings, Werner Spies, Gunter Metken and others, Paris 1978; *Photographen der 20er Jahre* by Karl Steinorth, Munich 1979; *Film und Foto der 20er Jahre,* exhibition catalog, by Ute Eskildsen and Jan Christopher Horak, Stuttgart 1979; Internationale Ausstellung des Deutschen Werkbundes ''Film und Foto'' *1929,* facsimile reprint, edited by Karl Steinorth, Stuttgart 1979; *Herbert Bayer: Recent Works,* exhibition catalog, New York 1979; *Herbert Bayer: Das kunstlerische Werk 1918–1938,* exhibition catalog, West Berlin 1982; *Herbert Bayer: The Complete Work* by Arthur A. Cohen, Cambridge, Massachusetts 1984; *Herbert Bayer and Modernist Design in America,* Ann Arbor, 1987; *Herbert Bayer Collection and Archive at the Denver Art Museum,* by Gwen F. Chanzit, Seattle, 1988; *The Imagery of Herbert Bayer's European Years, 1920–1938,* by Curit-Karin Anhold, New Brunswick, 1988; *Herbert Bayer: Collection and Archive at the Denver Art Museum,* Denver, 1988; *Word Becomes Image: Herbert Bayer, Pioneer of a New Vision in Book Design,* by Kathleen Marie Burnett, Berkeley, 1989. **Articles—**''The Last Paintings of Herbert Bayer'' by Marty Neumeier, in *Communication Arts,* vol. 30, pt. 5, September-October 1988; ''Herbert Bayer: Out of Austria'' by Rolf Sachsse in *Camera Austria,* no. 46, 1994.

*

I believe in a totality of art and design integrated with the life of our time. I have extensively collaborated with industry and other institutions toward the visual improvements in life.

—Herbert Bayer (1983)

* * *

Of all the artists who taught at the Bauhaus, Herbert Bayer was the most prone to the non-figurative-design way of life promoted by that institution. He himself was particularly active in the field of design, and much of what he produced at that time still influences the works of contemporary lay-out and functional design (and craft) as it is found in the notepaper, packaging and kindred requirements in bureaux of industry, commerce and trade today.

Something of this commercial ''awareness'' percolated through to his art works. Accuracy is exact. Almost over-exact. Techniques are manifold and he is the master of all of them. Neatness is the keyword to the entire oeuvre. The shapes and the compositions in which they find themselves cannot be faulted. Colours are chosen with unyielding care but not with love. Any one of Bayer's pictures could grace the boardroom without affront and without distracting attention from business. The words ''modern art'' would not pass through the head of any of the directors. Bayer is ''safe,'' efficient, and burdened with good taste, a kind of glyptothek taste that wounds none, however up-to-date in accent.

Can he claim a place in the ranks of Contemporary Artists? As a stylist and one whose influence on design is far from moribund—Yes. In the words of Will Grohmann, ''Bayer was first and foremost a graphic designer, and secondly a painter who, with patterns and metal foil, succeeded in transcending reality.''

—Sheldon Williams

BAYRLE, Thomas

Nationality: German. **Born:** Berlin, Germany, 11 November 1937. **Education:** Training in weaving at Goppeningen, 1956–58, and at Werkkunstschule Offenbach, 1958–61. **Family:** Married Helke Bayrle in 1962; children: Marielle and Yong-Chul. **Career:** Verlag Gulliverpresse, 1961–65; Bayrle and Kellermann, Frankfurt, 1968–70; Villa Massimo, Rome, 1970–71; instructor, Stadelschule, since 1975; lived in San Francisco, 1980–81; taught at Japanese schools, including Osaka University for Art, Kyoto Art Academy, and Yamagata Tohoku University, 1977, 1980, 1990, and 1996. **Awards:** Prix Ars Eletronica, Linz, Austria, 1995. **Agent:** Barbara Weiss Gallery, 10785 Berlin, Germany; UNAC-Tokyo, 1-1-20-112 Azabudai-Minato-Ku, Tokyo T 106, Japan. **Address:** Staedelschule Duerer St 10, 60596 Frankfurt, Germany.

Individual Exhibitions:

1968 Art Intermedia, Cologne
Galleria Apollinaire, Mailand
Mäntel, Galerie Thelen, Essen
1971 Studio S, Rome
1972 La Pochade, Paris
1973 Galerie Meyer-Ellinger, Frankfurt
1977 Wako, Tokyo
Galerie Camomille, Brussels
1981 Wako, Tokyo
1984 Museum am Ostwall, Dortmund
1987 Kunstverein Frankfurt
1988 Kunsthalle Innsbruck
1989 Kunstverein Freiburg
Seedhall, Tokyo
1990 Portikus, Frankfurt
Autobahnkopk, Galerie Buchholz, Cologne
Sint Lukas Galerij, Brussels
1991 Galerie Luis Campana, Frankfurt
1994 Portikus, Frankfurt
1995 Galerie Meyer-Ellinger, Frankfurt
1996 Kunsthalle St. Gallen, Switzerland
1997 Koriyama City Art Museum, Japan
Academy of Art and Design, Peking
Tassen Tassen, Museum für Moderne Kunst, Frankfurt
1998 Galerie Meyer-Ellinger, Frankfurt
Galerie Francesca Pia, Bern

Thomas Bayrle: *Lakecity,* 1977. Photo by v. Brauchitsch. ©Thomas Bayrle.

1999 Galerie Parduhn, Düsseldorf
2000 Galerie Barbara Weiss, Berlin
Museum in Progress, Wien

Group Exhibitions:

1963 *Schrift und Bild,* Kunsthalle Baden, Baden
Stedellijk Museum, Amsterdam
1964 *Documenta III,* Kassel
1965 *Between Poetry and Painting,* Institute of Contemporary Art, London
1966 *EXTRA,* Museum Wiesbaden
1967 *Serielle Formationen,* Universität Frankfurt
1970 *Sammulung Feelisch,* Museum am Ostwall, Dortmund
1977 *Documenta VI,* Kassel
1984 *von hier aus,* Messehalle Düsseldorf
1994 *La Ville,* Centre Pompidou, Paris and Barcelona
1995 *Priz,* Ars Electronica, Linz
Elastic Lights, Sidney Gallery
1996 *Grafik,* Galerie Klosterfeld, Berlin
Künstlerhaus Stuttgart
L'Art de Plastique, Ecole de Beaux Arts, Paris
1997 *Urban Space,* de Dingel, Antwerp
KünstlerInnen, Museum in Progress, Kunsthaus Bregenz, Bregenz
1998 *Technoculture,* FRI ART Centre Contemporaine, Friburg
Life Style, Kunsthaus Bregenz, Bregenz
Die Macht des Alters, Berlin, Bonn, and Stuttgart
Anticipation, Centre pour l'image Contemporain, Genf
Massornament, Brandts Klaedefabrik, Odense, Germany
1999 Laboratorium, Antwerp
Serien/Konzepte in Foto/Video, Museum Ludwig, Cologne
2000 *Herausforderung Tier,* Städtische Galerie, Karlsruhe
out of space, Kölnischer Kunstverein

Publications:

By BAYRLE: Films—*Auto,* 1979–80; *Autobahn-Kopf,* 1988–89; *Gummibaum,* 1993–94; *Sunbeam,* 1993–94; *Superstars,* 1993.

On BAYRLE: Books—*A, das geht ran,* with text by Bazon Brock, Bad Homburg 1963; *Druck,* with text by Bernhard Jäger, Darmstadt 1963; *Bloom Zeitung,* with text by Bernhard Jäger and Bazon Brock, Frankfürt 1963; *Weiss wie weiss, with Franz Mon,* Bad Homburg 1963; *Horen und Sehen,* with text by Wolfgang Maier, Stierstadt 1963; *Artmann Brief,* with text by H.C. Artmann, Bad Homburg 1964; *Hosianna,* with Horst Jandl and Bernhard Jäger, Bad Homburg 1965; *Egoist 16,* Frankfürt 1969; *Feuer im Weizen,* Frankfürt 1970; *My Journey,* The Hague 1971; *Zeichnungen,* Frankfürt 1976; *24 Postcards,* Tokyo 1977; *Rasterfahndung,* Frankfürt 1981; *Cities, Accumulations and Eros,* Tokyo 1983; *Druckgrahik 1960–83,* Wolfsburg; *Bayrle Big Book,* Cologne 1992; *Grafik 1967–72 und* *animierte Grafik von 1979–94,* Cologne 1995; *Thomas Bayrle Works,* Beijing 1997; *Subversion* by Marius Babias, Frankfurt am Main 2000.

*

Teaching is fundamentally linked to the question ''what am I / who am I?'' My own answer to that question goes something like this: I see myself as a kind of leavening, as an ''unquiet ferment'' that makes dough rise . . . as a rather unpleasant product, yeast, with no mass of its own, completely enclosed and constantly seeking a way out. This underlying feeling is connected to a hermetic and ''claustrophobic'' sense of space that has its roots in my own biography. At the age of 18 I learned weaving and textile finishing in two southern German firms. The fabric, the way 10,000 weft threads are combined with 10,000 warp threads, the forms of linkage they can represent—these are aspects that I used to muse on as I day-dreamed in front of the looms, applying them in my mind's eye to cities and urban spaces and even to the entire fabric of society. I saw them as rigid spatial systems in which millions of tiny spaces / apartments were enclosed . . . (the air pockets in a fabric determine its warmth). From the early 60s onwards, this notion of the social fabric as a woven textile, as I imagined it, had become inextricably linked in my imagination with Chinese culture and I tended to think of them in terms of real social models that were by no means totalitarian, but which enabled ''democracy on a tiny scale.'' The threads were individual and the textile collective (a single thread consists of many fibres and can be individually dyed; it can be as complex as a glass fibre carrying millions of data—it is more than something). The quality of the overall fabric—Heidegger—thus depends on the quality and the quantity of the individual parts of which it is made up. This hermetic image (which I admit I find terrifying) is something I have seen looming on the horizons of society for some time now. It is the primitive appropriation of land culminating in an equally primitive notion of freedom. (Considering the price per square yard of real estate in our cities, one either thinks immediately of street riots where every inch is fought for, or is reminded of an English advertisement that illusrates the space between hairs—both are examples of A the infinity of space—Mandelbrot—and B that spaces can be sought and found between occupied places). But to return to what I do: what I do when I am teaching—the spectacles one looks through are tinted by biographical experience one cannot escape—no matter how much one might wish to. The ''street riot'' approach to gaining new forms between forms is tough, but worth the effort. In a cramped space there are no ''long-term prospects.'' Working within such a space is like taking the microbe's view of the world, trying to get from the liver to the kidney . . . holes appear and close again immediately . . . bubbles . . . hollow volumes that burst again . . . I see myself, by force of circumstance, as an uncertain artistic existence that is constantly driven and can never ''rest''. . . . In this image, resting is somewhere between breathing in and breathing out. The social consequence of such a situation (as opposed to ''anything goes'') is a constant search for form that will make different patterns or keys compatible in order to create the next yard. . . . This ''need'' is the driving force behind my actions. By externalising that need and projecting it into other existences, I become something like a ''good teacher'' . . . a trainer who tries to continue the tasks he cannot solve himself . . . in the existence of further satellites—students—just as the liver sometimes has to delegate tasks to the kidney—because it cannot cope with them on its own. . . . A bunch of grapes . . . frogspawn . . . emerge . . . on equal terms . . . in a hermetic work situation . . . as friendship in a real collective.

OK—let's do it!

—Thomas Bayrle

* * *

Thomas Bayrle's raster pictures have been compared to Andy Warhol's serial screen printings and have unjustifiably been regarded as the European variation of American Pop-Art. But Bayrle's picture language is not so much dedicated to the American abstraction principle of seriality, but rather grounded in the European principle of the dialectic. Bayrle's works connect two developments that were paradigmatic for the German post-war avantgarde: the antagonism between abstraction and realism of the 1950s and the political activism of the 1960s.

Right after his training to be a weaver, Bayrle, together with Bernhard Jäger, founded a small experimental publishing house, the Gulliver Presse, which published concrete poetry by H. C. Artmann, Gerhard Rühm, Franz Mon, Helmut Heissenbüttel, and Ernst Jandl. Each volume was artistically designed by the publishers. In his position as a weaver, small publisher, and political activist in the periphery of the outer-parliamentary opposition ''APO,'' Bayrle looked at art as something bourgeois, even reactionary. It was the friendship with his companion Peter Roehr, who died in 1968, which inititated Bayrle's central mind figure, the raster. From then on it permutatively found its way into his graphics, pictures, wall papers, curtains, into movies and, beginning in the mid-1990s, also into computer animations.

Bayrle, who since the mid-1960s has dealt with Mao's political theory of the ''permanent revolution'' and with the teachings of the main and side discrepancies of capitalism, was interested in the growth and forms of accumulation, whether he was dealing with mass production or mass society, the Third Reich, China or Vietnam, consumer articles or people. Mass gatherings—whether military parades, political rallies or rock concerts—awakened both fascination and fright within him. Totalitarism and individualism became the antipodes of his creative thinking. In the act of weaving, which is a mechanical pre-form of the computer and consists of creating a woven fabric by binding and crossing yarn (in connection with computer science one could speak of a binary code), Bayrle found the aesthetic equation which allowed him to work on the political fabric. That is how the raster emerged—the ideal crossing point between the whole and the detail, between the mass and the individual. ''I wanted to continue the raster via a subraster until the cellular,'' Bayrle told me in *Subversion.* ''First there were pictograms, then small figures, later photos and films. Through my dealings with political theory, I discovered the radical-democratic reality that it is all about balance. The point is not that the raster emancipates itself until the ultimate excess and thus destroys the whole, the society.'' His individual handwriting that could still be detected in his motorized consume actions built from 1964–65, such as ''Zähne putzen'' (''Brushing Teeth'') was pushed back in favor of half-mechanical production processes and the use of industrial finish parts.

The raster has remained Thomas Bayrle's central artistic construction principle since 1967. First pictograms, then pictures of daily-life objects were reproduced half-mechanically and attached to each other until a raster surface, a matrix emerged. This matrix was serially screen-printed and inumerable rasters formed a whole of the same object. This created various ox-, shoe-, tulip-, or cup-rasters that have been printed on pictures, wall papers, curtains, or coats.

The maxim formulated in German romanticism (Goethe, Novalis) and in German idealism (Hegel) that the detail is reflected in the whole (namely the godly in the earthly) experienced with Bayrle a dialectic turn in the mechanical reproduction. God became logorithmetized to a measurement unit that, many times reproduced, still represented a super form, but a cloned one. Bayrle invented and declinated an impressive aesthetic formula with far-reaching political consequences: the individual becomes part of a collective. While it is included into the superform, society, its individuality is only partly revealed. The superform thus suspends individuality, but promises a collective identity model. The dialectic fine mechanics form the core of societal life and for Bayrle steer the relationship between society and the individual.

Bayrle also picks up this theme when he makes use of computerized means of reproduction: the pixels in his computer animations, which came into existence in the mid-1990s. For Bayrle, who always kept up with technological developments, pixels became raster points in a digital garment. His mapped computer animations are critical picture analyses in times of gene and biotechnology, which are aesthetically prepared and supported in the cultural picture production. Bayrle reactivates a subversive strategy of the 1960s: the existing art ideology needs to be questioned in exactly those forms for which it has the greatest admiration.

Bayrle's works, almost forgotten in the 1980s during the postmodernism discussion, prove to be anticipatory and highly up-to-date. As a professor at the Städelschule in Frankfurt, Bayrle founded a second Frankfurt School.

—Marius Babias

BEAL, Jack

Nationality: American. **Born:** Richmond, Virginia, 25 June 1931. **Education:** Norfolk Division of William and Mary College, Virginia, 1950–53; studied at the Art Institute of Chicago, under Briggs Dyer, Isobel MacKinnon and Kathleen Blackshear, 1953–56; University of Chicago, 1955–56. **Family:** Married Sondra Freckelton. **Career:** Lives and works in New York. Artist-in-residence/visiting lecturer, University of Indiana, Bloomington, 1966; Purdue University, Lafayette, Indiana, 1967; University of Wisconsin, Madison, 1967; and Cooper Union, New York, 1968; Board of Trustees, La Napoule Art Foundation, 1983–1989; Endowed Chair, College of William and Mary, 1992. **Awards:** First Prize, *University of Chicago Arts Festival,* 1955; Wild Award. *70th American Exhibition,* Art Institute of Chicago, 1972; National Endowment for the Arts Grant, 1972; Honorary Doctorate, Hollins College, 1994; American Artist Achievement Award, 1994. **Address:** c/o George Adams Gallery, 41 West 57th Street, New York, New York 10019, U.S.A.

Individual Exhibitions:

1965 Allan Frumkin Gallery, New York (2 exhibitions)
1966 Allan Frumkin Gallery, Chicago
1967 Allan Frumkin Gallery, New York
1968 *Recent Paintings by Jack Beal,* Allan Frumkin Gallery, New York
1969 Allan Frumkin Gallery, Chicago
1970 Allan Frumkin Gallery, New York
1972 Allan Frumkin Gallery, New York
Miami-Dade Junior College, Florida
1973 Allan Frumkin Gallery, New York
Galerie Claude Bernard, Paris
Virginia Museum, Richmond (retrospective; travelled to Boston University, and the Museum of Contemporary Art, Chicago, 1974)
1974 Allan Frumkin Gallery, Chicago
1975 Allan Frumkin Gallery, New York
1978 Allan Frumkin Gallery, New York
1980 Allan Frumkin Gallery, New York
Reynolds' Minor Gallery, Richmond, Virginia
1988 Frumkin/Adams Gallery, New York
1993 Frumkin/Adams Gallery, New York

Selected Group Exhibitions:

1968 *Whitney Annual,* Whitney Museum, New York (and 1969)
1969 *Aspects of a New Realism,* Milwaukee Art Center (toured the United States)
1971 *New Realism,* Art Gallery of the State University of New York at Postdam (travelled to the Delaware Art Museum, Wilmington)
1973 *American Realism: Post Pop,* Oakland University, Rochester, Michigan
1975 *Drawings: Techniques and Types,* William Benton Museum of Art, University of Connecticut, Storrs
Portrait Painting 1970–75, Allan Frumkin Gallery, New York
1976 *America 1976.* United States Department of the Interior travelling Exhibition (toured the United States, 1976–78)
1979 *100 Artists/100 Years: Alumni of the School of the Art Institute of Chicago,* Art Institute of Chicago
1981 *Contemporary American Realism since 1960,* Pennsylvania Academy of Fine Arts, Philadelphia
1985 *American Realism,* San Francisco Museum of Modern Art (travelled to Lincoln, Massachusetts; Austin, Texas; Evanston, Illinois; Williamstown, Massachusetts; Akron, Ohio; Madison, Wisconsin)
1998 *Embodied Fictions,* Boyden Gallery, St. Mary's College, Maryland

Collections:

Whitney Museum, New York; Museum of Modern Art, New York; Neuberger Museum, Purchase, New York; University of Vermont, Burlington; Delaware Art Museum, Wilmington; University of North Carolina, Chapel Hill; Art Institute of Chicago; Minneapolis Institute of Art; Walker Art Center, Minneapolis; Museum of Modern Art, San Francisco; San Francisco Museum of Fine Arts; National Gallery of Art, Washington, D.C.

Publications:

On BEAL: Books—*Recent Painting by Jack Beal,* exhibition catalog, with an introduction by R. C. Kenedy, New York 1968; *Aspects of a New Realism,* exhibition catalog, with texts by Sidney Tillim and

William Wilson, Milwaukee 1969; *22 Realists,* exhibition catalog, New York 1970; *Jack Beal,* exhibition catalog, with text by Mark Strand, Paris 1963; *Jack Beal,* exhibition catalog, with text by Peter Schjeldahl, Norfolk, Virginia 1973; *Jack Beal,* exhibition catalog, with text by Gerrit Henry, New York 1975; *100 Artists/100 Years: Alumni of the School of the Art Institute of Chicago,* Chicago 1979. **Articles**—''Is Jack Beal Still a Figurative Painter?'' by Scott Burton in *Art Scene* (Chicago), April 1969; ''Facts of Life'' by Nancy Grimes in *ARTnews,* vol. 87, no. 10, December 1988; ''Jack Beal's Portraits of Life'' by Stephen M. Doherty in *American Artist,* vol. 63, no. 681, April 1999.

*

Make art like life—make life like art—that's become my motto. As a student my training was confined to modernist aesthetics and practices, which I finally found too restrictive. I began to paint from *Life,* and realized that I could use everything I had learned from modernism, *and* all that study of great representational art had taught me, to make paintings about the best of life as we live it. This purpose grew as I understood that the arts had influenced my own life at least as much as the experience of life itself had done. I hope to contribute to that tradition.

—Jack Beal

* * *

Among the diverse painters who arose during the late 1960s under the banner of 'New Realism,' Jack Beal lies somewhere towards the middle. Over the years his work has been more closely aligned with that of Philip Pearlstein and Alfred Leslie than that of the Photo-Realists. Beal concentrates on tightly controlled organization, structuring his complex composition with clarity of detail, intricate articulation of contour, color and light in a manner which implies the mentality of a post-Pop, post-formalist abstraction context. He is most noted for his compositions of the figure (many of them nudes) in interior environments filled with complexly patterned fabrics, which stress a dynamically diagonal thrust and a point of view slightly below eye level.

Among the best of these is Beal's ''Danae'' (1972) which skillfully incorporates flesh, figure, pattern and sharp light and shadow in an intimate interior, conveying a sense of presence yielded by its deliberately dispassionate ordering. Beal, like Pearlstein, stresses the objectivity of his analysis which treats the figure as one element among the many in the composition. Yet despite the sense of distancing and the anti-narrative leaning, there is always a psychological element which reads as content beyond the formal in Beal's pictorial analyses. It is evoked by the very openness of the forms whose blank, nonjudgmental qualities constitute a state of mind as concrete as it is aesthetic. The title, ''Danae,'' is suggestive of Beal's involvement with Renaissance to Baroque themes and structures which have lately come even more into the forefront of his painting.

In 1977 Beal completed a series of four murals commissioned by the General Services Administration for the Department of Labor Building in Washington, D.C. on the given theme of the History of American Labor. For help in accomplishing this complex task, Beal turned to the art historical past, specifically to Caravaggio, the Italian Mannerists and Benjamin West, for various elements of dramatic realism, composition and figure drawing. The murals, titled ''Settlement,'' ''Colonization,'' ''Industry'' and ''Technology,'' are 12 by 12 foot, monumental statements of a sweeping moral nature which have earned Beal the position of being called the most prominent Social Realist in America since the 1930s generation.

Although Beal continues to paint his more intimate studies of figures and textured surroundings, he has also produced works of a more directly traditional thematic kind. In a series titled ''Vices and Virtues'' (Envy, Sloth, Prudence, Avarice, Lust, Anger, Justice, Fortitude), Beal makes his contemporary models into allegorical figures who symbolize the traditionally moral themes. As always, the compositions are tight and complex, stressing diagonal motion which is more violent in the painting of ''Anger'' and more meditatively dynamic in ''Fortitude.'' In his large paintings ''The Farm'' (1979) and ''Harvest'' (1980), Beal takes on a more bucolic subject matter. Painted on his farm in Oneonta, New York, these two pictures combine two figures in a rural setting which is highly idealized. The man and woman in ''The Farm'' are painting some pigs in the company of a dog/companion and in a setting filled with some flowers and sun and blue skies. People, animals, art and nature working in harmony, the details of which are given tender loving care which is reminiscent of the Hudson River School painters and, even more, of the Pre-Raphaelite William Holman Hunt. However, there is the basic difference of context, relevance and artifice, and, although Beal is a master technician, the pictures come across as a kind of adaptation from the past which remains more in the realm of the formal than the social real or meaningful real, whether as art or as nature.

—Barbara Cavaliere

BEARDEN, Romare (Howard)

Nationality: American. **Born:** Charlotte, North Carolina, 2 September 1914. **Education:** Public School 139, New York, until 1925; Peabody High School, Pittsburgh, Pennsylvania, 1925–29; New York University, 1932–35, B.S. 1935; studied under George Grosz, at the Art Students League, New York, 1936–37; studied advanced mathematics at Columbia University, New York, 1943, and philosophy and art history at the Sorbonne, Paris, 1951. Served in the 372nd Infantry, United States Army, 1942–45. **Family:** Married Nanette Rohan in 1954. **Career:** Case Worker, New York City Department of Social Services, 1938–42, 1946–49, and 1952–66. Travelled in Italy, Switzerland, Algiers, and Morocco, 1950; concentrated on song writing, 1951–54; established studio on Canal Street, New York, 1956; Art Director, Harlem Cultural Council, New York, since 1964; Co-Founder, with Norman Lewis and Ernest Crichlow, Cinque Gallery in New York Public Theater, 1969; Set and Costume Designer for Alvin Ailey Ballet Company, New York, 1977. Artist-in-residence, Spelman College, Atlanta, 1968; visiting lecturer in African and Afro-American Art, Williams College, Williamstown, Massachusetts, 1969; artist-in-residence, University of Delaware, Newark, 1970; instructor, Yale College, New Haven, Connecticut, 1980. **Awards:** American Academy of Arts and Letters Painting Award, 1966; National Institute of Arts and Letters Grant, 1966; Guggenheim Fellowship, 1970; Ford Foundation Fellowship, 1973; Medal of the State of North Carolina, 1976; Frederick Douglas Medal, New York Urban League,

1978; James Weldon Johnson Award, Atlanta Chapter of the National Association for the Advancement of Colored People (NAACP), 1978. Honorary Doctorates: Pratt Institute, New York, 1973; Carnegie Mellon University, Pittsburgh, 1975; Maryland Institute of Art, Baltimore, 1976; North Carolina Central University, Durham, 1977; Davidson College, North Carolina, 1978. Member, American Academy of Arts and Letters. **Agent:** Cordier and Ekstrom Inc., 980 Madison Avenue, New York, New York 10021. **Died:** 12 March 1988.

Individual Exhibitions:

1935 ''G'' Place Gallery, Washington, D.C.
1940 A. D. Bates Studio, New York
1944 *10 Hieroglyphic Paintings,* ''G'' Place Gallery, Washington, D.C.
1945 Galerie John Duvuloy, Paris (with Pietro Lazzari) ''G'' Place Gallery, Washington, D.C.
Samuel Kootz Gallery, New York
1946 Samuel Kootz Gallery, New York
1947 Samuel Kootz Gallery, New York
1948 Niveau Gallery, New York
1955 Barone Gallery, New York
1960 Michel Warren Gallery, New York
1961 Cordier and Ekstrom Gallery, New York
1964 *Projections,* Cordier and Ekstrom Gallery, New York
1966 Carnegie Institute, Pittsburgh
6 Panels on a Southern Theme, Bundy Art Gallery, Waitsfield, Vermont
Corcoran Gallery, Washington, D.C.
1967 Fine Arts Building, Spelman College, Atlanta
Collages, J. L. Hudson Gallery, Detroit
Cordier and Ekstrom Gallery, New York
1968 *Paintings and Projections,* State University of New York at Albany
1969 Williams College, Williamstown, Massachusetts
Iowa State University, Iowa City
1970 Cordier and Ekstrom Gallery, New York
Tricia Karliss Gallery, Provincetown, Massachusetts
The Prevalence of Ritual, Museum of Modern Art, New York (retrospective; toured the United States, 1971–72)
Cordier and Ekstrom Gallery, New York
1973 Cordier and Ekstrom Gallery, New York
1974 Galerie Albert Loeb, Paris
Madison Art Museum, Wisconsin
Everson Museum, Syracuse, New York
Of the Blues, Cordier and Ekstrom Gallery, New York
1976 Firehouse Gallery, Nassau College, New York
Graphics Gallery, Toronto
Cordier and Ekstrom Gallery, New York
1977 Union College, Cranford, New Jersey
Odysseus: Collages, Cordier and Ekstrom Gallery, New York
1978 Cordier and Ekstrom Gallery, New York
Davidson College, North Carolina
1980 *Retrospective: 1970–1980,* Mint Museum, Charlotte, North Carol (travelled to the Mississippi Museum of Art, Jackson; Baltimore Museum of Art; and the Virginia Museum of Fine Arts, Richmond, 1981)
1981 *Collages: Profile: The 30's,* Cordier and Esktrom Gallery, New York
1982 Birmingham Museum of Art, Birmingham
New Orleans Contemporary Art Center, New Orleans
Hunter Museum of Art, Chattanooga
1988 North Carolina Museum of Art, Raleigh
1989 ACA Galleries, New York
1991 *Romare Bearden: The Human Condition,* ACA Galleries, New York
Memory and Metaphor: The Art of Romare Bearden 1940–1987, Studio Museum of Harlem, Harlem, New York
ACA Galleries, New York
1997 *Romare Bearden in Black-and-White: Photomontage Projections 1964,* Whitney Museum of American Art, New York Madison Art Center, Madison, Wisconsin

Selected Group Exhibitions:

1945 *Annual Exhibition,* Whitney Museum, New York (and 1946, 1955, 1969)
1948 6 American Painters, Galerie Maeght, Paris
Abstract and Surrealist American Art, Art Institute of Chicago
1951 *Survey of American Art,* Metropolitan Museum of Art, New York
1968 *30 Contemporary Black Artist,* Minneapolis Institute of Art (toured the United States, 1968–70)
1969 *New American Painting and Sculpture,* Museum of Modern Art, New York
1970 *5 Famous Black Artists,* Museum of the National Center of Afro-American Arts, Boston
1981 *6 Black Americans,* New Jersey State Museum, Trenton
The Human Form, Maryland Institute College of Art, Baltimore
24 Black American Artists, Goucher College, Baltimore

Collections:

Metropolitan Museum of Art, New York; Museum of Modern Art, New York; Whitney Museum, New York; Rochester Memorial Art Gallery, New York; Museum of Fine Arts, Boston; Princeton University, New Jersey; Newark Museum, New Jersey; Philadelphia Museum of Art; High Museum of Art, Atlanta; Madison Art Center, Wisconsin; Akron Art Institute, Ohio; Brooklyn Museum; Albright-Knox Art Gallery, Buffalo; Mint Museum of Art, Charlotte; Davidson College, North Carolina; Flint Institute of Arts, Michigan; The Wadsworth Atheneum, Hartford; Honolulu Academy of Arts, Honolulu; Studio Museum of Harlem, New York.

Publications:

By BEARDEN: Books—*The Painter's Mind, with Carl Holty, New York 1969; 6 Black Masters of American Art,* with Harry Henderson, New York 1972; *Prevalence of Ritual,* portfolio of 5 silkscreens, New York 1977. **Articles—**''The Negro Artist and Modern Art'' in *Opportunity,* December 1934; ''Problems of the Negro Artists'' in *Critique,* October 1948; ''Rectangular Structure in My Montage Paintings'' in *Leonardo* (Paris), January 1969; ''The Artist and His Education'' in *Harvard Art Review* (Cambridge, Massachusetts), Spring 1969.

On BEARDEN: Books—*Romare Bearden: Paintings and Projections,* exhibition catalog, with text by Ralph Ellison, Albany, New York 1968; *Romare Bearden: The Prevalence of Ritual,* exhibition catalog, with an introduction by Carroll Greene, New York 1971; *The Art of Romare Bearden* by John Williams and Bundie Washington, New York 1974; *Of the Blues,* exhibition catalog, with text by Albert Murray, New York 1975; *Romare Bearden: Odysseus: Collages,* exhibition catalog, with an introduction by Calvin Tomkins, New York 1977; *Romare Bearden: Collages: Profile: The 30's,* exhibition catalog, edited by Albert Murray, New York 1981; *Romare Bearden* by Lowery Stokes Sims, New York, 1993; *Romare Bearden in Black-and-White: Photomontage Projections 1964,* exhibition catalog, with text by Gail Gelburd and Thelma Golden, New York 1997. **Articles—** ''Romare Bearden—Projections'' by Dore Ashton in *Quadrum* (Brussels), no. 17, 1965; ''Black Persephone'' by Ralph Pomeroy in *Artnews* (New York), October 1967; ''Romare Bearden—Paintings and Projections'' by Ralph Ellison in *New Yorker,* 28 November 1977; ''Romare Bearden: 'I Paint Out of the Tradition of the Blues''' by Avis Berman in *Artnews* (New York), December 1980; ''Romare Bearden'' in *Vogue* (New York), February 1981; ''Romare Bearden'' in *Smithsonian* (Washington, D.C.), March 1981; ''Romare Bearden'' in *Newsweek* (New York), 30 March 1981; ''Romare Bearden: Rites and Riffs'' by M. S. Campbell in *Art in America* (New York), December 1981; ''Cut and Paste: Romare Bearden's Collages Reflect His Life in Many Worlds'' in *Art and Antiques,* vol. 9, May 1992; ''A Look at Romare Bearden and the Textile Metaphor'' in *Fiberarts,* vol. 19, September/October 1992; ''Ralph Ellison, The Collage of Romare Bearden and Race: Some Speculations'' in *International Review of African American Art* (Hampton), vol. 11, no. 3, 1994; ''Bibliographic Essay on Three African American Artists: William H. Johnson, Romare Bearden, and Jacob Lawrence'' by Beth Anne Margolies in *Art Documentation,* vol. 13, pt. 1, Spring 1994; ''Signifying Identity: Art and Race in Romare Bearden's Projections'' in *The Art Bulletin* (New York), vol. 76, September 1994; ''Romare Bearden: In Tune With Jazz'' in *Art News* (New York), vol. 94, September 1995; ''Romare Bearden at the Whitney'' by Mario Naves in *New Criterion,* vol. 15, pt. 7, March 1997.

* * *

Part of Romare Bearden's originality lies in his application of the formal means discovered by the Cubist masters at the beginning of the century to the world of the American black. Negro himself, he simply re-thought the subject matter that interested and involved him most in such a way that he was able to ''distance'' it as an artist and, instead of some negative form of protest, to take the history and life of his race and present it anew in works of high artistic sophistication. He has looked fully and found Aphrodite in a vegetable patch, ''The Three Musicians'' in the apartment next door.

His themes run to jazz and folk music, urban and rural Negro life, rituals of baptism and voodoo, home life and street action. He prefers the archetypal and the not-too-specific image. He combines fragments of photostats and torn and cut paper which he has painted and mounts them on canvas. Usually he draws the composition beforehand in charcoal in the traditional manner. There is something especially ''right'' about his large collages in their mix of African imagery with Cubist space—a moving backwards as it were through art history past the discoveries of African art that led to the invention of Cubism. It is this formal strength that sets Bearden apart from many of his contemporaries. He is not afraid of the strong traditional qualities in his pictures. In fact he strives for them. By being so much a part of something already established in terms of time he is able to surmount the merely fashionable and enter a larger span of time. It is also a way of placing at the proper distance whatever it is he wants to show us. His sense of the largeness of his themes enables him not only to equate a field hand with a god, but to mix the races: It is no surprise in his work to come upon, say, a hand that has both black and white fingers. This way he avoids being pinned down to the over-simplified and the over-stressed. Because he has taken unexpected routes, he has succeeded in arriving at new realms of dignity.

—Ralph Pomeroy

BECHER, Bernhard and Hilla

Nationality: German. **Born:** Bernhard Becher born in Siegen, 20 August 1931; Hilla Becher born Hilla Wobeser in Potsdam 2 September 1934. **Education:** Bernard studied painting and lithography at the Staatlichen Kunstakademie, Stuttgart, 1953–56, and typography at the Staatlichen Kunstakademie, Dusseldorf, 1957–61; Hilla studied photography in Potsdam, and painting at the Staatlichen Kunstakademie, Dusseldorf. **Career:** Bernhard and Hilla Becher married in 1961; they have worked together as freelance photographic artists, concentrating on industrial photography, Dusseldorf, since 1959. Both are instructors in photography at the Staatlichen Kunstakademie, Dusseldorf. **Awards:** British Council Photo Study Grant, 1966; Fritz-Thyssen-Stiftung grant, West Germany, 1967–68. **Agents:** Galerie Konrad Fischer, Platanenstrasse 7, Dusseldorf; Nigel Greenwood Inc., 4 New Burlington Street, London WIX 1FE, England; and Sonnabend Gallery, 420 West Broadway, New York, New York 10012, U.S.A. **Address:** Wittlauer 4, Am Muhlenkamp 16, Dusseldorf, West Germany.

Individual Exhibitions:

1963 Galerie Ruth Nohl, Siegen, West Germany
1965 Galerie Pro, Bad Godesburg, West Germany
1966 Staatliche Kunstakademie, Dusseldorf
1967 Staatliches Museum, Munich
Technische Hochschule, Karlsruhe
Bergbau-Museum, Bochum, West Germany
Kunstakademie, Copenhagen
1968 Wachsman Institute, University of Southern California, Los Angeles
Goethe Center, San Francisco
Stedelijk Van Abbemuseum, Eindhoven, Netherlands
Galerie Ruth Nohl, Siegen, West Germany
Städtisches Museum, Monchengladbach, West Germany
1969 Städtische Kunsthalle, Dusseldorf
1970 Städtisches Museum, Ulm, West Germany
Form genom Funktion, Moderna Museet, Stockholm
Galerie Konrad Fischer, Dusseldorf
1971 Kabinett für Aktuelle Kunst, Bremerhaven, West Germany
Gegenverkehr, Aachen, West Germany
1972 Sonnabend Gallery, New York
Bennington College, Vermont
1973 Galleria Forma, Genoa
Nigel Greenwood Inc., London

Sonnabend Gallery, New York
1974 Institute of Contemporary Arts, London (toured the U.K.)
La Jolla Museum of Contemporary Art, California
Sonnabend Gallery, New York
1975 *Fotografien* 1957–1975, Rheinisches Landesmuseum, Bonn
Galleria Castelli, Milan
Museum of Modern Art, New York
Sonnabend Gallery, New York
1976 Kunsthalle, Tübingen, West Germany
1977 Sonnabend Gallery, New York
1978 Sonnabend Gallery, New York
Milwaukee Art Center, Wisconsin
Von der Heydt Museum, Wuppertal, West Germany
1979 Galerie Sonnabend, Paris
Kunstbibliothek Tranegarden, Copenhagen
Galleria Massimo Valsecchi, Milan
Kunstraum Munich
1981 Stedelijk Van Abbemuseum, Eindhoven, Netherlands (Retrospective)
Kunstverein, Siegen, West Germany
Sonnabend Gallery, New York
Carl Taylor Gallery, Dallas
1982 Sonnabend Gallery, New York
1985 Museum Folkwang, Essen, West Germany
Musée d'Art Moderne, Paris
Musée d'Art Moderne, Liége, Belgium
1986 Architekturmuseum, Basle
1989 Dia Center for the Arts, New York
1995 *Bernd & Hilla Becher: Industrial Buildings,* Westfalisches Landesmuseum fur Kunst und Kulturgeschichte, Munster (traveled to IVAM Centre Julio Gonzalez, Valencia) (catalog)
1996 *Bernd and Hilla Becher,* Albright-Knox Gallery, Buffalo (catalog)
Works 1963–1995, IVAM Centro Julio Gonzalez, Valencia
Bernd & Hilla Becher: A Survey, Frankel Gallery and Daniel Weinberg Gallery, San Francisco

Selected Group Exhibitions:

1969 *Prospekt '69,* Städtische Kunsthalle, Dusseldorf
1970 *Information,* Museum of Modern Art, New York
1974 *Art and Image in Recent Art,* Art Institute of Chicago
1975 *New Topographics: Photographs of a Man-Altered Landscape,* International Museum of Photography, George Eastman House, Rochester, New York (travelled to the Otis Art Institute, Los Angeles, and Princeton University Art Museum, New Jersey)
1977 *Documenta 6,* Museum Fridericianum, Kassel, West Germany
1979 *Photographie als Kunst 1879–1979/Kunst als Photographie 1947–1979,* Tiroler Landesmuseum Ferdinandeum, Inssbruck, Austria (travelled to the Neue Galerie an Wolfgang Gurlitt Museum, Linz, Austria; Neue Galerie am Landesmuseum Joanneum, Graz, Austria; and Museum des 20.Jahrhunderts, Vienna)
Concept, Narrative, Document, Museum of Contemporary Art, Chicago
1981 *Photos der 70er Jahre,* Galerie Wilde, Cologne
1983 *The Medium is Photography,* San Francisco Museum of Modern Art
1987 *Photography and Art 1946–86,* Los Angeles County Museum of Art
1988 *Artists Use Photography—Today,* John Hansard Gallery, Southampton, England (catalog)
1990 *Bernd und Hilla Becher: Typology and Typologies,* Venice Biennale, Italy (catalog)
1991 *Tyrologies: Nine Contemporary Photographers,* Newport Harbor Art Museum, Newport Beach, California (catalog)
1992 *Einsamkeit: A German Sensation,* Sala de Exposiciones de la Fundacion 'La Caixa', Madrid (catalog)
Special Collections: The Photographic Order from Pop to Now, International Center of Photography, New York (catalog)
Bernd and Hilla Becher, Jannis Kounellis, Susana Solano, Musee d'Art Contemporain, Bordeaux, France (catalog)
1992 *Becher, Mapplethorpe, Sherman 1977–1992,* Museo de Monterrey, Mexico (catalog)
1994 *The Epic and the Everyday: Contemporary Photographic Art,* Hayward Gallery, London (catalog)
1995 *Witness: Photoworks from the Collection,* Tate Gallery, Liverpool (catalog)
From Icon to Irony: German and American Industrial Photography, Boston University Art Gallery (catalog)
1996 *Photography in Contemporary German Art,* Claudia Gian Ferrari Arte Contemporanea, Milan (catalog)
1997 *Positions in Art Photography in Germany Since 1945,* Martin-Gropius-Bau, Berlin (catalog)
1998 *Degrees of Stillness: Photographs from the Manfred Heiting Collection,* Photographische Sammlung der SK Stiftung Kultur, Cologne
Artranspennine98: An Exhibition of International and Contemporary Art, Tate Gallery, Liverpool (traveling exhibition) (catalog)
Veronica's Revenge: Photographic Works from the Lambert Collection in Hamburg, Deichtorhallen, Hamburg
1999 *Mechanics and Expression: The Ann and Jurgen Wilde Collections—Photographs from the 20th Century,* Sprengel Museum Hannover, Germany (catalog)

Collections:

Wallraf-Richartz Museum, Cologne; Moderna Museet, Stockholm; Tate Gallery, London; Museum of Modern Art, New York; Metropolitan Museum of Art, New York; Allen Memorial Art Museum, Oberlin College, Ohio; Art Gallery of Ontario, Toronto; International Museum of Photography at George Eastman House, Rochester, New York.

Publications:

By the BECHERS: Books—*Anonyme Skulputuren: Eine Typologie Technische Bauten,* Dusseldorf 1970; *Die Architektur der Förder- und Wasser-Türme,* with text by W. Schoenberg, J. Werth and T. Aachen, Munich 1971; *Industrial Buildings, portfolio of 14 photos, Munich 1975; Framework Houses of the Siegen Industrial Region,* Munich 1977; *Blast Furnaces,* Cambridge 1990; *Pennsylvania*

Coal Mine Tipples, Munich 1991; *Gas Tanks,* Cambridge 1993; *Grundformen,* Munich 1993; *Industrial Façades,* Cambridge 1995; *Mineheads: Bernd and Hilla Becher,* Cambridge 1997. **Articles—** interview, with Lynda Morris, in *Bernhard and Hilla Becher,* exhibition catalog, London 1974; ''Photographing Industrial Architecture,'' interview, with Angela Graverholz and Anne Ramsden, in *Parachute* (Montreal), Spring 1981; interview with James Lingwood in *Art Press* (Paris), no. 209, January 1996.

On the BECHERS: Books—*Bernhard och Hilla Becher: form genom Funktion,* exhibition catalog, Stockholm 1970; *Visuelle Kommunikation,* edited by Hermann K. Ehmer, Cologne 1971; *Bernhard and Hilla Becher,* exhibition catalog, edited by Lynda Morris, London, 1974; *Berhard and Hilla Becher,* exhibition catalog, with text by Germano Celant, LaJolla, California 1974; *Bernhard and Hilla Becher: Fotografien 1957–1975,* exhibition catalog, with text by Klaus Honnef, Bonn 1975; *New Topographics: Photographs of a Man-Altered Landscape,* exhibition catalog, with text by William Jenkins, Rochester, New York 1975; *Documenta 6/Band 2,* exhibition catalog, edited by Klauf Honnef and Evelyn Weiss, Kassel and Cologne 1977; *Geschichte der Fotografie im 20. Jahrhundert/Photography in the 20th Century* by Petr Rausk, Cologne 1977, London 1980; *Typologien Industrieller Bau 1963–1975,* exhibition catalog, Sao Paulo 1977; *Photographie als Kunst 1879–1979/Kunst als Photographie 1949–1979,* exhibition catalog, 2 vols., by Peter Weiermair, Innsbruck, Austria 1979; *Bernd und Hilla Becher,* exhibition catalog, Essen 1985; *Photography and Art 1946–86,* exhibition catalog by Andy Grundberg and Kathleen M. Gauss, Los Angeles 1987. **Articles—**''Bernd and Hilla Becher: The Function Doesn't Make the Form'' by Liliane Touraine in *Artefacum,* vol. 6, no. 28, April-May 1989; ''Reinhard Mucha und Bernd und Hilla Becher'' by Doris von Drathen in *Kunstforum International,* no. 109, August-October 1990; ''Bernd et Hilla Becher ou la photographie monumentaire'' by Thierry de Duve in *Cahiers du Musee National d'Art Moderne* (Paris), no. 39, Spring 1992.

* * *

The age of industrialization brought with it vast collections of documentation which depicted all the elements of mechanical subjects in the clearest detail. Towards the eighteenth century when smokestacks, factories and bridges became an almost inseparable part of the landscape, this documentation, once a singular expression of scientific reality, had also become a statement of new sociological realities. Since 1959 Hilla and Bernd Becher, upholding a tradition of archeological-industrial documentation, have salvaged testimonies of past developments for future cultural historians.

Their medium is photography, one that ignores every expressionistic component and concentrates on the real subject. The anonymous nature of photography gives the viewer the possibility of perceiving the reality of a rational and conceptual process, which produces two results: the first, the industrial monument, and the second, an artistic composition. This monument will derive a decorative value because it exists as a testimony to itself without the artists in any way adding a personal setting. It is with great perseverance that the Bechers have traced a variety of objects, simply because they exist. They began photographing in Germany, then travelled to the industrial regions of Belgium, France, Luxembourg, Holland, England and the United States. Their artistic endeavors are propelled as much by their interest in the technical qualities of these areas as by the strange fascination of the ''anonymous'' buildings, many of which, having been recently demolished, remain only as a visual record.

To organise the overwhelming quantity of their work, the Bechers have developed a consistent, methodological photographic approach. Irrespective of the photograph's subject, a certain legibility has to be maintained. The photographs have to be neutral images rather than the artists' interpretation. Each shot is equal in light intensity: grayish, overcast, even skies, no dramatic cloud effects producing photographs at once factual and objective and simultaneously enhanced by the details unfolding around the subject. Equally important to the Bechers' approach is the concept of comparability, since the true character of an object gains explicitness when compared with other objects of the same kind. Thus by means of a comparison of all available structures of a particular type and by means of offering different angles and different points of view, they reveal their subject. The visual association of the same subjects, specifically industrial monuments, provides a ''reading system'' for visual comparison, enabling artifacts of apparent anonymity and banality to be seen in terms of notable decorative and typological differences. The Bechers are chiefly interested in photographing a sequence of heavy drills, silos, gas tanks, water towers and other structures. Each structural ''family'' disposes itself throughout the sequences of illustrations to form typological catalogs whose variations are grouped according to their material and formal similarities. But these are presented in a way that offers contrasting images characterized by symbols and ornamentation of different styles. Thus the visual result (in the same category of object) glows with differences, paradoxes and contradictions, likening it to sculpture.

The Bechers' photographs underline environmental and social differences between cultures. They show the industrial monuments of England as being cold, resolved to mere practical uses and devoid of aesthetic value. Those of Continental Europe, however, are quietly symbolic as if to negate their function by masquerading as buildings either Romanesque or Renaissance. The typological correlation of different structures of different periods or countries has become not just a source of information of different areas of knowledge (history, technology), but also a new kind of vision. In this sense Bernd and Hilla Becher are making significant visual and intellectual contributions to our knowledge of the environment.

—Carrie Barker

BECKLEY, Bill

Nationality: American. **Born:** Hamburg, Pennsylvania, 11 February 1946. **Education:** Kutztown State College, Pennsylvania, B.F.A. (studied with James Carroll), 1968; Temple University, Philadelphia, M.F.A. (studied under Italo Scanga and Stephen Green), 1970. **Family:** Married to Laurie Johenning. **Career:** Instructor in semiotics, School of Visual Arts, New York, since 1971. **Awards:** Creative Artists Program Service Grant, New York, 1972, 1973, 1974, 1975; National Endowment for the Arts Grant, Washington, D.C., 1979; New York Foundation of the Arts Grant, 1987. **Agent:** Hans Mayer, Grabbeplatz 2, 4000 Düsseldorf, Germany. **Address:** 155 Wooster Street, New York, New York 10012, U.S.A.

Individual Exhibitions:

1969 Wabash Transit Gallery, Chicago
1971 93 Grand Street, New York (performance)
1972 98 Green Street, Holly Solomon New York (performance)
112 Green Street Gallery, New York
Galerie Rudolf Zwirner, Cologne (performance and installation)
Galerie 20, Amsterdam
Galleria Francoise Lambert, Milan
1973 John Gibson Gallery, New York
Nigel Greenwood Gallery, London
Galerie Konrad Fischer, Düsseldorf
1974 Galerie 20, Amsterdam
Galleria Francois Lambert, Milan
John Gibson Gallery, New York
1975 Galerie Yvon Lambert, Paris
Galerie Patric Verelst/Marc Poitier dit Caulier, Antwerp
Galleria Francois Lambert, Milan
Steinway Hall, New York (performance)
Galerie 20, Amsterdam
1976 Galleria d'Allessandro, Ferranti, Rome
John Gibson Gallery, New York
Galleria Lucio Amelio, Naples
1977 Nigel Greenwood Gallery, London
Galerie Denise René/Hans Mayer, Düsseldorf
Galerie Daniel Templon, Paris
1978 Museum of Modern Art, New York
Studio G7, Bologna
Art in Progress, Munich
1979 Galerie Vera Munro, Hamburg
Nigel Greenwood Gallery, London
Galerie Denise René/Hans Mayer, Düsseldorf
1980 Galerie Loyse Oppenheim, Geneva
Nigel Greenwood Gallery, London
1981 Annina Nosei Gallery, New York
Marian Deson Gallery, Chicago
Galerie Daniel Templon, Paris
International Center of Photography, New York
1982 Studio Cannaviello, Milan
Bonlow Gallery, New York
1983 John Gibson Gallery, New York
Galerie Hans Mayer, Düsseldorf
1984 Freidus/Ordover Gallery, New York
Städtisches Museum, Abteiberg Mönchengladbach, West Germany (retrospective)
1986 Galerie Daniel Templon, Paris
John Gibson Gallery, New York
Galleria Trisorio, Naples
1987 Toni Shafrazi Gallery, New York
Galerie Hans Mayer, Düsseldorf
1988 Ace Contemporary Exhibitions, Los Angeles
1989 Galleria Milano, Italy
Studio G7, Bologna
1990 Galerie Daniel Templon, Paris
1991 John Gibson Gallery, New York
Ace Contemporary Exhibitions, Los Angeles
1992 American Opera Projects, New York (performance)
Galleria Trisorio, Naples
1993 Galeria Pedro Oliveira, Pôrto, Portugal
1994 Galerie Hans Mayer, Düsseldorf
Foundation du Chateau de Jau, Cases de Pene
1997 John Gibson, New York

Selected Group Exhibitions:

1971 *Projects Piers 18,* Museum of Modern Art, New York
1976 *Biennale,* Venice
1977 *Documenta 6,* Kassel, West Germany
1979 *Whitney Biennial Exhibition,* Whitney Museum, New York
1980 *Photographic Art,* Museum of Modern Art, Paris
1983 *Kunst mit Photographie,* Nationalgalerie, West Berlin (travelled to Cologne, Munich and Kiel)
1985 *A New Beginning,* Hudson River Museum, Yonkers, New York
1986 *New Painting and Sculpture,* Indianapolis Museum, Indiana
1988 *Large Scale Photography,* Los Angeles County Museum
1993 *Building a Collection,* Museum of Fine Arts, Boston

Collections:

Museum of Modern Art, New York; Guggenheim Museum, New York; Whitney Museum, New York; Kunstmuseum, Basel; Städtisches Museum, Abteiberg Mönchengladbach, Germany; Victoria and Albert Museum, London; La Jolla Art Museum, California; Museum of Fine Arts, Boston; Wexner Center for the Arts, Ohio State University, Columbus; Morton Neuman Collection, Chicago; Victoria and Albert Museum, London

Publications:

By BECKLEY: Articles—"Bill Beckley: Pink, I Think" in *Art Press,* no. 200, March 1995.

On BECKLEY: Exhibition Catalogs—*Art in the Mind* by Athena Spear, Oberlin, Ohio 1969; *Narrative Art,* Brussels 1974; *In Progress 5* (with text by Achille Bonita Oliva), Livoro, Italy 1975; *Bill Beckley,* Mönchengladbach, West Germany 1984; *Bill Beckley,* Paris 1986; *Image World, Art and Media Culture,* Whitney Museum of American Art, 1989; *Bill Beckley,* Galleria Milano, 1989; *Galerie Mit Bleistift,* Galerie Konrad Fischer, 1993; catalog by Hans Bayer, Chateau de Jau, 1994. **Articles**—"Bill Beckley" in *Heute Kunst* (Düsseldorf), July/August 1973; "Bill Beckley" in *Interfunctionen* (Cologne), no. 10, 1973; "Bill Beckley" by M. Jochimsen in *Kunst* (Mainz, West Germany), September 1974; "Narrative Art" by Peter Schjeldahl in *Domus* (Milan), February 1976; "Bill Beckley's Lies" by E. Cameron in *Artforum,* February 1977; "Bill Beckley: L'Archeologie du Tableau" by Anne Dagbert in *Art Press* (Paris), June 1985; "Bill Beckley" by Jane Bell in *Art News,* January 1988; review by Jude Schwendenwien in *Art News,* vol. 87, February 1988; review by David Shapiro in *Art Scribe,* November/December, 1988; "Marathon Autor de Beauborg" by Michel Uridsany in *Le Figaro,* 11 September, 1990; "Books in Artist's Lives" by Alan Jones in *Arts Magazine,* January 1991; "Image World, Art and Media Culture" by Lisa Phillips in *New Art,* edited by Andreas Papadakis, New York, Rizzoli, 1992; "Bill Beckley at John Gibson" by Jonathan Goodman in *Art in America* (New York), vol. 85, no. 9, September 1997.

* * *

Born in 1946, Bill Beckley is not only one of the youngest proponents of the new "Narrative Art," but also one who has produced one of the most solid bodies of work in a relatively short time. Like other artists whose work has been linked to the grass-roots "Story Art" movement, such as James Collins, William Wegman, and even John Baldessari, Beckley concerns himself with three interrelationships; time, relationships between objects, humans, animals and natural or urban phenomena, and process. Also like them, Beckley spices his technically brilliant, sleek series of photographs and texts with a gleeful wit ranging from the subtly self-deprecating to the patently absurd. As a result, his work tends to be more immediately accessible than, for example, David Askevold's or Peter Hutchinson's.

Formerly, Beckley presented his stories in a shaggy dog style, beginning and ending with deliberately pointless incidents—sometimes an encounter between a young man (the artist) and a groundhog, sometimes an erotic encounter more obviously based in fantasy than in reality, though the confessional spirit seems to be an underlying thematic device. Beckley's "shaggy dog stories" have been from his first shows immensely popular (though never populist), because they never propound theory but present faintly ridiculous incidents via one or two mysteriously selected photographs and a dead-pan, non-editorializing simple text. Because of this tersely poetic presentation, his stories frequently take on the characteristics of entertaining myths or children's tales once told to prove or otherwise, unpalatable point.

Beckley's work since 1975 shares this mythologizing aspect, but has become less accessible and perhaps consequently stronger in its formal aspects. It has become, in fact, a work hinging more directly on the manipulation of mood in a progressively more theatrical (or contrived) context. Beckley depends less on the unconscious and more on establishing a formal situation, while replacing the explicit story/subject with an implicit one. The "characters" in his stories—which rely almost entirely on large panels of color prints—now tend to be almost exclusively domestic objects, engaged in an anthropomorphic visual dialogue. Two color-coded faucets, for example, drip and meet in a single stream down a yellow drain; a broom relentlessly follows a dust ball until it is, literally, swept "under the rug"; two equally lovely professional photographic models wordlessly enact the vainglorious theme of Snow White, in his panel, "The Fairest of Them All"; even a hamburger and its condiments are "actors" in a Beckley scenario. Because of the increased visualization of Beckley's narrations, the trick ending so frequently used to effect in his shaggy dog period has been deliberately sacrificed for a harder, more sophisticated statement; the slyly innocent inanities in the early work are making way for greater formal impact in the exquisite staging of objects photographed in lush flat colors, and an increasingly mysterious iconographic power.

—Jane Bell

BEDEL, Jacques

Nationality: Argentine. **Born:** Buenos Aires, Argentina, 7 August 1947. **Education:** University of Buenos Aires, School of Architecture and Urbanization (1965–71). **Family:** Divorced; father of four children. **Career:** Painter and sculptor since 1968; architect since 1972; founding member of the Group of Thirteen/CAYC Group, 1972—; creator, along with Luis Benedit and Clorindo Testa, of the Buenos Aires Cultural Center, 1980; visiting fellow, Cornell University, New York, 1982. **Awards:** Braque Prize, French Government Grant, Paris, 1969; British Council Grant, West Surrey College of Art, 1974; Gold Medal, United Nations Exhibition, Slovenj Gradec, 1975; Grand Prize 14th Sao Paulo International Art Biennial, 1977; Grand Prize, 1st Montevideo International Art Biennial, 1980; Fulbright Grant, Cornell University, New York, 1982; Gold Medal, 2nd Buenos Aires International Architecture Biennial, 1987; Latin American Grand Prize, 8th Buenos Aires International Architecture Biennial, National Museum of Fine Arts, Buenos Aires, 1987. **Agent:** Ruth Benzacar Art Gallery, Florida 1000 (1005) Buenos Aires, Argentina. **Address:** Santiago del Estero 1148 (1075) Buenos Aires, Argentina.

Individual Exhibitions:

1968 Galatea Gallery, Buenos Aires, Argentina
1973 Martina Céspedes Gallery, Buenos Aires, Argentina
1977 Center for Art and Communication (CAYC), Buenos Aires, Argentina
1979 Ruth Benzacar Gallery, Buenos Aires, Argentina
1980 García Bes Gallery, Salta, Argentina
1983 Union Carbide Gallery, Buenos Aires, Argentina
1984 Museum of American Art, Maldonado, Uruguay
1986 Ruth Benzacar Gallery, Buenos Aires, Argentina
1989 *Instituto de Cooperación Iberoamericana,* Buenos Aires, Argentina
1991 Simon Watson Gallery, New York, USA
1992 Ruth Benzacar Gallery, Buenos Aires, Argentina
1996 Ruth Benzacar Gallery, Buenos Aires, Argentina

Selected Group Exhibitions:

1969 6th Paris Biennial, *Musée d'Art Moderne de la Ville de Paris.*
Kunstsystemen in Latinjs-America 1974, Paleis vor Schöne Kunsten, Brussels.
Art Systems in Latin America, Institute of Contemporary Art, London
Latin America 76, Joan Miro Foundation, Barcelona, Spain.
Group of Thirteen, 16th Sao Paulo International Biennial
Arte Agora III/América Latina. Geometria Sensivel. Museum of Modern Art, Rio de Janeiro
1980 CAYC Group, ROSC' 80, Bank of Ireland, Dublin
Contemporary Art in Latin America and Japan, The National Museum, Osaka, Japan
CAYC Group, Cantonal Museum of Fine Arts, Lausanne, Switzerland
CAYC Group, 42nd International Art Exhibition, Venice Biennial, Venice, Italy
Ideas and Images from Argentina, Alvar Aalto Museum, Jyväskylä.
Missões 300 anos. A visão do artista, Sao Paulo Art Museum, Brazil
Ideas and Images from Argentina, The Bronx Museum, New York.
CAYC Group, 21st Sao Paulo International Biennial.
1993 *Latin American Artists of the 20th Century,* Museum of Modern Art, New York
CAYC Group, The Striped House Museum, Tokyo

CAYC Group. National Museum of Fine Arts, Santiago, Chile
1st Mercosur Visual Arts Biennial, Museum of Contemporary Art, Rio Grande do Sul, Brazil.
Terra Incognita, Banco do Brasil Cultural Center, Rio de Janeiro, Brazil
48th International Art Exhibition, Venice Biennial, Venice, Italy
1st Buenos Aires International Art Biennial, National Museum of Fine Arts, Buenos Aires

Collections:

Museum of Modern Art, Buenos Aires, Argentina; Paris National Library; Chase Manhattan Collection, New York; National Museum of Fine Arts, Caracas, Venezuela; Citibank Collection, Buenos Aires; Museum of Contemporary Art, Montevideo, Uruguay. Art Gallery of Western Australia, Perth, Australia; Chase Collection of Argentine Contemporary Art, Buenos Aires; Museum of Art of Rio Grande do Sul, Porto Alegre, Brazil; Civic Gallery of Modern Art, *Palazzo dei Diamanti,* Ferrara, Italy; Experimental Museum of Modern Art, Saint-Etienne, France; National Museum of Fine Arts, Buenos Aires; University of Palermo, Buenos Aires; Municipality of Maldonado, Uruguay; Bank of Boston Collection, Buenos Aires.

Publications:

On BEDEL: Books—*Jacques Bedel—La Arqueología del Saber* (Jacques Bedel—The Archeology of Learning) by Jorge Gumier Maier, Buenos Aires 1979; *Jacques Bedel—Art in Argentina* by Jorge Glusberg, Milan 1986; *Los monumentos de Jacques Bedel* (The Monuments of Jacques Bedel) (exhibition catalog) by Jorge Glusberg, Buenos Aires, 1986; *Los tiempos de Jacques Bedel* (The Times of Jacques Bedel) (exhibition catalog) by Jorge Glusberg, Buenos Aires, 1992; *Jacques Bedel* (exhibition catalog) by J.A. Farmer, Seville 1996; *Latin American Art of the Twentieth Century,* London, 1996; *Jacques Bedel y el día de la ira* (Jacques Bedel and the Day of Rage) (exhibition catalog), Buenos Aires 1996; *Talleres de Artistas Argentinos* (Argentine Artistas' Workshops) edited by Alejandra Longo, Buenos Aires 2000; *Tesoros del Museo Nacional de Bellas Artes* (Treasures of the National Museum of Fine Arts) by Jorge Glusberg, Buenos Aires 2000. **Articles**—''Los Incunables de Bedel (Bedel's Incunabula)'' by Hugo Monzón in *Confirmado* (Buenos Aires), no. 506, 13 September 1979; ''La indagación estética del artista Jacques Bedel (Artist Jacques Bedel's Aesthetic Inquiry)'' in *La Opinión,* 11 January 1981; ''Jacques Bedel o la Preparación de la Eternidad (Jacques Bedel or Preparing Eternity)'' by Miguel Briante in *El Porteño* (Buenos Aires), no. 2, June 1982; ''En busca de la síntesis (In Search of Synthesis)'' by Lala Méndez Mosquera in *Summa+* (Buenos Aires), no. 3, October-November 1993; ''El tiempo es todo (Time is Everything)'' by Miguel Briante in *Writings on Art and Artists* (Buenos Aires), November 1996; ''Jacques Bedel en el Sol (Jacques Bedel in the Sun)'' by Albino Dieguez Videla in *La Prensa* (Buenos Aires), 13 October 1996; ''Jacques Bedel'' by Jorge Glusberg in *D'Ars* (Milan), no. 154, July 1998; ''Opus Bedel'' by Alfonso Corona-Martínez in *Summa+* (Buenos Aires), no. 34, December-January 1999; ''El universo de Jacques Bedel (Jacques Bedel's Universe)'' by Isabel Estrada in *Living* (Buenos Aires), no. 1, August-September 1999; ''Entrevista exclusiva a Jacques Bedel (Exclusive Interview with Jacques Bedel)'' by Delia Miler in *Moradas* (Buenos Aires), no. 2, January/February/March 2001.

* * *

Sculptor, painter, and architect Jacques Bedel obtained a French government grant in 1968 to carry out studies in Paris in the field of visual research. The following year, he was invited to take part in the 10th International Congress of Architects, as a delegate for the *Association Internationale des Arts Plastiques,* an agency of UNESCO. In 1974, the British Council awarded him a grant to study sculpture in London and in 1980, he received a Fulbright grant to carry out research at the U.S. National Astronomy and Ionosphere Center at Cornell University and NASA in Washington D.C. As of 1971, he became a member of the CAYC (Center for Art and Communication) Group, participating along with its other members in the Venice Biennial and obtaining the Sao Paulo Biennial's Grand Prize in 1977. The members of the CAYC Group were Jacques Bedel, Luis Benedit, Víctor Grippo, Leopoldo Maler, Alfredo Portillos, Clorindo Testa and, yours truly, Jorge Glusberg.

In Paris, Bedel initiated his research into mirrored planes and acrylics, as a means of obtaining superimposed, multiplied images. The mirror, on reflecting its surroundings, captures and transmits movement. Later, he utilized parabolic mirrors in his proposals as a means of achieving a greater field of reflection. So he began to move away from flat works to develop spheres within geometric bodies (spheres and cubes). Slowly, he worked his way into the field of sculpture, when—within the framework of his research into reflection of images—he began to use polished stainless steel. Working with stainless steel permitted him to start creating works of greater size, without risk of the mirrored surfaces breaking. Later, he began to work with iron sheet metal with tiny perforations.

The book is the symbol of culture. It is, *par excellence,* the object that *encloses* feelings. The *Books* created by Bedel, in polyester, vacuum-coated with metallic powder, contain three-dimensional objects: landscapes, ruins, remains. The closed book/open book contrast in his proposal also carries multiple meanings. The closed book, like Pandora's Box, holds hidden within it unknown and disconcerting elements. The open book is no longer a book at all, but an icon-like piece of ecological reality, a semblance of something pre-existent, quite often ignored by those who see it. One of the most singular is *Ciudad del Plata.*

He also makes cubes with the same material used for his archeological remains—polyurethane resins—in 0.50 x 0.50 x 0.50-meter modules. His landscapes are foreshortened within the cubes and offer an appearance of depth, thanks to a chiseled effect.

Bedel encloses his forms within books or frees them in cubes. His activity might well be described as meta-sculpture: one sculptural language about another, an identical spatial discourse contained in different forms: books and cubes.

The artist re-combines natural elements taken from different areas of the country and subjects them to the same chemical processes they suffered over the course of time. The difference here is that he controls and experiments with the process throughout the different creative stages. In this way, he recreates fossilizations, carbons, and incrustations from mineral waters that are integrated into his representations by means of soils, oxides, and silicates.

In 1992, he initiated his *Rollos* (Scrolls) series, and since then has been recovering the *divine scriptures* penned by Man. In these works, as in earlier ones, there is no mysticism or theological end, but rather, an interest in the interminable human enterprise of learning about himself and his destiny. Man, for Bedel, is the spirit of Mankind in every time and place. John was banished to Patmos as a result of the violent persecution ordered against the incipient Christian Church by the Roman Emperor Domitian. The Apocalypse describes God's struggle against the impiety and barbarity of the Romans, with the aim of vanquishing His enemies and establishing the Holy City, the definitive Celestial Kingdom. The Greek term *apocalipsis* signifies ''revelation,'' and the Old Testament contains several examples of apocalyptic literature, so dear to the Jews, the paradigm of which is the Book of Daniel. Every revelation is, in the end, a prophecy, and the Apocalypse is a prophetic text: It reveals/prophesies how the wicked world of war and death will be annihilated and how a new world of peace and love will be built. But if all revelations are prophecies, all prophecies contain hope. ''The Apocalypse,'' says the Bible of Jerusalem, ''is the great epic of hope.''

So it is that Bedel has chosen quotes that are related to hope and not to the disasters narrated by John—disasters that have led the word apocalypse to be synonymous with death and destruction. These texts, which manifest the majesty of the indecipherable and His plan for the future as well, as symbolized in ''life-giving water,'' can only be seen when the spectators' eyes are parallel to the ray of light that illuminates this work. That is to say, two observers standing close together will have a different perception of the work, depending on how they are situated. From a theological point of view, when the spectator's eye coincides with the ray of light, he or she is enlightened and can read the sacred text. What Bedel has done, in alluding to the end of time with the Book of John and the new millennium, is to reveal a revelation: His quotes are only made visible by the light that Yahweh created on the first day. (Genesis, I:3).

Another series of scrolls is *Ignis* (Fire), the realization of which is based on graphs indicating the shockwave of the huge fireball and energy intensity created when the U.S. spacecraft Skylab recorded a powerful solar explosion. The data recorded by Skylab today serve as a means to research the future—a future announced in the yesterdays of cosmogonies, religions and philosophical thought.

The 12 *Ignis* scrolls are along the same conceptual lines as the *Verbum* series. If in the latter, what the works recomposed was the interminable dialog between Man and the Absolute, in *Ignis* the artist deduces and suggests the extreme forms that might possibly hold a dialog with the Absolute in its relationship with Man.

—Jorge Glusberg

BEDNARSKI, Krzysztof M(aria)

Nationality: Polish. **Born:** Kraków, Poland, 25 July 1953. **Education:** Akademia Sztuk Piêknych (Academy of Fine Arts), Warsaw, 1973–1978. **Career:** Collaborates with Jerzy Grotowski Teatr Laboratorium, 1976–1981; designs film posters and appears in supporting parts in films, 1981–1987; visiting professor, Sculptural Department, Fine Arts Academy, Warsaw, 1996–97; artist in residence, Daniel Spoerri's ''Il Giardino,'' Seggiano, Italy, 1998–99. **Address:** 02–010 Warszawa, ul. Nowowiejska 28 m.55, Poland, and 00–186 Roma, Via dei Banchi Vecchi 134, Italy.

Selected Individual Exhibitions:

1978 *Portret totalny Karola Marksa* (diploma show), Galeria Repassage, Warsaw
1981 *Święto ziemi,* 7-day action at the Festival "Teatro in Piazza," Santarcangelo di Romagna, Italy
1982 *Niobe,* Genoa, Italy
Presenza/Durata, Centro Culturale del Levante, Genua, Italy
Mostra Laboratorio di Krzysztof Bednarski, Centro Culturale del Levante, Genoa
1982–83 *Luogo di nascita,* (with Ambrogio Ferrari), Circolo Culturale "Carlo Perini," Milan, Italy
1985 "Spalenie wnętrzności Sfinksa (Wielkim budowniczym)," Academy of Fine Arts, Warsaw
1986 *La rivoluzione siamo Noi—J. Beuys,* Galeria Stowarzyszenia Historyków Sztuki, Warsaw
1987 *Pomiêdzy czarnym i bia'ym,* Instytut Kultury Francuskiej, Warsaw
Moby Dick, Muzeum of the Academy of Fine Arts, Warsaw
1988 *Dzieci Wielkiej Niedÿwiedzicy,* Galeria Promocyjna, Warsaw
Moby Dick, Centro Di Sarro, Rome
Thanatos polacco, Studio E, Rome
Incubazione fredda, Gruppo 10 C.E.P.A., Rome
1989 *Altre stelle,* Galleria dell'Immagine, Palazzo Gambalunga, Rimini
Wurzeln treiben (with Leon Tarasewicz and Andrzej Szewczyk), Kutscherhaus, Berlin
1990 *Trzy Pasaże,* Galeria Studio, Warsaw
Pasaż Vision & Prayer, Centrum Sztuki Współczesnej, Warsaw
1991 *Hiny,* (with *Joseph Beuys from the Collection of Muzeum Sztuki in Łódź*), Watari Museum of Contemporary Art, Tokyo
1992 *Unsichtbar/Niewidzialne,* Pañstwowa Galeria Sztuki, Sopot
Laska Edypa, Galeria Przyjaciółk Akademii Ruchu, Kinoteatr Tęcza, Warsaw
1997 *Trawa, tylko trawa,* Galeria Przyjaciół Akademii Ruchu, Kinoteatr Tęcza, Warsaw
Tombstone on the grave of Krzysztof Kieslowski, Warsaw.
1998 *L'orto dei frutti dimenticati/Ogród owoców zapomnianych,* Galeria Potocka, Kraków, Poland
1999 *Buty włoskie* and *Scarpe italiane,* (retrospective) Centrum Sztuki Współczesnej, Warsaw
Artistinvetrina—Krzysztof M. Bednarski, Fendissime, Via Fontanella di Borghese, Rome

Public installations:

Orto dei Frutti Dimenticati, Pennabilli, Italy; Statue of St. Phillipe Neri, Chiesa Nuova (Santa Maria in Vallicella) church, Rome; Xawery Dunikowski Muzeum, Warsaw.

Publications:

On BEDNARSKI: Books—*Krzysztof M. Bednarski: Ritratto totale di Karl Marx 1977–1989* (exhibition catalog), with text by Achille

Bonito Oliva, Lidia Reghini di Pontremoli, Waldemar Baraniewski, and Piotr Szubert, Rome 1991; *De Europa* by Achille Bonito Oliva, Milan 1991; *Krzysztof M. Bednarski: Dark Passage* (exhibition catalog), with text by Anda Rottenberg and Waldemar Baraniewski, Warsaw 1993; *Moby Dick Krzysztofa M. Bednarskiego* by Jaromir Jedliñski, Łódź 1994; *Krzysztof M. Bednarski: Prace z lat 1976–1995* (exhibition catalog), with text by Piotr Szubert, Maryla Sitkowska, Achille Bonito Oliva, Waldemar Baraniewski, Lidia Reghini di Pontremoli, Angelika Stepken, Marek Goydziewski, Piotr Rypson, and Jan Stanislaw Wojciechowski, Warsaw 1995; *Krzysztof M. Bednarski: Passaggio ''Scarpe italiane.'' Works from the years 1976–1999* (exhibition catalog), with text by Maryla Sitkowska, Achille Bonito Oliva, and Waldemer Baraniewski, Warsaw 1999.

* * *

Krzysztof Bednarski's oeuvre is not easily labeled. As a sculptor occupied with ideas rather than a particular style or current, he works simultaneously in different media, producing both representational and non-representational works. A solid academic background enables him to work with ease in stone, resins, or metal, and he chooses his means according to a concept that usually comes first. Exceptions to this rule include his pieces inspired by found objects, the best examples of which are *Moby Dick* (1992), a hulk turned upside down and cut into segments, the assemblage sculpture *Polish Thanatos* (1984), depicting a crucified dead tree in a rowboat (dedicated to Bednarski's deceased friends who were members of Jerzy Grotowski's theater), or a more recent installation titled *L'orto dei frutti dimenticati* (1998), which consists of picture frames lying on the floor and filled with fruit wrapping paper picked up from the ground after a street market.

Since his diploma installation, *Portrait of Karl Marx* (exhibited at a graduate show at the Academy of Fine Arts in Warsaw in 1978), which brought him a sort of *succès de scandale,* Bednarski has been recognized as one of the most innovative young artists in Poland. In the work (followed closely by *Total Portrait of Karl Marx,* 1978) the young artist dared to trivialize one of the holy icons of state ideology: the face of the founding father of Communism. The piece was a partial presentation of the process used in making multiple copies of a plaster head of the idol. The work prevented Bednarski from graduating with honors despite having scored excellent grades throughout his studies. Later in his career, he would return to the face of Karl Marx using it, among other things, in common objects like lamps (*La rivoluzione siamo Noi—J. Beuys* and *Mars Galaxy,* both 1986).

In 1979 Bednarski produced another significant political work, *Ticket*—a big stone fist proudly holding a bus ticket. The piece, originally situated in front of a typical blue-collar housing block, was a monument to the mediocrity of the people's life in a system which called itself the workers' dictatorship and in which only members of a narrow privileged class could afford to purchase automobiles. Later on he returned several times to the motif of a fist, which also appears in one of his best marble works, *Victoria-Victoria* (1983). The two fingers of the fist forming a ''V'' are truncated, cut off. A smaller version of the sculpture, originally created in Digne-les-Bains, France, was presented at an underground exhibition in Warsaw in 1984. At that time Bednarski took an active part in the independent art movement, whose members protested against the imposition of Martial Law by General Jaruzelski by rejecting state owned galleries in favor of exhibiting in their studios, private apartments, and churches.

Bednarski often makes references to people who have influenced his life. By coincidence, most of them bear the initials JB: his father, Joseph Beuys, Josif Brodski. One of the artist's most important personal works seems to be *Fuga da Bisanzio* (1987), dedicated to Brodski. The main element of this installation is a pyramid (symbolizing totalitarianism) made up of old rugs taken from his family's home. Bednarski also had memories of his father in mind when he created this piece.

Since the mid-1980s Bednarski has lived and worked in Italy, although he has never severed his close links with Poland. Of his Italian works, the most spectacular is a project for a Federico Fellini monument (*Meeting with Fellini,* 1994) to be built in Rimini, hometown to both the filmmaker and the artist's wife. Once a year this abstract sculpture, lit by sunlight, will cast a shadow in the shape of Fellini's profile. The same effect would be achieved at night using a beam of artificial light. Unfortunately, this project, originally accepted by city officials, was contested by some of the citizens and has been postponed, although there is still a chance that it will eventually be built at a different site. Bednarski has also designed a tombstone for his friend, the distinguished Polish film director, Krzysztof Kieslowski. This is one more mark of his strong attachment to the world of film and theater, a relationship which is reflected in the strong narrative qualities of many of his works.

—Marcin Giżycki

BEECROFT, Vanessa

Nationality: Italian. **Born:** Genoa, Italy, 1969. **Education:** Studied architecture at Civico Liceo Artistico Nicolo' Barabino, Genoa, 1983–87; painting at Accademia Ligustica di Belle Arti, Genoa, 1987–88; and stage design at Accademia di Belle Arti di Brera, Milan, 1988–93. **Career:** Lives and works in Brooklyn, New York. **Agent:** Deitch Projects, 76 Grand Street, New York, New York 10013. **Web site:** http://www.vanessabeecroft.com.

Selected Individual Exhibitions:

1994 *Ein blonder Traum,* Galerie Schipper & Krome, Cologne
Jane bleibt Jane, Courtesy Fac-Simile, Milan
VH5, Giacinto di Pietrantonio, Milan
Mädchen in Uniform, Galerie Massimo De Carlo, Milan; Andrea Rosen Gallery, New York
1995 *Play,* Galerie Analix, Geneva
1998 *Show,* Solomon R. Guggenheim Museum, New York; Galerie Ghislaine Hussenot, Paris
1999 *US Navy VB39/VB42,* Deitch Projects, New York
VB42 Intrepid: The Silent Service in Cooperation with The Undersea Warfare Community, Deitch Projects, New York
2000 *VGBDW,* Deitch Projects, New York

Selected Group Exhibitions:

1994 *Winter of Love II,* P. S. 1 Museum, New York
Incertaine Identité, Galerie Analix, Geneva

Soggetto-Soggetto, Castello di Rivoli, Turin
Prima linea, Trevi Flash Art Museum, Italy

1995 *Campo 95,* Corderie, Venice
Aperto Italia, Trevi Flash Art Museum, Italy
Fuori Uso 95, ex Aurum, Pescara, Italy

1996 *Truce: Echoes of Art in an Age of Endless Conclusions,* Site Santa Fe, New Mexico (catalog)
ID: An International Survey on the Notion of Identity in Contemporary Art, Stedelijk Van Abbemuseum, Eindhoven, The Netherlands (catalog)
Persona, Renaissance Society at University of Chicago; Kunsthalle Basel, Switzerland (catalog)

1997 *Fatto in Italia,* Centre d'Art Contemporain, Geneva (catalog)
Ein Stück vom Himmel-Some Kind of Heaven, Kunsthalle Nürnberg, Nuremberg; South London Gallery (catalog)
BV 97 Future, Present, Past, XLVII Esposizione Internazionale d'Arte, Venice Biennale
Arte Italiana, Ultimi Quarant'anni Materiali Anomali, Galleria d'Arte Moderna, Bologna (catalog)

1998 *Wounds: Between Democracy and Redemption in Contemporary Art,* Moderna Museet, Stockholm (catalog)
Shoes: A Lexicon of Style, Museum at the Fashion Institute of Technology, New York (catalog)
Kritische Elegantie (Critical Elegance), Museum Dhont-Dhaenens Duerle, Belgium (catalog)
Ontom, Galerie für Zeitgenössische Kunst, Leipzig, Germany (catalog)

1999 Museum of Contemporary Art, San Diego
Museum of Contemporary Art, Sydney
Examining Pictures, Like Hands Stuck in a Mattress, Whitechapel Art Gallery, London (catalog)
The 3rd Art Life 21-Spiral TV, Spiral/Wacoal Art Center, Tokyo (catalog)

2000 *Whitney Biennial,* Whitney Museum of American Art, New York (catalog)
Présumés innocents: L'art contemporain et l'enfance, Musée d'art contemporain de Bordeaux, France (catalog)
Biennale of Sydney 2000 (catalog)
What's the Ideal Woman, Arts Show, New York (catalog)

2001 *Exposure: Recent Acquisitions, The Doron Sebbag Art Collection,* Tel-Aviv Museum of Art, Israel (catalog)
I am a Camera, The Saatchi Gallery, London (catalog)

Publications:

By BEECROFT: Book—*VB 08–36: Vanessa Beecroft Performances,* Stuttgart 2000. **Articles—**''Interview with Vanessa Beecroft'' by Giacinto Di Pietrantonio in *Flash Art* no. 183, Summer 1995; ''I Prefer Nudity: An Interview with Vanessa Beecroft'' by Munro Galloway in *Art Press,* no. 265, February 2001.

On BEECROFT: Articles—''Vanessa Beecroft'' by Elizabeth Janus in *Artforum International,* May 1995; ''Vanessa Beecroft: Deitch Projects'' by Martha Schwendener in *New Art Examiner,* no. 23, April 1996; ''Models of Fashion'' by Daryl Chin in *PAJ,* September 1998; ''Vanessa Beecroft'' by Giacinto Di Pietrantonio in *Flash Art,* Summer 1995; ''Vanessa Beecroft'' by Brad Killiam in *New Art Examiner,* no. 25, October 1997; ''Bikini Brief'' by Wayne Koestenbaum in *Artforum,* vol. 36, no. 10, Summer 1998; ''Thin-Skinned and Ambiguous: Uncanny Beauty, Uncanny Familiarity, and Uncanny Everydayness'' by Urs Stahel in *Unheimlich/Uncanny,* Winterthur 1999; ''Classic Cruelty'' by Keith Seward in *Parkett,* 1999; ''US Navy Seals'' by Norman Bryson in *Parkett,* no. 56, September 1999; ''Let the Picture do the Talking'' by Jan Avgikos in *Parkett,* no. 56, September 1999; ''Classic Cruelty'' by Keith Seward in *Parkett,* no. 56, September 1999; ''Vanessa Beecroft at the Museum of Contemporary Art, San Diego'' by Doug Harvey in *Art Issues,* no. 59, September-October 1999; ''Adventures in the Skin Trade'' by Gloria Fisk in *feedmag* (www.feedmag.com/feature/fr314lofi.html), accessed 31 March 2000;''Vanessa Beecroft: VB43'' by Claire Bishop in *Make: The Magazine of Women's Art,* no. 88, June-August 2000; ''Vanessa Beecroft: Deitch Projects'' by Barry Schwabsky in *Artforum,* vol. 39, no. 3, November 2000.

* * *

Few contemporary artists divide critics like performance artist—or, more correctly, performance director—Vanessa Beecroft. Descriptions of her *tableaux vivants* of hired, creatively blocked models, often wearing little more than designer underwear, range from ''symbolically layered'' to ''fantastically shallow.'' But few critics or audiences would deny that her human installations conjure uncomfortable emotions that force one to confront the interrelation of art, commercialism, and voyeurism, regardless of whether they feel the artist's work critiques or is complicit in this relationship.

Beecroft's study of architecture and stage design are apparent in her performance pieces, where a group of models is precisely arranged in a gallery environment like so many set pieces. Their decorative nature is underscored through Beecroft's demand that they avoid movement, expression, and eye contact with the audience or one another. Since 1994 these installations were comprised of all-female ensembles that, through the use of costumes, wigs, and body paint, became increasingly uniform. Considering her view of these women as her ''army,'' it seems logical that Beecroft would eventually look literally to the military as an ideal of such uniformity, and has since arranged several exhibitions of Navy personnel in the same manner as her better-known arrangements of female fashion and art models. Although the meanings of these different ''casts'' inevitably evoke wildly different interpretations, in all cases the setting was the same: the models, unresponsive and passively still, would hold positions dictated by the artist—allowing for an occasional rest, if they remain in place—for a period of two to four hours, during which time the audience mills about the living sculpture.

Since the earliest of Beecroft's performances, such as *VB08* at New York's P.S. 1 Contemporary Art Center, she has demonstrated a twin interest in three-dimensional composition and audience-performer dynamics that betray her theatre background. In this particular work a group of ten attractive young women—wearing sensible underwear and cartoonish, red yarn wigs braided Pippi Longstocking-style—took over a corner of P.S. 1 and lounged with a disinterest in their surroundings that seemed to parody the cool affectations of the New York art audience taking in the performance itself. By the presentation of *VB16* at Deitch Projects just two years later, Beecroft had completely shrugged off the openly comical undertone of the earlier work. Here, her models far more closely resembled—in both costume and physique—the ''supermodels'' of popular fashion magazines. In this work, however, the glamorous veneer of the slim, platinum-bobbed women was designed to fade. The longer the audience stared, the more likely they were to confront the models' and their own vulnerabilities: the models' bodies distorted through the control-top pantyhose worn over underpants; the longer the women stood in their strappy high heels the less perfect their pose and swollen their ankles; and the mere fact of the audience's necessary meditation on this human installation forced them to confront their own inappropriate notice and judgment of these imperfections.

It is just this time-based aspect of Beecroft's installations that is often forgotten in the sensationalistic imagery through which most are introduced to her work. Naturally, the documentation of her performances reminds us of the disturbing nature of her "objects." In photographs the often rail-thin physiques of certain exhibition's models, and her increased association with prominent fashion houses like Prada and Gucci—her 1998 *VB 35: SHOW* exhibition at the Solomon R. Guggenheim museum in New York being the best known example—immediately remind the viewer of similar, ubiquitous imagery with which one is assaulted through fashion journalism and advertising. Of course, her very choice to use these body types and brand names only add credence to interpretations of her work that lament its shallowness and commercialism. The performances themselves, however, are an exercise in the power of that which arguably defines postmodernity—theatricality. In the tradition of Fluxus, the performance/installation itself almost becomes secondary to the process unfolding and the audience reacting—under the blazing theatrical lights the charge of the mere potential for a taboo breaking rupture between audience and artwork is palpable, even though the audiences are almost uncontrollably compelled to keep their distance. Perhaps the most telling aspect of a Beecroft performance is the inevitable projection of identity upon the anonymous, seemingly homogeneous models; the longer each audience member lingers over the work, the more one overhears the increasingly comfortable audience speculating on their identities, as if they were so many ambiguously attributed, classical caryatids.

In much the same way that audience projection plays a crucial part in Beecroft's work, so does the artist's own, similar approach to her conception of the performances. In fact, her tendency to project her own identity and neuroses upon her doll-like models was perhaps clearest in her first solo exhibition in 1993, based on a journal the artist had kept for eight years. The journal, which obsessively chronicled the artist's eating habits, battle with anorexia, and revelations through psychiatric counseling, was displayed alongside drawings inspired by its contents, and only viewed by a small, all-female audience that she had hand-picked based on each woman's resemblance to the artist herself. Once the audience arrived, the relevance of their resemblance became clear as the artist went immediately about "correcting" her guests' appearance or composure, arranging them around the gallery into something of an ideal, multiple self-portrait. In an almost shamanistic act of catharsis and self-healing, the artist effectively transfers her own issues with self-control and rigid order from her body to another's. Whereas many of critics address the impersonal nature of her homogenous, passive subjects, others recognize this very human tendency in her performances, whereby the models become both her medium and her surrogates. The disconcerting nature of her work is in Beecroft's invitation to her audiences to similarly indulge in this neurotic, voyeuristic scenario in the safe and amoral theatrical space she has constructed.

—Maria Elena Buszek

BELL, Larry

Nationality: American. **Born:** Chicago, Illinois, 6 December 1939. **Education:** Birmingham High School, Eureka, California, 1953–57; Chouinard Art Institute, Los Angeles, 1957–59. **Family:** Married 1) Gloria Jean Neilsen, 1967 (divorced, 1971); daughters: Zara Augusta and Rachel Victoria; son: Oliver; has lived with Janet Ruth Burns, since 1973. **Career:** Worked as a bowling alley maintenance engineer, truck driver and picture framer, Los Angeles, 1957–59; general manager, The Unicorn saloon-cabaret, Hollywood, 1957–65. Full-time artist since 1965. Instructor, University of California, Berkeley, 1972, and University of South Florida, Tampa 1973. **Member:** Founder-Member, with Bob Irwin, Newton Harrison, Joshua Young, Ed Wirtz, and Frank Geary, Don Quixote Collective, California, 1974. **Awards:** William Noma Copley Foundation Prize, 1963; Guggenheim Fellowship, 1969; National Endowment for the Arts grant recipient, 1975; Governor's Award for Excellence and Achievement in the Arts (Visual Arts), State of New Mexico, 1990. **Address:** Box 4101, Taos, New Mexico 87571, U.S.A.

Selected Individual Exhibitions:

1962 Ferus Gallery, Los Angeles
1963 Ferus Gallery, Los Angeles
1965 Ferus Gallery, Los Angeles
Pace Gallery, New York
1967 Galerie Sonnabend, Paris
Pace Gallery, New York
Stedelijk Museum, Amsterdam
1969 Mizuno Gallery, Los Angeles
1970 Pace Gallery, New York
Ace Gallery, Los Angeles
1971 Pace Gallery, New York
Helman Gallery, St. Louis
Mizuno Gallery, Los Angeles
Ace Gallery, Los Angeles
Galerie Rudolf Zwirner, Cologne
1972 Pace Gallery, New York
Felicity Samuel Gallery, London
Pasadena Art Museum, California
Wilmaro Gallery, Denver
1973 Oakland Art Museum, California
Pace Gallery, New York
Bonython Gallery, Sydney
1974 Marlborough Galleria d'Arte, Rome (toured Italy)
Galleria La Citta, Verona
Galleria Il Cavallino, Venice
Salone Annunciata, Milan
1975 Marlborough Galleria d'Arte, Rome (toured Italy
Galleria Il Cavallino, Venice
Tally Richards Gallery, Taos, New Mexico
Recent Works, Fort Worth Art Museum, Texas
1976 Washington University, St. Louis
Santa Barbara Museum of Art, California
Art Museum of South Texas, Corpus Christi
1977 Hayden Gallery, Massachusetts Institute of Technology, Cambridge
University of Massachusetts, Amherst

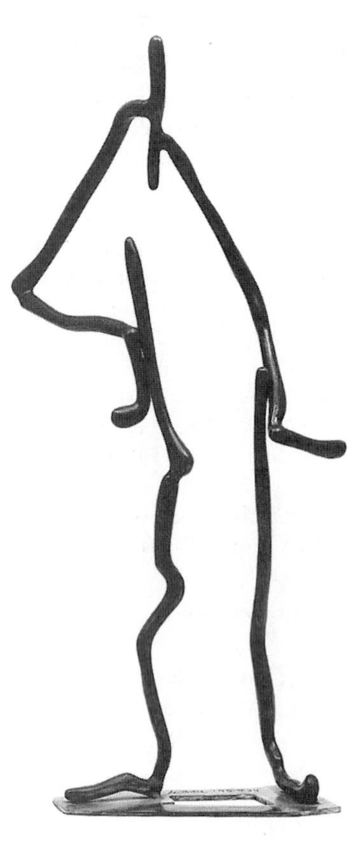

Larry Bell: *Stickman #24,* 1994. Photo by Paul O'Connor. ©Larry Bell.

Federal Reserve, Boston
Fort Worth Art Museum, Texas (with Eric Orr)
1978 Multiples Gallery, New York
Delahunty Gallery, New York
Texas Gallery, Houston
Erica Williams-Anne Johnson Gallery, Seattle
University of New Mexico, Albuquerque
Roswell Museum and Art Center, New Mexico
Tally Richards Gallery, Taos, New Mexico
1979 Roswell Museum and Art Center, New Mexico
Multiples Gallery, New York
Sebastian-Moore Gallery, Denver
Hill's Gallery of Contemporary Art, Santa Fe, New Mexico
Hansen Fuller Gallery, San Francisco
Tally Richards Gallery, Taos, New Mexico
Janus Gallery, Venice, California
Marian Goodman Gallery, New York
1980 Sebastian-Moore Gallery, Denver
Hill's Gallery of Contemporary Art, Santa Fe, New Mexico
Tally Richards Gallery, Taos, New Mexico
Marion Goodman Gallery, New York
1981 Hudson River Museum, Yonkers, New York
Marion Goodman Gallery, New York
Ann Jacob Gallery, Atlanta, Georgia (with Eric Orr)
L. A. Louver Gallery, Venice, California
Wildine Galleries, Albuquerque, New Mexico
Tally Richard Gallery, Taos, New Mexico
University of Ohio, Athens
1982 Newport Harbor Art Museum, Newport Beach, California
Marion Goodman/Multiples Gallery, New York
Ruth S. Schaffner Gallery, Santa Barbara, California
Erica Williams/Anne Johnson Gallery, Seattle, Washington
Milwaukee Art Museum, Wisconsin
Museum of Fine Arts, Santa Fe, New Mexico
Tally Richards Gallery, Taos, New Mexico
Detroit Institute of Arts, Michigan
1983 University of Nebraska, Lincoln
Advanced Art Gallery, Riconada, New Mexico
Arco Center for Visual Art, Los Angeles
Wildine Gallery, Albuquerque, New Mexico
1984 Colorado springs Fine Arts Center, Colorado
Museum of Contemporary Art, Los Angeles
The Works Gallery, Long Beach, California
1985 Dord Fitz Gallery, Amarillo, Texas (with Lee Mullican)
The Works Gallery, Long Beach, California
L. A. Louver Gallery, Venice, California
1986 Braunstein Gallery, San Francisco
Boise Gallery of Art, Idaho
The New Gallery, Houston
Amarillo Art Center, Texas
1987 Galerie Gilbert Brownstone, Paris
Braunstein/Quay Gallery, San Francisco (with Peter Voulkos)
1988 Laguna Art Museum, Laguna Beach, California
Gemini Editions Limited, Los Angeles, California
1989 Musée d'Art Contemporain, Lyon, France
1990 Galerie Rolf Ricke, Köln, Germany
Galerie Montenay, Paris
1991 Tony Shafrazi Gallery, New York
Tucson Museum of Art, Tucson, Arizona
1992 Tampa Museum of Art, Tampa, Florida
1996 Art et Industrie Gallery, New York
1997 The Albuquerque Museum, Albuquerque, New Mexico
Reykjavik Muncipal Art Museum, Reykjavik, Iceland
1998 Bergen Kunstmuseum, Bergen, Norway
1999 Museum Moderner Kunst Landkreis Cuxhaven, Otterndorf, Germany
2000 Center Galleries, Center for Creative Studies, Detroit, Michigan
2001 Gallery Gan, Tokyo, Japan

Selected Group Exhibitions:

1964 *California Hard-Edge Painting,* Pavilion Gallery, Balboa, California
1966 *Primary Structures,* Jewish Museum, New York
1972 *USA West Coast,* Kunstverein, Hamburg (travelled to Hannover, Cologne and Stuttgart)
1976 *200 Years of American Sculpture,* Whitney Museum, New York
1977 *Painting and Sculpture in California: The Modern Era,* Washington Collection of Fine Arts, Smithsonian Institution, Washington D.C.

1979 *Contemporary Sculpture: Selections from the Collection of MOMA,* Museum of Modern Art, New York
1980 *Beyond Object,* Aspen Center for the Visual Arts, Colorado
1982 *One Hundred Years of California Sculpture,* Oakland Museum, California
1984 *Americans in Glass,* Woodson Art Museum, Wausau, Wisconsin (toured Europe)
1987 *Art and the West,* University of Wyoming, Laramie
1987 Pheonix Art Museum, Pheonix, Arizona
1988 Guggenheim Museum, New York
Spaso House, Moscow
1989 Galerie Joan Prats, Barcelona
1992 *Sculpturen und Projectionen,* Arolsen, Germany
1993 Musee du Palais du Luxembourg, Paris
1995 Galerie Nächt St. Stephen, Vienna, Austria
1997 Kunstmuseum Wolfsburg, Germany
1999 Norton Simon Museum, Pasadena, California
2000 Guggenheim Museum, Bilbao, Spain
San Francisco Museum of Modern Art

Collections:

Whitney Museum, New York; Guggenheim Museum, New York; Museum of Modern Art, New York; National Collection of Fine Arts, Smithsonian Institution, Washington, D.C.; Fort Worth Art Center, Texas; Museum of New Mexico, Santa Fe; Roswell Museum and Art Center, New Mexico; Los Angeles County Museum of Art; Norton Simon Art Museum, Pasadena, California; Tate Gallery, London; Stedelijk Museum, Amsterdam; Stedelijk Museum, Rotterdam; Albright-Knox Gallery, Buffalo, New York; Albuquerque Museum, Albuquerque, New Mexico; Art Gallery of New South Wales, Sydney, Australia; Art Institute of Chicago, Chicago, Illinois; Australian National Gallery, Canberra, Australia; The Berardo Collection, Funchal, Portugal; Centre Georges Pompidou, Paris, France; City of Albuquerque Public Arts, Albuquerque, New Mexico; The Contemporary Museum, Honolulu, Hawaii; Corning Museum of Glass, Corning, New York; Dallas Museum of Fine Arts, Dallas, Texas; Denver Art Museum, Denver, Colorado; Metropolitan Bronco Football Stadium District and City of Denver, Denver, Colorado; Des Moines Art Center, Des Moines, Iowa; Detroit Institute of Arts, Detroit, Michigan; The Archer M. Huntington Art Gallery, University of Texas, Austin, Texas; Massachusetts Institute of Technology, Cambridge, Massachusetts; The Menil Collection, Houston, Texas; Milwaukeee Museum of Art, Milwaukee, Wisconsin; Minneapolis Art Institute, Minneapolis, Minnesota; Musée Saint-Pierre Art Contemporain, Lyon, France; Museum of Contemporary Art, Caracas, Venezuela; Museum of Contemporary Art, Los Angeles, California; Museum of Fine Arts, Houston Texas; Museum Ludwig, Köln, Germany; Oakland Museum of Art, Oakland, California; Roswell Museum and Art Center, Roswell, New Mexico; San Francisco Museum of Modern Art, San Francisco, California; University of Arizona, Tucson, Arizona; Victoria and Albert Museum, London, England; Walker Art Center, Minneapolis, Minnesota.

Publications:

By BELL: Articles—Statement in ''Saint Andy'' by Philip Leider in *Artforum* (New York), 1965; statement in *A New Esthetic,* exhibition catalog, Washington, D.C. 1967; interview in *Los Angeles 6,* exhibition catalog, by John Coplans, Vancouver 1968; interview in *Transparency, Reflection, Light Space,* exhibition catalog, by Frederick S. Wight, Lost Angeles 1971; ''Larry Bell,'' interview with Alastair Mackintosh, in *Art and Artists* (London), January 1972; ''The Iceberg'' in *Vision* (Oakland, California), September 1975. **Film—** *Larry Bell, Watching the Watcher—The Creation of Summer,* 1996.

On BELL: Books—*Larry Bell,* exhibition catalog, with texts by Raphael Sorin and Annette Michelson, Paris 1967; *American Art since 1900* by Barbara Rose, London 1967, *6 Artists: 6 Exhibitions,* exhibition catalog, Milwaukee 1968; *West Coast 1945–1969,* exhibition catalog, by John Coplans, Pasadena, California 1969; *Kompas IV-West Coast U.S.A.,* exhibition catalog, Amsterdam 1969; *Larry Bell, Robert Irwin, Doug Wheeler,* exhibition catalog, by M. Compton and N. Reid, London 1970; *Larry Bell,* exhibition catalog, by Barbara Haskell, Pasadena, California 1972; *USA West Coast,* exhibition catalog, Hamburg 1972; *Possibilities for Glass Sculpture,* exhibition catalog, Sydney 1973; *Larry Bell,* exhibition catalog, Rome 1974; *Sunshine Muse: Contemporary Art on the West Coast* by Peter Plagens, New York 1974; *Readings in America Art 1900–1975,* edited by Barbara Rose, New York 1975; *Larry Bell: Recent Works,* exhibition catalog, Fort Worth, Texas 1975; *Larry Bell: New Work,* exhibition catalog with introduction by Robert Creeley, New York 1981. **Articles—**''A Lot of Talent . . .'' by Henry J. Seldis in the *Los Angeles Times,* 21 October 1973; ''American in Paris: 1974'' by Melinda Wortz in *Arts Magazine* (New York), 1975; ''Larry Bell'' in *Art News* (New York), March 1975; ''A Hotbed of Advanced Art'' by E. Perlmutter in *Art News* (New York), January 1976; ''Larry Bell on New York'' by David Rush in *Artweek* (Oakland, California), 15 May 1976; ''The Grip of the Iceberg'' by Kenneth Baker in the *Boston Phoenix,* 8 February 1977; ''A Glass Menagerie'' by R. Talor in the *Boston Globe,* 16 June 1977; ''Larry Bell and Eric Orr'' by Gerrit Henry in *Art News* (New York), April 1978; article by Gerrit Henry in *Art News* (New York), May 1979; ''Larry Bell'' by Jon Meyer in *Arts Magazine* (New York), September 1982; ''Art Vapor Made'' by Jody Jacobs in the *Los Angeles Times,* 14 October 1985; ''Larry Bell's Lights'' by Kenneth Baker in *San Francisco Chronicle,* 14 June 1986; ''Sixties Sculpture Relieves Summer Doldrums'' by Christopher Knight in *Los Angeles Herald Examiner,* 17 July 1987; ''Through A Glass Brightly: Meet a High-Tech Romantic'' by Susan Chadwick in *Houston Post,* 17 April 1988; ''Artist Larry Bell Proves Making Magic is Still Viable'' by Sandy Ballatore in the *Albuquerque Journal,* 30 April 1989; ''Cirrus Offers Minimalism with a West Coast Slant'' by Kristine McKenna in *Los Angeles Times,* 12 December 1990; ''Larry Bell at Shafrazi'' by Eleanor Heartney in *Art in America,* July 1991; ''Larry Bell'' by Todd Baron in *ArtScene,* vol. 11, no. 7, 1992; ''Ask Not for Whom the Bell Toils'' by Wesley Pulkka in *Art Review,* 24–30 January 1994; ''The Shapes of Things to Come'' by David Greene in *Los Angeles Reader,* 1 July 1994; ''Sculptural Renaissance in Bronze'' by Wesley Pulkka in *Albuquerque Journal,* 4 June 1995; ''Is This Any Way to Make a Living?'' by B. J. Foreman in *Sculpture Magazine,* April 1996; ''Arist-Alchemist Takes Viewer on Mystical. . .'' by Wesley Pulkka in *Albuquerque Journal,* 2 March 1997; ''Larry Bell at Kiyo Higashi'' by David Pagel in *Art Issues,* January/February 1998; ''Larry Bell at Kiyo Higashi'' by Mary Kay Lombino in *Artweek,* January 1998; ''Larry Bell's Evolving Vision'' by Phaedre Greenwood in *Taos News,* 4 February 1999; ''Bell's Minimalist Art Reflects Major Talent'' by Donald

Miller in *Pittsburgh Post-Gazette,* 3 April 1999; ''Bit by Bit, 'Fractions' Creates an Absorbing Irresistible Whole'' by David Pagel in *Los Angeles Times,* 13 August 1999. **Film—***A Video Portrait: Larry Bell* by John Hunt, 1976.

*

I used to think that a person got what he wanted, and that was all he got, 'cause that's all there was. Everything was very simple. If you didn't know what you wanted, you still got what you set up for yourself, but you may not know that you got what you wanted. In a recent conversation with a friend, he suggested that maybe you get what your character dictates, and you spend most of your life trying to make sense out of the chaos of your character; finding your rational explanation to yourself, of what it's all about. I like to look at it like this. And I am responsible for my acts, for the things I say and do, just like everybody else. My rational mind is fighting the same chaotic battle that everyone fights every day, who either thinks that they know what they want, or don't think about it at all. I think it's a terrible delusion to believe that a person is the master of his character.

—Larry Bell

* * *

In all the art capitals of the world, the artists jostle for their place in the hierarchy of reputation, eyeing the other contenders and marshalling their supporting forces of critics and other hangers-on: In all the capitals except Los Angeles, where Larry Bell is undisputed king.

There are of course many West Coast artists with high reputations and an international following, and it would be foolish to pretend at this stage of history that one could say who will or will not be remembered. Anyway, status has little to do with quality; it stems rather from the stance or image of the artist, and the consistency and self-confidence of the work.

Bell has achieved his position of pre-eminence by matching his work exactly to the ethos of Los Angeles. Art from New York tends to have an intellectual and slightly paranoid edge, that from San Francisco a colourful messiness associated with psychedelia—the art matches the city from whence it grows. L.A. is the blandest, least intellectual and most stylish of American cities, the worst place on earth to be poor. Economic extravagance is an aesthetic quality in L.A., and nothing matters more than effect.

This may sound like a condemnation, but any quality can become a virtue in the hands of a skilful artist, and there is no denying Bell's skill. His art may depend on great technical ability based upon a high cost of production, but it is also successful. Who complains at the cost of a high budget movie as long as it succeeds at box office, and Bell's work has certainly done that.

His work, since it first became widely known in 1964, has all been variations on a single idea. The earlier examples were glass cubes with 15–30 cm sides, upon which were imposed patterns by an aluminising process, which caused delicate interference when one side was seen against another. Soon, however, Bell was finding this technique too crude, and he switched to vacuum coating, which allowed him to introduce extremely subtle variations of transparent colour onto the surface of the glass. After experimenting with various colour effects, he settled mainly on the use of greys, some of which were so slight as to be almost non-existent.

The reductive quality of these works has led to Bell's being associated with minimalism, an essentially East Coast school of art. But the differences are far greater than the similarities. Minimalism is an intellectual system; art is reduced to the bare essentials for theoretical reasons and any visual impact is a subsidiary bonus. Bell's work is extremely sensuous and the reduction is made to increase the sensuality, not for any theoretical reason. It is minimal only in the sense that the whiteness of Jean Harlow's satin dresses is minimal, as an increase of visual impact.

In 1968, Bell started to work on a large scale, evolving techniques that would allow him to make pieces big enough for the viewer to walk through. The equipment necessary to achieve this was very expensive, and this had a concomitant effect on Bell's prices. On the East Coast there is still a feeling that art should cost little to make (whatever price it is sold for) and that blatantly industrial techniques are somehow cheating; but in Los Angeles this attitude is considered absurd. In a city where you can buy a gold-plated toothbrush, vacuum coated sculpture is perfectly logical.

There is no denying that Bell's work is possibly the most sheerly beautiful and elegant of the post-war period. Its flawless finish combined with great simplicity makes it seductively attractive compared to the ''unfinished'' aesthetic of most contemporary art. Critics have tended to underrate Bell because there is no theory to his art for them to bite on; it is there, you look at it and that is that, and in a period where art is weighed down by the verbiage that surrounds it, this is a highly satisfactory quality.

Bell's best pieces are probably those constructed in the form of simple mazes. The sheets of glass, six feet high, are coated with grey, and this is further treated with a mirroring process which fades evenly top to bottom. The viewer finds himself in a web of reflections, sometimes seeing himself in a mirrorized part of the glass and sometimes seeing through the surface to a further series of reflections beyond. It is like entering a multiple exposure photograph. The effect is not at all disturbing, but rather of pure visual pleasure, in which the analytical part of the mind becomes servant to the sensuous, and problems of form and content do not exist; a Los Angeles aesthetic par excellence, and one that is perfectly legitimate for that.

—Alastair Mackintosh

BELLEGARDE, Claude

Nationality: French. **Born:** 18 July 1927 in Paris, France. **Education:** University of Paris I, Panthéon-Sorbonne, Doctorate in Art. **Military:** Special Ski Commandos, French Military, in occupation army in Austria after World War II, 1948–49. **Family:** 1) Jacqueline Neumann, 1950 (died 1960); 2) Hnina Illouz, 1962 (divorced 1978); 3) Marquita Doassans (partner since 1974); children: Stephane and Veronique. **Awards:** Lissonne, Milan, 1959 and 1961; Biennale of San Marino, 1965; Chevalier des Arts and Letters, Paris, 1983. **Agent:** Galerie Larock-Granoff, 13 Quai Conti, 75006 Paris, France. **Address:** 67 Rue Vergniaud, 75013 Paris, France.

Collections:

Tate Gallery, London; R.S. Guggenheim Museum, New York; Centre National des Arts Contemporains, Paris; Musée des Beaux-Arts, Lille; Musée des Beaux-Arts, Wuppertal, Germany; Musée des

Claude Bellegarde: *les 4 éléments,* 1991. ©2001 Artists Rights Society (ARS), NY/ADAGP, Paris.

Beaux-Arts, San Marino; Musée d'Art et d'Histoire, Geneve; Bibliotheque Nationale, Paris; Musée Cantini, Marseille; Musée du Montparnasse, Paris.

Publications:

On BELLEGARDE: Books—*Claude Bellegarde ''Achromatisme 1953–1957,''* Paris 1989; *L'Art Contemporain en France,* by Catherine Millet, Paris 1989; *L'Affiche d'Art en Europe,* by Mustapha Chelbi, Paris 1990; *Le Regne Imaginal,* by Jean-Clarence Lambert, Paris 1991; *Le Coeur et la Raison,* by Pierre Restany, Paris 1991; *Le Regard des Mots,* by Jean-Clarence Lambert, Paris 1995; *La Couleur d'Origine,* by Jean-Clarence Lambert, Sochaux 1995; *La Peinture Monochrome,* by Denys Riout, 1996; *Musique et Arts Plastiques,* by Jean-Yves Bosseur, 1998; *ART, l'Age Contemporain,* by Paul Ardenne, 1998; *Vocabulaire des Arts Plastiques du 20 Siecle,* by Jean-Yves Bosseur, 1999. **Visual Media—***Bellegarde* (television) by Madame Haas, France Panorama, March 1973; *Claude Bellegarde* (video) by César Sunfeld, Encyclopédie Audiovisuelle de l'Art Contemporain, 1998.

*

I belong to the generation of Frenchmen born in the period between the two World Wars. Born of a Jewish mother and having lost my father at a very early eage, I lived in hiding in a town nearby Paris during the German occupation. In my late teens after my school years, I took drawing lessons before joining a spiritual community where for a period of two years I was initiated to sculpture. Called into the army, I served with the Alpine Ski Commandos as part of the post war occupation forces in Austria. Discharged from the Army and ill with tuberculosis I was sent to a Swiss sanatorium in the mountains. I began painting white spaces which became known as ''Achromatisme'' or ''White Period.'' My spiritual quest was thus actualized in my paintings.

This experience led me to discover, as my illness faded, the dreamlike power of colors.

My creation was embodied in a renaissance where red stood for vitality, blue for space, yellow for radiance and intelligence, green for creation, orange for sensations, violet for spirituality. . .

My paintings expressed the lyrical song of nature. . . . . I then created abstract portraits (psy-color) based on human character and personality analysis and physical appearance. Then in collaboration with medical doctors, I built chromatic booths using both color and sound for therapeutic treatments of specific illnesses.

Enriched by this research and experience, I returned to pure painting, experimenting with the effects of color on different materials—aluminum, wood, glass. . . . .

From then on I centered my work around such themes as ecology and the relationship between the four elements—water, air, fire and earth—which led to large canvases with very vivid colors evoking large expanses.

Today my pictorial research questions man's interior vision for it carries the legacy of mankind and its ancient animality, like a ray of light that passes through us.

—Claude Bellegarde

* * *

From the outset, Claude Bellegarde makes an option for informal, tachist and lyrical abstract art, then for total abstraction through his white monochrome paintings which were shown for the first time in Paris in 1953, thus preceding the blue monochrome pictures of Yves Klein. Far from being satisfied with this revolutionary contribution to the history of art in France, Bellegarde introduced the whole of the colour spectrum into his paintings and recently even a highly symbolic form, that of the human eye.

When Bellegarde created his first white monochromatic paintings some art theoreticians saw in them a sequel to Malevich's White Square pictures; however it is equally possible to see in them a conscious or unconscious influence from a painting by Monet, *The Magpie,* in which the bird, just a small black point, is less the subject of the picture than the texture and scintillation of the landscape covered by snow. In fact, the formal preoccupations of Malevich do not seem to have been the same as those of Bellegarde who said having painted his first white pictures on the occasion of his stay, for health reasons, in an Alpine village in the midst of winter, in order to ''materialize his meditations after a number of trials.'' From this stay in a high altitude, Bellegarde hoped not only to recover his health, but also to begin a new physical and spiritual life. It is possible also that he hoped to turn over a leaf both as a person and as an artist and to deliver the history of abstract art from the excesses of gestural painting at that moment.

Yet Bellegarde was never sufficiently ingenuous for wanting to annihilate painting altogether, and similarly his white monochrome

Claude Bellegarde: *les Traces du Temps,* 1956. ©2001 Artists Rights Society (ARS), NY/ADAGP, Paris.

paintings are far from having been conceived with a nihilistic intention, but once their double autotherapeutic and regenerative function had been accomplished, all the colours of the spectrum reappeared in the work of the artist. To begin with, iridescent colour trails emerge in the white areas of the pictures followed by graphic works in basic colours giving rise to the first typograms or ''psychochromatic'' likenesses.

Just as the white pictures had not been painted in front of the motif, the portrait-typograms have not been painted before a model. They are the outcome of a play between horizontal, vertical and oblique lines and circles arranged according to the principle of simultaneous contrasts as practised by Robert and Sonia Delaunay. Bellegarde's typograms can be considered as some sort of psychophysical equations of the chosen personality. The artist who conceives painting as a physical and psychological relationship with elementary nature never finds himself in the position of a describer of reality but as a transcriber of natural and human energy.

The expressive force of the colour, of absolute white as well as that of the chromatic scale he uses in thinking of the palette of Matisse, have led Bellegarde quite rapidly to utilize colour as a healing medium. Between 1965 and 1970, he created some chromatic and therapeutic cabins in the shape of living spaces in human dimensions which were conceived ''for a voyage of the spirit in a different temporal dimension'' by means of a stimulating and soothing colour spectrum. Bellegarde's chromatic dwelling-places occupy a position somehow parallel to the lumino-kinetic environments where the participation of the public is solicited.

Between 1970 and 1980, Bellegarde employed new supports, aluminium, glass and wooden lathing, in order to multiply the effects of virtual movement created by the colours playing on the undulatory and mirroring surfaces. The artist, more than ever convinced of the energetic and dynamic powers of the colours, began to take an interest in the relationship between colour and sound, in this case that of the natural elements—earth, water, air and fire. From this emerged around 1990 the ''organic and telluric'' compositions that precede the ecological preoccupations of many of the artists of the young generation. Among Bellegarde's ecological paintings let us single out *Gaia,* a gigantic red sphere turning into indigo blue and crossed by yellow and white flashes—a spectacular and expressive way to remind us that the earth is a living being ready to implode or to explode at any moment. With this new series of works, still within the orbit of abstract art but making reference to the ultraconcrete, Bellegarde's metaphysical preoccupations are receding.

Since about 1995, the artist, always in a state of alertness, has engaged himself on the path of the memory of his origins, those of humanity and those of art, through a series of paintings on the subject of the eye which could send us back among other symbols to the eye of the Father or that of the Law, or to the third eye of Surrealism, that of the unconscious. As a matter of fact, it seems that for Bellegarde the eye rather represents an organ of scopic pulsion which engenders a desire to see and to know.

Claude Bellegarde is among the artists who have continued the modern French painting tradition and have given it a new perspective while his personal mark and his originality reside more particularly in the fact that he operates a plastic synthesis between his metaphysical, physical and scientific options.

—Aline Dallier-Popper

BENAYOUN, Maurice

Nationality: French. **Born:** Mascara, Algeria, March 1957. **Career:** Instructor, ''Video Art and New Images,'' Université de Paris 1 (Panthéon-Sorbonne), since 1984; invited artist, Ecole Nationale Supérieure des Beaux Arts, Paris; co-founded Z-A Production, 1987; art director, Z-A Production; created and directed, in collaboration with François Schuiten, *The QUARXS,* the first 3D CG high definition 35mm series based on an original script, 1993; first tele-interactivity project, *The Tunnel Under the Atlantic,* in 1995; participant in many conferences, including Colloque International, University Lyon 2, 1994; French/American Animation Conference, New York, 1995; Second Worldwide Symposium on Information Technology (FWS), Futuroscope, Poiters, France; current activities focus on developing the artistic potential of virtual reality and interactive projects. **Awards:** 1st place communication image, Tech Image Contest, Paris, 1990; 1st place credits category, Prix Pixel INA, Imagina 93, Monte Carlo, Morocco, 1993; Villa Médicis Hors Les Murs, from the French Foreign Ministry, 1993; Golden Nica Award, interactive art category, Ars Electronica, Linz, Austria, 1998; Medaille de Chevalier des Arts et Lettres, for contributing to French culture in the field of interactive digital art, 2000; José Abel Prize, Best European Animation Film, CINANIMA, Animation Film Festival of Espinho, Portugal, 1994. **Web site:** http://www.benayoun.com.

Selected Individual and Group Exhibitions:

1986 *ARC,* Musée d'art moderne de la ville de Paris
1990 Tech Image, Paris
1991 Galerie 172, Paris
Paris Cité, Parc floral, Vincennes, France
1992 Galerie Sabrina Grassi, Paris

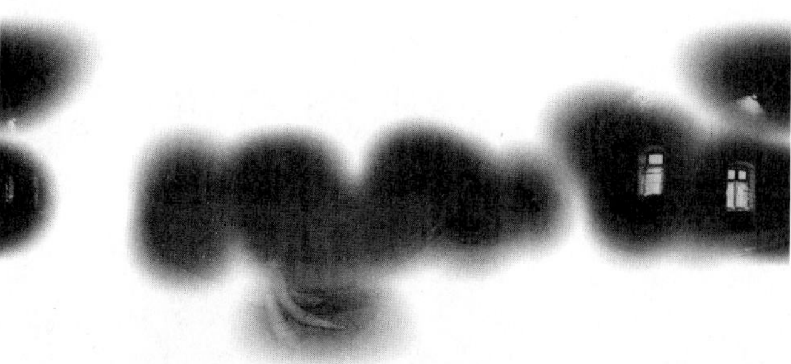

Maurice Benayoun: *Art Impact, Collective Retinal Memory.* ©Maurice Benayoun.

Les Cités Obscures, Schuiten/Peeters, Brussels
1993 *Animation in the Pixel Land,* Musée Château, Annecy, France
1994 Siggraph 94, Art and Design Show, Orlando
3D image and animation films, Le Grand huit / T. N. B., Rennes, France
1995 *The Tunnel Under the Atlantic,* Musée d'art contemporain de Montréal; Centre Georges Pompidou, Paris
Is the Devil Curved? MIM, Montréal; Imagina, Monte Carlo, Morocco
Is God Flat? Salon International d'art contemporain de Strasbourg; MILIA, Cannes; Salle de la Légion d'Honneur, Saint Denis; MIM, Montréal
Unlimited Mirage, Machida Museum of Graphic Arts, Tokyo
1996 *And What About Me?* Kahanamoku and Beyond, Sidney
Is the Devil Curved? Vidéothèque de Paris
1997 *Version Originale,* Musée d'Art contemporain de Lyon
1998 *World Skin,* KTH, Stockholm; Ars Electronica, Linz, Austria; Imagina 98, Monte Carlo, Monaco
Transarchitectures 03, Missing Matter, DEAF, Rotterdam; UQAM, Montreal; Galerie AEDES, Berlin

Maurice Benayoun: *World Skin.* ©Maurice Benayoun.

Paris-New Delhi Tunnel, Cité des sciences et de l'industrie de la Villette, Paris; Virtual Gallery, Pragati Magdan, New Delhi, India
Navigation Room, Cité des sciences et de l'industrie de la Villette, Paris
1999 *Crossing Talks,* Forum des Images, États Généraux de l'écriture interactive, Paris
World Skin Web site, Biennale do Mercosul, Brazil
Crossing Talks, ICC Biennale '99, Tokyo

Publications:

On BENAYOUN: Article—''Maurice Benayoun: Parallel Worlds and Virtual Tunnels'' by Pier Luigi Capucci in *Domus,* July-August 1996.

* * *

Maurice Benayoun began his long itinerary as video and multimedia artist with a number of photographic works and short video films. His first real success came in 1985 when Benayoun realised a series of video projects, *Pièces à conviction,* which permitted him to work in certain well-defined situations after placing the spectator into a state of immersive interactivity. In 1992–1993, he selected a number of artists who would produce works using a virtual reality technique. Later he applied the artists' material as a principle in some virtual reality installations. The works of these artists were gathered together in a Collection of Contemporary Art, which Benayoun named *Art after the Museum.* For him, the museum is generally the dead memory of art whereas in his Collection he was trying to create a living memory by including only works which represented a sequel to the practice of each artist and by taking into account the peculiarities of their environment. These realisations by Benayoun involved already the notion of virtual space which led him to explore the possibilities of the digital image and of the interactivity of the spectator.

Influenced visually by the cartoonists and intellectually by the writers of science fiction and of the literature of the fantastic, he had started, in 1989, the series of *The QUARXS,* which involved more advanced animation techniques such as 3-D high-definition images and 35 mm film. The Quarxs, purely imaginary and invisible odd beings that are supposed to be found anywhere in our environment, served Benayoun as pretext to explore with the aid of a new technique the immediate environment and the limits of the scientific understanding of reality. If Benayoun explores since the 1980s the areas of communication and technology in an attempt to cross—in a facetious manner—the territories shared between art and reality, he leaves relatively quickly the digital images in favour of some installations employing networks and virtual reality devices.

In 1994 he asks his Big Questions, a series of interactive virtual reality installations and Internet realisations. The first of these, *Is God Flat?,* is followed a year later by *Is the Devil Curved?* In the first, which is a playful and labyrinthic quest for the image of God, participants are invited to dig into brick walls, whereas in *Is the Devil Curved?,* which includes voluminous figures with intense seductive qualities, the user intervenes in a blue sky littered with clouds.

Both of these works of virtual reality are based on the same principle: We are in a closed room from which we can only escape if we pass diggingly through some corridors in real time and in a three-dimensional material. The base of the architectural elements is reconstructed by each image. The spectator can choose any direction on a horizontal level. The constructed corridors remain in the memory and can be arranged in such a way as to constitute an architectural space of great complexity. The fundamental idea is that the digging should be interpreted as a metaphor for a participation of the spectator in the creation of a world which he explores. In other words, the visitor benefits from his overall power—due to the fact that the world he explores is being constructed around his movements—but, at the same time, he is confronted with the impossibility to find an exit, a way to escape from the fatality of a world which is only a trace of what he himself produces.

A third question is asked by Benayoun: And what about me? This interactive work on the Internet does not involve any foraging, but presents the world from a two-dimensional aerial point of view. One can freely choose a part of the world and throw oneself on it like a small pebble or a grain of sand which, in falling on the earth, deforms the continent it touches. Thus the world is provisionally modified by our presence. In a second part of And what about me?, the possibility to participate in the rewriting of the creation of the world is given to everyone.

Among the multiple other realisations of Maurice Benayoun who is concerned with the aesthetic specificity of artistic endeavours in a highly technical environment and who puts the stress on the processes and not onto the final result, one could mention his series of Virtual Tunnels, and his installations and Internet realisations *World Skin, Crossing Talks,* and *Art Impact.*

The Tunnel under the Atlantic Ocean, a televirtual event presented simultaneously at the Pompidou Centre in Paris and at the Museum of Contemporary Art in Montreal in September 1995, is a manifestation which favors the dialogue between different people. The voice of the interlocutor here is not only an instrument for an individual message but rather a compass that leads to an ultimate goal which is an encounter. In this work the participants delve into the images of the past in order to provoke this encounter.

Both *The Tunnel around the World* and a project *The World Nerve Tunnel (Far Near) (e-motion),* an installation of local televisual reality, which forms part of it, induce people to meet each other in the same space, through images and sounds.

Whereas the *Tunnel under the Atlantic* linked "diggers" thousands of miles away, *Far Near* functions as a network in such a way as to create a technological distance between people actually in the same place. This network operates like a huge nervous system, making the diggers sensitive to human pain and to humanity's anguishing trouble zones. A signal linking the diggers will follow a random path around the planet via the Internet. Through war areas, terrorist sites, and places marked by famine, misery, drought, and dictatorships, the signal's path will be projected on the wall of the tunnel. When the Internet signal passes through one of these troubled zones, graphically represented by colours, a communication between the diggers is established.

One of the most impressive works created in the same spirit by Benayoun, *The World Skin: A Safari into the Land of War,* was first shown at the Ars Electronica exhibition in Linz, Austria, in 1997. In this work, the visitor/tourist/participant armed with cameras, is making his way through a three-dimensional space. The landscape before his eyes is scarred by war: demolished buildings, armed men, tanks and artillery, piles of rubble, the wounded and the maimed. This arrangement of photographs and news pictures from different zones and theaters of war depicts a universe filled with mute violence. Benayoun claims that by taking photographs one can rip the skin off the body of the world. This work is intended to show the status of the image in the process of getting a grip on the world. The rawest and most brutal realities can be reduced to an emotional superficiality in our perception. Acquisition, evaluation and understanding of the world constitute a process of capturing it.

As regards the sound in this work one can note that in sharp contrast to the video games that transform people into passionate warriors, here the audio unmasks the true nature of apparently harmless gestures and seeks to provide rather a form of experience than a form of comprehension. Some things cannot be shared. Among them are the pain and the image of our remembrance. The worlds to be explored here can bring these things closer to us, but always simply as metaphors, never as a simulacrum.

Crossing Talks immerses us in a space of non-communication, but takes as a model the exchanges occurring on the Internet. This is a complex device which closely resembles a communications process on a network and gives the opportunity to the user to find himself with others in cyberspace. Yet its purpose is not to justify the status of the exchanges on the Internet but rather to reassess the problems of representation and communication with regard to the world as a whole and to stage settings that provoke a world-wide dialogue.

On the other hand, *Art Impact, Collective Retinal Memory,* an installation presented at the Centre Pompidou, Paris, in November 2000, and simultaneously on the Internet as a window opening on the possibilities of spherical photography, gave the visitor the feeling that he found himself in the midst of an exhibition, in this case the Beauty and its sequels (La beauté et après) show, held in Avignon, France. Whereas this latter exhibition juxtaposed artistic creations and fragments of nature chosen by man for their aesthetic qualities, *Art Impact* added to it such other places in the neighbourhood lacking totally any aesthetic connotation, such as supermarkets and slaughter-houses. *Art Memory* was conceived as a collective retinal memory, an original and amalgamating device that allowed the visitor to construct by the displacement of his regard, a new visual space.

If Maurice Benayoun is an artist preoccupied with war, destruction and their images and more so with new forms of exchanges and encounters on a world-wide scale and with new definitions of space as architecture constructed by displacement or by the regard of the visitor who is constantly placed in the center of the world, it is an enquiry of the relationship between the virtual and the real that accompanies his whole production. For him, the virtual and its vicissitudes can offer, beyond any worship of digital simulation, a possibility to discover and to experience a new deciphering of the real.

—Frank Popper

BENGLIS, Lynda

Nationality: American. **Born:** Lake Charles, Louisiana, 25 October 1941. **Education:** Newcomb College, New Orleans, with Zoltan Buki, Harold Carney, Ida Kolhmeyer, Patrick Trivigno, 1960–64, B.F.A. 1964; Yale Summer School, Norfolk, Connecticut, 1963; Brooklyn Museum Art School, Max Beckmann Scholarship Class, 1964–65. **Career:** Assistant professor of sculpture, University of Rochester, New York, 1970–72; assistant professor, Hunter College, New York, 1972–73; visiting professor, California Institute of the Arts, Valencia, 1974; visiting professor, Princeton University, New Jersey, 1975; visiting professor, California Institute of the Arts, Valencia, 1976; visiting artist, Kent State University, Ohio, 1977; visiting artist, Skowhegan School of Painting and Sculpture, Maine, 1979; Visiting Professor, University of Arizona, Department of Art, Tucson 1982; visiting professor, School of Visual Arts, Fine Arts Workshop, New York, 1985–87. **Awards:** Guggenheim Fellowship, 1975; Artpack Grant, 1976; Australian Arts Council Award, 1976; National Endowment for the Arts Grant, 1979; Avery Distinguished Professor Award, Bard College, Annandale-on-Hudson, New York, 1987; Olympiad of Art Sculpture Park Award, 1988; Delphi Art Symposium Award, 1988; Mino Beach Art Symposium Award, 1988; National Council of Art Administration Award, 1989. **Agent:** Paula Cooper Gallery, 155 Wooster Street, New York, New York, 10012. **Address:** 222 Bowery, New York, New York, 10012, U.S.A.

Individual Exhibitions:

1969 University of Rhode Island, Kingston
1970 Paula Cooper Gallery, New York
Janie C. Lee Gallery, Dallas
Virginia Polytechnic Institute, Rockwell
1971 Kansas State University, Manhattan
Paula Cooper Gallery, New York
Hayden Gallery, Massachusetts Institute of Technology Cambridge
1972 Hansen-Fuller Gallery, San Francisco
1973 Hansen-Fuller Gallery, San Francisco
Portland Center for the Visual Arts, Oregon
The Clocktower, New York
1974 Hansen-Fuller Gallery, San Francisco
Texas Gallery, Houston
Paula Cooper Gallery, New York
1975 Texas Gallery, Houston
Physical and Psychological Monuments in Time, State University of New York, at Oneonta (retrospective)
The Kitchen, New York
Paula Cooper Gallery, New York
1976 Paula Cooper Gallery New York
1977 Margo Leavin Gallery, Los Angeles
Hansen-Fuller Gallery, San Francisco
Douglas Drake Gallery, Kansas City
1978 Paula Cooper Gallery, New York

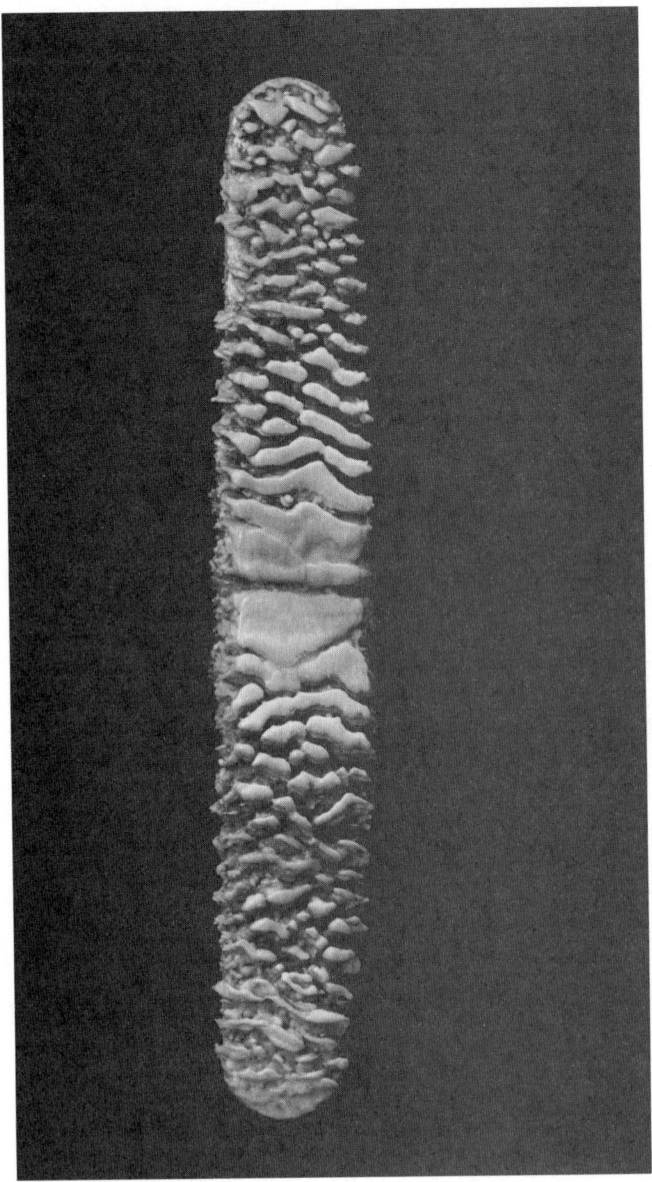

Lynda Benglis: *Excess,* 1971. ©Lynda Benglis/Licensed by VAGA, New York, NY.

1979 Texas Gallery, Houston
Dart Gallery, Chicago
Real Art Ways, New Haven, Connecticut
Hansen-Fuller Gallery, San Francisco
Georgia State University, Atlanta
Galerie Albert Baronian, Belgium
Suzanne Hilberry Gallery, Birmingham, Michigan (with Ron Gorchov)
1980 Galerie Albert Baronia, Belgium
Texas Gallery, Houston
Lynda Benglis: 1968–1979, University of South Florida, Tampa
Lowe Art Museum, Miami
Margo Leavin Gallery, Los Angeles
Portland Center for the Visual Arts, Oregon

Lynda Benglis: *Cloak-Wave/Pedmarks,* 1998. ©Lynda Benglis/Licensed by VAGA, New York, NY.

Paula Cooper Gallery, New York
David Heath Gallery, Atlanta
Chatham College, Pittsburgh
Suzanne Hilberry Gallery, Birmingham, Michigan
1981 University of Arizona, Tucson
Galerie Albert Baronian, Brussels
Dart Gallery, Chicago
Texas Gallery, Houston
Jacksonville Art Museum, Florida
1982 Okun-Thomas Gallery, St. Louis, Missouri
Margo Leavin Gallery, Los Angeles
Paul Cooper Gallery, New York
Fuller Goldeen Gallery, San Francisco
1983 Susan Hilberry Gallery, Birmingham, Michigan
Dart Gallery, Chicago
1984 Paula Cooper Gallery, New York
Texas Gallery, Houston
Tilden-Foley Gallery, New Orleans
1985 Margo Leavin Gallery, Los Angeles
Dart Gallery, Chicago
Susan Hilberry Gallery, Birmingham, Michigan
Heath Gallery, Atlanta, Georgia
1986 Fuller Goldeen Gallery, San Francisco
Tilden-Foley Gallery, New Orleans
1987 Paula Cooper, New York
1989 Margo Leavin Gallery, Los Angeles
1990 Richard Gray Gallery, Chicago
1991 *Lynda Benglis: Dual Nature,* High Museum of Art, Atlanta (traveling exhibition) (catalog)
1993 *Lynda Benglis, from the Furnace,* Auckland City Art Gallery (catalog)
1997 Galerie Michael Janssen, Cologne
1999 Cheim & Read Gallery, New York

Selected Group Exhibitions:

1977 *Recent Acquisitions,* Guggenheim Museum, New York
1978 *Art at Work: Recent Art from Corporate Collections,* Whitney Museum, Downtown Branch, New York
1979 *Contemporary Sculpture: Selections from the Collection of The Museum of Modern Art,* Museum of Modern Art, New York
1980 *Extensions: Jennifer Barlett/Lynda Benglis/Robert Longo/ Judy Pfaff,* Contemporary Arts Museum, Houston
1981 *Decorative Sculpture,* Whitney Museum, New York
1982 *Postminimalism,* Aldrich Museum of Contemporary Art, Ridgefield, Connecticut
1983 *Back to the U.S.A.,* Rheinisches Landesmuseum, Bonn (travelled to Lucerne and Frankfurt)
1984 *American Art Since 1970,* Whitney Museum, New York
1985 *New York Now: Correspondences,* Laforet Museum, Tokyo (travelled to Tochigi and Kobe, Japan)
1986 *Between Geometry and Gesture,* Palacio de Velazquez, Madrid
1987 *Fifty Years of Collecting: An Anniversary Selection (Sculpture of the Modern Era),* Solomon R. Guggenheim Museum, New York
1988 *Lynda Benglis, John Chamberlain, Joel Fisher, Mel Kendrick, Robert Therrien,* Magasin 3, Stockholm (catalog)
From the Collection of Dorothy & Herbert Vogel, Arnot Art Museum, Elmira, New York (catalog)
Eleven Artists from Paula Cooper, Mayor Rowan Gallery, London (catalog)
Life Forms: Contemporary Organic Sculpture—Lynda Benglis, Tom Butter, Petah Coyne, Bruce Edelstein, Heide Fasnacht, Carol Hepper, Freedman Gallery, Albright College, Reading Pennsylvania (catalog)
1989 *First Impressions,* Walker Art Center, Minneapolis
Sculptural Intimacies: Recent Small-Scale Work, Security Pacific Gallery, Costa Mesa (catalog)
1990 *The New Sculpture 1965–1975: Between Geometry and Gesture,* Whitney Museum of American Art, New York
SOLO Impressions Inc., College of Wooster Art Museum (catalog)
1993 *The First Generation: Women and Video, 1970–75,* Musee d'Art Contemporain, Montreal (catalog)
1996 *More Than Minimal: Feminism and Abstraction in the '70s,* Rose Art Museum, Brandeis University, Waltham (catalog)
1997 *Plastic,* Wurttembergischer Kunstverein, Stuttgart (catalog)

Collections:

Museum of Modern Art, New York; Guggenheim Museum, New York; Philadelphia Museum of Art, Detroit Institute of Arts; Walker Art Center, Minneapolis; Milwaukee Art Center; National Gallery of Australia, Canberra; National Gallery of Victoria, Melbourne; San Francisco Museum of Modern Art.

Publications:

By BENGLIS: Articles—"Interview 99/Lynda Benglis," with Karen Edwards, in the *Sunday Herald* (New York), 13 June 1971 "Lynda Benglis in Conversation with France Morin" in *Parachute* (Montreal), Spring 1977; "Intensity of Form and Surface: An Interview with Lynda Benglis" in *Sculpture* (Washington, D.C.), vol. 19, no. 6, July/August 2000. **Videotapes—***Totem 1971,* New York, 1971; *Document 1972,* Castelli-Sonnabend exhibition catalog, New York, 1972; *Collage,* Castelli-Sonnabend exhibition catalog, New York, 1973; *Female Sensibility,* Castelli-Sonnabend exhibition catalog, New York, 1974; *Videoworks of Lynda Benglis Vol 1,* Chicago; *Lynda Benglis: Dual Natures,* Chicago 1990.

On BENGLIS: Books—*Physical and Psychological Monuments in Time,* exhibition catalog, by Robert Pincus-Witten, Oneonta, New York, 1975; *Video Art,* exhibition catalog, with essays by David Antin, Lizzie Borden, Jack Burnham, and John McHale, Philadelphia 1975; *From the Center* by Lucy Lippard, New York, 1976; *American Artists '76: A Celebration,* exhibition catalog, with an essay by Alice Simkins, San Antonio, Texas 1976; *The 1976 Biennale of Sydney,* exhibition catalog, Sydney 1976; *Artculture* by Douglas Davis, New York, 1977; *1977; Video-Visions: A Medium Discovers Itself* by Jonathan Price, New York 1977; *Postminimalism* by Robert Pincus-Witten, New York 1977; *5 from Louisiana,* exhibition catalog, supplement to the *Times-Picayune* (New Orleans), 30 January 1977; *A View of a Decade* exhibition catalog, Chicago 1977; *Made by Sculptors,* exhibition catalog, Amsterdam 1978; *American Portraits of the 60's and 70's,* exhibition catalog, Aspen, Colorado 1979; *Painting: 5 Views,* exhibition catalog, Wayne, New Jersey 1979;

Contemporary Sculpture: Selections from the Collection of the Museum of Modern Art, exhibition catalog, New York 1979; *Extensions: Jennifer Bartlett/Lynda Benglis/Robert Longo/Judy Pfaff,* exhibition catalog, Houston 1980; *Sculpture on the Wall* exhibition catalog, Amherst, Massachusetts 1980; *Lynda Benlis: 1968–1979,* exhibition catalog, Tampa, Florida 1980; *Current/New York,* exhibition catalog, Syracuse, New York 1980; *Painting in Relief,* exhibition catalog, New York 1980; *Painting in Environment,* exhibition catalog, Milan 1980; *Drawing: The Pluralist Decade,* exhibition catalog, introduction by Janet Kardon, Philadelphia 1980; *With Paper, About Paper,* exhibition catalog, with an essay by Charlotta Kotik, Buffalo, New York 1980; *Lynda Benglis: Works in Glass,* exhibition catalog, with essay by David Shapiro, Los Angeles, 1985; *Making Their Mark: Women Artists Move Into the Mainstream,* exhibition catalog, New York 1989; *Lynda Benglis: Dual Nature* by Susan Krane, Atlanta 1991; *Sexual Politics: Judy Chicago's Dinner Party in Feminist Art History,* edited by Amelia Jones, Los Angeles and Berkeley, California 1996; *Body Art: Performing the Subject* by Amelia Jones, Minneapolis 1998. **Articles—**''Lynda Benglis: The Frozen Gesture'' by Robert Pincus-Witten in *Artforum* (New York), November 1974, ''The New Sexual Frankness: Good-bye to Hearts and Flowers'' by Dorothy Seiberling in *New York Magazine,* 17 February 1975; ''Lynda Benglis: Sculptural Knots'' by Suzanne Muchnic in *Artweek* (Oakland, California), 4 June 1977; ''Artpeople'' by John Russel in the *New York Times,* 17 February 1975; ''Lynda Benglis'' by Ellen Lubell in *Arts Magazine* (New York), January 1979; ''Cosmetic Transcendentalism: Surface Light in John Torreano, Rodney Ripps and Lynda Benglis'' by Donal Kuspit in *Artforum* (New York), October 1979; ''Painting in New York: An Illustrated Guide'' by Thomas Lawson in *Flash Art* (Milan), October/November 1979; ''Women Artists'' by John Gruen in *Working Women* (New York), July 1980; ''Ramshackle Kennels Glimpsed by Moonlight'' by John Ashbery in *New York Magazine,* 6 October 1980; ''Lynda Benglis'' by Douglas Welch in *Arts Magazine* (New York), November 1980; ''Knot-Theme Sculptures by Lynda Benglis'' by Vivien Raynor in the *New York Times,* 26 November 1982; ''A Girl of the Zeitgeist'' by Janet Malcolm in *The New Yorker,* 20 October 1986; ''Lynda Benglis at Paula Cooper'' by Holland Cotter in *Art in America* (New York), July 1987; ''Materials Girl: Lynda Benglis in Atlanta'' by Amy Jinkner-Lloyd in *Arts Magazine,* vol. 65, no. 9, May 1991; ''Knots, Glitter, and Funk'' by Marcia E. Vetrocq in *Art in America,* December 1992; ''Lynda Benglis'' by Francesco Bonami in *Flash Art,* vol. 29, no. 187, March-April 1996; ''Lynda Benglis'' by Monroe Denton in *Arti,* no. 34, May-June 1997; ''Lynda Benglis, Jackson Pollock and Process'' by Jeanne Siegel in *Arti,* no. 34, May-June 1997; ''Lynda Benglis: Videos'' by Pamela Markham in *Arti,* no. 34, May-June 1997; ''Linda Benglis at Cheim and Read'' by Maura Reilly in *Art in America,* November 1998; ''Linda Benglis: Cheim and Read'' by Michael Klein in *Sculpture,* 18, no. 5, June 1999; ''Intensity of Form and Surface: An interview with Lynda Benglis'' by Erica-Lynn Huberty in *Sculpture,* 19, no. 6, July-August 2000.

*

I am interested in work that depends on technology, that is visually exciting, and that hasn't been experienced in art or technology. Through genetic engineering, science is re-creating nature. Artists also do this. Only recently has science been able to understand nature in order to re-create it (e.g., using fusion research to create a star and genetic engineering to create new forms of life). Art ideas that are really inventive do not repeat each other. They re-create the nature of art.

The allusion to and the imitation of nature are the substance of art. I like to think that I mime the spirit of nature in re-creating it. Adjustments to gravity, weightlessness, hardness, softness, and motion are felt. Painting led me to sculpture; I wanted to free color of its flat form on canvas or board and to free form of much-used flat planes. I work with the probable and stretch it to the possible by using contradictions in material and context. Each work exists in its right scale and motion within the contextual rules I've set up.

Perhaps these rules exist as I make them (that's my illusion), or perhaps they exist as they have always existed and I only allude to them. I am definitely bound by traditional concepts of classicism and beauty, while using technology, and wish to enter the contemporary spirit with this personal game.

—Lynda Benglis

* * *

Lynda Benglis' interests in a wide range of materials, structures and modes of presentation have produced some of the most sensuous and provocative sculpture in contemporary American art. With the first execution of the organic latex and foam floor pieces in the late 1960s that boasted blob-like and spreading structures and intensely garish colors, she began the explorations of an issue that proved to be a major concern of hers in the 1970s and that continues to occupy many artists in the 1980s: the relationship of painting and sculpture. Benglis created these works by pouring the liquid substances onto the floor and mixing in fluorescent tones; this method, by the late 1960s was associated with the ''poured'' paintings, say, of Morris Louis. In the early 1970s the forms moved off the floor onto the wall and took on more specific shapes. Made of various combinations of materials they offered a more concentrated experience of color and form. Two examples are ''Sparkle Totem'' (1971–72), a narrow tube consisting of cotton bunting, plaster, pigment and sparkles; and ''Valencia'' (1972) a vertical bar with a corrugated surface of beeswax and damar resin on masonite. Staying of the wall, the works that followed explored various formats. Some of them continued to develop the narrow tubular shape; they include the cord-like ''Zulu'' (1970) a mixed mediums piece that features a central knot and the columnar-like ''Volt'' (1977), gold leaf and mixed mediums. Among the others that explored eccentric gestural shapes are ''Pinto'' (1971), the serial, polyurethane foam piece whose wing-like, curved appendages appear to fly-off-the-wall and penetrate the viewer's space, and ''Omega'' (1973), and asymmetrical multiple layered surface, containing folds and various protuberances.

In the middle 1970s Benglis also made videos in which she focused on female sexuality. Perhaps her most controversial statement on this subject was the announcement card she did for the May 1985 show she had at the Paula Cooper Gallery in New York. It featured a color photograph of the artist herself nude except for the jeans dropped to below her knees and a pair of platform shoes. With head turned toward the viewer and back-side aimed at the same, she is offering a provocative take-off on the ''classic'' pin-up pose.

Benglis is continuing to explore the issue of the female in the abstract relief sculptures she has done since the late 1970s. The sensual curves of the female body are brought to mind in a number of the gold leaf pieces whose volumetric sections swell out at top and bottom from a narrow center. ''Figure #2'' (1978) is an example. In the cast metal pieces with repetitive elements reminiscent of pleats and fanning structures there is strong reference made to the tradition of the draped female figure in classical scripture. In ''Essex'' (1986) and ''Lozier'' (1985) the vivid sensations of movement produced by the contrasting rhythms of each composition's dynamic parts are heightened by the intensely reflective metallic surfaces to give the illusion of glorious presence.

—Ronny Cohen

Considering Benglis' career-long interest in infusing her abstract sculptures with the very human qualities of action and sensuality, it should come as no surprise that the artist refers to her recent sculptural works as iconic of physical ''hot spots.'' Ranging from modest ceramic works suggestive of human brains or torsos to large, gravity-defying bronzes that call to mind monumental, twirling dancers, Benglis' work addresses human motion from the molecular level up. Her insistent physicality—in both her sculpture and performance—has recently found a new group of admirers in the form of young feminist artists and scholars interested in reclaiming her work for the continuing women's movement. Although deemed controversial (and even anti-feminist) in the early 1970s, Benglis' comedic and blatantly sexual video work and pin-up self-portraiture have been adopted by Third Wave feminists for whom Benglis—like her contemporaries Hannah Wilke and Carolee Schneemann—symbolizes Third Wave philosophy before the fact. Along with retrospectives of the artist's work in 1991 and 1999, these feminist reinvestigations have resulted in much new interest in and writing about the artist's oeuvre.

—Maria Elena Buszek

BENGSTON, Billy Al

Nationality: American. **Born:** Dodge City, Kansas, 7 June 1934. **Education:** Studied at Los Angeles City College, 1953–54; Los Angeles State College, 1954–55; California College of Arts and Crafts, San Francisco, 1955–56; and Los Angeles County Art Institute, 1956–57. **Career:** Independent Artist since 1957; founder of Artist Studio, Venice, California, 1960; instructor, Chouinard Art Institute, Los Angeles, 1961; lecturer, University of California at Los Angeles, 1962–63; guest artist, University of Oklahoma, Norman, 1967; guest professor, University of Colorado, Boulder, 1969; guest instructor in ceramics and painting, University of California at Irvine, 1973; executive director, Westfall Art, Venice California, 1996–1998. **Awards:** National Foundation for the Arts Grant, 1967; Tamarind Fellowship, Tamarind Lithography Workshop, Los Angeles, 1968, 1982; Guggenheim Fellowship, 1975. **Address:** 805 Hampton Drive, Venice, CA 90291–3020.

Individual Exhibitions:

1958 Ferus Gallery, Los Angeles
1960 Ferus Gallery, Los Angeles
1961 Ferus Gallery, Los Angeles
1962 Martha Jackson Gallery, New York
Ferus Gallery, Los Angeles
1963 Ferus Gallery, Los Angeles
1968 *Motel Dracula,* San Francisco Museum of Art (toured the United States and Canada)
1969 Utah Museum of Fine Arts, Salt Lake City
1970 Santa Barbara Museum of Art, California
Mizuno Gallery, Los Angeles
Galerie Neuendorf, Hamburg
Galerie Neuendorf, Cologne
1971 Margo Leavin Gallery, Los Angeles
La Jolla Museum of Art, California
Contract Graphic Associates, Houston
Galerie Neuendorf, Cologne
1972 Felicity Samuel Gallery, London
Galerie Neuendorf, Hamburg
1973 Corcoran and Corcoran Gallery, Miami
Nicholas Wilder Gallery, Los Angeles
Pollock Gallery, Southern Methodist University, Dallas
Contemporary Arts Museum, Houston
Texas Gallery, Houston
1974 John Berggruen Gallery, San Francisco
Jared Sable Gallery, Toronto
Texas Gallery, Houston
Nicholas Wilder Gallery, Los Angeles
1975 Pyramid Gallery, Washington, D.C.
Seder/Creigh Gallery, Coronado, California
Tortue Gallery, Santa Monica, California
Dootson-Calderhead Gallery, Seattle
1976 Texas Gallery, Houston
Dobrick Gallery, Chicago
Portland Center for the Visual Arts, Oregon
1977 Texas Gallery, Houston
University of Montana, Missoula
James Corcoran Gallery, Los Angeles
1978 James Corcoran Gallery, Los Angeles
Security Pacific Bank Building, Los Angeles
John Berggruen Gallery, San Francisco
Sarah Campbell Blaffer Gallery, University of Houston
Texas Gallery, Houston
Mizuno Ceramics Gallery, Los Angeles
1979 James Corcoran Gallery, Los Angeles
Texas Gallery, Houston
Conejo Valley Art Museum, Thousand Oaks, California
Acquavella Contemporary Art Gallery, New York
Cantor-Lemberg Gallery, Birmingham, Michigan
1980 James Corcoran Gallery, Los Angeles
Malibu Art and Design, California
Honolulu Academy of Arts
1981 Corcoran Gallery, Washington, D.C.
Acquavella Contemporary Art, New York
San Diego University, California
Thomas Babeor Gallery, La Jolla, California
James Corcoran Gallery, Los Angeles
Texas Gallery, Houston
1982 James Corcoran Gallery, Los Angeles
Thomas Babeor Gallery, La Jolla, California
Linda Farris Gallery, Seattle, Washington
1983 James Corcoran Gallery, Los Angeles
John Berggruen Gallery, San Francisco
Thomas Babeor Gallery, La Jolla, California
Acquavella Contemporary Art, New York

1984 Smith Anderson Gallery, Palo Alto, California
Douglas Drake Gallery, Kansas City, Kansas
James Corcoran Gallery, Los Angeles
Thomas Babeor Gallery, La Jolla, California
Texas Gallery, Houston
1985 James Corcoran Gallery, Los Angeles
Angles Gallery, Santa Monica, California
Thomas Babeor Gallery, La Jolla, California
1986 James Corcoran Gallery, Los Angeles
Thomas Babeor Gallery, La Jolla, California
Smith Anderson Gallery, Palo Alto, California
1987 James Corcoran Gallery, Santa Monica, California
Thomas Babeor Gallery, La Jolla
1988 Contemporary Arts Museum, Houston, Texas
Thomas Babeor Gallery, La Jolla
James Corcoran Gallery, Santa Monica
1989 Cirrus Gallery, Los Angeles
Kaleidoscope Gallery, Boulder, Colorado
The Works Gallery South, Costa Mesa, California
1990 James Corcoran Gallery, Santa Monica
1991 The Works Gallery South, Costa Mesa
The Works Gallery, Venice, California
James Corcoran Gallery, Santa Monica
1992 Valerie Miller Fine Art, Palm Desert, California
1993 Galerie Neuendorf, Frankfurt, Germany
1997 James Corcoran Gallery, Santa Monica
2001 Rosamund Felsen Gallery, Santa Monica

Selected Group Exhibitions:

1957 *Los Angeles Annual,* Los Angeles County Museum of Art
1963 *Pop Art USA,* Oakland Art Museum, California
1969 *New Media: New Methods,* Museum of Modern Art, New York (toured the United States)
1972 *Working in California,* Albright-Knox Art Gallery, Buffalo, New York
1976 *The Last Time I Saw Ferus,* Newport Harbor Art Museum, Newport Beach, California
1979 *1979 Biennial Exhibition,* Whitney Museum, New York
1980 *Fabrications,* Lowe Art Museum, University of Miami
1983 *On and Off the Wall,* Oakland Museum, California (toured the United States)
1985 *Poly-Eclecticism:* Humano Institute, Tokyo
1986 *Tamarind Impressions: Recent Lithographs,* Tamarind Institute, Albuquerque, New Mexico
1989 *L.A. Pop in the Sixties,* Newport Harbor Art Museum, California
1992 *Kustom Kulture,* Laguna Museum of Art, Laguna, California
1993 *Hand Painted Pop American Art in Transition, 1951–62,* Museum of Contemporary Art, Los Angeles (travelled to Chicago and New York)

Collections:

Los Angeles County Museum of Art; Newport Harbor Art Museum, Newport Beach, California; La Jolla Museum of Contemporary Art, California; University of California at Los Angeles; San Francisco Museum of Modern Art; Guggenheim Museum, New York; Museum of Modern Art, New York; Whitney Museum, New York; Museum of Fine Arts, Houston; Art Institute of Chicago; Fort Worth Art Center Museum; National Gallery, Washington, D.C.

Publications:

By BENGSTON: Book—*Business Cards,* with Ed Ruscha, Los Angeles 1968. **Articles—**''Late 50's at the Ferus'' in *Art-forum* (New York), January 1969; ''Los Angeles Artists' Studios'' in *Art in America* (New York), November/December 1970.

On BENGSTON: Books—*Pop Art* by Lucy Lippard, New York 1966; *Sunshine Muse,* by Peter Plagens, New York 1974; **Exhibition Catalogs—***Billy Al Bengston* by James Monte, Los Angeles 1968; *Billy Al Bengston,* Los Angeles 1977; *Billy Al Bengston: Paintings of the 70's* by Fredericka Hunter, Los Angeles 1978; *Billy Al Bengston: Paintings of Three Decades* by Jane Livingston, Karen Tsujimoto, Henry T. Hopkins and Maurice Tuchman, Houston 1988; *Billy Al Bengston,* Frankfurt am Main 1993. **Articles—**''Billy Al Bengston'' by John Coplans in *Artforum* (New York), June 1965; ''Billy Al Bengston's Dentos'' by Fidel Danieli in *Artforum,* May 1967; ''Bengston in Los Angeles'' by James Monte in *Artforum,* November 1968; ''Billy Al Bengston, Vancouver Art Gallery'' by Charlotte Townsend in *Artscanada* (Toronto), August 1969; ''Billy Al Bengston, Felicity Samuel Gallery'' by Peter Fuller in *Connoisseur* (London), December 1972; interview with William Robinson in *Art in America* (New York), March/April 1973; ''Bengston's Recent Work'' by R. H. MacDonald in *Artweek* (Oakland, California), March 1974; ''Billy Al Bengston's New Paintings'' by Peter Piagens in *Artforum,* March 1975; ''Billy Al Bengston Framed by Joan Quinn'' in *Interview* (New York), October 1979; ''The Decorative Impulse'' by Jeff Perrone in *Artforum,* November 1979; ''Billy Al Bengston'' by Ruth Bass in *Artnews* (New York), November 1979; ''Billy Al Bengston: Sensuality and Structure'' by Susie Kahil in *Artweek,* 22 December 1979; ''Billy Al Bengston'' by Elise Miller in *San Diego Magazine,* May 1981; ''New Editions'' in *Artnews,* October 1983; ''Los Angeles: The New Mecca'' by Barnaby Conrad III in *Horizon* (New York), January/February 1987; ''Billy Al Bengston in Venice: The Artist's Hand Animates His Residence and Studio'' by Susan Cheever in *Architechtural Digest* (Los Angeles), vol. 48, May 1991; ''Showroom for Westfall Interiors, Fountain Valley, California'' by Marilyn Zelinsky in *Interiors* (New York), vol. 156, January 1997.

*

It's the best I can do.

—Billy Al Bengston

* * *

Undeservedly, there may yet hover about Bengston's works a ''tough guy'' image. If so, it remains from the textbook use, to illustrate early 1960s Pop art, of his paintings which prominently featured a centralized motif of chevron bars. Of course these were taken, as in *Buster* (1962) as military iconography. What was forgotten is that the chevrons were centered on a gently hazy sprayed lacquer surface surrounded by glowing balls of light. While Bengston himself is a physical person, with life-long interests in gymnastics, surfing, and motorcycle racing, his art has always been, like Los Angeles Pop art, easy-going and non-aggressive. His oeuvre may in fact be taken as almost a cliche of California Art: light-filled, vaporously-hued, Japanese influenced both in calligraphic concerns, and more importantly in the wider sense of elegant finesse. (His memory of the on-set of the chevron bar element is simply a personal fascination with the motif-pattern; and such thinking has permeated his art since, as he continues to fasten upon a particular shape or object—for no outward reason and with no intent to indicate an incisive daily life involvement.) And so there appear in his body of works, long series of paintings which show bars, circles, fish, the Iris, et. al. In their decorative, collage-like flat pattern, his paintings in recent years have come to resemble silk-screened fabrics. Bengston clearly foreshadows the Pattern and Decoration movement and may be linked to those artists who coalesced that idiom through contact with the Art Department at the University of California at San Diego—M. Schapiro, Kushner, Zakanitch, and MacConnel.

—Joshua Kind

BEPPLER, Lucie

Nationality: German. **Born:** Wetzlar, 4 July 1961. **Education:** Studied art and literature, Justus-Liebig-University, Gießen, 1981–86; studied art with M. Croissant, U. Rückriem, L. Weiner, and T. Bayrle, Städel School, Frankfurt, 1985–93. **Family:** One child: Jakob. **Awards:** One year stipendium from city of Frankfurt am Main, 1993; studio stipendium for Budapest, office for Art and Science, Frankfurt am Main, 1999. **Agent:** Museum für Moderne Kunst, Domstrasse 10, D-60311 Frankfurt am Main, Germany; Dr. Mario Kramer, Galerie de Ligt, Oppenheimer Strasse 34a, D-60594 Frankfurt am Main, Germany. **Address:** Scheidswaldstrasse 53, D-60385 Frankfurt am Main, Germany; e-mail: mail@moskitosoft.de.

Exhibitions:

1987 Kunstverein, Limburg
1988 Feddersen, Laule Stroth and Partner, Frankfurt am Main
1989 Collection ''Contemporary Art,'' Deutsche Bank, Frankfurt am Main
1992 *Art in Frankfurt: Medium Drawing,* Frankfurter Kunstverein, Frankfurt am Main
1994 Karmeliterkloster, Frankfurt am Main
1995 Gallery Fenster, Frankfurt am Main
1996 Haus am Lützoplatz, Berlin
1997 Gallery Oberländer, Augsburg
Gallery Braas, Frankfurt am Main
1998 Gallery Kornhaus, Stuttgart
1999 Auswärtskunstraum, Frankfurt am Main
Grammonphonfabrik, Hannover
2000 Gallery de Ligt, Frankfurt am Main
Museum for Photography, Budapest
Selected Photography, Seoul
2001 *Change of Scene XIX,* Museum for Modern Art, Frankfurt am Main

* * *

The oeuvre of Frankfurt artist Lucie Beppler reveals a surprisingly broad range of media and styles. It includes drawings of various kinds, clay figures, photographs, and paintings. Yet her true passion is for drawing, and it is the drawings which constitute the largest part of her work.

Most of her works are not much bigger than A5 size. What is remarkable is that the small format proves to be no obstacle—thanks to the intensity of what is depicted in many of the works. When Lucie Beppler draws, it is as though she is listening to an inner voice in order to transform what she hears into a score of lines, structures, and forms. The drawings are the result of a constant probing of the self as regards emotionality, a realm which is real, yet neither visible nor measurable in its qualities. The drawings resemble seismographic recordings that detect the slightest movement or sensation. She terms this realm an emotional store that can grow and change. Her images originate in a state of mind that understands sensation and emotion as organic properties—as an entity which grows along with the self and is so alive and conscious of being alive that it also always bears decay within it. Thus the drawings waver between the two poles of growth and transience. Beppler herself states: ''Every moment is fleeting and essentially cannot be captured by some material or other. My attempts are to capture that moment, but in terms of its fragility.''

At times the works are composed of fine mazes of branches, twists and twirls, confusions of forms or lines. Sometimes they are small circles lined up so closely and so threaded with swirls as to be reminiscent of a galaxy. Sometimes the pages are filled with fine pencil lines, or structures drawn in thick ink, or voluptuous lines and forms painted with oils. And in others, it is scratches which form the structures on the paper. Heads or organ-like forms appear, shimmering, within the lines or are spun in their web. The independent status the lines assume may well play a role but nothing is coincidental. Rather, they appear to be organized, like formations which become extremely dense, expand or dissipate.

To apply the term ''abstract'' to these drawings is only correct to a limited extent as it touches the topic of stylistic information without specifying what generates it. The question is: How does one go about ''describing'' that inner cosmos in such a way that the object (drawing) contains the specific sensation or the inner reality? The answer is probably to be found in this short text which appears on an invitation card: ''At another time she asked, 'What is a soul?,' 'No one knows,' I replied: 'but we know it is not the body, and it is that part of us which thinks and loves and hopes, and is invisible.' 'But if I write what my soul thinks,' she said, 'then it will be visible, and the words will be its body.''' (Invitation card sent out by Galerie Christian Nagel/Cologne for the exhibition ''Catherine Sullivan,'' 2001). No matter how much you dissect the body and decipher its individual parts you will not discover either the location of the self or what the self is.

Lucie Beppler's approach has as little to do with a lack of reality as has the woman's perception in this little dialogue. In her drawings, Beppler focuses on giving a ''body'' to what is invisible. The same is true of the clay sculptures and photographs except that here, the intangible is tied to something ''realistic'' or to purportedly ''realistic'' models, i.e., the human body and illustrations from a magazine.

The sculptures, all of unfired clay, record various moments: moments of sexual desire, contemplation, absorption in thought, and rest. All figures are molded with great precision and devotion to bodily detail. The torsos are stretched out and extremely fine-limbed. They are stylized rather than individualized figures. These portraits depict specific moments to a far greater extent than specific people.

Thus, the elaboration of the figures in clay corresponds to that infinitely detailed re-creation of exceptionally intense or more appositely existential moments in which humans are not just depicted as sentient beings, but also as physical i.e., biologically determined beings. For instance, there is the reclining female figure: given her already aged, emaciated body her state of rest vacillates between sleep and death. Alongside her, there are other no less intense portrayals of passion for life and physical desire as can be seen in the couple embracing in the 69-position, or the woman masturbating.

In formal terms, the photographs entail a category very much of their own within Lucie Beppler's oeuvre, if only because they are based on already existing illustrative material. In terms of content, this wall of photos likewise depicts a condensed view of man, although here the image is somber if not degenerate.

Beppler took her cue for the photographs from images in *Der Spiegel* magazine. She crops a section from the pictures which range in size from about 4 x 6 cm to a half page, photographs it with a macro-lens and then blows the shot up to make prints of about 20 x 30 cm. For the artist, the photographs are an inventory of human existence or of what humans are today in various walks of life. Mostly we see pictures of war, destruction, poverty, and suffering but also some of high society, of the red-light world, of religious and other dignitaries, the "fitness industry," and the ultimate megaparty. Everybody has seen the likes of these illustrations in newspapers, magazines and TV—but as visual accoutrements to factual information and by way of background. However, here the information level is absent. Torn from its context, bereft of accompanying copy, and in this format the contents of the pictures have a very different, much more direct impact. And it becomes clear just how much the images express on their own, without commentary or concrete classification. Indeed, it becomes overly apparent just how drastic they are and how extremely man can treat things—including himself. When viewing these pictures we are robbed of those filters of perception that create remoteness, and by this I mean not just spatial distance. In this sense, all things individual vanish, as they do with the sculptures. Thus the meaning to be seen here spills over into the realm of the universal and commingles with the existential: in other words, here we can sense everywhere that existential level bereft of specific attributes such as event, time, place, and culture.

If we regard Lucie Beppler's oeuvre through to the present, then for all the various means of expression she chooses it always comes back to one and the same issue: what we really are, how and why we think, feel, and act. Beppler is particularly concerned with the unfathomable in man, in both the positive and the negative sense—as playwright/poet Botho Strauß recently put it in *Die Zeit* (20 December 2000), "that which continues to abound in this world and which can not be driven out even by the most refined deciphering methods."

—Natalie de Ligt

BERTHOT, Jake

Nationality: American. **Born:** Niagara Falls, New York, 30 March 1939. **Education:** Studied at the New School for Social Research, New York, 1960–61; Pratt Institute, Brooklyn, New York, 1960–62. **Career:** Independent artist, New York, since 1962; taught at Cooper Union, New York, 1974–81; resident artist, Skowhegan School, Skowhegan, Maine, 1982; artist-in-residence, Yale University, New Haven, Connecticut, 1982; taught at School of Visual Arts, New York since 1992. **Awards:** Guggenheim Fellowship, 1981; National Endowment for the Arts Grant, 1982; American Academy of Arts and Letters, Academy Institute Award in Art, 1992; National Academy of Design, New York, Academician, 1994; Elizabeth Foundation Grant, 1995. **Agent:** David McKee Gallery, 41 East 57th Street, New York, New York 10022. **Address:** 105 Bowery, New York, New York 10002, U.S.A.

Jake Berthot, *Shag Bark,* 1997. ©Jake Berthot, courtesy of McKee Gallery, New York.

Individual Exhibitions:

1970 O.K. Harris Gallery, New York
1971 Michael Walls Gallery, San Francisco
1972 O.K. Harris Gallery, New York
Michael Walls Gallery, San Francisco
1973 Portland Center for the Visual Arts, Oregon
Galerie de Gestlo, Hamburg
Cunningham Ward Gallery, New York
1974 Locksley-Shea Gallery, Minneapolis
1975 O.K. Harris Gallery, New York
Daniel Weinberg Gallery, San Francisco
1976 David McKee Gallery, New York
1977 Galerie de Gestlo, Hamburg
Brandeis University, Waltham, Massachusetts
1978 David McKee Gallery, New York
1979 Nigel Greenwood Gallery, London
Nina Nielsen Gallery, Boston
1982 David McKee Gallery, New York
1983 David McKee Gallery, New York
1984 University of California, Berkeley

Nina Nielsen Gallery, Boston
1985 Southern Methodist University, Dallas
1986 David McKee Gallery, New York
1987 Cava Gallery, Philadelphia
David McKee Gallery, New York
1988 Galleri Olsson, Stockholm
Rose Art, Waltham, Massachusetts
David McKee Gallery, New York
Nielsen Gallery, Boston
1989 David McKee Gallery, New York
1990 Gallery Gunnar Olson, Stockholm
1991 David McKee Gallery, New York
1992 Pamela Auchinsloss Gallery, New York
Neilsen Gallery, Boston
Tony Oliver Gallery, Sydney
1994 Gallery Paule Anglim, San Francisco
The Kristin Paintings and Works on Paper, McKee Gallery, New York
1995 *Red Paintings,* Nina Nielsen Gallery, Boston, Massachusetts
Jake Berthot, Jaffe-Friede and Strauss Galleries, Hopkins Center, Dartmouth College, Hanover, New Hampshire
1996 *Jake Berthot—Works on Paper,* Nielsen Gallery, Boston, Massachusetts
Jake Berthot—Drawings and Paintings, The Phillips Collection, Washington D.C.
McKee Gallery, New York
1997 *Jake Berthot,* Galleri Gunnar Olsson, Stockholm, Sweden
McKee Gallery, New York
1998 Nielsen Gallery, Boston, Massachusetts
1999 *Jake Berthot Trees: Drawings and Texts,* Cooper Union, New York
2000 *Jake Berthot,* Nielsen Gallery, Boston, Massachusetts

Selected Group Exhibitions:

1972 *8 New York Painters,* University of California Art Museum, Berkeley
1974 *Recent Abstract Painting,* Pratt Institute, Brooklyn, New York
1976 *Critical Perspectives in American Art,* at the *Bienale,* Venice
1977 *8 Abstract Painters,* Institute of Contemporary Art, Philadelphia
1979 *New Painting/New York,* Hayward Gallery, London
1980 *L'Amerique aux Indépendents 1944–1980,* Grand Palais, Paris
1981 *New Works on Paper,* Museum of Modern Art, New York (travelled to the Museum of Fine Arts, Houston; La Jolla Art Museum, California; and the Art Museum of South Texas, Corpus Christi)
1984 *International Survey of Recent Painting and Sculpture,* Museum of Modern Art, New York
1985 *Landscape and Abstract Art,*Colby College, Waterville, Maine
1988 *Contemporary American Art,* Sara Hilden Art Museum, Tampere, Finland (travelled to Oslo)
1989 *The 1980s: Prints from the Collection of Joshua P. Smith,* National Gallery of Art, Washington D.C.
1991 *Works on Paper,* Nigel Greenwood Gallery, London
1992 *American Institute Invitational Exhibition of Painting and Sculpture* (for recipients of the Award in Art), American Academy and Institute of Arts and Letters, New York
1993 *Drawings, 30th Anniversary Exhibition for the Foundation for Contemporary Performance Arts,* Leo Castelli Gallery, New York
1994 *Isn't it Romantic,* On Crosby Street, New York
1995 *The Small Painting,* O'Hara Gallery, New York
1996 *Ut Pictura Poesis: Berthot, Jensen, Lees, Quaytman, and Walker,* Galleri Gunnar Olsson, Stockholm
1997 *Founders and Heirs of the New York School,* Museum of Contemporary Art, Tokyo (travelled to Miyagi Museum of Art, Museum of Modern Art, Ibaraki, Japan)
1998 *In the Spirit of Landscape III,* Nielsen Gallery, Boston, Massachusetts
1999 *The Power of Drawing,* Westbeth Gallery, New York
2000 *Group Show,* McKee Gallery, New York

Collections:

Museum of Modern Art, New York; Whitney Museum, New York; Guggenheim Museum, New York; Fogg Art Museum, Harvard University, Cambridge, Massachusetts; Museum of Art, Carnegie Institute, Pittsburgh; Philadelphia Museum of Art; High Museum of Art, Atlanta; Dallas Museum of Fine Arts; Australian National Gallery, Canberra; Boston Museum of Fine Arts, Boston, Massachusetts; Metropolitan Museum of Art, New York; Moderna Konsthall, Malmo, Sweden; Phillips Collection, Washington, D.C..

Publications:

By BERTHOT: Article—Comment in ''Points of View: A Taped Conversation with 4 Painters'' by Willoughby Sharp in *Arts Magazine* (New York), December 1971.

On BERTHOT: Books—*Jake Berthot,* exhibition catalog, with text by Dore Ashton, Minneapolis 1974; *Painting Endures,* exhibition catalog, Boston 1975; *Critical Perspectives in American Art,* exhibition catalog, Venice 1976; *Jake Berthot,* exhibition catalog, with text by Bonnie Saulnie, Waltham, Massachusetts 1977; *8 Abstract Painters,* exhibition catalog, with text by Dore Ashton, Philadelphia 1977; *Silence and Slow Time,* exhibition catalog, by Robin Karson, South Hadley, Massachusetts 1977; *New Painting/New York,* exhibition catalog, with text by C. Lampert, London 1979; *New Works on Paper,* exhibition catalog, New York 1981; *American Art Since 1945* by Dore Ashton, New York 1984; *Jake Berthot,* exhibition catalog, Hanover, New Hampshire 1995; *Jake Berthot—Drawings and Paintings,* exhibition catalog, New York 1996; *Jake Berthot,* exhibition catalog, Boston 2000. **Articles—**''Jake Berthot Paints Quietness'' by Dore Ashton in *Arts Magazine* (New York), November 1971; ''Jake Berthot'' by C. Baret in *Art Press* (Paris), September/October 1973; ''Jake Berthot: Recent Works'' by Stephen Kasher In *Artforum* (New York), September 1978; ''Jake Berthot'' by Dore Ashton in *Arts Magazine* (New York), January 1979; ''Jake Berthot'' by Oswell Blakeston in Arts *Review* (London), 27 April 1979; ''Jake Berthot'' by B. Lemarche-Vadel in *Artistes* (Paris), April 1981; ''Jake Berthot's Order'' by Dore Ashton in *Arts Magazine* (New York), March 1982; ''Jake Berthot'' by Grace Glueck in the *New York Times,* 25 November 1983; ''A Return to the Basics: Jake Berthot's Recent Paintings'' by John Yau in *Arts* (New York), March 1984; ''Fancy Geometry'' by Kay Larson in *New York Magazine,* 21 October 1985; ''Talking Abstract'' by Lilly Wei in *Art in America,* July 1987; ''Jake Berthot'' by John Yau in *Artforum,* Summer 1988; ''Without You, We're Nothing'' by William Heller in *Avenue Magazine,* February 1991; ''Jake Berthot Paints from Palette of Emotion'' by Nancy Stapen in *Boston Globe,* 20 April 1995; ''Powerful Expressions, Recent American Drawings'' by J. Bowyer Bell in *Review,* 1 December 1996; ''Exhibition Notes, Jake Berthot: New Paintings and Drawings'' by David Cohen in *New Criterion,* February 1998; ''Jake Berthot'' by Alexi Worth in *ARTnews,* April 1998.

* * *

Jake Berthot's poetic abstractions result from a sustained give and take between the hand and eye, a search for the essence of things. In an unmediated confrontation with the act of painting, Berthot lifts away the ''veil'' of premature solutions, uninflected geometries, associations and memories, to uncover the irreducible elements, ''the bare-boned, raw experience'' of painting. For Berthot the meaning of the painting thus becomes, however unfashionably, inextricably bound up in the forms and surfaces that constitute its particularity. Berthot's paintings do not rely for their existence on the artist's conception, rather, they encapsulate ''the reality of the moment,'' achieving a kind of palpable presence.

Berthot's early paintings coincided with the heyday of Minimalism, with its emphasis on rationality, coolness, and detachment. While sharing a Minimalist simplicity of means, Berthot's early paintings nonetheless recalled the Abstract Expressionist antecedents of Barnett Newman and Mark Rothko, with their large, thinly stained fields of color, meditative hues, and hints of suffused light. While not painting in a strictly gestural manner, Berthot worked ''for the moment when the painting would be there,'' (JB) when it could exist on its own terms. The artist was attempting to deal with the void, the visual experience of the emptied field. Many of Berthot's early paintings, such as *Lovella's Thing,* 1969, made use of a framing device of narrow strips of dark color around a centralized, resonant space, ''so that space was framed out,'' (JB), signified but emptied.

As such, Berthot was attempting to investigate the relationship between ''the visual and the physical, the seen and the experienced.'' (John Yau, ''Human Encounters,'' in *Jake Berthot: Recent Work 1988–89,* the catalog for an exhibition at David McKee Gallery, New York.) It is this persistent preoccupation that has characterized his continued evolution as a painter. Berthot's paintings from the seventies would begin with a sort of loose geometrical understructure, which would then undergo a process of painterly sedimentation. This method of working from the generalized to the specific yielded images of compositional austerity with quietly charged, richly tactile surfaces. In the large painting *Yellow Bar with Red* (1977), a tall, cadmium yellow rectangle hovers near a pair of smaller rectangles, one a dirty white-and-ocher, the other, a scumbled cadmium red, on a gray-ocher field. The simplicity of the painting's format is belied by its densely articulated surface, which suggests a process of slow accretion, and lends the rectangular forms, especially the dominant yellow bar, an uncanny immanence.

By the early 80s, Berthot's rectangular bars had softened into single ovals with thick, corporeal presences. The intimacy and inwardness implied by the paintings' heavily worked surfaces were matched by their smaller scale. Sometimes the oval would elongate into a skinny lozenge, as in *A Turning To, A Turning From,* from 1984–85, where an orange-red lozenge converses with it subdued, dark-brown cousin against an enveloping warm gray ground. By the late eighties, the oval had ripened into a fuller lozenge of lusciously applied paint, which hovered in the foreground of a deep space. These centralized figures, and the compositions as a whole, gradually became less refined and less balanced. The restrained beauty of the earlier ovals now gave way to paintings that were simultaneously elegant and raw, with surfaces ranging from loosely veiled, translucent washes to coagulates of chunky impasto or rough scumblings fraught with rich undercolor. The warm, yellow-white lozenge in *Conrad* (1989) emanates a chalky, crepuscular light, which seems refracted by the cool, blue-gray ground in which it appears, off-center at upper left, like the moon seen through smoke, clouds, or fog. *Untitled (Woman)* (1989) has a more overt figurative reference, with its lozenge of fleshy de Kooning pinks and reds set against a warm green ground. Here the painting's field is inflected with a few sparse, calligraphic strokes of black, which serve to push against its deep space, and to move Berthot's figure-ground investigations in a new direction.

This element of linear black marks literally comes to the fore in Berthot's newest work, resulting in a shift of emphasis to the painting's surface. It's as if the artist scraped away the accumulated layers of paint from his previous works to reveal the complex infrastructures beneath them. In *Triangle for William Carlos Williams* or *Lakes Measure*, both from 1991, the lozenge shape still appears, as do triangles, vertical bars, and ovals. Color asserts itself more urgently, is less carefully blended. In *Triangle for William Carlos Williams*, a number of triangles are disposed along the outer edges of the canvas, in intense and unadulterated primary hues, creating a displacement away from center. These elements are fused together by a wiry scaffolding of black lines that stretches across the picture plane, asserting its flatness, at times allowing a momentary glimpse of deep space, at others seeming to submerge the forms altogether. This oscillation between flatness and depth is furthered by the range in texture and weight of Berthot's surfaces, which ultimately rely on the black webbing to coalesce into a unified whole. In *Lake's Measure*, the dominant bright-red oval dissolves into the ground, elsewhere, the black lines which outline it undermine its integrity as form because they relate more emphatically to the overall linear network.

In these paintings Berthot seems to return to his beginnings, to Resnick and Cezanne. The paintings share a syntax with the scratchy linear drawings he has produced throughout his career. As searching as his more emblematic paintings, these newer works show Berthot to be an artist who continues to strip away the conventions of his own painting. Private and hermetic, deeply bound to painting's long continuum, Berthot eschews mere style or facility for the stubborn and subtle revelations of a hard-won art.

—Dorothy Valakos

BERTRAND, Jean-Pierre

Nationality: French. **Born:** Paris, 11 January 1937. **Education:** Studied filmmaking at the Ecole Technique du Cinéma, Paris, 1955–57; mainly self-taught in drawing. **Military Service:** Served in film section, French Army, in Senegal, Algeria and West Germany, 1958–60. **Family:** Married Christa Anna Seidl in 1963 (divorced, 1975); daughter: Viana. **Career:** Worked as cameraman in several film productions in France, 1960–63; television cameraman, O.R.T.F., Paris, 1963–69; freelance cameraman, in Buenos Aires, Rome, Hamburg and Madrid, 1969–72; independent artist, Paris, since 1972. **Address:** 27 rue Titon, 75011 Paris, France.

Individual Exhibitions:

1970 Kunstsammlungen, Ludwigshafen, West Germany
1972 Galerie Sonnabend, Paris
1975 Galerie Eric Fabre, Paris
1976 Chapelle de la Salpetriere, Paris
Fine Arts Building, New York
1977 Galerie Eric Fabre, Paris
1978 Galleria Nuovi Strumenti, Brescia, Italy
1979 C Space, New York
Galerie Jacques Donguy, Bordeaux
1980 Galerie Eric Fabre, Paris
1981 Musée de Toulon, France
1982 Galleria Luigi Deambrogi, Milan
Galerie Camomille, Brussels
1983 Galerie de France, Paris
1992 Musee des Beaux-Arts, Nantes, France
1993 Musée d'Art Moderne de la Ville de Paris, France

Selected Group Exhibitions:

1972 *International Art Festival,* Spoleto, Italy
1973 *Contemporanea,* Parcheggio Villa Borghese, Rome
1974 *Pour Memoires,* Entrepots Laine, Bordeaux
1975 *Photography as a Medium,* Maison de la Culture, Rennes, France
Memoire d'un Pays Noir, Musée des Beaus Arts, Charleroi, Belgium
1978 *Boites,* Musée d'Art Moderne de la Ville, Paris
Aspects de l'Art en France, at *Art 9, '78,* Basle
1979 *Europa 79,* Stuttgart
1982 *Trente Ans de Cinema Experimentale en France,* Centre Georges Pompidou, Paris
1991 *Individualities: 14 Contemporary Artists from France,* Art Gallery of Ontario, Toronto
Drawings and Drawings: First Shutter, Musee des Beaux-Arts, Mulhouse, France
1999 *48th Venice Biennale,* Italy

Collections:

Centre Georges Pompidou, Paris; Musée de Toulon, France.

Publications:

By BERTRAND: Articles—Interview with Liliana Albertazzi in *Art Press,* no. 131, December 1988; Interview with Doris von Drathen in *Kunstforum International,* no. 133, February-April 1996; Interview with Doris von Drathen in *Kunstforum International,* no. 147, September-November 1999.

On BERTRAND: Books—*Pour Memoires,* exhibition catalog, with text by Jean Clair and others, Bordeaux 1974; *Jean-Pierre Bertrand,* exhibition catalog, Toulon, France 1981; *Jean-Pierre Bertrand: El Volumen Rojo* by Carmen Alborch Bataller and Francois Deck, Valencia 1991; *Jean-Pierre Bertrand,* exhibition catalog with text by Henry-Claude Cousseau, Daniel Soutif and Bernard Marcade, Nantes 1992. **Articles—**''Jean-Pierre Bertrand'' by C. Bouyere in *Opus International* (Paris), June 1974; ''In Memoriam'' by Effie Stephano in *Art and Artists* (London), July 1974; ''L'obscure Clarté de J. P. Bertrand'' by Michel Nuridsany in *Le Figaro* (Paris), 19 June, 1981; ''Jean Pierre Bertrand in Milano'' in *Domus* (Milan), June 1982; ''Jean-Pierre Bertrand: solution de continuite'' by Jacques Soulillou in *Art Press,* no. 136, May 1989; ''Jean-Pierre Bertrand: la fabrique du rouge'' by Maiten Bouisset in *Beaux Arts Magazine,* no. 93, September 1991; ''Les codes secrets de Jean-Pierre Bertrand'' by Nadine Gayet-Descendre in *Beaux-Arts Magazine,* no. 144, April 1996; ''Jean-Pierre Bertrand: Neue Arbeiten'' by Doris von Drathen in *Kunstforum International,* no. 141, July/September 1998; ''Jean-Pierre Bertrand: Traversing the Body'' by Ann Hindry in *Art Press,* no. 247, June 1999; ''Jean-Pierre Bertrand'' by Philippe Piguet in *L'Oeil* (Lausanne), no. 507, June 1999; ''Jean-Pierre Bertrand: Licht wird zu Materie'' by Doris von Drathen in *Kunstforum International,* no. 147, September/November 1999.

*

Perhaps my work began during this summer morning when, entering in my room, I saw a book opened in front of the window, between outside and outside, sun and darkness. With the sun, the two pages seemed to be white for a short time I was in the whiteness; the magic world revealed in His absence-presence. The book was the memorandum of Robinson Crusoe on the island. During fifty-four days I began to copy each day a day of Crusoe at the present form (the original text is at past) and took each day a photo of the book opening more and more to the end laying by the window. A few years after I noticed that Crusoe left the island when he was fifty-four years old. My last show was a sentence of which Crusoe has a strange relation with my own life.

I try to be available and vigilant with the magic world. Sometimes art makes me wink. Sometimes I wink at art. As Defoe says ''serious reflections during the life and surprising adventures of Robinson Crusoe.'' The solitary man is between the ''real'' man and his emblematic original.

—Jean-Pierre Bertrand

* * *

The art of Jean-Pierre Bertrand recalls attitudes typical of the seventies. This aspect of his work appears spontaneously and without inhibition in his choice of materials—a choice which ultimately makes way for the unpredictable and extra-artistic element. Objects, natural products, photographs, paper drawings or ready-mades all provide the ideal vehicle for the realization of Bertrand's concepts, through which the chemical components intrinsic to these materials find their expression.

Bertrand's works and installations thus become a theatre of phenomena, revelations of nature and hidden decay, which at the same time are visualizations of the artist's attention to those materials through which he can find the most appropriate metaphor. Here we have honey or lemon juice sprinkled onto paper, and, in time, changing back to their original colour; salt placed in a metal box will corrode, or may be used to form a star on the floor of a room; a dark area drawn around the edge of a sheet of white paper, then covered by a pane of glass (which then protects it) takes on the character of the missing frames from around drawings in series of diptychs, and thus becomes a part of the work.

In certain respects, Bertrand's work has similarities to those processes typical of 'Arte Povera,' in particular those of Gilberto Zorio, where the work is an event occurring within the duration of the time taken to construct it. In other respects, he recalls Beuys, who employed every means available, even his own body, to expound his own ideology and elaborate symbolism. Bertrand also institutes the symbolic language of the Cabala, which for this French artist redefines and renews specific aspects of Hebraic mysticism. This complex system transforms the work—canvases or performances—resulting in a freedom and sensibility which is essentially contemporary while contributing a timeless and precise significance.

—Giorgio Verzotti

BEUYS, Joseph

Nationality: German. **Born:** Krefeld, 12 May 1921. **Education:** Rindern, near Kleve, 1930–39; preparatory medical studies, Kleve, 1940; studied art, under Joseph Enseling and Ewald Matare. Staatliche Kunstakademie, Dusseldorf, 1947–51. **Military Service:** Served as a radio-operator and fighter pilot, German Air Force, in Posen, Erfurt and Pardobitz, 1940–45; injured in plane crash in Russia, 1943; prisoner-of-war, Cuxhaven, 1945. **Family:** Married Eva Wurmbach, 1959, children Wenzel and Jessyka. **Career:** First concentrated on art, Kleve, 1946; independent artist, Dusseldorf and Kleve, 1951, until his death in 1986. First "actions" and contact with Fluxus artist, Dusseldorf, 1962–65. Professor of sculpture, Staatliche Kunstakademie, Dusseldorf, 1961–72; guest professor, Hochschule für Bildende Kunste, Hamburg, 1974–75. Founder, German Students Party, Dusseldorf, 1967, and Non-Voting Free Referendum Party for Direct Democracy, Dusseldorf, 1970; candidate, Joint Action Party for Independent Germans, Dusseldorf, 1976; candidate for the Green Party, West Germany, 1979. **Awards:** Lichtwark-Preis, Hamburg, 1977; Thorn-Prikker-Ehrenplakette, Krefeld, 1978; Kaiserring Award, Goslar, 1979; Honorary Citizen Award, Bolognano, 1984; Wilhelm-Lehmbruck Prize, Duisburg, 1986. Honorary doctorate, Nova Scotia College of Art and Design, 1976; **Member:** Akademie der Kunste, West Berlin, 1978; Royal Academy of Fine Arts, Stockholm, 1980. **Died:** Of heart failure, Düsseldorf, Germany, 23 January 1986.

Individual Exhibitions:

1952 Kunstmuseum, Wuppertal, West Germany
1953 Kunstmuseum, Nijmegen, Netherlands
1961 Städtische Museum, Kleve, West Germany
1963 Staatliche Kunstakademie, Dusseldorf
Haus van der Grinten, Kranenburg, West Germany
1965 Galerie Schmela, Dusseldorf
1966 *Joseph Beuys . . . mit Braunkreuz,* Galerie René Block, West Berlin
Galerie St. Stephan, Vienna
Galerie Schmela, Dusseldorf
1967 Galerie Franz Dahlem, Darmstadt
Wide White Space Gallery, Antwerp
Beuys und das weisse Kreuz von Malewitsch, Städtische Museum, Mönchengladbach, West Germany
1968 Stedelijk Van Abbemuseum, Eindhoven, Netherlands
Kunstmuseum, Hamburg
Neue Pinakothek, Munich
Intermedia Galerie, Cologne
Staatliche Kunstakademie, Dusseldorf
1969 Galerie Schmela, Dusseldorf
Galerie René Block, West Berlin
Nationalgalerie, West Berlin
Akademie der Künste, West Berlin
Städtisches Museum, Mönchengladbach, West Germany
Werk aus der Sammlung Stroher, Kunstmuseum, Basle
1970 Galerie Nachst, St. Stephan, Vienna
Herzog Anton-Ulrich Museum, Braunschweig, West Germany
Louisiana Museum, Humlebaek, Denmark
Kunsthalle, Dusseldorf
Zeeuws Museum, Middleburg, Netherlands
Kunstmuseum, Lucerne
Kunstverein, Ulm, West Germany
1971 *Sammlung Hans und Franz Josef van der Grinten,* Galerie im Taxispalais, Innsbruck
Zeichnungen und Objekte 1937–1970 aus der Sammlung van der Grinten, Moderna Museet, Stockholm
Galerie Schellmann, Munich
Von-der-Heydt Museum, Wuppertal, West Germany
Kunsthalle, Kiel, West Germany
Galerie Schmela, Dusseldorf
Galerie Seebacher, Nuziders, Austria
1972 Staatliche Graphische Sammlung, Munich
Galerie René Block, West Berlin
Art Information Agency, Naples
Harcus-Krakow Gallery, Boston
Museum Folkwang, Essen
Tate Gallery/Whitechapel Art Gallery, London
"Friedenfeier," Mönchengladbach, West Germany
Centro d'Informazione Alternativa, Rome
Videogalerie Gerry Schum, Dusseldorf
Galerie Schmela, Dusseldorf
Hessisches Landesmuseum, Darmstadt
Galleria L'Attico, Rome
Tate Gallery, London
1973 Ronald Feldman Fine Art, New York
John Gibson Gallery, New York
Galerie Loehr, Frankfurt
Studio Marconi, Milan
Galerie Klein, Bonn
Galerie Grafikmeyer, Karlsruhe, West Germany
Eat-Art Galerie, Dusseldorf
Daytons Gallery 12, Minneapolis
Kaiser-Wilhelm-Museum, Krefeld, West Germany

Galerie René Block, West Berlin
1974 Ronald Feldman Fine Art, New York
René Block Gallery, New York
John Gibson Gallery, New York
Centre d'Art Contemporain, Bordeaux
The Secret Block for a Secret Person in Ireland, Museum of Modern Art, Oxford, (travelled to National Gallery of Modern Art, Edinburgh; Institute of Contemporary Arts, London; Municipal Gallery of Modern Art, Dublin; Arts Council Gallery, Belfast)
Zeichungen 1946–1971, Museum Haus Lange, Krefeld, West Germany Galerie Bama, Paris
Galleria Lucrezia De Domizio, Pescara, Italy
1975 Studio Brescia, Brescia, Italy
Galleria Lucrezia De Domizio, Pescara, Italy
René Block Gallery, New York
Ronald Feldman Fine Art, New York
Schwarzes Kloster, Freiburg, West Germany
Kestner-Gesellscha ft, Hannover
Kunstverein, Kassel, West Germany
Fecoman Gallery, New York
1976 Kunstforum, Munich
Galerij Albert Baronian, Brussels
Kaiser-Wilhelm-Museum, Krefeld, West Germany
Wasserfarben 1936–1963, Kunstverein, Frankfurt
1977 Galerie Bama, Paris
Galleria Lucrezia De Domizio, Pescara, Italy
Museum Folkwang, Essen
Richtkrafte, Nationalgalerie, West Berlin
Kunstmuseum, Basle
Galerie Marika Malacorda, Geneva
Galerie Konrad Fischer, Dusseldorf
Galerie Schellmann und Kluser, Munich
Tekeningen, Aquarellen, Gouaches, Collages, Olieverven, Museum van Hedendaagse Kunst, Ghent
Galleria Saman, Genoa, Italy
1978 Kleine-Grafik-Galerie, Bremen, West Germany
Museo Diego Aragona Pignatelli Cortes, Naples
Galleria Ferrari, Verona, Italy
Kunstverein, Bremerhaven, West Germany
Galerie Polit-Art/o42, Nijmegen, Netherlands
University of California, Riverside
Studio Cavalieri, Bologna, Italy
Galerie Cuenca, Ulm, West Germany
Universitatsmuseum, Marburg, West Germany
Landesmuseum Joanneum, Graz, Austria
Galerie Schmela, Dusseldorf
1979 Galerie Nachst St. Stephan, Vienna
Kunstverein, Gottingen, West Germany
Galerie Puschel, Bielefeld, West Germany
Monchehaus-Museum, Goslar, West Germany
Galleri Per Sten, Copenhagen
Museum Boymans-van Beuningen, Rotterdam (travelled to Berlin, Bielefeld and Bonn)
Guggenheim Museum, New York
Galerie Schmela, Dusseldorf
1980 Galerie Schellmann and Kluser, Munich
Galleria Piero Cavellini, Brescia, Italy
Galleria Delta, Salerno, Italy
Anthony D'Offay Gallery, London
Richard Demarco Gallery, Edinburgh
Stadtisches Kunstmuseum, Bonn
Badischer Kunstverein, Karlsruhe, West Germany
Galerie Holtmann, Cologne
Stadtische Galerie, Erlangen, West Germany
1981 Ink Halle fur internationale Kunst, Zurich
Kunstvrein, Mannheim, West Germany
Heath Gallery, Atlanta, Georgia
Kunstraum, Munich
Galleria del Cortile, Rome
Galleria Schellmann und Kluser, Munich
Stadtische Galerie im Lenbachhaus, Munich
Museum Commanderie van St. Jan, Nijmegen, Netherlands (travelled to Dusseldorf and Ulm)
Sammlung Ulbricht, East Berlin
1982 Ronald Feldman/Schellmann und Kluser, New York
Galerie Durand-Dessert, Paris
Forum fur aktuelle Kunst/Galerie Krinzinger, Innsbruck, Austria
Henie-Onstad Kunstsenter, Hovikodden, Norway
Galerie Klein, Bonn
1983 City Art Gallery, Leeds, Yorkshire (travelled to Cambridge and London)
Galerie Konrad Fischer, Dusseldorf
Galerie Schmela, Dusseldorf
Europaisches Forum, Alpbach, Austria
Stadelschen Kunstinsitut, Frankfurt
Anthony D'Offay Gallery, London
Galerie Stahlberger, Weil am Rhein, West Germany
Musee Cantonal des Beaux-Arts, Lausanne (travelled to Winterthur; Calais; St. Etienne; Linz; Oslo; Marseille)
1984 Galerie Konrad Fischer, Dusseldorf
Galerie Durand-Dessert, Paris
Stadtsparkasse, Wuppertal, West Germany
Galerie Schellmann und Kluser, Munich
Mittelrhein-Museum, Mainz, West Germany
Busch-Reisinger Museum, Harvard University, Cambridge, Massachusetts
Seibu Museum of Art, Tokyo
Kunsthalle, Tubingen, West Germany
Kunstlerhaus Eisenturm, Mainz, West Germany
Neue Galerie der Stadt Linz, Austria
Stadtische Galerie, Wurzburg, West Germany
1985 Galerie Beaubourg, Paris
Galerie Cuenca, Ulm, West Germany
Edition Schellmannn, Munich
Nassauischer Kunstverein, Wiesbaden, West Germany
Museum und Museumsverein, Aachen, West Germany
Commanderie van St. Jan, Nijmegen, Netherlands
Suermondt-Ludwig-Museum, Aachen (travelled to Ratingen)
Museum am Ostwall, Dortmund, West Germany
John Gibson Gallery, New York
Galerie Bernd Kluser, Munich
Anthony D'Offay Gallery, London
Edizione Lucio Amelio, Naples (travelled to New York)
Fundacion Caja de Pensiones, Madrid
Museo di Capodimonte, Naples

1986 Stadtische Galerie im Lenbachhaus, Munich
Galerie Gogger und Murrer, Munich
1990 Fundacio Joan Miro, Barcelona
1991 Bayerische Staatsbibliothek, Munich
1993 Tate Gallery, Liverpool
Circolo degli Artisti, Turin
1994 Museo Nacional Centro de Arte Reina Sofia, Madrid
1995 Ludwig Muzeum, Budapest
1996 Ludwig Muzeum, Budapest
1998 Walker Art Center, Minneapolis
1999 Royal Academy of Arts, London

Selected Group Exhibitions:

1963 *Festum Fluxorum Fluxus,* Staatliche Kunstakademie, Dusseldorf
1964 *Documenta 3,* Museum Fridericianum, Kassel, West Germany (and *Documenta 4,* 1968; *Documenta 5,* 1972; *Documenta 7,* 1982)
1973 *Contemporanea,* Parcheggio Villa Borghese, Rome
1974 *Projekt 74,* Kunsthalle, Cologne
1976 *Biennale,* Venice
1977 *Art of the 60s.* Städtisches Kunstmuseum, Bonn
1982 *Arte Povera et Anti-Form,* Centre d'Arts Plastiques Contemporains, Bordeaux
1983 *Museums by Artists,* Art Gallery of Ontario, Toronto
1985 *Kunst in der Bundersrepublik 1945–85,* Nationalgalerie, West Berlin
1987 *Berlinart 1961–87,* Museum of Modern Art, New York (travelled to San Francisco)
1988 *The Objects of Sculpture,* Arts Club of Chicago, Chicago
1989 *Departures: Photography 1924–1989,* Hirschl and Adler Modern, New York
1991 *Wilhelm Lehmbruck, George Minne, Joseph Beuys,* Museum voor Schone Kunsten, Ghent
The Interrupted Life, New Museum of Contemporary Art, New York
1995 *Revolution: Art of the Sixties from Warhol to Beuys,* Hara Museum of Contemporary Art, Tokyo
Dons 1989–1994, Musee d'Art Contemporain, Montreal
1996 *The Froehlich Foundation: German and American Art from Beuys and Warhol,* Tate Gallery, London
1997 *Images of Artists: Portraits from Tischbein to Beuys,* Staatliche Museen, Kassel, Germany
Lehmbruck/Beuys, Galerie Michael Werner, Cologne (traveled to Michael Werner Gallery, New York
Haupstrom Jupiter, Beuys und die antike, Glypothek, Munich

Collections:

Stroher Collection, Hessiches Landesmuseum, Darmstadt; Kaiser-Wilhelm-Museum, Krefeld, West Germany; Städtisches Museum, Mönchen gladbach, West Germany; Louisiana Museum, Humlebaek, Denmark; Kunstmuseum, Basle; Centre Georges Pompidou, Paris.

Publications:

By BEUYS: Books—*I a gebraten Fischgrate,* West Berlin 1972; *Die Leute sind ganz prima in Foggia,* Naples 1973; *Lotta Poetica; 3 Pots Action, Edinburgh,* Brescia 1975; Zeichnungen zu "Codices Madrid" von Leonardo da Vinci, Stuttgart 1975; *Joseph Beuys: Series of 90 Paintings,* Munich 1976. **Articles—**"Plastik und Zeichnung" in *Kunst* (Mainz), 1965; "Winterlager" in *Christ und Welt* (Dusseldorf), no. 37, 1968; "Direkte Demokratie; Joseph Beuys Talking at Documenta 5" in *Avalanche* (New York), 1972; "Joseph Beuys: Public Dialogue" in *Avalanche* (New York), May/June 1974; "Joseph Beuys" in *New Observations* (New York), no. 118, Spring 1998.

On BEUYS: Books—*Joseph Beuys . . . mit Braunkreuz,* exhibition catalog, edited by René Block, West Berlin 1966; *Beuys und das weisse Kreuz von Malewitsch,* exhibition catalog, with text by Johannes Cladders, Mönchengladbach, West Germany 1967; *Wat Bedoelt Beuys?* by Tom-Frenken, Eindhoven, Netherlands 1968; *Beuys' Boys* by Per Kirkeby, Copenhagen 1968; *Beuys,* exhibition catalog, with text by Otto Maurer, Eindhoven, Netherlands 1968; *Joseph Beuys: Werk aus der Sammlung Stroher,* exhibition catalog, with text by Dieter Koepplin, Basle 1969; *Joseph Beuys* by Gotz Adriani, Winfried Konnertz and Krain Thomas, Cologne, 1970; *La Rivoluzione siamo noi* by Achille Bonito Oliva, Naples 1971; *Joseph Beuys: Sammlung Hans und Franz Josef van der Grinten,* exhibition catalog, with an introduction by Hans van der Grinten, Innsbruck 1971; *Uber Beuys* by Rolf Wedewer and Lothar Romain, Dusseldorf 1972; *Joseph Beuys: Zeichnungen 1947–1959,* with text by Hagen Lieberknecht, Cologne 1972; *Joseph Beuys: Bleistiftzeichnungen aus den Jahren 1946–1964* by Franz Josef and Hans van der Grinten, West Berlin 1973; *Tod im Leben, gedicht für Joseph Beuys* by Heiner Bastian, Munich 1972; *Joseph Beuys: Zeichnungen 1946–1971,* exhibition catalog, with text by Paul Wember, Krefeld, West Germany 1974; *Joseph Beuys: The Secret Block for a Secret Person in Ireland,* exhibition catalog, with foreword by Nick Serota, Oxford 1974; *Joseph Beuys, Jeder Mensch ein Kunstler* by Clara Bodenmann-Ritter, Frankfurt, West Berlin and Vienna 1975; *Joseph Beuys,* exhibition catalog, with text by Paul Wember, Hannover 1975; *Joseph Beuys: Wasserfarben 1936–1963,* exhibition catalog, with text by Franz Josef and Hans van der Grinten, Frankfurt 1976; *Soziale Plastik, Materialen zu Joseph Beuys* by Volker Harlan, Rainer Rappmann and Peter Shata, Achberg 1976; *Joseph Beuys: Coyote,* with text by Caroline Tisdall, Munich 1976; *Joseph Beuys: Tekeningen, Aquarellen Gouaches, Collages, Olieverven,* exhibition catalog, with text by R. Vandenwege, Jan Hoet and Clair van Damme, Ghent 1977; *Prophete rechts, Prophete links: Joseph Beuys* by Ingrid Burgbacher-Krupka, Stuttgart 1977; *Joseph Beuys: Richtkrafte,* exhibition catalog, West Berlin 1977; *Joseph Beuys: Multiples—catalog raisonne,* Munich 1977; *Beuys tracce in Italia* by Germano Celant, Naples 1978; *Joseph Beuys: Spuren in Italien,* exhibition catalog, with text by Martin Kunz, Lucerne 1979; *Joseph Beuys,* exhibition catalog, with text by Caroline Tisdall, New York 1979; *Beuys/Burri,* exhibition catalog, edited by Italo Tomassoni, Perugia, Italy 1980, *Joseph Beuys: Multiplizierte Kunst 1965–1980* with text by Willi Bongard, Dusseldorf 1980; *Joseph Beuys: Zeichnungen Begleitende Texte,* with foreword by Ulrich Weisner, text by Heribert Heere, Bielefeld, West Germany 1980; *Joseph Beuys: Zeichnungen, Bildobjekte, Holzschnitte,* exhibition catalog, with texts by Michael Schwarz and Dieter Koepplin, Karlsruhe 1980; *Joseph Beuys: Dernier Escape avec Introspecteur 1964–1982* by Caroline Tisdall, London 1982; *The Interrupted Life,* exhibition catalog, New York 1991; *Joseph Beuys: Is It About A Bicycle?,* exhibition catalog with text by Bernard Lamarche-Vadel, New York 1985; *Beuys and Warhol: the Artist as*

Shaman and Star, exhibition catalog, Boson 1991; *Joseph Beuys: the Revolution in Us,* exhibition catalog, (text by Nicholas Serota, Lewis Biggs, Charles Stephens, Richard Demarco, Sean Rainbird), Liverpool, 1993; *Thinking is Form: the Drawings of Joseph Beuys,* by Ann Temkin and Bernice Rose, London 1993; *Joseph Beuys: Drawings, Objects and Prints,* exhibition catalog, Budapest 1995; *Revolution: Art of the Sixties from Warhol to Beuys,* exhibition catalog, Tokyo 1995; *Lehmbruck/Beuys,* exhibition catalog, Cologne 1997; *The Use and Abuse of the Sublime: Joseph Beuys and Art After Auschwitz* by Gene Ray, Miami 1997. **Articles—**''Joseph Beuys: a Private Collection'' by Heiner Stachelhaus and Gotz Adriani, Munich, 1990; ''Back to Beuys'' by Christopher Phillips in *Art in America,* vol. 81, September 1993; ''Conference Report: Joseph Beuys: Then and Now'' by Brian Hatton in *Art Monthly,* no. 172, December 1993–January 1994; ''Le B.A. ba de Beuys: Lexicon of Joseph Beuys' Art Concepts'' in *Beaux Arts Magazine,* no. 125, July/August 1994; ''Buys: Eastern Front'' by Olga Sviblova in *Art Press,* no. 194, September 1994; ''Joseph Beuys' Pedagogy and the Work of James Hillman: the Healing Art and the Art of Healing'' by Shelley Sacks in *Issues in Architecture, Art and Design,* vol. 4, no. 1, 1995; ''How to Explain Joseph Beuys to Peter Fuller'' by Robert Lamb, vol. 8, Winter 1995; ''Tom Patchett: Beverly Hillbilly Meet Joseph Beuys'' by Peter Clothier in *Art News* (New York), vol. 94, February 1995; ''Archaic Thought and Ritual in the Work of Joseph Beuys'' by Annie Suquet in *Res* (Cambridge), no. 28, Autumn 1995; ''Democracy is Fun! Joseph Beuys and the Aesthetics of Activism'' by Richard A. Schindler in *New Art Examiner,* vol. 24, October 1996; ''Beuys' Voice and the Coyote's Spirit'' by Terry Atkinson in *Collapse,* no. 2, December 1996; ''A Balancing Act'' by George Baker and Christian Philipp Muller in *October* (Cambridge), no. 82, Fall 1997; ''Wilhelm Lehmbruck/Joseph Beuys'' by Jurgen Kisters in *Kunstforum International,* no. 139, December 1997–March 1998; ''Joseph Beuys: Exhibit'' by Katy Siegel in *Artforum,* vol. 36, no. 8, April 1998; ''The Century's 25 Most Influential Artists'' in *Art News,* vol. 98, no. 5, May 1999; ''Joseph Beuys'' by David Jeffreys in *Burlington Magazine* (London), no. 1158, vol. 141, September 1999; ''Beuys Will Be Beuys'' by Michael Archer in *Arts Monthly,* no. 231, November 1999; ''Beuys' Own Story'' by Isabel Carlisle in *Royal Academy Magazine,* no. 63, Summer 1999; ''Every Artist Can Be a Man: The Silence of Beuys Is Understandable'' by Francesco Bonami in *Parkett,* no. 59, 2000.

* * *

Of all the hagiographies of 20th century art, none has seemed more secure than that of Marcel Duchamp. It has been argued that the style and subject matter of most post-war art can be traced to his influence, that he set up the pieces of the game which everybody else is now playing. To question Duchamp's status is like attacking the Pope if you're Catholic.

Yet Duchamp's influence has been largely negative. There was nothing forward looking in his art; rather, it was an attempt to close the book before the barbarians arrived. He belonged to the old European tradition of artists—elegant, sensitive, aristocratic. If the language of art were tainted, then the only thing a gentlemen could do was lapse into enigmatic silence. Duchamp's art is one of defeat.

So it is apt that it was a barbarian who called this deadly silence. One thinks of Luther nailing his theses on the church door: enough of this southern pomp and circumstance, enough of this Frenchness. So the barbarian, dressed like a poacher, bearing the scars of a war that destroyed Duchamp's country writes in chalk across a blackboard:

THE SILENCE OF DUCHAMP IS OVERRATED.

Joseph Beuys was not interested in enigma: come to that he was not interested in Dada, Happenings, Situations, Environments, Performances or any of that Latinate epicenity. I suspect he had suffered too much to think that art was anything else but a life and death matter.

Duchamp had destroyed the language of art; Beuys would create a new one; one that was based, as are all languages of art in their new born state, on the emotions used raw, on pain and pleasure, on the senses used as reasoning devices, on the mind used as a sense.

In Dusseldorf, he sat in a bar room, surrounded by the salient textures of his universe: felt, fat, wires, wood, cradling in his arms a dead hare. The piece was called ''How to explain art to a Dead Hare.'' The urgent whispering shattered Duchamp's silence, and here, for those prepared to follow him was a solution; go back to your own experience, to your own agony if necessary, for there the fountainhead of art was still bubbling.

The art of Beuys then is, like all great developments, a move towards realism. In recent years, that word has been much in vogue, but it has usually been applied to painting of a clearly revisionist tendency, or to the rather shallow use of ''real'' objects à la Duchamp. Beuys used reality in the form of his favourite textures and objects, or his own body and personality—not for theoretical or stylistic reasons, but for honesty. They were important to him, as important as perspective was to Piero or chiaroscuro to Caravaggio, and I think he believed that they are important also to everyone else. We may not all be felt freaks or butter fetishists, but we all have our obsessions. Upon these, Beuys suggests, our humanity rests.

Robert Morris also uses felt in large rolls, but for their abstract, sculptural quality. Beuys reacts against abstraction; he used such materials because they made up his world, his real world, a world in which theory has become debased but in which real people still live and die, as happy or miserable as they have always done.

One must not hope to understand Beuys if one has seen him only in the centres of culture, the great museums, the private dealers. One had to catch him somewhere where people still talk to each other, still get drunk to forget, where they couldn't give a damn about modern art. There he made sense, there people would warm to him, but not in New York, Paris or London.

I saw him first in Scotland, home of last stands and hopeless causes. In a huge bare room he went through a series of motions, sitting, drawing, sticking globs of fat to a wall and picking them off again, finally standing motionless. The first day he spent three hours doing this, by the fifth and last the whole procedure took nearer five. Yet people looked in and stayed. He had the ability to convince one of the significance of his actions. Each of his moves seemed like an element of meaning and by putting them together he was creating a new syntax. The resulting sentence was not written in any existing syntax, and its meaning can not be exactly transcribed, but as far as I am able to put it into words, I would say that its basic ingredients were to do with passion, courage and nobility, not exactly words one would associate with most contemporary art.

There was a moment when it seemed as if Beuys was destined to become a cult figure with a pathetic band of imitators trailing behind him. He refused, however, to act in the way expected of him, and frequently offended his defenders by offering unfashionable views. He remains, though, the most avant-garde of artists, in the true sense of the word, the one who most convincingly forged a new language, and a new method. His real influence has been to suggest that artists must rely upon themselves rather than upon any one style. One cannot imitate Beuys, but one can follow his method.

—Alastair Mackintosh

BIDLO, Mike

Nationality: American. **Born:** Chicago, Illinois, 20 October 1953. **Education:** University of Illinois, Chicago, B.A. 1973; Southern Illinois University, M.F.A. 1975; Teachers College, Columbia University, M.A. 1978. **Career:** Painter, conceptual artist; Chase Mangattan Bank, New York; New York Stock Exchange, New York; Sezon Museum, Tokyo; Omaha National Bank, Nebraska; Modern Museum, Stockholm; Fashion Institute of Technology, New York, University of Colorado, Boulder. Guest lecturer: Art Center, Pasadena, 1978; Pratt Institute, New York, 1984; University of Colorado, Boulder, 1985; University of California, Los Angeles, 1988; Otis Art Institute, Los Angeles, 1988; Bard College, 1989; and State University of California, Fullerton, 1991. **Awards:** Fellowship, National Endowment of the Arts. **Address:** 432 W 38th Street, New York, New York 10018–2816.

Selected Individual Exhibitions:

1989 Grey Art Gallery, New York
1990 Daniel Templon, Paris
1991 Sezon Museum, Tokyo
Saatchi Collection, London
1992 Bruno Bischofberger Gallery, Zurich

Publications:

On BIDLO: Books—Exhibition catalog, with text by Robert Rosenblum, Zurich 1989; Exhibition catalog, with text by Olivier Zahm and Joe Masheck, Paris 1990; Exhibition catalog, with text by Thomas McEvilley and Francis Naumann, Zurich 1992; *Duchamp* by Calvin Tomkins, New York 1996. **Articles—**''Art in the Park: Paterson, New Jersey'' in *Ceramics Monthly,* vol. 30, February 1982; ''X Equals Zero, as in Tac-Tac-Toe'' by N.-A Moufarrege in *Arts Magazine,* vol. 57, February 1983; ''Neo-Pop Strategy'' by D. Glaser in *Arts Magazine,* vol. 58, November 1983; ''Slouching Toward Avenue D'' by Walter Robinson and Carlo McCormick in *Art in America,* Summer 1984; ''Two Blasts-from-the-Past in Picasso, and, Yes, Marcel, You Too: notes on retroactive influence'' by Joseph Masheck in *Arts Magazine,* vol. 59, March 1985; ''Tendering Rendering: Nine Notes Apropos Still Lifes by Giorgio Morandi by Mike Bidlo'' by Joseph Masheck in *Arts Magazine,* vol. 60, March 1986; ''Wessel O'Connor Gallery, Rome'' by Ida Panicelli in *Artforum International,* vol. 24, April 1986; ''China Trade: Discourse with W. D. Barnes'' by Joseph Masheck in *Arts Magazine,* vol. 61, September 1986; ''Massimo Audiello, New York'' by Eleanor Heartney in *Art News,* vol. 85, October 1986; ''New Look and Newer Look: The Commutation of Jackson Pollock by Cecil Beaton and Mike Bidlo'' by Richard Martin in *Arts Magazine,* vol. 62, March 1988; ''Bidlo's Monstrous Eggs'' by Robert Costa in *Arts Magazine,* vol. 62, April 1988; ''Returning the Origin to the Antioriginal'' by Amelia Jones in *Artweek,* vol. 19, 2 April 1988; ''Leo Castelli Gallery, New York'' by Donald Kuspit in *Artforum International,* vol. 26, May 1988; ''Bidlo's Pablo'' in *Art in America,* vol. 76, May 1988; ''Untitled: Antique Torso and Bananas'' in *Artforum International,* vol. 28, Summer 1990; ''Amerikanische Malerei Heute: Der Neubeginn der achtziger Jahre'' by Udo Kultermann in *Pantheon,* vol. 49, 1991; ''Waking up and Warming up'' by Paul Gardner in *Art News,* vol. 91, October 1992; ''Swiss Court Bars Bidlo Exhibition'' in *Art in America,* vol. 80, December 1992; ''Meeting His Match'' by Barbara MacAdam in *Art News,* vol. 96, March 1997; ''Fountain Drawing (Polymer on paper, 1998)'' in *Art in America,* vol. 86, no. 9, September 1998; ''Letter from New York: November 1998'' by Dena Shottenkirk in *C Magazine,* no. 60, November 1998-January 1999; ''Mike Bidlo: Remedos y copias'' by Monica Yoldi in *Goya,* no. 268 January-February 1999; ''Mike Bidlo: Tony Shafrazi'' by Nico Israel in *Artforum International,* vol. 37 no. 5, January 1999; ''Bidlo's Shrines'' by Robert Rosenblum in *Art in America,* vol. 87 no. 2, February 1999.

* * *

Mike Bidlo began his public art career creating uncannily exact recreations of modern art masterpieces including works by Pollock, Schnabel, Warhol, Duchamp, and Brancusi. He produced these replications in conjunction with historical reenactments of events from the lives of the artists—a kind of modern Vasari. This body of work, falling under the general rubric of homage, questions the origins of imagination and re-imagines the question of originality. Moreover, as an oeuvre that takes as its central tenet the artist's relationship to history, the pieces catch in their net a panoply of psychological, aesthetic, and social issues surrounding contemporary artists in a post-Duchampian universe.

In his replications, Bidlo explores the relationship between, and by extension responsibility toward, created objects and their creator. Yet this is never strictly as an observer, although he brings formidable technical skills to his works. By creating already created pieces he traces a literal and figurative connection between himself and a pioneering generation of modern artists. It is in homage and also in askance. For example, one of his series of Morandi bottles is entitled ''Not Morandi (Natura Morta, 1948) 1985.'' The negative is instructive for the pieces consist primarily in what they are not—they are not forgeries, they are not original works of art, and they are not even copies in a strict historical sense. Although Joseph Masheck has suggested they place Bidlo as Morandi's ''ideal viewer'' he functions even more as a kind of Doppelganger or reverse muse, turning inside out the notion of the artist as a vessel through which creative impulses pass. Bidlo often chooses to replicate artists marked by an obsessional return to certain subjects and for whom repetition constitutes a hallmark, i.e., Pollock and Warhol.

As if to underscore the many questions raised by duplication Bidlo also authors performance pieces of famous or (in his understanding) important moments in contemporary art history. Some of these are like the reproduced artwork. For example, in an East Village storefront Bidlo recreated Duchamp's chess match with a naked woman, producing a photograph similar to the 1963 match. However he also reenacts less self-conscious acts, for example certain behaviors of the painter Jackson Pollock at Peggy Guggenheim's, now part of contemporary art legend.

Sometimes the artist finds fodder by reenacting the inadvertent or chance collisions of popular and art culture. A 1960 *Vogue* magazine fashion shoot in which models posed against a background of Jackson Pollock paintings was the catalyst for Bidlo's 1982 ''Jackson Pollock Wardrobe.'' These paint-splattered pieces of clothing appear to make the marriage of art and commerce complete. Yet though Bidlo may seem prescient in showcasing the increasingly blurred lines between fashion and art, his is not an instance of political protest against the social pollution of artistic purity. Rather the artist utilizes the conjunction to explore the nature of surface and allusion. Bidlo doesn't seek to denigrate the Pollock by making it into a dress but to re-vision it; citing different intentions for the viewer one could say *Vogue* magazine had the same motive. For Bidlo, the worn image (even the fear that it will become a ''worn'' image) creates another sort of action painting.

Perhaps no artist looms more massively over Bidlo's aesthetic world than Marcel Duchamp. As Calvin Tomkins has pointed out, though Duchamp is considered the father of most modern art movements—performance art, conceptual art, installation, and environmental art, to name a few—he is curiously without heirs. The fact that he has spawned mostly imitators may have been Bidlo's initial point of reference. However, there remain many other sympathies between the two artists. Not least of these are Duchamp's interest in mining the aesthetic implications of chance. So too Bidlo's totemistic recreations of historical events—say, Pollock's lack of control in a social sphere—reenacted with aforethought do not lose their randomness. In the same way that the paintings cannot be truly painted again, the recreated events, once placed in history, cannot really be shaken free. One could argue that such actions ''replaced'' the actual artist in the same way Bidlo has ''replaced'' the actual art.

In 1997 Bidlo's ''St. Duchamp,'' an exhibition of recreated ready-mades, included a replica of his infamous urinal. Most recently the artist showed ''The Fountain Drawings'' consisting of some 3,000 drawings of the urinal. The artist displayed the work salon-style, floor to ceiling. The urinal graced every sort of paper, including newspaper and textbook and in a widely diverse vocabulary of brush styles. The fact that Bidlo drew the pieces, rather than created replicas, may signal a subtle change in direction for the artist. Yet the sheer bulk of the work while speaking to Bidlo's feeling for the stature of Duchamp, also remains true to particularly Dadaist causes. The effect of 3,000 drawings on the same theme is curiously similar to the effect of the original ready-mades. So that it might be regarded in a new light Duchamp singled out one object. Here Bidlo has duplicated a single object so many times it takes on an entirely new life.

—Merridawn Duckler

BIGGERS, Sanford

Nationality: American. **Born:** Los Angeles, California, 22 September 1970. **Education:** Morehouse College, Atlanta, Georgia, B.A. 1992; Syracuse University (Department of International Programs Abroad), Florence, Italy, 1990–1991; Maryland Institute College of Art, 1996–97; Skowhegan School of Painting and Sculpture, Skowhegan, Maine, 1998; School of the Art Institute of Chicago, M.F.A. 1999. **Career:** English and art instructor, Nagoya, Japan, 1992–94; painting and drawing instructor, California Afro-American Museum, 1995, and Youth Opportunities Unlimited, 1996; teacher-in-residence, Chelsea Vocational High School (Eyebeam/New York City Annenberg Challenge for Arts Education), New York, 2000; Co-Director of Cooper Union Saturday Program, New York, 2000—. Artist-in-Residence: Socrates Sculpture Park, New York, 2001; World Trade Center, New York, 2001; Studio Museum in Harlem, New York 2000; and P.S. 1 Studio Residency, New York, 2000. **Awards:** Second place, Central Metals Sculpture Competition, Atlanta, Georgia, 1990; Santa Fe Public Art Fund Grant, Los Angeles, California, 1996; Camille Hanks-Cosby Scholarship, Skowhegan School of Painting and Sculpture, Skowhegan, Maine, 1998; James Nelson Raymond Fellowship, School of the Art Institute of Chicago, 1999; Graduate Incentive Scholarship, School of the Art Institute of Chicago, 1999. **Address:** 146 West 132 St. #4, New York, New York, 10027 U.S.A.

Individual Exhibitions:

1993 *In the Mind's Eye,* Wight Gallery, UCLA, Los Angeles, California
1996 *Gomi no Tendankai,* Cabaret Mago, Nagoya, Japan

Selected Group Exhibitions:

1991 *Studenti di Savonarola,* Piazza Savanarola, Florence, Italy
1992 *Foreign Artists' Exhibition,* International Center, Nagoya, Japan
1997 *Magical, Mythical, Monumental,* Green Street Space (MICA), Baltimore, Maryland
1998 *Doing Our Own Thang,* Christopher Art Gallery, Prairie State College, Chicago, Illinois
1999 *Dialog,* Krasl Art Center, St. Joseph's Harbor, Michigan
Altered Objects, Hyde Park Art Center, Chicago, Illinois
2000 *P.S. 1 Artist-in-Residence Exhibition Part 2,* P.S. 1 Museum, Long Island City, New York
Artists-in-Residence 2000, Studio Museum in Harlem, New York
2001 *Freestyle,* Studio Museum in Harlem, New York
Rapper's Delight, Yerba Buena Center for the Arts, San Francisco, California
Mesh, Project, New York

Collections:

Altoid Curiously Strong Collection, New York; Doron Sebbag Art Collection, Israel; Studio Museum in Harlem, New York.

Publications:

On BIGGERS: Articles—''Power Spins'' by Carly Berwick in *ARTnews,* November 2000; ''Picking Out Distinctive Voices in a Pluralistic Chorus'' by Holland Cotter in *New York Times,* 18 August 2000; ''Dharma on the Dancefloor'' by Brian Keith Jackson in *Paper Magazine,* September 2000; ''From the Studio: Artists in Residence 2000'' by Franklin Sirmans in *Time Out New York,* 3–10 August 2000; ''A Condensed International Melange'' by Holland Cotter in *New York Times,* 6 May 2000; ''Power Enormous'' by Thomas Girst

Sanford Biggers: *OM,* 2000. ©Sanford Biggers.

in *NY Arts,* April 2001. **Video**—*Art Beat Chicago,* WTTV, Chicago, Illinois, 1999.

*

My work is based on materials and the meanings that I can interpret or assign to them. My process usually begins with an attraction to an object or to objects. I then make an association between the intended purpose of the object and my own philosophical system which celebrates the spirituality of the banal and the demystification of popular icons.

The spiritual practices of diverse cultures inspire me. In particular, the altars of Haitian Vodou (a fusion between the beliefs of African Yoruba and Catholicism) have informed the process of my work. A Haitian altar infuses icons and an amalgam of elements from popular culture that, when combined, unify and consequently increase exponentially in power. Through the incorporation of diverse materials and references, these ''power objects'' act as crossroads for seemingly incongruous ideas. This syncretism forms the ideological core of my work.

I begin with found and mass produced materials that bespeak a pre-existing history and a point of reference. However seemingly abstract or distant, I transform them. The challenge becomes discovering a methodology to bring forth a new dialogue from the extant information. I achieve this by changing the context of and the relationships between the objects. The results are sculptures and installations with elements that range from poetic to nostalgic to humorous. Most of the works are site-specific installations that are informed or transformed by the environment, yet some works must go even further and be reintroduced into the real-time world via performance. It is important to me to create a strong balance of visually compelling and didactic elements in the work. In this respect, these objects operate as small anecdotal vignettes.

—Sanford Biggers

* * *

At the foundation of Sanford Biggers art practice is an economy of material and a vernacular gesture that serves to elevate the mundane object into the realm of high art. In this transformation of material and object, Biggers reasserts the sacredness of simplicity, bringing under scrutiny a western disposition to privilege complex materialism over that of those works that have been appropriated from other banal usages. His work presents an addendum to larger historical questions that continue to assert themselves in our contemporary culture concerning ethnographic exploration and cultural translation.

In his work *Mandala,* a linoleum floor installation created to visually mimic the Buddhist or Hindu sacred iconography, Biggers invites break dancers to duel, effectively presenting an urban and culturally-specific meditation. Biggers ability to infuse this ''power object'' created from mundane material with that of an urban secular ritual serves to elevate the banality of linoleum as a material into a realm of reverence fortified by the residual traces of ritualized energy. As such, Biggers not only creates a sacred urban territory, but an object that embodies the cultural ethos.

Biggers' interest lies in mining the ambiguous territory of cultural signifiers and the means by which our capitalistic society has effectively commodified the sacred, determining what is an authentic cultural expression. By querying the marketing of both Eastern cultural traditions (Fung Shei and Zen) and an evolving sacred urban culture (hip-hop, black hair styles and the iconography of the Black Power Movement of the 1970s), Biggers' work exposes the unfortunate by-product of recycling culture—the consumption and eventual regurgitation as tasteless objects devoid of original context. It is not a territory that Biggers treads without a sense of his own complicity. After all, he digests culture as a participant and extends this ''authentic'' experience to others equally willing to consume and cannibalize. We have all been implicated as voyeurs in Biggers' own experiences, and to some degree we have brought with us the fetishizing of a culture to which we are not connected. Our desire to experience the other without a sense of shame or fear clearly points to the pathology of lure and loathing that Stanley Crouch speaks so eloquently toward.

In the recent piece *The Chronicle* (2000), a ten-foot rendering of an afro-pick onto which images of ancient African civilizations are projected, Biggers seeks to teach by narrating the historical legacy of the marketed object. Biggers makes visible the historical and cultural narratives associated with this object in Africa, its transference from Africa into the Americas during slavery, and its resurgence in the 1970s as a symbol of black pride—all of which have been buried in the effort to market the afro-pick as the new hot consumer item. The viewer becomes an unsuspecting pupil, learning the rich history and culture embedded deeply within the sculptural object.

However hard-hitting, Biggers' work does not compromise its formalistic qualities even as it backs the viewer into a corner. Quite to the contrary, Biggers' work is unapologetically seductive and formally beautiful, while remaining exceptionally conceptual. His language is deliberate in its evidence of code-switching, its movement from vernacular to mainstream and back again. As such, there is a purposefulness to the work. It is the elevation of the discarded, the refusal to accept decay, and the reappropriation/reassertion/re-presentation of what we no longer embrace that allows us to see the beauty of what lies abandoned among us. Perhaps this effort forces us to see the value of our own humanity through a ritualistic act that elevates and pays homage to our everyday existence as exemplified in the ancient Japanese tradition of *wabi-sabi*, a quiet and demur utterance in the wake of hyper-consumption.

Biggers' work humors the western philosophies that drive the evolutionary progress of contemporary art production and materials. His work convincingly rejects the elevation of western constructions of art production established in the 19th century, and unveils the complete articulation of the ''primitive'' gesture. Biggers' work repositions this simplistic gesture as an organic and complex philosophy that has a proven longevity and one that prevails in contemporary society. Biggers' artistic expression continues to question of the commodification of art, particularly the pathological commodification of cultural artifacts and sacred iconography.

Biggers provides us with new myths by projecting a narrative that essentially chronicles his own sense of history, urgency, and hope. His practice, unlike any within his generation, is as visually fluid in its ability to move between the sacred and mundane as is the music of legend Al Green in its ability to traverse between soulful crooning and cries of sacred bliss.

—Valerie Cassel

BILL, Max

Nationality: Swiss. **Born:** Winterthur, 22 December 1908. **Education:** Trained as silversmith, Kunstgewerbeschule, Zurich, 1924–27; studied art, Staatliche Bauhaus, Dessau, Germany, 1927–29. **Military Service:** Served in the Swiss Army, 1939–45. **Family:** Married 1) Bibia Spoerri in 1931 (died 1988); 2) Angela Thomas, 1991; sons: Johann, Jakob. **Career:** Independent architect, painter, sculptor and graphic artist, Zurich, since 1929, and industrial designer, since 1944. Lecturer on the Theory of Form, Kunstgewerbeschule, Zurich, 1944–45; Co-Founder and Rector, Hochschule für Gestaltung, Ulm, Germany, 1951–56; Professor of Environmental Design, State Institute of Fine Arts, Hamburg, 1967–74. **Awards:** Grand Prize, *Triennale di Milano,* Milan, 1936, 1951, 1954, Kandinsky Prize, 1949; First Prize for Sculpture, *Bienal,* Sao Paulo, 1951; Gold Medal, Verucchio, Italy, 1966; City of Zurich Art Prize, 1968. Honorary Fellow, American Institute of Architects, 1964; Extraordinary Member, Akademie der Künste, West Berlin, 1972; Honorary Member, Royal Flemish Academy of Sciences, Literature and Arts, 1973; Piepenbrock Prize for Sculpture, Osnabrueck, West Germany, 1990; Honorary award, 1991, and Grand Prize, 1993, International Graphics Biennial, Llubljana; Grand Prize, Chevalier de la Légion d'Honneur, 1993; Imperial Prize, Japan, 1993; honorary doctorate, Swiss Technical College, Zürich, 1994. **Member:** Communal Council, City of Zurich, 1961; National Councillor, Swiss Parliament, 1967–74. Central Board, Schweizerische Werkbund, 1952–62; Swiss Federal Art Commission, 1961–69; Member of the Board, Geschwisten-School Foundation, Ulm, 1964; Member of the Superior Council (Creation Esthetique Industrielle), French Ministry of Industrial and Scientific Development, 1971–73. Abstraction-Creation group, Paris, 1932–36; Allianz, Zurich 1937; CIAM (Congrés Internationaux d'Architecture Modernes), 1938; UAM (Union des Artistes Modernes), Paris 1949; Deutscher Werkbund 1956. **Agent:** Marlborough Fine Art, 6 Albemarle Street, London, WIX 3HF, England. **Died:** In Berlin, Germany, 9 December 1994.

Individual Exhibitions:

1928 Staatliche Bauhaus, Dessau, Germany (with Albert Braun)
1929 Atelier des Kunstlers, Zurich
1939 Kunstmuseum, Basle
1946 Galerie des Eaux-Vives, Zurich
1948 Herber Hermann Galerie, Stuttgart (with Josef Albers and Jean Arp)
1949 Galerie d'Art Moderne, Basle
Kunsthaus, Zurich (with Antoine Pevsner and Georges Vantongerloo)
1950 Museu de Arte Moderna, Sao Paulo
1951 Kunstverein, Freiburg im Breisgau, West Germany (with Julius Bissier and Georges Vantongerloo)
1956 Ulmer Museum, Ulm, West Germany (toured Germany)
1957 Helmhaus, Zurich

1958 Galerie Suzanne Bollag, Zurich
1959 Galerie Gelbes Haus, St. Gallen, Switzerland
Städtisches Museum, Leverkusen, West Germany Studio F., Ulm, West Germany
1960 Staatsgalerie, Stuttgart
Kunstmuseum, Winterthur, Switzerland
Galerie Suzanne Bollag, Zurich
Galerie im Ronca-Haus, Lucerne
1961 Galerie de Perron, Geneva
Galerie Anna Roepke, Wiesbaden, West Germany
1962 Galerie Hilt, Basle
1963 Galerie Suzanne Bollag, Zurich
Gimpel & Hanover Galerie, Zurich
Staempfli Gallery, New York
Pace Gallery, Boston
Studio F., Ulm, West Germany
1964 Galleria Cadario, Milan
Galleria del Deposito, Genoa
Galleria dell'Accademia, Rome
Galleria Suzanne Bollag, Zurich
1965 Galerie Aktuell, Berne
Op-Art Galerie, Esslingen, West Germany
Galleria Flaviana, Locarno, Switzerland
Galerie 58, Rapperswil, Switzerland
Gemeindehaus, Uster, Switzerland
Galerie Suzanne Bollag, Zurich
1966 Staempfli Gallery, New York
Galerie Hilt, Basle
Hanover Gallery, London
Galerie Suzanne Bollag, Zurich
1967 Galerie im Erker, St. Gallen, Switzerland
1968 Kunsthalle, Berne
Kestner-Gesellschaft, Hannover
Kunstverein für die Rheinland und Westfalen, Dusseldorf
Haags Gemeentemuseum, The Hague
Musée des Beaux-Arts, La Chaux de Fonds, Switzerland
Kunsthalle, Nuremberg, West Germany
Kunsthaus, Zurich
Galerie Suzanne Bollag, Zurich
1969 Arts Club of Chicago
Galleria La Bertesca, Genoa
Galleria La Polena, Genoa
Galleria Vismara, Milan
Galerie Godard Lefort, Montreal
Staempfli Gallery, New York
Galerie Denise René, Paris
Galleria Martano/Due, Turin
Galerie Bischofberger, Zurich
Centre National d'Art of Contemporain, Paris
Musée de Peinture et de Sculpture, Grenoble, France
1970 Galerie Bischofberger, Zurich
Galerie Loeb, Berne
Galerie im Weissen Haus, Winterthur, Switzerland
San Francisco Museum of Art
Galerie Appel und Fertsch, Frankfurt
Galleria del Cavallino, Venice
White Gallery, Lutry, Switzerland
Galleria Arte Studio, Macerata, Italy
Galerie Design II, Hamburg
Galleria d'Arte Peccolo, Livorno, Italy
Galleria del Cortile, Rome
Galerie Kludschule, Zurich
Staempfli Gallery, New York
1971 Galerie Reckermann, Cologne
Galerie Denise Rene, Paris
Galerie Suzanne Bollag, Zurich
Galerie im Erker, St. Gallen, Switzerland
1972 Musée Rath, Geneva
Galleria Lorenzelli, Milan
Marlborough Galerie, Zurich
Kunstmuseum, Aarhus, Denmark
Galerie Hausdewell, Baden-Baden, West Germany
Marlborough-Godard Gallery, Toronto (travelled to the Marlborough Gallery, Montreal)
1973 Galerie 58, Rapperswil, Switzerland
Galerie Ziegler, Geneva
1974 Marlborough Fine Art, London
Galleria Lorenzelli, Bergamo, Italy
Galerie Media, Neuchâtel, France
Galleria Medea, Milan
Marlborough Galerie, Zurich
Watari Gallery, Tokyo
Albright-Knox Art Gallery, Buffalo, New York (toured the United States)
1975 Comsky Gallery, Los Angeles
Art Institute, San Francisco
Marlborough Gallery, New York
Galleria Effereridi, Bologna
1976 Museum für Kunst und Gewerbe, Hamburg (toured Germany)
Akademie der Künste, West Berlin
Galleria Lorenzelli, Milan
1977 Universita di Parma, Italy
1978 Moderne Galerie, Bottrop, West Germany
1979 *Pinturas, Esculturas, Grafica,* Museo de Bellas Artes, Caracas
Galerie Bossin, West Berlin
Gallery Watari, Tokyo
1980 Galerie Seestrasse, Rapperswil, Switzerland
Galerie Bossin, West Berlin
Artline, The Hague
1981 Galerie Buhler, Biel, Switzlerland
Gallery Watari, Tokyo
1982 Galerie Bossin, West Berlin
Galerie Denise Rene, Paris
Gimpel-Hanover-Andre Emmerich Galerie, Zurich
1983 Galleria Narciso, Turin
Galerie Bertram, Burgdorf, Switzerland
Gimpel-Hanover-Andre Emmerich Galerie, Zurich
1984 Galerie Henz, Munich
Galleria Narciso, Turin
Deutsche Bank, Hamburg
1985 Galerie Wolfgang Ketterer, Munich
Galerie Teufel, Cologne
Galleria Lorenzelli, Milan
Galerie Edith Wahlandt, Stuttgart
1986 Mucsarnok Art Gallery, Budapest
1987 National Gallery, Belgrade
Kunsthalle, Frankfurt
1988 Galleria Comunale Arte Moderna, Bologna

1990 Galerie Denise René, Paris
1991 *Internationalen Grafik-Biennale,* Llubljana
Casa Rusca, Locarno, Switzerland
Max Bill, Lorenzelli Arte, Milan
Max Bill, Edward Totah Gallery, London
1993 Julian Barran Ltd. Gallery, London
1994 *Raumplastik*—Berlin Dankt Frankreich, Berlin
Rhythm in Space: Max Bill, Europaisches Patentamt Munchen, Munich
1995 *Max Bill: The Graphic Series,* Landratsamt Esslingen, Germany

Selected Group Exhibitions:

1930 *Bill/Valloton/Probst/Steck/Von May,* Kunsthalle, Berne
1944 *Konkrete Kunst,* Kunsthalle, Basle
1951 *Bienal,* Sao Paulo
1952 *Monument to the Unknown Political Prisoner,* Institute of Contemporary Arts, London
1958 *Biennale,* Venice
1960 *Concrete Art: 50 Years of Development,* Kunsthaus, Zurich
1971 *La Peinture Non-Objective 1924–1939,* Galerie Jean Chauvelin, Paris (travelled to Annely Juda Fine Art, London, and Galleria Milano, Milan)
1972 *Konstruktivismus,* Galerie, Grmurzynska + Bargera, Cologne
1973 *Kunst in Deutschland 1898–1973,* Kunsthalle, Hamburg (travelled to Städtisches Galerie im Lenbachhaus, Munich)
1982 *Acquisition Priorities: Postwar European Painting,* Guggenheim Museum, New York
1989 *Selected by Max Bill,* Kunsthaus, Zurich
1990 *Concrete Art,* Ulmer Museum, Ulm, Germany
1991 *Swiss Open-air Sculpture 1960–91,* Foundation Pierre Gianadda, Martigny, Switzerland
1993 *20th International Biennial of Graphic Art,* Moderna Galerija, Ljubljana
Masterpieces from the Museum of Fine Arts Berne, Daimaru Museum, Tokyo (traveling exhibition)
1994 *Line+Movement,* Annely Juda Fine Art, London
1996 *Max Bill, Georges Vantongerloo: A Working Friendship—50 Years of Sculpture, Painting and Drawing,* Annely Juda Fine Art, London
1997 *The Magic of Number in the Art of the 20th Century,* Staatsgalerie Stuttgart, Germany
1998 *The Thirties: Influences on Abstract Art in Britain,* Annely Juda Fine Art, London
2000 *All Sculpture: From Medardo Rosso to the Threshold of the Millennium,* Circolo La Scaletta, Matera, Italy

Collections:

Kunsthaus, Zurich; Kunstmuseum, Winterthur, Switzerland; Musée d'Art et d'Histoire, Geneva; Musées Royaux des Beaux-Arts, Brussels; Centre Georges Pompidou, Paris; Wilhelm-Lehmbrock Museum, Duisburg, West Germany; Galleria Nazionale d'Arte Moderna, Rome; Art Institute of Chicago; Albright-Knox Art Gallery, Buffalo, New York; Hirshhorn Museum and Sculpture Garden, Washington, D.C.

Bill's architectural works, including his own house and studio at Zumikon/Zurich, are extant throughout Europe in Aargau, Ulm, Rhinfall, Leverkusen, Cologne, Tamins, Dusseldorf and Esbly.

Publications:

By BILL: Books—*Quinze variations sur un meme theme,* Paris 1938; *Le Corbusier: Oeuvre Complete,* volume 3, editor, Zurich 1939, London 1964; *Konstruktionen + 5 Kompositionen,* Zurich 1941; *10 Original Lithos,* Zurich 1941; *X + X,* Zurich 1942; *Leo Luppi: 10 Kompositionen,* Zurich 1943; *Konkrete Kunst,* exhibition catalog, with others, Basle 1944; *Hans Arp: 11 Configurations,* with others, Zurich 1945; *Wiederaufbau,* Zurich 1945; *Wassily Kandinsky: 10 Farbige Reproduktionen,* Basle 1949; *Robert Maillart: Brucken und Konstruktionen,* Zurich 1949, New York 1969; *Moderne Schweizer Architektur 1925–1945,* Basle 1950; *Wassily Kandinsky,* editor, Paris 1951; *Form: A Balance Sheet of Mid-20th Century Trends in Design,* Basle 1952; *Uber des Geistige in der Kunst,* editor, Berne 1952; *Mies van der Rohe,* Milan 1955; *Essays uber Kunst und Kunstler,* editor, Stuttgart 1955, Berne 1963; *Die Gute Form,* Winterthur 1957; *Punkt und Linie zu Flache,* editor, Berne 1959; *Enzo Mari,* with Bruno Munari, Milan 1959; *Konkrete Kunst: 50 Jahre Entwicklung,* exhibition catalog, Zurich 1968, 1969; *11 x 4,* Zurich 1970; *Jahresgabe 1972,* Berne 1972; *System mit funf vierfarbigen Zentren,* St. Gallen Switzerland 1972; *8 = (2 x 4/4) = 8,* Neuchâtel, Switzerland 1974; *16 Constellations,* Paris 1974; *7 Twins,* Neuchâtel, Switzerland 1977. **Articles—**Interview with Dalmazio Ambrosioni in *Giornale dell-Arte,* vol. 9, no. 94, November 1991; ''Max Bill: The Early Years—An Interview'' with Angela Thomas in *Journal of Decorative and Propaganda Arts* (Miami Beach), no. 19, 1993.

On BILL: Books—*Max Bill,* Buenos Aires 1955; *Max Bill* by Max Bense and others, Teufen, Switzerland 1958; *Max Bill* by Margit Staber, St. Gallen, Switzerland 1971; *Max Bill* by Eduard Huttinger, Zurich 1977, 1978; *Max Bill,* exhibition catalog, edited by Arturo Carlo Quintavalle, Parma 1977; *Max Bill: Pinturas, Esculturas, Grafica,* exhibition catalog, by Carlos Silva and Ricardo Axel Stein Nunex, Caracas 1979; *Contemporary Architects,* edited by Muriel Emanuel, London and New York 1980; *Max Bill,* exhibition catalog, Bologna 1988; *Max Bill,* exhibition catalog, Milan 1991; *Max Bill,* exhibition catalog, London 1991; *Max Bill: The Graphic Series,* exhibition catalog, Esslingen 1995. **Articles—**''Max Bill: Perpetuating the Bauhaus Ideal'' by Michael Peppiatt in *Architectural Digest* (Los Angeles), vol. 44, August 1987; ''Das Apollinische in der Kunst: Max Bill zum 80'' by Karl Gerstner in *Du* (Zurich), no. 10, 1988; ''Max Bill's Birthday Blues'' by Ernest Beck in *Art News,* vol. 88, February 1989; ''Le Rythme: Max Bill'' by Serge Lemoine in *Beaux Arts Magazine,* no. 117, November 1993; Obituary in *Art in America* (New York), vol. 83, February 1995.

*

One often speaks of the mathematics, the structure, the systems in art. I also did so. Looking for a non-individualistic approach to so-called art problems. I did different kinds of research, and I wrote a few statements which were publicized and interpreted worldwide. As life—and so ideas and art as one of the human activities—is in constant motion, and we hope permanent development, my ideas have also developed and become clearer. This because of more experience and an accumulation of knowledge.

When I wrote a quarter of a century ago about ''the mathematical approach in contemporary art'' this was a new way to see art which until then had been considered mostly as the more or less uncontrolled experience of an individual.

Today I know better that mathematics are only a part of the methods to be adapted for the regulation of so-called works of art. I know that a concept has to conform to its inner organization and its visual existence. This means that a concept and the finally executed work have to be a unity. This unit is the result of the logical approach to the solution of the problem and its realization.

I prefer today to describe this process as the logical approach to the problems of art. This means that every part of the creative process consciously follows step by step a logical analysis and feedback. This is the way I hope to best realize my vision.

—Max Bill

* * *

Among the painters of the 20th century Max Bill is one of the few who represents and puts into effect the Renaissance principle of the *uomo universale.* It is true that he is presented officially as an architect, but his painting and sculptural work is at least as important as his buildings. He is equally instigator and publicist, organizer, man of letters and teacher; he is versed in philosophy and involves himself in the cultural politics of his country. Judgment—the balance between rationalism and emotion—and order—the demonstration of law in the world—form the basis of his multiple activities. As an artist he became the most important representative of ''concrete art'' which he himself defined as follows: ''We call those works of art concrete art which have arisen by virtue of their original means and laws—without external support from natural appearances or their transformation, therefore without abstraction . . . they are of that sharp, unequivocal and perfect nature as must be expected from works of the human intellect.'' The striving after perfection evident in the definition marks all Bill's creative work. In the realization of his buildings, sculptures and pictures, mathematics is, to him, not the only but the most important medium. A large part of his work could be understood as mathematics become visible, although not exhaustively. Bill himself speaks of an ''application of logical thought processes in the organization of rhythms and relationships, of laws that have individual origins . . . . '' In this emphasis on the individual is hidden the allusion to creative fantasy which Bill develops as much in purpose-free as in purposeful problems, perhaps in the design of a poster or a memorial.

His life's work presents itself as an explanation of the aesthetic principles he has himself defined. It possesses a chronology, yet hardly any development in the sense that no stylistic groups or periods are discernable in his work. A theme which preoccupies the artist can again be taken up by him after a number of years and varied with new methods of realization without any apparent breach.

Bill's work stands in a tradition which follows directly on Stijl and the Bauhaus. It continues this tradition in that it systematically and methodically pursues the experiments which had begun there. This aim was also served by the ''Design School'' in Ulm, which despite its short life after 1945 gained greater international influence than all other didactic art institutes of the last decades.

When in 1975–76 a comprehensive retrospective of Bill's pictures, sculpture, graphics and models was mounted in the USA and Germany, he himself spoke of certain modifications to his principles in the sense that he described the ''design process as that of logical method'' and made a clear differentiation between purposeful and purpose free activity: ''While the problems of building, of the form of an object, of education or political decision must be solved in relation to their complex functions, the function of painting and sculpture is unequivocal: Their usefulness rests on their intellectual/spiritual usefulness.''

—Heinz Spielmann

BIRNBAUM, Dara

Nationality: American. **Born:** New York, 29 October 1946. **Education:** Carnegie Mellon University, Pittsburgh, Pennsylvania, B.A. in architecture 1969; San Francisco Art Institute, B.F.A. 1972; New School of Social Research, New York, 1976. **Career:** Video artist; instructor, School for Visual Arts, New York, 1983–86; Princeton University, New Jersey, 1987–88; Hunter College, New York, 1990–91; Bildende Kunst and Institute, Frankfurt, 1992. **Awards:** Maya Deren Award, American Film Institue, 1987; Louis XIII de Remy Martin Award of Excellence, 1987; Harvard University Special Jury Prize, 1988. Recipient of numerous grants and awards for video work from the National Endowment for the Arts, the New York State Council on the Arts, Creative Artists Public Service, and others. **Address:** 140 Thomson Street, Apt. 3A, New York, New York 10012, U.S.A.

Selected Individual Exhibitions:

1977 Artist Space, New York
1978 The Kitchen, New York
1981 Museum of Modern Art, New York
1982 Hudson River Museum, New York
Institute of Contemporary Art, London
1983 Musee d'Art Contemporain, Montreal
1989 Forum de Arte Contemporanea, Lisbon
1990 IVAM Centre del Carme, Valencia, Spain
1991 Rhona Hoffman Gallery, Chicago
Australian International Video Festival, Sydney
1994 Portikus, Frankfurt
CAPC Museum of Art and Contemporary Entrepot, Bordeaux
X Works at l'Esec, Paris
Rena Bransten Gallery, San Francisco
Paula Cooper Gallery, New York
1995 Kunsthalle Wien, Vienna

Selected Group Exhibitions:

1987 *A Post-modern Perspective,* Moderna Museet, Stockholm
1988 *Film/Video Arts: 21 Years of Independents,* Museum of Modern Art, New York
The World of Art Today, Milwaukee Art Museum
1989 *Image World: Art and Media Culture,* Whitney Museum, New York

A Forest of Signs, Museum of Modern Art, New York
The Arts for Television, Museum of Modern Art, New York
1990 *Life-Size,* Israel Museum, Jerusalem
1991 *Inaugural Exhibition,* Irish Museum of Modern Art, Dublin
1992 *Video: Two Decades,* Museum of Modern Art, New York
Trans-Voices, Whitney Museum, New York
1995 *Cinema Effect,* Musee d'Art Contemporain, Montreal

Publications:

By BIRNBAUM: Books—*Playground (The Damnation of Faust),* 1985; *Rough Edits: Popular Image Video Works 1977–1980,* Halifax, Nova Scotia 1987; *Every TV Needs Revolution,* Gand 1992. **Articles—** ''Out of the Blue'' in *Discourses: Conversations in Postmodern Art and Culture,* 1990; ''The RIO Experience'' in *Illuminating Video: An Essential Guide to Video Art,* New York 1990; ''An Interview with Dara Birnbaum'' in *Media Arts,* Winter 1990; ''Interview'' with susan Canning in *Art Papers,* November–December 1991; ''Overlapping Signs'' in *War after War,* San Francisco 1992; ''Every TV Needs a Revolution'' in *IMSCHOOT,* 1992; ''Reversing Angles: Talking Back to the Media'' (interview with Sina Najafi and Sven-Olov Wallenstein) in *Material,* no. 25, 1995. **Videotapes—***Kiss the Girls: Make Them Cry,* 1979; *Pop-Pop Video,* 1980; *Remy/Grand Central: Trains and Boats and Planes,* 1980; *Fire!/Hendrix,* 1982; *PM Magazine/Acid Rock,* 1982; *Damnation of Faust: Evocation,* 1983; *Damnation of Faust: Will-o-the-Wisp (A Deceitful Goal),* 1985; *Artbreak,* 1987; *Damnation of Faust: Charming Landscape,* 1987; *Canon: Taking to the Streets, Part One: Princeton University—Take Back the Night,* 1990; *Canon: Taking to the Streets, Part Two: Rutgers University—1988 National Student Convention,* 1991.

On BIRNBAUM: Books—*Dara Birnbaum,* Dijon, France 1986; *Dara Birnbaum,* Valencia, Spain 1991; exhibition catalog, Vienna 1995. **Articles—**''Mixed Blessing'' in *Afterimage,* May 1982; ''Phantasmagoria of the Media'' by C. Owens in *Art in America,* May 1982; ''Allegorical Procedures; Appropriation and Montage in Contemporary Art'' in *Artform,* September 1982; ''Dara Birnbaum'' by S. Gorney in *Juliet,* April/May 1988; ''Dara Birnbaum'' by S. Hapgood in *Contemporanea,* May 1990; ''Dara Birnbaum'' by K. Hixson in *Flash Art,* May/June 1991; ''DB'' by Judith Kirshner in *Forum Internation,* March/April 1993; ''Dara Birnbaum'' by Giorgio Verzotti and Antonella Russo in *The Collection: Castello di Rivoli Museo d'Arte Contemporanea,* Milan 1995; ''Mirrors and Memesis: An Examination of the Strategies of Image Appropriation and Repetition in the Work of Dara Birnbaum,'' by Dot Tuer in *N.Paradoxa,* issue 3, May 1997.

* * *

Video artist Dara Birnbaum was one of the first to use overt appropriation of television images to directly critique the mass media and its messages. Her works deconstruct and recontextualize materials, creating a subversive message through repetition and variations in speed. Birnbaum works primarily with images of pop icons and news footage to engage viewers in new ways with common visual information.

Birnbaum's 1978 *Technology/Transformation: Wonder Woman* took images of the female superhero from the popular television drama and used them to critique the construction of gender in such an arena. Birnbaum said the purpose of this project was one of ''attempting to slow down the 'technological speed' of television and arresting moments of TV time for the viewer, which would then allow for examination and questioning.'' This critical examination sought to illustrate the shifts in gender roles inherent in the cultural and technological changes occurring in the world. This critical examination continued in the 1979 work *Kiss the Girls and Make Them Cry,* a video which looked at the representation of women in such shows as *Kojak* and the popular soap opera *General Hospital.*

In the 1980s, Birnbaum's work evolved into a more lyrical style in which the potential of video as an expressive tool was explored. The *Damnation of Faust* trilogy included *Evocation* (1983), *Will o' the Wisp* (1985), and *Charming Landscape* (1987). These works were far more concerned with metaphor and the interactions between people and spaces of everyday life. The piece as a whole seeks to rearticulate the Faustian myth through a female voice. Images are slowed down, showing a study of the struggle between the inner and outer worlds. Here the metaphorical aspects of image placement are at the forefront. In 1987, Birnbaum entered the realm of mainstream television when she did work featured on MTV's *Art Break* segments. The American Film Institute honored Birnbaum in 1987 with the Maya Deren Award, a prestigious citation for film and video art.

Birnbaum began a more direct involvement with art in public spaces when she won a design competition for what was to be the first permanent video wall in the United States. Her background in architecture and painting were employed in this work commissioned by the city of Atlanta, Georgia, for a new shopping mall. The *Rio Videowall* project was physically created from 1987–1989 (when the work ''opened'' at the mall). The structure was comprised of twenty-five video monitors in a five-row grid. When the mall is empty, the outdoor video wall shows recorded images of the landscape which existed in the space prior to the construction of the mall. When people are inside, milling around in hallways and stores, two live surveillance cameras capture silhouettes of their bodies. These are then keyed into the landscape images, creating matts which then become filled with live satellite feeds from CNN, Ted Turner's Atlanta-based news organization. The human interface with the elaborate signs of technology and globalization make the piece a constantly changing artwork with significant symbolism.

Birnbaum continued to examine the interplay of the personal and the political with her 1990 work *Canon: Taking to the Streets.* The piece features footage from the April, 1987 ''Take Back the Night'' rally at Princeton University. The annual rally is held nationally to call attention to the plight of women in the world and to demand an atmosphere of safety, a freedom from fear of rape and violence. This contemporary action is juxtaposed to images from and hints at the student uprising in Paris in May, 1968. The volatility of the political struggles of the 1960s emphasizes the intensity of more small-scale but equally important battles. Birnbaum continued this critical approach with her 1991 work *Tiananmen Square: Break-in Transmission.* This piece explores the role of the media in the much-publicized Chinese student uprisings against governmental oppression. Continued work in this area brought the 1994 *Hostage,* a six-channel video installation which takes a 1977 German hostage crisis as its subject. Again images from the news appear in a context which is critical of the media's inability to provide solutions in its constant coverage of political strife. Birnbaum sees this as a sign of irresponsibility and concrete proof of the voyeurism inherent in the medium of television.

Birnbaum began work in 2000 on an interactive piece for a new government center in Austria, returning once again to large-scale public art. In the autumn of that year, the Seoul Metropolitan Museum featured Birnbaum's work in their conference, ''The Architectures of Video Imagery'' (1978–2000). She has exhibited installations in such reputable venues as the Pompidou Centre in Paris and the Whitney Museum and the Museum of Modern Art in New York. Birnbaum continues to challenge notions of social responsibility and the power of the media.

—Tammy A. Kinsey

BISHOP, James

Nationality: American. **Born:** Neosho, Missouri, 7 October 1927. **Education:** Syracuse University, New York, 1946–50, B.A. 1950; Washington University, St. Louis, Missouri, 1951–54; studied under Esteban Vicente, Black Mountain College, North Carolina, 1953; Columbia University, New York 1955–56. **Career:** Independent artist: lived and travelled in France, 1957–66; now lives and works in New York. Editorial associate, *Artnews,* New York, 1969–70. Artist-in-residence, Cooper Union, New York, 1969–70; University of California at Irvine, 1970; Carnegie-Mellon University, Pittsburgh, 1971; School of Visual Arts New York 1972. **Awards:** Guggenheim Fellowship, 1970. **Agent:** Margarete Roeder Gallery, P.O. Box 317, Prince Street Station, 545 Broadway, New York, New York 10021. **Address:** 5 Lispenard Street, New York, New York 10013, U.S.A.

Individual Exhibitions:

1963 Galerie Lucien Durand, Paris
Galerie Smith, Brussels
1964 Galerie Lawrence, Paris
1966 Fischbach Gallery, New York
Galerie Fournier, Paris
1968 Fischbach Gallery, New York
1970 Fischbach Gallery, New York
1971 Galerie Fournier, Paris
1972 Fischbach Gallery, New York
1973 Galerie Fournier, Paris
The Clocktower, New York
1974 Rosa Esman Gallery, New York
1975 Galleria D'Alessandro-Ferranti, Rome
1976 Galerie Annemarie Verna, Zurich
Galerie Fournier, Paris
1977 Galerie Françoise Lambert, Milan
Galerie Rüdiger Schöttle, Munich
1979 Droll/Kolbert Gallery, New York
Galerie Annemarie Verna, Zurich
1980 Frank Kolbert Gallery, New York
1981 Galerie Annemarie Verna, Zurich
1986 Galerie Annemarie Verna, Zurich
1987 Simon/Neuman Gallery, New York
1993 *James Bishop: Paintings and Works on Paper,* Kunstmuseum Winterthur
1994 Galerie nationale du Jeu de Paume, Paris
Musée du Jeu de Paume, Paris

Selected Group Exhibitions:

1965 *Promesses Tenues,* Musée Galliera, Paris
1967 *Expo '67* Montreal
1968 *Painting Annual,* Whitney Museum, New York
1970 *One Man's Choice,* Dallas Museum of Fine Arts
1971 *Award Invitational,* National Institute of Arts and Letters, New York
1973 *Options and Alternatives: Some Directions in Recent Art,* Yale University Art Museum New Haven, Connecticut
1982 *Accrochage,* Musée d'Art Moderne de la Ville de Paris
1986 *Trends in Geometric Abstract Art,* Tel Aviv Museum
1990 *Radical auf Papier,* Aargauer Kunsthaus, Aarau, Germany
1992 *Yvon Lambert collectionne,* Musée d'Art Moderne de la Communauté de Lille and Musée des Beaux-Arts, Tourcoing, France
1995 *American Drawings and Graphic Works: From Sol LeWitt to Bruce Nauman,* Kunsthaus, Zurich
1997 Annemarie Verna Gallery, Zurich

Collections:

San Francisco Museum of Modern Art; Centre Georges Pompidou, Paris; Kunstmuseum, Zurich.

Publications:

By BISHOP: Articles—Statement in *Art Now,* vol. 4, no. 2, 1972; interview in *Art in America,* October 1983.

On BISHOP: Books—*Options and Alternatives: Some Directions in Recent Art,* exhibition catalog, with texts by Anne Coffin Hanson, Klaus Kertess, and Annette Michelson, New Haven, Connecticut 1973. **Articles—**''An Experiment in Reality: The Painting of James Bishop'' by Marcelin Pleynet in *Art and Literature* (Paris), March 1964; ''La Peinture et Son Sujet?'' by Philippe Sollers in *Tel Quel* (Paris), Winter 1965; ''Paris Letter'' by Annette Michelson in *Art International* (Lugano, Switzerland), March 1965; ''Post-Painterly Quattrocento'' by John Ashbery in *Artnews* (New York), December 1966; ''Symbol Lurking in the Wings'' by Dore Ashton in *Studio International* (London), February 1967; ''James Bishop: Reason and Impulse'' by Robert Rosenblum in *Artforum* (New York), February 1967; ''A Dying Style?'' by Peter Schjeldahl in the *New York Times,* 3 May 1970; ''New York Letter'' by Carter Ratcliff in *Art International,* Summer 1970; ''Pourquoi la Peinture?'' by Marcelin Pleynet and Peinture sur Peinture: James Bishop'' by Philippe Sollers in *Peinture Cahiers Théoriques,* Winter 1972; ''James Bishop'' by Kenneth Baker in *Artforum* (New York), June 1972; ''Once More, With Feeling'' by Carter Ratcliff in *Artnews* (New York), Summer 1972; ''Action in the North Atlantic'' by John Ashbery in *New York Magazine,* 21 May 1979; ''Towards A Theory and Practice of Painting: Abstract Expressionism and the Surrealist Discourse'' by P. Rogers in *Artforum,* March 1980; ''Mostly Monochrome'' by Carter Ratcliff in *Art in America,* April 1981; ''James Bishop: Remembering How to See'' by Carter Ratcliff in *Artforum,* May 1988; ''The

Acceptable Apple of Painting'' by Lucio Pozzi in *Tema Celeste,* January-March 1992; ''James Bishop'' by Eric Amouroux in *Beaux Arts Magazine,* no. 120, February 1994; ''Bishop's Gambit'' by Holland Cotter in *Art in America,* vol. 82, no. 5, May 1994; ''James Bishop'' by Eric Amouroux in *Beaux Arts Magazine,* no. 120, February 1994.

* * *

Since the Second World War the character of art and artists has changed dramatically. Kandinsky's semi-abstract and abstract work of the years 1911–14 provided a major impetus for the rediscovery of Abstract Expressionism in the 50s. This rediscovery also served as a response to the horrors made so familiar by the war: the destruction of cities and individuals, the barbarity of concentration camps and mass annihilation, found expression in paintings that spoke of violence and wounds. What started as an imperative art of protest developed into a style, or rather a whole range of styles unified by being more or less abstract or expressionist in its free, almost vehement handling of paint and colour.

American James Bishop was among the first generation of post-war abstract expressionists who, though under the auspices of his group, is not without individual sensibility or the diversity of vision which affirms the vitality of contemporary art. Having studied at the famous Black Mountain College, Bishop was exposed to the leading figures in every domain of the avant-garde. He was also familiar with the latest artistic developments from first-hand experience in New York which were then labeled ''Abstract Expressionism.'' During the late 1950s in New York, he attempted to assimilate the important elements of Abstract Expressionism to modern art while avoiding the flamboyant splashes and dribbles of the de Kooning followers. As a result Bishop developed a pictorial organisation derived from the structure of the painting as a means of both controlling the flamboyance and to anchor his painting more firmly in the formal properties of its material. A contributing factor to his success is his strict insistence on using oil paint during a period when his contemporaries were relying on ubiquitous acrylics.

Bishop's method of painting is clearly his own. He first pours the oils onto a canvas placed flatly on the ground; then he tilts the stretcher so that the paint runs up to, and encroaches on, the painting's pictorial organisation, spilling over its delineations. After the paint has been applied in this manner, he reverts to a more traditional method of brushwork which allows him to control his surface, building up successive coats and paying meticulous attention to underpainting. The delicate tidal interaction between free-moving paint and the boundaries of pictorial organisation shows how Bishop plays off the gestural manner of abstract Expressionism against the more linear and structural approach of later painting.

Bishop distinguishes himself from his contemporaries by placing the crucial issue of ''automatism'' at the centre of his art. The notion of ''psychic automatism,'' introduced by Breton from his reading of Freud, is the process of purging the unconscious, a preoccupation found in virtually all art, music and literature in the twentieth century. Automatism plays a key role in Bishop's paintings because it answers for the mysterious disappearance in his subject matter, indeed in that of most modern art. Ironically, a close survey of his work reveals a new ''subject'' in the unravelled line of the classical figure.

Breton provided Bishop with the necessary technique to unveil the new ''subject.'' According to this method, the painter begins his picture with an automatic gesture in an effort to make contact with the world of his unconscious mind. First, his canvas is marked by the spontaneous impulse of the artist. Next, he uses this mark to prompt associations in his imagination so that the subject of the picture emerges in an embellishment of vivid imagery. Thus Bishop's subject seems to emanate from the interior of his painting.

In all of Bishop's paintings, his central preoccupation falls in his manipulation of rich and subtle tones of colour in a discreetly changed flow of liquid energy resulting in an intimate and withdrawn art. Collectively, these elements seem to hint at the perception of an underlying presence. The result, ironically, likens him to de Kooning, an artist primarily concerned with making and confronting an image. For Bishop, subject and image were one. Being an abstract expressionist in the 1950s meant working without apparent constraints whilst retaining something of a brand image that separated his work from another's. His art proved itself capable of remarkable refinement noting the marks made and the materials used.

—Carrie Barker

BLAKE, Peter (Thomas)

Nationality: British. **Born:** Dartford, Kent, 25 June 1932. **Education:** Studied at Gravesend Technical College, and Gravesend School of Art, Kent, 1946–51; and Royal College of Art, London, 1953–56. **Military Service:** Served in the Royal Air Force, 1951–53. **Family:** Married the artist Jann Haworth. **Career:** Painter and graphic artist, London, since 1956. **Awards:** Leverhulme Research Award, 1956; Guggenheim Painting Award, 1958; First Prize, *John Moores Exhibition,* Liverpool, 1961. **Agent:** Waddington Galleries, 2 Cork Street, London W1. **Address:** 8 Esmond Road, London W4, England.

Individual Exhibitions:

1962 Portal Gallery, London
1965 Robert Fraser Gallery, London
1967 *3 Painters: Peter Blake/Jim Dine/Richard Hamilton,* Midlands Arts Centre, Birmingham (travelled to Arts Council Gallery, Cambridge
1969 Bristol City Art Gallery
Portal Gallery, London
Robert Fraser Gallery, London
Leslie Waddington Prints, London
1970 Waddington Galleries, London
Ashgate Gallery, Farnham, Surrey
1971 Peter M. David Gallery, Minneapolis
1972 Waddington Galleries, London
1973 Stedelijk Museum, Amsterdam (travelled to the Gemeentemusuem, The Hague, and the Gemeentemuseum, Arnhem, Netherlands)
Kunstverein, Hamburg
Palais des Beaux-Arts, Brussels
1974 Hayward Gallery, London
Festival Gallery, Bath (with Jann Haworth)
1977 Waddington/Tooth Galleries, London
1979 Bohun Gallery, Henley-on-Thames, Oxfordshire

1980 Galleria Documenta, Turin
1983 Tate Gallery, London
Kestner-Gesellschaft, Hannover
Olympus Gallery, London
1984 Galerie Claude Bernard, Paris
2000 *Peter Blake: About Collage,* Tate Gallery, Liverpool

Selected Group Exhibitions:

1954 *Summer Exhibition,* Royal Academy of Art, London
1958 *5 Painters,* Institute of Contemporary Arts, London
1964 *Carnegie International,* Carnegie Institute, Pittsburgh (and 1967)
1969 *Pop Art,* Hayward Gallery, London
1970 *Contemporary British Art,* National Museum of Modern Art, Tokyo
1976 *Arte Inglese Oggi 1960–76,* Palazzo Reale, Milan
1977 *British Painting 1952–1977,* Royal Academy of Art, London
1980 *Prints of the 70's by 6 British Artists,* National Art Gallery, Wellington (toured New Zealand)
1981 *The Brotherhood of Ruralists,* Arnolfini Gallery, Bristol (toured the U.K.)
1988 *The British Picture,* L.A. Louver Gallery, Venice, California
Exhibition Road: Painters at the Royal College of Art, Royal College of Art, London
1991 *From Bacon to Now: The Outsider in British Figuration,* Palazzo Vecchio, Florence
1992 *The Painter in Glass,* Glynn Vivian Art Gallery, Swansea, Wales
1993 *The Portrait Now,* National Portrait Gallery, London
1994 *Absolut RCA,* Royal College of Art, London
1995 *Peter Blake, Patrick Caulfield, Howard Hodgkin: Paintings from the 60's and 70's,* Waddington Galleries, London
1997 *Brancusi to Beuys: Works from the Ted Power Collection,* Tate Gallery, London
The Lois Beurman Torf Print Collection for the University of Massachusetts, University Gallery, University of Massachusetts, Amherst
Essence of Humour, Crane Kalman Gallery, London
Hockney to Hodgkin: British Master Prints 1960–1980, New Orleans Museum of Art
Drawing Distinctions: Twentieth-century Drawings and Watercolours from the British Council Collection, University Art Museum/Pacific Film Archive, University of California at Berkeley
1999 *Signature Pieces: Contemporary British Prints and Multiples,* Alan Cristea Gallery, London
2000 *Painted Pictures,* Michael Hoppen Photography Gallery, London

Collections:

Arts Council of Great Britain, London; British Council, London; Tate Gallery, London; Victoria and Albert Museum, London; Whitworth Art Gallery, Manchester; Bristol City Art Gallery; Museum Boymans-van Beuningen, Rotterdam; Wallraf-Richartz Museum, Cologne; Baltimore Museum of Art; Museum of Modern Art, New York.

Publications:

By BLAKE: Books—*Alphabet: A Series of 26 Screenprints, 1991—Peter Blake,* London 1991. **Articles—**''Homage to Holbein'' in *Art Quarterly,* Autumn 1997; ''Wrestling: Painter Peter Blake Describes his Fascination with Wrestling'' in *Art Review* (London), vol. 45, June 1993; ''Meeting the Magician'' with Holly Johnson in *Modern Painters* (London), vol. 13, no. 2, Summer 2000.

On BLAKE: Books—*Peter Blake,* exhibition catalog, with test by Robert Melville, London 1965; *3 Painters: Peter Black/Jim Dine/Richard Hamilton,* exhibition catalog, with test by John English, Birmingham 1967; *Image as Language; Aspects of British Art 1950–1968* by Christopher Finch, London 1969; *Movements in Art since 1945* by Edward Lucie-Smith, London 1969; *Peter Blake,* exhibition catalog, with text by Roger Coleman, Bristol 1969; *Pop Art Redefined* by John Russell and Suzi Gablik, London 1969; *Pop Art* by Michael Compton, London 1970 *English Pop Art: Figurative Art since 1945* by Robert Melville, London 1971; *Peter Blake,* exhibition catalog, with text by Rainer Crone, Amsterdam 1973; *Peter Blake,* exhibition catalog, with text by Uwe M. Schneede, Hamburg 1973; *Prints of the 70's by 6 British Artists,* exhibition catalog, with text by Anne Kirker, Wellington 1980; *The Brotherhood of Ruralists* by Nicholas Usherwood, London 1981; *The British Picture,* exhibition catalog with essays by Marina Vaizey, Catherine Lampert and William Feaver, Venice, California 1988. **Articles—**''Going No Place with Peter Blake'' by Roger Kimball in *The New Criterion,* vol. 12, January 1994; ''In Profile: Peter Blake'' by David Lee in *Art Review,* vol. 48, October 1996; ''Blake's Progress'' by Geordie Greig in *Modern Painters* (London), vol. 9, Autumn 1996; ''Planes, Trains, Bathing Beauties, and Elvis'' by William Feaver in *Art News,* vol. 99, no. 4, April 2000.

* * *

The small panel surfaced with gold-leaf sheets never quite all in juxtaposition, the caparison-richness of which is also occasionally disturbed by small abrasions betraying undercoating, is in no way typical, however early its creation date, of the actual enduring character of the British painter Peter Blake and the essence of his works. ''Painted'' possibly as a Pop-art spoof, it was offered to a dealer in barter for a picture by a naive fantasist that had caught Blake's fancy.

Yet in a way this anecdote unveils the dichotomy that invades the spirit (itself hydra-headed) of this artist's talent and personalized brilliance.

In his day Blake has given a tinpot (I was tempted to say tinsel) glitter to Pop Art at a time when it was reaching its English zenith. Not necessarily goldplated it is true, but none the less buoyant as he was neatly painting pop-realist images in carefully arresting colours on plaques of metal (seemingly tin, but probably copper) so as to meet art half-way between deliberate naivety and the echo of the old metal-based ads that used once to adorn sites where they were allowed to be nailed up (many decades before Blake was born), while at the same moment he was underlining the abiding simplicity that is the beguiling factor of so much ''innocent'' art.

One of the earliest of his paintings to catch the attention of the public had for subject a much-bemedalized self-portrait (again rendered in super-real hones exactitude), but this along with the sheets of metal in no fashion could place any limit on his inventiveness and the extent to which it could progress. If each of these avenues, taken together or apart, suggested an extraordinary marriage between Pop and Naïve—not Naïve in its true Art sense of course, because here was a highly sophisticated and fully-trained artist—such a quaint circumstance was to be still further expanded in near 3-dimensional set-ups with his *furniture* (Blake has always taken exceptional pleasure in the point-of-sale straight-forwardness of children's toys), and perhaps even more so with his decorated doors and their incorporated nooks and crannies alive with pin-ups, graffiti, scrappy press-cuttings even—all the pathetic short-lived enthusiast desiderata of the ''with-it'' poor.

In style and manner Blake had a culture break-through to population millions and was able to speak in visual terms in a voice that was at once direct, without art complications, and ''popular.''

Comes the interim . . . Since the heady days of *Swinging Britain* the artist has cooled down and, in doing so, he has joined the ranks of approved British Artists, acquiring all the rights, respect and relevance such acceptance implies. Career success assured, the quality of his works, the infusions of ''reality'' into them, the spontaneous innuendos (paradoxically subtle yet obvious) are untrammelled. Blake and his gifts have not been dislocated; it is the Times and the People who are out of joint.

—Sheldon Williams

BLUME, Peter

Nationality: American. **Born:** Smorgon, Russia, 27 October 1906; immigrated to the United States, 1911: naturalized, 1919. **Education:** Brooklyn public schools, and at the Educational Alliance School of Art, New York, until 1921; studied at the Art Students League, and the Beaux-Arts Academy, New York, 1921–24. **Family:** Married Grace Douglas Craton in 1931. **Career:** Worked briefly for a jewelry firm and a lithographic and engraving company, New York, 1920. Independent painter since 1924: established studio on 13th Street, New York, and subsequently in Patterson, New York, 1925; travelled in New England, 1926–27, and in Pennsylvania and South Carolina, 1930; established and maintains studio in Sherman, Connecticut, since 1930; travelled in Italy, France, and England, 1932; commissioned by United States Government to paint murals for Post Offices in Geneva, New York and Cannonsburg, Pennsylvania, and by local government to paint mural for the Court House in Rome, Georgia, 1941; travelled in Mexico, 1949, and in Italy and Sicily, 1952, 1956. Artist-in-Residence, American Academy, Rome, 1956, 1962, 1973. **Awards:** Guggenheim Fellowship, 1932–1936; First Prize, *International Exhibition of Painting and Sculpture,* Carnegie Institute, Pittsburgh, 1934; Artists for Victory Prize, Museum of Modern Art, New York, 1942; National Institute of Arts and Letters Grant, 1947. Associate, National Academy of Design; Member, National Institute of Arts and Letters Grant, 1947. Associate, National Academy of Design; Member, National Institute of Arts and Letters. **Agent:** Terry Dintenfass Gallery, 50 West 57th Street, New York, New York 10019. **Died:** New Milford, Connecticut, 31 November 1992.

Individual Exhibitions:

1930 *Paintings,* Daniel Gallery, New York
1936 Julien Levy Galleries, New York
1941 The Downtown Gallery, New York
1947 The Downtown Gallery, New York
Durlacher Brothers Inc., New York
1949 Durlacher Brothers Inc., New York
1954 Durlacher Brothers Inc., New York
1958 Durlacher Brothers Inc., New York
1964 *Paintings and Drawings in Retrospect 1925–1964,* Currier Gallery of Art, Manchester, New Hampshire (travelled to the Wadsworth Atheneum, Hartford, Connecticut)
1968 Kennedy Galleries, New York
Recollections of the Flood and Related Works, Danenberg Gallery, New York
1970 Danenberg Gallery, New York
1975 *Bronzes about Venus,* Coe Kerr Gallery, New York
1976 *A Retrospective Exhibition,* Museum of Contemporary Art, Chicago
New Britain Museum, Connecticut (retrospective)
1980 *From the Metamorphoses: Recent Paintings and Drawings,* Terry Dintenfass Gallery, New York
1993 Terry Dintenfass Gallery, New York

Selected Group Exhibitions:

1933 *Century of Progress Exhibition I,* Art Institute of Chicago
1934 *Century of Progress Exhibition II,* Art Institute of Chicago
International Exhibition of Painting and Sculpture, Carnegie Institute, Pittsburgh
1938 *American Painting and Sculpture Annual,* Art Institute of Chicago
1991 *Painting a Place in America: Jewish Artists in New York 1900–1945—A Tribute to the Educational Alliance Art School,* Jewish Museum, New York

Collections:

Metropolitan Museum of Art, New York; Museum of Modern Art, New York; Whitney Museum, New York; Museum of Fine Arts, Boston; Williams College, Williamstown, Massachusetts; Fogg Art Museum, Harvard University, Cambridge, Massachusetts; Wadsworth Atheneum, Hartford, Connecticut; Newark Museum, New Jersey; Randolph-Macon College, Lynchburg, Virginia; Gallery of Fine Arts, Columbus, Ohio; The Art Institute of Chicago, Illinois.

Publications:

By BLUME: Articles—Statements in *Peter Blume: Recollections of the Flood and Related Works,* exhibition catalog, New York 1970; statement in *Peter Blume: A Retrospective Exhibition,* catalog, Chicago 1976; *Peter Blume: Paintings and Sculpture,* New York 1987.

On BLUME: Books—*Painting in America: The Story of 450 Years* by E. P. Richardson, New York 1956; *Modern Art and the New Past* by James Thrall Soby, Norman, Oklahoma 1957; *From Realism to Reality in Recent American Painting* by Virgil Barker, Lincoln, Nebraska 1959; *Mainstreams of Modern Art* by John Canaday, New York 1959; *Paintings in the 20th Century* by Werner Haftman, 2 vols., New York 1960; *A History of American Art* by Daniel M. Mendelowitz, New York 1961; *Art: U.S.A.: Now,* edited by Lee

Nordness, 2 vols., Lucerne 1962; *Peter Blume: Paintings and Drawings in Retrospect 1925–1964,* exhibition catalog, with an introduction by Charles E. Buckley, Manchester, New Hampshire 1964; *American Art since 1900: A Critical History* by Barbara Rose, New York, 1967; *Peter Blume,* exhibition catalog, with text by Frank Getlein, New York 1968; *Peter Blume: Recollections of the Flood and Related Works,* exhibition catalog, New York 1970; *Peter Blume: Bronzes about Venus,* exhibition catalog, with an introduction by Gordon Hendricks, New York 1974; *Peter Blume: A Retrospective Exhibition,* catalog, with text by Dennis Adrian, Chicago 1976; Peter Blume: ''From the Metamorphoses'': Recent Paintings and Drawings, exhibition catalog, with text by John Paul Driscoll, New York 1980; *Peter Blume,* by Frank Anderson Trapp, New York, 1987. **Articles—**''Letters from Charles Daniel to Peter Blume'' by Julie Mellby in *Archives of American Art Journal,* vol. 33, no. 1, 1993; ''New England: Papers and Documents Received'' by Robert F. Brown in *Archives of American Art Journal,* vol. 33, no. 4, 1993; ''Slicing and Dionysian: Peter Blume's Vegetable Dinner'' by Mark Andrew White in *American Art,* vol. 14, no. 1, Spring 2000.

* * *

During the 1930s Peter Blume produced four major paintings, and it is for these Magic Realist works that he is still best known. ''Parade'' (1930), ''South of Scranton'' (1931), ''Light of the World'' (1932) and ''The Eternal City'' (1934–37) invest contemporary scenes with a bizarre allegorical element of surreality. They are painted with a highly precise, meticulously detailed technique, using smooth contours and clear outlines, which is related with the illusionistic surrealism of Dali. Blume's earlier work had been closer to the American Precisionist vein, and his subsequent painting continued to be characterized by a detailed preparation and long term experimentation carried on with numerous sketches. Blume pursues complicated compositional schema and dramatically heightened imagery to portray humanity's struggles with a hostile world. The narrative element is unabashedly present in his works, and reality tends toward the horror/science fiction levels, especially those types of the genres which make the real into the animistic.

Most of Blume's paintings are on a rather generalized level, such as that in ''Light of the World'' (1932) which is a critical statement about the new technology as symbolized in the foreground and about the dark, church dominated past as depicted in the background. ''The Eternal City'' is Blume's most overtly political painting, directly portraying the ruthless menace of Fascism with an attitude of passionate hostility and very specific protest. In a wildly perverse and complicated setting which combines ancient Roman ruins with contemporary Roman ruins, the jack-in-the-box head of a green faced Mussolini with scowling red lips arises on his accordion-pleated ''body.'' It is purposefully dissonant visualization of the perversities of Italian Fascism, including two people looking toward the grotesque effigy of their leader as they come out of a primitive bomb shelter. Blume spent nearly four years exclusively developing this picture, whose combination of powerful human drama and highly skilled technique shows him at his best level of pictorial satire.

After ''The Eternal City,'' Blume concentrated on more general human themes of struggle, always pursuing the long, slow route which produces fastidiously composed and executed paintings, in a relatively small number because each is the result of sustained periods of preparation. ''The Rock'' (1948) becomes the symbol of life and death, with man before it as if in judgment. ''Man of Sorrows'' (1951) communicates the sufferings of war.

Subsequent paintings portray Blume's more and more fervent involvement with Quattrocento techniques, and, in works such as ''Hadrian's Villa'' (1957), he lapses dangerously into dependence on the past, losing much of the potent satirical edge he had achieved earlier and remaining more in the realm of the mundane despite his always thoughtfully well-composed execution. This kind of prosaic pastorale quality continued to plague Blume's works, even in his most ambitious compositions such as ''Recollection of the Flood'' (1967) which, although it is skillfully composed in every detail, remains more sentimental than socially relevant, more an exercise in formal prowess than a conveyor of the human struggle. Perhaps there is a certain frustration underlying Blume's move to sculpture in the early 1970s, but his series of ''Bronzes About Venus'' remain virtuoso displays of the classic Greek theme, refined and elegant, but beneath the level of Blume's achievements of earlier times.

—Barbara Cavaliere

BOCHNER, Mel

Nationality: American. **Born** in Pittsburgh, Pennsylvania, in 1940. **Education:** Studied painting and philosophy at the Carnegie Institute of Technology, Pittsburgh, B.F.A. 1962. Now lives and works in New York. Instructor, School of Visual Arts, New York, since 1965. **Awards:** Recipient of Academic Institution Award for Art, 1990. **Agent:** c/o Sonnabend Gallery, 420 West Broadway, New York, New York 10012.

Individual Exhibitions:

1966 Visual Arts Gallery, New York
1968 Galerie Konrad Fischer, Dusseldorf
Bykert Gallery, New York
1969 Galerie Heiner Friedrich, Munich
Ace Gallery, Los Angeles
Yale University, New Haven, Connecticut
1970 Art and Project, Amsterdam
Galleria Sperone, Turin
Galleria Toselli, Milan
1971 112 Green Street Gallery, New York
University of Rhode Island, Kingston
Centro de Arte y Communication, Buenos Aires
Museum of Modern Art, New York
1972 Galerie Sonnabend, Paris
Sonnabend Gallery, New York
Lisson Gallery, London
Hartford Art School, Connecticut
Galerie MTL, Brussels
Galleria Bonomo, Bari, Italy
Galleria Toselli, Milan
1973 Galerie Sonnabend, Paris
Sonnabend Gallery, New York
1974 Galerie Sonnabend, Paris
Galleria Schema, Florence
University of California Art Museum, Berkeley
1975 Sonnabend Gallery, New York

Galerie Ricke, Cologne
1976 Sonnabend Gallery, New York
Number and Shape, Baltimore Museum of Art
1977 Bernier Gallery, Athens
Acconci/Bochner/LeVa, Sonnabend Gallery, New York
1978 Sonnabend Gallery, New York
Daniel Weinberg Gallery, San Francisco
Galleria Schema, Milan
Galleria Schema, Florence
Gallerie Sonnabend, Paris
1979 Galerie Art in Progress, Dusseldorf
1980 Sonnabend Gallery, New York
Mel Bochner/Richard Serra, Massachusetts Institute of Technology, Cambridge
1981 Texas Gallery, Houston
Daniel Weinberg Gallery, San Francisco
1982 Sonnabend Gallery, New York
Centre de Creation Artistique, Abbaye de Senanque, Gordes, France
Med a Mothi Galerie, Montpellier, France
1983 Sonnabend Gallery, New York
Yarlow/Salzman Gallery, Toronto
Daniel Weinberg Gallery, Los Angeles
Pace Editions, New York
Carol Taylor Gallery, Dallas, Texas
1984 Roger Ramsay Gallery, Chicago
1985 Sonnabend Gallery, New York
Carnegie-Mellon University, Pittsburgh
1988 *Mel Bochner: Drawings,* David Nolan Gallery, New York (catalog)
1990 Kornblatt Gallery, Washington, D.C.
David Nolan Gallery, New York
Mel Bochner: Drawings, Galerie Jahn und Fusban, Munich (catalog)
1991 SteinGladstone Gallery, New York
1994 Sonnabend Gallery, New York
1995 *Mel Bochner: Handpainted, Engraved, and Embossed Monoprints,* Betsy Senior Gallery, New York
1996 *Mel Bochner: Thought Made Visible 1966–1973,* Yale University Art Gallery, New Haven (international traveling retrospective) (catalog)
Palais des Beaux-Arts, Brussels
1998 *Working Drawings and Other Visible Things on Paper Not Necessarily Meant to Be Viewed as Art,* Drawing Center, New York
Printed Works, Betsy Senior Gallery
Drawings 1966–1973, Lawrence Markey Gallery (catalog)

Selected Group Exhibitions:

1970 *Information,* Museum of Modern Art, New York
1974 *Art and Image in Recent Art,* Art Institute of Chicago
1975 *Bochner/LeVa/Rochburne/Tuttle,* Contemporary Arts Center, Cincinnati, Ohio
1976 *Drawing Now,* Museum of Modern Art, New York
1977 *Whitney Biennale,* Whitney Museum, New York
1978 *Contemporary Drawing/New York,* University of California Museum, Santa Barbara
1979 *The Decade in Review,* Whitney Museum, New York
1981 *Murs,*Centre Georges Pompidou, Paris
1983 *Minimalism to Expressionism,* Whitney Museum, New York
1985 *New Abstraction,* Milwaukee Art Museum, Wisconsin
1988 *The Sonnabend Collection: 25 Years of Selection and Activity by Ileana and Michael Sonnabend,* Cenre d'Arts Plastiques Contemporains de Bordeaux, France (catalog)
1989 *Lines and Geometry: Martin Ball, Mel Bochner, Karl Heinz Strohle,* Ricky Renier Gallery, Chicago (catalog)
1990 *American Drawing in the 1980s,* Graphische Sammlung Albertina, Vienna (catalog)
1996 *Drawing on Chance: Selections from the Collection,* Museum of Modern Art, New York (catalog)
New Art on Paper, Philadelphia Museum of Art (catalog)
1997 *Laying Low,* Kunstnernes Hus, Oslo
The Magic of Number in the Art of the 20th Century, Staatsgalerie Stuttgart (catalog)
1999 *Circa 1968,* Serralves Museum of Contemporary Art, Oporto, Portugal

Collections:

Los Angeles County Museum of Art; Musée National d'Art Moderne, Paris; Whitney Museum of American Art, New York.

Publications:

By BOCHNER: Books—*Working Drawings and Other Visible Things on Paper,* New York 1966; *The Singer Notes,* New York 1968; *10 Misunderstandings (A Theory of Photography),* New York 1970; *Notes on Theory,* Kingston, Rhode Island 1971; *11 Excerpts,* Paris 1972; *Primer,* Milan 1973; *(Toward) Axiom of Indifference,* New York 1975. **Articles—**''Less Is Less (for Dan Flavin)'' in *Art and Artists* (London), 1966; ''Primary Structures'' in *Art Magazine* (New York), June 1966; ''Domain of the Great Bear (Hayden Planetarium)'' in *Art Voices* (New York), Summer 1966; ''Art in Process'' in *Arts* (New York), October 1966; ''The Beach Boys—100%'' in *Arts Magazine* (New York), March 1967; ''Serial Art (Systems: Solipsism)'' in *Arts Magazine* (New York), Summer 1967, reprinted in *Minimal Art,* edited by Gregory Battcock, New York 1968; ''The Serial Attitude'' in *Artforum* (New York), December 1967; ''Compilation for Robert Mangold'' in *Art International* (Lugano), April 1968; ''Alphaville, Godard's Apocalypse'' in *Art International* (New York), May 1968; ''7 Discrete Tiers'' in *Aspen Magazine* (Colorado), June 1968; ''Background Is Not the Margin'' in *Art in Process* (New York), no. 4, 1969; ''No Thought Exists . . .'' in *Arts Magazine* (New York), April 1970; ''Excerpts from Speculation'' in *Artforum* (New York), May 1970; ''3 Conditions'' in *Art and Project Bulletin 27* (Amsterdam), September 1970; ''10 Hypotheses de Travail'' in *VH* (Paris), Fall 1970; ''Bullshit'' in *Artforum* (New York), October 1970; ''Mental Exercise: No.1 Counting'' in *Data* (Milan), February 1972; ''Concerning the Art of Dorothea Rockburne'' in *Artforum* (New York), March 1972; ''Parenthetical Reflections on 5 Earlier Statements'' in *Flash Art* (Milan), May 1972 and in *Arts Magazine* (New York), Summer 1972; statement in *Some Recent American Art,* exhibition catalog, by Jennifer Licht, New York 1973; ''Interview,'' with L. Haller, in *Flash Art* (Milan), June 1973; ''Book Review'' in *Artforum* (New York), June 1973; ''On Malevich,'' interview with John Coplans, in *Artforum* (New York), June 1974; ''Statement on My Prints'' in *Prints,* exhibition catalog, Toronto 1975; interview with Paul Cummings in *Drawing,* vol. 10, no. 1, May-June 1988;

interview with Frederic Valabregue in *Artefactum,* vol. 5, no. 24, June-August 1988; ''Out of Context: Mel Bochner'' edited by Melissa Marks in *Tema Celeste,* vol. 7, no. 3, July-September 1989; ''Statement on Abstraction'' in *Tema Celeste,* Autumn 1991; interview with James Meyer in *Flash Art (International Edition),* no. 177, Summer 1994; interview in *Art Press,* Special Issue, no. 17, 1996. **Films**—*Walking a Straight Line Through Grand Central Station,* 1965; *NYC Windows,* 1965; *Dorothea in 15 Positions Stasis,* 1970.

On BOCHNER: Books—*Mel Bochner,* exhibition catalog, Milan 1971; *Mel Bochner,* exhibition catalog, Buenos Aires 1972; *Line as Language: 6 Artists Draw,* exhibition catalog, by Rosalind Krauss, Princeton, New Jersey 1974; *Mel Bochner/Barry LeVa/Dorothea Rockburne/Richard Tuttle,* exhibition catalog, Cincinnati, Ohio 1975; *Drawing Now,* exhibition catalog, by Berenice Rose, New York 1976; *Mel Bochner: Number and Shape,* exhibition catalog, by Brenda Richardson, Baltimore 1976; *Mel Bochner 1973–1985,* exhibition catalog, Pittsburgh 1985. **Articles**—''Reverse Continuity: The Prints of Mel Bochner'' by Barry Schwabsky in *The Print Collector's Newsletter,* vol. 25, July/August 1994. **Films**—*Mel Bochner: Language Is Not Transparent* by Richard Field and Yve Alain Bois, 1997.

* * *

The trajectory of Mel Bochner's artistic practice—from his 'floor sculptures' of the sixties and seventies, which explored issues of framing, context, and function, to the painterly geometric abstractions he has created since the early eighties—seems to confound the neat critical oppositions by which most contemporary art is categorized and interpreted. As an artist who appears to have engaged in both conceptual and formalist practice, and whose works might be described variously as analytic or expressionist, Bochner has used seemingly disparate means to explore concerns that have in fact remained consistent. His shifting presentation does not represent a kind of postmodernist commentary on signification or style, rather, it is the result of what the artist has called ''a kind of research based on the idea of bracketing and *unbracketing*. . . . When you bracket you set something aside, you don't eliminate it.'' He states, ''When you recognize that my work is an analytic attempt to rethink painting's functions and meanings, you realize that it is all one continuous investigation.''

Bochner's early work poked holes in Greenberg's formalist theory of painting as a bounded and pure activity, whose meaning was inextricably derived from process and solely dependent upon its outward form. *Theory of Painting,* 1969, consists of four large, roughly rectangular clusters of newspapers on a gallery floor, portions of which have been masked off and then sprayed with blue spray paint. In two of these, the newspapers have been arranged so as to form neat rectangles. One has a spray painted blue rectangular field within it—a sort of debased Albers or Reinhardt. In the other, the spray paint defines a series of notched, irregular geometric shapes. The remaining two ''paintings'' have irregular edges achieved by the more haphazard placement of the newspapers. In one, the blue spray painted rectangle neatly imposed on the sheets of newspaper contrasts with their irregular outer edge. In the other, smaller blue rectangles abound on the newspaper pages, which have been placed on the floor at diagonals to the overall rectangular shape of the gallery.

Theory of Painting clearly owes much to a hybrid of Minimalist and Conceptualist strategies—the use of common, non-art materials, the serial repetition of geometric forms, the emphasis on procedure rather than esthetics—of which Bochner himself was one of the main formulators. More specifically, the artist's wry comment on the Modernist grid here addresses our received notions of boundaries and frames, both those that define the artwork itself, and those that define our perception and experience of the artwork. With its playful inversions of order and instability, rationality and arbitrariness, inside and outside, the transcendent and the commonplace, *Theory of Painting* subverts our need to have artworks affirm fixed definitions and prescribed categories. Bochner wrote in 1970, ''Boundaries. . . are only the fabrication of our desire to detect them. . . a tradeoff between seeing something and wanting to enclose it.''

Axiom of Indifference, from 1973, addresses the phenomenology of boundaries and chance more directly. Four small rectangles on the gallery floor have been taped off and then labeled ''Some Are Not In,'' ''Some Are In,'' ''All Are Not In,'' and ''All Are In,'' respectively. Coins appear scattered within or without the taped boundaries, accordingly, like a perverse version of the school yard coin toss. The work's title suggests that the random workings of chance are ineluctable, beyond human control, but its visual appearance, the labeled boxes on the floor, attests to our persistent need to give events meaning through processes of ordering, naming, and shaping. According to Bochner, the piece addresses questions ''of how language and space intersect.'' The work carries implications of how rules of inclusion and exclusion operate in any number of systems—social, scientific, and philosophical. *Which* are indifferent or intractable, the phenomena that refuse to cooperate with the limitations imposed by human categories, or the boundaries themselves? Bochner thus posits the act of ''reframing'' to include the artwork's relationship to the larger psychological and physical space that contains it.

By the mid-eighties Bochner's examination of the conditions by which a work of art exists led him to painting itself. He wrote: ''How does mental space intersect with physical objects? The issue now is how to put the knowledge gained from earlier investigations back into the language of art. Not to make paintings-about-painting but to *make* paintings. Can a critical language be embedded inside a painting? Can ideas be infected by experience? And if they can. . . what will the paintings look like?'' In Saturn, a shaped canvas from 1983, thick, layered lines of white create a kind of geometric, crystalline scaffolding that seems to project forward in space, even as the underlying pentimenti of black lines and the painting's agitated, red-brown ground imply a deep spatial recession. Here Bochner's investigation of the viability of the art object, its questionable autonomy as it relates to physical and mental space, moves from the conceptual to the perceptual. The illusionism of his shifted gridded planes, with their simultaneous movement forward and back, occurs on a canvas that is in actuality flat. Further complicating our spatial reading of the painting is the fact that the canvas is shaped, which underscores its presence as a concrete physical object, rather than the traditional 'window' into space. The painting is thus a bound record of the artist's mental and physical processes played out in time, and a contradiction of those processes, a static, flat object in real space.

Domain, a large oil on canvas from 1987, is installed so that its two panels intersect in the corner of the gallery. Here again, Bochner's gestural application of paint to depict simple geometrical cubes turning in a densely articulated space—his intuited geometry, is offset by the cool logic of the painting's placement at the right angle intersection created by the actual cube of the gallery space. Spatial illusionism, painting's *lingua franca,* is thus posited and then deemed ultimately inaccessible. Bochner has stated, ''The pictorialization of space and the way in which it's outside experience is, for me, equivalent to the way in which one's mind is inaccessible. Illusionism represents the irrational, the place where logic surrenders. Only in painting have I been able to foreground these ideas.''

In recent years, Bochner has exhibited his large abstract paintings and his 'floor sculptures' together. New conceptual pieces, such as *5 x 4,* from 1993, continue Bochner's exploration of art as a set of functions derived from a series of interrelationships. In each of four chalk circles inscribed on the floor, Bochner has placed five hunks of blue glass slag, which are in turn inscribed with chalk to create different numerical equations each totaling five: four hunks of glass in one circle, plus one hunk of glass in another, or three hunks of glass in one circle and two in another, etc. Here Bochner's ''framing'' of elements, his circles within circles, once again allows for the assignment of meaning. Works such as *5 x 4* are juxtaposed with paintings like *Optic Chiasma,* from 1992–3, which consists of four panels arranged around a central empty square of wall. The panels themselves depict Bochner's familiar cubes tumbling forward and back in space against perspectival grids. This deep illusionism is foiled by the concrete presence of the wall in the piece's center, precisely where, in Renaissance one-point perspective, the vanishing point would occur. Instead, it is real space that becomes enclosed by imaginary space. In both his painting and floor pieces, Bochner's framing devices, in concrete and formal terms, ''suggest that the problem of how 'vision is structured' has everything to do with how we choose to define what we are looking at.'' (Jan Avigkos, *Artforum,* March 1994). As such, Bochner's ''theory of boundaries'' collapses the distinctions between visual modes of inquiry usually deemed antithetical in contemporary theory and practice, forcing us to reclaim and reintegrate that which is 'bracketed out' by our accepted habits of perception.

—Dorothy Valakos

Continuing to play with perceptions and boundaries, Bochner's work has sustained these themes of measurement and geometry. His ''Counting and Measuring Pieces'' have been on-going since the 1960s, and have now been translated onto canvas. Bochner has created a painterly language that is both critical and formally restrained—the result of his exploration, begun in the 1980s, into the possibility of simply *making.* Bringing together minimalist formalism and conceptual process has resulted in a recent body of work entitled simply *Measurement* from 2001. These rectangular, monochrome red canvases are conceptualized through the introduction of a consistent 12'' square. Sometimes removed completely from the canvas, leaving a void, or consisting of the 12'' square itself in various configurations, the text ''12"'' with arrows remains the same. Like chalk on a building site, these works reference space and construction, but also real and virtual space, a methodology of how we might relate to the world around us.

This desire to document our surroundings, particularly that which is both unquantifiable and seemingly mundane, has been a preoccupation for Bochner since his first major piece in 1966: *Working Drawings and Other Things on Paper Not Necessarily Meant to Be Viewed as Art.* As this work experiences a revival, being both exhibited and published in 1997 and 1998 respectively, Bochner's entire body of work is undergoing a re-evaluation, particularly as we assess how the first artwork made with a Xerox machine may translate in our digital age. As we disseminate vast bodies of information over the Internet, have the ability to precisely measure, compute, and quantify seemingly everything, Bochner's work slows us down as we realize the appeal of uncertainty, the fine line between order and disorder.

—Carly Butler

BOETTI, Alighiero E.

Nationality: Italian. **Born:** Turin, 16 December 1940. **Family:** Married Anne Marie Sauzeau; children: Matteo and Agata. **Career:** Independent artist, Turin, 1965–72, and in Rome since 1972. Established the ''One Hotel,'' Kabul, Afghanistan, 1971–73. **Agent:** Galleria Christian Stein, Via Lazzaretto 15, 20124 Milan. **Died:** Of brain cancer, Rome, 24 April 1994.

Individual Exhibitions:

1967 Galleria Christian Stein, Turin
Galleria La Bertesca, Turin
1968 Galleria De Nieuborg, Milan
Galleria Sperone, Turin
Galleria Christian Stein, Turin
1970 Galleria Toselli, Milan
Galleria Acme, Brescia, Italy
Aktionsraum I, Munich
1971 Galerie Konrad Fischer, Dusseldorf
Galleria Sperone, Turin
1972 Galleria Toselli, Milan
1973 Galleria Marilena Bonomo, Bari, Italy
John Weber Gallery, New York
Galleria Sperone-Fischer, Rome
Galerie MTL, Brussels
Art and Project, Amsterdam
Galleria Toselli, Milan
1974 Kunstmuseum, Lucerne
Galleria Sperone, Turin
1975 John Weber Gallery, New York
Galerie Annemarie Verna, Zurich
Galleria Sperone, Rome
Galleria Pascuala Trioprio, Naples
Galleria Area, Florence
Zwei Area Galerie, Munich
Saman Gallery, Genoa
1976 Studio Marconi, Milan
Galleria Lia Rumma, Naples
Galleria d'Alessandro Ferranti, Rome
Galleria Banco, Brescia, Italy
1977 Galleria Marlborough, Rome
Galleria dell'Ariete, Milan
Centre d'Art Contemporain, Geneva
Galerie Annemarie Verna, Zurich
1978 Kunsthalle, Basle
Galleria Christian Stein, Turin
Galleria Mario Diacono, Bologna
Galerie Paul Maenz, Cologne

Galleria il Cortile, Rome
Galleria Giuliana de Crescenzo, Rome
1979 Chiostro di Voltorre, Gavirate, Italy
1980 Salvatore Ala Gallery, New York
Art Agency Gallery, Tokyo
Galleria Banco, Brescia, Italy
1981 Galerie Chantal Crousel, Paris
Galleria LP220, Turin (twice)
Galleria Banco, Brescia, Italy
1982 Galleria Mario Diacono, Rome
Galerie Annemarie Verna, Zurich
Galleria Franco Toselli, Milan
1983 Galleria Mario Pieroni, Rome
Galleria LP 220, Turin
Galleria Giorgio Persano, Turin
Galleria Enzo Cannaviello, Milan
1984 Faculty of Architecture, University of Rome
Galerie Eric Franck, Geneva
Galleria LP 220, Turin
John Weber Gallery, New York
Pinacoteca di Ravenna, Italy
1985 Galleria Il Cortile, Rome
Galleria Marilena Bonomo, Bari, Italy
Galleria Pero, Miozawo, Italy
Galleria Chisel, Genova
1986 Le Nouveau Musée, Lyon, France
Galerie Pietro Sparta, Chagny, France
Michael Klein Inc., Amsterdam
Galerie Susan Wyss, Zurich
Van Abbemuseum, Eindhoven, Netherlands
Villa Arson, Nice, France
1987 Galleria Lucio Amelio, Naples
Galleria Christian Stein, Milan
Galleria Sergio Casoli, Milan
Galleria Alessandra Bonomo, Rome
1989 Toselli Gallery, Milan
1990 Esso Gallery, New York
1995 Kunstverein, Bonn
1999 Esso Gallery, New York
Laure Genillard Gallery, London
Galerie Artra, Milan
2000 Whitechapel Art Gallery, London

Selected Group Exhibitions:

1967 *Arte Povera,* Galleria La Bertesca, Genoa (toured Italy)
1968 *Prospect 68,* Städtische Kunsthalle, Dusseldorf (and *Prospect 69)*
1969 *When Attitudes Become Form,* Kunsthalle, Berne (toured Europe)
1970 *Conceptual Art/Arte Povera/Land Art,* Galleria Civica d'Arte Moderna, Turin
1972 *Documenta 5,* Kassel, West Germany
1974 *8 Contemporary Artists,* Museum of Modern Art, New York
1978 *La Traccia del Racconto,* Villa Comunale Ormond, San Remo, Italy
1981 *Identité Italienne,* Centre Georges Pompidou, Paris
1984 *Il Modo Italiano,* California State University, Northbridge
1987 *Arte Povera,* Galerie Durand Dessert, Paris
1995 *Worlds Envisioned,* Dia Gallery, New York

Collections:

Museo Sperimentale, Turin: Galleria Civica d'Arte Moderna, Turin; Stedelijk Museum, Amsterdam; Museum of Modern Art, New York.

Publications:

By BOETTI: Books—*Insicuro Noncurante,* Genoa 1976; *Classifying the Thousand Longest Rivers in the World,* with Anne Sauzeau Boetti, Rome 1977; *Alighiero Boetti,* exhibition catalog, with Guido Fuaga, Rome 1977; *Alighiero & Boetti,* exhibition catalog, Milan 1979; *Da uno a dieci,* edited by Rosellina Archinto, Milan 1980.

On BOETTI: Books—*Alighiero Boetti,* exhibition catalog, with texts by Henry Martin, Germano Celant and Tomasso Trini, Turin 1967; *Nuove Dimensioni della Scultura* by Udo Kultermann, Milan 1968; *7th Paris Biennale: Italy,* edited by Archille Bonito Oliva, Rome 1971; *Documenta 5: Befragung der Realität,* edited by Harald Szemann and others, Kassel, West Germany 1972; *Art Annual 73–74,* edited by Willem Sandberg, Cologne 1973; *6 Years: The Dematerialization of the Art Object* by Lucy R. Lippard, New York 1973; *8 Contemporary Artists,* exhibition catalog, New York 1974; *Alighiero E. Boetti,* exhibition catalog, with text by Jean-Christophe Ammann, Lucerne 1974; *Segni e disegni: Alighiero e Boetti 1976,* exhibition catalog, Rome 1977; *Alighiero Boetti, La festa dell'immaginario visivo,* exhibition catalog, edited by Tommaso Trini, Gavirate 1979; *Boetti,* exhibition catalog, edited by Alberto Boatto, Ravenna 1984. **Articles**—''Toselli Gallery, Milan; Exhibit'' by Shaun Caley in *Flash Art International* (Milan), no. 148, October 1989; ''Obituary'' in *Art in America,* vol. 82, June 1994; ''Alighiero e Boetti & Frédéric Bruly Bouabré: Dia Center for the Arts, New York; Exhibit'' by Robert Farris Thompson, vol. 33, March 1995; ''Alighiero e Boetti'' by Lisa Panzera in *Art News,* vol. 94, January 1995; ''Worlds Envisioned'' by Michael Oren in *Third Text,* no. 33, Winter 1995–1996; ''Alighiero e Boetti and Frederic Bruly Bouabre'' by Robert Farris Thompson in *Artforum International,* vol. 33, March 1995; ''Alighiero E. Boetti'' by Barry Schwabsky in *Artforum International,* vol. 36, no. 9, May 1998; ''Alighiero e Boetti; Claudia Losi: Galerie Artra, Milan'' by Gabi Scardi in *Art Press* (Paris), no. 246, May 1999; ''Alighiero e Boetti: Whitechapel Art Gallery, Laure Genillard Gallery'' by Nina Mehta in *Art Monthly* (London), no. 231, November 1999; ''Legnetti e fasci: Alighiero e Boetti'' by Dorian Ker in *Third Text* (Abingdon), no. 49, Winter 1999–2000; ''London, Oxford and Halifax: Post-war Italian Art'' by Mark Francis in *The Burlington Magazine* (London), vol. 142, no. 1162, January 2000; ''Alighiero e Boetti: Whitechapel Art Gallery, London'' by Barry Schwabsky, in *Artforum International,* vol. 38, no. 6, February 2000; ''Alighiero e Boetti: Esso Gallery, New York'' by Jonathan Goodman in *Art On Paper* (New York), vol. 4, no. 5, May–June 2000.

* * *

In 1969 Alighiero Boetti produced his ''Little Traced Squares,'' a work which epitomizes his basic principles as an artist. Here he has taken a sheet of paper and traced on it, in pencil, a series of squares, thereby giving us an elemental situation which invites an endless series of interpretations, each with its own formal effect.

In all of his work Boetti uses this basic device of a minimalist whole with functional parts. Each work contains a secret, but a secret which is full of mysteries and possibilities. He has given us ''Ping Pong,'' two signs placed close to each other which light up in turn and read, first ''ping,'' then ''pong.'' The spaces opened up by such works permit the perception of different units which are infinitely suggestive; and his works also set up elaborate cross-references among themselves which we are meant to recognize.

Different rhythms, gestures, repetitions, deliberate artifice—all of these are the basic elements of Boetti's experiments, and each work is designed to reflect a certain kind of mental operation or thought-process; for him art is really the manifestation of these processes.

In some instances the results are analytical and follow the pattern of elementary mathematical operations. This is the case, for example, with his ''Alternating From 1 to 100'' (1970) and ''The Four Operations'' (1980), in which the play of numbers and letters is reduced to a minimum: the end result is always the same, whether the process involved is addition, subtraction or multiplication. In other works—''Producing the World,'' for example, or ''Other and Disorder''—he suggests an underlying creative, cosmic force. The basic elements remain the same but they now contain a much broader range of implications.

Recently Boetti has perfected a technique which synthesizes his earlier, more abstract concerns with a new regard for colour and subject matter. By incorporating bits of pre-existing objects (coins, stamps, and so forth) he has produced collages which give us a new, expressive symbolic language.

—Roberto G. Lambarelli

BOEZEM, Marinus

Nationality: Dutch. **Born:** Leerdam, 28 January 1934. **Education:** Attended the Akademie Artibus, Utrecht; Vrije Akademie, The Hague. **Family:** Married Maria-Rosa Busato in 1966; daughter: Natasja. **Career:** Professor of art, architecture section, Technical University of Delft, since 1979. **Address:** Molenwater 125, 4331 SG Middelburg, Holland, The Netherlands.

Individual Exhibitions:

1964 *Hommage à Marilyn Monroe,* Galerie de Ruif, Leiden, Netherlands
Galerie Punt 31, Dordrecht, Netherlands (with Jan van Munster)
1965 Galerie 845, Amsterdam (with Jan van Munster)
Dromedaris, Enkhuizen, Netherlands (with Jan van Munster)
1968 *Air Environment* Galerie Swart, Amsterdam
Boezem/Van Elk, Galleria d'Arte la Nuova Loggia, Bologna (with Ger Van Elk)
1969 *Korenveld,* Kunstkring, Rotterdam (with Ger Van Elk)
1970 Studium Generale, Economics High School, Rotterdam
Galleria Lucio Amelio, Naples
Art and Project, Amsterdam
Boezem/Panamarenko, Stedelijk Van Abbemuseum, Eindhoven, Netherlands
1971 Yellow Now Gallery, Liège, Belgium
1975 Galerie Het Badhuis, Gorinchem, Netherlands
1976 Gomeentemuseum, The Hague
1978 Galerie Media, Neuchâtel, Switzerland
Art Fair, Bologna
Multi Art Points, Amsterdam
Galleria Ferrari, Verona
1979 *Space Sculptures,* De Vleeshal, Middelburg, Netherlands
1980 Kunstcentrum Het Badhuis, Gorinchem, Netherlands
1981 Galerie Media, Neuchâtel, Switzerland
1982 Provinciaal Museum, Hasselt, Belgium
De Vleeshal, Middelburg, Netherlands
Musée Grenoble, France
De Keus van de Kunstenaar, Haags Gemeentemuseum, The Hague, Netherlands
1983 *Toren-Project,* at the *Festival De Stad,* Armheim, Netherlands
Galerie Media, Neuchatel, Switzerland
1984 Galerie Muller-Roth, Stuttgart
1985 Galerie Peter van Beveren, Rotterdam
Anthony Reynolds Gallery, London
Galerie Waalkens, Finsterwolde, Netherlands
1986 Galerie Muller-Roth, Stuttgart
1987 Wilhelm-Hack-Museum, Ludwigshafen, Germany
1988 Musée d'Art Contemporain, Lyon
1989 Museum de Beijerd, Breda, Holland
Degli Uccelli, De Vleeshal, Middelburg, Netherlands
XX Bienal de Sao Paolo, Sao Paolo
Reflection 1/2/3, Chapelle des Carmelites, Toulouse
1991 Ram Galerie, Rotterdam
Museum voor Hedendaagse Kunst, Ostende, Belgium
1992 Galerie Langer Fain, Paris
1993 Aleph, Almere, Holland
Corcoran Gallery of Art, Washington, D.C.
Kunstvereniging Diepenheim, Diepenheim, Netherlands
Green Cathedral, Differentes Natures, La Défense, Paris
1995 *Tectona Grandis,* Provinciaal Museum Hassetl, Belgium
1996 Ram galerie, Rotterdam, Netherlands
2001 *Panorama—Via Aurelia Antica,* Chateau-Gontier, France

Selected Group Exhibitions:

1968 *Les Structures Gonflables,* Musée d'Art Moderne de la Ville, Paris
1969 *When Attitudes Become Form,* Kunsthalle, Berne
1970 *Tokyo Biennale '70: Between Man and Matter,* Biennale, Metropolitan Museum of Modern Art, Tokyo (travelled to the Kyoto Municipal Art Museum, and the Aichi Prefectural Art Gallery, Nagoya)
1979 *Photography als Kunst 1879–1979, Kunsts als Photography, 1949–1979,* Museum des Jahrhunderts, Vienna (travelled to Innsbruck, Linz)
1981 *Contemporary Art from the Netherlands,* Museum of Contempory Art, Chicago (travelled to the Brooklyn Museum, New York; Little Rock Museum, Arkansas, La Jolla Museum, California; and the Art Gallery of Ontario, Toronto)

1983 *Ruimtelijk Werk,* Gemeentemuseum, Arnhem, Netherlands
1986 *Tu es Pierre,* Fonds Regional d'Art Contemporain, Limoges, France
1987 *Flags of 12 Artists,* Musée d'Art et d'Hisoire, Geneva
1988 *Zeitlos,* Hambrger Bahnhof, Berlin
1990 *National Garden Festival,* Gateshead, England
1991 *Kunst und Kanal,* Wettbewerb zur Markierung der Europaischen Wasserscheidung, Nuremberg, Germany
1993 *Differentes Natures,* La Défense, Paris
1995 *Paris Ville Lumiere, Projects d'Artistes pour l'espace public Parisien,* Espace Electra, Paris
Insomnie, Le Domaine de Kerhguehennec, Centre d'art contemporain, Bignan, France
1997 *De Verborgen Stad,* De Vleeshal, Middelburg, Netherlands
1998 *Waves Breaking on the Shore: Ad Dekkers in his Time,* Stedelijk Museum, Amsterdam
The Inflatable Moment: Pneumatics and Protest in 1968, Architectural League, Urban Center, New York (traveled to Paris and London)
2000 *Narcisse Blessé: Autoportraits Contemporains 1970–2000,* Passage de Retz, Paris
De Voorstelling, Nederlandse Kunsts in Het Stedeijk Paleis, Stedelijk Museum, Amsterdam, Netherlands
Tuin van Verbeelding, Van Gimborn Arboretum, Doorn, Netherlands
2001 5th International Sofia Film Festival, Euro-Bulgarian Cultural Centre, Bulgaria

Collections:

Museum Boysmans van Beuningen, Rotterdam; Haags Gemeentemuseum, The Hague; Stedelijk Museum, Amsterdam; Van Abbemuseum, Eindhoven, Netherlands; Kunsthaus, Zurich; Musée Cantonal des Beaux Arts, Lausanne, Switzerland; Musée de Grenoble, France; Musée d'Art Moderne, Lyon, France.

Permanent Public Installations:

Podio del Mondo per l'Arte, Middelburg, Netherlands, 1975—; *Gothic Growing Project, Green Cathedral Almere,* Almere, Netherlands, 1978—; *Abri,* Flood Barrier Neeltje Jans, Netherlands, 1994—; *Land Art Project in Crown Property,* Het Loo, Netherlands, 2000—.

Publications:

By BOEZEM: Books—*Boezem Airobjects,* 1966 *Paper-Events,* Antwerp 1970; *Anti-Art and Visual Education,* photo book, The Hague 1970; *Press-Art-Project,* Gorinchem, Netherlands 1974; *Podio del Mondo per l'Arte,* Middelburg, Netherlands 1975. **Films—***Sand-Fountain,* 1969; *Breathing Upon the TV-Screen,* 1971; *Project Hooglandse Kere Leiden,* 1971; *A Gentle Breeze in May,* 1974; *Cartographia,* 1996; *Panorama: Via Aurelia Antica,* 1998.

On BOEZEM: Books—*Boezem/Van Elk,* exhibition catalog, with text by Renato Barilli, Bologna 1968; *Op Losse Schroeven,* exhibition catalog, text by W. Beeren, Amsterdam 1969; *Von Hodler zur Antiform* by Harold Szeeman, Berne 1970; *Boezem-Panamarenko,* exhibition catalog, Eindhoven, Netherlands 1970; *Contemporary Art from the Netherlands,* exhibition catalog, Chicago 1981; *Marinus Boezem,* exhibition catalog, Grenoble, France 1982; *Marinus Boezem: La lumière cistercienne clairvaux,* exhibition catalog, Ludwigshafen 1987; *Skywriting: The Work of Marinus Boezem,* exhibition catalog with text by Thomas McEvilley, Washington, D.C. 1993; *Marinus Boezem: Catalogue Raisonne* by Edna van Duyn and Frans Witteveen, Bussum 1999. **Articles—**''Dall 'Olanda''' by Piero Gilardi in *Flash Art* (Milan), June 1968; ''Primary Energy and the Micromotive Artists'' by Piero Gilardi in *Artsmagazine* (New York), September–October 1968; ''Imagination Takes Command'' by Tommaso Trini in *Domus* (Milan), February 1969; ''Dutch Artists on Television'' by Carel Blotkamp in *Studio International* (London), June 1971; ''Education and Art'' by Frans Haks in *Museumjournaal* (Amsterdam), December 1974; ''Narrative Art'' by Liesbeth Brandt Corstius in *Museumjournaal* (Amsterdam), March 1975; ''Double Dutch: Realism & Visual Fraud from the Netherlands'' by Jonathan Turner in *Art and Text,* no. 47, January 1994; ''Mother Nature's Church: Full-scale Floorplan of Reims Cathedral Made from Trees'' by Jonathan Turner in *Art News,* vol. 95, December 1996.

*

The world as the complement of the work of art.

In the course of years an image of my work has grown which cannot be described on formal grounds of conformity of form and/or material. The basic theme of these works is, over and over again, the search for a new concept in which art becomes art: the context of the work of art as its necessary complement.

The works all have much in common; they evoke a new ''environment,'' interacting with the work. Both components thus form the work of art. The works do not refer to themselves. They endeavor to formulate a new context. As such, I do not make a ''profile'' of reality to reach a specialization of it, but place the spectator himself in the process of searching for that reality.

The works that originated in the 60s already point in this direction: both ''Wind-Tables'' (1968) and the photographic work ''To Sign the Sky by an Aeroplane'' (1968).

In the more recent works, this idea of interaction between the work and the spectator is materialized again, such as in the mirror-project ''space-sculpture'' (1978), in which two large mirrors are placed in the center of the exhibition room, the reflecting sides facing each other. Space and time are here expressed in themselves, not dependent on the surrounding architecture. This work, on the one hand, is a materially space-determining sculpture: dividing the physical space; on the other hand, it creates its own context as a concept.

The ''wallpaper-project'' (1970), later realized at the Gemeentemuseum in The Hague, also reacts to the physical quality of the museum room. For me, this means searching for expression and significance in the classical conception of sculpture as illustrated in a later work titled ''Jump'' (1981), in which I try to epitomize a classical sole.

This sole, placed in space with only my shoes on it, is in front of a wall which has a life-size photograph of myself, seen as background. Here, then, is a connection between plastic art and flat level. Hopefully, a dimension is created out of the shoes to the wall to sculpture.

In recent years, I was also engaged in studying gothic space, which apart from its specific form and rhythm, develops its own mythology as a metaphor. Such metaphors are used as a datum to suggest new spaces and to evoke new dimensions of them. The ground-plan as a given structure is used here to attain a new interpretation of sculpture.

My works try to illustrate a process of research in which the staging and interim results are shown by means of the works of art. That is why these works lack the stamp of a trademark. They attempt to approximate my own obsessions with relation to reality from a plural point of view, as if answers could be found.

—Marinus Boezem

* * *

From the very start, Marinus Boezem has made clear that his artistic activities were not to be hampered by the traditional painter's and sculptor's materials. In the year 1966, in a privately published booklet, he states that already in 1963 he discovered air ''as a purification, as a reality, as a conquest of space.'' Boezem identifies air with freedom and he considers man himself ''as an object of art.''

In 1968 he shows his famous *Windtables,* covered with light-weight white cloth that is moved to wave by a ventilator. The atmosphere created by these Tables is poetically suggestive and, because of the empty cloth, brings some good painterly associations to the fore. During these years, around 1970, Boezem's work can be seen at international exhibitions like *Op Losse Schroeven* (Stedelijk Museum, Amsterdam, 1969). For this show he proposed to give a number of gigantic white sheets some airing by opening the huge first floor windows of the museum and let these hang over the window-sill out in the open.

Contrary to his colleagues Jan Dibbets and Ger van Elk, Boezem's work has retained a process-like character; he has not chosen a production of traditionally framed objects. Already in 1969 he demonstrated the expansive but at the same time substantially non-permanent status of an individual signature in a piece called *Sign the sky above the port of Amsterdam with an aeroplane.* Another piece, dating from 1967 and realised in 1981, illustrates the possibility of combining a heavy, unmovable form with a never ending process. Boezem measures the outline of the shadow of a given tree, at a certain time of a certain day, and fills this with a black granite. As the tree in the course of time grows and changes, and correspondingly the shadow, the granite form becomes autonomous as a three-dimensional piece of sculpture.

From 1980 onwards Boezem has concentrated on a new project, the ''Etude Gothique.'' At its starting point is the groundplan of a gothic cathedral, a continuously recurrent motif that functions as the vehicle for various images, including many self-portrayals. A recent manifestation is the planting of poplars literally following the lines of a cathedral plan. Within a number of years the trees will touch the sky and sheep will graze among its pillars. This project has been realised in the newly developed Ysselmeer-polders, where one will find some other large-scale works of art, for instance Robert Morris' Observatiorium, originally proposed for the important outdoor exhibition *Sonsbeek buiten de Perken* in 1971.

Boezem works at the fringe of the artistic scene in Holland, in the quiet provincial town of Middelburg in Zealand. In this city, together with his wife Maria-Rosa, he yearly organizes a symposium where artists, critics and audience meet in a well motivated and concentrated atmosphere.

—A. F. Wagemans

BOLTANSKI, Christian

Nationality: French. **Born:** Paris, 6 September 1944. **Education:** Self-taught in art. **Career:** Professional photographer and artist, Paris, since 1969. **Agent:** Sonnabend Gallery, 420 West Broadway, New York, New York 10012, U.S.A. **Address:** 746 Boulevard Camelinat, 92240 Malakoff, France.

Individual Exhibitions:

1970 Galerie Templon, Paris (with Jean Le Gac)
Musée d'Art Moderne, Paris
1971 Galerie Sonnabend, Paris
Galerie M. E. Thelen, Cologne
1972 Galerie Folker Skulima, Berlin
Studio Santandrea, Milan
1973 Galleria Lucio Amelio, Naples
Kunsthalle, Baden-Baden, West Germany
Sonnabend Gallery, New York
Museum of Modern Art, Oxford
Israel Museum Jerusalem
1974 *Saynette Comique,* Westfalischer Kunstverein, Münster, West Germany
Louisiana Museum, Humlebaek, Denmark
Centre National d'Art Contemporain, Paris (with Jacques Monory)
1975 Sonnabend Gallery, New York
Kunsthalle, Kiel, West Germany
Centre d'Art Contemporain, Geneva
Wurttembergische Kunstverein, Stuttgart
Galerie Seriaal, Amsterdam
1976 Musée d'Art Moderne, Paris
Rheinischer Landesmuseum, Bonn
1977 Museum of Contemporary Art, La Jolla, California
Galleria Bruno Soletti, Milan
Galerie Sonnabend, Paris
1978 Badischer Kunstverein, Karlsruhe, West Germany
Galerie Jollenbeck, Cologne
Galerie Malacorda, Geneva
Galerie Foksal, Warsaw
1979 *Compositions,* Musée de Peinture, Calais
Galerie Sonnabend, Paris
Carpenter Art Center, Harvard University, Cambridge, Massachusetts
1981 Musée d'Art Moderne, Paris (retrospective)
1982 Sonnabend Gallery, New York
Le Nouveau Musée, Lyon, France
1983 Aldrich Museum of Contemporary Art, Ridgefield, Connecticut
1984 Centre Georges Pompidou, Paris
Kunsthaus, Zurich
Staatliche Kunsthalle, Baden-Baden, West Germany
Galerie 't Venster, Rotterdam
1985 Galerie Optica, Montreal
Galerie Crousel-Hussenot, Paris
Le Consortium Centre d'Art Contemporain, Dijon, France
1986 Galerie Elisabeth Kaufmann, Zurich
Galerie Crousel Hussenot, Paris
Galerie des Ponchettes, Nice, France

Kunstverein, Munich
1988 *Christian Boltanski: Lessons of Darkness,* Museum of Contemporary Art, Chicago
Centro de Arte Reina Sofia, Madrid
Maria Goodman Gallery, New York
Museum of Contemporary Art, Los Angeles
1989 Galerie Ghislaine Hussenot, Paris
Vancouver Art Gallery
Museum of Contemporary Art, Basel
Jean Bernier Gallery, Athens
Marika Malacorda Gallery, Geneva
Art Museum of the University of California at Berkeley
Israel Museum, Jerusalem
Folksal Museum, Warsaw
1990 Galerie des Beaux-Arts, Brussels
Elisabeth Kaufmann Gallery, Basel
Reconstitution: Christian Boltanski, Whitechapel Gallery, London
Musée de Grenoble, France
Institute of Contemporary Arts, Nagoya, Japan
1991 *Christian Boltanski: Inventory,* Kunsthalle, Hamburg
Lisson Gallery, London
Marion Goodman Gallery, New York
1994 *Lost Property,* Tramway Gallery, Glasgow
The Reserve of the Dead Swiss, CCA Gallery, Glasgow
Glasgow School of Art, Scotland
Obala Art Center, Sarajevo
1995 Marion Goodman Gallery, New York
Kunsthalle Wien, Vienna
1996 Galerie Yvon Lambert, Paris
Neues Museum Weserburg, Bremen, Germany
1997 Galleria d'Arte Moderna, Bologna, Italy
1998 *Christian Boltanski: Dernières années,* Musée d'Art Moderne de la Ville, Paris
Christian Boltanski: Nightfall, Anthony D'Offay Gallery, London
2000 *Landscapes,* Yvon Lambert Gallery, Paris

Selected Group Exhibitions:

1969 *Biennale de Paris,* Musée d'Art Moderne, Paris
1971 *Prospekt 71,* Kunsthalle, Dusseldorf
1972 *Documenta 5,* Museum Fridericianum, Kassel, West Germany (and *Documenta 6,* 1977)
1974 *Pour Memoire,* Centre d'Art Plastique Contemporain, Bordeaux, France (travelled to Paris)
1977 *Malerei und Photographie im Dialog,* Kunsthaus, Zurich
1979 *3rd Biennale of Sydney,* Art Gallery of New South Wales, Sydney
1980 *Artist and Camera,* Mappin Art Gallery, Sheffield, Yorkshire (travelled to Stoke, Durham and Bradford)
1983 *Kunst mit Photographie,* Nationalgalerie, West Berlin
1986 *Photography as Performance,* Photographers' Gallery, London
1990 *France Today,* Muzeum Narodowe, Warsaw
1991 *The Interrupted Life,* New Museum of Contemporary Art, New York
Individualities: 14 Contemporary Artists from France, Art Gallery of Ontario, Toronto
1993 *Danse Macabre: Photographic Portraits,* FRAC Basse-Normandie, Caen, France (traveling exhibition)
1994 *Even If It's Night-time,* Musee d'Art Contemporain, Bordeaux, France
The Absence of Photography, Goethe-Institute, Montreal
1995 *Take Me (I'm Yours),* Serpentine Gallery, London
Through a Glass Darkly, Art Gallery of New South Wales, Sydney
1996 *Islands,* National Gallery of Australia, Canberra
1997 *Thirty-Five Years at Crown Point Press,* National Gallery of Art, Washington, D.C.
Havana Bienal, Cuba
1998 *From Remembrance to Renewal,* Contemporary Art Center of Virginia, Virginia Beach
1999 Musée d'Art et d'Histoire du Judaïsme, Paris
Berlin/Berlin, Akademie der Kunste, Berlin
2000 *Voila le monde dans la tete,* Musee d'Art Moderne de la Ville, Paris
L'Ombra della Ragione: l'Idea del Sacro nell'Identita Europea, Galleria d'Arte Moderna, Bologna, Italy

Collections:

Musée d'Art Moderne, Paris; Musée d'Art, Dijon, France; Kunsthalle, Hamburg; Kunsthalle, Kiel, West Germany; Neue Galerie, Aachen, West Germany; Louisiana Museum, Humlebaek, Denmark; Boymans-van Beuningen Museum, Rotterdam; Museum of Fine Arts, Lodz, Poland; Israel Museum, Jerusalem; Art Institute of Chicago; Fine Art Houston; Galerie Ghislaine Husseno, Paris; Suermondt-Ludwig-Museum, Aachen, Germany.

Publications:

By BOLTANSKI: Books—*Tous ce que reste de mon enfance,* Paris 1969; *Reconstitutions des Gestes,* Paris 1971; *10 Portraits Photographiques,* Paris 1972; *Album Photographique,* Hamburg 1972; *Inventaire,* Münster, West Germany 1973; *Quelques Interpretations,* Paris 1974; *20 Regles et Technique,* Copenhagen 1975; *Les Morts pour Rire,* Antibes, France 1975; *Modellbilder,* with others, Bonn 1976. **Articles**—Interview with Stuart Morgan in *Artscribe International,* November/December 1988; interview with Bernard Goy in *Journal of Contemporary Art,* fall/winter 1989; interview with Georgia Marsh in *Parkett,* December 1989; interview with Mark Durden and Lydia Popadimitriou in *Creative Camera,* April/May 1992; interview with Leslie Camhi in *Print Collectors Newsletter,* vol. 23, January/February 1993; interview with Bruno Villien in *Beaux Arts Magazine,* no. 121, March 1994; interview with Debra Bricker Balken in *Art New England* (Brighton, MA), vol. 16, April/May 1995; interview with Sandrine Malinaud in *Cimaise,* vol. 45, no. 255, Summer 1998. **Film**—*La Vie Impossible de Christian Boltanski,* 1968.

On BOLTANSKI: Books—*L'Art en France: Une Nouvelle Generation* by Jean Clair, Paris 1973; *Saynette Comique,* exhibition catalog, by Klaus Honnef, Münster, West Germany 1974; *Reconstitution* by Andreas Franke, Paris 1978; *Les Modeles* by Paull-Hervé Würz, Paris 1979; *Spurensicherung* by Günter Metken, Cologne 1979; *Compositions,* exhibition catalog by Dominique Vieville, Calais 1980; *Christian Boltanski,* exhibition catalog, Baden-Baden 1984; *Christian Boltanski: Lessons of Darkness,* exhibition catalog by Lynn Gumpert and Mary Jane Jacob, Chicago 1988; *Christian Boltanski* by Lynn

Gumpert, 1994; *Christian Boltanski: Neuter,* exhibition catalog, Vienna 1995; *Christian Boltanski,* exhibition catalog, Bremen 1996; *Christian Boltanski,* exhibition catalog, Bologna 1997. **Articles—** ''An Artist of Uncertainty'' by Semin Dedier in *Parkett,* December 1989; ''Resisting the Obscure Art of Light'' by Therese Grisham in *Art Criticism,* vol. 8, pt. 2, 1993; ''Time After Time: Photograph and Allegory'' by David Green in *Creative Camera,* no. 328, June/July 1994; ''Christian Boltanski: Portfolio'' in *Kunstforum International,* no. 128, October/December 1994; ''The Aesthetics of Mourning'' by T.J. Demos in *Flash Art (International Edition),* no. 184, October 1995; ''Christian Boltanski'' by Laura Falls and Lynn Sloan in *Occasional Readings in Photography,* no. 6, 1996; ''Monuments to Darkness: Portfolio of Photographs from Installations'' in *Aperture,* no. 142, Winter 1996; ''Mourning or Melancholia: Christian Boltanski's Missing House'' by Abigail Solomon-Godeau in *Oxford Art Journal,* vol. 21, no. 2, 1998; ''Memory, Commemoration, and the Photograph'' by Martin Golding in *Modern Painters* (London), vol. 12, no. 1, Spring 1999; ''Du temps perdu'' in *Art On Paper,* vol. 3, no. 5, May/June 1999; ''Christian Boltanski: Traces of the Dead'' by Carol Rosen in *Sculpture* (Washington, D.C.), vol. 18, no. 5, June 1999; ''Christian Boltanski: Yvon Lambert'' by Laurie Attias in *Art News,* vol. 99, no. 2, February 2000.

* * *

Try as they may to dodge their forebears, artists continually circle back to common themes—not because they grow timid but because, if lucky, they rediscover art's inherently treasonous mission in the ongoing wars between fiction and reality (as Picasso said, ''Art is the lie that makes us realize the truth'') and between death and life (as Boltanski says, the ''more a painter works, the less he lives''). When we call an artist original, we usually mean that he or she has found a new path to the same old place.

The advent of photography promised to some a relief from painting's knack for misrepresentation, but, from the beginning, the technology was used for purposes other than straight documentation. Because of unendurably long exposure times, the first photographic portraits were memorial images of corpses propped upright and with their eyes opened so they appeared natural. Boltanski's deceptively authentic tales of everyday life are a compelling fulfillment of photography's potential because they present falsehoods that are utterly plausible. Having a disposition that enables him to view life clinically and compassionately at the same time, he turns his gaze on the clothing and utensils of children, deliberately cloaking whether he is showcasing one person or many, a living being or one recently dead.

If Boltanski is to be believed, the historical subject that has provided him with the most stirring material for his approach also strikes close to his own history. Boltanski's father was a Jewish doctor whom his Catholic mother allowed to hide in the basement of her Parisian home during the Occupation. (Boltanski was born in 1944 on the day of the liberation.) Eradicating so many individual lives by a massive racist, that is, an indiscriminate campaign, the Holocaust offers a fruitful if horrifying chance to puzzle together the connection between possessions and identity. Boltanski's projects have many intended parallels with the Central German Museum, a project begun in Prague by Nazis eager to document an extinct people. The Museum assembled, categorized, and displayed quotidian artifacts of European Jews. François C., nominal subject of *Les habits de François C.,* and the family documented in *Album de photos de la famille D., 1939—1964,* could easily be Nazi casualties.

Boltanski is as willing to fudge the data on his own life as he is those of the anonymous members of the Mickey Mouse Club whom he commemorates in *Les 62 membres de Club Mickey en 1955.* Entranced, along with other *Nouveaux Realists* including Arman and Marcel Broodthaers, by the specimen-filled vitrines of the *Musée de l'Homme* in Paris, he has created museum displays of toys, clothing, homework, and snapshots that he says came from his own childhood. He often supplies anecdotes and fragments of memory to bolster their authenticity, but he has also confessed to engaging in so much deception about his early years that he no longer knows what the truth is. If that is true, he has succeeded at the ultimate in self-effacement. From the start, Boltanski's willingness to toy with his memories has been synonymous with his inhuman numbness toward his own existence: in January of 1970, he mailed sixty identical letters complaining of depression and forecasting his imminent demise.

In addition to mail art, he has created short films and eerie installations made from such simple but suggestive items as candles and miniature skeletons, often staged in interiors other than museums and galleries. Furthermore, he insists that his occupation is *painter,* asking only that a more flexible definition of the word be applied. Typically, he is playing fast and loose with the evidence, the great part of which identifies him as a photographer. Beyond trickery and subterfuge, however, the stance testifies to his awareness of the persistent assumption that photography is a lesser art form, perhaps more in the European mind than the American. Boltanski, though he denies having read French poststructuralist anthropology, linguistics, and aesthetics, practices a photography that harmonizes with all three, particularly with their assertion that the facts and realms of existence considered to be most absolute are in reality constructed by culture. Focusing on death, the most impenetrable of absolutes, he creates from monochromatic rectangles, small light bulbs, and photographs of children's faces, works that he calls *Monuments.* The most prominent of his artistic output in the 1980s and 90s, they inquire in an original yet familiar manner into our perceptions and myths about the dead and demonstrate Roland Barthes's observation that being photographed somehow feels just like dying.

—Mark Swartz

BOOTH, Peter

Nationality: Australian. **Born:** Sheffield, England, in 1940; immigrated to Australia in 1958. **Education:** Sheffield College of Art, 1956–57, and National Gallery School, Melbourne, 1962–65. **Career:** Painter: lives and works in Melbourne. **Agent:** Pinacotheca, Richmond. **Address:** c/o Pinacotheca, 10 Waltham Place, Richmond, Victoria 3121, Australia.

Individual Exhibitions:

1969 Pinacotheca, Melbourne
Central Street Gallery, Sydney
1970 Pinacotheca, Melbourne
1972 Pinacotheca, Melbourne
1973 Chapman Powell Gallery, Melbourne
1974 Chapman Powell Gallery, Melbourne
1975 Pinacotheca, Melbourne
1976 Monash University Gallery, Melbourne

Project 12: Peter Booth, Art Gallery of New South Wales, Sydney
Pinacotheca, Melbourne
1977 Pinacotheca, Melbourne
1978 Pinacotheca, Melbourne
1979 Pinacotheca, Melbourne
1980 Pinacotheca, Melbourne
1981 Pinacotheca, Melbourne
1982 *Works by Peter Booth and Rosalie Gascoigne,* at the *Biennale,* Venice
1984 Museum of Modern Art, New York
Guggenheim Museum, New York
1987 CDS Gallery, New York
1988 Albemarle Gallery, London
1990 *Peter Booth: Recent Painting,* Deutscher Brunswick Street Gallery, Fitzroy, Australia
1994 *Peter Booth: Paintings & Works on Paper 1992–1994,* Deutscher Fine Art, Malvern, Australia
1995 *Peter Booth: Works on Paper,* Rex Irwin Art Dealer, Woollahra, Australia
Peter Booth: Small Paintings 1992–1995, Deutscher Fine Art, Malvern, Australia
1996 *Peter Booth: Recent Paintings and Drawings,* Deutscher Fine Art, Malvern, Australia

Selected Group Exhibitions:

1968 *The Field,* National Gallery of Victoria, Melbourne (travelled to the Art Gallery of New South Wales, Sydney)
1973 *Recent American Art,* Gallery of New South Wales, Sydney
1976 *Minimal Art,* National Gallery of Victoria, Melbourne
Drawing: Some Definitions, Ewing and George Paton Galleries, University of Melbourne
1979 *Third Biennale of Sydney: European Dialogue,* Art Gallery of New South Wales, Sydney
1981 *Australian Perspecta 1981: A Biennial Survey of Contemporary Australian Art,* Art Gallery of New South Wales, Sydney
1982 *Eureka! Artists from Australia,* Serpentine Gallery, London
1988 *Advance Australian Painting,* Auckland City Art Gallery, Auckland, New Zealand
1989 *Fables and Fantasies,* Duke University Museum of Art, Durham, North Carolina
1991 *The Sublime Imperative,* Australian Centre for Contemporary Art, South Yarra, Australia
1996 *Australian Drawing 1940–1996,* Niagara Gallery, Richmond, Australia
Art of this Century, CDS Gallery, New York (catalog)
1998 *The Age of Drawing: An International Scene,* CDS Gallery, New York (catalog)

Collections:

Australian National Gallery, Canberra; National Gallery of Victoria, Melbourne; Monash University Art Gallery, Melbourne; Geelong Art Gallery, Victoria; Ballarat Fine Art Gallery, Victoria; Bendigo Art Gallery, Victoria; Mornington Peninsula Art Gallery, Mornington, Victoria; Art Gallery of South Australia, Adelaide; Art Gallery of New South Wales, Sydney; Queen Victoria Museum and Art Gallery, Launceston, Tasmania.

Publications:

On BOOTH: Books—*Project 12: Peter Booth,* catalog broadsheets, with text by Frances Lindsay, Sydney 1976; *Australian Perspecta 1981,* exhibition catalog, with text by Bernice Murphy, Sydney 1981; *Australia: Venice Biennale 1982: Works by Peter Booth and Rosalie Gascoigne,* exhibition catalog, with an essay by Gary Catalano, Sydney 1982; *Eureka! Artists from Australia,* exhibition catalog, with essays by Nancy D. H. Underhill, Ian Burn and Paul Taylor, London 1982; *Peter Booth: Recent Painting,* exhibition catalog with text by Robert Lindsay and John Embling, Fitzroy 1990; *Peter Booth: Paintings & Works on Paper 1992–1994,* exhibition catalog, Malvern 1994; *Peter Booth: Works on Paper,* exhibition catalog, Woollahra 1995; *Peter Booth: Small Paintings 1992–1995,* exhibition catalog, Malvern 1995; *Peter Booth: Recent Paintings and Drawings,* exhibition catalog, Malvern 1996. **Articles—**''Peter Booth'' by Frances Lindsay in *Art and Australia* (Sydney), vol. 16, no. 1, 1978; ''Images of Tradition'' by Gary Catalano in *The Australian Arts Today,* edited by John Colmer, London 1980; ''Empathetically Painterly'' by Katherine Hattam in *Art Monthly Australia,* no. 82, August 1995; ''Madness and Landscape: The Art of Peter Booth in the Age of Unreason'' by Helen McDonald in *Art and Australia,* vol. 33, Spring 1995.

*

I feel that my work has to speak for itself, and that the viewer should be free to make his/her own interpretations.

—Peter Booth

* * *

Like those of many Australian artists who began to exhibit in the late 1960s, Peter Booth's early works were decidedly minimal in appearance. Characteristically his paintings of the time often contained nothing more than a black rectangle bounded on its upper horizontal and two vertical sides by a thin strip of lighter-toned canvas. During the past six or seven years the appearance of his work has greatly altered. Figurative images are now to the fore. Yet in one important sense Booth's concerns have not changed, for human society is still the major theme of his work. While the blank facades of his early paintings gave symbolic form to the alienating power of society, his more recent paintings present a more direct image of society's tensions and conflicts.

This change has certainly been facilitated by his obsessive graphic activity. Born in the English industrial city of Sheffield, Booth has continually sketched the industrial landscapes of his adopted Melbourne. Even an unpractised eye can see the similarities between the proportions of his early minimal paintings and those found in the facades of the factories and warehouses which he has sketched. A further influence on his work stems from his interest in certain romantic and symbolist writers of the 19th century. William Blake is of particular importance to him. The influence of Blake's graphic illustrations can be discerned in Booth's drawings of the mid-1970s. In these drawings Booth first unveiled many of the specific images to be found in his current paintings—the winding roads, the fire-engulfed monoliths, the totemic symbols.

For a number of years now Booth has recorded his dreams in pictorial form. His recent paintings can often be traced back to these dream images. By combining such material with scenes or incidents directly experienced, Booth attempts to show what it is like to be alive in our day and age. His is the ambition of most romantic artists: to be true to one's self, to be true to one's time.

—Gary Catalano

BORGES, Jacobo

Nationality: Venezuelan. **Born:** Caracas, 1931. **Education:** School of Fine Arts, Caracas, 1949–1951. **Career:** Worked a variety of jobs, including the Free Art Workshop, Caracas; exhibited first paintings, 1952; traveled to Paris on a scholarship and lived there until 1956; joined the Young Painters Group, 1956; stopped painting for five years to concentrate on multimedia work, 1965–1970; scenery and costume designer for plays including *El Tintero,* 1979, *Los Angeles Terribles,* 1985, *Lo que dejó Tempestad,* and *Sand,* New York, 2001; taught art, Internationale Sommerakademie Für Bildende Künst, Salzburg, 1994, and School of Fine Arts, Caracas and Valencia. **Awards:** Jose Loreto Arismendi prize and honorable mention, Sao Paulo Biennial, 1957; first prize, Salon Michelena, Valencia, and first prize, Museum of Fine Arts, Curacao, Dutch Antilles, 1960; Pueblo de Bolivar and Antonio Esteban Frias prizes, Salon Caracas, 1962; first prize for Drawing, Drawings and Etchings Salon, Universidad Central de Venezuela, Caracas, 1963; Guggenheim International Award, Solomon R. Guggenheim Museum, New York, 1964; First Armando Reveron prize, Asociación Nacional de Artistas Plasticos, 1983; Guggenheim Fellowship, 1985 and 1986. **Address:** 118 East 25th Street, 9th., New York, New York 10010, U.S.A.

Selected Individual Exhibitions:

1956 Galería Lauro and Museum of Fine Arts, Caracas
1976 *Magia de un Realismo Crítico,* Museum of Modern Art, México City, and the Museum of Fine Arts, Caracas
1985 *Jacobo Borges, A Draftsman,* CDS Gallery, New York
1987 *Jacobo Borges: From Fishing. . . to Mirror of Waters, 60 paintings from 1956–1986,* Museo de Monterrey, Mexico (traveled to Berlin, Bogota, Caracas)
1988 CDS Gallery, New York
Jacobo Borges, Obra Reciente, Galería Arvil, Mexico City
1989 *Berliner Bilder,* Gallerie Eva Poll, Berlin, Germany
Art Museum at Florida International University, Miami, Florida
1991 *Jacobo Borges, Itinerario de Viaje,* Centro Cultural Consolidado, Caracas
1992 *Ubërgange,* Galerie Poll, Berlin
Jacobo Borges, A Propos de Romantisme Baroque, Vasarely Foundation, Aix en Provence, France
1993 *Jacobo Borges,* Casa de América, Granada, Spain
1995 *Es ist die Seele ein Frendes auf Erden,* Galerie Traklhauss, Salzburg, Austria
1998 *Der Himmel senkte sich,* Residenz Gallery, Salzburg, Austria
1999 *El Paraiso Perdido,* Galeria Freites, Caracas
2000 *EL BOSQUE,* Museo de Arte Contemporaneo, Sofia Imber, Caracas

Selected Group Exhibitions:

1957 *Sao Paulo Biennial*
1958 *Venice Biennial*
1964 *The Guggenheim International Award Exhibition,* Solomon R. Guggenheim Museum, New York
1966 *The Emergent Decade: Latin American Painters and Paintings in the 1960s,* Guggenheim Museum, New York.
1984 *First Biennial Wifredo Lam,* La Havana, Cuba
1987 *Fantastic Art of Latin America,* Indianapolis Museum of Art, Indianapolis
Fifty Years of Collecting: An Anniversary Selection, Guggenheim Museum, New York
1988 *Olympiad of Arts,* Seoul Olympic Games, Seoul, Korea
Venice Biennale, Venice
1993 *Latin American Artists of the Twentieth Century,* Museum of Modern Art, New York
1999 *A REBOURS, The Informal Rebellion,* Museo Nacional Centro de Arte Reina Sofia, Madrid, Spain (traveled).
America Latina: Las Vanguardias de Fin de Milenio, Lisbon, Portugal.

Public Installations:

''EL BOSQUE'' Museo de Arte Contemporaneo, Sofia Imber, Caracas, and Museo de Arte Contemporaneo del Zulia, 2000.

Publications:

By BORGES: Books—*The Great Mountain and Its Era,* Caracas, 1979. **Articles**—''El canto de la muerte'' in *Cal* (Caracas), 23 June 1962; ''El grito'' in *Cal* (Caracas), no. 26, 24 January 1964; ''El arte no es ya una actividad pasiva sino forzosamente agresiva'' in *Clarin* (Caracas), 26 April 1968; ''El arte no puede nacer a partir de una elaboración sólo racional'' in *Excelsior* (Mexico), 28 July 1976. **Films**—*Cine-Urgente*; *IMAGEN DE CARACAS* (multimedia spectacle-performance); *22 de Mayo.*

On BORGES: Books—*Guggenheim International Award* (exhibition catalog) with text by Laurence Alloway, New York 1964; *El Avila: Guaraira Repano,* Caracas 1978; *Jacobo Borges,* by Dore Ashton, Caracas 1982; *Jacobo Borges* (exhibition catalog), Staatliche Kunsthalle, Berlin 1987; *El Espectáculo Continua: Theatre and the Paintings of Jacobo Borges* (unpublished Master's Thesis) by Marguerite K. Mayhall, University of Texas at Austin 1993; *Der Himmel senkte sich/Se vino abajo el cielo* (exhibition catalog), Residenzgalerie, Salzburg 1996, Museo Jacobo Borges, Caracas 1998, and the Haus der Kulturen der Welt, Berlin 1998. **Articles**—''Latin America and International Art'' by Laurence Alloway in *Art in America,* no. 3, 1965; ''Jacobo Borges'' by Ruth Bass in *Art News,* 1987; ''Jacobo Borges. La pintura: un río de agua en el que me ahogo'' by Mercedes Garcia Ocejo in *Activa,* vol. 12, no. 20, 1987; ''Agua, muros, espejos. El sueño de Jacobo Borges'' by Guillermina Olmedo in *Casas Gente,* vol. 4, no. 34, 1989; ''Jacobo Borges: la pintura como identidad latinoamericana'' by Osiris Chierico in *El Nacional* (Caracas), 21 May 1990.

* * *

Primarily a painter, Jacobo Borges's paintings and work in other modes demonstrate his attempt to reconcile being Latin American and Venezuelan in a country with strong cultural, political, and racial ties to Europe. In his most well-known works, Borges concocts elaborate critiques of Western history (including Venezuela's), paeans to lost relatives, windows framing vanished urban panoramas, glimpses of childhood memories, and tableaux of invented figures and objects in oversize paintings that engulf the viewer both physically and emotionally. The theatrical qualities of these paintings enable them to work on many levels, making them accessible to international audiences, but reading them within the painter's local and personal context amplifies their meaning. As Borges has said, ''I am a communicator much more than I am a painter. A painter is a medium, a communicator is a conscious man. A painter is absorbed by his own instrument. A communicator reflects on it,'' according to Dore Ashton in *Jacobo Borges.* As such, Borges's oeuvre encompasses more than painting and includes drawing, film, theatre, and installation.

Borges's painting in particular demands discussion of ''influences,'' as at various times he has made use of elements of German Expressionism, geometric abstraction, and hard-edged Pop, the work of Rembrandt, Goya, Velasquez, and Hokusai, as well as references from film and theater. More than appropriation, these stylistic and cultural references are a way for Borges to upend time and space; these ''pictorial quotations,'' among other things, enable the painter to create images in which space is ambiguous and shifting, and time is simultaneous and fluid.

After early attempts to reconcile geometric abstraction (then the rage in 1950s Venezuela) and Venezuelan themes, and a four year sojourn to study art in Paris, Borges startled the Caracas art world with a series of paintings highly critical of contemporary society. Executed in a harsh Expressionist style reminiscent of Ensor and De Kooning, these works culminated in two masterpieces, *The Show Has Begun,* 1964, and *The Show Continues,* of the same year. Technically and thematically, the paintings in this series contain other elements significant in the artist's oeuvre: the use of a triptych format, multiple layers of paint and other expressionist techniques such as cuts, erasures, marked out passages, incised lines, and grotesquely deformed figures, and a sense of time and space that refers both to the contemporary caraqueño context and to a broader and more historical one.

The theatrical titles of the 1964 paintings presage Borges's decision to give up painting in 1965 to direct a multidisciplinary team of artists, writers, composers, playwrights, architects, and filmmakers in the creation of the 1968 multimedia spectacle *Imagen de Caracas.* Ostensibly designed as part of the quatricentenary celebration of the founding of Caracas, and funded by the municipal government, the project took the history of the city as its theme. Film, music, live action, kinetic labyrinths, and slide projections created a multimedia experience, one in which the public was both spectator and participant. *Imagen*'s ''manifesto'' outlined the team's attempts to create a ''new space'' in which the spectator/spectacle/actor relationship would be reconfigured to allow total spectator participation and collaboration, and the participants' sense of past, present, and future suspended. Although the spectacle was closed down by police action after two months, its influence on Venezuelan painting, theatre, and film has been profound. It is clear, for example, that the return in Venezuelan painting to the subject of the Avila during the 1970s took inspiration from *Imagen de Caracas.*

Disappointed, but not yet disillusioned with art's power to effect social change, Borges began painting again, this time incorporating more hard-edged elements such as color planes and historical photographs into shadowy expressionist interiors. The two signature works of this period, *Meeting with Red Circle* of 1973 and *Nymphenburg* of 1974, continue his critical examination of political institutions, but they depart from the early works in making clearer references (to a local audience) to their specifically Venezuelan context: *Meeting* is based on a group photograph of an official meeting during the regime of the dictator Juan Vicente Gomez (1908–1935), while the space within *Nymphenburg* seems to suggest a Bavarian Baroque palace interior, but the paintings lining the walls are Borges's own, and the hazy figures kicking a prostrate figure in a room beyond the foreground could be German, Chilean, Venezuelan, Serbian, or Argentine.

Photography became a major source for Borges in a series of smaller works that explored personal rituals and situations such as weddings and first communions in the mid to late 1970s. In the early 1980s he introduced his self-portrait into large-scale paintings that began to work toward the creation of a kind of personal history. Still expressionist in execution, works such as *The Real Mountain,* 1981, and *Landscape from This End,* 1982, incorporated images of deformed and misshapen dolls he had created for stage sets, the silhouette of Caracas's defining landmark, Mount Avila, architectural elements, posed family groups rendered as ghostly apparitions, and reproductions of Borges's earlier paintings. The spaces within these works are completely irrational, but entirely believable in their depiction of landscapes and interiors dominated by memory rather than history. As the decade progressed, Borges's paintings became darker in palette as well as theme and lost their expansiveness of space and time to instead focus on what the painter has called, after Donald Kuspit, ''potential space.'' *Swimmers in the Water Mirror* and *Mirror of Waters,* both of 1986, focus on the painter's long-standing obsession with water as a way to once again address the issue of simultaneous time, this time in the context of personal history.

Toward the end of the decade these ''water'' paintings become looser to the point of abstraction. Their size increases as well, making them approach the environmental in feeling. The culmination of this strain is the 2001 work *El cielo se vino abajo (The Sky Fell Down),* a multi-room installation based on the theme of the Deluge and inspired by the five part cycle of Noah paintings (1568) by Kaspar Memberger located in the Residenzgallerie Salzburg. The expressionist marks, cuts, and distorted figures of Borges's early work are here exploded into fragments, then blown up, and used as backdrops, envelopes, and stage sets for the retelling of the ancient myth of the Flood in various texts: the *Atra-Hasis* (Babylonian), *Gilgamesh* (Ancient Mesopotamian), the Bible (Judeo-Christian), and the Tamanaco (Venezuelan) Indian text the *Amalivaca.*

—Marguerite K. Mayhall

BOROFSKY, Jon(athan)

Nationality: American. **Born:** Boston, Massachusetts, 24 December 1942. **Education:** Carnegie Mellon University, Pittsburgh, B.F.A.

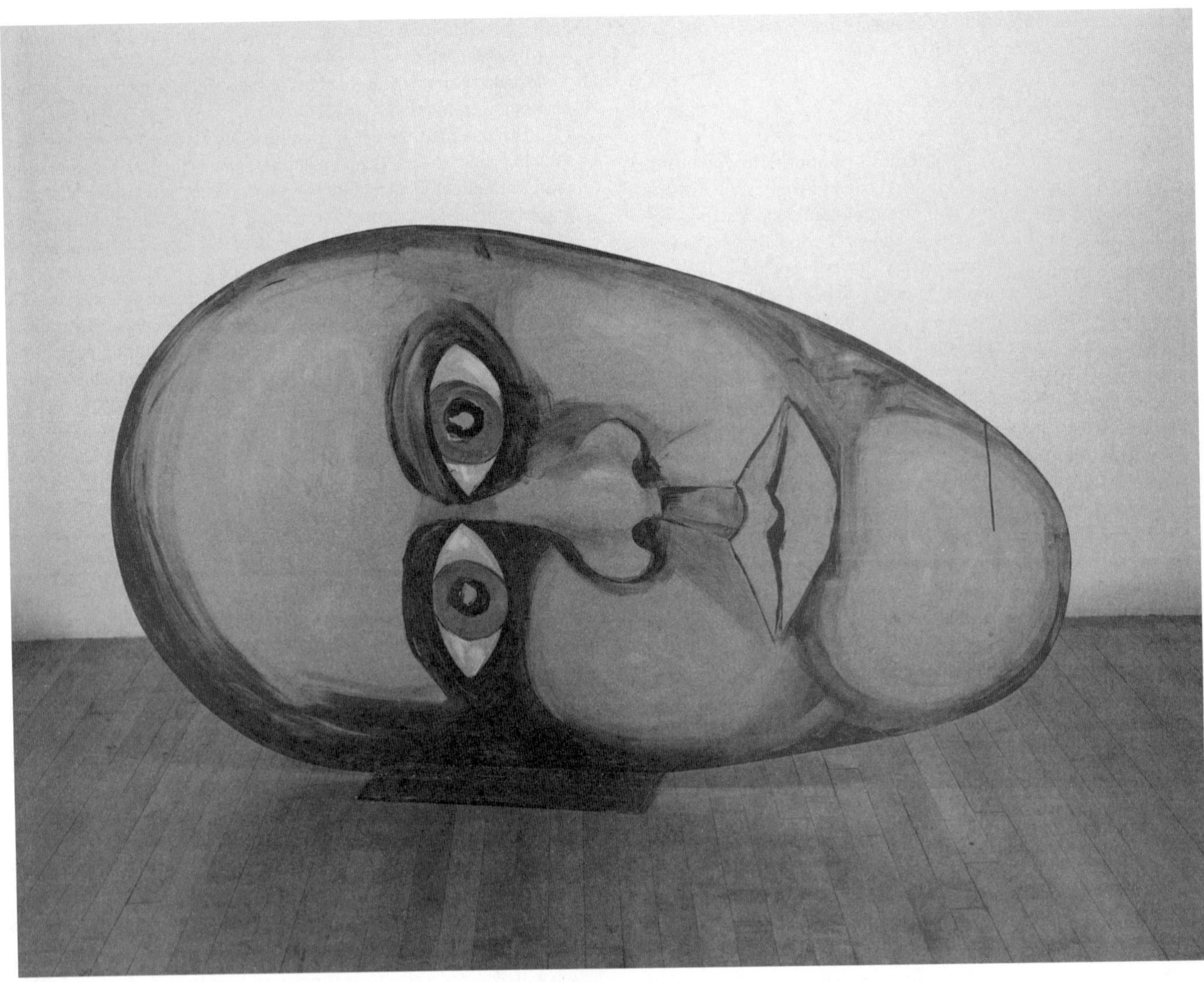

Jonathan Borofsky: *Self-Portrait at 2,719,997,* 1981. ©Geoffrey Clements/Corbis.

1964; Ecole de Fontainebleau, France, Summer 1964; and Yale School of Art and Architecture, New Haven, Connecticut, M.F.A. 1966. **Career:** Independent artist, New York and California, since 1966. Teacher, School of Visual Arts, New York, 1969–77, and California Institute of the Arts, Valencia, since 1977. **Agent:** Paula Cooper Gallery, New York. **Address:** c/o Paula Cooper Gallery, 155 Wooster St., New York, New York 10012–3159, U.S.A.

Individual Exhibitions:

1975 Paula Cooper Gallery, New York
1976 *Matrix 18,* Wadsworth Atheneum, Hartford, Connecticut
Paul Cooper Gallery, New York
1977 University of California at Irvine
1978 Protech-McIntosh Gallery, Washington, D.C.
Thomas Lewallen Gallery, Los Angeles
University of California Art Museum, Berkeley
Corps de Garde, Groningen, Netherlands
Projects Gallery, Museum of Modern Art, New York
1979 Paula Cooper Gallery, New York
INK: Halle für Internationale Neue Kunst, Zurich
Portland Center for the Visual Arts, Oregon
1980 Paula Cooper Gallery, New York
Hayden Gallery, Massachusetts Institute of Technology, Cambridge
1981 Contemporary Arts Museum, Houston
Galerie Rudolf Zwirner, Cologne
Kunsthalle, Basel
Institute of Contemporary Arts, London
1982 Museum Boymans-van Veuningen, Rotterdam
Museum van Hedendaagse Kunst, Ghent, Belgium
Paula Cooper Gallery, New York
Gemini G.E.L., Los Angeles
Friedrich Gallery, Berne
1983 Kunstmuseum, Basel
Galleria dell'Ariete Grafica, Milan
Akron Art Museum, Ohio
Paula Cooper Gallery, New York
Gemini G.E.L., Los Angeles
1984 University of Miami, Coral Gables

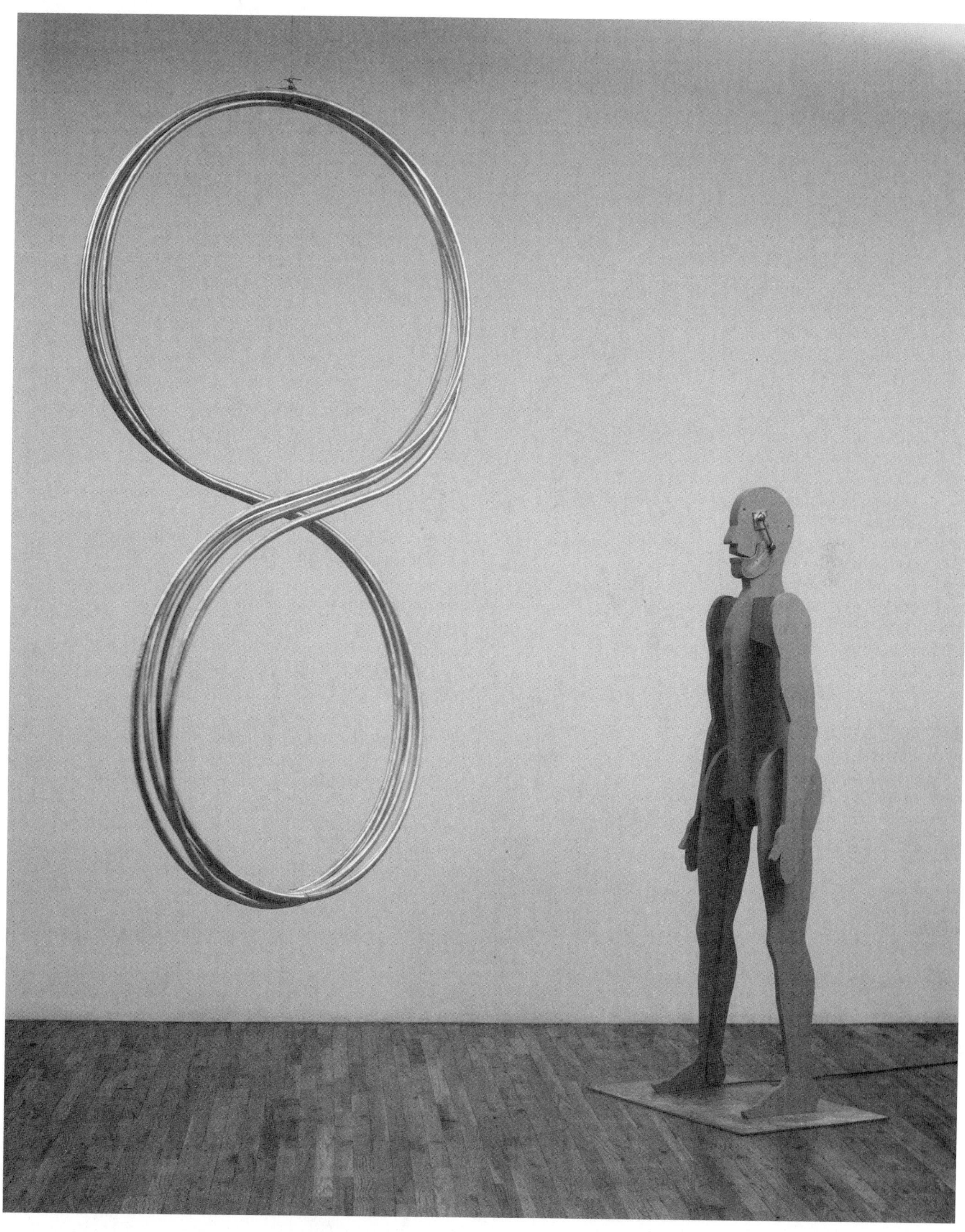

Jonathan Borofsky: *Installation with Chattering Man,* ca. 1983. ©Geoffrey Clements/Corbis.

Louisiana Museum, Humlebaek, Denmark
Israel Museum, Jerusalem
Moderna Museet, Stockholm
Kunsthalle, Bielefeld, West Germany
Carl Solway Gallery, Cincinnati
Seattle Art Museum, Washington
Philadelphia Museum of Art, Pennsylvania
Gallery Watari, Tokyo
Galerie Susanna Kulli, St. Gallen, Switzerland
1985 Philadelphia Museum of Art, Pennsylvania (travelled to New York; Berkeley, California; Minneapolis; Washington, D.C.; Los Angeles, 1985–86)
Gemini G.E.L., Los Angeles
1986 St. Louis Art Museum, Missouri
Gemini G.E.L., Los Angeles
Harvard University Art Museum, Cambridge, Massachusetts
Paula Cooper Gallery, New York
Heath Gallery, Atlanta, Georgia
Milwaukee Art Museum, Wisconsin (travelled to Des Moines Art Center, Iowa)
1987 Cathedral of St. John the Divine, New York
Metropolitan Museum of Art, Tokyo (travelled to Shiga, Japan)
Galerie Yvon Lambert, Paris
Gallery Watari, Tokyo
1990 Glenn-Dash Gallery, Los Angeles
1992 Margo Leavin Gallery, Los Angeles
Georgia-Pacific Center, Atlanta
1993 Hudson River Museum, Yonkers, New York
Remba Gallery, Santa Monica, California
String of Consciousness #3, Paula Cooper Gallery, New York
1995 Paula Cooper Gallery, New York
1997 *Jonathan Borofsky: The God Project,* Rose Art Museum, Brandeis University, Waltham (catalog)
2000 *RSVP: Jonathan Borofsky,* Museum of Fine Arts, Boston

Selected Group Exhibitions:

1974 *Drawing and Other Work,* Paula Cooper Gallery, New York
1976 *Soho,* Akademie der Kunste, West Berlin (travelled to the Louisiana Museum, Humleback, Denmark)
1977 *New York: The State of Art,* New York State Museum, Syracuse
Surrogates/Self-Portraits, Holly Solomon Gallery, New York
1978 *Contemporary Drawing, New York,* University of California Art Museum, Santa Barbara
1979 *Visionary Images,* Renaissance Society, University of Chicago
1983 *Back to the USA,* Rheinisches Landesmuseum, Bonn (travelled to Lucerne and Stuttgart)
1985 *Modern Machines: Recent Kinetic Sculpture,* Whitney Museum, New York
1987 *Berlinart,* Museum of Modern Art, New York (travelled to San Francisco Museum of Modern Art)
1992 *Documenta IX,* Kassel, Germany
Both Art and Life, Newport Harbor Art Museum, Newport Beach, California (catalog)
1993 *Yale Collects Yale,* Yale University Art Gallery, New Haven (catalog)
The Body of Drawing: Drawings by Sculptors, Graves Art Gallery, Sheffield (catalog)
1994 *Drawing Rooms,* Modern Art Museum of Forth Worth (catalog)
1995 *Prison Sentences: The Prision as Site/The Prison as Subject,* Eastern State Penitentiary, Philadelphia (catalog)
1996 *Group Show,* Paula Cooper Gallery, New York
Inside, California Center for the Arts Museum, Escondido (catalog)
1997 *Travel & Leisure,* Paula Cooper Gallery, New York
Identity Crisis: Self-Portraiture at the End of the Century, Aspen Art Museum, Colorado (catalog)
2000 Monte Carlo International Sculpture Festival: Contemporary American Sculpture

Collections:

Whitney Museum, New York; Museum of Modern Art, New York; BankAmerica Corporation, San Francisco; Philadelphia Museum of Art, Pennsylvania; Commodities Corporation, Princeton, New Jersey; Tate Gallery, London.

Permanent Public Installations:

Ballerina Clown, Venice, California; Los Angeles Subway System.

Publications:

By BOROFSKY: Books—*Jonathan Borofsky: Dedicated to the Audience* with Udo Kittelmann, Stuttgart 1993; *Signifying Art: Essays on Art After 1960* by Marjorie Welish, Cambridge 1999.

On BOROFSKY: Books—*6 Years: The Dematerialization of the Art Object from 1966 to 1972* by Lucy Lippard, New York 1973; *Jon Borofsky: Matrix 18,* exhibition catalog, with text by Mark Rosenthal, Hartford, Connecticut 1976; *Contemporary Drawing, New York,* exhibition catalog, Santa Barbara, California 1978; *Drawings: A Contemporary Approach* by Claudia Betti and Teel Sale, New York 1980; *Drawing: The Pluralist Decade,* with an introduction by Janet Kardon, Philadelphia 1980; *20 Artists: Yale School of Art 1950–1970,* exhibition catalog, by Irving Sandler, New Haven, Connecticut 1981; *Jonathan Borofsky: Dreams 1973–81,* exhibition catalog with essay by Joan Simon, London and Basel 1981; *Jonathan Borofsky: Zeichnungen 1960–1983,* exhibition catalog with texts by C. Geelhaar and D. Koepplin, Basel 1983; *Jonathan Borofsky,* exhibition catalog with essays by Mark Rosenthal and Richard Marshall, Philadelphia and New York 1984; *Jonathan Borofsky: New Works,* exhibition catalog with introduction by Peter Nisbet, Cambridge Massachusetts 1986; *Jonathan Borofsky: Dreams,* Tokyo 1987; *Borfosky: Drawings, Printings and Multiples,* exhibition catalog with essay by Mark Rosenthal, Tokyo 1987; *Le Tramway de Strasbourg: Jonathan Borofsky, Gérard Collin-Thiébaut, Barbara Kruger, Mario Merz, L'Oulipo* by Catherine Grout, Paris 1995. **Articles—**"Jonathan Borofsky at 2,096,974" in *Artforum* (New York), November 1974;

''Before the Reason of Images: The New Work of Jon Borofsky'' in *Arts* (New York), October 1976; ''Jon Borofsky's Dream Language'' in *Artweek,* 23 April 1977; ''Jon Borofsky'' by Philip Smith in *Arts Magazine* (New York), March 1978; ''Energism: An Attitude'' by Romy H. Cohen in *Artforum* (New York), September 1980; ''Art: Transformations of Jonathan Borofsky'' by John Russell in the *New York Times,* 24 October 1980; ''Strike: A Project by Jonathan Borofsky'' in *Artforum* (New York), February 1981; ''A Walk Through Borofsky's Brain'' by Nancy Grimes in *Artnews* (New York), Summer 1985; ''The Disquieting Mind of Jonathan Borofsky'' by Joseph Jarrell in *Sculpture,* September/October 1990; ''Jonathan Borofsky: What Is Dragging Me?'' by Rhonda Lieberman in *Artforum International,* vol. 32, September 1993; ''Living Outside His Own Shell: Jonathan Borofsky'' by Hunter Drohojowska-Philp in *The Los Angeles Times,* 24 October 1999; ''Jonathan Borofsky, The Art-Making Man'' by Christine Temin, *The Boston Globe,* 22 October 2000; ''Perspectives: Borofsky's Vision One of Repression'' by Christine Temin in *The Boston Globe,* 7 March 2001.

* * *

Jonathan Borofky's installation at the L.A. County Museum, 1981, included a large figure painted on both wall and ceiling. The image had giant rabbit ears, a haunted face, and eyes which were circled in a deadened, exacerbated state. He presented a flying man at Basel's Kunsthalle, and a running man in the Hayden Gallery, M.I.T. At Paula Cooper Gallery he painted legions of black-streaked humans which hurried over the wall. Also installed was a ping-pong table set in the middle of the space, along with assorted debris, a stooped black human form, large scissors, and 80 to 100 other strewn objects attached to the installation. Also at Basel: a 26 foot high, two-dimensional planar sculpture, which is Borofsky's hammering man, with a hand-held object, head-hung, feet plodding, a techno-cave man, an emblematic cut-out.

Borofsky's work is shadowy. At first one thinks the work could be a mistake, since the painting is often done on the gallery walls. Even in his sculptural work, objects generally appear awry. Soon, though, the relationship between the clear, interior lit gallery space becomes apparent against the underlife of Borofsky's mammoth figures. The images and the people are private possessions of Borofsky's; therein lies their unfocused dream-like reference. They are exposed interior beings in which a particular imagination chooses as it wants, rather than as it dreams.

For years Borofsky worked with numbers, counting incessantly. He literally wrote out numbers onto pieces of paper, reaching over two million in several years. This pile of sheets of numbers was exhibited in Borofsky's first New York show at Artists Space. Later Borofsky learned to use numbers as numerical signification, as a ''signature'' next to his imagery. This impersonal quality of signature assisted in placing his imagery within a larger opus, similar to the type of posthumous textual studies usually written and cataloged by scholars. In a sense, Borofsky was creating the categorization of his work, if not the analysis, at an early stage.

Most of Borofsky's work belies bourgeois scale and therefore ''civilized'' dwellings. The rooms and buildings are appropriately the wrong size for the work; either they are too small or misshaped for the quantity of strewn objects exhibited. The work is not hesitant, though obviously the sign of odd inward intelligence, a fulfilled combination of form turning into crazed function. The rational mind explains itself inside out in Borofsky's work. ''Self-Portrait in Closet at 2490197'' was shown at the Morgan Thomas Gallery in Los Angeles, painted over and also inside of a closet, with the closet door ajar. The blunt, dark markings picture Borofsky with a downcast gaze, a hat and its brim, closed and tight lips, and the closet door which opens and closes through the portrait, suggesting certain transparencies. The portrait is softer in tone than the rest of the work.

—John Robinson

Borofsky still occasionally returns to counting, and he can safely be credited as the inventor of that art form. Now that he is well into the millions, it somehow seems appropriate that his relatively more traditional art works have a monumental aspect. *Man Walking to the Sky* featured a life-size figure confidently striding up a nearly vertical painted pole of stainless steel that reached high above the rooftop of the Museum Fridericanum in Kassel, Germany, the site of Documenta IX (1992).

—Mark Swartz

BOSHIER, Derek

Nationality: British. **Born:** Portsmouth, Hampshire, in 1937. **Education:** Studied at the Yeovil School of Art, Somerset, 1953–57; Royal College of Art, London, 1959–62. **Military Service:** Served in the British Army, 1957–59. **Career:** Lecturer, Central School of Art and Design, and Hornsey College of Art, London, since 1963. Visiting lecturer, University of Victoria, 1975; and University of Houston 1980–81. **Awards:** Arts Council Young Contemporaries Award, 1961; Indian Government Scholarship, 1962; Peter Stuyvesant Foundation Travel Bursary to the United States, 1964; British Government Cultural Exchange Programme Grant, 1968; Minister of Affairs Prize, *7th Print Biennale,* Tokyo, 1970; Film Grant, Arts Council of Great Britain, 1970. **Agents:** Angela Flowers, London; Robin Cronin, Houston, Texas. **Address:** 25 Ladbroke Gardens, London W11, England.

Individual Exhibitions:

1962 *Image in Revolt,* Grabowski Gallery, London (with Frank Bowling)
1965 Robert Fraser Gallery, London
Galerie Aujourd'hui, Brussels
1967 Galerie Bischofberger, Zurich
1968 Robert Fraser Gallery, London
1970 Edizioni O, Milan
Nigel Greenwood Gallery, London
Galerie Bucholtz, Munich
Galerie Varenne, Paris
1971 Hayward Gallery, London
1972 Arnolfini Gallery, Bristol (toured the U.K., 1972–73)
1974 Angela Flowers Gallery, London
1975 Art Net, London
Whitworth Art Gallery, Manchester
Angela Flowers Gallery, London
1976 Angela Flowers Gallery, London

1977 Peterloo Gallery, Manchester
1979 Felicity Samuel Gallery, London
1980 Angela Flowers Gallery, London
1981 Angela Flowers Gallery, London
Painting 1980–81, Contemporary Art Museum, Houston
Muzeum Sztuki, Lodz, Poland
1982 Cronin Gallery, Houston, Texas
Institute of Contemporary Arts, London
1983 Bluecoat Gallery, Liverpool, Merseyside
Texas Gallery, Houston
1985 Edward Totah Gallery, London
Texas Gallery, Houston
1986 Totah-Stelling Art, New York
1987 Edward Totah Gallery, London
Texas Gallery, Houston
1993 *Derek Boshier,* Galerie du Centre, Paris
The Sixties Art Scene, Barbican Art Gallery, London
1995 *Derek Boshier: The Texas Years,* Contemporary Art Museum, Houston
1996 *Derek Boshier: Recent Works,* Connaught Brown Gallery, London
2000 *Derek Boshier: New Work,* Shakespeare Fine Art, Islington

Selected Group Exhibitions:

1963 *3rd Biennale des Jeunes,* Paris
1964 *The New Generation,* Whitechapel Art Gallery, London
1967 *New Shapes of Color,* Stedelijk Museum, Amsterdam (toured the Netherlands)
1969 *12 British Artists,* Kunstlerhaus Galerie, Vienna
1973 *Henry Moore to Gilbert and George,* Victoria and Albert Museum, London
1977 *British Painting 1952–1977,* Royal Academy of Art, London
1979 *A Generation,* Scottish National Gallery of Modern Art, Edinburgh
1982 *The Human Figure,* Contemporary Arts Center, New Orleans
1984 *Content: A Contemporary Focus,* Hirshhorn Museum, Washington, D.C.
1987 *Still-Life: Theme and Variation,* Glassel School of Art, Houston, Texas
1995 *3 Ways: An Exhibition of Contemporary British Painting,* South African National Gallery, Cape Town
1997 *Hockney to Hodgkin: British Master Prints 1960–1980,* New Orleans Museum of Art
2000 *Live in Your Head,* Whitechapel Art Gallery, London

Collections:

Arts Council of Great Britain, London; Victoria and Albert Museum, London; City Art Gallery, Manchester, National Museum of Wales, Cardiff; Museum of Modern Art, New York.

Publications:

By BOSHIER: Books—*16 Situations,* London 1971; *6 Cities* (series of postcards), London 1972. **Articles**—''Derek Boshier on His Constructed Prints: A Suite of Three, in Conversation with Christopher Fox'' in *Studio International* (London), December 1970; statement in *Studio International* (London), November 1973; ''The Artist's Eye: Derek Boshier Discusses His Painting Possibilities of Nature'' in *Art Review* (London), vol. 48, March 1996. **Films**—*Link,* 1970; *Circle,* 1971; *Reel,* 1973; *Watch,* 1975.

On BOSHIER: Books—*Derek Boshier,* exhibition catalog, London 1973; *Boshier,* exhibition catalog, Manchester 1975; *Lives: An Exhibition of Artists Whose Work Is Based on Other People's Lives,* selected by Boshier, exhibition catalog, London 1979; *Derek Boshier: Painting 1980–81,* exhibition catalog, by Cheryl Brutvan, Houston 1981; *Derek Boshier: The Texas Years,* exhibition catalog, with text by Lynn M. Herbert, Marti Mayo and Guy Brett, Houston 1995; *Derek Boshier: Recent Works,* exhibition catalog, with text by Mel Gooding, London 1996; *Derek Boshier: New Work, 31 March-16 May 2000,* exhibition catalog, London 2000. **Articles**—''Derek Boshier: Hayward Gallery'' by Eddie Wolfram in *Arts Review* (London), December 1970; ''Derek Boshier Situations'' in *Creative Camera* (London), June 1971; ''The Impossibility of Sculpture'' by Paul Overy in *The Times* (London), June 1973; ''It's All in Your Mind'' by Barry Schwabsky in *Art in America,* September 2000.

* * *

Of the class of 1962 at the Royal College of Art, taking his diploma with David Hockney and Peter Phillips, Derek Boshier was one of the successes of the Pop movement in England. With Frank Bowling he showed under the title *Image in Revolt* at the Grabowski Gallery, London, in the same year. In large canvases he expressed his personal rejection of the conventional format for pictures. Chiefly the motives were those of printed symbols, many of them from commercial packaging and cheap comics.

This employment of ready-made and widely known characters from the media aligned the work with the proletarian connection in Pop art, though this aspect was bent by Boshier to narrative content concerned with S.F. and a fanciful quasi-surrealist effect. Large-scale compositions emphasized the repetitive elements, mostly tiny figures representing mankind in situations of symbolic compulsive direction or motivation.

Fascinated by ambiguities, Boshier saw some of his earlier Pop paintings as embodying social comment based on autobiographical experience, though this was not always explicit. Strangely enough, after he had gone to India for a year on a scholarship, he completely rejected the figurative element in his painting. In *The New Generation* exhibition at the Whitechapel Gallery in 1964, Boshier's post-Indian paintings echoed more the eye-dazzling stripes and hard-edge patterns of Bridget Riley and Frank Stella than any assimilated visual data from the East. The use of shaped stretchers for surfaces that projected beyond the usual rectangular enclosure implied a possible allegorical meaning in the shape of the canvas. The colour bands, stepped and curbed, alternately straight and diagonal, embody a symbolism more subtle than any exercise in abstract Op organization. The Pop allusion (that of a giant table game akin to ''Monopoly'') is played down in a cool context, but the metaphors can be no less than intentional. Traffic signs, painted wall and street insignia and directions—these are all part of the universal eye-reaction vocabulary.

In common with several of his generation, Boshier is concerned less with a medium for its own character than for its capacity to carry the message he loads into it. Experiments in plastic constructions, though inconclusive, indicated his versatility and adaptability in approach. He says: ''Art is about ideas, and your medium is the medium that is best suited to your ideas.'' As a friend of poets and writers, he is interested in film-making and in writing for communication—e.g., fiction. He has written a novel, and—as he demonstrates—his approach to art is open-ended.

—G. S. Whittet

BOTERO, Fernando

Nationality: Colombian. **Born:** Fernando Botero Angulo in Medellin, Antioquia, 19 April 1932. **Education:** Attended primary and secondary schools in Medellin, 1938–49; Liceo de la Universidad de Antioquia, Medellin, 1950, baccalaureate; studied at the Real Academia de Bellas Artes, San Ferdinando, Spain, and copied paintings of Goya, Veláquez, and others at the Museo del Prado, Madrid, 1952; studied fresco painting at the Accademia San Marco, and art history, under Roberto Longhi, at the Università degli Studi, Florence, 1953. **Family:** Married Gloria Zea in 1955 (divorced, 1960); children: Fernando, Lina, and Juan Carlos; married Cedilia Zambrano in 1964 (divorced, 1975); son: Pedro (died in auto crash, 1974). **Career:** Worked as an illustrator for the Sunday Literary Supplement of *El Colombiano,* Medellin, 1948–51; worked briefly as a set designer for the Compania Lope de Vega touring Spanish theatre group, 1950. Independent artist since 1951: lived in Bogota, then moved to Tolu on the Gulf of Morrosquillo, also painting at Covenas and the islands of San Bernardo, 1951; returned to Bogota, then travelled to Barcelona, and lived in Madrid, 1952–53; spent summers in Paris, 1953–54; lived and established studio in Florence, and travelled throughout northern Italy to study fresco sites, 1953–54; influenced strongly by exhibition of the works of Piero della Francesca, Paolo Uccello, Andrea del Castagno, and Domenico Veneziano, Florence, 1954; returned to Bogota, 1955; lived in Mexico City, 1956–57; travelled to New York and Washington, D.C., 1957, 1958; lived in Bogota, 1957–60; commissioned by Banco Central Hipotecario to paint a fresco in its Medellin branch, 1960; lived in New York, 1961–73: rented a loft studio at MacDougal and Third Streets in Greenwich Village, 1961–64, moved to Tomkins Square on Lower East Side, 1963–71, built summer house and studio on Stephen's Hand Pass Road, Easthampton, Long Island, and established a studio at 214 West 14th Street, 1964–72, moved to 30 Fifth Avenue, 1971; rented an apartment in Paris, and established studio in Bogota, 1971; rented studio on rue Monsieur-le-Prince, Paris, and bought house in which to spend summers in Cajicà, north of Bogota, 1972; has lived in Paris since 1973; concentrated almost entirely on sculpture, 1976–77; established Sala Pedro Botero, with 16 of his works, at the Museo de Zea, Medellin, 1977; established and maintains studio on rue du Dragon in building formerly housing the Académie Julian, Paris, since 1978. Professor of painting, Escuela de Bellas Artes, Universidad Nacional, Bogota, 1958–60. **Awards:** First Prize for Painting, *Salon Anual de Artistas Colombianos,* Bogota, 1958; Colombian Section Award, *Guggenheim International Award Exhibition,* New York, 1960; Andrés Bello Award, President of Venezuela, 1975. Cruz de Boyacá for service to Colombia, Government of Antioquia, 1977. **Agent:** Marlborough Fine Art, New York. **Address:** 900 Park Avenue, #22A, New York, New York, 10021–0231.

Individual Exhibitions:

1951 Galerias de Arte Foto-Estudio Leo Matiz, Bogota
1952 Galerias de Arte de Leo Matiz, Bogota
1955 Biblioteca Nacional, Bogota (travelled to Club de Profesionales, Medellin, Colombia)
1957 Galeria Antonio Souza, Mexico City
Fernando Botero of Colombia, Pan American Union, Washington, D.C.
1958 *Oleos,* Galeria Antonio Souza, Mexico City
Recent Oils, Watercolors, Drawings, Gres Gallery, Washington, D.C.
1959 *Obras Recientes,* Biblioteca Nacional, Bogota
1960 Gres Gallery, Washington, D.C.
1961 Galeria de Arte El Callejón, Bogota
1962 Gres Gallery, Chicago
The Contemporaries, New York
1964 *Obras Recientes,* Museo de Arte Moderno, Bogota
Bosquejos Realidades, Galeria Arte Moderno, Bogota
1965 *Recent Works,* Zora Gallery, Los Angeles
1966 Staatliche Kunsthalle, Baden-Baden, West Germany (travelled to the Galerie Buchholz, Munich)
Ölbilder und Zeichnungen, Galerie Brusberg, Hannover
Recent Works, Milwaukee Art Center
1968 Galeria Juana Mordó, Madrid
Paintings by Fernando Botero and Leopold Richter, Walter Engel Gallery, Toronto
Galerie Buchholz, Munich
1969 Center for Inter-American Relations, New York
Peintures, Pastels, Fusains, Galerie Claude Bernard, Paris
1970 *Bilder 1962–1969,* Staatliche Kunsthalle, Baden- Baden, West Germany (travelled to Haus am Waldsee, Berlin; Städtische Kunsthalle, Dusseldorf; Kunstverein, Hamburg; and Kunsthalle, Bielefeld)
Botero/Coronel/Rodon, Museo de la Universidad de Puerto Rico
Hanover Gallery, London
Botero/Cuevas: Paintings, Drawings. Walter Engel Gallery, Toronto
1971 *Botero/Lindner/Wesselmann: Ausgewähte Bilder, Zeichnungern und Grafik.* Galerie Brusberg, Hannover
1972 Marlborough Gallery, New York
Bleisftzeichnungen, Sepiazeichnungen, Aquarelle, Galerie Buchholz, Munich
Pastels, Fusains, Sanguines, Galerie Claude Bernard, Paris
1973 *Retrospectiva 1948–1972,* Colegio San Carlos, Bogota
Marlborough Galleria d'Arte, Rome
Botero/Akawie, Pyramid Galleries, Washington, D.C.
1974 *Aquarelle und Zeichnungen,* Galerie Brusberg, Hannover
Sala de Arte, Biblioteca Publica Piloto, Medellin, Colombia
Marlborough Galarie, Zurich
1975 Museum Boymans-van Beuningen, Rotterdam
Galeria Adlec Castillo, Caracas
Marlborough Gallery, New York (travelled to Marlborough Godard, Toronto; and Marlborough Godard, Montreal, 1976)
1976 *Aquarelles et Dessins,* Galerie Claude Bernard, Paris
Museo de Arte Contemporaneo, Caracas

Pyramid Galleries, Washington, D.C.
Arte Independencia, La Galeria de Colombia, Bogota
1977 *Las Sala Pedro, Botero,* Museo de Arte Medellin, Colombia
Sculptures, at *FIAC,* Grand Palais, Paris
1978 *Das Plastische Werk,* Galerie Brusberg, Hannover (travelled to Skulpturenmuseum der Stadt Marl, West Germany)
1979 Galerie Isy Brachot, Knokke, Belgium
Musée d'Ixelles, Brussels (travelled to Konsthall, Lund, Sweden; and Sonja Henie-Neils Onstad Foundations, Oslo)
Galerie Claude Bernard, Paris
Galerie Brusberg, Hannover
Hirshhorn Museum and Sculpture Garden, Smithsonian Institution, Washington, D.C. (travelled to the Art Museum of South Texas, Corpus Christi, 1980)
1980 *Aquarelles, Dessins, Sculptures,* Galerie Beyeler, Basle
1981 Marlborough Gallery, New York
Betsy Rosenfield Gallery, Chicago
1982 *Sculpture and Drawings,* Hokin Gallery, Chicago
1983 Galerie Beyeler, Basle
Thomas Segal Gallery, Boston
1984 Proctor Institute, Utica, New York
Everhart Museum, Scranton, Pennsylvania
Cornell University, Ithaca, New York
Purdue University, Lafayette, Indiana
Botero, at the *International Art Expo.* Chicago
1985 National Museum, Bogota, Colombia
Museo de Ponce, Puerto Rico
Marlborough Gallery, New York
1986 Museum of Contemporary Art, Caracas, Venezuela
Kunsthalle der Hypo-Kulturstiftung, Munich
Kunsthalle, Bremen, West Germany
Tokyo Art Gallery, Tokyo
Daimaru Museum, Osaka, Japan
City Art Museum, Niigata, Japan
1990 Fondation Pierre Gianadda, Martigny, Switzerland
Marlborough Gallery, New York
1991 Forte di Belvedere, Florence
Marlborough Fine Art, Tokyo
1992 Champs Elysees, Paris
Pallazo delle Fesposizioni, Rome
Kunst Haus Wein, Vienna
Galeries Nationales du Grand Palais, Paris
Palais des Papes, Avignon
Pushkin Museum, Moscow
Hermitage Museum, St. Petersburg
1994 Grant Park, Chicago
Museo Nacional de Bellas Artes, Buenos Aires
Paseo de Recoletos, Madrid
1996 Museo de Arte Contemporaneo de Caracas Sofia Imber, Caracas
Galerie Brusberg, Berlin

Selected Group Exhibitions:

1948 *Exposición de Pintores Antioqueños,* Instituto de Bellas Artes, Medellin, Colombia
1952 *Salón Anual de Artistas Colombianos,* Biblioteca Nacional, Bogota (and 1957, 1958, 1959)
1956 *Gulf-Caribbean Art Exhibition,* Museum of Fine Arts, Houston (toured the United States, 1956–57)
1958 *Guggenheim International Award,* Guggenheim Museum, New York (and 1960)
1959 *Botero/Grau/Obregón/Ramirez/Villegas/Wiedemann,* Galeria de Arte Callejón, Bogota
Arte de Colombia, Galleria Nazionale d'Arte Moderna, Rome (travelled to Liljevalchs Konsthall, Stockholm; Rautenstrauch-Joest-Museum, Cologne; Staatliche Kunsthalle, Baden-Baden, and the Sociedad Española de Amigos del Arte, Madrid)
1965 *The Emergent Decade: Latin American Painting,* Guggenheim Museum, New York (toured the United States and Canada, 1965–67)
1970 *Latin American Paintings and Drawings from the Collection of John and Barbara Duncan,* Center for Inter-American Relations, New York (toured the United States, 1970–72)
1971 *12 Artists from Latin America,* Ringling Museum of Art, Sarasota, Florida
1977 *Recent Latin American Drawings 1969–1976: Lines of Vision,* Center for Inter-American Relations, New York (toured the United States and Philippines, 1977–79)
1989 *Sculpture by Abakanowicz, Botero, Bruskin, Davies, Grooms, Mason,* Marlborough Gallery, New York
1995 *3 Continents: Fernando Botero, Claudio Bravo, Larry Rivers, Manolo Valdes,* A.M.S. Marlborough, Santiago

Collections:

Museo de Zea, Medellin, Colombia: Museo de Arte Moderno, Bogota; Museo de Bellas Artes, Santiago; Museum of Modern Art, New York; Guggenheim Museum, New York; New York University; Baltimore Museum of Art; Neue Pinakothek, Munich; Museo d'Arte Moderno del Vaticano, Rome; Museo de Arte Contemporaneo, Madrid; Walrat-Richarts Museum, Cologne; Hirshhorn Museum and Sculpture Garden, Washington, D.C.; National Museum, Tokyo; Metropolitan Museum of Art, New York.

Publications:

By BOTERO: Books—*Botero,* portfolio of 20 black-and-white reproductions, with an introduction by Walter Engel, Bogota 1952; *Botero: New Works on Canvas,* interview by Ana Maria Escallon, New York 1997. **Articles—**"Picasso y la Inconformidad en el Arte" in *El Colombiano* (Medellin), 17 July 1949; ''Anatomia de Una Locura'' in *El Colombiano* (Medellin), 7 August 1949; interview, with Wibke von Bonin, in *Fernando Botero,* exhibition catalog, New York 1972; interview, with Titia Berlage, in *Fernando Botero,* exhibition catalog, Rotterdam 1975.

On BOTERO: Books—*Fernando Botero,* exhibition catalog, Bogota 1951; *Botero,* exhibition catalog, Bogota 1952; *Botero* by Walter Engel, Bogota 1952; *Gulf-Caribbean Art Exhibition,* catalog, with foreword by Lee Malone and an introduction by José Gómez-Sicre, Houston 1956; *Fernando Botero of Colombia,* exhibition catalog, Washington, D.C. 1957; *Fernando Botero; Recent Oils, Watercolors,*

Drawings, exhibition catalog, Washington, D.C. 1958; *Botero: Obras Recientes,* exhibition catalog, Bogota, 1959; *Botero,* exhibition catalog, Chicago 1962; *Botero; Recent Works,* exhibition catalog, Los Angeles 1965; *Fernando Botero,* exhibition catalog, with text by Daniel Robbins, Baden-Baden, West Germany 1966; *Fernando Botero: Recent Works,* exhibition catalog, with a foreword by Tracy Atkinson, Milwaukee 1966; *The Emergent Decade: Latin American Painters and Painting in the 1960's,* Ithaca, New York 1966; *Paintings by Fernando Botero and Leopold Richter,* exhibition catalog, Toronto 1968; *Fernando Botero,* exhibition catalog, with foreword by Stanton Catlin, and essay by Klaus Gallwitz, New York 1969; *Botero: Peintures, Pastels, Fusains,* exhibition catalog, with text by Fernando Arrabal, Paris 1969; *Botero* by Klaus Gallwitz, Munich 1970; *Botero: Pastels, Fusains, Sanguines,* exhibition catalog, with an introduction by Jean Paget, Paris 1972; *Fernando Botero: Retrospectiva 1948–1972,* exhibition catalog, with text by Tracy Atkinson, Bogota 1973; *Botero* by Marta Trata, Mexico City 1973; *Fernando Botero* by German Arciniegas, Madrid 1973, translated by Gabriela Arciniegas, New York 1977; *Botero,* exhibition catalog, by Antonio Hernandez Barrera, Medellin, Colombia 1974; *Fernando Botero,* exhibition catalog, with an introduction by R. Hammacher-van der Brande, Rotterdam 1975; *Fernando Botero,* exhibition catalog, with an introduction by Sam Hunter, New York 1975; *Los Intocables: Botero, Grau, Negret, Obregón, Ramirez V.* by Fausto Panesso, Bogota 1975; *Botero: Aquarelles et Dessins,* exhibition catalog, with an introduction by Severo Sarduy, Paris 1976; *Fernando Botero,* exhibition catalog, with an introduction by Sofia Imber, Caracas, Venezuela 1976; *Botero,* exhibition catalog, with text by Robert Pinzón, Bogota 1976; *Fernando Botero* by Klaus Gallwitz, New York, London, and Stuttgart 1976; *Modern Art* by Sam Hunter and John Jacobus, New York 1976; *La Sala Pedro Botero,* exhibition catalog, with text by Belisario Betancur, Medellin, Colombia 1977; *Recent Latin American Drawings 1969–1979: Lines of Vision,* exhibition catalog, with essays by Barbara Duncan and Damián Bayón, New York 1977; *Fernando Botero: Das Plastische Werk* by Ursula Bode, Hannover 1978; *Fernando Botero,* exhibition catalog, with text by Marie-Franccoise Carolus-Barré, Brussels 1979; *Fernando Botero,* exhibition catalog, by Cynthia Jaffee McCabe, with foreword by Abram Lerner, Washington, D.C. 1979; *Fernando Botero: Malerier, Tegninger, Skulpturer,* exhibition catalog, with texts by Marianne Nanne-Brahammar and Ole Henrik Moe, Oslo 1979; *Botero: Aquarelles, Dessins, Sculptures,* exhibition catalog, with an introduction by Ernst Beyeler, Basle 1980; *Botero* by Carter Ratcliff, New York 1980; *Botero,* exhibition catalog, Martigny 1990; *Fernando Botero: Recent Sculpture,* exhibition catalog, New York 1990; *Botero* by Gerard Durozoi, Paris 1992; *Fernando Botero,* edited by Werner Spies, Munich 1992; *Botero in Buenos Aires,* exhibition catalog, Buenos Aires 1994; *3 Continents: Fernando Botero, Claudio Bravo, Larry Rivers, Manolo Valdes,* exhibition catalog, Santiago 1995; *Fernando Botero: ''The Inverted Kolumbus,''* exhibition catalog, Berlin 1996; *Botero: Donation by the Artist to the Museo de Arte Contemporaneo de Caracas Sofia Imber,* exhibition catalog, Caracas 1996. **Articles—**''The Bullfight: Fernando Botero'' by Maria Elvira Triarte in *Art Nexus,* no. 9, June-August 1993; ''Botero on the Avenue'' by Brooks Adams in *Art in America* (New York), vol. 81, no. 11, November 1993; "Site: Botero on Park Avenue" by George Melrod in *Sculpture* (Washington, D.C.), vol. 13, no. 2, March-April 1994.

* * *

Fernando Botero is one of those fortunate artists whose subject or style becomes immediately recognizable. His pneumatic nudes and overdressed, adipose children form a personal, fantasy world of undeniable conviction. The combination of obese, exaggerated, human forms, elaborately decorative costumes and the oversweet colours of South American peasant art results in images in which wit and sympathy are undermined by an aggressive irreverence.

It must be noted that the two major influences in Botero's art are Goya and Veláquez. Born in the industrial centre of Colombian life, Medellin, he moved to Bogota, where he held his first exhibitions, and then entered the Academia in San Ferdinando, Spain. Here the work of the two great Spanish masters had their effect; from Goya he absorbed a critical view of the human comedy, whilst in the meticulously painted, realistic still-lifes, one recognizes the influence of Velázquez. In Europe Botero also studied fresco techniques in Florence, especially impressed by the famous series of wall paintings by Piero della Francesca in Arezzo. These disparate forces in his development were bound into an artistic whole by Botero's love for his native Colombia, whose daily life, religious myths and folk art, descended from the Indians, remain his basic subjects.

The resultant images are curiously enigmatic; he is neither as open a commentator as Goya, nor as willing a participant as Velázquez. On the other hand, nor is he merely a recording camera. Whilst the real world is Botero's point of departure, he feels at liberty to use anti-natural devices common to native art—or to the ''primitive'' painters of Christian Europe—his own depiction as a tiny figure, carrying palette and brushes, beside a full-length portrait, or his self-portrait on Communion Day, with two tiny devils whispering into his ear

—Charles Spencer

BOTO, Martha

Nationality: Argentinian. **Born:** Buenos Aires, 27 December 1925. **Education:** Studied drawing, Academy Prilidiano Pueyrredon, Buenos Aires, 1942–43; Ernesto de la Cracova Superior Academy of Fine Arts, Buenos Aires, 1944–46. **Family:** Married to Gregorio Vardanega. **Career:** Independent artist since 1946, producing kinetic sculptures and installations that alter light; has lived and worked in Paris since 1959. Founding member, Groupe Artistes Non-Figurative Argentins, 1956. **Awards:** Painting Prize, Museo Quinquella Martin, Buenos Aires, 1947. **Agent:** Galerie Denise René, 196 Boulevard Saint-Germain, 75007 Paris, **Address:** Atelier 127, 21 rue de l'Amiral-Roussin, 75015 Paris, France.

Individual Exhibitions:

1951 Galerie van Riel et Krayd, Paris (and each year through 1955)
1957 Galeria Galatea Pizarro, Buenos Aires
1960 Galerie H. Buenos Aires
1969 Galerie Denise René, Paris
1970 Galerie Thelen, Essen
1972 La Belle Epine, Val de Marne, France
1976 Centre Culturel, Sceaux, France
1996 Galerie Argentine, Paris
1997 Poste St. Lambert, Paris

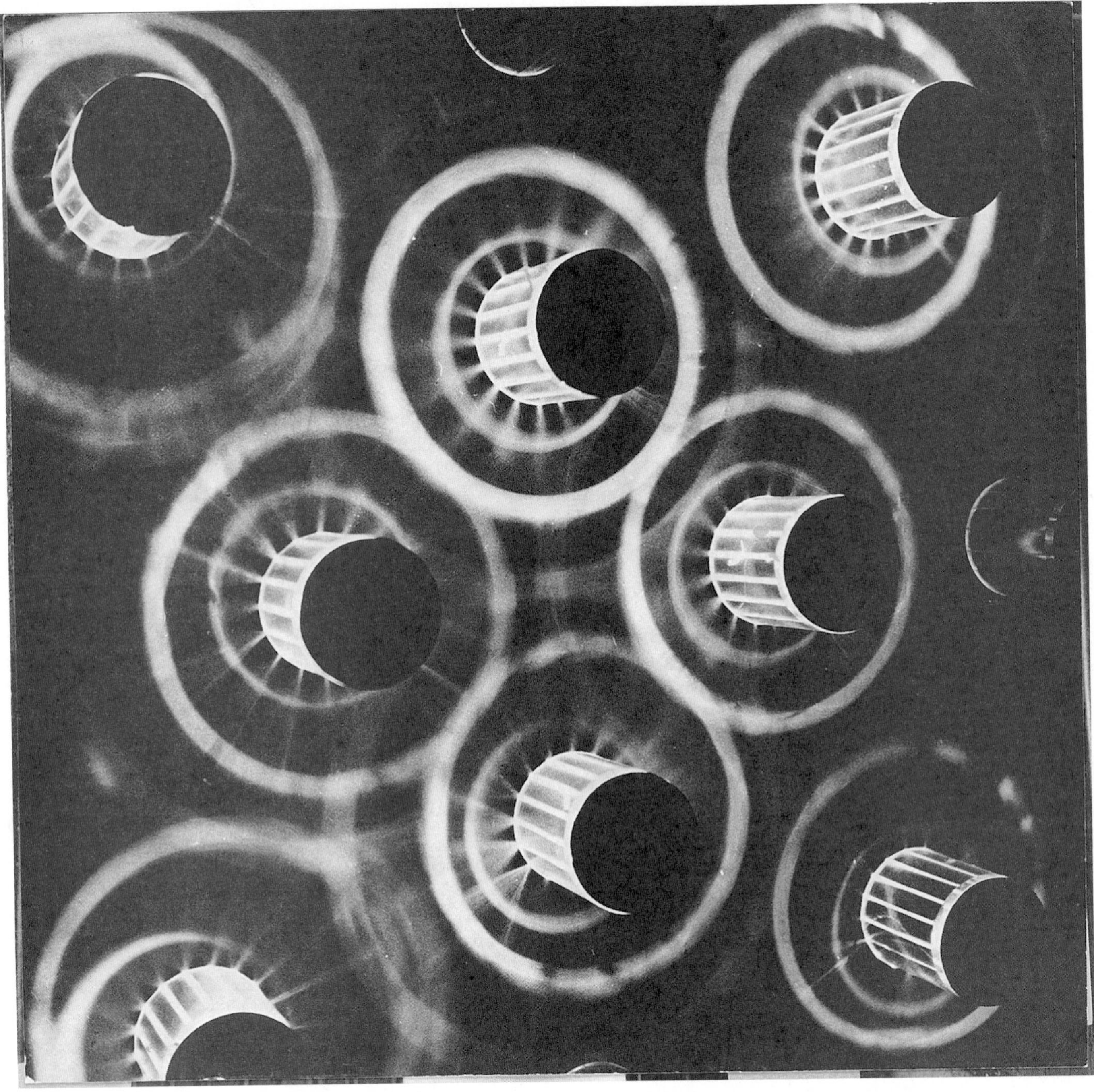

Martha Boto: *Dilatations Chromatiques,* 1967. ©Martha Boto.

Selected Group Exhibitions:

1967 *Lumiére et Mouvement,* Musée d'Art Moderne de la Ville, Paris
1973 *Art Cinétique,* Bagneaux, France
1981 *Grands et Jeunes d'Aujourd'hui,* Grand Palais, Paris
1983 *Electra,* Musée d'Art Moderne de la Ville, Paris
1987 *Féerie Cinétique,* Monte Carlo, Monaco
1988 *Fête Bleue,* Grand Palais, Paris
1989 *Art Constructif: Lumiére et Mouvement,* Galerie Denise René, Paris
1990 *Abstraction Géométrique,* Galerie Denise René, Paris
1992 *L'Art en Mouvement,* Fondation Maeght, Saint Paul de Vence, France
1993 *UAPA,* Espace Bateau Lavoir, Paris
1995 *Transparences,* Musée des Beaux Arts, André Malraux, Le Havre, France
1996 *Chimériques-Polymères,* Musée d'Art Moderne et d'Art Contemporain, Nice
1997 Hommage à Denise René, Musée SZTUKI, Wieckowskiego, Lódz, Poland
1998 *Intuition Pure,* Galerie Denise René, Espace Marais, Paris

Martha Boto, Paris, 1970.

1999 *Art Construit et Cinétique d'Amerique Latine,* Galerie Denise René, Espace Marais, Paris
2000 *Formes et Mouvements d'Art au 20th Siecle,* Hommage à Denise René, Japan
2001 Hommage à Denise René, au Centre Georges Pompidou, Paris

Collections:

Musée d'Art Moderne de la Ville, Paris; Prefecture of Paris; Fonds National d'Art Contemporain, France; Museo Nacional de Bellas Artes, Buenos Aires; Museo de Arte Contemporaneo, Buenos Aires; Recklinehausen Museum, Germany; Albright Knox Gallery, Buffalo; Milwaukee Art Museum; Art Museum of New South Wales, Sydney; Rembrandt Art Foundation, Le Cap, South Africa; Fondation Guggenheim, Venice; Tel-Aviv Museum, Israel.

Permanent Public Installations:

Centre Commercial de Belle Epine, Thiais, France; Centre Commercial de Metz Borny; Galerie Point Show, Paris; Centre Commercial Créteil Soleil, Créteil, France; Centre Commercial les Arcades, Marne la Valée; Passage de l'Horloge, Paris.

Publications:

On BOTO: Books—*Artes y Letras Argentinas* by Cordova Iturburu, Buenos Aires 1961; *Naissance de l'Art cinétique* by Frank Popper, Paris 1966; *Art et Mouvement,* exhibition catalog, by Denys Chevalier, Montreal 1967; *Martha Boto,* exhibition catalog, by Michael Ragon, Paris 1969; *L'Art Actuel* by Tronche, Paris 1973; *L'Art Abstrait,* vol. 4, by Michel Ragon and Michel Seuphor, Paris 1975. **Articles—**''L'Art de la lumiére artificielle'' by Frank Popper in *L'Oeil* (Paris), December 1966; ''Buenos Aires, nouvelle capitale artistique'' by Michel Ragon in *Jardin des Arts* (Paris), April 1967; ''Dalla Francia con amore'' by Ettore Sottsas in *Domus* (Milan), July 1967; ''Lumiére et mouvement'' by Frank Popper in *Art Cinétique a Paris,* exhibition catalog, Paris 1967.

*

I have always been fascinated by the laws of harmony and equilibrium that govern the cosmos in all its relations, to light and movements, space, time, colors. The necessity of applying these laws in the plastic arts has taken me in different directions in painting: impressionism, expressionism, surrealism, and abstraction.

Buenos Aires, 1958: Mobile Structures

This was the beginning of my concern with three-dimensional space, which resulted in the creation of structure and mobiles suspended in space, transparent plexiglas with colored water (natural movement).

Paris, 1960: Kinetic Art

The necessity of controlling, in real space, light and movement, led me to manipulate them technically by means of electricity and mechanics (motors, lamps), and gave birth to my kinetic works: *Light and Movement,* in the form of electric boxes with projections on screens—movement of objects by themselves—or with light and colors incorporated into programs.

Paris, 1979: Sculptures

Families of white forms, unified by flowing rhythms, sometimes colored graphisms accentuating the sensuality of the new language.

Paris, 1983: Painting

Interpretation of energy in permanent movement in virtual space, by means of a swarm of small points in flight, which invade the entire canvas, climbing on graphisms of unprecedented decoration.

My most recent inquiries are oriented toward undulatory rhythms, the intimate and parallel language of a dialogue between two forces: volume and space, complementarily, expressed in painting with abstract synthesis.

Paris, 1991: *Mémoires Végétales*

In reality, my inquiries in painting are oriented toward the luminous expression of lyrico-abstract color and form, in free-flight, sometimes full, sometimes empty, sometimes horizontal, sometimes vertical.

—Martha Boto

* * *

Martha Boto belongs to the tradition of South American Constructivism and has taken a prominent part in its conversion into kinetic art. Light and movement appear in all their purity and dynamism in her art, but there is always an underlying formal structure which can be seen or sensed.

Boto's works concentrate upon such features as rapid movement, circular forms and intense luminous effects. The light source itself is constantly moving in many of her works, and this results in a strong impression of contraction and expansion in the interplay of circles and planes, as well as a tendency for forms to appear and disappear, ranging from intensity to diffusion.

Martha Boto's investigation leads from the principle of repetition into the world of reflection and the progressive transformation of the image. In her ''chromokinetic'' works she has rarely used more than one colour, usually an ultramarine blue or a transparent rose. But the variations of the hues are many. They allow her to add an individual sense of completeness to the distinctive arrangements of movement through the manipulation of transparent light and enable the graphic properties inherent in the circle to emerge.

Boto's environment works realized since 1971 in and around Paris reflect all the accomplishments of the earlier research, yet in these works the sensuality of the rhythm, the hypnotizing variations of speeds, the subtle programmation of form transformation and the original treatment of colour and space take on a new dimension and most clearly demonstrate the interrelationship between the artist's technical/aesthetic achievements and her distinctive personality.

—Frank Popper

BOURGEOIS, Louise

Nationality: American. **Born:** Paris, France, 25 December 1911. **Education:** Lycée Fenelon, Paris, 1932; Sorbonne, Paris, 1932–35; Ecole de Louvre, Paris, 1936–37; Académie des Beaux-Arts, Paris 1936–38; Atelier Bissière, Paris, 1936–37; Académie Julian, Paris, 1938; Atelier Fernand Léger, Paris, 1938; also studied with Marcel Duchamp in New York. **Family:** Married Robert Goldwater in 1938; children: Michel, Jean-Louis and Alain. **Career:** Independent artist, New York, since 1938. Taught at the Academie de la Grande Chaumière, Paris, 1937–38; Great Neck Public Schools, New York, 1960; Brooklyn College, New York, 1963, 1968; and Pratt Institute, New York, 1965–67. Professor of Sculpture, School of Visual Arts, New York; lecturer, Lebanon College, New York University; critic, New York Studio School. **Awards:** National Endowment for the Arts Grant, 1973; Outstanding Visual Arts Achievement Award, Women's Caucus for Art, New York, 1980; Skowhegan Medal, Skowhegan School of Painting and Sculpture, Maine, 1984; MacDowell Medalist, MacDowell Colony, Peterborough, New Hampshire, 1990; The Sculpture Center Award for Distinction in Sculpture 1990, The Sculpture Center, New York; Lifetime Achievement Award, International Sculpture Center, Washington D.C., 1991; Grand Prix National de Sculpture by the French Ministry of Culture, 1992; NORD/LB art prize 1992; Mayor's Awards for Art & Culture, New York City, 1993; Maison Francaise, New York University, 1993; Biennial Award, The Ueno Royal Museum, Tokyo, and The Hakone Open-Air Museum, Kanagawa-ken, Japan, 1995; First Annual Urban Glass Award for Innovative Use of Glass by a Non-Glass Artist, 1996; National Medal of Arts, 1997; Academician of the National Academy, New York, 1998; Citation from the National Association of Schools of Art and Design, 1998; Wexner Prize, Wexner Center for the Arts, Ohio State University, 1999; Golden Lion, for a living master of contemporary art, LaBiennale di Venezia, 1999; Praemium Imperiale Award, Japan Art Association, 1999; Honorary Member, Akademie Der Bildenden Kunste Wien, 2000. Honorary doctorates: Yale University, New Haven, Connecticut, 1977; Bard College, Annandale-on-Hudson, New York, 1981; Massachusetts College of Art, Boston, 1983; Maryland Art Institute, Baltimore, 1984; The New School, New York, 1987; Pratt Institute, Brooklyn, New York, 1993; Art Institute of Chicago, 1995; Harvard University, 1999; Art Institute of Boston, 2000. **Address:** c/o Cheim & Read Gallery, 521 West 23rd Street, New York, New York 10011, U.S.A.

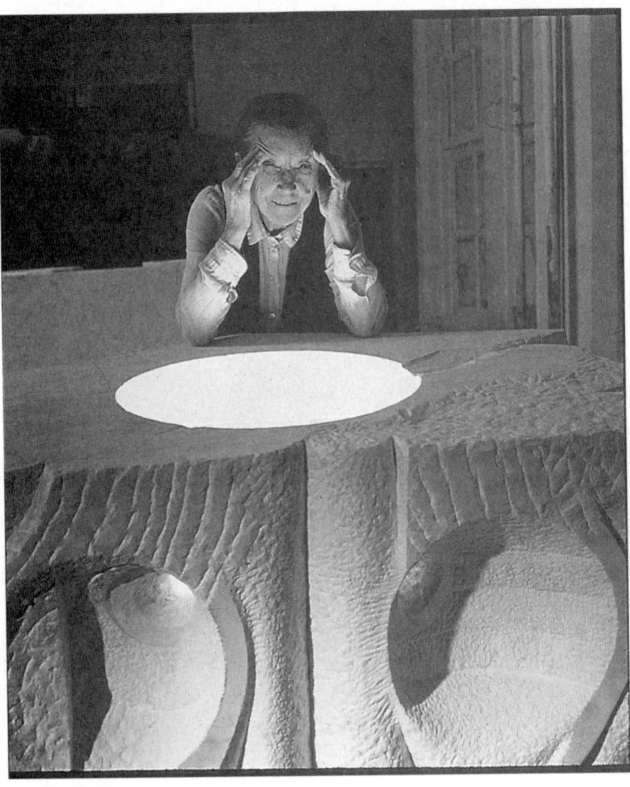

Louise Bourgeois in her studio with PASS, 1988. Photo by Claudio Edinger. ©Louise Bourgeois/Licensed by VAGA, New York, NY.

Individual Exhibitions:

1945 Bertha Schaefer Gallery, New York
1947 Norlyst Gallery, New York
1949 Peridot Gallery, New York
1950 Peridot Gallery, New York
1953 Peridot Gallery, New York
Allan Frumkin Gallery, Chicago
1959 Cornell University, Ithaca, New York
1964 The Stable Gallery, New York
Rose Fried Gallery, New York
1974 112 Greene Street Gallery, New York
1975 Stable Gallery, New York
1978 *Structures,* Xavier Fourcade Inc., New York
Confrontations, Hamilton Gallery, New York
1979 *Sculptures 1941–53,* Xavier Fourcade Inc., New York
Art Museum, University of California, Berkeley
1980 *The Iconography of Louise Bourgeois,* Max Hutchinson Gallery, New York
Sculpture: The Middle Years 1955–1970, Xavier Fourcade Inc., New York
1981 University of Chicago
1982 Robert Miller Gallery, New York
Museum of Modern Art, New York (retrospective; travelled to Chicago and Akron, Ohio, 1983)
1984 Daniel Weinberg Gallery, Los Angeles
Daniel Weinberg Gallery, San Francisco
Robert Miller Gallery, New York
1985 Serpentine Gallery, London

Louise Bourgeois: *Cell XIV (Portrait),* 2000. ©Louise Bourgeois. Licensed by VAGA, New York, NY.

Galerie Maeght-Lelong, Zurich
Galerie Maeght-Lelong, Paris (retrospective)
1986 Eyes Gallery, Doris Freedman Plaza, New York
Texas Gallery, Dallas
1987 Robert Miller Gallery, New York
Yares Gallery, Scottsdale, Arizona
Taft Museum, Cincinnati (toured the United States, 1987–90)
1989–91 *Louise Bourgeois: A Retrospective Exhibition,* Frankfurter Kunstverein, West Germany (traveled to Stadtische Galerie im Lenbachhaus, Munich, Musée d'art Contemporain, Lyon, France, Fondacion Tapies, Barcelona, Spain, Kunstmuseum, Berne, Switzerland, and Kröller-Muller-Museum, Otterlo, The Netherlands)
1990 Musée d'Art Contemporain, Lyon (retrospective)
1993–96 American Pavilion, Venice Biennale, Italy (expanded as *The Locus of Memory* and traveled to the Brooklyn Museum of Art, New York, The Corcoran Gallery of Art, Washington, D.C., Galerie Rudolfinum, Prague, Czech Republic, Musée d'Art Moderne de la Ville de Paris, France, Deichtorhallen, Hamburg, Germany, and Musée d'Art Contemporain de Montreal, Canada)
1994 *Louise Bourgeois: The Personages,* The Saint Louis Art Museum, St. Louis, Missouri (traveled to Nelson-Atkins Museum of Art, Kansas City)
Louise Bourgeois: Sculptures, Kestner-Gesellschaft, Hannover, Germany
1994–96 *Louise Bourgeois: Print Retrospective,* Museum of Modern Art, New York (traveled to the Bibliotheque Nationale, Paris, Musée du Dessin et de l'Estampe Originale, Gravelines, France, The Museum of Modern Art, Oxford, England, and Bonnefanten Museum, Maastricht, The Netherlands)
1995 *Louise Bourgeois: Pensée Plumes,* Musée National d'art Moderne, Centre Georges Pompidou, Paris, France (traveled to Helsinki City Art Museum, Finland)
1995–96 *Louise Bourgeois,* MARCO, Monterrey, Mexico (traveled to Centro Andaluz de Arte Contemporaneo, Seville, Spain, and Museo Rufino Tamayo, Mexico City)
1996 *Louise Bourgeois: Drawings,* University Art Museum, University of California, Berkeley (traveled to The Drawing Center, New York, and the List Visual Art Center, Massachusetts Institute of Technology, Boston)
1997 *Louise Bourgeois: Ode a Ma Mere,* Contemporary Arts Center, Cincinnati, Ohio
Louise Bourgeois, Galerie Karsten Greve, Cologne
Louise Bourgeois: Blue Days and Pink Days, Prada Foundation, Milan, Italy
1997–98 *Louise Bourgeois: Homesickness,* Yokohama Museum, Tokyo, Japan
1998 *Sacred and Fatal: The Art of Louise Bourgeois,* North Carolina Museum of Art, Raleigh
Louise Bourgeois: Topiary, Whitney Museum of American Art, New York, ''(4/15–4/26/98)
1998–99 *Louise Bourgeois,* Musee d'Art Contemporain, Bordeaux, France (traveled to Foundation Belem, Lisbon, Portugal, Malmo Konsthall, Malmo, Sweden, and Serpentine Gallery, London, England)
1999–2000 *Louise Bourgeois: Architecture and Memory,* Museo Nacional Centro de Arte-Reina Sofia, Madrid, Spain
2000 *Louise Bourgeois: Inaugural Installation of the Tate Modern Art at Turbine Hall,* Tate Modern, London
Louise Bourgeois: The Space of Memory, National Museum of Contemporary Art, Kyungki-do, Korea
2001 *Louise Bourgeois: The Insomnia Series,* Tate Modern, London
Louise Bourgeois, The State Hermitage Museum, St. Petersburg, Russia (travelled to Helsinki City Art Museum, Finland)

Selected Group Exhibitions:

1945 *Whitney Annual,* Whitney Museum, New York (and regularly until 1973)
1969 *International Sculpture Biennale,* Carrara, Italy
1975 *200 Years of American Sculpture,* Whitney Museum of American Art, New York
1977 *Permanent Collection of American Art,* Whitney Museum, New York
1980 *The Originals: Women in Art,* Graham Gallery, New York
1981 *Decade of Transition 1940–50,* Whitney Museum, New York

1982 *Sculpture 1982: 20 American Artists,* San Francisco Museum of Modern Art
1983 *Portrait Sculpture,* State University of New York, Buffalo
1985 *Traces: Sculpture and Monuments,* Kunsthaus, Zurich
1987 *Von Chaos un Ordnung der Seele,* Universitat Mainz, West Germany

Collections:

Australian National Gallery, Canberra, Australia; British Museum, London, England; Brooklyn Museum, New York; Denver Art Museum, Denver; Detroit Institute of the Arts, Detroit, Michigan; Guggenheim Museum, New York; Hirshhorn Museum, Washington, D.C.; Metropolitan Museum of Art, New York; Museum of Modern Art, New York; Museum of Modern Art, Vienna, Austria; Musée d'art Contemporain de Montreal, Canada; Musée d'art Moderne de la Ville de Paris, France; Musée National d'Art Moderne, Centre Georges Pompidou, Paris, France; National Gallery of Art, Washington, D.C.; New York Public Library, New York; Tate Gallery, London, England; Uffizi Museum, Florence, Italy; Whitney Museum of American Art, New York.

Installations:

Musee d'Art Moderne, Choisy le Roi, France, 1996; *Toi Et Moi,* Bibliotheque Nationale de Paris, 1997; *The Welcoming Hands,* Jardin des Tuileries, Paris, 2000.

Publications:

By BOURGEOIS: Books—*Louise Bourgeois: Drawings & Observations,* with Larry Rinder, Berkeley, California, 1995; *Destruction of the Father/Reconstruction of the Father (Writings and Interviews 1923–1997),* edited and with texts by Marie-Laure Bernadac and Hans-Ulrich Obrist, London, 1998. **Articles—**''Louise Bourgeois: A Search for Gravity,'' interview with Marcia Pels, in *Art International,* October 1979.

On BOURGEOIS: Books—*Nature in Abstraction* by John Baur, New York 1958; *American Art of Our Century,* exhibition catalog, by Lloyd Goodrich and John Baur, New York 1961; *Form and Space; Sculpture in the 20th Century* by Eduard Trier, New York 1968; *The Iconography of Louise Bourgeois,* exhibition catalog. New York 1980; *Louise Bourgeois* by Deborah Wye, New York 1982; *Louise Bourgeois: The Locus of Memory, 1982–1993* by Charlotta Kotik and others, New York, 1994; *Louise Bourgeois Sculptures and Installations,* edited by Carl. Haenlein, Hannover, Germany, 1994; *Louise Bourgeois* by Marie-Laure Bernadac, Paris 1995; *Louise Bourgeois: Blue Days and Pink Days* by Pandora Tabatabai Asbaghi and Jerry Gorovoy, Milan, 1997; *Louise Bourgeois: The Secret of the Cells,* by Rainer Crone, Rainer, Munich, 1998; *Louise Bourgeois: Architecture and Memory,* exhibition catalog, Madrid, Spain, 1999; *Louise Bourgeois Prints: 1989–1998* by Carol Smith, Lynchburg, Virginia, 1999; *Louise Bourgeois,* exhibition catalog with text by Frances Morris and Marina Warner, London, 2000; *Louise Bourgeois: The Insomnia Drawings,* by Marie-Laure Bernadac and Elisabeth Bronfen, New York and Zurich, 2000. **Articles—**''Some Reflections Prompted by the Recent Work of Louis Bourgeois'' by William S. Rubin in *Art International,* April 1969, ''Louise Bourgeois'' by J. P. Marandel in *Art International,* December 1971; ''Louise Bourgeois from the Inside Out'' by Lucy Lippard in *Artforum* (New York), March 1975; ''Louise Bourgeois'' by Carter Ratcliff in *Art International,* November/December 1978; ''The Discreet Charm of Louise Bourgeois'' in *Art News,* February 1980; ''Louise Bourgeois'' by Carter Ratcliff in *Vogue,* October 1980; special issue of *Oxford Art Journal,* vol. 22, no. 2, 1999.

*

My childhood has never lost its magic, it has never lost its mystery, and it has never lost its drama. All my work of the last fifty years, all my subjects, have found their inspiration in my childhood.

—Louise Bourgeois

* * *

A study of Louise Bourgeois' work from the late thirties to the present indicates that style and the evolution thereof are not fundamental to her character as an artist. Rather, it reveals the struggle of an individual actively attempting to define herself through her art. Bourgeois looks to herself for inspiration; consequently her work is personal and deeply autobiographical in content. Art functions for her as a psychological outlet, for making art is the process of giving tangible form to, and thus exorcising, the gripping, subconscious states of being that fill one with anxiety. Bourgeois' greatest achievement has been her ability to capture—and animate—the depth of the human psyche within a wide range of inventive and meaningful images.

Most of her prominent themes can be traced back to her years in France when a series of unresolved psychological conflicts governed her imagination. Her art belies the tension of her family life as created by the opposition of a clear-thinking, calm, and nurturing mother, and a powerful, volatile, and oppressive father. The polarity exacted anxiety, pain and anger, emotions that became the sources of Bourgeois's art. The psychological trauma of the war years, during which time her father was wounded, also had an impact on her work. After the war an English tutor caused the Bourgeois family additional problems because of her eventual liaison with Louise's father. The complications inherent in that triangle, the betrayals and primordial jealousies, seem to constitute a convincing origin for the implicit violence in a significant part of her oeuvre.

Bourgeois' career began to take form in the mid-1940s after studying at several schools in France, including the Academie Ransom, the Academie Julian, the Academie de la Grande-Chaumiere, and the École des Beaux-Arts, from 1934 to 1938. Stylistically, by the end of 1944 a grid scheme began to dominate the compositions of her paintings. She has related her use of this surface structure to her early family connections with tapestries and the delineation of their weave. During this period she developed an interest in balancing the formal issues of abstraction with the depiction of symbolic subject matter, a concern which she shared with the Abstract Expressionist tradition. As the decade progressed, Bourgeois's painting began to evolve toward a more personal, quasi-figurative imagery, with an underlying spirit of Surrealism. Her work moved toward the exploration of the reality of the subconscious. In effect, Surrealism encouraged her to tap the complex texture of her personal life as a source for her art.

The ''Femme-Maison'' paintings of 1947, portrayals of women with houses perched on their bodies in place of heads, are among her most powerful images. They are also symbols, moving in thematic directions that preoccupy the rest of her career. In them, a woman's sign of identity, her face, has been replaced by a house, implying that domesticity becomes the very definition of these women, since they have no other means by which to speak. Interestingly, the feminist dimension of her early imagery was not recognised until 30 years later.

In 1949 Bourgeois abandoned painting as a medium and began to explore the possibilities of sculpture, with the greater level of substantiality and physical impact afforded by its three-dimensional nature. By 1950 she had made over thirty sculptures and had achieved a surprising breadth of emotion through an increasingly formal sophistication. Her 1953 piece ''Foret'' embodied a new sculptural concept that would characterize her formal and thematic development of wood sculpture in the fifties. In this piece Bourgeois crowded a large assemblage of unusual elements together on a single base, suggesting a primordial group of plants. Due to the group's placement on the floor, it seems to be growing, as if sprouting seeds or pods. Furthering the theme of growth, Bourgeois exhibited *One and Others* in 1955. With its colourful, separate spools, this piece appears as a garden or bouquet. Yet viewed from certain angles, it takes on the form of a single flower whose blooming petals crate an organic symbol of health and burgeoning fecundity. The title, however, brings the sculpture back to the human world, suggesting individuals of various shapes and sizes huddling in mutual support and interdependence. This technique of clustering and crowding elements on a base is one that Bourgeois has employed persistently as a visual counterpart or symbol for the interactions of groups.

After 1953, Bourgeois participated in no solo shows until 1964 in New York. The highly politicized atmosphere of the 60s may have contributed to the transition of her formal development, as she was actively involved with certain issues. Her work was still an investigation of psychological and symbolic meaning. Yet the entire decade represented a time of wide experimentation with plaster, cement, rubber, latex, plastics, marble, and bronze. She toyed with twisted arrangements, labyrinthine formations, and amorphous masses of plaster or cement. With these eccentric pieces she tried to animate such psychological states as fear, vulnerability, and loss of control. She revived her favourite themes of withdrawal, hiding, protection, sheltering and nurturing. ''Lairs,'' cavernous plaster structures resembling cocoons, illustrate these themes. The 1967 ''Landscape'' series expanded the format of ''Lair,'' yet they bear the suggestions of human contours which are the beginnings of the sexual works that follow.

During the 60s and 70s, when feminism was gathering strength, sexuality finally emerged explicitly in her work. Her previous definition of woman—that of being helpless, expendable, and utterly without identity beyond the domestic realm—gradually gave way to a new conception tending toward a greater aggressiveness, sophistication, and elegance.

Her work in the 70s seemed to fill a distinct aesthetic need for personal content and meaning well beyond her earlier achievements. ''The Destruction of the Father,'' 1974, a continuation of her earlier preoccupation with the hidden recesses of the plaster ''Lairs,'' was the loudest personal statement of her career. The reincarnation of a perverse childhood fantasy in which the members of her family dismembered and devoured their self-important, domineering father, the piece consists of a cluster of bulbous, feminine latex forms that hang menacingly over a group of phallic shapes which rest on a table-like structure. The overtly psychological and sexual content of Bourgeois' work from this period on attests not only to the artist's resolute faithfulness to the intimate emotional sources of her work, but is all the more remarkable given the prevailing aesthetics of the Minimalist and Conceptual art of the time, which emphasized instead detachment, intellect and reserve.

In the last decade and a half, Bourgeois has produced some of her most powerful and ambitious work. The return to more personal and expressive modes of artistic production in the eighties and the thematics of the body in nineties art has meant increased recognition for Bourgeois's long career. She has continued to produce sculptures in materials as diverse as plaster, wood, latex, bronze, marble, and found objects, creating visceral biomorphs or startlingly realistic marble renderings of discrete human body parts that are at once sensual and foreboding. Flesh-like polyps of highly polished marble emerge from the roughly hewn base of *Untitled (with Growth)* from 1989, suggesting the fecund origins of both nature and sculpture. On a larger scale, *Needle (Fuseau)* from 1992 alludes to Bourgeois's family trade of tapestry restoration and hints at a reconciliation of male-female dichotomies. As an instrument used for mending, the shape of the needle suggests both a masculine piercing and, with its eye to hold thread, a feminine receptivity. Here a spool of raw, soft flax, placed on a mirror, rises up from the floor to thread a thinly arched steel needle which is flanked by testicle-like wooden spheres.

Increasingly, Bourgeois has created large and striking installations which amplify existential themes of privacy, dislocation, loneliness, and fear. The *Cells* series from 1989–93 consists of six rooms made from welded steel window frames and wooden doors. Placed in each cell is an enigmatic tableaux. In *Cell (Eyes and Mirrors),* round mirrors and looking glasses reflect back both the viewer and the cell's steel structure, creating complex interpenetrations of gaze and reflection, distortion and refraction. In another, glass spheres placed on chairs surround a pair of exquisitely rendered marble hands lying clutched together in pain or consternation on a table. In *Cell (Choisy),* an intricate marble replica of Bourgeois's childhood home sits below a suspended steel guillotine which acts as a sort of menacing gate. For Bourgeois the *Cells* title refers to both organic units of growth and self-contained, autonomous realities, all containing objects of memory. With their allusions to fragility, disease, and death, they extend the psychological themes of Bourgeois's oeuvre to the social realm.

Bourgeois's body of work is monumental in its range of materials and visions and in the depth of its commitment to revealing intimate, visceral conditions of self. Her endless resourcefulness and energy, her wit, her profound sense of inner strength, and her pioneering explorations of the body, of taboo subjects, and of installation have made her work germane to other women artists and to many younger artists working today.

—Essay by Carrie Barker; updated by Dorothy Valakos

Louise Bourgeois has remained artistically productive during the past decade. As always, her work is diverse in both style and media, and resists easy categorization; if anything, in recent years she has expanded her range of both imagery and materials. She has expanded upon the *Cells* series, large multimedia constructions of psychologically resonant roomlike spaces, ''the locus of memory,'' as they were aptly called in the 1994 catalogue that accompanied a major retrospective of her work. Recently, as in ''Cell XVI'' (2001), Bourgeois has added discarded clothing to the assemblage, consistent with her use of patched material in other new work as in ''Why have you run so far away'' (1999).

The spider is a major motif that was present in her early works, particularly her drawings, but greatly expanded in her later ones, as in her commission for the inauguration of the Tate Gallery for Modern

Art in 2000. ''Maman'' (1999) is a thirty-five foot black spider that filled the Tate's central turbine hall. Bourgeois has explained that her mother was ''(as) clever, patient, and neat as a spider; she could also defend herself.'' In ''Nest'' a maternal figure hunkers down over several smaller spiders. Psychologically ambiguous, these spider figures are both nurturant and threatening, presenting a complex construction of the maternal.

During the last decade Bourgeois has been the subject of numerous traveling and retrospective exhibitions, including representation in the XXIII Sao Paolo exposition. In these shows, and in several publications, she has paired drawings and prints with excerpts from her diaries, expanding upon the autobiographical nature of her explorations into the human psyche. Bourgeois's themes remain rich and large: memory, sexuality, childhood, home.

—Mara Witzling

BOYD, Arthur (Merrick Bloomfield)

Nationality: Australian. **Born:** Murrumbeena, near Melbourne, Victoria, 24 July 1920. **Education:** State School, Murrumbeena 1927–35; mainly self-taught in art from 1935. Served as cartographic field surveyor, Australian Army, in Melbourne and Bendigo, 1940–43. **Married:** Yvonne Hartland Lennie in 1945; children: Polly, Jamie and Lucy. **Career:** Worked in paint factory, Melbourne, 1934–36; as potter, Melbourne, 1943–48; independent artist, concentrating exclusively on painting, Melbourne 1948–55, in Beaumaris, Victoria 1955–59, in Nowra, New South Wales, and in London and Woodbridge, Suffolk, since 1959: first theatre decors, Edinburgh, 1963; decor and Costumes *Electra,* Royal Opera House, London, c. 1969; designed tapestry installed in Parliament House, Canberra, Australia, 1988. **Awards:** *Encyclopedia Britannica* Award, 1971; Fellowship in Creative Arts, Australian National University, Canberra, 1971–72. Officer, Order of the British Empire (O.B.E.), 1970; Officer, Order of Australia (A.O.), 1979; Companion of Australia (A.C.). **Agent:** Fischer Fine Art, St. Johns Wood, London. **Died:** Melbourne, Victoria, 24 April 1999.

Individual Exhibitions:

1937 Westminster Gallery, Melbourne
1939 Royden White Library, University of Melbourne (with Jo Bergner)
1940 Athenaeum Gallery, Melbourne
1949 Kozminsky Galleries, Melbourne
1950 David Jones Gallery, Sydney (retrospective)
1951 Princes Gallery, Melbourne (retrospective, travelled to the Marodian Gallery, Brisbane)
John Martin's Gallery, Adelaide
1952 Princess Gallery, Melbourne
Peter Bray Galleries, Melbourne
Macquarie Galleries, Sydney
1953 Peter Bray Galleries, Melbourne (retrospective)
Johnstone Gallery, Brisbane
1954 Peter Bray Galleries, Melbourne
1958 Australian Galleries, Melbourne
South Australian Society of Arts, Adelaide
Terry Clune Gallery, Sydney
David Jones Gallery, Sydney
1960 Zwemmer Gallery, London
1962 Whitechapel Art Gallery, London (retrospective)
1963 Australian Galleries, Melbourne
Terry Clune Gallery, Sydney
Ceramic Paintings by Arthur Boyd, Zwemmer Gallery, London
1964 National Gallery of South Australia, Adelaide (retrospective)
Museum of Modern Art and Design, Melbourne (retrospective)
Bear Lane Gallery, Oxford
1965 Skinner Gallery, Perth
Australian Galleries, Melbourne
1966 Hungry Horse Art Gallery, Sydney
1969 *Retrospective Exhibition,* Richard Demarco Gallery, Edinburgh
Arthur Tooth & Sons, London
Hamet Gallery, London
Maltzahn Gallery, London
1971 Australian National University, Canberra Skinner Gallery, Perth
1973 *Recent Paintings,* Fine Art, London
1977 Fischer Fine Art, London
1980 Folkstone Arts Centre, Kent
Fischer Fine Art, London
1981 Britten-Pears School, Aldeburgh, Suffolk
1982 Queensland University, Brisbane
Australian Galleries, Melbourne
1983 Fischer Fine Art, London
1984 Art Gallery of South Australia, Adelaide
1986 Fischer Fine Art, London
1988 *Four Australian Modern Masters: Arthur Boyd, Sidney Nolan, Brett Whiteley, Fred Williams,* Savill Galleries, Paddington, New South Wales
Venice Biennale
1990 Fischer Fine Art, London
1991 *Arthur Boyd: ''The Magic Flute'' Series and Other Paintings; ''Mars'' Drawings and Graphics,* Wagner Art Gallery, Sydney
Arthur Boyd: Five Decades, Savill Galleries, Paddington, New South Wales
1993 *Arthur Boyd: Works Dating from 1937 to 1989,* Savill Galleries, Paddington, New South Wales
Sydney Art Gallery, Sydney
National Gallery of Victoria, Tasmania, Western Australia
Arthur Boyd Retrospective, Art Gallery of New South Wales, Sydney
1994 *Arthur Boyd: 30 Paintings 1985–1994, 23 Etchings 1993,* Australian Galleries, Collingwood, Victoria

Selected Group Exhibitions:

1955 *Australian Contemporary Painting.* National Gallery of Victoria, Melbourne (toured Australia)
1956 *Biennale,* Venice (and 1958)
1963 *Australian Painting and Sculpture in Europe Today,* New Metropole Arts Centre, Folkstone, Kent (toured West Germany and the Netherlands)

1966 *Australian Painters 1964–66.* Corcoran Gallery, Washington, D.C.
1972 *Australian Prints,* Victoria and Albert Museum, London
1981 *Australian Drawings of the 30s and 40s,* Victoria and Albert Museum, London
1983 *The Boyd Family,* Arts Council Gallery, Canberra
1985 *Representations Abroad,* Hirshhorn Museum, Washington, D.C.
1987 Ipswich County Gallery, Suffolk (with son, Jamie)
1988 Gillian Jackson Gallery, London (with son, Jamie)
Hayward Gallery, London (with Sidney Nolan)
1991 Chirstchurch Mansion, Ipswich, England (with Jamie Boyd)
1997 *Arthur Boyd & John Olsen: Two Great Australian Painters,* Savill Galleries, Paddington, New South Wales
2000 *Arthur Boyd & John Olsen: Journeys Through the Landscape,* Savill Galleries, Paddington, New South Wales

Collections:

Department of External Affairs, Canberra; Australian National University, Canberra; National Gallery of Victoria, Melbourne; Art Gallery of New South Wales, Sydney; National Gallery of Queensland, Brisbane; National Gallery of South Australia, Adelaide; Art Gallery of Western Australia, Perth; Museum and Art Gallery of Tasmania, Hobart; Contemporary Art Society, London; Rhodes House Trust, Oxford; Victoria and Albert Museum, London; Arts Council of Great Britain.

Publications:

By BOYD: Books—*Saint Francis of Assisi,* with text by T. S. R. Boase, London 1968; *Nebuchadnezzar: 34 Paintings and 18 Drawings by Arthur Boyd,* with text by T. S. R. Boase, London 1972; *Jonah,* with poems by Porter, London 1973; *Arthur Boyd at Bundanon* with Janet McKenzie, London 1994; *Arthur Boyd Prints,* London 1995; *Arthur Boyd: Portraits,* with Anderew Sayers, Canberra 1999; *The Lady and the Unicorn,* with poems by Peter Porter; *Pushkin's Fairy Tales,* translated by Janet Dalley; *Lysistrata,* translated by Lack Lindsay; *Mars,* poems by Peter Porter; *The Drifting Continent,* poems by A. D. Hope; *Persistent Images,* by Grazia Gunn; *The Painter and the River,* by Sandra McGrath.

On BOYD: Books—*Arthur Boyd,* exhibition catalog, with text by Bryan Robertson, London 1960; *Australian Painting* by Bernard Smith, Melbourne 1962, rev. ed. as *Australian Painting 1788–1970,* Melbourne 1971; *Arthur Boyd,* exhibition catalog, with text by Bryan Robertson, London 1962; *Ceramic Paintings by Arthur Boyd,* exhibition catalog, with text by T. S. R. Boase, Oxford 1964; *Day of My Delight* by Martin Boyd, Melbourne 1965; *Arthur Boyd* by Franz Philipp, London 1967; *Encyclopaedia of Australian Art* edited by Alan Mac Culloch, Melbourne 1968, 1993; *Arthur Boyd: Retrospective Exhibition* catalog with texts by T. G. Rosenthal and Cordelia Oliver, Edinburgh, 1969; *Art in Britain 1969–1970* by Edward Lucie-Smith and Patricia White, London 1970; *Arthur Boyd: Etchings and Lithographs* by Imre von Maltzahn, London 1971; *Arthur Boyd: Drawings 1934–1970,* with a foreword by Laurie Thomas, London 1973; *Arthur Boyd: Recent Paintings,* exhibition catalog, with text by Robert Melville, London 1973; *Outlines of Australian Art: The Joseph Brown Collection* by Daniel Thomas, Melbourne and Sydney 1973, London 1974; *Arthur Boyd,* exhibition catalog, with an introduction by Robert Melville, Folkestone, Kent 1980; *The Art of Arthur Boyd* by Ursula Hoff, London 1986; *The Works of Arthur Boyd,* exhibition catalog, Paddington 1998; *Arthur Boyd & John Olsen: Journeys Through the Landscape,* exhibition catalog, Paddington 2000; *Arthur Boyd: Art & Life* by Janet McKenzie, London 2000. **Articles—**''Arthur Boyd (1920–1999)'' by Tom Rosenthal in *Art Review* (London), vol. 51, November 1999; ''Arthur Boyd: Paintings in the Studio'' by Fred Cress in *Art and Australia,* vol. 38, no. 2, 2000. **Films—***Understanding the Art of Arthur Boyd* by Traudi Allen, 1994; *Arthur Boyd: Testament of a Painter* by Don Bennetts, 1994; Arthur *Boyd* by Don Featherstone, 1997; *Arthur Boyd Tribute* by Peter Waley, 1999.

* * *

Arthur Boyd was a distinguished member of the remarkable generation of Australian artists who transferred to Britain in the post-war period and made a profound impact on European art. He also typifies the curious phenomenon (discernible in many other artists who move away physically from their origins) whereby aspects of native culture and subject-matter become more profoundly realised as a result of transplantation. Thus as with Sidney Nolan, Boyd remained deeply influenced by the richly diverse landscape of his native country and the equally strange mythology rooted in the original settlement of the country by criminals and other exotic characters.

Boyd comes from a long line of Australian artists; his parents and grandparents included popular painters, and various aunts and uncles are also represented in national collections. His brother David Boyd is a successful painter, also resident in England.

Arthur Boyd's first important paintings, in the immediate post-war period, depicted the charming Victorian architecture of Melbourne, but soon after, as a result of his admiration for the Flemish masters Breugel and Bosch, a series of religious paintings emerged, subjects such as ''The Assumption'' and ''The Prodigal Son'' being used in architectural murals, and also on a brilliant series of ceramic tiles. Pottery led to sculpture, still on religious themes, re-interpreting Flemish expressionism in the new medium. Picasso and Chagall influenced this period of Boyd's career, coinciding with this earliest absorption with the Australian folk hero, Ned Kelly.

The Chagallian strain then emerged to dominate Boyd's series of ''Bride'' paintings in which a small white-faced female figure accompanies her aboriginal husband. Whilst residence in England has heightened the painter's involvement in Australian themes, the urgency of the ''Bride'' series, with their anatomy of inter-racial problems, has never been repeated or surpassed.

Boyd's technical control remained impressive, and his versatility extended to designing for theatre, lithography and etching.

—Charles Spencer

BOYLE, Mark

Nationality: British. **Born:** Glasgow, Scotland, 11 May 1934. **Education:** Studied law at Glasgow University 1955–56; mainly self-taught in art, from 1956. **Military Service:** British Army, 1950–53.

Family: He has lived with the artist Joan Hills since 1958; children: Sebastian and Georgia. **Career:** Worked as labourer, Stewarts and Lloyd steelyard, Parkhead, Glasgow, 1953–54; as park keeper, office clerk, barman and head-waiter, all London, 1955–58. Independent artist, London, since 1958; collaborated on light-environments for theatrical events, 1960–65; co-director, with Joan Hills, Sensual Laboratory, London, since 1966; light-shows for U.F.O. Club, London, 1967; light-environments for music groups Jimi Hendrix Experience and Soft Machine, U.S.A., 1968–69; has worked on Earth Pieces since 1964, and Journey to the Surface of the Earth since 1967. Instructor, Waterford School of Art, 1966–67. **Awards:** Painting Prize, *5th Biennale de Paris,* 1967; Painting Prize, *15th Premio Lissone,* Italy, 1967; Painting Prize, *Zagreb International,* Yugoslavia 1968. **Agent:** A National Gallery, Greenwich, London. **Address:** c/o A Notional Gallery, Hillside House, Crooms Hill, Greenwich, London SE10, England.

Individual Exhibitions:

1963 Woodstock Gallery, London
Traverse Gallery, Edinburgh
Citizens' Gallery, Glasgow
1964 *Suddenly Last Supper,* South Kensington, London (event)
Richard Demarco Gallery, Edinburgh
Exit Music, Strand Electric Theatre, London (with Ken Dewey and Charles Marowitz)
The Street, London (event)
1965 *O, What A Lovely Whore,* Institute of Contemporary Arts, London (event)
Any Plan or No Play, Theatre Royal, Stratford East, London (event)
1966 Indica Gallery, London
Dig, Shepherd's Bush, London (event)
Son et Lumiére far Earth, Air, Fire and Water, Cochrane Theatre, London (event)
Son et Lumiére for Insects, Reptiles and Water Creatures. Cochrane Theatre, London (event)
Bodily Fluids and Functions, Roundhouse, London (event)
1967 Bluecoat Gallery, Liverpool
1969 Institute of Contemporary Arts, London
1970 Gemeentemuseum, The Hague
Bela Centre, Copenhagen
Institute of Contemporary Arts, London
1971 Henie-Onstad Kunstsenter, Oslo
Requiem for an Unknown Citizen, Rotterdam (event)
Galerie Paul Maenz, Cologne
1972 Henie-Onstad Kunstsenter, Oslo
Galerie Paul Maenz, Cologne
1973 Kelvin Hall, Glasgow
Galerie Müller, Stuttgart
McRoberts Centre, Stirling, Scotland
1974 Galerie Paul Manez, Cologne
1975 Serpentine Gallery, London
1977 Felicity Samuel Gallery, London
1978 British Pavilion, at the *Biennale,* Venice
Kunstmuseum, Lucerne
Kulturhuset, Stockholm
Seattle Museum of Art
Henie—Onstad Kunstsenter, Oslo
1979 Louisiana Museum, Humlebaek, Denmark
Museum am Ostwall, Dortmund, West Germany (with Joan Hills)
1980 Charles Cowles Gallery, New York
Kunstmuseum, Lucerne
Art Gallery of South Australia, Adelaide
Richard Hines Gallery, Seattle, Washington
1981 Seattle Art Museum, Washington
Newport Harbor Art Museum, Newport Beach, California
1982 Institute of Contemporary Art, Boston
San Francisco Museum of Modern Art
1983 Nishimura Gallery, Tokyo
1985 Henie-Onstad Kunstsenter, Hovikodden, Norway
A Notional Gallery, London
1986 Cornerhouse Arts Centre, Manchester, Lancashire
Hayward Gallery, London
1987 City Art Gallery, Southampton, Hempshire
Glasgow Art Gallery and Museum, Scotland
Museum of Modern Art, Oxford
Muzeum Sztuki, Lodz, Poland (travelled to Sopot)
British Pavilion, *Bienal de Sao Paulo,* Brazil
Gardner Centre, Brighton, Sussex
Warwick Arts Centre, Warwickshire
Turske und Turske Galerie, Zurich
Turske and Whitney Gallery, Los Angeles
1988 Galerie Lelong, Paris
Paco Imperial, Rio de Janeiro

Selected Group Exhibitions:

1967 *Biennale de Paris,* Musée d'Art Moderne de la Ville, Paris
1968 *International Exhibition,* Zagreb, Yugoslavia
1973 *Magic and Strong Medicine,* Walker Art Gallery, Liverpool
1976 *Arte Inglese Oggi 1960–76,* Palazzo Reale, Milan
1980 *British Art 1940–80,* Hayward Gallery, London
1981 *Approaches to Landscape,* Tate Gallery, London
1983 *Aspects of British Art,* Metropolitan Art Museum, Tokyo (toured Japan)
1985 *Exhibition Dialogue,* Fundaco Calouste Gulbenkian, Lisbon
1986 *Between Object and Image: British Contemporary Sculpture,* Palacio de Velazquez, Madrid (travelled to Barcelona and Bilbao)
1987 *British Air in the Twentieth Century,* Royal Academy, London (travelled to Stuttgart)
1990 *Down to Earth: Boyle Family in New Zealand,* City Art Gallery, Auckland
1991 *Atlas: Curatorial Project #7,* Art Gallery of Hamilton, Ontario
Boyle Family: Dockland Series—London, Runkel-Hue-Williams Gallery, London
1994 *This Object, That Object: To Reveal the Hidden Meaning of Things—An Exhibition of Contemporary European Art from the Permanent Collection of the McMaster University,* McMaster University Art Gallery, Hamilton, Ontario
1995 *Fluxus and the Nouveaux Realistes: The Cremer Collection for the Hamburger Kunsthalle,* Hamburger Kunsthalle, Germany

1996 *In the Limelight: Photography in the 20th Century from the Collections in the Kunsthaus Zurich,* Kunsthaus Zurich

Collections:

Tate Gallery, London; British Council, London; Ulster Museum, Belfast; Scottish National Gallery of Modern Art, Edinburgh; Städtisches Museum, Bochum, West Germany; Kaiser-Wilhelm Museum, Krefeld West Germany; Gemeensemuseum, The Hague; Sonja Henie-Nils Onstad Kunstsenter, Oslo; Australian National Gallery, Canberra; Seattle Museum of Art.

Publications:

By BOYLE: Books—*Journey to the Surface of the Earth: Mark Boyle's Atlas and Manual,* with introduction by J. L. Locher, The Hague 1970; *Boyle Family Archives,* Oslo 1985; *Familia Boyle: 19a, Bienal de Sao Paulo,* Sao Paulo 1987.

On BOYLE: Books—*Art in Britain 1969–70* by Edward Lucie-Smith and Patricia White, London 1970; *Art Without Boundaries 1950–1970* by G. Woods, P. Thompson and J. Williams, London 1972; *Magic and Strong Medicine,* exhibition catalog, with text by Norbert Lynton, Liverpool 1973; *Projekt 74: Aspekte Internationaler Kunst am Anfang der 70er Jahre,* exhibition catalog, with texts by Dieter Rönte, Evelyn Weiss, Marlis Gruterich and others, Cologne 1974; *Venice Biennale: Mark Boyle,* exhibition catalog, with text by Michael Compton, London 1978; *Mark Boyle's und Joan Hills' Reise um die West 3: Schweizer Serie,* exhibition catalog, with text by Martin Kunz, Lucerne 1980. **Articles—**"Avant-garde v. Traditional" by Linda Heywood in *The Artist* (Tenterden), vol. 104, August 1989; "Boyle Family" by Richard Cork in *Kunstforum International,* no. 107, April-May 1990; "Art and the Natural Environment" in *Art & Design,* vol. 9, May/June 1994.

*

In a condition of adamant doubt you are asked for explanations when all you want is for someone to explain anything. And you are asked for purposes when you are learning to accept that a purpose is not going to emerge ever. And you are asked for a statement of intent when the head seethes with all your fluctuating statements of the past instantly and meticulously taken down and which you use constantly, with increasing derision, in evidence against yourself. And you remember years ago deciding that art, if the work had any meaning, should be waged like war and how, according to all the strategists, you had to locate the enemy and evaluate your own forces and assess the terrain and clarify your objectives and work out your strategy and your tactics and, whatever you do, do not forget your logistics, and how after months of thinking you succeeded with point one and it's not the dealers or the critics or the intellectuals or the government or the rich or the bourgeoisie or "them" and it's not even like Father Xmas your father all the time but the only enemy is yourself and maybe it doesn't matter too much whether you win or lose.

—Mark Boyle

* * *

Journey to the Surface of the Earth is the unwavering conceptual excursion of Mark Boyle and his collaborator/wife, Joan Hills. This "journey" is Boyle's ongoing series of "earthprobes," the literal mapping in every minute detail of 6-ft. square sections of the earth's surface.

In 1970 Boyle handed visitors to his studio a dart to throw at a large Mercator projection map of the world. Eventually a thousand sites were randomly selected for the Boyles to document. A closely guarded and painstaking procedure lifts topographical surface texture, extraneous natural or man-caused materials, and whatever surface deformations are present (shifting beach sands, tire tracks, railroad ties, ploughed fields, ablating rock formations, etc.), onto a molded fiberglass shell. Real and ersatz materials are added to achieve verisimilitude. Full documentation includes the surface casting, a cast vertical sampling of the substrata, and photographic enlargements of microscopic details of plants and insects gathered on-site, hair, and fluid wastes from the artist's body, all revealed as crustaceous or crystalline molecular patterns of structure.

The meticulous factuality of these relief panels are presented in the rarified space of the gallery. They demand and invite scrutiny. The works are not intended as abstractions of nature, though formal relationships of texture, shape and compositional balance can be readily ascertained in the patterns of wavetossed sand, tilled soil and geologic outcroppings. Rather, the viewer is re-sensitized by the direct immediacy of these panels, to look at nature in terms of Boyle's process, product and attitude. The moral and ethical imperative is to heighten and engage, in a non-militant yet forceful way, a greater sensitivity to ecological matters. The "grand scheme" of nature merges in the macro-and-micro-cosmic units of reality: the flecks of stone, the crusty exoskeleton of a mite, the kaleidoscopic rainbow colors of crystals and molecules. The world beneath one's feet seems more real, more solid and palpable, after seeing the work of Mark Boyle.

—Ron Glowen

BRANDMEIER, Monika

Nationality: German. **Born:** Kamen, Germany, 19 January 1959. **Education:** Studied design at Fachhochschule Dortmund, 1977–82; studied visual art at Hochschule für Bildende Künste, Braunschweig, and Staatliche Kunstakademie Düsseldorf, M.F.A., 1986–1991. **Career:** Professor of Sculpture, Hochschule für Bildende Künste Dresden, since 2001; lives and works in Berlin. **Awards:** Residency/grant, Deutsch-Französiches Jugendwerk, Paris, 1983; Wilhelm Fabry Award of the City of Hilden, Germany, 1985; grant of the Pollock-Krasner Foundation, New York, 1987; residency, Djerassi Foundation, Woodside, California, 1989; grant of Kunstfonds e.V., Bonn, Germany, 1990; residency/grant, Philip Morris Art Foundation, Berlin, 1990; award for Visual Art of the Westfälischer Kunstverein, Münster, Germany, 1991; award for Visual Art of the City of Nordhorn, Germany, 1992; residency/grant, Künstlerdorf Schöppingen, Germany, 1992; Art/Omi residency, Ghent, New York, 1998. **Web site:** http://www.monikabrandmeier.de.

Selected Individual Exhibitions:

1989 *Und ein paar Schuhe wie Anführungsstriche (unten),* Schuetz Gallery, Frankfurt am Maine

Monika Brandmeier: *Streber, Seele, Teleskope, [striver, soul, telescopes]*. ©2001 Artists Rights Society (ARS), NY/VG Bild-Kunst, Bonn.

1990 *Joint Exhibition: Floating Scale,* Spiral Art Center, Tokyo (with Emiko Kasahara) (catalog)
1991 Conrads Gallery, Neuss
1992 Gebauer und Günther Gallery, Berlin
Otto Schweins Gallery, Cologne
R-5,0, L-6,0, James Hockey Gallery, Farnham, United Kingdom (catalog)
Der normale Aufenthalt im Freien, City Gallery, Nordhorn, Germany (catalog)
1993 Albrecht Dürer Gesellschaft Nürnberg, Nürnberg (catalog)
Conrads Gallery, Düsseldorf
1994 Gebauer und Günther Gallery, Berlin
Mark Mueller Gallery, Zürich
1995 *Dinge Dinger,* Otto Schweins Gallery, Cologne
No Ideas But in Things, Keine Ideen ausser in Dingen, Zadnych idei poza Rzeczami, Artists´ Museum, Lodz, Poland (with Hartmut Böhm)
Mueller-Roth Gallery, Stuttgart
1996 *Raum verpflichten (und vier Stuetzen),* City Gallery, Ravensburg, Germany (catalog)
1997 *21 Zeichnungen,* Otto Schweins Gallery, Cologne
1998 *Untertage,* Mark Mueller Gallery, Zürich
More lies and a line, Mario Flecha exhibition space, Girona, Spain (with Jordan Baseman)
In Vitro-Künstliche Bedenken, Otto Schweins Gallery, Cologne
1999 Staatliche Museen, Hamburger Bahnhof; Museum für Gegenwart, Berlin (catalog)
Conrads Gallery, Düsseldorf, Germany
2001 Dioezesanmuseum Cologne
Mueller-Roth Gallery, Stuttgart, Germany (catalog)

Selected Group Exhibitions:

1985 *Kunst mit Eigensinn,* Museum des 20 Jahrhunderts, Vienna (catalog)
1987 *BRD: Abstract Tendencies in New German Art,* Carl Bornstein Gallery, Los Angeles
1988 *Papier Paper,* Stalker, Breda, The Netherlands
1989 *Niemandsland/No Mans Land,* Kunsthalle Recklinghausen, Germany (catalog)
La Biennal de Barcelona (catalog)
1990 *Künstlerinnen des 20 Jahrhunderts/ Women Artists of the 20th Century,* Museum Wiesbaden (catalog)
Construction in Process: Back in Lodz, Museum Kinematografii, Lodz, Poland
1991 *Europaeische Werkstatt Ruhrgebiet,* Ikonenmuseum Recklinghausen (catalog)
Förderpreis 1991, Westfälischer Kunstverein, Münster (catalog)
Im Lärm der Stadt, Niedersachsen Foundation, Hannover (catalog)
1992 *Tiefgang: Bildräume im Schlossbunker,* Shelter under the Castel in Mannheim, Germany (catalog)
1993 *The Humpty Dumpty's Kaleidoscope: A New Generation of German Artists,* Museum of Contemporary Art, Sydney (catalog)
Die Subversion des Lachens, Museum am Ostwall, Dortmund, Germany
1994 *Übergangsraum,* Gesellschaft für Aktuelle Kunst, Bremen, Germany
Site-ations, Mowlems Factory, Cardiff, Wales
1995 *Construction in Process: Co-existence,* Mitzpe-Ramon, Israel
Tapko: A Space, Overgaden, Copenhagen
La Prima idea, Eugen Lendl Gallery, Graz, Austria
Palast der Künste, Kölnischer Kunstverein, Cologne
1996 *Fishing for Shapes? Photography by Sculptors,* Projektraum Voltmerstrasse, Hannover; Künstlerhaus Bethanien, Berlin
1997 *Augenzeugen,* Kunstmuseum im Ehrenhof, Düsseldorf (catalog)
In den Raum gestellt, oder, Helmhaus Zürich, Zurich (catalog)
1998 *Tapko: A Sunday Morning Walk,* Brandts Klædefabrik, Odense, Denmark
1999 *Fairy-tale,* Center for Metamedia, Plazy, Czech Republic
Zoom: Ansichten zur Deutschen Gegenwartskunst, Villa Merkel, Esslingen, Germany (catalog)
Projections, David Pestorius Gallery, Berlin
Paradise 8: Permanent Resident, Exit Art, New York
2000 *Kabinett der Zeichnung,* Kunstverein für die Rheinlande und Westfalen, Düsseldorf; Kunstverein Lingen, Germany; Kunstsammlungen Chemnitz, Germany; Württembergischer Kunstverein, Stuttgart (catalog)

Keine zwei Eier sind gleich: Über Wahrnehmung, Mueller-Roth Gallery, Stuttgart
Construction in Process: This Earth is a Flower, Muzeum Okregowe im Leona Wyczolkowskiego, Bydgoszcz, Poland
From Here to There: Passageways at Solitude, Akademie Schloss Solitude, Stuttgart
2001 *Once, Then Something,* Sculpture Center, New York

Public Collections:

Staatliche Museen zu Berlin, Kupferstichkabinett, Berlin; Deutsche Ausgleichsbank, Bonn; Collection of the Federal Republik of Germany, Berlin; Kunstmuseum im Ehrenhof, Düsseldorf, Germany; Villa Merkel, Esslingen a. Neckar, Germany; Landesmuseum Pfalzgalerie, Kaiserslautern, Germany; Neues Museum Nürnberg—Staatliches Museum fur Kunst und Design, Nürnberg, Germany; City Gallery, Nordhorn, Germany; Kunsthalle Recklinghausen, Recklinghausen, Germany; Staatliche Museen, Schwerin, Germany; Collection of the City of Stuttgart, Germany; Landesbank Baden-Württemberg, Stuttgart, Germany; Foundation Collection Koenig, Zollikon, Switzerland; Kunstraum Buchberg Foundation, Castle of Buchberg, Austria; Neue Galerie am Landesmuseum Joanneum, Graz, Austria; Statens Konstrad, Stockholm; Weatherspoon Art Galery, University of North Carolina at Greensboro; Busch-Reisinger Museum, Cambridge, Massachusetts.

Publications:

On BRANDMEIER: Books—*Dinge Dinger,* edited by Städtische Galerie Ravensburg, Ravensburg 1996; *Monika Brandmeier Zeichnungen,* edited by Alexander Dückers and Eugen Blume, Nürnberg 1999. **Articles—**''Richtung ist interessanter als Position: Ein Gespräch'' by Alexander Braun in *Kunstforum International,* vol. 145, 1999.

* * *

Monika Brandmeier is a sculptress, draughtswoman, and photographer. Her room-filling works neither make opulent use of materials, nor do they have a representational and narrative dimension in the traditional sense. They do not tell of anything taking place outside of themselves. The reduction that is characteristic to them invites the digressing and fidgety glance to halt and note the precise. But it would be wrong to assume that we are dealing with a minimalistic concept. Minimalism is a questionable conceptual construction. If anything from the various definitions is useful in our context, it would be the attempt to view the form in complete identity with itself and without associative and narrative possibilities. Monika Brandmeier casually remarked in 1992: ''I want to create certain things because I have never seen them. I want to create them for the purpose of their existence.''

The artist creates her work out of a context that is derived from the potential of things and their materialism. She is sensitized to an aesthetics of coincidence, which inevitably occurs in our thing world, and to an unwatched world of events not necessarily belonging to our seeing culture. This discovery most pointedly reveals itself in Monika Brandmeier's photographs because photography, in contrast to things built or drawn, is not mere invention but directly reflects reality.

Her sculptures are often brought into connection with a wall. The wall as a prerequisite for a sculpture is an unusual decision because a free-standing sculpture is usually connected to the room, and traditionally the wall is only needed for the relief. Because of her decision to relate them to the wall, Monika Brandmeier's wall works change between firmness and weakness, between presence and absence, between existence and dissolution. Their ''staging'' implicitly acts as a necessity involving both the placing against the wall and the taking it away from it. The sensation of these acts is an essential process during the observation. This process disconnects itself from the perception of merely a reality of geometrical forms or sometimes expands them.

The primary event in the sculptures is the act of placing them rather than the work with the material itself. The material plays an important role, but the relationship between the formed shape and the wall, other things, and itself is the decisive move. The works do not narrate, but mostly consist of different elements that are related to each other as a form. A form that has been included into the ensemble because of its form, its assignment, and its distance to the other forms appears to have been mathematically calculated. Deviation does not occur. The sense of a possible deviation equals the deconstruction of the work. The precise placing of a figure, to which we cannot simply assign an experience, most of all needs to achieve one thing: to be convincingly present.

Glass or plastic cases as well as zippers often occur in Monika Brandmeier's works. Glass is a material suggesting invisibility. When the light falls in, its edges form fine lines that resemble pencil lines. Things are often placed into these hardly visible bodies, for instance a colored string that starts from the upper third and continues backwards between wall and backwall like a freely drawn colored pen. These enigmatic compositions rather remind us of poems and of the sometimes disparate word choice of poetry, which allows a picture, a very distinct sound, to emerge from its secret. In her artistic position, Monika Brandmeier is closer to poetry than to music. If syntheses occur, it is the sound of words. What unites her sculptures, her photographs, and her pictures is the special way of adding words that sound even where other works can go without words. A poetic sculpture is in this sense characterized by its closed and at the same time open form. The suspense, which we may well call poetic, is grounded in its discrepancy.

Her sculptures oscillate between the insistence on the flat surface and its erection to a three-dimensional figure. In their linearity and character of surface, the works resemble the drawings. What is the relation between the pictures and the works that unfold in the room? The imagination that these room-taking works are based on cannot lets us expect sculpture sketches in a traditional sense. For Monika Brandmeier, drawing rather is a parallel process. Just like the linear and graphic view of the sculpture prevails in the plastic works, the drawings on the other hand are very close to the plastic works and the photographs. The third form is the video film, the moving picture, that is also mostly thought of as coming from the drawing. The slow closing of a zipper, for example, very strongly associates the movement of the pencil during the act of drawing. The observation of water finding its way along and beside a streak of hair is viewed as the emergence of a drawing.

The metamorphosis of the idea into a representation is the task of both the plastic works and the drawings. Thus the drawing emerges out of the idea, out of the spirit, not out of the reality of the material. Illusion does not play an important role in the drawing. It is rather the layers of lines that move from the edge or the center of the paper, closely together or open, that now possess their own materialism. They achieve their highest level of abstraction in a mathematical association, in which we start to count. The special character of the drawings has emerged from a number of works, which had the wall as their basic surface. Writings on the wall, drawings, poles, lines, and bodies placed before them also point to the occurrence that the drawings as well as some of the sculptures have unhinged themselves from the wall in an attempt to exist independently from now on. But in some works the return occurs, the interplay between wall and room. Suspense starts at the wall and continues onto the floor. Sensitized to the graphic view, one repeatedly finds things in the sculptures that act as drawings.

—Eugen Blume

BRAUER, Erich (or Arik)

Nationality: Austrian. **Born:** Vienna, 4 January 1929. **Education:** Attended elementary schools in Vienna, 1935–42; studied art under Robin Anderson and Albert Paris Gütersloh, Academy of Fine Arts, Vienna, 1945–51; also studied singing at the City Conservatory, Vienna, 1949–53. **Family:** Married Naomi Dahabany in 1955; daughters: Timma, Talija and Ruth. **Career:** Served in underground resistance, Vienna, 1942–45. Bicycled to Paris to work as folk singer; travelled to Algeria, stayed in Sahara Desert, 1950; travelled to France, Spain, Greece, Israel and Austria, earned living as folk-singer, 1951–58; settled in Paris, performed as folk-singer, with wife Naomi, 1958; former friendship, with Hundertwasser, Paris, 1958; has painted full time in Vienna, since 1960, and in Ein Hod, Israel, since 1964; has also worked as a costume and set designer for operas, in Zurich, Vienna and Paris, since 1970. **Address:** Colloredogasse 30, 4180 Vienna, Austria.

Individual Exhibitions:

1956 Neue Gallerie, Vienna
1957 Artist's House, Jerusalem
1958 Galerie Ernst Fuchs, Vienna
Galerie Wolfgang Gurlitt, Munich
1959 Galerie La Cour d'Ingress, Paris
Artist's House, Jerusalem
1960 Galerie Delta, Basle
1961 Galerie Brochstedt, Hamburg
Galerie Sydow, Frankfurt
Galerie Raymond Cordier, Paris
1963 Galerie Karl Flinker, Paris
1964 Galerie Sydow, Frankfurt
Galerie Karl Flinker, Paris
1965 Galerie Peithner-Lichtenfels, Vienna
Felix Landau Gallery, Los Angeles
1966 Galerie Sydow Fine Art, Frankfurt
1967 Felix Landau Gallery, Los Angeles
Landau Gallery, New York
1968 Galerie 3 + 2, Paris
Kunstlerhaus Peithner, Vienna
Galerie Sydow, Frankfurt
Galerie Sydow, West Berlin
1969 Marlborough New London Gallery
Galerie Haas, Vaduz, Lichtenstein
Galerie Passerpartout, Copenhagen
Galerie 3 + 2, Paris
Galleria La Vetrina, Rome
Galerie Wolfgang Ketterer, Munich
1970 Galerie Wendtorf, Dusseldorf
Buhler Graphics, Stuttgart
Galerie Le Grenier d'Art, Geneva
Galleria Vicotti, Turin
1971 Galerie des 20, Jahrhunderts, Vienna
Galerie Peithner-Lichtenfels, Vienna
Galerie d'Halluin, Dusseldorf
Galerie Hartmann, Munich
Oils, Goaches, Watercolors and Etchings, Marlborough-Gerson Gallery, New York
1973 Galerie Hartmann, Munich
Galerie Wolfrum Vienna
Galerie Lochte, Hamburg
Marlborough Galerie, Zurich
1974 *Das Graphische Werk 1951–1974,* Die Graphische Sammlung Albertina, Vienna (toured Norway, Yugoslavia and Latin America 1977–78, Turkey, 1979, Germany 1980–81, and France, 1982)
1975 Museum for Culture and Fine Arts, University of Marburg, West Germany
1976 Kurpfalzisches Museum Heidelberg
Kunst und Kulturverein, Esslingen, West Germany
Museum Mazowiecki, Plock, Poland (toured Poland)
Galerie Facchetti, Paris
Städtische Galerie, Rosenheim, West Germany
Osterreichische Galerie im Oberen Belvedere, Vienna
Oberbach Fine Art, New York
1977 St. Mary's University Art Gallery, Halifax
Galerie Facchetti, Paris
Galerie in der Staatsoper, Vienna
1978 Goldmann Fine Art, Basie
Beethovenhaus, Schwenningen, West Germany
Kunstverein Hochrhein, Sackingen, West Germany
1979 *Austria Presents Brauer to the Continents,* The Jewish Museum, New York (and world tour, 1979–83)
1985 Jack Rutberg Gallery, Los Angeles
1985–94 Vienna Sezession
Brauer-House, Vienna
Wiener Schule des Phantastischen Realismus, Japan
Motorway rest station, Lindach, Austria
1986 *Timna and Arik Brauer,* Galerie Rolandseck, Bonn
1989 *Arik Brauer: Fantastic Visions,* Jack Rutberg Gallery, Los Angeles
1991 Galerie Georges and Lesaar, Düsseldorf
Der Phantastische Mozart, Galerie Weihergut, Salzburg
1997 *Arik Brauer: Ein Lebenswerk,* Schloß Burgau

Selected Group Exhibitions:

1961 *Micro Salon,* Tokyo Gallery
Der Gegenstand in Der Osterreichischen Malerei und Plastik Secession, Vienna
1962 *Surrealismus, Phantastiche Malerei der Gegenwart,* Kunslerhaus, Vienna

Graphik aus Osterreich, Ljubljana, Yugoslavia
1963 *Grands et Jeunes d'Aujourd'hui,* Musée d'Art Moderne de la Ville, Paris
1964 *Salon de Mai,* Paris
1965 *Bienal,* Sao Paulo
1968 *Die Entwicklung der Wiener Schule,* Kunstlerhaus, Vienna
1972 *Die Wiener Schule des Phantastischen Realismus,* Museum des 20, Jahrhunderts, Vienna
1975 *22nd Biennale Premia Del Fiorina,* Palazzo Strozzi, Florence

Collections:

Albertina, Vienna; Historisches Museum der Stadt Wien, Vienna; Osterreichische Galerie des 19th and 20th, Jahrhunderts, Vienna; City of Vienna; Moderne Galerie und Graphische Sammiung Rupertinum, Salzburg; Des Moines Art Center, Iowa; The Jewish Museum, New York; Tel Aviv Museum, Israel.

Publications:

By BRAUER: Books—*Human Rights,* portfolio, New York, London and Paris 1975; *Die Zigeunerziege,* Munich 1976; *Das Rundle Fliegt,* Munich 1983; *Monography,* Harenberg, West Germany 1984; records—*Arik Brauer,* Vienna 1971; *Alles was Flugel Hat Fliegt,* Vienna 1974; *Poesie mit Krallen,* Vienna 1984; television show—*Alles was Flugel Hat Fliegt,* Vienna 1973; *Brauer Bunte Mauer,* Munich 1975; *Die Pessach-Haggadah,* Munich 1979; *Dreibändiges Werkverzeichnis,* Dortmund 1984; *Der Phantastische Mozart,* Munich 1991; *Die Zauberflöte,* Stuttgart 1998; *Arik Brauer,* with text by Naomi Brauer, Rudolf Buchbinder, Irenäus Eibl-Eibesfeld, Ernst Fuchs, Ulrich Gansert, Friedensreich Hundertwasser, Walter Koschatzky, Hugo Portisch, and Ernst Steinkellner, Vienna 1998; *Satiricon,* Vienna 2000.

On BRAUER: Books—*Brauer,* exhibition catalog by Wieland Schmied, Frankfurt 1964; *Brauer: Malerei des Phantastischen Realismus,* Munich 1968; *Brauer,* exhibition catalog, London 1969; *Art in Britain 1969–70* by Edward Lucie-Smith and Patricia White, London 1970; *Brauer: Oils Goaches, Watercolors and Etchings,* exhibition catalog, by Wolfgang Fischer, New York 1971; *Brauer: Monographie mit Werkkatalog* by Wieland Schmied, Vienna 1972; *Erich Brauer: Morgenrot, Morgengrau,* Vienna 1972; *Brauer,* exhibition catalog, by Gustav Rene Hocke, Zurich 1973; *Brauer Small Monography,* Salzburg 1973; *Malerie aus Bereichen des Unbewussten; Kunstler experimenteeren unter LSD* by Richard P. Hartmann, Cologne 1974; *Brauer: Das Graphische Werk 1951–1974* by Walter Koschatzky, Vienna 1974; *Die Wiener Schule des Phantastischen Realismus* by Johann Muschik, Vienna and Munich 1974; *Brauer's Bunte Mauer* by Erich Lessing, Munich 1975; *Brauer: New York,* Glarus, Switzerland 1975; *Brauer: Paris,* Glarus, Switzerland 1976; *Austria Presents Brauer to the Continents,* Glarus, Switzerland 1979; *Brauer Retrospective: Paintings, Drawings, Graphics,* exhibition catalog, Glarus, Switzerland 1979; *Arik Brauer, Werkverzeichnis,* exhibition catalog, Dortmund 1984; *Arik Brauer,* exhibition catalog, Vienna 1998. **Articles**—''Erich Brauer'' in *Mizue* (Tokyo), 1969; ''Brauer'' by Wieland Schmied in *Graphis* (Zurich), December 1973/January 1974.

*

I have been painting ever since I can remember, and I have done so from seven to eight hours a day over the past 30 years. Even though I painted more or less always the same, painting has never lost its fascination for me.

My first studio was the windowsill in my father's workshop. He was a bootmaker. The window was on the ground floor and I could thus sit astride, one leg inside the shop and the other dangling outside into the street. It gave me a grand feeling of commanding the crossroads of two worlds.

On the other side of the street lived a charcoal-dealer. His door was decorated with faggots and coalsacks. There were many cats around his place. I believe that those cats made me understand movement and sequences of motion. For years I drew the cats and admired their well-rounded grace. I even played at cats myself and prowled around on all fours between the bundles of leather. I slid down the big pile of solo-leather and mewed. I understood the cats. My father hummed yiddish songs and asked: ''And what are you today?'' He did not ask: ''What do you paint today?'' My movements and my painting had become as one.

Next to motion, my paintings' second base is colour. I discovered my true colours rather late and quite suddenly, from one day to the next. I had finished my studies at the Academy in Vienna and was on my first visit to Israel. One evening I sat on the beach and looked at a small shell. In a flash I suddenly realized that a colour appears luminous when it is enhanced by a second colour; a reddish-brown leaf, for example, turns red at the edge, a yellow ball turns white around the middle.

To know and to realize are not the same in painting. My ''realization'' of this intensification of colour was certainly not new then and is known to every better commercial artist. But I alone can make use of it in my own way. The sudden realization found me ready, encountered a subjective inclination, which changed mere knowledge into creative understanding. There and then I went home and started painting. My head grew hot, and I understood what impact the little shell had had upon my life.

For the next twenty years, the cat's movements and the shimmering shell were my spiritual baggage. Sometimes, and out of mere curiosity, I tried different styles of painting, perhaps a plainer surface, or a harder contour, but all such attempts ended in crisis. I have not understood that one man can do one painting only, even if he seems to pass through different periods. Other paintings, other painters.

My own painting has always been figurative and literary. In my graphic work in particular, I have often illustrated stories or followed a theme. Every artist has certain objects and forms suited to his style. The topics of his paintings may therefore quite often grow out of these objects. When painting a given subject, the situation is reversed: the painter is confronted with the difficult but exciting task of fitting the literary content to his personal forms. If, for instance, a painter's style is particularly apt for the representation of plaints, an interesting tension ensues if he tries to do buildings or machinery. I do not believe that the theme can enhance the quality of a painting, but I do believe that a subject can provide an added impetus and trigger the artist's best effort.

Among the many ways which lead towards painting, one passes through story-telling. Jewish history has almost never been painted. Those who should have created the images did not do so for religious reasons. Only the future will show whether I was big enough to fill that gap.

The history of oppression and persecution of a minority is the same for all nations. I have therefore quite often used the symbols and signs of other oppressed nations. I do not care whether the stories and contents of all the details and all the backdrops are seen my way. The subjects are unequivocal, but my paintings are resilient and open to interpretation. They ought to stimulate the imagination. Every spectator should continue to think them to their very conclusion.

Painting is influenced by so many unconscious, subconscious processes that it really cannot be learnt. It will always remain an exciting, risky endeavour, full of attraction for a lifetime. In painting there are no recognizeable, generally valid laws. One painter's quality is the other's weakness. The art of painting cannot be stolen. The purloined artistic gold turns to pitch in the hands of the thief. This holds equally true for the painter who steals from his own painting, that is who tries to repeat his own, old ideas over and over without inner need. It is impossible to fake an idea and even untrained spectators can tell an artist's living work from his empty, barren products. A visitor who approaches an exhibit with a total lack of understanding, even with disgust, will nevertheless arrive at a relatively correct judgement of the works of art. Painting is a veritable hour of truth, and one may lie with words but not with images.

The idea that strikes the artist is at the core of every work of art. The word "strike" suggests something which hits one from the outside, as if an artist could not do anything by himself but would have to wait until "art" comes to him. This is not so. I am convinced that nothing ever comes from waiting alone. I believe, on the contrary, that "being struck" is a spiritual act which a gifted person can bring about by concentration. These basic ideas, the very essence of a painting, of its forms and colours, are usually so simple that, once executed, they seem self-evident, almost two-dimensional eggs of Columbus.

Painting, unlike language, knows no frontiers in space and time. Looking at works of art created many thousand years ago, one can still re-live the artists' efforts and feelings. One can experience the same, deep understanding for the works of foreign cultures, for Chinese or African art. The fine arts seem to express something that is common to all mankind, something everybody can understand. Potentates and dictators of all kind react to painting with astounding irritability. The poetic world of forms and colours may be a closed book to them; but with the heightened senses of the wrongdoer they understand the psychological and, even more so, the political impact of painting. It is not the light-hearted art it might seem at first glance.

Painting must become a mass-activity, like speaking. Professional painters should stop feeling like miracle-workers whose magic is inaccessible to the average person. They should become examples and stimuli, almost like top-athletes in sport. The painting on houses and public institutions should not be forbidden, but should be promoted and rewarded. Industry ought to produce objects of daily use with a surface that lends itself to colouring. Children in particular should be encouraged to paint their schools inside and out.

Painting is a mysterious and singular activity that cannot be replaced by anything else and may well have the power to solve problems of our time.

—Erich Brauer

* * *

There is a school in Vienna, a school with very few pupils. It is dedicated to the teaching of *misch-tecknik,* a kind of melding of the ancient painting craft (from the times before oils and canvases became the natural raw materials for aspiring artists) and its mysteries—some of them far from easy to comprehend and then be able to harness effectively—together with antique lore and alchemies. Ernst Fuchs could be regarded as a champion of this "other" art; but the misch-technik school is not the only source of painted magic in contemporary Vienna. It is quoted here because it is an important part of his magico-medieval cultural atmosphere in which so many exotic flowers bloom. Side by side with these unexpected outcrops of archaic imagination and learning there is the Vienna School of Phantastic Realism of whose artists perhaps the best known in Erich Brauer, painter and erstwhile lute-player, folk-singer and dancer.

The fluttering petals that invade so many of Brauer's pictures recall in imagery some of the details in paintings by Naumowski, except that the Yugoslav has none of the finesse of the Austrian, nor does he impart any of the same romantic strangeness.

Even though the majority of Brauer's paintings, watercolours and etchings tend to have titles that have an everyday ring about them like "Naomi on Friday Evening," this picture suggests a parallel unreality with "The Angel Tree" or "The Flying Saucers Weep." In all three can be found a kindred iridescence. The cuffs of Naomi's dress are like the flowers of "The Redheaded King." The Orpheus-figure in "Looking Back" is accompanied by a dog whose ears are like diaphanous wings. Every image sprouts vegetally, whether through its limbs or its garments or out of the landscape itself. A world of articulated Turkish delight, except that everything is more delicately rendered and the colours are not the pale evanescences of pastel, but the burnished hues expanded in an imaginative furnace.

These are narrative pictures. The stories they tell are in a visual language for the sensitive eye. They are beguiling, a natural mirror for children's dreams. Brauer treats luxury with respect.

—Sheldon Williams

BRAVO, Claudio

Nationality: Chilean. **Born:** Valparaiso, Chile, 8 November 1936. **Education:** Studied with Miguel Venegas, 1949–48. **Career:** Lived in Spain, 1961–72. Has lived in Tangier since 1972. **Awards:** Gold Medal of Honor, Casita Maria settlement house, New York, 1996.**Agents:** Galeria Vandres, Don Ramon de la Cruz 26, Madrid 1, Spain; Marlborough Fine Art, 40 West 57th Street, New York, New York 10019, U.S.A. **Address:** 49 rue du Village, Marshan, Tangier, Morocco.

Individual Exhibitions:

1970 Gallery Staempfli, New York
1971 Galeria Egam, Madrid
1972 Gallery Staempfli, New York
Galeria Vandres, Madrid
1980 F.I.A.C. Paris
1981 Marlborough Gallery, New York
1982 Marlborough Gallery, New York
Museum of Monterrey, Mexico
1983 Marlborough Fine Art, London
1984 Marlborough Gallery, New York
Galeria Quintana, Bogota, Colombia

1985 Marlborough Gallery, New York
1989 *Claudio Bravo: Recent Paintings and Pastels,* Marlborough Gallery, New York
1990 *Claudio Bravo: Works on Paper,* Marlborough Gallery, New York
1994 Museo Nacional de Bellas Artes, Santiago, Chile (retrospective; catalog)
1997 *Claudio Bravo: Recent Works,* Marlborough Gallery, New York (catalog)
1998 *Wrapped Packages,* The Bass Museum of Art, Miami
Marlborough Gallery, New York
1999–2000 *Claudio Bravo: New Works,* Marlborough Gallery, Madrid (traveling exhibiton)

Selected Group Exhibitions:

1972 *Documenta 5,* Kassel, West Germany
Relativerend Realisme Stedelijk Van Abbemuseum, Eindhoven, The Netherlands
1973 *Artistes Hyper-realistes,* Galerie des Quatre Mouvements, Paris
1974 *Ars 74: Alternatives of Realism,* Fine Arts Academy of Finland, Helsinki
1976 *Modern Portraits: The Self and Others,* Wildenstein Galleries, New York
1981 *International Contemporary Art,* Museo Rufino Tamayo, Mexico City
1983 *48th Carnegie International,* Carnegie Institute, Pittsburgh
1984 *The Classic Tradition in Painting and Sculpture,* Aldrich Museum of Contemporary Art, Ridgefield, Connecticut
1985 *Contemporary Narrative Figure Painting,* Moravian College, Bethlehem, Pennsylvania
1995 *3 Continents: Fernando Botero, Claudio Bravo, Larry Rivers, Manolo Valdes,* A.M.S. Marlborough, Santiago
A Changing Exhibition: 20th Century Modern and Contemporary, James Goodman Gallery, New York
1997 *FIA'97,* Caracas Hilton Hotel, Venezuela

Collections:

University of Pennsylvania Art Museum, Philadelphia; Princeton University Art Museum, New Jersey; Ponce Art Museum, Puerto Rico; Museo de Arte Abstracto, Cuenca, Spain; Museum Boymans-van Beuningen, Rotterdam; Museum of Art, Helsinki.

Publications:

On BRAVO: Books—*Documenta 5,* exhibition catalog, Kassel, West Germany 1972; *Relativerend Realisme,* exhibition catalog, Eindhoven, Netherlands 1972; *Claudio Bravo: Recent Paintings and Pastels,* exhibition catalog, New York 1989; *Claudio Bravo: Wrapped Packages,* exhibition catalog, Miami 1997; *Claudio Bravo: Paintings and Drawings,* exhibition catalog, New York 1997; *Claudio Bravo: New Works,* exhibition catalog, New York 1999. **Articles—**''Lettre de New York: Claudio Bravo, Staempfli Gallery'' by J. P. Marandel in *Art International* (Lugano, Switzerland), January 1971; ''Flashback su Kassel'' in *Flash Art* (Milan), September/October 1972; ''The New Spanish Realists'' by W. Dyckes in *Art International* (Lugano, Switzerland), September 1973; ''Claudio Bravo in Tangier: Moroccan Tranquility Inspires the South American Artist'' by Edward J. Sullivan in *Architectural Digest* (Los Angeles), vol. 47, March 1990.

*

At present nothing interests me except the resurrection. I don't want movements or fashions. Art is something so subtle that these things do not last. They are poor flowers that test the brightness and quickly fade.

One had to be forgotten, and work as an honest labourer, perhaps for some years, not to be mistaken as the follower of a trend. Neither Leonardo nor Vermeer knew anything about tendencies; they did what they had to do and what they believed in—alone, very alone and quietly.

One has to be forgotten, like the dead—to disappear.

I live beside a Moroccan cemetery that I see every morning when I open my window to let the sun into my place on the bed. My experiences each day are so long and serene that I don't have even a moment to think of the neurotic involvements of other artists in big cities. I am apart from time in my beautiful Arabian palace, quiet and white like a dove sitting next to a rose.

Hyperealism, realism, superrealism and other isms will pass; they fly far above my studio and only come to visit. I am shut in, painting, and don't open my windows to them; like Abel with the Angel I will fight to be alone.

One day will come the resurrection.

—Claudio Bravo

* * *

Claudio Bravo is a painter, draughtsman, sculptor and lithographer of exhaustive accurate realism. Although it is hard to believe that some of the subjects of his works could—in real life—exist with the same dust-free stillness, this in no way invalidates the effect of his achievement. Quite rightly he holds himself to be aloof from all art movements past and present. His work is carried out in a condition of seclusion that might well be compared with that of an anchorite, and perhaps like the more successful hermits, who found both lack of company and the failure of the world to impinge upon their solitude was conducive to practical meditation, perhaps like them Claudio Bravo has been able to create a distillation (of vision, in his case) that would be difficult for an actively involved member of human society to imitate.

The ''artificiality'' of Bravo's works might be said to measure up to the improbability of a character without stain; the famous ointment has no fly in it.

And yet, with all this respectable attitude of withdrawal, Bravo slots neatly into place amongst contemporary artists. He might not like his exquisitely packed and strung parcels, marvels of painted observation, to be hung beside the packages of Christo and Manzoni, yet—for all their difference in construction—they would be fit companions. He would be appalled if his elegant drawings of boots shared exhibition with pop-art metal castings of the same subject, and yet both are part of the modern art scene.

Works by Bravo have been shown in the black museum at Cuenca, normally a venerated show-place for nonfigurative art, but such an action merely underlies the proof, if underlining were necessary, that the accomplished artist ought never to be hidebound by the dictates of contemporary taste. The unrecognisable can be the ineffable just as easily as can exact representation. Claudio Bravo might not agree with such a statement, but to substantiate it the whole history of mankind's creativity ought to be enough.

—Sheldon Williams

BRECHT, George

Nationality: American. **Born:** New York City, 7 March 1926. **Education:** Philadelphia College of Pharmacy and Science, 1946–50, B.Sc. 1950; New School for Social Research, New York, 1958–59. **Military Service:** United States Army, 1943–45. **Family:** Married Marceline Allemand in 1951 (divorced); son: Eric. **Career:** Worked as analytical chemist and quality control supervisor, Chas. Pfizer and Co., Brooklyn, New York; quality control supervisor, research chemist, engineer and inventor, Johnson and Johnson, New Brunswick, New Jersey; research inventor, chemist and engineer, Mobil Chemicals, New Brunswick, New Jersey. Independent artist active in areas including performance, artists' writings and conceptual art; early associate of Fluxus group; founded *Sight Unseen* journal: has lived and worked in Cologne since 1972. Research fellow, Leeds College of Art, England, 1968–69. **Agent:** Arturo Schwarz, via Gesu 17, Milan 20121, Italy.

Individual Exhibitions:

1959 *Toward Events,* Rueben Gallery, New York
1965 *The Book of the Tumbler on Fire,* Fischbach Gallery, New York
1967 Galleria Schwarz, Milan
1969 Galleria Schwarz, Milan
1970 Galerie Michael Werner, Cologne
Galerie Hansjörg Mayer, Stuttgart
Los Angeles County Museum of Art
1973 Galerie Onnasch, New York
1978 *Beyond Events,* Kunsthalle, Bern

Selected Group Exhibitions:

1961 *The Art of Assemblage,* Museum of Modern Art, New York
1962 *Fluxus International Festival,* New York
1965 *11 From the Reuben Gallery,* Guggenheim Museum, New York
1967 *Poems to be Seen, Paintings to be Read,* Museum of Contemporary Art, Chicago
1968 *Chemistry of Music,* Moderna Museet, Stockholm
1969 *La Cedille Qui Sourit,* Städtisches Museum, Monchengladbach, West Germany
1970 *Art in the Mind,* Allen Art Museum, Oberlin College, Ohio
1972 *Documenta 5,* Kassel, West Germany
1984 *Salvaged: Altered Everyday Objects,* Project Studios One, Long Island City, New York
1986 *Europa-Amerika,* Museum Ludwig, Cologne
1989 *Museum of Contemporary Art, Lyons: Works from the Collection,* Stadtische Galerie, Groppingen, Germany
1990 *Fluxus Subjective,* Galerie Krinzinger, Vienna
1991 *FluxAttitudes,* New Museum of Contemporary Art, New York
1992 *Fluxus,* Galerie Hundertmark, Cologne
1997 *Art Games: The Little Boxes of the Fluxus Artists,* Staatsgalerie Stuttgart, Cologne
1999 *Off Limits: Rutgers University and the Avant-Garde, 1957–1963,* Newark Museum, New Jersey
2001 *How's Your Cow?,* Musee d'Art Contemporain, Lyon

Collections:

Museum of Modern Art, New York; Städtisches Museum, Monchengladbach, West Germany; Archiv Sohm, Markgroningen, West Germany; Staatsgalerie, Berlin; Centre Georges Pompidou, Paris; Fluxus West Collection, San Diego.

Publications:

By BRECHT: Books—*Chance Imagery,* New York 1966; *Games at the Cedillas or the Cedilla Takes Off,* with Robert Filliou, New York 1967; *Vicious Circles and Infinity,* with Patrick Hughes, New York 1975; *Hsin-hsin-ming,* Cologne 1987. **Articles—**''3 Dances'' in *New Departures* (London), no 4, 1962; ''Chance Imagery'' in *Collage* (Palermo, Italy), December 1964; ''Conversation sur Autre Chose,'' with Ben Vautier, in *Identities* (Nice, France), no. 11–12, 1965; ''Dances, Events and Other Poems'' in *Something* (New York), vol. 1, no. 2, 1965; ''An Interview,'' with Henry Martin in *Art International* (Lugano, Switzerland), November 1967; ''From the Brecht/Lovell Motto Board'' in *Big Venus* (London), no. 3, 1969; ''George Brecht: An Interview'' by Robin Page and others in *Art and Artists* (London), October 1972; ''George Brecht: Sure, We Had Reasons, but We Had No Goals'' by Giancarlo Politi in *Flash Art (International Edition),* no. 167, November/December 1992.

On BRECHT: Books—*Postface* by Dick Higgins, New York 1964; *Assemblage, Environments and Happenings* by Allan Kaprow, New York 1966; *An Introduction to George Brecht's Book of the Tumbler on Fire* by Henry Martin, Milan 1978. **Articles—**''Environments, Situations, Spaces at Martha Jackson Gallery'' by J. Kroll in *Artnews* (New York), September 1961; ''The Value of Didactic Art'' by Barbara Rose in *Artforum* (New York), August 1967; ''Non-Games'' by Jasia Reichardt in *Studio International* (London), March 1968; ''An Art of Multiple Dimensions'' by Jan van der Marck in *Art in America* (New York), July/August 1974; ''Gepatenteerde Archeology Patentiert Marginale Dates: From George Brecht's Notebook of 1959'' by Dieter Daniels in *Mediamatic,* vol. 4, no. 1–2, Fall 1989; ''George Brecht: Interkulturelles Denken'' by Jurgen Raap in *Kunstforum International,* no. 144, March-April 1999; ''The Rutgers Group: Garden State Avant-Garde'' by Richard Kalina in *Art in America,* December 1999; ''Flux Generations'' by Janet A. Kaplan in *Art Journal,* Summer 2000.

*

To paraphrase Satie: ''I was born unborn into a very young world.''

—George Brecht

* * *

George Brecht is always mentioned as one of the original members of the Fluxus group, and like many of the others he had participated in the composition course that John Cage held at New York's New School for Social Research in 1958 and 1959. But Brecht's own attitude to the movement (or ''non-movement'') that claims him is, ''I say, let it go. After all, FLUXUS is a Latin word Maciunas dug up. I never studied Latin. If it hadn't been for Maciunas nobody would ever have called it anything. We would all have gone our separate ways like the man crossing the street with his umbrella, and a woman walking a dog in another direction.''

After an initial period of splashing liquid paint on canvases that he then folded up so as to allow the colors to blot and bleed, Brecht went on to begin to work with the idea of the ''event.'' Some of his events are performance pieces, and some of them are not, and with some it is a little difficult to say. One hundred or so of these events were all printed on small squares of paper and published in 1962 in a box called ''Water Yam.'' One card, for example, says ''Three aqueous events: ice, water steam.'' Another says ''Table: on a white table, glasses, a puzzle, and (having to do with smoking).'' Still another requires a performer to make a vertical pile of playing blocks on the strings of an open grand piano until one or more of the blocks fall off.

Many of these events were later to find a more physical and permanent form as assemblages, and as such they entered that continuing and ever-growing collection of experiences that's entitled *The Book of the Tumbler on Fire.* Though later dated retroactively to include certain works from as early as 1962, it was begun in 1964 and contains almost all the work that Brecht has done since. Its various chapters consist of series of assemblages of odds and ends in shallow cotton-filled specimen boxes (like the ones for presenting collections of butterflies), other assemblages in deeper boxes that allow the objects in them to move, various arrangements of chairs or tables with specific objects placed upon them (a glove, for example, or a pepper-mill, or a blind man's black-and-white cane and an orange) and sometimes associated as well with quotations from the *Guinness Book of Records.* One chapter consists of signs that say things like ''No Smoking,'' or ''Sans Issue,'' or ''Silence'' spelled out in cork letters on canvas; another is dedicated to an aerodynamic redesigning of the letters of the alphabet; another is a translation of a book by Robert Filliou. There's also a collection of paradoxes (the first in the history of philosophy) done in collaboration with Patrick Hughes and published by Doubleday and Company: this is Part III of Volume III of the *Book* . . . Part I is a work called ''Donna dei Nodi'': a full-sized reclining figure of a naked woman carved in marble by a tomb-stone sculptor and holding in her hand a large monkey's paw knot at the end of a rope the strands of which separate to end in a series of other knots at her side and feet. The artist has also made maps containing proposals for the displacement of various land-masses from one part of the earth to another. Other works are crystals grown in Petri dishes and housed in leather boxes that may also have a row of smaller lateral compartments for objects such as keys, dice, pieces of wood, and tiny spheres of marble. He has also done an English translation of the Chinese original of Seng-ts'ans's *Hsing-Hsing Ming,* the first of the classical texts of Zen Buddhism. Some of Brecht's most recent works have been stones, large and small, inscribed with the word ''Void.''

The internal logic of George Brecht's work is entirely impossible to describe, since his problem as an artist is always and only to work towards an intuitive grasp of the problems of knowledge and awareness that are central to his own individual being in the universe. He has written, ''Science tells us that the universe is what we conceive it to be, and chance enables us to determine what we conceive it to be (for the conception is only partly conscious). The receptacle of forms available to the artist thus becomes open-ended, and eventually embraces all of nature, for the recognition of significant form becomes limited only by the observer's self.'' His works, then, are simply things that he has *done* in the course of trying to clarify his relationship to the rest of existence, and they don't try to posit themselves as symbolic expressions with which the artist has established any simple kind of psychological identification. Brecht's works, like many of Marcel Duchamp's, seem marvelously arbitrary. They're about that experience of inner freedom that *allows* an individual to be arbitrary—arbitrary with respect to any and all previous conditioning. This is to say that Brecht stands behind his work much as we can stand in front of it: he, the work, and we are all a part of a larger arrangement in which both artist and spectator have the potential to realize a condition in which they're of entirely equal status. We can do with Brecht's works whatever we like: but to discover that they are beautiful is not to fall in line with an artist's revelation of a definition of beauty; it's rather to discover that the discovery of beauty is itself an entirely personal event of which all of us are individually capable.

—Henry Martin

BREER, Robert C.

Nationality: American. **Born:** Detroit, Michigan, 30 September 1926. **Education:** Detroit University School, 1932–43; Stanford University, California, 1943–45, 1947–49, B.A. 1949. Served in the United States Army, 1945–47. **Family:** Married Frances Foote in 1955; children: Julia, Emily, and Harriet. **Career:** Lived in Paris, 1949–59, now resident in New York State. Adjunct to Carnegie Professor, Films and Kinetics, Cooper Union, New York City, since 1972; co-designer, Pepsi-Cola Pavilion, *Expo '70,* Osaka, Japan, 1970. **Member:** Board of Directors, Filmmakers Cooperative, New York 1967–72. **Awards:** Annual Painting Award, Stanford University, 1949; Creative Film Foundation Award, 1957–61; Diplome Speciale, Bergamo, Italy, 1962; Max Ernst Award, Oberhausen, West Germany, 1968; Film Culture Award, New York, 1972; Guggenheim Fellowship, 1978. **Agents:** Cinegate Ltd., 70 Portobello Road, London W11, England; Projection Galerie Ursula Wevers, Am Rinkenpfulh 20–26, 5000 Cologne 1, West Germany; and Filmmakers Cooperative, 175 Lexington Avenue, New York, New York 10016. **Address:** 80 Sparkill Avenue, Tappan, New York 10983, U.S.A.

Individual Exhibitions:

1956 Palais des Beaux-Arts, Brussels
American Students and Artists Center, Paris
1960 Gallery Mayer, New York
1961 Charles Cinema, New York (film retrospective)
1962 Bleecker Cinema, New York
1963 Dwan Gallery, Los Angeles (film retrospective)
1965 Galeria Bonino, New York
1966 Galeria Bonino, New York
1968 Galerie Ricke, Cologne
1969 Museum of Contemporary Art, Chicago
1970 Galeria Bonino, New York

Museum of Modern Art, New York
1972 J. L. Hudson Gallery, Detroit
Millenium Film Workshop, New York
1973 Hammarskjold Plaza, New York
1974 IBM Plaza, New York
Michael Berger Gallery, Pittsburgh
1975 Film Forum, New York (film retrospective)
Museum of Modern Art, New York (film retrospective)
Whitney Museum, New York (film retrospective)
1977 Whitney Museum, New York
1979 St. Louis Art Museum
Walker Art Center, Minneapolis
1980 Whitney Museum, New York (film retrospective)
Albright Knox Art Gallery, Buffalo, New York
Art Institute of Chicago
1981 Exterior Film Forum, New York (mural painting)
1990 *Robert Breer: A Painter in Paris 1949–1959,* Galerie 1900–2000, Paris (catalog)
2000 Staff USA, New York

Selected Group Exhibitions:

1976 *Une Histoire du Cinema,* Centre Beaubourg, Paris
1977 *Paris-New York,* Centre Beaubourg, Paris
1978 *Filmex: American Independent Animation,* Hollywood, California
1979 *Contemporary Sculpture,* Museum of Modern Art, New York
Film as Film, Arts Council of Great Britain, London
Biennial Exhibition, Whitney Museum, New York
Americans in Paris: The 50's, California State University at Northridge
1980 *The Pleasure Dome: American Experimental Film 1939–79,* Moderna Museet, Stockholm
1981 *Biennial Exhibition,* Whitney Museum, New York

Collections:

Museum of Modern Art, New York; New York Public Library; Anthology Film Archives, New York; Institute of Contemporary Art, London; Musée National d'Art Moderne, Paris; Austrian Film Archives, Vienna; Moderna Museet, Stockholm; National Film Archives, Canberra, Australia.

Publications:

By BREER: Books—*A Critical Cinema 2: Interviews with Indepented Filmmakers* by Scott MacDonald, Berkeley 1992. **Articles**—"On 2 Films" in *Film Culture* (New York), Summer 1961; "What Happened" in *Film Culture* (New York), Fall 1962; "Interview with Robert Breer," with Guy Cote, in *Film Culture* (New York), Winter 1962; "A Statement" in *Film Culture* (New York), Summer 1963. **Films**—*Form Phrases I,* 1952; *Form Phrases II,* 1953; *Form Phrases III,* 1953; *Form Phrases IV,* 1954; *Images by Images I,* 1954; *Un Miracle,* 1955; *Image by Images II,* 1955; *Image by Images III,* 1955; *Image by Images IV,* 1966; *Cats,* with Frances Breer, 1956; *Recreation I,* with spoken text by Noel Burch, 1956–57; *Recreation II,* 1956–57; *Jamestown Baloos,* 1957; *A Man and His Dog Out for Air,* 1957; *Par Avion,* 1958; *Eyewash,* 1958–59; *Homage to Jean Tinguely's 'Homage to New York',* 1960; *Blazes,* 1961; *Horse Over a Tea Kettle,* 1962; *Pat's Birthday,* 1962; *Breathing,* 1963; *Fistfight,* 1964; *66,* 1966; *69,* 1968; *OBL No. 2,* 1968; *70,* 1970; *Gulls and Buoys,* 1972; *Fuji,* 1974; *Rubber Cement,* 1975; *77,* 1977; *LMNO,* 1978; *TZ,* 1979.

On BREER: Books—*Robert Breer* by Michel Seuphor, Paris 1956; *Hard Center* by Nicholas and Elena Calas, New York 1964; *Film: A Montage of Theories* by Richard Dyer, New York 1966; *Animation in the Cinema* by Ralph Stephenson, London 1967; *An Introduction to the American Underground Film* by Sheldon Renan, New York 1967; *The New American Cinema* by Gregory Battcock, New York 1967; *Art of Time* by Michael Kirby, New York 1969, *The American Independent Film* by P. Adams Sitney, Boston 1971; *Experimental Cinema* by David Curtis, New York 1971; *Pavilion* by Nilo Lindgreen, Barbara Rose, and Calvin Tomkins, New York 1972; *Experimental Animation* by Robert Russett, New York 1976; *Robert Breer* by Sandra Moore, Minneapolis 1980; *Robert Breer: A Study of His Work in the Context of the Modernist Tradition* by Louis Mendelson, Ann Arbor, Michigan 1981; *Robert Breer—A Critical Cinema 2* by Scott MacDonald, Berkeley 1992. **Articles**—"Four artists as Film-Makers" by Adrienne Mancia and Willard Van Dyke in *Art in America* (New York), January 1967; "The Experience of Kinesis" by Michael Kirby in *Art News* (New York), February 1968; "Onward and Upward with the Arts," by Calvin Tomkins, in *The New Yorker,* October 1970; "Gulls and Buoys" by Scott Hammen in *Afterimage* (Rochester, New York), December 1974; notes by Lucy Fischer in *Museum of Modern Art Circulating Films,* exhibition catalog, New York 1976; "The Other Cinema" by Noel Carroll in *Soho Weekly News* (New York), 25 January 1979; "Robert Breer's LMNO" by Elena Simons in *Millenium Film Journal* (New York), nos. 4 and 5, 1979; "On A Breer Day" by Amy Taubin in *Soho Weekly News* (New York), 28 May 1980; "Robert Breer's Animated World" by J. Hoberman in *American Film* (Washington, D.C.), September 1980; "Robert Breer, Whitney Museum" by Amy Taubin in *Artforum* (New York), September 1980.

* * *

The art of traditional animation—with very modest means—has been the medium in which Robert Breer has invented filmic language paralleling the evolution of recent attitudes towards form and content in the visual arts. His oft-quoted statement best approaches the long-evolved, and even anti-animation, effect of his films: "I'm interested in the domain between motion and still pictures . . . the single frame is the basic unit of film, just as bricks are the basic unit of brick houses." And thus his films have generally offered a sense of the sequence of separate images that compose the film rather than a continuous flow. His art has been described as an animated film variant comprising the Pop art use of everyday accessories, especially as in Dine and Oldenburg; the color fields and geometric hard edge of Ellsworth Kelly; pictorial collage and stream-of-consciousness flow as in Rauschenberg; and cubist-like line found in the paintings of Stuart Davis.

The son of an engineering prodigy then working in Detroit, Breer himself first studied engineering. In 1949 he went to Paris intending to be a painter, but soon became interested in documenting the process by which his final work was achieved. With his father's borrowed Bolex, he began to construct films as geometric abstraction paralleling and reviving the pre-World War II graphic cinema tradition of Richter and Eggeling—with which Breer was then only little acquainted. In 1954 he began a loop work *Image by Image,* which became a series where single framing became the structural and ideational base. In this manipulation, although unknown to one another at that time, Breer has been likened to the Viennese Peter Kubelka. With *Recreation I* (1956–57), Breer began his use of the collage of actual objects, and thus referred to the type of graphic cinema originated in Léger's *Le Ballet Mechanique;* and then a year after, Breer began to produce film based upon a combination of literal figure collage and abstract geometric patterns as in *Jamestown Baloos.* During the years 1957–64, he produced essentially animated cartoons in this manner, including *Man and His Dog Out for Air* (1957) which through long commercial run in New York spread his reputation beyond the avantgardist film community. At that time, he also began to use 3 by 5 inch flip cards to construct his films, and has since offered mutoscopes—a device that permits the hand-cranking of these flip cards—in his public exhibitions, e.g., his retrospectives at the Whitney Museum of American Art in 1977 and 1980.

Breer returned to the U.S. in 1959, and absorbed at first the open vulgarity of Pop—perhaps best felt in the autobiographical *Fist Fight* (1964); and then the abstract vigor of Minimalism. Under the influence of the latter, he reworked his earliest films *Form Phases* (1952–53), and then went on to create his finest abstract films, each setting itself specific problems of color, illusion, and image control, *66* (1966), *69* (1969), and *70* (1970). At this time, which coincided with a strong rise of interest in the United States in a Tech-art, Breer also became known as the maker of extremely slow-moving abstract geometric, motorized, sculptures; less well-known were the violently moving mylar sheet constructions. In the next decade Breer's films made more liberal use of literal content as he began the use of the rotoscope which permits a frame-by-frame tracing of live action footage. With it, he continued his exploration of the connections between figuration and abstraction through retarded movement and figure-dissolution. His most recent works, such as *LMNO* and *T.Z.* (1978 and 1980), continue his long-time synthesis of literal subject and geometric pattern.

—Joshua Kind

BREHMER, K. P.

Nationality: German. **Born:** Berlin, 12 September 1938. **Education:** Studied applied graphics at the Werkkunstschule, Krefeld, West Germany, 1959–60, and printmaking at the Staatliche Kunstakademie, Dusseldorf, 1961–63. **Family:** Married Monika Aich in 1963; children: Sebastian and Jelle. **Career:** Worked as photographic technician, Carl Lange Verlag publishers, Duisburg, West Germany, 1957–59. Independent graphic artist, Dusseldorf, 1963–71, Hamburg, 1971–74, and in West Berlin, since 1974; also filmmaker, since 1959. Professor, Hochschule für Bildende Künste, Hamburg, 1971–74. Lives in West Berlin, Hamburg and Vietze an der Elbe, West Germany. **Agent:** Galerie René Block, Schaperstrasse 11, 1000 Berlin 12. **Addresses:** Lerchenfeld 2, 2000 Hamburg 76, West Germany; Regensburgerstrasse 27, 1000 Berlin 30, West Germany.

Individual Exhibitions:

1964 Graphisches Kabinett der Freien Galerie, West Berlin
1965 Galerie René Block, West Berlin
1966 Galerie Patio, Frankfurt
1967 Galerie Rudolf Zwirner, Cologne
Galerie René Block, West Berlin
1969 Galerie René Block, West Berlin
1970 Goethe-Institut, Athens
Galerie Centro, Oldenburg, West Germany
Deutsch Bibliothek, Rome
1971 *Produktion 1962–1971,* Kinstverein, Hamburg (retrospective)
1972 Galerie Bama, Paris
1973 Galerie René Block, West Berlin
Galerie Magers, Bonn
Galerie Inge Baecker, Bochum, West Germany
1975 René Block Gallery, New York
1976 René Block Gallery, New York
Museum Wiesbaden, West Germany
1977 Galerie René Block, West Berlin
1985 DAAD-Galerie, West Berlin
1986 Stadtgalerie Saarbrucken, West Germany
Buro Orange, Munich
1987 Galerie Vorsetzen, Hamburg
1998 Museum Fridericianum Kassel, Germany

Selected Group Exhibitions:

1964 *Kapitalistischer Realismus,* Galerie René Block, West Berlin
1966 *Kritische Kunst,* Dum panu z kunstatu, Brno, Czechoslovakia
1968 *Ars Multiplicata,* Kunsthalle, Cologne
1970 *Information,* Museum of Modern Art, New York
1972 *Documenta 5,* Kassel, West Germany
1974 *Art into Society/Society into Art,* Institute of Contemporary Arts, London
1979 *Kunstler/Sozialarbeiter/Eremit/Forscher,* Kunstverein, Hamburg
1981 *Art Allemagne Aujourd'hui,* ARC/Musee d'Art Moderne, Paris
1984 *Der Mang zum Gesamtkunstwerk,* Akademie der Kunste, West Berlin
1987 *Berlinart,* Museum of Modern Art, New York (travelled to San Francisco Museum of Modern Art)
1991 *Capitalist Realism: Print Portfolio,* Ars Multiplicata, Surry Hills, Australia
1992 *Beuys, Brehmer, Cage, Filliou, Paik, Thomkins, Weiner, Williams 1985–86,* Ars Multiplicata, Surry Hills, Australia

Collections:

Kaiser-Wilhelm Museum, Krefeld, West Germany; Museum of Modern Art, New York; DAAD-Buro, West Berlin.

Publications:

By BREHMER: Films—*Madame Butterfly,* 1969; *Ideale Landschaft,* 1969; *Musikfilm—Stumm,* 1969; *Die geschiedene Frau,* 1969; *Walkings,* 1969; *Nr. 1 (Sieg),* 1969; *Nr. 2 (Mauer),* 1969; *Nr. 3 (Stanley Brouwn),* 1969; *Nr. 4 (Passer),* 1969; *Nr. 5 (Parallel/ Identitat),* 1969; *Nr. 6 (Out/ In—Imaginar),* 1969; *Die Welt im

Kopf—Skala, 1970; Helmut von Florenz, 1970; *MA MA,* 1970; *Fernshoper,* 1970.

On BREHMER: Books—*Ars Multiplicata,* exhibition catalog, Cologne 1968; *K. P. Brehmer: Produktion 1962–1971,* exhibition catalog, with an interview by Werner Rohde, Hamburg 1971; *Documenta 5: Befragung der Realitat,* exhibition catalog, edited by Harald Szeemann and others, Kassel, West Germany 1972; *Kunst im Politischen Kampf,* exhibition catalog, Hannover 1973; *Art into Society/Society into Art,* exhibition catalog, London 1974; *Tampons d'Artistes,* edited by Herve Fischer, Paris 1974; *K. P. Brehmer: Wie mich die Schlange sieht,* exhibition catalog, with text by Bernd Schulz, Munich 1986.

*

It is my view that the only progress achieved by art is that represented by the transference of its whole intensity from ''I'' to ''we.'' Through ideological kleptomania, so to speak, we must intervene in bourgeois culture, whereby the value of personal possessions, which is inherent in artistic creation, is reduced. This is possible by withholding ''creativity'' and substituting ''imitation.'' This modification consists of the reduction of ''artistic language'' to apparent theft and adoption of collective symbols.

The transformation of art from the ideology of self to a social plane signifies stepping away from the private act of individual creation in favour of a collective and anonymous stance, in order to recognize reality through a frame of reference and to provide an orientation for oneself and the on-looker.

In this way the artist develops from a lone hero to an active participant.

—K. P. Brehmer

BRISLEY, Stuart

Nationality: British. **Born:** Haslemere, Surrey, in 1933. **Education:** Guildford School of Art, Surrey, 1949–54; Royal College of Art, London, 1956–59; Akademie der Bildenden Künste, Munich, 1959–60; and Florida State University, Tallahassee, 1960–62. **Career:** Independent artist, concentrating on performance and installation works, London since 1963: Artist in Residence, Imperial War Museum, London, 1987. Founder-Member, Arts Information Registry, London, 1967, and Artists' Union, London, 1972. **Member:** Artists Placement Group, London, 1967–71. **Awards:** Bavarian State Stipendium, 1959–60; Fulbright Travel Award, to Florida, 1960–64; Deutscher Akademischer Austauschdienst (D.A.A.D) Scholarship, West Berlin, 1973; British Council grant, 1976, 1977. **Address:** 28 Oakhill Road, London SW15, England.

Individual Exhibitions:

1960 Galerie Deutscher Bucherbund, Munich
1961 Studio F. Ulm, West Germany
1962 Cornell University, Ithica, New York
1963 Washington and Jefferson College, Washington, Pennsylvania
Cornell University, Ithica, New York
1965 New Vision Centre, London
1966 McRoberts and Tunnard Gallery, London
1967 Museum of Modern Art, Oxford (with Bill Culbert)
Herbert Art Gallery, Coventry (with Bill Culbert; travelled to Trinity College, Dublin, and the University of Bristol)
1968 *Bromsgrove Festival,* Worcestershire (with Bill Culbert)
Tate Gallery, London (with Peter Sedgeley)
Camden Arts Centre, London (with Bill Culbert)
Madame Tussaud's Waxworks, London (with Bill Culbert)
1969 Camden Arts Centre, London
1970 *Guest of Honour,* New Arts Laboratory, London
Sigi Krauss Gallery, London
1971 Centro de Arte y Communicacion, Buenos Aires
1972 *You Know It Makes Sense,* Ikon Gallery, Birmingham
Zl656395C, Gallery House, London
Artist as Whore, Gallery House, London
1973 *10 Days,* Paramedia Editions, West Berlin
1975 *12 Days,* Kunsforum, Rottweil, West Germany
Moments of Decision.Indecision, Palac Kultury i Nauki, Warsaw
1976 Battersea Arts Centre, London
Northern Arts Gallery, Newcastle upon Tyne
1981 Institute of Contemporary Arts, London (travelled to Ikon Gallery, Birmingham)
Acme Gallery, London (with Iain Robertson)
1986 Orchard Gallery, Derry, Northern Ireland
1987 Imperial War Museum, London
1996 *Black,* South London Gallery, London
The Naples Arrangement (In Bits and Pieces) (performance), Hereford Salon, London
1999 Mission Gallery, Swansea
2000 *Voices from Everywhere,* Arthouse, London

Selected Group Exhibitions:

1953 *Young Contemporaries,* R.B.A. Galleries. London (and 1957, 1958, 1959)
1960 *Grosse Sommer Ausstellung Neue Gruppe,* Haus der Kunst, Munich
1965 *The London Group,* Art Federation Galleries, London
1968 *Artists for Czechoslovakia,* Camden Arts Centre, London
1970 *Come Together,* Royal Court Theatre, London
1972 *A Survey of the Avant-Garde in Britain,* Gallery House, London
1973 *Magic and Strong Medicine,* Walker Art Gallery, Liverpool
1976 *Arte Inglese Oggi 1960–76,* Palazzo Reale, Milan
1978 *Spring Show 2,* Serpentine Gallery, London
1982 *Group Exhibition,* Lewis Johnstone Gallery, London
1990 *Signs of the Times,* Museum of Modern Art, Oxford
1991 *The Cenotaph Project: Stuart Brisley and Maya Balcioglu,* Orchard Gallery, Londonderry, Northern Ireland
1998 *Out of Actions: Between Performer and the Object, 1949–1979,* Museum of Contemporary Art, Los Angeles (catalog)
1999 *Intimate House,* South London Gallery, London
2000 *Live in Your Head,* Whitechapel Art Gallery, London (catalog)

Publications:

By BRISLEY: Books—*Interviews with the Artists,* compiled and edited by Nicholas Wegner and Sarah Batiste, Teddington 1992. **Articles**—''Wanted: A New Deal in Art Schools?'' in *Penrose Annual,* London 1969; ''Environments'' in *Studio International* (London), June 1969; ''Physical Situations,'' interview with Simon Field, in *Art and Artists* (London), August 1971; ''No, It Is Not On'' in *Studio International* (London), March 1972; ''Anti-Performance Art'' in *Arte Inglese Oggi 1960–76,* exhibition catalog, Milan 1976; Stuart Brisley,'' interview with John Roberts, in *Artlog* (London), April/May 1981; interview with Nicholas Wegner in *CV: Journal of Art and Craft,* vol. 3, no. 1, March 1990; interview with William Furlong in *Audio Arts,* vol. 16, no. 1, 1996.

On BRISLEY: Books—*Play Orbit,* edited by Jasia Reichardt, with texts by several authors, London 1969; *Art Event and Happenings* by Udo Kultermann, London 1971; *A Survey of the Avant-Garde in Britain,* volume 1, with an introduction by Rosetta Brooks, London 1972; *Magic and Strong Medicine,* exhibition catalog, with text by Norbert Lynton, Liverpool 1973; *Stuart Brisley,* exhibition catalog, with texts by Paul Overy and John Roberts, London 1981. **Articles**—''The Body Politic—In the Ring with Brisley and Barney'' in *DPICT,* no. 1, April/May 2000; ''It's All in Your Mind'' by Barry Schwabsky in *Art in America,* 1 September 2000.

* * *

The work of Stuart Brisley is concerned with pain.

In a period when art has upped stakes and moved from its position of lofty detachments to set up its own stall at the Vanity Fayre, when painters celebrate the latest fashions in automobiles, ladies' shoes or pop singers in a joyful and colourful discord, when sculptors rush to imitate the recent inventions of a mechanical age, when artists of all persuasions are glad to see their work sold to the highest bidder with all the television and champagne razzmatazz of the big gallery opening, Brisley has taken it upon himself to be the conscience of the art world, reminding it that art also contains a more somber tradition of horror and disgust, protest and pain.

Such a role is difficult to sustain; it could easily become strident or embarrassing, which is possibly why Brisley has always been meticulous about his techniques, about what is and what is not permissible, and is certainly why in his work the pain is transmitted to the audience via himself. To paint pictures of the ills of society could easily become mere preaching, but to use himself as the illustration safeguards the artist from such a tendency.

A typical Brisley piece, and one of his best, was his ''Bath'' performance at Gallery House in London, This, now sadly defunct, avant-guard gallery invited Brisley to take part in a survey of recent British art and followed its usual policy of allowing the artists to choose their own space. The gallery had once been a private house and Brisley chose the bathroom.

On the day the exhibition opened, visitors, drawn to the location by the gathering crowd, could see Brisley lying fully clothed in the bath with only his nose and mouth above water. He had put dye in the water which gave it a stagnant look and had not attempted to clean the room, which had been unused for sometime. On the floor were scattered pieces of raw meat.

The image was powerful, with overtones of police state torture or lonely suicide. It worked as well as a photograph of the real thing might do and clearly had a strong effect on the spectators. But Brisley was not yet finished: the exhibition ran for three weeks and every day he spent lying in the bath just able to breathe. After about three days the flies in the neighborhood woke up to the fact that a magnificent free meal was available to them in the form of the now rotting flesh; after 10 the stench was unbearable, and Brisley's fellow artists had to ask him to terminate the performance.

The effect of such a work is shock, but because Brisley is careful to do work slowly and submit his own mind and body to far greater pressure than he inflicts on his audience, it avoids being mere shock and becomes instead archetypal and thought provoking.

Brisley's earliest performances took place in gridlike sculptural settings and featured large casts dressed in white medical-looking clothes and bandages. This phase of working with others reached its culmination in an exhibition in Edinburgh where the artist worked in a disused car saleroom on one of the main streets. In this the grid was replaced by wrecked cars, some of which still were capable of movement, and Brisley spent the exhibition driving them headlong into each other until the whole area was littered with wreckage. He eventually had to stop this when affected by carbon monoxide poisoning from the exhaust fumes.

Since that time Brisley has realized that he cannot ask others to take part in his art and has worked alone. In one recent piece he had himself locked for five days in a room containing just one chair and one lightbulb continuously burning; the floor was swimming in water. Visitors to the exhibition could see him through a small barred window.

There are other artists who are working in similar fields of self-inflicted pain and humiliation, but only Brisley brings to this highly questionable type of activity a dignity and an ability to relate the images he creates to the wider issues of society. Where others indulge in exhibitionistic masochism, Brisley by carefully removing his individuality from the situation and by using his own body as if it were inert sculpture, often achieves the difficult feat of enabling the spectator to overcome his feelings of shock and embarrassment and, in their place, to contemplate the creepy-crawlies that still lurk under the stone of our affluent and somewhat complacent society.

—Alastair Mackintosh

BROUWN, Stanley

Nationality: Dutch. **Born:** Paramaribo, Surinam, in 1935. **Education:** Attended schools in Paramaribo; self-taught in art. **Career:** Independent artist, Amsterdam, since 1960; first ''This Way Brouwn'' works, Amsterdam, 1960; associated with the Fluxus performance artists, Amsterdam, from 1962. **Address:** Willem de Zwygerlaan 60–1, Amsterdam, Netherlands.

Individual Exhibitions:

1970 Stedelijk Museum, Schiedam, Netherlands
Städtisches Museum, Mönchenglabach, West Germany
1971 Zentrum fur Aktuelle Kunst, Aachen, West Germany
1976 Van Abbemuseum, Eindhoven, Netherlands (travelled to the Kunsthalle, Berne)
1977 Whitechapel Art Gallery, London
1997 *Presentation new publication,* Van Abbemuseum entre'acte, Eindhoven

Selected Group Exhibitions:

1970 *18 Paris iv 70,* Paris
1972 *Documenta,* Kassel, West Germany
1978 *Werke aus der Sammiung Crex,* Ink, Zurich (travelled to the Louisiana Museum, Humieback, Denmark, Städtische Galerie in Lenbachhaus, Munich, and the Van Abbemuseum, Eindhoven, Netherlands)
1979 *Mit Zeichnerischen Mittein gemacht,* Stadtschloss, Fulda, West Germany
1992 *Interventions,* Art Gallery of Ontario, Toronto
1996 *An Eternity With Boundaries,* Genesta Gallery, London
1997 *With Tuning Up #4,* Kunstmuseum Wolfsburg, Germany
1999 *Collected Works 1: Contemporary Art sine 1968,* Kunstmuseum Wolfsburg

Collections:

Van Abbemuseum, Eindhoven, Netherlands; Stedelijk Museum, Amsterdam; Kunsthalle, Berne.

Publications:

By BROUWN: Books—*This Way Brouwn,* Cologne and New York 1971; *Afghanistan/Zambia,* Aachen, West Germany 1971; *Stanley Brouwn,* Eindhoven 1997. **Articles—**''Stanley Brouwn'' in *Forum International,* vol. 3, no. 13, May-August 1992.

On BROUWN: Books—*18 Paris iv 70,* edited by Michel Claura, Paris 1970; *Concept Art* by Klaus Honnef, Cologne 1971; *Documenta 5: Befragung der Realiat Bildwelten huete,* exhibition catalog, edited by Harald Szeeman and others, Kassel, West Germany 1972; *Stanley Brouwn,* exhibition catalog, edited by Coosje van Bruggen and Rudi H. Fuchs, Eindhoven, Netherlands 1976; *Werke aus der Sammlung Crex,* exhibition catalog, by Cristel Sauer and Urs Raussmuller, Zurich 1978; *Mit Zeichnerischen Mitteln gemacht,* exhibition catalog, with text by Michael Lingner, Fulda, West Germany 1979; *Interventions,* exhibition catalog, Toronto 1992; *Stanley Brouwn: 1M x 1M,* exhibition catalog, Frankfurt am Main, 1993. **Articles—**''Dutch Artists on Television'' by Carel Blotkamp in *Studio International* (London), June 1971; ''Stanley Brouwn: Door Kosmischestralen Lopen'' by J. Cladders in *Museumjournaal* (Amsterdam), July 1971; ''Stanley Brouwn: Steps'' in *Avalanche* (New York), Spring 1972; ''The Clocktower, New York: Exhibit'' by Joshua Decter in *Arts Magazine* (New York), vol. 63, Summer 1989; ''Cartes et Territoires'' by Marie-Ange Brayer in *Parachute* (Montreal), no. 83, July-September 1996; ''An Eternity With Boundaries'' by Michael Archer in *Art Monthly* (London), no. 200, October 1996.

BROWN, Larry

Nationality: American. **Born:** New Brunswick, New Jersey, 1 June 1942. **Education:** Washington State University, Pullman, WA, B.A. 1967; University of Arizona, Tucson, M.F.A. 1970. **Family:** Margaret A. Brown; daughter: Gabrielle. **Career:** Painter and sculptor; has taught as a professor or visiting artist at several universities, since 1970. **Awards:** National Endowment for the Arts Fellowship Grant, 1979. **Agent:** Bernard Toale Gallery, Boston, MA; Morgan Gallery, Kansas City, MO; Butters Gallery, Ltd., Portland, OR; Davis and Hall, Hudson, NY. **Address:** 54 Franklin St., New York, NY 10013, U.S.A.; P.O. Box 336, Hobart, NY 13788, U.S.A.

Larry Brown: *Primary Particles,* 1999. ©Larry Brown.

Individual Exhibitions:

1971 Clarke College, Dubuque, Iowa
University of Minnesota, Morris
1973 Washington State University, Pullman
University of Wisconsin, Whitewater
1974 Rhode Island School of Design, Providence
St. Lawrence University, Canton, New York
1975 Lamagna Gallery, New York
Montana State University, Bozeman
1976 Missoula Museum of the Arts, Missoula, Montana
1977 O.K. Harris, Works of Art, New York
1978 Morgan Gallery, Kansas City, Missouri
State University of New York, Potsdam
1979 O.K. Harris, Works of Art, New York
1980 Morgan Gallery, Kansas City, Missouri
University of Wisconsin, La Crosse
1982 O.K. Harris, Works of Art, New York
Iowa State University, Ames
1985 Morgan Gallery, Kansas City, Missouri
1986 Carlo Lamagna Gallery, New York
1987 Carlo Lamagna Gallery, New York
Ann Jaffe Gallery, Bay Harbor Island, Florida

1988 G.H. Dalsheimer Gallery, Baltimore
Elliot Smith Contemporary Art, St. Louis
Ivory/Kimpton Gallery, San Francisco
Muhlenberg College Center for the Arts, Allentown, Pennsylvania
1989 Edward Thorden Gallery, Goteborg, Sweden
Carlo Lamagna Gallery, New York
1990 Carlo Lamagna Gallery, New York
Ann Jaffe Gallery, Bay Harbor Island, Florida
Focus Gallery, University of Florida, Gainsville
R.F. Brush Gallery, St. Lawrence University, Canton
1992 Morgan Gallery, Kansas City
1993 Helander Gallery, New York
1997 Bernard Toale Gallery, Boston
1998 Davis and Hall, Hudson, New York
1999 Butters Gallery Ltd., Portland
2000 Davis and Hall, Hudson, New York
2001 Morgan Gallery, Kansas City

Selected Group Exhibitions:

1970 *Drawing Invitational: California, Arizona, Nevada, Utah,* University of California, Santa Barbara
1971 *56th Wisconsin Painters and Sculptors Exhibition,* Milwaukee Art Center
1974 *Invitation '74,* Walker Art Center, Minneapolis, Minnesota (traveled to Tweed Museum of Art, Duluth)
1975 *Abstraction: Alive and Well,* State University of New York, Potsdam
1976 *66th Annual Exhibition,* The Carnegie Museum of Art, Pittsburgh
1978 *The Forward Edge of Twentieth Century Painting,* University of North Texas, Denton
1979 *Variety and Quest in Current Painting,* Zolla/Lieberman Gallery, Chicago
1984 *The Lewis and Clark Collection,* Portland Center for the Visual Arts, Portland
1986 *New Work, New York,* Helander Gallery, Palm Beach, Florida
1987 *New Year, New Work,* Ann Jaffe Gallery, Bay Harbor Island, Florida
1988 *Modern Masters for the '40s to the '80s,* Morgan Gallery, Kansas City
Ten Americans, The Carnegie Museum of Art, Pittsburgh, Pennsylvania
1989 *Artists of the '80s* (selected works from the Maslow Collection), Sordoni Art Gallery, Wilkes College, Wilkes-Barre, Pennsylvania
1990 *Mind and Matter/New American Abstraction* (traveling exhibition), South Korea and New Zealand
1991 *Mind and Matter/New American Abstraction* (traveling exhibition), Singapore, Taiwan, Malaysia, and Philippines
1991–94 *Collaborations: Artists + Printers* (traveling exhibition) Central and South America
1993 *Painting: Larry Brown, Joseph Haske, David Schoffman,* Helander Gallery, New York
1994 *Larry Brown and Mark Williams,* Lindblad and Thorden Gallery, Goteborg, Sweden
1995 *Tamarind: Into the Nineties* (traveling exhibition), North Carolina, Massachusetts, New Hampshire, New Mexico
2000 *Ambiguity: Layers of Information,* Contemporary Gallery, Marywood University, Scranton, Pennsylvania

Collections:

Indianapolis Museum of Art, Indianapolis; Minnesota Museum of Art, St. Paul; University of New Mexico, Albuquerque; The Newark Museum of Art, Newark, New Jersey; The Norton Museum of Art, West Palm Beach, Florida; Portland Museum of Art, Portland; St. Lawrence University, Canton; University of Wisconsin, Stevens Point; University of Wisconsin, La Crosse; Walker Art Center, Minneapolis; and many corporate collections.

Publications:

On BROWN: Books—*Drawings 1979: California, Arizona, Nevada, Utah,* exhibition catalog, by David Gebhard, Santa Barbara 1970; *Abstraction: Alive and Well,* exhibition catalog, by Anthony Boyle, Potsdam, New York 1975; *Painting and Sculpture Today,* exhibition catalog, edited by Hillary D. Bussett, Indianapolis Museum of Art 1978; *Ten Americans,* exhibition catalog, Pittsburgh 1988; *Artists of the '80s, Selected Works from the Maslow Collection,* exhibition catalog, Wilkes-Barre, Pennsylvania 1989; *Mind and Matter/ New American Abstraction,* exhibition catalog, by Leslie Luebbers, World Print Council, San Francisco 1990; *Collaborations: Artists + Printers,* exhibition catalog, Tamarind Institute, Arts America, and USIA, 1991; *Tamarind: Forty Years* by Marjorie Devon, Albuquerque, 2000. **Articles—**''Human Touch Happily Returns to Art'' by Mike Steel in *Minneapolis Tribune,* 26 May 1974; ''Artists Enliven Mellon Galleries'' by Donald Miller in *Pittsburgh Post Gazette,* 13 February 1976; ''Four Artists, O.K. Harris Gallery'' by John Perrault in *Soho News,* 29 December 1977; ''Larry Brown at the Morgan Gallery'' by Victoria Kirsch Melcher in *Kansas City Star,* 19 November 1978; ''Larry Brown'' by Donald Hoffman in *Kansas City Star,* 9 October 1980; ''Larry Brown'' by Susan Gill in *Art News,* December 1986; ''Larry Brown'' by Ellen Lee Klein in *Arts Magazine,* April 1986; ''Larry Brown'' by Stephen Westfall in *Arts Magazine,* May 1986; ''Larry Brown'' by John Sturman in *Art News,* December 1987; ''Larry Brown'' by Ellen Handy in *Arts Magazine,* December 1987; ''Larry Brown'' by Ronny Cohen in *Artforum,* January 1988; ''Larry Brown'' by Ellen Lee Klein in *Arts Magazine,* February 1988; ''S.F. Galleries Showing 'New' Work—Larry Brown at Ivory/Kimpton'' by Kenneth Baker in *San Francisco Chronicle,* 14 July 1988; ''At Dalsheimer, Larry Brown's Abstract Paintings Have Real Pull'' by Steve Purchase in *Baltimore Evening Sun,* 2 December 1988; ''Art Journal—Larry Brown'' by Alice Thorson in *Kansas City Star,* 1 March 1992; ''Painter Larry Brown's arcane Regions of Space'' by Peter Barton in *Register Star/Hudson Valley Newspapers,* 9 June 2000.

* * *

An Uneasy Truce Between Medium and Illusion

Across the last three decades of formal critique aimed at the tradition and relevance of painting in a Post Modern society, artist Larry Brown has clung steadfastly to his craft. While there appear to be dramatic style shifts from one series of canvases to another in response to this critical evaluation, two expressive factors intrinsic to the act of painting itself are always in evidence to refute this notion.

In the first case, the assertive force of wet paint and the aggressive application of scraping and scratching tools create a suffusive maelstrom that reads as the essence of emotion—an outcry in paint. In the second case, the articulate and careful depiction of geometry by means of traditional drafting techniques is stridently emblematic of a sophisticated reasoning—a calculating intellection.

Psychology informs us that these dual motivations come from separate parts of the brain, distinct impulses of the imaginative process requiring wholly different mental faculties and, as a consequence, painterly technique. In this manner the immediate experience when approaching this work is to be caught in an uncertain middle ground right along with the artist, between two expression theories wrestling equally for autonomy. The viewer *feels* the emotional ground of agitated planes and eructations of color and, simultaneously, is motivated to *think* about this insertion of adroitly crafted geometric elements that modify and amplify the scene.

What we witness is at the heart of the existential thesis. Impulses from imagination are thrown down on the abstract plane of the canvas, which receives them in passionate even confrontational response. These impulsions are let loose from the ethereal dimension of the mind and take form in the plastic dimension of the world. It is a forceful outburst of activity into which, after the paint has dried and the emotion has settled down, dismaying objects are born, crystallize and take root.

We cannot be certain as to the why or wherefore of their appearance other than to experience an uneasy awareness that each belongs to the other—each exists in consequence, deference or opposition to the other—and each in its own way is meant to be there. In the Zen sense, emotion accommodates the illusion of reality.

Transforming a surface essentially abstracted by the expressive use of paint into a pictorial landscape that was capable of giving the illusion that objects inhabit that space was an inconceivable notion to Late Modernist painters. Until the end of the 1970s, it could be said that monochromatic Minimalist dogma had stalled painting and mired abstraction in a stagnant process of covering square surfaces. Expressive factors and pictorial space were banned. ''Flat, frontal and depthless'' were the three pillars of this post-painterly abstraction and one exhibition after another represented contemporary paint practices as little more than the mounting of pristine colored squares on stark white walls.

Brown was not alone in breaking out of this *cul de sac* to reclaim esthetic issues rejected by Minimalists as ''antique modes.'' In his peer group were painters like David Row, David Reed and Sean Scully. All these artists risked censure by cracking open surfaces and installing pictorial elements within their color fields. But Brown always kept himself apart. Not prone to settle into any sort of *genre,* the artist infused a literal and personal interpretation into the forms of his geometry going further than any of this master clan.

Energetic spirals, for example, have been a favorite subject for the artist through the years. Etched and scratched on the surface of the painting, Brown's spirals are visually electric and often dominate the picture's plane with such intimacy that they can be seen as a portrait of an actual occurrence of physical law taking place somewhere in the universal landscape. That creative interlude may in fact be nothing other than what took place in the artist's studio. Its significance may rest in its existence as the visual end result the artist's own painterly activity. The effect is of an enhanced uncertainty.

When deftly articulated globes, balls and spheres appear, they look like actual structures. Painted with a still life sensibility, there is a personal representational bias to these forms which gives us cause to wonder about their true nature. Do these curious and contemplative iconic figures exist as representations of higher physical law or are they part of the artist's common memory and personal acquaintance—every day stuff? In either event, this array of uncertain meanings is the unmistakable stamp of this artist.

The detailing method and skillful manipulation of materials along with an impressive array of visual vocabulary clearly demonstrate that Brown has colonized this spatial frontier for some time now—and on his own terms. But the territory is far from civilized. The tension in that eternal *pique*—the beast in the jungle—continues to obsess his method with primal uneasiness and to grip his viewers with a similar sensation of existential *angst.* Like human experience itself, these artworks are less definitive points or moments, and more vacillating junctions where, in a thrust and parry code, cross purposes meet and affinities diverge.

It is between eye and canvas where the active ground of this work lies. Across that animated divide of impulse and action an important documentation of the last quarter century of American abstract painting has arisen and perhaps more than any other artist Brown's paintings are literal colophons of this particular era.

—Peter Barton

BRUGUERA, Tania

Nationality: Cuban. **Born:** Havana, Cuba, 1968. **Education:** Academia de Artes Plásticas San Alejandro, Havana, 1983–87; Escuela Elemental de Artes Plásticas 20 de Octubre, Havana, 1980–83; Instituto Superior de Arte, Havana, 1987–92; Art Institute of Chicago, M.F.A. Performance, 2001. **Career:** Professor, painting department, Instituto Superior de Arte, Havana, 1992–96; coordinating director, project for children with behavioral difficulties, Tomas Sánchez Foundation, 1992–93; curator of group exhibition ''Una Brecha Entre el Cielo y la Tierra'' (in conjunction with the V Havana Biennial), Centro de Artes Plástica y Diseño, Havana, 1994; teacher, workshop and exhibition ''Juego de Imagenes,'' XVII Festival of New Latin American Film, Instituto de Arte e Industria Cinematografica, Havana, 1995; artist in residency, The Gasworks Studios, London, 1995; artist in residency, Slade College of Art, printmaking department, London, 1995; artist in residency, ART/OMI International Workshop, Hudson, New York, 1995; artist in residency, Xamaca Workshop, Crystal Spring, Jamaica, 1995; teacher, interdisciplinary creativity workshop, Comunidad Las Terrazas, Pinar del Río, Cuba; artist in residency, ''1990's Art from Cuba,'' a national residency and exhibition program, 1997; Art in General, Bronx Council for the Art, The Andy Warhol Foundation, Art Institute of Chicago, 1997; artist in residency, Western Front, media department, Vancouver, 1997; artist in residency, Ephemeral Sculpture International Workshop, VI Havana Biennal, Soroa, Pinar del Rio, Cuba, 1997; artist in residency, Headlands Centers for the Arts, Sausalito, California, 1998; artist in residency, Fundación Museo de Arte Contemporáneo de Maracay Mario Abreu, Maracay, Venezuela, 1998. **Awards:** Fellowship, John Simon Guggenheim Memorial Foundation, New York, 1998; Merit Scholarship, School of The Art Institute of Chicago, Illinois, 1999.

Selected Individual Exhibitions:

1986 *Marilyn Is Alive,* Galería Leopoldo Romañach, Academia de Artes Plásticas San Alejandro, Havana

1992 *Ana Mendieta,* Sala Polivalente, Centro de Desarrollo de las Artes Visuales, Havana (catalog)
1993 *Memoria de la Postguerra,* Galería Plaza Vieja, Fondo Cubano de Bienes Culturales, Havana
1995 *Soñando,* with Fernando Rodriguez, Gasworks Studios Gallery, London, England
1996 *Cabeza abajo,* Espacio Aglutinador, Havana (catalog)
1997 *Anima,* Base Space, School of the Art Institute of Chicago, Illinois
1999 *Colloquia,* Ciudad Guatemala, Guatemala (catalog)
2001 Casa de las Américas, Havana, Cuba
2001 The Kitchen, New York

Selected Group Exhibitions:

1986 *Proteo,* Galería Leopoldo Romañach, Academia de Artes Plásticas San Alejandro, Havana
1988 *No por Mucho Madrugar Amanece más Temprano,* Fototeca de Cuba, Havana
1993 *XI International Drawing Biennial,* Middlesbrough Fine Arts Museum, Cleveland, England
1994 *Una Brecha Entre el Cielo y la Tierra,* Centro Provincial de Artes Plásticas y Diseño, Havana (catalog)
1995 *1st Contemporary Art Competition,* Museo Nacional de Bellas Artes, Havana (catalog)
New Art from Cuba, Whitechapel Art Gallery, London.
1996 *23rd Sao Paolo International Biennial,* Parque do Ibirapuera, Sao Paolo, Brazil (catalog)
1997 *Trade Routes,* 2nd Johannesburg Biennale, Electric Workshop, Johannesburg, South Africa (catalog)
1998 *The Garden of Forking Paths,* Helsinski City Art Museum, Helsinski, Finland (traveled to Kunstforeningen, Copenhagen, Denmark; EdsuikKunst & Kultur, Stockholm, Sweden) (catalog)
La Dirección de la Mirada, Stadhaus, Zürich (traveled to Musée de Beaux Arts, La Chaux-des-Fonds, Switzerland) (catalog)
De Discretas Autorías: Cuba y Venezuela: Nuevas Poéticas, Museo de Arte Contemporáneo Mario Abreu, Maracay, Venezuela (catalog)
1999 *Looking for a Place,* III International Biennial, SITE Santa Fe, New Mexico (catalog)
2000 *Exotica Incognita,* 3rd Kwangju Bienale, Kwangju, South Korea (catalog)
VII Havana Bienal, Havana, Cuba (catalog)
2001 Performance Festival, Odense, Denmark

Collections:

Museo Nacional de Bellas Artes, Havana; Centro de Arte Contemporaneo Wifredo Lam, Havana; New Museum for Latin American Art, Essex, England; Colección Barro de America, Maracaibo, Venezuela.

Publications:

By BRUGUERA: Books—*Corpus Delecti: Performance Art of the Americas,* with text by Tania Bruguera and Coco Fusco, London and New York, 1999. **Videos—***Cabeza Abajo (Head Down),* 1997; *Juego con los Sentimientos (Playing with Feelings); El Peso de la Culpa (The Burden of Guilt),* 1999; *Tania Bruguera, Performances 1994–1999 (Selection),* 1999.

On BRUGUERA: Books—*New Art of Cuba* by Luis Camnitzer, Austin, Texas 1994; *Performance Live Art since 1960* by Roselee Golberg, New York 1998. **Articles—**''Art in Cuba'' by Judy Cantor in *Miami New Times,* 8 June 1994; ''Art in Cuba, The Mask: Utopia and Ideology'' by Engenio Valdés Figueroa in *Flash Art,* vol. 192, no. 30, January-February 1997.

* * *

Electing not to emigrate from her native Cuba as have many other contemporary artists, Tania Bruguera works instead to heal the breach between those who stayed and those who fled Castro's despotic régime. Even more fundamental, however, is her overarching aim to probe those levels of the psyche yet unexplored. Conflating sculpture with installations and performance, Bruguera has brought her message of cultural reconciliation and healing around the world.

A memorial installation dedicated to Cubans who perished attempting to flee their homeland, *Tabla de Salvación* (*Table of Salvation*), 1994, was a kind of boat made from the wooden ribs of a vessel and marble slabs suggesting funerary steles. In a related performance titled *Miedo* (*Fear*), the artist lay for hours in a battered skiff, like those in which the *balseros,* or boat people, lost their lives. She was surrounded by personal things: letters from friends living outside Cuba, treasured books, maps, and old drawings. Before getting into the boat, Bruguera caulked *Tabla de Salvación* with cotton, a substance used for bandages and therefore for healing.

In Chicago, Bruguera's performance piece, *Art in America (The Dream)* (1997) probed the analogy between America's homeless and Cuba's émigrés: neither have a resting place. Crouching on the floor amidst candles, the artist whispered the fortunes of viewers from Tarot cards. Nearby, a wraithlike figure enacted a move, mechanically transferring boxes from one location to another, while participants impersonating U.S. customs officials questioned other observers as though they were communist agents, even goading a few to intone the ''Star-Spangled Banner.''

Bruguera's sculpture is similarly interactive. A response to a rash of deaths at sea among those fleeing Cuba, *Dedalo* or *Imperio de Salvación (Empire of Salvation),* 1996, is a series of ''flying'' contraptions, symbolic means of escape. Functioning as the participant ''puts it on'' and moves its parts, each conveyance takes on organic life from the one who sets it into motion. To open and close one of these machines, for example, the participant has to bow—compliance or homage? Equally as provocative, *Ilusión (Illusion)* can be activated only with clenched fists and elevated arms, the accepted stance of confrontation—gesture and object working in tandem. Accenting the work's message of protest is a palm tree, Cuba's national symbol.

Deeply influenced by Ana Mendieta's life and art, Bruguera not only replicates the older artist's work from reproductions, but also creates pieces in her ''spirit.'' Brought to the United States only three years into the Castro era, when she was barely thirteen, Mendieta suffered from an ever-increasing sense of alienation, having been ''taken from the womb.'' Her fall from a New York apartment building in 1985 ended a frenzied attempt ''to become one with the earth'' through her art. Like all those who left Cuba, Mendieta was banished from official history. In an effort to revive her memory and to reinstate her life and art into the national consciousness, Bruguera created a series of works and performances titled *Homenaje a Ana Mendieta (Tribute to Ana Mendieta),* 1987–96. At the same time that they paid homage to Mendieta, these works sought to memorialize the countless Cubans who had been forced to flee the island.

In a particularly audacious performance for the Seventh Havana Biennial (2001), Bruguera positioned five naked figures in a wide tunnel. Entering the darkened space, participants tread on freshly picked sugar cane leaves, releasing a heavy, sweet fragrance, suggestive both of tropical delights and of sexuality. They then see video fragments from old newsreels of Castro, edited to highlight his godlike appeal. Women reach toward his face and hair; men hug him; the masses fall at his feet. The striking contrast between Castro's allure—at once heroic and sexual—and the obvious, abashed nudity of the performers throws into relief Bruguera's thesis: reduced and victimized by the dictator, Cubans have ''fallen'' from grace and have been banished from ''Eden.''

Bruguera's's work must be understood in the context of today's art scene in Cuba. What Luis Commitzer has termed an ''untidy revolution'' has created a climate that, despite sporadic repressions, has generally allowed for a good measure of artistic freedom. During the 1980s when artists were seeking to break away from sclerotic academic formulae and socialist propaganda exported from Russia, they turned to the inherently mystical syncretism of their Afro-Cuban forebears. The climate changed dramatically a decade later, however, when young artists adopted an overtly defiant stance, challenging the government in satirical street performances. Authorities expectedly imposed strict censorship and closed galleries. Many artists left for good. Others began to travel—as does Bruguera—discovering that the outside world was eager not only to see but also to buy their works. Today tourists flock to Cuba with money to spend on art. Driven by the need for dollars and recognizing that art makes money, the government is now allowing artists a surprising degree of freedom.

An amalgam of contemporary trends and native traditions, Bruguera's's art is both personal and political. Her aim ''to transform work into a personal therapy and cure, useful to others'' is the deeply felt goal of a woman who has experienced the emotional wrenching of the Cuban Diaspora. But at the same time, she raises her arms in protest against the causes of these social wounds.

—Dorothy Joiner

BRUS, Günter

Nationality: Austrian. **Born:** Ardning, 27 September 1938. **Education:** Volkschule and Hauptschule, Mureck, 1944–50; Hauptschule, Stainz, 1950–56; studied at the Kunstgewerbeschule, Graz, 1953–57; Akademie der Angewandten Kunst, Vienna, 1957–60. **Military Service:** Served in the Austrian Federal Army, 1961. **Family:** Married Anna Steiner in 1962; daughter: Diana. **Career:** Independent artist; has lived and worked in Vienna, 1960–69, West Berlin, 1969–79, and in Graz, Austria, since 1979; produced first action works and self-painting works, Vienna, 1964; Founder member, with Hermann Nitsch, Otto Muehl and Rudolf Schwarzkogler, Wiener Aktionismus group, Vienna, 1964; founder, with Otto Muehl, Institut für Direkte Kunst, Vienna, 1966; founder, with Arnulf Meifert, *Deutsche Trivialeum,* West Berlin, 1974; founder editor, with Arnulf Meifer, *Die Schastrommel,* later *Die Drossel* newspaper of the Osterreichische Exilgierung, West Berlin, 1969–76. **Awards:** Wurdigungspreis für Bildende Kunst, Bundesministerium für Unterricht und Kunst, Vienna, 1982; Kunstpreis, City of Graz, 1986; Kunstpreis, City of Vienna, 1986. **Agent:** Galerie Heike Curtze, Citadellstrasse 11, D-4000 Dusseldorf 1, and Seilerstätte 15/14, A-1010 Vienna. **Address:** Einspinnergasse 3, 8010 Graz, Austria.

Individual Exhibitions:

1961 *Aktionsmalerei,* Galerie Junge Generation, Vienna (with Alfons Schilling)
1965 *Malerie-Selbstbemalung-Selbstverstümmelung,* Galerie Junge Generation, Vienna
1971 *Handzeichnungen,* Galerie Michael Werner, Cologne
1973 *Zeichnungen,* Galerie Grünangergasse, Vienna
Fotos von Aktionen, Galleria Diagramma, Milan
1974 *Zeichnungen,* Galerie Krauthammer, Zurich
Fotos von Aktionen, Studio Morra, Naples
Der Vollschmerz, Galerie Springer, Berlin
1975 *Das Namenlos,* Galerie Wiener and Würthle, Berlin
Der Vollschmerz und Arbeiten von 1973 und 1975, Galerie Van de Loo, Munich
Nachtfreudenwalzer, Galerie Grünangergasse, Vienna
1976 *Nachtfreudenwalzer,* Galerie Stummer und Hubschmid, Zurich
Auszüge aus dem laufenden Werk, Galerie Gaëtan, Carouge, Geneva
Zeichnungen, Galerie Klein, Bonn
Brus: Werke, Galerie Kalb, Vienna
Zeichnungen und Schriften, Kunsthalle, Berne
1977 *Zeichnungen, Bücher und Mappenwerke,* Galerie A, Amsterdam
Bilder aus Gebenedeitanien, Galerie Springer, Berlin
Die Gärten in der Exosphäre, Galerie Van de Loo, Munich
Herzeigung, Galerie Jörg Stummer and Galerie Gysin, Zurich
1978 *Die Pracht der hellsten Freude,* Goethe-Institut, Amsterdam
Amorphophallus Titanum, Studio Morra, Naples
1979 *Franz Schreker: Die Gezeichneten,* Oper, Städelsches Kunstinstitut, and Städtische Galerie, Frankfurt am Main; and Staatsoper and Galerie Heike Curtze, Vienna
Reizfluten, Galerie Heike Curtze, Vienna
Bild-Dichtungen, Whitechapel Art Gallery, London; Kunstverein, Hamburg; and Kunstmuseum, Lucerne
Bild-Dichtungen, Galerie Heike Curtze, Dusseldorf
Des Knaben Wunderhorn, daad galerie, Berlin
Abendwerke und Nachtarbeiten, Galerie Jörg Stummer, Zurich
1980 *Schädelschrei-Romantik,* Galerie Van de Loo, Munich
Augenmusik, Galerie Heike Curtze, Dusseldorf
Augenmusik: Trugschttengewächse, Galerie Bloch, Innsbruck
1981 *Bild-Dichtungen,* Kulturhaus, Graz, Austria
Traumentziehungskur, Galerie Heike Curtze, Vienna
Weisser Wind, Gallerie Jörg Stummer, Zurich
1982 *Unruhe nach dem Sturm,* Galerie A, Amsterdam
Blaues Herz im Nerveninfernal, Galerie Zell am See, Austria

Zyankal-Zyklamen, Galerie Van de Loo, Munich
1983 *Rasende Geduld,* Maximilianverlag Sabine Knust, Munich
Lichtsprache—Le langage de la lumière, Galerie Farideh Cadot, Paris
Risba-Risiko. Vom Risiko, zu zeichnen, Galerija Meduza, Koper, Slovenia
Die Gärten in der Exosphäre und andere Bild-Dichtungen, Rupertinum, Salzburg
Blindes Brot, Petersen Galerie, Berlin
Trunkene Triebe, Galerie Heike Curtze, Dusseldorf
1984 *Horchposten des Pulsschlags,* Galerie Jörg Stummer, Zurich
Sonata Domestica, Galerie Bleich-Rossi, Graz, Austria
Augensternstunden, Van Abbemuseum, Eindhoven, Netherlands
Franz Schreker: Die Gezeichneten, Rupertinum, Salzburg
La Croce del Veneto, Galerie Heike Curtze, Vienna
Eisblut, blauer Frost, Ausstellungsraum Edition Hundertmark, Cologne
1985 *Astres de la nuit—Nachtgestirne,* Galerie Maeght Lelong, Paris
Eisblut, blauer Frost, Galerie A, Amsterdam
Bühnenbild-und Kostümentwürfe zu G. Roth, Kulturhaus, Graz, Austria
1986 *Der Uberblick,* Museum des 20. Jahrhunderts, Vienna; Lenbachhaus, Munich; and Kunsthalle, Dusseldorf
Der Ausblick, Galerie Heike Curtze, Vienna (and Galerie Zell am See, Austria)
Stichproben, Maximilianverlag Sabine Knust, Munich
Stumme Gewitter, Galerie Jörg Stummer, Zurich
1987 *Ballungsträume,* Galerie Thaddaeus Ropac, Salzburg
Berichte von der Hoffnungsdauer, Galerie Beaumont, Luxembourg
1988 *Nachtgewitter/Friedrich von Schlegel: Zehn Sonette,* Galerie Heike Curtze, Vienna
Vor dem akzentfreien Schweigen, Galerie Heike Curtze, Dusseldorf
1989 *Staubgemälde,* Studio d'Arte Cannaviello, Milan
Naturschauplätze und Satzgebilde, Maximiliansverlag Sabine Knust, Munich
Leibvertreib, Galerie Heike Curtze, Dusseldorf
1990 *Im Dunstkreis der Lichtmaschinen,* Deweer Art Gallery, Ostende, Belgium
Bild-Dichtungen, Galerie Hubert Klocker, Vienna
Bildfluchtwege, Galerie Beaumont, Luxembourg
1991 *Blick-Dichtungen,* Galerie Bleich-Rossi, Graz, Austria
Part of the Oeuvre-Machine, Schmidt & Dean Gallery, Philadelphia
Faustkeile im Glashaus, Galerie Michael Haas, Berlin
1992 *Holde Muse, gib mir Kunde,* Heinrich-Heine-Institut, Dusseldorf
Sichtweiten. Sichtweisen. Lichtnotstand, Galerie Fortlaan, Ghent
1993 *Sichtgrenze-Limite de vue,* Centre Georges Pompidou, Paris
Tremor, Galerie Heike Curtze, Dusseldorf
1994 *Atmosphärisch undicht wie Sprache,* Galerie Sabine Knust, Munich
1996 *Günter Brus: The World View Turbine—Sketches and Picture-Poems 1996,* Galerie Heike Curtze, Dusseldorf
1999 *Colored Brainbow,* Klemens Gasser & Tanja Grunert, New York

Selected Group Exhibitions:

1972 *Documenta 5,* Kassel, West Germany
1975 *Bodyworks,* Museum of Contemporary Art, Chicago
1978 *11 Artists Working in Berlin,* Whitechapel Art Gallery, London
1980 *Kunst der Siebziger Jahre,* at the *Biennale,* Venice
1982 *Biennale,* Sydney
1983 *New Art* Tate Gallery, London
1987 *Berlinart 1961–87,* Museum of Modern Art, New York (travelled to San Francisco Museum of Modern Art)
1988 *Aktionsmalerei-Aktionismus,* Museum Friedericianum, Kassel, Germany
1989 *Aktionsmalerei-Aktionismus,* Museum für Angewandte Kunst, Vienna
1991 *Of Flesh & Blood,* Stedelijk Museum Schiedam, Netherlands
1994 *Couplet 2,* Stedelijk Museum, Amsterdam
1996 *L'art au corps,* MAC, Galeries Contemporaines des musées de Marseille, France
Ese Oscuro Interior, Salsa Parpallo, Valencia, Spain
1998 *Out of Actions: Between Performance and the Object 1949–79,* Museum of Contemporary Art, Los Angeles
1999 *Speck Collection,* Museum Ludwig, Cologne
2000 *Günter Brus & Hermann Nitsch,* White Box Gallery, New York

Collections:

Uno-City, Vienna; Tate Gallery, London; Museum of Modern Art, New York; Musée d'Art Moderne, Paris; Van Abbemuseum, Eindhoven, Netherlands; Kunsthalle, Hamburg; Kunstmuseum, Winterthur, Switzerland; Festspielhaus, Bregenz; Landessammlungen Rupertinum, Salzburg; Staatsgalerie, Stuttgart.

Publications:

By BRUS: Books—*Malerei-Selbstemalung-Selbstverstrümmelung,* Vienna 1965; *b & m—direkte kunst,* with Otto Muehl, Vienna 1967; *Brus/Muehl: Direkte' Theatre,* Vienna 1967; *Patent Urinoir,* Vienna 1968; *Patent Merde,* Vienna 1969; *Unter dem Ladentisch,* Berlin 1969; *Die Schastrommel* no. 1–12, Berlin 1969–74; *Brus: Bausch-und-Bogen-Scheisse,* Cologne 1970; *Korperanalyse,* Berlin 1970; *Handzeichnungen,* Cologne/New York 1971; *Irrwisch* Frankfurt 1971; *Der Balkon Europas,* Berlin 1972; *Die Neue Dekadenz,* Berlin 1972; *Art des Giftes, Dauer der Vergiftung, Sitz der Schmerzer,* Berlin 1973; *Zereissprobe,* Berlin 1974; *Nacht freudewalzer,* Berlin 1975; *Das Namelos, Die Drossel, Nr. 14,* Berlin 1975; *Circannual, Die Drossel Nr. 16,* Berlin 1976; *Die Lachende Verwesung,* Berlin 1976; *Hohes Gebrechen,* Altona and Hohengebraching 1976; *Der Frackzwang,* Altona and Hohengebraching 1976; *Das Aulicht,* Stuttgart 1977; *Jeden jeden Mittwoch,* with D. Steiger, Berlin 1977; *Farbige Zeichnungen aus dem Jahren 1970–77,* Altona and Hohengebraching 1977; *Phantom-Palaste,* Berlin 1978; *Gestirn-Abzeichan,* Altona and Hohengebraching 1978; *Die Falter des Vorschlafs,* Altona and

Hohengebraching 1978; *Die Gärten in der Exosphäre,* Altona and Hohengebraching 1979; *Das Rufwort,* Altona and Hohengebraching 1979; *Die Herbsttrompete,* Vienna and Munich 1981; *Zyankal-Zyklamen,* Munich 1982; *Rasende Geduld,* Munich 1983; *Stillstand der Sonnenuhr,* Vienna and Munich 1983; *Die Geheimnistrager,* Salzburg 1984; *Die Wundharmonika,* Eindhoven 1984; *Die Ruine,* Paris 1985; *Stumme Gewitter,* Zurich 1986; *Amor und Amok,* Salzburg 1986; *Gebrauchsmystik,* Vienna and Munich 1986; *Picturepoems,* London 1991; *Holde Muse, gib mir Kunde,* Dusseldorf 1992; *Tremor,* Dusseldorf 1993. **Films**—*Ana,* with Kurt Kren, 1964; *Silber,* 1965; *Selbstverstümmelung,* 1965; *Wiener Spaziergang,* 1965; *Starrkrampf,* 1965; *Transfusion,* 1965; *2. Totalaktion,* 1966; *Vietnamparty,* 1966; *Pullover/Osmose/Einatmen und Ausatmen,* 1967; *20 September,* 1967; *Direct Art Festival,* 1967; *Mit Schwung ins Meue Jahr,* with Otto Muehl and Rudolf Schwartzkogler, 1967; *Fountain,* 1968; *Satisfaction,* 1968; *Kunst und Revolution,* 1968; *Strangulation,* Vienna 1968; *Blumenstück,* 1969; *Impudenz im Grunewald,* 1969; *Intelligenztest,* Berlin 1969; *Körperanalyse 1,* 1969; *Psycho-Dramolett,* Munich 1970; *Zerreissprobe,* Munich 1970.

On BRUS: Books—*Günter Brus: Zeichnungen und Schriften,* exhibition catalog, with text by Johannes Gachnang and Arnulf Meifert, Berne 1976; *Die Gärten in der Exosphäre,* exhibition catalog, Munich 1977; *Die Pracht der hellsten Freude,* exhibition catalog, Amsterdam 1978; *Amorphophallus Titanum,* exhibition catalog, Naples 1978; *11 Artists Working in Berlin,* exhibition catalog, London 1978; *Franz Schreker: Die Gezeichneten,* exhibition catalog, Frankfurt 1979; *Reizfluten,* exhibition catalog, Vienna 1979; *Des Knaben Wunderhorn,* exhibition catalog, with text by Wieland Schmied and Arnulf Meifert, Berlin 1979; *Kunst der 70er Jahre,* exhibition catalog, Venice 1980; *Günter Brus: Bild-Dichtungen,* exhibition catalog, with text by Arnulf Meifert, London 1980; *Günter Brus: Arbeiten auf Papier 1987,* exhibition catalog, with introduction by Helga Kocher, Salzburg 1987. **Articles**—''Gunter Brus'' by Heinz-Peter Schwerfel in *Beaux Arts Magazine,* no. 116, October 1993; ''Gunter Brus: Kindheit ist wie eine Wunde'' by Gunter Engelhard in *ART: das Kunstmagazin,* no. 8, August 1994; ''Modern Art's Excrement Adventure'' by Catherine Millet in *Art Press,* no. 242, January 1999.

* * *

It is perhaps no great surprise that the vehemence of Günter Brus's art has generated a good deal of extreme commentary. On the one hand he has been called neurotic, obsessive; on the other, a hero, an artist of ''titanic temperament.'' As an unashamed Romantic, Brus would no doubt claim that the former was in some way bound up with the latter.

Brus gave up live work in 1970 for the state of his own mental health after being hounded out of Austria by the police for offending public decency. Threats were also made against his life. Exiled in West Berlin, he began to draw and paint and write poetry. The self-image of the outcast, which in the ''Aktions'' took the extreme form of public purging (the ''Suffering Servant'') today is reflected in work which is uncompromisingly conventional. In rejecting modernism Brus has turned to traditional forms of representation (the fairy tale) as a form of Aktionismus.

The tradition of the seer or visionary is very important to him. Blake, Munch, Bosch. It is Blake who has been the most direct influence. The unity of word and image. The mythic struggle between good and evil. The utopianism. Brus's first drawings, coming directly after the Aktions and his work with Nitsch, Muehl and Schwarzkogler, were very much retaliatory, Sadian fantasies of unremitting horror and degradation. ''A successful drawing . . . shocks the sufferer back into life.'' In the fairytale drawings this Nietzchian combativeness (in a world without religion, it is the artist who must take on the ills of the world) takes on an obverse, festive side. If the earlier drawings showed the horror that prevents beauty, the new drawings, or ''Soul Screens'' as he calls them, celebrate the creation of new worlds—an idyllic vision of arbours and gardens, peopled by weird and wonderful creatures (pixies, homuncules) from his vivid imagination.

Brus's creation of a ''world apart,'' like Blake's, is a moral stand. Nostalgia doesn't come into it. Whatever one thinks of Brus's millenarianism (in a sense it is only by accepting such extremes that Brus can create such an ''extreme'' art), he has created a formidable body of work.

—John Roberts

BUCKLEY, Stephen

Nationality: British. **Born:** Leicester, 5 April 1944. **Education:** University of Newcastle, 1962–67; University of Reading, 1967–69. **Family:** Married Stephanie Buckley in 1973; children: Scarlet, Matilda and Felix. **Career:** Independent painter, London, since 1969. Part-time Lecturer, Canterbury College of Art, Kent, 1969–71; and Leeds College of Art, Yorkshire, 1969–71; visiting artist-in-residence, King's College, Cambridge, 1972–74; professor of fine art, Reading University. **Awards:** Painting Prize, *John Moores Exhibition,* Liverpool, 1974; Prize, Chichester National Art Exhibition, 1975; Painting Prize, Tolly-Cobbold Exhibition 1977. **Agents:** Brooke Alexander, 20 West 57th Street, New York, New York 10019; and Knoedler Gallery, London. **Address:** c/o Knoedler Gallery, 22 Cork Street, London WIX 1HB, England.

Individual Exhibitions:

1966 University of Durham
1970 Nigel Greenwood Gallery, London
1972 Galerie Neuendorf, Cologne
Kasmin Gallery, London
1973 Gallerie dell'Ariete, Milan
1974 Kettles Yard Gallery, Cambridge
Garage Art, London
1975 Galerie Jacomo Santivero, Paris
Museum of Modern Art, Oxford
1976 Waddington Galleries, London
1977 Arnolfini Gallery, Bristol (travelled to the Aberdeen Art Gallery, Scotland, and the Turnpike Gallery, Leigh, Lancashire)
1978 Knoedler Gallery, London
Robert Alkon Gallery, New York
Gallery Malmgran, Gothenburg, Sweden
Hobson Gallery, Cambridge
Arnolfini Gallery, Bristol
1980 Knoedler Gallery, London
Amano Gallery, Osaka, Japan

Bernard Jacobson Gallery, London
1981 Brooke Alexander Gallery, New York
Knoedler Gallery, London
1982 L. A. Louver Gallery, Los Angeles
Knoedler Gallery, London
1983 Brooke Alexander, New York
Knoedler Gallery, London
1984 Thorden-Wetterling Galleries, Goteborg, Sweden
1985 Museum of Modern Art, Oxford
Walker Art Gallery, Liverpool
Brooke Alexander, New York
Clock Tower, New York
Yale Center for British Art, New Haven, Connecticut
1988 Knoedler Gallery, London

Selected Group Exhibitions:

1969 *6 at the Hayward,* Hayward Gallery, London
1972 *Objects and Documents,* Arts Council Gallery, London (toured the U.K.)
1973 *La Peinture Anglaise d'Aujourd'hui,* Musée National d'Art Moderne, Paris
1975 *3rd Triennale—India,* La Kit Kala Akademi Rabindra Bhavan, New Delhi
1976 *The Human Clay,* Hayward Gallery, London (toured the U.K.)
1977 *British Painting 1952–1977,* Royal Academy of Art, London
1979 *Un Certain Art Anglais,* Musée d'Art Moderne de la Ville, Paris
1981 *Baroques '81,* Musée d'Art Moderne de la Ville, Paris
1983 *Twentieth-Century Art from the Metropolitan Museum,* Queens Museum, Flushing, New York
1985 *14th John Moores Exhibition,* Walker Art Gallery, Liverpool, Merseyside
1994 *British Abstract Art Part 1: Painting,* Flowers East, London

Collections:

Tate Gallery, London; Arts Council of Great Britain, London; Victoria and Albert Museum, London; Walker Art Gallery, Liverpool; Cambridge University; Aberdeen Art Gallery, Scotland; National Art Gallery of New Zealand, Wellington; Metropolitan Museum of Art, New York.

Publications:

On BUCKLEY: Books—*Objects and Documents,* exhibition catalog, London 1972; *La Peinture Anglaise Aujourd'hui,* exhibition catalog, by Edward Lucie-Smith, Paris 1973; *British Abstract Art Part 1: Painting,* exhibition catalog, London 1994. **Articles**—''London Letter'' by William Feaver in *Art International* (Lugano, Switzerland), January 1973; ''Stephen Buckley'' by L. Morris in *Art Press* (Paris), September 1973; ''Profile of Stephen Buckley'' by Peter Fuller in *Arts Review* (London), 3 May 1974; Buckley in Midstream'' by John McEwan in *The Spectator* (London), 11 October 1975; ''Who Will Be Who in the 1980s'' in *Sunday Times Magazine* (London), 2 April 1978; ''Four British Painters'' by John McEwan in *Artforum* (New York), December 1978; ''Serenity and Restlessness'' by Neal Menzies in *Artweek* (Oakland), 24 April 1982; ''Knoedler Gallery, London: Exhibit'' in *The Burlington Magazine* (London), vol. 130, December 1988.

* * *

As an art student in the 1960s Stephen Buckley came under the influence of surrealism, pop art (through Richard Hamilton) and abstract expressionism. Today one sees traces of this background in the grand scale of much of his work, the willingness to let chance take a part in the creation of his objects and in the use of discarded ''popular'' items. There are also elements of the ''L.A. Look'' as seen in the work of, for example, Charles Christopher Hill, who weaves together found materials, then buries, washes or pounds them.

Drawing upon these influences but keeping strongly to his own view of his environment, Stephen Buckley selects raw materials autobiographically. Discarded stretchers from a friend's attic, his mother's curtains, paintings by himself or others, his own personal clothing are transformed and renewed in his hands.

Once selected, Buckley does not treat these things gently. They are torn, scorched, twisted or stretched to their limits, then woven or stitched together. The actual process of creation is important enough to Buckley for him to share it with us so the worked-upon materials are often partially turned over to show the back side of the work. The stretchers—whether found or made—are also revealed or even placed on the front of the painting. And it is important to remember that Buckley sees himself specifically as a painter. Having provided himself with sensuously textured surfaces, he works in warm, earthy colours. A conservationist's nightmare, he also may add plaster, floor polish, wax or even yoghurt to his oils, acrylics, watercolours and enamels.

Since 1977 Buckley has created several sets of etchings, building the finished image with several plates arranged for printing on one sheet—using the medium with a painter's rather than merely a printmaker's eye—a continuation of his exploration into colours, textures and materials.

—Marlee Robinson

BURDEN, Chris

Nationality: American. **Born:** Boston, Massachusetts, 11 April 1946. **Education:** Pomona College, Claremont, California, B.F.A. 1969; University of California at Irvine, 1970–71, M.F.A. 1971. **Career:** Conceptual artist and sculptor. Instructor in avant-garde art, LaVerne College, California, 1973–74; visiting artist, Fresno State University, California, 1974; professor of art, University of California, Los Angeles, 1978-present. **Awards:** New Talent Award, Los Angeles County Museum of Art, 1973; National Endowment for the Arts Grant, 1974, 1976; John Simon Guggenheim Foundation Fellowship, 1978; National Endowment for the Arts grants, 1980, 1983; Artist of the Year, Armand Hammer Art Museum, Los Angeles, 1994. **Agent:** Gagosian Gallery. **Address:** c/o Gagosian Gallery, 980 Madison Avenue, New York, New York 10021, U.S.A.

Individual Exhibitions:

1971 *Five Day Locker Piece,* University of California at Irvine
Bicycle Piece, University of California at Irvine
1972 *Bed Piece,* Market Street, Venice, California
Math Piece, Pomona College, Claremont, California
Jaizu, Newport Harbor Art Museum, Newport Beach, California
Riko Mizuno Gallery, Los Angeles
1973 *Movie on the Way Down,* Oberlin College, Ohio
Through the Night Softly, Main Street, Los Angeles
1974 Riko Mizuno Gallery, Los Angeles
Ronald Feldman Fine Arts, New York
Hansen-Fuller Gallery, San Francisco
1975 Riko Mizuno Gallery, Los Angeles
Ronald Feldman Fine Arts, New York
1979 Ronald Feldman Fine Arts, New York
1983 Ronald Feldman Fine Arts, New York
1984 Rosamund Felsen Gallery, Los Angeles
Art Park, New York
1985 Lowe Art Museum, Miami, Florida
Lawrence Oliver Gallery, Philadelphia
Wadsworth Atheneum, Hartford, Connecticut
1986 New Langton Arts, San Francisco
1987 Hoffman Borman Gallery, Santa Monica
Los Angeles Contemporary Exhibitions
Rosamund Felsen Gallery, Los Angeles
Christine Burgin Gallery, New York
1988 Newport Harbor Art Museum, Newport Beach, California (travelled to Institute of Contemporary Art, Boston, and Carnegie Mellon University Art Gallery, Pittsburgh)
1989 Kent Fine Art, New York
Josh Baer Gallery, New York
Christine Burgin Gallery, New York
1990 Galerie Juergen Becker, Hamburg
Daniel Buchholz Gallery, Cologne
1991 Brooklyn Museum
Josh Baer Gallery, New York
1992 Miller Nordenhake Gallery, Cologne
Lannan Foundation, Los Angeles
Josh Baer Gallery, New York
1993 Gagosian Gallery
1994 Le Consortium, Dijon
FRAC Champagne-Ardenne, Reims, France
Galerie Anne de Villepoix, Paris
The Fabric Workshop, Philadelphia
Gagosian Gallery
1995 Musée de Marseille
Fundacio Espai Poblenou, Barcelona
FRAC Languedoc-Roussillon, Montpellier
1996 Museum fur Angewandte Kunst, Vienna
Chris Burden: Beyond the Limits, Museum für Angewandte Kunst, Vienna
London Projects Gallery, London
Chris Burden: Selected Works, Bonakdar Jancou Gallery, New York (catalog)
Three Ghost Ships, Gagosian Gallery, New York (catalog)
1999 *When Robots Rule: The Two-Minute Airplane Factory,* Tate Gallery, London
Magasin 3 Stockholm Konsthall, Stockholm
2000 *Structures,* Crown Point Press, San Francisco

Selected Group Exhibitions:

1971 *Body Movements,* La Jolla Museum of Contemporary Art
1975 *Projects Video,* Museum of Modern Art, New York
1977 Biennial Exhibition, Whitney Museum of American Art
Documenta, Kassel, Germany
1985 *Modern Machines: Recent Kinetic Sculpture,* Whitney Museum of American Art, New York
1986 *Individuals,* Museum of Contemporary Art, Los Angeles
1989 *Image World,* Whitney Museum of American Art, New York
1992 *Helter Skelter,* Museum of Contemporary Art, Los Angeles
1994 *Virtual Reality,* National Gallery of Australia, Canberra
Hors Limites, Centre Georges Pompidou, Paris
1995 *Made in L.A.: The Prints of Cirrus Editions,* Los Angeles County Museum of Art, Los Angeles
1996 *L'art au corps,* MAC, Galeries Contemporaines des Musées de Marseille, France
1997 *Sunshine and Noir,* Louisiana, Humlebaek, Denmark
The 1997 Biennale Exhibition, Whitney Museum of American Art, New York (catalog)
1999 *48th Venice Biennale,* Venice, Italy
Tate Gallery, London
The End: An Independent Vision of Contemporary Culture, 1982–2000, Exit Art/The First World, New York (catalog)

Collections:

Museum of Modern Art, New York; Whitney Museum of American Art, New York; Los Angeles County Museum of Art; Museum of Contemporary Art, Los Angeles; La Jolla Museum of Contemporary Art; Dallas Museum of Art; Musée de Marseille, France; FRAC Languedoc-Rousillon, Montpellier, France; Magasin 3 Konsthall, Stockholm; Albertina Museum, Vienna.

Publications:

By BURDEN: Articles—''Interview: Chris Burden'' in *Art Papers,* September/October 1991; ''Chris Burden: Another World'' in *Art Press,* no. 197, December 1994.

On BURDEN: Books—*Sunshine Muse: Contemporary Art on the West Coast* by Peter Plagens, New York 1974; *The Shock of the New* by Robert Hughes, New York 1980; *Chris Burden: The Artist and His Models,* exhibition catalog, Miami, Florida, 1986; *Chris Burden: A Twenty Year Survey,* exhibition catalog, Newport Beach, California, 1988; *Breaking the Mind Barrier* by Todd Siler, New York 1990; *Chris Burden: LAX,* exhibition catalog, Vienna 1992; *Chris Burden,* Stockholm 1999. **Articles**—''Church of Human Energy'' by Sharp and Bear in *Avalanche,* Summer/Fall 1973; ''Young Sadhu'' in *Time Magazine,* 24 February 1975; ''Through the Night Softly'' by Jan Butterfield in *Arts Magazine,* March 1975; ''Risk as the Practice of Thought'' by Francois Pluchart in *In the Art of Performance,* edited by Gregory Batcock and Robert Nikas, New York 1984; ''Chris Burden'' by Dennis Cooper in *Art Forum International,* March 1988;

''Best of Burden'' by Kay Larson in *New York,* 18 September 1989; ''Peace on Earth? Chris Burden's Investigation'' by Lucy Hughes-Hallet in *Performance,* November 1990; ''Unmasking Chris Burden'' by Kristine McKenna in *Los Angeles Times Magazine,* 29 November 1992; ''Chris Burden: Another World'' by Paul Schimmel in *Art Press,* December 1994; ''Chris Burden: America's Darker Moments'' by Kim Levin in *Grand Street,* Spring 1995; ''Chris Burden's 'Uncollectable' Works'' by Suzanne Muchnic in *Art News,* vol. 97, no. 5, May 1998; ''Chris Burden and the Potential for Catastrophe'' by Christopher Knight in *Art Issues* (W. Hollywood), no. 52, March/April 1998; ''Chris Burden Transfixed: Between Public and Private'' by Frazer Ward in *Collapse,* no. 4, May 1999.

* * *

Chris Burden did his first Performances in 1971 while still a graduate student in Southern California. It was one of those rare cases when an artist going through the art educational system arrived at an individualistic, perceptive grasp of his own direction. In ''Five-Day Locker Piece,'' Burden interred himself in locker ''number 5'' for five days below five gallons of bottled water and above an empty five gallon bottle. It was the beginning of an artistic output which was to cause mixed feelings of consternation, attention, misinterpretation and praise over the next decade which brought more than 60 works from Burden's head.

Burden's performances and sculptures are about the fears and anxieties faced by the individual in the midst of the complex psychological and social context of the late twentieth century. Many earlier works, such as his (overly) notorious ''Shoot'' (1971, in which he had a friend shoot him in the arm) and ''220'' (which involved real dangers of electrocution for the participants), were rather overtly ''macho'' in attitude, but the vast majority of Burden's pieces which suggest real danger are very much under the artist's control. ''Transfixed'' (1974), for example, in which Burden had himself ''crucified'' on the back end of a Volkswagen with nails driven through his hands, was well researched and caused little real physical pain, expressing, rather, the symbolic element behind our attachments to the objects of our industrial environment.

In a number of works, Burden has used his body as a sculptural form to express the tensions we feel in trying to maintain our individuality as artists or as anybody else dealing with our already post-industrial age. In ''Bed Piece'' (1972) and in ''Wite Light/White Heat'' (1975), among other works, Burden placed himself in a state of isolation for long periods of time, assuming states of mental/physical deprivation with elements of withdrawal from contact and sight which both showed the benefits of introspective meditative states and caused anxious moments for viewers and friends in the process. Among his most seductively and frighteningly alluring works is ''Through the Night Softly'' (1973) in which Burden crawled through broken glass, incurring multiple small cuts on his almost naked body. Burden's quiet, controlled attitude, not unlike that of the Zen master, portrays more centrally the idea of risk sacrifice and atonement and the mental capacity to get through danger than it does a masochistic self-destruction.

Works since the mid-1970s have tended to be less dramatic, though no less involved in using self as conveyor of anxious mental states. In many, Burden opens up elements of his private life to prolong/dispel the personal ''myth'' of the artist built up over the past years of work. In his second television ''commercial'' (1976), Burden adds his own name to the list of the five most well-known (from survey) artists, in a listing which reads ''Leonardo da Vinci, Michaelangelo, Rembrandt, Van Gogh, Picasso, Chris Burden.'' Continuing in his continually dialectical fashion, Burden, in the same year, acted as unidentified ''Garcon'' throughout the duration of a gallery group show, and also charged admission for a tour of his studio in Venice, California. Along with the issues of confinement, time, fear, threat and control, Burden has also concerned himself with the state of the individual in relationship to technology and to the threat of nuclear war. In ''Art and Technology'' (1975) and ''Death Valley Run'' (1976), he created vehicles of transportation for one person which were fuel efficient, lightweight and capable of practical transport through space and, suggestively through personalized technology, into the mind. ''C.B.T.V.'' (1977) reconstructed the primitive television precursor of 1915 in an effort to show us the nature and origin of the medium which dominates us in the present.

Among Burden's recent works are those which are concerned with the weapons of war so imminently upon us. In an exposition of another prevalent anxiety, ''The Reason for the Neutron Bomb'' (1979) is a grid of 50,000 nickels, each with a match on top, emblematic of the number of tanks the Soviets have on the border between Eastern and Western Europe. It is a fascinating prediction of subsequently current events and a potent visual symbol as well. Burden's recent sculptural mini-environment, ''A Tale of Two Cities,'' incorporates a variety of toys. Medieval castles, modern buildings, airplanes and weapons of varied vintage, warriors including knights, soldiers and futuristic robots interact to create a tiny panorama of the persistence of human war, which shows no sign of abating in the foreseeable future. Looking at it through the spyglasses provided by Burden, one is forced to see us as we really are and as science fiction predicts the future. As always, there is a sardonic wit and topical pertinence in Burden's continual portrayals of our personae in this post-industrial time, in which there is more trouble than ever in dealing with psychological and sociological basics.

—Barbara Cavaliere

BUREN, Daniel

Nationality: French. **Born:** Boulogne-Billancourt, 25 March 1938. **Education:** Lycée Condorcet, Paris, 1946–56; studied at the Ecole Nationale Supérieurie des Métiers d'Art, Paris, graduated 1960. **Career:** Independent artist, Paris. Member, Buren Mosset, Parmentier (Michel) and Toroni association, 1967. **Address:** 21 rue de Navarin, 75009 Paris, France.

Individual Exhibitions:

1967 *Buren o Toroni o Chichessia,* Galleria Flaviana, Lugano Switzerland
1968 Musée d'Art Moderne de la Ville, Paris Galleria Apollinaire, Milan
1969 Wide White Space Gallery, Antwerp
Interruption, Galerie Yvon Lambert, Paris
Position/Proposition, Galerie Konrad Fischer, Dusseldorf
Galerie Eva Buren, Stockholm
1970 Galleria Francoise Lambert, Milan
Art and Project, Amsterdam
Une pièce/peinture, Bradford College, Massachusetts

Galerie MTL, Brussels
Galerie Yvon Lambert, Paris
1971 Wide White Space Gallery, Antwerp
Galerie Folker Skulima, Berlin
Galerie Michael Werner, Cologne
Städtisches Museum, Mönchengladbach, West Germany
1972 Modern Art Agency, Naples
Jack Wendler Gallery, London
Galleria Sperone, Turin
Peinture Affichée/Pittura Affisa, Incontri Internazional d'Arte, Rome
Theatre de la Ville, Belgrade
Wide White Space Gallery, Antwerp
1973 New Theatre, New York
Sanction of the Museum, Museum of Modern Art, Oxford
Fragment I, II and III, Mezzanine Gallery and Anna Leonowens Gallery, Halifax, Nova Scotia
Part 2, John Weber Gallery, London
California Institute of Art, Valencia
3 Paintings, Galerie Konrad Fischer, Dusseldorf
Within and Beyond the Frame, John Weber Gallery, New York
Démultiple, Städtisches Museum, Monchengladbach, West Germany
1974 *Trasposizione,* Galleria Toselli, Milan
Triptyque, Galerie Rolf Preisig, Basle
Transparency, Art and Project, Antwerp
3 Passages, Galerija Grada, Zagreb
Wide White Space Gallery, Antwerp
Transparency-Opacity, Max Protetch Gallery, Washington, D.C.
Between and Through, Cusack Gallery, Houston
On the Hang Up, 11501 West Rico, Los Angeles
Passage Between Inside and Outside, Portland Center for Visual Arts, Oregon
1975 Kunstmuseum, Lucerne
Akademie der Künste, Berlin
Galerie, Folker-Skulima, Berlin
Städtisches Museum, Mönchengladbach, West Germany
1976 *Hier,* Stedelijk Museum, Amsterdam
Rijksmuseum Kröller-Muller, Otterlo, Netherlands
Ailleurs/Elders, Stedelijk van Abbemuseum, Eindhoven, Netherlands
Institute of Contemporary Arts, London
1977 *3 Installationem,* Galerie Paul Maenz, Cologne
1978 Galerie Yvon Lambert, Paris
John Weber Gallery, New York
1979 National Galerie of Victoria, Melbourne
1980 *Il Est Encore Une Fois—Toile, Toile/Voile,* Kunstmuseum, Lucerne
Art Institute of Chicago
1981 Stedelijk van Abbemuseum, Eindhoven, Netherlands
1982 Krefeld Museum, West Germany
1984 Galerie Grewad, Ghent, Belgium
Galeria Zona, Florence
Galerie Arca, Marseille, France
Galerie Arca, Paris
1988 Capodimonte Museum, Naples
Ugo Ferranti Gallery, Rome
1990 John Weber Gallery, New York
Daniel Buren, Here and There—Works on Location, Staatsgalerie, Stuttgart
1991 *Daniel Buren: Site of the Flags,* Nykytaiteen Museo, Helsinki
Daniel Buren: Topical Arguments, Musee d'Art Contemporain, Bordeaux
Daniel Buren: Where? What? How?, Kunstverein, Hanover, Germany
1992 John Weber Gallery, New York
Galleria Tucci Russo, Turin
1995 Arts Club of Chicago
1996 *Daniel Buren: Appearing, Seeming, Disappearing,* Kunstsammlung Nordrhein-Westfalen, Dusseldorf (catalog)
Renn Espace d'Art Contemporain, Paris
John Weber Gallery, New York
1999 Château de Fraïssé, Fraïsse-des-Corbières, France
2000 *Une Traversée, 1964–99,* Musée d'Art Moderne, Villeneuve d'Ascq, France
Cabanes éclatées, Insititut d'Art Contemporain, Villeurbanne, France
Espace Méridien, Brussels

Selected Group Exhibitions:

1968 *Prospect '68,* Galerie Apollinaire, Dusseldorf
1970 *Conceptual Art and Conceptual Aspects,,* New York Cultural Center
1971 *Situation Concepts,* Galerie Nächst St. Stephan, Vienna
1972 *Documenta 5,* Kassel, West Germany
1973 *Contemporanea,* Villa Borghese, Rome
Bilder: Objekte: Filme: Konzepte, Städtische Galerie, Munich
1974 *Political Art,* Max Protetch Gallery, Washington, D.C.
Projekt '74, Kunsthalle, Cologne
1975 *Corridor Passage,* Museum of Modern Art, New York
12 x 1, Palais des Beaux-Arts, Brussels
Galerie Beaubourg, Paris (with Alain Jacquet)
1989 *Hirshhorn WORKS 89: Daniel Buren, Buster Simpson, Houston Conwill, Matt Mullican,* Hirshhorn Museum and Sculpture Garden, Washington, D.C.
The Presence of Absence: New Installations, University of Illinois at Chicago, Illinois
1990 *Christian Boltanski, Daniel Buren, Gilbert and George, Jannis Kounellis, Sol LeWitt, Richard Long, Mario Merz,* Musee d'Art Contemporain, Bordeaux, France
1991 *Individualities: 14 Contemporary Artists from France,* Art Gallery of Ontario, Toronto
1992 *Funny Dispatches: Mail Art—Art Postal,* Centre d'Animation Culturelle de Compiegne et du Valois, Compiegne, France
1994 *Gemini G.E.L.: Recent Prints and Sculptures,* National Gallery of Art, Washington, D.C.
Even If It's Night-Time, Musee d'Art Contemporain, Bordeaux, France
Wall to Wall, Serpentine Gallery, London
1996 *An Eternity With Boundaries,* Genesta Gallery, London
1997 *Sculpture Projects,* Münster, Germany

1998 *Minimal Maximal: Minimal Art and its Influence on the International Art of the 1990s,* Neues Museum Weserburg, Bremen, Germany

1999 *The Space Here is Everywhere,* Villa Merkel and Galerien der Stadt Esslingen, Esslingen, Germany
Wall Works: Site-Specific Wall Installations, Paula Cooper Gallery, New York

Collections:

Centre Georges Pompidou, Paris; Van Abbemuseum, Eindhoven; Netherlands; Stedelijk Museum, Amsterdam; Kunstmuseum, Lucerne; Neues Museum, Weimar, Germany.

Publications:

By BUREN: Books—*Daniel Buren: Legend, Vol. I and II,* London 1973; *5 Texts,* New York 1973; *Daniel Buren: Voile/ Toile, Toile/ Voile,* with Bernd Mahr and Horst Merten, Berlin 1975; *Daniel Buren: les ecrits (1965–1990),* compiled by Jean-Marc Poinsot, Bordeaux 1991; *Daniel Buren, Entretien avec Jerome Sans,* Paris 1998; *A force de descendre dans lar rue, l'art peut-il enfin y monster?,* Paris 1998. **Articles—**''Beware'' in *Studio International,* March 1970; ''Mise en Garde No. 3'' in *Vh 101,* Spring 1970; ''Extrait de Position-Proposition'' in *VH 101,* Spring 1971; ''Art Is Not Free'' in *Studio International,* June 1973; ''Daniel Buren: An Interview with Jean-Marc Poinsot'' in *Art and Artists,* July 1973; ''The Function of the Museum'' in *Artforum,* September 1973; ''The Function of an Exhibition'' in *Studio International,* December 1973; ''Site Works'' in *Artforum,* vol. 26, no. 7, March 1988; interview with Jerome Sans in *Forum International,* vol. 2, no. 9, September-October 1991; interview with Philippe Piguet in *L'Oeil* (Lausanne), no. 460, April 1994; interview with Jean-Jacques Lafaye in *Connaissance des Arts* (Paris), no. 515, March 1995; ''Daniel Buren'' in *Art Press,* special issue no. 17, 1996. **Film—***Identification,* London 1973.

On BUREN: Books—*Daniel Buren,* exhibition catalog, by Jean-Christophe Ammann, Lucerne 1975; *Daniel Buren: Hier,* exhibition catalog, with text by E. de Wilde, Michel Claura and Germano Celant, Amsterdam 1976; *Daniel Buren: 3 Installationen,* exhibition catalog, Cologne 1977; *Daniel Buren: Il est Encore Une Fois—Voile/Toile, Toile/Voile,* exhibition catalog, with text by Martin Kunz, Lucerne 1980; *Daniel Buren: Works* by Phyllis Rosenzweig, Washington, D.C. 1989; *Daniel Buren: Site of the Flags,* exhibition catalog, with text by Tuula Arkio, Helsinki 1991; *Daniel Buren: Where? What? How?,* exhibition catalog, Hanover 1991; *Daniel Buren: Appearing, Seeming, Disappearing,* exhibition catalog, with foreward by Armin Zweite, Doris Krystof and Seth Sieglaub, Dusseldorf 1996. **Articles—**''Paris Commentary: Buren at Prospect '68, Dusseldorf'' by Michel Claura in *Studio International,* January 1969; ''La Proposition de Buren'' by G. Gassiot-Talabot in *Opus International* (Paris), June 1969; ''Lettre de Paris: Daniel Buren'' by M. Pleynet in *Art International,* February 1971; ''Daniel Buren'' by Jean Clair in *Chroniques de l'Art Vivant,* April 1971; ''On Daniel Buren'' by R. Smith in *Artforum,* September 1973; ''Das Prinzip der Wiederholung'' by Georg. F. Schwarzbauer in *Magazin Kunst,* no. 4, 1974; ''Le Groupe BMPT'' by Otto Hahn in *Art Press,* June 1974; ''Daniel Buren'' by Alain Cueff in *Beaux Arts Magazine,* no. 92, July-August 1991; ''Daniel Buren'' by Jean-Pierre Criqui in *Artforum,* 1 January 2000; ''Time Unwrapped'' by Graham Bader in *Art On Paper,* vol. 4, no. 5, May/June 2000.

*

I have often been criticized for the almost absolute ''reductionism'' of my work. That was the criticism leveled at me when I began, and continues even now. The main reason of these criticisms, which is particularly revealing about those who express them, is that people are accustomed to looking at a painting or an object in an exhibit as the be all and end all. In other words, they look at the visual materials that I used as if they were a painting. I never have and never will respond to such absurd comments, for I have the impression that they are talking about something other than my work. Why should I have to defend something that is not being attacked? It is as though I were being criticized under the pretext that for the opening of every one of my shows, it rains . . .

Right from the start I have always tried to show as clearly as I could that indeed a thing never exists in itself, in a kind of ''en soi.'' A fortiori, this is true of all my work. Nothing that I show—the materials I use, to begin with—exists unrelated to something else that is clearly refined. Anyone who experiences my work directly—provided he agrees to make the minimum of effort required, of course—perceives that the ''reduction'' is in fact the widening of one's field of vision. Widening of such dimension that—for the very first time—what is being challenged in fact is the entire field of painting itself—nothing less—as being a reducing factor in art. From this stems the whole debate on art (criticism and history), based on the autonomy of a work of art; a debate which has also perforce a reducing effect, being simplistic and too good to be true. To reconsider works and their contexts, in fact to realize that their autonomy in a fable supported by an idealistic proportion, is not only to challenge the proposition itself but also, to a great extent, the works which it supports, that is, art in general.

The Marxist label, used by some who believe it offers a way to escape this debate, obviously does not change a thing. On the other hand, the concept of the non-autonomy of a work of art opens new doors to a field of study and work that is very vast and unexplored. Of course, this field has nothing to do with any sociological art nor a sociology of art. It is only with plastic means—to be completely overhauled—that it is possible to question and deal seriously with plastic problems and their implications.

—Daniel Buren

* * *

Daniel Buren is a Conceptual artist who sees his work as defining spaces where people circulate and expanding public vision from the art object itself to the space it inhabits. Using a signature stripe as a ''visual tool,'' the artist has applied his trademark to a variety of materials and architectural elements in site-specific installations throughout the world. The stripes themselves always alternate color with white, and are usually 8.7 centimeters wide, broad enough so their optical effect is kept to a minimum, though it may operate at a distance. Restricted, repetitious, and seemingly unpromising though this strategy may be, Buren manages to put it to an almost inexhaustible number of original uses. With these simple means he can produce all manner of visual effects.

In a gallery space or other interior he will adapt his stripes to the space and transform it. Sometimes this will mean exploiting the possibilities of an interesting and complex space, as, for instance, a succession of receding rooms opening on to one another. Here perspective plays a part, alters the stripes, and may even give an overall two-dimensional effect. At other times he will take an uninteresting gallery space and enhance it to the point of distorting its size and shape (as usually perceived).

These works he calls ''installations'' with the usual implication that they have to be installed and will later be taken away. In other words, they are ephemeral and not readily commodified, and even when permanently installed, they often disintegrate or fade, as have the painted pink-and-white stripes leading up to Spoleto's Piazza del Duomo, which Buren installed in 1980.

Like the project for the Spoleto festival, many of Buren's works seek to transform the outdoors or amplify the constructed environment. One of his practices is to paint steps or frieses or plinths of columns or parts of solemn buildings with black-and-white stripes. Another is to fly striped flags on important buildings, such as the Louvre or that ancient emporium, La Samaritaine, or drape striped banners around them. The point of this, as with Christo's wrapped buildings, is to draw attention to the building, to make it conspicuous, to draw attention to aspects of it, to make us look at it anew and to transform it. He even invades the streets with sandwich-boards in black-and-white stripes (a change from 'Prepare To Meet Your Doom' but possibly no less disturbing).

Buren has made installations the world over: *Chicago,* 1977, *Step by Step, Up and down, In and Out,* Sydney, 1979, *Upside Down* (!), and the same year, in Los Angeles, *Frost and Defrost,* and so on till the present day. Though most of these works are ephemeral, Buren carefully records them. He has done so since the 1960s with his 'photo/souvenirs'.

One of Buren's most prestigious and controversial projects was installed in 1986 in the Cour d'Honneur of the Palais Royal, Paris, at the invitation of the French Ministry of Culture. Called ''Deux Plateaux,'' meaning two levels or plains, it consists of striped columns of various heights, partly above ground or partly below (but still visible through a grating), which form elaborate patterns as one walks through the formal symmetry of the seventeenth century courtyard. This juxtaposition of old and new has enraged many Parisians who walk through to the beautiful gardens beyond, but it is precisely this public dialogue around the work that most interests Buren. Beyond creating a visual counterpoint to the garden itself, the incongruity of Buren's installation points to the layers of history embedded in the Palais Royal itself, which was destroyed by the Commune in 1871, and exists now as a nineteenth century reconstruction.

Another project by the Buren, a former anarchist, included installing variously colored striped canvas sails on the boats of a children's regatta, so that ''art show itself in full sail'', without the compromise, physical constraint, and commercialization of a museum or gallery setting.

Recently, Buren created an installation for the soon-to-be-demolished Arts Club of Chicago, whose interior was designed by the supreme Modernist architect, Mies van der Rohe. Playing off the Miesian grid of the building's white plywood interior, Buren created a checkerboard pattern of painted squares, overlaid with plexiglass sheets installed somewhat off-kilter, which had been painted on the back with white stripes oriented so as to compensate for the 'slippage' of the plexiglass. ''Simultaneously a homage and extension of Mies's project. . . Buren activated and energized [the] architectural space, transforming a beautiful if moribund site into a cacophony of reflection and refraction. . . energizing the grid to its limit, and as is the case with his own stripes, finding it capable of infinite application and unending permutation.'' (James Good) Here Buren's temporary installation, housed in a building that is itself impermanent, points to the sort of profound questions about the meaning of the built environment and about the nature of art itself that have characterized his restlessly productive career.

—Essay by D. C. Barrett; updated by Dorothy Valakos

BURGIN, Victor

Nationality: British. **Born:** Sheffield, Yorkshire, 24 July 1941. **Education:** Royal College of Art, London, 1962–65, A.R.C.A. (1st class) 1965; Yale University, New Haven, Connecticut, 1965–67, M.F.A. 1967. **Career:** Artist based in London, since 1967. Lecturer, Department of Fine Art, Trent Polytechnic, Nottingham, 1967–73. Senior Lecturer in the History and Theory of the Visual Arts, School of Communication, Polytechnic of Central London, since 1973. Picker Professor of Fine Arts, Colgate University, Hamilton, New York, 1980; Professor of Art History, University of California, Santa Cruz, 1989; artist residency, Adelaide Festival of the Arts, Australia 1988; artist residency, Simon Fraser University, British Colombia Canada 1989; ''Film in the Cities'' International Residency Program, Saint Paul, Minnesota 1989; artist residency, Institut Méditerranéen de Recherche et de Création, Marseille, France 1993; artist residency, C^3, Budapest, Hungary 1997. **Awards:** U.S./U.K. Bicentennial Arts Exchange Fellowship, 1976–77; Deutscher Akademischer Austauschdienst (DAAD) Fellowship, Berlin, 1978–79; Allocation de recherche et de séjour, Ministère de la Culture et de la Communication, Délégation aux Arts Plastiques, Paris 1991; NEA Regional Initiative Artists' Regranting Program Project Grant 1995. **Agents:** John Weber Gallery, 420 West Broadway, New York, New York 10012, U.S.A.; Liliane and Michel Durand-Dessert, 43 rue de Montmorency, 75003 Paris, France. **Address:** 25 St. Mary-le-Park Court, Albert Bridge Road, London SW11 4PJ, England.

Individual Exhibitions:

1970 Camden Arts Centre and Swiss Cottage Library, London (with Art and Language and Keith Arnatt)
1974 Galleria Banco, Brescia, Italy
1975 Musée d'Art et d'Industrie, St. Etienne, France (with Art and Language)
1976 Institute of Contemporary Arts, London
Robert Self Gallery, London
1977 *Victor Burgin: Work,* Stedelijk van Abbemuseum, Eindhoven, Netherlands (travelled to the John Weber Gallery, New York)
1978 Museum of Modern Art, Oxford

1979 Deutscher Akademischer Austauschdienst, Berlin (travelled to the John Weber Gallery, New York; Liliane and Michel Durand-Dessert Gallery, Paris; and Max Hetzler Gallery, Stuttgart)
1980 *Victor Burgin: US 77/ZOO 78,* Picker Art Gallery, Colgate University, Hamilton, New York
1981 Zwigzek Polskich Artstow Fotografikow, Warsaw
Musée de la Ville, Calais, France
1982 John Weber Gallery, New York
1983 National Gallery of Canada, Ottawa
1984 Galerie Durand-Dessert, Paris
1991 *Passages,* Musée d'Art Moderne Villeneuve d'Ascq, Villeneuve d'Ascq, France (traveled to Espace Poulain, Ville de Blois, France) (catalog)
1994 *The End,* John Weber Gallery, New York (traveled to State University of New York at Buffalo Art Gallery)
Les Quatres Saisons, Galerie Durand-Dessert, Paris
1996 *Love Stories,* John Weber Gallery, New York (traveled to Mûcsarnok Kunsthalle, Budapest)
2000 *Nietzsche's Paris,* Architectural Association, London

Selected Group Exhibitions:

1969 *When Attitudes Become Form,* Institute of Contemporary Arts, London
1970 *Idea Structures,* Camden Arts Center, London
Information, Museum of Modern Art, New York
1971 *6th Guggenheim International,* Guggenheim Museum, New York
1972 *Documenta,* Kassel, West Germany
The New Art, Hayward Gallery, London
1976 *Arte Inglese Oggi,* Palazzo Reale, Milan
1977 *Aspects of European Art in the 70's,* Art Institute of Chicago (toured the United States, 1977–79)
1980 *Kunst im Sozialen Kontext,* Badischer Kunstverein, Karlsruhe, West Germany
1987 *Berlinart 1961–87,* Museum of Modern Art, New York (travelled to San Francisco)
1988 *The Future of the Metropolis,* Triennale di Milano, Milan, Italy
1989 *New Acquisitions/New Work/New Directions,* George Eastman House, Rochester, New York
Malaise, Galeria La Máquina Española, Madrid
International Video Exhibition Tate Gallery, London
On the Art of Fixing a Shadow, Art Institute of Chicago (also National Gallery of Art, Washington, D.C.; Los Angeles County Museum of Art)
The Art of Photography: 1839–1989, Museum of Fine Arts, Houston (traveling exhibition)
1991 *Shocks to the System,* Northern Centre for Contemporary Art, Sunderland, England
1992 *The Power of Words: An Aspect of Recent Documentary Photography,* American Federation of Arts (touring exhibition)
1994 *Artists' Impressions,* Kettle's Yard, Cambridge, England (catalog)
1995 *Photography After Photography,* Siemens Kulturprogramm, Munich, Germany
L'Image Électronique, 3e Biennale d'Art, Musée d'Art Contemporain de Lyon, France
1996 *Spellbound: Art and Film Since 1945,* The Museum of Contemporary Art, Los Angeles
Face à l'Histoire 1933–1966, Centre Georges Pompidou, Paris
Lisson Gallery, London
1997 *La Stanza Degli Specchi: Arte e Film dal 1945,* Palazzo della Esposizioni, Rome
Biennale Internationale de l'Image: Instants de Ville, Palais de Congrès de Nancy, France
2000 *Sleuth,* Barbican Centre, London

Collections:

Tate Gallery, London; Victoria and Albert Museum, London; Arts Council of Great Britain, London; British Council, London; Walker Art Gallery, Liverpool; Graves Art Gallery, Sheffield; Museum of Modern Art, Oxford; Centre Georges Pompidou, Paris; Bibliothèque Nationale, Paris; Van Abbemuseum, Eindhoven, Netherlands; Museum of Modern Art, New York; New York Public Library; Los Angeles County Museum of Art; Walker Art Center, Minneapolis; Victoria and Albert Museum, London.

Publications:

By BURGIN: Books—*Work and Commentary,* London 1973; *Two Essays on Art, Photography, and Semiotics,* London 1976; *Family,* New York 1977; *Newcastle Writings,* with others, London 1977; *Thinking Photography: Essays in the Theory of Photographic Representation,* editor, London 1981; *Essays: Interview: Work,* Berlin 1981; *Contemporary British Art in Print* with introduction by Patrick Elliott, Jeremy Lewison and Duncan Macmillan, Edinburgh 1995; *19 Projects: Artists-in-Residence at the MIT List Visual Arts Center* by Marie Cieri, Dana Friis-Hansen, Katy Kline and Helaine Posner, Cambridge 1996. **Articles—**''Art Society Systems'' in *Control* (London), no. 4, 1968; ''Situational Aesthetics'' in *Studio International* (London), October 1969; reprinted in *Conceptual Art,* edited by Ursula Meyer, New York 1972; ''Thanks for the Memory'' in *Architectural Design* (London), August 1970; ''Rules of Thumb'' in *Studio International* (London), May 1971; ''Interview with Varsity'' in *Varsity* (Cambridge), October 1971; ''Margin Note'' and ''Interview'' in *The New Art,* exhibition catalog, edited by Anne Seymour, London 1972; ''In Reply'' in *Art-Language* (Leamington Spa, Warwickshire), Summer 1972; ''Photographic Practice and Art Theory'' in *Studio International* (London), July/August 1975; ''Socialist Formalism'' in *Studio International* (London), March/April 1976; ''Art, Common-Sense and Photography'' in *Camera-work* (London), no. 3, 1976; ''Modernism in the Work of Art'' in *20th Century Studies* (Canterbury, Kent), no. 15/16, 1976; ''Looking at Photographs'' in *Screen Education* (London), Autumn 1977; ''Images of People'' in *Studio International* (London), no. 2, 1978; ''Seeing Sense'' in *Artforum* (New York), February 1980; ''Photography, Fantasy, Function'' in *Screen* (London), Spring 1980; ''Yes, Difference Again: What History Plays the First Time Around as Tragedy, It Repeats as Farce'' in *Flash Art (International Edition),* no. 143, November/December 1988; interview with Geoffrey Batchen in *Afterimage,* vol. 16, February 1989; interview with Gregorio Magnani in *Flash Art (International Edition),* no. 149, November/December 1989; interview with Robin White in *Artweek,* vol. 22, 11 April 1991; interview with Laura Cottingham in *Journal of Contemporary Art,* vol. 4, no. 1, Spring-Summer 1991; interview in *Art Press,* Special Issue, no. 17, 1996; interview with Peter Suchin in *DPICT,* no. 5, December 2000/ January 2001. **Videos—***Fall, Video-Wall,* Tate Gallery, London 1989; *Venise,* Ville de Marseille, France 1993; *Ferenczi,* C^3, Budapest.

On BURGIN: Book—*Victor Burgin: Work,* exhibition catalog, Eindhoven, Netherlands 1977; *Notorious: Alfred Hitchcock & Contemporary Art* by Kerry Brougher, Michael Tarantino, and Astrid Bowron, Oxford 1999; *Victor Burgin: Shadowed,* London 2000. **Articles—**''Victor Burgin: La Representation par le Text'' by A. Pacquement in *Art Press* (Paris), no. 5, 1973; ''Victor Burgin'' by E. Tynan in *Studio International* (London), September/October 1976; ''Victor Burgin in Oxford'' by D. Reed in *British Journal of Photography* (London), March 1978; ''Victor Burgin: Double Space'' by Paul Smith in *Forum International,* vol. 2, no. 9, September-October 1991; ''Victor Burgin: The Space Man'' by Tony Godfrey in *Tate: The Art Magazine,* no. 13, Winter 1997.

* * *

From the early photo-essay *Work and Commentary* (with its rather formalist foray into semiotics) to the recent captioned advertisement style documentary panels, Vic Burgin has been involved with photography as a *signifying* practice, with its inseparability—as with all visual images—from language. In the 1970s this was called conceptualism. Today it offers—for Burgin at least, who has never found the artworld conducive to his own needs—the possibility of a wholly new practice. ''I feel I'm working across the fringe areas—for example . . . where ''art,'' advertising, ''documentary,'' ''theory'' etc. overlap.'' Burgin in fact makes no hierarchical distinction between his writing (which has been extensive) his activities as a teacher and lecturer and his photography; all are part of the same *political* education—Burgin's role as an artist is, in an old fashioned sense, pedagogic.

Burgin's involvement with photography as a language has been a critique of the notion of the ''purely visual,'' which art-historically has come to mean Greenberg's modernism, but which in reality covers a whole range of what Burgin sees as academic prephotographic art teaching. Like many artists who questioned the primacy of painting (or rather the primacy of post-war American painting), Burgin has attempted to give back image-making certain cultural responsibilities, to ''interfere,'' albeit peripherally, with dominant forms of representation. In the early 70s—when the Art and Society debates were at their height—Burgin attempted a populist approach, putting his images into circulation in the community itself. His poster campaign in Newcastle upon Tyne (the poster showed a young attractive couple embracing, underneath the slogan: 7% of the population own 84% of the wealth) came in for a good deal of criticism for its cosmeticism and somewhat condescending airs. It was not a success. Burgin's recent work though has been less tendentious. Series such as ''US 77'' and ''Zoo'' (shown at the *Hayward Annual* in 1979) show Burgin moving towards allegory; captions, almost poetic in their scansion, are superimposed over single shot photographs of predominantly urban scenes, some sparse and barren, some a welter of signs, symbols and narrative fragments.

Burgin's attempt to work on the margins of mainstream visual culture represents an important shift in thinking towards re-engagement with *culture as a whole;* the problem, though, still remains one of finding a broad audience for that engagement. Burgin's decision to work outside of what is notionally known as the ''artworld'' can only help to promote it.

—John Roberts

Over the course of the 1980s, Victor Burgin's practice became increasingly inflected with psychoanalytic theory. The ''Office at Night'' series of 1985–86 combines large-scale staged black and white photographs of a female office worker with loaded symbols drawn from a pictographic system developed in Germany in the 1930s. The piece grew out of Burgin's fascination with Edward Hopper's 1940 painting *Office at Night.* As Burgin describes it, Hopper's work provides a highly provocative point of departure; the painting ''may be read as an expression of the general problem of the organization of Desire Within the Law, couched in terms of the particular problem of the organization of sexuality within capitalism—symptomatically represented by those (dis)contents filed under 'working late at the office.'''

Burgin's interest in film came to the fore in *The Bridge* of 1984, a piece in which he used film stills, photography, and text to juxtapose Alfred Hitchcock's representation of women with Sigmund Freud's theorization of male desire. Burgin continues to pursue the highly-theorized meeting-place of psychoanalysis and filmic narrative. His recent work has taken the form of video installation, often with several channels of image and audio. These pieces tend to combine an anecdotal framework with historically specific materials in an evocative, idiosyncratic way. Merging fact with fiction in relation to specific moments and places, Burgin produces a kind of poetics of psychohistory and psychogeography.

Burgin's video installation *Love Letters,* for example, first shown in Budapest in 1999, juxtaposes the text of Freud's 1915 paper ''Observations on Transference-Love'' with the true story of Sándor Ferenczi, a Hungarian psychoanalyst and collaborator of Freud, whose life was torn apart by his simultaneous love for a young female patient and the patient's mother, whom he ultimately married. Burgin uses the devices of dream-production—condensation, displacement and association—to form and dissolve loose links among and between several video monitors and an eclectic soundtrack. Appropriated film footage of a young woman standing on Freud's doorstep in Vienna in 1938 intersects with music, the sound of Hungarian voices, fragments of psychoanalytic theory, and images of the landscape fleeting past the rain-spattered window of a moving vehicle. As in much of Burgin's later work, a viewer hoping to move beyond the suggestive surface of the piece to the undercurrents of historical and theoretical resonance can follow in the path of Burgin's research and contemplation by reading supplementary catalogue text.

—Lucy Soutter

BURRI, Alberto

Nationality: Italian. **Born:** Città di Castello, Umbria, 12 March 1915. **Education:** Studied medicine in Perugia 1934–39; mainly-self-taught in art, from 1944. **Military Service:** Served as medical officer in the Italian Army, in North Africa, 1940–43. **Family:** Married Minsa

Craig in 1955. **Career:** Independent artist, Perugia, 1945–48, and in Rome, 1948–53; lived in the United States, 1953–69; returned to Rome, 1960; first abstract paintings, 1949; member, with Colla, Capogrossi and Balloco, ''Gruppo Origine,'' Rome 1951. **Awards:** International Award, Carnegie International, Pittsburgh, 1958; Premio dell' Ariete, Milan 1959; Unesco Prize, 5th Biennal de Sao Paulo, 1959; Critics' Prize, Biennale, Venice, 1960; Premio Marzotto, 1964; Grand Prix, 8th Bienal de Sao Paulo, 1965; Feltrinelli Prize, Milan 1972; Italian Order of Merit, 1994. **Agent:** Fondazione Palazzo Albizzini, Città di Castello, Italy. **Died:** Of respiratory failure at Pasteur Hospital, Nice, France, 13 February 1995.

Individual Exhibitions:

1947 Galleria La Margherita, Rome
1948 Galleria dell'Angelo, Città di Castello, Italy
Galleria Margherita, Rome
1949 Galleria dell'Angelo, Città di Castello, Italy
1952 Galleria dell'Obelisco, Rome
Galleria d'Arte Contemporanea, Florence
1953 Fondazione Origine, Rome
Allan Frumkin Gallery, Chicago
Stable Gallery, New York
1954 Galleria dell'Obelisco, Rome
Allan Frumkin Gallery, Chicago
1955 Stable Gallery, New York
Colorado Springs Fine Arts Center
Oakland Art Museum, California
1956 Seligmann Gallery, Seattle
Galleria del Cavallino, Venice
Galerie Rive Droite, Paris (with Cesar)
1957 Galleria Del Naviglio, Milan
Galleria dell'Obelisco, Rome
Galleria La Loggia, Bologna
Galleria La Bussola, Turin
Carnegie Institute, Pittsburgh
1958 Arts Club of Chicago
Albright-Knox Art Gallery, Buffalo, New York
San Francisco Museum of Art
Galleria La Salita, Rome
Galleria Blu, Milan
Galleria Alberti, Brescia, Italy
1959 Galerie d'Art Moderne, Basle
Palais des Beaux-Arts, Brussels
Galleria La Loggia, Bologna
Galleria La Tartaruga, Rome
Museum Haus Lange, Krefeld, West Germany
Galerie Beyeler, Basle
Galerie Wiener Sezession, Vienna
Museum am Ostwall, Dortmund, West Germany
1960 Martha Jackson Gallery, New York
Hanover Gallery, London
Museo Nacional de Bellas Artes, Buenos Aires
Galerie Anne Abels, Cologne
1961 Galleria La Medusa, Rome
Galerie de France, Paris
1962 Castello Cinquecentesco, L'Aquila, Italy
Galleria Marlborough, Rome
1963 Marlborough New London Gallery
Museum of Fine Arts, Houston
1964 Walker Art Center, Minneapolis
Albright-Knox Art Gallery, Buffalo, New York
Pasadena Art Museum, California
Marlborough-Gerson Gallery, New York
1965 Galleria La Bussola, Turin
Galleria Toninelli, Milan (with Marino Marini and Afro)
1966 Galleria Il Segno, Rome
1967 Kunsthalle, Darmstadt
Museum Boymans-van Beuningen, Rotterdam
Museum of Modern Art, New York (with Lucio Fontana)
Galleria La Tartaruga, Rome
Palazzo Vitelli, Città di Castello, Italy
1968 Galleria Blu, Milan
1969 Galleria Notizie, Turin
Galleria Giussi, Turin (With Marini and Moreni)
Galleria San Luca, Bologna
1970 Galleria La Tartaruga, Rome
Galleria Acme, Brescia, Italy
Qui Arte Contemporanea, Rome
Transart, Milan
1971 Galleria Il Margutta, Rome
Galleria Civica d'Arte Moderna, Turin
Modern Art Agency, Naples
Libreria Stampatori, Turin
Libreria-Galleria Congrande, Verona
1972 Musée d'Art Moderne, Paris
1973 Galleria San Luca, Bologna
1974 Galerie Jacques Benador, Geneva
Galleria Grafica Oggi, Milan
1975 Sacro Convento di San Francesco, Assisi, Italy
Disegni, Tempere e Gragica, Galleria Il Segnapassi, Pesaro, Italy
1976 Galleria Nazionale d'Arte Moderna, Rome
1977 Fundacao Calouste Gulbenkian, Lisbon
Santa Barbara Museum of Art, California (toured the United States)
1978 P & P Galerie, Zurich
Marion Koogler McNay Institute, San Antonio, Texas
Milwaukee Art Center
Museo di Capodimonte, Naples
Guggenheim Museum, New York
1979 Galleria Lorenzelli, Milan
Studio Marconi, Milan
J. Corcoran Gallery, Los Angeles
Galleria D'Ascanio, Rome
Essiccatoio del Tabacco, Città di Castello, Italy
1980 Rocca Paolina, Perugia, Italy (with Joseph Beuys)
Staatsgalerie Moderner Kunst, Munich
Istituto Italiano di Cultura, New York
Istituto Italiano di Cultura, Madrid
Orsanmichele, Florence
1981 Galleria L'Isola, Rome
1982 Desert Museum, Palm Springs, California
Galleria San Luca, Bologna, Italy
Brooklyn Museum, New York
Columbus Museum of Art, Ohio
San Francisco Museum of Modern Art
1983 Cantieri Navali alla Guidecca, Venice
1984 Galerie Sapone, Nice, France

Galerie des Ponchettes, Musée de Nice, France
1985 Musée de Toulon, France
Galleria Sanluca, Bologna
Galerie Artcurial, Paris
Centro Congressi la Serra, Ivrea
Galleria Sprovieri
1986 Maison de la Culture, Amiens
DiLaurenti Gallery, New York
Accademia di Belle Arti, Reggio Calabria
Musée de l'Imprimerie, Lyon
Galleria d'Arte Il Sole, Bolzano
1987 Kunstverein, Ludwigshafen, Germany
Hahnentorburg, Cologne
Museo Laboratorio dell'Università degli Studi La Sapienza, Roma
1988 Museo Nazionale complesso San Vitale, Ravenna
M. Gallery, Tokyo
Mixografia Gallery, Los Angeles
Galleria Sprovieri, Rome
Murray and Isabella Rayburn Foundation, New York
Galleria Eva Menzio, Torino
1989 Galleria La Polena, Genoa
Galleria Lia Rumma, Naples
Museum Moderner Kunst, Vienna
1990 Salvatore Ala Gallery, New York
1991 Palazzo Pepoli Campogrande, Bologna
1992 *FIAC,* Grand Palais, Paris
1993 Galleria Niccoli, Parma
Museo delle Genti d'Abruzzo, Pescara
1994 National Gallery and Alexandros Soutzos Museum, Athens
1997 *Burri: Works 1944–95,* Palazzo delle Esposizioni, Rome (travelled to *Stadtische Galerie im Lenbachhaus,* Munich; *Palais des Beaux-Arts,* Paris; *Electa,* Milan)

Selected Group Exhibitions:

1951 *Gruppo Origine,* Fondazione Origine, Rome
1952 *Biennale,* Venice (and 1956, 1966, 1968, 1983)
1953 *Younger European Painters,* Guggenheim Museum, New York
1959 *Bienal,* Sao Paulo (and 1965)
1967 *Contemporary Italian Art,* Ulster Museum, Belfast (toured the U.K.)
1980 *Arte Astratta Italiana 1909–1959,* Galleria Nazionale d'Arte Moderna, Rome
1982 *Documenta 7,* Kassel, Germany
1985 *The European Iceberg,* Art Gallery of Ontario, Toronto
1992 *FIAC,* Grand Palais, Paris
Prints and Multiples by Contemporary Masters, Museo de Arte Moderno, Mexico City
1994 *The Italian Metamorphosis,* Guggenheim Museum, New York
1996 *Burri and Fontana, 1949–68,* Centro per l'Arte Contemporaneana Luigi Pecci, Prato, Italy; Skiro, Milan, Italy.
1997 *Italian Painting: Alighiero e Boetti, Anselmo, Arienti, Burri, Clement, de Maria, Griff, Lo Savio, Marisaldi, Merz, Pisani, Toderi,* Museo d'Arte Contemporanea, Milan

Collections:

Galleria Nazionale d'Arte Moderna, Rome; Nationalgalerie, Berlin; Centre Georges Pompidou, Paris; Carnegie Institute, Pittsburgh; Galleria delle Arte, Città di Castello; Museo Internazionale delle Ceramiche, Faience.

Publications:

On BURRI: Books—*Burri* by James Johnson Sweeney, Rome 1955; *Burri* by Herbert read, London 1960; *Burri* by Enrico Crispolti, Milan 1961; *I Ferri di Burri* by G. Marchiori and M. Drudi Gambillo, Rome 1961; *Alberto Burri* by Cesare Brandi, Rome 1963; *New Italian Art 1953–1971,* exhibition catalog, with text by Giovanni Carandente, Liverpool 1971; *Alberto Burri* by Maurizio Calvesi, Milan 1971; *Alberto Burri,* exhibition catalog, with texts by Enrico Crispolti, Nello Ponente, Giuseppe Marchiori and others, Rome 1971; *Art without Boundaries 1950–1970,* edited by Gerald Woods, Philip Thompson and John Williams, London 1972; *Alberto Burri,* exhibition catalog, with texts by Jean Leymarie, Aldo Passoni and others, Paris 1972; *Burri* by Vittorio Rubiu, Turin 1975; *Burri: Disegni Tempere e Grafica,* exhibition catalog, with text by Maurizio Calvesi, Pesaro 1975; *Burri,* exhibition catalog, with text by Bruno Mantura, Lisborn 1977; *Alberto Burri: Prints 1959–1977* by Vittorio Rubin and others, Rome 1977; *Burri: La Forma e l'Informe* by Flavio Caroli, Milan 1979; *Alberto Burri: Il Viaggio,* with text by Nemo Sarteanesi and Erich Steingraber, Milan 1980; *Alberto Burri* by G. Butterfield, Palm Springs 1982; *Burri: Sestante,* edited by Vanni Bramanti, with introduction by Giulio Carlo Argan, Milan 1983; *Burri: Works 1944–95,* exhibition catalog, with texts by Carolyn Christov-Bakargiev and Maria Grazia Tolomeo, Rome 1997; *Burri,* edited by Andreas Hapkemeyer and Chiara Sarteanesi, Vienna 1999. **Articles—**''Burri'' in *Flash Art (International Edition),* no. 147, Summer 1989; ''Alberto Burri's Umbrian Collage: the Artist's Multifaceted Realm Near Perugia'' in *Architectural Digest,* vol. 47, January 1990; ''Medium Hot: Alberto Burri'' in *Artforum International,* vol. 29, December 1990.

* * *

The work of Alberto Burri—one of the greatest artists of this century—is an endless game with material. Sacks, wood, iron, plastics, Cellotex; he burns these materials, twists them, tears them, or else gently arranges them into amazing, calm fifteenth-century compositions. And sometimes, dramatically, both these things are combined in a single design. With Burri the material is identified with space; it becomes pure presence, the affirmation of existence; first of all, it *is.* But (and this is a paradox to be found only in art) it is only when a human works it, forces it, building up an eminently, wholly erotic relationship with it, that it reaches the essential state. Memory, a great memory of impressionist and tonal painting, informs the whole of Burri's work, alive like no others to delicate shading (even when the material is most crushed and contaminated), to the spreading of tone within a particular colour—as in the ''sacks,'' where the splits, the stitching, the holes, the patches that stretch the coarse stuff to its limits tell of nothing but the violence and pain of the material (and the material is the World), yet also of the chromatic chances by which everything creates colour: the shadows, the protrusions, the different tissues of the texture and the broken lines they follow.

In his different series of works there is always a strong tension between the defined space of the picture's surface and the irruptions on one side and another made by the "wounds" in these materials, natural or artificial, always poor but redeemed in the passage from quantity to quality. The "irons" of the later 1950s, for example, jammed hard together against each other so as to cover the whole rectangular frame given them, at once respect and transgress the surface of the pictorial design. They respect it because they are bent by main force to conform with it, ruled by the formal command to adhere to the design; they transgress it because, being forced in this way, they protrude in menacing spikes which encroach on the space and create a volume with the shadows they project on the others still held at the level of the surface. The burns on plastic—in which we may see a "baroque" in Burri—and on wood relate to the primordial power of fire, seat and symbol of life and so also of destruction, of biological poetry. From the subtle ambiguities between abstraction and *trompe-l'oeil,* between artifice and nature in the "cracks" (like coagulated streams of lava in which there are endless splits and fissures), to the clear, bright oblong shapes and patches of colour in the great impaginations of the series in Cellotex (a compound derived from the scission of cellulose). Burri's journey remains unique. And here, stupendously incarnate, breathes the absolute.

—Massimo Carboni

Burri's game with Cellotex continues in his works of the late 1980s and early 1990s. In the first of two series of black on black paintings, *Annottarsi* ("Up to Nite,"), the Cellotex that supports the pigment creates subtle variations in the paint's tone and texture. Some of the surfaces suggest landscapes, others focus on the more abstract juxtaposition of varying shades of black. Observing the nine paintings of another black-on-black series, *Non ama il nero,* one first recognizes the varied tones of black created by the Cellotex surface and layering of paint. Eventually, the mirage of a geometric shape on a black surface shifts into stylized letters that, altogether, form an anagram of the series' title: six paintings contain single letters, while three paintings reveal the double letters *no, ne,* and *am.* As Massimo Carboni has observed, both *Annottarsi* and *Non ama il nero* invite the viewer to explore the tonal multiplicity of the color black (*Artforum,* December 1990). Both series are housed in the Palazzo Albizzini Foundation's Burri collection, located in the artist's hometown of Città di Castello, Umbria.

—Beth Duncan

BURSON, Nancy

Nationality: American. **Born:** St. Louis, Missouri, 1948. **Education:** Attended Colorado Women's College, Denver. **Awards:** CAST, in conjunction with the New York State Council on the Arts and Syracuse University, 1977; National Science Foundation Grant for "Composite" Machine exhibit, 1987; National Endowment for the Arts Award, Photography, 1990. **Address:** c/o Jayne H. Baum Gallery, 588 Broadway, New York, New York 10012, USA.

Nancy Burson: *The President.* ©Nancy Burson, 1989, courtesy of National Museum of American Art, Smithsonian Institution, museum purchase through the Smithsonian Institution Special Exhibitions Fund.

Individual Exhibitions:

1974 Bertha Urdang Gallery, New York
1977 Hal Bromm Gallery, New York
1978 C.W. Post College, Installation, Long Island University, Brookville, New York
1984 Holly Solomon Gallery, New York
Bruce Velick Gallery, San Francisco
1985 International Center of Photography, New York
Institute of Contemporary Art, Boston
Baker Gallery, Kansas City
1986 Greathouse Gallery, New York
Chrysler Museum, Norfolk, Virginia
1987 Holly Solomon Gallery, New York
Torino Fotographia, Turin, Italy
New Britain Museum of American Art, New Britain, Connecticut
Baker Gallery, Kansas City
1989 Jan Kesner Gallery, Los Angeles
1990 Museum of Contemporary Photography, Columbia College, Chicago
Massachusetts Institute of Technology, List Visual Arts Center, Cambridge, Massachusetts Jayne H. Baum Gallery, New York
1991 Galerie Michèle Chomette, Paris
Jan Kesner Gallery, Los Angeles

1992 Jayne H. Baum Gallery, New York
Faces, Contemporary Arts Museum, Houston, Texas (toured)
The New Museum, New York
1993 Jayne H. Baum Gallery, New York
University of Rhode Island, Fine Arts Center Galleries, Kingston, Rhode Island
1998 Ricco/Maresca, New York

Selected Group Exhibitions:

1976 Susan Caldwell Gallery, New York
Bertha Urdang Gallery, New York
1977 *Arte Fierra,* Hal Bromm Gallery, Bologna, Italy
1978 *Atypical Works,* Julian Pretto Gallery, New York
1979 *Big Drawing Show,* P.S.1, Long Island City, New York
1980 *Pool Show,* Artists Space, New York
1981 Julian Pretto Gallery, New York
New Acquisitions, Stadt Galerie in Lembachhaus, Munich, Germany
1982 *Androgyny,* Emily Lowe Gallery, Hofstra University, Hempstead, New York
Nuclear Disarmament, Ronald Feldman Gallery, New York
1983 London Regional Art Gallery, Ontario, Canada
*Invitational,*Bertha Urdang Gallery, New York
1984 *1984,* Ronald Feldman Gallery, New York
Seven Women Artists, Zurich Art Fair, Switzerland
1985 *Signs of the Times, Some Recurring Motifs in 20th Century Photography,* San Francisco Museum of Modern Art
Identity, Palais de Tokyo, Paris
Biennale, Sao Paulo, Brazil
1986 *Stills: Cinema and Video Transformed,* Seattle Art Museum
Television's Impact on Contemporary Art, Queens Museum, Flushing, New York
1987 *Fake,* The New Museum, New York
Portraits, Virginia Museum, Richmond, Virginia
Extending the Boundaries of Contemporary Photography, Museum of Contemporary Photography, Chicago
1988 *Two to Tango: Collaboration in Recent American Photography,* International Center of Photography, New York (travelled to the Center for the Fine Arts, Miami)
Fabrication: Staged, Altered and Appropriated Photographs, Carpenter Center, Harvard University, Cambridge, Massachusetts
Education and Democracy and Cultural Participation, Dia Art Foundation, New York
1989 *Photography Now,* Victoria and Albert Museum, London
Fotografie, Wissenschaft und Neuetechnologien, Kunstmuseum, Dusseldorf, Germany
AIDS and Democracy, Dia Art Foundation, New York
1990 *"Rien Que La Chose Exhorbitée. . . ,"* Galerie Michèle Chomette, Paris
Critical Realism, Perspektief, Rotterdam, Netherlands
Selections Five, at *Fifth Cologne Biennale,* Cologne, Germany
1991 *L'oeuvre photographique considérée comme un état de sculpture,* Galerie Michèle Chomette, Paris
Sculpter Photographier, Centre national de la photographie, Palais de Toyko, Paris
1992 *Numerical Proof,* Centre national de la photographie, Palais de Tokyo, Paris
The Evolution of the Portrait in Photography, The Photography Museum, The International Cultural Centre, Antwerp, Belgium
1993 *Konstruktion Zitat: Kollektive Bilder in der Fotografie,* Sprengel Museum, Hannover, Germany
Danse Macabre: Portraits Photographiques, Abbaye aux Dames, Caen, le FRAC, Basse-Normandie, France
1993–94 *Beyond Recognition: Contemporary International Photography,* Australian National Gallery, Canberra
1994 *Body and Soul: Contemporary Art and Healing,* DeCordova Museum, Lincoln, Massachusetts
Photography Now: Facts and Fantasies, Rye Arts Center, Rye, New York
Metamorphoses: Photography in an Electronic Age, Fashion Institute of Technology, New York (toured; catalog)
An American Century of Photography, Hallmark Photographic Collection, Hallmark Cards, Inc. (toured through 2001)
1995 *Temporarily Possessed,* New Museum of Contemporary Art, New York (catalog)
2000 *Paradise Now: Picturing the Genetic Revolution,* Exit Art/ The First World, New York (catalog)
2001 *Selections from the Photography Collection,* Chrysler Museum of Art, Norfolk, Virginia

Collections:

Allentown Art Museum, Oberlin, Ohio; Australian National Gallery, Canberra; Bayly Museum of Art, University of Virginia, Charlottesville, Virginia; Chrysler Museum, Norfolk, Virginia; Emily Lowe Gallery, Hofstra University, Hempstead, New York; Fonds National d'Art Contemporain, Paris; Fonds Regional d'Art Contemporain de Basse-Normandie, France; International Museum of Photography, George Eastman House, Rochester, New York; Library of Congress, Washington, D.C.; Los Angeles County Museum; The Metropolitan Museum of Art, New York; Musée National d'Art Moderne, Centre Georges Pompidou, Paris; Museum of Fine Arts, Houston, Texas; National Museum of American Art, Smithsonian Institution, Washington, D.C.; San Francisco Museum of Modern Art; Stadt Galerie in Lembachhaus, Munich, Germany; The Tampa Museum of Art; Victoria and Albert Museum, London.

Publications:

By BURSON: Books—*COMPOSITES Computer Generated Portraits,* with an introduction by William A. Ewing and Jeanne A. McDermott, New York 1986; *Nancy Burson: The Age Machine and Composite Portraits,* with an essay by Dana Friis-Hansen, Cambridge, Massachusetts 1990; *Faces—Nancy Burson,* with an essay by Jeanne A. McDermott, Santa Fe, New Mexico 1993.

On BURSON: Books—*Photography Now* by Mark Haworth-Booth, England 1989; *The Photography of Invention, American Pictures of* *the 1980s* by Joshua P. Smith, Cambridge, Massachusetts 1989; *About Faces* by Terry Landau, New York 1989; *Artificial Nature* by Jeffrey Dietch, Athens, Greece 1990; *Crisis of the Real: Writings on Photography 1974–1989* by Andy Grundberg, New York 1990; *The History of Photography, an Overview* by Alma Davenport, Stoneham, Massachusetts 1991; *The Reconfigured Eye: Visual Truth in the Post-Photographic Era* by William J. Mitchell, Cambridge, Massachusetts 1992. **Articles—**''Patents: A Method That Pictures a Person at Any Age'' by Stacy Jones in *The New York Times,* 14 July 1981; '''Age Machine' Evolves from Artist's Idea'' by David Olmos in *Computerworld,* 23 April 1984; ''Images in the Computer Age'' by Andy Grundberg in *The New York Times,* 14 April 1985; ''Face to Face, it's the Expression that Bears the Message'' by Jeanne A. McDermott in *Smithsonian Magazine,* March 1986; ''The Serious Implications of Digital Image Processing'' by Michael O'Connor in *Print Magazine,* March/April 1986; ''Books: Prodigies & Identities'' by Vicki Goldberg in *American Photographer,* vol. XVII, July 1986; ''New Faces'' by Art Kleiner in *Aperture,* Issue No. 106, 1987; ''Nancy Burson: Chimaeras'' in *European Photography,* January/February/March 1988; ''Photographing AIDS: Difficult Subject'' by Robert Atkins in *The Village Voice* (New York), 28 June 1988; ''Portraits with Bursonality'' by Owen Edwards in *American Photographer,* Vol. XXII, No. 5, May 1989; ''Images Abundant: Anything's Possible'' by Andy Grundberg in *The New York Times,* 12 January 1990; ''Choices'' by Vince Aletti in *The Village Voice* (New York), 24 January 1990; ''Ask No Questions the Camera Can Lie'' by Andy Grundberg in *The New York Times,* 12 August 1990; ''Nancy Burson Making Faces'' by Robert Atkins in *Contemporanea,* Vol. 24, January 1991; ''Figure de l'au-dela'' by Patrick Roegiers in *Le Monde* (Paris), 5 June 1991; ''VISION USA'' by Gianni Romano in *Zoom* (Italy), No. 116, March/April 1992; ''Composites of Reality'' by Sue Heinemann in *New Environment* (Tokyo), No. 2, 1992; ''About Face, Redefining Normality With Nancy Burson'' by Vince Aletti in *The Village Voice* (New York), 21 April 1992; ''Fast Forward, Art Goes High Tech'' by Mark Dery in *ARTnews* (New York), February 1993; ''Visions of the Future'' by Sue Alexander in *American Photo,* May/June 1994; ''A Defining Reality: The Photographs of Nancy Burson'' by Rebecca Busselle in *Aperture,* Summer 1994; ''Photography After Photography'' by Jeanne Nugent in *ARTnews,* December 1997; ''Nancy Buson at Ricco/Maresca'' by Grady T. Turner in *Art in America,* February 1998; ''Nancy Burson'' by Dennis Cooper in *Artforum,* January 2000.

* * *

When Nancy Burson saw the Museum of Modern Art exhibition *The Machine as Seen at the End of the Industrial Age* in 1968, she was compelled by the magical possibilities of nascent computer and video technologies. Her conception of a ''time machine,'' however, was forced to wait for technology to reach the needed level of sophistication for realization. When Burson approached Experiments in Art and Technology (EAT)—Robert Rauschenberg's project to pair artists with scientific expertise—she was effectively transformed from a ''painter'' to a ''conceptual artist,'' although she continued to work in ''manual'' forms of art throughout the 1970s.

Initially, Burson's goal was to allow a person to look in a ''mirror'' and see themselves at any age. Gradually, with increasing knowledge about the capabilities of the technology, she developed in cooperation with Massachusetts Institute of Technology (MIT) a method to translate photographed portraits into the digitized language of computers, allowing for mathematical manipulation of the images via a grid of pixels.

Burson—with her husband and collaborator David Kramlick—developed the software to systematically ''age'' faces. The aging images are achieved by what she described as ''a patented facial warping system.'' The premise is that aging in the eyes and mouth happens in a fixed number of ways, for example, for fat men, thin men, fat women, and thin women. The amount of variability is finite and somewhat subjective. Burson holds patent number 4,276,570 on ''The Method and Apparatus for Producing an Image of a Person's Face at a Different Age,'' along with Thomas D. Schneider, who worked with her at the Massachusetts Institute of Techonology on computer aspects of the invention. The age machine, as Burson calls it, simulates the aging process through computer graphics.

Burson's work in digital photographic cooperation was truly pioneering, and it looks somewhat as quaint as daguerreotypes did 25 years after their introduction. The pictures created by this process are formed by digital, on-off impulses rather than by the smooth and seamless tonalities of conventional photographic processes. The resolution is very low by today's standards. Close inspection reveals a somewhat pixilated and fuzzy image with vague areas of dark and light. Most home PCs now have color monitors that have the ability to view over a million colors at 1280 X 1024 pixels. Burson's images were photographs made from the black and white video screen that was 512 X 480 pixels.

Burson's computer-rendered photographic portraits were displayed in 1985 at the International Center of Photography, in an important exhibition called *Simulacra: Forms without Substance.* The works on display included the combinations of ''types'' into single archetypes: movie stars and businessmen, for example.

Warheads, a series of formula-driven works by Burson created in the 1980s, sum up the end of the Cold War era. The portraits contain content from world leaders' faces in proportion to their nation's reported number of nuclear warheads: Reagan 55%, Brezhnev 45%, Thatcher, Mitterand, and Deng less than 1% each, for example. Burson made one for each year from 1982 to 1985, showing the evolving identity of the nuclear ''person.'' *Big Brother*—a composite of world leaders Adolf Hitler, Ayatollah Khomeini, Mao Zedong, Benito Mussolini, and Joseph Stalin—was used in a CBS documentary titled *1984 Revisited.*

The media has, understandably, been interested in the applications of Burson's work, as her interest in aging, identity, popularity, and celebrity are largely the turf of television and magazines. *People* magazine featured the aged portraits of Lady Di and Brooke Shields and the artist's transformations were also featured on ABC's *That's Incredible* and other television programs. The media has inspired her conceptual portraits as well; movie stars including Jacqueline Bisset, Marilyn Monroe, Audrey Hepburn, and Jane Fonda were all combined into an ''ideal beauty.'' Burson also created a 1991 Madonna-Michael Jackson combination that was to represent the definitive celebrity.

Well beyond the confines of the art world, Burson and associates were commissioned by the Federal Bureau of Investigation to create composite renderings of missing children, assisting the authorities and public in identifying them. To do this, Burson used family photographs to create an amalgam image of what child kidnapping victims might look like years after the crime.

In a 1989 Los Angeles exhibition, Burson's computer shuffled invented faces that came from the photographed features of two or more portraits of mostly children. There were Victorian death portraits, physically deformed children, and porcelain play dolls. The gallery images, disquieting black and white Polaroids of sampled innocents, were both innocent and freakish.

For the past number of years, Burson has used a simple plastic camera to photograph children born with craniofacial conditions or progeria, whom Burson describes as having ''unusual, very special faces.'' In a 1997 New York exhibition, photographic portraits of these disfigured individuals appeared. Traditional in style and almost romantic, the pictures are bathed in a warm golden light against a black background. Many of the characters depicted are in the process of having operations to bring their appearance back from the ravages of disease. Burson's portraits are ultimately a representation of science's own imperfectly scarred face, an on-going examination of our desire and ability to alter our physical appearance and our response to the results.

—Deirdre Donohue

BURY, Pol

Nationality: Belgian. **Born:** Haine-Saint-Pierre, 26 April 1922. **Education:** Studied painting, drawing and decoration under Louis Buisseret and Louis Navez, Academie des Beaux-Arts, Mons, 1938–39. **Military Service:** Served in the Belgian resistance movement, Brussels, 1943. **Career:** Painter and sculptor, living and working in Belgium, La Louviére, 1939–61, in Fontenay-Aux-Roses, near Paris, 1961–65, in Saulx-les-Chartres, France, 1965–73, and in Perdreauville, Yvelines, France, since 1973: produced first abstract paintings, 1947; first mobile-kinetic sculptures, 1957. Founder-member, with Archille Chavée André Lorent, Group Rupture, La Louvière, 1939–40; Young Belgian Painters group, Brussels, 1947; member, with Christian Dotremont and Pierre Alechinsky, COBRA (Copenhagen-Brussels-Amsterdam) group, Brussels, 1949–51; member, Art Abstrait group, Brussels, 1952; founder, with André Balthazar, Academie de Montbliart and Verlag de Montbliart publishing house, Brussels, 1953. Designed sets for ballet *Der Spiegel;* also involved in filmmaking, since 1970. Instructor in sculpture, University of California, Berkeley, 1970; Minneapolis College of Art and Design, 1973; professor of monumental sculpture, Ecole Nationale Supérieure des Beaux-Arts, Paris, 1983. **Awards:** Marzotto Prize, 1964; Grand Prix National de Sculpture, Paris, 1985. Honorary Doctorate: Minneapolis College of Art and Design, 1973. **Addresses:** Vallée de la Taupe, Perdreauville, 78200 Mantes-la-Jolie, France; 236 boulevard Raspail, 75014 Paris, France.

Individual Exhibitions:

1953 Galerie Apollo, Brussels
1955 Galerie Les Contemporains, Brussels
1957 Galerie du Verseau, Brussels
1959 Galerie St. Laurent, Brussels
1960 Galerie St. Laurent, Brussels
1961 A.P.I.A.W., Liège, Belgium
1962 Galerie Iris Clert, Paris
1963 Galerie Iris Clert, Paris
1964 Lefebre Gallery, New York
1965 Felix Landau Gallery, Los Angeles
1966 *Twice Pol Bury: Cinetizations, Moving Sculptures,* Lefebre Gallery, New York
Galerie La Hune, Paris
1967 Kasmin Gallery, London
1968 Lefebre Gallery, New York
1969 Galerie Pierre, Stockholm
Galerie Maeght, Paris
1970 University of California, Berkeley (toured the United States)
1971 *A Way Out,* Lefebre Gallery, New York
Estudio Actual, Caracas
Gallery Moos, Toronto
Kestner-Gesellschaft, Hannover (travelled to the Nationalgalerie, West Berlin and the Kunsthalle, Dusseldorf)
1972 Palais des Beaux-Arts, Charleroi, Belgium (travelled to Centre National d'Art Contemporain, Paris)
Kunsthalle, Dusseldorf
1973 Museum Boymans-van Beuningen, Rotterdam
Louisiana Museum, Humlebaek, Denmark
1974 *25 Tonnes de Colonnes,* Foundation Maeght, St. Paul de Vence, France
1976 Musée d'Art Moderne, Brussels
Woodprints, Lefebre Gallery, New York
1977 Museo de Arte Moderno, Mexico City
1978 F.S. Wright Art Galleries, University of California at Los Angeles
University of Texas at Austin
Portland Art Museum, Oregon
University of Georgia, Athens
1979 Musée Saint-Georges, Liége, Belgium
Oeuvres de 1963 a 1978, Cloitre Saint-Trophime, Arles, France
1980 Guggenheim Museum, New York
1981 Herning Museum, Denmark (with Pablo Palazuelo)
1982 Musée d'Art Moderne de la Ville, Paris (retrospective)
1985 Galerie Maeght, Paris
1986 Galerie Ziegler, Zurich
1988 Galerie 1900–2000, Paris
Galerie Sapone, Nice
Palais Governor, Antwerp
Pol Bury: Sculptures 1959–88, Cinetizations 1962–88, Drawings, Grand Palais, Paris
1989 Galeria Tega, Milan
Joseph Albers Museum, Bottrop, Germany
Galerie Keeser, Hamburg
Prakapas Gallery, New York
1990 Arnold Herstand Gallery, New York
Galerie 1900–2000, Paris
1991 Centre de la Gravure, La Louviere, Belgium
Maison Balzac, Paris
Arnold Herstand & Company, New York
1994 Galerie Keeser, Hamburg
Pol Bury: Retrospektive 1939–1994, Museum am Ostwall, Dortmund, Germany
Maison de Balzac, Musée de la Ville de Paris, France
1999 *Pol Bury: Fountains and Other Intriguing Works,* Louis Stern Fine Arts, West Hollywood

Selected Group Exhibitions:

1945 *Surrealisme,* Galerie des Editions La Boetie, Brussels
1955 *Le Mouvement,* Galerie Denise René, Paris
1959 *Breer, Bury, Klein, Mack, Munari, etc.,* Hussenhuis, Antwerp
1964 *Biennale,* Venice
Documenta 3, Kassel West Germany
1967 *Dix Années de l'Art Vivant 1955–65,* Galerie Maeght, Paris
1972 *Douze Ans d'Art Contemporain en France,* Grand Palais, Paris
1973 *Hommage à Picasso,* Kestner-Gesellschaft, Hannover
2000 *Force Fields: Phases of the Kinetic,* Museu d'Art Contemporani, Barcelona (traveled to Hayward Gallery, London; catalog)

Collections:

Neue Nationalgalerie, West Berlin; Kaiser Wilhelm Museum, Krefeld, West Germany; Kunstmuseum, Dusseldorf; Stedelijk Museum, Amsterdam; Belgian State Collection, Brussels; Museum of Modern Art, New York; Guggenheim Museum, New York; Albright-Knox Art Gallery, Buffalo, New York; Menil Foundation, Houston.

Permanent Public Installations:

Fountain, Palais Royale, Paris; fountain, New Canaan, Connecticut; *Skycatcher,* Newark Airport, New Jersey; fountain for University of Art and Design, Yamagata, Japan.

Publications:

By BURY: Books—illustrations for *L'Aventure devorante,* with COBRA group, Brussels 1950; illustrations for *La Main heureuse,* Brussels 1950; *Dix Sérigraphies de Pol Bury,* with an introduction by R. V. Gindertael, La Louviére, Belgium 1955; *La Boule et le Trou,* Brussels 1961; *Le Petit Commencement,* La Louviére, Belgium 1965; *La Boule et le cube,* Brussels 1967; *Milano, cinetizzazioni,* Venice 1967; *Derrière le miroir,* Paris 1969; *Décalcomanies,* La Louviére, Belgium 1970; *L'Art à bicyclette et la revolution à cheval,* Paris 1972; *Art is too serious to be left in the hands of artists . . .,* Minneapolis 1973; *Douze Ramollissements du Président Mao,* Paris 1973; *Ramollissements de 17 corps,* Paris 1973; *Le petits Moutons blancs qui sorten en rang du Lavoir,* Montpellier 1976; *Infracritique de l'Oeuvre plastique de Prof. Froeppel,* La Louvière, Belgium 1976; *Le Vélo de Joseph Staline et le Circuit idéologique,* La Louvière, Belgium 1976; *Le Sexes des Anges et celui des Géomètres,* Paris 1976; *Léon III, l'Isaurien, dit l'Iconomaque, Essai d'Iconophobie,* Brussels 1976; *Les Horribles mouvements de l'immobilité* (collected writings), Paris 1977; *L'Art inopiné dans les Collections publiques,* La Louvière 1982; *Les Gaietés de l'Esthétique,* Paris 1984. **Article—**"Tribune Libre" in *Chroniques de l'Art Vivant* (Paris), December 1970. **Films—***Tour Eiffel,* with Clovis Prevost, 1971; *8,500 Tonnes de Fer,* with Clovis Prevost, 1971; *Une Leçon de Geometrie plane,* with Clovis Prevost, 1972; *135 kilometres-heure,* with Clovis Prevost, 1972; *25 Tonnes de Colonnes,* with Clovis Prevost, 1973; *L'Art illustre,* 1975; *L'Oeuvre plastique du Professeur Froeppel,* with Claude Gaspari, 1976.

On BURY: Books—*Pol Bury,* exhibition catalog, with texts by Roger Bordier and André Balthazar, New York 1964; *Twice Pol Bury: Cinetizations, Moving Sculptures,* exhibition catalog, with text by Eugene Ionesco, *New York* 1966; *Pol Bury* by André Balthazar, Milan 1967; *Pol Bury,* exhibition catalog, with interview by Peter Selz, introduction by Eugene Ionesco, essay by André Balthazar, Berkeley 1970; *Pol Bury* by Dore Ashton, Paris 1970; *Pol Bury,* exhibition catalog, with text by Clara Diament de Sizo, Caracas 1971; *Pol Bury,* exhibition catalog, edited by André Balthazar, Hannover 1971; *Icons and Images of the 60's* by Nicolas and Elena Calas, New York 1971; *Pol Bury,* exhibition catalog, edited by André Balthazar, Paris 1972; *Douze Ans d'Art Contemporain en France,* exhibition catalog, Hannover 1973; *Pol Bury: 25 Tonnes de Colonnes,* exhibition catalog, with an interview by André Balthazar, St. Paul de Vence, France 1974; *Pol Bury: Oeuvres de 1963 à 1978,* exhibition catalog, with texts by Michael Moutashar, Anne Tronche, Roger Brodier, Dore Ashton and others, Arles, France 1979; *Les Fontaines de Pol Bury* by Pierre Descargeus, La Louviere 1986; *Pol Bury,* exhibition catalog, New York 1991; *Pol Bury* by Rosemarie E. Pahlke, Brüssel 1994; *Pol Bury: Fountains and Other Intriguing Works,* exhibition catalog, West Hollywood 1999. **Articles—**"Pol Bury: décaler le sourire de la joconde" by Claude Bouyeure in *L'Oeil* (Lausanne), no. 465, October 1994; "Force Fields: Phases of the Kinetic" by Yve-Alain Bois in *Artforum,* November 2000; "All the Right Moves" by Lynn Macritchie in *Art in America,* February 2001.

* * *

Until 1953 when he gave up easel painting completely, Pol Bury was one of the most enterprising young Belgian painters. He studied at the Mons Academy of Art from 1938 to 1939, when he joined the experimental surrealist group formed locally by two poets. He was a member of the Jeune Peinture Belge group, and until 1951 was associated with the COBRA group. His first experiments with mobile constructions were exhibited at Galerie Apollo, Brussels, in 1953, a series of *plans mobiles,* flat planes of black and white that could be fitted together to produce a variety of patterns. With Calder, Soto, Tinguely and Vasarely, Bury showed in the 1955 "Mouvements" exhibition at Galerie Denise René in Paris.

Electric motors were first used in Bury's works in 1957. *Multiplans,* flat rectangles set edge to edge, were painted with an overall abstract design that changed by minute degrees when moved by the power. These were succeeded in 1959 by his "Ponctuations" shown at the Galerie St. Laurent, Brussels, where perforated black and white discs performed constantly changing patterns and rigid and pliable stems rose and fell according to their phasing by the current. His show at Galerie Iris Clert showed a further development in "Entités erectiles" of 1963, where the spheres and globes appeared for the first time setting up subtle and almost imperceptible shudders. This contrast with rapid movement imposed its own intrinsic character in the work. Bury described it: "Speed limits space, slowness multiplies it." The sensuous associations suggested by the nudging of the globes are summarised by Bury: "Two slownesses gently grazing each other even go so far as to rub against each other. We dare henceforward speak of such activity no longer in terms of geometry but almost in the language of the boudoir."

From kinetics Bury progressed to constructions of finely carved and painted wooden objects comprising balls, cylinders and other cubes assembled in apparent disarray on flat ramps. Other works of hammered copper in freely curving arabesques fixed in panels carried hints of shock in their end tremors. Such is the reputation acquired by Bury's almost immobile mobiles that a structure of his designed for permanent static life can produce an hallucinatory effect on the onlooker, who easily imagines that it *does* move. As Bury insists, the difference is so slight.

Following representations at the Venice *Biennale* in 1964 and at exhibitions in the U.S.A. and Europe, Bury is to be seen in most major museums of the world. Swerving of bodies in space and the frailty of seemingly fixed galactic systems is further illustrated by analogy in Bury's ''Cinematisations'' where photographs and reproductions have circular details cut out and replaced in collages only slightly awry so that the Eiffel Tower or a Gothic cathedral seems ominously out of true, less obviously than the Tower of Pisa, but on that account all the more nerve-tingling.

—G. S. Whittet

A 1991 exhibition at the Arnold Herstand Gallery, New York, showcased sixteen new sculptures by Bury. Like his previous fountains, a new sculpted fountain of stainless steel seems to sculpt the water itself, making it an integral part of the sculpture, rather than a merely decorative element. In another group of sculptures, bunches of geometric shapes move slightly on their copper pedestals. A table piece, *72 Squares in a Rectangle* (1990), is arguably the most striking work. The 16-by-48-inch rectangular top is inlaid with seventy-two stainless-steel moving cubes. Reflections from the moving cubes throw a constantly changing, nongeometric picture onto a wall behind the table. These new works show that Bury, while still using some of the same themes, continues to create unique and surprising pieces that invite the viewer to consider the world from a new perspective.

—Beth Duncan

BUTHE, Michael

Nationality: German. **Born** in Sonthofen, Allgau, 1 August 1944. **Education:** Studied at the Werkkunstschulle, Kassel, 1962–64; under Arnold Bode, Hochschule fur bildende Kunste, Kassel, 1964–66. **Career:** Independent painter and environmental artist, in Kassel, 1966–68, in Cologne, 1969, and in Marrakesh beginning 1970: adopted pseudonym Michel de la Sainte Beaute, 1971. Professor, Akademie der Kunste, Dusseldorf, 1982 (resigned, 1982). **Awards:** Villa Romana Prize, Florence, 1976. **Agents:** Moderne Kunst Dietmar Werle, Spichernstrasse 44, 5000 Cologne 1; Galerie Bama, 40 rue Quincampoix, 75004 Paris; Galerie Toni Gerber, Gerechtigkeitsgasse 74, 3011 Berne. **Died:** 1994.

Individual Exhibitions:

1968 Galerie Ricke, Kassel, West Germany
1969 Galerie Ricke, Cologne
Von-der-Heydt-Museum, Wuppertal, West Germany
1970 Galerie Kuhn, Aachen, West Germany
Kabinett für Aktuelle Kunst, Bremerhaven, West Germany
Galerie Renée Ziegler, Zurich
Galerie Ernst, Hannover
1971 Galerie Toni Gerber, Berne
Galerie Renée Ziegler, Zurich
1972 Galerie Mollenhoff, Cologne
1973 Galerie Onze, Brussels
Kunstverein, Cologne
Kunstmuseum, Lucerne
Galerie Pablo Stahli, Lucerne
Galerie Oppenheim, Cologne
1974 Galerie Loeb, Berne
Galerie Vandres, Madrid
Galerie Oppenheim, Cologne
1975 Galerie Magers, Bonn
Oppenheim-Studio, Cologne
1976 Atelier des Kunstlers, Cologne
1977 Galerie AK, Frankfurt
Tarahumaras, Statisches Museum Schloss Morsbroich, Leverkusen, West Germany
Kunstmuseum, Dusseldorf
1978 Galerie Gerhild Grolitsch, Munich
Galerie Toni Gerber, Berne
Stadtisches Galerie, Ravensburg, Germany
1979 Galerie Bama, Paris
Galerie 't Venster, Rotterdam
Galerie Harlekin Art, Wiesbaden, Germany
1980 *Die endlose Reise der Bilder,* Museum Folkwang, Essen
Kunstverein, Kassel, Germany
1981 Galerie Munro, Hamburg
Galerie Bernier, Athens
Galerie Bama, Paris
Galerie Toni Gerber, Berne
Galerie Nachst St. Stephan, Vienna
1982 Galerie Krinzinger, Innsbruck, Austria
Galerie Art in Progress, Munich
Galerie Baronian/Lambert, Ghent, Belgium
Villa Romana, Florence
Holly Solomon Gallery, New York
1983 Galerie Toni Gerber, Berne
1984 Galerie Munro, Hamburg
Galerie Bama, Paris
Museum Villa Stuck, Munich
1987 Moderne Kunst Dietmar Werle, Cologne
1989 Wurttembergischer Kunstverein, Stuttgart
1999 Kunstmuseum Dusseldorf, Germany
Kunstmuseum Bielefeld, Germany
Michael Buthe: Early Drawings, Collages and Diaries, Kunsthalle Bielefeld, Germany

Selected Group Exhibitions:

1968 *Programm I,* Galerie Ricke, Kassel, West Germany
1969 *When Attitudes Become Form,* Kunsthalle, Berne (toured Europe)
1970 *14 x 14,* Staatliche Kunsthalle, Baden-Baden, Germany
1972 *Documenta 5,* Museum Fridericianum, Kassel, Germany (and *Documenta 6,* 1977; *Documenta 7,* 1982)
1973 *Yes, Sir, That's My Baby(etween),* Gallery House, London
1975 *Dessins: Beuys/Biel/Buthe/Filliou/Polke,* Gallerie Bama, Paris
1978 *Hammer I,* Galerie Handschin, Basle
1979 *Soft Art,* Kunsthaus, Zurich
1981 *Art Allemagne Aujourd'hui,* ARC/Musee d'Art Moderne de la Ville, Paris

1983 *Sculpture from Germany,* San Francisco Museum of Modern Art (toured the United States)
Michael Buthe & Marcel Odenbach, Walter Phillips Gallery, Banff Alberta, Canada
1997 *German Art in Singapore: Contemporary Art from the Collection of the Kunstmuseum Bonn,* Singapore Art Museum, Singapore

Collections:

Kunstmuseum, Dusseldorf; Kunstmuseum, Lucerne; Centre Georges Pompidou, Paris; Museum des 20. Jahrhunderts, Vienna; Museum der Stadt, Linz; Museum Ludwig, Cologne; Von-der-Heydt-Museum, Wuppertal; Stadtisches Museum, Ulm; Kunsthalle, Kiel; Nationalgalerie, Berlin.

Publications:

By BUTHE: Books—*Freunde/Friends,* Dusseldorf 1971; *Lukretia bagann damals gerade von der Kuste weg zu ziehen,* Zurich 1971; *Die Wunderlose Reise des Saladin Ben Ismael,* Cologne 1977; *Der Vortrag uber die Schonheit des absoluten Positivismus: le dernier Empire,* Essen 1980.

On BUTHE: Books—*Deutsche Kunst: eine neue Generation* by Rolf-Günter Dienst, Cologne 1970; *Bis Heute* by Karin Thomas, Cologne 1971; *Michael Buthe: Le Dieux de Babylon,* exhibition catalog box with pamphlets, Cologne 1973; *Michael Buthe: Tarahumaras,* exhibition catalog, with text by Rolf Wedewer, Leverkusen, West Germany 1977; *Weich und Plastiche/Soft-Art,* exhibition catalog edited by Erika Billeter, Zurich 1979; *Michael Buthe: Die endlose Reise der Bilder,* exhibition catalog, with text by Zdenek Felix, Essen 1980; *Michael Buthe & Marcel Odenbach,* exhibition catalog, introduction by Lorne Falk, Banff 1983; *Michael Buthe: Pompeian Spring,* text by Tilman Osterwold, Noemi Smolik, Stephan von Wiese and Juliane Schulze, Stuttgart 1989. **Articles—** ''Michael Buthe: the Best Thing is That We Are Alive At All'' by Jurgen Glaesemer in *Kunstforum International,* no. 93, February-March 1988; ''Galerie Dietmar Werle, Cologne; Exhibit'' by Peter Winter in *Art International,* no. 11, Summer 1990; ''Nationalgalerie Berlin; Exhibit'' by Peter Winter in *Art International,* no. 12, Autumn 1990; ''The Sorcerer of Vingst'' by Gerard A. Goodrow in *Art News,* vol. 92, March 1993.

* * *

Michael Buthe's oeuvre is primarily a convincing performance of creative intelligence. It can be regarded as a self-realization of the contextual and formal potential of his early journals (since 1963) and his collage books.

While his early drawings on paper (1967–69) are imaginary, conceptually related blueprints for spatial projects, he presented his stripe drawings on canvas in combination with plastic cushions and wooden elements like sticks and boxes as an installation (Kassel, 1968). In his drawings, line movement and colors are direct emotion and afterthought and are experienced as process and recollection. His fabrics, torn with delicate aggression and later sewn together and colored in red, violet, or turquoise, are in a physical and psychological sense a journey within the material itself. Buthe presented them as paintings on stretchers, as tapestries on walls, and as robes. Distancing himself from minimal art, he explored a kind of anthropomorphism by showing a close relationship between artwork, body, and space.

After 1970 Buthe continued to work on the integration of his inner reality and the inner context of his studio with the outer reality of his journeys to Africa and Persia. The journeys brought about the experience of landscape and people, resulting in an invasion of colour and of gold. The environmental aspect of his work started with the *Homage to the Sun* and *The God of Babylon,* when Buthe covered the walls with red fabrics to create a special milieu for the presentation of his drawings, paintings, and objects. In 1972, Harald Szeeman characterized his contributions to the *Documenta 5* as an ''individual mythology.'' Throughout the 1970s Buthe was involved with ritual forms as a means to give his environments a meaningful framework. The exhibition *Museum of Echnaton,* in his studio in Cologne in 1976, can be regarded as a summary of ten years' work, of his store of experience, as well as of the contextual aspect of his work. In 1984 he gave another retrospective view of his work with his exhibition *Inch Allah* (Ghent), which included his Florentine paper works (1976), *Babylonian Writings* (1982–83), and installations such as *I ono l'amoro preciöse after Caspar David Friedrich* (1984).

For Buthe, ''journey'' became journey via myth. ''Stories'' were stories of demons, angels, gods, and witch doctors. Buthe remained close to them because for him they were beings whose realm he wished to make his own. It is significant that Buthe did not use myth as an ideological frame for a ''better future,'' but experienced it through others and transformed it into artistic reality. Materials were brought together to evoke a crocodile or a ship. They are not there for purposes of representation but rather are sculptural forms which the function of crocodile or ship approaches. The canvas stretched over a massive circular frame, coated with beeswax and splattered with gold is picture/object and sun. The vast red-colored fabrics are painting and firmament, roof of heaven and home. The rectangular structure built from branches, covered with wax and rose leaves—an element of the environment *Homage to the Sun*—is sculpture and bed. The significance of these objects proceeds first from something produced by the artist not in any particular context, even thought they apparently fit seamlessly into it.

The works of his exhibition *Primavera Pompejana* (Stuttgart, 1991) were connected by his witty artistic animism. The gestural aspect and dancelike presentation of his objects and the drifting structure of his paintings cannot be regarded as a reconsidered primitivism but as an artistic form of consent to the ''necessary unity of mind and body'' (Gregory Bateson). Another exhibition which was dedicated to the topographical aspect of his work (Köln, 1992) opened the view for the ''absurd work of art'' as described by Albert Camus in ''The Myth of Sisyphus'' (1942). The life of an artist is drifting between ''the harmony of life and human being'' as it could be experienced in a landscape and the reversion to isolation and despair. Buthe's belief in the power of artistic progress as a spiritual process refuses any judgement about art in terms of good or bad. The form and colors of his late paintings (1994) are as multifaceted as they are dedicated to the ideal of emptiness.

—Jean-Christophe Amman and Marietta Franke

C

CADMUS, Paul

Nationality: American. **Born:** New York, 17 December 1904. **Education:** Townsend Harris High School, New York, 1917–19; at the National Academy of Design, New York, with Charles Hawthorne, Charles Curran and William Auerbach-Levey, 1919–26; Art Students League, New York, with Joseph Pennell and Charles Locke, 1928. **Career:** Worked for Blackman and Company advertising agency, New York, 1928–31; lived and worked with Jared French, who was an important influence, Majorca, and travelled in Europe, 1931–33; returned to the United States, and worked for the Public Works of Art Project, New York, 1933; designed costumes and set for the ballet *Filling Station,* New York, 1938. Vice-President, Arts Students League, New York, 1935. **Awards:** Witkowsky prize, Art Institute of Chicago, 1945; American Academy of Arts and Letters grant, 1961; Benjamin West Clinedinst Memorial Medal, 1989; Gerard Manley Hopkins Award for Visual Arts, Fairfield University, 1990; Doctor of fine Arts, State University of New York at Oswego, 1994. **Member:** American Academy of Arts and Letters, 1975; Associate, 1979, and Academician, 1980, National Academy of Design. **Agent:** Midtown Payson Galleries, 745 Fifth Avenue, New York, New York 10151. **Died:** Weston, Connecticut, 12 December 1999.

Paul Cadmus. ©Oscar White/Corbis.

Individual Exhibitions:

1937 Midtown Galleries, New York
1942 *3 American Painters,* Baltimore Museum of Art
1945 Midtown Galleries, New York
1949 Midtown Galleries, New York
1956 Midtown Galleries, New York
1967 Palm Beach Galleries, Florida
1968 Midtown Galleries, New York (retrospective)
1976 Midtown Galleries, New York
1977 Midtown Galleries, New York
1979 *75th Birthday Exhibition,* Midtown Galleries, New York
1981 *Paul Cadmus: Yesterday and Today,* Miami University Art Museum, Oxford, Ohio (retrospective; travelled to the Ulrich Museum of Art, Wichita, Kansas; Gribbes Art Gallery, Charleston, South Carolina; and the William Benton Museum of
1983 Midtown Galleries, New York
1985 *Eightieth Birthday Celebration,* Midtown Galleries, New York
1986 Louis Newman Galleries, Beverly Hills, California
1992 Midtown Galleries, New York
1993 *The Artist as Subject: Paul Cadmus,* Midtown Galleries, New York
1997 *Paul Cadmus: Visionary Realist,* Yale University Art Gallery, New Haven (catalog)

Selected Group Exhibitions:

1935 *Whitney Annual,* Whitney Museum, New York
1936 *Murals in Federal Art,* Corcoran Gallery, Washington, D.C.
1939 *Art in Our Time,* Museum of Modern Art, New York
1942 *20th Century American Portraits,* Museum of Modern Art, New York
1950 *American Symbolic Realism,* Institute of Contemporary Arts, London
1966 *Art of the United States 1670–1966,* New York Cultural Center
1972 *Collectors Anonymous,* New York Cultural Center
1975 *Work by Newly Elected Members,* American Academy of Arts and Letters, New York
1986 *Treasures from the National Museum of American Art,* Seattle Art Museum, Washington (travelled to Minneapolis, Fort Worth, Atlanta and Washington, D.C.)
1987 *Twentieth Century American Art,* Whitney Museum at the Equitable Center, New York

Collections:

Metropolitan Museum of Art, New York; Whitney Museum, New York; Museum of Modern Art, New York; Sara Roby Foundation Collection, New York; Fogg Art Museum, Harvard University,

Paul Cadmus: *The Shower.* ©Christie's Images/Corbis.

Cambridge, Massachusetts; National Museum of American Art, Smithsonian Institution, Washington, D.C.; Library of Congress, Washington, D.C.; J. B. Speed Art Museum, Louisville, Kentucky; Georgia Museum of Art, Atlanta; Los Angeles County Museum of Art.

Publications:

By CADMUS: Book—*Ballet Alphabet: A Primer for Laymen,* with Lincoln Kirstein, New York 1939. **Articles—**interview with Geoffrey Batchen in *Afterimage,* vol. 16, February 1989.

On CADMUS: Books—*Art U.S.A. Now,* edited by Nordness, Lucerne 1962; *Paul Cadmus: Prints and Drawings* by Una E. Johnson, New York 1968; *Paul Cadmus: Yesterday and Today,* exhibition catalog, by Philip Eliasoph, Oxford, Ohio 1981; *Paul Cadmus* by Lincoln Kirstein, New York 1984, revised edition 1992; *The Drawings of Paul Cadmus* by Guy Davenport, New York 1989; *Collaboration: The Photographs of Paul Cadmus,* Margaret French and Jared French, Santa Fe, New Mexico 1992. **Articles—**''Paul Cadmus: Enfant Terrible'' by Harvey Salpeter in *Esquire* (Chicago), July 1937; ''Paul Cadmus: Etcher'' by Childe Reece in *Magazine of Art* (New York),

November 1937; ''Paul Cadmus of Navy Fame Has His First Art Show'' in *Life* (New York), March 1937; ''Paul Cadmus Continues'' by Ralph Pomeroy in *After Dark* (New York), December 1970; ''The Figure Drawings of Paul Cadmus'' by Diane Casella Hines in *American Artist* (New York), November 1972; ''Profile on Paul Cadmus'' by Raymond J. Steiner in *Art Times* (Woodstock, New York), May 1986; ''Paul Cadmus'' in *American Artist* (New York), February 1987; ''Cruising with Paul Cadmus'' by Jonathan Weinberg in *Art in America,* November 1992; ''Paul Cadmus'' by Richard Meyer in *Art Journal,* Fall 1998; obituary in *The New York Times,* 15 December 1999; ''Scout's Honor: Justin Spring on Paul Cadmus'' in *Artforum,* vol. 38, no. 7, March 2000. **Film—***Paul Cadmus: Enfant Terrible at 80* by David Sutherland, 1984.

*

A poet is not expected to give an exegesis of a poem. I don't think that a painter should do one of a painting. (*Aims* differ with each work.) I have made statements in the past, now I know better. Let art majors, art historians, etc. say their says.

In 1987 a continuing aim is clarity, a clarity that does not preclude mystery but does eschew mystification; also a technique that is delicate, precise and unobtrusive—no matter what the subject matter be.

—Paul Cadmus

* * *

Before he was 10 years old, Paul Cadmus had decided to become an artist. Although he produced a number of paintings in the 1930s and 40s, it is an interest in drawing which began as a teenager that Cadmus has sustained throughout his career. Working in a tightly rendered style, using masses of figures in motion and perspective schemes akin to those of the Italian Renaissance, Cadmus concentrated on contemporary social issues in his paintings, drawings, and etchings. The effects of densely populated city life on human behavior particularly interested the artist during the 1930s, and he chose to paint social interaction among the sexually promising.

A scandal arose in 1934 when a Cadmus painting, ''The Fleet's In!,'' attracted negative attention from the U.S. Navy. Done as a Public Works of Art Project, ''The Fleet's In!'' depicted sailors smoking, drinking, and carousing with women who were behaving similarly. The Navy was outraged by Cadmus' satirical view and denounced the painting as ''undignified, sordid, and depraved.'' Newspapers nationwide covered the incident. Cadmus, wise to the ways of Renaissance artists in pre-photography days, made an etching of the painting, pulled 50 prints, and thereby disseminated the image through his own devices, a fortunate move since the painting itself was ''misplaced.'' Cadmus was not deterred from satire and social realism, however, and went on to paint ''Hinkey-Dinkey Parlez-Vous'' and ''Sailors and Floosies,'' perhaps his best known work.

In keeping with his interest in artistic concerns of the Renaissance, Cadmus occasionally painted in egg tempera, and when he turned primarily to drawing in the mid 1950s he again used Renaissance methods—light colored strokes on toned paper. Cadmus takes his drawing seriously, regarding it as a fulfilling discipline rather than a casual study. His style and content have changed, however. ''To the Lynching,'' 1935, for example, shows a swirling mass of horseflesh and humanity at its ugliest, while more recent drawings emphasize a single nude figure, carefully modeled. The interest in muscular tensions and dramatic foreshortening remains although the view of humanity has grown gentler.

—Mary Stofflet

Although Cadmus' production continued to be interspersed with the satirical paintings for which he had become famous in the 1930s—for example, *See No Evil, Speak No Evil, Etc.* of 1985 with its Reagan-esque central character—the later years of his career also saw more straightforward depictions of an all-male domestic life. The *Haircut,* 1986 (executed in the same exacting medium of tempera used for many of his earlier paintings), showed Jon Anderson acting as barber for the artist. Anderson, an actor-singer and Cadmus' longtime companion, often served as his model. He was subject of a number of drawings produced over the thirty-five years of their relationship. Although specific portraits, the images, often nude, were also celebrations of idealized male beauty. As in many of Cadmus' works, there was something of an inherent contradiction between the frank sensuality of the figure and the fact that it had been rendered with academic precision.

A number of intersecting social and cultural currents led to a resurgence of interest in Cadmus' work in the final three decades of his career. Post-Stonewall, the homosexual community publicly embraced the artist as an important role model, both for his uncloseted adult life and for his specific depictions of gay men. With an increased interest in representational work, especially in the 1980s, the art world—which had generally celebrated Cadmus' production in the middle years of the century but then tended to ignore it in the 1960s and 1970s—began to reposition it as a significant part of a continuous tradition of carefully executed figurative images. Around the same time, scholars not only increasingly acknowledged his importance as a figurative artist, also recognized his groundbreaking treatment of homosexual themes.

—Paula Wisotzki

CAGE, John

Nationality: American. **Born:** Los Angeles, California, 5 September 1912. **Education:** Primary schools in Los Angeles and Los Angeles High School, until 1928 (class valedictorian); studied piano privately, 1920–28; studied at Pomona College, Claremont, California, 1928–30; studied architecture, and piano under Lazare Levy, Paris, 1930–31; studied composition, under pianist Richard Bühlig, Los Angeles, and under composers Adolph Weiss and Henry Cowell, New York, 1931–34; studied counterpoint and analysis, under Arnold Schönberg, at the University of Southern California, Los Angeles, and at the University of California at Los Angeles, 1934; studied philosophy and traditional music of India, under Gita Sarabhai, and attended lectures on Zen Buddhism by Daisetz T. Suzuki, Columbia University, New York, 1945–47. **Family:** Married Xenia Andreyevna Kashevaroff in 1934 (separated, 1945). **Career:** Independent composer, painter, printmaker, and writer, since 1931; travelled to Paris, Biskra, Majorca, Madrid and Berlin, painting and writing poetry, also began to compose music, 1930–31; composed chromatic music, and became increasingly interested in percussion music and rhythmic structure, 1935–36; Composer-Accompanist, dance classes of Bonnie Bird, Cornish School, Seattle, where he met Merce Cunningham, then a student at the school, also composed and performed percussion music with groups and performed percussion music with groups that he organized, collecting various types of instruments, including ''junk'' objects, 1937–39; commissioned by CBS-Radio to create a score, *The City Wears a Slouch Hat,* with the poet Kenneth Patchen, Chicago, 1941; moved to New York and began a lifelong collaboration with Merce Cunningham, 1942; commissioned by the New York Ballet Society to score *The Seasons,* with choreography by Cunningham and sets by Isamu Noguchi, 1947; influenced by the thought of R. Buckminster Fuller, 1948; travelled to Europe, 1949; began collaboration with pianist David Tudor on many performances and projects, 1950; worked with Tudor, and composers Morton Feldman, Christian Wolff, and later, Earle Brown, to free sounds from memory, taste and fixed relationship to each other, making experiments and discoveries in the area of electronic music, 1950; influenced by Abstract Expressionist painters, 1950; introduced to the *I Ching* (Chinese *Book of Changes*), which became very important to the composition of his music and printmaking, 1951; moved with friends to a small cooperative community near Stony Brook, New York, where he became interested in nature, and concentrated on the study of mushrooms, 1954–72; made European concert tour with David Tudor, which influenced experimental music abroad, 1954; travelled to Europe with David Tudor, 1958; commissioned by the Montreal Festival Society to write major orchestral work, *Atlas Eclipticalis,* composed with astronomical charts, 1961; travelled to Japan on concert tour with David Tudor, 1962; travelled with Merce Cunningham on world tour, 1964; became interested in working with language: letters, syllables, words, and phrases free from syntax and meaning, 1969; became interested in lecture/performance for voice and tape, influenced by the writings of Mao Tse-Tung, 1971; moved back to New York, 1972; commissioned by Canadian Broadcasting Corporation to create a work related to the Bicentennial, *Lecture on the Weather,* 1975; commissioned by Seiji Ozawa and the Boston Symphony Orchestra to create a work for the Bicentennial, *Renga,* and *Apartment House 1776,* 1976; became intensely preoccupied with *Finnegans Wake,* 1976; invited by Kathan Brown to begin printmaking sessions at Crown Point Press, Oakland, California, 1978; devised way of ''translating'' any book into music, which he put to use on *Finnegans Wake,* 1979. Musical Director, Cunningham Dance Company, 1944–66, and President, Cunningham Dance Foundation, since 1965. Co-Founder, New York Mycological Society, 1962; Director, Foundation for Contemporary Performance Arts, since 1965. Visiting Instructor of Experimental Music, at invitation of László Moholoy-Nagy, Institute of Design, Chicago, 1941; Black Mountain College, North Carolina, 1948, 1952; New School for Social Research, New York, intermittently 1956–60; Darmstadt, West Germany, 1958; University of Hawaii, Honolulu, 1964; Fellow, 1960–61, 1970, and Associate, 1968–69, Center for Advanced Studies, Wesleyan University, Middletown, Connecticut; Composer-in-Residence, University of Cincinnati, 1967; Artist-in-Residence, University of California at Davis, 1969. **Awards:** Guggenheim Fellowship, 1949; Award, American Academy of Arts and Letters and National Institute of Arts and Letters, 1949; Grand Honor, *International Biennial of Prints,* Tokyo, 1979. **Member** American Academy of Arts and Sciences, 1979. **Agent:** Margarete Roeder Fine Arts, 545 Broadway, New York, New York 10012. **Died:** 12 August 1992.

Individual Exhibitions:

1958 Stable Gallery, New York
1971 Galleria Schwarz, Milan
1977 *Renga,* Museum of Modern Art, New York (score)
1978 Museum Folkwang, Essen
Städtisches Museum, Mönchengladback, West Germany
Kunstverein, Cologne
1979 Kunstforum, Bonn
1982 *John Cage: Scores and Prints,* Whitney Museum, New York (travelled to the Albright-Knox Art Gallery, Buffalo, New York and the Philadelphia Museum of Art)

Performances:

1937 *The Future of Music: Credo,* Seattle (lecture)
1943 Museum of Modern Art, New York (concert of percussion music)
1944 Joint recital, Merce Cunningham Dance Company, New York
1950 *Lecture on Nothing,* Artist's Club, New York
1952 Untitled ''event,'' Black Mountain College, North Carolina (with Merce Cunningham, Robert Rauschenberg, David Tudor, and poets Charles Olson and Mary Caroline Richards)
1955 Joint recital, Clarktown High School, New York City (with Merce Cunningham)
1958 *Concert for Piano and Orchestra,* Town Hall, New York (retrospective)
Lecture on Indeterminacy, at *World's Fair,* Brussels (30 ''amusing'' stories, read 1/minute)
Water Walk, Milan (concert of theatre and music)
Sounds of Venice, Milan (concert of theatre and music)
1963 *Vexations, With 840 Repetitions,* by Erik Satie, New York (director)
1967 *1st Musicircus,* University of Illinois, Urbana (simultaneous performances of as much unrelated music as possible)
1968 *Reunion,* Toronto (with others; game of chess on an amplified board in which moves activate sound systems created by various musicians)
1969 *HPSCHD,* Assembly Hall, University of Illinois, Urbana (multi-media audio-visual performance)
1970 *Musicircus,* at *Paris Music Week*
1972 *Mesostics* and *Mureau,* European tour (with David Tudor; latter is mix of writings of Thoreau, superimposed on electronic music of Tudor)
1974 *12 Haiku,* Stony Brook, New York
1975 *Lecture on the Weather,* Canadian Broadcasting Corporation studios, Toronto (chanted texts derived from Thoreau with film and recordings of breeze, rain, and thunder)
1976 *Renga and Apartment House 1776,* Boston (with Boston Symphony, conducted by Seiji Ozawa; incorporated live or recorded songs, calls, and hollers)
1978 *Roaratorio: An Irish Circus on Finnegans Wake,* IRCAM recording studios, Paris (uses several thousand sounds found in *Finnegans Wake)*

1981 *Empty Words,* National Public Radio, United States
Compositions in Retrospect, at *Computer Music Conference,* Denton, Texas
30 Pieces for 5 Orchestras, Pont-á-Mousson, France
1982 *Roarotorio,* Toronto
New Music America Festival, Chicago
1990 *John Cage: New River Watercolors,* Washington, D.C.
1991 Bayerische Staatsgemaldesammlungen, Munich

Selected Group Exhibitions:

1979 *International Biennial of Prints,* National Museum of Modern Art, Tokyo
1980 *Print Publishing in America,* Stedelijk Museum, Schieldam, Netherlands
1989 *Dancers on a Plane: Cage, Cunningham, Johns/Susan Sontag, In memory of their feelings; Richard Francis . . . [et al],* Anthony d'Offay Gallery, London
1990 Tate Gallery, Liverpool

Collections:

Metropolitan Museum of Art, New York; Museum of Modern Art, New York; Whitney Museum, New York; Museum of Fine Arts, Houston; San Francisco Museum of Modern Art; Stedelijk Museum, Amsterdam.

Selected Compositions:

For piano—*Music for Xenia,* 1934; *2 Pieces,* 1935; *Metamorphosis,* 1938; *A Room,* 1943; *Experiences I,* 1945–48; *Ophelia,* 1946; *2 Pieces,* 1946; *Dream,* 1948; *In a Landscape,* 1948; *Suite for Toy Piano,* 1948; *Music of Changes,* 1951; *For M. C. and D. T.,* 1952; *Music for Piano I,* 1952; *7 Haiku,* 1952; *Waiting,* 1952; *Music for Piano 2,* 1953; *Music for Piano 3,* 1953; *Music for Piano 4–19,* 1953; *Music for Piano 20,* 1953; *Music for Piano 21–36, 37–52,* 1955; *Music for Piano 53–68,* 1956; *Music for Piano 69–84,* 1956; *For Paul Taylor and Anita Dencks,* 1957; *Winter Music,* 1957; *TV Koeln,* 1958; *Electronic Music for Piano,* 1964; *Cheap Imitation,* 1969; *Etudes Australes,* 1974–75. **For prepared piano—***Bacchanale,* 1938; *Amores,* 1943; *Meditation,* 1943; *Totem Ancestor,* 1943; *A Book of Music,* 1944; *The Perilous Night,* 1944; *Prelude for Meditation,* 1944; *Root of an Unfocus,* 1944; *A Valentine out of Season,* 1944; *Daughters of the Lonesome Isle,* 1945; *Mysterious Adventure,* 1945; *3 Dances,* 1945; *Sonatas and Interludes,* 1946–48; *Music for Marcel Duchamp,* 1947; *2 Pastorales,* 1951. **For voice—***20 Years After,* 1932; *Is It as It Was,* 1932; *At Eat and Ingredients,* 1932; *5 Songs for Contralto,* 1938; *Forever and Sun-smell,* 1942; *The Wonderful Widow of 18 Springs,* 1942; *Experiences II,* 1945–48; *A Flower,* 1950; *Aria,* 1958; *Solo for Voice 1,* 1958; *Solo for Voice 2,* 1960; *Song Books 1 & 2,* 1970; *Litany for the Whale,* 1980; *Empty Words,* 1981. **For strings—***Nocturne for Violin and Piano,* 1947; *6 Melodies for Violin and Keyboard (Piano),* 1950; *String Quartet in 4 Parts,* 1950; *Freeman Etudes,* 1977. **For winds—***Sonata for Clarinet (Solo),* 1933; *3 Pieces for Flute Duet,* 1935; *Music for Wind Instrument,* 1938. **For harp—***In a Landscape,* 1948. **For carillon—***Music for Carillon No. 1,* 1952; *Music for Carillon No. 2* 1954; *Music for Carillon No. 3,* 1954; *Music for Carillon No. 4,* 1961; *Music for Carillon No. 5,* 1967. **For various solos and ensembles—***6 Short Inventions,* 1933; *Solo with Obbligato Accompaniment of 2 Voices in Canon, and 6 Short Inventions on the Subject of the Solo,* 1933; *Sonata for 2 Voices,* 1933; *Composition for 3 Voices,* 1934; *3 Pieces for Flute Duet,* 1935; *She Is Asleep,* 1943; *16 Dances,* 1951; 4'33'', 1952; *59 1/2 for a String Player,* 1953; 31'57.9864'' for a Pianist, 1954; 34'46.776'' for a Pianist, 1954; 26'1.499'' for a String Player, 1955; 27'10.554'' for a Percussionist, 1956; *Variations I,* 1958; *Variations II,* 1961; 0'00'', 1962; 0'00'' No. 2, 1968; *Sound Anonymously Received,* 1969; *Score (40 Drawings by Thoreau) and 23 Parts,* 1974; *12 Haiku,* 1974. **For orchestra and chamber orchestra—***The Seasons,* 1947; *Concerto for Prepared Piano and Chamber Orchestra,* 1951; *Concerto for Piano and Orchestra,* 1957–58; *Atlas Eclipticalis,* 1961–62; *30 Pieces for 5 Orchestras,* 1981; *Atlas Borealis* (with chorus), 1982. **For percussion (and electronic devices)—***Quartet,* 1935; *Trio,* 1936; *First Construction (in Metal),* 1939; *Imaginary Landscape No. 1,* 1939; *Living Room Music,* 1940; *Second Construction,* 1940; *Double Music,* with Lou Harrison, 1941; *Third Construction,* 1941; *Credo in Us,* 1942; *March (Imaginary Landscape No. 2),* 1942; *Imaginary Landscape No. 3,* 1942; *Imaginary Landscape No. 4 (March No. 2),* 1951; *Imaginary Landscape No. 5,* 1952; *Speech,* 1955; *Radio Music,* 1956; *Cartridge Music,* 1960; *Music for Amplified Toy Pianos,* 1960; *Variations III,* 1963; *Variations IV,* 1964; *Variations VI,* 1967; *Variations VII,* 1967; *Variations VIII,* 1968; *Child of Tree,* 1975; *Branches,* 1976; *Renga,* 1976; *Apartment House 1776,* 1976; *A Dip in the Lake,* 1976; *Roaratorio, An Irish Circus on Finnegans Wake,* 1979. **For magnetic tape—***Williams Mix,* 1952; *Fontana Mix,* 1958; Music for ''The Marrying Maiden,'' 1960; *WBAI,* 1960; *Rozart Mix,* 1965. **For audio-visuals—***Water Music,* 1952; *Music Walk,* 1958; *Sounds of Venice,* 1959; *Water Walk,* 1959; *Theatre Piece,* 1960; *Variations V,* 1965; *Musicircus,* 1967; *Newport Mix,* 1967; *Reunion,* 1968; *HPSCHD,* with Lejaren Hiller, 1969; *Lecture on the Weather,* 1975. Many of these scores have been published by Henmar Press, New York; over 40 recordings of various works have been made since 1933.

Publications:

By CAGE: Books—*Virgil Thomson,* with Kathleen Hoover, New York, 1959; *Silence,* Middletown, Connecticut 1961; *A Year from Monday*, Middletown, Connecticut 1967; *Diary: How to Improve the World (You Will Only Make Matters Worse) Continued 1967*, pamphlet, New York 1967; *Diary: Part III,* New York 1967; *Diary: Part IV,* New York 1968; *Notations,* with Alison Knowles, New York 1969; *To Describe the Process of Composition Used in Not Wanting to Say Anything about Marcel,* Cincinnati 1969; *Mushroom Book,* with Lois Long at Alexander H. Smith, New York 1972; *Writings '67-'72,* Middletown, Connecticut 1973; *Writing Through Finnegans Wake,* New York 1978; *Empty Words: Writings '73-'78,* Middletown, Connecticut 1979; *Changes and Disappearances,* portfolio of prints, New York 1982; *On the Surface,* portfolio of prints, New York 1982; *The Mud Book,* with Lois Long, New York 1982. **Articles—**''Goal: New Music, New Dance'' in *Dance Observer,* December 1939; ''Chavez and the Chicago Drouth'' in *Modern Music,* March/April 1942; ''For More New Sounds'' and ''South Winds in Chicago'' in *Modern Music* May/June 1942; ''Grace and Clarity'' in *Dance Observer,* November 1944; ''Summer Music: The Parks'' in *Modern Music* November/December 1944; ''Dreams and Dedications of George Antheil'' in *Modern Music,* January 1946; ''East in the West'' in *Modern Music* April 1946; ''Forerunners of Modern Music'' in *Tiger's Eye,* March 1949; ''Contemporary Music Festivals

Held in Italy'' in *Musical America,* June 1949; ''Satie Controversy'' in *Musical America,* December 1950; ''A Few Ideas about Music and Films'' in *Film Music News,* January/February 1951; ''Letters to the Editors: More Satie'' in *Musical America,* 1 April 1951; ''Manifesto on Music'' in *Living Theatre Program* (New York), 1952; ''Letter to Peter Yates'' in *Arts and Architecture* (Los Angeles), November 1953; ''Manifesto on Painting of Bob Rauschenberg'' in the *New York Herald Tribune,* 27 December 1953; ''Music Lover's Field Companion'' in *United States Lines Parts Review,* 1954; ''Experimental Music'' in *The Score,* June 1955; ''In This Day . . .'' in *Dance Observer,* January 1957; ''2 Pages, 122 Words on Music and the Dance'' in *Dance Magazine,* November 1957; ''To Describe the Process of Composition Used in 'Music for piano 21–52''' in *Die Reihe,* vol. 3, 1957; ''Morris Graves,'' introduction to exhibition catalog, Ogunquit, Maine 1957; ''Erik Satie'' in *Art News Annual,* New York, 1958; ''Composition as Process: Interdeterminacy'' in *Das Neue Forum,* vol. 8, nos. 4, 6, 8, 1958; ''Composition as Process: Communication'' in *The Village Voice* (New York), April 1958; ''Roster on Varèse'' in *Nutida Musik* (Stockholm), Fall 1958; ''History of Experimental Music in the United States'' in *Beiträge zur Neuen Musik* (Darmstadt), vol. 4, 1959; ''Unbestimmtheit'' in *Die Reihe,* vol. 5, 1959; ''Lecture on Nothing'' in *Incontri Musicali,* August 1959; ''Lecture on Something'' in *It Is,* 1959; ''Form Is a Language'' in *Artnews* (New York), April 1960; ''On Robert Rauschenberg, Artist, and His Work'' in *Metro* (Milan), May 1961; ''Where Are We Going? and What Are We Doing?'' in *Ring des Arts,* Summer 1961; ''Where Do We Go from Here?'' in *Dance Perspectives,* vol. 16, 1962; ''26 Statements re Duchamp'' in *Mizue* (Tokyo), September 1962; ''Jasper Johns: Stories and Ideas'' in *Jasper Johns* by Alan R. Solomon, New York 1964; ''Nam June Paik: A Diary'' in *Nam June Paik,* exhibition catalog, Rio de Janeiro 1965; interview, with Michael Kirby and Richard Schechner in *Tulane Drama Review* (New Orleans), Winter 1965; interview, with Ilhan Mimaroglu in *Discoteca,* November 1965; ''Diary: Emma Lake Music Workshop 1965'' in *Canadian Art,* January 1966; ''Letters to the Editor: Electronic Souls'' in the *Village Voice* (New York), 20 January 1966; ''Seriously Comma'' in *Preuves* (Paris), March 1966; ''Rhythm'' in *Module, Proportion, Symmetry, Rhythm,* edited by Gyorgy Kepes, New York 1966; ''Diary: How to Improve the World (You Will Only Make Matters Worse) 1965'' in *Joglars,* vol. 1, no. 3, 1966; ''A Lethal Measurement,'' interview, with Michael Zwerin, in the *Village Voice* (New York), 6 January 1966; ''Diary: How to Improve the World (You Will Only Make Matters Worse) 1966'' in *Paris Review,* Spring 1967; ''Diary: Audience 1966'' in *Arts: Planning for Change,* 1967; ''Remarks about Merce Cunningham'' in *Dance Perspectives,* Summer 1968; ''John Cage,'' interview, with Richard Kostelanetz, in *The Theatre of Mixed Means,* New York 1968; ''HPSCHD,'' interview, with Larry Austin, in *Source,* vol. 2, no. 2, 1968; ''Soixante Résponses a Trente Questions,'' interview, with Daniel Charles, in *Revue d'Esthetique* (Paris), 1968; ''How to Improve the World (You Will Only Make Matters Worse) 1968 (Revised 1969)'' in *TriQuarterly* (Evanston, Illinois), no. 18, 1970; essay in *Sound on Paper: Music Notation in Japan,* exhibition catalog, New York 1981; ''John Cage: An Interview,'' interview, with Vincent Katz, in *The Print Collector's Newsletter,* vol. 20, January/February 1990; ''In the Form of a Thistle: A Conversation Between John Cage and Thomas McEvilley'' in *Artforum International,* vol. 31, October 1992; ''Life can be so Excellent: Interview with John Cage,'' interview, with Irmeline Lebeer, in *Cahiers du Musee National d'Art Moderene,* no. 52, Summer 1995.

On CAGE: Books—*Zen and American Thought* by Van Meter Ames, Honolulu, Hawaii 1962; *Happenings,* edited by Jurgen Becker and Wolf Vostell, Hamburg 1965; *The Bride and the Bachelors: 5 Masters of the Avant-Garde (Duchamp, Tinguely, Cage, Rauschenberg, Cunningham)* by Calvin Tomkins, New York 1965; *The New Art,* edited by Gregory Battock, New York 1966; *Die Unvermeidliche Musik des John Cage* by Werner Bartsch and others, Kolb, Switzerland 1969; *The New Music,* edited by Gregory Battcock, New York 1970; *Print Publishing in America,* exhibition catalog, Schiedam, Netherlands 1980; *Cage, Cunningham, Johns: Dancers on a Plane* by Susan Sontag, Richard Francis, Mark Rosenthal, Anne Seymour, David Sylvester, and David Vaughan, London 1990; *John Cage: New River Watercolours,* exhibition catalog, Washington, D.C. 1990; *John Cage: Scores and Prints,* exhibition pamphlet, New York 1982; *Into the Light of Things: the Art of the Commonplace from Wordsworth to John Cage* by George L. Leonard, Chicago 1994; John *Cage: Composer in America,* edited by Marjorie Perloff and Charles Junkermann, Chicago 1994; Happenings *and Other Acts,* edited by Mariellen R. Sandford, London 1995; *Difference/Indifference: Musings On Postmodernism, Marcel Duchamp And John Cage* by Moira Roth and Jonathon D. Katz, Amsterdam 1998. **Articles—**''Cage, Composer, Shows Calligraphy of Note'' by Dore Ashton in the *New York Times,* 6 May 1959; ''Figure in an Imaginary Landscape'' by Calvin Tomkins in *The New Yorker,* 28 November 1964; ''Poets and Kings'' by Jill Johnston in the *Village Voice* (New York), 8 November 1967; ''Social Concern'' by Calvin Tomkins in the *New York Times Book Review,* 21 January 1968; ''Cage—Wissenschaftlich Betrachlet'' by Hans Rudolf Zeller in *Zur Theorie der Offenen Form,* edited by Konrad Boehmer, Frankfurt 1968; ''The American Avant-Garde, Part II: John Cage'' by Richard Kostelanetz in *Stereo Review* (New York), May 1969; ''John Cage: Some Random Remarks'' by Richard Kostelanetz in *Denver Quarterly,* Winter 1969; ''The New River Watercolors of John Cage'' by Ray Kass in *Drawing* (New York), vol. 10, no. 3, September-October 1988; ''Cage, Cunningham and Johns: Participation and Collaboration'' in *Journal of Art,* vol. 2, no. 2, November 1989; ''John Cage: Perception and Reception'' by Dick Higgins in *Art Papers* (Atlanta), vol. 15, no. 6, November-December 1991; ''John Cage's 4'33'': Using Aesthetic Theory to Understand a Musical Notion'' by Mark Robin Campbell, vol. 26, Spring 1992; ''John Cage (1912–1992)'' by David Sylvester, Roger Smalley, and Arlynn Nelhaus in *High Performance,* vol. 15, no. 2–3, Summer-Fall 1992; ''The Boulez-Cage Correspondence: Selections'' in *October* (Cambridge), no. 65, Summer 1993; ''Finishing School: John Cage and the Abstract Expressionist Ego'' in *Critical Inquiry,* vol. 19, no. 4, Summer 1993; ''John Cage: Music for Museums'' by Jill Johnston in *Art in America* (New York), vol. 82, January 1994;''John Cage: Music for Museums'' by Jill Johnston in *Art in America* (New York), vol. 82, no. 1, January 1994; ''John Cage at Crown Point Press'' by David Ryan in *Printmaking Today* (London), vol. 3, no. 1, Spring 1994; ''Cage and Philosophy'' by Noel Carrol in *The Journal of Aesthetics and Art Criticism,* vol. 52, Winter 1994; ''Flux Acts'' in *Art in America,* vol. 82, June 1994; ''Chance Collection'' by Deidre Stein in *Art News,* vol. 93, September 1994; ''John Cage'' by Nicholas Zurbrugg, in *Art and Design,* vol. 10, November/December 1995; ''Mobius/Boston: Cage for Trombone'' by Joel Segel in *Art New England,* vol. 17, August/September 1996; '''Concerts of Everyday Living': Cage, Fluxus and Barthes, Interdisciplinarity and Inter-media Events'' by Simon Shaw-Miller in *Art History* (Oxford), vol. 19, no. 1, March 1996; ''From the 'Aesthetics of Indifference' to 'Negative Aesthetics': John Cage and Germany 1958–1972'' by Ian

Pepper in *October* (Abingdon), no. 82, Fall 1997; ''John Cage and the Architecture of Silence'' by Branden Joseph in *October* (Abingdon), no. 81, Summer 1997; ''Reflections of a Progressive Composer on a Damaged Society'' by Hans G. Helms in *October* (Abingdon), no. 82, Fall 1997; ''Chance as Ideology'' by Konrad Boehmer in *October* (Abingdon), no. 82, Fall 1997; ''John Cage, or Liberated Music'' by Heinz Klaus Metzger in *October* (Abingdon), no. 82, 1997; ''The Silence of Nothingness and American Abstraction'' by Wilfrid Mellers in *Modern Painters* (London), vol. 11, no. 1, Spring 1998.

* * *

John Cage was born September 5, 1912, in Los Angeles. In his long career as composer he encompassed many interests, delighted many people and enraged or antagonized a number of others. Best known as a guiding force of the avant-garde in America since the end of World War II, Cage's influence on composers, poets, dancers and painters has been as extensive as his work output has been prolific. Yet people at large are not so familiar with his music. His reputation for levity and eccentricity has served to obscure the seriousness of his inventions and perhaps limited the audience for his teachings.

Central to Cage's teaching is the view that art should imitate nature in its multiplicity and synchronous operations. He saw his music as a means of awakening people to the world around them; he exhorted people to listen to the sounds, or noises of their everyday lives, as worthy of attention in themselves, not just as they might be structured in a composition, where they tend to lose their inherent self-sufficient value. One of Cage's most infamous pieces, called 4' 3'', consisted of the performer or performers playing nothing—the sounds of the piece were the sounds of the audience and the environment. But Cage deployed a number of methods in serving his phenomenological interests.

His earliest acclaimed invention was the ''prepared piano''—a piano turned into a kind of percussion orchestra (played by one) by the placement of screws and other materials between the strings. By then, in the 1940s, Cage's deviant concern for ''noise'' as proper material for music had been established. As a young man in California he had studied with Arnold Schoenberg whose traditional base for musical structure, dividing the whole into parts by means of tonality and harmony, provided a point of departure for the independent Cage. To include noises in his work Cage first devised rhythmic structures, which also resulted from his work with dancers. Since the early 1950s Cage had worked closely with dancer/choreographer Merce Cunningham, as composer, mentor, friend and performer.

In the 1940s Cage moved to New York, becoming interested in Zen Buddhism and Indian aesthetic theory. He studied with D.T. Suzuki at Columbia, an association that led him to his lifelong obsession with removing his ego (conscious taste and memory) from his work. His introduction to the *I Ching,* or *Chinese Book of Changes,* gave him the tool for implementing this removal of self, as he saw it, from composition. Since 1950 he had used the *I Ching* continuously, though not exclusively, to determine, by tossing coins, the sequence of events or specific order of sounds, and sometimes even materials, in his work. It is these ''chance operations'' that have impressed so many other artists in their own quests for the unfamiliar. Akin to them are the various methods of Indeterminacy by which Cage has left or instructed his performers to supply aspects of his compositions that he has not himself. Things left to the performer's discretion, however, are not to be confused with improvisation, which remains dependent on personal likes and dislikes, taste and memory, etc: rather they are determined by the performers in advance of performance, in the creation of the score.

During the 1970s Cage united his chance methodology with his admiration for Henry Thoreau and James Joyce, creating literary Dada-like variations on the famous texts: *Walden* and *Finnegans Wake.*

He also pioneered the use of tape and electronic music, and is known for producing the prototypical ''happening''—at Black Mountain College in 1952.

—Jill Johnston

CAHN, Miriam

Nationality: Swiss. **Born:** Basel, 21 July 1949. **Education:** Grafikfachschule and Kunstgewerbeschule, Basel, 1968–73; Atelier der Stadt Basel, Paris, 1978–79. **Career:** Independent artist; lives and works in Basel. **Awards:** Förderpreis des Landes Baden-Württemberg, 1984; DAAD, Berlin, 1985; Preis der Hypothekenbank, Geneva, 1988; stipden from Landis & Gyr, London, 1996; Karl Ströher Preis, Frankfurt, 1997; Käthe Kollwitz Preis, Berlin, 1998. **Address:** Giessliweg 1, CH-4057 Basel, Switzerland.

Individual Exhibitions:

1977 Stampa, Basel
1979 Stampa, Basel
1981 Stampa, Basel
1982 *Wach Raum 1,* Konrad Fischer, Zurich
1983 *Das Klassische Lieben,* Kunsthalle Basel
Stampa, Basel
1984 *Das Wilde Lieben,* Musée la Chaux-de-Fonds
Das Wilde Lieben, Galerie Grita Insam, Vienna
Das Wilde Lieben, Stampa, Basel
1985 *Strategische Orte,* Kunsthalle Baden-Baden, and Kunstmuseum, Bonn
Strategische Orte, Elisabeth Kaufmann, Zurich
1986 *Strategische Orte,* DAAD, Berlin
Strategische Orte, Stampa, Basel
1987 *Lesen in Staub/Strategische Orte,* Galerie Schmela, Dusseldorf
Centre Culturel Suisse, Paris
Galerie Vorsetzen, Hamburg
Stampa, Basel
1988 Elisabeth Kaufmann, Zurich
Van de Loo, Munich
Lesen in Staub, Gemeentemuseum, Arnhem
Lesen in Staub, Haus am Waldsee, Berlin
Lesen in Staub/Weibliche Monate, Kunstverein Hannover
Musée Rath, Geneva
1990 *Verwandschaften,* Stampa, Basel
Verwandschaften, Art Frankfurt
Verwandschaften, Cornerhouse, Manchester
1991 *Verwandschaften,* Galerie Espace, Amsterdam
1992 *Nachkrieg-Vorkrieg (Was Fehlt),* Stampa, Basel
Museum für Moderne Kunst, Frankfurt am Main
1993 *Sarajevo,* Stampa, Basel
1994 Stampa, Basel
1995 Museum für Moderne Kunst, Frankfurt am Main

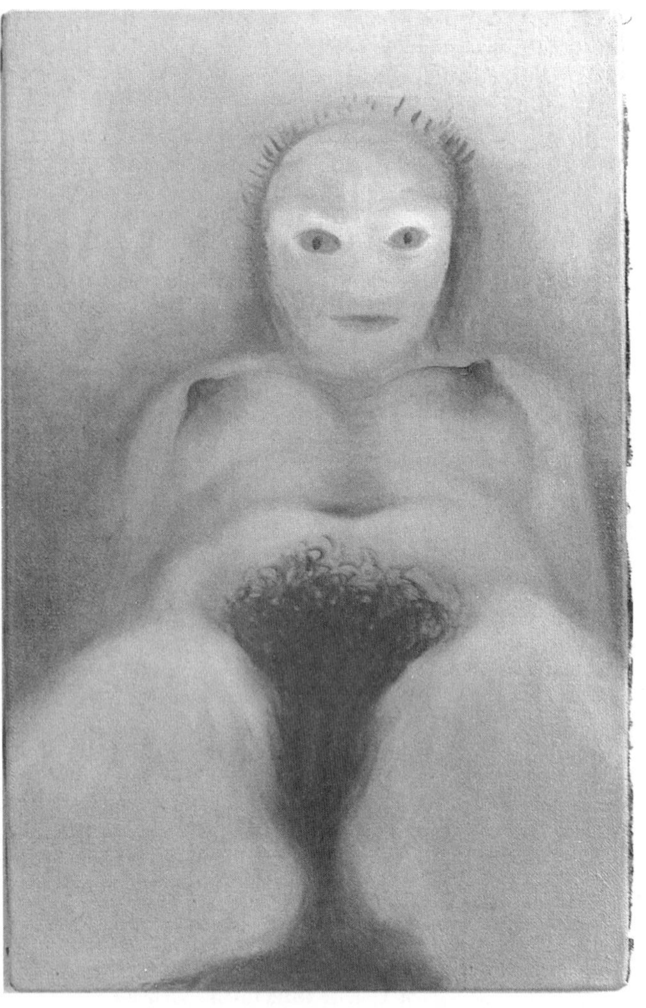

Miriam Cahn: *stilwechsel,* 1999. ©Miriam Cahn, courtesy of Museum für Moderne Kunst, Frankfurt am Main.

Obala Art Centar, Sarajevo
1996 Kunstverein Bonn, Stadtgalerie Saarbrücken
1997 Galeri Jon Dobloug, Oslo
1998 Museum für Moderne Kunst, Frankfurt am Main
Akademie der Künste, Berlin
1999 Castello di Rivara, Italy
Galeri Jon Dobloug, Oslo
Zeno X Gallery, Antwerp

Selected Group Exhibitions:

1979 *Feministische Kunst International,* Frauenzimmer, Basel
1982 *Documenta,* Kassel, Germany
1984 Museum of Modern Art, New York
Crosscurrents in Swiss Art, Serpentine Gallery, London
1986 Biennial, Sydney
1989 *Triennal de Dibuix,* Fundació Joan Miró, Barcelona
1990 *Zur Sache Selbst,* Künstlerinnen des 20. Jahrhunderts Museum, Wiesbaden
1994 Centre d'Art Contemporain, Geneva
From Beyond the Pale, Irish Museum of Modern Art, Dublin
1995 *Where Is Abel, Thy Brother?,* National Gallery of Contemporary Art Zacheta, Warsaw
1997 *Alpenblick,* Kunsthalle, Vienna
2000 Museum für Moderne Kunst, Frankfurt

Collections:

Museum für Moderne Kunst, Frankfurt; Museum of Modern Art, New York; Museum für Gegenwartskunst, Basel; Kunstmuseum, Basel; Kunstmuseum, Bern; Kunsthaus, Zurich; Kunsthaus, Aargau; Kunstmuseum, Chur, Switzerland.

Publications:

On CAHN: Books—*Lesen in Staub,* exhibition catalog, Berlin and Hannover 1988; *Was Mich Anschaut,* exhibition catalog, Darmstadt 1993; *Miriam Cahn,* exhibition catalog, Oslo, 1997; exhibition catalog, Berlin, 1998; *Katalog Miriam Cahn,* exhibition catalog, Italy, 2000. **Articles—**''New Painting in Switzerland'' by B. Curiger in *Flash Art,* no. 102, 1981; ''Miriam Cahn'' by Jean-Christophe Ammann in *Kunstbulletin,* no.3, 1985; ''A Female Way and a Male Way'' in *Art Link,* August/September 1986; ''Miriam Cahn'' by E. Beck in *Art News,* October 1988 and March/April 1989; ''Miriam Cahn'' by H. Thiel in *Noema,* no. 22, 1989; ''Miriam Cahn'' in *Lettre* (Berlin), no. 37, 1997.

* * *

The works of Miriam Cahn are representational of our everyday experiences. The artist answers the question that she herself poses—what she sees around her; and her works investigate the various methods of perception. In addition, Miriam Cahn has also developed painterly process, one in which the human form plays an essential role. Her methods reflect the rhythm of the body itself, something she has further developed into a singular visual vocabulary. Such energy is readily apparent in the lines of the drawing.

Central to Cahn's work is a concept of space. In her earliest works a way of considering art as a future representation of a spatial whole was already apparent, and the multilayered levels of meaning within a work develop only completely in a specific exhibition situation. One such early conceptual work is ''Silent Sister,'' which Cahn constructed in the Kunsthalle of Basel, Switzerland.

One important theme running through Cahn's creations is gender identity and the relationship with the representation of the human form. In the series ''the wild life,'' the artist works in the rhythm and energy of work, concepts that have resulted in the historically constricted gender differences. Cahn questions the preconceived notions of roles played, and the nondiscursive picture of the female form, with her marks of abridgment and deformation. Through the steady repetition of motifs, and a method geared toward inclusion in specific series, she is successful is letting loose, and indeed even placing into question, preconceived notions of human figure representation. Attempting to formulate a frank body image, and the sexual implications thereof, was what gained Cahn international recognition with her entry in the Venice *Biennale.* The artist explored, in drawings centered around the theme ''Children, Women, and Animals,'' the typical cultural representations of the human form with her characteristic style. The process of painting this related series of themes, that at the same time can be seen through the fixed way of the process of perception itself, is readable in the black dabs of chalk upon the surfaces of the art.

The relationship with violence and war has been, from the outset, yet another apparition in Cahn's body of work. The ''Atomic Bombs'' series are watercolors, noteworthy for colors that are firmly planted meanings of disciplinary categories. Here art is a process, one which is apparent in the analogy to nature and science. The destructive capability of modern science, as well as the fascination with this science, is an ambiguity explored in the work. The dangers and consequences of this technological research are accompaniments to Cahn's work around the themes of women and animals—the ''flashes of light'' of the bombs also serve to destroy life. In this context the ''process'' can also be settled. There are near-photographic quality oil paintings of chemical factories, nuclear reactors, and similar lairs of destruction.

The 1991 war in the Persian Gulf marked a turning point in Cahn's artistic career. At that point, applied procedures and thought processes were reconsidered. The view righted itself, away from more inner concerns, that which only one person saw, and towards the ideas and events that were developing. From these Cahn carried away a changed perception of the present. The work ''War Room'' in the Galerie Stampa further mirrored this upheaval. In Cahn's more current work in the series ''Couches'' the relationship with death becomes urgently expressed. The drawings under the title ''Unnamable'' seek to explore the frank, the intangible, of this theme.

Cahn's landscapes are also part of a relationship with nature. ''Reading in Dust'' and ''With Closed Eyes'' are two works in executed in chalk that explore this process. ''Sight'' concerns itself with the movement of the body of landscape, and the act of imagining or remembering. Just as control over the eyes is abolished is an exact visual experience possible, one that doesn't take over older examples of painting. Following through on this theme, a preoccupation with the effluvium of nature, arises the thematic possibility of understanding as responsibility. Landscapes in ''movement'' are Cahn's own films of sorts, stills in which water, the force of nature, or plants and animals are holding still, frozen. Her monumental drawings of cities, ''Strategic Places,'' are also landscapes, from the perspective of one who is dreaming or fleeing.

Her first object pieces arose parallel to the earlier lines in Cahn's work. In such objects Cahn works over materials such as found pieces of wood. The noise of the process itself determines the final form of the object. In her newer works Cahn reaches back to the subconscious; an example is ''Prayer Shawl,'' an object that originated directly from a dream image. The working process, such as the throw of the ceramic material, and the creation of the objects, are documented on video.

The objective of the art of Miriam Cahn is ''something found, that had been lost, or forgotten. . . that had disappeared,'' as the artist has said. Her work is a search for a visual language with a new comprehension of perception and time. A search for the unnameable, the revelatory.

—Sabine Gebhardt

CAI Guo-Qiang

Nationality: Chinese. **Born:** Quanzhou City, Fujian, China, 1937. **Education:** Studied in the Fine Arts Department of the Shanghai Theatrical University, 1981–85. **Career:** Traveled extensively in the Tibetan Plateau, Dunhuang, 1980–86; lived in Japan, 1986–95; gave a series of lectures on contemporary art in Japan at Beijing Central Art Collegem, 1989; stayed in Paris under a grant from Fondation Cartier pour l'Art Contemporain, 1993; moved to New York in 1995. **Awards:** Benesse Corporation Prize of Transculture Exhibition, 46th Venice Biennale, Italy, 1995; Japan Cultural Design Prize, 1995; Oribe Awards, Japan, 1997.

Selected Individual Exhibitions:

1990 *Works 1988/89,* Osaka Contemporary Art Center, Japan
1991 *Primeval Fireball: The Project for Projects,* P3 Art and Environment, Tokyo
1992 *Wailing Wall: From the Engine of Four Hundred Cars,* IBM Kawasaki City Gallery, Japan
1993 *Long Mai,* P3 Art and Environment, Tokyo
1994 *Chaos,* Setagaya Museum, Tokyo
To Flame, Tokyo Gallery
From the Pan-Pacific, Iwaki City Art Museum, Fukushima, Japan
Calendar of Life, Gallery APA, Nagoya, Japan.
1996 *The Century with Mushroom Clouds: Projects for the 20th Century,* Nevada
Nuclear Test Site, Salt Lake City, Utah; New York
1997 *Cultural Melting Bath: Projects for the 20th Century,* Queens Museum of Art, New York
1998 *No Destruction No Construction: Bombing Taiwan Museum of Art,* Taichung, Taiwan
1999 *Hiriya in the Museum,* Tel Aviv Museum of Modern Art, Israel (catalog)
Cai Guo-Qiang: I am the Y2K Bug, Kunsthalle Wein (catalog)
2000 *Cai Guo-Qiang,* Fondation Cartier pour l'art contemporain, Paris (catalog)

Selected Group Exhibitions:

1985 *Wuyi-shan Open Air Exhibition,* Fujian, China
The Shangai and Fujian Youth Modern Art Joint Exhibition, Fuzhou City Museum, China
1989 *Project for Extraterrestrials n.1: Human Abode,* Tama River Fussa Art Exhibition, Tokyo
1990 *Project for Extraterrestrials n.5: Fetus Movement,* 7th Japan Ushimado International Art Festival, Okayama, Japan
Project for Extraterrestrials n. 4: I'm an Extraterrestrial—Project for Meeting with Tenjin, Museum City Tenjin, Fukuoka, Japan
The 7th Japan Ushimado International Art Festival, Okayama, Japan
Chine Demain pour hier, Pourriers, France
1991 *Project for Extraterrestrials n. 11: The Immensity of Heaven and Earth,* Fukuoka, Japan
Waves of Asia: Three-Men Exhibition, Tokyo Gallery
Exceptional Passages, Fukuoka, Japan
1992 *Encountering the Others,* The Kassel International Art Exhibition, Hann-Munden, Germany
1993 *Project for Extraterrestrials n. 10: Project to Add 10,000 Meters to the Great Wall of China,* Jiayuguan, China

History of the Rocket, Museum of Modern Art, Sakama, Japan
Project for Extraterrestrials n. 12: Myth of Humanity, Vienna, Austria
Silent Energy, Museum of Modern Art, Oxford
1994 *Project for Heiankyo 1200th Anniversary: Celebration from Changan,* Kyoto, Japan
Heart of Darkness, Rijksmuseum Kroller-Muller, Otteerlo, Holland
Creativity in Asian Art Now, Hiroshima City Museum
Well Spring, Bath Festival Exhibition, England
1995 *East Asia,* The HO-AM Art Museum, Seoul
Bringing to Venice What Marco Polo Forgot, 46th Venice Biennale
The Orient: San-jo Tower, Museum of Contemporary Art, Tokyo
Project for Extraterrestrials n. 25: Restrained Violence-Rainbow, The 1st Johannesburg Biennial, Turbine Hall Building/ Johannesburg Power Station
1996 *The Hugo Boss Prize 1996,* Guggenheim Museum Soho, New York
The Red Gate, Museum van Hedendaagse kunst, Gent, Belgium
Between Heaven and Earth: Aspects of Contemporary Japanese Art II, Nagoya City Art Museum, Japan; Tamayo Museum, Mexico City
In the Ruins of the Twentieth Century, Institute for Contemporary Art, P. S. 1, New York
1997 *Cities on the Move,* Secession, Vienna; Museum of Contemporary Art, Bordeaux, France
On Life, Beauty, Translation, and Other Difficulties, 5th International Istanbul Biennial, Turkey
Future, Past, Present, 47th Venice Biennale
Performance Anxiety, Museum of Contemporary Art, Chicago; Museum of Contemporary Art, San Diego; SITE Santa Fe
1998 *Crossings,* National Gallery of Canada, Ottawa (catalog)
Global Vision: New Art from the 90s, Part II, Deste Foundation, Athens
Taipei Biennial ''Site of Destre,'' Taipei Fine Arts Museum, Taiwan
Where Heaven and Earth Meet, Art Museum of the Center for Curatorial Studies, Bard College, New York

Publications:

By CAI: Articles—''Portfolio'' with Octavio Zaya in *Grand Street,* Winter 1999.

On CAI: Books—*Performance Anxiety,* exhibition catalog, Chicago 1997; *Cai Guoqiang,* by Dawei Fei and Andrei Ujica, London 2000. **Articles**—''The Explosive Drawings of Cai Guo-Qiang'' by Robert M. Murdock in *Drawing,* Summer 1998; ''Cai Guo-Qiang: Between Heaven and Earth'' by Evelyne Jouanno and Christopher Martin, Jr. in *Flash Art,* November-December 2000.

* * *

Cai Guo-Qiang is best known for his use of explosives as the primary medium in large public performances. In the series ''Project for Extraterrestrials,'' produced since 1989, Cai creates predetermined configurations of crackling fire by means of controlled detonations. In Denmark in 1997, a 100-meter long paper kite in the shape of a dragon was outfitted with gunpowder fuses in ''Project for Extraterrestrials No. 29: Flying Dragon in the Heavens.'' As it was being blasted from head to tail, the dragon burst to life in an awesome conflagration illuminating the night sky. Lasting merely seconds, this and other pieces in the series challenge the concept of art as tangible and permanent objects. Cai describes the process as an attempt to ''rediscover eternity through the ephemeral'' and to awaken ''primordial emotion.'' Echoing new age mysticism, he also expresses the hope of using his art as a vehicle for communicating with alien life forms from outer space.

The adoption of fire, dragon, and other symbols of primordial forces relates to what the artist calls his ''subjective culture,'' something he equates with ancient Chinese belief systems. At the same time, he aspires to bring this ''subjective culture'' closer to the universal through science and technology. This simultaneous evocation of the past and the present (and the future) is firmly rooted in the discourse of Chinese modernism of the past century and in particular the desire to reconcile cultural self-preservation with modern progress. The multisensory art events at times assume the guise of scientific and physiological experiments. ''Project for Extraterrestrials No. 9: Fetus Movement II,'' staged in Germany in 1992, measured seismic activities and the artist's heart rate and brain waves as the earth flared up around him. In 1997, Cai incorporated foot reflexology and Chinese herbal medicine in an installation in the Museum of Contemporary Art in Chicago. The medicine dispensed from a state-of-the-art, American-made vending machine. Called ''A Cure When Ill, A Supplement When Healthy,'' this piece was another fusion of ancient Chinese practices with Western technology, emphasizing their mutually empowering utility.

The reliance on technology notwithstanding, aesthetics remains an important goal of Cai's art. He derives great pleasure from the formal beauty of his work, from the pure impact of sight and sound. He especially relishes the unpredictability inherent in the medium of explosives, an element captured in videos and in his ''gunpowder drawings.'' The latter, reminiscent of the highly expressive splashed-ink paintings in the Zen tradition, refers to the charred patterns on two-dimensional surfaces set on fire by gunpowder fuses. ''The Project for Projects,'' ''Project for Humankind,'' and ''The Vague Border at the Edge of Time/Space Project'' were among his ''gunpowder drawings,'' which he completed on folding screens in Japan during the early 1990s. In 1998 Issey Miyake invited Cai to collaborate on his line of *haute couture*, called Pleats Please. Serpentine imageries of the dragon were blasted onto the Japanese fashion designer's signature crinkled garments, which were then presented in a runway show at the Fondation Cartier pour l'art Contemporain. As a medium of destruction, explosives symbolize an iconoclastic reaction against the narrative constraints of social realism, the official style of art in Communist China between the 1960s and the 1980s. Cai's great achievement is his ability to turn destruction into creation, the fleeting into memorable statements rich with cultural significance.

—Aida-Yuen Wong

CALLE, Sophie

Nationality: French. **Born:** Paris, 1953. **Agent:** Donald Young Gallery, 933 W. Washington Blvd., Chicago, Illinois 60607; Paula Cooper Gallery, 534 West 21st St., New York, New York 10011.

Individual Exhibitions:

1981 Galerie Canon, Geneva
1983 Galerie Chantal Crousel, Paris
1984 Galerie Formi, Nîmes, France
1985 A.P.A.C., Nevers, France (catalog)
1986 Ecole des Beaux-Arts, Dunkerque, France
Centre d'Art Contemporain, Orléans, France
De Appel, Amsterdam, The Netherlands
1987 Centre d'Art de Flaine, Cluses, France (catalog)
Muséotrain du F.R.A.C. Limousin, Limoges, France
1988 Galeria Montenegro, Madrid, Spain
1989 Fred Hoffman Gallery, Los Angeles, California
1990 Institute of Contemporary Art, Boston, Massachusetts
Matrix Gallery, University of California at Berkeley
Galerie Crousel-Robelin, Paris
1991 *Sophie Calle: à suivre . . . ,* ARC Musée d'Art Moderne de la Ville de Paris (catalog)
Sophie Calle. . . in under skinnet, Kulturhuset, Stockholm, Sweden
1992 Donald Young Gallery, Seattle, Washington
Sophie Calle—Les Tombes, Galerie Sollertis, Toulouse, France
1993 *Last Seen,* Leo Castelli, New York
Sophie Calle: Proofs, Hood Museum of Art, Dartmouth College, Hannover, New Hampshire (catalog)
1994 *Sophie Calle: Romances,* Contemporary Arts Museum, Houston, Texas (catalog)
Absence, Museum Boymans van Beuningen, Rotterdam, The Netherlands
Absence, Musée Cantonal des Beaux-Arts, Lausanne, Switzerland (catalog)
Sophie Calle: Proofs, Contemporary Arts Center, Cincinnati, Ohio
1995 *Last Seen,* Portalen, Koge Bugt Kulturhus, Copenhagen, Denmark
Proofs, University Art Museum, University of California, Santa Barbara, California; travelled to Cleveland Center for Contemporary Art, Cleveland, Ohio; David Winton Bell Gallery, Brown University, Providence, Rhode Island
1996 *True Stories,* Tel Aviv Museum of Art, Israel
High Museum of Art, Atlanta, Georgia
1997 *Relatos,* Centre Cultural de la Fundación *la Caixa,* Barcelona, Spain (catalog)
Donald Young Gallery, Seattle, Washington
1998 *The Birthday Ceremony,* The Tate Gallery, London
Double Game, Site Gallery, London
1999 *Souvenirs de Berlin-Est,* Musée de Strasbourg, Strasbourg, France
Double Game, Camden Arts Centre, London
1999–2000 *Exquisite Pain,* Harra Museum of Contemporary Art, Tokyo
2000 *The True Stories of Sophie Calle,* Museum Fridericianum, Kassel, Germany; Staatliche Kunsthalle Baden-Baden, Baden-Baden, Germany
2001 *Double Game,* Paula Cooper Gallery, New York
Portraits d'artistes, Sophie Calle, Museé d'Art et d'Histoire de Provence, Grasse, France
Public Places—Private Spaces, The Jewish Museum, San Francisco

Selected Group Exhibitions:

1980 11th Biennale des jeunes, Paris
Une Idée en l'Air, The Clocktower, New York, and Fashion Moda, New York
1981 *Autoportraits,* Centre Georges Pompidou, Paris
Acquisitions Récentes des Collectionneurs Genevois, Musée d'Art et d'Histoire, Geneva, Switzerland
1983 *Il n'y a pas à proprement parler une histoire. . . ,* Maison de la Culture, Rennes, France
1984 *Nouvelles Acquisitions du F.N.A.C.,* Centre Georges Pompidou, Paris
La Chambre, Centre National de la Photographie, Palais de Tokyo, Paris
1987 *The New Who's Who,* Hoffman/Borman Gallery, Los Angeles, California
1988 *Art & Text,* First National Bank, Minneapolis, Minnesota
1989 Serpentine Gallery, London (toured England)
L'Invention d'un art, Centre Georges Pompidou, Paris
1990 *Autour de René Payant,* Musée d'Art Contemporain, Montréal, Canada
Sydney Biennale, Sydney, Australia
Seven Obsessions, Whitechapel Art Gallery, London
1991 *L'esprit nouveau: une exposition de l'art contemporain en France,* Musée d'Art Contemporain de Lyon, Lyon, France
Carnegie International, Pittsburgh, Pennsylvania
1992 *Doubletake: Collective Memory and Contemporary Art,* Hayward Gallery, London
1993 *Biennal Exhibition,* Whitney Museum of American Art, New York
Strange Hotel, Aarhus Kunstmuseum, Aarhus, Denmark
1994 *Some Went Mad. . . Some Ran Away,* Serpentine Gallery, London; Museum of Contemporary Art, Chicago, Illinois; Portalen, Copenhagen, Denmark
Taking Pictures, International Center of Photography, New York
1995 *Els límits del museu,* Fundació Antoni Tàpies, Barcelona, Spain
Photography and Beyond: New Expressions in France, The Boca Raton Museum of Art, Boca Raton, Florida; Museum of Contemporay Photography, Chicago, Illinois; Museum of Photographic Arts, San Diego, California; Bard College Museum, New York; The Israel Museum, Jerusalem
1996 *NowHere,* Louisiana Museum of Modern Art, Humlebaek, Denmark

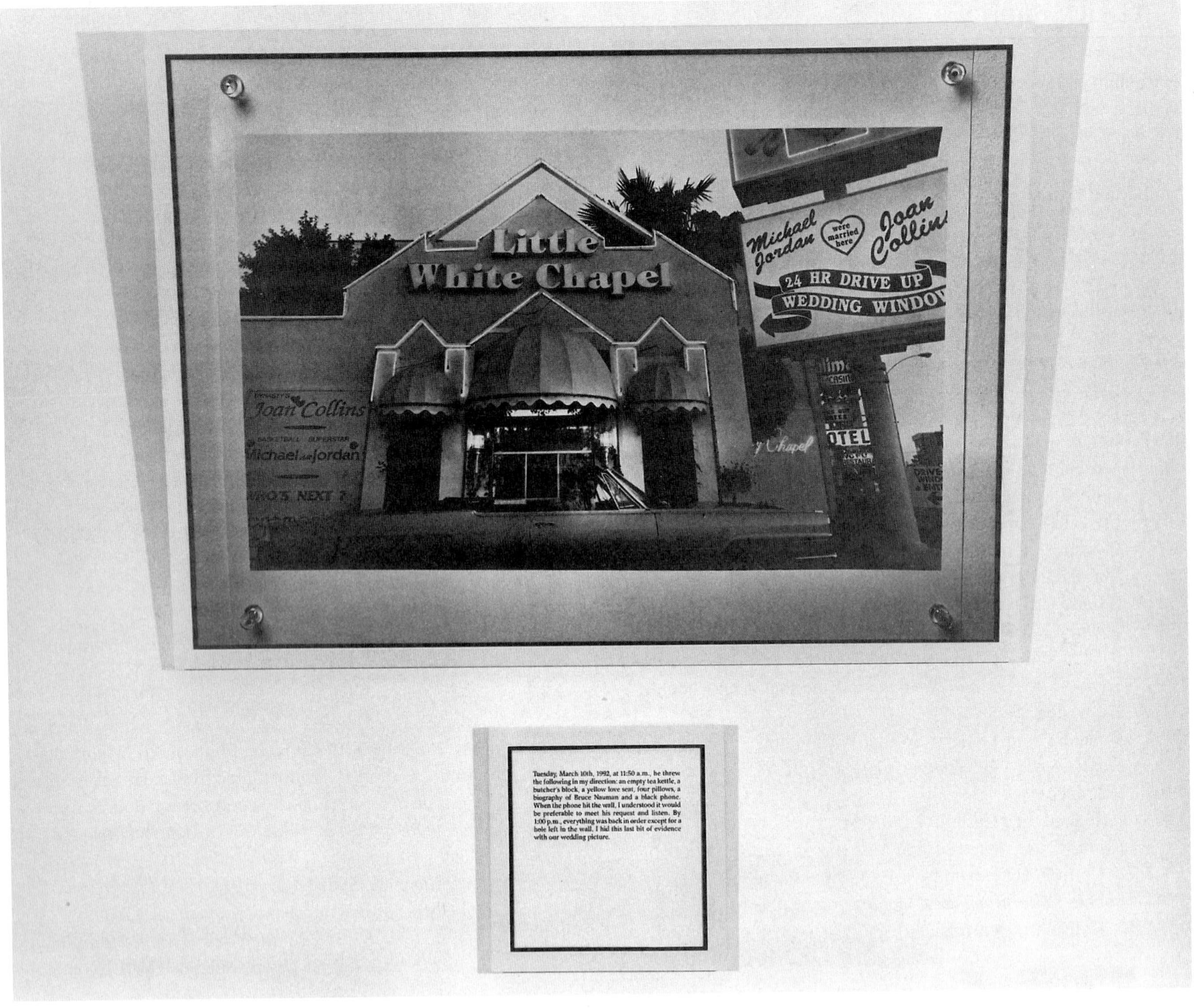

Sophie Calle: *Autobiographical Stories (The Dispute),* 1992. Photo by Eduardo Calderon. ©2001 Artists Rights Society (ARS), NY/ADAGP, Paris.

Imagined Communities, Oldham Art Gallery, Oldham; John Hansard Gallery; University of Southhampton: Firstsite at the Minorities, Colchester; Walsall Museum and Art Gallery; Royal Festival Hall, London; Gallery of Modern Art, Glasgow

Passions privées, Musée d'Art moderne de la Ville de Paris, Paris

Féminin-Masculin Cinéma, Centre Georges Pompidou, Paris

1997 *Veronica's Revenge: Photographs from the Lambert Art Collection,* Centre d'Art Contemporain, Geneva

Trade Routes: History and Geography, Johannesburg Biennale, Johannesburg, South Africa

1999 The Jewish Museum, New York

2000 *La Photographie Traversée, Résonances, Croisements, Disparitions,* XXXIèmes Rencontres Internationales de la Photographie, Arles, France

Around 1984: A Look at Art in the 80s, P.S.1, New York

2001 *Part Two (1988–1994),* Pat Hearn Gallery, New York

Video Screenings:

Kunsthalle, Vienna, Austria, 1993; Whitney Biennale, New York, 1993; Telluride Film Festival, Telluride, Colorado, 1993; New York Film Festival, New York, 1993; I.C.A., London, 1994; Festival of Belfort, France, 1994; Festival of Taormina, Italy, 1994; Tel Aviv Museum of Art, Tel Aviv, Israel, 1996.

Publications:

By CALLE: Books— *Suite venitienne/Please Follow Me,* Paris, Edition de l'etoile, Paris 1983; *Ecrit sur l'image,* Paris, Editions de l'Etoile 1984; *Des histoires Vrais,* Arles, Actes Sud/Galerie Sollertis 1994; *The Detachment,* Berlin, G&B Arts International/Arndt & Partner Gallery 1996; *Eruv,* Jerusalem Center for the Visual Arts

1996; *Sophie Calle: La Visite Guidee* (with an ''audioguide'' compact disc by Calle, with music by Laurie Anderson), Rotterdam, Museum Boymans-van Beuningen 1996; *Double-Jeux* (set of seven books, *De l'obeissance, Le rituel d'anniversaire, Les panoplies, A suivre. . . , L' hotel, Le carnet d' adresses, Gotham Handbook: New York, mode d'emploi*), Arles, Actes Sud 1998; *Double Game,* London, Violette Editions 1999; *L'Absence* (set of three books, *Souvenirs de Berlin-Est, Fantomes, Disparations*), Arles, Actes Sud 2000; *Appointment: Sophie Calle & Sigmund Freud,* London, Violette Editions 2001. **Articles—**''Room 25'' in *The Journal: A Contemporary Art Magazine,* Winter 1983; ''Provoking Arbitrary Situations Which Take on the Form of Rituals'' in *Art & Text,* March-May 1987; ''La Filature'' in *Autrement,* April 1988; ''Doublebind: An interview with Sophie Calle and Greg Shephard,'' by Lynne Cooke in *Art Monthly,* February 1993; ''Body Double,'' interview with Meghan Dailey in *Time Out New York,* 15–22 March 2001.

On CALLE: Books—*Sophie Calle: A Survey,* text by Deboar Irmas, Santa Monica, California, Fred Hoffman Gallery 1989; *Dislocations,* text by Robert Storr, New York, Museum of Modern Art 1991. **Articles—**''Le chichi de Sophie'' by Herve Guibert in *Le Monde,* April 1983; ''Sophie Calle: The Prying Eye'' by Robert L. Pincus in *Art in America,* October 1989; ''Sophie Calle's Uncertainty Principle'' by Luc Santé in *Parkett,* no. 36, 1993; ''Tombstones, Inscriptions, Photographs, Captions: The Hyperfication of Life and Death'' by Patrick Frey in *Parkett,* no. 36, 1993; ''Postcards to Sophie Calle'' by Joseph Grigely in *Parkett* no. 36, 1993; ''Paranoia by the Dashboard Light: Sophie Calle's and Gregory Shepard's 'Double Blind''' by Robert Beck in *Parkett,* no. 36, 1993; ''Sophie the Spy'' by Ginger Danto in *ArtNews,* May 1993; ''Double Game'' by Caryn Faure Walker in *Make: The Magazine of Women's Art,* no. 83, March-May 1999; ''Speeches of Display and the Museum Audioguides of Sophie Calle, Andrea Fraser, and Janet Cardiff'' by Jennifer Fisher in *Parachute,* no. 94, April/June 1999; ''Character Study'' by Yve-Alain Bois in *Artforum,* April 2000.

* * *

With no formal art training, conceptual artist Sophie Calle first came to the gallery world in 1979 through the suggestion of a critic and curator who had learned of Calle's obsessive-compulsive documentation of strangers' lives, whom she followed secretly through the streets of Paris. That year, feeling lost and directionless after returning to her now-unfamiliar hometown from seven years of travel abroad, she had begun trailing randomly chosen individuals in hopes of developing, like them, a comfortable routine. The photographs and notes she took on these excursions (in much the same style of Vito Acconci's earlier *Followings*) culminated in works such as her 1980 piece, *Suite Vénitienne.* In this piece, begun after she serendipitously met one of her city ''guides'' at a gallery opening, Calle secretly followed the subject on a trip to Venice. Using wigs to disguise herself and mirrored lens attachments to take photographs of her subject without his knowledge, she compiled her imagery and text from the two-week trip into an exhibition. She returned to Venice the following year for another fact-finding mission, this time serving as a chambermaid for three weeks at a hotel, during which time she documented and photographed the belongings of the guests whose rooms she cleaned. *L'Homme Au Carnet* (1983) took her spy ring to new extremes. After finding a lost address book on a Paris street, the artist photocopied its pages before sending it back to its owner, then began calling those within its pages, asking them for information about its owner, who had left the country to work in Norway. Calle then compiled her findings and photographs into monthly columns for the French newspaper *Liberation,* expanding outside participation in her work to include not only ''informants'' but a large, popular audience.

Recently, however, Calle has more frequently turned her spy lens toward herself, creating works in which the artist's own life and memories are presented for both the artist's and audience's scrutiny. *Double Blind* (1993), a video collaboration with her then-lover Gregory Shepard, documents each artist's perspective on their doomed romance during a cross-country trip across the United States. The exhibition and book *Double Game* (1998) repeats this *pas à deux,* this time through a call-and-response collaboration with writer Paul Auster, whose character Maria Turner in the novel *Leviathan* was inspired by Calle herself. The first section is a brief retrospective of the various Calle works that inspired Auster to invent Turner's in the novel; in the second section, Calle documents herself acting out her fictional alter-ego's performances from *Leviathan*; and in the third Calle documents her enactment of performances that Auster conceptualized specifically for her to enact for *Double Game. True Stories* (or *Personal Museum,* 1996) also opened up the artist's history as an object of study, this time in the form of a personal ''retrospective'' not of artworks she created but objects she accumulated that symbolize events in the artist's life—a shoe stolen as an adolescent, her first lover's bathrobe, a wig from her job as a stripper. The works are accompanied by intensely personal text on both the gallery walls and a script read by the artist on a personal audioguide, explaining the significance behind the objects. This interest in the museum as not only a repository for objects, but a site of memory and meaning led to the *Absence, Ghosts,* and *Last Seen* series, which address curatorial issues as well as the subject of loss, in their attempt to ''reconstruct'' removed or stolen objects from museum collections through wall texts comprised of museum visitors' and guards' memories of the works.

The significant constant in Calle's work is also that which inevitably makes its viewers most uneasy—her detached and highly formal presentation of the often unflattering and messy reality of life, even as she attempts to undermine that same reality through her cool, scientific tone. Although she superficially appears to master her subjects' or her own awkward lives, her efforts to do so are always thwarted—the detective is discovered, the chambermaid is caught peeping, the witness reveals too much—and the audience oscillates between cringing at the intimacy of her findings and at their own complicity in her voyeurism. Calle's dual role as an artist who both controls and is a victim to her own desire to look is often read as containing a feminist subtext, considering the Freudian belief in women's inability to take part in such scopophilic pleasures. By asserting the possibility of a female ''gaze'' in the economy of visual pleasure, Calle's work suggests the potential of women seizing its power.

—Maria Elena Buszek

CALZOLARI, Pier Paolo

Nationality: Italian. **Born:** Bologna in 1943. **Education:** Accademia di Belle Arti, Urbino, 1967. **Family:** Married, has one child. **Career:** Independent artist, Bologna, since 1967. **Agent:** Sonnabend Gallery,

420 West Broadway, New York, New York 10012, U.S.A. **Address:** Via San Felice 13, 40122 Bologna, Italy.

Individual Exhibitions:

1965 Sala Studio Bentivoglio, Bologna
1967 Sala Studio Bentivoglio, Bologna
1969 Galleria Sperone, Turin
1970 Galleria Sonnabend, Paris
Galleria Sperone, Turin
1971 Sonnabend Gallery, New York
Galerie Sonnabend, Paris
Modern Art Agencies, Naples
1973 Galerie Skulima, Berlin
1975 Galleria de Domizio, Pescara, Italy
1976 Galleria Toselli, Milan
1977 Galleria Tucci Russo, Turin
1978 Galleria San Ala, Milan
1979 Galerie Jean und Karen Bernier, Cologne
Galerie Tucci Russo, Cologne
1980 Stanze, Genazzano, Italy
LP 220, Turin
Galleria Paludetto, Turin
Cantieri Navali/Luigi De Ambrogi, Venice
Galleria di Capricorno, Naples
1981 Galerie Eric Fabre, Paris
Galerie Eric Schurr, Stuttgart
1982 Galerie Knoedler, Zurich
1983 Galleria Luigi De Ambrogi, Milan
1984 Galerie de France, Paris
Galerie Bernier, Athens
Galerie Pakesch, Vienna
1988 Barbara Gladstone Gallery, New York
1994 Jeu de Paume, Paris (retrospective; travelled to the Castello di Rivoli, Turin, and Musée d'Art Contemporain, Lausanne)
1999 Villa delle Rose, Bologne, Italy (catalog)
Galleria d'Arte Moderna di Bologna, Villa delle Rose, Italy

Selected Group Exhibitions:

1968 *Teatro delle Mostra,* Galleria La Tartaruga, Rome
1969 *Square Pegs in Round Holes,* Stedelijk Museum, Amsterdam
When Attitudes Become Form, Kunsthalle, Berne
1970 *Conceptual Art/Arte Poveral/Land Art,* Galleria Civica d'Arte Moderna, Turin
1971 *Biennale des Jeunes,* Paris
1974 *Projekt 74,* Cologne
1975 *Americans in Florence/Europeans in Florence,* Long Beach Museum of Art, California
1978 *Biennale,* Venice (and 1980)
1981 *A New Spirit in Painting,* Royal Academy of Art, London
1986 *Aspects of Italian Art 1960–85,* Kunstverein, Frankfurt

Publications:

On CALZOLARI: Books—*Calzolari,* exhibition catalog, by Alberto Boatta, Bologna 1967; *Teatro delle Mostra,* exhibition catalog, by Maurizio Calvesi, Rome 1968; *Documenta 5,* exhibition catalog, Kassel, West Germany 1974; *Pierpaolo Calzolari,* exhibition catalog with essay by Dieter Ronte, Vienna 1984; *Pier Paolo Calzolari,* exhibition catalog with text by Denys Zacharopoulos, Paris 1984; *Pier Paolo Calzolari* by Mario Bertoni and Bruno Cora, Turin 1999; *Pier Paolo Calzolari,* Hopefulmonster 1999. **Articles**—''Nuovo al Fabeto per Corpo e Materia'' by Tommaso Trini in *Domus* (Milan), no. 470, 1969, ''Pier Paolo Calzolari'' by Germano Celant in Studio International (London), July 1970; ''Pier Paolo Calzolari'' by Gregory Battcock in *Arts Magazine* (New York), February 1972; ''Pier Paolo Calzolari'' by Denys Ropp-Zacharopoulos in *Artistes* (Paris), October/November 1980; ''Pier Paolo Calzolari'' by Cecile Bourne in *Artfactum,* vol. 6, no. 31, November 1989-Jaunary 1990.

* * *

After some work in the field of ''poor art,'' in which he showed his main interest in ephemera and in fairytales (some significant works of the period were ''The Filter,'' ''Welcome to the Angel'' and ''Horoscope,'' 1967), Pier Paolo Calzolari moved on to painting. His first works in this field date from the 1970s. He did not abandon the object all at once; it is present as dramatic ''comment'' both in and outside the painting. He adds to the materiality of the painting, so that his all-embracing spatiality is also full of existential meanings. But what emerges most of all is the grandeur of the surface, abounding in grotesque multicoloured material. There is a sort of love-hate relationship between the object, essentially poor, and the positively opulent painting, as if the artist were struggling against the imaginativeness of his experience. For Pier Paolo Calzolari, art proceeds by metamorphoses; it faces destiny rather than the project, so that his work is always somewhat unfinished. His art is above all possessed of a violent gesturality, which unites differing significances; enigmatic symbols of a vitality that breaks down the whole surrounding reality, which is constantly changing and so seems unpredictable. Thus the artist is the one who meets reality in the space of an essay open to the shifting play of the elements between object and painting. If in his ''poor art'' he was exalting the contradiction of the ephemeral, in his recent painting he demonstrates the deflagration of the material of art. His fulfillment is achieved only in the gesture, through which he completes the picture's destiny.

Calzolari's painting distorts itself. A material in expansion and contraction dramatizes its striking quality, which takes in also the space outside the picture. The material of painting consists of paints—soft, mellow paints, responding to the light. It is their coagulation that is informal. The material colours are firmly obedient to the urgency of the gesture.

In his big pictures Calzolari's creative gesture has a primordial fury which breaks up the material, and with it any possible figuration. The abstraction is powerful, incontrovertible, hermetically closed/opened. It brings out obvious surprise effects in the wide surface of the picture. Calzolari thus comes near to a painting made by continual, striking attacks which break down the growth of the abstraction. It is only in appearance that this approaches the informal. But Calzolari is not a post-informal artist, and he possesses a creative density too firm to be channelled into the flow of the new painting. If anything he is looked on as the initiator of a ''diverse'' materiality of painting. In fact, his work, at once noble and terrifying, shows how painting can be liberated (especially from the material point of view). A movement prevails on the surface that spreads out in all directions (interrupted only by external elements—a dagger, for instance, thrust into the canvas). Calzolari is thus a ''visionary'' artist who materializes the secret magma contained in the creative gesture.

—Italo Mussa

Calzolari's first major retrospective debuted at the Jeu de Paume, Paris, in 1994. The exhibition, which spanned thirty years of the artist's career, featured paintings, sculptures, photographs of happenings and action-performances, and mixed-media installations, such as a margarine-smeared staircase bearing neon citations. Not having seen some of his works in nearly thirty years, the artist expressed some wariness about encountering them again. However, after seeing his collected works in Paris, Calzolari still found them ''very fresh and vital'' and ''light and lyric, but without being sentimental or melodramatic.''

—Beth Duncan

CAMPUS, Peter

Nationality: American. **Born:** New York City, 19 May 1937. **Education:** Ohio State University, Columbus, 1955–60, B.Sc. 1960. **Military Service:** United States Army, 1960–62. **Career:** Associated with artist Robert Grosvenor; began informal art studies, New York, 1960–62. Worked as production assistant and film editor, with William Shatner, on the television series *For The People,* Plantus Productions, New York; *Trials of O'Brien,* with Peter Falk, Filmways Inc., New York, 1962–70. Influenced by the work of Ian Wilson, Charles Ross, Robert Smithson, Nancy Holt, Yvonne Rainer and Joan Jonas, New York, 1962–70. First art works, New York, 1970. Video Consultant, Education Department, Metropolitan Museum of Art, New York, 1970–72. Instructor, Massachusetts Institute of Technology, Cambridge, 1976–80; Rhode Island School of Design, Providence, 1982–83. **Awards:** Guggenheim Fellowship, 1975–76; Advanced Visual Studies Fellowship, Massachusetts Institute of Technology, Cambridge 1975–76; National Endowment for the Arts Grant, 1976. **Address:** c/o Paula Cooper Gallery, 155 Wooster St., New York, NY 10012-3159.

Individual Exhibitions:

1972 Bykert Gallery, New York
1973 Bykert Gallery, New York
1974 *Closed Circuit Video,* Everson Museum of Art, Syracuse, New York
1975 Bykert Gallery, New York
1976 Leo Castelli Gallery, New York
Hayden Gallery, Massachusetts Institute of Technology, Cambridge
Projects Gallery, Museum of Modern Art, New York
1977 The Kitchen, New York
Ohio State University, Columbus
1978 Whitney Museum, New York
Sarah Lawrence College, Bronxville, New York
Atlantic Gallery, Boston
1979 Akron Art Institute, Ohio
Paula Cooper Gallery, New York
Protetch-McIntosh Gallery, Washington, D.C.
Kölnischer Kunstverein, Cologne
Neuer Berliner Kunstverein, West Berlin
1980 Centre Pompidou, Paris
1981 Paula Cooper Gallery, New York
McIntosh-Drysedale Gallery, New York
1982 Paula Cooper Gallery, New York
1983 Paula Cooper Gallery, New York
Hayden Gallery, Massachusetts Institute of Technology, Cambridge (with David Deutsch)
1985 Paula Cooper Gallery, New York
1986 Paula Cooper Gallery, New York
1987 Albright College, Reading, Pennsylvania (travelled to the Institute of Contemporary Art, Philadelphia)
1988 Whitney Museum of American Art, New York
1990 *Peter Campus: Slide Projections,* Stadtisches Museum Abteiberg, Monchengladbach, Germany
1995 *Recent Work,* Paula Cooper Gallery, New York (catalog)
1997 *Peter Campus By Degrees,* Paula Cooper Gallery, New York (catalog)
1998 Paula Cooper Gallery, New York

Selected Group Exhibitions:

1973 *Circuit: A Video Invitational,* Everson Museum of Art, Syracuse, New York (toured the United States and travelled to the Kunstverein, Cologne)
1975 *Bienal,* Sao Paulo
1976 *Autogeography,* Whitney Museum, New York
1977 *Documenta 6,* Kassel, West Germany
1978 *Biennale,* Venice
1979 *Art on Paper 1979,* Weatherspoon Art Gallery, University of North Carolina, Greensboro
1980 *Lynda Benglis/Jon Borofsky/Peter Campus/Michael Hurson,* Paula Cooper Gallery, New York
1982 *PostMinimalism,* Aldrich Museum of Contemporary Art, Ridgefield, Connecticut
1984 *Content: A Contemporary Focus 1974–84,* Hirshhorn Museum, Washington, D.C.
1987 *Photography and Art 1946–86,* Los Angeles County Museum of Art (travelled to Fort Lauderdale, Florida; Flushing, New York)
1988 *Identity: Representations of the Self,* Whitney Museum of American Art, New York
1991 Carnegie Museum of Art, Pittsburgh (traveling exhibit)
1996 *New Art on Paper: Acquired with Funds from the Hunt Manufacturing Co. 1989–1995,* Philadelphia Museum of Art
1997 *UTZ: A Collected Exhibition,* Lennon, Weinberg Gallery, New York (catalog)
Travel & Leisure, Paul Cooper Gallery, New York (catalog)
2000 *Alternative Realities,* Laurence Miller Gallery, New York

Publications:

By CAMPUS: Articles—statement in *Peter Campus: Closed Circuit Video,* exhibition catalog, Syracuse, New York 1974; in *Studio International* (London), May/June 1976; essay in *Peter Campus,* exhibition catalog, Cologne 1979; in *Studio International* (London), no. 1008, 1985; interview with John Hanhardt in *Bomb,* no. 68, Summer 1999.

On CAMPUS: Books—*Peter Campus: Closed Circuit Video,* exhibition catalog, with an introduction by Jane Harithas, essay by David A. Ross, Syracuse, New York 1974; *Video Art,* exhibition catalog, by Susan Delehanty, Philadelphia 1975; *Peter Campus,* exhibition catalog, Cologne 1979; *5 Artists, 5 Technologies,* exhibition catalog, Grand Rapids, Michigan 1979; *The Elusive Image,* exhibition catalog, Minneapolis 1979; *Peter Campus Photographs/David Deutsch Paintings and Drawings,* exhibition catalog, with essay by Kathy Halbreich and Katy Klein, Cambridge, Massachusetts 1983. **Articles—**''Video Is Being Invented'' by Bruce Kurtz in *Arts Magazine* (New York), December 1972; ''Fields: Peter Campus'' by Bruce Kurtz in *Arts Magazine* (New York), May 1973; ''Video Art by Peter Campus'' by John Perreault in the *Village Voice* (New York), 11 October 1973; ''Inference and Actuality'' by Robert Pincus-Witten in *Projected Images,* exhibition catalog, Minneapolis 1974; ''Beyond Flashing Lights'' by Mike Steele in *Art News* (New York), December 1974; ''Epistemological TV'' by Joseph Lorber in *Art Journal* (New York), Winter 1974–75; ''Video: The Aesthetics of Narcissism'' by Rosalind Krauss in *October* (New York), Spring 1976; ''The Ins and Outs of Video'' by Jeff Perrone in *Artforum* (New York), June 1976; ''About Faces: The New Work of Peter Campus'' by Roberta Smith in *Art in America* (New York), March/April 1977; ''Galleries: A Dark Series Portraits'' by Benjamin Forgery in the *Washington Star,* 28 March 1979; ''Inside Out: Peter Campus'' by Ingrid Sischy in *Artforum* (New York), March 1985; ''Peter Campus'' by Hearne Pardee in *Arts Magazine* (New York), May 1985; ''Durational Perception: The Art of Peter Campus'' by Hearne Pardee in *Arts Magazine,* vol. 63, no. 4, December 1988; ''Peter Campus: Faces'' in *Aperture,* no. 114, Spring 1989; ''The Video Public Sphere'' by David Joselit in *Art Journal,* Summer 2000.

*

I work in both closed circuit video installations and video tape. The close circuit installations include viewer participation where his/her image is projected in front of him/her in some altered state. This work concerns itself with: projections and confrontation of self, light, space and accumulations in time. My videotapes generally have me performing some activity that continuously alters the image. These tapes are more concerned with narrative, utilizing questions of figure-ground, surface, illusion, time and space.

—Peter Campus

* * *

Peter Campus is an artist who knows how to create psychologically charged visual fields. After working in commercial films and television, he decided in the late 1960s to change careers and become an artist. Video remained the dominant concern during the 1970s. He produced both videotapes and video environments in which a superbly precise and efficient mastery of this electronic technique was channeled to the creative investigations of the perceptual and emotional politics of seeing and knowing the self. In each medium time is an active and aggressive element.

Structured episodically, the videotapes, though of short duration, took the individual as the subject. Many of them featured a deep, dark spatially ambiguous background before which close-ups of faces, often in emotively laden split and repetitive structures, were highlighted. ''Three Transitions'' (1973) and ''East Ended Tapes'' (1976), both six minutes in length, are examples. In the video environments, time is a direct factor of the viewing, which, in turn, depends on the presence and participation of the audience. Usually composed of a basic set-up consisting of one or more video cameras and inflared lights, projectors and monitors in a darkened room, they are closed-circuit installations, ''closed'' or activated by the viewer's entry into the boundaries of the designated situation. Once in a camera view, the viewer, in essence, the viewer's image, is the piece. Each environment/installation is designed to reveal different aspects of the complex relationship involving the self and the image of the self. The image of the self is manipulated, for example in ''Interface'' (1972) to offer a confrontation between the projected video image and a reflected mirror image, and in ''Num,'' ''lus'' and ''aen'' (1976–77) the imagery consisted of enlarged, expressionistically shadowed and inverted pictures of the viewer's head.

In 1979, a projected slide-piece signalled a turning away from video towards photography. This development was a natural one dictated by the work in response to a lessening interest in time and a growing interest in what Campus has called ''tangible image.'' Photography has been the central concern since 1980.

In the silverpoint photographs he has done of various landscape subjects, reality is being reconstituted in the concreteness of the illusion these images give. Campus' careful modulation of light and dark values allows him to create a composition that conveys the material essence of forms. In Slow Tide (1987), a close-up of a rock on a pebble-covered ground, the luminous intensity of the surface is suggestive of metaphorical concerns.

—Ronny Cohen

CANE, Louis

Nationality: French. **Born:** Beaulieu-sur-Mer, Alpes-Maritimes, 13 December 1943. **Education:** Ecole Nationale des Arts Décoratifs, Nice, 1961–64; attends Ecole Nationale Superieure des Arts Décoratifs, Paris, from 1962; attends Ecole Nationale Supérieure des Beaux-Arts de Paris, from 1968. **Career:** Independent painter, Paris, since 1968. Co-founder and director of the review *Peinture,* Paris, from 1971. **Agent:** Galerie 14, 14 rue des Beaux Arts, 75006 Paris, France. **Address:** 37 rue d'Enghein, 75010 Paris, France.

Individual Exhibitions:

1969 Galerie Givaudan, Paris
1970 Galerie Daniel Templon, Paris
1971 Galerie Yvon Lambert, Paris
Galleria Francoise Lambert, Milan
1972 Galerie Yvon Lambert, Paris
1973 Galerie Daniel Templon, Paris
Institute of Contemporary Arts, London
Galleria Daniel Templon, Milan
Galleria Lia Rumma, Naples
1974 Galerie Rudolf Zwirner, Cologne
Galleria del Cortile, Rome
1975 Galerie D., Brussels

Louis Cane: *Roses Manet,* 1994. Photo by Laurent Lecat. ©2001 Artists Rights Society (ARS), NY/ADAGP, Paris.

Galerie Daniel Templon, Paris
Galleria Daniel Templon, Milan
Galerie Konrad Fischer, Dusseldorf
1976 Galerie Bischofberger, Zurich
Louisiana Museum, Humlebaek, Denmark
Musée d'Art Contemporain, Montreal
Kunstverein, Franfurt
1977 Galerie Daniel Templon, Paris
Galleria Spagnoli, Florence
Leo Castelli Gallery, New York
Galerie Arnessen, Copenhagen
Centre Georges Pompidou, Paris
1978 Galleria del Milione, Milan
Galerie Daniel Templon, Paris
Louis Cane 1968–1978: The First 10 Years of a Painter, Israel Museum, Jerusalem
Art 9'78, Basle
Kunsthalle, Bielefeld, West Germany
1979 Galerie Art in Progress, Dusseldorf
Galerie Art Line, The Hague
Galerie Charles Kriwin, Brussels
Musée d'Art Moderne, Strasbourg
Galleria Mantra, Turin
Galerie Daniel Templon, Paris
1980 Galerie Art in Progress, Munich
Galerie Artline, La Haye, Netherlands
1981 Galerie Daniel Templon, Paris
Galerie Ressle, Stockholm
Galerie Art in Progress, Dusseldorf
F.I.A.C., Grand Palais, Paris
1982 Leo Castelli Gallery, New York
Galerie Art in Progress, Munich
Inoue Gallery, Tokyo
Ecole National Superieure des Beaux-Arts, Paris
1983 Galerie J. Giraud, Toulouse, France
Fondation Maeght, St. Paul de Vence, France
1986 Galerie Reckermann, Cologne
1987 *Les inédits de Louis Cane,* Musée de Toulon
1988 Galerie Gill Favre, Lyon
Galerie des Ponchettes, Nice
Galerie de la Gare, Bonnieux
1989 Galerie Beaubourg, Paris
Galerie Haranobu Okada, Japan
1990 Chapelle Saint Louis de la Salpétrière, Paris
Galerie Reckermann, Cologne
Musée Saint-Roch, Issoudun
1991 Fondation Deutsch Belmont, Lausanne, Switzerland
Museo Municipal de Bellas Artes, Santander, Spain
Galerie Bjorn Olsson, Stockholm
1992 *Manifeste,* Centre Georges Pompidou, Paris
Tel Aviv Museum of Art, Israel
National Hungarian Gallery, Budapest, Hungary
1993 Museum der Bildenden Künste, Leipzig, Germany
Salon de Mars, Paris
Centre Culturel de Boulogne-Billancourt
1994 Musée de l'Orangerie, Jardin des Tuileries, Paris
Salon de Mars, Paris
Institut Français, Athens
1995 Musée d'Art Contemporain, Cambrai
Kawamura Memorial Museum, Japan
Municipal Museum, Kokkaido, Japan
F.I.A.C., Paris
Palais des Congrès, Paris
Galerie 29, New York
1996 Salon de Mars, Paris
Galerie Patricia Dorfman, Paris
Manoir de Cologny, Geneva
1997 Musée d'Art Moderne de Skopié, Macedonia
Galerie Hélène Trintignan, Monpelier
Galerie Rachelin-Lemarie, Paris
1998 Galerie Le rire bleu, Figeac
Galerie Piltzer, Paris
1999 *Décoration,* Musée Tecla Sala, Barcelona
Galerie ARKOS, Clermont-Ferrand
2000 Museu de Arte Moderna, Sao Paulo, Brazil
Centro Cultural Banco do Brazil, Rio de Janeiro, Brazil

Selected Group Exhibitions:

1968 *Salle Rouge pour le Vietnam,* Musée d'Art Moderne de la Ville, Paris
1969 *ABC Production,* Maison de la Culture, Montpellier, France
1971 *Biennale,* Paris
1973 *Réalite-Réalite,* Musée de Saint Etienne, France *Biennale,* Paris
1975 *Fundamental Painting,* Stedelijk Museum, Amsterdam
Europalia, Palais des Beaux-Arts, Brussels

1976 *Europa-America,* Bologna
1977 *Documenta 6,* Kassel, West Germany
1979 *Biennale,* Sydney
1991 Musée d'Art contemporain de Saint-Etienne
1993 Musée Denys Puech, Rodez, France (toured Japan)
1995 Musée de la Chartreuse, Douai, France
1998 Musée de Jeu de Paume, Paris
1999 *Les années Supports-Surfaces,* Maison de la Culture, Namur, Belgium (toured)
Le seuil de Peinture, Centre d'exposition *Della Rocca Paolina,* Province of Perugia, Italy
2000 Museum of Contemporary Art, Tokyo

Collections:

Centre Georges Pompidou, Paris: Musée d'Art Moderne de la Ville, Paris; Musée de Saint-Etienne, France; Musée de Grenoble, France; Louisiana Museum, Humlebaek, Denmark; Kunstmuseum, Basle; Ghent Museum; Musée d'Art Contemporain, Montreal; Museum of Modern Art, New York.

Publications:

By CANE: Book—*Paroles sur l'Art Moderne,* exhibition catalog with Camille Saint-Jacques, St. Paul de Vence 1983. **Articles—** ''Pour un programme théorique pictural,'' with Daniel Dezeuze, in *Peinture* (Paris), June 1971; ''Le peintre sans modéle'' and ''Vivela Chine révolutionnaire'' in *Peinture* (Paris), January 1972; ''Louis Cane,'' interview with Catherine Millet, in *Art Press* (Paris), March/April 1973; ''Sur le sol, pliée, avec lacouleur,'' introduction to a Don Judd interview with John Coplans, and Sur la peinture d'Alain Kirili'' in *Peinture* (Paris), April 1973; ''La Mort de Germanicus'' and ''Sur James Bishop'' in *Peinture* (Paris), February 1974; ''Marc Devade, piongée dans la couleur'' in *Art Press* (Paris), February 1974; ''Robert Ryman, peinture à tempera'' in *Art Press* (Paris), March/April 1975; ''Peinture fondamentale, une exposition au Stedelijk Museum d'Amsterdam'' in *Art Press* (Paris), July/August 1975; Le métier de peintre'' in *Peinture* (Paris, November 1975; ''James Bishop: Savoir le prés pour voir le loin'' in *Art Press* (Paris), March/April 1976; L'Hétérogenesous gene'' in *Peinture* (Paris), March 1977; ''A propos de Rubens'' in *Art Press* (Paris), January 1978; ''Philipe Sollers: Interview'' in *Peinture* (Paris), May 1978; ''Un peintre en analyse,'' interview with Catherine Millet, in *Art Press* (Paris), January 1979; ''Ce qui ira'' in *Skira Annuel,* Geneva 1980; ''L'âge mur de l'avant-garde,'' interview with Catherine Millet, in *Art Press* (Paris), January 1981; ''Cy Twombly'' in *Art Press* (Paris), March 1981; ''L'Art Moderne'' in *Spirali* (Milan), June 1982; ''Yves Klein'' in *art Press* (Paris), February 1983.

On CANE: Articles—''Notes sur un peintre opérant dans de beaux draps'' by Marc Devade and ''Les toiles systématiquement temponnées de Louis Cane'' by Daniel Dezeuze in *Louis Cane,* exhibition catalog, Paris, 1971; ''L'intervention picturale de Louis Cane'' by Marcelin Pleynet in *Art Vivant* (Paris), April 1971; Quelques problèmes de la peinture moderne: Louis Cane'' by Marcelin Pleynet in *Louis Cane,* exhibition catalog, Paris 1972; ''Forme et couleur découpées de la peinture de Louis Cane'' by Marcelin Pleynet in *Art Press* (Paris), March/April 1973; ''Louis Cane'' by Claire Stoulig in *Stoulig in Cimaise* (Paris), May-August 1974; *Louis Cane,* exhibition catalog, with text by Marcelin Pleynet, Paris 1977; *Louis Cane 1968–1978: The First 10 Years of a Painter,* exhibition catalog, with interview by Michael Pauseback, Jerusalem 1978; ''La rupture de l'avant-grade'' by Catherine Millet in *Connaissance des Arts* (Paris), January 1981; ''Report from New York: And Now—A French Wave'' by Ratliff Carter in *Art in America* (New York), September 1982; ''Louis Cane: la peinture et la loi'' by Michel Brandeau in *Art Press* (Paris), no. 70, 1983.

*

To tell the truth, I think that for the most part the type of painting which can be seen in galleries today is deliberately deluding itself. Sunk in ignorance, it pretends there is nothing to know. It shows nothing because there is nothing to show. Simplicity turns out to be over-simplification.

It is a fact, and I think a true one, that drawing and lines result in composition: i.e., a set of forms well adjusted together and also adjusted into a kind of unitary relation with my desire to paint. Adjusted so that the desire I cast into it will correspond to the desire I expect from it. In this sense, composition can't be but a compromise; even unfinished paintings cannot invalidate this. As a ''composer'' I am a subject who is calling upon and summoning himself as Another to be identified in the lines of the drawing. And I call myself into it to thwart somehow, to undo what unconsciously forces me to be me and not, if only for a moment, possessing the other. Drawing which orders form is the first stage in a process of identification of this other whom painting displays. More precisely, I think I have a certain conception of painting but finally ''Painting'' is nothing else than a certain conception I have of the ''other.'' The ''other'' could be the recollection of something: I remember an old art teacher used to give me the following piece of advice: ''Keep hold of forms with the lines and you'll have composition!''

The simple question today is to know whether our painter's means and ways, in a word our painter's craft, correspond to the end of naturalism or whether in the making of abstract painting, there's not still a conception of painting which comes too close to the old naturalist school. In his notes on painting, Shi Tao (1641–1717) says about receptivity and knowledge that receptivity comes first and knowledge follows. I think that Shi Tao is right. He is right not only because his statement has the truthfulness of practice but also because he seems to suggest that I give more attention to my own receptivity so that my knowledge be not limited to the knowledge of others. This is how, for me, time spent painting can become time spent learning.

—Louis Cane

* * *

The fundamental characteristic of every *avant-garde* movement has always been the trying out of new languages, of unfamiliar cultural situations, the production of subjects or ideas that, in their deepest significance, would violate the traditional orders to which the artistic experience of the time was subject. ''A drive towards the new'' is a phrase often used to describe this characteristic, with its significant Freudian references. For a painter like Louis Cane, the *avant-garde* coincided with the Support/Surface period, during which material features of painting were subjected to a rigorous critical-ideological analysis which tended to disclose things in them which had been kept quiet but which, for that very reason, were still operative. Later, the French artist—whose work as a painter has a strong background of theory—took up the history of art as a subject on which to set down his working reflections. This history became a really authoritative source, taking in all the multiple and contradictory interpretations of current artistic practice; the work was based essentially on an inextricable round of reading (of the sources) and writing (the production of a new authoritative text on painting). The architecture of Brunelleschi, 14th and 15th century Tuscan painting and the non-objective painting of the United States were the great reference points of these masterly paintings, evident in the pictorial quality and in the formal layout, always complex and thick with references.

More recently, making a decision which, for him, evidently cloaked a great, profound and ''philosophical'' significance, Louis Cane rediscovered the figure, the image, and there appeared his series of women in which we can see the influence of Picasso and Giaconmetti, of De Kooning and of primitive rock paintings. Here Man appears in his essential pristine nakedness—the anthropological body untouched by any cultural transformation belonging to the times. He appears as in Matisse (though the two men's methods and rhythms of composition are fundamentally different), isolated in a solitary expanse of colour which is neither background nor surroundings, and he assumes primitive, sometimes indecent, poses. But it is still the pictorial significance that is final and conclusive, arising as it does from the history of art which Louis Cane is still rewriting, taking on himself the responsibilities of the present time and its dramatic, neurotic conflicts.

—Massimo Carboni

CANOGAR, Rafael (Gomez)

Nationality: Spanish. **Born:** Toledo, 17 May 1935. **Education:** Madrid High School, 1945–50; studied with the painter Daniel Vazquez-Diaz, in Madrid, 1948–53. **Family:** Married Ann Jane McKenzie in 1960; children Susana, Daniel, Diego and Robert. **Career:** Independent painter, Madrid, since 1956. Founder-member, El Paso group, Madrid, 1957. Visiting Professor of Art, Mills College, Oakland, California, 1965–66; Guest artist, Tamarind Lithography Workshop, Los Angeles, 1969. **Awards:** Third Prize, *2nd International Festival of Painting,* Gagnes-sur-Mer, France, 1969; Grand Prize, *Bienal,* Sao Paulo, 1971; D.A.A.D. Artist in Residence, Berlin, 1972 and 1974; Grand Prize, International Triennial of Painting, Sofia, 1982; National Prize for Fine Arts, Madrid, 1982. Chevalier L'Ordre des Arts et des Lettres, France, 1985; Cross of the Order of Isabel la Catolica, Madrid 1991; Member of the San Fernando Royal Academy of Fine Arts, Madrid, 1996. **Address:** Menéndez Pelayo 11 duplicado, 3 Izda, 28009 Madrid, Spain.

Individual Exhibitions:

1954 Galeria Altamira, Madrid
1955 Galeria Fernando Fe, Madrid
1956 Galerie Arnaud, Paris
Galleria Numero, Florence
1959 Galleria L'Attico, Rome
Galleria Blu, Milan
1960 Galerie Aujourd'hui, Brussels
1961 Galleria L'Attico, Rome
Galerie Rive Gauche, Paris
1962 Galerie Anne Abels, Cologne
Galleria Naviglio, Milan
Galleria Il Cancello, Bologna
1963 Galerie Rive Gauche, Paris
Galeria Biosca, Madrid
1964 Galleria L'Attico, Rome
1965 Galeria Juana Mordo, Madrid
1966 Mills College Art Gallery, Oakland, California
De Young Memorial Museum, San Francisco
Salle Communali del Palazzo Constanzi, Trieste
Galleria 3, Pescara, Italy
1967 Bertha Schaefer Gallery, New York
1968 Galeria Grises, Bilbao, Spain
Galeria Juana Mordo, Madrid
1969 Silvan Simone Gallery, Los Angeles
Deson-Zaks Gallery, Chicago
Galleria Senior, Rome

Rafael Canogar: *El Caminante,* 1973. ©2001 Artists Rights Society (ARS), NY/VEGAP, Madrid.

Galerie Withofs, Brussels
Galleria Sanluca, Bologna
1970 Galerie Klang, Cologne
Galerie Poll, Berlin
1971 Istituto di Storia dell'Arte, Parma
Galeria Tolmo, Toledo
1972 Museo Espanol de Arte Contemporaneo, Madrid
Galeria Rayuela, Madrid
Silvan Simone Gallery, Los Angeles
Galleria Naviglio, Milan
Galerie Poll, Berlin
Galeria Punto, Valencia
Galeria Adria, Barcelona
Galeria Luzaro, Bilbao
1973 Galeria Alcoiart, Altea, Spain
Galeria Juana Mordo, Madrid
1974 Galeria Arte-Contacto, Caracas
Galerie Poll, Berlin
Galleria Bocchi, Milan
Galleria Bocchi, Parma, Italy
Galleria Brazia Bosser, Turin
1975 Silvan Simone Gallery, Los Angeles
Musée d'Art Moderne de la Ville, Paris
Sonia Henie Foundation, Oslo
Kunsthalle, Lund, Sweden
Galleria d'Art San Michele, Brescia, Italy
Pirkanpohja-75, Nykytaidetta, Ah-Tarissa, Finland
1976 Galeria Juana Mordo, Madrid
Galerie Christel, Stockholm
1977 Galerie Nordenhake, Malmo, Sweden
Galerie Nordenhake Rykken, Oslo
Galerie Benet Malmgram, Gothenburg, Sweden
1978 Galerie Nouvelles Images, The Hague
Galeria Punto, Valencia
1979 Galleria Esse Arte, Rome
Galeria San Diego, Bogota
1980 Galeria 3i5, Gerona, Spain
Colegio Oficial de Arquitectos, Canary Islands
Sala Luzan, Zaragoza, Spain
1981 Casa Municipal de Cultura, Aviles, Spain
1982 National Library of Spain, Madrid
Galeria Punto, Valencia
Caja de Ahorros, Alicante (travelled to Murcia)
1983 Casa de los Caballos, Caceres, Spain
Galeria Cadaques, Gerona, Spain
1984 Contemporary Art Museum, Madrid
Galeria Juana Mordo, at *Art 15/84,* Basel
1985 Galeria Bronda, Helsinki
Galeria Sala Gaspar, Barcelona
Galerie Poll, West Berlin
1986 Galeria Cadaques, at *Arco 86,* Madrid
Municipal Cultural Centre, Alcoy, Valencia (retrospective)
1987 Paris Art Center, Paris (retrospective; travelled to Museum Bochum, West Germany)
Bochun Museum, Alemania (retrospective)
1988 Palacio de Almudi, Murcia (retrospective)
1990 Museo de Bellas Artes de Bilbao (retrospective)
Galleria Civica d'Arte Moderna, Palazzo Dei Diamanti, Ferrara, Italy
1995 Galeria Barcelona, Barcelona
1997 Centro Cultural Casa del Cordon, Caja de Burgos, Burgos
Museo de Santa Cruz, Toledo (retrospective)
1999 Centro de las Artes, Alcorcon, Madrid
2000 Tardor Cultural, Villafamés

Selected Group Exhibitions:

1955 *3rd Biennale Hispano-Americana,* Barcelona
1956 *Biennale,* Venice
1959 *13 Peintres Espagnois,* Musée Des Arts Décoratifs, Paris
1960 *Junge Spanische Kunst,* Kunsthalle, Berne (toured Europe)
1971 *Bienal,* Sao Paulo
1973 *Tra Rivolta e Rivoluzione,* Museo Civico, Bologna
1977 *Exposition International des Arts Plastiques,* Modern Art Museum, Belgrade
1980 *Printed Art: A View of Two Decades,* Museum of Modern Art, New York
1984 *Arte Espanol Contemporaneo,* Pinacoteca Nacional, Athens
1986 *Spagna: 75 anni di protagonisti nell'arte,* Villa Malpensata, Lugano, Switzerland
1989 *Spanish Masterpieces of the 20th Century,* Seibu Museum of Art, Tokyo
1991 *ART'91,* Galeria BAT, Basilea
ARCO, Galeria Punto, Madrid
1992 *ARCO,* Galeria Punto, Madrid
1993 *ARCO,* Galeria Punto, Madrid
1997 *40 Aniversario Grupo El Paso,* Centro Cultural Caixavigo, Vigo
1998 *El Paso, 1957–1960, Antologica,* Museo Gustavo de Maeztu, Caja de Pamplona
1999 *Canogar-Feito,* Galería Darío Ramos, Oporto
2000 *Arte '92 Itinerario di un decennio,* Milan

Selected Collections:

Galleria Civica d'Arte Moderna, Turin; Galleria Civica d'Arte Moderna, Bologna; Museo de Arte Contemporaneo, Barcelona; Museo de Arte Contemporaneo, Seville; Contemporaneo de la Universidad, Sao Paulo; Staatliche Museum, Berlin; Haags Gemeentemuseum, The Hague; Carnegie Institute, Pittsburgh; Museum of Modern Art, New York; Art Institute of Chicago; Carnegi Institute, Pittsburgh, Pennsylvania.

Publications:

On CANOGAR: Books—*Rafael Canogar by Enrico Crispolti, Madrid 1959; Neue Kunst nach 1954* by U. Apollonio, Cologne 1959; *Canogar* by J. Dypreau, Cirlot and others, Rome 1962; *Canogar* by J. Castro Arines, Barcelona 1964; *Pintura Espanola: La Ultima Vanguardia* by J. Moreno Galvan, Madrid 1969; Arte Dopo II 1945 ''Spagna'' by U. Aguilera Cerni, Bologna 1970; *Canogar,* exhibition catalog, Parma 1971; *Treinta Anos de Arte Espanol* by Carlos A. Arean, Madrid 1972; *Canogar* by A. Garcia-Tizon, Madrid 1973; *Rafael Canogar: Evolution dans la Synthese,* exhibition catalog, with essay by J. M. Ballester, Paris 1975; *Rafael Canogar, pintor,* exhibition catalog by Daniel Giralt-Miracle, Madrid 1976; *Rafael Canogar,* with texts by Ante Glibota, Peter Spielmann and Gerard Xuriguera, Paris 1987; *Canogar, Monografia, Catalogo General,* Barcelona 1992; *Espagne 1945–1995* by Christine Cayol, Paris 1996; exhibition catalog, Lisbon 1998. **Articles—**''Still un Entwicklung bei R. Canogar'' by Juan Eduardo Cirlot in *Musee Labirinthe* (Aschaffenburg, Germany), no. 1, 1963; ''Reality and Silence'' by U. Aguilera Cerni in *Art International* (Lugano, Switzerland), January 1969; ''Rafael Canogar'' by D. W. Case in *Art and Artists* (London), February 1970; special Canogar issue of *Nueva Forma* (Madrid), December 1971; ''La Aventura Plastica de Rafael Canogar'' by F. Calvo Serraller in *El Pais* (Madrid), 25 September 1982; ''Rafael Canogar: Beyond Modernism'' by Keith Patrick in *Studio International* (London), no. 1007, 1984; Rafael Canogar, Sala Gaspar'' by Gloria Moure in *Artforum* (New York), September 1985; ''Rafael Canogar'' by Ben Milad Mondher in *Les Cahiers de la Peinture,* 1–15 April 1987; ''Obra Gráfica de Canogar'' by M. Rubio in exhibition catalog for Museo de Bellas Artes de Bilbao, July 1990; ''Ültimas tendencias'' by Lourdes Dirlot in *Planeta,* Barcelona 1993; ''Manifestación bajo el puente'' by Fernando Delgado in *El País,* Februray 1999; ''Tawassul, un puente artistico entre España y Marruecos'' ABC 2000.

* * *

Before 1962 Rafael Canogar's paintings and graphics bore a strong resemblance to the passionate churned-up images of Saura, and the matiere painting of the gifted, post-war Spanish school. He was then 27, and had developed from meticulous depictions of his native Toledo (following in the footsteps of El Greco), to Miro-like linear compositions. The powerful abstracts of the 60s, with their flashing, cutting, brush strokes, sombre colours, and sense of urgency, expressed a frustration with Spanish life. Saura, Millares and other compatriots were involved in similar imagery and similar situations.

By 1966 a return to figuration tentatively concerned itself with intimate, domestic matters, although there was already evidence in the gestural dominance of limbs, of the dramatic narrative manner of Canogar's now celebrated political paintings. In 1967 he began to use a mixture of media, both to encrust, so to speak, reality onto his canvas, and convey a sense of shock. Photography, often newspaper images of accidents or police confrontations, would be used, with isolated elements emerging from a solid black background, emphasized by collage, so that a pair of real trousers would be used with a drawn or painted figure.

Gradually the collage method developed into full-scale sculptural relief, so that the insistent gesture, present in all Canogar's work, became the movement of a simulated hand or leg. The protagonists were now openly political; demonstrating mobs versus uniformed members of the state; sometimes a group of raised hands symbolizing the demand for freedom and liberty; the titles ''Protest,'' ''Arrest,'' ''Desolation,'' ''Aggression,'' ''The Escape,'' ''Tumult,'' making no effort to disguise the inspiration or purpose of the impassioned images.

They are, of course, in the great tradition of Goya, sufficiently generalized to include all forms of state violence and denial, to be applicable to governmental systems and methods in many parts of the world. For this reason, perhaps, Canogar has been able to function and exhibit in his native Spain, as well as winning respect internationally.

—Charles Spencer

CARDIFF, Janet

Nationality: Canadian. **Born:** Brussels, Ontario, 1957. **Education:** Queen's University, Kingston, Ontario, B.F.A., 1980; University of Alberta, Edmonton, Alberta, M.V.A., 1983. **Agent:** Luhring Augustine, 531 West 24th Street, New York, NY 10011.

Individual Exhibitions:

1987 Glendon Art Gallery, York University, Toronto
1988 Macdonald Stewart Art Centre, Guelph, Ontario
1989 Latitude 53, Edmonton, Alberta
1990 Evelyn Amis Gallery, Toronto
1991 The New Gallery, Calgary, Alberta
1992 Eye Level Gallery, Halifax, Nova Scotia
YYZ, Toronto
1993 La Chambre Blanche, Quebec City
To Touch: An Installation by Janet Cardiff, The Edmonton Art Gallery, Edmonton, Alberta (catalog)
1994 The Powerplant Art Gallery, Toronto
The Southern Alberta Art Gallery, Lethbridge (catalog)
Randolph Street Gallery, Chicago
1995 Front Gallery, Vancouver, British Columbia (with George Bures Miller)
Eastern Edge Gallery, St. John's, Newfoundland
The Walter Phillips Gallery, The Banff Centre, Banff, Alberta (with George Bures Miller) (catalog)
1996 Gallerie Optica, Montreal
1997 Gallery Barbara Weiss, Berlin
Raum Aktueller Kunst, Vienna (with George Bures Miller)
Morris Healy Gallery, New York (with George Bures Miller)
1999 *London Walk,* Artangel, London
Side Street Project, Los Angeles (with George Bures Miller)
2000 Kunstraum Munich, Munich
Lakeside Walk, Oakville Galleries, Oakville, Ontario
2001 The Canadian Pavillion, Venice Biennial (with George Bures Miller)
Kunstmuseum des Kantons Thurgau, Warth, Switzerland
Janet Cardiff, P.S. 1, New York City
The Muriel Lake Incident, Southern Alberta Art Gallery (with George Bures Miller)

Selected Group Exhibitions:

1992 *Intimacies* (performance with Charles Cousins, Nelson Henricks, and Jon Winet), sponsored by The New Gallery, Calgary
Environment, The Photographers Gallery, Saskatoon
A Public Room, Cambridge Library and Art Gallery, Ontario; Whitby Arts Inc., Whitby, Ontario; McLaren Art Centre, Barrie, Ontario
1995 *A Night at the Show,* Zurich, Switzerland
1996 ''Thinking Walking and Thinking,'' *NowHere,* Louisiana Museum, Denmark
Alberta Biennial for Contemporary Art, Edmonton Art Gallery and The Glenbow Musuem

1997 *Present Tense: Nine Artists in the Nineties,* San Francisco Museum of Modern Art (catalog)
Sculpture: Projects in Münster, Westfälisches Landesmuseum, Münster (catalog)
Ear As Eye, Los Angeles Contemporary Exhibitions
1998 *Places in Gothenburg,* Kulturnämnden, Gothenburg, Sweden
1999 *The Carnegie International,* The Carnegie Museum of Art, Pittsburgh
6th International Istanbul Biennial, Istanbul, Turkey
The Museum as Muse: Artists Reflect, The Museum of Modern Art, New York (catalog)
III International Site Santa Fe Biennial, Santa Fe, New Mexico
6th International Istanbul Biennial, Instanbul, Turkey
2000 *Mixing Memory and Desire,* Kunstmuseum, Lucerne
Sculpture, Luhring Augustine Gallery, New York
Wonderland, St. Louis Art Museum, Missouri
La Ville, le Jardin, la Memoire—1998, 2000, 1999, Acadamie de France, Villa Medici, Rome (catalog)
Tate Modern Opening, London
2001 *100 Wishes,* Ludwig Museum, Cologne
Elusive Paradise, The National Gallery of Canada, Ottawa
Black Box, Museum of Fine Arts, Berne, Switzerland

Collections:

British Air; Wanas Art Foundation, Knislinge, Sweden; Westfälisches Landesmuseum, Germany; The Art Gallery of Ontario; The Edmonton Art Gallery; Louisiana Museum,Denmark; Musée D'Art Contemporain, Montreal; Alberta Foundation for the Arts; University of Lethbridge, Lethbridge, Alberta; Hart House, University of Toronto, Toronto; Air Canada, Montreal; Canada Council Art Bank; Central Guaranty Trust, Toronto.

Publications:

On CARDIFF: Articles—''Janet Cardiff: Evelyn Amis Gallery'' by Linda Genereux in *Artforum,* vol. 29, no. 3, November 1990; ''Janet Cardiff'' by Barbara Lounder in *Parachute,* no. 71, July-September 1993; ''Janet Cardiff: Power Plant'' by Laura U. Marks in *Artforum,* vol. 33, no. 7, March 1995; ''Mock Excursions and Twisted Itineraries: Tour Guide Performances'' by Jim Drobnick in *Parachute,* no. 80, October/December 1995; ''Louise Wilson and Janet Cardiff'' by Valerie Lamontagne in *Parachute Magazine,* no. 83, Summer 1996; ''Post Ironic Re-enchantments'' by David Garneau in *Border Crossings* (Winnipeg) Fall 1996; ''Janet Cardiff and George Bures Miller'' by David Garneau in *Art/Text,* no. 57, May-July 1997; ''In Deep: Janet Cardiff and George Bures Miller'' by Leslie Camhi in *The Village Voice,* 23 December 1997; ''Janet Cardiff: Whitechapel'' by Claire Bishop in *Flash Art,* vol. 32, no. 209, 1999; ''Janet Cardiff: Miami Art Museum'' in *Sculpture,* vol. 18, no. 1, January-February 1999; ''Janet Cardiff'' by Gary Michael Dault in *Canadian Art Magazine,* Spring 1999; ''Speeches of Display: The Musuem Audio Guides of Sophie Calle, Andrea Fraser and Janet Cardiff'' by Jennifer Fisher in *Parachute Magazine,* no. 94, 1999; ''Janet Cardiff the Missing Voice (Case Study B): An Audio Walk'' by Monica Biagioli in *Artfocus* (Toronto), Winter/Spring 2000; ''An Artist Who Travels With You (on Tape, That Is)'' by Sarah Boxer in *The New York Times,* 8 August 2000; ''Janet Cardiff'' by Iwona Blazwick in *Fresh Cream,* London, Phaidon Press 2001; ''Ghostly Footsteps: Voices, Memories and Walks in the City'' by David Pinder in *Ecumene: A Journal of Cultural Georgraphies,* vol. 8, no. 1, 2001.

* * *

Although Janet Cardiff is perhaps best-known for her audio-based artworks, her photographic installations of the early 1990s underscore an investigation of the construction of memory and reality that continues to be an integral part of her work. In these installations, Cardiff groups ethereal, foreboding black-and-white photographs to suggest strange alternate realities. Combinations of images, such as a dark house emerging through trees and a woman leaving a bed, spark viewers' memories. The works seem to suggest a truth that lies just out of reach.

More recent installations focus on the role the human body plays in constructing personal knowledge and memory. Recorded sound and speech are essential to these works. In *The Dark Pool* (1995–96), created in collaboration with George Bures Miller, participants explore a dimly lit room filled with battered furniture, abandoned science experiments, an open suitcase, and other strange contraptions. As they gradually learn about the fictitious inhabitants of the space, knowledge is linked directly to the physical body. Movement triggers tape loops containing snippets of music, conversations, and stories. Since there is no specific route, participants gradually obtain information that, like knowledge and memory, is ultimately only fragmentary.

While *The Dark Pool* underscores the haphazard process by which humans acquire information as they move through the world, Cardiff's installation *To Touch* (1993–95) demonstrates that memory is embedded in the human body and that touch and sound can elicit a flood of mental associations. The work consists of an old wooden carpenter's table situated in the center of a darkened room. As visitors pass their hands over the table, they trigger sensors hidden in its surface. These sensors activate various audio loops—including sound effects, descriptions of scenes, conversations, and music—that play in twenty small speakers located around the room. Sounds are mixed randomly by the participant who is completely in charge of the effect, with quick touches, sustained pressure, and sweeps of the hand eliciting different combinations of sound. In *To Touch,* Cardiff demonstrates how sound can convert to touch in the listener's mind, and touch to memory as the dreamlike voices and sounds trigger personal associations.

Absent viewer participation, Cardiff's installations remain passive and mute. The artist's recent invention of site-specific audio walks, therefore, is a logical outgrowth of her artistic production. For these pieces, individuals wear a headset connected to a stereo cassette player and are guided by Cardiff's voice along a predetermined path. Her narration alternates between real-time observations and memories with dream-like fluidity. Ambient sounds like the roar of an airplane or the honking of horns intercut the artist's spoken and whispered words. The result is an audio collage that makes participants intimately aware of their dependence on sound for their experience of the world.

Since the human ear is trained to differentiate between the sound of large and small spaces, between art galleries and airports, Cardiff records her audio walks on site. Additionally, she employs a binaural recording technique in which microphones are placed simultaneously on each side of either her head or that of a dummy as she traces the path the viewer will take. The resultant recordings register stereophonic sound with the full three-dimensionality perceived by human ears, seeming to capture the world exactly.

When out-of-context sounds are added to the track, the result is incredibly disjointing. In *The Missing Voice (Case Study B)* (1999), which takes places in the streets of London, participants become anxious as quickening footsteps follow them up a flight of stairs. Upon turning, however, they discover that no one is there. In this and many other examples, Cardiff forces participants to contemplate how they construct ''reality'' through their less-than-perfect senses.

—Joyce Youmans

CARO, Anthony (Alfred)

Nationality: British. **Born:** London, 8 March 1924. **Education:** Hampshire and Surrey primary schools; apprenticed to the sculptor Charles Wheeler during school vacations, 1937–42; studied engineering at Christ's College, Cambridge, 1942–44; attended Farnham's School of Art, 1944; studied sculpture, then drawing at the Royal Academy Schools, London, under Charles Wheeler, 1947–53. **Military Service:** Fleet Air Arm, 1944–45. **Family:** Married the artist Sheila Girling in 1949; sons: Tim and Paul. **Career:** Worked as a part-time assistant to Henry Moore, Much Hadham, Hertfordshire, 1951–53; settled in Hampstead, London, 1954; produced first abstract welded, bolted steel and aluminum works, 1959; visited Mexico and the United States, 1959; and continued working visits to the U.S. from 1965; worked in Kenneth Noland's studio, Shaftsbury, Vermont, 1970; worked with James Wolfe, Ripamonte Factory, Verduggio, Italy, 1972–73; worked on York Sculptures, York Steel Corporation, Ontario, Spring and Summer 1974. Part-time Lecturer, St. Martin's School of Art, London, 1952–53; Lecturer in Sculpture, Bennington College, Vermont, 1963–65; and St. Martin's School of Art, London, 1964–72; Artist-in-Residence, Summer Workshop, University of Saskatchewan, Emma Lake, 1977; Lecturer, Slade School of Fine Art, London, since 1982; Founder/Lecturer, Triangle Summer Sculpture Workshops, Pine Plains, New York, since 1982. **Awards:** Ford Foundation Travel Grant, 1959; Prize for Sculpture, *Paris Biennale,* 1959; David Bright Sculpture Prize, *Biennale,* Venice, 1966; Prize for Sculpture, *Bienal,* Sao Paulo, 1969. Honorary Fellow, Christ's College, Cambridge, 1979; honorary doctorate: University of East Anglia, 1979; University of York, 1979; Brandeis University, Waltham, Massachusetts, 1981; Cambridge University, 1985; Honorary Fellow: Royal College of Art, London, 1986; honorary degree: University of Surrey, Guildford, 1987. C.B.E. (Commander, Order of the British Empire), 1969; Knight Bachelor, 1987; Honorary Foreign Member, American Academy of Arts and Sciences, 1988; honorary degree: Yale University, Connecticut, 1989, and University of Alberta, Edmonton, 1990; Honorary Fellow, Wolfson College, Oxford, 1991; Henry Moore Grand Prize, First Nobutaka Shikanai Prize, Hakone Open Air Museum, Tokyo, 1991; Honorary Member, Accademia delle Belle Arte di Brera, Milan, 1992; Imperiale Prize for sculpture, Japan Art Association, Tokyo, 1992; honorary degree: Royal College of Art, London, 1994, University of Charles de Gaulle, Lille, 1996, Durham University, 1996; Chevalier des Arts et Lettres, France, 1996; Lifetime Achievement Award, International Sculpture Center, 1997; honorary degree: Flordia International University; Honorary Fellow, Royal Institute of British Architects, Royal Society of British Sculptors, London, 1997; Honorary Board of Trustees, International Sculpture Center, 1998; Honorary Fellow, Glasgow School of Art and Bretton Hall College, University of Leeds, 1998; honorary degree: University of Westminster, London, 1999; Order of Merit, 2000. **Member:** Royal College of Art, London, 1981–83; Trustee, Tate Gallery, London, since 1982. **Address:** 111 Frognal, London NW3 6XR, England. **Web site:** www.barford.org

Individual Exhibitions:

1956 Galleria del Naviglio, Milan
1957 Gimpel Fils, London
1963 Whitechapel Art Gallery, London
1964 André Emmerich Gallery, New York
1965 Gallery of Modern Art, Washington, D.C.
Kasmin Gallery, London
1966 André Emmerich Gallery, New York
David Mirvish Gallery, Toronto
Galerie Bischofberger, Zurich
1967 Kasmin Gallery, London
David Mirvish Gallery, Toronto (with Kenneth Noland)
Rijksmuseum Kröller-Müller, Otterlo, Netherlands
1968 André Emmerich Gallery, New York
Metropolitan Museum of Art, New York (with Kenneth Noland and Morris Louis)
1969 Hayward Gallery, London
Dayton's Gallery 12, Minneapolis (with Kenneth Noland and Frank Stella)
1970 André Emmerich Gallery, New York
1971 David Mirvish Gallery, Toronto
Kasmin Gallery, London
1972 André Emmerich Gallery, New York
Kasmin Gallery, London
1973 *Norfolk and Norwich Triennial Festival,* Norwich
André Emmerich Gallery, New York
1974 André Emmerich Gallery, New York
Kenwood House, London
David Mirvish Gallery, Toronto
Galleria dell'Ariete, Milan
1975 Museum of Modern Art, New York (toured the United States)
Watson de Nagy Gallery, Houston
1976 Richard Gray Gallery, Chicago
Lefevre Gallery, London
Galerie Wentzel, Hamburg
Museum of Fine Arts, Boston
1977 Galerie Piltzer-Rheims, Paris
Waddington and Tooth Galleries, London
Tel Aviv Museum (toured New Zealand, Australia and travelled to Ottawa, 1977–79)
1978 Knoedier Gallery, London
Galerie André Emmerich, Zurich (with Ben Nicholson)
Harcus-Krakow Gallery, Boston
Richard Gray Gallery, Chicago
Galerie Wentzel, Hamburg
Ace Gallery, Venice, California
Antwerp Gallery

Anthony Caro: *Goodwood Steps,* 1994–96. ©Anthony Caro, courtesy of Barford Sculptures Ltd.

1979 Kunstverein, Brunswick, West Germany
Gallery Kasahara, Osaka, Japan
Ace Gallery, Vancouver
Stadt Galerie im Lenbachhaus, Munich
Kunstverein, Frankfurt
Kunsthalle, Mannheim
1980 *The York Sculptures,* Christian Science Center, Boston
Aquavella Contemporary Art, New York
Galerie André, Berlin
1981 Kenwood House, London
1982 Hunterian Art Gallery, Glasgow (toured the U.K., 1982–83)
1983 Knoedler Gallery, London
Waddington Galleries, London
Galerie de France, Paris
1984 Knoedler Gallery, London
Galerie Wentzel, Cologne
Martin Gerard Gallery, Edmonton, Alberta
André Emmerich Gallery, New York
Acquavella Galleries, New York
Serpentine Gallery, London
Whitworth Art Gallery, Manchester
Leeds City Art Gallery, Yorkshire
Ordrupgaard Samlingen, Copenhagen
1985 Kunstmuseum, Dusseldorf
Fondacion Joan Miro, Barcelona
Galerie Wentzel, Cologne
Galerie André Emmerich, Zurich
Grimaldis Gallery, Baltimore, Maryland
Gallery One, Toronto
Galerie Blanche, Stockholm
Galleri Lang, Malmo, Sweden
Galerie Artek, Helsinki
Harcus Gallery, Boston
Galleria Stendhal, Milan
Norrkopings Kunstmuseum, Sweden
1986 Richard Gray Gallery, Chicago
André Emmerich Galery, New York
Acquavella Galleries, New York
Galeria Joan Prats, Barcelona
Comune di Bogliasco, Genoa, Italy
Knoedler Gallery, London

Waddington Galleries, London
Iglesia de San Esteban, Murcia, Spain
1987 La Lonja, Valencia, Spain
Galeria Soledad Lorenzo, Madrid
Grimaldis Gallery, Baltimore, Maryland
1988 Sylvia Cordish Fine Arts, Baltimore, Maryland
Galerie Renee Ziegler, Zurich
1989 Annely Juda Fine Art (and 1991, 1994, 1998)
Sala de Exposiciones del Banco Bilbao Vizcaya, Barcelona
Walker Hill Art Center, Seoul
Nabis Gallery, Seoul
Rutgers Barclay Gallery, Santa Fe, New Mexico
Sala d'Art Sebastia Jané, Girona, Spain
Galleria Fluxus, Porto, Portugal
Carl Schlosberg fine Art, Sherman Oaks, California
1990 Galeria Charpa, Gandia
Galeria Acquavella, Caracas
Galerie Lelong, Paris
Musée des Beaux-Arts, Calais
Paribas Bank, Huis Österrieth, Antwerp
Fuji Television Gallery, Tokyo
Gallery Pousse, Tokyo
Gallery Asuka, Tokyo
1991 Tate Gallery, London
Galerie Hans Mayer, Düsseldorf
1992 Veranneman Foundation, Kruishoutem, Belgium
Accademia Italiana, London
Trajan Markets, Rome
Galleria Oddi Baglioni, Rome
Studio Marconi, Milan
1993 Mucsarnok, Palme-Haz, Budapest (toured)
1994 Upstairs Gallery, Poole, Dorset
Kettle's Yard, Cambridge (toured)
Graves Art Gallery, Sheffield
Kukje Gallery, Seoul
Yorkshire Sculpture Park, Wakefield
Henry Moore Studio, Dean Clough, Halifax
1995 Museum of Contemporary Art, Tokyo
Galerie Josine Bokhoven, Amsterdam
Koffler Gallery, North York, Ontario
Metropole Arts Centre, Folkestone (toured)
1996 Chesil Gallery, Portland, Dorset (with Sheila Girling) (toured)
1997 Dorset County Museum, Dorchester
French Institute, Thessaloniki
National Gallery, Athens
Middelheim Sculpture Park, Antwerp
1998 National Gallery, London
Marlborough Gallery, Boca Raton, Florida
Garth Clark Gallery, New York (toured)
1999 Venice Biennale
Marlborough Gallery, Boca Raton, Florida
2000 Ameringer Howard, New York (toured)
Venice Design, Venice
Museo des bellas artes, Bilbao
Galleri Weinberger, Copenhagen

Selected Group Exhibitions:

Sir Anthony Caro has been in hundreds of group exhibitions.

1955 *New Sculptors and Painter-Sculptors,* Institute of Contemporary Arts, London
1958 *Pittsburgh International,* Carnegie Institute, Pittsburgh
1959 *1st Biennale des Jeunes,* Musée d'Art Moderne, Paris
1954 *Painting and Sculpture of a Decade: 1954–1964,* Tate Gallery, London
1968 *New British Sculpture and Painting,* University of California, Berkeley (toured the United States and Canada)
1970 *Contemporary British Art,* Museum of Modern Art, Tokyo
1974 *The Great Decade of American Abstract Art,* Museum of Fine Arts, Houston
1980 *Hayward Annual,* Hayward Gallery, London
1983 *Aspects of British Art,* Guggenheim Museum, New York
1987 *British Painting and Sculpture in the 1980s,* Museum of Modern Art, Oxford (toured Hungary, Poland, Czechoslovakia)

Collections:

Tate Gallery, London: Arts Council of Great Britain, London; Kunsthaus, Zurich; Museum of Modern Art, New York; National Gallery of Art, Washington, D.C.

Publications:

By CARO: Articles—''The Master Sculptor'' in *The Observer* (London), 27 November 1960; ''Conversation with Anthony Caro, Ken Noland and Jules Olitski'' by David Thompson in *Nonad* (London), January 1964; statement in *Art Now* (New York), September 1969; ''Some Thoughts after Visiting Florence'' in *Art International* (Lugano, Switzerland), May 1974; ''An Interview with Anthony Caro,'' with Phyllis Tuchman, in *Anthony Caro* by Richard Whelan and others, London 1974; ''Conversations with Anthony Caro'' by Lutz Haufschile in *Arts Magazine* (New York), June 1978; interview, with Christopher Andreae, in the *Christian Science Monitor* (Boston), August 1980; ''A Conversation with Anthony Caro,'' with Yorick Blumenfeld, in *Architectural Digest* (Los Angeles), September 1981.

On CARO: Books—*Anthony Caro,* exhibition catalog, by Michael Fried, London 1969; *Anthony Caro* by Richard Whelan and others, London 1974; *Anthony Caro* by William Rubin, New York and London 1975; *The York Sculptures,* exhibition catalog, Boston 1980; *Anthony Caro,* exhibition catalog, New York 1980: *The Sculpture of Anthony Caro: Catalog Raisonné,* 5 vols, edited by Dieter Blume, Cologne 1981–86; *Anthony Caro: Sculptures,* exhibition catalog with text by Karen Wilkin, New York 1981; *Anthony Caro* by Diane Waldman, Oxford and New York 1982 (includes bibliography); *Anthony Caro Sculpture 1969–84,* exhibition catalog with foreword by Joanna Drew and Catherine Lampert, London 1984; *Anthony Caro* by Terry Fenton, London and Barcelona 1986; *Aspects of Anthony Caro* edited by Ian Barker, London 1989; *Anthony Caro: Sculpture towards Architecture* by Paul Moorhouse, London 1991; *Caro* by Karen Wilkin, London 1991; *Anthony Caro: The Cascades* by Ken Johnson, London and New York 1991; *Anthony Caro* by Giovanni Carandente, Sonzogno 1992; *Caro by Anzai* by Shigeo Anzai, Tokyo

1992; *Caro at the Trajan Markets, Rome* by Giovanni Carandente, London 1993; *Modernism with a Vengeance, 1957–1969* by Clement Greenberg, Chicago and London 1993; *The Trojan War: Sculptures by Anthony Caro* by Julius Bryant and John Spurling, London 1994; *Anthony Caro: Sculptures et dessins figuratifs des années cinquante et des années quatre-vingt* by Patrick Le Nouene, Angers 1996; *The Caros, A Creative Partnership: Sheila Girling and Anthony Caro* by Julie Summers, Portland 1996; *Anthony Caro* by Tim Marlow, Antwerp 1997; *Art and Objecthood* by Michael Fried, Chicago and London 1998; *Caro at the National Gallery: Sculpture from Painting* by John Golding, London 1998; *The Last Judgment: Sculpture by Anthony Caro* edited by Ian Barker, 1999; *Anthony Caro and Twentieth-Century Sculpture* by Giovanni Carandente, 1999; *Sculptors Talking: Anthony Caro-Eduardo Chillida* by Andrew Dempsey, Paris 2000.

*

You cannot explain abstract art in ten minutes, and you cannot expect yourself to like it on the very first glance, any more than you'll like a piece of unfamiliar serious music on the first hearing. It takes a lot of listening and a lot of looking to get the rewards of difficult art, but it is worthwhile in the end.

—Anthony Caro

* * *

Anthony Caro's reputation was established by his superb welded steel pieces of the 1960s. He is rightly acclaimed as having pushed sculpture even further into abstraction, by eliminating any lingering figurative references and by freeing it completely from the constraints of the pedestal.

Caro's works of the '60s usually develop horizontally, appropriating the viewer's own space. They claim and animate that space simply by looking like nothing other than themselves. They are built of industrial materials—I-beams, stock angles, expanded metal mesh and the like—but in spite of the literal strength and weight of their components, they appear weightless, like disembodied drawings which hover above the floor rather than resting heavily upon it. This is partly due to the thinness of their members; they are sculptures of plane, edge, and line, not of mass. It results, too, from Caro's practice of painting these works in uniform, often rather light colors, which homogenizes the disparate components and makes the sculptures declare themselves as single, unified objects. More importantly, the apparent weightlessness of Caro's work depends on his habit of deliberately confusing supporting and pictorial elements. He often establishes elevated surrogate horizon planes, and disposes forms above and below them, so that these elements appear to float freely.

Caro's sculptures of the '60s expanded our notions of what sculpture could be, picking up, as they did, the implications of Picasso and Gonzalez's metal constructions as well as those of David Smith's work, and making them still more abstract and more optical. For once, the over-used term ''drawing in space'' seems apt. Caro's sculptures of the period were conceived as transparent three-dimensional objects. Their eloquent gestures and comfortable human scale made us aware of our own bodies' ability to move, yet at the same time, they were purely visual structures.

The small scale Table sculptures of more or less the same time were equally remarkable. In these, Caro at first established scale by incorporating real grips and handles (in ungraspable positions) to instantly give a sense of the hand. Later, perhaps to contradict this reference to ordinary objects on a table, which were distinguished because they *could* be picked up, Caro eliminated the handles. Instead, he established scale through positioning. The Table Pieces often spring over the edges of their supporting bases, appearing as weightless and animated as their larger counterparts, but perceived differently because of their small size. We tend to see each of their component parts as something of great importance, since we are so close to them.

If Caro had done nothing but the linear painted pieces and the Table Pieces, his place in the history of contemporary sculpture would still be secure, but in the '70s and early '80s, he has retained his pre-eminence with a body of inventive work which explores new territory and new materials. In the early '70s, Caro seemed to fall in love with the properties of his chosen material, with the surface inflections of steel, its weight and mass, after years of dissembling. A series of extremely painterly, relatively massive sculptures, made of rolled sheets, revelled in the particularities of magnificent pieces of metal. As if to emphasize his pleasure in the individual sheet, Caro often presented them vertically, for the viewer's inspection, rather than horizontally, as in earlier works. Works of this type began with the Verduggio series, made in Italy, and continued with the Durham series, after Caro found a British rolling mill which could provide him with the irregular sheets and folded slabs which come at the end of a run, or when the mill makes a mistake. They culminated in the York Pieces of 1974–75, Caro's first very large scale works. Previously, his improvisatory approach demanded that his sculptures be kept within a scale which he could manipulate himself, or with a minimum of assistance. Larger scale implied using maquettes or fabricators, intermediaries antithetical to his working methods. But in making the York Pieces, he had at his disposal, for the first time, men and equipment which allowed him to work on big sculptures without altering his approach. The York series, for all their size and the sheer weightiness of their tilted, layered slabs, have all the immediacy of his early work, albeit with a new solemnity and dignity.

Similarly, Caro had not worked in bronze since abandoning figuration in the late '50s. Again, the medium seemed too indirect, to require too much preconception. In the early '70s, however, an invitation to make sculpture in clay at Syracuse University led Caro back to bronze without forcing him to give up his usual collage method. By having forms made in clay (or other equally manipulable material) which he could then alter and have cast in bronze, Caro assembled a lexicon of eccentric personal elements. He used these in combination with brass rods and sheets, to make bronzes as directly and spontaneously as he did works in steel, assembling and constructing unique works, rather than preparing maquettes for casting. The resulting sculptures have ranged from intimate Table Pieces which evoke Chinese temple bronzes as much as they do the tradition of modernism, to large scale ''Screens'' built of cascading planes which spring against vertical walls in the same way that the horizontal drawing of earlier works skimmed the floor.

Despite his interest in new formal concerns, such as verticality and mass, and new materials, such as lead, silver and bronze. Caro has continued to make expressive linear sculptures in steel. The Emma Lake pieces of 1977–78 are large scale, drawing-like works which recall earlier sculptures but are developed in the round in ways relatively new to Caro. It is as though their slender configurations had been informed by the density and substance of his painterly ''slab'' pieces of the early '70s. The Writing Pieces, small calligraphic works of 1978, and a recent series of larger, rather densely packed steel sculptures, both make free use of found objects from small tools to bollards. In the recent steel pieces, as well as the bronzes, Caro has begun to make use of color in new ways, varying tones and patinas to enhance structure and emphasize form, rather than applying a uniform and unifying skin of color.

Small calligraphic sculptures continued this linear vein well into the 1980s, while the most extreme examples of the persistence of this mode were a group of sculptures made at an international artists' workshop in Barcelona, in 1987, perhaps as a response to the omnipresent Catalan ironwork balconies and railings.

Yet mass and implied volume, along with an intense physical presence, have characterized much of Caro's sculpture since 1980. His steel constructions, whether polychromed or unpainted, are often very large, (within the context of his preference for human scale), massive accretions of thick members; some incorporate huge, sliced marine floats that, because of their size and hollowness, have inevitable associations with architecture and shelter. Caro acknowledges that he has been looking hard at medieval and Renaissance churches, in recent years, but as always, his best works declare themselves independently of literal allusions.

Most surprisingly, the man who long maintained that, for him, sculpture had to be abstract if was to be "real"—that is, to have the same intensity and authority as anything in the existing world—has been working from the model since the early '80s. His richly inflected cast bronze figures are a clear homage to Matisse, but they owe as much to Caro's own abstract sculpture as to any of the figurative sculptors whose work interests him; certainly they are articulated in ways that have little to do with Caro's thickest figures of the 1950s, made before he began to work abstractly in steel. The bronze figures seem to have, in turn, influenced a recent series of abstract bronzes whose swelling, sensuous forms are abutted in a manner that is typical of Caro—whose work always depends upon placement—and at the same time, evokes classic Indian sculpture, which Caro admires greatly.

Knighted in 1987, at 63, in recognition of his past achievement, Caro continues to make challenging and original sculpture. Most impressive is his enduring ability to respond to new notions and to reexamine his conception of what sculpture can be.

—Karen Wilkin

CARR-HARRIS, Ian

Nationality: Canadian. **Born:** Victoria, British Columbia, 12 August 1941. **Education:** Studied modern history, Queen's University, Kingston, Ontario, 1959–63; library science, University of Toronto, 1963–64; sculpture, Ontario College of Art, Toronto, 1967–71. **Family:** Married in 1966 (divorced); daughter: Lisa Renee. **Career:** Independent sculptor, Toronto, since 1971. Director of Library Services since 1972, and Instructor in Art Theory and Practice since 1975, Ontario College of Art, Toronto. Board member, A Space Gallery, Toronto, 1970–71, 1982–83, and The Power Plant (formerly, The Art Gallery at Harbourfront), Toronto, 1983–87; Member of the Contemporary Acquisitions Committee, Art Gallery of Ontario, Toronto, 1987–88. Contributor to the periodicals *Parachute, Vanguard* and *C Magazine,* since 1975. **Member:** Royal Canadian Academy, 1976. **Agent:** Carmen Lamanna Gallery, 988 King Street West, Toronto, Ontario M5V 1N6. **Address:** 68 Broadview Avenue, 4th floor, Toronto, Ontario M4M 2E6, Canada.

Individual Exhibitions:

1971 A Space, Toronto
1972 Nova Scotia College of Art and Design, Halifax
1973 Carmen Lamanna Gallery, Toronto (and annually, since 1973)
1981 Yajima/Galerie, Montreal
1982 Dalhousie University, Halifax, Nova Scotia Scarborough College, Toronto
1983 49th Parallel Centre, New York
1987 London Regional Art Gallery, Ontario
1988 *Ian Carr-Harris, 1971–1977,* Art Gallery of Ontario, Toronto
1993 *Ian Carr-Harris: Early Works,* Oakville Galleries, Ontario
1994 *Ian Carr-Harris: Indices,* Galeria Carles Poy, Barcelona (traveling exhibition)

Selected Group Exhibitions:

1970 *Concept '70,* Nightingale Gallery, Toronto
1974 *Investigations,* Mount Allison University, Sackville, New Brunswick
1977 *Another Dimension,* National Gallery of Canada, Ottawa
1978 *Kanadische Kunstler,* Kunsthalle, Basle
1979 *Confrontations,* Vancouver Art Gallery, British Columbia
1981 *Canada in Birmingham,* Ikon Gallery, Birmingham, England
1984 *41st Biennale,* Venice
1986 *Luminous Sites,* Western Front and Video Inn, Vancouver
1987 *Documenta 8,* Museum Fridericianum, Kassel, West Germany
1989 *Canadian Biennial of Contemporary Art,* National Gallery of Canada, Ottawa
1993 *Visual Evidence,* Dunlop Art Gallery, Regina, Saskatchewan
1995 *Ian Carr-Harris: Sphere of Influence/Mouvance,* Susan Hobbs Gallery, Toronto and Galerie Optica, Montreal
1996 *Reading and Re-reading: Selections from the Permanent Collection,* Centennial Gallery, Oakville, Ontario, Canada

Collections:

Art Gallery of Ontario, Toronto; Canada Council, Ottawa; National Gallery of Canada, Ottawa.

Publications:

By CARR-HARRIS: Articles—"John Greer" in Parachute (Montreal), December/February 1982–83; "Museums in the 80s", with Goldie Rans, in *Vanguard* (Vancouver), March 1983; "Philip Monk, Sentences on art" and "Vincent Tangredi" in *Parachute* (Montreal), March/May 1983; "A. R. Penck" in *Parachute* (Montreal), June/August 1983; "From Here to Zero: Stephen Horne" in *C Magazine* (Toronto), no. 1, 1983; "Sex and Representation" in *Vanguard* (Vancouver), November 1984; "Women's Work" in *Vanguard* (Vancouver), December 1987.

On CARR-HARRIS: Books—*Art in Boxes* by A. Mogelin and N. Laliberte, New York 1974; *Another Dimension,* exhibition catalog with text by Mayo Graham, Ottawa 1977; *Confrontations,* with text by Ann Pollock, Vancouver 1979; *Ian Carr-Harris: Recent Work,* exhibition catalog with text by Linda Milrod, Halifax 1982; *Visions: Contemporary Art in Canada* by Diana Nemiroff, Toronto 1983; *Ian Carr-Harris/Liz Magor: Canada, XLI Biennale di Venezia 1984,* exhibition catalog with text by Jessica Bradley, Ottawa 1984; *Toronto: A Play of History,* exhibition catalog with text by Louise Dompierre, Toronto 1987; *Ian Carr-Harris, 1971–1977,* exhibition catalog, with text by Philip Monk, Toronto 1988; *Ian Carr-Harris: Early Works,* exhibition catalog with text by Carolyn Bell Farrell, Oakville 1993; *Ian Carr-Harris: Sphere of Influence,* exhibition catalog, with text by Diane Gagné, Toronto 1995; *Moving & Storage,* exhibition catalog, Hull 1999. **Articles**—''Democratiser'' by Richard Rhodes in *C Magazine,* no. 21, March 1989; ''Ian Carr-Harris'' by Christina Ritchie in *Canadian Art* (Toronto), vol. 12, Spring 1995.

*

I have a number of concerns about what artworks can accomplish, and they fall roughly into two intersecting categories. These have to do on the one hand with their suggestiveness and the meanings they can construct dialectically in the imagination of the viewer by virtue of their permissiveness; and on the other hand with the intentions of the artist—who at least holds responsibility for the existence of the work—in directing meaning and presenting to the social consciousness of the viewer particular codes of value. When taken together—and all artworks exhibit both these categories—they act to define and to counter our own individual productions of meaning. They both produce and deny those productions: this is what artworks accomplish.

—Ian Carr-Harris

CARRINGTON, Leonora

Nationality: British. **Born:** Chorley, Lancashire, England, 6 April 1917. **Family:** Lived with surrealist painter Max Ernst in France until the German occupation forced her to flee the country; married Renato Leduc in 1941 to flee Europe for America (divorced 1942); married photographer Chiqui Weisz in 1946; two sons with Weisz. **Education:** At age nine sent to Catholic convents (one, called Newhall, had been a palace of Henry VIII, king of England) for education and finishing; presented to the court at age seventeen. Instead of becoming a socialite she entered Mrs. Penrose's Academy of Art, Florence, Italy; Chelsea School of Arts, London; and Academy of Amedée Ozenfant, London. **Career:** One of the most important surrealist painters. Numerous exhibits in Mexico City, New York, San Francisco, Paris, London, Munich, and Tokyo. **Agent:** Brewster Arts Limited, 41 West 57th Street, New York, New York 10019, U.S.A. **Web site:** http://members.nbci.com/lecarrington/

Selected Individual Exhibitons:

1948 Pierre Matisse Gallery, New York
1960 Museo Nacional de Arte Moderno, Mexico City
1979 Center for Inter-American Relations, New York
1991 Serpentine Gallery, London
1994 Museum of Contemporary Art, Monterrey, Mexico.

Selected Group Exhibitions:

1991 *Women in Mexico,* National Academy of Design, New York

Publications:

By CARRINGTON: Books—*The Oval Lady, Other Stories: Six Surreal Stories,* Santa Barbara, California, 1975; *The Hearing Trumpet,* New York 1975; *The Stone Door,* 1977; *The Seventh Horse and Other Tales,* New York 1988; *The House of Fear* with introduction by Marina Warner, New York 1988.

On CARRINGTON: Books—*Leonora Carrington. A Retrospective Exhibition* (exhibition catalog) with texts by Edward James and Inés Amor, New York, 1975; *The Theater of the Marvelous* by Gloria Feman Orenstein, New York 1975; *Women Artists and the Surrealist Movement,* by Whitney Chadwick, Boston 1985; *The Reflowering of the Goddess* by Gloria Feman Orenstein, New York 1990; *Surrealism and Women* edited by Mary Ann Caws, Rudolf E. Kuenzli, and Gwen Raaberg, Cambridge, Massachusetts, 1990; *Leonora Carrington: Paintings, Drawings and Sculptures 1940–1990* (exhibition catalog) edited by Andrea Schleiker, London 1991; *Leonora Carrington. The Mexican Years 1943–1985,* exhibition catalog with texts by Holly Barnet-Sanchez and Whitney Chadwick, San Francisco, 1991; *Leonora Carrington. Una Retrospectiva* (exhibition catalog) with texts by Fernando Treviño Lozano Jr., Lourdes Andrade, and Luis Carlos Emerich, Monterrey (Mexico) 1994; *Magnifying Mirrors. Women, Surrealism, and Partnership,* by Renée Riese Hubert, Lincoln, Nebraska, and London, England 1994; *Women, Art, and Society (World of Art)* by Whitney Chadwick, London 1997; *Surrealist Women: An International Anthology* edited by Penelope Rosemont, Austin, Texas 1998; *Mirror Images: Women, Surrealism and Self-Representation,* (exhibition catalog) edited by Whitney Chadwick and Dawn Ades, Cambridge, Mass. 1998. **Articles**—''Leonora Carrington's Whimsical Dreamworld: Animals Talk, Children Are Gods, a Black Swan Lays an Orphic Egg'' by Bettina L. Knapp in *World Literature Today: A Literary Quarterly of the University of Oklahoma* (Norman), 1977; ''Humor at the Service of the Revolution: Leonora Carrington's Feminist Perspective on Surrealism'' by Nancy B. Mandlove in *Perspectives on Contemporary Literature* (Lexington, KY), no. 7, 1981; ''Women Surrealists'' by Maurice Poirier and Jeffrey Hoffeld in *Art News,* vol. 84, October 1985; ''The Muse as Artist: Women in the Surrealist Movement'' by Whitney Chadwick in *Art in America,* vol. 73, July 1985; ''Surrealism in Mexico'' by Serge Fauchereau in *Artforum,* vol. 25, September 1986; ''Leonora Carrington: Evolution of a Feminist Consciousness'' by Whitney Chadwick in *Woman's Art Journal,* vol. 7, Spring/Summer 1986; ''Surrealism and Esoteric Feminism in the Paintings of Leonora Carrington'' by Janice Helland in *RACAR, (Revue d'Art Cannadienne, Canadian Art Review),* vol. 16, no. 1, 1989; ''The Methodology of the Marvelous'' by Gloria Feman Orenstein in *Symposium: A Quarterly Journal in Modern Literatures* (Washington, D.C.), vol. 42, no. 4, Winter 1989; ''Women in Mexico'' by Ronny Cohen in *Artforum,* vol. 29, no. 5, January 1991; ''Leonora Carrington and Max Ernst:

Artistic Partnership and Feminist Liberation'' by Renee Riese Hubert in *New Literary History: A Journal of Theory and Interpretation,* vol. 22, no. 3, Summer 1991; ''Gardens of Delight: Or, What's Cookin'? Leonora Carrington in the Kitchen'' by Sonia Assa in *Studies in Twentieth Century Literature* (Manhattan, KS), vol. 15, no. 2, Summer 1991; ''Beasties and Ghosties'' by Sue Hubbard in *New Statesman & Society,* vol. 5, no. 184, 10 January 1992; ''From an Occult Realm, Mexican Museum'' by Marcia Tanner in *Artweek,* vol. 23, 23 January 1992; ''The Bird Superior meets the Bride of the Wind: Leonora Carrington and Max Ernst'' by Susan Rubin Suleiman in *Significant Others. Creativity and Intimate Partnership,* edited by Whitney Chadwick and Isabelle de Courtivron, London 1993; ''Voyages of Discovery: Leonora Carrington's Magical Prose'' by Debora B. Gaensbauer, *Women's Studies,* vol. 23, no. 3, July 1994; ''The Martyred Muse: Silencing the Female Creator in *Breton's Nadja*'' by Ilona Chessid in *Synthesis: An Interdisciplinary Journal* (Knoxville, TN) Fall 1995; ''Leonora Carrington's Mexican Vision and the European Circle of Surrealists Active in Mexico'' by Clare Kunny in *Museum Studies,* vol. 22, no. 2, 1996; ''The Bestial Fictions of Leonora Carrington'' by Annette Shandler Levitt in *Journal of Modern Literature* (special issue), vol. 20, no. 1, Summer, 1996; ''Art and the Conditions of Exile'' by Linda Nochlin in *Poetics Today,* vol. 17, no. 3, Fall 1996; ''Leonora Carrington'' by Salomón Grimberg in *Art Nexus,* no. 26, October/Decemer 1997; '''Something to See': Spectacle and Savagery in Leonora Carrington's Fiction'' by Rachel Carroll in *CRITIQUE: Studies in Contemporary Fiction,* vol. 39, no. 2, Winter 1998.

* * *

Leonora Carrington is a Surrealist painter and writer, one of the few women participating in the Surrealist exhibitions in 1937 and 1942. Educated in Florence and in the London Art Academy of Amedée Ozenfant, she brought into her work the love of colors and the structural devices of the Italian trecento and quattrocento from her Florentine experience and mastery of drawing acquired in London. In her work the influence of Surrealism merges with the Celtic mythology she knew from her Irish mother and with the Mexican myths she had come to know since she immigrated to Mexico in 1942.

She began her career with paintings such as the self-portraits painted in 1936–1937, *The Horses of Lord Candlestick* (1938), and the portrait of Max Ernst (1939). Peggy Guggenheim, who met Carrington at that time, called her an artist ''full of imagination in the best Surrealist manner'' in *Confessions of an Art Addict.* In her early works the presence of a white horse predominates, originating in the Goddess Epona in Celtic mythology as her personal emblem. The self-portraits entitled *Inn of the Dawn Horse* (1936–1937) and *Woman and Bird* (1937) show the artist with mane-like hair. In *Inn of the Dawn Horse* a liberated horse gallops outside the window and a hobby-horse can be seen behind the seated artist. In Carrington's short story *Little Francis* (1937) she represented herself in the form of a boy who, out of love for his uncle (Max Ernst's alter ego), changes into a creature with a horse head. In *The Oval Lady* from the same year she writes of a friendship between a little girl and a hobby horse; when burned by the girl's despotic father, the hobby-horse cries out in a human voice. In Carrington's paintings and writings the human and animal worlds overlap, and half-human, half-animal hybrids are frequent inhabitants of her imagery. Mexican Indian mythology, with its belief in the human and animal components of the human soul, further strengthened this interest.

Carrington's early works also satirized the upper-class. In *The Meal of Lord Candlestick* (1938) a group of society ladies voraciously devour a lavish cannibal feast. Carrington's contempt for aristocratic *savoir-vivre* found its literary expression in the story *The Debutante* in which the author's alter ego avoids going to her first ball by sending a befriended hyena in her place. The macabre ending—the hyena tears the maid to pieces and disguises itself in her face which it eventually eats—made Breton include *The Debutante* in his *Anthology of Black Humor* (1941). The only woman included in it, Carrington is today its only surviving author.

Several dramatic flights that punctuated Carrington's life exerted a strong influence on her work. In *Crookhey Hall* (1947) a female figure flees a gloomy mansion which looks like the Carrington family house in England—the same house the artist fled to start an independent life in London and then in France with Max Ernst. Her spirit of revolt and the subsequent flights—to Spain and Mexico during World War II—had an impact on other paintings, such as *Adelita Escapes* (1987) in which a ghost-like figure is about to fly out of the room, watched with approval by a little boy. A written and then painted account of her breakdown and descent into madness—both entitled *Down Below*—reflect upon the need to escape any patriarchal power.

In Mexico Carrington moved towards more complex compositions often containing Bosch- and Breughel-like landscapes. Her interest in alchemical transformations, as exemplified in *Inn of the Dawn Horse* in the figure of a hyena being born of a cloud of plasma, provoked her to start painting with egg tempera she mixed herself. Study of the occult, of Tibetan Buddhism, and of the philosophy of Jung further enriched her work.

Her passion for the indigenous culture of Mexico brought her a governmental commission to execute a mural for the Museum of Anthropology in Mexico City. *The Magical World of the Maya* (1963) reflects Carrington's respect for the Chiapas Indians' traditional way of life and her preoccupation with ecological issues.

Carrington's feminist consciousness matured in Mexico where she took an active part in the formation of the women's movement. Under the influence of Robert Graves's *White Goddess* she formulated her philosophical stand about female power suppressed by patriarchal institutions. She typically pays tribute to female power by representing the figure of an old crone whose wisdom is deeply inaccessible, such as the old woman with a malicious smile in *The Magdalens* (1986). In her novel *The Hearing Trumpet* (first published in 1974) it is the ninety-two-year-old heroine who finds the Holy Grail to give it back to its original owner—a primal Goddess robbed by patriarchal religions. In *The Naked Truth* (1962) a naked woman with a little booklet in her hand is contrasted to a group of bearded sages, who are unable to grasp her essential knowledge despite their enormous library.

In Carrington's paintings and stories a kitchen and a nursery play important roles of places where women cook, care for children, and exercise magic at the same time. In her paintings *The House Opposite* (1947) or *Grandmother Moorhead's Aromatic Kitchen* (1975) cooking a meal is analogous to preparing a magic potion. The search for magic in everyday life is a Surrealist preoccupation that Carrington enriched with her humor and unorthodox style of feminism.

Carrington's sculptures—such as the recent fountain in Chapultapec Park in Mexico City—develop in three dimensions the familiar elements known from her paintings.

Carrington had an important influence on her friend and artistic collaborator, the painter Remedios Varo. She continues to inspire other artists through her complex iconography, technical mastery, perverse irony, and piercing intelligence.

—Agnieszka Taborska

CASCELLA, Pietro

Nationality: Italian. **Born:** Pescara, Italy, 2 February 1921. **Education:** With his father Tommaso, and at the Accademia di Belle Arti, Rome. **Family:** Married; children: Benedetta, Tommaso, Susanna and Jacopo. **Career:** Sculptor. **Awards:** First Prize, Monument to Auschwitz Competition, 1960; Prize, *Biennale di Carrara,* 1967. **Address:** Castello della Verrucola, Fivizzano, Italy.

Individual Exhibitions:

1950 Galleria l'Obelisco, Rome (with Andrea Cascella)
1954 Galleria del Naviglio, Milan
1955 Galleria Cavallino, Venice
1957 Galleria Selecta, Rome
1960 Galleria del Milione, Milan
1962 Galleria l'Obelisco, Rome
1963 Galerie du Dragon, Paris
1965 Bonino Gallery, New York
Galleria Milano, Milan
1966 *Biennale,* Venice
Galleria Milano, Milan
1967 Galleria Milano, Milan
1968 Galerie du Dragon, Paris
Galleria Milano, Milan
Musée d'Ixelles, Brussels
1969 Galleria Arte Borgogna, Milan
Galleria Nuova Pesa, Rome
1971 Palais des Beaux-Arts, Brussels
Galleria Arte Borgogna, Milan
Musée d'Art Moderne de la Ville, Paris
Rotonda di via Besana, Milan
1972 *Biennale,* Venice
1973 Galleria Goethe, Bolzano, Italy
Galleria Etrusculundens, Rome
1974 Galleria Forni, Bologna
Galleria Giulia, Rome
1975 Galleria Forum, Trieste
1976 Galleria Niccoli, Parma, Italy
Kloster Camiore di San Lazzaro, Italy
Galleria Salotto, Como, Italy
Galleria Nove Colonne, Trento, Italy
1977 Galleria Stendhal, Milan
Grafica Club, Milan
Centro Arte Moderna, Pisa
Centro Storico, Rimini, Italy
1979 Galerie Godula, Buchholz, West Germany
1980 Galleria del Naviglio, Milan
1983 Galleria Bergamini, Milan
1984 Galleria Gian Ferrari, Milan
1984 Palazzo Pubblico, Magazzini, Del Sale Siena
1986 Galleria Comunale, Forte Del Marmi
1991 Museo di Suzzara
1993 Galleria Dantesca, Torino
Galleria Fioretto, Padua
Galleria La Sanseverina, Parma
1996 *Porta del Terzo Millennio,* Accademia di San Luca, Rome
1998 *Cascella, Pietro e la Famiglia: una Lunga Vocazione Artistica,* Fondazione Monte, Parma
1999 *Progetti e Sculture,* Galleria Giulia, Rome
2000 *Le Rive Congiunte,* Chiesa di San Samuele, Venice
Pietro Cascella, Camera del Deputati, Rome

Selected Group Exhibitions:

1948 *Biennale,* Venice
1950 *Consorso Internazionale,* Rome
1952 *Consorso per il Monumento di Albisola,* Italy
1960 *Auschwitz Monument Competition Exhibition,* Auschwitz, Poland
1964 *Pittsburgh International,* Carnegie Institute, Pittsburgh
1973 *Middelheim Sculpture Biennale,* Antwerp
1975 *Disegni di 34 Scultori,* Salone delle Conference, Milan
1977 *Arte in Italia 1960–77,* Galleria Civica d'Arte Moderna, Turin
1981 *Linee della Ricerca Artistiche in Italia 1960–80,* Palazzoelle Esposizioni, Rome
1983 *Memoria dell'Uomo: La Grande Metafora,* Villa Pacchiani, Santa Croce sull'Arno, Italy
1986 *I Biennale di Scultura d'Asti,* Asti
1987 *Ipotesi per un Museo,* la Versiliana, Pietrasanta
1989 *Nei Labirinti della Materia,* Palazzo Farnese, Ortona
1990 *Scultura a Milano,* Palazzo della Permanente, Milan
1991 *Scultori a Pietrasanta,* Studio d'Arte La Subbia, Pietrasanta
1994 *Per un Amico: 27 Scultori Ricordano Pier Carlo Santini,* Fondazione Ragghianti, Lucca
1995 *Oro d'Autore,* Museo Nacional de Bellas Artes, Buenos Aires
1996 *VIII Biennale Internazionale di Scultura ''Città di Carrara,''* Carrara, Italy
1997 *L'Arte Nella Città,* Triennale, Milan
1998 *Il Tempo del Marmo e Quello del Bronzo,* Museo del Marmo, Carrara, Italy (travelled to Willy Brandt-Haus, Berlin; Hôtel de Ville, Neuchâtel)
1999 *XIII Quadriennale,* Palazzo delle Esposizioni, Rome
2000 *X Biennale Internazionale ''Città di Carrara,''* Carrara, Italy

Collections:

Museo d'Arte Moderna, Bologna; Middelheim Museum, Antwerp; Museo Cascella, Pescara; University of Chieti; City of Parma.

Permanent Public Installations:

War Memorial, Albissola, Italy, 1956; *Auschwitz Memorial,* with Andrea Cascella and the architect Lafuente, Auschwitz, Poland 1960; *Mazzini Monument,* Piazza della Republica, Milan 1974; *Berlusconi family mausoleum,* Milan; *Nave,* Pescara, 1987; *Volta Celeste,* Milan 1990; *Via Emilia Monument,* Parma 1990; *Porta della Sapienza,* Pisa 1995; *Scrigno,* Parma 1997; *Luogo dell'Incontro,* Isernia, 1998; *Teatro della Germinazione,* Parco Nazionale d'Abruzzo 1998; *L'Acqua*

Pietro Cascella: *Nave.* Photo by Aurelio Amendola. ©Pietro Cascella.

e la Pietra, Fontana per la Baraclit in Casentino 1999; *Fontana nella Città di Chiavari,* Pistoia 2000; *Porta del Mediterraneo,* Nuoro 2000.

Publications:

On CASCELLA: Books—*Il Monumento di Auschwitz,* exhibition catalog, by Mario de Michel, Milan 1960; *Pietro Cascella* by Cesare Vivaldi, Milan 1966; *Mostra dell Besana* by Guido Ballo, Milan 1971; *Pietro Cascella* by Guido Vegani, Milan 1974; *Maestri Contemporanei: Pietro Cascella* by Roberto Sanesi, Milan 1983; *Pietro Cascella* by Enrico Crispolti, Florence 1984; *Distesa Estate,* exhibition catalog with introduction by Marcello Polacci, 1986; *Nei Labirinti della Materia,* exhibition catalog with text by Corrado Marsan, 1989; *Pietro Cascella: Opere Monumentali* by Mario de Micheli, Rossana Bossaglia, and Pietro Toesca, Firenze 1993; *Per un Amico: 27 Scultori Ricordano Pier Carlo Santini,* exhibition catalog with introduction by Rossana Bossaglia, 1994; *Nello Specchio di Mozart,* exhibition catalog with text by Enrico Bellati, Firenze 1995; *Scultori del Libro,* exhibition catalog with text by Vittorio Vettori and Mario Guidotti, Vicenza 1997; *Cascella: Pietro e la Famiglia: una Lunga Vocazione Artistica,* exhibition catalog with introduction by Tommaso Paloscia and text by Carlo Franza, Parma 1998; *Progetti e Sculture,* exhibition catalog with text by Tommaso Paloscia, Rome 1999; *Accadde in Toscana,* exhibition catalog by Tommaso Paloscia, Firenze 1999; *Le Rive Congiunte,* exhibition catalog with text by Mario Luzi, Venice 2000; *Pietro Cascella alla Camera dei Deputati,* exhibition catalog with text by Fred Licht, Rome 2000.

*

My works are a great stone-dream, a dream which crosses the time, if it answers the requests of the time we're living in, if it is a mirror of our time in which everybody recognizes himself. I'm interested in large town-spaces. I'm interested in human communities, in meeting places and public spaces. In order to confer poetry on the suburbs of great cities, art may be a good advisor against violence.

—Pietro Cascella

* * *

From a distinguished family of sculptors, Pietro Cascella and his brother Andrea have emerged as two of the most gifted practitioners in contemporary Italian art. The two brothers are similar in their media preference and imagery, but Pietro can be identified principally for his choice of more monumental conceptions, in which scale, simplicity, and in particular rough unfinished marble are basic components.

Stone carvers are comparatively rare in modern art but for an Italian it is both a challenge and a reference to national history and the natural scene. Cascella has said that one cannot consider the process ''in terms of the consumer society; the method of working, and the time required, belongs to a former age; it is an art of patience.'' He prefers to confront a huge block of marble (a la Michelangelo, perhaps).

Two distinct forms emerge in Pietro Cascella's work; rounded, feminine, sexual shapes, similar in a generalised way to the shapes found in Henry Moore's reclining females; but with Cascella there is no evocative comparison of the nude body to a gentle, rolling landscape. He is more involved in the complexities of the body, sexually curious, isolating and examining details, so that the emergent sculptures are enlarged combinations of rounded forms and orifices. They do not resemble landscape, or indeed nature in general, except that their organic nature evokes memories and references. Enormously enlarged, physically dominating, and abstracted beyond original inspiration, they manage to promote the idea of intimacy and inevitability.

His sculptures neither provoke nor disturb. More open to doubt is the development from these organic, intimate, sensual conceptions, to extended public monuments, some of which he has worked on with his brother Andrea. These include the ''Auschwitz Monument,'' the Gate of Peace'' at Tel Aviv, the ''National Congress Monument'' at Strasbourg and the Mazzini commemoration in Milan. One can see the reason for such commissions since it is difficult to think of other modern sculptors who can undertake such portentous requests. Individual characteristic works by sculptors are often commissioned as public monuments, and no doubt enhance the space they occupy; Cascella, in the great Mediterranean tradition, produces massive public celebration, partly architecture, part landscape, partly sculpture. They inevitably lack the personal involvement of the more intimate works, combining with the intimate rounded forms, the more architectural details of flat pavements and geometrical intersections.

—Charles Spencer

CASTELLANI, Enrico

Nationality: Italian. **Born:** Castelmassa, Rovigo, Italy, 4 August 1930. **Education:** Novara and Milan; studied painting and sculpture at the Académie Royale des Beaux-Arts, Brussels, 1952–56, and architecture at the Ecole Nationale Supèrieure de la Cambre, Belgium, 1956. **Career:** Has lived and worked in Milan since 1956: Founder, with Piero Manzoni, *Azimuth* journal, Milan, 1959; associated with the Zero Group, Milan, 1962. **Awards:** Painting Prize, Nagaoka Museum, Tokyo, 1967; Gold Medal, *Biennale di San Marino,* 1967. **Agent:** Galerie M, Haus Weitmar, Bochum, West Germany. **Address:** 01010 Cellere, Vitterbo, Italy.

Individual Exhibitions:

1959 Galerie Kasper, Lausanne, Switzerland
1960 Galleria Azimut, Milan
1961 New Vision Centre, London
Galleria La Tartaruga, Rome
1962 Galerie Aujourd'hui, Brussels
1963 Galleria dell'Ariete, Milan
1964 Galleria La Polena, Genoa
Galleria Notizie, Turin
Galleria del Leone, Venice
Gallerie Wulfengasse, Klagenfurt, Austria
1965 Galleria La Tartaruga, Rome
Galerie Lawrence, Paris
1966 Galleria Notizie, Turin
Betty Parsons Gallery, New York
Tokyo Gallery
1968 *Documenta,* Kassel, West Germany
1970 Galerie M. Bochum, West Germany
1971 Artestudio, Macerata, Italy
1972 Galleriaforma, Genoa
1988 Kodama Gallery, Osaka
1989 Niccoli Gallery, Parma
1994 Museo Laboratorio di Arte Contemporanea, Rome
1999 Lia Rumma Gallery, Milan
Galleria Civica di Arte Contemporanea, Trento

Selected Group Exhibitions:

1960 *Monochrome Malerei,* Städtisches Museum, Leverkusen, West Germany
1961 *Nove Tendencije I,* Zagreb
1962 *Zero,* Stedelijk Museum, Amsterdam
1964 *Guggenheim International,* Guggenheim Museum, New York
1965 *The Responsive Eye,* Museum of Modern Art, New York
1966 *Third Exhibition,* Nagaoka Museum, Tokyo
1968 *Many Italian Artists,* Jewish Museum, New York
1971 *11 Italiener Heute,* Museum am Ostwall, Dortmund, West Germany
1981 *Artee Critica,* Galleria Nazionale d'Arte Moderna, Rome
1986 *Aspects of Italian Art 1960–85,* Kunstverein, Frankfurt
1996 *ARS AEVI 2000: 10 International Artists,* Centro per l'Arte Contemporanea Luigi Pecci, Prato, Italy

Collections:

Galleria Nazionale d'Arte Moderna, Rome.

Publications:

On CASTELLANI: Books—*Visites d'Atelier* by Giulia Veronesi, Lausanne, Switzerland 1959; *La Linea dell'Arte Italiana* by Guido Ballo, Milan 1964; *Testo del Libro Castellani Pittore* by Vincenzo Agnetti, Milan 1968; *Op Art* by Cyril Barrett, London 1970; *Enrico Castellani: 1 June-30 June, 1988,* exhibition catalog, Osaka 1988; *Enrico Castellani: The Minimum Travel, the Minimum Change,* exhibition catalog, Rome 1994; *ARS AEVI 2000: 10 International Artists,* exhibition catalog, Milan 1996. **Articles—**''La Peinture Objet dans l'Art Italien Contemporain'' by Gillo Dorfles in *L'Oeil*

(Paris), no 121, 1965; Il Purismo di Castellani'' by M. F. dell Arco in *L'Avanti* (Milan), no. 6/8, 1966; ''Enrico Castellani: Portrait by Armin Lake'' by Kay Heymer in *Du,* no. 1, January 1994; ''Enrico Castellani: Palazzo Fabroni'' by Massimo Carboni in *Artforum* (New York), vol. 35, no. 2, October 1996; review in *Flash Art (International Edition)* (Milan), no. 146, May/June 1989; ''Enrico Castellani'' in *Artforum* (New York), vol. 37, no. 10, Summer 1999.

* * *

By 1956, when he and Piero Manzoni founded the review *Azimuth,* Enrico Castellani had already worked out the basic principles which have governed his artistic experiments ever since. The Monochromatic surfaces which he now began to produce were essentially reactions against his earlier irrationalist exercises, with their explosive colors and violent imagery. Thus his later work is basically abstract in character: in intensity and aim he comes close to the conceptualism of an artist like Lucio Fontana.

In his monochromatic surfaces Castellani has explored new areas of painting, yet he also wishes to work within the tradition which leads back to the neo-plastic origins of art, as Gestalt psychological theory defines them. These red, yellow, blue, white and silver canvases are hung over projecting nails of varying lengths, so that the surface is contoured. And over these surfaces lights play, half-lights corresponding to the convexities, shadows to the concavities. These chiaroscuro effects give his work some affinity with the early Op-Art of the early 1960s, but the intensity of Castellani's work goes far beyond those cold experiments.

At the corner of his work lies the quintessentially modern concern with space and time. He expresses the problem by means of his contoured surfaces—''spatial modulators,'' as Dorfles calls them—which both contain and liberate space. Castellani wishes us to grasp the flexibility of space; and the lights which play over the surfaces at varying rates of speed are designed to express the continuity of time and the relationship which exists between time and space themselves. His experiments have opened up new vistas.

—Roberto G. Lambarelli

CASTELLI, Luciano

Nationality: Swiss. **Born:** Lucerne, 28 September 1951. **Education:** School of Art and Design, Lucerne, 1969. **Career:** Lived and worked in Lucerne until 1977, Rome, 1977–78, and in Berlin since 1978. **Awards:** Kiefer Hablitzel Stipendium, 1970–71; Bundes Stipendium, 1973–75. **Agents:** Galerie Stahli, 39 Gruezgasse, Zurich 8008, Switzerland; Galerie de Appel, 196 Brouwersgracht, Amsterdam, Netherlands. **Address:** Reckenbuhlstrasse 17, 6005 Lucerne, Switzerland.

Individual Exhibitions:

1971 Galerie Toni Gerber, Berne
1975 Galerie Stahli, Zurich
Galerie de Appel, Amsterdam
Galerie t'Venster, Rotterdam
Salle Municipal Palino, Geneva
1978 Galerie Handschin, Basle
1979 Galerie Stahli, Zurich
1981 Centre d'art contemporain, Geneva
Galerie Farideh Cadot, Paris
Annina Nosei Gallery, New York
1983 CAPC/Musee d'Art Contemporain, Bordeaux, France (with Fetting and Salome)
1984 Galerie Farideh Cadot, Paris
1987 Harcourts Contemporary Gallery, San Francisco
1989 *Luciano Castelli: Images,* Musée Cantonal des Beaux-Arts Lausanne, Switzerland
Luciano Castelli: Images 1972–1988, Musee Cantonal des Beaux-Arts, Lausanne, Switzerland
1990 Raab Galerie, Berlin
Luciano Castelli: New Paintings, Richard Gray Gallery, Chicago
1991 *Luciano Castelli,* Galerie Fischer, Lucerne, Switzerland
1996 *Le miroir du désir: Luciano Castelli,* Maison Européenne de la Photographie, Paris
1998 Musée Edgar Mélik, Cabriès

Selected Group Exhibitions:

1971 *Biennale des Jeunes,* Paris
1972 *Documenta 5,* Museum Fridericianum, Kassel, West Germany
1974 *Transformer-Aspekte der Travestie,* Kunstmuseum, Lucerne
1975 *Biennale des Jeunes,* Paris.
1980 *Biennale,* Venice
1981 *Schweizer Kunst '70-'80.* Kunstmuseum, Lucerne
Im Westen nichts Neues, Kunstmuseum, Lucerne
12 Kunstler aus Deutschland, Kunsthalle, Basle
1982 *A l'Ouest rien de Nouveau,* Centre d'Art Contemporain, Geneva
1987 *Berlinart 1961–87,* Museum of Modern Art, New York (travelled to San Francisco)
1991 *Painter/Sculptor,* Raab Galerie, Berlin (traveled to Raab Gallery, London)
1994 *Neue Wilde aus Berlin,* Schleswig-Holsteinisches Landesmuseum, Schleswig, Germany
Einstellung 25: Photography of the 1990s in Germany, Raab Galerie, Berlin
1997 *38th Swiss Art and Antiquities Fair, IAM,* Messehallen, Zurich

Collections:

Kunstmuseum, Basle, Kunstmuseum, Lucerne.

Publications:

By CASTELLI: Articles—interview by Jean-Christophe Ammann in *Rapport der Innerschweiz,* exhibition catalog, Zurich 1974; interview by Jean-Christophe Ammann in *Transformer-Aspekte der Travestie,* exhibition catalog, Lucerne 1974; interview by Jacques Clayssen in *Identité/Identifications,* exhibition catalog, Paris 1976.

On CASTELLI: Books—*Visualierte Denkprozesse,* exhibition catalog, by Jean-Christophe Ammann, Lucerne 1971; *Giovanne Arte Svizzera,* exhibition catalog, by W. Schonenberger and Theo Kneubuhler, Milan 1972; *Aspekte der Travestie,* exhibition catalog, Lucerne 1974; *9th Biennale,* exhibition catalog, Paris 1975; *Fundatie,* exhibition catalog, Amsterdam 1979; *Schweizer Kunst '70-'80,* exhibition catalog, Lucerne 1981; *12 Kunstler aus Deutschland,* exhibition catalog, Basle 1982; *A l'Ouest rien de Nouveau,* exhibition catalog, with texts by Martin Kunz and Eberhard Roters, Geneva 1982; *Luciano Castelli: Images=Bilder,* exhibition catalog, Lausanne 1989; *Luciano Castelli: Pictures 1972–88,* exhibition catalog with text by Erika Billeter, Lausanne 1989; *Luciano Castelli: New Paintings,* exhibition catalog, Chicago 1990; *Luciano Castelli,* exhibition catalog with text by Erika Billeter, Lucerne 1991; *Luciano Castelli: The Dreamed Woman,* exhibition catalog, Bern 1993.

* * *

Luciano Castelli's painting is painting for effect; it shows off its colours with unbridled eroticism and aestheticism. Between the rapid brush-strokes there appear fragments or details of an image, "prisoner" of the swift play set in motion by the colour-shape itself. The result is a surface abstraction/figuration, with no spatial depth. It is the emotive effect of an instant projected towards a chance pleasure. The artist gives free rein to the gesture, to the sensual peacefulness of his becoming, to the eclecticism of his deviations. The artist has only love of himself; his "inner emotions" last only a moment and are therefore exploited to the full. It would be sheer hypocrisy to emerge from this perverted state of grace; he has rather to enter freely into it, to make clearer the duration of the gestural orgasm.

Castelli is an artist by vocation; his daily prayers are made to beauty and to exhausting pleasure. Hedonism is the unknown, to be violated, to be gratified. Hence the screaming density of the colour-shape, the fragments of image exposed in the grip of excitement. The surface, crowded in this way, looks like a film show which we attend as *voyeur.* The artist, moving within the transient multicoloured light, creates unexpected situations; his movements (posed or dancing), charged with exhibitionism, let that self-love shine through above all.

Castelli's painting (like that of Rainer Fetting, Helmut Middendorf and Salome) is pervaded with auto-erotism. With or without the self-portrait, the artist always portrays a little of himself. Painting is thus a marvelous, exhilarating, freethinking, ambiguous medium to exalt or satisfy the call to be an artist. It does not aim at surprise effects; any that are produced are only apparent. It is actually the appearance, and the wonderful melancholy of it, that attract and seduce the artist. In the self-portrait he seems to see how deviation changes aspect, obedient to an implacable fate that inexorably deforms the reality. But the self-portrait is disconcerting to anyone who looks for the logic of the likeness in it. Instead, the artist thirsts for extravagance; he is filled with an urge to follow the irreverent, shocking path of his narcissism in order to hide the true, fleeting image. Luciano Castelli disguises himself in order to fling out something disturbing through the medium of a painting whose very facility makes it pungent and enigmatic. It may be that his painting reflects a tendency to deja vu, and why ever should it represent the invisible? An enervating scepticism does not consort with the art of the self-portrait.

—Italo Mussa

CATTELAN, Maurizio

Nationality: Italian. **Born:** Padua, Italy, 1960. **Education:** Self-taught. **Career:** Independent artist, New York. **Agent:** Galerie Emmanuel Perrotin, 30 rue Louise Weiss, 75013 Paris.

Selected Individual Exhibitions:

1990 *Strategie,* Galleria Neon, Bologna; Studio Oggetto, Milan; Leonardi V-Idea, Genoa
1991 *Stand abusivo,* Arte Fiera Bologna, Italy (action)
1992 *Edizioni dell'Obbligo,* Juliet, Trieste, Italy
Doppiogioco, Serre di Rapolano, Italy (action)
Fondazione Oblomov, Accademia di Brera, Milan (action)
Rassegna piccoli editori, Castello di Belgioioso, Italy (action)
1993 Galleria Massimo De Carlo, Milan
Galleria Raucci Santamaria, Naples
1994 Laure Genillard Gallery, London
Daniel Newburg Gallery, New York
Daniel Buchholz, Cologne
Galerie Analix, Geneva
1995 *Errotin, le vrai lapin,* Galerie Emmanuel Perrotin, Paris
Choose your destination, how to get a Museum-paid vacation, University of South Florida Contemporary Art Museum, Tampa (action)
1996 Ars Futura Galerie, Zurich
Laure Genillard Gallery, London
Galleria Massimo De Carlo, Milan
1997 *Maurizio Cattelan,* Castello di Rivoli, Turin (catalog)
Maurizio Cattelan, Wiener Secession, Vienna (catalog)
Moi-Même-Soi-Même, Galerie Perrotin, Paris
Maurizio Cattelan, Espace Jules Verne, Centre d'Art de Bretigny-sur-Orge, France (catalog)
1998 Institute of Visual Arts (INOVA), Milwaukee
Project #65, The Museum of Modern Art, New York
1999 Anthony d'Offay Gallery, London
Maurizio Cattelan, Kunsthalle Basel, Switzerland (catalog)
Massimo De Carlo, Milan
6th Caribbean Biennial, St. Kitts, British West Indies (co-curated with Jens Hoffmann)
2000 Migros Museum für Gegenwartskunst, Zurich
Artpace, San Antonio
Forum, Centre Georges Pompidou, Paris
Maurizio Cattelan, Marian Goodman Gallery, New York

Selected Group Exhibitions:

1990 *Existenz Maximum,* Instituto degli innocenti, Florence
Improvvisazione libera, Museo Pecci, Prato, Italy
Take Over, Galleria Inga Pin, Milan; Landau Gallery, Los Angeles
Ipotesi d'arte giovane, Faqbbrica del vapore, Milan
1991 *Loro,* Castello Visconteo, Trezzo, Italy
Briefing, Galleria Inga Pin, Milan
Anni 90, Galleria d'Arte Moderna, Bologna, Italy
Medialismo, Galleria Vitolo, Rome
1992 *Twenty Fragile Pieces,* Galleria Analix, Geneva

Maurizio Cattelan: *The Ninth Hour,* 2001. ©AFP/Corbis.

Ottovolante, Museo d'Arte Contemporanea, Bergamo, Italy
Una Domenica a Rivara, Castello di Rivara, Italy
1993 *Aperto 93,* Venice Biennale (catalog)
1994 *Incertaine Identité,* Galerie Analix, Geneva
Prima Linea, Flash Art Museum, Trevi, Italy
L'hiver de l'amour, ARC/Musée d'Art Moderne de la Ville de Paris
P. S. 1/Institute for Art and Urban Resources, Long Island City, New York
1995 *Photomontage,* Le Consortium, Dijon, France
Das spiel in der Kunst, Neue Galerie, Graz, Austria; Arlge Kunst, Bolzano, Italy
Kwangju Biennial, Kwangju, Korea
Caravanserraglio, Ex Aurum, Pescara, Italy
1996 *Fool's Rain,* Institute of Contemporary Art, London
Le Magasin, Centre d'Art Contemporain de Grenoble, France
L'Ameus Corps, Musée d'Art Contemporain, Marseille, France
Crap Shoot, De Appel, Amsterdam
1997 *Skulpture Project,* Landesmuseum, Münster, Germany
Fatto in Italia, Centre d'Art Contemporain, Geneva, Switzerland; Institute of Contemporary Art, London, England
Moment Ginza, Le Magasin, Centre d'Art Contemporain de Grenoble, France; Fargfabriken, Stockholm
47th Venice Biennale (Italian Pavilion with Cucchi and Spalletti), Italy (catalog)
1998 *Artificial,* Museu d'Art Contemporani de Barcelona, Spain
Wounds, Moderna Museet, Stockholm
Manifesta 2, European Biennale of Contemporary Art, Luxemburg
Wiener Secession, Vienna, Austria
1999 *La Ville, le Jardin, la Memoire,* Villa Medici, Rome
Abracadabra, Tate Gallery, London (catalog)
Let's get together, Kunsthalle Wien, Vienna
Aperto Over All, Venice Biennale
2000 *Apocalypse: Beauty and Horror in Contemporary Art,* Royal Academy of Art, London (catalog)
Presumed Innocent, CAPC Musée d'Art Contemporain de Bordeaux, France
Age of Influence: Reflections in the Mirror of American Culture, Museum of Contemporary Art, Chicago
Expo 2000, Hannover, Germany
2001 *Home is where the heArt is,* Museum van Loon, Amsterdam
Let's Entertain, Walker Art Center, Minneapolis; Musée National d'Art Moderne-Centre Georges Pompidou,

Paris; Museo Rufino Tamayo, Mexico City; Miami Art Museum

Publications:

By CATTELAN: Articles—''Everybody Must Get Stoned'' interview by Alicia Bona in *Christie's Contemporary catalog,* 17 May 2001.

On CATTELAN: Books—*Projects 65: Maurizio Cattelan* (brochure), by Laura Hoptman, New York 1998; *Maurizio Cattelan,* with text by Frank Bonami, B. Vanderlinden, with interview by Nancy Spector, London 2000; *Maurizio Cattelan,* London 2000. **Articles—** ''Maurizio Cattelan'' by Olivier Zahm and Warren Niesluchowski in *Artforum International,* summer 1995; ''Maurizio Cattelan . . . Went Home'' by Jeff Rian in *Flash Art,* October 1996; ''Maurizio Cattelan: The Village Idiot'' by David Perreau in *Art Press,* 1998; ''Maurizio Cattelan'' (3 article special section) in *Parkett,* 2000; ''The Witz Kid'' by Jean-Yves Jouannais, Christophe Kihm, and Jacques Demarcq in *Art Press,* February 2001.

* * *

Maurizio Cattelan is one of the best-known Italian artists to have emerged internationally in the 1990s. He has had exhibitions at Site Santa Fe and Skulptur Projeckte in Münster in 1997, at the Tate Gallery in London in 1999, and has participated in the 1993, 1997, 1999, and 2001 Venice Biennales. Unusual for an artist of his renown, Cattelan did not follow the professional route of training at art school, but entered the art system through the side door of happenstance. The words ''trickster,'' ''jester,'' and ''thief'' appear in almost every article written about him. His installations and actions disrupt civic laws, religious tenets, and societal conventions. From the preparatory drawings to the finished products, Cattelan employs the services of other artisans to complete his works and continues to deny that he is, in fact, an artist at all.

His most controversial work to date, *La Nona Ora* (The Ninth Hour), executed in 1999 features a lifesize, realistically styled wax figure of the Pope that has fallen down and is being crushed under the weight of a large meteor. The scene is complete in all the details, with lush red carpet, scattered broken glass, and the hole that the meteor presumably created in the glass ceiling. Cattelan intended to make the work so realistic that it ''dissolves into pure communication,'' as he told Alicia Bona. While he thinks of this piece as an exercise in absurdity, Cattelan also used the icon of the Pope as a pretext for a metaphor of the meeting of the sacred and the profane in daily life. Perhaps the most surprisingly comical aspect of the Pope's figure is that Cattelan has given the Pope tube socks, and as Cattelan told Alicia Bona in an interview: ''comedy can be an easy way out from the boredom of living.''

Costumed characters are a recurring theme in Cattelan's work. For a project at The Museum of Modern Art in 1998, Cattelan hired an actor wearing an enormous, cartoony head of the 20th century's most famous artist, Pablo Picasso, to stand at the door and greet visitors as they came in to the museum. Curator Laura Hoptman places his use of masquerade in the tradition that includes *commedia dell'arte,* Pirandello, Dario Fo, and Roberto Benigni. Picasso functions as a kind of logo for the museum, but in the end, as Hoptman writes, ''Who is the target of this joke anyway? It is The Museum of Modern Art? Picasso? The audience? Cattelan himself?'' The fact that Cattelan does not take sides but involves all is the successful equation of his project. In *Tarzan and Jane,* 1993, he convinced two gallerists, on whom he relies to sell his work, to wear full-body lion costumes during the run of his exhibitions. In *Errotin, Le Vrai Lapin,* 1994, Cattelan persuaded French gallerist, Emmanuel Perrotin, to sell his work for one month dressed as a phallus shaped rabbit.

Not only animal costumes but actual animals play an important part in Cattelan's oeuvre. At his first New York exhibition, *Warning! Enter at your own risk. Do not touch, do not feed, no smoking, no photographs, no dogs, thank you,* 1994, Cattelan placed a live donkey in the gallery with a crystal chandelier. He intended the donkey to be a stand-in for himself, the buffoon in the world of high culture. For *La Ballata di Trotski* (The Ballad of Trotsky), 1996, Cattelan suspended a taxidermied horse from the ceiling. In this unnatural state, the horse represents the impossibility of action and becomes a symbol for loss, absence, and death. Cattelan plays on the anthropomorphic qualities of animals, and while cartoon animals are used to make human stories more mild, these are not cartoons but actual dead animals that contribute an uneasy level of grossness to the work. *Bidibidobidiboo* from 1996 is diorama of a squirrel suicide, where Cattelan has posed a stuffed squirrel slumped over a formica table with a mini revolver at its feet. To complement the surrealism of the scene, Cattelan adds tiny domestic touches such as a little glass of water on the table and dirty dishes still in the sink.

Another one of Cattelan's guises is that of the criminal or thief. *Il Super Noi* (Super Us), 1992 features portraits of himself as a missing person done by police sketch artists based on descriptions of Cattelan by friends and family. As a modern day art world Robin Hood, Cattelan created the piece *Fondazione Oblomov* in 1992. He solicited money from a series of donors and created a prize that he awarded to an artist provided that he or she did not exhibit their work for at least a year. No one accepted. Cattelan is also a thief of ideas. In *Untitled,* 1996, he carved a delicate ''Z'' shape into a canvas, thus humorously conflating Lucio Fontana, a leading Italian artist of the 1960s who painted monochromes and then elegantly slashed the surfaces, and Zorro, the artful dodger. On other occasions he has both filed a police report for a ''stolen'' artwork and exhibited that instead and hijacked a complete gallery show by another artist and installed it as his own at a gallery in Amsterdam. Cattelan's magazine, *Permanent Food,* published irregularly since 1995 consists solely of pages taken from other magazines that are chosen by other artists and friends.

Hoptman refers to Cattelan's work as "legalized but unofficial subversion." While he hires stand-ins for interviews and assumes the role of the anti-heroic artist, Cattelan acknowledges his dependence on the very system he parodies. ''How can I contest the system if I'm totally inside it?,'' he asked Nancy Spector in an interview. Besides, even if he does not acknowledge himself as an artist, he has the right to earn a living.

—Sarah Wagner

CAULFIELD, Patrick

Nationality: British. **Born:** London in 1936. **Education:** Chelsea School of Art, London, under Jack Smith, 1956–60, and at the Royal College of Art, London, 1960–63. **Career:** Painter and printmaker: lives and works in London. Lecturer, Chelsea School of Art, 1963–71. **Awards:** Prix de Jeunes Artistes (graphics), 1965. **Agent:** Waddington

Galleries, London. **Address:** c/o Waddington Galleries, 11 Cork Street, London W1, England.

Individual Exhibitions:

1965 Robert Fraser Gallery, London
Galerie d'Aujourd'hui, Brussels (with Derek Boshier)
1966 Robert Elkon Gallery, New York
1967 Studio Marconi, Milan
Robert Fraser Gallery, London
1968 Robert Elkon Gallery, New York
1969 Waddington Galleries, London
1971 D. M. Gallery, London
Waddington Galleries, London
1972 Galerie Stadler, Paris (with Howard Hodgkin and Michael Moon)
Sweeney Reed Galleries, Victoria, Australia
1973 Waddington Galleries, London
Europalia, Brussels
1974 O. K. Harris Gallery, New York
Kinsman Morrison Gallery, London
1975 Waddington Galleries, London
Scottish Arts Council Gallery, Edinburgh
1976 Arnolfini Gallery, Bristol
1977 Tortue Gallery, Santa Monica, California
1978 Tate Gallery, London
1979 Waddington Galleries, London
1980 Hughes Gallery, Brisbane
IAC, Basle
Tolarno Galleries, Melbourne
Gardner Center for the Arts, University of Sussex, Brighton (travelled to the Oriel Gallery, Cardiff, and the Midland Group Gallery, Nottingham)
1981 Walker Art Gallery, Liverpool (travelled to the Tate Gallery, London, 1982)
Waddington Galleries, London
1982 Nishimura Gallery, Tokyo
1983 Arnolfini Gallery, Bristol
1985 Waddington Galleries, London
Bernardelli Gallery, Rio de Janeiro (toured South America, 1985–87)
1989 Waddington Galleries, London (travelled to Tony Shafrazi Gallery, New York)
1990 Music Theatre Gallery, London
1993 Claudine Papillon Gallery, Paris
Serpentine Gallery, London
1997 Waddington Galleries, London
1998 Waddington Galleries, London
1999 Hayward Gallery, London (travelled to Musee National d'Histoire et d'Art, Luxembourg; Centro de Arte Moderna Jose de Azeredo Perdigao, Lisbon; Yale Center for British Art, New Haven)
Fundacao Calouste Gulbenkian, Lisbon
Alan Cristea Gallery, London

Selected Group Exhibitions:

1964 *The New Generation,* Whitechapel Art Gallery, London
1965 *Biennale des Jeunes,* Musée National d'Art Moderne, Paris
1966 *Recent Still Life,* Rhode Island School of Design, Providence
1967 *Jeunes Peintres Anglais,* Palais des Beaux-Arts, Brussels
1969 *Marks on a Canvas,* Museum am Ostwall, Dortmund, West Germany
1971 *Junge Englander,* Kunststudio Westfalen, Bielefeld, West Germany
1974 *British Painting 74,* Hayward Gallery, London
1976 *Arte Inglese Oggi,* Palazzo Reale, Milan
1982 *Aspects of British: Art Today,* Metropolitan Art Museum, Tokyo (toured Japan)
1984 *British Artists' Books 1970–83,* Atlantis Gallery, London
1992 *Ready Steady Go: Painting of the Sixties from the Arts Council Collection,* Royal Festival Hall, London
1995 *Peter Blake, Patrick Caulfield, Howard Hodgkin: Paintings from the 60's and 70's,* Waddington Galleries, London
1997 *British Art: A Selection From Waddington Galleries,* Foire Internationale d'Art Contemporain, Paris (travelled to Tokyo International Art Festival; Art Cologne; Art Miami '98; European Fine Art Fair, Maastrict)
Hockney to Hodgkin: British Master Prints 1960–1980, New Orleans Museum of Art, Louisiana
Drawing Distinctions: Twentieth-Century Drawings and Watercolours from the British Council Collection, University Art Museum/Pacific Film Archive, University of California at Berkeley

Collections:

Arts Council of Great Britain, London: Tate Gallery, London; Walker Art Gallery, Liverpool; Whitworth Art Gallery, Manchester; Hirshhorn Museum and Sculpture Garden, Washington, D.C.: Virginia Museum of Fine Arts, Richmond; Art Gallery of Ontario, Toronto.

Publications:

By CAULFIELD: Books—''Patrick Caulfield: The Poems of Jules Laforgue,'' with introduction by Sean O'Brien, London 1995. **Articles—**''Why Do Artists Make Prints?'' in *Studio International* (London), June 1967; ''Questionnaire'' in *London Magazine,* April/May 1979.

On CAULFIELD: Books—*Paintings by Patrick Caulfield, exhibition catalog, London 1967; Patrick Caulfield* by Christopher Finch, London 1971; *Patrick Caulfield,* exhibition catalog, London 1975; *Patrick Caulfield: Paintings and Prints,* exhibition catalog, by Norbert Lynton, Edinburgh 1975; *Patrick Caulfield Print Retrospective: Complete Works 1964–1976,* exhibition catalog, Santa Monica, California 1977; *Patrick Caulfield: Paintings 1963–81,* exhibition catalog by Marco Livingston, London 1981; *Patrick Caulfield,* exhibition catalog edited by the Waddington Galleries, London 1985; *Patrick Caulfield* by John McEwan, London 1987; *Patrick Caulfield,* exhibition catalog, London 1989; *Patrick Caulfield: Paintings 1963–1992,* with foreword by Andrea Schlieker, London 1992; *Peter Blake, Patrick Caulfield, Howard Hodgkin: Paintings from the 60's and 70's,* exhibition catalog, London 1995; *Patrick Caulfield: New Paintings,* exhibition catalog, London 1997; *Patrick Caulfield: Works on Board,* exhibition catalog, London 1998; *Patrick Caulfield: The Complete Prints 1964–1999* by Mel Gooding and Alan Cristea,

London 1999; *Patrick Caulfield,* exhibition catalog, with text by Mel Gooding, London 1999. **Articles—**''From Illusion to Allusion'' by Christopher Finch in *Art and Artists* (London), April 1966; ''Comic Strip Pop'' by John Loring in *Arts Magazine* (New York), September 1974; ''Patrick Caulfield'' by William Feaverin *The Observer* (London), 30 November 1975; ''A Talent in English Painting'' by James Burr in *Apollo* (London), July 1979; ''Patrick Caulfield'' by Mel Gooding in *Art Monthly* (London), no. 163, February 1993; ''London: Caulfield, Scott, Oulton, Riley'' in *Burlington Magazine* (London), vol. 139, no. 1131, June 1997; ''Patrick Caulfield: The Artist Who Looked at a Pipe'' by Colin Martin in *The Lancet,* vol. 353, no. 9158, 27 March 1999; ''Happy Hour: David Bussel on Patrick Caulfield'' by David Bussel in *Frieze* (London), no. 45, March-April 1999; ''Patrick Caulfield'' by Rachel Withers in *Artforum* (New York), vol. 37, no. 8, April 1999; ''Patrick Caulfield'' by Norbert Lynton in *Burlington Magazine* (London), vol. 141, no. 1157, August 1999; ''The Not-So-Happy Hours of Patrick Caulfield'' by Barry Schwabsky in *Art in America* (New York), vol. 87, no. 11, November 1999; ''Bonjour Monsieur Caulfield'' in *Contemporary Visual Arts* (London), no. 22, 1999.

* * *

Patrick Caulfield is a deceptive artist. At first glance his work looks easy, unimaginative, almost childlike. When you examine it more closely, things look very different. The comparisons with Lichtenstein and other ''Pop'' artists are ridiculous. Caulfield is a profoundly European painter who never seeks to glamourise or depict American merchandise. Caulfield selects everyday objects and sometimes juxtaposes them with exotic ones. In ''Still Life with Dagger'' a dull jug stands next to an exotic turquoise dagger from the Victoria and Albert Museum. Banality is linked with sophistication such as in ''Still Life on a Table.'' Highly decorative china is placed against a background of a parody of modern art. In ''Pony'' the horse has taken an imposing Stubbs pose but looks as though it had been painted by numbers. In ''Still Life with Candle'' the vanitas theme without the skull appears. The candle is burnt out, the bread is being eaten by a mouse and the glass has fallen over. In ''View of the Rooftops'' Caulfield has become romantic. The flame red background is reminiscent of the great fire in *Gone with the Wind.* In the successful ''Bend in the Road'' the bend is executed in the corniest of ways by leading the viewers' eye into the canvas—similar to the children walking down the road into the sunset advertising Start Rite shoes. Sometimes Caulfield makes perverse subject choices such as the ''Smokeless Coal Fire'' or the room divider.

Humans are rarely present but their presence is felt. In ''Window at Night'' a window is open and a light is on. The contrast between the warm glow of the room and the blackness of the night is superbly portrayed. Caulfield makes little attempt at shading or modelling, but the familiar black lines create vitality. In the painting ''Inner Office'' there is again a contrast between the external and internal world. The desk is silhouetted, and the objects lying on it are highly defined—the little bronze picture of the wife and so on. In ''Paradise Bar'' it looks as though one would never have to go outside. Plastic vines cascade from the ceiling, food and wine are plentiful, art is present in the form of a mural—nothing else is needed, except real life maybe. In ''Office Party'' the traces of life can certainly be seen. Empty Verdicchio bottles and wine glasses are placed against the background of Spoleto Cathedral. Against a background of such grandeur the objects would normally seem meaningless but Caulfield has turned the tables.

Caulfield has said that ''nothing is stranger than life itself.'' In his brilliantly executed visions he certainly proves it.

—Carine Maurice

CAVALIERE, Alik

Nationality: Italian. **Born:** Rome, 5 August 1926. **Education:** University of Milan, and at the Accademia di Belle Arti, Milan, 1956. **Career:** Sculptor: lived and worked in Milan. Lecturer and assistant to Marino Marini, later professor of sculpture, Accademia di Belle Arti, Milan. **Died:** Milan, 5 January 1998.

Selected Individual Exhibitions:

1951 Galleria Colonna, Milan
1953 Galleria La Bussola, Turin
1955 Galleria Il Pincio, Rome
1959 Galleria Bergamini, Milan
Galleria Il Pincio, Rome
1962 Piemonte Artistico e Culturale, Turin
1963 Galleria Levi, Milan
1964 Galleria Schwarz, Milan
1965 Gallery 12, Minneapolis
Galerie Ad Libitum, Antwerp
Martha Jackson Gallery, New York
1966 Galleria Narciso, Turin
Galerie Aujourd'hui, Brussels
Palais des Beaux-Arts, Brussels
1967 Galleria del Minotauro, Brescia, Italy
Gallerie de Foscherari, Bologna
Galleria La Medusa, Rome
Gemeentemuseum, The Hague
Galleria Schwarz, Milan
Galleria Laminima, Turin
1968 Galleria Schwarz, Milan
Castello dell'Aquilla, Italy
Kunstammlungen, Nuremberg
1969 Galerie Withofs, Brussels
Studio Condotti 85, Rome
1970 Galleria de Foscherari, Bologna
Galleria Il Segnapassi, Pesaro, Italy
1971 Galleria Caprotti, Monza, Italy
Museo de Bellas Artes, Caracas
3 Environments, Galleria Schwarz, Milan
1987 *Galatea, lo Specchio di Pigmalione,* Studio Nadia Bassanese, Trieste, Italy
Il Pimmalione, Museo Butti, Viggiù
Voyage, Pinacoteca e Musei Comunali, Macerata, Italy
1989 *Riflessione,* Unimedia, Genoa
Studio d'Arte, Venice
Opere Recenti, Mara Coccia, Rome
1990 *Opere dal 1946 al 1972,* Mara Coccia, Rome
Lo Studio e le Opere, Galleria Milano, Milan
I Giardini della Memoria, Galleria Milano, Milan
1992 *I Luoghi Circostanti,* Palazzo Reale, Milan
1993 *Le Leggi Eterne dell'Arte,* Sala Napoleonica dell'Accademia di Brera, Milan

1994 *Res Enim est Amor Quae Ipsam Imitatur Naturam,* Galleria Arcadia Nuova, Milan
Il Fioretto, Padua, Italy
Accademia di San Luca, Rome
1995 Cultura Mercato, Mostra di Antiquariato, Sarnano, Macerata, Italy
1996 *Pian Cordova, Romagnano Sesia 28078,* Studio Nadia Bassanese, Trieste, Italy
Riflessi e Riflessioni, Nuova Pinacoteca, Scuola Comunale, Scuderie di Villa Piccolo, Capo D'Orlando
Elogio della Scultura, Parco di San Sebastiano, Perugia, Italy
1999 *Le Storie: i Processi,* Fondazione Stelline, Sala del Collezionista, Milan
Natura e Racconto, Naturarte 1999, Lodi, Italy

Selected Group Exhibitions:

1955 *Premio Internazionale,* Varese, Italy
1956 *Quadriennale,* Rome
1964 *Pittsburgh Internatinal,* Carnegie Institute, Pittsburgh
1965 *Neue Realisten und Pop art,* Akademie der Kunst, Berlin
1966 *Italian Artists of Today,* Bucharest
1971 *New Italian Art 1953–1971,* Walker Art Gallery, Liverpool
1972 *Scultori Italiani Contemporanei,* Palazzo Reale, Milan
1977 *La Traccia del Raconto,* Villa Comunale Ormond, San Remo, Italy
1982 *Arte Italiana 1960–82,* Hayward Gallery, London
1983 *Il Segno della Pittura e della Scultura,* Palazzo della Permanente, Milan
1984 *Arte Italiana 1960/80,* Banca Commerciale Italiana, New York
1985 *Arte, Dio, Cucina, Consumo,* Circolo Bertold Brecht, Milan
1986 *Per Nanni Valentini,* Circolo Culturale Koh-i-Noor, Milan
1987 *Poesia per la Vita,* Galleria San Fedele, Milan
1988 *Sculture in Cemento,* Palazzo del Municipio, Ternate, Italy
1989 *Milano Punto 1,* Galleria Mara Coccia, Rome (travelled to Galleria Nicola Verlato, Bologna; Galleria La Polena, Genoa)
1990 *Exposition Programme,* Galleria Sonia Berryer, Brussells
1991 *Bildhauerei in Mailand,* Kunsthalle, Darmstadt, Germany
1992 *Creazione: Milano,* Odakyu Museum, Japan (travelled to Museum of Modern Art, Toyama; Hiroshima City Museum of Contemporary Art)
1993 *Scultori a Confronto, il Modo e i Modi,* Farsettiarte, Milan
1994 *Artedesign,* Spazio Vivre, Milan
1995 *Patafisica, la Scienza delle Soluzioni Immaginarie,* Palazzetto Eucherio Sanvitale, Parma, Italy
1996 *Miramare, Scultura ne Parco,* Parco del Castello di Miramare, Trieste, Italy
1997 *Dadaismo, Dadaismi, da Duchamp a Warhol,* Palazzo Forti, Verona, Italy
1998 *L'Arbre que Cache la Forêt,* Musée d'Art Moderne et d'Art Contemporain, Liège, Belgium
1999 *Arte a Milano 1946–1959,* Galleria Gruppo Credito Valtellinese, Galleria San Fedele, Galleria Centre Culturel Français, Milan
2000 *Miracoli a Milano, Artisti, Gallerie, Tendenze 1955–1965,* Palazzo della Permanente, Milan

Collections:

Galleria Nazionale d'Arte Moderna, Rome; Gemeentemuseum, The Hague; Carnegie Institute, Pittsburgh.

Publications:

By CAVALIERE: Books—*Il Pimmalione,* exhibition catalog, Viggiù 1987; *Lo Studio,* with text by Alik Cavaliere and Roberto Sanesi, Milan 1990; *Alik Cavaliere, I Luoghi Circostanti,* with text by Alik Cavaliere, Guido Ballo, Emilio Tadini, Roberto Sanesi, Bruno Canino, Jean Dypréau, and Al Nodal, Milan 1992; *I Luoghi Circostanti,* exhibition catalog, Milan 1992. **Article—**''Notes for a Dialogue Beyond the Work'' in *Alik Cavaliere: 3 Environments,* exhibition catalog, Milan 1971.

On CAVALIERE: Books—*Alik Cavaliere,* exhibition catalog, by Enrico Crispolti, Milan 1967; *Alik Cavaliere,* by Guido Ballo, Turin/ Milan, 1967; *New Italian Art 1953–1971,* exhibition catalog, by Giovanni Carandente, Liverpool 1971; *Voyage,* exhibition catalog with text by Rossana Bossaglia, Macerata 1987; *Elogio della Scultura,* exhibition catalog with text by Roberto Sanesi, Perugia 1996; *Le Storie: i Processi,* exhibition catalog with text by Rossana Bossaglia and Roberto Sanesi, Milan 1999. **Article—**''Cavaliere'' by Guido Ballo in *Art and Artists* (London), May 1971.

* * *

Alik Cavaliere thought of sculpture as entertainment. Sculpture to him was an inversion of reality, a variant repetition that thumbs its nose at the world of experience. His aim was to reconstruct a habitat that fits the technique. Art remakes the world, and remakes it as a false construction, a nihilist deception.

Cavaliere did not want to erect monuments, to use form to celebrate events; his works were real life experiences, able to stage events. So his sculpture was no longer a restricted form, defined and complete, no longer a super-object to be gazed at; it became a stage technique able to act its own plays and its own tricks.

For Cavaliere, the sculptor's work is not a formally enclosed territory, a formal event crystallized, but a mini-world made by the play of skilled hands; it is the space where the performance takes place.

The works comprised in the 1959/1962 series called ''The Adventures of G. B.'' are all carried out on multiple levels of interpretation. They give life to little things, to a number of happenings, using scenery made up from simple elements, very small but still essential, as are the people that populate them. They look to us like little stage plays in which the producer—the sculptor, in this case—has amused himself by directing a theatre made up of random extracts, familiar happenings punctuated by continual surprises.

At the time he was producing these works Cavaliere occupied a studio in an area of ill repute at the heart of Milan—an area that has now disappeared. The room where he worked was like a maze, a network of doors and windows, dark areas and light areas; and it may be that this extraordinary place is to some extent reflected in his work, for that too is all played out in a space with a great many scenes.

Later that artist moved into a sort of oasis, still in Milan; his studio was completely surrounded by a huge, luxuriant garden in which nature seemed to produce every known plant. Cavaliere's interest in nature, its theatricality and the manifold formal possibilities that it offers, dates from that time.

The tree and the forest became then the dominant themes of all works. First he examined the roots (and it was a surprise to Cavaliere to discover how spectacular those hidden parts, the basis of his sculpture in some ways, can be), then the trunk, the leaves and the fruit.

Playing as they do on the artificiality of nature, these works, carried out in bronze like the earlier ones, do not try to take over the natural element; they do not want to play with the actual properties but to play a game of substitution and repetition.

Interest in theatrical invention is evident in these works too; falsehood is introduced, and with it purely theatrical mechanisms are activated. Nature becomes artifice, opening itself up to complex combinations, to endless games.

—Loredana Parmesani

CELMINS, Vija

Nationality: Latvian. **Born:** Riga, Latvia, 1939; moved to Indianapolis, Indiana in 1949. **Education:** John Herron Art Institute, Indianapolis, Indiana, B.F.A. 1962; University of California, Los Angeles, M.F.A. 1965. **Career:** Painter and sculptor. **Awards:** Cassandra Foundation award, 1968; National Endowment for the Arts, 1971 and 1976; MacArthur Foundation Fellowship, 1997; Guggenheim Fellowship, 1980; American Academy of Arts and Letters Award in Art, 1996. **Address:** 49 Crosby Street, New York, New York 10012, U.S.A.

Selected Individual Exhibitions:

1965 Dickson Art Centre, University of California at Los Angeles
1966 David Stuart Gallery, Los Angeles
1973 Whitney Museum of American Art, New York
1980 *Vija Celmins: A Survey Exhibition,* Newport Harbor Art Museum, Newport Beach, California; travelled (catalog)
1983 McKee Gallery, New York
1988 McKee Gallery, New York
1992–94 *Vija Celmins Retrospective,* Institute of Contemporary Art, Philadelphia; Walker Art Center, Minneapolis; Whitney Museum of American Art, New York; Museum of Contemporary Art, Los Angeles; and others (catalog)
1995 *Vija Celmins,* Foundation Cartier pour l'art contemporain, Paris (catalog)
1996 *Vija Celmins Works 1964–1996,* Institute of Contemporary Arts, London (catalog)
1997 *Vija Celmins Works 1964–1996,* Museo Nacional Centro de Arte Reina Sofia, Madrid; Kunstmuseum Winterthur, Switzerland; Museum für Moderne Kunst, Frankfurt, Germany (catalog)

Selected Group Exhibitions:

1970 *Annual of Contemporary American Sculpture,* Whitney Museum of American Art, New York
1972 *California Prints,* Museum of Modern Art, New York
1976 *America 1976,* Corcoran Gallery of Art, Washington, D.C. (toured)

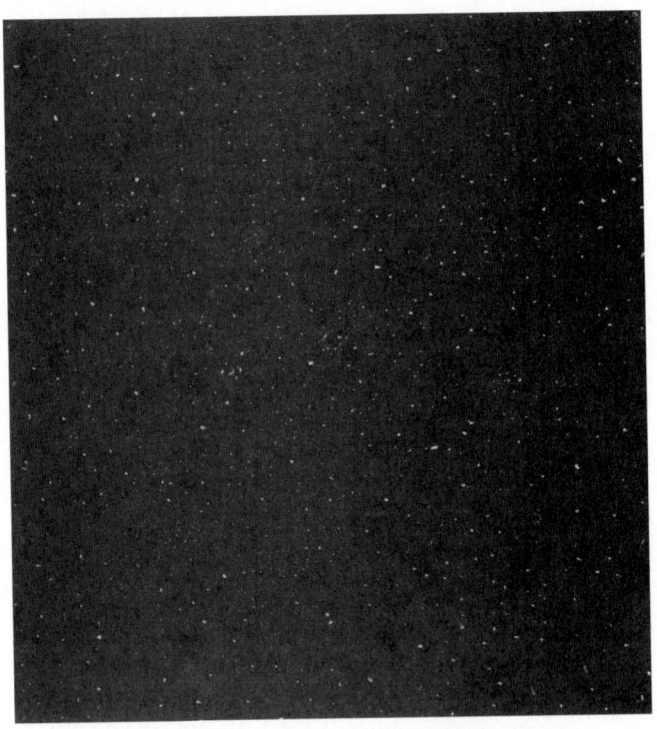

Vija Celmins: *Night Sky,* ca. 1980s. ©Geoffrey Clements/Corbis.

1983–84 *American Still Life 1945–1983,* Contemporary Arts Museum, Houston, Texas (toured) (catalog)
1989 *Making Their Mark: Women Artists Move into the Mainstream,* Cincinnati Art Museum, Ohio (toured) (catalog)
1994 *Love in the Ruins: Art and Inspiration of L.A.,* Long Beach Museum of Art, Long Beach, California
1996 *About Photography,* Tokyo Metropolitan Museum of Photography, Japan (catalog)

Publications:

On CELMINS: Books—*Vija Celmins: A Survey Exhibition* (exhibition catalog) with introduction by Susan C. Larsen, Los Angeles 1979; *Vija Celmins* edited by William S. Bartman, New York 1992; *Vija Celmins: Works 1964–96* edited by James Lingwood, London 1996. **Articles—**''Los Angeles Exhibition'' by R.G. Wholden in *Arts Magazine,* vol. 39 December 1964; ''Exhibition in Los Angeles'' by P. Plagens and T.H. Garver in *Artforum,* vol. 8, March 1970; ''Exhibition in Los Angeles'' by J.E. Young in *Art International,* vol. 14, March 1970; ''West Coast Report: Four Los Angeles Artists'' by Jane Livingston in *Art in America,* vol. 58, September 1970; ''Mizuno Gallery, Los Angeles'' by P. Plagens in *Artforum,* vol. 9, October 1970; ''Los Angeles, 1971'' by Elizabeth C. Baker in *Art News,* vol. 70, September 1971; ''Riko Mizuno Gallery, Los Angeles'' in *Arts Magazine,* vol. 48, September 1973; ''Vija Celmins'' by M. Kozloff in *Artforum,* vol. 12, March 1974; ''Felicity Samuel Gallery, London'' in *Art International,* vol. 19, June 1975; ''Felicity Samuel Gallery, London'' in *Studio,* vol. 190, July 1975; ''New Editions (Suite of Four Images—The Sky, The Desert, Stars and Ocean)'' in *Art News,* vol. 75, March 1976; ''Visceral Aesthetic of a New Decade's Art; American Artists: A New Decade (Exhibition on

Recent American art)'' by Janet Kutner in *Arts Magazine,* vol. 51, December 1976; ''Reductionist by Nature'' by G.J. Hazlitt in *Art News,* vol. 77, February 1978; ''Objects and Illusions: Newport Harbor Art Museum, Newport Beach, California'' by M. Ball in *Artweek,* vol. 11, January 12 1980; ''Newport Harbor Art Museum, Balboa, California'' by C. Knight in *Artforum,* vol. 18, March 1980; ''Newport Harbor Art Museum, Los Angeles'' in *Art News,* vol. 79, Apr 1980; ''Hudson River Museum, Yonkers, N.Y.'' in *Art News,* vol. 79, October 1980; ''Of Earthly Objects and Stellar Sights: Vija Celmins'' by Richard Armstrong in *Art in America,* vol. 69, May 1981; ''David McKee Gallery, New York'' in *Arts Magazine,* vol. 57, June 1983; ''Prints and Photographs Published'' in *The Print Collector's Newsletter,* vol. 14, July-Aug 1983; ''David McKee Gallery, New York'' by R. Armstrong in *Artforum,* vol. 21, Summer 1983; ''Vija Celmins: Drawing Without Withdrawing'' by K. Baker in *Artforum,* vol. 22, Nov 1983; ''Vija Celmins: An Art of Reclamation'' by Carter Ratcliff in *The Print Collector's Newsletter,* vol. 14, January-February 1984; ''The Aeroplane in art'' by Julie H. Wosk in *Art and Artists,* no. 219, December 1984; ''Prints and Photographs Published'' in *The Print Collector's Newsletter,* vol. 16, May-June 1985; ''Multiples and Objects and Books'' in *The Print Collector's Newsletter,* vol. 16, January-February 1986; ''David McKee Gallery, New York'' by Dennis Cooper in *Artforum International,* vol. 27, February 1989; ''David McKee Gallery, New York'' by Gerard Haggerty in *Arts Magazine,* vol. 63, March 1989; ''David McKee Gallery, New York'' by Ken Johnson in *Art in America,* vol. 77, March 1989; ''David McKee Gallery, New York'' by Gregory Galligan in *Art International,* no. 6, Spring 1989; ''Prints and Photographs Published'' in *The Print Collector's Newsletter,* vol. 23, May-June 1992; ''McKee Gallery, New York'' by Terry-R Myers in *Flash Art,* (International Edition) no. 165, Summer 1992; ''McKee Gallery, New York'' by Lisa Liebmann in *Artforum International,* vol. 30, Summer 1992; ''McKee Gallery, New York'' by Eleanor Heartney in *Art News,* vol. 91, September 1992; ''McKee Gallery, New York'' by Richard Kalina in *Art in America,* vol. 80, September 1992; ''Waking up and Warming up'' by Paul Gardner in *Art News,* vol. 91, October 1992; ''Institute of Contemporary Art, Philadelphia'' by Judith E. Stein in *Art News,* vol. 92, February 1993; ''Vija Celmins: A Spiritual Descendant of Hopper Creates Mysterious Intimations of the Sublime'' by Scott Gutterman in *Art and Antiques,* vol. 15, February 1993; ''University of Pennsylvania, Institute of Contemporary Art, Philadelphia'' in *Drawing,* vol. 14, March-April 1993; ''Institute of Contemporary Art, University of Pennsylvania, Philadelphia'' by Lynne Cooke in *The Burlington Magazine,* vol. 135, March 1993; ''Out of this World'' by Lois Allan in *Artweek,* vol. 24, May 6 1993; ''Earth to Vija Celmins'' by Lane Relyea in *Artforum International,* vol. 32, October 1993; ''Visionary Realist'' by Brooks Adams in *Art in America,* vol. 81, October 1993; ''Museum of Contemporary Art, Los Angeles'' by Marlena Donahue in *Sculpture,* (Washington, DC) vol. 13, May-June 1994; ''Vija Celmins'' in *Parkett,* no. 44, 1995; ''Vija Celmins: Material Fictions'' by Nancy Princenthal in *Parkett,* no. 44, 1995; ''Night, Sleep, Death and the Stars: Twelve Exercises in Honor of Vija Celmins'' by Jim Lewis in *Parkett,* no. 44, 1995; ''Vija Celmins in Conversation with Jeanne Silverthorne'' by Jeanne Silverthorne in *Parkett,* no. 44, 1995; ''Vija Celmins's Play of Imitation'' by Richard Shiff in *Parkett,* no. 44, 1995; ''Vija Celmins'' by Eric Gibson in *Art News,* vol. 95, June 1996; ''Vija Celmins at David McKee'' by Nancy Princenthal in *Art in America,* vol. 84, July 1996; ''Vija Celmins: Vastness in Flatland'' by Jeff Rian in *Flash Art,* (International Edition) no. 189, Summer 1996; ''Vija Celmins'' by Melissa E. Feldman in *Art Monthly,* no. 202, December 1996-January 1997; ''First Time Here'' by Kathy Kubicki in *Make, The Magazine of Women's Art,* no. 74, February-March 1997; ''Vija Celmins'' by Gilda Williams in *Art Text,* no. 57, May-July 1997; ''Explosion at Sea, 1966'' by Andrea D. Barnwell in *Museum Studies,* vol. 25, no. 1, 1999; ''Vija Celmins'' by Cherry Smyth in *Art Monthly,* no. 229, September 1999.

* * *

The work of the Latvian-born American artist Vija Celmins is most immediately noticeable for its deadpan lack of affectation, narrow color range that is reminiscent of grisaille, and unusually intense exploration of a limited number of themes. Celmins has worked in painting, drawing, and sculpture, her subjects vacillating between the extremes of familiar, banal household objects and far-away galaxies.

Celmins' early paintings are generally of single domestic objects presented against flat gray backgrounds and given fittingly blunt titles like *Heater, Hot Plate,* and *Fan* (all 1964). The style of the paintings is not crisp enough for them to be grouped with any sort of photorealism; likewise, they lack the flipness and commercial edge of Pop. Surrounded by large areas of plain background, the household items seem at once forlorn and slightly menacing. At the same time, the subject matter of these paintings speaks to basic human needs like food and relief from the elements. In fact, the objects were taken from Celmins' own studio in Venice, California.

Other paintings from the 1964–65 period introduce an element of violence more clearly, such as *Pistol* (1964), of a hand firing a gun, and *German Plane* and *Flying Fortress* (both 1966), of World War II fighter planes. These latter paintings may be taken as a reference to Celmins' early childhood years, which were marred by the war in Europe, the cause of her family's fleeing Latvia for Germany and settling later in the United States. Yet despite the strong emotional associations we might expect Celmins to express in relation to these warplanes, they are depicted in as affectless a style as her studio objects.

Celmins soon moved from dealing with isolated, discrete objects to vistas of various sorts. The earliest is *Freeway* of 1966, an oil painting taken from a photograph snapped by Celmins from across the dashboard of her car while making her commute from Venice to her teaching position at the time in Irvine.

Then, for more than a decade, Celmins abandoned painting for graphite drawing, her habitual subjects being lunar surfaces, ocean waves, the desert floor, and constellations. In interviews, Celmins has spoken about her absorption with the graphite medium and the gradual building-up of marks on the paper surface. While these images are rendered in painstaking detail, experimentation with the process of drawing seems to have been Celmins' primary motivation: in some of the drawings, a string placed across the surface of the paper has resulted in a blank line that disrupts the illusionistic space of the drawing, and, in one series, Celmins drew the same image of waves seven times, but with a different lead each time. The artist has described her task as slowing or stilling time and adapting vast space to the two-dimensional plane.

One of Celmins' most ambitious projects is the sculpture *To Fix the Image in Memory* of 1977–82, a set of eleven stones paired with near-identical counterparts fashioned by Celmins in acrylic-painted cast bronze. The sculpture is a rigorous exercise in looking and making. Emotion or expression on the part of the artist has been purged.

In the 1980s, Celmins began painting again, doing (among other subjects) a series of night skies that recall her earlier graphite drawings of galaxies. The artist has cited a wide range of influences, including Cézanne, Matisse, Jasper Johns, Willem de Kooning, and Giorgio Morandi. Although perhaps surprising initially, the Cézanne comparison seems particularly apt with respect to Celmins' drawings, with Celmins' careful building-up of graphite marks echoing the structured network of the French painter's brushstrokes.

Celmins, who relocated to New York in 1980, continues to live and work there today.

—Jennifer A. Smith

CEROLI, Mario

Nationality: Italian. **Born:** Castelfrentano, Chieti, Italy, 17 May 1938. **Military Service:** Italian Army, 1961. **Career:** Worked in a studio with Leoncillo, Ettore Colla and Pericle Fazzini. Designed scenery for Pier Paolo Pasolini's *Orgia,* Teatro Stabile, Turin, and Giordano Bruno's *Candelaio,* Festival Theatre, Venice, 1962–64. Independent sculptor and performance artist, Rome since 1964. **Awards:** Prize, *Mostra Nazionale di Termoli,* Italy, 1964; Third Prize, *Biennale d'Arte Metallo,* Gubbio, Italy, 1965; Gollin Prize, *Biennale,* Venice, 1966; Bolaffi Prize, Turin, 1972. **Agent:** Galleria Il Naviglio, via Manzoni 45, Milan. **Address:** Via della Pisana 1138, Rome, Italy.

Individual Exhibitions:

1964 Galleria La Tartaruga, Rome
1965 Galleria La Tartaruga, Rome
1966 Galleria del Naviglio, Milan
1967 Galleria del Naviglio, Milan
Modern Art Agency, Naples
Bonino Gallery, New York
Galleria Sperone, Turin
Galerie Thomas, Munich
Galerie Schmela, Dusseldorf
Galleria de Foscherari, Bologna
Mana Art Market, Rome
1969 Galleria del Naviglio, Milan
Modern Art Agency, Naples
Kunstverein, Karlsruhe, West Germany
Galerie René Block, Berlin
Galerie Brusberg, Hannover
Salone delle Scuderie, Parma, Italy
Kunsthalle, Hannover
Palais des Beaux-Arts, Brussels
Palazzo Ducale, Pesaro, Italy
Albright-Knox Art Gallery, Buffalo, New York (with Michelangelo Pistoletto)
1970 Galleria La Tartaruga, Rome
Galleria de Foscherari, Bologna
Galleria Ferrari, Verona
Museum Folkwang, Essen
1971 Kunstverein, Frankfurt
Museum am Ostwall, Dortmund, West Germany
Galleria Colophon, Milan
Galleria La Tartaruga, Rome
Haus am Waldsee, Berlin
1972 Galleria Forma, Genoa
Palazzo Ducale, Pesaro, Italy
1974 Betty Parsons Gallery, New York
Studio Marconi, Milan
Galleria Plurima I, Udine, Italy
1975 Galleria Graziussi, Venice
Galleria de'Foscherari, Bologna
1976 Centro Colombo Amricano, Bogota, Colombia
Nova Arte Moderna, Prato, Italy
Galleria La Tartaruga, Rome
Galleria Marin, Turin
Fundacion Eugenio Mendoza, Caracas, Venezuela
1977 Galeria Sandiego, Bogota, Colombia
1978 Galleria Plurima I, Udine, Italy
1979 Galleria Il Centro, Naples
Galleria Aries, Bari, Italy
Galleria de'Foscherari, Bologna
Galleria San Soaze, Treviso, Italy
Galleria Franca Mancini, Pesaro, Italy
1980 Galleria Mario Diacono, Rome
Galleria Torbandena, Trieste, Italy
1981 Galleria Editalia, Rome
Galleria La Chiocciola, Padua, Italy
Galleria Meta, Florence
1982 Galleria La Tartaruga, Rome
Galleria de'Foscherari, Bologna
Studio Marconi, Milan
Mario Ceroli, at the *Biennale,* Venice
1983 Banco di Santo Spirito, Rome
Forte Belvedere, Florence
1984 *Mario Ceroli,* at the *Biennale,* Venice
1985 Galleria de'Foscherari, Bologna
1986 Palazzo degli Alessandri, Viterbo, Italy
Galleria 2RC, Milan
1989 *Omaggio alla Rivoluzione Francese,* Spazio Arte RENAULT, Rome
Il Teatro di Ceroli, Festival de Teatro Italiano, Fondi
Curve di livello dell'Uomo, Chiesa di San Paolo, Macerata
1990 Galleria Editalia, Rome
Museo Archeologico, Teramo
Mangiafuoco, Galleria Cleto Polcina Arte Moderna, Rome
1995 *L'Albero della Vita—Il Seme dell'Uomo,* Kirim Beer Village, Yokohama
1996 Museum of Art, Fukuyama, Japan
Museum of Art, Asahikawa, Japan
Galleria Sprovieri, Rome
1997 Galleria (Mudima Fondazione), Milan
1998 *I Discorsi Platonici sulla Geometria,* Palazzo Vecchio, Sala d'Arme, Firenze
Biennale del Cinema, Venice
1999 Tempio di Confucio, Museo della Capitale, Pechino

Selected Group Exhibitions:

1960 *Quadriennale,* Galleria Nazionale d'Arte Moderna, Rome
1965 *8 Italienischer Kunstler,* Kunsthaus, Zurich
1968 *Young Italians,* Institute of Contemporary Art, Boston
1971 *New Italian Art 1953–71,* Walker Art Gallery, Liverpool

1973 *Il Ritratto Oggi,* Villa Faraggiana, Albissola, Italy
1977 *XIV Bienal de Sao Paulo,* Brazil
1980 *One Hundred Years of Italian Art,* Museum of Modern Art, Tokyo
1982 *Arte Italiana 1960–82,* Hayward Gallery, London
1985 *Italia Oggi,* Villa Arson, Nice, France
1986 *Aspekte Italienischen Kunst 1950–85,* Kunstverein, Frankfurt
1988 *Italian Figurative Sculpture of the Twentieth Century,* Museum of Fine Arts, Gifu
L'Autoritratto non Ritratto nell'Arte contemporanea italiana, Arte Fiera, Bologna
Scultori ai giardini, XLIII Biennale Internazionale d'Arte, Venice
Mostra su Lello Basso, Rotonda della Besana, Milan
1989 *Verso l'Arte Povera,* Pad. Arte Contemporanea, Milan
Contemporary Sculpture Center, Tokyo
Acquisizioni 1988, Galleria d'Arte Moderna, Bologna
XX Biennal do Brasil, San Paolo
Italian Technology, Austria Center for World Technology, Vienna
1990 *Off Side,* Spazio Arte Renaul, Rome
La otra Esclutura. 30 anos de Escultura Italiana, Palacio de Cristal, Madrid
L'incrocio dei venti. Omaggio dell'Arte alla Vita, Accademia delle Arti del Disegno, Firenze
1991 *Rome anni Sessanta. Al di là della Pittura,* Palazzo delle Esposizioni, Rome
1992 *Profili. 1950–1990,* Palazzo delle Esposizioni, XII Quadriennale d'Arte, Rome
Arte Rome 92, Palazzo dei Congressi, Rome
Il mondo di Snoopy, Spazio Flaminio, Rome
FIAC, Galleria Cleto Polcina Arte Moderna, Parigi
Galleria Cleto Polcina Arte Moderna, Rome
Groma, Exposition Universal, Siviglia
Uomo Gaffeggiante, Colombiadi, Genova
1993 *Tutte le strade portano a Rome,* Palazzo delle Esposizioni, Rome
Macchine per la pace, Biennale, Venice
1994 *Giorgio de Chirico. Confronti neometafisici,* Galleria nazionale d'Arte, Rome
1995 *Il mito e il classico,* Fortezza Firmafede Sarzana, Sarzana
1996 *Collezioni d'Artista,* Palazzo Cuttica
Qui Arte contemporanea trenta anni, Galleria Edieuropa, Rome
Biennale scultura Carrara, Carrara
1997 Arte Fiera, Bologna
Materiali Anomali, Galleria d'Arte Moderna, Bologna
Minimalia da Giacomo Balla a. . . , Palazzo Guerrini Dubois
Dadaismo—Dadaismi da Duchamp, Palazzo Forti, Verona
Opera, Palazzo delle Esposizioni, Rome
1998 *Minimalia da Giacomo Balla a. . . ,* Palazzo delle Esposizioni, Rome
Mostra presenza del Mito, Villa Cattolica Baghera, Palermo
1999 Alitalia per l'Arte, Umbria Jazz
Chiostro del Bramante, Rome
Dall'informale alla Pop Art, Castello cinquecentesco, L'Aquila
Proiezioni 2000: lo spazio delle Arti visive nella civiltà multimediale, XIII Quadriennale, Palazzo delle Esposizioni, Rome
Galleria Diagonale, Rome
Galleria Marescalchi, Cortina

Collections:

Galleria Nazionale d'Arte Moderna, Rome; Kaiser-Wilhelm Museum, Krefeld, West Germany; Kunstmuseum, Dusseldorf.

Installations:

Casa Nettuno, Palazzo d'Accursio, Bologna, 1988; Teatro, Portorotondo, 1989; *''GOAL'' Italia '90,* Palazzetto dello Sport e Foro Italico, Rome, 1989–1990; *Squilibrio,* Centro Direzionale, Napoli, 1990; Malindi African Dream Village, Kenya, 1994; Portone Palazzo Comunale, Trappeto (Palermo), 1998.

Publications:

On CEROLI: Books—*Ceroli,* exhibition catalog with text by Gillo Dorfles, Milan 1966; *4 Artistes Italiens plus que Nature,* exhibition catalog by Maurizio Calvesi, Paris 1969; *Ceroli,* exhibition catalog with essay by Arturo Carlo Quintavalle, Parma 1969; *Mario Ceroli / Michelangelo Pistoletto,* exhibition catalog with text by Robert M. Murdock, Buffalo, New York 1969; *New Italian Art 1953–1971,* exhibition catalog by Giovanni Carandente, Liverpool 1971; *Le Due Avanguardie,* 2 vols., by Maurizio Calvesi, Bari 1971; *Kunst um 1970,* edited by Wolfgang Becker, Aachen 1972. **Articles—**''Mario Ceroli'' by G. Schoenenberg in *Art International* (Lugano), June 1968; ''Ceroliade'' by Tommaso Trini in *Domus* (Milan), April 1969; ''Ceroli,'' special issue of *Flash Art* (Milan), January 1971; ''Mario Ceroli a Pesaro'' in *Data* (Milan), Summer 1972.

* * *

Following a brief period of works characteristic of the 'informal' movement after his military service, Mario Ceroli produced the first work marking his personal style. From this first period lasting little more than four years from 1956 to 1961 comes the sculpture *Legno con Chiodi* (1958), constructed out of a tree trunk pierced by large nails. This work in some respects anticipates Arte Povera, the movement with which Ceroli was briefly associated.

From 1962 comes the piece *Lettere,* whose title is descriptive of the row of letters roughly hewn out of wood: A.S.O.Z., a partial alphabet in which is anchored in a poetry opposed to the then ubiquitous informal. *Lettere* fomulates the ideas soon to be seen in his best works. *Adam and Eve* and *Leonardo's Man* are explicitly based on classical themes or the artistic culture of the past. At the same time, Ceroli created works which refer to objects of daily use, as in *Clock* and *Telephone.* In these and successive works we see his poetry ripen as his techniques reaches full maturity.

Maurizio Calvesi has written of *Adam and Eve* and the related works: ''The plastic marquetry is complicated by the employment of empty spaces where shadows are modelled as if they were solid matter, and settle into a cunning play of relationships between empty and full areas; the first Cerolian silhouettes occur springing and taut, produced through a system of alternating projections of image or shadow.'' The works which follow attain a formal coherence. The rhythms of fullness and emptiness and of light and dark are intensified, as in *Casa di Dante* (1965), which, like subsequent pieces, reveals a new element. This element is a ladder which extends forward as an invitation to climb in and enter the sculpture. Not only does this element aspire to involve the spectator, as in *La Scala* (1965), but its three-dimensionality adds a new constituent to the work's expressive possibilities. In *Casa Sistina* (1966), the diverse tendencies of the preceding works are clarified. From the outside, the work looks like a huge packing case with two small doors located on opposite walls, inviting the spectator to enter the interior whose walls are covered with silhouettes and woodcut figures standing erect at balconies. This work, a prize-winner at the Venice Biennale, is indubitably one of Ceroli's most important creations to date. Here, contemporary and historical memories meet to become one with the space and the spectator.

This creative period is followed by another phase which takes on a conceptual accent. In a 1967 exhibition, *Lo Spazio dell'Immagine,* Ceroli exhibited the piece *Centoucelli.* Three cubes inserted into one another recall early works of abstraction and minimalism, a trend which was to continue into successive works, such as *Primavera di Daria* (1968), where the juxtaposition of an infinite number of wooden poles, each square in section, were built up to form a large, tightly packed, parallelepiped structure. It was during this phase that Ceroli took part in the first Arte Povera exhibition, and in this climate is to be found his work produced for the cultural fair *Teatro delle mostre* promoted in 1968 by the Galleria La Tartaruga. This work, entitled *Dal caldo al freddo,* was conceived as the experience of travelling through a series of wooden doors until one arrived in front of a wall of ice.

Very soon, Ceroli was to turn to re-working and inventing themes with that originality that has always been his distinguishing mark. Additionally, his work as a scenographer, notably for Luca Ronconi's production of *Richard III* in 1968, has brought him recognition most importantly for his vocation as a sculptor.

—Roberto Lambarelli

CESAR (Baldaccini)

Nationality: French. **Born:** Marseilles, 1 January 1921. **Education:** Ecole des Beaux-Arts, Marseilles, 1935–43; Ecole des Beaux-Arts, Paris, 1943–50. **Military Service:** French Army 1939–40. **Family:** Married Rosine Groult in 1960; daughter: Anna. **Career:** Sculptor, Paris, since 1950: first ''compressions'', 1960; first polyester ''expansions'', 1967. Instructor in Sculpture, Ecole Nationale Supérieure des Beaux-Arts, Paris, 1968–86. **Awards:** Prix des trois arts, Ecole des Beaux-Arts, Marseilles, 1954; Sculpture Prize, *Biennale of Carrara,* Italy 1957; Silver Medal, *Exposition Universal,* Brussels, 1958; Grand Prix National de Sculpture, France, 1980; Chevaliere de la Legion d'Honneur, 1976; Officier de l'Ordre National du Merite, France, 1982; Commandeur de l'Ordre des Arts et Lettres, France, 1984. **Died:** Of cancer, 6 December 1999.

Individual Exhibitions:

1954 Galerie Lucien Durand, Paris
1955 Galerie Rive Droite, Paris
1957 Galerie Creuzevalt, Paris
Hanover Gallery, London
1959 Galerie Claude Bernard, Paris
1960 *Recent Sculpture,* Hanover Gallery, London
1961 Saidenberg Gallery, New York
Galleria Apollinaire, Milan
1966 Stedelijk Museum, Amsterdam (travelled to the Wilhelm-Lehmbruck-Museum, Duisburg, West Germany)
Outdoor Expansions, Kunstmuseum, Munich (travelled to Sao Paulo, Rio de Janeiro, and Montevideo)
Musée Cantini, Marseilles (retrospective)
Galleria Il Fante di Spade, Rome
Galleria Galatea, Turin
1968 Galleria Buren, Stockholm (travelled to the Konstmuseum, Gothenburg)
Outdoor Expansions, Tate Gallery, London (and European tour)
1969 Musée des Arts Décoratifs, Paris
Galerie Mathias Fels, Paris
1970 Centre National d'Art Contemporain, Paris
Galerie Creuzevalt, Paris
Galleria del Leone, Venice (travelled to Galleria Schwarz, Milan)
Galleria del Naviglio, Milan
Galleria Victor Emmanuel, Milan
Galerie Rive Gauche, Brussels
Galerie Argos, Nantes, France (with Pavlos and Miralda)
Galerie Soisson, Nice (with Farhi and Arman)
1971 Palais des Beaux-Arts, Brussels
Kunsthalle, Hamburg
Galerie Semiha Huber, Zurich
Galerie Rive Gauche, Brussels
Eat-Art Gallerie, Dusseldorf
Galerie Municipale A. M. Douet, Montreuil, France
Galleria Il Centro, Naples
Henie-Onstad Kunstsenter, Oslo
Galerie Creuzevalt, Paris
Maison de la Culture, Rennes, France
1972 Musée Cantini, Marseilles
Galerie Mathias Fels, Paris
Galerie Lucien Durand, Paris
Cesar á Nice, Galerie des Ponchettes, Nice
Gallerie Fred Lanzenberg, Brussels
1973 *Tete á Tete,* Galerie Creuzevalt, Paris
Cesar en Arles, Cloitre Saint Trophine, Arles, France
Galerie Semiha Huber, Zurich
Theatre Municipal, Angers, France
Centre Culturel, Romainville, France
1974 Rotonda della Besana, Milan (travelled to the Galerie L'Expression, Strasbourg)
Galleria Il Fauno Due, Turin
1975 Galerie Sapone, Nice
1976 *Retrospective des Sculptures,* Musée Rath, Geneva (travelled to the Musée des Beaux-Arts, Grenoble, France; Casino Communal, Knokke, Belgium; Museum Boymans-van Beuningen, Rotterdam; and the Musée d'Art Moderne de la Ville, Paris)
Galerie Semiha Huber, Zurich
Galerie Beaubourg, Paris
1977 Galerie Kriwin, Brussels

1978 Musée Picasso, Antibes, France
Galerie Sapone, Nice
Galerie Bornand, Marseilles
1979 Chateau de Jau, Perpignan, France (with Arman)
Les Expansions, Galerie Daniel Templon, Paris
Galerie Olga, Stockholm
1980 Galerie Beaubourg, Paris
Galerie Kriwin, Brussels
1981 Fondation Veranneman, Kruishoutem, Belgium
Musée de Cabriès-en-Provence, France (retrospective; travelled to Brest and Roubaix)
Musée d'Art Moderne, Liège, Belgium
Galerie Zanetacci, Geneva
1982 Espace nicois d'art et de culture, Nice, France (retrospective)
Fondation Seibu, Tokyo (retrospective)
Museum of Ohara, Japan (restrospective)
Yoshibi Gallery, Tokyo
Galerie Beaubourg, Paris
Musée de Villetaneuse, France
Galerie Asbaeck, Copenhagen
1983 Musée Picasso, Antibes, France
Pavillon des Arts, Paris (retrospective)
Christian Fayt Art Gallery, Knokke-le-Zoute, Belgium
Galerie Verrière, Lyon, France
Galerie Cupillard, Saint-Tropez, France
1984 Musée de la Poste, Paris
Galleria Forni, Bologna, Italy
Fondation Cartier, Jouy en Josas, France
Palazzo Grassi, Venice
1985 Musée d'Art Contemporain, Dunkerque, France
Galerie Artio, Athens
Galerie Beaubourg, Paris
Chateau de Brecey, France
1986 Art Centre, Hong Kong
Fondation Cartier, Jouy en Josas, France
Galerie Zanetacci, Geneva
1987 Musée d'Aix en Provence, France (retrospective)
Musée de Montbélliard, France
Cesar, at the *Salon d'Automne,* Brive, France
Galerie Beaubourg, at *FIAC 87,* Paris
Musée de Middelheim, Antwerp, Belgium
1997 Jeu de Paume, Paris (retrospective)
1998 Palazzo Reale, Milan

Selected Group Exhibitions:

1956 *Biennale,* Venice
1957 *Bienal,* Sao Paulo
1958 *Carnegie International,* Carnegie Institute, Pittsburgh
1959 *Documenta 2,* Kassel, West Germany
1961 *L'Objet,* Musée des Arts Décoratifs, Paris
1967 *Superlund,* Konsthall, Lund, Sweden
1974 *Jewerly as Sculpture as Jewerly,* Institute of Contemporay Art, Boston
1976 *L'Animal—de Lascaux á Picasso,* Musée d'Histoire Naturelle, Paris
1984 *Peinture en France,* Palazzo Sagredo, Venice
1986 *Les Nouveaux Realistes,* Musée d'Art Moderne, Paris

Collections:

Centre Georges Pompidou, Paris; Musée Cantini, Marseilles; Tate Gallery, London; Scottish National Gallery of Modern Art, Edinburgh; Rijksmuseum Kröller-Müller, Otterlo, Netherlands; Musée Royal des Beaux-Arts, Brussels; Moderna Museet, Stockholm; Galleria Nazionale d'Arte Moderna, Rome; Museum of Modern Art, New York; Carnegie Institute, Pittsburgh.

Publications:

By CESAR: Book—*Cesar par Cesar,* edited by Pierre Cabanne, Paris 1971; *César,* Milan 1998.

On CESAR: Books—*Cesar,* exhibition catalog, with text by John Russell, London 1957; *Cesar: Recent Sculpture,* exhibition catalog, with text by Pierre Restany, London 1960; *Cesar* by Douglas Cooper, St. Gallen, Switzerland 1960; *Cesar,* exhibition catalog, with text by Gerhard Handler, Duisberg, West Germany 1966; *Cesar,* exhibition catalog, with texts by Francois Mathey and Douglas Cooper, Marseilles 1966; *Cesar Balaccini,* exhibition catalog, with text by Luigi Carluccio, Rome 1966; *Cesar,* exhibition catalog, with text by Luigi Carluccio, Turin 1966; *Cesar,* exhibition catalog, with text by Francois Mathey, Amsterdam 1966; *Cesar: Compressions,* exhibition catalog, with text by Pierre Restany, Paris 1969; *Cesar Expansions Controlées,* exhibition catalog, with text by Pierre Restany, Gothenburg 1969; *Cesar: Plastiques,* exhibition catalog, with texts by Francois Mathey and Pierre Restany, Paris 1970; *Cesar,* exhibition catalog, with text by Pierre Restany, Milan 1970; *Cesar à Nice,* exhibition catalog, with texts by Jacques Medecin and Daniele Giraudy, Nice 1972; *Cesar,* exhibition catalog, with text by Daniele Giraudy, Marseilles 1972; *Cesar en Arles,* exhibition catalog, with texts by Douglas Cooper, Arles, France 1973; *Tête à Tête,* exhibition catalog, with text by Pierre Restany, Paris 1973; *Cesar: Compressions d'Or,* with text by J. Baldwin Paris, 1973; *Cesar,* exhibition catalog, with text by Janus, Turin 1974; *Cesar,* exhibition catalog, with text by Pierre Restany, Milan 1974; *Cesar* by Pierre Restany, Munich and New York 1975; *Cesar: Retrospective des Sculptures,* exhibition catalog, edited by Rainer Michaed Mason, Geneva 1976; *Cesar: Les Expansions,* exhibition catalog, with text by Catherine Millet, Paris 1979; *Cesar,* exhibition catalog, with text by Pierre Restany, Tokyo 1982; *Les Fers de Cesar,* exhibition catalog, by Marie-Claude Beaud, Pierre Restany and Catherine Franchlin, Jouy en Josas, France 1984; *Cesar 1955–1985,* exhibition catalog, Dunkerque 1985; *César: Catalogue Raisonné,* exhibition catalog, with text by Denyse Durand-Ruel, Paris 1994; *César,* exposition catalog, Paris 1997. **Articles—**"The Mature Richier, the Young Cesar: Expressionist Confluences in French Postwar Sculpture" by Michele C. Cone in *Art Journal,* vol. 53, no. 4, Winter 1994; "César Bows Out" by Penelope Rowlands in *Art News,* vol. 94, April 1995; "César (César Baldaccini) 1921–1999" in *Art Monthly* (London), no. 223, February 1999; "Obituaries" in *Art in America* (New York), vol. 87, no. 2, February 1999.

*

I would say that I am, above all, a man in love with art, and yet I can't explain what I do since one doesn't explain art. It's a question of feeling and sensibility. What I can explain are practical things: how to make a mould, what glue to use, different techniques. I am not an intellectual artist, but I create my own bit of culture. I have my own deep-rooted culture with respect to my experiences, to the life I have led, to the training I have undergone, to the work I have executed. People may identify me with ''Compressions'', but curiosity has led me to make other discoveries too, to use a whole variety of materials: leather, iron, steel, bronze, marble, crystal, polyurethane, gold . . . . But behind every material there's the same person at work. Each day one can start the same piece of work again and each day it can be different.

There's also the question of conviction: if you believe in it, you don't make a product, you're aiming at creating something. But what does create mean? Is one creative because one has a lot of imagination? Am I creative because I've compressed cars? People will tell me that I've got imagination, but sometimes it seems to me that I haven't got any at all. I think physically and I feel a physical need to sculpt. I'm not a person who can think abstractly, who can foresee or make plans. Circumstances, events, encounters with the material, ''accidents'' sometimes make me look at my work differently. But then, nobody creates anything in fact! We simply receive the heritage of one person or another, of all those who were here before us. As far as I am concerned it's the work of, among others, Duchamp and Picasso which has enabled me to progress. I should add that sculpture today is a confused notion. Anything that occupies a place in space is called sculpture. But just because it's three-dimensional an object isn't necessarily a piece of statuary. I think of my compressions, for example, as objects and not as sculptures. I've simply quoted this example at random, but it brings us back to the sculptor/artist debate, for a sculptor isn't necessarily a creator of statuary and may in fact never reach that level. A sculptor may make a torso and if it reaches the level of statuary, that torso will be enough in itself, will need no explanation, no story. The work will exist like a piece of sculpture dug up in Greek soil. It may be a fragment of a human body, without head or legs. No one will ever know who made it or when, but it will have the evocative power of Greek sculpture. It will be useless to restore it or to attach a story to it. It exists and that is enough, whereas a section of my ''compressions,'' for example, cannot be elaborated on by being read about. My *Venus de Villetaneuse,* in contrast, even without a head lacks nothing, and nothing can be added to it. Even if my signature is removed, and even if it's mutilated by an earthquake, my *Centaure* will continue to exist. I disown nothing that I've done, I ask simply that my work be given several ''readings.''

—Cesar

* * *

Cesar is the sculptor's sculptor. After his long studies, like many of his fellows, he was forced into another activity in order to earn his living while continuing to pursue his art in his spare time as far as possible. Which was not very far, for materials were not only difficult to obtain, they were also expensive. His choice of ready-made scraps of metal that he welded together was forced on him by economic necessity, yet at the same time the method of construction had its provocative challenge. His early constructions of insects, animals and fish are rich in improvised invention and humorous in their juxtaposition of diverse parts. His unique combination of passionate and pawky styles developed from the consistent forming of elements into a work such as the life size ''Seated Nude'' (1954) where the skeletal figure has a skin of emaciated iron strips.

By 1956 the sensitive modelling of the human prototype had made evident the underlying humanism of Cesar. It was humanism that not only showed itself of the tactile shaping of the torso, in the plastic tributes to birdman Leo Valentin, but also in the symbolic winged men and central figures against a background of facetted metal akin to the placing of a statue of a saint against a stained glass window in an old chapel. His use of screens lent mystic, almost religious, presence to universal imagery.

His temporary detour into the sphere of ''compressions'' when he enjoyed the new sensation of surface obtained by crushing cars in an hydraulic press was but one of his investigations into the possibilities available in the treatment of the ready-made. Its significance rested in this explosive moulding of the metal in exciting an exploratory system rather than arriving at an end product of sculptural finality; they represent milestones instead of wayside shrines built in celebration of life. The same could be said of his plastic works when the liquid hardens to its ultimate form in three minutes. Captivated by the accidental results possible, similar to Jackson Pollock's poured pigment, Cesar enjoyed the speed in which a form would arrive in brilliant colour. Plastic expansions like ''The Thumb,'' as large as its creator, marked further steps in the continuous quest, though in retrospect some appear as self-indulgence. Cesar defended their appearance as examples of automatic and subconscious gestalts.

For Cesar the 1960s were shadowed by personal setbacks, but his ebullient spirit was not to be subdued for long, and he returned to the fray with elan and resource. His reliefs of metal junk and scrap were full of quirky formal jokes like ''Portrait of Patrick Waldberg'' (1961). Some of the early welded figures were now translated in bronze casts that reflected in the sympathetic metal the rigidity and angularity of the movements of cocky chickens and poised insects. His self-identification and his commitment to material came through with characteristic vitality in the series of 30 masks in bright bronze he called ''Tête a tête.'' Self-portraits: he shows himself in them as an actor of roles having their formal roots in art history from the Roman senatorial to the caricatural; by turns he is the clown, the tragic fate-doomed sufferer, yet each work has its thumbmark of mercurial, almost primitive, power. It is scarcely accidental that, of the race of Michelangelo and Donatello, Cesar also reflects in his sculpture much of the droll worldly humour of his birthplace; Marseilles.

—G. S. Whittet

CHADWICK, Lynn (Russell)

Nationality: British. **Born:** London, 24 November 1914. **Education:** schools in London; trained as an architectural draughtsman; mainly self-taught in art. **Military Service:** Served as a pilot in the Fleet Air Arm, 1941–44. **Family:** Married Charlotte Ann Secord in 1942: one son; Frances Mary Jamieson in 1959 (died, 1964): two daughters; Eva Reiner in 1965: one son. **Career:** Sculptor since 1948; in private practice as architectural draughtsman, 1946; worked with the architect Rodney Thomas, 1947; settled in Upper Coberley, 1947; made first metal mobiles in the early 1950s; executed three works commissioned for the *Festival of Britain,* London, 1951; now lives and works in Gloucestershire. **Awards:** Prize, International Competition for Unknown Political Prisoner, 1953; International Sculpture Prize,

Lynn Chadwick. Photo by Sophie De Martino.

Biennale, Venice, 1956; First Prize, *Consorso Internazionale del Bronzetto,* Padua, 1959; Prize, *International Exhibition of Drawings and Engravings,* Lugano, Switzerland, 1960. C.B.E. (Commander, Order of the British Empire), 1964; Officier, Ordre des Arts et Lettres, France, 1986; Order of Andres Bello, First Class, Venezuela, 1988; Commandeur, Ordre des Arts et Lettres, France, 1993; Associate, Academie Royale de Belgique, Belgium, 1995; Honorary Fellow, Cheltenham and Gloucester College of Higher Education, 1995; Honorary Fellow, Bath Spa University College, 1998. **Address:** Lypiatt Park, Stroud, Gloucestershire, England.

Individual Exhibitions:

1950 Gimpel Fils, London
1952 Gimpel Fils, London
1956 *Biennale,* Venice (with Ivon Hitchens; toured Europe, 1956–57)
1957 Saidenberg Gallery, New York
Palais des Beaux-Arts, Brussels (travelled to the Arts Council Gallery, London)
1958 Galerie Daniel Cordier, Paris
1959 Galerie Charles Lienhard, Zurich
Galerie Daniel Cordier, Frankfurt
1960 Kestner-Gesellschaft, Hannover (with Kenneth Armitage)
1961 Marlborough Fine Art, London
Knoedler Galleries, New York
Bienale, Sao Paulo
1963 Forum Gallery, Bristol
Carborundum Company, New York
1964 Galerie Wilhelm Grosshennig, Dusseldorf
1965 Knoedler Galleries, New York
Sunsvall Museum, Hasten, Sweden
1966 Galerie Grosshennig, Dusseldorf
Marlborough Fine Art Gallery, London
Galerie Gunther Franke, Munich
1968 Galerie Gerald Cramer, Geneva
Galleria Blu, Milan
Waddington Gallery, Montreal
Galerie d'Eendt, Amsterdam
1969 Dorsky Gallery, New York
Galerie Withofs, Brussels
1970 Galerie d'Eendt, Amsterdam
Court Gallery, Copenhagen
Galerie Blu, Stockholm
Louisiana Museum, Humlebaek, Denmark
1971 Dorsky Gallery, New York
Galerie Zodiac, Geneva
1972 Gallery Moos, Toronto
Galerie Zodiac, Geneva
Gloucester City Museum
Galleria Blu, Milan
Waddington Gallery, Montreal
1974 Marlborough Fine Art Gallery, London
Galerie Farber, Brussels
Marlborough Galerie, Zurich
Marlborough Galleria d'Arte, Rome
1975 Galleria Toninelli, Milan
Galleria Contacto, Caracas
Marlborough-Godard Gallery, Toronto
Hokin Gallery, Chicago
Wolpe Gallery, Cape Town
Goodman Gallery, Johannesburg
Court Gallery, Copenhagen
Galerie Carlssen, Gothenburg, Sweden
1976 Galerie d'Eendt, Amsterdam
Galerie Farber, Brussels
JPL Fine Arts, London
1978 Court Gallery, Copenhagen
Marlborough Fine Art, London (travelled to the Marlborough Galerie, Zurich)
1979 Galerie 99, Bay Harbor Island, Florida
Century Gallery, Henley-on-Thames, Oxfordshire
The Keys Gallery, Londonderry, Northern Ireland
Arts Council Gallery, Belfast
Galerie D'Eendt, Amsterdam
1980 Galerie Regards, Paris
Galerie Farber, Brussels
Waddington/Shell Galleries, Toronto
Fondation Veranneman, Kruishoutem, Belgium
1981 Galeria Freites, Caracas, Venezuela
Theo Waddington Galleries, Montreal
1982 Christie's Contemporary Art, New York (with Victor Pasmore)
1983 Mercury Gallery, Edinburgh
Gallery Ueda, Tokyo (with Victor Pasmore)
Galerie Herbage, Cannes, France
Artcurial, Paris

Margaret Fisher Gallery, London
1984 Theo Waddington Galleries, Montreal
Marlborough Fine Art, London
1991 Yorkshire Sculpture Park, Wakefield
Museo de Arte Contemporaneo, Caracas
Museum of Modern Art, Toyama
Museum of Modern Art, Saitama
The Hakong Museum
The Museum of Kyoto
1993 Cheltenham Art Gallery and Museum
Millfield School, Street
1993 The Economist Plaza, London
1994 Lillian Heidenberg Gallery, New York
Beaux Arts Gallery, Bath, England
1995 The Minories, Colchester, England
Cleveland Gallery, Middlesborough, England
1996 Gimpel Fils and Berkeley Square Gallery, London
Yeh Gallery, Seoul, South Korea
Soho Square, Golden Square, Mount Street Gardens, London
1997 Philharmonic Center for the Arts, Naples, Florida
Fondation Veranneman, Kruishoutem, Belgium
Galeria Freites, Caracas, Venezuela
Freites Revilla Gallery, Coral Gables, Florida
Galleria Blu, Milan
1998 Edwin A. Ulrich Museum of Art, Wichita State University, Kansas
A Selection of Sculptures from the Collection of the Philip and Muriel Berman Museum of Art, Knoxville Museum of Art, Tennessee (travelled to Ball State University Museum of Art, Muncie, Indiana; Butler Institute of American Art, Youngstown, Ohio; Zoellner Arts Center, Lehigh University, Bethlehem, Pennsylvania)
1999 Beaux Arts, London
2000 Buschlen Mowatt Gallery, Vancouver, Canada

Selected Group Exhibitions:

1947 *Building Trades Exhibition,* London
1951 *International Open-Air Exhibition of Sculpture,* Battersea Park, London
1952 *Biennale,* Venice
1955 *The New Decade,* Museum of Modern Art, New York
1958 *10 Young British Sculptures,* Museo de Arte Moderno, Rio de Janeiro
1962 *British Art Today,* San Francisco Museum of Art
1964 *Painting and Sculpture of a Decade 1954–1964,* Tate Gallery, London
1967 *Expo '67,* Montreal
1982 *Chadwick/Cuevas/Manzu/Matta/Moore,* Tasende Gallery, La Jolla, California
1983 *International Art Exposition,* Navy Pier, Chicago
1993 *Chelsea Harbour Sculpture 93,* London
A British Vision of World Art, City Art Gallery, Leeds
1994 *Modern British Sculpture,* Beaux Arts Gallery, London
1995 *Europa Despues del Diluvio, Arte de la Postguerra (1945–1965),* Fundacio La Caixa, Barcelona
1996 *Les Champs de la Sculpture,* Champs Elysee, Paris
1997 *Noi non Abbiamo Paura del Blu,* Galleria Blu, Milan
1998 *Monumental Sculpture in the Elements,* Kaoshiung Museum of Fine Arts, Taipei, Taiwan, Republic of China
1999 *Iron and Steel,* Duveen Galleries, Tate Gallery, London
2000 *Bronze: Contemporary British Sculpture,* Holland Park, London

Collections:

Tate Gallery, London; Victoria and Albert Museum, London; Musée Royaux des Beaux-Arts, Brussels; Middelheim Sculpture Park, Antwerp; Rijksmuseum Kröller-Müller, Otterlo, Netherlands; Centre Georges Pompidou, Paris; Kunsthaus, Zurich; Louisiana Museum, Humlebaek, Denmark; Museum of Modern Art, New York; Art Institute of Chicago; Art Gallery of South Australia, Adelaide; Nationalgalerie-Staatliche Museen zu Berlin; Tel Aviv Museum, Israel; Galleria Nazionale d'Arte Moderna e Contemporanea, Rome; Museum of Modern Art, Toyama, Japan; Museo Rufino Tamayo Arte Contemporaneo Internacional, Mexico; Scottish National Gallery of Modern Art, Edinburgh; Albright Knox Art Gallery, Buffalo, New York; Hirshhorn Museum and Sculpture Garden, Smithsonian Institution, Washington D.C.; Museo de Arte Contemporaneo Sofia Imber, Caracas, Venezuela.

Publications:

By CHADWICK: Articles—''A Sculptor and His Public'' in *The Listener* (London), October 1954; statement in *The New Decade,* exhibition catalog, New York 1955.

On CHADWICK: Books—*Contemporary Sculpture: An Evolution in Volume and Space* by Carola Giedion-Welcker, London 1956; *Lynn Chadwick,* exhibition catalog, by Robert Melville, Venice 1956; *Lynn Chadwick* by Herbert Read, Amriswill, Switzerland 1960; *Sculpture of This Century: Present-Day Sculpture in Great Britain* by Michel Seuphor, London 1960; *Lynn Chadwick* by J. P. Hodin, Amsterdam and London 1961; *Lynn Chadwick* by Alan Bowness, London 1962; *Chadwick,* exhibition catalog edited by Marborough Fine Art, London 1984; *Lynn Chadwick, the Sculptor and His World* by Nico Koster and Paul Levine, Leiden; *Lynn Chadwick, Sculptor* by Dennis Farr and Eva Chadwick, Oxford 1990; *Lynn Chadwick,* exhibition catalog by Dennis Farr, Kyoto 1991; *Lynn Chadwick, Sculpture,* exhibition catalog by Andrew Causey, Wakefield, West Yorkshire 1991; *Chadwick* by Edward Lucie-Smith, 1997.

* * *

Lynn Chadwick was one of the prominent group of young British sculptors who were enthusiastically acclaimed, internationally, following the discovery that in Henry Moore Britain had produced a major sculptor. Like many artists of this generation, his studies and activities were delayed by war-time service, so that he was 36 years old before he held a one-man exhibition at Gimpel Fils. With Moore winning the Venice *Biennale* Sculpture Prize in 1948, the British Council promoted the younger generation, and in the group exhibition at the 1952 *Biennale* launched a large group of new sculptors, including Armitage, Butler, Paolozzi, Turnbull, on to exciting international careers. Chadwick was in some senses the most successful of them all, returning to Venice in 1956 to win the International Sculpture Prize. His exhibition was then toured throughout Europe, with Chadwick showing his work in the leading museums in Vienna, Munich, Paris, Amsterdam, Brussels, as well as in London. There followed important international contracts, and for the next ten years Chadwick's work continued to excite wide-spread attention.

It is, however, significant that in recent years he has rarely exhibited in London. His work, in fact, has shown little development. Like a number of modern sculptors, Chadwick's roots lie in architecture, and there is also reason to assume that his experience as a wartime pilot influenced his sculpture. Movement in space, the example of Calder, inspired his earliest efforts, and his work in defining space took on menacing, animalistic forms with spiky legs and antennae. Eventually more recognizable, though still aggressive, bird-like creatures emerged, and the bleak desperation of their stance seemed to symbolize the experience of war and its aftermath. Gradually the dramatic, worrying aspects of these forms were weakened in the employment of smoother surfaces and less aggressive extensions, and by the evolution of human or animal forms less in conflict with themselves, or us.

Stylistic formulas of pyramid shapes or wingspans have now been reduced to anecdotal, almost sentimental symbols; seated couples, walking figures, or standing forms, reminiscent of the gentler imagery of his contemporary, Kenneth Armitage.

—Charles Spencer

John Chamberlain: *Untitled,* 1965. ©2001 John Chamberlain/Artists Rights Society (ARS), NY.

CHAMBERLAIN, John (Angus)

Nationality: American. **Born:** Rochester, Indiana, 16 April 1927. **Education:** Art Institute of Chicago, 1950–52; University of Illinois; and Black Mountain College, North Carolina, 1955–56. **Career:** Independent artist, New York and Florida. First works used crushed automobile motor and body parts, 1957–63; moved next to painting, urethane, galvanized metals and later plexiglass. **Awards:** Guggenheim Fellowship, 1966, 1977; Art in Architecture Award, United States General Services Administration, 1978; Brandeis University Creative Arts Award, 1984; election to American Academy and Institute of Arts and Letters, 1990; Lifetime Achievement Award, International Sculpture Center, Washington, D.C. 1993; Skowhegan Medal for Sculpture, Skowhegan School of Painting and Sculpture, 1993. **Agent:** Pace Wildenstein, 32 E. 57th St., New York, New York 10022. **Address:** Ten Coconut Inc., 1315 Tenth Street, Sarasota, Florida 34236, U.S.A.

Individual Exhibitions:

1957 Wells Street Gallery, Chicago
1958 Davida Gallery, Chicago
1960 Martha Jackson Gallery, New York
1962 Leo Castelli Gallery, New York (with Frank Stella)
Dilexi Gallery, Los Angeles
Dilexi Gallery, San Francisco
1963 Robert Fraser Gallery, London (with Richard Stankiewics)
1964 Leo Castelli Gallery, New York
Galerie Ileana Sonnabend, Paris
Pace Gallery, Boston
1965 Leo Castelli Gallery, New York
1966 Dwan Gallery, Los Angeles
1967 Cleveland Museum of Art
Galerie Rudolf Zwirner, Cologne
1968 Contemporary Arts Center, Cincinnati
1969 Leo Castelli Warehouse, New York
Mizuno Gallery, Los Angeles
1970 Lo Giudice Gallery, Chicago
Locksley-Shea Gallery, Minneapolis
1971 Leo Castelli Gallery, New York
Guggeneheim Museum, New York
1972 Taft Museum, Cincinnati, Ohio (with Peter Alexander)
1973 Leo Castelli Gallery, New York
Dag Hammarskjolk Sculpture Plaza, New York
1974 Walter Kelly Gallery, Chicago
1975 Contemporary At Center, Houston
Ronald Greenberg Gallery, St. Louis
Locksley-Shea Gallery, Minneapolis (with Cy Twombly)
Minneapolis Institute of Art
1976 Leo Castelli Gallery, New York
1977 Margo Leavin Gallery, Los Angeles
Dia Art Foundation Installation, Ward's Island, New York
Heiner Freidrich Gallery, New York
1979 Kunsthalle, Berne
Galerie Heiner Friedrich, Cologne
1980 Van Abbemuseum, Eindhoven, Netherlands

John Chamberlain: Installation model for *McNamara's Band,* 1979. ©2001 John Chamberlain/Artists Rights Society (ARS), NY.

1982 Leo Castelli Gallery, New York
1983 Ringling Museum of Art, Sarasota, Florida
Butler Institute of American Art, Youngstown, Ohio
Robert L. Kidd Galleries, Birmingham, Michigan
Dia Art Foundation, New York
Multiples/Marian Goodman Gallery, New York
L.A. Louver Gallery, Los Angeles
1984 Palacio de Cristal, Madrid
Xavier Fourcade Inc., New York
Marian Goodman Gallery, New York
University of California, Santa Barbara (with Alan Saret)
1985 Margo Leavin Gallery, Los Angeles
1986 Galerie Fred Jahn, Munich (travelled to Cologne and New York)
Museum of Contemporary Art, Los Angeles
1987 Xavier Fourcade Inc., New York
Galerie 10, Munich
Fabian Carlsson Gallery, London
Fruit Market Gallery, Edinburgh
De Menil Foundation, Houston, Texas
Albright Knox Art Gallery, Buffalo, New York
Galerie Pierre Huber, Geneva
1988 Margo Leavin Gallery, Los Angeles
1989 Pace Gallery, New York
Greenberg Gallery, St. Louis
1990 Waddington Galleries, London
Dia Art Foundation, New York
1991 Galerie Fred Jahn, Stuttgart
Pace Gallery, New York
Pace Editions, New York
Staatliche Kunsthalle, Baden-Baden (retrospective; travelled to Staatliche Kunstsammlungen, Dresden)
Galerie Karsten Greve, Paris
1992 Daniel Weinberg Gallery, Los Angeles
Albert Totah, Milan
Galleria Seno, Milan
Laura Carpenter Fine Art, Santa Fe
Dia Center for the Arts, Bridgehampton, New York
Galerie Meyer-Ellinger, Frankfurt am Main
Pace Gallery, New York

1993 Mira Mar Gallery, Sarasota
Galerie Sonia Zannettacci, Geneva
Galerie Karsten Greve, Paris
Parrish Art Museum, Southampton, New York (travelled to Tampa Museum of Art and Indianapolis Museum of Art
Barbara Krakow Gallery, Boston
1994 Daniel Weinberg Gallery, San Francisco
John Chamberlain: Recent Sculpture, Pace Wildenstein, New York
Biennale, Sao Paulo
1995 Pace Wildenstein, New York
1996 *John Chamberlain: Current Work and Fond Memories—Sculptures and Photographs, 1967–1995,* Stedelijk Museum, Amsterdam
1998 *John Chamberlain: Chamberlain's Fauve Landscape,* Pace Wildenstein, New York
1999 Galerie Academia, Salzburg
2000 *John Chamberlain: Recent Sculpture,* Pace Wildenstein, New York

Selected Group Exhibitions:

1987 Biennial Exhibition, Whitney Museum of American Art, New York
1988 *The Oliver-Hoffman Collection,* Museum of Contemporary Art, Chicago
Paintings and Sculpture of the 1960s, Whitney Museum of American Art Downtown, New York
Contemporary American Art, Ho-Am Gallery, Seoul, and Seibu Museum of Art, Tokyo
1990 *Paradox of Process,* Museum of Temporary Contemporary Art, Los Angeles
Seoul Art Festival, Seoul
1991 *Abstract Sculpture in America,* travelled to Lowe Art Museum, Coral Gables; Museum of Arts and Sciences, Macon; Akron Art Museum; Fort Wayne Museum of Art; Musée de Quebec; Terra Museum of American Art, Chicago
Constructing American Identity, Whitney Museum of American Art Downtown, New York
1993 *American Art in the Twentieth Century,* Martin-Gropius-Bau, Berlin and Royal Academy of Arts, London
1994 *The Tradition of the New,* Guggenheim Museum, New York
Recycled, Galerie Reckermann, Cologne, Germany
Country Sculpture, l'Usine le Consortium, Dijon, France
Material and Idea, Kunstsammlung Nordrhein-Westfalen, Dusseldorf
1995 Galerie Ludwig, Krefeld, Germany (with Willi Kopf)
1996 *The Froehlich Foundation: German and American Art from Beuys and Warhol,* Tate Gallery, London (traveling exhibition)
2000 Indiana Museum of Art, Indianapolis

Collections:

Museum of Modern Art, New York; Whitney Museum, New York; Guggenheim Museum, New York; Hirshhorn Museum, Washington, D.C.; Dallas Museum of Fine Arts; Fort Worth Museum, Texas; Museum of Contemporary Art, Los Angeles; Indianapolis Museum of Art; Gallery of Modern Art, Rome; Moderna Museet, Stockholm.

Permanent Public Installations:

First Bank Place, Minneapolis

Publications:

By CHAMBERLAIN: Books—*Conversation with Myself,* New York 1992. **Articles—**''Conversation Between Elizabeth C. Baker, John Chamberlain, Donn Judd and Diane Waldman,'' (excerpts) in *John Chamberlain,* exhibition catalog, New York 1971; ''Interview with John Chamberlain,'' by Phyllis Tuchman, in *Artforum,* January 1972; ''An Interview with John Chamberlain'', with Michael Auping, in *Art Papers,* January/February 1983; interview with Munro Galloway in *Art Press,* special issue no. 17, 1996. **Films—***Wedding Night,* 1967; *The Secret Life of Hernando Cortez,* 1968; *Wide Point,* 1968; *Thumbsuck,* 1971.

On CHAMBERLAIN: Books—*The New Art Scene* by Alan Solomon and Ugo Mulas, New York 1967; *A Report on the Art and Technology Program of the Los Angeles County Museum of Art 1967–1971* by Maurice Tuchmann, Los Angeles 1971; *John Chamberlain: A Retrospective Exhibition,* exhibition catalog by Diane Waldman, New York 1971; *John Chamberlain,* exhibition catalog by Johannes Gachnang and R. H. Fuchs, Berne 1979; *John Chamberlain: A Catalog Raisonne of the Sculpture, 1954–1985* by Julie Sylvester, New York and Los Angeles 1986; *Structure to Resemblance* by Michael Auping, New York 1987; *Sculpture: John Chamberlain 1970s and 1980s* by Walter Hopps, Houston 1987; *John Chamberlain: Recent Sculpture,* exhibition catalog with text by Brian O'Doherty, New York 1994; *John Chamberlain: Current Work and Fond Memories—Sculptures and Photographs,* exhibition catalog, Amsterdam 1996; *John Chamberlain: Current Works and Fond Memories,* exhibition catalog, Amsterdam 1996; *John Chamberlain: Chamberlain's Fauve Landscape,* exhibition catalog, New York 1998; *John Chamberlain: Recent Sculpture,* exhibition catalog, New York 2000. **Articles—**''Chamberlain: Another View'' by Brian O'Doherty and ''How To Look at John Chamberlain's Sculpture'' by Barbara Rose in *Art International,* January 1964; ''John Chamberlain'' by Robert Creely in *Recent American Sculpture,* exhibition catalog, New York 1964; ''A New Medium for John Chamberlain'' by Phillip Leider in *Artforum,* February 1967; ''The Secret Life of John Chamberlain'' by Elizabeth C. Baker in *Art News,* April 1969; ''The Vicissitudes of Sculpture'' by Peter Schjeldahl in the *New York Times,* February 1969; ''Fashions in Living: John Chamberlain's Environment'' in *Vogue,* April 1970; ''John Chamberlain's Sculptures'' by John Canaday in the *New York Times,* April 1971; ''The Chamberlain Crunch'' by Elizabeth C. Baker in *Art News,* February 1972; ''An Important Sculpture by John Chamberlain'' by E. B. Henning in *Bulletin of The Cleveland Museum of Art,* October 1973; In the Heart of the Tinman: An Essay on John Chamberlain'' by Duncan Smith in *Artforum,* January 1984; ''His Sculpture Transforms Scrap into Steel Poems'' by John Russell in the *New York Times,* 17 August 1986; ''The Year of John Chamberlain'' by William Agee in *The New Criterion,* November 1987; ''A Rare Sculptor Who Suceeds with Color'' by Hilton Kramer in *The New*

York Observer, 13 March 1989; ''John Chamberlain'' by Joshua Dector in *Arts Magazine,* May 1989; ''Self-Portrait in Steel'' by Fielding Dawson and ''Troubled Titan'' by Donald Kuspit in *Arts Magazine,* April 1990; ''John Chamberlain'' by Suzanne Ramljak in *Sculpture,* September/October 1993. **Films**—*John Chamberlain: Modern Sculpture Part I & II* by Allan Stone, 1999; John *Chamberlain: Modern Sculpture* by Paul Tschinkel, 1999.

* * *

Towards the end of the 1950s John Chamberlain exhibited sculptures fashioned largely from steel pipes and noticeably under the influence of David Smith. He next used bent and welded metal sheets from old discarded automobiles. In the 1960s he found his place within the ambit of the movement for which the critic Lawrence Alloway coined the term ''Junk art.'' In order to avoid any suggestion of deliberate craftsmanship the artists in this movement drew their materials from demolition yards, junk piles and refuse heaps of urban waste. In this they followed a trend which had its origins in the ''hautes pâtes'' of Dubuffet and was exemplified in the ''combines'' of Robert Rauschenberg. Within this aesthetic context Chamberlain, like the Italian artist César, made his specialty polychrome ''sculptures'' from crushed automobile bodies.

Analogies are often made between the techniques of ''Junk'' sculpture, those of Chamberlain in particular, and the free brushstrokes of Willem de Kooning. But there is a world of difference between the apparently random but controlled effects of Action Painting and the deliberate randomization of Richard Stankiewicz and Chamberlain.

Much has been written, too, about the social and philosophical implications of putting to aesthetic use the discarded materials and scrap of modern urban civilisation. But the interest of Chamberlain himself has usually been in the formal qualities of his finished work rather than in any implicit social comment. Although the element of serendipity inevitably features largely in an art which relies on mechanical crushing, Chamberlain in most of his works allows suggestions from the shapes of his metal sheets to guide the composition and structure of his work. This is evident in such pieces as *Sweet William* (1962). About the mid-1950s Chamberlain also began to use brightly painted pieces of automobiles brand new from the factory. Later he worked with such materials as urethane, transparent plastic and fibreglass, moving on to galvanized steel and aluminum. Examples in these techniques are *Héng* (1967, urethane) and *Tippecanoe* (1967, galvanized steel and aluminum).

—Harold Osborne

In his earlier pieces, Chamberlain's use of scale and structure maintained the material identity of the automobile parts from which they were constructed. Color, too, was applied in broad, unmodulated passages, with patches of rust, broken edges, and areas of the original paint showing through to reaffirm the sculpture's origins. More recently, the artist has experimented with these formal elements, creating works imbued with a luscious organic energy that refers less to the industrial scrap heap and more to aspects of a visually-saturated contemporary culture at large. One group of sculptures from 1992 measures under a foot high and features jewel-like glazes and bits of highly-polished chrome. Other works feature surfaces that are packed with dazzling permutations of intense color, gesture, and pattern, including marbelization, stenciling, splattering, and spraying done with glossy, matte, translucent, and opaque finishes. Like color, freed from its automobile reference, form too has assumed an almost non-metallic, buoyant effect—the artist twists and coils his steel compositions, rather than crushing them, lacing them with ribbons of shiny chrome. Working within the long-established boundaries of his materials and processes, Chamberlain shows himself to be an artist of great formal invention, freshness, and vitality.

—Dorothy Valakos

CHARLTON, Alan

Nationality: British. **Born:** Sheffield, Yorkshire, 26 February 1948. **Education:** Sheffield School of Art, 1963–66, Camberwell School of Art, London, 1966–69, and the Royal Academy Schools, London, 1969–72. **Family:** Married in 1966; son: Emile. **Career:** Painter: lives and works in London. **Agent:** Konrad Fisher, Dusseldorf. **Address:** 15 Mossford Street, London E3 4TH, England.

Individual Exhibitions:

1972 Galerie Konrad Fischer, Dusseldorf
Nigel Greenwood, London
Whitechapel Art Gallery, London
1973 Galerie Konrad Fischer, Dusseldorf
Nigel Greenwood, London
1974 Galleria Gian Enzo Sperone, Turin
Sperone-Fischer Gallery, Rome
Art and Project, Amsterdam
1975 Galerie Konrad Fischer, Dusseldorf
Galerie Bischofberger, Zurich
Museum of Modern Art, Oxford (travelled to the Stedelijk van Abbemuseum, Eindhoven, Netherlands, 1976)
1976 Leo Castelli Gallery, New York
Lisson Gallery, London
1977 Durand-Dessert, Paris
Art and Project, Amsterdam
Galerie Konrad Fischer, Dusseldorf
1978 Lisson Gallery, London
Rolf Preisig, Basel
Graeme Murray, Edinburgh
1979 Gallerie Konrad Fischer, Dusseldorf
I.N.K., Zurich
1980 Michele Lachowsky, Brussels
Art and Project, Amsterdam
Durand-Dessert, Paris
1981 Lisson Gallery, London
1982 Stedelijk van Abbemuseum, Eindhoven, Netherlands
Galerie Konrad Fischer, Dusseldorf
1983 Galerie Konrad Fischer, Dusseldorf
Art and Project, Amsterdam
Durand-Dessert, Paris
1984 Galerie Konrad Fischer, Dusseldorf
1985 John Hansard Gallery, Southampton
Graeme Murray, Edinburgh
1986 Art and Project, Amsterdam
Victoria Miro, London
Durand-Dessert, Paris

Gallery S.65, Aalst, Belgium
Galerie Konrad Fischer, Dusseldorf
1987 Musée St. Pierre, Lyon, France
Delfryd Celf, Caernarfon, Wales
1988 Victoria Miro Gallery, London
Art and Project, Amsterdam
Michael Klein, New York
Palais des Beaux-Arts, Charleroi, Belgium
1989 Musée d'Art Moderne de la Ville, Paris
Durand-Dessert, Paris
Galerie Konrad Fischer, Dusseldorf
Victoria Miro, London
Galerie Tschudi, Glarus, Switzerland
Castello di Rivoli, Turin
Dorrie Priess, Hamburg
1990 Pierre Huber, Geneva, Switzerland
Grasslin-Erhardt, Frankfurt
Alfonso Artiaco, Naples
Victoria Miro, Florence
Galerie Nächst St. Stephan, Vienna
Galerie S.65, Aalst, Belgium
1991 Louver Gallery, New York
Jean Bernier, Athens
Hallen für Neue Kunst, Schaffhausen, Switzerland
Galerie Tschudi, Glarus, Switzerland
Institute of Contemporary Art, London
Victoria Miro, London
1992 Galerie Konrad Fischer, Dusseldorf
Alfonso Artiaco, Naples
Cairn Gallery, Nailsworth, England
Museum Haus Esters, Krefeld, Germany
Burnett Miller Gallery, Los Angeles
1993 Victoria Miro, London
Durand-Dessert, Paris
Galerie Tschudi, Glarus, Switzerland
Kunsthaus Glarus, Glarus, Switzerland
1994 Foksal Gallery, Warsaw
Pino Casagrande, Rome
John Gibson Gallery, New York
Galerie Nächst St. Stephan, Vienna
1996 Annely Juda Fine Art Gallery, London
Cairn Gallery, Nailsworth, England
Sammlung Goetz, Munich, Germany
1997 Studio d'Arte Contemporanea Pino Casagrande, Rome
Alan Charlton, Carré d'Art, Nîmes, France
Ridinghouse Editions, London

Selected Group Exhibitions:

1973 *Prospekt '73,* Kunsthalle, Dusseldorf
1974 *Painting Exhibition,* Scottish Arts Council Gallery, Edinburgh
1975 *Fundamental Paintings,* Stedelijk Museum Amsterdam
1982 *Documenta 7,* Kassel, Germany
1986 *Falls the Shadow,* Hayward Gallery, London
1988 *Color Alone,* Musée St. Pierre, Lyon
1990 *Interventions,* Art Gallery of Ontario, Toronto
1992 *Das Offene Bild,* Westfalisches Landesmuseum, Münster
1993 *Singular Dimensions in Painting,* Guggenheim Museum, New York
1994 *Conversation Pieces,* Institute of Contemporary Art, Philadelphia
1995 *Contemporary British Art in Print,* Scottish National Gallery of Modern Art, Edinburgh
1998 *Waves Breaking on the Shore: Ad Dekkers in His Time,* Stedelijk Museum, Amsterdam
1999 *Here and Now,* Henry Moore Institute, Leeds, England
2000 Galerie Liliane, Paris
Michel Durand-Dessert, Paris

Collections:

Centre Georges Pompidou, Paris; Tate Gallery, London; Guggenheim Museum, New York; Musée d'Art Contemporain, Lyon; Stedelijk Museum, Amsterdam; Muzeum Sztuki, Lodz, Poland; Castelli di Rivoli, Turin; Viennese Museum für Moderne Kunst, Vienna; Kaiser Wilhelm Museum, Krefeld, Germany; Winterthur Kunstmuseum, Switzerland.

Publications:

By CHARLTON: Articles—interview with Giancarlo Politi in *Flash Art (International Edition),* no. 183, Summer 1995. **Video**—*I Am an Artist Who Makes a Grey Painting,* 1990.

On CHARLTON: Books—*Alan Charlton,* exhibition catalog, Eindhoven, Netherlands 1982; *Alan Charlton,* exhibition catalog edited by the John Hansard Gallery, Southampton 1985; *Alan Charlton,* exhibition catalog by Emile Charlton, Schaffhausen, Switzerland 1991; *Alan Charlton,* exhibition catalog, Warsaw 1994; *Alan Charlton,* exhibition catalog with introduction by Guy Tosatto, Nimes 1997. **Articles**—''Alan Charlton'' by Lynda Morris in *Art Press* (Paris), July/August 1973; ''European Cool Painting'' by Germano Celant in *Domus* (Milan), October 1973; ''Alan Charlton'' by H. Einzig in *Arts Review* (London), July 1981.

* * *

Curiously, the uniform monochrome painting appeared in caricatures of modern art before the 1914 war, some years before it appeared in art itself with Rodchenko in 1918. However, the evolving traditions of art resurrected this form of the medium in the late 1950s with Klein and Manzoni, later, for quite different reasons, Ryman and Marden.

The problem of a painting which is to be abstract to the point of eliminating any illusion whatever is to put a second colour, layer, or texture on any part of the surface. The reductionist tendency of art must lead to this crux.

Alan Charlton's painting has been monochrome, but it is not reductive in this way. His works have consisted now for many years of canvases painted uniformly grey. The precise shade of grey varies from work to work and may relate to the scale and configuration of the work. Very often rectilinear slots appear in the canvas, lined with a separate stretcher corresponding in depth to the main stretcher, which is about two inches deep—that is, deep enough to give the canvas the air of being an object. It is also deep enough to produce a distinct shadow on the wall in normal conditions of lighting. Canvases may be adjoined, or arranged in such a way that they form an overall configuration which includes the wall space between them. In certain cases a slot may form a complete margin in a canvas so that an island canvas remains in the centre. In each case the treatment of the inner and outer returns of the canvas over the stretcher are the same, so that the enclosure of an inner space implies the exclusion of the outer wall space. I hope it will not appear a paradox if I assert that this has the effect of comprising the outer space in the definition of the work just as the sea around it is necessary to define an island.

This discrimination deals with the formal characteristics of Charlton's work, but his is not a purely formal art—it is not tautological, like that of Lewitt or Andre, for example. It seems rather to be an art of feeling—closer in spirit to that of Rothko.

Charlton's painting, like the art of several of his contemporaries, has been much more highly estimated in continental Europe and the United States than in Britain.

—Michael Compton

CHATONSKY, Grégory

Nationality: French. **Born:** Paris, France, 4 May 1971. **Education:** Master of Aesthetics and Visual Arts, Paris I—Panthéon Sorbonne, 1995; Post Graduate Diploma in Aesthetics and Visual Arts, Paris I—Panthéon Sorbonne, 1996; Masters of Hypermedia and Multimedia, ENSBA, ENST, 1998–99. **Career:** Independent artist, Paris, 1999—; Web site artist since 1994, sites include ''Isme, ideology stories'' (www.is-me), ''Ion, network affectivity'' (www.io-n.net), ''Revenances'' (www.revenances.net) with Reynald Drouhin, Integral Ruedi Baur & Associes (www.integral.ruedi-baur.com), ''Sous Terre, the subnetwork'' (www.sous-terre.net), ''Nervures to Rhizome'' (www.incident.net), ''Centre Pompidou'' (www.centrepompidou.fr), ''The Speed of Silence'' (www.incident.net/works/silence/vitesse/), ''Disoriented Frontiers'' (www.cicv.fr/3rives), ''Incident of the Last Century 1999—Sampling Sarajevo'' (www.cicv.fr/incident), ''Villa Medici'' (www.villamedici.it), and ''Incident, affect and percept datasystem'' (www.incident.net); Interactivity aesthetics professor, CESI; scenario writer and designer of the CD-Rom ''Memories of Deportation,'' 1995–98. **Awards:** SoundSpace, 1999; SACD Interactive Fiction Prize, 1999; Mobius Prize, 1999. **Address:** 8, rue de l'adjudant réau, 75020 Paris, France.

Individual Exhibitions:

1998 *Art Virtuel et créations multisensorielles,* Boulogne, France
1999 *Festival multimédia d'arts urbains,* Belfort, France
2000 RATP, Paris
Revenances, Other World, Montreal Biennal, Montreal, Canada
Revenances, French Institute, Budapest, Hungary
Revenances, Electrohappening, Rennes, France
Interferences, Belfort, France
Sous Terre, Belfort, France
Sous Terre, VRML 99, San Franscico, California

Publications:

On CHATONSKY: Books—*L'envoutement de nos distances et de nos solitudes* by Anne-Clotilde Boussand, Paris 2001. **Articles—**''Pour que memoire s'ensuive'' by Nathalie Levisalles in *Libération* (Paris), November 1998; ''Incident of the Last Century'' by P. Sorge in *Canal+* (Paris), May 1999; ''Art virtuel'' by Frank Popper in *Supérieur Inconnu* (Paris), June 1999; ''Grégory Chatonsky: Artiste et Concepteur Multimédia'' by Patrice Faudot in *Citoyenne TV* (Paris), August 2000; ''Internet et le cinéma'' by Olivier Martinez in *Nawak* (France), September 2000; ''Mourir sur le net'' by Karine Portrait in *Transfert* (France), October 2000; ''Des artistes 100% internet?'' by Jean-François Berthet in *Stribe* (Paris), December 2000; ''Créer l'interférence'' by Jérôme Duval in *Canal+* (France), January 2001; ''L'Image manipulee'' in *Télérama* (Paris), 2 January 2001; ''Nectar de net art'' in *Télérama* (Paris), 10 January 2001; ''Temps forts'' by Marc de Suzzoni in *Create* (Paris), February 2001; ''Revenances'' by Valérie Lamontagne in *Mobilegaze* (Montreal), 1 February 2001; ''Gregory Chatonsky, Artiste des nouveaux médias'' by Valérie Lamontagne in *Archee* (Montreal).

* * *

Grégory Chatonsky is a young video and communication artist who has already realized a considerable number of projects that illustrate the enormous potentialities of the new technological media and in particular those connected with the Internet.

Since 1989, Chatonsky has produced various video art works and video installations and become a founding member of the experimental web platform entitled ''www.incident.net.'' Between 1995 and 1998 he took a leading part in the creation of the CD-ROM *Mémoires de la déportation* (*Memory of the Deportation*) which received the Mobius Prize in 1999 and contained a considerable amount of information regarding the vicissitudes of the arrest, internment, and deportation of French citizens of the Resistance groups and of those who were branded as Jews by the German Nazis and their French collaborators during World War II. But this CD-ROM contains also a number of references to the nature of the Nazi regime and to the fate of those other European citizens who were exterminated under their racial pretexts. Chatonsky's critical commitment is open to the scientific, social, and technological issues of the twenty-first century but cannot be entirely isolated from this dramatic event that marked the twentieth century.

One of the most telling examples of this can be seen in the web installation entitled ''Incident of the Last Century, Sampling Sarajevo,'' in which the artist asks in which ways human beings and their new technologies have become inseparable. By going back yet another century, into the nineteenth century and its visual and technological inventions and by introducing a human element, a true or fictional encounter between two persons, a man and a woman, Chatonsky produces a narrative in which several independent tales progress on the screen. As in the history of the twentieth century, here the technical control of the narrative development is always subject to an incident, an incident which, in the mind of the artist, forms always part of any technical or human commitment and consequently of any human destiny.

In another web site, ''Revenances,'' created in collaboration with the artist Reynald Drouhi, Chatonsky enters the realm of the fantastic without abandoning his basic commitment to the memory and reassessment of the tragic aspects of the twentieth century. In this site the artists give their own version of one of the most widespread beliefs about the afterlife, i.e. the belief that a person can return to the world in another shape—as a ghost, a spectre, or a wraith, the invisible double of the deceased taking over after death. According to these

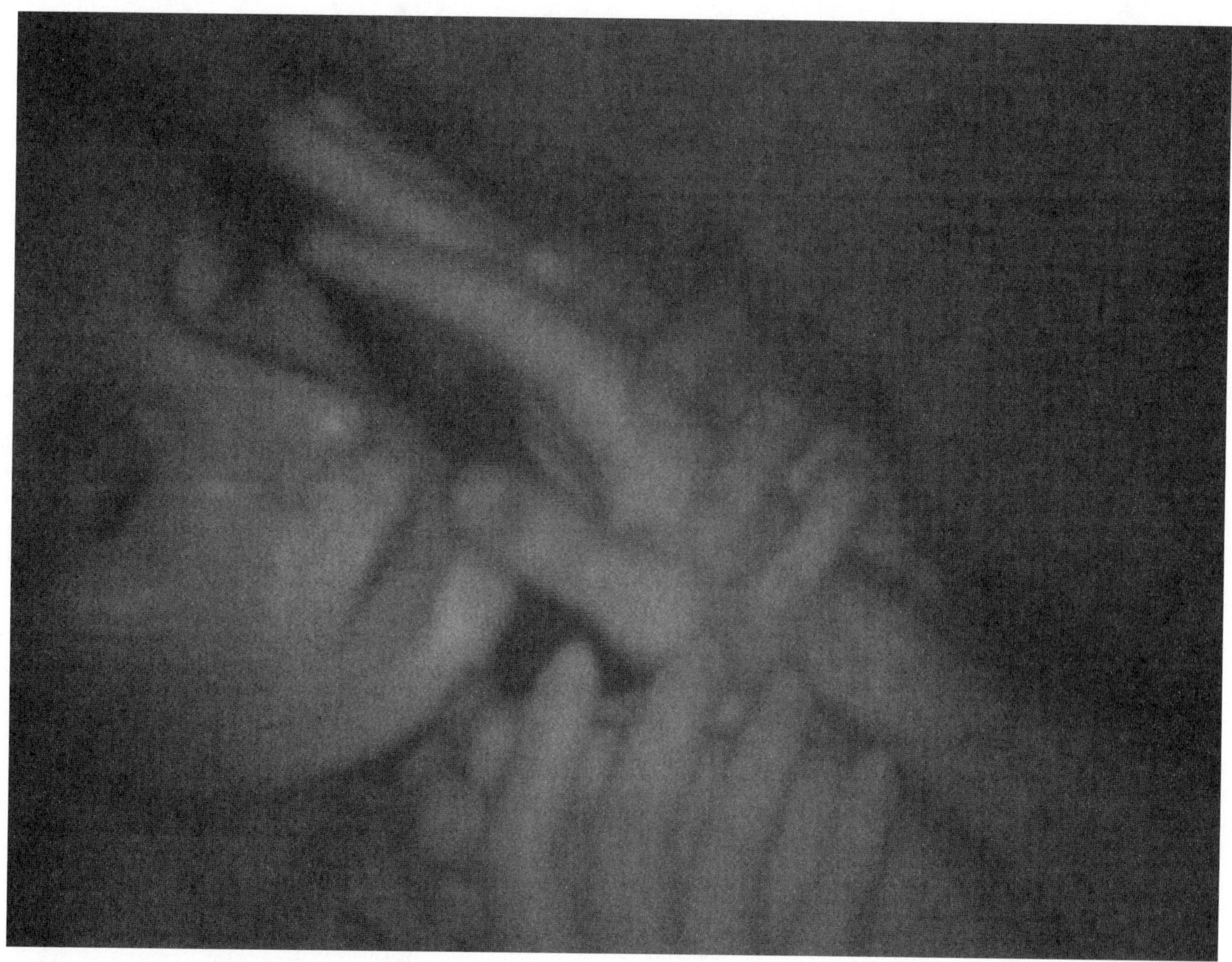

Gregory Chatonsky: *Revenances.* ©Gregory Chatonsky.

beliefs, although ghosts are not of this world and are invisible and intangible to the living, they are still present and can reveal themselves through a medium, in a topical space of communication between the living and the dead. Chatonsky alludes here to and creates a narrative of the characteristics of the technological nightmare, the ''original iterability'' and the ''irreductible virtuality of space and time,'' if one follows Jacques Derrida's thought.

A particular way of dealing with present-day problems concerning space can be discovered in a web site and installation named ''The Last Stone,'' in which Chatonsky juxtaposes a consultable web site with two installations, one situated in Japan and the other in France. This work is based on the idea that virtual space is a paradox and that an interlocutor who is walking in a digital garden can discover another, a real garden of whom he was not aware, and which only became visible through his own displacement. In fact Chatonsky reconstructs on the Internet a famous garden in Kyoto which is composed of fifteen stones but where the visitor wherever he is placed cannot see more than fourteen stones and who needs to move in order to know that there is in reality a fifteenth stone to be discovered.

Chatonsky's intimate knowledge of the internet informs most of his projects. In his web realisation called ''Sous-Terre,'' produced for the Paris subway, a close parallelism between the Metro system and the Internet is established by treating carefully what is similar and what is different in their specificity as networks, a term that applies to both of them. According to Chatonsky, they are different and distant in so far as the subway is marked by the history of the last century with its utopian ideas, but they are close and similar to each other since they favour relationships between human beings: in the case of the subway below ground and in the case of the Internet all over the world with its binary system. Both offer the same possibility of encounters between ''travellers.''

Travellers in a sense are also the inhabitants of a town like St. Petersburg who confer an identity to the town by their walking on the streets and their different ways of displacement. In Chatonsky's web installation site entitled ''Reparation'' the user moving in the streets of St. Petersburg advances pace by pace, click by click, each frame being constituted by a fragment of a street. The sky, the ground, the horizon in front of him, the house fronts on the right and on the left of him can be changed and manipulated. Through the multiple movements and interventions of the ''interactor,'' a new way to ''communicate'' is established, conferring its present identity to St. Petersburg. It is in fact the inhabitants of the town who, by their appropriation and movements, have deviated the original town plan and have thereby created a different topography, a parallel space which exists only in passing, in flux and which is only perceptible through a web site on a network like the Internet.

On two other web sites ''La Vitesse de Silence'' and ''Double Vue,'' the interactivity with the spectator-participant is related to the speed of light, the speed of sound, and the duration of life. In the first of these web sites the silence resides in the distance of conversation, in the interval the sound needs to become audible to a distant interlocutor. The second, ''Double Vue,'' is based on the photographic interstice and the doubling of the narrative, between the voice of thought and the voice of speech that haunts all fiction.

Silence, memory, human presence in an age of motion, of new media, of new ways of life—this is the artistic message of Chatonsky, who is ready to accept the past, the present, and the future with their paradoxes on the condition that one remains aware of all their implications.

—Frank Popper

CHIA, Sandro

Nationality: Italian. **Born:** Florence, 20 April 1946. **Education:** Accademia di Belle Arti, Florence, 1965–69. **Family:** Divorced; has 2 children. **Career:** Independent painter, in Ronciglione, near Rome, 1970–85, in New York since 1980, and in Montalcino, near Siena since 1985; worked in Monchengladbach, West Germany, 1980–81; lives and works between New York City and Montalcino, Italy. **Agent:** Galerie Daniel Templon, 30 rue Beaubourg, 75003 Paris, France. **Addresses:** Castello Romitorio, Montalcino, Siena, Italy; care Sperone Westwater, 142 Greene St., New York, New York 10012–3236. **Web site:** http://www.sandrochia.com/.

Individual Exhibitions:

1971 Galleria La Salita, Rome (and 1972, 1973, 1975)
1975 Galleria Lucrezia de Domizio, Pescara, Italy
Galleria L'Attico, Rome
1976 Galleria Paolo Marinucci / Tucci Russo, Turin
Galleria La Salita, Rome (and 1977)
1977 Galleriaforma, Genoa, Italy
Galleria Gian Enzo Sperone, Rome
1978 Galleria dell'Oca, Rome
Galleria Guiliana de Crescenzo, Rome
Studio Antonio Tucci Russo, Turin
Framart Studio, Naples
Galerie Paul Maenz, Cologne (and 1979)
1979 Galleria Mario Diacono, Bologna, Italy
Galleria Gian Enzo Sperone, Rome
1980 Art and Project, Amsterdam
Galerie Paul Maenz, Cologne
Sperone Westwater Fischer, New York (and 1981)
1981 Galerie Bruno Bischofberger, Zurich
Galleria Mario Diacono, Rome
Anthony D'Offay / Gian Enzo Sperone, London
1982 James Corcoran Gallery, Los Angeles
Sperone Westwater, New York
1983 Stedelijk Museum, Amsterdam
Galleria Mario Diacono, Rome
Leo Castelli Gallery, New York
Palazzo Grassi, Venice
Galerie Bruno Bischofberger, Zurich
Fruitmarket Gallery, Edinburgh
Galerie Daniel Templon, Paris
Galerie Natalie Seroussi, Paris
Galleri Five, Stockholm
Galerie Silvia Menzel, West Berlin
Stadtische Museum, Monchengladbach, West Germany
Kestner-Gesellschaft, Hannover
1984 Staatliche Kunsthalle, West Berlin
Musée d'Art Moderne de la Ville, Paris
Mathildenhohe, Darmstadt, West Germany
Kunstverein, Dusseldorf
Akira Ikeda Gallery, Tokyo
Metropolitan Museum of Art, New York
Galerie Schellmann und Kluser, Munich
Galerie Daniel Templon, Paris
Galleria Sima, Venice
Museum des 20. Jahrhunderts, Vienna
Galerie Ascan Crone, Hamburg
James Corcoran Gallery, Los Angeles
1985 Galerie Michael Haas, West Berlin
Leo Castelli Gallery, New York
Galerie Bruno Bischofberger, Zurich
Galerie Thaddaus Ropac, Salzburg, Austria
1986 Staatsgalerie moderne Kunst, Munich
Akira Ikeda Gallery, Tokyo
Kunsthalle, Bielefeld, West Germany
1987 Akira Ikeda Gallery, Tokyo
Sperone Westwater, New York
Fishcher Fine Art, London
1988 Galerie Daniel Templon, Paris
Sperone Westwater, New York
Ex Chiesa di San Nicolo, Spoleto, Italy (catalog)
1989 Museum Moderner Kunst, Vienna (catalog)
1991 Palazzo Medici Riccardi, Florence (catalog)
1992 Galerie Carola Mosch, Berlin
Staatliche Museen Preussischer, Berlin (catalog)
1993 Galerie Thaddaeus Ropac, Paris
Studi d'Arte Raffaeli
1994 Kohn Abrams Gallery, Los Angeles
Grand Salon, New York
Waddington Galleries, London (catalog)
65 Thompson Street, New York
1995 *Elektra,* Galerie Thaddaeus Ropac, Salzburg
Sandro Chia, Academie de France, Villa Medici, Rome
1996 *Sandro Chia: New Paintings,* Sidney Janis Gallery, New York (catalog)
Sandro Chia: Recent Work, Galerie Thaddaeus Ropac, Paris
1997 Galeria Civica, Siena Palazzo Sforzesco, Milan

Sandro Chia: *April 20th 40 Years,* 1985. ©Sandro Chia/Licensed by VAGA, New York, NY.

M.O.M.A., Boca Raton, Florida
Galerie Thaddaeus Ropac, Salzburg
1998 Pepperdine University, Weismann Foundation, Malibu, California
1999 Tony Shafrazi Gallery, New York
Magazzini D'Arte Contemporanea, Italy
Sandro Chia: New Paintings, Frederick R. Weisman Museum, Malibu (catalog)
2000 Museo di Ravenna, Italy
Velge & Noirhomme, Brussels
Galleria Civica d'Arte Contemporanea, Trento (catalog)
2001 Gallery Enrico Navarra, Paris

Selected Group Exhibitions:

1977 *10e. Biennale de Paris,* Musée d'Art Moderne de la Ville, Paris
1979 *XV Bienal de Sao Paulo,* Brazil
1980 *The Cut-Off Hand,* Kunstverein, Bonn (travelled to Wolfsburg and Groningen)
1981 *A New Spirit in Painting,* Royal Academy of Arts, London
1982 *Aspects of Italian Art Now,* Guggenheim Museum, New York
1983 *La Transavanguardia,* Caja de Pensiones, Madrid
1984 *Six in Bronze,* Williams College, Williamstown, Massachusetts
1985 *700 Eichen,* Kunsthalle, Tubingen, West Germany (travelled to Bielefeld)
1986 *40 Ans: Une Generation Mondiale,* Palais de l'UNESCO, Paris
1988 The Marshall Frankel Collection, Museum of Contemporary Art, Chicago (catalog)
Fables and Fantasies, From the Collection of Susan Kasen and Robert D. Summer, Duke University Museum of Art, Durham, North Carolina (catalog)
1989 *Italian Art,* Royal Academy of Arts, London
S. Chia/E. Cucci, Akira Ikeda Gallery, Nagoya
Meta-Menphis, Fondazione Querini Stampalia, Venice
1990 *Number One 1990,* Galeria Dau al Set, Barcelona
Artists for Amnesty, Blum Helman Gallery
Dreams of Artists' Furniture, Art Gallery, Antwerp
1991 *Festival of Salzburg,* Austria

Sandro Chia: *Sitting Boy Inspired,* 1984. ©Sandro Chia/Licensed by VAGA, New York, NY.

1992 *Transavanguardia: Chia, Clemente, Cucci, De Maria, Paladino: Works from 1977–90,* Gian Ferrari Arte Contemporanea, Milan

1993 *Chia, Clemente, Paladino, Salvo: Works on Paper,* Galerie Delta, Rotterdam

Utopia: Arte Italiana 1950–1993, Galerie Thaddaeus Ropac, Salzburg (also Galerie Thaddaeus Ropac, Paris)

1994 *Chia, De Maria, Paladino,* Galleria Cardi, Milan

New Prints by Contemporary Masters, Salama-Caro Gallery, London

1995 *Die Muse?,* Galerie Thaddaeus Ropac, Salzburg (also Galerie Thaddaeus Ropac, Paris)

Art After Art, Nassau County Museum of Art, Roslyn Harbor, New York (catalog)

1996 *Pablo Picasso: A Contemporary Dialogue,* Galerie Thaddaeus Ropac, Salzburg (also Galerie Thaddaeus Ropac, Paris) (catalog)

1997 Galerie Thaddaeus Ropac

1998 Museum Wurth, Kunzelsau-Gaisbach, Germany (catalog)

1999 *Tony Shafrazzi Gallery,* New York

2000 Museum of Modern Art, New York

Collections:

Museum of Modern Art, New York; Guggenheim Museum, New York; Hirshhorn Museum, Washington, D.C.; Tate Gallery, London; National Gallery of Scotland, Edinburgh; Stadtisches Museum, Monchengladbach; Kunsthalle, Bielefeld; Stedelijk Museum, Amsterdam; Groninger Museum, Groningen; Musée d'Art Moderne, Paris.

Publications:

By CHIA: Book—*Monchengladbach Journal,* with afterword by Johannes Cladders, Monchengladbach 1983. **Articles—**interview with Wolfgang Fischer in *Studio International,* vol. 201, no. 1019, April 1988; interview with Thomas West in *Art International,* no. 12, Autumn 1990; interview with Jade R. Dellinger in *Printmaking Today,* vol. 4, no. 4, Winter 1995; ''Post-apocalypse Experience'' in *New Observations,* no. 119, Summer-Fall 1998.

On CHIA: Books—*La Transavantgarde Italienne* by Achille Bonito Oliva, Milan 1980; *The Draught of Dr. Jekyll: An Essay on the Work of Sandro Chia* by Anne Seymour, London 1981; *Sandro Chia / Enzo Cucchi: Scultura Andata / Scultura Storna,* edited by Emilio Mazzoli, Modena 1982; *Sandro Chia,* exhibition catalog with introduction by Carter Ratcliff, Edinburgh 1983; *Sandro Chia,* exhibition catalog edited by Edy de Wilde and Alexander von Gravenstein, Amsterdam 1983; *Sandro Chia: Bilder 1976–1983,* exhibition catalog with texts by Henry Geldzahler, Carl Haenlein and Anne Seymour, Hannover 1983; *Sandro Chia: New Paintings,* exhibition catalog edited by Akira Ikeda Gallery, Tokyo 1984; *Sandro Chia,* exhibition catalog with text by Heiner Bastian, Salzburg 1985. **Articles—**''Art in the Belly of the Whale: Sandro Chia'' by Demetrio Paparoni in *Tema Celeste,* no. 29, January-February 1991; ''Sandro Chia at Enterprise Farm: The Artist's Spirited Restoration of his Hudson Valley House and Studios'' by Steven M. L. Anderson in *Architectural Digest* (Los Angeles), vol. 48, June 1991. **Videos—***A New Spirit in Paintings: Six Painters of the 1980s* by Michael Blackwood and Donald B. Kuspit, New York 1990.

*

Sometimes I ask myself which artists of the past have had an influence on my work and the answer that comes to mind is that any true artist would have to make his own the theoretical revolutionary statement from the beginning of this century: ''It is necessary to burn the museums.''

In fact the artist must not for anything in the world lose his sense of this spirit of revolt and of freedom because it is the essence of art. Free of all restriction and submission the artist participates in the conquest of this lost universe. Since the time when a man's skin ceased to be his limit, the soul has never again been the prisoner of death nor has beauty of aesthetics.

Even though today the museums are asking for nothing but to be ''burned,'' and the spreading of freedom constitutes a new order, without the realization of the great alchemical or artistic dream coming true, it is imperative that the artist consider in a more subtle and sophisticated manner the concept of ancestry, the concept of autonomy and the concept of rebellion if he wants to be something other than the ape of modernity. In these years of intensive work, of torment and of joy, I have learned the truth of some things in metaphysics and in physics which I could also call ''the passion for art.''

Every man has two kinds of memory: the exterior memory of the things of the world and the interior memory of the things of the spirit, but the spirit is not, and even less are the angels, capable of seeing the world with their own eyes. If one really wants to know the reason for those eyes in spiral form on the face of the sculpture, the answer is that if works of art are not the eyes of the spirit and of the angels, at least they are their eyeglasses! The angel, a free thinking artist, looks, remembers and learns through the spectacles of art, but art, which has never been an objective instrument, obsessively weaves itself into civil, moran and strategic thinking. It is the struggle between the eyes and the head: the eyes are the superior party for looking at this civilization of the head, which the more it advances the more it deteriorates. There is a given definition of rebellion against which the angel rebels. Let us listen to his song in peace and avoid the damnation of prejudice: the soul of the whole world will reap the profit.

I think about what kind of thing art really is, and time stands still and slowly turns backwards. Yesterday Joseph Beuys died. Twenty-five years ago I decided in the glory of one night to consecrate my life to painting and to art. Meanwhile the enigmatic faces of a hundred artists are emerging from the density of time. They are a group of men fleeing from conventional history in order to attempt another way, and however much the world strives to capture them, they are beacons, they are lights, they are something which can in no way be completely hidden. To be born and to die are the same thing, to merge and to separate are the same thing, but man was not made to bear the burden of being bound for a long time without suffering or losing heart. The passion for art is identical with the passion for separation, for difference and for divorce, and if necessary I am aware that I must also be ready to divorce myself from the conventions of this contemporary art.

We were made for the plough, for hunting, for music, and for God, and instead we find ourselves with a pile of photographs in our hands, and a mistaken idea of success insists on wanting to govern us.

Conscious neither of having received from nature, nor of having subsequently acquired any superior quality, I have only the love of art, and on this absolute premise, I have believed it legitimate to negotiate my existence with my contemporaries, but I have never lied, nor have I ever sought to spare myself by choosing the easiest way.

Nevertheless, it is as if I had forgotten to do something important, like killing the pig which is inside me and which dictates to me certain actions, certain formal solutions. Experience alone will teach me if my complex testimony is anything other than the dominance of mind over matter or of matter over sensuality or of sensuality over logic. Anyway one thing is certain, art can probably do without the beautiful, but not without the sublime.

This coming April twentieth I will be forty years old and in pain I would be able to write a treatise on how to break up friendships, to offend those one holds dear and perhaps to be ruined. After all, what was to be expected from someone who educated himself by reading the life of Cellini. But that is not sufficient, and does not explain for example this real pain provoked by something only a phantom.

It is clear that the voices which come from the world—be they those of censure or of praise—proceeding from either friendship or enmity, are phantoms. Sometimes these phantoms have the power to cause real suffering: An unbearable inhuman suffering, which lacerates the soul to its depths and devours the body with remorse. One decides then to change, but not even the will seems to have the power to break the stone of which we are made. If to understand, to repent, to suffer, to lose, is of absolutely no use and does not teach anything, so be it!

—Sandro Chia

* * *

In the first half of the 1980s, the Italian transavantgarde formed and imposed a style and taste on an entire epoch. It was the vital energy of this explosive pictorial figuration that was responsible for the outpouring of expressionism that rapidly spread and became an international style. Its success is based on the fact that the transavantgarde corresponds to a current need—the necessity to reconsider traditional ways of making art and to posit questions centred on disquiet.

Sandro Chia has taken radical steps within this movement. Arising from his experience related to concept and performance art and reminiscent of precedents set by Merz and Kounellis, around 1978 Chia turned to the pictorial, to design and sculpture of a rigorous figuration. His figuration, however, is not that of the Realists. Any conflict between realism and abstraction in his picture dissolves. In no way does Chia share any ideological element forming the cornerstone of that Realism whose role is to re-present the ''real.'' Chia operates with an awareness that the picture is a system of self-referential signs which find their own truth in their own reality. He is particularly concerned to accentuate this character of *hortus conclusus* pertinent to the picture, while dismantling the idea of an external reality. The picture is the language of its history.

Chia's work adopts the role of ''citationist'': that is, the work is the fruit of a reflection on the pictures of the past. These he reads with a freely elective affinity and sentiment—an approach to the history of painting which is, of consequence, a purely ideological project. The explicit citation or quotation is evident only in rare cases—for example in *Bar Tintoretto* and *Natura Morta,* both of 1981. In the first picture, Chia reproduces not only the dominant chromatic green (precisely recording the Tintoretto original), the broken line and the fiery reds of the enflamed clouds which hang suspended above two mysterious figures in the foreground, but is also similar to certain features of Boccioni. In the distance, however, Chia has painted sketchy, agitated silhouettes which are inevitably associated with the dynamic figures of *Rissa in galleria.* In the second picture, quotation from Morandi is more openly declared, although the original lacks Chia's warm and enveloping light. In general, while Chia often retains a dynamic rhythm of broken and whirling Futurist marks, he does so without deconstructing the composition. Rather, Chia's marks form a foundation of tiny particles like a tissue of molecules, which is an irresistible cosmic force going so far as to contaminate the image, thereby rendering it uncertain and difficult to recognize.

In Chia's iconography where the protagonist is the human figure, we also find that the ancestry is derived from something between the Metaphysical painters and those of the 1990s, between the coloration of Matisse and the structure of a Picasso, Carra, De Chirico, and—above all—Savinio appear to be the preferred sources of his inspiration. Chia shares with Savinio a certain ironic (when not completely satirical) character which, while shrouding the images with mystery, at the same time de-dramatizes them. If Savinio gave the heads of flamingoes to his noblewomen, Chia paints his people with a cartoonist's humour, though without diminishing their enigmatic nature.

The dominant literary and cultural references in Chia's work are expressed with a certain flavour of disenchantment. As Bonito Oliva has noted, Chia's thoughts are organically linked to the present. He doesn't forget that he lives in a world under continual bombardment by the mass-media and ''images of the masses''; in this way he introduces into his work an omnivorous desire for signs that are iconic and heterogenous. The picture becomes a meeting-ground for images from high culture, stereotypes from pop culture and products of an industrial culture.

Chia in fact reveals the expression of the epoch's needs that he himself is answering to. Following the neo-avantgarde's break with tradition, and the dematerialization of the object as in conceptual art, art today measures up to the values of a subjectivity immersed in a high technology where sensuality is being reclaimed as a vehicle for a new and uninhibited sensibility

—Giorgio Verzotti

In a departure from his previous work, Chia showed in 1994 a series of diminutive, decidedly atypical sculptures. Gone were his usual sensuous, voluminous forms, replaced by what Deidre Stein described as awkward, flat figures. Chia's style, however, remained highly allusive: the worked surfaces of the pieces suggested Rodin, their elongated silhouettes resembled those of Giacometti, and the amorphous spaces formed by connecting body parts evoked images of Henry Moore's works. Also reflective of Chia's earlier style was the suggestive imagery of the pieces, as in *By the Sea,* where a twisting, eel-like form metamorphoses into a woman.

—Joan Oleck

CHICAGO, Judy

Nationality: American. **Born:** Judy Cohen in Chicago, Illinois, 20 July 1939. **Education:** University of California at Los Angeles, 1960–64, B.A. 1962, M.F.A. 1964; influenced by the work of Emily Carr, Georgia O'Keeffe, Barbara Hepworth, and Louis Nevelson. **Family:** Married 1) Jerry Gerowitz in 1961 (died, 1963); 2) Lloyd Hamrol in 1969. **Career:** Instructor, University of California Extension, Los Angeles, 1963–69; Painting Instructor, University of California Institute Extension, Irvine, 1966–69; Assistant Professor, California State University at Fresno (started first women's art program), 1969–71; Faculty Member and Co-Founder, Feminist Art Program, California Institute of Arts, Valencia, 1971–73; Artist-in-Residence, Western Washington State College, Bellingham, 1973. Co-Director, Womanhouse, Los Angeles, 1972; Co-Founder, Woman-Space Art Gallery, Los Angeles, 1972; Co-Founder and Instructor, Feminist Studio Workshop, Los Angeles, 1973–74; Co-Founder, Woman's Building, Los Angeles, 1974. **Awards:** Woman of the Year Award, *Mademoiselle* magazine, New York, 1973; Individual Artist Grant, 1976, and Services to the Field Grant, 1977, National Endowment for the Arts; Woman of Achievement of the World award, Women's Pavilion in the Louisiana world Exposition, 1984; grant for *The Birth Project,* California Arts Commission, 1984; grant for *The Holocaust Project,* Threshold Foundation, 1988; Vesta Award, Los Angeles Women's Building, 1990; grant for *The Holocaust Project,* Streisand Foundation, 1992; International Friends of Transformative Arts, 1992. Honorary Doctorate in Fine Arts, Russell Sage College, Troy, New York, 1992. **Address:** Office, PO Box 1327, Belen, NM 87002–1327.

Individual Exhibitions:

1966 Rolf Nelson Gallery, Los Angeles
1969 Pasadena Art Museum, California
1970 Faculty Club, California State College, Fullerton
Fresno State College, California
1972 Jack Glenn Gallery, Corona de Mar, California
1973 Grandview Gallery, Woman's Building, Los Angeles
1974 Kenmore Galleries, Philadelphia
Artemisia Gallery, Chicago
Coe College, Cedar Rapids, Iowa
Judy Chicago and Lloyd Hamrol, Western Washington State College, Bellingham
1975 College of St. Catherine, St. Paul, Minnesota
Fe/Vision, Los Angeles
JPL Fine Arts, London
1976 Quay Ceramics, San Francisco
Anne Hughes and Friends, Portland, Oregon
1977 Schaffner Gallery, Los Angeles
1979 Schaffner Gallery, Los Angeles
Anhalt-Barnes Gallery, Los Angeles
1979–88 *The Dinner Party,* San Francisco Museum of Modern Art (toured the world)
1980 Hadler-Rodriguez Gallery, Houston
Parco Gallery, Tokyo
Parco Gallery, Osaka
1983–88 *Birth Project,* Multi-Cultural Art Institute, San Diego (sponsered by Dimensions Network and travelled throughout U.S.)
1984 Robertson Galleries Ltd., Ottawa, Ontario, Canada
ACA Galleries, New York
1985 Marilyn Butler Fine Art, Scottsdale, Arizona
Marilyn Butler Fine Art, Santa Fe, New Mexico
ACA Galleries, New York
1986 Shindoni Gallery, Santa Fe, New Mexico
ACA Galleries, New York
1987 Wallace-Wentworth Gallery, Washington, D.C.
1988 Jan Baum Gallery, Los Angeles
Andrew Smith Gallery, Santa Fe, New Mexico
1990–92 *One Hundred Years,* organized by Nassau City Museum of Fine Art (toured by the Gallery Association of New York)
1991 Nemiroff-Deutsch Gallery, Santa Monica, California
1992 Robbin Lockett Gallery, Chicago
Arlene LewAllen Gallery, Santa Fe, New Mexico
1993 Joy Horwich Gallery, Chicago
Holocaust Project, Spertus Museum, Spertus College of Juaica, Chicago (currently touring the U.S.)
2000 *Resolutions for the Millennium: A Stitch in Time,* American Craft Museum, New York City
Butler Institute of American Art, Youngstown, Ohio

Selected Group Exhibitions:

1967 *Sculpture of the Sixties,* Los Angeles County Museum of Art (Travelled to the Philadelphia Museum)
1968–69 *West Coast Now,* travelling exhibition organized by the Los Angeles Municipal Art Gallery
1969 *American Drawings,* Fort Worth Museum of Art, Fort Worth, Texas
1972 *Color as Structure,* Whitney Museum, New York
1977 *Frauen machen Kunst,* Galerie Magers, West Germany
Overglaze Imagery: Cone 019 to 016, California State University at Fullerton Art Gallery
1979–80 *The 1970's: New American Painting,* organized by the New Museum, New York (toured Eastern Europe)
1979–82 *Creativity: A Human Resource,* organized by Chevron Corporation Pacific Science Center, Seattle (toured the United States and Canada)
1984 *Containers of Culture: Ceramics of Four Continents,* Santa Barbara Museum of Art, Santa Barbara, California
1984–87 *Art and the Law,* organized by West Publishing Company
1985–86 *American Art: American Women,* Stamford Museum and Nature Center, Connecticut
1995 *Made in L.A.: The Prints of Cirrus Editions,* Los Angeles County Museum of Art
1996 *The Holocaust Project: From Darkness Into Light,* Cleveland Center for Contemporary Art, Ohio

Collections:

Museum of Modern Art, New York; Albuquerque Museum of Art; Arkansas Art Center, Little Rock; Asher Library, Spertus Museum, Chicago; Brooklyn Museum, New York; Museum of Fine Arts, Santa Fe; Oakland Museum of Art, California; San Francisco Museum of Modern Art; Virginia Museum of Fine Art, Richmond; Los Angeles County Museum of Art.

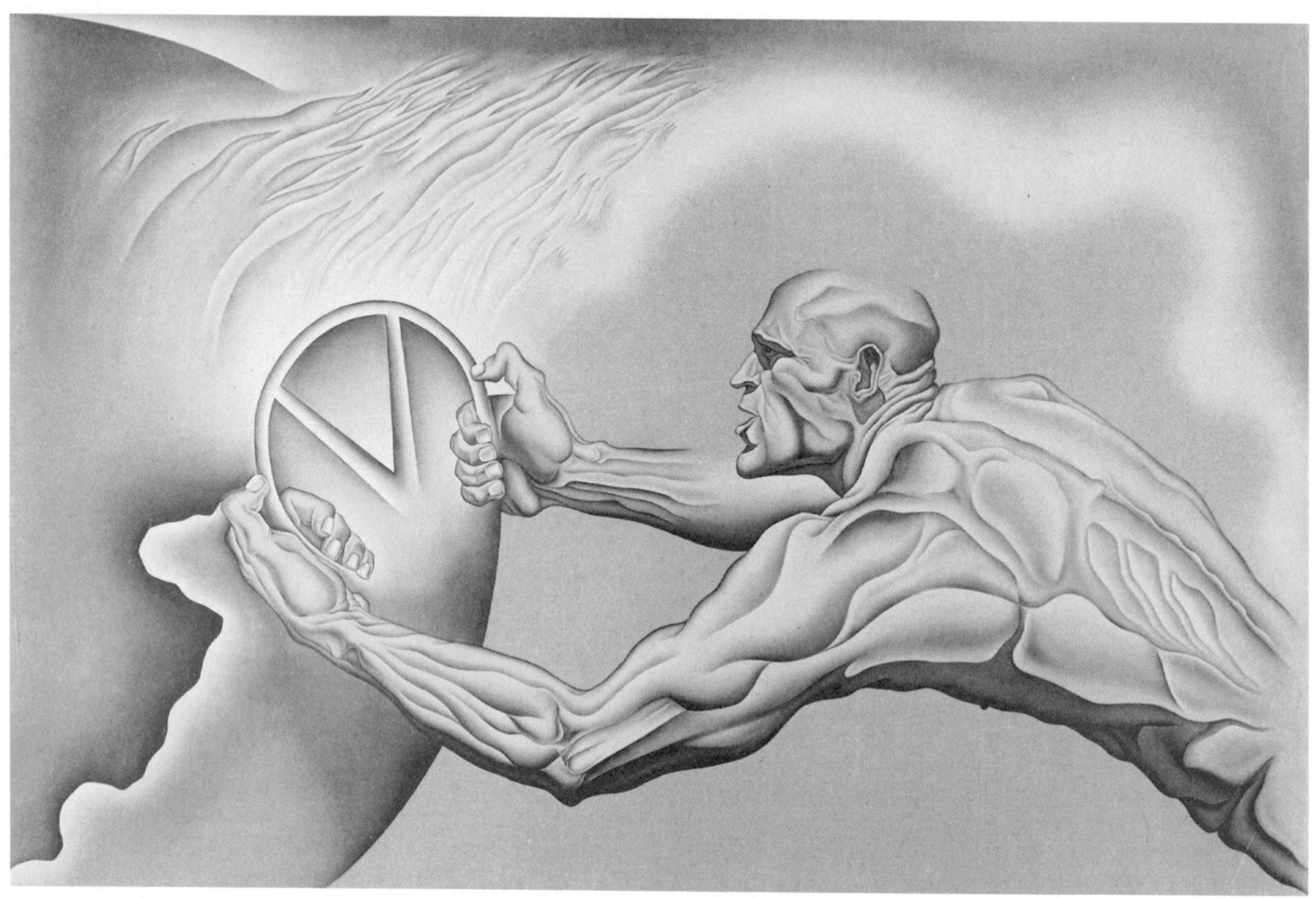

Judy Chicago: *Driving the World to Destruction from Powerplay,* 1985. Photo ©Donald Woodman. Through the Flower.

Publications:

By CHICAGO: Books—*Through the Flower: My Struggle as a Woman Artist,* New York 1975; *The Dinner Party: A Symbol of our Heritage,* New York 1979; *Embroidering Our Heritage: The Dinner Party Needlework,* New York 1980; *The Birth Project,* New York 1985; *Judy Chicago: The Dinner Party,* Germany, 1987; *Connecting Conversations: Interviews with 28 Bay Area Women Artists,* edited by Moira Roth, Oakland 1988; *Holocaust Project: From Darkness into Light,* New York 1993; *Judy Chicago: The Dinner Party,* New York 1996; *Beyond the Flower: The Autobiography of a Feminist Artist,* New York 1996; with Edward Lucie-Smith, *Judy Chicago, An American Vision,* New York 2000. **Articles**—statement in *Everywoman Newspaper* (Los Angeles), 7 May 1971; statement and introduction, with Miriam Shapiro, in *Womanhouse,* exhibition catalog, Los Angeles 1972; introduction to *Invisible/Visible,* exhibition catalog, Long Beach, California 1972; ''Let Sisterhood Be Powerful'' in *Womanspace Journal* (Los Angeles), February/March 1973; ''Female Imagery,'' with Miriam Shapiro, in *Womanspace Journal* (Los Angeles), Summer 1973; ''Letter to A Young Woman Artist,'' with Arlene Raven, in *Anonymous Was A Woman,* Valencia, California 1974; ''2 Artists Interview Each Other,'' with Lloyd Hamrol, in *Criteria* (Vancouver), 1974; ''Interview with Judy Chicago,'' with Arlene Raven and Susan Rennie, in *Chrysalis* (Los Angeles), no. 4 1977. **Films**—*Judy Chicago and The California Girls,* with J. Dancoff, Los Angeles 1971; *Womanhouse,* with Johanna Demetrakis, Los Angeles 1972.

On CHICAGO: Books—*Primary Structures,* exhibition catalog, by Kynaston McShine, New York 1966; *Painting, Sculpture, Photographs of Judy Chicago,* by Dextra Frankel, Fullerton, California 1970; *Voicing Today's Visions: Writings by Women Artists* by Mara Witzling, New York and London 1991, 1992; *The Power of Feminist Art: The American Movement of the 1970s,* edited by Norma Broude and Mary D. Garrard, New York 1994; *Sexual Politics: Judy Chicago's Dinner Party in Feminist Art History,* edited by Amelia Jones, Berkeley 1996. **Articles**—''Thru The Feminist Looking Glass with Judy Chicago'' by Susan Stocking in the *Los Angeles Times,* July 1972; ''Woman's Art: A Theoretical Perspective'' by Arlene Raven in *Womanspace Journal* (Los Angeles), February/March 1973; ''Judy Chicago at Kenmore'' by Judy Stein in *Art in America* (New York), July/August 1974; ''Judy Chicago Talking to Luch R. Lippard'' in *Artform* (New York), September 1974; ''Judy Chicago and Trials of 'Dinner Party''' by Grace Glueck in the *New York Times,* 30 April 1977; ''Judy Chicago: World of China Painter'' in *Ceramics Monthly* (Columbus, Ohio), May 1978; ''Publishing: Judy Chicago Speaking in Volumes'' by Herbert Mitgang in the *New York Times* (New York), September 1980; ''The Womanly Art of Judy Chicago'' by Gwenda Blair in *Mademoiselle* (New York), January 1982; ''The State of Feminism in the Visual Arts: Judy Chicago's Dinner Party—White Elephant or Trojan Horse'' by Helen Topliss in *Art Monthly: Australian and International,* no. 9, April 1988; ''Judy Chicago's Fiber Art: Revising History, Changing Society'' by Sandy Ballatore in *Fiberarts,*

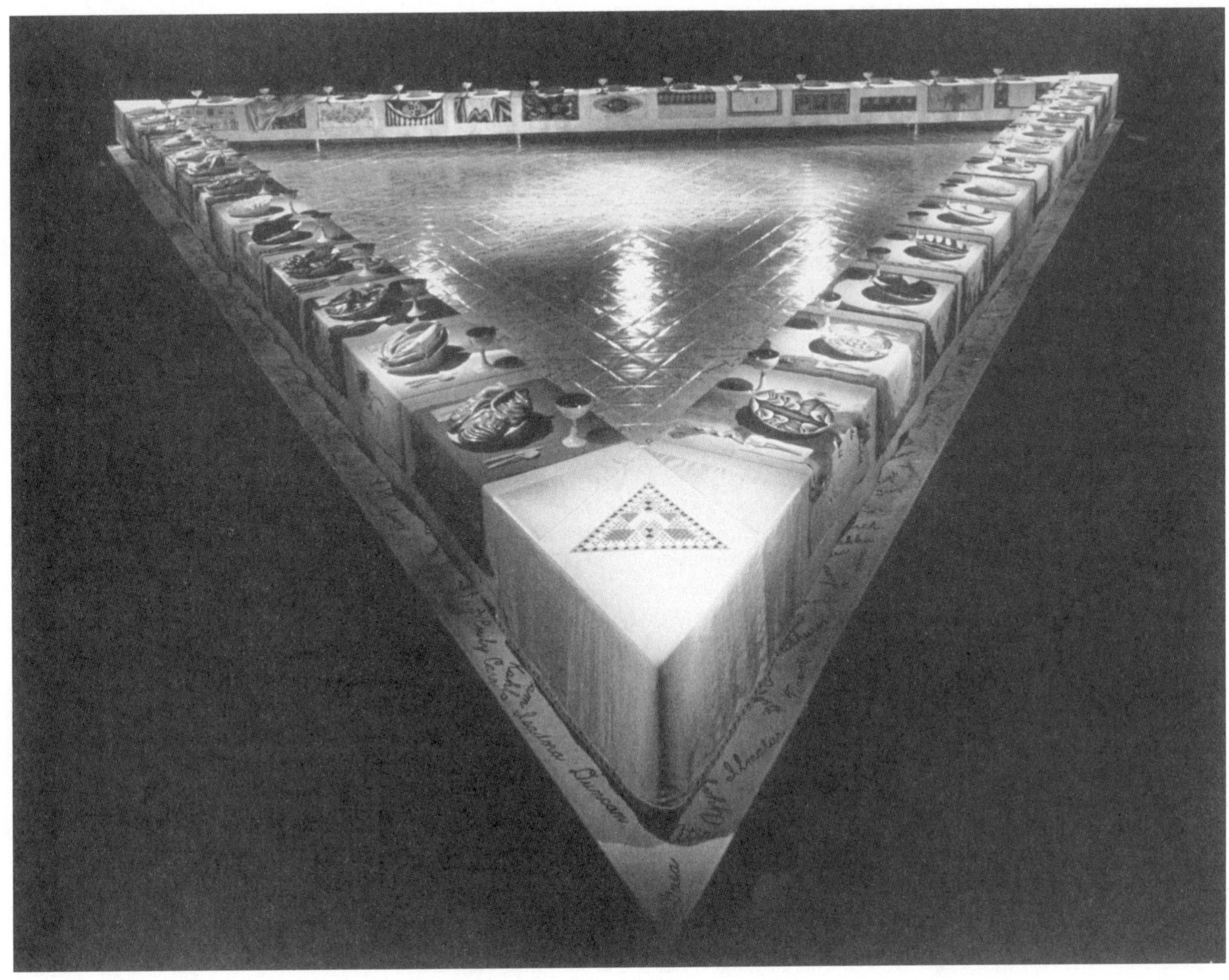

Judy Chicago: *The Dinner Party.* Photo ©Donald Woodman. Through the Flower.

vol. 17, Summer 1990; ''Entertaining Judy'' in *Women Artists News,* vol. 15, Fall 1990; ''No Sexual Perversion in (Judy) Chicago'' by Nancy McCauley in *Art Documentation,* vol. 11, no. 4, Winter 1992; ''Being in the Presence of the Truth: An Interview With Judy Chicago'' by Nancy Jo Hoy in *The Ear,* Spring 1994; ''Exclusive Interview With Judy Chicago'' by Guy Cross in *THE Magazine,* March 1994; ''Judy Chicago: Exploitation or Art?'' by Audrey Farrell in *Art Criticism,* vol. 10, no. 2, 1995; ''The Chicago Resolutions'' by Paula Harper in *Art in America* (New York), vol. 88, no. 6, June 2000. **Films—***Right Out of History: The Making of The Dinner Party* by Johanna Demetrakas, New York, 1979; *Birth Project* by Vivian Kleiman, 1985; *Holocaust Project,* Albuquerque; *A Family of Women* by Vu Productions, 1994.

*

I organized the first feminist art program in America in 1970 and have been instrumental in developing the Women's Building in Los Angeles, which is committed to a feminist perspective in art-related professions. I am a feminist artist, interested in making the female experience stand for an aspect of the human condition which has been shrouded in mythology and fantasy. I am committed to expanding the perspective of my world through breaking the historical silence of women. I believe in art that is connected to real human feeling, that extends itself beyond the limits of the art world to embrace all people who are striving for alternatives in an increasingly dehumanized world. I am trying to make art that relates to the deepest and most mythic concerns of human kind and I believe that, at this moment of history, feminism is humanism. I believe that art, if authentic, can reach across all gaps between people and create understanding.

—Judy Chicago

* * *

''I wanted to wed my skills to my real ideas and to aspire to the making of art that could clearly reveal my values and point of view as a woman . . . integrating my art and my feminism.''

—Judy Chicago, from *Through the Flower*

Painter, sculptor, teacher, director, organizer, political activist, writer, Judy Chicago is all these.

She originally studied traditional painting and sculpture. Later—struggling for male acceptance—she learned spray painting in an auto body shop, taught herself carpentry, discovered how to use machinery in an industrial arts shop, studied pyrotechnology, made a lithograph—''toughing it out.'' Her autobiography, *Through the Flower,* is partly an attempt to escape that search for masculine approval and to resolve the conflict of how to be a woman *and* an artist.

Chicago's early work was often labelled ''Judy's cunts,'' but she soon hid her aggressive female imagery in minimalism. In painting series she explored ''hard'' and ''soft'' interactions through colour relationships. In sculpture three-domed shapes represented both her physical self and the family of mother/father/child.

Driven to share her experiences, Chicago initiated an art class for women in Fresno, California, then created ''Womanhouse'' with a group of working female artists. ''Womanhouse'' involved renovating a dilapidated house—so learning ''male'' skills and crafts—then transforming it into environmental statements. The women, working alone or in teams on individual rooms, emerged stretched emotionally, mentally and artistically. Chicago grew and learned with them.

''Womanhouse'' taught Chicago that a woman's art benefits from being shown with art of other women—in context, so to speak. It also stimulated her to ''wave a red flag'' at the bull of the male-dominated art community with renewed emphasis in her work on recognizable female imagery. ''Red Flag'' is the title of her first lithograph—an overt highly-coloured image of a used Tampax being withdrawn from a woman.

In 1973 Chicago began a major five-year project—''The Dinner Party.'' A ''symbolic history of women's achievements and struggles,'' it is an evolutionary summation of Chicago's own achievements begun with the inspiration of a single hand-painted plate. Thirty-nine women are honoured with a full place at Chicago's triangular-shaped table. Each place setting is marked by an embroidered runner and a ceramic plate. The strong three-dimensional plate designs, reminiscent of Chicago's early specific imagery, fight to rise from their bases—trapped butterflies straining for freedom. The entire work stands on a porcelain floor of triangles painted in gold with names of 999 ''supporting'' women. A feminist statement is made using traditional female crafts and activities.

''The Dinner Party,'' which has been travelling since its completion, is both a celebration and a challenge—a celebration of accomplishments from the primordial goddess of ancient religions to Katherine Hepburn. It celebrates women's successes in art, politics, science and religion. ''The Dinner Party'' would, however, be a beautiful failure if it did not also challenge, demanding of men and women a better knowledge of and interest on contributions of women to every facet of life—and a demand that women continue to answer the challenge. That is the reason for ''The Dinner Party''—and for the art and life of Judy Chicago.

—Marlee Robinson

Chicago's art continued to evolve after ''The Dinner Party.'' Her later works are marked by some of the approaches to art and art-making that characterized her earlier endeavors. She continued to use materials not usually considered part of the high art canon, particularly needlework media; she continued to collaborate with other art-workers in the production of her images; and she worked on ''projects'' that consisted of multiple pieces and images.

Perhaps because she had so much trouble getting museums to exhibit ''The Dinner Party'' (which remained in storage after the early 1980s, with the exception of a major exhibition at UCLA in 1996), Chicago decided to construct her next major opus, ''The Birth Project'' (1980–85), so that pieces of it could be exhibited in multiple locations simultaneously. This project was also a collaborative work, in which Chicago designed about 100 panels which were then rendered in varying forms of needle arts by needle-workers who were credited for their contributions. She chose the theme of birth specifically to redress its lack of depiction in Western art. Many of the images expand upon the central core imagery that was so important to her earlier work, placing it in a more broadly conceived context, as in ''The Creation of the World'' (1984) in which a birthing woman becomes the landscape, the sky, the sun.

After ''The Birth Project'' Chicago decided to lay aside her exploration of ''female'' imagery. In ''Powerplay'' (1980–86), she explores images of masculinity, especially those of the heroic male nude. This series, consisting of drawings, oil paintings, and bronze reliefs, explores the way in which masculinity is marked by the violence in our culture. In ''The Holocaust Project: From Darkness to Light'' (1985–93, in collaboration with her husband Donald Woodman), she drew upon her Jewish identity to create a multi-media epic based on the Holocaust, with the goal of ''healing and repairing the world'' through her art. ''Resolutions: A Stitch in Time'' (1994–2000) consists of painted and needle-worked images that deconstruct some of the aphorisms that predominate in western culture. In recent years Chicago's work has been more widely exhibited than in the past; most significant was the display and re-evaluation of ''The Dinner Party'' in 1996. ''Trials and Tributes: A Judy Chicago Retrospective'' has traveled to various venues in 2000 and 2001.

Chicago donated her archives to the Arthur and Elizabeth Schlesinger Library at Radcliffe College, where they are available for consultation. Her work still remains controversial (people objected to the use of Holocaust imagery, as they had found the central core imagery difficult twenty years earlier) but there is no doubt that she is a major artist with a keen, unique vision.

—Mara Witzling

CHILLIDA, Eduardo

Nationality: Spanish. **Born:** San Sebastian, 10 January 1924. **Education:** Classical High School, San Sebastian, 1930–42; studied architecture at the University of Madrid, 1943–47, and painting at a private art school, Madrid, 1947. **Family:** Married Pili de Belzunce in 1950; children: Guiomar, Pedro, Ignacio, Carmen and Suzanna. **Career:** Independent artist, in Paris, 1948–49, in Villaines-sous-Bois, France, 1950, in Hernani, Spain, 1951–58, in San Sebastian, since 1959. Visiting professor, Carpenter Center, Harvard University, Cambridge, Massachusetts 1971; elected Honorary Member of the American Academy of Arts and Letters, New York, 1993; nominated as Honorary Member of the Real Academia de Bellas Artes de San Fernando, Madrid, 1994; Chillida Leku Museum, 2000. **Awards:**

Eduardo Chillida (center) next to his sculpture *Berlin*, located near the German Chancellor's Office in Berlin. ©2001 Artists Rights Society (ARS), NY/ VEGAP, Madrid.

Eduardo Chillida, 2000. ©2001 Artists Rights Society (ARS), NY/ VEGAP, Madrid.

Diploma of Honour, *Triennale di Milano,* 1954; Sculpture Prize, Comune di Venezia, 1958; Kandinsky Prize, 1960; Carnegie Sculpture Prize, Pittsburgh, 1964; Nord-Rhein Prize, Dusseldorf, 1966; Wilhelm-Lehmbruck Sculpture Prize, Duisburg, West Germany, 1966; Rembrandt Prize, San Sebastian, 1975; Engraving Prize, Japanese Ministry of Culture, 1976; Peach Prize, Victor Seix Institute, 1978; Andrew W. Mellon Prize, with Willem de Kooning, Carnegie Institute, Pittsburgh, 1978; Gold Medal of Merit for Fine Arts, Madrid, 1981; European Plastic Arts Prize, Strasbourg, 1983; Grand Prix des Arts et des Lettres, Paris, 1984; Wolf Foundation Prize, Herzlia, Israel, 1985; Kaiserring Award, Goslar, West Germany, 1985; *Revista Euzkadi* Prize, Bilbao, Spain, 1986; Premio de Asturias, Madrid, 1987; Premio Lorenzo il Paris Magnifico, Florence, 1987; Order of Merit for Science and Art, Bonn, 1987; Praemium Imperiale Award, Japan Art Association, 1991; Medal de Andres Bello, 1992; Gold Medal, City of Donostia, 1992; Assn. Espanola Critica Arte, 1995; Cross, Portuguese Order Merit Mario Soares, Freedom Prize, 1995; Doctor Honoris Causa, University of Alicante, Spain 1996; ISC Lifetime Achievement Award, Chicago, 1998; Golden Rose Prize, Palermo, 1998, Engraving's National Prize, Calcografía Nacional, Madrid, 1998. **Agents:** Sala Gaspar, Consejo de Ciento 323, Barcelona, and Galerie Maeght, 13 rue do Tehran, 75008 Paris, France.

Address: Tasende Gallery, 8808 Melrose Ave, West Hollywood, CA 90069–5604. **Web site:** www.eduardo-chillida.com.

Individual Exhibitions:

1954 Galeria Clan, Madrid
1956 Galerie Maeght, Paris
1961 Galerie Maeght, Paris
1962 Kunsthalle, Basle
1964 McRoberts and Tunnard Gallery, London
1966 Galerie Maeght, Paris
Wilhelm-Lehmbruck-Musuem, Duisburg, West Germany
Galerie Buchholz, Munich
Museum of Fine Arts, Houston
1967 Munson-Williams-Proctor Institute, Utica, New York
City Art Museum, St. Louis
Alex Galerie, Dusseldorf
Konstsalongen Samlaren, Stockholm
1968 Galerie Maeght, Paris
Galerie Im Erker, St. Gallen, Switzerland
1969 Kunstmuseum, Basle
Kunsthaus, Zurich
Stedelijk Museum, Amsterdam
Galerie-Verein München e. V, Munich
Galerie Buchholz, Munich
Galerie im Erker, St. Gallen, Switzerland
1970 Kunstkabinett, Frankfurt
Galerie Maeght, Paris
Librairie-Galerie La Hune, Paris
Galerie Renée Ziegler, Zurich
1971 Sala Gaspar, Barcelona
1972 Galeria Iolas-Velasco, Madrid
Konsthall, Lund, Sweden
Ulmer, Museum, Ulm, West Germany
1973 Galerie Maeght, Paris
Caja de Ahorros, Pamplona, Spain
Caja de Ahorros, Sorguesa, Spain
Caja de Ahorros, Estella, Spain
Galerie Wünsche, Hamburg
1974 Hastings Gallery/Spanish Institute, New York
Galeria 42, Barcelona
Galeria Juana de Aizpuru, Seville
Galeria Turner, Madrid
Chateau de Ratilly, France
Galleria d'Art Serfontana, Morbio Inferiore, Italy
Galerie d'Art Moderne, Basle
1975 Galerie Nouvelle Images, The Hague
Galerie Numaga, Neuchâtel, Switzerland
Galeria Internacional de Arte, Madrid
1976 Kulturhuset, Hellerup, Denmark
1977 Galeria Iolas-Velasco, Madrid
Museo de Durango, Spain
Caja de Ahorros, Pamplona, Spain
FIAC 77, Grand Palais, Paris
Carpenter Center, Harvard University Cambridge. Massuchesetts
Galerie Art in Progress, Munich
1978 Staatliche Kunsthalle, Baden-Baden, West Germany
Galerie Maeght, Zurich
Galerie Schmela, Dusseldorf

Galerie Artek, Helsinki (with Luginbuhl and Tinguely)
1979 Landau-Alexander Gallery, Los Angeles
National Gallery, Washington, D.C.
Carnegie Institute, Pittsburgh
1980 Galerie Maeght, Paris
Guggenheim Museum, New York (retrospective)
Palacio de Valezquez, Madrid
Esculturas/Obra Grafica, Galeria Maeght, Barcelona
Galerie Maeght, Paris
1981 Museo de Bellas Artes Bilbao
Skulpturen, Kestner-Gesellschaft, Hannover
Galerie Maeght, Zurich
Frances Aronson Gallery, Atlanta, Georgia
Galerie Marghescu, Hannover
Galerie Hans Ostertad, Frankfurt
1982 Galerie Beyeler, Basle
Galerie Maeght, Zurich
1983 Maison de Goya, Bordeaux, France
Galeria Maese Nicolas, Leon, Spain
Erker Galerie, St. Gallen, Switzerland
Galerie Herbert Meyer-Ellinger, Frankfurt
1984 Sala Celini, Madrid
Galerie Kaj Forsblom, Helsinki
Galerie Grariart, Turku, Finland
Galerie Brusberg, Hannover
Galerie Adrien Maeght, Paris
M.A. Martin Gallery, New York
Tasende Gallery, La Jolla, California
1985 Caja Ahorros Municipal, Elgoibar, Spain
Anne Berthoud Gallery, London
Galerie Biedermann, Munich
Caja Laboral Popular, Portugalete, Spain
Caja Laboral Popular, Algorta, Spain
Galerie Beaumont, Luxembourg
Abadia Montmajour, Arles, Franch
Musee d'Art Moderne, Brussels
Galerie Maeght-Lelong, Zurich
1986 Fondacion Miro, Barcelona
Caja Laboral Popular, Aretxabaleta, Spain (toured Spain)
Centro de Arte Reina Sofia, Madrid
Neue Galerie der Stadt, Linz, West Germany
Galerie Meyer-Ellinger, Frankfurt
Dresdner Bank, Frankfurt
Museo de Bellas Artes, Bilbao, Spain
Tasende Gallery, La Jolla, California
Ospedale degli Innocente, Florence
Fondacion Miro, Barcelona
1987 Galeria Joan Prats, Barcelona
Galerie Ulysses, Vienna
Galeria Ederti, Bilbao, Spain
Stadtmuseum, Pforzheim, West Germany
1988 *Chillida at Gernika: Birth of a Monument Gure Aitaren Etxea/Our Father's House,* Navy Pier, Chicago
1989 Städtische Kunstmuseum, Bonn (retrospective; travelled to Westfälisches Landesmuseum, Munster)
Chillida in New York, Sydney Janis Gallery, New York
Chillida, Adams-Middleton Gallery, Dallas
1990 *Eduardo Chillida: Prints and Drawings,* Staatliche Graphische Sammlung, Munich
Hayward Gallery, London (retrospective)
Galerie Lelong, Paris
1991 *Eduardo Chillida,* Kunsthalle, Basle
Neuer Berliner Kunstverein, Berlin
Real Academy, Madrid
Palacio de Revillagigiedo, Gijon (travelled to Bilbao, Spain, and Caracas, Venezuela)
Galerie Lelong, Paris
Eduardo Chillida: Sculptures and Works on Paper, Galerie Springer, Berlin
Chillida, Martin-Gropius-Bau, Berlin (retrospective)
1992 Palacio de Miramar, San Sebastian (retrospective)
Eduardo Chillida: Sculpture and Works on Paper, Annely Juda Fine Art, London
Chillida, Galerie Tokoro, Tokyo
1993 *Eduardo Chillida: A Retrospective,* Schirn Kunsthalle, Frankfurt (retrospective)
1995 Galerie Ellen, Paris
Chillida: Petits Poids, Galerie Lelong, Paris
Eduardo Chillida: Sculpture and Works on Paper, Annely Juda Fine Art, London
1996 *Chillida: Drawings, Collages, Forces of Gravity 1947–96,* Galerie Lelong, Zurich
Eduardo Chillida: Sculptures in Clay, Museum Bellerive, Zurich (traveled to Stadtgalerie, Sundern; Lunds Konsthall, Sweden; Hetjens-Museum, Dusseldorf)
Chillida and Goethe, Kunstverein, Osnabruck, Germany
1997 Tasende Gallery, Los Angeles
Remba Gallery, Los Angeles
Chillida and the Music, Sinclair-Haus, Bad Homburg, Germany
Museo Bellas Artes, Bilbao (traveling exhibition)
1998 Galería Elvira González, Madrid
Bach Book—Homage to Bach, Real Academia de Bellas Artes, Madrid
Chillida—Elogio del Hierro—Años 50, IVAM, Valencia
Museo Nacional Centro de Arte Reina Sofía, Madrid
1999 *Eduardo Chillida: 1948–1998,* Guggenheim Bilbao Museum, Bilbao, Spain
Eduardo Chillida: Tension of Line, Penetration of Space, Guggenheim Museum, Bilbao, Spain
Murales, Galerie Lelong, Paris

Selected Group Exhibitions:

1949 *5th Salon de Mai,* Musée d'Art Moderne, Paris
1954 *10th Triennale di Milano*
1958 *Biennale,* Venice
1964 *Documenta 3.* West Germany (and *Documenta 4,* 1968; *Documenta 6,* 1977)
1967 *Guggenheim International,* Guggenheim Museum, New York
1974 *9th Biennale of Prints,* National Museum of Modern Art, Tokyo (travelled to the Museum of Modern Art, Kyoto)
1975 *Contemporary Spanish Painters,* Cultural Center, New York
1983 *Arte abstracto espanol,* Fundacion Juan March, Madrid
1987 *Monumenta,* Middelheim Museum, Antwerp, Belgium
1989 *From Goya to Tinguely: Watercolours and Drawings from a Private Collection,* Kunstmuseum, Berne

The Artist's Book: The Most Beautiful Artists' Books from the Collection of the Herzog August Library in Wolfenbuttel, Kestner-Gesellschaft, Hanover, G.F.R.

1990 *44th Biennale,* Venice

Iron Sculptures from Spain, Stadtische Kunsthalle, Mannheim, Germany

1993 *The Body of Drawing: Drawings of Sculptors,* Graves Art Gallery, Sheffield

Directions in Modernism: The Beyeler Collection, Nationalgalerie, Staatliche Museen Preussischer Kulturbesitz, Berlin

1995 *FIAC: Foire Internationale d'Art Contemporain,* Paris

European Plastic Informal Art 1945–65, Wilhelm-Lehmbruck-Museum, Duisburg, Germany

1996 *Black is a Color,* Galerie Maeght, Barcelona, Spain

Masterpieces of the Twentieth Century: The Beyeler Collection, Art Gallery of New South Wales, Sydney

1997 Kroller-Müller Museum, Otterlo, Netherlands

Collections:

Wilhelm-Lehmbruck-Museum, Dusburg, West Germany; Kunstmuseum, Basle; Kunsthaus, Zurich; Tate Gallery, London; Galleria, Nazionale d'Arte Moderna, Rome; Museo Civico, Turin; Museum of Modern Art, New York; Guggenheim Museum, New York; Art Institute of Chicago; Museum of Fine Arts, Houston; Nestlé Contemporary Art Collection, Vevey, Switzerland.

Permanent Public Installations:

Porthania Place, Helsinki; Unesco Headquarters, Paris; Parc Albert Michallon, Grenoble; Thyssen Building, Dusseldorf; Taunus Anlage, Frankfurt; Rathaus Innenhof, Munster; City of Tehran; Basilica de Aranzazu, Spain; Plaza del Rey, Madrid; Paseo de la Castellana, Madrid; Fundacion Juan March, Madrid; Monte Urgull, San Sebastian; Real Golf Club, Feunterrabia, Spain; Iglesia Santa Maria, San Sebastian; Peine del Viento, San Sebastian; Cadenas de San Gregorio, Valladolid, Spain; Plaza de los Fueros, Vitoria, Spain; Plaza del Rey, Barcelona; Creueta del Coll, Barcelona; Recinto Historico, Guernica; Cerro de Santa Catalina, Gijon; Paseo de la Concha, San Sebastian; Muelle de la Sal, Seville; Parque de Bonaval, Santiago Compostela, Spain; Parque Rodriguez Sahagun, Madrid; Musée Olympique, Lausanne; Market Place, Lund, Sweden; Museum of Art, Houston; World Bank, Washington, D.C.; Symphony Hall, Dallas; Pei's Morton Symphony Center, Dallas; Cerro de Santa Catalina, Gijón, Spain; Sinclair House Garden, Bad Homburg; Landeszentral Bank Square, Trier, Germany.

Publications:

By CHILLIDA: Books—*Hommage à Georges Braque,* Paris 1964; *Chillida,* portfolio, with foreword by Carola Giedion-Welcker, Paris 1964; *Chillida: Sculptures,* with foreword by Juan Daniel Fullaondo, Paris 1968. **Books Illustrated—***Le Chemin des Devins/Menerges* by André Frenaud, Paris 1966; *Meditationen in Kastillien* by Max Holzer, St. Gallen, Switzerland 1968; *Die Kunst und der Raum* by Martin Heidegger, St. Gallen, Switzerland 1969; *Poetes-Peintres-Sculpteurs,* Paris 1960; *Mas alla* by Jorge Guillen, Paris 1973; *Die Penser* by Aeschylus, Madrid 1978; *Ce maudit moi* by E. M. Cioran, Paris 1983. **Articles—**interview with Anthony O'Hear in *Modern Painters* (London), vol. 3, no. 3, Autumn 1990; interview with Maite Lores in *Art Line* (London), vol. 5, no. 4, March-April 1991; interview with Tim Marlow in *Modern Painters* (London), vol. 5, no. 4, Winter 1992; interview with Jorge Garcia in *Kalias,* no. 9, vol. 5, 1993; interview with Sandra Wagner in *Sculpture* (Washington, D.C.), vol. 96, October 1997.

On CHILLIDA: Books—*Contemporary Sculpture: An Evolution in Volume and Space* by Carola Giedion-Welcker, London 1961; *Chillida,* exhibition catalog, with text by Franz Meyer, Basle 1962; *Eduardo Chillida,* exhibition catalog, with text by James Johnson Sweeney, Houston 1966; *Chillida* by Pierre Volboudt, Paris 1967; *Form and Space* by Eduard Trier, London 1968; *Vingt-Cing Ans d'Art Vivant* by Michael Ragon, Paris 1968: *The Eye and the Hand of the Sculptor* by Paul Waldo Schwartz, London 1969; *Chillida* by Claude Esteban, Paris 1971; *Los Espacios de Chillida* by Gabriel Celaya, Barcelona 1974; *Hablando con Chillida, escultor vasco* by Marin de Ugalde, San Sebastian 1975; *Chillida* by Luis Figuerola-Ferretti, Madrid 1976; *Cuaderno Chillida,* edited by Revista de Occidente, Madrid 1976; *Eduardo Chillida: Akte-Hande-Formen* by Werner Schmalenbach, West Berlin 1977; *Chillida: Oeure Graphique* by Julien Clay, Paris 1978; *Chillida* by Octavio Paz, Paris 1979; *Chillida,* exhibition catalog, with text by Octavio Paz, New York 1980; *Chillida: Esculturas/Obra Grafica,* exhibition catalog, with text by Santiago Amon, Barcelona 1980; *Eduardo Chillida: Skulpturen,* exhibition catalog, with text by Carl-Albrecht Haenlein, Hannover 1981; *Chillida,* exhibition catalog, with text by Octavio Paz, Zurich 1981; *Eduardo Chillida: Graphic Works,* exhibition catalog with text by R. Hohl, La Jolla, California 1984; *Eduardo Chillida,* exhibition catalog by Michael Semff, Pforzheim, West Germany 1987; *Chillida at Gernika: Birth of a Monument Gure Aitaren Etxea/Our Father's House,* exhibition catalog, Chicago 1988; *Chillida in New York,* exhibition catalog with text by Thomas M. Messer, New York 1989; *Chillida,* exhibition catalog with text by Francisco Calvo Serraller, Dallas 1989; *Omaggio a Eduardo Chillida,* exhibition catalog, Venice 1990; *Chillida,* exhibition catalog, Paris 1990; *Eduardo Chillida: Prints and Drawings,* exhibition catalog with text by Richard Harprath and Wolfgang Holler, Munich 1990; *Chillida,* exhibition catalog, Berlin 1991; *Chillida,* exhibition catalog, Berlin 1991; *Chillida Elogio del Horizonte,* exhibition catalog, Gijon 1991; *Chillida Intimo,* exhibition catalog, Madrid 1991; *Eduardo Chillida: Sculpture and Works on Paper,* exhibition catalog with text by William Packer, London 1992; *Chillida,* exhibition catalog with text by James Johnson Sweeney and Gabriel Celaya, Tokyo 1992; *Chillida Oeuvre Grave* by Julien Clay and Jorge Guillen, Paris 1993; *Chillida: Zeichnungen, Collagen, Gravitationen 1947–96,* exhibition catalog, Zurich 1996; *Eduardo Chillida: Sculptures in Clay,* exhibition catalog, Zurich 1996; *Chillida* by Matthias Barmann, Milan 1999. **Articles—**''Chillida's Monument to Peace'' by Peter Howard Selz in *Arts Magazine,* vol. 63, September 1988; ''Viva Chillida'' by Peter Buchanan in *The Architectural Review,* vol. 188, October 1990; ''Chillida: Body and Space'' by Katherine Chacon in *Art Nexus* (Bogota), no. 8, April-June 1993; ''Asking Questions in Steel and Stone: Sculptor Eduardo Chillida'' by Suzanne Muchnic in *Art News,* vol. 96, October 1997.

* * *

Since the deaths of Gonzalez and Picasso, Eduardo Chillida is the most distinguished living Spanish sculptor. He is, however, a

Basque, and does not share with those two great compatriots, and many other Spanish artists, a concern for surrealistic fantasy or narrative necessity. Cubism and Constructivism seem to be part of his formal inheritance, but from his native background he also brings the influence of artisanship, in the use of heavy metals and the making of positive, forged shapes. A slow, contemplative artist, Chillida has always preferred to live and work away from international centres.

It was not until the early 60s that Chillida established a positive style. Earlier work in wood and forged iron, elaborated from heavy, gestural, twisted forms, is reminiscent, at times, of Gonzalez, but, in the eclectic change of manner, clearly searching for a final, personal form. Since then Chillida's sculptures have become more and more ascetic and controlled, the twisted, writhing, interlocking forms, carefully articulated into rhythmic definitions of space. This maturity is the result of a return, both physically and emotionally, to his native soil. His drawings, on paper, or the lead-inlaid marble calligraphy, as well as the attenuated sculptures, are deeply involved in the landscape of a mountainous country which plunges into a turbulent ocean. The division and meeting of these natural elements are vigorously delineated by Chillida, with a mixture of energy and elegance which brings to mind the stylised images of Japanese landscape painting. His sculptures further explore natural forces, through a medium which has roots in Spanish artisanship. They are concerned with flow, not conflict; he avoids intersections which interfere with the monumental rhythms of his forms.

Chillida says his subject is the relationship between time and space, defined by three-dimensionality: ''the two elements of space, one which might be called negative, the other positive, are in a relationship which I call a dialogue.'' This dialogue is concerned with poetic values, not scientific definitions, and derives from the observation of nature.

—Charles Spencer

CHLANDA, Marek

Nationality: Polish. **Born:** Cracow, 12 November 1954. **Education:** Graduated from the Academy of Fine Arts, Cracow, 1978. **Career:** Draftsman, sculptor and performance artist. Taught at Academy of Fine Arts, Cracow, 1980 and 1892; at the Vestlandetskunstakademie, Bergen, Norway, 1983–84; and at the Silesain University, Cieszyn, Poland, 1986–88. **Agent:** Starmach Gallery. **Address:** c/o Starmach Gallery, Rynek Glowny 45, 31–013 Cracow, Poland.

Individual Exhibitions:

1976 Dorn Polski, Cieszyn, Poland
1978 Galeria Maly Rynek, Cracow
1979 Galeria Kanonicza 5, Cracow
1980 Galeria Krytykow, Warsaw
1981 Galeria Studio, Warsaw
Galleri St. Agnes, Roskilde, Denmark
Galerie Kanal 2, Copenhagen
1982 Galerie Asbaek, Copenhagen
1983 Galleri St. Agnes, Roskilde, Denmark
Kunstforeningen, Bergen, Norway
1985 Muzeum Sztuki, Lodz
Herning Kunstmuseum, Herning, Denmark
1986 Moltkerei, Cologne
Galeria Krzysztofory, Cracow
Galleri St. Agnes, Roskilde, Denmark
Galeria Uniwersytecka BWA, Cieszyn, Poland
1987 Fyns Kunstmuseum, Odense, Denmark
1988 Galerie S. and H. de Buck, Ghent, Belgium
1989 Galeria Potocka, Cracow
1990 Galerie S. and H. de Buck, Ghent, Belgium
Starmach Gallery, Cracow
Galeria Wschodnia, Lodz
Muzuem Sztuki, Lodz
Budapest Galeria, Budapest
Galeria Na Pude, Teski Tesin
1991 Galerie van der Crommenacker, Arnhem
Galeria Krzysztofory, Cracow
Galeria Grodzka BWA, Lublin, Poland
1992 Galerie in Situ, Aalst, Belgium
Galerie Thomas Gehrke, Hamburg
Galeria Miejsce, Cieszyn, Poland
1993 Galerie de Zaal, Delft, Holland
Tel Aviv Museum of Art
Galeria Arsenal, Bialystok, Poland
Galeria Krzysztofory, Cracow
1994 Galerie Thomas Gehrke, Hamburg
Curt Marcus Gallery, New York
Narodowa Galeria Sztuki Wspolczesnej Zacheta, Warsaw
1996 *Good Night-sculpture,* Center for Contemporary Art, Warsaw

Selected Group Exhibitions:

1978 *Grands et Jeunes d'Aujourdhui,* Grand Palais, Paris
1979 *Polish Modern Art,* Galerie Asbaek, Copenhagen
1980 *Biennale,* Musée d'Art Moderne de la Ville, Paris
1981 *New Art from Poland,* Kunstlerhaus, Stuttgart
1986 *Biennale,* Sydney
1988 *Polish Realities: New Art from Poland,* Third Eye Centre, Glasgow
1990 *Verzameling II,* Museum van Hedendaagse Kunst, Antwerp
1992 *Muzeum Sztuki Lodz, 1931–1992,* Muzeum Sztuki, Lodz, and Musée d'Art Contemporain de Lyon and Espace Lyonnais d'Art Contemporain, Lyon
1993 *Identity Today,* Centre de Conferences Albert Borschette, Brussels
1994 *Biennale,* Sao Paulo
1995 *Where Is Your Brother Abel?,* Narodowa Galeria Sztuki Wspolczesnej Zacheta, Warsaw
1999 The Bunkier Sztuki Gallery, Kraków (retrospective)

Collections:

Muzeum Sztuki, Lodz; Muzeum Narodowe, Warsaw; Muzeum Gornoslaskie, Bytom, Poland; Narodowa Galeria Sztuki Wspolczesnej Zacheta, Warsaw; Albertinum-Kupferstich Kabinett, Dresden; Billedgalerie, Bergen, Norway; Kunsthalle, Neremberg; Museum van Hedendaagse Kunst, Antwerp; Museum van Hedendaagse Kunst, Ghent.

Publications:

By CHLANDA: Books—*Marek Chlanda: Dobranoc,* Warsaw 1996.

On CHLANDA: Books—*Marek Chlanda: Seria XIII,* exhibition catalog with text by Wojciech Sztaba, Cracow 1978; *Marek Chlanda: Rzezby Reliefy Rysunki,* exhibition catalog with texts by Ryszard Stanislawski and Maria Morzuch, Lodz 1985; *Marek Chlanda: Den Unulige Kaerlighet/ The Impossible Love,* exhibition catalog with text by Lise Lotte Blom, Odense 1987; *Polish Realities: New Art from Poland,* exhibition catalog, Glasgow 1988; *Marek Chlanda: Selection for Budapest,* exhibition catalog with text by Jaromir Jedlinski, Budapest 1990; *Marek Chlanda: Sculptures and Drawings,* exhibition catalog with texts by Yona Fischer and Jaromir Jedlinski, Tel Aviv 1993; *Marek Chlanda: Rzezba/Sculpture,* exhibition catalog with text by Jaromir Jedlinski, Warsaw 1994; *Where is Abel, Thy Brother?,* exhibition catalog with text by Anda Rottenberg, Warsaw 1995. **Articles—**''Confrontations des generations et des tendences'' by Jean Raoul Moulin in *L'Humanite,* 19 September 1978; ''Koncert'' by W. Sztaba in *Literatura IX,* 1980; ''Cielesnose rysunku/The Sensuality of Drawing'' by B. Madra in *Projekt,* December 1981; ''Marek Chlanda'' by J. Borgen in *Herning Kunstmuseum Bulletin,* no. 2, 1985; ''Marek Chlanda'' by J. Fonce in *Forum International,* January/February 1990; ''Marek Chlanda'' by P. Vanrobayes in *Arte Factum,* no. 33, 1990; ''Marek Chlanda'' by Marek Bartelik in *Art Forum,* December 1994; ''Marek Chlanda'' by Gregory Volk in *Art News,* January 1995; ''Marek Chlanda: The Bunkier Sztuki Gallery'' by Elaine A. King in *Sculpture* (Washington, D.C.), vol. 18, no. 10, December 1999.

*

Dream:

If you manage to produce two good sculptures, then your greatest dream is to make two more. This is a precondition. The more good sculptures, the better for everyone.

Hopes and Aspirations:

In terms of filiations, I am indebted to realism. I just hope I am a realistic artist. I regard art as the echo of being in the most elementary sense. The mode in which my works exist, the way they are placed and made, is fragmentary and arbitrary (technically). They are about orientation and disorientation, and about balance. This refers to the process going on in my brain, which is itself fragmented and arbitrary.

Needless to say, thoughts and obsessions should collide in order to keep their balance. To keep the integrity that is of prime importance to sculpture.

—Marek Chlanda

CHRISTO and JEANNE-CLAUDE

Nationality: American. CHRISTO: **Born:** Christo Javacheff in Gabrovo, Bulgaria, 13 June 1935; emigrated to the United States, 1964: naturalized, 1973. **Education:** Fine Arts Academy, Sofia, Bulgaria, 1953–56; Fine Arts Academy, Vienna, 1957. JEANNE-CLAUDE: **Born:** Jeanne-Claude de Guillebon in Casablanca, 13 June 1935, raised in France and Switzerland; emigrated to the United States, 1964. **Education:** University of Tunis, BA 1952. BOTH: **Family:** Son: Cyril, born 1960. **Career:** Environmental artists who create temporary works of art in urban and rural environments. Lived in Paris 1958–64; moved to New York, 1964. The couple worked under the name Christo until 1994; have continued their collaborative work as Christo and Jean-Claude since 1994. Select projects include: *Wrapping of a Public Building,* 1961; *Stacked Oil Barrels* and *Dockside Packages,* Cologne Harbor 1961; *Iron Curtain-Wall of Oil Barrels,* Paris 1962; *Stacked Oil Barrels,* Gentilly 1962; *Wrapping a Girl,* London 1962; *Showcases,* 1963; *Store Fronts,* 1964; *Air Package* and *Wrapped Tree,* Stedelijk van Abbemuseum, Holland, 1966; *42,390 Cubic Feet Package,* Walker Art Center 1966; *Wrapped Fountain and Wrapped Medieval Tower,* Spoleto 1968; wrapping of Kunsthalle Berne, 1968; *5600 Cubicmeter Package,* Documenta 4, Kassel, 1968; *Corridor Store Front,* 1968; *1240 Oil Barrels Mastaba* and *Two Tons of Stacked Hay,* Philadelphia Institute of Contemporary Art 1968; *Wrapped Museum of Contemporary Art,* Chicago 1969; *Wrapped Floor and Stairway,* Museum of Contemporary Art, Chicago, 1969; *Wrapped Coast, Little Bay, One Million Square Feet, Sydney Australia,* 1969; *Wrapped Monuments,* Milan 1970; *Wrapped Floors,* Kaiser Wilhelm Haus Lange, Krefeld, Germany, 1971; *Valley Curtain, Grand Hogback, Rifle, Colorado,* 1970–72; *The Wall,* Rome 1974; *Ocean Front,* Newport, Rhode Island, 1975; *Running Fence,* Sonoma and Marin Counties, California, 1972–76; *Wrapped Walk Ways,* Kansas City 1978; *The Mastaba of Abu Dhabi,* 1977—; *The Gates: Project for Central Park,* 1979—; *Surrounded Islands,* Biscayne Bay, Greater Miami, 1980–83; *Wrapped Floors and Stairways,* Architecture Museum, Basel, 1984; *The Pont Neuf Wrapped,* Paris, 1975–85; *The Umbrellas, Japan-USA,* 1984–91; *Over the River, Project for the Arkansas River,* Colorado, 1992—; *Wrapped Floors and Stairways and Covered Windows,* Museum Würth, Künzelsau, Germany, 1995; *Wrapped Reichstag, Berlin, 1971–95,* 1995; *Wrapped Trees, Fondation Beyeler and Berower Park,* Riehen-Basel, Switzerland 1997–98; *The Wall, 13,000 Oil Barrels, Gasometer, Oberhausen, Germany,* Oberhausen, Germany, 1999. **Awards:** Numerous awards. **Address:** 48 Howard Street, New York, New York 10013, U.S.A.

Individual Exhibitions: (Christo only, until 1972)

1961 Galeria Haro Lauhus, Cologne
1962 Galerie J. Paris
1963 Galerie Schmela, Dusseldorf
Galleria Apollinaire, Milan
Galleria de Leone, Venice
1964 Gallerie Schmela, Dusseldorf
Galleria del Leone, Venice
Galerie Ad Libitum, Antwerp
Galleria G.E. Sperone, Turin
Galleria La Salita, Rome
1966 Stedelijk van Abbemuseum, Eindhoven, Netherlands
Leo Castelli Gallery, New York
1967 Wide White Space Gallery, Antwerp
Galerie Der Spiegel, Cologne
1968 John Gibson Gallery, New York
Museum of Modern Art, New York
Galleria del Leone, Venice
1969 John Gibson Gallery, New York
Lo Giudice Gallery, Chicago
Wide White Space Gallery, Antwerp
Central Street Gallery, Sydney
National Gallery of Victoria, Melbourne

Galerie der Spiegel, Cologne
1970 The New Gallery, Cleveland
Galerie Francoise Lambert, Milan
Galerie Rene Ziegler, Zurich
Kaiser-Wilhelm Museum, Krefeld, West Germany
1971 Annely Juda Gallery, London
Galerie Yvon Lamberg, Paris
Haus Lange Museum, Krefeld, West Germany
Museum of Fine Arts, Houston
Kunstsammlungen-Stadt Nurnberg, Nuremberg
Galerie Victor Loeb, Berne
Kunsthaus, Hamburg
Colophon Galleria, Milan
Centro La Capella, Trieste
Ars Studeo, Copenhagen
Galerie Mikro, Berlin
Centro de Arte y Communicacion, Buenos Aires
1972 The New Gallery, Cleveland
La Jolla Museum of Contemporary Art, California
Santa Barbara Museum of Art, California
The Friends of Contemporary Art, Denver
Joslyn Art Museum, Omaha, Nebraska
Contemporary Arts Center, Cincinnati, Ohio
The Morgan Gallery, Kansas City
1973 Stedelijk Museum, Amsterdam
Seriaal Galerie, Amsterdam
Alan Frumkin Gallery, New York
Miami Dade Junior College
Ball State University, Muncie, Indiana
University of Washington Art Museum, Seattle
La Rotonda, Milan
Galeria Francoise Lambert, Milan
Galerie Charles Kriwin, Brussels
Neue Pinakoteck, Munich
Max Protetch Gallery, Washington, D.C.
Museu La Tertulia, Cali, Columbia
Kalamazoo Institute of Arts, Michigan
Rosa Esman Gallery, New York
Kunsthaus, Zurich
Kunsthalle, Dusseldorf
Kroller-Muller Museum, Otterlo, Netherlands
Kansas State University, Manhattan
Galleria d'Arte Vinciana, Milan
1974 Louisiana Museum, Humleback, Denmark
Sonja Henie-Niels Onstad Foundation, Oslo
Galerie W. Aronowitsch, Stockholm
Millersville State College, Pennsylvania
Annely Juda Gallery, Ondon
Hatton Gallery, University of Newcastle-upon-Tyne, England
Musée de Peinture et de Sculpture, Grenoble, France
1975 Musée Rath, Geneva
White Gallery, Lutry, Switzerland
Galeria Conkreight, Caracas
Galerie Gimpel Hanover, Zurich
Princeton University Art Museum, New Jersey
Galleria d'Alesandro-Ferranti, Rome
Galerie J. Benador, Geneva
La Jolla Museum of Contemporary Art, California
Oakland Museum, California
Institute of Contemporary Art, Boston
Musée Jenisch, Vevey, Switzerland
M. H. de Young Memorial Museum, San Francisco
Alberta College of Art Gallery, Calgary
Memorial Union Art Gallery, University of California at Davis
Grinnell College, Iowa
Galeria Ciento, Barcelona
Fabian Fine Arts, Cape Town
Harcus-Krakow-Rasoen-Sonnabend Gallery, Boston
Galerie Der Spiegel, Cologne
Galleria Buonaparte, Milan
1976 Foundation Veranneman, Kruishoutem, Belgium
Museum des 20. Jahrhunderts, Vienna
San Francisco Museum of Modern Art
Museum of Contemporary Art, La Jolla, California
Pasadena City College, California
Fine Arts Center, University of Massachusetts, Amherst
Broxton Gallery, Los Angeles
Art Association, Newport, Rhode Island
1977 Colorado Springs Fine Arts Center
Galeria Juan Prats, Barcelona
Galeria Trece, Barcelona
Israel Museum, Jerusalem
Newcomb College Art Department, Tulane University, New Orleans
Metropolitan Museum, Miami
Museum Boymans-van-Beuuingen, Rotterdam
Landische Museum, Bonn
Kestner Gesellschaft, Hannover
Minami Gallery, Tokyo
Annely Juda Fine Arts, London
American Center, Kyoto
1978 Louisiana Museum, Humlebaek, Denmark
Sonja Henie-Niels Onstad Foundation, Oslo
The American Foundation for the Arts, Miami
Western Michigan University, Kalamazoo
Murray State University, Kentucky
Galerie Art in Progress, Munich
Kunstgewerbe Museum, Zurich
Palais des Beaux-Arts, Brussels
Musée de Grenoble, France
Atkins Museum, Nelson Gallery of Art, Kansas City, Missouri Wadsworth Atheneum, Hartford, Conneticut
University of Arkansas, Little Rock
1979 Weiner Secession, Vienna
Appalachian State University, Boone, North Carolina
Greenville County Museum of Art, South Carolina
Institute of Contemporary Arts, London
Institute of Contemporary Art, Boston
Kunstverein, Freiburg, West Germany
Annely Juda Fine Arts, London
Wright State University, Dayton, Ohio
Hunter Museum of Art, Chattanooga, Tennessee
Laguna Gloria Museum, Austin, Texas
Corcoran Gallery, Washington, D.C.
Nash Gallery, University of Minnesota, Minneapolis
Galerie Catherine Issert, Saint Paul de Vence, France
1980 Newport Harbor Museum, Newport Beach, California
The New Gallery, Cleveland

Swen Parson Gallery, Northern Illinois University, DeKalb
Midwest Museum of American Art, Elkhart, Indiana
Mississippi Museum of Art, Jackson
Winnipeg Art Gallery
Hatton Gallery, Colorado State University, Fort Collins
French Cultural Center-Alliance Francaise, Abu Dhabi
Artspace, Peterborough, Ontario
Cabrillo College Gallery, Aptos, California
Sonoma Arts Council, Santa Rosa, California

1981 American Graffiti Gallery, Amsterdam
Hokin Gallery, Miami, Florida
Metropolitan Museum, Miami, Florida
Tennessee Tech University, Cookeville
Albuquerque Museum, New Mexico
Musee d'Art Contemporain, Montreal
Santa Monica City College, California
Community College of Lancaster, Pennsylvania
University of Texas, El Paso
Ludwig Museum, Cologne
Juda-Rowan Gallery, London
Portland Center for the Visual Arts, Oregon
La Jolla Museum of Contemporary Art, California
Madison Art Center, Wisconsin
Conejo Valley Art Museum, Thousand Oaks, California

1982 Nickle Arts Museum, University of Calgary, Alberta
University of Maine, Orono
Colby College of Museum of Art, Waterville, Maine
Stadel Museum, Frankfurt
Kunstlerhaus Bethanian, Berlin
Biuro Wystaw Artystycznych, Krakow, Poland
Art Gallery of Hamilton, Ontario
Miami-Dade Public Library, Florida
Galerie Catherine Issert, St. Paul de Vence, France
Elvehjem Museum of Art, University of Wisconsin, Madison
Dumont-Landis Gallery, New Brunswick, New Jersey
Hara Museum of Contemporary Art, Tokyo

1983 Snite Museum of Art, University of Notre Dame, Indiana
Fukuoka Municipal Museum of Art, Japan
National Museum of Osaka, Japan
Contemporary Arts Center, Cincinnati, Ohio
Art Museum of Santa Cruz County, Soquel, California
Delahunty Gallery, Dallas
Galleria Pero, Milan

1984 Hartnell College, Salinas, California
Luther Burbank Center for the Arts, Santa Rosa, California
Herron School of Art, Indiana University, Indianapolis
Satani Gallery, Tokyo
Nationalgalerie, Berlin
Annely Juda Fine Art, London
Sun Valley Center for the Arts and Humanities, Idaho
Henie-Onstad Foundation, Oslo
Westport-Weston Arts Council, Connecticut
Boston Atheneum, Massachusetts

1985 University of West Florida, Pensacola
Kunsthalle, Hamburg
New Britain Museum of American Art, Connecticut
Fondation Maeght, St. Paul de Vence, France
Rijksmuseum Kroller-Muller, Otterlo, Netherlands
Carpenter + Hochman Gallery, Dallas

1986 Florida State University, Tallahassee
Fundacion Caja de Pensiones, Madrid
Galeria Joan Prats, Barcelona
Southern Illinois University, Carbondale
Bass Museum, Florida
Alternative Work Site, Omaha, Nebraska
Barrett Art Gallery, Utica College, New York
Satani Gallery, Tokyo
College of Saint Rose, Albany
Real Art Ways, Connecticut

1987 Musee Cantonal des Beaux-Arts, Lausanne Switzerland
Lehman College, Bronx, New York
Aldrich Museum of Contemporary Art, Ridgefield, Connecticut
Elizabeth Galasso Fine Art, Ossining, New York
Halsey Gallery, College of Charleston, South Carolina
Museum van Hedendaagse Kunst, Ghent, Belgium
Seibu Museum of Art, Takanawa, Japan
Le Centre d'Art Nicolas de Staël, Braine-l'Alleuv, Belgium
Long Island University, Brooklyn

1988 Seibu Museum of Art, Tokyo
Satani Gallery, Tokyo
Schneider Museum, Southern Oregon State College, Ashland
Annely Juda Fine Art, London
Toa Road Gallery, Kobe, Japan
Hyogo Prefectural Museum of Modern Art, Kobe, Japan
Taipei Fine Arts Museum, Taiwan
Szentendrei Mühely Galeria, Szentendrei, Hungary

1989 Labirynt 2 Gallery, Lublin, Poland
Deutsches Theater, Berlin
Art Gallery at Kendall College of Art and Design, Grand Rapids, Michigan
Laage-Salomon Gallery, Paris
Gallery Guy Pieters, Knokke-Zoute, Belgium
Stanford University Museum of Art
Skidmore College Art Gallery, Saratoga Springs, New York
Galerie des Kulterbundes, Schwazenberg, Germany
Galerie Catherine Issert, St. Paul de Vence, France
Musée de Nice, France
Museu de Arte Contemporanea da Universidade de Sao Paolo, Brazil
Cleveland Center for Contemporary Art

1990 De Saisset Museum, Santa Clara, California
Henie-Onstad Foundation, Norway
Hiroshima City Museum of Contemporary Art
Art Gallery of New South Wales, Sydney
Hara Museum of Contemporary Art, Shibukawa, Japan
Bogerd Fine Arts, Amsterdam
Akron Art Museum, Ohio
Magidson Fine Art, New York
Gallery Seomi, Seoul
Satani Gallery, Tokyo

1991 Annely Juda Fine Art, London
Galerie Eric van de Weghe, Brussels
Southwestern College Art Gallery, Chula Vista, California
Galeria Joan Prats, Barcelona

Reykjavik Municipal Museum, Iceland
Cunningham Art Gallery, Bakersfield, California
Sapporo Art Park, Sapporo, Japan
Contemporary Art Gallery, Mito, Japan
Bakersfield College Art Gallery, Bakersfield, California
Todd Madigan Gallery, Bakersfield, California
Seomi Gallery, Seoul
Satani Gallery, Tokyo
Arternatives Gallery, San Luis Obispo, California
Kunsthallen Brandts Klaedefabrik, Odense, Denmark

1992 Shiga Museum of Modern Art, Japan
Westmont College, Santa Barbara, California
Pepperdine University Center for the Arts, Malibu, California
Galerie 63, Klosters, Switzerland
Gallery Seomi, Seoul
Gallery Hyundai, Seoul
Marugame Genichiro Inokuma Museum of Contemporary Art, Kagana, Japan
Hanson Art Galleries, Beverly Hills, California
Hanson Art Galleries, San Francisco
Galerie Alex Lachmann, Cologne
Exhibition Hall of Toyota City Hall, Nagoya, Japan
Visual Arts Gallery, University of Alabama at Birmingham

1993 Berlin Akademie der Kunste Galerie, Berlin
Art Front Gallery, Tokyo
Kunsthaus, Vienna
Museum of Contemporary Art, Skopje, Macedonia
Kunstmuseum, Bonn, Germany
Galerie Kaj Forsblom, Zurich

1994 Brownson Gallery, Manhattanville College, Purchase, New York
Villa Stuck, Munich
Johannbau, Dessau, Germany

1995 Museum Würth, Künzelsau, Germany
Annely Juda Fine Art, London
Kunstverein, Emsdetten, Germany
Suermondt-Ludwig Museum, Aachen
Podsreda Castel, Kozjanski Park, Podsreda, Slovenia
Sonja Henie-Niels Onstad Kunstsenter, Høvikodden, Norway
Kunstforum, Berlin
Galerie Georg Nothelfer, Berlin
Obalne Galerije Piran, Piran, Slovenia
Schloss Bonndorf, Bonndorf, Germany
Richmond Museum, Indiana
Ostergötlands Länsmuseum, Linkøping, Sweden
Cankar Center Gallery, Ljubljana, Slovenia
Tølgyfa Galeria, Budapest, Hungary
The College of Saint Rose, Albany, New York
Art Front Gallery, Tokyo
Laura Carpenter Fine Art, Santa Fe, New Mexico

1996 Amos Andersons Art Museum, Helsingfors, Finland
Fort Wayne Museum of Art, Indiana
One West Art Center, Fort Collins, Colorado
Kulturhaus Graz, Graz, Austria
Adelson Art Gallery, Aspen Institute, Colorado
Macy Gallery, Columbia University, New York
Eric Dean Gallery and Permanent Collection Gallery, Wabash College, Crawfordsville, Indiana
Gallerie Fabien Boulakia, Paris
Sheldon Memorial Art Gallery, University of Nebraska, Lincoln
Robischon Gallery, Denver, Colorado

1997 Denver Art Museum, Denver, Colorado
Gallerie Stephanie Hollenstein, Lustenau, Switzerland
Rupertinum Museum of Modern Art, Salzburg, Austria
Holderbank, Switzerland
Art Gallery Varna, Bulgaria

1998 University of Wyoming Art Museum, Laramie
Vero Beach Art Museum, Vero Beach, Florida
Colorado Springs Fine Arts Center, Taylor Museum, Colorado
Musée du Château, Noirmoutiers-en-L'Ile, France
Guy Pieters Gallery, Knokke Le Zoute, Belgium
Western Colorado Center for the Arts, Grand Junction, Colorado
Longmont Center for the Arts, Longmont, Colorado
Muzeum Narodowe Warszawie, Warsaw
Willanow Muzeum, Warsaw
Galerie Beyeler, Basel

1999 Hong Kong Arts Center, Hong Kong
Guang Dong Museum of Art, Guangzhou, China
Lafayette College Art Gallery, Easton, Pennsylvania
Gasometer, Oberhausen, Germany
Sangre de Cristo Arts Center, Pueblo, Colorado
Musée d'Art Moderne et d'Art Contemporain, Nice, France
Savannah College of Art and Design, Savannah, Georgia
Centre Cultural de la Fundació ''la Caixa,'' Barcelona

2000 Sonoma County Museum, Santa Rosa, California
Galeria Joan Prats, Barcelona
Haus Wittgenstein, Bulgarian Culture Institute, Vienna
New Britain Museum of American Art, New Britain, Connecticut
Annely Juda Fine Art, London
Baldwin Gallery, Aspen
Galerie Vonderbank, Frankfurt
Mønchehaus für Moderne Kunst, Goslar, Germany
Pritchard Art Gallery, University of Idaho, Moscow
Block Museum of Art, Northwestern University, Evanston, Illinois

2001 Kennesaw State University Art Gallery, Georgia
Palazzolo sull'Oglio, Brescia, Italy
Neue Berliner Kunstverein, Berlin
Martin-Gropius-Bau, Berlin
Regione Sicilia, Palermo, Italy
Fondacao Armando Alvares Penteado, Sao Paulo, Brazil

Publications:

By JEANNE-CLAUDE: Books—*Erreurs les plus Fréquentes,* Paris 1998.

On CHRISTO and JEANNE-CLAUDE: Books—*Christo,* text by David Bourdon, Otto Hahn and Pierre Restany, Milan 1965; *Christo: 5600 Cubic Meter Package,* Munich 1968; *Christo,* text by Lawrence

Alloway, New York 1969; *Christo: Wrapped Coast, One Million Square Feet,* Minneapolis 1969; *Christo,* text by David Bourdon, New York 1970; *Christo: Projekt Monschau* by Willi Bongard, Cologne 1971; *Christo: Valley Curtain,* New York 1973; *Christo: Ocean Front,* texts by Sally Yard and Sam Hunter, Princeton, New Jersey 1975; *Environmental Impact Report: Running Fence,* Santa Clara 1975; *Christo: The Running Fence,* text by Werner Spies, New York and Paris 1978; *Christo: Running Fence,* text by Calvin Tomkins and David Bourdon, New York 1978; *Christo: Wrapped Walk Ways,* New York 1978; *Christo: Complete Editions,* New York and Munich 1982; *Christo: Works 1958–83,* text by Yusuke Nakahara, Tokyo 1984; *Christo: Der Reichstag,* compiled by Michael Cullen and Wolfgang Volz, Frankfurt 1984; *Christo, Surrounded Islands, Biscayne Bay, Greater Miami, Florida, 1980–83,* with text by Werner Spies, New York 1985; *Christo,* text by Dominique Laporte, New York 1986; *Christo, Surrounded Islands, Biscayne Bay, Greater Miami, Florida, 1980–83,* with commentary by David Bourdon and essay by Jonathan Fineberg, New York, 1986; *Le Pont-Neuf de Christo, Ouvrage d'Art, Oeuvre d'Art* by Nathalie Heinich, 1987; *Hat Fel I Paris* by Pelle Hunger and Jaokim Stromholm, Fromme, England, 1987; *Christo: Prints and Objects,* introduction by Werner Spies, New York 1988; *Christo: The Pont Neuf Wrapped,* with texts by David Bourdon and Bernard de Montgolfier, New York 1990; *Christo* by Yusuke Nakahara, Tokyo 1990; *Christo* by Marina Vaizey, New York 1990; *The Accordion-Fold Book for the Umbrellas,* foreword and interview by Masahiko Yanagi, San Francisco 1991; *Christo: The Reichstag and Urban Projects,* edited by Jacob Baal-Teshuva, 1993; *Christo and Jeanne-Claude: Der Reichstag und Urbane Projekte,* edited by Jacob Baal-Teshuva, Munich 1994; *Christo and Jeanne-Claude* by Jacob Baal-Teshuva, Cologne 1995; *Christo, Jeanne-Claude, Der Reichstag dem Deutschen Volke* by Michael S. Cullen and Wolfgang Volz, Bergisch-Gladbach, Germany 1995; *Christo and Jeanne-Claude, Prints and Objects 1963–95* exhibition catalog, edited by Jörg Schellmann and Joséphine Benecke, Munich 1995; *Christo and Jeanne-Claude, PostcardBook,* Cologne 1995; *Christo and Jeanne-Claude, Poster Book* by Thomas Berg, Cologne 1995; *Christo and Jeanne-Claude: Wrapped Reichstag, Berlin, 1971–95,* Cologne 1995; *Christo and Jeanne-Claude, Wrapped/Verhüllter Reichstag, Berlin 1971–95,* Cologne 1996; *Christo and Jeanne-Claude Projects selected from the Lilja Collection,* London 1996; *Christo and Jeanne-Claude, The Umbrellas, Japan-USA, 1984–91,* Cologne 1998; *Christo and Jeanne-Claude, Wrapped Trees, 1997–98,* Cologne 1998; *XTO + J-C,* with Burt Chernow and Wolfgang Volz, Cologne 2000. **Films**—*Wrapped Coast,* Blackwood Productions 1969; *Christo's Valley Curtain,* Maysles Brothers and Ellen Giffard 1972; *Running Fence,* Maysles Brothers and Charlotte Zwerin 1977; *Wrapped Walk Ways,* Blackwood Productions 1978; *Islands,* Maysles Brothers and Charlotte Zwerin 1985; *Christo in Paris,* David and Albert Maysles, Deborah Dickson, and Susan Froemke 1990; *Umbrellas,* Albert Maysles, Henry Corra, and Graham Weinbren 1996; *Christo und Jeanne-Claude: Dem Deutsche Volke, Verhüllter Reichstag 1971–95,* Wolfram and Jorg Daniel Hissen 1996; *Christo and Jeanne-Claude, Wrapped Trees,* Gebrüder Hissen 1998.

* * *

In all of his packages, Christo transforms familiar objects into ambivalent presences, sometimes rendering them unrecognizable and often raising doubts about their past, present, and future identity and function. In his more epic endeavors, he questions the relationship of art at both the urban and natural environments. In a materialistic age, his art is a profound comment on the chronic expectations and frustrations aroused by the increasing number of consumer products and services that are ''enhanced'' through packaging.

No other artist so fully illuminates the twentieth century's preoccupation with packaging. By appropriating and wrapping familiar objects, buildings and sites, making them visible in a new way, he has created a wide range of disturbing and strangely beautiful art works that collectively call for a double take.

—David Bourdon

In the 1990s, Christo acknowledged that his French-born wife Jeanne-Claude does and had always contributed substantially enough to his artistic projects that she deserved to be known as his co-creator. Her ability to organize and manage the bureaucrats and laborers required for the spectacles of landscape and architecture has helped realize two especially massive projects of the 1990s. Envisioning whole countrysides dotted with twenty-foot-tall umbrellas, Christo and Jeanne-Claude simultaneously opened 1,340 blue ones in Japan and 1,760 yellow ones in California. The *Umbrellas* project made headlines after a Japanese worker was electrocuted and another person was crushed under an umbrella that had toppled in high winds. The tragedies interfered with the twenty-year-long negotiations to wrap Berlin's Reichstag, a building that stands for democracy in post-reunification Germany despite its violent history. At a cost of more than 11 million deutschmarks, Christo and Jeanne-Claude finally achieved this dream in June 1995; they announced it would be the end of their legendary wrapping career.

—Mark Swartz

Since 1995, Christo and Jeanne-Claude have continued to work on many of their as-yet-unrealized projects. They have completed about 19 projects since their first artistic collaboration in 1961; 21 remain unrealized. The main projects they have in the development stage include, ''The Mastaba of Abu Dhabi, Project for the United Arab Emirates,'' started in 1977; ''The Gates, Project for Central Park, New York City,'' begun in 1979; and ''Over the River, Project for the Arkansas River, Colorado,'' first started in 1992. The artists see which project is more likely to receive permission and they marshal all their resources, time, and efforts into promoting that particular project, while the others continue to wait for sufficient permissions for the artists to proceed.

The artists continue to finance their artworks themselves through the sale of preparatory works, collages, and early works by Christo. Christo's early experiences in his Communist homeland left him with a profound distaste for state funding. Jeanne-Claude similarly believes in the value of the entrepreneurial spirit and embraces the artistic freedom permitted by independently funding their projects. Since the mid-1970s, the artists have maintained a private corporation to manage the financial responsibility of each project.

Christo and Jeanne-Claude's large-scale projects function as subtle disturbances in a landscape, like carnivals or circuses which only come to town for a brief period and never exist again in exactly the same way. Their projects are designed to encourage the viewer to experience a place in a slightly different manner. The projects require active audience involvement because they do not stay on exhibit like an object in a museum collection. Effort is required to see the works while they are installed, usually only for a period of about three weeks, never to exist again.

—Anne Swartz

CHRYSSA

Nationality: American. **Born:** Athens, Greece, 31 December 1933. **Education:** Académie de la Grande Chaumiére, Paris, 1953–54; California School of Fine Arts, San Francisco, 1954–55. **Career:** Has lived and worked in New York since 1955. **Awards:** Guggenheim Fellowship, 1973. **Address:** c/o Albright-Knox Art Gallery, 1285 Elmwood Avenue, Buffalo, New York 14222, U.S.A.

Individual Exhibitions:

1961 Betty Parsons Gallery, New York
Guggenheim Museum, New York
1962 Cordier and Ekstrom, New York
1963 Museum of Modern Art, New York
1965 Institute of Contemporary Arts, Philadelphia
1966 Pace Gallery, New York
1968 Pace Gallery, New York
Harvard University, Cambridge, Massachusetts
Walker Art Center, Minneapolis
Galerie Rive Droite, Paris
1969 Galerie der Spiegel, Cologne
Obelisk Gallery, Boston
1970 Graphics Gallery, San Francisco
Galleria d'Arte Contemporenea, Turin
1973 Galerie Denise René, New York
Galerie Denise René,-Hans Mayer, Dusseldorf
1974 Galerie Denise René, Paris
Musée d'Art Contemporian, Montreal
Andre Emmerich Galerie, Zurich
1976 Galerie Denise René, New York
1978 Galerie Denise René, New York
1979 *Oeuvres Rècentes,* Musée d'Art Moderne de la Ville de Paris
1980 National Pinacotheque Museum Alexander Soutsos, Athens
1982 Albright-Knox Art Gallery, Buffalo, New York
1988 Leo Castelli Gallery, New York
1991 Leo Castelli Gallery, New York

Selected Group Exhibitions:

1966 *68th American Exhibition,* Art Institute of Chicago
1967 *Light-Motion-Space,* Walker Art Center, Minneapolis
Art of the 60's Los Angeles County Museum of Art (travelled to Philadelphia Museum of Art)
1968 *Documenta 4,* Kassel, West Germany
1969 *Bienal,* Sao Paulo
1970 *Annual Exhibition of Contemporary American Sculpture,* Whitney, Museum, New York
1971 *Annual Exhibition of Contemporary American Sculpture,* Whitney Museum, New York
1972 *Biennale,* Venice
1998 *New Glass Review 20,* Corning Museum of Glass, New York

Collections:

Museum of Modern Art, New York; Guggenheim Museum, New York; Whitney Museum, New York; Albright-Knox Art Gallery, Buffalo, New York; Walker Art Center, Minneapolis; Corcoran Gallery of Art, Washington D.C.; Hirshhorn Museum and Sculpture Garden, Washington D.C.; Musée d'Art Contemporain, Montreal; Tate Gallery, London; Pinacotheque Nationale, Athens; Chase Manhattan Bank, New York; Boise Cascade Corporation, Boise.

Publications:

By CHRYSSA: Articles—statement in "The Artists Say—Chryssa" in *Art Voices* (New York), Fall 1965; interview with John Gruen in the *New York Herald Tribune,* 27 March 1968.

On CHRYSSA: Books—*Pop Art* by Lucy Lippard, New York 1966; *Chryssa,* exhibition catalog, New York 1966; *Chryssa,* exhibition catalog, with text by Pierre Restany, Paris 1968; *Minimal Art: A Critical Anthology,* edited by Gregory Battcock, New York 1968; *Chryssa: Selected Works 1955–57,* exhibition catalog, New York 1968; *Icons and Images of the 60's* by Nicolas and Elena Calas, New York 1971; *Art Without Boundaries 1950–1970,* edited by Gerald Woods, Philip Thompson and John Williams, London 1972; *Chryssa,* exhibition catalog, New York 1973; *Chryssa* by Sam Hunter, London and New York 1974; *Chryssa* by Pierre Restany, New York 1977; *Chryssa: Oeuvres Récentes,* exhibition catalog, Paris 1979. **Articles**—"The Role of the Inscription in Painting" by James Reaney in *Canadian Art* (Toronto), October 1966; "Chryssa" by Don Cyr in *School Arts* (Cherry Hill, New Jersey), March 1967; "Light Art" by Nan R. Piene in *Art in America* (New York), May/June 1967; "Torino: Chryssa" in *NAC* (Milan), February 1971; "New York Letter" by Carter Ratliff in *Art International* (Lugano), December 1972; "Chryssa" by Sam Hunter in *Art News* (New York), 3 May 1973; "Chryssa: Some Observations: by V. Campbell in *Art International* (Lugano), April 1973; "Chryssa Sculptures with Neon Tubes" by James Mellow in the *New York Times,* 21 April 1973; "Mysteries of Neon" by Robert Hughes in *Time* (New York), 4 June 1973; "Chryssa: Cityscapes and Icons" by Miranda McClintic in *Arts Magazine,* vol. 62, Summer 1988; "Leo Castelli Gallery, New York; Exhibit" in *Artforum International,* vol. 29, April 1991; "Chryssa at Castelli" by David Ebony in *Art in America* (New York), vol. 84, no. 10, October 1996; "Artists and Objects: New Glass Review 20" in *Neues Glas,* no. 2, 1999.

* * *

Birthright and nationality are not necessarily built in to the thumbprint of an artist. Chryssa, for all her Hellenic origins, cannot claim—as she does, and as others have done for her—to have inherited a cultural legacy from Ancient Greece. This is sheer lunacy. If she wants a public to be impressed with the classical Greek accent of her ''Cycladic Books'' (sculpture which she made in the 1950s), then she could expect that public to trace the same influence in Brancusi's ''Kiss.'' Of course the Greek civilization (and the Roman) left its mark on Europe, but it was a mark not a last-will-and-testament.

This point needs to be established because if Chryssa the artist is not *typically Greek,* neither can she claim to have become Americanized after naturalization. For all her New World methods and media, this sculptor/constructor/luminator retains a European character. After she abandoned her early experiments with lay-out moulds on newsprint scale or blown up even larger and began investigating the potentialities of the alphabetical confusion of shop signs, she was continuing the outcome of the cubist papier-collé rather than exploring variants of Jasper Johns' interest in the same field. From the refuse dumps and demolition years, like many European artists before her, she was able to extract and reassemble material of more than object-trouvé stature. Scrap of this kind can be on a large scale and at this time of her development her works often had a monumentality that derived their dimensions more from origins than from invention.

The change, in size as well as importance, came when she started examining the opportunities afforded by neon lightning. If at first this new medium came about as the result of chance encounter, it was soon to be a matter of far less casual concern. Chryssa studied the nature of neon and how it could be made subservient to her will. Today, a brilliant technician, she is capable of discussing the science of illuminated signs with people whose entire business lies in that field.

Her neon works she calls *luminates,* but she is not wholly concerned with light and colour. She parallels her views with those of a maker of mobiles. If an Alexander Calder mobile looks beautiful when it is still and in repose, why cannot a luminate claim just as fine an appearance when the lights have been extinguished as when it blazes with colour? This is an issue she takes up with anyone who complains about the limited longevity of neon tubing. Either have the tube replaced or live with your Chryssa in the dark.

—Sheldon Williams

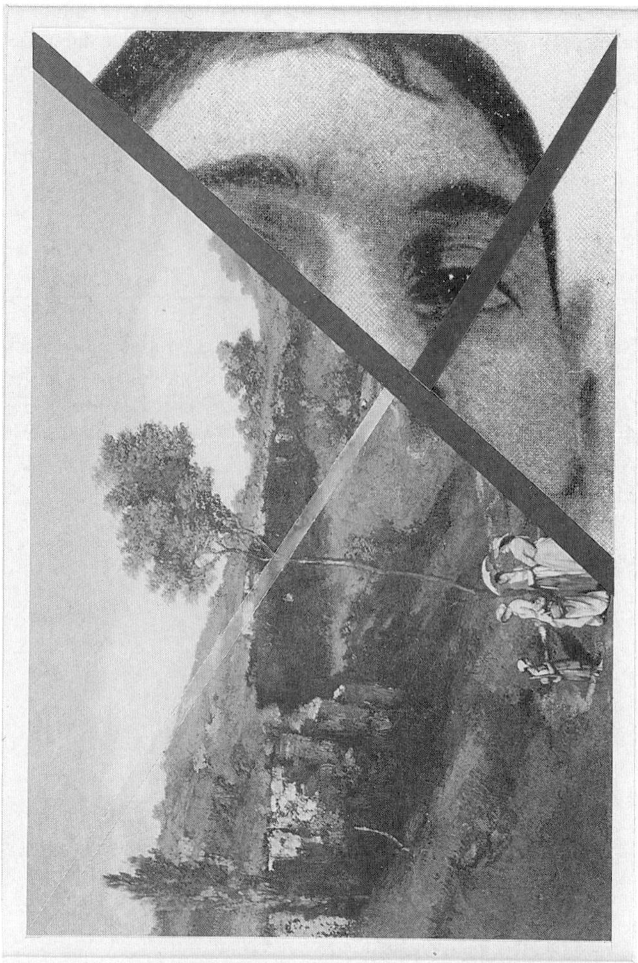

Roman Cieslewicz: *Les dieux ont soif* [*The Gods are Thirsty*], 1988. Photo by Jean-Claude Planchet. ©2001 Artists Rights Society (ARS), NY/ADAGP, Paris.

CIESLEWICZ, Roman

Nationality: French. **Born:** Lvov, Poland, 13 January 1930; immigrated to France, 1963; naturalized, 1971. **Education:** Academy of Fine Arts, Cracow. **Career:** Independent graphic artist, working for several magazines and book publishers, Warsaw, 1955–62, in Paris since 1963; art director, *Elle* magazine 1964, 1966–69, Vogue magazine 1966, and M.A.F.I.A. publicity agency, 1969–72; designer, *Opus International* magazine, 1967–69, *Kitsch* magazine, 1970–71, *Musique en Jeu* magazine, 1970–73, *CNAC-Archives* publications, 1971–74, *Kamikaze* magazine 1976, and *XX Siècle* magazine, 1976; graphics designer, *Festival d'Automne,* 1976–77. Instructor, Ecole Nationale Supérieure des Arts Graphiques, Paris, 1973–75; Ecole Supérieure des Arts Graphiques, Paris, from 1975. **Awards:** Trepkowski Prize, Poland 1955; Grand Prix, Czech Cinema Posters Awards, 1964; Grand Prix, *4th Biennale of Posters,* Warsaw, 1972; Special Prize for Cinema Poster, Cannes, 1973; Grand Prix, *4th Biennale of Photomontage,* Poland, 1979; Grand Prix, *Affiche Francaise,* Paris, 1980. **Address:** c/o *Elle,* 100 rue Réaumur, 75002 Paris, France.

Individual Exhibitions:

1959 Salon d'Ecran, Warsaw
1960 Salon CBWA-ZPAP, Cracow
1961 Galerija Likovnih Umjetnosti, Rijeka, Yugoslavia
1963 Goethe-Institut, Frankfurt
Librairie Mandragore, Paris
1964 Club Synergie, Paris
1965 Théâtre de la Cité, Villeurbanne, France
Salon CBWA-ZPAP, Szczecin, Poland
Galerie in der Biberstrasse, Vienna
1967 Salon CBWA-ZPAP, Warsaw
1968 Galerie Aurora, Geneva
1971 *Wystawa Foto-grafiki 1962–1971,* Muzeum Sztuki, Lodz, Poland
Galerie Aurora, Geneva
1972 *Graphismes,* Musée des Arts Décoratifs, Paris
Musée du Grenoble, France
1973 Stedelijk Museum, Amsterdam
Hotel de Ville, Dieppe, France
Galerija Suvremene Umjetnosti, Zabreg

Razstavno Salon Ratzovz, Maribor, Yugoslavia
1974 Galerie l'Oeil de Boeuf, Paris
Musée de l'Affiche, Vilanov, Poland
Galerie Saluden, Quimper, France
1975 Salon G.V.N., Amsterdam
Mala Galeria, Wroclaw, Poland
Galerie Baumeister, Munich
Galerie Aurora, Geneva
Galerie 13/Theatre Municipal, Angers, France
1976 Centre Jean Prevost, Saint-Etienne-du-Rouviray, France
Cantieri Navali, at the *Biennale,* Venice
1977 Galerie l'Oeil de Boeuf, Paris
Martinischule am Rhein, Emmerich, West Germany
French Institute, Stockholm
1978 Konsthall, Lund, Sweden
Galeria Stu, Teatr Stu, Wroclaw, Poland
Galeria Fotografii, Wroclaw, Poland
B.W.A. Salon Krytykow, Lublin, Poland
Palais Rihour, Lille, France
Galerie Baumeister, Munich
Stedelijk Museum, Amsterdam
1979 Maison de la Culture, Grenoble, France
Librairie-Galerie La Hune, Paris
Maison du Tourisme, Auxerre, France
1980 Centre Choreographique, Nancy, France
House of Culture, Legnica, Poland
Teatr Narodowy, Warsaw
FNAC—Montparnasse, Paris
Centre Dramatique, Nanterre, France
Théâtre National Populaire, Villeurbanne, France
Centre Dramatique, Nice
FNAC, Toulouse
Photomontages, Maison de la Culture, Grenoble, France
1981 *Photomontages,* Chelsea School of Art, London
1993 Pompidou Center, Paris (retrospective)

Selected Group Exhibitions:

1962 *International Poster Exhibition,* Smithsonian Institution, Washington, D.C.
1963 *Bienal,* Sao Paulo
1964 *Documenta 3,* Kassel, West Germany
1965 *Internationale Buchkunstausstellung,* Messehaus, Leipzig
1967 *Affischer ur Tekniska Museet,* Fagersta Stadsbibliothek, Fagersta, Sweden
1968 *Experimental 4,* Casino, Knokke-le-Zoute, Belgium
1970 *4th Biennale of Graphic Arts,* Moravska Galerie, Brno, Czechoslovakia
1971 *Word and Image,* Museum of Modern Art, New York (toured the United States)
1972 *Biennale,* Venice
International Graphic Exhibition Arkcenter, London
1993 *The Lahti X Poster Biennial,* Lahti, Finland
1997 *17th International Biennale of Graphic Design,* Brno, Czech Republic

Collections:

Stedelijk Museum, Amsterdam, Moderna Museet, Stockholm, Umelecko-Proumyslove Muzeum, Prague; Musée des Arts Décoratifs, Paris; Museum Narodowe, Warsaw; Museum Narodowe, Poznan, Poland; Muzeum Sztuki, Lodz, Poland; Museo de Arte Moderna, Sao Paulo; Museum of Modern Art, New York; Library of Congress, Washington, D.C.

Publications:

By CIESLEWICZ: Articles—interview with Margo Rouard-Snowman in *Eye,* no. 9, vol. 3, 1993; interview with Joanna Sitkowska in *Projekt,* no. 202–203, 1995.

On CIESLEWICZ: Books—*Polnische Plakatkunst* by Jozek Mroszczak, Dusseldorf 1962; *Das Plakat* by Anton Sailer, Munich 1965; *Roman Cieslewicz* by Aleksander Wojciechowski, Warsaw 1966; *Roman Cieslewicz: Wystawa Fotografiki 1962–1971,* exhibition catalog, with text by Ursula Czartoryska, Lodz, Poland 1971; *Les Chefs-d'Oeuvre du Kitsch* by Jacques Sternberg, Paris 1971; *Roman Cieslewicz: Graphismes,* exhibition catalog, with text by Alain Jouffroy, Paris 1972; *Histoire Concise de l'Affiche* by John Barnicoat, Paris 1972; *Roman Cieslewicz,* exhibition catalog, with text by Roland Topor, Amsterdam 1973; *Roman Cieslewicz: Photomontages,* exhibition brochure, with text by Yann Pavie, Grenoble, France 1980; *Roman Cieslewicz: Photomontages,* exhibition brochure, with text by Nick Wadley, London 1981; *Dans la peau du miroir,* by Marcel Mariën, Bruxelles 1988; *Roman Cieslewicz* by Margo Rouard-Snowman, New York 1993.

* * *

Roman Cieslewicz, the Polish graphic artist who has lived in Paris since 1963, operates on the ''borderline'' between two areas of artistic exploration—popular art addressed to the consumer of mass media and art with cognitive pretensions, that of creating images of modern man's spiritual experiences.

Since his debut in 1955 Cieslewicz has succeeded in appealing both to the man in the street and to an elitist audience. At the same time as his work appeared at the 1976 Venice *Biennale,* every passerby in Paris (and perhaps elsewhere) carried his shopping in a bag or paper decorated with a Cieslewicz collage. With the help of Cieslewicz and a few more artists of similar ilk, the graphics of mass media was ennobled into a tool—a tool that would spread the visions of today.

Cieslewicz had several revelations along his artistic path: they made a great impression on everything that lay within his sphere of capability. While still in Warsaw, he discovered the possibilities that collage offered to 20th century art, in particular expressionist and surrealist collages as understood by Max Ernst. As a result, he decided to part with all traditional graphical equipment—brushes, paint, pen and ink. Instead, he began to use scissors, glue, a rule, photographic paper and a darkroom. Under what came to be called photomechanical technique, his dramatic theatrical and operatic posters came to life. The collage, in fact, remains the basis of Cieslewicz's artistry, though it now appears in many forms.

Another result of the time spent in the darkroom was a series of experiments with photographic materials. ''I am trying,'' he said, ''to obtain something that has nothing to do with photographic technique—a screen, the network of thread that is . . . the polygon which opens all possibilities.'' By means of this work without a camera, the joint structures of photographics (the separation of the two words is important) were born. Rooted in photography, these structures laid the foundations for the pictures that were to appear. A few methods worthy of mention were: the separation of an image by the use of a screen with a varied gradation of points; the use of contrast with no half-shades; reflections and rotations; multiple images; plain colour (grounds) and other sallies by colour into black-and-white photography.

His next artistic adventure was the discovery of the originality of expression of a repeated image. These images were an offshoot of his photo-graphical work. Developed in an epoch of mass media, they revealed man's lack of defense against the aggression of his visual surroundings.

His last revelation came as a result of contact and identification with Pop Art as a universal style. ''I not only thought, but was quite certain,'' he said in an interview, ''that this would be a never-ending style. That it would register reality forever.'' This, of course, was not to be. But—until it fizzled out—Pop, which added the whole of consumer life to art—mass production, fashion, sex, amusements, advertisements, the lights and shadows of the great metropolis, rape, kitsch and horror—all became Cieslewicz's sources of ideas and inspiration. He was infected by Pop's dynamism—as were most young people keen on rock and pop music. He acted as Artistic Director of *Elle* and *Vogue,* edited such exclusive periodicals as *Kitsch* and *Kamikaze* and *Opus International,* designed theatrical posters and programmes (for Arabal, among others), and founded a new kind of visual publication.

The second half of the 1970s saw a ''change of climate'' in Cieslewicz's work. This is the title that he gave to the cycle of photomontage exhibited at the Galerie l'Oeil de Boeuf in Paris. The critics pointed to the artist's spiritual evolution, his tendency toward contemplation and metaphysics. As shown in these colorful pictures reminiscent of the old masters, the world is full of peace and harmony. The artist no longer interferes with it as brutally as before but offers a modern interpretation, a new and possible way of reading the representational.

—Szymon Bojko

CLAUS, Jürgen

Nationality: German. **Born:** Berlin, 28 May 1935. **Education:** Studied theater, philosophy, and art at Universities of Marburg and Munich, 1954–60. **Career:** Artist, author, and educator. Artist-in-residence, Institute for Humanistic Studies, Aspen, 1972; artistic collaborator, Olympic Games, Munich, 1970–72; fellow and research associate, Center for Advanced Visual Studies, MIT, Cambridge, 1983–88; lecturer in art and technology, Academy of Fine Arts, Munich, 1986—; editorial advisor and international co-editor, *Leonardo, International Journal,* MIT Press, 1987—; director, Centre Overoth, Baelen, Belgium, 1989—; professor, Academy of Media Arts, Cologne, 1991–2000; coordinator and participant, SolArt Global Network '95 (with Nora Claus), 1993—; task leader, European Community Project, BIOMODE-Development of bi-functional photovoltaic modules for building integration, 1997–2000. **Awards:** Werkstipendium, Kunstfonds e.V., Bonn, 1983; Werkstipendium, Institute for Foreign Relations, Stuttgart, 1987; Prix Lago Maggiore, Videoart Festival, Locarno, 1988; European Solar Prize, Bonn, 1995 (with Nora Claus); Deputy Governor, American Biographical Insititure, Raleigh. **Address:** Centre Overoth, Overoth 5, B-4837 Baelen, Belgium. **Web site:** www.khm.de/∼SolArt/artClaus.html. **E-mail:** jurclaus@euregio.net.

Jürgen Claus: *Solar Icosahedron,* 1997–98. ©Jürgen Claus.

Individual Exhibitions:

1958 Galerie Krauch and Fincke, Giessen
1963 Galerie S Ben Wargin, Berlin
1967 Galleria 111, Lisbon
1968 *Strukturelles Ornament,* Galerie Mike Cullen, Berlin
Galerie Kümmel, Cologne
Galleria Il Giorno, Milan
Strukturelles Ornament, Galerie Klaus Lüpke, Frankfurt
L'Ornamento Struttural, Galleria SM, Rome
Galleria Il Salotto, Como
1972 *Planet Ocean,* Institute for Humanistic Studies, Aspen
1975 *Planet Meer—Celebration of the Ocean,* Kunsthalle Nuremberg
University of the Arts, Osaka
1979 *Welt unter Wasser,* Natur Museum, Lucerne
Autoren Galerie, Munich
1982 *Aus der Tiefsee,* boot Düsseldorf
Aus der Tiefsee, Torhaus Galerie, Münster
1986 *Kreativität Wasser,* Vienna
1988 *Planète Océan,* Galerie Experimentale, Cité des Sciences et de l'Industrie, La Villette, Paris

1990 *Solarskulpture—Bildtagebucher,* Autoren Galerie 1, Munich
1991 *Solarkunst,* Itertal Klinik, Aachen
1992 *Solarkunst—Parallele Raume,* Kultuskulum, Aachen
1994 *SonnenMeer,* Haus Basten, Geilenkirchen
1996 *Solarkunst—Sonnenprojekte,* Katholische Akademie, Freiburg
1999–2000 *Kristallwelten,* SIG Combibloc, Linnich

Selected Group Exhibitions:

1966 *Deutscher Künstlerbund,* Essen
1968 *From Collage to Assemblage,* Kunsthalle Nuremberg
1975 *Arttransition,* CAVS/MIT, Cambridge
1981 *Sky Art,* CAVS/MIT, Cambridge
1983 *Sky Art,* Galerie BMW, Munich
Electra, Musee d'Art Moderne, Paris
1984 *Art and Technology,* Federal Ministry for Research and Technology, Bonn
1986 *Terminal Art, ars electronica,* Linz
1988 *European Media Festival,* Dominikanerkirche, Osnabrück
Computer Art '88, Städtisches Museum Gladbeck
1989 *40 Years Art in the Federal Republic of Germany,* Stadtische Kunsthalle, Recklinghausen, Berlin, Rostock
1991 *Artist and the Light,* Manège, Rheims
1993 *68—Art and Culture,* Bauhaus Dessau
1996 *Solar Year—Sculptura,* Ulm, Germany
1997 *Solar Art,* Rathaus, Leonberg, Germany
1999 *Lumia,* Charlottenborg Museum, Copenhagen
2000 *Nachbarshaftsgäste,* Centre d'Art Contemporain du Luxembourg Belge, Jamoigne

Collections:

Wilhelm Lehmbruck Museum, Duisburg; Städtische Sammlung, Lenbachhaus, Munich, Collection Pansa di Biumo; Atlantic Richfield Company, Los Angeles; Solar Crystal, Fachhochschule Aachen-Jülich; Solar Icosahedron, Geislingen, Germany.

Publications:

By CLAUS: Books—*Theorien zeitgenössischer Malerei* (Theories of Contemporary Painters), Rowohlt, Hamburg 1963, new edition, Ullstein, Berlin 1986; *Kunst heute* (Art Today), Rowohlt, 1965, new edition, Ullstein, Berlin 1986; *Expansion der Kunst* (Expansion of Art), Rowohlt, Hamburg 1970, new edition, Ulstein, Berlin 1982; *Planet Meer* (Planet Ocean), DuMont Schauberg, Colgone 1972; *Treffpunkt Kunst* (Meeting Point Art), Keil Editor, Bonn 1982; *Umweltkunst* (Environmental Art), Edition Interfrom, Osnabruck 1982; *Das elektronische Bauhaus* (The Electronic Bauhaus), Edition Interfrom, Zurich 1987; *Elektronisches Gestalten in Kunst und Design* (Electronic Creating in Art and Design), Rowohlt, Hamburg 1991; *Kulturelement Sonne—Das Solare Zeitalter* (Cultural Element Sun—The Solar Age), Zürich 1997. **Films—***Planet Meer—Unterwasserkunst von Jürgen Claus,* ARD, 1980; *Planet Ocean—Underwater Art by Jürgen Claus,* 1983; *Solar Energy Sculptures,* 1986; *SolArt Expert System,* 1987; *Mind in Man in Universe,* 1992; *Solar Energy—Art Energy,* 1993.

On CLAUS: Books—*SonnenMeer* (SunOcean), Wienand, Cologne 1995.

* * *

The faith in nature and the dynamic preservation of its powers in a context dominated by High-Tech inventions is at the base of the work of ''eco-technological'' artist and theoretician Jürgen Claus. At an early stage, Claus was principally concerned with artistic events in which water, as one of the fundamental elements of the physical universe, was predominant. In the second half of the 1960s he began to develop spaces using electricity and electronics. He wanted to install a ''fluid space'' in which images from film and slide projections appeared simultaneously in order to create multi-dimensionality. When he began to work in the naturally multi-dimensional space of underwater his experiences affected his artistic concepts. He used electricity and electronics as extensions of human sensory organs; light was as important as acoustics and both related to his physiological reactions.

In his *Planet Ocean* project, Claus was concerned with the ecologization of technology based on the physical sciences. It involved, besides water, two lasers, two video cameras, neon light and a mirrored sphere representing the Earth. The work attempted to act as a metaphor for the profound changes in our perceptions of our planet and planetary system as we move towards holistic awareness of the physical universe.

After having explored the elements of earth and water, Claus turned his attention to the relationship between water and light, particularly by creating solar energy sculptures using photo-electric cells. This eco-technology is intended to take us into the solar age.

In his *Sun Sculptures I, II, and III,* Claus used solar energy to produce electricity under water from photovoltaic cells mounted on floating platforms on the ocean's surface. The cells transform natural solar energy into electricity, which was then stored in batteries. This electricity was used to bring light to the 24-hour cycle of light-blue and dark-blue illumination of *Planet Ocean.* Thus natural light was needed to evoke visually the complex structures and colours of an underwater environment.

These ''sun sculptures'' on which Claus has been working for several years, are vertical constructions with a projected height of approximately 30 metres in their final stage. They have wings furnished with solar cells that follow the position of the sun by means of a computer ''brain,'' which he calls a Solart expert system. This is a computer graphics interaction system through which images and information can be called up. The data-bank contains technical and environmental information, for instance about light, photovoltaics, and the distribution of natural energies in the landscape. This facility is necessary since these sculptures are in a real sense responsive, environmental, energy-transforming systems.

As regards the outlook for artistic expert systems, according to Claus one has to search for new and more specific connotations within the artistic and scientific matrix. In his view such basic connotations—indeed a new kind of paradigm or metaparadigm—are related to the fact that ''organic'' machines made by artists, engineers, and scientists using electronic technology at its most advanced stage (including responsive interaction in an ecologically responsible way) could serve human and natural survival and/or vital reconstruction as metaphors, symbols, realities.

In his *Carousel of Suns,* created in collaboration with his wife, Nora, for the exhibition *Artists and Light* at the Manège of Rheims,

France in 1991, Claus occupied a space with a surface area of 530 square metres. This installation was bathed in a bluish light, and argon gas writing served as a metaphor announcing the Solar Age. Two circles made up of three suns rotated slowly, intersecting with each other in a radiancy of yellow light. A laser beam travelled across this space at different points. This beam was not only the result of its material source, argon or krypton, but as much an outcome of the manner in which it lingered in a veil of mist—in other words, it was also the result of the way it blended into the environment. This work, produced by various technological means, was intended to be perceived and interpreted as a single form and as an illustration of the unity between natural and man-made environments.

Jürgen Claus's multiple eco-technological activities as artist, writer, educator, and organizer culminated, after two years of preparation and several preliminary events, in the summer of 1995, in a SolArt Global Network, conceived as a collective cosmic rally, a model of humanization.

—Frank Popper

CLEMENTE, Francesco

Nationality: Italian. **Born:** Naples, 1952. **Family:** Married to Alba Clemente: has two children. **Career:** Independent painter, since 1973; lives and works in New York, Rome and Madras. **Agents:** care Gagosian Gallery, 980 Madison Avenue, New York, New York, 10021–1848; Sperone Westwater, 142 Greene Street, New York, New York 10012–3236, U.S.A. **Address:** Via dei Riari 59, 00165 Rome, Italy.

Individual Exhibitions:

1974 Galleria Area, Florence
1975 Galleria Gian Enzo Sperone, Rome
Galleria Gian Enzo Sperone, Turin
Galleria Massimo Minini, Brescia, Italy
Galleria Franco Toselli, Milan
1976 Galleria Gian Enzo Sperone, Rome
Galleria Lucrezia de Domizio, Pescara, Italy
1977 Galleria Paolo Betti, Milan
1978 Centre d'Art Contemporain, Geneva
Art and Project, Amsterdam
Galerie Paul Maenz, Cologne
1979 Gian Enzo Sperone, Turin
Art and Project, Amsterdam
Galerie Paul Maenz, Cologne
Lisson Gallery, London
Galerie Annemarie Verna, Zurich (with Mimmo Paladino and Nicola de Maria)
Galleria Emilio Mazzoli, Modena, Italy
Galleria Guiliana de Crescenzo, Rome
Galleria lucio Amelio, Naples
1980 Galleria Gian Enzo Sperone, Rome
Art and Project, Amsterdam
Galerie Paul Maenz, Cologne
Sperone Westwater Fischer Gallery, New York
Padiglione d'Arte Contemporanea, Milan
Galleria Mario Diacono, Rome
1981 Vereniging voor het Museum van Hedendaagse Kunst, Ghent
Anthony d'Offay Gallery, London
Sperone Westwater Fischer Gallery, New York
Galerie Bruno Bischofberger, Zurich
University of California, Berkeley (travelled to Long Beach, California, Hartford, Connecticut)
1982 Galerie Daniel Templon, Paris
Galerie Paul Maenz, Cologne
Galleria Mario Diacono, Rome
Galleria Bruno Bischofberger, Zurich
1983 Whitechapel Art Gallery, London (travelled to Groningen, Karlsruhe, Stockholm and Nice)
Galleria Mario Diacono, Rome
A Space, Toronto
Kunsthalle, Basle
James Corcoran Gallery, Los Angeles
Arts Council Gallery, Belfast
1984 Nationalgalerie, West Berlin (travelled to Essen, Amsterdam and Tubingen)
Kestner-Gesellschaft, Hannover
Akira Ikeda Gallery, Tokyo
Riverside Studios, Hammersmith, London
1985 Sperone Westwater/Leo Castelli Gallery, New York
Metropolitan Museum of Art, New York
Ringling Museum of Art, Sarasota, Florida (travelled to Minneapolis, Dallas, Berkeley, Buffalo and Los Angeles)
Museum für Gegenwartskunst, Basle
1986 Akira Ikeda Gallery, Tokyo
Anthony d'Offay Gallery, London
Sperone Westwater, New York
Museum of Modern Art, New York
1987 Galerie Ascan Crone, Hamburg
Museum fur Gegenwartskunst, Basle
Galerie Bruno Bischofberger, Zurich (twice)
Art Institute of Chicago
Ulmer Museum, Ulm, West Germany
Kunstmuseum, Basle (travelled to Groningen, Ulm, Cologne, Lausanne, Frankfurt and Nice)
1988 Winnipeg Art Gallery
1989 Paul Maenz Gallery, Cologne
1990 *Francesco Clemente: Three Worlds,* Philadelphia Museum of Art (catalog)
1990 Sperone Westwater, New York
1991 Kunst Museum, Basel
Royal Academy, London
San Francisco Museum of Modern Art
1992 Gagosian Gallery, New York
Perry Rubenstein Gallery, New York
1993 Anthony d'Offay Gallery, London
1994 *Black Paintings,* Gagosian Gallery, New York
Centre National d'Art et de Culture Georges Pompidou, Paris
Bruno Bischofberger Gallery, Zurich, Switzerland
1995 Château de Chenonceau, France
Jablonka, Cologne, Germany
Francesco Clemente: Helsinki Festival, Helsingin Taidehalli (catalog)

Francesco Clemente: *Hunger,* 1980. ©Philadelphia Museum of Art/Corbis.

Francesco Clemente, Galerie Rigassi, Berne (catalog)
1996 Peter Blum Gallery, New York
1997 *Anamorphosis,* Gagosian Gallery, New York
The Paintings at the Gate, Jerome de Noirmont, Paris
Galerie Jérôme de Noirmont, Paris
1998 *Francesco Clemente: Indian Watercolours,* Indianapolis Museum of Art
1999 *Der Stachel der Lebendigkeit,* Kunstsammlung NRW, Düsseldorf
Solomon R. Guggenheim Museum, New York (retrospective) (catalog)
Galleria d'Arte Moderna di Bologna, Italy
2000 Galerie Dominion, Montreal

Selected Group Exhibitions:

1973 *Italy Two,* Civic Center Museum, Philadelphia
1975 *Bienal,* Sao Paulo

Francesco Clemente, 1986. ©Marianne Haas/Corbis.

1977 *X Biennale de Paris,* Musée National d'Art Moderne, Paris
1979 *Europe '79,* Stuttgart
1980 *Die Enthauptete Hand: 100 Zeichnungen aus Italien,* Kunstverein
1981 *Westkunst,* Cologne
1982 *Documenta 7,* Kassel, West Germany
1984 *Content: A Contemporary Focus 1974–84,* Hirshhorn Museum, Washington D.C.
1985 *India and the Contemporary Artist,* Museum of Modern Art, New York
1987 *Avant-Garde in the Eighties,* Los Angeles County Museum of Art
1990 *Culture and Commentary: An Eighties Perspective,* Hirshhorn Museum and Sculpture Garden, Washington, D.C. (catalog)
1992 *Works on Paper by Andy Warhol, Anselm Kiefer and Francesco Clemente,* KunstHal, Rotterdam
Drawing Redux, San Jose Museum of Art (catalog)
1995 46th Venice Biennale, Italy
1996 *Picasso: A Contemporary Dialogue,* Galerie Thaddaeus Ropac, Paris (catalog)
Surrealism: Dream of Centuries, Galerie Beyeler, Basel (catalog)
Collaborations: Warhol, Basquiat, Clemente, Museum Fridericianum, Kassel, Germany (catalog)
1997 *Italian Painting,* Castello di Rivoli, Museo d'Arte Contemporanea, Rivoli, Italy (catalog)
Contemporary Prints, Yvonne Andrews Gallery, London (catalog)
1998 *Trans Avan Guardia,* Museum Wurth, Kunzelsau-Gaisbach, Germany
Beyond Belief: Modern Art and the Religious Imagination, National Gallery of Victoria, Melbourne (catalog)

Publications:

By CLEMENTE: Books—*The Pondicherry Pastels,* London and Madras 1986; *India,* with John Wieners, Altadena, California 1987. **Articles**—''An Interview with Francesco Clemente'', with Achille Bonito Oliva, in *Flash Art,* Summer 1980; ''Francesco Clemente at the Metropolitan'', interview with Danny Berger, in *Print Collector's Newsletter,* March/April 1982; ''Francesco Clemente'', interview with Edit deAk, in *Interview,* April 1982; ''Samtale me Francesco Clemente'', interview with Heiner Bastian, in *Louisiana Revy* (Humlebaek), June 1983; ''A Project for Artforum'', in *Artforum,* March 1987; interview with Sarah Kent in *Artscribe International,* no. 77, September-October 1989; interview with Ingrid Sischy in *Interview,* vol. 27, no. 7, July 1997.

On CLEMENTE: Books—*The Different Avantgarde: Europe/America,* by Achille Bonito Oliva, Milan 1976; *The Italian Trans Avantguarde* by Achille Bonito Oliva, Milan 1980; *Francesco Clemente: il viaggiatore napoletano,* exhibition catalog with essay by Reiner Crone, Cologne 1982; *Francesco Clemente: The Fourteen Stations,* exhibition catalog edited by Mark Francis, London 1983; *Currents: Francesco Clemente,* with text by Elisabeth Sussman, Boston 1984; *Francesco Clemente: Pastelle 1974–83,* with texts by Rainer Crone, Zdenek Felix and Lucius Grisebach, Munich 1984; *Francesco Clemente,* exhibition catalog with texts by Mark Ormond and Marianna Adams, Sarasota 1985; *Francesco Clemente* by Michael Auping, New York 1985; *Francesco Clemente CVIII,* with text by Dieter Koepplin, Basle 1987; *Francesco Clemente: Testa Coda* with introduction by Dieter Koepplin and Michael McClure, New York 1991. **Articles**—''Francesco Clemente: Spiritual Kinship Between the Italian Artist and Hinduism'' by Holland Cotter in *Parkett,* no. 40/41, 1994; ''Francesco Clemente and a Memory of His Childhood'' by Mary Elizabeth Karoll in *Art Criticism,* vol. 13, no. 1, 1998; ''Clemente: il nomade dell'arte'' by Luisa Perlo in *Arte,* no. 320, April 2000.

* * *

Francesco Clemente has made an impression as one of the most significant personalities in the panorama of ''new tendencies'' characterized by the renewed interest in the image and in traditional painting techniques. The preeminence of the concept in art, with the consequent tendency to dematerialism, is being seriously re-examined in the work of the younger artists, those whose work began to take shape at the end of the 1970s. The optimistic, evolutionist theory of *avant-garde* ideology starts to decline; together with the revival of techniques hitherto regarded as obsolete, artists are trying out the end of ideologies as a theory of a new cultural orientation, pointing to a reinterpretation of the past and a revival of local cultures. There is an established international movement which no longer wants to model itself on a parallel ''international style,'' but prefers to stimulate the differences between one culture and another in a free cross-fertilization of ideas.

Clemente has adopted the stylistic eclecticism that is the most significant outcome of these tendencies and the consequence of an aesthetic attitude that argues the case for the values of subjectivity. Like a number of others, the artist has moved on from photographic media and has abandoned them in favour of manual techniques (collages, oil painting, pastels, tempera, fresco, mosaic, drawing . . .) giving more immediate access to the objects of an ambiguously expressed expressiveness. Clemente's pictures are, as it were, intrinsically ambivalent; they allude to an explicit perverted erotic phantasmagoria, yet at the same time escape from recognizability, closed in the blazons of a private heraldry (''emblems'' is the title of a series of works by Clemente). Clemente has often expressed a lively interest in esoteric ideas, in astrology, the history of religion and Indian civilization, from whose symbolism he has drawn inspiration for his own pictorial language. In addition, his painting explicitly recalls the world of late Roman culture, an era of surprising cultural and stylistic eclecticism. This purpose can be recognized especially in Clemente's self-portraits, which have become a recurrent theme with him. A common enough theme in the pictorial tradition, here the self-portrait becomes an elaboration of the idea of self through a self-denigrating rhetoric with a literary flavour, near to the influence of an Egon Schiele, near in short to an ''accursed'' nature, strongly intellectualized.

The identity loses its familiar features and becomes an unreal, iridescent apparition, organically degenerate, connected with the world of impulses. The artist depicts himself as a convulsed body, an eroticized object ready for any metamorphosis. The image in Clemente springs from the encounter between this body, the cheerful intensity, and objects and entities transformed by a similar tension into emblems, enigmatic fragments, already completely detached from the totality. The figures are flattened on to the surfaces, suspended in an irrationally defined spatiality. With no depth, a caricature of itself, the picture no longer tries to come to terms with reality, and the painting becomes an example of excess. The excess lies in the recourse to ambiguity. It even dictates the selection of forms: sometimes the drawing looks ugly, crude, like ''anti-graceful'' graffiti, deliberately elementary, but at other times its studied elegance and surprising fastidiousness are astonishing. The painting fluctuates between a ''neo-savage,'' aggressively *brut* style, even in the choice of colours, and a style that is courtly and sumptuous, with background of delicately evanescent colour.

The painter's knowledge is there to see in his virtuoso skill, or else lies hidden in coprophilia; it becomes clear in the stylistic polymorphism of one who, in his painting, wishes not to find an identity but to lose himself. As Edit deAk has written, Clemente is a clever chameleon cynically content with his own state of grace.

—Giorgio Verzotti

CLOSE, Chuck

Nationality: American. **Born:** Monroe, Washington, 5 July 1940. **Education:** Everett Community College, Washington, 1958–60; University of Washington, Seattle, 1960–62; B.A. 1962; Yale Summer School of Art and Music, Norfolk, Connecticut, 1961; Yale University, New Haven, Connecticut, 1962–64, B.F.A. 1963, M.F.A. 1964; Akademie der Bildenden Künste, Vienna, 1964–65. **Family:** Married Leslie Rose in 1967; daughters: Georgia Molly and Maggie Sarah. **Career:** Independent Artist, since 1966; has lived and worked in New York since 1967. Instructor, University of Massachusetts, Amherst, 1965–67; School of Visual Arts, New York, 1967–71; New York University, 1970–73; University of Washington, Seattle, Summer 1970; Yale Summer School of Art and Music, Norfolk, Connecticut, 1971–72. **Awards:** Fulbright Grant, 1964; National Endowment for the Arts Grant, 1973; 6th Annual Infinity Award for Art, International Center for Photography, 1990; Skowhegan Arts Medal, 1991; Academy-Institute Award in Art, Academy of Arts and Letters, 1991; Academy of the Arts Award for Lifetime Achievement in the Visual Arts, 1995; New York State Governor's Award, 1997; Friends of Art in Embassies Citation, The White House, Washington, D.C., 1998; American Academy in Rome Centennial Award, New York, 2000. Honorary doctorates from Yale University, University of Massachusetts, Amherst, University of Washington, and several others. **Address:** c/o PaceWildenstein, 32 East 57th Street, New York, New York 10022, U.S.A.

Individual Exhibitions:

1967 University of Massachusetts Art Gallery, Amherst
1970 Bykert Gallery, New York
3 Young Americans: A Biennial, Allen Memorial Art Museum, Oberlin College, Ohio (with Ron Cooper and Neil Jenney)
1971 *Recent Work,* Los Angeles Country Museum of Art
Bykert Gallery, New York
1972 Museum of Contemporary Art, Chicago
1973 Museum of Modern Art, New York
Akron Art Institute, Ohio
Bykert Gallery, New York
1974 *3 Realists: Estes, Raffael,* Worcester Art Museum, Massachusetts
1975 Edwin Ulrich Museum, Wichita State University, Kansas
Mint Museum of Art, Charlotte, North Carolina
Ball State University Art Museum, Muncie, Indiana
Phoenix Art Museum, Arizona
Laguna Gloria Art Museum, Austin, Texas
Texas Gallery, Houston
Art Museum of South Texas, Corpus Christi
Minneapolis Institute of Arts
Center for Visual Arts, Portland, Oregon
San Francisco Museum of Modern Art
Bykert Gallery, New York
1976 Contemporary Art Center, Cincinnati, Ohio
Baltimore Museum of Art
Richard Artschwager/Chuck Close/Joe Zucker, David Weinberg Gallery, San Francisco (travelled to the La Jolla Museum of Art, California, and the University of California at Davis)
1977 Matrix 35, Wadsworth Atheneum, Hartford, Connecticut
Recent Work, Pace Gallery, New York
1979 Kunstraum, Munich
New Painting of Mark and Recent Drawings, Pace Gallery, New York
1980 *Close Portraits,* Walker Art Center, Minneapolis (retrospective 1968–80; travelled to the St. Louis Art

Museum, Missouri; Museum of Contemporary Art, Chicago; and the Whitney Museum, New York, 1981)
1982 *Photographs,* California Museum of Photography, Riverside (travelled to Berkeley, California)
Paperworks, Richard Gray Gallery, Chicago (travelled to Minneapolis; Jacksonville; St. Louis)
1983 *Recent Work,* Pace Gallery, New York
1984 *Paper Works,* Herbert Palmer Gallery, Los Angeles (travelled to Cheney, Washington; Milwaukee; De-Kalb, Illinois: Columbia, South Carolina)
1985 *Works on Paper,* Contemporary Arts Museum, Houston
Fuji Television Gallery, Tokyo
Photographs, Pace/MacGill Gallery, New York
Large Scale Photographs, Fraenkel Gallery, San Francisco
1986 *Maquettes,* Pace Gallery, New York
Recent Works, Pace Gallery, New York
1987 *Polaroids,* Aldrich Museum of Contemporary Art, Ridgefield, Connecticut
1994 *Retrospektive,* Staatliche Kunsthalle, Baden-Baden (traveled to Lenbachhaus Stadtische Gallery, Munich; catalog)
1997 *Large Scale Photographs,* PaceWildensteinMacGill Los Angeles, Beverly Hills, California
1998 *Chuck Close,* Museum of Modern Art, New York (traveled to Museum of Contemporary Art, Chicago; Hirshhorn Museum and Sculpture Garden, Washington, D.C.; Seattle Art Museum; and Hayward Gallery, London)
2000 *Recent Paintings,* PaceWildenstein, Los Angeles (catalog)

Selected Group Exhibitions:

1969 *Annual Exhibition,* Whitney Museum, New York
1970 *22 Realists,* Whitney Museum, New York
1971 *Prospect 71,* Städitische Kunsthalle, Dusseldorf
1972 *Documenta 5* Kassel, West Germany (and *Documenta 6,* 1977)
1974 *Hyperréalistes Américans/Réalistes Européens,* Center National d'Art Contemporain, Paris (toured Europe)
1978 *American Painting of the 1970's,* Albright-Knox Art Gallery, Buffalo, New York
1980 *Printed Art: A View of 2 Decades,* Museum of Modern Art, New York
1982 *Great Big Drawings,* Massachusetts Institute of Technology, Cambridge
1984 *Drawings 1974–84,* Hirshhorn Museum, Washington, D.C.
1986 *Nude, Naked, Stripped,* Massachusetts Institute of Technology, Cambridge
1991 *Biennial,* Whitney Museum of Art, New York
1993 Venice Biennial
1995 Venice Biennial
Screen, Friedrich Petzel Gallery, New York (catalog)
1996 Jill Kempner Fine Art, New York (catalog)
Photorealism's Greatest Hits, Louis K. Meisel Gallery, New York (catalog)
IN-FORM, Bravin Post Lee Gallery, New York (catalog)
Systematic, Karen McCready Fine Art, New York (catalog)
1997 *Project Painting,* Basilico Fine Arts and Lehmann Maupin, New York (catalog)
The Artist's Eye: Will Barnet Selects from the Collection, National Academy Museum, New York (catalog)
1998 *Portraits,* Trans Hudson Gallery, New York (catalog)
1999 *The American Century: Art and Culture 1900–2000,* Whitney Museum of American Art, New York (catalog)
2000 *About Faces,* C&M Arts, New York (catalog)

Collections:

Museum of Modern Art, New York; Whitney Museum, New York; Allen Memorial Art Museum, Oberlin College, Ohio; Walker Art Center, Minneapolis; National Museum of Canada Ottawa; Art Galery of Ontario, Toronto; Neue Gallery, Aachen, West Germany; Museum Boymans-van Beuningen, Rotterdam; Australian National Gallery, Canberra.

Publications:

By CLOSE: Articles—''An Interview with Chuck Close,'' with Cindy Nemser, in *Artforum* (New York), January 1970; interview, in ''Photo-Realists: 12 Interviews'' by Linda Chase and Ted McBurnett in *Art in America* (New York), November/December 1972; statement in ''The Artist and the Face: A Modern American Sampling'' by Gerrit Henry in *Art in America* (New York), January 1975; statement in ''The Art of Portraiture in the Words of 4 New York Artists'' in the *New York Times,* 31 October 1976; interview in ''The 20th Century Artists Most Admired by Other Artists'' by Grace Glueck in *Artnews* (New York), November 1977; ''An Interview with Chuck Close,'' with Barbara Harshman, in *Arts Magazine* (New York), June 1978; interview, with Barbaralee Diamonstein, in *Inside New York's Artworld,* New York 1979; ''An Interview with Chuck Close,'' with Jane Cottingham, in *American Artist* (New York), May 1983; ''New York in the Eighties: A Symposium'' in *The New Criterion* (New York), Summer 1986.

On CLOSE: Books—*22 Realists,* exhibition catalog, with text by James Monte, New York 1970; *3 Young Americans: A Biennial,* exhibition catalog, with text by Athena Spear, Oberlin, Ohio 1970; *Chuck Close: Recent Work,* exhibition catalog, with text by Gail R. Scott, Los Angeles 1971; *The Painter and the Photography* by Van Deren Coke, Albuquerque, New Mexico 1972; *American Art since 1900* by Barbara Rose, New York 1972; *Neue Formen des Realismus* by Peter Sager, Cologne 1973; *Photo-Realism: The Ludwig Collection,* exhibition catalog, London 1973; *3 Realists: Close, Estes, Raffael,* exhibition catalog, Worcester Massachusetts 1974; *Super Realism: A Critical Anthology,* edited by Gregory Battcock, New York 1975; *History of Modern Art* by H. H. Arnason, New York 1977; *Chuck Close/Matrix 35,* exhibition catalog, Hartford, Connecticut 1977; *Chuck Close: Recent Work,* exhibition catalog, New York 1977; *Super-Realism* by Edward Lucie-Smith, New York 1979; *What Is Art?* by John Canaday, New York 1980; *Printed Art: A View of 2 Decades,* exhibition catalog, New York 1980; *Close Portraits,* exhibition catalog, with texts by Lisa Lyons and Martin Friedman, Minneapolis 1980; *Contemporary American Realism Since 1960* by Frank H. Goodyear, Jr., New York 1981; *Realists at Work* by John Arthur, New York 1983; *Chuck Close,* exhibition catalog with text by John Perreault, New York 1983; *The Revenge of the Philistines: Art and Culture 1972–1984* by Hilton Kramer, New York 1985; *Chuck Close: Recent Work,* exhibition catalog with text by Arnold Glimcher,

New York 1986; *50 New York Artists* by Richard Marshall and Robert Mapplethorpe, San Francisco 1986; *Chuck Close* by Lisa Lyons and Robert Storr, New York 1987; *Chuck Close: Life and Work, 1988–1995* by John Guare, New York 1995; *Chuck Close* by Robert Storr, New York 1998. **Articles**—Article by Donald Kuspit in *Art New England,* June/July 1998; article by Lyle Rexer in *Aperture,* Summer 2000.

*

Portraiture is very important to my work, but not for what would seem like the most obvious reasons. Everyone knows something about the way people look—we have certain ideas about what's right and what's wrong. If the complexion is too green, all of a sudden it's not acceptable—whereas, if I were painting a tree, and it were a little too green or too red, no one but a botanist would know or care. I wanted to paint something that people cared about—a face contains very specific information that people can sense is either right or wrong. That keeps me on my toes, keeps me from letting well enough alone, or saying, this is close enough—no pun intended.

Likeness is an important by-product of what I do, but only to the extent that if the photograph I paint from looks like the person, the painting will look like the photograph. But the photograph may not look like the person and if it doesn't, it can be bothersome. I suppose I'd like to make the image like the person, but I've always felt it necessary to maintain a certain distance from the subject. When I painted myself, I always referred to it as ''him''—I somehow couldn't deal with the fact that it was me and whether I looked ugly or handsome or whatever.

I have a hard time dealing with my work in terms of the history of portraiture—I don't know how it fits. A lot of great paintings, when I think about it, happen to be portraits, but I have a hard time with it—when I think of something called portrait painting. I think of how all portraits by Rembrandt look like paintings by Rembrandt—that would seem to be shortcoming of portraiture.

I'm not really interested in photography, but one thing I like about photographs is the snapshot or mugshot quality of a California driver's license. It's got such an immediacy and a strong reason to exist in terms of nailing down what a certain driver looks like. It doesn't have anything to do with vanity, it doesn't have anything to do with the ego of the sitter or whatever. I've never done commissioned portraits because I never wanted to get involved with those ego problems. If somebody wants a nine-foot-high picture of their head, they must be involved with how they look. I'd hate to have the feeling that I needed to straighten teeth.

As to sitters, I just photograph my friends. Most of the people are relatively anonymous when I photograph them; sometimes they don't stay too anonymous, but I don't try and paint art stars or anything like that.

I never see someone and say, oh, you'd be great to paint. What I do is, get together a whole bunch of people and shoot them, and some of them turn out to be interesting photographs. I don't really think about interesting *people.* I scan a contact sheet and try to imagine what it would be like to paint from that photograph. Some of them seem better than others, not in terms of the overall iconography but in terms of what kind of painting experience they would be—how sharp and how blurry.

But I do care that they are people. I think sometimes it sounds like I don't care, or for that matter, that I don't think they're people. But if you're going to spend three to six months on a painting, you can't just worry about the image and say, gee, I just want this to be a picture of so-and-so. The workaday problems of making a painting tend to take over in my mind. Of course, for the last six or seven years, at least, I haven't really felt like painting anything else, so there must be something there.

—Chuck Close

* * *

A key to the work of Chuck Close lies in his statement: ''I liked the fact that I wasn't thinking of the cheek in relation to the ear and trying to decide which was closer and which farther away . . . if a person were simply panning across or scanning the cheek and some informational change took place, he would realize that he was moving back and forth in space....'' Close achieves this detachment from his subject through the huge scale that breaks free of the normal human facial confrontation; through his success at keeping the visage impersonal yet of course recognizable; through the tight 'sandwich' of clear focus that Close establishes when he blurs the nose tip in the frontally positioned heads which he himself photographs with a 190mm lens so that clarity reigns only in a zone ending at the back of the cheeks; through the melange of non-gestural marks that comprise all his works both the very large and small; and through the grids left visible in the watercolors, pastels, and prints, but not present in the large paintings. (''By breaking—the grid—down this way, I can make the act of painting exactly the same all the way through.'') All such attitudes and processes have led to Close being labelled quite rightly a Minimalist and Conceptualist—his subject matter thus disregarded.

Close appeared at a time when a photographic style in painted art was ostensibly logical because of the triumph of Pop Art and photography's importance there. He had worked on *Big Nude,* a 20-foot-long, black-and-white canvas based on his photograph, but found that he had to avoid 'hot' subject matter. And so as he worked, in the late 1960s, to develop an anthology of techniques to avoid any gestural pictorialism and subjective color, he turned to spray painting, rag smearing, and razor markings. (''My invention is an invention of means, rather than an invention of shape and other things.'') Close was then a pioneer Photo-Realist, using only his own features in these early large works, and he remains one of the few Photo-Realists to use the figure. When be began to use color in the early 70s, he wished to continue without palette because of his satisfaction with the previous monochromatic images where no color mixing was involved as the black was diluted on the white picture surface. From his color photographs, Close had three color-separation prints made which he then matched in three painting campaigns (magenta, cyan, yellow) across the canvas from the top down. He thus avoided traditional paint-mixing as he produced a handcrafted image based upon the chemical-mechanical photographic process. At this time as well, since he wished neither to change his image nor his asubjective approaches, he changed the nature of his studio practice in order to maintain his interest in the experience of the technical process. He developed the use of a grid which allowed him to present the same kind of marking unit throughout the image: i.e., the title of the work gave the specific number of grid points, even when as in large works, *Robert 104,072,* 1973–74, 108 by 84 inches, they are not visible as a grid. With smaller works, where there might be but 2760 grid points and they were left clearly distinct as individual, unblended marks, there is a striking resemblance to computer-generated, digital images. In yet another variant of such attempts at a relatively depersonalized creative process, Close has also used dyed paper pulp, cut into tiny curved-edged chips, glued onto the picture surface to produce some of the most tactile work of his mature career.

—Joshua B. Kind

Close's earlier work was usually appreciated as a fusion of Pop Art and Minimalism. Using as his chosen subject the human face as seen by a camera, the artist also anticipated questions about the nature and limits of photographic representation that were to preoccupy many artists working in the 1980s and '90s. Inventing out of necessity a pictorial means to achieve in his large works both a photographic clarity and a Minimalist, purist surface, Close's portraits forced the notion of traditional identification and its concomitant search for sentiment.

In the eighties, Close's portraits became more impressionistic. Continuing to produce work despite the effects of a debilitating illness that in 1989 left him paralyzed, Close has made in recent years some of the most exuberant and painterly works of his career. Gone is the precision of his earliest work; Close's grid now seems almost intuited. In the newest works it seems to shimmer and at times dissolve, allowing areas of the image to shift in and out of focus as the viewer moves in the space before it. In some paintings, the grid runs diagonally or becomes enlarged, creating a loose, undulating rhythm. Like tiny abstractions, the paint applied within the grid appears in multiform variety—in gestural loops, crosshatches, plaidlike strokes, or tiny targets. Color too is generally richer and sometimes unabashedly brilliant.

Softer and warmer in overall effect, Close's latest works achieve a kind of abstract realism, suggesting a different kind of involvement with the act of portraiture, one that is less detached. "Each painting is a different experience. And they're more personal today. They look more *like* the person than the photographs I work from." (CC) The paintings convey more than ever the sense of the artist's touch, a physical involvement with the work that has gained in import even as the artist's mobility has radically decreased. Close's art has thus evolved from a phenomenological reduction to an emblem of consciousness.

—Dorothy Valakos

For the larger art public, if not beyond this relatively small demographic, Close has achieved an almost mythic status in the recent past. The breadth and magnetic force of all his art—but especially the large scale work—had become fused with the image of his seemingly super-human return to creative vigor as if to deny his grave paralysis. The large retrospective exhibition of 1998 at the Museum of Modern Art, New York, which then travelled cross-country to Chicago, Washington, D. C., and Seattle, of course only enhanced such views of Close. For example, Donald Kuspit wrote in *Art New England* that ''...the fashionable inhumanity of Close's portraits bespeaks the inhumanity of our age, which makes them emotionally telling despite their spectacular character.'' As if in reaction to such critique, and to acknowledge his career-long dependence upon the photograph, Close collabaratively produced a series of daguerreotypes of the human body: ''Torsos'' in 1999–2000. Close told Lyle Rexer that ''both photography and painting are highly artificial...I translate between the two.''

—Joshua B. Kind

COFFEY, Susanna

Nationality: American. **Education:** Studied painting, University of Connecticut, B.F.A., 1976; studied painting and printmaking, Yale University, M.F.A., 1982. **Career:** Artist. F. H. Sellers Professor of Painting and Drawing, The School of the Art Institute of Chicago, 1982—; visiting professor or instructor at Royal College of Art, London, New Haven Correctional Center, Boston Museum School of Fine Arts, Rhode Island School of Design, Parsons School of Design, Cooper Union, Vermont Studio School, since 1983. **Awards:** Individual Artists grantee, Connecticut Committee on the Arts, 1980; Ragdale Foundation Residency grantee, Lake Forest, Illinois, 1984; Illinois Arts Council grantee, 1985, 1992; SAIC Faculty Enrichment grantee, 1987, 1990, 1991; Chicago Artists Abroad grantee, 1990; Marie Walsh Sharpe Foundation Studio Program grantee, 1992; National Endowment for the Arts grantee, 1993; Louis Comfort Tiffany Foundation Award, 1993; Academy Award in Art, American Academy of Arts and Letters, 1995; Guggenheim fellow, 1996. **Address:** School of the Art Institute of Chicago, 37 S. Wabash Ave, Chicago, Illinois 60603–3002, U.S.A.

Individual Exhibitions:

1986 The Cultural Center of the Chicago Public Library
1989 Sazama Gallery, Chicago
1993 Gallery Three Zero, New York
1994 K & E Gallery, New York
1995 Alpha Gallery, Boston
1996 Tibor De Nagy Gallery, New York
1999 *Susanna Coffey Recent Paintings,* Tibor de Nagy Gallery, New York (catalog)
Strauss Galleries, Dartmouth College, New Hampshire
2000 Alpha Gallery, Boston
2001 Weatherspoon Art Gallery, University of North Carolina at Greensboro

Selected Group Exhibitions:

1995 Galeria Alejandro Sales, Barcelona
1997 *About Face,* Rosenberg + Kaufman Fine Art, New York (catalog)
LA TRADICION The Tradition: Performing Painting, Exit Art/The First World, New York (catalog)
Self Portraits: Susanna Coffey, Susan Hauptman, and Daniel Leary, Elaine L. Jacob Gallery, Detroit
1999 *The End: An Independent Vision of Contemporary Culture 1982–2000,* Exit Art/The First World, New York (catalog)

Collections:

Northwestern University, Evanston, Illinois; Art Institute of Chicago; Minneapolis Museum of Art; Bryn Mawr (Pennsylvania) College; Vanderberg Foods; and private collections.

Publications:

On COFFEY: Articles—''Chicago: Susanna Coffey'' by Sue Taylor in *ARTnews,* January 1987; ''Portrait of the Artists'' by Joanne

Trestrail in *Chicago,* November 1988; ''Susanna Coffey at the K&E Gallery'' by Eileen Myles in *Art In America,* July 1994; ''Susanna Coffey at Tibor de Nagy'' by Nicole Krauss in *Art in America,* July 1994; ''Jaffe Friede and Strauss Galleries Hopkins Center, Dartmouth College/Hanover: Susanna Coffey: Paintings'' by Charles Davenport in *Art New England,* February 1999; ''Alpha Gallery/ Boston: SUSANNA COFFEY, SELF-PORTRAITS'' by Joshua Meyer in *Art New England,* April-May 2000.

* * *

For the past 20 years Susanna Coffey has devoted her career to mining the psychological, sociological, and aesthetic territory of the self-portrait. Painting primarily in oil on linen, panels, and canvas, in a nearly square ground, Coffey paints and re-paints her own face, head, and upper body. The portraits are not only uniform in subject matter but also in style though each exhibit subtle and important differences in placement, light source, and compositional relationships.

Coffey paints in thick, confident brushstrokes using a rich, dramatic palette of highly charged colors, as in such pieces as ''Self-Portrait (St. James Red),'' where the artist sports nearly neon blue eye shadow. Although initially her work seems reminiscent of other women artists absorbed in pictorial self-analysis, such as the photographer Cindy Sherman, they primarily overlap in the use of costume and make-up. Both women use clothing and ornamentation that, especially in the traditionally feminine arena of make-up, clothing, and hair color, suggest they are either in disguise or the inventors of other persona. Contemplation of the self, especially a multiplicity of selves, has been fertile ground for contemporary artists, as it speaks to the politics of seeing. However, due to distinctive aspects of Coffey's oeuvre, her effect is, at heart, very different from Sherman's.

Accessories and narrative detail change from portrait to portrait but Coffey retains a largely formal compositional style. In the paintings her head, face (and occasionally upper torso) makes up the lower portion of the painting against a single field of color or sometimes pattern. Coffey has said she produces these works by looking into a mirror. Indeed the placement of her face on the canvas—nearly always in the lower quadrant—replicates the way an ordinary woman sees her own face in a mirror. The pieces italicize this sensation or even directly refer to it as in ''Self-Portrait (St. Marks Glasses)'' in which Coffey's own face reflects from sunglasses worn by the artist. The work itself also functions as a mirror; albeit one that the viewer looks into only to see the artist peering out. It is this highly specified relationship that ultimately propels the psychological implications of such a repetitious and exact body of work.

Self-portraiture, of course, has a long provenance in the history of art. It is in a way, the first subject of all artists. Coffey may be slightly disingenuous in stating, ''I paint self-portraits because it would be hard to find another model as available.'' Yet the statement may be more accurate than wry. The availability of the artist in an emotional sense does carry a potent narrative force. For example, the portraits remain true to life, showing the artist clearly aging from canvas to canvas. Yet Coffey's images are actually less about the revelation of self than the significance of the one visage controlled in every aspect, including costume and personality, and the other entirely uncontrollable. Both the specter of duplication and the mirror-like compositional arrangement clearly indicate the artist-viewer relationship as a fundamental subject of the work. Since Coffey has a single subject—her own face—the dialog further inferred between the beheld and the beholder is one in which Coffey plays both roles.

The politics of image, self-image, and female countenance act similarly to the exotic colors that Coffey utilizes in the paintings' details—they bring an electric charge to the seemingly innocuous formal material. The dramatic cropping of the face underscores the complicated relationship between the beheld and the beholder. In this way, the work also addresses issues of gaze, an issue of particular interest to women, who have historically more often been the objects than the subject of art. Coffey brings a formidable arsenal of confident technique and masterful manipulation of color to these explorations to which the viewer is invited to make the congruence complete.

—Merridawn Duckler

COHEN, Bernard

Nationality: British. **Born:** London, 28 July 1933. **Education:** Schools in London; studied shorthand and typing at Clark's College, Leytonstone, London, 1947, and art at South West Essex Technical College and School of Art, 1949–50, St. Martin's School of Art, London, 1950–51, and Slade School of Fine Art, London 1951–54. **Family:** Married Jean Britton in 1959. **Career:** Lives and works in London. Lived in Paris and travelled in France, 1954–56; spent several months in Rome, 1956; lived in Hertfordshire, 1959; returned to London, and shared house with William Turnbull, 1961–63, then settled in Putney, South London, 1963; worked on design for stage curtain, Theatre Royal, Stratford, East London, 1965; built studio in Kingston-on-Thames, Surrey, 1967. Part-time lecturer, Hammersmith School of Art, London, 1957–60; lecturer, Ealing School of Art, London, 1961–64; guest lecturer, St. Martin's School of Art, London 1963–64; lecturer, Chelsea School of Art, London, 1966–68, and Slade School of Fine Art, 1967–73 and since 1977. Visiting professor, Department of Art, University of New Mexico, Albuquerque, 1969–70. **Awards:** French Government Travel Scholarship, 1954; Boise Scholarship, University of London, 1955. **Address:** 17 Leyborne Park, Kew, Surrey, England.

Individual Exhibitions:

1958 Gimpel Fils, London (with James Tower)
Midland Group Gallery, Nottingham
1960 Gimpel Fils, London
1962 Molton Gallery, London
1963 Kasmin Gallery, London
1964 Kasmin Gallery, London
1967 Kasmin Gallery, London
Arnolfini Gallery, Bristol
Betty Parsons Gallery, New York
Lady Margaret Hall, Oxford
1972 Arnolfini Gallery, Bristol
Hayward Gallery, London
Waddington Galleries, London
Studio LaCitta, Verona
Hester van Royen Gallery, London
1973 Galleria Annunciata, Milan
Waddington Galleries, London
1974 Waddington Galleries, London

1977 Waddington Galleries, London
1979 Waddington Galleries, London
1980 Amano Gallery, Osaka, Japan
1990 Waddington Galleries, London
1998 *Bernard Cohen: Paintings of the Nineties,* Flowers East, London

Selected Group Exhibitions:

1958 *Abstract Impressionism,* Arts Council Gallery, London
1960 *Situation,* Federation of British Arts Galleries London
1964 *Painting and Sculpture of a Decade,* Tate Gallery, London
1965 *London: The New Scene,* Walker Art Center, Minneapolis
1967 *Jeune Peintres Anglais,* Palais des Beaux-Arts, Brussels
1969 *Marks on Canvas,* Museum am Ostwall, Dortmund, West Germany
1970 *British Painting,* National Gallery, Washington, D.C.
1973 *New British Painting,* Musée National d'Art Moderne, Paris
1976 *Arte Inglese Oggi,* Palazzo Reale, Milan
1982 *Carnegie International,* Pittsburgh
1992 *Ready Steady Go: Painting of the Sixties from the Arts Council Collection,* Royal Festival Hall, London

Collections:

Tate Gallery, London: Arts Council of Great Britain, London; Whitworth Art Gallery, Manchester; Museum am Ostwall, Dortmund, West Germany; Museum of Modern Art, New York; Walker Art Center, Minneapolis; Museum of Modern Art, Caracas.

Publications:

By COHEN: Articles—''Gesture and Style'' in *Gazette* (London), no. 2, 1961; ''International Union of Architects Congress Buildings, South Bank, London'' in *Architectural Design* (London), November 1961; ''Observations about the Photograph of the Painting Generation'' in *Cambridge Opinion,* January 1964; interview, with Denis Bower, in *Arts Review* (London), December 1964; The Art That Launched a Thousand Ships'' in the *Sunday Times Colour Magazine* (London), November 1965; statement in *Bernard Cohen,* exhibition catalog, Bristol 1967; statement in *Recent British Painting* by Alan Bownes, London 1968; statement in *Arte Inglese Oggi,* exhibition catalog, Milan 1976; ''For My Eyes Only'' in *Art Review* (London), vol. 46, November 1994.

On COHEN: Book—*Bernard Cohen: Paintings and Drawings 1959–71,* exhibition catalog, by Richard Morphet, London 1972; *Bernard Cohen,* exhibition catalog, London 1990; *Bernard Cohen: Paintings of the Nineties,* exhibition catalog, London 1998. **Articles—** ''Bernard Cohen and Harold Cohen: From Gesture to Symbol'' in *London: The New Scene,* exhibition catalog by Martin Friedmann, Minneapolis 1965; ''Bernard Cohen'' by David Thompson in *5 Young Painters,* exhibition catalog, Vence, France 1966; ''Bernard Cohen'' by Andrew Forge in *The Listener* (London), April 1972; ''The Work of Bernard Cohen'' by B. Bernstein in *Studio International* (London), June/July 1972.

* * *

There has been a dramatic change in Bernard Cohen's paintings; in the 1960s they resembled highly colored spaghetti, arranged on the canvas in a mixture of meticulous care and free association. One could see why he pointed to their narrative quality, since, in Klee's immortal phrase, they were rather like taking a line, or a tube, for a walk. The churned-up, intestinal association of the imagery also suggested intense, emotional elements, and there were indications that the paintings were, so to speak, graphs of both the process of painting and the physical experience before the canvas.

Cohen is a member of that English generation of artists whose greatest influences came from the United States; whilst he refers to his admiration for such artists as Fontana, Dubuffet, Miró and Dali—and one certainly notes the mixture of informality and surrealism in this early period—there can be little doubt that the most relevant example is Jackson Pollock. The American painter's famous drip paintings are precisely images which record the effort of creation, as well as being monuments to that creativity: They are facts and sequences of time. Cohen's narratives clearly sought to experience the same direct intensity of creation, and to record that experience on canvas. He also refers to his liking for *art nouveau,* which relates to the sinuous convolution of these painted linear graphs.

More recently he has pushed his way through the morass of neo-organic matter, into the fresh air, into uncluttered space; the result is a series of almost white canvases, arranged in a series of oblong areas, against acid-colored backgrounds, in which pale, distantly burning, lunar symbols float in corners of space. Meticulously conceived and painted, this new phase is immediately more elegant and sophisticated, suggesting a search for idealistic physicality, for a mediative stance through which to reflect metaphysical notions of the physical world and human life. Most recently Cohen has returned to the undisturbed space of a single canvas, in which the clinically white surface is broken not by single sums, but galaxies of colored spots, floating, drifting rhythmically through space. Perhaps they suggest the smallness of individual man, the non-uniqueness of the earth, the remote mystery of the universe.

—Charles Spencer

COLEMAN, James

Nationality: Irish. **Born:** in Ballaghaderreen, County Roscommon, 6 July 1941. **Education:** Studied at the Ecole des Beaux-Arts, Paris, 1960–61, Central School of Arts and Crafts, London, 1961–63, National College of Art and Design, Dublin, 1963–66, and Accademia di Belle Arti, Milan, 1966–71. **Career:** Lives and works in Dublin and Milan. **Awards:** Arts Council of Ireland grant, 1968, 1970; Irish-American Cultural Institute Award for the Arts, 1977; Irish Arts Counsil Award, 1979. **Agents:** Studio Marconi, via Tadino 15,20124 Milan; David Hendricks, 119 St. Stephen's Green, Dublin, Ireland; and Nigel Greenwood Inc., 4 New Burlington Street, London W1, England. **Address:** 189 Emmet Road, Inchicore, Dublin 8, Ireland.

Individual Exhibitions:

1965 Molesworth Gallery, Dublin
1967 Design Studio, Amsterdam
1970 Studio Marconi, Milan
1972 *Projections,* Galleria Toselli, Milan

1973 *Habitual Object,* David Hendricks Gallery, Dublin
Habitual Object, Studio Marconi, Milan
1974 Ulster Museum, Belfast
Slide Piece, Studio Lia Rumma, Naples
Installation for Location and Slide Piece, Galerie t'Venster, Rotterdam
2 Seagulls; or, One Seagull Twice, Cork Arts Society, Ireland
1975 *Clara and Dario,* Studio Marconi, Milan
1978 *Strongbow,* Project Arts Centre, Dublin
1979 *Box,* Galleria Schema, Florence
Box, Nigel Greenwood Inc., London (with Marc Chaimowicz)
1980 *Connemara Landscape,* University College Art Gallery, Galway, Ireland
So Different . . . and Yet, Nigel Greenwood Inc., London
Douglas Hyde Gallery, Dublin
1981 *Now and Then, So Different . . . and Yet,* Project Arts Centre, Dublin
So Different . . . and Yet, Franklin Furnace, New York
1982 *Slide Piece,* John Hansard Gallery, Southampton, England
Nigel Greenwood Inc., London
Douglas Hyde Gallery, Trinity College, Dublin (travelled to the Arts Council of Northern Ireland Gallery, Belfast)
Ignotum per Ignotius, Lantaren Theatre, Rotterdam (toured Netherlands)
1983 Whitechapel Art Gallery, London
Orhard Gallery, Derry, Northern Ireland
Teatro Estudio Citac, Coimbra, Portugal (travelled to Lisbon)
1984 Douglas Hyde Gallery, Dublin
David Bellman Gallery/Art Metropole, Toronto
1985 Dungaire Castle, County Clare, Ireland
Renaissance Society, Chicago (retrospective; travelled to Institute of Contemporary Arts, London)
1987 Galerie Rudiger Schottle, Munich
Galerie Johnen und Shottle, Cologne
1988 Galerie des Beaux-Arts, Brussels
1989 Musée d'Art Moderne de la Ville de Paris, Paris
1990 Van Abbemuseum, Eindhoven, Netherlands
1991 Lisson Gallery, London
Marian Goodman Gallery, New York
1994 *James Coleman: Projected Images 1972–1994,* Dia Center for the Arts, New York (catalog)
1996 *James Coleman,* Centre National d'Art et de Culture Georges Pompidou, Paris
Centre Georges Pompidou, Paris
Musée National d'Art Moderne, Paris
1997 Wiener Secession, Vienna
Stedelijk Van Abbemuseum, Eindhoven
1998 *Lapsus Exposure,* Rüdiger Schöttle, Munich, Germany
2000 *James Coleman: Mannerist Photographer,* Galerie Marian Goodman, Paris
Marian Goodman Gallery, New York
Fundació Antoni Tàpies, Barcelona, Spain

Selected Group Exhibitions:

1972 *Living Art,* Project Arts Centre, Dublin
1973 *Biennale de Paris,* Musée d'Art Moderne de la Ville, Paris
1976 *Living Art,* National Gallery of Ireland, Dublin
1977 *ROCS '77,* Hugh Lane Municipal Gallery of Modern Art, Dublin
1978 *Milano '80,* Palazzo Reale, Milan
Biennale, Venice
1980 *Without the Walls,* Institute of Contemporary Arts, London
1982 *Biennale,* Sydney
1986 *In De Maalstroom,* Palais des Beaux-Arts, Brussels
1987 *From the Europe of Old,* Stedelijk Museum, Amsterdam
1988 Artists Space, New York (with Michael Asher)
1990 *Culture and Commentary: An Eighties Perspective,* Hirshhorn Museum and Sculpture Garden, Washington, D.C.
1991 *Projected Identities,* San Francisco Museum of Modern Art
1993 *Acquisitions 1989–1993: A Selection,* Stedelijk Van Abbemuseum, Eindhoven, Netherlands
1994 Ydessa Hendeles Foundation, Toronto
1999 *Moments in Time: On Narration and Slowness,* Stadtische Galerie im Lenbachhaus, Munich

Collections:

Ulster Museum, Belfast; Arts Council of Northern Ireland, Belfast; Municipal Gallery of Dublin.

Publications:

By COLEMAN: Articles—statement in *VIII Biennale de Paris,* exhibition catalog, Paris 1973; article in *Art Press* (Paris), September 1973; articles in *Prospect* (Milan), March/April 1973; "Essay from Coleman" in *Art in Ireland* (Dublin), vol. II, no. 3, 1974; article in *Data* (Milan), Summer 1974; "Flash Piece 1970 and Slide Piece 1972/73" in *Bollaffi Selected Artists,* Turin 1974; statement in *Rotterdam Arts News,* September/October 1974.

On COLEMAN: Books—*Installation Made for Location and Slide Piece,* exhibition catalog, by Achille Bonito Oliva, Rotterdam 1974; *Europe-America: The Different Avant Gardes* by Achille Bonito Oliva, Milan 1976; *James Coleman,* exhibition catalog, by Jean Fisher, Dublin 1982; *The Enigma of the Hero in the Work of James Coleman* by Jean Fisher, Londonderry 1983; *James Coleman: Selected Works,* exhibition catalog with essays by Anne Rorimer and Michael Newman, Chicago and London 1985; *James Coleman: Projected Images, 1972–1994,* exhibition catalog, New York 1994; *The Life & Works of James Coleman* with introduction by Kenny Loggins, text by Mark Doyle, Westlake Village 1995; *James Coleman,* exhibition catalog with text by Raymond Bellour and Jean Fisher, Paris 1996; *James Coleman,* exhibition catalog with essay by Rosalind E. Krauss, Vienna 1997. **Articles—**"James Coleman à la Tête de l'Avant-garde à la Biennale de Paris" by George Astalos in *Nouvelle Europe* (Paris), no. 6, 1973; "Causality and the Interpretation of Information" by Ricardo Luccio in Data (Milan), May/June 1976; "Review from Dublin" by Dorothy Walker in *Art Monthly* (London), November 1978; "Installations and Performances in Ireland" by Dorothy Walker in *Flash Art* (Milan), October/November 1979; "James Coleman" by Friedemann Malsch in *Artefactum,* vol. 8, no. 39, June-August 1991; "James Coleman: Call to Mind" by Peggy Gate in *Parachute,* no. 63, July-September 1991; "James Coleman: Charon and the Paradox of Time" by Eric de Bruyn in *Forum International,* no. 12, vol. 3, March-April 1992; ''James Coleman: The Detective and the Secret'' by Marie-Ange Brayer in *Art Press,* no. 179, April 1993; ''Inexorable Dissolve: James Coleman Blindsides Art'' by Jean Fisher in *Artforum International,* vol. 32, December 1993; ''Narratives Of No Return: James Coleman's guaiRE'' by Luke Gibbons in *Artforum,* vol. 32, no. 4, December 1993; '''And Then Turn Away?': An Essay on James Coleman'' by Rosalind E. Krauss in *October* (Cambridge), no. 81, Summer 1997; ''The Living Dead'' by Raymond Bellour in *Circa,* no. 79, Spring 1997; ''Rhythm, Repetition and Reproduction: Re-experiencing the Art of James Coleman'' by Paula Murphy in *Irish Arts Review Yearbook,* vol. 14, 1998; ''Sight(s) and/or Sound(s): sur trois oeuvres de James Coleman'' by Jacinto Lageira in *Parachute,* no. 95, July/September 1999; ''James Coleman: Photograph, 1998–99—Opening Lines'' by David Frankel in *Artforum,* vol. 38, no. 9, May 2000.

* * *

In the theatre the audience interpret what they see and hear to reconstruct the narrative and its meaning. James Coleman foregrounds this process of interpretation in his work which has taken a variety of forms since the early 1970s including slide projection, tapeslide, film, video, installation, and performances using actors. By constructing the work as an enigma, by fragmenting the narrative and making the relation of images to text not an obvious or illustrative one, Coleman draws attention to the way in which the viewer or audience is drawn into the work by the interpretative act. The way in which images and text intersect to constitute the position of the interpreter becomes a subject of the work. Through the process of interpretation the subject—the interpreter—is constituted within Language.

Coleman builds into his works allusions to different codes. The slide projection *Connemara Landscape* (1980) deconstructs the implications of romantic depictions of the Irish landscape by simultaneously providing clues for and frustrating intepretation. The video work *So Different . . . and Yet* (1980) could be interpreted according to the discourse of psychoanalytic theory: This would focus on the fetishistic pose of the woman, and the fetishism of the green dress and woman as an object of desire in the fragmented romantic-fiction narrative. For those familiar with the code of Irish national and literary history the green dress and the proper names of the characters take on additional symbolic functions. Yet another intepretation, this time according to the code of mythology, is hinted at by the horns on the head of the pianist in the video image—a possible reference to Cernunnos, the horned god of pre-Christian Irish myth—as well as the structural relationships within the narrative. Yet while the act of interpretation is continually provoked it is never allowed to be conclusive, to terminate in a ''transcendental signified.'' The fragmentation of the linear chain of the narrative—where one thing would otherwise lead smoothly to another—opens the space for the ''vertical'' metaphorical substitutions of interpretation. Yet, like the needle of a record player which jumps to another track, these possible interpretations don't lead outside Language to the signified as thing-in-itself, whether artist's intention, viewer's experience, or enclosing context. One signifier only leads to another, and yet another. The title invites completion: ''So different, and yet—the same.'' But this ''same'' is suspended as absence, as an identity that cannot be provided, as the void or lack which instigates the desire which motivates the play of signifiers.

One of the features which contributes to the extraordinary richness of Coleman's work is that it involves a modern reworking of age-old themes. While he employs contemporary media and techniques of handling text and images, Coleman draws on such central texts of the Western tradition as Sophocles' *Oedipus the King* and the Irish epic the *Táin Bó Cuailnge.* Not only his works thematize interpretation, they are also reinterpretations of tradition—interpretations in terms of the interpretative act itself. In this sense they are reflexive—analytical—allegories of the theatrical scent of interpretation with the interpreter—the viewer or member of the audience—as protagonist, both victim and murderer.

To see identity as something which is constituted in a process and involved with interpretation is to prise it away from what is often to be its natural relation to the fully rounded character. Coleman uses theatricality to deconstruct the identification of the actor with character as if he or she were a real person. Rather the figures in the narrative of *So Different . . . and Yet* and in the tableaux of *Living and Presumed Dead* (1983–85) serve as what V. Propp in *The Morphology of the Folktale* called ''functions'' in a narrative structure. Just as the figures in a dream are not real characters but elements in a structure which expresses, in a distorted form, a repressed unconcious wish, so the functions in *So Different . . . and Yet and Living and Presumed Dead* only become interpretable (in a way that is always problematic and reflexive) in terms of their interrelationship and, in this process of allegorical reading, construct a position for the interpreter.

In *Living and Presumed Dead* the narrative of identity is also a story of a secret discovered, of a search for the father or the hero, of murder and of revenge. The murderer turns out to be an obscure figure without face who is unnamed in the action and listed only as ''Mr.'' This designation functions linguistically as a shifter, like ''I'' or ''You,'' a syntactical position filled by whoever performs the utterance or is designated by it. This is the point where the act of enunciation encounters the symbolic order, where the living speaker assumes a position within language, in a sense ''dying'' into representation. It could be said that the interpreter is both the murderer and the victim of the interpretation, in that he or she both constructs a symbolic order and takes a position within it, freezing being—the living flow of desire—into meaning.

—Michael Newman

(from *The Analytical Theatre,* Independent Curators Inc., 1987)

COLESCOTT, Robert

Nationality: American. **Born:** Oakland, California, 1925. **Education:** Student of Fernand Léger, Paris, 1940–50; University of California, Berkeley, B.A. 1949; University of California, Berkeley, M.A. 1952. **Career:** Associate professor of art, Portland State University, Oregon, 1957–66; visiting professor, American University of Cairo, 1966–67; professor of art history, American College, Paris, 1967–68; professor of art, College Art Study Abroad, Paris, 1967–69, California State College, Stanislaus, California, 1970–74; visiting lecturer of painting and drawing, University of California, Berkeley, 1974–79; visiting professor of art, University of Arizona, Tucson, 1983–84; instructor of painting and drawing, San Francisco Art Institute, 1976–85; professor of art, University of Arizona, Tucson, 1985–90. Since 1990 regents' professor of art, University of Arizona, Tucson. Since 1984 public lecturer throughout the United States. **Awards:** Visual Arts Award, SECCA Winston-Salem; American Research Center grant, 1964–65; National Endowment for the Arts grant, 1976,

1980 and 1983; Guggenheim Foundation grant, 1985; Roswell Foundation Artist's Residency grant, 1987; "Robert Colescott Day" declaration, City of Houston, December 2, 1988; Tamarind Institute Resident Artist grant, 1989; Marie Walsh Sharpe Foundation award, 1991. **Agent:** Phyllis Kind Gallery, 136 Greene Street, New York, New York 10012, U.S.A.

Individual Exhibitions:

1953 Miller Pollard, Seattle
1957 Zoe Dusanne, Seattle
1958 Portland Art Museum, Oregon
1960 Portland Art Museum, Oregon
Museum of Art, Eugene, Oregon
Fountain Gallery, Portland, Oregon
1961 Salem Art Museum, Oregon
Reed College Art Gallery, Portland, Oregon
1965 Victoria Municipal Art Gallery, British Columbia
1966 Fountain Gallery, Portland, Oregon
Portland Art Museum, Oregon
1972 Friedlander Gallery, Seattle
1973 Spectrum Gallery, New York
1975 Razor Gallery, New York
1977 Razor Gallery, New York
1978 John Berggruen Gallery, San Francisco
1979 Hamilton Gallery, New York
1981 Semaphore Gallery, New York
1982 Semaphore Gallery, New York
1983 Freedman Gallery, Albright College, Reading, Pennsylvania
1985 Institute of Contemporary Art, University of Pennsylvania, Philadelphia
Hadler/Rodriguez Gallery, Houston, Texas
Greenville County Museum of Art, Greenville, South Carolina
Semaphore Gallery, New York
Dart Gallery, Chicago
Knight Gallery, Charlotte, North Carolina
1986 Koplin Gallery, Los Angeles
Semaphore East Gallery, New York
1987 Roswell Museum and Art Center, San Francisco
Semaphore Gallery, New York
Phyllis Kind Gallery, Chicago
Robert Colescott: A Retrospective, 1975–1986, San Jose Museum of Art (traveling)
1988 *The Eye of the Beholder: Recent Work by Robert Colescott,* Marsh Gallery, Modlin Fine Arts Center, University of Richmond, Virginia (traveling)
1989 Phyllis Kind Gallery, New York
Robert Colescott: A Retrospective, Seattle Art Museum
Greg Kuccra Gallery, Seattle
University of Texas, El Paso
1990 Overholland Museum, Amsterdam, Holland
Arthur Roger Gallery, New Orleans
Phyllis Kind Gallery, Chicago
Linda Cathcart Gallery, Los Angeles
Howard Yezerski Gallery, Boston
1991 Phyllis Kind Gallery, New York
University of Colorado Museum, Boulder
1992 G.R. N'Namdi Gallery, Birmingham, Mississippi
Phyllis Kind Gallery, New York
1993 Laura Russo Gallery, Portland, Oregon
Linda Cathcart Gallery, Santa Monica, California
Phyllis Kind Gallery, New York
1994 Phyllis Kind Gallery, New York
1995 Scottsdale Center for the Arts, Arizona
Horwitch LewAllen Gallery, Santa Fe, New Mexico
Katonah Museum of Art, Westchester County, New York
1996 G.R. N'Namdi Gallery, Birmingham, Mississippi
1997 *Works on Paper,* Van Every Gallery, Davidson College, North Carolina; toured
1998 Phyllis Kind Gallery, New York
Howard Yezerski Gallery, Boston
1999 Laura Russo Gallery, Portland, Oregon
Recent Work, G.R. N'Namdi Gallery, Chicago
1998–2000 *Robert Colescott: Recent Paintings, 1987–1997,* Venice Biennale, Venice, Italy; toured to Walker Art Center, Minneapolis, SITE Sante Fe, New Mexico, University of Arizona Museum of Art, and other museums
2000 *Recent Work,* G.R. N'Namdi Gallery, Birmingham, Michigan
Recent Work, Phyllis Kind Gallery, New York

Selected Group Exhibitions:

1991 Aldrich Museum of Art, Ridgefield, Connecticut
1992 *Spirit Made Visible,* John Natsoulas Gallery, Davis, California
Museum of Modern Art, New York
1993 Brooklyn Museum, New York
The Purloined Image, Flint Institute of Arts, Flint, Michigan
Arthur Roger Gallery, New Orleans
1994 Corcoran Gallery of Art, Washington, D.C.
Whitney Museum of Contemporary Art, New York
1995 Aspen Art Museum, Colorado
Horwitch LewAllen Gallery, Santa Fe
Temporarily Possessed: The Semi-Permanent Collection, New Museum of Contemporary Art, New York (catalog)
1998 *Brand New Editions,* Karen McCready Fine Arts, New York (catalog)
2000 *The End: An Independent Vision of Contemporary Culture, 1982–2000,* Exit Art/The First World, New York (catalog)

Collections:

Akron Art Museum, Ohio; Boston Museum of Fine Art; Brooklyn Museum of Art, New York; Columbia College, Portland, Oregon; Contemporary Museum of Art, Honolulu; Corcoran Gallery of Art, Washington, D.C.; Delaware Museum of Art, Wilmington; Denver Museum of Art; Greenville County Museum of Art, South Carolina; High Museum of Art, Atlanta, Georgia; Hirshorn Museum, Washington, D.C.; Indianapolis Art Museum, Indiana; Kresge Art Museum, Michigan State University, East Lansing; Metropolitan Museum of Art, New York; Museum of Modern Art, New York; Newark Museum of Art, New Jersey; Oakland Art Museum, California; Portland Art Museum, Oregon; Reed College, Portland, Oregon; Rose Art Museum,

Brandeis University, Waltham, Massachusetts; Roswell Museum, New Mexico; San Francisco Museum of Modern Art; Seattle Art Museum; Tucson Museum of Art, Arizona; University of Massachusetts, Amherst; University of Oregon, Eugene; Victoria Art Gallery, British Columbia; Whitney Museum of American Art, New York.

Publications:

By COLESCOTT: Articles—''Cultivating a Subversive Palette,'' in *Reimaging America: The Arts of Social Change,* edited by Mark O'Brien and Craig Little, Philadelphia, New Society Publishers, 1990.

On COLESCOTT: Books—*Those Africans Look Like White Elephants: An Interview with Robert Colescott,* exhibition catalog, New York, Semaphore Gallery and Joe Lewis, 1982; *Here and Now, Robert Colescott,* exhibition catalog, South Carolina, Greenville County Museum of Art and Thomas W. Styron, 1984; *Robert Colescott: The Artist and the Model* by Gerald Silk, Philadelphia: Institute of Contemporary Art, University of Pennsylvania, 1984; *In Celebration of Black History Month: Twelve Artists and Their Work* by Dennis Evans, Sowder and Associates, Incorporated, Minneapolis, Minnesota, 1984; *Robert Colescott: Another Judgment,* exhibition catalog, Charlotte, North Carolina, Night Gallery, Kenneth Baker and Anne Shengold, 1985; *Robert Colescott: A Retrospective 1975–1986,* exhibition catalog, California, San Jose Museum of Art, Lowery S. Sims and Mitchell D. Kahan, 1987; *The Eye of the Beholder: Recent Work by Robert Colescott,* exhibition catalog, Virginia, University of Richmond, Katherine Weiss and Susan Arnold (interview), 1988; *Paris Connections: African American Artists In Paris,* exhibition catalog, San Francisco, Bomani Gallery and Q.E.D. Press, 1992; *African American Visual Aesthetics: A Postmodernist View*, edited by David Driskell, Washington, D.C. and London 1995; *Robert Colescott: Recent Paintings*, exhibition catalog, text by Miriam Roberts, Sante Fe, New Mexico 1997. **Articles—**''Bob Colescott Ain't Just Misbehavin''' by Lowery S. Sims in *Artforum*, March 1984; ''Robert Colescott: Pride and Prejudice'' by Mitchell Kahan in *Art Papers,* May/June 1985; ''Colescott Sees Humor in Human Behavior'' by Suzanne Muchnic in *Los Angeles Times,* 24 April 1986, part VI; ''Robert Colescott: Saints and Other Stereotypes'' by Merle Schipper in *Artweek,* 10 May 1986; ''Invented Stereotypes: The Painting of Robert Colescott'' by M. VanProyon in *Artweek,* vol. 18, no. 15, 18 April 1987; ''Ironic, Irreverent, Confrontational Robert Colescott: A Retrospective'' by E. Wright in *The Baltimore Afro-American,* 16 January 1988; ''Robert Colescott's Perspectives on Black and White'' by Paul Richard in *Washington Post,* 20 January 1988; ''Picasso Was Here: Five Contemporary Artists Mine the Master'' by Matthew Diehl in *Art and Antiques,* vol. 6, February 1989; ''Robert Colescott's Searing Stereotypes: Perceptions and Perspectives'' by Robert L. Douglas in *New Art Examiner,* vol. 16, June 1989; ''Colescott on Black and White'' by Ken Johnson in *Art in America,* vol. 77, June 1989; ''The Mirror, the Other'' by Lowery Stokes Sims in *Artforum International,* vol. 28, March 1990; ''L'Ecole de Paris Is Burning: Robert Colescott's Ironic Variations'' by Faye Hirsch in *Arts Magazine,* vol. 66, September 1991; ''The Figure Returns'' by Robert G. Edelman in *Art in America,* vol. 82, March 1994; ''Robert Colescott: Christina's Day Off (Down in the Dumps II), 1983'' by Charles Wylie in *Saint Louis Art Museum Bulletin,* vol. 21, Winter 1995; ''From Picasso to Sepik River: An Interview with Robert Colescott'' by Faye Hirsch in *On Paper,* vol. 1, May-June 1997; ''One-two Punchinello'' by Sally Eauclaire in *Art News,* vol. 96, June 1997; ''Robert Colescott'' by Jim Waltzer in *Art and Antiques,* vol. 20, June 1997; ''Robert Colescott Rocks the Boat'' by Sharon Fitzgerald in *American,* Visions vol. 12, June-July 1997; ''Reconstitucion pictorica de la historia negra: la obra de Robert Colescott'' by Udo Kultermann in *Goyano,* no. 259–260, July-October 1997; ''Americans Show Robert Colescott'' in *Flash Art* (International Edition), no. 195, Summer 1997; ''Who Killed Sandra Fisher?'' by Rosalin Sadler in *Modern Painters,* vol. 10, Autumn 1997; ''Robert Colescott'' in *Art Papers,* vol. 21, November-December 1997; ''Robert Colescott's Acerbic Brush'' by Francine Koslow Miller in *Art New England,* vol. 19, December 1997-January 1998; ''San Francisco Fax: April. 10 '98'' by Marchia Porges in *Art Issues,* no. 53, Summer 1998; ''Don't Worry, Be Happy?'' by Odili Donald Odita in *Art Papers,* vol. 22, no. 6, November-December 1998; ''Robert Colescott at the Portland Art Museum'' by Kate Bonansinga in *Artweek,* vol. 30, no. 3, March 1999; ''New Orleans'' by D. Eric Bookhardt in *Art Papers,* vol. 24, no. 3, May-June 2000. **Recordings—** ''David D'Arcy Interview with Robert Colescott'' on *Morning Edition, National Public Radio,* 14 March 1989; ''Video Interview,'' Linda Freeman Productions, March 1991.

* * *

Sometimes referred to as a forerunner of postmodernism, Robert Colescott is known for his highly expressive and gestural paintings which address a wide range of social and cultural themes. In producing satirical paintings with layers of meaning, Colescott seeks to challenge and debunk a variety of cultural stereotypes and, consequently, leads viewers to question what is presented to them, whether it is literature, history, art, or popular culture. Most frequently, Colescott achieves his goal of rewriting history by inserting black figures into scenes from which they were previously excluded. Formally, his highly expressive style is indebted to European modernism, particularly Cubism and Expressionism, but he undermines this tradition by incorporating elements from African sculpture, the long history of African-American art, and post-World War II American styles.

Colescott's early years and artistic training profoundly impacted the style and content of his paintings. A California-born artist, Colescott grew up in a musical family; his mother was a pianist and his father was a classically-trained violinist who was also a jazz musician. Drawn to the visual arts more than music, he often found himself surrounded by creative individuals as he was growing up, such as the sculptor Sargent Johnson who was a family friend and served as an artistic mentor. Colescott received his bachelor of arts in 1949 from the University of California at Berkeley, where he trained in the styles of European abstraction. This training continued when he studied with Fernand Léger in Paris from 1949 to 1950. An artist whose worked combined the styles of Cubism and Futurism and emphasized the human figure, Léger renewed Colescott's interest in figurative art. By 1952, Colescott had earned his masters degree from Berkeley. While Abstract Expressionist artists were moving away from representing the figure, Bay area artists were integrating figures in paintings with expressive gestures.

Colescott's painting style continued to evolve considerably over the next decade before arriving at his mature style. Colescott moved to the Pacific Northwest, settling first in Seattle and then in Oregon to teach at Portland State University. His first solo exhibition occurred in 1963 at Fountain Gallery in Portland. His painting style was dramatically influenced by his stay in Cairo, Egypt—first as a fellow at the American Research Center in Cairo and then as a professor at the American University. There, Colescott was exposed to ancient art and absorbed its graphic quality, monumentality, and color. Inspired by his stay in Egypt, Colescott moved away from European modernism by initiating a critique of contemporary American culture from his African-American perspective through the use of irony and satire. Like other 1960s artists, Colescott began pulling subjects from popular culture, but highlighted their expressive potential.

In the 1970s, Colescott began synthesizing these earlier influences into his characteristic style. Predating the emergence of multiculturalism, postmodernism, and neo-exressionist painting of the 1980s, Colescott produced satirical interpretations of contemporary culture by appropriating images from the history of art and popular culture. His paintings sought to subvert stereotypes through racial and gender reversals. Colescott's training in the modes of European modernism enabled him to critique not only the content of these ubiquitous works, but also their style. Due to the controversial and sensitive issues that Colescott addressed, his paintings were not always well-received. However, Colescott's reputation was somewhat buoyed by the rising popularity of feminist artists, many of whom utilized similar revisionist strategies.

Colescott was especially interested in inserting African Americans into history and the history of art. For example, *George Washington Carver Crossing the Delaware: Page from an American History Textbook* (1975) quotes Emmanuel Leutze's nineteenth-century painting, but Colescott re-stages the historical event with the scientist Carver as General Washington accompanied by historical black stereotypes, such as cooks, mammies, and banjo players. Similarly, Colescott targeted the exclusion of African Americans from the history of art by rendering figures from canonical paintings in ''blackface.'' Some of the best known images that Colescott appropriates include Jan van Eyck's *Giovanni Arnolfini and his Wife*, Edouard Manet's *Dejeuner sur l'herbe*, and Willem de Kooning's *Woman I*. *I Gets a Thrill Too When I Sees de Koo* (1978) superimposes a smiling Aunt Jemima face on de Kooning's figure. This alteration and the title, influenced by Mel Ramos's 1977 pinup version of the same painting, serves as a critique of both de Kooning's and Ramos's paintings and highlights the problematic representation of women in the history of art and popular culture.

By the mid-1980s, Colescott continued to utilize a figurative-narrative style infused with humor, but his paintings became more gestural. Additionally, the content of his work moved toward universal concepts and allegorical subjects based on religion, mythology, and literature. Through these changes Colescott questioned broader concepts such as beauty and power to delve deeper into issues like race. His work began to find a wider audience in the late 1980s with the emergence of neo-expressionist artists such as Sandro Chia and Francesco Clemente, who used an expressive figurative style in combination with explorations of identity, and appropriation artists like Jeff Koons and Sherrie Levine, who questioned fixed meaning and notions of authority and genius. Similarly, 1980s multiculturalism opened a dialogue on issues of identity, including African-American identity. Of course, Colescott's forays into these arenas predated the current trends by about ten years. Following his individual approach to art rather than the popular modes of postmodernism, Colescott's paintings from the late 1980s turned towards the moral and ethical issues surrounding artistic production through a heightened use of color and painterly gestures.

In the 1990s, Colescott continued to reflect on the role of the artist in American society along with concerns of race, gender, and power. In 1997, Colescott was selected to represent the United States with nineteen paintings from the previous ten years at the 47th Venice *Biennale*, making him the first African-American artist to have a solo exhibition at the *Biennale*. Colescott continues to live and work in Tucson where he is Emeritus Professor of Art at the University of Arizona.

—Sharon Matt Atkins

COLLINS, James

Nationality: British. **Born:** In Northampton, England, 1939; emigrated to United States, 1970. **Education:** Studied at St. Martins School of Art, London, 1959–63; Hornsey School of Art, London, 1963–64. **Career:** Independent artist; lives and works in both New York and London. Taught at London College of Printing, High Wycombe and Epsom Schools of Art, England, 1964–69; taught at New York University, 1970–75; taught at Hartford University, Connecticut, 1976–77. **Awards:** Prix de Rome Scholarship (Painting), 1964; National Endowment for the Arts Fellowship, 1977.

Individual Exhibitions:

1975 Galleria Francoise Lambert, Milan
Galerie Gaetan, Geneva
John Gibson Gallery, New York
Patrick Verelst Gallery, Antwerp
1976 Galleria Il Capricorno, Venice
York University Gallery, Toronto
Galleria Renzo Spagnoli, Florence
Galerie Folker Skulima, Berlin
Galleria Peirgriorgio Firinu, Turin
Galleria Pasquale Trisorio, Naples
Galerie Ingrid Oppenheim, Cologne
1977 Palomar College, San Marcos, California
Galerie Isy Brachot, Brussels
Galleria Pasquale Trisorio, Naples
Galerie Tanit, Munich
Akron University, Ohio
Galerie Krinzinger, Innsbruck, Austria
Galeria Stampa, Basel
Western Front Gallery, Vancouver
Galleria Cicconi, Macerata, Italy
Galleria Ginevra Grigolo, Bologna
A Space Gallery, Toronto
Galleria Arte Verso, Turin
University of California at Santa Barbara
1978 Arnolfini Gallery, Bristol
Institute of Contemporary Arts, London
University of Wisconsin, Menomonie
Emily Carr College, Vancouver
1979 Washington Project for the Arts, Washington, D.C.
University of South Florida, Tampa
University of Iowa, Iowa City
Max Protetch Gallery, New York
Galleria Paolo Tonin, Turin
Glen Hanson Gallery, Minneapolis
University of Florida, Miami

Galleria Arte Borgogna, Milan
1980 Pallazzo dei Diamanti, Ferrara, Italy
Galerie Linssen, Bonn
Galleria Arte Borgogna, Milan
Galleria Pasquale Trisorio, Naples
L'Incontro Galleria d'Arte, Imola, Italy
1981 Hans Redman Gallery, Berlin
''123'' Gallery, Antwerp
Galleria Anna D'Ascanio, Rome
Mississippi Museum of Art, Jackson
1982 Anne van Horenbeeck Gallery, Brussels
Galleria Paolo Tonin, Turin
Galleria Pasquale Trisorio, Naples

Selected Group Exhibitions:

1976 *Foto & Idea,* Comune di Parma, Italy
1977 *Documenta 6,* Kassel, West Germany
Contemporary Figuration, Ohio State University, Columbus
1979 *AA on Paper,* University of North Carolina, Greensboro
Concept, Narrative, Document, Museum of Contemporary Art, Chicago
1980 *Presences: The Figure and Man-Made Environments,* Albright College, Reading, Pennsylvania
Refigurations, Max Protetch Gallery, New York
1981 *Genius Loci,* Ferrara, Italy
1982 *Facons de Peindre,* Chalon-sur-Saone, France

Publications:

By COLLINS: Book—*Narrative Art,* exhibition catalog, Brussels, 1974. **Articles—**''Things and Theories'' in *Artforum* (New York), May 1973; Pointing, Hybrids and Romanticism: John Baldessari'' in *Artforum* (New York), October 1973; ''Remarks on Romanticism'' in *Flash Art* (Milan), June 1975; ''The Importance of Not Being Earnest About Photography'' in *Skira 76,* Geneva 1976; The Rise of Europe'' in *Flash Art* (Milan), October 1981; ''Bald But Blonde: Notes of a Not-So-Gentle Cultural Chameleon—James Collins'' in *Flash Art (International Edition),* no. 30, October/November 1986.

On COLLINS: Books—*6 Years* by Lucy Lippard, New York 1973; *Europa/America* by Achille Bonita Oliva, Milan 1979; *James Collins,* edited by Giancarlo Politi and Helana Kontova, with an essay by Sarah Kent, Milan 1978. **Articles—**''The Semantics of Concept Art'' by Gopnik in *Artscanada* (Toronto), April 1970; review by David Bourdon in the *Village Voice* (New York), September 1975; review by Romano Giachetti in *L'Express* (Paris), October 1975: ''The Boulevard of Soho Dreams'' by Mona Da Vinci in the Soho *Weekly News* (New York), 18 September 1975; review by Walter Robinson in *Art in America* (New York), December 1975; ''The Erotic and the Didactic'' by Robert Pincus-Witten in *Arts Magazine* (New York), January 1976; ''James Collins Voyeuredonista'' by Angelo Calabrese in *Documentioggi* (Naples), March 1976; ''Photography: A Specific Communication for Artistic Research'' by Ilaria Bignamini in *Flash Art* (Milan), June 1976; ''New Movements in Conceptual Art'' by Margaret Sheffield in *Studio International* (London), November/December 1976; ''James Collins'' by Werner Lippert in *Kunstforum* (Mainz), June 1976; ''James Collins Double Portraits'' by Margaret Sheffield in *Artforum* (New York), April 1977; review by A. A. Bronson in *Artscanada* (Toronto), May 1977; review by Anne-Sargent Wooster in the *New York Arts Journal,* no. 15, 1979; review by John Russell in the *New York Times,* July 1979; ''An Art Collector's Dream'' in *Wildlife Art* (Edina), vol. 15, no. 7, December 1996.

*

My 1973 essay, ''Things and Theories'' was really a corrective attack against the extremes of conceptual art and a defense of then beleagured ''painting,'' and I say painting in inverted commas because at that time I was interested in the idea of promoting a very open kind of situation, and I've always looked at my photographs as just one kind of painting, but I must say recently I'm interested in painting in perhaps more traditional terms—some kind of mark.

When I started photographs in late 1968, it was an avant-garde activity—at least as a kind of painting. The history of people using photographs in fine arts was short, and photographs seemed a new area not explored. I didn't know the history of photography, and it was an interesting new way of working. Now the whole art world is full of people using photographs, and it no longer has those avant-garde ramifications. This is one complaint. My other complaint is the limited visual things you can do with photographs; it's a kind of ''a priori'' activity. You set the situation up, you photograph it, you can manipulate the photograph afterwards to some extent, but you can't manipulate it the same way you can manipulate a drawing or an image. What I like about drawing particularly, for example, is that it's a kind of fiction where you can bring together very disparate elements, whereas in a photograph you have to actually get hold of the elements and then photograph them. It's a different kind of activity.

I started off as a painter, and I still consider myself a painter. And what's interesting about painting is its limitations: All you have is a surface and marks to move people with. That's it! What puts me off about so many other art areas is the apparatus. Never could I imagine myself being a filmmaker just because of the Mickey Mouse organization stuff. You have to orchestrate the lives of 50 people for six months, raise money, etc., etc. Activities interesting perhaps sociologically—but they are not my main interests. I'm an image maker: My passion is making images to move people. Photography was merely a way to make those images quickly. Now I'm finding that photographs do move people, but they move them within certain limitations.

You run into big problems any time you make marks on canvas, however you make those marks. I'm interested in trying to find the visual equivalent to the speed of photography—images almost like handwriting, having some reference to the world, having the speed of handwriting, but getting information across quickly. I wouldn't mind mixing the sensuousness of Morris Louis with the subjects of Richard Pryor.

—James Collins

* * *

James Collins's work is comprehensively characterized by the intermixed use of the media, from abstract and figurative painting to conceptual photography. Even if the changes of media are often caused by external events and by artistic fashions, there is a persisting continuity around which his work is built. He has in fact been concentrating for the past ten years on a single theme, ''Watching

Women,'' a sort of intellectual voyeurism which is represented in a number of variations: on the beach, on the grass, in bed or in the artist's studio, but always as observer. The only one who can observe the girl is in fact someone at the front, in front of the picture.

Voyeurism, which the artist says has been a lifetime obsession, has since 1973 become his basic poetry.

As early as 1969–71 his ''Introduction Pieces'' were based on his introducing himself to unknown people whom he had met casually. All that was necessary was to change the situation from one of sexual indifference to one of eroticism to bring about the different result. His photography, which looked at first like something from the newspapers or the police records, turned into a photography directly executed by the artist, becoming much more evocative and esthetic.

Later works left simple photo-documentation even further behind and moved towards formal solutions, such as the segmentation of the panels, symmetry between objects and person (i.e. the woman and the artist), the use of a monochromatic background, and painting. The situations photographed became increasingly artificial and composed until they formed a meticulous design.

The pastels of girls or of voyeuristic situations done in the last years are mostly based on photographic portraits collected from time to time during a journey, in the street or in an art gallery. Certain details in the figure, standing out against the monochrome field, are highly focused so as to emphasize the eroticism of the model. The extremely elegant and controlled painting, like that of Balthus or Klossowski, whom Collins greatly admires, with its startling contrasts of light and colour, succeeds in maintaining the tension of an aloof eroticism.

—Helena Kontova

COLOMBO, Gianni

Nationality: Italian. **Born:** Milan, 1 January 1937. **Education:** Self-educated in art. **Career:** Began artwork using various materials, 1954; produced first monochrome reliefs, 1958; first changeable objects, 1959. Co-founder, with Giovanni Anceschi, Davide Boriani and others, Gruppo T, 1959. Organized Nouvelle Tendance, 1963. Lecturer, Faculty of Architecture, University of Berlin, 1982. **Awards:** Gold Medal for Industrial design, *13th Triennale,* Milan, 1964; Gold Medal, *14th Covegno Internazionale Artisti,* Rimini, 1964; First Prize, *34th Biennale,* Venice, 1968; Giolli Prize, 1980; First Prize, *Kunst am Bau* Bau competition, West Berlin, 1981. **Died:** 1993.

Individual Exhibitions:

1960 Galleria Pater, Milan
1965 Galleria Vismara, Milan
Galleria La Salita, Rome
1966 Gallerie Loehr, Frankfurt
1967 Galleria del Deposito, Genoa
Galleria Flaviana, Locarno, Switzerland
1968 Galleria Schwarz, Milan
Galleria L'Attico, Rome
Galleria Guida, Naples
Biennale, Venice
Gallerie Tony Gerber, Berne
Studio di Informazione Estetica, Turin
1969 Galleria del Leone, Venice
1970 Studio Marconi, Milan
Kunstlersiedlung Halfmannshof, Gelsenkirchen, West Germany
Galerie Suzanne Bollag, Zurich
Galleria La Città, Verona
1971 Galerija Suvermeni Umjetnosti, Zagreb
Galleria La Polen, Genoa
Neue Galerie am Landesmuseum, Graz, Austria
Plus-Kern, Ghent (with Morellet and Stein)
1972 Galerie Thomas Keller, Munich
Palazzo dei Diamanti, Ferrara, Italy
Galerie M, Bochum, West Germany
Galerie Suzanne Bollag, Zurich
1973 Sineron, Brescia, Italy
Studio Marconi, Milan
Studio Casati, Merate, Italy
1974 Galerie Swart, Amsterdam
Galerie Lydia Megert, Berne
Centro Serre Ratti, Como, Italy
1975 Studio V, Vigevano, Italy
Galleria Giuli, Lecco, Italy
Galerie Media, Neuchatel, Switzerland
Galleria Uxa, Novara, Italy
Studio Marconi, Milan
Galerie Muller-Roth, Stuttgart
Stadtisches Museum, Leverkusen, West Germany
1976 Kunsthalle, Baden-Baden, West Germany
Kunsthalle, Kiel, West Germany
Galleria G7, Bologna
Galleria A, Parma, Italy
1977 Studio Marconi, Milan
Galleria Solferino, Milan
1978 Arte Struktura, Milan
Galleria 2000, Bologna
Centro Culturale, Fara d'Adda, Italy
1981 Van Abbemuseum, Eindhoven, Netherlands
Studio Grosetti, Milan
Centro Serre Ratti, Como, Italy
1982 Nuovo Spazio Metropolitano, Milan
Raad Galerie, West Berlin
1983 Galleria Civica d'Arte Contemporanea, Suzzara, Italy
1984 Padiglione d'Arte Contemporanea, Milan
Italian Pavilion, *XLI Biennale,* Venice
1985 Galleria Pero, Milan
Galerie Hoffman, Friedberg, West Germany
Galerie Scholler, Dusseldorf

Selected Group Exhibitions:

1960 *Contemporary Italian Art,* Institute of Design, Chicago
1965 *Licht und Bewegung,* Kunsthalles, Berne (toured Europe)
1966 *Kunst-Licht-Kunst,* Stedelijk van Abbemuseum, Eindhoven, Netherlands
1970 *Kinetic Art,* Hayward Gallery, London
1974 *Fotomedia,* Museum am Ostwall, Dortmund, West Germany

1976 *Biennale,* Sydney
1978 *Metafisica del Quotidiano,* Galleria d'Arte Moderna, Bologna
1980 *Pier and Ocean,* Hayward Gallery, London (travelled to the Rijksmuseum Kroller-Muller, Otterlo, Netherlands)
1983 *Electra,* Musée d'Art Moderne de la Ville, Paris
1987 *Mathematik in der Kunst,* Wilhelm-Hack-Museum, Ludwigshafen, West Germany

Collections:

Galleria Nazionale d'Arte Moderna, Rome; Museo Sperimentale, Turin; Museum des 20. Jahrhunderts, Vienna; Städtisches Museum, Bochum, Germany; Museum of Modern Art, New York; Columbia University, New York.

Publications:

By COLOMBO: Books—*Miriorama I,* Milan 1960; *After Structures,* exhibitions catalog, Genoa 1967; *Lo Spazio dell'Immagne,* Foligno, Italy 1967. **Articles—**''Im Elastichen Raum'' in *Trigon,* exhibition catalog, Graz 1967; ''Spazioelastico-Ambiente'' in *Studio V* (Vigevano, Italy), 1975. **Films—***Vobulazione e Bieloquenza Neg,* with Vicento Agnetti, Milan 1970; *Arte programmata,* Milan 1972.

On COLOMBO: Books:—*Nature and Art of Motion* by Gyorgy Kepes, New York 1965; *Gianni Colombo* by Gillo Dorfles, Rome 1965; *Rapporto 60* by Maurizio Fagiolio dell'Arco, Rome 1966; *L'Art Cinetic* by Frank Popper, Paris 1967; *Constructivism: Origins and Evolution* by George Rickey, New York 1967; *Gianni Colombo,* exhibition catalog by Guido Balla, Venice, 1968; *Gianni Colombo,* exhibition catalog, by Rolf Wedewer, Gelsenkirchen, West Germany 1970; *Gianni Colombo,* exhibition catalog by Guilio Carlo Argan, Ferrara, Italy 1972; *Gianni Colombo,* exhibition catalog by Antije von Graevenitz, Eindhoven, Netherlands 1981; *Gianni Colombo,* exhibition catalog by Marco Meneguzzo, Suzzara, Italy 1983; *Gianni Colombo,* exhibition catalog by Jean Louis Scheffer, Milan 1984. **Articles—**''Art and Design: Joe and Gianni Colombo: Gallery of Modern and Contemporary Art, Bergamo; Exhibit'' by Francesco Pagliari in *Domus,* no. 770, April 1995; ''Joe and Gianni Colombo, Designer and Architect'' by Fulvio Irace, Stephano Casciani and Alessandro Mendini in *Arbitare,* no. 339, April 1995; ''The Colombo Brothers'' by Lisa Licitra Ponti in *Domus,* no. 771, May 1995; ''I Colombo'' by Giorgio Verzotti in *Art and Text,* no. 51, May 1995.

*

To construct is that particular dimension of a work (not only the work of art) that implies a coming into contact with the manifold inventory of materials. It is work carried out through a 'culture of materials' which technology continuously develops through time. It is the universe of technologies that consigns to us not only materials but also the ways to put them together in order to concretise 'the construction'.

Once we understand art as something to do with construction, materials, and technology as the 'working supervisor', does the presentation of such materials represent a 'technological universe'?

As far as the relationship with the technological is concerned, in many cases it is just a question of multiplying the usage of different techniques toward concentrating on the opposite ends of technology—i.e., the impact it has on man's behavior. My art means placing the notion of behavior within the operation of environmental planning, where 'environment' is understood as the visualization of the specific condition of planning itself.

—Gianni Colombo

* * *

Gianno Colombo's earliest works (1954) were nonfigurative, 'multimaterial' (sort of collage) pieces. From these he went on to make monochrome pieces, reliefs composed of rectangles arranged vertically in rows. By 1959 these had become mobile. They were either moveable by the spectator or on their own account. In either case they moved rhythmically, the rectangular elements coming out and going in: *In and Out or Pulsating Structures.* This was the beginning of his interest in kinetic art. In that year he became a founder member of Gruppo T and four years later the group joined the Nouvelle Tendence.

The next year, 1960, he began to make 'Fluid Structures'. These consisted of moving, transparent plastic tapes that writhed within an enclosed space. In 1964, like many of the Nouvelle Tendence, he turned to optical-kinetic and enviromental art. This began with his 'Roto-optic' work which produced strange moving luminous forms, like X-rays of organs pulsating with life. Pulsation and rhymthmic, organic movement means much to him and he finds various ways of displaying it.

But his most adventurous light structures were his 'Elastic Spaces', begun in the mid-1960s. These consisted of cubes of elastic florescent cords, subdivided into regular sections and lit by ultra-violet light. The cords either distort themselves rhythmically or are distorted by the spectator walking through them.

In the 1970s Colombo turned from kinetic and light works to lopsided structures of various kinds, mostly interiors. These seem to have been inspired by a house built by Buster Keaton in the film *A Week* (1920). Everything about the house—roofs, windows, the door—is askew, but it holds together; and Keaton stands back, saw in hand, looking at it admiringly. Colombo sometimes uses pillars arranged at odd angles and looking like the ruins of an ancient city that had been struck by an earthquake. At other times he constructs interiors rather on the lines of the rooms constructed by the psychologist, Ames *(Ames room)*, to illustrate illusions of space. The floor is tilted, possibly the ceiling also; in consequence the walls are inevitably out of kilter. He calls these works 'Topestesia' or 'Architettura Cacogonimetrica', which loosely translates as fruitfully bad architecture, but the words themselves are lopsided and strictly meaningless.

These are among the most original works to come from Colombo's fertile imagination. The source of inspiration he acknowledges, but he alone exploited it. Hitherto he had tended to swim with the tide that flowed: kinetic-optical-light art. But in these later works he has struck out on his own. Not that he was not original when swimming with the tide. He invariably was. Three things seem to obsess him: A striving for purity and clarity of expression, characteristic of the Nouvelle Tendence; a feeling for and love of the fluctuations and pulsations and the rhythms of living forms; and the oddness of our perception of the world around us.

—D. C. Barrett

COLVILLE, Alex

Nationality: Canadian. **Born:** David Alexander Colville in Toronto, Ontario, 24 August 1920. **Education:** Under Stanley Royle, at Mount Allison University, Sackville, New Brunswick,1938–42, B.F.A. 1942. **Military Service:** Served in Canadian Infantry, 1942–46: Lieutenant, then Captain; War artist, 1944–46. **Family:** Married Rhoda Wright in 1942; children: Graham, John, Charles, and Ann. **Career:** Independent painter, Nova Scotia, since 1963. Commissioned to design Canadian centennial coinage, 1967. Assistant to associate professor, Mount Allison University, 1946–63. Visiting artist, University of California of Santa Cruz, 1967–68; Kunstler program, West Berlin, 1971. **Member:** Canada Council, 1966–72. **Awards:** Dunn International Award, 1963; Canada Council Award, 1975; Officer, 1967, and Companion, 1982, Order of Canada, Privy Councillor, 1993. Honorary degrees: Trent University, Peterborough, Ontario; Dalhousie University, Halifax, Nova Scotia; Simon Fraser University, Burnaby, British Columbia; University of Windsor, Ontario; Acadia University, Wolfville, Nova Scotia; Mount Allison University, Sackville, New Brunswick; Memorial University, St. John's, Newfoundland; University of Calgary; University of King's College, Halifax; University of Manitoba, Winnipeg; Bishop's University, Quebec; Nova Scotia College of Art and Design, Halifax. **Agent:** Mira Godard Gallery, 22 Hazelton Ave. Toronto M5R 2E2, Ontario, Canada. **Address:** Box 550, Wolfville, Nova Scotia, Canada.

Individual Exhibitions:

1951 New Brunswick Museum, St. John
1953 Hewitt Gallery, New York
1955 Hewitt Gallery, New York
1963 Banfer Gallery, New York
1966 Hart House, University of Toronto
1969 Kestner Gesellschaft, Hannover
1970 Marlborough Fine Art Gallery, London
1971 *Serigraphs,* University of Moncton, New Brunswick (toured Canada,1971–73)
1976 Fischer Fine Art, London
Norman Mackenzie Art Gallery, Regina, Saskatchewan
Lynnwood Arts Center, Simcoe, Ontario
1977 *Bilder und Zeichnungen 1970–1977,* Kunsthalle, Dusseldorf (travelled to Fischer Fine Art, London)
1978 Mira Godard Gallery, Toronto
1983 Art Gallery of Ontario, Toronto
Staatliche Kunsthalle, West Berlin
Museum Ludwig, Cologne
1984 Museum of Fine Arts, Montreal
Dalhousie Art Gallery, Halifax, Nova Scotia
Vancouver Art Gallery, British Columbia
Exhibition Hall, Beijing, China
1985 University of Hong Kong
Teien Art Museum, Tokyo
Canada House, London
1992 Drabinsky Gallery, Toronto
1993 *Selected Drawings,* Mount Allison University, Sackville
1994 *Graphics, 1955–1993,* Carleton University, Ottawa
Paintings, Prints, Processes, Museum of Fine Arts, Montreal
1999 *Alex Colville,* Mira Godard Gallery, Toronto
2000 *Alex Colville: Milestones,* National Gallery of Canada

Selected Group Exhibitions:

1964 *Canadian Painting,*Tate Gallery, London
1967 *Statements: 18 Canadian Artists,* Norman Mackenzie Art Gallery, Regina, Saskatchewan
1973 *Kunst nach Wirklichkeit,* Kunstverein, Hannover (toured Europe)
Ekstrem Realisme, Louisiana Museum, Humleback, Denmark
1974 *Hyperréalists Américains/Réalistes Européens,* Centre National d'Art Contemporain, Paris (toured Europe)
1975 *Realismus und Realitadt,* Kunsthalle, Darmstadt
Der Einzelne und die Masse, Städtische Kunsthalle, Recklinghausen, West Germany
1976 *Aspects of Realism,* Rothman's of Pall Mall travelling exhibition, Stratford Art Gallery, Ontario (toured Canada, 1976–78)

Collections:

National Gallery of Canada, Ottawa; Art Gallery of Hamilton, Ontario; Art Gallery of London, Ontario; Montreal Museum of Fine Arts; New Brunswick Museum, St. John; Beaverbrook Museum, Fredericton, New Brunswick; Museum of Modern Art, New York; Kestner Gesellschaft, Hannover; Museum Boymans-van Beuningen, Rotterdam; Centre National d'Art Contemporain, Paris; Nova Scotia Art Gallery, Halifax.

Publications:

On COLVILLE: Books—*Statements: 18 Canadian Artists,* exhibition catalog, Regina Saskatchewan 1967; *Neue Formen des Bildes* by Udo Kultermann, Tübingen, 1969; *The Art of Alex Colville* by Helen J. Dow, Toronto 1972; *Neue Formen des Realismus* by Peter Sager, Cologne 1973; *Der Neue Realismus* in *Amerika* by Linda Chase, Berlin 1973; *High Realism in Canada* by Paul Duval, Toronto 1974; *Hyperréalistes Américains/Réalistes Européens,* exhibition catalog, Paris 1974; *Colville* by David Burnett, Toronto 1983; *Alex Colville: The Observer Observed* by Mark Cheetham, 1994; *Alex Colville Paintings, Prints and Processes, 1983—1994* by Philip Fry, Montreal 1994; *A Biographical Sketch of Alex Colville* by J.R.C. Perkin, Hantsport, Nova Scotia 1995; *Colville* by Tan Kaijun and Jiang Dake, Shanghai 2000. **Articles—**''Realism, Surrealism and Celebration: The Paintings of Alex Colville in the National Gallery of Canada'' by Patrick Hutchings in *National Gallery of Canada Bulletin* (Ottawa), vol. 4, no. 2, 1966; ''For Real'' by Robert Melville in *New Statesman* (London), January 1970; ''Alex Colville'' by Peter Kipphoff in *Die Zeit* (Hamburg), October 1970; ''Alex Colville as Image Maker'' by Helen J. Dow in *The British Journal of Aesthetics* (London), Summer 1972; ''Alex Colville: La Perfection dans le Realisme'' by Virgil G. Hammock in *Vie des Arts* (Montreal), Autumn 1976; ''Modes of Representational Art'' by Michael Greenwood in *Artscanada* (Toronto), December 1976/January 1977; ''Alex Colville'' by Jeffrey Meyers in *Modern Painters* (London), Autumn 2000.

* * *

Born in Toronto and brought up in the salty atmosphere of the Maritimes, Alex Colville studied at the Mount Allison University School of Fine Art until 1942, when he joined the Canadian Army. He served in Europe as a war artist, painting and drawing scenes and action in Belgium, Holland and Germany. On demobilization, Colville returned to Mount Allison as professor of painting, though now he paints only professionally.

Colville is a realist painter who aims at epitomising Jung's definition by attempting a synthesis of total experience. Details from life are observed and noted; then they are articulated within a setting composed for the purpose of making evident a sensation of fact.

''Magic Realism'' is the term that covers Colville's approach, but though it verges on a noncommital lack of emphasis common to Photo-Realism, its precise definition and lighting, together with the purposeful focus on individuals and objects, create an irresistible atmosphere of significance. The square of canvas reveals a segment of actuality, often of the most commonplace aspect, and it paradoxically endows this chosen viewpoint with a singular intensity. Unlike Impressionism, his intention is not to capture light in the division of the spectrum. Colville imposes a universality of tone across the whole field of vision.

Often there is an implied aura of loneliness akin to some of Andrew Wyeth's works such as ''Christina's World.'' ''Hound in a Field'' of 1958 shows Colville's grasp of drama in the selection of an incident or a moment of time, freezing it within the framework of the canvas. Sometimes the realism is as airless as a still life *trompe l'oeil,* but the scale again distorts its presence.

The freezing may take place on a large oil-on-masonite, such as ''Elm Tree at Horton Landing'' of 1965, representing its own environmental tragedy. This once handsome tree standing alone is now flawed and damaged, some of its branches stricken and bleached. It nonetheless retains some original dignity in its upright stance. Viewed from ground level, it becomes more than a tree preserved for its lost beauty. It has the pathetic note of a graceful creation singled out for accidental violation; whether by vandalism or act of God is unknown. The effect, however, is endowed with Colville's unique paint touch, immaculate in strength and balance of tone.

Often the import is meteorological. The cold sterility of a winter day clarifies a landscape of snow in one even tone of whiteness, shadowed and pocked by changes of contour. The sky is a level blue, and the chill almost strikes our bones. In the human figures, the blood seems frozen too, as they stand immersed in suspended action. One aspect runs through Colville's painting; it is the stillness of the final scene. No words pass between his people, mute in the trivial commonplaces of the day, silent evidence of the unremarkable, miraculously immobilized in clinical antiseptic objectivity.

—G. S. Whittet

CONNER, Bruce

Nationality: American. **Born:** McPherson, Kansas, 18 November 1933. **Education:** Kansas City Art Institute, Missouri, summer, 1951; Wichita State University, Kansas, 1951–52; University of Nebraska, Lincoln, B.F.A. 1956; Brooklyn Museum Art School (with Reuben Tam), 1956–57; University of Colorado, Boulder, 1956–57. **Family:** Married Jean Sandstedt in 1957; son: Robert. **Career:** Artist working in many media, including painting, print making, conceptual art, watercolor, assemblage artwork, photography, drawing, and wood engraving collages, since the 1940s; independent filmmaker, since 1957. Taught 8mm filmmaking, California College of Arts and Crafts, Oakland, 1965; taught life drawing, 1966–67, and painting and sculpture, 1972, at the San Francisco Art Institute; taught ''The Art of Assemblage'' at UCLA Extension, 1973; taught beginning and advanced painting, San Jose State University, California, 1974; taught filmmaking, San Francisco State University, 1976. **Awards:** Ann Bremer Award, San Francisco Art Association, 1958; second prize, Church Art Today, San Francisco Episcopal Diocese, 1960; first prize, Art Competition of the National Council of Churches, 1960; Neallie Sullivan Award, San Francisco Art Association, 1963; Ford Foundation Fellowship, 1964; Tamarind Lithography Workshop Fellowship Grant, 1965; Copley Foundation Award 1965; Gold Medal, *Sesta Biennale D'Arte,* San Marino 1967; National Endowment for the Arts Grant 1973; American Film Institute Grant, 1974; Francis Scott Key Award, 1975; Guggenheim Fellowship, 1975; citation in film, Brandeis University Creative Awards, Waltham, Massachusetts, 1979; named honorary doctor of fine arts, San Francisco Art Institute, 1987; Maya Deren Award for Independent film, American Film Institute, 1988. **Agent:** c/o Smith/Anderson Gallery, 200 Homer St., Palo Alto, California 94301, U.S.A.

Individual Exhibitions:

1956 Rienzi Gallery, New York
1958 East West Gallery, San Francisco
Designers Gallery, San Francisco
1959 Spatsa Gallery, San Francisco
1960 Alan Gallery, New York
Batman Gallery, San Francisco
1961 Alan Gallery, New York
1962 Batman Gallery, San Francisco
Glantz Gallery, Mexico City
Antonio Souza Gallery, Mexico City
1963 Neallie Sullivan Award Show, San Francisco
Wichita Art Museum, Kansas
Alan Gallery, New York
Swetzoff Gallery, Boston
1964 Batman Gallery, San Francisco
Alan Gallery, New York
George Lester Galleria, Rome
Robert Fraser Gallery, London
1965 University of British Columbia Art Gallery, Vancouver
Rose Art Museum, Brandeis University, Waltham, Massachusetts
Galerie ''J'', Paris
Alan Gallery, New York
1966 Quay Gallery, San Francisco
Western Association of Art Museums (travelling show)
1967 Institute of Contemporary Art, Philadelphia
San Francisco Art Institute
1971 San Francisco Art Institute
Molly Barnes Gallery, Los Angeles
Reese Palley Gallery, San Francisco
1972 Reese Palley Gallery, San Francisco
Martha Jackson Gallery, New York

Willis Gallery, San Francisco
Texas Gallery, Houston
Nicholas Wilder Gallery, Los Angeles
1973 Texas Gallery, Houston
1974 Quay Gallery, San Francisco
Tyler Art Museum, Texas
Smith/Andersen Gallery, Palo Alto, California
DeYoung Museum, San Francisco (retrospective; toured United States)
1977 Denver Art Museum, Colorado
University of Colorado, Boulder
1980 North Point Gallery, San Francisco
1983 Fraenkel Gallery, San Francisco
1984 Smith/Andersen Gallery, Palo Alto
1985 *Bruce Conner Photograms,* The Art Museum Association of America (traveling exhibition)
1986 Smith/Andersen Gallery, Palo Alto
Fraenkel Gallery, San Francisco
1987 University of California Art Museum, Berkeley
Pink and Pearl Gallery, San Diego
1988 56 Bleecker Gallery, New York
1989 Smith/Andersen Gallery, Palo Alto
1990 Michael Kohn Gallery, Santa Monica, California
1991 Smith/Andersen Gallery, Palo Alto
Michael Kohn Gallery, Santa Monica
1992 San Francisco Museum of Modern Art
Feigen Gallery, Chicago
Curt Marcus Gallery, New York
Smith/Andersen Gallery, Palo Alto
1993 Zabriskie Gallery, New York
Gallery Paule Anglim, San Francisco
Kohn/Abrams Gallery, Los Angeles
1996 *15 Beautiful Mysteries,* Curt Marcus Gallery, New York
Susan Inglett Gallery, New York
1997 Kohn Turner Gallery, Los Angeles
Wichita Art Museum, Kansas
1999 *Looking for Mushrooms: Bruce Conner Drawings 1960 to 1968,* Kohn Turner Gallery, Los Angeles
2000 *2000 BC: The Bruce Conner Story Part II,* M.H. de Young Memorial Museum, San Francisco (traveling exhibition)

Selected Group Exhibitions:

1961 *The Art of Assemblage,* Museum of Modern Art, New York
1963 *IV Biennale Internationale d'Art Contemporanea,* Republic of San Marino
1964 *Annual Exhibition: Contemporary American Sculpture,* Whitney Museum, New York
1967 *American Sculpture of the Sixties,* Los Angeles County Museum of Art
1969 *Human Concern/Human Torment,* Whitney Museum, New York
1972 *Poets of the Cities: New York and San Francisco, 1950–1965,* Dallas Museum of Fine Arts (travelling exhibition)
1973 *Family Show of Work by Robert, Jean and Bruce Conner,* Jacqueline Anhalt Gallery, Los Angeles
1975 *Poets of the Cities,* Museum of Fine Arts, Dallas (travelled to San Francisco Museum of Modern Art, and the Wadsworth Atheneum, Hartford, Connecticut)
1976 *California Painting and Sculpture: The Modern Era,* San Francisco Museum of Modern Art (travelling exhibition)
1979 *Biennial Exhibition,* Whitney Museum, New York
1981 *Remember It's Only Art,* Civic Arts Gallery, Walnut Creek, California
1986 *Seven Artists in Depth: The Creative Process,* San Francisco Museum of Modern Art
1987 *Made in U.S.A.,* University of California Art Museum, Berkeley
1988 *Different Drummers,* Hirshhorn Museum, Washington, D.C.
1993 *Talking Heads: Conversations,* Jan Turner Gallery, Los Angeles
1994 *Crossing the Lines,* Barn Gallery, Middle Tennessee State University, Murfreesboro, Tennessee
1997 *1997 Whitney Biennial,* Whitney Museum of American Art, New York

Collections:

Museum of Modern Art, New York; Whitney Museum, New York; Los Angeles County Museum of Art; San Francisco Museum of Modern Art; Oakland Art Museum, California; University of Art Museum, University of California, Berkeley; Norton Simon Museum of Art, Pasadena, California; Rockhill Nelson Gallery, Kansas City, Missouri; Art Institute of Chicago; Centre Georges Pompidou, Paris; Guggenheim Museum, New York; Rose Art Museum, Waltham, Massachusetts; Waltham Addison Gallery, Andover.

Publications:

By CONNER: Articles—''Bruce Conner Makes a Sandwich'' in *Artforum* (New York), September 1967; ''Bruce Conner: A Discussion at the 1968 Flaherty Film Seminar'' in *Film Comment* (New York), No. 4, 1969; interview with Elizabeth Armstrong in *October* (Cambridge), no. 70, Fall 1994; interview with Paul Cummings in *Drawing,* vol. 16, September/October 1994; interview with John Yau in *On Paper,* vol. 2, no. 5, May/June 1998; interview with Juan Rodriguez in *Artweek,* vol. 31, no. 7/8, July/August 2000. **Films—***A Movie,* 1958; *Cosmic Ray,* 1961; *Looking for Mushrooms,* 1961–67; *Report,* 1963–67; *Vivian,* 1964; *Breakaway,* 1966; *White Rose,* 1967; *Permian Strata,* 1969; *5 X Marilyn,* 1973; *Crossroads,* 1976; *5:10 to Dreamland,* 1976; *Valse Triste,* 1977; *Mongoloid,* 1978; *America Is Waiting,* 1981. **Books illustrated—***The Adventures of a Novel in Four Chapters* by Michael McClure, San Francisco, Limestone Press, 1991.

On CONNER: Exhibition catalogs—*Bruce Conner,* New York 1960; *Bruce Conner,* New York 1965; *Bruce Conner* (with text by Thomas Garver), Waltham, Massachusetts 1965; *Bruce Conner* (with text by Joan C. Siegfried and Stephen S. Prokopoff), Philadelphia 1967; *Assemblage in California: Works from the Late 50s and Early 60s* (with texts by John Coplans, Walter Hopps, Philip Leider, and Hal Glicksman), Irvine, California 1968; *Bruce Conner: Drawings 1955–1975,* San Francisco 1974; *Bruce Conner* by Anthony Reveaux, St. Paul, Minnesota 1981; *Bruce Conner: Assemblages, Paintings,*

Drawing, Engraving Collages (foreword by Dennis Hopper; interview by Robert Dean), Michael Kohn Gallery, 1990; *Bruce Conner: Films* (with text by Christoph Setele, Anthony Reveaux, Scott MacDonald, Robert A. Haller, James Peterson, and others), Lucern, Switzerland, 1992; *2000 BC: The Bruce Conner Story Part II,* with text by Peter Boswell, Joan Ruthfuss, and Bruce Jenkins, Minneapolis 1999. **Articles—**''Bruce Conner'' by Cecile McCann in *Artweek* (Oakland, California), March 1974; ''The Artist as Dactylographer'' by Peter Selz in *Art in America* (New York), July/August 1974; ''Bruce Conner's Cinematic Drawings'' by A. Flanagan in *Artweek,* November 1974; ''Fallout: Some Notes on the Films of Bruce Conner'' by W. Moritz and B. O'Neill in *Film Quarterly* (Berkeley, California), summer 1978; ''A Tribute to Bruce Conner'' by Tony Reveaux in *Artweek,* vol. 20, 23 September 1989; ''Bruce Conner: The Gnostic Strain'' by Griel Marcus in *Artforum International,* vol. 31, December 1992; ''Documents for a Secret Tradition: Bruce Conner & His Inkblot Drawings'' by Barry Schwabsky in *The Print Collector's Newsletter,* vol. 24, November/December 1993; ''Bruce Conner'' by Kristin M. Jones in *Artforum International,* no. 34, March 1996; ''Bruce Conner'' by Alexi Worth in *Art News,* no. 95, March 1996; ''Up Above My Head: Consciousness and Habitation in the Graphic Work of Bruce Conner'' by Faye Hirsch in *Parkett,* no. 48, 1996; ''The Bruce Conner Story Continues'' by John Bowles in *Art Journal,* vol. 59, no. 1, Spring 2000; ''Keeping Up with Conner'' by Michael Duncan in *Art in America* (New York), vol. 88, no. 6, June 2000.

* * *

Bruce Conner has long been acknowledged as a seminal force behind the collage and assemblage movement of the early 1960s. Yet, he is probably one of the most misunderstood and underexposed artists of his generation. Although drawing has been his primary form of artistic expression since 1964, he is still recognized mainly for his collages and small sculptures and for the films that grew out of his collage sensibility. At times, even they are overlooked because of their iconoclastic content or dismissed on the basis of their heterodoxy, when they could best be appreciated in stylistic terms—for example, ''Last Supper'' (1961), or ''Couch'' (1963), two sculptures whose mordantly satirical subject matter obscured their fundamental contribution to an expressionistic tradition that reaches back to Bosch, Bruegel, Goya, Daumier and, more recently, George Grosz.

In 1974 and 1975, in recognition of Conner's skill with the medium, San Francisco's de Young Museum organized a traveling exhibition of his drawings, highlighting the various factors that influenced their development over a period of some seventeen years. Unfortunately, by focusing entirely on the drawings instead of showing them in the context of his other works, and despite a comprehensive catalog essay stressing the connection, the exhibition isolated the drawings visually instead of emphasizing their relationship to other aspects of the artist's repertoire. Since then, he has been included in many museum group shows but, save for a limited retrospective at the North Point Gallery (San Francisco), the totality of his oeuvre has never been fully explored or documented. As a result, the significance of his contribution to the history of American art in the realm of mysticism has been greatly diluted. For, by taking a separative rather than combinative approach, curators have missed the opportunity to demonstrate both the correlation that exists between his handling of various media and the continuity of his style over a period of some twenty-five years.

That mysticism is at the core of Bruce Conner's vision is obvious from the entire body of his drawings and from the photograms and paintings of the 1970s. Drawn from such variant sources as religious symbolism, ethnic mythology, and private spiritual experience, their iconography often alludes to the cosmos—to distant stars and galaxies whose suggested forms seem to be undergoing visionary transmutations into geometrical and metaphysical shapes. The mystical implications of the collages and assemblages of the 1960s are not as readily apprehensible. More intellectual than visual, their content is based upon philosophically esoteric notions that portend cataclysmic events and challenge our concepts of God, life, and death.

The seeds of an expressionist revival scattered in the late 1970s throughout the art scene of Western Europe and the United States are currently being nurtured by the depressing financial condition of the world. Talented young artists anxious to ride the wave of avant-garde breakthroughs are, in increasing numbers, trading ultimate objectivity for emotionally charged subjectivity. But it takes time and experience to become a master—someone who not only understands the lessons of the past, but who also has the ability to press those lessons into service of the present. Bruce Conner is such an artist. A veteran expressionist, he has demonstrated his ability to grow and change within the continuity of a highly mystical vocabulary. In his custody, the future of the medium is in good hands.

—Andrée Maréchal-Workman

Though he is certainly most famous for his assemblages and films, in the 1980s and 1990s Conner returned to two media for which he is less well known: collage and drawing. His engraving collages, a medium he had begun exploring as early as 1959, have often been compared to similar collages produced by Max Ernst in the early decades of the twentieth century. These surrealistic collages include scenes of biblical, philosophical, and mystical imagery, many of which are believed to be complex allegorical self-portraits. Conner also resurrected his ''Star'' drawings from the 1970s, produced by looping a felt-tip pen on a sheet of paper leaving thousands of tiny white points, the *horror vacui* of which revealing a sense of obsession, pessimism, and doom. Conner produced what one critic called ''fantastic nocturnal landscapes'' by incorporating photocopies of the ''Star'' drawings into his engraving collages.

Though significantly less dense than his previous line and ''Star'' drawings, his intricate and highly detailed inkblot drawings, which he began producing in the mid-1990s, present symmetrical, nonhierarchical images resembling ''mysterious hieroglyphics, or images of insects, or collections of objects.'' Conner denies any relationship between his inkblots and those designed by Rorschach, whose blots were presented as homogenous images, whereas Conner, through multiplicity and an all-over composition, ''neutralizes the propensity of any one blot to become a complete organism generating definitive interpretations.''

Most of Conner's energies in the 1980s, however, were spent working on an unfinished documentary about a gospel quartet called The Soul Stirrers, titled *By and By*. The documentary, through which Conner sought to promote the influence of gospel on pop music, is composed much like his assemblages and collages, with low production values and a ''jarring rawness.'' In the 1990s, Conner re-edited and reprocessed two of his films, *Television Assassination* and *Looking for Mushrooms*, as well as adding or replacing sound tracks. In 1999, Conner was given his first major retrospective, *2000 BC: The*

Bruce Conner Story Part II, organized by the Walker Art Center in Minneapolis.

—Bradley Bailey

CONSAGRA, Pietro

Nationality: Italian. **Born:** Mazara del Vallo, Sicily, in 1920. **Education:** Studied at the Accademia di Belle Arti, Palermo, 1938–44. **Career:** Lives and works in Rome, since 1944; founder, with Piero Dorazio, Achille Perilli, Giulio Turcato and others, Forma I, Rome, 1947. **Awards:** Second Prize, *Biennale del Bronzetto,* Padua, 1955; Metallurgica Prize, *Bienal,* Sao Paulo, 1955; Premio Einaudi, *Biennale,* Venice, 1956; Belgium Critics Prize, 1958; First Prize for Sculpture, *Bienale,* Venice, 1960. **Agent:** Marlborough Galleria d'Arte, via Gregoriana 5, 00187 Rome. **Address:** Via Cassia 1162, 00189 Rome, Italy.

Individual Exhibitions:

1947 Galleria Mola, Rome
1948 Galleria Sandri, Venice
1949 Galleria del Secolo, Rome
1951 Galleria del Pincio, Rome
1953 Galleria del Naviglio, Milan
1956 *Biennale,* Venice
1958 Palais des Beaux-Arts, Brussels
Galleria Tartaruga, Rome
1959 Galerie de France, Paris
Bienal, Sao Paulo
1960 *Biennale,* Venice
1961 Galleria Blu, Milan
Mostra di Disegni di Pietro Consagra, Galleria Odyssia, Rome
Galerie Charles Lienhard, Zurich
1962 Staempfli Gallery, New York
Bonino Gallery, Buenos Aires
1963 Pace Gallery, Boston
1964 Odyssia Gallery, New York
1965 Galleria dell'Ariete, Milan
1966 Marlborough Galleria d'Arte, Rome
1967 Galleria dell'Ariete, Milan
Boymans van Beuningen Museum, Rotterdam
Marlborough-Gerson Gallery, New York
1969 Marlborough Galleria d'Arte, Rome
Galleria dell'Ariete, Milan
Galleria Rampa, Naples
Grafica Romera, Rome
1971 Galleria dell'Ariete, Milan
1972 Marlborough Galleria d'Arte, Rome
Galleria Peccolo, Livorno
1973 Galleria Editalia, Rome
Palazzo dei Normanni, Palermo
Qui Arte Contemporanea, Rome
Salone Annunciata, Milan
1974 Galleria del Bibliofili, Milan
Marlborough Galleria d'Arte, Rome
Galleria Ferrari, Treviglio, Italy
1975 Galleria Annunciata, Milan
1976 Marlborough Galleria d'Arte, Rome
1977 *Disegni 1945–1977,* Galleria Stendhal, Milan
Museo di Castelvecchio, Verona
Galleria Il Disegno, Rome
Studio L'Arco, Rome
1981 Galleria Editalia, Rome
Palazzo dell'Arengo, Rimini
Museo d'Arte Grafica, Gibellina, Italy
1984 Bottega dell'Incisione, Turin
1985 Qui Arte Contemporanea, Rome
1996 *Consagra: Scultura e Architettura,* Palazzo Brera, Milan
1998 Institut Mathiuldenhohe, Darmstadt, Germany
2000 *Pietro Consagra,* Credito Valtellinese Galery, Palazzo Sertoli, and Palazzo Pretorio, Sondrio

Selected Group Exhibitions:

1946 *Group Exhibition,* Rome
1950 *Biennale,* Venice
1953 *Junge Italienische Kunst,* Kunsthaus, Zurich
1959 *European Art Today,* Minneapolis Museum of Art (toured the United States)
1964 *Decade 1954–1964,* Tate Gallery, London
1966 *Moderne Kunst aus Italien,* Museum am Ostwall, Dortmund, West Germany
1971 *New Italian Art 1953–71,* Walker Art Gallery, Liverpool
1977 *Disegni 1945–77,* Galleria Scheiwiller, Milan
1981 *Omaggio a Serpotta,* Galleria dell-Arco, Rome
1983 *Giornale di Manovra,* Galleria della Cometa, Rome
1984 *Crossings: Lines in the New Contemporary Italian Art,* Rocca Paolina, Perugia

Collections:

Galleria Nazionale d'Arte Moderna, Rome; Tate Gallery, London; Musée Royaux des Beaux-Arts, Brussels; Centre Georges Pompidou, Paris; Middelheim Sculpture Park, Antwerp; Gallerija Suvremene Umjetnosti, Zagreb; Museo d'Arte Moderna, Sao Paulo; Museum of Modern Art, New York; Guggenheim Museum, New York; Art Institute of Chicago; Carnegie Institute, Pittsburgh; Museum of Fine Arts, Minneapolis.

Publications:

By CONSAGRA: Books—*Necessita della Scultura,* Rome 1952; *L'Agguato c'e,* Rome 1960; *LaCitta Frontale,* exhibition catalog, Rome, Milan and Bari, Italy 1969; *Poema Frontale,* Milan 1973; *Fotografia L'Arte,* Milan 1973; *Mallumore,* Milan 1974; *Welcome to Italy,* Milan 1974; *La Ruota Quadrata,* Milan 1976; *Approssimativamente,* Milan 1977; *Vita Mia,* Milan 1980. **Articles—** "Teorema dell Scultura" in *Forma I* (Rome), March 1947; "Disegno" in *Traits* (Paris), no. 6, 1947; "Mangeri" in *Noi Donne* (Rome), July 1951; "Scultura" in *Domus* (Milan), no. 2, 1951; "Plastico" in *Spazlo* (Milan), December 1951; "In Difesa dell'Astratismo" in *Calendario del Popolo* (Milan), September 1951; "Design for Sculpture" in *Contemporary Drawings from 12 Countries,* exhibition catalog, Chicago 1952; "Autoritratto" in *Arte Libera* (Naples),

October 1952; ''La Fiamma Issidrica'' in *Paese Sera* (Rome), March 1953; ''Der Eiserne Arm'' in *Junge Italinische Kunst,* exhibition catalog, Zurich 1953; ''Inchieste sull-Arte Contemporanea'' in *Il Nuovo Corriere* (Florence), February 1954; ''Colloqui'' in *Paese* (Rome), January 1955; ''Uno Scultore guidica l'Architettura'' in *L'Architettura* (Rome), May 1956; ''Intervista a Pietro Consagra,'' with Lonzi, in *Pietro Consagra,* exhibition catalog, Milan and Rome 1967; ''Una Lezione di Scultura'' in *Civilta delle Macchine* (Rome), vol. XVIII, 1970; ''L'Oggetto'' in *Consagra,* exhibition catalog, Milan 1971; ''Avere di me'' in *Consagra,* exhibition catalog, Rome 1972; statement in *Pietro Consagra,* exhibition catalog, Rome 1974; ''Io Consagra'' in *Bolaffiarte* (Turin), October 1980.

On CONSAGRA: Books—*Pietro Consagra* by Umbro Apoliono, Rome 1956; *Mostra di Disegne Pietro Consagra,* exhibition catalog by Marisa Volpi Orlandini, Rome 1961; *Pietro Consagra* by Giulio Carlo Argan, Neuchâtel, Switzerland 1962; *Consagra,* exhibition catalog by Giovanni Carandente and others, Palermo 1973; *Pietro Consagra* by Marisa Volpi Oraldini, Milan 1977; *Pietro Consagra: Disegni 1945–1977,* Milan 1977; *Pietro Consagra,* exhibition catalog, by Guido Ballo, Rimini, Italy 1981; *Consagra,* exhibition catalog with essay by Lorenza Trucchi, Rome 1985. **Articles—**''Sicily'' by Vivana Trapani in *Designer's Journal,* no. 68, June 1991; '''Down with Modern Architects': Urban Renaissance: Second Architecture Triennale: Consagra, Sculpture and Architecture: Various Locations, Bologna'' by Maria Giulia Zunino in *Abitare,* no. 354, September 1996; review in *Sculpture* (Washington, D.C.), vol. 17, no. 8, October 1998.

* * *

One of Pietro Consagra's distinctions is that, unlike most Italian sculptors of his generation, he originates from Sicily, arriving in Rome at the age of twenty-four; it is however interesting to note that the painter Guttuso, his senior by eight years, was also born in Sicily. In some senses the term sculptor does not quite fit Consagra; he is a maker of icons rather than an investigator of three-dimensional space, a manufacturer of screens rather than sculptural volumes. Whilst there may be some original preoccupation with Sicilian Baroque architecture or the richly decorated mosaic walls of some of the island's famous chapels, Consagra's more obvious influence derives from Cubist definition of space.

Consagra belongs to the important post-war movement in Italian sculpture which sought a new language, a renewal in the face of the relaxed inheritance of classical forms which marked the older generation, Marini, Manzu, Greco, or the achievements of the Futurists. It is one of the fascinations of modern Italian art that in addition to brilliant craftsmanship, inventive form, striking intelligence and undeniable elegance and taste, many of the most gifted artists have felt the need to adopt mannerisms or styles which suggest violence or self-hatred. It is as though they distrust the very gifts which Italian civilization and taste have given them; hence the violation of space and form in Fontana, the torn and scratched techniques of Burri, the satire of Baj, the aggressive calligraphy of Capogrossi, Colla's spiky gestures, and the variations of bruised bronze surfaces or penetrated images found in Cavaliere, Arnaldo Pomodoro and Mastroianni.

Consagra is of this school. His standing screens, often brightly colored, are images of aggression and destruction, giving the impression of torn fabric, scarred wood, or disintegrated matter. The starting point is a simple square, manipulated out of all recognition. Consagra is a brilliant technician, working in every variety of material: bronze casting, welded steel, oxidizing, aluminium forms either cut into strange, oriental patterns, or elaborating a Calderesque hanging manner, each misshapen petal suspended by wire. Consagra is more organic than his fellow Italians, sometimes building up webbed or comb-like structures, patterned on some natural system of growth or development. His famous polemical manner—the author of numerous essays and manifestos on sculpture—is evident in the sculptures, and saves them from the more obviously over-designed decorativeness of some of his compatriots.

—Charles Spencer

COPLEY, William Nelson (CPLY)

Nationality: American. **Born:** New York City, 24 January 1919. **Education:** Philips Academy, Andover, Massachusetts, until 1938; Yale University, New Haven, Connecticut, 1938–42. **Military Service:** Served in the United States Army, in Africa, Sicilly, and Italy, 1942–46. **Family:** Married Chuang-Hua. **Career:** Began painting in 1946; director, with John Ployardt, Copley Galleries, showing the work of Magritte, Cornell, Matta, Tanguy, Man Ray, and Ernst, Beverly Hills, California, 1946–48; lived in Paris, associating with Max Ernst, Man Ray, and Marcel Duchamp, 1951–64; returned to the United States and lived in New York since 1964. **Agent:** Phyllis Kind Gallery, New York and Chicago. **Died:** Sugar Loaf Key, Florida, 7 May 1996, of complications from a stroke.

Individual Exhibitions:

1947 Royer's Bookstore, Los Angeles
1953 Galerie Nina Dausset, Paris
1954 Galerie Monte Napoleone, Milan
1956 *Peintures Récentes,* Galerie du Dragon, Paris
Iolas Gallery, New York
1958 Iolas Gallery, New York
1959 Galerie Furstenberg, Paris
1960 Galleria Naviglio, Milan
Galleria Cavallino, Venice
Iolas Gallery, New York
1961 *Recent Paintings by CPLY,* Institute of Contemporary Arts, London
Galleria Schwarz, Milan
Galerie Iris Clert, Paris
1963 *Paintings,* Hanover Gallery, London
Les Suffragettes Erotiques, Galerie Iris Clert, Paris
Iolas Gallery, New York
1964 David Stuart Gallery, Los Angeles
1965 Louisiana Gallery, Houston
Southwestern College, Chula Vista, California
Allan Frumkin Gallery, Chicago
1966 *Projects for Monuments to the Unknown Whore,* Galerie Iolas, Paris (travelled to the Iolas Gallery, New York)
Entertainment for Men, Stedelijk Museum, Amsterdam
1967 *Homage to Robert W. Service,* Iolas Gallery New York (travelled to the Galerie Iolas, Paris)
1968 Bodley Gallery, New York

1969 Merida Gallery, Louisville, Kentucky
1970 Galerie Neuendorf, Cologne
Project for a Dictionary of Platitudes, Galleria Iolas, Milan (travelled to Iolas Gallery, New York)
CPLY, *Magritte and Brauner,* Louisiana Gallery, Houston
1972 Galerie Springer, West Berlin
Galerie Aspects, Brussels
David Stuart Gallery, Los Angeles
Mail Order, Galleria Iolas, Milan (travelled to the Iolas Gallery, New York)
1973 CPLY, Galeria Anselimo, Turin
1974 X-Rated, New York Cultural Center
Western Songs, Onnasch Gallery, New York (retrospective; travelled to Moore College of Art, Philadelphia, and Galerie Onnasch, Cologne)
Galerie Iolas, Paris
Nounes, Galleria Ioals, Milan (travelled to the Iolas Gallery, New York)
1975 Erik Nord Gallery, Nantucket, Massachusetts
1976 Iolas Gallery, New York
1978 Iolas Gallery, New York
Galerie Fassbinder, Munich
Galerie Springer, West Berlin
Galerie Zwirner, Cologne
1979 Iolas Gallery, New York
Reflections on a Past Life, Institute for the Arts, Rice University, Houston
1980 Iolas Gallery, New York
Museum of Fine Arts, St. Petersburg, Florida
Kunsthalle, Berne (travelled to the Centre Georges Pompidou, Paris, and the Stedelijk Van Abbemuseum, Eindhoven, Netherlands)
1981 Iolas Gallery, New York
Sierra Nevada Museum of Art, Reno
Colorado Springs Fine Arts Center
1982 Phyllis Kind Gallery, Chicago
1983 Reinhard Onnasch Ausstellugen, West Berlin
1985 Galerie Susanna Kulli, St. Gallen, Switzerland
1987 Kewenig Galerie, Frechen-bachem, Germany
Phyllis Kind Gallery, New York
1988 Galerie 1900/2000, Paris
1990 Phyllis Kind Gallery, Chicago
Galerie Klewan, Munich
1991 *CPLY: William N. Copley,* David Nolan Gallery, New York (catalog)
Phyllis Kind Gallery, New York and Chicago
Galerie Fred Jahn, Munich
1993 Galerie Zell am See, Schloss Rosenberg, Austria
Techniques of Fornication, Haus Am Lutzowplatz, Berlin (catalog)
1994 Nolan/Eckman Gallery, New York
1995 *William N. Copley, Bilder 1951–1994,* Kestner-Gesellschaft, Hannover (retrospective)
Galerie Lelong, Zurich
1996 Nolan/Eckman Gallery, New York
1997 Ulmer Museum, Ulm
Galerie Fred Jahn, Munich
1998 Galerie Lelong, Zurich
Galerie Onrust, Amsterdam
Nolan/Eckman Gallery, New York
1999 *William N. Copley,* Galerie Fred Jahn, Munich (catalog)
L.A.C., Lieu d'Art Contemporain, Sigean, France (catalog)
2000 *Copley Collects Copley,* Phyllis Kind Gallery, New York

Selected Group Exhibitions:

1962 *Collage out of California,* Pasadena Art Museum, California
L'Antagonisme de l'Objet, Musée des Arts Decoratifs, Paris
1964 *New Directions in American Painting,* Brandeis University, Waltham, Massachusetts
Surrealism: Sources/History/Affinities, Galerie Charpentier, Paris
1966 *Surrealist Exhibition,* University of California at Santa Barbara
1972 *Humor in Art,* New School for Social Research, New York
1973 *Erotic Art,* New School for Social Research, New York
1975 *3 Generations of American Nudes,* New York Cultural Center
1977 *Artists' Rendering of Paintings,* Brera Museum, Milan (travelled to Le Louvre, Paris)
1999 *Bad—Bad: That is a Good Excuse,* Staatliche Kunsthalle Baden-Baden, Germany

Collections:

Museum of Modern Art, New York; Whitney Museum, New York; New York Cultural Center; Philadelphia Museum of Art; Art Institute of Chicago; Los Angeles County Museum of Art; Tate Gallery, London; Centre Georges Pompidou, Paris; Stedelijk Museum, Amsterdam; Nagaoka City Museum, Japan.

Publications:

By COPLEY: Books—*The Evil Story of My Life,* New York 1965; *CPLY: Project for a Dictionary of Platitudes,* exhibition catalog, Milan and New York 1970; *Notes on a Project for a Dictionary of Ridiculous Images,* Cologne and New York 1972; *Variations on a Theme by Francis Picabia,* New York 1979. **Articles—**''Introducing the Paintings of Serge Charchoune'' in *Artnews* (New York), March 1960; ''Man Ray: The Dada of Us All'' in *Portfolio* (New York), Winter 1963; interview with Alan Jones in *Flash Art (International Edition),* no. 140, May/June 1988; interview with Alan Jones in *Art Press,* no. 254, February 2000.

On COPLEY: Books—Copley: *Peintures Récentes,* exhibition catalog with text by Patrick Waldberg, Paris 1956; *William Copley: 470, Mostra del Cavallino,* exhibition catalog with text by Roberto Rossellini, Venice 1960; *History of Surrealist Painting* by Marcel Jean, New York 1960; *Recent Paintings* by CPLY, exhibition catalog, London 1961; *Bill Copley,* exhibition catalog with text by Roland Penrose, Milan 1962; *W.N. Copley: Paintings,* exhibition catalog with text by Robert Melville, London 1963; *Les Suffragettes Erotiques de Bill Copley,* exhibition catalog with texts by Marcel Duchamp and others, Paris 1963; *CPLY: Projects for Monuments to the Unknown Whore,* exhibition catalog with text by Julien Levy, Paris and New York 1966; *Copley: Entertainment for Men,* exhibition catalog with text by Roland Renrose, Amsterdam 1966; *CPLY: Homage to Robert W.*

Service, exhibition catalog, New York and Paris 1967; *Pop Art* by Lucy Lippard, New York 1967; *CPLY: Mail Order,* exhibition catalog, Milan and New York 1972; *CPLY,* exhibition catalog with text by Janus, Turin 1973; *CPLY: Nounes,* exhibition catalog, Milan and New York 1974; *CPLY: X-Rated,* exhibition catalog with an introduction by Sam Hunter, New York 1974; *CPLY: Western Songs,* exhibition catalog, Cologne 1974; *CPLY: Reflections on a Past Life,* exhibition catalog, Houston 1979; *William N. Copley,* exhibition catalog with texts by Johannes Gachnang and Marianne Schmidt, with an introduction by R.H. Fuchs, Berne 1980; *William N. Copley,* exhibition catalog with essay by Ilonah Lindenburg, West Berlin 1983; *William N. Copley: Heed Greed Trust Lust: Bilder=Paintings, 1951–1994,* exhibition catalog, Hannover 1995; *William N. Copley: True Confessions,* exhibition catalog, New York 1997. **Articles—** Obituary in *Art in America* (New York), June 1996.

* * *

Though born a full generation after the original Surrealists, William Copley—a.k.a. CPLY—called himself a Surrealist, lived as a Surrealist, painted as a Surrealist, in fact, was a Surrealist. At first glance this may seem a retrogressive role for a post–World War II American artist. But the important paradox in Copley's career is that he saw and, without chauvinism, *admitted* the influence of classic European Surrealism on American art while simultaneously in his own work anticipated some of the directions in which American art has grown from these historic roots.

As early as 1946 Copley (with a brother-in-law) was running a Surrealist gallery in Los Angeles. There, the first Surrealist they met was Man Ray, who said, "There's more Surrealism rampant in Hollywood than all the Surrealists could invent in a lifetime." Through Man Ray, Copley met Duchamp in New York, Max Ernst in Arizona, and gradually other surviving Dadaists, Surrealists, and modern masters. He bought their work—first for the gallery, then for himself, for pleasure and as a sort of visual reference library. At the same time, he taught himself to paint innocently and playfully, absorbing the Surrealists' improvised, free-associative spirit and abandoning (as they did) aesthetic and moral prejudices.

Copley's theme was and is sex—sex in its most cheerful, anxiety-free form, dirty but not filthy, erotic but not pornographic. By the late '40s he developed an iconography of curvy, cartoon-like women who cavort through his paintings, often being chased, kissed, ogled, mounted, etc. by a small man in a derby who is not only closely related to Copley himself but to the Keystone Cops and other heroes of silent film, and to the bourgeois males in the work of Magritte. Authority, when it appears, is an equally playful and cartoon-like French cop (un flic). As Duchamp said, "Cops pullulate, Copley copulates." A painting like Copley's "Capella sextina" (1961) makes Delacroix's "Le bain turque" look spare and monogamous.

While raiding the zaniness of comic strips and Hollywood (Mae West, W.C. Fields, and the Marx Brothers are other Copley favorites), he also reinvented popular images from advertising (THINK), newspapers (the crossword puzzle), Robert Service's ballads (the Yukon bars and whorehouses), patriotic symbols (the flag, the Liberty Bell), slogans (BEAT YALE, Copley's university), etc. All of his very large production of drawings and paintings are flat, non-illusionistic, "American." As Julien Levy said, Copley was "a Pop of Pop in 1948." That's true, and so is the fact, which Copley is the first to acknowledge, that the grandparents of Pop (and Abstract Expressionism) were Dada and Surrealism. In recent years, Copley has shown regularly at the Phyllis Kind Gallery in New York City and Chicago, in addition to travelling shows in the United States and abroad.

—B. H. Friedman

CORNEILLE

Nationality: Dutch. **Born:** Cornelis Guillaume Beverloo, in Liege, Belgium. 3 July 1922; emigrated to the Netherlands 1940; subsequently naturalized. **Education:** Studied drawing at the Rijksakademie, Amsterdam, 1940–43, etching, under S. W. Hayter, at Atelier 17, Paris, 1953, and ceramics, with Mazzotti, at Albisola Mare, Italy, 1954–55. **Career:** Independent painter and graphic artist, Amsterdam, 1943–53, and in Paris since 1950; co-founder, Dutch Experimental Group, Amsterdam 1948, and COBRA (Copenhagen-Brussels-Amsterdam) group, with Appel, Jorn, Constant, Alechinsky, Pedersen, etc., 1949–51; worked in Mallorca and Cadaques, Spain, 1961–66. **Awards:** Guggenheim Netherlands Prize, 1956; Graphics Prize, Ibiza, 1972, **Agent:** Galerie Krikhaar, Spuistraat 330, 1012 VX Amsterdam, Netherlands. **Address:** 58 Rue Vieille du Temple, 75003 Paris, France.

Individual Exhibitions:

1946 Het Beerenhuis, Groningen, Netherlands
1947 Europai Iskola, Budapest
1950 Galleri Birch, Copenhagen
1951 Martinet en Michels, Amsterdam
Galerie t'Venster, Rotterdam
1953 Kunstkabinett Horemans, Antwerp
1954 Galerie Colette Allendy, Paris
1956 Galerie Craven, Paris
Palais des Beaux-Arts, Brussels
Stedelijk Museum, Amsterdam
Stedelijk Museum, Schiedam, Netherlands
1957 Museum of Curacao, Dutch Antilles
1959 Galerie Espace, Haarlem, Netherlands
Galerie Le Gendre, Paris
1960 *Tekening van Corneille,* Stedelijk Museum, Amsterdam
1961 Galerie Ariel, Paris
Haags Gemeentemuseum, The Hague
Stedelijk Van Abbemuseum, Eindhoven, Netherlands
Brook Street Gallery, London
K.B. Gallerie, Oslo
1962 Lefebre Gallery, New York
Galerie Mathias Fels, Paris
1963 Galleria del Naviglio, Milan
Musée d'Antibes, France
Gallerie Blanche, Stockholm
Galerie Le Point Cardinal, Paris
Galerie Creuzevalt, Paris
1964 Galeria Souza, Mexico City
Lefebre Gallery, New York
Galleria Schwarz, Milan, Italy
1965 Cultureel Centrum, Hilversum, Netherlands
Galerie Stangl, Munich
Lefebre Gallery, New York

1966 Stedelijk Museum, Amsterdam
Kunsthalle, Dusseldorf
Galeria Relevo, Rio de Janeiro
1967 Galerie Kaleidoskoop, Ghent
Lefebre Gallery, New York
1968 Galerie Espace, Amsterdam
Galerie Casse, Paris
1969 Galerie Stangl, Munich
Galeria Ivan Spence, Ibiza, Spain
1970 Galerie Ariel, Paris
Galerie La Pochade, Paris
Lefebre Gallery, New York
Galeria Ivan Spence, Ibiza, Spain
1971 Galerie Rive Gauche, Paris
Palais Walderdorf, Trier, West Germany
Galeria Ivan Spence, Ibiza, Spain
Galleria d'Arte, Trieste
Kunstverein, Salzburg
Lefebre Gallery, New York
1972 Galleria 70, Potenza, Italy
Schillerhof, Graz, Austria
1974 Galleria La Medusa, Rome
The Quartier Rose of Amsterdam, Lefebre Gallery, New York
Galerie Montjoie, Brussels
Palazzo Buonacorsi, Macerata, Italy
Palais des Beaux-Arts, Chaleroi, Belgium
Retrospective Tentoonstelling: Corneille, Museum voor Schone Kunsten, Ghent
Studio Erre, Rome
Galleria La Medusa, Rome
1975 Galleria del Cavallino, Rome
Petite Galerie, Rio de Janeiro
Galerie l'Oeil de Boeuf, Paris
Meseu de Arte Moderno, Sao Paulo
Galerie Espace, Amsterdam
Institut Neerlandais, Paris
Galleria Gian Ferrari, Milan
Galerie Krikhaar, Amsterdam
Galleria M. Arte, Milan
Galleria C.M., Rome
Carnegie Institute, Pittsburgh
Lefebre Gallery, New York
Galleria Gregory, Rome
1976 Galleri Documenta, Copenhagen
Centro d'Arte, Sarono, Italy
Galerie Riis, Trondheim, Norway
Galerie Fabien Boulakia, Paris
Galerie Moderne, Silkeborg, Denmark
Lefebre Gallery, New York
1977 Galerie Espace, Amsterdam
Galleri Documenta, Copenhagen
Maison Bernard, Caracas, Venezuela
1978 Galerie Orientale, Geneva
Galleri Kanda Malare, Jonkoping, Sweden
Galleria Bonaparte, Milan
1979 Galerie Fabien Boulakia, Paris
Galerie L'Oeil de Boeuf, Paris
New Gallery, Jabbeke, Belgium
Galerij Maeyaert, Ostend, Belgium
1980 Galerie Delta, Rotterdam
Galerie Michel Casse, Paris
Galerie Reflex, Amsterdam
1981 Galerie Fabien Boulakia, Paris
Galleri Hammerlunds, Osla
Galerie de Kuil, The Hague
Galerie Jas, Utrecht, Netherlands
1982 Galerie Krikhaar, Amsterdam

Selected Group Exhibitions:

1946 *Junge Schilders,* Stedelijk Museum, Amsterdam
1949 COBRA, Stedelijk Museum, Amsterdam
1951 *Salon de Mai,* Musée d'Art Moderne, Paris
1953 *Bienal,* Sao Paulo
1956 *Carnegie International,* Carnegie Institute, Pittsburgh
1959 *Documenta 2,* Kassel, West Germany (and *Documenta 3,* 1964)
1964 *Guggenheim International,* Guggenheim Museum, New York
1973 *Hommage à Picasso,* Kestner-Gesellschaft, Hannover
1978 *Cobra 1948–78,* Statens Museum for Konst, Copenhagen
1983 *Cobra 1948–51,* Musée d'Art Moderne, Paris
1999–2000 *From Kandinsky till Corneille: Linoleum in Art during the 20th Century,* Cobra Museum, Amstelveen

Collections:

Stedelijk Museum, Armsterdam; Stedelijk Museum, Schiedam, Netherlands; Stedelijk Van Abbemuseum, Eindhoven, Netherlands; Palais des Beaux-Arts, Brussels; Musée de Liege, Belgium; Collection de la Ville de Paris; Museum Charlottenborg, Copenhagen; Nasjonalgalleriet, Oslo; Brooklyn Museum, New York; Museum of Djakarta, Indonesia.

Publications:

By CORNEILLE: Book—*Journal de la Tour,* Paris 1981.

On CORNEILLE: Books—*Corneille,* exhibition catalog, with text by Charles Estienne, Paris 1954; *Corneille,* exhibition catalog, with text by Edouard Jaeger, Amsterdam 1956; *Tekening van Corneille,* exhibition catalog, with text by Imre Pan, Amsterdam 1960; *Corneille,* exhibition catalog, with texts by Lawrence Alloway and E.L.L. de Wilde, London 1961; *Corneille,* exhibition catalog, with text by A. M. Hammacher, The Hague 1961; *Corneille,* exhibition catalog, with text by Karl K. Ringstrom, Oslo 1961; *Corneille,* exhibition catalog, with text by Lawrence Alloway, New York 1961; *Corneille,* exhibition catalog, with text by Willem Sandburg, New York 1964; *Corneille,* exhibition catalog, with text by Werner Haftmann, New York 1965; *Corneille,* exhibition catalog, with text by Max Loreau, Amsterdam 1966; *Corneille,* exhibition catalog, with an interview by Christian Bussy, New York 1967; *Ariel 17: Corneille,* exhibition catalog, with texts by D. H. Lawrence, Octavio Paz and Malcolm Lowry, Paris 1970; *Corneille,* exhibition catalog, with text by Andre Laude, New York 1970; *Corneille,* exhibition catalog, with text by Gunnar Jespersen, New York 1971; *Hommage a Picasso,* exhibition catalog, with texts by Wieland Schmied, Werner Haftmann and Daniel H. Kahnweiler, Hannover 1973; *Corneille Le Roi—Image* by Andre Laude, Paris 1973; *Corneille et la Vie* by Elvirio Maurizi, Macerata, Italy 1974; *Corneille: The Quartier Rose of Amsterdam,* exhibition catalog, New York 1974; *Corneille,* exhibition catalog, with text by Elvirio Maurizi, Rome 1974; *Retrospective Tentoonstelling: Corneille,* exhibition catalog, Ghent 1974; *Corneille Aujourd'hui* by Andre Laude, Stockholm 1978; *Corneille* by Daniel Marchesseau, Paris 1980. **Articles—**''A Young Painter Named Corneille'' by Margot Welle in *Cimaise,* vol. 45, no. 256, October/December 1998; ''Numero Special Cobra: 7 Article Special Section'' in *Cimaise,* vol. 45, no. 256, October/December 1998.

* * *

COBRA was a nest of poets as well as artists. Corneille, a co-founder of the group, even if he is now wholly concerned with painting, injects into all his work the haunting suggestion of half-heard verse.

In his way he is a cyclic artist. Starting, as so many COBRA painters did, with what Lawrence Alloway has described as a ''hectic display of birds and moonheads in free-fall,'' he later departed from this style of imagery and concentrated on a series of compacted landscapes, pictures in which every tiny facet of color was bounded by a rugged edge of paint in contrasting tone. All these areas of color came together in a crowded amalgam like a delicious many hued fruit of random shape. These paintings were veritable banquets.

Yet about 15 years ago he came back to his figures and figuration, albeit retaining the painted outline of every fragment of the picture. Color areas increased in size. The sheer glutinous gravity of the landscapes was replaced by puckish humor. Mankind and the other creatures met once again, and they would be seen to be a in world which, if not real in the orthodox recognizable way, was still a world sprouting grass and trees and flowers under the canopy of a sky (however quirkily populated).

With or without COBRA affiliations, he stands out as an important artist of Northern Europe. His rejection of latin geometry and equal disinterest in a classical devotion to composition and style, has left him free to let the gamut of emotion in figures—or landscapes—run riot.

—Sheldon Williams

COSTA, Claudio

Nationality: Italian. **Born:** Tirana, Albania, 22 June 1942; moved with his family to Italy, 1944. **Education:** Studied architecture at the Polytechnico, Milan, 1963–65; studied engraving, Atelier Hayter, Paris, 1965–67. **Family:** Married Anita Zeiro in 1967; daughter: Marisol. **Career:** Independent artist, Genoa, since 1967. **Agents:** Galleria Massimo Valsecchi, Via S. Marta II, Milan; Galleria Unimedia, Vico dei Garibaldi I, Genoa. **Address:** Vico dei Garibaldi 1, 16123 Genoa, Italy.

Individual Exhibitions:

1969 Galleria La Bertesca, Genoa
1970 Galleria Modulo, Milan
1971 *Il Cervello sul Muro,* Modern Art Agency, Naples
Galleria Barozzi, Venice
Produzenten Galerie, Berlin
Tele Acide:Tele Acidate, Galleria Ferrari, Verona
1972 Galleria Duemila, Bologna
Galleria del Leone, Venice
1973 Galleria La Bertesca, Genoa
1974 *In the Company of the Human Brain and Prehistoric Man,* Neue Galerie, Aachen, West Germany
Galerie Klang, Cologne
Gallerie Nuovi Strumenti, Brescia, Italy
1975 Galleria Massimo Valsecchi, Milan
Foundation of the Museum of Anthropology, Monteghirfo, Genoa
1976 Galleria Arteverso, Genoa
Galleria Civica, Moderna, Italy
1977 Galleriaforma, Genoa
Studio di Via Crugoni, Genoa
Studio Torelli, Ferrara, Italy
1978 Galleria Arte Moderna, Portofino, Italy
Fabjbasaglia Galleria, Bologna
Galleria Arte Moderna, Alessandria, Italy
Galleria Nuova 13, Alessandria, Italy
1979 Galleria Nuovi Strumenti, Brescia, Italy
Galleria R. Rotta, Genoa
Galleria Unimedia, Genoa
Galleria Arco d'Alibert, Rome
Galleria II Luogo di Gauss, Milan
1980 Galleria De Amicis, Florence
Galleria II Gabbiano, La Spezia, Italy
Studio Cesare Manzo, Pescara, Italy
Salone Villa Romana, Florence
1981 Galleria Massimo Valsecchi, Milan
Galeria Andata-Ritorno, Geneva
1982 Galleria R. Rotta, Genoa
Galleria del Cavallino, Venice
Galleria Unimedia, Genoa
2000 *The Order of Things Upside Down,* Villa Croce, Genoa

Selected Group Exhibitions:

1969 *Rassegna Biennale,* Galleria di Tendenza, Modena, Italy
1973 *8th Biennale,* Paris
1974 *Spruensicheerung: Archaelogie und Erinnerung,* Hamburg and Munich
1976 *Identité: Identification,* CAP, Bordeaux
1978 *Arte e Cinema negli Anni 70,* Pinacoteca Civica, Ravenna, Italy
1979 *Metafisica del Quotidiano,* Galleria d'Arte Moderna, Bologna
1980 *Work in Process,*Galleria Arte Moderna, Genoa
1981 *Mythos and Ritual,* Kunsthaus, Zurich
1982 *Deserto,* Comune di Bergamo, Italy

Collections:

Neue Galerie, Aachen, West Germany

Publications:

By COSTA: Books—*Interpretazione Intera,* Genoa 1970; *Sintomi di un Lavoro,* Naples 1971; *Evolution: Involution,* Berlin and Genoa

1971; *Due Esercizi di Antropologia,* Brescia, Italy 1974; *Materiale e Metaforico,* Genoa 1979; *Sublimato Potabile,* Milan 1981.

On COSTA: Books—*Il Cervello sul Muro,* exhibition catalog, by Corrado Maltese, Naples 1971; *Tele Acide: Tele Acidate,* exhibition catalog, by Renato Barili, Verona 1971; *In the Company of the Human Brain and Prehistoric Man,* exhibition catalog, by Wolfgang Becker, Aachen, West Germany 1974; *Maori's Eyes Reflect the Latent Colours of the Forest* by Lorenza Trucchi, Rome 1974. **Articles—**''Metodologia del fare'' by Edda Gazzero in *Due Esercizi di Antropoliga,* Brescia, Italy 1974; ''Noi i Primitivi'' by Franco Torriani in *Gala* (Milan), February 1975; ''Il Museo Attivo delle Forme Inconsapevoli'' by Antonio Slavich in *Terzo Occhio,* vol. 18, no. 3, September 1992.

*

After a period of quite general activity, I turned to experimentation in the most difficult means of expressions: I slowly acquired the use of the ''substance'' as a means referring to itself and to its history. At that time I worked particularly on acid and acidified canvas.

In the meantime I had acquired a consciousness of a precise interest in man. I then ideally reconstructed the brain and the brain-pan, assimilating it to the polar skull-cap: this interest produced a big file of engravings and of other works.

My intention was the definition of an ''absolute'' geographical place as an ambiguous sign of existence. At that time I began to make use of chalk and afterwards of raw clay.

And I also worked, at that time, on research into man's memory. Works such as ''portraits by heart'' are of this category.

To be more exact, the work about man's evolution began in 1971. The book *Evolution: Involution* is of this period too. In it I also tried to present the idea, which I consider as fundamental, of recovering the past in a critical perspective: I started the work as research into the ''possibilities of space and of time'' which man has altered and lost during his evolution.

I studied pre-historic man, and I extracted and reproduced his peculiar traits. The casts of living persons, reconstructed according to the different periods of evolution, belong to this period. Then I studied primitive cultures that have preserved their original way of life and original tools. I have also been interested in man's ''habitat'', and some of my works have to be considered as studies of its changes.

Afterwards I recognized in the objects used by man signs of his way of life: The object reveals the relationship it has with man. The reconstructions on which I work or the appropriation of certain objects, inserted into the works, have precisely this purpose: They are a sign of reality; they propose it again as directly as possible.

In the work of reconstruction of the ''Active Museum of Monteghirfo'' it was my intention to collect and preserve in their original setting these objects of use-signs of a culture crushed by our consumer civilization.

Through this work I have identified things, persons, places, nuclei of families, the human aggregate and the environment—an exact and fated living mosaic. A certain number of document-works have been the results of this interest. In these works the materials used are photographic enlargements of environments or of objects and the objects themselves, which I have covered with clay.

I make use of anthropology as a means of knowing, but in my work it is only a tool aiding my intuition and emotion, which more decidedly are the means to urge me to operate and perform.

I believe that man, as all the things on earth, must be perceived in himself, in what he is in his totality beyond and outside scientific knowledge, which ends by concealing, by darkening our lives and the existence of things.

—Claudio Costa

* * *

In the making of a work, Claudio Costa behaves according to a methodology of ''doing,'' which is typical of that kind of contemporary conceptual art of which he is certainly a prominent practitioner. His work consists of perfectly identifiable images or objects, and they can be ''placed'' historically: They are documents (both real and faithfully reconstructed) of periods prior to contemporary life. Annotations explaining the cultural references are inserted into the works. Thus, the construction has form and functions as a channel for communication in a typically contemporary particularization of inquiry and expression.

However, this description is not sufficient to convey the fundamental characteristics of his art. Costa's work is not complete within itself or within the conceptual/rational reference in which it places itself as praxis (which is, more or less, the characteristic of the art-concept), for it is his intention to establish a relationship of knowledge as from the objects as facts. A relationship of this kind, as realized by Costa, does not exhaust itself in mere rational fact; it aims to go further, to become a kind of feedback on man facing his history—in a process analogous in its psychic mechanism to that of the emotional, nonformal genesis of classic expressionism.

As for the composition of the work: The chosen object—identified, indicated—is not used for the image it offers of itself, nor as an indication, a reference, of external reality to be analyzed for ethical or social values. Claudio Costa's ''object'' is, as it were, a laboratory finding, a cognitive moment in itself, to be regarded as such. In this sense the artist is a kind of anthropologist—not only in his interests but also in his methods. He reports his findings without loading them with symbols or myths; he does not report according to some basic cultural perspective.

His form of analysis is a propaedeutic methodology, and therefore neutral. And his work should be regarded in its entirety, so as to differentiate it from that of those contemporaries who also use historical, archaeological or anthropological findings in their works. For Costa such findings do not involve an occasional fact or a chance discovery of an unusual source of images and objects. Rather, they are the result of a constant ''observation'' of man and his natural habitat.

In the past Costa has edited the memory of man; he has proposed a relation with Cromus; he has analyzed ''lived'' space in relation to ''possible'' space. He has investigated the materiality, the availability, the modifications of habitat. From the relationship between man and space-time, as well as habitat, he has extracted the ''object''—an object which, however, does not report on itself but on something other than itself.

If for most artists one can speak of the object-as-code or the sign-as-code, for Costa one must speak perhaps of some primary, preliminary code in the sense that the significant means are external to the object and to its meaning. These ''means'' rest between object and observer, and they are constituted not as conventional signs but as evocations of a relationship. It is a code composed of object/man means, in which the sign is not the object nor the man but the action occurring between the two and modified (i.e., further codified) by the remote, philogenetic, and consequently, present experience. Costa uses this relationship as an art object, an intuitive means of knowledge, and, paradoxically, his work is characterized by the absence of real time: What he proposes is proposed always in the present, without temporal references.

Costa's analysis proceeds synchronically (that is, descriptively); the sign juxtapositions of another type which he also uses do not actuate a diachronism (that is, comparison with different systems) but are notes in a thought progress within the work, which thus are taken for single cognitive moments: he proceeds by simple elements to which he juxtaposes in a differentiated and conscious manner more complex cultural indications, which are, however, always placed *a posteriori* as regards the single cognitive moment. Thus Costa injects himself, by a route of his own, into the context of contemporary thought, which recognizes man's sources of knowledge as contingent and contained within himself as well as within his biologically delimited being. Through his work Costa creates a cognitive, intuitive/emotional, biologically recognizable moment.

—Edda Gazzerro

COTTINGHAM, Robert

Nationality: American. **Born:** Brooklyn, New York, 26 September 1935. **Education:** Studied at the Pratt Institute, Brooklyn, 1959–64, Associate Degree in Advertising Art 1962. **Military Service:** Served in the United States Army, in Com-Z Unit, Orleans, France, 1955–58: Specialist 3rd Class. **Family:** Married Jane Marie Weismann in 1967; daughters: Reid Ann, Molly Jane and Kyle Annie Bliss. **Career:** Art Director, Young and Rubicam Advertising Inc., New York, 1959–64, and Los Angeles, 1964–68. Independent painter, since 1968. Instructor, Art Center College of Design, Los Angeles, 1969–70. **Awards:** National Endowment for the Arts Grant, 1974. **Agent:** Forum Gallery, 745 5th Ave., New York, New York 10151, U.S.A. **Address:** P.O. Box 604, Blackman Road, Newtown, Connecticut 06470, U.S.A.

Selected Individual Exhibitions:

1968 Molly Barnes Gallery, Los Angeles
1969 Molly Barnes Gallery, Los Angeles
1970 Molly Barnes Gallery, Los Angeles
1971 O.K. Harris Gallery, New York
1974 O.K. Harris Gallery, New York
1975 D.M. Gallery, London
Galerie de Gestlo, Hamburg
1976 O.K. Harris Gallery, New York
John Berggruen Gallery, San Francisco
1977 Landfall Press Gallery, Chicago
1978 Morgan Gallery, Kansas City, Missouri
Bethel Art Gallery, Connecticut
O.K. Harris Gallery, New York
1979 Aldrich Museum, Ridgefield, Connecticut
Beaver College, Glenside, Pennsylvania
Landfall Press Gallery, Chicago
Galerie de Gestlo, Cologne
Delta Gallery, Rotterdam
Getler-Pall Gallery, New York
Dean Junior College, Franklyn, Massachusetts
1980 University of Bridgeport, Connecticut
Thomas Segal Gallery, Boston
Ball State University, Muncie, Indiana
Madison Art Center, Wisconsin
1981 Fendrick Gallery, Washington, D.C.
Mattatuck Museum, Waterbury, Connecticut
Swain School of Design, New Bedford, Massachusetts
1982 Coe Kerr Gallery, New York
1983 Signet Arts, St. Louis, Missouri
Modernism Gallery, San Francisco
Wichita Art Museum, Kansas
1984 Coe Kerr Gallery, New York
Fendrick Gallery, Washington, D.C.
Springfield Art Museum, Missouri
Palace Theatre, New Haven, Connecticut
1985 The Art Guild, Farmington, Connecticut
Abilene Christian University, Texas
Roger Ramsay Gallery, Chicago
Reynolda House Museum of American Art, Winston-Salem, North Carolina
Arkansas Arts Center, Little Rock (travelled to Washington, D.C.; St. Louis, Missouri; Odessa, Texas)
1986 Signet Arts, St. Louis, Missouri
Museum of Art, Science and Industry, Bridgeport, Connecticut
Gallery Karl Oskar, Westwood Hills, Kansas
Brenda Kroos Gallery, Columbus, Ohio
1986–91 *Robert Cottingham: A Print Retrospective, 1972–1986,* Springfield Art Museum, Springfield, Missouri (toured, with extensions, for six years in museums throughout the United States)
1987 Union Station, Hartford, Connecticut
Gimpel and Weitzenhoffer, New York
1988 Fendrick Gallery, Washington, D.C.
Roger Ramsay Gallery, Chicago
1989 Gimpel and Weitzenhoffer, New York
Fendrick Gallery, Washington, D.C.
1990 Roger Ramsay Gallery, Chicago
1991 Harcourts Contemporary, San Francisco
1992–93 *Robert Cottingham: Rolling Stock Series*, Brenda Kroos Gallery, Cleveland, Ohio (traveled to Butler Institute of American Art, Youngstown, Ohio, and Central Connecticut State University, New Britain)
1993 Marisa del Re Gallery, New York
Robert Cottingham: 27 Heralds, Bruce R. Lewin Gallery, New York
1994 Louis K. Meisel Gallery, New York
Harcourts Contemporary, San Francisco
Takada Gallery, San Franciso
Robert Cottingham, Triton Museum, Santa Clara, California
Struve Gallery, Chicago
1996–97 *Robert Cottingham: An American Alphabet,* Montgomery Museum of Fine Arts, Alabama (traveled to Forum

Robert Cottingham: *Blues,* ca. 1989. ©Geoffrey Clements/Corbis.

Gallery, New York, and Aldrich Museum of Contemporary Art, Ridgefield, Connecticut)

1997–98 *Hollywood Stills: House Portraits by Robert Cottingham,* Long Beach Museum of Art, California

1999 Works on Paper Gallery, Philadelphia

Eyeing America: Robert Cottingham Prints, National Museum of American Art, Washington, D.C. (toured; catalog)

2000 Forum Gallery, New York

Cline Gallery, Santa Fe, New Mexico

Selected Group Exhibitions:

1970 *The Highway,* Institute of Contemporary Art, University of Pennsylvania, Philadelphia (travelled to the Institute for the Arts, Rice University, Houston, and the Akron Art Institute, Ohio.)

1971 *Radical Realism,* Museum of Contemporary Art, Chicago

1972 *Documenta 5,* Kassel, West Germany
1973 *Photo-Realism: The Ludwig Collection,* Serpentine Gallery, London
1974 *Hyperréalistes Américains/Réalistes Européens,* Centre National d'Art Contemporain, Paris (toured Europe)
1978 *Art About Art,* Whitney Museum, New York (travelled to the North Carolina Museum of Art, Raleigh; Frederick S. Wright Art Gallery, University of California at Los Angeles; and the Portland Museum, Oregon)
1981 *Contemporary American Realism since 1960,* Pennsylvania Academy of Fine Arts, Philadelphia
1983 *Painting New York,* Museum of the City of New York
1985 *American Realism: The Precise Image,* Isetan Museum Tokyo (travelled to Osaka and Yokohama, Japan)
1986 *Hollywood: Legend and Reality,* Smithsonian Institution, Washington, D.C. (toured the United States)
1989–90 *Trains and Planes: The Influence of Locomotion in American Painting,* Sherry French Gallery, New York (travelling exhibition)
1990–91 *Word as Image: American Art 1960–1990,* Milwaukee Art Museum, Wisconsin (travelling exhibition)
1991–92 *American Realism and Figurative Art, 1952–1990* (toured Japan)
1995–96 *Printmaking in America: Collaborative Prints and Presses, 1960–1990,* Northwestern University, Evanston, Illinois (travelling exhibition)
1999 *Twentieth Century American Drawings,* Arkansas Art Center, Little Rock (travelling exhibition)

Collections:

Whitney Museum, New York; Metropolitan Museum of Art, New York; Guggenheim Museum, New York; Syracuse University, New York; Hirshhorn Museum and Sculpture Garden, and National Museum of American Art, Smithsonian Institution, Washington, D.C.; Indianapolis Museum of Art; Cleveland Museum of Art, Ohio; Walker Art Center and Minneapolis Sculpture Garden, Minneapolis, Minnesota; Honolulu Academy of Art; Museum of Modern Art, New York; Art Institute of Chicago; Arts Council of Great Britain, London; Boymans-van Beuningen Museum, Rotterdam; Hamburg Museum, Germany; Utrecht Museum, Netherlands.

Publications:

By COTTINGHAM: Article—interview in Photo-Realists: 12 Interviews'' by Linda Chase and Ted McBurnett in *Art in America* (New York), November/December 1972.

On COTTINGHAM: Books—*New Realism* by Udo Kultermann, Tübingen, West Germany 1972; *Photo-Realism: The Ludwig Collection,* exhibition catalog, London 1973; *Hyperréalistes Américains/Réalistes Européens,* exhibition catalog, Paris 1974; *Realists at Work* by John Arthur, New York 1983; *Robert Cottingham-A Print Retrospective 1972–86,* edited by John Arthur, Springfield, Missouri 1986. **Articles**—''Too Easy to Be Art'' by Peter Schieldahl in the *New York Times,* May 1974; ''Robert Cottingham: The Capers of the Signscape'' by Toni del Renzio in *Art and Artists* (London), February 1975; ''Cottingham's Air: Letter Perfect'' in *New Art Examiner* (Chicago), December 1985; ''Photorealism by Design'' by Stanley Marcus in *Artweek,* 12 April 1986; ''Capturing the Fading Signs of America as Art'' by William Zimmer in *New York Times,* 11 September 1988; ''Who's Who in Realism . . . Readers and Experts Choose'' by Laura Silver in *U.S. Art,* July-August 1989; ''Cottingham Makes Fresh Tracks in His 'Rolling Stock Series''' in *Antique and Arts Weekly,* 9 April 1993; ''Who's Afraid of Photorealism?'' by James F. Cooper in *American Arts Quarterly,* Summer-Autumn 1993; *Architectural Digest,* July 1995; ''Who Hails from Hopper?'' by Ann Landi in *Art News,* vol. 97, no. 4, April 1998; ''Eyeing America: Robert Cottingham Prints'' in *Antique and Arts Weekly,* 16 October 1998; ''Keeping It Real'' by Robin Cambe in *Art & Auction,* Summer 2000.

*

For more than twenty years now I have been painting and drawing a uniquely American subject—the neon signs, shop fronts and movie marquees of our cities and downtown neighborhoods.

My interest in these cultural icons seems to derive from my Brooklyn upbringing, my fascination with letter forms as symbols and my interest in society's use of language as a means of persuasion.

During the four year period from 1983 through 1986, I became particularly intrigued by a row of shop fronts that included such diverse commercial establishments as a barber shop, a hotel, a bar, a news-stand, a liquor store, and a Mexican restaurant named Barrera-Rosa's. This panorama of facades and messages struck me as an image rich with aesthetic possibilities, not only as a singular, unified vision, but as a network of separate and overlapping compositional fragments. I began an extensive exploration of this image, dissecting and analysing its parts, in an attempt to reveal its abstract underpinnings. This pictorial foray resulted in an output of 45 individual works executed in a multitude of media, including watercolor, acrylic, gouache, ink, graphite, woodcut, linoleum cut, etching, lithography and oil.

The three prints in the *Barrera-Rosa* portfolio played an important part in this exploration. Each deals with a specific means of visual expression: line (dry-point etching), mass (linoleum cut), and color (lithograph). Each print, while a finished graphic work in its own right, contributes significantly to the overall investigation of the image's substructure; its abstract patterns, the formal relationships of interlocking shapes, the nuances of line, value and color-in short, the fundamental components of composition.

And beyond these formal issues there is, of course, the subject matter itself. I like to think of these prints and my work in general as a celebration of the signs and urban iconography that have given American cities their peculiar energy. Monumental, poignant, absurd, and surreal, these structures stand as vivid testimony to the vitality and variety of contemporary American life.

—Robert Cottingham

* * *

Robert Cottingham ascribes to Pop Art the essential permissiveness that allowed him to paint images of mundane urban reference, with an emphasis upon a display of letter types in commercial signs, and clearly based upon the photograph. Although Cottingham has always used photographs—which he himself takes in carefully planned forays to various American cities—he has likewise always handpainted his images without the use of compressed air spray techniques. He thus joins Richard Estes and others among prominent ''Photo-Realists'' who ironically enough combine the traditional liking for the handicraft and brushed facture of easel painting with the apparently antithetical feel of the mechanically-produced photographic print. His etchings and lithographs are also handwork, and not photo-transcriptions of painted works.

After an earlier career in advertising and a move from the East Coast to California, Cottingham's first exhibition in Los Angeles, in 1968, already presented the themes and compositional orderings which have remained constant throughout his career.

These early works, of city landmarks from the pre-World War II era, such as ''Ralph's Market'' and the ''Pan Pacifica Auditorium'' (the latter still one of his largest works at 10 feet in width), presented a passerby's view of the building's upper parts; while lettering was already a clear intent in these works, the structures were seen broadly against the sky. At the onset of the next decade, Cottingham had painted one of his most often reproduced works, ''Art,'' 1971, a closely cropped—the photo terminology clearly appropriate—view of a theatre marquee which goes on beyond the picture frame. Although the light bulbs are missing and have been replaced by neon light strips and the letter character is clearly inter-war, nostalgia and good-humored word play are only infrequently the clear goal of the artist. More pointedly, these paintings are intended as brilliantly hued, abstracted plays of line and movement.

Cottingham himself has affirmed that it is not the social character of the letters as much as their visual interest that led him initially to those parts of American cities (sections which he has found often changed in his subsequent returns). In interviews he has spoken of his calculated use of three lenses on the cameras with which he gathers materials for his studio production. And his paintings have easily reflected this photographic practice—the use of telephoto lenses with their close-up, ''zoom'' focus. Although Cottingham's best-known works have been signage seen at sharp angles from below, he has also produced more relaxed, less camera-referential and more personal, perceptual work. The omnipresence of the photographic image in our culture has neither diminished his productivity nor style qualities. His mid-decade work is still based upon the ''fading'' urban neighborhood. There may now more often appear a dazzling, even mannered, interplay of a multitude of elements, but perhaps more often presented both more parallel and more perpendicular to the picture plane. A touch of the long American love for *trompe l'oeil* has been added to another Populist tradition—the neighborhood realism of the Ash Can School of the early twentieth century—and modernist abstraction is like-wise touched with pre-modern attitudes. Cottingham has said of his particular poignant formalism: ''I'm not primarily interested in documentation, although I think there is a certain documentary aspect to my work. It's unavoidable because of the degree of realistic depiction involved and by the nature of the subject matter. It's a vision exclusive to the century and is fading fast.''

Within the last decade, Cottingham has been accorded two large museum exhibitions where, strikingly, his ''signature'' and quite well-recognized image—''urban iconography''—was not present. *An American Alphabet,* seen in Houston, New York, and Connecticut, while based upon the artist's long-time focus upon signage, used only single letters and so of course encompassed twenty-six paintings. The series was begun at the MacDowell Colony (New Hampshire), where these works evolved from original photographs; they all evolved as well through the traditional process of graphite drawing for value study and compositional order and gouche paintings for color pattern (some of these accompanied the final paintings in exhibition). The ''cropping'' strategy—the omnipresent photographic reference in Cottingham's art—of necessity became even tauter in this series; and the presentation of a lengthy traditional handicraft process for works so seemingly ''photographic'' may have been surprising as it made somewhat problematic the label of Photo-Realist for Cottingham.

Another seeming departure from his focus in the larger body of his work was *Hollywood Stills: House Portraits,* seen in California at the Long Beach Museum of Art. His older and well-known images were also presented in a retrospective at the Museum of American Art in Washington, D.C., called *Eyeing America: Robert Cottingham's Prints.*

—Joshua Kind

CRAGG, Tony

Nationality: British. **Born:** Liverpool, in 1949. **Education:** Studied art, Gloucestershire College of Arts and Technology, Cheltenham, 1968–70; painting, Wimbledon School of Art, London, 1970–73; sculpture, Royal College of Art, London, 1973–77, MA 1977. **Family:** Married Ute Uberste-Lehn in 1977; sons: Daniel and Thomas. **Career:** Worked as a laboratory technician, Natural Rubber Producers Research Association, Liverpool, 1966–68. Independent sculptor, in Wuppertal, Germany, since 1977. Instructor in sculpture, Ecole des Beaux-Arts, Metz, France, 1976; instructor, Kunstakademie, Dusseldorf, since 1979. **Agents:** Galerie Crousel-Robelin, 40 rue Quincampoix, 75004 Paris, France; and Lisson Gallery, London. **Address:** c/o Lisson Gallery, 67 Lisson Street. London NW1, England.

Individual Exhibitions:

1979 Lisson Gallery, London (and 1980)
Lutzowstrasse Situation, West Berlin
Kunstlerhaus Weidenallee, Hamburg
1980 Arnolfini Gallery, Bristol
Galerie Konrad Fischer, Dusseldorf
Galerie Chantal Crousel, Paris
Lutzowstrasse Situation, Buro Berlin
Galleria Lucio Amelio, Naples
Galleria Franco Toselli, Milan
Saman Galleria, Genoa, Italy
1981 Galerie Schellmann und Kluser, Munich
Musee d'Art et d'Industrie, St. Etienne, France
Whitechapel Art Gallery, London
Front Room, London
Nouveau Musee, Lyon, France (and 1982)
Von der Heydt Museum, Wuppertal, West Germany
Galerie Vacuum, Dusseldorf
1982 Badischer Kunstverein, Karlsruhe, West Germany
Kanransha Gallery, Tokyo
Nisshin Gallery, Tokyo
Marian Goodman Gallery, New York (and 1983)
Galerie Chantal Crousel, Paris
Buro Berlin
Lisson Gallery, London
Galerie Konrad Fischer, Dusseldorf
Museum Kroller-Muller, Otterlo, Netherlands
Galerie Schellmann und Kluser, Munich

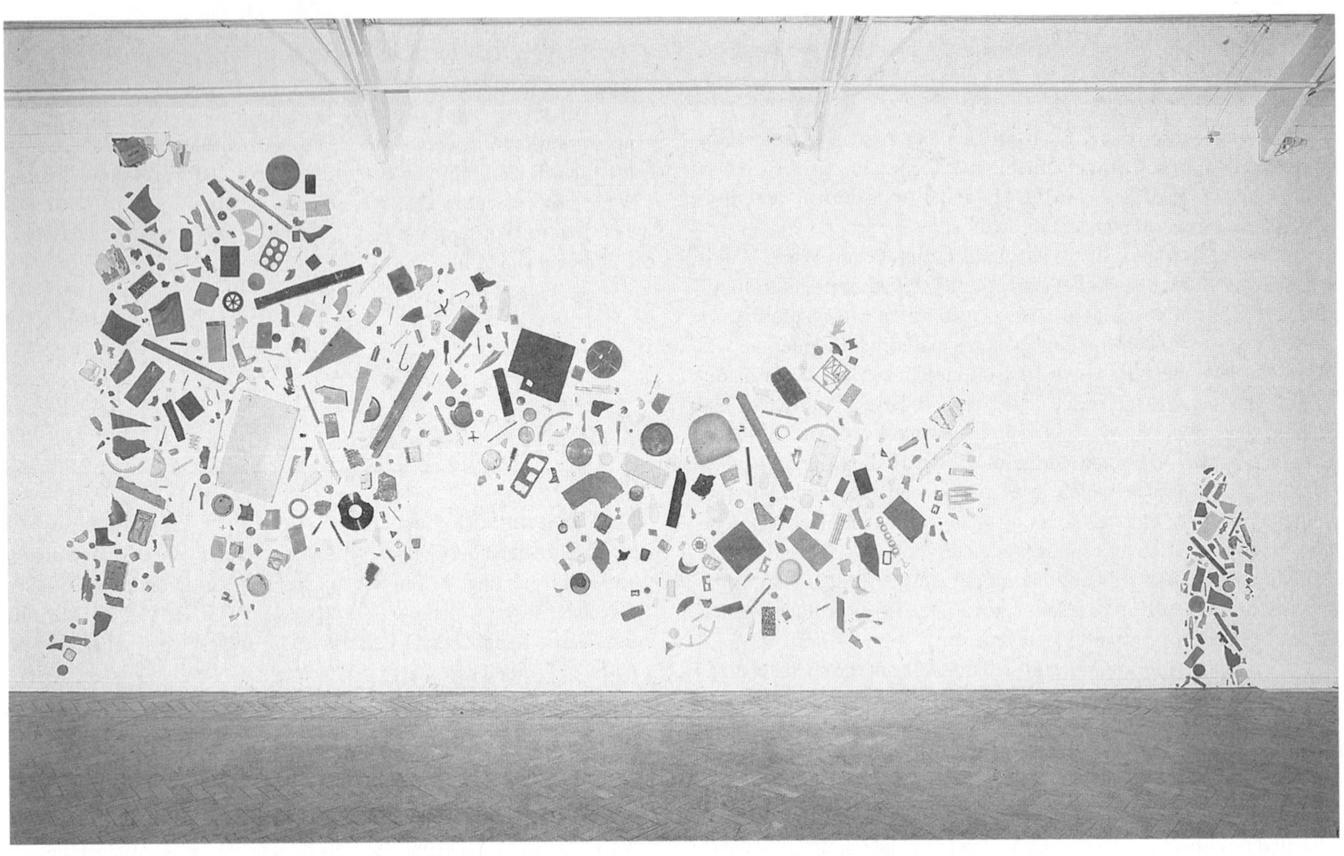

Tony Cragg: *Britain Seen from the North,* 1981. ©Tate Gallery, London/Art Resource, NY; courtesy of Tate Gallery.

1983 Galleria Lucio Amelio, Naples
Kunsthalle, Berne
Art and Project, Amsterdam
Galeria Thomas Cohn, Rio de Janeiro
Galleria Franco Toselli, Milan
Galerie Buchmann, St. Gallen, Switzerland
1984 Yarlow and Salzmann, Toronto
De Vleeshal, Middelburg, Netherlands
Louisiana Museum, Humlebaek, Denmark
Galerie Schellmann und Kluser, Munich
Marian Goodman Gallery, New York
Kanransha Gallery, Tokyo
Galerie Crousel-Hussenot, Paris
Kunstverein, Cologne
Galleria Tucci Russo, Turin
1985 Kunsthalle Waghaus, Winterthur, Switzerland
Staatsgalerie Moderner Kunst, Munich
Donald Young Gallery, Chicago
Lisson Gallery, London
Art and Project, Amsterdam
Palais des Beaux-Arts, Brussels
ARC/Musee d'Art Moderne de la Ville, Paris
1986 Kestner-Gesellschaft, Hannover
Galerie Bernd Kluser, Munich
Galerie Joost Declercq, Ghent, Belgium
Brooklyn Museum of Art, New York
Galerie Pierre Huber, Geneva
University of California, Berkeley
1987 Hayward Gallery, London
Galleria Tucci Russo, Turin
Marian Goodman Gallery, New York
1988 Galeria Marga Paz, Madrid
Galerie Buchmann, Basle
Galerie Crousel-Robelin, Paris
Lisson Gallery, London
1989 Tate Gallery, London
1990 *Tony Cragg: Recent Work,* The Kunstsammlung Nordrhein-Westfalen, Düsseldorf
Marian Goodman Gallery, New York
1991 Newport Harbor Art Museum, Newport Beach, California
1992 Centre d'Art Contemporain, Locminé, France
Marian Goodman Gallery, New York
Musee Departemental d'Art Contemporain de Rochechouart, France
Tony Cragg: Sculpture, Centre for Contemporary Arts, Glasgow (also Lisson Gallery, London)
1994 Marian Goodman Gallery, New York
Tony Cragg: Drawings, Musee des Beaux-Arts, Nantes, France (traveling exhibition) (catalog)
1995 Museo Nacional Centro de Arte Reina Sofia, Madrid (catalog)
1996 Centre Georges Pompidou, Paris
Openluchtmuseum voor Beeldhouwkunst Middelheim, Antwerp, Belgium (catalog)
1997 *Tony Cragg: Sculpture,* Whitechapel Art Gallery, London (catalog)

Art Gallery of New South Wales, Sydney (traveled to Queensland Art Gallery, Brisbane and Wellington City Gallery, Wellington) (catalog)

1998 Makslas Musejs Arsenals, Riga (catalog)

2000 *A New Thing Breathing: Recent Work by Tony Cragg,* Tate Liverpool, England

2001 Marian Goodman Gallery, New York

Selected Group Exhibitions:

1977 *RCA Degree Show,* Royal College of Art, London

1980 *Kunst in Europa na '68,* Museum van Hedendaagse Kunst, Ghent, Belgium

1981 *British Sculpture in the 20th Century,* Whitechapel Art Gallery, London

1982 *Kunst wird Material,* Nationalgalerie, West Berlin

1983 *Edges and Shadows: Sculpture in Britain,* Hayward Gallery, London (and Serpentine Gallery, London)

1984 *The British Art Show,* City Art Gallery, Birmingham (and Ikon Gallery, Birmingham; travelled to Edinburgh, Sheffield and Southamption)

1985 *Mobel—Objekte und Installationen,* Von der Heydt Museum, Wuppertal, West Germany

1987 *A Quiet Revolution: British Sculpture since 1965,* San Francisco Museum of Modern Art (travelled to Newport Beach; Washington, D.C.; Buffalo)

1988 *Brittanica: Vingt-cinq ans de sculpture,* Musee des Beaux Arts, Le Havre, France (travelled to Evreux, Rouen and Antwerp, 1988–89)

1990 *Culture and Commentary: An Eighties Perspective,* Hirshhorn Museum and Sculpture Garden, Washington, D.C. (catalog)

1991 *To Return to Base,* Deweer Art Gallery, Otegem, Belgium (catalog)

1993 *Tony Cragg,* Monderna Galerija, Ljubljana (catalog)

1995 *Here & Now,* Serpentine Gallery, London (catalog)
British Abstract Art Part 2: Sculpture, Flowers East, London (catalog)

1997 *On the Edge,* Museum of Modern Art, New York (catalog)
Material Culture: The Object in British Art of the 1980s and '90s, Hayward Gallery, London (catalog)

1998 *Art Treasures of England: The Regional Collections,* Royal Academy of Arts, London (catalog)

1999 30th Art Basel, Switzerland

2000 Tate Gallery, London
Conversation: An Exhibition of Figurative Sculpture, Milton Keynes Gallery, England (catalog)

Collections:

Tate Gallery, London; British Council, London; Arts Council of Great Britain, London; Museum of Modern Art, New York; Fonds Regional d'Art Contemporain Rhone-Alpes, France.

Publications:

By CRAGG: Books—*Tony Cragg: Skulpturen,* exhibition catalog, with others, Hannover 1985; *Tony Cragg,* exhibition catalog, with Lynne Cooke, London 1987; *Sculptures on the Page: Tony Cragg,* Halifax 1997. **Articles**—interview with Robert Hopper in *Tate: The Art Magazine,* no. 11, Spring 1997; interview with David Sylvester in *Modern Painters* (London), vol. 13, no. 2, Summer 2000.

On CRAGG: Books—*Tony Cragg,* exhibition catalog with foreword by Bernard Ceysson, St. Etienne 1981; *Tony Cragg,* exhibition catalog with text by Ursula Peters, Wuppertal 1981; *Tony Cragg: Skulpturen,* exhibition catalog with essay by Michael Newman, Karlsruhe 1982; *Tony Cragg,* exhibition catalog with text by Nobuo Nakamura, Tokyo 1982; *Tony Cragg,* exhibition catalog with texts by Jean-Hubert Martin and Germano Celant, Berne 1983; *Tony Cragg: Zwei Landschaften,* exhibition catalog with text by Armin Wildermuth, St. Gallen 1984; *Tony Cragg,* exhibition catalog with essay by Armin Wildermuth, Cologne 1984; *Tony Cragg,* exhibition catalog with texts by Anneliese Pohlen and Demosthenes Davvetos, Brussels and Paris 1985; *Tony Cragg* by Germano Celant, London 1996. **Articles**—''Laboratory Still Lives: 35 Prints by Tony Cragg'' by Susan Tallman in *Arts Magazine,* vol. 63, February 1989; ''Tony Cragg'' by Euan McArthur in *Art Monthly,* no. 160, October 1992; ''Tony Cragg: Under the Skin'' by Annie Claustres in *Art Press,* no. 209, January 1996; ''Latent Tectonics in the Work of Tony Cragg'' by Jesse Reiser in *Art & Design,* vol. 12, July/August 1997.

* * *

Tony Cragg is a part of that generation of artists who, following Philip King, Richard Long and Barry Flanagan, have renewed the scope of English sculpture by insisting on a critical rereading and one sensitive to the value of the object in the contemporary plastic arts. Though close to the trends of the seventies, Cragg's work nevertheless departs from the rigorous formulas and strictly 'objectual' criteria of minimal art in order to address itself to the crisis of our modern consumer society.

Cragg, who has lived in West Germany since 1979, was trained as a biologist and later worked in a research laboratory, which taught him to consider ''art as an extension of science'' (T. C.). From the time of his first artistic creations, while he was still a student at London's Royal College of Art, he discovered and utilised the formal, emotional and narrative potential of the industrial object, serving as an 'archaeologist' of the technical era.

All the products of consumption, used and discarded, those reject materials which clutter our daily world, are retrieved by the artist near his place of work, then 'staged' in the exhibition area. The materials are displayed without modifications according to a system of accumulation which demonstrates the complex interactions that take place between man and his creations, the object being the projection and the receptacle of socio-economic interests and of individual pretensions. ''I think that objects have the capability to carry valuable information for us, to be important to us, but the fact is that most objects are made in ways which are irresponsible and manipulative. Irresponsible because people—the makers of this or that—don't really consider in any metaphysical way the meanings of the objects that they are making; and manipulative because things are made for a variety of commercial and power-based reasons'' (T. C.). In his work Cragg ignores the functional aspect of objects. The plastic unity of his assemblages is subjectively determined by the preliminary choice of a form (one of his first pieces, *Staple,* 1977, is made up of planks, stones and diverse other materials which together build up a perfect cube) or of a colour (for *Spectrum,* 1984, the materials have been put together in series of blues, reds, yellows, and greens). For his first compositions Cragg primarily used plastic objects that had been worn out by time or use, along with bits and pieces of artificially coloured synthetic materials, placing them one beside the other so that they filled out the human figures which he had outlined on walls or the ground. A veritable critical cartography of society, these assemblages represent life-size human silhouettes (self-portraits, group portraits, *Britain Seen from the North,* 1981, *Polizist,* 1981, *Riot,* 1987 . . .) which have the quality of historical and metaphysical symbols. Some of the figures take on the magnified shape of one of the objects of the composition (*Green bottle,* 1980) or of a natural element (*Red skin,* 1979), or of an object-type in the artistic (*Palette,* 1982) or poetic vocabulary (*Blue moon,* 1980).

From 1982 Cragg's working methods became more diversified. By covering objects with a uniform layer of white or speckled paint and thereby obscuring the qualities of the material, he accorded particular importance to the form and to the equilibrium of the work as a whole (*Lens,* 1985, *No place for a rabbit,* 1985, *Aquaduct,* 1986).

From 1982 Cragg also developed an interest in organic objects and in hand-crafted objects, in a pretechnological mode of production where manual work plays a direct part in the transformation of the material. *Axe Head,* 1982, for example, in which an axe figures as part of the overall image, brings into contact with one another certain wooden objects of varying volume and complexity which, in view of the means of their production, carry within themselves this very axe.

The tool as symbol of man's creative capacities and of his control over matter became the subject of a number of Cragg's sculptures. Chosen for the purity of their volumes, various tools were magnified and worked in wood, glass or steel in works which underline the interaction between form and function (*Mortar and pestle,* 1986, *Eye bath,* 1986). With the series entitled *Landscape* (1982, 1983) Cragg distances himself once again from industrial society in order to linger over the organization of natural elements, in the face of which man abandons rationalism and returns to his ancient role as creator of images and inventor of myths. The austere compositions of *Landscape* seem to be insisting still on the arbitrary forms and structures of stones, the result of fractures to the original block from which they have split. Certain compositions in which crude materials are assembled are then exploded by the introduction of a geometric shape symbolising the intrusion of architecture into the landscape (*Installation in Cadillac,* 1985, *Jurassic landscape,* 1986). With *Echo,* 1984, a piece which is made up of large geometric volumes uniformly covered with repetitive and depersonalising graffiti, the artist analyses urban architecture. The degradation and dehumanisation of the natural and urban environment occupy a prominent place in Cragg's work as a whole.

—Dominique Liquois

In the past decade Cragg has extended his themes based on the interpenetration nature and culture in a virtuostic array of materials and forms. In works such as *Bacchus Drops* (1985) and *Inverted Sugar Crop* (1987), Cragg alludes to the chemical processes which form the basis for the manufacture of certain food products like sugar and wine. The cast bronze and steel used in these pieces, traditional sculptural materials, point to the realm of culture, of high art, but the organic forms they represent suggest culture's dependency on nature. Thus Cragg considers the creative function, in both scientific and artistic terms, in its alchemical capacity as a transformative power.

Other works suggest a sort of archeology in reverse. *Three Cast Bottles,* from 1989, represents three bottles, of the common plastic variety, blown up to huge proportions in cast iron, the throw-away as monument. *Formnifera,* 1988, consists of a bottle and other ambiguous forms, both industrial and organic in association, whose cast plaster surfaces appear eroded and pock-marked, as if salvaged from the sea. Cragg's recurrent wit is demonstrated in *Fruit Bottles,* 1989, a grouping of seven bottles of the kind that usually hold a fruity sugar-water that appeals to children, enlarged in cast steel, their rusted forms both residually goofy and surprisingly elegant.

Loco, 1988, with its eccentric jointed wood parts, features an outsized double head which is laminated to appear blurred as if in rapid motion. The piece typifies the increasing formal and philosophical complexity of Cragg's work. Its title alludes to the movement or locomotion implied by the falsely mechanized, anti-monumental head and the variously jointed wood components, and also the Spanish word for 'crazy.' This layered reading and perversely menacing quality recurs in *Untitled,* 1993, in which a painted upright piano, grouped with some wooden chairs, planks, and shaved logs, appears overtaken by the shiny metal hardware hooks protruding from every surface—even the inside of the piano, like some fuzzy mold or wormy parasite.

Cragg's sheer inventiveness and his dexterity with materials belies the pervasive philosophical underpinning of his work, with its recurrent scientific, social and historical associations that blur the boundaries between what is natural and manmade. "People say there's a great deal of variety in my work, but I'm not so sure that's true . . . It's like making a complete landscape with all the parts in it: there's the urban world, architecture and so on, there's the organic world, there's the atmosphere, and there's the geological structure." (TC) "In a sense, it's obvious that in terms of the physical world scientists make the more fundamental statements, but artists and philosophers don't have a less important job. They humanize, they find out what the significance of science is for human beings. . . . I think you have to make images of objects which are like thinking models to help you get through the world" (TC).

—Dorothy Valakos

Becoming increasingly prolific as a public sculptor, Cragg's sculptural statements, these "thinking models" as he calls them, have reached a larger audience as he is frequently commissioned to make works for public spaces and the outdoors. Continuing his experimentation with organic forms, Tony Cragg has recently developed more monumental works that function as a type of personal "organic architecture." For the British Embassy in Berlin in 2000, for example, Cragg created two large sandstone works entitled *Dancing Columns.* Like living fluid forms, the work belies its stone solidity as the columns appear to melt and bend as if made of rubber. Again we see Cragg pushing the boundaries of materials—engaging with space and scale as well as form.

This on-going research into the actual process of creating, as well as the nature and language of materials, continues to inspire Cragg. While the sculptures themselves have often become more refined, he has not abandoned the use of detritus or found objects that first inspired him. *Pacific* and also *Cumulus* from 1998 use glass bottles and containers, but the sculptures created are more complex and controlled than earlier work, becoming about the total object rather than focussing our attention on the recycling of individual elements. This increased formality, while still playful, sees Cragg developing an increasingly sophisticated dialogue between artist, material and audience, as he reaches his goal as a sculptor: "to fill up the meaning around objects."

—Carly Butler

CRAIG-MARTIN, Michael

Nationality: British. **Born:** Dublin in 1941; moved with his family to the United States, 1946; returened to Britain, 1966. **Education:** Yale University, New Haven, Connecticut, 1961–63; studied at the Yale School of Art and Achitecture, 1964–66. **Family:** Divorced; has one daughter. **Career:** Settled in Corsham, Wiltshire, 1966–68; lived in London, 1968–70, and since 1972. Lecturer, Bath Academy of Art and Canterbury College of Art, 1970–72; principal lecturer, 1973–88, and professor, since 1993, Goldsmiths' College, London. Trustee, Tate Gallery, London, 1989–99. **Agent:** Waddington Galleries, London. **Address:** c/o Waddington Galleries, 2 Cork Street, London WIX 1PA, England

Individual Exhibitions:

1969 Rowan Gallery, London
1970 Rowan Gallery, London
1971 Arnolfini Gallery, Bristol
Richard Demarco Gallery, Edinburgh
1972 Rowan Gallery, London
1973 Rowan Gallery, London
1974 Rowan Gallery, London
Galerie December, Münster, West Germany
1975 Rowan Gallery, London
1976 Rowan Gallery, London
Selected Works 1966–1975, Turnpike Gallery, Leigh, Lancashire (toured the U.K.)
1977 Third Eye Centre, Glasgow
Oliver Dowling Gallery, Dublin
1978 Galerie December, Dusseldorf
Institute of Modern Art, Brisbane (toured Australia)
Rowan Gallery, London
1979 Galerie Foksal, Warsaw
Galerie Akmulatory, Poznan, Poland
Oliver Dowling Gallery, Dublin
1980 Rowan Gallery, London
Galerie BaMa, Paris
1981 Galerija Suvremene Umjetnosti, Zagreb
1982 Waddington Galleries, London
1983 Waddington and Shiell Galleries, Toronto
1985 Waddington Galleries, London
1988 Waddington Galleries, London
1989 *Michael Craig-Martin: A Retrospective, 1968–1989,* Whitechapel Art Gallery, London
1991 *Michael Craig-Martin*, Musée des Beaux-Arts, Le Havre (catalog)
16 Objects, Ready of Not, Museum of Modern Art, New York, and David Nolan Gallery, New York
1997 *Innocence and Experience*, Waddington Galleries, London (catalog)
1998 Kunstverein Stuttgart (installation)
1999 *and sometimes a cigar is just a cigar* (installation), Wurttembergischer Kunstverein Stuttgart, Stuttgart (catalog)

Selected Group Exhibitions:

1966 *First II,* Jewish Community Center, New Haven, Connecticut
1970 *Critics' Choice,* Tooths Gallery, London
1972 *The New Art,* Hayward Gallery, London
1973 *Henry Moore to Gilbert and George,* Palais des Beaux-Arts, Brussels
1974 *Idea and Image in Recent Art,* Art Institute of Chicago
1975 *Bienal,* Sao Paulo
1976 *Sydney Biennale,* Art Gallery of New South Wales, Sydney
1979 *Un Certain Art Anglais,* Musee d'Art Moderne de la Ville, Paris
1980 *ROSC,* University College Gallery, Dublin (travelled to the Crawford Gallery, Cork)
1982 *Aspects of British Art Today,* Metropolitan Art Museum, Tokyo (toured Japan)
1984 *When Attitudes Became Form 1965–72,* Kettle's Yard Gallery, Cambridge (travelled to Edinburgh)
1986 *Esculturas sobre la Pared,* Galerie Juana de Aizpuru, Madrid
1995 Southampton City Art Gallery, England
1996 *Un siècle de sculpture anglaise,* Jeu de Paume, Paris
1998 XXIV Bienal de São Paulo, Brazil
2000 *Intelligence: New British Art 2000*, Tate Gallery, London (catalog)

Collections:

Tate Gallery, London; Arts Council of Great Britain, London; Victoria and Albert Museum, London; Fitzwilliam Museum, Cambridge; Australian National Gallery, Canberra; Baltimore Museum of Art; City Art Gallery, Southampton, Hampshire; Allen Art Museum, Oberlin College, Ohio; Swindon Art Gallery, Wiltshire.

Publications:

By CRAIG-MARTIN: Articles—"Acquisitions" in *The Tate Gallery Biennial Report 1968–70,* London 1970; "A Procedural Proposition: Selection, Repetition, Extension, Exchange" in *Studio International* (London), September 1971; "An Interview with Simon Field" in *Art and Artists* (London), May 1972; "Acquisitions" in *The Tate Gallery Biennial Report 1970–71,* London 1972; interview with Anne Seymour in *The New Art,* exhibition catalog, London 1972; "Acquisitions" in *The Tate Gallery Biennial Report 1972–74,* London 1974; statement in *Michael Craig-Martin,* exhibition catalog,

Zagreb 1981; ''Wall to Wall'' interview in *Audio Arts Magazine,* January 1994; ''Signing Off'' in *tate: the art magazine,* no. 2, Spring 1994; ''The Teaching of Josef Albers: A Personal Reminiscence'' in *The Burlington Magazine,* April 1995.

On CRAIG-MARTIN: Books—*Michael Craig-Martin: Selected Works 1966–75,* exhibition catalog, by Anne Seymour, Leigh, Lancashire 1976; *Michael Craig-Martin,* exhibition catalog with text by Richard Stone, London 1985. **Articles—**''Michael Craig-Martin'' by Merete Bates in *The Guardian* (London), March 1976; ''Best of British'' by Marina Vaizey in the *Sunday Times* (London), 31 July 1977; ''Sculptor's Visit Is Bound to Have an Impact'' by Gertrude Langer in *Courier Mail* (Brisbane), 17 February 1978; ''The State of British Art: It's a Bewilderment'' by William Feaver in *Art News* (London), January 1980; ''Michael Craig-Martin: A Retrospective, 1968–1989'' by David Batchelor in *New Statesman & Society,* 17 November 1989; ''An Artist's Secrets: Drawing'' in *The Economist,* 28 January 1995; ''Art on the Line'' by Sue Hubbard in *New Statesman & Society,* 14 April 1995.

*

I have a thought, not clearly formulated, but a sense of the possibility of a particular meaning.

I am focusing my attention, seeking the words to express this thought, to give it form. I am using words I know. (My vocabulary is not static, new words enter it, others fall from use.)

These words are in common usage. They have immediacy and flexibility. Each word carries great associative resonance.

I am employing the grammar I know, putting the words together to make phrases and sentences, simple and complex.

I am stating facts, expressing opinions, making allusions, drawing comparisons, revealing values.

I have used these words many times, but this is the first time I have used them to express this thought in this way.

This is how I do my drawings.

—Michael Craig-Martin

* * *

Like a number of other ''post-object'' artists (to use the then-fashionable phrase) who took part in the *New Art* show at the Hayward Gallery in 1972, Michael Craig-Martin has been preoccupied with how we see and judge the veracity of a picture. What constitutes a picture? In what ways do words anchor or interfere with images? During the 1970s, of course, these concerns were for the most part the basis for reflections on photography. Craig-Martin's work, though, has had little to do—in any formal sense—with photography.

Trained as a sculptor, Craig-Martin's investigations into ''ways of seeing'' have been based—until recently—on the manipulation of objects and words. In an early installation work he involved the spectator in a simple experiment on the limits of our field of perception (what we take in, what we lose). Using numerous mirrors, Craig-Martin re-presented a composite view of the spectator. Craig-Martin has been called an illusionist. These powers are perhaps no better illustrated than by a piece he did in 1973. A glass of water was exhibited on a shelf as an oak tree. Here our partial or subjective perception of things is troubled by an obvious conflict between the sign and the signifier. But besides acting as a kind of visual example of Sausserian linguistics, the work achieved something else. In the most simple of ways it tapped the transforming powers that artists claim as magic (or rather the institutions from within which artists operate, label magic). It is charming work and takes its place alongside other object-pieces of the same period which test the limits of the real.

In the recent work (post-78) this gap between a present and an absent object, or rather the gap between picture and pictured, has shifted away from objects to images—isometric drawings of domestic objects projected onto the gallery wall. These large scale objects are superimposed over each other, creating a dense jungle of projecting lines. Ambiguity here is based on a static simultaneity of objects. In the mirror piece, simultaneity was the result of the breakup of a single image; the mirrors acted very much like a camera, panning around the object. In these drawings, the play between absence and presence becomes a kind of half-way house. Objects hover in and out of view. The eye can only take in one object at a time. Although visible, the other objects remain half-hidden, submerged. This has a lot to do with the scale of the objects. All the objects are uniform in size. We are therefore unable to read off objects according to their normal scale.

Picturing for Craig-Martin has nothing to do with interpretation, but rather with establishing a framework for inquiry. Each set of works adopts (adapts) a perceptual model which decentres the single and unitary vantage point of the viewer. In principle, Craig-Martin's work could be said to be structuralist in origin. It works on the interstices between things, between names, pictures and signs.

—John Roberts

In recent work, Craig-Martin has continued his investigation into the linguistic nature of art and representation through the deployment of his lexicon of images. While the work of the 1970s and 1980s was characteristically austere and cool, moving from objects to drawings executed in black, occasionally red, tape on a white wall, the work of the 1990s, and since, is spectacularly colourful and has developed from painting on canvas into ambitious museum scale installations. In the latter, whole sequences of gallery spaces are painted, floor to ceiling, in unmodulated vivid colours—magenta, yellow, red, blue, purple, green—across which representations of objects float, drawn in simple black outline and filled in with the same brilliant colours. The images are of objects which are instantly recognisable: chairs, step-ladders, globes, cameras, light-bulbs, selected from a bank of more than 200 such images which Craig-Martin has created. The objects are chosen for their ordinariness and the timelessness of their form which is determined by their function. Craig-Martin has described them as ''pictorial readymades.'' The pictured objects are free of narrative, emotion, and expression as is Craig-Martins's use of line and colour. The fascination is in how we can effortlessly read a ten-foot high flat pattern of pink and green paint as a glass of water, with which it shares no qualities, and that we can construct a narrative out of the relationship of one image to another. It is the viewer who brings information to the work and completes it.

What distinguishes this work is its clarity of form and thought: Craig-Martin elegantly demystifies art by his completely straightforward means of representation, stripping away all inessentials and showing exactly what he has done. He once said that he thought there was too much meaning in art and the difficulty was in getting rid of it. Mystification is dispensed with: what remains is the mystery and thrill of a transcendent, visual experience.

—Richard Salkeld

CRANDALL, Jordan

Nationality: American. **Born:** Detroit, Michigan, 1960. **Career:** Editor, *Blast,* since 1990; Director, X Art Foundation, New York, since 1990; visiting critic, Hani Rashid and Lise Ann Couture (Asymptote), School of Architecture, Columbia University, 1996; visiting critic, Advanced Studio VI, with Keller Easterling, School of Architecture, Columbia University, 1997; visiting professor, Multimédia, École Nationale Supérieure des Beaux-Arts, Paris, 1999; visiting professor, École Supérieure d'Art Normandie, Caen, France, 2001. **Awards:** Wittenborn Award, Art Libraries Society of North America, presented at the Museum of Contemporary Art, Montreal, 1994; Design Excellence Award, 44th Annual Type Directors Club Exhibition, 1998; ''The 50 best,'' Internationaler medienkunstpreis, Germany, 2000; SÜDWEST TV, International Media Art Award, Germany, 2000. **Agent:** Sandra Gering Gallery, 534 West 22nd Street, New York, New York 10011. **Web site:** http://www.blast.org/crandall.

Selected Individual Exhibitions

1994 Sandra Gering Gallery, New York (in association with X Art Foundation)
1995 Galerie des Archives, Paris (in association with X Art Foundation)
Javier Lopez Gallery, London (in association with X Art Foundation)
Koelnischer Kunstverein, Cologne (in association with X Art Foundation)
1996 Sandra Gering Gallery, New York (in association with X Art Foundation)
1998 *Blast,* Galleria Figure, Torino, Italy (catalog)
Sandra Gering Gallery, New York
2000 *Drive,* Neue Galerie am Landesmuseum Joanneum, Graz; The Kitchen, New York; Centre d'art contemporain de Basse-Normandie, France; Museo de arte Carillo Gil, Mexico City; ARTLAB-Prospect4 Spiral Gallery, Tokyo (catalog)
2001 Galeria Baro Senna, São Paulo, Brazil
Drive, TENT Centrum Beeldende Kunst, Rotterdam (in collaboration with V2 Organization) (catalog)
Heatseeking, Sandra Gering Gallery, New York

Selected Group Exhibitions:

1992 *The Spatial Drive,* New Museum of Contemporary Art, New York
Multiplicity, Robbin Lockett Gallery, Chicago
1993 *States of Mind,* University of California Library, San Diego
1994 The Museum für Zukunft, Friesenwall 116, Cologne
TZ'Art & Co Gallery, New York
Depart, Bernard Toale Gallery, Boston
Inside/Outside, in situ, Cincinnati
1995 *Temporarily Possessed: The Semi-Permanent Collection,* New Museum of Contemporary Art, New York
Inaugural Exhibition, Richard Heller Gallery, Los Angeles
Take Me (I'm Yours), Serpentine Gallery, London
SMS, Susan Inglett Gallery, New York
1996 *In the Flow: Alternate Authoring Strategies,* Franklin Furnace, New York
Alem da Agua, Museo de Arte Extremeno e Iberoamericano, Badajoz, Portugal
Interplace Access, Viafarini, Milan
Baumgartner Gallery, Washington, D.C.
1997 *Documenta X,* Kassel (catalog)
Revisions II, Karl Ernst Osthaus Museum, Hagen, Germany
Selections from the Ruth and Marvin Sackner Archive, Rosenwald Gallery, University of Pennsylvania, Philadelphia
Works from the Collection of the Edward P. Taylor Research Library, Art Gallery of Ontario
1998 *Bureau Des Videos: Bricks and Kicks,* Vienna and Espace des Arts, Chalon-Sur-Saone
1999 *Rewind to the Future,* Neuer Berliner Kunstverein, Berlin (catalog)
Net Condition, ZKM Zentrum für Kunst und Medientechnologie, Karlsruhe
Montreal International Festival of New Cinema and New Media, Ex-Centris, Montreal
Graz Biennial on Media and Architecture, Austria
2000 *InSITE,* San Diego and Tijuana
Die nominierten medienkünstlerischen Internationaler medienkunstpreis, Galerie K + S, Berlin
Greater New York, P. S. 1 Institute for Contemporary Art, New York; Museum of Modern Art, New York
Particle Accelerators, Photographic Resource Center at Boston University
2001 *The Future of Cinema,* ZKM Zentrum für Kunst und Medientechnologie, Karlsruhe
Optical Verve, The Ottawa Art Gallery, Canada
Bitstreams, Whitney Museum of American Art, New York
Transmediale International Media Art Festival, Berlin

Collections:

ZKM Zentrum für Kunst und Medientechnologie, Karlsruhe; Neue Galerie am Landesmuseum Joanneum, Graz; Karl Ernst Osthaus Museum, Hagen; New Museum of Contemporary Art, New York; Koelnischer Kunstverein, Cologne.

Publications:

By CRANDALL: Articles—''Transactional Space'' in *M/E/A/N/I/N/G,* May 1993; ''Forum'' in *M/E/A/N/I/N/G,* Spring 1994;

''Netzprojekte: The Thing'' in *Ars Electronica 95,* Wein 1995; ''Alignment and Informatic Form'' in *Art Papers,* May-June 1995; ''Pages and Spaces'' in *Documenta Documents 3,* March 1997; ''Convertible Vehicles'' in *TRANS>arts.cultures.media,* Summer 1997; ''On Suspension'' in *X Mal Documenta X,* Kassel 1998; ''Eyebeam-Blast'' and ''Ass in Gear'' in *Readme: The Nettime Book,* New York 1998; ''Tech Ass in Gear'' in *European Media Art Festival,* Osnabruck, Germany 1999; ''Drive: Project for Atlantica'' in *Atlantica,* February 1999; ''Machine Image'' in *Ohm,* June 2000; ''Drive, Track 3'' in *Net Condition: Art and Global Media,* Cambridge, Massachusetts 2000; ''Introduction'' in *Interaction: Artistic Practice in the Network,* New York 2001.

On CRANDALL: Articles—''Monitoreando Biotecnologia: Entrevista con Jordan Crandall'' by Masa Adherida in *Sputnik,* 2000; ''Jordan Crandall: Driving Images'' by Brian Holmes in *Parachute,* October-December 2000.

CREMONINI, Leonardo

Nationality: Italian. **Born:** Bologna, 26 November 1925. **Education:** Studied at the Accademia delle Belle Arti, Bologna, under the painters Alfred Protti and Giuglielmo Pizzirani and sculptor Luciano Minguzzi, 1932–36; attended art classes, Paris, 1951. **Career:** Moved to Milan, 1945; settled in Paris, 1951, but worked often in Forio d'Ischia, until 1955; spent in Douarnenez, Finistere, 1956; lived in Panarea, Eolian Islands, 1958–59. Professor, Ecole des Beaux-Arts, Paris, Lives in Florence and Paris. **Agent:** Galerie Claude Bernard, 7 rue des Beaux-Arts, 75006 Paris. **Address:** 11 rue de Buci, 75006 Paris, France.

Individual Exhibitions:

1951 Centre d'Art Italien, Paris
1952 Catherine Viviano Gallery, New York
1954 Galleria dell'Obelisco, Rome
Frank Perls Gallery, Beverly Hills, California
Catherine Viviano Gallery, New York
1955 Hanover Gallery, London
1957 Catherine Viviano Gallery, New York
1960 Galleria del Milione, Milan
Galleria Galatea, Turin
Galerie du Dragon, Paris
Galerie Lacloche, Paris
1962 Catherine Viviano Gallery, New York
Galerie du Dragon, Paris
1963 Gallerie Galatea, Turin
1964 Galerie du Dragaon, Paris
Biennale, Venice
1966 Galerie du Dragon, Paris
1967 Galleria Il Fante di Spade, Rome
1969 Palais des Beaux-Arts, Brussels
National Gallery, Prague
Kunsthalle, Basle
Konsthall, Lund, Sweden
Museum Civico, Bologna (retrospective)
Galleria Il Bisonte, Florence
Musée d'Art Moderne de la Ville, Paris
1970 Kunsthalle, Darmstadt
1971 Galleria Giulia, Rome (toured Italy, Brussels, Paris)
1972 Galerie du Dragon, Paris
Galleria dei Lanzi, Milan
Galleria Il Gabbiano, Rome
1973 Galerie du Dragon, Paris
Maison des Arts et Loisirs, Montbeliard, France
Maison de la Culture, Rennes
Musée d'Art Moderne, Strasbourg
1974 Galerie du Dragon, Paris
Galleria Il Portico, Cesena, Italy
Maison de la Culture, Grenoble
Galleria Eidos, Milan
Maison de la Culture, Amiens, France
1975 Galerie Jan Krugier, Geneva
1976 Galerie Forni, Amsterdam
Maison de la Culture, Gretil, France
Maison de la Culture, Corbeil, France
1977 Galleria Il Gabbiano, Rome
Galleria Forni, Bologna
Galleria Santacroce, Florence
Galleria Adelphi, Padua
1978 Galleria Santacroce, Florence
Galleria Communale, Prato, Italy
Galleria Communale, San Gimignano, Italy
1979 Galerie Claude Bernard, Paris
1980 Galleria Forni, Bologna
Seibu Museum, Tokyo
Galerie La Hune, Paris
Musée Dechelette, Roanne, France
1982 Centre Culturel Le Parvis, Tarbes, France
La Chartreuse, Villeneuve-les-Avignon, France
1983 Galerie Claude Bernard, Paris
Musée de Grenoble, France
Tours Narbonnais, Carcassonne, France
Galerie Jean Claude David, Grenoble, France
1984 Palazzo Racani-Arroni, Spoleto, Italy
1985 Palazzo Pubblico, Siena, Italy
1986 Galleria Tentadue, Milan
Institut Culturel Francais, Athens
Spedale di Santa Maria della Scala, Siena, Italy
Castello Aragonese, Ischia, Italy
1987 Galerie Claude Bernard, at *FIAC 87,* Grand Palais, Paris

Selected Group Exhibitions:

1952 *Pittsburgh International,* Carnegie Institute, Pittsburgh
1956 *Modern Italian Art,* Tate Gallery, London
1961 *Italian Contemporary Art,* Museum of Kamakura, Japan
1967 *Le Monde en Question,* Musée National d'Art Moderne, Paris
1971 *Aspetti della Nuova Figurazione,* Palazzo Reale, Naples
1977 *Arte in Italia 1960–1977,* Galleria d'Arte Moderna, Turin

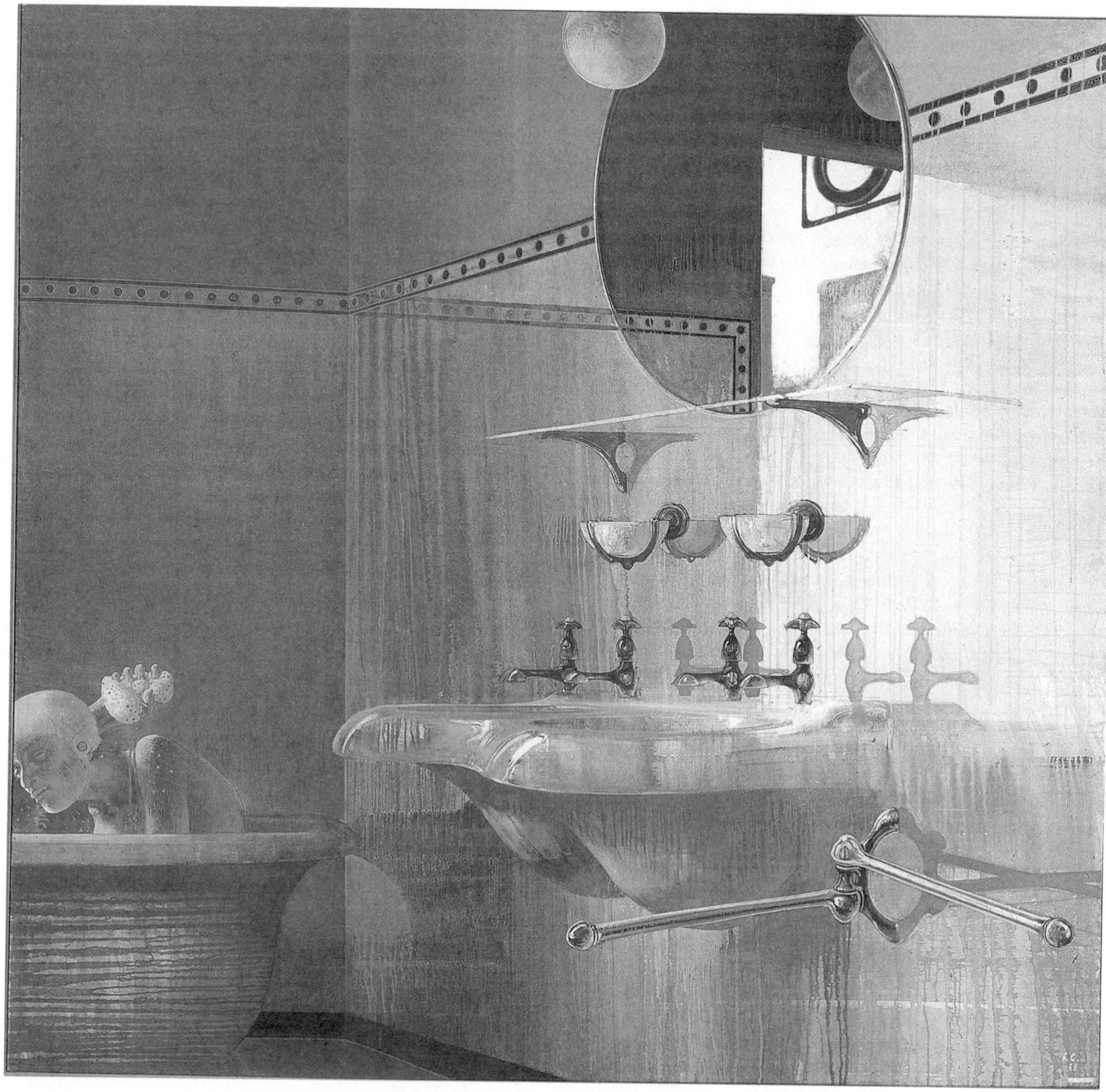

Leonardo Cremonini: *Parenthesis of Water (Les parentheses de l'eau),* 1968. ©2001 Artists Rights Society (ARS), NY/ADAGP, Paris.

1978 *Biennale,* Venice
1981 *Il Materiale delle Arte,* Castello Sforzesco, Milan
1984 *L'Immagine e il suop Doppio,* Palazzo Bagatti-Valsecchi, Milan (travelled to Galleria Rondanini, Rome)
1986 *Il Viaggio del Dialogo,* Villa Medici, Rome

Collections:

Museum of Modern Art, New York; Albright-Knox Art Gallery, Buffalo, New York; Carnegie Institute, Pittsburgh; Hirshhorn Museum and Sculpture Garden, Smithsonian Institution, Washington D.C.; Princeton University, New Jersey; Israel Museum, Jerusalem; Galleria d'Arte Moderna, Bologna; Galleria d'Arte Moderna, Milan; Centre Georges Pompidou, Paris; Musée d'Art Moderne de la Ville, Paris

Publications:

By CREMONINI: Articles—''Artisanat Populaire et Artisanat Colonise'' in *Revolution* (Paris), no. 3, 1963; ''Picasso? 13 Peintres Respondent'' in *Le Jardin des Arts* (Paris), October 1970; ''Dialogue avec Michel Troche'' in *La Nouvelle Critique* (Paris), December 1970; ''Nature bien ordonnee,'' with Marc le Bot, in *Traverses* (Paris), October 1976; Art et Machine: Entretien a propos du Multiple avec Cremoni et Cueco'' in *ATAC Informations* (Paris), April 1978;

La Commande Sociale dans les Arts Plastiques Seminaire du Creusot'' in *Cracap Informations* (Le Creusot), May 1978; ''Biennale '78: Il Pluralism o la Cattava Coscienza dell-Avanguardia'' in *La Loggia dei Mercanti* (Milan), May 1978; ''La Pudeur n'est pas Parole: L'Image Autobiographique'' in *Skira Annuel,* Geneva 1978; ''Modeles de l'Histoire'' in *Skira Annuel,* Geneva 1979.

On CREMONINI: Books—*Cremonini* by Marco Valsecchi, Milan 1962; *Cremonini* by Franco Solmi, Michel Butor and Louis Althusser, Bologna 1969; *Cremonini: 80 Dessigni* by Giuliano Briganti, Florence 1970; *Leonardo Cremonini* by Jacques Brosse and others, Bologna and Paris 1979 (includes bibliography); *Das kritische Engagement in Leonardo Cremoninis Malerei 1965–1980,* thesis by Petra Spatazza, Ruprecht Karl University, Heidelberg 1981; *Approche des peintures et dessins (1953–1978) de Leonardo Cremonini et des discours du peintre,* thesis by Jean Louis Fauthoux, University of Tolouse Le Mirail 1981; *Om relationemmellan rummet, objekten och Manniskan i Leonardo Cremoninis Maleri,* thesis by Carina Heden, University of Goteborg 1981; *Leonardo Cremonini,* with texts by William Rubin, Italo Galvino, Alain Jouffroy and others, Geneva 1987. **Articles—**''Artists Against Apartheid'' in *Arts Magazine,* vol. 60, October 1985; ''Lucida realta con ombra di follia'' by Mario de Micheli in *Arte,* no. 199, vol. 19, September 1989; ''Leonardo Cremonini: The Unconfessable in Painting'' by Gerard Xuriguera in *Cimaise,* no. 242, vol. 43, July-August 1996. **Films—***Grand Portrait: Leonardo Cremonini ou les jeux sans regle* by Jean Louis Roy, 1973; *Peintre de notre temps: Cremonini* by Georges Paumier, 1977.

* * *

Leonardo Cremonini is one of the group of Italian artists who were influenced and inspired by Picasso's ''Guernica'' to develop a dramatic, realistic style, enabling them to translate a concern for everyday life and human tragedy into a stylized, illustrative manner. It is no wonder, therefore, that in 1951, in his mid-30s, Cremonini transferred himself to Paris, where he has remained ever since, though he maintains regular contact with Italy; in 1960 he was honored with a major retrospective at the Museo Civico in his native Bologna.

His work, apart from the example of Picasso, reveals the profound influence of such Renaissance artists as Giotto, Masaccio and Piero della Francesca, especially in the balance that he has struck between rounded, almost sculptural human depiction, and an anti-natural, linear, geometrical form of composition. His preoccupations, however, have always been more dramatic and tense than these masters, almost theatrical in the investigation of torture, accidents, and the like, at the same time investing even the most innocent setting (figures in the interiors of autobuses, children at play, lovers in a park, or the wall furniture of a bathroom) with strange, nervous overtones. Cremonini is a brilliant draughtsman, and there are aspects of his figures, in their doll-like rounded stylization, which are reminiscent of such fellow Italians as Campigli and Manzu. His stated subject is ''l'homme social,'' or man in existentialist relationship to the world. Certainly there is usually present a sense of uncertainty, as though one were waiting for the catastrophe to occur.

In his earlier work, often landscapes, isolating vegetation as huge, fleshy forms, he used paint in deep impasto with bright, brash colour. Gradually, as he adopted the idea of the figure in landscape, albeit urban landscape, he refined both his draughtsmanship and thinned down his palette. The early 1960s saw violent subjects, tortures, road accidents, often involving children (reminiscent of the Yugoslav painter Velickovic). Although the superficial drama of these subjects was eventually abandoned, precisely the same sense of unease is contained in the interior views of buses, with the bulbous heads barely in view, or in the beach-scenes and domestic interiors. There is something cinematic in Cremonini's visual definitions, as if he were seeking to place his figures at odd angles to their architectural settings. Throwing them, and us, so to speak, off balance.

—Charles Spencer

CRUZ-DIEZ, Carlos

Nationality: Venezuelan. **Born:** Caracas, 17 August 1923. **Education:** Studied at the School of Plastic and Applied Arts, Caracas, 1940–45, diplomas in artistic education and manual arts, 1945; studied advanced techniques of art and publicity, New York, 1947. **Career:** Publications designer, Creole Petroleum Corporation, 1944–45; art director McCann-Erickson Advertising Agency, Venezuelan Subsidiary, 1946–51; illustrator, *El Nacional,* Caracas, 1953–55; travelled to Barcelona, and to Paris to study physical qualities of color, 1955–56; Designer of Publications, Ministry of Education, and Designer, *El Disco Anaranjado,* Caracas, from 1957; lived in Paris, 1960–80, before returning to Caracas. Teacher, 1953–55, professor and assistant director, School of Arts, Caracas, 1958–60; professor, School of Journalism, Central University of Venezuela, Caracas, 1959–60; professor, 1972–73, and juror, 1973–80, Ecole Superieur des Beaux-Arts, Paris. **Awards:** First Prize, Alphabetization Poster Contest, Caracas, 1946; José Loreto Arismendi Prize, 1950, Artistides Rojas Prize, 1952, and Enrique Otero Vizcarrando Prize, 1953, Official Exhibition of Venezuelan Art; Emilio Boggio Prize, Ateneo de Valencia Exhibition, Venezuela, 1950; First Prize, *Bienal,* Cordóba, Argentina, 1966; Subsecretaria de la Cultura Award, Cordoba, 1966; International Painting Prize, *Bienal,* Sao Paulo, 1967; First Prize, *Nacional de Artes Plasticas,* Venezuela, 1971; Premio de Intervención del Arte en la Arquitectura, *Bienal de Arquitectura,* Venezuela, 1976. **Agents:** Galerie Denise René, 124 rue de la Boetie, 75008 Paris, France; Galeria Adler Castillo, Edificio Galipan Avenida Francisco de Miranda, Caracas 106. **Address:** 23 rue Pierre Semard, Paris 75009, France.

Individual Exhibitions:

1947 Instituto Venezolana Americano, Caracas
1955 Museum of Fine Arts, Caracas
1956 Galeria Buchholz, Madrid
1960 Faculty of Architecture, Central University of Venezuela
Museum of Fine Arts, Caracas
1965 Galleria La Polena, Genoa
Galleria Il Punto, Turin
Signals Gallery, London
Physichromies de Cruz-Diez: Oeuvres do 1954 a 1965, Galerie Kerchache, Paris
1966 Galerie M.E. Thelen, Essen
Galerie Fundacion Mendoza, Caracas
1967 Galerie Corkright, Caracas
1968 Galerie Art Intermedia, Cologne
Galerie Accent, Brussels

Gallerie K.B., Oslo
Museum am Ostwall, Dortmund, West Germany
1969 *Cruz-Diez et les 3 Etapes la Couleur Moderne,* Galerie Denise René, Paris (Rive Droite and Rive Gauche)
Galerie Corkright, Caracas
1970 Galerie Ursula Lichter, Frankfurt
Artestudio Macerata, Macerata, Italy
1971 *Physichromies, Couleur Additive, Induction Chromatique, Chromointerferences,* Galerie Denise René, New York
Galerie Corkright, Caracas
1972 Galerie Buchholz, Munich
Galerie Formes et Muraux, Lyons
1973 Galleria Falchi, Milan
Galerie Denise Rene, Paris
Galleria Christian Stein, Turin
Galeria Cadafe, Caracas
1974 Galleria Trinita, Rome
Génesis, Eclosión y Absoluto del Color, Galeria Corkright, Caracas
1975 Galeria Aele, Madrid
Galerie Denise René, Paris
Museo de Arte Contemporáneo, Bogota
Galeria Barbie, Barcelona
Museo La Tertulia, Cali, Colombia
Artiste et Ville, Caracas
1976 Galeria de Arte Mikeldi, Bilbao, Spain
Museo de Arte Moderno, Mexico City
Pabellón de Arte de la Ciudadela, Pamplona, Spain
Galerie Denise René, New York
Musée de la Chaux des Fonds, Switzerland
1977 Galerie Latzer, Kreuzlingen, Switzerland
Allianza Francesa, Caracas
Galerie Venezuela, New York
Galerie Noroit, Arras, France
Art in the Street, Imperial College, London
1978 *Art in the Street,* University of Reading
Ausbildungszentrum USB, Wolfsberg, Switzerland
Pavillon Werd, Zurich
Umjetnik i Grad, Galerija Suvremene, Zagreb
Ibero-Amerikansiches Institut, West Berlin
1979 Arte Contacto, Caracas
Galerija Zgraf, Sarajevo, Yugoslavia
1980 Universidad Simon Bolivar, Caracas
Art in the Street, University of Liverpool
Casa de las Americas, Havana
1981 *Didactica y Diálectica del Color,* at *Triennale,* Caens (travelled to the Museo de Bellas Artes, Pordenone, Italy; and Museo de Arte Contemporáneo, Caracas)

Selected Group Exhibitions:

1950 *Official Exhibition of Venezuela Art,* Caracas (and 1952, 1953)
1953 *Bienal,* Sao Paulo (and 1963, 1967, 1979)
1962 *Biennale, Venice*
1964 *Mouvement II,* Galerie Denise René, Paris
1965 *Anthology of Kinetic Sculpture and Perceptual Art,* Signals Gallery, London
1966 *Licht und Bewegung,* Kunstverein, Dusseldorf
1968 *Art Vivant,* Foundation Maeght, St.-Paul-de-Vence, France
1972 *12 Ans d'Art Contemporain en France,* Grand Palais, Paris
1977 *3 Villes, 3 Collections,* Centre Georges Pompidou, Paris
1979 *Modern Latin American Art,* Lowe Art Museum, University of Miami

Collections:

Museo de Bellas Artes, Caracas; Casa de la Cultura, Havana; Museum of Modern Art, New York; Museum of Contemporary Art, Chicago; Musée d'Art Contemporain, Montreal; Victoria and Albert Museum, London; Städtisches Museum, Leverkusen, West Germany; Museum des 20. Jahrhunderts, Vienna; Centre National d'Art Contemporain, Paris, Musée d'Art Moderne de la Ville, Paris; Museum Ludwig, Cologne; Modern Art Lambert Collection, Dublin.

Publications:

On CRUZ-DIEZ: Books--*Physichromies de Cruz-Diez: Oeuvres de 1954 a 1965,* exhibition catalog, with text by Frank Popper, Paris 1965; *Carlos Cruz-Diez,* exhibition catalog, with text by Carlos Dorante, Caracas 1967; *Cruz-Diez et les 3 Etapes de la Couleur Moderne,* exhibition catalog, with text by Jean Clay, Paris 1969; *Relief and 3-Dimensional Structures* by Cyril Barrett, London 1970; *An Introduction to Opitcal Art* by Cyril Barrett, London 1971; *The Techniques of Kinetic Art* by John Tobey, New York 1971; *12 Ans d'Art Contemporain en France,* exhibition catalog, with text by Jean-Luc Allerant, Paris 1972; *Carlos Cruz-Diez: Génesis, Eclosión y Absoluto del Color,* exhibition catalog, with text by Roberto Guevara, Caracas 1974; *Cruz-Diez* by Alfredo Boulton, Caracas 1975; *Cruz-Diez: Didactia y Dialectica del Color,* exhibition catalog, with text by Umbro Apollonio, Caracas 1981. **Articles—**''Karuptures: A Symposium on Monumental Sculpture in Lamentin (Guadeloupe)'' in *Cimaise,* no. 230, vol. 41, June-August 1994; ''Carlos Cruz-Diez: A Venezuelan in Paris'' by Valère Bertrand in *Cimaise,* vol. 41, November/December 1994.

* * *

Cruz-Diez's main preoccupation is to set up ''situations'' of various kinds which in their turn give rise to certain sequences of events whose interest lies in an intense experience of colour. These ''chromatic events'' are obtained by transforming ''concepts'' into sensory phenomena and in this way colour, which is traditionally subordinate to subject or form, acquires an existence of its own and pursues its own evolution in space and time.

All of Cruz-Diez's chromatic propositions—*Physichromies, Chromointerferences, Chromosaturations, Transchromies*—are based on this particular theoretical position, but the artist expresses a different aspect of the problem in each type of work.

The *Physichromies* are changing structures which project colour from a surface into space. They set up an atmosphere of coloured light which varies with the intensity and the position of the light source and with the position and the distance of the spectator. These statements combine three modalities of colour: addition, reflection and subtraction. The *Chromointerferences* are formal networks which bring into the foreground the phenomenon of chromatic waves produced by interference. While these works are based in general on a plane surface, the *Chromosaturations,* on the contrary, are conceived in terms of the appropriation of three-dimensional space for the purpose of bringing the experience of pure colour into the foreground. The *Transchromies* differ from the other colour experiments by Cruz-Diez through the use of effects which derive from the superimposition of various different chromatic scales and the accent is placed specifically on transparency, on optical mixture and the instability of the chromatic vision.

All of these researches by Carlos Cruz-Diez have given rise to large-scale architectural and environmental applications in-and outside private dwellings, industrial plants, administrative buildings and town squares in his native Venezuela and in Europe. Outstanding among Cruz-Diez's achievements in Venezuela are the giant cylinders of chromatic induction for the grain elevators of the port of La Guaira, the walls of additive colour on the left bank of the Guaire river, and the multiple environmental chromatic works in the two vast rooms where the machinery of the hydroelectric power station at Guri is located and which were realized between 1977 and 1986. An impressive environmental work, the *Radial Chromostructure* or *Homage to the Sun,* at Barquisimeto, elaborated between 1982 and 1987, consists of thirty-two multicoloured elements placed in a circle on high ground, whereas the *Double-Faced Chromostructure* at the Centro Plaza and the gigantic *Physichromie* at the Banco Consolidado in Caracas are good examples of urban integration. At the same time, Cruz-Diez has realized a number of environmental works in Europe. Among these one can mention another *Double-Faced Chromostructure* at the Place du Venezuela in Paris, a new version of which was installed at Oleron-Sainte-Marie some twelve years later. A chromatic interior installation can be found at a Bank in Zurich and two giant *Physichromies* in Lyons and Cambrai in France, as well as an additive coloured wall at Arras and a *Chromostructure* at Jouy-en-Josas. In Spain, a dynamic *Chromostructure* was installed at the Rey Juan Carlos Park, Recinto Ferial, in Madrid, in 1991 and several works of chromatic induction, transition and saturation were shown at the Venezuelan pavilion of the World Exhibition at Sevilla in 1992.

With this impressive array of large-scale works applied to internal and external architecture in an advanced social and industrial context, Carlos Cruz-Diez can be considered as one of the principal artists who have traced a route from the environmental art of the 60s and 70s to the techno-ecologically concerned art of the end of the twentieth century.

The artist has also undertaken a number of chromatic ''actions'' in public places involving the spectator both physically and psychologically in the creative process. In fact, in all his statements involving space and taking place in time, Cruz-Diez aims through the intermediacy of the public, to achieve perpetual transformation of both event and colour.

—Frank Popper

CUCCHI, Enzo

Nationality: Italian. **Born:** Morra d'Alba, near Ancona, in 1950. **Family:** Married to Brunella Cucchi. **Career:** Independent painter, living and working in Ancona and Rome; co-designed (with Mario Botta) Chapel Santa Maria degli Angeli, Monte Tamaro, Italy, 1996. **Agents:** Joseph Helman Gallery, 20 West 57th Street, New York, New York, 10019; Galerie Kaess-Weiss, Grüneisenstrasse 19, D-70184, Stuttgart, Germany; Petersburg Press, P.O. Box 2238, New York, New York, 10101.

Individual Exhibitions:

1977 Incontri Internazionali d'Arte, Rome
1978 Galleria de Crescenzo, Rome
1979 Galleria Mario Diacono, Bologna
Galleria Tucci Russo, Turin
Galleria Mozzoli, Modena, Italy
1980 Galerie Paul Maenz, Cologne
1981 Gallery Sperone/Westwater/Fischer, New York
Galleria Sperone, Rome
Galerie Bruno Bischofberger, Zurich
Galleria Mario Diacono, Rome
Galerie Paul Maenz, Cologne (travelled to Art and Project, Amsterdam, 1982)
1982 Galerie Beyeler, Basle
Kunsthaus, Zurich (travelled to the Groningen Museum, Netherlands)
1983 Museum Folkwang, Essen, West Germany
Galerie Schellmann und Kluser, Munich
Sperone-Westwater, New York
1984 Akira Ikeda Gallery, Tokyo
Anthony D'Offay Gallery, London
Sperone-Westwater, New York
Kunsthalle, Basle
1985 Galerie Daniel Templon, Paris
Galerie Bernd Kluser, Munch
Kunstmuseum, Dusseldorf
Louisiana Museum, Humlebaek, Denmark
1986 CAPC/Musee d'Art Contemporain, Bordeaux, France
Guggenheim Museum, New York
Centre Georges Pompidou, Paris
1987 Galerie Beyeler, Basle
1994 *Idoli,* Galerie Artiscope, Brussels
1995 *Enzo Cucchi,* Palazzo Reale-Arengario, Milan (catalog)
Cucchi, Sara Hildenin Taidemuseo, Tampere, Finland (catalog)
1996 Sezon Museum, Japan
Simm'Nervusi, Magazzino d'Arte Moderna, Rome (catalog)
1997 Museum of Capodimonte, Italy
Città d'Ancona: Enzo Cucchi, Mole Vanvitelliana, Ancona (catalog)
Bruno Bischofberger Gallery, Zurich
Closer to the Light, Suermondt-Ludwig-Museum, Aachen, Germany (catalog)
Simm'nervusi, Tony Shafrazi Gallery, New York (catalog)
1999 *Decades,* Artcore Gallery, Toronto
Berge, Menschen, Licht—Gemälde un Zeichnungen 1995–1999, Deichtorhallen, Hamburg (catalog)
Works on Paper, The Italian Cultural Institutes, Los Angeles
2000 Tony Shafrazi Gallery, New York (catalog)
Cucchi: Chi Cucca Chi, Cucchi?, Galleria Poggiali & Forconi, Firenze (catalog)

Selected Group Exhibitions:

1979 *Alternativa del Nuovo,* Palazzo delle Esposizioni, Rome
1980 *Die Enthauptete Hand: 100 Zeichnungen aus Italien, Kunstverein,* Bonn (travelled to the Städtische Galerie,

Wolfsberg, West Germany, and the Groningen Museum, Netherlands)
1981 *Westkunst: Zeitgenossiche Kunst seit 1939,* Rheinhallen, Cologne
1982 *'60-'80: Attitudes, Concepts, Images,* Stedelijk Museum, Amsterdam
1983 *New Art,* Tate Gallery, London
1984 *International Survey of Recent Painting and Sculpture,* Museum of Modern Art, New York
1985 *The European Iceberg,* Art Gallery of Ontario, Toronto
1987 *Avant-Garde in the Eighties,* Los Angeles County Museum of Art
1994 *Imprimateur,* Galerie Graff, Montreal (also Centre Saidye Bronfman, Montreal, and Galerie de l'Université de Québec à Montréal)
Mario Botta—Enzo Cucchi: La Cappella del Monte Tamaro, Museo d'Arte, Lugano (catalog)
1996 *23rd São Paulo Biennale,* Brazil
Enzo Cucchi, Martial Raysse: Dei, Santi e Viandanti=Dieux, Sanits et Pèlerins, Museo Civico Medievale, Bologna (catalog)
1997 *47th Biennale,* Venice, Italy (catalog)
Balla, De Chirico, Savinio, Picasso, Paolini, Cucchi, Museo d'Arte Contemporanea, Castello di Rivoli, Italy (catalog)
1998 *Artenergie,* Pitti Imagine, Florence
Transavanguardia: Sandro Chia, Enzo Cucchi, Francesco Clemente, Mimmo Paladino, Museum Wirth, Kunzelsau-Gaisbach, Germany (catalog)
Enzo Cucchi, Mimmo Paladino: Opere Sue Carta, Galleria Cesarea, Genova (catalog)
2000 *Arte al Centro,* Cittadellarte-Fondazione Pistoletto, Biella, Italy

Publications:

By CUCCHI: Books—*Treo Quattro Artisti Secchi,* exhibition catalog, Modena, Italy 1979; *Canzone,* Modena, Italy 1979; *Enzo Cucchi,* exhibition catalog, Basle 1984; *Enzo Cucchi; Italia,* London 1984; *La Cappella del Monte Tamaro,* with Mario Botta, Torino 1994; *Enzo: Scritti Scelti dal 1983 al 1993,* with Ida Gianelli and Mario Codognato, Torino 1995; *Enzo Cucchi: Piu Vicina Alla Luce,* Milan 1997; *Enzo Cucchi: The Tel Aviv Mosaic,* with Mordechai Omer, Milan 1999. **Articles—**''Designo Finto'' in *Enzo Cucci,* exhibition catalog, Rome 1978; ''Die Hauser fullen sich alle bis auf halbe Höne'' in *Sieben Junge Kunstler aus Italien,* exhibition catalog, Basle 1980; ''Di Certo Communque ce che l'Immagine'' in *Enzo Cucchi,* exhibition catalog, Cologne 1981; interview with Ernö P. Szabó in *Új Müvészet,* vol. 5, no. 10, October 1994; interview with Rahel Hartmann in *Kunst und Kirche,* no. 2, 1996.

On CUCCHI: Books—*Enzo Cucchi,* exhibition catalog, Rome 1978; *Enzo Cucchi,* exhibition catalog, Cologne 1981; *Die Enthaupieie Hand: 100 Zeichnungen aus Italien,* exhibition catalog, with W. M. Faust, Bonn 1980; *The Italian Trans-Avantgarde* by Achille Bonito Oliva, Milan 1980; *Seiben Junge Kunstler aus Italien,* exhibition catalog, by Jean-Christophe Ammann, Basle 1980; *Mythe/Drame/Tragedie,* exhibition catalog, by Achille Bonito Oliva and others, Saint-Etienne, France 1982; *Enzo Cucchi: Zeichnungen,* exhibition catalog with texts by Ursula Perucchi and Frans Haks, Zurich 1982; *Baldessari/Borofsky/Chia/Clemente/Cucchi/Disler/Penck/Winnewisser,* with foreword by Frans Haks, introduction by Steven Kolsteren, New York and Groningen 1982; *Enzo Cucchi,* exhibition catalog with essay by Diane Waldman, New York 1986. **Articles—**''Enzo Cucchi: Portrait by Armin Linke'' by Jean-Christophe Ammann in *Du,* no. 1, January 1994; ''Enzo Cucchi, Maria Papadimitriou'' by Miltos Manetas in *Flash Art,* vol. 27, no. 174, January-February 1994; ''Roma: Enzo Cucchi: Studio Home'' by Stefano Casciani in *Abitare,* no. 335, December 1994; ''Die Kapelle Santa Maria degli Angeli auf dem Monte Tamaro'' by Ludger Fischer in *Munster,* vol. 50, no. 3, 1997; ''Cucchi'' by Alessandro Riva in *Arte,* no. 283, March 1997; ''A Living and Work Space'' by François Burkhardt in *Domus,* no. 803, April 1998; ''Conservation'' by Allan Byrne in *Artonview,* no. 20, Summer 1999–2000; ''Steady Demand for Cucchi'' by Daniel Grant in *Art News,* vol. 100, no. 3, March 2001.

* * *

Towards the end of the 1970s there were a number of Italian painters who were looking for new foundations for their work, new horizons, and new ways of dealing with the artistic problems of the recent past. By using some of their experiments Enzo Cucchi was able to realize a poetic style of his own, although his debt to these artists is apparent in those first works of his which clearly reveal a kind of tension between form and content. These are works which bear his own personal signature and yet still reflect a general preoccupation with the problematic relationship between a work of art and the space it occupies. More precisely, Cucchi is interested in the conflicts which characterize such relationships.

Two of his exhibitions are particularly relevant here. In the first of these, *Alla lontana alla francese* (January, 1979), Cucchi gave us a canvas, loosely hung from the wall, which depicted an ordered series of houses in silhouette. In the foreground is a large cane, curved at the top, and a white-enamel ceramic form. And further away is another canvas, bearing the artist's signature, which depicts a series of repeated animal forms. In the second exhibition, *Lacavalla, Azzura* (February, 1979), there is an unbleached canvas, thickly overlaid with earthy, red-orange pigment, one corner of which has been curled up to reveal a large terracotta ladle, resting on two easels below. The aim here is to establish a rapport among the canvas, the paint, and the objects themselves.

After these two exhibitions, Cucchi turned his attention to the pictorial image, which until now had played a secondary role in his work. There is a kind of transitional period, in which he moves from his earlier concern for relationships to works in which the images themselves carry the full burden of his meaning. In many works, the object to be depicted is still placed nearby. One example, a 19' canvas from 1980 called *Teste di Terra Cotta* (''Terracotta Heads''), typifies the ongoing interrelationship of drawing, painting, and sculpture in Cucchi's oeuvre. It depicts a floating sideways figure awkwardly rendered in charcoal, whose head touches a group of four disembodied heads in the corner of the canvas, all bearing outstretched tongues and unfocused eyes. A large dark ovoid floats in the space at the figure's rear—a rock, a shadow? On the floor to the left of the canvas rests a simple terracotta oval the same shape and scale as the heads. Elemental and somewhat crude, the piece illustrates the fundamentally intuitive, primitivist impulse of Cucchi's work.

Paintings from only a few years later tend to be blatantly apocalyptic in tone, with huge, densely painted, swirling compositions depicting fires or deluges, populated with roosters, skulls, or struggling heroic figures. *A Sigh of a Wave,* 1983, with its surging whites, blacks, and terracotta reds, depicts a conflagration of elemental forces loaded with traditional Christian associations of mortality and judgment.

In the last decade, the archaic and visionary themes of Cucchi's work have remained constant even while his emblems and palette have become more enigmatic and sophisticated. His fantastical visions become touched with whimsy and irony. He continues to use many different techniques in a single piece—oil on canvas, collage, ceramic, pencil—giving his work great textural range. In *Untitled (Roma),* 1990, strange elongated figures hover over a mystical landscape. A centralized flame, cut from a sheet of metal and affixed to the canvas, bursts forth like a quirky plant, the source of light and subsequent life thus literalized like a talisman. Drawing has continued to occupy an important role in Cucchi's work; small drawings from the artist's archives often accompany his exhibitions, amplifying his themes. The drawings may be appreciated independently for their qualities of tactile immediacy, their awkward lyricism, and the associative richness they impart to Cucchi's free-ranging methods.

The artist currently designs frescoes for churches, casts large-scale bronzes, carves marble sculptures, and creates fountains for public squares in his native Italy, but within this diversity of means he returns again and again to the ancient mythic sources of human history and culture, expressing them in emotive, poetic symbols of simple mystery and strange beauty.

—Essay by Robert G. Lambarelli; updated by Dorothy Valakos

CUEVAS, José Luis

Nationality: Mexican. **Born:** Mexico City, 26 February 1934. **Education:** Studied at the School of Painting and Sculpture, La Esmeralda, Mexico City, 1944–47; studied engraving with Lola Cueto, Mexico City, 1948; **Family:** Married Bertha Lilian in 1961; children: Mariana, Zimena and Marie-Jose. **Career:** Independent painter and graphic artist, Mexico City and New York, professor of drawing, Latin American University, Mexico City, 1956–57; artist-in-residence, Philadelphia Museum School of Art, 1957–58, San Jose State College, California, 1970, and Fullerton College, Los Angeles, 1975. **Awards:** First International Drawing Award, *Bienal,* Sao Paulo, 1959; First Prize, *Mostra Internazionale di Bianco e Nero,* Lugano, Switzerland, 1962; ''Madeco'' Prize, *Bienal de Santiago,* Chile, 1965; First International Award, *Triennale,* New Delhi, 1968; First Prize, *Bienal de Grabado Latinoamericano,* San Juan, Puerto Rico, 1977; National Fine Arts Award, Mexico, 1981. **Agents:** Galeria de Arte Mexicano, Milan 18, Mexico City; Marisa Del Re Gallery, 41 East 57th Street, New York, New York 10019; Tasende Gallery, 820 Prospect Street, La Jolla, California 92037. **Address:** Galeana 109, San Angel, Mexico City 20, Mexico; 14 West 17th Street, New York, New York 10011, U.S.A; and Tasende Gallery, 820 Prospect St., La Jolla, CA 92037–4248.

Individual Exhibitions:

1953 Galeria Prisse, Mexico City
1954 Pan American Union, Washington, D.C.
1955 Galerie Edouard Loeb, Paris
1956 Galeria Proteo, Mexico City
Palacio de Bellas Artes, Havana
1957 Aenille Gallery, New York
1958 Instituto de Arte Contemporáneo, Lima, Peru
Galeria de Arte Contemporáneo, Caracas
1959 Galeria Bonino, Buenos Aires
1960 David Herbert Gallery, New York
Silvan Simone Gallery, Los Angeles
Fort Worth Art Center, Texas (retrospective)
1961 Galleria L'Obelisco, Rome
University of Texas at Austin
Santa Barbara Museum of Art, California
1962 Galleria Sixtina, Milan
Jerrold Morris Gallery, Toronto
Occidental College, Toronto
1963 Pan American Union, Washington, D.C. (graphic works retrospective, 1947–62)
Andrew Morris Gallery, New York
228 Gallery, St. Louis
Galleria Antonio Souza, Mexico City
1964 Galleria Profili, Milan
Silvan Simone Gallery, Los Angeles
Biblioteca Luis Angel Arango, Bogota
1965 Grace Borgenicht Gallery, New York
Munson-Williams-Proctor Institute, Utica, New York
Cuevas antes de Cuevas, Galeria Mer-Kup, Mexico City
1966 Galeria Misrachi, Mexico City
Silvan Simone Gallery, Los Angeles
1967 Walter Engel Gallery, Toronto
1969 Glade Gallery, New Orleans
1970 Galeria Misrachi, Mexico City
San Francisco Museum of Art
University Museum, Ciudad Universitaria, Mexico City
1971 Grace Borgenicht Gallery, New York
La Sala Nacional de Exposiciones, San Salvador
Galeria El Morro, San Juan, Puerto Rico
Museo de Bellas Artes, Toluca, Mexico
1972 Michael Wyman Gallery, Chicago
Museo de Arte Moderno, Mexico City
1973 Rothman Galleries, Toronto
Museo de Arte Moderno, Bogota
Galeria Aele, Madrid
Galeria Pecanins, Barcelona
1974 Palais de Beaux Arts, Brussels
Galeria Multipla, Sao Paulo
Museo de Arte Contemporáneo, Caracas
1975 San Diego Museum of Fine Arts, California
Phoenix Art Museum, Arizona
Palace of the Legion of Honor, San Francisco
Fullerton College, Los Angeles
Bienal, Sao Paulo
Museum of Modern Art, Gothernburg, Sweden
1976 Museo de Arte Moderno, Mexico City
Musée d'Art Moderne, Paris (restropective)
1977 Galeria Estudio Actual, Caracas
Musée des Beaux-Arts, Chartres, France
Galeria Misrachi, Mexico City
Galerie de Seine, Paris
1978 Grace Borgenicht Gallery, New York
1979 Museo de Arte Moderno, Mexico City
Tasende Gallery, San Diego, California

1980 Museo de Monterrey, Mexico (retrospective)
1981 Meeting Point Gallery, Miami
Galeria Joan Prats, Barcelonia
Museo de Ponce, San Juan, Puerto Rico
1982 Marisa del Re Gallery, New York
1991 *Twenty Five Years with Jose Luis Cuevas,* Tasende Gallery, La Jolla, California
1993 *On the Erotic Diaries of Jose Luis Cuevas,* Museo Jose Luis Cuevas, Mexico City
Jose Luis Cuevas: Recent Work—Large-Scale Paintings, Large-Scale Drawings, Prints, Sculpture, Ceramics, Illustrated Books, Museo Jose Luis Cuevas, Mexico City
1997 *Jose Luis Cuevas: Travelling Through the Studios,* Fondo de Cultura Economica, Mexico City

Selected Group Exhibitions:

1957 *Quatre maitres de la ligne: José Luis Cuevas, Alexander Calder, Stuart Davis and Morris Graves,* Napoule Museu, Napoule, France
1967 *Rosc 67,* Dublin
1970 *Collection of José Gómez Sicre,* College Art Gallery, State University of New York at New Paltz
1972 *Biennale,* Venice
1978 *Documenta,* Kassel, West Germany
1987 *Images of Mexico: Mexico's Contribution to the Art of the 20th Century,* Schim Kunsthalle, Frankfurt am Main, Germany
1991 *Homage to Catalonia and Mexico,* Pinacotecade Nuevo Leon, Monterrey, Mexico
1994 *Painters in Mexico in the XXth Century,* Luis Angel Arango Library, Bogota

Collections:

Museum of Modern Art, New York; Hirshhorn Museum, Smithsonian Institution, Washington, D.C.; Pan American Union Art Collection, Washington, D.C.; Munson Williams-Proctor Institute, Utica, New York; Fine Arts Gallery of San Diego, California; Art Gallery of Ontario, Canada; Museo de Arte Moderno, Mexico City; Museo de Bellas Artes, Caracas; Museo de Arte Moderno, Bogota; Museum of Art, Tel Aviv.

Publications:

By CUEVAS: Books—*Cuevas por Cuevas,* Mexico City 1965; *Cuevario,* Mexico City 1973; **Books illustrated—***The World of Kafka and Cuevas,* Philadelphia 1959; *Recollections of Childhood,* Los Angeles, 1962; *Cuevas-Charenton,* Los Angeles 1966; *Crime by Cuevas,* New York 1968; *Homage to Quevedo,* San Francisco 1969; *Cuevas Comedies,* San Francisco 1972; *La Rue des Mauvais Garcons,* Paris 1972; *Cuaderno de Paris,* Mexico City 1977; *Zarathustra,* Milan 1979; *Les obsesions noires de J.-L. Cuevas,* Paris 1982; *Letters to Tasende,* San Diego 1982.

On CUEVAS: Books—*José Luis Cuevas* by Jean Cassou, Philippe Soupault, and Flores Sanchez, Paris 1955; *José Luis Cuevas* by Carlos Valdes, Mexico City 1967; *El Mundo de José Luis Cuevas* by Carlos Fuentes, Mexico City 1969; *Confesiones de José Luis Cuevas* Alaide Foppa, Mexico City 1975; *Revelando a José Luis Cuevas* by Daisy Ascher, Mexico City 1979; *Cuevas: Ipotesi per una lettura* by Roberto Sanesi, Milan 1979; *Cartas para una exposicion,* Mexico City 1981; *José Luis Cuevas* by José Gomez Sicre, Barcelona 1982; *Twenty Five Years with Jose Luis Cuevas,* exhibition catalog, La Jolla 1991; *De los diarios eroticos de Jose Luis Cuevas,* exhibition catalog, Mexico City 1993; *Jose Luis Cuevas: Obra Reciente—Pinturas de Gran Formato, Dibujos de Gran Formato, Grabados, Esculturas, Ceramica, Libros Ilustrados,* exhibition catalog, Mexico City 1993; *Jose Luis Cuevas: Homanaje,* Mexico City 1997; *Jose Luis Cuevas: Viajando Por Los Talleres,* exhibition catalog, Mexico City 1997. **Articles—**''Painters in Mexico in the XXth Century: Luis Angel Arango Library, Bogota'' in *Art Nexus,* no. 14, October/December 1994; ''Mixed Fortunes in Mexico'' by Catalina Duran in *Printmaking Today,* vol. 8, no. 1, Spring 1999.

*

I hate accident, improvisation, play with materials for their own sake. I believe in ''originality'' only when it comes from the very essence of tradition. I believe an artist is original only when he shows his own accent or his full voice through materials given by his predecessors.

Today my main interest is the work of the great artists of the past: Van Eyck, Hals, Velazquez, Zurbaran, etc., and above all the great Chinese draftsmen of the 16th and 17th centuries.

—José Luis Cuevas

* * *

José Luis Cuevas is one of this century's most expressive draftsmen. His expressive power stems from a tension between the monstrous crudeness of the people he portrays: deformed, distorted, seamed and ridged, and an extreme delicacy of touch and technical skill. Like Leonardo, he sets down the line very swiftly, and should the stroke in a slightly different place seem better to him, leaves the first and adds the second, to produce an impression of the artist's hand, sure and immediate. His line, most often done with the pen, combines with a system of washes in greys and blacks, or a spectrum of watered down hues, pale, evoking faded things like dried flowers under glass, lavender in keepsakes, whatever has no juice. The vital is drained. By choosing to work in the desiccated colors of the funeral wreath, the artist calls up sensations of mortality, a modern-day *memento mori,* which fixes the moment before transition to another stage.

The presence of death has been constant with Cuevas since, at the age of 9, he was bedridden for a year with rheumatic fever. During that time he read intensely in European literature, which gave him a background in that culture and an understanding of its history coupled with respect, and he drew. His images have, ever since, reflected that background and the hallucinatory quality of the fevered sickbed.

They reflect as well his familiarity with the life of the miserable poor. Born himself in a poor quarter of Mexico City, living in rooms above his grandfather's pencil factory, he came to know intimately the lives of people society has trained us not to see: the old and sick, the cripple, the prostitute, the criminal. Through the remarkably compelling quality of his art he brings the observer to a head on confrontation with these subjects, at once marvelous and grotesque.

The frequency of the *autoretrato* in his oeuvre makes it clear that it was the artist himself who was first forced to this confrontation and to this fascination, in the end. As with the image of death, which he has often, through continuing ill health, been forced to contemplate. His contemplation ends in an erotic embrace: ''When the last heartbeat stops pounding, my good lady will bend down and give me a kiss.'' Death the Sweet Sister.

This attitude is very much in tune with the Mexican obsession with death, evident in the ritual festivities in the cemetery, the sweet candy skulls of the Day of the Dead, the cult of mutilation and sacrifice in the ancient religions of Mexico. Indeed, the bulbous heads in his drawings hark back to Olmec ancestors, yet Cuevas is no Mexican nationalist in his art. He abhors ''the Cactus Curtain'' and insists that art must build on the European tradition which has gone before, feeling a special affinity with many of the European masters, especially Rembrandt and Velazquez. This affinity has much to do with the international status which has always been accorded him, and much of his art has to do with European cities as well as his own.

But neither the European past nor echoes from ancient Mexico really determine his choice of subject, but rather the present day reality of the streets, the jails, cafes, brothels, where the struggle from day to day is all too real. It is this continual, brooding concern with the tragedy of life in this century, the conviction that life is not only absurd but a waste, a conviction born of experience, which makes his art ring true.

—Barbara Cortright

CURNOE, Greg

Nationality: Canadian. **Born:** London, Ontario, 19 November 1936. **Education:** Wortley Road Public School, London 1940–50; South Collegiate Institute, London, 1950–54; studied art at H.B. Beal Technical School, London, 1954–56; Doon School of Art, Ontario, 1956; Ontario College of Art, Toronto, 1957–60. **Family:** Married Sheila Curnoe in 1965; children: Owen, Galen, and Zoe. **Career:** Worked with survey crew, London, 1957–60; worked as a trucker for Coca Cola Company, London, 1961. Independent artist in London since 1960: established studio on Richmond Street, 1960–63, on King Street, 1963–68, and on Weston Street, since 1968. Founder, Garrett Gallery artists' cooperative Toronto, 1957–59; Region Gallery, London, 1961–63; 20/20 Gallery, London 1966–70; and Forest City Art Gallery, London, since 1973. Founder-editor, *Region* magazine, London, 1961–78; contributing editor, *20 Cents Magazine,* London, 1967–70. Member, Société pour l'Etude du Mouvement Dada, London, 1954; president, Nihilist Party of Canada, since 1961; kazoo manufacturer, and member, Nihilist Spasm Band, since 1966; member, and former Racing Secretary, London Centennial Wheelers Club, since 1971; founder, Association for the Documentation of Neglected Aspects of Culture in Canada popular culture group, since 1972; Spokesman, Canadian Artists Representation, Ontario, 1974–75. Artist-in-residence, University of Western Ontario, London, 1975–76. **Died:** London, Ontario, due to injuries sustained during a cycling accident, 14 November 1992.

Individual Exhibitions:

1961 *Exhibition of Things,* Richard E. Crouch Branch Library, London, Ontario
Isaacs Gallery, Toronto
McIntosh Memorial Art Gallery, London, Ontario Region Gallery, London, Ontario
1962 *Greg Curnoe/Larry Russell,* Region Gallery, London, Ontario
McIntosh Memorial Art Gallery, London, Ontario
1963 McIntosh Memorial Art Gallery, London, Ontario
Greg Curnoe/Brian Dibb, Region Gallery, London
1964 *Imports and Local Works: Curnoe/Urquhart,* McIntosh Memorial Art Gallery, London, Ontario
David Mirvish Gallery, Toronto
Norman MacKenzie Art Gallery, Regina, Saskatchewan
1965 David Mirvish Gallery, Toronto
1966 *Paintings by Greg Curnoe,* Vancouver Art Gallery (travelled to Edmonton Art Gallery)
New York from Sowesto Greg Curnoe, Isaacs Gallery, Toronto
Recent Collages, New Design Gallery, Vancouver
1967 *Series,* 20/20 Gallery, London, Ontario
Time Series, Isaacs Gallery, Toronto
Chambers/Curnoe, Mc Intosh Memorial Art Gallery, London, Ontario
1969 *Bienal,* Sao Paulo
1970 *Drawings,* McIntosh Memorial Art Gallery, London, Ontario
Collages 1961–70, Isaacs Gallery, Toronto
Views of Victoria Hospital and Wings over the Atlantic, Isaacs Gallery, Montreal
1971 Waddington Galleries, Montreal
1972 *Display of Water Colours, Measurements and Clockings,* London House, Ontario
1973 Isaacs Gallery, Toronto
Watercolours and Drawings, Polyglot Gallery, London, Ontario
1974 *The Great Canadian Sonnet,* Drawings, National Gallery, Ottawa (toured Canada)
Watercolours, Forest City Art Gallery, London, Ontario
1975 *Recent Watercolours,* Isaacs Gallery, Toronto
Some Lettered Works 1961–69, London Art Gallery, Ontario
Greg Curnoe—Artist With His Work, Art Gallery of Ontario, Toronto, Canada
1976 *Biennale,* Venice
1982 Art Gallery of Ontario, Toronto, Canada (retrospective)
2001 *Life & Stuff,* Art Gallery of Ontario, Toronto, Canada

Selected Group Exhibitions:

1967 *Statements: 18 Canadian Artist,* Norman Mackenzie Art Gallery, Regina, Saskatchewan
1969 *Canada: Art d'Aujourd hui,* Centre Georges Pompidou, Paris (toured Europe)
The Heart of London, National Gallery of Canada, Ottawa (toured Canada, 1968–69)
Canada 101, at the Edinburgh Festival
1973 *Realism: Emulsion and Omission,* Kingston, Ontario

1974 *Bienal Americana de Arts Graphics,* at Colombia Art Mart, Kitchener-Waterloo Art Gallery, Ontario
1993 *Book Ends & Odd Books: Publications Refuting Conventional Form from the Banff Centre Library Collection,* Walter Phillips Gallery, Banff Centre, Banff, Alberta
1999 *A Century of Canadian Drawing: Selected from the Permanent Collection of the Dalhousie Art Gallery,* Dalhousie Art Gallery, Halifax, Nova Scotia

Collections:

University of Western Ontario, London; London Public Library and Art Gallery, Ontario; The Canada Council, Ottawa; National Gallery of Canada, Ottawa; Art Gallery of Ontario, Toronto; Art Institute of Ontario, Toronto; Museum of Fine Arts, Montreal; Vancouver Art Gallery; City Trust, Vancouver, Norman Mackenzie Art Gallery, Regina Saskatchewan.

Publications:

By CURNOE: Books—*Deeds/Abstracts: The History of a London Lot,* edited by Frank Davey, London, Ontario, 1995. **Articles—** ''Greg Curnoe'', in *ArtViews,* vol. 14, no. 1, Winter 1987–88.

On CURNOE: Books—*Paintings by Greg Curnoe,* exhibition catalog, Vancouver 1966; *Chambers and Curnoe,* exhibition catalog, London, Ontario 1967; *Statements: 18 Canadian Artists,* exhibition catalog, Regina, Saskatchewan 1967; *Canada: Art d'Aujourd hui,* exhibition catalog, Paris 1968; *The Heart of London,* exhibition catalog, Ottawa 1968; *Greg Curnoe: Canada,* exhibition catalog, Sao Paulo 1969; *Canadian Art Today* by William Townsend, London 1970; *Realism: Emulsion and Omission,* exhibition catalog, with text by M. Kluyver-Cluysenaer, Kingston, Ontario 1973; *Greg Curnoe,* exhibition catalog, Venice 1976; *A Century of Canadian Drawing: Selected from the Permanent Collection of the Dalhousie Art Gallery,* exhibition catalog, Halifax 1999. **Articles—**''More Words on Curnoe's Worldly World'' by John Chandler in *Artscanada* (Toronto), April 1969; ''The Language of the Eyes: Windows and Mirror'' by Ross Mendes in *Artscanada* (Toronto), October 1969; ''Painting from Life: Greg Curnoe at the Isaac Gallery'' by J. N. Chandler in *Artscanada* (Toronto), June 1971; ''Knowing: The Surface'' by V. Coleman in *Artscanada* (Toronto), February 1972; ''Sources, Resources: Greg Curnoe'' by J. N. Chandler in *Artscanada* (Toronto), February 1973; ''The Typography of Art'' by Mark Critoph in *Studio Magazine,* vol. 11, no. 2, March-April 1993; ''Local Colour: Colour and Technique in the Work of Joanne Tod, Greg Curnoe and Jaan Poldaas'' in *C Magazine,* no. 38, Summer 1993; ''Studio View'' in *Canadian Art,* vol. 14, no. 2, Summer 1997.

*

I frequently work in series, but what I do does not come from any general concept or framework of ideas. I work with people, places and things. Any ideas that I have and conclusions that I make come from the people, places and things I know.

I assemble all kinds of materials. Assembling, sorting, listing and collecting has been the basis of most of my work.

I have strong feelings about where I was born, about living in a relatively small city slightly over 200 km away from a large one, about living in a sparsely populated large country beside a heavily populated large one. I live in an extended family and that makes me think a lot about the shared culture in my community contrasted with other cultural activities that only a small number of people are aware of. My work operates in both of theses contexts. I also think a lot about eroticism and pornography and about how they relate to community and individual tastes.

My work is about resisting as much as possible the tendency of American culture to overwhelm other cultures. I also resist, as much as possible, any attempt to elevate what I do to the level of high art.

—Greg Curnoe

* * *

''The world is your own backyard,'' says Greg Curnoe. More important, he might add, your own background is your world. For Curnoe, a sense of Regionalism is the key to authentic work. His is based in London, Ontario (he was born there in 1936), more humid in summer and colder in winter than other parts of southern Ontario. It's a place with its own confident, dynamic creative milieu, to some extent associated with the University of Western Ontario. It's a breeding ground for artists, most of whom, like Curnoe, receive a firm foundation at H. B. Beal Technical School where he studied from 1954 to 1956.

Curnoe first came into contact with Dada through his teachers at Beal in 1954. In 1961, he participated with Michael Snow and Joyce Wieland in a Neo-Dada exhibition. His work is remarkable for its bold design sense, bright primary flat colours, clean outlines, a complete rejection of modelling. His work is spare and deft.

From 1964, Curnoe has expressed his concerns in works like ''Springs on the Ridgeway,'' using words to describe the real world around the edge, and in the picture space, a real curtain, metal rod and yoyo. Combined with these ''real'' objects are a cut-out of a radio and a lushly painted and flat nude seen from the back. In later works, like his masterpiece, the mammoth ''View of Victoria Hospital, Second Series,'' 1969–1971, Curnoe adds wires and electric lights. Here, his fine, harmonious colour is modelled on Robert Delaunay and county town carnivals, strident oranges and greens or rainbow tints.

In works expanded from his journals, wordscapes, he records what he sees in lettered words that seem almost compulsive. At times, the results are bland and overly earnest, but they are personal documents too, perhaps even the most personal, recording the pattern of his life, his trips, his thoughts, his conversations.

Curnoe is an original. But his kind of painting always had the feel of the real, ''Made in Canada.'' ''I am afraid of art,'' he once said. ''It could still kill me.''

—Joan Murray

CUTFORTH, Roger

Nationality: British. **Born:** Sleaford, Lincolnshire, 29 October 1944. **Education:** Nottingham College of Art, 1962–63; and the Ravensbourne College of Art, England, 1963–66. **Career:** Independent conceptual artist and photographer, since 1966; moved to New York City in 1968, concentrated on making films of women in landscapes, 1973–75; now lives and works in Texas. **Award:** National Endowment for the Arts Photography fellowship, Washington, D.C.,

1984. **Agent:** Hal Bromm Gallery, 90 West Broadway, New York, New York 10007. **Address:** HC65, Box 276D, Alpine, Texas 79830.

Individual Exhibitions:

1969 Pinacothea Gallery, Melbourne
1971 Lisson Gallery, London
Nova Scotia College of Art, Halifax
1972 Pinacotheca Gallery, Melbourne
1974 John Gibson Gallery, New York
Galerie Kornblit, Amsterdam
Studio Cannaviello, Rome
1975 Galerie Kornblit, Amsterdam
1976 Galerie Gaetan, Geneva
John Gibson Gallery, New York
Studio Cannaviello, Rome
1977 Galleria II Diaframma, Milan
Studio 46, Turin
1978 John Gibson Gallery, New York
Studio Cannaviello, Milan
1979 Unimedia, Genoa
Studio Cannaviello, Milan
1981 Hal Bromm Gallery, New York
1983 Hal Bromm Gallery, New York
1986 Dos Amigos Gallery, Terlingua, Texas
Hal Bromm Gallery, New York
1987 University of Texas, El Paso
AIR Gallery, Austin, Texas
1988 Bauer House, Austin, Texas
1991 San Angelo Museum of Fine Arts, San Angelo, Texas

Selected Group Exhibitions:

1970 *Information,* Museum of Modern Art, New York
1971 *Prospect 71,* Studtische Kunsthalle, Dusseldorf
1972 *Artists Using Photographs,* Inhiborderss, Sydney
1975 *Artists' Bookworks,* British Council travelling exhibition, London (toured West Germany)
1976 *Photo as Art,* Contemporary Art Museum, Zagreb, Yugoslavia
1979 *New Acquisitions,* Wallraf-Richartz Museum, Cologne
1980 *Printed Art,* Museum of Modern Art, New York
1981 *Biennale,* Sydney
1986 *Ten,* Hal Bromm Gallery, New York (catalog)
1987 *This Is Not a Photograph,* Ringling Museum, Sarasota, Florida
1988 *Manipulations,* Frances Wolfson Art Gallery, Miami, Florida
1999 *Contemporary American, European, and Russian Painting, Sculpture, Drawing and Photography,* Hal Bromm Gallery, New York
2001 *Snapshot,* Beaver College, Fine Arts Gallery, Glenside, Pennsylvania

Collections:

Museum of Modern Art, New York; Metropolitan Museum of Art, New York; Wallraf-Richartz Museum, Cologne; Stadtisches Museum Abteiberg, Monchengladbach.

Publications:

By CUTFORTH: Books—*The Empire State Building: A Reference Work,* New York 1969, *The Visual Book,* New York 1970; *Cleopatra's Needle/Eiffel Tower/Empire State Building,* London 1971.

On CUTFORTH: Books—*Situation de l'Art Conceptual* by Catherine Millet, Paris 1970; *Conceptual Art* by Ursula Meyer, New York 1971; *6 Years: The Dematerialization of the Art Object* by Lucy Lippard, New York 1973; *La Linea Analitica de Arte Moderna* by Menna Filiberto, Turin 1975; *Skira Annuel,* Geneva 1977; *Skira Annuel,* Geneva 1980; *The Gallery of World Photography: New Directions,* edited by Weston Naef, New York 1984; *Thought Objects,* edited by Barbara Ess and Glenn Branca, New York 1987. **Articles—** ''Personal Spaces'' by James Collins in *Artforum* (New York), September 1973; ''Roger Cutforth'' by Valentin Tatransky in *Arts Magazine* (New York), September 1978; article by Loredana Parmesani in *Segno* (Pescara, Italy), no. 13, 1979, ''Roger Cutforth'' by Jean Fisher in *Aspects* (Newcastle upon Tyne), no. 13, 1981.

*

My portrait work began as a group of experimental photographic works in 1984. They grew out of a feeling of frustration with conventional photography, i.e., single image lying behind a glasslike surface in which any presence of the artist is excluded. For me, photography was always a sequence of images connected either in time, or in the consciousness of the person who had taken them. What follows is an outline of some of the problems I saw in photography. The notes begin by referring to painting. I was, and still am, a painter, though I've worked mainly in photography for the last fifteen years.

In painting it is not so much an issue about how things look as about how things feel. Photography is almost exclusively about how things look. I'm cutting up photographs and sticking them together so that I can get details from different frames all into one picture. The photographs are portraits of people I know. One thing can be said in favor of photography in this respect: it is revealing. Most of us have lots of trouble with photographs of ourselves. I search all the frames of the films for details that really interest me. These details of various images become a key for me as to what is interesting about this medium. Thoughts on the portrait of Kim Gordon work fast so that ideas stay ahead of the medium. By this I mean, what interests me in the images should stay ahead of any consideration of them as photographs. Think about the irrational. Is it possible to subvert the rational construction of the world, that the camera constantly hands to us? One of the things wrong with conventional photography is that the medium speaks for itself and tells us next to nothing. Yet, another picture of the world (the direct photography of the nineteenth century, where the world was seen freshly through photographs) only exists for us today in the family snap-shot album. I think it was Carl Andre who once said, ''Photographs are like rumors'' (i.e. unverified information of uncertain origin). What I want from photography is the possibility of working creatively with the medium after the pictures have been taken. I want the process by which a picture is constructed to show in the end result. Photography, as a mechanical means of reproduction, naturally avoids this issue. This, plus the fact that there's no visible presence of the artist, is the reason photography has such a shaky footing as an artform.

I want the work to reveal something that was not previously known. The psychology of the photographer or artist must come forward and play a role in the finished work. ''Sometimes you can hide behind a photograph but you can't hide behind a line.'' (Paulette Nenner)

Man Ray set us a good example but we have regressed.

What the world doesn't need is another pretty picture.

Some friends are rephotographing photographs. I see this not only as a comment on our media-based culture, but also as a reflection of the fact that everything has been photographed a hundred times over. Photographs no longer bear any relationship to anything other than an endless, ongoing series of visual statements. The issue of photography is a false track. The medium is invisible; forget it. Lift from the film whatever interests you and follow your intuition; it's the only route to whatever power there is left in the process in its relation to life. I tell Dan Graham I know what I'm trying to do with photography. I want to show a certain kind of truth about it that's contained in what I consider the dross of my existence, test strips. The strips, made of the most interesting part of the image, accumulate in piles on my floor. I catch myself thinking that they probably contain a more interesting picture than the finished print on the wall. Bethany Jacobson asks me why I don't use the test strips? Because I think I may hate what the work made up of them looks like. I think I may hate what really interests me. I constantly have to tell myself to go ahead and make a mess, to subvert the idealized perfection of the photographic image. ''Photographs are always presented as if the photographer doesn't exist. You are reinstating the photographer in the picture.'' (Jean Fisher) The portrait work is becoming even more unpredictable, the result of a performance between the person photographed, myself, and the camera. I want the finished work to reflect these aspects. It's odd that we think portraits can reveal something hidden about the person portrayed, yet do not see that they speak just as much of the person who made the portrait. It's impossible for me not to see the portraits as mirroring my own desire, of being equally that which I want to see, as well as that which is shown to me. Photographing women the camera obviously becomes a phallic extension through which I am intimate with them and take what I wish. But what about the men? The portrait with Jean Fisher makes me realize that the missing element in the construction of these works is myself. Jean plays me off against myself. Before the camera she displays an embarrassed prostituted image of femininity, then turning the camera on me, forces me into being a parody of my own expectations of her. This work is hard for me to take. I feel I am naked in it both physically and symbolically.

From this work I realize I can no longer handle the images I collect without being aware that they are also references to an unconscious meaning that is demanding to be brought out.

—Roger Cutforth

D

DADO

Nationality: Yugoslav. **Born:** Miodrag Djuric in Cetinjie, Montenegro, 4 October 1933. **Education:** School of Fine Art, Hercognovi, Montenegro, 1947–52; Academy of Fine Arts, Belgrade, 1952–56. **Career:** Worked as a lithographic printer, Paris, 1956–58. Independent painter, draughtsman and printmaker, Paris and Courcelles, France, since 1958. **Agent:** Galerie Beaubourg, Château Notre-Dame des Fleurs.

Individual Exhibitions:

1958 Galerie Daniel Cordier, Paris
1960 Galerie Daniel Cordier, Frankfurt
1962 Galerie Daniel Cordier, Paris
1964 Galerie Daniel Cordier, Paris (2 shows)
1965 Cordier and Ekstrom Gallery, New York
1967 Galerie d'Aujourd'hui, Brussels
1970 Byron Gallery, New York
Centre National d'Art Contemporain, Paris (retrospective)
1971 Galerie Jeanne Bucher, Paris
Galerie Therese Roussel, Perpignan, France
1973 Galerie Jeanne Bucher, Paris
1974 Museum Boymans-van Beuningen, Rotterdam (retrospective)
Aberbach Fine Art, New York
Galerie Jeanne Bucher, Paris
1975 Galerie Isy Brachot, Brussels
Galerie Jeanne Bucher, Paris
1976 Aberbach Fine Art, New York
1978 *Dessins,* Galerie Isy Brachot, Paris
Malningar teckningar grafik, Konsthall, Lund, Sweden
1979 Galerie Isy Brachot, Knokke, Belgium
Galerie Isy Brachot, at *Art 10, '79,* Basle
1979 Foundation Veranneman, Kruishoutem, Belgium
Aberbach Fine Art, New York
Galerie Isy Brachot, Paris
1981 Galerie André-Francois Petit, Paris
1982 Centre Georges Pompidou, Paris
1991 Galerie Beaubourg, Château Notre-Dame des Fleurs (catalog)
1994 *Travaux Récents,* Musée Denys Puech, Rodez, France (catalog)
Galerie Beaubourg, Château Notre-Dame des Fleurs (catalog)
1996 Galerie Alain Margaron, Paris
Galerie Rachlin-Lemarié, Paris
2000 Galerie Rachlin Lemarie Beaubourg, Paris (catalog)
2001 Galerie Beaubourg, Château Notre-Dame des Fleurs

Selected Group Exhibitions:

1960 *Antagonismes,* Musée des Arts Décoratifs, Paris
1963 *Carnegie International,* Carnegie Institute, Pittsburgh (and 1967)
1964 *Documenta 3,* Kassel, West Germany
1965 *European Drawings,* Guggenheim Museum, New York
1968 *The Obsessive Image,* Institute of Contemporary Arts, London
1969 *Malerei des Surrealismums,* Kunstverein, Hamburg
1972 *Creation Artistique en France 1960–72,* Grand Palais, Paris
1976 *Les Espaces Insolites,* Palais des Congress, Strasbourg
Contemporains IV, Musée d'Art Moderne, Paris
1978 *FIAC 78,* Grand Palais, Paris
1994 Musée des Beaux-Arts Denys Puech, Rodez, France (with Bernard Dufour)
1996 *Biennial,* Cetinje, Montenegro

Collections:

Centre Georges Pompidou, Paris; Centre National d'Art Contemporain, Paris; Stedelijk Museum, Amsterdam; Museum Boymans-van Beuningen, Rotterdam; Guggenheim Museum, New York; Art Institute of Chicago.

Publications:

By DADO: Articles—''Dado: Painting, Those Successive Bereavements'' with Philippe Piguet in *Cimaise,* vol. 45, January/February 1998.

On DADO: Books—*Dado,* exhibition catalog, with text by Georges Limbour, Frankfurt 1960; *Dado,* exhibition catalog, with text by Patrick Waldberg, Paris 1967; *Dado,* exhibition catalog, with text by Daniel Cordier, Paris 1970; *Dado,* exhibition catalog, with text by Gaeton Picon, Paris 1971; *Dado,* exhibition catalog, with text by Richard E. Friedman, New York 1974; *Dado,* exhibition catalog, with an introduction by R. Hammacher-van den Brande, text by Francois Mathey, Rotterdam 1974; *Dado,* exhibition catalog, with text by Michael Peppiatt, Paris 1975; *Dado: Dessins,* exhibition catalog, with text by Bernard Noel and an interview by Michael Peppiatt, Paris, 1978; *Dado: Malningar teckninger grafik,* exhibition catalog, with texts by Marianne Nanne-Brahammer and Jacques Adelin Brutaru, Lund, Sweden 1978; *Dado; L'Exasperation de Trait,* exhibition catalog, with texts by Christian Derouet and others, Paris 1981. **Articles—**''Dado: January 13, 1943: Flashback Forward'' by Alain Jouffroy in *Art Press,* no. 248, July/August 1999.

* * *

Dado cannot be classified, neither in his times and its isms of art, nor in a country, nor in a culture. He cites Martin Schongauer, Konrad Witz and Durer as his great ideals and loves the Renaissance painting of the North. From the richly historical Montenegrin alpine landscape of his native country the artist has withdrawn—with occasional excursions to the pygmies in Africa and to New York—to a Norman watermill in France, as far away as possible from the Parisian art world; he prefers to maintain contact with his surroundings through his children.

Dado came at an early stage to his own style—in the manner of the old masters—which achieved its perfect expression in the graphic works. To him, drawings are always of specific value; they are never sketches or designs for paintings whose themes they in any case share. The impetus to Dado's creative activity starts from obsessions which are so intense that only extreme precision in their portrayal is able to liberate the artist from them momentarily. In 1973–74 Dado destroyed a large number of earlier drawings in order to form the pieces into an assemblage showing in one picture the total horror of his vision. Since 1973 his frightening images have grown ever larger. In correlation with the consequent slowdown in the production of paintings, there is a simultaneous intensification of graphic activity. From 1976, as the paintings were undergoing a stylistic change, the most remarkable feature of which is in a new distribution of light, the drawings also show larger free zones in front of which on various planes and in detail passing images unite to form an exciting style.

The fascinating effect of Dado's style lies in the juxtaposition of detailed realistic images and indefinable fantastic scenes. The viewer is attracted by a seemingly hazy painting which often seems bathed in luminous rosy colours—and is deceived by the changing play on perception, appearance and reality. Behind the delicate haze graphic elements appear in various places, and on closer inspection one sees them condense to form gruesome images. Yet the details cannot be identified precisely. If one thinks that one sees pictures of the atrocities of concentration camps or Hiroshima, after longer inspection one finds that the scenery blurs to a vision of unutterable horror which as yet has no name in contemporary art and which perhaps as a vision of the future constitutes the originality of Dado's work. There one discovers children ''in limbo'' to whom no life is allotted and an ''ancestral gallery'' of old people who have outlived themselves, drawn by one who ''above all sees in nature not life but death'' and who dreads one day the loss of the seeing eye. Idyllically painted children are disfigured with repulsive hydrocephalus, animals with bodies torn open turn into hideous legendary creatures, plants are destructively rampant, and poisonous mushrooms develop dangerous explosive matter. Walls and buildings crumble away beneath the spectator's gaze and fall in ruins. In the midst of putrefaction arise monstrosities, terrifying mutants are born of dislocated and mutilated beings. The Book of Job, the interpretation of which Dado has pursued since the 1950s, always with a fresh technical approach, gains in his hands an added contemporary dimension. Mankind's frightful primeval visions couple with contemporary anxieties about organ transplants in living bodies, the fear of cancer and the bomb—without any hope of salvation.

Dado produces pictures of anxiety, superbly crafted with the precision of an old master, on which the eye cannot rest but in confusion wanders from one scene to another. It is only at first sight that one thinks to have discovered the work of a modern Brueghel (he has, after all, an acquaintance with Hans Bellmer, Max Ernst, Magritte and Dali). Yet Dado does not see the world with the same eyes as the old masters in the Christian Occident; he also does not view it with the profound psychologically acute vision of a contemporary adult, who perhaps delights in cruelties; he looks with the wide open eyes of a terrified child who sometimes (with the help of diluted ink) artificially ''ages'' his drawings so that he is relieved of his visions, a child who refuses to learn to suppress the dread of being devoured or turned to stone, who regards the old and the sick with dread and mortal terror, who stares with horror at deformity, a child who perhaps frightens others with terrifying spiders but does not himself tear off the legs of insects.

—Dagmar Sinz

DAHN, Walter

Nationality: German. **Born:** St. Tonis bei Krefeld, 8 October 1954. **Education:** Studied art under Joseph Beuys, Kunstakademie, Dusseldorf, 1971–77. **Career:** Painter, in Cologne, since 1976; Professor, Hochschule für Bildende Künst, Braunschweig, since 1995. **Agent:** Galerie Paul Maenz, Bismarckstrasse 50, 5000 Cologne 1. **Address:** Klapperhof 33, 5000 Cologne 1, Germany.

Individual Exhibitions:

1982 Galerie Paul Maenz, Cologne (and 1983)
Galerie Helen van der Meij, Amsterdam
Galerie 't Venster, Rotterdam (with Georg Dokoupil)
Galerie Hetzler, Stuttgart
1983 Galerie Chantal Crousel, Paris
Produzentengalerie, Hamburg (with Georg Dokoupil)
Galerie Six Friedrich, Munich (with Georg Dokoupil)
Mary Boone Gallery, New York
1984 Galerie Six Friedrich, Munich (and 1985)
Groninger Museum, Groningen, Netherlands (with Georg Dokoupil)
Galerie Paul Maenz, Cologne (and 1985)
Marian Goodman Gallery, New York
Galerie Crousel-Hussenot, Paris (and 1985)
1985 Galerie Barbara Jandrig, Krefeld, West Germany
Galerie Paul Maenz, Cologne (with Georg Dokoupil)
Galerie Vera Munro, Hamburg (with Georg Dokoupil)
Gallery Paule Anglim, San Francisco
Asher/Faure, Los Angeles
Rheinisches Landesmuseum, Bonn
Groninger Museum, Groningen, Netherlands
1986 Museum fur Gegenwartskunst, Basle
Kaiser Wilhelm Museum, Krefeld, West Germany
Kunsthalle, Basle
Museum Folkwang, Essen, West Germany
Galerie Paul Maenz, Cologne
Galerie Six Friedrich, Munich
1987 Van Abbemuseum, Eindhoven, Netherlands
Galerie Roger Pailhac, Marseille, France
Neuer Aachener Kunstverein, Aachen, West Germany
Galerie Luis Campana, Stuttgart
1988 Galerie Paul Maenz, Cologne
Galerie F.C. Gundlach, Hamburg
Galerie Six Friedrich, Munich
1994 Monika Sprüth Galerie, Cologne
Alles Wird Gut, Anlässlich der Ausstellung in der Kunsthalle zu Kiel, Germany
1996 Monika Sprüth Galerie, Cologne
1997 *Another Time, Another Place,* Stedelijk Museum of Modern Art, Amsterdam

Selected Group Exhibitions:

1980 *Auch wenn das Perlhuhn leise weint,* Hahnentorburg, Cologne
1981 *Phoenix,* Alte Oper, Frankfurt
1982 *La Giovane Pittura in Germania,* Galleria d'Arte Moderna, Bologna
1983 *Expressionisten—Neue Wilde,* Museum am Ostwall, Dortmund, West Germany
1984 *International Survey of Recent Painting and Sculpture,* Museum of Modern Art, New York
1985 *Koln-Kunst,* Kunsthalle, Cologne
1987 *Avant-Garde in the Eighties,* Los Angeles County Museum of Art
1995 *Growing Up and Coming Down,* Jörn Bötnagel Projekte, Cologne
1996 Hansa-Gymnasium, Cologne

Collections:

Museum Folkwang, Essen; Hessisches Museum, Darmstadt; Bonnefantenmuseum, Maastricht; Groninger Museum, Groningen; Van Abbemuseum, Eindhoven; Staatsgalerie, Stuttgart; Kaiser Wilhelm Museum, Krefeld; Museum fur Gegenwartskunst, Basle; Museum am Ostwall, Dortmund.

Publications:

By DAHN: Books—*Walter Dahn im Gespräch mit Wilfried Dickhoff, Bettina Pauly und Johannes Stüttgen,* Cologne 1993; *Walter Dahn: Mirror-Image Ritual America #1,* Cologne 1999; *After Nihilism: Essays on Contemporary Art,* with multiple authors, Cambridge 2000. **Articles**—interview with Jens Rönnau in *Kunstforum International,* no. 127, July/September 1994; interview with Richard Prince in *Journal of Contemporary Art,* vol. 7, Summer 1994.

On DAHN: Books—*10 Junge Kunstler aus Deutschland,* exhibition catalog with text by Zdenek Felix, Essen 1982; *Walter Dahn,* exhibition catalog with text by Patrick Frey, Cologne 1982; *Dahn und Dokoupil: Die Afrika-Bilder,* exhibition catalog with text by Wilfried Dickhoff, Groningen 1984; *Walter Dahn: Zeichnungen, 12 Skulpturen,* exhibition catalog with text by Dieter Koepplin, Basle 1986; *Walter Dahn: Gemalde 1981–1985,* exhibition catalog edited by Wifried Dickhoff, Basle 1986. **Articles**—''Ten Artists to Watch WorldWide'' in *ARTnews,* vol. 94, no. 1, January 1995; ''Hommage an ein Stilles Amerika'' by Joachim Hauschild in *ART: Das Kunstmagazin,* no. 9, September 1996.

* * *

The first unequivocal manifestation of Walter Dahn's independent position was his painting, in 1981, *Maler ohne Idee* (Painter without Idea), undoubtedly a self-portraiture. This title is a paradox that, for those who do not recognize it as such, seemed to confirm the common presumption that Dahn and his former Mullheimer Freiheit colleagues (Adamski, Bommels, Dokoupil, Kever, Naschberger) were merely a bunch of naive 'wild painters'. It is important to realize that these Cologne-based artists were very keen to distinguish themselves from the group of Berlin expressionists that included among others Fetting and Salome.

After the dissolution of Mullheimer Freiheit, Dahn went his own way, although he regularly worked together with Georg Dokoupil. In 1982–83 both did the series of Ricki-paintings, based on the motif of a shower splashing water over various objects such as an oven, a transistor radio, a pair of gloves, an armchair. These paintings might be considered as playful ironies of Fetting's expressionist Dusche-Bilder. However, the following collaboration project is of a different character. These Afrika-paintings from the end of 1983 show a sincere respect towards the visual qualities of primitive painting.

Like Dokoupil, Dahn produces in considerable quantity, although in less chameleontic fashion. While Dokoupil, above all, seems to be involved with continuous comment and irony concerning the artworld's codes and conventions, Dahn, on the other hand, concentrates on his own personal impulse in relation to the relics of other cultures. He tries to balance direct emotional response with the reproduction techniques through which we learn about the existence of these relics. For him there exists a correlation between his own imagery and the things from the past, not in terms of subconscious mythology but in those of potential subject-matter to be painterly reproduced.

From 1985 onwards he has put a lock to his spontaneous way of painting by complicating his procedure. This resulted in a series of monotype silkscreens on cloth, where there is no relief in the paint at all, a technique also employed by the American artist Robin Winters in his Bonaparte's Party series (1984).

From 1986–87 dates a group of large paintings, among these a painting that shows the figure of an Australian native. On a monochrome ground there is a multitude visible of massive black forms, blow-ups of photographic mass-reproduction. This painting demonstrates two complementary ways of seeing and enjoying. Nearby the expression is a painterly one. It is only at a distance that the image appears. The subject matter is not anecdotal and, by its archaism, brings the viewer into a state that conflicts with his sheer aesthetic pleasure.

Dahn has also done a group of small bronzes with subject matter that includes a large number of self-portraits. He also shows photopieces taking his friends, street life and shop windows for subjects. Altogether Dahn seems to grow as a painter, as an artist who does not depend on the circumstantial evidence of the current art world.

—A.F. Wagemans

DALI, Salvador

Nationality: Spanish. **Born:** Salvador Felipe Jacinto Dali y Domenech, in Figueras, Gerona, 11 May 1904. **Education:** Marist Friars School, Figueras, 1914–18; San Fernando Academy of Fine Arts, Madrid, 1921–25. **Family:** Married Gala Eluard in 1930. **Career:** Worked as a book and magazine illustrator, Figueras, 1919–21; independent artist, in Sitges, 1925–30, Paris, 1930–40, Pebble Beach, California, 1940–48, and in Port-Lligat, Spain, since 1948; worked on films with Luis Bunuel, 1929; member, André Breton's Surrealist Group of artists and writers, Paris, 1930–34; first theatre decors, 1939; first classical and religious paintings, 1948; first 3-dimensional works, 1964; established Dali Museum, Figueras, 1973. Editor, *L'Amic des Arts* magazine, Sitges, 1926–29, and *Manifest Groc,* with S. Gasch and L. Montanya, Sitges, 1928. **Awards:** Huntington Hartford Foundation award, 1957; Gold Medal of the City of Paris, 1958. **Agent:**

Salvador Dali: *Metamorphosis of Narcissus,* 1934. ©Art Resource/Tate Gallery.

Knoedler and Co., 21 East 70 Street, New York, New York 10021, U.S.A. **Died:** From complications of pneumonia, in Figueras, Spain, 23 January 1989.

Individual Exhibitions:

1925 Galeria Dalmau, Barcelona
1927 Galeria Dalmau, Barcelona
1929 Galerie Goemans, Paris
1931 Galerie Pierre Colle, Paris
1932 Julien Levy Gallery, New York
Galerie Pierre Colle, Paris
1933 Galeria d'Art Catalunya, Barcelona
Julien Levy Gallery, New York
Galerie Pierre Colle, Paris
1934 Julien Levy Gallery, New York
Galeria d'Art Catalunya, Barcelona
Zwemmer Gallery, London
Galerie Quatre Chemins, Paris
Galerie Jacques Bonjean, Paris
1936 Alex Reid and Lefevre Gallery, London
Julien Levy Gallery, New York
1939 Dali Studio, Paris
Julien Levy Gallery, New York
1941 Museum of Modern Art, New York
Julien Levy Gallery, New York
Julien Levy Gallery, Hollywood, California
1942 Museum of Modern Art, New York
1943 M. Knoedler and Co., New York
1945 Bignon Gallery, New York
1946 M. Knoedler and Co., New York
1947 Cleveland Museum of Art
Bignon Gallery, New York
1948 Bignon Gallery, New York
1950 Carstairs Gallery, New York
1951 Galerie David Weill, Paris
Alemany and Ertman, New York
Lefevre Gallery, London
1952 Carstairs Gallery, New York
Alemany and Ertman, New York
1953 Santa Barbara Museum of Art, California
1954 Palazzo Pallaricini-Rospigliosi, Rome
Carstairs Gallery, New York
1955 Philadelphia Museum of Art
Denver Art Museum
1956 Casino Communal, Knokke, Belgium
Carstairs Gallery, New York
1958 M. Knoedler and Co., New York
Carstairs Gallery, New York
1959 French and Co., New York
1960 Musée Galliera, Paris
Finch Gallery, New York

Salvador Dali with his painting, *The Face of War.* ©AP/Wide World Photos.

Carstairs Gallery, New York
1963 M. Knoedler and Co., New York
1964 Prince Hotel Gallery, Tokyo (travelled to Prefectural Museum of Art, Nagoya and the Municipal Art Gallery, Kyoto)
Los Angeles Municipal Art Gallery
1965 M. Knoedler and Co., New York
Phyllis Lucas Gallery, New York
1966 Gallery of Modern Art, New York
1967 Hotel Meurice, Paris
Galerie D, Prague
Staempfli Gallery, New York
1968 Palais des Beaux-Arts, Charleroi, Belgium
London Graphic Art Gallery
Phyllis Lucas Gallery, New York
1969 Galerie Les Heures Claires, Paris
Hiram College, Ohio
Galerie Knoedler, Paris
Zachary Walker Gallery, Los Angeles
1970 Museum Boymans-van Beuningen, Rotterdam (retrospective)
M. Knoedler and Co., New York
Galleria Guissi, Turin
Musée de l'Athenée, Geneva
Galerie Andre-Francois Petit, Paris
M. Knoedler and Co., New York
Karl-Ernst-Osthaus Museum Hagen, West Germany
1971 *Gemalde, Zeichnungen, Objekte Schmuck,* Staatliche Kunsthalle, Baden-Baden, West Germany
Art-in-Jewels Exhibition, Whitechapel Art Gallery, London
Museum Boymans-van Beuningen, Rotterdam
1972 *Holograms Conceived by Dali,* M. Knoedler and Co., New York
Museum Boymans-van Beuningen, Rotterdam
Galerie Isy Brachot, Brussels
1974 Städtisches Galerie/Stadelsches Kunstinsitut, Frankfurt
1977 *Bilder, Gouachen, Zeichnungen, Skulpturen,* Sammlung Levy, Hamburg
1979 *Retrospective 1920–1980,* Centre Georges Pompidou, Paris
1980 Tate Gallery, London
1982 *Obra Grafica,* Caja de Ahorros, Madrid
1984 Galeria Surrealista, Barcelona

1987 Galerie 1900–2000, Paris
1988 Salvador Dali Museum, St. Petersburg
1989 Staatsgalerie, Stuttgart
1990 Centro de Arte Reina Sofia, Madrid
1991 Museo d'Arte Contemporanea, Genoa
1992 IVAM Centre Julio Gonzalez, Valencia
1994 Hayward Gallery, London
1996 Tate Gallery, London
1999 Tate Gallery, Liverpool
Salvador Dali Museum, St. Petersburg

Selected Group Exhibitions:

1921 *Group Exhibitions,* Galeria Dalmau, Barcelona
1933 *Exposition Surrealiste,* Galerie Pierre Colle, Paris
1936 *Fantastic Art, Dada & Surrealism,* Museum of Modern Art, New York
1940 *Exposicion Internacional del Surrealismo,* Galeria de Arte Mexicano, Mexico City
1951 *Surrealisme en Abstractie,* Stedelijk Museum, Amsterdam
1959 *Exposition Internationale du Surrealisme,* Musée d'Art Moderne, Paris
1965 *Bienal,* Sao Paulo
1968 *Dada, Surrealism and Their Heritage,* Museum of Modern Art, New York
1970 *Surrealism,* Moderna Museet, Stockholm
1982 *A Century of Modern Drawing,* British Museum, London (travelled to the Boston Museum of Fine Arts, and the Cleveland Museum of Art)
1989 *Modern Paintings,* Franco Semenzato, Milan
1990 *Antiquity/Modernity in 20th Century Art,* Fundacio Joan Miro, Barcelona
1991 *Picasso, Miro, Dali and the Origins of Contemporary Art in Spain,* Schim Kunsthalle, Frankfurt am Main
1993 *Masterpieces from the Museum of Fine Arts Berne,* Daimaru Museum, Tokyo
1995 *The Surrealist Word,* Museo Nacional Centro de Arte Reina Sofia, Madrid
Surrealism in Spain: 1924–34, Stadtische Kunsthalle, Dusseldorf
1996 *Drawing on Chance: Selections from the Collection,* Museum of Modern Art, New York
1997 *Annees 30 en Europe: le Temps Menacant,* Musee d'Art Moderne de la Ville de Paris, Paris
Surrealism and After: The Gabrielle Keiller Collection, Scottish National Gallery of Modern Art, Edinburgh
Exiles and Emigres: The Flight of European Artists from Hitler, Los Angeles County Museum of Art, Los Angeles

Collections:

Salvador Dali Museum, Figueras, Spain; Centre Georges Pompidou, Paris; Nationalgalerie, West Berlin; Stedelijk Museum, Amsterdam; Museum Boymans-van Beuningen, Rotterdam; Kunsthaus, Zurich; Tate Gallery, London; Museum of Modern Art, New York; Guggenheim Museum, New York; Cleveland Museum of Art (A guide to Dali's work in public museums is published by Cleveland Museum of Art, 1974).

Publications:

By DALI: Books and pamphlets—*La Femme Visible,* Paris 1930; *L'Amour et al Memoire,* Paris 1931; *Conquest of the Irrational,* Paris 1935; *The Metamorphosis of Narcissus,* 1937; *Declaration of the Independence of the Imagination and the Rights to His Own Madness,* 1938; *Hidden Faces,* New York 1944; *The Secret Life of Salvador Dali,* London 1948; *Mystical Manifesto,* 1951; *Dali's Moustache,* 1954; *The Cuckolds of Old Modern Art,* 1956; *The Tragic Myth of Millet's Angelus,* 1963; *Diary of a Genius,* 1964; *Dali de Draeger,* Paris 1968; *Dali by Dali,* New York 1970; *Les Diners de Gala,* New York 1963; *The Unspeakable Confessions of Salvador Dali,* New York 1976; *The Collected Writings of Salvador Dali,* edited and with commentary by Haim Finkelstein, Cambridge, 1998. **Films—***Un Chien Andalou,* with Luis Bunuel, 1929; *L'Age d'Or,* with Luis Bunuel, 1930; *The Prodigious History of the Laceworker and the Rhinoceros,* with Robert Descharnes, 1954.

On DALI: Books—*Dickens, Dali and Others: Studies in Popular Culture* by George Orwell, New York 1946; *Salvador Dali* by James Thrall Soby, New York 1946; *Catalog of Works by Salvador Dali* by A. Reynolds Morse, Cleveland 1956; *Dali* by Michel Tapie, Paris 1957; *Dali,* edited by Linda Livingstone, Greenwich, Connecticut 1959; *The Case of Salvador Dali* by Fleur Cowles, London 1959; *A New Introduction to Salvador Dali* by A. Reynolds Morse, Cleveland 1960; *The Salvador Dali Museum* by A. Reynolds Morse, Cleveland 1962; *Dali Exhibition-Japan 1964,* exhibition catalog, edited by Shuzo Takiguchi, Yoshiaki Tono and Shin Ohoka, Tokyo 1964; *Salvador Dali 1910–1965,* exhibition catalog, with an introduction by Carl J. Weinhardt Jr., New York 1965; *Dali: Miró* by Paul Walton, New York 1967; *Dali,* edited by Max Gerard, New York 1968; *In Quest of Dali* by C. Lake, New York 1969; *Dada and Surrealist Art* by William S. Rubin, London 1970; *Dali,* exhibition catalog, with texts by Patrick Waldberg, Robert Descharnes and Gerrit Komrij, Rotterdam 1970; *A Short Survey of Surrealism* by David Gascoyne, London 1970; *Dali: The Masterworks* by A. Renolds Morse, Cleveland 1971; *Dali: Gemalde, Zeichnungen, Objekte, Schmuck,* exhibition catalog, with a foreword by Klaus Gallwitz, texts by Patrick Waldberg, Gerrit Komrij and others, Baden-Baden, West Germany 1971; *Dali: Art-in-Jewels Exhibition,* exhibition catalog, London 1971; *The Surrealists* by William Gaunt, London 1972; *Antologie Grafica del Surrealismo* by Maurice Henry, Milan 1972; *Holograms Conceived by Dali,* exhibition catalog, with an introduction by Dennis Gabor, New York 1972; *Salvador Dali: Catalog of a Collection—93 Oils 1917–1970,* edited by A. Reynolds Morse, Cleveland 1972; *The World of Salvador Dali* by Robert Descharnes, London 1972; *The History of Surrealism* by Maurice Nadau, London 1973; *Salvador Dali/Pablo Picasso* by A. Reynolds Morse, Cleveland 1973; *Surrealisme et Sexualité* by Xaviere Gauthier, Paris 1971; *Dictionnaire de la Peinture Surrealiste* by Sarane Alexandrian, Paris 1973; *Malerei des Surrealismus* by Uwe M. Schneede, Cologne 1973; *A Dali Primer* by A. Reynolds Morse, Cleveland 1970; *The Draftsmanship of Dali,* with an introduction by A. Reynolds Morse, Cleveland 1970; *Dali,* edited by David Larkin, with an introduction by J. G. Ballard, London 1974; *Dali: A Guide to His Works in Public Museums* by A. Reynolds Morse, Cleveland 1974; *Salvador Dali,* exhibition catalog, with a foreword by Klaus Gallwitz, texts by several authors, Frankfurt 1974; *Salvador Dali: Bilder, Gouachen, Zeichnungen, Skulpturen* exhibition catalog, Hamburg 1977; *Salvador Dali: Retrospective 1920–1980,* exhibition catalog, with texts by Daniel Abadie and others, Paris

1979; *Salvador Dali,* exhibition catalog, with text by Simon Wilson, London 1980; *Dali: Obra Grafica,* exhibition catalog, with texts by Javier Tusell, Ramon Gomez de la Serna and others, Madrid 1982; *Salvador Dali,* exhibition catalog with essay by Robert Descharnes, Paris 1987; *Surrealist Drawings,* exhibition catalog, St. Petersburg, 1988; *Salvador Dali: The Surrealist Jester* by Meryle Secrest, London, 1988; *Salvador Dali, or the Art of Spitting on Your Mother's Portrait* by Carlos Rojas, University Park, 1993; *Doubling and Dedoublement: Gala in Dali* by Fiona Bradley in *Art History* (Oxford), vol. 17, no. 4, December 1994; *Salvador Dali 1904–1989,* by Gilles Neret, Cologne 1994; *Dali* by Christopher Masters, London 1995; *Salvador Dali* by Dawn Ades, London 1995; *Salvador Dali* by O.B. Duane, London 1996; *Dali and Postmodernism: This is Not an Essence* by Marc LaFountain, Albany 1997; *Dali* by Robert Radford, London 1997; *Salvador Dali: A Mythology* edited by Dawn Ades and Fiona Bradley, London 1998. **Articles—**''Salvador Dali's Anthropomorphic Landscapes'' by Haim Finkelstein in *Pantheon,* vol. 46, 1988; ''From Breton to Dali: The Adventures of Automatism'' by Laurent Jenny in *October* (Cambridge), no. 51, Winter 1989; ''Solving a Spellbound Puzzle: Salvador Dali Designed Dream Sequence in Hitchcock's Film'' by James Bigwood in *American Cinematographer,* vol. 72, June 1991; ''Report from Mexico II: Reassessing Dali'' by Brook Adams in *Art in America* (New York), vol. 79, no. 10, October 1991; ''An Amusing Lack of Logic: Surrealism and Popular Entertainment'' by Keith L. Eggener in *American Art,* vol. 7, Fall 1993; ''Dali'' by Wendy Beckett in *Modern Painters* (London), vol. 7, Spring 1994; ''Political Action and 'Paranoid-Critical' Analysis: The Mother Image in Max Lingner and Salvador Dali'' by Jutta Held in *Oxford Art Journal,* vol. 19, no. 2, 1996; ''Aurel Kolnai's 'Disgust': A Source in the Art and Writing of Salvador Dali'' by Robert Radford in *Burlington Magazine* (London), no. 1150, vol. 141, January 1999; ''The Century's 25 Most Influential Artists'' with introduction by Robin Cembalest in *ARTnews,* vol. 98, no. 5, May 1999; ''Doubling and Dedoublement: Gala in Dali'' by Fiona Bradley in *Art History,* vol. 17, December 1994; ''A Spellbinding Scenario'' by Lilly Wei in *Art News,* vol. 98, no. 11, December 1999; ''Dali in the Land of the Snowbirds'' by Jordan Simon in *Art and Antiques,* vol. 22, no. 11, December 1999.

* * *

After faltering Impressionist and then Cubist beginnings, Salvador Dali settled rapidly on a world and language of his own and on a style of painting not unlike that of the old masters. At the age of 25, in 1929, he was in full control of his art. It is for that reason that he went through the entire Surrealist era an absolute master. Furthermore, the theory he had just developed, labeled ''paranoiac critical method,'' made it possible for him to present all his erotic, libidinous and scabrous obsessions in a fairy-tale-like context, thus transcribing visually everything Freud had expressed in words. André Breton wrote that in this method, Dali had provided the Movement with ''an instrument of the utmost importance.'' Dali was to apply it with equal care and success to painting, to poetry, to film-making *(Un Chien Andalou, L'Age d'Or,* made with Luis Buñuel), to the construction of the familiar surrealist objects (the telephone with receiver in the shape of a lobster, the Venus of the drawers, the sofa in the shape of Mae West's lips), to fashion (he designed for Elsa Schiapparelli) and to any sort of exegesis (for instance, his theories on the emperor Trajan and Romania). Later on, Dali maintained that the greatest of his discoveries was doubtless still the paranoiac critical method. He doesn't know exactly what the term means, but he's sure it has brought him millions and millions of dollars.

All joking aside, it is the Surrealist period which clearly dominates his works, and which gives us a master of the art of painting: ''The Great Masturbator'' (1929), ''The Enigma of Desire'' (1929), ''The Persistence of Memory: Limp Watches'' (1933); watches can be anything, even limp, provided they show the correct time, says the artist. The power of words (reinforcing as they do the pictorial image, while the image sends us back to the title) nearly takes us outside the limits of painting: the artist becomes a medium. This period is also that of Dali's historical intuitions represented by such magnificent canvases as ''The Enigma of William Tell'' (1933), showing a figure with tentacle-like legs and a raw chop on one knee, and the *shapka* (Russian hat) picture, held up by a crutch, showing a Lenin who had already sacrificed the children of his Revolution. There are also works foretelling the Spanish Civil War: ''Prémonition de la Guerre Civile'' (1936).

The 1950s marked the gradual disappearance of this emotion-filled, profoundly upsetting content, so full of eccentricities, sadism, solitude, and those complexes necessarily a part of Dali's erotically based universe. The images of Christ, where Dali is trying to leave the spectator breathless through his panoramic, plunging views, are the reflection of a different world.

As everybody knows, Dali did more than anyone else to make himself an object of discussion, giving a tragic example to the new generations. ''I want people to talk about me, even if they say nice things,'' he declared in that period of his youth when he was already formulating the following principle: ''Painter, if you wish to take your place in society, you must at a very tender age launch a terrific kick at its left leg.'' Such violence began as instinctive and was later refined; Dali was, doubtless, the first to evaluate to the status of doctrine a notion which was to become one of the signs of our times. Increasingly ''different,'' increasingly eccentric, forever doing the opposite of what others did in order to set himself apart, and forever calling into question his position as madman or genius, Dali left a lifeless and declining bourgeoisie increasingly astounded, and he made them pay the outrageous price for his psychological maneuverings.

The story of his eccentricities is a long one, and has been brilliantly told by Dali himself in his books. The most important of them is a literary masterpiece, as well as one of the most entertaining pieces one could hope to encounter: *The Secret Life of Salvador Dali* by Salvador Dali. Its first chapter is cleverly entitled ''Am I a Genius?'', a question which he answers repeatedly throughout the book, and which is treated again in a sequel. Of course he's a genius. The title of the second volume, by the way, is highly revelatory: *Diary of a Genius* by Salvador Dali. What can we learn from these books concerning the most celebrated of living artists? At six years of age, he wanted to be a cook, and at seven, Napoleon. Since then, he assures us, his ambition has never ceased to grow; nor his megalomania.

Dali has gone about building his universal kingdom and temple of ''genius'' in a number of different ways. He has been doing so in his mind since his birth on May 11, 1904, or perhaps even before if one takes into account the intrauterine memories he has continued to describe in minute detail right up to present day. Along more concrete lines he has built, ten years ago, a theater-museum in his birthplace, Figueras, for the self-glorification of his genius.

The persistent nature of Dali's torment has led to a curious identification with the ultimate incarnations of power, be they Lenin,

Stalin, Hitler, Mao, Franco, King Juan Carlos; money (the Dollar) or Science. But the same Dali who tried to assimilate all new discoveries, all forms of power, and who never hesitated to use extravagant forms of provocation to establish his position as ''genius,'' has at the same time, as a rule, been obsessively strict when it came to painting. In painting he is against ''freedom'' and for restraint. He favors form. ''Classicism stood for integration, synthesis, cosmogony, instead of breakup, experimentation or scepticism'' wrote this enemy of the ''old modern art.''

The specter of Picasso constantly confronts Dali. It is undeniable that just as the former revolutionized painting, the latter revolutionized the behavior of the painter. Seeing the two juxtaposed in this way, we can notice how very different their work has been. ''Picasso,'' says Dali, ''pushed ugliness to its furthest extreme.'' Breaking up the shape of reality and yet continually clashing with objects, Picasso remained a prisoner to his perceptions. Having broken up the universe, with his tireless worker's hands, he put it back together, using the smashed pieces. Dali did just the opposite. The two geniuses are mutually exclusive in their fundamental approach. Interested rather in beauty and in the hidden harmony of things, Dali stands as the great manipulator of myths in our time—of myths and not simply of media. That is perhaps the most interesting thing about him, and certainly the most important as well, at a period in history when people are satisfied with myths which have been debased or made caricatures, which are useless in helping us to live.

In person, Dali is touching, serious, well-informed. He is infinitely charming. The persona he has created for himself, on the other hand, demonstrates an egotistical inflation without parallel and is devouring, cruel, extravagant and provocative. Now if this persona has been able to endure and to continue to be identified with the notion of *genius* for more than 50 years, it is because Dali has simultaneously cultivated a second art—that of *galateo,* the art of laughing at oneself invented in 16th century Tuscany, of finding one's weaknesses, of publicly identifying them and of blowing them up to such proportions that we are forced to regard him with tenderness and humor rather than with what might have been hatred. For we will have recognized something of ourselves in this hero who up till then had seemed sublime and without weakness.

The concept of *genius,* peculiar to the 19th century, was applied above all to the *artist*—that person who could not prove his place in society and who was subject to both divine grace and disgrace. He was chosen by the gods and damned by society, whence the helpless rebellion expressed his Alfred de Vigny in *Moise:*—''Why me?'' However, no one has done as much as Dali to amass unto himself the advantages of being chosen.

The notion of genius has suffered a loss of favor since 1930, but has remained in use from Napoleon right up through Dali. (Remember that he wanted to be Napoleon as a child.) We have learned from Zielsel and Isac Kapuano that the concept of genius cannot exist without that of flaw or Achilles heel. Dali seems to have sensed this instinctively in his perpetual effort to call attention to his own weaknesses (''How cowardly I am,'' ''At any rate, I'm completely impotent,'' ''I used to read Kant and understand nothing''). One might also conclude that genius is necessarily eccentric, that is *ex-centric.* But it remains to be known whether genius can coexist in the same person as the initiate who, by definition, is supposed to be *the center.*

—Radu Varia

DANBY, Ken

Nationality: Canadian. **Born:** Sault Sainte Marie, Ontario, 6 March 1940. **Education:** Studied under Jock MacDonald, Ontario College of Art, Toronto, 1957–60. **Family:** Married 1) Judith E. Harcourt, 1965; 2) Gillian M. Rumble, 1988; sons: Sean, Ryan, Noah. **Career:** Worked in mining tower construction, Wawa, Canada, 1958; set designer, CJIC-TV, Toronto, 1960; promotions designer, *The Telegram* newspaper, Toronto, 1960–62; Independent artist: influenced by Andrew Wyeth exhibition, New York, 1962; moved to Speed River, Guelph, Ontario, 1967; commissioned to design Series III Olympic Coinage, 1976. **Member:** Canada Council, 1985. **Awards:** Purchase Award, *Four Seasons Exhibition,* Toronto, 1962; Jessie Dow Best Painting Award, Museum of Fine Arts, Montreal, 1964; Drawing Award, *Hadassah Exhibition,* Toronto, 1965; R. Tait McKenzie Chair for Sport Award, National Sport and Recreation Centre and Labatt Breweries, Ottawa; Ontario Arts Council Award, 1976; Queen's Canadian Silver Jubilee Medal, 1977; Member, Royal Canadian Academy of Arts, 1976; Ontario UNICEF Medal, 1983; 125th Anniversary Commemorative Medal of Canada, 1992; City of Sault Ste. Marie Award of Merit, 1995; Nominated for Canada's Walk of Fame. Honorary doctorate from Algoma University College/ Laurentian University, 1997. **Agent:** Gallery Moos Ltd., 136 Yorkville Avenue, Toronto, Ontario M5R 1C2. **Address:** R.R. 4, Guelph, Ontario NIH 6JI, Canada.

Individual Exhibitions:

1964 Gallery Moos, Toronto
1965 Gallery Moos, Toronto
1966 Gallery Moos, Toronto
Galerie Agnes Lefort, Montreal
1967 Gallery Moos, Toronto
1968 Gallery Moos, Toronto
1969 *Kunstmarkt,* Cologne
Gallery Moos, Toronto
1970 Gallery Moos, Toronto
1971 Gallery Moos, Toronto
1972 William Zierler Gallery, New York
Gallery Moos, Toronto
Images Gallery, Toledo, Ohio
1973 Galerie Allen, Vancouver
Fleet Gallery, Winnipeg
Continental Art Agencies, Vancouver
William Zierler Gallery, New York
1974 *Brown/Danby/Forrestall,* Canadian Consulate, New York
Gallery Moos, Toronto
Wallack Gallery, Ottawa
Galerie Moos, Montreal
Kitchener-Waterloo Gallery, London, Ontario (retrospective; toured Southern Ontario)
1975 *Algoma Arts Festival,* Sault Ste. Marie, Ontario
Galerie Allen, Vancouver
Gallery Moos, Toronto
1976 Gallery Moos, Toronto
1977 Canadian Consulate, New York
Arras Gallery, New York
de Vooght Galleries, Vancouver
Gallery Moos, Toronto

1978 Gallery Moos, Toronto
1979 Gallery Moos, Toronto
1980 *Ken Danby: The Graphic Work: Lithographs and Serigraphs,* Art Gallery of Hamilton, Ontario (toured Canada, 1980–82)
De Vooght Galleries, Vancouver
1982 Gallery Moos, Toronto
1983 Galerie Mihalis, Montreal
Americas Cup Gallery, Newport, Rhode Island
1985 Gallery Moos, Toronto
Kenneth G. Heffel Fine Art, Vancouver
1986 Halton Hills Cultural Centre, Georgetown, Ontario
1987 *25 Year Retrospective,* MacDonald Stewart Art Centre, Guelph, Ontario
1989 Gallery Moos, New York
1990 *Graphic Retrospective,* Harris Gallery of Fine Art, Ottawa, Ontario
1997 *Retrospective: Drawings and Watercolours,* Art Gallery of Algoma, Sault Ste. Marie, Ontario
1998 *Ken Danby: New Paintings,* Joseph D. Carrier Art Gallery, Toronto, Ontario
1999 *Ken Danby: True North,* South River Festival of the Arts, South River, Ontario
Manitoba Art Expo, Winnipeg, Manitoba
2000 *Trail 2000,* Masters Gallery, Calgary, Alberta
Rails' End Gallery, Haliburton, Ontario

Selected Group Exhibitions:

1964 *Drawings and Watercolours,* National Gallery of Canada, Ottawa
1966 *Magic Realism in Canadian Art,* London Art Gallery, Ontario
1970 *Survey 70: Realisms,* Art Gallery of Ontario, Toronto (travelled to the Museum of Fine Arts, Montreal)
1971 *Biennale,* Paris
1972 *Silk Screen: History of a Medium,* Philadelphia Museum of Art
1974 *Canadian Realists,* Canadian Cultural Centre, Paris (toured Europe)
1976 *Aspects of Realism,* Rothman's of Pall Mall travelling exhibition, Stratford Art Gallery, Ontario (toured Canada, 1976–78)
1980 *Canadian High Realism,* Bayard Gallery, New York
1981 *Champions of American Sports,* National Portrait Gallery, Washington, D.C. (travelled to Los Angeles, Chicago, New York)
1985 *A Celebration of Amateur Sport,* Queen's Park, Toronto
1993 ACA Galleries, New York
1996 *Wildlife,* Koffler Gallery, Koffler Centre of the Arts, North York, Ontario
Celebration of Jerusalem's 300th Anniversary, International Conference Centre, Jerusalem, Israel
They Shoot. . . They Score, Ils Lancent et Comptent, Canadian Embassy, Washington, D.C.
1997 *Our Hockey Legends,* Bruce County Museum, Southampton, Ontario
1999 *The Sporting Life,* Gallery Stratford, Stratford, Ontario
2000 *Fragile Embrace,* Burlington Art Centre, Burlington, Ontario

Collections:

National Gallery of Canada, Ottawa; Visual Arts Bank, Canada Council, Ottawa; Museum of Fine Arts, Montreal; Art Gallery of Vancouver, Vancouver, B.C.; Mendel Art Gallery, Saskatoon, Saskatchewan; Museum of Modern Art, New York; Museum of Fine Arts, Indianapolis, Indiana; Art Institute of Chicago, Chicago, Illinois; University of California, Berkeley; Bradford City Art Gallery and Museum, England; Saskatoon Art Centre, Saskatoon, Saskatchewan; C.I.L. Collection, Montreal, Quebec; Power Corporation of Canada Ltd., Montreal, Quebec; The Toronto-Dominion Bank, Toronto, Ontario; United States Steel Company, New York; White-Weld and Company, New York; Pittsburgh National Bank, Pittsburgh, Pennsylvania; National Sport and Recreation Centre, Ottawa, Ontario; Norman MacKenzie Art Gallery, Regina, Saskatchewan; The Art Gallery of Hamilton, Hamilton, Ontario; Sportdevco, Vanier, Ontario; Shell Canada, Calgary, Alberta; University of Guelph, Guelph, Ontario; Canada Sports Hall of Fame, Toronto, Ontario; The Governor General of Canada, Ottawa, Ontario; The Hockey Hall of Fame, Toronto, Ontario; The Brooklyn Museum, New York; University of British Columbia, Vancouver, B.C.

Publications:

By DANBY: Article—interview, with Andrew J. Oka, in *Ken Danby: The Graphic Work: Lithographs and Serigraphs,* exhibition catalog, Hamilton, Ontario 1980; *Ken Danby: New Paintings,* exhibition catalog, text by Ken Danby, with essays by W. Chandler Kirwin and David Moos, foreword by Flavio Belli, Guelph 1998.

On DANBY: Books—*Ken Danby,* exhibition catalog, with texts by Russell J. Harper and Paul Duval, Toronto 1967; *Ken Danby,* exhibition pamphlet, by Mario Amaya, New York 1972; *4 Decades* by Paul Duval, Toronto 1972; *High Realism in Canadian Art* by Paul Duval, Toronto 1974; *Neue Formen des Realismus* by Peter Sagel, Cologne 1974; *Ken Danby* by Paul Duval, Toronto, deluxe edition 1974, trade edition 1976; *Danby Images of Sport* by Hubert de Santana, Toronto 1978; *Super Realism* by Edward Lucie-Smith, London 1979; *Siebdruck: Technick, Praxis, Geschichte* by Wolfgang Hainke, Cologne 1979; *Ken Danby: The Graphic Work: Lithographs and Serigraphs,* exhibition catalog, with a foreword by Glen E. Cumming, Hamilton, Ontario 1980; *Contemporary Canadian Art,* by David Burnett and Marilyn Schiff, Toronto 1983; *Ken Danby: The New Decade* by Paul Duval, Toronto 1984. *Horizons, Contemporary Canadian Landscapes* by Marci and Louise Lipman, Toronto 1985; *The Best Contemporary Canadian Art* by Joan Murray, Edmonton 1987; *Adventures in the Abstract: The Paintings of Ken Danby,* exhibition catalog, with text by David Moos, New York 1989; *Ken Danby Retrospective Drawings and Watercolours,* exhibition catalog, with text by Michael Burtch, Sault Ste. Marie 1997; *Home Truths—A Celebration of Family Life by Canada's Best-Loved Painters* by Joan Murray, Toronto 1997. **Film—***Ken Danby,* produced by Rex Bromfield, Toronto 1971; *Ken Danby—Behind the Mask* by Brian Vallee, 1998.

*

Throughout the history of art, we have witnessed a great metamorphosis taking place, which continues to alter and expand our appreciation of art. A constant exploration, into the various elements of the visual world, together with individual interpretation, has always been at the core of fine art.

As important discoveries and insights have been offered, the posture of the ''art community'' has been unsettled and then adjusted over a period of time, according to the degree of accommodation necessary. For example, for centuries, a great effort was made to resolve the applications of simple perspective, in drawing and painting. Equally so, was the attempt to create form and dimension through the use of strong light and shade: chiaroscuro.

While acknowledging that continued experimentation is essential, I also feel that it is time to integrate that which we have learned; in a cohesive and constructive manner, as well as in an experimental one. The individual entities of art; colour, shape, light, dimension, texture, etc., are but the pieces of the whole. Rather than continue the procedure of assessing these elements separately, I prefer to utilize their particular assets collectively, in creating a complete statement—a total integration of all I have learned and am learning. Only in this way, can I hope to communicate successfully, and be satisfied with the results.

—Ken Danby

* * *

Born in Sault Ste. Marie, Ontario, Ken Danby studied at the Ontario College of Art in Toronto from 1958 to 1960 with the well-known abstractionist, J. W. G. (Jock) MacDonald, and began his own career as an abstract painter, but soon returned to his first love, realism, The palette of his early abstractions with their colours of coral, grey and brown set the tone for later work. Nor did he forget the techniques he'd learned as an abstract artist—he used them later. But in the meantime, the subjects of his paintings changed to carefully posed, snapshot-like views, often of rural Ontario. In 1962 a visit to an Andrew Wyeth exhibition at Buffalo, N. Y., confirmed for Danby that a realist artist could be respected. In his maturity as an artist Danby enjoyed painting personal friends and family, and anonymous sports figures. In his *At the Crease* (1972), the masked ice-hockey goalie recalls knights of an earlier day. For many in Canada that painting has become something of a national symbol.

In its mix of abstraction and realism, Danby's work recalls that of Christopher Pratt, but Danby's atmosphere is not so rarefied and cerebral. He did not hesitate to deal with almost Caravaggesque low-life, as in *Motel* (1971) which recounts the cigarettes, coffee, and crumpled pillow of the lonely motel room. Over the last decade, he has increasingly sought poetic, simple, effects; the almost invisible division between water and land in *The Sculler* (1976); the way the water in *Acapulco* (1985) is abstractly treated while the woman seated on the diving board, and the setting, are realistic. ''The symmetrical design was challenging, as was the need to created a sensuous and luminous light,'' said Danby of *Acapulco*. ''I was intrigued by the fact that the work combines both a confrontational thrust with a peaceful calm.''

—Joan Murray

DAPHNIS, Nassos

Nationality: American. **Born:** a United States citizen, in Krokeai-Sparta, Greece, 23 July 1914; settled in the United States, 1930. **Education:** Art Students League, New York 1946–49; Académie Frochot, Paris, 1950–51; Institute Statale d'Arte, Florence, 1951–52. Served in the United States Army, 1942–45. **Married:** Helen Avlonitis in 1956; children: Artemis, Demetrios. **Career:** Independent artist, New York, since 1938. **Member:** American Abstract Artists, New York, since 1957; Member of the Board, City Walls Incorporated, New York, since 1969. **Awards:** Ford Foundation Award, 1962; Purchase Award, Whitney Museum , New York, 1962; National Foundation of Art and Humanities Award, 1966; National Endowment of the Arts grant, 1971; Prize, New England 350th Celebration Exhibition, 1972; A. P. Saunders Medal 1973; Tree Peony Award 1973; Guggenheim Fellowship, New York, 1977; Francis J. Greenburger Foundation Award, New York, 1987; Pollock/Krasner Foundation grant, New York, 1987; The Richard A. Florsheim Art Fund Award, 1993; Arts Achievement Award, Queens Museum of Art, New York 1999. **Agent:** Leo Castelli Gallery, 420 W. Broadway, New York, New York 10021. **Address:** 362 West Broadway, New York, New York 10013, U.S.A.

Individual Exhibitions:

1938 Contemporary Arts Gallery, New York
1947 Contemporary Arts Gallery, New York
1949 Contemporary Arts Gallery, New York
1950 Colette Allendy Galerie, Paris
1959 Leo Castelli Gallery, New York
1960 Leo Castelli Gallery, New York
1961 Leo Castelli Gallery, New York
Toninelli Arte Moderna, Milan
1962 Galerie Iris Clert, Paris
1963 Leo Castelli Gallery, New York
1965 Leo Castelli Gallery, New York
1967 Franklin Siden Gallery, Detroit
1968 Leo Castelli Gallery, New York
1969 Albright-Knox Museum, Buffalo, New York (retrospective)
Everson Museum, Syracuse, New York
1970 Brockton Art Center, Massachusetts
1971 Leo Castelli Gallery, New York
1973 Leo Castelli Gallery, New York
1974 Ande Zarre Gallery, New York
1975 Leo Castelli Gallery, New York
1980 *Paintings of the 50's,* Leo Castelli Gallery, New York
Phillips Gallery, Salt Lake City
Eaton-Shoen Gallery, New York
1983 Leo Castelli Gallery, New York
Andre Zarre Gallery, New York
1985 Kouros Gallery, New York
Leo Castelli Gallery, New York
Eaton-Shoen Gallery, San Francisco
Andre Zarre Gallery, New York
1986 Leo Castelli Gallery, New York
1988 Leo Castelli Gallery, New York
1990 *Nassos Daphnis: Thirty Years with Leo Castelli,* Leo Castelli Gallery, New York

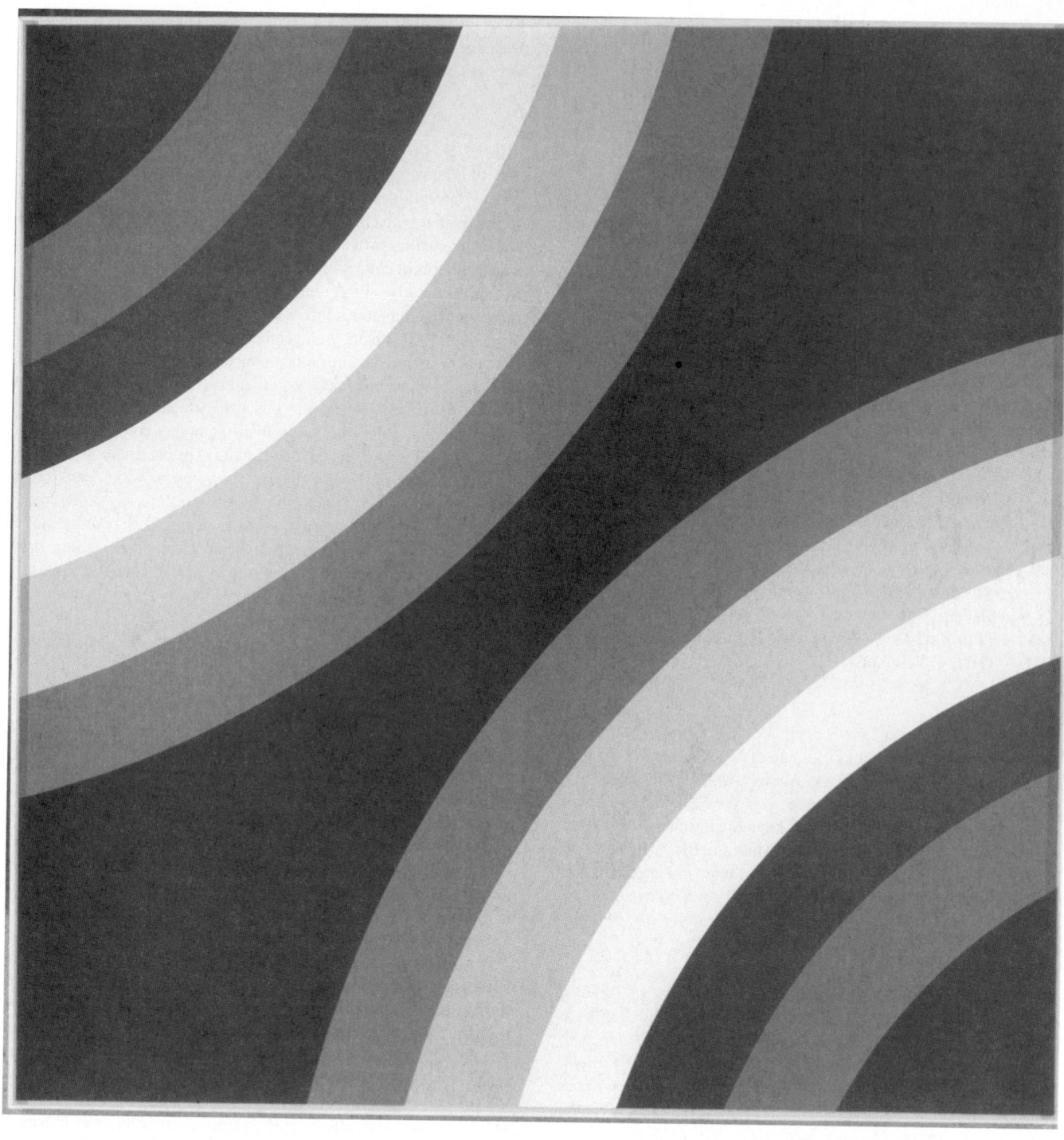

Nassos Daphnis: *2–68,* 1968. ©2001 Nassos Daphnis/Artists Rights Society (ARS), NY.

Raynolds Gallery, Pittsburgh
1991 Illeana Tounta Contemporary Art Center, Athens
Nassos Daphnis: Biomorphic Watercolors of 1947–48, Sid Deutsch Gallery, New York
1992 Berto Walker Gallery, Provincetown, Massachusetts
1993 *Nassos Daphnis: Color and Form,* Boca Raton Museum, Boca Raton, Florida
Butler Institute of American Art, Youngstown, Ohio
1994 Butler Institute of American Art, Youngstown, Ohio
1995 *Energies in Outer Space,* Leo Castelli Gallery, New York
1996 *Matter in Outer Space,* Andre Zarre Gallery, New York

Selected Group Exhibitions:

1960 *International Art of a New Era,* Museum of Fine Arts, Osaka, Japan
1963 *Formalists,* Washington Gallery of Modern Art, Washington, D.C.

1965 *White on White,* DeCordova Museum, Lincoln, Massachusetts
1967 *10 Years,* Leo Castelli Gallery, New York
1972 *Monoprints,* Trica Karlis Gallery, Provincetown, Massachusetts
1974 *Drawings,* Leo Castelli Gallery Downtown, New York
1980 *The Geometric Tradition in America,* Marilyn Pearl Gallery, New York
1982 *Modern American Paintings,* National Museum, Athens
1987 *Leo Castelli y sus Artistas,* Centro Cultural Arte Contemporaneo, Mexico City
1989 *From Mondrian to Minimalism,* Marilyn Pearl Gallery, New York
1995 *The Fifties,* Anita Shapolsky Gallery, New York
1997 *Artists of the 1950s,* Anita Shapolsky Gallery, New York
Special Collection, Anita Shapolsky Gallery, New York
Fourty Years of Exploration and Innovation: The Artists of the Castelli Gallery 1957–1997 Part Two, Leo Castelli Gallery, New York
1998 *Abstract 1950–2000,* Yellow Fellow Foundation, Woudrichem, The Netherlands
The Abstract Expressionist Tradition, Anita Shapolsky Gallery, New York
1999 *Modern Odysseys,* Queens Museum of Art, New York
Artists of the Fifties—Still Working!, Anita Shapolsky Gallery, New York
2000 *Art For Art's Sake—Credo of the 50s,* Anita Shapolsky Gallery, New York

Collections:

Whitney Museum, New York; Museum of Modern Art, New York; Guggenheim Museum, New York; Albright-Knox Gallery, Buffalo, New York; Everson Museum, Syracuse, New York; Baltimore Museum of Art; Museum of Art, Pittsburgh; Akron Art Institute, Ohio; Utah Art Museum, Salt Lake City; Tel Aviv Museum, Israel; Boca Raton Museum of Art, Florida; The Butler Institute of American Art, Youngstown, Ohio; Queens Museum of Art, New York.

Publications:

On DAPHNIS: Books—*Nassos Daphnis: Paintings of the 50s,* exhibition catalog, by April Kingsley, New York 1980; *Nassos Daphnis: Biomorphic Paintings 1947–48,* exhibition catalog with essay by John Gruen, New York 1985; *Thirty Years with Leo Castelli,* exhibition catalog with essay by Robert M. Murdock, New York 1990; *Nassos Daphnis,* exhibition catalog with text by Dore Ashton, Athens 1991; *Nassos Daphnis Biomorphic Watercolors 1947–48,* New York 1991; *Nassos Daphnis Color and Form: A Retrospective,* introduction by Barbara Rose, essay by Louis A. Zona. **Articles—** ''Nassos Daphnis: A Perennial Order'' by James R. Mellow in *Art International* (Lugano, Switzerland) March 1969; ''Nassos Daphnis'' by A. Brunelle in *Art News* (New York), April 1973; ''Nassos Daphnis: Wall Painting at 620 West 47th Street, New York'' in *Art Now: New York* (New York), 1973; review in *Art Forum* (New York), June 1973; ''New York'' by April Kingsley in *Art International* (Lugano, Switzerland), Summer 1973; ''Nassos Daphnis at Leo Castelli'' by Elizabeth Frank in *Art in America* (New York), Summer 1980; ''Nassos Daphnis'' by Mary Anne Staniszewski in *Art News* (New York), Summer 1980; ''Organic Geometry'' by Blair T. Birmelin in *Art in America* (New York), October 1985; ''Nassos Daphnis, Butler Institute of American Art'' by Joan Seeman Robinson: review in *Art Forum* (New York), February 1994.

*

For the past few years, I have been searching for images which convey the energies that permeate the universe. I try to portray the forces of energy itself, its wavelengths, its movement through space and its interaction with other waves as their paths intersect. While the visual patterns of color which I use are free of content, my intention is to express creative, life-giving forces, although, from time to time, more violent, ambiguous forces come into play.

Since 1952, I have used geometric forms to express my ideas. I have concentrated on pure color, using only the primaries—blue, red, yellow, white and black. By so doing, I can achieve the most vibrant qualities inherent in each color. It is also extremely important for me to try to liberate color from form. In my paintings, color is an element in and of itself, eloquent and independent in its presentation. In 1957, I developed my own color theory, according to which each color exists relative to the planal space which it occupies. I order colors according to their characteristic spatial depth. This permits me to create visual space without using perspective or modelling, and contributes simultaneously to the complex interactions of forces in conjunction or tension with each other.

—Nassos Daphnis

* * *

When Nassos Daphnis began hybridizing exotic tree peonies, crossing rare Chinese species with hardy native varieties, he had to outsmart the nearly insurmountable sterility of the hybrid to reestablish the line of offspring that may extend into the future. This need to circumvent dead ends, to predate dogmatic trends, has characterized Daphnis' work since the beginning of his career. Paying homage to the pure and simple during the freewheeling period of expressionism in the 50s, he precociously hybridizes a blunt forthrightness to create a strain of geometric abstraction that has borne fruit ever since.

More than a painter, Daphnis is a pioneer. His work has been a succession of experiments, surviving complex alterations to achieve the degree of simplification encompassed in his recent paintings. Yet through each phase, his attention to purity of color and image has remained consistent. In 1938 Daphnis began painting landscapes that made direct, legible statements in bold, intense colors neatly bound within hard edges. In 1947 critics noticed a change in style when he exhibited quasi-surrealistic representations of charred trees in barren landscapes. His work in camouflage and relief maps during the war years may have been responsible for the new forms and textures in his paintings. His 1950 travels to Greece, where the light ''flattened everything,'' slanted his perspective towards abstraction. The effect eliminated texture and surface incident, prompting Daphnis to research optical properties of color and the activities of planes.

His commitment to ''pure'' color resulted in a color theory which has sustained the basic structure of his subsequent work. Visualizing an arbitrary scale of 1 to 100, he gave each color a value: black, the most intense color, occupies planes 0–10; blue from 10–70 followed by red, yellow and finally white, being ''without substance but an expanding essence'' from 90–100. The color planes extend back to infinity behind the picture plane. A color becomes a tonal value and loses the energy of pure color whenever it goes beyond its limit.

Around 1955 his painting became highly complex in design in efforts to overcome the strict limitations of ''pure'' art. The adherence to his color theory nevertheless remained tenacious. Yet the seeming arbitrary change from one approach to the next suggests a consistent trend which moves, cyclically—and cathartically—from complex design to simplified, reductive purity. In 1958 he discovered acrylic paints. First by applying the paint consistently with rollers, then by masking and spraying his canvases, Daphnis achieved effects of uniformity and geometric precision while maintaining pure bands of colors. He increased his scale, creating nearly wall-sized surfaces, and engendered a feeling of absorption into the paintings by choosing red for its intensity and strength. The viewing experience bore obvious comparisons to that of Abstract Expressionist work, though Daphnis himself is reluctant to acknowledge any analogy to the gestural approach of this school.

Daphnis added another variable to his work with the introduction of wood reliefs, physical planes which compliment and augment the painted ones. Plastics, which succeeded this phase in 1962, included the elements of translucency and transparency to the now three-dimensional bands. The interaction between actual and painted elements produced color vibrations and spatial constituencies stronger than those in earlier paintings. This relief method allowed Daphnis to incorporate color into sculpture. His red and black column is best known in this series. Large in scale, it commands space and absorbs light. The core of the piece is clear plastic which calls attention away from its mass creating spatial ambiguity and intensifying color contrasts. It suggests change and is an architectural statement of structure and continuation.

In pursuit of pure abstraction, his ingenuity captured critical attention around 1960 with his invention of a large, compass-like instrument used to delineate arcs with perfect precision. The arcs appear to continue on their great trajectories out of the picture space on either side indefinitely with the same exactitude. Yet the unsettling behavior of the arc's position on the canvas within the soothing geometric order creates the vital energy of his paintings.

Having earned a place in recent history, Daphnis is also likely to receive exposure as an important artist of the future. His devotion to purity predicted '60s Minimalism; his systematic approach predated systematic painting. Now, another phase of his work completed, he is ever exploring new possibilities. His art resists stagnation, for it is still developing, still anticipating new experiments.

—Carrie Barker

DARBOVEN, Hanne

Nationality: German. **Born:** Munich, 29 April 1941. **Education:** Studied art at the Hochschule für Bildende Kunst, Hamburg. **Career:** Independent artist, working with number-concepts, Hamburg and New York, since 1966. **Agent:** Leo Castelli Gallery, 420 Broadway, New York, New York 10012; Dia Center for the Arts (SOHO), 548 West 22nd Street, New York, New York, 10011; Sperone Westwater, 142 and 121 Greene Street, New York, New York, 10012. **Address:** Am Burgberg 20, 2000 Hamburg 90, Germany.

Individual Exhibitions:

1967 Galerie Konrad Fischer, Dusseldorf
1968 Galerie Konrad Fischer, Dusseldorf
1969 Städtisches Museum, Mönchengladbach, West Germany
Galerie Heiner Friedrich, Munch
1970 Galerie Michael Werner, Cologne
Galerie Konrad Fischer, Dusseldorf
Art & Project, Amsterdam
Galleria Sperone, Turin
1971 Westfälischer Kunstverein, Münster, West Germany
Galerie Konrad Fischer, Dusseldorf
1972 Galerie Heiner Friedrich, Cologne
Galerie M.T.L., Brussels
Galleria Toselli, Milan
Galleria Marilena Bonomo, Bari, Italy
Studio Lia Rumma, Naples
Kabinett für Aktuelle Kunst, Bremerhaven, West Germany
Museum für Kunst und Gewerbe, Hamburg
1973 Galerie Yvon Lambert, Paris
Leo Castelli Gallery, New York
1974 Art & Project/M.T.L., Antwerp (travelled to Amsterdam and Brussels)
Palais des Beaux-Arts, Brussels
Museum of Modern Art, Oxford
Kabinett fur Aktuelle Kunst, Bremerhaven, West Germany
Leo Castelli Gallery, New York
Ein Monat, ein Johr, ein Jahrhundert: Arbeiten von 1968 bis 1974, Kunstmuseum, Basle
Sonnabend Gallery, New York
1975 *Een Maand, een Jaar, een Eeuw: Werken van 1968 tot en met 1974,* Stedelijk Museum, Amsterdam
Leo Castelli Gallery, New York
Kunstmuseum, Lucerne
1976 *For Jean-Paul Sartre,* Leo Castelli, New York
1978 Leo Castelli/Sperone-Westwater-Fischer, New York
1988 Kunstraum Munchen, Munich
1990 *Primitive Zeit/Uhrzeit: Primitive Time/Clock Time,* Goldie Paley Gallery, Moore College of Art and Design, Philadelphia (catalog)
1991 Ydessa Hendeles Foundation, Toronto
1993 Leo Castelli Gallery, New York
1994 *Hanne Darboven, Constructed, Literary, Musical, the Sculpting of Time,* Goethe Institut, London (catalog)
Musée d'Art Moderne de la Ville, Paris
1995 *Hanne Darboven,* Leo Castelli Gallery (SOHO), New York
1996 *Kulturgeschichte 1880–1983,* Dia Center for the Arts, New York
Ausstellungsgesellschaft Zeche Zollverein, Essen
Dia Center for the Arts, New York
Neue Bildende Kunst, Berlin
Hanne Darboven: Evolution Leibniz, 1986, Sprengel Museum Hannover, Hannover (catalog)
Stone of Wisdom/Stein der Weisen 1996, Sperone Westwater Gallery, New York
1997 *Hanne Darboven: Children of this World,* Staatsgalerie Stuttgart, Germany (catalog)
Hanne Darboven: Kulturgeschichte 1880–1983, Dia Center for the Arts, New York (catalog)

1999 Hallen für Neue Kunst, Schaffhausen
Hamburger Kunsthalle, Hamburg
Hanne Darboven: A Century Dedicated to Johann Wolfgang von Goethe, Museum für Moderne Kunst, Frankfurt am Main
Hommage à Picasso, Deichtorhalle, Hamburg (catalog)
Hanne Darboven: Works 1969, 1972, 1983, Harvard University Art Museums, Cambridge

Selected Group Exhibitions:

1967 *Normal Art,* Lannis Museum of Normal Art, New York
1968 *Language II, Dwan Gallery,* New York
1969 *When Attitudes Become Form,* Kunsthalle, Berne (toured Europe)
1970 *Conceptual Art/Arte Povera/Land Art,* Galleria Civica, Turin
1971 *7th Biennale de Paris,* Musée d'Art Moderne de la Ville, Paris
Guggenheim International, Guggenheim Museum, New York
1972 *Documenta 5,* Kassel, West Germany (and *Documenta 7,* 1982)
1973 *Bienal,* Sao Paulo
1974 *Project 74,* Kunsthalle, Cologne
1985 *The European Iceberg,* Art Gallery of Ontario, Toronto
1994 *BILD: Photography in Germany Contemporary Art,* Louisiana Museum, Humlebaek, Denmark (catalog)
1996 *Inside the Visible,* Institute of Contemporary Art, Boston (catalog)
Collage, Leo Castelli Gallery, New York
1997 Staatsgalerie Stuttgart
Forty Years of Exploration and Innovation: The Artists of the Castelli Gallery 1957–1997 Part Three, Leo Castelli Gallery (SOHO), New York
4e Biennale de Lyon, Germany
Hanne Darboven/John Cage, Staatsgalerie Moderner Kunst, Munich (also Bayerische Staatsgemäldesammlungen Pinothek der Moderne, Munich) (catalog)
1999 *Chronos & Kairos,* Fridericianum, Kassel, Germany
Global Conceptualism: Points of Origin 1950s-1980s, Queens Museum of Art, New York
2000 *Diary,* Cornerhouse, Manchester, England
Carnegie International, Carnegie Museum of Art, Pittsburgh

Collections:

Stedelijk Museum, Armsterdam; Kaiser-Wilhelm-Museum, Krefeld, West Germany.

Publications:

By DARBOVEN: Books—*Ein Jahrhundert,* Amsterdam 1971; *Hanne Darboven: Briefe aus New York 1966–68 an zu Hause,* Ostfildern 1995; *Conceptual Art: A Critical Anthology,* with multiple authors, Cambridge 1999. **Articles—**''6 Manuskripte '69'' with others, in *Kunstzeitung* (Dusseldorf), no. 3, 1969, ''Words'' in *Avalanche* (New York), Spring 1972; interview with Mark Gisbourne in *Art Monthly,* no. 181, November 1994; *Hanne Darboven/John Cage: A Dialogue of Artworks,* Munich 2000; *Hanne Darboven: Schreibzeit,* Köln 2000. **Film—***6 books, 68–6,* 1971. **CD—***Sprechzeit: Hanne Darboven im Gespräch mit Gerwig Epkes,* 1999.

On DARBOVEN: Books—*Arte Povera* by Germano Celant, Milan, Tübingen and New York 1970; *Hanne Darboven* by Ingrid Krupka, Cologne 1972; *Hanne Darboven,* exhibition catalog with texts by Klaus Honnef and Johannes Cladders, Munster, West Germany 1971; *Guggenheim International Exhibition 1971,* catalog with texts by Thomas M. Messer, Diane Waldman and Edward F. Fry, New York 1971; *Was Die Schonheit sei, das Weiss ich Nicht, Kunstler, Theori, Werk,* Nuremberg 1971; *Documenia 5: Berfragung der Realiät,* exhibition catalog, edited by Harald Szeemann and others, Kassel, West Germany 1972; *Six Years: The Dematerialization of the Art Object* by Lucy R. Lippard, London and New York 1973; *Bilder, Objekei, Filme, Konsepte,* exhibition catalog, with texts by J. Herbig, M. Petzet and A. Sweite, Munich 1973; *Projekt 74: Aspekte internationaler Kunst am Anfang der 70er Jahe,* exhibition catalog, with texts by Dieter Ronte, Evelyn Weiss, Marlis Gruterich and others, Cologne 1974; *Hanne Darboven: ein Monat, ein Jahr, ein Jahrhundert: Arbeiten von 1968 bis 1974,* exhibition catalog, with text by Franz Meyer, Basle 1974; *Hanne Darboven: Een Maand, een Jaar, een Eeuw: werken van 1968 tot en met 1974,* exhibition catalog, with text by Franz Meyer, Amsterdam 1975; *Hanne Darboven: For Jean-Paul Sartre,* exhibition folder, New York 1976; *Hanne Darboven,* exhibition folder, New York 1978. **Articles—**''On a Number of Things: Hanne Darboven's Kulturgeschichte 1880–1983'' by Dorothea Dietrich in *On Paper,* vol. 2, September/October 1997; ''Darboven in Concert'' by Andreas Denk in *Kunstforum International,* no. 145, May-June 1999; ''Das Labyrinth der Geraden Linie: Uber die Zeit bei Hanne Darboven'' by Doris von Drathen in *Kunstforum International,* no. 150, April-June 2000.

* * *

In many regards Hanne Darboven is unique in the annals of contemporary art. Externally her work bursts open the dimensions of the customary from the onset. A thousand-plus drawings seem pregnant witnesses to the cultural history of the trivial, as do the occasional photographic images united with, from time to time, a single self-contained work. Yet the drawings do not correspond to traditional standards. They resemble literary notes of the past, and the frequently appearing numbers, some in digits, others in words or with their numerical value written out, seem to replace the language of literature. The numbers arrange themselves into a fixed system. This system goes astray in a spiral movements and falls back at the end toward the previous century in almost every case, orienting itself through the traditional calendar. A mathematical operation—the formation of crossed sums of the month—and the count of years—provides the formal ''arrangement.'' Nevertheless, in the perception of the aesthetic of Hanne Darboven's work the knowledge of numerical systems stems not from decisive meaning. The artist is not a numerologist. Instead, the numeric system lends the artistic work merely aesthetic structure. Within this aesthetic structure takes place the ''real'' of the artistic work. Darboven's work is unique in contemporary art, especially in the way in which it counts up, through the details, an insight into the connection between the universe and existence. The most extensive, complex examples of her work embody a piece of subjective experience of life and at the same time represent a successful attempt in breaking from the seemingly senseless universal birth of meaning.

Although the person of the artist shapes the focus of the experience, the work of Hanne Darboven transgresses the individual horizon of subjective reflection. In her work the empirical is represented, unbroken, alongside the imaginative, both connected through a mixture of free association and montage-heavy construction. In certain ways Hanne Darboven enlivens the once-aristocratic historical province painting of art anew, by sometimes unusual methods and without any direct reference back toward the tradition of art. The diagrams and graphic paper that came to be misunderstood as contributions to ''conceptual'' art since the last half of the 1960s, has instead developed into a vast ''panorama'' of sensual, experience-rich ''universe-personification'' and ''universe-explanation.'' At first sight the work of Darboven appears likewise also so imperceptible and impenetrable as the universe; however the perception as also a means of assistance of intellectual insight opens up toward careful ''readings'' of the core, a core into which the work of Hanne Darboven reaches. Through her work the body and spirit of the observer become equally seized, while the decisiveness of her aesthetic principals prove themselves at the end not through the transposition in filmic and musical forms. Hanne Darboven strives for nothing less than a ''total work of art.'' In spite of all the suggestivity that radiates out of the work, in its optical version just as in its acoustic, the rational lesson remains constantly recognizable. The relation between the parts of the whole are easily clear, even when the perimeter of some works transgress the familiar proportions of art. Somehow the crystalline forms of the works remind one of the hundreds and thousands of carefully written-upon sheets on the metaphorical level of the filigreed buildings of gothic cathedrals, and the trivial objects which the artist inserts into it, secular monuments to the art of numbers. Hanne Darboven has created a singular universe, a world, however, that from the empirical reality of everyday experience is only one step removed from the aesthetic penetration.

—Klaus Honnef

DAVIE, Alan

Nationality: British. **Born:** Grangemouth, Scotland, in 1920. **Education:** Studied at the Edinburgh College of Art, 1937–40. **Family:** Married Janet Gaul in 1947; daughter: Jane. **Military Service:** Served in the Royal Artillery, 1941–46. **Career:** Worked as a jazz musician, 1947; travelled extensively in Europe, 1947–49; worked as a jeweller, 1949–53; visited New York, 1956; Gregory fellow, University of Leeds, 1956–59; lecturer, Central School of Arts and Crafts, London, 1959–60; performed at public recital, Gimpel Fils Gallery and Tate Gallery, London: first record issued, 1971; Member, Tony Oxley group: gave concerts and broadcasts, 1973–75; travelled in the West Indies, 1976; frequently lectures at universities, colleges and art institutes; visiting professor at Brighton University, October 1993; now lives in Hertfordshire and in St. Lucia, West Indies. **Awards:** Guthrie Award, Royal Scottish Academy, Edinburgh, 1942; Prize, *Bienal,* Sao Paulo, 1953; Critics' Choice Award, London, 1956, 1958, 1960; Prix Guggenheim, Musée d'Art Moderne, Paris, 1956; First Prize, *International Graphics Exhibition,* Cracow, 1966; Saltine Award, Edinburgh, 1976; Honorary Royal Scottish Academician, 1976; C. B. E. (Commander, Order of the British Empire), 1972; Order of the Southern Cross, Brazil, 1987; Senior Fellow, Royal College of Art Convocation, 1991. Honorary doctorates from Heriot-Watt University, 1994, and University of Hertfordshire, 1995. **Agent:** Gimpel Fils, London. **Address:** Gamels Studio, Rush Green, Hertford SG13 7SB, England.

Alan Davie: *Meditation on Jain Cosmology No. 6,* 1985. ©Alan Davie.

Individual Exhibitions:

1946 Grant's Bookshop, Edinburgh
1948 *Art and Inspiration,* Galleria Michelangelo, Florence
The Forest, Galleria Sandri, Venice
1950–55 Gimpel Fils, London
1956 Catherine Viviano Gallery, New York
1957 Catherine Viviano Gallery, New York
1958 Wakefield City Art Gallery, Yorkshire (travelled to Whitechapel Art Gallery, London, and the Walker Art Gallery, Liverpool)
University of Nottingham
1960 Gimpel Fils, London
Galerie Charles Lienhard, Zurich
1961 Gimpel Fils, London
Galleria del Naviglio, Milan
Galerie Rive Droite, Paris
Martha Jackson Gallery, New York
Carnegie Institute, Pittsburgh
Esther Robles Gallery, Los Angeles
1962 FBA Gallery, London (travelled to the Stedelijk Museum, Amsterdam)

Carnegie Institute, Pittsburgh
Esther Robles Gallery, Los Angeles
Kunstnernes Hus, Oslo
1963 Galleria La Medusa, Rome
Gimpel Fils, London
Commercial Centre of the Brazilian Embassy, London
Kunsthalle, Berne
Kunsthalle, Baden-Baden, West Germany
1964 Gimpel and Hanover Galerie, Zurich
Crestline Galerie, Edinburgh
1965 Gimpel Fils, London
Martha Jackson Gallery, New York
Galerie Rudolf Zwirner, Cologne
Graves Art Gallery, Sheffield (toured the U.K.)
Court Gallery, Copenhagen
Galerie d'Aujourd'hui, Brussels
1966 Gimpel Fils, London
Commonwealth Institute Gallery, Edinburgh
Castle Museum, Norwich
Kunstkring, Rotterdam
Usher Gallery, Lincoln
Queen Square Gallery, Leeds
1967 Gimpel Fils, London
Gimpel and Hanover, Zurich
Galerie de France, Paris
Arts Club of Chicago (travelled to University of Minnesota, Minneapolis)
Kestner-Gesellschaft, Hannover
1968 Kunstverein, Dusseldorf
Galerie Overbeck-Gesellschaft, Lubeck
Richard Demarco Gallery, Edinburgh
Hudson Gallery, Detroit
1969 Gimpel Fils, London
Kunstmuseum, Basle
Galleria La Medusa, Rome
Gimpel Fils, New York
1970 Gimpel Fils, London
Galleria La Medusa, Rome
Galerie Stangl, Munich
1971 Gimpel Fils, London
Galerie Lambert Monet, Geneva
Gimpel and Hanover Galerie, Zurich
1972 Gimpel Gallery, New York
Gimpel and Weitzenhoffer Gallery, New York
Royal Scottish Academy Edinburgh (travelled to the Kunstverein, Brunswick, and the Badischer Kunstverein, Karlsruhe, West Germany)
1973 Gimpel Fils, London
Galleria d'Arte Rotta, Genoa
1974 Gimpel Fils, London (travelled to Gimpel and Hanover Galerie, Zurich)
Gimpel and Weitzenhoffer Gallery, New York
Playhouse Gallery, Harlow, Essex
1975 Gimpel Fils, London
Galleria d'Arte Rotta, Milan
Galerie de France, Paris
Arte '75, Basle
Comskey Gallery, Los Angeles
1976 Galleria La Medusa, Rome
Chateau de Lucens, Switzerland
Allan Rubiner Gallery, Royal Oak, Michigan
Hokin Gallery, Chicago
1977 Gimpel Fils, London
Zoumbarakis Galleria, Athens
Caronne Gallery, Fort Lauderdale, Florida
Le Demeure, Paris
Art Galerie and Museum, Aberdeen, Scotland
1978 Kunsthandel Brinkman, Amsterdam
Gimpel and Hanover Galerie, Zurich (travelled to the Galerie am Palmengarten, Frankfurt, and Gimpel Fils, London)
Maercklin Galerie, Stuttgart
Galerie Cour St. Pierre, Geneva
Lister Gallery, Perth, Western Australia (travelled to the Art of Man Gallery, Sydney, and the Ray Hughes Gallery, Brisbane)
1979 Aitken Dott, The Scottish Gallery, Edinburgh
Gimpel Fils, London
Galerie Ado, Bonheiden, Belgium
1980 Gimpel and Weitzenhoffer, New York
Gimpel and Hanover, Zurich
Lister Gallery, Perth, Western Australia
1981 Gimpel Fils, London
Galerie van Loe, Frankfurt
1982 Rosenberg Fine Art, Toronto
The Scottish Gallery, Edinburgh
Arcade Gallery, Harrogate, Yorkshire
Arts Centre, Hong Kong
Galerie de Raam, Breda, Netherlands
Gimpel Fils, at *FIAC 82,* Grand Palais, Paris
1983 Galerie de'Eendt, Amsterdam
Gimpel Fils, London
1984 Festival Gallery, Bath, Avon
Community Arts Centre, Windsor, Berkshire
Galerie Van Loe, Frankfurt
Bede Gallery, Jarrow, Durham
Loft Gallery, Ware, Hertfordshire
1985 Galerie Apicella, Bonn
Gimpel Fils, London
Yares Gallery, Scottsdale, Arizona
1986 Gimpel and Weitzenhoffer, New York
1987 Gimpel Fils, London
Moray House Gallery, Edinburgh
Galerie Louis Carre, Paris
Gimpel Fils, at *FIAC 86,* Grand Palais, Paris
1988 *Magic Fountains,* Gimpel Fils Gallery, London
South West Arts Association, Scotland (touring Scotland 1988–89)
1989 Scottish Gallery, Edinburgh
Galerie G, Helsinborg, Sweden
Gimpel Fils Gallery, London
1990 Madrid Art Fair, Madrid
Galerie Louis Carre, Paris
Alan Davie in the 70s, Galerie G, Helsinborg, Sweden
Major Work of the 60s, Gimpel Weitzenhoffer Gallery, New York
1991 Bath Art Fair, Bath, England
Galerie M, Krakow, Poland
Wolf at the Door Gallery, Penzance, England
Gimpel Fils Gallery, London

Galerie Bork, Copenhagen

1992 *Retrospective Exhibition,* McLennan Galleries, Glasgow (toured United Kingdom)
Print Gallery, Edinburgh
Compass Gallery, Edinburgh
B.P. Gallery, Brussells

1993 *The Quest for the Miraculous,* Hastings Museum and Art Gallery, Hastings, England (travelled to Ramsgate Gallery, Ramsgate; University Gallery, Newcastle; University Arts Gallery, Nottingham and Smith Art Gallery and Museum, Stirling)
Retrospective Exhibition, Barbican Gallery, London
Retrospective Exhibition, Butler Gallery, Kilkenny Castle, Kilkenny, Ireland
A.C.A. Gallery, New York
Eva Cohon Gallery, Chicago

1993–95 *British Council Circulating Exhibition (number 887),* Brazil (toured South and Central America)

1994 Bineth Gallery, Tel Aviv, Israel
Wolf at the Door Gallery, Penzance, England
A.C.A. Gallery, Munich
Gimpel Fils at FIAC, Paris
Galeria Fernando, Santos Oporto, Portugal
Galeria Quadrum, Lisbon, Portugal
Centro de Arte Moderna, Almada, Portugal

1995 Gimpel Fils Gallery, London
Isis Gallery and Education Trust, Essex, England

1996 Pallant House Gallery, Chichester, England

1997 *Retrospective Drawing Exhibition,* Scottish National Gallery of Modern Art, Edinburgh
Gouaches, 1993–1996, Gimpel Fils Gallery, London
Oils and Gouaches Retrospective, A.C.A. Gallery, New York
Inverness Festival, Inverness Museum and Art Gallery, Scotland
Gouaches and Drawings, Joseph Rickards Gallery, New York

1998 *Paintings 1993–1998,* Pier Arts Centre, Stromness, Orkney
Works on Paper, 1950s-1970s, Faggionato Fine Arts, London

1999 Gimpel Fils Gallery, London
Cobra Museum, Amsterdam
Hertfordshire University, Hertfordshire, England
Gimpel Fils Gallery at Bologna Art Fair, Bologna, Italy

2000 *Small Paintings Retrospective,* Brighton University, Brighton, England
Alan Davie Collection, National Gallery of Modern Art, Edinburgh

2001 Gimpel Fils Gallery at Bologna Art Fair, Bologna, Italy
Galeria Morine Milano, Milan, Italy

Selected Group Exhibitions:

1950 *Aspects of British Art,* Institute of Contemporary Arts, London

1958 *50 Ans d'Art Moderne,* Palais des Beaux-Arts, Brussels

1960 *British Painting 1720–1960,* Pushkin Museum, Moscow (travelled to The Hermitage, Leningrad)

1961 *Pittsburgh International,* Carnegie Institute, Pittsburgh

1966 *International Graphics Exhibition,* Cracow

1970 *British Painting and Sculpture 1960–1970,* National Gallery of Art, Washington, D.C.

1973 *Hommage à Picasso,* Kestner Gessellschaft, Hannover

1977 *British Painting 1952–1977,* Royal Academy of Art, London

1985 *Recalling the Fifties,* Serpentine Gallery, London

1987 *British Art in the 20th Century,* Royal Academy, London
20th Century Scottish Painting, 369 Gallery, Edinburgh

1988 *The Romantic Tradition in Contemporary British Painting,* Icon Gallery, Birmingham, England (travelled to Spain)
Athena Exhibition, Barbican, London

1989 *The Broader Canvas,* Gimpel Fils Gallery, London
Galerie C Exhibition, Stockholm Art Fair, Sweden
Images of Paradise, Harewood House, Yorkshire, England
Scottish Art Since 1900, Scottish National Gallery of Modern Art, Edinburgh

1990 *Annual Exhibition of Royal Scottish Society of Painters in Watercolour,* R.S.A. Galleries in Edinburgh
Scottish Art Since 1900, Barbican, London
Scottish Art 1900–1990, Scottish Gallery, London

1991 *Scottish Art in the 20th Century,* Royal West of England Academy, Bristol
Focus of Attention, Hamburger Kunsthalle, Germany

1993 *Scottish Painting,* Flowers East Gallery, London

1995 *The Discerning Eye,* Mall Gallery, London
Gimpel Gallery at FIAC Exhibition, Paris
Royal Scottish Academy, Edinburgh
The Stuff of Dreams, Australian High Commission London Gallery, London

1996 Mappin Art Gallery, Sheffield, England

1997 *Eight by Eight,* Pallant House, Garden Gallery, Chichester, England

Collections:

Tate Gallery, London; Victoria and Albert Museum, London; Stedelijk Museum, Amsterdam; Museum des 20, Jahrhunderts, Vienna; Museum of Modern Art, Tel Aviv; Museum of Modern Art, New York; Albright-Knox Art Gallery, Buffalo, New York; Carnegie Institute, Pittsburgh; Museum of Fine Arts, Boston.

Publications:

By DAVIE: Books—*Alan Davie: Major Works of the Fifties,* exhibition catalog, London 1987; *Lithographs, Drawings, and Magic Reader* (18 Original Lithographs), published by Charles Booth-Clibborn, 1992; *Small Paintings, 1949–2000,* 1999. **Articles—**statement in *Art and Inspiration,* exhibition catalog, Florence 1948; statement in *The Forest,* exhibition catalog, Venice 1948; statement in *Statements: British Abstract Art in 1956,* London 1957; statement in *Notes by the Artists,* exhibition catalog, London 1958; ''Notes on Teaching'' in *The Developing Process,* exhibition catalog, London 1959; ''Towards a New Definition of Art: Some Notes on Now Painting'' in *New Departures* (London), April 1960; ''Personal Thoughts'' in *Times Educational Supplement* (London), June 1960; ''I Confess'' in *Visone Colore,* exhibition catalog, Venice 1963.

On DAVIE: Books—*Contemporary British Art* by Herbert Read, London 1951; *Space in Colour,* exhibition catalog, by Patrick Heron, London 1953; *Private View* by Bryan Robertson, John Russell and

Lord Snowdon, London 1965; *Alan Davie* by Alan Bowness, London 1967; *The Art Scene* by Barrie Stuart-Penrose, London 1967; *Alan Davie,* exhibition catalog, by Alan Bowness, London 1972; *Alan Davie,* catalog with text by Dore Ashton, London 1984; *Alan Davie,* exhibition catalog with essay by Jacques Roche-Villiers, Paris 1987; *Alan Davie* by Douglas Hall, with introduction by Alan Davie, essay by Michael Tucker, 1992; *Alan Davie: The Quest for the Miraculous,* exibition catalog, edited and with an introduction by Michael Tucker, with text by Lynne Green, London 1993; *Alan Davie Drawings,* Paragon Press, 1997.

*

Images are not used as art objects, but as channels of communication with the Divine.

—Allan Davie

* * *

Writing about Alan Davie's painting makes you feel like Sisyphus pushing that huge boulder up the mountain. Just when you think you have attained a certain understanding, something else catches your eye, and you are thrown off balance yet again. This is what is so fascinating and at the same time frustrating about Davie's art. In many ways his work is reminiscent of a jam session by the saxophonist John Surman: constant improvisation, then settling down on one particular theme, then suddenly changing tracks.

Davie has made up his own world of signs and symbols. Each viewer is bound to have varying interpretations. Various images remain firmly embedded in the mind—such as the highly defined scarab which represents resurrection, the ankh which symbolises life or royal authority; dragons, serpents and birds are also always present. The influence of early Christian art can clearly be seen, and Davie's admiration for Bosch, Brueghel and Uccello is also very clear.

Davie's style is wild, exuberant, free. He paints just as if he were gliding—swooping here and there finally reaching a destination. Life is seen amid a flurry of colors: reds, mauves, pinks, greens and yellows go hand in hand in "Feathers for a Serpent" of 1963. In "Phantom in the Room" a wonderful vibrant red, pink and green room is set alight; the chessboard and hand of Fatima symbolize fate and the game of life.

Davie paints almost as if he were guided by some mysterious force. Some of his paintings give the impression that they were painted in a trance: Images cascaded into his mind, and he could not get them down quickly enough. In fact, Davie has said, "We must confront a painting empty and open-hearted"—but not completely empty, as when a Japanese monk enquired of his Zen master, "What would you advise if a man came to you with nothing." The master immediately replied: "Throw it away." Davie has also said that he practices art for enlightenment and that a picture "must happen in spite of me rather than because of me."

After long and meticulous preparation Davie puts on his painting boots and sets off into the canvas. He is not one of the self-satisfied group who sits back and thinks that is another canvas finished. One senses that he worries endlessly and returns to past works—for him they are alive, still part of him, and it is this concern that gives the paintings their vitality. For Arp art was "a fruit grown on the tree of man." For Davie the fruit never stops growing.

There is no doubt that much of Davie's imagination and vision springs from his Celtic heritage. As one wanders about Scotland, one sees many of Davie's images, but they are usually seen against a dour grey backcloth. Davie has surrounded them with brilliant color, which remains in the mind. "Like a bird I shall take up my color and my brush, and I shall paint as the bird sings"—and so he does.

—Carrie Maurice

DAVIES, John

Nationality: British. **Born:** Cheshire, 14 July 1946. **Education:** Painting at Hull and Manchester Colleges of Art, 1963–67; studied sculpture, Slade School of Fine Art, London, 1967–69; Gloucestershire College of Art and Design, Cheltenham (Sculpture Fellowship), 1969–70. **Career:** Sculptor, London and Kent, since 1970. **Award:** Sainsbury Award, 1970. **Agent:** Marlborough Fine Art Ltd., London. **Address:** c/o Marlborough Fine Art (London) Ltd., 6 Albemarle Street, London WLX 4BY, England.

Individual Exhibitions:

1972 Whitechapel Art Gallery, London
1975 Whitechapel Art Gallery, London
1980 *Recent Sculpture and Drawings,* Marlborough Fine Art, London
1981 Kunstverein, Hamburg (travelled to the Wilhelm Lehmbruck Museum, Duisburg, and the Kunstverein, Karlsruhe, 1981–82)
1982 Ferens Art Gallery, Hull, Yorkshire
1984 Marlborough Fine Art, London
1985 Sainsbury Centre, University of East Anglia, Norwich, Norfolk
1987 Prema, Gloucestershire
1989 Marlborough Gallery, New York
1992 Marlborough Graphics, London
1993 Marlborough Fine Art, London
1995 Centro de Arte Palacio Almundi, Murcia, Spain
1996 Whitworth Art Gallery, Manchester
1997 Marlborough Fine Art, London
1998 Purdy Hicks Gallery, London
1999 University Gallery, Newcastle-upon-Tyne, England
Plymouth Arts Centre, Plymouth, England

Selected Group Exhibitions:

1973 *Biennale des Jeunes,* Musée National d'Art Moderne, Paris
1974 *12 Views of Mankind,* MacRobert Centre, University of Stirling, Scotland
1976 *Biennale,* Venice
1977 *Documenta,* Kassel, Germany
1979 *Europaische Realistische Plastik,* Kunsthalle, Bremen, Germany
1981 *British Sculpture since 1900: Part II, 1950–1980,* Whitechapel Art Gallery, London
1982 *Aspects of British Art Today,* Metropolitan Museum of Art, Tokyo (toured Japan)

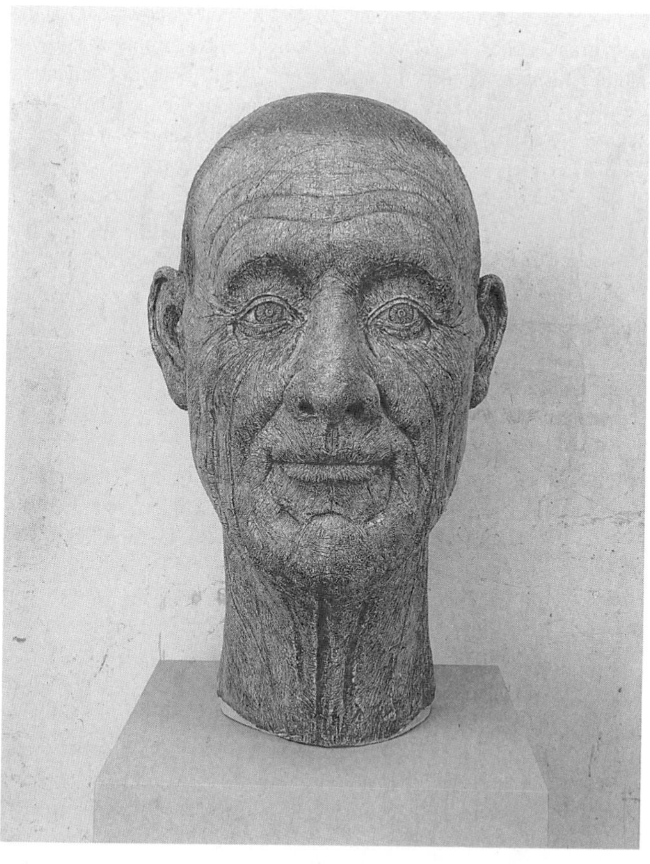

John Davies: *Head like my Father,* 1985–88. Photo by James Austin. ©John Davies.

1984 *The British Art Show,* Museum and Art Gallery, Birmingham (and Ikon Gallery, Birmingham; toured Britain)
The Hard-Won Image, Tate Gallery, London
From the Figure, Ikon Gallery, Birmingham
Sculptor's Drawings, British Council, Circulating Exhibition
Masterpieces of Modern Sculpture, Marlborough Fine Art, New York
1985 *A Singular Vision: Paintings of the Figure by Contemporary British Artists,* Arts Council Travelling Exhibition Human Interest
Fifty Years of British Art about People, Cornerhouse, Manchester
1986–87 *The Foundation Veranneman Invites Marlborough,* Foundation Veranneman, Kruishouten, Belgium
1987–88 *Viewpoint,* Koninklijke Musea voor Schone Kunsten van België, The British Council, Belgium
1988 *The Face,* The Arkansas Art Centre, Arkansas
Introducing with Pleasure, Gardener Art Centre and Arts Council tour
Works on Paper by Contemporary Artists, Marlborough Fine Art, London
1988–89 *100 Years of Art in Britain,* Leeds City Art Gallery
1995 *Kent Artists,* Canterbury City Art Gallery
Altars, Canterbury Festival
1997 *Bodyworks,* Kettles Yard, Cambridge
Surrealism and After, Scottish National Gallery of Modern Art, Edinburgh
Claude Bernard Gallery, Paris
1999 Den Haag Sculptuur, Holland
2000 *Elogio de lo Visible,* International Figuration Exhibition, Galeria Marlborough, Madrid (travelled to Centro Cultural Las Claras, Murcia; Centro Cultural Casa del Cordon, Burgos; Cultural Rioja, Logroño)
Le Brun, Campbell, Oulton, Davies, Raab Galerie, Berlin

Collections:

Tate Gallery, London; Arts Council of Great Britain, London; Contemporary Arts Society, London; Sainsbury Centre for the Visual Arts, Norwich; Wigan Art Gallery, Lancashire; Ulster Museum, Belfast; Wilhelm Lehmbruck Museum, Duisburg; McCrory Corporation, New York; Queensland Museum, Brisbane, Australia; The British Council; Art Gallery of Western Australia; Caracas Museum of Contemporary Art; City of Kingston-upon-Hull Museums and Art Galleries; Bolton Museum and Art Gallery; University of the Punjab, India; Scottish National Gallery of Modern Art, Edinburgh; Tokushima Museum, Japan; Whitworth Art Gallery, University of Manchester; Art Gallery of Western Australia, Perth.

Publications:

By DAVIES: Article—Discussion with Nicholas Wadley in *John Davies: Recent Sculpture and Drawings,* exhibition catalog, London 1980.

On DAVIES: Books—*John Davies: Recent Sculpture and Drawings,* exhibition catalog, London 1980; *Surrealism and After,* exhibition catalog by Elizabeth Cowling, 1997; *Bodyworks,* exhibition catalog by Michael Harrison, 1997. **Articles—**''A Show to Be Seen'' by Edward Lucie-Smith in the *Sunday Times* (London), 25 June 1972; ''The Human Condition'' by Robert Melville in *Architectural Review* (London), September 1972; ''The Bald Facts'' by Michael Shepherd in the *Sunday Telegraph* (London), 23 November 1980; ''The Sculpture of John Davies'' by Nicholas Wadley in *Art International* (Lugano, Switzerland), February 1981; ''John Davies'' by Heidi Bürklin in *Art Das Kunstmagazin,* May 1984; ''John Davies Portfolio'' in *NWT Nieuw Werldtydschrift,* July 1984; ''John Davies'' by Simon Corbin in *What's on in London,* 7–14 April 1993; ''This Life and Others'' by Michael Simpson in *Still,* exhibition catalog, 1996.

* * *

In his search to create ''something very real'' John Davies soon found that mimeticism was not the answer: something, and often something drastic, had to be done to the figures in order to wrench them from the realm of art, from looking too much like sculpture and too little like human beings:

''I used to think that there was no limit to what I'd have to make the figures do to get something out of them, anything that extraordinary or novel, which—however strange it might have seemed—created something very real: making sense.''

In an effort to secure this quality he placed ''devices,'' nose-bags or other kinds of masks or wire mesh cones over his carefully modelled or life-cast heads. The attention required to by-pass the mask in order to ''read'' the head better brings the face into sharper focus, making it more vivid than otherwise. This approach is closer to Francis Bacon's distorting of the sitter's features in an attempt to capture the truth than it is to a surrealist delight in the bizarre or shocking.

Since Davies found that the gaze was a key ingredient in eliciting the sense of animation and presence he desired, he sought to establish contact with the viewer by displaying these life-size heads on thin poles, at eye-level.

Recently he has eliminated the devices without losing the intense vitality. The heads have become tiny, often not more than a couple of inches high and the coloring less naturalistic, yet they are more potent. Given their size, the scrutiny normally accorded art objects does not reveal an excess of detail, like that found in a photograph: what is revealed is all that is given in just looking—the content of any ordinary glance.

In those works which contain life-size figures engaged in activities ranging from the extreme to the ordinary, Davies has sought a similar kind of reality:

''There is always a conflict for me between the qualities of made sculpture and what one might see on the street, but I strive to make the figures display the qualities of a human being rather than those of sculpture.''

Yet the means by which this is achieved clearly belong to the realm of art. For example, the figures often have a frozen quality, but this is very different from that found in snap-shots. They seem much closer to Egyptian sculpture where movement is conveyed through stasis. As one concentrates on these figures the props and other devices which accompany them gradually dissolve and the figures take on the immediacy and immutability of ancient sculpture. They are never merely genre or anecdotal works.

—Lynne Cooke

DAVIS, Douglas (Matthew)

Nationality: American. **Born:** Washington, D.C., 11 April 1933. **Education:** Abbott Art School, Washington, D.C., 1948–50; American University, Washington, D.C., 1952–56, B.A. 1956; Rutgers University, New Brunswick, New Jersey, 1956–58, M.A. **Family:** Married Mary Virginia Miller (divorced, 1967); children: Laura and Mary; married art critic Jane Bell in 1970. **Career:** Painter until 1969; since then has concentrated on video-performance work. Teaching fellow in English, Douglass College, 1957–60; freelance editor and writer, 1961–67; art critic, *National Observer,* Silver Spring, Maryland, 1965–69; contributing editor, *Art in America,* New York, 1968–70; art critic, *Newsweek,* New York, 1970–76 (now senior writer), visiting artist-in-video, Corcoran Gallery, Washington, D.C., 1970–71; artist-in-residence, Television Laboratory, WNET-TV, New York, 1972; visiting artist, Northwood Experimental Art Institute, Dallas, 1972; Artistic director, International Network for the Arts; Visiting Professor, Columbia University, 1990; Adjunct Professor of Fine Art, University of Southern California, Los Angeles, 1992–93; Fulbright Lecturer, Russia, 1994; Fulbright Scholar, Moscow State University, 1995; Distinguished Visiting Artist, Ramapo College, 1996; Lecturer, Parsons School of Design, 1998. **Awards:** New York State Council on the Arts grant, 1970; National Endowment for the Arts grant, 1971, 1975; DAAD Exchange Fellowship, Berlin, 1977; National Endowment for the Arts grant, 1981; Graham Foundation Fellow, 1988; Trust for Mutual Understanding Grant, 1989, 1991; Fulbright Scholar, 1995. **Agents:** Galleria Forma, Largo San Giuseppe 18, 16121 Genoa, Italy; Ronald Feldman Fine Arts, 33 East 74th Street, New York, New York 10012; and Electronic Arts Intermix, 100 Fifth Avenue, New York, New York 10011. **Address:** 80 Wooster Street, New York, New York 10012, U.S.A.

Individual Exhibitions:

1970 Reese Palley Gallery, New York
1972 *Events, Drawings, Objects, Videotapes 1967–72,* Everson Museum of Art Syracuse, New York
1973 DeSaisset Museum, University of Santa Clara, California
1975 *Videotapes,* San Francisco Museum of Modern Art
1976 *3 Silent and Secret Acts,* The Kitchen Center for Video and Music, New York
1977 *4 Places, 2 Figures, 1 Ghost,* Whitney Museum, New York
1978 *Arbeiten 1970–77,* Neue Berliner Kunstverein and Kunstlerhaus Bethanien, Berlin (travelled to Basel and Essen)
1979 *Drawings, Objects and Soundboxes,* PS 1, New York
1980 *Double Entendre,* Whitney Museum, New York (objects and drawings, accompanied by satellite telecast between the Whitney and the Centre Georges Pompidou, Paris, broadcast on WNYC-TV and via satellite to National Public Radio Stations in the United States)
1981 *The Wizard of Malta and The Moving Obscura* (3-screen film and room-sized installation), Ronald Feldman Fine Arts, New York
1982 *Video, Objects, Graphics,* Museum Sztuki, Lodz, Poland (retrospective)
1986 Guggenheim Museum, New York
1988 Guggenheim Museum, New York
1994 Lehman College Art Gallery, New York
1995 *Douglas Davis: Redness,* Muzeum Sztuki, Lodz, Poland
Digital Salon Exhibition of Computer Art, School of Visual Arts, New York

Selected Group Exhibitions:

1971 *10 Videotape Performances,* Finch College Museum of Contemporary Art, New York
1974 *L'Art Video,* Musée de l'Art Moderne de la Ville de Paris
1975 *Video Art,* Institute of Contemporary Art, Philadelphia
Projected Video, Whitney Museum, New York
Questions: Moscow-NY-NY-Moscow, San Francisco Museum of Modern Art
Bodyworks, Museum of Contemporary Art, Chicago
1976 *Biennale,* Venice
1977 *Documenta,* Kassel, West Germany (installation and satellite telecast, ''The Last 9 Minutes,'' with Nam June Paik and Joseph Beuys, broadcast to 25 countries)
1982 *Counterparts: Form and Emotion in Photography,* Metropolitan Museum of Art, New York

Collections:

Metropolitan Museum of Art, New York; Everson Museum of Art, Syracuse, New York; DeSaisset Museum, University of Santa Clara, California; Museo de Arte Contemporaneo, Caracas; Wallraf-Richartz Museum, Cologne; Museum Sztuki, Lodz, Poland; Centre Georges Pompidou, Paris; Hirschorn Museum, Washington, D.C.; Ludwig Museum, Cologne; Victoria and Albert Museum, London; Wadsworth Atheneum, Hartford; Dahlem Museum, Berlin; Guggenheim Museum, New York.

Publications:

By DAVIS: Books—*Art and the Future,* New York and London 1973, Cologne 1975; *Fragments for a New Art of the 70s* with Robert Stefanotty, Los Angeles 1975; *Artculture: Essays on the Post-Modern,* New York 1977; *Photography as Fine Art,* New York 1983. **Articles**—numerous critical essays in the *National Observer, Art in America,* and particularly *Newsweek* (since 1970), and ''For a New Esthetic'' in *American Scholar,* March/April 1966; ''Media Art Media'' in *Arts Magazine,* April 1972; ''A Conversation with Douglas Davis,'' with Marc Sapporta, in *Information and Documents,* May 1973; ''Filmgoing/Videogoing: Making Distinctions'' in *American Film Institute Journal,* May 1973; ''What is Content? Notes toward an Answer'' in *Artforum,* October 1973; ''Time! Time! Time! The Context of Immediacy'' in the *Museum of Modern Art Newsletter,* January 1974; ''Interview with Douglas Davis,'' with David Ross, in *Flash Art,* May 1975; ''Artpolitics: Thoughts against the Prevailing Fantasies'' in the *New York Arts Journal,* May 1975; ''Video in the Mid-70's: Prelude to an End/Future'' in *Video Art,* edited by Beryl Korot and Ira Schneider, New York 1976; ''The Idea of a 21st Century Museum'' in *Art Journal of the College Art Association,* January 1976; ''The Size of Non-Size'' in *Artforum,* December 1976; ''The End of Video: Black Death/White Vapor'' in *Video End,* edited by Horst Gerhard Haberl, Graz, Austria 1976; ''Die Euro American Generation'' in *Favored-Forever?,* edited by Werner Hofer, Dusseldorf 1976; ''Post-Modern Form: Stories Real and Imagined/Toward a Theory'' in the *New York Arts Journal,* January/February 1978; ''The Post-Modernist Dilemma,'' dialogue with Suzi Gablik, in the *Village Voice,* 27 March 1978, 3 April 1978 and 10 April 1978; ''How to Make Love to Your Television Set'' in the *New York Arts Journal,* May/June 1975; ''Post Post-Art Where Do We Go from Here?'' in the *Village Voice,* 25 June 1979; ''Post Post-Art II: Symbolismo, Come Home'' in the *Village Voice,* 13 August 1979; ''Post Post-Art III: Symbolismo Meets the Faerie Queen'' in the *Village Voice,* 17 December 1979; ''Dialogue with David Schapiro'' in the *New York Arts Journal,* February 1980; ''Post Everything'' in *Art in America,* February 1980; ''After Photography'' in the *Village Voice,* February 1981; ''Post-Performance ISM'' in *Artforum,* October 1981.

On DAVIS: Books—*Douglas Davis: Drawings, Objects, Videotapes 1967–72,* exhibition catalog by James Harithes, Nam June Paik and David Rose, Syracuse, New York 1972; *The Videotapes of Douglas Davis* by John Hanhardt, New York 1977; *Video Art,* edited by Beryl Korot and Ira Schneider, New York 1977; *Douglas Davis: Arbeiten 1970–77,* exhibition catalog, with essays by Wulf Herzogenrath, Wieland Schmied and Ann Sargent-Wooster, Berlin 1978; *Douglas Davis: Video, Objects, Graphics,* with essays by Ryszard Stanislawski, Ursula Czartoryska, Irving Sandler, and John G. Hanhardt, Lodz, Poland 1982; *Douglas Davis* by Donald Kuspit, New York 1988; *Douglas Davis: Redness,* exhibition catalog, Lodz 1995. **Articles**—''Explorations in Video'' by Gregory Battcock in *Art and Artists,* February 1973; ''The Davis Tapes'' by Alfred Frankenstein in the *San Francisco Chronicle,* 6 October 1973; ''Douglas Davis: Video Against Video'' by David Ross in *Arts Magazine,* January 1974; ''Douglas Davis'' by Walter Robinson in *Art-Rite,* Autumn 1974; ''Fragments for a New Art of the 70's'' by Pierre Restany in *Domus,* December 1975; ''Douglas Davis'' by Cynthia Nadelman in *Artnews,* May 1980; ''Douglas Davis'' by Jean-Paul Fargier in *Art Press,* July 1981; review in *Art in America,* vol. 83, December 1995; ''The Art World & I Go Online'' by Robert Atkins in *Art in America* (New York), vol. 83, no. 12, December 1995; ''Gallery Artworks: Computer Animations: Net-works: Exhibiting Artists: The Jury'' in *Leonardo* (Cambridge), vol. 28, no. 5, 1995; ''Collecting On-Line: ''A Leap of Faith"'' by Barbara Pollack in *Art News,* vol. 96, March 1997.

*

The medium (video) is at once of no importance and of the greatest importance. It is simply the latest tool to be adopted by contemporary art, which has been since Duchamp reaching for new means of expression. Video is thus like film, light, sound, movement, linguistics. But it is far more profound in its implication than these tools because it can communicate instantly, everywhere. And it is related to the social-power complex, very directly. Art in a gallery or a museum, or even in a film theatre, is confined. Art on television is loose, free, and dangerous.

I think that the central problems that are attached to my work are two: 1) how to communicate on a very intense, private and personal level through a public medium (videotape is public whether broadcast or seen in a gallery); and 2) how to engage in a two-way dialogue with the eye and the mind of the viewer that goes beyond Duchamp—who simply said first that art needs the viewer to complete itself.

From these two points, it is clear that the overall direction in my work is ''against video'' in the sense that I am assaulting what the medium *is* and *has been* (that is, bland, stupid, silly, and stiff). Video is simply the latest step in a process that is destroying the spectator ritual in art—the going-out to the temple to see it—but by no means the last. The next step is to get rid of the intervening structure, the cameras, the monitors, and telecasting circuitry.

My first thought about the television set was to activate it, as a link in a live sending as well as receiving link. We are almost blind to the two-way nature of television. Bertold Brecht wrote an astounding essay, ''Theory of Radio,'' in 1929. He correctly pointed out that the decision to manufacture radio sets as receivers only was a political decision, not an economic one. The same is true of television. It is a conscious (and subconscious) decision that renders it one way. My attempt was and is to inject two-way metaphors—via live telecasts—into our thinking process. All my early two-way telecasts were structural invasions, then, very different from work I am doing now, though I hope that the two kinds of investigation will finally merge.

I don't even think of video as a medium anymore, but as an extension of myself, like drawing or speaking. The ideas expressed in my prints, drawings, performances and writings are all present in my work in television—and vice-versa.

Unless you use the camera as you use your hand, or a pencil—poking it wherever you want it to poke—the work will never come out like a drawing can, that is, close to your primal self. Art is a two-way process for me, whether it is printmaking, performance, drawing or video—knowing that I am involved in the evolution of a deeper, more diversified system of communication, between myself and the world and back.

—Douglas Davis

* * *

Television is the most influential mass medium of the modern world and a major icon of our culture. It has also managed to isolate and pacify a great majority of its target markets as a direct result of its de facto one-way nature. On the other hand, television has motivated a number of American, Asian and European visual artists, poets and writers towards the redevelopment of the video form and the re-structuring of the world information network. Douglas Davis is one of these contemporary artists whose refined ideas and philosophy has changed the face of mass communications.

Important to the understanding of Davis' work is the artistic and social climate out of which he developed. He was born and raised in Washington, D.C., a city whose informational system involves global communication. His videotaping began in 1970 after he moved to New York City where media-orientation is thoroughly insular. These tapes emerged from the City's increasingly open-minded techniques. His first tape, ''Look Out'' (1970), documented exchanges with large numbers of people he met on the streets for 24 hours. In 1971 he produced ''Electronic Hokkadim,'' in which thousands of viewers participated in a telephone to television direct access experiment, and ''Talk-Out!'' an open input dialogue allowing the artist both to send and receive messages from the viewing public.

Davis regarded the television as an archetypal form projecting light radiation in such a way as to reach primary levels of communication. At the same time what interested him about the screen is that it constitutes a barrier between him and the viewer, between his image in the television space and the viewer sitting in front of the screen. Consequently we see the theme ''Breaking the Barrier'' recurring in his work whether it be the television screen, the Iron Curtain, or Outer Space. Sometimes the barrier is the difficulty of communication itself. In making these videotapes, Davis' goal has been to relate, interpenetrate, juxtapose, and oppose different spaces at different times in a different media.

His performances explore the illusionistic properties of video space and time both by recording actions in different locations and by manipulating stored (taped) and real (live) time. Further, they offer the process of broadcast and reception as a tactile, visual and aural experience that the viewer completes before his own television set in the perception of the work. The television becomes the viewer's medium of self-awareness. For instance, in the ''Austrian Tapes'' (1974) Davis asks each viewer: ''Please come to the television set in front of you. Place your hands against my hands. Think about our touching each other.'' The viewer is then asked to touch cheeks, lips, and so on, bringing him or her to the screen. In another work Davis succeeds in arranging a conversation between his own ''live'' person and his own ''pre-recorded'' person (a ghost).

Again in 1981 he treated the public perception of broadcast and reception by exploiting the ambiguities and myths of live transmission when he carried out a ''long-distance'' dialogue with a female performer speaking from the Centre Pompidou in France. The work entitled ''Double Entendre: Two Sites Two Times (for Roland Barthes)'' incorporated live and taped audio and video linked by satellite. The dialogue plied with the duality of the sexes and sites, with the difference in language, with radio and television, and with living persons. Both the paradoxes and the ultimate achieving of unity in spite of the distance constitute the strength of the performance. The point at which the two merge summarizes Davis' concern and vision for re-shaping the television medium, as they declare in their own and each other's language: ''Male and female, left and right, New York and Paris seem to become one figure, one line.'' By actively engaging the viewer in the work, by utilizing the ambiguity and complexity of real-time transmission, and lastly, by layering images and sound tracks, Davis' work becomes a multiple discourse, an unfolding narrative in which the self of the artist is expanded in the collective presence of the viewers.

—Carrie Barker

DAVIS, Gene

Nationality: American. **Born:** Washington, D.C., 22 August 1920. **Education:** University of Maryland, College Park, 1938–40; Wilson Teachers College, Washington, D.C., 1941. **Family:** Married Florence Coulson in 1960. **Career:** White House correspondent, Transradio Press, Washington, D.C., 1942–52; worked as copy boy for the *New York Times;* reporter for United Press International, Jacksonville, Florida; congressional correspondent for Newhouse Newspapers; and as a sports writer for the *Washington Daily News,* 1952–66. Assistant professor, Corcoran Gallery School of Art, Washington, D.C., 1967–68, 1970–85; instructor in painting, American University, Washington, D.C., 1968–70; artist-in-residence, Skidmore College, Saratoga Springs, New York, Summer 1969; artist-in-residence, University of Virginia, Charlottesville, 1972. **Awards:** Bronze Medal, *Biennial Exhibition of American Painting,* Corcoran Gallery of Art, Washington, D.C., 1965; National Endowment for the Arts grant, 1967; Guggenheim Fellowship, 1974–75. **Agent:** Charles Cowles Gallery, 420 West Broadway, New York, New York 10012. **Died:** 6 April 1985, in Washington D.C.

Individual Exhibitions:

1952 Dupont Theatre Gallery, Washington, D.C.
1953 Catholic University, Washington, D.C.
1955 American University, Washington, D.C.
1956 Jefferson Place Gallery, Washington, D.C.
1961 Jefferson Place Gallery, Washington, D.C.
1963 Jefferson Place Gallery, Washington, D.C.
Poindexter Gallery, New York
1964 Corcoran Gallery of Art, Washington, D.C.
1965 Poindexter Gallery, New York
1966 Poindexter Gallery, New York
Hofstra University, Hempstead, New York
1967 Poindexter Gallery, New York
Jefferson Place Gallery, Washington, D.C.
Massachusetts Institute of Technology, Cambridge
Galerie Ricke, Cologne
Art Center, Des Moines, Iowa
Fischbach Gallery, New York (and yearly until 1975)
1968 Corcoran Gallery of Art, Washington, D.C.

Gene Davis: *Stripe Painting,* ca. 1965–85. ©Geoffrey Clements/Corbis.

Museum of Art, San Francisco
Washington Gallery of Modern Art, Washington, D.C.
Jewish Museum, New York
Henri Gallery, Washington, D.C.
Kunstmarkt 68, Cologne

1969 Atelier Chapman Kelley, Dallas
Henri Gallery, Washington, D.C.
Axiom Gallery, London
Boymans Museum, Rotterdam
Yale University, New Haven, Connecticut

1970 *Early Paintings 1950–60,* Corcoran Gallery, Washington, D.C.
Fendrick Gallery, Washington, D.C.
Nova Scotia College of Art, Halifax
Annamaria Verna Galerie, Zurich
Dunkelman Gallery, Toronto

1972 Dunkelman Gallery, Toronto
J. L. Hudson Gallery, Detroit
Museum of Fine Arts, University of Utah, Logan
Friends of Contemporary Art, Denver
Joslyn Art Museum, Omaha, Nebraska
Max Protetch Gallery, Washington, D.C.

1973 Michael Berger Gallery, Pittsburgh
Quay Gallery, San Francisco

1974 New Gallery, Cleveland
Tibor de Nagy Gallery, Houston

1975 Reed College, Portland, Oregon

1976 Harcus-Krakow Gallery, Boston

1977 Corcoran Gallery of Art, Washington, D.C.
Fischbach Gallery, New York
Max Protetch Gallery, Washington, D.C.
Paris Art Fair

1978 Corcoran Gallery of Art, Washington, D.C.
Fischbach Gallery, New York
Walker Art Center, Minneapolis
Dayton Art Institute, Ohio
Protetch-McIntosh Gallery, Washington, D.C.

1979 Droll-Kolbert Gallery, New York

1980 Droll-Kolbert Gallery, New York
Protetch-McIntosh Gallery, Washington, D.C.
Arts Gallery, Baltimore, Maryland

1981 Frank Kolbert Gallery, New York
Feldman Galleries, Sarasota, Florida
McIntosh/Drysdale Gallery, Washington, D.C.

1982 Charles Cowles Gallery, New York
Brooklyn Museum, New York

1983 Middendorf/Lane Gallery, Washington, D.C.
Delaware Art Museum, Wilmington
Washington Project for the Arts, Washington, D.C.

1984 Charles Cowles Gallery, New York
U.M.K.C. Gallery of Art, Kansas City, Missouri
Middendorf Gallery, Washington, D.C.
Charles Cowles Gallery, New York

1986 Charles Cowles Gallery, New York

1987 National Museum of American Art, Washington, D.C. (memorial exhibition)

1988 Charles Cowles Gallery, New York

Selected Group Exhibitions:

1967 *The 60's,* Museum of Modern Art, New York

1971 *The Structure of Color,* Whitney Museum, New York

1974 *Within the Decade,* Guggenheim Museum, New York

1975 *34th Biennial of American Painting,* Corcoran Gallery of Art, Washington, D.C.

1977 *Summer Exhibition of the Permanent Collection,* Guggenheim Museum, New York

1979 *Selections from the Permanent Collection,* Museum of Modern Art, New York

1980 *American Art 1900–1980,* Guggenheim Museum, New York

1982 *Thirty Painters: Given and Promised,* Metropolitan Museum of Art, New York

1984 *Generations of the Washington Color School,* George Washington University, Washington, D.C.

1986 *The Window in Twentieth Century Art,* Neuberger Museum, State University of New York, Purchase

1989 *Abstraction, Geometry, Painting,* Albright-Knox Art Gallery, Buffalo

Collections:

Museum of Modern Art, New York: Whitney Museum, New York; Metropolitan Museum of Art, New York; Guggenheim Museum,

New York; Albright-Knox Art Gallery, Buffalo, New York; National Gallery of Art, Washington, D.C.; Hirshhorn Museum, Washington, D.C.; Corcoran Gallery, Washington, D.C.; Art Institute of Chicago; Walker Art Center, Minneapolis; Tate Gallery, London; Akron Art Museum, Ohio; Museum of Fine Arts, Boston; Denver Art Museum, Colorado; High Museum of Art, Atlanta; Massachusetts Institute of Technology, Cambridge; Art Gallery of Toronto, Canada; Washington Museum, St. Louis, Missouri; Princeton University, New Jersey; Wellesley College, Massachusetts; Yale University, Connecticut.

Publications:

By DAVIS: Articles—''Preoccupation with Colour: Conversations with Gene Davis and Albert Stadler'' by Gene Baro in *Studio International* (London), November 1967; ''Statement by the Artist'' in *Art Now* (New York), February 1970; ''A Conversation with Gene Davis'' by Barbara Rose in *Artforum* (New York), March 1971; ''Random Thoughts on Art'' in *Art International* (Lugano, Switzerland), November 1971; ''Gene Davis on Gene Davis,'' in collaboration with Donald Wall, in *Art in America* (New York), May 1973; ''Gene Davis and the Stripe as Subject Matter,'' interview with Walter Hopps, in *Art News* (New York), February 1975; ''Painter's Reply'' in *Artforum* (New York), September 1975; ''Gorky Taught Me That—A Remembrance of Arshile Gorky'' in *Art Magazine* (New York), March 1976; ''Starting Out in the 50's'' in *Art in America* (New York), July/August 1978; interview with David Tannous in *Art in America* (New York), July/August 1978; ''Of Stripes on Canvas: A Conversation with Gene Davis'' by Jean Lawlor Cohen in the *Washington Star* (Washington, D.C.), 17 December 1978; ''An Interview with Gene Davis'' by Mary Swift in *Washington Review* (Washington, D.C.), December/January 1979/80; interview with Percy North in *Abstractions from the Phillips Collection,* exhibition catalog, Fairfax, Virginia 1983.

On DAVIS: Books—*Gene Davis: New Paintings and Drawings,* exhibition catalog with essay by Tom Haulik, Baltimore 1980; *Gene Davis Drawings* by Gene Baro, New York 1982; *Gene Davis* by Steven W. Naifeh, New York 1982; *Gene Davis: The Random and the Ordered,* exhibition catalog, with essay by Pinky Kase, Kansas City 1984; *Gene Davis,* exhibition catalog with essay by Jacquelyn Days Serwer, Washington, D.C. 1987. **Articles**—''Gene Davis'' by Ralph Pomeroy in *Arts Magazine* (New York), March 1970; ''Gene Davis: New Paintings'' by Donald Wall in *Arts Magazine* (New York); ''Gene Davis: The Drawn Image'' by Gene Baro in *Arts Magazine* (New York), September/October 1976; ''Gene Davis at the Corcoran and the Protech'' by Davis Tannous in *Art in America* (New York), May/June 1977; ''Gene Davis: A Review'' by Norman Turner in *Arts Magazine* (New York), September 1977; ''Art: New Drawings by Gene Davis'' by Hilton Kramer in the *New York Times,* 9 March 1979; ''Classical Shoppers'' by William Zimmer in *The Soho Weekly News* (New York), 15 March 1979; ''Out of Left Field'' by John Ashbery in *New York Magazine,* 2 April 1979; ''Single-Idea Art, Singularly Filmed'' by Benjamin Forgey in *Washington Star News* (Washington, D.C.), 6 January 1980; ''Reading Stains and Stripes: Morris Louis and Gene Davis Reconsidered'' by Stephen Westfall in *Arts Magazine,* vol. 63, April 1989; ''Papers of Gene Davis'' by Liza Kirwin in *Archives of American Art Journal* (Washington, D.C.), vol. 31, no. 3, 1991; ''Reading Stains & Stripes: Morris Louis and Gene Davis Reconsidered'' by Stephen Westfall in *Arts Magazine* (Forest Hill), vol. 63, no. 8, April 1998.

* * *

As an artist renowned for his majestic paintings of stripes, Gene Davis has left an impressive legacy of works, including early abstract expressionist oils, collages, gestural drawings, and prints. In the early 1960s, Davis emerged as a prominent member of the Washington Color School, whose artists explored painting's basic elements and the technique of straining raw canvas with thin washes of color. Like many painters of his generation, Davis fathomed the essential properties of color and space as the subject, form, and content of his work.

In creating his broad repertoire of stripe paintings, Davis likened himself to a jazz musician, ''playing by eye''. He felt the music of the stripes and painted them intuitively. Davis' complex and expansive investigation of the stripe format yielded numerous series, among which are hard-edge, free-hand or ''bleed'' stripes and broad, narrow, or pin-striped bands. Intrigued by the impact of scale, Davis challenged established perceptions of architectural space by creating minuscule ''micro'' paintings in 1967, countered by two monumental ''street'' paintings, one in front of the Philadelphia Museum in 1977 and the other at New York Artpark in 1979. He also designed a pattern of colored tubes of water for a solar wall at the College of William and Mary's Muscarelle Museum in Williamsburg, Virginia. In the early 1980s, Davis exhibited a provocative series of large black silhouette self-portrait heads (in conjunction with ''micro'' replicas of the same) and offered a new investigation of interval in contrast with his brilliant stripe palette.

Davis' remarkable versatility is highlighted by a vast number of works on paper (ink, collage, colored pencil, pastel, and crayon), which were produced as drawings in themselves rather than painting studies. Among his late works are a collaborative project in 1983 which juxtaposes a series of his drawings with those of children and a number of drawings which combine his pattern of stripes with pictographs, symbols, and collage, bringing together all the components of his artistic expression.

—Percy North

DAVIS, John

Nationality: Australian. **Born:** Ballarat, Victoria, in 1936. **Education:** Melbourne State College, Caulfield Institute of Technology, Melbourne University, and Royal Melbourne Institute of Technology, 1955–57; studied sculpture under Lenton Parr and Vincent Jomantis, R.M.I.T., 1946–66. **Family:** Married Shirley Heberle in 1961; children: Penelope and Martin. **Career:** Instructor in art, Queenscliff High School, 1958; instructor in woodcraft, Numurkah High School, 1959–60; instructor in art, Mildura High School, 1961–62; instructor, Highett High School, 1963–66; lecturer in 3D design and sculpture, Caulfied Institute of Technology, 1967–71; tutor in sculpture, Monash University, 1969–70; lecturer in charge of sculpture and 3D design, Prahan College of Advanced Education, 1973–80; senior lecturer in charge of sculpture, 1975–80, and coordinator of postgraduate studies, Victoria College of the Arts, 1981;

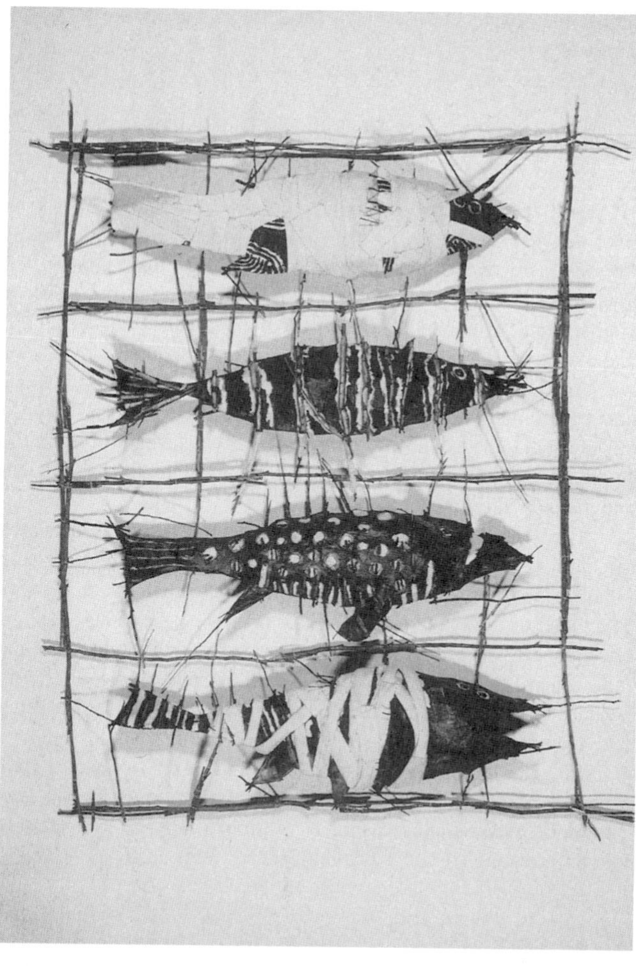

John Davis: *Inventory of Four,* 1992. ©2001 Artists Rights Society (ARS), NY/VISCOPY, Sydney.

artist-in-residence at Monash University, Melbourne, 1976, University of Southern California, 1984, Djerassi Foundation, Woodside California, 1986 and 1987, School of Art, Canberra, 1989, Eltham College, Melbourne, 1994, and Cheney Cowles Museum, Spokane, Washington, 1994; Muka Studio and Gallery, Auckland, New Zealand, 1997; visiting professor, Nagoya University of the Arts, Nagoya, Japan, 1995. **Awards:** Comalco Invitation Award, Melbourne, 1970; Artist Development Grant, Visual Arts Craft Board of the Australia Council, 1992; Blake Prize for Religious Art, 1993. **Died:** Melbourne, Australia, 17 October 1999.

Individual Exhibitions:

1969 Strines Gallery, Melbourne
1971 Watters Gallery, Sydney
1972 Gallery One Eleven, Melbourne
1974 Pinacotheca Gallery, Melbourne
1975 C.A.S. Gallery, Adelaide
Monash University, Melbourne
1977 Watters Gallery, Sydney
1978 National Gallery of Victoria, Melbourne
Art Gallery of New South Wales, Sydney
1979 Art Projects, Melbourne
Watters Gallery, Sydney
1980 Institute of Modern Art, Brisbane
Wollongong City Gallery, New South Wales
Q Space Annex, Brisbane
1981 Art Projects, Melbourne
Watters Gallery, Sydney
1982 Ina Gallery, Tokyo
Ryo Gallery, Kyoto, Japan
1983 Art Projects, Melbourne
Gallery Anri, Nagoya, Japan
1984 University of Southern California, Los Angeles
1985 Watters Gallery, Sydney
Avago Gallery, Sydney
1986 Space Gallery, Los Angeles
Inax Gallery, Tokyo
Inax Gallery, Osaka, Japan
1988 Watters Gallery, Sydney
Heide Park and Art Gallery, Melbourne
1989 Kohji Ogura Gallery, Nagoya, Japan
Seiganji Temple, Nagoya
Luba Bilu Gallery, Melbourne
1990 Watters Gallery, Sydney
1992 Luba Bilu Gallery, Melbourne
1993 Watters Gallery, Sydney
T.A.B. Office, Bendigo, Victoria
1994 Swan Hill Regional Gallery for Contemporary Art, Victoria
Cheney Cowles Museum, Spokane, Washington
Space Gallery, Los Angeles
1995 *Rivers,* Robert Lindsay Gallery, Melbourne
1996 *Continuum (White),* Robert Lindsay Gallery, Melbourne
1997 *My Country,* Muka Studio and Gallery, Auckland, New Zealand
1998 *Kōan: Nomads, Rivers, and a Presence,* Robert Lindsay Gallery, Melbourne
2000 *Kōan,* Robert Lindsay Gallery, Melbourne

Selected Group Exhibitions:

1981 *First Australian Sculpture Triennial,* Latrobe University, Melbourne
1983 *Continuum,* Lunami Gallery, Tokyo
1984 *Australia: Nine Contemporary Artists,* Los Angeles Institute of Contemporary Art
1985 *Common Earth, Alive and Unfired,* University of Tasmania
1987 *Field to Figuration, Australian Art 1960–1986,* National Gallery of Victoria, Melbourne
1990 *Pacific Currents,* Muckenthaler Center, Fullerton, California
1991 *Contemporary Art of the 80's, 100 Forms,* Inax Gallery, Tokyo
1992 *Review 1992,* Luba Bilu Gallery, Melbourne
1993 *Innerland, Exhibition of Australian Contemporary Art,* Soko Gallery, Tokyo
1994 *Fifth International Shoebox Sculpture Exhibition,* University of Hawaii
1995 *The River,* Swan Hill Regional Art Gallery, Australia (toured Mildura, Mount Gambier, Shepparton, Benalla, Albury, Sale)

1996 *Toolangi International Sculpture Event,* Toolangi, Victoria
1997 *The Sixth International Shoebox Sculpture Exhibition,* University of Hawaii at Manoa Art Gallery (toured United States)

Collections:

Australian National Gallery, Canberra; Art Gallery of New South Wales, Sydney; Shepparton City Art Gallery, Victoria; National Gallery of Victoria, Melbourne; Hobart Art Gallery, Tasmania; Brisbane Art Gallery; Art Gallery of Western Australia, Perth; Wollongong City Art Gallery, New South Wales; Kawasaki City Art Museum, Japan; Seiganji Temple, Nagoya, Japan; Australian Chancery, Riyadh, Saudi Arabia.

Public Installations:

Beach Work, Cholamandal, India 1978; *Observatory,* Barmah Forest, Victoria 1980; *Place Two,* Latrobe University, Victoria 1981; *Conversation,* University of Tasmania, Hobart 1985; *Another Time, Another Place (and a River),* Cheney Cowles Museum, Spokane, Washington 1994; *Passage,* Toolangi, Victoria 1996; *A Hill, a River, Two Rocks and a Presence,* Melbourne International Festival Herring Island Project, Melbourne, Victoria 1997; *Kõan,* Robert Lindsay Gallery, Melbourne 2000.

Publications:

On DAVIS: Books—*Contemporary Australian Sculpture* by Graeme Sturgeon, Craftsman House, 1991; *The Yellow Lady—Australian Impressions of Asia* by Alisa Broinowski, Oxford Press, 1992. **Exhibition catalogs—***Place* by Noel Hutchison, Melbourne 1975; *Skira Annual Special Issue 1970–1980,* Geneva 1975; *John Davis, Landscape as Subject and Source,* by Robert Berlind, Spokane, Washington 1994. **Articles—**article by Elwyn Lynn in *Art International* (Lugano, Switzerland), July 1977; ''Quadrant'' in the *Venice Biennale,* exhibition catalog, Venice 1978; ''The Venice Biennale'' by Henry Martin in *Art International* (Lugano, Switzerland), October 1978; article by Elwyn Lynn in *Art International* (Lugano, Switzerland), vol. XXLL/5–6, 1978; ''Report from Australia'' by Suzi Gablik in *Art in America* (New York), ''Mildura Rides Again'' by Graeme Sturgeon in *Art and Australia* (Sydney), summer 1981; ''Report from Australia'' by Suzi Gablik in *Art and Australia* (Sydney), autumn 1981; ''In'' in *Exchange of Contemporary Art* (Tokyo), December 1981; ''Asian Interface, Australia-Japan'' by Peter Emmett in *Craft Australia,* summer 1983/84; ''Continuum '83 Review'' by Tadashi Akatsu in *Art Network,* spring 1984; ''Places and Locations'' by Geoffrey Edwards in *Art and Australia,* winter 1989; ''Suspended Animation'' by Jenny Zimmer in *The Sunday Herald,* 12 November 1989; ''Getting Recycling Down to a Fine Art'' by Rebecca Lancashire in *The Age,* 20 November 1990; ''Figuring Out Fun of the Fair'' by Robert Rooney in *The Weekend Review,* 10 October 1992; ''Report from Australia'' by Robert Berlind in *Art in America,* April 1993; ''Melbourne Sculptor Takes Prize'' by Ava Hubble in *The Age,* 10 December 1993; ''East and West in the Art of John Davis'' by J. S. M. Willette in *Visions Art Quarterly,* Winter 1994; ''John Davis at Cheney Cowles Museum'' by Frances De Vuono in *Artweek,* 18 August 1994; ''Sculpting the Life Force of Old Man Murray'' by Rebecca Lancashire in *Age,* 1 September 1998.

*

A Sense of Place

In 1976 I rediscovered an informal education in the Australian Bush denied to me through urbanization and formal education. It is as relevant to my understanding of what it is to be an Australian in 1982 as is my interpretation of European and Aboriginal histories. In other words, I have attempted to establish within myself a sense of place and of time, eventually transferring this into the work.

And like all people, I am bound to carry certain aspects of history about with me. In my response to the impulse to make art, I refer to this consciously and subconsciously so that whatever evolves in the 'work space' is somehow an amalgamation of that which is ancient and that which is a new experience.

The beginning is in the tying of two twigs. Then it takes its own direction, full of inconsistencies, contradictions, ambiguities and alliances, moving as nature does; or how Australian country towns eventuate; or how themes in music or poetry evolve into metaphor. Each piece is part of a larger on-going work, a specific and at the same time general occurrence, a mass of detail demanding close scrutiny because of its close approximation and juxtaposing; it demands that the viewer step back to encompass 'the view.'

Like all things in nature, it is fragile and subject to easy destruction; each part is dependent on another for its identity and difference, eventually indicating its position in another place, moving into or retreating from the location where it finds itself.

—John Davis

* * *

John Davis was an Australian. He inhabited, with the majority of his fellow Australians, the small crescent of coastal land in the south-eastern corner of a massive continent. He lived in a pleasant house in a residential suburb of Melbourne. He was married, with children. He was a convivial man, who loved the bush and the sea and believed in the sanctity of Saturdays. John Davis was in many ways a very typical Australian.

In other respects, John Davis belongs to a wider community. He was idealistic, humanist, passionate, socialist and, in the very best sense of the word, nationalistic. Most atypical of all, he chose to make manifest his beliefs, his hopes and, his fears in sculptures that are at one and the same time delicate and monolithic. The fragile bindings of twigs and paper, into brooding towers and mountains or spaced marks on an endless plain, echo the fragility of the environment. The spatial relationships which characterise Davis's sculptures reflect his awareness of and empathy with landscape on a monumental scale. Davis's sculptures may not be physically large, but emotionally and conceptually they embrace the dimensions of a continent.

Davis's sculptures grow, like living organisms. In this sense too, Davis was concerned with nature. But this concern is devoid of romantic notions. Australia is a difficult and complex land from a Western standpoint. The Australian Aborigines learned, in the Dreamtime, that the means by which man might live in this contradictory land was by accepting and accommodating nature rather than trying to improve upon it. Many of the political conflicts that exist in contemporary Australia are conflicts between ecologically conservative forces and those which would seek to perpetuate the exploitative philosophies of the Industrial Revolution. Davis believed in the possibilities of a harmony (of sorts) between these two attitudes.

The Melbourne critic, Robert Rooney, coined the deathless phrase ''twiggery folkery'' in response to the work of John Davis and other artists who employ natural materials in their art. In so doing, Rooney was revealing a commonly held fear of a sentimental response to the Australian landscape and a parochial sense of identity rather than making serious criticism. The fear is that a cloying romanticism towards the landscape (perhaps a hangover from the champagne days of Tom Roberts et al) will reveal Australians as intellectually barren land-lovers. The gum-tree school of painting is an embarrassment: we often seek to legitimise our artistic status by adopting a preference for international modes in art and in rejecting that which smacks of the ''pretty'' or of sources closely identified with heroic concepts of landscape art. ''Nature,'' in Australian art terms, can often appear to be a euphemism for cliché and corn. Yet the ''natural'' pattern of Australia is a violent one—fire is needed for the germination of some plant seeds; drought and floods re-occur, often within one season. Balance does exist, but often between extremes. John Davis's sculptures are a lucid and loving attempt to recreate not only the balances and relationships that exist in this most unorthodox of climes, but also, through his own experience, the balances and relationships of those who live in the environment and who choose to be affected by it.

In so doing Davis transcended his ''Australianness'' and offers concepts and statements that can be recognized and understood on an international level. By embracing an accessible specific, Davis speculates on the universal.

—Alison Fraser

DEACON, Richard

Nationality: British. **Born:** Bangor, Caernarvonshire, Wales, 1949. **Education:** Somerset College of Art, Taunton, 1968–69; Saint Martin's School of Art, London, 1969–72; Royal College of Art, London, 1974–77; part-time, Chelsea School of Art, London, 1977–78. **Career:** Independent sculptor, London, since 1978. Instructor, Central School of Art, London, 1981—. **Awards:** Turner Prize, Tate Gallery, London, 1987. **Agent:** Lisson Gallery, London; Marion Goodman Gallery, New York. **Address:** c/o Lisson Gallery, 67 Lisson Street, London NW1 5DA, England.

Individual Exhibitions:

1975 Royal College of Art, London
1976 Royal College of Art, London
1978 Acre Lane Studio, Brixton, London
1980 Acre Lane Studio, Brixton, London
1981 Sheffield City Polytechnic Gallery, Sheffield
1983 Lisson Gallery, London
Orchard Gallery, Londonderry, Northern Ireland
1984 Riverside Studios, London
Chapter Arts Centre, Cardiff, Wales
Fruitmarket Gallery, Edinburgh (travelled to Le Nouveau Musée, Lyon-Villeurbanne, France

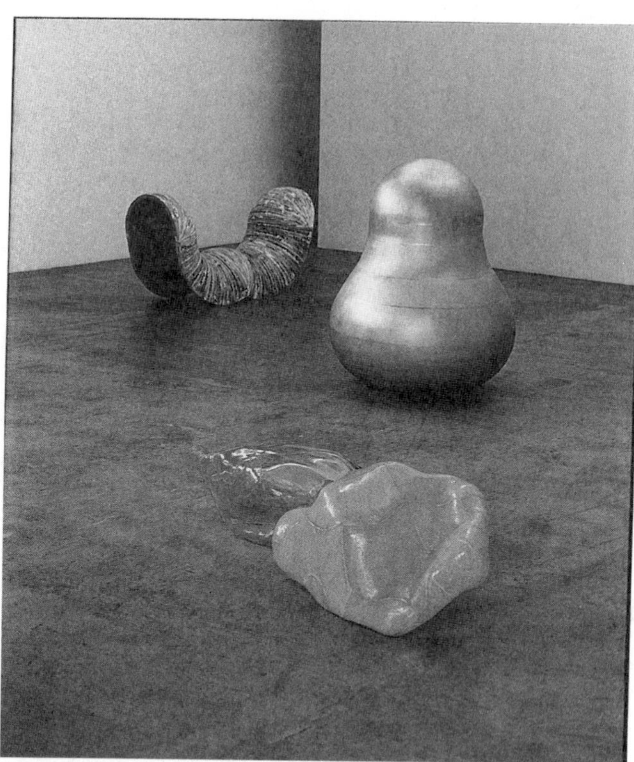

Richard Deacon: *Beauty and the Beast* [front], 1995, *Dumb Bell* [middle], 1998, *Eat Me* [back], 1998. ©Richard Deacon.

1985 Donald Young Gallery, Chicago (with Tony Cragg)
Tate Gallery, London
Margarete Roeder Fine Arts, New York (with Jackie Winsor)
Serpentine Gallery, London (with Richard Rogers and John Tchalenko)
1986 Marian Goodman Gallery, New York
Interim Art, London
Galerie Artlogos, Nantes, France
Aberystwyth Arts Centre, Wales (toured Britain)
1987 Lisson Gallery, London
Bonnefanten Museum, Maastricht, Netherlands (travelled to Lucerne, Madrid, Antwerp)
1988 Lisson Gallery, London
Carnegie Museum of Art, Pittsburgh (travelled to St. Louis, Los Angeles, and Toronto)
Marian Goodman Gallery, New York
Whitechapel Art Gallery, London
1989 Musée National d'Art Moderne de la Ville, Paris
Plymouth Arts Centre, Plymouth
1990 Kunstnernes Hus, Oslo
Marian Goodman Gallery, New York
Galleria Locus Solus, Genoa
Moderna Galerija, Mala Galerija, Ljubljana, Slovenia
1991 Mead Gallery, University of Warwick, Coventry
Museum Haus Lange and Museum Haus Esters, Krefeld
Galerie Konrad Fischer, Dusseldorf
1992 Lisson Gallery, London
Musée d'Art Moderne, Villeleuve d'Ascq, France
Marian Goodman Gallery, New York

Stadtische Galerie, Nordhorn, Germany
Museum der Stadt, Waiblingen, Germany
1993 Galerie Artlogos, Nantes
Chisenhale Gallery, London (with Bill Woodrow; travelled to Portsmouth and Brussels)
Kunstverein Hannover and Orangerie, Herrenhauser Garten, Hannover, Germany
Accademia Britanica, Rome
1994 L.A. Louver Gallery, Los Angeles, California
1995 Customs House, South Shields, England
Museo de Arte Contemporaneo de Caracas Sofia Imber, Caracas, Venezuela (travelled to Havana, Buenos Aires, Santiago, and Mexico City)
Lisson Gallery, London
1997 Marian Goodman Gallery, New York
Musée Departmentale de Rochechouant, France
1998 SCAI, The Bathhouse, Tokyo
1999 Tate Gallery, Liverpool
Lisson Gallery, London
Galleri Susanne Ottesen, Copenhagen
2000 L.A. Louver Gallery, Los Angeles
Fig. 1, London

Selected Group Exhibitions:

1981 *Objects and Sculpture,* Institute of Contemporary Arts, London (travelled to Bristol)
1982 *Englische Plastik Heute,* Kunstmuseum, Lucerne
1983 *Transformations,* Biennale de Sao Paolo (travelled to Rio de Janeiro, Mexico City, and Lisbon)
1984 *International Survey of Recent Painting and Sculpture,* Museum of Modern Art, New York
1985 *Carnegie International,* Carnegie Museum of Art, Pittsburgh
1986 *Correspondentie Europa,* Stedelijk Museum, Amsterdam
1987 *A Quiet Revolution,* Museum of Contemporary Art, Chicago (travelled to San Francisco; Newport Harbor; Washington, D.C.; and Buffalo)
1992 *Documenta 9,* Kassel, Germany
1993 *New Sculpture,* Middelheim Park, Antwerp
1994 *Till Brancusi,* Malmo Kunsthall, Sweden
1995 *ARS '95,* Helsinki, Finland
1996 *Un Siecle de Sculpture Anglaise,* Jeu de Paume, Paris
1997 *Material Culture—The Object in British Art of the 80s and 90s,* Hayward Gallery, London
1998 *Towards Sculpture,* Gulbenkian Foundation, Lisbon
1999 *At Home with Art,* Mind Zone, Millenium Dome, London (travelled to various locations in England and Kaiser Wilhelm Museum, Krefeld)
2000 *The Eye of the Storm,* La Mandria, Turin, Italy
10 Instensita in Europa, Museo Luigi Pecci, Prato, Italy

Collections:

Tate Gallery, London; British Council, London; Arts Council of Great Britain, London; Fonds Regional d'Art Contemporain Rhone-Alpes, France; Museum of Modern Art, New York; Carnegie Institute, Pittsburgh; San Francisco Museum of Modern Art; Art Gallery of New South Wales, Sydney; Musée Beauborg, Paris; Kaiser Wilhelm Museum, Krefeld; Stedelijk Museum, Amsterdam; Sprengel Museum, Hannover; Kiasma, Helsinki; Fondacao Caixa de Pensiones, Barcelona; Kröller-Müller Museum, Otterloo; Moca, Tokyo; Muhka, Antwerp.

Publications:

By DEACON: Books—*Stuff Box Object,* London 1972, Cardiff 1984; *Jacqui Poncelet: New Ceramics,* exhibition catalog, London 1981; *Carol McNicol,* exhibition catalog, London 1984; *For Those Who Have Ears No. 2,* London 1985; *For Those Who Have Eyes,* exhibition catalog, Aberystwyth 1986; *Atlas: Gondwanaland & Laurasia,* Oslo 1990; *What Car?,* with Lynne Cooke, Paris 1992; *Only the Lonely* with Bill Woodrow, London 1993; *In Praise of Television,* 1997.

On DEACON: Books—*Objects and Sculpture,* exhibition catalog with text by Iwona Blaszcwyk, Lewis Biggs and Sandy Nairne, London 1981; *Englische Plastik Heute,* exhibition catalog with text by Martin Kunz and Michael Newman, Lucerne 1982; *Richard Deacon: Sculpture,* exhibition catalog with text by Lynne Cooke, Londonderry 1983; *Richard Deacon: Sculpture 1980–84,* exhibition catalog with text by Michael Newman, Edinburgh 1984; *Richard Deacon: Recent Sculpture,* exhibition catalog with text by Charles Harrison, Maastricht 1987; *Richard Deacon,* exhibition catalog with text by Peter Schjeldahl, New York 1988; *Richard Deacon,* exhibition catalog with text by Marjorie Allthorpe Guyton and Lynne Cooke, London 1988; *Let's Not Be Stupid,* exhibition catalog with text by Katherine Eustace and Michael Newman, Coventry 1991; *Skulpturen und Zeichungen,* exhibition catalog with text by Julian Heynen, Krefeld 1991; *Art for Other People,* exhibition catalog with texts by Jean de Loisy and Joelle Pijaudier, Villeneuve d'Ascq 1992; *Richard Deacon Skulpturen 1987–93,* exhibition catalog with text by various authors, Hannover 1993; *Richard Deacon* by Pier Luigi Tazzi, Peter Schjeldahl, and Jon Thompson, 1995; *New World Order,* exhibition catalog, Liverpool 1999.

* * *

Richard Deacon is one of the younger generation of British sculptors who have won international acclaim in the last few years. He himself prefers the term ''fabricator'' as a more accurate description of what he does as he is neither a modeler nor a carver. The materials he works with, such as laminated wood, linoleum, galvanised steel or aluminum, are chosen primarily for their structural potential rather for any intrinsic value or sensual properties.

As an undergraduate at St. Martin's School of Art in the 1970s he was much involved in Performance Art, but even then he was not using his own body as the basic material as had his immediate predecessors, Bruce McLean or Gilbert and George. In Deacon's performances he used materials which underwent a transformation or were resolved into a final object, so though he was accepted for the experimental post-graduate course at the Royal College of Art on the basis of his performance art, process became of much less importance than the object in mind. The works he made about this time were strong, architectonic shapes with emphasis on integration of surface and structure. There is no hidden armature in these works, no distraction of surface detail from the spare, angular shapes. Already the young artist seems to be pondering on the centuries-old preoccupations of sculptors—the relationships of skin and structure, inner and outer surfaces, mass and volume and edge conditions—and this exploration continued when he went to the United States in 1978. After his return from America his ideas started to cohere in a series of confident and mature constructions. Some of Deacon's work is reminiscent of the moving parts of machinery—of mills and steam engines—and others are evocative of propellers and conic sections. There is often the suggestion of potential movement. There are forms which remind one of navigation aids in preradar days—those spherical, open basket shapes on top of high poles at harbour mouths. Other works indicate that Deacon enjoyed and was inspired by the geometry of conic sections—the ellipse, the circle, the parabola and the hyperbola—but he then became increasingly interested in organic and biomorphic forms and the expressive content of his work deepened accordingly.

While he was in the States he had made a series of drawings entitled *Orpheus When There's Singing* which were inspired by *Sonnets to Orpheus* by Rainer Maria Rilke. Deacon says that these drawings started with a geometric figure with parts linked by a spiral. "A series of arcs and curves build up a network or ground against which specific shapes are allowed to emerge." That is an accurate description of the series *For Those Who Have Ears.* The Orpheus myth is about music, both the making of music and the hearing of music. In *For Those Who Have Ears No. 2* (1983), which is made of curving loops of laminated wood, the shapes can suggest both ears and also lyres—the ears to hear and the lyres to make music. The forms in this work are open, generous and flowing; the luxuriant curves are sensuous and suggest sexual imagery. It is a large sculpture, 9 x 13 x 13 feet, but Deacon can handle large-scale works which never become monumental. It sits lightly on the ground and is particularly pleasing in its balance and poise and its subtle delineation of shifting forms expressed in a linear context. The process of the making is indicated by the glue which oozed out when the strips of wood were pressed together.

His work from the mid-eighties seems to have certain basic themes which deal with growth processes and a continuing concern with orifices and the sense organs; sexual imagery and the penetration of forms becomes more evident. Works which appear initially to have a limpid simplicity develop a haunting and mysterious presence. The titles with their references to vernacular speech, poetry, and literature remind us of the artist's recurrent search for the balance between form and content and the need to synthesize abstraction and nature.

Many of Deacon's most recent sculptures are characterized by greater solidity and mass but, conversely, do not neatly resolve either formally or in terms of meaning. Often hugging the floor, they suggest human scale but remain indeterminate, subtly disquieting monoliths. Deacon's surfaces reveal the almost obsessive touch of a consummate craftsman, only to be offset by drilled holes or dabs of epoxy glue that emphasize the ordinary nature of the materials used. The low, undulating surface and simple shape of *Dummy*, 1992, made from sanded slats of wood covered with clear polyvinyl resin, give the piece a gently implacable presence. *Pipe*, 1991, is made from bolted aluminum ribbing. With its skin constructed so as to externalize structure, it resembles earlier works, but its blocked ends suggest that the pipe refers here to quotidian materials of building and plumbing, not musical instruments or biological passageways. A series called *The Interior Is Always More Difficult*, 1992, makes more explicit these contradictions, while suggesting new directions for Deacon. Made of corrugated polycarbonate and aluminum, the pieces feature oblong bases supporting rectangular windows with ribbed patterns and shapes. The tensions created by the windows—with their references to two-dimensionality and their patterned relief surfaces—and the fully sculptural bases is relieved only by the similarity of the materials use throughout.

—Essay by Mary Ellis; updated by Dorothy Valakos

DE ANDREA, John (Louis)

Nationality: American. **Born:** Denver, Colorado, 24 November 1941. **Education:** University of Colorado, Boulder, 1961–65, B.F.A. 1965; University of New Mexico, Albuquerque, 1966–68 (an art assistantship). **Career:** Lives and works in Denver. **Agent:** O.K. Harris Gallery, 383 West Broadway, New York, New York 10012; Louis K. Meisel Gallery, 141 Prince Street, New York, New York, 10012. **Address:** 4646 Grove Street, Denver, Colorado 80211, U.S.A.

Individual Exhibitions:

1970 O.K. Harris Gallery, New York
1971 O.K. Harris Gallery, New York
1972 Wilmaro Gallery, Denver
1973 O.K. Harris Gallery, New York
1976 O.K. Harris Gallery, New York
1981 Tortue Gallery, Santa Monica, California
1982 Aspen Center for the Visual Arts, Colorado
1995 *Fragments,* The Singer Gallery, Denver
1996 Denver Art Museum
1997 *Female Figures 1991–96,* O.K. Harris Gallery, New York

Selected Group Exhibitions:

1970 *Annual Exhibition,* Whitney Museum, New York
1971 *Biennale,* Paris
1972 *Documenta 5,* Kassel, West Germany
1974 *Hyperréalistes Américains/Réalistes Européens,* Centre National d'Art Contemporain, Paris (toured Europe)
1976 *Aspects of Realism,* Rothman's of Pall Mall traveling exhibition, Stratford Art Gallery, Ontario (toured Canada, 1976–78)
1977 *The Nude: Avery and the European Master,* Borgenicht Gallery, New York
1979 *7 on the Figurine,* Pennsylvania Academy of Fine Arts, Philadelphia
1981 *Contemporary American Realism since 1960,* Pennsylvania Academy of Fine Arts, Philadelphia
1982 *Real, Really Real, Super Real,* San Antonio Museum of Art, Texas (travelled to Indianapolis, Tucson and Pittsburgh)
1988 *Figure It Out: Visual Body Language,* Helander Gallery, Palm Beach, Florida
1994 *Portraits de Femmes,* Château Notre-Dame des Fleurs, Vence, France
1997 *Body,* Art Gallery of New South Wales, Sydney
2000 *The Photorealists,* The Center for the Arts, Vero Beach, Florida

Collections:

Everson Museum, Syracuse, New York; Neue Galerie, Aachen, West Germany.

Publications:

By DE ANDREA: Article—"The Verist Sculptors: 2 Interviews: Duane Hanson and John De Andrea," with J. Masheck, in *Art in America* (New York), November/December 1972.

On DE ANDREA: Books—*Hyperréalistes Américans/Realistes Européens,* exhibition catalog, Paris 1974; *Aspects of Realism,* exhibition catalog, Stratford, Ontario 1976; *Neue Formen des Realismus* by Peter Sager, Cologne 1974; *John De Andrea: Sculptures 1978–81,* exhibition catalog with essay by Philip Yenaivine, Aspen, Colorado 1982. **Articles—**"A New Realism in Sculpture" by Grace Glueck in *Art in America* (New York), November/December 1971; "Downtown Uptown, Not 10th Street" by John Perreault in the *Village Voice* (New York), December 1971; "Art in the Artist" by Emily Ganauer in the *New York Post,* December 1971; "Neutral Style" by Edward Lucie-Smith in *Art and Artists* (London), August 1975; "Hyper-Realistic Dreiklang" in *Du* (Zurich), July 1979; "Cherchez la Femme!" by Gilles Plazy in *Cimaise,* vol. 41, June/August 1994.

* * *

John De Andrea casts his figures straight from life, an equivalent of Photo Realism in 3-D. Still, however much his painted polyvinyl seems at first like living flesh, one would never take them for the people in the street. The people in the street are not young, untarnished, gracefully formed nudes. They have, besides, a beauty of gesture; they present a dynamic, rhythmic, harmonious composition of torso and limb as they leave or enter embrace, play ball, lie easily asleep. It is this carefully caught grace of body and motion which has led to the classification of De Andrea's nudes as classic and ideal, in spite of his disclaimer: "How can you idealize from casts?"

It is true that he practices total honesty. Every fold of skin, every pore, every broken capillary, shows, yet in the models that he chooses there are few of these. By opposing the present, transitory beauty of the model's flesh to the imagined beauty of the classic past, the work comes off as emphasizing a transcendent loveliness in the here and now. The idealization lies in selection, of gesture and of model, just as with Pheidias the ideal form, the ideal act, was the one portrayed.

Seemingly unposed, these figures appear as studiedly dispassionate, objectified. They never address the observer directly through the gaze of their real-seeming eyes, and by this means a distance is created which sets off the work as art, not life, even more effectually than a frame would do. They are not nature caught as if by the camera, with all the attendant out-of-jointedness which accident, while freezing motion, can create, but something based on life, distilled and offered as apart from it.

As his work has developed in recent years, De Andrea has widened it to include, beside the recreation of single figures, the figure in dialog with another, sometimes as becoming itself, as for example in the artist—De Andrea complete with spattered jeans and beard—painting the sculpted model, Pygmalion catching himself in the act. There are also quotations from other works, like the *Déjeuner sur l'herbe,* into which the artist enters, a tableau in which the author joins.

By this means De Andrea has allied himself with the twentieth-century tradition of offering the work of art as comment on art, as in, say, Duchamp, but the difference seems to be that De Andrea still believes in and affirms the beauty of the human form.

—Barbara Cortright

DE DOMINICIS, Gino

Nationality: Italian. **Born:** Ancona, Italy, in 1947. **Career:** Lives and works in Rome (since 1965). **Address:** c/o Galleria L'Attico, via del Babuino 114, 00187 Rome, Italy.

Individual Exhibitions:

1969 Galleria L'Attico, Rome
1970 Galleria Toselli, Milan
Galleria L'Attico, Rome
1971 Galleria L'Attico, Rome
1979 Galleria Mario Pieroni, Rome (with Jannis Kounellis and Ettore Spalleti)
1988 Lia Rumma Gallery, Naples
1990 Rayburn Foundation, New York
1998 Galleria Nazionale D'Arte Moderna, Rome (retrospective)

Selected Group Exhibitions:

1970 *Biennale d'Arte Contemporanea,* Bologna
Group Exhibition, Galleria L'Attico, Rome
1971 *Comportamento e cose di 13 Uomini che invecchiano e muoiano,* Munich
1978 *Biennale,* Venice
1982 *Documenta,* Kassel, West Germany
1990 *Biennale,* Venice
1999 *Biennale,* Venice

Collections:

Stedelijk Museum, Amsterdam.

Publications:

On DE DOMINICS: Book—*L'Arte Moderna* by Renato Barili, Milan 1975. **Articles—**review in *Flash Art (International Edition),* no. 143, November/December 1988; review in *Art in America* (New York), vol. 78, May 1990; "Gino de Dominicis: Le Sourire Crepusculaire" in *Art Press* (Paris), no. 147, May 1990; "Gino De Dominicis: On the Trail of Gilgamesh" by Nicolas Bourriaud in *Flash Art (International Edition),* no. 153, Summer 1990; "What Will Become of Our Sensitive Skin: 44th Biennale di Venezia" by Bojana Pejic, Giorgio Verzotti, Lars Nittve in *Artforum International,* vo. 29, September 1990; "Gino de Dominicis" by Marco Meneguzzo in *Artforum International,* vol. 34, February 1996; review in *Art News,* vol. 98, no. 11, December 1999.

* * *

As one critic has observed, by 1970 Gino De Dominicis had become the most important ''find'' of the Galleria L'Attico where a year before he had held his one-man exhibition of ''invisible'' objects. ''Invisible Pyramid'' may serve as an example: Here we have the square base of a pyramid drawn on the floor, while nearby there is a placard which gives the title of the work and the date. In 1970, at the same gallery, he exhibited ''The Zodiac,'' a large work which demonstrates his own particular imaginative powers: Here he has provided a very literal and concrete version of the zodiac in which a lion stands for Leo, a young woman for Virgo, and so forth. And in the same year De Dominicis participated in two group shows and made a statement which sums up his aesthetic: ''To have true existence, things must be eternal and immortal.'' ''Invisibility'' and ''ubiquity'' are also key concepts rendered in mythic terms: It is immortality which is the greatest attribute of the gods, and as was the case with ''The Zodiac,'' artistic representation involves a kind of anthropomorphism. He asserted his position once again in the Venice *Biennale* of 1972 and caused a scandal by placing a mongoloid on display as the symbol of a particular attitude towards death. This goes to the center of De Dominicis' work: The victory over death which proves man's genuine existence. His basic assumption is that without immortality there is no true life. Thus the mongoloid became a symbol of the triumph of life over death: He is indifferent to fate or change or death—he simply exists.

The boundaries of De Dominicis' art are the cosmic and the mythic. He uses archetypal images to provoke esoteric sensations and emphasizes once again the ability to overcome the laws of nature. To this end he also uses the discoveries of technology and the efforts of science to conquer death. In ''Greeting Card'' (1971) he seems to be wishing immortality of the body for everyone. For him immortality means the capacity to overcome nature, in terms drawn from myth and evolutionary struggle. ''Attempt at Flight,'' for example, is a video tape produced by Gerry Schum in 1970 in which the artist makes repeated attempts to fly. Once more De Dominicis is struggling to overcome the natural order and limits of things: The laws of nature are what bind man to one place and time and force him to grow old. To transcend even one of these limitations would be to prove the possibility of attaining the great goal of immortality.

—Roberto G. Lambarelli

DEEM, George

Nationality: American. **Born:** Vincennes, Indiana, 18 August 1932. **Education:** School of the Art Institute of Chicago, B.F.A. 1957; under Willi Baumeister, Stuttgart. 1951–52. **Military Service:** Served in the United States Army, 1952–54. **Career:** Independent artist since 1960; lives and works in New York City; spent 1970–77 living and working in Cortona, Italy. Painting instructor, College of Art and Technology, Leicester, England, 1966–67, and University of Pennsylvania, Philadelphia, 1968; Artist-in-Residence, Evansville Museum of Arts and Science, Indiana, 1979; Visiting Artist, Illinois State University, Normal, 1982; The Branson School, Ross, California, 1995. **Agent:** Nancy Hoffman Gallery, 429 West Broadway, New York, New York 10012. **Address:** 10 West 18th Street, New York, New York 10011, U.S.A.

Individual Exhibitions:

1962 Allan Stone Gallery, New York
1963 Allan Stone Gallery, New York
1964 Allan Stone Gallery, New York
Merida Gallery, Louisville, Kentucky
1965 Goodman Gallery, Buffalo, New York
Allan Stone Gallery, New York
1966 Allan Stone Gallery, New York
1968 Allan Stone Gallery, New York
Merida Gallery, Louisville, Kentucky
1969 Ferrier Gallery, Houston
Allan Stone Gallery, New York
1974 *Paintings and Drawings,* Indianapolis Museum of Art (travelled to the Witte Memorial Museum, San Antonio, Texas)
1975 Allan Stone Gallery, New York
1979 *The Making of a Masterpiece: Recent Paintings,* Evansville Museum of Arts and Sciences, Indiana
1980 Sneed Gallery, Rockford, Illinois
1981 Sneed Gallery, Rockford, Illinois
1983 Merida Gallery, Louisville, Kentucky
1986 On View Downtown Gallery, Indianapolis, Indiana
1993–94 *The School of. . . : Paintings by George Deem,* Evansville Museum of Arts and Science, Evansville, Indiana (travelled to museums in Gainesville, Florida; Mount Vernon, Illinois; Lakeland, Florida; Indianapolis, Indiana; and Wichita, Kansas)
1994 Eckert Fine Art Gallery, Indianapolis, Indiana
Capricorn Galleries, Bethesda, Maryland
2000 Nancy Hoffman Gallery, New York
2001 *George Deem and Peter Angelo Simon: Paintings and Photographs in Conversation,* Evansville, Indiana

Selected Group Exhibitions:

1969 *Painting and Sculpture Today,* Indianapolis Museum of Art
1974 *Contemporary American Painting and Sculpture 1974,* Krannert Art Museum, University of Illinois, Champaign
1978 *Artists Look at Art,* Spencer Museum of Art, University of Kansas, Lawrence
Art about Art, Whitney Museum of American Art, New York (travelled to museums in Raleigh, North Carolina; Los Angeles, California; and Portland, Oregon)
1981 *Contemporary American Realism since 1960,* Pennsylvania Academy of Fine Arts, Philadelphia (travelled to museums in Richmond, Virginia; Oakland, California; Lisbon, Portugal; Madrid, Spain; and Nuremberg, Germany)
1984 *Indiana Influence,* Inaugural Exhibition, Fort Wayne Museum of Art, Fort Wayne, Indiana
1985 *Chicago International Art Exposition,* Nancy Hoffman Gallery, Chicago, Illinois
1990 *Winter Gold,* Nancy Hoffman Gallery, New York
1993 *The Purloined Image,* Flint Institute of Arts, Flint, Michigan
1994 *Art after Art,* Nassau County Museum of Art, Roslyn, Long Island, New York

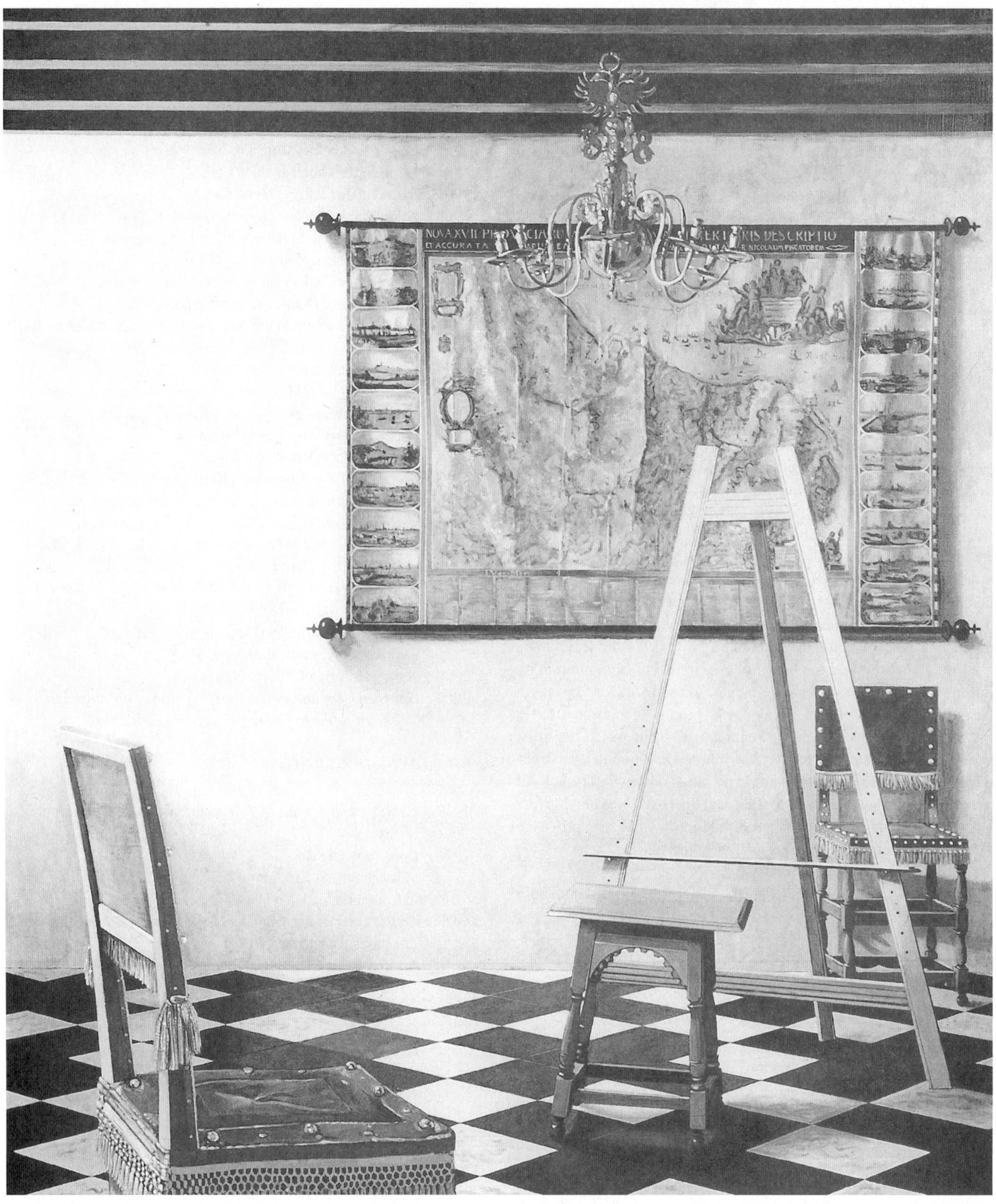

George Deem: *Vermeer's Easel,* 1999. Photo by Edward Peterson, Jr. Courtesy of the artist.

1996 *The New Traditionalists,* University of Oregon Museum of Art, Eugene
2000 *The Revolutionary War: Founding the New Nation,* Nassau County Museum of Art, Roslyn Harbor, New York
Dance, Dance, Dance, Nassau County Museum of Art, Roslyn Harbor, New York
Fortieth Anniversary Exhibition, Allan Stone Gallery, New York
2002 *The Mona Lisa,* Herbert F. Johnson Museum of Art, Cornell University, Ithaca, New York

Collections:

Allen Memorial Art Museum, Oberlin College, Ohio; American General Finance, Inc., Evansville, Indiana; American National Bank and Trust Company, Rockford, Illinois; Arizona State University Art Museum, Tempe; Becton-Dickinson and Company, Paramus, New Jersey; Chase Manhattan Bank, New York; Cleary Gottlieb Steen and Hamilton, New York; Evansville Museum of Arts and Sciences, Indiana; Law Art Collection, First National Bank of Boston; Hallmark Cards, Inc., Kansas City, Missouri; Houston Museum of Fine Arts; Indianapolis Museum of Art; J.B. Speed Art Museum, Louisville; Miami University Art Museum, Oxford, Ohio; MGM/Mirage Resorts, Inc., Las Vegas, Nevada, and Biloxi, Mississippi; Museum Ludwig Donation, The State Russian Museum, St. Petersburg; Paul Weiss Rifkind Wharton and Garrison, New York; Memorial Art Gallery, Rochester, New York; Rockford Art Museum, Illinois; San Francisco Museum of Modern Art; Stiftung Ludwig, Aachen, Germany; University of Nebraska Art Galleries, Lincoln; University of North Carolina Art Gallery, Greensboro; Vassar College Art Gallery, Poughkeepsie, New York; Wellington Management Company, Boston.

Publications:

By DEEM: Books—*Bruna Seviri, Sun and Moon,* with Ronald Vance, 1978; *Aanababcac, Sun and Moon,* 1979; *Mona Lisa Washington, Zone,* 1980; *Extra Genre, White Walls,* 1981; *Art School: An Homage to the Master/Paintings by George Deem,* London and San Francisco 1993.

On DEEM: Books—*Aspects of a New Realism* exhibition catalog, Milwaukee 1969; *The New Realism* by Udo Kultermann, New York 1972; *Recent Accessions 1966–1972,* exhibition catalog, Indianapolis 1972; *Deem: An Exhibition of Paintings and Drawings,* exhibition catalog, Indianapolis, 1974; *The New Painting* by Udo Kultermann, Tübingen, West Germany 1975; *Art-School, An Homage to the Masters, Paintings by George Deem* introduction by Irene McManus, London and San Francisco, 1993; *The Purloined Image* exhibition catalog, Flint, Michigan 1993; *Art After Art* exhibition catalog, Roslyn Harbor, New York 1994; *Quoting Caravaggio: Contemporary Art, Preposterous History* by Mieke Bal, Chicago 1999; *George Deem and Peter Angelo Simon: Paintings and Photographs in Conversation* exhibition catalog, Evansville, Indiana 2001. **Articles—**''Painting Lists'' by Ronald Vance in *Art and Artists* (London), February 1968; ''George Deem'' by Edgar Buenaquiro in *Arts Magazine* (New York), November 1977; ''Vermeer and Contemporary American Painting'' by Udo Kultermann in *American Art Review* (Los Angeles), November 1978; ''Masterworks and 'The Work of the Master''' in *Collier's Encyclopedia* (New York), 1990; ''Back to the Classroom: The American Painter George Deem'' by Geroge Melly in *The Independent Magazine* (London), 1 May 1993; ''Bilder von der Letzten Bank'' (Picture from the Last Row, Paintings by George Deem) by Dorothea Friedrich in *Frankfurter Allgemeine Magazin* (Frankfurt, Germany), 2 July 1993; ''An Artist's New Take on the Old Schools of Art: George Deem in a class by himself'' by Constance Bond in *Smithsonian Magazine,* July 1993; ''Be True to Your School? Artist George Deem. . .'' by Arthur McCune in *The Lakeland Ledger* (Lakeland, Florida), 9 March 1994; ''George Deem at Nancy Hoffman'' by Reagan Upshaw in *Art in America* (New York), July 2000. **Video—**Documentary video portrait titled ''George Deem: A Conversation'' by Calvin Kimbrough and distributed by Evansville Museum of Arts and Science (Evansville, Indiana), 1993.

*

In 1960 I was painting calligraphic images of cursive script on a one-color ground. The ''writing'' was not readable. I began adding images of well-known paintings, sometimes repeating the same image more than once on a single canvas, sometimes juxtaposing various quoted paintings. I quoted familiar paintings so that the quoted image would be recognizable: Millet's *The Man With A Hoe,* Raeburn and Frans Hals portraits, Chardin still-lifes, Constable landscapes. The image: calligraphic paragraphs with illustrations. By about 1965 I had dropped the abstract calligraphic paragraphs and was quoting familiar paintings by themselves on a one-color ground.

During the 1970s I came to include in my work the style and technique of the painters whose works I was quoting, but not their color. I made a series of Vermeer paintings in which I combined two or more Vermeers into new compositions. In 1974, this series of Vermeer paintings was the subject of a solo exhibition at the Indianapolis Museum of Art and at the Allan Stone Gallery in New York. By 1978 many artists were working with quotations, and in that year the Whitney Museum in New York organized an exhibition *Art About Art* which included paintings from my Vermeer series. Among the artists participating in that exhibition were Dottie Attie, John Clem Clarke, Josef Levi, Roy Lichtenstein, and Larry Rivers.

In 1984, thinking about the question of attribution of paintings, I arrived at my painting *School of Vermeer.* I painted a school room with blackboard and wooden desks, an image out of my childhood, but with a Vermeerian black-and-white tile floor. In my schoolroom I placed figures from several Vermeer paintings: *Woman With Her Maidservant Writing a Letter, Woman Pouring Milk, Woman Weighing Gold,* etc. *School of Vermeer* opened the way to a series of about fifty ''School of. . .'' paintings, from *Ashcan School* and *Barbizon School* to *School of Velazquez.* These paintings were the subject of a book *Art School: Paintings by George Deem,* published in 1993 by Thames and Hudson in London and by Chronicle Books in San Francisco, and of a travelling exhibition organized in that same year by the Evansville Museum of Arts and Science in Evansville, Indiana.

In 1991 I began a series of paintings about painting and picture-making and the painter's traditional subject matter of landscape, interiors, portraits, and still life. The photographer Peter Angelo Simon joined me in this project in 1993, and we developed a collaborative exhibition, ''Paintings and Photographs in Conversation,'' which took place at the Evansville Museum of Arts and Science in Evansville, Indiana, in 2001, an exhibition documented by a catalogue with an essay by Mieke Bal.

During the 1990s I continued working with Vermeer imagery, which remains a major focus of my work. In 2000, at Nancy Hoffman Gallery in New York, I showed a series of paintings of Vermeer interiours with Vermeer's figures and furniture removed.

—George Deem

* * *

The paintings of George Deem are devoted to the exploration and rediscovery of prefigurated themes of art from the past. He uses images of paintings by artists such as Vermeer, Caravaggio, Rubens and Rogier van der Weyden as subject matter to express a contemporary sensibility revitalizing and translating the themes of the old masters. It is, therefore, necessary for the viewer to have a preknowledge of the original work in order to fully appreciate the fresh adaptation. The recycling and complexity of dealing with the source is a serious form of contemporary painting and reflects the historic dimension in contemporary art.

One of the major thematic sources for Deem is the work of Vermeer van Delft, whose paintings are often used by Deem as a point of departure from which new and exciting results are achieved. Vermeer's images are transformed to a contemporary level which finds an equivalent in Deem's masterly painting technique. In several of his works Deem identifies with the artist from the past by translating past centuries into the 20th century. Through this identification new aspects of the content are introduced, thereby constituting the earlier work into a more complex one in which old and new are combined.

In other paintings by Deem new aspects of serial art have emerged. Following the pioneering examples by Jasper Johns and Andy Warhol, Deem added a new variation to the theme in paintings such as ''Eight Women'' (1967). Another innovative aspect of his work can be seen in a complex combination of historic images. One such example is ''Mona Lisa Washington'' of 1972, which is a combination of two images from different sources painted into one new complex form inaugurating an interpersonal figuration. The dimension of this complex image has yet to be fully appreciated.

The work of George Deem is of consistent character in its exploration of thematic prefigurations which relate art of our time to art of the past. His work transcends the concept of the avantgarde and is one of the many parallels in the spectrum of contemporary art.

—Udo Kultermann

DE KEYSER, Raoul

Nationality: Belgian. **Born:** Deinze, 29 August 1930. **Education:** Studied art at the Academie of Deinze, 1963. **Military Service:** Served as adjunct in the welfare section, Belgian Army, in West Germany, 1950–51. **Family:** Married Dina Baudoneq in 1952; children: Luc, Piet and Jan. **Career:** Independent painter; lives and works in Deinze, Belgium. Non-teaching adjunct advisor, University of Ghent, since 1970. **Awards:** Jeune Peinture Belge Prize, Brussels, 1967. **Agent:** Brooke Alexander, 59 Wooster Street, New York, New York, 10012, U.S.A. **Address:** Kouterlosstraat 118, 9800 Deinze, Belgium.

Individual Exhibitions:

1965 Galerie Drieghe, Wetteren, Belgium
Kaleidoskoop, Ghent
1966 Galerie Les Contemporains, Brussels
3 Vlaamse Schilders, Groninger Museum, Groningen, Netherlands (with Elias and Raveel)
1967 Celbeton, Dendermonde, Belgium
M.A.S., Deinze, Belgium
1968 Galerie Contour, Brussels
Galerie Kaleidoskoop, Ghent
1969 Galerie Les Contemporains, Brussels
1970 Galerie Denise-Emmanual, Brussels
Korrekelder, Bruges
Galerie Richard Foncke, Ghent
Museum, Antwerp
Groninger Museum, Groningen, Netherlands
Museum, Haarlem, Netherlands
Museum, 'sHertogenbosch, Netherlands
1971 Galerie de Vaart, Hilversum, Netherlands
Galerie Plus-Kern, Ghent
1972 Galerie Ado, Bonheiden, Belgium
Galerie Grafiek 50, Wakken, Belgium
Galerie Plus-Kern, Ghent
1973 Galerie Aksent, Waregem, Belgium
Provincial Begijnhof, Hasselt, Belgium
1974 Van Abbemuseum, Eindhoven, Netherlands (with Amedee Cortier)
Galerie de Mangelgang, Groningen, Netherlands
1975 Galerie Aksent, Waregem, Belgium
E v H Loringhoven Galerie, Ghent
Neue Galerie, Aachen, West Germany (with Norbert Heyers)
1976 Galerie de Mangelgang, Groningen, Netherlands
Galerie Grafiek 50, Wakken, Belgium
1977 Galerie Drieghe, Wetteren, Belgium
Witterpoppetoren, Hasselt, Belgium (with Hugo Duchâteau)
1978 Galerie Jeanne Buytaert, Antwerp
Galerie Jean Leroy, Paris
Museum van Hedendaagse Kunst, Ghent
1979 Galerie Waalkens, Finsterwolde, Netherlands
Bilder 1976–1978, Belgisches Haus, Cologne
1980 Galerie Declercq, Knokke, Belgium
Galerie Jeanne Buytaert, Antwerp
International Cultureel Centrum, Antwerp
1982 Kunsthandel Lambert Tegenbosch, Heusden aan de Maas, Netherlands
Galerie Richard Foncke, Ghent
1983 Vereniging Aktuele Kunst Gewad, Ghent
1984 Villa des Roses, Ghent
1985 Dam 43, Middelburg, Netherlands
Galerie Drieghe, Wetteren, Belgium
Ado, Bonheiden, Belgium
1986 Museum Mw. J. Dhondt-Dhaenens, Deurle, Belgium
Paleis voor Schone Kunsten, Brussels
1987 Vereniging voor het Museum van Hedendaagse Kunst, Ghent
Villa des Roses, Ghent
1988 Galerie Minnen, Dessel

Zeno X Gallery, Antwerp
1989 Groeningemuseum, Bruges
Zeno X Gallery, Antwerp
1990 Wewerka Galerie, Berlin
Museum van Deinze en de Leiestreek, Deinze
1991 Kunsthalle, Bern
Portikus, Frankfurt am Main
Kunstverein, Arnsberg
Zeno X Gallery, Antwerp
1992 Galerie Rüdiger Schöttle, Munich
Galerie Rüdiger Schöttle, Paris
Wewerka & Weiss Galerie, Berlin
Zeno X Gallery, Antwerp
1993 Galerie Karlheinz Meyer, Karlsruhe
Galerie Barbara Weiss, Berlin
1994 *Leervluchten,* Zeno X Gallery, Antwerp
Twee Cellen, Stedelijk Museum Het Toreke, Tienen, Belgium
1995 Raum Aktueller Kunst, Vienna
Brooke Alexander Gallery, New York
DAAD, Berlin
Galerie Béla Jarzky, Cologne
1996 *Leervluchten 1992–1994,* PMMK Museum voor Moderne Kunst, Oostende (catalog)
Landing, Galerie Karlheinz Meyer, Karlsruhe
1997 *Schilderijen 1995,* MUHKA Museum voor Hedendaagse Kunst, Antwerp (catalog)
Training Flights 1992–1994, Museum voor Moderne Kunst, Ostend, Belgium
Raum Aktueller Kunst, Martin Janda, Wein, Austria (catalog)
1998 *Arbeiten auf Papier,* Galerie Karlheinz Meyer, Karlsruhe
Galerie Barbara Weiss, Berlin
1999 *Raoul De Keyser 1991–1998,* Kunstmuseum Luzern, Luzem (catalog)
Retour, Zeno X Gallery, Antwerp
2000 *Tachtig Luchten,* Academie Leon, Roborst (catalog)
Gallagher Gallery, Dublin
Goldie Paley Gallery, Philadelphia
Renaissance Society, Chicago
2001 David Zwirner Gallery, New York
Goldie Paley Gallery, Moore College of Art and Design, Philadelphia (catalog)

Selected Group Exhibitions:

1967 *Premio Lissone,* Milan
1968 *Alternative Attuali 3,* L'Aquila, Italy
1971 *Bienal,* Sao Paulo
1973 *Fortunately There Is Still Some Grass,* Camden Arts Centre, London
1974 *3rd Triennale,* Bruges
1975 *Concerning Painting,* Museum van Bommel—Van Dam, Venlo, Netherlands (toured the Netherlands)
1980 *Beervelde 1966—nu,* De Vieeshal, Middelburg, Netherlands
Belgie-Nedeland: Kunst na '45, Palais des Beaux-Arts, Brussels (travelled to the Museum Boymansvan Beuningen, Rotterdam)
1986 *Een keuze/un choix,* KunstRAI, Amsterdam
1992 *Documenta 9,* Kassel, Germany
1994 *Unbound: Possibilities in Painting,* Hayward Gallery, London (catalog)
1995 *Dialoog aan de Leie,* Musea, Deurle, Belgium
Raoul De Keyser, Désirée Dolron, Fabrice Hybert, Mark Manders, Zeno X Gallery, Antwerp
Een Actuele Privé-Verzameling, Sint-Lukasgalerij, Brussels
1996 *Ver na Vermeer,* Museum van Hedendaagse Kunst, Antwerp
1997 *Artcologne 1997,* Zeno X Gallery, Rheinhalle, Köln
La Pittura Fiamenga e Olandese da Van Gogh, Ensor, Magritte, Modrian ai Contemporanei, Centre D'Art Santa Monica, Barcelona
Arte del '900, Palazzo Grassi, Venice
Maakt Kunst Staat, Provinciaal Museum Hasselt, Belgium
1998 *The Fascinating Faces of Flanders,* Centro Cultural de Belém, Lisbon (catalog)
Art Forum Berlin, Messe Berlin, Berlin
Shopping the Stars, Zeno X Gallery, Antwerp
1999 *La Consolation,* Magasin, Centre National d'Art Contemporain, Grenoble (catalog)
De Opening, SMAK, Stedelijk Museum voor Aktuele Kunst, Ghent (catalog)
Undercurrents and Overtones, CCAC, Oliver Art Center, Oakland
2000 *Opening,* Kunstmuseum Luzern (catalog)
Luc Tuymans and Raoul de Keyser, Stedelijk Museum voor Aktuele Kunst, Ghent, Belgium

Collections:

Museum van Hedendaages Kunst, Ghent; Groeninge Museum, Bruges; Museum voor Schone Kunsten, Courtrai, Belgium; Provinciaal Museum, De Lakenhalle, Ypres, Belgium; Gemeentekrediet van Belgie, Brussels; Museum, Dienze, Belgium; Groninger Museum, Groningen, Netherlands; Museum voor Moderne Kunst, Brussels.

Publications:

By DE KEYSER: Book—*More Is Less,* with Roland Jooris, Deinze 1972; *Paintings 1980–1999,* with Steven Jacobs, Ghent 2000.

On DE KEYSER: Books—*Raoul De Keyser,* exhibition catalog, with text by Roland Jooris and Paul Vries, Groningen, Netherlands, 1970; *Raoul De Keyser: Het samengaan van gegeven en schilderij* by Roland Jooris, Wakken, Belgium, 1972; *Raoul De Keyser: Nota najaar 73* by Roland Jooris, Deinze, Belgium, 1973; *Amedée Cortier and Raoul De Keyser,* exhibition catalog, with text by Yves De Smet and Roland Jooris, Eindhoven, Netherlands, 1974; *Raoul De Keyser* with text by Roland Jooris, Antwerp 1978; *Raoul De Keyser,* exhibition catalog, with text by Jan Hoet, Marc Callewaert and Roland Jooris, Ghent 1978; *Raoul De Keyser: Bilder 1976–1978,* exhibition catalog, with text by Roland Jooris, Cologne 1979; *Raoul De Keyser,* exhibition catalog, with text by Roland Jooris, Heusden, Netherlands, 1982; *Raoul De Keyser,* exhibition catalog with text by Bart De Baere, Deurle 1986; *Raoul De Keyser,* exhibition catalog with text by Olivier Hamerlynck, Ghent 1987. **Articles—**"'Leervluchten' und 'Aircraft-Retour': Ereignisse in Raoul De Keysers Malerei" by Hans Rudolf Reust in *Kunst-Bulletin,* no. 6, June 1999.

DEKKERS, Ger(rit Hendrik)

Nationality: Dutch. **Born:** Borne, 21 August 1929. **Education:** At secondary school in Hangelo, 1942–46; studied graphics at the Academie voor Kunst en Industrie, Enschede, 1950–54. **Military Service:** Served in the Dutch Army, in Indonesia, 1948–50. **Family:** Married Hilda Hartsuiker in 1954; children: Henriette and Jose. **Career:** Freelance artist and photographer, Enschede, 1954–73, and in Giethoorn, since 1973. **Awards:** Dutch Ministry of Culture Grant, 1970, 1971, 1975, 1976; City of Amsterdam Stipendium, 1976. **Member:** Photo Section, Gebonden Kunstenfederatie (GKf), since 1969. **Agents:** Galerie M., Haus Weitmar, 463 Bochum-Weitmar, West Germany; and Galerie Nouvelles Images, Westeinde 22, The Hague, Netherlands. **Address:** Dwarsgracht 31, 8355 CV Giethoorn, Netherlands.

Individual Exhibitions:

1972 *Landscape Perception,* Rijksmuseum Kröller-Müller, Otterlo, Netherlands
1973 *Landscape Perception,* Museum Bochum-Kunstsammlung, Bochum, West Germany
Landscape Perception, Neue Galerie-Kunstsammlung Ludwig, Aachen, West Germany
1974 *Landscape Perception,* Stedelijk Museum, Amsterdam
Landscape Perception 1968–1975, Gemeentemuseum, The Hague
1975 *Landscape Perception,* Palais des Beaux-Arts, Brussels
Landscape Perception, Galleria del Cavallino, Venice
1976 *Landscape Perception,* Kunstmuseum, Aarhus, Denmark
Landscape Perception, Print Gallery Peiter Brattinga, Amsterdam
Landscape Perception, Galerie M. Bocum, West Germany
1977 *Planned Landscapes,* Rijksmuseum Kröller-Müller, Otterlo, Netherlands
Plastic, Museum Boymans van Beuningen, Rotterdam
1978 *Plastic,* Gemeentemuseum, Arnhem, Netherlands
Planned Landscapes, De Vishal, Haarlem, Netherlands
1979 *New Dutch Landscape,* Hayden Gallery, Massachusetts Institute of Technology, Cambridge
Planned Landscapes, Print Gallery Pieter Brattinga, Amsterdam
Planned Landscapes, Provincial Begijnhof, Hasselt, Belgium
1980 *Planned Landscapes,* Kunstcentrum Markt 17, Enschede, Netherlands
Planned Landscapes, Rijksplanologische Dienst, The Hague
1981 *Planned Landscapes,* Stadium Generale, Wageningen, Netherlands
Planned Landscapes, Städtische Galerie, Nordhorn, West Germany

Selected Group Exhibitions:

1969 *Atelier 6,* Stedelijk Museum, Amsterdam
1971 *Sonsbeek 71,* Central Station, Amsterdam
1974 *Projekt 74,* Kunsthalle, Cologne
1977 *Sequenzen,* Kunstverein, Hamburg
Documenta 6, Kassel, West Germany
Museum of Drawers, Kunsthaus, Zurich (now permanent installation)
1978 *Fotografie in Nederland 1940–75,* Stedelijk Museum, Amsterdam
Fotografie als Kunst/Kunst als Fotografie 2, Fotoforum der Gesamthochschule, Kasel, West Germany (toured Germany, Poland, Portugal, Spain and the United States)
1979 *To Do With Nature,* travelling exhibition (toured the Netherlands, Sweden, Belgium, West Germany, Denmark, and Portugal)
Kunst als Fotografie 1949–79, Tiroler Landesmuseum Ferdinandeum, Innsbruck (travelled to the Neue Galerie am Wolfgang Gurlitt Museum, Linz, Austria; Neue Galerie am Landesmuseum Joanneum, Graz, Austria; and the Museum des 20, Jahrhun, Vienna)

Collections:

Rijksmuseum Kröller-Müller, Otterlo, Netherlands; Stedelijk Museum, Amsterdam; Frans Halsmuseum, Haarlem, Netherlands; Museum Boymans van Beuningen, Rotterdam; Gemeentemuseum, The Hague; Gemeentemuseum, Arnhem, Netherlands; Ministry of Culture, The Hague; Sammlung Ludwig, Cologne; Kunsthalle, Hamburg; Museum Bochum-Kunstsammlung, Bochum, Germany.

Publications:

By DEKKERS: Book—*Planned Landscapes: 25 Horizons,* with an introduction by R. W. D. Oxenaar, Amsterdam 1977; *Graven en begrave in Overijssel,* editor, with H. Schelhaas and B. Molenaar, Zwolle 1980.

On DEKKERS: Books—*Ger Dekkers: Landscape Perceptions,* exhibition catalog, with text by R. W. D. Oxenaar, Otterlo, Netherlands 1972; *Ger Dekkers: Landscape Perceptions,* exhibition catalog, with text by Peter Spielmann, Bochum, West Germany 1973; *Ger Dekkers: Landscape Perceptions,* exhibition catalog, with text by Wolfgang Becker, Aachen, West Germany 1973; *Ger Dekkers: Landscape Perceptions 1968–1975,* exhibition catalog, with text by J. L. Locher and Manfred Schneckenburger, The Hague 1974; *Fotografie in Nederland 1940–1975,* exhibition catalog, with text by Els Barents, Ingeborg Leyerzapf and others, The Hague 1978; *New Dutch Landscape,* exhibition catalog, by Marc S. Gerstein, Cambridge, Massachussetts 1979; *The Artist as Photographer* by Marina Vaizey, London 1982. **Articles—**''Ger Dekkers'' in *Flash Art* (Milan), December 1974/January 1975; ''Ger Dekkers'' by A. Van Berswordt-Wallrabe in *M-Bochum* (Bochum, West Germany), no. 3, 1976, ''Ger Dekkers'' by Betty van Garrel in *Volker Post* (Rotterdam), no. 4, 1978; ''Ger Dekkers'' by Dolf Welling in the *Holland Herald* (Amsterdam), July 1979; ''Ger Dekkers'' by Fred Hazelhoff in *Foto* (Hilversum, Netherlands), September 1980; ''Ger Dekkers'' by Herman v. Buuren in *Bijvoorbeeld* (Amsterdam), no. 2, 1981.

*

My actual subject is the effect that our culture has on landscape. The Dutch landscape with its polders provides an excellent example.

I am aware that my work is a personal expression, in which my personality is one factor. My principal action—to record a situation that I encounter—I experience myself as an intruder.

My concern with the subject and its surroundings does not go further than emotionally choosing the angle of the camera and focussing it, and later on making a selection and carefully completing the process.

The horizon acts as a middle line in the square pictures: This gives a continuous line that runs throughout the series and thus the whole project.

The medium I use is another factor.

I find only a limited number of phototechnical possibilities important. It is not the gimmicks of photography that mean most to me but its very irrevocability, its inevitability. From these factors, but mainly, I hope, from its essence, my work derives its validity.

—Ger Dekkers

* * *

In his works Ger Dekkers makes visible the way in which the Dutch landscape reveals itself to the observer as a continuous series of organized data—although a simple disclosure itself is not necessarily an ordered achievement. Thus it is no accident that around 1972 the color photographs of Ger Dekkers were at the center of a debate about the differences between photography as a means of recording reality and as a plastic art.

Dekkers' large exhibition at the Rijksmuseum Kröller-Müller gave the distinguished critic Rudi Fuchs an occasion to consider the nature of photography. For Fuchs, the most important elements of photography are the possibilities afforded by direct manipulation, especially by the deliberate placing of objects and the process of excision. But he goes on to accuse Dekkers of using the medium in an unnatural way, of denying the history of photography and structuring his work according to the aesthetic of a particular trend of the moment, in this case Minimal Art. He accuses Dekkers of going beyond the bounds of his medium, of borrowing from the plastic arts without giving anything in return: Dekkers does not even bother to acknowledge that the boundaries are problematic. On another occasion Fuchs defended those works by Jan Dibbets in which there is a living relationship between an impersonal medium and the artist's individuality. But in general Dekkers is an artist because he *makes,* and Dibbets, because he merely *registers,* is not.

The importance of Ger Dekkers' work is that its quality is apparent whether it is a photograph, a slide or a book. For example, in cooperation with the Art Animation in Groningen (since 1977 the Corps de Garde) he produced a series of carefully planned catalogs. These are particularly relevant to the question raised by Conceptual Art: Is plastic art necessarily confined to particular forms and occasions? No doubt the particular qualities of the Dutch landscape are especially suited to the point of view of constructivism and minimalism. That Dekkers has been influenced by them is itself unimportant: What matters is what he has done with dikes, the forests and fields of grain and playgrounds. The special realms of the gallery and museum are not for him. Much more appropriate, in fact, are busy public buildings—the Netherlands railway stations, for example, where some of his photographs now appear.

—A. F. Wagemans

de KOONING, Willem

Nationality: American. **Born:** Rotterdam, Netherlands, 24 April 1904, emigrated to the United States as stowaway on a ship, 1927. **Education:** Studied at the Akademie voor Beeldende Kunsten en Techischen Wetenschappen, Rotterdam, 1916–24, 1926–27. **Family:** Married Elaine Marie Catherine Fried in 1943; daughter; Lisa. **Career:** Apprentice to the commercial artists Jan and Jaap Gidding, Rotterdam 1916; assistant to Bernard Romein, art director of a Rotterdam department store, 1920–23; worked as house painter, Hoboken, New Jersey 1927; moved to New York and held various commercial art jobs, 1927–28; met John Graham, Arshile Gorky and Studart Davis, New York, 1928–29; full time painter from 1935; shared studio with Arshile Gorky, New York 1937; designed and painted murals, Federal Arts Project, New York, 1935–39. Instructor, Black Mountain College, Beria, North Carolina, 1948, and Yale University, New Haven, Connecticut, 1950–51, 1959–60. **Awards:** Logan Medal and Purchase Prize, Art Institute of Chicago, 1951; President's Freedom Award Medal, 1964; Talens Prize International, Amsterdam 1968; Gold Medal, American Academy of Arts and Letters, New York, 1975; Artist of the Year Award, Fairfield Arts Festival, Connecticut, 1978; Mellon Prize (with Eduardo Chillida), Carnegie Institute, Pittsburgh, 1979; Max Beckman Prize, Frankfurt, 1984; Kaiser Ring Award, Goslar, 1984; National Medal of Arts, Washington, D.C., 1986; Mayor's Liberty Medal, New York, 1986; Praemium Imperiale of Japan Art Association, 1989; CAA Distinguished Artist Award for Lifetime Achievement, 1993. **Member:** National Institute of Arts and Letters, 1960; Royal Academy of Fine Arts, Stockholm, 1986. **Died:** From complications of Alzheimer's Disease, East Hampton, New York, 19 March 1997.

Individual Exhibitions:

1948 Charles Egan Gallery, New York
1951 Charles Egan Gallery, New York
De Kooning/Pollock/Shahn, Arts Club of Chicago
1953 Sidney Janis Gallery, New York
Boston Museum Art School (retrospective; travelled to the Workshop Art Center, Washington, D.C.)
1955 Martha Jackson Gallery, New York
1956 Sidney Janis Gallery, New York
1959 Sidney Janis Gallery, New York
1961 Paul Kantor Gallery, Beverly Hills, California
1962 *Barnett Newman and Willem de Kooning,* Allan Stone Gallery, New York
1964 Allan Stone Gallery, New York
'Woman' Drawings by Willem de Kooning, James Goodman Gallery, Buffalo, New York
1965 Paul Kantor Gallery, Beverly Hills, California
Smith College Museum of Art, Northampton, Masschussetts (retrospective; travelled to the Massachussetts Institute of Technology, Cambridge)
1966 *De Kooning's Women,* Allan Stone Gallery, New York
1967 M. Knoedler and Company, New York
Allan Stone Gallery, New York
1968 *Peintures Récentes,* M. Knoedler et Cie, Paris
Stedelijk Museum, Asmterdam (retrospective; travelled to the Tate Gallery, London)
1969 Museum of Modern Art, New York (retrospective)

Willem De Kooning: *Woman Singing II,* 1966. Tate Gallery, London/Art Resource. ©2001 Willem de Kooning Revocable Trust/Artists Rights Society (ARS), New York.

M. Knoedler and Company, New York
1971 M. Knoedler and Company, New York
Allan Stone Gallery, New York
1972 Allan Stone Gallery, New York
Baltimore Museum of Art
Sidney Janis Gallery, New York
1974 University of Alabama, University (toured the United States)
Walker Art Center, Minneapolis (toured the United States and Canada)
Richard Gray Gallery, Chicago
1975 *New Works: Paintings and Sculpture,* Xavier Fourcade Inc., New York
Paintings, Drawings, Sculpture 1967–75, Norton Gallery of Art, Palm Beach, Florida
1976 Seattle Art Museum
Stedelijk Museum, Amsterdam
Collection d'Art, Amsterdam
Gimpel Fils, London
Gimpel Fils, Zurich
New Paintings 1976, Xavier Fourcade Inc., New York
Blaffer Gallery, University of Houston
1977 Collection d'Art, Amsterdam
Xavier Fourcade Inc., New York
Wilheim Lembruck Museum, Duisburg, West Germany
Musée de Grenoble, France
The Sculpture of de Kooning with Related Paintings, Drawings and Lithographs, Arts Council of Great Britain, London
Galerie Templon, Paris
Museum of Modern Art, Belgrade
Museum of Modern Art, Ljubljana, Yugoslavia
1978 *Willem de Kooning in East Hampton,* Guggenheim Museum, New York
Museum of Art, Science and Industry Bridgeport, Connecticut
Romanian National Museum of Art, Bucharest
Branch Post, Cracow
Helsinki National Museum of Art
America House, East Berlin
University of California Art Museum, Berkeley
De Kooning 1969–1978, University of Northern Iowa, Cedar Falls
1979 St. Louis Art Museum
Contemporary Arts Center, Cincinnati, Ohio
Akron Art Institute, Ohio
March Foundation, Alicante, Spain
Fundación Juan March, Madrid
Norwegian National Gallery of Art, Oslo
Dordrechts Museum, The Netherlands
Pittsburgh International Series, Museum of Art, Pittsburgh
1980 Richard Hines Gallery, Seattle
Richard Gray Gallery, Chicago
Galerie Hans Strelow, Dusseldorf
1981 Janie C. Lee Gallery, Houston
Guild Hall, East Hampton, New York
1982 C. Grimaldis Gallery, Baltimore
Xavier Fourcade Inc., New York
1983 *The North Atlantic Light 1960–63,* Stedelijk Museum, Amsterdam (travelled to Denmark and Sweden)
Xavier Fourcade Inc., New York
De Kooning Drawings, Whitney Museum, New York (travelled to West Berlin and Paris)
Retrospective Exhibition, Whitney Museum, New York (travelled to West Berlin and Paris)
De Kooning Sculpture, Josef-Haubrich-Kunsthalle, Cologne
Sculpture Court, Philip Morris, New York
Galerie Maeght Lelong, New York
1984 Colorado State University, Fort Collins
Intimate Gallery, Lincoln Center, Fort Collins, Colorado
Stadelsches Kunstinstitut, Frankfurt
Xavier Fourcade Inc., New York
Das Moenchehaus Museum, Goslar, West Germany
Galerie Daniel Templon, Paris
Galerie Hans Strelow, Dusseldorf
Anthony D'Offay Gallery, London
1985 Studio Marconi, Milan
Xavier Fourcade Inc., New York
Margo Leavin Gallery, Los Angeles
1986 Fabian Carlsson Gallery, London
Anthony D'Offay Gallery, London
1987 Margo Leavin Gallery, London
C. Grimaldis Gallery, Baltimore
Richard Gray Gallery, Chicago
1990 Salander-O'Reilly Galleries, New York
1993 C&M Arts, New York
Hirshhorn Museum, Washington, D.C.
1994 National Gallery of Art, Washington, D.C.
1995 Thomas Ammann Fine Art, Zurich
San Francisco Museum of Modern Art, San Francisco
1996 Whitney Museum of American Art, New York
C&M Arts, New York
Kunstmuseum Bonn, Bonn
1997 Matthew Marks Gallery, New York
Museum of Modern Art, New York
2001 C&M Arts, New York (catalog)

Selected Group Exhibitions:

1945 *Group Show,* Charles Egan Gallery, New York
1950 *Biennale,* Venice
1951 *60th Annual of American Painting and Sculpture,* Art Institute of Chicago
1954 *Biennale,* Venice
1969 *Festival of 2 Worlds,* Spoleto, Italy
1978 *Sculpture and Works on Paper from the 1930's and 1940's,* Washburn Gallery, New York
1981 *A New Spirit in Painting,* Royal Academy, London
1982 *New York School: Four Decades,* Guggenheim Museum, New York
1985 *Flying Tigers: Painting and Sculpture in New York 1939–46,* Brown University, Providence, Rhode Island (travelled to Worcester, Massachussetts; Southampton, New York)
1987 *L'Epoque, la mode, la morale, la passion,* Centre Georges Pompidou, Paris
1989 *The Alice and Harris Weston Collection of Post-war Art,* Cincinnati Art Museum, Cincinnati

1988 *Abstract Expressionist Drawings 1941–1955,* Janie C. Lee Master Drawings
Contemporary Drawings: The Collection of Prince Franz of Bavaria, Staatliche Graphische Sammlung, Neue Pinakothek, Munich
1990 *Willem De Kooning, Jean Dubuffet: The Women,* Pace Gallery, New York
1995 *Sculpture,* Anthony d'Offay, London
1997 *The New York School: de Kooning, Gorky, Kline, Newman, Pollock, Rothko, Smith, Still,* Gagosian Gallery, New York
XIX & XX Century Master Paintings and Sculptures: An Exhibition, Acquavella Galleries, New York
1998 *Drawing Exhibitions,* Drawing Center, New York; Armand Hammer Museum of Art in Los Angeles; Matthew Marks Gallery, New York.
The New York School: Selections from the Collection, Museum of Modern Art, New York
2000 *Pasted Pictures: Collage and Abstraction in the 20th Century,* Knoedler & Company, New York (catalog)

Collections:

Museum of Modern Art, New York; Metropolitan Museum of Art, New York; Guggenheim Museum, New York; Whitney Museum, New York; Art Institute of Chicago; Carnegie Institute, Pittsburgh; National Gallery, Washington, D.C.; Centre Georges Pompidou, Paris; Tate Gallery, London; Stedelijk Museum, Amsterdam; Bayerische Staatsgemaldesammlung, Munich; Baltimore Museum of Art, Baltimore; Brooklyn Museum, New York; Albright-Knox Art Gallery, Buffalo, New York; Australian National Gallery, Canberra; The Hirshhorn Museum and Sculpture Garden, Washington, D.C., Los Angeles County Museum of Art; National Gallery of Canada, Ottawa; Art Gallery of Toronto, Canada; Vassar College, Poughkeepsie; Moderna Museet, Stockholm, Sweden; Washington University, St. Louis.

Publications:

By de KOONING: Articles—letter to the editor, on Arshile Gorky in *Art News* (New York), January 1949; interview, with Martha Boudrez, in *The Knickerbocker* (New York), May 1950; ''Artists' Sessions at Studio 35 (1950)'' in *Modern Artists in America,* edited by Robert Motherwell and Ad Reinhardt, New York, 1951; ''The Renaissance and Order'' in *Transformation* (New York), vol. 1, no. 2, 1951; ''What Abstract Art Means to Me'' in *Museum of Modern Art Bulletin* (New York), spring 1951; interview in *Conversations with Artists* by Selden Rodman, New York, 1957; ''Is Today's Artist with or Against the Past?,'' interview, with Thomas B. Hess in *Artnews* (New York) June 1958; film-script in *Sketchbook No. 1:3 Americans,* (New York), 1960; ''Content is a Glimpse . . .'' interview with David Sylvester in *Location* (Easthampton, New York), 1963; interview with James T. Valliere in *Partisan Review* (New York), fall 1957; interview in *Vrij Nederland* (Amsterdam), 5 October 1968; ''A Desperate View'' in *Willem de Kooning* by Thomas B. Hess, New York, 1969; ''Interview with Willem de Kooning,'' with Harold Rosenberg, in *Artnews* (New York), September 1972; ''What Abstract Art Means to Me'' in *Art Newspaper,* vol. 5, May 1994.

On de KOONING: Books—*De Kooning Retrospective,* exhibition catalog, with a foreword by Clement Greenberg, Boston 1953; *De Kooning,* exhibition catalog, New York 1955; *Willem de Kooning* by Thomas B. Hess, New York 1959; *De Kooning* by Harriet Janis and Rudi Blish, New York and London 1960; *Willem de Kooning,* exhibition catalog, with text by Clifford Odets, Beverly Hills, California 1961; *Willem de Kooning,* 3 volume unpublished collection of photographs, critical commentaries and annotations, complied by William C. Agee, New York 1962; *De Kooning-Newman,* exhibition catalog, with comments by Allan Stone, New York 1962; *Woman Drawings by Willem de Kooning,* exhibition catalog, with a preface by Merle Goodman, Buffalo, New York 1964; *Willem de Kooning,* exhibition catalog, with preface by William Inge, Beverly Hills, California 1965; *De Kooning's Women,* exhibition catalog, New York 1966; *De Kooning: Recent Paintings,* exhibition catalog, by Thomas B. Hess, New York 1967; *De Kooning: Peintures Récentes,* exhibition catalog, Paris 1968; *Willem de Kooning,* exhibition catalog, with an introduction by Thomas B. Hess, Amsterdam 1968; *De Kooning: January 1968—March 1969,* exhibition catalog by Thomas B. Hess, New York 1969; *Drawings of Willem de Kooning* by Thomas B. Hess, Greenwich, Connecticut 1972; *Willem de Kooning* by Gabriella Drudi, Milan 1972; *De Kooning* by Harold Rosenberg, New York 1974; *American Masters: The Voice and the Myth* by Brian O'Doherty, New York 1974; *De Kooning: Paintings, Drawings, Sculpture 1967–1975,* exhibition catalog, Palm Beach, Florida 1975; *De Kooning: New Works, Paintings and Sculpture,* exhibition catalog, New York 1975; *Willem de Kooning,* exhibition catalog, Amsterdam 1976; *De Kooning: New Paintings, 1976,* exhibition catalog, New York 1976; *The Sculpture of de Kooning with Related Paintings, Drawings and Lithographs,* exhibition catalog, with text by Andrew Forge, foreword by David Sylvester, London 1977; *American Art at Mid-Century: The Subjects of the Artist* by E. A. Carnean, Jr. and Eliza R. Rathbone, Washington, D.C. 1978; *Willem de Kooning in East Hampton,* exhibition catalog, by Diane Waldman, New York 1978; *De Kooning 1969–1978,* exhibition catalog, edited by Sanford Shman, with text by Jack Coward, Cedar Falls, Iowa 1978; *Willem de Kooning: Pittsburgh International Series,* exhibition catalog, Pittsburgh 1979; *Willem de Kooning: The North Atlantic Light 1960–83,* exhibition catalog, Amsterdam 1983; *Willem de Kooning: Skulpturen,* exhibition catalog, Cologne 1983; *Willem de Kooning: Drawings, Paintings, Sculpture,* exhibition catalog, New York 1983; *Willem de Kooning, Retrospective,* exhibition catalog, West Berlin and Paris 1984; *Willem de Kooning,* by Diane Waldman, London 1988; *Willem De Kooning: an Exhibition of Painting,* exhibition catalog, New York 1990; *Willem De Kooning: an Exhibition of Paintings,* exhibition catalog, New York 1990; *Willem De Kooning: Transcending Landscape Paintings 1975–1979,* exhibition catalog, New York 1993; *Willem de Kooning from the Hirshhorn Museum Collection,* exhibition catalog, Washington, D.C. 1993; *Willem De Kooning: Paintings,* Washington, D.C. 1994; *Willem de Kooning: The Late Paintings, the 1980s,* exhibition catalog, San Francisco 1995; *Willem de Kooning,* exhibition catalog, Zurich 1995; *Willem de Kooning: Paintings 1982–1986,* exhibition catalog, New York 1996; *Willem de Kooning's Door Cycle,* exhibition catalog, New York 1996; *Willem de Kooning: Paintings 1983–84,* exhibition catalog, Matthew Marks Gallery, New York 1997; *Willem de Kooning (1904–1997),* exhibition catalog, Richmond 1997. **Articles**—''Willem de Kooning'' by Rose C.S. Slivka in *Art Journal* (New York), vol. 48, no. 3, Fall 1989; ''Conversations with Willem de Kooning'' by Irving Sandler in *Art Journal* (New York), vol. 48, no. 3, Fall 1989; ''Willem de Kooning, On His

Eighty-fifth Birthday'' in *Art Journal,* vol. 48, Fall 1989; ''The Conundrum of Willem de Kooning—Painting Masterfully with Alzheimer's Disease: Mystery, Miracle, or Myth?'' by Catherine Barnett in *Art and Antiques,* vol. 6, November 1989; ''The Angel and the Demoiselle: William de Kooning's Black Friday'' by Sally Yard in *Record of the Art Museum,* vol. 50, no. 2, 1991; ''Seeing the Face in the Fire'' by Robert Hughes in *Time*, 30 May 1994; ''The Incomparable De Kooning'' by William Feaver in *Art News,* vol. 93, May 1994; ''The Ghost of Willem de Kooning'' in *Modern Painters,* vol. 7, Summer 1994; ''Willem and Elaine de Kooning: An Appreciation'' by Vincent Katz in *The Print Collector's Newsletter,* vol. 25, November/December 1994; ''Body of Evidence: Willem de Kooning'' in *Artforum International,* vol. 33, November 1994; ''De Kooning's Changes of Climate'' by Paul Branch in *Art in America,* vol. 83, January 1995; ''The de Kooning Dilemma'' by Kay Larson in *ARTnews,* vol. 94, no. 10, December 1995; ''The Birth of Woman I: Willem DeKooning's Painting'' by David Sylvester in *The Burlington Magazine,* vol. 137, April 1995; ''Willem de Kooning: Clam Diggers, 1964'' by Paul Muldoon in *Artforum International,* vol. 34, November 1995; ''Different Strokes: The Late Work of Willem de Kooning'' by Peter Schjeldahl in *Artforum International,* vol. 35, January 1997; ''Willem de Kooning's Late Paintings'' by Mario Naves in *The New Criterion,* vol. 15, April 1997; ''Meeting de Kooning'' by David Sylvester in *Modern Painters* (London), vol. 10, no. 4, Winter 1997; ''Dispatches: Late de Kooning'' by Michael Klein in *Artnet.com Magazine*, 14 February 1997; ''Willem de Kooning'' by Alexi Worth in *Slate Magazine*, 26 February 1997; ''Desire at Full Stretch'' by Robert Hughes in *Time*, 31 March 1997; ''Willem de Kooning: 'The Hilariousness of It''' by Arthur C. Danto in *Art News,* vol. 96, May 1997; ''De Kooning's 'Women' and the Performance of Femininity'' by Fionna Barber in *Make, The Magazine of Women's Art,* no. 77, September/November 1997; ''Identifying Willem de Kooning's Reclining Man'' by Judith Zilczer in *American Art* (Washington, D.C.), vol. 12, no. 2, Summer 1998; ''De Kooning With Attitude'' by Bill Berkson in *Modern Painters,* vol. 13, no. 3, Autumn 2000.

* * *

The de Kooning style of work has spread itself across a variety of influences, not all of them comfortable bedfellows.

His successful childhood apprenticeship with the commercial artists' company run by the decorators Jan and Jaap Gidding in Holland prompted Jaap to arrange for him to enter the Rotterdam Academy of Fine Arts and Techniques where he remained a student for eight years absorbing the breadth of a wide curriculum which was nevertheless strict in its determination to give every aspirant a stern academic training in the arts and a mastercraftsman's proficiency in craft techniques. During this time he also became aware of what the de Stijl group of Mondrian and van Doesburg believed creative art should achieve.

Later on when, after several vain attempts, he left Holland behind and entered the United States, he was able to bring with him the balance of a training that gave him an aptitude for both painting and making things. He was practical as well as accomplished.

When he started to paint seriously—as an artist—his first development was in the direction taken by Arshile Gorky (in his early portraits), but these de Kooning paintings of the 1930s were in double-harness with untitled, non-figurative works which may have owed something to de Stijl (but had none of the hard edge of the Dutch School) and something also to the later and more fantastic Gorky. At all events, in both categories there lurked a strong flavor of the United States.

In the mid-1940s the character of his paintings took on two other aspects. A number of them (generally based on figures and usually those of women) seemed to transmute at least a part of what Jackson Pollock had discovered. Rarely with Pollock's random attack (most of them, but by no means all, were very carefully strung together in professionally correct composition), they still inspired the same effect of splintered or sprawling confusion—an emotional confusion rather than a visual one. For all their frequent and decorous attention to expert tailoring, these pictures—full of pastel tints and black outlines or dark areas edged with white—were moving proof that here was an artist who combines taste with passion.

Side by side with them, and with increasing frequency, appeared the figure studies. No hint of early Gorky this time. These paintings are a fascinating mixture of picassoid distortions with Cobra School vehemence and vibrant coloring (a curious, if long-delayed legacy from the Netherlands where he was born). The Spaniard's part in all this alchemy at the hands of a contemporary art apothecary has been gradually phased out, but the Cobra element remains and has since entered the near-abstract landscapes and pictures of atmosphere like ''Rosy-Fingered Dawn at Louse Point.''

Without question Willem de Kooning was a well-organized modern artist. He worked steadily and never totally rejected what he has been able to glean from experience. His latest development had been to try his hand—with some success—at sculpture. He could make things.

—Sheldon Williams

Willem de Kooning's work shifted in style after about 1980. His flirtation with sculpture never approached the successes he had known with his paintings and drawings, and age brought new concerns to the artist. Critical opinions of his late work are widely varied and show a public often baffled by the changes in his technique and approach.

In the early 1980s, de Kooning's work displayed a gradual transition in color pallette and emotional tone. The earlier paintings often used vibrant reds, yellows, and blues and had an urgency in their content. By 1982, de Kooning was using orange, brown, purple, and beige much more frequently and often placed these shades within fields of creamy whites. The late works are much more calm in tone, less intense but perhaps more lyrical. Curator Michael Klein described the late de Kooning work as a kind of natural progression. ''The rough surface has become unusually serene, as if the subject matter is no longer a soul-searching enterprise, but a glimpse of a glorious rapture.'' Klein's summation of the later work is more accommodating than most. The exhibition catalog which accompanied the 1997 Museum of Modern Art retrospective attributes the changes in de Kooning's work in the 1980s to his mental deterioration from Alzheimer's disease. Art historian Robert Hughes echoed this sentiment about the paintings created in the 1980s: ''These spectral, vacuous confections of ribbony paint are among the saddest things ever made by a once major artist.'' Regardless of the reasons for the stylistic changes in de Kooning's work, it is impressive that this man painted until he could paint no more. In the years 1982–83, it is estimated that he completed about one picture per week, and he continued to work furiously, even as his body and mind failed. Willem de Kooning had a great passion for painting.

—Tammy A. Kinsey

DELVAUX, Paul

Nationality: Belgian. **Born:** Antheit, near Huys, 23 September 1897. **Education:** in Brussels; studied architecture, 1916–17, then painting under Constant Montald and Jean Delville, 1919–21, Academie des Beaux-Arts, Brussels. **Military Service:** Served in the Belgian Army, Brussels, 1920–21. **Family:** Married Anne-Marie (Tam) DeMartelaere in 1952. **Career:** Painter from 1921; established studio in Brussels, 1924; visited Paris, 1926; travelled in Italy, 1938, 1939; worked in seclusion during the German occupation, 1940–44; worked on designs for *Adame Mirroir,* ballet by Jean Genet, Theatre Marigny, Paris, 1948; lived in Choisel, France, 1949. Professor of Painting, Ecole Nationale Supérieure d'Art et d'Architecture, Brussels, 1950–62. President, Académie Royale des Beaux-Arts, Brussels, 1965. **Awards:** Prix de l'Académie Picard, Brussels, 1938; Prix de Reggio Emilio, 1955; Grand Prize for Painting, Province of Liège, 1961; Rembrandt Prize, Amsterdam, 1969; Prix Septemnnal, Province of Liège, 1987. Honorary Doctorate: Free University of Brussels, 1979. Member, Institut de France, 1977; Honorary Citizen, Town of Furnes, 1978. Foundation Paul Delvaux established, 1980; Musée Paul Delvaux. Saint-Idesbald, established, 1982. **Address:** Foundation Paul Delvaux, 42 Kabouterweg, 8460 Saint-Idesbald, Belgium. **Died:** In Veurne, Belgium, 20 July 1994.

Individual Exhibitions:

1925 Galerie Breckpot, Brussels (with Robert Giron)
1926 Galerie Manteau, Brussels
1927 Galerie Manteau, Brussels
1928 Galerie Manteau, Brussels (with Robert Giron)
Palais des Beaux-Arts, Brussels
1929 Galerie Manteau, Brussels
1930 Palais des Beaux-Arts, Brussels
1933 Atelier de la Grosse-Tour, Brussels
1934 Palais des Beaux-Arts, Brussels
1936 Palais des Beaux-Arts, Brussels (with Rene Magritte)
1937 Palais des Beaux-Arts, Brussels
Galerie Esher Surrey, The Hague
1938 Palais des Beaux-Arts, Brussels
London Gallery
1940 Palais des Beaux-Arts, Brussels
1943 Galerie Lou Cosyn, Brussels
1944 Palais des Beaux-Arts, Brussels
1946 Julien Levy Gallery, New York
Redfern Gallery, London
1948 Julien Levy Gallery, New York
APIAW, Liège, Belgium
Galerie René Drouin, Paris
Sidney Janis Gallery, New York
1949 Palais des Beaux-Arts, Brussels
Société Royale des Beaux Arts, Verviers, Belgium
1952 Casino Communal, Knokke-le-Zoute, Belgium (with Rene Magritte)
1955 Atelier Verannaeman, Courtrai, Belgium
Het Atelier, Deurne, Antwerp
1956 Atelier Veranneman, Courtrai, Belgium
1957 Maison Haute, Boitsfort, Belgium
Cercle Royal, Charleroi, Belgium (with Marc Chagall)
1959 Staempfli Gallery, New York
1962 APIAW, Liège, Belgium
Musée des Beaux-Arts, Ostende, Belgium
Renée Lachowsky and Lou Cosyn, Brussels
1963 Staempfli Gallery, New York
1964 Galerie Helikon, Hasselt, Belgium
Staempfli Gallery, New York
1965 Musée des Beaux-Arts, Mons, Belgium
Galerie Luttece, Paris
1966 Galleria del Naviglio, Milan
Gallerie del Naviglio, Turin
Gallerie Krugier, Geneva
Palais des Beaux-Arts, Lille, France
1967 Galerie Bateau-Lavoir, Paris
New Smith Galerie, Brussels
Musée d'Ixelles, Brussels
1968 Société Royale des Beaux Arts, Verviers, Belgium
Belgisches Haus, Cologne
1969 Staempfli Gallery, New York
Musée des Arts Décoratifs, Paris
1970 Musée de Peinture et de Sculpture, Grenoble, France
1971 Staempfli Gallery, New York
1972 Atelier Veranneman, Courtrai, Belgium
1973 Casino Knokke-Heist, Belgium
Museum Boymans-van-Beuningen, Rotterdam
1974 Art Salon Ginza Nova, Tokyo
Museo de Arte Moderno, Mexico City (with James Ensor and Rene Magritte)
Cultural Center, New York
Galerie Isy Brachot, Brussels (with Domenico Gnoli and Rene Magritte)
1975 Museum of Modern Art, Tokyo (travelled to the Museum of Modern Art, Kyoto)
Galerie Isy Brachot, Brussels
Palais des Beaux-Arts, Brussels (with James Ensor)
1976 Palais de l'Europe, Menton, France
1977 Galerie Isy Brachot, Brussels
Galerie Isy Brachot, Basle
Ilot St. Georges, Liège, Belgium
Musée Royaux des Beaux-Arts, Brussels
1978 Galerie Isy Brachot, Paris
1980 Gentre Cultural de la Communaute Francaise de Belgique, Paris
San Francisco Museum of Modern Art
Museum of Fine Art, Montreal
1981 Museum of Art, Newport Beach, California
La Chataigneraie, Flemmalle, Liège, Belgium
Bienal, Sao Paulo
1982 Museum of Modern Art, Rio de Janeiro
Museum of Modern Art, Caracas
1989 *Paul Delvaux,* Kunsthalle der Hypo-Kulturstiftung, Munich
1990 Galerie Isy Brachot, Paris
1997 *Paul Delvaux 1897–1994,* Musee d'Art Moderne, Brussels (travelled to Musees Royaux des Beaux-Arts de Belgique, Brussels; Musées d'Art Ancien, Brussels)

Paul Delvaux: *Women of the Telephone.* ©P. Delvaux Foundation—St. Idesbald, Belgium/Licensed by VAGA, New York, NY.

1998 *Delvaux,* Fundacion Juan March, Madrid

Selected Group Exhibitions:

1924 Le Sillon, Brussels
1935 *Exposition Internatinale d'Art Moderne,* Brussels
1938 *Internationale du Surrealisme,* Galerie des Beaux-Arts, Paris
1942 *Surrealist Exhibition,* 451 Madison Avenue, New York
1948 *Biennale,* Venice
1952 *Contemporary Belgian Art,* Mitsikoshi Department Store, Tokyo
1961 *Midwestern Exhibition of Belgian Painters,* Arts Club of Chicago (toured the Midwestern states)
1968 *Dada, Surrealism and Their Heritage,* Museum of Modern Art, New York
1972 *Peintures de l'Imaginaire: Symbolistes et Surrealists Belge,* Grand Palais, Paris
1982 *A Century of Modern Drawing,* British Museum, London
1988 *The Marshall Frankel Collection,* Museum of Contemporary Art, Chicago
Paul Delvaux, Rene Magritte, Robert Elkon Gallery, New York
Foundation Giannada, Martigny, Switzerland
1990 *Art in Belgium: Flanders and Wallonia in the 20th Century—A Point of View,* Musee d'Art Moderne de la Ville de Paris, Paris
1994 *The Joseph Winterbotham Collection,* The Art Institute of Chicago
1996 *From Ensor to Delvaux: Ensor, Spilliaert, Permeke, Magritte, Delvaux,* Museum voor Moderne Kunst, Ostend, Belgium
1997 *Flemish and Dutch Painting: From Van Gogh, Ensor, Magritte and Mondrian to Contemporary Artists,* Palazzo Grassi, Venice
From Ensor to Delvaux, Museum voor Moderne Kunst, Ostend, Belgium

Collections:

Delvaux Museum, St. Idesbald, Belgium; Musee Royaux des Beaux-Arts, Brussels; Musee Royaux des Beaux-Arts, Antwerp; Musee d'Art Moderne, Brussels; Musee des Beaux-Arts, Charleroi, Belgium; Gemeentemuseum, The Hague; Tate Gallery, London; Centre Georges Pompidou, Paris; Museum of Modern Art, New York; Art Institute of Chicago.

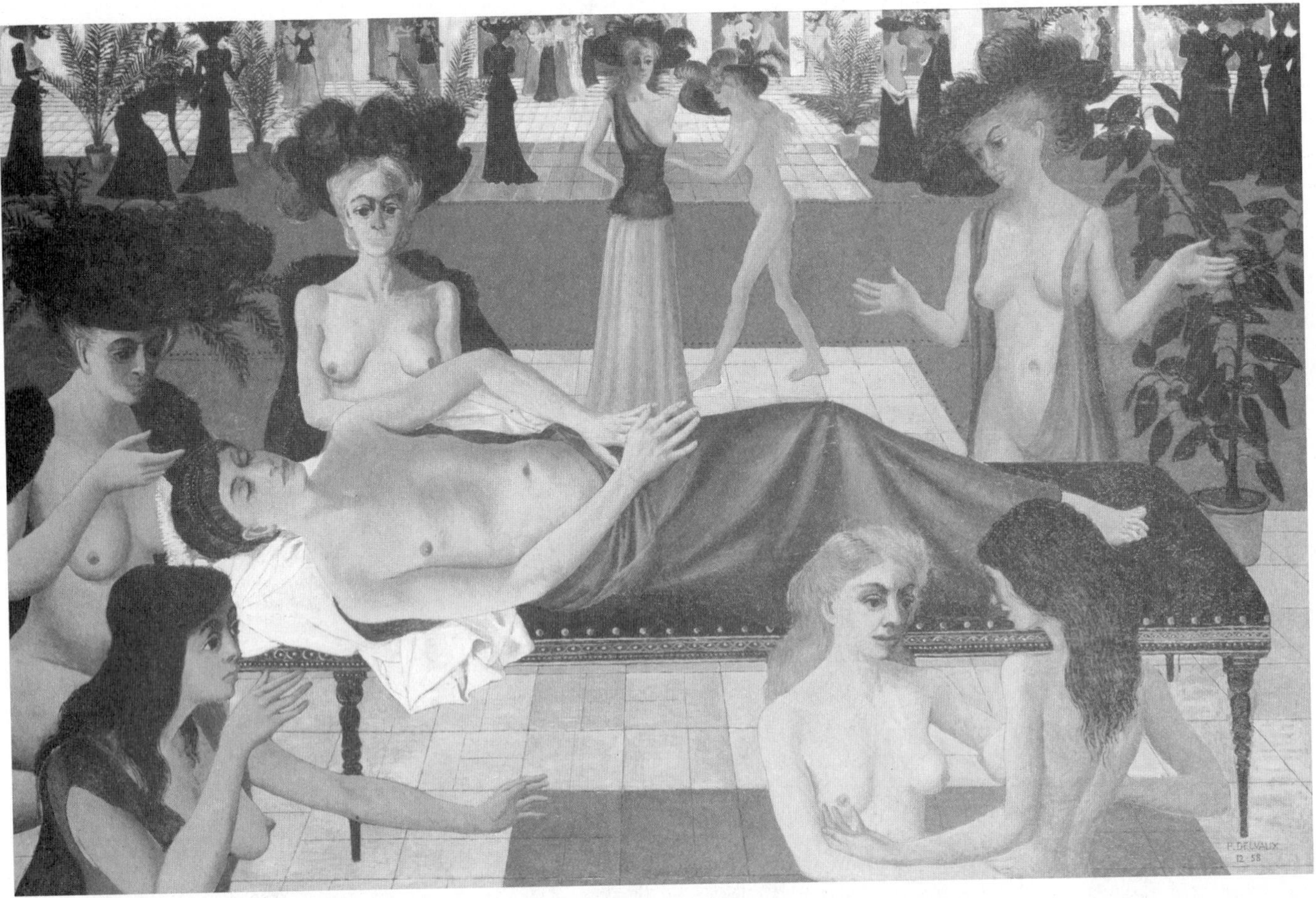

Paul Delvaux: *Antinous,* 1958. ©P. Delvaux Foundation—St. Idesbald, Belgium/Licensed by VAGA, New York, NY.

Publications:

By DELVAUX: Book—*Sept Dialogues avec Paul Delvaux, Accompagnes de Sept Lettres Imaginaires,* with Jacques Meuris, Paris 1971. **Articles**—''Notice sur James Ensor'' and ''Notice sur Alfred Bastien'' in *Annuaire de l'Académie Royale de Belgique,* Brussels 1963; ''A propos d'un Voyage en Greece'' in *Bulletin de l'Academie Royale de Belgique,* Brussels 1965.

On DELVAUX: Books—*Paul Delvaux ou les Rêves Eveillés* by Rene Gaffe, Brussels 1945; *Paul Delvaux* by Claude Spaak, Antwerp 1948; *Paul Delvaux: Der Mensch, her Maler* by Paul Aloise de Bock, Hamburg 1965, as *Paul Delvaux: L'Homme. Le Peintre: Psychologie d'Un Art,* Brussels 1967; *Cahiers Paul Delvaux I: Premières Lithographies,* Paris 1969; *Paul Delvaux II: L'Oeuvre Grave 1966–69,* Paris 1969; *Paul Delvaux* by Antoine Terrase, Paris 1972; *Paul Delvaux: Catalog Raisonne* by Michel Burton and Jean Clair, Brussels 1974; *Paul Delvaux: Catalog de l'Oeuvre Peint* by Michel Butor, Jean Clair and Suzanne Houbart-Wilken, Brussels 1975; *Paul Delvaux, Graphic Work* by Mira Jacob, Paris 1976; *Delvaux* by P. Emerson, Antwep 1985; *Paul Delvaux, Rene Magritte,* exhibition catalog, New York 1988; *Paul Delvaux* by Marc Rombaut, New York 1989; *Paul Delvaux 1897–1994,* exhibition catalog, Brussels 1997; *Flemish and Dutch Painting: From Van Gogh, Ensor, Magritte and Mondrian to Contemporary Artists,* New York 1997; *From Ensor to Delvaux: Ensor, Spilliaert, Permeke, Magritte, Delvaux,* exhibition catalog, with introduction by Willy van den Bussche, Ostend 1996; *Delvaux,* exhibition catalog, Madrid 1998. **Articles**—review in *Arts Review* (London), vol. 43, 1991–1992; review in *Apollo* (London), vol. 144, November 1996; ''Delvaux Feted at Last Back Home'' by Martin Bailey in *Art Newspaper* (Denville), vol. 8, April 1997; ''Paul Delvaux and the Empire of Women'' by Dale Mackenzie Brown in *Art News,* vol. 96, June 1997; ''Paul Delvaux'' by Tom Rosenthal in *Modern Painters,* vol. 10, Summer 1997; review by Fiona Bradley in *Burlington Magazine* (London), no. 1132, vol. 139, July 1997.

* * *

Paul Delvaux' earliest paintings belong to the Post-Impressionist mode. ''Holy Cross Square'' (1923) is a typical cityscape in the style of Utrillo, while ''Promenade on the Isle of Huy'' (1926) derives from Cézanne's landscape studies. In the late 1920s Delvaux adopted a primitive style reminiscent of Henri Rousseau. Depicting stylized nude figures in sylvan settings, ''Figures in the Forest'' (1928) and ''Pink and White'' (1929) achieve a remarkable serenity through simplicity of line and color. Over the next few years this style became increasingly expressionistic, focusing on crowd scenes in urban settings and culminating in ''Sleeping Venus'' (1932) and ''The Spitzner Museum'' (1933). In both works a supine female nude is juxtaposed with clothed figures in a museum environment of skeletons and display cases. As the artist later explained, their source was a bizarre exhibit he had encountered at the *Brussels Fair.* ''I was struck by an extraordinary display by the Spitzner Museum,'' he noted, ''with red velvet draperies at the window, two skeletons and a mechanical sleeping Venus . . . which was very sad and strange amid the hubbub of the merry-go-rounds and the frantic fun-seeking characteristic of such large carnivals.'' That this display deeply affected him is evidenced by the many skeletons and sleeping Venuses in his later work.

Toward 1934, fortified by his experience at the museum, Delvaux discovered Giorgio de Chirico—an encounter that was to leave a lasting impression on his work. Among other things, it precipitated his conversion to Surrealism which was to occupy him for the rest of his life. To some extent his preexisting iconography was superimposed on de Chirico's. His sleeping Venuses resemble the latter's reclining Ariadnes, while his skeletons correspond to various de Chirico statues and mannequins. In general he borrows freely from the Italian master, appropriating his vast, deserted public squares, his architectural settings, his claustrophobic interiors (''The Mirror,'' 1936), and his old-fashioned trains. Like the latter, and pursuant to Surrealist doctrine, he devotes himself to the ''marvelous''—revelatory—experience springing from the unconscious. Whence the supreme importance of mystery and enigma.

Drawing on this background and on his own experience, Delvaux creates paintings that are profoundly original, exerting a strange hypnotic power on the viewer. His scenes, which often take place at twilight, are essentially dramas of the mind in which figures, objects, and settings are juxtaposed according to the processes of dream. In this context his aesthetics revolve around incongruity and contradiction. Delvaux' characters are also uniquely his own. To some extent the skeleton illustrates the traditional mortality theme, especially in the late 1940s and 1950s when it appears in a series devoted to Christian subjects. In many cases, however, it simply represents the armature of the body and as such acquires a purely architectural significance. Beginning in 1939 the artist introduced a character taken from Jules Verne's *Journey to the Center of the Earth,* the heroic scientist Prof. Otto Liedenbrock (Prof. von Hardwigg in the English translations). In painting after painting, including ''The Phases of the Moon'' (1939), we see the good professor intent on examining a mineral specimen, totally oblivious to the bevy of nude beauties surrounding him. This is a frequent theme in his work: the impossibility of significant connection between the sexes. Certainly it reflects the artist's own ambivalence toward women, springing from a childhood shaped by a domineering mother. This explains why all the women in his paintings look the same—they are all equally seductive, all equally threatening. Part of the fascination of a Delvaux painting resides in its violation of the taboo against public nudity. Typically he places his nude or semi-nude female protagonists in a public setting where they remain totally unaffected by the experience, distracted, even aloof. Undeniably attractive, they seem impervious to our stares. In the analysis Delvaux specializes in tantalizing his audience—and himself—with unattainable dreams. Above all, he is the master of frigid eroticism.

—Willard Bohn

The artist's extraordinarily long life—he died in 1994 at the age of 96, having painted actively until blindness forced him to desist in 1986—enabled him to outlast those cycles of critical opinion which devalued the figurative tradition. In the current reappraisal of academic or academic-seeming painting, his enduring preoccupation with the female nude was reaffirmed. Although throughout most of his life his renown was limited for the most part to Europe, in his later years a series of important exhibitions in New York and Tokyo in addition to those on the continent, as well as ascending prices at auction, allowed him to witness an international extension of his reputation.

—Barbara Cortright

DEMAND, Thomas

Nationality: German. **Born:** Munich, Germany, 1964. **Education:** Studied at Akademie der Bildenden Künste, Munich, 1987–89; studied at Kunstakademie Düsseldorf, 1989–92; studied at Cité des Arts, Paris, 1992; Goldsmiths College, London, M. A. in Fine Arts, 1994; studied at Rijksakademie van Beeldende Kunsten, Amsterdam, 1995. **Career:** Lives and works in Berlin.

Selected Individual Exhibitions:

1991 Galerie Guy Ledune, Brussels
1992 Galerie Tanit, Munich
Förderkoje Art, Cologne
1994 Galerie Tanit, Cologne
Galerie Blancpain-Stepcynski, Geneva
1995 Victoria Miro Gallery, London
Galerie Guy Ledune, Brussels
1996 Galerie de l'ancienne poste, Le Channel, Calais, France
Galerie Tanit, Munich
Max Protetch Gallery, New York
1997 Victoria Miro Gallery, London
Thomas Demand, Galerie de l'ancienne poste, Le Channel; Calais, France; Centre d'art contemporain de Vassivière en Limousin, Beaumont-du-lac, France (catalog)
Galerie Monika Sprüth, Cologne
1998 *Thomas Demand,* Kunsthalle, Zurich; Kunsthalle Bielefeld, Germany (catalog)
Galleria Monica de Cardenas, Milan
303 Gallery, New York
Galerie Schipper & Krome, Berlin
1999 *Tunnel,* Art Now 17, Tate Gallery, London (catalog)
2000 *Thomas Demand,* Fondation Cartier pour l'art contemporain, Paris; Actes Sud, Arles (catalog)
Victoria Miro Gallery, London
Galerie Peter Kilchmann, Zurich
Galerie Monika Sprüth, Cologne

Selected Group Exhibitions:

1990 *Gezeigt in sieben Mosigwellen,* Galerie Löhrl, Monchengladbach
1991 *Quellen und Ergänzungen,* Galerie der Künstler, Munich
1993 *Het intelectuele Geweeten van de Kunst,* Galerie D'Eendt, Amsterdam
1994 *Scharf im Schauen,* Haus der kunst, Munich
1995 *Ars Viva 1995,* Anhaltische Gemäldegalerie, Dessau, Germany; Frankfurter Kunstverein, Frankfurt; Nürnberger Kunsthalle, Nuremberg
Le paysage retrouvé, Galerie Renos Xippas, Paris

Temples, Victoria Miro Gallery, London
Ulrich Meister und Thomas Demand, Galerie Christian Gögger, Munich
1996 *New Photography 12,* Museum of Modern Art, New York
Campo 6: The Spiral Village, Galleria Civica d'arte contemporaneo, Turin, Italy; Bonnefanten Museum, Maastricht, The Netherlands
Raumbilder-Bildräume, Museum Folkwang, Essen, Germany
Radical Images, Johanneum, Steir, Germany; Landesmuseum, Graz, Austria
1997 *Positionen Künstlerischer Photographie in Deutschland Seit 1945,* Berlinische Gallery, Berlin; Martin Gropius Bau, Berlin (catalog)
Elsewhere, Carnegie Museum of Art, Pittsburgh (catalog)
Stills: Emerging Photography in the 1990s, Walker Art Center, Minneapolis (catalog)
Making It Real, Reykjavik Municipal Museum, Iceland; ICI/The Aldrich Museum of Contemporary Art, Ridgefield, Connecticut
1998 *Etre nature,* Fondation Cartier pour l'art contemporain, Paris; Actes Sud, Arles (catalog)
Every Day, 11th Biennale of Sydney, Museum of Contemporary Art (catalog)
Vollkommen gewöhnlich, Kunstverein Freiburg im Marienbad, Germany; Germanisches Nationalmuseum Nürnberg, Nuremberg; Kunstverein Braunschweig, Germany; Kunsthalle zu Kiel, Germany; Kunstsammlung Gera, Germany
Artificial, MoCBA, Barcelona
1999 *Grosse Illusionen: Thomas Demand, Andreas Gursky, Edward Ruscha,* Kunstmuseum Bonn, Germany; Museum of Contemporary Art, Miami (catalog)
The Mirror's Edge, Vancouver Art Gallery; Castello di Rivoli, Turin, Italy; Tramway, Glasgow (catalog)
The Carnegie International, Carnegie Museum of Art, Pittsburgh (catalog)
Photography: An Expanded View, Recent Acquisitions, Solomon R. Guggenheim Museum, New York
2000 *Vision and Reality,* Louisiana Museum of Modern Art, Humlebaek, Denmark (catalog)
The Age of Influence, Museum of Contemporary Art, Chicago
Supermodel, Massachusetts Museum of Contemporary Art
Small World: Dioramas in Contemporary Art, Museum of Contemporary Art, San Diego/La Jolla (catalog)

Publications:

By DEMAND: Articles—''Notion of Space: A Conversation'' with Vik Muniz in *Blind Spot,* Fall-Winter 1996.

On DEMAND: Articles—''Thomas Demand: Catastrophic Space'' by Stephen Horne in *Parachute,* October-December 1999; ''Thomas Demand: Paper Chases'' by Nancy Princenthal in *Art/Text,* November 1999-January 2000; ''Thomas Demand: Foggy Intersections of Photography and Truth'' by Martha Schwendener in *Flash Art,* October 2000; ''Les espaces improbables de Thomas Demand'' by Philippe Nolde in *Beaux Arts Magazine,* January 2001.

* * *

DE MARIA, Nicola

Nationality: Italian. **Born:** Foglianise, near Benevento, Italy, 6 December 1954. **Career:** Lives and works in Turin. **Agent:** Galerie Kaess-Weiss, Grüneisenstrasse 19, D-70184, Stuttgart; Galerie Lelong, 20 West 57th Street, New York, New York, 10019; Galerie Iris Wazzau, Promenade 79, CH-7270, Davos. **Address:** Corso G. Agnelli 46/12, 10137 Turin, Italy.

Individual Exhibitions:

1975 Galleriaforma, Genoa
1976 Galleria Amelio, Naples
1977 Galleria Toselli, Milan
1978 Galleria Toselli, Milan
Galerie Maenz, Cologne
Galleria Persano, Turin
1979 Galleria Mario Diacono, Bologna
Galerie Annemarie Verna, Zurich (with Francesco Clemente and Mimmo Paladino)
1980 Galleria Toselli, Milan
Galerie Maenz, Cologne
Galleria Persano, Turin
Galerie Annemarie Verna, Zurich
1983 Kunsthalle, Basle
1992 *Musica del Mare,* Galerie Lelong, Paris (catalog)
1994 Galerie Lelong, New York
Mario Diacono Gallery, Boston
Galleria Col, Osaka
Kunstverein Ludwigsburg
Galleria Alberto Valerio, Brescia
1995 Galleria Col, Osaka
Galleria Cardi, Milano
1996 Galleria Cardi, Bologna
Galerie Lelong, Zurich
Portside Gallery, Yokohama
Galleria Cardi, Turin
Galerie Lelong, Paris
1997 Galerie Borkowki, Hannover
Galerie Beck & Eggeling, Dusseldorf
Galleria Col, Osaka
Galleria Cardi, Basel
Galleria Cardi, Milan

Selected Group Exhibitions:

1980 *Arte e Critica 1980,* Galleria Nazionale d'Arte Moderna, Rome (and 1981)
1981 *Identité Italienne,* Centre Georges Pompidou, Paris
1985 *The European Iceberg,* Art Gallery of Ontario, Toronto
1986 *Aspects of Italian Art 1960–85,* Kunstverein, Frankfurt
1996 *Contemporary Italian Painting,* Galerie Kaess-Weiss, Stuttgart

Color and Structure: De Maria, Mangold, Swanger, Tuttle, Thursz, Galerie Lelong, New York
1997 *Minimalia: An Italian Vision in 20th-Century Art,* Palazzo Querini Dubois, Venice (traveled to Rome and New York)
100 Giorni del 1992, Cardi Galleria d'Arte, Milan
Giorni, Parole, Stelle, Fiori, Musée et Centre d'Art Contemporain de Montbéliard (also Kunstverein Ludwigsburg) (catalog)

Publications:

On DE MARIA: Books—*The Italian Trans-Avantgarde* by Achille Bonito Oliva, Milan 1980; *Nicola De Maria,* exhibition catalog with text by Jean-Christophe Ammann, Basle 1983. **Articles—**''Nicola de Maria'' by M. Bandini in *Data* (Milan), October/November 1976; ''Espansivo Eccessivo: Osservazioni sulla Giovane Arte Italiana'' by Jean-Christophe Ammann in *Domus* (Milan), April 1979; ''Il Primo Catalogo degli Artisti Nuovi'' by F. Alinovi, R. Barilli and R. Daolio in *Bolaffiarte* (Turin), March 1980; ''Restaurant im Bundestag Bonn'' by Ingeborg Flagge in *Baumeister,* vol. 91, March 1994; ''Nicola De Maria'' by Thomas McEvilley in *Artforum,* vol. 32, no. 7, March 1994; ''Nicola de Maria'' by Hervé Vanel in *Beaux Arts Magazine,* no. 126, September 1994.

* * *

Among the artists of the *Transavantgarde,* Nicola De Maria certainly has the least recourse to ''quotation.'' His pictorial lyricism is extravagant, devoid of figuration and abstraction and relative designs. Nearly always conceived in relation to the surroundings (and so beyond the borders of the picture), his painting, always annotated in a symbolic writing, is wholly manifested in a space that seems as far distant as the heavenly vault. The space of his painting, a vision of the void, is crowded with moments of color, very thin forms and evanescent shapes freely interwoven and generating rich ''contaminations.'' In this respect Nicola De Maria comes close to the compositional balances of Paul Klee, particularly to those that alternate the visible and the invisible.

As early as 1978, in a work with the significant title of ''Philosophy of Magic and of Works of Art,'' De Maria had stressed his rapport with the liberation of painting. The form and color indicated a vision made of distances, of chromatic improvisations. Their spatiality was something enigmatic and impalpable.

Ut pictura poesis might be De Maria's motto. Painting as a poetry of silence, of something constantly changing in the infinity of light, animates his noble work through beauty of design and color. The artist paints as if he were digging in the transcendental splendor of an eternal sunset. But the sunset—not the decline—of art presages a new dawn. Its own shadow or reflection, De Maria's changeful painting is the most complete manifestation of that. He concentrates regard on it until it is lost, for the changing of the colors is at once visible and hidden.

De Maria loves the unaccustomed and the exotic: indeed, one of his works is called ''I Am African, I Am Asian'' (1980).

In another work, ''Quore'' (1982), he portrays an environment that might be called a (provisional) exposition of the work of art, a study of the rich path taken by responses between the single parts of a work and the spatiality of the work as a whole. The single elements of which it is composed (a big painted card, a handbag also painted, and a series of little squares) have a clear meaning in themselves and, of course, in the context in which they are found. In ''Quore'' the spatiality of the colors expands their specificity, setting the real significant symbols of the painting at an almost unattainable distance. The inimitable visual evolution seems to take place somewhere else, somehow outside the visual range of the eye. It is a magical moment, colored by painting that continually changes even when it displays subtle material thicknesses and spontaneous writing. The ensemble is in unstable equilibrium, which extends the moment in contemplative rapture. Invisible at the center of the work, there dominates the fantasy of the artist (or the heart of art); the shifts of his imagination recognizable in the colors and the writing can be vaguely seen. The effect of the writing, the handmaid of the work, leads to the heart of art, to the rediscovery of an unsullied grace of color and symbol. But it is the existential abyss that gives them their beauty; to paraphrase Ungaretti, when Nicola De Maria finds a color or a symbol it is as if it were discovered in the abyss of the starry heavens. Thus his work, an esoteric work, is a sort of maze, not walled at all but open to the far distance of an interior light, visible only to the veiled eye of poetry.

—Italo Mussa

DE MARIA, Walter (Joseph)

Nationality: American. **Born:** Albany, California, 1 October 1935. **Education:** University of California, Berkeley, 1953–59, B.A. in history 1957, M.A. in art 1959. **Career:** Organized ''happenings'' at the University of California and at the California School of Art, San Francisco, 1959–60; drummer with the group Velvet Underground, 1965. Now lives and works in New York. **Awards:** Guggenheim fellowship, 1969; Mathew Sculpture Prize, Art Institute of Chicago, 1976. **Address:** c/o Gagosian Gallery, 555 West 24th St., New York, New York 10011, U.S.A.; Dia Center for the Arts (Chelsea), 548 West 22nd Street, New York, New York 10011.

Individual Exhibitions:

1963 9 Great Jones Street, New York
1965 Paula Cooper Gallery, New York
1966 Cordier Ekstrom Gallery, New York
1968 Nicholas Wilder Gallery, Los Angeles
Galerie Heiner Friedrich, Munich
1969 Dwan Gallery, New York
1972 Kunstmuseum, Basel
1974 Heinrich Friedrich Inc., New York
Hessisches Landesmuseum, Darmstadt
1977 *The New York Earth Room/The Equal Area Series,* Heiner Friedrich Gallery, New York
1979 *The Broken Kilometer,* Heiner Friedrich Gallery, New York
1981 *360° I Ching/64 Sculptures,* Centre Georges Pompidou, Paris
1982 Centre Georges Pompidou, Paris
1986 Xavier Fourcade Inc., New York
2000 *The 2000 Sculpture,* Kunsthaus, Zurich (traveling exhibition) (catalog)
Walter De Maria: 1900 Milano 2000, Fondazione Prada, Milan (catalog)

Selected Group Exhibitions:

1968 *Directions 1: Options,* Milwaukee Art Center
1969 *When Attitudes Become Form,* Kunsthalle, Berne (toured Europe)
1970 *Information,* Museum of Modern Art, New York
1971 *Guggenheim International,* Guggenheim Museum, New York
1972 *Diagrams and Drawings,* Kunstverein, Stuttgart (toured Switzerland and the Netherlands)
1973 *Medium Fotografie,* Stadisches Museum, Leverkusen, West Germany
1975 *Masterworks in Wood: The 20th Century,* Portland Art Museum, Oregon
1976 *Rooms, P.S. 1:* Institute for Art and Urban Resources, New York
1977 *Biennale,* Venice
1994 *Exhibition: Anna & Bernhard Blume, Walter de Maria,* Museum Moderner Kunst Stiftung Ludwing Wein, Wien (catalog)
1997 *Documenta 10,* Kassel, Germany
1999 *Von Beuys bis Cindy Sherman,* Stadtische Galerie im Lenbachhaus, Munich
Histoire d'Are, Versailles, France
2000 *Le Desert,* Fondation Cartier, Paris

Collections:

Museum of Modern Art, New York; Whitney Museum, New York; Dia Art Foundation, New York; Kunstmuseum, Basel.

Publications:

By DE MARIA: Articles—text in *The New Avant-Garde,* New York and London 1972; ''Project for Munich'' in *Domus* (Milan), August 1973; ''The Lightning Field'' in *Artforum* (New York), April 1980; ''The Owner's Choice—Some Words About Private Viewing'' with Jan van Adrichem and Martin Visser in *Jong Holland,* vol. 13, no. 2, 1997.

On DE MARIA: Books—*Changing: Essays in Art Criticism* by Lucy Lippard, New York 1971; *The New Avant-Garde* by Gregoire Muller, New York and London 1972; *6 Years: The Dematerialization of the Art Object* by Lucy Lippard, New York and London 1973; *Walter De Maria,* exhibition catalog, with text by H. H. Schmidt, Darmstadt 1974; *Walter De Maria,* exhibition catalog edited by Xavier Fourcade, New York 1986. **Articles—**''Walter DeMaria'' by Jill Johnston in *Artnews* (New York), February 1963; ''Walter De Maria: Word and Thing'' by Dennis Adrian in *Artforum* (New York), January 1967; ''A Sedimentation of the Mind: Earth Projects'' by Robert Smithson in *Artforum* (New York), September 1968; ''Walter De Maria: The Singular Experience'' by David Bourdon in *Art International* (Lugano, Switzerland), December 1968; ''Walter De Maria'' by Germano Celant in *Casabella* (Milan), March 1969; ''Drawing Lines in the Desert'' by Eric Cameron in *Studio International* (London), October 1970; ''Artworks on the Land'' by Elizabeth C. Baker in *Art in America* (New York), January 1976; ''De Maria: Elements'' by Roberta Smith in *Art in America* (New York), May 1978; ''Walter De Maria's 'The Broken Kilometer''' by Brian Wallis in *Arts Magazine* (New York), February 1980; ''Walter De Maria: Les Danger de l'Art'' by Jean-Marc Poinsot in *Art Press* (Paris), May 1981; ''Exertzitien in der Wuste: Eine Reise zu Walter De Maria's 'Bitzfeld' nach Neu-Mexiko'' by Gunter Metken in *Die Zeit* (Hamburg), 9 April 1982; ''Walter De Maria: The Broken Kilometer'' by Ludger Derenthal in *Kunst und Antiquitäten,* no. 9, September 1994; ''Walter de Maria: Measure and Substance'' by Neville Wakefield in *Flash Art (International Edition),* no. 182, May/June 1995; ''Passer la Nuit Avec une Oeuvre: Quelques Notes à Propos d'Un Voyage au Lightning Field de Walter de Maria'' by Rober Racine in *Parachute,* no. 80, October-December 1995; ''The Illuminarti'' by Chris McAuliffe in *World Art,* no. 2, 1996; ''The Lightning Field'' by Bruce Grierson in *Saturday Night,* vol. 111, no. 10, December 1996.

*

I feel proud to have started minimal art and land art.

—Walter De Maria

DENES, Agnes (Cecilia)

Nationality: American. **Born:** Budapest, Hungary, 31 May 1938; left Hungary with parents to live in Stockholm, 1948; moved to the United States, 1954. **Education:** New School for Social Research, New York, 1959–63; City College of New York, 1961–62; Columbia University, New York (M. L. Robinson Scholar), 1964–66. **Career:** Independent artist; lives and works in New York. Instructor of fine arts: School of Visual Arts, New York, 1974–79; Skowhegan School of Painting and Sculpture, Maine, 1979; University of Genoa, Italy, 1986; School of Architecture, University of Pennsylvania, 1991. Has lectured at over 100 universities in the United States and abroad and speaks at global conferences. **Awards:** New York State Council of the Arts, 1972, 1974, 1980, 1984; National Invitational Purchase Award, Albion College, Michigan, 1973; National Endowment for the Arts fellowship, 1974, 1975, 1981, 1989; National Invitational Purchase Award, Rutgers University, New Brunswick, New Jersey, 1975; International Women's Year Award, 1976; Museum of Modern Art Purchase with CAPS matching grant, 1976; Berthe Von Moschzisker Prize, 1980; Donald McPhail Award, Print Club of Philadelphia, 1982; Purchase Award, American Academy and Institute of Arts and Letters, New York, 1985; Thord-Gray Memorial Fund Grant, American Scandinavian Foundation, 1987; Eugene McDermott Achievement Award, M.I.T., 1990; Purchase Grant, Herbert F. Johnson Museum of Art, 1993; Watson Award for Transdisciplinary Achievement in the Arts, Carnegie Mellon University, 2000. Fellow at Massachusetts Institute of Technology, Carnegie-Mellon Institute, and DAAD. Honorary doctorate, Ripon College, Wisconsin. **Address:** 595 Broadway, New York, New York 10012, U.S.A.

Individual Exhibitions:

1965 Columbia University, New York
1966 Granite Gallery, New York
1967 New Masters Gallery, New York

Agnes Denes: *Wheatfields—A Confrontation, two acres of wheat planted and harvested by the artist, Battery Park landfill, downtown Manhattan—Summer, 1982 (with Statue of Liberty).* ©Agnes Denes.

1968 Ruth White Gallery, New York
1972 A.I.R. Gallery, New York
1974 Ohio State University, Columbus
Perspectives, Corcoran Gallery, Washington, D.C. (toured the United States)
1975 Stefanotty Gallery, New York
Galleria Forma, Genoa
Sawyer Gallery, San Francisco
University of California Art Museum, Berkeley
Long Beach Art Museum, California
1976 Douglass College, Rutgers University, New Brunswick, New Jersey
Newport Harbor Art Museum, Newport Beach, California
Sculptures of the Mind, University of Akron, Ohio
1977 Tyler School of Art, Temple University, Philadelphia
Animi Pathema—The Emotional Animal, 112 Greene Street Gallery, New York
1978 Amerika Haus, West Berlin
Ikon Gallery, Birmingham, England
Franklin Furnace, New York
Sculptures of the Mind, Centre Culturel American, Paris
1979 Institute of Contemporary Arts, London
Studio d'Arte Cannaviello, Milan
1980 Hayden Gallery, Massachusetts Institute of Technology, Cambridge
Lund Galleriet, Sweden
Galerie Aronowitsch, Stockholm
Anima/Persona—The Seed, Elise Meyer Gallery, New York
1981 Elise Meyer Gallery, New York (print retrospective)
1982 Kunsthalle, Nuremberg, West Germany
1985 University of Hawaii, Honolulu
Northern Illinois University, Chicago
1986 Ricardo Barreto Arte Contemporaneo, Guadalajara, Mexico
1990 *Agnes Denes: Concept Into Form—Works 1970–1990,* Arts Club of Chicago
Anselmo Alvarez Galeria de Arte, Madrid
1992 Herbert F. Johnson Museum of Art, Ithaca, New York (retrospective)
1994 Wynn Kramarsky, New York
1996 *The Visionary Art of Agnes Denes,* Gibson Gallery, State University of New York at Potsdam
2000 *Poetry Walk—Refections: Pools of Thought (With Time Capsule 2000–3000 A.D.),* University of Virginia, Charlottesville

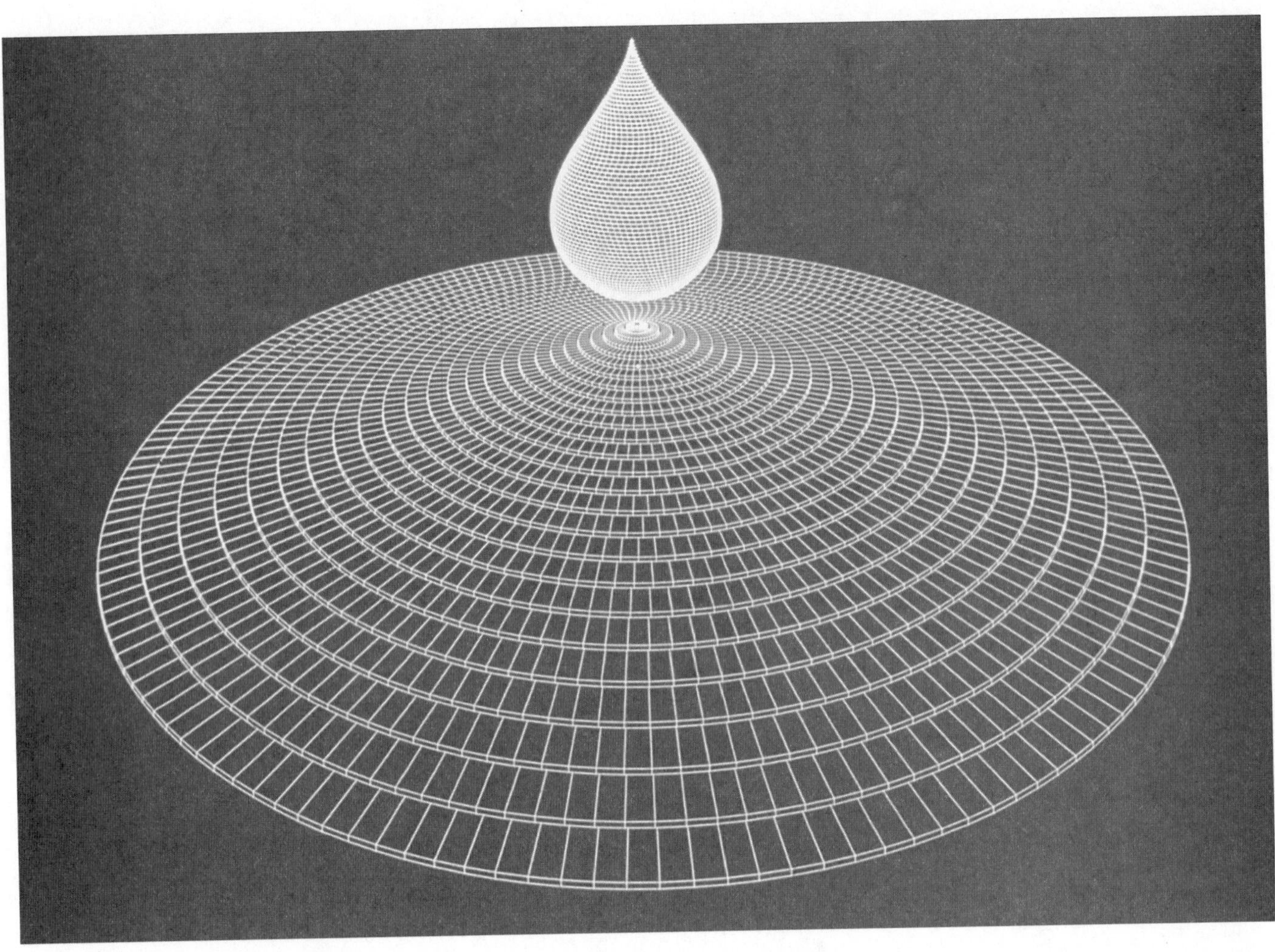

Agnes Denes: *Teardrop—Monument to Being Earthbound,* 1984. Photo by the artist. ©Agnes Denes.

Selected Group Exhibitions:

1980 Museo de Arte Contemporanea da Universidade de Sao Paolo
Drawings: The Pluralist Decade, Institute of Contemporary Art, Philadelphia (travelled to Denmark, Norway, Spain, and Portugal)
Cartes et Figure de la Terre, Musée d'Art Moderne, Paris
1983 *World Print Four,* San Francisco Museum of Modern Art (travelled throughout the United States and to Japan)
1985 Moderna Museet, Stockholm
1987 *International Art Show for the End of World Hunger,* Minnesota Museum of Art, St. Paul (travelled throughout the United States, Europe, and South America)
1989 *Making Their Mark,* Cincinnati Art Museum (travelled to New Orleans, Denver, and Philadelphia)
1991 *The Contemporary Drawing: Existence, Passage and the Dream,* Rose Art Museum, Waltham, Massachusetts
Atlas: Curatorial Project #7, Art Gallery of Hamilton, Ontario, Canada
1992 *Strata,* Museum of Contemporary Art, Helsinki, and The Art Museum of Tampere, Finland
1993 *Différentes Natures,* La Defense, Paris
1996 *Map,* Beaconsfield, London, and Institute of International Visual Arts, London
1999 *Afterimage: Drawing Through Process,* Museum of Contemporary Art, Los Angeles

Collections:

Museum of Modern Art, New York; Whitney Museum, New York; Metropolitan Museum of Art, New York; University of Massachusetts, Amherst; National Museum of American Art, Washington, D.C.; Corcoran Gallery, Washington, D.C.; Allen Memorial Art Museum, Oberlin College, Ohio; Israel Museum, Jerusalem; Moderna Museet, Stockholm; Kunsthalle, Nuremberg.

Permanent Public Installations and Environmental Sculptures:

Wheatfield, New York 1982; *Stelae,* Santa Maria di Castello, Italy; *Hypersphere,* First National Bank of Chicago Headquarters, New York; *Introspection 1: Evolution,* Harold Washington Library Center, Chicago; *Circle of Megaliths with Sundial,* Colombus, Ohio; *Tree Mountain—A Living Time Capsule,* Ylöjärvi, Finland.

Publications:

By DENES: Books—*Sculptures of the Mind,* Akron, Ohio 1976; *Paradox and Essence,* Rome 1977; *Isometric Systems in Isotropic Space—Map Projections,* Rochester, New York 1979; *Book of Dust: The Beginning and the End of Time, and Thereafter,* Rochester, New York 1988. **Articles—**''Pyramid Series'' in *Skira Annual,* Geneva 1979; ''Rice/Tree/Burial Project'' in *White Walls,* Chicago 1978; ''Organic Notebooks'' in *Konstnarsbocker—Artists' Books—Kaledoskop,* Sweden; ''Notes on a Visual Philosophy'' in *Symmetry: Unifying Human Understanding,* London 1986; ''The Dream'' in *Critical Inquiry,* vol. 16, no. 4, Summer 1990; ''Daring to Dream: Art in the Public Sphere'' in *Critical Inquiry 16,* Chicago 1990; ''Notes on Eco-Logic'' in *Leonardo,* vol. 26, no. 5, 1993; ''Entropy II—Amorphous Continents'' in *New Observations* (New York), no. 105, March-April 1995; ''Artistic Vision and Molecular Genetics'' in *Art Journal* (New York), vol. 55, Spring 1996.

On DENES: Books—*6 Years: The Dematerialization of the Art Object* by Lucy Lippard, New York 1973; *Agnes Denes: Perspectives,* exhibition catalog, with texts by Roy Slade, Lawrence Alloway, and Susan Collins, Washington, D.C. 1974; *Agnes Denes: Sculptures of the Mind,* exhibition catalog, with an introduction by Thomas Deecke, West Berlin 1978; *Agnes Denes: Work 1968–78,* exhibition catalog, Birmingham, England 1978; *Agnes Denes: Drawings, Objects, Graphics, Photos,* exhibition catalog, Lund, Sweden 1980; *Investigations: Probe, Structure, Analysis,* exhibition catalog with texts by Lynn Gumpert and Allan Schwartzman, New York 1980; *Agnes Denes 1968–1980,* exhibition catalog with text by Garry Garrels, Cambridge, Massachusetts 1980; *American Artists on Art* edited by Ellen Johnson, New York 1980; *Art in a Turbulent Era* by Peter Selz, Ann Arbor, Michigan 1985; *Agnes Denes at the Herbert F. Johnson Museum of Art,* with text by Denes and essays by numerous others, Ithaca, New York 1992; *Agnes Denes,* edited by Jill Hartz, Ithaca 1992; *The Visionary Art of Agnes Denes,* exhibition catalog, Potsdam 1996. **Articles—**''Agnes Denes'' by Barbara Reise in *Studio International* (London), December 1974; ''Agnes Denes: The Visual Presentation of Meaning'' by Peter Selz in *Art in America,* March 1975; ''Dynamic Visual Systems in Process: The Works of Agnes Denes'' by Phillip Smith in *Arts Magazine,* December 1975; ''Agnes Denes: The Ironies of Comprehension'' by Donald Kuspit in *Arts Magazine,* December 1981; ''Agnes Denes: The Triumph of the Will'' by Ronny Cohen in *Print Collectors Newsletter,* November 1982; review in *Art in America,* 3 April 1992; ''Opposites Attract: An Interview with Agnes Denes'' by S. Wallstein and E. van der Heeg in *Material 6,* Stockholm 1992; ''Agnes Denes at the Herbert F. Johnson Museum of Art, Cornell University'' by Eleanor Heartney in *Art in America* (New York), vol. 81, no. 4, April 1993; ''Which Public? Whose Art?'' by John K. Grande in *Espace* (Montreal), no. 29, Autumn 1994; ''Agnes Denes'' by Donald B. Kuspit in *Artforum International,* vol. 34, February 1996; ''Fields for Thought: The Art of Agnes Denes'' by James M. Clark in *Public Art Review* (St. Paul), vol. 8, no. 2, Spring-Summer 1997; ''Sculptural Conceptualism: A New Reading of the Work of Agnes Denes'' by Ricardo D. Barreto in *Sculpture* (Washington, D.C.), no. 4, May 1999; ''Afterimage: Drawing Through Process: The Museum of Contemporary Art'' by Charlene Roth in *New Art Examiner,* vol. 27, no. 3, November 1999; review by Peter Selz in *Sculpture* (Washington, D.C.), vol. 19, no. 10, December 2000.

*

All my work up to now seems to culminate in my environmental art. From the early poetry to the philosophical drawings, from the abandonment of painting to working without color for eleven years—a self-imposed discipline that allowed concepts to dictate the mode of presentation—this complex body of work I have created: the art put out into the world is perhaps the most fully realized.

My work that always reached beyond the boundaries of the art area to bring about a flow of communication among alien disciplines and address controversial global issues questioning the status quo and the endless contradictions we seem to accept into our lives. It touches on ecological, territorial, social, and cultural issues, celebrating our achievements, calling attention to our misconceptions and the most endearing of all human traits—our follies.

It is important to put art out into the world where it loses its preciousness but not its beauty, so it can touch all levels—elevate, communicate, be mysterious, provocative, ask disturbing questions and have a conscience. And be realized on a monumental scale when necessary. The art is freed to be true to itself. Before, I allowed it to dictate the mode of presentation; now I let it breathe and touch people's lives. Whether permanent or temporary, these are fully realized works that live and evolve in the environment.

In a time when the intelligent restructuring of our environment is imperative, this art can assume an important role. It can bring people together and it can effect meaningful communication. A well-conceived work can motivate people and influence how a place is perceived. Artistic vision, image, and metaphor are powerful tools of communication that can become expressions of human values with profound impact on our consciousness and collective destiny.

—Agnes Denes

* * *

Although her work bears no likeness to Moholy-Nagy's, Agnes Denes shares his awareness that science and philosophy can be used in the service of art for the purpose of sensitizing the individual and society. Like the brilliant earlier modernist, Denes does not fit into any art movement or school. Although she has been described as a Conceptual artist by some critics, and although like certain Conceptualists she deals with a variety of intellectual problems, she gives palpable form and specific aesthetic beauty resulting from the visual clarification of complexity to her scientific and/or philosophic probes. Her work brings new thoughts and insights into the art arena, stretching its boundaries, toward a new breadth of thought and vision.

Increasingly, as many artists have rejected formalist aesthetics, they have absorbed and appropriated material from other disciplines for art (or non-art) purposes, and Denes has turned to philosophy and science. But this is where we may easily misunderstand her. Denes is not interested in providing new scientific information. What she does rather is use the latest stages of scientific knowledge for the enrichment of artistic possibilities. She extends art, which traditionally had dealt with life and nature, into the realms of science; she is drawn to the enormous significance and creative energy in scientific thought. She also sees parallels between the structure of science and the structure of art.

At first encounter with Denes' work, one wonders about the relationship between X-ray photographs of the underlayers of famous paintings, diagrammatic studies of time and truth, the visualization of Pascal's triangle, concern with dust and bones, a visual presentation of human evolution, the exploration of organic cells through extreme magnification, a psychograph of artists' ''Profiles'' based on questionnaires, various ''abstract'' studies of the meaning of language and communications, and many other such analytical works. Yet a certain unity of concept and form slowly emerges.

In all her forays, Denes is attracted to the most basic of questions—the structure of matter and idea, the void, the meaning of life, the place of humanity in the world, the mysteriousness of human existence. It may be useful to point out that while her subject matter is essentially a unified one when viewed in terms of her broadest concerns, it is expressed in several different ways. Like much new and innovative art, some of it may be difficult to grasp. We are not accustomed to art which is presented in a philosophical/mathematical form. Her physical investigations (X-rays of paintings, magnifications of cell tissue, etc) or those which use anthropological and psychological material are, of course, more immediately accessible.

In 1968–69 Denes created her first major environmental project when she planted rice seeds to represent life and growth, chained trees to indicate interference with life and imply death, and buried her own Haiku poetry to symbolize the dialectical synthesis: human intellectual power. Since that time she has continued with important outdoor projects, outstanding among which was *Wheatfield—A Confrontation* (1982): the planting of a two-acre wheatfield at Battery Park in Lower Manhattan and the harvesting of 1,000 pounds of wheat. In 1987 she embarked on a commission for the Tamiami Airport in Florida of three large fields of green shrubs, wild flowers and poured concrete in the shape of *Flying Pyramids.* Also in 1987 she completed *Hypersphere—The Earth in the Shape of the Universe,* a lobby environment in New York's Equitable Tower of 144 panels of carved, frosted glass to form the ceiling which represents one of her earlier map projections.

Denes brings new philosophic insight into the abundance of available information, dealing with man's ''importance or insignificance in the universe.'' Her work is analytic in the Kantian sense. Her singular contribution is in the fact that her symbols remain visual, her attitude romantic, her approach intuitive. Denes' unique position in today's art is at the place where systematic and intuitive knowledge intersect.

—Peter Selz

DE VRIES, Herman

Nationality: Dutch. **Born:** Alkmaar, 11 July 1931. **Education:** Horticultural College, Hoorn, 1949–52. **Family:** Married in 1956 (divorced 1968); children: Mirjam, Marc, Dirk, Merik and Harmen Vincent. **Career:** Worked in the plant protection service, at the Institute for Applied Biological Research in Nature, Arnheim, 1952–68. First art activities, Alkmaar, 1953; first mobile works, 1954; first monochrome paintings and collages, 1956; participated in Zero group exhibitions, 1961–63; researched random systems, 1962–75; experimental language and poetry, 1965; chance and change processes, 1970. Published *NUL=Zero* magazine, Amsterdam, 1961–64; *Revue Integration,* Amsterdam, 1965–72; and Eschenau Summer Press (temporary travelling press), since 1974; editor of *Integration,* 1991-. **Agents:** Galerie Mueller-Roth, Christophstrasse 40–42, Stuttgart, Germany; Galerie Conrads, Poststrasse 3, 40213 Dusseldorf, Germany; Galerie Elke Dröscher, Grotinsweg 79, 22587 Hamburg, Germany; Galerie Aline Vidal, Rue Bonaparte 70, 75006 Paris, France; Art Affairs, Wittenburgergracht 313, 1082zl, Amsterdam, Holland. **Address:** Eschenau 29, 97478 Knetzgau, Germany.

Individual Exhibitions:

1959 Galerie 31, Dordrecht, Netherlands
1960 Mensa, Delft
1963 Galerie Wulfengasse 14, Klagenfurt, Austria
Metz and Company, Amsterdam
1964 Galerie D, Frankfurt
1965 Galerie Knoll, Basle
Galerie Akruell, Berne
Galerie Loehr, Frankfurt (with Colombo)
1967 'tVenster, Rotterdam
't Ouwe Tientje, Arnhem
Galerie Julicher, Mönchengladbach, West Germany
Galerie Hansjorg Mayer, Stuttgart
1968 Gemeentemuseum, The Hague
Nederlandse Kunststichting, Zeist, Netherlands
Felison, Ijmuiden, Netherlands
1969 Art Academy, Copenhagen
1970 Galerie Swart, Amsterdam
Galerie Swart, Amsterdam (with Frieder Nake)
Kunsthistorisch Instituut, Amsterdam
Galerie M., Bochum, West Germany
1971 Utrechtse Kring, Utrecht
Galerie Swart, Amsterdam
Galerie Lichter, Frankfurt
I.K.I., Dusseldorf
1972 Galerie Teufel, Koblenz
Aktionsgalerie, Berne (with Sarenco)
I.K.I./Modern Art Galerie, Dusseldorf
1973 Galerie Swart, Amsterdam
1974 Lucy Milton Gallery, London
Galerie Swart, Amsterdam
Galerie Lydia Megert, Berne
Galerie am Wochenende, Feldkirchen, West Germany
1975 Galerie Hermanns, Furstenfeldbruck, West Germany
Stedelijk Museum, Amsterdam
1976 *At Random,* Kunstcentrum Badhuis, Gorinchem, Netherlands
Galerie Swart, Amsterdam
1977 Galerie Lydia Megert, Berne
Galerie Muller-Roth, Stuttgart
Galerie Magazijn, Groningen, Netherlands
1978 Lieftinghsbroek Nature Reserve, Groningen, Netherlands
1979 De Vleeshal, Middelburg, Netherlands
Galerie Lydia Megert, Berne
Galerie Muller-Roth, Stuttgart
1980 *Werken 1954–1980,* Groninger Museum, Groningen, Netherlands
Galerie Swart, Amsterdam
Galerie Magazijn, Groningen, Netherlands
Kunsthistorisch Instituut, Groningen University Netherlands
1981 Van Reckum Museum, Apeldoorn, Netherlands
Het Apollonius, Eindhoven, Netherlands
1982 Gemeentemusuem, The Hague
Gomera, Canary Islands

1983 *From Earth,* Galerie Megert, Bern
1984 *Natural Relations,* Galerie Mueller Roth, Stuttgart
1989 *Natural Relations,* Osthaus Museum, Hagen, Germany
1990 *Natural Relations,* Silkeberg Kunstmuseum, Denmark
Art Affairs, Amsterdam
Galerie Mueller Roth, Stuttgart
1991 *Terre, vie, et poésie,* Espace de l'art Concret, Mouans-sartoux, France
Flora, Royal Botanic Garden, Edinburgh
1992 Durhammer Galerie, Frankfurt
Documents of a Stream, Royal Botanic Garden, Edinburgh
1993 Galerie Conrads, Dusseldorf
Gute Hofnung, Kunstverein, Essen
Galerie Mueller Roth, Stuttgart
Durhammer Galerie, Frankfurt
Städt Galerie, Würzburg, Germany
Städt Sammlungen, Schweinfurt, Germany
1994 Art Affairs, Amsterdam
Kunst im Gang, Bamberg, Germany
Galerie Kornfeld, Zurich
1995 Städtische Galerie, Erfurt
Karl-Ernst Osthaus Museum, Hagen
1996 Museum Scription, Tilburg
Galerie Conrads, Düsseldorf
Durhammer Galerie, Frankfurt
1997 Galerie Kunst im Gang, Bamberg
Art Affairs, Amsterdam
1998 Susan Inglett Gallery, New York
Rijksmuseum Twenthe, Enschede
Galerie Aline Vidal, Paris
Art Affairs, Amsterdam
Librairie du Musée d'art moderne, Paris
1999 Refusalon, San Francisco
Kunsthaus, Nürnberg
2000 Centre for Artist Books, Visual Research Centre, Dundee
Galerie Aline Vidal, Paris
Galerie Müller Roth, Stuttgart
2001 Museum für Konkrete Kunst, Ingolstadt
Galerie Conrads, Düsseldorf
Galerie Elke Dröscher, Hamburg

Selected Group Exhibitions:

1957 *Natuur en Kunst,* Stedelijk Museum, Amsterdam
1962 *Nul,* Stedelijk Museum, Amsterdam
1965 *Licht und Bewegung,* Kunsthalle, Berne
1970 *Konkrete Poesie,* Stedelijk Museum, Amsterdam
1974 *Basically White,* Institute of Contemporary Arts, London
1975 *Poesia Concreta 1952–1967,* Biblioteca Nazionale, Florence
1979 *Zero,* Kunsthaus, Zurich
1987 *The Unpainted Landscape,* Scottish National Gallery of Modern Art, Edinburgh
1989 *The European Movement 1958–1989,* Central Artists House, Moscow
1992 *From the Silence. . . ,* Zacheta, Warsaw
1996 Trilogy-kunst-natur-videnscap, Botanisk Have, Copenhagen
1997 Sculpture Projects, Münster
Livres d'artistes 1960–1980, Bibliothèque Nationale, Paris
Konkrete poesie konzept kunst, Städtische Galerie Rosenheim
1999 *Natural Reality,* Ludwig Forum für Internationale Kunst, Aachen
2000 *Kunstraum Deutschland,* Institut für Auslandsbeziehungen, Stuttgart

Collections:

Sammlung Albertina, Vienna; Haags Gemeentemuseum, The Hague; Stedelijk Museum, Amsterdam; Van Abbemuseum, Eindhoven, Netherlands; Kröller-Müller Museum, Otterlo, Netherlands; Kunstmuseum, Dusseldorf; Staatsgalerie, Stuttgart; Kunsthaus, Zurich; Museum Sztuki, Lodz, Poland; Museum of Modern Art, New York; Bibliothèque Nationale, Paris; Bayerische Staatsbibliothek, Munich; National Galerie, Berlin; Victoria and Albert Museum, London; and many others.

Publications:

By DE VRIES: Books—*Wit is overdaad,* Amsterdam 1960; *Manifest van de gecastreerde werkelijkheid,* Amsterdam 1960; *Wit,* with introduction by J. C. Van Schagen, Amsterdam 1962; *Permutierbard Text,* Stuttgart 1967; *Wit/Weiss,* Stuttgart 1967; *Change,* Amsterdam 1970; *Random Objectivations,* Brescia, Italy 1972; *Chancefields/Chancefelder: An Essay on the Topology of Randomness,* Dinkelscherben 1973; *The Wittgenstein Paper, I and II,* Berne 1974; *To Be All Ways to Be,* Katmandu 1974; *Vijf Manifesten over Taal—en een Gedicht,* Berne 1975; *Asiatische und Eschenauer Texte,* portfolio, Berne 1975; *October, February, June,* Eschenau 1977; *The Dust of Some Roads and Leaf from a Tree,* Eschenau 1977; *Some Early Change Projects/Einige fruhe anderungs Projekte 1963–1967,* portfolio with tape cassette, Berne 1977; *16 dm2, an Essay,* Berne 1979; *Documents of a Stream,* Eindhoven, Netherlands 1981; *From Here,* Gorinchem, Netherlands 1982; *Von Wirlichkeit und Sprache,* Eschenau 1986; *Collecting Notes,* Eschenau 1987; *Von Groningse Aarde,* Groningen 1988; *Natural Relations,* 1989; *Remember Gustav Theodor Fechner,* Eschenau 1994; *Terrae Petrinsulares,* Bern 1995; *To be.textetextarbeiten-textilder,* Stuttgart 1995; *Botanische werke: Distelsamen,* Eschenau 1995; *This,* Eschenau 1996; *Green?,* Paris 1997; *De Tuindorpcollecties,* Tilburg 1998; *Watergoed de kop van overijasel,* Amsterdam 1998; *Red!/Rouge!—From Red Earth,* Paris 1998; *Wörter,* Eschenau 1999; *Tutto,* Eschenau 1999; *108 x.,* Paris 2000; *Grey & Greay—From Earth,* Paris 2000; *Different & Identic,* 2000; **Films—***Look Out of Any Window,* 1972; *100 Ansichten von grossen Knetzberg,* 1972; *Chance and Change,* 1973; *A Letter from James,* 1977; *The Flower-Sutra,* 1979; *Film-Notes,* 1979; *Water Pictures,* 1980. **Sound-recordings—***Natura Artis Magistra,* tape-cassette, 1967; *Humanae Vitae,* tape-cassette, 1967; *Natura Artis Magistra and Humanae Vitae,* tape-cassette with drawing, 1971; *Water—The Music of Sound,* 1977; *Belladonna,* 1983.

On DE VRIES: Books—*Herman De Vries* by Walter Aue, Cologne 1966; *Constructivism: Origins and Evolution* by George Rickey, New York 1967; *Herman De Vries,* exhibition catalog, with text by Herbert V. Franke, Bochum, West Germany 1970; *Konkret Dichtung* by Siegfried J. Schmidt, Munich 1972; *Asthetik als Informationsverarbeitung* by Frieder Nake, Vienna and New York 1974; *Programmi Sistematici* by Jean Leering, Milan 1975; *Herman De Vries: At Random,* exhibition catalog, with an introduction by Antoinette Hilgemann-de Stiger, Gorinchem, Netherlands 1976;

Konstruktive Konzepte by Willy Rotzler, Zurich 1977; *Nederlandse Kunstenarsboeken* by Flip Bool and G. J. de Rook, The Hague 1978; *Herman De Vries: Werken 1954–1980,* exhibition catalog, with an introduction by Frans Haks, and essays by Urs and Ros Graf, Groningen, Netherlands 1980; *Honey from a Weed* by Patricia Gray, London 1986; *The Unpainted Landscape* by David Reason, Edinburgh 1987; *From Earth* by David Reason, Nailsworth 1990; *Herman De Vries,* exhibition catalog with essay by Paul Nesbitt, Edinburgh 1992; *Différentes natures* by Liliane Albertazzi, Lindau 1993; *Herman De Vries: Mein Poesie Ist die Welt,* exhibition catalog with essays by Erich Schneider, Britta Buhlman, and Paul Nesbitt.

*

Around 1960, my grey-white informal paintings changed slowly to empty white canvases under the influence of the Buddhist thought of emptiness.

Some years later, I was looking for structure without giving up the objectivity, the emptiness of limited and limiting meaning I had gained in the white paintings with homogenous surfaces.

In my biological work I used randomness as a means for leaving out the influence of the researcher in the research series, and discovered that this system was very useful to come to form again and not to have to say anything. In the following 14 years I was mainly occupied with ''random objectivations''—researching visual relationships in random programs. During this work, I became interested in the nature of randomness and chance: the existing definitions were not satisfying nor did they coincide with the results of my work. By following definitions of randomness and of art and always having to change them again and again, I realized that there are limits to the intellect. In this period, I also found that the patterns of *chance* were connected to *change:* they were all around in everyday reality. I tried to document them, first in photo-series at the beginning of the 70s, and later in the facts of reality itself—works which I now call ''actuality as a document of itself.''

Last year I crossed the border between art and non-art, between art and actuality, so becoming free of an important contradiction. My parallel ongoing preoccupations with philosophy and poetry all became integrated.

A final statement is not possible to give. When I say ''all,'' I include the negation ''not all''; so I prefer to leave it open. (1989)

At present I work almost exclusively with the real works—of nature, as nature is our primary reality. (1994)

—Herman de Vries

* * *

From 1949 to 1952 Herman de Vries was a student at the Montpelier Ecole des Beaux-Arts. Even that was for him a period when he was intensely caught up with the patterning wrought by geometric fragments hanging together as mobiles but subsequently conjured into monochrome oil paintings which proved a short step to collages of the same character.

In 1965 he made his first experiments with *concrete poetry* and by 1968 had become an active contributor to the Edition Hansjörg Mayer's great anthology exhibition at The Hague's Gemeentemuseum with a number of exhibits which (besides unnumbered blank or patterned pages) included a wild conglomeration of interwoven linear triangles with title: ''empty space for an empty space prepared for you by herman de vries this one is for him.''

Ten years after found him at work upon pocket-multiples (white squares each with ten black spots, dots would be a more accurate description of them, in quasi-casual disarray on their surfaces) and—rather larger—1 decimeter in dimension and when fully assembled stretching 16 decimeters in extent. These were not only bigger than the pocket-multiples, the black images set central on each part of the full assembly of squares were non-figurative, of course but more complicated than those of the pocket-multiples and were richly different, each from each.

Herman de Vries, in his casual economy of means, with a predominant desire to establish what imagery he does employ in implied boundless space, has somehow translated the freedom of the mobile onto a two-dimensional surface.

In doing so he has endowed his works with an enduring character of liberty.

—Sheldon Williams

DEWASNE, Jean

Nationality: French. **Born:** Lille, 21 May 1921. **Education:** Studied music, the classics and architecture, at the Ecole des Beaux-Arts, Paris. **Career:** Produced first abstract paintings, Paris, 1943; member, Abstract art group, with Hartung, Schneider, de Staël, Poliakoff and Deyrolle, Paris, 1945; founder-member with Jean Arp, Antoine Pevsner, Sonia Delaunay and others, Salon des Réalités Nouvelles, Paris, 1945; painted first large mural commission, Paris, 1948; founder-director, Studio of Abstract Art, Paris, 1950–53. Has travelled and lectured extensively in Europe and America, since 1951. **Awards:** Kandinsky Award, Paris 1945. **Address:** 18 rue du Bourg-Tibourg, 75004 Paris, France.

Individual Exhibitions:

1949 Arne Bruun-Rasmussen Galerie, Copenhagen
1955 Palais des Beaux-Arts, Brussels
Arne Bruun-Rasmussen Galerie, Copenhagen
1956 Galerie Cordier, Paris
1959 Palais des Beaux-Arts, Brussels
1961 Galleria Lorenzelli, Milan
1962 Carrefour Galerie, Brussels
1963 Galerie Cordier, Paris
Galerie Hybler, Copenhagen
Esbjerg Museum, Denmark
1965 Cordier-Ekstrom Gallery, New York
1966 Kunsthalle, Berne (restrospective)
1967 Galleria Lorenzelli, Bergamo, Italy
1969 Musée d'Art Moderne, Paris
Palais des Beaux-Arts, Brussels
1971 Galerie Creuzevalt, Paris
1972 Lefebre Gallery, New York
Galerie Janssen, Brussels
1973 Galerie Francoise Tournier, Paris
Galerie Artel, Geneva
Soto Museum, Ciudad Bolivar, Venezuela
1974 Louisiana Museum, Humlebaek, Denmark

Jean Dewasne: *Moving Forces,* 1970–80. Photo by Jacques Faujour. ©2001 Artists Rights Society (ARS), NY/ADAGP, Paris.

Nordyllands Kunstmuseum, Aalborg, Denmark
Orly Airport, Paris
1975 Galerie Mark, Zurich
Centre d'Art et Loisirs, Privas, France
Maison des Arts et Loisirs, Sochaux, France (toured France)
Musée d'Art Moderne de la Ville, Paris
Carnegie Institute, Pittsburgh (toured the United States)
Musée d'Art Moderne, Paris
Galerie Remarque, Trans en Provence, France
Esbjerg Kunstforening, Denmark (toured Denmark)
Idées Contemporaines, Pontaven, France
Galerie Attali, Paris
Jean Dewasne, Muraliste, Kunstverein, Hannover
Centre Culturel Pablo Neruda, Corbeil, France
Centre Action Culturel, Macon, France
1976 Centre d'Art et Communication, Vaduz, Liechtenstein
Galeria d'Arte Contacto, Caracas
1977 *Gouches et Dessins,* Galerie Asbaek, Copenhagen
Galerie Groninger, Groningen, Netherlands
Antisculptures et Gouaches, Nordjyllands Kunstmuseum, Aalborg
1978 *Antisculptures, Maxi-Peintures, Gouaches,* Henie Onstad Museum, Oslo
Conceptions, Institute Francais, Stockholm
1979 Galerie Sapone, Nice
Museum of Modern Art, Caracas
1980 Grand Palais, Paris
1981 *La Longue Marche,* Centre Georges, Pompidou, Paris

Selected Group Exhibitions:

1945 *Salon des Réalités Nouvelles,* Paris
1968 *Biennale,* Venice
1972 *The Non-Objective World 1939–1955,* Annely Juda Fine Art, London (toured Europe)
Douze Ans d'Art Contemporain en France, Grand Palais, Paris
1975 Kunstmesse Art 6/75, Basle
Art Fair, Cologne

Jean Dewasne: *Project for the Apotheosis of Marat,* 1951. ©2001 Artists Rights Society (ARS), NY/ADAGP, Paris.

1976 *Artist from France,* Covent Garden, London
1981 *Paris—Paris 1937–1957,* Centre Georges Pompidou, Paris

Collections:

Nordyllands Kunstmuseum, Aalborg, Denmark; Louisiana Museum, Humlebaek, Denmark; Boymans van Beuningen Museum, Rotterdam; Musée des Beaux-Arts, Brussels; Centre Georges Pompidou, Paris; Musée de Grenoble, France, Carnegie Institute, Pittsburgh; Guggenheim Museum, New York; Museum of Modern Art, New York.

Permanent Public Installations:

Grande Arche de la Fraternité, La Défense, Paris.

Publications:

By DEWASNE: Books—illustrations for *Preface to a Future Book* by Lautreamont, Copenhagen 1949; *Robert Jacobsen,* Copenhagen 1950; *Vasarely,* Paris 1952; *Traité de la peinture* (written in 1949), Paris 1972. **Articles**—''Mathematical Space and Abstract Art'' in *20th Siècle,* no. 2, 1952; ''The Paintings of the Cuzco School'' in *Lettres Francaises,* September/October 1952; ''Visit to the Secret City of Macchu-Picchu'' in *Lettres Francaises,* March 1956; ''Romanesque Paintings and Gothic Painting in Denmark'' in *Lettres Francaises,* October 1956; ''Andrea del Castagno'' and ''The Gods of Saint Augustine'' in *Letters Francaises,* August 1957; ''What Is Avant-Garde in 1958'' in *Lettres Francaises,* June 1958; ''Reflections on Abstract Art'' in *Quadrum,* no. 7, 1959; ''Abstract Art and Objectivity'' in *Nouvelle Critique,* September 1968; ''The Problem of the Wall'' in *L'Oeil,* September/October 1971; ''De la Theorie au Concept'' with E. Mavrommatis, in *Opus,* no 37, 1972; ''Dedie au spectateur'' in *Galerie des Arts,* March 1977; ''Une creation mathématisée'' in *Gazette des Beaux-Arts,* September 1977.

On DEWASNE: Books—*Jean Dewasne* by Pierre Descargues, Paris 1952; *Jean Dewasne,* exhibition catalog, with text by several authors, Milan 1961; *Dewasne,* exhibition catalog, with text by Daniel Cordier, New York 1965; *Dewasne,* exhibition catalog, with text by Daniel Cordier, New York 1972; *The Mondial Art 1960–1975,* edited by Germain Viatte, Geneva 1975; *From Thorvaldsen to the Atomic Age,* edited by Sigurd Schultz, Copenhagen 1975; *Art Actuel: Skira Annuel 75,* Geneva 1975.

*

Here is a general theory of aesthetic creation:

The artist begins by formulating dynamic currents in order to express the drama of plastic happenings. Because of this, the assemblies cannot be isolated from their liaisons. The rhythm of these liaisons gives the work its main meanings. The dynamic currents and the filiations impose the sittings and the positions.

The positions, within the currents, give rise to other plastic assemblies which momentarily hold the spectator's attention. This period of contemplation and analysis permits the spectator to experience mental speculations which can ensure and multiply his pleasure. They prepare him to then throw himself into the torrent of the current; this, in its turn, can be considered as a significant assembly, one that can be analysed, a detectable one. The relative positions, the situations, the combinations triumph over the form-colour elements that were visible at first. The structure of association will liberate from the constellations and, indirectly, as a result, from the configurations of the fabric of the messages.

The adagios, the lentos intermingle with the baroque ''fortes,'' taking support in invisible outlines that are very complex in themselves, submitting to the topological laws of the situation.

In the course of the formulation of the work, the artist knowingly runs the maximum of possible dangers: many errors are voluntarily touched upon; many losses envisaged. In the choices constantly incited by the creation, the artist opts for risks. His strategy of decision always leads him towards the uncomfortable, the unknown. When the evolution of the happenings of the creation at its various levels seems too sober, he voluntarily provokes skidding. If the position shows itself to be unmaintainable, the creator has the opportunity to advance towards some interesting result.

The work of art does not have to search for a maximum probability. It would quickly become banal and boring. It must deliberately opt for the most unforeseen probability. When a fairly improbable plastic thought provokes a new solution, it immediately acquires the most powerful affective charge. Here, logic does not control creation; it is at its service: it does not close, it opens.

The overall effects of the creation do not at all depend on the overall initial conditions, but on the interactions, the correlations, the feed-back effects, rebounds and ricochets of the creative action.

It is to be wished that the phenomena intensify from the beginning to the end of the plastic happening. The total work incites a cumulative phenomenon.

—Jean Dewasne

* * *

After training as a sculptor Jean Dewasne turned to painting in the hard-edged geometrical styles associated with Vasarely and Herbin. From easel paintings he has enlarged his formats to long and continuously evolving patterns in which channels of colours follow their progressive rhythms in interchanging directions to arrive at their starting point, repeating in two-dimensional equivalents the perimeter of a building or the track of a stadium.

In 1949 Dewasne wrote *Traité de la peinture,* reflections on the creative process of painting which he expresses thus: ''The work results from contact between two facts acting according to their own laws and which coincide in one: the material and the artist—the work says more than its creator.'' His development has stressed the mural potential in painting beyond the rectangular format of traditional character and more towards the architectural domination of the environment by dynamically placed areas of strong colour. These murals such as that for the ice stadium at Grenoble which is 3 metres high and 60 metres wide and the ''Longue marche'' that measures 2 metres high and 100 metres long become by themselves backgrounds and curtain walls whose space exercises optical control over everything before it assumes the proportions of natural phenomena such as a cliff or ski run.

While Optical art has generated the climate of acceptance of his massive composition, Dewasne has achieved a unique synthesis of the formal motives embodied in his paintings and their progressive unfolding of the basic knots of formal design in a formal unity, suggestive of landscape gardening and the mosaics of Moresque architecture. Something of modern technological plotting is inherent in the boldly hued strips running parallel and crossing and interchanging in their progressive journey, yet their inevitable structure implies a movement time has arrested. Curved, triangular and stepped conjunctions move to and fro in balanced harmonies of weight and contrast. The eye is not dazzled as in a Bridget Riley painting; the continuity of strips in associations of width and space achieve an empathy with the spectator leaving a neutral reaction in terms of individual shapes, but their linking produces a feeling of satisfaction in regard to evolution in time.

Eminently expressive of the artist's theories relating to spatial control of an environment no matter how limited, Dawasne's work is capable of great expansion in its role in dictating the mood and planar atmosphere of buildings or boundary surfaces. His ''Antisculptures,'' in which he took parts of automobile bodies and erected them as freestanding objects that he proceeded to paint in patterns breaking up their outlines in the fashion of wartime camouflage, were somewhat equivocal in their results in as much as their effects were to some extent controlled by their backgrounds and angles of viewing—less successful than his mural colour tracks where painting becomes its own background and thus dominates the casual objects that come before it.

—G. S. Whittet

DEZEUZE, Daniel

Nationality: French. **Born:** Ales-Gard, 1 February 1942. **Education:** Ecole Nationale des Beaux-Arts, Montpellier, 1959–62; studied Spanish literature at the Faculté des Lettres, University of Montpellier, 1959–62 (Licence-és-Lettres, 1962, Diplome d'Etudes Supérieures, 1965); also studied at the School of Architecture, Mexico University, 1964–65, and at the Sorbonne, Paris, 1967–70 (Doctorat 1970). **Family:** Married Karen Nesbitt in 1974. **Career:** Served as assistant in charge of cultural affairs, French Consulate, Toronto, 1965–66. Instructor, Alliance Francaise, Avila Spain, 1962–63; lecturer, French Department, University of Toronto, 1966–67, and French summer school, McGill University, Montreal, summers 1969–1970; instructor, Ecole des Arts Décoratifs, Nice, 1973–74, and Ecole Nationale des Beaux-Arts, Bourges, 1974–77; professor, Ecole des Beaux-Arts, Montpellier, since 1978. **Agents:** Daniel Templon, 30 rue Beaubourg, 75003 Paris, France; Albert Baronian, 20 Boulevard Barthélémy, 1000 Brussells, Belgium. **Address:** Villa Lucia, Chemin de Saint Clair, Impasse du Hérisson, 34200 Sète, France.

Individual Exhibitions:

1971 Galerie Yvon Lambert, Paris
1973 Galerie Yvon Lambert, Paris
1974 Galerie Albert Baronian, Brussels
1975 Galerie Yvon Lambert, Paris
1976 Galerie Maillard, St. Paul de Vence, France
Galerie D'Allessandro-Ferranti, Rome
Maison de la Culture, Bourges, France
1977 Julian Pretto Gallery, Fine Arts Building, New York
Galerie Yvon Lambert, Paris
1978 Galleria Artra, Studio, Milan
Galerie Rudolf Zwirner, Cologne
Foundation M.L. Jeanneret, Boisssano, Italy
Galerie Albert Baronian, Brussels
1979 Galerie Meda-Mothi, Montpellier, France
Musée du Parc de la Boverie, Liège, Belgium
1980 Galerie Artline, The Hague
Musée d'Art et d'Industrie, Saint-Etienne, France
Musée de l'Abbaye Sainte-Croix, Les Sables d'Olonne, France
1981 Galerie Yvon Lambert, Paris
1982 Artra Studio, Milan
1983 Galerie Yvon Lambert, Paris
1985 Galerie Yvon Lambert, Paris
1986 Galerie des Arenes, Nimes, France
1987 Galerie Yvon Lambert, Paris
Gemeentemuseum, The Hague
1988 Galerie Athanor, Marseilles

Daniel Dezeuze: *Par une forêt obscure I,* 1991. Photo ©2001 Artists Rights Society (ARS), NY/ADAGP, Paris.

1989 Centre National des Arts Plastiques, Paris
1990 Galerie Marthe Carreton, Nîmes
Musée des Beaux-Arts, Nantes
1991 Galerie Yvon Lambert, Paris
Galerie A. Baronian, Brussels
1992 Galerie J. Girard, Toulouse
Galerie Armarium, Liepzig
Institut Français, Thessalonika, Greece
1993 Cabinet d'Art Graphique du Centre Georges Pompidou, Paris
Institut Français, Tel Aviv
Musée Crozatier, Le Puy-en-Velay
Galerie Athanor, Marseilles
1994 Musée d'Art et d'Histoire, Annecy
1996 Galerie Hélène Trintignan, Montpellier, France
1997 Galerie Jaques Girard, Toulouse, France
1998 Galerie Albert Baronian, Brussels
Musée d'Art Contemporain, Nîmes, France
1999 Galerie Daniel Templon, Paris
2000 Ancien Collège des Jésuites, Reims, France

Selected Group Exhibitions:

1969 *Biennale,* Paris
1970 *Supports/Surfaces,* Musée d'Art Moderne de la Ville, Paris
1975 *Europalia 12 x 1,* Palais des Beaux-Arts, Brussels
1978 *Aspects de l'Art en France,* Kunstmesse, Basle
1979 *Tendances de l'Art en France 1968–1979,* Musée d'Art Moderne de la Ville, Paris
1981 *The Subject of Painting,* Museum of Modern Art, Oxford (travelled to the Arnolfini Gallery, Bristol)
1984 *Ecritures dans la Peinture,* Villa Arson, Nice, France
1986 *Pictura Loquens,* Villa Arson, Nice, France (travelled to Palazo Reale, Milan)
1992 *Manifeste,* Centre Georges Pompidou, Paris
1996 *Monuments et Modernité,* Musée du Luxembourg, Paris

1998 *Rendez-vous,* Guggenheim Museum, New York
1999 *Le Soglie della Pittura,* Perugia, Italy
2001 *As Painting: Division and Displacement,* Wexner Center for Arts, Columbus, Ohio

Collections:

Musée d'Art et d'industrie, Saint Etienne, France; Musée Cantini, Marseille, France; Musée Sainte Croix, Les Sables d'Olonne, France; Musée Fabre, Montpellier, France; Musée Picasso, Antibes, France; Musée National d'Art Moderne, Paris; Australian National Gallery, Canberra; Musée d'Art Moderne, Ghent, Belgium; Musée de la Ville de Paris; Musée d'Art Contemporain, Nice.

Publications:

By DEZEUZE: Books—*Les toiles systématiquement tamponnées de Louis Cane,* Paris 1971; *Note sur le systéme euclidien et le dessin,* Paris 1971; *Brève relation d'un lointain voyage,* Melun, France 1983; *S-Clavo,* Paris 1986; *Textes et Notes,* Paris 1991; *Au-delà de Penetang,* Saint-Benoît-du-Sault 1993; *Le Livre Noir de la Chevalerie Errante,* Saint Benoît-du-Sault 1993; *La Disquette de Tuchan,* Annecy 1996; *Chine, Jardins Nouveaux et d'Autrefois,* Auvers-sur-Oise 1996; *Relevés et Commentaires,* Saint-Benoît-du-Sault 1996; *Colophons,* Marseilles 1998; *L'Art de la Solitude,* Marseilles 2000; *Vade-Mecum Pour Gnostiques Avancés,* Saint-Benoît-du-Sault 2000. **Articles—** essay in *Support/Surfaces,* exhibition catalog, Paris 1970; ''Les Toiles Systématiquement Tamponnées de Louis Cane'' in *Louis Cane,* exhibition catalog, Paris 1971; ''Situation et Travail du Groupe Supports/Surfaces'' in *VH 101,* Spring 1971; ''Pour un Programme Théorique Pictural,'' with Louis Cane, and ''Note Complementaire'' in *Peinture: Cahiers Théoriques,* no. 1, June 1971; ''Sans Titre'' in *Actualité d'un Bilan,* exhibition catalog, Paris 1972; ''Lecture d'un Texte de Thomas Herbert'' in *Peinture: Cahiers Théoriques,* no. 2–3, January 1972; ''La notion de nonrepresentation chez Tchouang Tseu'' in *Spirali,* no. 1, 1978; ''Daniel Dezeuze: entretien'', with E. Grazioli, in *Flash Art,* April 1987; ''Entretien avec H. C. Cousseau'' in *Art/Cahier 9,* Paris 1989; ''Entretien avec G. G. Lemaire'' in *Verso,* no. 4, Paris 1996.

On DEZEUZE: Books—*Le Nouveau Grand Espace* by Marcelin Pleynet, Paris 1971; *Art en France, Une Nouvelle Generation* by Jean Clair, Paris 1972; *L'Art Actuel en France* by Anne Tronche and Hervé Gloaguen, Paris 1973; *Daniel Dezeuze* by E. Grazioli, Milan 1978; *Daniel Dezeuze,* exhibition catalog, with text by Bernard Ceysson, interview by Jacques Beauffet, Saint-Etienne, France, 1980; *Comme la Peinture/Like Painting (Daniel Dezeuze)* by Christian Prigent, Paris 1983; *Support/Surface* by J. Poinsot, Paris 1983; *Daniel Dezeuze,* exhibition catalog with text by P. Javault, The Hague 1987; *Daniel Dezeuze* by J. Pijaudier, O. Kaeppelin, and A. Pacquement, Paris 1989; *Daniel Dezeuze* by Georges Duby, Clermont-Ferrand 1993. **Articles—**''Daniel Dezeuze, La Peinture et son Espace'' by Christian Prigent in *Art Press,* March/April 1975; ''Du Differe d'un Discours'' by Marcelin Pleynet in *Europalia,* exhibition catalog, Brussels 1975; ''D'un Trait'' by Alain Coulagne in *Gramme,* no. 6, 1977; ''Daniel Dezeuze'' by B. Ceysson in *Catalog Blickfelder 81,* exhibition catalog, Bielefeld 1981; ''Daniel Dezeuze'' by Claude Minière in *L'art en France,* Paris 1995; ''Daniel Dezeuze en Perspectives'' by Patrick Javault in Musée d'Art Contemporain exhibition catalog, Nîmes 1998; ''Daniel Dezeuze'' by Alfred Pacquement in *Rendez-vous,* exhibition catalog, New York 1998.

*

What's happened to the empty space that was so central to your previous work?

It's true that emptiness was an important feature in the sense that it recurred as part of a geometrical repetition; it was rhythmical, exposed by repetition and by a geometrical infrastructure. Here, it's true, there are far fewer empty spaces, particularly with regard to the wooden assemblages which are on the contrary extremely compact and heavily grounded. But I wasn't in any sense trying to do the opposite of what I'd done before; that's not it at all. I think that when I was working with masses I concentrated on the cut of the outline in the way that I'd done to a large extent with gauzes, but, obviously, I abandoned the notion of emptiness in order to create something very concentrated, something which wasn't about to disappear or disperse into thin air, but which was on the contrary extremely dense and closed in on itself.

A weapon is an object which very often takes up very little space and has at the same time the maximum potency; that's often its secret and in that sense it's an exemplary object—only in that sense, of course!

—Daniel Dezeuze (from an interview, 1987)

DI SUVERO, Mark

Nationality: American. **Born:** Shanghai, China, 18 September 1933. **Education:** San Francisco City College, 1953–54; University of California, Santa Barbara, 1954–55; University of California, Berkeley, 1956. **Career:** Sculptor; lives and works in New York. Built ''Tower of Peace'' as protest against Vietnam War, Los Angeles, 1966. **Agent:** Oil and Steel Gallery, 30–30 Vernon Boulevard, Box 2216, Long Island City, New York 11102, U.S.A.

Individual Exhibitions:

1960 Green Gallery, New York
1964 Park Place Gallery, New York
1965 Dwan Gallery, Los Angeles
1966 Park Place Gallery, New York
1967 Park Place Gallery, New York
1968 Lo Guidice Gallery, Chicago
1972 Stedelijk van Abbemuseum, Eindhoven, The Netherlands
Wilhelm-Lembruck Museum, Duisburg, West Germany
1974 La Ville de Chalon-sur-Saone, France
1975 Jardin des Tuileries, Paris
Whitney Museum of American Art, New York (retrospective)
1978 *New Sculpture,* Janie C. Lee Gallery, Houston
1979 ConStruct Gallery, Chicago
1980 *Inner Search,* Northwestern Operations Center, Minneapolis (permanent installation)
Ace Gallery, Venice, California
1983 Oil & Steel Gallery, New York

Esprit Park, San Francisco
1985 Oil & Steel Gallery, New York
Storm King Art Center, Mountainville, New York
1986 Hill Gallery, Birmingham, Michigan
1987 Akira Ikeda Gallery, Tokyo
1988 Wurttembergischer Kunstverein, Stuttgart
1990 Valence, France
Galerie de France, Paris
L. A. Louver Gallery, Venice, California
1991 Musee d'Art Moderne et d'Art Contemporain de Nice, Nice
Akira Ikeda Gallery, Tokyo
1992 Chalon sur Saone, France
Galerie Heike Curtze, Vienna
Verein fur Heimatpflege, Viersen, Germany
1993 Musée de Beaux-Arts and Passerelle, Brest, France
Gagosian Gallery, New York
Rettig y Martinez Gallery, Santa Fe, New Mexico
Esprit Park, San Francisco
1994 Berggruen Gallery, San Francisco
IVAM Centre Julio Gonzalez, Valencia, Spain
1995 Storm King Art Center, Mountainville, New York
Venice Biennale, Italy
1996 Weigand Gallery, Belmont, California
Galerie Jeanne-Bucher, Paris, France
1997 Gagosian Gallery, New York
1998 Orange County Museum of Art, Newport Beach, California
Mark Moore Gallery, Santa Monica, California
The Hiroshima Museum of Contemporary Art, Hiroshima, Japan
1999 John Berggruen Gallery, San Francisco

Selected Group Exhibitions:

1962 *Continuity and Change,* Wadsworth Athenaeum, Hartford, Connecticut
1964 *Recent American Sculpture,* Jewish Museum, New York
1968 *Documenta,* Kassel, West Germany
1969 *Sculpture of the 60s,* Los Angeles County Museum of Art
New York Painting and Sculpture 1940–70, Metropolitan Museum of Art, New York
1970 *Monumental Art,* Contemporary Art Center, Cincinnati, Ohio
1971 *Works for New Spaces,* Walker Art Center, Minneapolis
1974 *Public Sculpture/Urban Environment,* Oakland Museum, California
1975 *Biennale,* Venice
1980 *Sculpture in California 1975–1980,* San Diego Museum of Art, California
Homage to Picasso, Walker Art Center, Minneapolis, Minnesota
American Sculpture: Gifts of Howard and Jean Lipman, Whitney Museum of American Art, New York
1981 *Contemporary Painting/Sculpture I,* Oil & Stelel Gallery, New York
1982 *Contemporary Painting/Sculpture II + III,* Oil & Steel Gallery, New York New York
20 American Artists: Sculpture 1982, San Francisco Museum of Modern Art, California
1983 *The First Show: Painting and Sculpture from Eight Collections, 1940—1980,* The Museum of Contemporary Art, Los Angeles, California
1985 *International Exhibition VII,* Solomon R. Guggenheim Museum, New York
The Third Dimension: Sculpture of the New York School, Whitney Museum of American Art, New York
1986 Oil & Steel Gallery, Long Island City, New York
An American Renaissance: Painting and Sculpture Since 1940, Museum of Art, Fort Lauderdale, Florida
Individuals: A Selected History of Contemporary Art, 1945–1986, The Museum of Contemprary Art, Los Angeles, California
1987 *Aspects of Collage, Assemblage and the Found Object in the 20th Century,* Solomon R. Guggenheim Museum, New York
1988 *Sculpture Since the Sixties from the Permanent Collection of the Whitney Museum of American Art,* Whitney Museum of American Art at Equitable Center, New York, New York
1989 Oil & Steel Gallery, Long Island City, New York
The ''Junk'' Aesthetic: Assemblage of the 1950's and Early 1960's, Whitney Museum of American Art at Equitable Center, New York
1993 *The Second Dimension: Twentieth Century Sculptor's Drawings from the Brooklyn Museum,* The Brooklyn Museum, Brooklyn, New York
1994 *Le Temps d'un Dessin,* Galerie de l'Ecole des Beaux Arts de Lorient, France
1995 *Twentieth Century American Sculpture II,* The White House, Washington D.C.
1996 San Francisco Museum of Modern Art, San Francisco, California
The Philip Johnson Collection, Museum of Modern Art, New York
1998 *100 Years of Sculpture: From the Pedestal to the Pixel,* Walker Art Center, Minneapolis, Minnesota
1999 *The American Century: Art and Culture 1900–2000,* Whitney Museum of American Art, New York

Permanent Public Installations:

Moderna Museet, Stockholm; St. Louis Art Museum; High Park, Toronto; Nathan Manilow Sculpture Park, Monee, Illinois; Kroller-Muller Museum, Otterlo, Netherlands; Los Angeles County Museum of Art; Bradley Foundation, Milwaukee, Wisconsin; Dallas Museum of Fine Arts; La Ville de Chalon sur Saone, France; Le Musée de Grenoble, France; Western Washington State College, Bellingham; Oakland Museum of Art, California; Akron Art Museum, Ohio; Grand Rapids, Michigan; Muhlenberg College, Allentown, Pennsylvania; Century Center, South Bend, Indiana; Inner Harbor, Baltimore, Maryland; Toledo Museum of Art, Ohio; Storm King Art Center, Mountainville, New York; Dartmouth College, New Hampshire; Bluff Park, Milwaukee, Wisconsin; National Gallery, Canberra, Australia; Museum of Contemporary Art, Los Angeles; Northwestern Bank, Minneapolis, Minnesota; Minneapolis Sculpture Garden, Minnesota; Baylor Medical Center, Houston; Wells Fargo Bank Building, Los Angeles; Cincinnati Art Museum, Ohio; Menil Collection, Houston; Baltimore Museum of Art, Maryland; Sheldon Memorial Art

Gallery, Lincoln, Nebraska; Stuttgart, Germany; Viersen, Germany; Valance, France; Brest, France.

Collections:

New York University; Hirshhorn Museum and Sculpture Garden, Smithsonian Institution, Washington, D.C.; Landesmuseum fur Teknik und Arbeit, Mannheim, Germany; Los Angeles County Museum of Art, California; Moderna Museet, Stockholm, Sweden; The Museum of Contemporary Art, Los Angeles, California; The Museum of Modern Art, New York; Walker Art Center, Minneapolis, Minnesota; Whitney Museum of American Art, New York; Wadsworth Athenaeum, Hartford, Connecticut; Rhode Island School of Design, Providence; Massachusetts Institute of Technology, Cambridge; Art Institute of Chicago; St. Louis Art Museum; University of Iowa City.

Publications:

By DI SUVERO: Books—*Mark di Suvero: Open Secret, Sculpture 1990–92, Poems Selected by the Artist,* New York 1993. **Article—** ''Mark di Suvero a Chalon-sur-Saone,'' interview, in *Art Press* (Paris), December/January 1974; ''Letter to the World: Tendresse'' in *Grand Street,* Summer 1991.

On DI SUVERO: Books—*Mark di Suvero,* exhibition catalog, by James K. Monte, New York 1975; *Mark Di Suvero: New Sculpture,* exhibition catalog, with text by Barbara Rose, Houston 1978; *Sculpture in California 1975–1980,* exhibition catalog, San Diego, California 1980; *Mark di Suvero,* exhibition catalog, Los Angeles 1982; *Mark di Suvero at Storm King Art Center,* exhibition catalog, New York 1996. **Articles—**''Mark di Suvero'' by Jill Johnston in *Recent American Sculpture,* exhibition catalog, New York 1964; ''Di Suvero: The Pressures of Reality'' by H. Rothenstein in *Artnews* (New York), February 1967; ''Mark di Suvero'' by Max Kozloff in *Artforum* (New York), Summer 1967; ''Mark di Suvero'' by Carter Ratcliff in *Artforum* (New York), November 1972; ''Mark di Suvero's Burgundian Season'' by E. C. Baker in *Art in America* (New York), May/June 1974; ''Mark di Suvero: An Epic Reach'' by Donald Goddard in *Artnews* (New York), January 1976; ''Idealism Realized: Two Public Commissions by Mark di Suvero'' by J. Klein in *Arts Magazine* (New York), December 1981; ''Mark di Suvero'' by Kenneth Baker in *ARTnews,* January 1994; ''Socratic Dialogue'' by Barbara A. Macadam in *ARTnews,* May 1997; ''A Season of Steel in the City of Light: The Works of Sculptor Mark di Suvero on Display in Paris, France'' by Raphael Rubinstein in *Art in America,* July 1998; ''Mark di Suvero at Danese'' by Edward Leffingwell in *Art in America,* February 2001.

* * *

It is difficult for any art historian to avoid the dialectic of Hegelism. From a distance the confusion of art movements and isms can be seen to settle into patterns of thesis, antithesis, and synthesis, a slow (and nowadays, not so slow) swing of the pendulum backwards and forwards. Every new development that occurs can be seen as a historical necessity, and the new artists are not original thinkers but players carrying out the dictates of the role that history has assigned them.

Such a view leads to a skepticism where originality among artists is concerned. A development that seemed revolutionary at the time it first became manifest, now takes its place as a small variation in the continuous rhythm of action and reaction. Artists are no longer seen as free agents, breaking new ground with every advance, but as manifestations of the process, needed by history to carry out a particular role.

Hence the critical acclaim lavished on any particular artist is absurd; one might as well praise winter for coming after autumn. This publication contains hundreds of examples of meaningless acclamation. claims made on the behalf of artists which have no validity, which are, in the end, ridiculous.

I make these remarks because I am not going to say that Mark Di Suvero is the greatest sculptor since Michaelangelo, or that his work has ''seminal'' influence, or that it is the best or the biggest or the most important around. Personally I like what I have seen, but that in itself is insignificant; my liking something means nothing.

What one can do, however, is explain where Suvero fits into the dialectical pattern of recent American art, what is the historical necessity of his work, because his sculpture inhabits a turning point, a corner in the process, where one idea became another one.

Suvero inherited a dilemma. Fifties art concerned itself with the emotional level of the human being. It tended to do so more successfully in painting than in sculpture, probably because sculpture is a slow process and much 50s art depended on the instant release of emotion on to the canvas. There is no real school of Abstract Expressionist sculptors.

In the 60s through the influence of David Smith, a native style of sculpture emerged. It began as essentially constructivist, and then, through the discovery of symmetry, became monumental. Artists such as Bryden, Tony Smith, Judd and Morris established a massive style, based upon straight lines used in a balanced and symmetrical way.

The problem was that sculpture began to look more and more like office blocks. The associations of the new style were certainly not human but mechanical and artificial. The sculpture contained no accidents, no reference to the random nature of life and of human emotion. They were too controlled.

Suvero was among those who tried to solve the problem, and his solution remains the best to date. He retained the concept of ''presence,'' which is found among the monumental school. His work is usually on a large scale and forces itself upon the viewers' attention. He also retained the constructivist element; his work has ''parts'' which have been put together, but in a manner that is much more fluid than one would expect from the minimalists.

The most significant change is in choice of materials. Here he seems to have learnt from the 50s fashion for ''objects trouvé.'' Instead of using the polished and enamelled steel so beloved of minimal sculptors, he employs bits of rusty chain, old wooden beams, punctured tires. The style is a rhetoric of the vernacular, a synthesis of the 50s and 60s.

An inevitable and necessary development perhaps; but one may be glad that it has been done so well.

—Alastair Mackintosh

DIAS, Antonio

Nationality: Brazilian. **Born:** Campina Grande, Paraiba, 22 February 1944. **Family:** Married Iole de Freitas. **Career:** Painter; lives and works in Milan. **Awards:** Acquisition Prize, *Salao de Arte Moderna,* Belo Horizonte, Brazil, 1962; First Prize for Drawing, *Salao do*

Parana, Brazil, 1963; ''Hors Concours,'' *Salao Nacional de Arte Moderna,* Rio de Janeiro, 1964; International Painting Prize, *Biennale,* Paris, 1965; Drawing Prize, *Young National Drawing Exhibition,* Sao Paulo, 1965; Critics Prize, *Resumo,* Rio de Janeiro, 1965; Acquisition Prize, *Salao de Abril,* Rio de Janeiro, 1966; Critics Prize, *Resumo JB,* Rio de Janeiro 1968; P. Favro Prize San Fedele Award, Milan, 1968; Guggenheim Fellowship, 1971; Drawing Prize, *International Exhibition,* Rijeka, Yugoslavia, 1972. **Agent:** Galeria Luisa Strina, Rua Padre João Manoel 974A, São Paulo, Brazil 01411–000.

Individual Exhibitions:

1962 Galeria Sobradinho, Rio de Janeiro
1964 Galeria Relèvo, Rio de Janeiro
1965 Galerie Houston-Brown, Paris
1966 Galeria Guignard, Belo Horizonte, Brazil
1967 Galerie Delta, Rotterdam
Galeria Relèvo, Rio de Janeiro
1969 Galleria Acme, Brescia, Italy
Studio Marconi Grafica, Milan
Studio Marconi, Milan
Galleria La Chiocciola, Padua
1970 Galerie Richard Foncke, Ghent
1971 Galleria Breton, Milan
Studio Marconi, Milan
1972 Galerie Stampa, Basel
Galleria Toselli, Milan
1973 Galeria Ralph Camargo, Sao Paulo
Galeria Delta, Brussels
Bolsa de Arte, Rio de Janeiro
Centro de Arte y Communicacion, Buenos Aires
Galerie Stampa, Basel
1974 Galerie Nächst St. Stephan, Vienna
Galleria Nuovi Strumenti, Brescia, Italy
Museu de Arte Moderna, Rio de Janeiro
1976 Galerie Albert Baronian, Brussels
Galleria Lucio Amelio, Naples
Galleria Nuovi Strumenti, Brescia, Italy
Galerie Eric Fabre, Paris
Palais des Beaux-Arts, Brussels
1978 Arte Global, Sao Paulo
Coleman/Dias/Nespolo, Palazzo Reale, Milan
Gravura Brasileira, Rio de Janeiro
Galeria Luisa Strina, Sao Paulo
1979 Nucleo de Arte Contemporanea, Joao Pessoa, Brazil
Galeria Saramenha, Rio de Janeiro
1980 Galerie Walter Storms, Munich
Galleria Nuova Strumenti, Brescia, Italy
Biennale, Venice
1982 Gravura Brasileira, Rio de Janeiro
Galerie Walter Storms, Munich
1983 Galerie Albert Baronian, Brussels
Thomas Cohn Arte Contemporanea, Rio de Janeiro
Galerie Beatrix Wilhelm, Leonberg, West Germany
1984 Stadtische Galerie im Lenbachhaus, Munich
1985 Taipei Fine Arts Museum, Taiwan
1986 Galleria Piero Cavellini, Milan
1994 *Trabalhos,* Mathildenhöhe Institute, Darmstadt, Germany (catalog)
Galerie Pablo Stahli, Zurich
1995 Studio Marconi, Milan
1996 Galeria Luisa Strina, São Paulo
Galeria Paulo Fernandes, Rio de Janeiro
Paço Imperial, Rio de Janeiro
1999 Centro de Arte Hélio Oiticica, Rio de Janeiro (catalog)
Fundação Calouste Gulbenkian, Lisbon (retrospective)
Galerie Walter Storms, Munich
2000 Galeria Luisa Strina, São Paulo
2001 *The Invented Country,* Museum of Modern Art, São Paulo (also Museum of Modern Art, Rio de Janeiro) (catalog)

Selected Group Exhibitions:

1965 *Biennale,* Paris
1969 *Dialogue between East and West,* National Museum of Modern Art, Tokyo
1971 *International Exhibition,* Guggenheim Museum, New York
1973 *Record as Artwork,* Galleria Forma, Genoa (travelled to the Galleria Francoise Lambert, Milan, and the Royal College of Art, London)
1974 *Projekt '74,* Wallraf-Richartz Museum, Cologne
Video Art, Institute of Contemporary Art, Philadelphia (travelled to the Museum of Contemporary Art, Chicago)
1977 *Art and Cinema,* Centro Internazionale di Brera, Milan (travelled to the *Biennale,* Venice, 1978)
1981 *Kunstlerbucher,* Kunstverein, Frankfurt
1984 *International Survey of Recent Painting and Sculpture,* Museum of Modern Art, New York
1985 *Italian Contemporary Art,* Porin Taidemuseo, Pori, Finland
1996 *Transparências,* Museu de Arte Moderna, Rio de Janeiro
1997 *Impressões Itinerantes,* Casa Do Brasil, Madrid
1998 *Re-Aligning Vision: Alternative Currents in South American Drawing,* The Archer M. Huntington Art Gallery, Austin
Terra Incógnita, Centro Cultural Banco De Brasil, Rio de Janeiro
1999 *XXIV Bienal de São Paulo,* Brazil
Das Vanguardas Ao Fim Do Milênio, Culturgest, Lisbon
2000 *Heterotipias,* Centro de Arte Reina Sofia, Madrid
Global Conceptualism: Point of Origin 50's-80's, Miami Art Museum
ICON + GRID + VOID: Art of the Americas from the Chase Manhattan Collection, Americas Society Art Gallery, New York

Collections:

Museu de Arte Contemporanea, Sao Paulo; Museu de Arte Moderna, Rio de Janeiro; Museu de Arte, Campina Grande, Brazil; Museu de Arte, Belo Horizonte, Brazil; Museum of Modern Art, New York; Wallraf-Richartz Museum, Cologne; Power Gallery, Sydney; Chase Manhattan Collection, New York.

Publications:

By DIAS: Books—*The Illustration of Art: Art,* Buenos Aires, 1972; *Some Artists Do, Some Don't,* Milan 1974; *The Illustration of Art: The Meaning of Production Models,* with text by Paulo Sergio, Milan 1974; *The Illustration of Art: A Public Portrait,* Milan 1974; *The Art of Transference,* Milan 1974; *The Illustration of Art: Economy (Model),* Cologne 1974; *Untitled,* Rio de Janeiro 1974; *Landscapes,* with João Candido Galvão and Izabel Burbridge, São Paulo 1994. **Article—**''The Illustration of Art'' in *Kunst Nachrichten* (Lucerne), April 1973. **Recording—***The Space Between,* Milan 1971. **Films and videotapes—***The Illustration of Art No. 1,* Milan 1971; *The Illustration of Art No. 2,* Milan 1971; *The Illustration of Art No. 3,* Milan 1971; *The New York Information System,* New York 1972; *The Illustration of Art: GIMMICK,* Milan 1972; *The Illustration of Art: Working Class Hero/Eating/Washing,* Milan 1972; *The Illustration of Art: Conversation Piece,* Milan 1973.

On DIAS: Books—*Antonio Dias,* exhibition catalog, with an essay by Pierre Restany, Rio de Janeiro 1964; *Antonio Dias,* exhibition catalog, with an essay by Helio Oiticica, Rio de Janeiro 1967; *Record as Artwork,* exhibition catalog, with an essay by Germano Celent, London 1973; *Antonio Dias,* exhibition catalog, with an essay by Ronaldo Brito, Rio de Janeiro 1974; *Antonio Dias,* exhibition catalog, with text by Sérgio Duarte, Venice 1980; *Antonio Dias: The Invented Land,* exhibition catalog with essay by Helmut Friedel, Munich 1984. **Articles—**''Cannibals All (24th Sao Paulo Bienal)'' by Edward Leffingwell in *Art in America* (New York), May 1999.

* * *

A Brazilian artist living in Italy, Antonio Dias has become, since the end of the 1960s, distinguished in the field of Conceptual Art. Among his early works were the series of *Trame* (1968), woodcuts of essentially linear graphic outlines, abandoned at an elementary stage. These pieces *(Evergreen Monument to Agriculture/Grass Covered Pyramid)* had the appearance of projects that remained unrealizable because of the paucity of available data. In these and other works, the predicative function of the arts that constituted the input—i.e., the intention of the work—was underlined by the anonymity of its making, and by the constant supportive function which Dias assigned to the work's subtitle.

Dias considers art as a system (ideological and economical), and his study of it revolves around those aspects of art most compromised by ideology (*The Illustration of Art,* 1970–74). He then broadens his field of investigation to take into account the most widespread channels of mass-communication. He deals with newspapers as if they were 'tazebao' (handwritten mural papers of the Chinese Cultural Revolution), whereas magazine illustrations are treated as material for the study of their signifying functions. He then continues to analyse the relationship, however recondite, between the macrosystem of cultural industries and the microsystem of contemporary art. The object of his analysis is the specific iconic quality of language, investigated by means of long, painstaking work on handmade paper onto which he organizes a series of dots to form a constellation. In addition, he has investigated the legitimizing codes that art has produced for itself in order to become an autonomous discipline.

In the cycle *The Illustration of Art/Model Society* (1974), Dias gives us an ensemble of black squares, each marked by a smaller white square in the upper right corner. The inscription of one figure within another is to be found in several examples of Dias' work. Besides being a metonymic representation of art (as a system that produces ideas), the work opens up a specific relationship with space. The white rectangle determines an ambiguous perception inasmuch as it may be perceived by the viewer as part of the whiteness of the wall behind—and so become a sign open to the continuity of the space; at the same time Dias uses the white rectangle in a structure that can represent a map of the gallery in which it is exhibited. The viewer is here offered the opportunity to reflect on the complexity of a particular system, signified by the different meanings he can attribute to the concept of space. Space, in this case, can be understood either as proper painted space, or as wall-space, both in their physical, not symbolic, functions. Alternatively, such space may be understood as that sociological space defined according to its function, or as symbolic space in which communicative exchange takes place, touching on such matters as sociability and the commodity value of signs.

This elaboration of the picture as agent of semantic displacements is present in Dias' most recent work, too. Handmade paper has now become his preferred material, chosen after a long journey to Nepal, where the artist worked with the local craftsmen. Since the paper is entirely handmade, from the very beginning it is already speckled with impurities—minimal materic 'events'. The colours subsequently used by the artist are entirely of vegetable origin, so that nature becomes the first and foremost ambience of the picture, the primordial space that the picture carries inscribed within itself.

The signs drawn on the paper, all the more conforming to allusive symbols, at times repeat the structure of the rectangle inscribed within the square, or else suggest it—in a negative sense—as empty space. The visual repertoire is now open to an array of symbols from a variety of sources (the dollar, a bone, a flag, or some other abstract form). These often allude to the differences between Western cultures (from which a number of symbolic stereotypes are derived) and Eastern cultures, understood as the 'primary' sources from which archetypal symbols are quoted.

Thus, meanings are displaced and interchanged, or at least made relative. At times, they are even totally transformed. The images, uprooted from their original context and rendered as heraldic figures on the fragmented surfaces of the paper, are at the same time both ironically treated and ennobled by the sumptuousness of the artefact.

—Giorgio Verzotti

DIBBETS, Jan

Nationality: Dutch. **Born:** Gerardus Johannes Marie Dibbets, in Weert, 9 May 1941. **Education:** Studied at Bisschoppelijk College, Weert, 1953–59; art education, Academie voor Beeldende en Bouwende Kunsten, Tilburg, 1959–63; private painting studies under Jan Gregoor,

Eindhoven, 1961–63; Saint Martin's School of Art, London, 1967. **Family:** Married Bianka Francisca de Poorter in 1967; daughter: Hiske Karool. **Career:** Independent artist, in Antwerp 1964, in Enschede 1964–67, in Amsterdam since 1968; abstract paintings 1964–68; photographic works, since 1967. Co-founder, with Reinier Lucassen and Ger Van Elk, International Institute for the Re-education of Artists, Amsterdam 1968. Art instructor, Enschede, 1964–67; and Ateliers 63, Haarlem, since 1968; visiting artist, Nova Scotia College of Art and Design, Halifax, 1971; professor, Staatliche Kunstakademie, Dusseldorf, since 1983. **Awards:** British Council Scholarship, 1967; Heineken Prize, The Hague 1969; Cassandra Foundation Award, 1971; Rembrandt Prize, Goethe-Stiftung, Basle, 1979. **Agents:** Barbara Gladstone Gallery, 515 West 24th Street, New York, New York 10011, U.S.A.; Waddington Galleries, 11 Cork Street, London WIX 1PD, England; Galerie Konrad Fischer, Platanenstrasse 7, 4000 Dusseldorf, West Germany. **Address:** Boerhaaveplein 6, 1091 Amsterdam, Netherlands.

Individual Exhibitions:

1965 Galerie 845, Amsterdam
Galerie Swart, Amsterdam
1966 Galerie Swart, Amsterdam
1967 *Demontable Multiples,* Galerie Swart, Amsterdam
1968 Galerie Konrad Fischer, Duseldorf
1969 Seth Siegelaub Gallery, New York
Videogalerie Gerry Schum, Dusseldorf
Art and Project, Amsterdam
Museum Haus Lange, Krefeld, West Germany
1970 Galerie Yvon Lambert, Paris
Galleria Francoise Lambert, Milan
Zentrum für Aktuelle Kunst, Aachen, West Germany
Aktionstraum 1, Munich
1971 Galleria Sperone, Turin
Galerie Konrad Fischer, Dusseldorf
Art and Project, Amsterdam
Stedelijk Van Abbemuseum, Eindhoven, Netherlands
1972 Galerie MTL, Brussels
Galerie Yvon Lambert, Paris
Jack Wendler Gallery, London
Galleria Toselli, Milan
Bezalel National Museum, Jerusalem
Dutch Pavilion at the *Biennale*, Venice
Stedelijk Museum, Amsterdam
1973 Leo Castelli Gallery, New York
Jack Wendler Gallery, London
Galleria Sperone-Fischer, Rome
Galerie Konrad Fischer, Dusseldorf
Art and Project, Amsterdam
Kabinett für Aktuelle Kunst, Bremerhaven, West Germany
1974 Galleria Sperone, Turin
Galerie Konrad Fischer, Dusseldorf
Galerie Rolf Preisig, Basle
Galerie Yvon Lambert, Paris
1975 Galerie MTL, Brussels
Galleria Marilena Bonomo, Bari, Italy
Art and Project, Amsterdam
Autumn Melody, Kunstmuseum, Lucerne
Cusack Gallery, Houston
Claire Copley Gallery, Los Angeles
Leo Castelli Gallery, New York
1976 Scottish Arts Council Gallery, Edinburgh (travelled to the Arnolfini Gallery, Bristol; Chapter Arts Centre, Cardiff; and the Museum of Modern Art, Oxford)
Galerie Konrad Fischer, Dusseldorf
1978 Leo Castelli Gallery, New York
Galerie Charles Kriwin, Brussels
1979 INK, Zurich, Switzerland
1980 Stedelijk Van Abbemuseum, Eindhoven, Netherlands (travelled to the Musée d'Art Moderne de la Ville, Paris; and the Kunsthalle, Berne)
1981 Galerie Konrad Fischer, Dusseldorf
Galleria Christian Stein, Turin
1982 Museum Fodor, Amsterdam
Anthony d'Offay Gallery, London
Centre International de Création Artistique, Paris
Kamakura Gallery, Tokyo
Galerie Karen and Jean Bernier, Athens
Leo Castelli Gallery, New York
1984 Galerie Dam 43, Middelburg, Netherlands
Waddington Galleries, London
1985 Galerie Maeght Lelong, Paris
Van Abbemuseum, Eindhoven, Netherlands
Muzej Savremene Umetnosti, Belgrade (travelled to Galerija Suvremene Umjetnosti, Zagreb)
1987 Galerie Konrad Fischer, Dusseldorf
Guggenheim Museum, New York (travelled to Minneapolis, Detroit, West Palm Beach, and Eindhoven, Netherlands)
1991 FRAC, Le Grand Jardin, Reims
1995 Kunstverein Ludwigsburg, Ludwigsburg
Bonnefantenmuseum, Masstricht, The Netherlands
1996 Galerie Lelong, Paris
1997 Städlische Kunstsammlungen, Chemnitz, Germany
1999 Barbara Gladstone Gallery, New York
2000 Bawag Foundation, Vienna
Quelques Fenetres, Galerie Lelong, Paris
2001 Barbara Gladstone Gallery, New York

Selected Group Exhibitions:

1967 *Serielle Formationen,* Universität Frankfurt, Frankfurt
1970 *10th International Biennale of Art,* Tokyo
1971 *Guggenheim International,* Guggenheim Museum, New York
1972 *Konzept-Kunst,* Kunstmuseum, Basle
1974 *Contemporanea,* Parcheggio Villa Borghese, Rome
1977 *Europe in the 70's,* Art Institute of Chicago
1979 *European Dialogue,* at the *3rd Biennale of Sydney,* Art Gallery of New South Wales, Sydney
1982 *Documenta,* Kassel, West Germany
1984 *La Grande Parade,* Stedelijk Museum, Amsterdam
1987 *Photography and Art 1946–86,* Los Angeles County Museum of Art

1991 *Conceptual Art,* Musée d'Art Moderne de la Ville de Paris
1995 *Considering the Object of Art, 1965–1975,* Museum of Contemporary Art, Los Angeles
1996 *Turning Up 1–4,* Kunstmuseum Wolfsburg, Germany
1997 *Art in the 20th Century,* Martin-Gropius, Berlin
Venice Biennale
1999 *The Museum as Muse,* Museum of Modern Art, New York
Stedelijk Museum, Amsterdam
2000 *Postmedia, Conceptual Photography in the Guggenheim Museum Collection,* Solomon R. Guggenheim Museum, New York
Changing Perceptions: The Panza Collection at the Guggenheim Museum, Guggenheim Museum, Bilbao, Spain

Collections:

Stedelijk Museum, Amsterdam; Stedelijk Van Abbemuseum, Eindhoven, Netherlands; Museum Boymans-van Beuningen, Rotterdam; Tate Gallery, London; Centre Georges Pompidou, Paris; Louisiana Museum, Humlebaek, Denmark; Kunstmuseum, Basle; Museum Ludwig, Cologne; Museum of Modern Art, New York; Walker Art Center, Minneapolis.

Publications:

By DIBBETS: Books—*Robin Redbreast's Territory; Sculpture 1969, April-June,* Cologne and New York 1970. **Films and video—***Land Art,* edited by Gerry Schum, 1968; *Fire/Feuer/Feu/Vuur,* 1968; *12 Hours Ride/Objects with Correction of Perspective,* 1969; *Painting 1,* 1970; *Painting 2,* 1970; *Vertical-Horizontal-Diagonal-Square,* 1970; *Horizon I—Sea, Venetian Blinds,* 1971; *Horizons II—Sea,* 1971; *Horizon III—Sea,* 1971; *Vibrating Horizon,* 1971; *Video—2 Diagonals,* 1971; *Video—3 Diagonals,* 1971.

On DIBBETS: Books—*Jan Dibbets: Demontable Multiples,* exhibition folder, with text by Marcel Vos, Amsterdam 1967; *Jan Dibbets,* exhibition catalog, with text by Paul Wember, Krefeld, West Germany 1969; *Jan Dibbets,* exhibition catalog, with text by Klaus Honnef, Aachen, West Germany 1970; *Jan Dibbets,* exhibition catalog, with text by Rudi H. Fuchs, Eindhoven, Netherlands 1971; *Jan Dibbets,* exhibition catalog, with texts by E. de Wilde, Rini Dippel and Marcel Vos, Amsterdam 1972; *Jan Dibbets; Autumn Melody,* exhibition catalog, with text by Jean-Christophe Ammann, Lucerne 1975; *Jan Dibbets,* exhibition catalog with texts by Barbara Reise and M.M. Vos, Edinburgh and Cardiff 1976; *Jan Dibbets,* exhibition catalog, with text by Rudi H. Fuchs, Eindhoven, Netherlands 1980; *Jan Dibbets,* exhibition catalog, with texts by Suzanne Page, M.M. Vos and Carole Naggar, Paris 1980; *Jan Dibbets,* exhibition catalog, with texts by Martin Friedman, M.M Vos and Rudi Fuchs, New York, Minneapolis and Amsterdam 1987.

* * *

Jan Dibbets' work springs from the relationships between human sight, camera perspective, and nature, as defined by the flatness of the Dutch landscape. Working on and between these three levels since 1968, Dibbets began to create what he called ''Perspective Corrections.'' In these works, he introduced geometric forms into the landscape and studio, subsequently photographing them with a perspective that in the final image, rendered them as different shapes entirely. Hence, an ellipse becomes a circle, and a trapezoid, a perfect square. The photograph, seemingly natural, collides with nature as experienced by the human eye. A tension arises between the two systems of sight, placing the viewer in a state of uncertainty.

Dibbets' works acknowledges that both ways of seeing are equally ''true.'' This play between the reality of ''nature'' and the ''reality'' of illusionistic space is clearly depicted in *Fireplace,* 1968, in which two events are presented: a film about a fire that burnt a television screen, and an actual fire which burns the screen on which the former event was shown. Here, reality appears as illusion repeated. The fact of the actual incident, and the fact of its registration are different, yet regarded equally.

In pieces such as *The Shadows in My Studio Photographed Every Ten Minutes* and *The Shortest Day at the Van Abbemuseum,* Dibbets used photography to show the progressive transformation of place in relation to time and light. Presented as a multiple-frame grid piece, each frame in the grid represents a select photographic view of a particular moment in the time sequence. The works have a certain formal cohesion uncharacteristic of the random manner with which we experience the passage of light and time. Here again, the photographic representation presents a different reality, i.e., light and time viewed in compressed form, as a geometric grid.

Dibbets' strategies disturb our conventional trust in photographs. At times, his photographic manipulations are a convincing illusion, as in the *Perspective Corrections.* However, in pieces like *Dutch Mountains,* in which the selectivity of framing and movement are deliberately apparent, we are less fooled. Here the artist relies on the assumption of photographic objectivity to create the tension between the camera representations and the contrived shape of the sequenced prints. In the end, the work convinces us by its cohesive form alone, aided by scientific-looking hand-applied diagrams. The photographic view of nature remains fragile.

In his more recent work, Dibbets combines painting (acrylic and watercolor) with photographs of architecturally extraordinary windows in various international cities, as in *The Barcelona Windows,* 1989–90, and *Montreal,* 1988–89. The windows, photographed from skewed angles and cropped into abstract fragments that include only the pane and the frame, are suspended in a painted field. The depth of the view through the window to the natural world contrasts with the flat painted field, which, lacking in depth of perspective, nevertheless vibrates with a surface energy. The windows, architectural mediators between interior and exterior space, provide a view to the natural world. But the distorting angles Dibbets adopted while photographing them distract from the promise of reality, thus creating a fragile tension. Here, as in the previous work, the photographic image is the uncertain element, whereas the painted field, with its added diagrammatic lines, provides a sort of rational/spiritual refuge.

Dibbets regards natural and artificial perspectives as occurrences of equal ontological status. Rather than devaluing ''natural'' reality, Dibbets's manipulations deepen our relationship to it by challenging conventions of perspective. The confounding of customary ways of looking ultimately intensifies sight itself. Thus, we receive from the artist what one might call a ''new pair of eyes.''

—Essay by Alicja Kepinska; updated by Audrey Mandelbaum

DIEBENKORN, Richard (Clifford Jr.)

Nationality: American. **Born:** Portland, Oregon, 22 April 1922. **Education:** Stanford University, California, 1940–43, B.A. 1949; University of California, Berkeley, 1943–44; California School of Fine Arts, San Francisco, 1946–47; University of New Mexico, Albuquerque, 1950–52, M.A. 1952. **Military Service:** Served in the United States Marines, 1943–45. **Family:** Married Phyllis Gilman in 1943; children: Gretchen and Christopher. **Career:** Independent artist, California, since 1952. Taught at California School of Fine Arts, San Francisco, 1947–50; University of Illinois, Urbana, 1952–53; California College of Arts and Crafts, Oakland, 1955–60; and San Francisco Arts Institute, 1961–66; Artist-in-residence, Stanford University, 1963–64; professor of art, University of California at Los Angeles, 1966–73. **Awards:** Rosenberg Travelling fellowship 1959; National Institute of Arts and Letters Award, 1962; Tamarind fellowship, 1962; Cultural Exchange Grant, to Europe and U.S.S.R., United States Department of State, 1964; Beck Gold Medal, Pennsylvania Academy of Fine Arts, Philadelphia, 1968; Edward MacDowell Medal, MacDowell Colony, Peterborough, New Hampshire, 1978; Skowhegan Medal for Painting, Skowhegan School of Art, Maine, 1979; National Medal of Arts Award, National Endowment for the Arts, 1991; Gold Medal for Painting, AAAL, 1993. **Member:** National Council on the Arts, Washington, D.C., 1966–69; National Institute of Arts and Letters, 1967; American Academy of Arts and Letters, 1985. **Agent:** M. Knoedler and Company Inc., 19 East 70th Street, New York, New York 10021. **Address:** 334 Amalfi Drive, Santa Monica, California 90402, U.S.A. **Died:** Of respiratory failure, in Berkeley, California, 30 March 1993.

Richard Diebenkorn, 1992, photo by Christopher Felver. ©Archive Photos, Inc.

Individual Exhibitions:

1948 California Palace of the Legion of Honor, San Francisco
1951 University of New Mexico, Albuquerque
1952 Paul Kantor Gallery, Los Angeles
1954 Paul Kantor Gallery, Los Angeles
San Francisco Museum of Art
Allan Frumkin Gallery, Chicago
1955 University of California, Berkeley
1956 Poindexter Gallery, New York
Oakland Art Museum, California
1957 Swetzoff Gallery, Boston
1958 Poindexter Gallery, New York
1960 *Recent Paintings by Richard Diebenkorn,* California Palace of the Legion of Honor, San Francisco
Pasadena Art Museum, California (retrospective)
1961 Phillips Collection, Washington, D.C.
Poindexter Gallery, New York
1962 National Institute of Arts and Letters, New York
1963 M.H. de Young Memorial Museum, San Francisco
Poindexter Gallery, New York
1964 Washington Gallery of Modern Art, Washington, D.C. (retrospective)
Stanford University Art Gallery, California
1965 Jewish Museum, New York
Pavilion Art Gallery, Newport Beach, California
Waddington Galleries, London
Paul Kantor Gallery, Los Angeles
Poindexter Gallery, New York
1967 Waddington Galleries, London
National Institute of Arts and Letters, New York
Stanford University Art Gallery, California
Peale House, Pennsylvania Academy of Fine Arts, Philadelphia
1968 Peale House, Pennsylvania Academy of Fine Arts, Philadelphia
Nelson-Atkins Art Gallery, Kansas City, Missouri
Richmond Art Center, California
Poindexter Gallery, New York
1969 *The Ocean Park Series,* Poindexter Gallery, New York
New Paintings of Richard Diebenkorn, Los Angeles County Museum of Art
1971 Irving Blum Gallery, Los Angeles
Poindexter Gallery, New York
The Ocean Park Series: Recent Work, Marlborough Gallery, New York
Gallerie Smith-Andersen, Palo Alto, California
1972 *Paintings from the Ocean Park Series,* San Francisco Museum of Art
Lithographs, Gerald John Hayes Gallery, Los Angeles
Herbert Mondavi Gallery, Oakville, California
The Ocean Park Series: Recent Work, Marlborough Fine Art, London
Marlborough Galerie, Zurich
1974 *Drawings 1944–1973,* Mary Porter Sesnon Gallery, University of California at Santa Cruz
1975 *Early Abstract Works 1948–1955,* James Corcoran Gallery, Los Angeles

Richard Diebenkorn: *Pouring Coffee,* 1958. ©Burstein Collection/Corbis.

John Berggruen Gallery, San Francisco
Marlborough Gallery, New York
1976 *Monotypes,* Wight Art Gallery, University of California at Los Angeles
Albright-Knox Art Gallery, Buffalo, New York (toured the United States)
Museum of Contemporary Art, Chicago
1977 M. Knoedler and Company, New York
1979 M. Knoedler and Company, New York
1980 M. Knoedler and Company, New York
1981 *Matrix/Berkeley 40,* University of California Berkeley
Etchings and Drypoints 1949–80, Minneapolis Institute of Arts, Minnesota (toured the United States, 1981–83)
Marlborough Gallery, New York
1982 M. Knoedler and Company, New York
Crown Point Gallery, Oakland, California
Intaglio 1961–80, Brooklyn Museum, New York
1983 *Works on Paper,* John Berggruen Gallery, San Francisco
Paintings 1948–83, San Francisco Museum of Modern Art
1984 M. Knoedler and Company, New York
Etchings and Drypoints 1965, L.A. Louver Gallery, Venice, California
1985 Sheldon Memorial Art Gallery, University of Nebraska, Lincoln (travelled to Brooklyn Museum, New York)
Etchings and Drypoints, Patricia Heesy Gallery, New York
M. Knoedler and Company, New York

1986 Crown Point Press, New York
1989 Hara Museum of Contemporary Art, Tokyo
1991 *Richard Diebenkorn: New Work,* Knoedler, New York
1992 Whitechapel Art Gallery, London (retrospective) (travelled to Juan March Fondacion, Madrid; Frankfurter Kunstverein, Frankfurt am Main)
1994 *Richard Diebenkorn: Small Format Oil on Canvas—Figures, Still Lifes and Landscapes,*
1995 *Richard Diebenkorn: Abstraction,* Galerie Lawrence Rubin, Zurich
1997 *The Art of Richard Diebenkorn,* Whitney Museum of American Art, New York (travelled to Modern Art Museum of Forth Worth; Phillips Collection, Washington, D.C.; San Francisco Museum of Modern Art)

Selected Group Exhibitions:

1964 *Paintings and Sculpture of a Decade 1954–1964,* Tate Gallery, London
1966 *Art of the United States 1970–1966,* Whitney Museum, New York
1968 *Biennale,* Venice
1969 *Annual Exhibition,* Whitney Museum, New York
Kompass, Stedelijk van Abbemuseum, Eindhoven, Netherlands
1972 *70th American Exhibition,* Art Institute of Chicago
1973 *Biennial of Contemporary American Painting,* Corcoran Gallery of Art, Washington, D.C.
1978 *Biennale,* Venice
American Paintings of the 1970's, Albright-Knox Art Gallery, Buffalo (toured the United States, 1978–79)
1979 *Works on Paper,* Knoedler Gallery, London
1980 *American Drawing in Black and White,* Brooklyn Museum, New York
1984 *The Figurative Mode: Bay Area Paintings 1956–66,* Grey Art Gallery, New York University (travelled to Newport Harbor Art Museum, California)
1986 *After Matisse,* Queens Museum, Flusing, New York (toured the United States, 1986–88)
1988 *Painting from the San Francisco Bay Area,* North Carolina Museum of Art, Raleigh
Twentieth Century Paintings and Sculpture: Avery, Chia, Cucchi, De Kooning, Diebenkorn, Dubuffet, Francis, Gottlieb, Hockney, Hofmann, Leger, Lichtenstein, Lipchitz, Miro, Picasso, Smith, Vuillard, Warhol, Richard Gray Gallery, New York
1989 *Bay Area Figurative Art 1950–1965,* San Francisco Museum of Modern Art
Illustrious Alumni, Art Museum, University of New Mexico, Albuquerque
Richard Diebenkorn, Jim Dine, Sam Francis, Associated American Artists, New York
1990 *Gifts of the Associates: 1975–1990,* Museum of Modern Art, New York
1991 *Image and Likeness: Figurative Works from the Permanent Collection of the Whitney Museum of American Art,* New York
American Masters of the '60s: Early and Late Works, Tony Shafrazi Gallery, New York
1996 *The San Francisco School of Abstract Expressionism,* Laguna Beach Museum of Art, California (travelled to San Francisco Musuem of Modern Art)
1997 *American Abstract Expressionist Painting,* Centro Cultural de Arte Contemporaneo, Mexico City
Sunshine & Noir: Art in L.A. 1960–1997, Louisiana Museum of Modern Art, Humlebaek, Denmark (travelled to Kunstmuseum Wolfsburg, Germany; Museo d'Arte Contemporanea, Turin; Armand Hammer Museum of Art and Cultural Center, Los Angeles)

Collections:

California Palace of the Legion of Honor, San Francisco; Los Angeles County Museum of Art; Albright-Knox Art Gallery, Buffalo, New York; Metropolitan Museum of Art, New York; Whitney Museum, New York; Museum of Modern Art, New York; Guggenheim Museum, New York; Corcoran Gallery, Washington, D.C.; Hirshhorn Museum, Smithsonian Institution, Washington, D.C.; Art Institute of Chicago; Brooklyn Museum, New York; Nelson Gallery, Kansas City; Phoenix Art Museum; Pasadena Art Museum.

Publications:

By DIEBENKORN: Books—*Drawings,* edited by Lorenz Eitner, Stanford, California 1965; *41 Etchings, Drypoints,* Berkeley, California 1965; *The Artist Observed: 28 Interviews with Contemporary Artists,* with interviews with John Gruen, Chicago 1991.

On DIEBENKORN: Books—*Recent Paintings by Richard Diebenkorn,* exhibition catalog, introduction by Howard Ross Smith, San Francisco 1960; *Richard Diebenkorn,* exhibition catalog with an introduction by Thomas B. Leavitt, Pasadena, California 1960; *Richard Diebenkorn,* exhibition catalog, with an essay by Gifford Phillips, Washington, D.C. 1961; *The Collector in America,* edited by Jean Lipman and others, New York 1961; *A Short History of Painting in America* by E. P. Richardson, New York 1963; Richard *Diebenkorn,* exhibition catalog, London 1965; *50 Years of Modern Art 1916–1966,* by Edward P. Henning, Cleveland 1966; *American Art since 1960* by Barbara Rose, New York 1967; *History of Modern Art: Painting, Sculpture, Architecture* by H. H. Armason, New York 1968; *Richard Diebenkorn,* exhibition catalog, Richmond, California 1968; *New York Painting and Sculpture 1940–1970* by Henry Geldzahler, New York 1969; *New Paintings of Richard Diebenkorn,* exhibition catalog, with an essay by Gail Scott, Los Angeles 1969; *The Ocean Park Series,* exhibition catalog, New York 1969; *A History of American Art* by Daniel M. Mandelowitz, New York 1970; *The Ocean Park Series: Recent Work,* exhibition catalog, with an essay by Gerald Nordland, New York 1971; *Richard Diebenkorn: Lithographs,* exhibition catalog, Los Angeles, 1972; *Contemporary Art 1942–72: Collection of the Albright-Knox Art Gallery,* New York 1972; *Richard Diebenkorn: Paintings from the Ocean Park Series,* exhibition catalog, essay by Gerald Nordland, San Francisco 1972; *The Genius of American Painting,* edited by John Wilmerding, London 1973; *Richard Diebenkorn, The Ocean Park Series: Recent Work,* exhibition catalog, essay by John Russell, London 1973; *American Impressionism* by Richard J. Boyle, Boston 1974; *Richard Diebenkorn: Drawings*

1944–1973, exhibition catalog, with an essay by Philip Brookman and Walker Melion, Santa Cruz, California 1974; *Early Abstract Works 1948–1955,* exhibition catalog, Los Angeles 1975; *Richard Diebenkorn: Monotypes,* exhibition catalog, essay by Gerald Nordland, Los Angeles 1976; *Richard Diebenkorn,* exhibition catalog, New York 1979; *Richard Diebenkorn: Paintings and Drawings 1943–80,* New York 1980; *Richard Diebenkorn, Etchings and Drypoints 1949–80,* Houston 1981; *Richard Diebenkorn: Works on Paper,* edited by Richard Newlin, Houston 1987; *Painting from the San Francisco Bay Area,* exhibition catalog, Raleigh 1988; *Richard Diebenkorn, Jim Dine, Sam Francis,* exhibition catalog, New York 1989; *Illustrious Alumni,* exhibition catalog, Albuquerque 1989; *Richard Diebenkorn,* exhibition catalog, London 1991; *Richard Diebenkorn: New Work,* exhibition catalog, New York 1991; *Richard Diebenkorn: Ocean Park* by Jack Flam, New York 1992; *Richard Diebenkorn: Small Format Oil On Canvas—Figures, Still Lifes and Landscapes,* New York 1994; *Richard Diebekorn: Abstraction,* exhibition catalog, Zurich 1995; *The Art of Richard Diebenkorn,* exhibition catalog, with texts by multiple authors, New York 1997. **Articles—** ''Caro/Diebenkorn: In a Scale Apart'' by William Peterson in *Artspace,* vol. 16, no. 1–2, January-April 1992; ''Richard Diebenkorn'' by Donald Kuspit in *Artforum* (New York), vol. 31, no. 5, January 1993; ''Observations on Richard Diebenkorn's Later Drawings'' by Joseph R. Goldyne in *Drawing* (New York), vol. 15, no. 6, March-April 1994; ''Richard Diebenkorn at Knoedler'' by Stephen Westfall in *Art in America* (New York), vol. 83, no. 4, April 1995; review by David Anfam in *Burlington Magazine* (London), vol. 139, no. 1127, February 1997; ''Transformations'' by Jed Perl in *The New Republic,* vol. 217, no. 22, 1 December 1997; review by David Carrier in *Burlington Magazine* (London), vol. 139, no. 1137, December 1997; ''God is in the Vectors: The Luminous Architecture of Richard Diebenkorn's Paintings'' by Robert Hughes in *Time,* vol. 150, no. 24, 8 December 1997; ''Richard Diebenkorn at the Whitney'' by Mario Naves in *New Criterion,* vol. 16, no. 5, January 1998; ''Richard Diebenkorn'' by Peter Plagens in *Artforum* (New York), vol. 36, no. 6, February 1998; ''A Window on a World of Shape & Color'' by Kenneth Baker in *Smithsonian* (Washington, D.C.), vol. 28, no. 12, March 1998; ''Richard Diebenkorn: A Seasoned Sensuality'' by Stephen Westfall in *Art in America* (New York), vol. 86, no. 10, October 1998.

* * *

Since he began painting during the 1940s, California painter Richard Diebenkorn evolved through three distinct phases, moving from early work in an abstract vein related to Abstract Expressionism of the de Kooning, Clyfford Still variety, to a period of gestural figuration, arriving finally at his Ocean Park Series of abstracted, painterly landscapes.

During the period covering the years between 1943 and 1955, Diebenkorn developed his basic concern, to abstract from his perceptions of things seen: painterly, atmospheric, lightfilled distillations of the Western American landscape. From the beginning, the work was rooted in visual impressions of his environment which he translates in terms of painterly areas of colored light accompanied by geometrical framing. Diebenkorn's central concerns are formal, and he uses his considerable skills to develop a vocabulary which is not autobiographical in the sense of stressing private associational meanings but is rather more broadly evocative of outer and inner realms.

In 1954 Diebenkorn began working directly from the model, along with his teacher, David Park, and another painter, Elmer Bischoff, in San Francisco. In a 1957 exhibition, national recognition came for this group of figurative, gestural painters whose work is characterized by slapdash brushstrokes, sensuous color and a generally rough and lush atmosphere. Diebenkorn's figuration of the late 1950s and early 60s is exemplified by ''Girl On A Terrace'' (1956). The expressionistic figure is part of a setting combining indoors and outdoors: Her bodily form acts as part of an implied window frame which both separates and links the overall atmosphere. She is more a formal element in the composition than a suggestion of particular subject matter. Her presence is used as an element to complete the structural tensions and it also enhances the pervasive mood of sober contemplation.

In pictures such as ''Cityscape I'' and ''Landscape I'' (both 1963), the figure disappears. Housetops, terraced hillsides, lots are undergoing a process of schematization, becoming geometrical patternings, defining spaces inhabited only by atmospheric colors awash with a kind of energetic quietude. In 1966 Diebenkorn moved to Santa Monica, California, and in 1967 he made the first of his Ocean Park Series pictures, named for a section of that area which borders on the ocean. It was a series he would develop throughout the 70s finding multiple variations in a schema which consists of a highly formalized conjunction of geometry and painterly field, enlivened by the misty light which emanates from the areas of soft off-colors. These areas are variously sized, shaped and activated by subtle remnants of the painting process to achieve the feeling of what Diebenkorn called the ''tension beneath calm.'' Colored borders act both to divide and conjoin the translucent spaces, adding additional tension to the illusion that there is an active presence hidden within the emotively empty fields. Sometimes the viewpoint is that of looking upward, and often it suggests aerial sittings from a great distance below. Always there is the tense balance of inside/outside, and always there is the sense of ultimate origination from things perceived analytically and at a remove which borders between alienation and intimacy.

The Ocean Park Series is the outgrowth of Diebenkorn's persistence over many years to refine his painter's skills. The pictures are informed by a quality of color as light which is highly personal and grows out of studious perception. Diebenkorn is by no means a revolutionary painter. His are steps out of earlier masters, Matisse, Mondrian, Monet and Abstract Expressionism, and present in his pictures are the souvenirs gathered from these precursors. Yet, by sticking to his own experience, so particularly Western American, he has managed to distill things from each of them and translate them into a visualization which is quite his own.

—Barbara Cavaliere

DIEHL, Hans-Jurgen

Nationality: German. **Born:** Hanau/Main, 22 May 1940. **Education:** Studied art at Akademie für Bildenden Künste, Munich, 1959–62; Ecole National Supérieur des Beaux-Arts, Paris, 1959–62; and at the Hochschule für Bildende Künste, Berlin, 1962–66; M.A. 1966. **Family:** Married Margrit Wiebe in 1966; son: Hannes. **Career:** Painter since 1966; Professor, Hochschule für Bildende Künste, Berlin, since 1977. **Member:** Founder-Member, Grossgorchen 35, Berlin 1964; Cooperative 10/9, Munich, since 1972; Member, Deutscher

Painting by Hans-Jürgen Diehl. ©2001 Artists Rights Society (ARS), NY/VG Bild-Kunst, Bonn.

Kunstlerbund, Bonn, 1972. **Agent:** Galerie Limmer, Cologne, Germany. **Addresses:** 47 Clinton Street, New York, New York 10002, U.S.A.; and Halberstädter Strasse 7, 10711 Berlin, Germany.

Individual Exhibition:

1964 Galerie Grossgorchen 35, West Berlin
1966 Galerie Groosgorchen 35, West Berlin
1967 Galerie Junge Generation, Hamburg
1968 Galerie Schmucking, Braunschweig, West Germany
Galerie Ostentor, Dortmund
1969 Galerie Niepel, Dusseldorf
1970 Diehl/Petrick/Sorge: Malerei, Grapnik, Material, Haus am Waldsee, West Berlin (travelled to Badischer Kunstverein, Karlsruhe)
Galerie Brusberg, Hannover
Galerie Kerlikowsky und Kneiding, Munich
1971 Kunstverein, Dusseldorf

Kunstmuseum, Ludwhigshafen, West Germany (with Wolfgang Petrick)
Galerie 2000, West Berlin
1972 Institut fur Moderne Kunst, Nuremberg, West Germany
1973 Karl-Ernst-Osthaus Museum, Hagen, West Germany (with Wolfgang Petrick)
Galerie Wolfgang Ketterer, Munich
1974 Galerie 2000, West Berlin
1976 Galerie Poll, West Berlin
1977 Ulmer Museum, Ulm, West Germany (travelled to the Kunstverein, Hannover)
1980 Galerie Poll, West Berlin
1981 Galerie Lucklum, West Germany
1984 Galerie Friedrich, Cologne
1985 Staatliche Kunsthalle, West Berlin
1989 Galerie Poll, Berlin
1992 Galerie Limmer, Freiburg, Germany
1993 Galerie Limmer, Freiburg, Germany
1995 Galerie Limmer, Freiburg, Germany
1997 Galerie Tammen & Busch, Berlin
1999 Galerie Limmer, Cologne, Germany
2000 Kesselhaus, Hannover, Germany

Selected Group Exhibitions:

1964 *Kunstpreis Junger Western,* Recklinghausen, West Germany (and 1965)
1966 *Junge Berliner Kunstler,* Kunsthalle, Basle
1967 *Neuer Realismus,* Haus am Waldsee, West Berlin (toured Germany)
1970 *Berliner Realisten,* Bädischer Kunstverein, Karlsruhe, West Germany
1972 *Prinzip Realismus,* Deutsche Akademischer Austauschdienst, West Berlin (toured Germany, Sweden, Norway, Italy, and Greece, 1972–74)
1975 *Deutsche Grafik,* Lawrence Gallery, Kansas City, Missouri
1976 *Deutsche Grafik im 20. Jahrhundert,* Kestner-Gesellschaft, Hannover
1977 *Berlin Now,* New School for Social Research, New York
1978 *Ugly Realism,* Institute of Contemporary Arts, London
1985 *Fifteen Berlin Artists in Brazil,* toured Brazil
1987 *Momentaufnahme, Staatl,* Kunsthalle, Berlin
Ich und die Stadt, Berlinische Galerie, Berlin
1989 *Zeitbilder, Mannheimer Kunstverein,* Mannheim, Germany
1988 *Stationen der Moderne,* Berlinische Galerie, Berlin
1990 *Berliner Kunststücke,* Altes Museum Berlin, Leipzig
1991 *Interferenzen, Riga,* St. Petersburg
Um 68, Kunsthalle Düsseldorf (travelled to Zurich, Berlin, Hugh Lane Municipal Gallery of Modern Art, Dublin)

Collections:

Nationalgalerie, Berlin; Landesmuseum, Hannover; Kestner-Gesellschaft, Hannover; Karl-Ernst-Osthaus Museum, Hagen, Germany; City Art Museum, Helsinki; Hessisches Landesmuseum, Darmstadt, Germany; Museum Witten, Germany; Staatliche Museen Preussischer Kulturbesitz, Nationalgalerie and Kupferstichkabinett, Berlin.

Publications:

On DIEHL: Books—*Pop und die Folgen* by Heinz Ohff, Dusseldorf 1968; *Kunstjahrbuch I,* edited by Jurgen Harten and others, Hannover 1970; *Diehl, Petrick, Sorge: Malerie, Graphik, Material,* exhibition catalog, West Berlin 1970; *Kritischer Realismus,* exhibition catalog, with text by Heinz Ohff, West Berlin 1971; *Deutsche Kunst der 60er Jahre: Malerie, Collage, Op-Art, Graphik,* edited by Juliane Roh, Munich 1971; *Kunst ist Utopie* by Heinz Ohff, West Berlin 1974; *Hans-Jurgen Diehl: Bilder und Zeichnungen 1963–1977,* exhibition catalog with text by Johann Karl Schmidt and Eberhard Roters, Ulm, West Germany 1977; *Diehl,* exhibition catalog, with text by Dore Ashton and J. K. Schmidt, West Berlin 1985; exhibition catalog, with text by B. Weyergraf, Freiburg, 1992; *L'Art en Allemagne 1945–1995* by Violette Garnier, Paris 1997.

* * *

If Hans-Jürgen Diehl were a novelist, he would be Joyce. His natural instinct is to work in the time-honoured approach of free association, which allows for compendious abstractions adding up to reality. The results are demonic, almost apocalyptic paintings: A sudden flash of insight revealing the implications of a culture estranged from the world and so utterly without a unifying identity since the Thirty Years' War.

Diehl had several reasons to feel alienated as a modern German artist. First, being a painter, he had to deal with art history—a history that in Germany, with its special historic circumstances, is riddled with significant ruptures and turbulent debates. He chose to live in Berlin during a period when Berlin painters were accused of being unimaginative realists. Diehl rejected this prosaic, realist tradition. Second, during the post-war years when the Americans began rebuilding the country, they brought with them a culture that was anything but German. Subsequently Diehl's preoccupation with his own heritage was tinctured with considerations of foreign traits. His tradition and state of mind being splintered, the "fragment" emerged as the central leitmotif of his work.

Since the mid-60s, Diehl's paintings have been a response to this uprooted, mechanized, fragmented and manipulated existence which epitomized Berlin. His work is generated on an impulse of beauty, always present in Diehl, in spite of everything, and a need to speak of this wound. The human figures in his early paintings are truncated, mutilated, damned: puppets impaled on a wall, mounds of bodies on a grid. He lovingly models his figure, recording the details of unkempt pleats and folds, cracks in damp leather jackets in photographic precision. However he omits their life-imbuing qualities, leaving them helplessly without heads or faces, imprisoned by their cruel surroundings. The figures appear embryonic; it is as if by trying to climb out of the canvas, they'll find their missing parts and achieve wholeness. So unresolved are the paintings that they often resemble a photograph taken out of the developer when only bits and pieces have begun to appear.

In 1966, under the impact of the Wirtschaftswunder and all its ugly implications, Diehl abandoned the sensuous, allusive approach and harnessed an idiom that carries unmistakable references to the recent past. The careful attention to detail interrupted by deliberate fragmentation was a technique employed during the Weimar period.

He favored urban settings until the mid-70s whose undertone of shame and scandal became a kind of exorcism. During the 70s Diehl moved to New York where, living in a slum of the Lower East Side, he experienced loneliness, disorientation, and, above all, chaos. Capturing both German and American urban ambiance, these subtle feelings of alienation enter in his New York paintings.

This fermenting chaos, this monstrous mutant of social organism that New York is, severing, killing biting off its own limbs, unhesitantly sprouting new shoots out of the cadaver, spills onto Diehl's canvases. It is these new shoots that deliver a secondary theme: evolvement. Diehl subtly reminds us of the latencies, possibilities and repressed realities embodied in his figures. Often the fragmented, truncated bodies never realize their potential because of other bodies crowding, imposing, occupying their space on the canvas. Diehl relies on an even more effective technique to convey this message: Completely developed figures stand behind crossbars, as behind prison bars, looking out at other bodies still undeveloped, still in a state of latency on the other plane of the picture. The sharp polarity of each distinct reality is forced to coincide. Like Kafka, Diehl records the particulars of both sides with ghastly precision, yet put together, they lack coherence and unity, a metaphor for a society thoroughly rationalized and administered in its single segments but perfectly irrational as a whole.

Upon his return to Berlin in 1983 he completed the diptych, The Bath, a painting which became one of his key works. The painting, on first glance, is a harmonious, vernal scene. Yet it is riddled with hidden meaning and bears definite historical resonances. Diehl's returns to the lake country of Berlin, as did early 20th century German painters, for his setting. Merging two images, he first conjures a past: on the left, the bather, absorbed by nature into the shadows. The scene with its rustic hues recalls early 19th-century German landscape painters, notably Karl Rottmann. Then to break the continuity, he strategically places a car of another era in the triangular axis in the center of the painting. The triangular crux highlights the gloom of nature implying both the inaccessibility of his ambiguous paradisical vision and the distancing that history demands.

During the 80s Diehl diffused the intensity of his earlier paintings. His colors, once harsh dissonant, take on more earthy and natural tones. More than ever he uses light to unfold space. Even the figures, previously estranged from the often layered backgrounds, are a more integral part of the now textured and animated environment. Diehl has opened dialogue between them by capturing gestures in motion rather than locking the figures in fixed, rigid positions. The resulting dialogue is a more open-ended narration than a revelation. As in the past the figures remain mere adumbrations of bodies. Yet the missing parts are deemphasized: Rather they seem to have slipped back into the canvas and fused themselves into their surroundings. Consequently, Diehl's use of space has become obfuscated by its expansion and various ''layers'' within the picture.

Diehl's return to Berlin seems only befitting to polish the themes of his career. The paintings which so aptly express alienation—both individual and cultural, artistic and political, historical and current—must be contained in Berlin. It is a city of exile—physical exile from a German nation psychological exile, reinforced by the formal occupation of other nations. Diehl has found means to express this mood of inner exile, for his paintings re-poses history, confronting the ruins that lie in memory if not in the city itself.

—Carrie Barker

DIETMANN, Erik

Nationality: Swedish. **Born:** Malmo in 1937. **Career:** Has lived and worked in Paris since 1960. **Agent:** Galerie Brama, 40 rue Quincampoix, 75004 Paris, France.

Individual Exhibitions:

1964 Galleria Sperone, Turin
1966 Galerie Mathias Fels, Paris
Galleria L'Elefante, Venice
Galerie 20, Amsterdam
1967 Galleri Hedenius, Stockholm
1968 Galerie 20, Amsterdam
Galleria Apollinaire, Milan
Galleria Christian Stein, Turin
1969 Galerie Mathias Fels, Paris
1970 Galerie Mathias Fels, Paris
1971 Galleri Buren, Stockholm
Jysk Kungstgalleri, Copenhagen
1972 Eat-Art Galerie, Dusseldorf
1973 Galerie Bama, Paris
1974 Galleria Massimo Valsecchi, Milan
Galerie Bama, Paris
1975 Hotel d'Angleterre, Copenhagen
Musée d'Art Moderne de la Ville, Paris (retrospetive)
1976 Galerie Bama, Paris
Galerie Tanit, Munich
Galerie Valois, Paris
Galleria Massimo Valsecchi, Milan
Academie Royale, Copenhagen
Moderna Museet, Stockholm
1977 Galleria Arte Verso, Genoa, Italy
Galerie Bon Valois, Paris
1978 Galerie Lucien Durand, Paris
1979 Galerie Herta Klang, Cologne
Nordjyllands Kuntsmuseum, Aalborg, Denmark
1980 Galleri Ahlner, Stockholm
Galerie Leger, Malmo, Sweden
1981 Galerie Gerzli Konstsalong, Goteborg, Sweden
Galerie Forum, Stockholm
Galerie Arnesen, Copenhagen
1982 Jonkoping Museum, Sweden
Galerie Sonia Zannettacci, Geneva
1983 Lunds Galleriet, Lund, Sweden
1984 Galerie Aronowitsch, Stockholm
Galerie Bama, Paris
1985 Fundacao Gulbenkian, Lisbon
Lilla Galleriet, Helsinki
Galerie Asbaek, Copenhagen
Anthony Reynolds Gallery, London
1987 Moderna Museet, Stockholm
1994 *Sans Titre. Pas un Mot. Silence,* Galerie Sud, Centre Georges Pompidou, Paris
A toi Rabelais qui a su Boire Avant la Soif, Fonds Régional d'Art Contemporain Champagne-Ardennes, Reimes, France
Galerie Aronowitsch, Stockholm
1995 *Trait Portrait,* Galerie Jacques Barbier, Paris

Injures, Galerie Claudine Papillon, Paris
Pique-nique dans mon âme, Belvédère du Château de Prague et Institut Français de Prague
1996 *Sculptor Classicus,* Musée d'Art Moderne, St. Etienne, France
1997 *Verres d'Hiver,* Union Centrale des Arts-Décoratifs, Paris
1998 *200 Sculptures de Verre,* Galerie d'Etat, Banska Bystrica, Slovakia
Double Sauce Périgueux, ADDC Espace Centre Culturel François Mitterrand, Périgueux
1999 *Les Arbres d'Odile et Autres Nouvelles,* Centre Culturel Suédois, Paris
För Fulla Glas, National Museum, Stockholm
Ceramic-mac, Le Parvis 3, Pau
2000 *Un Nez das le Verre, un Verre Dans le Nez,* Musée des Beaux-Arts, Nancy
Galerie Catherine Issert, St Paul de Vence
Galerie José Martinez, Lyon
2001 *Praise of the Desire,* Musee D'Art Moderne et D'Art Contemporain, Nice (catalog)
Château de Tanlay, Bourgogne
Galerie Papillon-Fiat, Paris
Musée d'Art Contemporain, Turin

Selected Group Exhibitions:

1967 *Superland,* Konsthall, Lund, Sweden
1980 *Malmo,* Malmo Konsthall, Sweden
1981 *Autoportraits Photographiques,* Centre Georges Pompidou, Paris
1982 *Transes a la Van Garde,* Galerie Bama, Paris
1983 *Sculptures,* Galerie Camomille, Brussels
1984 *Ceramiques,* Galerie Camomille, Brussels
1985 *Sculpture,* Fondation Cartier, Jouy-en-Josas, France
1995 *1995 Foire Internationale d'Art Contemporain,* Paris
1999 *Biennale d'Art Contemporain,* Venice

Collections:

Moderna Museet, Stockholm; Centre Georges Pompidou, Paris; Louisiana Museum, Humlebaek, Denmark.

Publications:

On DIETMANN: Books—*Hommage à Dietmann* by F.T. Bidlake, Ole Granath and Outil O'Toole, Paris 1975; *Erik Dietmann,* exhibition catalog with essay by Roland Topor, London 1985; *Erik Dietmann,*exhibition catalog with essay by Olle Granath, Stockholm 1987. **Articles—**''Comedic Mass'' by Anne Rochette and Wade Saunders in *Art in America* (New York), vol. 82, December 1994.

* * *

When Erik Dietmann wishes to refer to other artists, in order to illuminate his work, he will choose authors like the Swedish poet Gunnar Ekelöf, or Raymond Roussel and James Joyce, rather than other figurative artists. In his capacity as a multilingual maker of objects he feels more at home in Paris, where he has lived since 1960, than in Sweden. Language is for him an unlimited theatrical wardrobe, which allows practically any disguise. He lets his personality break through the language, or rather languages, as through a prism. The word-play and the multiplicity of meaning transform his literary objects into picture-puzzles, the solution of which turns out to be an absurdity. Art in his case does not answer any questions; it is rather a temporary arrangement, which constitutes a fragile support in daily life. He has, loosely based on Dali, described it as a crutch of a ''BUT,'' which in French means an aim or a support, while in English it becomes an objection.

Vulnerability is a theme in Dietmann's art. The absurd and the meaningless do not arouse his aggression, but rather his tenderness. This emotion was already present in his early objects, which were all carefully coated with plaster. Far removed from all large gestures, he is a gentleman who stands with clumsy awkwardness in the entrance-hall, dressed in a bowler and tie, with a tulip in his hand—all scrupulously covered in plaster. He has described the situation like this: ''Your qualities surpass your charms.'' Even though he addresses the spectators with this statement, it still contains a description of himself. Through all he does there also runs a warm stream of light and diverting humor, somewhat like peeing one's name in the snow, an action which he also recorded in one of his objects.

His attitude contains a disassociation from the ratrace, which enables him to let others take in the making of a work of art. Art is finally an attempt to fill a vacuum with a dialogue. In the considerably older poet and connoisseur of life, Fabian Tommyrot Bidlake, who in many cases has contributed ideas and texts to the works, Dietmann has found a kindred spirit. Their collaboration has nourished both of them.

Dietmann's gestures and sometimes breakneck wordgames have from the beginning helped to establish ''guarded crossings'' (in French *Passage Cloutee*) between the real events on the one hand and art-language on the other. As a pacifist in exile, he was in 1962 employed building a sea-side restaurant in Sainte Maxime, when he committed a symbolic act: He swallowed a couple of metres of gauze bandage, as a complement to that gauze bandage required for the external injuries of the inexperienced building worker. He was well aware that the aims of pacifism should never be limited to avoiding the external injuries to man and his surroundings. The root of the evil lies in the already inflicted internal injuries, in a language which is so tattered and torn, that acts of violence replace communication.

Dietmann made, for Pierre Restany's exhibition *Superlund* in Lund's Konsthall in Sweden 1967, a ''guarded crossing'', which was a ''demonstration dependent on you, just like the future.'' In front of the entrance to the gallery was a small wooden hut with a plexi-glass box, through which one could put nickel balls. They rolled down through a labyrinth which made up the word VOLVO (I roll). In order to pass from the hut into the exhibition one had to walk through another labyrinth, which made one write the word WALK with one's body. That is how a guarded crossing looks, as does a picture of a dream: the action and the language as one invisible unit.

—Olle Granath

DIMITRIJEVIĆ, Braco

Nationality: Yugoslavian. **Born:** Sarajevo, 18 June 1948. **Education:** Gymnasium, Sarajevo, 1962–66; studied at the Academy of

Fine Arts, Zagreb, 1968–71, and St. Martin's School of Art, London, 1971–73. **Family:** Married Nena Bal in 1969. **Career:** Independent artist, in Zagreb 1968–71, in London since 1971. **Awards:** 300th Anniversary Painting Prize, University of Zagreb, 1969; British Council Grant, 1971–72; Skoj Fine Arts Award, Zagreb, 1975; D.A.A.D. Fellowship, West Berlin, 1975; Arts Council Award, London, 1978; Prix Jean Dominique Ingres, Paris, 1979. **Address:** 25 Somers Road, London SW2, England.

Individual Exhibitions:

1968 Radnicki Univerziter, Sarajevo
1969 Galeria Studio Centre, Zagreb
1970 Veza Frankopanska 2a, Zagreb
Galeria 212, Belgrade
Salon Tribine Mladih, Novi Sad, Yugoslavia
Aktionsraum 1, Munich
1971 Galeria Suvremene Umjetnosti, Zagreb
Modern Art Agency, Naples
1972 Situation Gallery, London
Galerie Konrad Fischer, Dusseldorf
Galeria Jabuka, Zagreb
1973 Museum of Contemporary Art, Zagreb
Situation Gallery, London
1974 Galleria Sperone, Turin
Museum of Temporary Art, Lauterbach, West Germany
Galleria Francoise Lambert, Milan
1975 Palais des Beaux-Arts, Brussels
Museo del Arte Temporanea, Albioli, Italy
Städtisches Museum, Mönchengladbach, West Germany
Sperone, Gallery, New York
Galeria Nova, Zagreb
P.M.J. Self Gallery, London
1976 Galleria Sperone, Turin
Galerie René Block, West Berlin
Kabinett für Aktuelle Kunst, Bremerhaven, West Germany
1977 Galleria Civica d'Arte Moderna, Modena, Italy
Nuovi Strumenti, Brescia, Italy
Hetzler + Keller, Stuttgart
Robert Self Gallery, Newcastle upon Tyne
1978 Centre d'Art Contemporain, Geneva
Galerie Ecart, Geneva
MTL Gallery, Brussels
1979 Museum & Garden Charlottenburg, West Berlin
Arbeiten/Works 1968–1978, Badischer Kunstverein, Karlsruhe, West Germany
Stedelijk Van Abbemuseum, Eindhoven, Netherlands
Underground Train Stations, London
Kunsthalle, Tübingen, West Germany
Institute of Contemporary Arts, London
1980 Peter Velebit Factory, Belgrade
1981 *New Culturescapes,* Waddington Galleries, London
1982 Galerija Roman Petrovic, Sarajevo
Deweer Art Gallery, Otegem, Belgium
1983 Zoological Garden, Sarajevo
1984 Museum Ludwig, Cologne
Kunsthalle, Berne
Galerie Ingrid Dacic, Tubingen, West Germany
Galerie Marika Malacorda, Geneva
1985 Tate Gallery, London
Galerie Philomene Magers, Bonn
1986 Galerie Ingrid Dacic, Tubingen, West Germany
1987 Galerie de Paris, Paris
Le Consortium Centre d'Art Contemporain, Dijon
Hillman Holland Fine Arts, Atlanta, Georgia
Wilhelm-Hack-Museum, Ludwigshafen, West Germany
1994 *Slow as Light, Fast as Thought,* Museum Moderner Kunst, Stiftung Ludwig, Vienna (catalog)
Israel Museum, Jerusalem
Galerie de France, Paris
1995 *Against Historic Sense of Gravity,* Hessisches Landesmuseum, Darmstadt (catalog)
1996 Kunsthalle, Dusseldorf
The Man of Lascaux, Museum of Modern Art, Ljubljana (catalog)
1998 Gallery Arogos, Paris
Made in France 1947–97, Centre Georges Pompidou, Paris
Sarajevo 2000, Museum Moderner Kunst, Stiftung Ludwig, Vienna
Ménagerie du Jardin des Plantes, Paris
1999 Galerie Michael Jansen, Cologne

Selected Group Exhibitions:

1970 *Bitef 4,* Galeria 212, Belgrade
1971 *7th Biennale de Paris,* Musée d'Art Moderne de la Ville, Paris
1972 *Documenta 5,* Museum Fridericianum, Kassel, West Germany (and *Documenta 6,* 1977)
1976 *Biennale,* Venice (and 1982)
1978 *The Record as Artwork,* Museum of Contemporary Art, Chicago
1979 *Biennale of Sydney,* Art Gallery of New South Wales, Sydney (and 1986)
1980 *British Art 1940–80,* Hayward Gallery, London
1982 *Aspects of British Art Today,* Metropolitan Museum, Tokyo (toured Japan)
1985 *Promenades,* Centre d'Art Contemporain, Geneva
1987 *Vis a Vis,* Musee Saint-Denis, Rheims, France
1994 *Kommentar zu Europa,* Museum Moderner Kunst, Stiftung Ludwig, Vienna
L'Art du Portrait en France, Shoto Museum, Tokyo
L'Artiste à la Place de l'Oeuvre, Centre des Expositions de Moscou, Russia
The Ossuary, Luhring Augustine Gallery, New York
Europa-Europa, Bundeskunsthalle, Bonn
1995 *SITE Santa Fe,* Santa Fe, New Mexico
Kwangju Biennale, South Korea
1996 *Biennial,* Sao Paulo
Wadsworth Atheneum, Hartford
NowHere, Louisiana Museum of Modern Art
Exhibition of Visual Art, Limerick, Ireland
1997 *6th Biennial of Havana,* Cuba
1999 *Les Champs de la Sculpture 2000,* Champs d'Élysees, Paris
Zeitwenden Kunstmuseum, Bonn, Germany
2000 *L'Autre Moitie de l'Europe,* Galerie Nationale du Jeu de Paume, Paris

Collections:

Museum of Contemporary Art, Zagreb; Museum of Modern Art, Belgrade; Arts Council of Great Britain, London; Centre Georges Pompidou, Paris; City of Cologne, West Germany; Museum and Garden Charlottenburg, West Berlin; Städtisches Museum, Mönchengladbach, West Germany; Museum van Hedendaagse Kunst, Ghent; Cincinnati Museum of Art, Ohio.

Publications:

By DIMITRIJEVIĆ: Books—*Interview Book,* Zagreb 1974; *Tale of an Artist and a Castle,* Bremerhaven, West Germany 1976; *Tractatus post Historicus,* Tübingen 1976; *Self Portrait After Rembrandt and Miguel Perez,* Geneva 1978; *An Obelisk Beyond History,* West Berlin 1979. **Articles—**"Grupa penzioner Tihomir" in *Novine GSC* (Zagreb), no. 2, 1969; "Some Changes" in *Aktionsraum 1* catalog, Munich 1970; "Just as Piano Is Not Music, Painting Is Not Art," in *Dimitrijevic* exhibition catalog, Zagreb 1973; "Why I Paint Like Pollock" in *Tendencije 5* exhibition catalog, Zagreb 1973; "Towards a New Way of Behavior" in *Studio International* (London), February 1974; "My Mind is Between Sociology and Sculpture" in *Flash Art* (Milan), no. 46–47, 1974; All'Inizio dell'Alfabeto dell'Arte" in *Data* (Milan), October 1974; "Three Museum Exhibitions of Braco Dimitrijević" in *Dimitrijević* exhibition catalog, Zagreb 1975; "Status Historicus—Status Post Historicus", in +-(Brussels), no. 18, 1977; "Three Museum Exhibitions," in *Studio International* (London), no. 990, 1980; record—*His Pencil's Voice,* 1973; "Nobel Prize Stories: Part of a Collection Yet to be Published by the Artist" in *Art Press,* no. 193, July/August 1994; "Braco Dimitrijević: Louvre is my Studio, Street is My Museum" with Jean-Hubert Martin in *Flash Art (International Edition),* no. 186, January/February 1996.

On DIMITRIJEVIĆ: Books—*7e Biennale de Paris,* exhibition catalog, with texts by Jesa Denegri and others, Paris 1971; *Braco Dimitrijević,* exhibition catalog, with text by Caroline Tisdall, Zagreb 1973; *6 Years:The Dematerialization of the Art Object* by Lucy R. Lippard, New York and London 1973; *Happenings and Environments* by Adrian Henri, London 1973; *Braco Dimitrijević,* exhibition catalog, with text by Johannes Cladders, Mönchengladbach, West Germany 1975; *Off Media* by Germano Celant, West Berlin 1977; *The Record as Artwork: From Futurism to Conceptual Art,* exhibition catalog, with text by Germano Celant, Chicago 1978; *Braco Dimitrijević,* exhibition catalog, with text by Sarah Kent, London 1979; *Braco Dimitrijević,* exhibition catalog, with text by Clara Weyergraf, Tubingen 1979; *Braco Dimitrijević: Arbeiten/Works 1968–1978,* exhibition catalog, with texts by Michael Schwarz and Manfred Schmalriede, Karlsruhe, West Germany 1979; *Braco Dimitrijević: New Culturescapes,* exhibition catalog, with text by David Brown, London 1981; *Braco Dimitrijević,* exhibition catalog with text by David Brown, London 1985; *Braco Dimitrijević,* exhibition catalog with essays by Bernhard Holeczek, Richard Gassan and Lida von Mengden, Ludwigshafen 1987; *The Life of Braco Dimitrijević* by Jonathan Watkins, Antwerp 1991; *Branco Dimitrijević* by Michael Gauthier, Paris 1998. **Articles—**"Accidental History: Braco Dimitrijević" by Lynn Gumpert in *Art in America,* (New York), vol. 79, June 1991; "Braco Dimitrijević: Nature Meets Culture" by Catherine Millet in *Art Press,* no. 238, September 1998.

*

I have attempted to change our customary relationships and reactions in our encounters with everyday reality. Since it would be impossible to consider this relationship in its entirety, it is necessary to restrict attention to certain fragments of the whole: my interest is in specific, rather than in general, information. By "specific information" I mean information transmitted by contemporary mass media as well as by "historical" media: monuments, memorial plaques, books, pictures, photographs, etc. On the other hand, general information is usually understood to consist of a wealth of data which the environment offers in its totality.

The first intention of my work is to establish a new qualitative relationship between man and specific information, then, secondly, between man and his exterior reality. It is important to change that with which, as a result of acquired and inherited experience, we have a definite and established *a priori* relationship. I refer primarily to our automatic acceptance of particular forms of information dispersal (while disregarding its real content) and to the passive and negative attitude which is passed through education from one generation to the next. We accept the messages transmitted through these channels automatically and unconsciously as important historical and social facts. As we discover new content within old forms of presentation, it is possible that in the future we may doubt the exclusiveness of one-way information. This may also result in the creation of a new system of associations well outside the established forms. Realizing that the faces and names on the posters and memorial plaques were selected at random and presented for the sole purpose of making an artistic statement, it is possible that we might also question that data received earlier through similar channels. The moment we begin to doubt the *a priori* value of information offered to us, we necessarily create a criterion for accepting it. In a wider sense, this new criterion makes for a new relationship with our environment and results in a different sort of behavior and activity.

It is interesting to observe the mechanism which creates art history, the methods of selection, the influence of information systems, on the creation of concepts and names. Using the same forms of presentation, I have deliberately emphasized the element of chance in selecting subjects of my monuments, memorial plaques, photographs, etc. The purpose of these activities is not to make some people famous, but rather to point out the relativity of criteria for promoting some individuals/ideas instead of others.

The aesthetic and visual characteristics of the means I employ to realize this programme are unimportant. The work can be presented through any form of communication, and its idealistic intensity is increased through repetition.

In 1976 I started working in several European museums on a series of works entitled "Triptychos Post Historicus." These are triadic compositions consisting of an original master painting, an object of everyday use, and a product of nature. All three are presented on a plinth which at the same time promotes and questions all the elements involved. One Triptychos was described by John del Bosna as a "universe in small, represented with three objects only."

—Braco Dimitrijević

* * *

Throughout his career as an artist Braco Dimitrijević has concerned himself with provoking the viewer to question the criteria with which we assign importance to objects, events, or people. So much of what we think of as important or famous is a result of our cultural conditioning. Dimitrijević has frequently demonstrated how history, fame and notoriety, as well as obscurity, are, perhaps, matters of chance. To illustrate this view he once made a marble bust of an 'unknown' and placed it on a plinth with the sitter's name carved and gilded, and installed it for several weeks in the center of a famous London square. By focusing on the anonymous, seemingly unimportant individual, Dimitrijević has tried to subvert conventional values and also, perhaps, to suggest that a potential for greatness and creativity may exist in masses of unknown people. In an ongoing series called ''Casual Passerby'' begun in 1969, Dimitrijević has displayed large black and white photographs (reminiscent of the Eastern European political tradition of glorifying political leaders by publicly displaying their photographs) on various facades, including a short, incomplete biography of the subject.

The first of the ''Casual Passerby'' series, shown at the Pat Hearn Gallery in March 1990, originally displayed in a main square of Zagreb, Croatia, consisted of three highly unlikely and incongruous photographs—a middle-aged man, an older woman bundled in winter clothes, and a young woman. ''The form of the personality cult was familiar, but in this case the personalities were not.'' (Lynn Gumpert, ''Accidental History'' *Art in America,* June, 1991). Other examples of the ''Passerby'' series include one portrait mounted on the facade of an administrative building for the 1976 Venice Biennale, which, because of the public's overwhelming, questioning response, was moved to a less conspicuous location. Another portrait displayed on the Boulevard St. Germain in Paris, 1971, was taken down after two weeks by the police and firefighters because ''it upset the Parisians.'' The accompanying, sketchy, biographies, for example, 'someone that the artist met in Berlin, 1976 at 2:25 P.M.', enhance the apparent absurdity of the composition because it challenges the viewer's sense of orientation. While the ''Casual Passerby'' photographs may remind the viewer of Douglas Hueber's intention to ''photograph everyone alive'' or Dennis Adam's photos of socially invisible immigrant workers, Dimitrijević's originality lies in his effort to force the viewer to become aware of the conscious and subconscious mechanisms that make us automatically accept exterior reality.

In the installation of the series ''Status Post Historicus'', exhibited at Nicole Klagsbrun Gallery, 1989, Dimitrijević displayed six bronze busts perched upon marble pedestals. Three of the busts were recognizable, famous, artists such as Da Vinci, Michelangelo, and Dürer, and the other three were 'unknowns.' Dimitrijević emphasized his point by including a parable that tells of the chance ''discovery'' of da Vinci over another painter. *Once upon a time, far from cities and towns, there lived two painters. One day the King, hunting nearby, lost his dog. He found him in the garden of one of the two painters. He saw the works of that painter and took him to the castle. The name of that painter was Leonardo da Vinci. The name of the other disappeared forever from human memory.* Working in the 20th century Duchampian tradition Dimitrijević's work jolts pre-conceived ideas and overturns the accepted values of the art world and the conditioned responses of the gallery goer.

In his ongoing series, *Triptychos Post Historicus* which he started in 1976, the title refers to ''the time which escapes the 'objectivity' of traditional history; time when, it is realized, different qualities co-exist on a equal basis'' (David Brown, Triptychos Post Historicus, Tate Gallery, 1985). The installations are composed of three-part still life arrangements of a well-known painting, an object belonging to a specific person, and an arrangement of something organic such as fruits or vegetables. Originally this series existed as photographs, but Dimitrijević was eventually given permission to ''compose'' his arrangements in museums. Viewers react with incredulity at the sight of a garden rake casually propped against Cezanne's ''Gardener'' with a scatter of fruits at its base or the Modigliani ''Little Peasant'' negligently placed half in and half out of a shabby wardrobe with a pumpkin on the top shelf. Usually the viewer assumes that the painting must be a reproduction and then reacts with irritation and anxiety when he or she realizes that the painting is the real thing. In the ''Triptychos'' series Dimitrijević challenges the museum goer's assumptions about the museum as a protector and defender of social and cultural values.

Dimitrijević's choice and arrangements of the objects are by no means random. The chosen fruit and objects are very symbolic and often cannot be understood without various historical and cultural contexts. A good example is the combination of Malevich's ''Dynamic Suprematism'' displayed with an iron (which represents suprematist technology as well as a flattening device) and two precariously positioned apples (perhaps forbidden fruit). Another provocative piece in the ''Triptychs'' series was composed and arranged in the Gallery Runny Van de Veld in Antwerp, Belgium, 1990. Dimitrijević borrowed a painting of a commander from Belgium's Royal Guard from a private collection. The painting was partially placed inside a vintage Citroën along with oranges and lemons strategically arranged. While viewing the composition at a certain angle, one corner of the painting appeared to be perched on top of one of the oranges. This combination ''functioned as pointed reminders of Belgium's not too distant past as a colonial presence in the African Congo, now Zaire''(Lynn Gumpert, ''Accidental History'' *Art in America,* June 1991).

—Essay by Mary Ellis; updated by Christine Miner Minderović

DINE, Jim

Nationality: American. **Born:** Cincinnati, Ohio, 16 June 1935. **Educated:** University of Cincinnati, Ohio; Boston Museum School; and Ohio University, Athens 1953–57, B.F.A. 1957. **Family:** Married Nancy Minto in 1957; has 3 sons. Settled in New York, 1958; now lives and works in New York and Putney, Vermont. **Career:** Visiting lecturer, Yale University, New Haven, Connecticut, 1965; artist-in-residence, Oberlin College, Ohio, 1965; visiting critic, Cornell University, Ithaca, New York, 1967. **Awards:** Norman Harris Silver Medal, Art Institute of Chicago, 1964. **Agent:** Pace Gallery, New York, 32 East 57th Street, New York, New York, 10022, U.S.A. **Address:** 59 Barrow Street, New York, New York 10014–3701.

Individual Exhibitions:

1959 *The Smiling Workman,* Judson Gallery, New York
1960 *Car Crash,* Reuben Gallery, New York
Jim Dine's Vaudeville, Reuben Gallery, New York
1962 Galleria dell Ariete, Milan
Martha Jackson Gallery, New York
1963 Galerie Zwirner, Cologne
Galerie Sonnabend, Paris
Palais des Beaux Arts, Brussels
Sidney Janis Gallery, New York
1964 Sidney Janis Gallery, New York

1965 Galleria Gian Enzo Sperone, Turin
Natural History (The Dreams), First New York Theatre
Allen Memorial Art Museum, Oberlin College, Ohio
Robert Fraser Gallery, London
1966 Robert Fraser Gallery, London
1967 Galerie Ricke, Kassel, West Germany
Galerie Zwirner, Cologne
Gallery Upstairs, Buffalo, New York
Harcus-Krakow Gallery, Boston
Museum of Modern Art, New York
Sidney Janis Gallery, New York
Stedelijk Museum, Amsterdam
White Museum of Art, Cornell University, Ithaca, New York
1969 Galerie Sonnabend, Paris
Kunstverein, Munich
Kunsthalle, Nuremberg
Robert Fraser Gallery, London
1970 Whitney Museum, New York
Kesner-Gesellschaft, Hannover
Galerie Milkro, Berlin
Galerie van der Loo, Munich
Sonnabend Gallery, New York
Dunkelman Gallery, Toronto
Palais des Beaux-Arts, Brussels
Museo Civico Galleria d'Arte Moderno, Turin
Neue Galerie der Stadt, Liz, Austria
Wolfgang Gurlitt Museum, Linz, Austria
1971 Museum Boymans-van-Beuingen, Rotterdam
Nationalgalerie, Berlin
Staatliche Kunsthalle, Dusseldorf
Staatliche Kunsthalle, Baden-Baden, West Germany
Galerie Sonnabend, Paris
Sonnabend Downtown Gallery, New York
D.M. Gallery, London
Kunsthalle, Berne
Contract Graphics, Houston
1972 Galerie Sonnabend, Paris
Sonnabend Downtown Gallery, New York
Gimpel and Hanover Galerie, Zurich
Aronson Gallery, Atlanta
Jack Glenn Gallery, Newport Beach, California
1973 John Berggreum Gallery, San Francisco
Galerie Gerald Cramer, Geneva
Gimpel Fils, London
D.M. Gallery, London
Dine/Kitaj Cincinnati Museum of Art, Ohio
Felicity Samuel Gallery, London
Sonnabend Gallery, New York
1974 Sonnabend Gallery, New York
Knoedler Prints Gallery, New York
Institute of Contemporary Arts, London
Museum of Contemporary Art, La Jolla, California
Galerie Ileana Sonnabend, Geneva
Hopkins Center Art Galleries, Dartmouth College, Hanover, New Hampshire
1975 Sonnabend Gallery, New York
Galerie Sonnabend, Paris
Centre Culturel Americain, Paris
Centre d'Arts Plastiques Contemporains, Bordeaux
1976 Neue Galerie, Graz, Austria
1977 *Paintings, Drawings, Etchings 1976,* Pace Gallery, New York
Jim Dine Works on Paper 1975–1976, Waddington and Tooth Galleries, London
Galleria Civica d'Arte Moderna, Ferrara, Italy
Prints 1970–1977, Williams College Museum of Art, Williamstown, Massachusetts
1978 *New Painting,* Pace Gallery, New York
Makler Gallery, Philadelphia
Pace Gallery, Columbus, Ohio
Jim Dine's Etchings, Museum of Modern Art, New York
1979 *Jim Dine: The Animate Objects,* Katonah Gallery, Katonah, New York
Jim Dine, Oeuvres sur Papier 1978–79, Galerie Cluade Bernard, Paris
Jim Dine: Figure Drawings 1975–1979, California State University at Long Beach (toured the United States)
1980 Pace Gallery, New York
Galerie Alice Pauli, Lausanne
Janie C. Lee Gallery, Houston
Harcus Krakow Gallery, Boston
1981 *Jim Dine: An Exhibition of Recent Figure Drawings 1978–1980,* Richard Gray Gallery, Chicago
1982 Waddington Galleries, London
1983 Richard Gray Gallery, Chicago
Los Angeles County Museum of Art
1984 Walker Art Center, Minneapolis
John Berggruen Gallery, San Francisco
Barbara Krakow Gallery, Boston
Fay Gold Gallery, Atlanta, Georgia
Cantor Leinberg Gallery, Detroit
Thorden Wetterling Galleries, Goteborg, Sweden
1985 Toni Birkhead Gallery, Cincinnati, Ohio
Akron Art Institute, Ohio
Albright-Knox Art Gallery, Buffalo, New York
Hirshhorn Museum, Washington, D.C.
Pace Gallery, New York
1986 University of Texas, Austin
Los Angeles County Museum of Art
Toledo Museum of Art, Ohio
Des Moines Art Center, Iowa
Williams College of Art, Williamstown, Massachusetts
Pace Gallery, New York
Galerie Baudoin Lebon, Paris
Fuji Televesion Gallery, Tokyo
Galerie Alice Pauli, Lausanne
1994 Pace Gallery, New York
Jim Dine: Walldrawing, Kunstverein Ludwigsburg, Ludwigsburg (catalog)
1995 *Jim Dine: Winter Dream,* Alan Cristea Gallery, London (catalog)
1996 *Jim Dine: The Body and Its Metaphors,* Miyagi Museum of Art, Japan (traveled to Sapporo, Kagawa, Gifu) (catalog)
Jim Dine: Raven on White Paper, Davidson Art Center, Wesleyan University, Middletown, Connecticut
Jim Dine: Venus, Civico Museo Revoltella, Milan (catalog)
1997 Galerie de Bellefeuille, Westmount, Montreal

1999 *Walking Memory: 1959–1969,* Cincinnati Art Museum, Ohio (also Solomon R. Guggenheim Museum, New York) (catalog)
Pace Wildenstein Gallery, New York
2000 *Jim Dine: Photographs,* UCR/California Museum of Photography, University of California, Riverside (catalog)
Jim Dine in Italia, Centro Arte Contemporanea, Siena (catalog)
Subjects, Alan Cristea Gallery, London (catalog)
2001 *New Drawings and Sculpture,* Richard Gray Gallery, Chicago (catalog)
Bentley Art Gallery, Scottsdale

Selected Group Exhibitions:

1969 *International Exhibition,* Carnegie Institute, Pittsburgh
1973 *Annual Exhibition,* Whitney Museum of American Art, New York
Modern Art in Prints, Museum of Modern Art, New York
1974 *Poets of the Cities: New York and San Francisco 1950–1965,* Museum of Fine Arts, Dallas
1976 *The Human Clay,* Hayward Gallery, London
1977 *Documenta 6,* Kassel, West Germany
Drawings of the 70's, Art Institute of Chicago
1979 *Drawings about Drawing: New Directions 1968–1978,* Ackland Memorial Art Center, Chapel Hill, North Carolina
Emergence and Progression: 6 Contemporary Artists, Milwaukee Art Center
1984 *Olympian Gestures,* Los Angeles County Museum of Art
1994 *American Art in Italian Private Collections,* American Academy in Rome (catalog)
Dine in Detroit, Detroit Institute of Arts, Detroit (catalog)
1996 *Charles H. Carpenter, Jr.: The Odyssey of a Collector,* Carnegie Museum of Art, Pittsburgh (catalog)
Art to Art, Toledo Museum of Art, Ohio (catalog)
1997 *47th Venice Biennale,* Italy
Still Life: The Object in American Art 1915–1995, Marsh Art Gallery, University of Richmond (traveling exhibition) (catalog)
Amerikanische Pop Art in der Hamburger Kunsthalle, Galerie der Gegenwart, Hamburger Kunsthalle, Hamburg (catalog)
Hockeny to Hodgkin: British Master Prints 1960–1980, New Orleans Museum of Art, New Orleans (catalog)
1998 *Mois de la Photo,* multiple galleries, Paris
2000 *Anna and Bernhard Blume, Sophie Calle, Mat Collinshaw, Jim Dine, Flor Garduño, Candida Höfer,* Museum of Contemporary Photography, Chicago
Monte-Carlo International Sculpture Festival: Contemporary American Sculpture, Casino, Monte Carlo, Monaco (catalog)

Collections:

Museum of Modern Art, New York: Metropolitan Museum of Art, New York; Guggenheim Museum, New York; Whitney Museum, New York; Williams College Museum of Art, Williamstown, Massachusetts; Hirshhorn Museum and Sculpture Garden, Smithsonian Institution, Washington, D.C.; Art Institute of Chicago; Museum of Contemporary Art, Chicago; Carnegie Institute, Pittsburgh Museum of Fine Arts, Dallas.

Publications:

By DINE: Books—*Jim Dine Designs for A Midsummer Night's Dream,* New York 1968; *Picture of Dorian Gray,* stage script after Oscar Wilde, London 1968; *Work from the Same House* with Lee Friedlander, London 1969; *Welcome Home Lovebird,* London 1969; *Adventures of Mr. and Mr. Jim and Ron,* with Ron Padgett, London 1970: *Letters to Nancy,* New York 1970; *Drawings from the Glyptothek,* with Ruth E. Fine and Stephen Fleischman, Hudson Hills 1993; *Jim Dine: The Alchemy of Images,* with Marco Livingstone, New York 1998. **Articles**—''What Is Pop Art,'' interview with G.R. Swenson in *Artnews* (New York), November 1963; statement in *American Drawings* exhibition catalog, New York 1964; ''Eye to I,'' interview with Charlotte Willard in *Art in America* (New York) March/April 1966; ''Dining with Jim'' interview with Robert Fraser in *Art and Artists* (London), September 1966; answers to ''Test in Art,'' prepared by Kenneth Koch, in *ARTnews* (New York), October 1966; statement in ''Jim Dine's Red Mural for the United States Pavilion'' by William C Lipke in *Artscanada* (Toronto), October 1976; ''Lithographs and Original Prints: Two Artists Discuss their Recent Work'' in *Studio International* (London), June 1968; interview, with Thomas Krens, in *Jim Dine Prints 1970–1977,* by Riva Castleman, New York 1977; interview with Meeka Walsh (with introduction by Robert Enright) in *Border Crossings,* fall 1993; ''The Name Game: Jim Dine Walks Down Memory Lane'' in *Border Crossing,* vol. 18, no. 2, May 1999; interview with Fiamma Arditi in *Ars,* vol. 3, no. 5, May 1999.

On DINE: Books—*Jim Dine: Drawing from the Glyptothek* by Ruth E. Fine, Hudson Hill Press, 1993; *In Company: Robert Creeley's Collaborations* by Robert Creeley, Elizabeth Licata and Amy Cappellazzo, Niagara Falls 1999. **Exhibition catalogs**—*6 Painters and the Object,* by Lawrence Alloway, New York, 1963; *The Popular Image Exhibition,* with an essay by Alan R. Solomon, Washington, D.C. 1963; *The New American Realism,* with an introduction by Martin Carey, preface by Daniel Catton Rich, Worcester, Massachusetts 1965; *Pop Art and the American Tradition,* by Tracy Atkinson, Milwaukee 1965, *Prints by 5 New Artists,* New York 1969, *Jim Dine,* New York 1970; *Jim Dine: Complete Graphics* by John Russell and others, London 1970; *Dine/Kitaj,* by R.F. Boyle and R.F. Kitaj, Cincinnati 1973; *Jim Dine,* Bordeaux 1975; *The Human Clay,* by R. B. Kitaj, London 1976; *Drawing Now,* by Bernice Rose, New York 1976; *Jim Dine,* by Paola Serra Zanett, Ferrara, Italy 1977; *Jim Dine Works on Paper 1975–1976,* by R. B. Kitaj, London 1977; *Jim Dine: Paintings, Drawings, Etchings 1976,* New York 1977; *Jim Dine Prints 1970–1977* by Riva Castleman, New York 1977; *Jim Dine Prints 1970–1971,* Williamstown, Massachusetts 1977; *Jim Dine's Etchings by Riva Castleman, New York 1978; Jim Dine: New Painting,* New York 1978; *Jim Dine: Figure Drawings 1975–1979* by Constance W. Glenn, New York 1979; *Jim Dine,* text by James R. Mellow, New York 1980; *Jim Dine: An Exhibition of Recent Figure Drawings 1978–1980,* with text by David Shapiro, Chicago 1981; *Jim Dine Prints 1977–1985,* with texts by Ellen G. D'Oench and Jean E. Feinberg, Los Angeles 1986; *Jim Dine: Une Exposition pour Paris,* with essay by Anne Dagbert, Paris 1986; *Jim Dine: Walking Memories, 1959–1969* by Germano Celant, Clare Bell and Julia Blaut, New York 1999. **Articles**—''Dine Unrobed'' by Ann Landi in *ARTnews,* vol. 95, no. 2, February 1996; ''Jim Dine: Le Moment de la Métamorphose'' by Jean-Jacques Bernier in *Vie des Arts,* vol. 40, no. 166, Spring 1997; ''Making OO LA LA'' by Rod Padgett in *Modern Painters* (London), vol. 12, no. 1, Spring 1999; ''Schonheit, Tod und Melancholie: Jim Dine'' by Ivo Kranzfelder in *Neue Bildende Kunst,* no. 4, June-July 1999; ''Symbols for the Self'' by Vincent Katz in *Art in America* (New York), vol. 87, no. 12, December 1999.

* * *

Though Jim Dine has been loosely associated with Pop by some critics, his work is essentially personal and expressionistic. Throughout his career, the prolific painter, sculptor, and printmaker has reworked a number of motifs, which include hearts, bathrobes, tools, Venuses, and skulls. His earlier work owed much to the climate created by Jasper Johns and Robert Rauschenburg—especially recognizable in works which incorporated everyday objects (the tool paintings, e.g.), universally recognizable signs (hearts), and words. But unlike the neo-Dadaists and the stars of Pop, Dine eventually eschewed the cool irony and mass-media references characteristic of those movements in favor of a more introspective and expressionistic style.

In the early 1960s, Dine was an active organizer of happenings, *Car Crash* (1960), being perhaps the best known. Concurrently, he began to produce paintings which incorporated everyday objects, thus extending the boundaries of high modernist flatness both dimensionally and metaphorically. In *Lawnmower* (1962), a lawnmower on a pedestal leans up against a canvas which is partially covered with slashes of paint in landscape-like hues. As in Rauschenburg's work, the painterly marks recall gestural abstraction, while the lawnmower irreverently honors the tradition of the Duchampian ready-made. From this time on, clothing and common household objects continued to bulk large amongst his subjects, though his style in depicting them progressively revealed Dine as an artist who took seriously the expressive potential of paint.

Dine's depictions of his central themes succeed best when the objects themselves exude both personal significance and formal grace, as in the case of his suite of tool drawings from the 1970s. These sensual graphite renditions of clamps, wrenches, hammers and saws evoke a surprisingly emotional response. Each tool is bathed partially in light and partially in a murky patch of dark shading, thus creating intriguing and subtle variations of depth and weight in each object that rivals the psychological complexity of humans. The work invites anthropomorphic comparisons and leads one to reflect on how we invest personal meaning in inanimate objects.

Dine's ever-growing series of heart paintings, though exemplary of both Dine's virtuosity as a painter and his exploitation of what Max Kozloff calls ''entertainment psychology,'' fails to produce a comparable tension. Like language, the heart shape is a sign which gains meaning from the emotional weight attached to that which it signifies. Even as an abstract form, it is overpowered by sentimentality, begging for the type of cool treatment given by Johns to his American flags. With some exceptions, Dine's heart canvases—with their bright color schemes, unchallenging brushwork, and inclusion of other cliche-laden symbols (skulls, moons, eyes)—seem to confirm what we already know. One brilliant exception would be *Romancing Late Winter* (1981). Here the artist balances patina-green, coppery-gold, blue, and black using subtle and varied brushstrokes. Delicate drips of dark paint run from a warm black patch on the left side of the heart down to the lower edge of the canvas, revealing a deeper, darker significance to the motif.

Sculpture is an arena in which the artist has diverged from his most recognizable subjects to explore a broader range of thematic and material concerns. Particularly striking are two recent yet very different sets of works: the life-sized *Venus* sculptures (1990–91) and the *Ape and Cat* series (1992–93). The Venuses (a motif Dine has used since the early 1980s) include carved wood, cast bronze, and marble versions of the classic form—only here they are crudely hacked in the style of backwoods ''chain saw'' sculpture in what may be a uniquely American homage to Rodin. The marble work is the most striking, owing to a powerful contrast between the milky-whiteness of the stone and the roughness of its surface.

The *Ape and Cat* series of bronze and wood sculptures, inspired by a found Victorian statuette, is perhaps Dine's most disturbing and ambiguous work to date. The ape and cat are depicted as a heterosexual couple, with animal heads and humanoid bodies. The cat clutches her partner's chin in what appears to be a gesture of possessive longing, while the monkey bears an expression of passive bliss. A blending of human desire with anachronistic anthropomorphism, the effect of the figures is simultaneously campy and tragic. Dine's expressionistic style, which has served him well in the transition from paint to bronze, rescues the work from being pure postmodern nostalgia.

—Essay by Lavinia Learmont; updated by Audrey Mandelbaum

DISTEFANO, Juan Carlos

Nationality: Argentine. **Born:** August 1933, Villa Celina, Buenos Aires Province. **Family:** Married the writer Griselda Gambaro in 1955; two children. **Education:** Drawing professor at the Manuel Belgrano School of Fine Arts, Buenos Aires. **Career:** Graphics designer since 1956 and sculptor since 1966. **Awards:** Francesco Romero Grant, Rome, 1969. **Agent:** Ruth Benzacar Gallery, Florida 1000, (1005)-Buenos Aires, Argentina. **Address:** Benito Pérez Galdós 311, PB, (1155)-Buenos Aires, Argentina.

Individual Exhibitions

1964 Rioboó-Nueva Gallery, Buenos Aires
1966 Rubbers Gallery, Buenos Aires
1976 Artemúltiple Gallery, Buenos Aires
1980 Jacques Martínez, Buenos Aires
1987 Del Retiro Gallery, Buenos Aires
1991 Fundación San Telmo, Buenos Aires
1991 Ruth Benzacar Gallery, Buenos Aires
1998 Juan Carlos Distéfano in the National Museum of Fine Arts, Buenos Aires.

Selected Group Exhibitions

1964 *Premio ''Ver y Estimar''* (View and Appraise Awards), National Museum of Fine Arts, Buenos Aires
1966 3rd American Art Biennial, Cordoba, Argentina — Lima, Peru
1967 *Surrealismo en la Argentina* (Surrealism in Argentina), *Instituto Torcuato Di Tella,* Buenos Aires
9th Sao Paulo Biennial, Sao Paulo, Brazil

1970 *Panorama de la Pintura Argentina 3* (Perspectives in Argentine Painting 3), National Salons, Buenos Aires
1971 *El desnudo en los siglos XIX y XX* (The Nude in the 19th and 20th Centuries), National Museum of Fine Arts, Buenos Aires
1974 *Actuelles Tendences de lArt´Argentine* (Current Trends in Argentine Art), *Centre Artistique de Recontres Internationales,* Nice, France
1978 *Argentine Art 78,* National Museum of Fine Arts, Buenos Aires
1979 *Twelve Argentine Sculptors,* San Martín Cultural Center, Buenos Aires
1981 Augusto Palanza National Arts Fund Prize, National Museum of Fine Arts, Buenos Aires
1987 *Arte Argentina dalla Independenza ad oggi 1810–1987* (Argentine Art from Independence until the Present Day 1810–1987), Rome
1994 *Contemporary Argentine Art,* Permanent Collection, National Museum of Fine Arts, Madrid
1994 *Ver y Estimar,* (See and Appraise), National Museum of Fine Arts, Buenos Aires
1996–97 *Otro mirar* (Another View), Contemporary Argentine Art, National Museum of Fine Arts, Buenos Aires and Barcelona, Spain

Collections:

National Museum of Fine Arts, Buenos Aires; Museum of Modern Art of the Autonomous City of Buenos Aires; The First National Bank of Boston, U.S.A.; Mundus Artium Collection, Pittsburgh, U.S.A.; Villa Ciani Art Museum, Lugano, Switzerland; various private collections in Europe, the United States, and South America.

Publications:

On DISTÉFANO: Books—*Aventura Plástica Hispanoamericana* (Adventures in Hispano-American Plastic Art) by Carlos Bayón, Mexico 1979; *Rescate del arte: Ultimos 100 años de escultura y de pintura en occidente* (Recovering Art: The Last 100 Years in Occidental Sculpture and Painting) by Jorge Romero Brest, Buenos Aires 1981; *La moderna escultura figurativa* (Modern Figurative Sculpture) by Jorge López Anaya, Buenos Aires 1983; *Del Pop Art a la Nueva Imagen* (From Pop Art to the New Image) by Jorge Glusberg, Buenos Aires 1985; *Abismos privados, infiernos cotidianos* (Private Voids, Daily Hells) by Martha Nanni, Buenos Aires 1998. **Articles—** ''Juan Carlos Distéfano—Talento de creador, humildad de artesano (Juan Carlos Distéfano—The Talent of a Creator, The Humility of a Craftsman)'' by Elba Pérez in *Panorama,* Buenos Aires, 1977; ''Tras larga ausencia Juan Carlos Distéfano ha vuelto a Buenos Aires (After a Long Absence, Juan Carlos Distéfano Is Back in Buenos Aires)'' by Jorge Feinsilver in *Ambito Financiero,* Buenos Aires, 1980; ''Ser y cuerpo (Being and Body)'' by Samuel Paz in *Clarín,* Buenos Aires, 1980; ''Distéfano visto por Romero Brest, (Distéfano as Seen by Romero Brest)'' by Jorge Romero Brest in *El Colombiano,* Medellín, Colombia, 1981; ''Escultura en el Premio Palanza (Sculpture in the Palanza Awards)'' by Rosa Brill in *Competencia,* Buenos Aires, 1981; ''Clásicismo y nostalgia en la obra de Juan Carlos Distéfano (Classicism and Nostalgia in the Work of Juan Carlos Distéfano)'' in *La Nación,* Buenos Aires, 1987; ''Encuentros y desencuentros entre obras y textos (Matches and Mismatches between Works and Texts)'' in *Pagina 12,* Buenos Aires, 1989.

* * *

Juan Carlos Distéfano (1933) is one of the truly great contemporary Argentine artists. His works have been exhibited sporadically since 1964. His work is not that of a *preacher* in the religious sense: Distéfano avoids delivering sermons and proclaims no revealed truths.

If we recall, however, that one meaning of the verb *to preach* is to ''urge acceptance or abandonment of something'' by noting it publicly or making it patently clear, then it is no exaggeration to say—nor should the idea be rejected out of hand—that Distéfano's sculptures do indeed *preach,* since they allegorically and metaphorically note and make patently clear Man's situation in the world of today.

The recurrence of the word ''pain'' is hardly arbitrary: Pain is (one might say) Distéfano's theme. Says he: ''There is a part of my work that was carried out during a pretty sinister period, the '70s, which certainly does not elicit joy.'' Perhaps, it is a way of subtly insisting on this idea of ''not eliciting joy.'' And there is nothing and no one that prohibits the artist from awakening this feeling, of inspiring sorrow, sadness, affliction. Schiller's *Ode to Joy,* which Beethoven adopted as a theme for his *Ninth Symphony,* doesn't spawn joy. Rather, it yearns for it, which, of course, does not invalidate the excellence of the poem.

Torture (which forms part of this pain) has hardly fallen into disuse; we Argentines have witnessed its prevalence until just a decade and a half ago. And one of Distéfano's most heart-rending sculptures—*El Mudo* (The Mute; 1973)—is a testimony to this reality, which would later become systematic, with the terrifying addition of ''the disappeared,'' the monstrous name given to the fatal victims of State terrorism as of 1976. This is the framework, indeed, the backdrop, for Distéfano's sculptures. The multiplication of the physical pain caused to some—plus the moral pain of famine, unemployment, economic inequality, injustice, and racial disdain—while the fields of medicine, biology, and genetics seek solutions that tend not only to prolong life, but also to make life possible via alternative means, to erase the lines of aging or at least to soften them.

Having started out in graphic design in 1951—an area in which he was to achieve international renown—he had his first painting exhibition in 1964, where he showed paintings from that year and the year before (all but one of which he would later destroy, in what he would eventually refer to as ''an act of pity, but also of arrogance,'' because he was no longer in agreement with them.

He left graphic design entirely in 1976 to devote all of his energy to art. And following the then-military dictatorship's decision to ban the novel *Ganarse la muerte* (Beating Death), whose author was Distéfano's wife, Griselda Gambaro, he and his family took the pathway of exile, living and working in Barcelona from 1977 through 1980.

Distéfano put on his first show in the days of Neo-figuration, in the proximity of which he himself works. In a passage from his writings of 1974, he maintains that this movement, led by Ernesto Deira, Rómulo Macció, Luis Felipe Noé, and Jorge de la Vega, ''was fundamental and powerfully renewed the artistic scene in Buenos Aires. My own work from those years reveals its influence, to which I should add the influence of the CoBrA movement and that of Britain's Alan Davie.''

But the first person to recognize Distéfano's originality was Aldo Pellegrini, who included his paintings in the exhibition titled *Surrealism in Argentina,* organized in 1967, for the *Instituto Torcuato di Tella*'s Visual Arts Center. Distéfano was that Center's Graphics Director from 1960 through 1970. Also in 1967, in his *Overview of Argentine Contemporary Painting,* Pellegrini said of Distéfano that, "based on the work he has already done, he should right now be considered one of the most original and major Neo-figurative artists of the day."

But his Neo-figurative style, now as then, is unique and by no means surreal. The Neo-figurative school maintains that "today's Man is not tucked away behind his own image." Perhaps Distéfano, like no other Neo-figurative artist, and like few of his other Argentine colleagues, zealously and vigilantly seeks to express this certainty, to tear down the last vestiges of pretense that today's Man places between himself and his image in the field of art.

Seen from a strictly material and technical angle, Distéfano's work can be broken down into three stages:

1) In the first stage, he painted in relief, carrying the work out in polyester reinforced with spun fiberglass, on canvas, pressed wood or stainless steel. The type of paint used was oil-based or acrylic.

2) In the second stage came his first sculptures, carried out in polyester of uniform color, reinforced with spun fiberglass and partially painted using an epoxy resin base, which meant *adding* paint afterward.

3) With the third stage came his definitive sculptures, the product of a more significant solution: the adding of paint beforehand. Now the paint, which is a polyester resin, is the first thing applied in the mold, *painting in reverse,* as one might paint a window. In other words, from the outset he paints what will appear later on, and then what comes after and so on, giving the work as many coats, front-to-back, as the sculpture has colors, until he reaches the one or two base coats. Afterward comes lamination, and so the sculpture emerges with the color already *included.*

Distéfano's system of expression is resolved, therefore, in a veritable amalgam of painting and sculpture. Seen in this way, the artist went from sculpted painting to flat painting and from incipient volume to declared volume, as well as from pictorial space to general space. In the end, it is a matter of the obvious conquest of greater freedom of both diction and expression. His works are a gallery of exteriorizations of a sensitive awareness, alert to the infinite labyrinths of an ever more destructive world.

—Jorge Glusberg

DOKOUPIL, Jiri Georg

Nationality: Stateless. **Born:** Krnov, Czechoslovakia, 3 June 1954; immigrated to West Germany, 1968. **Education:** Studied fine arts in Cologne and Frankfurt, and under Hans Haacke at the Cooper Union, New York, 1976–78. **Career:** Independent painter and sculptor, Cologne, from 1978; currently lives in Cologne and Santa Cruz de Tenerife, Canary Islands. Instructor, Staatliche Kunstakademie, Dusseldorf, 1983–84. **Agent:** Galerie Paul Maenz, Bismarckstrasse 50, 5000 Cologne 1. **Address:** Aachener Strasse 21, 5000 Cologne 1, West Germany.

Individual Exhibitions:

1982 Galerie Paul Maenz, Cologne
Galerie 't Venster, Rotterdam (with Walter Dahn)
Galerie Magers, Bonn (with Walter Dahn)
Galerie Chantal Crousel, Paris
Galerie Helen van der Meij, Amsterdam
1983 Galerie Paul Maenz, Cologne
Galerie Six Friedrich, Munich
Produzentgalerie, Hamburg (with Walter Dahn)
Galerie Six Friedrich, Munich (with Walter Dahn)
Galerie Paul Maenz, Cologne (with Walter Dahn)
Mary Boone Gallery, New York
Galerie Chantal Crousel, Paris
1984 Galerie Schurr, Stuttgart
Groninger Museum, Groningen, Netherlands (with Walter Dahn)
Galerie Paul Maenz, Cologne
Museum Folkwang, Essen, West Germany
1985 Kunstmuseum, Lucerne, Switzerland
Galerie Crousel-Hussenot, Paris
Galerie Leyendecker, Santa Cruz de Tenerife
Galerie Paul Maenz, Cologne (with Walter Dahn)
Groninger Museum, Groningen, Netherlands
Galerie Paul Maenz, Cologne
Espace Lyonnais d'Art Contemporain, Lyon, France
Galerie Vera Munro, Hamburg
Paule Anglim Gallery, San Francisco
Asher/Faure Gallery, Los Angeles
Heinrich Erhardt Galerie, Frankfurt
Leo Castelli Gallery, New York
1986 Galerie 121, Antwerp
Galleria Marilena Bonomo, Bari, Italy
Sonnabend Gallery, New York
1987 Galerie Paul Maenz, Cologne
Galeria Leyendecker, Santa Cruz de Tenerife
Galerie Six Friedrich, Munich
Galerie Swart, Amsterdam
Galerie Dacic, Tubingen, West Germany
Studio Marconi, Milan
Galerie Bischofberger, Zurich
1988 Galleria Marilena Bonomo, Bari, Italy
Galeria Juana de Aizpuru, Madrid
1989 Robert Miller Gallery, New York
1990 *Jiri Georg Dokoupil: New Paintings,* Edward Totah Gallery, London
1991 *Jiri Georg Dokoupil: Fruit Architecture* 1991, Galerie Krinzinger, Vienna
Jiri Georg Dokoupil: Candle Paintings 1990–1991, Galerie Krinzinger, Vienna
1997 *Jiri Georg Dokoupil: Something Strange and Fantastic,* Palais Liechtenstein, Vienna

Selected Group Exhibitions:

1980 *Auch wenn das Perlhuhn leise weint,* Hahnentorburg, Cologne
1981 *Die Seefahrt und der Tod: Mulheimer Freiheit,* Kunssthalle, Wilhelmshaven, West Germany (travelled to Wolsburg)

1982 *Documenta 7,* Museum Fridericianum, Kassel, West Germany
1983 *Expressionisten-Neue Wilde,* Museum am Ostwall, Dortmund, West Germany
1984 *International Survey of Recent Painting and Sculpture,* Museum of Modern Art, New York
1985 *Kunst in der Bundesrepublik 1945–85,* Nationalgalerie, West Berlin
1986 *Wild, Visionary, Spectral: New German Art,* Art Gallery South Australia, Adelaide
1987 *Avant-Garde in the Eighties,* Los Angeles County Museum of Art
1988 *Art and Language: The 1980s—Selected Works,* Centre d'Histoire de l'Art Contemporain, Rennes
1991 *To Return to Base,* Deweer Art Gallery, Otegem, Belgium

Collections:

Van Abeemuseum, Eindhoven; Neue Galerie/Sammlung Ludwig, Aachen; Groninger Museum, Groningen; Staatsgalerie, Stuttgart; Museum Boymans-van Beuningen, Rotterdam; Kunsthaus, Zurich; Museum Folkwang, Essen; Nationalgalerie, West Berlin; Museum am Ostwall, Dortmund; Emmanuel Hoffman Stiftung, Basel.

Publications:

By DOKOUPIL: Book—*Neue Kolner Schule,* exhibition catalog, Cologne 1982. **Articles—**''Swings of the Pendulum,'' interview with Thomas West in *Art International,* no. 9, Winter 1989; Interview with Philip Pocock in *Journal of Contemporary Art,* vol. 4, no. 2, Fall-Winter 1991.

On DOKOUPIL: Books—*Das Bilderbuch,* edited by Karl Pfefferle, Munich 1981; *Junger nach Bildern: Deutsche Malerei de Gegenwart* by Wolfgang Max Faust and Gerd de Vries, Cologne 1982; *10 junge Kunstler aus Deutschland,* exhibition catalog with text by Zdenek Felix, Essen 1982; *Walter Dahn und Georg Dokoupil,* photographs by Roman Soukup, foreword by Paul Maenz, Cologne 1982; *Die Sammlung FER—The FER Collection* by Christel Sauer, Cologne 1983; *Die Afrika—Bilder: Dahn/Dokoupil,* exhibition catalog with texts by Frans Haks and Wilfried W. Dickhoff, Groningen 1984; *Dokoupil: Arbeiten 1981–84,* exhibition catalog with texts by Zdenek Felix, Frans Haks, Martin Kunz and Thierry Raspail, Cologne 1984; *Jiri Georg Dokoupil: Corporations and Products—The Sculpture,* edited by Paul Maenz, Cologne 1985; *Jiri Georg Dokoupil,* exhibition catalog with texts by Ernst A. Busche and Paul Maenz, Cologne 1987; *Art and Language: The 1980s—Selected Works,* exhibition catalog, Rennes 1988; *Jiri Georg Dokoupil,* exhibition catalog, New York 1989; *Jiri Georg Dokoupil: New Paintings,* London 1990; *Jiri Georg Dokoupil: Fruit Architecture,* Vienna 1991; *Jiri Georg Dokoupil: Candle Paintings 1990–1991,* Vienna 1991; *To Return to Base,* exhibition catalog, Otegem 1991; *Jiri Georg Dokoupil: Something Strange and Fantastic,* exhibition catalog, Vienna 1997. **Articles—**review by Lise Holst in *Art News,* vol. 88, December 1989; ''Jiri Georg Dokoupil'' by Maiten Buisset in *Beaux Arts Magazine,* no. 88, March 1991; ''By Kitsch Possessed: Jiri Georg Dokoupil's Satirical Art'' by Donald B. Kuspit in *Arts Magazine,* vol. 66, no. 4, December 1991; review in *Artforum International,* vol. 30, Summer 1992; review in *Art in America* (New York) by Reagan Upshaw, vol. 82, May 1994.

* * *

The artist Jiri Georg Dokoupil has manifested himself as a versatile and chameleonic painter, as one gifted with the talent to take a central position in the art debate of the day while at same time he forfeits current expectations.

Already for six years now he plays the game successfully. It is virtually impossible to circumscribe his already enormous oeuvre in a few lines, just as it does not make much sense to deal with some of the paintings individually. As his self-designed catalog (Folkwang Museum, Essen; Groninger Museum, Groningen and others, 1984), shows, he works in groups of paintings, very often done for particular gallery exhibitions. His production scheme seemed especially fit to match any number and size of exhibitions. By continuously changing his themes and by applying a wide range of painting techniques he is able to make each show look different. In this respect Dokoupil gives one the impression of being the artist par excellence for a commercial market system, precisely because his method allows for marketable surprise. To him the commercial system has never been a bondage; on the contrary, it is a stimulus. Critical doubt about superficiality or lack of seriousness, the traditional claim that a painting should show a certain struggling with its materials and its subject matter does not hold here. His way of painting allows for no doubts and hesitations, in its mechanical character it reminds one of many of Picasso's achievements. Despite his great success Dokoupil has retained something of an anarchistic and combative spirit.

Around 1980 Dokoupil was part of the Cologne-based artist group Mullheimer Freiheit (with Adamski, Bommels, Dahn, Kever, Naschberger). From 1982–83 onwards, from the moment that the young German painter's generation rapidly became successful, in Germany as well as abroad, Dokoupil has made clear that the art from Cologne should not be confused with the expressionist ''wild painting'' from Berlin (Fetting, Salome) or even Hamburg (Oehlenbrothers, Büttner).

Possibly, one of Dokoupil's reasons for collaborating intensively with Walter Dahn (1982/83) has been the need to demonstrate the relativity of an individual, ''expressive'' signature. For him the year 1982 was a very productive one; witness the *Amsterdam-Bilder* that deals with schizophrenic painting as well as the gigantic *History of the Universe* that seems to be a monumental and public translation of microscopic-cosmic fertilization.

Remarkable as well is the series of *Frotee-Bilder* from 1983–84, framed sweat-cloth supplied with buttons and zippers, workshop-products that associate themselves with Fontana's spatial, eroticizing cuts. A group of ceramics called *Corporations and Products* (Paul Maenz Gallery, Cologne, 1985) offers all the potentials of a well-organized firm. The gallery show consisted of a large amount of baked logos of international firms, all reduced to one (Dokoupil) vocabulary. Recently Dokoupil started a new collaboration, with the young Dutch artist Rob Scholte.

—A. F. Wagemans

DOMELA, César

Nationality: Dutch. **Born:** César Domela Nieuwenhuis in Amsterdam, 15 January 1900. **Education:** Gymnasium in Hilversum, Netherlands, 1913–18. **Married:** Ruth Deremberg in 1928; children: Lie and Anne. **Career:** Visited Henri Laurens' Paris atelier, 1914; began drawing, 1918; moved to Ascona, 1920, to Berlin, 1923; met Piet Mondrian and Theo van Doesburg; joined De Stijl group, 1925; moved to Amsterdam, 1925; returned to Berlin, 1927; advertising photographer, with own commercial studio, Berlin-Wilmersdorf, 1928–33; joined Ring Neue Werbegestalter group, founded by Schwitters, 1929; lecturer, Berlin, Munich and Stuttgart typography companies, 1931; burned personal anarchist literature and returned to Paris, 1933; opened silkscreen studio, with Frederick Kann; founded *Plastique* magazine, with Jean Arp and Sophie Täuber-Arp, 1937; worked with jewelry, 1941; lived and workd in Paris. Visiting instructor, Skowhegan School of Painting, Maine, 1977. **Member:** Cercle at Carré/Abstraction-Création groups, Paris, 1934. **Died:** Paris, December 1992.

Individual Exhibitions:

1924 Galerie d'Audretsch, The Hague
1934 Galerie Pierre, Paris
1936 Museum of Living Art, New York
1939 Galerie Pierre, Paris
1947 Galerie Denise René, Paris
1948 Galerie Apollinaire, London
1949 Galerie Allendy, Paris
1950 Galerie Huinck en Scherjon, Amsterdam
1951 Galerie Allendy, Paris
1952 Galerie de Babylone, Paris
1953 Galerie Cahiers d'Art, Paris
1954 Museu de Arte Moderna, Rio de Janeiro (retrospective; travelled to the Museu de Arte Moderna, Sao Paulo)
1955 Stedelijk Museum, Amsterdam
1956 Galerie 93, Paris
1959 Galerie Simone Heller, Paris
1960 Gemeentemuseum, The Hague
1961 Chalette Gallery, New York
1962 Galerie Simone Heller, Paris
1964 Galerie d'Eendt, Amsterdam
Galerie Cahiers d'Art, Paris
1965 Institut Neerlandais, Paris
1967 Galerie Cahiers d'Art, Paris
1968 Galerie Klihm, Munich
1969 *Retrospective 1922–1969,* Galerie Verrière, Lyons
Galerie Simone Heller, Paris
1970 Maison de la Culture, St. Etienne, France (retrospective)
1971 Galerie de Seine, Paris
1972 *Werke 1922–1972,* Kunsthalle, Dusseldorf (retrospective)
Institut Goethe, Paris
1973 Galerie Weiler, Paris
Galerie Klihm, Munich
Collection d'Art, Amsterdam
Retrospective, Annely Juda Fine Art, London
1974 Maison de la Culture, Bourges, France
1978 Galerie Dobbelhöff, Antwerp
1979 Birla Museum, Calcutta

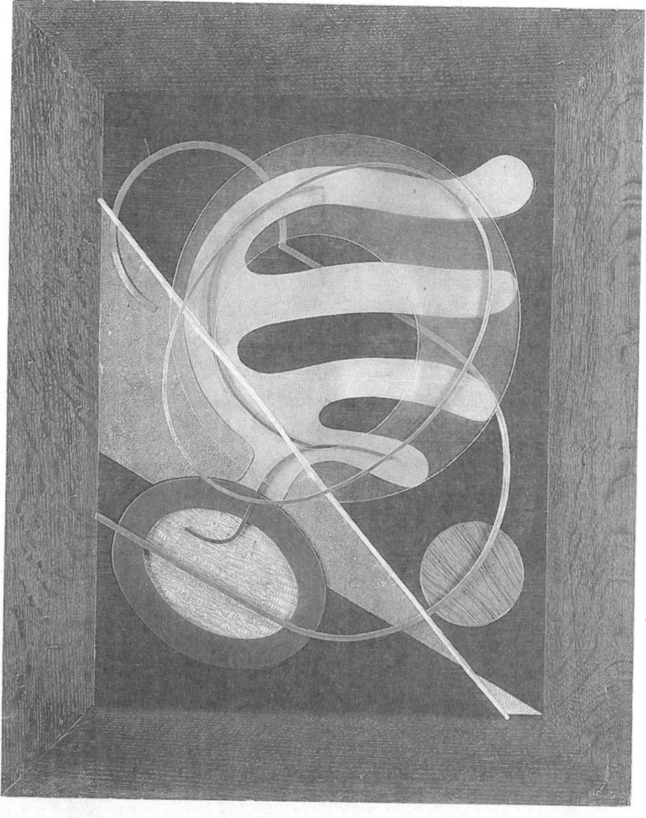

César Domela: *Relief No. 17,* 1943. Photo by Michèle Bellot. ©2001 Artists Rights Society (ARS), NY/ADAGP, Paris.

1980 Galerie de Seine, Paris
Schilderijen, Reliefs, Beelden, Grafiek, Typografie, Fotos, Gemeentemuseum, The Hague
1981 Galerie Carmen Martines, Grand Palais, Paris
Galerie Martini and Ronchetti, Geneva
1984 Modern Museum, Dordrecht, Netherlands
Modern Museum, Apeldoorn, Netherlands
Galerie Tanit, Munich
1985 Galerie Susanna Kulli, St. Gallen, Switzerland
1986 Galerie Spiess, Paris
1987 Musée d'Art Moderne de la Ville, Paris
Musée de Grenoble, France
1988 Stedelijk Museum, Amsterdam
1990 Gemeentelijke van Reekummuseum, Apeldoorn

Selected Group Exhibitions:

1932 *Exposition Internationale de la Photographie,* Palais des Beaux-Arts, Brussels (travelled to Lakenhal, Leiden)
1936 *Cubism and Abstract Art,* Museum of Modern Art, New York
1938 *Abstrakte Kunst,* Stedelijk Museum, Amsterdam
1954 *Contour Beeldende Kunst,* Museum Prinsenhof, Delft, Netherlands
1955 *Artistes Etrangers en France,* Petit Palais, Paris
1957 *Art Abstrait Premières Generations 1910–39,* Musée d'Art et d'Industrie, St. Etienne, France
1970 *Leger and Purist Paris,* Tate Gallery, London

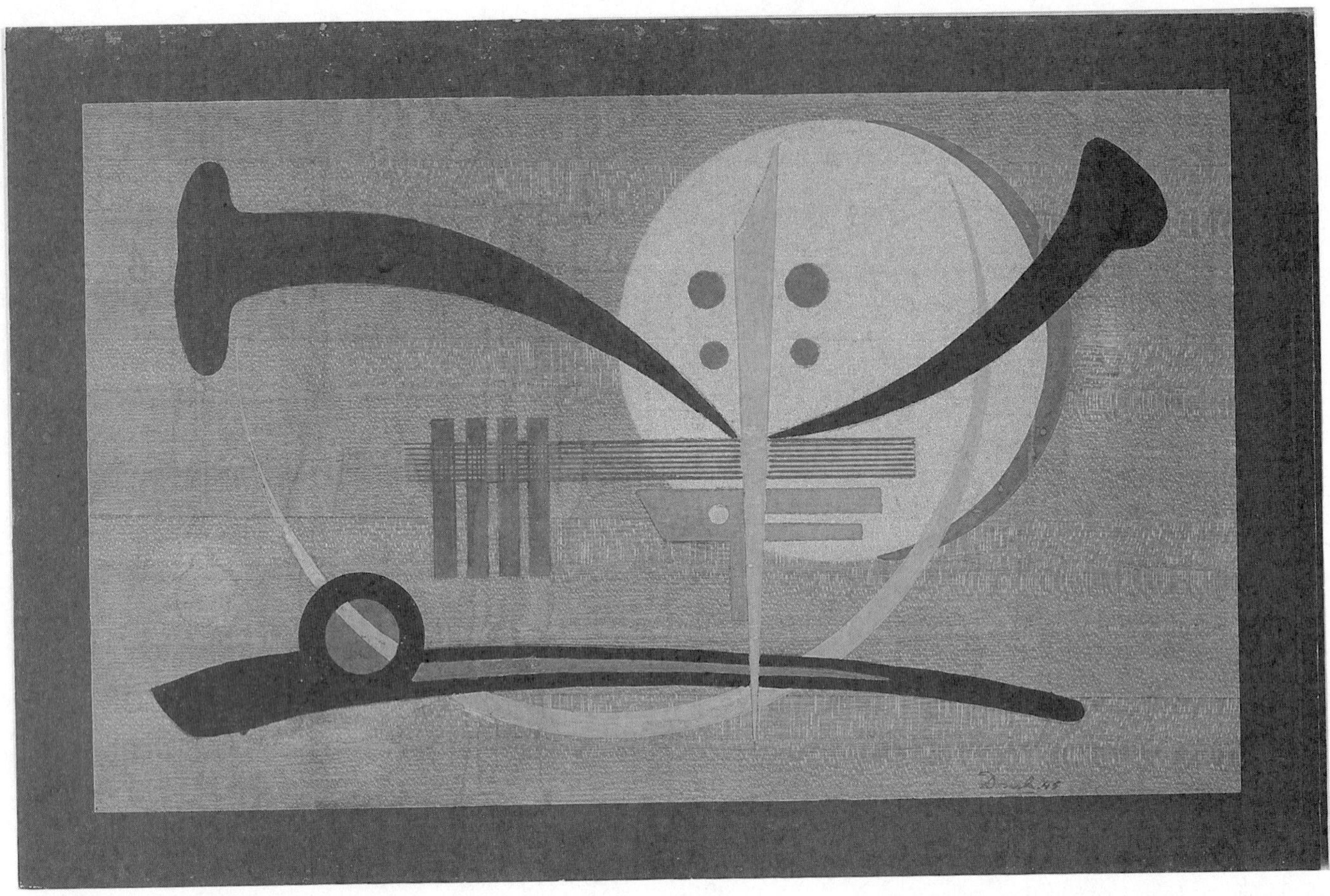

César Domela: *Untitled,* 1945. Photo © Bertrand Prévost. ©2001 Artists Rights Society (ARS), NY/ADAGP, Paris.

1976 *Art 7, 76,* Kunstmuseum, Basle
1979 *Fotografie in Nederland 1920–40,* Gemeentemuseum, The Hague
1980 *Abstraction 1910–40,* Annely Juda Fine Art, London
1981 *The Classical Moderns,* Galerie Gmurzynska, Cologne

Collections:

Staatsgalerie, Stuttgart; Bayerische Staatlichen Sammlungen, Munich; Stedelijk Musem, Amsterdam; Gemeentemuseum, The Hague; Centre Georges Pompidou, Paris; Museum of Modern Art, Jerusalem; Museu de Arte Moderna, Rio de Janeiro; Guggenheim Museum, New York; Philadelphia Museum of Art; Hirshhorn Museum, Washington, D.C.

Publications:

By DOMELA: Articles—''Entretien avec César Domela,'' with Roger van Gindertael, in *Cimaise* (Paris), November/December 1970; ''Quelques Apercus et Conceptions sur l'Art Moderne'' in *Domela,* exhibition catalog, Paris 1971; Entretien avec César Domela,'' with Henry Galy-Carles, in *Les Lettres Francaises* (Paris), December 1971.

On DOMELA: Books—*Domela* by Wassily Kandinsky, Paris 1943; *Presentation de l'Oeuvre de Domela* by Roger van Gindertael, Paris 1951; *Domela* by Marcel Brion, Paris 1961; *Domela* by Marcel Pobe, Hilversum, Netherlands 1965; *Domela* by Christian Zervos, Amsterdam 1965; *Functional Graphic Design in the 20's* by Eckhard Neumann, New York 1967; *Domela: Retrospective 1922–1969,* exhibition catalog, with text by Marcel Brion and others, Lyons 1969; *Domela,* exhibition catalog, Paris 1971; *César Domela: Werke 1922–1972,* exhibition catalog, with foreword by Karl-Heinz Hering, text by Jean Laude, Dusseldorf 1972; *César Domela: Retrospective,* exhibition catalog, with introduction by Gerhard Weber, London 1979; *Domela: Catalog Raisonnée de l'Oeuvre,* edited by Alain Clairet, Paris 1978; *Fotografie in Nederland 1920–1940,* exhibition catalog, by Flip Bool and Kees Broos, The Hague 1979; *Domela: Schilderijen, Reliefs, Beelden, Grafiek, Typografie, Fotos,* exhibition catalog, with text by Kees Broos, Flip Bool and Mathilde Visser. The Hague 1980; *Domela* by H. C. L. Jaffe, Paris 1980; *César Domela: Fotografie, Fotomontaggi, Disegni* by G. B. Martini and A. Ronchetti, Genoa 1981; *Domela: 65 Ans d'Abstraction,* exhibition catalog, Grenoble 1987; *Transparency as Art: Acrylic Glass as a Medium,* by Anca Arghir, Cologne, 1988; *Domela: Paintings, Reliefs, Prints,* exhibition catalog, Apeldorn, 1990; *The Ideal as Art: De Stijl 1917–1931,* by Carsten-Peter Warncke, Cologne, 1998. **Articles—**''What Links Domela's Work with Bert Boogaard's Graceful Scrolls?'' by Evert van Straaten in *Dutch Art & Architecture Today,* no. 23, June 1988; ''Domela'' by Renate Puvogel in *Das Kunstwerk,* vol. 41, February 1988; ''Construction (Oil and metal on panel, ca 1929)'' in *Bulletin* (Philadelphia), vol. 89, Winter/Spring 1994; ''Construction (1929)'' in *The Structurist,* no. 35/36, 1995/1996; ''Strasbourg.

Musee d'Art moderne et contemporain'' by Nadine Lehni in *La Revue du Louvre et des Musees de France,* vol. 46, October 1996.

*

I, for my part, should like my reliefs to be structurally the exact and absolute expression of the inner reality which gives rise to them. The message I should like them to convey is one of the repose, and I should like to think of them as the concrete representation of a certitude of a knowledge that fills the soul and is the reflection of a strict order.

This strict order, without which the meditation behind a work of art is impossible, makes it necessary for me to have a method enabling me to put into a work the maximum of intensity. When I set out to work on a relief, I try to find my gravitational field, then the laws governing come into play, lines are given a direction, colors are brought in, a rhythmic pattern orders the dynamic units of the composition and takes command of the nascent work.

—César Domela

* * *

The full name of this Dutch-born artist is Domela Nieuwenhuis. He left Holland in 1919, for Switzerland, and in his early years was a landscape painter. In the 1920s he became interested in Russian Constructivist ideas and made his first attempts at abstraction. Contact with Mondrian and Van Doesburg in Paris brought him back to Dutch activities, leading to an exhibition in The Hague and membership in the de Stijl group in 1925. The close connections between de Stijl and the Bauhaus were reinforced by his long stay in Berlin, 1927 to 1933, during which he turned from flat painting to the construction of reliefs, searching for subtle forms. In Paris, where he worked after the rise of Hitler, he began experiments in multi-colored reliefs, exploiting the contrasting effects of different materials.

Domela, whilst enormously influenced by Mondrian and Van Doesburg, can only be regarded as a peripheral member of de Stijl. His earlier work reveals considerable originality in applying to the rigid, balanced confrontation of simple geometrical shape and primary colors, a new sense of space and decoration. In particular he produced a three-dimensional basis, developing the basic elementarism into new forms of neo-plasticism, largely by the superimposed layers of different materials. This was clearly at variance with strict de Stijl principles, even though Domela's reliefs have much in common with the movement's functional designs and architecture. But in his case the moral and social basis of de Stijl is somewhat undermined by the tendency to picture-making for its own sake, rather than as philosophical or social statements. Domela, incidentally, was also a typographer of considerable achievements.

It is little wonder that in about 1930 Domela's association with de Stijl became tenuous and that in time he left the movement. His later reliefs are increasingly multi-colored, bordering on the decorative, introducing curved linear elements into his compositions, which reveal the influence of Jean Arp. It must, however, be said that, as a survivor of the de Stijl generation, Domela, with Vordemberg-Gildewart and Herbin, has kept alive the great achievements of the Dutch group and their contribution, no matter how diluted, to the abstract movement. In fact it was only Mondrian who remained devoted to the ascetic, original principles of de Stijl. Domela's long, active career has recently been rewarded by renewed interest in his work, part of the re-investigation of the purposes and achievements of the great experimental movements early in the century, and their striving for a new relationship between art and society.

—Charles Spencer

DOMPÉ, Hernán

Nationality: Argentinian. **Born:** Buenos Aires, Argentina, 1946. **Education:** Graduated from the Prilidiano Pueyrredón National School of Fine Arts, 1972. **Career:** Sculpture professor. **Awards:** First Prize, Sculpture, ESSO Foundation Drawing and Sculpture Prizes, Eduardo Sívori Museum of Plastic Arts, Buenos Aires, 1982; Young Artist 1985, Argentine Association of Art Critics, Buenos Aires, 1985; First Prize, Young Sculptor, Fundación Alfredo y Amalia Fortabat, Buenos Aires, 1986; Second Prize, 17th Sur Neige International Sculpture Contest, Quebec, Canada, 1989; First Prize, 10th International Wood Sculpture Contest, Cortina D'Ampezzo, Italy, 1990; Konex Platinum Prize, 1992 Konex Awards, Konex Foundation, Buenos Aires, 1992; First Prize, Second International Wood Contest, Resistencia, Chaco Province, Argentina, 1992; Second Prize, Henry Moore Institute Prize, Buenos Aires, 1998; Jorge Luis Borges Acquisition Grand Prize, Palais de Glace, Buenos Aires, 1999.

Selected Individual Exhibitions:

1985 Jacques Martínez Gallery, Buenos Aires
1989 *Obras 1979–1989* (Works 1979–1989), Fundación San Telmo, Buenos Aires
1991 *Nuevas Esculturas* (New Sculptures), Der Brücke Gallery, Buenos Aires (catalog)
1993 *Expresiones Arte Latinoamericano* Gallery, Guayaquil
1994 *La obra escultórica* (The Sculptural Work), Ramis Barquet Gallery, Monterrey (catalog)
1995 National Museum of Fine Arts, Buenos Aires
1996 *Una luz en el cerro* (A Light on the Mountain), Der Brücke Gallery, Contemporary Art, Buenos Aires (catalog)
Raleigh Gallery, Boca Raton, Florida
1997 *Yaco García Arte Latinoamericano,* Panama

Selected Group Exhibitions:

1990 *Artistas de Buenos Aires,* Museum of Modern Art, Mexico
1991 *2nd Sud del Mondo,* Civic Contemporary Art Gallery, Marsala, Sicily
1993 *La otra cara,* Das andere Gesicht, Dock 4, Kassel
Decouvertes '93, Der Brücke Gallery, Grand Palais, Paris
1994 *El arte de la Instalación,* National Museum of Fine Arts, Buenos Aires
ARCO '94, Der Brücke Gallery, Crystal Pavilion, Casa de Campo, Madrid
ARCO '96, Der Brücke Gallery, Contemporary Art, Juan Carlos I Fairgrounds, Madrid
1995 *70–80-90,* National Museum of Fine Arts, Buenos Aires

1995 Trabucco Acquisition Prize, Fundación Alberto J. Trabucco, National Academy of Fine Arts, Museum of Modern Art, Buenos Aires
Fuera del Centro?, Caracas Fine Arts Museum, Venezuela
1996 *Buenos Aires, la ciudad agredida,* National Museum of Fine Arts, Buenos Aires
MIRARTE '96, Latin American Fair of International Art, Der Brücke Gallery, Contemporary Art, Santafe de Bogota
Puente Aéreo II, Cultural Affairs Office, Argentine Foreign Relations Ministry, Chilean Museum of Contemporary Art, Santiago
Artistas Argentinos en Art Chicago '96, Der Brücke Gallery, Contemporary Art, Buenos Aires
1997 Sofía Imber Museum of Contemporary Art, Caracas
International Festival of the City of Medellín, Colombia
Art Chicago '97, Der Brücke Gallery, Contemporary Art, Buenos Aires, and Navy Pier, Chicago
ARCO '97, Der Brücke Gallery, Contemporary Art, Juan Carlos I Fairgrounds, Madrid
1998 *Art Miami '98,* International Art Exposition, Der Brücke Gallery, Miami Beach Convention Center, Miami
1999 *FIAC '99,* Diana Lowenstein Fine Arts, Pavillon du Parc-Porte de Versailles, Paris
Artist's Presentation NE2, Diana Lowenstein Fine Arts, Miami
Art Chicago 2001, Diana Lowenstein Fine Arts, Navy Pier, Chicago
Art Palm Beach 2001, Diana Lowenstein Fine Arts, Palm Beach, Florida

Publications:

On DOMPÉ: Books—*Cinco Años* (Five Years), Guayaquil 1994; *Panorama de la Escultura Argentina Contemporánea* (A Look at Contemporary Argentine Sculpture), Buenos Aires 1998.

* * *

Hernán Dompé studied in Spain, France, and Italy. Ten years later he returned to Italy, later visiting Holland, Germany, and Switzerland. All of these travels informed his work, but the most crucial trip he ever made was, without a doubt, the one that took him to Peru and Mexico in 1980, where he made contact with the works of the Aztecs, Mayas, Quiches, and Incas. Shortly afterward, in 1982, he would go to the United States on a scholarship, settling for a year in New York.

The path Dompé took would lead him from ancient America to the present day, in close communication with the invading Europe of the 16th century and with the United States that grew within a vast territory with no great Indian cultures. Like the Maya and Aztec pyramids, Dompé's *Testigo* (Witness) suggests persistence in the face of future destruction. The choice of wood and lead as a medium is no accident. These materials are found in nature and both serve, when transformed by culture, to both protect and harm man, their transformer.

Dompé recreates ancient forms and methods that allude to archaic Latin American societies, using techniques that produce objects capable of *updating* pre-Columbian regionalism. Incas, Aztecs, Mayas: everything Dompé felt in Peru and Mexico—the nature, the architecture, the clay works, the stone sculptures, the arms derived from artistic craft—have worked as catalysts in his search for a regional identity.

The first thing that astonishes one about Dompé's sculptures is their consummate execution—so carefully precise and yet so imaginative. The wood, the iron, and the bronze to which most of his most recent works have been circumscribed, and the earlier marble and granite, surrender entirely to the hands of this artist without producing forced or discordant situations. He also resorts to the use of some of the strangest of elements and articles, many of which were, however, used in ancient society (and are still used today) as adornments or amulets: animal bones, teeth and skulls, antlers, bristle and shells but also things like chain links, nails, keys, hides, rope, keyhole covers and violin necks.

His *Barcas* (Vessels) have decks and keels bristling with sharp points, but they are svelte and haughty in their lively quietude. And then there are *Ballestas* (Bows), *Cuchillos* (Knives) *Hachas* (Axes) and *Herramientas Agrícolas* (Farming Implements), characterized by their enormous height and enigmatic presence. And then, the *Totems. . . .* His totems are tall (as tall as 2.50 meters, or a little over 8 feet) and it is in them that the artist provides the full measure of his creativity. It is no exaggeration to suppose that the arms, implements, and even the vessels constitute, beyond their formal appearances, still another totem-like presence.

According to Dompé himself, the totems are "the basic symbols of the link between earth and sky." The totem (a word that comes from the language of the Ojibwas, natives of the territory that is today the United States and Canada) is almost always some sort of animal or vegetable species (and is seldom the representation of an inanimate or manmade object), to which tribe members paid (and in some aboriginal societies still pay) a kind of superstitious respect, believing that between themselves and the totem there existed some indissoluble tie of parentage.

The men and women of the tribe worshipped the totem, of whom they believed themselves to be blood descendents and whose name they took in periodic ritual ceremonies. Defender and spirit of well-being, the totem also foresaw the future of the faithful and led them in their actions. He who killed the totem animal, destroyed the totem vegetable, or damaged the totem as such would lose his life.

Totem worship was then (and still is where practiced) a religious system, perhaps the first among mankind in chronological terms. But it was, at the same time, a social system, since it was the investiture of the spiritual beliefs of the tribe (which carried the name of the totem as the surname of the dynasty, since the totem was hereditary). And it was from these beliefs that the tribe derived its legal, political, and ethical standards.

From a contemporary and personal perspective, Dompé recovers the religious and social aptitude of "totemism." There is a sacred-like resonance in his sculptures, and a leaning toward a moral tone. He himself has indicated that his totems encompass an earthly proposal (one that is highly held in our time): namely, that of impeding and halting the destruction of our environment. But this objective emerges from the spiritual character of the these *Totems*: the man of today, as yesterday, is the incarnation of that duality.

Dompé represents this duality in his *Totems,* the basic material for which is wood—a natural substance *par excellence*—but iron too participates in them, be it totally or partially. The form of the sculptures responds to a model: a column with a base and a crown—a bird, a set of half moons, a trident, a helmut, a ball. The columns are carved and faceted. Some seem to suggest a human figure (two eyes, a nose, a mouth). Many present a toothy contour (like the *Blue Totem,* from 1991, one of Dompé's most attractive totems). Still others culminate in elements taken from weapons (the arc of a bow, the blade of a knife).

In short, these *Totems* rise like the prayers of man—in his dual role as maker and predator—offered up to Providence, to the center from which emanates his transcendence, his ultimate sense of life and death. In a world where nature is deteriorating by the day and where, in so many places, such insult is inflicted on human dignity, the discourse of any Dompé exhibit is the unfolding of works that are outstanding for the inventive capacity of their forms and the spiritual space that they create. It is a surreal space, where the myths of America float, redeemed by this artist for the here and now.

—Jorge Glusberg

DONO, Heri

Nationality: Indonesian. **Born:** Jakarta, 1960. **Education:** Graduated from Indonesia Institute of the Arts (ISI), Yogyakarata, 1987; studied traditional puppetry, wayang kulit. **Career:** Participant, International Artists Exchange Programme, Basel, Switzerland, 1990–91; artist-in-residence, Canberra School of Art, ACT, Australia, 1993; artist-in-residence, 24 Hr ART Gallery, Northern Territory Centre for Contemporary Art, Darwin, Australia, 1994; artist-in-residence, Museum of Modern Art, Oxford, United Kingdom, 1995. **Awards:** Best painting, Indonesian Institute of the Arts (ISI), Yogyakarta, Indonesia, 1981, 1985; I Gusti Nyoman Lempad Prize, Sanggar Dewata, Yogyakarta, 1986; Prince Claus Award, Prince Claus Fund for Culture and Development, Netherlands, 1998. **Address:** Ronodigdayan Dn. 5, No. 263, Yogyakarta, Indonesia.

Selected Individual Exhibitions:

1988 Cemeti Contemporary Art Gallery, Yogyakarta, Indonesia
Mitra Budaya Indonesia Gallery, Jakarta, Indonesia
Bentara Budaya Gallery, Yogyakarta, Indonesia.
1991 *Unknown Dimensions,* Museum für Völkerkunde, Basel, Switzerland
1993 Canberra Contemporary Art Space, ACT, Australia
1996 *Blooming in Arms,* Museum of Modern Art, Oxford, England
2000 *Dancing Demons and Drunken Deities,* Japan Foundation Asia Center, Tokyo

Selected Group Exhibitions:

1986 *5th Biennale of Indonesian Young Artists,* TIM, Jakarta, Indonesia
1987 *Sandiwa,* Kulay-Diwa Art Galleries/Cultural Centre of the Philippines, Manila, Philipines.
1988 *Wayang Legenda,* shadow play, Seni Sono Gallery, Yogyakarta, Indonesia
Hendendaagse Indonesische Kunst, Volkenkundig Museum Nusantara, Delft, Holland
1989 *Young Indonesian Artists,* L'Alliance Franceise and Institute of Technology, Bandung, Indonesia
1990–91 *Modern Indonesian Art: Three Generations of Change,* traveling exhibition in United States
1991 *Wayang: From Gods to Bart Simpson,* University of British Columbia, Vancouver, Canada
Man and Human Expression, Tropen Museum, Amsterdam, Holland
Wayang Top (performance), International Cultural Camp, Desa Apuan, Tabanan, Bali, Indonesia
1992 *Sanggar Dewata Indonesia Art Exhibition,* Museum Nyoman Gunarsa, Yogyakarta, Indonesia
New Art from Southeast Asia 1992, Tokyo Metropolitan Art Space
Hiroshima City Museum of Contemporary Art
1993 *Modern Art/Indonesian Painting Since 1945,* Gate Foundation, De Oude Kerk, Amsterdam, Holland
International Festival of Puppetry in the World, Taman Budaya, Yogyakarta, Indonesia
1st Asia-Pacific Triennale of Contemporary Art Space, Queensland Art Gallery, Brisbane, Australia
1994 *Indonesia's Excellence,* Grand Hyatt, Jakarta, Indonesia
9th Asian International Art Exhibition, National Museum of History, Taipé, Taiwan
4th Asian Art Show Fukuoka, Fukuoka Art Museum, Japan
Jakarta International Art Exhibition 1994, The Indonesian Fine Arts Foundation, Jakarta, Indonesia
1995 *Visions of Happiness—Ten Asian Contemporary Artists,* Japan Foundation Art Forum, ASEAN Cultural Centre, Akasaka, Tokyo
Orientasi, National Gallery, Jakarta, Indonesia
Beyond the Border, 1st Kwangju Biennale, Kwangju, South Korea
1996 *Traditions/Tensions,* New York (toured in United States, Australia, and Japan through 1999)
Drawing, Institute of International Visual Arts, London, England
Orientation, Stedelijk Museum De Lakenhal, Leiden, Holland
Modernity and Beyond, National Heritage Board, Singapore Art Museum, Singapore
1996 Sao Paulo Biennale, Brazil
1997 *Cities on the Move,* Vienna, Austria (toured)
1998 *50 Years Anniversary of Human Rights,* Boijmann Museum of Art, Rotterdam, Netherlands
Rupa Seni-Seni Rupa, Museum Benteng Vredeburg, Yogyakarta
1999 *Asia-Pacific Triennial of Contemporary Art,* Queesland Art Gallery, Brisbane, Australia
Media within Media, National Gallery, Jakarta
Art Biennial, Art Centre Purna Budaya, Yogyakarta

Collections:

Fukuoka Art Museum, Fukuoka, Japan; Queensland Art Gallery, Brisbane, Australia; Indonesian Institute of the Arts, Yogyakarta, Indonesia; National Heritage Board, Singapore Art Museum, Singapore; Museum für Völkerkunde, Basel, Switzerland; Cemeti Contemporary Art Gallery, Yogyakarta, Indonesia; Artoteek den haag, The Hague, Netherlands.

Publications:

By DONO: Articles—Interview with Larry Polansky in *Sounding Sphere* (booklet and CD-ROM), Japan 1998; interview with Hans Ulrich Obrist in *ChineseArt.com,* vol. 2, no. 6, 1999.

On DONO: Articles—''Heri Dono'' by Tsutomu Mizusawa at http://www.uol.com, 1996; ''Interview With Heri Dono'' by Larry Polansky at http://music.dartmouth.edu, 1997; ''Low Tech Magician'' by Carol Lutfy in *Artnews,* 1999; ''The Ever-Increasing Colonization of Time'' by Hans-Ulrich Obrist in *Flash Art,* 2000; ''Heri Dono: Low-Tech Wizard, Postmodern Puppeteer and Hilarious Satirist'' by Apinan Poshyananda in exhibition catalog, Japan Foundation Asian Center, Tokyo 2000; ''Positioning Contemporary Asian Art'' by Apinan Poshyananda in *Art Journal,* Spring 2000.

* * *

If there exists an aesthetic equivalent of globalization, it is artist Heri Dono. The Indonesian-born painter, who currently resides in Yogyakarta, marries centuries old art and craft forms to modern-day causes such as subversive political activity. Part of a recent explosion of vitality and expressiveness in the Asian art world, Dono's art applies aspects of Javanese craft, including puppetry and gamelan, to modern video, performance, mixed media installation, and public art. The artist consciously utilizes a traditional aesthetic to explore the transformational nature of art whether this is transfiguring by masks or transfiguring by toppled regimes. His vibrant, often political, artworks act as a running commentary on historical and contemporary Asian culture. His work, in whatever incarnation, is marked by humor, the use of low-tech gadgetry and, increasingly, a sense of multitude and ceremony.

Although Dono began as a painter, his early vivid and frequently animistic pictures owe as much to Kandinsky and Picasso as they do to the traditional forms they ostensibly resemble. In 1991 Dono apprenticed under a master of *wayang kulit,* the shadow puppet theater intimately identified with Indonesian culture. He is known in his own country primarily for puppet shows that utilized folkloric legends to political effect, and further afield his work is also marked by a sense of theater. His installations, as theater in stasis, borrow from theatrical narrative and spectacle and even mimic a proscenium with objects commonly arranged in rows.

Some Western doctrines such as distinctions between ''high'' and ''low'' art and the purpose of a canon have proved problematic for contemporary artists. Dono's unique hybrids consciously refer to the aspects of traditional art making which speak to such entanglements. His puppet shows become a precursor of collaborative enterprise. The use of recycled materials is a continuation of a tradition of ''native'' materials, that is, whatever comes to hand, whether teak tree or a television circuitry. Dono says he finds little distinction between the screen behind which the wayang kulit takes place and a computer screen. To him, it is all animation. In the 1992 ''Bad Man,'' a line of dangling fiberglass puppets with outsized lips and bright red boots follow a single beckoning puppet. Electronic screens comprise their chest and bellies. Although there are strong political overtones about corruption and gullibility, the piece could be equally referring to Dono's role as a *Punakawan,* a kind of court clown. If the artist's mission is to communicate through formal usage, it has been Dono's particular gift to transmogrify those elements of ancestral forms that also answer to contemporary interests within the art world.

Since Dono created his first installation in 1982 the form has been increasingly his chosen arena. In the 1997 ''Animal Journey'' a row of bicycles festooned with shadow puppets, masks, and heads have animal sounds emanating from small radios attached to the bikes. As with any piece of guerrilla theater, there is a fluid blend of genres and materials. This fluidity (''Animal Journey'' has several versions) echoes in the mode of transportation, the organic, animal origins of the masks, and the placement of the bikes in regular rows. Their arrangement is both orderly, in a formal sense, and chaotic in color and texture. So too are the cities in which these animal-bicycles live. In the 1994 ''Fermentation of the Mind'' dozens of fiberglass casts of the artists own head sit atop Indonesian school desks. The heads nod and emit chants by virtue of a modest electrical device. Such installations refer on many levels to Dono's philosophical belief that the adaptation of materials itself carries a potent commentary. In an interview Dono has spoken of the ''spiritual energy of electricity'' that acts less as a scientific tool than as a cultural or even religious icon. Collective imagination and adaptability as a cultural necessity continues in his work no differently than the way painted objects, spoken objects, and performed objects served similar functions as folk paintings, folk theater, or folk dance in past centuries.

—Merridawn Duckler

DOUGLAS, Stan

Nationality: Canadian **Born:** Vancouver, 1960. **Education:** Graduated from Emily Carr College of Art, Vancouver, 1982. **Career:** Film and Video Projects: *Monodramas,* 1991; *Horchamps,* 1992; *Pursuit, Fear, Catastrophe: Ruskin, B.C.*, 1993; *Evening,* 1994; *Der Sandmann,* 1995; *Nu-tka,* 1996; *Win, Place, or Show,* 1998. Photography Projects: *Nootka Sound Series,* 1996, *Strathcona Series,* 1998, *Detroit Photos,* 1999. **Address:** 613 Union Street, Vancouver, British Columbia V6A 2C1, Canada.

Individual Exhibitions:

1981 Jericho Beach Air Station, Jericho Beach, Vancouver, Canada
1983 Ridge Theatre, Vancouver, Canada
1985 Or Gallery, Vancouver, Canada
1986 Western Front, Vancouver, Canada
1987 Art Gallery of Ontario, Toronto, Canada
Contemporary Art Gallery, Vancouver, Canada
Artspeak Gallery, Vancouver, Canada
1989 YYZ Gallery, Toronto, Canada
1990 Ambassade du Canada, Services Culturels, Paris, France
1991 Galerie Nationale du Jeu de Paume, Paris, Frances
1992 Art Metropole, Toronto, Canada
University of British Columbia Fine Arts Gallery, Vancouver, Canada
1993 Galerie Christian Nagel, Cologne, Germany
Transmission Gallery, Glasgow, Scotland
World Wide Video Centre, Den Haag, Netherlands
David Zwirner Gallery, New York, New York
1994 Milwaukee Art Museum, Milwaukee, Wisconsin
Centre for Contemporary Art, Rotterdam, Netherlands
Institute of Contemporary Art, London, England

Musée national d'art moderne, Centre Georges Pompidou, Paris, Frances
Museo Nacional Centro de Arte Reina Sofia, Madrid, Spain
Kunsthalle Zurich, Switzerland
DAAD, Berlin, Germany
1995 David Zwirner Gallery, New York, New York
Neueraachenerkunstverein, Aachen, Germany
DAAD, Berlin, Germany
Walter Phillips Gallery, Banff, Canada
1996 Musée d'Art contemporain Montréal, Montréal, Canada
Museum Haus Lange & Museum Haus Esters, Krefeld, Germany
Zeno X Gallery, Antwerp, Belgium
David Zwirner Gallery, New York, New York
1997 Freedman Gallery, Albright Center for the Arts, Reading, Pennsylvania
Museum of Contemporary Art, Chicago, Illinois
Centre genevois de gravure contemporaine, Geneva, Switzerland
Museo Alejandro Otero, Caracas, Venezuela
1998 Salzburger Kunstverein, Salzburg, Austria
David Zwirner Gallery, New York, New York
1999 Vancouver Art Gallery, Vancouver, Canada
Edmonton Art Gallery, Edmonton, Alberta, Canada
The Power Plant, Toronto, Ontario
De Pont Museum, Tilburg, Netherlands
Museum of Contemporary Art, Los Angeles, California
DIA Center for the Arts, New York
2000 Art Institute of Chicago, Chicago, Illinois
Museo do Chiado, Lisbon, Portugal
Ormeau Baths Gallery, Belfast, Ireland
2001 Kunsthalle Basel, Basel, Switzerland
Perth International Arts Festival, Australia
Winnipeg Art Gallery, Winnipeg, Canada
Neue Gesellschaft für bildende Kunst, Berlin, Germany
Kestner Gesellschaft, Hannover, Germany

Selected Group Exhibitions:

1990 Biennale di Venezia, Venice, Italy
1992 Documenta IX, Kassel, Germany
1995 Carnegie International, The Carnegie Museum of Art, Pittsburgh, Pennsylvania
Whitney Biennale, The Whitney Museum of American Art, New York, New York
1996 Hugo Boss Prize, Solomon R. Guggenheim Museum, New York, New York
1997 '97 Kwangju Biennale, Kwangju, Korea
Documenta X, Kassel, Germany
1998 Images Festival of Independent Film and Video, Toronto, Canada
Berlin Biennale, Berlin, Germany
1999 The Liverpool Biennale, Tate Gallery, Liverpool, England
2000 Media City Seoul 2000, Seoul, Korea

Publications:

By DOUGLAS: Books—*Link Fantasy,* Vancouver 1988; editor, *Samuel Beckett: Teleplays,* Vancouver 1988; *Photofile,* Fall 1990; *Joanne Tod,* Toronto/Saskatoon 1990; *Parachute,* January-March 1991; editor, *Vancouver Anthology: The Institutional Politics of Art,* edited by Stan Douglas, Vancouver 1991; *WestCoast Line,* Burnaby, Fall 1992; *Frieze,* September 1993; *Jahresring 41: Jahrbuch für moderne Kunst,* edited by Christiane Schneider, 1994; *Art Metropole,* April 1996; *Art Recollection. Artists, Interviews and Statements in the Nineties,* 1997.

On DOUGLAS: Books—*Perspective 87: Stan Douglas,* with text by Barbara Fischer, Toronto, Ontario 1987; *Stan Douglas. Television Spots,* with text by Miriam Nichols, Vancouver, British Columbia 1988; *Stan Douglas,* with text by Christine van Assche, Jean-Christophe Royoux, Peter Culley, Paris 1993; *Stan Douglas, Douglas Gordon, Joachim Koester,* with text by Simon Sheikh, Copenhagen, Denmark 1994; *Stan Douglas,* Guelph and Toronto, Ontario 1994; *Stan Douglas,* with text by Christine van Assche, Madrid 1994; *Stan Douglas. Potsdamer Schrebergarten. Der Sandmann,* with text by Stan Douglas and Julian Heynen, Krefeld, Germany 1996; *Stan Douglas,* with text by Gilles Godmer, Montréal 1996; *Stan Douglas,* with text by the artist, Diana Thater, Scott Watson, Carol J. Clover, London 1998; *Stan Douglas,* with text by Daina Augaitis, George Wagner, and William Wood, Vancouver, Canada 1999; *Stan Douglas: Der Sandmann,* Chiado, Portugal 2000. **Articles—** "Fleeting Phantoms: the Projected Image at SFMOMA" by Tony Reveaux in *Artweek,* 28 March 1991; "Projected Identities" by David Joslit in *Art in America,* November 1991; "The Creation of the African-Canadian Odyssey" by Nkiru Nzegwu in *The International Review of African American,* vol. 10, no. 1, Spring 1992; "Vancouver Anthology" by John O'Brian in *Parachute,* no. 66, April-June 1992; "Broadcast Views. Stan Douglas interviewed by Lynne Cooke" in *Frieze,* September 1993; "Stan Douglas" by Elisabetta Luca in *Juliet Art Magazine,* no. 64, October/November; "Stan Douglas: Christian Nagel" by José Stals Lebrero in *Flash Art,* no. 173, November/December 1993; "Stan Douglas" by Daniel Barb in *Vanguard,* September 1982; "Camera Works" by Michael Lawlor in *Parachute,* June-August 1987; "Television Spots" by Karen Henry in *Parachute,* July-August 1988; "Zweimal Canada Dry—Sechs Künstler aus Vancouver" by Scott Watson in *Wolkenkratzer Art Journal,* March-April 1988; "Stan Douglas" by Mark Harris in *C Magazine,* Spring 1989; "Stan Douglas Talks at YYZ" by Mike Hoolbloom in *Independent Eye,* vol. 10, no. 2, Winter 1989; "Stan Douglas Review at the ICA" by Catherine Elwes in *Art Monthly,* no. 180, October 1994; "Stan Douglas" by Ben Lewis in *What's On,* September 23, 1994; "Resonance: Stan Douglas & Olivier Cadiot" by Jean-Christophe Royoux in *Galeries Magazine.* no. 58, April 1994; "Douglas Loops and Splits in Guelph and Downsview" by Harry Rudolfs in *Excalibur,* 16 March 1994; "Lesen auf der Rückseite der Bilde" by Sabine Vogel in *Frankfurter Allgemeine Zeitung,* Nr. 222, Friday, 23 September 1994; "Making History" by Scott Watson in *Canadian Art,* vol. 11, no. 4, Winter 1994; "Stan Douglas" by Sarah Curtis in *World Art,* February 1995; "Stan Douglas at David Zwirner" by Tom Eccles in *Art in America,* October 1995; "Fehlgeschlagene Utopien: Interview mit dem Videokünstler Stan Douglas" by Sabine B. Vogel in *Zitty,* March 1995; "Global Warming" by Dan Cameron in *Artforum.* vol. XXXVI, no. 4, December 1997; "Eyes on the Prize" by Ken Johnson in *Art in America,* April 1997; "Stan Douglas" by Ronald Jones in *Frieze,* March-April 1997; "Stop the Train: Stan Douglas, Beat Streuli, Bruce Nauman, and Gary Hill" by Rainald Schumacher in *Flash Art,* May-June 1997; "Stan Douglas" by Martha Schwendener in *Time Out/New York,* 2–9 January 1997;

''Stan Douglas'' by Noemi Smolik in *Kunstforum International,* February-March 1997; ''Stan Douglas: Detroit Photos'' by Ann Doran in *Time Out,* 19–26 November 1998; ''Stan Douglas at David Zwirner'' by Christopher Phillips in *Art in America,* December 1998; ''Stan Douglas'' in *Weltkunst,* 15 July 1998; ''Stan Douglas/Douglas Gordon: Double Vision'' in *Artforum,* January 1999; ''Stan Douglas Stays Behind the Lens'' by Robin Laurence in *The Georgia Straight,* 25 February-4 March 1999; ''Stan Douglas'' by Sarah Milroy in *Canadian Art,* Fall 1999; ''Stan Douglas'' by Reid Shier in *National Post,* 16 February 1999; ''Stan Douglas'' in *ART/TEXT,* August-October 1999; ''The Art of Stan Douglas'' in *Artforum,* January 2000; ''Stan Douglas'' by Ingrid Chu in *Frieze,* March/April 2000; ''Stan Douglas: Alienation and Proximity'' by Robert Monk Storr and Georg Imdahl in *Artpress,* November 2000.

* * *

In his video, film, and still photography, Stan Douglas comments on cultural spaces and time and how representation determines experience. Known primarily for his video work, Douglas has been steadily producing a body of work since 1983. Initially, he became known for his series of television interventions and explorations. In these works, Douglas utilized video as a method to mine the hegemony of television for its vocabulary, effects, and commentary. Having come of age during the 1960s and 1970s, he was clearly a product of the television generation. Like many artists employing video or film, Douglas is concerned with how media shapes and influences observation and representation, as well as how it defines a notion of time. He explored this idea extensively in *Evenings* (1994), a work utilizing three simultaneous projections of two broadcasts to show the leveling effect of the evening news and its ''even-ing'' effect on the events of the day. No matter how grotesque or distressing, the broadcasters relied on ''happy-talk,'' which involves presenting all stories with smiles on their faces.

After these television-focused works, Douglas's gallery installations have become increasingly elaborate. His photographs usually precede the videos or films and function as a way for Douglas to locate himself in preparation for the time-based work. He fluctuates between scrutinizing the contemporary lingua-franca of television and the perceived orthodox form of the cinema. In both film and video, Douglas looks at how memory, narrative, and representation are constructed.

Much of Douglas's art explores the theoretical realities of history and media in shaping cultural notions of space, place, and time. He frequently relies on a simultaneous production of distinct voices as a way to synthesize the experience of many into a collective whole. His work addresses narratives of forgotten places and overlooked people. Much of this cross-referencing, accomplished through simultaneous projection of image and sound, permits an interesting synthesis to occur. Arguably, much of the imposed identification demanded by media saturation is Douglas's method of exploring the experience of African-Americans in North America. Douglas has remarked that he is very interested in how simultaneous alienation and connection happens, as well as the difference between lived experience, exterior identification, and external events. These factors are all ways for him to investigate living through being black in a dominantly white culture.

In his art, Douglas explores the isolated schemes and unites them into synthetic commentary in terms of both form and content. Douglas has readily played with the construction of time and space in television and cinema in his video and film works. In his work, he willfully experiments with the viewer's expected notions of how television and cinema exist within culture and plays with those presumptions.

—Anne Swartz

DURHAM, Jimmie

Nationality: American/Cherokee. **Born:** Arkansas, 1940. **Education:** Studied sculpture, École des Beaux-Arts, Geneva, graduated 1972. **Career:** Artist. Co-founder, Adept Art Center and *Adept Magazine,* Houston, Texas, 1963; performed, wrote, and edited poetry in Houston, Texas, late 1960s; worked for the American Indian Movement as head of the International Indian Treaty Committee at the United Nations, 1973–80; Executive Director, Foundation for the Community of Artists (FCA), 1982; editor, *Art and Artists Newspaper,* 1982–86; writer and critic. **Agent:** Galeria Micheline Szwajcer, Verlatstraat 14, 2000 Antwerpen, Belgium.

Selected Individual Exhibitions:

1967 Adept Gallery, Houston, Texas
University of Texas, Austin, Texas
1971 Circa Gallery, Geneva, Switzerland
Centre des Rencontres, Geneva, Switzerland
1972 Circa Gallery, Geneva, Switzerland
Ecole des Beaux-Arts, Geneva, Switzerland
1985 Alternative Museum, New York
22 Wooster Gallery, New York
1986 John Jay College, New York
1988 Matt's Gallery, London
Orchard Gallery, Derry, North-Ireland
1989 Exit Art, New York
1990 Western Washington University, Belligham, Washington
1991 The Luggage Store, San Francisco, California
Museum of Civilization, Hull, Québec, Canada
1992 Nicole Klagsbrun, New York
1993 Palais des Beaux-Arts, Brussels, Belgium
Institute of Contemporary Arts, London
L.A. Louver, Venice, California
1994 Galerie Micheline Szwajcer, Antwerp, Belgium
1995 Nicole Klagsburn Gallery, New York
Modulo Centro Diffusor de Arte, Lisboa, Portugal
The Center of the World, De Vleeshal, Middelburg, Netherlands
Resurrection, Haus of Prints, Multiples and Drawings, Antwerp, Belgium
1996 *La porte de l'Europe (Les bourgeois de Calais),* Galerie de l'Ancienne Poste, Calais, France
Der Verführer und der Steinerne Gast, Haus Wittgenstein, Vienna, Austria
Le leçon d'anatomie (A Progress Report), FRAC Champagne-Ardenne, Reims, France
10 Voyages Conceptuels, Haus of Prints, Multiples and Drawings, Antwerp, Belgium
L'Atelier, M.A.J.T., Lille, France
Anders Tornberg Gallery, Lund, Sweden

1997 *Jimmie Durham Ordnung (for A.T.),* Galerie Nordenhake
Via Farini, Milan, Italy
Museum of Contemporary Art, Porri, Finland
Galerie Micheline Szwajcer, Antwerp, Belgium
Shelter, Kunstakademie & Environs, Trondheim, Norway
1998 *Between the Furniture and the Building (Between a Rock and a Hard Place),* Kunstverein München, München, Germany
1999 *Incoming Mail,* CBKM, Maastricht, Netherlands
Drawings, Anders Tornberg Gallery, Lund, Sweden
Semi-Precious, Lumentravo, Amsterdam, Netherlands

Selected Group Exhibitions:

1991 *Savoir-vivre, savoir-faire, savoir-etre,* Centre international d'art contemporain, Montréal, Québec
Souvenirs of Site-Seeing: Travel and Tourism in Contemporary Art, Whitney Museum of American Art, New York
1992 *Land, Spirit, Power,* National Gallery of Canada, Ottawa, Ontario
1993 *Will/Power,* Ohio State University, Columbus, Ohio
On Taking a Normal Situation and Retranslating it into Overlapping and Multiple Readings of Conditions Past and Present, Antwerp Cultural Capital of Europe, Antwerp
Biennial Exhibition, Whitney Museum of American Art, New York
1993–94 *Original Re-runs,* ICA, London
A Certain Lack of Coherence, Palais des Beaux-Arts, Brussels, Belgium
1994 *Economies: Une exposition, des logiques d'investissement,* Galerie Roger Pailhas, Marseille, France
Cocida y Crudo, Mueso National Centro de Arte Reina Sofia, Madrid, Spain
States of Loss: Migration, Displacement, Colonialism, and Power, Jersey City Museum, New Jersey
1996 *Eurasian Project, Stage One: La Porte de l'Europe,* Galerie de l'Ancienne Poste, Galerie Micheline Szwajcer, Champagne-Ardenne; Calais; Anvers
Transformers, Illingworth Kerr Gallery, Alberta College of Art and Design, Calgary
1998 *Crossings,* National Gallery of Canada, Ottawa, Ontario
Do It, Surrey Art Gallery, British Columbia (traveled)
1999 *Indoor,* Musée d'Art Contemporain, Lyon, France
Expériences du divers, Galerie Art et ''Essai,'' Université de Rennes II, Campus Villejean, Rennes, France
2000 *Micropolitiques,* Magasins, Centre National d'Art Contemporain, Grenoble, France

Publications:

By DURHAM: Books—*We the People: Pena Bonita, Jimmie Durham, Harry Fonseca,* New York 1987; *Jimmie Durham: The Bishop's Moose and the Pinkerton Men,* New York 1990; *Elaine Reichek—Native Intelligence,* New York 1992; *Columbus Day,* Albuquerque, New Mexico 1993; *A Certain Lack of Coherence: Writings on Art and Cultural Politics,* London 1993. **Articles—**''On the edge of town'' in *Art Journal,* vol. 51, no. 2, 1992; ''Geronimo!'' in *Partial Recall: Photos of Native North Americans,* edited by Lucy R. Lippard, New York 1992; ''Interview at the ICA'' by Mark Gisbourne in *Art Monthly,* no. 173, 1994; ''Artist's project'' in *Blocnotes,* no. 8, 1995; ''Attending to words and bones: An interview with Jean Fisher'' in *Art and Design,* vol. 10, nos. 7–8, 1995; ''The Centre of the World Is Several Places, Part I'' interview by Beverly Koski and Richard William Hill in *FUSE Magazine,* vol. 21, no. 3, Summer 1998.

On DURHAM: Books—*Ni'Go Tlung A Doh Ka* by Jean Fisher, New York 1986; *Jimmie Durham: The Bishop's Moose and the Pinkerton Men* by Papo Colo et al, New York 1990; *Souvenirs of Site-Seeing: Travel and Tourism in Contemporary Art* by Jonathon Caseley, Karin M. Higa, and Pamela M. Lee, New York 1991; *Mixed Blessings: New Art in a Multi-cultural America* by Lucy R. Lippard, New York 1993; *Indians are Us? Culture and Genocide in Native North America* by Ward Churchill, Toronto 1994; *Jimmie Durham* by Laura Mulvey et al, London 1995. **Articles—**''In Search of the 'Inauthentic': Disturbing Signs in Contemporary Native American Art'' by Jean Fisher in *Art Journal,* vol. 51, no. 3, Fall 1992; ''The Necessity of Jimmie Durham's Jokes'' by Richard Shiff in *Art Journal,* vol. 51, no. 3, Fall 1992; ''Jimmie Durham: Postmodernist 'Savage''' by Lucy R Lippard in *Art in America,* February 1993; ''Beyond the Pale: Art in the Age of Multicultural Translation'' by Homi K. Bhabha in *Kunst & Museum Journal,* vol. 5, no. 4, 1994; ''Sovereignty: A Line in the Sand'' by Jolene Rickard in *Art and Design,* vol. 10, nos. 7/8, 1995; ''Ceci n'est pas Jimmie Durham'' by Laura Turney in *Critique of Anthropology,* vol. 19, no. 4, 1999.

* * *

Jimmie Durham is a visual artist, writer, poet, and performer whose works contest derogatory stereotypes of Native Americans. Since European exploration and colonization of the Americas, Euro-Americans have invented a Native American ''authenticity'' that reduces native peoples to silence, relegating them to the past and denying them a future. In this schema, native art comprises works that belong to a romanticized, vanishing peoples who live in an ''ethnographic past.'' By using a combination of humor, anger, irony, and satire in his sculptures, installations, and performances, Durham destabilizes the notion of the ''authentic'' Native American.

In *Self Portrait* (1987), a large, two-dimensional figure topped by a mask-like wooden head, Durham explores identity construction. While statements written on the work embody stereotypical assumptions about Durham as a Cherokee Indian (including notions that he is unemployed, an alcoholic, etc.), they reveal nothing about him as an individual. Durham's body is alienated from itself. Its outside ''skin'' has no corresponding inside or substance, and its inside lacks representation. Nevertheless, this travestied body is funny in a satirical way. For example, in one inscription Durham writes: ''My skin is not really this dark, but I am sure that many Indians have coppery skin.''

The installation *On Loan from the Museum of the American Indian* (1985) protests the oftentimes-ignorant museum display practices of Euro-Americans. Durham presents to the viewer an odd assortment of objects purported to illustrate the natural history of the Native American. These items include a toothbrush, family photographs, ''An Indian Leg Bone,'' and ''Real Indian Blood.'' When exhibited both on the wall and in a vitrine and juxtaposed with captions about the ordinary life of present-day Native Americans, the installation seeks to reveal the ludicrous and irresponsible nature of ethnographic museum displays.

Durham investigates Native American history and identity in his performance art. In a 1985 piece, a deadpan Durham told stories and enacted rituals against a background of projected slides showing maps of ''trends in Indian land ownership.'' As Native American land in North America slowly diminished in the chronological slides, Durham ironically distributed gifts, including stones, feathers, and a ribbon shirt, to the audience.

In the early 1990s, Durham began producing large, abstract sculptures. One of these works, a 100-foot-long snake titled *Banks of the Ohio* (1992), consists of a mud-formed head and a body made of the green PVC pipe used for industrial and domestic plumbing. The body itself undulates along the gallery space, set off by white walls smeared with brown paint. Seen from a distance, the brown marks resemble elegant vegetal forms. Close-up, however, the smears look like human excrement. In this way, the work may be interpreted as an exposed sewage system. The works' title refers to the Serpent Mound, one the most impressive of the Native American mounds that dates to the year 1000 B.C. and stretches 1,348 feet along the valley of the Ohio River. Since the locations of the mounds were natural vantage points, early European settlements often formed on them. Many of the mounds were destroyed and currently contain sewage systems like the one represented in *Banks of the Ohio*.

Durham forces Westerners to re-evaluate their basic beliefs and values about Native American peoples. He inscribes some of his works with words in both Cherokee and English. Although the Cherokee relays simple, punning jokes, Westerners cannot understand them. Durham has no desire to explain the jokes; he wants Westerners to recognize their own exclusion and concomitant failure to control Native Americans and their identity.

—Joyce Youmans

DYE, David

Nationality: British. **Born:** Ryde, Isle of Wight, 23 October 1945. **Education:** Studied sculpture at St. Martin's School of Art, London, 1967–71; Goldsmith's College, London, 1984–86, M.A. 1986. **Career:** Artist, working with film and photography, London, since 1971. Lecturer, Brighton Polytechnic, 1972–76. Part-time lecturer, Newcastle Polytechnic, since 1979. Artist-in-residence, University of Reading, 1982. **Awards:** Arts Council of Great Britain Film Grant, 1973, and Arts Council Award, 1976. **Addresses:** (studio) 6A Peacock Yard, Iliffe Street, London SE17, 3LH; (home) 76 Burton Road, Myatts Fields, London SW9 6TQ, England.

Individual Exhibitions:

1972 Institute of Contemporary Arts, London
1975 Lisson Gallery, London
1976 Robert Self Gallery, London
1977 Arnolfini Gallery, Bristol

Selected Group Exhibitions:

1971 *The English Avant-Garde,* Cultural Center, New York
1972 *The New Art,* Hayward Gallery, London
1974 *Beyond Painting and Sculpture,* Leeds City Art Gallery (toured the U.K.)
1975 *Biennale de Paris,* Musee National d'Art Moderne, Paris
1976 *Arte Inglese Oggi,* Palazzo Reale, Milan
1977 *Time, Words and the Camera,* Kunstlerhaus, Graz, Austria (toured Austria and West Germany)
1978 *Scale for Sculpture,* Serpentine Gallery, London (toured the U.K., 1978–79)
1981 *Extended Photography,* Vienna Secession
1984 *When Attitudes Became Form,* Kettle's Yard, Cambridge (travelled to Fruitmarket Gallery, Edinburgh)
1987 *Under the Sign of Saturn,* Nigel Greenwood Gallery, London

Collections:

Arts Council of Great Britain, London; Victoria and Albert Museum, London.

Publications:

By DYE: Articles—''Interview with David Dye'' with Simon Field, in *Art and Artists* (London), December 1972; interview, with Anne Seymour, in *The New Art,* exhibition catalog, London 1972; ''The Big O,'' with Stuart Morgan in *Art Monthly* (London), no. 144, March 1991. **Films—***Mirror,* 1971; *Two Cameras,* 1971; *Cross Reference,* 1972; *Projection/Introjection,* 1972; *Window,* 1972; *Unsigning I,* 1972; *Hand Piece,* 1972; *Unsigning 2,* 1972; *Unsigning 3,* 1972; *Unsigning for Eight Projectors,* 1972; *Overlap,* 1973; *Open/Close,* 1973; *Western Reversal,* 1973; *4 Slide Projector Piece,* 1973; *Static, Contracted, Vertical/Moving, Stretched, Horizontal,* 1973; *Western Reversal,* 1974; *4 Slide Projector Piece,* 1975; *Edges Guess,* 1975; *Throw,* 1975; *Light Interruptions,* 1975; *Commercial Break,* 1975; *Scan,* 1976; *Letter to Rita,* 1978; *Man in Space,* 1979; *3-D* (installation), 1979–80.

On DYE: Articles—''Artists Seeking the Potential of Film'' by Richard Cork in the Evening News[eu] (London), 4 May 1972; ''Artist as Film-Maker'' by Annabel Nicolson in *Art and Artists* (London), December 1972; ''David Dye, Artist/Film-Maker?'' by Alan Sheridan in *Studio International* (London), November/December 1975; ''David Dye'' by Hugh Adams in *Studio International* (London), September/October 1977; ''David Dye: 3-D'' in *Aspects* (London), Spring 1980; ''David Dye'' by Stuart Morgan in *Artscribe International,* no. 72, November-December 1988.

*

For many years I have been using film and photography as a medium. I'm not interested in making ''film'' into ''art,'' an idea which I feel is closely aligned to the ''consumer'' ''novelty'' culture, but I use film and photography because perhaps they are more transparent and less individuated than painting or sculpture. No, my concern has not been about the medium itself as such; although some of my works seem ''self-referential,'' it is because they reject conventional notions of film as exemplified in the commercial cinema, and can only be understood in terms of that rejection.

My work has always been ambiguous, dualistic, paradoxical, or any other words that signify a contradiction or ambivalence of stance or intention.

Ambivalence, because I am aware of the way art is relative to a particular culture at a particulare time. We are, in a sense, locked into our time. I am also aware that our culture has created the myth of subjectivity, self-expression, and individualism.

This myth of the romantic outsider could be seen to relate directly to the status-quo; if you see art as art only, isolated pure, ideal, then that naturally blinkers you to the institutions and economics that uphold it. The ideology of ''art for art's sake'' is a conservative viewpoint that eschews relations and upholds territoriality.

This ''pedestal'' viewpoint links up to the myth of the artist as ''knower,'' ''seer,'' ''God,'' an internalization of paternalism. I believe that the interpersonal and conventional systems which traverse the individual make him a space in which forces and events meet rather than individuated essence.

All my work has been done in relationship to the ''art'' situation I find myself in—most of it ironic and self-deprecatory. I try to embody contradictions which I feel exist in myself, and by definition, our Western culture.

—David Dye

DZUBAS, Friedel

Nationality: American. **Born:** Berlin, Germany, 20 April 1915; emigrated to the United States in 1939, and subsequently naturalized. **Education:** Berlin Gymnasium until 1931; Prussian Academy of Fine Art and Kunstgewerbeschule, 1931–33; studied with Paul Klee in Dusseldorf, 1933–36. **Family:** Married four times, all ended in divorce; three children, Hannele Dzubas Brooks, Morgan Dzubas and Adam Dzubas. **Career:** Painter. Artist-in-Residence, Dartmouth College, Hanover, New Hampshire, 1962–63; visiting artist, University of South Florida, Tampa, 1962; artist-member, Symposium on Art Education, New York University, 1965; artist-in-residence, Institute for Humanistic Studies, Aspen, Colorado, 1965, 1966; visiting artist-critic, Cornell University, Ithaca, New York, 1967, 1969–74; visiting artist-critic, University of Pennsylvania, Philadelphia, 1968. **Awards:** Guggenheim Creative Painting Fellowship, 1966, 1968; National Council on the Arts grant, 1968. **Address:** c/o Long Fine Art, 24 West 57th St., New York, New York 10019, U.S.A. **Died:** After a long illness in Newton, Massachusetts, 11 December 1994.

Individual Exhibitions:

1952 Tibor de Nagy Gallery, New York
1958 Leo Castelli Gallery, New York
1959 French and Company Gallery, New York
1960 Dwan Gallery, Los Angeles
1961 Robert Elkon Gallery, New York
1962 Robert Elkon Gallery, New York
1963 Robert Elkon Gallery, New York
1964 Kasmin Gallery, London
Robert Elkon Gallery, New York
1965 Kasmin Gallery, London
Robert Elkon Gallery, New York
1966 Nicholas Wilder Gallery, Los Angeles
Andre Emmerich Gallery, New York
1967 Andre Emmerich Gallery, New York
1968 Andre Emmerich Gallery, New York
1971 Galerie Hans Strelow, Dusseldorf
Jack Glen, Corona del Mar, California
Lawrence Rubin Gallery, New York
Galerie Hans Strelow, Cologne
1972 Lawrence Rubin Gallery, New York
Galerie Hans Strelow, Cologne
1973 Lawrence Rubin Gallery, New York
David Mirvish Gallery, Toronto
1974 Knoedler Contemporary Art, New York
David Mirvish Gallery, Toronto
Museum of Fine Arts, Houston (retrospective)
1975 Museum of Fine Arts, Boston
Knoedler Contemporary Art, New York
David Mirvish Gallery, Toronto
1976 David Mirvish Gallery, Toronto
Watson/de Nagy Gallery, Houston
Margo Leavin Gallery, Los Angeles
Tibor de nagy Gallery, New York
Knoedler Contemporary Art, New York
1977 John Berggruen Gallery, San Francisco
M. Knoedler and Company, New York
Kunsthale, Bielefeld, West Germany
1978 Dart Gallery, Chicago
M. Knoedler and Company, New York
1979 M. Knoedler and Company, New York
John Berggruen Gallery, San Francisco
1980 M. Knoedler and Company, New York
1982 Robert Elkon Gallery, New York
M. Knoedler and Company, New York (twice)
Gallery One, Toronto
Ochi Gallery, Boise, Idaho
1985 M. Knoedler and Company, New York
Gallery One, Toronto
1986 Hokin Gallery, Palm Beach, Florida
M. Knoedler and Company, New York
1987 Andre Emmerich Gallery, New York
Nassau County Museum of Fine Arts, New York
Herbert F. Johnson Museum of Art, Ithaca, New York
Meredith Long & Co., Houston
1988 Rose Art Museum, Waltham, Massachusetts
Harcus Gallery, Boston
Garner Tullis, New York
1989 Andre Emmerich Gallery, New York
1990 Ann Jaffe Gallery, Bay Harbor Islands, Florida
Gallery One, Toronto
Andre Emmerich Gallery, New York
1991 Museum of Fine Art, Inc., Fort Lauderdale, Florida
Friedel Dzubas: Four Decades 1950–1990, Andre Emmerich Gallery, New York
1993 *Friedel Dzubas: The Early Years,* Elkon Gallery, New York
1994 Louis Newman Galleries, Beverly Hills, California
Jaffe Baker Blau, Boca Raton, Florida
1996 Andre Emmerich Gallery, New York
1997 Anita Shapolsky Gallery, New York
1998 *Friedel Dzubas: Critical Painting,* Tufts University Gallery, Medford, Massachusetts

Selected Group Exhibitions:

1957 *U.S. Painting; Recent Directions,* Stable Gallery, New York

1961 *Abstract Expressionists and Imagists,* Guggenheim Museum, New York
1964 *Post-Painterly Abstraction,* Los Angeles County Museum of Art
1967 *Form, Color, Image,* Detroit Institute of Arts
1970 *Color and Field,* Albright-Knox Art Gallery, Buffalo, New York (toured the United States)
1974 *The Great Decade of American Abstraction,* Museum of Fine Arts, Houston
1977 *18 Contemporary Masters,* United States Embassy, Ottawa
1986 *Garner Tullis Workshop: Monotypes,* Pace Editions, New York
1987 *39th Annual Academy-Institute Purchase Exhibition,* American Academy and Institute of Arts and Letters, New York
1989 *The Flat Side of the Landscape: The Emma Lake Artists' Workshop,* Mendel Art Gallery, Saskatoon, Saskatchewan
1990 *The Great Decade: The 1960s,* Andre Emmerich Gallery, New York
1994 *Reclaiming Artists of the New York School: Toward a More Inclusive View of the 1950s,* Sidney Mishkin Gallery, New York
1999 *Abstraction: New Directions for a New Millennium,* Robert Kidd Gallery, Birmingham

Collections:

Metropolitan Museum of Art, New York; Guggenheim Museum, New York; Whitney Museum, New York; White Museum of Art, Cornell University, Ithaca, New York; Museum of Fine Arts, Boston; Baltimore Museum of Art; Phillips Collection, Washington, D.C.; City Art Museum, St. Louis; Museum of Fine Arts, Houston; San Francisco Museum of Modern Art.

Publications:

By DZUBAS: Articles—''Panel: All-Over Painting'' in *It Is* (New York) Autumn 1958; ''Discussion: Is There a New Academy'' in *Artnews* (New York), September 1959; ''An Interview with Friedel Dzubas,'' with Max Kozloff, in *Artforum* (New York), September 1965; ''Sensibility of the 60s'' in *Art in America* (New York), January/February 1967; statement in *Art Now: New York,* December 1971; ''A Conversation with Friedel Dzubas,'' with Ken Carpenter, in *Studio International* (London), July/August 1974.

On DZUBAS: Books—*Friedel Dzubas: A Retrospective Exhibition,* exhibition catalog, by E.A. Carmean, with an introduction by William C. Agee, Houston 1974; *Friedel Dzubas,* exhibition catalog, by Kenworth Moffett, Boston 1975; *Friedel Dzubas* by Charles W. Millard, Washington, D.C. 1983; *Friedel Dzubas,* exhibition catalog with introduction by Karen Wilkin, New York 1987; ''Color is Lifeblood of Dzubas'' by Joanne Silver in *The Boston Herald,* September 30, 1988; *Friedel Dzubas: Four Decades,* exhibition catalog by Karen Wilkin, New York, 1990; *Friedel Dzubas: The Early Years,* exhibition catalog, New York 1993; *Reclaiming Artists of the New York School: A More Inclusive View of the 1950s,* exhibition catalog by Sandra Kraskin, New York, 1994; *Friedel Dzubas: Critical Painting,* exhibition catalog, Medford 1998. **Articles**—Obituary in *Art in America* (New York), vol. 83, February 1995.

* * *

Friedel Dzubas is not a newcomer. A painter with a long and distinguished career, he has as a background both traditional European training and participation in the rethinking of traditional values which took place in New York in the 1940s. He has been respected as an abstract painter for many years, but recently interest in his work has increased, especially in his paintings since the 1970s. This interest has been generated not only by the excellence of individual works, but also by the implications of Dzubas's special brand of abstraction. His paintings since about 1972 have been highly dramatic, depending upon colliding masses of brushy, varied color, and upon sumptuous contrasts of dark and light. They make full use of the range of his experience.

Most abstract color painters, such as Kenneth Noland and Jack Bush, found that they had to forgo strong tonal contrast in order to keep their paintings unified. Clearly bounded areas of different hues, such as Noland's bands or Bush's strokes, seemed to require close-valuing, if the pictures were not to split apart. It's a lesson they learned from the Impressionists and the Fauves, as well as from their own experience. Jules Olitski's seamless expanses of color offered a way of salvaging the play of dark and light and making use of it for abstraction, but it meant that internal divisions of the picture had to be suppressed. For many younger painters, Olitski's example has seemed all but insurmountable, but Dzuba's successful use of both discrete color areas *and* rich tonal variation offers new alternatives.

These are, of course, qualities we take for granted in traditional painting, qualities which reinforce illusion and defy the flatness which modernism has pursued, consciously or unconsciously, for the last century. Dzubas, too, apparently felt that he had to avoid this kind of allusive drama in his earlier works. His paintings of the late 50s and 60s were fine examples of the possibilities of juxtaposing close-valued color shapes, stained into the canvas. The swelling bands of color were clear and smoothly bounded, the application of paint uniform and fairly anonymous. They were well-crafted, handsome pictures, and, at their best, a lot better than that, but they seemed slightly impersonal. By 1969, however, the color areas in these paintings had become more inflected and more intense. At the same time, Dzubas allowed his handwriting to become more evident, and to take advantage of a sensuous touch which has become one of the outstanding characteristics of his work of the past ten years. The paintings lost none of the clarity of the earlier work, but they became far more complex and subtle, and gained a new alert tenseness.

The sense of the handmade, of the painting being the result of a particular individual's gesture, like the play of chiaroscuro, links these pictures with historical tradition. Dzubas's floating blocks of color are obviously made with an energetic scrubbing gesture, a movement of the arm and hand which forces layers of thin paint into the surface of the canvas. Denser, more opaque areas are clearly built up with repeated scrubbings. It is a very different approach from that of many of Dzubas's contemporaries, who have used a variety of overscaled tools expressly to manipulate paint in ways impossible to the hand. In Dzubas's pictures the evident handmadeness of the color blocks seems willful in relation to their large expanse and adds to the impact of the paintings.

Since the early 1980s Dzubas has made monotypes, using presses that allow him to make prints as large as his mid-sized canvases. The unpredictability of the medium fascinates him and the eccentric imagery of his monotypes has begun to appear in his paintings. His frayed-off color blocks, once regularly aligned in horizontal rows, now float, and tumble, swirl and curve. Dzuba's abstraction has entered its Baroque phase.

It goes without saying that Dzubas's pictures are noteworthy for reasons other than their connection with an older tradition, but their reclaiming of that tradition for modernism is part of their fascination. Their lushness and richness evoke old master painting, without any sense of illusion or narrative. Critics writing about Dzubas have compared him to the artists of German romanticism or the Venetian Renaissance, but his paintings are free of the nostalgia for the past which has provoked so many recent pastiches, among lesser painters. This is, of course, part of Dzubas's strength. His best pictures reverberate with overtones of the grand manner, but he remains a unique 20th century individual.

—Karen Wilkin

E

EDDY, Don

Nationality: American. **Born:** Long Beach, California, 4 November 1944. **Education:** University of Hawaii, Honolulu, 1965–69, B.F.A. 1967, M.F.A. 1969; did postgraduate work at the University of California at Santa Barbara, 1969–70. Served in the United States Naval Reserve, 1967–68. **Family:** Married Nancy Lee Walker in 1968 (divorced, 1975); daughter: Sarah. **Career:** Painter: lives and works in New York. Lecturer in Art, University of Hawaii, 1967–79; Assistant Professor, New York University, since 1972. **Agent:** Nancy Hoffman Gallery, 429 West Broadway, New York, New York 10012. **Address:** 543 Broadway, New York, New York 10012, U.S.A.

Individual Exhibitions:

1968 Ewing Krainin Gallery, Honolulu
1970 Molly Barnes Gallery, Los Angeles
Ester Bear Gallery, Santa Barbara, California
Galerie M. E. Thelen, Essen
1971 Molly Barnes Gallery, Los Angeles
Galerie de Gestlo, Bremen, West Germany
French and Company, New York
1973 Nancy Hoffman Gallery, New York
Galerie Petit, Paris
1974 Nancy Hoffman Gallery, New York
1975 Williams College Museum of Art, Williamstown, Massachusetts
1976 Miami-Dade Community College, Florida
Nancy Hoffman Gallery, New York
1979 Nancy Hoffman Gallery, New York
1982 University of Hawaii at Manoa, Honolulu
1983 Nancy Hoffman Gallery, New York
1986 Nancy Hoffman Gallery, New York
1990 Nancy Hoffman Gallery, New York
1992 Nancy Hoffman Gallery, New York
1994 Nancy Hoffman Gallery, New York
Scarabb Gallery, Cleveland, Ohio
1996 Nancy Hoffman Gallery, New York
Huntington Museum of Art, West Virginia
1998 Nancy Hoffman Gallery, New York
2000 *From Logic to Mystery,* Duke University Museum of Art, Durham, North Carolina (travelled to Boca Raton Museum of Art, Florida; Contemporary Arts Center, New Orleans)
Nancy Hoffman Gallery, New York

Selected Group Exhibitions:

1970 *Beyond the Actual,* Pioneer Museum, Stockton, California
1972 *Documenta,* Kassel, West Germany
1974 *Hyperréalisme Américain/Realisme Européen,* Centre National d'Art Contemporaian, Paris
1976 *Super Realism,* Baltimore Museum of Art
1978 *Things Seen,* Sheldon Memorial Art Gallery, University of Nebraska, Lincoln (toured the United States)
1982 *Spiegel Bilder,* Kunstverein, Hannover (travelled to Duisburg and West Berlin)
1984 *Visions of Childhood,* Whitney Museum, New York
1986 *Landscape, Seascape, Cityscape 1960–85,* Contemporary Arts Center, New Orleans, Louisiana
1991 *Amerikansk Kunst efter 1960,* G. I. Holtegaards, Copenhagen
1993 *The Purloined Image,* Flint Institute of Arts, Michigan (toured the United States)
1994 *A Bouquet for Juan,* Nancy Hoffman Gallery, New York
1995 *The Poetic Image in American Realism,* Sun Valley Center Gallery, Ketchum, Idaho
1996 *Summer Pleasures, Summer Treasures,* Nancy Hoffman Gallery, New York
1997 *Forces of Nature: Contemporary Paintings,* Taipei Gallery, New York
1998 *From Diptychs to Polytychs,* Nancy Hoffman Gallery, New York
1999 *Realism Knows No Bounds,* van de Griff Gallery, New York
2000 *The Creative Surround: The Framed Image,* Nancy Hoffman Gallery

Collections:

Storm King Art Center, Mountainville, New York; Fogg Art Museum, Harvard University, Cambridge, Massachusetts: Cleveland Museum of Art; Toledo Museum of Art, Ohio; Oklahoma Art Center, Oklahoma City; Santa Barbara Museum of Art, California; Neue Galerie, Aachen, West Germany; Musée d' Art, St.-Etienne, France; Museum of Modern Art, New York; Solomon R. Guggenheim Museum, New York; Israel Museum, Tel Aviv; Museo de Arte Moderno, Bogota, Colombia; Utrecht Museum, Belgium; Whitney Museum of American Art, New York.

Publications:

By EDDY: Article—''The Photo-Realists: 12 Interviews,'' with Linda Chase, Nancy Foote and Ted McBurnett, in *Art in America* (New York), November 1972.

On EDDY: Books—*The New Realism* by Udo Kultermann, New York 1972; *Hyperrealisme* by Isy Brachot, Brussels 1973; *Le Monde des Grands Musées: L'Hyperréalisme Américain,* with an introduction by Linda Chase, Paris 1973; *Neue Formen des Realismus* by Peter Sager, Cologne 1973; *Don Eddy* exhibition catalog, with a foreword by S. Lane Faison Jr., and an introduction by John Hallmark Neff, Williamstown, Massachusetts 1975; *Forces of Nature,* exhibition catalog by Ronny Cohen, New York 1997; *Art of the 20th Century* by Karl Ruhrberg, Cologne 1998; *Get Real, Contemporary American Realism from the Seavest Collection* by Virginia Anne Bonito, Durham, North Carolina 1998; *Together/Working,* exhibition catalog with essay by Barry Schwabsky, 1999; *Conversations with*

Don Eddy: *Seasons of Water,* 1999–2000. ©Don Eddy. Courtesy of Nancy Hoffman Gallery.

Don Eddy by Leda Cempellin, Padua, Italy 2000; *Dreams 1900–2000, Science, Art, and the Unconscious Mind,* Ithaca, New York 2000; *Don Eddy, From Logic to Mystery,* exhibition catalog, Durham, North Carolina 2000. **Articles—**''Rent Is the Only Reality'' by Ivan Karp in *Arts Magazine* (New York), December 1971; ''Documenta 5: A Critical Preview'' by Bruce Kurtz in *Arts Magazine* (New York), Summer 1972; ''The Connotation of Denotation'' by Linda Chase in *Arts Magazine* (New York), February 1974; ''Don Eddy: A Complete Approach'' in *Artist's Magazine,* November 1999; ''Don Eddy e L'Universo Nell'Arte'' by Leda Cempellin in *Art Leader,* December/February 1999–2000; ''Eddy's Photo-Realism Reflects New View'' by Blue Greenberg in *Herald-Sun,* 18 February 2000.

*

My art is about tension—the development and maintenance of tension: the tension created by the desire to transcend my limitations and possibilities while simultaneously recognizing the futility of that venture. It is about the tension created by the necessity to make an art that spills over its social, cultural and environmental barriers. It is about the tension between the spiritual and the material dimension of being.

In its specific formal problems, the paintings are about the development and maintenance of spatial tensions: the tension that results from the creation of a space that is both logical and illogical, a space that simultaneously strains toward illusionary depth and flatness.

—Don Eddy

* * *

Each artist attempts, within a formal system which he develops for the purpose, to interpret the world whose reality is only the sum total of the laws which establish it. Hyper-realism—sometimes called ''photographic realism'' in the United Stated—seems, in its apparent objectivity, to be only a mirror held up to aspects of reality. The image, immediately recognizable, does not seem to create a problem. So for a long time, in the eyes of both critics and amateurs, Don Eddy has been the painter of automobile coachwork whose reflections distort surrounding objects.

But the most important part of Don Eddy's work when, in 1969, he discovered in the car one of his preferred props in his analysis of reality, is not so much the object actually depicted on the canvas as that which is there only by allusion. In these works, in fact, fragments of coachwork give him the opportunity to portray on the chromium plated elements of the bumper or hub-cap the distorted image of the world. Reality, given direct recognition and proclaimed as a self-evident truth in this painting appears, in its entirely, only in the form of a distorted halo, outside of the image and having no other reality than that of the painting, since the reflection portrayed no longer corresponds to that which should appear—the immediate surroundings of the spectator—on the object depicted, thus obviously displaced. This visual use of the synecdoche has progressively led Don Eddy to reproduce no longer a revelatory part of reality, but reality in its entirety. Without doubt the most significant work of this period is the diptych ''Bumper Section'' (1970) which, on two canvases of identical format and painted from the same initial photographic document, proposes an image which, by the play of focus, presents in one of the versions a foreground distinctly defined at the expense of the background and in the other version an inverted depth of field allowing precise perception of background details.

This play on focus permits Don Eddy to introduce a questioning of reality into the evidence of the image: the photographic document, automatically accepted in a society conditioned by audio-visual methods of information, is an accepted method of reading against which the painter can revel. As a matter of fact all the work of the American hyperealists contains a critical dimension—misunderstood because it does not coincide with a political purpose—which brings their work closer to that of the minimalists than to any other form of representation.

The latest works of Don Eddy: shop windows of fruiterers, bazaars or shoe merchants take to their extreme consequences the premises contained in ''Bumper Section.'' The shop window, a transparent surface which allows one to see the space it both reveals and encloses and at the same time to peruse, in its reflections, the outside animation of the street, can be considered as a metaphor for the act of painting. Indeed the glass relates to the blank surface of the canvas which the painter enters into, according to the laws of perspective, while remaining outside of the space which he creates. In this way emerges the profound analogy between the blank canvas and the glass which separates two worlds of images—that of the street and that of the shop: both are neutral sites where an unexpected relationship among a variety of different images can be shown. By bringing into coincidence the focus which presents in their greatest clarity the objects contained in the shop window with that which allows one to identify with maximum precision the reflections of the street, Don Eddy provokes a syncope of spatial relationships and brings together, without restraint and closely overlapping, unrelated objects: individuals and water-melons, cooking pots and cars. Beneath the apparent simplicity of the photographic image the neutral space where the image takes shape comes to light. We are dealing here with an ABC of vision.

—Daniel Abadie

ELIASSON, Olafur

Nationality: Icelandic. **Born:** Denmark, 1967. **Education:** Studied at Royal Academy of Arts, Copenhagen, 1989–95. **Career:** Lives and works in Berlin. **Agent:** Bonakdar Jancou Gallery, 521 West 21st Street, New York, New York 10011.

Selected Individual Exhibitions:

1991 Overgarden Galleri, Copenhagen
1994 Stalke Out of Space, Copenhagen
Einige erinnern sich, daß sie auf dem Weg waren diese Nacht, Lukas & Hoffmann, Cologne
No Days in Winter, No Nights in Summer, Forumgalleriet, Malmö, Sweden
1995 *Eine Beschreibung einer Reflexion, oder aber eine angenehme Übung zu deren Eigenschaften,* neugerriemschneider, Berlin
Künstlerhaus, Stuttgart, Germany
Thoka, Hamburger Kunstverein, Hamburg
Tommy Lund Galerie, Odense, Denmark
1996 Kunstmuseum, Malmö, Sweden
Your Foresight Endured, Galleria Emi Fontana, Mailand, Italy
Your Strange Certainty Still Kept, Tanya Bonakdar Gallery, New York
Tell Me about a Miraculous Invention, Galeri Andreas Brändström, Stockholm
1997 Stalke Out of Space, Copenhagen
Your Sunmachine, Marc Foxx, Los Angeles
The Curious Garden, Kunsthalle Basel (catalog)
1998 Bonakdar Jancou Gallery, New York
Kjarvalstadir Museum, Iceland
Galerie Peter Kilchmann, Zurich
Yet Untitled, neugerriemschneider, Berlin; Kunstverein Wolfsburg, Germany (catalog)
1999 *Your Position Surrounded and Your Surroundings Positioned,* Contemporary Arts, Dundee, Great Britain
Your Double Day Diary, Frankfurter Kunstverein, Frankfurt
Your Circumspection Disclosed, Castello di Rivoli, Italy
Beauty, Marc Foxx, Los Angeles
2000 *Surroundings Surrounded,* Neue Galerie Graz, Austria
The Curious Garden, Irish Museum of Modern Art, Dublin

Selected Group Exhibitions:

1989 *Ventilator Projects,* Charlottenborg Konsthall, Copenhagen
1990 *Street Signs,* BIZART, Copenhagen
1991 *Young Scandinavian Art,* Stalke Out of Space, Copenhagen
1992 *Paradise Europe,* Copenhagen
Overdrive, 10 Young Nordic Artists, Copenhagen
Lightworks, Demonstrationslokalet for Kunst, Copenhagen
1993 *1700 CET,* Stalke Out of Space, Copenhagen
Black Box, GLOBE Kuratorengruppe, Copenhagen
1994 *Europa,* Ausstellung Münchner Galerien, Munich (catalog)
1995 *Landschaft,* Mittelrheinmuseum Koblenz, Haus am Waldsee, Germany (catalog)
Campo 95, Venedig, Italy (traveled to Turin; Malmö) (catalog)
Kunst & Okologie, Kunstverein Schloß Plön, Germany
1996 *Views of Icelandic Nature,* Kjarvalsstadir Museum, Reykjavik
The Scream; Nordic Fine Arts, 1995–96, Arken Museum, Ishøj, Denmark
Glow: Sublime Projected and Reflected Light, New Langton Art, San Francisco
Remote Connections, Neue Galerie, Graz; Wäino Aaltonen Museum of Art, Turku, Finland; Artfocus, Tel Aviv

1997 *Heaven,* P. S. 1, New York
On Life, Beauty, Translations and Other Difficulties, 5th International Istanbul Biennal, Turkey (catalog)
Trade Routes, 2nd Johannesburg Biennale, South Africa
Truce: Echoes of Art in an Age of Endless Conclusions, Site Santa Fe, New Mexico (catalog)
1998 *Light x Eight: The Hanukkah Project,* The Jewish Museum, New York
New Photography 14, Museum of Modern Art, New York
Nuit Blanche, Musée d'Art Moderne de la Ville de Paris (traveled to Reykjavik Municipal Art Museum; Bergen Billedgalleri, Norway; Porin Taidemuseo, Finland; Göteberg Konstmuseum, Sweden) (catalog)
Sightings: New Photographic Art, ICA, London (catalog)
1999 *Panorama 2000,* Central Museum, Utrecht, Netherlands (catalog)
dAPERTutto, 48, International Exposition of Art, Venice Biennale (catalog)
Photography: An Expanded View, Recent Acquisitions, Solomon R. Guggenheim Museum, New York
German Open, Kunstmuseum Wolfsburg, Germany (catalog)

Publications:

On ELIASSON: Books—*Wonderland* by Rochelle Steiner and Guiliana Bruno, Saint Louis 2000; *Olafur Eliasson* by Jessica Morgan and Lars Lerup, Boston and Ostfildern, Germany 2001. **Articles—**''The Iceman Cometh'' by Christian Haye in *Frieze,* issue 40, May 1998; ''Olafur Eliasson'' by Jan Winkelmann in *Art/Text,* February-April 1998; ''Olafur Eliasson: Poetry in Motion'' by Simon Grant in *Tate: The Art Magazine,* issue 19, winter 1999; ''Olafur Eliasson'' by Jan Winkelmann in *Metropolis M,* no. 1, February-March 1999.

* * *

Olafur Eliasson is best known for his spare, site-specific installations that invite viewers to explore their embodied, subjective, memory-laden, and always incomplete processes of perceiving. Eliasson's installations, like many in the 1990s, are minimally-inspired environments in which viewers are forced to actively search out a way to experience and understand the subtle variations and changes they perceive. Eliasson cites 1970s minimalist artist Robert Morris's exploration of the phenomenological basis of perception as an important precedent for his own work. His artistic project is equally inspired by the writings of Danish physicist Niels Bohr, who posited that our understanding and measurement of natural phenomena is highly dependent on our position and perspective. Eliasson begins conceptualizing each new art project from the imagined perspective of the viewers, asking himself what kinds of experiences he wants to offer them. His titles, many beginning with ''your,'' emphasize the importance of the viewer's role in the actualization of his installations. He calls his installations ''machines'' because they require activation by the viewer. But in use, Eliasson's ''machines'' always mediate and distort the viewer's perceptions of the natural and cultural environment.

Eliasson's ''machines'' are designed to create a contradictory understanding of the distinction between nature and culture. Although Eliasson repeatedly employs natural elements such as fire, light, water, steam, and earth commonly associated with the vast, empty, and volcanically active Icelandic and Scandinavian environments of his youth, his installations are far from sublime or mystical. In fact, the point of much of Eliasson's work is to demystify the viewer's relationship to nature by consistently foregrounding the low-tech mechanisms and industrial materials that frame his use of natural elements. Even in his earliest pieces, these ''natural'' elements are made ambiguous. *No nights in summer, no days in winter,* 1994, is a ring of fire; but it is not an all-consuming or destructive presence. Rather, it is a small Bunsen burner ring of blue gas fire mounted vertically on the wall that gives off a bit of warmth and a gassy vapor reminiscent of a gas stove. Over the past decade, Eliasson's ''machines'' have become more open-ended in order to accommodate the complexity of the way we perceive the boundaries between nature and culture.

Many of his outdoor installations, what he calls ''pollution machines,'' call attention to our experience of nature as always mediated by technological machines of one sort or another. *Double Sunset,* 1999, is a large artificially illuminated billboard of a false sunset that mirrors the actual sunset. It inspires a series of questions about what is real and what is represented and how our experience of the real sunset is framed by our cultural understanding and representations of sunsets. Eliasson also ''polluted'' the Strömmen River that flows through Stockholm in 2000 with a bright green biodegradable pigment, making the river more ''natural'' looking through artificial coloring. *The very large ice floor,* an installation constructed in 1998 for the Biennial at Sao Paulo, consisted of a thin layer of ice in the middle of the gallery that extended through the glass wall to the exterior of the building. Visitors were encouraged to walk and play on the ice in the gallery and local residents came to play on the exterior portion of the ice. A glass wall separated those who had paid admission and those who had not, literally making the economic exclusiveness of the museum visible. Like many of Eliasson's installations that use glass walls and mirrors, *The very large ice floor* breaks down barriers of interior and exterior, culture and nature, and the object and subject of art. These contradictory elements and situations transform the act of spectatorship into the object of scrutiny, creating a space in which viewers can reflect on the ways they perceive their relationship to the environment.

The obvious technological mechanisms with which Eliasson creates his representations of nature—ice machines, tanks of natural gas, chemicals, neon lights, mirrors, plastics—make us aware of how our technology frames, appropriates, and even constructs nature. These concerns, present in most of his ''machines,'' also inform Eliasson's interest in photography. Each season, he returns to Iceland to photograph the slow geological changes in the landscape. Like the installation, the camera is simply another machine that mediates our perception of our environment, selecting and framing our personal, cultural, and geologic time and space. Eliasson likes to separate his photography from his installations during their exhibition so that his installations are not perceived as attempts to merely capture and translate the natural sublime into the gallery context. Instead, he uses both types of ''machines'' to explore how our personal and cultural memory, our past experiences and our expectations of the future are all part of the complicated process of perceiving and acquiring knowledge of our world.

—Jaimey Hamilton

ELLER, Thomas

Nationality: German. **Born:** Coburg, Germany, 1964. **Education:** Studied visual arts at HdK Berlin, 1985; studied religion, art history, and philosophy at FU Berlin, 1986–89. **Career:** Internship at Institut für Asthetische Grenzbereiche, Nuremberg, 1984; scientific assistant at Science Center Berlin for Social Research (WZB), 1987–95; moved to New York, 1995. **Awards:** Förderkoje, Art Cologne, 1990; grant from Senate for Cultural Affairs, Berlin, 1991; grant from Karl Schmidt-Rottluff Foundation, 1996; grant from Stiftung Kulturfonds, 1996; residency at Landeskulturzentrum, Salzau, 1997; Villa Romana, Florence, Italy, 2000. **Address:** Lindower Strasse 18, 13347 Berlin, Germany.

Selected Individual Exhibitions:

1990 *Warum ich Kunst mache,* ID-Galerie, Düsseldorf (catalog)
THE Sublime-SELBST, Galerie Anselm Dreher, Berlin
1991 *THE Künstler-SELBST (aus Nürnberg),* Galerie Defet, Nuremburg
1992 *THE Arbeit-SELBST,* Galerie vier, Berlin
1993 *THE Material-SELBST,* ID-Galerie, Düsseldorf
THE Jerusalem-SELBST (oder Babylon?), Sürmondt-Ludwig Museum, Aachen, Germany (catalog)
1994 *THE!-SELBST,* Wilhelm-Hack Museum, Ludwigshafen, Germany
THE People of Europe-SELBST, Contemporary Art Center of Lithuania, Vilinius
1995 *Was ist en Bild?* Galerie Schütz, Frankfurt am Main
YOU!, Rum, Malmo, Sweden (with Andreas Kaufmann)
THE Maß?-SELBST, Städtische Galerie Wolfsburg, Germany
1997 *THE Passage—SELBST,* Munich (catalog)
1998 *THE Objektil-SELBST,* Galerie Defet, Nuremberg
Resident Alien, Neuer Berliner Kunstverein, Berlin (catalog)
1999 *THE Kitchen,* Kitchen Gallery, Seoul, Korea
THE Moi-SELBST, Museum of Installation, London (catalog)
2000 *Presence,* Antonella Nicola Galleria, Turin, Italy
THE Bounty, Galerie Holtmann, Cologne
Contemporaries, Ackland Art Museum, University of North Carolina at Chapel Hill
2001 *THE . . . . (with love),* DeChiara/Stewart Gallery, New York

Selected Group Exhibitions:

1991 *The Colors of Money,* Fondacion Cartier, Paris
Interferenzen: Westberlin 1960–90, Riga, Russia; St. Petersburg, Russia
1992 *TIEFGANG: Bildräume im Schloßbunker,* Mannheim, Germany (catalog)
Korrespondenzen: Zwölf Künstler aus Florenz und Berlin, Berlinische Galerie, Berlin; Casa Masaccio, San Giovanni Valdarno, Italy (catalog)
1993 *Ich-4mal vielmals,* Städtische Ausstellungshalle am Hawerkamp, Muenster (with Philip Akkerman, Cary S. Leibowitz, Harald Falkenhagen)

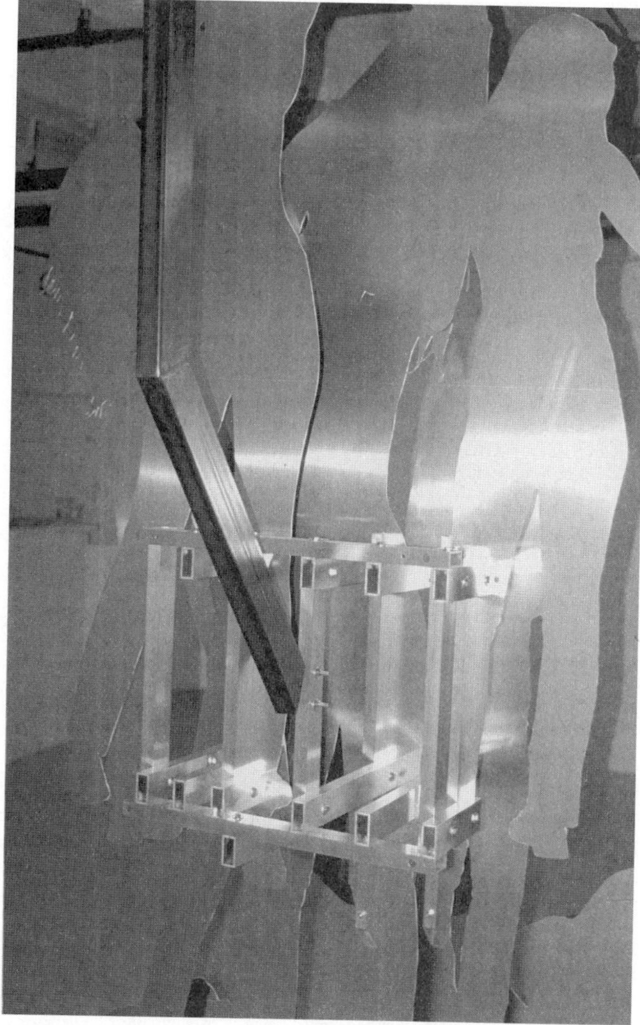

Thomas Eller: **THE** .... *thinking: — — — (with love) 2001.* ©2001 Artists Rights Society (ARS), NY/VG Bild-Kunst, Bonn.

1994 *Thomas Eller, Thomas Florschuetz, Nan Goldin, Thomas Ruff,* Galerie Nikolaus Sonne, Berlin
A Midsummer Night's Dream: Rauma Biennale Balticum, Rauman Taidermuseo, Finland (catalog)
MEMENTO-Positionen zeitgenössischer Kunst aus Berlin, Galerie hlavniho mesta Prahy, Prague, Czech Republic (catalog)
1995 *Gegengewichte,* Kunsthalle Nürnberg, Nuremburg (catalog)
(Landschaft) mit dem Blick in die 90er Jahre, Mittelrhein-Museum Koblenz, Germany (catalog)
MEMENTO: Kunst-Geschichte-Gedenken, Haus am Waldsee, Berlin
1996 *fast nichts/almost invisible,* Umspannwerk Singen Hohentwiehl
Grenzenlos, Moscow Fine Art
Noch nie gezeigt, Berlinische Galerie, Berlin
1997 *Musée Imaginaire,* Museum of Installation, London
1998 *International House and Garden,* Pusan Metropolitan Art Museum, Korea (catalog)
Skulptur Berlin: Positionen der Neuziger, Kunsthaus Dresden

100 Jahre Kunst im Aufbruch, Kunst und Ausstellunghalle der BRD, Bonn (catalog)
Personal Touch, Art in General, New York (catalog)
1999 *Untold Stories,* DeChiara/Stewart Gallery, New York
Three Suitcases, Art and Idea, Mexico City
2000 *Solitude au Musée,* Musée d'Art Moderne, Saint Etienne, France
Brooklyn ZOO, Staatsgalerie Stuttgart
Karl Schmidt-Rottluff Grant, Akademie Dresden and Kunsthalle/Kunstverein, Düsseldorf
I Believe in Dürer, Kunsthalle Nürnberg, Nürnberg (2000)

Publications:

By ELLER: Articles—''Schönheit—einige Randnotizen'' in *Macht der Verführung: Schönheit Geheimnis in der aktuellen Kunst,* Berlin 1996; ''Everything Is Essentially Possible'' in *Gerhard Mayer, NUOVA ICONA,* Venice 1998; ''U-Kunst und E-Kunst: Wie die Industrialisierung der Kunst eine Spaltung hervorbringen wird'' in *BE: Yearbook of Künstlerhaus Bethanien,* Berlin 2000.

On ELLER: Book—*Wer ist Thomas Eller?,* edited by Jan Winkelmann, Ludwigshafen 1994. **Articles—**''Young Artist Thomas Eller'' by Kim Hyun-Ji in *In: Art,* February 2000; ''Simultaneous Vision'' by Sam Rose in *Thomas Eller,* Berlin 2000; ''Thomas Eller e Simon Vogel'' by Joachim Burmeister in *Firenze Fotografia,* Florence 2000.

* * *

Thomas Eller belongs to a generation of contemporary artists for whose art a convenient label has not yet been created. Ever since his first body of work got a public showing—at Galerie Ohne Ort in West Berlin, Germany, in 1987—Eller has been addressing the issue of the self, customarily abbreviating this reference by using THE (i.e. the initials of his first and last name, THomas Eller) as a prefix to titles such as *THE Künstler—SELBST (aus Nürnberg),* i.e. *THE Artist—SELF (from Nuremberg),* dated 1991. In addition, THE is of course the definite article in the English language. In the specific context of Thomas Eller's artwork, the implicit function of THE is comparable to an index finger pointing to something to identify oneself with.

While his earliest pieces frequently included hand-made, oversized objects such as a monumental palette, measuring eight feet in height in *THE Kunst—SELBST, Palette* (*THE Art—SELF, palette,* 1990), Eller soon ventured into the exclusive usage of photographic processes to render his oeuvre. Utilizing the achievements of generating and manipulating photographic images on a computer, Eller's signature objects frequently sport a black-and-white image of the artist himself. This is exemplified in his first solo exhibition in a museum, *THE Jerusalem—SELBST''* at Suermondt-Ludwig-Museum in Aachen, Germany, in 1993.

Venturing into color imagery, Eller started introducing color photographs and cibachromes by the mid-1990s. While the actual image of the artist is increasingly replaced by lusciously colored depictions of a plethora of objects, ranging from coins to lipsticks to butterflies, Eller has constantly been refining the technique of laminating cibachromes onto aluminum supports. This offers him the possibility to create gigantic, three-dimensional wall sculptures (as in *THE . . . . an intense moment (with love),* 2001, a cibachrome on aluminum, measuring 80 by 78 feet).

His frequent juxtaposition of large and small images creates complex visual experiences, perpetually animating the spectators to re-adjust their focus and to find a new perspective in the room where the works are exhibited. Due to the employment of unconventionally dimensioned objects and the simultaneous utilization of photography and its rendering as sculpture, Eller creates a medium that is both sculptural and photographic. ''We become participants by immediately choosing an angle of vision and by establishing our own physical relation to the images as well as a spontaneous emotional one,'' wrote Sabine Russ in the catalog for the *Resident Alien* exhibition in 1998.

His refined choice of the articles depicted, the subtle selection of titles, and the decision to render objects in disproportionate dimensions all feed into Thomas Eller's investigation of identity, ''not through the thing itself, but rather by stressing the importance of outside influences on the self,'' wrote Nicolas de Olivera in the *THE Moi-SELBST* exhibition catalog in 1999. One characteristic and recurring query in his oeuvre, as noted by the critic Sam Rose, reads: ''Who would that be—me? The most redundant question turns out to be the most tricky one.'' Despite their aesthetically pleasing yet frequently challenging appearances, such existential overtones invariably link Eller's pieces to contemporary philosophical discourse, as exemplified by the writings of Derrida or Foucault, among others. Over the years, Eller has devised a flexible, comprehensible, and recognizable canon of images which may at the same time be deciphered as marker, identification device, and ornament, as well as picture and portrait. Quite apart from their sheer beauty and their meticulously pristine surfaces, these installation pieces of photographic sculpture, along with their inherent discursive interrogations into the realm of self and identity, never cease to perplex their audiences, be it in private or public settings.

—Daniel Kletke

ELLIS, Stephen

Nationality: American. **Born:** High Point, North Carolina, 1951. **Education:** Boston University Art Program at Tanglewood, Lenox, Massachusetts, 1969 and 1973; Cornell University, Ithaca, New York, B.F.A., 1973; New York Studio School, 1973–74. **Career:** Adjunct Instructor in Painting, State University of New York at Old Westbury, 1982–83; Visiting Artist, Louisville Arts Council, Louisville, Kentucky, 1988; Instructor in Introduction to Painting, New York University, 1988; Studio-Seminar in Painting for Graduate Students, New York University, 1988–92; Associate Editor, Art in America, 1988–89; Editorial assistant, *Parkett,* 1989; Visiting Artist, University of Tennessee, Knoxville, 1989; Contributing Editor, *Art in America,* 1989–94; Visiting Artist, Kent State University, Kent, Ohio, 1990; conducted Seminar in Contemporary Art Criticism, Rhode Island School of Design, Providence, Rhode Island, 1992; Instructor in Foundation Drawing, New York University, 1992 to present; gave lecture on ''Abstract Art: End or Beginning?'' at the Museum of Modern Art, New York, 1993; Editorial assistant, *ArtForum,* 1993–96; Visiting Artist (Graduate Sculpture), Rhode

Island School of Design, 1994; Artist's Lecture Series, Institute of Fine Art, New York University, 1994; Painting Instructor, Summer Graduate Program, Bard College, 1994; Visiting Artist (Graduate Painting), Rhode Island School of Design, 1995; Multimedia Instructor, Summer Graduate Program, Bard College, Annandale-on-Hudson, New York, 1995; Instructor in Foundation Drawing, School of Visual Arts, New York, 1995; Visiting Artist, Parsons School of Design, New York, 1995 and 1996; Visiting Artist, Akademie voor beeldende Kunst, Enschede, Netherlands, 1996; Junior Independent Painting Projects, School of Visual Arts, New York, 1997; Visiting Artist, Ecole regionale des Beaux-Arts de Valence, Valence, France, 1997; Visiting Artist (Graduate Painting), California Institute of the Arts, Valencia, California, 1997; lectured on ''Does Abstraction Exist?'' at the Carpenter Center for Visual and Environmental Studies, Harvard University, Cambridge, Massachusetts, 1999; Visiting Artist, Department of Visual and Environmental Studies, Harvard University, Cambridge, Massachusetts, 1999–2000. **Awards:** New York Foundation for the Arts Grant in Painting, 1985; National Endowment for the Arts Grant in Painting, 1991.

Selected Individual Exhibitions:

1982 Baskerville and Watson Gallery, New York
1986 *Drawings,* Galerie Alfred Kren, Cologne, Germany
1987 *Paintings,* Galerie Alfred Kren, Cologne, Germany
1988 Galerie 86, Europäische Akademie fur Bildende Kunst, Trier, Germany
1989 Koury Wingate Gallery, New York
1990 Galerie Ascan Crone, Hamburg, Germany
Koury Wingate Gallery, New York
1991 Elizabeth Koury Gallery, New York
1992 Galerie Ascan Crone, Hamburg, Germany (catalog)
Baumgartner Gallery, Washington, D.C.
Elizabeth Koury Gallery, New York
1993 Galerie Nathalie Obadia, Paris, France
1995 André Emmerich Gallery, New York
Galerie Thomas von Lintel, Munich, Germany
1996 *Paintings,* Max Planck Institute, Munich, Germany
Galerie Nathalie Obadia, Paris, France
André Emmerich Gallery, New York
1997 Galerie Thomas von Lintel, Munich, Germany
Marella Arte Contemporanea, Sarnico, Italy (catalog)
1998 Patrick De Brock Gallery, Knokke, Belgium
1999 Galerie Thomas von Lintel, Munich, Germany
2000 Von Lintel & Nusser Gallery, New York
Marella Arte Contemporanea, Milan, Italy
Niels Borch Jensen Verlag und Druck, Berlin, Germany, and Copenhagen, Denmark

Selected Group Exhibitions:

1989 *Three Portfolios—Stephen Ellis, Sol Lewitt, Fred Sandback,* Galerie Alfred Kren, Cologne, Germany
Projects and Portfolios, Brooklyn Museum, New York (catalog)
Herbstsalon, DuMont Kunsthalle, Cologne, Germany (catalog)
Drawings, Daniel Newburg Gallery, New York
1990 *Group Show,* Lawrence Oliver Gallery, Philadelphia, Pennsylvania
Token Gestures, Scott Hanson Gallery, New York
Christian Eckart, Stephen Ellis, Alain Kirili, Imi Knoebel, Koury Wingate Gallery, New York
1991 *New Generations: New York,* Carnegie Mellon University Art Gallery, Pittsburg, Pennsylvania (catalog)
Architectures, Galleria in Arco, Turin, Italy (catalog)
La Metaphysica de la Luce, John Good Gallery, New York (catalog)
Conceptual Abstraction, Sidney Janis Gallery, New York (catalog)
1992 *Abstract Painting Between Analysis and Synthesis,* Galerie Nachst St. Stephan, Vienna, Austria (catalog)
Group Exhibition, Mars Gallery, Tokyo, Japan
Who's Afraid of Duchamp, Minimalism, and Passport Photography? Annina Nosei Gallery, New York (catalog)
Stephen Ellis, Nicholas Rule, Madella Simoni, Shoshana Wayne Gallery, Santa Monica, California
1993 *Sailing to Byzantium with Disenchantment,* Sergio Tossi Arte Contemporanea, Prato, Italy (catalog)
Prospect 93, Kunstverein Frankfurt, Germany (catalog)
Group Exhibition, Galerie Weber, Munster, Germany
Italia-America/l'astrazione ridefinita, Museo di Stato, San Marino, Italy (catalog)
1994 *Promisory Notes,* Artifact Gallery, Tel Aviv, Israel (catalog)
Just a Story from America, Galleria in Arco, Turin, Italy
Group Exhibition, Albert Baronian Gallery, Brussels, Belgium
1995 *Stephen Ellis and Lydia Dona,* Baumgartner Gallery, Washington, D.C.
New York Abstraction, MacDonald Stewart Art Center, Guelph, Canada
Transatlantica: The American-European Nonrepresentational, Museo de Artes Visuales Alejandro Otero, Caracas, Venezuela (catalog)
1996 *Nuevas Abstractiones,* Museo Nacional Centro de Arte Reina Sofia, Madrid, Spain (catalog)
1997 *After the Fall: Aspects of Abstract Painting Since the 1970s,* Snug Harbor Cultural Center, Staten Island, New York (catalog)
Abstraction/Abstractions: Conditional Geometries, Musee d'Art Moderne de Saint Etienne, St. Etienne, France (catalog)
Vertical Painting, P.S.1 Contemporary Art Center, Long Island City, New York
1998 *New York Stories,* Diatonia, Commune di Faenza Assessorato alla Cultura, Faenza, Italy (catalog)
Six Painters (Baroque Geometry), Marlborough Chelsea Gallery, New York (catalog)
1999 *Four Painters,* Carpenter Center, Harvard University, Cambridge, Massachusetts
Do Paintings Dream of Veronese Green? Elga Wimmer Gallery, New York
2000 *Deep Field Painting,* Hunter College Art Gallery, New York
Paintings, Art Club Berlin, Berlin, Germany

Publications:

By ELLIS: Articles—''At Order's Edge'' in *Art in America* (New York), July 1986; ''The Elusive Gerhard Richter'' in *Art in America* (New York), July 1986; ''Theory of Practice/Practice of Theory'' in *Code* (Amsterdam, The Netherlands), 1987; ''Expanded Pictograms'' in *Art in America* (New York), April 1987; ''Something Different'' in *Bomb* (New York), Spring 1987; ''Metaphorical Morphologies'' in *Art in America* (New York), September 1988; ''The Boys in the Bande'' in *Art in America* (New York), December 1988; ''Spleen and Ideal'' in *Parkett* (Zurich, Switzerland), Summer 1989; ''After the Fall'' in *Tema Celeste* (Milan, Italy), December 1991; ''Dialogo tra S.P. e S.E.'' in *Juliet Art Magazine* (Trieste, Italy), December 1998/ January 1999.

On ELLIS: Articles—''Dike Blair, Stephen Ellis, General Idea'' by Joshua Decter in *Arts Magazine* (New York), March 1989; ''Stephen Ellis'' by Richard Kalina in *Arts Magazine* (New York), December 1989; ''Stephen Ellis'' by Lise Holst in *ARTnews,* vol. 88, no. 10, December 1989; ''Stephen Ellis'' by Holland Cotter in *Art in America* (New York), December 1989; ''Stephen Ellis'' by Michael Brenson in *New York Times* (New York), 23 November 1990; ''Stephen Ellis'' by Demetrio Paparoni in *Tema Celeste* (Milan, Italy); ''Stephen Ellis'' by Brooks Adams in *Art in America,* vol. 79, no. 4, April 1991; ''Abstract Monsters'' by Patrick McGrath in *Parkett* (Zurich, Switzerland), December 1992; ''A New Lost Generation'' by Steven Henry Madoff in *ARTnews,* vol. 91, no. 4, April 1992; ''Stephen Ellis'' by Jones K. Marriott in *Artforum,* vol. 31, no. 6, February 1993; ''Stephen Ellis'' by Sue Scott in *ARTnews,* vol. 92, no. 1, January 1993; ''Add-Venture'' by Maia Damianovic in *Abstraction: Journal of Philosophy and Visual Arts* (New York), no. 5, 1995; ''Stephen Ellis'' by Michael Kimmelman in *New York Times* (New York), 16 February 1996; ''Stephen Ellis at André Emmerich'' by Richard Kalina in *Art in America* (New York), May 1996; ''Stephen Ellis at André Emmerich Gallery'' by Thad Ziolkowski in *ArtForum* (New York), May 1996; ''De Amerikaanse abstracten van de jaren negentig'' by Joannes Kesenne in *Kunst & Cultur* (Amsterdam, Netherlands), May 1996; ''Abstraction at the End of the Millenium'' by John Good in *Speak* (San Francisco, California), Fall 1997; ''Time and the Grid: The Paintings of Stephen Ellis'' (unpublished manuscript) by Aruna D'Souza and Tom McDonough Numark Gallery, Washington, D.C. 2000; ''Stephen Ellis, The Grid Unlocked'' by Jessica Dawson in *Washington Post,* 19 April 2001; ''Haber's Art Review: Abstraction since 1970 at Snug Harbor'' by John Haber, online at: http://www.haberarts.com/snugharb.htm (accessed May 2001).

* * *

Stephen Ellis became a prominent painter in the late 1980s, after having started to exhibit his work regularly around 1980. He was one of several painters who established their reputations in the 1980s by painting austere, emotionally detached geometric abstractions. In so doing, Ellis was returning to the principles of Minimalism and Color-Field Painting of the 1960s. Ultimately, the sources for his work are in the very beginnings of geometric abstraction, the pioneer of which was Piet Mondrian and Analytic Cubism, without which Mondrian's Neoplastic paintings would have been impossible.

Ellis began his geometrically abstract paintings in the 1980s by creating compositions consisting of small and narrow geometric shapes evenly distributed across the picture surface with gradually shifting colors and tones spread over these usually flat, empty shapes. Although color varies in these early works, it is often subdued, pale and tonal. These works are reminiscent of the staunchly geometric and seemingly non-emotional abstract paintings of the 1960s, especially the blandly colored paintings of Brice Marden and Agnes Martin. Most of Ellis' paintings are untitled; if they are individualized by title it is only by the combination of letters and numbers which the artist sometimes assigns them. If for no other reason, such basic labeling is useful to differentiate works in cataloguing and selling them.

By the early 1990s, Ellis was creating geometric abstractions based on grid structures placed flatly across the picture surface, and he is now best known for his use of grids as the fundamental compositional devices of his paintings. Since then, Ellis has continued to work with clearly delineated lines or quadrilaterals of various lengths and widths in strictly vertical and horizontal arrangements scattered across the picture plane in more or less even distribution. Such compositional structures are destined to be compared to Mondrian, Theo van Doesburg, and any number of Color-Field Painters of the 1960s. Fortunately, Ellis can survive the comparison, for he holds his own in technical, aesthetic, and creative possibilities. Ellis was clearly looking back at these profoundly important precedents in establishing his basic mode of composing and executing his works, but he has usually been able to creatively depart from his sources and find his own aesthetic and expressive path. In the aftermath of Performance Art, Earth Art, Conceptual Art and the rise of Post-Modernism, he has proven that pure painting is not dead after all. He has found himself in the heart of abstract painting of the last quarter of the twentieth century.

Ellis varies the width, length and color of the horizontal and vertical lines, strips and quadrilateral shapes that constitute the compositional structure of his paintings. Their number, size and shape vary considerably from painting to painting and often within individual works. Their colors also very greatly. The grid components do not always extend the length of the entire canvas nor are all of them identical in any single painting, although they are usually evenly and symmetrically distributed across the composition. Ellis' geometric grids have become more diverse and complex during the 1990s. Whereas the lines and strips are often painted smoothly and flatly with sharply cut edges, the spaces they enclose are often much thicker and rougher in texture. Ellis often combines smooth, crisply defined lines in his grid structures with thickly smeared, blurred, scraped off, and stained areas of color existing in the supposed or apparent voids between the linear framework. He sometimes gives the geometric shapes, strips and linear forms which comprise the grid structures the same variety of rich, tactile textures. Frequently, a contrast in textures is created; the forms that construct the grid and the spaces in between them feature a contrast between smoother and rougher textures. The natural textures of paint are usually obscured in favor of artificially manipulated textures which are more polished or more tactile than ordinary paint application would create. The fact that one might question which are the lines, strips and quadrilaterals, in other words the forms, and which are the voids around and between them, reveals how Ellis has modified the geometric abstraction that inspired him.

Since the mid-1990s, Ellis' paintings have tended to be more diversely, vividly, and brightly colored. Vibrant oranges, hazy sky blues, eerie purples, glowing yellows, deep ceruleans, and sensuous crimsons, among other colors, are seen often in the more recent work. Ellis' use of color is extraordinary subtle, evocative, and beautiful. In some works it is coldly mechanical; in others, it is full of emotional possibilities. The somewhat enclosed areas in his grids often seem to be about to burst with diverse, vibrant, sensuous colors. Yet these same semi-enclosed areas can often appear fastidious in their geometry and linearity.

This variety of shapes, colors, and texture was virtually never seen in Mondrian's Neoplastic paintings nor in geometric abstraction of the 1960s. Ironically, the one noteworthy, famous exception to this in Mondrian's oeurve is his final painting, *Broadway Boogie-Woogie,* of 1944. It seems fitting that Mondrian's last work would be the prototypes in his oeurve for Ellis' paintings; it is almost as if Ellis has engaged the same challenges that Mondrian may have been unable to deal with fully in his lifetime. The variety of shapes, colors and surfaces in Ellis' grid abstractions as his work has evolved during the 1990s and early 2000s can sometimes situate his work as a link between or merger of the gestural abstraction of the 1950s and the sedate, methodical, geometric abstraction that followed it.

The strict and complex geometry and diverse and often vivid color in Ellis' paintings have been interpreted, more or less convincingly, as references to the digital imagery and vibrant colors of computer monitors, to the images recorded on deteriorated films and photographs, to universal product codes and other computer generated, coded images, and vaguely industrial, metallic constructions. Many of his grid forms suggest close-up, slowed-down views of individual frames on reels of motion picture film, although once the viewer has carefully examined these works, the purely abstract color and texture of these grids becomes apparent. The variety within repetition and the expressive power of diverse, vivid colors within the calm, intellectual use of shape and picture surface found in Ellis' grid abstractions create a vibrant, pulsating, sometimes glitzy quality that does seem vaguely, uncertainly industrial, commercial, and technological. Many of Ellis' paintings seem to be abstract celebrations or explorations of the visually overloaded, image-inundated environment of highly commercial, technological, late twentieth-century life. They often make the viewer ponder the gap between the theoretical idealism of early abstraction and the imagery of mass-media, technology and our capitalist, consumer-driven culture. As a result of this fragmentary, fleeting references to real, tangible aspects of everyday experience, there is in Ellis' work a self-conscious examination of the nature of the content and expressive function of painting, of the awareness of painting as painting and of the historical lineage to which late twentieth-century abstraction such as this belongs.

—Herbert R. Hartel, Jr.

ENDO, Toshikatsu

Nationality: Japanese. **Born:** Takayama, Gifu Prefecture, 1950. **Education:** Nagoya Junior College of Art and Design, graduated 1972.

Selected Individual Exhibitions:

1975 *Code of Water I,* Lunami Gallery, Tokyo
1977 *Code of Water III,* Tokiwa Gallery, Tokyo
1978 *Water Erosion II,* Sato Gallery, Tokyo
1980 *Constellation IV,* Tamura Gallery, Tokyo
1982 Independent Gallery, Tokyo
1984 *Allegory I,* Gallery Yo, Tokyo
1986 *Epitaph,* Gallery Yo, Tokyo
1988 *Fountain,* Galerie Gutharc Ballin, Paris
1989–90 *Toshikatsu Endo,* Nordic Art Center, Helsinki, Finland (traveled to Malmo Konstmuseet, Malmo, Sweden; Hafnarborg, Reykjavik, Iceland; Henie Onstad Art Centre, Oslo, Norway; Charlottenborg Art Exhibition Hall, Copenhagen, Denmark)
1991 *Toshikatsu Endo,* Touko Museum of Contemporary Art, Tokyo
1991–92 *Earth:Air:Fire:Water—The Sculpture of Toshikatsu Endo,* Oriel Mostyn, Llandudno, Wales (traveled to Douglas Hyde Gallery, Dublin, Ireland; Yorkshire Sculpture Park, Halifax, United Kingdom; I.C.A., London)
1993 *Two Walls,* Gallery Yamaguchi, Osaka

Selected Group Exhibitions:

1984–85 *Metaphor and/or Symbol: A Perspective on Contemporary Art,* National Museum of Modern Art, Tokyo (traveled to National Museum of Art, Osaka)
1986 *New Trends in Contemporary Sculpture—10 New Outstanding Sculptors of America and Japan,* Contemporary Sculpture Center, Tokyo (traveled to Contemporary Sculpture Center, Osaka; Art Park Center Art Lobby, Sapporooto)
1987 Venice Biennale, Italy
1989 *Art of the Showa Period,* National Museum of Modern Art, Tokyo
1990–91 *Japanische Kunst der Achtziger Jahre,* Frankfurter Kunstverein, Frankfurt (traveled to Bonner Kunstverein, Bonn; Museum Moderner Kunst, Vienna; Bregenzer Festspiele, Bregenzer, Austria)
A Primal Spirit—The Contemporary Japanese Sculptors, Hara Museum ARC, Gunma (traveled to Los Angeles County Museum of Art, Los Angeles, California; Museum of Contemporary Art, Chicago, Illinois; Fort Worth Museum of Modern Art, Texas; National Gallery, Ottawa, Canada)
1991–92 *Zones of Love,* Art Gallery of Western Australia, Perth (traveled to Art Gallery of South Australia, Adelaide; Waikato Museum and Art Gallery, Hamilton, New Zealand; Dunedin Public Art Gallery, Dunedin, New Zealand; Museum of Contemporary Art, Sydney, Australia)
1993 *Archetypy,* Manes, Prague, Czechoslovakia

Publications:

On ENDO: Articles—''New Trends in Contemporary Sculpture'' by Timothy Cohrs in *ARTnews,* vol. 86, no. 9, November 1987; ''Gaining Face: Japan's Artists Emerge'' by Carol Lutfy in *ARTnews,* vol. 89, no. 3, March 1990; ''Vexed in Venice'' by M. Vetrocq in *Art in America,* no. 78, October 1990; ''A Primal Spirit: Ten Contemporary Japanese Sculptors'' by Kathryn Hixson in *Arts Magazine,* vol. 65, no. 6, February 1991; ''Toshikatsu Endo at Akiyama'' by Janet Koplos in *Art in America,* vol. 88, no. 10, October 2000.

* * *

ENGELS, Pieter

Nationality: Dutch. **Born:** Rosmalen, 3 December 1938. **Education**: Studied painting, drawing and material research at the Koninklijke Academie, The Hague, 1955–58, and painting, sculpture, drawing, architecture and art history, Rijksakademie, Amsterdam, 1958–62. **Family:** Married Liesbeth Vandergraaf in 1961; children: Manuela and Wladimir. **Career:** Independent artist, Amsterdam, since 1962: founder, Engels Products Organization, Amsterdam, 1964–69; Engels New Interment Organization, Amsterdam, 1968–69; Engels Third Institute for Research in Subcultural Brainbuilding, Amsterdam, 1969–74; and Engels Genesis Foundation, Amsterdam, 1974. **Awards:** Koninklijke Subsidy, 1959; Dutch Government grants, 1967, 1969, 1970, 1971, 1974; Cassandra Foundation Award, Philadelphia, 1971. **Agent:** Galerie Yaki Kornblit, Willemsparkweg 69, Amsterdam. **Address:** Willem Nuijenstraat 26, Amsterdam; or Grote Wittenburgstraat 37, Amsterdam, Netherlands.

Individual Exhibitions:

1963 Galerie Orez, The Hague
Galerie t'Venster, Rotterdam
De Krabbedans, Eindhoven, Netherlands
1965 Galerie 845, Amsterdam
Galerie A. Arnhem, Netherlands
Galerie Arti Schunck, Maastricht, Netherlands
1966 Galerie Swart, Amsterdam
Koninklijke Academie, The Hague
Gemeentemuseum, The Hague
Galerie 20, Amsterdam
Galerie 845, Amsterdam
1967 Wide White Space Gallery, Antwerp
Galerie Waalkens, Finsterwolde, Netherlands
1968 Galerie 20, Amsterdam
Galerie Kuckels, Bochum, West Germany
Galerie Jalmar, Amsterdam
1969 *Self-Portrait of This Century,* Stedelijk Museum, Amsterdam (travelled to the Van Abbemuseum, Eidhoven, Netherlands)
1970 Galerie 20, Amsterdam
Galerie Toni Gerber, Berne
1971 Stichting Utrechtse Kring, Utrecht
Galerie 20, Amsterdam
1972 Kunststichting, Rotterdam
Galerie 20, Amsterdam
Galerie Dorothea Loehr, Frankfurt
Self-Portrait of This Century, Stedelijk Museum, Amsterdam
1973 International Cultureel Centrum, Antwerp
Galerie Yaki Kornblit, Amsterdam
Yodfat Gallery, Tel-Aviv
1974 Galerie Yaki Kornblit, Amsterdam
1975 *Self-Portrait of This Century,* Museum Boymans-van Beuningen, Rotterdam (retrospective)
Galerie Yaki Kornblit, Amsterdam
1981 *Recent Work,* Stedelijk Museum, Amsterdam
1987 *Pieter Engels: Ahead to the Roots,* Galerie Brinkman, Amsterdam (catalog)
1988 LedisFlam Gallery, New York
1991 LedisFlam Gallery, New York
Pieter Engels: Parallel Landscape, Remembrandt, Nijmeegs Museum Commanderie van Sint Jan, Nijmegen, Netherlands
1997 Arti et Amicitiae, Amsterdam
Galerie Scheper, Amsterdam

Selected Group Exhibitions:

1965 *Manifestatie Zeist,* Nederlandse Kunststichting, Zeist, Netherlands
1967 *5th Biennale de Paris,* Musée d'Art Moderne, Paris
1968 *Documenta 4,* Kassell, West Germany
1970 *Art by Projects,* Kunsthalle, Berne
1971 *Metamorfose van het Object,* Palais des Beaux-Arts, Brussels (toured Europe)
1973 *Nytt fra Nederland,* Henie-Onstad Kunstsenter, Osla
1974 *11 Dutch Artists,* Fruit Market Gallery, Edinburg
1976 *Schuhwerke,* Museum Stadt, Nuremberg
1998 *Art in Nature,* ALP Academia Foundation, Huilversum, Netherlands

Collections:

Stedelijk Museum, Amsterdam; Stedelijk Van Abbemuseum, Eindhoven, Netherlands; Gemeentemuseum, The Hague; Museum Boymans-van Beuningen, Rotterdam; Centraal Museum, Utrecht; International Cultureel Centrum, Antwerp; Bank Lambert, Brussels; McCrory Corporation, New York.

Publications:

By ENGELS: Books—*Engels New Interment Organization,* with Simon Es, Amsterdam 1968; *Resurrection of Art,* Amsterdam 1974. **Articles—**''Engels: Image of an Image,'' with Simon Es, In *Museumjournaal* (Amsterdam), no. 1, 1967; ''Engels: (pre) Hume Ghost Writer of a Non-Existent Vanguard,'' with Simon Es, in *Engels: Self-Portrait of This Century* exhibition catalog, Amsterdam 1972. **Films—***Paramarche,* television film, 1972; *Oral Signature,* 1972; *Self Portrait,* 1972. **Records—***Oral Signature,* Rotterdam 1972.

On ENGELS: Books—*Engels: Self-Portrait of This Century,* exhibition catalog, Amsterdam 1969; *De Eksplosie van het Intellekt* by Jan Donia, Hilversum, Netherlands 1968; *Metamorfose van het Objekt,* exhibition catalog, with text by Jean Dypreau, Brussels 1971; *Pieter Engels,* exhibition catalog, with text by Carel Blotkamp, Amsterdam 1972; *11 Dutch Artists,* exhibition catalog, with text by Caroline Tisdall, Edinburgh 1974; *Engels: Self-Portrait of This Century,* exhibition catalog, with an introduction by R. Hammachervan den Brande, Rotterdam 1975; *Pieter Engels: Recent Work 1979–1980,* exhibition folder, with texts by Tijmen van Grootheest and Dirk Pieters, Amsterdam 1981. **Articles—**''Economics and Memory: The Art of Pieter Engles'' by Ellen Handy in *Arts Magazine,* vol. 65, February 1991.

* * *

For many years, Pieter Engels has been producing a steady stream of works in a variety of media which define his own particular gifts as an artist and also make a comment on the position of the artist in society. As a person he seemed to retreat, at first, behind the facade of EPO (the Engels Product Organization, founded in 1964), whose skillful sales manager was Simon Es. By this time Engels had also produced some of his *materieachtig* work (''Dirty Picture,'' for example, from 1961).

In 1964 EPO created a stir with an exhibition held in Galerie A in Arnhem. Included here were ''Restored Furnishings,'' groupings of functionless pieces of furniture which seemed to be conversing with each other. And in 1966 there was ''Girl's Coat-Piece,'' a rain-slicker stretched on a canvas which was also a kind of comment on the work of the American artist Jim Dine.

In 1968 Engels founded ENIO: Engels' New Interment Organization (New Methods for the Interment Field). Here the aim was to dispel any notion that a funeral had to be a sad occasion. In its brochure ENIO offers cheerful alternatives and concludes with the enticing invitation to ''Think it over—have a good ending for your life .... We will prepare you. Our funerals are gorgeous and luxurious—and so are our prices.''

In 1969 and 1970 Engels exhibited aural works in Galerie 20 in Amsterdam (in one of these works you can hear street noises recorded simultaneously from each of the four floors of the building). In 1972 he produced an important photographic work which can be regarded as his first venture into the field of painting. The ''Painting Piece for Four Hands'' consists of three photographs, the last of which has a caption which explains helpfully ''painting of Engels' left hand painted blue by Engels' blue-painted right hand.'' In this same year Engels also made a brief statement which sums up his intentions as an artist: ''The artist is a cat among the pigeons.''

There is a series of particularly concentrated works from 1974, including portraits and still-lifes, which Engels painted in the dark or while blindfolded. He also founded the Engels Genesis Foundation in 1974, the mission of which was to construct a monumental work (completed in 1977) in de Bijlmeer, a suburb of Amsterdam. Underground there are boxes which contain tape recordings and collections of objects over which cement has been poured. Above ground are images of the objects buried below. Here according to Engels is a cross section of the urban life of the three cities of the ''Randstad''—Amsterdam, Utrecht and Rotterdam.

Despite the continually changing nature of his work, Engels succeeded in coming to a prominent place in the Dutch art world of the 1980s. Since 1970 his work has won a place in private collections and museums as well, reaching a kind of high point in the *Self-Portrait of the Century* exhibition at the Boymans-van Beuningen Museum in Rotterdam in 1975.

—A. F. Wagemans

ERRÓ, (Gudmundur Gudmundsson)

Nationality: Icelandic. **Born:** Olafsvik, 19 July 1932. **Education:** Academy of Art, Reykjavik, 1949–51 (Art Professor's Diploma, 1951); painted frescoes, Academy of Art, Oslo, 1952–54; studied fresco painting, Academy of Art, Florence, 1954. **Family:** Married Myriam Bat-Yosef in 1956 (divorced, 1964); married Vilai Permchit in 1972. **Career:** Worked on frescoes and mosaics, Reykjavik, 1955–58; moved to Paris, 1958; produced first Catastrophe Happenings, with Jean Jacques Lebel, Paris, 1962; travelled in the United States, performing happenings, 1963; lived and worked in New York, 1962–68; lived in New York and Paris, 1962–68; in Thailand and the Far East, 1972–2000. **Agents:** Galerie Montenay-Giroux, 8 rue Charlot, 75003 Paris; Galerie Zannettacci, 16 rue des Granges, Geneva 1204, Switzerland **Address:** 39 rue Fondary, 75015 Paris, France.

Individual Exhibitions:

1955 Galerie Saint Trinity, Florence
1956 Galerie Montenapoleone, Milan
Galerie Schneider, Rome
1957 Maison des Artistes, Reykjavik
1958 Bezalel National Museum, Jerusalem
Museum of Modern Art, Tel Aviv
Museum of Modern Art, Haifa
1960 Galerie Chirvan, Paris
Maison des Artistes, Reykjavik
1961 Galleria del Cavallino, Venice
Galleria del Naviglio, Milan
1962 Galerie J. Dols, Liège, Belgium
1963 Galerie Sydow, Frankfurt
Galerie St. Germain-des-Pres, Paris
1964 Gertrude Stein Gallery, New York
Galleria Edouard Smith, Milan
Galleria Schwarz, Milan
1965 Galerie L'Attico, Rome
Maison des Artistes, Reykjavik
Galerie St. Germain, Paris
1966 Galerie Kaleidoscope, Ghent
1967 Galleria Schwarz, Milan
Galerie Krikhaar, Amsterdam
1968 Galerie Givaudan, Paris
Galerie Mendoza, Caracas
1969 Musée d'Art Moderne, Paris
Galerie Heland, Stockholm
Galerie Givaudan, Paris
Galerie M. E. Thelen, Essen
1971 Galerie André, Berlin
Galerie 3 Laplace, Paris
Kerlikowsky Galerie, Munich
1972 Galerie Boulakia, Paris
1973 Galerie Buchholz, Munich
Galleria d'Arte Borgogna, Milan
Galerie Benador, Geneva
Kunstmarkt, Cologne
Galerie Buchholz, Munich
1974 D. K. Bookhouse, Bangkok
1975 Musée des Beaux-Arts, Brest, France
Palais des Papes, Avignon, France
Sigma, Bordeaux
Tableaus Chinois, Kunstmuseum, Lucerne
Galerie Buchholz, Munich
Galerie Fred Lanzenberg, Brussels
Galleria d'Arte Borgogna, Milan
Neue Galerie, Aachen, West Germany
1976 Musée Despiau et Wlerick, Mont-de-Marsan, France
Kunstichting Lijnbaancentrum, Rotterdam
Galerie Beaubourg, Paris
O. K. Harris Gallery, New York

Erró: *The French Comicscape,* 1985. ©2001 Artists Rights Society (ARS), NY/ADAGP, Paris.

Maison de la Culture, Amiens, France
Musée d'Ethnographie, Bastia, Corsica
1977 Beaux-Arts Angoulème, Centre d'Art, Flaine, France
Centre d'Art Contemporain, Chelles, France
Galerie Fred Lanzenberg, Ibiza, Spain
Galerie Beaubourg, Paris
Reykjavik Art Festival
1978 Galerie Sven Hanssen, Copenhagen
Galerie Buccholz, Munich
1979 Galerie Beaubourg, Paris
Galerie Claude Givaudan, Geneva
Galleria d'Arte Borgogna, Milan
Galerie Fred Lanzenberg, Brussels
1980 Galerie Impact, Vannes, France
1981 Galerie Maeght, Zurich
Lunds Konsthall, Lund Sweden (travelled to the Kunstforeningen, Bergen; Nordisk Konstcentrum, Sveaborg; Pohjoismainen taidekeskus, Helsingfors; and the Kunstforeningen, Copenhagen)
1982 Galerie Jan Six, Paris
Maison de la Culture, Chalon-sur-Saone, France
Salle Demangel, Montpellier, France
Musée Rigaud, Perpignan, France
Musée des Beaux-Arts, Nîmes, France
Tour Narbonnaise, Carcassonne, France
Musée Fabrégal, Béziers, France
Galerie le Dessin, at *FIAC 82,* Grand Palais, Paris
Art Front Gallery, Tokyo
Museum voor Hedendaagse Kunst, Utrecht, Netherlands
1983 Miroir d'Encre, Brussels
Galerie Jaqueline Storms, Lille, France
Galerie Municipale, Gennevilliers, France
Galerie Fernand Leger, Ivry-sur-Seine, France
Piscine Municipale, Le Pré, Saint-Gervais, France
Galerie Electrochoc 2, Caen, France
1984 Centre Culturel Gérard Philippe, Brétigny-sur-Orge, France
Galerie Zannettaci, Geneva
Centre Culturel Pablo Neruda, Corbeil-Essonnes, France
Espace des Cordeliers, Châteauroux, France
Galerie d'Art Contemporain, Tours, France
Galerie Poll, West Berlin (with Arroyo and Monory)
Miroir d'Encre, Brussels
1985 Galerie Loft, Paris
Galerie Gilbert Brownstone, Paris
ARC/Musée d'Art Moderne de la ville, Paris
Musée du Dole, France
Centre d'Art Contemporain, Montbeliard, France
Stadmuseum, Rattingen, West Germany
Centre d'Art Contemporain, Annecy, France
1986 Norreina Husid, Reykjavik

Erró: *Pol-Pot,* 1992. ©2001 Artists Rights Society (ARS), NY/ADAGP, Paris.

Maison de la Culture, Le Havre, France
Maison de la Culture, Bourges, France
Galerie Municipale, Saint-Priest, France
Chateau de Belfort, France
Abbaye de Montmajour, Arles, France
Venice Biennale
Galerie Jacqueline Storme, Lille, France

1987 Galerie Montenay, Paris
Festival International de la Bande Dessiné, Sierre, Switzerland
Galerie Sonia Zannettacci, Geneva

1988 *Huit Paysages,* Galerie Jacqueline Storm, Lille, and Le Mirroir d'Encre, Brussels
Centre d'Art Contemporain, Rouen
Galerie Medaine, Rouen
Carré Vert, Rouen

1989 Galerie Vincent Saint Pierre, Reunion Island
Kjarvalshus, Reykjavik
Galerie Montenay, Paris

1990 FNAC, Rouen
Galerie Sonia Zannettacci, Geneva
Centre d'Art Contemporain de Mont de Marsan
Les Fresques, les Savants, et les Ingénieurs, La Vilette Cité des Sciences et de l'Industrie, Paris
Gaberret, Peyrehordade
Saint Sever, Hagetman

1991 Centre Gérard Philippe, Cergy Pointnoise, France
Galerie 1900–2000, Paeis
Galeria Leorica, Milan
Biennale, Lyon
Galeria Fandos, Valencia, Spain
Galerie Storme, Lille

1992 Galerie Berggruen, Paris
Centre Culturrel, Issoire
Pavillion Français, Seville
Bergen Billedgalleri, Bergen, Norway
Galerija Graficki Kolektiv, Belgrade

1993 Nordisk Ministerrad, Copenhagen
Charlottenborg, Copenhagen
Pori Taide Museoon, Finland
Kunstmuseum, Goteborg, Sweden
Galerie Aveny, Goteborg, Sweden

1994 Hall Palais des Congrés, Paris
Galerie Sonia Zannettacci, Geneva
Fruitmarket Gallery, Edinburgh
Karolina Ceske Museum Vytvarnych, Umeni, Prague

1995 Galerie Jacqueline Storme, Lille, France
''Quoi de Neuf Docteur?,'' Erró: ğuvres Graphiques, Le Salon d'Art, Brussels
L.A.C. Lieu d'Art Contemporain, Sigean, France
Galeria 56, Budapest

1996 *Erró: Von Mao bis Madonna,* Museum Moderner Kunst Stiftung Ludwig, Vienna
Erró: Les Femmes Fatales, Galerie Selart, Stockholm
Erró: Political Painting, Orangerie Herrenhausen, Wilhelm-Busch-Museum, Hannover (travelled to Aktionsforum Praterinsel, Munich; Kunsthaus, Hamburg; Haus am Waldsee, Berlin; Galéria mesta Bratislavy, Bratislava, Slovenia)
Galerie F. Miliani, Marseille, France
Galerie Galax, Göteborg, Sweden

1997 *Erró: Les Femmes Fatales,* Galerie Montenay-Giroux, Paris (travelled to Galerie Sonia Zannettacci, Geneva)
Faroe Islands Art Gallery, Thorshavn, Denmark
Erró—Mixt Paintings, Galerie der Stadt, Kornwestheim
Galerie Frédéric Storme, Lille, France

Museum of Modern Art, Belgrade
Erró 1974–1996, Palácio Galveias, Lisbon
Galerie Galax, Göteborg, Sweden
1998 *Se Non e Vero, e Ben Trovato,* Le Salon d'Art, Brussels
Sævar Karl Gallery, Reykjavik Arts Festival, Reykjavik, Iceland
Erró, Konur, Women, Musée d'Art de la Ville de Reykjavik, Musée Erró, Reykjavik, Iceland
Erró: Political Painting, Villa Tamaris, La Seyne-sur-Mer, France
Galerie Municipale Julio Gonzalez, Arcueil
5th Biennale d'Art Graphique, Belgrade
1999 Katuaq, Nuuk, Greenland
Erró. . . Renault, Espace Culturel Hippolyte Mars, Equeurdreville-Hainneville
Erró: Images du Siècle, Galerie Nationale du Jeu de Paume, Paris (travelled to Musée d'Art Contemporain, Marseille)
2000–01 Galerie Sonia Zannettacci, Geneva
Stord Kunsthalle, Norway
Bibliothèque Municipale et Ancienne Mairie, Audincourt, France
Château Prieural, Monsepron-Libos
Erró, A Critical Vision, Bergen Kunstmuseum, Bergen, Germany
Norskvasskraft Og Industristad Museum, Odda, Norway
Musée des Beaux-Arts, Charleroi, France
Trabinos Recente, Galeria Atlantica, Porto, Portugal
Erró, Tributo A, Galeria Nasoni, Porto, Portugal
Les Femmes Fatales, Musée des Beaux-Arts, Le Château, Caen, France
Hong Kong Arts Center, Pao Galleries, Hong Kong
Galeria Antonio Prates, Lisbon
Fylkes Galleriet I Sogn, Og Fjordane, Norway
Helsinki City Art Museum, Helsinki, Finland

Selected Group Exhibitions:

1963 *Biennale,* Musée d'Art Moderne, Paris
1964 *Biennale,* Museum of Modern Art, Tokyo
1966 *L'Art Fantastique Contemporain,* Musée d'Antibes, France
1967 *Le Monde en Question,* Musée d'Art Moderne, Paris
1968 *Surrealismus in Europa,* Galerie Baukunst, Cologne
1969 *Kunst und Politik,* Kunstverein, Karlsruhe
1975 *Biennale,* Venice
1980 *Science au Futur,* Palais Rameau, Lille, France
1982 *Printed Art since 1965,* Museum of Modern Art, New York
1985 *Figuration Narrative 1960–80,* Galerie des Arènes, Nîmes, France

Collections:

Moderna Museet, Stockholm; National Museum, Jerusalem; Temperas Museum, Tel Aviv; Museum de la Révolution, Algiers; National Museum, Reykjavik; Nationalgalerie, West Berlin; Musée National d'Art Moderne/Centre Georges Pompidou, Paris; Hara Museum, Tokyo; National Air and Space Museum, Washington, D.C.; Museum of Modern Art, New York; Louisiana Museum, Denmark.

Publications:

By Erró: Book—*Mecanifest,* Venice 1962; *Macanfest 2,* Venice 1963. **Films—***Mecamorphoses,* with Eric Duvivier, 1962; *Grimaces,* 1964; *Stars,* 1966.

On Erró: Books—*Erró* by Gilbert Brownstone, Paris 1972; *Erró,* exhibition catalog, with text by Udo Kultermann, Munich 1973; *Erró: Tableaux Chinois,* exhibition catalog, with text by Jean-Christophe Ammann, Lucerne 1975; *Erró: Catalog General,* Milan and Paris 1976; *Erró* by Pierre Tilman, Paris 1976: *Erró* by B. Asgeirsson and M. Johannesson, Reykjavik 1978; *Erró* by Philippe Sergent, Paris 1979; *Erró* by Jehiro Hairu, Tokyo 1979; *Erró,* exhibition catalog, by Marianne Nanne-Brahammar and Jacques Adelin Brutaru, Lund, Sweden 1981; *Erró* by Xavier Moreau, New York and Paris 1983; *Erró, 1974–1986; Catalog General II,* Paris 1986; *Erró* by Adalsteinn Ingólfsson, Reykjavik 1991; *Erró, Peintre Mythique* by Marc Augé, Paris 1994; *Science Fiction,* exhibition catalog by Jean-Christophe Ammann, Edinburgh 1994; *Erró n'a Pas Peur des Images. . . ,* exhibition catalog by Bernard Marcadé, Paris 1994; *A Pantheon of Images,* exhibition catalog by Graeme Murray, Edinburgh 1994; *Jenseits der Montage—Zurück zur Malerei,* exhibition catalog by Hans Joachim Neyer, Hannover 1996; *Erró, Political Paintings* by Gunnar B. Kvaran and Hans Joachim Neyer, Stuttgart 1996; *Von Mao Bis Madonna—Das Bild als Entmythologisierung* (From Mao to Madonna—The Image as Demythologisation), exhibition catalog by Lóránd, Hegyi, Vienna 1996; *Erró, un Artiste Transculturel* by Élisabeth Mabin, 1997; *L'ğuvre d'Erró de L'Atelier à L'Exposition* by Zoé Rumeau, Paris 1997–98; *Erró,* exhibition catalog with text by Catherine Francblin and Itzhak Goldberg, Paris 1999. **Films—***Les Femmes Fatales* by Jean Pierre Noury, 1997; *Rencontre avec Erró Une Pécheur d'Images* by Jean Pierre Noury, 2000; *L'ğuvre et L'Artiste Erró* by Catherine Terzieff, 2000.

*

My greatest problem, as a painter, is to talk about my work. I am not interested in a painting the moment I finish it. I do not want to talk about it. I would like better to be told why a certain person does like it or does not like it. Even when I try to cast some light on my work, I have the impression that I indulge in unnecessary explanations, I have the impression that I do not act in good faith.

A painter explained that he was driven by the necessity to make order in chaos. An author whom I respect said that he worked for his own pleasure. Another one suggested that the results of this work were symptoms of a neurosis.

A painter spends a major part of his time alone, which makes relations—other than friendly relations—difficult. I adore being alone; silence is to me a substance, a quality in itself, like music.

My motivations are not mysterious; they are multiple, contradictory, and they frequently surprise me. My pictures are inadapted, hesitant companions, with all kinds of defaults.

I am never satisfied with what I already achieved, and I would like, in one way or another, to correct my work, to complete it, to suggest other solutions. Solutions which could by termed as negative, dormant, chained, paralyzed. Often against the language, pictorial or not, because of excesses or abuse.

I work in the interior of a composition, well aware of the fact that my painting is my vicious circle. My dismantlings and my recompositions do not affect the composition, the substance, they count on its permanence. I think that if some paintings are silent, they are silent in order to let others speak. The pretension to make the unspeakable speak, or to convert paintings into action guides, according to my opinion, leads to uncertainty and to the lack of modern. I like paintings more as an exercise of lyricism. A kind of alchemy of senses, which finally becomes a combination of pictorial signs. This is because the world of fiction intrigues me: the circulation of stories, the disguise of forms give us the power to believe.

Painting is the laboratory of the possible: a place where one can experiment, make old out of new. I paint because painting is a private form of Utopia, the pleasure to contradict, the happiness to be alone against everybody, the joy to provoke. I like playing with forms, I like the rhythm of composition, I like constructing my own world, a world in which I live during a certain time. I like my capacity to "give for seeing" what I saw, plus a little boring, a little vanity.

Painting is a means of trying to discover the significance of a confused world. Each painting is to me "an old story," a story I tell to myself in order to fill the obsessions of a child—I never ceased being a child.

Painting reacts to necessity by pleasure. And if I harvest a certain amount of anguish, I know very well that it is a price I have to pay. The painting helps me share my loneliness.

To make paintings is a work which is like any other work: with its problems, its difficulties, its technical solutions, its obscure zones, and its moments of routine.

Painting is an artisanship where the best one can experience is to acquire a professional conscience equal to that of an artisan which makes a pair of shoes or a night table. With, of course, a nuance: a carpenter knows, at least approximately what piece of furniture he will make: the painter, at the other hand, almost never. . .

When painting, one discovers that painting is sometimes a boring job, exasperating and tiring. What makes us perverse? In a way, the same thing that makes a carpenter continue to be a carpenter: it is difficult to abandon a job in the apprenticeship of which one invested so much time and efforts.

One gives different answers, depending on different moments and different persons one talks to. I think that all answers could be almost true, but none of them could be absolutely true. Nor an absolute truth.

I visited the factory of fireworks Ruggieri. I saw small, light huts, ready to fly away after the smallest explosion. Strange chemists mixed, in tubes, powders of different colors, which should eventually become rockets, suns, and other fireworks. A painting is something similar to that.

Stories one tells are too long to be told by voice. When I paint, I never imagine that I should subordinate my work to some standard or to a formula imposed, nor to the rules of any kind of doctrine. Painting is an investigation of existence; it means fixing the flux of intuition by a system of symbols which can be submitted to analysis. It is a test of conscience without rules, without the anesthesia of oblivion. It is also a work which makes it possible to ascend to the pleasure of being an individual in the present world which is depersonalized. Work is a false ideology which steals the appearances from the reality, or, better to say, a sad story, with dialogues and symbols, capable of becoming a Utopia.

The confessions of a painter cannot provide additional information; they consist almost entirely of lies: another occasion to be ostensibly modest, to add a supplementary detail to a scenography, or to hide some secret imperfections. The true reasons must remain mysterious; there are things that must not be said, there are others not to be discussed.

An idea, a character, a theme come to my mind; they take away my peace. When one succeeds in getting rid of those elements, one feels much better.

The satisfaction linked to the work accomplished comes later—if it ever comes. The satisfaction is obviously something less powerful.

Always when I finish a painting, I say to myself that that one could be the end. The last one.

What makes me paint, is not the wish to teach others about things I think I have learned; it is the wish to show the broadness of my incompetence. Is maybe my first impulsion to pretend that I recognized myself? But even for pretending, one has to gather information, knowledge, observations: I must succeed in imagining the slow accumulation of an experience.

Painting consists in overcoming silence and shock. Like an observer without religion, without ideology, a passer-by, a tourist. There is an amount of perception, a collective conscience which can be enlarged and enriched by art.

This gives me something to do while dying; this makes it possible to sense the infinite in all its variations.

—Erró

* * *

Erró paints with a demoniacal frenzy and intensity, as if the world were being held in suspense. His output comprises several thousand pictures and collages mostly in large format. "Holding the world in suspense" is no chance metaphor. In the process of producing and reproducing societies of all degrees of latitude through picture worlds, in the rhythm of the productive imagination of his own pictures, his work has the significance of a crucible.

Like no other painter Erró has traversed the "World of Painting" within an incomparable campaign of conquest, seemingly effortlessly, because he assigns to these picture worlds of his no deeper significance. They form a closed system, regenerate and fertilize themselves according to an intrinsic dynamic, and what they contain by way of allusions to reality stands in an inverse relationship to what they express. To put it even more strongly, Erró must have clearly recognized that the statements of a code of painting inherent in mass culture primarily state nothing but themselves, and are formulated only on the plane of the portrayal of specific objects, whilst reference to reality is of general banal character.

So it is not surprising that the most capricious things come together in a purely associative undertaking. Erró does not explain things. And yet he unmasks stereotyped *Leitbilder* with stalwart pleasure; but not according to a "didactic" method, rather through the spontaneous blending of insignificant features which demonstrate all the more the characteristic nature of the image and of its effect.

Thus at first sight one is often inclined to consider Erró's paintings to be as stupid as the material upon which they are based. Often it is not easy to separate oneself from the individual factors of the content and look at them in their connection as standpoint and painting of Erró's. Already the circumstance that Erró makes a point of maintaining neutrality towards his material, that he manipulates it in accordance with is own laws, and reduces it ad absurdum, makes his pictures lose sight of their original aim. For the criterion of kind of picture and the way it is painted is not decisive. Erró paints just as well as the copy—always a collage—demands; with highest precision and differentiated tonalities or just summarily with coarse textures, Erró's art lies in the intuitive grasp of the possibilities lying dormant in the material itself, possibilities of a contentual, formal or syntactic nature; he makes the most of it, and places it without protection, utilizes it constantly at the same time to tell its own story (and this impetus knows no bounds). Not that he sets it up vicariously; he trains his protagonists, whether human or animal, for a game of life and death, fetches out of the reserve bank whatever he needs and finally drives the whole pack into the cockpit when he has finished a picture-series.

—Jean-Christophe Ammann

ESTES, Richard

Nationality: American. **Born:** Keewane, Illinois in 1932. **Education:** Art Institute of Chicago, 1952–56. **Career:** Lived in Evanston, Illinois, and worked as illustrator for publishing and advertising layout work; moved to New York, 1959; lived and painted in Spain, 1962; full-time painter from 1966: now lives and works in New York and Maine. **Award:** National Council of the Arts Fellowship 1971. **Agent:** Marlborough Gallery, 40 West 57th Street, New York, New York 10019; Louis K. Meisel Gallery, 141 Prince Street, New York, New York 10012. **Address:** 300 Central Park West, New York, New York 10024–1513, U.S.A.

Individual Exhibitions:

1968 Allan Stone Gallery, New York
Hudson River Museum, Yonkers, New York
1969 Allan Stone Gallery, New York
1970 Allan Stone Gallery, New York
1972 Allan Stone Gallery, New York
1974 Allan Stone Gallery, New York
3 Realists: Close, Estes, Rafael, Worcester Art Museum, Massachussets
Museum of Contemporary Art, Chicago
1978 Museum of Fine Arts, Boston
Museum of Contemporary Art, Chicago
Museum of Art, Toledo, Ohio
Nelson Gallery-Atkins Museum, Kansas City, Missouri
1979 Hirshhorn Museum, Smithsonian Institution, Washington, D.C.
1983 Museum of Fine Arts, Boston
Allan Stone Gallery, New York
1985 Louis K. Meisel Gallery, New York
1990 *Richard Estes: The Complete Prints and the Japan Paintings,* Sert Gallery, Carpenter Center for the Visual Arts, Harvard University, Cambridge, Massachusetts
Richard Estes 1990, Isetan Museum of Art, Tokyo; Museum of Art, Kintetsu, Osaka; Hiroshima City Museum of Contemporary Art, Hiroshima
1991 *Richard Estes: Urban Landscapes,* Portland Museum of Art, Portland, Maine
Foster Goldstrom Gallery, New York
1992–95 *Richard Estes: The Complete Prints,* The Museums at Stony Brook, Stony Brook, New York; Canton Art Institute, Canton, Ohio; Middlebury College Museum of Art, Middlebury, Vermont; Louisiana Arts & Science Museum, Baton Rouge, Louisiana; Columbia Museum of Art, Columbia, South Carolina; Nelson-Atkins Museum of Art, Kansas City, Missouri; Huntsville Museum of Art, Huntsville, Alabama; Hunter Museum of Art, Chattanooga, Tennessee; and other venues
1993 *Richard Estes: New York Cityscapes,* Marlborough Gallery, New York (catalog)
1994 *Paintings: 1967–1993,* Louis K. Meisel Gallery, New York
1995 *Richard Estes: New York Paintings,* Marlborough Gallery, New York (catalog)
1997 *Richard Estes: Small Paintings,* Marlborough Gallery, New York (catalog)
1998 *Richard Estes: Six New Paintings,* Marlborough Gallery, New York (catalog)
2000 *Richard Estes: Recent Works,* Marlborough Gallery, London (catalog)

Selected Group Exhibitions:

1975 *Trends in Contemporary American Realist Painting,* Museum of Fine Arts, Boston
1976 *America 1976,* Corcoran Gallery, Washington, D.C. (toured the United States)
America as Art, National Collection of Fine Arts, Smithsonian Institution, Washington, D.C.
American Master Drawings and Watercolors, Whitney Museum, New York
1977 *Biennial,* Whitney Museum, New York
1981–82 *Contemporary American Realism since 1960,* Pennsylvania Academy of Fine Arts, Philadelphia; Virginia Museum of Fine Arts, Richmond; Oakland Museum, California; Gulbenkian Museum, Lisbon; Germanisches Nationalmuseum, Nuremberg, West Germany
Super Realism From the Morton G. Neumann Family Collection, Kalamazoo Institute of Arts, Michigan; the Art Center, Inc., South Bend, Indiana; Springfield Art Museum, Springfield, Missouri; Dartmouth College Museum and Galleries, Hanover, New Hampshire; De Cordova and Dana Museum, Lincoln, Massachusetts; Des Moines Art Center, Iowa.
1985 *American Realism: The Precise Image,* Isetan Museum, Tokyo; Daimaru Museum, Osaka; Yokohama Takashimaya, Tokohama
1991 *American Realism & Figurative Art: 1952–1990,* The Miyagi Museum of Art, Sendai; Sogo Museum of Art, Yokohama; The Tokushima Modern Art Museum, Tokushima; The Museum of Modern Art, Shiga; and Kochi Prefectural Museum of Art, Kochi
1992 *Six Takes on Photo-Realism,* Whitney Museum of American Art at Champion, Stamford, Connecticut
1994 *Review of the Season,* Louis K. Meisel Gallery, New York
1996 *Paper Work,* Louis K. Meisel Gallery, New York
Attention to Detail, Louis K. Meisel Gallery, New York
1997 *Photorealism,* Jaffe Baker Gallery, Boca Raton, Florida
Photorealists, Savannah College of Art and Design, Savannah (catalog)
Landscape: The Pastoral to the Urban, The Center for Curatorial Studies Museum, Bard College, Annondale-on-Hudson

City Scapes: A Survey of Urban Landscape, Marlborough Gallery, New York
Photorealism's Greatest Hits, Louis K. Meisel Gallery, New York
1998 *Against the Grain: Contemporary Woodcuts,* Jim Kempner Fine Arts, New York
1999 *To Celebrate the South Carolina Aquarium,* Gibbes Museum of Art, Charleston (also Mobile Museum of Art, Alabama and Leigh Yawkey Woodson Art Museum, Wausau, Wisconsin) (catalog)
Radical Realism, McLean Project for the Arts, Emerson Gallery, Virginia

Collections:

Metropolitan Museum of Art, New York; Whitney Museum of American Art, New York; Museum of Modern Art, New York; Hirshhorn Museum and Sculpture Garden, Smithsonian Institution, Washington, D.C.; Art of Institute of Chicago; Toledo Museum of Art, Ohio; Centre Georges Pompidou, Paris; Kaiser Wilhelm Museum, Krefeld, West Germany; Teheran Museum of Contemporary Art, Iran; Neue Galerie der Stadt Aachen, Ludwig Collection, Aachen, West Germany; Museum of Contemporary Art, Chicago, Illinois; High Museum of Art, Atlanta, Georgia; Solomon R. Guggenheim Museum, New York; Erie Art Museum, Pennsylvania.

Publications:

By ESTES: Book—*Urban Landscape, Portfolio,* New York 1971. **Articles—**interview in ''The Photo-Realists: 12 Interviews'' in *Art in America* (New York), November/December 1972; ''The Real Estes,'' interview, with Herbert Raymond, in *Art and Artists* (London), August 1974. **Film—***Richard Estes: A Film Documentary,* Southwest Harbor 1998.

On ESTES: Books—*Richard Estes* by Lois Meisel, New York 1986; *Painting and Prints* by John Arthur, 1993. **Articles—**''Rent is the Only Reality: or, the Hotel Instead of the Hymns'' by Ivan Karp in *Arts Magazine* (New York), December 1971/January 1972; The Real Thing'' by Gerrit Henry in *Art International* (Lugano, Switzerland) Summer 1972; ''A Critic's Valedictory: The Americanization of Modern Art and Other Upheavals'' by John Canady in the *New York Times,* 8 August 1972; ''Pop-Art Inspired Objective Realism'' by Mary Lou Kelley in *Christian Science Monitor* (Boston), 1 April 1974; ''An Unnatural Silence'' by John Russell in the *New York Times,* 25 May 1974; ''Treacle and Trash'' by Barbara Rose in *New York Magazine,* 27 May 1974; ''Estes'' by Chris Hempbill in *Andy Warhol's Interview* (New York), October 1974; ''The Neutral Style'' by Edward Lucie-Smith in *Art and Artists* (London), August 1975; ''Photo-Realism: Post Modernist Illusionism'' by Linda Chase in *Art International* (Lugano Switzerland), March/April 1976; ''Realism Rules: O.K.?'' by Edward Lucie-Smith in *Art and Artists* (London), September 1976; ''Richard Estes: New York i Focus'' by Søren Elgaard in *Hrymfaxe,* vol. 25, no. 3, September 1995.

* * *

Superficially Richard Estes is seen as one of the new American hyper or photo-realists and, indeed, his imagery does parallel that of members of that movement. But, as is true for one or two other new realists, his is a far more painterly approach than that of the majority of artists so labelled. (The danger of just such labels is once again made evident.) One has only to look closely at a work by Estes to see how richly painted it is. The pigment is applied with considerable painterly elan, with virtuoso handling of the brush here and there—as seductive as touches in a Guardi or Vermeer. Just because Estes refers to photographs for pictorial information does not preclude his profound interest in composition, drawing, color and form.

This interest in picture-making has caused him to edit a great deal. In no way is he a slave to the images captured by his camera. He applies geometry to his compositions. And balances out his complex subjects through careful counterpointing of forms, color, tonality and line. He does a nice bit of spatial footwork as well—in and out, up and down—on the canvas plane. The movement is so overall that the pictures appear harmonious, even quiet, without remaining static or in any way inert. Estes deals with perspective, but plays around with it. Like one of Cezanne's typical tables with the edge starting at one place and coming out from behind a vase or pile of fruit at another, a street is shifted as it recedes making the viewer aware of space beyond whatever it is that comes between it and his perception of it. Estes' use of reflections accomplishes much the same thing: in one of his front-on store windows we become aware of what is *behind* us, outside of the painting altogether, through the multiple imagery recorded in the glass. In a painting where the store window is viewed from the side, we are given visual information about what's on the other side of the street. In a way it is all like three-dimensional tic-tac-toe.

Estes' interest in and use of buildings is akin to that of Sheeler and O'Keeffe in the 30s. Buildings are, after all, already abstract in their forms as are many man-made objects. Thus does a ''new realist'' redefine our ideals about the process of abstracting.

—Ralph Pomeroy

F

FABRO, Luciano

Nationality: Italian. **Born:** Turin, 20 November 1936. **Career:** Lives and works in Milan.

Individual Exhibitions:

1965 Vismara Arte Contemporanea, Milan
1967 Galleria Notizie, Turin
Teatro Stabile, Turin
1968 Qui Arte Contemporanea, Rome (with Jannis Kounellis and Giulio Paolini)
1969 Galleria Notizie, Turin
Galleria La Salita, Rome
Galleria Toselli, Milan
Galleria de Nieubourg, Milan
1970 Aktionstraum I, Munich
1971 Galleria Il Leone, Venice
Arte Borgogna, Milan
Galleria Notizie, Turin
1973 Arte Borgogna, Milan
Galleria Sperone Fischer, Rome
Modern Art Agency, Lucio Amelio, Naples
Salle Patino, Geneva
1974 Galleria Notizie, Turin
1975 Galleria Christian Stein, Turin
Galleria Pieroni, Pescara, Italy
Galleria Area, Florence
1976 Galleria del Cortile, Rome
1977 Framart Studio, Naples
1978 Galleria Il Collezionista, Rome
Galerie Paul Maenz, Cologne
1979 Galleria Mario Pieroni, Rome
1980 Galleria Christian Stein, Turin
Padiglione d'Art Contemporanea, Milan
Salvatore Ala Gallery, New York
1981 Museum Folkwang, Essen West Germany (travelled to the Museum Boymans-van-Beuningen, Rotterdam)
Galleria Mario Pieroni, Rome
1986 Galleria Christian Stein, Milan
1988 Galleria Christian Stein, Turin
Galleria Marion Pieroni, Rome
Palais des Beaux-Arts, Brussels
Kunstverein, Munich
1989 Galerie Micheline Szwajcer, Antwerp
Galerie Elisabeth Kaufmann, Basel
Castello di Rivoli, Turin
Museo di Capodimonte, Naples
Stein Galdstone Gallery, New York
1990 Fundació Joan Miró, Barcelona
Galleria Christian Stein, Milan
1991 Museo Casa Bianca, Malo, Italy
Kunstmuseum, Lucerne
Galleria Elisabeth Kaufmann, Basel
1992 San Francisco Museum of Art (catalog)
Galerie Durand-Dessert, Paris
1994 Galerie Micheline Szwajcer, Antwerp
Sisifo, Micheline Szwajcer Gallery, Antwerp
FabroNiOpera—Luciano Fabro, Palazzo Fabroni, Pistoia
Luciano Fabro: Sisyphus, Gegen Wartskunst Museum, Basel
1995 *Il Giorno mi pesa Sulla Notte,* Barbara Gladstone Gallery, New York
Portikus, Frankfurt am Main, Germany
1996 Centre Georges Pompidou, Paris, France
1997 Galleria Helia Oiticica, Rio de Janeiro, Brazil
Tate Gallery, London (catalog)

Selected Group Exhibitions:

1967 *Italian Contemporary Art,* Museum of Modern Art, Tokyo
1968 *Cento Opere d'Arte Italiana del Futurismo ad Ogge,* Galleria Nazionale d'Arte Moderna, Rome
1971 *New Italian Art 1953–1971,* Walker Art Gallery, Liverpool
1972 *Documenta 5* (and *Documenta 9,* 1992), Kassel, Germany
1975 *Bienal,* Sao Paulo
1979 *100 Anni d'Arte Italiana,* Museum of Art, Osaka, Japan
1980 *Kunst in Europa na '68,* Centrum voor Kunst en Cultuur, Ghent
1981 *Art Italien 1960–1980,* Centre Georges Pompidou, Paris
1985 *The European Iceberg,* Art Gallery of Ontario, Toronto
1993 *Biennale,* Venice
1995 ARS 95 Helsinki, Museum of Contemporary Art, Finland (catalog)
1996 *Dessins,* Centre Georges Pompidou, Paris
Contemporanea, Capo di Monte, Naples, Italy
1997 *Face A L'Histoire, 1933–1996,* Centre Georges Pompidou, Paris (catalog)
Arti et Amicitiae, Amsterdam, Netherlands
Venice Biennale (catalog)
1998 *Arte Italiana 1945–95,* Aichi Prefectural Museum of Art, Nagoya; Museum of Contemporary Art, Tokio; Yonoga City Museum of Art. Tottori; Hiroshima City Museum of Contemporary Art, Hiroshima

Collections:

Galleria Nazionale d'Arte Moderna, Rome; Galleria d'Arte Moderna, Turin; Castello di Rivoli, Turin; ARC 2, Paris; Centre Georges Pompidou, Paris; Museum of Modern Art, New York; Museum of Modern Art, San Francisco; Kunstmuseum, Lucerne; Art Gallery of Ontario, Toronto.

Publications:

By FABRO: Books—*Letture Parallele,* Milan 1973; *Letture Parallele II,* Geneva 1974; *Attaccapanni,* edited by A. Izzo, Naples 1977; *Attaccapanni,* Turin 1978; *Regole d'Arte,* Milan 1980. **Articles—** "Vorrei far rilevare" in *Lucio Fabro,* exhibition catalog, Milan 1965; "Sto trattendo contemporaneamente" in *Documenta 5,* exhibition catalog, Kassel, West Germany 1972; "Miracolo a Milano" with I.

Nagasawa, F. Torrello and A. A. Trotta, in *Data* (Milan), Spring 1975; ''Testi,'' with S. Vertone and J. de Sanna, in *Flash Art* (Milan), no. 72 / 73, 1977; ''Lucio Fabro ad Antoine Laurent Lavoisier'' in *La Citta di Riga II,* Pollenza, Italy 1977; ''Intervista con Lucio Fabro'' by L. L. Ponti in *Domus* (Milan), June 1977; ''Tempo tendenze paura dell Arte: Intervista con Lucio Fabro'' in *Domus* (Milan), no. 604, 1980.

On FABRO: Books—*Il Problema della Nascita delle Idee* by S. Ceccato, Milan 1965; *Arte Povera* by Germano Celant, Milan 1969; *Precronistoria 1966–69* by Germano Celant, Florence 1976; *Lucio Fabro* by B. Risso, Turin 1980; *Lucio Fabro,* exhibition catalog, Essen, Germany 1981; *Fabro: Works 1963–1986,* exhibition catalog, Edinburgh 1987; *Arte Povera* by Germano Celant, New York 1989; *Luciano Fabro,* exhibition catalog, San Francisco 1992. **Articles—** ''Luciano Fabro'' by Jole De Sanna in *Artforum,* January 1987; ''Luciano Fabro: The Image that Isn't There'' by Germano Celant in *Artforum,* October 1988; ''A Message from Luciano Fabro'' by Gay Morris in *Art in America,* March 1993.

* * *

The first we heard of Luciano Fabro was in May 1965, when the artist showed his ''elaborati'' for the first time in Milan, accompanied by a poetry recital. The working climate of those days was in line with the teaching of Piero Manzoni or Yves Klein; the aim was to define the work of the artist as a purely imaginative process, leaving to the materials the ordinary role of tangible residue of the process itself. This radical attitude, the shifting of interest from the object to the subject of the operation, was continued through Manzoni's and Klein's different development of Concept Art.

Fabro is more a follower of Lucio Fontana, through that artist's determination to abstract nothing from the recognizable values that can be inferred from the physical shape, the material and the logical relation with the environment. Fabro works with things; all his work aims to establish a relationship between thought and that irreducible element that the thing, with its ''encumbrances,'' opposes to it, according to a view opposite to that of, say, Malevich. The objects used by the artist are not the natural elements; his work does not shed light on the existential demand. Nor does his interest in the object mean the reappearance of the ready-made, or a return to representative art. Fabro constructs object-emblems which he offers as logical propositions relating to the dynamic investigation of the environment, using a factual technique that visualizes the structure of the object itself (*Hole, Round and Square, Wheel*). The work constitutes the topos which the logos originates (to use the artist's own terms), finding its proof in the effect made at the other pole, on the viewer.

Fabro is against ideologies; he is ready to criticize any component element in the organized teaching of art. The viewer is physically involved in bewildered sensory adventures (in *Cube, Theatrical Production,* 1966–1967) while the work emphasizes its inability to be reduced to ''interpretation.'' The tautologies are outside the dialectic, propositions approaching the irony of paradox, inhibitions of the creative act, neutralized, ambiguous events generated by a thought that aims to induce criticism of the conventions (*Contact,* 1967; *Object with Device to Reduce Its Weight, Sky,* 1968 . . .).

A similar ''debunking'' intention animates the works that Fabro carried out after the tautologies. The opposite of the conventions of ''elevated'' culture are the banal ideas of familiar shapes, the non-scientific value of common sense elements that Fabro makes use of by ''tripping them up,'' as he put it himself (see *Attacapanni,* Turin 1978). The discarding of logic is emphasized by a formal elaboration of the materials that sometimes approaches the limits of sumptuousness. Some of these works are intended as iconographic themes on which the artist insists by treating them as visual modules (the ''Italies,'' 1968–1975) or which he works out starting from recognition of their symbolic functions (*Feet,* 1971, *Iconographies,* 1975). These works are devised in the light of a memory of the classics and the myths, of what can perhaps be defined as the ontological dimension of the artist's research.

In such works, be they single or serial pieces, the image recalls subtle and profound notions that form the base layers of the collective imagination. The materials employed often underline, through combination and form, the metaphorical function conferred on the work, as in *Io* and *Tu* (1978), *Il Guidizio di Paride* (1979), or *Cristo-Buddha-Zaratustra* (1981). Matter is analysed for its autonomous, signifying potential, and is therefore exhibited in its raw state; at the same time, it is dealt with as a matrix of form through which the image emerges as the sign of a harmonic order forged from primordial or natural chaos—as in *La Dialettica* (1985), *Efeso* (1986), or in the numerous *Italia* pieces.

In recent years, Fabro has produced installations which physically involve the spectator, as in the case of *Baldacchino* (1980), *Enfasi* (1982 and 1983), right up to the enigmatic *Proteo* (1986).

—Giorgio Verzotti

FAVRO, Murray

Nationality: Canadian. **Born:** Huntsville, Ontario, 24 December 1940. **Education:** Beal Technical School, London, Ontario, 1958–64. **Career:** Independent artist, lives and works in London, Ontario. **Agent:** Christopher Cutts Gallery, 21 Morrow Avenue, Toronto, Ontario, Canada M6R 2H9.

Individual Exhibitions:

1968 20/20 Gallery, London, Ontario
Carmen Lamanna Gallery, Toronto
1971 Carmen Lamanna Gallery, Toronto
1972 *Country Road,* Carmen Lamanna Gallery, Toronto
1973 *Synthetic Lake,* Carmen Lamanna Gallery, Toronto
Forest City Gallery, London, Ontario
1974 London Public Gallery, Ontario
1975 *News,* Forest City Gallery, London, Ontario
1976 *Inventions,* Carmen Lamanna Gallery, Toronto
1977 *The Flying Flea,* Carmen Lamanna Gallery, Toronto
1978 Carmen Lamanna Gallery, Toronto
1980 Carmen Lamanna Gallery, Toronto
1981 Forest City Gallery, London, Ontario
1982 *18 Preparation Drawings to Construct a 55% Scaled Sabre Jet,* Whitewater Gallery, North Bay, Ontario
1983 Art Gallery of Ontario, Toronto (retrospective; toured Canada)
1991 *Murray Favro: The Guitars 1966–1989,* MacKenzie Art Gallery, Regina (catalog)
1994 Christopher Cutts Gallery, Toronto
1996 Christopher Cutts Gallery, Toronto
1998 Christopher Cutts Gallery, Toronto

Murray Favro, London Regional Art and Historical Museum, Ontario (also McIntosh Gallery, London, Ontario) (retospective) (catalog)

Selected Group Exhibitions:

1968 *Heart of London,* National Gallery of Canada, Ottawa (toured Canada)
1971 *Canadian National Exhibition,* Toronto
1973 *Canada Trajectories 73,* Musée d'Art Moderne, Paris
Boucherville, Montreal, Toronto, London, National Gallery of Art, Ottawa
1974 *Projekt '74,* Wallraf-Richartz Museum, Cologne
1975 *Carmen Lamanna Gallery at the Owens Art Gallery,* Mount Allison University, Sackville, New Brunswick
A Response to the Environment, Rutgers University Art Gallery, New Brunswick, New Jersey
1976 *Changing Visions: The Canadian Landscape,* Art Gallery of Ontario, Toronto
1977 *Another Dimension I & II,* National Gallery of Canada, Ottawa
1980 *10 Canadian Artists in the 1970s,* Art Gallery of Ontario, Toronto (toured Europe)
1994 *Christmas Show,* Christopher Cutts Gallery, Toronto
1995 *Chinese New Year Show,* Christopher Cutts Gallery, Toronto
1996 *Inaugural Exhibition at 21 Morrow Avenue,* Christopher Cutts Gallery, Toronto
1997 *Track Records,* Canadian Museum of Contemporary Photography, Ottawa
Works on Paper, Christopher Cutts Gallery, Toronto
1998 *Bealart: 80 Years of Experiment 1912–1992,* London Regional Art and Historical Museum, Ontario
Track Records: Trains and Contemporary Photography, Kerr Gallery, Calgary
Art Forum Berlin, Germany
1999 *Art Forum Berlin,* Germany
2000 *Toronto International Art Fair,* Canada

Collections:

National Gallery of Canada, Ottawa; Montreal Museum of Fine Arts, Montreal; Art Gallery of Ontario, Toronto; London Regional Art and Historical Museum, London; McIntosh Art Gallery, University of Western Ontario, London; Oakville Art Gallery, Oakville; Owens Art Gallery, Halifax; Transport Canada; Bell Canada; Carleton University Art Gallery; Winnipeg Art Gallery; Art Gallery of Windsor.

Publications:

By FAVRO: Articles—''Notes'' in *Region* (London, Ontario), Summer 1966; ''Ron Martin's Conclusions and Transfers at 20/20 Gallery'' in *20 Cents* (London, Ontario), September 1967; text in *Heart of London,* exhibition catalog, Ottawa 1968; ''Murray Favro's Journal'' in *20 Cents* (London, Ontario), December 1969.

On FAVRO: Books—*Realism: Emulsion and Omission,* exhibition catalog, by M. Kluyver-Cluysenaer, Kingston, Ontario 1972; *Canada Trajectories 73,* exhibition catalog, Paris 1973; *Boucherville, Montreal, Toronto, London,* exhibition catalog, Ottawa 1973; *Projekt '74,* exhibition catalog, Cologne 1974; *Murray Favro: Retrospective Exhibition,* catalog with texts by Mari Fleming, Michael Snow and Greg Curnoe, Toronto 1983. **Articles—**''Exhibit by 2 London Artists Draws Praise'' by Leonore Crawford in *London Free Press* (Ontario), December 1966; ''A New Regionalism'' by Ross Woodman in *Artscanada* (Toronto), August 1967; ''The Heart of London'' by G. James in *Vie des Arts* (Montreal), Winter 1968; ''Murray Favro, Carmen Lamanna Gallery'' by Gary Dault in *Artscanada* (Toronto), February 1969; ''Form-image Replicas: Murray Favro'' by K. Dewdney in *Artcanada* (Toronto), December 1973; ''Opening Doors'' by Roni Feinstein in *Art in America* (New York), November 1994; ''A Full Context for Self'' by James Campbell in *C Magazine,* Winter 1995; ''Favro Tracks the Feel of the Real'' by Christopher Hume in *Toronto Star* (Toronto), 14 March 1996; ''Reverie Track'' by Gary Michael Dault in *Border Crossing,* Summer 1996; ''Murray Favro: Auto Pilot'' by Bryne McLaughlin in *Canadian Art,* vol. 16, no. 1, Spring 1999.

* * *

Murray Favro's stance as guileless model-maker and inventor appears too playful to contain heroic ambitions. But appearances are only partial, and in truth Favro's wryly mock-primitive mechanistic investigations of natural phenomena or man-made things are a subtle strategy for posing profound questions about the nature of our contact with the world.

Favro traces the way he works to the influence of his brother, an innovative and versatile Mr. Fix-it, and to watching his ''Uncle Walter (full-time inventor) trying to perfect his power-developing machine (which never worked).'' From the latter, Favro recalls he ''learned to value the activity of an inventor regardless of whether his inventions were useful or worked properly.''

''Van Gogh's Room'' is one of a group of ''Projected Reconstructions'' which Favro began to make in 1970. These are made of a slide or film loop projected on an uncoloured three-dimensional mock-up of the subject matter of the slide or film, and thus constitute synthetic reconstructions of the physical world from its component sensory and material parts. Favro's first successful projected reconstruction was ''Still-Life (The Table),'' 1970, which consisted of a slide of a number of objects—books, boxes, a battery lying on a table top—projected onto a duplicate table top, its contents made of wood covered with canvas and painted white. The slide projector was angled from the same position as the camera which took the slide. Unexpectedly, the projected image and its reconstructed counterpart were not congruent, and in subsequent works Fabro learned to rebuild the objects to incorporate the distortions which arose from projecting onto three-dimensional objects. An especially elaborate ''projected reconstruction'' recreated an expansive external view looking down a country road with a parked car, a tree stump, plants and a cliff.

''Van Gogh's Room'' in at least three interrelated ways compounds the problem of the preceding works. It is a reconstruction, not of the real world, but of the work of art. It is a three-dimensional reconstruction of what was originally a flat image (which before that was based on physical reality). The slide image itself already incorporates distortions, so that a three-dimensional reconstruction of space and objects must be devised which will coincide with a projection of a ''subjective'' space rendered on a flat surface, further, if objectively, distorted in the projection itself because it is projected through various depths of space.

"Synthetic Lake," 1973, attempted to reconstruct actual natural motion by projecting a film of waves breaking on a beach onto an elaborate mechanical "wave machine" made from a hinged and roped wooden lattice-work construction whose slats rise and fall underneath a length of eight-foot-wide canvas moving to the even rhythm of a motor-driven, spiral fiberglass rotating shaft running the length of the machine.

Favro, of course, never achieves perfection in his constructions—and would rather not. The illusion always remains partial, and does so critically, so as to lay open the absurdity of this particular way of taking the world apart and putting it back together again. But if there are here metaphors at play which ultimately point to the entire gamut of disjunctions between experience and systematic knowledge, there is also an immediate inquisitiveness and fascination with things themselves and how they work or how they could work, provided the questions are cunning enough.

—Roald Nasgaard

FERRARA, Jackie

Nationality: American. **Born:** Detroit, Michigan, in 1929. **Career:** Independent sculptor and environmental design artist, New York, since 1970. **Member:** Policy, funding and planning panels for the National Endowment for the Arts, New York State Council on the Arts, The Bush Foundation, Ohio Arts Council, since 1977. **Awards:** New York State Council on the Arts grant, 1971, 1975; National Endowment for the Arts Grant, Washington, D.C., 1973, 1977, 1987; Guggenheim Foundation Grant, New York, 1976; Award for Excellence in Design, the Art Commission of the City of New York, 1988; Institute Honor, American Institute of Architects, 1990. **Agent:** Frederieke Taylor Gallery; 535 West 22 Street 6th Floor, New York, New York 10011. **Address:** c/o Max Protetch Gallery, 560 Broadway, New York, New York 10012, U.S.A.

Individual Exhibitions:

1973 A. M. Sachs Gallery, New York
1974 A. M. Sachs Gallery, New York
1975 Daniel Weinberg Gallery, San Francisco
Protetch-McIntosh Gallery, Washington, D.C.
Max Protetch Gallery, New York
1976 Max Protetch Gallery, New York
1977 Ohio State University, Columbus
1978 Minneapolis College of Art and Design
Max Protetch Gallery, New York
1979 University of Rhode Island, Kingston
Glen Hanson Gallery, Minneapolis
Max Protetch Gallery, New York
1980 Okun-Thomas Gallery, St. Louis
University of Massachusetts, Amherst
1981 Max Protetch Gallery, New York
University of Southern California, Los Angeles
Marianne Deson Gallery, Chicago
Laumeier International Sculpture Park, St. Louis
1982 Max Protetch Gallery, New York
Lowe Art Museum, Coral Gabels, Florida

Belvedere, 1988, cedar constructions/sculptures by Jackie Ferrara. Collection Walker Art Center, Minneapolis, Gift of the Butler Family Foundation, 1988.

1983 Lunds Gallerriet, Sweden
Janus Gallery, Los Angeles
University of North Carolina, Chapel Hill
Max Protetch Gallery, New York
1984 Susan Montezinos Gallery, Philadelphia
Max Protetch Gallery, New York
1987 San Antonio Art Institute, Texas
Moore College of Art, Philadelphia
1991 Michael Klein, Inc., New York
1992 *Jackie Ferrara Sculpture: A Retrospective,* John and Mable Ringling Museum of Art, Sarasota, Florida (traveled to Indianapolis Museum of Art) (catalog)
Museum of Art, Indianapolis
1994 *Wallworks & Tableworks,* Michael Klein Inc., New York
2000 Frederieke Taylor/TZ' Art, New York (retrospective)

Selected Group Exhibitions:

1972 *GEDOK American Woman Artist Show,* Kunsthaus, Hamburg
1973 *Biennial Exhibition,* Whitney Museum, New York
1974 *7 Sculptors,* Institute of Contemporary Art, Boston
1976 *New York-Downtown Manhattan: Soho,* Akademie der Kunst, Berlin
1979 *Biennial Exhibition,* Whitney Museum, New York
1980 *Drawings: The Pluralist Decade,* at the *Biennale,* Venice
1982 *Postminimalism,* Aldrich Museum of Contemporary Art, Ridgefield, Connecticut
1984 *Drawings by Sculptors,* Seagram Collection, New York (toured the United States)
1985 *Artists and Architects,* Cleveland Center for Contemporary Art, Ohio

1986 *Sculpture of the Eighties,* Queens Museum, Flushing, New York
1990 *First Tyne International Exhibition of Contemporary Art,* National Festival Garden, Newcastle-upon-Tyne, England
1996 *More Than Minimal: Feminism and Abstraction in the '70s,* Rose Art Museum, Brandeis University, Waltham (catalog)

Collections:

Museum of Modern Art, New York; Guggenheim Museum, New York; Whitney Museum, New York; Carnegie Institute, Pittsburgh; Cincinnati Art Museum, Ohio; High Museum of Art, Atlanta; St. Louis Art Museum, Missouri; Louisiana Museum, Humlebaek, Denmark; Stuart Collection, University of California, San Diego.

Permanent Public Installations:

Meeting Place, Seattle Convention Center; *Stone Court,* General Mills Sculpture Garden, Minneapolis; *Meeting Place,* Washington Convention and Trade Center, Seattle; Fulton County Government Center, Atlanta (with M. Paul Friedberg); *Hamm Plaza,* St. Paul, Minnesota; *Paths,* Greater Pittsburgh International Airport; *Lenox Park,* Silver Springs, Maryland; *Covered Walkway* and *Kiosk,* Lehman College, Bronx, New York; *Floor,* Massachusetts Institute of Technology, Cambridge; *Lap Pool and Bath House,* Coconut Grove, Florida (with William Bialosky); *Amphitheater* and *Seat Wall and Half Moon,* Los Angeles County Museum of Art; *Stepped Tower,* University of Minnesota, Minneapolis; *Baruch Benches,* Baruch College, New York; *Copper Tower,* University of Connecticut; *Flushing Bay Promenade,* Flushing Meadow Corona Park, Queens, New York; *Grand Central Arches, Towers, Pyramids,* Metropolitan Transportation Authority Arts for Transit, New York; *Canal Demonstration Project,* Phoenix, Arizona (with M. Paul Friedberg and Douglas Hollis).

Publications:

By FERRARA: Book—*Jackie Ferrara: Drawings, June and July 1977,* New York 1977. **Articles—**''Sculptors Talk on Art'' in *Women Artists News,* vol. 16–17, 1991–92.

On FERRARA: Books—*Jackie Ferrara,* exhibition catalog with text by Michael Klein, Amherst, Massachusetts 1980; *Jackie Ferrara: Benches, Thrones, and a Table,* exhibition catalog with text by Elsa Weiner Longhauser, Philadelphia 1987. **Articles—**review by Laurie Anderson in *Artforum* (New York) January 1974; review by Edit DeAk in *Art in America* (New York) March/April 1975; ''Jackie Ferrara: On the Cutting Edge of a New Sensibility'' by David Bourdon in *Arts Magazine* (New York) January 1976; review by Nancy Foote in *Artforum* (New York) January 1976; ''Jackie Ferrara: The Feathery Elevator'' by Robert Pincus-Witten in *Arts Magazine* (New York) November 1976; review by Jeff Perrone in *Artforum* (New York) January 1977; review by Robert Berlind in *Art in America* (New York) March/April 1979; ''Jackie Ferrara's II-lusions'' by Kate Linker in *Artforum* (New York) November 1979; ''Jackie Ferrara'' by Grace Glueck in the *New York Times* November 30, 1979; review by Richard Whelan in *Artnews* (New York) February 1980; ''Jackie Ferrara's Views from Stage'' by Shoichiro Higuchi in *Idea,* vol. 40, no. 231, March 1992; ''Jackie Ferrara'' by Judith Page in *Scultpure* (Washington, D.C.), vol. 16, January 1997.

*

My work is about: the process of building form; the space within and surrounding the form; responding to site and situation; a quality of timelessness, so there is no historical certainty.

—Jackie Ferrara

* * *

Jackie Ferrara is known for her ''Post-Minimalist'' wood pyramidal structures composed of variously stacked, horizontally layered ''steps.'' She has used this vocabulary and system of construction since the early 1970s to find multiple variations in a sequence of sculptures which admit quirky irregularities into a basically geometric and architectural pattern.

During the 1950s, Ferrara made ceramics and pottery in a primitivizing, crafty vein. By 1961 she was making small, Max Ernst-like works, and by the late 1960s she was creating fetishistic sculptures made from the type of hairy, raw flax which is used as packing material. These either hung from the ceiling or came up from the floor. What at first looked like weird heads became what she has described as ''tails'' and then turned into more abstracted but equally eccentric and metaphoric rope pieces. On the surface, there seems to be little connection between these earlier works and Ferrara's neater and cooler constructs of the 70s. There is, however, a connection in the continual development of an idiosyncratic personalized approach and a finely honed craft sensibility which persist in her mature works. These tendencies enter into Ferrara's concerns with the building process and with meticulous care for craft and fastidious attention for precise detail. They also relate to Ferrara's choices of specific configurations that are a bit off from the geometrically precise.

Ferrara's works are consciously pre-planned, worked out in detail in gridded drawings, precisely showing the shape of the structure and sometimes also indicating the quality of the surface down to the texture and direction of the wood grain. On one hand, the pyramidal stacks are extremely neat, clean, clear and simple, and on the other hand, they are informed by a individualized intellect, sensitized toward the hermetic and the ritualistic. The works show connections with a long-range cultural tradition, with the architecture of Egypt and Meso-America, and they are also strangely warped to change into something more irregularly hand made. The combined occurrences of slats and openings imply psychological readings involving inner and outer realms.

All of these elements add up to much more than the minimalist's concentration on literal presence and all-at-onceness. Along with others who matured around 1970, Ferrara refused the hard-nosed formalism of 60s Minimalism and used systems to build a morphology which suggests extra-art connections.

Until a few years ago, her work remained within the scale of sculpture despite its relationships with architectural antecedents. In 1979, Ferrara built ''Tower and Bridge for Castle Clinton,'' a more architecturally scaled piece with site-specified qualities. Composed of two rectangular structures made by stacking cedar two-by-fours, the work was placed in the court of the almost circular early American fortress located in Battery Park in Lower Manhattan. It bears resemblances both to log cabins and to Indian tepees, constructs particularly harmonious in their setting. Access into "Tower and Bridge" adds another interior space to the site. Ferrara has since completed numerous site-specific public commissions such as *Meeting Place,* a stepped plaza set into a hillside, which she designed for the Seattle Convention Center in 1989. These large-scale installations allow the viewer to actively experience the intervals and spatial topographies of Ferrara's work in full-scale. Other sculptural works remain on the scale of models or maquettes, objects of contemplation that force no less profound considerations of the spectator's relationship to space. These small works and Ferrara's larger sculptures have been given in recent years delicate stains of color, which articulate changes in their structural patterning, or operate at variance with the underlying form.

Despite its seemingly endless extrapolations of mathematic scale from the minute to the monumental, Ferrara's visionary towers, pyramids, and ziggurats appear human and eccentric. The artist's abstract conceptions are realized only through a process so labor-intensive as to be almost ritualistic, piece by small piece. As such, Ferrara's work reconfigures the relationship between logic and imagination in both artistic practice and the larger human environment.

—Essay by Barbara Cavaliere; updated by Dorothy Valakos

FERRER, Rafael

Nationality: American. **Born:** Santurce, Puerto Rico, 1933. **Education:** Staunton Military Academy, Virginia, 1948–51; Syracuse University, New York, 1951–52; University of Puerto Rico, Mayaquez, under E. Grannell, 1952–54. **Family:** Married Irene Alvarez in 1962; children: Theresa, Diego. **Career:** Worked as a drummer in a Latin band, Syracuse, 1951–52; visited Europe; associated with Surrealist group, Paris 1953; worked as a drummer in Spanish Harlem, New York, 1957; full-time painter from 1959; moved to Philadelphia, 1965; visited Germany, 1969, Amsterdam, Barcelona and Cologne, 1970, first Body Art exhibitions, Amsterdam, 1970. Instructor, Philadelphia College of Art, 1967, and School of Visual Arts, New York, 1977–79; Visiting Professor, Youngstown State University, Ohio, 1981; Visiting Professor, University of Pennsylvania, 1984–1989; Visiting Professor, Anderson Ranch Art Center, Snowmass, Colorado, 1990; Visiting Professor, Tyler School of Art, Elkins Park, Pennsylvania, 1992. **Awards:** Guggenheim Award, 1975; National Endowment for the Arts, Artist Fellowship, 1972, 1978, 1989; Pew Fellowship in the Arts, Fellow, 1993. **Agent:** c/o Nancy Hoffman Gallery, 429 West Broadway, New York, New York, 10012.

Individual Exhibitions:

1964 University of Puerto Rico Museum, Mayaquez
1966 Pan American Union, Washington, D.C.
1968 Leo Castelli Gallery, New York
1969 Galerie M. E. Thelen, Essen
Eastern Connecticut State College, Hartford
1970 Leo Castelli Gallery, New York
Galerie Mickery, Amsterdam
Philadelphia Museum of Art
Galerie M. E. Thelen, Cologne
University of Hartford, Connecticut
1971 University of Rhode Island Fine Art Center, Kingston
University of Pennsylvania, Philadelphia
Whitney Museum, New York
1972 Pasadena Museum of Art, California
1973 Contemporary Art Center, Cincinnati, Ohio
1974 Nancy Hoffman Gallery, New York
Museum of Modern Art, New York
1975 Nancy Hoffman Gallery, New York
1977 Albright-Knox Art Gallery, Buffalo, New York
Marianne Deson Gallery, Chicago
Galerie Dorothea Speyer, Paris
Fort Worth Art Museum, Texas
1978 Nancy Hoffman Gallery, New York
The New Gallery, Cleveland
1980 Hamilton Gallery of Contemporary Art, New York
Frumkin Struve Gallery, Chicago
1982 Nancy Hoffman Gallery, New York
1988 Nancy Hoffman Gallery, New York
1989 Nancy Hoffman Gallery, New York
1990 Nancy Hoffman Gallery, New York
Mangel Gallery, Philadelphia
1992 Nancy Hoffman Gallery, New York
1994 Marta Gutierrez Fine Arts, Key Biscane, Florida
Nancy Hoffman Gallery, New York
1995 *Drawing,* Nancy Hoffman Gallery, New York (catalog)
2000 Nancy Hoffman Gallery, New York

Selected Group Exhibitions:

1970 *Whitney Annual,* Whitney Museum, New York
1971 *Depth and Presence,* Corcoran Gallery, Washington, D.C.
1973 *Whitney Biennial,* Whitney Museum, New York
1977 *Drawings of the 70s,* Art Institute of Chicago
Narrative Arts, Contemporary Art Museum, Houston
A View of a Decade, Museum of Contemporary Art, Chicago
1978 *Private Myths,* Queens Museum, New York
Masks, Tents, Vessels, Talismans, Institute of Contemporary Art, Philadelphia
1980 *The Pluralist Decade: Venice Biennale,* Institute of Contemporary Art, Philadelphia
1994 *Collector's Exhibition,* Arkansas Arts Center, Little Rock
46th Annual Academy Purchase Exhibition, American Academy of Arts and Letters, New York
1995 *Pennart,* Myerson Hall Galleries, University of Pennsylvania, Philadelphia
American Art Today: Night Paintings, The Art Museum at Florida International Museum, Miami (catalog)
Collector's Choice, Center for the Arts, Vero Beach, Florida
Collector's Show, The Arkansas Arts Center, Little Rock
1996 *Large Drawings and Objects: Expressive Voices of the Meaningful,* Arkansas Arts Center, Little Rock (catalog)
Latin Viewpoints: Into the Mainstream of Art, Nassau County Museum of Art, Roslyn Harbor, New York
Modern and Contemporary Art of the Dominican Republic, The Spanish Institute, New York
The Boat, Object and Metaphor, Pratt Institute, Pratt Manhattan and Schafler Gallery, Brooklyn

Collections:

Metropolitan Museum of Art, New York; Whitney Museum, New York; Museum of Modern Art, New York; Albright-Knox Art Gallery, Buffalo, New York; Philadelphia Museum of Art; Museum of Contemporary Art, Chicago; Lehmbruck Museum, Duisburg, West Germany; Museo de Art Moderno, Bogota, Columbia; Museo de Ponce, Puerto Rico; The Ackland Art Museum, Chapel Hill, North Carolina; Baltimore Museum of Art, Maryland; Butler Institute of American Art, Youngstown, Ohio; Denver Art Museum.

Publications:

By FERRER: Book—*Deseo: An Autobiography,* Cincinnati, Ohio 1973. **Article—**''Rafael Ferrer: An Interview,'' with Stephen Prokopoff, in *Art and Artists* (London), April 1972; essay in *Drawing,* exhibition catalog, New York, Nancy Hoffman gallery 1995; ''Rafael Ferrer'' in *Art Press Special Issue,* no. 17, 1996.

On FERRER: Articles—''New York: Rafael Ferrer, Leo Castelli Gallery'' by B. Vinklers in *Art International* (Lugano, Switzerland), March 1970; ''A Different Drummer'' by K. Levin in *Artnews* (New York), December 1971; ''New York: Rafael Ferrer, Whitney Museum'' by Kenneth Baker in *Artforum* (New York), March 1972; ''Rafael Ferrer'' by J. L. Dunham in *Artweek* (Oakland, California), November 1974; ''Ferrer's Sun and Shade'' by Carter Ratcliff in *Art in America* (New York), March 1980; ''Rafael Ferrer'' by Hearne Pardee in *Art News,* vol. 94, November 1995; ''Neurotic Imperatives: Contemporary Art from Puerto Rico'' by Marimar Benitez in *Art Journal,* vol. 57, no. 4, Winter 1998.

* * *

Rafael Ferrer's art has been a continuing attempt both to resolve his inherent sense of visual expression away from the Hispanic-American modernist tradition—surreal-expressionism—and incorporate more North American style. As well, Ferrer's entire career can be taken as a concerted effort to see how far the vein of primitivizing modernism might be stretched. In order to accomplish these ostensible aims, Ferrer—who is essentially self-taught after an earlier career as a professional musician—has formed, from the fragments of the abstract and anti-form traditions of the 1960s, his own humane and often poignant art.

He first came to prominence during the heady years and culmination of the protean inventiveness of the late 1960s. As an acquaintance of Morris, Serra, Italo Scanga, and others of similar inclination, Ferrer naturally participated in the free-form, ''Process art'' orientation of that moment. And thus he manipulated in free and non-referential patterns, such materials as grease, hay, ice, corrugated metal, and wooden poles, in transient installations. Perhaps his decisive insight was his understanding of the oddly clear Romantic possibilities inherent in the interaction of these natural industrial products, should a more clearly thematic element be introduced into the installations. Ferrer accomplished this within an archeo-anthropological frame—in this akin to artists of quite distinct stylistic bent, such as Jud Fine and Charles Simonds. And so specific geographic place names became the titles of his environmental groupings—Celebes; Patagonia; Sudan. The poignance of such names, often given as neon signs in darkened interiors, was supported by the intensity of the ensemble which typically included kayak-like boats, explorers' equipment and furniture—all assembled raggedly by Ferrer; exotic groupings of animal skins and over-painted printed maps, and the well-known masks of human heads drawn on brown paper bags; and the equally well-known sewn-canvas, hanging, tent-like structures. Whatever calligraphic marking or drawing occurred on these surfaces was rendered with high naivete.

Since 1978, Ferrer has produced no installations, and instead has turned exclusively to easel painting. Nonetheless, the heroic adventurer aura which overlaid those earlier works can still be felt even though Ferrer's subject matter is predominantly contemporary life in Puerto Rico. Sexuality has been pervasive, with many images featuring naked women, at times mysteriously tangential to the other action. (One of Ferrer's ongoing fantasies centers upon the interaction of two unclothed women observed by others.) He seems to present an elemental ''Paradisical'' world, and it has been observed that his paintings apparently challenge Puritanical tradition.

Unlike his work of the 1970s, Ferrer has evolved his representational style beyond mere naiveté in a figurative and spatially coherent art. He has used a variety of photographic source material as an access to posture and psychology in figures and scenic views, often collaging together the cut-outs as working supports for the larger paintings. More recent work has moved toward direct observation in an attempt to achieve a more fluid poetic atmosphere and perhaps to create his distinctive sensuality through a study of the literal effects of light, color and texture.

It may be that Ferrer's continuing personal triumph lies in his knack for hiding his pictorial knowledge and control within his outwardly free-seeming and unmeditated expressivity: that faux naive aura so false and affected when found in other artists. Like Jacob Lawrence and William Johnson, Ferrer has for some time—from the installation period until the present—made perhaps a self-conscious effort, via his idiom of seemingly unself-conscious immediacy, to communicate with those he depicts, if not with others equally far removed from the art world.

And so it is that his richly compassionate art, filled only then with pictorial guile, has been warmly received by the wide-ranging critical community and art audience in New York City, as if in appreciation for Ferrer's continuing modernist hopefulness. Utterly artful when looked at closely, Ferrer's images can be seen as filled with a working knowledge of Western art—from ancient Cycladic to Munch; from Matisse and Gauguin; from Hartley to Alex Katz, and many more. In his recent exhibitions Ferrer made such attachments clear in a series of small gouaches and large paintings which celebrated the studios of artists powerfully influential in his career: Giacometti, Lam, and David Smith. Earlier in the decade, large drawings of Lam had prefigured the later works. With such images, Ferrar removed himself from his perennial focus upon the Caribbean which had lasted into the first years of the 1990s. Those paintings, from photographs and drawings made in Dominican Republic where the artist had for long lived half the year, already displayed a break with Ferrer's long held approach to his tropical subject matter. Although dark, they had let go of the sensuality and the action, if not as well the violence that characterized the tropical work of the 1980s decade.

If there was a prevailing nostaglia about the work through the last decade, it came to clear view in 90 works on paper gathered together from the previous 25 years. For that 1995 exhibit, Ferrer himself wrote a lengthy memoir for the gallery brochure.

—Joshua Kind

FETTING, Rainer

Nationality: German. **Born:** Wilhelmshaven, West Germany, in 1949. **Education:** Attended schools in Wilhelmshaven, 1959–66; apprentice journeyman carpenter, working in theatres, 1968–72; studied painting at the State Academy of Art, West Berlin 1972–76. **Career:** Painter, lives and works in Berlin and New York; also filmmaker, since 1975: founder, with Helmut Middendorf, Salomé and Bernd Zimmer, Galerie am Moritzplatz artists' co-op, West Berlin, 1977. Lives in Berlin-Kreuzberg. **Awards:** D.A.A.D. Scholarship, Berlin, to New York, 1978–79. **Agents:** Galerie Silvia Menzel, Kurfurstendamm 195, 1000 Berlin 15; Galerie Raab, Potsdamer Strasse 58, Berlin-Tiergarten (am Kulturforum), D-10785, Germany.

Individual Exhibitions:

1977 Galerie am Moritzplatz, West Berlin
1978 Galerie am Moritzplatz, West Berlin
1979 Interni Galerie, West Berlin (with Bernd Zimmer and Helmut Middendorf)
1981 Anthony D'Offay Gallery, London
Mary Boone Gallery, New York (with Helmut Middendorf)
Galerie Bruno Bischofberger, Zurich
Mary Boone Gallery, New York
1982 Anthony D'Offay Gallery, London
1983 Studio Cannaviello, Milan
Galerie Yvon Lambert, Paris
Galerie Silvia Menzel, West Berlin
Galerie Raab, West Berlin
Galerie Helen van der Meij, Amsterdam
Galerie 5, Stockholm
Galerie Maier-Hahn, Dusseldorf
CAPC/Musee d'Art Contemporain, Bordeaux, France (with Salome and Castelli)
1984 Marlborough Gallery, New York
Galerie Raab, West Berlin
1985 Galerie Daniel Templon, Paris
Galerie Raab, West Berlin
Galerie Thomas, Munich
1986 Museum Folkwang, Essen, West Germany
Kunsthalle, West Berlin
Studio Cannaviello, Milan
Gallery Paule Anglim, San Francisco
Marlborough Gallery, New York
Kunsthalle, Basel
1994 *Rainer Fetting: Paintings and Works on Paper,* Grace Borgenicht Gallery, New York (catalog)
1995 *4 x Fetting,* Stadtgalerie im Elbeforum, Germany (catalog)
Schim Kunsthalle, Frankfurt am Main
Berlinische Galerie, Berlin
Museum der Bildenden Künste, Leipzig
Staatliches Russisches Museum, St. Petersburg
1996 Museum Würth, Günzelsau-Gaisbach
Schloss Charlottenborg, Copenhagen
Museum of Contemporary Art, Tokyo
Willy Brandt Skulptur für Neue SPD Zentrale, Berlin
Willy Brandt: Die Skulptur von Rainer Fetting, Galerie Tammen & Busch, Berlin (catalog)
1997 National Arts Center, Moscow
Museum Würth, Künzelsau
Georg-Kolbe-Museum, Berlin
Kunstverein Eislingen
Kunsthalle Wilhelmshaven
1999 *Self Portraits 1973–1988,* Neuer Berliner Kunstverein, Berlin (catalog)
Fifty Years, Galerie Peter Borchardt, Hamburg (catalog)
Berlinische Galerie, Berlin
Galerie Michael Schultz, Berlin
2000 *New Pictures—New Sculptures,* Galerie Karl Pfefferle, Munich

Selected Group Exhibitions:

1977 *Die zwanziger Jahre,* Hochschule der Künste, West Berlin
1978 *Photographien,* Galerie am Moritzplatz, West Berlin
1980 *Heftige Malerei,* Haus am Waldsee, West Berlin
1981 *Après le Classicisme,* Musée d'Art et d'Industrie, St.-Etienne, France
A New Spirit in Painting, Royal Academy of Arts, London
1982 *10 Judge Kunstler aus Deutschland,* Museum Folkwang, Essen
1984 *The European Attack,* Galerie Barbara Farber, Amsterdam
1985 *Moritzplatz,* Kunstverein, Bonn
1987 *Berlinart 1961–87,* Museum of Modern Art, New York (travelled to San Francisco)
1994 *Neue Wilde aus Berlin,* Holsteinisches Landesmuseum, Schleswig (catalog)
1997 *Violent Painting,* Museum Wurth, Kunzelsau-Gaisbach, Germany (catalog)
1998 *Luciano Castelli, Rainer Fetting,* Musée Edgar Mélik, Cabriès (catalog)

Publications:

By FETTING: Article—interview with Stefan Koldehoff and Heiz Peter Schwerfel in *ART: Das Kunstmagazin,* no. 3, March 1999. **Films**—several short films, 1975–79; *Geburstag 76,* 1976; *R. und s. in B.,* 1977; *Brooklyn 11238,* 1978–79.

On FETTING: Books—*Im Westen nicht Neues,* exhibition catalog, with text by Martin Kunz, Lucerne 1981; *10 Junge Kunstler aus Deutschland,* exhibition catalog, with text by Zdenek Felix, Essen 1982; *12 Kunsler aus Deutschland,* exhibition catalog, with text by Jean-Christophe Ammann, Basel 1982; *Rainer Fetting,* exhibition catalog, by Anne Seymour, London 1982; *Rainer Fetting,* exhibition catalog with text by Norman Rosenthal, New York 1986; *Rainer Fetting,* exhibition catalog with texts by Jean-Christophe Ammann, Zdenek Felix and others, Basel 1986. **Articles**—''Rainer Fetting'' by Silvio R. Baviera in *Du,* no. 1, January 1994; ''Rainer Fetting'' by Ingo Arend in *Kunstforum International,* no. 130, May/July 1995; ''Rainer Fetting'' by Flora Fischer in *Art News,* vol. 94, December 1995.

* * *

From the 1940s through the 1960s, as the abstract painters of Europe and America were perfecting the modernist aesthetic, they chose jazz as their soundtrack. The music represented for them a new kind of virtuosity, a sophisticated handling of abstract forms, and an affinity for what they perceived as the primal force of African American artistic expression. Since the 1970s, however, rock music has had an increasing influence on visual culture. The rhythms, comparatively more urgent and repetitious, the appeal to youth, and, above all, the explicit and implicit sexuality of rock have inspired painters to seek out new forms in their quest for personal expression.

"If I had studied guitar," Rainer Fetting has said, "today I would be a rock star." Fetting profited from the rock and punk playing on Berlin radio at the start of his career, applying its immediacy to his already sure capability with Germany's expressionist tradition (his palette, meanwhile, derived from the Fauves). Where the German expressionists from earlier in the century attempted to render such predicaments as alienation, angst, and ennui in general terms, to emphasize their universal character, Fetting situates the human drama in specific locales, often night clubs and public bathrooms. His "Shower" series focuses on sexual relations between men in community bath houses.

Because of rock's sometimes macho posturing and the bombast that often accompanies the music, people often overlook its confessional side. Rock music relies more on the songwriters' personal lives than do popular styles of the past, and as a result much light is shed on the comparatively grimmer and grittier urban settings where it tends to flourish. Fetting, similarly, chronicles in paint and on film his own relationships and exploits. His friends and fellow artists often make appearances in paintings. Fetting has indicated that he admires the English duo Gilbert and George for making their personal lives a crucial element of their art.

Fetting and his friends, Helmut Middendorf, Bernd Zimmer, and Salomé (né Wolfgang Cielarz) were young punks who founded an artistic community in the Kreuzberg district of Berlin in the late 1970s and developed a loosely defined movement, *heftige malerei,* or "violent painting." Where Salomé portrayed transvestites and the others painted other unconventional and marginal subjects, Fetting distinguished himself by his obsession with Vincent van Gogh. Relocating Gogh to contemporary surroundings, he strenuously asserts his identification with the expressionist master in both his life and his art.

Fetting further distanced himself from his Berlin contemporaries by moving to New York in 1983. The move resulted in a more symbolic and mythic presentation of his concerns: He envisions New York as a city populated by wolves and fish. *Empire Fish* (1989) shows two giant fish in front of the city's most famous building. The fish appear to be fighting—or else they are dancing to a particularly brutal rock song.

—Mark Swartz

FILLIOU, Robert

Nationality: French. **Born:** Sauve, Garde, 17 January 1926. **Education:** Lycee d'Ales, Gard, 1938–44; studied economics and science, University of California, Los Angeles, 1948–51, M.A. 1951; self-taught in art from 1950. **Military Service:** Served in the French Resistance, 1944–45. **Family:** Married Marianne Staffeldt in 1967; children: Bruce and Marcelle. **Career:** Worked for the United Nations Korean Reconstruction Agency, Seoul, 1952–54; independent playwright, in Cairo, Barcelona, Copenhagen, London and Paris, 1954–60. Independent artist since 1960: action-poetry performances, from 1960; 'Galerie Legitimate' events, from 1962; associated with Fluxus artists, from 1962; worked with Emmett Williams, 1962–65; La Cedille qui Sourit and Eternal Network projects, with George Brecht, from 1965; Poupoidrome works, with Joachim Pfeufer, 1963 and 1975–78; Genial Republic works, 1971–73. Artist-in-Residence, Akademie fur bildenden Kunste, Hamburg, 1982–83. **Awards:** DAAD fellowship, West Berlin, 1974; Arts Council of Canada grants, 1977, 1979, 1980. **Died:** 2 December 1987.

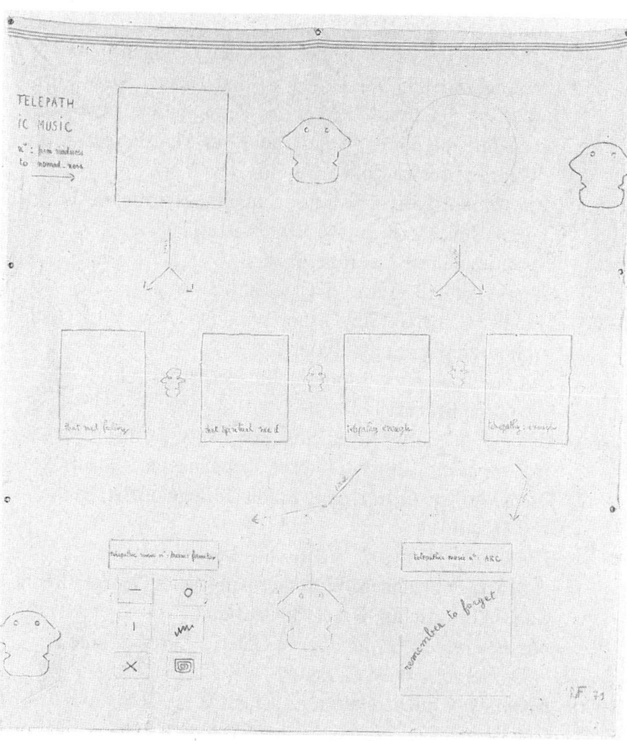

Robert Filliou, ©Marianne Filliou: *Telepathic music no: from madness to nomad-ness,* 1979. ©CNAC/MNAM/Dist. Réunion des Musées Nationaux/ Art Resource, NY; courtesy of Musee National d'Art Moderne, Centre Georges Pompidou, Paris, France.

Individual Exhibitions:

1960 *Performace Piece,* several locations, Paris (with Peter Cohen)

1961 *Poi-Poi,* Koepcke, Copenhagen
A 53 Kilos Poem, Lille Kirkestrade no. 1, Copenhagen

1962 *Galerie Legitime,* street event, in Paris, Frankfurt and London
Pere Lachaise no. 2, Librairie-Galerie Le Fleuve, Paris
13 Ways to Use Emmett Williams' Skull, street event, Paris (with Emmett Williams)

1963 *Poem Collectif,* Musee de la Ville, Arras, France (with Emmett Williams)
Le Poipoidrome, Liege, Belgium (with Joachim Pfeufer)
Au Comptoir, Galerie Raymond Cordier, Paris (with Emmett Williams)
Whispered Art History for a Jukebox, Kunstbiblioteket, Copenhagen

1964 *Soumission au Possible,* Cafe Theatre de la Vieille Grille, Paris

Platitudes en Relief, Galerie J., Paris (with Daniel Spoerri; travelled to Galerie Rudolf Zwirner, Cologne)

1965 *Streetfighting Singing Sade,* East End Theater, New York
Key Event, East End Theater and Penn Station, New York
La Cedille qui Sourit, Villefranche-sur-Mer, France (with George Brecht) Cafe a Go-Go, New York

1966 *Exposition Intuitive,* Galerie Jacqueline Ranson, Paris
Galerie Renee Ziegler, Zurich, Switzerland
Librairie-Galerie La Hune, Paris
Galerie Aktuell, Berne, Switzerland

1967 *The Key to Art,* Tiffany's shop windows, New York (with photographer Scott Hyde)
The Poetic Science, Moderna Museet, Stockholm (with George Brecht)

1968 Galerie Hansjorg Mayer, Stuttgart, West Germany
Streetfighting, Kunsbiblioteket, Copenhagen

1969 *Leeds: A New Card Game,* Royal College of Art, Leeds, England
The Eternal Network, Stadtisches Museum, Monchengladbach, West Germany (with George Brecht)
Galerie Handschin, Basel, Switzerland
The Principle of Equivalence, Galerie Alfred Schmela, Dusseldorf, West Germany

1970 *Commemor,* Neue Galerie, Aachen, West Germany
Galerie Michael Werner, Cologne, West Germany
Galerie Alfred Schmela, Dusseldorf, West Germany
Kabinett fur Aktuelle Kunst, Bremerhaven, West Germany

1971 Eat-Art Gallery, Dusseldorf, West Germany
Galerie Muller, Dusseldorf, West Germany
Galerie Michael Werner, Cologne, West Germany
Jount Works with . . ., Galerie Rene Block, West Berlin
15 Works for the 3rd Eye, Wide White Space Gallery, Antwerp, Belgium
Artiste d'Avril, Galerie BDDT, Nice, France
Research at the Stedelijk, Stedelijk Museum, Amsterdam

1972 *9 Weeks Research: The Genial Republic,* Wide White Space Gallery, Antwerp, Belgium
Galerie Alfred Schmela, Dusseldorf, West Germany
Gallery House, London
3 Samples of the Work of Robert Filliou, Galerie Magers, Bonn, West Germany

1973 *The Genial Republic: 9 Weeks of Futurology,* Galerie Alfred Schmela, Dusseldorf, West Germany
Galerie Roberto Medici, Solothurn, Switzerland
Recherche en Pre-Biologie, Galleria Multipla, Milan, Italy
Studio Ferrero, Nice, France
Galerie Buchholz, Munich, West Germany
Neue Berliner Kunstverein, West Berlin
Der 1000010 Geburstag der Kunst, Neue Galerie, Aachen, West Germany

1974 *Recherche sur le pas fait,* Galerie Bama, Paris
Erforschung des Ursprungs, Stadtische Kunsthalle, Dusseldorf, West Germany
The Act of God Act, Museum of Modern Legislation, Copenhagen

1975 *Recherchen sur l'Origine,* Kunstmuseum, Lucerne, Switzerland

1976 *Pantogrammes,* Galerie Handschin, Basel, Switzerland (with Andre Thomkins)
Telepathic Music, John Gibson Gallery, New York
Le Poipoidrome, Maison des Jeunes Artists, Budapest (with Joachim Pfeufer)
The Eternal Network, Galerie Bama, Paris

1977 *Le Poipoidrome,* Ecole d'Art, Nantes, France (with Joachim Pfeufer)
La Boutique Aberrante, Centre Georges Pompidou, Paris
Anton's, Calgary, Alberta
Western Front Society, Vancouver, British Columbia

1978 *Le Poipoidrome,* Reykjavik Art School, Iceland (with Joachim Pfeufer)
The Eternal Network, Partecipazione Arte Contemporanea, Genoa, Italy
La Fondation Poipoi, Centre Georges Pompidou, Paris (with Joachim Pfeufer)
Galerie Bama, Paris

1979 *Dessins sans Desseins,* Galerie Bama, Paris
Galerie Marika Malacorda, at *Art 10 '79,* Basel, Switzerland

1980 Musee d'Art Contemporain, Montreal, Quebec (with Ben Vautier and Dick Higgins)

1981 *Seeing on All Sides,* Galerie Catherine Issert, St. Paul de Vence, France
Galerie Bama, Paris

1982 Galleria Mercato del Sale, Milan, Italy
Galerie Marika Malacorda, Geneva, Switzerland

1983 Galerie Bama, Paris

1984 Sprengel-Museum, Hannover
Musee d'Art Moderne de la Ville, Paris

1985 Kunsthalle, Berne

1990 Galerie des Arnes, Musee d'Art Contemporain de Nimes, Carre d'Art, Nimes

1991 Centre National d'Art et de Culture Georges Pompidou, Paris
Kunsthalle, Basle
Kunstverein, Hamburg

1995 Morris and Helen Belkin Art Gallery, Vancouver

1998 Musee de Perigord, Perigueux

Selected Group Exhibitions:

1960 *Festival d'Art d'Avant-garde,* Palais des Expositions, Porte de Versailles, Paris

1962 *Festival of Misfits,* Gallery One, London

1965 *First World Congress: Happenings,* St. Mary's of the Harbor, New York

1970 *Happening and Fluxus,* Kolnischer Kunstverein, Cologne

1972 *Documenta 5,* Museum Fridericianum, Kassel, West Germany

1973 *Artists' Books,* Moore College of Art, Philadelphia

1977 *Bookworks,* Museum of Modern Art, New York

1979 *Fluxus and Chaos,* Espace Lyonnais d'Art Contemporain, Lyon, France

1982 *Fluxus 1962–1982,* Nassauischer Kunstverein, Wiesbaden, West Germany

1987 *Berlinart 1961–87,* Museum of Modern Art, New York (traveled to San Francisco)

1990 *Fluxus S.P.Q.R.,* Galleria Fontanella Borghese, Rome

1992 *Beuys, Brehmer, Cage, Filliou, Palk, Thomkins, Weiner, Williams 1985–86,* Ars Multiplicata, Surry Hills
1999 *The Museum as Muse: Artists Reflect,* Museum of Modern Art, New York (traveled to Museum of Contemporary Art, San Diego)

Collections:

Kaiser-Wilhelm Museum, Krefeld; Stadtisches Museum, Monchengladbach; Westfalischer Landasmuseum, Munster; Neue Galerie/Sammlung Ludwig, Aachen; Museum am Ostwall, Dortmund; Museum Moderner Kunst, Vienna; Centre Georges Pompidou/Musee National d'Art Moderne, Paris; Musee de la Ville de Toulon; Musee de la Ville de Calais.

Publications:

By FILLIOU: Books—*A Five Year Plan for the Reconstruction and Development of South Korea,* with Robert Nathan, New York 1953; *Ample Food for Stupid Thought,* New York 1965; *Je Disais a Marianne,* Basel 1965; *L'lmmortelle Mort du Monde,* New York 1967; *A Filliou Sampler,* New York 1967; *14 Songs and One Riddle,* Stuttgart 1968; *Teaching and Learning as Performance Arts,* with contributions by John Cage, Allan Kaprow, George Brecht and others, Cologne 1970; *A Thousand Japanese Poems,* Cologne 1970; *Le Siege des Idees,* with Edwige Regenwetter, Brussels 1977; *La Boite Futile,* Malmo 1978; *Je Meurs Trop,* Brussels 1979; *Musical Economy no.1,* Florence 1980; *A New Way to Blow Out Matches,* Malmo 1980; *Le Livre Etalon,* Reykjavik 1981.

On FILLIOU: Books—*Happenings, Fluxus, Pop Art, Nouveau Realisme,* edited by J. Becker and Wolf Vostell, Hamburg 1965; *Notations* by John Cage, New York 1969; *Happening and Fluxus,* exhibition catalog compiled by Hanna Sohm, Cologne 1970; *Mail Art: Communication a Distance, Concept* by Jean-Marc Poinsot, Paris 1971; *Fluxshoe,* exhibition catalog edited by David Mayor, Cullompton 1972; *Le Geste a la Parole* by Jacques Donguy, Paris 1981; *Fluxus 1962–1982,* exhibition catalog with texts by George Brecht, Ludwig Gosewitz, Geoffrey Hendricks and others, Wiesbaden 1982; *Robert Filliou,* exhibition catalog, Hannover 1984; *Robert Filliou,* exhibition catalog, Nimes, 1990; *Robert Filliou: From Political to Poetical Economy,* exhibition catalog, Vancouver, 1995. **Articles**—''From Madness to Nomadness'' by Claude Gintz in *Art in America,* vol. 73, June 1985; ''The Four Lives of Robert Filliou'' by Pierre Tilman in *Art Press* (Paris), no. 233, March 1998;''Robert Filliou: Poet'' by Alexander Braun in *Kunstforum International,* no. 140, April-June 1998; ''The Four Lives of Robert Filliou'' by Pierre Tilman in *Art Press,* no. 233, March 1998; ''How's Your Cow?: Musee d'art contemporain, Lyon,'' by Amanda Crabtree in *Art Monthly,* no. 242, December/January 2001.

* * *

The majority of contemporary artists in the West, while rejecting the traditional forms of art, have accepted the traditional role of the artist. That is to say, they see their products as being part of a continuous and historically legitimate process with its own internal logic and development. The artist will justify his work in terms of its relationship to work in the immediate past and his role, seen from this point of view, is to develop ''Art.''

As ''Art,'' in this sense, is a somewhat limited activity, with little or no interest to anyone outside the art world, contemporary Western art is prone to academicism and the art-for-art's-sake fallacy. It tends to lose contact with the other half of the creativity equation-life-and concentrate rather on essentially sterile problems of style.

Artists who have become aware of this have invented various strategies to overcome the huge gap that now separates art from life. One can catalog these strategies as Marxist, participatory, popular, anti-art and so on, although none of these has yet succeeded in evolving a convincing solution, as they all tend to rely upon the idea of bringing Art, as it is currently understood, to the people.

A more interesting and fertile approach can be found among those artists who, while retaining the idea that art is a metaphorical description of reality, have attacked the traditional role of the artists. Instead of trying to dilute contemporary art to a point where everybody can understand it, they defend the right to be ''difficult'' and self-indulgent, without claiming that anything they do has any relevance to contemporary art structures. Robert Filliou is one such artist.

Filliou's success has been based on failure. He has almost invariably failed to carry out any of the strategies he has invented to overcome what he considers to be the impossible position of the artist today. Faced with the problem of how to sell work and to make a living without being absorbed in the system of values, market prices and critical reputations, he invented ideas which could not possibly work: an art gallery in his hat, a shop that was never open, books which were too expensive to buy or in editions too small to make any impact. As a result he has retained an enigmatic position which has allowed him freedom to experiment in any direction he chooses without being pinned down by the art public's expectations (of course, though, it hasn't solved the problem of income).

Strategies such as the above are clearly ''absurd'' and reflect the principal influence upon his art: Zen. The Zen koan of the ''what is the sound of one hand clapping'' variety, or the ridiculous answers given by Zen patriarchs to the earnest questions of their pupils are designed to explode the accepted categories of language and meaning, thus clearing the mind for the entrance of intuitively understood truth. The absurdity is not the absurdity of despair, in the existentialist mode, but a destructive technique which is seen as a necessary preliminary to reconstruction.

In the Zen tradition, Filliou's work is not only absurd; it also contains its positive elements based upon an optimism about the potential creativity of all people (his piece in the Edinburgh/Dusseldorf show was actually created by visitors, Filliou providing the framework only in the form of a game without rules). But for everybody to be creative, we must first destroy the idea that only a small proportion of people, artists in fact, have the right to creation. Filliou argues that this elitist attitude is not due to the artists themselves but the structures that surround them, thus the absurd attacks upon the ideas of galleries and marketing.

Filliou has also taken from Zen the idea of delicacy. Where most artists with a social or political point to make galumph into the arena like elephants who think they have discovered the Secret of Life, he works silently, stating as little as possible. There is a sense of poetry in his work, the idea that concepts are better illustrated than described. For instance, he takes a sheet of those red spots that galleries use to indicate a sale and writes across the top, ''each morning wear a new brain in the centre of the forehead'' and signs it Robert Filliou, gaga-yogi, taoist de gauche. The idea came to him, he records, when he saw his wife slip into a pair of paper panties.

Possibly his best known images are the words ''innocence'' and ''imagination,'' often made in neon tubing and attached to objects or environments that one would not normally consider as having anything to do with Art: a tool box, for instance, or a garden shed. The results of such juxtapositions are mysterious and poetical, seeming to contain meaning yet resisting classification by the mind, just far enough within the boundaries of contemporary art to be recognized as such, but containing implications of a much more interesting territory beyond.

Because of his aesthetic of failure, Filliou will probably never achieve wide recognition in the orthodox art world. As most of his art is fragile and transitory in nature, it will not be found in the major art collections. I doubt if he would wish it otherwise, as this very elusiveness gives him a potency that would soon be lost in the glare of critical acclaim. He is one of those underground artists, the secret molders of the future, and when the history of 20th century art can be seen clearly, unaffected by market values, Filliou will emerge as one of the more important and honest artists of our time.

—Alastair Mackintosh

FINLAY, Ian Hamilton

Nationality: British. **Born:** Nassau, Bahamas, of Scottish parents, 28 October 1925. **Education:** Studied at Mackintosh's School of Art, Glasgow. **Family:** Married Susan Finlay; children: Eck and Ailie. **Career:** First short stories published, Edinburgh, 1961–66, Easter Ross, 1966–69, and Dunsyre, since 1969. First concrete poems, 1963; first graphic images, 1967. Founder, Society for the Protection of the Arts against the Arts Council, 1974, and Free Arts Society, 1978. **Awards:** Scottish Arts Council bursary, 1966, 1967, and 1968; Atlantic-Richfield Award, Boston, 1968. **Address:** Stonypath, Dunsyre, Carnwath, Lanarkshire, Scotland.

Individual Exhibitions:

1963 Ledlanet House, Fife, Scotland
1968 Axiom Gallery, London
1969 Pittencrieff House and Park, Dunfermline, Scotland
1970 Coelfriths Bookshop Gallery, Sunderland, County Durham
1971 Winchester College of Art, Hampshire
1972 Scottish National Gallery of Art, Edinburgh (travelled to the MacRobert Centre, University of Stirling, and Laing Art Gallery, Newcastle-upon-Tyne)
1974 National Maritime Museum, London
1975 Hamilton Technical College, Lanarkshire, Scotland
1976 Coracle Press, London
Graeme Murray Gallery, Edinburgh
Art Gallery, Civic Centre, Southampton, Hampshire
1977 Serpentine Gallery, London
Kettles Yard, Cambridge
1980 Graeme Murray Gallery, Edinburgh
Collins Exhibition Hall, University of Strathclyde, Scotland
1981 Graeme Murray Gallery, Edinburgh
1986 Aberdeen Art Gallery, Scotland
1987 Victoria Miro Gallery, London
ARC, Paris
1988 Claire Burrus Gallery, Paris
Galerie Jule Kewenig, Cologne
1990 Victoria Miro Gallery, London
Kunsthalle, Basel
Christine Burgin Gallery, New York
Graeme Murray Gallery, Edinburgh
1991 Graeme Murray Gallery at the Fruitmarket Gallery, Edinburgh
Wadsworth Athenaeum, Hartford, Connecticut
1992 Institute of Contemporary Arts, London (travelled to Henry Moore Centre for the Study of Sculpture, Leeds City Art Gallery; and Yorkshire Sculpture, West Bretton, Wakefield)
1993 *Wild Flowers,* Städtische Galerie im Lenbachhaus, Munich
1995 *Works, Pure and Political,* Deichtorhallen Hamburg (catalog)
1996 *Reef-Points,* Nolan/Eckman Gallery, New York (catalog)
1997 Nolan/Eckman Gallery, New York
Ian Hamilton Finlay: Prints 1963–1997, Museum am Ostwall, Dortmund, Germany (traveling exhibition)
1998 *Little Sparta,* National Galleries of Scotland, Edinburgh (catalog)
1999 *Variations on Several Themes,* Fundacio Joan Miro, Barcelona
A Posey: Selected Works by Ian Hamilton Finlay, National Gallery of Canada, Ottawa (catalog)

Selected Group Exhibitions:

1964 *Cambridge International Exhibition of Concrete Poetry*
1976 *Inscape: Works by Contemporary Scottish Artists,* Fruitmarket Gallery, Edinburgh
1978 *Exhibition of Concrete Poetry,* Battersea Art Centre, London
1982 *Inner Worlds,* E. M. Flint Gallery, Walsall, Staffordshire (toured the U. K., 1982–83)
1984 *The British Art Show,* City Art Gallery, Birmingham (and Ikon Gallery, Birmingham; travelled to Edinburgh, Sheffield, and Southampton)
1985 *Promenades,* Parc Lullin, Genthod, Geneva
1987 *Skulptur/Projeket/Munster,* Munster
1994 *East of Eden,* Museum Schloss Mosigkau, Dessau-Mosigkau, Germany
Translokation, Haus der Architektur, Graz (catalog)
1995 *Where is Abel, Thy Brother*?, Galeria Zacheta, Warsaw (catalog)
1996 *Public Works,* Van Abbemuseum, Eindhoven, Holland (catalog)

Perfect Unity: Sculptors and Living Forms 1990–1994, Laumeier Sculpture Park and Museum, St. Louis (catalog)

1997 *Wortwechsel,* Künstlerwerkstatt Münich, Munich (catalog)

Collections:

Tate Gallery, London; Towner Art Gallery, Eastbourne, Sussex; Gallery of Modern Art, Lodz, Poland; Kröller-Müller Museum, The Netherlands; The Stuart Collection, University of California, San Diego.

Publications:

By FINLAY: numerous cards and folding cards, poem/prints, published by Wild Hawthorn Press, Edinburgh/Easter Ross/Dunsyre, Scotland, since 1963, and numerous books and booklets, including *The Sea-Bed and Other Stories,* 1958; *The Weed Boat Masters Ticket, Preliminary Text, Part Two,* 1971; *Jibs,* 1972; *Poems to Family,[e],* 1973; *Butterflies,* 1973; *Exercise X,* 1974; *A Book,* 1977; *Heroic Emblems,* 1977; *The Boy's Alphabet Book,* 1977; *Woods and Seas,* 1979; *Romances, Emblems, Enigmas,* 1981; *3 Developments,* 1982; *A Celebration of the Grove,* 1984; *The Desmoulins Connection,* 1988; *The Ian Hamilton Finlay Printed Archive,* Richmond 1994; *Ian Hamilton Finlay,* Longhouse 1995; *Anthology,* with multiple authors, Edinburgh 1997; *Et in Arcadia Ego,* Den Haag 1999. **Articles:** interview with Paul Crowther in *Art & Design,* vol. 9, May/June 1994; interview with Nicholas Zurbrugg in *Art & Design,* vol. 10, November/December 1995; interview with Udo Weilacher in *Kunstforum International,* no. 146, July/August 1999.

On FINLAY: Books—*Ian Hamilton Finlay,* exhibition catalog, by Stephen Bann, Edinburgh 1972; *Ian Hamilton Finlay,* exhibition catalog, by Stephen Scobie, Southampton, Hampshire, 1976; *Ian Hamilton Finlay,* exhibition catalog, by Stephen Bann, London 1977 (includes bibliography); *Ian Hamilton Finlay* by Francis Edeline, Paris 1978; *Coincidence in the Work of Ian Hamilton Finlay,* exhibition publication by Christopher McIntosh, Edinburgh 1980; *Ian Hamilton Finlay: A Visual Primer* by Yves Abrioux, Edinburgh 1985, New York 1986; *Homage to Ian Hamilton Finlay,* exhibition catalog with essay by Yves Abrioux, London 1987; *Wood Notes Wild: Essays on the Poetry and Art of Ian Hamilton Finlay* by Alec Finlay, Edinburgh 1995; *Contemporary Sculpture in Scotland* by Andrew Patrizio, Sydney 1999. **Articles—**''A Forgotten Art: A Conversation with Ian Hamilton Finlay,'' by Everett Potter in *Arts Magazine,* September 1987; ''Neoclassical Rearmament: The Poetic-Philosophic Garden in Scotland Cultivated by Ian Hamilton Finlay,'' by Claude Gintz in *Art in America* (New York), February 1987; ''The Inscription in the Garden: Ian Hamilton Finlay and the Epigraphic Convention,'' by Stephen Bann in *Apollo,* August 1991; ''The Divided Meadows of Aphrodite,'' by Michael Archer in *Artforum,* November 1991; ''A Luton Arcadia: Ian Hamilton Finlay's Contribution to the English Neo-Classical Tradition,'' by Stephen Bann in *Journal of Garden History,* January/June 1993; ''Ian Hamilton Finlay's Garden'' by Anne Barclay Morgan in *Sculpture* (Washington, D.C.), vol. 13, January/February 1994; ''Ian Hamilton Finlay: Classicism, Piety and Nature (An Interview),'' by Paul Crowther in *Art and Design* (London), May/June 1994; ''Ian Hamilton Finlay'' by Wout Nierhoff in *Kunstforum International,* no. 132, November 95/January 96; '''Live Unknown': The Garden Art of Ian Hamilton Finlay'' by Stephen Bann in *Lotus International,* no. 88, 1996; ''O.M. Ungers and Ian Hamilton Finlay: Buildings Which Depict a Better World'' by Harry Gilonis in *Architecture Design* (London), vol. 67, July/August 1997; ''Dans la Lande Sculptée de Ian Hamilton Finlay'' by Jerome Coignard in *L'Oeil* (Lausanne), no. 489, October 1997; ''A Circumnavigation of Little Sparta: Portfolio of Photographs'' in *Art & Design,* vol. 12, November/December 1997; ''Ian Hamilton Finlay: Die Kraft des Wortes'' by Alexander Braun in *Kunstforum International,* no. 142, October/December 1998.

* * *

The Scottish poet Ian Hamilton Finlay has established himself as the major exponent of concrete poetry in the British Isles, producing work which has influenced many younger poets in the United States and Canada as well as Britain. But more recently he has moved on to produce his own unique and distinctive form of environmental art.

Concrete Poetry explores the common ground between poetry and painting by using words or letters as a graphic medium. It thus becomes a visual as well as a verbal art, because it is poetry in which the writer tries to give greater meaning to the words by forming them into a particular shape, either on the printed page or, in Finlay's case, often by laying them out on the ground, in for instance a garden, on a large scale.

Such ideas are far from being new, going back through Lewis Carroll's pictorial typography for the mouse's tale in the shape of a mouse's tail, to the egg-shaped poem written by the Greek poet Simmias around 300 B.C. But the modern rise of concrete poetry has its roots in the experiments of the Futurists and Dadaists.

Finlay's poems include all sorts of visual experiments. He too has in fact written a pear-shaped poem, made up of repetitions of the phrase ''au pair girl''—a sort of visual pun. In ''Acrobats'' the letters of this word arranged repeatedly in a rectangular shape become a sort of Op Art poem, with the word springing out across the various diagonals, like actual acrobats in a circus. The ''XM Poem'' is rather like Lewis Carroll's mouse tail, a Scottish stream swaying down the page, with different kinds of type suggesting the altering nature of the water as it flows. ''Pleur—pleut'' is a poem which by repetitions gives the effect of rain splashing down a window, so much so that it ends with a para-pluie to provide the reader with an umbrella. A collage made up of the poetic names of actual trawlers suggests, and almost becomes, a traditional sea lyric: Green Waters Blue Spray Grayfish etc.

The poem ''wave/rock,'' originally executed on glass, combines a picture of sea and rocks with the repeated letters of the word ''wave,'' which seem to move from left to right, where they come up against the massed letters of the word ''rock,'' thus successfully combining visual and verbal symbols. Finlay has also made a series of standing poems as well as large poem-constructions in glass and concrete. And he also makes effective use of colour to add another dimension or to emphasize an analogy, as in a poem made up of such simple elements as ''fish,'' ''nets,'' ''stars,'' ''night,'' where the actual words glow in yellow ink while the enclosing elements reach around them coloured in deep blue. Finlay has also sculpted words in neon.

In 1960 Finlay founded the Wild Hawthorn Press, producing his own highly individual prints and cards; and he also edits the magazine *P.O.T.H., Poor Old Tired Horse.* Such publication of his own work and that of many other experimental poets has made him an indispensable agent in the spreading and promotion of concrete poetry.

Finlay's more recent work has been a progressive elaboration of the environment around his Lanarkshire farm, Little Sparta. Inscriptions on carved stones, constructions such as sundials and weathercocks, or other alterations show the interaction of the poet with the landscape, so that in place of individual works this becomes a continuous form of permanent artistic activity in which the poet creates (and responds to) his own environment. Finlay's efforts at Little Sparta have met with considerable opposition from the Strathclyde Regional Council since the early 1980s. The Council objected to the artist's description (for ordinance and taxation purposes) of a built structure as a "garden temple." This essentially bureaucratic controversy has obscured the true significance of Finlay's project.

In addition to the ongoing work at Little Sparta, Finlay intervenes in urban environments as well. In 1990 he installed a monumental inscription from Plato's *Republic* on the Bridge Piers (stone blocks which once supported a railway bridge) in the center of Glasgow. He also works internationally, designing gardens and installations suited to the material and historical context of the particular environment. In 1989 the French government commissioned a garden from Finlay to commemorate the bicentennial of the French Revolution; the commission was withdrawn based upon the misinterpretation of certain forms in a 1987 work, "Osso," as anti-Semitic.

In Finlay's view the controversies surrounding the French commission and his work at Little Sparta point to a disturbing trend of moralizing secularization in contemporary society, a process he hopes to contend by breaking down divisions between the real and the idea, thereby revealing the lyricism in the world. Finlay has depicted many versions of his vision of arcadia, and he challenges his audience to do the same.

—Essay by Lavinia Learmont; updated by Britt Salvesen

FISCHL, Eric

Nationality: American. **Born:** New York City, 9 March 1948. **Education:** Studied at California Institute of Arts, Valencia, B.F.A. 1972. **Career:** Independent painter, in California, 1972–74, in Nova Scotia, 1974–78, and in New York, since 1978. Assistant professor, Nova Scotia College of Art and Design, Halifax, 1974–78. **Agent:** Mary Boone Gallery, 417 West Broadway, New York, New York 10012.

Individual Exhibitions:

1975 Dalhousie Art Gallery, Halifax, Nova Scotia
1976 Galerie B, Montreal
The Studio, Halifax, Nova Scotia
1978 Galerie B, Montreal
1980 Edward Thorp Gallery, New York
University of Akron, Ohio
1981 Edward Thorp Gallery, New York
Sable-Castelli Gallery, Toronto
1982 Edward Thorp Gallery, New York
Sable-Castelli Gallery, Toronto
University of Colorado, Boulder
1983 Larry Gagosian Gallery, Los Angeles
Galleria Mario Diacono, Rome
Multiples/Marian Goodman Gallery, New York
Nigel Greenwood Gallery, London
Saidye Bronfman Centre, Montreal
Concordia University, Montreal
1984 Mary Boone Gallery, New York
1985 Mendel Art Gallery, Saskatoon, Saskatchewan (travelled to Eindhoven, Basle, London, Toronto, Chicago and New York, 1985–86)
1986 California State University, Long Beach (travelled to Berkeley, Honolulu, Baltimore and St. Louis, 1986–87)
1987 Walker Art Center, Minneapolis (with Vernon Fisher and Laurie Simmons)
1989 *Eric Fischl: New Paintings,* Waddington Galleries, London (catalog)
1990 Walker Art Center, Minneapolis
Yale University Art Gallery, New Haven
Koury Wingate, New York
Eric Fischl: Paintings and Drawings, Musee Cantonal des Beaux-Arts, Lausanne, Switzerland (catalog)
1991 *Eric Fischl: Drawings,* Milwaukee Art Museum, Wisconsin (catalog)
Kunstmuseum, Aarhus, Denmark (catalog)
1992 Montgomery Museum of Fine Arts, Alabama
Center for Fine Arts, Miami
1993 Galeria Soledad Lorenzo, Madrid (catalog)
Mary Ryan Gallery, New York
Mary Boone Gallery, New York
1994 Galerie Daniel Templon, Paris
1996 Mary Boone Gallery, New York (catalog)
1998 *Eric Fischl: Sculpture,* Gagosian Gallery, New York (catalog)
1999 Mary Boone Gallery, New York
2000 Gagosian Gallery, London

Selected Group Exhibitions:

1975 *The Canadian Canvas,* Time Canada Ltd., Toronto
1976 *17 Artists: A Protean View,* Vancouver Art Gallery, British Columbia
1978 *Neun Kanadische Kunstler,* Kunsthalle, Basle
1979 *The Great Big Drawing Show,* Project Studio One, Queens, New York
1981 *The Reality of Perception,* Rutgers University, Newark, New Jersey
1982 *Focus on the Figure: Twenty Years,* Whitney Museum, New York 1984*Paradise Lost, Paradise Regained,* at the *Biennale,* Venice
1985 *The Allegorical Image in Recent Canadian Painting,* Agnes Etherington Art Centre, Kingston, Ontario

Eric Fischl: *Untitled,* 1992. ©Smithsonian American Art Museum, Washington, D.C./Art Resource, NY; courtesy of Smithsonian American Art Museum.

1987 *Avant Garde in the Eighties,* Los Angeles County Museum of Art

1988 *Contemporary American Art,* Sara Hilden Art Museum, Tampere, Finland (travelled to Oslo)

1991 Cleveland Center for Contemporary Art, Ohio

1992 *Four Friends: Eric Fischl, Ralph Gibson, April Gornik, Bryan Hunt,* Aldrich Museum of Contemporary Art, Ridgefield, Connecticut (catalog)

1994 *Printer,* Galerie Graff, Montreal (catalog)

1995 *A New York Time: Selected Drawings of the Eighties,* Bruce Museum, Greenwich, Connecticut

1997 *Singular Impressions: The Monotype in America,* National Museum of Art, Washington, D.C.

2000 *A Plurality of Truths,* Schick Art Gallery, Skidmore College, Saratoga Springs, New York (catalog)

Collections:

Museum of Modern Art, New York; Metropolitan Museum of Art, New York; Art Institute of Chicago; Museum of Contemporary Art, Los Angeles; Whitney Museum, New York; Des Moines Art Center, Iowa; De Menil Foundation, Houston; California State University, Long Beach; National Gallery of Canada, Ottawa.

Public Installations:

Arthur Ashe, Arthur Ashe Stadium, Queens, New York.

Publications:

By FISCHL: Books—*Eric Fischl: Bridge, Shield, Shelter,* exhibition catalog, Halifax 1975; *Sketchbook with Voices,* with Jerry Saltz, New York 1986; *Speak Art!: The Best of Bomb Magazine's Interviews with Artists* by Betsy Sussler, Suzan Sherman and Ronalde Shavers, New York 1997; *Eric Fischl, 1970–2000,* with Arthur Coleman Danto, New York 2000. **Articles—**''Eric Fischl'' in *Neun Kanadische Kunstler,* exhibition catalog, Basle 1978; ''Picasso: A Symposium'' in *Art in America* (New York), December 1980; ''Eric Fischl'' in *Impressions* (New York), Winter 1982; ''Figures and Fiction'' in *Aperture* (Millerton, New York), Winter 1985; ''The Man Who Exposes Himself to Women'' in *Normal* (Illinois), Summer 1987; interview with Tazmi Shinoda and Constance Lewallen in *View,* vol. 5, no. 5, Fall 1988; interview with Paul Cummings in *Drawing,* vol. 14, January/February 1993; interview with A. M. Homes in *Bomb,* no. 50, Winter 1994–1995; interview with Frederic Tuten in *Art in America* (New York), vol. 84, no. 11, November 1996; interview with Bruce Ferguson in *Art Press,* no. 191, May 1994; interview in *Art in America,* November 1996; interview with Frederic Tuten in *Art in America,* vol. 84, November 1996; ''The Pleasure of Their Company'' with Robert Enright in *Border Crossings,* vol. 19, no. 3, August 2000.

On FISCHL: Books—*Eric Fischl: Dessins,* exhibition catalog with text by Bruce W. Ferguson, Montreal 1983: *Eric Fischl: Birthday Boy* by Mario Diacono, Rome 1983; *Eric Fischl: Paintings,* exhibition catalog with texts by Sandra Paikowsky and Bruce W. Ferguson, Montreal 1983; *Eric Fischl: Paintings,* exhibition catalog with texts by J. C. Ammann, D. Kuspit and B. Ferguson, Saskatoon 1985; *Eric Fischl: Scenes before the Eyes,* exhibition catalog by Constance W. Glenn and Lucinda Barnes, Long Beach 1986; *Fischl* by Donald B. Kuspit, New York 1987; *Eric Fischl* by Peter Schjeldahl, New York 1988. **Articles—**''Portrait of the Artists: Eric Fischl and April Gornik on Long Island'' in *Architectural Digest* (Los Angeles), vol. 46, April 1989; ''Eric Fischl's Dream Screen'' by Richard S. Field in *American*

Eric Fischl: *Boaters,* ca. 1970s. ©Geoffrey Clements/Corbis.

Art, vol. 6, no. 4, Fall 1992; ''Fear and Desire: The Paintings of Eric Fischl'' in *ARTnews,* September 1994; ''Eric Fischl'' by Lilly Wei in *ArtNews,* September 1999; ''Eric Fischl at Mary Boone'' by Edward Leffingwell in *Art in America,* March 2001.

* * *

Eric Fischl's paintings reflect the suburban, middle-class cultural climate of contemporary America. His huge, figurative canvases depict popular suburban leisure subjects, e.g. beach scenes, swimming pools, picnics, and family outings. Other subjects disrupt the homogeneity of suburban culture by depicting images of interracial and homosexual encounters, and scenes from the artist's trips abroad. His characters, painted with a kind of unpleasant severity, seem alienated in spite of their apparent position of privilege. Having stated once that the best art in the United States derives from a crisis of American identity, Fischl's most striking work succeeds in revealing the rough underbelly of the American middle class.

That Fischl's characters seem neither particularly beautiful nor happy contradicts the expectation of pleasure to be derived from the activities in which they partake. In his paintings, leisure rituals such as sunbathing take on the quality of social habit, emptied of their emotional contents. In *Close Up,* 1982, five nude beach-goers crowd the canvas. Not one person makes eye contact with another, and their bland expressions reveal their boredom. One woman focuses the lens of her camera on an unidentifiable spot—possibly the knee of a reclining nude man. The sexuality is simultaneously overt and repressed, and the camera, presumably a tool for mediating relationships, represents a sort of alienated voyeurism.

A certain consistency of theme and context contributes to the narrative quality of Fischl's work. Several paintings involving the figure of a young adolescent boy contain an undercurrent of suppressed anger and sexual taboo. In *Sleepwalker,* 1979, a boy stands alone in a plastic kiddie pool, masturbating. In *Squirt,* 1982, a boy points a water pistol in the direction of a couple reclining at the beach, presumably his parents. In *Bad Boy,* 1981, a mother's genitals are exposed to her son as he steals from her purse. Though the physical appearance of the boy varies, each painting is a fragment of a greater story about adolescent rebellion and sexual awakening against a suburban middle-class backdrop.

A discussion of Fischl's painting style is essential to any debate about his work. Often deemed haphazard and careless, Fischl's earlier canvases contained large flat patches of color, hard color and light contrasts, imprecise figure outlines, and unsettling spatial dislocations. Though Fischl is now more optimistic about the role of painting in art, his earlier work reflects an ambivalence about painterly tradition, most likely influenced by the ''painting is dead'' ethos of the 1960s and 70s. In recent works, such as *Why the French Fear Americans,* 1992, and *Scene I,* 1994, the sense of light is softer and the colors more harmonious, thus presenting a contrast between style and subject characteristic of the artist's maturing sensibilities. The direct emotional edge once so recognizable in his earlier work appears in more his recent paintings of people engaged in leisure activities, but less so in the series about India, and the more recent *Scenes.*

Fischl improvised his earlier compositions directly on canvas without previous sketches, later moving on to use of the photograph as a pictorial source. Both techniques result in an ambiguous play between flatness and depth that undermines the naturalism achieved by traditional figurative painting. In contrast with modernists such as Cezanne, Fischl's pictorial strategy serves to shed light on his subjects, and to produce the effect of social discomfort and emotional uncertainty. In *Untitled,* 1992, the image is composed from what appears to be two separate photographs. The foreground figures look ''pasted on'' to the background scene. Fischl disturbs the viewer's sense of ''natural'' depth by dramatically varying the size of the foreground and background figures in relation to one another.

—Essay by Alicja Kepinska; updated by Audrey Mandelbaum

Over the course of his career, Fischl's work has shown a remarkably consistent vision. Many of his paintings still suggest a dark narrative that prompt a sense of discomfort, making viewers feel like they have stumbled upon something they shouldn't see.

In 1999, Fischl departed from his usual modus operandi and showed a body of work that used familiar subjects, rather than anonymous figures. In addition to a self-portrait, these paintings featured the actor Steve Martin, an avid collector of contemporary art; Fischl's dealer Mary Boone; and his wife, the painter April Gornik.

The following year, Fischl exhibited a group of large oil paintings whose titles all begin *The Bed, The Chair*, with additional words further describing the scene. These works show a single scene, in contrast to works of the past decade that split the canvas in half to show two different scenes concurrently. *The Bed, The Chair* series includes single or double figures, often nude, and makes dramatic use of shadow and light. The furniture almost becomes anthropomorphized, playing a role in the narrative along with the human figures.

—Tara Reddy Young

FISCHLI, Peter, and David WEISS

Nationality: Swiss. **Born:** Fischli: Zürich, 8 June 1952; Weiss: Zürich, 21 June 1946. **Education:** Fischli: Studied at Accademia di Belle Arti, Urbino, 1975–76; Accademia di Belle Arti, Bologna, 1976–77. Weiss: Vorkurs, Kunstgewerbeschule, Zürich, 1963–64; Kunstgewerbeschule Basel, Bildhauerklasse, 1964–65; studied sculpture with Alfred Gruber and Jaqueline Stieger. **Career:** Began working together in 1979.

Selected Joint Exhibitions:

1987 University Art Museum, Berkeley, California
List Visual Arts Center, Massachusetts Institute of Technology, Cambridge (catalog)
1988 The Museum of Contemporary Art, Los Angeles
Portikus, Frankfurt am Main (catalog)
1992 Musée National d'Art Moderne, Centre Georges Pompidou, Paris (catalog)
Siedlungen, Agglomeration, Kunsthalle, Zürich (catalog)
1994 Museum für Gegenwartskunst, Basel
Raum unter der Treppe, Museum für Moderne Kunst, Frankfurt am Main (catalog)
Portikus, Frankfurt am Main
Documenta VIII, Kassel
1995 Swiss Pavilion, XLVI Venice Biennale
Monika Sprüth Galerie, Cologne
Kölnischer Kunstverein, Cologne
1996 Institute of Contemporary Art, Philadelphia
Kunsthaus, Zürich
Galerie für Zeitgenössische Kunst, Leipzig
Serpentine Gallery, London
Peter Fischli and David Weiss: In a Restless World, San Francisco Museum of Modern Art, California, and Walker Art Center, Minneapolis (catalog)
1997 Saint-Gervais Galerie, Genèva
Institute of Contemporary Art, Boston
Centro d'Arte Contemporanea, Bellinzona
Dany Keller Galerie, Münich
San Francisco Museum of Modern Art, California
Städtische Galerie für Gegenwartskunst, Dresden
1998 Monika Sprüth Galerie, Cologne
White Cube-Jay Jopling, London
Galerie Hauser & Wirth, Zürich
Galerie Ghislaine Hussenot, Paris
Mary Boone Gallery, New York

Matthew Marks Gallery, New York
1999 James Cohan Gallery, New York
Friedrich Petzel Gallery, New York
Marianne Boesky Fine Art, New York
Chac Mool Gallery, Los Angeles
Matthew Marks Gallery, New York
ARC Musée d'Art Moderne de la Ville de Paris Paris
2000 *Visible World, Suddenly This Overview, Big Questions—Small Questions,* Museum of Contemporary Art, Basel
Zwirner & Wirth, New York
Sammlung Goetz, Münich (catalog)
Städtische Galerie Nordhorn, Nordhorn
James Cohan Gallery, New York
Bonakdar Jancou, New York
Dundee Contemporary Art, Dundee
Tate Modern, London

David Weiss Solo Exhibitions:

1976 Galerie Stähli, Zürich
1979 Galerie Gugu Ernesto, Cologne, and Galerie t'Venster, Rotterdam

Selected Group Exhibitions:

1984 *An International Survey of Recent Painting and Sculpture,* Museum of Modern Art, New York
1985 The Serpentine Gallery, London
1988 Video Installations, Institute of Contemporary Arts, London
1991 Metropolis International Art Exhibition, Martin-Gropius-Bau, Berlin
1992 Swiss Pavilion, World's Fair, Seville, Spain
1998 Kunsthaus, Zürich

Publications:

By FISCHLI and WEISS: Books—*Peter Fischli, David Weiss: Bilder, Ansichten,* Zürich 1991; *Sichtbare Welt,* Cologne 2000. **Video—***The Ways Things Go,* 1987.

By WEISS: Books—*Sketches,* Bern 1970; *Drei Geschichten,* Zürich 1974; *Up and Down Town,* Zürich 1975; *The Desert is Across the Street* (with Urs Lüthi and Elke Kilga), Zürich 1975.

On FISCHLI and WEISS: Books—*Lehrgeld: Zqanzig Künstler-Portraits* by Renate Puvogel, Oktagon 1995. **Articles—**''Masters of the Glum 'Eureka!''' by Carter Ratcliff in *Art in America,* January 1987; ''Collaboration Peter Fischli/David Weiss'' (special issue) in *Parkett* (Zürich), no. 17, 1988; ''Peter Fischli and David Weiss: *The Way Things Go*'' by Jerry Saltz in *Arts Magazine,* April 1988; ''Peter Fischli and David Weiss'' by Massimo Carboni in *Artforum,* January 1992; ''Through the Looking Glass, Darkly: Fischli/Weiss'' by Dan Cameron in *Artforum,* September 1992; ''Real Time Travel'' interview by Rirkrit Tiravanija in *Artforum,* Summer 1996; ''Suddenly It All Makes Sense'' by Virginia Rutledge in *Art in America,* June 1997.

* * *

Swiss artists Peter Fischli and David Weiss have collaborated since 1979, producing two interrelated strands of work: painstaking sculptural recreations of everyday objects, and deadpan photographic and video representations of the world around them. Like Marcel Duchamp's readymades of the 1910s, these works insert banal items into an art context. Unlike Duchamp, however, Fischli and Weiss are deeply invested in the perceptual and aesthetic qualities of these icons of ordinariness. Their sculptural work engages with late 20th-century debates on realism via Fluxus, Nouveau Réalisme, and Pop Art. Frequently shot in and around Zürich, their videos and photographs also reflect a fascination with the landscape, architecture, and lifestyle of their native Switzerland.

In their first joint project, ''Wurstserie'' of 1979, Fischli and Weiss produced whimsical photographic tableaux. Bits of carved and sliced sausage acted as cars, carpets, and mountaineers. The artists continued to explore these playful impulses throughout the 1980s, using a range of household objects as their protagonists. The 1984–85 photographic series ''Quiet Afternoon,'' sometimes known as ''The Equilibrium Series,'' features bottles, hammers, chairs, shoes, and ladders, balanced and counterbalanced against each other in assemblages with portentous, evocative titles such as ''Dark Impulse,'' ''Honor, Courage, Confidence,'' and ''Ben Hur'' (a saucepan chariot pulled by a spray can horse). As a climax of their use of actual household objects, the artists spent two years producing a 16mm film ''The Way Things Go'' (1985–87). The piece documents an elaborate continuous chain-reaction of objects in the studio, triggered by a Swiss cuckoo clock and fueled by fire, gas, and gravity. Without function or goal, the film harnesses physical comedy in the service of entropy.

In the early 1990s Fischli and Weiss turned to a new sculptural material, and with it introduced a new level of realism to their work. Polyurethane provides a malleable, lightweight base for life-size recreations of household objects which the artists paint in full detail with acrylic and emulsion paint. First seen in a presentation entitled ''The Table'' at the ZUrich Kunsthalle in 1992–93, this mode of trompe l'oeil sculptural production has led to site-specific installations such as ''Room Under the Staircase'' at the Museum of Modern Art in Frankfurt in 1995, and a gallery in the inaugural installation of the Tate Modern in London in 2000. In both these sites the artists have created the illusion of an area recently abandoned by janitorial or construction workers. Ersatz buckets, cigarette butts, and food wrappers are barely distinguishable from the real thing, both amazing and dismaying museum visitors.

The artists produced their first major video installation for the Swiss Pavilion at the Venice Biennale in 1995. Incorporating 12 monitors and 96 hours of video, the piece includes real time footage of a range of banal activities, mostly taking place in the Alpine region around Zürich. The activities of a dentist, construction workers, cheesemakers, sewage system cleaners, and woodcutters play alongside images of sunsets, pets, and airports. In each video the camera wanders idiosyncratically around the scene, evoking the artists' fluctuating attention and interest, and paralleling the experience of viewers confronted with the array of videos.

In all their works, Fischli and Weiss use humor and cliché to produce contemplations on the relationship between art and life. Whether reproducing the effects of machinework with elaborate handwork, or creating permanent records of everyday moments, they explore the territory where the mundane meets the marvelous.

—Lucy Soutter

FISHER, Ebon

Nationality: American. **Born:** Harrisburg, Pennsylvania, 4 August 1959. **Education:** Carnegie-Mellon University, Pittsburgh, Pennsylvania, B.F.A. in Visual Art, 1982; Massachusetts Institute of Technology, Cambridge, M.S. in Visual Studies, 1986. **Family:** Quaker. **Career:** Instructor in Outreach Program, Boston Children's Museum, 1984; instructor, Massachusetts Institute of Technology, Cambridge, 1985–87; instructor, Massachusetts College of Art, Boston, 1987–88; instructor of digital imaging and cultural studies, New School University, New York, 1989–98; assistant professor and developer of Digital Worlds program, School of Art and Art History, University of Iowa, 1998–2001; associate professor, Department of Film and Media Studies, Hunter College/CUNY, New York, 2001—. Radio co-host, ''Art Bridge,'' WMBR, Cambridge, Massachusetts, 1987–88; computer graphics specialist, Eye Research Institute, Boston, 1987–89; media artist in residence, Downtown Community Television, New York, 1989–90; media director, Test-Site Gallery, Brooklyn, New York, 1991–92; computer imaging for a variety of clients including Young & Rubicam, Berlitz, the Boston Consulting Group, and Ford Motor Company, 1989–98. **Address:** Film and Media Studies, Hunter College, 695 Park Ave., New York, NY 10021, U.S.A.. **Web site:** www.olulo.net

Selected Individual Exhibitions:

1981–83 Graffiti projects, Pittsburgh, Pennsylvania and Cambridge, Massachusetts
1992 Test-Site Gallery, Williamsburg, Brooklyn
1999 Pixel Gallery (online at www.theglobe.com)

Selected Group Exhibitions:

1986–93 *The Limelight, The Roxy, Keep Refrigerated, Room Temperature, El Sensorium, The Rat,* and *The Channel* (nightclub installations in Boston and New York)
1992–93 *Apartment Store* and *The Opium Den,* Exit Art, New York
1993 *Out of Town: The Williamsburg Paradigm,* Krannert Art Museum, University of Illinois, Champaign
1994 *Bioinformatica,* Sandra Gering Gallery, New York (travelled to Kölnischer Kunstverein, Köln, Germany)
1996 *One Hundred Days of Contemporary Art,* Centre International d'Art Contemporain de Montréal, Quebec
Can You Digit?, Postmaster's Gallery, New York
Greene/Naftali Gallery, New York
1997 *Féile 97,* St. Eugene's Parish Hall, Derry, Northern Ireland
1998–99 *Transatlantic Connections,* Royal Scottish Academy, Edinburgh, Scotland
2000 *Summer Projects,* P.S. 1/Museum of Modern Art, New York

Media Projects and Performances:

1985 *Chekov* (choreographer and performer for Stuart Sherman), List Visual Arts Center, Massachusetts Institute of Technology, Cambridge
1987 *Existence* (creator and performer), Dupont Gym, Massachusetts Institute of Technology, Cambridge
An Offering to the Heart (creator and performer), Eventworks Performance Festival, Massachusetts College of Art, Boston
1988 Carpenter Center for the Arts, Harvard University, Cambridge
Evolution of the Grid (creator and performer), Institute of Contemporary Art, Bates Art Resource Center, The Channel, Boston
1991–92 Phone-in prose and poetry system, (718) SUBWIRE, Williamsburg, Brooklyn, New York
1993 *Organism* (instigator and coordinator of multimedia ''web jam''), Williamsburg, Brooklyn, New York
1995–96 Music/media performances (creator and performer), The Kitchen, New York
1997 *Port* (co-organizer, internet and site-based event), List Visual Arts Center at the Media Lab, Massachusetts Institute of Technology, Cambridge
2000 Computer projections for rave with DJ Ritchie Hawtin (Plastikman), University of Iowa Ballroom, Iowa City

Publications:

By FISHER: Articles—''Quivering Amidst the Cultural Organisms of Our Own Construction'' in *Out of Town: The Williamsburg Paradigm,* exhibition catalog, Champaign, Illinois 1993; ''Web Jam Manifesto'' in *Utne Reader,* 1995; ''Visionaries of the New Millennium'' in *Java Magazine* (Phoenix), 1997; ''The Future of Wiggling Things'' in Digital Creativity (London), Summer 1998; ''Pioneers of Digital Art Education'' in *Artbyte Magazine,* Summer 1999. **Musical recording—**''Circulate All Sensation'' in *State of the Union* (CD anthology), produced by Elliott Sharp, 1996; ''Jodi x 2'' in *Beyond Interface* web project, Walker Arts Center, Minneapolis.

On FISHER: Books—*The Best Graphic Art on the Web* by The Internet Design Project, New York 1998; *Art since 1940: Strategies of Being* by Jonathan Fineberg, Prentice Hall, New York 2000. **Articles**—Appeared as eyeball in comic strip ''Medea's Weekend'' by Tony Millionaire in *Waterfront Week,* 1992; ''Where Do We Go After the Rave?'' in *Newsweek,* 26 July 1993; ''The New York Cyber Sixty'' in *New York,* 13 November 1995; ''Absorb into Memory: Ebon Fisher's Media Organisms'' by Peter Boerboom in *Mute* (London), 1997; ''Vis-a-vis Manhattan'' by Claudia Steinberg in *Die Zeit,* 1997; ''Go with the Flow: Eight New York Artists and Architects in the Digital Era'' by Suzan Wines in *Domus,* 1998; ''Ebon Fisher's AlulA Dimension'' by Jennifer Dalton in *Performing Arts Journal,* 1998; ''Mr. Meme,'' by Matt Haber in *Wired,* 1995. **Internet**—''Bionic Codes: The World's First Biocybernetic Ballet,'' *Word.com,* 1995; ''The Web's Best Sites,'' *Encyclopaedia Britannica* (Britannica.com), August 2000; ''Bionic Codes'' by Aaron Paul in *Now.com,* 18 September 2000; ''Ebon Fisher Explores Subversive Play'' by Mike Tanner in *Wired News* (wired.com), 8 May 1997; ''CyberAtlas'' by Laura Trippi and Jon Ippolito in Guggenheim Museum website (guggenheim.org), 1996–2001.

* * *

Ebon Fisher is an artist whose ''Media Organisms''—artificial life forms cultivated in the plasma of popular culture—and ''Bionic Codes''— subjective ecosystems existing over the internet—constitute a highly original contribution to the latest developments in technological art.

Fisher collectively named his creations and the world they inhabit the ''OlulO Dimension,'' after the alula, the spurious, ''bastard'' feathers on a bird's wing. This is a bionic world, in which many of the codes operate as ritual elements. OlulO was born when Fisher, while still living in Pennsylvania, began spray-painting simplified drawings of nerve cells on surfaces around Pittsburgh. At an early stage, Ebon Fisher had already decided to abandon traditional art for science and technology in order to search for more universal meanings. He considered that art had lost touch with everyday life. When in 1981 he ''tagged'' Pittsburgh with diagrams of neurons, this crude displacement of biological science into the streets marked the beginning of a long fascination with the living properties of information.

In the following years, Fisher experimented with a variety of ''Media Rituals.'' These rituals focused on the immediacy of body-experience and on community-based culture, as Fisher organized massive participatory art events in gyms, nightclubs and neighborhoods. They were also efforts at exploring new ways to build vital convergences of humans and media technology.

In the beginning of the 1990s, Ebon Fisher lived in the close-knit artists' neighborhood of Williamsburg, Brooklyn. His work involved the interface of media, technology, and industry with the human environment of a small community and with the individual. He was thrilled by the many possibilities of mixing global communication with the intimacy of the small artists' community. In 1993, he instigated the Brooklyn ''Web Jam.'' This was, according to Netlingo, ''a weblike layering of music, media, performers, audience, and the surrounding ecosystem into a rhythmic 'jungle.' The objective was to celebrate an expanded sense of nature inclusive of culture and technology. With roots in African American jazz and 1990s rave culture, the web jam takes an improvisational, 'emergent' approach to cultural, political, and ecological systems. The first web jam, known as 'Organism,' was instigated by Ebon Fisher in collaboration with 120 artists, musicians, and children from Williamsburg. Over 2000 people attended—jamming from 6:00 at night until 9:00 the next morning.'' This nightlong temporary organism in an abandoned mustard factory incubated within a creative community involved huge overlapping webs of media, sound, performance, and sculptural systems.

Since 1992, Fisher has also been cultivating the bionic codes. A bionic code is defined in Netlingo as a ''problem-solving routine for human behavior as it is exercised in the realm of networks and cyberspace. The first bionic codes were developed by Fisher based on a series of his theatrical experiments involving communication systems amongst audience members. Fisher's bionic codes have been formalized as a series of diagrams and statements which 'float' in the infosphere in a variety of media.'' They can be found in museum installations, art magazines, projections in New York night clubs and performance spaces, as well as on t-shirts, stickers, and diagrams of computer networks and in other media.

In Fisher's first mature bionic code, ''Equalize with Other Beings,'' an installation placed in Williamsburg, Brooklyn's seminal art gallery, Test-Site, the bionic code was projected from the ceiling onto people below who had triggered motion detectors. Illuminated within one of the circles that compose the code, these impromptu participants were thrust into interaction not only with other human beings, but with the code itself, and with the mechanism of its display.

As Peter Boerboom states in *Mute,* ''Each bionic code is a stand-alone program designed to trigger patterns of behavior and processes of thought. In other words, the bionic codes act as moral operators on biological operands. They are modules designed to hack into culture's core and rewrite some of its basic routines. Unlike many moral systems, the codes do not indulge in dogmatism. They do not demand allegiance nor do they make promises. Above all they make no claim of exclusive truth. As routines available to the operating system of society, they assert themselves as beneficial options.''

Although Fisher's bionic codes also draw upon numerous spiritual and romantic traditions, he states that ''these codes are not meant to be prudish or to invoke sin. Rather they are fertilized by wild invention, and a need, in this cynical age, to unleash some positive disturbances. They are not rules. They are an optional and flexible system of social algorithms, problem-solving devices, to be utilized in any combination.''

The bionic codes grew out of Fisher's media rituals and have mutated again into ''Zoacodes,'' which are beginning to appear in OlulO, a world Fisher has begun to grow in the media with the intention of becoming a live TV show for the web.

As to Fisher's ''Wigglism Manifesto,'' a project which started in 1996, it followed Fisher's abandonment of the concept of ''integration'' as a philosophy of organic fusion, in favor of ''Wigglism'' with its reflexive emphasis on lively movement, which is a quality possessed by many healthy, integrated systems and organisms. Wigglism can be considered as an effort at moving our collective gaze away from both art and science and towards the nurturing of ''life'' in the broadest, non-objective, and non-human sense. It is an attempt to seed a form of ''subjective ecology.'' This leads, among other things, to a de-centered authorship where one creates with the community, with the medium, and with nature. Many Eastern traditions, such as the Japanese tea ceremony, extend authorship and identity into the mists of the tea garden. Wigglism is also indebted to the elegant call-and-response method of many African cultures, a long-standing tradition which our North European cultures are just beginning to emulate. Underground rock and hip hop, at their best, build intimate communities using variations of call-and-response, including analog and electronic forms of voice integration.

All these codes, processes, and ''world breeding'' efforts by Ebon Fisher can be interpreted as the artist's commitment to life as it is perceived at the beginning of the new century.

—Frank Popper

FISHER, Joel

Nationality: American. **Born:** Salem, Ohio, 6 June 1947. **Education:** Kenyon College, Gambier, Ohio, 1965–69. **Family:** Married Pamela Robertson-Pearce, 1977, son: Noah, born 1977. **Career:** Started painting, Salem, Ohio, 1956; first paintings purchased by Butler Institute, Youngstown, Ohio, 1965; moved to New York and began paper works 1969; occasional work as bartender, furniture remover, jobbing painter, in New York, 1969–71; lived in Berlin 1974–75; lived in London, 1976–83; began exhibiting sculpture in 1979; moved to New York; educator, School of Visual Arts, New York, 1988; educator, Parsons School of Design, New York, 1990;

guest professor, Ecole des Beaux-Arts, Paris 1991–99. **Awards:** Kress Foundation Awards in Art History, 1967, 1968; Thomas J. Watson Travelling Fellowship, 1969; Berliner Kunstlerprogram (D.A.A.D.), 1974; National Endowment Fellowship (Sculpture), 1984; George & Eliza Gardner Howard Foundation, 1986–87, J. Simon Guggenheim Fellowship, 1993; Pollock-Krasner Foundation, 1993; The Adolf and Esther Gottlieb Foundation Grant, 2000. **Agents:** Bellas Artes Gallery, 653 Canyon Road, Santa Fe, New Mexico 87501; Lawrence Markey, 55 Vandam Street, New York, New York 10013; Karen McCready Fine Art, 425 West 13th Street, New York, New York 10014; Stefan Stux Gallery, 529 West 20th Street, New York, New York 10011. **Address:** Home, PO Box 349, North Troy, VT, 05859–0349; Office, 99 Commercial Street, Brooklyn, New York 11222–1078.

Individual Exhibitions:

1970 Mansfield Fine Arts Center, Ohio
Whitney Art Resource Center, New York
1971 Victoria and Albert Museum, London
Nigel Greenwood Inc., London
1972 Galerie Ileana Sonnabend, Paris
Galleria Marilena Bonomo, Bari, Italy
1973 New Gallery, Cleveland
Galerie Stampa, Basle
1974 Galerie Folker Skulima, Berlin
Neue Galerie, Aachen, West Germany
Galerie Ileana Sonnabend, Paris
1975 Max Protetch Gallery, Washington, D.C.
112 Greene Street, New York
Galerie Ernst, Hannover
Stadtische Museum, Monchengladbach, West Germany
1976 Nigel Greenwood Inc., London
1977 Max Protetch Gallery, New York
Palais des Beaux Arts, Brussels
Museum of Modern Art, Oxford
1978 Stedelijk Museum, Amsterdam
Galeria Foksal PSP, Warsaw
Salvatore Ala, Milan
1984 Matt's Gallery, London
1986 Nigel Greenwood Gallery, London
1987 Galerie Susanna Kulli, St. Gallen, Switzerland
1988 Gallery Shimada, Yamaguchi, Japan
Diane Brown Gallery, New York
1989 Nigel Greenwood Gallery, London
Galeria Comicos, Lisbon
1990 Farideh Cadot Gallery, Paris
Farideh Cadot Gallery, New York
1991 Galerie Raymond Bollag, Zurich
Barbara Gross Galleris, Munchen
1992 C. Grimaldis Gallery
1993 Gallerij S-65 Aalst, Belgium
Art Affairs/Antoinette de Stigter, Amsterdam
1994 Lawrence Markey Gallery, New York
Hubert Winter Gallery, Vienna
Text, Ben Shahn Gallery, William Patterson College, New Jersey (catalog)
Circle, Farideh Cadot Gallery, Paris
1997 *Mosaic Evolution,* Antoinette de Stigter Gallery, Amsterdam

Selected Group Exhibitions:

1972 *Documenta,* Kassel, Germany
Small Series, Paula Cooper Gallery, New York
1973 *Seven,* Museum of Modern Art Penthouse Gallery, New York
Drawings, Sonnabend Gallery, New York
Aspects de l'Art Actuel (Festival d'Automne), Museé Galliera, Paris
1974 *Separation,* Amerika Haus, Berlin
1986 *Europa-Amerika,* Museum Ludwig, Cologne
Sculpture Sein, Kunsthalle, Dusseldorf
1987 *Sculpture to Resemblance: Eight Sculptors,* Albright-Knox Gallery, Buffalo, New York
The New Poverty, John Gibson Gallery, New York
1989 *4 Americans—Aspects of Current Sculpture,* The Brooklyn Museum, New York
1990 *Within: A Sculpture Exhibition,* Baumgartner Galleries, Washington, D.C. (catalog)
1994 *5th Paper Biennale,* Leopold Hoesch Museum, Duren, Germany
1998 *Not Nothing,* Todd Gallery, London

Collections:

Arts Council of Great Britain, London; Art Complex Museum, Duxbury, Massachusetts; Australian National Gallery, Sydney; Kunstmuseum Bern, Switzerland; The Brooklyn Museum, New York; Butler Institute of Art Youngstown, Ohio; Chase Manhatten Bank, New York; Cincinnati Art Museum, Ohio; Castellani Art Museum, Niagara University; Coburn Gallery, Kenyon College, Gambier, Ohio; FRAC Picardie, Amiens; Fogg Art Museum, Harvard University; Museum of Contemporary Art, Ghent, Belgium; Georgia Museum of Fine Arts, Athens, Georgia; Groninger Museum, Groningen, Holland; Kunstmuseum Luzern, Lucern, Switzerland; Malmo Museum, Malmo, Sweden; Moderna Museet, Stockholm, Sweden; Museum of Modern Art, New York; Museum Sztuki W Lodzi, Lodz, Poland; Musee d'Art Contemporain de Rochechouart, France; Municipal Art Gallery, Leeds, England; New York Stock Exchange, New York; Neues Museum Weserburg Bremen, Germany; Center Georges Pompidou, Paris; Prudential Life Museum of Fine Art, Richmond, Virginia; Museum of Fine Arts, Charlotteville, Virginia; Staatliche Museum, Berlin; Stadisches Museum, Monchengladbach, Germany; Stedelijk Museum, Amsterdam; Tate Gallery, London; Tehran Museum of Contemporary Art, Tehran; The Tokushima Museum of Art; Musee d'Art e Architecture, Toulon; Victoria and Albert Museum, London; Wadsworth Atheneum, Hartford; Weatherspoon Art Gallery, Greensboro, North Carolina.

Publications:

By FISHER: Books—*An Image in Blankness,* Oxford 1977; *The Second Furlong,* London 1984. **Articles—**''On Paper,'' interview by Simon Field, in *Art and Artists* (London), January 1972; ''Joel Fisher,'' interview, with Lisa Bear, in *Avalanche* (New York), December 1974.

*

In the beginning the idea of paper was the idea of ground. Over and over again I watched the paper rise from the water. The materials I used were simple: 1. a tub of water in which the paper pulp floated in dispension; 2. a wooden frame with a filter mesh stretched over it; and 3. some squares of felt to which the wet and fragile paper could be transferred until it was strong enough to be picked up.

The filter screen is drawn through the water. Water falls back, and the tiny cellulose fibers interlock, fiber upon fiber, each holding in place and in turn being held by others. There is no glue, for it is unnecessary; it is a self-structuring surface maintaining itself.

For me papermaking is not only an activity but also an event. The paper forms at that instant when its constituent fibers are pulled from the water and enter the air. The surface of the water is a plane which creates a plane. A tension is established; the substance is differentiated. In its creation each sheet is separated from the materials which is itself. It remains a subsidiary only of itself; a surface connecting by identity to its base. The paper is not an idea itself but contains an idea—almost as a cognate to thought. Always and throughout, what is meant is equal to what is not meant. Within the sheet of paper there is great structural homogeneity; back, front, inside, and outside are all equal. Although paper is not a *carte blanche* (contrary to my original expectations), it still remains a balanced and adequate ground for experience.

A sheet of paper can be repaired by returning it to its liquid state and making it anew (much as the mud pies of children can be repaired and reformed eternally by adding water). The form and structure of the material is perceived as beyond all barriers of separate objects with beginnings and ends. It is a fugitive with a history of other manifestations. As one of the most polymorphous of materials, paper goes back and forth between its structured and unstructured states with relative ease. One senses an inherent potential in this general fluidity. Conscious of the nature of a pulp which constantly allows itself to renew and define, I concern myself only with those acts which establish a simple, fugitive, structuring relationship.

On spun lines: Several years ago I went to Scotland in order to learn to spin. A strange old lady taught me using a stone she picked up from the beach and a thick clump of wool which was clinging to a low shrub. As a shepherdess, years ago, she would save the wool which clung to fences and shrubs by spinning it in this manner—one stone for white wool, one for the black—the process is simply this: after the wool is gathered it is picked apart, allowing any small particles of dirt to fall out. This increases the volume but not the weight. Usually the next step is to ''card'' the wool using wire brushes. This aligns the fibers in roughly parallel lines. The carded fibers are then rolled along one's thigh into long rolls called ''rolags.'' From these rolags a thread is spun pulling out a few fibers at a time. This is called ''drawing'' or ''drafting'' and the resultant line is really a thread; the tension between the fibers which was destroyed by pulling the fibers apart is now re-established. The fibers spin around each other in a linear spiral—holding themselves together—drawing a line. When shorter fibers have been twisted together into a long strand, this strand becomes stronger than the cumulative strength of the untwisted fibers. The spinning operation combines two separate movements: a twisting and longitudinal movement away from the drafting or drawing zone. These two forces—the twisting and the pulling—must always be kept in balance.

—Joel Fisher

* * *

Joel Fisher's creative activity is strongly involved with the processes of vital functions: it is tied to experiencing the kind of work that one decides to carry out alone, from the start, with one's own hands. The artist produces his own paper (occasionally from scraps of his own clothes), which then becomes the basis for his thought processes and for their formulations.

On receiving a clean piece of paper, the artist stands simultaneously in the presence of both a void and its disturber. The paper is full of irregularities: the edges of the sheets are uneven. One can also notice the fibers that remain after the sheet has been dried—on a layer of felt. Sometimes, the artist pays attention to one of these fibers, which then takes on a meaning and stands out as a form. This fiber may then be enlarged, drawn onto paper and become a sign (''Apographs''). It can also lose its background and be transferred onto a wall as a pattern, newly created from repetition of the original.

The moment that the artist notices and chooses the fiber, and the attention paid to the unevenness of the sheet edges, don't, however, form a clear boundary from whence the creative act begins. This includes the whole work, beginning with the decision to produce one's own paper. Thus is paper not a ''background'' to the expression, but itself takes part in its construction. That is why all that the clean sheet offers becomes so important. Equally as important is the actual birth of the paper's surface, at the moment it emerges from water—this is where the idea of a ''return'' to the watery womb comes from. It becomes identified with a retrieval of the original moment in the process of creation (in a Happening in the Mönchengladbach Museum, the artist dissolved his previous works in water). ''By making paper, I take part in the potential of the world,'' says Fisher.

The artist therefore attaches importance to the most basic ontological issues, those at the heart of human philosophy: he wishes to touch the original state of the material and to be at the heart of the first impulse, setting into motion thoughts and things. In this way, he wishes to take part in the ''whole,'' in the actual core of the world. The philosophical attitude is contained in the artistic attitude and is expressed by means of art.

Paper treated in this way becomes the carrier of many reflections. Above all, by being ordinary and mundane, it seems to become invisible; it is ''everywhere.'' The sheet of paper becomes a free space; ''it absorbs and demarcates ends of the world.'' a reflection, on that place and its existence in time, then follows. It appears to us as a clean area, still unmarked, as the beginning of the day. It also foretells the end of the day's promise, of the advent of ''evening,'' of darkness. The clean sheet that is ''everywhere'' thus begins to succumb to the action of linear time. We cannot free ourselves from a feeling for history: an empty place is its announcement, the promise of its fulfillment. An empty place is also the promise of the unknown—it gives us no certainty, not even the knowledge that it will still exist when we look at it again. This uncertainty becomes for the artist sui generis a guarantee of creativity, since certainty does not engage us at all; it is uncreative.

Clean paper also holds out the possibility of uninhibited expansion. It is true that the edges of the sheet make us aware of the limits of possibility, but they also identify the area that they enclose. That is why the edges become important: the artist sees them as lines that have a control over the actual interior of the paper. He thus draws into the paper the shape of these uneven edges; he repeats these lines in the direction of the center of the sheet; he fills the inside with them so that he reaches the limits of possibility—going from emptiness to fullness. The paper loses its area, ceases to accept anything, ''speaks but does not listen.'' It becomes filled just as the world becomes filled with things, our thoughts and fancies. The movement from the edge to the center of the paper suddenly makes the boundaries appear elsewhere: they move aside from the edges, they carry their uncrossability to the center. Now the center becomes a threshold that must be crossed.

Crossed in order to recover the empty space. This is a very difficult step since even pointing out an empty space spoils its excellence, fills it with our intentional acts. That is why the artist suggests obtaining a distance by ignoring the spots and the flaws. By setting up a certain threshold below which we will not notice visual material, one calls to mind the experience of seeing the earth at a great distance, when it appears to be uninhabited. The capacity to achieve an empty space is very important, just as one needs to recover the ''beginning''; it becomes a condition of working, forcing one's will onto the material world.

Joel Fisher's art comes from the simplest of acts—and facts so obvious that they are almost ''invisible.'' The artist notices possibilities of sublimation in them and turns them into such excellent ideas in the flesh that the beginning and end of the process become as one: the covered piece of paper regains its innocence, the day—the promise of a new beginning; the regained ''empty place'' makes the continued process of creation possible.

—Alicja Kepinska

FLANAGAN, Barry

Nationality: British. **Born:** Prestatyn, North Wales, 11 January 1941. **Education:** Attended schools in Sussex; studied at the Birmingham College of Art, 1957–58, then briefly at various art schools, 1958–63; studied advanced sculpture, under Anthony Caro, Phillip King and William Tucker, at St. Martin's School of Art, London, 1964–66. **Family:** Married Susan Lewis in 1963; children: Samantha and Tara; children with Renate Widman: Alfred and Annabelle. **Career:** Lives in Dublin; first stone carvings, Birmingham, 1958; spent several months in Devon and London, visited Montreal, then settled in Bristol; first structures using sand, with canvas and other fibres, 1966; first etchings made at St. Martin's School of Art, 1970, and later in his own studio; travelled in the United States, 1970; returned to stone carvings, in Italy, 1973; began bronze casting in London at A&A Sculpture Casting (now AB Fine Art Foundry); moved to Ibiza, Spain, 1987. Lecturer, Central School of Art and Design, London, 1967–71, St. Martin's School of Art, 1967–71, and Omaha Municipal University, Nebraska, 1971–75. **Awards:** Dover Street Materials Award, Institute of Contemporary Arts, London, 1965; Gulbenkian Foundation grant, 1972; Arts Council Award, 1975; Charles Wollaston Award for *The Cricketer.* **Address:** c/o Waddington Galleries, 11 Cork Street, London W1X 2LT, England.

Individual Exhibitions:

1966 Rowan Gallery, London
1968 Rowan Gallery, London
Galerie Ricke, Kassel, West Germany
Galleria dell'Ariete, Milan
1969 Museum Haus Lange, Krefeld, West Germany
Fischbach Gallery, New York
1970 Rowan Gallery, London
1971 Rowan Gallery, London
Galleria del Leone, Venice
1972 Rowan Gallery, London
1973 Rowan Gallery, London
1974 Rowan Gallery, London
Museum of Modern Art, New York
Bluecoat Gallery, Liverpool
Museum of Modern Art, Oxford
1975 Hogarth Galleries, Sydney
Art and Project, Amsterdam
1976 Hester van Royen Gallery, London
1977 Art and Project, Amsterdam
Appledorn Museum, Netherlands
Stedelijk van Abbemuseum, Eindhoven, Netherlands
Arnolfini Gallery, Bristol
1978 Serpentine Gallery, London
1980 Waddington Galleries, London
New 57 Gallery, Edinburgh
1981 *60s and 70s Prints and Drawings by Barry Flanagan,* Mostyn Art Gallery, Llandudno, Wales (toured Wales and England)
Waddington Galleries, London
1982 *Stone and Bronze Sculptures,* at the *Biennale,* Venice (travelled to the Whitechapel Gallery, London)
1983 Centre Georges Pompidou, Paris
Waddington Galleries, London
1985 Richard Gray Gallery, Chicago
Waddington Galleries, London
1986 Tate Gallery, London
1987 Laing Art Gallery, Newcastle-upon-Tyne (travelled to Belgrade, Zagreb, and Ljubljana)
1988 Galerie Durand-Dessert, Paris
1990 Waddington Galleries, London
1992 Galerie Durand-Dessert, Paris
1993 Fundacion ''La Caixa,'' Madrid (retrospective; travelled to Nantes, France)
1994 *Recent Sculpture,* Richard Gray Gallery, Chicago (catalog)
Waddington Galleries, London (catalog)
Recent Sculpture, Pace Gallery, New York (catalog)
Galerie Hans Mayer, Dusseldorf
1995 RHA Gallagher Gallery, Dublin
Galerie Thaddaeus Ropac, Salzburg
University of Iowa Museum of Art, Iowa City
Barry Flanagan on Park Avenue, 54th to 59th Street, New York
1996 *Barry Flanagan: Sculpture in Grant Park,* Chicago
Galerie Durand-Dessert, Paris
Galleria Karsten Greve, Milan
Musée des Beaux-Arts, Caen
Estampes, Bibliothèque Nationale de France, Paris (retrospective) (catalog)
1997 Centre Cultural La Tecla Sala, Barcelona
Galerie Hans Mayer, Dusseldorf
Barry Flanagan: Bronzes, Dibuixos I Gravats, Edicions T Galeria D'Art, Barcelona (catalog)
1998 *Sculpture,* Richard Gray Gallery, Chicago (catalog)
Galerie Thaddaeus Ropac, Salzburg
Barry Flanagan: Sculptures and Ceramics, Galerie von Bartha, Basel

Barry Flanagan and Pataphysics, Crestet Centre d'Art, Valréas, France
Waddington Galleries, The Economist Plaza, London (catalog)
1999 Galerie Xavier Hufkens, Brussels
2000 Tate Gallery, Liverpool
2001 *Seeing Round Corners,* Waddington Galleries, London (catalog)

Selected Group Exhibitions:

1972 *The New Art,* Hayward Gallery, London
1975 *Biennale,* Musee National d'Art Moderne, Paris
1978 *Made by Sculptors,* Stedelijk Museum, Amsterdam
1980 *Pier + Ocean,* Hayward Gallery, London (travelled to the Rijksmuseum Kroller-Muller, Otterlo, Netherlands)
1982 *Aspects of British Art Today,* Metropolitan Art Museum, Tokyo (toured Japan)
1984 *The British Art Show,* City Art Gallery, Birmingham (and Ikon Gallery, Birmingham; travelled to Edinburgh; Sheffield; Southampton)
1987 *A Quiet Revolution: British Sculpture since 1965,* San Francisco Museum of Modern Art (travelled to Newport Beach, California; Washington, D.C.; Buffalo, New York)
1988 *Starlit Waters,* Tate Gallery, Liverpool
1993 *Gravity and Grace,* Hayward Gallery, London
1994 *Biennale Skulptur '94,* Amsterdam
1995 *Wasser & Wein: Zwei Dinge des Lebens,* Kunsthalle Krems, Austria
Here and Now, Serpentine Gallery, London
Of the Human Form, Waddington Galleries, London
Revolution: Art of the Sixties from Warhol to Beuys, Museum of Contemporary Art, Tokyo
Feminin-Masculin, Centre Georges Pompidou, Paris
1996 *Un Siècle de Sculpture Anglais,* Jeu de Paume, Paris
Summer Exhibition, Royal Academy of Arts, London
Sculpture in the Close, Jesus College, Cambridge
Made New, City Racing, London
1997 *Treasure Island,* Calouste Gulbenkian Foundation, Lisbon
Barely Made, Norwich Gallery, Norwich School of Art and Design
RHA Annual Exhibition, Royal Hibernian Academy, Dublin
Surrealism and After: The Gabrielle Keiller Collection, Scottish National Gallery of Modern Art, Edinburgh
KölnSkulptur 1, Skulpturenpark Köln, Gesellschaft der Freunde des Skulpturenparks Köln, Cologne
1998 *Dix ans de Commandes Publiques,* Centre Européen d'Actions Artistiques Contemporaines, Strasbourg
New Displays, Duveen Galleries, Tate Gallery, London
British Figurative Art Part Two: Sculpture, Flowers East, London
Up to 2000, Southampton City Art Gallery
1999 *RHA Annual Exhibition,* Royal Hibernian Academy, Dublin
Pierwalk Exhibition, Navy Pier, Chicago
Les Champs de la Sculpture 2000, Champs d'Élysées, Paris
2000 *Summer Exhibition,* Royal Academy of Arts, London
UBU in UK, Mayor Gallery, London
Nijinsky (1889–1950), Musée d'Orsay, Paris

Collections:

Museum van Hedendaagse Kunst, Ghent, Belgium; National Gallery of Canada, Ottawa; Musée des Beaux-Arts, Calais; City of Douai, France; F.R.A.C. Rhône-Alpes, Lyon; C.E.A.A.C., Strasbourg; Kaiser Wilhelm Museum, Krefeld, Germany; Hugh Lane Municipal Gallery, Dublin; Israel Museum, Jerusalem; Fuchu City, Tokyo; Nagaoka Contemporary Art Museum, Japan; Nagoya Museum, Japan; Setagaya Museum, Tokyo; Tochigi Prefectural Museum of Fine Arts, Japan; Tokyo Metropolitan Art Museum; Stedelijk Museum, Amsterdam; Van Abbemuseum, Eindhoven, Netherlands; Rijksmuseum Kröller Müller, Otterlo, Netherlands; Sintra Museum of Modern Art, Portugal—The Berardo Collection; Kunsthaus, Zurich; Ulster Museum, Belfast; National Museum of Wales, Cardiff Leeds City Art Gallery; Leicestershire Education Authority; Rawlins Upper School and Community College, Quorn, Leicestershire; Walker Art Gallery, Liverpool; Arts Council of Great Britain, London; British Council, London, Manchester and Madrid; Contemporary Art Society, London; Government Art Collection, London; Phoenix Community Garden, London; Tate Gallery, London; Victoria and Albert Museum, London; Peterborough Development Corporation; Southampton City Art Gallery; Baltimore Museum of Art; Beverly Hills City Council; Art Institute of Chicago; Museum of Modern Art, New York; Virginia Museum of Fine Arts, Richmond; San Francisco Museum of Modern Art; National Gallery of Art, Washington D.C.; Museo de Arte Contemporaneo de Caracas, Venezuela.

Public Installations:

Beverly Gardens Park, Beverly Hills, California; Park Avenue, New York; Grant Park, Chicago.

Publications:

By FLANAGAN: Article—''Sculpture Made Visible,'' discussion with Gene Baro, in *Studio International* (London), October 1969. **Films—***Hole in the Sea,* videotape, 1969; *The Works I,* 1970; *Atlantic Flight,* 1970; *Bus Ride,* 1970; *The Phantom Sculptor,* 1971; *The Lesson,* 1971; *Sand Girl,* 1971; *Line on Holywell Beach,* 1971.

On FLANAGAN: Books—*Barry Flanagan,* exhibition catalog, by Catherine Lampert, London 1980; *Barry Flanagan,* exhibition catalog, by David Brown, Edinburg 1980; *60s and 70s Prints and Drawings by Barry Flanagan,* exhibition catalog, by Catherine Lampert, Llandudno, North Wales 1981; *Barry Flanagan: Stone and Bronze Sculptures,* exhibition catalog, by Michael Compton and Tim Hilton, Venice and London 1982; *Barry Flanagan,* exhibition catalog with text by Shinichi Nakaazawa, Tokyo 1985; *Barry Flanagan: A Visual Invitation,* exhibition catalog, Newcastle 1987; *Sculpture in the Close,* exhibition catalog with text by Colin Renfrew, Cambridge, England, 1988; *Barry Flanagan,* exhibition catalog with text by Enrique Juncosa, Madrid and Nantes 1993; *Barry Flanagan,* exhibition catalog, London 1994. **Articles—**''British Sculpture: The Developing Scence'' by Gene Baro in *Studio International* (London),

October 1966; ''British Sculpture Today'' by Christopher Finch in *Art and Artists* (London), May 1967; ''Doubts, Dilemmas, Eyelines: Some Leaves from Barry Flanagan's Notebook'' by Anthony Fawcett in *Art and Artists* (London), April 1968; ''Barry Flanagan's Sculpture'' by Charles Harrison in *Studio International* (London), May 1968; ''Barry Flanagan'' by Catherine Lampert in *Studio International* (London), December 1974; ''Barry Flanagan'' by William Feaver in *Vogue,* December 1981; review by Lynne Cooke in *Art in America,* March 1983; ''Barry Flanagan: Always the Unexpected'' by Catherine Francblin in *Art Press,* December 1993; ''Les Chimères de Barry Flanagan'' by Didier Ottinger in *Beaux Arts Magazine,* no. 119, January 1994; ''Barry Flanagan: Alles Ernste Liegt dem Hasen Fern'' by Hans Pietsch in *ART: Das Kunstmagazin,* no. 4, April 1995; ''Une Insolente Légèreté: Les Gravures de Barry Flanagan'' by Geneviève Meunier in *Nouvelles de l'Estampe,* no. 145, March 1996.

* * *

Barry Flanagan's oeuvre is marked by its diversity of appearance. Yet the absence of family likeness (a signature style) signifies neither loss of directions nor a rampant eclecticism, for Flanagan's approach to sculpture has been informed by a singleness of vision, one which is perhaps best summarized in his statement: ''within the sculpture there are carried its own solutions; we invest it with problems, ideas and excitements. One merely causes the things to reveal themselves to the sculptural awareness. It is the awareness that develops, not the agents of the sculptural phenomena.''

Trained, in part, at St. Martin's School of Art during the heyday of its sculptural activity. Flanagan gained the habit of questioning all dogmas and preconceptions: from the beginning his work has been made against the grain. ''aaing j gni aa,'' for example, in which brightly colored Miroesque turds have been clumped insouciantly together, struck a dada note at odds with the prevailing climate of more solemn inquiry. Others, like ''Heap,'' ''Pile,'' ''Stack,'' and ''Bundle,'' examined the nature of those concepts, their titles named through such unorthodox materials as dyed hessian filled with paper, foam or sand. Later works, including ''Untitled '70,'' resemble nomadic tents, and like such transitory phenomena seem to stake a minimum claim to space and permanence.

In the 70s Flanagan turned increasingly to traditional materials—stone and bronze—and conventional techniques—casting and carving—but, typically, he diverted them to new ends. In pieces like ''a nose in repose,'' the nose appears to be a found form, its contours given, not shaped, by the artist; the carving element consists of a line etched into the surface of this stone, a line which appears to have little in common with the form in which it is imbedded. Flanagan's characteristic wit took a new turn in a series of more recent stone works, like ''Carving no. 13,'' 1981, which were executed by assistants enlarging small clay maquettes whose forms had been arrived at by Flanagan simply squeezing a lump of clay in his hand. In the process of transforming the model into the large stone version, the original forms had to be reinterpreted into a different material, one for whom such squashy, spongy shapes are far from natural. Yet the irony deepens; the final image has taken on an organic naturalness, but it is a different kind of naturalness from that of the maquette, not at all reminiscent of its gestural beginnings.

Such witty yet profound questioning underlies most of Flanagan's work. In recent bronzes based on the image of a hare he has once again reinvigorated traditional concerns, for he has managed to introduce an anthropomorphic content in such a way that sculpture can at least return to tragic themes without heroics or self-consciousness.

—Lynne Cooke

FLAVIN, Dan

Nationality: American. **Born:** New York, 1 April 1933. **Education:** Cathedral College of the Immaculate Conception, Douglastown, New York, 1947–52; United States Air Force Meteorological Technician's Training School, 1953; University of Maryland Extension Program, Korea, 1954–55; New School for Social Research, New York, 1956; and Columbia University, New York, 1957–59; self-taught in art. **Career:** Artist; lecturer, graduate faculty, University of North Carolina, Greensboro, 1967; Albert Dorne Visiting Professor, University of Bridgeport, Connecticut, 1973. **Awards:** William and Noma Copley Foundation Grant, 1964; Skowhegan Medal for Sculpture, Maine, 1976. **Address:** Dan Flavin Art Institute, Corwith Ave., Bridgehampton, New York 11932, U.S.A. **Died:** In Riverhead, New York, 29 November 1996.

Individual Exhibitions:

1961 Judson Gallery, New York
1964 Kaymar Gallery, New York
Green Gallery, New York
1965 Ohio State University, Columbus
1966 Galerie Rudolf Swirner, Cologne
Nicholas Wilder Gallery, Los Angeles
1967 Kornblee Gallery, New York
Galleria Sperone, Milan
Museum of Contemporary Art, Chicago
1968 Galleria Sperone, Turin
Galerie Heiner Friedrich, Munich
Pennsylvania State University, University Park
Dwan Gallery, New York
1969 Galerie Konrad Fischer, Dusseldorf
Irving Blum Gallery, Los Angeles
Galerie Bruno Bischofberger, Zurich
Fluorescent Light, etc., National Gallery of Canada, Ottawa
Vancouver Art Gallery
1970 The Jewish Museum, New York
Dwan Gallery, New York
Leo Castelli Gallery, New York
Los Angeles County Musuem of Art
Galerie Heiner Friedrich, Munich
1971 Leo Castelli Gallery, New York
Galerie Heiner Friedrich, Munich
John Weber Gallery, New York
Janie C. Lee Gallery, Dallas
Galerie Heiner Friedrich, Cologne
1972 Leo Castelli Gallery, New York
Rice University, Houston
Albright-Knox Art Gallery, Buffalo, New York
1973 John Weber Gallery, New York
Leo Castelli Gallery, New York
City Art Museum, St. Louis

Dan Flavin: *Untitled,* ca. 1965–96. ©Estate of Dan Flavin/Artists Rights Society (ARS), NY.

3 Installations in Fluorescent Lights, Galerie Heiner Friedrich, Cologne
University of Bridgeport, Connecticut
Locksley Shea Gallery, Minneapolis
Lisson Gallery, London
1974 Leo Castelli Gallery, New York
The Greenberg Gallery, St. Louis
Jared Sable Gallery, Toronto
Galleria Pasquale Trisorio, Naples
Daniel Weinberg Gallery, San Francisco
1975 Leo Castelli Gallery, New York
Musuem Boymans-Van Beuningen, Rotterdam
Fort Worth Art Museum, Texas
Funf Installationen in Fluoreszierendem Licht van Dan Flavin, Kunstmuseum, Basel
1976 Leo Castelli Gallery, New York
Fort Worth Art Museum, Texas
Charlotte Square Gallery, Edinburgh
Scottish National Gallery of Modern Art, Edinburg
Portland Center for the Visual Arts, Oregon
Heiner Friedrich Gallery, New York
1977 Heiner Friedrich Gallery, New York
Otis Art Gallery, Los Angeles
Ace Gallery, Los Angeles
Art Institute of Chicago
Ace Canada, Vancouver
Contemporary Arts Center, Cincinnati, Ohio (with Michael Venezia)
1978 Heiner Friedrich Gallery, New York (twice)
University of California Art Museum, Berkeley
Leo Castelli Gallery, New York
Parrish Art Museum, Southampton, New York
Galerie Heiner Friedrich, Cologne
1979 Leo Castelli Gallery, New York
Hudson River Musuem, Yonkers, New York (travelled to the Laguna Gloria Art Museum, Austin, Texas)
National Gallery of Canada, Ottawa
1981 Leo Castelli Gallery, New York
1985 CAPC Musée d'Art Contemporain, Bordeaux, France
Rijksmuseum Kröller-Müller, Otterlo, Netherlands
1990 *Dan Flavin,* Waddington Galleries, London (catalog)
Dan Flavin: Four Works of Art in Fluorescent Light from the Reinhard Onnasch Collection, Stadtisches Museum Abteiberg, Monchengladbach, Germany (catalog)
1996 *Dan Flavin (1962/63, 1970, 1996),* Dia Center for the Arts, New York
Guggenheim Museum, New York
PaceWildenstein, New York
2000 *Dan Flavin: Nine Works,* The Dan Flavin Art Institute, Bridgehampton, New York

Selected Group Exhibitions:

1957 *Roslyn Air Force Station Art Exhibit,* North Shore Community Center, Roslyn, New York
1964 *Black, White and Grey,* Wadsworth Atheneum, Hartford, Connecticut
1966 *Primary Structures,* Jewish Museum, New York
1971 *Art and Technology,* Los Angeles County Museum of Art
1975 *Sculpture: American Directions 1945–1975,* National Collection of Fine Arts, Smithsonian Institution, Washington, D.C.
1976 *Drawing Now,* Museum of Modern Art, New York
1977 *Early Work: André/Flavin/Judd/LeWitt,* Sperone, Westwater, Fischer Inc., New York
1979 *The Reductive Object: A Survey of the Minimalist Aesthetic in the 1960s,* Institute of Contemporary Art, Boston
1980 *91st Exposition Société des Artistes Indépendants,* Grand Palais, Paris
1984 *Reflections: Contemporary Art since 1964,* National Gallery of Canada, Ottawa
1988 *Sculpture Since the Sixties,* Whitney Museum of American Art, Equitable Center, New York (catalog)
1989 *Minimalism,* Tate Gallery Liverpool, England (catalog)
1990 *Object and Content: Meaning in Minimal Art,* Australian National Gallery, Canberra (catalog)
1991 *Immaterial Objects,* Whitney Museum of American Art, New York (catalog)
1992 *Sculpture,* Waddington Gallery, London (catalog)
1993 *Lighworks from the National Gallery of Australia,* Museum of Contemporary Art, Sydney (catalog)
1994 *American Drawings and Graphic Works: From Sol LeWitt to Bruce Newman,* Kunsthaus, Zurich (catalog)

1995 *The Marzena Collection: Arte Povera, Minimal Art, Concept Art, Land Art,* Museum Moderner Kunst, Vienna (catalog)
1968, National Gallery of Australia, Canberra
1996 *The Froehlich Foundation: German and American Art from Beuys and Warhol,* Tate Gallery, London (traveling exhibition) (catalog)
1997 *The Hirshhorn Collects: Recent Acquisitions,* Hirshhorn Museum and Sculpture Garden, Washington, D.C. (catalog)
1998 *Waves Breaking on the Shore—Ad Dekkers in His Time,* Stedelijk Museum, Amsterdam (catalog)
Minimal Maximal: Minimal Art and Its Influence on the International Art of the 1990s, Neues Museum Weserburg, Bremen, Germany (catalog)
1999 *Wall Works: Site-Specific Wall Installations,* Paula Cooper Gallery, New York (catalog)
2000 *A Century of Lights,* Fondation Beyeler, Reihen, Switzerland

Collections:

Museum of Modern Art, New York; Metropolitan Museum of Art, New York; Guggenheim Museum, New York; Whitney Museum, New York; Philadelphia Art Museum; La Jolla Museum of Contemporary Art, California; Pasadena Art Museum, California; National Gallery of Canada, Ottawa; Stedelijk Museum, Amsterdam.

Public Installations:

Kunstmuseum, Basel, Switzerland, 1975; Grand Central Station, New York City; Kroller Muller Museum, Eindhoven, Netherlands; U.S. Courthouse, Anchorage.

Publications:

By FLAVIN: Articles—letter to the editor in *Artnews* (New York) April 1963; ''... In Daylight or Cool White: An Autobiographical Sketch'' in *Artforum* (New York), December 1965; ''Flavin Speech'' in *Blockprint* (Providence, Rhode Island), 21 March 1966; statements in *Artforum* (New York), December 1966; letter to the editor in *Arts Magazine* (New York), February 1967; ''Some Other Comments. . .'' in *Artforum* (New York), December 1967; statements in *Don Judd,* exhibition catalog, New York 1968; letters to the editor in *Artforum* (New York), March 1968, April 1968, October 1968; letter to the editor in *Artnews* (New York), Summer 1968; ''. . . In Daylight or Cool White'' in *Fluorescent Light, etc.,* exhibition catalog, Ottawa 1969; ''Dan Flavin'' in *Art Now: New York,* March 1969; statement in *Studio International* (London), April 1969; ''Fluorescent Light, etc. from Dan Flavin: A Supplement,'' with Brydon Smith, in *Artscanada* (Toronto), October 1969; ''Untitled, To Dear Durable Sol from Stephen, Sonja and Dan'' in *Sol LeWitt,* exhibition catalog, The Hague 1970; ''Correspondence: The Guggenheim Affair'' in *Studio International* (London) July/August 1971; letter in *Artforum* (New York), October 1971; statement in ''Around Barnett Newman'' by Jeanne Siegel in *Artnews* (New York), October 1971; ''Comment by the Artist'' in *Studio International* (London), December 1972; ''Address Delivered by Dan Flavin at the National Gallery of Canada for Don Judd's Retrospective Exhibition'' in *Studio International* (London), September 1975.

On FLAVIN: Books—*Dan Flavin,* exhibition catalog, Turin 1968; *Late Modern: The Visual Arts since 1945* by Edward Lucie-Smith, New York 1969; *Dan Flavin, Fluorescent Light, etc.,* exhibition catalog, by Brydon Smith, Ottawa 1969; *Modern Painting: The Movement, the Artists and Their Work* by Burton Wasserman, New York 1970; *Art and Technology,* Los Angeles 1971; *Icons and Images of the 60s* by Nicolas and Elena Calas, New York 1971; *The New Avant Garde: Issues for the Art of the 70s* by Gregoire Muller, New York 1972; *Dan Flavin: 3 Installations in Fluorescent Lights,* exhibition catalog, Cologne 1973; *Funf Installationen in Fluoreszierendem Licht van Dan Flavin,* exhibition catalog, Basel 1975; *Dan Flavin,* exhibition catalog, Otterlo 1985; *Dan Flavin: Installationen in Fluoreszierendem Licht 1989–1993,* edited by Klaus Gallwitz, Stuttgart 1993. **Articles—**''Dan Flavin: Situations'' by Madeleine Deschamps in *Art Press,* no. 121, January 1988; ''L'espace au Neon de Dan Flavin'' by Maiten Bouisset in *Beaux Arts Magazine,* no. 90, May 1991; ''Lighting by Dan Flavin'' by Jeffrey Kastner in *Art Monthly,* no. 191, November 1995; ''Dan Flavin: Specifying Light'' in *Trans,* vol. 1, no. 2, 1996; ''In Another Light'' in *Art in America* (New York), June 1996; ''Dan Flavin, Posthumously'' by Tiffany Bell in *Art in America* (New York), vol. 88, no. 10, October 2000.

* * *

When Dan Flavin began exhibiting his rhythmic arrangements of fluorescent tubes of light in the early 60s, the New York art world shuddered with delight. Though minimal painting and sculpture were well on their way to solving every art-making problem (or so it seemed), Flavin's sculptures opened up a Pandora's box of new considerations. Not that the art establishment wasn't ripe for this kind of intrusion. After all, Flavin wasn't the only one making waves. But he was one of very few making waves with light waves. The sculptures were hard to pin down. Though they satisfied all the requirements of minimalism, they were more contradictory, more vulnerable, less static than their close cousin of the era. The fact that they were store-bought, ready-made items which were arranged in only one geometrical composition out of the infinite possibilities from which a particular arrangement could be made was central to Flavin's concept. It was therefore unnecessary for one to pay heed to the eerie light which they shed. But one could hardly help noticing the light by which they were engulfed upon entering these subtly manipulated spaces. In this way, the pieces were more intuitive, less self-referential than Judd's or Lewitt's or Andre's.

Flavin used the tubes as neutral lines of light much in the same way, he proposed, that a painter used line. Predetermining their configurations, Flavin pointed and watched while each construction was installed by electricians. They were parallel, adjacent groupings flush against walls, stretching across corners, tunneling through hallways or pointing away from walls at varying angles. Though Flavin made no attempt to compose these tubes with any respect to a particular environment, they filled any room from wall to wall, sometimes negating the room entirely with their eerie illumination, isolating their own essence from the walls, ceilings and floors. Though they shared with other minimal art of the era a radical independence of the artist's touch, this quality of illumination made them ironically dependent upon the variables inherent in any gallery with natural light. Thus, they necessarily developed a partnership with their environment, even though they did not help to define or enhance it. Also, the idea of their need for an electrical outlet brought inevitable questions of how these disparate concepts (light and form) were interrelated. Where did the art stop and start, and, indeed, what exactly was the art?

Flavin's work has not changed much in the last 20 years. Much of his older work, like icons or a rich tradition from the past, is exhibited around the world.

—Janet Goleas

Unchanged in form throughout his career, Flavin's consistency did indeed make the fluorescent tube a minimalist icon. His development of its installation, however, particularly in terms of its ability to transform space, maintained dialogue and criticality in his work. While early installations were focussed on the light tube as a radical form in itself, Flavin began engaging the space of the gallery once the idea of light as an art-object had been fully integrated. Using the fluorescent tube as both a sculptural object and light source with which to transform space, Flavin expanded its possibilities. With the site itself becoming increasingly important, the notion of "site-specific" art became a new and ground-breaking concern, pioneered in part by Flavin's integration of object, light, and the space of the gallery.

Using seemingly limitless configurations, as well as introducing colour, Flavin re-invented the context of the minimalist fluorescent, as well as the spaces in which it was shown. One of his most dramatic installations in 1992 at the Guggenheim Museum, New York, literally highlighted the architecture with light; each circular bay in the rotunda was lit, and the space itself reconfigured through the construction of an immense light tower running from floor to ceiling in the atrium. Other installations had similar intent as Flavin used light to transform architecture and the way we experience an otherwise familiar environment. Whether through subtle interventions such as changing the colour of already existing fluorescents, or by creating dramatic sculptural forms, Flavin's work continually challenged our perceptions of light and space.

—Carly Butler

FLINZER, Jochen

Nationality: German. **Born:** Bad Harzburg, Germany, 16 June 1959. **Education:** Studied art education at the Hochschule für Bildende Künste, Hamburg, 1977–82; studied the Japanese language at the Tokyo School of the Japanese Language, 1984–86. **Career:** Artist-in-residence, Ibaraki, Japan, 1997. **Awards:** Jugendförderpreis Bad Harzburg, 1982; DAAD scholarship, 1984; Hamburger Arbeitsstipendium für Bildende Kunst, 1988; Ernst Barlach Preis, Wedel, Germany, 1996. **Agents:** Dörrie*Priess, Admiralitätstraße 71, D-20459 Hamburg, Germany; Galerie Anita Beckers, Frankenallee 74, D-60327 Frankfurt/Main, Germany; Galerie Karin Sachs, Buttermelcherstraße 16, D-80469 Munich, Germany; Thomas Rehbein, Maria-Hilf-Straße 17, D-50677 Köln, Germany. **Address:** Postfach 306 140, D-20327 Hamburg, Germany.

Selected Individual Exhibitions:

1990 *53 Wochen Pech,* Galerie Tröster und Schlüter, Frankfurt am Main, Germany (catalog)
1992 *Ärsche und Tassen,* Galerie Tröster und Schlüter, Frankfurt am Main, Germany
1994 *Klein, aber oho!,* Elisabeth-Schneider-Stiftung, Freiburg im Breisgau, Germany
1996 *Jetzt noch sinnloser,* Galerie Andreas Schlüter, Hamburg, Germany
1998 *Grüße aus Moriya,* Institut für Moderne Kunst, Nuremberg, Germany
6 x 6, Galerie Andreas Schlüter, Hamburg, Germany
1999 *Indianerspiele,* Galerie Anita Beckers, Frankfurt am Main, Germany
2001 *Sonntag ist der Beste Tag im Tom's,* Galerie Karin Sachs, Munich

Selected Group Exhibitions:

1983 *Hamburg-Ulm,* Kunstverein Ulm, Germany
1992 *Szenenwechsel II,* Museum für Moderne Kunst, Frankfurt am Main, Germany
1994 *Szenenwechsel V,* Museum für Moderne Kunst, Frankfurt am Main, Germany
1995 *Szenenwechsel VIII,* Museum für Moderne Kunst, Frankfurt am Main, Germany
1996 *Views from Abroad—European Perspectives on American Art 2,* Whitney Museum of American Art, New York (catalog)
Wunderbar, Kunstverein Hamburg, Hamburg, Germany
1997 *ARCUS—Project Rooms,* Moriya, Japan (catalog)
Szenenwechsel XII, Museum für Moderne Kunst, Frankfurt am Main, Germany
1998 *Loose Threads,* Serpentine Gallery, London (catalog)
Lifestyle, Kunsthaus Bregenz, Austria
2000 Bill Maynes Gallery, New York
Szenenwechsel XVII, Museum für Moderne Kunst, Frankfurt am Main, Germany
2001 *Blondies and Brownies,* Aktionsforum Praterinsel, Munich
Hausarbeiten, Städtische Galerie, Nordhorn

Collections:

Museum für Moderne Kunst, Frankfurt am Main, Germany; Kunsthalle, Hamburg.

Publications:

On FLINZER: Books—*Bewegung im Kopf: Vom Umgang mit der Kunst* by Jean-Christophe Ammann, Regensburg 1993; *Welsh, Wolfgang: Die Aktualität des Asthetischen* by Jean-Christophe Ammann, Munich 1993; *Annäherung: Die Notwendigkeit von Kunst* by Jean-Christophe Ammann, Regensburg 1996; *Jochen Flinzer,* Nürnberg 1996. **Articles—**"Dorothea Baer-Bogenshütz über Jochen Flinzer" in *Artist Kunstmagazin,* no. 27, 1996; "Jochen Flinzer. Himmel, Arsch und Zwirn" interview with Stephan Trescher in *Jahrbuch '96* (Nürnberg), 1996; "Jochen Flinzer" by Cornelia Gockel in *Kunstforum Band 149,* 2000.

* * *

Handicraft has been the main theme of Jochen Flinzer's work since the early 1980s. His main focus point is dedicated to the

Jochen Flinzer: *Der Teppich von Atlanta* [*The Atlanta Tapestry*], 1997–99, in the Museum Für Moderne Kunst, Frankfurt am Main, 2000. ©Jochen Flinzer.

relationship between script and picture, whereby figuration and abstraction are inseparably connected with each other. The basic structure of his work repeatedly appears as an embroidered motif, topography, or picturesque design on the front part of the picture and its abstract counterpart on the back. His themes are mostly taken from the daily life of mass culture, such as television, sports, consumer products, personal ads, pornography, comics, crossword puzzles, or the sign language of tattoos. These different societal codes lead Jochen Flinzer to an artistic argument.

Our world is shaped by sign language, not only in the highly specialized job fields, but first of all in our recreational behavior. Behavior codes determine our lives from childhood on. Societal norms and cultural awareness determine what is to be feminine or masculine and what is considered high or low culture. The ones who know the codes belong; those who do not are outsiders. Jochen Flinzer is always concerned with the personal within the collective. He puts the markedly masculine domains into contrast with the rather domestic act of embroidering, a tender ''female'' activity. The noisy emotional is seen against the quiet simple-mindedness. The element of boredom, of pastime, but also the futile act are themes in many of Jochen Flinzer's works.

The picture motifs chosen for the front part of his works are always followed by a ''negative'' on the back. This structure, usually considered irrelevant and thus devalued, is put into the same position as the one on the front. Jochen Flinzer's works always have two picture sides. The orderly progression of the line (yarn) is at the same time followed by a chaotic entanglement of zigzag cross hatches on the back. This does not mean that the back side has been created less consciously or even at random. Jochen Flinzer follows the constraints of the front side, but also pays a lot of attention to the creation of the second picture on the back. The two sides of the picture are inseperable, thus there is no main picture view.

The two-sidedness of the pictures and objects has dominated the work of Jochen Flinzer from its very beginning. The carrier material for the embroidery, whether canvas, cloth, or paper, together with the mostly colored yarn, have very subtly been attuned to the pictures' contents.

Over and over again it is the power and strength of language and its codes that Jochen Flinzer is concerned with. The imaginations and fantasies connected with that idea of language are created in painstaking topography on the fromt of the picture and experience their neutralization on the back. Jochen Flinzer lived in Tokyo from 1984 to 1986, where he studied the Japanese language and calligraphy. During this time he developed a very pronounced preference for the relationship between script and picture. Here we also find the connecting points to the form of picture carpets, scrolls, and paravents that repeatedly appear in his work. They are the pictures of human longings and their contrasting images.

The work of Jochen Flinzer is multi-layered and profound. He challenges us to question the unsaid meaning of pictures, words, and rooms.

—Mario Kramer

FOREST, Fred

Nationality: French. **Education:** University of Paris, Sorbonne, Ph.D., 1985. **Career:** Media artist and educator; lives and works in Nice. Professor, University of Nice Sophia-Antopols, Nice. Director of the aesthetics of communication laboratory, Centre de Recherches et d'Etudes en Anthropologie, Communication, and Creation. **Awards:** Prize in Communications, *Biennale,* Venice, 1976; Distinction Vidéo, Festival International du Film d'Art, Paris, 1987; Prix Laser d'Or, Video Festival, Locarno, Switzerland, 1990; First Prize of the City of Locarno, Video Festival, Locarno, 1995; Silver Trophy, Art and Culture, F.A.U.S.T., Toulouse, France, 1996. **Member:** Société Française des Sciences de l'Information et de la Communication. **Address:** 147 Promenades des Anglais, 06200 Nice, France.

Individual Exhibitions:

1969 Galerie Sainte-Croix, Tours
1982 Centre Georges Pompidou
1988 Galerie Friedrich, Cologne
1989 Galerie Jacqueline Felman, Paris
Galerie Donguy, Paris
1990 Galerie Jacqueline Rivolta, Lausanne
1994 *The Square Meter Territory,* Galerie Donguy, Paris

Selected Group Exhibitions:

1976 *Biennale,* Venice
1977 *Documenta VI,* Kassel, Germany
1987 *Documenta VIII,* Kassel, Germany
1990 Usine Ephémère, Méru, France
1991 *The Electronic Bible,* Center of Contemporary Art, La Base, Levallois, France
Artists and Light, Center of Art and Technology, Reims, France
1992 *Fill in a container by phone,* A.R.S.L.A.B. Arts and Science Technology, Mole Antonelliana, Turin, Italy

Public or Internet Actions:

Fred Forest, President of Bulgarian TV, 1991; *The Miradors of Peace,* 1993; *From Casablanca to Locarno,* with National Swiss TV, 1995; *The Web Territory,* 1996.

Publications:

By FOREST: Books and Pamphlets—*Bourse de l'imaginaire,* Paris 1982; *100 actions,* Nice 1995; *Pour un art actuel, L'art à l'heure de l'Internet,* Paris, 1998; *Fonctionnement et dysfonctionnements de l'art contemporain,* Paris, 2000. **Articles—**''Manifeste de l'esthétique de la communication, plcs moins-zero'' in *Oktober,* no. 43, 1985; ''Esthétique de la communication'' in *Art Press,* February 1988; ''For an Aesthetics of Communication'' in *Design Issues,* 1988.

* * *

Fred Forest is an artist who operates on the edges of the artistic field. He devotes himself to what can be called the art of communication. It is certain that here we are fairly far from the idea we have of painters and sculptors in general. In Fred Forest's case we can even say that art has left its own area to enter that of the media, even advertizing.

Yet a careful analysis of Forest's itinerary and activities shows us that he is a veritable artist, his options and behaviour being those of a creator of new values of an aesthetic order obtained through the work on communications, provocative work for sure but sensitive nevertheless. This process is not illustrated by the production of tangible and physically realized objects but by the production of communications systems and diverse situations.

To grasp the meaning of the relationship between subjective and social factors in Fred Forest's background, it should be said that from 1954 to 1970 he was Postal and Telecommunications Inspector in Algeria, which, as we see, oriented his artistic career in that the latter took place in parallel with the former (he was then a painter) and ended in 1970 with his making a decisive step. From employee at the Post and Telecommunications, Fred Forest became an artist of communications, inaugurating inventive and creative work in human networks and relations.

Such an existential transformation is not entirely miraculous. It has to be inserted into the context of 1968 to 1970, a period when counter-culture movements assimilated life with art and highlighted each person's daily creativity. This existential transformation in Forest was also linked with the introduction of advanced technology in his art. He was among the first in France to use video and closed-circuit television. In 1970 he realized an audio-visual show at the Universal Exhibition at Osaka before directly interceding in the press and other mass medias just about everywhere in the world. His communication systems utilize the telephone, radio, television, telematics and the cable.

Among the numerous events organized by Fred Forest I shall single out his *Sociological Walk in Brooklyn-Sao Paolo,* in Brazil in October, 1973. After placing daily advertisements in the local newspapers and on local radio urging the residents of Brooklyn-Sao Paolo to phone the Art Museum in order to sign up for this walk in his company, Fred Forest invited the participants to walk through the district according to a pre-planned itinerary. At different stages the group visited the local music shop, the fruit vendor, the cobbler, the bank, the supermarket, the church and an art gallery. Fred Forest was aiming to investigate a localized urban area through its different business, administrative and cultural vocations. With the participants' help he wanted to experience daily reality, reveal their internal relationships and create micro-communication events enabling the establishment of information-circulation through direct intervention in the milieu.

Fred Forest's artistic career has also been marked by his belonging to the Sociological Art Collective, active until the end of the 1970s, then to the Communication Aesthetic Group. Each of these movements united plastic artists and theoreticians (sociologists and aesthetic thinkers) and gave them the chance to show individually as practicing artists after having tried to work out a common theory.

Forest has recently devoted himself to producing electronic-diode newspapers that unite two characteristics of his procedure: limited appearances in the mass medias and the use of advanced technology. One of his latest works of this type, *The Bible Culled from the Sands,* originally called *The Electronic Bible and the Gulf War,* shows a luminous parade of quotes from the Old Testament simultaneously with excerpts from newspaper articles reporting the fighting in the Gulf War. Long lists of military equipment are juxtaposed with long genealogies taken from the Bible. Forest thereby wants to draw our attention to the fact that history can repeat itself through similar speeches. He obviously does not care about the stereotypical statements made by politicians and military leaders.

All of Fred Forest's manifestations that can be inserted into socio-political news are provocative and critical by nature, but they incite to think, even if they grate because of their aggressivity. In the end they work as questions, communications and interactivity that confirm Forest's artistic aims. This is also the case in his most recent works, such as ''La Machine à travailler le temps,'' where he offers an opportunity to the spectator/manipulator to shorten or to accelerate the flux of time both in the physical space of an installation and in the virtual cyberspace of the Internet.

—Frank Popper

FOX, Terry (Alan)

Nationality: American. **Born:** Seattle, Washington, 10 May 1943. **Education:** Studied at Cornish School of Allied Arts, Seattle, and Academia di Belle Arti, Rome 1962. **Awards:** Adaline Kent Annual Award for Californian Artists, 1977; DAAD Artists Fellowship, West Berlin, 1982. **Agent:** Ronald Feldman Fine Arts, 31 Mercer Street, New York, New York 10013. **Address:** 71 rue Maghin, B-4000 Liège, Belgium.

Individual Exhibitions:

1970 Reese Palley Gallery, San Francisco
Museum of Conceptual Art, San Francisco
Richmond Art Center, California
1971 Reese Palley Gallery, New York
Reese Palley Gallery, San Francisco
1972 Galerie Ileana Sonnabend, Paris
Reese Palley Gallery, San Francisco
Modern Art Agency Lucio Amelio, Naples
1973 University of California, Berkeley
1974 Everson Museum of Art, Syracuse, New York
1975 Galleria Schema, Florence
Long Beach Museum of Art, California
And/Or Gallery, Seattle, Washington
1976 The Kitchen, New York
1977 Site, San Francisco
The Kitchen, New York
Galerie De Appel, Amsterdam
Galerie Krinzinger, Innsbruck, Austria
1978 Podio del Mondo per l'Arte, Middelburg, Netherlands
San Francisco Art Institute
1979 Galerie Nachst St. Stephen, Vienna
Galerie Dany Keller, Munich
1980 Museum of Modern Art, New York
1982 Kunstmuseum, Lucerne, Switzerland
Galleria Fernando Pellegrino, Bologna, Italy
Museum Folkwang, Essen, West Germany
Daad-Galerie, West Berlin
1983 Galerie Grita Insam, Vienna
1984 Ronald Feldman Fine Arts, New York
1985 Kunstraum Munchen, Munich
Galleria del Cavallino, Venice
1986 Galerie Löhrl, Mönchengladbach, Germany
1987 University Art Museum, University of California, Berkeley
Primo Piano, Rome
1988 Via Toscanella, Florence
Gesellschaft fur Aktuelle Kunst, Bremen, Germany
1991 Galerie Löhrl, Mönchengladbach, Germany
Syndikat Halle, Bonn
1992 *Articulations (Labyrint/Text Works),* Paley/Levy Galleries, Moore College of Art and Design, Philadelphia (traveled to Otis Gallery, Los Angeles)(catalog)
1993 Ronald Feldman Fine Arts, New York
1995 Galerie Lohrl, Monchengladbach, Germany (traveled to Pfalzgalerie, Kaiserslautern, German) (catalog)
1997 *Elementary Parallelism,* Gesellschaft für Aktuelle Kunst, Bremen (catalog)
1998 *Echoes, Shadows and Reflections,* Stadt Galerie Saarbrucken, Germany
Metronom Gallery, Barcelona
2000 Paula Anglim Gallery, San Francisco

Selected Group Exhibitions:

1969 *The Return of Abstract Expressionism,* Richmond Art Center, California
1970 *The 80s,* University of California Art Museum, Berkeley
1971 *Project: Pier 18,* Museum of Modern Art, New York
1972 *Documenta 5,* Museum Fridericianum, Kassel, West Germany (and *Documenta 6,* 1977)
1978 *Adaline Kent Awards,* San Francisco Art Institute
1980 *Space, Time, Sound,* San Francisco Museum of Modern Art
1983 *Site Strategies,* Oakland Museum, California
1984 *Content: A Contemporary Focus 1974–84,* Hirshhorn Museum, Washington, D.C.
1986 *California Sculpture 1959–80,* San Francisco Museum of Modern Art
1987 *Berlinart 1961–87,* Museum of Modern Art, New York (travelled to San Francisco)
1990 *Sydney Biennale,* Australia
1996 *Withdrawing,* Ronald Feldman Fine Arts, New York
1999 *Art 30 Basel,* Basel
Out of Actions: Between Performance and the Object, Museum of Contemporary Art, Los Angeles (traveling exhibition)
2001 *The Artists for Visual Sound, Part II,* Mattress Factory, Pittsburgh

Collections:

University of California Art Museum, Berkeley; San Francisco Museum of Modern Art; Museum Folkwang, Essen; Museum Moderner

Kunst, Vienna; Kunstmuseum, Lucerne; Kunstmuseum, Bern, Switzerland; Von Der Heydt-Museum, Wuppertal, Germany.

Publications:

By FOX: Books—*Catch Phrases and Hobo Signs,* Munich 1985; *Textum (Web),* Eindhoven, Netherlands, Het Appollohuis, 1989; *Articulations,* Philadelphia 1992; *Ocular Language: Terry Fox—30 Years of Speaking and Writing About Art,* edited by Eva Schmidt, Bremen 2000. **Articles**—''A Conversation with Terry Fox'' with Pat Leddy, Josef Woodard and M.A. Greenstein in *Artweek,* vol. 25, no. 4, 17 February 1994. **Films**—*If Marcia Ever Gets Back with the Butane, This Film Will Be a Gas,* with Willoughby Sharp, 1969; *Rain,* 1970; *Sweat,* 1970; *3-Minute Film,* 1970; **Videos**--*Taonguing,* 1970; *The Rake's Progress: In the Service of Art,* 1971; *Turgenscent Sex,* 1971; *Clutch,* 1971. **CD**—*Ataraxia,* Germany 1998.

On FOX: Books—*Outside the Frame: Performance and the Object: A Survey History of Performance Art in the USA Since 1950* by Gary Sangster, Cleveland 1994. **Exhibition catalogs**—*Terry Fox,* Essen 1982; *Terry Fox* (with essay by Christine Tacke), Munich 1985; *Terry Fox—OBJECTS (TEXTS)/DRAWINGS (TEXTS),* Mönchengladbach, Germany, 1991; *Terry Fox: Articulations,* Paley/Levy Gallery, Moore College of Art and Design, Philadelphia, 1992.

* * *

FRANCIS, Sam

Nationality: American. **Born:** in San Mateo, California, 25 June 1923. **Education:** Studied medical sciences at the University of California, Berkeley, 1941–43; began painting while a tuberculosis patient at hospitals in Denver and San Francisco, studying privately with David Park, 1944–47, and during convalescence at the Artists' Colony, Carmel, California, 1947; returned to the University of California as an art student, 1948–50, B.A. 1949, M.A. 1950, then studied at the Academie Fernand Leger, Paris, 1950. Served in the United States Army Air Corps, 1943–44. **Family:** married Mako Ioemitsu; son: Osamu; married Margaret Smith in 1986. **Career:** Full-time artist since 1950; worked in Paris, with travel to Mexico, Tokyo and throughout Europe, 1950–58; moved to New York, 1959; lived in Berne, 1960–61; moved to Santa Monica, California, 1962; lived in Tokyo, 1973–74; collaborated with the group ''Single Wing Turquoise Bird,'' 1968; established studio in San Leandro, California, 1981–83; founded Lapis Press, Santa Monica, California, 1984. **Awards:** *International Biennial Exhibition of Prints* Award, Tokyo, 1962; Dunn International Prize, 1963; Tamarind Fellowship, 1963. Honorary Ph.D.: University of California, Berkeley, 1969. **Agent:** Smith-Andersen Gallery, 200 Homer Street, Palo Alto, California 94301. **Died:** Of prostate cancer, 4 November 1994.

Individual Exhibitions:

1952 Galerie Nina Dausset, Paris
Galerie du Dragon, Paris
1955 Galerie Rive Droite, Paris
1956 Galerie Rive Droite, Paris
Martha Jackson Gallery, New York
1957 Martha Jackson Gallery, New York
Gimpel Fils Ltd., London
Kornfeld und Klipstein, Berne
1958 Kornfeld und Klipstein, Berne
Galerie Olaf Hudtwalcher, Frankfurt
Martha Jackson Gallery, New York
Zoe Dussane Gallery, Seattle
Kunstverein, Dusseldorf
1959 Pasadena Art Museum, California (travelled to the San Francisco Museum of Art and the Seattle Art Museum)
1960 Kunsthalle, Berne (travelled to the Modern Museet, Stockholm) David Anderson Gallery, New York
Galleria La Notizie, Turin
1961 David Anderson Gallery, New York
Galerie de Seine, Paris
Kornfeld und Klipstein, Berne
Grabowski Gallery, London
Galleria Il Segno, Rome
Galerie Jacques Dubourg, Paris
Minami Gallery, Tokyo
Galerie Alfred Schmela, Dusseldorf
Galerie St. Stephan, Vienna
1962 Galerie Benador, Geneva
Galerie Edwin Engelberts, Geneva
Esther Bear Gallery, Santa Barbara, California
Galerie Olaf Hudtwalcher, Frankfurt
Galerie Pauli, Lausanne
Galerie Brusberg, Hannover
1963 Kornfeld und Klipstein, Berne
Kestner-Gesellschaft, Hannover
Galerie Anderson-Mayer, Paris
Martha Jackson Gallery, New York
1964 Martha Jackson Gallery, New York
Galerie Ernst Hauswedell, Baden-Baden
Minami Gallery, Tokyo
Pasadena Art Museum, California
1965 Kornfeld und Klipstein, Berne
Auslander Gallery, New York
Württembergischer Kunstverein, Stuttgart
Arthur Tooth and Sons Ltd., London
Galerie Ricke, Kassel, West Germany
1966 Kornfeld und Klipstein, Berne
California State College at Fullerton
Minami Gallery, Tokyo
Galerie Edwin Engelberts, Geneva
Pasadena Art Museum, California
1967 Dom Galerie, Cologne
Pierre Matisse Gallery, New York
Museum of Fine Arts, Houston (travelled to the University of California Art Museum, Berkeley, and the San Francisco Museum of Art)
University of California at Los Angeles
Dickson Art Center, Los Angeles
Skupina Ceskoslovenskych Umelcu Orajiju-Hollar, Prague
1968 Martha Jackson Gallery, New York
Kunsthalle, Berne
Kornfeld und Klipstein, Berne
Minami Gallery, Tokyo
Badischer Kunstverein, Karlsruhe
Stedelijk Museum, Amsterdam

Sam Francis: *In Lovely Blueness,* 1955. Giraudon/Art Resource, NY. ©2001 Estate of Sam Francis/Artists Rights Society (ARS), New York.

Tokyo Central Gallery
Centre National d'Art Contemporain, Paris
Galerie du Bac, Paris
1969 University of Minnesota, Minneapolis
Andre Emmerich Gallery, New York
Felix Landau Gallery, Los Angeles
1970 Los Angeles County Museum of Art
Martha Jackson Gallery, New York
Minami Gallery, Tokyo
Nicholas Wilder Gallery, Los Angeles
1971 Andre Emmerich Gallery, New York
1972 Standford University, California
Albright-Knox Art Gallery, Buffalo, New York (retrospective; travelled to the Corcoran Gallery, Washington, D.C., Whitney Museum, New York; Museum of Fine Arts, Dallas; and the Oakland Museum of Art, California)
1973 Kornfeld und Klipstein, Berne
1974 Gimpels Fils, London
Minami Gallery, Tokyo
1975 Nicholas Wilder Gallery, Los Angeles
Galerie Jean Fournier, Paris
Andre Emmerich Gallery, New York
Richard Gray Gallery, Chicago
Kornfeld und Klipstein, Berne
Smith-Andersen Gallery, Palo Alto, California
1978 Nicholas Wilder Gallery, Los Angeles
1979 Galerie Jean Fournier, Paris
Andre Emmerich Gallery, New York
Brooke Alexander Inc., New York
1980 Riko Mizuno Gallery, Los Angeles
James Corcoran Gallery, Los Angeles
Smith-Andersen Gallery, Palo Alto, California
1981 Andre Emmerich Gallery, New York
Ace Gallery, Melrose, Los Angeles
Ruth Schaffner Gallery, Santa Barbara, California
Faith and Charity in Hope Gallery, Idaho
1982 Andre Emmerich Gallery, New York
Nantenshi Gallery, Tokyo
Richard Gray Gallery, Chicago
1983 Andre Emmerich Gallery, New York
Galerie Kornfeld, Berne
Smith-Andersen Gallery, Palo Alto, California
Fondation Maeght, St. Paul de Vence, France
Studio Marconi, Milan
Colorado State University, Fort Collins
Galerie Jean Fournier, Paris
Art Attack Gallery, Idaho
John Berggruen Gallery, San Francisco
Nantenshi Gallery, Tokyo
Art Museum Association, New York(toured the United States)
1984 André Emmerich Gallery, New York
Pamela Auchincloss Gallery, Santa Barbara, California
Brooke Alexander Inc., New York
Cantor/Lamberg Gallery, Michigan
Robert Elkon, Gallery, New York
1985 Galerie Kornfeld, Berne
Galerie Jean Fournier, Paris
Nantenshi Gallery, Tokyo
Richard Gray Gallery, Chicago
Smith-Andersen Gallery, Palo Alto, California
1986 André Emmerich Gallery, New York
Galerie Jean Fournier, Paris
Nantenshi Gallery, Tokyo
Angles Gallery, Santa Monica, California
1987 Knoedler Gallery, London
André Emmerich Gallery, New York
Pamela Auchincloss Gallery, Santa Barbara, California
Heland Thorden Wetterling Galleries, Stockholm
G. Dalsheimer Gallery, Baltimore
Galeria Eude, Barcelona

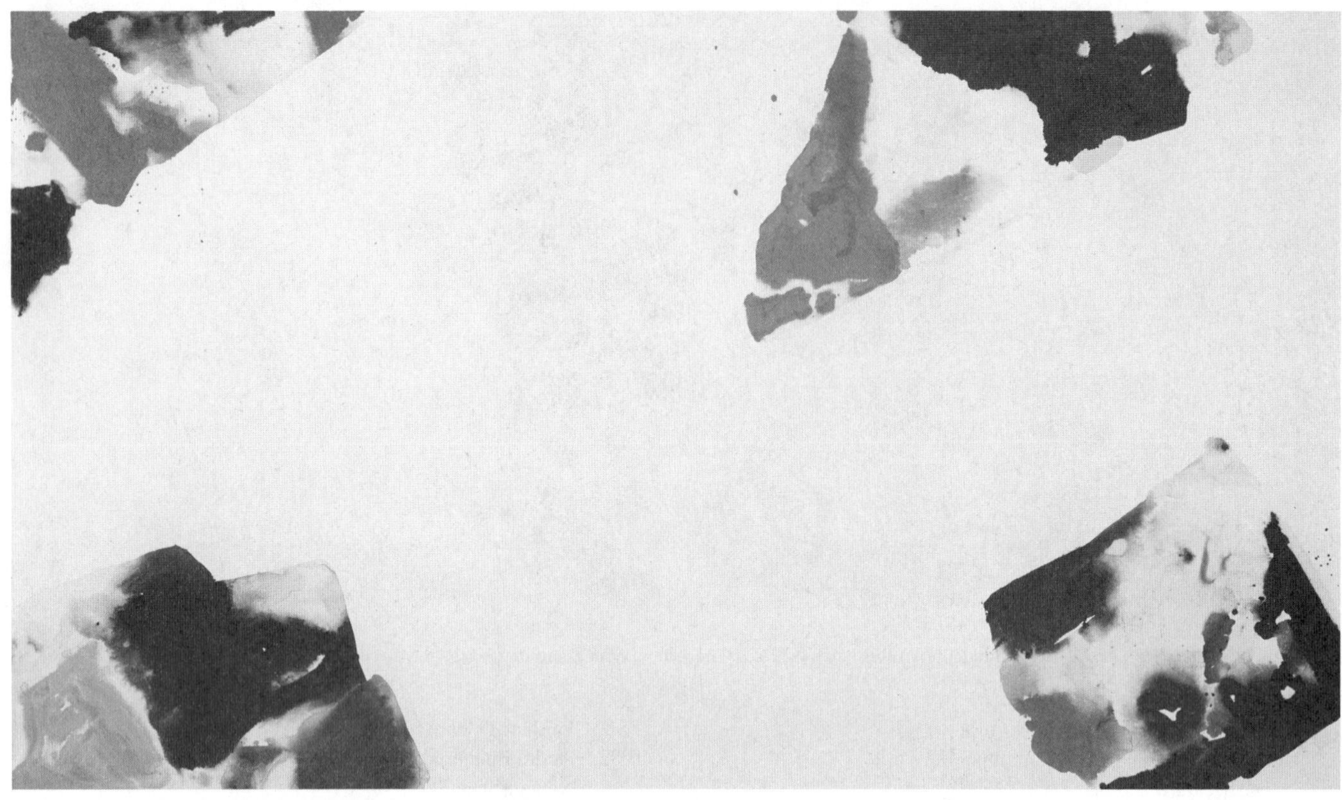

Color patches painting by Sam Francis, 20th century. ©2001 The Estate of Sam Francis/Artists Rights Society (ARS), NY.

Manny Silverman Gallery, Los Angeles
Galerie Pudelko, Bonn, East Germany;
Lever/Meyerson Galleries, New York
1988 André Emmerich Gallery, New York
Galerie Jean Fournier, Paris
Nantenshi Gallery, Tokyo
Smith/Andersen Gallery, Palo Alto
Greenberg Gallery, St. Louis, Missouri
Galerie de Seoul, Korea (travelled to Toyama Museum; The Museum of Modern Art, Seibu, Takanawa, Karuizawa; The Museum of Modern Art, Shiga; Ohara Musuem of Art, Murashiki; Setagaya Art Museum, Tokyo)
1989 André Emmerich Gallery, New York
Galerie Jean Fournier, Paris
Bernard Jacobson Gallery, London
Sun Valley Center Gallery, Idaho
Linda Farris Gallery, Seattle, Washington
Cantor/Lemberg Gallery, Birmingham, Michigan
Knoedler Gallery, London
1990 Associated American Artist, New York
Gallery Delaive, Amsterdam
Heland Wetterling Gallery, Stockholm
Ogawa Art Foundation, Tokyo
Ochi Gallery, Sun Valley, Idaho
Talbot Rice Gallery, Edinburgh
André Emmerich Gallery, New York
Smith/Andersen Gallery, Palo Alto
1991 Galerie Kornfeld, Bern
Galerie Jean Fournier, Paris
James Corcoran Gallery, Los Angeles
Angles Gallery, Los Angeles
Gana Art Gallery, Seoul, Korea
Associated American Artists, New York
Gagosian Gallery, New York
Centre Regional d'Art Contemporian Midi-Pyrenees, Toulouse-Labege, France
1992 Galerie Daniel Papierski, Paris
Museum van der Togt, Amsterdam
Kukje Gallery, Seoul
1993 Kunst-und Ausstellungshalle der Bundesrepublik Deutschland, Bonn
Galerie Pudelko, Bonn
Bobbie Greenfield Fine Art, Venice, California
M. Cohen Gallery, New York
Ochi Galleries, Ketchum, Idaho
Manny Silverman Gallery, Los Angeles
Galerie Iris Wazzau, Davos, Switzerland
1994 Long Fine Art, New York
Galerie Delaive, Amsterdam, Netherlands
Bobbie Greenfield Gallery, Venice, California
Galerie Jean Fournier, Paris
Galerie Proarta, Zurich, Switzerland
André Emmerich Gallery, New York
Richard Gray Gallery, Chicago
University Art Museum, University of California at Berkeley
1995 Kunstverein Ludwigsburg
Louisiana Museum of Art, Humlebaek
Stadtische Kunstsammlungen Chemnitz

1995 Galerie nationale du jeu de paume, Paris
1996 Galerie nationale du jeu de paume, Paris
1997 Museo d'arte Mendrisio
1999 Museum of Contemporary Art, Los Angeles
Lawrence Rubin Greenberg Van Doren Fine Art, New York

Selected Group Exhibitions:

1950 *Salon de Mai,* Musée National d'Art Moderne, Paris
1955 *Tendances Actuelles,* Kunsthalle, Berne
1956 *12 Americans,* Museum of Modern Art, New York (toured the United States)
1958 *50 Ans d'Art Moderne,* Palais des Beaux-Arts, Brussels
1973 *25 Years of American Painting,* Des Moines Art Center, Iowa
1974 *Variations of Abstractions,* Andre Emmerich Gallery, New York
1987 *American Painting: Abstract Expressionism and After,* San Francisco Museum of Modern Art
1990 *Watercolors from the Abstract Expressionist Era,* The Katonah Museum of Art, New York
1991 *Recent Acquisitions,* National Museum of American Art, Washington, D.C.
1993 *Azure,* Foundation Cartier pour l'art contemporain, Jouyen Josas, France

Collections:

Museum of Modern Art, New York; Whitney Museum, New York; Albright-Knox Art Gallery, Buffalo, New York; National Gallery, Washington, D.C.; Los Angeles County Museum of Art; Musée National d'Art Moderne, Paris; Nationalgalerie, Berlin; Ohara Museum, Okayama, Japan; St. Louis Art Museum, Missouri; National Collection of Fine Arts, Smithsonian Institution, Washington, D.C.; Stedelijk, Amsterdam; Offentliche, Basel; Ulster Museum, Belfast, Northern Ireland; Carnegie Institute of Technology, Pittsburgh; Dallas Museum of Fine Arts, Dallas, Dayton Art Institute, Ohio; Kunstsammlung Nordrhein-Westfalen, Düsseldorf, Germany; Stedelijk van Abbe-Museum, Eindhoven, Holland; Hamburger Kunsthause, Hamburg, Germany; Kestner-Gesellschaft, Hannover, Germany; National Museum of Western Art, Tokyo; Art Gallery of Toronto, Canada; Washington University, St. Louis; Yale Univeristy, New Haven.

Murals: Sogetsu School of the sculptor and flower arranger, Sofu Teshigahara, Tokyo, 1957; Chase Manhattan Bank, New York, 1959; Kunsthalle, Berne, 1960; Weinstock's Department Store, Sacramento, California, 1980; General Services Administration Building, Anchorage, Alaska, 1980.

Publications:

On FRANCIS: Book—*Sam Francis,* exhibition catalog, by James Johnson Sweeney, Houston 1967; *Sam Francis,* by Pontus Hulten, Stuttgart, 1993; *Sam Francis: les annees parisiennes 1950–1961,* exhibition catalog, Paris, 1996. **Articles—**''Summer Events: Paris: Sam Francis,'' by Pierre Schneider in *Art News* (New York), Summer 1955; ''Sam Francis'' by Berto Moruccio in *Aujourd'hui* (Paris), May 1963; ''Sam Francis'' by C. H. in *Werk* (Winterthur, Switzerland), June 1968; ''New York Letter'' by Carter Ratcliff in *Art International* (Lugano), January 1970; ''Sam Francis: From Field to Arabesque'' by Lawrence Alloway in *Artforum* (New York), February 1973; ''New Editions'' in *Art News* (New York), November 1974; ''Sam Francis: Light, Colour and Space'' by Philippe Piguet in *Cimaise* (Paris), vol. 42, November/December 1995; ''Sam Francis, the Paris Years 1950–1961'' by Anne Bertrand in *Art Press*, no. 211, March 1996; ''In Lovely Blueness, 1955–56'' in *Museum Studies*, vol. 25, no. 1, 1999; ''Sunny Side Up'' by Daniel Schulman in *Artforum* (New York), vol. 37, i7 March 1999; ''Sam Francis'' by David Carrier in *Burlington Magazine* (London), no. 1155, vol. 141, June 1999.

* * *

Francis studied medicine and psychology at the University of California at Berkeley from 1941–43. After the war he studied painting with David Park at the California School of Fine Art in San Francisco (1948–50), and received his B.A. (1949), and M.A. (1950) from the University of California. In 1950 he went to Paris where he became friendly with the Canadian abstract painter Jean-Paul Riopelle and had his first solo show in 1952. From 1950–58 he worked in Paris, with travels to other European countries and, further afield, to Mexico and Japan. Dubbed by Barbara Rose in *American Art since 1900* a second-generation Abstract Expressionist, his work at this time was characterized by a cool palette and the compression of elements into segments of the canvas. The pigment was kept thin, which allowed for delicate dripping. By the late 1950s his paintings were composed of masses of brilliant colour floating on expanses of unpainted canvas.

His career has been well punctuated with inclusion in major international exhibitions and retrospectives (Sao Paulo Bienal and Kassel Dokumenta in 1959; The Museum of Fine Arts, Houston and the University of California, Berkeley in 1967; Los Angeles County Museum of Art in 1970; Albright-Knox in Buffalo in 1972).

Francis lived and exhibited in Tokyo from 1973–74 which strengthened his interest in Oriental simplicity. By the late 1970s Francis's paintings had become more obviously structured, with large multicoloured grids dominating the picture surface. The surface was then covered with splashes and drips, all thinly laid on and 'blooming' out of each other. Also at this time came an interest in the monotype, with a major exhibition of these at the Los Angeles County Museum of Art in 1980. The monotypes used, often all at the same time, watercolour, gouache, dry pigment, inks, acrylic and oil, laid on a copper plate and put through a press. Since the early 1980s Francis has been producing both large monotypes and paintings characterized by their glowing colours. He has said of his attitude to colour: ''Color is light on fire. Each color is the result of 'burning', for each substance burns with a particular color.''

—Victoria Keller

FRANKENTHALER, Helen

Nationality: American. **Born:** New York City, 12 December 1928. **Education:** Dalton School, New York, with Rufino Tamayo; Bennington College, Vermont, with Paul Feeley, 1945–49, B.A. 1949; Art Students League, New York, with Vaclav Vytlacil, 1946; privately with Wallace Harrison, New York, 1948; privately with Hans Hofmann, New York, 1950. **Family:** Married Robert Motherwell, *q.v.*, in 1958; married Stephen DuBrul, 1994. **Career:** Independent painter, since 1950: lives and works in New York. Instructor, New York University, 1958–59; painting instructor, Yale University, New Haven, Connecticut, 1962; Princeton University, New Jersey, Hunter College, New York, 1970; University of Rochester, New York 1971; Bennington College, 1972; Brooklyn Museum Art School, New York, 1973; Swarthmore College, Pennsylvania, 1974; Drew University, Madison, New Jersey, 1975; Bard College, Annandale-on-Hudson, New York, 1977; University of Arizona, Tucson, 1978; Art Institute of Chicago, 1983; Skowhegan School of Painting and Sculpture, Maine, 1986. Trustee, Bennington College, Vermont, 1967–82; Fellow of Calhoun College, Yale University, since 1968. **Member:** Corporation of Yaddo, Saratoga Springs, New York, 1974–78; National Council on the Arts, Washington, D.C., 1985; National Institute of Arts and Letters, 1974; the American Academy, 1990; Vice-Chancelor of the American Academy, 1991; the American Academy of Arts and Sciences, 1991; the Advisory Committee to the Board, Santa Fe Institute of Fine Arts, 1992–93. **Awards:** First Prize, *Biennale,* Paris, 1959; Gold Medal, *International Graphics Biennale,* Catania, Italy, 1972; Garrett Award, Art Institute of Chicago, 1972; National Conference of Christians and Jews Award, 1978; Bennington College Alumni Award, 1979; Mayor's Award of Honor, New York 1986. DHL: Skidmore College, 1969; DFA: Smith College, 1973; Moore College of Art, 1974; Bard College, 1946; Radcliffe College, 1978; Amherst College, 1979; New York University, 1979; Harvard University, 1980; Philadelphia College of Art, 1980; Williams College, 1980; Yale University, 1981; Brandeis University, 1982; University of Hartford, 1983; Syracuse University, 1985; Dartmouth College, 1994; Parsons School of Design, 1996; University of Pennsylvania, 1996; Rhode Island School of Design, 1996; Tufts University, 1998. Connecticut Arts Award, 1989; Distinguished Artist Award for Lifetime Achievement, College Art Association, New York, 1994; Lotos Medal of Merit, 1994; Artist of the Year Award, 1995; Jerusalem Prize, 1999; Lifetime Achievement Award, 1999. **Agent:** Knoedler & Co., Inc., 19 East 70th Street, New York, New York 10021.

Individual Exhibitions:

1951 Tibor de Nagy Gallery, New York
1952 Tibor de Nagy Gallery, New York
1953 Tibor de Nagy Gallery, New York
1954 Tibor de Nagy Gallery, New York
1956 Tibor de Nagy Gallery, New York
1957 Tibor de Nagy Gallery, New York
1958 Tibor de Nagy Gallery, New York
1959 André Emmerich Gallery, New York
1960 Jewish Museum, New York
1961 André Emmerich Gallery, New York
Everett Ellin Gallery, Los Angeles
Galerie Lawrence, Paris
Neufville Galerie, Paris
1962 Galleria dell'Ariete, Milan
André Emmerich Gallery, New York
Bennington College, Vermont
1964 Kasmin Gallery, London
1965 David Mirvish Gallery, Toronto
André Emmerich Gallery, New York
1966 Windham College, Putney, Vermont
André Emmerich Gallery, New York
1967 Nicholas Wilder Gallery, Los Angeles
Gertrude Kasle Gallery, Detroit
1968 André Emmerich Gallery, New York
1969 Whitney Museum, New York (retrospective)
Whitechapel Art Gallery, London
André Emmerich Gallery, New York
Kongress-Halle, Berlin
Kunstverein, Hannover
1970 André Emmerich Gallery, New York
1971 Heath Gallery, Atlanta
André Emmerich Gallery, New York
Galerie Godard Lefort, Montreal
David Mirvish Gallery, Toronto
1972 Fendrick Gallery, Washington, D.C.
John Berggruen Gallery, San Francisco (print retrospective)
André Emmerich Gallery, New York
Portland Art Museum, Oregon
1973 David Mirvish Gallery, Toronto
André Emmerich Gallery, New York
Waddington Gallery, London
Janie C. Lee Gallery, Dallas
Metropolitan Museum of Art, New York
1974 Galerie Emmerich, Zurich
1975 André Emmerich Gallery, New York
Waddington Gallery, London
Corcoran Gallery, Washington, D.C. (retrospective)
David Mirvish Gallery, Toronto
Guggenheim Museum, New York
ACE Gallery, Vancouver
Rosa Esman Gallery, New York
1976 Diane Gilson Gallery, Seattle
Janie C. Lee Gallery, Houston
1977 Greenberg Gallery, St. Louis
André Emmerich Gallery, New York
Jacksonville Art Museum, Florida
Galerie Wentzel, Hamburg
1978 Knoedler Gallery, London
International Communications Agency, World Tour (retrospective)
Bennington College, Vermont
Nelson Gallery of Art, Kansas City
Janie C. Lee Gallery, Houston
1979 André Emmerich Gallery, New York
John Berggruen Gallery, San Francisco
Fendrick Gallery, Washington, D.C.
1980 *Helen Frankenthaler: Works of the 70s,* Saginaw Art Museum, Michigan (travelled to Grand Rapids Art Museum and Kalamazoo Institute of Arts, Michigan)
Phillips Collection, Washington, D.C.
Janie C. Lee Gallery, Houston
1981 André Emmerich Gallery, New York
Knoedler Gallery, London
Thomas Segal Gallery, Boston
Toledo Museum of Art, Ohio
1982 Janie C. Lee Gallery, Houston
André Emmerich Gallery, New York
John Berggruen Gallery, San Francisco
Getler/Pall Gallery, New York
1983 Rosa Esman Gallery, New York

Gallery One, Toronto
Knoedler Gallery, London
Dana Reich Gallery, San Francisco
1984 André Emmerich Gallery, New York
Katonah Gallery, New York
1985 Guggenheim Museum, New York (travelled to Edmonton, Alberta; Toronto; Milwaukee; Baltimore; San Francisco; Houston; and Cambridge, Massachusetts, 1985–86)
Knoedler Gallery, London
1986 John Berggruen Gallery, San Francisco
André Emmerich Gallery, New York
1987 John Berggruen Gallery, San Francisco
1989 Museum of Modern Art, New York (retrospective; travelled to Los Angeles; and Fort Worth, Texas, 1989–90)
1990 André Emmerich Gallery, New York,
1991 André Emmerich Gallery, New York
Kukje Gallery, Seoul, Korea
Rosa Esman Gallery, New York
1992 Associated American Artists, New York
Knoedler and Co., New York
1993 Meredith Long and Company, Houston
André Emmerich Gallery, New York
The Century Association, New York
National Gallery of Art, Washington, D.C (travelled to: San Diego Museum of Fine Arts; Museum of Fine Arts, Boston; Cincinnati Contemporary Arts Center; Machida City Museum of Graphic Arts, Japan)
1994 Knoedler and Co., New York
Meredith Long and Company, Houston
1995 *Recent Prints and Paintings on Paper,* Bobbie Greenfield Gallery, Santa Monica (catalog)
Woodcuts 1973–1994, Dennos Museum Center, Traverse City (catalog)
New Work, Knoedler & Company, New York (catalog)
1996 *Spring Run Monotypes,* Knoedler & Company, New York
1997 *Paintings and Works on Paper,* Tasende Gallery, Los Angeles (catalog)
1998 *After Mountains and Sea: Frankenthaler 1956–1959,* Solomon R. Guggenheim Museum, New York
Frankenthaler: A Selection of Paintings from the Collection of the Artist 1951–1992, Neuberger Museum of Art, Purchase (catalog)
The Darker Palette, Savannah College of Art and Design, Georgia (catalog)
Helen Frankenthaler: 'Mountains and Sea' and the Years Afterwards (1956–59), Deutsche Guggenheim Berlin, Germany
2000 *On Paper: 1990–1999,* Bernard Jacobson Gallery, London (catalog)
2001 *The Prints of Helen Frankenthaler 1970–2001,* Greg Kucera Gallery, Seattle (also Connecticut Graphic Arts Center, Norwalk)

Selected Group Exhibitions:

1961 *Abstract Expressionist and Imagists,* Guggenheim Museum, New York
1970 *American Artists of the 1960s,* Boston University
1971 *The Structure of Color,* Whitney Museum, New York
1974 *Abbott/Frankenthaler/Grossman/Nevelson,* Smith College Museum of Art, Northampton, Massachusetts
1978 *Two Decades of American Abstraction,* University of Tampa, Florida
1980 *Woman: Artist and Image,* Columbus Museum of Art, Ohio
1983 *The American Artist as Printmaker,* Brooklyn Museum, New York
1986 *After Matisse,* Queens Museum, Flushing, New York (travelled to Norfolk, Virginia; Miami Beach, Florida; Washington, D.C.; Dayton, Ohio; and Worcester, Massachusetts, 1986–88)
1990 *The Unique Print,* Museum of Fine Arts, Boston
1994 *The New York School: Five Decades of Abstraction,* Gallery One, Toronto, Ontario
Western Artists/African Art, Museum of Modern Art, New York
2000 *A Theater of Art III,* Riva Yares, Santa Fe

Collections:

Metropolitan Museum of Art, New York; Museum of Modern Art, New York; Whitney Museum, New York; Brooklyn Museum, New York; Cleveland Museum of Art; Art Institute of Chicago; San Francisco Museum of Modern Art; Museum of Fine Arts, Boston; Museum of Fine Arts, Houston; Solomon R. Guggenheim Museum, New York; National Gallery of Art, Washington, D.C.

Publications:

By FRANKENTHALER: Books— *Frankenthaler: A Catalogue Raisonné: Prints 1961–1994* by Pegram Harrison, New York 1996. **Articles—**''Discussion: Is There a New Academy?'' in *Artnews* (New York), June 1959; ''An Interview with Helen Frankenthaler,'' with Henry Geldzahler, in *Artforum* (New York), October 1965; ''A Conversation with Helen Frankenthaler,'' with Donald J. Cyr, in *School Arts* (Worcester, Massachussets), April 1968; ''An Interview with Helen Frankenthaler,'' with Hilton Kramer in *Partisan Review,* vol. 61, Spring 1994; '''Making a Message; Giving a Message': Interview with Helen Frankenthaler,'' with Tim Marlow in *Art Newspaper,* vol. 11, no. 104, June 2000.

On FRANKENTHALER: Books—*Helen Frankenthaler,* exhibition catalog, by Frank O'Hara, New York 1960; *Helen Frankenthaler* by Eugene C. Goossen, New York 1969; *Helen Frankenthaler* by Barbara Rose, New York 1971, 1975; *Frankenthaler: The 1950s* by Carl Belz, Waltham, Massachusetts 1981; *Frankenthaler: Works on Paper 1949–1984* by Karen Wilkin, New York 1984; *Helen Fankenthaler* by John Elderfield, New York 1987; *Abstract Expressionist Women Painters: An Annotated Bibliography* by Françoise S. Puniello and Halina Rusak, Lanham 1996; *Originals: American Women Artists* by Eleanor C. Munro, New York 2000. **Articles—** ''The Art Galeries'' by Robert M. Coates in *The New Yorker,* November 1951; ''Helen Frankenthaler'' by E. C. Goossen in *Art International* (Zurich), October 1961; ''Poet of the Surface'' by William Berkson in *Arts Magazine* (New York), May/June 1965; ''The Achievement of Helen Frankenthaler'' by Gene Baro in *Art International* (Lugano, Switzerland), September 1967; ''Painting within the Tradition: The Career of Helen Frankenthaler'' by Barbara Rose in *Artforum* (New York), April 1969; ''Frankenthaler'' by

J. Goldman in *Artnews* (New York), November 1974; ''Helen Frankenthaler: The Moment and Distance'' in *Arts Magazine* (New York), April 1975; ''Helen Frankenthaler at the Guggenheim'' by Phyllis Tuchman in *Art in America* (New York), September/October 1975; ''Helen Frankenthaler's Art in the 50s'' by Hilton Kramer in the *New York Times,* 7 June 1981; *Helen Frankenthaler: A Paintings Retrospective,* exhibition catalog with essays by E.A. Carmean, Jr., New York, Harry N. Abrams, Inc., in association with the Modern Art Museum of Fort Worth, 1989; *Helen Frankenthaler: Prints,* exhibition catalog with essay by Ruth E. Fine, New York, Harry N. Abrams, Inc, in association with the National Gallery of Art, Washington, D.C., 1993; ''Helen Frankenthaler: Theme and Variation'' by Eric Gibson in *ARTnews,* vol. 95, no. 10, November 1996; ''Frankenthaler at the Guggenheim'' by Karen Wilkin in *New Criterion,* vol. 16, no. 7, March 1998; ''Helen Frankenthalers Ubergrosse Wasserfarben'' by Christopher Knight in *Texte zur Kunst,* vol. 8, no. 31, September 1998. **Film—***Frankenthaler: Toward a New Climate,* produced and directed by Perry Miller Adato, 1978.

* * *

Helen Frankenthaler's first mature pictures were produced, astonishingly, when she was in her 20s. This is rare for an abstract artist, since most don't hit their stride until their 40s, but it's clear that Frankenthaler's early paintings are marked not only by audacity and ambition (in the best sense) but also by pure ability. We see her taking on the artists she admired, not by imitating their manner, but by examining the substances of their work. If, for example, we are sometimes reminded of Pollock or Miró, it is because of the fluidity of Frankenthaler's gesture or the multiplicity of her evocative images; it is not because the paintings evoke existing Pollocks or Mirós.

From Pollock, she took the notion of fusing drawing and painting, translating this idea into her own suggestive, mysterious calligraphy. There is a now-famous litany which accompanies these early works: Frankenthaler stained paint directly into unprimed canvas, and achieved, on a large scale, the immediacy and transparency of watercolor. The white of the canvas set off her expansive drawing and led to greater openness, more disembodied color and more purely optical painting. The litany continues with the legendary visit of Kenneth Noland and Morris Louis to Frankenthaler's studio, which spurred their own investigations into the possibilities of staining with close-valued color, and changed the course of American abstraction.

Frankenthaler's early work has been the subject of a good deal of recent re-interpretation, which links its symbolic allusive qualities to an earlier generation of Abstract Expressionists, rather than stressing its evident connections with later-blooming members of Frankenthaler's own generation, such as Noland, Louis and Jules Olitski. Veiled references to personal experience and observation certainly pervade the early works, but like the artists she stimulated, Frankenthaler, too, gradually abandoned overt allusion for a no less moving, but more painterly and less specific kind of radiant color painting. Her pictures of the '60s and early '70s are distinguished by pools and flows of transparent color which paradoxically seem both to have their own shape and to have been manipulated by a very specific individual. It is impossible to separate color and drawing in these works; the floods of color seem self-determined because subtle adjustments of density and hue combine to make the result seem inevitable, but at the same time the shapes formed by these pools appear personal and expressive, never accidental or arbitrary. The continuous expanses of the areas of stained color are stiffened by drawn lines and drawing created by the edges of the color areas.

Since the mid-70s Frankenthaler's paintings have become denser and even lusher. The drama of color is intensified by the drama of surfaces. She reveals her debt to Hans Hofmann in a range of paint applications which vary from thick encrustations to transparent washes, but the imagery and drawing are unmistakably her own. She still insists on our awareness of paint as a fluid, spreading liquid, but her paintings of the past five years or so no longer depend upon staining. Instead, we are given layers of transparent color, floating ''clumps'' of paint, and sensuous puddles. Small incidents of painting, set against broad sweeps of layered color, become as important as the allusive images of earlier works. These evocative palimpsests of paint have considerable spatial complexity; at the same time they are clearly about matter on a surface, and considerable emotional complexity as well.

Frankenthaler's work since about 1985 has been characterized by a new daring and a new emphasis on drawing. While she is still capable of lush layerings and transparencies, her recent work has relied on broad, relatively uninterrupted expanses of color against which she plays large scale drawn strokes and patches of varied textures and contrasting hues. The paintings have a startling clarity and immediacy.

Frankenthaler has explored many media in the 1980s. She has continued her investigation of print-making techniques, producing monotypes, acquatints, and working with a master woodblock maker in Japan. She has done sets and costumes for the ballet, renewed her interest in making sculpture, and produced a large body of works on paper, some as rich and complex as her canvases.

There is high risk of failure in Frankenthaler's mature work. There is the danger that the superimposed layers of her paintings of the early '80s can become opaque and clotted, or that the bold sheets of color in her more recent work can appear too inert and uninflected; units of drawing and thick paint can look too artful, too placed, rather than spontaneously achieved. But at their best, Frankenthaler's canvases are simultaneously lyrical, intensely romantic and uncompromisingly tough. At the risk of overstatement, they invite comparison with the tradition of Delacroix and Turner, perhaps of Beethoven. Like that of her distinguished predecessors, Frankenthaler's recent works achieve extraordinary resonance through richness of color and density of texture. Most impressive, however, in a career that spans more than 50 years, Frankenthaler has continued to evolve, to take new risks and to respond to new challenges.

—Karen Wilkin

FRASER, Donald Hamilton

Nationality: British. **Born:** London, 30 July 1929. **Education:** St. Martin's School of Art, London, 1949–52; studied in Paris, 1952–54. **Military Service:** Served in the Royal Air Force, 1947–49. **Family:** Married the illustrator Judith Wentworth-Shields in 1954; daughter: Catherine Jane. **Career:** Tutor in Painting, Royal College of Art, London, 1958–84. Honorary Secretary, 1975–81, and Chairman, 1981–87, Artists General Benevolent Institution, London; Member of the Royal Fine Arts Commission, London, 1986–99. **Member:** Royal Academy of Art, London, Associate, 1975, Royal Academician, 1986, Honorary Curator, 1992–99, Trustee, 1993–99. Fellow of the Royal College of Art, London, 1981; Royal Overseas League, London, vice-president, 1988-. **Address:** Bramham Cottage, Remenham Lane, Henley-on-Thames, Oxon. RG9 2LR, England.

Individual Exhibitions:

1953 Gimpel Fils, London
1957 Gimpel Fils, London
Galerie Craven, Paris
1958 Paul Rosenberg, New York
1959 Gimpel Fils, London
1960 Paul Rosenberg, New York
1961 Gimpel Fils, London
1963 Gimpel Fils, London
Paul Rosenberg, New York
1964 Paul Rosenberg, New York
1965 Gimpel Fils, London
1966 Paul Rosenberg, New York
1967 Gimpel-Hanover, Zurich
1968 Gimpel Fils, London
Paul Rosenberg, New York
1969 Gimpel Fils, London
1970 Paul Rosenberg, New York
1971 Gimpel Fils, London
1973 Paul Rosenberg, New York
1975 Paul Rosenberg, New York
1976 Paul Rosenberg, New York
1977 Bohun Gallery, Henley-on-Thames, Oxfordshire
1978 Paul Rosenberg, New York
1979 Bohun Gallery, Henley-on-Thames, Oxfordshire
1980 Gallery Ten, London
1981 Scottish Gallery, Edinburgh
Bohun Gallery, Henley-on-Thames, Oxfordshire
1982 Gallery Ten, London
1983 Bohun Gallery, Henley-on-Thames, Oxfordshire
1984 Gallery Ten, London
1985 Christies' Contemporary Art, London
Christies' Contemporary Art, New York (travelled to Tulsa, Oklahoma, Oklahoma City; Kansas City, Missouri; and Carmel, California, 1985–86)
1987 CCA Galleries, London
1988 Kingfisher Gallery, Edinburgh
Gallery 10, London
1989CCA Gallery, London
1990 Bunkamura Gallery, Tokyo
1991 CCA Gallery, London
1992 Bunkamura Gallery, Tokyo
Gallery 10, London
1993 Flying Colours Gallery, Edinburgh
Beaux Arts Gallery, Bath
1994 CCA Gallery, London
1996 A.T. Kearney Corporation, London
1997 New Academy Gallery, London
1998 City Gallery, London
2000 W.H. Patterson Fine Art, London
Print Retrospective, CCA Gallery, London

Selected Group Exhibitions:

1953 *British Romantic Painting in the 20th Century,* National Museum of Wales, Cardiff (toured Wales)
1957 *6 British Painters,* Art Club of Chicago (travelled to the Albright-Knox Art Gallery, Buffalo, New York and National Gallery of Canada, Ottawa, 1957–58)
1964 *Englische Kunst der Gegenwart,* Städtische Kunstgalerie, Bochum, West Germany
1967 *Pittsburgh International,* Carnegie Institute, Pittsburgh
1973 *Earth Images,* Scottish Gallery of Modern Art, Edinburgh
1977 *British Painting 1952–77,* Royal Academy of Arts, London
1980 *Israel Observed: 10 British Painters,* Israel Museum, Jerusalem
1983 *Print Biennial,* Taipei
1984 *100 Years of Scottish Painting,* Edinburgh Fine Art Society
1985 *Six British Painters,* Toronto
1997 *Six British Painters,* Museum of Modern Art, Dubrovnik, and Royal Academy of Arts, London

Collections:

Arts Council of Great Britain, London; Hirshhorn Museum and Sculpture Garden, Washington, D.C.; Museum of Fine Arts, Boston; Albright-Knox Art Gallery, Buffalo, New York; Carnegie Institute, Pittsburgh; Yale University, New Haven, Connecticut; National Gallery of Canada, Ottawa; National Gallery of Victoria, Melbourne; H.M. The Queen; Desert Art Museum, Palm Springs, California; Wadsworth Athenaeum, Hartford, Connecticut.

Publications:

By FRASER: Books—*Gauguin's "Vision after the Sermon,"* London, 1969; *"Dancers" Extracts from a Ballet Notebook,* Phaidon Press, 1988.

On FRASER: Books—*Conversations with Artists,* by Neal Barber, London 1964; *Private View,* by Lord Snowdon, John Russel and Bryan Robertson, London, 1968. **Article—**"Donald Hamilton Fraser's Dance Drawings" by Nicholas Usherwood in *R.A. Magazine* (London), September 1987.

*

There has always been a sort of painting that resists the written word. It is drawn simply from the eye and the heart, and is about the experience of the present moment. I suppose my own work is of that kind.

—Donald Hamilton Fraser

* * *

Donald Hamilton Fraser lies in a direct line of image response to de Stael. Physical reality is intensified by the transference of an original visual experience, through the mind, in intervening layers of time and reflection, to the point where emotionally the painting acquires an identity as of itself alone. The affinity is heightened by the choice of scenes in the Mediterranean littoral de Stael loved. Fraser, however, makes his own decision in regard to elaboration of the picture plane, both by linear perspective, and a subtle and sensitive manipulation of paint in both color and texture.

In the late 1950s the paintings were of a liquescent spread, so that still-life subjects confined on the two opposing planes of table top and background wall became enlivened in a suggestion of space fired in varied strengths of hue, reflecting and contrasting with each other in aerial vibrations. Later work thickened in pigment, with accents placed more firmly in context, though the over-painting and adjustment of tone, together with a glow of halation on outlines, preserve the depth and shadow of the mass.

Something of the classic formula of planar division of the perspective gives Fraser's work a link with tradition, but, though he denies chance as a factor in conception he rejects also the possibility of self-analysis. It is true that recreation of a visual experience is implicit in his art. He has said: ''A stretch of seashore, a pot of flowers in the sun, a patch of hillside, almost anything may suddenly seem to become almost inconceivably significant.'' This significance belongs to Fraser's make-up where painting and poetry are insoluble ingredients conditioning his outlook. It may be dismissed as of little experimental or progressive importance, yet in itself it constitutes a personal refinement of shared artistic climates with Paris having a powerful sway.

Transparency from solid medium, space from physical enclosure, light from shadow-casting substance—the triumph over those contradictory imponderables are Fraser's constant preoccupation with an emotional rather than a rational basis for his figurative intention is summed up by him as having the basic impulse 'to create a recognizable image in terms of paint.'

In the French lineage of ''la belle facture'' his painting is, nonetheless, its own contemporary animus. It could scarcely be otherwise, considering the exposure of the artist to new work in London and on the Continent, work that has taken its place for assessment and effect in the attitudes of a consistent number of the middle post-war generation of British artists, coming to maturity through operative as opposed to conceptual activity. Material involvement with oils, and occasionally acrylic, and his appreciation of its depth of capacity in the historic process leads one to believe that Fraser will surprise only by his own maturing in a purity of achievement disregarding any accusation of anachronism.

—G. S. Whittet

FREUD, Lucian

Nationality: British. **Born:** Berlin, 8 December 1922; son of the architect Ernst Freud, and grandson of Sigmund Freud; immigrated to England in 1932; naturalized, 1939. **Education:** Studied at the Central School of Arts and Crafts, London, 1942; studied drawing, part-time, at Goldsmiths College, London, 1942–43. Served in the Merchant Marine, 1941. **Family:** Married Kathleen (Kitty) Garman Epstein in 1947 (divorced 1952); 2 children; Married Caroline Maureen Blackwood (divorced 1957). **Career:** Painter; spent time in Wales, associating with Stephen Spender and David Kentish, 1939;

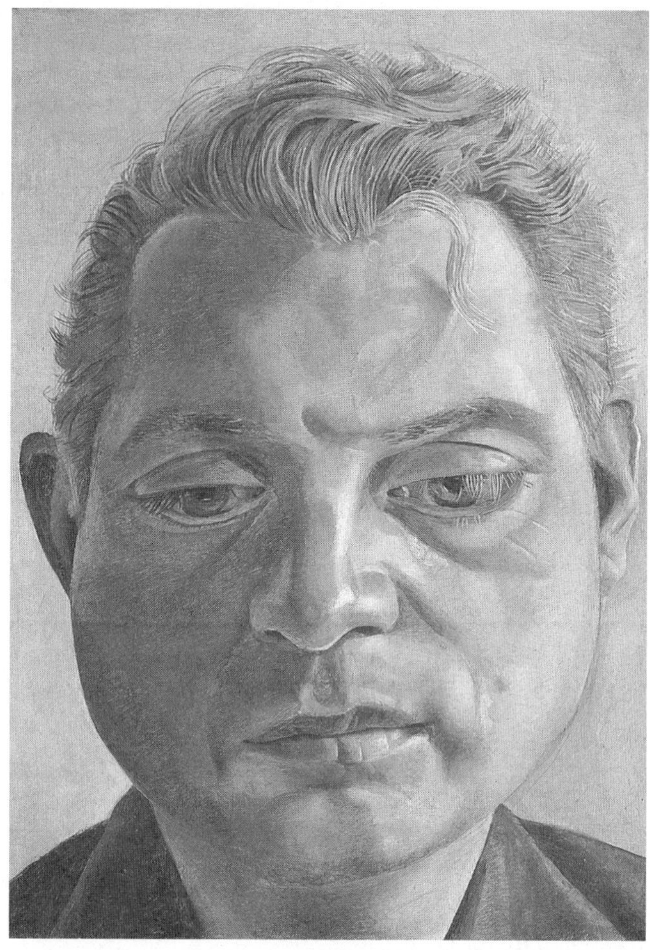

Lucian Freud: *Portrait of Francis Bacon,* 1952. ©Tate Gallery, London/Art Resource, NY; courtesy of Tate Gallery.

has lived and worked in London since 1941; close friendship with the painter Francis Bacon, from 1945; Honorary member of the Academy and Institute of Arts and Letters. **Awards:** Arts Council Prize, 1951; Companion of Honour, 1993; Order of Merit, 1993. **Agent:** Anthony d'Offay Gallery, 9 Dering Street, London W1. **Address:** c/o James Kirkman, 46 Brompton Square, London, SW3 2AF, England; c/o Acquavella Galleries Inc., 18 East 49th Street, New York 10021.

Individual Exhibitions:

1944 Lefevre Gallery, London (with Julian Trevelyan and Felix Kelly)
1947 London Gallery, (with John Craxton)
1950 Hanover Gallery, London (with Roger Vieillard)
1951 London Gallery
1952 Hanover Gallery, London (with Martin Gray)
1954 Hanover Gallery, London
Biennale, Venice
1956 Hanover Gallery, London
1958 Marlborough Fine Art, London
1963 Marlborough Fine Art, London
1968 Marlborough Fine Art, London
1972 Gray Art Gallery, Hartlepool, County Durham

Lucian Freud: *Girl with White Dog,* 1950–51. ©Tate Gallery, London/Art Resource, NY; courtesy of Tate Gallery.

Anthony d'Offay Gallery, London
1974 Hayward Gallery, London (toured the U.K.)
Anthony d'Offay Gallery, London
1977 Tate Gallery, London (with Francis Bacon)
1978 Anthony d'Offay Gallery, London
1982 Anthony d'Offay Gallery, London
1988 Hayward Gallery, London (retrospective)
Lucian Freud: Works on Paper, Ashmolean Museum, Oxford (catalog)
1991 *Lucian Freud: The Complete Etchings 1946–1991,* Thomas Gibson Fine Art, London (catalog)
1992 *Lucian Freud: Paintings and Works on Paper, 1940–91,* Castello Sforzesco, Milan (traveling exhibition) (catalog)
1993 Metropolitan Museum of Art, New York (retrospective)
1995 Dulwich Picture Gallery, London
1945: The End of the War, Annely Juda Fine Art, London (catalog)
1996 Tel Aviv Museum
Lucian Freud: Paintings and Etchings, Abbot Hall Art Gallery, Kendal, England
1997 Scottish Gallery of Modern Art, Edinburgh (catalog)
The Hirshhorn Collects: Recent Acquisitions, Hirshhorn Museum and Sculpture Garden, Washington, D.C. (catalog)
1998 Tate Gallery, London
1999 *Lucian Freud: Etchings from the Paine/Webber Art Collection,* Yale Center for British Art, New Haven (catalog)
2000 Acquavella Gallery, New York

Selected Group Exhibitions:

1946 *Recent Paintings,* Lefevre Gallery, London
1948 *La Jeune en Grand Bretagne,* Galerie René Drouin, Paris
1951 *21 Modern British Painters,* Vancouver Art Gallery
1977 *British Painting 1952–1977,* Royal Academy of Arts, London
1981 *8 Figurative Painters,* Yale Center for British Art, New Haven, Connecticut
1982 *Aspects of British Art Today,* Metropolitan Art Museum, Tokyo (toured Japan)

1987 *A School of London,* Louisiana Museum, Humlebaek, Denmark (travelled to Venice and Dusseldorf)
1988 *The British Picture,* L.A. Louver Gallery, Venice, California
1989 *School of London: Works on Paper,* Odette Gilbert Gallery, London (catalog)
1991 *The Transformation of Appearance,* Sainsbury Center for the Visual Arts, Norwich, England (catalog)
1995 *From London,* Scottish National Gallery of Modern Art, Edinburgh (catalog)
1997 *Contemporary Prints,* Yvonne Andrews, London (catalog)
XIX & XX Century Master Paintings and Sculptures: An Exhibition, Acquavella Galleries, New York (catalog)
1998 *The School of London from Bacon to Bevan,* Fondation Dina Vierny-Musee Maillol, Paris (catalog)
Art Treasures of England: The Regional Collections, Royal Academy of Arts, London (catalog)
2000 *Encounters—New Art from Old,* National Gallery, London

Collections:

Tate Gallery, London; Arts Council of Great Britain, London; Walker Art Gallery, Liverpool; Museum of Modern Art, New York; Beaverbrook Foundation, Fredericton, New Brunswick, Canada; National Portrait Gallery, London; Fitzwilliam Museum, Cambridge; National Museum of Wales, Cardiff; Scottish National Gallery of Modern Art, Edinburgh; Hartlepool Art Gallery, Liverpool; Walker Art Gallery, Liverpool; Centre Georges Pompidou, Paris; Bibliotheque Nationale, Paris; Victoria and Albert Museum, London; Centro Cultural Arte Contemporaneo, Mexico City; National Gallery, Capetown; Art Institute of Chicago; Carnegie Institute, Pittsburgh; Hirshhorn Museum and Sculpture Garden, Washington, D.C.

Publications:

By FREUD: Book—*The Artist Observed: 28 Interviews with Contemporary Artists* by John Gruen, Chicago 1991.

On FREUD: Books—*Lucian Freud,* exhibition catalog by John Russell, London 1974; *Lucian Freud* by Lawrence Gowing, London 1982; *Lucian Freud: Six Etchings 1984–85,* edited by James Kirkman and Brooke Alexander, London and New York 1986; *Lucian Freud* by Bruce Bernard and Derek Birdsall, New York 1996; *Lucian Freud: Some New Paintings—Display Guide* with William Feaver, London 1998; *Lucien Freud: Etchings from the PaineWebber Art Collection* by Donald Marron, et al., New Haven 1999. **Articles—** ''Lucian Freud: Clairvoyeur'' by John Russell in *Art in America,* January/February 1971; ''Lucian Freud'' by William Feaver in the *Sunday Times Magazine* (London), February 1974; ''In the Flesh: Lucian Freud'' by Robert Storr in *Art in America* (New York), vol. 76, no. 5, May 1988; ''The Migration of Lucian Freud'' by Grey Gowrie in *Modern Painters* (London), vol. 1, no. 1, Spring 1988; ''Lucian Freud: A Ruthless Master'' by Robin Duthy in *Connoisseur,* vol. 218, no. 914, March 1988; ''Leading Talent: The Phenomenon of Lucien Freud'' by Giles Auty in *Apollo* (London), vol. 135, no. 361, March 1992; ''The Flaying of Freud'' by Wendy Beckett in *Modern Painters* (London), vol. 6, no. 4, Winter 1993; ''Inside Freud's Mind'' by William Feaver in *ARTnews,* vol. 92, no. 7, September 1993; ''Flesh for Phantasy: Frayed Fraud'' by Linda Nochlin in *Artforum,* vol. 32, no. 7, March 1994; ''Fresh Freud'' by Donald Kuspit in *Artforum,* March 1994; ''The Misfit: The Particular Apotheosis of Lucian Freud'' by Sanford Schwartz in *The New Republic,* vol. 210, no. 7, 14 February 1994; ''Anguished Vision'' by Jeffrey Meyers in *Virginia Quarterly Review,* vol. 71, no. 1, 1995; ''Flesh and Ink: The Etchings of Lucian Freud'' by Nathan Kernan in *Art on Paper,* vol. 3, no. 5, May-June 1999.

* * *

Lucian Freud's father Ernest Freud, architect, was the younger son of the famous Sigmund Freud. With his family, Lucian Freud came to England when he was nine. He had a precocious commitment to be an artist. Drawing was his earliest love, and a full frontal treatment of the human face was even then inescapable from his images. In his pictures of around 1940 to 1942 there is a stylised distortion in the figure with a barbed comment akin to that of Grosz. By the early 1950s he had acquired an assurance in the delineation of physiognomy, instilling a factual presence from paint unequivocal and demanding in its essence. More frequently the models were nameless, but their identity is never in doubt. In the named portraits of his friends John Minton and Francis Bacon of 1952, physical characteristics are projected with an emphasis almost embarrassing in close-up. An early success was the prize-winning ''Interior at Paddington,'' a major painting surprise of the 1951 Festival of Britain competition, suggesting the trapped defiance of ordinary people in ordinary circumstances.

Often mistaken for surrealist juxtapositions, household objects in his paintings assume significance by implication rather than intention. Broadly speaking, Freud is a realist of uncompromising devotion to what he sees. This sense of truth to object retreated in the 1960s from stress on the linear elements to reliance on texture and modelling that resulted from greater involvement with paint. Pigment, however, was never allowed to obtrude more than was necessary, and tone remains the constant of his value-treatment, particularly in the paintings of factories and waste ground amidst Paddington slums in the early 1970s.

Colour is restrained to the extent that a monochrome reproduction of a Lucian Freud painting loses a minimum amount as compared with, say, an Ivon Hitchens. This total basis exudes a coldness of attitude, not from lack of feeling, but from the implied avoidance of sentiment as an influence in responding to purely visual stimulus. Thus his unclothed models are never titled as nudes, but as ''naked girl'' or ''naked child,'' because the nude calls into consideration a relationship with all other known paintings of the subject. For Freud, the only parameter is the model herself and the painting she induces. Nakedness is thus the key to what Freud is about.

His series of small portraits of his mother 1971–73 varies only in expression and slightly in posing. Their unsmiling truth to appearance is never in doubt. They are paintings of an individual as impersonal as it is possible to be without tipping the delicate balance to a caricature. They are not portraits. Freud is no more capable of portraiture in the conventional way than was Cézanne.

He has, he says, a horror of the idyllic and, by inference, of art itself. To transpose the appearance and the nature of people whom he knows becomes a continuous nagging dialogue between his brush and the canvas. His mind, to a worrying degree, is a distracting factor as well as a filter and reactor. It is not accidental that pictures of people will always outnumber those of still life or townscape. The latter do not stare at the spectator, though the leaves and the curtains may conceal the peering face of ''someone else.''

—G. S. Whittet

A career retrospective at the Metropolitan Museum of Art in 1993 brought to a head the longstanding debate surrounding Freud's approach to the figure. His advocates view him as an inheritor of a tradition that includes Watteau and Ingres, painters who managed to capture the elegance of the human form without losing its earthy qualities, while his opponents dismiss him as a skilled draftsman too mired in solipsism and egomania to express anything other than a monotone conception of depressing and humiliating sexuality. Reclusive and unswayed by art trends of the past forty years, Freud is unlikely to change either his style or obsessions.

—Mark Swartz

Lucien Freud's primary subject remains the human body. He applies paint thickly, underscoring the fleshy tactility of his sitters. His unidealized, often awkward figures are not nudes, a term that suggests a kind of romanticism. They are, simply and unapologetically, naked people. One of Freud's favorite subjects in the past decade has been the late performance artist Leigh Bowery. Bowery's large stature and fascinating physical details (like the holes for piercings in his cheeks) are particularly jarring in the large format paintings.

In 1999–2000, a retrospective exhibition of Freud's etchings traveled throughout the United States. These works included etchings from early in his career, and works created after a break of more than thirty years. The etchings bring out Freud's skill as a draftsman, and with their quiet intimacy, provide an antidote to the often-unsettling nature of the paintings.

—Tara Reddy Young

FRIEDMAN, Tom

Nationality: American. **Born:** Massachusetts, 1965. **Address:** James Cohen Gallery, 41 West 57th Street, New York, New York 10019, U.S.A.

Individual Exhibitions:

1995 Museum of Modern Art, New York (catalog)
1996 *Affinities* (with Chuck Close), Art Institute of Chicago, Chicago
Stephen Friedman Gallery, London
1997 Christopher Grimes Gallery, Los Angeles
Saint Louis Art Museum, Missouri (catalog)
1998 Dorsky Gallery, New York
Tomio Koyama Gallery, Tokyo
2000 Museum of Contemporary Art, Chicago (toured)
2001 Aspen Art Museum, Aspen
Southeastern Center for Contemporary Art, Winston-Salem (catalog)
New Museum of Contemporary Art, New York

Group Exhibitions:

1994 Richard Telles Fine Art, Los Angeles
2000 *Art on Paper,* Weatherspoon Art Gallery, Greensboro, North Carolina
2001 *Almost Warm and Fuzzy: Childhood and Contemporary Art,* P.S. 1 Gallery, New York

Publications:

On FRIEDMAN: Books—*Waste Management* (exhibition catalog), Art Gallery of Ontario, Toronto 1999; *Tom Friedman* by Dennis Cooper, Bruce Hainley, and Adrian Searle, London, 2001. **Articles—** ''Connecting Incongruities'' by Wolf Kahn in in *Art in America,* November 1992; ''Next to Nothing: The Art of Tom Friedman'' by Bruce Hainley in in *Artforum International,* no. 34, November 1995; ''Friedman's Flea Circus'' by Ken Johnson in in *Art in America,* May 1996; ''X-acto Science'' by David Frankel in in *Artforum International,* vol. 38, no. 10, Summer 2000.

* * *

Continuing the exploration of the intersection of art and life, Tom Friedman integrates references to Dada, Pop, and Minimalism with a conceptualist vision and a use of nontraditional materials. Friedman subjects his media—taken from the home and grocery store—to a technical rigor that renders them extraordinary, while at the same time underscoring their familiarity. With a scientist's gift for observation and investigation, Friedman tests his own limits and the limits of his materials. His obsessive/compulsive attention to detail is tempered with a deadpan humor that makes his work complex, yet easily accessible.

Working in a bare, windowless studio reminiscent of a laboratory, a practice he began in graduate school, Friedman executes his drawings and sculpture in a neutral context, divorcing his materials from their immediate associations. One of his earliest works, a large trapezoid of toothpaste applied to the wall in a painterly manner, invites comparison to Abstract Expressionism and Yves Klein's *Blue Monochrome*, but with the added sensual dimension of the instantly recognizable minty odor. His postmodern recreations of seminal moments in Post-World War II art, such as his erased Brillo box, which simultaneously references Warhol and Rauschenberg's *Erased de Kooning Drawing*, and his identically folded pieces of paper, recalling Rauschenberg's critique of Abstract Expressionist originality in *Factum I* and *Factum II*, reveal an encyclopedic knowledge of art history and a wry, subversive sense of mischief. His self-portrait carved out of an aspirin pill is rendered with minute precision, invoking thoughts of classical sculpture and elevating the chalky, white material to the canonical status of marble. His most rigorous project, the three-year task of inscribing every word in the dictionary on a three-square-foot piece of paper, exemplifies the phenomenal focus and concentration Friedman applies to his efforts, and causes the viewer to ponder how and why such a monumental project was undertaken.

Friedman's interest in binary relationships like cosmic/microscopic and public/private is explored throughout his work. He arranges pubic hairs on a bar of soap in a perfect concentric spiral, taking the common, random condition of personal hygiene product and imputing to it a galactic configuration of geometric order and perfection. His fascination with numbers and measurement is seen in ''My Foot'' (1991), for which he attempted to create a foot-long ruler by memory, transforming a universal standard into a unique and personal statement, as well as pointing out the arbitrary and relative issues involving units of length and distance. A tiny ball of his own feces presented on a white, Minimalist plinth, a metonymic representation of the debased and abject, is deprived of its appearance and odor, and is transformed into a pure Minimalist object.

Underlying the aesthetic and theoretical implications of Friedman's sculptures is the subtle yet undeniable presence of consumer and cultural commentary. An upside-down map with the names of the states printed right-side up presents the nation from a different perspective, questioning the notion of the United States' cultural hegemony. Indeed, the powerful presence of his sculptures, drawings, and photographs, though most immediately credited to the apparent originality and complexity of their creation, can be attributed to his deft incorporation and critique of past art styles and a keen awareness of his socio-cultural environment.

—Bradley Bailey

FRINK, Elisabeth

Nationality: British. **Born:** Thurlow, Suffolk, 14 November 1930. **Education:** Guildford School of Art, Surrey, 1947–49; The Chelsea School of Art, London, 1949–53. **Married:** Michel Jammet in 1956 (divorced, 1963); Edward Pool in 1970 (divorced, 1972); Alexander Csaky in 1974. **Career:** Sculptor: lived in France, 1969–73; now lives and works in Dorset. Lecturer in sculpture, Chelsea School of Art, 1951–61, and St. Martin's School of Art, London, 1954–62; visiting lecturer, Royal College of Art, London, 1965–67. Member, Royal Fine Art Commission, 1977. Trustee of the British Museum, London, since 1975. **Awards:** Associate, 1972, and Royal Academician, 1977, Royal Academy of Arts; Honorary Fellow, St. Hilda's College, Oxford, 1986; D.B.E. (Dame Commander, Order of the British Empire), 1982. **Agent:** Waddington Galleries, 31 Cork Street, London W1X 1HB, England. **Died:** 1993.

Individual Exhibitions:

1955 St. Georges Gallery, London
1959 Waddington Galleries, London
Bertha Schaefer Gallery, New York
1961 Felix Landau Gallery, Los Angeles
Waddington Galleries, London
Bertha Schaefer Gallery, New York
1963 Waddington Galleries, London
1967 Waddington Galleries, London
1968 Waddington Galleries, London
1969 Waddington Galleries, London
1971 Waddington Galleries, London
1972 Waddington Galleries, London
1974 Maltzahn Gallery, London
1976 Waddington Galleries, London
1977 Waddington Fine Arts, Montreal
Galerie D'Eendt, Amsterdam
1979 Terry Dintenfass Gallery, New York
1981 Winchester Great Hall, Hampshire
1982 Dorset County Museum, Dorchester
Beaux-Arts Gallery, Bath, Avon
1983 Bohun Gallery, Henley-on-Thames, Oxfordshire
Yorkshire Sculpture Park, Bretton Hall
Terry Dintenfass Gallery, New York
1984 University of Surrey, Guildford
St. Margaret's Church, King's Lynn, Norfolk
1985 Royal Academy of Art, London
Fitzwilliam Museum, Cambridge
1989 New Grafton Gallery, London
1990 *Elisabeth Frink: Sculpture and Drawings, 1950–1990,* National Museum of Women in the Arts, Washington, D.C.
Compass Gallery, Glasgow
1992 *Elisabeth Frink: Etching, Lithographs and Screenprints, 1965–1992,* Lumley Cazalet, London
Elisabeth Frisk: Sculpture and Drawings, 1969–1990, Lumley Cazalet, London
1993 *Elisabeth Frink: A Celebration,* Beaux Arts, London
1994 *Elisabeth Frink: Sculpture and Drawings 1965–1993,* Lumley Cazalet, London
1995 *Twentieth Century Drawings: Sculpture and Drawings by Elisabeth Frink—Late Nineteenth Century and Twentieth Century Prints,* Lumley Cazalet, London
Elisabeth Frink: Sculptures, Drawings, and Prints, Beaux Arts, London
1997 *Elisabeth Frink: Sculptures, Graphic Works, Textiles,* Salisbury Library and Galleries, England (travelled to Salisbury Cathedral and Close; Dorset County Museum, Dorchester; Edwin Young Trust, Salisbury)

Selected Group Exhibitions:

1951 *London Group,* Beaux-Arts Gallery, London
1952 *Biennale,* Venice
1954 *Holland Park Open Air Exhibition,* London
1956 *Aldeburgh Festival,* Suffolk
1957 *Open Air Exhibition,* Sonsbeek, Netherlands
1959 *Biennale,* Middelheim, Antwerp
1971 *Summer Exhibition,* Royal Academy of Arts, London
1977 *Jubilee Exhibition,* Waddington and Tooth Galleries, London
1982 *Hayward Annual 1982: British Drawing,* Hayward Gallery, London
1984 *Man and Horse,* Metropolitan Museum of Art, New York

Elisabeth Frink: *Horse and Rider IV* 1970–71. ©Tate Gallery, London/Art Resource, NY.

1990 *Exhibition of Modern Paintings,* Jonathan Clark, London
1993 *The Byker Art Show,* Byker Art Show, Newcastle-upon-Tyne, England
1995 *Victor Waddington: A Tribute,* Waddington Galleries, London
1997 *Artists of Fame and Promise: 1997,* Beaux Arts, London

Collections:

Tate Gallery, London; National Gallery of Victoria, Melbourne; Museum of Modern Art, New York; Hirshhorn Museum, Washington, D.C.; British Museum, London; Walker Art Gallery, Liverpool; Fitzwilliam Museum, Cambridge; Brisbane Art Gallery, Queensland; South African National Gallery, Cape Town.

Publications:

By FRINK: Books illustrated—*Aesops Fables,* London 1968; *Canterbury Tales,* London 1972; *The Iliad and The Odyssey,* London 1975. **Articles—**''Elisabeth Frink: A Conversation with Dulan Barber'' in *Transatlantic Review* (London), Summer 1973; ''Elisabeth Frisk Talks About Art and the Church'' with George Pattison in *Modern Painters,* vol. 2, no. 3, Autumn 1989; ''The Monumentality of Elisabeth Frink'' with Claudine Jan in *Women's Art Magazine,* no. 39, March-April 1991.

On FRINK: Books—*The Art of Elisabeth Frink* by Edwin Mullins, London 1972; *Elisabeth Frink,* exhibition catalog with text by Sarah Kent, Dorchester 1982; *Elisabeth Frink,* exhibition catalog with essay by Sarah Kent, London 1985; *Elisabeth Frink,* exhibition catalog, Glasgow 1990; *Elisabeth Frink: Sculpture and Drawings, 1950–1990,* exhibition catalog, National Museum of Women in the Arts, Washington, D.C. 1990; *Elisabeth Frink: Etchings, Lithographs and Screenprints, 1965–1992,* exhibition catalog, London 1992; *Elisabeth Frink: A Celebration,* exhibition catalog, London 1993; *Twentieth Century Drawings: Sculpture and Drawings by Elisabeth Frink—Late Nineteenth and Twentieth Century Prints,* exhibition catalog, London 1995; *Elisabeth Frink: Sculptures, Drawings, and Prints,* exhibition catalog, London 1995; *Elisabeth Frink: Sculptures, Graphic Works, Textiles,* exhibition catalog, Salisbury 1997; *Elisabeth Frink: Original Prints—Catalogue Raisonne,* preface by Lin Jammet, London 1998. **Articles—**''Goggle-Eyed Obsession'' by Paul Savage in

Elisabeth Frink with *Tribute 1976* at Silver Jubilee Exhibition, Battersea Park. ©Hulton-Deutsch Collection/Corbis.

the *Daily Telegraph Magazine* (London), January 1970; ''Elisabeth Frink: Sculpture and Drawings'' by Hilton Kramer and Sarah Kent in the *Massachusetts Review* (Boston), Spring 1980; ''Art, Faith and Vision'' in *Modern Painters,* vol. 2, no. 3, Autumn 1989; ''Making It Like a Woman'' by Marina Warner in *Women's Art Magazine,* no. 48, September-October 1992; ''Dame Elisabeth Frink 1930–1993: An Appreciation'' by Edward Lucie-Smith in *Art Review,* vol. 45, June 1993; obituary in *Art in America* (New York), vol. 81, July 1993; ''Frink Again: Representational Curse on Elisabeth Frink'' by Emma E. Roberts in *Women's Art Magazine,* no. 62, January/February 1995.

* * *

Heavy, but without being grotesquely monumental, the sculpture of Elisabeth Frink started by swinging to and fro between the lepidoptera imagery of Germaine Richier and the sort of forceful presentation that was later to be associated with Ipousteguy. To which point of the compass did she eventually turn?

Perhaps to neither. A very sincere feeling for nature, horses (not the Marino Marini kind), birds and beasts in general cut across her other subjects like archaic figures and astronauts in goggles. This nature period was also given extra emphasis because of the subject matter she found, and created, in her graphics.

Elisabeth Frink later settled for a reality that married comfortably with her contemporary style. The roughness of 1954 (a seated man betraying no emotion), the warrior of 1957 (in which the war-weary head has become one with the helm), or the spinning man of 1960 (more a baby than a man, and perhaps that is a telling fact), or even the Dead King of the early 1960s; progress has been steady and logical. There are those who miss the grating edge and the mute drama of these early pieces, but they were a part of her development and the impression reached later is that Elisabeth Frink finally found her true nature as a sculptor and, more important, the way in which she would mould it.

Frink herself looked like a sculptor, someone capable of wrestling from irascible materials shapes and imagery that would teeter on the brink of the archaic or of unmelodramatic science fiction with nature somewhere in the middle ground acting as referee.

—Sheldon Williams

FRITSCH, Katharina

Nationality: German. **Born:** Essen, 1956. **Education:** Studied art history in Münster; took drawing classes with Hermann Josef Kuhna, Münster Volkschochschule; studied with Fritz Schwegler, Kunstakademie Düsseldorf, 1978–84. **Agent:** Matthew Marks Gallery, 522 West 22nd Street, New York, New York 10011.

Selected Individual Exhibitions:

1987 Kaiser Wilhelm Museum, Krefeld, Germany
1988 *Katharina Fritsch,* Kunsthalle, Basel, and Institute of Contemporary Art, London
1989 *Katharina Fritsch 1979–1989,* Westfälischer Kunstverein, Münster
1993 *Rat King,* Dia Center for the Arts, New York
1996 *Katharina Fritsch* (retrospective), San Francisco Museum of Modern Art, San Francisco, California, and Museum für Gegenwartskunst Basel, Switzerland
Katharina Fritsch New Work and *The Complete Multiples,* Matthew Marks Gallery (Uptown), New York (catalog)
2001 *Katharina Fritsch,* Museum of Contemporary Art, Chicago
Tate Modern, London

Selected Group Exhibitions:

1986 *A Distanced View: One Aspect of Recent Art from Belgium, France, Germany, and Holland,* New Museum of Contemporary Art, New York
1987 *Skulptur Projekte,* Münster
1990 *Culture and Commentary: An Eighties Perspective,* Hirshhorn Museum and Sculpture Garden, Washington, D.C.
OBJECTives: The New Sculpture, Newport Harbor Art Museum, Newport Beach, California
1991 Luhring Augustine Gallery, New York
1995 Venice Biennale, Venice
1997 *Curiosity Room: Cross-Cultural Arts and Artifacts,* Jack Shainman Gallery, New York (catalog)
1998 *Maverick,* Matthew Marks Gallery, New York (catalog)
1999 *Selections from the Permanent Collection,* Walker Art Center, Minneapolis, Minnesota
Venice Biennale, Venice

Publications:

On FRITSCH: Books—*Katharina Fritsch* by Jean-Christophe Ammann, Basel and London 1988; *BiNATIONALE: German Art of the Late '80s,* Düsseldorf 1988; ''Interview with Katharina Fritsch'' by Marie Luise Syring and Christiane Vielhaber in *Katharina Fritsch 1979–1989,* Münster and Frankfurt am Main 1989; *Culture and Commentary: An Eighties Perspective,* exhibition catalog with text Kathy Halbreich, Washington, D.C. 1990; *OBJECTives: The New Sculpture,* exhibition catalog with text by Stephan Schmidt-Wulffen, Newport Beach, California, 1990; *Katharina Fritsch*, New York 1993; *Katharina Fritsch*, San Francisco and Basel 1996. **Articles—** Special edition of *Parkett,* no. 25, September 1990; ''Art That Goes Bump in the Night'' by Amanda Zonia in *ARTnews,* November 1996; ''Katharina Fritsch'' by Glen Helfand in *Sculpture* (Washington, D.C.), February 1997.

* * *

Although Fritsch is best known as a sculptor, her body of work—now stretching over more than twenty years—also includes prints, designs for gardens and cemeteries, and staged events incorporating sounds and smells. Her work depends for its bold effect on a combination of immediate visual impact and an opacity that makes it resistant to easy interpretation. She relies frequently on the tension between psychologically or emotionally charged imagery and a rational, ordered presentation. Since attracting widespread critical and popular attention in the late 1980s, she has established herself as one of the most important and provocative figures in contemporary German art. Her work draws on the legacies of minimalism, pop, conceptualism, and the sort of humor and obliqueness found in the work of Richard Artschwager.

Fritsch's early works, done while a student at the prestigious Kunstakademie Düsseldorf (Düsseldorf Art Academy) under the direction of Fritz Schwegler, show the beginnings of themes that would continue to have relevance throughout her career. For example, a number of her student pieces are radically simplified sculptural copies of common sights such as an upright piano, a tunnel, a chimney, and a car and trailer. Some of these objects took on unexpected colors, such as the 1979 ''Dunkelgrüner Tunnel'' (''Dark Green Tunnel'') made of colored wax. Thus, early in her career, Fritsch's marriage of the banal and the unexpected was established. Over time, she has moved from a miniaturized to a monumental scale.

The large-scale sculpture ''Elefant'' (''Elephant,'' 1987) launched Fritsch to widespread notice in both the art press and the popular press. Made for and exhibited at the Kaiser Wilhelm Museum in Krefeld, Germany, the work was a lifesize model of a female elephant fabricated from a stuffed elephant at a museum in Bonn. ''Elefant'' is full of naturalistic detail, except for one striking feature—its deep blue-green color. In the same year, Fritsch presented her ''Madonnenfigur'' (''Madonna Figure'') as part of the outdoor scupture show *Skulptur Projekte* (*Sculpture Projects*) in Münster. This figure is patterned after the sort of small figures available for sale in devotional shops and at religious sites. However, this ''Madonnenfigur'' (a motif she had already used in earlier projects) was presented life-size and painted a brilliant yellow. The Münster work provoked controversy and was destroyed several times, although apparently by vandals and not by people who found the work religiously offensive.

In addition to experimentation with color and scale, commerce and display are issues that repeatedly surface in Fritsch's work. For example, the Lourdes Madonna figure of ''Madonnenfigur'' was also used in ''Warengestell mit Madonnen'' (''Display Stand with Madonnas,'' 1987–89). In this piece, nine circular tiers of bright yellow Madonna figurines were on display like bottles of detergent in a supermarket. Similar themes are handled in the work ''Warengestell mit Vasen'' (''Display Stand with Vases,'' also 1987–89) and the earlier works ''Warengestell'' (''Display Stand,'' 1979–84) and ''Werbeblatt I'' (''Advertising Leaflet I,'' 1981), in which the artist advertised small works for sale which she could create in multiples. Although her preoccupation with display and commerce has led some to link her work with Jeff Koons', Fritsch lacks entirely the glibness so prevalent in Koons and well as his taste for personal publicity.

More recent works have dealt with large-scale, pared-down forms that elicit a strong emotional response, such as the humorous yet nightmarish ''Mann und Maus'' (''Man and Mouse,'' 1991–92), in which a giant black mouse sits on the sleeping, solid white form of a man in bed. In a similar vein is the work ''Rattenkönig'' (''Rat-King,'' 1991–93), in which a ring of sixteen rats, each identical and over nine feet tall, look out menacingly while their tails are entwined in a knot in the ring's center. The work draws upon folklore (much of it German) in which startled rats are said to create a ''rat king'' through the tangling of their tails. Fritsch has also expressed a more spiritual aspect and a strong faith in the transformative power of art in her work ''Museum, Modell 1:10'' (1995), a large sculptural design for an octagonal art museum set amidst a forest clearing. This work, both in its formal aspects and in its function as a place of aesthetic and spritual contemplation, draws on the tradition of romantic expressionism seen in Germany in the earlier twentieth century, such as in some of Bruno Taut's projects. The artist has specifically discussed the ethereal ''Museum'' as a symbol of hope as opposed to her earlier work ''Tischgesellschaft'' (''Company at Table,'' 1988), which she has described as a symbol of hopelessness. ''Tischgesellschaft'' sets pairs of stark, mannequin-like men staring at each other down the span of a long, narrow table with a bright, red-and-white tablecloth. The work uses the artist's familiar tactics of repetition and simplified forms to create an oppressive environment that can be taken as an indictment of conformity.

What ties together Fritsch's work over the span of her career is a sense that her sculptural objects are like the ideas of things—distilled, archtypal forms—rather than the things themselves. She frequently takes commonplace objects and perfects, abstracts, or gives them surprising new colors or scales. And despite her preference for the rational, ordered presentation of her works (often involving rings or rows of identical things), her work contains a strong undercurrent of the irrational via its connection to the world of childhood memories, fairy tales, myths, and dreams.

—Jennifer A. Smith

FROST, Terry

Nationality: British. **Born:** Leamington Spa, Warwickshire, 13 October 1915. **Education:** Educated in Leamington Spa until 1929; attended evening classes at Birmingham Art College, 1945; studied at the St. Ives School of Painting, Cornwall, under Richmond and Harry Rowntree and John Park, 1945–47, at Camberwell School of Art, London, under Victor Pasmore, William Coldstream and Lawrence Gowing, 1947–50, and at Penzance School of Art, Cornwall, 1950–51. **Military Service:** Served in the British Army, 1939–45, in France and Palestine, and with the Commandos in Sudan, Abyssinia, Egypt, and Crete, 1941; prisoner-of-war in Salonika, Poland and Germany, 1941–45. **Family:** Married Kathleen Clarke in 1945; 5 sons and 1 daughter. **Career:** Took up painting while a prisoner-of-war; after the war worked for electrical wholesalers, 1945, then became ill and settled in St. Ives; worked with his wife as domestic servants, 1947; returned to London, 1947; first abstract paintings, 1949, and low-relief constructions in the early 1950s; worked as an assistant to Barbara Hepworth on *Festival of Britain* sculptures, St. Ives, 1951; lived in Leeds, 1955–57; began to paint full-time in St. Ives, 1957; with Peter Lanyon opened art school, St. Peters Loft, St. Ives, 1957–60; visited the United States and met the American abstractionists, 1960; lived in Banbury, Oxfordshire, 1963–67, then settled in Newlyn, Cornwall. Lecturer in Life Drawing, Bath Academy, 1952–54; part-time lecturer in painting and anatomy, Willesden, London, 1953–54; lecturer in basic design, Leeds School of Art, 1956–57; part-time lecturer, Conventry Art College, 1963; lecturer, San Jose University, California, Summer 1965; lecturer, Voss Summer School, Norway, 1967, and Banff Summer School, Alberta, 1975. Part-time lecturer in painting, 1964, full-time lecturer, 1965–70, reader in painting, 1970–77, professor, 1977–81, and professor emeritus since 1981, University of Reading. **Awards:** Gregory Fellowship in Painting, University of Leeds, 1954; Fellowship in Fine Art, University of Newcastle upon Tyne, 1964; Painting Prize, *John Moores Exhibition,* Liverpool, 1965; Painting Prize, *Open Painting Exhibition,* Ulster Museum, Belfast, 1966. LLD: Council for National Academic Awards, 1977. **Agents:** Angela Flowers Gallery, 11 Tottenham Mews, London W1; Gillian Jason Art Gallery, 42 Inverness Street, London NW1. **Address:** Gernickfield Studio, Tredavoe Lane, Newlyn, Penzance, Cornwall TR18 5DL, United Kingdom.

Individual Exhibitions:

1944 Leamington Spa Public Library, Warwickshire
1947 G. R. Downing's Bookshop, St. Ives, Cornwall
1952 Leicester Galleries, London
1956 Leicester Galleries, London
1958 Leicester Galleries, London
1960 Bertha Schaefer Gallery, New York
1961 Waddington Galleries, London
1962 Bertha Schaefer Gallery, New York
1963 Galerie Charles Lienhard, Zurich
Gallery 5, Reading, Berkshire
1964 Laing Art Gallery, Newcastle upon Tyne (toured the U. K. and United States)
1966 Waddington Galleries, London
1967 Queen Square Gallery, Leeds
Lincolnshire Association Centre, Lincoln
1968 Bear Lane Gallery, Oxford
1969 Museum of Modern Art, Oxford
Waddington Galleries, London
Gallery Caballa, Harrogate, Yorkshire
1970 City Art Gallery, Plymouth, Devon
Bear Lane Gallery, Oxford
1971 Waddington Galleries, London
Dartington Hall, Totnes, Devon
Peterloo Gallery, Manchester
Institute of Contemporary Arts, London
1972 Arnolfini Gallery, Bristol
1973 Leeds Playhouse Gallery
Waddington Galleries, London
1974 Oxford Gallery (with Denis Mitchell and Ronald Searle)
1976 Plymouth City Museum and Art Gallery, Devon (toured the U. K., 1976–77)
1978 Compass Gallery, Glasgow
Oxford Gallery
1980 New Art Centre, London
Franz Wynan Art Core, Vancouver
1981 Rufford Craft Centre, Ollerton, Nottinghamshire
London Regional Art Gallery, Ontario
1983 New Art Centre, London
1986 University of Reading, Berkshire
Angela Flowers Gallery, London
1988 Gillian Jason Gallery, London
1989 Belgrave Gallery, London
1990 *Terry Frost: Paintings 1948–89,* Mayor Gallery, London
1994 Peter Scott Gallery, Lancaster University
Burston Gallery, Brighton College
Mayor Gallery, London
Belgrave Gallery, London
Adelson Gallery, New York

1999 *Spotlight: Terry Frost,* Peter Scott Gallery, Lancaster; South Bank Centre, London
2000 *Terry Frost,* Royal Academy, London
Terry Frost: New Work, Beaux Arts, London
Terry Frost, Peterborough Museum and Art Gallery

Selected Group Exhibitions:

1944 *Exhibition of Arts and Crafts of Prisoners of War,* Daily Telegraph Newspaper Offices, London
1955 *Pittsburgh International,* Carnegie Institute, Pittsburgh
1964 *Contemporary British Painting and Sculpture,* Albright-Knox Art Gallery, Buffalo, New York
1967 *Recent British Painting,* Tate Gallery, London
1970 *British Paintings 1960–1970,* National Gallery of Art, Washington, D.C.
1974 *British Painting,* Hayward Gallery, London
1977 *British Painting 1952–1977,* Royal Academy of Arts, London
1980 *Art in the Making,* King Street Gallery, Bristol (travelled to Bath, Avon)
1985 *St. Ives 1939–64,* Tate Gallery, London
1989 *A Century of Art in Cornwall 1889–1989,* Newlyn Orion Galleries, Perizance, England
1992 *The Poetic Trace: Aspects of British Abstraction Since 1945,* Adelson Galleries, New York
1994 Tate Gallery, London
Paintings from Cornwall 1945–1975, Montpelier Studio, London
British Abstract Art Part 1: Painting, Flowers East, London
1995 *The Urban Scene: Paintings, Drawings and Prints by 20th Century British Artists,* 4 New Burlington Street, London
Porthmeor Beach: A Century of Images, Tate Gallery, St. Ives, England
1997 *Artists of Fame and Promise: 1997,* Beaux Arts, London
1998 *Twentieth Century British Art: From Sickert to Hirst,* Spink-Leger Pictures, London
The Fifties: Art From the British Council Collection, British Council, London
20th Century Art, Adam Gallery, Bath
Terry Frost, Barbara Hepworth, Patrick Heron, Roger Hilton, Peter Lanyon, William Scott, Beaux Arts, London

Collections:

Tate Gallery, London; Victoria and Albert Museum, London; Arts Council of Great Britain, London; Vancouver Art Gallery; National Gallery of Canada, Ottawa; Tel-Aviv Museum; Christchurch Art Gallery, New Zealand; Art Gallery of South Australia, Adelaide; West Australian Art Gallery, Perth; Art Gallery of New South Wales, Sydney.

Publications:

By FROST: Articles—Statement in *9 Abstract Artists: Their Work and Theory* by Lawrence Alloway, London 1954; ''Writings of Terry Frost'' in *Terry Frost: Paintings, Drawings and Collages,* exhibition catalog, London 1976; introduction to *Terry Frost,* exhibition catalog, Ollerton, Nottinghamshire 1982; ''Still Crazy After All These Years'' with Mike Von Joel in *Art Line,* vol. 4, no. 8, 1989; ''Terry Frost and the Lorca Suite'' with Sheila Oliner in *Printmaking Today* (London), vol. 5, no. 3, Autumn 1996.

On FROST: Books—*9 Abstract Artist: Their Work and Theory* by Lawrence Alloway, London 1954; *Terry Frost: Paintings, Drawings and Collages,* exhibition catalog, by David Brown, London 1976; *Terry Frost: Painting in the 1980s,* exhibition catalog with texts by Dennis Farr and Adrian Heath, Reading, Berkshire 1986; *Terry Frost,* edited by Elizabeth Knowles, Aldershot 1994; *Terry Frost,* by David Lewis; *Terry Frost, Barbara Hepworth, Patrick Heron, Roger Hilton, Peter Lanyon, William Scott,* exhibition catalog, London 1998; *Spotlight: Terry Frost,* exhibition catalog, Lancaster 1999. **Articles—**''Frost and the Duende'' by Linda Saunders in *Green Book,* vol. 3, no. 3, 1989; ''Terry Frost'' by Frank Ruhrmund in *Arts Review* (London), vol. 41, 22 September 1989; ''In Profile: Terry Frost'' by David Lee in *Art Review* (London), vol. 45, June 1993; ''Terry Frost'' by Joseph Williams in *Modern Painters* (London), vol. 7, Autumn 1994; ''Plain Dwelling'' by Trevor Boddy in *The Canadian Architect,* vol. 43, no. 7, July 1998; ''A Touch of Frost'' by Michael Bird in *Art Review* (London), vol. 52, October 2000.

* * *

St. Ives, the charming Cornish fishing village where Ben Nicholson lived for some time and near which Barbara Hepworth set up her famous studio, is the centre of the only regional movement in modern British art. In the past, particularly related to the 18th and 19th century landscape tradition, different areas of Britain, such as Norfolk, produced important and distinctive provincial styles. St. Ives was never the centre of locally-born painters, concerned with a traditional way of life, or identifying with a particular landscape; the painters who came to live in the area—including Heron, Hilton, Lanyon, Bell, Bryan Wynter—did so not out of aesthetic or philosophic unity, but either for purely practical reasons or because they enjoyed the quasi-romantic isolation but, at the same time, because they did, in fact, find something of common interest locally. They certainly shared a very British involvement in landscape, as a means of identification, as the source of their work. They also shared a form of abstraction which inclined towards expressionism, in larger, more gestural shapes, more overblown color than, say, you would find in Nicholson, or for that matter Pasmore.

Terry Frost's work reveals an effort to impose formality and severity on this kind of temperamental abstraction; the earlier works, whose titles referred to their color harmonies—often high-pitched Yellows or Oranges—were loose arrangements of linear forms, dialogues between stiff, almost puritanical elements, and more sensuous curves, with, beneath these arrangements, a positive sense of land and sea. He gradually imposed firmer, overall formality, in quasi-geometrical shapes, spheres, verticals, V-shaped wedges, still maintaining the sense of dialogue, perhaps now of conflict.

Most recently he has reconciled these opposed forces into kinetic arrangement of oval shapes, cunningly arranged to suggest uniformity, whilst in fact very different in weight and substance. The intense, emotional colors of the past have been put aside for the simplicity of blue and black on white. This may be the result of a less passionate middle-age, or the refinement of the artist's relationship to his subject-matter.

—Charles Spencer

FUCHS, Ernst

Nationality: Austrian. **Born:** Vienna, 13 February 1930. **Education:** Studied painting privately with Emmy Steinböck, Vienna; also studied at Fröhlich's Painting School, St. Anna, Vienna, 1943–45, and with Albert Paris von Gütersloh at the Academy of Fine Arts, Vienna, 1945. **Career:** Painter and graphic artist, in Paris, 1949–60, in Vienna since 1962; associated with the ''school of fantastic realism,'' together with Anton Lehmden, Erich Brauer, Rudolf Hausner, Wolfgang Hutter and others, Vienna; designs stage sets for opera houses, 1974–78; living and working in Monaco 1986-. **Awards:** Painting Prize, *Bienal,* Sao Paulo, 1969; Art Prize, City of Vienna, 1972. **Address:** Atelier Ernst Fuchs, 6 Quai Antoine 1er, 98000 Monaco. **Web site:** www.ernstfuchs-center.com. **E-mail:** ernst.fuchs.privatstiftung@netway.at.

Individual Exhibitions:

1946 Galerie Halm und Goldmann, Vienna
1949 Galerie du Siècle, Paris
1950 Galleria La Bussola, Turin
Galerie Wolfgang Gurlitt, Munich
1951 Neue Galerie der Stadt, Linz, Austria
1952 Galeria Buchholz, Madrid
Galerie 55, Paris
1954 Galerie Allard, Paris
1957 Fuchs' House, Jerusalem
Galerie Nächst St. Stephan, Vienna
1958 Galerie Wolfgang Gurlitt, Munich
St. George's Gallery, London
Galerie Nächst St. Stephan, Vienna
1960 Galerie Raymond Cordier, Paris
Galerie Ernst Fuchs, Vienna
1962 Galerie Die Insel, Worpswede, West Germany
1963 Banfer Gallery, New York
1964 Galerie Willy Verkauf, Vienna
1965 Aoki Gallery, Tokyo
1966 Galerija Kolektiva, Belgrade
Sphinx, Galerie Snow, Frankfurt
1967 Galleria El Carpino, Rome
Kiko Gallery, Houston
Galerie Wolfgang Ketterer, Munich
Galerie Sydow, Frankfurt
Galerie Peithner-Lichtenfels, Vienna
1968 Pintorarium Harmann, Munich
Galerie Toni Brechbuhl, Bern
Rathaus Tempelhof, West Berlin
Kärntner Landesgalerie, Klagenfurt, Austria
Aoki Gallery, Tokyo
Galerie 6, Vienna
Galerie Koch, Hannover
Galerie Haas, Vaduz, Lichtenstein
Felix Landau Gallery, Los Angeles

Ernst Fuchs: *Der Anti-Laokoon,* 1965. ©2001 Artists Rights Society (ARS), NY/VBK, Vienna.

Graphische Sammlung Albertina, Vienna
1969 Galerie Gmurzynska, Cologne
Galerie Wentdorf, Düsseldorf
1970 Galerie von der Holm, Hamburg
Galleria Viotti, Turin
Galerie Ariadne, Vienna
Galerie d'Halluin, Düsseldorf (toured Germany and Austria)
Zeichnungen und Druckgraphik, Galerie Welz, Salzburg
Paintings and Drawings, Felix Landau Gallery, Los Angeles
Aoki Gallery, Tokyo
Bühler Graphics, Stuttgart
1971 Kunstverein, Heidelberg
Goethe-Institut, Marseilles
Galerie Commeter, Hamburg
Galerie Romanum, Vienna
Galerie Heismann, Essen
Galleria Don Chisciotte, Rome
Galerie Moser, Graz, Austria
1972 Die Galerie, Mannheim
Galerie Hippolyt, St. Pölten, Austria
Neufeld-Galerie, Lustenau, Austria
Galerie Herzmansky, Vienna
Odaky Department Store, Tokyo

Museum of Modern Art, Hyogo, Japan
Museum of Modern Art, Aichi, Japan
Museum des 20. Jahrhunderts, Vienna
1973 Baukunst, Cologne
1974 Aberbach Fine Art, New York
1975 *Oeuvre Grave,* Musée d'Art et d'Histoire, Fribourg, Switzerland
Galleria Don Chisciotte, Rome
Palazzo Costanzi, Trieste
Kuperion, Murano, Italy
1976 Galleria del Naviglio, Milan
1977 Galleria Forni, Bologna
Galleria Viotti, Turin
Stamperia della Bezuga, Florence
1979 Galleria La Medusa, Rome
1981 Kulturgeschichtliches Museum, Osnabruck, West Germany
1995 Château de Vascoeuil, France
Galerie am Steinweg, Passau, Germany
1997 Galerie Lehar, Vienna, Austria
Palais de L'Europe, Menton, France
Stadtgalerie Bamberg, Villa Dessauer, Germany
1998 Sabatier-Gruppe, Verden, Germany
1999 Kunstamt Zitadelle Spandau, Berlin
Kunstverein zu Hochenaschau, Germany

Selected Group Exhibitions:

1969 *Bienal,* Sao Paulo
1972 *Phantastischer Realismus,* Tiroler Landesmuseum Ferdinandeum, Innsbruck
1974 *19. und 20. Jahrhunders,* Galerie Wolfgang Ketterer, Munich
1992 *Videnska Skola Fantazijniho Realismu,* Stredoceska Galerie, Muzeum Moderniho Umeni, Prague
1994 *Du Fantastique au Visionnaire,* LLE Zitedelle, Centro Culturale, Venice
1996 *Kunst aus Österreich 1896–1996,* Kunst und Ausstellungshalle der BRD, Germany
2000 *Phantastik am Ende Der Zeit,* Stadtmuseum Erlangen, Germany

Publications:

On FUCHS: Books—*Ernst Fuchs: Sphinx,* exhibition catalog, with an introduction by Heinrich von Sydow-Zirkwitz, Frankfurt 1966; *Ernst Fuchs: Paintings and Drawings,* exhibition catalog, with an introduction by Johann Muschik, Los Angeles 1970; *Ernst Fuchs: Zeichnungen und Druckgraphik,* exhibition catalog, with text by Johann Muschik, Salzburg 1970; *Phantastischer Realismus: Malerei und Graphik aus dem Besitz der Stadt Wien,* exhibition catalog, with text by Robert Waissenberg, Innsbruck 1972; *Le Réalisme Fantastique* by J. C. Guilbert, Paris 1973; *Ernst Fuchs,* exhibition catalog, with text by Gustav René Hocke, Cologne, 1973; *Ernst Fuchs: Oeuvre Grave,* exhibition catalog, with text by Michel Terrapon, Fribourg, Switzerland 1975; *Ernst Fuchs,* exhibition catalog, Osnabruck 1981; *Ernst Fuchs—Fantasia,* exhibition catalog by Herausgeber Igor Jassenjawski and J. Kiblitski (with text by Ernst Fuchs), Munich 1993; *Du Fantastique au Visionnaire* by M. Albarelli, M. Random, G. di Genova, Bologna 1994; *Die Bibel (Altes und Neues Testament)* by Prof. Karl Matthäus Woschitz, Augsburg, Germany 1996; *Ernst Fuchs, Malerei und Graphik,* exhibition catalog by Klaus Jörg Schönmetzler, Hohenaschau, Germany 1999; *Ernst Fuchs, Mythos, Phantasie, Realismus,* exhibition catalog by Dr. Beate Zimmermann, Berlin 1999; *Phantastik am Ende der Zeit* by Thomas Engelhardt, Christine Ivanovic, and Markus May, Erlangen, Germany 2000.

* * *

Ernst Fuchs in Vienna, and in many other places as well, stands for a kind of imagery that is a mixture of sex, medievalism, mysticism and modernism that is hard to parallel in the work of any other artist. Perhaps in the recent past his closest cousin, in feeling and story if not in appearance, is Odilon Redon.

A master of the *mischtechnick,* he is also a brilliant graphics artist utterly capable as investigator into litho techniques with all the contemporary variants plus some that he has invented for himself; an etcher, a dry-pointer, aquatinter, mezzotinter, prolific graphics producer apparently untroubled by any challenge to his skills.

What does Fuchs choose as imagery? The basilisk in all his complications, the carnal sphinx, the Venus/Aphrodite/Hecate, young love, idolatry, and all the esoteric and occult mysteries of centuries past.

Nor is this all. Fuchs not only has the ability to make whatever he likes out of his subject matter, he also has a seemingly boundless range in feeling, able to evoke the refrigerated majesty of ancient days with the same puissance as he can convey the hot passion of erotic loveplay.

And the methods he uses . . . equally comfortable before the easel or at the drawing board, this Viennese not only extracts the best possible out of the traditions of the past, he also has few difficulties when it comes to expanding the means of graphic presentation.

Colour. Fuchs has a natural taste for exotic tinting, frequently of a twilight kind, but he is as variable with his colours as he is with his choice of subjects—sometimes proposing a near monochrome subtlety of tints, at others, in another mood, allowing violent clashes.

Where does Fuchs fit into the world of contemporary artists? His work and his styles find a warm response not only from those interested in art, but also from a great number who have looked for so long in vain for a master craftsman who could revivify the world of magic and ancient lore and do this in such a way that it would avoid becoming a pale copy of the past. Ernst Fuchs has supplied this want and, by so doing, has opened up a new area of art appreciation.

—Sheldon Williams

FULTON, Hamish

Nationality: British. **Born:** London in 1946. **Education:** Hammersmith School of Art, London, 1964–65; St. Martin's School of Art, London, 1966–68; Royal College of Art, London, 1968–69. **Career:** Professional artist since 1970. Lives in Canterbury, Kent. **Address:** c/o Waddington Galleries, 2 Cork Street, London W1, England. **Web site:** http://www.hamish-fulton.com.

Individual Exhibitions:

1969 Galerie Konrad Fischer, Dusseldorf
1970 Galleria Sperone, Turin
1971 Galerie Konrad Fischer, Dusseldorf

Situation, London
Richard Demarco Gallery, Edinburgh
1972 Galleria Sperone, Turin
Art and Project, Amsterdam
Galleria Toselli, Milan
Galerie Konrad Fischer, Dusseldorf
Museum of Modern Art, Oxford
Galerie Yvon Lambert, Paris
1973 Kabinett für Aktuelle Kunst, Bremerhaven, West Germany
Stedelijk Museum, Amsterdam
Galleria Sperone-Fischer, Rome
Situation, London
Galerie Yvon Lambert, Paris
Art and Project-M.T.L., Antwerp
1974 Galleria Marilena Bonomo, Bari, Italy
Museum of Modern Art, Oxford
Galleria Sperone, Turin
Galerie Konrad Fischer, Dusseldorf
1975 Art and Project, Amsterdam
Galerie Rolf Preisig, Basel
P.M.J. Self Gallery, London
Kunstmuseum, Basel
1976 Sperone-Westwater-Fischer Gallery, New York
Cusack Gallery, Houston
Institute of Contemporary Arts, London
Hester van Royen Gallery, London
Robert Self Gallery, London
Claire Copley Gallery, Los Angeles
1977 Galerie Rolf Preisig, Basel
City Museum, Canterbury, Kent
Stedelijk van Abbemuseum, Eindhoven, Netherlands
Robert Self Gallery, London
Sonnabend Gallery, New York
1978 Galerie Konrad Fischer, Dusseldorf
Galerie Nancy Gillespie/Eliszabeth de Laage, Paris
Museum of Modern Art, New York (project exhibition)
Centre d'Art Contemporain, Geneva
Galerie Tanit, Munich
1979 Whitechapel Art Gallery, London
Galerie Rolf Preisig, Basel
Art and Project, Amsterdam
1980 Galerie Gillespie de Laage, Paris
Thackrey and Robertson Gallery, San Francisco
Sperone-Westwater-Fischer Gallery, New York
Graeme Murray Gallery, Edinburgh
Kanransha Gallery, Tokyo
Waddington Galleries, London
1981 Galleria Massimo Valsecchi, Milan
Centre Georges Pompidou, Paris
1982 Waddington Galleries, London
Orchard Gallery, Londonderry, Northern Ireland
1983 Galerie Gillespie-de Laage-Salomon, Paris
Kanransha Gallery, Tokyo
Galleria Massimo Valsecchi, Milan
John Weber Gallery, New York
Coracle Gallery, London
1984 Waddington Galleries, London
Centre d'Art Contemporain, Geneva
1985 Stedelijk van Abbemuseum, Eindhoven, Netherlands (travelled to Le Nouveau Musee, Lyon; Fruit Market Gallery, Edinburgh; Mendel Art Gallery, Saskatoon; Castello di Rivoli, Turin; Coracle Gallery, London)
1986 Galerie Tanit, Munich
Galerie Dietmar Werle, Cologne
Kanransha Gallery, Tokyo
Galerie Gillespie-de Laage-Salomon, Paris
1987 Victoria Miro Gallery, London
1994 John Weber Gallery, New York
Galerie Lydie Rekow, Crest, France
Galleria Luis Serpa, Lisbon
Galleri Riis, Oslo
1995 Centre d'Art Contemporain, Geneva
Gallerie Tschudi, Glarus, Switzerland
Thirty-One Horizons, Lenbachhaus, Munich (catalog)
Galerie Tanit, Munich
1996 Second Floor, Reykjavik, Iceland
Le Musee de Valence, France
John Weber, New York
Walking from Wakayama in the Kii Peninsula, Museum of Modern Art, Wakayama, Japan (catalog)
Galerie Stadtpark, Krems, Austria (catalog)
Galerie Artek, Helsinki, Finland
Olga Korper Gallery, Toronto, Canada
1997 Cairn Gallery, Nailsworth, England
Galerie Mueller-Roth, Stuttgart
Texas Gallery, Houston
Art Museum, Missoula, Montana
1998 *Walking Beside the River Vechte,* Stadtische Galerie, Nordhorn (catalog)
Galerie Nishida Nara, Japan
Galerie Koyanagi, Tokyo
Annely Juda Fine Art, London (catalog)
John Weber Gallery, New York
1999 *Hill Walk—Bergwanderung,* Palais Thurn und Taxis, Bregenz, Austria (catalog)
Crawford Arts Centre, St. Andrews, Scotland
Anchorage Museum of Art and History, Alaska
Galerie Tschudi, Glarus, Switzerland
Galleri Riis, Oslo
2000 *Walking is the Constant, the Art Medium is the Variable,* Danese Gallery, New York
Galerie Mueller-Roth, Stuttgart, Germany
Patrick de Brock Gallery, Knokke, Belgium
Chesa Planta, Samedan, Switzerland
Magpie, Southern Alberta Art Gallery, Lethbridge, Canada (catalog)
Hausler Kulturmanagement GmbH, Munich
2001 Sainsbury Centre for the Visual Arts, Norwich, England

Selected Group Exhibitions:

1969 *Konzeption/Conception,* Städtisches Museum, Leverkusen, West Germany
1970 *Information,* Museum of Modern Art, New York
1972 *Documenta 5,* Kassel, West Germany
1973 *Medium Fotografie,* Städtisches Museum, Leverkusen, West Germany
1974 *Project 74,* Kunsthalle, Cologne
1975 *Artists over Land,* Arnolfini Gallery, Bristol

1978 *Art as Photography, Photography as Art,* Institute of Contemporary Arts, London
1980 *The British Art Show,* Mappin Art Gallery, Sheffield (toured the U.K.)
1982 *Approaches to Landscape,* Tate Gallery, London
1984 *Photographs in Contemporary Art,* National Museum of Modern Art, Tokyo
1994 *Conversation Pieces,* Institute of Contemporary Art, University of Pennsylvania, Philadelphia (catalog)
1996 *A Series of Twelve Prints by Six Artists,* Alan Cristea Gallery, London (catalog)
1997 *Timeframes,* Freedman Gallery, Albright College, Center for the Arts, Reading, Pennsylvania (catalog)
1998 *Hamish Fulton und Peter Hutchinson,* Kunstverein, Dusseldorf (catalog)
Conceptual Photography from the 60s and 70s, David Zwirner Gallery, New York
Landschaft, Kunsthalle zu Kiel, Bielefeld (catalog)
1999 *Circa 1968,* Serralves Museum of Contemporary Art, Oporto, Portugal

Collections:

Museum of Modern Art, New York; The Brooklyn Museum, New York; Princeton Art Gallery, New Jersey; Philadelphia Museum of Art; Los Angeles County Museum of Art; Eastman House, Rochester, New York; National Gallery of Canada, Ottawa; Metropolitan Museum, Tokyo; National Museum, Osaka; Victoria and Albert Museum, London; Biblioteque National, Paris; Australian National Gallery, Canberra; Stedelijk Museum, Amsterdam; The Tate Gallery, London; Stedelijk Van Abbemuseum, Eindhoven; Art Gallery of Ontario, Toronto; National Gallery of Scotland, Edinburgh; British Council, London; Kunstmuseum, Basel; Centro Cultural Arte Contemporaneo, Mexico City; Centre d'Art Contemporain, Geneva; Musee de Grenoble; Musee St. Pierre, Lyon; FRAC, Rennes, France; Museum of Modern Art, Wakayama.

Publications:

By FULTON: Books—*Hollow Lane,* London 1971; *The Sweet Grass Hills of Montana,* Turin 1971; *10 Views of Brockmans Mount,* Amsterdam 1973; *Hamish Fulton,* Milan 1974; *Skyline Ridge,* London 1977; *Nepal 1975,* Eindhoven, Netherlands 1977; *Nine Works, 1969–73,* London 1977; *Roads and Paths,* Munich 1978; *Wild Flowers,* Paris 1981; *Song of the Skylark,* London 1982; *Horizon to Horizon,* Londonderry 1983; *Twilight Horizons,* Bordeaux 1983; *Camp Fire,* Eindhoven 1985; *Coast to Coast Walks,* London 1985; *Cloud River,* 1985; *Thirty One Horizons,* Munich 1995; *Higurashi,* Kitakyushu 2000; *Wildlife,* Edinburgh 2000; *Hamish Fulton, Walking Artist,* Dusseldorf 2001.

On FULTON: Books—*Photography as Art* by Volker Kahmen, Tubingen 1973, London 1974; *Concept/Narrative/Document* by Judith Tannenbaum, Chicago 1979; *The Artist as Photographer* by Marina Vaizey, London 1982; *Earth-works* and *Beyond,* New York 1984. **Articles—**''Hamish Fulton'' by Hal Foster in *Artforum* (New York), February 1978; ''Richard Long and Hamish Fulton'' by Allan Davies in *Art Monthly* (London), April 1979; ''Moral Landscapes'' by Michael Auping in *Art in America* (New York), February 1983; ''Hamish Fulton'' by Charles Fagan in *Artforum* (New York), January 1984; ''Walks Are Like Clouds They Come and Go: Hamish Fulton'' by Adachiara Zevi in *L'Architettura,* vol. 39, September 1993; ''In Winchester, a Modern Day Medici'' by Christine Temin in *Boston Globe,* 26 October 1994; ''Hamish Fulton: Transition'' by Roger Marcel Mayou in *Kunstforum International,* no. 137, June-August 1997; ''Hamish Fulton at Texas'' by Colpitt Frances in *Art in America* (New York), January 1998; ''Images After the Fact'' by John Haldane in *Modern Painters* (London), vol. 11, no. 3, Autumn 1998; ''Strutting His Stuff'' by Blake Gopnik in *The Toronto Globe and Mail,* 24 October 2000.

*

My work is about the experience of walking. The framed artwork is about a state of mind—it cannot convey the experience of the walk. A walk has a life of its own; it does not need to be made into art. I am an artist and choose to make my artworks from real life experiences. All the walks I make are easy. I prefer to go out into the world and be influenced and changed by events rather than work from my imagination in one fixed place.

—Hamish Fulton

* * *

Hamish Fulton's gallery works consist of a photograph or photographs together with a caption and brief explanatory text. The essential point to register in looking at these works is that they come from a 'walking' experience. The starting point of all of Fulton's work is just that—the walk. It is a walk that may last for a few hours or go on for days. It may be over the smooth Downs of southern England, the hills and crags of Scotland, or further afield in the lonely vastnesses of places such as Iceland. It may be only a few hours scrambling up a hillside or a long steady trek over a flat countryside. The scenery around him may be full of historical associations or an untouched wilderness, but whatever it may be, on his walk he seems able to absorb its particular resonances and encapsulate them in the photograph, the artwork which is the final result. The walking, that most natural of human rhythms, provides the gestation period for his response. His cool, black and white photographs with their laconic accompanying text have a quiet, but nevertheless emotional impact.

Walking—looking—photographing. During these walks Fulton takes photographs of what lies before him, sometimes a bare handful of shots, but on other occasion he may take hundreds. The one which seems particularly appropriate to his feelings is usually one which selects itself on the walk and rarely from later viewing of all that he has taken. He does not process his own shots, nor does he often choose to touch up or make many changes in the prints. Should using the camera on a blustery day result in a blurred and grainy print then that is accepted if that is the view which best represents what he has experienced.

The texts which accompany his photographs are of equal importance and though they may appear at first to be only straightforward, factual captions, when read in conjunction with the picture they can provide a rich stimulus to the imagination. In FRANCE ON THE HORIZON (1975) Fulton adds the following information: ''21 MILES ACROSS THE CHANNEL/ A ONE DAY 50 MILE WALK BY WAY OF THE WHITE CLIFFS OF DOVER/ ENGLAND SUMMER 1975.'' The photograph itself, which was taken about 5:00 a.m.

shows the coast line of France, barely visible in the far distance, a white fringed diagonal line or waves breaking on the English beach which lies far beneath a rough patch of grass at the cliff top. The artist says that as he stood there he was reminded of the historic associations of that nearest point between the two countries, the Second World War song, ''The White Cliffs of Dover,'' and the evacuation from Dunkirk.

In a print entitled NO DARKNESS which resulted from a week-long trek through Iceland the title can be taken to refer to the white nights of the Icelandic summer. Below that SOFT GROUND probably refers to the thawing out of the icebound earth while TRACKS OF AN ARCTIC FOX and LATE SPRING convey their own meaning. The mysterious DRIFTWOOD FROM SIBERIA, the artist has revealed, refers to driftwood washed up on the Icelandic coast that summer and the Russian lettering on some of the wood proved what great distances it had travelled.

Asked if he had studied landscape painting of past centuries Fulton replied that he was not interested in Western landscape painting but that he did study Oriental landscape painting, and this influence may be seen in the spareness and elegance of his compositions.

—Mary Ellis

FURNIVAL, John

Nationality: British. **Born:** London, 29 May 1933. **Education:** Attended schools in London; studied at Wimbledon College of Art, London, 1952–56, and Royal College of Art, London, 1958–60. **Military Service:** Served in the Royal Fusiliers, London, 1955; studied Russian at the Joint Services School for Languages; worked as an Intelligence Officer in the War Office, London, 1956–57. **Family:** Married Astrid Hennig in 1960; children: Eve, Jack and Harry. **Career:** Independent artist, Gloucestershire, since 1960. Editor, with Dom Sylvester Houedard and Edward Wright, Openings Press, since 1964. Lecturer in Painting, Gloucestershire College of Art and Gloucester City College, 1960–65; lecturer in Graphic Design, Bath Academy of Art, 1965 to present. Founder, Dorothy's Umbrellas environmental group, Woodchester, Gloucestershire, 1972 (now Dorothy's Umbrellas Dining Society), and Saties Faction, group perpetuating the works of Erik Satie, 1975. **Awards:** First Prize, Arnolfini Gallery Open Competition, Bristol, 1962; Prize, *Bradford Print Biennale,* Yorkshire, 1972. **Agent:** Thumb Gallery, 20–21 D'Arblay Street, London W1. **Address:** Rooksmoor House, Woodchester, Gloucestershire, England.

Individual Exhibitions:

1964 Arnolfini Gallery, Bristol
Piccadilly Gallery, London
1966 Arnolfini Gallery, Bristol (with Dom Sylvester Houedard and Ken Cox)
Midland Group Gallery, Nottingham (with Dom Sylvester Houedard)
1967 Galerie Riquelme, Paris
1968 Ikon Gallery, Birmingham
1971 Laing Art Gallery, Newcastle upon Tyne
1972 Arnolfini Gallery, Bristol
1974 Thumb Gallery, London
1979 Thumb Gallery, London (with Tom Phillips)
1987 Galerie Hoss, Stuttgart
1994 *The Locative Case,* Cairn Gallery, Nailsworth
1997 Green Park Gallery, Bath

Selected Group Exhibitions:

1965 *Between Poetry and Painting,* Institute of Contemporary Arts, London
1966 *Concrete/Spatial Poetry,* Midland Group Gallery, Nottingham
1967 *Aktual Art International,* San Francisco Museum of Art
1969 *Multiples Unlimited,* Ikon Gallery, Birmingham
1970 *The World as Image,* Jewish Museum, New York
Concrete Poetry, Stedelijk Museum, Amsterdam (toured Europe)
1979 *The Open and Closed Book,* Victoria and Albert Museum, London
1980 *Mazes,* Rochdale Art Gallery, Lancashire (travelled to the Ferens Art Gallery, Hull, Yorkshire
1982 *Le Livre-Objet,* Centre Georges Pompidou, Paris
1986 *The Bordeaux Collection,* Thumb Gallery, London
1995 *L'Ultima Avanguardia,* Spoleto, Italy
1996 *Visual Poetry,* Novgorod, Russia
2000 *Flags/Drapeaux,* Liège, Aachen , Knokke

Collections:

Arnolfini Trust, Bristol; McAlpine Collection, London; Sammlung Cremer, Stuttgart; Pinakothek, Munich; Arts Council of Great Britain, London; Staatsgalerie, Stuttgart; Roswell Museum, New Mexico; British Council, London; Tate Gallery, London; Getty Foundation, Santa Barbara, California.

Publications:

By FURNIVAL: Books—Numerous publications in small editions by Openings Press, Woodchester, Gloucestershire, since 1965, also *Teapoth,* Dunsyre, Lanarkshire 1967; *The Bang Book,* with Rom Meyer, Highlands, North Carolina 1971; *Erick Satie,* with Stuart Hodges and Gary Birch, Corsham, Wiltshire 1976. **Illustrated books**—*Sport and Divertissements* by Ronald Johnson, Dunsyre, Lanarkshire 1965; *Ten and the Ox Eye Daisy* by Ronald Johnson, Dunsyre, Lanarkshire 1965; *The Lucidities* by Jonathan Williams, London 1967; also, contrubutions to *Concrete Poetry,* edited by Stephen Bann, London 1967; *Anthology of Concrete Poetry,* edited by Emmett Williams, New York 1967; *Anthology of Concretism,* Chicago 1967; *Concrete Poetry: A World View,* edited by Mary Ellen Solt, Terre Haute, Indiana 1968; *Group and Woup,* edited by Bob Cobbing, Gillingham, Kent 1974; *The Deck of Card,* London 1979; *Blind Date,* with Thomas Meyer, London 1980; *Letters to the Great Dead,* with Jonathan Williams, Woodchester, Gloucestershire 1984; *The Bordeaux Collections,* suite of 4 etchings, Nailsworth, Gloucestershire 1986; *St. Swithin's Swivet,* with Jonathan Williams, 1998. **Articles**—''Openings'' in *Baseline,* 1994.

On FURNIVAL: Books—*Experimentalni Poezie,* Prague 1967; *Once Again,* edited by Jean Francois Bory, Paris 1968; *Der Kunstliche Baum* by Ernst Jandl, Berlin 1969; *Svetova Literatura '68,* Prague 1968; *The World as Image,* edited by Berjouhi Bowler, London 1970;

Imaged Words and Worded Images by Richard Kostelanetz, New York 1970; *Signal 2–3* by Miroljub Todorovic, Belgrade 1971; *John Furnival; Ceolfrith 14,* Sunderland, County Durham 1971; *John Furnival: Selected Works of the Last Twenty Years,* exhibition catalog, Verona 2000. **Article—**''John Furnival'' by K. Power and J. Williams in *Arts Review* (London), October 1978.

*

I continue to work in the same manner—developing, I hope. I spent a year in Roswell, New Mexico, between 1983 and 1984, and this gave me a welcome break from teaching, upon which I rely for my basic income. That year, apart from anything else, enabled me to earn enough money to extend my studio facilities in England, including the setting up of a proper etching studio. I seem to be able to just about exist without being too much involved with the regular art establishment, which suits me perfectly, Most of my sales are to the United States, although I have recently been making incursions into Germany; and the establishment of Wine Arts in 1986 has widened my catchment area considerably.

Until 1986 I taught at the Bath Academy of Art, Corsham—which has since been moved into Bath proper, and is now euphemistically entitled ''Bath Spa University College''—B.SVC for short! College song: ''Where the B.SVC's, there suck I.''

—John Furnival

* * *

Although they have worked together, John Furnival's concrete poetry is, in its imagery, far removed from that of Dom Sylvester Houedard, co-editor with him of Openings Press. Furnival's actual use of words, whether printed or cursive, is also much more congested than that of the monk's, and the scale upon which he works is frequently far larger. Nevertheless, both believe in the effiency of the ''obvious'' (*obvious,* as Furnival puts it, in the sense that Vincent van Gogh's sunflowers are *obvious*). There is a kind of classical control running through his work that is not always evident in the ''poetry'' of his contemporary Henri Chopin, for instance, yet this is not the sort of scholarly discipline that infuses the output of the concrete poets of Munich—not sources upon which to draw if the spirit moves him: he has a classical background of Latin and Greek, very clearly a wide knowledge of English literature and has also managed—as a paradoxical bonus—to pick up Russian. An unfulfilled ambition of his—possibly not serious—is to acquire fluency in Chinese at one time or another. And this is easily perceptible in his work for those who are prepared to take on the intellectual challenge of assessing the textual meanings in the poems, although he himself is on record as saying that his ''tower'' pictures are for looking at, not for reading.

Furnival loots trash rather in the same way as Kurt Schwitters kept a wary eye open for valuable *Merz* material. There the resemblance between the performances of the two artists ends. Whatever he may say, Furnival is on the look-out for lyrical impact, whereas Schwitters, if he often produced works in poetic vein, did so more by a series of *happy incidents* because he had an eccentric genius for emancipating rubbish from the threat of the ecological incinerator.

Furnival declares that the term ''artist'' is an archaism born out of the Renaissance and overdue for retirement. Not without practical verity, he asserts that he wants to pull alongside the dustman and keep the postman busy. For one so productive, insofar as print and poetry are concerned, the rising cost of any volume of mail must have a baleful ring about it. After all, ''Mail Art,'' as Jean-Marc Poinsot points out in his book of that title—which illustrates Furnival's ''Watch Warranty'' and ''From your soldier boy''—this particular corner of contemporary art is expanding rapidly. It would be sad if this development were killed by cost.

—Sheldon Williams

FUSSMANN, Klaus

Nationality: German. **Born:** Velbert, Rhineland, 24 March 1938. **Education:** Studied drawing, under Karl Klode, Essen, 1950–53; Folkwang-Schule, Essen, 1957–61; art, under Professor Lortz, Hochschule fur bildende Kunste, West Berlin, 1962–66. **Family:** Married Barbara Gordon in 1971. **Career:** Independent painter, in Berlin, since 1966. Professor, Hochschule der Kunste, West Berlin, since 1974. Lives in Berlin and in Gelting. **Awards:** Villa-Romana-Prize, Florence, 1971; Bottcherstrasse Prize, Bremen, 1972; Kunstpreis, City of Darmstadt, 1979. **Member:** Free Academy Hamburg, 1989. **Agents:** Galerie Lange, Wielandstrasse 26, 10707 Berlin, Germany; Galerie Ludorff, Koningshalle 22, III, 40212 Dusseldorf, Germany; Galerie Peerlings, Friedriechstrasse 49, 47798 Krefeld, Germany; Galerie Zwang, Paulinenallee 28, 20259 Hamburg, Germany; Galerie Rosenbach, Walderseestrasse 24, 30177 Hannover, Germany; Galerie Kruse, Rotestrasse 22–24, 24937 Flensburg, Germany; Galerie Nickel, Plobenhofstrasse 4, 90403 Nuremberg, Germany; Galerie Steinrötter, Rotenburgstrasse 16, 48143 Munster. **Address:** Grainauer Strasse 19, 10777 Berlin, Germany.

Individual Exhibitions:

1968 Galerie 6, West Berlin
1969 Galerie Schuler, West Berlin
1970 Baukunst-Galerie, Cologne
1971 Paula-Becker-Modersohn-Haus, Bremen, West Germany
Nationalgalerie, West Berlin (with Hoffmann and Waldenburg)
1972 Villa Hammerschmidt, Bonn
Galerie Gunzenhauser, Munich
Galerie Schuler, West Berlin
1973 Kunsthalle, Darmstadt (and the Kunstverein and Magistrat, Darmstadt)
Galerie am Steinernen Tor, Frankfurt
1974 Galerie Kornfeld, Zurich
Galerie Lietzow, West Berlin
1975 Galerie Schuler, West Berlin
Galerie Kammer, Hamburg
Baukunst-Galerie, Cologne
1976 Galerie Gunzenhauser, Munich
Lefebre Gallery, New York
Galerie Nickel-Zadow, Nuremberg, West Germany
1977 Overbeck-Gesellschaft, Lubeck, West Germany
Galerie Schuler, West Berlin
Baunkunst-Galerie, Cologne
Galerie Walther, Dusseldorf
1978 Lefebre Gallery, New York
Galerie im Kirschgarten, Mainz, West Germany

Klaus Fussman: *Death of a Hare,* 1993. ©Klaus Fussman.

Achim Moeller Gallery, London
Galerie Schuler, West Berlin
Kunsthandel Lambert Tegenbosch, Netherlands
Galerie Haus II, Karlsruhe, West Germany
Galerie im Winter, Bremen, West Germany (with Albert Held)
1979 Galerie Pudelko, Bonn
Galerie Gierig, Frankfurt
Lefebre Gallery, New York
Galerie Internie, West Berlin
Galerie Nickel-Zadow, Nuremberg, West Germany
1980 Suermondt-Ludwig-Museum, Aachen, West Germany
Galerie Roedel, Mannheim, West Germany
Galerie Landesgirokasse, Stuttgart (with Albert Held)
1981 Lefebre Gallery, New York
Galerie Haus II, Karlsruhe, West Germany
Galerie Thomas, Munich
Galerie Hartwig und Bethke, West Berlin
Galerie Peerlings, Krefeld, West Germany
1982 Kunsthandel Lambert Tegenbosch, Netherlands
Galerie Schuler, West Berlin
Mathildenhohe, Darmstadt, West Germany
Galerie Thomas, Munich
1983 Lefebre Gallery, New York
Baukunst-Galerie, Cologne
1984 Lefebre Gallery, New York
1985 Galerie Timm Gierig, Frankfurt
Lefebre Gallery, New York
1986 Baunkunst Gallery, Cologne
Galerie Steinrotter, Munster, West Germany
1987 Schleswig-Holsteinisches Landesmuseum, Schleswig, West Germany
Galerie Zwang, Hamburg
Galerie Schuler, West Berlin
Achim Moeller Fine Arts, New York
1988 ZDF-Galerie, Mainz-Lerchenberg, West Germany
Henri Nannenmuseum, Emden, West Germany
Galerie Rieder, Munich
1990 Worthington Gallery, Chicago
Galerie Ludorff, Dusseldorf
1991 Anthony Ralph Gallery, New York
Campbell/Thiebaud Gallery, San Francisco
Staatliche Kunstsammlung, Dresden
1992 Kunsthalle Bremen
Landesmuseum Schleswig-Holstein
Galerie Steinrötter, Munster
Galerie Zwang, Hamburg
1993 Galerie Peerlings, Sylt
1994 Galerie Ludorff, Dusseldorf
Galerie Lange, Berlin
1996 Bundeskanzleramt, Bonn
Kunstverein Uelzen, Germany
1997 Zweites Deutsches Fernsehen
Deutsches Historisches Museum, Berlin
1998 Galerie Peerlings, Kampen, Sylt, Germany
Schleswig-Holsteinische Landesbibliothek, Kiel, Germany
Schloß Hardenberg, Velbert-Neviges, Germany
SAP, Walldorf
1999 Galerie Ludorff, Düsseldorf
Galerie Thomas, Munich
2000 Galerie Peerlings, Kampen, Sylt, Germany

Selected Group Exhibitions:

1985 *Representations Abroad,* Hirshhorn Museum, Washington, D.C.

Collections:

Albertina, Vienna; Kupferstichkabinett, West Berlin; Nationalgalerie, West Berlin; Rheinisches Landesmuseum, Bonn; Kunsthalle, Bremen; Stadtische Sammlung, Darmstadt; Neue Pinakothek, Munich; Wurttembergischer Staatsgalerie, Stuttgart; Metropolitan Museum of Art, New York; Landesmuseum Schleswig-Holstein; Suermondt-Ludwig-Museum, Aachen, Germany; Berlinische Galerie, Berlin; Bundeskanzleramt, Bonn; Landesmuseum, Darmstadt.

Publications:

By FUSSMANN: Books and portfolios—*Zwergnase,* portfolio of 5 lithographs, West Berlin 1964; *Spuren,* portfolio of 7 lithographs, with text by Peter O. Chotjewicz, West Berlin, Frankfurt and Vienna 1974; illustrations to *Die Gegenstande der Gedankenstille* by Peter O. Chotjewicz, Dusseldorf 1976; *Tage, 7 Gedichte,* 7 lithographs with text by Wittich Rohleder, Karlsruhe 1977; *Grossere Versuche uber den Schmutz,* 7 lithographs with text by Christian Enzensberger, West Berlin 1980; *Die verschwundene Malerei,* West Berlin 1985; *Die Schuld der Moderne,* Berlin 1991; *Du Bekommst Bestimmt eine Antwort,* Hamburt 1993. **Articles—**''Alle Kunst ist Allegorie, Ein Maler Schaut Zurück: Pop-art Zwanzig Jahre Später'' in *Frankfurter*

Allgemeine Zeitung, 1978; ''Die Kunst, die Sich Selbst Suchte'' in *Frankfurter Allgemeine Zeitung,* 1984; ''The Color of Dirt. Lovis Corinth'' in *Artforum,* May 1986; ''Die Blaue Unendlichheit'' in *Die Zeit,* 1988; ''Sie Malten und Verschwanden von der Erde'' in *Frankfurter Allgemeine Zeitung,* 1992; ''Strandleben am Styx'' in *Frankfurter Allgemeine Zeitung,* 1994; ''Die Auferstehung des Fleisches'' in *Frankfurter Allgemeine,* 1995.

On FUSSMANN: Books—*Klaus Fussmann: Gemalde und Gouachen,* exhibition catalog with text by Bernd Krimmel, Darmstadt 1973; *Klaus Fussmann* by Werner Haftmann, West Berlin, Frankfurt and Vienna 1976; *Klaus Fussmann: Gemalde, Gouachen, Aquarelle, Zeichnungen,* exhibition catalog with essays by Joachim Fest, Bernd Krimmel and Elisabeth Krimmel, Darmstadt 1982; *Klaus Fussmann: Self-Portraits and Landscapes,* exhibition catalog with introduction by Kenneth Baker, New York 1985; *Ansichten: Klaus Fussmann,* with foreword by Siegfried Salzmann, Bremen 1992.

*

Art is almost as great an illusion as religion, has as much to do with sophistry as philosophy has, and remains mysteriously bound up with both. Art has its own metaphysics, and with this sign language can penetrate that particular darkness where words can no longer follow. But that is necessarily problematic and quickly leads, as we have seen in the late modern period, to misunderstandings and to interpretations that no longer make sense. And yet, despite so many imponderables, art remains the medium whereby man in all his complexity can express himself. In and through art man mirrors his being and the world, and he keeps creating this mirror of art for himself anew—in the hope of finally discovering something about what determines his being. And now and then a transfiguration is thus effected, showing man in harmony with nature. Such a situation—however shortlived—brings such new-found meaning and is so inspiring in its effects that it repays every effort.

—Klaus Fussmann

G

GAGNON, Charles

Nationality: Canadian. **Born:** Montreal, 23 May 1934. **Education:** Parsons School of Design, New York School of Design, New York University, Art Students League, 1955–59. **Career:** Independent artist. Professor, Loyola/Concordia University, 1967–75; University of Ottawa, 1975–95. **Awards:** Canada Council Arts Grants, 1962, 1968, 1978, 1993; Banff Centre School of Fine Arts National Medal, 1981; Donald Cameron Medal, Banff Centre, 1981; Chevalier, Ordre du Quebec, 1991; honorary doctorate, University of Montreal, 1991; Quebec Government Arts Grant, 1992. **Agents:** Yajima/Galerie, 307 Ste. Catherine West, Montreal, Quebec H2X 2A3, Canada; Sable/Castelli Gallery, 33 Hazelton Ave., Toronto, Ontario, Canada M5R 2E2. **Address:** 3510 Addington Avenue, Montreal, Quebec H4A 3G6, Canada.

Individual Exhibitions:

1959 Galerie Artek, Montreal
1961 Galerie Denyse Delrue, Montreal
1962 Galerie Denyse Delrue, Montreal
Jerrold Morris International Gallery, Toronto
1963 Musée des Beaux-Arts, Montreal (with John Fox)
1964 Galerie Camille Hébert, Montreal
1966 Galerie Agnés Lefort, Montreal
1969 Galerie Godard/Lefort, Montreal
1971 Vancouver Art Gallery
Edmonton Art Gallery
1972 Mendel Art Gallery, Saskatoon
Sir George Williams University Art Gallery, Montreal
Yellowknife Library and Art Center, Yellowknife
Moose Jaw Art Gallery, Moose Jaw
Vincent University Art Gallery, Halifax
1973 Université de Sherbrooke, Quebec (travelled to Toronto and Sackville, New Brunswick)
1974 Marlborough-Godard Gallery, Toronto
Marlborough-Godard Gallery, Montreal
1975 Yajima/Galerie, Montreal
1978 Musée des Beaux-Arts, Montreal
1979 National Gallery of Canada, Ottawa (travelled to Vancouver, Toronto, and Winnipeg)
1982 Yajima/Galerie, Montreal
1983 Equinox Gallery, Vancouver
1988 Sable-Castelli Gallery, Toronto
1989 Galerie René Blouin, Montreal
1991 Sable/Castelli Gallery, Toronto
1992 Galerie René Blouin, Montreal
1993 *Charles Gagnon: Recent Work,* Edmonton Art Gallery, Edmonton
1994 Galerie René Blouin
Sable/Castelli Gallery, Toronto
2000 *Charles Gagnon: Observations,* Canadian Museum of Contemporary Photography, Ottawa (catalog)
2001 *Charles Gagnon: A Retrospective,* Montreal Museum of Contempoary Arts (catalog)

Selected Group Exhibitions:

1961 *Biennale,* Paris
1964 *Salon du Printemps,* Musée des Beaux-Arts, Montreal
1969 *Biennale,* Paris
1978 *Canadian Contemporary Painting,* Centre Culturel Canadien, Paris (travelled throughout Australia and New Zealand)
1981 *Canadian Painting in the Twentieth Century,* National Museum of Modern Art, Tokyo (travelled to Sapporo and Oita, Japan)
1983 *The Mountain: A Survey of Photography,* International Center of Photography, New York
1984 *Reflections,* National Gallery of Canada, Ottawa
1987 *A Second Look,* Confederation Centre Museum, Charlottetown, Prince Edward Island (travelled to Wolfville and Halifax, Nova Scotia; Fredericton, New Brunswick; and St. Johns, Newfoundland)
1988 *Ewen, Gagnon, Gaucher, Hurtebise, McEwen: Concerning Painting of the 1960s,* Musee d'Art Contemporain, Monreal
1992 *Independent Eyes,* Festival of Festivals, Toronto
1993 *The Crisis of Abstraction in Canada,* National Gallery of Canada, Ottawa (travelled to Regina, Saskatchewan; Calgary, Alberta; Hamilton, Ontario; and Quebec)
1995 *Donations 1989–94,* Musee d'Art Contemporain, Montreal

Collections:

National Gallery of Canada, Ottawa; Musée des Beaux-Arts, Montreal; Vancouver Art Gallery; Art Gallery of Ontario, Toronto; Hirshhorn Museum, Washington D.C.; Musée du Quebec; Banff Centre, Alberta; University of Saskatchewan, Regina; University of Guelph, Ontario; Université de Montreal; Canada Council Art Bank, Ottawa; Department of External Affairs, Ottawa; Owens Art Gallery, Mount Allison University, Sackville, New Brunswick.

Publications:

By GAGNON: Book—*Incidences: Projets Photographiques,* Montreal 1992.

On GAGNON: Books—*La peinture canadienne des origines à nos jours* by J. R. Harper, Quebec 1964; *Canadian Art Today* edited by W. Townsend, London 1970; *An Inquiry into the Aesthetics of Photography* by Geoffrey James, Toronto 1975; *Charles Gagnon* by P. Fry, Montreal 1978; *Seize Peintres du Quebec dans leur milieu* by A. Paradis, Montreal 1978; *The Banff Purchase* by P. Cousineau, Toronto 1979; *Visions: Contemporary Art in Canada* by R. Bringhurst, G. James, and R. Keziere, Vancouver and Toronto, 1983; *Contemporary Canadian Art* by D. Burnett and M. Schiff, Toronto 1983;

Parmenidean Puzzles: Paradox and Discovery in the Paintings of Charles Gagnon by James Campbell, Montreal 1989; *Masterpieces of Canadian Art from the National Gallery* by David Burnett, Toronto and Edmonton 1990; *Charles Gagnon: Recent Work,* exhibition catalog, preface by Elizabeth Kidd, Edmonton 1993; *La collection Lavalin du Musée d'Art Contemporain de Montreal* by G. Walsh and M. Held, Montreal 1994; *Dons 1989–1994,* exhibition catalog, preface by Marcel Brisebois, Montreal 1995. **Articles—**''Charles Gagnon'' by C. Jasmin in *Canadian Art,* March/April 1962; ''Charles Gagnon'' by N. Thériault in *Vie des Arts,* winter 1968–69; ''Charles Gagnon: The Ambiguous Object'' by D. Burnett in *Vanguard,* June/July 1979; ''Charles Gagnon's Point of View'' by Dore Ashton in *Artscanada,* August/September 1979; ''Charles Gagnon'' by Ann Duncan in *Art News,* vol. 94, February 1995; '''A' Lyric'' by Jennifer Couëlle in *Canadian Art,* vol. 14, no. 1, Spring 1997; review by Franceska Gnarowski in *Vie des Ars,* vol. 44, no. 178, Spring 2000.

* * *

Charles Gagnon of Montreal has long been in the first rank of Canadian painters. Since the mid-1950s, he has developed his own daunting vocabulary as an abstract painter. A gifted medium of surfaces, his work is nonetheless fraught with depth—structures and paradoxes that reward our continued perceptual and mental acquaintance. Gagnon's is a painterly abstraction preoccupied with enigmas that make it a genuine catalyst for thought.

Born in Montreal, Gagnon spent his formative years (1955–60) in New York, where he studied and became aware of the ground-breaking work of composer John Cage, dancer Merce Cunningham, painter Robert Rauschenberg, among others. Gagnon painted and photographed while in New York, and his first wholly mature work dates from this period. By the time he returned to Montreal, in 1960, he was producing exceptionally cerebral abstract paintings in a very cool, spontaneous Zen idiom.

Gagnon as a creative artist is impossible to pigeonhole. Gifted filmmaker and photographer (he has been photographing actively for over 40 years) as well as a painter, Gagnon has sought to subvert the staid conventions of painting by importing sets of concerns and structural devices from these other media. The paradox is that he has also, in the process, been able to reinvigorate a painting practice that has always demonstrated a high level of formal invention. The psychological iconography of his 1950s abstractions evolved, in the 1960s and 70s and beyond, into works of consummate painterliness—the brushstroking is startling in its sensuousity—that were still notable for the tenor of their resolute intelligence and structural austerity.

In his *Cassations* series of the 1970s, for instance, Gagnon places a rectangle within a rectangle that suggests a window perspective (or viewfinder or cinema screen), but the brushstroking is continuous within and without the rectangles, suggesting a Magritte-like conundrum at work in the painting's surface. The lively—and enlivening—brushwork, the rich colours (this smoky violet, that froth-smeared cerulean blue) and the drips of paint spattered across the composition, remind us of the dynamism of process in Gagnon's work—and, above all, the physicality of paint; the factuality of a painted surface.

In the late 1980s, Gagnon would stencil words at the center of his abstract compositions (textual fragments have often found their way into his otherwise abstract work), and the relation of the word to the painting generates further enigmas. These iconic signs seem to embody a hidden and perhaps ineffable truth of painting, which we are encouraged to seek out. Gagnon's signature brushstroking and understanding of colour and form make these works at once engaging and provocative.

Perhaps because of the unlikely combination of seductive brushwork and cool sobriety of subject matter—sundry enigmas and paradoxes abound—in his paintings, Gagnon has always been seen as an artist's artist.

Observing one of Gagnon's paintings means coming to terms with the paradoxes they offer, and with our own propensities in looking at paintings. Gagnon works to make us think—and to undermine our unthinking assumptions. Simply put, he constructs enigmas that are nourishing food for thought.

Through the use of ambiguous structures that could not occur in respect of natural objects, a sensuous but deceptively serene brushstroking that plays off canons of structural continuity and discontinuity, a beguiling use of incompatible and ambiguous depth-cues, and Wittgensteinian language games, Gagnon renders his paintings thresholds that we are entreated to cross. And crossing such thresholds means crossing the chalk-line between reality and illusion, because his paintings are not only windows that open outward, but open inward as well, capturing the mind as well as the eye.

More recently, Gagnon has sought to reconcile his painting and photography in works which wed the most compelling aspects of both. These photoworks bring together enlarged photographic images that are framed together with monochromatic paintings in a variety of formats. The photographic images are generally of seized fragments of nature while the abstractions, which are sensuous and austere at once, invoke nature in its carnal essence.

In the work entitled *Histoire Naturelle I (MARE)* from 1991, Gagnon juxtaposes an enlarged silverprint with three small oil-on-masonite paintings, each framed separately but abutting to form one unified work. We immediately search out any affinity between the seascape of the photograph and the three sombre monochromes stacked vertically and numbered 1, 2, and 3 respectively. These low-key bluish panels perhaps allude to the possible colours of water. But a feeling for the strong affinity between them stems readily from our own imaginations. (The stencilled numbers relate to linear perspective. They differ from other numeric sequences he uses in his work that are based on purely mental progressions—Fibonacci sequences which relate, for him, to the mental perception of depth.)

In transforming what painting and photography are by showing what, together, they can be, Gagnon seems to be telling us that we are all completely prejudiced. Our biases have to do with how we, in the Western tradition, are disposed to think of photographs (or paintings, for that matter) in terms of representation. This artist makes us ask ourselves which is the more abstract mediation, the photograph or the painting? Gagnon deals with the role of acculturation here—how what we've been taught influences our outlook. He explores the essential relation of photography and painting to the world, to the ground plane of representation itself. Few abstract painters in the 1990s could be said to do the same. Fewer still could hope to broach highly original art in so doing.

Claude Monet held that a painting was best understood as a window opening on nature. Gagnon, too, understands paintings as windows; he wants to understand nature/culture in new ways. As witnesses to that ongoing project of understanding and exploration, which Gagnon would perhaps aver has only just begun, he opens those windows for us.

—James D. Campbell

GARCÍA, Daniel

Nationality: Argentine. **Born:** Rosario, Santa Fe Province, Argentina, 18 January 1958. **Education:** Graduated as Chemical Technician, Instituto Politécnico Superior (Advanced Polytechnical Institute), Rosario, Argentina, 1971–77; studied chemical engineering, National Technical University, Rosario, 1976–80; studied color theory with Eduardo Serón, Rosario, 1981; studied literature, School of Humanities and Arts, Rosario National University, Rosario, 1985–87; studied at workshop coordinated by Guillermo Kuitca, Buenos Aires, 1991–92. **Military Service:** Served in the Argentine Army, 1978–79. **Family:** Married Elina Heredia, 1986 (divorced 1994); married María Eugenia Spinelli, 1996. One son: Joaquín. **Career:** Worked at chemical laboratory, 1974–1977; painter since 1981; graphics designer, 1990–91; graphics designer and cover artist, *Beatriz Viterbo* Publishing, 1991—. Secretary of A.P.A. (Associated Plastic Artists), Rosario, 1984. **Awards:** Second Prize, George Braque Award, Museum of Modern Art, Buenos Aires, 1991; Scholarship, Antorchas Foundation, Buenos Aires, 1991; Scholarship, Antorchas Foundation, Buenos Aires, 1992; *Nuevo Mundo* Foundation Prize, National Museum of Fine Arts, Buenos Aires, 1994; Grant for Artistic Creation, Antorchas Foundation, Buenos Aires, 1996; First Prize, Austria Award, National Museum of Fine Arts, Buenos Aires, 1996; Young Artist of the Year, Association of Argentine Art Critics, Buenos Aires, 1995; First Regional Prize, Mayorazgo Foundation Award, National Museum of Fine Arts, Buenos Aires, 1996; Second Prize, Costantini Collection Award, National Museum of Fine Arts, Buenos Aires, 1997. **Agent:** Sicardi Gallery, 2326 Kipling #101, Houston, Texas 77098. **Address:** Friuli 160, Rosario 2000, Argentina.

Selected Individual Exhibitions:

1982 Buonarotti Gallery, Rosario
1984 Miró Gallery, Rosario
1985 Miró Gallery, Rosario
1987 Architects Center, Rosario
1989 Santillán Gallery, Rosario
1990 *Argentina* Library, Rosario
1991 Recoleta Cultural Center, Buenos Aires
Castagnino Gallery, Harrods, Buenos Aires (catalog)
1993 Sara García Uriburu Gallery, Buenos Aires
1994 Fredric Snitzer Gallery, Coral Gables, Florida
1995 Ruth Benzacar Gallery, Buenos Aires (catalog)
1996 Banco Patricios Foundation, Buenos Aires (catalog)
Museum of Contemporary Art, Bahía Blanca (catalog)
1997 Recoleta Cultural Center, Buenos Aires (catalog)
1998 OMR Gallery, Mexico City
1999 Sicardi Gallery, Houston, Texas (catalog)
2000 Blue Star Art Space, San Antonio, Texas (catalog)
Pinturas, Parque de España Cultural Center, Rosario (catalog)
Ramis Barquet Gallery, New York (catalog)
2001 Sicardi Gallery, Houston, Texas (catalog)
2002 Museum of Fine Arts, Rosario (catalog)

Selected Group Exhibitions:

1992 *Les Allumées* Exhibition, Nantes, France
La Conquista—500 años, 40 artistas, Recoleta Cultural Center, Buenos Aires (catalog)
1993 *Pictorica,* Art Museum of the Americas, Washington, D.C. (catalog)
De la Tierra del Fuego al Otro Polo, Arte Actual Mexicano Gallery, Monterrey
1994 *La Pasión de Pintar,* Ruth Benzacar Gallery, Buenos Aires (catalog)
1995 *70–80-90,* National Museum of Fine Arts, Buenos Aires (catalog)
El objeto de los 90, Museum of Fine Arts, Rosario
1996 *América Latina 96*, National Museum of Fine Arts, Buenos Aires (catalog)
de Sagastizábal/García/González Perrín, Museum of American Art, Maldonado, Uruguay (catalog)
1997 *1st Mercosur Biennial,* Porto Alegre, Brazil (catalog)
6th Havana Biennial (catalog)
47th Venice Biennial (catalog)
1999 *America Latina: das vanguardas ao fim do milénio,* Culturfest, Lisbon (catalog)
2nd Mercosur Biennial (catalog)
El Horizonte se corre diez pasos más acá, Bryggens Museum, Bergen, Norway (catalog)
34 ARC, Museum of Fine Arts, Rosario (catalog)
The Eye of the Millennium: Arts of the Americas, Art Museum of the Americas, Washington, D.C. (catalog; toured Buenos Aires)
2000 *Group Show,* Ramis Barquet Gallery, New York
1st Buenos Aires International Biennial, Buenos Aires (catalog)

Collections:

Museum of Latin American Art, Buenos Aires (MALBA); Juan B. Castagnino Museum of Fine Arts, Rosario; Antorchas Foundation, Buenos Aires; Museum of Contemporary Arts, Bahía Blanca, Buenos Aires Province, Argentina; Queen Sofía National Art Center, Madrid.

Publications:

By GARCÍA: Articles—''Daniel García. Dialogue Beyond Image'' interview with Edward Shaw in *D & D Diseño y Decoración en la Argentina,* no. 35, September 1995; ''Daniel García—Interview with Luis Sagasti and Gustavo López in *VOX arte + literatura* (Buenos Aires), no. 3–4, April 1997.

On GARCÍA: Books—*Daniel García,* exhibition catalog with text by Fabián Lebenglick, Buenos Aires 1995; *Cuatro Aspectos de la Pintura Argentina Contemporánea,* exhibition catalog with text by Guillermo Whitelow, Madrid 1997; *El ojo del que mira—artistas de los noventa* by Victoria Verlichack, Buenos Aires 1998; *Daniel García,* exhibition catalog with essay by Edward J. Sullivan, New York 2000. **Articles—**''Daniel García—Con la pintura por la cabeza'' by Fabián Lebenglick in *Página 12* (Buenos Aires), 10 December 1991; ''Daniel García en La Boca'' by Carlos Basualdo in *Rosario 12* (Rosario), 10 February 1993; ''Beyond Heaven and Hell'' by Edward Shaw in *Buenos Aires Herald,* 8 October 1995; ''Daniel Garcia'' by Jorge Glusberg in *Cultura* (Buenos Aires), no. 55, March 1996; ''Il male come 'altro''' by Jorge Glusberg in *D'ars Periodico D'arte Contemporanea* (Milan), no. 149, December 1996; ''Daniel García, y sigue la pintura'' by Marcelo Pacheco in *Magazine Literario* (Buenos Aires), no. 6, December 1997; ''Pablo Suárez y Daniel Garcia según Edward Sullivan'' by Edward Sullivan in *Cultura,* no. 61–62, 1998; ''Paintings Reflect Anguish Suffered by Argentines'' by Dan R. Goddard in *San Antonio Express-News* (San Antonio, Texas), 20 April 2000; ''Daniel García da una lección de pintura en el Parque de España'' by Fernando Farina in *Diario La Capita* (Rosario), 24 July 2000.

* * *

In the exhibition catalog for *70–80-90,* Daniel García said that ''Painting is a process, like that of an illness—a process to which one submits. There is a certain inevitable character about the process and I am forever painting the same way. Perhaps that's why references to the different states of the body, to the organs, are recurrent in my work.'' But what is sick is the world—sick, at any rate, with anguish and loneliness. García has been an attentive reader of Thomas Bernhard (1931–89), the Austrian writer whose works of poetry, theater, and prose fiction delve deeply into madness, destruction and death. Within this framework, he seeks the symptoms of the ills that our societies suffer, as doctor-patient and as artist-''mythophile''.

Philosophers and theologians divide ills into three classes: physical, moral, and metaphysical. We think that Daniel García's work has to do with all three and, at the same time, none of them, because the meanings that emerge from—or that are incarnate in—his surreal paintings go beyond the limits of the established, beyond appearance, beyond the presupposed. The physical ill is pain and suffering: hence its synonymity with infirmity. The moral ill has often been identified with sin in religion and with crime in law. The metaphysical ill is the root of all evil, a more subjective issue.

García quite often resorts to symbolisms of the sacred and the profane, of evil and sin as proposed by intellectuals in May of 1968. In ''Freak''—a term that refers to counter-natural living beings, to monsters, but also to things that are extravagant or rare—a snake emerges from a young human's forehead. In ''Heaven and Hell,'' two serpents that are biting each other's tails appear intertwined. And finally, in ''Memoria del Paraíso'' (''Memory of Paradise''), there are branches interlaced like a decorative arabesque, from which hang dozens of red apples. In the first case, the serpent is the devil, who tempts Eve in the Garden of Eden, according to the mosaic narration, in which the snake is described as ''the most astute of the creatures of the field that Yahweh had ever made.'' So it was that besides expelling Adam and Eve from Paradise, Yahweh also condemned the snake: ''On thy belly shalt thou walk and dust shalt thou eat all the days of thy life. Enmity shall I place between thee and woman, and man shall tread upon thy head. . .'' (Genesis, III).

By giving a woman's head to the serpent in his work and by making the snake emerge from the head of a man in ''Freak,'' García proposes variations on the biblical story we have just cited. And so too does he proceed in ''Memoria del Paraíso,'' where he turns to popular tradition, taking the apple as the ''fruit forbidden by Yahweh,'' and so, precisely, ''the tree of the science of Good and Evil.'' In ''Heaven and Hell,'' biblical references are taken to the extreme, as it were, since the serpent becomes the symbol of Heaven, the dwelling place of God and Paradise itself in the Christian religion. To this must be added the Greek myth about the serpent that bites its own tail, an allegorical representation of Eternity (and in Christian law, eternal is life in both Heaven and Hell). The condition of the snake—a theme taken up in almost every culture—is not always negative. Even Moses manages to save a lot of his brethren using the Brass Serpent that Yahweh orders him to make.

García's message tends to touch on the political, as in the early 1990s, when his paintings were done on the canvas of army cots (in an allusion to war, violence, the tending of the wounded and the transporting of the dead—indeed, an unusual framework). ''Death Mask'' is a symptomatic work: the face is severe and gazes attentively at the observer. From it emerge three legs of a swastika and on the surface of its skin, the image of a skull is repeated again and again. The antithesis is ''Durmiente'' (''Sleeper'')—another human face, with eyes closed, but with open eyes crying tears of blood covering the forehead and cheeks. If ''Death Mask'' takes its cue from the technique used in billboard ads and wanted posters, in the second work one sees something of popular illustrations of religious scenes or miracles.

Be that as it may, there are no religious or miracle-maker impulses in García's pictures: the swastika that in pre-Christian times was the symbol of life; in the days of the Nazis became the symbol of death. The eyes that cry tears of blood in the sleeper's face are those that see the pain and crime scorned by the protagonist. Of similar orientation is ''Olvídame'' (''Forget Me''), in which some old bathtubs are filled with blood. ''La alegría de vivir'' (''The Joy of Living'') shows an enormous mouth with perfect, white teeth. ''Evening Star'' shows a jail, and around it, four chimneys, broken at the base, but with their plume of smoke in the form of a swastika. And finally, there is ''Vidas ejemplares'' (''Exemplary Lives''), in which the face is hairless and eyeless but covered, as if in contusions or sores, with crowns of thorns, while the rest of the canvas repeats boxing and martial arts scenes.

In all of García's paintings, like some sign, the surface appears to be upholstered in stain-like patches. These are a metaphor for the three forms of ills the artist approaches: patches of pain, patches of violated ethics, and patches of time—that immense space of life and death.

—Jorge Glusberg

GASTINI, Marco

Nationality: Italian. **Born:** Turin in 1938. **Education:** Accademia Albertina di Belle Arti, Turin. **Career:** Independent painter, Turin, since 1964. **Agents:** Galleria Martano, Via Cesare Battisti 3, 10123 Turin; Carlo Grossetti, Salone Annunciata, via Manzoni, 20121 Milan. **Address:** Strada del Nobile 37/3i, 10131 Turin, Italy.

Individual Exhibitions:

1964 Galleria del Falo, Alba, Italy
1967 Galleria della Steccata, Parma, Italy
Galleria il Girasole, Rome

1968 Galleria Pozzi, Novara, Italy
Galleria Il Punto, Turin
1969 Salone Annunciata, Milan
1970 Galleria Gap, Rome
1971 Galleria LP 220, Turin
Salone Annunciata, Milan
Galleria Wspolczesna, Warsaw
Galerie Arges, Brussels
1972 Galleria Flori, Florence (with Giorgio Griffa)
Galleria Benjamino, San Remo, Italy
Les Halles, Bruges, Belgium
Salone Annunciata, Milan
1973 Galleria Primo Piano, Rome
Galerie Arges, Brussels
Galerie Annemarie Verna, Zurich
1974 Galleria Banco, Brescia, Italy
Galerie M. Bochum, West Germany
Galleria Il Sole, Bolzano, Italy
Galerie D + C/Müller-Roth, Stuttgart
Galerie Swart, Amsterdam
Galleria Perrari, Verona
Galleria Claudio Bottello, Turin
Nova Arte Moderna, Prato, Italy
1975 Salone Annunciata, Milan
Cirrus Gallery, Los Angeles
Galleria Peccolo, Livorno
1976 Galleria Sperone, Rome
Salone Annunciata, Milan (with Giuseppe Spagnulo)
Galleria Primo Piano, Rome
Galerie Baronian, Brussels
Galerie Annemarie Verna, Zurich
Biennale, Venice
1977 Galleria Christian Stein, Turin
Galerie Müller-Roth, Stuttgart
Galleria Forma, Genoa
John Weber Gallery, New York
Galleria Spagnoli, Florence
1978 Galerie Water Storms, Munich
Studio Grossetti, Milan
1979 *Marks and/on Spaces,* John Weber Gallery, New York
Galerie Baronian, Brussels
Studio G7, Bologna
1980 Galerie Walter Storms, Villingen West Germany
Galerie Annemarie Verna, Zurich
Centre d'Art Contemporain, Geneva
1981 Galleria Taide, Salerno, Italy
Galleria Martano, Turin
Galerie Appel und Fertsch, Frankfurt
Karmeliter-Kloster, Frankfurt
Villa Romana, Florence
Galleria Vigato, Alessandria, Italy
1982 Galleria d'Arte Moderna, Bologna, Italy
Studio G.7, Bologna, Italy
Stadtische Galerie, Munich
John Weber Gallery, New York
Galleria Meta, Bolzano, Italy
1983 Olsson Gallery, Stockholm
Galleria I'Isola, Rome
Galleria Civica, Modena, Italy
Galleria Plurima, Udine, Italy (with Mario Nigro)
Ariete Grafica, Milan
Galerie Muller-Roth, Stuttgart
1984 Galerie Susanna Kulli, St. Gallen, Switzerland
Padiglione d'Arte Contemporania, Milan
Galleria Plurima, Udine, Italy
Studio Dossi, Bergamo, Italy
Galerie Krohn, Badenweiler, West Germany
Studio Grosetti, Milan
1985 Olsson Gallery, Stockholm
Galleria Martano, Turin
Gallery Nordenhake, Malmo, Sweden
1986 Galerie Appel and Fertsch, Frankfurt
Krista Miola Gallery, Helsinki
John Weber Gallery, New York
Galerie Edition E, Munich
Galerie Walter Storms, Munich
1987 Galerie Susanna Kulli, St. Gallen, Switzerland
Galleria Martano, Forum, Zurich
Studio Grossetti, Milan
Arte ed Altro, Milan
Galleria Rossanaferri, Modena, Italy
1992 *Marco Gastini,* Galleria Comunale d'Arte Moderna, Bologna
1993 *Marco Gastini: Works 1967–1993,* Frankfurter Kunstverein, Frankfurt am Main

Selected Group Exhibitions:

1968 *Alternative attuali 3,* Castello Spagnolo, L'Aquila, Italy
1970 *Arte e Critica '70,* Galleria Civica, Modena, Italy
1972 *Vers le Blanc* at the *Festival International du Livre,* Nice
1974 *Italy Two:Art Around '70,* Civic Center, Philadelphia
1977 *Apparent Contrast:16 Italian Artists,* Museum Boymans van Beuningen, Rotterdam
1980 *Arte e Critica '80,* Galleria Nazionale d'Arte Moderna, Rome
1982 *Arte Italiana 1960–1982,* Hayward Gallery, London
1984 *Confronto per opera,* Galleria d'Arte Moderna, Bologna, Italy
1986 *Aspekte italienischer Kunst 1960–85,* Kunstverein, Frankfurt
1987 *La struttura del gesto,* Sala 1, Rome
1990 *Temperamenti: Contemporary Art from Italy—Anselmo, Gastini, Icaro, Mattiacci, Nagasawa, Paolini, Parmiggiani, Penone, Spagnulo, Zorio,* Tramway, Glasgow
1991 *Marco Gastini, Paolo Patelli,* Studio La Citta, Verona

Collections:

Galleria Nazionale d'Arte Moderna, Rome; Museo d'Arte Moderno, Milan; Galleria Civica d'Arte Moderna, Turin; Museo Civico, Bologna; Museum of Modern Art, New York; Museum Boymans van Beuningen, Rotterdam; Moderna Museet, Stockholm; Kontshall, Malmo.

Publications:

By GASTINI: Books—*(in) Spaxio,* Turin 1971; *Progetto,* Turin 1971; Progretto, Milan 1974; *New York project/ten possibilities,* New York 1977; *Parete,* New York 1977; *Pantomina,* Turin 1978; *21/29, 7=71/100=435/640=paesaggio,* Munich 1979, Bologna, 1980; *La parete e l'angolo,* Lugo 1982.

On GASTINI: Books—*Ricerche dopo l'Informale* by Enrico Crispolti, Rome 1969; *Ultime Tendenze dell'Arte d'Oggi* by Gillo Dorfles, Milan 1973; *Marco Gastini* by Paolo Fossati, Turin 1976; *Europe/America: The Different Avant-Gardes* by Achille Bonito Oliva, Milan 1976; *Il Divenire della Critica* by Gillo Dorfles, Turin 1976; *Marco Gastini: Marks and/on Spaces,* exhibition catalog, New York 1979; *Marco Gastini,* exhibition catalog, by Peter Weiermair and Pier Giovanni Castagnoli, Frankfurt 1981; *Marco Gastini: Come di un Respiro che preme nei Polmoni* by Tommaso Trini, Turin and Munich 1981; *Marco Gastini,* exhibition catalog, by Paolo Fossati and Flaminio Gualdoni, Bologna 1982; *Marco Gastini,* exhibition catalog with text by Flamino Gualdoni, Modena 1983; *Marco Gastini: Milano 1984,* exhibition catalog with texts by Paolo Fossati and Flaminio Gualdoni, Milan 1984; *Marco Gastini, Paolo Patelli,* exhibition catalog, with text by Mario Bertoni, Verona 1991; *Marco Gastini,* exhibition catalog, Bologna 1992; *Marco Gastini: Works 1967–1993,* exhibition catalog, with texts by Peter Weiermair and Mrio Bertoni, Frankfurt am Main 1993. **Articles—**''Marco Gastini at John Weber'' by Raphael Rubinstein in *Art in America* (New York), vol. 83, no. 1, January 1995; ''Marco Gastini'' by Anthony Iannacci in *Artforum International,* vol. 33, March 1995.

*

I have always painted very large pictures, so large that I couldn't see them properly even by standing back in the far recesses of my studio. I felt a compulsion to paint this way because I wanted to call into play the space in which I move. It was a kind of 'being inside it', a total immersion in that space, as if living through the entire complex of different realities that surround me and constitute the world of my work. In short, I aimed at fixing onto the canvas the continuity between the act of painting and the painting itself.

I talk about painting as 'becoming immersed'. One cannot isolate just one part of it: as soon as one begins, suddenly painting is everything—very much like a fever. But whilst one sees everything, one simultaneously perceives each fragment of that everything: like vertigo.

Spaces are many: the moment you focus on a landscape and attain a definition of one specific field of vision, then the tension between you and space, of 'you' and of 'outside yourself', generate other spaces infinitely. It is not a matter of dimension, but of immersion. You feel as if your want to be part of an all-and-sundry space. Time does not flow with its own inexorable logic: it simply does not exist. The very slowest or fastest speed of the marks you are drawing have the duration and viscosity of total immersion, as if your were stretching yourself inside it. Duration of working becomes one with space—a space constrained only by one's own dimensions. It is the space that you are using: you meet it, and it comes forward to you. It is a kind of space/time that entirely embraces you, an objective, tangible reality. Such is the picture, *the work;* what I call ''the work'' is what I produce and exhibit.

A number of other realities come into play, though I don't know whether they really belong to the work; they are just things seen or merely thought. But they all enter that space. The picture takes on the form of an autonomous entity, even though it is born out of oneself. I would like the work to always be in motion, moving off its own accord. It is necessary for the picture to contradict the basic formal structure and stability I have conferred on during the act of painting. I want it to be transient in regard to that aspect of formalization. Everything strives to reach its own potential, either by reaching outward or pressing back into its own constraints. It has to unbalance and compromise the intentionality, that moves the picture toward a specific, predetermined direction. I believe that my painting must be precisely that.

Is any of this attainable? Is it possible to make visible both the immersion and the tension? I wish it were, and with sensitively.

—Marco Gastini

* * *

Painting is carried out, it takes shape, in space. Other fields, other dimensions may—and should—be born from it, but it is still in space that it occurs.The work of Marco Gastini reminds us all the time of this simple, irrefutable, Kantian reality. He actually speaks of ''infinite spaces,'' which interact, reflecting and reacting on each other. In the complex, technically skilful pattern of streaks and blots, signs and spots, a dynamic is created and developed, generated by progressive additions which involve the conventional space of the canvas (which is also ''worked'' in Gastini, analysed, decomposed and recomposed) with the physical nature of the environment, of life in osmosis with art. The perceptive intuition—itself intimately dynamic—does not, therefore, stop at the discovery of what happens within the frame of the canvas, but expands to absorb the environmental development and to draw attention to it.

It is an illusion to try to define and specify the ''discipline'' (painting sculpture) in which Gastini's work is carried out; there is an air of totality all round the whole work, involving every aspect of it. Interactions: for Gastini (who here echoes a train of thought that may or may not be contemporary) being is purely a matter of relationships. A thing—a gesture, a spot, a material, a brush-stroke—is related to other things not only in the spatial field but also in the conceptual. It is only in this way that a thing—a being—passes from mere existence to being, to action in the world, and it is only thus that it becomes an object to be perceived.

The more fields there are, then, the more languages: that is what the antimony, the lead, tin, carbon, parchment and mother-of-pearl are that are used in his work. Materials, of course; but each has a specific language of its own, which can be made clear to the extent to which it is interwoven with the language of the other material, and united with that to form that totality in variety that seems to be one of the essential keys to Gastini's work—work that also takes in organic, vitalistic components (a tree trunk, for instance), all then reconnected in the single dimension of the painting but all still agents of emotive, physical tensions. And at the end of the journey (but there is no real end), perceived instinctively at the heart of the work, sealing all the material, gestural and spatial—and also, mental—stratifications, there is energy in the pure state, which, when fully unfurled, reveals the intimate, essential nature of the work.

—Massimo Carboni

GAUCHER, Yves

Nationality: Canadian. **Born:** Montreal, Quebec, in 1934. **Education:** Ecole des Beaux-Arts, Montreal, 1954–56. **Family:** Married Germaine Chausse in 1965; sons; Benoit and Denis. **Career:** Painter and printmaker: lives and works in Montreal (first intaglio printing, 1960; concentrated exclusively on printmaking, 1964–65). Assistant professor of fine arts, 1966–69, and since 1970 associate professor, Sir George Williams University, Montreal. **Awards:** Graphics Award, *Salon de la Jeune Peinture,* Montreal, 1959; First Graphics Prize, Province of Quebec Competition, 1961, 1963; Second Prize, National Print Competition, Vancouver, 1961; First Prize, National Print Competition, Burnaby, British Columbia, 1961; Purchase Prize, *Winnipeg Biennial,* 1962; Canada Council Grant, 1962, 1967, 1972; Purchase Prize, *Montreal Spring Exhibition,* 1963; *Thomas More Institute Exhibition* Prize, 1963; Hadassah Exhibition Prize, Montreal, 1964; Second Prize *International Triennale of Coloured Prints,* Grenchen, Switzerland, 1964; Grand Prize, *Sandage '68,* Montreal Museum of Fine Arts, 1968. **Agent:** Mira Godard Gallery, 22 Hazelton Avenue, Toronto M5R 2E2. **Died:** Of throat cancer, in Montreal, Canada, 8 September 2000.

Individual Exhibitions:

1957 Galerie l'Echange, Montreal
1963 Galerie Godard Lefort, Montreal
Galerie Moos, Toronto
Martha Jackson Gallery, New York
1965 Galerie Godard Lefort, Montreal
1966 Martha Jackson Gallery, New York
Winnipeg Art Gallery
Galerie Moos, Toronto
1967 Galerie Godard Lefort, Montreal
1969 Galerie Godard Lefort, Montreal
Paintings and Graphics, Vancouver Art Gallery
Edmonton Art Gallery
Whitechapel Art Gallery, London
1970 Sir George Williams University, Montreal
Galerie Moos, Toronto
1971 University of Manitoba, Winnipeg
1972 Galerie Godard Lefort, Montreal
Marlborough Godard Gallery, Toronto
1973 Marlborough Godard Gallery, Montreal
1975 Marlborough Godard Gallery, Toronto
New York Cultural Center
1976 Musée d'Art Contemporian, Le Havre, France
1979 Art Gallery of Ontario, Toronto (retrospective)
1984 Canada House Gallery, London
1990 Olga Korper Gallery, Toronto
1992 *Aspects of Yves Gaucher's Art 1978–1992 (Abstract Practices II),* Power Plant, Toronto
1995 *Yves Gaucher: Recent Work,* Leonard & Bina Ellen Art Gallery, Concordia University 1995
1992 *Yves Gaucher,* Olga Korper Gallery, Toronto

Selected Group Exhibitions:

1961 *Bienale,* Paris
Exposition Internationale de Gravures, Ljubljana, Yugoslavia (and 1962, 1963)
1963 *American Biennial of Prints,* Santiago, Chile
1964 *Contemporary Painters as Printmakers,* Museum of Modern Art, New York
1966 *Biennale,* Venice
1967 *Canadian '67,* Institute of Contemporary Art, Boston
1968 *Canada: Art d'Aujourd'hui,* Palais des Beaux-Arts, Brussels
1970 *Expo '70,* Osaka, Japan
1974 *Aspects of Canadian Art,* Albright-Knox Art Gallery, Buffalo, New York
13 Artists from Marlborough Godard, Marlborough Gallery, New York
1988 *Ewen, Gagnon, Gaucher, Hurtebise, McEwen: Concerning Painting of the 1960s,* Musee d'Art Contemporain, Montreal
1991 *25 Years of the Council: 25 Years of Painting,* Maison de la Culture Côte-des-Neiges, Montreal
Space Drawing, Saidye Bronfman Centre, Montreal
1992 *Montreal, 1942–1992: The Splendid Anarchy of Painting,* Galerie de l'Université de Quebec, Montreal
1994 *From the Permanent Collection: A Selection of Recent Acquisitions,* Leonard & Bina Ellen Art Gallery, Concordia University, Montreal
The Festival de Peinture in Mascouche: Abstraction in Montreal, 1950–1970, Hotel de Ville, Mascouche, Quebec
The Lavalin Collection of the Musee d'Art Contemporain in Montreal: The Sharing of a Vision, Musee d'Art Contemporain, Montreal
1998 *Home Base: Notes to an Installation,* Kamloops Art Gallery, British Columbia

Collections:

Musée d'Art Contemporain, Montreal; Museum of Fine Arts, Montreal; Sir George Williams University, Montreal; National Gallery of Canada, Ottawa; Art Gallery of Ontario, Toronto; Vancouver Art Gallery; Museum of Modern Art, New York; Library of Congress, Washington, D.C., Art Institute of Chicago; Tate Gallery, London.

Publications:

By GAUCHER: Book—*The Empirical Presence: Six Essays—Barbara Caruso, Jean-Marie Delavalle, Yves Gaucher, Ron Martin, Jaan Poldaas, Henry Saxe,* Montreal 1992. **Article—**''Des Artistes Sans Galerie'' with Lawrence Sabbath in *Vie des Arts,* no. 136, vol. 34, September 1989.

On GAUCHER: Books—*Yves Gaucher: Paintings and Graphics,* exhibition catalog, by Doris Shadbolt, Vancouver 1969; *Canadian*

Art Today by William Townsend, London 1970; *Contemporary Canadian Painting* by William Withrow, Toronto 1972; *Aspects of Yves Gaucher's Art: 1978–1992 (Abstract Practices II),* with text by James D. Campbell, Toronto 1992; *Yves Gaucher,* exhibition catalog, with text by Roald Nasgaard, Toronto 1992; *Depth Markers: Selected Art Writings, 1985–1994, Volume One* by James D. Campbell, Toronto 1995; *Yves Gaucher: Recent Work,* exhibition catalog, with text by Karen Antaki and Anna Carlevaris, Montreal 1995. **Articles—** ''Eminence Grise at Edinburgh'' by Bryan Robertson in the *Spectator* (London), August 1968; ''A Canadian Scene'' by David Thompson in *Studio International* (London), October/November 1968; ''A Kind of Silence'' by Nigel Gosling in *The Observer* (London), October 1969; ''Seeing Is Believing: Yves Gaucher's New Paintings'' by M. and I. Gopnik in *Artscanada* (Toronto), October/November 1971; ''Reverie de l'Absolu'' by Michael Ragon in *Vie des Arts* (Montreal), Spring 1973; ''Canadian Art in Review'' by Dore Ashton in *Artscanada* (Toronto), December 1974; ''All About Yves'' in *Canadian Art,* vol. 17, no. 2, Summer 2000; ''Passages'' in *Maclean's,* September 25, 2000.

* * *

Yves Gaucher's art matured in the 1960s when in North America the modernist imperative was requiring an uncompromising purification of painting's means of expression. Though his work, like postpainterly abstraction in the United States, turned on the activation of colour planes, Gaucher, working in Montreal, made formal choices which countered not so much the dictums as the taste of dominant American criticism. Where, for example, stain painting kept its preference for the personal and lyrical touch, Gaucher's practice of working with sprayed or rolled-on surfaces obliterated personal touch, signs of process and evidence of surface support. His impersonal art seemed to embrace too much of the idealist tradition of geometric abstraction, and was suspected of being European, which then meant regressive.

The general preconditions for Gaucher's work were, however, entirely North American. Gaucher has remarked on his realization, during his first visit to Paris in 1962 (his first purely abstract work appeared in 1963), that he was not French, but a French-speaking North American, with affinities not with current Europeans but with contemporary New York painters such as Jasper Johns and Morris Louis. The reference to Barnett Newman in the ''Jericho'' paintings of 1977 is also a reassertion of Gaucher's partiality for an art which, though rooted in the European abstract tradition, above all in Mondrian, was, in North America, to expand its theatre of action into a monumental arena for personal struggle and moral and existential affirmation.

Gaucher's way of composing has been called ''algebraic'' because of its requirements that successive moves be made, and that these moves in turn be successively compensated for. This is in the tradition of Mondrian and of relational painting such as Newman claimed to overthrow; though as Gaucher agrees, Newman did not abandon relational painting, he merely changed the terms by reducing the components so that the remaining elements could function in a more complex manner. It is a kind of painting, which even within its strict formal limit requires the full play of intuition and judgement. Gaucher has consequently never deferred decision making in his work to predetermined givens. He would quarrel with those of his contemporaries who have adopted standards and repeatable compositions in order to focus on other problems or with Albers' admonition not to worry about colour because what it does happens without you. ''What happens in my colours,'' insists Gaucher, ''happens because I put it there.'' In the various phases of his work Gaucher has consequently never proceeded towards reduction or simplification but towards increased complexity. In practice this has meant that in all the stages of his career over the last two decades he has moved from relative symmetry to increasing asymmetry. A handwritten text signed and dated 29/1/79 hanging on Gaucher's studio wall reads: ''l'asymétrie est l'affirmation d'un esprit indepéndent.''

To understand a Gaucher painting requires seeing it, almost simultaneously from several perspectives, each of which, of course, is incomplete. If, for example, looking at one of the large ''Jericho'' paintings, we take the lead of the upward and lateral thrusts of the truncated triangle in order to attempt to complete its gestalt, the leftover white ''ground'' begins to fall away. If, on the contrary, we scan the canvas laterally, it divides down the vertical white band and the outward pressures of the coloured wedges threaten to split the painting asunder. At the same time, however, we discover that the white ''ground'' shapes which were so reticent before now assert themselves as precisely measured surface shapes calculated to resist the outward forces of the coloured shapes, which we discover, as well, are gripped together across the centre by their subservience to the gestalt of the original triangle. Finally, because both colour and structure are perfectly turned, equilibrium prevails and each thrust, however complex and multi directional, is checked by another, and the surface of the painting attains a breathtaking tautness right to its very edges. It is this visual holding together in face of imminent discord and break that keeps our attention and speaks of spiritual victory over disruptive forces.

—Roald Nasgaard

GAUL, Winfred

Nationality: German. **Born:** in Dusseldorf, 9 July 1928. **Education:** Cologne University, 1949–50; studied at the Kunstakademie, with Baumeister, Stuttgart, 1950–53. **Family:** Married Barbara Jeckstadt in 1969. **Career:** Independent painter, since 1955: lives and works in Dusseldorf; lived in New York, 1962; worked in Antwerp, 1967–69; in Genoa, 1969–70. Guest lecturer, Staatlische Kunstschule, Bremen, 1965; visiting lecturer, Bath Academy, England, 1965; visiting lecturer, Regional College, Hull, England, 1966. **Awards:** Confederation of German Industrialists' Painting Prize (B.D.I.), 1958; Villa Romana Painting Prize, Florence, 1964; Lovis Corinth Prize, Regensburg, 1994. **Agents:** Roberto Peccolo, Piazza della Republica 12, Livorno, Italy; Galerie Hennemann, Poppelsdorfer Allee 17, 5300 Bonn, Germany. **Address:** An St. Swidbert 56–58, D-4000 Dusseldorf-Kaiserwerth, Germany.

Individual Exhibitions:

1956 Galerie NRZ, Duisburg, West Germany
Contra-Kreis, Bonn
Galerie Gurlitt, Munich
1957 Galerie 22, Dusseldorf
Galerie Nohl, Siegen, West Germany
Galerie 33, Berne, Switzerland

Galerie Schüler, Berlin (with O.H. Hajek)
Galeria Apollinaire, Milan
1958 Galerie St. Laurent, Brussels
Galerie Inge Ahlers, Mannheim
1959 Galerie Aujourd'hui, Palais des Beaux-Arts, Brussels (with K.F. Dahmen)
1960 Galerie Anne Abels, Cologne
Galerie St. Stephan, Vienna
1961 Kunstkring, Rotterdam
Galleria Blu, Milan
1963 Galerie Müller, Stuttgart
1964 Galerie J. Dumay, Paris
Galerie Niepel, Dusseldorf
Städtische Museum, Wiesbaden, West Germany
1965 Galerie René Block, Berlin
Galleria del Deposito, Genoa
1966 Institute of Contemporary Arts, London
Städtische Kunsthalle, Mannheim
1967 Karl-Ernst-Osthaus Museum, Hagen, West Germany
Galerie Swart, Amsterdam
Galerie Orez International, The Hague
Galerie Brechbühl, Grenchen, Switzerland
Galerie Räber, Lucerne, Switzerland
Galerie Tobiès and Silex, Cologne
Galerie Springhornhof-Falazik, Neuenkirchen, West Germany
Palais des Beaux-Arts, Brussels
1968 Galerie Niepel, Dusseldorf
Galerie Nickel, Bad Godesberg, West Germany
Galerie Rewolle, Bremen, West Germany
Galerie Foncke, Ghent
Zentrum für aktuelle Kunst, Aachen, West Germany
1969 Galleria il Segnapassi, Pesaro, Italy
Studio 2B, Bergamo, Italy
Galleria Arco d'Alibert, Rome
Galleria La Polena, Genoa
Galerie Fürneisen, Hamburg
Galerie Mutzenbach, Dortmund, West Germany
1970 Overbeck-Gesellschaft, Lübeck, West Germany (with K.L. Schmaltz and H. Sundhaussen)
Galleria del Cavallino, Venice
1971 Galerie Wilbrand, Cologne
Galleria Sincron, Brescia, Italy
Kunstverein, Münster, West Germany
Kunstverein, Weidenbruck, West Germany
Kunststudio, Bielefeld, West Germany
Galerie Apfelbaum, Karlsruhe
1972 Galleria II Segnapassi, Pesaro, Italy
Studio Kausch, Kassel, West Germany
Galleria Peccolo, Livorno, Italy
1973 *Restrospektive 1953–1973,* Westfälischer Kunstverein, Münster, West Germany (travelled to Ludwigshafen, Ulm, and Bielefeld, 1973–74)
1974 Galleria Peccolo, Livorno, Italy
Galleria La Polena, Genoa
Stufidre Arte Contemporanea, Turin
Galerie Karsten Greve, Cologne
1975 Galleria II Milione, Milan
Malerei 1959–1961, 1974–1975, Wilhelm-Lehmbruck Museum, Duisburg, West Germany

Galleria Seconda Scala, Rome
1977 Galerie Peccolo, Cologne
Galerie Wintersberger, Cologne
Zeichen + Malen, Karl-Ernst-Osthaus Museum, Hagen, West Germany
Paula-Becker-Modersohn-Haus, Bremen, West Germany
1978 Galleria La Polena, Genoa
Werkverzeichnis der Druckgraphik und Objekte, Kunsthalle, Kiel, West Germany
1979 Kunstverein, Heidelberg
Galerie Schönbrunn, Frankfurt
Galerie Wintersberger, Cologne
Arbeiten 1953–1961, Galerie Hennemann, Bonn
Galerie Karsten Greve, Cologne
1981 Galleria Sincron, Brescia, Italy
1982 Dibbert Galerie, Berlin
Lavori Su Carta 1956–1981, Pinacoteca di Macerata, Italy (retrospective of drawings)
Galerie Hennemann, Bonn
Galerie 44, Kaarst, West Germany
1983 Galerie Wintersberger, Cologne
Galleria Morone 6, Milan
1984 Galleria Martano, Turin
Galleria Peccolo, Livorno, Italy
Galleria Peccolo, Livorno, Italy
Galerie Lupke, Frankfurt
Stadtische Galerie, Quakenbruck, West Germany
1985 Galerie im Winter, Bremen, West Germany
Galerie Gruppe Grun, Bremen, West Germany
Galerie Hennemann, Bonn
Galerie Beck, Erlangen, West Germany
1986 Galerie Schuppenhauer, Essen, West Germany
Hans-Thoma-Gesellschaft, Reutlingen, West Germany
1987 Kunstverein, Freiburg, West Germany
Kunstverein, Emmerich, West Germany
1988 *Works on Paper 1955–87,* toured West Germany 1988–89
Malerei in 2.3.n. Phasen, Galerie Schüppenhauer, Cologne
Dialog mit Claude Monet, Galerie Hennemann, Bonn
1989 *Deutsche Bank, Münster*, Deutsche Bank, Bielefeld
Dialog mit Claude Monet, Galerie Winkelmann, Düsseldorf
1991 *Shaped Canvas*, Galerie Schüppenhauer, Cologne
Galerie Dorn, Stuttgart
Galerie Pages, Baden-Baden
Frammenti per una retrosspettiva opere 1960–1983, Palazzo Martinengo, Brescia, Italy
Forum Kunst, Rottweil
Bilder und Blätter der fünfziger Jahre, Galerie Viertel, Frankfurt
1993 *Painter's Diary*, Galerie Winkelmann, Düsseldorf
Dialog mit Henry Matisse, Galerie Hennemann, Bonn
1994 Galerie Viertel, Frankfurt
Galerie Hoffmeister, Lüdenscheid
Kunstgalerie Kaliningrad, Russia
Ostdeutsche Galerie, Regensburg, Germany
1997 *Das Frühwerk,* Märkisches Museum, Witten and Städt, and Galerie am Buntentor, Bremen, Germany
Paintings and Works on Paper, Galerie Bengelsträter, Iserlohn, Germany

Works on Paper, Galerie Nicols, Düsseldorf
1998 *Painting 1956–1998,* Kunstverein Emsdetten, Germany
Works of the Sixties, Galerie Brüning and Zischke, Düsseldorf
Galerie Marianne Hennemann, Bonn
Ohne rechten Winkel, Von der Heydt-Museum, Wuppertal, Germany
Big Size Paintings, Studio Galerie Busse, Worpswede, Germany
Galerie Dorn, Stuttgart
1999 *Works on Paper,* Galerie Schloss Mochental
2000 *Recycling,* Galleria Peccolo, Livorno, Italy
Recycling, Galerie Bengelsträter, Iserlohn, Germany
2001 *Recycling,* Galerie Zischke, Düsseldorf
Recycling, Galerie Neue Kunst, Konstanz, Germany

Selected Group Exhibitions:

1959 *Documenta 2,* Kassel
1965 *Pop Art, Nouveau Realisme, etc.,* Palais des Beaux-Arts, Brussels
1970 *Klischee und Anti-klischee,* Neue Galerie, Aachen, West Germany
1977 *Documenta 6,* Kassel
1979 *5 x 30: Düsseldorfer Kunstszene aus 5 Generationen,* Kunstverein and Kunsthalle, Dusseldorf
1983 *Kunst nach '45,* Kunstverein, Frankfurt
1985 *1945–85: Kunst in der Bundesrepublik,* Nationalgalerie, West Berlin
1987 *Analytische Malerei—ein Ruckblick,* Galerie Schuppenhauer, Cologne
1993 *Kunst und Kultur '68,* Bauhaus Museum, Dessau
1994 *Meisterwerk von Turner bis zur Gegenwart,* Galerie Brigitte Wagner, Bonn
Gruppe 53, Arbeiten 1953–1959, Galerie Heseler, Munich
Brüning, Fürst, Gaul, Hoehme, Galerie Dorn, Stuttgart
1995 *Here Comes the Sun,* Galerie Brigitte Wagner, Bonn
Kunst in Deutschland 1945–1995, Museum Ostdeutsche Galerie, Regensburg, Germany
1996 *Kontraste XII,* Galerie Hoffmeister, Lüdenscheid, Germany
Aufbruch einer Szene, Bremen 1963–1967, Städtische Galerie Bremen, Germany
1997 *Solo artisti stranieri,* Centro culturale d'arte contemporanea sincron, Brescia, Italy
Positionen des Informel und Abstrakte Positionen, Galerie Dorn, Stuttgart
1998 *25 Jahre Galerie Marianne Hennemann,* Bonn
Rot-Red-Rouge-Rosso, Galerie Brigitte Wagner, Bonn
1999 *Vive L'Art,* Galerie Hoffmeister, Lüdenscheid, Germany
Licht, Farbe, Raum, Galerie Dorn, Stuttgart

Collections:

Städtisches Kunstmuseum, Bonn; Städtisches Kunstmuseum, Dusseldorf; Staatliche Museen Preußischer Kulturbesitz, Kupferstichkabinett, Berlin; Rheinisches Landesmuseum, Bonn; Landesgalerie, Hannover; Museum of Modern Art, New York; Carnegie Institute, Pittsburgh; Stedelijk Museum, Amsterdam; Museum Zeitgenössischer Kunst, Belgrade; Kolekcja Jürgena Wiechardta, Museum Okregowe, Chelm, Poland; Museum van Hedendaagse Kunst, Gent, Belgium; Pinacoteca e Musie Comunali, Macerata, Italy; and many other galleries and museums in Germany.

Publications:

By GAUL: Books—*First Quibb-Manifesto,* with H. P. Alvermann, Dusseldorf 1962; *Opinioni Eretiche di un Produttore d'Arte,* Florence 1972. **Articles**—Statement in *Das Kunstwerk* (Baden-Baden, West Germany), no. 11, 1962; ''Die Welt der Slogans und der Phrasen'' in *Die Welt* (Hamburg), January 1963; ''Amerika has du es besser'' in *Das Kunstwerk* (Baden-Baden, West Germany), no. 9, 1963; ''Segni e Segnali Stradali'' in *Marcatre* (Milan), no. 11–13, 1965; ''Picasso und die Beatles'' in *Frankfurter Allgemeine,* December 1966; ''Traffic Signs and Signals'' in *ICA Bulletin* (London), January 1966; ''Gutes Deutsch auf der Strasse'' in *Tragesspiegel* (Berlin), February 1968; ''Verkehrszeichen als Totem'' in *Frankfurter Allgemeine,* January 1969; ''Traffic Signs and Signals'' in *Gebrauchsgraphik* (Munich), no. 11, 1970; statement in *Seit 45* (Brussels), vol. 1, 1970; ''Due Esempi della mia Pittura'' in *Data* (Milan), no. 4, 1974; ''Sulla Pittura'' in *Paint 1,* Milan 1974, reprinted in *Winfred Gaul,* exhibition catalog, Livorno 1974; *Winfred Gaul,* exhibition catalog, Turin 1974; *Winfred Gaul,* exhibition catalog, Genoa 1974; *Winfred Gaul,* exhibition catalog, Milan 1974; ''Uber Malerei'' in *Winfred Gaul,* exhibition catalog, Duisburg, West Germany, 1975; ''Uber Malerie'' in *Magazine Kunst* (Mainz, West Germany), no. 4, 1975; statement in *Catalog Documenta 6,* exhibition catalog, Kassel, West Germany 1977; ''Ein verfuhrerischer Traum, zur gesellschaftlichen Integration des Kunstlers'' in *Mitteilungen des Institut für Moderne Kunst* (Nuremberg), August 1981; ''Disegnare e Dipingere'' in *Winfred Gaul: Lavor Su Carta 1956–1981,* exhibition catalog, Macerata, Italy 1982; *Picasso und die Beatles,* Verlag Quensen, Lamspringe 1987; *Notizen und Bilder,* Eremitenpresse, Düsseldorf, 1989; *Die Malerei ist eine eifersuchtige Geliebte,* Eremitenpresse, Düsseldorf, 1992; ''In Memoriam Jean-Pierre Wilhelm'' in *Düsseldorfer Aventgarden,* Düsseldorf 1995; *Recycling,* exhibition catalog by Winfred Gaul and Claudio Cerritelli, Livorno, Italy 2000.

On GAUL: Books—*Geschichte der Deutschen Kunst von 1900 biz zur Gegenwart,* by Franz Roh, Munich 1958; *Lyrisme et Abstraction* by Pierre Restany, Milan 1960; *Deutsche Malerei von 1900, bis heute* by Franz Roh, Munich 1962; *Abstract Painting: 50 Years of Accomplishment from Kandinsky to the Present* by Michel Seuphor, New York 1961; *Happenings, Pop Art, Nouveau Realisme etc.,* by Hans Joachim Dietrich, Dusseldorf 1965; *Winfred Gaul,* exhibition catalog, with text by Heinz Fuchs, Mannheim 1966; *Deutsche Kunst—eine Neue Generation* by Rolf Günter Dienst, Cologne 1970; *Deutsche Kunst der sechziger Jahre* by Juliane Roh, Munich 1971; *Kunst Praxis Heute* by Karin Thomas, Cologne 1972; *Verkehrskultur* by Klaus Honnef, Recklinghausen, West Germany 1972; *Geschichte der Deutschen Malerei im 20. Jahrhundert* by Paul Vogt, Cologne 1972; *Art without Boundaries 1950–70* by Gerald Woods, London 1972; *Winfred Gaul—20 Jahre Malerei,* exhibition catalog, by Klaus Honnef, Bielefeld, West Germany 1973; *Winfred Gaul: Retrospektive 1953–1973,* exhibition catalog, with text by Klaus Honnef and others, Münster 1973; *Deutsche Druckgraphik seit 1960* by Juliane Roh, Munich 1974; *Geschichte der deutschen Malerei im 20.*

Jahrhundert by Paul Vogt, Cologne 1974; *Winfred Gaul: Malerei 1959–1961, 1974–1975,* exhibition catalog, with texts by Manfred de la Motte and Karlheinz Nowald, interview by Klaus Honnef, Duisburg, West Germany 1975; *Winfred Gaul: Zeichen + Malen,* exhibition catalog, with text by Johann H. Müller, Hagen, West Germany 1977; *Winfred Gaul: Werkverzeichnis der Druckgraphik und Objekte,* with texts by Jens C. Jensen and Eberhard Freitag, Kiel, West Germany 1978; *Winfred Gaul: Arbeiten 1953–1961,* with texts by Manfred de la Motte, Pierre Restany, Will Grohmann and others, Bonn 1979; *Winfred Gaul: Arbeiten auf Papier aus der Serie Recycling,* exhibition catalog with introduction by Jurgen Weichardt, Bremen 1985; *Winfred Gaul: Arbeiten des Informel,* exhibition catalog with text by Diethelm Rohnisch, Emmerich 1987; *Brockhaus Enzyklopädie,* Brockhaus edition 1989; *W.G. catalog raisonné,* Concept Verlag, Düsseldorf 1993; Horst Richter: *Geschichte der Malerei im 20.Jahrh.,* Verlag DuMont, Cologne 1990; Herbert Read: *Künstlerlexikon,* Verlag DuMont, Cologne 1991; Heinz Thiel: "Interview with W.G." in *Kunstforum International,* Cologne 1988; Jürgen Weichardt: *Künstler-kritisches Lexikon der Gegenwartskunst, Ausgabe 14,* München 1991; Elisabetta Longari: *W.G.,* ritratti monografici, edizione Roberto Peccolo, Livorno, Italy 1992; *Kunst in Deutschland, Werke zeitgenössicher Künstler aus der Sammlung des Bundes,* exhibition catalog, Bonn 1995; *Graphik der2: Hälfte des 20 Jahrhunderts aus der Sammlung Jürgen Weichardt,* exhibition catalog, Perm 1995–96; *Kunst des Westens—Deutsche Kunst 1945–1960* by Ferdinand Ullrich, Cologne 1996; *L'Art en Allemange,* Paris 1997; *Winfred Gaul—das Frühwerk, Märkische,* exhibition catalog, by Siegfried Gnichwitz and Walter Israel 1997; *German Marks* by Erika G. Költzsch, Cambridge, Massachusetts 1998; *Kunst im Aufbruch,* exhibition catalog, Ludwigshafen 1998; *Die Informellen—von Pollock bis Schumacher,* exhibition catalog, Morsbroich 1998; *Brennpunkt Informel—Quellen, Strömungen, Reaktinen* by Christoph Zuschlag, Köln 1998; *Von Beuys bis Cindy Sherman,* exhibition catalog, Munich 1999; *Informel—der Anfang nach dem Ende,* Dortmund 1999; *Wege zum deutschen Informel,* exhibition catalog, with text by Wolgang Zemter, Witten 1999; *Word and Image,* exhibition catalog, with text by Samuel Becket, Atlanta 1999; *Die Farbe, Psycologie für Alle* by Gisla Gniech and Michael Aurel Stadler, Bremen 2000.

*

When I was twenty, I wanted to be a sculptor. I worked with wood, plaster and ceramics, but also tried to paint in a semi-abstract way influenced by reproductions I had seen in catalogs.

It was only in 1953 when I decided that painting was the right thing for me. I've stuck to it ever since, and I'm still curious to find out what painting is all about.

Compared with other media which have become so attractive to other artists recently, painting might seem to be rather old fashioned, restricted in its means and loaded with the burden of tradition. It is, but it does not make painting less attractive to me.

I think a painter who dedicates himself seriously to his medium sooner or later will find himself a part of that big "stream" called tradition and will learn to appreciate it.

As far as I'm concerned, I accept the conditions of painting as any chess player accepts the rules of the game, knowing that within the rules there are infinite chances to win or lose.

For me as a painter it is even more exciting since I cannot rely on the same rules twice. If there *are* rules in painting they are valid only for a given series of works. After a series is finished, these rules are replaced by new ones which will fit into a new series.

What I mean is: I do not want to restrict my painting to one particular style or formal device, but to keep it open to all ends, to make use of the full range of possibilities offered by the medium and my own capacities.

Right from the start, my main interest was the materials of painting. Instead of artist's colours, I preferred to work with non-artistic or "poor" materials such as printing ink, industrial varnish or house paint. I replaced the brush with sponge, roller or rags soaked into paint. I used knives and razor blades, children's crayons, blackboard chalk or my fingers and hands. I still like to change the tools, the colours, the scale as well as concept. When I have worked for a certain period, with the full range of spectrum, I have always felt a need to work exclusively with black and white and vice versa. The variety of materials used and their application to the process of painting determines the variety of linguistic means.

—Winfred Gaul

* * *

An artist who conceives of the purpose of art as "an incessantly-renewed aesthetic subversion" is difficult to describe. His works do not in the long term admit of being squeezed into the narrow confines of preconceived judgments; they slip out just when they seem to have been stored in one of thought's many filing drawers. Such an artist is Winfred Gaul. For many years he has been producing paintings that are characterized on the one hand by what appear to rapid radical shifts of style, on the other by an immense consistency, especially when one considers them from the perspective of his central themes.

Gaul's field of artistic operations was from the beginning painting. He has never limited himself to a partial treatment, but has always attempted to explore manifold expressive possibilities of painting, at the same time confirming their essential theoretical and practical postulates. It is not surprising, therefore, that his artistic work has always been accompanied by constant reflection, which he has set out in numerous essays. Even less surprising is Gaul's gradual turning toward the analysis of the most elementary procedures and relationships of the medium of painting, after he had dedicated himself years before to his diverse images and stylistic changes. Gaul has in recent years become a leading exponent of "analytical painting." This form of painting leads those artistic efforts, from Claude Monet's water-lily picture via Matisse's collages to Fontana's radical gestures and Ryman's artistic refusals, which determine modern painting, back to fundamental essence.

For the analytical painter, painting is, to quote Gaul, "one specific method, among other specific methods, of making art." It plumbs the depths, as it were, of the linguistic dimensions of the medium of painting, and in doing so it forcibly restricts this inquiry to taking as its object the medium of painting. An artistic process is facilitated thereby which has no need of reference to extra-medial categories. The object and the means of examination are identical.

In the exhibition *Planned Painting* in Milan, 1974, Gaul exhibited a triptych. In this picture one can not only distinguish the separate stages of his productive process, but also discern the goals of Analytic Painting as a whole.

The first decisions which the artist took concerned the materials. The materials consist of the canvas, the paint, and the tools with which the colour is applied to the canvas.

Gaul selected as a base brown, coarsely textured canvas. This he stretched on wedge-shaped frames. As a carrier of artistic operations other backgrounds are also conceivable, for example walls.

After the question of background had been disposed of, Gaul produced an artistic programme. This programme is always so widely laid out that it permits various possible methods of realization. Of course the expressive possibilities are already decisively preconditioned by the choice of background.

A further limitation occurs through the choice of kind of colour. Gaul decided to use a synthetic resin solution, thinned with water, to which, from one part of the picture to the other, he from time to time added a small percentage of black colour. Through the various kinds of colour application, the individual parts of the picture experienced differentiated coloration. The colouration can result from various instruments.

In the case in question Gaul used sheepskin paint rollers, such as home decorators use. He used several layers of colour one over another, so that there occurred an inter-penetration of the individual layers of colours.

The colorization is nevertheless only one component of the picture. To this is added a second: the hatching. The hatching develops a dialectical relationship with the colour. Gaul makes use of hatching as horizontal, or vertical, sometimes also diagonal lines, in a stage therefore where it has not yet constructed itself into a sign-figure. In the triptych the signs manifest themselves as a black perpendicular dividing line with thoroughly differentiated content. In the blackest part of the picture the line almost wholly disappears.

"Analytic Painting," as another of its exponents, Gianfranco Zappetini sums it up, is "a question of looking afresh at the data of painting from a more radical perspective; it concerns the problem of painting in that it explores the fundamental linguistic uniformities in their relation one to another." The result of analytic painting is therefore not limited to the enumeration of structural elements but broadens itself out over the structural relationships of these elements. The object of inquiry is the structuring process. It is this which Gaul brings to the fore.

—Klaus Honnef

GECCELLI, Johannes

Nationality: German. **Born:** Königsberg, 14 October 1925. **Education:** Kunstakademie, Dusseldorf, 1947–51, Dip. Art Teaching 1953; Universität Koln, 1952. **Military Service:** Served as signals operator, German Army, in Poland, Czechoslovakia and Yugoslavia, 1943–45; prisoner-of-war, Austria and Britain, 1945–47. **Family:** Married Audrey Morris in 1953 (died, 1972); children: Markus, Nina, Martina and James; married Regina Hendel in 1974. **Career:** Independent artist, Dusseldorf, 1952–65, West Berlin, since 1965. Worked as teacher in Gymnasium, Dusseldorf, and in Mulheim-Ruhr, 1952–65; guest professor, Hochschule für Bildende Kunst, Hamburg, 1964; professor, Hochschule für Bildende Künste, West Berlin, 1965; visiting professor, Hunter College, New York, 1980. **Awards:** Forderpreis, North Rhine/Westphalia, 1958; Villa Romana Prize, Florence, 1960; Ruhr-preis, Mulheim-Ruhr, 1963. **Agents:** Galerie Appel und Fertsch, Taunuslange 21, 6000 Frankfurt, Germany; Galerie Niepel, Grabenstrasse 11, 4000 Dusseldorf, Germany. **Address:** Bayerischer Platz 4, 1000 Berlin 30, West Germany.

Individual Exhibitions:

1957 Abendatelier Pieng, Dusseldorf
1959 Galerie Niepel, Dusseldorf
1960 Galerie Parnass, Wuppertal, West Germany (retrospective)
1961 Galerie Springer, West Berlin
1962 Galerie Muller, Stuttgart
1963 Von-der-Heydt Museum, Wuppertal, West Germany
Galerie Niepel, Dusseldorf
1964 Galerie Springer, West Berlin
Kunstverein, Oldenburg, West Germany
1965 Galerie Brusberg, Hannover
Staatliche Kunsthalle, Mannheim (retrospective)
Galerie Niepel, Dusseldorf
1967 Galerie Brusberg, Hannover
1968 Galerie Klang, Cologne
Galerie Rothe, Heidelberg
1970 Galerie Defet, Nuremberg
1971 Galerie Appel und Fertsch, Frankfurt
Kunstverein, Kassel, West Germany (retrospective)
1973 Museum, Mulheim-Ruhr, West Germany (retrospective)
Kunstverein, Heidelberg (retrospective)
1974 Galerie Niepel, Dusseldorf
1975 Galerie Appel und Fertsch, Frankfurt
1977 Galerie Niepel, Dusseldorf
1978 Neuer Berliner Kunstverein, West Berlin
Kunsthalle, Kiel, West Germany
1979 Galerie Appel und Fertsch, Frankfurt
Galerie Bossin, West Berlin
1980 Galerie Suzanne Fischer, Baden-Baden, West Germany
1981 *Bilder 1978–81,* Westfälischer Kunstverein, Münster, West Germany
1982 Galerie Braunbehrens, Munich
1983 Galerie Schoeller, Dusseldorf
1984 Galerie Bossin, West Berlin
1985 Galerie Dobele, Stuttgart
Onnasch Galerie, West Berlin
1989 Galerie Hans Strelow, Düsseldorf

Selected Group Exhibitions:

1960 *Monochrome Malerei,* Städtisches Museum, Leverkusen, West Germany
1964 *Carnegie International,* Carnegie Institute, Pittsburgh
1966 *Junge Generation,* Akademie der Künste, West Berlin
1968 *Menschenbild,* Kunsthalle, Darmstadt
1977 *Rationale Konzepte 77,* Stadtische Kunstsammlungen, Gelsenkirchen, West Germany
1978 *Konkrete Konzepte,* Galerie Bossin, West Berlin
1979 *20 Jahre Ausstellung,* Galerie Appel und Fertsch, Frankfurt
1982 *Hommage a Barnett Newman,* Nationalgalerie, West Berlin
1985 *Kunst in der Bundesrepublik 1945–85,* Nationalgalerie, West Berlin

Collections:

Neuer Berliner Kunstverein, West Berlin; Kunsthalle, Mannheim; Kunsthalle, Recklinghausen, West Germany; Stadtmuseum,

Ludwigshafen, West Germany; Städtisches Museum, Mulheim-Ruhr, West Germany; Landesmuseum, Oldenburg, West Germany; Städtisches Museum, Witten-Ruhr, West Germany; Stadtisches Kunstsammlungen, Augsburg, West Germany; Guggenheim Museum, New York.

Publications:

On GECCELLI: Books—*Malerei und Plastik* by Alfons Hoffmann and others, Essen 1960; *Junge Kunstler 1962/63* by John Anthony Thwaites, Cologne 1963; *Johannes Geccelli,* exhibition catalog with text by Heinz Fuchs, Mannheim 1965; *Deutsche Kunst: eine neue generation* by Rolf-Günter Dienst, Cologne 1970; *Deutsche Kunst der 60er Jahre: Malerei, Collage, Op-Art, Graphik* by Juliane Roh, Munich 1971; *Bis Heute* by Karin Thomas, Cologne, 1971; *Johannes Geccelli,* exhibition catalog with text by Helmut Heissenbuttel, Mulheim-Ruhr, West Germany 1973; *Malerei nach 1945* by Wieland Schmied, West Berlin 1976; *Johannes Geccelli: Bilder 1978–81,* exhibition catalog with texts by Thomas Deecke and Gottfried Boehm, Münster, West Germany 1981; *Johannes Geccelli,* exhibition catalog with essay by Bernd Growe, West Berlin 1985.

*

Among the diffuse, visual supply of colours and structures, man seeks the shape of his own kind. He has an evolutionary need to recognize friend or foe in his surroundings. The preservation of the species, among other things, depends on this reaction. So his perception requires only a few clues in order to make out a human form.

With the emancipation of painting from all extra-artistic requirements, man's way of seeing was also gradually liberated from those earlier constraints. As painting developed towards the abstract and concrete, every blurred factor, every objective association, had to be eliminated in order to develop the liberated colour as a function of light. If the free colour in its pure interactions was brought into the picture, the structure determining it must arouse no memory of the objective.

The impossibility of abandoning the objective brings the form into the picture. It derives from the action of the ''free'' colour. This contradiction remains.

A shadow under the hem of a coat, a faint difference in colour from the surroundings, slight shifts of angle, a few structures definable by their contents, suffice to recognize the human form.

Even the slightest changes in surface texture—of skin or fabric—which attract the attention of the senses, set in motion a practised recognition-mechanism. Only a few contrasts are necessary in order to recognize the human form: the rest is taken care of by accumulated knowledge: the picture that we already have of it.

I am always at the mercy of this picture. It is true that I need it in everyday life, to stay on my feet. I know it well. It was drummed into me. I could draw its outline. But I must insist that it isn't true, that I can't identify with it. Painters have chosen not to reproduce the old picture, rather than be untruthful.

''Natural'' perception wants contrasts. I don't give them where they are wanted. They predominate on the edge of the picture. Complimentary contrasts. Stable colour-relations. Well suited, in fact, for distinguishing the figure from the background. RED-GREEN. Towards the centre, where it is least expected, they both flow together. Red will no longer be the same red that it was at the edges, because the green has imperceptibly changed it at the same time. It's turning into blue. The eye perceives that the red is losing its unequivocalness because of the gradual changes taking place in its vicinity. It has to be redefined according to circumstances. Where stability should be, there is ambiguity. The colour is taking itself to the centre, to an area where, close together, it scarcely moves on from one contrast to another. The colour is in motion. What it reveals is not yet determined; it struggles against the outline. A constellation in the colour continuum: the figure.

The painter's centuries-long relations with pigments, tints, pastels, hinders our understanding of colour. It still prevents the necessary thinking-through of the phenomenon. But the knowledge that colours are ''the acts and creatures of light'' should have altered the artistic process. The mixing and application of pigments is an intermediary activity of light.

It is misleading to talk about colour as if it were a thing. It is not an object for a subject. You can't talk about it without considering the perceiver. It is neither external to the seer, nor wholly internal. (Dualistic thinking must dissolve in the experience of colour???)

Colour is the experience of a dialectical occurrence. It is not wholly given, but always mediated. The experience of colour is the reflection of a mediation which is constantly taking place. It is the process, the continuum, in which we are united with all visible things. Colour is the outward sign of an undeniable mediation between man and the whole of creation.

—Johannes Geccelli

GENOVÉS, Juan

Nationality: Spanish. **Born:** Valencia, 1930. **Education:** Studied art at the Escuela Superior de Bellas Artes San Carlo, Valencia, and in Madrid. **Career:** Painter and graphic artist, Valencia, since 1950: member, Grupo Parpallo, and Gruppo Hondo; founder-member, *Exposicion de Primavera,* Madrid, 1953. **Awards:** First Prize, *15th Salon del Circulo de Bellas Artes,* Madrid, 1955; Gold Medal, *6th Biennale di San Marino,* 1967; Premio Marzotto, Italy, 1968; Premio Nacional de Artes Plasticas, 1984. **Agent:** Marlborough Fine Art, 6 Albemarle Street, London W1, England, **Address:** Arandilla 17, Aravaca, 28023 Madrid, Spain.

Individual Exhibitions:

1956 Galeria Alfil, Madrid
1957 Museo de Arte Moderno, Havana
Galerie Dintel, Santander, Spain
1958 Ateno, San Juan, Puerto Rico
1960 Ateneo, Madrid
1962 Galeria Diario de Noticia, Lisbon
Galeria El Corsario, Ibiza, Spain
1965 Sala de Bellas, Artes Moderno, Madrid
Galerie Relevo, Rio de Janeiro
1966 Sal de San Eloy, Salamanca, Spain
Museo de Arte Moderno, Bilbao, Spain
1967 Marlborough-Gerson Gallery, New York
Marlborough Fine Art, London

1969 Tokyo Gallery
Marlborough Galleria d'Arte, Rome
Galleria La Bussola, Turin
1971 Kunstverein, Frankfurt
Haus am Waldsee, West Berlin
1972 Württembergischer Kunstverein, Stuttgart
Städtisches Kunsthalle, Recklinghausen, West Germany
Fundacio Eugenio de Mendoza, Caracas
Museo d'Arte Moderno, Bogota
Museum Boymans-van Beuningen, Rotterdam
1973 Galeria Val i 30, Valencia, Spain
Galeria Vandres, Madrid
Galerie Marlborough-Godard, Montreal
Marlborough Gallery, New York
1974 *Mostra Retrospectiva,* Galeria Alcoiarts, Alicante, Spain
1976 Marlborough Galerie, Zurich
1977 Galeria Arte Comtacto, Caracas
1980 Marlborough Gallery, New York
1981 Galeria Theo, Valencia, Spain
1982 Museo de Arte Contemporaneo, Caceres, Spain
Palacio de la Lonja, Zaragoza, Spain
Colegio de Arquitectos, Murcia, Spain
Galeria Rayuela, Madrid
Sala Posada del Potro, Cordoba, Spain
1983 Centro de la Villa, Madrid (retrospective)
Museo de Vitoria, Gasteiz, Spain
Ayuntamiento de Valencia, Spain
1984 Marlborough Gallery, New York
1985 Museo de Albacete, Spain
Arco '85, Stand Marlborough, Madrid
Galeria Punto, Valencia, Spain
1986 Galeria Quintana, Bogota, Colombia
1987 Galeria Atxerri, San Sebastian, Spain
1989 Galeria El Coleccionista, Madrid
Galeria Punto, Valencia, Spain
Centre Municipal de Cultura, Madrid
1990 Galeria Barcelona
1991 Museo de San Telmo, San Sebastian, Spain
Galerie Patrice Trigano, Paris
Sala Unicaja, Malaga, Spain
Fundación Caixa Galiza, A Coruña, Spain
1992 Palacio Revillagigedo, Gijon, Spain
1993 *Genoves,* Centre Julio Gonzalez, Valencia, Spain
1994 Galeria Pelaires, Palma de Mallorca, Spain
Fundación Marcelino Botín, Santander, Spain

Selected Group Exhibitions:

1954 *Bienal Hispano-Americana,* Casa de las Americas, Havana
1964 *World's Fair,* New York
1965 *Bienal,* Sao Paulo
1966 *Biennale,* Venice
1967 *Carnegie International,* Carnegie Institute, Pittsburgh
1970 *Kunst and Politik,* Badischer Kunstverein, Karlsruhe, West Germany
1974 *Contemporary Spanish Art,* Marlborough Fine Art, London (toured Europe)
1984 *Dreams and Nightmares,* Hirshhorn Museum, Washington, D.C.
1989 *Object and Concept,* Guggenheim Museum, New York
1993 *El Aire* (toured New York, Caracas, Havana, and Buenos Aires)
1996 *City Scapes: A Survey of Urban Landscape,* Marlborough Gallery, New York

Collections:

Museo Nacional de Arte Contemporaneo, Madrid; Galleria Nazionale d'Arte Moderna, Rome; Museum Boymans-Van Beuningen, Rotterdam; Kulturministerium Baden-Württemberg, Stuttgart; Centre National d'Art Contemporain, Paris; Musée Royal des Beaux-Arts, Brussels; Museo de Arte Moderno, Rio de Janeiro; Museum of Modern Art, New York; Guggenheim Museum, New York; South African National Gallery, Cape Town.

Publications:

On GENOVÉS: Books—*Genovés,* exhibition catalog with text by José M. Moreno, Lisbon 1962; *Kunst and Politik,* exhibition catalog with texts by Robert Kudielka, Geráld Gassiot-Talabot, Herbert Marcuse and others, Karlsruhe, West Germany 1979; *Juan Genovés,* exhibition catalog with texts by Alfonso Sastre and G. Bussmann, Frankfurt 1971; *Juan Genovés,* exhibition catalog with text by J. van der Wolk, Rotterdam 1972; *Art without Boundaries 1950–1970* by Gerald Woods, Philip Thompson and John Williams, London 1972; *Kunst um 1970/Art around 1970,* exhibition catalog with text by Wolfgang Becker, Aachen, West Germany 1972; *Juan Genovés,* exhibition catalog, New York 1973; *Juan Genovés: Mostra retrospectiva,* exhibition catalog, Alicante, Spain 1974; *Genovés,* exhibition catalog with text by Vicente Aguilera Cerni, Madrid 1982; *Genovés,* exhibition catalog with text by Francisco Candel, Barcelona 1991; *Genovés,* exhibition catalog with text by Pierre Cabanne, Paris 1991; *Genovés,* exhibition catalog with text by Teresa Posada, Eduardo Subirats, and Manuel Vincent, Valencia 1993; *Juan Genovés,* exhibition catalog with text by Andrés Aberasturi, Santander 1994; *Secuencias: 1996–97,* Madrid 1997.

* * *

Juan Genovés once described himself as a ''pictorial journalist,'' by which I imagine he regards himself as someone providing the public with facts and images as reportage on current events. Perhaps Goya would have similarly described himself. Genovés, like his Spanish contemporary Canogar, is part of the second wave of postwar Spanish artists, who were prepared to express themselves in realistic terms, rather than define opposition to the state through passionate abstract images.

After his impressive exhibition at the 1966 Venice *Biennale,* Genovés was launched on an international career by the Marlborough Galleries, preceding the photo-realistic school. Photographic images have been used by artists for a hundred years, and, in particular, Muybridge's pioneering records of human and animal movement have inspired numerous artists, notably Francis Bacon. Genovés was influenced by the films of Eisenstein. His paintings are based on photographic records of crowd scenes, or remembered images. They look like enlarged photographs of frightened, fleeing crowds, strangely anonymous, without reference to place or purpose, to attitude or objective. In that sense they have a Kafkaesque atmosphere, and whilst one assumes they relate to Spain, they could equally, even more relevantly, apply to many other countries and many other conflicts. Genovés, in fact, is far more motivated by visual ideas than by social comment; the critic Robert Melville commented, after his 1967 London exhibition, "His interest in crowds may well be more philosophical than political." In 1966 Genovés saw the films of Eisenstein, *Potemkin* and *October,* at a film club in Madrid, and then recalled having seen them before, in Valencia, as a boy. It would appear that the impact of those disturbing, often horrific, scenes of threatened, hysterical crowds remained in his memory.

Born in Valencia, he studied in Madrid, and started to paint the crowd scenes in 1964, seven years after his first one-man show. Earlier, in complete contrast, he worked in collage, usually on single figures, concerned, he says "with the problems of solitude," sometimes depicting men in prison. He passionately believes that the artist must be involved in the human situation, and in adapting film techniques to image making he regards "the cinema as the art form of our times. I wanted to adopt the language of films, of television, and photography, in order to reach more people." To do so, he had to invent a complex technique of exactly articulated tiny forms in narrative sequences, incorporating the art of cutting and montage, as well as a highly skillful use of draughtsmanship and paint.

—Charles Spencer

GENZKEN, Isa

Nationality: German. **Born:** Bad Oldesloe, 27 November 1948. **Education:** Studied painting, under Alvir Mavignier, Hochschule fur bildende Kunste, Hamburg, 1969–71; photography and graphics, Hochschule fur bildende Kunste, West Berlin, 1971–73; painting, under Gerhard Richter, Staatliche Kunstakademie, Dusseldorf, 1973–77. **Family:** Married the artist Gerhard Richter in 1982. **Career:** Independent painter, sculptor and photographer, Dusseldorf, 1977–82, and in Cologne since 1983, currently lives and works in Berlin. Instructor in sculpture, Staatliche Kunstakademie, Dusseldorf, 1977–78; instructor in design, Fachhochschule Niederrhein, Krefeld, 1978–79. **Awards:** Karl-Schmidt-Rottluff Scholarship, West Berlin, 1978; Kunstpreis, West Berlin, 1980. **Agent:** c/o Jack Shainman Gallery, 513 West 20th Street, New York, New York 10011.

Individual Exhibitions:

1976 Galerie Konrad Fischer, Dusseldorf
1978 Kabinett fur aktuelle Kunst, Bremerhaven, West Germany
1979 Museum Haus Lange, Krefeld, West Germany (with H. Schuler)
1980 Galerie Max Hetzler, Stuttgart
Galerie Van Krimpen, Amsterdam
1981 Galerie Konrad Fischer, Dusseldorf
1982 Kolnischer Kunstverein, Cologne (with W. Nestler and H. Schuler)
1983 Galleria Pieroni, Rome (with G. Richter)
1985 Galerie Van Krimpen, Amsterdam
1986 Galerie Fred Jahn, Munich
Galerie Konrad Fischer, Dusseldorf
Galerie Jean Bernier, Athens
1987 Galerie Harald Behm, Hamburg
Galerie Daniel Bucholz, Cologne
Galleria Pieroni, Rome (with G. Richter)
1988 Galerie Ghislaine Hussenot, Paris
Rheinisches Landesmuseum, Bonn (travelled to the Kunstmuseum, Winterthur, Switzerland, and Museum Boymans-van Beuningen, Rotterdam)
1992 Marian Goodman Gallery, New York
Renaissance Society, Chicago
1993 Kunsthalle, Bremen
Marion Goodman Gallery, New York
1994 Galerie Daniel Buchholz, Cologne
Xavier Hufkens Gallery, Brussels
1995 Galerie Daniel Buchholz, Cologne
1996 *MetLife, Isa Genzken,* EA-Generali Foundation, Wien (catalog)
1998 Galerie Daniel Buchholz, Cologne
INIT Kunst-Halle, Berlin
2000 *You Are My Happiness,* Kunstverein Braunschweig (retrospective) (catalog)
Urlaub, Kunstverein, Frankfurt
AC Project Room, New York

Selected Group Exhibitions:

1979 *Schlaglichter,* Rheinisches Landesmuseum, Bonn
1981 *Art Allemagne Aujourd'hui,* Musée d'Art Moderne de la Ville, Paris
1982 *Documenta 7,* Museum Fridericianum, Kassel, West Germany
1983 *Standort Dusseldorf,* Kunsthalle, Dusseldorf
1984 *Ein anderes Klima,* Kunsthalle, Dusseldorf
1985 *Schwarz-Weiss,* Galerie Holtmann, Cologne
1986 *Bodenskulptur,* Kunsthalle, Bremen, West Germany
1987 *Juxtapositions: Recent Sculpture from England and Germany,* Institute for Art and Urban Resources, New York
1988 *Biennale of Sydney,* Art Gallery of New South Wales, Sydney
1994 Frith Street Gallery, London
1995 *Bodily Logos: 14 Women Artists from Germany,* Staatsgalerie, Stuttgart, Germany (catalog)
Haus der Kunst, Munich
Aargauer Kunsthaus, Aarau
Nationalmuseum für Monderne Kunst, Oslo
1997 *Skulptur Projekte,* Munster
Sammlung Hoffmann, Berlin
Kunst in der Leipziger Messe, Leipzig
Villa Merkel, Esslingen
1998 *Ecstasy,* Jack Shainman Gallery, New York
Flash Art Berlin 3001, Berlin
Fast Forward—Image on Show, Kunstverein, Hamburg, Germany
Kunsthalle, Cologne
1999 *Gif en Goerde Vorm,* Museum voor Moderne Kunst, Arnheim, Netherlands
Lenbachhaus, Munich
2000 *Central House of the Artist,* Expo Park, Moscow

Collections:

Nationalgalerie, West Berlin; Staatsgalerie, Stuttgart; Stedelijk Van Abbemuseum, Eindhoven; Rijksmuseum Kroller-Muller, Otterlo.

Publications:

By GENZKEN: Articles—interview in *Schlaglichter,* exhibition catalog, Bonn 1979; "Die Objekte liegen . . ." in *Kunstforum International* (Mainz), no. 36, 1979; "Ein Preis oder ein Arbeitsstipendium . . ." in *Junge Kunst in Deutschland,* edited by Dieter Honisch, West Berlin 1982; "Isa Genzken: Sketches for a Movie, and Other Writings" in *Journal of Contemporary Art,* vol. 7, Summer 1994.

On GENZKEN: Book—*Isa Genzken* by Klaus Honnef, Dieter Schwartz, and Jan van Adrichem, Munich 1988. **Exhibition catalogs—** *Isa Genzken/Horst Schuler,* with texts by Birgit Pelzer and Marianne Stockebrand, Krefeld 1979; *5 Deutsche,* with text by Paul Groot, Amsterdam 1981; *Art Allemagne Aujourd'hui,* with text by Bernhard Kerber, Paris 1981; *Isa Genzken/Horst Schuler/Wolfgang Nestler,* with text by Bernhard Kerber, Cologne 1982; *Isa Genzken/Gerhard Richter,* with text by Rudi H. Fuchs, Rome 1983; *Isa Genzken,* with text by Paul Groot, Munich 1986; *Juxtapositions: Recent Sculpture from England and Germany,* with text by Joshua Decter, New York 1987. **Articles—**"Le Point de Gravite: Les Sculptures d'Isa Genzken" by Birgit Pelzer in *Parachute,* no. 94, April-June 1999; "Isa Genzken" by Astrid Wege in *Artforum,* vol. 39, no. 2, October 2000; "Isa Genzken at AC Project Room" by Gregory Volk in *Art in America* (New York), vol. 89, no. 3, March 2001.

*

Concrete is forced nature. When I visit a museum and enter a room full of bad pictures but then suddenly find a picture I can linger in front of for a while, I forget the others. Public sculpture is today located in the area of tension between a modern house and a traditional monument. I find the rough brickwork construction of new buildings more interesting than the routine concealment of facades with pseudoprecious materials, since with the former the engineer's rational thinking is more closely concerned with truth.

—Isa Genzken

* * *

Though Le Corbusier and Mies van der Rohe were arguably the most influential architects of the industrial era, their influence subsided during the 1980s and 1990s, as ornate and irreverent postmodern styles started to replace their efficient and monumental plans. In the hands of Isa Genzken, a fine artist, however, the forms of modernist architecture thrive again, this time as a postmodernist strategy. In her reinforced concrete public and gallery-sized sculpture, she recontextualizes the material exalted by Le Corbusier and retains its grave force and brutal texture. From the outside, a work such as *Bild* (*Painting,* 1989) resembles a ruined fortress, a miniature stronghold perched with unlikely sturdiness atop a fragile-looking steel base. Sheltered by this stark exterior, however, are materials of almost dainty splendor: smooth walls encrusted with mica, glass, and ornamental porcelain.

Genzken's feminism-informed concern for the political and metaphysical connotations of interiors and exteriors dates back to her earliest widely exhibited works, a series of photographs of women's ears from 1980. The familiar yet fascinating shapes, simultaneously inside and outside the body, decorated by jewelry or wisps of hair, suggested forms that were almost architectural.

Genzken's penchant for rethinking the forms and meanings of modernist architecture has led her time and again to Chicago, its American center, where she held her 1992 miniretrospective, titled "*Jeder braucht mindestens en Fenster*" ("Everyone needs at least one window"), at the University of Chicago's Renaissance Society. In *X* (1992), she re-presents the familiar motif of the exterior of the John Hancock Center in epoxyed resin and steel. *Chicago Window* (1991) alludes to the sash windows promoted by Daniel Sullivan. And *Mies* (1987) pays homage to Genzken's countryman and longtime Chicago resident Mies van der Rohe.

Along with less well-known artists, including Georg Herold, Imi Knoebel, Reinhard Mucha, and Meuser, Genzken has made the sculptural reworking of architectural motifs into a recognizably German art form. These artists explore in different ways the relationship between architecture and national identity, attempting to invent lasting structures that utilize the building blocks of the past as raw material in the construction of brand new ideals and realities.

—Mark Swartz

GERSTNER, Karl

Nationality: Swiss. **Born:** Basel, 2 July 1930. **Education:** Primary school and gymnasium in Basel, 1937–44; studied graphic design and typography at the Allgemeine Gewerbeschule, Basel, 1945–46; mainly self-taught in art from 1947, but influenced by Georges Vantongerloo, Marcel Duchamp, Josef Albers, Max Bill, Camille Graeser and Richard Paul Lohse. **Military Service:** Served in the Swiss Army. **Family:** Marrried Inge Hoechberg in 1958; daughter: Muriel. **Career:** Painter, Basel, from 1947: first interchangeable paintings 1952, first programmed paintings 1953; also worked as a typographer, graphic designer and photographer, Basel, 1947–60; founder-director, with Markus Kutter and Paul Gredinger, GGK Advertising Agency, Basel, 1959–70; full-time painter, Basel, Paris and Hippoltskirch, Alsace, since 1970. Visiting lecturer, Royal College of Art, London; Massachusetts Institute of Technology, Cambridge; University of California, Berkeley; University of Hawaii, Honolulu; and other institutions, from 1970. **Agents:** Galerie Denise René, 196 Boulevard Saint-Germain, 75007 Paris; Galerie Hans Mayer, Grabbeplatz 2, 4000 Dusseldorf; Marlborough Fine Art (London) Ltd., 6 Albemarle Street, London W1S 4BY, United Kingdom, and Staempfli Gallery, 47 East 77th Street, New York, New York 10021. **Address:** Mönchsbergerstrasse 10, CH-4024 Basel, Switzerland.

Individual Exhibitions:

1957 Club Bel Etage, Zurich
1961 Galerie Suzanne Bollag, Zurich

1962 Galerie Denise René, Paris
1963 Galerie Der Spiegel, Cologne
Haus am Lutzowplatz, West Berlin
1965 Staempfli Gallery, New York
1966 Op-Art-Galerie Hans Mayer, Esslingen, West Germany
Tokyo Gallery
Galerie Der Spiegel, Cologne
1967 Galerie Denise René, Paris
Staempfli Gallery, New York
1969 *D'ou vous est venue cette idée?,* Galerie Denise René, Paris
Programmierte Bilder, Karl-Ernst-Osthaus Museum, Hagen, West Germany
Galerie Denise René/Hans Mayer, Dusseldorf
1970 Galerie Swart, Amsterdam
Haus am Lutzowplatz, West Berlin
1971 Galerie Denise René/Hans Mayer, Dusseldorf
1973 Museum of Modern Art, New York
Galerie Liatowitsch, Basel
Denise René Gallery, New York
1974 Kunstmuseum, Dusseldorf
Galerie Denise René, Paris
1975 Galeria Arte/Contacto, Caracas
Galerie Jasa, Munich
Galerie Liatowitsch, Basel
Color Sounds, Denise René Gallery, New York
1977 Galerie 58, Rapperswill, Switzerland
1978 Galerie Denise René/Hans Mayer, Dusseldorf
Quadrat-Bottrop Moderne Galerie, Bottrop, West Germany
Kunstmuseum, Solothurn, Switzerland
1979 *Bericht über den Versuch: Karl Gerstner anzugehen,* Galerie Brigitte Lopes, Zurich
1981 *Color Forms,* Galerie Denise René/Hans Mayer, Dusseldorf
Studio Bombelli, Cadaques, Spain
1982 Galerie Denise René, Paris
1984 Galerie Der Spiegel, Cologne
1985 Staempfli Gallery, New York
1986 Galerie Denise René, Paris
Galerie Appel und Fertsch, Frankfurt
1988 Holderbank, Switzerland
1990 Galerie Hans Mayer, Dusseldorf
1992 Museum für Gegenwartkunst, Basel
Galerie Littmann, Basel
Galerie am Lindenplatz Schaan, Lichtenstein
Kunsthalle, Tubingen, Germany
Galerie APC, Zurich
1993 Kunstmuseum Solothurn, Switzerland
Kunsthalle Weimar, Germany
Von der Heydt Museum, Wuppertal, Germany
1994 *Neue Color Fractals,* Galerie ACP Zürich, Switzerland
1996 *Color Fractals und Mehr,* Galerie Susanne Kulli, Bern
Synchromien, Galerie Beyeler, Basel (catalog)
1997 Galerie Gmurzynska, Cologne (catalog)
Synchromies, Marlborough Gallery, New York (catalog)
1998 *Synchromies,* Fondation Saner Studen, Biel (catalog)
Synchromies, Centro Cultural Recoleta, Buenos Aires
1999 Galerie Denise René, Paris
First London Exhibition, Marlborough Fine Art, London (catalog)
40 Years of Painting, Galerie Jamileh Weber, Zurich
2000 *Genesis,* Neues Museum Weserburg, Bremen

Selected Group Exhibitions:

1960 *Konkrete Kunst,* Helmhaus, Zurich
1965 The Responsive Eye, Museum of Modern Art, New York
1968 *Documenta 4,* West Germany
1969 *Freund, Freunde, Friends,* Kunsthalle, Dusseldorf
1971 *Dusseldorf Art Scene,* at the *Edinburgh Festival*
1974 *Aspekte der Düsseldorfer Kunstszene,* Neue Galerie am Wolfgang Gurlitt Museum, Linz, Austria
1977 *Kunst, was ist das?,* Kunsthalle, Hamburg
1980 *Schweizerische Plastik-Ausstellung,* Biel, Swizerland
1982 *Vor 150 Jahren: Goethe. . . ,* Kunstverein, Hannover
1986 *Biennale,* Venice
1994 *Der Traum vom Absoluten/The Dream of the Absolute,* Galerie Beyeler Basel, Basel
1995 *Who is Afraid of Red...?,* Galerie Beyeler Basel, Basel
Constructivism and Kinetic Art from the Collection of the Galerije Suvremene Umjetnosti, Galerie Suvremene Umjetnosti, Zagreb
1996 *Lumière et Mouvement,* Galerie Denise René, Paris
1997 *Product: Art! Where is the Original?,* Kunstmuseum Solothurn, Switzerland (traveling exhibition) (catalog)
Produkt: Kunst! Wo Bleibt das Original, Kunstmuseum Solothurn (also Neues Museum Weserberg, Bremen)
Denise René: Sztuka Konkretna, Muzeum Sztuki Lodzi
1998 *Regel und Abweichung: Schweiz Konstruktiv 1960–1997,* Haus für Konstruktive und Konkrete Kunst, Zurich
1999 *Kunst im Aufbruch: Abstraktion Zwischen 1945 und 1959,* Wilhelm-Hack-Museum Karlsruhe

Collections:

Kuntsmuseum, Solothurn, Switzerland; Kunstmuseum, Dusseldorf; Leopold-Hoesch-Museum, Duren, Germany; Kunsthalle, Nuremberg, Germany; Staatsgalerie, Stuttgart; Museum des 20, Jahrhunderts, Vienna; Museum of Modern Art, New York; Albright-Knox Art Gallery, Buffalo, New York; Arco Center, Los Angeles; Tate Gallery, London.

Publications:

By GERSTNER: Books—*Kalte Kunst?,* Teufen, Switzerland 1957; *Programme entwerfen/Designing Programs,* Teufen, New York, Tokyo and Barcelona 1963; *Mit dem Computer Kunst produzieren,* Zagreb 1968; *Do-it-yourself Kunst,* Cologne 1970; *Kompendium für Alphabeten/Compendium for Literates,* Teufen 1970, Cambridge, Massachusetts 1972; *Typographisches Memorandum,* St. Gallen, Switzerland 1972; *Think Program,* New York 1973; *André Thomkins: Inspiration und Methode,* Hannover 1974; *15 Variationen über einen Satz von Max Bill,* Ulm, West Germany 1978; *Gute Kunst, schlechte Kunst,* Hamburg 1981; *Der Wert der Kunst,* Basel 1982; *Kunst in der Demokratie—eine Utopie,* Frankfurt 1981; *Der Kunstler und die Mehrheit,* Frankfurt 1986; *The Forms of Color,* Cambridge, Massachusetts 1986; *Kunst=Gestaltung,* Zurich 1988; *Uber das Apollinische in der Kunst,* Zurich 1988; *Karl Gerstner's Avant Garde Küche,*

Stuttgart, Germany and Teufen, Switzerland 1990; *Die Sammlung Karl Gerstner,* with Christine Breyhan and Katerina Vatsella, Bremen 1991; *Vilém Flusser und die Farben,* Basel 1992; *Kosmos, Chaos, Fraktale,* Hamburg 1992; *Visuelle Logik: Die Kunst von Karl Gerstner—In Zeugnissen uber Ihn und von Ihm,* with multiple authors, Cologne 1997. **Articles—**''Unser Erbe aus der Steinzeit'' in *Basler Magazin,* no. 25, 1995; ''Expedition in die Vorzeit der Kunst'' in *ART: Das Kunstmagazin,* no. 4, April 1997.

On GERSTNER: Books—*Karl Gerstner: d'ou vous est venue cette idée?,* exhibition catalog, Paris 1969; *Karl Gerstner: Programmierte Bilder,* exhibition catalog, Hagen, West Germany 1969; *Prinzip seriell,* exhibition catalog, by Friedrich W. Heckmanns, Dusseldorf 1974; *Karl Gerstner: Color Sounds,* exhibition catalog, with interview by Wibke von Bonin, New York 1975; *Bericht über den Versuch: Karl Gerstner anzugehen,* exhibition catalog, Zurich 1979; *Karl Gerstner: Color Forms,* exhibition catalog, with text by Grace Glueck, Dusseldorf 1981; *Der Geist der Farbe: Die Kunst von Karl Gerstner/L'Esprit des Couleurs: L'Art de Karl Gerstner/The Spirit of Color: The Art of Karl Gerstner,* edited by Henri Stierlin, Stuttgart, Geneva, Paris and Cambridge, Massachusetts 1981; *Karl Gerstner's Private Pinakothek,* Solothurn, Switzerland 1983; *Herr über tausend Farben* by Dieter Bachmann, Hamburg 1983; *Science + Art* by Ans von Berkum and Tom Blekkenhorst, Utrecht 1985; *Gerstners Muhle,* Hamburg 1985; *Karl Gerstner* by Vilém Flusser, Dusseldorf 1990; *Karl Gerstner im Gesprach,* Bremen 1991; *Ein Gesprach mit Karl Gerstner* by Dieter Koepplin, Basel 1992; *Karl Gerstners Werk* by Götz Adriani, Tubingen 1993; *Bausteine zum Verstandnis von Karl Gerstners Kunst* by Sabine Fehlemann, Wuppertal 1993; *Begegnungen: An Architect Meets an Architect* by Werner Blaser, Basel 2000. **Articles—**''Ein Mass für das Unermessliche Finden, Karl Gerstner'' by Hans-Joachim Müller in *Du,* no. 10, October 1988; ''Ein Tag im Leben von Karl Gerstner'' by René Ammann in *Tagesanzeiger Magazin Zürich,* 1 April 1995; ''Primary Colours: Jennifer Higgie on Karl Gerstner'' in *Frieze,* no. 47, June-July 1999.

*

Kandinsky was concerned with the correlation between geometric forms and primary colors. This being granted, his correlations can also be reproduced. But is it correct to proceed from given primary colors or basic forms?

With regard to color it has not yet been possible to fix a norm. And even in the case of the undisputed primary colors yellow/red/blue it remains undecided which yellow, which red and which blue satisfy the quality of the primary color.

And with regard to forms the case is anything but unequivocal. True, there are the platonic figures which are defined by the same length of side. The triangle is quite definitely a basic form with sides of the same length and equal angles. The same goes for the square. And the pentagon. But what about polygons having 17,18, 19 and so on sides? Is there any dividing line between polygons which are basic forms and those which are basic forms no longer? Or do polygons with an increasing number of sides diminish in quality as a basic form? Right up to the pre-eminent case of the circle, which has an infinite number of corners, that is to say none at all.

I am concerned in my speculations neither with physically defined primary colors nor with basic geometric forms—even if there were norms for them. I am interested solely in colors and forms which are elementary in respect of the sensation they evoke.

My intention: to design a model in which the correspondence between the elementary colors and elementary forms (elementary as just defined) contains the sum of all that I could learn and have myself experienced: the color form continuum. It is not a fixed construction but a variable (computer generated) structure. This structure is conclusive, transforms (and/or transcolors) colors and forms in continuous steps.

—Karl Gerstner

* * *

Karl Gerstner advanced from advertisement art to that form of Construction to which the name Cold Art *(Kalte Kunst)* was given. Like Kenneth Martin and his associates later in England, Max Bill, the founder of Concrete Art in Switzerland, had maintained that works of art can be constructed in accordance with mathematical formulae, claiming that mathematical thought is one kind of rational thought and that ''it is by rational thought that we are able to arrange the sensorial values in such a way as to produce a work of art.'' Following in Max Bill's footseps, Karl Gerstner, together with Richard Lohse, applied his principles to the realm of colour, advocating the use of sequential systems to generate colour patterns. From an initial formula he derived whole series and sequences of hues and tones. Consistently with these principles, he quite logically advocated Multiple or Programmatic art, since any number of identical art works can obviously be generated from one and the same mathematical programme. Nothing was lost by mechanical reproduction. Allied to all this he lent his support and encouragement to the idea of Modular or Generative art of the kind in which art works are composed of identical units put together in a variety of ways like a child's building blocks. Finally, he has been an enthusiastic advocate of spectator participation, and at an exhibition of the Nouvelle Tendance in 1964 he declared: ''Our aim is to make you a partner . . . our art depends on your active participation. What we are trying to achieve is your joy before the work of art, that it may be no longer that of an admirer but of a partner.'' Whether this squares with the recondite mathematical basis of his *Kalte Kunst* is not clear.

In his writings on *Kalte Kunst* Gerstner has made few concessions to traditional aesthetic ideas of composition, balance, harmony, etc. This is not what he was aiming at. When his own works are exhibited and seen in bulk they give the impression of some obscure scientific demonstration or advertisement display. They do not invite visual enjoyment. Appreciation and enjoyment must be intellectual, based upon understanding of the mathematics involved, and for this reason the mathematical systems are exhibited along with the works derived from them. How far if at all this comes within the scope of what is commonly understood by ''art'' is an open question.

—Harold Osborne

GERTSCH, Franz

Nationality: Swiss. **Born:** Moerigen, Berne, 8 March 1930. **Education:** Sekundarschule, Berne, 1940–47; studied painting at the

Franz Gertsch: *Silvia II,* 1999–2000. Photo by Peter Suter. ©Franz Gertsch.

Malschule Max von Muehlenen, Berne 1947–50. **Family:** Married Maria Meer in 1963; has five children. **Career:** Painter, since 1947. **Awards:** DAAD Fellowship, Berlin, 1974. **Agent:** M. Knoedler Zurich AG, Kirchgasse 24, 8001 Zurich. **Address:** Huslistatt, 3154 Ruschegg-Heubach, Switzerland.

Individual Exhibitions:

1968 Galerie Martin Krebs, Bern
1969 Galerie Riehentor, Basel
1970 Galerie Toni Gerber, Bern
Galerie Stampa, Basel
1971 Galerie Verna, Zurich
1972 Kunstmuseum, Lucerne
Galerie Mikro, Berlin
1973 Nancy Hoffman Gallery, New York
1975 Akademie der Künste, Berlin (travelled to the Kunstverein, Brauschweig, West Germany; Kunsthalle Dusseldorf; and the Palais des Beaux-Arts, Brussels)
Kunsthalle, Basel
Galerie Turske, Cologne
1976 Galerie Turske, Cologne
1977 Galerie Turske, Cologne
1979 Galerie Turske, Cologne
1980 Kunsthaus, Zurich
Kunstmuseum, Hannover

1981 Louis K. Meisel Gallery, New York
1982 M. Knoedler Zurich AG, Zurich
1986 Kunsthalle, Basel
Museum Moderner Kunst, Vienna
Johanna II, Kunsthalle, Bern
1987 Galerie Turske and Turske, Zürich
1988 Galerie Michael Haas, Berlin
1989 *Bois Gravés Monumentaux,* Cabinet des Estampes and Musée Rath, Geneva
Large Scale Woodcuts, Perimeter Gallery, Chicago
Galerie Friedman-Guiness, Frankfurt
1990 *Woodcuts in the Series 'Projects,'* Museum of Modern Art, New York
Nine Large Scale Woodcuts, Hirshhorn Museum, Smithsonian Institution, Washington, D.C.
1991 *Large Scale Woodcuts,* Museum of Art, San José, California
Holzschnitte, Städtische Galerie im Lembachhaus, Munich
1992 Galerie Patrick Roy, Lausanne
1993 *Landschaften,* Graphische Sammlung ETH, Zürich
Städtische Galerie im Städelschen Kunstinstitut, Frankfurt
1994 *Holzschnitte und Malerei auf Papier,* Kunstmuseum, Berne (travelled to Aichi Prefectural Museum of Art, Nagoya, Japan)
Holzschnitte 1986–1994, Galerie Kornfeld, Bern
Staatliche Kunsthalle Baden-Baden, Germany
1997 *Holzschnittwerk,* Hamburger Bahnhof, Berlin
Holzschnitte, Kunsthalle Burgdorf (Maxe Sommer), Germany
Mönchehaus-Museum für Moderne Kunst, Austellung zur Verleihung des Kaiserrings, Goslar, Germany
1999 *Holzschnitte and Malerei 1987–97,* Kleve, Germany
Kunstmuseum Thun, Thun, Switzerland
Hess Collection at Vinopolis
2000 *Graser Holzschnitt,* Galerie Berlin

Selected Group Exhibitions:

1972 *Dokumenta 5,* Museum Fridericianum, Kassel, West Germany
1973 *Prospect,* Kunsthalle Dusseldorf
The Super-Realist Visions, De Cordova Museum, Lincoln, Massachusetts
1974 *Hyperrealistes Americains-Realistes Europeens,* Centre National d'Art Contemporain, Paris
1976 *Aspects of Realism,* The Gallery, Stratford, Ontario (toured Canada)
1977 *Malerie und Photographieim Dialog,* Kunsthaus, Zurich
1978 *Dalla Natura all'Arte, dall'Arte alla Natura,* at the *Biennale,* Venice
1979 *Bilder einer Ausstellung,* Kunsthalle, Bern
1980 *Printed Art,* Museum of Modern Art, New York
1981 *Art 12, '81 (Turske Fine Art),* Kunstmesse, Basel
1997 *Biennale Lyon,* France
Biennale Kwangjn Korea
1999 *Biennale Venice*
Face to Face to Cyberspace, Fondation Beyeler
2000 *Das Gedächtnis der Malerei,* Aarauer Kunsthaus, Switzerland

Collections:

Museum Moderner Kunst, Vienna; Museum Ludwig, Cologne; Bayerische Staatsgemaldesammlung, Munich; Kunsthalle, Kiel; Nationalgalerie, Berlin; Kunstmuseum, Hannover; Kunstmuseum Bern; Kunstmuseum, Lucerne; Kunsthaus, Zurich; National Gallery of Australia, Canberra.

Publications:

By GERTSCH: Articles—''Interview mit Franz Gertsch,'' with P. Killer, in *Abendezeitung* (Zurich), February 1971; ''Entretien entre Franz Gertsch et Urs Graf'' in *L'Art Vivant* (Paris), March 1973; ''Ein Statement'' in *Projekt '74,* exhibition catalog, Cologne 1974; ''Meine Strategie des Malens'' in *Franz Gertsch,* exhibition catalog, Berlin 1975; interview, with Jürgen Glaesemer, in *Franz Gertsch,* exhibition catalog, Zurich 1980.

On GERTSCH: Books—*Neue Formen des Bildes* by Udo Kultermann, Tübingen 1969, 1975; *Franz Gertsch,* exhibition catalog, with texts by Jean-Christophe Ammann, Timothy Leary, Harald Szeemann and others. Lucerne 1972; *Neue Formen des Realismus* by Peter Sager, Cologne 1973; *Super-Realism: A Critical Anthology,* edited by Gregory Battcock, New York 1975; *Franz Gertsch,* exhibition catalog, with texts by Karl Ruhrberg, Harald Szeeman, Jean-Christophe Ammann and others, Berlin 1975; *Franz Gertsch* exhibition catalog, with texts by Jean-Christophe Ammann, Erika Billeter, Joachim Buchner and others, Zurich 1980; *Franz Gertsch—Holzschnitte, mit einem Oeuvrekatalog der Druckgraphik der Jahre 1972–1991* by Rainer Michael Mason, Munich 1991; *Franz Gertsch: Landschaften,* exhibition catalog with text by Margret Stuffmann and Paul Thanner, Zürich 1993; *Sinn für Farbe—Franz Gertsch, Raimer Jochims, Ricardo Saro,* exhibition catalog by Gudrun Thiessen, with text by Michael Bockemühl, 1995; *Annäherung—Die Notwendigkeit von Kunst (darin: Ansprache zur Eröffnung der Ausstellung von Franz Gertsch* by Jean-Christophe Ammann, Regensburg, Germany 1996; *Franz Gertsch: Landschaften und Porträts 1986–1995,* exhibition catalog with text by Alexander Dückers, Berlin 1997/98; *Franz Gertsch: Silvia—Chronik eines Bildes* by Norberto Gramaccini, Baden, Switzerland 1999. **Articles—**''Franz Gertsch'' by Jean-Christophe Ammann in *Art International* (Lugano, Switzerland), vol. 12, no. 10, 1968; ''Franz Gertsch'' by Leonardo Bezzola in *Werk* (Basel), February 1972; ''Franz Gertsch at Nancy Hoffmann'' in the *Village Voice* (New York), 20 September 1973; ''Bilder von Bildern von Bildern'' by Francois Grundbacher in *Berner Zeitung* (Berne), 11 August 1979; ''Wozu die virtuose Fleissarbeit des Franz Gertsch: Art pour art?'' by Hans Jurg Kupper in *Basler Zeitung,* 10 May 1980; ''A Newer Objectivity: Franz Gertsch's Photo-Realist Paintings'' by Agnes von Borch in *Arts Magazine* (New York), December 1981; ''Franz Gertsch—Vom Ereignis zum Wesen'' by Christian Huther in *Künstler-Kritisches,* vol. 31, no. 18, 1995; ''Zwischen den Gräsern—Drei Neue Bilder von Franz Gertsch'' by Hans Rudolf Reust and Ulrich Loock in *Kunst-Bulletin,* April 1998.

*

Seven times painting has been declared dead, but as yet painters are not extinct; in fact, they still stand at the crossroads: is painting's exclusive purpose to refer to itself, or would it be better advised to deal with reality? I chose the radical way: reality as painting. Mankind is unlikely to find a conceptual and rational answer to the question as to what this reality actually means. Even Leonardo da Vinci failed in this respect, he who had reflected most extensively on art in all its complexities. As a matter of fact, artists will never wholly reach that goal for all its apparent simplicity and banality. They do not have any ready-made solutions at hand, nor do they possess a master key, but ever since painting came into existence, they have been searching for a solution to the mystery that remains as baffling as the Sphinx.

Extract from Franz Gertsch's epilogue in *Franz Gertsch—Silvia Chronik eines Bildes* by Norberto Gramaccini, Baden 1999.

—Franz Gertsch

* * *

Swiss born painter Franz Gertsch is the best known European exponent of the Photo-Realist approach. Gertsch has been making portraits since he was a child and has always been attracted to representation in painting. In 1952 he was already painting from photographs and working to reach an element of "objectivity" and "stylelessness" in his pictures. It wasn't until 1969, however, that he reached his characteristic method and started painting from projected slides.

Gertsch's working method is almost excruciating meticulous and painstakingly slow, especially considering that he works with small, extra-fine brushes rather than with the air brush employed by many of the American Photo-Realists. Gertsch begins with photographs which he takes himself, and he chooses his models for the paintings from among a large number taken of each subject. His subjects are mainly either himself or family and friends, people with whom he is highly familiar and who usually reflect a lifestyle which is a bit off-center from the regular and ordinary work-a-day populace. His compositions seem to lie somewhere between the candid spontaneous and the posed, as if they were the result of pointing the camera, saying "smile" and rapidly snapping. Probably because the subjects are people he knows relatively well, he captures characteristic personality traits recognizably individualistic and yet relatable as types. It is a combination of intimacy and remove which gives life to his works as a whole, with little need for detailed surrounding environment. Consider, for example, the portrait of "Franz and Luciano" (1973) which, with very little extra paraphernalia surrounding the subjects, amply communicates their connections with painting and rather "hip" way of life by the inclusion of portions and paintings behind them and by their style of hair and dress, almost but not quite rock star in appearance. A later and more developed example is Gertsch's large (100 x 154") painting of "Irene" (1980), which reveals a lot about her character within the limiting context of the head and shoulder view. Her aggressive, almost scowling expression, heavy makeup, large sword earrings and campily natural, severe hairdo are enough to portray a type of "New Wavey," *Cabaret* character who, by the way, is also the sustained subject for a number of penetrating watercolor studies.

It is such persistently tough and individualistic subjects which Gertsch seems to prefer, perhaps because they display a literal quality equal to his own pertinacious approach to the canvas. His apt blending of the ruggedly literal and the straightforwardly emotive is amplified by one of the most striking features of his painting. It is the way the images break up on closer scrutiny, revealing the painterly brushstoke quality of the handmade. It's a quality which gives the work a physicality as paint on a level beyond that of the literal Photo-Real, bringing visual satisfaction too often missing in the genre and suggesting that Gertsch's slow methodology is somehow worth it.

—Barbara Cavaliere

GERZ, Jochen

Nationality: German. **Born:** Berlin, 4 April 1940. **Education:** Gymnasium, Dusseldorf, 1951–58; studied American and German literature and Sinology, University of Cologne, 1959–60; English language, St. Mary College, London, 1961–62; German literature and pre-history, University of Basel, 1963–64. **Family:** Married Veronika von Buren in 1963; daughter: Francis Jan. **Career:** Worked as news agency volunteer, Dusseldorf, 1956–59; lived and worked as a journalist in London, 1960–61; salesman and public relations for Gerstner and Kutter, Basel, 1962–66; correspondent for a news agency, Paris, 1968–73. Began writing poetry in 1958; has produced visual texts since 1966, performances since 1967; and photo texts since 1969; has worked in video since 1972; collaborations with Esther Shalev-Gerz, from 1984; Professor/Senior Research Fellow, Coventry University, 1999–2000; Artist in Residence, Chelsea College of Art and Design and London Institute of Art; lives and works in Paris. **Awards:** Roland Preis, Bremen, 1990; Deutscher Kritikerpreis, Berlin, 1996; Ordre National du Mérite, Paris, 1996; Peter Weiss-Preis, Bochum, 1996; Grand Prix National des Arts Visuels, Paris, 1998; Artistic Contribution Award, Festival of Films on Art, Montréal, March 1999; 1.Preis der Helmut-Kraft-Stiftung, Stuttgart, 1999; Honorary Chair, Braunschweig Art Academy. **Agent:** Galerie Crousel Robelin Bama, 40 rue Quincampoix, 75004 Paris. **Address:** 4 rue René Villermé, 75011 Paris, France.

Individual Exhibitions:

1968 Galleria Rinascita, Modena, Italy (with Jean-Francois Bory)
1969 Galerie Groh, Oldenburg, West Germany (with K. H. Krull)
Aktionstraum I, Munich
1970 Galleria la Communes, Brescia, Italy
Galerie Ben Doute de Tout, Nice
Galerie Yellow, Liège, Belgium
Galerie Mediacontact, Dusseldorf
1971 Galleria Tool, Milan
Galerie NW 8, Beindersheim, West Germany
1972 Galerie Bama, Paris
Danert Galeriet, Copenhagen
Galerie Stampa, Basel
1973 German Institute, Amsterdam
German Institute, Bordeaux
Centro Diffusione Grafica, Florence
Galerie Delta, Brussels
1974 Studio Gap, Rome
Kunsthalle, Kiel, West Germany
Galerie Stampa, Basel

Galerie S. Press, Hattingen, West Germany
Kunstmuseum, Bochum, West Germany
Galerie Entre, Paris
Galerie Klein, Bonn
Galerie Bama, Paris
1975 Kunstverein, Karlsruhe
Musée d'Art Moderne de la Ville, Paris
Musée d'Art et d'Industrie, St. Etienne, France
Galerie Nächst St. Stephan, Vienna
Wilhelm-Lehmbruck Museum, Duisburg, West Germany
1976 Tranegarden Kunstbibliothek, Hellerup, Denmark (with Paul-Armand Gette)
Foto/Texte und Stucke, Kunstverein, Braunschweig, West Germany
Galerie Art in Progress, Dusseldorf
German Pavilion, at the *Biennale,* Venice (with Joseph Beuysand Reiner Ruthenbeck)
Kunstraum V, Munich
1977 Studio d'Arte Cannaviello, Rome
Painting Box, Zurich
Association pour Musée d'Art Actuel, Ghent
Galerie Stampa, Basel
Galerie André, Berlin
Video-Studio Mike Stein, Berlin
Galerie Bama, Paris
Galerie Art in Progress, Munich
Stätische Galerie in Lenbachhaus, Munich
1978 Bundner Kunstmuseum, Chur, Switzerland
Der Stein will zuruck zur Schleuder, Landesmuseum Joanneum, Graz, Austria
Galerie Klein, Bonn
Foto/Texte 1975–1978, Kestner-Gesellschaft, Hannover
Kulchur Pieces 1,2,3, Westfälischer Kunstverein, Münster, West Germany
Centro de Arte Contemporaneo, Oporto, Portugal (travelled to the Fundaco Calouste Gulbenkian, Lisbon)
1979 *The Depot: Kulchur Piece No. 4,* Ikon Gallery, Birmingham, England
1980 *5 Installations,* Frankfurter Kunsterverein, Frankfurt
Galerie Stampa, Basel
Galerie Bama, Paris
Jochen Gerz, Nachtbilder, Kasseler Kunstverein, Kassel, West Germany
1981 *Mit 1 Publikum (Performances 1968–80),* Kunsthalle, Bielefeld, West Germany
The Flat, Copenhagen
1982 *Le Grand Amour,* Kunstverein, Freiburg, West Germany
Fotografien und Texte 1980–81, Galerie Dany Keller, Munich
Galerie AK, Frankfurt
Galerie A, Amsterdam
Galerie Bama, Paris
Galerie Stampa, Basel
1983 Maison de la Culture, Chalon-sur-Saone, France
Galerie Stampa, Basel
1984 Galerie Holtmann, Cologne
Banff Arts Centre, Alberta
Yuill/Crowley Gallery, Sydney (travelled to the Australian Center for Contemporary Art, Melbourne)
Wilhelm-Hack-Museum, Ludwigshafen, West Germany
Kunstverein, Heidelberg, West Germany
1985 Galerie Bama, Paris
Museum fur Photographie, Braunschweig, West Germany
Neuer Berliner Kunstverein, West Berlin
Stadglaerie, Saabrucken, West Germany
Or Gallery, Vancouver
1986 Kunstraum, Munich
Passages Centre d'Art Contemporian, Troyes, France
Musee des Beaux-Arts, Calais, France
Galerie de l'ancienne Poste, Calais, France
Musee des Beaux-Arts, Chartres, France
Galerie Cora Holzl, Dusseldorf
Espace Lyonnais d'Art Contemporain, Lyon, France
Coburg Gallery, Vancouver
1987 La Criee, Rennes, France
Galerie Optica, Montreal
Yuill/Crowley Gallery, Sydney
Galerie Kicken/Pauseback, Cologne
1988 Galerie Crousel-Robelin Bama, Paris
Galerie AK, Frankfurt
Kunstsammlung Nordrhein-Westfallen, Dusseldorf (travelled to Vienna, Paris, Saint-Etienne, and Hamburg)
Ruibe der Künste, Berlin
Galerie Anselm Dreher, Berlin
Gallery Löhrl, Mönchengladbach
1989 Gallery Shimada, Yamaguchi, and Sagacho Exhibit Space, Tokyo
Galerie Harald Behm, Hamburg
Galerie Ursula Ehrhardt, Nuremberg
Dany Keller Galerie, Munich
1990 Galerie Kicken/Pauseback, Cologne
Galerie Modulo, Lisbon
Galeria Potochka, Cracow
FRAC Champagne-Ardennes, Reims, and Museum Morsbroich, Leverkusen
1991 Galerie Modulo, Porto
Hirschl & Adler, New York
Kunstverein Ruhr, Essen
Galerie Anselm Dreher and Galerie Vier, Berlin
Galerie Crousel-Robelin Bama, Paris
Galerie Cora Hölzl, Dusseldorf
Gallery Löhrl, Mönchengladbach
1992 Richard L. Nelson Gallery, Davis, California
Galerie AK, Frankfurt
Galerie Sandmann & Haak, Hannover
Pascal de Sarthe Gallery, Los Angeles
Neues Museum Weserburg Bremen und Forum Langenstrasse, Bremen (travelled to Karlsruhe, Manchester, Saarbrucken, Altenburg, and Potsdam)
Yuill/Crowley, Sydney
1993 Centre Saidye Bronfman, Montreal (travelled to Musée Bossuet, Meaux, France)
Galerie Lallouz & Waterson, Montreal
Galerie von Witzleben Edition, Karlsruhe
Galerie Sima, Neremberg
City Art Gallery, Manchester
1994 Musée d'Art Moderne, Strasbourg
Galerie Gandy, Prague
Galerie Löhrl, Moenchengladbach
Vancouver Art Gallery, Vancouver

1995 Newport Harbor Art Museum, Newport Beach, California
Tel-Aviv University Gallery, Tel-Aviv
Galerie Guy Ledune, Brussels
Galerie Chantal Crousel, Paris
Neuberger Museum, Purchase, New York
Galerie Bernd Lutze, Friedrichshafen
Gallery of Contemporary Art, Warschau
1996 Galerie Cora Hoelzl, Düsseldorf
Gallery CRG, New York
ADDC, Périgueux
Galerie Sandmann+Haak, Hannover
Galerie Ernst Busche, Berlin
1997 Germanisches Nat. Museum, Nürnberg
Kunstmuseum Düsseldorf , Düsseldorf
Museum Wiesbaden, Wiesbaden
Musée d'Art Moderne, Saint-Etienne
Catriona Jeffries Gallery, Vancouver
1998 Berkeley Art Museum, Berkeley, California
Kunstmuseum Thurgau, Ittingen, Czechoslovakia
1999 ZKM, Zentrum für Kunst und Medientechnologie, Karlsruhe
Galerie Kerry Crowley, Sydney, Australia
Museum Bolzano, Bolzano, Italy
2000 Kunsthalle zu Kiel, Kiel
Gallerie Cora Hölzl, Düsseldorf
Art Gallery of Windsor, Windsor, Ontario
Sonderjyllands Kunstmuseum, Tonder
Dany Keller Galerie, München
Galerie Sandmann + Haak, Hannover
Glasmuseum Marl, Marl

Performances: *Rufen bis zur Erschopfung,* Paris, *Der Saal, die Wiedergabe,* Paris, and *Schreiben mit der Hand,* Frankfurt, 1972; *Das was sich beschreiben last,* Rome, and *Thomas Jefferson,* Florence, 1973; *Leben,* Kunstmuseum, Bochum, West Germany, and *Das Vergehen von Hoven und Sehen,* Kunstmuseum, Bochum, West Germany, 1974; *Das Auto-Portrait,* Galerie Nachst St. Stephen, Vienna, *Ich bin gleich zuruch (Eurydike),* Kunstverein, Karlsruhe, *Prometheus,* Lembruck Museum, Duisburg, West Germany, and *Nacht, lass den Jager schlafen,* Kunstverein, Braunschweig, West Germany, 1975; *Marsyas,* Kunstmarket, Basel, and *Snake Hoods and Dragon's Dreams,* Videogalerie Steiner, Berlin, 1977; *Marsyas,* Stadpark Forum, Graz, Austria, *Marsyas,* Kunstmarket, Cologne, *Raum mit Grabrelief und Jager,* at the *Bremen Performance Festival,* 1978; *Purple Cross for Absent Now,* Centre d'Art Contemporain, Geneva, *Nice to Meet You,* and the *Lyons Performance Festival, ABC of Reading,* Centre Georges Pompidou, Paris, and *Letter to Jane,* Palazzo Grassi, Venice, 1979; *Welcome Home,* Basel, and *We Are Coming,* Centre Georges Pompidou, Paris, 1980; *Die Reise,* Kunstverein, Heidelberg, 1981; *Pionniers!,* Off Centre, Calgary, Alberta, 1982; *Chinook,* Stadtisches Museum, Monchengladbach, 1985; *Purple Cross for Absent Now no. 2,* at *Documenta 8,* Kassel, West Germany, 1987; *The Plural Sculpture* (web site), Ada Web, New York 1995; *The Berkeley Oracle* (web site), Berkeley Art Museum, Zkm Karlsruhe, and Ada Web, 1997–99.

Selected Group Exhibitions:

1970 *Concrete Poetry,* Stedelijk Museum, Amsterdam
1976 *Biennale,* Venice
1977 *Documenta 6,* (and *Documenta 8,* 1987), Kassel, Germany
Words, Whitney Museum, New York
1979 *Biennale,* Sydney (and 1992)
1980 Rosc, Dublin
1986 *Behind the Eyes,* Museum of Modern Art, San Francisco
1988 *De Facto,* Royal Academy, Copenhagen
1990 *Um 1968 Konkrete Utopien in Kunst und Gesellschaft,* Kunsthalle Dusseldorf
1994 *Hors limites, l'art et la vie,* Centre Georges Pompidou, Paris
1995 *Where Is Abel, Thy Brother?,* Zacheta Gallery of Contemporary Art, Warsaw
1996 *Face à l'histoire,* Centre Georges Pompidou, Paris
1997 *Made in France,* Centre Georges Pompidou, Paris
Deutschlandbilder, Martin-Gropius-Bau, Berlin
1998 *Out of Actions,* MOCA, Los Angeles
Premises: Art in France, 1960 to 2000, Guggenheim Museum, New York
1999 *Das 20. Jahrhundert,* Nationalgalerie Berlin
2000 *Das Gedächtnis der Kunst,* Schirn Kunsthalle, Frankfurt

Collections:

Kunsthalle, Kiel, West Germany; Kunstmuseum, Dusseldorf; Städtisches Museum, Bonn; Centre Georges Pompidou, Paris; Bibliothéque Nationale, Paris; Kunsthaus, Zurich; Kunstmuseum, Lucerne; Museum for Contemporary Art, Livorno; Australian National Gallery, Canberra; Art Gallery of Ontario, Toronto.

Permanent Public Installations:

Monument against Fascism, Hamburg 1986; *Monument against Racism,* Saarbrucken 1993; *The Bremen Questionnaire,* Bremen 1995; *Le Monument Vivant de Biron,* Biron 1996; *Why Did It Happen?,* Berlin 1997–98; *Die Berliner Ermittlung* (with Esther Gerz), 1998; *Les Temoins,* Cahors 1998; *Kunstlers Traum: Goethe In Buchenwald,* Weimar 1999; *My Word,* 1999–2000; *Money, Love, Death, Freedom—What Counts In The End?,* Court Of Honour, Ministry Of Finance, Berlin 2000; *Les Mots de Paris,* Notre Dame de Paris 2000; *Le Vote de Barbirey,* Barbirey-sur-ouche 2000.

Publications:

By GERZ: Books—*Footing,* Paris 1968; *Replay,* Paris 1969; *Resurrection,* Brescia, Italy 1970; *Recto Verso,* Florence 1971; *Annoncenteil,* Berlin 1971; *Die Beschreibung des Papiers,* Darmstadt 1973; *Contacts,* Toronto 1974; *Die Schwierigkeit des Zentaurs beim vom Pferd Steigen,* Munich 1976; *A Danish Exorcism,* Ringkobing 1976; *Das zweite Buch (Die Zeit der Beschreibung).* Lichtenberg 1976; *Exit/Das Cachau-Projekt,* Frankfurt 1978; *The Fuji-Yama-Series,* Saarbrucken 1981; *Le Grand Amour,* Saarbrucken 1982; *Das vierte Buch (Die Zeit der Beschreibung),* Spenge 1983; *Von der Kunst/De l'art,* Dudweiler 1985; *Texte,* Bielefeld 1985. **Articles—**''The Arts in the Museum of Illiteracy'' in *Klepht,* Swansea, Wales 1970; ''Pour un langage du faire'' in *Opus International* (Paris), no. 40–41, 1972; ''Kritik an der Gesellschaftlichen Produktion auf dem Gebiet der Kultur'' in *Kunst Praxis Heute,* Cologne 1972; ''Bedingungen der Visuellen Poesie'' in *Nachrichten des Instituts fur Moderne Kunst* (Nuremberg), no. 4, 1972; ''La difficulte du centaure a descendre du cheval'' in *Monsieur*

Bloom (Paris), no. 3, 1979; ''Le Voyage'' in *Travereses* (Paris), no. 33/34, 1985; ''Objects Are Withdrawing from Me More and More'' in *Acts* (San Francisco), no. 5, 1986.

On GERZ: Books—*Neue Bucher* by Helmut Heisenbuttel, Hamburg 1971; *Jochen Gerz,* exhibition catalog, Rome 1974; *Jochen Gerz,* exhibition catalog, Kiel, West Germany 1974; *Jochen Gerz,* exhibition catalog, St. Etienne, France 1975; *Jochen Gerz: Foto/Texte und Stucke,* exhibition catalog, Braunschweig 1976; *Jochen Gerz: Biennale Venedig 76,* Venice 1976; *Jochen Gerz,* exhibition catalog, Chur, Switzerland 1978; *Jochen Gerz: Der Stein will zuruck zur Schleuder,* exhibition catalog, Graz, Austria 1978; *Jochen Gerz: Foto/Texte 1975–1978,* exhibition catalog, edited by Carl-Albrecht Haenlein, Hannover 1978; *Jochen Gerz,* exhibition catalog, Lisbon 1978; *Jochen Gerz: Kulchur Pieces 1, 2, 3,* exhibition catalog with texts by Fernando Pernes, Carl-Albrecht Haenlein and Thomas Deecke, Münster 1978; *The Depot: Kulchur Piece No. 4,* exhibition catalog, with text by R. C. Kenedy, Birmingham 1979; *Jochen Gerz: 5 Installations,* exhibition catalog, Frankfurt 1980; *Jochen Gerz, Nachbilder,* exhibition catalog, Kassel, West Germany 1980; *Jochen Gerz: Mit 1 Publikum (Performances 1968–80),* exhibition catalog, Bielefeld, West Germany 1981; *Jochen Gerz: Le Grand Amour,* exhibition catalog, Freiburg 1982; *Jochen Gerz; La Chasse/The Strip,* exhibition catalog with text by Christine Tacke, Munich 1986; *Eine Ausstellung=An Exhibition,* exhibition catalog with texts by Demosthenes Davvetas, Ulrich Krempel, and Friedmann Malsch; *Jochen Gerz,* exhibition catalog with text by Irit Rogoff, Davis, California 1992; *Jochen Gerz: Life after Humanism,* exhibition catalog, Bremen 1992; *Jochen Gerz: It Was Easy,* exhibition catalog with texts by Regine Basha and Bojana Pejic, Montreal 1993; *Les Images,* exhibition catalog, Strasbourg 1994; *People Speak,* exhibition catalog, Vancouver 1994; *The French Wall,* exhibition catalog, Nürnberg 1996; *Get Out Of My Lies,* exhibition catalog, Museum Wiesbaden, 1997; *The Berkeley Oracle, Questions Unanswered,* exhibition catalog, Karlsruhe, 1999; *Catalogue Raisonné,* 3 Volumes, edited by Verlag Moderner Kunst Nürnberg/ Museum Wiesbaden 1999–2001.

*

What does art represent for you today?

It's something fragile. If I think of art, I don't think of any particular time or place or rectangular thing. I don't even think about *making* something. Sooner or later, I think about being. So art stays in touch with its origin, being, for me. In that sense, it's fragile. It's also the most radical manifestation of the unsaid you can produce, if not actually be—and the most opposite to us. Perhaps you make what you cannot be. It's emotionally disturbing that man is capable of making art. Criticizing this possibility is the same as criticizing oneself. No detour or consolation seems possible, or even necessary.

Do you think that works of art should have some sort of usefulness in our society?

And what if they weren't *for* anything…? I like things that are useful, but isn't being *for nothing* already being good for something? Today, every single thing seems conceived and conceivable only in the function of its finality. Everything is useful, profitable, explainable. In a useful world, art is a spoon. It's through misunderstanding or ignorance that it's good *for nothing,* rather than out of some elaborate strategy of refusal. More out of indifference. Every strategy has its season. Afterwards, it has no object and becomes a kind of decoration . . .

Art shows or hides, maybe, above all, the social consensus about the gratuitous, useless games, solitude, intensity . . . it does that more than all the *ritual places:* movies, casinos, churches, stadiums. Isn't this consensus based on the fact that we were all kids once?

The gratuitous aspect of love, of all life, right to the end—what else would make these things relevant? This gratuitous thing is a real provocation in a civilization that is separated into users and tools.

—Jochen Gerz (from an interview with Patrick Le Nouëne)

* * *

Suppression of pictures is one of Jochen Gerz's main categories of creation. In addition, there is also suppression of writing. Pictures, as they emerge, are concealed, painted over with brown paint remover, brushed over or produced in such an indistinct and washed-out manner that they necessarily remain irrecognizable. He writes with the left hand or in mirror script so that the text is illegible, or rather it is composed in such a way that the words with which something is described merely revolve round the subject or the event, approach it cautiously as if it were about to disappear or were only a vague memory. Whether in pictures or in words, Jochen Gerz manages to hold fast to nothing, to establish nothing, which in any case and by definition would not be a reality, a life lived, but a recapitulation of it.

To imprison, photograph or manufacture pictures is like a hunt for life which kills life. In his opinion all art is reproduction, duplication, a tombstone, the beginning of disintegration; unless, and that seems to Gerz to be the only way out. Its means of expression were fundamentally to contradict its original function. The best texts are, therefore, those that neutralize themselves through the indifference of their language, the best pictures those that suppress themselves, as Gerz made clear in an exhibition in Saint-Étienne in 1975. He showed canvases without pictures, with the paradoxical challenge to the spectator: ''Don't look at me,'' ''Don't remember me.'' As in this case, Jochen Gerz uses an essential part of his work to expose a genuine negative dialectic of art. Pictures appear as seducers which do not lead to reality but turn away from it until we are incapable of recognizing it at all. Instead of this, art should serve to refer the viewer to himself and his times, to the here and now of his life. Pictures as well as words have this effect of course only when they deny themselves. The main point is rather to discover fresh possibilities, to avoid altogether the conventional forms of expression and to uncover new artistic languages, which Gerz has attempted by performances, by the use of video and by his installations. An art which does not want to betray life should take place in a zone between reality and reproduction, in a fluctuating zone which functions beyond all permanently fixed forms. Languages have to be discovered which would not or could not be adopted by the culture industry and which will be used outside of the mass media. All communication today seems perverted into a mere barter system for contemporary myths and phantasms, and, in order to escape this system, Gerz invents languages which will not be spoken in it. He prefers to use his body and his gestures, and the space which surrounds him, his voice, physical exertion, even pain and exhaustion.

By all these means he tries to turn the viewer away from the beautiful illusion, from the aura of the work of art, and to bring him to himself. Whenever Gerz gathers the themes of his actions from Greek myths or even from the new myths which are closer to us and more dreadful in memory, as perhaps the ''Concentration Camp,'' he does so to strike at the fundamental conditionally of art. In all these actions and intallations it becomes clear: art exists only on condition that it bows to its own negation. In this way Gerz follows the tradition of language criticism which was characterized in Germany by Wittgenstein and Karl Kraus, but which, after the Second World War, Theodor Adorno enchanced and enlarged into a new universal examination of the present culture industry.

Initially there is in Jochen Gerz a declaration of mistrust in relation to the use of language and pictures which is equally complaisant to all political and ideological aims, the suspicion of ideas and signs which had served Fascism and continued to be used without reflection. What he, who is likewise obliged to use pictures and signs, is able to propose in opposition is either negation or destruction or artful evasion. Gerz has made use of all possibilities in his works. He has decomposed and disowned pictures and texts, has himself renounced and replaced them. In renouncing a picture and in its place making actions, spaces, art with the body and the public, it can result that something of the present time prior to suffocation and something of the world prior to the final violence will be preserved through culture.

—Marie Luise Syring

GIBSON, Ralph

Nationality: American. **Born:** Los Angeles, California, 16 January 1939. **Education:** Studied photography in the U.S. Navy, 1956–60; San Francisco Art Institute, San Francisco, California, 1960–62. **Career:** Worked as assistant to photographers Dorothea Lange (1961–62) and Robert Frank (1967–68). **Awards:** National Endowment for the Arts Fellowship, 1973, 1975, 1986; New York State Council of the Arts Fellowship, 1977; D.A.A.D., West Berlin, Germany, 1977; John Simon Guggenheim Memorial Fellowship, 1985; Decorated, Officier de l'Ordre des Arts et des Lettres de France, 1986; Leica Medal of Excellence Award, 1988; ''150 Years of Photography'' Award, Photographic Society of Japan, 1989; Eastman Kodak Grant for photography, 1989; Honorary Doctor of Fine Arts, University of Maryland, College Park, Maryland, 1991; Grand Medal of the City of Arles, France, 1994; Doctor of Fine Arts, Ohio Wesleyan University, Delaware, Ohio, 1997. **Web site:** http://www.ralphgibson.com.

Selected Individual Exhibitions:

1975 Hoesch Museum, Duren, West Germany
Galerie Agathe Gaillard, Paris, France
1976 Baltimore Museum of Art, Maryland
Focus Gallery, San Francisco, California
Light Impressions, Rochester, New York
1977 Fotografiska Museet, Stockholm, Sweden (catalog)
Museum of Modern Art, Oxford, England
1978 Robert Self Gallery, London, England
Camera Obscura, Stockholm, Sweden
1979 ICAF Museum of Art, Richmond, Virginia
1980 Kunstmuseum, Düsseldorf, West Germany
1981 Sprengel Museum, Hannover, West Germany
Museum Folkwang, Essen, West Germany
1982 Centre Georges Pompidou, Paris, France
Castelli Graphics, New York
Olympus Gallery, London, England
1983 Seattle Art Museum, Seattle, Washington
1984 Weston Gallery, Carmel, California
1985 Leo Castelli Gallery, New York
1986 Musée Carnavalet, Paris, France
1987 Leo Castelli Gallery, New York
International Center of Photography, New York
1988 The Photographer's Gallery, London, England
Bibliotheque Nationale, Paris, France
1989 The Arts Club of Chicago, Illinois
Moderno Museet, Fotografiska Museet, Stockholm, Sweden
1990 *Quatrieme Triennale Internationale de la Photographie,* Musee de la Photographie, Charleroi, Belgium
Musee Nicephone Niefice, Chalon Sur Soane, France
Drew University Art Gallery, Madison, New Jersey
1991 Castelli Graphics, New York
Oklahoma City Art Museum, Oklahoma City, Oklahoma
Princessehof Museum, Leuwardern, Netherlands
1992 Galerie Antoine Candau, Paris, France
Pictures of Peace, Louise Jones Brown Gallery, Duke University, North Carolina
1993 *L'Aire de Bourgogne,* Espace des Arts, Chalon sur Saone, France (catalog)
Women, Boca Museum of Art, Boca Raton, Florida (catalog)
Landscapes, Light Impressions, Rochester, New York (catalog)
1994 Butler Institute of American Art, Youngstown, Ohio
25eme Anniversaire, Les Rencontres d'Arles, Arles, France
Art Jonction, Leo Castelli, Cannes, France
1995 Tampa Museum of Art, Florida
Cantor Art Gallery, College of the Holy Cross, Worcester, Massachusetts
1996 Whitney Museum of American Art, New York
Leo Castelli Gallery, New York
1997 High Museum of Art, Atlanta, Georgia
1998 Museum für Moderne Kunst, Frankfurt, Germany
Tower Gallery, Yokohama, Japan
Greenville County Museum of Art, Greenville, South Carolina
1999 Maison Européenne de la Photographie, Paris, France
High Museum of Art, Atlanta, Georgia
Howard Greenberg Gallery, New York
2000 Kereva Art Museum, Kereva, Finland
Galerie Lucie Weil Seligman, Paris, France
Through a Glass Darkly: Ralph Gibson, A Retrospective, Michael Hoppen Gallery, London, England

Selected Group Exhibitions:

1967 *12 Photographers: The American Social Landscape,* Poses Institute of Fine Arts, Brandeis University, Waltham, Massachusetts
1972 *5 Photographers,* Portland Museum of Art, Portland, Maine
1974 *New Images in Photography,* Lowe Art Museum, Miami, Florida
1975 *4eme Rencontres International,* Arles, France

Photography for Collectors, Museum of Modern Art, New York
1977 *Rooms,* Museum of Modern Art, New York
Contemporary American Photography, Target Collection, Museum of Fine Art, Houston, Texas
1978 *40 American Photographers,* E.B. Crocker Gallery, Sacramento, California
American Photographers, Museum des 20, Vienna, Austria
The Great American Foot, American Crafts Museum, New York
1979 *Mirrors and Windows,* Cleveland Art Museum, Cleveland, Ohio; travelled to Walker Art Center, Minneapolis, Minnesota; J.B. Speed Museum of Art, Louisville, Kentucky; Museum of Modern Art, San Francisco; University of Illinois, Champaign; Museum of Fine Arts, Richmond, Virginia
1980 *Old and Modern Masters of Photography,* Victoria and Albert Museum, London, England
1981 *Self-Portraits,* Centre Georges Pompidou, Paris, France
1982 *20th Century Photographs from the Museum of Modern Art,* Seibu Museum, Tokyo, Japan
Counterparts: Form and Emotion in Photography, Metropolitan Museum of Art, New York
1983 *Particulars,* Philadelphia Museum of Art, Philadelphia, Pennsylvania
1984 *Acquisitions Recents,* Museum of Modern Art, Paris, France
1985 *American Images: Photography 1945–1980,* Barbican Art Gallery, London, England
Signs of the Times, San Francisco Museum of Modern Art, San Francisco, California
1986 *Views and Visions: Work from the Permanent Collection,* International Center of Photography, New York
Recent Acquisitions, Corcoran Gallery, Washington, D.C.
1987 *Contemporary American Figurative Photography,* Center for the Fine Arts, Miami, Florida
Photography and Art: Interactions Since 1946, Los Angeles County Museum of Art, Los Angeles, California
1988 *Photographic Memories,* The Ludwig Museum, Cologne, Germany
Legacy of Light, National Portrait Gallery, Washington, D.C.
Splendeurs et Miseres du Corps: Triennale Internationale de la Photographie, Friebourg, Germany, and Musee de l'Art Moderne, Paris, France
1989 *Landscape Photographs from the Permanent Collection,* Corcoran Gallery, Washington, D.C.
Center for Creative Photography, Tucson, Arizona
1990 *The Indomitable Spirit,* International Center of Photography Midtown, New York, and Los Angeles Municipal Art Gallery, Los Angeles, California
Focus: Photographs from the Collection of Helen Johnson, De Saisset Museum, Santa Clara, California
Expo '90, Osaka Museum, Osaka, Japan
1991 Museum of Modern Art, Rio de Janeiro, Brazil
Museum of Modern Art, Buenos Aires, Argentina
1992 *About Face: Portraits from the Permanent Collection,* International Center of Photography Midtown, New York
Decouvertes 1992, Grand Palais, Paris, France
Works from the Permanent Collection, Seattle Art Museum, Seattle, Washington
1993 *LaForet Museum,* Harajuku, Tokyo, Japan
Against AIDS, Festival du Cinema, Cannes, France
Photographers Who Created a New Age, Tokyo Metropolitan Museum of Photography, Tokyo, Japan
1994 *Dialogues with Photography: The Mexican Collection,* The Henry Art Gallery, University of Washington, Seattle, Washington
New Acquisitions/New York/New Directions 2: Photography from the Collection, Los Angeles County Museum of Art, Los Angeles, California
Four Friends, Oklahoma City Art Museum, Oklahoma City, Oklahoma
1995 *100 Yahre-100 Bidler,* Frankfurter Kunstverein, Frankfurt, Germany
Art Institute of Chicago, Chicago, Illinois
Photographies en Fetes, Galerie Suzel Berna, Paris, France
1996 Weston Gallery, Carmel, California
1997 *Collection in Context: Selected Photographs from the Buhl Collection,* Parrish Art Museum, Southampton, New York, and Ohio Wesleyan University, Delaware, Ohio
Autoportrait: The Calligraphy of Power, Exit Art, New York
The Body in the Lens, Musee des Beaux-Arts de Montreal, Montreal, Canada
Masterpieces from the Collection, Ho-Am Art Museum, Seoul, Korea
1998 *The Desiring Eye,* Moderna Museet, Stockholm, Sweden (catalog)
Before the Lens: Images of the Imagemakers, Charles Schwartz Collection,New Hampshire Institute of Art (catalog)
Faces: Photographic Portraits from the Collection, Columbus Museum of Art, Columbus, Ohio
Edifice, Denver Art Museum, Denver, Colorado

Collections:

Museum of Modern Art, New York; Metropolitan Museum of Art, New York; Whitney Museum of American Art, New York; John Simon Guggenheim Memorial Foundation, New York; National Gallery of Art, Washington, D.C.; Dallas Museum of Art, Dallas, Texas; High Museum of Art, Atlanta, Georgia; San Francisco Museum of Modern Art, California; Fogg Museum, Boston, Massachusetts; Bibliotheque Nationale, Paris, France; and many other museums.

Publications:

By GIBSON: Books—*A.C.L.U. Agenda,* Los Angeles, California, 1966; *The Strip,* Los Angeles, California, 1967; *The Hawk,* New York, 1968; *The Somnambulist,* New York, 1970; *Deja Vu,* New York, 1973; *Days at Sea,* New York, 1975; interview in *Photography Between Covers by Thomas Dugan,* Rochester, New York, 1979; *Syntax,* New York, 1983; *L'Anonyme,* New York and Paris, 1986; *Tropism,* New York and Paris, 1987; *Les cahiers de la photographie,* no. 22, Paris, 1988; *In Situ,* Paris, 1988; *Archive 24: Ralph Gibson,*

Early Work, Tucson, Arizona, 1988; *Apropos de Mary Jane,* Paris, France, 1990; *Chiaroscuro,* Paris, France, 1990; *L'Histoire de France,* New York and Paris, 1991; *Bookworks: Four Projects,* Paris, France, 1992; *Women,* Boca Raton, Florida, 1993; *Tropical Drift,* New York, 1994; *L'Aire de Bourgogne,* Paris, France, 1994; *Pharonic Light,* Southampton, New York, 1995; *Infanta,* New York and Tokyo, 1995; *Licht Jahre,* Zurich, Switzerland, 1996; *Eric Fischl: Sculpture,* New York, 1998; *Overtones,* Zurich, Switzerland, 1998; *Courant continue,* Paris, France, 1999; *Deus ex Machina,* Cologne, Germany, 1999; *Ex Libris,* New York, 2001. **Articles**—''A Statement on the Photographic Print Market'' in *Print Letter* (Zurich, Switzerland), September/October 1979; ''Interview with Ralph Gibson'' in *Camera International* (Paris), November 1984.

On GIBSON: Books—*Counterparts: Form and Emotion in Photographs* by Weston Naef, New York, 1982; *An American Century of Photography: From Dryplate to Digital* by Keith F. Davis, Kansas City, Missouri, 1999. **Articles**—''Ralph Gibson: The Somnambulist'' in *Creative Camera* (London), November 1971; ''Ralph Gibson'' in *Photography Annual 1992* (New York); ''Ralph Gibson: Deja-Vu'' by A.D. Coleman in *The New York Times* (New York), 25 February 1973, reprinted in *Coleman's Light Readings: A Photography Critic's Writings 1968–1978,* New York, 1979; ''Ralph Gibson: Pictures from Deja Vu'' by H.M. Kinzer in *35mm Photography* (New York), Spring 1973; ''Ralph Gibson'' in *Photo* (Paris), September 1973; ''Ralph Gibson'' in *Modern Photography Annual* (New York), 1973; ''Ralph Gibson: The Future Returns'' in *US Camera/Camera 35 Annual* (New York), 1973; ''Ralph Gibson'' by Douglas Davis in *Newsweek* (New York), 18 November 1974; ''Ralph Gibson'' in *British Journal of Photography* (London), 20 December 1974; ''Ralph Gibson'' by William Wilson in *Los Angeles Times* (Los Angeles, California), 13 June 1975; ''Ralph Gibson: How He Creates His Fractional Images'' in *Popular Photography* (New York), April 1977; ''An Imaginary Interview with Ralph Gibson'' in *Camera* (Lucerne, Switzerland), April 1979; ''Ralph Gibson's Early Work'' by Cynthia Gano Lewis in *Center for Creative Photography* (Tucson, Arizona), October 1979; ''Formalism Stretched to Vacuity'' by Hal Fischer in *Artweek* (Oakland, California), 12 January 1980; ''Tropism and Sophism'' in *British Journal of Photography* (London), 14 April 1988; ''Ralph Gibson'' in *Art News* (New York), November 1996.

* * *

Ralph Gibson was born in Los Angeles in 1939, and now resides in New York. He studied photography while he was in the U.S. Navy from 1956–1960, and then at the San Francisco Art Institute. While in San Francisco, Gibson worked as an assistant to Dorothea Lange before moving to Los Angeles to work as a freelance photographer. In 1966, Gibson moved to New York where he worked for Robert Frank. Gibson's experience with Frank, especially their collaboration on Frank's films, was crucial to Gibson's development as a photographer.

Frank's seminal book, *The Americans,* greatly influenced Gibson's work, as it did the work of many other young photographers when it was published in 1959. Gibson himself produced several photographic book projects, beginning in 1966. In 1969, Gibson founded Lustrum Press and published several books, including the trilogy of *The Somnambulist, Deja-Vu,* and *Days at Sea,* that brought his work into the spotlight. Perhaps the best known of these is *The Somnambulist,* a group of obscured images that evoke a sense of mystery and appear in a dream-like sequence. The placement of the photographs in relation to each other often contributes an additional layer of meaning in Gibson's books, evoking an idiosyncratic narrative.

Establishing his own press allowed Gibson complete control over the entire creation of each book. In addition to Gibson's own work, Lustrum Press published books by other photographers, including Larry Clark, Mary Ellen Mark, and Robert Frank, until it ceased operating in the mid-1980s.

During the course of his long career, Gibson has published more than twenty volumes. The most recent of these is *Ex Libris* (2001), a publication featuring images of books and starting off with the principle that ''libraries are as sacred as churches.'' The photographs in *Ex Libris* are representative of Gibson's work overall: they are simple, pared down images that show objects from a close range and use shadow and light deftly. For the most part, the text within the books is not legible, but is reduced to its formal elements of line and shape.

One of Gibson's frequent subjects over the course of his career has been New York City. In these images, Gibson has managed to pare away much of the visual noise of the city. He has often equated photography and archaeology, describing his working process as one that strips away the layers that obscure the true essence of an object. Many of Gibson's images of the city show its inhabitants obliquely; rather than photograph people head-on, Gibson often focuses on a particular part of their bodies, often not showing the face at all. While most of the city images, like the majority of Gibson's work overall, demonstrate his masterful use of black and white photography, Gibson has also photographed the city in color.

In addition to his books, Gibson has shown his photographs in countless exhibitions over the course of his career, from 1962 to the present. His images are also included in the permanent collections of many national and international museums.

—Tara Reddy Young

GILARDI, Piero

Nationality: Italian and Swiss. **Born:** 8 August 1942. **Education:** Liceo Artistico di Torino, 1952–58. **Career:** Performance, environmental, and electronic artist; sculptor. **Address:** Cso. Casale 121, 10132 Turin, Italy.

Individual Exhibitions:

1963	Galleria L'Immagine, Turin
1966	Galleria Sperone, Turin
1967	Galerie Sonnabend, Paris
	Piper Club, Turin
	Galerie Aujourd'hui, Brussels
	Galleria Sperone, Milan
	Galerie Neuendorf, Hamburg
	Galerie Zwirner, Cologne
	Galleria del Leone, Venice
	Fishbach Gallery, New York
	Galerie Michery, Amsterdam
	Galleria la Nuova Loggia, Bologna
1975	Galleria la Nuova Citta, Brescia
1976	Galleria la Nuova Citta, Verona
1977	Galleria Plura, Bologna

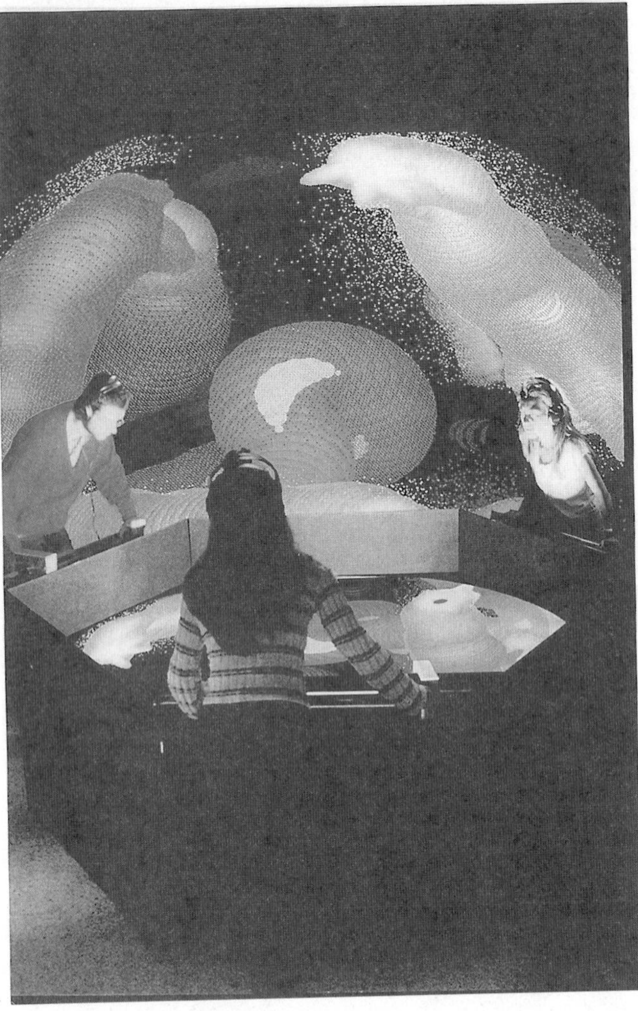

Piero Gilardo (cooperated by Ennio Bertrand): *Connected ES,* Bionic Interface Installation, 1998. ©Piero Gilardo.

1979 Galleria Serre Ratti, Como
1980 Galleria Persano, Turin
1981 Galleria Persano, Turin
1982 Galleria Persano, Turin
1984 Galleria Toselli, Milan (retrospective)
1985 Palazzo dei Diamanti, Ferrara
Palazzo Massari, Ferrara
1986 Galleria Seno, Milan
Galeria Pio Monti, Rome
1987 Galleria dei Banchi Nuovi, Rome
Galerie Lucien Bilinelli, Brussels
Galleria Eva Menzio, Turin
1988 Galleria Lara Vincy, Paris
1989 Galleria Toselli, Milan
Studio Marconi, Milan
Percorso della Scultura, Comune di Milano
Musée d'Art Decoratif, Paris
1990 Salone Villa Romana, Florence
Galleria Santo Ficara, Florence
Galleria Il Campo, Rome
1991 Galerie Di Meo, Paris
Sperone-Westwater Gallery, New York
Studio d'Arte Raffaelli, Trento
1993 Studio Duomo, Terni
Studio Spaggiari, Milan
1994 Galerie Di Meo, Paris
Galleria Ficara, Florence
Galerie Le Chanjour, Nice
1995 Stefano Fumagalli Gallery, Bergamo
1996 Galleria Ficara, Firenze
1997 Galleria ''Altri lavori in corso,'' Rome
Calleria B & D, Milan
1998 Galleria M. Minini, Brescia
1999 Retrospective, Loggetta Lombardesca, Comune di Ravenna
2000 Galleria Guastalla, Livorno

Selected Group Exhibitions:

1967 *Arte Povera,* Trieste
1968 Walker Art Center, Minneapolis
1981 *Registrazione di frequenze,* Galleria Communale d'Arte Moderna, Bologna
1985 *Il museo sperimentale della Galleria d'Arte Moderna di Torino,* Castello du Rivoli, Turin
1988 *East Meets West,* Los Angeles Convention Center
1989 *Aspetti dell'arte povera,* Galerie Willy D'Huysser, Knokke, Belgium
1991 *Landscape As Stage,* Locks Gallery, Philadelphia
1992 *Artifice,* St. Denis, Paris
1993 *Artec 93, Biennale,* Nagoya, Japan
Biennale, Venice
1995 *Multimediale 4,* ZKM, Karlsruhe
La grande scala, Galleria Civica d'Arte Moderna, Bergamo
Oltre il Villagio Globale, Triennale, Milan
1996 *Cybernauti 3,* Futurshow, Bologna
Espaces Interactifs—Europe, Pavillon de Bercy, Paris
Art at Home, Copenhagen
1997 *Arte italiana: Materiali anomali,* Galleria d'Arte Moderna, Bologna
Segnali d'opera: Arte e digitale in Italia, Civica Galleria Città di Gallarate
1998 *Mediamorfosi,* Corte San Donato, Pisa
1999 *XIII Esposizione Nazional Quadriennale d'Arte di Roma,* Palazzo delle Esposizioni, Rome
Techne: Tra arte e tecnologia, Spazio Oberdan, Milan
Il sentimento del 2000: Dalla vita all'arte, dall'arte alla vita, Triennale di Milan
2000 *There Is No Spirit in Painting,* Le Consortium, Dijon

Collections:

Moderna Museet, Stockholm; Museo Sperimentale di Cagliari; Fondazione Giorgio Morandi, Bologna; Galleria Comunale d'Arte Moderna, Milan; Galleria Civica d'Arte Moderna, Turin; Galleria Civica d'Arte Moderna, Milan; Museo Rufino Tamayo, Mexico City; Museum of Modern Art, New York; Museum HedenDaagse, Ghent, Belgium; Museo Rufino Tamayo, Mexico City; Museum Hedendaagse, Ghent; Museum fur Gegenwartskunts, Karlsruhe; Cité des Sciences et de l'Industrie, Paris; Galerie d'Art Moderne, Dunkirk.

Publications:

By GILARDI: Books—*Dall'arte alla vita, dalla vita all'arte,* Paris and Milan, 1981; *Not for Sale,* Milan, 2000. **Articles**—"Primary Energy and Microemotive Artists" in *Arts Magazine,* no. 43, 1968; "Nicaragua 1983" in *Flash Art,* no. 111, 1983; "Il filo dell rappresentazione" in *Alfabeta,* October 1984; "Arte e impregno" in *Flash Art,* no. 141, 1987.

On GILARDI: Books—*Piero Gilardi,* exhibition catalog by Galleria Sperone, Turin 1966; *Attraverso l'Arte* by L. Vergine, Milan 1972; *Il principo d'anarchia* by Pierre Restany, Ferrara 1985; *Piero Gilardi* by Achille Bonita Oliva, Rome 1987; *Alfabeto Urbano* by Pierre Restany, Paris 1988; *Le project Ixiana de Piero Gilardo* by Pierre Restany, Paris 1989. **Articles**—"Piero Gilardi" by E. Sottsass in *Domus,* no. 445, 1966; "Piero Gilardi" by R. C. Kennedy in *Art International,* February 1967; "Arte povera, appunti per una guerriglia" by G. Celant in *Flash Art,* November 1967; "Piero Gilardi" by Loredana Parmesani in *Flash Art,* March 1985; "Piero Gilardi" by A. Iannacci in *Artforum,* summer 1989.

* * *

The present anthropological mutation—induced by immaterial production and communication technologies—places us in front of a crossroads between a totalitarian-like society, in which technological communication patterns turn individuals into a complete homogenized capitalistic economic and production system, and a wholly communicable heterogeneous community, where individuals unceasingly and autonomously recreate the meaning of life.

Art is, therefore, the place where variety and abundance of human interactions allow the development of the necessary awareness to control the appropriation of "meaningful" technologies, the crossing over of identity logic, and the acquisition of a "common peculiarity" within a new cooperative community.

Piero Gilardi's principal aim is to reconcile apparently irreconcilable terms like 'nature' and 'technique' (or 'ecology' and 'technology'). This concern was already visible at the beginning of the 1960s in a first sculptural phase in which he produced what he calls his *Tappeti-natura.* The 'natural carpet' is seen as a rectangular block of polyurethane covered by a rubbery crust that was cut out in a forest, a river bed or a pebble beach. In short, a piece more real than nature but not 'realistic'. This means an ecological awareness before its time that took the form of humour, fiction and, especially, artistic creation. A little later he would extend his 'natural carpets' to environmental dimensions directly in the landscape.

This phase of countryside creations, comparable to *Land Art,* was followed by a phase entirely devoted to the theoretical analysis of the period's other new tendencies: *Arte povera* and *Antiform,* as well as aesthetic-political events in Third World countries.

It was around 1985 that Gilardi was to resume his plastic activities as such after an excursion into therapeutic art in different Italian psychiatric hospitals. He introduced advanced technology in his procedure for the working out of a technological megasculpture project entitled *Ixiana,* which was to take the form of a gigantic 'bionic doll' on the inside of which visitors would be able to exercise their creativity on interactive equipment involving the use of the body and the senses. The project was never carried out because of its costs, but Gilardi continued his work in the same direction, especially with the 'installation' called *Inverosimile (Unlikely)* in which the spectator can circulate between three rows of artificial vines that react to his movements.

The dramatic, allegoric and ecological intentions of Gilardi can be gathered from the fact that, throughout the performance of *Inverosimile,* the audience becomes in a certain way co-author of an electronic choreography. This comes about by means of an interactive programme which converts the spectator's gestures into a series of sounds, lights and movements of the vines. The choreography thus provoked lends meaning to the undercurrent of sounds which flow on until the final "dance" of the vines. These sounds are reinforced by a series of projected images which allow the free development of a psychodramatic group experience: from dread of night at the beginning (moon) to a day-time action (sun) which transcends the conflict (fire), a rebirth into the world (water) is achieved and hence a new sense of kinship with mankind is born. Making simulation an active principle in this work, Gilardi composes events that bear the trace of a manipulation: that of artificial intelligence, while reminding us of the refinement with which baroque theater organized a world dominated by the seeing eye, precipitated into the vertigo of metamorphoses.

In his interactive installation *North versus South* (1992), Gilardi developed the principle of transformation, simulation and interactivity still further, but this time with an added political flavour. *North versus South* is essentially a symbolic system simulating the possible developments of the general imbalance, as regards political and military control, the technolological monopoly and cultural hegemony, between Northern countries and those situated in the South. In order to become familiar with this installation, the public has to climb onto a spherical platform in constant rotation symbolizing the world. There the visitor can identify six different zones of audition which he can utilize in the manner of radio sets and which illustrate the possible evolution and involution of the different problems raised in this context.

In a still more recent project entitled *Survival* (started in 1994), Pietro Gilardi wants, with the aid of a game environment in which the psychophysical subjectivity of the individual interacts with a computer programme which simulates the construction of a simultaneously evolving urban living quarter, test the possibilities of making future cities not only the site of conflicts or a resonance box of geopolitical inequalities, but also the site for satisfying the inhabitants' various intellectual and affective ambitions and desires while at the same time liberating them from their narrow dependence on economic contingencies.

Like other artists of this tendency interested in techno-ecology in its widest sense, Piero Gilardi highlights the irreplacable qualities of our environment by using the natural forces as a model for our urban life and adds to it the sophistication of the most advanced technologies in order to bring out the strength of artistic expression in a contemporary context. Whether a matter of simulation or a recreation of the natural elements, of a combination between natural and artificial factors, we are always in the presence of an attempt to reconcile two apparently contradictory terms: scientific or technological progress against biological and spiritual survival for mankind.

—Frank Popper

GILBERT and GEORGE

Nationality: British. Gilbert: **Born:** Gilbert Proesch, in San Martino, the Dolomites, Italy, in 1943. **Education:** Studied at the Wolkenstein

Gilbert and George: *England,* 1980. ©Tate Gallery, London/Art Resource, NY; courtesy of Tate Gallery.

School of Art, and Hallein School of Art, Austria, and the Akademie der Kunst, Munich. George: **Born:** George Passmore, in Plymouth, Devon, England, in 1942. **Education:** Darlington Adult Education Centre, Devon; Darlington Hall College of Art; and Oxford School of Art. **Career:** Met while they were students at the St. Martin's School of Art, London, and have lived and worked together in London since 1968. **Awards:** Turner Prize, Tate Gallery, London, 1986. **Agents:** Anthony d'Offay, London; Sonnabend Gallery, New York; Art and Project, Amsterdam; and Konrad Fischer Galerie, Dusseldorf. **Address:** Art for All, 12 Fournier Street, London El, England.

Individual Exhibitions:

1968 Frank's Sandwich Bar, London
St. Martin's School of Art, London
Allied Services Bacon Factory, London
1969 Frank's Sandwich Bar, London
Geffrye Museum, London
Royal College of Art, London
Slade School of Fine Art, London
Ripley, Bromley, Kent (with David Hockney)
Studio International Office, London
National Jazz and Blues Festival, Plumpton, Sussex
Institute of Contemporary Arts, London
Stedelijk Museum, Amsterdam
1970 Fournier Street, London
Art and Project, Amsterdam
Konrad Fischer Galerie, Dusseldorf
Museum of Modern Art, Oxford
Kunsthalle, Dusseldorf
Kunstverein, Hannover
Museo d'Arte Moderna, Turin
Kunstverein, Krefeld, Germany
1971 Galleria Sperone, Turin
Sonnabend Gallery, New York
Whitechapel Art Gallery, London
Stedelijk Museum, Amsterdam
Kunstverein, Dusseldorf
1972 Museum voor Schone Kunsten, Antwerp
Oh the Grand Old Duke of York, Kunstmuseum, Lucerne
Galleria L'Attico, Rome
Konrad Fischer Galerie, Dusseldorf
Gerry Schum Video Galerie, Dusseldorf
1973 Sonnabend Galerie, Paris
Galleria Sperone, Turin
National Gallery of New South Wales, Sydney (travelled to the National Gallery of Victoria, Melbourne)
1974 Konrad Fischer Galerie, Dusseldorf
Art and Project/MTL Galerie, Antwerp
1975 Sonnabend Galerie, Paris
Sonnabend Galerie, Geneva
Lucio Amelio Galleria, Naples
Art Agency, Tokyo
1976 Sonnabend Gallery, New York
Albright-Knox Art Gallery, Buffalo, New York
Konrad Fischer Galerie, Dusseldorf
Robert Self Gallery, London
1977 Art and Project, Amsterdam
Konrad Fischer Galerie, Dusseldorf
Galleria Sperone, Rome
Art Fair, Sperone/Fischer, Basel
Stedelijk Museum, Amsterdam
1978 Darlington Hall Gallery, Devon
Sonnabend Gallery, New York
Art Agency, Tokyo
1980 Art and Project, Amsterdam
Konrad Fischer Galerie, Dusseldorf
Sonnabend Gallery, New York
Gilbert and George 1968–1980, Stedelijk van Abbemuseum, Eindhoven, Netherlands (travelled to the Kunsthalle, Dusseldorf; Kunsthalle, Berne; Centre Georges Pompidou, Paris; and the Whitechapel Gallery, London, 1980–81)
1981 Galerie Chantal Crousel, Paris
1982 Anthony d'Offay Gallery, London
Galerie Gewad, Ghent, Belgium
1983 Sonnabend Gallery, New York
David Bellman Gallery, Toronto
Crousel-Hussenot Galerie, Paris
1984 Baltimore Museum of Art, Maryland
Contemporary Arts Museum, Houston
Norton Gallery of Art, West Palm Beach, Florida
Anthony d'Offay Gallery, London
Galerie Schellmann und Kluser, Munich
Galleria Pieroni, Rome
1985 Milwaukee Art Museum, Wisconsin
Guggenheim Museum, New York
Sonnabend Gallery, New York
1986 CAPC Musee d'Art Contemporain, Bordeaux, France
Fruit Market Gallery, Edinburgh
Kunsthalle, Basel
1987 Palais de Beaux-Arts, Brussels

Gilbert and George, ca. 1970–97. ©John Garrett/Corbis.

Palacio Velazquez, Madrid
Stadtisches Museum im Lenbachhaus, Munich
Hayward Gallery, London
Anthony d'Offay Gallery, London
Sonnabend Gallery, New York

1989 *Gilbert and George for AIDS,* Anthony d'Offay, London (catalog)

1990 *11 Worlds by Gilbert and George and Antique Clocks,* Feuerle, Cologne (catalog)
Gilbert and George: Post-Card Sculptures and Ephemera, 1962–1981, Hirschl and Adler Modern, New York (catalog)

1991 *Gilbert & George: The Cosmological Pictures,* Palac Sztuki, Cracow, Poland (catalog)

1992 *Gilbert & George: New Democratic Pictures,* Kunstmuseum, Aarhus, Denmark (catalog)

1993 *Gilbert & George: China Exposition 1993,* National Art Gallery, Beijing (traveled to Art Museum, Shanghai) (catalog)

1995 *Gilbert & George: The Naked Shit Pictures,* South London Art Gallery, London (catalog)

1996 *Gilbert & George,* Galleria d'Art Moderna, Bologna (catalog)

1997 Musée d'Art Moderne de la Ville de Paris (30-year retrospective) (catalog)

1999 *Gilbert & George: The Rudimentary Pictures 1998,* Milton Keynes Gallery, England (traveled to Gagosian Gallery, Los Angeles) (catalog)

Selected Group Exhibitions:

1969 *Conception,* Stadtisches Museum, Leverkusen, West Germany

1970 *Information* Museum of Modern Art, New York

1972 *The New Art,* Hayward Gallery, London

1973 *From Henry Moore to Gilbert and George,* Palais des Beaux-Arts, Brussels

1976 *Arte Inglese Oggi,* Palazzo Reale, Milan

1979 *Un Certain Art Anglais,* Musee d'Art Moderne de la Ville, Paris

1981 *British Sculpture in the Twentieth Century,* Whitechapel Art Gallery, London

1983 *Photography in Contemporary Art,* National Museum of Modern Art, Tokyo

1985 Biennale de Paris, Grande Halle de La Villette, Paris

1987 *British Art in the Twentieth Century,* Royal Academy of Art, London

1989 *British Sculpture 1960–1988,* Museum voor Hedendaagse Kunst, Antwerp, Belgium (catalog)
The Nightingale's Lesson, Kunstlerhaus, Stuttgart (catalog)

1990 *Donation by Karin and Jules Schyl, 1900,* Konsthall, Malmo, Sweden (catalog)
Twenty-five Worlds by Gilbert and George, Robert Miller Gallery, New York (catalog)
Blue: Colour of Distance, Heidelberger Kunstverein, Germany (catalog)
Musee d'Art Contemporain, Bordeaux, France (catalog)
1992 *For the Future of the World: Notebook—Statements and Works,* Musee d'Art Contemporain, Montreal (catalog)
The Portrait in Contemporary Art, 1945–92, Musee d'Art Moderne et d'Art Contemporain, Nice (catalog)
1994 *Sculpture,* Anthony d'Offay, London (catalog)
1995 *Femininmasculin: The Sex of Art,* Centre National d'Art et de Culture Georges Pompidou, Paris (catalog)
Take Me (I'm Yours), Serpentine Gallery, London (catalog)
Minky Manky, South London Art Gallery, London (catalog)
1996 *The Art of the Body: The Body Exposed from Man Ray to Today,* MAC, Galeries Contemporaines des Musees de Marseille, France (catalog)
1998 *Art Treasures of England: The Regional Collections,* Royal Academy of Arts, London (catalog)
1999 *Wall Works: Site-Specific Wall Installations,* Paula Cooper Gallery, New York (catalog)

Collections:

Stedelijk Museum, Amsterdam; Arts Council of Great Britain, London; Kunstmuseum, Lucerne; Guggenheim Museum, New York.

Publications:

By GILBERT and GEORGE: Books—*Side by Side,* London 1971; *The Paintings (with Us in Nature) of Gilbert and George: The Human Sculptors,* Amsterdam 1971; *Dark Shadow,* London 1974; *Gilbert & George: The Singing Sculpture,* with introduction by Robert Rosenblum, London 1993; *The Words of Gilbert & George,* edited by Hans-Ulrich Obrist and Robert Violette, London 1997. **Articles**—''A Magazine Sculpture'' in *Studio International,* May 1970; ''Underneath the Arches'' in *Interfunktionen,* no 4, 1970: ''A Day in the Life of Gilbert and George'' in *Flash Art,* May 1972; ''Gilbert and George,'' interview with Anne Seymour in *The New Art,* exhibition catalog, London 1972; interview with Nicky Bird in *Arts Review,* vol. 41, no. 8, 21 April 1989; interview with Andrew Wilson in *Art Monthly,* no. 135, April 1990; interview with Andrew Wilson in *Journal of Contemporary Art,* vol. 6, no. 2, Winter 1993; interview with Catherine Mayer in *Tate: The Art Magazine,* no. 5, Spring 1995; interview with Martin Gayford in *Modern Painters* (London), vol. 8, no. 4, Winter 1995; interview with David Sylvester in *Modern Painters* (London), vol. 10, no. 4, Winter 1997; ''Gilbert and George Flicker Movie'' in *Everything,* vol. 2, no. 1, July 1997.

On GILBERT and GEORGE: Books—*Oh the Grand Old Duke of York,* exhibition catalog by Jean-Christophe Ammann, Lucerne 1972; *Gilbert and George 1968–1980,* exhibition catalog by Carter Ratcliff, Eindhoven, Netherlands 1980; *Gilbert and George,* exhibition catalog with essay by Brenda Richardson, Baltimore 1984; *Gilbert and George: The Charcoal on Paper Sculptures,* exhibition catalog with introduction by Demosthenes Davvetas, Bordeaux 1986; *Gilbert and George: The Paintings 1971,* with text by Wolf Jahn, Edinburgh 1986; *Gilbert and George: The Complete Pictures 1971–85,* with text by Carter Ratcliff, London 1986; *The Art of Gilbert and George* by Wolf Jahn, London 1989; *With Gilbert and George in Moscow* by Daniel Farson, London 1991; *Gilbert & George: A Portrait* by Daniel Farson, London 1999. **Articles**—''Beastly Bad Taste'' by Roger Scruton in *Modern Painters* (London), vol. 1, no. 1, Spring 1988; ''Gilbert & George'' by David Lee in *Arts Review,* vol. 45, January 1993; ''Gilbert & George: Deux Garcons Bien Eleves'' by Ian McMillan in *Beaux Arts Magazine,* no. 161, October 1997.

*

We are:

Unhealthy, middle-aged, dirty-minded, depressed, cynical, empty, tired-brained, seedy, rotten, dreaming, badly behaved, ill-mannered, arrogant, intellectual, self-pitying, honest, successful, hard-working, thoughtful, artistic, religious, fascistic, blood-thirsty, teasing, destructive, ambitious, colourful, damned, stubborn, perverted and good. We are artists.

—Gilbert and George

* * *

The wholly original art form of which Gilbert and George themselves form a vital part is unique. As they push their art to borderlines of bad taste and pornography, however, these artists have increasingly attracted controversy and censure.

Meeting as sculpture students at London's Saint Martins School of Art in 1967, alongside contemporaries Bruce McLean, Richard Long and Victor Burgin, they began collaborating in an era when Conceptual Art was the dominant vogue. The rejection of the art-for-art's sake aesthetic that gained currency in the late 1960s took the form of a rigorous investigation into the nature of the art-object itself, and a movement in favour of content and figuration rooted in social reality: a revolt against elitism.

Gilbert and George amalgamated both forms. Taking the conceptualist argument to its logical conclusion, they designated themselves ''living sculptures,'' utilizing both their public and private lives as part of their work.

''To be with art is all we ask,'' they declared. The aim was to become artists of their era: ''We are modern times artists. We have to devise a vocabulary which reflects this age. We don't want to hide our weaknesses, our sexual behaviour, our thinking, our suffering, and all that belongs to mankind.'' They moved into the working class neighborhood of Spitalfields, from which they took much of their art's material, labelled their Fournier Street home ''Art for All,'' and daily wore identical bland, grey suits, ''the responsibility suits of our art.'' Early works included the ''singing sculpture'' *Underneath the Arches* (which they revived in 1994), a non-music hall version of the Flanagan and Allen number performed for several hours until the song itself was rendered numbingly meaningless and the viewer became strongly aware of the ''sculpture'' (Gilbert and George, in their grey suits, with hands and faces painted silver) alone.

Such ''performance'' pieces were drastically reduced over subsequent years, and in 1977 their prolific output encompassed a wide range of media: books, videotapes, photographs, drawings, as well as just *being* sculptural objects. The first black-and-white photo pieces appeared in 1971, beginning as individual photographs placed together on the wall to form loose assemblages. In 1974, red colouring was introduced to heighten the expressive quality of work, and later photo pieces became combinations that formed a grid-like autonomous whole. The series of 1976 and 1977, *Mental, Dirty Words, and Red Morning,* were the most overtly political and included some of Gilbert and George's best work to date, operating both as moral comment and as neutral reportage. The images dealt with physical dereliction, power and oppression, religion, graffiti, and other manifestations of the culture of urban decay.

By 1981–82, vivid hues were being employed in the photo works in the service of a cartoon-style narrative along explicitly sexual themes. Personal fears and concerns appeared to be replacing any broader social issues. Forms of human excretion were relentlessly examined under such titles as *Sperm Eaters* and *Hard Cocks,* until such titles held more force than the images they described. These works developed into long friezes featuring somewhat overworked images of the artists alongside young men, the familiar icons now bearing cliché titles like *Life without End.*

The award of the 1986 Turner Prize was followed by a major exhibition of Gilbert and George's work at the Hayward Gallery. Critical opinion reacted with doubts about the award and a certain jaded quality permeating much of the exhibition. The use of glamourized violence from slick porno movies for an immediate, and ultimately personal, sensation made the work seem too superficial—but the most controversial aspect of Gilbert and George's imagery had always been the naked young males. Vulnerable or menacing, the youths were finally as vacuous as the traditional female pin-up they here supplanted. Gilbert and George's lavatorial and homosexual iconography had left critics floundering on the hurdle of moral concern. Cheap personal thrills or works of great aesthetic and ideological power?

—Sharon Lancer

Gilbert and George have aroused controversy in England with their Tory politics, even though they have explained that their mission is a populist one, and, simply, most English happen to be Tories. They broadened their political outlook during the 1990s, exhibiting their large-scale photomontages in Russia and China, where they intended not merely to shock those societies where artistic expression has been stifled, but also to make an impact on contemporary debates over national identity. Recognizing the poverty of many of the Chinese who would be attending their show, Gilbert and George distributed catalogs at no charge.

—Mark Swartz

GILLIAM, Sam

Nationality: American. **Born:** Tupelo, Mississippi, in 1933. **Education:** Madison Junior High School, Louisville, Kentucky; studied at the University of Louisville, 1952–56, 1958–61, B.A. 1955, M.A. 1961. **Military Service:** Served in the United States Army, 1956–58. **Family:** Married Dorothy Buller in 1962; has 3 daughters. **Career:** Painter. Lives and works in Washington, D.C. **Awards:** National Endowment for the Arts Individual Artist Grant, 1967, 1973, 1974; Artist's Fellowship, Washington Gallery of Modern Art, 1968; Norman B. Harris Prize, Art Institute of Chicago, 1969; Longview Foundation Award, 1970; Guggenheim Fellowship, 1971; Activities Grant, National Endowment for the Arts, 1973–75; Individual Artists Grant, NEA, 1989. D.Litt.: University of Louisville, Louisville, Kentucky; Memphis College of Art and Design, Georgia; Corcoran Gallery and School of Art, Washington, D.C.; Northwestern University, Evanston, Illinois. **Address:** Annie Gawlak, 1750 Lamont Street NW, Washington, D.C., 20010–2602; 1900 Quincy St. NW, Washington, D.C., 20011.

Individual Exhibitions:

1956 University of Louisville, Kentucky
1963 Frame House Gallery, Louisville, Kentucky
Adam Morgan Gallery, Washington, D.C.
1964 Adam Morgan Gallery, Washington, D.C.
1965 Jefferson Place Gallery, Washington, D.C.
1966 Jefferson Place Gallery, Washington, D.C.
1967 Jefferson Place Gallery, Washington, D.C.
Phillips Gallery, Washington, D.C.
1968 Jefferson Place Gallery Washington, D.C.
Byron Gallery, New York
1969 *Gilliam/Krebs/McGowin,* Corcoran Gallery, Washington, D.C.
1970 Jefferson Place Gallery, Washington, D.C.
Galerie Darthea Speyer, Paris
1971 Museum of Modern Art, New York
1972 Jefferson Place Gallery, Washington, D.C.
1973 Jefferson Place Gallery, Washington, D.C.
New Gallery, Cleveland
Greenburg Gallery, St. Louis
Howard University, Washington, D.C.
University of California at Irvine
Maison de la Culture, Rennes, France
1974 Fendrick Gallery, Washington, D.C.
Linda Farris Gallery, Seattle
Gilliam/Edwards/Williams: Extensions, Wadsworth Atheneum, Hardford, Connecticut
Phoenix Gallery, Seattle
Carl Solway Gallery, Cincinnati, Ohio
1975 Fendrick Gallery, Washington, D.C.
Linda Farris Gallery, Seattle
Philadelphia Museum of Art
Collectors Gallery, Baltimore
1976 J. B. Speed Art Museum, Louisville, Kentucky
Nina Freudenheim Gallery, Buffalo, New York
Rutgers University Art Gallery, New Brunswick, New Jersey
Fendrick Gallery, Washington, D.C.
1977 Pennsylvania State University, University Park
Artpark, Lewiston, New York
1978 Fendrick Gallery, Washington, D.C.
University of Kentucky, Lexington
Virginia Commonwealth University, Richmond
University of Massachusetts, Amherst
Galerie Darthea Speyer, Paris
Solway Gallery, New York
1979 Nina Freudenheim Gallery, Buffalo, New York
Middendorf/Lane Gallery, Washington, D.C.

Sam Gilliam. ©Klein Art Works.

Hamilton Gallery, New York
1980 Middendorf/Lane Gallery, Washington, D.C.
Hamilton Gallery, New York
1981 Nina Freudenheim Gallery, Buffalo, New York
Middendorf/Lane Gallery, Washington, D.C.
Nexus Galleries, Atlanta
Hamilton Gallery, New York
Carl Solway Gallery, Cincinnati, Ohio
1982 Dart Gallery, Chicago
1983 Galerie Darthea Speyer, Paris
Modern Painters at the Corcoran: Sam Gilliam, Corcoran Gallery of Art, Washington, D.C.
1984 Middendorf/Lane Gallery, Washington, D.C.
1985 Monique Knowlton Gallery, New York
Seuferer Chosy Gallery, Madison, Wisconsin
1986 Davis/McClain Gallery, Houston, Texas
Alice Simsar Gallery, Ann Arbor, Michigan
1987 Klein Gallery, Chicago
Robert Kidd Gallery, Birmingham, Michigan
1988 Iannetti-Lanzone Gallery, San Francisco
1989 Middendorf Gallery, Washington, D.C.
Fendrick Gallery, New York
1990 Koplin Gallery, Los Angeles
Middendorf Gallery, Washington, D.C.
1991 Gallery Simone Stern, New Orleans
Gallery Darthea Speyer, Paris
Nancy Drysdale Gallery/de Andino Fine Arts, Washington, D.C.
Walker Hill Arts Center, Seoul, Korea
The American Craft Museum, New York
1992 Smith Anderson Gallery, Palo Alto
Michael H. Lord Gallery, Milwaukee, Wisconsin
1993 Nancy Drysdale Gallery, Washington, D.C.
Brandywine Workshop, Philadelphia, Pennsylvania
1993–95 *Golden Windows Inside Gold* (installation), Whitney Museum of American Art at Philip Morris, New York
1994 Galerie Simmone Stern, New Orleans, Louisiana
Baumgartner Galleries, Washington, D.C.

Sam Gilliam: *In Celebration,* 1987. ©Smithsonian American Art Museum, Washington, DC/Art Resource, NY; courtesy of Smithsonian American Art Museum.

1995 Imago Gallery, Palm Desert, California
44th Biennial Exhibition of Contemporary American Painting, Corcoran Gallery of Art, Washington, D.C.
1996 *African-American Art: 20th Century Masterworks, III,* Michael Rosenfeld Gallery, New York (catalog)
1997 Klein Art Works, Chicago
African-American Art: 20th Century Masterworks, IV, Michael Rosenfeld Gallery, New York (catalog)
1998 *Constructions,* Jaffe Baker Gallery, Boca Raton, Florida
Gilliam in 3-D, Kreeger Museum, Washington, D.C.
2000 Marsh Mateyka Gallery, Washington, D.C.

Selected Group Exhibitions:

1964 *9 Contemporary Painters U.S.A.,* Pan-American Union, Washington, D.C.
1970 *Works on Paper,* Museum of Modern Art, New York
1971 *Works for New Spaces,* Walker Art Center, Minneapolis
1972 *Biennale,* Venice
1973 *Works for Spaces,* San Francisco Museum of Art
1986 *Abstraction-Abstraction,* Carnegie-Mellon University, Pittsburgh
1987 *The Afro-American Artist in the Age of Cultural Pluralism,* The Anacostia Museum of the Smithsonian, Washington, D.C.
1988 *Prints: Washington,* The Phillips Collection, Washington, D.C.
1989 *Looking South Continual,* Memphis Brooks Museum, Memphis
The Blues Aesthetic, Washington Project for the Arts, Washington, D.C.
Traditions and Transformations: Contemporary Afro-American Sculpture, Bronx Museum, New York (catalog)
1990 *African American Art from the Collection,* Philadelphia Museum of Art, Philadelphia, Pennsylvania

1994 *New Acquisitions,* Studio Museum in Harlem, New York
Tandem Press: Five Years of Collaboration and Experimentation, Elvejhem Museum of Art at the University of Wisconsin, Madison
1996 *Painting Outside of Painting,* Corcoran Gallery of Art, Washington, D.C.
1999 Kreeger Museum, Washington, D.C.

Collections:

Museum of Modern Art, New York; Baltimore Museum of Art; Corcoran Gallery, Washington, D.C.; Phillips Gallery, Washington, D.C.; National Gallery of Art, Smithsonian Institution, Washington, D.C.; Art Institute of Chicago; Walker Art Center, Minneapolis; Boymans van Beuningen Museum, Roterdam; Tate Gallery, London; Centre Georges Pompidou, Paris; Whitney Museum of American Art, New York; Rockefeller Collection, New York; Gallery of Modern Art, Washington, D.C.; Museum of African Art, Washington, D.C.; Carnegie Institute, Pittsburgh; Musee d'Art Moderne de la Ville de Paris; Boymans Museum, Rotterdam.

Publications:

By GILLIAM: Articles—Statement in *Gilliam/Edwards/Williams: Extensions,* exhibition catalog, Hartford, Connecticut 1974; ''Solid and Veils'' in *Art Journal,* Spring 1991.

On GILLIAM: Books—*Art in Washington* by Leslie Judd Ahlander, Washington, D.C. 1968; *Art and Ideas* by William Fleming, New York 1973; *The Great American Salt Works* by Jack Burnham, New York 1974; *Sam Gilliam,* exhibition catalog, Louisville, Kentucky 1976; *Modern Painters at the Corcoran: Sam Gilliam* by John Beardsley, Washington, D.C. 1983. **Articles**—''Meet the Artist: Sam Gilliam'' by Cornelia Noland in *The Washingtonian,* October 1965; ''A Gallery without Walls'' by Barbara Rose in *Art in America* (New York), March/April 1968; ''Painting Is Alive and Well'' by Barbara Rose in *Vogue* (New York), November 1969; ''3 Washington Artists'' by Walter Hopps and Nina Felshin Osnos in *Art International* (Lugano, Switzerland), May 1970; ''Energy Is the Catalyst in Sam Gilliam's Formula'' in the *Washington Star,* 19 October 1975; ''Sam Gilliam: Recent Black Paintings'' by Jay Kloner in *Arts Magazine* (New York), February 1978; ''Skin Deep'' by Kay Larson in *New York Magazine,* 23 March 1981; ''Amplifications'' by Marjorie Welish in *Art in America* (New York), November 1981; ''Letting Go'' by Jane Addams Allen in *Art in America,* January 1986; ''Sam Gilliam: Abstraction as Identity'' by Barbara Rose in *International Review of African American Art,* vol. 13, no. 3, 1996; ''Gaining Self-Confidence and Patience'' by Daniel Grant in *American Artist,* November 1990; ''Sam Gilliam: Abstraction as Identity'' by Barbara Rose in *The International Review of African American Art,* Summer 1996; ''Seeing and Thinking About the Unexpected in American Art'' by Richard J. Powell in *American Visions,* February 1999.

* * *

Gilliam is best known for—if not indeed forever to be identified with—his variant of color field paints; loosely spattered, almost automatist stained canvas, unstretched, and then freely manipulated through folding, draping, or hanging. As if in reaction to the limitation of post-painterly abstraction, he began to work with these arranged displays in the late 1960s, and worked so exclusively for about a decade, with the technique then remaining occasionally active in his repertoire. Gilliam, who came to Washington, D.C. in 1962, had been influenced by and himself became representative of the lyrical abstract art fostered by the stain painting of Louis, Noland, and Downing. And so the typical look of his first mature style was a canvas stained by soaking, spattering, and folding to achieve a depth of translucent hues. Such surfaces then became but a background for his presentation, since Gilliam would then take the canvas and manipulate it to produce sculptural effects as the material fell from vertical, overhead, and floor-based supports. It is felt that Gilliam thinks in terms of landscape imagery, and so his work has been likened to the heroic American landscape tradition. His sense of the impermanent positioning of the canvas may have been inspired by the process and anti-form attitudes of that time; in fact, his works have been labelled ''a painterly form of process art.'' His critics have faulted him for a too-great dependence upon these three-dimensional effects, and have remarked on the lack of invention in the paint markings themselves. The style reached its apex quickly so that *Autumn Surf* (1974) was not at all unusual in its 75-foot length. It appears that the polyphony of such work in the interplay of structure and improvisaton was to be a matured creative motif felt throughout his career.

In 1977, he gave up his long usage of stain technique, and unstretched works, to work with a thick acrylic surface with various painterly approaches, including graining. He also began to produce, as in a series of circular paintings in 1976, images collaged with wedges cut from others of his pictures. Such juxtaposition of clearly edged and differing surface treatments, in fairly rapid sequence, remains a Gilliam signature to the present. Like his use, in 1980, of irregular rectangular formats on rigid beveled supports, Gilliam seems to wish—as in his draped works—to break up the planarity and evoke a three-dimensional variety and movement. During the 1980s, Gilliam produced several very large public works in major American cities. The style of these planar painted constructions in traditional stabilizing compositional modes is reminscent of Frank Stella's 70s works; and yet, despite Gilliam's constant search for means to energize his essentially quietist vision, his imagery remains elegantly modernist.

And through the ultimate decade of the century, Gilliam's art continued to display the variety available within his long-established sensual and coloristic idiom—a sculpted painting and a painted-sculpture.

The draped paintings were in effect continued as soft sculptures composed of stained and shaped canvas; often the application of color was a heavy impasto—in contrast to the staining's flatness—with streaked edges through combing. Wall-hung works inevitably included reference to the artist's passion for layering and collage, and so then movement both implied and literal. For instance, painted canvases had a collage of three-dimensional wood fragments attached to one side which allude to the forms of both edge and color of the canvas. Very often these collages—for a time Gilliam used birch wood alone as the support and for both painted and unpainted collaged layering—would would appear as reassembled portions of other works, again then echoing earlier approaches. At times, a piano-lid hinge was used to attach side panels to the central support: these panels were painted on both sides and when moved; a total alteration of a first impression of the pictorial order was intended. New to this decade—arguably post-modern in its drive for a nuance of narrative—was the artist's use of computer-composed figurative images, a map or a flower, for instance, inserted behind the streams of color and collage. As well, the decade contained free-standing wood sculpture with cut-through sections to be viewed entirely in the round. Gilliam's clearly undiminished energy in seeking a non-cinematic yet time-involved color phantasmagoria continues.

—Joshua Kind

GILLICK, Liam

Nationality: British. **Born:** Aylesbury, England, 1964. **Education:** Studied at Hertfordshire College of Art, 1983–84; Goldsmiths College, University of London, B.A. (with Honors) 1987. **Career:** Taught at Columbia University, New York, 1999; Royal Academy, Copenhagen, 1999; Ecole des Beaux Arts de Lausanne, 1999; Central St. Martin's School of Art, London, 1997–98; Goldsmiths College, University of London, 1994–98; Ecole des Beaux Arts, Grenoble, 1997; Kunst Akademie, Hamburg, 1996; Royal Academy, Copenhagen, 1995; lives and works in London and New York. **Award:** Paul Cassirer Award, Berlin, 1998. **Agent:** Basilico Fine Arts, 26 Wooster Street, New York, New York 10013.

Selected Individual Exhibitions:

1989 *84 Diagrams,* Karsten Schubert Ltd., London (catalog)
1991 *Documents,* Karsten Schubert Ltd., London; A.P.A.C. (traveled to Nevers; Gio Marconi, Milan; CCA, Glasgow; Ars Futura, Zurich; Kunstverein ElsterPark, Leipzig; Schipper & Krome, Cologne) (with Henry Bond) (catalog)
1993 *An Old Song and a New Drink,* Air de Paris, Paris (with Angela Bulloch)
1994 McNamara, Schipper & Krome, Cologne
Liam Gillick, Interim Art, London
1995 *Ibuka! (Part 1),* Air de Paris, Paris
Ibuka! (Part 2), Künstlerhaus, Stuttgart (catalog)
Ibuka!, Galerie Emi Fontana, Milan
Part Three, Basilico Fine Arts, New York
1996 *Erasmus Is Late 'versus' The What If?* Scenario, Schipper & Krome, Berlin
Liam Gillick, Raum Aktuelle Kunst, Vienna
The What If? Scenario, Robert Prime, London
1997 *Discussion Island—A What If?* Scenario Report, Kunstverein, Ludwigsburg, Germany (catalog)
A House In Long Island, Forde Espace d'art contemporain, L'Usine, Geneva (catalog)
Another Shop in Tottenharn Court Road, Transmission Gallery, Glasgow (catalog)
McNamara Papers, Erasmus and Ibuka Realisations, The What If? Scenarios, Le Consortium, Dijon, France (catalog)
1998 *Liam Gillick,* Kunstverein in Hamburg (catalog)
Big Conference Center, Orchard Gallery, Derry (catalog)
Révision: Liam Gillick, Villa Arson, Nice (catalog)
When do we need more tractors? Schipper & Krome, Berlin
1999 *Liam Gillick,* Kunsthaus Glarus, Switzerland (catalog)
Liam Gillick, Rüdiger Schöttle, Munich
''David,'' Frankfurter Kunstverein, Frankfurt (catalog)

Selected Group Exhibitions:

1990 The Multiple Projects Room, Air de Paris, Nice
1991 *No Man's Time,* CNAC, Villa Arson, Nice (catalog)
1992 *Molteplici Culture,* Folklore Museum, Rome (catalog)
Lying on top of a building the clouds look no nearer than they had when I was lying in the street, Monika Sprüth, Cologne; Esther Schipper, Cologne; Le Case d'Arte, Milan
Manifesto, Daniel Buchholz, Cologne; Castello di Rivoli, Turin, Italy; Wacoal Arts Centre, Tokyo; Urbi et Orbi, Paris (catalog)
Etats Specifique, Musée d'art moderne, Le Havre, France (catalog)
1993 *Claire Barclay, Henry Bond, Roderick Buchanan, Liam Gillick, Ross Sinclair,* Gesellschaft für Aktuelle Kunst, Bremen, Germany (catalog)
Travelogue, Hochschule für Angewandte Kunst, Vienna (catalog)
Manifesto, Hohenthal und Bergen, Munich (catalog)
Backstage, Kunstverein in Hamburg; Kunstmuseum Luzern, Lucerne, Switzerland (catalog)
1994 *Surface de Réparations,* FRAC Bourgogne, Dijon (catalog)
Public Domain, Centro d'Art Santa Monica, Barcelona (catalog)
Lost Paradise, Kunstraum, Vienna (catalog)
The Institute of Cultural Anxiety, Institute of Contemporary Arts, London (catalog)
1995 *Faction,* Royal Danish Academy of Arts, Copenhagen (catalog)
Stoppage, CCC, Tours; Villa Arson, Nice (catalog)
New British Art, Museum Sztuki, Lodz, Poland (catalog)
Brilliant, Walker Art Center, Minneapolis (catalog)
1996 *Traffic,* CAPC, Bordeaux (catalog)
Nach Welmar, Landesmuseum, Weimar, Germany (catalog)
Life/Live, Musée d'Art Moderne de la Ville de Paris (catalog)
Itinerant Texts, Camden Arts Centre, London (catalog)
1997 *Enter: Audience, Artist, Institution,* Kunstmuseum Luzern, Lucerne, Switzerland (catalog)
504, Kunsthalle Braunschweig, Braunschweiger, Germany (catalog)
Documenta X, Kassel, Germany (catalog)
Enterprise, Institute of Contemporary Art, Boston (catalog)
1998 *Fast Forward,* Kunstverein in Hamburg (catalog)
Artist/Author: Contemporary Artists' Books, Weatherspoon Art Gallery, Greensboro, North Carolina; Emerson Gallery, Clinton; Museum of Contemporary Art, Chicago; Lowe Art Museum, Coral Gables, Florida; Western Gallery, Bellingham, Washington; University Art Gallery, Amherst, Massachusetts (catalog)
Minimal-Maximal, Neues Museum Weserburg, Bremen, Germany (catalog)
Dijon/Le Consortium, Centre Georges Pompidou, Paris (catalog)
1999 *Continued Investigation of the Relevance of Abstraction,* Andrea Rosen Gallery, New York

12 Artists, 12 Rooms, Galerie Thaddeaus Ropac, Salzburg, Austria
Le Capitale, Centre regionale d'art contemporain, Sete, France (catalog)
Get Together/Art As Teamwork, Kunsthalle, Vienna (catalog)

Publications:

On GILLICK: Books—*Brilliant! New Art from London* by Richard Flood et al., Minneapolis 1995; *Intelligence: New British Art 2000* by Virginia Button and Charles Esche, London 2000; *Liam Gillick* by Susanne Gaensheimer, Cologne 2000. **Articles**—''Liam Gillick'' by Alison Sarah Jacques in *Flash Art,* January-February 1993; ''David Batchelor and Liam Gillick: Monochromes of the Everyday'' by Alex Coles in *Parachute,* October-December 2000.

* * *

Who Controls the Near Future? (2000) is the title of an *Applied Complex Screen,* a simple rectangular aluminum frame with vertical and horizontal internal subdivisions containing sheets of coloured Plexiglas, which was installed by Liam Gillick in front of an office window in London's Hayward Gallery. It is also a question which permeates Gillick's sculptures, writings, designs, installations, and collaborative projects. The question is concerned not with power-wielding individuals but with the structures and spaces in which negotiations take place and decisions are made. While his concerns may well be informed by a Foucauldian analysis of power, the work itself demonstrates a deftness, humour, and lightness of touch which makes discourse theory visible. *Who Controls the Near Future?* elegantly draws attention to an otherwise anonymous corner of the gallery complex and viewers find themselves looking, not at the screen, but through it, into the curator's office: a site of discussion and decision-making with respect to the future of the gallery.

Gillick's work is characteristically de-centred and de-centreing. While Gillick is clearly the ''author'' of the work, he is largely absent as a personality. The work itself is an art of distraction: meanings constantly slip out of grasp. The work, typically, draws attention to itself only to divert attention to the spaces in which it exists and to the structures and contexts which inhabit that space. Much of Gillick's work, from very early pieces, such as *Quad Rail (Blue)* (1989) to recent work, *Consultation Filter* (2000), looks like classic modernist art, a meeting of De Stijl and Don Judd; however, the work, despite offering considerable formal pleasures, consistently denies the modernist orthodoxy of autonomy by insisting that meaning is determined by context. *Quad Rail (Blue),* for example, not only resists the modernist demand for ''truth to materials'' by featuring aluminum brackets with oak veneer, but the whole work is accompanied by a description and statement of purpose: ''Four round rails fabricated into a low wall-mounted structure that is constructed in order to emphasise otherwise over-looked areas of a chosen space,'' according to Susanne Gaensheimer in *Liam Gillick.*

Documents (1990–94), produced in collaboration with Henry Bond, are curious news photographs and reports which consistently miss the action. Gillick and Bond, posing as journalists, infiltrated the media structure which effectively sets the news agendas and determines our image of the world. They collected the Press Association list of scheduled photo-calls and press conferences and attended the events that had been pre-ordained as news. The resulting *Documents* are precisely annotated, but oblique and seemingly perverse views which miss the centre of attention: *2 August 1991 London England 10.30 Sentencing of teenager Mark Acklom, bogus stockbroker accused of obtaining money and goods by deception. Inner London Crown Court.* The accompanying photograph shows an anonymous gaggle of reporters and cameramen walking purposely from left to right across the frame in pursuit of their quarry. Here, as with *Quad Rail,* the text constructs meanings and references which are not actually visible but which inescapably become part of our reading of image and object.

As *Applied Complex Screen, Quad Rail,* and *Documents* draw our attention to overlooked spaces and turn our gaze away from the main event, so Gillick's fictional writings are peopled by overlooked, ''secondary'' historical characters, people at the edge of historical events. *Erasmus Is Late* (1995) is a novel in which Erasmus Darwin, grandfather of the more famous Charles, is the absent host of a dinner party attended, anachronistically, by Beach Boy Brian Wilson's father; Marshall McLuhan's mother; a co-founder of Sony, Masaru Ibuka; and others. *McNamara* (1993), a novel based on a screenplay, revolves around Robert McNamara, Secretary of Defence under John F. Kennedy. The action, featuring real figures in a fictionalised account of events, mostly takes place in the system of tunnels underneath the White House. Underground, off-stage, invisible, these are individuals described by Gillick as ''not at the centre of power, but central to power,'' as quoted by Gaensheimer. And the texts, themselves, are elements in a complex web of possibilities which has spawned a variety of gallery works. *Ibuka!* (1995) is a book borne out of a character in *Erasmus* and the basis for a projected musical in relation to which several gallery installations have been produced, for example, *Prototype Ibuka! Coffee Table/Stage (Act 3)* (1995). *McNamara* has produced a poster, furniture, a neon sign (*McNamara Motel* (1997) applied to the old Debtor Prison in Dublin), and a two-minute animation of the opening scene of the fifth draft of the screenplay viewed on a Brionvega Algol TVC 11R television which was first produced in the early 1960s, the period in which the film is set.

The texts and objects are individually self-sufficient but also clearly interconnected; the specific relations, however, remain ungraspable. Gillick's work is characterised by an open endedness: ''If there were conclusions or the end of a set of thinking [the work] would fail. There is a provisional quality to things and that is important for me,'' as quoted by Virginia Button and Charles Esche in *Intelligence: New British Art 2000.* This is most evident in the screens and platforms, begun in the mid 1990s, and the related text, *Big Conference Centre* (1997). The screens and platforms, usually either freestanding, extending from a wall or suspended from the ceiling, are constructed from rectangular aluminum frames fitted with coloured Plexiglas or Formica panels. The colours of the panels are determined by whatever happens to be available from local suppliers. In particular installations viewers are confronted with interventions into architectural spaces that appear as bold, abstract geometric structures furnished with titles such as *Delay Screen* (1999), which is ''a large screen that defines a space where it might be possible to reassess the speed of decision making,'' according to Gaensheimer, or *Consultation Filter* (2000). The viewer is forced to grapple with the apparent incompatibility of form and function and in doing so engages in the very process of discourse which informs the work and will, at a micro level, affect the near future.

—Richard Salkeld

GIOVANELLI, Jean-Pierre

Nationality: French. **Born:** Monaco, 30 December 1936. **Education:** Secondary studies completed in Venice, 1946; earned diploma from l'Ecole d'Horticulture d'Antibes, 1954; studied at Ecoles Nationales d'Ingénieurs, Montargis, 1955; attended l'ISTOM au Havre, 1958; studied at l'Ecole des Beaux Arts, Havre, 1958; studied painting with Luthier Danois and B. L. Knudsen at l'Acoustique, 1961; took courses at l'Ecole des Beaux Arts, Nice, 1961; studied opera at Conservatoire de Nice, 1961. **Military Service:** Served with the Chasseurs Alpinsin in Algeria on the Tunisian border, 1959–61. **Family:** Married to Maria Franco de Oliveira; one son, Julien. **Career:** Moved to St. Jeannet, France, 1963; begins painting and architecture projects, 1965; artistic director for the journal *Artitudes,* 1973–77; developed an intervention process on art criticism at Fine Arts Museum in Nice, 1978; traveled in Spain, 1982; collaborated with architect and professor Yonna Friedman on the project *Intervention sur le dechet,* 1984; developed intervention system in the field of communication networks, 1985; became a communication and installation artist and architect, 1985; participated in a symposium about Victor Hugo and his ideology at Université de Lettres de Nice, 1985; collaborated with Derrick De Kherkove on the project *Les Interactists,* 1986; participated in a symposium about the aesthetics of communication at the University of Salerno, Italy, 1986; participated in the first edition of the journal *Epiphaneia,* 1995; installation *IO* premiered in Genoa, Italy, 1996; installation *MA* premiered in Turin, Italy, 1998; participated in conference at Palais Ducal, Ecole d'architecture et des beaux arts, 1999. Professor at l'Université Paul Valéry de Montpellier; legal expert for the European Community. **Agent:** Immediart International, St. Jeannet 06640, France. **Address:** La Ferrage, St. Jeannet 06640, France.

Selected Individual Exhibitions:

1977 *Le message 'au' bocal aux sculptures,* Nice
1978 *Nous sommes tous des écrivans,* Festival International du livre, Nice
1979 *Critique sur la critique d'art,* Musée Jules Cheret, Nice
1980 *L'objet anthropomorphique,* Biennial of Portugal
1982 *La célebrite,* Cannes art vivant
1985 *Le dialogue,* Galerie d'art contemporain de Nice
1986 *L'imaginaire etalon,* Centre national d'art contemporain, Nice
1994 *Sos tiers monde,* Musée d'Art Moderne et d'Art Contemporain de Nice (catalog)
1996 *IO,* Gallery Leonardo V-Idea, Genoa, Italy (catalog)
Stable mouvant (25 serigraphs), Galerie Lola Gassin, Nice
1997 *Le monochrome perpetual,* Galerie Satellite, Paris (catalog)
1998 *Stable mouvant* (installation), Espace Landowski, Boulogne-Billancourt, France
1999 *Olea nostra,* Rome Biennale
2000 *Global Jackpot: Black and White,* Art Jonction, Nice (catalog)
Arte visive 3, Genoa, Italy

Selected Group Exhibitions:

1976 Fondation Maeght, St. Paul de Vence, France (with George Brecht and Dorotée Iannone)
1977 *Images and Words,* Centro de Arte y Comunicación, Buenos Aires, Argentina
1978 *Art is a Prison,* Edition Exposition, Rome
Biennale de Papier, Art Présent, Paris
1979 *Les senteurs de la dictature,* Galerie Calibre 33, Nice
1980 Artists' books, Metronom, Barcelona (catalog)
1981 *Epargnons ça a notre pays,* Cairn, Paris (catalog)
La France en bleu en blanc en rouge, Quebec
1982 Biennial of Portugal
1983 *Art et Societé,* Art Intermediare, Salerno, Italy (catalog)
1984 Biennial of Portugal
ARCOM 84, Jerusalem
L'art dans les musées, Galerie d'art contemporain de Nice (catalog)
1986 *Autour de la letter,* Château musée de cagnes sur mer (with Michel Butor and Bartomome Ferrando)
Biennial of Portugal
Biennial of Greece
1988 European Film Festival, Viborg, Denmark
Musée d'Iselp, Brussels (catalog)
Pages d'artistes hors mesure, Ecole d'art de Douai, France
1990 *A chacun son diable,* Galerie caliber 33, Nice
L'art á la page, Château Musée, Cagnes sur mer, France
1991 *Le rhinoceros,* Château dif, Marseille
1993 *Ecole de Nice,* Galerie Satellite, Paris; Galerie Artnold, Nice
Mediterranean Biennial, Taranto, Italy
1994 *L'art riquiqui,* Gallery Satellite, Paris
1996 *Ouvres et Lectures,* Galerie Lavoir Moderne Parisien, Paris
Ateliers d'artistes, Casa di Giorgione, Castelfranco Veneto, Italy
Le corps dans tous ses etats, Espace Belleville, Paris (catalog)
Happy End, Galerie Satellite, Paris
1998 *Maisons,* Galerie Satellite, Paris
L'instant et la memeoire, Spazio della Volta, Genoa, Italy (catalog)
Historie d'o, Parc Phenix, Nice
Video Evento, Turin, Italy
1999 Les arts virtuels, Espace Landowski, Boulogne-Billancourt, France (catalog)
Venice Biennale
Artevideo Biennale de Rome
2000 *World Wild Flags,* Echevinat de Liege, Belgium; New York
Arte Visive 3: L'occhio in ascolto, Sala dei gradi, Genoa, Italy (catalog)

Publications:

By GIOVANELLI: Articles—''Sculptures sieges: maquettes et croquis'' in *Artitudes,* January-May 1976; ''Les cendres de la construction'' in *Artitudes,* April 1977; ''Critique sur critique'' in *Le Figaro,* April 1979; ''Victor Hugo et l'urbinisme, vision passeiste ou moderne'' in *Hugoliennes: actes,* Nice 1985; ''Intervention sur l'identité'' in *Artemedia,* May 1986; ''Art communication technologique'' with Karen O'Rourke and others in *Incidences,* 1995.

On GIOVANELLI: Articles—''Intervention en art'' by D. Kaisergruber in *Maintenant Culture,* April 1979; ''Creer pour survivre''

Jean-Pierre Giovanelli: *Stable Movement,* 1999. ©2001 Artists Rights Society (ARS), NY/ADAGP, Paris.

by J. Usetowski in *ICI,* 1981; ''Art and Communication'' by D. Dewaele in *Intermedia Art,* 1985; ''Giovanelli á l'ere post-esthetique'' by René Cenni in *Nice Matin,* January 1994; ''Le verbe'' by M. C. de Oliveira Franco in *Flux News,* April 1995; ''Giovanelli et sa poetique technologique'' by Lino Polegato in *Cyber Flux News,* 1996; ''Giovanelli e le metafore tecnologiche'' by Mario Costa in *IO* (exhibition catalogue), Genoa 1996; ''*IO*'' by Viana Conti in *Flux News,* February 1997; ''*MA*: installation multimédia'' by René Berger in *Flux News,* June-July 1998; ''Art Virtuel: Créations interactives et multisensorielles'' by Richard Leydier in *Art Press,* March 1999; ''Preface'' by Francis Parent in *Global Jackpot: Black and White* (exhibition catalogue), Nice 2000.

* * *

Jean-Pierre Giovanelli is not only an artist who intervened and participated in different artistic movements but is an architect of multimedia installations.

From 1977 onwards, he is the author of a number of *Interventions* which are based on his commitment as a member of two collective undertakings: the Sociological Art and the Aesthetics of Communication groups.

In 1978, Giovanelli developed an intervention process on art criticism at the Fine Arts Museum in Nice, France, followed by a critical attack on all structural myths such as authenticity, identity, and celebrity.

From 1985, Giovanelli's intervention system approached the specific field of communication networks. It was then that the sociological operator transformed himself into a communication and installation artist and architect. His first important environmental work was entitled ''SOS Third World'' and was shown at Nice in 1994. In it sand silts up a television screen displaying satellite images of our advanced technological world, which the onlooker must ceaselessly sweep aside. Giovanelli invites us to share the thought that the proliferation of satellite images broadcast on television screens should legitimately give a direct and comprehensive grasp on reality, which is constantly subjected to the feverish investigation and accumulation of information.

In 1996, Giovanelli created an installation called ''IO'' (''Myself,'' in Italian) which was first shown at Genoa and which could be considered as a technological materialisation of a metaphor where the image of a drop of water, ceaselessly falling, is projected on a dark, oily surface overhung by a heavy rock, while on the same surface the reflection of a mouth is reading the wise texts of Lao-tse's Tao philosophy. According to Mario Costa, three levels of meaning and interpretation can be established with regard to this installation: the sociological, psychological, and metaphysical levels. Sociologically speaking, one can suppose that ''IO'' makes an allusion to the binary substance of the digital universe which is about to substitute itself for the human one. On a psychological or symbolic level it can be thought that this installation refers to an eternal maternal archetype or symbol.

Jean-Pierre Giovanelli: *SOS Tiers Monde.* ©2001 Artists Rights Society (ARS), NY/ADAGP, Paris.

Whereas on an ontological or metaphysical level ''IO'' could constitute a meditation on several aspects of time: real time through the falling drops of water, simulated time through tape recordings, the time of perception and the metaphoric time of being.

Two years later, Giovanelli exhibited his multimedia installation ''MA'': on Milk, Mother and Death, in Turin, Italy. This video event took place in a cubic shaped darkroom which was crossed from top to bottom by a cone. The opening of the cone was plunging on a round of old men's faces seized in a gyratic movement of milk contained in a semi visible tub; traces of light on the ground composed a kind of pearl necklace.The circular movement of the necklace took up the milk movement while one could hear continuous children babbles through hidden loudspeakers. ''MA'' was an installation which not only made an appeal to vision, but also to hearing and taste. The milk basin installed with audio effects received the projected image of an old man who could be the symbol of knowledge. The spectator who entered this installation could symbolically drink with his hands by destroying the image which immediately reconstructed itself. The whole of the installation could in fact be considered as a ''Mother.'' The visitor had at his disposal several possible entrances and exits from which he could choose and this choice had a meaning: that of death which he saw in front of him if he were to follow a circular direction or, on the contrary, that of life if he took a straight path in space/time celebrating our material existence. The symbolic meaning of this installation as a modern oracle could also be interpreted as one that has immortality as its subject. In any case an appeal is made to the spectator not only to meditate on this theme but also, by the very fact of being invited to drink images of milk, to require him to participate physically in this work of art.

Later in the same year 1998, Giovanelli creates his digital image installation ''Stable Mouvant,'' at Boulogne-Billancourt near Paris during the exhibition *Virtual Art: interactive and multisensorial creations.* The basic, complex theme of this installation is treated in its most essential and reduced form: tissue papers, some real, others simulated in a computer, are respectively presented as surging out from a box and projected on a screen. However, as stressed by the likeness between the real tissue papers and the simulated ones, the artist's approach does not favour any confusion between the real and the virtual objects. This subtle but fundamental point makes all the difference between Jean-Pierre Giovanelli's installation and laboratory experiences on ''virtual reality'' or illusionistic entertainments one can find in so many amusement parks. Giovanelli's installation stresses the dichotomy between the two states of reality. As regards the sound on one of the real sides (the real/real side) of the installation it is that of an improbable tornado and on the other (the virtual/real side) we hear the rumour of creased papers. The final aim of the installation is to establish a clear distinction between the categories of reality and virtuality.

In yet another multimedia installation, ''Olea Nostra'' (Oil Civilization), conceived in 1998 and shown at a biennial event in Rome one year later, Giovanelli is treating oil as a paradoxical liquid. In his earlier installation ''IO,'' this liquid, black and dirty, residue of oil change, was treated as a symbol of our surroundings soiled by a disturbed industry, by pollution of the factories and the machines. In ''Olea Nostra,'' oil is clean and transparent, and symbolizes the fatty juice that, under plural forms, has fed the people of the Mediterranean basin for millennia. The purpose of this installation is to make us think of many contradictory aspects of our society. This is also the case in the multimedia installation, ''Black and White Global Jackpot,'' exhibited by Giovanelli in May 2000 at Nice, where two dustbins full of garbage (in fact empty packages) place us symbolically before the unsolvable contradiction of the consumer society. The writings we discover when opening the lids (''black'' on one, ''white'' on the other) are referring less to a racial problem than to the famous whisky label and hence to a world economy advertisement where the only way that is proposed to us is the world-wide consumerism. As Francis Parent remarks, what is in question here is not only our present-day society, but also that of the future. In fact, a type of society where human beings, whatever the colour of their skin or their sex, are worth less than garbages, a society in which the paradoxical ''buying'' will be the jackpot we are bound to win, also invites us to intervene. It is here that Giovanelli's socio-critical art can play a role by allowing the public to question itself and perhaps to modify the course of events.

—Frank Popper

GIRONCOLI, Bruno

Nationality: Austrian. **Born:** Villach, Carinthia, 27 September 1936. **Education:** Villach primary school, 1942–46, and high school, 1946–51; apprentice metal-worker, Innsbruck, 1953–58; studied art at the Kunstakademie, Vienna, 1958; painting, under E. Baumer, Akademie dur Angewandte Kunst, Vienna, 1960–62. **Family:** Married Christi Melichar in 1961 (divorced, 1970); married Edith Matuskovics in 1970 (divorced, 1974); married Indrig Kedren in 1974 (divorced, 1975); daughter: Ina. **Career:** Independent artist, Vienna, since 1962. **Agent:** Kurt Kalb, Vienna. **Address:** c/o Kurt Kalb, Grunangergasse 12, 1010 Vienna, Austria.

Individual Exhibitions:

1967 Galerie Heide Hildebrand, Klagenfurt, Austria
1968 Galerie Nachst St. Stephan, Vienna
1969 Galerie Im Taxispalais, Innsbruck
Galerie Nachst St. Stephan, Vienna
1970 Galerie Appel und Fertsch, Frankfurt
Museum des 20. Jahrhunderts, Vienna
1971 Studentenhaus, Graz, Austria
Galerie Nachst St. Stephen, Vienna
Austrian Pavilion, at the *Bienal,* Sao Paulo (with Arnulf Rainer) Galerie Appel und Fertsch, Frankfurt
1972 Galerie Krinzinger, Bergenz, Austria
Galerie Krinzinger, Innsbruck
1973 Galerie Franzius, Munich
1974 Galerie Dorothea Leonhardt, Munich
Galerie Kalb, Vienna
Karntzer Landesgalerie, Klagenfurt, Austria (with F. X. Olzant)
Kulturhaus, Graz, Austria (with F. X. Olzant)
1975 Schloss Porcia, Spittal/Drau, Austria
Galerie Grunangergasse, Vienna
1976 Galerie Schapira und Beck, Vienna
1977 Museum des 20. Jahrhunderts, Vienna (travelled to Städtische Galerie im Lenbachhaus, Munich; Gallerieim Taxispalais, Innsbruck; Kunstverein, Salzburg; and Kulturhaus, Graz)
Galerie Schapira und Beck, Vienna
1978 Galerie Krinzinger, Innsbruck
1991 Galerie Patrice Trigano, Paris

Selected Group Exhibitions:

1966 *Konfrontation 66,* Galerie Heide Hildebrand, Klagenfurt, Austria
1968 *Profile 8: Osterreichische Kunst heute,* Stadtisches Museum, Bochum, West Germany
1970 *14 x 14,* Kunstverein, Baden-Baden, West Germany
1973 *The Austrian Exhibition,* Richard Demarco Gallery, Edinburgh (travelled to the Institute of Contemporary Arts, London)
1974 *Zeichnungen der Osterreichischen Avantgarde,* Innsbruck (travelled to Leverkusen, Basel and Geneva)
1975 *Plastik in Schloss Eggenburg,* Graz, Austria
1976 *Attersee/Gironcoli/Pichler/Rainer/Steiger,* Galerie Schapira und Beck, Vienna
Parallelaktion: neue kunst aus Osterreich, Von-der-Heydt Museum, Wuppertal, West Germany
1984 *Arte Austriacca 1960–84,* Galleria d'Arte Moderna, Bologna, Italy
1988 *Another Climate: Positions in Contemporary Art from Vienna,* Stadtische Kunsthalle, Düsseldorf
1999 *Lineamente International,* Neue Galerie, Linz
2000 *Versus 2000,* Museion, Bolzano
2001 *Objects,* Augarten, Austria

Collections:

Museum des 20. Jahrhunderts, Vienna.

Publications:

On GIRONCOLI: Books—*Gironcoli,* exhibition catalog with text by Alfred Schmeller, Vienna 1970; *Austria; Bruno Gironcoli-II Bienal de Sao Paulo,* exhibition catalog with text by Hermann Schurrer, Vienna 1971; *Osterreichische Kunst von heute,* edited by Oswad Oberhuber and Kurt Sotriffer, Vienna and Munich 1971; *Bruno Gironcoli,* exhibition catalog with text by Peter Weiermair and Armin Zweite, Vienna 1977. **Articles**—''Bruno Gironcoli'' by Otto Mauer in *Alte und Moderner Kunst* (Vienna), May-June 1969; ''New Tendencies in Austrian Art'' by Peter Weiermair in *Studio International* (London) May 1972; ''Uber Bruno Gironcoli'' by Jurgen

Morschel in *Das Kunstwerk* (Baden-Baden, West Germany), May 1974; ''Dossier: Vienna'' by Anne Barclay Morgan in *Sculpture* (Washington, D.C.), vol. 15, no. 10, December 1996.

GLASER, Milton

Nationality: American. **Born:** New York City, 26 June 1929. **Education:** High School of Music and Art, New York, 1943–46; studied at Cooper Union, New York, graduated 1951; Accademia di Belle Arti, Bologna, 1952–53 (Fulbright scholarship). **Family:** Married Shirley Girton in 1957. **Career:** Founder, with Seymour Chwast and Edward Sorel, 1954, and President, 1954–74, Push Pin Studios, New York; President, Milton Glaser, Inc., New York, from 1974, responsible for redesigning the magazines *Paris Match, Cue, New West, L'Express, L'Europe, Jardin des Modes,* and *Esquire*; founding partner, with Walter Bernard, of the publication design firm WBMG, New York, from 1983, responsible for redesigning *L'Espresso* (Rome), *Alma* (Paris), Rizzoli's *Journal of Art, Magazine Week, The Washington Post, La Vanguardia* (Barcelona), *Manhattan, Inc., Family Circle, Adweek, U.S. News, New York Law Journal,* and *Lire.* Founder, with Reynold Ruffins and Seymour Chwast, 1955, and co-art director, 1955–74, *Push Pin Graphic* magazine, New York; founder, with Clayton Felker, president, and design director, *New York Magazine,* 1968–77; vice-president and design director, *Village Voice* magazine, New York, 1975–77. Lecturer, Pratt Institute, Brooklyn, New York, and School of Visual Arts, New York, from 1961. Board member, Cooper Union, School of Visual Arts, and Aspen Design Conference (president, 1990–91); former vice-president, American Institute of Graphic Arts, New York. **Awards:** Society of Illustrators Gold Medal, 1979; St. Gaudens Medal, Cooper Union, New York, 1979; Hall of Fame Award, Art Directors Club of New York, 1979; Prix Savignac for World's Most Memorable Poster, 1996. Honorary doctorates from Minneapolis Institute of Arts, 1971; Moore College, Philadelphia, 1975; Philadelphia Museum School, 1979; School of the Visual Arts, New York, 1979; Queens College, CUNY; New York University at Buffalo; and Royal College of Art, London. Honorary Fellow, Royal Society of Arts, London, 1979. **Address:** Milton Glaser Inc., 207 East 32nd Street, New York, New York 10016, U.S.A.

Exhibitions:

1970 *The Push Pin Style,* Musée des Arts Décoratifs, Paris
1975 Museum of Modern Art, New York
Portland Visual Arts Center, Oregon
1977 Centre Georges Pompidou, Paris (toured)
1980 Carl Solway Gallery, Cincinnati
1981 Peabody Gallery, Harvard University, Cambridge, Massachusetts
Lincoln Center Gallery
1984 Houghton Gallery, Cooper Union, New York
1989 Vicenza Museum
Giorgio Morandi/Milton Glaser, Galleria Communale d'Arte Moderna, Bologna
1991 Tribute to Piero della Francesca, Arezzo and Milan, Italy; travelled to The Cooper Union, New York, 1994
1992 *The Imaginary Life of Claude Monet,* Nuages Gallery, Italy
1995 Art Institute of Boston
Ravello, Italy
The Imaginary Life of Claude Monet, Creation Gallery, Japan
1997 Retrospective, Suntory Museum, Japan
2000 Retrospective, Fondazione Bevilacqua La Masa, Venice, Italy

Collections:

Museum of Modern Art, New York; Israel Museum, Jerusalem; Chase Manhattan Bank, New York; National Archive, Smithsonian Institution, Washington, D.C.

Publications:

By GLASER: Books—(with Shirley Glaser) *If Apples Had Teeth,* New York, 1960; (with Jerome Snyder) *The Underground Gourmet,* New York, 1968, 1970; *Milton Glaser: Graphic Design* edited by Peter Mayer, New York and London, 1973; *The Milton Glaser Poster Book,* with introduction by Giorgio Soavi, New York, 1977; *Art is Work*, New York 2000. **Articles—**''A Letter to Monet'' in *Graphis*, March-April 1993.

On GLASER: Books—*Variations on a Theme: Fifty Years of Graphic Design in America* New York 1966; *Quality: Its Image in the Arts* edited by Louis Kronenberger, New York 1969; *The Push Pin Style Book,* exhibition catalogue, Palo Alto, 1970; *History of the Poster* by Josef and Shizuko Muller-Brockmann, Zurich, 1971; *Graphic Designers in the USA: 3* edited by Henri Hillebrand, London, 1972; *Milton Glaser: Graphic Design,* Woodstock, New York 1973; Who's Who in Graphic Art edited by Walter Amstutz, Dubendorf, 1982; *The Conran Directory of Design* edited by Stephen Bayley, London, 1985; *New American Design* by Hugh Aldersley-Williams, New York, 1988; *Six Chapters in Design: Bass, Chermayeff, Glaser, Rand, Tanaka, Tamaszewski,* with foreword by Philip B. Meggs, San Francisco 1997; **Articles—**''Milton Glaser of Push Pin Studios'' by Dorothy Waugh in *American Artist*, June 1966; ''Push Pin studios'' by Jerome Snyder in *Graphis,* no. 133, 1967; ''What Milton Glaser Really Saw'' by W. Feaver in *Design* (London), June 1978; ''Milton Glaser'' by Marshall Blonsky in *Graphis*, November-December 1990; ''Milton Glaser: Always One Jump Ahead'' by Patrick Argent in *CSD,* August-September 1999; ''Milton Glaser: Taking the Long View'' by Pete Hamill in *Graphis*, November-December 1999; ''Blast from the Past'' in *Design Week*, 10 November 2000; ''Design: The Man Who Drew Bob Dylan'' by Dominic Lutyens in *The Independent* (London), 6 January 2001; ''Milton Glaser: American Institute of Graphic Arts'' by Victoria C. Rowan in *Art News*, January 2001.

* * *

Injecting the fine art idiom into quotidian commerce, Glaser justly deserves the universal recognizability that his powerful avant-garde design and illustration have garnered in the past 40 years. His 1975 I♥NY logo is as familiar throughout the world as the Mona Lisa.

Meanwhile, the ''work,'' a term Glaser prefers to the semantically over-wrought ''art,'' is infused with a medley of influences ranging from Piero della Francesca to comic strips. He has been called the ''Picasso of Graphic Design,'' which contains a hierarchical distinction he flatly rejects. Indeed, Glaser studied painting in Bologna on a Fulbright Fellowship with Giorgio Morandi after graduating from Cooper-Hewitt in the early 1950s.

He is a proficient and prolific draftsman, as can be seen in the portraits that he executes of a vast array of contemporary and historic figures, and the illustrations he has executed for a variety of literary works by Dante, Shakespeare, Gogol, Baudelaire and Asimov, among others. For the 500th birthday of della Francesca in 1991, Glaser created a series of drawings and watercolors as meditations on the painter, with whom he has felt an affinity since discovering works of his at New York's Frick Collection as a teen. Glaser has preferred for his preparatory sketches to be published or exhibited alongside his finished products, displaying evidence of the artist, client, and marketplace dialog. In such a way, he indicates the very self-consciousness of his creative process and its relationship with the history of art making.

Glaser possesses a thoroughgoing knowledge of art that he applies to everything from portraits to beer bottles. The iconic 1966 poster of Bob Dylan, a bold black silhouette crowned with candy-colored strands of hair, was inspired not by psychedelic drugs, as many thought, but by Islamic miniatures and a cut-out self-profile by Marcel Duchamp. Besides the reservoir of art, he has said, ''I've always been a great believer in the world as your visual resource.''

Glaser has redefined the way that print media look through his designs for *Paris Match*, *New York* and, recently, *The Nation* and *Modern Maturity*. His influence is also seen through all of his former ''paste-up kids'' who are now art directors and editors at *Vogue*, *Esquire*, *Time*, *Life*, *Fortune*, *Atlantic Monthly*, among others. His other influence on subsequent generations of designers and artists has been through his long association with New York's School of Visual Arts.

In fact, New York City would seem to have been wholly design directed by Glaser in the period between the 1960s and the 1980s, from stores, to paperback books, posters for everything, shopping bags, restaurants, subway murals, and every type face in a city steeped in text and images.

He asserts that the Italian term *disegno,* which means both drawing and design, is his preferred common term. It has been art exhibitions that have joined the two definitions coherently, as in the MoMA retrospective in 1975 and The Centre Georges Pompidou monographic exhibition at the Beauborg in 1977, as well as the expansive recent one at the Philadelphia Museum of Art.

Indeed, it is a gauge of his fruitfulness that he has produced so much fine work not just for clients, all while a partner of two independent design firms and leading his own eponymous firm. The personal artistry has invaded the simplest typeface, and the professional acumen at intuiting what appeals to the viewer has entered the toolbox of the artist. His ''tool box'' remains traditional, as he literally still conceives at the drawing board. While acknowledging that computers are used in his firm, he still maintains that the eye, hand, and brain coalesce more readily in a pencil than a Macintosh. Nevertheless, Glaser's firm is, of course, designing for the web.

In a 1996 article, Glaser cautioned that computers were replacing invented form with assembled form. He expressed ambivalence about the benefit of democratization versus suspicion about any form of expression easily achieved. In the end, he decides that history has shown that each new technology develops its own standards.

In an age of specialization, Glaser remains a ''general practitioner,'' allowing for his wide variety of projects to cross-fertilize. Glaser's oeuvre covers many styles and movements, from classically illusionistic graphite renderings of the figure to industrial enamel tile murals. Whether this catholic output diminishes his significance as a fine artist is a matter of much introspection. Glaser, himself, says, ''All through history, fine art had a purpose just as commercial art does now. Renaissance artists painted with a specific purpose for a specific client and produced work that we now say is fine art.''

—Deirdre Donohue

GOBER, Robert

Nationality: American. **Born:** Wallingford, Connecticut, 12 September 1954. **Education:** Graduated Middlebury College, Vermont 1976. **Career:** Started with drawing, moved into photography, painting, and sculpture. **Address:** Lives in New York City.

Selected Individual Exhibitions:

1984 *Slides of a Changing Painting,*Paula Cooper Gallery, New York
1990 *Robert Gober,* Museum Boymans-Van Beuningen, Rotterdam and Kunsthalle Bern (catalog)
1991 Galerie Nationale du Jeu de Paume, Paris
1992 *Lockdown,* DIA Center for the Arts, New York
1999 *Robert Gober: Sculptures and Drawings,* Walker Art Center, Minneapolis (traveled to Malmo, Sweden; Washington D.C.; and San Francisco)

Selected Group Exhibitions:

1988 *Exposition Art at the End of the Social—38 artists from New York,* Rooseum, Center for Contemporary Art, Malmö
1990 Museum Boymans-van Beuningen, Rotterdam
1991 *Katharina Fritsch, Robert Gober, Reinhard Mucha, Charles Ray, and Rachel Whiteread,* Luhring Augustine Gallery, New York
1992 *Documenta IX,* Kassel
1995 *Masculin-Féminin, le sexe de l'art,* Georges Pompidou Centre, Paris
1996 *The Human Body in Contemporary American Sculpture,* Gagosian Gallery, New York
Try a Little Tenderness, Apex Art Curatorial Program, New York
1997 *Objects of Desire: The Modern Still Life,* Museum of Modern Art, New York
A House Is not a Home: Everyday Objects in Contemporary Sculpture, Rooseum, Center for Contemporary Art, Malmö
WOOD NOT WOOD / WORK NOT WORK, A/D Gallery, New York

Robert Gober: *Altered Door,* ca. 1989–95. ©Geoffrey Clements/Corbis.

1998 *Double Trouble: The Patchett Collection,* San Diego, Museum of Contemporary Art
Change of Scene XIV, Museum für Moderne Kunst, Frankfurt
100 Years of Sculpture: From the Pedestal to the Pixel, Walker Art Center and Minneapolis Sculpture Garden, Minneapolis
Travel & Leisure, Paula Cooper Gallery, New York
On the Edge: Contemporary Art from the Werner and Elaine Dannheisser Collection, Museum of Modern Art, New York, Painting and Sculpture Galleries, New York
2000 *Figure in the Landscape,* Lehmann Maupin Gallery, New York
Extra Ordinary, James Cohan Gallery, New York
Biennial Exhibition, Whitney Museum of American Art, New York
2001 Venice Biennale, Venice

Collections:

Whitney Museum of American Art, New York; Solomon R. Guggenheim Museum, New York; Museum of Modern Art, New York.

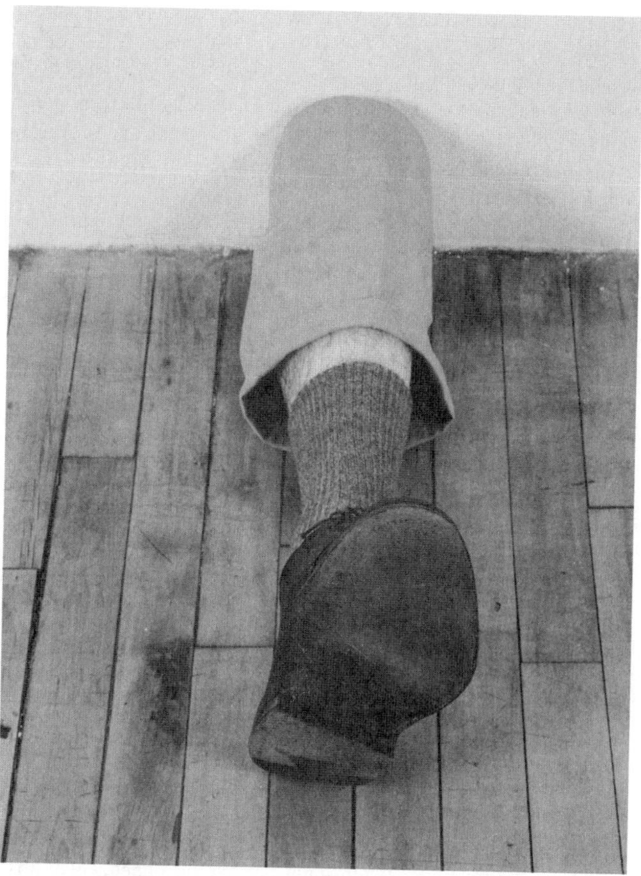

Robert Gober: *Untitled,* ca. 1989–93. ©Geoffrey Clements/Corbis.

Publications:

By GOBER: Articles—''Cumulus'' *Parkett,* no. 19, 1989; ''Robert Gober: Special Editions, An Interview'' by Richard Flood in *The Print Collector's Newsletter,* March-April 1990.

On GOBER: Books—*Robert Gober* (exhibition catalog), with text by Trevor Fairbrother, Karel Schampers, and Ulrich Loock, Rotterdam 1990; *Robert Gober* (exhibition catalog), with text by Catherine David and Joan Simon, Paris 1991; *Robert Gober* (exhibition catalog) edited by Karen Marta, with text by Dave Hickey, Detroit 1992. *Robert Gober: Sculpture + Drawing* (exhibition catalog) by Richard Flood et al., Minneapolis 1999. **Articles—**''Robert Gober'' by Joe Scanlan in *Dialogue,* September/October 1988; ''Arcadian Elegy: The Art of Robert Gober'' by Maureen P. Sherlock in *Arts,* September 1989; ''The House of Fiction,'' by Matthew Weinstein in *Artforum,* vol. 27, no. 6, February 1990; ''Louise Bourgeois & Robert Gober,'' by Gregg Bordowitz, Nancy Spector, Harald Szeemann in *Parkett* (special edition), no. 27, March 1991; ''Lockdown: Robert Gober at Dia'' in *Artforum,* February 1993; ''Poetics of the Drain'' *Art in America,* 1 December 1997; ''Robert Gober'' in *Artforum,* December 1997; ''On Art—Our Dadaist'' in *The New Republic* 17 April 2000; ''Our Man in Venice: Can U.S. Sculptor Robert Gober's Show at the Art World's 'Oscars' Take Him to the Top?'' *Newsweek,* 4 June 2001.

* * *

Domestic objects like sinks, drains, cribs, and windows punctuate Robert Gober's work. Gober takes inspiration from Marcel Duchamp (specifically the readymade urinal *Fountain,* 1915), and from minimalism, conceptualism, and surrealism. Unlike these precedents, in which the object was usually machine-made and secondary to the idea, Gober prizes the handmade object.

Gober was born in Wallingford, Connecticut, in 1954. He attended Middlebury College in Vermont, where he studied drawing. Upon moving to New York City in 1976, Gober worked as a studio assistant for painter Elizabeth Murray. Soon after arriving in New York, Gober began to use his camera as a way to capture his exhilarating new surroundings.

Gober used photography in his first mature work, *Slides of a Changing Painting* (1982–1983). More interested in the process of painting than in the finished product, Gober made this work by painting, scraping off, and repainting the same small board hundreds of times. He photographed the board throughout this process, then selected eighty-nine images from the group. He showed the slides to a small audience at the Paula Cooper Gallery in New York in 1984. This work has proved to be the foundation of Gober's art: nearly every image that has surfaced in his sculpture first appeared in *Slides of a Changing Painting.*

In 1983, Gober began creating the sink sculptures that would become his signature. He made dozens of these sculptures, evoking a minimalist aesthetic by repeating a simple form multiple times. Gober made the sinks by hand, applying plaster and layers of enamel paint over a wire armature. Later that decade, he extended the series to include urinals and pewter casts of sink drains. In Gober's hands, these objects are rendered useless: the sinks and urinals have no plumbing fixtures; the pewter drains are likewise unattached, often embedded absurdly in the wall. Water appears throughout Gober's oeuvre as a purifying element; its pointed absence in the non-functional sinks, urinals, and drains refers to society's inability to cleanse itself of the AIDS virus.

In 1986, Gober's work began to refer to the body as the sinks referred to water—through absence. One motif he used was the child's crib. These cribs were not only useless, but they also presented a disquieting view of childhood. In *X Crib* (1987), for instance, the walls of the crib meet in the center of the structure, creating a hostile and unwelcoming space.

During the same period, Gober made a series of dog beds. Like all of Gober's works, these sculptures were entirely handmade, from the woven basketry to the hand-painted fabric on the cushion. The fabric motif on the last of the dog beds, *Untitled* (1988), made it Gober's most notorious work. It features two alternating images: a white man asleep (from a Bloomingdale's advertisement) and a lynched black man (from a 1920s image in the New York Public Library Picture Collection).

Gober reused this imagery in a 1989 installation at the Paula Cooper Gallery, the first of many times that Gober would create an entire environment in a gallery space. In that exhibition, the sleeping man/lynched man imagery appeared as wallpaper behind a freestanding wedding dress. Hand-painted bags of cat litter—which have been compared to Warhol's silk-screened Brillo boxes—lined the walls. In an adjacent space hung wallpaper bearing images of male and female genitalia, with pewter drains mounted in the wall. At the center of the room, a pedestal held a bag of donuts. True to his obsession with the hand-made, Gober constructed the paper bag, drew the logo, fried the donuts, and had the grease removed and a preservative injected. While the objects and images are familiar, the reasons for Gober's juxtapositions often remain unclear. He has said that this installation referred in part to marriage vows, with the kitty litter suggesting the messy reality evoked in the phrase ''in sickness and in health.''

In 1990, Gober introduced the body that had until then been conspicuously absent, making sculptures of a man's leg, wearing cuffed pants, a sock and a shoe, and showing a bit of hairy flesh between the sock and the cuff. These wax legs, shown on the floor against a wall, took a variety of forms: for example, a leg with three candles sprouting from the shin (part of a 1991 exhibition at the Galerie Nationale du Jeu de Paume in Paris), and the disturbing sculpture of a woman's lower torso giving birth to a fully clothed and shod leg (*Man Coming Out of the Woman,* 1993–1994). The legs' disembodiment makes them unsettling, as if the viewer had just happened upon the scene of a horrific crime.

In 1992, Gober mounted an installation at the Dia Center for the Arts in New York. The previously useless sinks were now fully functional, with water flowing in an unending stream. Among other elements, the installation included stacks of newspapers with hand-collaged front pages of fictional ''news'' reports; boxes of rat bait; a painted mural of a forest on the walls; and a barred prison window, a motif that recalls the confining crib sculptures.

The Geffen Contemporary gallery of the Museum of Contemporary Art served as the venue for Gober's major 1997 installation. Here, the central figure was a six-foot tall concrete Madonna statue (cast by the artist) bisected by a large bronze drainage pipe. The Madonna stood on a storm drain above a pool of water containing coins inscribed with the artist's year of birth. The installation also included a forceful stream of water cascading down a flight of stairs; two suitcases whose bottoms were storm drains; and tide pools in which a man's legs dangled a baby's legs over the water. Raised Catholic, Gober brought together and reinvented elements of his religious upbringing in this installation.

Gober and his work resist classification. He merges elements of minimalism and surrealism yet uses images that are almost banal in their familiarity. Not one to let us off easy, his dark sense of humor puts just enough of a twist on these images to leave us disconcerted, even horrified. Gober's examination of the fundamental elements of our lives—sexuality, birth, childhood, religion, marriage, death, and the body—links his works and makes them relevant to us.

—Tara Reddy Young

GOERITZ, Mathias

Nationality: German. **Born:** Danzig, 4 April 1915; moved to Mexico, 1949. **Education:** Kaiserin-Augusta-Gymnasium, Charlottenburg, Berlin, 1924–34; Friedrich-Wilhelms-Universitat, Berlin, 1934–40; Ph.D. 1940. **Family:** Married Marianne Gast in 1942 (died, 1958); married Ida Rodriquez Prampolini in 1960; son: Daniel. **Career:** Professor, Centro de Estudios Marroquies, Tetuan, Spanish Morocco, 1940–44; painter in Granada, Spain, 1945–47, and Madrid, 1947–49; Professor of Visual Education and Design, Escuela de Arquitectura, Universidad de Guadalajara, Jalisco, Mexico, 1949–54. From 1953, painter, sculptor and architect in Mexico City, and founder/professor, Department of Basic Design, Universidad Nacional Autonoma de Mexico, Mexico City. Founder/director, Escuela de Artes Plastics y Escuela de Diseno Industrial, Universidad Iboamericana, Mexico City, 1957–60; artist-in-residence, Aspen Institute for Humanistic

Studies, Aspen, Colorado, 1970–72. Editor, art section, *Arquitectura Mexico,* Mexico City, from 1958. Founder, la Escuela de Altamira movement, Santillana del Mar, Santander, Spain, 1948, and Los Hartos movement, with Jose Luis Cuevas, Pedro Freideberg, Jesus Reyes Ferreira, and others, Mexico City, 1961. **Member:** GIAP (Group International d'Architecture Prospective), from 1965. **Awards:** Zeev Rechter Prize for Architecture, Israel, 1987. Member, Akademie der Kunste, Berlin, 1973; Honorary Fellow, Royal Academy of The Hague, 1976; Honorary Academician, Academia Nacional de Arquitectura, Mexico, 1984; Academia Mexican de Diseno, 1985; Academia de Artes, Mexico, 1986. Chevalier, Ordre des Arts et des Lettres, France, 1984. **Agent:** Caleria Mer-Kup, Moliere 328-C, Col. Polanco, Mexico D.F.-5. **Died:** 4 August 1990.

Individual Exhibitions:

1946 Sala Clan, Madrid
1948 Salon Alerta, Santander, Spain
1949 Galeria Palma, Madrid
1950 Galeria Camarauz, Guadalajara, Mexico
Galeria Clardecor, Mexico City
1952 Galeria Sapi, Palma de Majorca
Galeria Jardin, Barcelona
Galeria de Arte Mexicano, Mexico City
1953 El Eco Museo Experimental, Mexico City
1955 Galeria Proteo, Mexico City
1956 Carstairs Gallery, New York
1959 Galeria de Arte Mexicano, Mexico City (retrospective)
1960 Carstairs Gallery, New York
Galerie Iris Clert, Paris
Galeria de Antonio Souza, Mexico City
1961 Galeria de Arte Mexicano, Mexico City
1962 Carstairs Gallery, New York
1980 Israel Museum, Jerusalem
1984 Museo de Arte Moderno, Mexico City
1998 Antiguo Colegio de San Lldefonso, Mexico City

Selected Group Exhibitions:

1960 *New Media/New Forms,* Martha Jackson Gallery, New York
Aspects de la Sculpture Americaine, Galerie Claude Bernard, Paris
New Europeans, Contemporary Arts Museum, Houston
1961 *Art of Assemblage,* Museum of Modern Art, New York
1962 *Carnegie International,* Pittsburgh
1992 *Prints and Multiples by Contemporary Masters,* Museo de Arte Moderno, Mexico City
From 1962 Goeritz ceased active participation in many of the one-man and group exhibitions of his work.

Collections:

Museo de Arte Moderno, Mexico City; Museum of Modern Art, New York; Israel Museum, Jerusalem; Kunsthalle, Hamburg.

Publications:

By GOERITZ: Books—*Manifesto of the School of Altamira,* Santander, Spain 1948; *Manifesto: Estoy Harto,* Mexico City 1960; *Manifesto: Estamos Hartos,* Mexico City 1961. **Articles—**''Manifesto arquitectura Emocional'' in *Cuadernos de Arquitectura* (Guadalajara), no. 1, 1954; ''Statement'' in the catalog for his one-man show, Carstairs Gallery, New York 1962.

On GOERITZ: Books—*Art in Latin American Architecture* by Paul F. Damaz, New York 1964; *Mathias Goeritz* by Oliva Zuniga, Mexico City and New York 1963, 1964; *Arquitectura Contemporanea Mexicana* by Israel Katzman, Mexico City 1964; *Bouwmeesters van morgen* by J. J. Beljon, Amsterdam 1964; *El Arte Contemporaneo* by Ida Rodriquez Prampolini, Mexico City 1964; *Les Cites de l'Avenir* by Michael Ragon, Paris 1966; *Builders in the Sun* by Clive B. Smith, New York 1967; *The Aesthetic of Contemporary Architecture* by Michael Ragon, Neuchatel 1968; *A History of Latin American Art and Architecture* by Leopoldo Castedo, New York 1969; *Histoire Mondiale de l'Architecture et de l'Urganisme Modernes* by Michael Ragon, Paris 1972; *Mathias Goeritz* by Frederico Morais, Mexico City 1982; *Mathias Goeritz* by Lily Kassner, Mexico City 1984; *Arquitectura Emocional* by Rita Eder, Mexico City 1984. **Articles—**''El Eco: Ein Experimental-Museum in Mexico'' in *Baukunst und Werkform,* no. 4, 1954; ''Architektur in Mexiko'' by Helmuth Borcherdt in *Baumeister* (Munich), November 1959; ''Mathias Goeritz'' by Michel Ragon in *Cimaise* (Paris), no. 106, 1972; ''Expressionism and Emotional Architecture in Mexico: Luis Barragan's Collaborations with Max Cetto and Mathias Goeritz'' by Keith L. Eggener in *Architectura,* vol. 25, no. 1, 1995; ''Mathias Goeritz'' by Issa Maria Benitez Duenas in *Art Nexus* (Bogota), no. 28, May/July 1998.

*

Aesthetics without a secure ethical background may produce interesting, even beautiful results, but not art. Art is a service. As long as art has no spiritual function all our efforts are condemned to lead to nothing but a kind of egocentric folk art, done by intellectuals for intellectuals. The over-emphasis on individual expression has, in the end, destroyed its importance. The artist, instead of concentrating on his independent and nonconformist genius, should admit that his works are actually nothing but isolated, temporary designs or expressive spots on the wall, and that all the rest is vanity, propaganda or business.

When people asked me to define my own work, I used to say that I considered it an experiment of poetry in space. The truth is that it is a rather desperate attempt to find the right language for a prayer.

—Mathias Goeritz

* * *

Following his studies of philosophy in Berlin Goeritz became involved in the history of art, and after his travels in Europe he gradually became engaged in its practice. He frequented the circle of the German Expressionists and took some of the experimental spirit of modern sculptors such as Arp.

He spent the war years in Morocco before settling in Spain where he founded the School of Altamira, a group that influenced the younger artists emerging with interests expressed in the abstract idiom.

In 1949 he was invited to teach at the University of Guadalajara in Mexico. His sculptures and mural decorations aroused opposition from the native artists including Rivera and Siqueiros. His best known works are the Five Towers in the Square of that name built at the entrance to a satellite town in Mexico in 1957–58. This group of giant monoliths ranging in height from 120 to 185 feet combines five units three in white, one in yellow and the other in orange.

This daring concept with its affinity to the modern architecture of skyscrapers and to the grouping of ancient menhirs created its own mystique of pure form and mysteriously poised relationship with space and the surrounding environment. In the various fields of education, writing, poetry, architecture and sculpture, Goeritz always maintained a philosophical attitude to the visual forms of art seeking to express something of the physical presence to convey spiritual messages. Biblical subjects became refined from Expressionist and emotional figures to a simpler abstract iconography where unconventional materials were used to form assemblages. His series called ''Clouages'' are large panels on which cut-out-shapes of tin, plastic and other metals are nailed in patterns of symbolic intent. One such work ''Message XI'' (1958) measuring 63 by 71 inches and based on a text from the Book of Job ''I shall be condemned: why do I then labour in vain?,'' has its unique impact in its severe and secret metaphor of the written words.

Through the language of free form, Goeritz maintained a link with the conventionally recorded stories of the Old Testament, and in such series as ''Realisations'' and ''Commentaries,'' he substituted his own epigrammatic rhymes of nail-heads and shape outlines in monumental ''tablets'' striking lyrical responses from the imagination. His sensitive recycling of ready-made materials into reliefs of compulsive power was achieved by concentration on spacing and texture of the various elements arriving at formal conclusions seemingly pre-ordained. They present the ultimate in significant parables of the spirit expressed in dramatic non-allusive terms of materials whose properties are transmuted by the strength of the artist's numinous purpose.

—G. S. Whittet

Ralph Goings: *Pam II,* late 20th Century. ©Christie's Images/Corbis.

GOINGS, Ralph (Ladell)

Nationality: American. **Born:** Corning, California, 9 May 1928. **Education:** California College of Arts and Crafts, Oakland, 1950–53, B.F.A. 1953; California State University, Sacramento, 1965–66, M.A. 1966. **Military Service:** Served as Corporal in the United States Army, 1946–48. **Family:** Married Shanna Leslyn in 1951; children: Mark, Cameron, Drew and Kevin. **Career:** Independent artist known for photo-realist paintings. Instructor, Del Norte High School, Crescent City, California, 1955–59; chairman of art department, La Sierra High School, Carmichael, California, 1959–70; instructor, California State University, Sacramento, 1971; instructor, University of California at Davis, 1972. Lives in Charlotteville, New York. **Agent:** c/o O. K. Harris Works of Art, 383 West Broadway, New York, New York 10012, U.S.A.; **Address:** HCR Box 27, Charlotteville, NY 12036.

Individual Exhibitions:

1960 Artists Cooperative Gallery, Sacramento, California
1962 Artists Cooperative Gallery, Sacramento, California
1968 Artists Cooperative Gallery, Sacramento, California
1970 O. K. Harris Works of Art, New York
1973 O. K. Harris Works of Art, New York
1977 O. K. Harris Works of Art, New York
1980 O. K. Harris Works of Art, New York
1983 O. K. Harris Works of Art, New York
1985 O. K. Harris Works of Art, New York
1987 Tampa Museum of Art, Florida (with Chuck Close)
1990 Butler Institute of American Art, Youngstown
1992 O.K. Harris Works of Art, New York
1994 *Ralph Goings: A Retrospective View of Watercolors, 1972–1994,* Jason McCoy Gallery, New York
1996 *Paperwork,* Louis K. Meisel Gallery, New York

Selected Group Exhibitions:

1969 *Directions 2: Aspects of a New Realism,* Milwaukee Art Center
1970 *The Highway,* University of Pennsylvania, Philadelphia (toured the United States)
1971 *Radical Realism,* Museum of Contemporary Art, Chicago
1972 *Documenta V,* Kassel, West Germany
1974 *Tokyo Biennale 74*
1976 *American Master Drawings and Watercolors,* Whitney Museum, New York

1977 *Representations of America,* Metropolitan Museum, New York (travelled to Moscow, Leningrad and Minsk)
1981 *Contemporary American Realism Since 1960,* Pennsylvania Academy of Fine Arts, Philadelphia
1984 *Automobile and Culture,* Museum of Contemporary Art, Los Angeles (travelled to Detroit)
1986 *Boston Collects,* Museum of Fine Arts, Boston
1991 *In Sharp Focus: Super-realism,* Nassau County Museum of Art, Roslyn Harbor, New York
1996 *A Survey of Contemporary American Realism,* Posco Gallery, Seoul, South Korea
Photorealism's Greatest Hits, Louis K. Meisel Gallery, New York
van de Griff Gallery, Santa Fe, New Mexico
1997 *Photorealists,* Exhibit A Gallery, Savannah College of Art and Design, Georgia

Collections:

Museum of Modern Art, New York; Guggenheim Museum, New York; Neue Galerie, Aachen, West Germany; Whitney Museum, New York; Museum of Contemporary Art, Chicago; Tampa Museum of Art, Florida; Portland Museum of Art, Oregon; Sheldon Memorial Art Museum, University of Nebraska, Lincoln.

Publications:

By GOINGS: Article—''The Photo Realists: 12 Interviews'' by Brian O'Doherty in *Art in America* (New York), November/December 1972.

On GOINGS: Books—*Directions 3:8 Artists,* exhibition catalog by John Taylor, Milwaukee 1971; *New Realism* by Udo Kultermann, Tübingen, West Germany 1972; *Man Made Nature Vol. 5* by Yusuke Nakahara, Tokyo 1972; *Topics in Modern Art* by Lawrence Alloway, New York 1975; *Super Realism* by Edward Lucie-Smith, New York 1979; *Late Modern: The Visual Arts since 1945* by Edward Lucie-Smith, New York 1980; *Surrealist Painting and Scuplture* by Christine Lindey, New York 1980; *Art in the 70s* by Edward Lucie-Smith, New York 1980; *Photorealism* by Louis Meisel, New York 1980; *Realist at Work* by John Arthus, New York 1983; *Ralph Goings* by Linda Chase, New York 1988; *Ralph Goings: A Retrospective View of Watercolors, 1972–1994,* exhibition catalog, New York 1994. **Articles—**''Ralph Goings'' by Jean-Louis Bourgeois in *Artforum* (New York), November 1970; ''The Real and the Artificial'' by William Seitz in *Art in America* (New York), November/December 1972; ''New York'' by Peter Schjeldahl in *Art in America* (New York), September/October 1973; ''The Connotation of Denotation'' by Linda Chase in *Arts Magazine* (New York), February 1974; ''Ralph Goings at O. K. Harris'' by Pepe Karmel in *Art in America* (New York), May 1980; ''A Photorealist's Farmhouse: The Greek Revival Residence of Artist Ralph Goings'' by Carter Ratcliff in *Architectural Digest* (Los Angeles), vol. 45, June 1988.

* * *

Ralph Goings is one of the many Photo-Realist painters who came into prominence at the beginning of the 1970s. His pictures are characteristically clearcut, illusionistically precise transpositions from 35mm slides. His favored subject matter is the synthetic American scene, and he chooses things such as pickup trucks, franchised hamburger stands, California banks and deserted airports, all cool, and obviously artificial and timebound views, located in ''Anywhere U.S.A.''

Like Richard Estes, Robert Cottingham and a few others, Goings is aggressively anti-expressionist and emphasizes the glossiness of mass-produced industrial objects in non-hieratic compositions stressing painstaking craftsmanship and description of visual fact. Out of the artificiality of the industrial location come pictures emanating with static, undisturbed order and anonymity. Goings' attitude is anti-style; his aim, to suppress individuality and limit interpretation in terms of stylistic analysis and emotive content. How one can read these meticulously handmade reduplications of the photographic becomes an open-ended question. All this suppression and consciously accurate stress on visual elements of texture, light and reflection sets Goings in a new category of ''realism,'' one which connects with mass culture and the industrial environment but not with Nature, with what's new now and not relatable with past art. There are elements of Hopper and William Harnett, but with a large difference. The closest connections are with Pop Art, but the subject mattter is not rearranged as it is with 1960s Pop, and the deadpan is achieved by Goings through faithfulness to the photographically seen as counterfeited by arduous craftsmanship.

Goings's pictures are matter-of-fact, deductive, frontal depictions of visual fact. But when one views paintings such as ''Rose Bowl Parade,'' ''Bank of America'' or ''Dick's Union General,'' feelings of irony, lament or celebration creep in. What is depicted is glossy, so inhuman, so populist neat and available. But what is depicted is also quick to get old, becoming yesterday's signs of industrialized, mass-produced vigor. Goings's trucks and his franchised fast food stands are ''period pieces,'' even now turning America's hopes for fastly achieved equal opportunity into reminders of their temporary status and boring sameness. The slow, laborious process of painting these scenes, already rendered doubly artificial, brings heightened consciousness of painting's relationship with the new Nature that surrounds us in our present environment. Once you get over the initial awe of Goings' technical abilities at reduplication, you're left with his choice of subject matter with a definitely individualistic eye and mind. Consider, for instance, that in Goings' ''Burger Chef Interior'' the traditionally mystical dodecahedron is a hanging light, illuminating formica booths and dispensing machines and co-habiting equally with the latest-model bus and Wonder Bread truck. All will soon become outdated in favor of next year's mass-made models.

—Barbara Cavaliere

GOLDBERG, Ken

Nationality: United States. **Born:** Ibadan, Nigeria, 6 October 1961. **Education:** Studied art, Edinburgh University, Scotland, 1982; studied electrical engineering, University of Pennsylvania, B.S.E., 1984; visiting researcher, Center for Manufacturing Systems and Robotics, Israel Institute of Technology (Technion), 1986; studied computer science, Carnegie Mellon University, M.S. and Ph.D., 1990. **Family:** Married Tiffany Shlain. **Career:** Independent artist, San Francisco. Assistant Professor of Computer Science, University of Southern California, 1991–95; Assistant Professor of Computer Science,

1995–97, and Associate Professor of Industrial Engineering and Operations Research, University of California, Berkeley, 1997—. Co-founder and organizer, Art, Technology, and Culture Colloquium, University of California, Berkeley, 1996—; co-founder, Net Work exhibition program, New Langton Arts, 1998; board member and curator, New Langton Arts, 1999—; visiting professor, San Francisco Art Institute, 1999, and MIT Media Lab, 2000; co-organizer, CRASH: Symposium on Critical and Historical Issues in Net Art, University of California, Berkeley, 2000. **Awards:** Presidential Faculty Fellow, The White House and the National Science Foundation, 1995; Kobe Prize, Interactive Media Festival, 1995; First Prize, Festival for Independent Visual Arts Interactive, Montreal, 1995; Joseph Engelberger Award, Robot Industries Association, 2000. **Address:** 4135 Etcheverry Hall, University of California, Berkeley, California 94720–1777. **Web site:** http://www.ieor.berkeley.edu/ ∼goldberg.

Individual Exhibitions:

1990 Forbes Gallery, Pittsburgh, Pennsylvania
1992 *Power and Water* (with Margaret Lazzari), Fisher Gallery, The Los Angeles Biennial
1995 *The Telegarden,* Ars Electronica Center, Linz, Austria
2000 *Matrix Series (186),* Berkeley Art Museum, Berkeley, California

Selected Group Exhibitions:

1991 *Siggraph '91,* Las Vegas
1992 Onyx Gallery, Los Angeles
Siggraph '92, Chicago
1993 Moscone Center, San Francisco
Downey Museum of Art, Downey, California
Siggraph '93: Machine Culture, Anaheim, California
Pauline Hirsh Gallery, Los Angeles
1995 *Festival for Visual Arts (FIVA) Online '95,* Montreal
Siggraph '95, Los Angeles
Site Gallery, Los Angeles
Interactive Media Festival, Los Angeles
Digital Alchemy, San Francisco
Los Angeles Art Fair, Los Angeles Convention Center
1996 *Artifices 4,* La Villette, Paris
Dutch Electronic Art Festival '96, Rotterdam
Contemporary Art Center, New Orleans
Blasthaus Gallery, San Francisco
1997 Beyond Architecture, Chicago Art Institute, Chicago
Real World, New Langton Arts, San Francisco
Review Virtuelle (CD-ROM), Centre Georges Pompidou, Paris
1998 *Interiors,* San Francisco International Art Expo, Catharine Clark Gallery, San Francisco
Shock of the View, Walker Art Museum, Minneapolis
Ninth International Symposium on Electronic Art, Liverpool and Manchester, United Kingdom
Beyond Interface, International Conference on Museums and the Web, Toronto
Interface: Art + Tech in the Bay Area, Duke University Art Museum, Durham, North Carolina
CyberAtlas: Intelligent Life, Guggenheim Art Museum Online, http://cyberatlas.guggenheim.org
1999 *Mori,* ICC Biennale, Tokyo
School of Visual Arts: Digital Salon, New York
The Net Condition, ZKM, Karlsruhe, Germany
Rhizome Artbase, ongoing
2000 *Dystopia and Identity in the Age of Global Communications,* Tribes Gallery, New York
FILE: Festival Internacional de Linguagem Eletronica, Museu da Imagem e do Som, Sao Paulo, Brazil
Whitney Biennial, Whitney Museum of American Art, New York
Kwangju Biennial, South Korea.
High Touch High Tech, Refusalon, San Francisco
Art Entertainment Network, Walker Art Center, Minneapolis
Arte Red, El Pais Digital, Madrid
Particle Accelerators: At the Intersection of Science, Technology, and Photography, Photographic Resource Center, Boston
2001 *Telematic Connections,* San Francisco Art Institute, Art College of Art and Design Pasadena, Austin Museum of Art, and Atlanta College of Art and Design

Selected Internet Installations:

(See http://www.ieor.berkeley.edu/∼goldberg for links) *The Mercury Project* (telerobotic excavation), 1994–95; *The Telegarden* (telerobotic garden), Ars Electronica Center, Linz, Austria, 1995—; *Legal Tender* (telerobotic laboratory), 1996–97; *Dislocation of Intimacy* (telerobotic camera obscura), 1998—; *Mori* (internet-based earthwork), 1999—; *Ouija 2000* (telerobotic Ouija board), 2000—.

Collections:

Homage to Moholy-Nagy, Long Beach Museum of Art; *Ouija 2000,* Berkeley Art Museum.

Publications:

By GOLDBERG: Books—Editor, with others, *Workshop on the Algorithmic Foundations of Robotics,* Wellesley, Massachusetts, 1995; editor, *The Robot in the Garden: Telerobotics and Telepistemology in the Age of the Internet,* Cambridge, MIT Press 2000; editor, with Roland Siegwart, *Beyond Webcams: An Introduction to Online Robots,* Cambridge, MIT Press 2001. **Articles**—''Rationalizing the Irrational'' in *Framework: The Journal of Images and Cultures,* 1993; ''Data Dentata'' (with Richard Wallace) in *Plazm,* vol. 7, 1994; ''Rendering Text: The Web As Hybrid Community'' (with Peter Lunenfeld) in *Siggraph Visual Proceedings,* 1995; ''The Telegarden'' in *Ars Electronica Festival Catalog,* 1996; ''Telepistemology'' in *WIRED,* 1996; ''Virtual Reality in the Age of Telepresence'' in *Convergence,* 1998.

On GOLDBERG: Articles—''Can You Dig?'' by Andrew Rozmiarek in *WIRED,* 1994; ''Aperto: Technofornia'' by Peter Lunenfeld in *Flash Art,* 1996; ''The Invisible Cantilever'' by David Pescovitz in *WIRED,* 1997; ''The Robotic Billfold: Counterfeits and Telepistemology'' by Justine Herbert in *Mondo 2000,* 1997; ''Virtual

Community in a Telepresence Environment'' by Margaret McLaughlin, Kerry Osborne, and Nicole Ellison in *Virtual Culture: Identity and Communication in Cybersociety,* 1997; ''Foundation and Development of Electronic Art'' by Eduardo Kac in *Art Journal,* 1997; ''Shadows and Dirt, Telerobotic Art on the Net by Ken Goldberg'' by Jillian Burt in *Ars Telematica,* 1997; ''Web Robots Offer Hands-On Experience from Afar'' by David Kushner in *New York Times,* 1998; ''Ken Goldberg: Keeping Technology Grounded'' by Reena Jana in *ArtByte,* 1999; ''The Science of the Sleeper'' by Malcolm Gladwell in *The New Yorker,* 1999; ''Replacing Place'' by William Mitchell in *The Digital Dialectic: New Essays on New Media,* 1999; ''State of the (On-Line) Art'' by Robert Atkins in *Art in America,* 1999; ''Beyond the Image: New Directions in Interactive Art'' by Eduardo Kac in *Blimp Film Journal,* 1999; ''Ken Goldberg's Research Is about Facts, but His Online Works Challenge Viewers' Reality'' by Lawrence Biemiller in *Chronicle of Higher Education,* 17 March 2000.

* * *

Ken Goldberg is a multiple threat: one of the foremost roboticists in the world, a professor of Engineering and Operations Research at the University of California at Berkeley, and an artist of international reputation and historic import. His art work, involving robotics and networks and what he has come to refer to as ''telepistemology,'' has been featured in shows around the world, including the ICC in Tokyo; Ars Electronica in Linz, Austria; and the Whitney Biennial in New York. His work performs an investigation of the effects on the ways we think (our epistemologies) brought about by the emergence of the ability to manipulate the world at a vast distance (the tele-action made possible by the convergence of networks and robotics). As Goldberg puts it: ''What can you know when the knowing is at a distance, especially when the knowing is mediated by the distance?''

Goldberg's art works instantiate his technical and theoretical investigations and function as unique aesthetic and phenomenological experiences. He is perhaps best known for his telerobotic installation, *The TeleGarden* (1995–96), now on permanent exhibition at the Ars Electronica Center in Linz. A follow up to the 1995's *The Mercury Project*—the first telerobotic art on the World Wide Web—*The TeleGarden* is a living garden, a small plot of petunias, peppers, and marigolds tended to by a robot arm which seeds and waters the plants and a live video feed to keep watch and monitor the garden. *The Telegarden,* like so many of his later projects, embraces the paradox of immaterial physical environments, transforming what most would consider a fit of over-engineering into a subtle rumination on the nature of the commons. Anyone with a Web browser can access the site, and the rights to water and plant are given to those willing to make their e-mail public to others in the co-operative.

Both *The Mercury Project* and *The Telegarden* combine schematic mappings of physical space, video feedback in real time, and actual robotic movement. As Jillian Burt has noted, ''the sites advance the technical possibilities of human/machine interface over the Web, while simultaneously interrogating the human dimensions of what it means to have control via the Internet of actual motion and physical agency.'' Since then, his work has moved to confront the telepistemology of scale, with 1996's *Invisible Cantilever,* a nano-manufactured model of Frank Lloyd Wright's Fallingwater; the ethics and legalities of counterfeiting, with 1996–97's *Legal Tender,* which offered users the chance to destroy actual currency (a federal crime in the United States) via tele-robotic action; to the mapping of data in real time with 1998's *Mori,* which featured an installation and Java interface to a live seismograph; and most recently to the union of the technical and the mystical imaginaries with *Ouija 2000,* which allows for multiple users around the world to access a Ouija board together via telerobotic, distributed control.

The World Wide Web generated quite a bit of heat in the art world over the past half dozen years, but not that much light. Too few artists working with new technologies are able to penetrate beneath the shell of our culture's intertwined fascination with and repulsion from the machine in the studio. Ken Goldberg's utter mastery of that machine has allowed him the space—both technically and, even more importantly, conceptually—to develop a series of connected yet discrete aesthetic interventions. One need not believe in the myth of the Renaissance man to acknowledge that there are indeed certain individuals who, by virtue of their truly vast interests, skills, and accomplishments, can come to embody the spirit of an age. To do justice to our moment of computation-driven interconnectivity, someone would have to be a renowned scientist, a nuanced artist, and a thinker of subtly and depth. This is not a wish list. Instead, it is a modest description of Ken Goldberg.

—Peter Lunenfeld

GOLUB, Leon (Albert)

Nationality: American. **Born:** Chicago, Illinois, 23 January 1922. **Education:** University of Chicago, 1940–42, B.A. in art history 1942; School of the Art Institute of Chicago, under Paul Wieghardt, Kathleen Blackshear, Robert Lifuendahl, 1946–50, B.F.A. 1949, M.F.A. 1950. **Military Service:** Served as Sergeant in the 942nd Engineers, Aviation Typographic Battalion, in Europe, 1943–46. **Family:** Married the artist Nancy Spero, *q.v.,* in 1951; sons: Stephen, Philip, and Paul. **Career:** Independent artist, since 1950. Art instructor, Wright Junior College, Chicago, 1950–55, and Illinois Institute of Technology, Chicago, 1955–56; travelled in Europe, and lived in Italy, 1956–57; assistant professor of Art, Indiana University, Bloomington, 1957–59; lived in Paris, 1959–64; lecturer, Tyler School of Art, Temple University, Philadelphia, 1965–66; instructor, School of Visual Arts, New York, 1966–69; assistant professor of Art, Fairleigh Dickinson University, Rutherford, New Jersey, 1969. Professor, 1970–84, and John C. Van Dyck Professor of Visual Art since 1984, Mason Gross School of the Arts, Rutgers University, New Brunswick, New Jersey. **Awards:** Florsheim Memorial Prize, *61st American Exhibition,* Art Institute of Chicago, 1954; Ford Foundation grant, 1960; Watson F. Blair Purchase Prize, *65th American Exhibition,* Art Institute of Chicago, 1962; Tamarind Lithography Grant, 1965; Cassandra Foundation grant, 1967; Guggenheim grant, 1968; National Institute of Arts and Letters Award, 1973; Rutgers University Research Council Faculty Fellowship, 1975–76; Bartels-Cahn-Campana Award, Art Institute of Chicago, 1986; Hiroshima Art Prize, 1996. **Agents:** Ronald Feldman Fine Art, 31 Mercer St., New York, New York 10013; Rhona Hoffman Gallery, 215 West Superior Street, Chicago, Illinois 60610; Barbara Gross Galerie, Thierschstr, 51, 8000 Munich 22, Germany; Galerie Darthea Speyer, 6 rue Jacques Callot, 75006 Paris, France. **Address:** 530 La Guardia Place, New York, New York 10012, U.S.A.

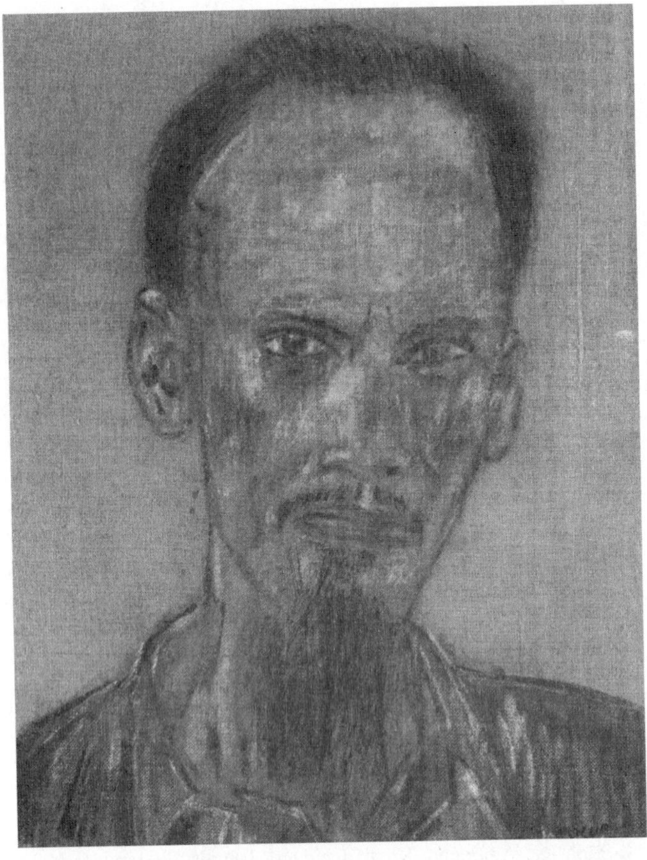

Leon Golub: *Three of Three Portraits of Ho Chi Minh,* 1967. ©Christie's Images/Corbis.

Individual Exhibitions:

1950 Contemporary Gallery, Chicago
1951 Purdue University, West Lafayette, Indiana
1952 Wittenborn and Company Gallery, New York
1954 Artists Gallery, New York
Wittenborn and Company Gallery, New York
1955 Feigl Gallery, New York
Allan Frumkin Gallery, Chicago
1956 Feigl Gallery, New York
Allan Frumkin Gallery, Chicago
Pomona College, California
Pasadena Museum of Art, California
1957 Allan Frumkin Gallery, Chicago
Institute of Contemporary Arts, London
1958 Allan Frumkin Gallery, Chicago
Indiana University, Bloomington
1959 Allan Frumkin Gallery, Chicago
1960 Allan Frumkin Gallery, Chicago
Centre Culturel Americain, Paris
1961 Allan Frumkin Gallery, Chicago
1962 Allan Frumkin Gallery, Chicago
Galerie Iris Clert, Paris
Hanover Gallery, London
1963 Allan Frumkin Gallery, Chicago
Gallery A, Melbourne
1964 Allan Frumkin Gallery, Chicago
Tyler School of Art, Temple University, Philadelphia (retrospective)
Galerie Iris Clert and Galerie Europe, Paris (joint exhibition)
1966 Cliffdwellers Gallery, Chicago
University of Chicago (retrospective)
1968 10 Downtown, New York (studio exhibition)
1970 LoGiudice Gallery, Chicago
Hayden Gallery, Massachusetts Institute of Technology, Cambridge
National Gallery of Victoria, Melbourne
1971 Galerie Darthea Speyer, Paris
1972 Herbert Lehman College, New York
Bienville Gallery, New Orleans
1973 Musée de l'Abbaye Sainte Croix, Sable d'Olonne, France
1974 *Leon Golub: The Development of His Art,* Museum of Contemporary Art, Chicago (retrospective)
1975 State University of New York at Stony Brook
New Jersey State Museum, Trenton
1976 Haverford College, Pennsylvania
San Francisco Art Institute
1977 Bienville Gallery, New Orleans
Olympia Galleries, Philadelphia
Walter Kelly Gallery, Chicago
1978 State University of New York at Stony Brook
Portraits of Power, Colgate University, Hamilton, New York
1979 Visual Arts Museum, School of Visual Arts, New York
1980 Protetch-McIntosh Gallery, Washington, D.C.
1981 *Leon Golub/Nancy Spero,* Swarthmore College, Pennsylvania
1982 Susan Caldwell Inc., New York
Vietnam War, Tweed Arts Group, Plainfield, New Jersey (with Nancy Spero)
Kipnis Works of Art, Atlanta
Young Hoffman Gallery, Chicago
Institute of Contemporary Arts, London
1983 University of California, Berkeley
University of New Mexico, Albuquerque (with Nancy Spero)
Honolulu Academy of Arts, Hawaii
Mercenaries, Interrogations and Other Works, University of Houston, Texas (travelled to Portland, Oregon; Tucson, Arizona; Oxford, Ohio; Storrs, Connecticut; Syracuse, New York)
College of Art and Design, Detroit (with Nancy Spero)
1984 Installation Gallery, San Diego, California
Susan Caldwell Inc., New York
Gallery Paule Anglim, San Francisco
New Museum of Contemporary Art, New York (retrospective; travelled to La Jolla, California; Chicago; Montreal; Washington, D. C.; and Boston, 1985)
Galerie Darthea Speyer, Paris
1985 Institute of Contemporary Art, Boston
Rhona Hoffman Gallery, Chicago
Printworks, Chicago
Donald Young Gallery, Chicago
Stanford University, California
1986 Barbara Gladstone Gallery, New York

Greenville County Museum of Art, South Carolina
Appalachian State University, Boone, North Carolina
1987 Kunstmuseum, Lucerne
Kunstverein, Hamburg
Orchard Gallery, Derry, Northern Ireland
1991 Dickinson College, Carlisle, Pennsylvania
Chicago Cultural Center
Brooklyn Museum, New York
1992 Musee d'Art Contemporaine de Montreal, Quebec
Institute of Contemporary Art, Philadelphia
Malmo Konsthall, Sweden
1993 Akron Art Museum, Ohio
Ulmer Museum, Ulm, Germany
Kunstverein Ulm, Germany
von der Heydt Museum, Wuppertal, Germany
1994 The American Center, Paris
1995 *Violence Zone: The Weimar Installation,* OrangerieSchlob Belvedere, Weimar
Snake Eyes, Ronald Feldman Fine Arts, New York
1996 *Leon Golub and Nancy Spero,* Hiroshima City Museum of Contemporary Art, Hiroshima City
Sphinx and Other Enigmas, Ronald Feldman Fine Arts, New York
1998 *Leon Golub and Nancy Spero,* Museo Jacobo Borges, Caracas (traveled to Ronald Feldman Fine Arts, New York)
1999 *Leon Golub,* Bucknell Art Gallery, Bucknell University, Lewisberg, Pennsylvania
2000 *Leon Golub Paintings,* Stedelijk Museum vor Actuele Kunst, Ghent, Belgium
Leon Golub, Irish Museum of Modern Art, Dublin

Selected Group Exhibitions:

1954 *Young American Painters,* Guggenheim Museum, New York (toured the United States)
1959 *Images of Man,* Museum of Modern Art, New York
1968 *The Obsessive Image 1960–68,* Institute of Contemporary Arts, London
1977 *Paris-New York,* Centre Georges Pompidou, Paris
1985 *Nouvelle Biennale de Paris,* La Villette, Paris
1987 *Documenta 8,* Museum Fridericianum, Kassel, West Germany
1991 *As Seen by Both Sides: American and Vietnamese Artists Look at War,* Boston University Art Gallery (travelled in U.S. and Vietnam 1991–94)
1992 *Parallel Visions: Modern Artists and Outsider Art,* Los Angeles County Museum of Art (travelled to Madrid, Basel and Tokyo)
1993 *43rd Biennial Exhibition of Contemporary American Painting,* The Corcoran Museum of Art, Washington, D.C.
1994 *Black Male,* The Whitney Museum of American Art, New York
1995 *Murder,* Thread Waxing Space, New York (also Bergamot Station Arts Center, Santa Monica)
25 Americans: Paintings in the 90s, Milwaukee Art Museum
1996 *Multiple Identity: Selections from the Whitney Museum of Art,* New York
Thinking Print: Books to Billboards, 1980–95, Museum of Modern Art, New York
1997 *Envisioning the Contemporary,* Museum of Contemporary Art, Chicago
1998 *Presence of the Greek Myth,* Instituto di Storia dell'Arte, Palermo, Italy
Extensions: Aspects of the Figure, Joseloff Gallery, University of Hartford, West Hartford, Connecticut
1999 *Coming to Life: The Figure in American Art, 1955–1965,* Henry Art Gallery, University of Washington, Seattle
To the Rescue: Eight Artists in an Archive, International Center for Photography Midtown, New York

Collections:

Museum of Modern Art, New York; Smithsonian Institution, Washington, D.C.; Art Institute of Chicago; Museum of Contemporary Art, Chicago; Los Angeles County Museum of Art; National Gallery of Victoria, Melbourne; Seattle Art Museum, Washington; Musee des Beaux-Arts, Montreal; Brooklyn Museum, New York; Metropolitan Museum of Art, New York; Tate Gallery, London; Uffizi Gallery, Florence; Whitney Museum of American Art, New York.

Publications:

By GOLUB: Articles—''A Critique of Abstract Expressionism'' in *College Art Journal* (Bloomington, Indiana), Winter 1955; ''The Artist as an Angry Artist'' in *Arts Magazine* (New York), April 1967; ''Bombs and Helicopters: The Art of Nancy Spero'' in *Caterpillar I* (New York), 1967; ''An Interview with Leon Golub,'' with Irving Sandler, in *Arts Magazine* (New York), February 1970; ''Regarding the Lehman and Rockefeller Gifts to the Metropolitan Museum'' in *Artforum* (New York), November 1970; ''Utopia/Anti-Utopia'' in *Artforum* (New York), May 1972; ''2D/3D'' in *Artforum* (New York), March 1973; ''16 Whitney Museum Annuals of American Painting: Percentages 1950–1972'' in *Artforum* (New York), March 1973; ''Art Politics and Ethics: Interview with Leon Golub and Nancy Spero,'' with Derek Guthrie, in *New Art Examiner* (Chicago), April 1977; ''The Mercenaries: An Interview with Leon Golub,'' with Matthew Baigell, in *Arts Magazine* (New York), May 1981; ''On Being Taken for Granted'' in *New Art Examiner* (Chicago), October 1981; ''Leon Golub,'' interview with Suzanne Davies, in *Art-Network* (Sydney), Autumn 1985.

On GOLUB: Books—*Leon Golub,* exhibition catalog by Lawrence Alloway, Chicago 1957; *Leon Golub,* exhibition catalog by Robert Melville, London 1957; *New Images of Man* by Peter Selz, New York 1959; *Art: USA: Now* by Allan Weller, Lucerne 1962; *Leon Golub: Retrospective Catalog* by A. James Speyer, Philadelphia 1964; *The Arts and the Public* by James E. Miller and Paul Herring, Chicago 1967; *Leon Golub,* exhibition catalog by Barbara Klein, Cambridge, Massachusetts 1970; *Leon Golub,* exhibition catalog by Corinne Robbins, Melbourne 1970; *Fantastic Images: Chicago Art since 1945* by Franz Schulze, Chicago 1972; *Leon Golub: The Development of His Art,* exhibition catalog by Lawrence Alloway, Chicago 1974; *Leon Golub,* exhibition catalog by Dennis Adrian, Trenton, New Jersey 1975; *Portraits of Power,* exhibition catalog by Edward Bryant, Hamilton, New York 1978; *The New York School* by Irving

Sandler, New York 1978; *Golub,* exhibition catalog by Lynn Gumpert and Ned Rifkin, New York 1984; *Leon Golub: Existential/Activist Painter* by Donald Kuspit, New Brunswick 1985; *Leon Golub 1986,* exhibition catalog by Peter Schjeldahl, New York 1986; *Leon Golub: Selected Paintings 1967–1986,* exhibition catalog, Derry 1986; *Leon Golub,* exhibition catalog by Donald Kuspit, Lucerne and Hamburg 1987; *Leon Golub,* exhibition catalog with text by Thomas McEvilley, Malmo 1992 (text reprinted in *The Exiles Return: Toward a Redefinition of Painting for the Post-Modern Era,* Cambridge, England, 1993); *Leon Golub: While the Crime is Blazing, Paintings and Drawings, 1994–1999* by Stuart Horodner, Bucknell University 1999. **Articles—**''A New Imagery in American Painting'' by Peter Selz in *College Art Journal* (Bloomington, Indiana), Summer 1956; ''Leon Golub'' by Robert Pincus-Witten in *Art International* (Lugano, Switzerland), February 1962; ''Chicago Letter'' by Franz Schulze in *Art International* (Lugano, Switzerland), 20 January 1967; ''Styles of Radical Will'' by Susan Sontag in *Caterpillar* (New York), October 1969; ''Golub: Mythes a l'heure de Napalm'' by G. Gassiot Talabot in *Opus International* (Paris), March 1971; ''Leon Golub: Art and Politics'' by Lawrence Alloway in *Artforum* (New York), October 1974; ''Majestic Existentialism'' by Franz Schulze in *ARTnews* (New York), October 1974; ''Golub's Assassins: An Anatomy of Violence'' by Donald Kuspit in *Art in America* (New York), May/June 1975; ''Aesthetics of Mutilation'' by Harold Rosenberg in *The New Yorker,* 12 May 1975; ''Leon Golub: The Faces of Power'' by Corinne Robbins in *Arts Magazine* (New York), February 1977; ''Leon Golub'' by Peter Fuller in *Beyond the Crisis in Art,* London 1980; ''Leon Golub's Gigantomachies: Pergamon Revisited'' by Joseph Dreiss in *Arts Magazine* (New York), May 1981; ''Leon Golub's Murals of Mercenaries'' by Donald Kuspit in *Artforum* (New York), May 1981; ''Leon Golub'' by Joseph Dreiss in *Arts Magazine* (New York), January 1982; ''Leon Golub's Mean Streets'' by Gerald Marzorati in *Arts News* (New York), February 1985; ''Riddled Sphinxes'' by Robert Storr in *Art in America* (New York), March 1989; ''Undercover Agent'' by Rosetta Brooks in *Artforum* (New York), January 1990; ''Nancy Spero und Leon Golub: Ars sine Scientia Nihil Est'' in *Artis, das Aktuelle Kunstmagazin,* April 1990; ''A Conversation with Leon Golub'' in *Worldwide,* traveling exhibition catalog by Barbara Diduk and David Robertson, 1992; ''Infuitabile fatum: Leon Golub's History Painting'' by Jon Bird in *Oxford Art Journal,* no. 20, 1997.

*

The ''Mercenaries'' (1979-), the ''Interrogations'' (1980-), ''White Squads'' (1982-), and ''Blacks'' (1985-) occur on a public scale; the figures are approximately twice life size. (The paintings range from 10 feet in height to 12 to 16 feet in length.) Despite the enormous scale, the figures are intended to be viewed directly, confrontationally, intimately. The mercs and police agents intervene (move into) our space, and we are *inserted* into their space, their actions. This ''intimacy'' pinpoints our direct awareness of the possibilities and consequences of such actions and events, part of the history of these times. The black individuals are seen as alerted to or resistant to the viewer, our presence in their space.

''Irregular'' actions occur at the peripheries of public or government control. Power is control, and governmental agencies or political groups will use extra-legal means when it suits their purposes, that is, when they can get away with it. This occurs to varying and changing degrees in all societies.

The mercs or interrogators are observed directly. We publicly acknowledge and voyeuristically observe them. They are raunchy, irritable, mocking, imply racial hostility and/or sexual ambivalence. Violence and implied violence are immediate and instantaneous, and the mercs and interrogators indicate no compunction in their actions. They are casually self-conscious and eye us, alerted to our observation and interest in their actions. The ''Black'' paintings continue this point of view but from the context of blacks in contact or tension with whites, a seared presence.

—Leon Golub

* * *

Leon Golub, a native Chicagoan, found his earliest influences as a painter at a time when the Abstract Expressionism of Kline, Pollock, de Kooning and others had achieved a total breakthrough to public acclaim. But unlike the action painters, whose historical lineage could be traced from nineteenth-century French painting, Golub felt a strong connection to tribal art and German Expressionism, which offered him an avenue away from painterly tradition towards ''different conceptions of the human body, other materials and techniques, directness.''

From the start, Golub's preoccupation was the human psyche, its power and vulnerability. His subject was not heroic man, but man at odds with his self and his civilization. Of ''Thwarted,'' 1953, Peter Selz has written that the painting depicts a creature of Herculean strength who nonetheless ''lacks the instruments by which [he] assumes control over his environment. . . . no neck to turn and view, no arms. . . an image of tragic frustration.'' The surfaces of Golub's early paintings were similarly scarred, heavily layered and scraped, with patches of turgid pigment bulked together, scarcely relieved by patches of white. Golub depicted shamans, mythical figures, sphinxes, and seers, personifications of the artist's role, then solitary heads, charred figures, colossuses, and reclining nudes, which gradually took on greater existential overtones.

Slowly the tilt of Golub's vision drew closer to that of Hellenistic art and late Roman sculpture, with their depictions of human figures in action, and emphasis on musculature and anatomy. *Gigantomachy I,* from 1965, depicts a large group of male nudes in battle. As in a classical relief, the scraped white, black, and red modeling of the figures plays against the simplicity of the thinly scrubbed, reddish brown ground. It is impossible to discern which of the agitated figures, in their frieze-like massing, are aggressors, and which are victims. In scale and subject, the five paintings of the *Gigantomachy* series point the way to Golub's mature depictions of violence and torture, but the nude figures here remain timeless and anonymous, locked in an eternal, mythic struggle.

In the early seventies, with the Vietnam war still raging, Golub experimented by giving his victims and victimizers identities: specific faces, physiognomies, weapons, and clothing. In *Vietnam I,* from 1972, the treatment of the figures is more visceral than before—even the flesh of the aggressors has a flayed, bloody quality, though their gestures seem strangely suspended, weightless and puppet-like. The background surrounding the figures has been left in large part completely bare; one huge piece of canvas it is simply cut away, like a war-torn fragment, though in the far right, where the main act of savagery takes place, the stained ground gives the suggestion of an architectural setting, and washes of rusty reds and blacks resemble clouds of smoke and flame. Gone is the psychological ambiguity of the earlier, classicized paintings, and while the "Vietnam" series may be too specific, too didactic, to be wholly effective, Golub's use of news photos and military handbooks for his source imagery had important implications for his ensuing work.

Throughout the mid-seventies, Golub worked on a number of small portraits based on news photographs of leaders of state: Henry Kissinger, Ho Chi Minh, Nelson Rockefeller, and the like. What fascinated Golub was how the media images distanced and flattened our perception of those in power. By removing them from their original context, Golub could address our relationship to these media images, to show how conditioned we are by them. As Gerald Marzorati has written, "What happens to these faces when they are lifted from the news columns and painted in dumb-rote fashion? They lose their gloss and immediacy. Unmoored, the meaning and intention of the images drift. The 'power' of the original photograph—and thus the power of the man-in-the-news photographed—is deflated." (Gerald Marzorati, "Leon Golub's Mean Streets, *Art News,* February 1985.)

With the *Mercenaries* series, begun in 1979, Golub forced the viewer into an uneasy identification with his subject, confronting us with a spectacle of brutality enacted by antagonists who appeared strangely detached from their actions. In *Mercenaries II,* from 1979, the figures with their stop-action gestures push against the front of the picture plane, threatening to enter our space. The unstretched canvas is meant to be hung low, implicating us further, forcing us to consider the nature of our involvement with the scene depicted. The exquisite facility and earthy beauty of Golub's paint handling—its richly textured colorations and luminous red oxide ground—only reinforce the feeling of discomfort, compelling us to look, to stay with and in the experience of the painting, thus serving as a stark contrast to its aura of impending violence. Here the seductive nature of the violent images with which we are so inundated as a society is arrested and enlarged, forcing us to question our perverse fascination and simultaneous detachment from them, in short, our own morality. The apparent ease of the mercenaries is excruciating, their matter-of-factness evincing our tacit approval. In *Interrogation II,* 1981, this discomfort is even more pronounced. The goons leer at us, their casual gestures seem to mock our unease, while their victim sits naked, masked, and bound, a mute symbol of our unspoken complicity. It is this ability to provoke our palpable anxiety, to encourage our identification with his figures of power and violence, and to implicate us in the barbarity that underlies their sensual surfaces, that gives Golub's work its rare authority as political art.

In the *Riots, Interrogations, White Squad,* and *Horsing Around* series that followed, there is an increased sense of physical identification with the painted thugs, assassins, and soldiers—a sort of enforced intimacy, that heightens our awareness of our shared vulnerability. Golub makes greater use of spatial recession and foreshortening, and figures become cropped, implying their continuation into real space. Golub has stated, "The glance is like the furthest extension of our nerve endings. . . One of the peculiar characteristics I have developed has to do with body awareness. It started with my notions about skin, which are not so different from those about the gaze. It's the way I paint, scraping down to the skin of the canvas. . . . The skin is a curious inside/outside membrane; it wraps us, it is between us and everything else out there."

Women now appear, as victims of rape and torture (*Interrogation III,* 1981), or willing sexual accomplices, as disturbingly vacant as their sinister macho counterparts (*Horsing Around I, II,* and *III,* 1982–83). Like the *Horsing Around* series, the *Patriot* series from the early 90s brings Golub's critique closer to home—the characters no longer allow us the comfort of geographical remove. Brawny working-class men wearing T-shirts emblazoned with patriotic imagery and slogans (an American flag with the text, "Try Burning This One. . . ASSHOLE") partake in aggressive sexual posturing, revealing the anxiety and acute sense of powerlessness underlying their bravado.

Recent paintings, such as *Agent Orange,* 1993, are more equivocal in tone, with crude graffiti-like inscriptions and stenciled text ("Will Allegory Kill Art?") overlaid on thin, almost vaporous layers of painted imagery, "as though glimpsed abruptly, but unforgettably, through bright flashes of stroboscopic light. . . These new paintings possess a kind of demonic beauty that is new to Golub's work." (Barry Schwabsky, *Artforum,* November 1993.) In a decade in which political art has proliferated, Golub's work, even at its most strident, has avoided the elitist, self-congratulatory and ultimately self-defeating strategy of preaching to the converted that diminishes so much well-intentioned work (after all, there is nothing the art world likes better than to think of itself as more enlightened than the rest of society). By relying on the intrinsic expressive power of his painted imagery to move us, and by locating his scenes of violence and torture within the dimensions of our own morality, Golub avoids those traps, eliciting real pathos and consternation from a too often desensitized and indifferent audience.

—Dorothy Valakos

Perhaps as a result of his advancing age, Golub's recent work has dealt more with abstract themes, and metaphors of suffering and death have replaced the images of implied violence which dominated the paintings of the 1970s and 1980s. Also absent is the narrative quality of the earlier works. Instead, the compositions are fragmentary, bringing together symbols, especially dogs and human skulls, often combined with phrases of text—for example, a quote from Nietzsche: "I have given a name to my pain and call it 'DOG.'" The dogs may serve as surrogates for the aggressive figures of his early series such as the "Mercenaries" or "Interrogations," and the skulls as remnants of their victims, but the sense of responsibility thrust upon the viewer is now more philosophical in nature, as each must find an individual path to meaning among the elements. Although the works continue to be formally ambitious in their scale and technical facility there is a graffiti-esque quality to the patches of color and transparent washes applied to raw linen.

—Paula Wisotzki

GÓMEZ-PEÑA, Guillermo

Nationality: Mexican. **Born:** Mexico City, 1955; moved to United States, 1978. **Career:** Founding member, Border Arts Workshop/Taller de Arte Fronerizo (binational arts collective), 1985–90; editor, *The Broken Line/La Línea Quebrada* (experimental arts magazine), 1985–90; contributor, *Crossroads* national radio program, 1987–90; regular contributor, *All Things Considered* radio program; author of essays for newspapers and magazines; contributing editor, *The Drama*

Guillermo Gómez-Peña: as *El Mad Max.* Photo by Eugenio Custro. ©Guillermo Gómez-Peña.

Review, Massachusetts Institute of Technology, Boston. **Awards:** Prix de la Parole, International Theatre of the Americas, Montreal, 1989; Bessie Award, New York, 1989; first prize, ''Performance Film,'' Cine Festival, San Antonio, Texas, 1991, and first prize, National Latino Film and Video Festival, 1991, for film version of performance *Border Brujo* (with Isaac Artenstein); Silver Award in Performance/Spoken Word Category, Corporation for Public Broadcasting, 1991, for ''Border Notebooks'' (radio performance); MacArthur Fellowship, 1991–1996; Viva Los Artistas Award, Los Angeles Music Center, 1993; first prize, National Association of Community Radios, 1993, for ''We Don't Speak English Only, Vato!'' (radio performance); named to *The Utne Reader*'s ''List of 100 Visionaries,'' 1995; Golden Reel Award, 1995, for ''Menage-à-Trade'' (radio performance); first prize, Cine Festival, San Antonio, Texas, 1996, for *El Naftazteca: Cyber Aztec TV for 2000,* and 1998, for *Temple of Confessions*; American Book Award for *The New World Border,* 1997; Cineaste Lifetime Achievement Award, Taos Talking Pictures Film Festival, 2000; ''best performance video,'' Vancouver Video Poetry Festival, 2001, for *Borderstasis.* **Agent:** Nola Mariano, Circuit Network, 2940 16th Street, Ste. 110, San Francisco, California 94103.

Public Performances:

1988 The International Theatre Festival of the Americas, Montreal
1989 The Demons of Los Angeles, France, Spain, and Sweden
1990 Bienal de la Habana, The Decade Show, New York
Time Festival, Gante, Belgium
EDGE '90, Newcastle, England
The Los Angeles Festival,
1991 The Next Wave Festival, Brooklyn Academy of Music, New York
The Festival of the Worlds, Finland
1992 EDGE '92, Madrid and London
The Sydney Biennale, Australia
1993 The Los Angeles Festival, Los Angeles
Whitney Biennale, New York
Fundación Banco Patricios, Buenos Aires
Rompeforma, Puerto Rico
The Hamburg Theatre Festival, Germany
LIFT, London
1994 3er Festival de Performance, Mexico City
Ante-América, Colombia, Dominican Republic, Mexico, and United States
1995 Helsinki Act, Finland
LIFT, London
1996 5Cyberconf, Madrid
Polverigi Theatre Festival, Italy
Szene Festival, Salzburg, Austria
1997 ARS Electronica, Lintz, Austria
Root/less Festival, Hull, England
1998 Inroads, Arts International, Miami
1999 Caribe 2000, San Juan, Puerto Rico
Sonart, Barcelona, Spain
Diaspora, Oviedo, Spain
2000 Eventa 5, Sweden
Encontro Hemisferico, Rio de Janeiro, Brazil
2001 Experiencias: Barcelona Art Report, Spain
International Theater Festival, Havana, Cuba
The Performance Space, Sydney, Australia

Publications:

By GÓMEZ-PEÑA: Books—editor, with Philip Brookman, *Made in Aztlán,* San Diego, California, Centrol Cultural de la Raza 1986; *Warrior for Gringostroika: Essays, Performance Texts, and Poetry,* St. Paul, Minnesota, Graywolf 1994; *The New World Border: Prophecies, Poems, and Loqueras for the End of the Century,* San Francisco, City Lights 1996; *Friendly Cannibals,* with art by Enrique Chagoy, San Francisco, Artspace 1996; *Mexican Beasts and Living Santos* (includes CD), with Roberto Sifuentes and others, New York, PowerHouse 1997; *Codex Spangliensis: From Columbus to the Border Patrol,* with Enrique Chagoya and Felicia Rice, San Francisco, City Lights 2000; *Dangerous Border Crossings: The Artist Talks Back,* New York, Routledge 2000. **Articles**—Interview in *Aspects of Resistance* by Rupbert Garcia, New York 1994; ''The Artist as Criminal'' in *Drama Review,* vol. 40, Spring 1996. **Audio**—*Borderless Radio* (spoken-word CD), Toronto, Word of Mouth 1995.

On GÓMEZ-PEÑA: Books—*English is Broken Here: Notes on Cultural Fusion in the Americas* by Coco Fusco, New York 1995; *Guillermo Gómez-Peña: An Introduction* by Lisa Wolford, Bowling Green (Ohio) University Press 1998. **Articles**—''On Nationality: 13 Artists'' by Lilly Wei et. al. in *Art in America,* September 1991; ''The Art of Ethnic Tensions: Guillermo Gómez-Peña Uses Theatrics to Ease Borders'' by Miriam Horn in *U.S. News and World Report,* 30 December 1991; ''Recent Latin American Art'' by Luis Camnitzer in *Art Journal,* Winter 1992; ''Guillermo Gómez-Peña: True Confessions of a Techno-Aztec Performance Artist'' by Scott T. Cummings in *American Theatre,* November 1994.

* * *

Guillermo Gómez-Peña's writings and performances have been recognized with numerous honors, yet only a small portion of his artistic and political activities have taken place within the confines of the art world. A visionary artist and cultural theorist who refuses to let his work be defined within pre-existing categories, Gómez-Peña is as likely to be found performing in community centers or marginally funded alternative arts spaces as in the museums and galleries of Mexico City, New York, and London. Whether working as a commentator for National Public Radio, engaging in street interventions at Ellis Island, or organizing performative town meetings, Gómez-Peña epitomizes the role of the artist as citizen diplomat and public intellectual, using performance as a tool to initiate dialogue on a range of issues, including immigration, global capitalism, and Anglo-American attitudes toward Latinos and indigenous peoples. He is committed to making art that is politically engaged, theoretically informed, and yet highly accessible, addressing multiple constituencies and communities.

Gómez-Peña's work is characterized by a type of artistic and political strategy that he describes as ''reverse anthropology.'' Both in his performance texts and his critical writings, Gómez-Peña seeks to appropriate and reverse the direction of the ethnographic gaze. To this end, his work explores situations of radical historical, political, and cultural contingency, strategically occupying a mythical center from which he is able to explain the dominant culture to itself. His performances alternately invoke and interrogate familiar images of the ''rrrrroomantic Mexican'' as seen on picture postcards and in tourist brochures, using humor and irony to guide his audiences through the millennial cartography of his ''performance universe,'' a world in which essentialist notions of identity collapse and geopolitical borders fade in the wake of an irreversible process of cultural hybridization.

Gómez-Peña first came to national attention as a solo artist in the late 1980s as a result of his celebrated performance *Border Brujo*, a bilingual, disnarrative piece in which he embodied a range of personae incarnating various archetypes associated with the U.S./Mexican border region. Along with his contributions to the influential Border Arts Workshop/Taller de Arte Fronterizo, a collective of activist-artists based in San Diego/Tijuana, *Border Brujo* helped to establish Gómez-Peña as a primary figure in the border arts movement. The movement—which began as a grass roots initiative that incorporated visual art, site-specific performance, experimental journalism, and various forms of political intervention— was eventually co-opted by mainstream institutions and Anglo impressarios at the expense of the visions and intentions of its originators, a development that led Gómez-Peña to distance himself from the label of ''border artist.''

In the early 1990s, Gómez-Peña worked primarily with postcolonial theorist and filmmaker Coco Fusco. Their collaboration gave rise to various projects, most significantly the diorama performance *Two Undiscovered Amerindians Visit. . .*, an interactive installation piece in which the artists appeared as two pre-contact natives from the fictional island of Guatinaui. Performing in natural history museums and historically charged sites rather than in traditional arts venues, Gómez-Peña and Fusco sought to reach a broad range of spectators, many of whom accepted the metafictional premise of the exhibit, viewing the artists as ''authentic primitives'' caged for their own protection. Comprised of highly charged images and physical tableaux without spoken dialogue, the performance functioned as a catalyst, inviting interventions and responses from audience members. Observers who failed to recognize the heavy irony of the performance responded variously to the spectacle of caged primitives, expressing outrage, amusement, or chagrin.

The interactive dimension of the diorama performances has remained central to Gómez-Peña's subsequent explorations of the genre. In *The Temple of Confessions*, one of Gómez-Peña's first major collaborations with interdisciplinary artist Roberto Sifuentes, the performers exhibited themselves inside Plexiglas boxes as ''living border saints.'' Visitors to the *Temple* installation entered an exotic and perversely sanctified space in which Sifuentes was displayed as a martyred Latino gang member, and Gómez-Peña as a hyperexoticized curio shop shaman. Performance docents costumed as nuns encouraged visitors to approach the persecuted saints and confess their fears and desires regarding Mexico, Mexicans, and people of color. A soundscape projected through the gallery included selections from the most provocative audience confessions, ranging from graphic sexual fantasies and descriptions of violent acts involving men and women of color to sensitive and highly nuanced reflections on the consequences of Anglo-American imperialism and affirmations of the rights of Mexicans and indigenous peoples. In conjunction with the *Temple* installation, Gómez-Peña and Sifuentes constructed a ''cyber-confessional'' inviting anonymous internet users to articulate their responses to a series of questions on race, immigration, language, and sexuality. Materials gathered by means of both the live and virtual confessions provided the point of departure for the creation of personae central to subsequent diorama performances such as *The Mexterminator Project* and *The Museum of Fetishized Identities,* created in collaboration with Sifuentes, dancer Sara Shelton-Mann, and performer Juan Ybarra, along with a range of contributing artists.

Gómez-Peña's exploration of digital technologies in selected performance projects, along with his influential writings on the relation of Latinos to virtual culture, constituted a significant intervention into the racially unmarked field of cyberstudies. He refers to the personae that populate his most recent interactive performances as ''ethno-cyborgs,'' a term that can be understood to suggest the extent to which ethnic identity is mediated through technologies of representation. These highly parodic, hybridized figures reflect the commodification of ethnic identities and the primitivizing rhetoric of dominant cultural discourse rather than the lived experience of subaltern groups: a pachuco space alien, an emasculated shaman, a transvestite Anglo mariachi, and a martyred Latino Christ.

Concurrent with his work on interactive diorama installations, Gómez-Peña has continued to develop both spoken-word performances and large-scale scripted pieces, along with theoretical writings and experimental fiction. He is currently collaborating with composer Guillermo Galindo and librettist Elaine Katzenberger on an experimental opera, *Califas 2000: Jurassic Aztlán.* Set in a distant future where ethnic difference has been genetically bred out of the human species, the performance takes the form of a ''memoryscape expo'' detailing the wrongs of humanity's past.

—Lisa Wolford

GONZALEZ, Tony

Nationality: Puerto Rican. **Born:** New York, New York, 9 November 1965. **Education:** Cooper Union, B.F.A. 1987; Yale University, M.F.A. 1989. **Family:** Married Hedy Roma. **Career:** Artist, since 1991; instructor, Burlington County College, 1989–91; adjunct instructor, 1991–97, and adjunct assistant professor, 1997—, Cooper Union, New York; visiting artist, Pratt Institute, 1998—; adjunct assistant professor, New York University, 1999—; photography consultant to a number of non-profit organizations, including the Ford Foundation, the Edna McConnell Clark Foundation, and the American Indian College Fund. **Awards:** Ford Foundation Fellowship, 1987–89; Ward Cheney Memorial Award, 1989; Honorable Mention, City Without Walls Gallery, 9th Annual Metro Juried Small Works Show, 1990; Award of Excellence, *Photographers Forum Magazine,* 11th Annual Spring Photography Contest, 1991; En Foco Inc. grant, 1996. **Address:** 720 Second Avenue, #9, New York, New York 10016, U.S.A.

Individual Exhibitions:

1991 Germantown Academy, Ft. Washington, Pennsylvania
1996 Sam Houston State University, Huntsville, Texas
1997 View Point Gallery, Sacramento, California
1998 El Museo Francisco Oller y Diego Rivera, Inc., Buffalo, New York
1999 Germantown Academy, Ft. Washington, Pennsylvania

Cheryl McGinnis Gallery, New York
Passaic County Cultural Council, Paterson, New Jersey
2001 Numina Gallery, Princeton, New Jersey

Group Exhibitions:

1990 *Ellarslie Open IX,* Trenton City Museum, New Jersey
Mercer County Photography, Holman Art Center, Trenton, New Jersey
1991 *Photography 10,* Perkins Center for the Arts, Moorestown, New Jersey
Undead Artists, City Without Walls Gallery, Newark, New Jersey
1996 *25 Valentines,* Pearl Street Gallery, New York
1997 *Shaded Voices: CU Alumni of Color,* The Cooper Union, New York
1999–2000 *A Tribute to En Foco,* El Museo del Barrio, New York (travelled to Bronx Museum of Arts, New York)
2000 *Share the Vision,* The Cooper Union, New York

Collections:

En Foco Inc., Bronx, New York; Mercer County Cultural and Heritage Commission, Trenton, New Jersey; Center for Photography, Woodstock, New York.

Publications:

On GONZALEZ: Books—*Best of Photography Annual: 1991 Photographer's Forum,* San Francisco, California 1992; *Is Progress Speeding Up?* by John Marks Templeton, Radnor, Pennsylvania 1997. **Articles—**'''Undead Artists', Gallery's Choice of Works by New Members'' by Vivien Raynor in *New York Times,* September 1991; ''Newark Gallery Flourishes Despite Bleak Climate Elsewhere'' by Eileen Watkins in *Star Ledger,* September 1991; ''A Place Where Time Stands Still: Tony Gonzalez Captures Life on the Jersey Shore'' by Stephanie Boozer in *Professional Photographer,* June 2000.

*

The New Jersey Shore

From 1991 to 1996 my work centered on exploring and documenting the people and places that populate the boardwalk towns along the New Jersey Shore.

To me, these places offered more than just the cheap thrill of riding a rollercoaster or a wave; they promised an endless diversion from everyday existence, a stage on which people play out specific rituals. Initially, I began this project using a Leica camera and my goal was to capture the gestures and expressions of the people and to describe a sensual quality of light as was reflected, distorted, and illuminated against various surfaces such as water, sand, flesh, etc.

Eventually, I expanded the project to extend beyond the intimate situations between people, and focused more on the man-made environments, such as the water parks' giant serpentine structures that rise out of the sand and uniquely defined the landscape. Along the boardwalk these giant skeletal forms of tubes and slides had an organic quality. However, in order to describe the smallest details within such images, I needed to use a larger format and thus began using a Crown Graphic 2x3 camera. The larger negative allowed for a bigger print capable of expressing the larger-than-life quality of these places.

Towards the end of the project, I decided to describe this subject matter in color. The use of color offered another layer of the experience, not possible in black and white. The artificiality of certain man-made objects was made more apparent and the use of color could also transform the natural into the surreal.

—Tony Gonzalez

* * *

GORDON, Douglas

Nationality: Scottish. **Born:** Glasgow, Scotland, 1966. **Education:** Glasgow School of Art, 1984–88; Slade School of Art, London, 1988–90. **Awards:** Turner Prize, London, 1996; Hugo Boss Prize, Guggenheim, New York, 1997; Winner, ''Premio 2000'' at the Venice Biennial, 1998.

Selected Individual Exhibitions:

1993 *Migrateur,* ARC, Musée d'Art Moderne de la Ville de Paris (catalog)
1994 Lisson Gallery, London
1995 *Entr'Acte 3,* Van Abbemuseum, Eindhoven (catalog)
The End, Jack Tilton Gallery, New York
Centre Georges Pompidou, Paris
1996 *The Turner Prize 1996,* Tate Gallery, London (catalog)
24 Hour Psycho, Akademie der Bildenden Künste, Vienna
1997 *Leben Nach dem Leben Nach dem Leben. . . ,* Deutsches Museum, Bonn
1998 Kunstverein Hannover, Hanover, Germany
1999 Centro Cultural de Belém, Lisbon (catalog)
Feature Film, The Atlantis Gallery, London (traveled to Kolnischer Kunstverein, Cologne) (catalog)
Through a Looking Glass, Gagosian Gallery, New York (catalog)
2000 *Sheep and Goats,* ARC-Musée d'Art Moderne de la Ville de Paris
2001 Retrospective, Museum of Contemporary Art, Los Angeles

Publications:

By GORDON: Books—*The Missing Text,* edited by Marysia Lewandowska, London 1991; *In Love in Vienna,* edited by Jérôme Sans and Karin Schorm, Vienna 1993; *Feature Film: A Book by Douglas Gordon,* 1999. **Articles—**''Lost, Then Found, Then Lost Again: A True Story, After Samuel Beckett'' in *Witte de With Cahier,* no. 2, June 1994; ''Project'' in *Index,* no. 3–4, 1995; ''Sailing Alone Around the World—A Correspondance Between Douglas Gordon and Liam Gillick'' in *Parkett,* no. 49, 1997.

On GORDON: Books—*Feature Film* by Raymond Bellour, Artangel 1999. **Articles—**''Windfall'' by Liam Gillick in *Artscribe,* 1989;

''Sites/Positions'' by Euan McArthur in *Artscribe,* 1991; ''London Calling'' by Eric Troncy in *Flash Art,* vol. XXV, no. 165, 1992; ''Hello, It's Me'' by Thomas Lawson in *Frieze,* March/April 1993; ''Collaborators'' by Michael Archer in *Art Monthly,* no. 178, July-August 1994; ''Beyond the Lost Object: From Sculpture to Film and Video'' by Michael Newman in *Art Press,* no. 202, May 1995; ''Trigger Happy'' by Marina Benjamin in *British Journal of Photography,* 17 May 1995; ''L'Immobilité Hypnotique de Douglas Gordon'' by Jean-Paul Fargier in *Le Monde,* 6 January 1996; ''The Big Screen'' by Catherine Elwes in *Art Monthly,* no. 199, September 1996; ''De Spectaculis or Who is Kim Novak Really Playing?'' by Tobia Bezzola in *Parkett,* no. 49, 1997; ''Douglas Gordon'' by Boris Groys in *Artforum International,* February 1999; ''Up and Down'' by Jerry Saltz in *Village Voice,* 30 March 1999; ''Rewind the Future'' by Dan Fulcher in *Contemporary Visual Arts,* 1999.

* * *

Scottish artist Douglas Gordon is up and running on the contemporary international exhibition circuit. Over the course of the last five years, he has won England's Turner Prize (1996), the Primo 2000 at the 1997 Venice Biennale, and the New York Guggenheim's Hugo Boss Prize (1998). The Museum of Contemporary Art in Los Angeles will be presenting his first U.S. retrospective in the fall of 2001, featuring his early photographic and text works, his video re-presentations of classic Hollywood films, special offsite projects, and new works.

Gordon studied at the Glasgow School of Art from 1984 to 1988 and at The Slade School of Art, London from 1988 to 1990. In 1990, he became one of the driving forces behind the artist-run Transmission Gallery in Glasgow. This group of Glaswegian artists had international ambitions and endeavored to define their own ways of making work and getting visibility. Due to lack of studio space, Gordon began working in 1990 on text-based art. In one piece, he listed all of the people, some 1440, he remembered ever having met on a Glasgow gallery wall. Gordon sent letters stating, ''I am aware of who you are and what you do'' to artists, dealers, critics, and museum people in his *List of Names,* 1991. While referencing earlier conceptual artists who worked with text such as Lawrence Weiner, for Gordon memory figures as the main theme of the text works, specifically how his private, personal space relates to the network of relationships in society and the art world.

In the mid-1990s Gordon became interested in the culture of cinema, and has since become linked with the genre of video and film installation art. Technology, including film, has transformed our way of doing things, and it profoundly conditions our experience of ourselves and others. Gordon treats film as a reservoir of collective memory. He uses it as a raw material that he slows down, speeds up, and selects fragments from which are repeated on loops, distorted and manipulated. His most notorious work to date, *24 Hour Psycho* (1993), consists of a silent, slow-moving projection of Alfred Hitchcock's classic film. Gordon has extended cinematic time by showing two frames per second, so that the story takes twenty-four hours to unfold. By uncondensing cinematic time, the original narrative disappears. In *5-Year Drive-By* (1995–2000), Gordon slows down a projection of John Ford's iconic Western *The Searchers* over a five-year period to correspond to the time in the movie it takes John Wayne to find a missing child.

Gordon is of the generation that grew up with television screens and movie theaters as backdrops to living, but most specifically his work serves as a fusion of installation art with VCR culture. In his native Glasgow, with high unemployment rates and little going on, Gordon notes that there is ''a different film culture, a replay culture, and a slow-motion take on things.'' In this context, a person could freeze a single frame of a movie and contemplate it or watch a favorite segment again. In addition to manipulating iconic Hollywood films, he has also sampled and appropriated bootleg concert footage and TV shows to create what he considers filmic versions of the readymade. A viewer would expect a film to have a narrative or documentary format in a theater, but in a gallery or art venue these expectations are waived. Here, there is a specific type of viewer who is in a different physical relationship to the video works than to a movie in the theater or private home.

The use of the split screen or mirror image reoccurs as a device in Gordon's video and photographic work. The basis of his work is rooted in the Western psychoanalytic concept of dualism, the distinction between something and its opposite, such as the boundary between normality and psychosis or good and evil. In *through a looking glass* (1999), Gordon creates an environment with two very large screens facing each other on opposite walls. On each of the screens, but slightly off sync, a 71 second clip from Martin Scorsese's *Taxi Driver* (1976) plays, showing the young Robert de Niro as Travis Bickle, a mentally unstable Vietnam veteran and New York City cab driver talking to himself in a mirror. The cult popularity of this particular monologue, with the often repeated ''Are you lookin' at me?'' line is part of Gordon's aim to amplify the phenomenon of a filmic moment that achieves a mythic life of its own independent from the intentions of its maker. The dual screens function as a manifestation of Bickle's split personality, and the viewer is caught in the uneasy space between a man's deranged conversation with himself. The screens are installed in a sculptural way, allowing for the viewer to look behind them to reveal the mechanisms of projection.

Gordon's first work as a director, *Feature Film* of 1999, shows James Conlon, director of the Paris National Opera and the Cologne Philharmonic, conducting Bernard Hermann's soundtrack to Alfred Hitchcock's *Vertigo* (1958). When installed, *Vertigo* is projected silently on a side wall, so that *Feature Film* becomes a large and independent footnote to the original ''text'' in the manner of Jorge Luis Borges. Combined with the tension of Hermann's music score, Gordon heightens the metaphor of neurosis by costuming Conlon in black in a darkened theater. Since neither the conductor's baton or the one hundred piece orchestra are visible, the viewer is left to wonder whether Conlon is actually conducting or just behaving madly.

Gordon's uses the diptych in his photographic works to create a narrative of dichotomy. In *Monster* (1996–97), he faces a photographic self-portrait next to a second self-portrait that features a deformed Gordon with his face hideously stretched and pulled with clear scotch tape. *Tattoo (For Reflection)* (1997) shows the backwards image of the word GUILTY, which Gordon had tattooed on a man's back, that becomes legible only in a mirror reflection.

—Sarah Wagner

GOSEWITZ, Ludwig

Nationality: German. **Born:** Naumburg/Saale, 20 January 1936. **Education:** Studied music at the Akademie für Tonkunst, Darmstadt,

1956–57; studied German literature, linguistics, history and philosophy at the Johann-Wolfgang-Goethe Universität, Frankfurt and Philipps Universität, Marburg/Lahn, 1957–65; studied glass-blowing at the Glasfachschule, Zwiesel, Bavaria, 1972. **Family:** Married Uta Lippert in 1958 (divorced, 1969); children: Aino and Valentin. **Career:** Independent artist, Berlin, since 1965. Public relations manager, Springer Verlag publishers, Berlin, 1967–68; worked as a glass-blower, Berlin-Kreuzberg, 1973–78, and in various glass studios in the United States, Austria, Sweden and Britain, since 1977. Guest instructor/artist-in-residence, Hochschule fur Bildende Künste, Hamburg, 1981. **Awards:** Will-Grohmann Prize, Akademie der Bildenden Kunste, Berlin, 1974; Forderpreis, Heitland Foundation, 1981. **Agents:** Rene Block, c/o DAAD, Berlin (West); Edition Hundertmark, Brusseler Strasse 29, 5000 Cologne 1, Germany; Galerie Marlene Frei, P.O. Box 72, 8042 Zurich, Switzerland.

Individual Exhibitions:

1971 Galerie Michael Werner, Cologne
Museum of Modern Art, Copenhagen
1972 Galerie Rene Block, Berlin
Galerie Michael Werner, Cologne
1973 Galerie Cornels, Baden-Baden, West Germany
Galerie Klein, Bonn
Galerie Michael Werner, Cologne
1975 Galerie Stampa, Basel
1976 Galerie Nachst St. Stephan, Vienna
Galerie A, Amsterdam
Galerie Loa, Haarlem, Netherlands
Galerie am Mehringdamm, Berlin
1980 Galerie Michael Werner, Cologne
Gessamelte Werke 1960–1980 und Neues Glas, DAAD-Galerie, Berlin
1983 Galerie Petersen, West Berlin
Galerie Fred Jahn, Munich
1985 Edition Hundertmark, Cologne
Galerie Fred Jahn, Munich
Galerie A, Amsterdam
1986 Galerie Marlene Frei, Zurich
Galerie Petersen, West Berlin
2000 *Ausgabe und Extra-Ausgabe,* 1976–1984, Galerie und Edition Hundertmark, Cologne
2001 *Fluxus in Germany 1962–1994,* Institut für Auslandsbeziehungen, Stuttgart

Selected Group Exhibitions:

1963 *Schrift en Beeld,* Stedelijk Museum, Amsterdam
1964 *Festival der Neuen Kunst,* Technische Hochschule, Aachen, West Germany
1970 *Visuelle Poesie,* Stedelijk Museum, Amsterdam
1972 *Fluxshoe,* Falmouth Art School, England (toured the U.K.)
1975 *8 from Berlin,* Fruit Market Gallery, Edinburgh
1978 *11 Artists Working in Berlin,* Whitechapel Art Gallery, London
1981 *Art Allemagne Aujourd'hui,* ARC/Musee d'Art Moderne de la Ville, Paris
1982 *Documenta 7,* Museum Fredericianum, Kassel, West Germany
1985 *Kunst in der Bundesrepublik 1945–85,* Nationalgalerie, West Berlin
1987 *Berlinart 1961–87,* Museum of Modern Art, New York (travelled to San Francisco Museum of Modern Art)

Collections:

Berlinische Galerie, West Berlin; Stadtisches Kunstmuseum, Bonn.

Publications:

By GOSEWITZ: Books—*Typogramme I,* Frauenfeld, Switzerland 1962; *Von Phall zu Phall,* with Tomas and Maruta Schmit, Berlin 1966, Cologne and New York 1971; *Anthology of Concrete Poetry,* edited by Emmet Williams, New York 1967; *Knud Pedersen: Der Kampf Gegen die Burgermusik,* Cologne 1973; *Teutonic Schmuck,* edited by David Mayor and Felipe Ehrenberg, Cullompton, Devon 1975; *Objets en Verre,* Berlin 1976; *Ludwig Gosewitz: Gesammelte Werke 1960–1980 und Neues Glas,* exhibition catalog, with Helga Retzer, Berlin 1980; *Von Phall zu Phall,* Cologne 1982; *Continue! Variations on op. 57,* Cologne 1985; *Konstellationen und astrologische Diagramme,* Zurich 1986; *Die Konstruktion der Rose (fur Joseph Beuys),* Heidelberg 1986. **Articles**—"3 Typograms" in *Experimentalni Poezie,* Prague 1967; "Something Written" in *Fluxshoe,* exhibition catalog, edited by David Mayor, Cullompton, Devon 1972; "Ludwig Gosewitz" in *Heute Kunst* (Dusseldorf), no. 6, 1974; "12 Zirkelkonstruktionen" in *8 from Berlin,* exhibition catalog, Edinburgh 1975; "Stammbaum oder die Plantanenlehre" in *16 Os—und Westdeutsche Kunstler,* East Berlin 1976; "Illustration zum I Ging" and "Sonne, Mond und Sterne" in *Ausgabenr.3* (Berlin), 1978; "7 Multiplications" in *11 Artists Working in Berlin,* exhibition catalog, London 1978; "In der Fremde Afrika?" in *Zweitschrift* (Hannover), no. 4–5, 1979; "Die Erinnerungen" in *Zehn Jahre Edition Hundertmark,* exhibition catalog, Berlin 1980; "15 unterschidlich verhaltnisse" in *Ludwig Gosewitz* in *Art Allemagne Aujourd'hui,* exhibition catalog, Paris 1981; "From my notebook" in *Ausgabe* (Cologne), no. 7, 1982/83; "Ing K. erzahlte . . ." in *Vom Zeichen,* exhibition catalog, Frankfurt 1985.

On GOSEWITZ: Book—*Konstellationen und astrologische Diagramme,* exhibition catalog with text by Dieter Schwarz, Zurich 1986. **Articles**—"Sonne, Monde und Sterne" by Heinz Ohff in *Der Tagesspeigel* (Berlin), September 1972; "Die Zeichen der Erinnerung" by Dieter Bucholtz in *Generalzeiger* (Bonn), March 1973; "Philosophie mit Glas, Farnen und Bleistift" by Rosemarie Frank in *Bonner Rundschau* (Bonn), March 1973; "Asthetik, Meditatives, ZeitkriVtisches" in *Wiener Zeitung* (Vienna), January 1976; "Ludwig Gosewitz in der Galerie Nächst St. Stephan" in *Kurier* (Vienna), January 1976; "Ein Mystiker mit Witz" by Heinz Ohff in *Der Tagesspeigel* (Berlin), November 1980; "20 Jahre Gosewitz" by Barbara Schnierle in *Tip* (Berlin), November 1980; "Irisierende Aaugenweide" in *Kolner Stadtanzeiger* (Cologne) February 1985.

*

Why in the world aren't we interested first and foremost in what we see? Why in the world don't we start recording the truth with our sense-brain, our eyes? There is no such thing as an optical illusion. The drawings that go by that name are the first harbingers of our wonderful world. Let's start taking them seriously and start basing the way we conceptualize the world on what our eyes tell us! It all began with careful drawings of objects, simple outline drawings, some of which I filled in with color later. I can't remember ever having felt so happy as in September 1968 when I transferred the shapes of a gas cigarette lighter, an ashtray, and two pears onto paper. I made use of that particularly human freedom to take an object, a thing, with identifiable characteristics, and add something completely new to it—its image. That is happiness.

At about this time I saw a drawing by Tomas Schmit which he had made using the so-called ''inversion of the circle'' formula. The figure enclosed in the circle is projected outside it by the square of the circle's diameter. Where the curved lines of the figure turn a corner, the straight lines of the ''squared'' figure outside form an angle. The transcendence of the infinite circle is transformed by means of the finite square. An image is formed that seems to give a human dimension to the mathematical constant Pi. A new and previously hidden meaning becomes visible. A human figure reveals its relationship to that of a butterfly; the body of a boy is held up physically by the emblem sewn onto his windbreaker.

What I am trying to do—is to ''detranscendentalize'' the transcendence of the concept Pi, which has had an absolute hegemony in saying something meaningful about the sphere up to now, but does not actually do so in a manner that is useful or understandable in human terms—in other words, my goal is to explain the infinity of the sphere in terms of the finity of the cube. These and similar thoughts moved me to project the spatial relationships of a face and a hand onto paper. I saw points in space as the points where two spheres (on paper, two circles) intersect. (This must have been the method—passed on to initiates for generations—used by the first icon painters to project round masses onto a plane.) There is a very special quality about the points at which two systems intersect. In one drawing using this method, a shape like the wing of a butterfly may appear (the butterfly—the space animal!); in another, the positions of the planets in the solar system, usually given in terms of a unicentered system, become visible with incredible plasticity. A new geometry of the eye! The old image of the isolated living being, set out by chance on a planetary body somewhere in the trackless void of space, is confronted with a new image—that of man learning to grasp his unique home in space as the incarnation of meaning itself.

—Ludwig Gosewitz

* * *

The work of Ludwig Gosewitz, which spans almost thirty years now, includes literary texts, essays, drawings, *objets d'art* and glassware. These various means of expression bespeak, if looked at more closely, great powers of concentration, which linger over the particular rather than straining towards the monumental. Using inconspicuous materials and limiting himself to small formats and even miniatures, Gosewitz sets out from a variety of different starting points but aims repeatedly at the same goal: a correct representation of phenomena with the means at our disposal.

But which phenomena? What is meant by ''correct''? And what means are there at our disposal? As an accomplished Germanist, Gosewitz does not disown his learned background. He always bears in mind the function and clarity of his designs and ignores the standards of conventional aesthetic art. His glassware is based on objects of everyday utility, as his horoscope drawings are based on experimental diagrams, and his geometric constructions on the investigation of hidden laws. This leads him to discoveries which infinitely extend the original function of his creations. During his studies of literature and philology, one branch of the latter had particularly interested Gosewitz: phonetics, which is concerned not with complex forms of speech, but with its simplest elements—sounds. Thanks to phonetics, we have methods for describing speech as abstract differentiated sounds or, conversely, for synthesising phonetic notation as speech utterances. The ''phenomena'' in this area are the physically perceptible acoustic speech utterances which can be taken up, dissected and represented in a formalised fashion by the speaker himself—a cycle in which the research remains constantly bound to the object being researched.

With regard to Gosewitz's drawings, the ''phenomena'' are located, in conformity with the medium, in the visible rather than the audible, and if speech sounds always come from the speaker, the thing seen always derives from the world that confronts the eyes. Everything visible is also capable of representation—we need not speak of what is invisible—or, in Gosewitz's words, ''Optical illusions do not exist.'' But in the same way that sounds cannot be transcribed but only analysed, so can a view not be copied but only reconstructed on paper. In drawing, Gosewitz's aim was that of art in general around 1960: to replace realistic representation with the realism of the object itself, a directly presented fragment of reality. So when Gosewitz draws something he sees, he treats the representation not as a reduction of three dimensions to a single plane; rather, he takes into account the stereoscopic qualities of seeing with two eyes and the curvature and area of the paper surface. A body appearing before one's eyes is transmuted into another body—on paper. Out of seeing comes a new conception, not in the sense of a mere positivistic recording of facts, but in the construction of concepts such as infinity or transcendence within the finite.

In the astrological drawings, the position of the planets at the time of birth of a given individual are represented by brightly coloured segments of spheres. This design is then thrown outwards over the edges of a square which has been placed around the circle; a new design is created which—though rigidly constructed—bears a surprising relationship to the sphere segment on which it is based. In this way the transformation of one body into another is demonstrated in the drawing as a model. The constellation of planets, instead of being submitted to a narrative interpretation, becomes a picture of crystal clarity. A vision of the stars, seeing in a metaphorical sense, is represented here in a way that neither explains nor transforms. This representation holds up for us to see and compare whatever Ludwig Gosewitz, on his journey of universal reportage, deems worthy of mention.

—Dieter Schwarz

GRAHAM, Dan

Nationality: American. **Born:** Urbana, Illinois, 31 March 1942. **Career:** Independent film, video, installation and performance artist. Lectured at University of California, San Diego, 1969–70; lectured at

Nova Scotia College of Art and Design, Halifax, 1970–71. **Awards:** New York State Creative Artists Public Service Program Multi-Media Grant, 1973–74. **Agent:** Marian Goodman Gallery, 24 West 57th Street, New York, New York 10019; Dia Center for the Arts (Chelsea), 548 West 22nd Street, New York, New York 10011. **Address:** P.O. Box 380, Knickerbocker Station, New York, New York 10002, U.S.A.

Individual Exhibitions:

1969 John Daniels Gallery, New York
1970 Anna Leonowens Gallery, Nova Scotia College of Art and Design, Halifax
1972 Fourth Floor Gallery, Halifax, Nova Scotia
Lisson Gallery, London
Protetch-Rivkin Gallery, Washington, D.C.
Galleria Toselli, Milan
Project, Inc., Cambridge, Massachusetts
1973 Galerie MTL, Brussels
Galerie Zwirner, Cologne
Galeria Schema, Florence
Gallery A 402, California Institute of the Arts, Valencia
1974 Galleria Marilena Bonomo, Bari, Italy
Galerie 17, Paris
Royal College of Art, London
Lisson Gallery, London
1975 Modern Art Agency, Naples
Galerie MTL, Brussels
John Gibson Gallery, New York
Palais des Beaux-Arts, Brussels
International Cultural Centrum, Antwerp
Otis Art Institute Gallery, Los Angeles
Griffiths Art Center, St. Lawrence University, Canton, New York
1976 Sperone Westwater Fischer, New York
Salle Patino, Geneva
Samangallery, Genoa
Galerie Vega, Liège, Belgium
Institute of Contemporary Arts, London
Galerie Anne-Marie Verna, Zurich
Galleria Banco, Brescia, Italy
Kunsthalle, Basle
1977 Leeds Polytechnic Gallery, England
René Block Galerie, Berlin
Van Abbemuseum, Eindhoven, Netherlands
Studio Terelli, Ferrara, Italy
Museum van Hedendaagse Kunst, Ghent
1978 Corps de Gard, Groningen, Netherlands
Museum of Modern Art, Oxford
1979 Franklin Furnace, New York
Galerie Rüdiger Schöttle, Munich
Galleria Paola Betti, Milan
Center for Art Tapes, Halifax, Nova Scotia
Locus Solus, Genoa
1980 Rüdiger Schöttle, Munich
Museum of Modern Art, New York
City of Los Angeles Central Library
Museum of Contemporary Art, Lisbon
Institute for Art and Urban Resources at P.S.1, New York
1981 Renaissance Society at the University of Chicago
Center for the Arts, Muhlenberg College, Allentown, Pennsylvania
Video at 30th Street Station, Institute of Contemporary Art, Philadelphia
Lisson Gallery, London
Galerie Durand-Dessert, Paris
1982 Hotel Wolfers, Brussels
1983 Kunsthalle, Berne
1984 Galeria del Calvino, Venice
Marianne Desan Gallery, Chicago
1985 Art Gallery of Western Australia, Perth
1986 Galerie Rüdiger Schöttle, Munich
Johnen & Schöttle, Galerie für Architektur und Kunst, Cologne and Munich
Galleria Lia Rumma, Naples
Galerie Durand-Dessert, Paris
Het Kijkhuis, The Hague
Cable Gallery, New York
Storefront for Art and Architecture, New York
1987 Marian Goodman Gallery, New York
Musée d'Art Moderne, Paris
Galerie Hufkens-Hoirhomme, Brussels
Le Consortium, Lyons, France
Centro de Arte Reina Sifia, Madrid
Fruitmarket Gallery, Edinburgh
1988 Kunsthalle zu Kiel, Kiel, Germany
Kunstverein, Munich
Musée d'Art Moderne, St. Etienne, France
1990 Yamaguchi Prefecural Museum of Art, Yamaguchi, Japan
Marian Goodman Gallery, New York
Galerie Bleich-Rossi, Graz, Austria
1991 Margo Leavin Gallery, Los Angeles
Galerie Fenster, Frankfurt am Main
Galerie Rüdiger Schöttle, Munich
Le Case d'Arte, Milan
Fondation pour l'Architecture, Brussels
Galerie Micheline Szwajcer, Antwerp
Galleria Pieroni, Rome
Galerie Roger Pailhas, Marseilles
Dia Center for the Arts, New York
1992 Wiener Secession, Vienna
Galerie Blech-Rossai, Graz, Austria
Musée Cantini, Marseilles
Witte de With Center for Contemporary Art, Rotterdam
Whitney Museum of American Art, New York
1992 Le Nouveau Musée/Institute d'Art Contemporain, Villerubanne, France
Walker Evans and Dan Graham, Witte de With Center for Contemporary Art, Rotterdam (travelled to Musée Cantini, Marseilles; Westfälisches Landesmuseum für Kunst und Kulturgeschichte, Munster; Whitney Museum of American Art, New York)
1993 Moore College of Art and Design, Philadelphia (travelled to MIT List Visual Arts Center, Cambridge, Massachusetts; Art Gallery of Ontario, Toronto; and Los Angeles Contemporary Exhibitions, Los Angeles)
1994 *Art and Architecture/Architecture and Art,* Villa Stuck, Munich

MAI 36 Galerie, Zurich
Nouveau Musée, Lyons, France

1995 *Rooftop Urban Park Project,* Dia Center for the Arts, New York
Video/Architecture/Performance, Generali Foundation, Vienna

1997 Camden Arts Centre, London

1998 *Centro Galego de Arte Contemporánea,* Santiago de Compostela, Spain

2000 Marian Goodman Gallery, New York
Heart Pavilion, Carnegie Art Institute, Pittsburgh

Selected Performances: *Lax/Relax,* Nova Scotia College of Art and Design, Halifax, 1969; *Video Camera/Monitor Performance,* Loeb Student Center, New York University, 1970; *Two Consciousness Projection(s)* and *Past Future Split Attention,* 98 Green Street Loft, New York, 1972; *Intention Intentionality Sequence I,* Lisson Gallery, London, 1972; *#7 and Nude,* Nova Scotia College of Art and Design, Halifax, 1975; *Performance/Audience Sequence,* Hallwalls, Buffalo, New York, 1975; *Performer/Audience/Mirror,* ''de appel,'' Amsterdam, 1977; *Eventworks,* Massachusetts College of Art, Boston, 1980; *New Wave and Feminism,* Institute of Contemporary Arts, London, 1980.

Selected Group Exhibitions:

1970 *Information,* Museum of Modern Art, New York

1971 *Sonsbeek 71,* Arnhem, Netherlands

1972 *Documenta,* Kassel, Germany

1974 *Video Art,* Institute of Contemporary Art, Philadelphia (travelled to the Museum of Contemporary Arts Center, Cincinnati, Ohio; Museum of Contemporary Art, Chicago; and Wadsworth Atheneum, Hartford, Connecticut)

1976 *Ambiente Arte,* at the *Biennale,* Venice

1979 *73rd American Exhibition,* Art Institute of Chicago

1982 *Documenta 7,* Kassel, Germany

1987 *Biennial Exhibition,* Whitney Museum of American Art, New York

1991 *Carnegie International,* Carnegie Museum of Art, Pittsburgh

1992 *Documenta 9,* Kassel, Germany

1994 *East of Eden,* Museum Schloss Mosigkau, Dessau-Mosigkau, Germany

1995 *Inside/Outside,* Laurence Miller Gallery, 138 Spring Street, New York
Light Construction, Museum of Modern Art, New York
Recaptured Nature, Marian Goodman Gallery, New York
Public Information: Desire, Disaster, Document, The San Francisco Museum of Modern Art

1996 Lisson Gallery, London (with Victor Burgin, Rodney Graham and John Hilliard)

1997 *1997 Biennial Exhibition,* Whitney Museum of American Art, New York

1999 *Architektonische Skulptur im 20. Jahrhundert,* Wilhelm Lehmbruck Museum, Duisburg, Germany

2000 *Let's Entertain: Life's Guilty Pleasures,* Portland Art Museum, Oregon (traveling exhibition)
Voici, Palais des Beaux-Arts, Brussels

Collections:

Allen Memorial Art Museum, Oberlin, Ohio; Museum of Fine Arts, Dallas; Tate Gallery, London; Van Abbemuseum, Eindhoven, Netherlands; Centre Georges Pompidou, Paris; Whitney Museum of Contemporary Art, New York; San Francisco Museum of Art.

Publications:

By GRAHAM: Books—*Selected Works, 1965–72,* New York 1972; Textes, Paris 1974; *For Publication,* Los Angeles 1975; *Films,* Geneva 1977; *Articles,* edited by R.H. Fuchs, Eindhoven, Netherlands 1978; *Video-Architecture-Television: Writings on Video and Video Works 1970–1978,* Halifax, Nova Scotia and New York, 1979; *Dan Graham/Static at Riverside Studios,* Audio Arts tape edition, London 1980; *Buildings and Signs,* Chicago 1981; *Illuminating Video: An Essential Guide to Video Art,* New York and Los Angeles, 1990; *Rock My Religion,* Cambridge, Massachusetts, 1993; *Two-way Mirror Power: Selected Writings by Dan Graham on his Art,* edited by Alexander Alberro, with introduction by Jeff Wall, Cambridge 1999; *Dan Graham: Works 1965–2000,* with Marianne Brouwer, Dusseldorf 2001. **Articles**—''Homes for America'' in *Arts Magazine* (New York), December/January 1966/67; ''Muybridge Moments'' in *Arts Magazine* (New York), February 1967; ''The Book as Object'' in *Arts Magazine* (New York), May 1967; ''Schema'' in *Aspen* (New York), no. 5–6, 1967; introductory text to *Dan Flavin,* exhibition catalog, Chicago 1967; ''Two Parallel Essays'' in *Artists and Photographs,* New York 1969; editorial note and contribution, *Aspen* (New York), no. 9, 1970; ''Pieces'' in *Interfunktionen* (Cologne), no. 5, 1970; ''Thoughts on Two Structures,'' in *Sol LeWitt,* exhibition catalog, The Hague 1970; ''Eleven Sugar Cubes'' in *Art in America* (New York), May/June 1970; ''Performance as a Perceptual Process'' in *Interfunktionen* (Cologne), no. 7, 1971; ''Film Pieces: Visual Field'' in *Interfunktionen* (Cologne), no. 8, 1972; ''Eight Pieces by Dan Graham'' in *Studio International* (London), May 1972; ''TV Camera/Monitor Performance'' in *DTR* (New York), June 1972; ''Intention Intentionality Sequence'' in *Arts Magazine* (New York), April 1973; ''Dan Graham I/Eve,'' with Tommaso Trini, in *Domus* (Milan), February 1973; ''Two Consciousness Projection(s)'' in *Arts Magazine* (New York), December 1974; ''The Book as Object and Notes on Income (Outflow) Piece'' in *Interfunktionen* (Cologne), no. 11, 1974; ''#7, Perfomance/Audience Sequnce, Notes on 'Income Piece''' in *Control Magazine,* no. 9 1975; ''The Glass Divider, Light and Social Division, Video Feedback, '+ 0''' in *Revue d'art contemporain* (Paris), September 1976; ''Interior Space/Exterior Space'' in *Video Art,* edited by I. Schneider and B. Korot, New York 1976; ''Elements of Video/Elements of Architecture'' in *Video by Artists,* edited by P. Gale, Toronto 1976; ''Public Space/Two Audiences'' in *Art Actuel, Skira Annual,* Geneva 1977; ''Art in Relation to Architecture/Architecture in Relation to Art'' in *Artforum* (New York), February 1979; '''Punk': Political 'Pop' ''in *Journal* (Los Angeles), March/April 1979; ''Dan Graham a Linao'' in *Domus* (Milan), no. 594, 1979; ''Dan Graham'' in *New Art* (Frisa, Italy), autumn 1980; ''L'Espace de la Communication'' in *Skira Annual '80,* Geneva 1980; ''Signs'' in *Artforum* (New York), April 1981; interview with Peter Doroshenko in *Journal of Contemporary Art,* vol. 7, no. 2, 1995; ''Not Post-Modernism'' in *Artforum* (New York), November 1981; interview with Mike Metz in *Bomb,* no. 46, Winter 1994; interview with Brian Hatton in *Zehar,* no. 29, October 1995;

interview with Peter Doroshenko in *Journal of Contemporary Art,* vol. 7, Winter 1995; interview with Marion Fricke and Roswitha Fricke in *Art Press,* Special Issue, no. 17, 1996; interview with Martin Kottering and Roland Nachtigäller in *Neue Bildende Kunst,* no. 2, April-May 1997; interview with Joerg Bader in *Art Press,* no. 231, January 1998; interview with Lief Skoog in *Paletten,* vol. 59, no. 4, 1998; interview with Ulrike Groos and Markus Muller in *Jahresring,* no. 45, 1998; ''Graham: Obra y Texto,'' with Valeria Gonzalez in *Artinf,* vol. 22, no. 101, Winter 1998; interview with David Brittain in *Creative Camera,* no. 360, October/November 1999; ''Dan Graham: Heart Pavilion, Bryn Mawr'' in *Casabella,* vol. 63, no. 673/674, December 1999/January 2000. **Video—***Two-Way Mirror Cylinder Inside Cube,* New York 1991.

On GRAHAM: Books—*Minimal Art,* edited by Gregory Batcock, New York 1968; *Conceptual Art* by Ursula Meyer, New York 1972; *6 Years: The Dematerialization of the Art Object* by Lucy Lippard, New York 1972; *Performance Art* by Rose Lee Goldbert, London 1980; *Dan Graham: Buildings and Signs,* exhibition catalog with text by A. Rorimer, Chicago 1981; *Dan Graham: Pavilions,* exhibition catalog, Bern 1983; *Dan Graham,* exhibition catalog, Perth, Australia, 1985; *Dan Graham: Art As Design—Design As Art,* exhibition catalog, Edinburgh 1987; *Dan Graham's Kammerspiel,* exhibition catalog with text by J. Wall, Toronto 1991; *Radical Scavengers: The Conceptual Vernacular in Recent American Art,* Museum of Contemporary Art, Chicago, 1994; *Dan Graham* by Alain Charre, Marie-Paule Macdonald and Marc Perelman, Paris 1995; *Dan Graham* by Mark Francis, Birgit Pelzer and Beatriz Columina, London 2001. **Articles**—''Quasi-Infinites and the Waning of Space'' by Robert Smithson in *Arts Magazine* (New York), November 1966; ''Serial Art'' by Mel Bochner in *Artforum* (New York), November 1967; ''Some Other Remarks'' by Dan Flavin in *Artforum* (New York), December 1967; ''Introduction'' by Terry Atkinson in *Art and Language* (London), vol. 1, no. 1, 1968; ''A Museum of Language in the Vicinity of Art'' by Robert Smithson in *Art International* (Lugano, Switzerland), March 1968; ''Dan Graham'' by David Antin in *Studio International* (London), July 1970; ''Body Art'' by Cindy Nemser in *Arts Magazine* (New York), September 1971; ''Pier 18'' by Robert Pincus-Witten in *Artforum* (New York), September 1971; ''Artist as Filmaker'' by Annabel Nicholson in *Art and Artists* (London), December 1972; ''Video'' by Wulf Herzogenrath and Marlis Gruterich in *Kunst Magazine* (Mainz), no. 4, 1974; ''A Space, A Thousand Words'' by Rose Lee Goldberg in *Architectural Design* (New York), May 1976; ''Pygmalion Reserved'' by Max Kozloff in *Artforum* (New York), November 1975; ''Past/Present'' by Rosemary Mayer in *Art in America* (New York), November-December 1975; ''Performance'' by Marc Chaimowicz in *Studio International* (London), January/February 1976; ''Dan Graham: Appearing in Public'' by Eric Cameron in *Artforum* (New York), November 1976; ''Moments of History in the Work of Dan Graham'' by B. H. D. Buchloh in *Articles,* Eindhoven, Netherlands 1978; introduction by Judith Tannenbaum to *Concept/Narrative/Docment,* exhibition catalog, Chicago 1979; ''Dan Graham, Paola Beti/Milano'' by Louisa Somaini in *Flash Art* (Milan), June/July 1979; ''Dan Graham at the Mudd Club'' by Amy Taubin in *SoHo Weekly News* (New York), 14 June 1979; ''Conceptual Art and the Continuing Quest for a New Social Context'' by Robert Morgan in *Journal* (Los Angeles), June/July 1979; ''Mirror and Text: Work of Dan Graham in Relation to Some Examples of the French Roman Nouveau'' by Adela Zeleznik in *M'Ars,* vol. 7, no. 3–4, 1995; ''Dan Graham: 'Die Muskik hat die Avantgardefunktion der Kunst übernommen''' by Justin Hoffmann in *Kunstforum International,* no. 135, October 1996–1997; ''Some Thoughts on Modeling: Dam Graham's Present Continuous Past(s)'' by Gordon Lebredt in *Parachute,* no. 86, April-June 1997; ''Dan Graham Glass Pavilion—Café Bravo in Berlin, Germany'' by Gerwin Zohlen in *Baumeister,* vol. 96, no. 4, April 1999; ''Un Panthéon des Enfants, Blois'' by Frédéric Bonnet in *L'Architecture d'Aujourd'hui,* no. 328, June 2000.

* * *

Dan Graham has used photography, architecture, sculpture, and video for his critical interventions into the discourse of Pop, Minimalist, and Conceptual art practice. His most recognizable achievement has been the use of the dialectics of these art movements—all of which were prominent during his early career—to address the issue of utopianism in urban planning and modern architecture. His projects reach beyond the rarified objecthood of Minimalist works and the cool ambivalence of Pop in order to pose questions about the role of aesthetics within the social environment.

Homes for America was one of Graham's first attempts at fusing the above-mentioned art movements into the format of a magazine layout. The piece incorporated photographs of tract housing developments with descriptive text, and appeared in the December 1966 issue of *Arts Magazine.* The photographs had a formal symmetry and an awareness of the rectangular frame which called attention to the homogenizing aesthetics of the developments. The text, in addition to describing the physical specifications of the homes (floorplan, color, overall design), discussed the prioritizing of ease of fabrication over quality craftsmanship and individual choice. The pedantic language style and straightforward image-text layout imitated the documentary page form, and represented Graham's overall strategy of working within (as opposed to against) the conventions of his chosen genre.

Graham intended this work to function not as criticism in the liberal humanist sense (of Farm Security Administration photographers, for example), but as a way of grounding the aesthetic discourses of the time in a social and economic context. *Homes For America* incorporated Minimalism by acknowledging basic forms and industrial materials, and Pop by its exploitation of print media and the treatment of the photographed homes as found ready-mades. Likewise, the documentary descriptiveness and the presentation of the 2038 possible color-style combinations for any given block referenced Conceptual art information systems. However, the real strength of this work lies not in the critical incorporation of normally opposing discourses, but in the revelation of possible relationships between aesthetic discourse and social reality-relationships bypassed by artists of those same movements in the rush to gain acceptance into the art commodity system.

With *Homes For America,* Graham implied the failure of modern form-follows-function architecture to achieve its original social ideals. Graham took this idea further in the 1970s and 1980s by designing site-specific structures, the *Pavilions,* which simultaneously mimic and critique the aesthetics of urban architecture. The *Pavilions* are free-standing enclosures which borrow the steel frame/glass skin construction from the modern skyscraper. They incorporate sliding glass or revolving glass doors as entrances, and often consist of two connected ''rooms'' separated by a sheet of glass that is both transparent and reflective. The majority of the works are located in parks, plazas, and other urban leisure settings, and serve as a recontextualization of functional urban design into idealized spaces.

The blending of artificiality with naturalism is essential to the irony of this work. Graham situates the *Pavilions* within the historical tradition of the various ''recreational'' architectural genres, e.g. the park gazebo, the shopping arcade, and the bus shelter. Yet the reduction of the genre to an interactive monument of questionable function, suspiciously reminiscent of the workplace, invites the viewer/participant to reflect on the social control aspect of leisure architecture. The *Pavilions* also serve as a vehicle for the contemplation of urban social relationships, as the reflective/transparent glass allows the viewer to identify the self and the Other superimposed. The effect on the viewer is unsettling, as when one passes by a mirrored exterior wall of an office building and must confront not only one's own image, but the theoretical gaze of the building's occupants.

Thus, the formal elegance of Graham's architectural pieces belies the deeper, more troubling questions they ask of the viewer. In addition to the eerie play of reflections, the scheme of entrances, exits, and glass dividers in these deceptively simple structures are actually maddeningly oblique. In his video, *Two-Way Mirror Cylinder in a Glass Cube and a Video Salon,* viewers' interactions with the structures reveal a certain discomfort with the experience. Though perhaps a typical reaction to public art, one cannot help but recognize the fine line the *Pavilions* tread between urban refuge and bureaucratic maze.

—Audrey Mandelbaum

GRAHAM, K. M.

Nationality: Canadian. **Born:** Hamilton, Ontario. **Education:** University of Toronto, B.A.; Royal Canadian Academy, 1973. **Family:** Married J. Wallace Graham, 1938, two children: John Wallace and Janet Howitt. **Career:** Independent artist; lives and works in Toronto. **Awards:** Honorary Fellow, Trinity College, University of Toronto, 1988.

Individual Exhibitions:

1967 Carmen Lamanna Gallery, Toronto
1968 Trinity College, University of Toronto
1970 Founders College, York University, Toronto
1971 Pollock Gallery, Toronto
1972 Art Gallery of Cobourg, Ontario
1973 Pollock Gallery, Toronto
1974 Toronto City Hall
1975 Pollock Gallery
1976 David Mirvish Gallery, Toronto
1979 Klonaridis Inc., Toronto
Frans Wynans Gallery, Vancouver
1980 Downstairs Gallery, Edmonton
Watson Willour, Houston
1981 Lillian Heidenburg Gallery, New York
Klonaridis Inc., Toronto
1982 Downstairs Gallery, Edmonton
Klonaridis Inc., Toronto
1983 Klonaridis Inc., Toronto
1984 Galerie Elca London, Montreal
Macdonald-Stewart Art Centre, Guelph, Ontario (travelled to Calgary, Alberta; Kingston, Ontario; Montreal; Windsor, Ontario; and Toronto)
1985 Klonaridis Inc., Toronto
1986 Lillian Heidenburg Gallery, New York
1987 Klonaridis Inc., Toronto
1988 Klonaridis Inc., Toronto
1989 Feheley Fine Arts Gallery, Toronto
1990 Klonaridis Inc., Toronto
1993 Douglas Udell Gallery, Vancouver
1994 Memorial University Art Gallery, St. Johns, Newfoundland (travelled to Beaverbrook Art Gallery, Fredericton, New Brunswick) (catalog)
Costin and Klintworth, Toronto
1997 Art Gallery of Ontario, Toronto
2001 *K. M. Graham: Selected Works on Paper,* Moore Gallery, Ltd., Toronto

Selected Group Exhibitions:

1974 *Canada x Ten,* Art Gallery of Ontario (toured Canada)
1975 *The Canadian Canvas,* organized by TIME Canada (toured Canada and the U.S.)
1976 *Changing Visions,* Art Gallery of Ontario and Edmonton Art Gallery (toured Canada and the U.S.)
1981 *Bolduc, Fournier, Graham,* Canada House, London, and Centre Culturel Canadien, Paris
The Heritage of Jack Bush, Robert McLaughlin Gallery, Oshawa, Ontario (toured Canada)
1982 *Selections from the Westburne Collection,* Edmonton Art Gallery (toured Canada)
1986 Associated American Artists, New York
1990 *Canadian Women Artists,* Kitchener-Waterloo Art Gallery, Ontario
1995 *Prosperity Returns,* Art Gallery of Hamilton, Ontario

Collections:

British Museum, London; National Gallery of Canada, Ottawa; Art Gallery of Ontario, Toronto; Musée d'Art Contemporain, Montreal; Art Gallery of Hamilton, Ontario; Vancouver Art Gallery; Edmonton Art Gallery; Art Gallery of Peterborough, Ontario; University of Toronto; MacDonald-Stewart Art Gallery, Guelph; Toronto City Hall; Agnes Etherington Art Centre, Kingston, Ontario; Musee d'Art Contemporain, Montreal; Beaverbrook Art Gallery, Fredericton, New Brunswick; Art Gallery of Newfoundland and Labrador; Robert McLaughlin Gallery, Oshawa, Ontario; Kitchener/Waterloo Art Gallery; McMichael Canadian Art Gallery; Hart House Art Gallery, Toronto.

Publications:

By GRAHAM: Book—*A Great Adventure in Art,* Toronto 1997.

On GRAHAM: Books—*Canada x Ten,* exhibition catalog by Karen Wilkin, Edmonton 1974; *The Heritage of Jack Bush,* exhibition catalog with text by Ken Carpenter, Oshawa, Ontario, 1981; *Horizons: Contemporary Canadian Landscapes* by Marci Lipman, Toronto 1985; *The Best Contemporary Canadian Art* by Joan Murray,

Toronto 1987; *K. M. Graham: Eternities of Space,* exhibition catalog with text by Lora Senechal Carney, St. Johns, Newfoundland, 1994.

* * *

K. M. Graham is an essentially self-taught painter of the natural world, a grandmother who began to make art only after the death of her husband. This description, however, while not inaccurate, is wholly misleading, since it suggests that Graham is a painter of naive landscapes. Nothing could be less true. In fact, she is an accomplished, sophisticated, and individual abstract artist who, in terms of both exhibition history and friendships, is a significant member of a generation of Toronto painters roughly half her age. Despite the differences in their formation as artists, Graham clearly has much in common with these younger Canadians and her pictures share many qualities with theirs, most notably, a dependence on meetings of unexpected colors and inventive shapes that seem jammed against the canvas by sheer will, an engaging eccentricity, and a sense of imagery's having been discovered, not preconceived. During the 1970s and early 1980s, these characteristics seemed to define much of Toronto painting, and they continue to exemplify how it differs from its more theoretical Montreal equivalent. That they are manifest in Graham's work is further evidence of her active role in at least one part of the aesthetic debate of the city where she has lived most of her adult life.

Graham's imagery is rooted in nature. Her palette and her vocabulary of forms are based on her observations of the world around her—vegetation, flowers, qualities of light, landscape forms—used not literally, but as the basis of free-wheeling improvisation. (She says she learned about color when she was an avid gardener, during her years as the wife of a well-known physician.) Since the 1960s, Graham has travelled extensively, particularly in the north, discovering in the apparent emptiness of snow-covered treeless plains and ice-dotted sea or in the brilliance of the ground-hugging wild flowers of the brief arctic summer, a lexicon of economical forms and radiant hues that she has incorporated into her pictorial language. Yet important as the intensity of the original experience is to Graham, the success of her pictures depends on her ability to fragment and recombine fondly remembered or briefly sketched images in new, unexpected ways. The whiplash curves and transparent washes of her early *Arctic Line* abstractions, for example, may have had their origins in the cloud formations, the cliff faces, and the light-diffusing expanses of snow that so fascinated her on her trips to the Canadian Arctic, just as other series may be based on her profound knowledge of the aquatic plants and shoreline trees of Algonquin Park, the changing snow patterns of wooded hillsides, or the bare-bones landscape of Newfoundland, but these sources are significant only as springboards for invention. Graham insists equally on the specificity of her stimuli and the freedom of her responses, as she distills her pleasure in the natural world into lyrical images that evoke the phenomena that triggered them without depicting them literally. She shifts scale, flattens space, clarifies hues, dissects and conflates images, translating everything into fluid touches of color, rapid lines, and detached shapes that drift across the surface of the canvas. When we are confronted by any of Graham's sources, both the accuracy of her perceptions and the boldness of her improvisations become immediately apparent. A recurring soft-edged, rounded shape and a dull bluish-red hue turn out to have their origins in a type of water lily pad with a red underside, common near her Algonquin Park cottage. In Graham's paintings, however, the shape can expand to fill the canvas and the color spread across the surface independently of any confining shape.

Graham is a knowledgeable observer of the art of the past and present, from the Venetians of the Renaissance to her younger Toronto colleagues, but her deepest connection is probably with Jack Bush. Bush was not only an artist whose paintings she admires greatly, but a close friend—long before she began to paint—whom she credits with encouraging her efforts and convincing her to take her work seriously. Matisse, both directly and filtered through Bush's example, has been a primary inspiration, as well, something immediately visible in Graham's fundamental conception of a painting as a flat expanse of uninflected color punctuated by articulate shapes. In a very real sense, however, Graham is best described as the heir to the long-standing tradition of Canadian landscape painting. Her ties to Algonquin Park, where she has summered since childhood, link her directly with the pioneer modernists, the Group of Seven, but she has profoundly altered their legacy. Her paintings are neither straightforward accounts nor nationalist exhortations, but rather, allusive abstractions, informed by the specifics of place, but not restricted by them. Graham often speaks of going from ''the particular to the universal''—of using, for example, her familiarity with the water lily growing in the shallows of the Algonquin Park lake to invent an image that, she hopes, will embody her affection and reverence for both particular places and nature in general, drawing intuitively upon her accumulated experience of nature and of art, and remaining alert to suggestions that present themselves in the course of working. In Graham's best work, she achieves these ambitious goals.

—Karen Wilkin

GRAHAM, Robert

Nationality: American. **Born:** Mexico City, 19 August 1938; naturalized U.S. citizen, 1950. **Education:** San Jose State College, California, 1961–63; San Francisco Art Institute, 1963–64. **Career:** Lived in Los Angeles and began making small art figures, 1964–69; lived and worked in London, 1969–70, then returned to Venice, California. Designed the ''National Medal of Arts'' award presented by the President of the United States; ''The Spirit of Liberty Award,'' People for the American Way; ''The California Governors' Award for the Arts'' and ''The John Huston Award'' for the Artists Rights Foundation. **Awards:** Freedom of Speech Award and California, ACLU, Governors' Award, for outstanding contribution to the Arts, both 1993. **Agent:** Robert Miller Gallery, 41E 57th St., Fl 2, New York, New York, 10022–1908. **Address:** 69 Windward Ave., Venice, CA 90291.

Individual Exhibitions:

1964 Lanyon Gallery, Palo Alto, California
1966 Nicholas Wilder Gallery, Los Angeles
1967 Nicholas Wilder Gallery, Los Angeles
Galerie Thelen, Essen
1968 Kornblee Gallery, New York
Galerie Neuendorf, Hamburg
Galerie Zwirner, Cologne
Galerie Neuendorf, Cologne
1969 Kornblee Gallery, New York

Social Programs by Robert Graham at the Franklin Delano Roosevelt Memorial, Washington, D.C., ca. 1991–97. ©James P. Blair/Corbis.

Nicholas Wilder Gallery, Los Angeles
1970 Galerie Neuendorf, Hamburg
Galerie Neuendorf, Cologne
Galerie Mollenhoff, Cologne
Galerie Rene Block, Berlin
Whitechapel Art Gallery, London
1971 Sonnabend Gallery, New York
Kunstverein, Hamburg
1972 Galerie Herbert Meyer-Ellinger, Frankfurt
Museum of Fine Arts, Dallas
Courtney Sale Gallery, Dallas
1974 Nicholas Wilder Gallery, Los Angeles
Galerie Neuendorf, Hamburg
Galerie Zwirner, Cologne
Felicity Samuel Gallery, London
Galerie Neuendorf, Cologne
Gimpel and Hanover Galerie, Zurich
Texas Gallery, Houston
1975 Felicity Samuel Gallery, London
Gimpel and Hanover Galerie, Zurich
Texas Gallery, Houston
Dorothy Rosenthal Gallery, Chicago
Gimpel and Hanover Gallery, at the *Basel Art Fair*
Nicholas Wilder Gallery, Los Angeles
1976 Greenberg Gallery, St. Louis
Galerie Neuendorf, Hamburg
Galerie Neuendorf, Cologne
Gimpel Fils, London
1977 Nicholas Wilder Gallery, Los Angeles
John Stoller Gallery, Minneapolis
Robert Miller Gallery, New York
Dorothy Rosenthal Gallery, Chicago, Illinois
1978 Robert Miller Gallery, New York
Dorothy Rosenthal Gallery, Chicago
Los Angeles County Museum of Art
1979 Robert Miller Gallery, New York
Galerie Neuendorf, Hamburg
Dag Hammarskjold Plaza, New York
1980 Dorothy Rosenthal Galllery, Chicago
1981 Los Angeles County Museum of Art
Walker Art Center, Minneapolis
Dorothy Rosenthal Gallery, Chicago
School of Visual Arts, New York
1982 Norton Gallery, West Palm Beach, Florida
Museum of Fine Arts, Houston
Joslyn Art Center, Omaha
Des Moines Art Center, Des Moines
San Francisco Museum of Modern Art
Robert Miller Gallery, New York
1984 Gemini G.E.L., Los Angeles

ARCO Center for Visual Arts, Los Angeles
1985 48 Market Street, Fragments Exhibition, Venice, California
1988 Los Angeles County Museum of Art
1989 Robert Miller Gallery, New York
1990 Galerie Neuendorf, Frankfurt
Galerie Fahenmann, Berlin
Earl McGrath Gallery, Los Angeles
48 Market Street, Venice, California
Mixografia Gallery, Los Angeles
Robert Miller Gallery, New York
1991 John Berggruen Gallery, San Francisco
1992 Robert Miller Gallery, New York
48 Market Street Gallery, Venice, California
1994 Gagosian Gallery, New York
1996 Gagosian Gallery, New York
Peter Blake Gallery, Laguna Beach

Selected Group Exhibitions:

1966 *Whitney Biennial,* Whitney Museum, New York (and 1969, 1971)
1971 *3 Americans,* Victoria and Albert Museum, London
1972 *West Coast U.S.A.,* Kunstverein, Hamburg (toured Germany)
1974 *Biennial,* Art Institute of Chicago
1975 *Sculpture: American Directions 1945–1975,* National Collection of Fine Arts, Smithsonian Institution, Washington, D.C.
1976 *L.A. 8: Painting and Sculpture 76,* Los Angeles County Museum of Art
Painting and Sculpture in California: The Modern Era, San Francisco Museum of Modern Art
1978 *Contemporary Artists Series, Number 1,* Rutgers University Art Gallery, New Brunswick, New Jersey
1980 *Aspects of the 70's: Directions in Realism,* Danforth Museum, Farmington, Massachusetts
1986 *California Sculpture 1959–80,* San Francisco Museum of Modern Art
1998 *Illusion/Allusion: Contemporary Sculpture,* Florida State University Museum of Fine Arts, Tallahassee
Art of this Century and of this Continent, CDS Gallery, New York
Aspects of Abstraction, Kirkland Art Center, Clinton, New York

Collections:

Museum of Modern Art, New York; Whitney Museum, New York; Hirshhorn Museum and Sculpture Garden, Washington, D.C.; Los Angeles County Museum of Art; Kuntsmuseum, Cologne; Kuntsmuseum, Hamburg; Dallas Museum of Fine Art; Walker Art Center, Minneapolis; Museum of Modern Art, Paris; Victoria and Albert Museum, London; Museum of Art, Rotterdam; National Museum of Wales, Cardiff.

Permanent Public Installations:

Monument to Joe Louis, Cobo Hall, Detroit; City of San Jose; *Column,* Federal Reserve Bank, San Francisco; *Great Bronze Doors,* Cathdral of Our Lady of the Angels, Los Angeles; *Franklin Delano Roosevelt,* FDR Memorial, Washington, D.C. in progress.

Publications:

By GRAHAM: Articles—''A Conversation with Robert Graham'' with Lane Barden in *Artweek,* vol. 24, April 8, 1993; ''Robert Graham's Casting Call'' with Steven Garbarino in *Interview,* vol. 24, no. 5, May 1994.

On GRAHAM: Books—*Robert Graham 1963–1969,* exhibition catalog, Cologne 1970; *Robert Graham: Statues by Graham* W.J. Beal and George W. Neubert, Minneapolis 1981; *Illusion/Allusion: Contemporary Sculpture* by James J. Murphy, Tallahassee 1998. **Articles—**''Through Western Eyes'' by Leo Rubinfien in *Art in America* (New York), September/October 1978; ''Robert Graham: Ignoring the Lessons of Modern Art'' by Barbara Isenberg in *ARTnews* (New York), January 1979; ''The Collectors: Contemporary Elan'' by Peter Carlsen in *Architectural Digest* (New York), March 1979; ''ART: American Figurative Sculpture'' by David Bourdon in *Architectural Digest* (New York), November 1979; ''Critic's Choice'' by Grace Glueck in the *New York Times,* 23 November 1979; ''Robert Graham'' by Jon R. Friedman in *Arts Magazine* (New York), January 1980; ''Robert Graham'' by Tomas Lawson in *Flash Art* (Milan), January/February 1980; '''Local' Art Hits the Big Time'' by Michael Tennesen and Richard B. Marks in *Los Angeles Magazine,* February 1980; ''Wheels and Deals Keep California Venice Spinning'' by Charles Lockwood in the *Smithsonian* (Washington, D.C.), March 1980; ''Studio: Robert Graham'' by Marlena Donohue in *Sculpture* (Washington, D.C.), vol. 13, May/June 1994; ''Dead or Alive: Molds, Modeling and Mimesis in Representational Sculpture'' by Robert Taplin in *Sculpture* (Washington, D.C.), vol. 13, May/June 1994; ''Robert Graham at Gagosian'' by Robert Taplin in *Art in America* (New York), vol. 82, no. 9, September 1994; review by Donald B. Kuspit in *Artforum International,* vol. 33, November 1994; ''Robert Graham'' by Pamela Hammond in *ARTnews,* vol. 94, April 1995.

* * *

The strength of Robert Graham's compelling bronzes derives from a series of subtle, overlapping oppositions. Though life-like in detail if not in size, the women he depicts are imbued with a distinct element of the hallucinatory. The effect holds the viewer at a psychological distance, who, as a matter of recourse, sees them as types rather than as individuals. With increasing accuracy Graham transposes his studio model into permanent form, maintaining that the sculptures serve not only as reproduction but also as ''a metaphor for the human spirit.''

Nearly all of Graham's career has been devoted to the human figure. During his early narrative stage in the sixties, when his medium was wax, the psychological tensions began to emerge from his work. Graham's wax miniature sybarites were applauded for their exquisite detail, yet covered by their Plexiglas from the viewer's world. They were kept in a vacuum, sealed from touch, offsetting the onlooker's sense of scale, forcing him into the role of voyeur. With the actual distance between sculpture and viewer indeterminate, the tiny personages were both approachable and distant.

Around 1970 Graham diverted his attention from narrative sculpture to experimenting with simultaneous views of the same figure. For the first time he employed a camera and a casting mold, two devices he found crucial for his subsequent work. Graham's first series of bronze pieces recalled the 19th-century Eadweard Muybridge photographs of figures in action. Engaged in simple movements—walking, bending, arising—Graham strove to make every gesture a simple and as immediate as possible, thereby eliminating the ambiguity of the earlier works. Graham's deepening interest in fusing motion into his composition resolved into a lengthy series of reference photographs. After photographing different models, each one executing basic actions in different ways, he derived a master figure from which the mold of subsequent figures was made.

Graham's wax figures progressed into bronze in 1971. With this came the departure of the Plexiglas covers and the descriptive coloring he applied to the wax. The ambiguities returned however. In his 1973 ''Single Head,'' Graham defiantly executes a ''bust'' whose portrayal of face and shoulders is sensitive and veristic, yet lacking in two important animating features—the head is hairless and the eyes have no pupils.

His 1973 ''Eight Heads,'' a piece in which each head bears a distinct facial expression, assumes classical overtones. With both hair and pupils still absent, the piece seems, paradoxically, complete within itself and, as one critic described, ''from another world.'' The Plexiglas that once separated onlookers physically has been replaced by a psychological barrier. Again the spectator is forced to become a voyeur.

Graham abandoned his eerie, science-fiction personages in the following years in pursuit of depicting specific individuals. This shift in focus necessitated a dramatic increase in scale. As his attention to detail heightened, the sense of real flesh and bone, of contours and dimples, intensified the reality of the bronze. Ironically the soothing order is disrupted by the abrupt, almost brutal truncation of the figure. The viewer is thus trapped between the astonishing realism and the drastic editing.

In 1977 Graham returned to a convention he still favours: a figure approximately three feet tall on a minimal geometric base. He introduced the anatomically precise ''Lise'' series whose poses range from the passivity of ''Lise I'' to the near swagger of ''Lise II,'' to the defiance of ''Lise III.'' For the first time the figures seem to be observing the viewer as he observes them. In this series, Graham delicately shifts the literal interpretations of the statues to meaphorical: by reducing the scale he has distilled the figure to its essence.

Graham uses oil paint to colour his statues. Flesh colour becomes less important to him as he moves to using his own black and white photos for research. His concern, instead, rests with tonal values and thus he opts for a narrow range of purples, grays and greens. The bloodless hues created by these colours disturb the realistic modeling of the nudes, further contributing to the emotional gap between viewer and figure.

—Carrie Barker

GRAHAM, Rodney

Nationality: Canadian. **Born:** Matsqui, British Columbia, Canada, 16 January 1949. **Education:** University of British Columbia, 1968–71. **Agents:** Donald Young Gallery, 933 West Washington Blvd., Chicago, Illinois 60607; Christine Burgin Gallery, 243 West 18th Street, New York, New York 10011; 303 Gallery, 525 West 22nd Street, New York, New York 10011; Lisson Gallery, 52–54 Bell Street and 67 Lisson Street, London, UK NW1 5DA; Galerie Micheline Szwajcer Verlatstraat 14, BE-2000 Antwerp, Belgium; Galerie Rudiger Schottle, Martiusstrasse 7, D-80802 Munich, Germany; Johnen & Schottle, Maria-Hilf-Strasse 17, D-50677 Cologne, Germany. **Address:** Rodney Graham Studios, #19–712 Robson Street, Vancouver, B.C. V6Z 1A2, Canada.

Selected Individual Exhibitions:

1986 Johnsen & Schottle Galerie, Cologne
1988 Vancouver Art Gallery, Vancouver, B.C. (catalog)
1989 Stedelijk Van Abbemuseum, Eindhoven, Netherlands (catalog)
1990 *Parsifal,* Johnsen & Schottle Galerie, Cologne (catalog)
1993 Galerie Micheline Szwajcer, Antwerp (catalog)
1996 Nicole Klagsbrun, New York
1999 *Rodney Graham—Cinema, Music, Video,* Kunsthalle, Vienna (catalog)
2000 *What Is Happy, Baby?,* Lisson Gallery, London (catalog)
2001 *Rodney Graham,* Hamburger Bahnhof, Berlin

Selected Group Exhibitions:

1986 *Ricochet,* Galleria Sala Uno, Rome (catalog)
1988 *Made in Camera,* Gallery Sten Eriksson, Stockholm (catalog)
1990 *Figure et Lecture,* Souma Samia Gallery, Paris
1991 *La Revanche de l'Image,* Galerie Pierre Huber, Geneva (catalog)
1992 *Camera Indiscretes,* Centre d'Art Santa Monica, Barcelona (catalog)
1994 *Des Objets sans Fondation,* Residence Secondaire, Carree Saint-Nicholas, Paris
1995 *Spirits at the Crossing,* Setagaya Art Museum, Tokyo (traveled to MOMA Kyoto, MOMA Hokkaido, MOMA Sapporo)
1997 *Citta/Natura,* Palazzo delle Exposizioni, Rome
1998 *Speed—Visions of an Accelerated Age,* Photographers Gallery and Whitechapel Art Gallery, London (catalog)
1999 *Regarding Beauty—A View of the Late Twentieth Century,* Hirshhorn Museum and Sculpture Garden, Washington, D.C.
2000 *The Greenhouse Effect,* Serpentine Gallery, London (catalog)

Publications:

By GRAHAM: Books—*Lenz* (edition of 10), Vancouver, B.C. 1983; *The Piazza 4.1* (edition of 25, signed and numbered), New York 1989; *Casino Royale* (edition of 15), Brussels 1989; *Freud et le cas Katharina (1990)* (edition of 300), Brussels 1991; *Reading Machine for Parsifal: One Signature* (edition of 12), Brussels 1992; *Oeuvres*

Rodney Graham: *City Self/Country Self (Paris Street Scene 1865),* 2000. Photo by Scott Livingstone. ©Rodney Graham.

Freudiennes/Oeuvres Wagneriennes, Brussels 1996. **Articles—**''Siting Vexation Island'' in *Art/Text,* no. 59, January 1998.

On GRAHAM: Books—*Cream—Contemporary Art in Culture* by Susan Kandel, London 1998. **Articles—**''Rodney Graham: Illuminated Ravine, Camera Obscura'' by R. Keziere in *Vanguard,* vol. 8, no. 9, November 1979; ''The Critic's Way'' by D. Kuspit, M. Wechsler, D. Cameron, P. L. Tazzi, and I. Rein in *Artforum,* vol. 26, no. 1, September 1987; ''Rodney Graham: Opening to Equivocal Strictures'' by Jeffrey Swartz in *Lapiz,* no. 67, April 1990; ''The Generic City and Its Discontents'' by Scott Watson in *Arts Magazine,* February 1991; ''Rodney Graham'' by Herve Legros in *Beaux-Arts Magazine,* no. 97, January 1992; ''Rodney Graham'' by Sarah Kent in *Time Out,* London, 1 January 1997; ''Dust Breeding'' by Kenneth Baker in *ARTnews,* November 1998; ''Video Show House'' by Polly Staple in *Art Monthly,* July-August 2000.

* * *

The most useful entrance to the work of Rodney Graham comes at the expense of the deep meaning we often expect from art. For if there is one thing that holds true in all of Graham's work it is this: it's good for a laugh. Take the third of Graham's so-called ''Hollywood style star vehicles,'' a 35mm film loop entitled *City Self/Country Self (Paris Street Scene 1865)*. Building narrative tension out of an easily recognizable set of 19th century costume conventions, this richly textured period piece turns on the coincidental encounter between a provincial rustic and a well-heeled dandy. At precisely the stroke of noon Graham's ''country self'' (played by himself) is unceremoniously booted in the ass by his ''city self'' (also played by himself). This ridiculous gag, which Graham singled out in the exhibition catalog for *What Is Happy, Baby?* as the ''injury laugh endemic to film comedy since Lumiere's *L'Arroseur Arrose (The Hoser Hosed)* of 1897,'' comes off without a hitch. The level of slapstick plumbed is so low, the lengths gone to stage the event so fantastic, that it is difficult not to laugh.

In the context of Graham's incredibly varied artistic practice, *City Self Country Self (Paris Street Scene 1865)* crytallizes something like a home-grown theory of irony: a theory in which Graham himself figures as nothing more or less than the principle fall guy or buffoon. The fact is that meaning in Graham's work is never entirely secure. Meaning always emerges by virtue of the artistic identity Graham performs. Whether he plays the part of the photo-conceptual artist, literary dandy, utopian architect, singer/songwriter, fashion designer, lecturer in Freud, independent filmmaker, or actor and executive producer in his own films matter little. In each case, meaning does not so much inhere in the media he employs as appear a function of the performance of a particular persona. One of the ways this operates in *City Self Country Self (Paris Street Scene 1865)* is that the two great clichés of artistic identity in the 19th and 20th century are both made a laughing stock. There is a laugh in seeing the artist in sync with popular forces as well as a chuckle in the supposed detachment of the artist from these forces.

Perhaps the main reason that Graham gets his laugh is that much of what transpires in the film turns on the fiction that the artist has been reading his social art history. The project is grounded in the form and circulation of an *Epinal* (a broad sheet type poster), the historical and ideological nature of 19th century costumery, peasant uprisings, class aspirations, the great Courbet, and the *petite creve*. That the work is not simply about becoming famous by starring in your own film, but rather about class—and further the nature of class (now), as the occulted matter of taste—might come as a shock to those familiar with Graham's typically detached aesthetic. Indeed Graham is perhaps best known for his highly intellectual or ''bookish'' conceptual art from the late 1980s and early 1990s. Nevertheless, it suggests a correspondence between the question of self-representation and that of meaning in Graham's art which consistently runs through his entire project.

In an important sense all of Graham's work hinges on a certain equation between the act of interpretation and the fact of getting some joke or other. His many artistic personae are so present in his art that in making sense of any one work, one invariably feels pressured into working alongside his self-conscious authorial presence. More often than not, this means that understanding presumes a certain humour or, more precisely, it presumes grasping the irony of the material as one presumes Graham himself has grasped it. A lot hinges on the way Graham uses visual, object-based, or acoustic languages. Thus, if his early conceptual art often begs an economy of meaning production associated with the early history of cinema, the rare book shop, that of minimalist sculpture and the science of optics, in his film works interpretation relies upon a relatively reduced and illustrative vocabulary. Interpretation counts on an act of meaning-making in synch with that of popular film and insinuated by the symbolic economy that a taste in the genre of film comedy entails.

It is in the flash of understanding when the meaning of Graham's work hits one like a punch line, that one broaches his peculiar notion of irony. For Graham, irony takes the certainty of meaning or the assumption of truth as its departure. In so doing his work shifts critical focus from the object as the bearer of meaning to the subject or viewer where meaning is produced. Getting the joke in Graham's work means accepting the fact that the joke is always on you: that within the moment of enlightenment itself, one is actually finishing off and polishing Graham's jokes for him through a kind of self-duplication of one's own making. Ultimately, for Graham irony turns on a problem located in the self; more specifically, of the self's belief in the truth with which one is continually confronted. If it were not for the fact that the act of interpretation is consistently deemed a laughing matter this would not be the case. Nor would it be possible for a light-hearted practice like Graham's to dramatize such a fugitive and melancholic process as that of meaning production.

—Shepherd Steiner

GRAU-GARRIGA, Josep

Nationality: Spanish. **Born:** San Cugat del Valles, near Barcelona, 18 February 1929. **Education:** Escuela de Artes y Officios, Barcelona, 1943–47; Escuela Superior de Bellas Artes, Barcelona, 1947–51. **Military Service:** Served in 1st Mountain Regiment, Spanish Army, Valle de Aran, 1952; soldier 2nd class. **Family:** Married Aurea Quintana Baules in 1960 (separated, 1969); children: Esther, Jordi, and Alexandra. **Career:** Worked in interior design studio, Barcelona, 1943–45, and in graphic design studio, Barcelona, 1945–47; in Jean Lurcat's tapestry studio, Paris, 1958. Painter and tapestry artist, Barcelona, since 1953. Director, Catalan School of Tapestry, San Cugat del Valles, Barcelona, from 1958; drawing instructor, Montserrat Monastery, Barcelona, 1958–62, and Eina School of Design, Barcelona, 1965–66; tapestry instructor, Esculade de Artes y Officios, Barcelona, 1968; University of Art and Architecture, Marseille-Luminy 1972; Rochester Institute of Technology, New York, 1974, and Workshop in Fiber Expression, Costa Mesa, California, 1974. **Agent:** Arras Gallery, 24 West 57th Street, New York, New York 10019, U.S.A. **Address:** 373 Travessera de las Corts, entresol 8–10, 08029 Barcelona, Spain.

Individual Exhibitions:

1953 Monastery, San Cugat del Valles, Barcelona
1964 Sal Gaspar, Barcelona
1967 Sala Mainel, Burgos, Spain
Casa del Siglo 15, Segovia, Spain
Amics de les Arts, Manresa, Spain

Painting by Josep Grau-Garriga, 2001. ©Josep Grau-Garriga.

Josep Grau-Garriga: *Senyor Important,* 1988. ©Josep Grau-Garriga.

Monastery, San Cugat del Valles, Barcelona
Museo de Arte Contemporaneo, Madrid
1968 Galerie La Demeure, Paris
Sala Domingo, Sao Paulo, Brazil
Sala Santa Catalina del Ateneo, Madrid
1969 Amics de l'Art, Terrassa, Spain
Galeria Galdeano, Zaragoza
Galerie La Demeure, Paris
1970 De Cordova Museum, Lincoln, Massachusetts
Galerie La Demeure, Paris
1971 *Retrospective Exhibit 1960–70,* Museum of Fine Arts, Houston
Arras Gallery, New York
Institute of International Education, New York
Birmingham Museum of Fine Arts, Alabama
1972 Galeria Antanona, Caracas
University of Marseille-Luminy, France
Pintures, Tapissos, Sala del Consell General de les Valls, Andorra
Maison de la Culture, Rennes, France
1973 Galeria Rene Metras, Barcelona
Hospital de la Santa Creu, Barcelona
Arras Gallery, New York
Museu Provincial Textil, Terrassa, Spain (retrospective)
1974 Banco de Granada, Spain
Los Angeles County Museum of Art (retrospective)
Arras Gallery, New York
Maison de Culture, Rennes, France (with Antoni Cumella; toured France)
1975 Galerie La Demeure, Paris
Oklahoma Art Center, Oklahoma City (retrospective)
Birmingham Museum of Fine Arts, Alabama
Ohio State University, Columbus
Centre Culturel de Marais, Paris
1976 Palacio de la Lonja, Zaragoza
Prisma Galeria, Zaragoza
Université d'Angerts, France
Arras Gallery, New York
Monastery of Montmajour, Angers, France
Chateau de Nascoil, France (with Olga de Amaral)
University of Wisconsin at Eau Claire
Sanctuari de Meritxell, Andorra
1977 Arras Gallery, New York
Galeria Atenas, Zaragoza
1978 The Gallery at 24, Miami
Galeria Febo, San Cugat del Valles, Barcelona
Ecole des Beaux-Arts, Lyons
1979 Galeria Ficares, Almagro, Ciudad Real, Spain
Grau-Garriga: Dibuixos del 1957 al 1978, Monastery, San Cugat del Valles, Barcelona
Galerie de l'Orangerie, Dieppe, France
Montgomery College, Washington, D.C.

Placa Sant Jaume, Barcelona
1980 Grau-Garriga-Studio Concept, Haarlem, Netherlands
Arras Gallery, New York
Galeria Brossoli, Barcelona
Hyatt Hotel, Dubai, United Arab Emirates (permanent installation)
1981 Galerie les Couteliers, Toulouse
Musée d'Art Moderne de la Ville, Paris
1982 Les Tours Narbonnaises, Carcassonne, France
Crocker Art Museum, Sacramento, California
Palais de Congres et Culture, Le Mans, France
Salle d'Expositions Permanentes, Andorra
1983 Maison de la Culture, Nantes, France
Maison de la Culture Le Parvis, Tarbes, France
Musee Goya, Castres, France
Musee Cambous, Montpellier, France
Galerie Margall, Montpellier, France
Caixa de Pensions, Valencia
Arras Gallery, New York
1984 Museo Gijon, Spain
Galeria Pinole, Gijon, Spain
Museo Oviedo, Spain
Casa Municipal de Cultura, Aviles, Spain
Galeria Parc, Andorra
Maison de la Culture Le Parvis, Tarbes, France
Palacio de los Cordovas, Granada, Spain
Institut Francais, Barcelona
Musee Hyacinthe Rigaud, Perpignan, France
Casa Pairal Le Castillet, Perpignan, France
Musee Puig-Cdacc, Perpignan, France
Musee de la Chartreuse, Douai, France
Centre Cultural Manuel de Falla, Granada
1985 Musee de Montbeliard, France
Cloitre du Monastere de San Cugat del Valles, Barcelona
Aula de Cultura, Alacant, Spain
Chateau de Benedormiens, Castell d'Aro, Spain
1986 Galerie Expo-Art, Girona, Spain
Maison de la Cultura, Alcoi, Spain
Musee de Granollers, Barcelona
Abbaye des Cordeliers, Chateauroux, France
1987 Museo Rufino Tamayo, Mexico
Palacio de la Lonja, Valencia
1988 Palau Robert, Barcelona
Museo Provincial, Teruel, Spain
1989 Musée des Beaux Arts, Angers
Musée Jean Lurcat, Angers
Abadia de Ronceray, Angers
Castillo de Angers, Angers
1990 Museo de Bellas Artes, Sabadell, Spain
Centro de Accion Cultural, Sant Avold
Casa de Cultura, Freyming-Merlebach
1992 Musée de la Chartreuse, Douai, France
Casa de Cultura des Princes, Perugia, Italy
Casa de Cultura del Gobierno Frances, Abidjan, Africa
1993 Casa de Cultura de Alcoi
Temple Romano de Vic
1994 Ayuntamiento de Saint Mathurin sur Loire, Angers
Centro de Arte Contemporaneo Bouvet Ladubay, Samur
1995 Centre Cultural de St. Cugat del Vallès, Spain
1996 Galeria Alba Cabrera, Valencia, Spain
1997 Galeria Can Marc, Girona, Spain
Centre d'Estudis Catalans, Paris
1998 *Homage a Grau-Garriga,* Galeria Canals, St. Cugat, Spain
Homage a Grau-Garriga, Como, Italy
1999 Galeria Blanquerna, Madrid
Salle Aragon, Trélazé, France
Maison des Arts, Châtillon, France
Galerie Askeo, Paris
Galeria Alba Cabrera and 6 de Febrero, Madrid
Galeria Benassar, Madrid
2000 Musée des Beaux-Arts de St. Lô, France
Galeria Daniel Duchoze, Rouen, France
Galeria Maria Villalba i Badia, Barcelona

Selected Group Exhibitions:

1961 *Tapissos Contemporanis,* Galeria Biosca, Madrid
1965 *2nd Biennale de la Tapisserie,* Lausanne, Switzerland
1968 *Contemporary Tapestries,* IBM Gallery, New York
1971 *Filet Fer,* Musée de la Tapisserie, Aix-en-Provence, France
1972 *Fiber Structures,* Denver Art Museum
1976 *Contemporary European Tapestries,* Museum of Contemporary Art, Tokyo (travelled to Museum of Contemporary Art, Kyoto)
1978 *L'Art Moderne dans les Musées de Province,* Grand Palais, Paris
1983 *Aspectes de la pintura contemporania a Europa 1945–83,* Conselleria de Cultura, Andorra
1986 *La Tapisserie en France,* Musee Departemental de la Tapisserie, Aubusson, France
1994 Instituto Frances, Barcelona

Collections:

Museo de Arte Contemporaneo, Madrid; Museo de Arte Contemporaneo, Seville; Museo Provincial Textil, Terrassa, Barcelona; Musée d'Art Moderne de la Ville, Paris; Musée Cantini, Marseilles; Musée Reattu, Arles, France; Metropolitan Museum of Art, New York; Museum of Fine Arts, Houston; Denver Art Museum; Museo Rufino Tamayo, Mexico City; Museo Salvador Allende, Santiago, Chile; Museu d'Art Moderne, Barcelona.

Publications:

On GRAU-GARRIGA: Books—*Grau-Garriga: Retrospective Exhibit 1960–70,* exhibition catalog with texts by Georges Boudaille, Alexandre Cirici-Pellicer and Philippe de Montebello, Houston 1971; *La Nouvelle Tapisserie* by A. Kuenzi, Geneva 1972; *Grau-Garriga: Pintures, Tapissos,* exhibition catalog with texts by J. Corredor Mattheos and Alain Ohnenwald, Andorra 1972; *Cumella/Grau-Garriga,* exhibition catalog/book by André Barey, Paris 1974; *Josep Grau-Garriga,* exhibition catalog with an introduction by George F. Kuebler, Oklahoma City 1975; *La Palabra del Arte* by Baltasar Porcel, Madrid 1976; *Textile Sculptures* by Irene Waller, London 1977; *Grau-Garriga* by Arnau Puig, Barcelona 1977; *Grau-Garriga en el Todo* by Baltasar Porcel, Barcelona 1978; *Grau-Garriga: Dibuixos del 1957 al 1978,* exhibition catalog with an introduction by José Maria Valverde, Barcelona 1979; *J. Grau-Garriga,* exhibition catalog with text by Alain Ohnenwald, Toulouse 1981; *Grau-Garriga* by Alain Ohnenwald, Paris 1982; *Josep Grau-Garriga,* exhibition catalog with texts by Bernadette Contensou and Alain Ohnenwald, Carcassonne, France 1982; *Grau-Garriga* by Arnau Puig, Barcelona 1985; *Grau-Garriga* by Enrique Llobregat, Gandia 1985; *Grau-Garriga a Chateauroux,* exhibition catalog with texts by Arnau Puig, Lucien Cruzi and others, Chateauroux 1986; *Grau-Garriga* by Pilar Parcerisas, Barcelona 1990; *Josep Grau-Garriga: Peintures, Papiers, Tapisseries,* exhibition catalog with text by Itzhak Goldberg and Christian Forestier, Paris 1999; *Grau-Garriga, Gravats 1950–2000,* exhibition catalog, Barcelona 2000; *Josep Grau-Garriga* by Christian Delacampagne and Michel Carduner, Barcelona 2000.

*

In my work, I make use of the object (specially in painting), that has personal connotations. It seems to me more valid and authentic to use simple forms than beautiful ones. I am much more interested in reality itself than its representation. In tapestry I use materials that are tied to my memories and the image of my land. I try to reaffirm their value so that they speak for themselves. I only want to make evident what is already there. I am very much in love with life, and it may be because of that I am frequently touched by its sarcastic dramatism.

To me the work of art should be the author's own reflexion. After it achieves liberty, it has to denounce injustice, to introduce new forms, to meet and to express itself as an absolute lover of beauty in all senses.

I believe that the most important thing that I can say about my work is that it is more than an intent of approach of my sensations to other people, that these intimate sensations are strengthened and motivated by the exterior world for which I feel a total love. Every factor of life affects me, especially when it is a problem. By natural inclination, I take sides for two persecuted minorities and for the revindications that I believe in. I cannot stay indifferent, and therefore take a partisan position. Therefore, in my work what I try to tell is more important than the way I tell it. I believe that the content in the work of art is what communicates the artist's feelings to people and so is everlasting. I am interested in formal problems, for they are useful to express myself in my own way, but I see very clearly the esthetic problems.

—Josep Grau-Garriga

* * *

Joseph Grau-Garriga is a painter and tapestry designer who should be described as a sculptor of soft forms. From his native Barcelona he came to Paris to work in the studio of Jean Lurcat, the basis of his understanding of the technique and future activities. Back in Catalonia he became a successful teacher of design and undertook a series of murals and stained glass windows in local buildings.

Appointment to the directorship of the Catalan School of Tapestry was followed by a series of teaching visits to the United States, Canada and Mexico. Grau-Garriga continues as a painter, and a print maker in lithography and lino-cuts, but his main creative technique is in tapestry hangings, or woollen murals. His approach is that of a painter, organizing powerful colours and contrasting textures to build up complex counterbalances of form. Whilst wool remains the basic material, he often incorporates thick ropes, hemp, threads of metallic materials, to enhance the drama and decorative potential of his compositions.

Grau-Garriga derives much of his style from Catalonian baroque. The weaving of the tapestries, at the Catalan School of Tapestry, has always enabled him to control the execution and to experiment with the traditional processes. Thus he has been able to incorporate knotted stiches, as in the manufacture of carpets, which result in tufts of wool, which can be modelled by hand. This relief technique results in a plastic density, a new dynamic contribution to the tapestry form. Compositionally, Grau-Garriga favours a central element around which he expands and builds up areas of colour or textural structure.

Recently he has experimented with plastics and the creation of free-standing woven structures. The incorporation of tiny plastic tubes in the woollen forms added elements of transparency and the conducting of light to otherwise solid images. In turn this suggested that flat, hanging ''reliefs'' limited the potential of additive possibilities, and the artist moved away from panels, or the flat picture image, to huge sculptures, exploring space both in an upright, vertical sense, as well as extending along the ground. In these works Grau-Garriga can be said to have enlarged the potential of his chosen medium.

—Charles Spencer

GRAUBNER, Gotthard

Nationality: German. **Born:** Erlbach, Vogtland, 13 June 1920. **Education:** Hochschule für Bildende Künste, Berlin, 1947–48; Kunstakademie, Dresden, 1948–49, 1951; Staatliche Kunstakademie, Dusseldorf, 1954–59. **Career:** Independent painter, Dusseldorf, since 1959. Art instructor, Lessing-Gymnasium, Dusseldorf, 1964–65; instructor, 1965–69, and since 1969 professor, Kunstakademie, Hamburg; professor, Staatliche Kunstakademie, Dusseldorf, 1976–1992; professor, Akademie der Künste, Hamburg, 1996; member, Sächsischen Akademie der Künste, Dresen, 1996. **Agent:** Galerie M Bochum, Haus Weitmar, 4630 Bochum, Germany. **Address:** Lohengrinstrasse 7, 4000 Dusseldorf-Oberkassel, Germany.

Individual Exhibitions:

1960 Galerie Schmela, Dusseldorf
1964 Galerie D, Frankfurt
1965 Op Art Galerie, Esslingen, West Germany
Galerie H., Hannover
1966 Galerie Schmela, Dusseldorf
Modern Art Museum, Munich
1967 Wide White Space Gallery, Antwerp
1969 Galerie Thomas, Munich
Kestner-Gesellschaft, Hannover
Stadtisches Museum, Leverkusen, West Germany
Kunsthalle, Dusseldorf
Kunstakademie, Braunschweig, West Germany
Galerie Ernst, Hannover
1970 Kunstverein für die Rheinlande und Westfalen, Dusseldorf
Kunsthalle, Cologne
1972 Galerie Schmela, Dusseldorf
Galerie Hans Meyer-Denise René, Dusseldorf
Galerie Elke Droscher, Hamburg
1974 André Emmerich Gallery, New York

1975 Galerie M, The Hague
Kunsthalle, Hamburg
Galerie Schellmann und Kluser, Munich
Galerie Elke Droscher, Hamburg
1976 Galerie André Emmerich, Zurich
Galerie René Ziegler, Zurich
Galerie Art in Progress, Munich
1977 Galerie M, Bochum, West Germany
Stadtische Kunsthalle, Dusseldorf
1978 Frankfurter Kunstverein, Frankfurt
Galerie Folker Skulima, Berlin
1979 Galerie Defet, Nuremberg
1980 Kunsthalle, Tübingen
Galerie Art in Progress, Munich
Kunsthalle, Baden-Baden, West Germany
1982 Stadtisches Museum, Monchengladbach, West Germany
1983 Kunstmuseum, Dusseldorf
Konsthall, Malmo, Sweden
1985 Galerie M, Bochum, West Germany
Kirche Sankt Markus-Nied, Frankfurt
Galerie Defet, Nuremberg, West Germany
Galerie Nordenhake, Malmo, Sweden
Raum fur Malerei, Cologne
1986 Stadtisches Kunstmuseum, Bonn
1987 Kunstsammlung Nordrhein-Westfalen, Dusseldorf
Galerie Schmela, Dusseldorf
1994 Galerie Walter Storms, Munich
Monoprints, Galerie Meyer-Ellinger, Frankfurt
1995 Galerie Karsten Greve, Cologne
Malerei, Saarland Museum, Stiftung Saarländischer Kulturbesitz, Saarbrücken (catalog)
Mestna Galerija, Ljubljana
1996 *Monoprints,* Kunstraum Falkenstein, Hamburg
1997 Kunstraum Fleetinsel, Hamburg
Malerei, Kunstsammlungen, Staatliches Museum Schwerin
Kunsthandel Wolfgang Werner, Berlin
Ausstellung des Instituts für Auslandsbeziehungen, Schwerin (catalog)
1998 Galerie Edith Wahlandt, Stuttgart
Neue Arbeiten, Galerie Karsten Greve, Cologne
Kunstverein Münsterland, Coesburg
1999 Kunstverein Münsterland, Coesfeld
Kunstmuseum, Städtisches Museum, Mühlheim a.d. Ruhr
Studio A, Museum Gegenstandsfreier Kunst des Landkreises Cuxhaven, Otterndorf
Radierungen: Unikate aus den Jahren 1969–1995, Kunstverein Münsterland, Coesfeld (catalog)
2000 *Zeichnung,* Gemäldegalerie Neue Meister, Staatliche Kunstsammlungen Dresden, Albertinum, Dresden
Malerei und Zeichnung, Museum Küpppersmühle, Sammlung Grothe, Duisburg (catalog)
2001 Instituts für Auslandsbeziehungen e.V., Stuttgart (traveled to Athens, Greece) (catalog)
Museum Wiesbaden
Staatliche Kunsthalle Karlsruhe

Selected Group Exhibitions:

1957 *Das Rote Bild,* Abendausstellung, Dusseldorf
1962 *Neue Tendenzen,* Galerie Orez, The Hague
1965 *Group Zero,* Washington Gallery of Modern Art, Washington, D.C.
1970 *Strategy: Get Arts,* Richard Demarco Gallery, Edinburgh
1971 *Bienal,* Sao Paulo
1974 *Geplante Malerei,* Westfalischer Kunstverein, Munster, West Germany
1977 *Documenta 6,* Museum Fridericianum, Kassel, West Germany
1979 *Soft-Art,* Kunsthaus, Zurich
1982 *Biennale,* Venice
1985 *Zeichner in Dusseldorf 1955–85,* Kunstmuseum, Dusseldorf
1987 *Der unverbrauchte Blick,* Martin-Gropius-Bau, West Berlin
1995 *Künstler Gegen die Folter,* Bündner Kunstmuseum, Chur
Sehnsucht nach Italien—Heute, Heidelberger Kunstverein, Heidelberg
Hans Arp, Joseph Beuys, Gotthard Graubner, A.R. Penck, Andreas Urteil, Stiftung Hans Arp und Sophie Taeuber-Arp e.V., Rolandseck
1996 *Kunst nach 1945,* Galerie Neher, Essen
1997 *Pro Lidice,* Tschechisches Museum für Bildende Kunst, Prag
Licht—Farbe—Raum, Galerie Gertrud Dorn, Stuttgart
Schilderijen on Papier, De Zonnehof, Amersfoort
1999 *Jean Arp, Gianfredo Camesi, Gotthard Graubner, Al Held: Arbeiten auf Papier,* Galerie Renée Ziegler, Zurich
Gesammelte Räume—Gesammelte Träume—Kunst aus Deutschland von 1960–2000, Martin-Gropius-Bau, Berlin
Zero aus Deutschland 1957 bis 1966—Und Heute, Galerie der Stadt Esslingen, Villa Merkel und Bahnwärtenhaus, Esslingen
Das XX. Jahrhundert—Ein Jahrhundert Kunst in Deutschland, Staatliche Museen zu Berlin—Preußischer Kulturbesitz, Berlin

Collections:

Nationalgalerie, Berlin; Wallraf-Richartz Museum and Museum Ludgwig, Cologne; Städtische Kunstmuseum, Dusseldorf; Neue Pinakothek, Munich; Kaiser-Wilhelm Museum, Krefeld, West Germany; Kunsthalle, Hamburg; Westfalisches Landesmuseum, Münster, West Germany; Rheinisches Landesmuseum, Bonn; Museum of Contemporary Art, Rio de Janeiro.

Publications:

By GRAUBNER: Articles—in *Europaische Avantgarde,* Frankfurt 1963; in *Zauber des Lichts,* Recklinghausen, West Germany 1967.

On GRAUBNER: Books—*Kunst Heute* by Jürgen Claus, Hamburg 1965; *Kunst unsere Zrit* by Will Grohmann, Cologne 1966; *Gedicht für Gotthard Graubner* by Franz Mon, Dusseldorf 1969; *Gotthard Graubner,* exhibition catalog with texts by Wieland Schmied and Volker Kahmen, Hannover 1969; *Noch Kunst* by Rolf-Günter Dienst, Dusseldorf 1970; *Deutsche Kunst* by Rolf-Günter Dienst, Cologne 1970; *Erotik in der Kunst* by Volker Kahmen, Tübingen 1971; *Kunst Heute* by Karin Thomas, Cologne 1971; *Gotthard Graubner* by

Dietrich Helms, Recklinghausen, West Germany 1974; *Malerei nach 1945* by Wieland Schmied, Berlin 1975; *Sammlung Nordrhein-Westfalen* by Werner Schmalenbach, Dusseldorf 1975; *Gotthard Graubner,* exhibition catalog with text by Werner Hofmann and others, Hamburg 1975; *Gotthard Graubner: Malerei und Arbeit auf Papier 1958–1975,* exhibition catalog with text by Margit Staber, Zurich 1976; *Gotthard Graubner,* exhibition catalog, with texts by H. A. Peters, K. Schmidt, M. Imdahl and V. Kahmen, Baden-Baden, West Germany 1980; *Gotthard Graubner,* exhibition catalog with texts by Max Imdahl and Volker Kahmen, Malmo 1983; *Gotthard Graubner,* exhibition catalog with essays by Max Imdahl and Joern Merkert, Dusseldorf 1986. **Articles—**''Color-space Bodies: The Art for Gotthard Graubner'' by Sabine Schülz in *Arts Magazine,* vol. 65, April 1991; ''Gotthard Graubner'' by David Galloway in *Art News,* vol. 94, May 1995; ''Sinfonien aus der Kraft der Farben'' by Angelika Kindermann in *ART: Das Kunstmagazin,* no. 5, May 1995; ''Gotthard Graubner: Le Corps de la Peinture'' by Caroline Naphegyi in *Beaux Arts Magazine,* no. 142, February 1996; ''Gotthard Graubner'' by Giorgio Verzotti in *Artforum International,* vol. 34, March 1996.

*

My paintings wax and wane depending on the light; beginning and ending are interchangeable. They describe no condition; they are a transition.

The action of the paint is crucial. At times, only one realm of color is necessary. The relationship between cold and warm values calls for tension and exchange. The paint spreads over the surface as if of its own volition. Its consistency dictates its movement, the way in which it runs its unconscious race. It arrives at dams; the color moves in the train of accumulations of pigment. The surface breathes.

The painter is responsible for this creation. He controls the execution of the painting's incidents and is thereby exalted to a process of meditation.

—Gotthard Graubner

GRAVES, Morris (Cole)

Nationality: American. **Born:** Fox Valley, Oregon, 28 August 1910; family moved to Seattle, 1920. **Education:** Self-taught in art. **Military Service:** Served in the United States Army, 1942–43. **Career:** Travelled as seaman in the Far East, 1928–31; visited Texas, 1931, and California, 1933; easel painter, Federal Art Project, 1936–37; met and became close friends with John Cage, 1937; built country house in San Juan Islands, 1938–39; instructor, Seattle Art Museum, 1940–42; visited Hawaii on Guggenheim Fellowship; studied at Honolulu Academy of Art, painting Oriental bronzes, 1946–47; travelled in France, 1948–49, Mexico, 1950, Japan, 1954, and Ireland, 1954–56; returned to Seattle, 1956; visited Europe on Windsor Award, 1957, then lived in Ireland; travelled in India and Japan, 1961–64; returned to United States, and settled in Loleta, California; travelled in Asia 1971, Africa and South America, 1972, and the Far East, 1973; Morris Graves Museum of Art, Eureka, California, opened 2001. **Awards:** Purchase Prize, Seattle Art Museum, 1933; Guggenheim Fellowship, 1946; Harris Medal, 1947, and Blair Prize, 1948, Art Institute of Chicago; Purchase Prize, University of Illinois, Urbana 1955; National Institute of Arts and Letters Grant, 1956; Duke and Duchess of Windsor Award, 1957. Honorary member, American Watercolor Society, 1968; Outstanding Contribution to the Arts Award, Humboldt Arts Council, 1989. **Agent:** Schmidt-Bingham Gallery, 41 East 57th Street # 5 fl, New York, New York 10022–1908. **Died:** Of stroke, Loleta, California, 5 May 2001.

Individual Exhibitions:

1936 Seattle Art Museum
1942 Willard Gallery, New York
1943 Willard Gallery, New York
University of Minnesota, Minneapolis (retrospective)
Arts Club, Chicago
Detroit Institute of Arts
Phillips Collection, Washington, D.C.
1944 Willard Gallery, New York
1945 Willard Gallery, New York
1946 Philadelphia Art Alliance
1948 Santa Barbara Museum of Art, California
California Palace of the Legion of Honor, San Francisco (retrospective)
Art Institute of Chicago
Los Angeles County Museum of Art
Willard Gallery, New York
1950 Margaret Brown Gallery, Boston
1951 Manchester Pierce Studio Gallery, Bellevue, Washington
1952 Beaumont Art Museum, Texas
1953 Willard Gallery, New York
1954 Willard Gallery, New York
Phillips Collection, Washington, D.C.
1955 Kunstforening, Oslo
Willard Gallery, New York
1956 Seattle Art Museum
Museum of Fine Arts, Boston (toured the United States)
1957 Bridgestone Museum of Art, Tokyo
La Jolla Art Museum, California
1959 Willard Gallery, New York
1960 Phoenix Art Museum, Arizona
1961 Roswell Museum and Art Center, New Mexico
Kalamazoo Institute of Arts, Michigan
1963 Pavilion Gallery, Balboa, California (retrospective)
1966 University of Oregon, Eugene (retrospective)
1969 Richard White Gallery, Seattle
1971 Willard Gallery, New York
1973 Willard Gallery, New York
1975 American Federation of Arts, New York (circulating exhibition)
1976 Willard Gallery, New York
1978 Willard Gallery, New York
1979 Charles Campbell Gallery, San Francisco
1981 Willard Gallery, New York
1982 University of Oregon, Eugene
1983 Phillips Collection, Washington, D.C.
Greenville County Museum of Art, South Carolina
Whitney Museum, New York
1984 Oakland Museum, California
Seattle Art Museum, Washington
San Diego Museum of Art, California
1996 *Retrospective,* Kurt Lidtke Galleries, Seattle

A Glimpse of Continuing, Schmidt Bingham Gallery, New York

1998 *Out of Darkness,* Schmidt Bingham Gallery, New York
The Five Seasons, Schmidt Bingham Gallery, New York
The Early Works, Whitney Museum of American Art, Stamford (traveling exhibition) (catalog)

1999 *Toward an Ultimate Reality,* Michael Rosenfeld Gallery, New York (catalog)

2000 *Instruments for a New Navigation,* Tacoma Art Museum (traveled to Museum of Art, Washington State University, Pullman; Gallery of Contemporary Art, Lewis & Clark College, Portland; Hearst Art Gallery, Saint Mary's College of California, Moraga) (catalog)
Paintings from the 1930s, Kurt Lidtke Galleries, Seattle

2001 *Still Life,* Schmidt Bingham Gallery, New York

Selected Group Exhibitions:

1963 *American Painting,* Tate Gallery, London

1966 *Birds in Contemporary Art,* Phillips Collection, Washington, D.C.
The Object Transformed, Museum of Modern Art, New York

1967 *Works on Paper,* Waddington Galleries, London

1963 *Painting and Sculpture Today,* Herron Museum of Art, Indianapolis

1969 *Art in America: Paintings, Drawings, Prints and Sculpture from the Museum's Collection,* Worcester Art Museum, Massachusetts

1971 *Drawings U.S.A. 71,* Minnesota Museum of Art, St. Paul

1973 *Drawing America 1973,* Museum of Art, St. Joseph, Missouri

1978 *Northwest Traditions,* Seattle Art Museum, Washington

1981 *Northwest Visionaries,* Institute of Contemporary Art, Boston

1994 *Perceivable Realities,* Michael Rosenfeld Gallery (catalog)
Morris Graves, Mark Tobey, Schmidt Bingham Gallery, New York (catalog)

1996 *Paintings and Sculpture 1845–1996,* Kennedy Galleries, New York

1997 *Twenty-five Treasures,* Campbell-Thiebaud Gallery, San Francisco (catalog)
Master Drawings in the Los Angeles County Museum of Art, Los Angeles County Museum of Art (catalog)

Collections:

National Institute of Arts and Letters, New York; Whitney Museum, New York; Metropolitan Museum of Art, New York; Museum of Modern Art, New York; Worcester Art Museum, Massachusetts; Phillips Collection, Washington, D.C.; Art Institute of Chicago; Seattle Art Museum; Portland Art Museum, Oregon; Tate Gallery, London.

Publications:

By GRAVES: Book—*Morris Graves: Flower Paintings,* with Theodore F. Wolff, Seattle 1994. **Articles—**''Mystic Painters of the Northwest'' in *Life* (New York), 28 September 1953; ''3 Kinds of Space'' in *Morris Graves: A Retrospective,* exhibition catalog, Eugene, Oregon 1966; interview with Katharine Kuh in *The Artist's Voice: Talks with Seventeen Modern Artists,* New York 2000.

On GRAVES: Books—*Morris Graves,* exhibition catalog by Frederick S. Wight, Berkeley and Los Angeles 1956; *Conversations with Artists* by Sheldon Rodman, New York 1957; *Morris Graves: A Retrospective,* exhibition catalog with foreword by Wallace S. Baldinger, Eugene, Oregon 1966; *The Drawings of Morris Graves* by Ida E. Rubin, Boston 1974; *Morris Graves: Vision of the Inner Eye* by Ray Kass, New York 1983. **Articles—**''Morris Graves at Schmidt Bingham'' by Ray Kass in *Art in America,* July 2000; obituary by Holland Cotter in *The New York Times,* 8 May 2001.

* * *

Morris Graves was a gentle visual poet of Oriental consciousness in a mechanical and secular world. Deeply influenced by Mark Tobey, Zen Buddhism and religious mysticism, Graves's delicate paintings aspire to the moment of awakening and enlightenment, the rasping of consciousness, by means of an animistic symbology.

Graves credited Tobey for inspiring his ''Bird'' paintings, and adapted Tobey's ''white writing'' and gouache washes on rice or mulberry paper as his medium. His iconography consists of invented representational forms with overt religious symbolism: chalices, birds, snakes, fishes, moon, and ''ritual bronze'' vessels. The fetishistic birds, for which Graves is best known, are the tokens of his transcendentalism. His inner vision conforms to Ananda Coomaraswamy's esthetic concepts of ''phenomenal space'' (the world outside the body), ''mental space'' (imagination and dreams), and the ''space of consciousness'' (symbolic, religious and spiritual thought). Lightly traced in calligraphic brush lines and filled with subtle washings, forms appear to assemble themselves out of the void. The ''space of consciousness'' is made manifest. A broader brushstroke reminiscent of *sumi* painting is sometimes used to outline form, lending an air of Oriental scrollwork. Concurrent with the animal paintings are unadorned still-lifes with simple vases, cups and flowers ceremoniously arranged.

For nearly his entire adult life, Graves lived in seclusion in the coastal wilds of the northwestern United States and, briefly, in Ireland during the late 1950's. The simple, unaffected and accidental occurrences of nature encountered there nourish his soul; the intrusions of man and technology are his anathema.

There is something almost painfully frail and awkward about his work, as if it might (spiritually) disintegrate under scrutiny. He seemed aware of this when he wrote in 1950, ''Secular and scientific 'art' is concerned with evolution . . . Religious art is concerned with involution.'' Graves demands an inwardness of experience. Within this deep devotion resides the implications of a transcendent universal expression of the inner self.

—Ron Glowen

GRAVES, Nancy

Nationality: American. **Born:** Pittsfield, Massachusetts, 23 December 1940. **Family:** Married Avery L. Smith. **Education:** Vassar College, Poughkeepsie, New York, 1958–61, B.A. 1961; School of Arts and Architecture, Yale University, New Haven, Connecticut,

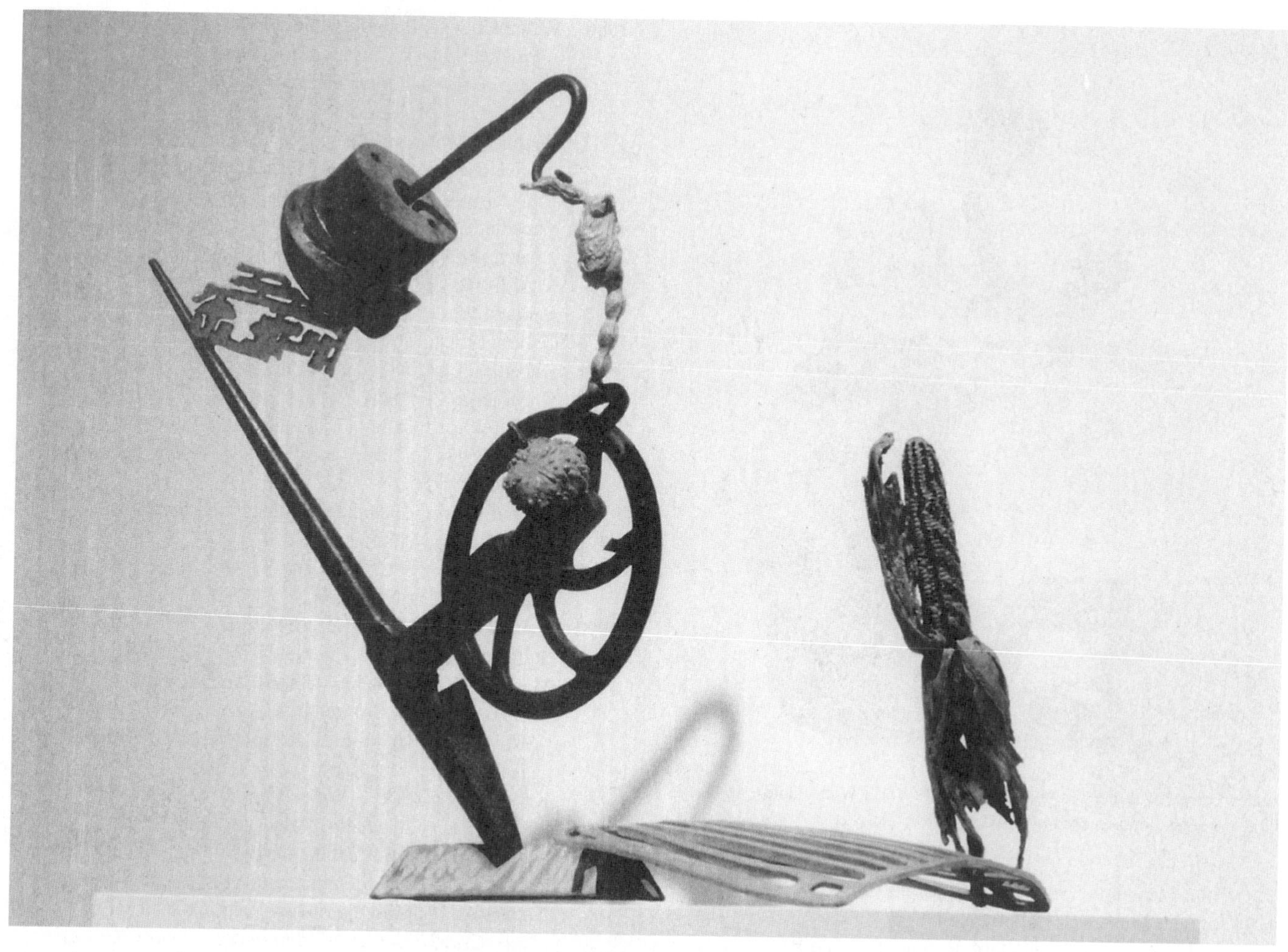

Nancy Graves: *Hindsight 1986.* ©Nancy Graves Foundation. Collection Walker Art Center, Minneapolis, Walker Special Purchase Fund, 1987/Licensed by VAGA, New York, NY.

1961–64, B.F.A. and M.F.A. 1964. **Career:** Independent artist, since 1966. Lived and worked in Florence, 1966; began making films, 1969. Resident, American Academy in Rome, 1979; currently lives and works in New York. **Awards:** Fulbright-Hayes Grant in Painting, Paris 1965; Vassar College Fellowship, 1971; Paris *Biennale* Grant, 1971; National Endowment for the Arts Grant, 1972; Creative Artists' Program Service Grant, New York, 1974; Skowhegan Medal for Drawing/Graphics, Maine, 1980; Yale Arts Award, New Haven, Connecticut, 1985; Distinguished Visitor Award, Vassar College, Poughkeepsie, New York, 1986; Award of American Art, The Pennsylvania Academy of Fine Arts, 1987; honorary degree, Skidmore College, Saratoga Springs, New York, 1989; Honorary Doctor of Fine Arts Degree, University of Maryland, Baltimore, and Yale University, New Haven, Connecticut, 1992. **Member:** American Academy and Institute of Arts and Letters, 1990. **Agent:** M. Knoedler and Company, 19 East 70th Street, New York, New York 10021, U.S.A. **Died:** Of cancer in New York, 21 October 1995.

Individual Exhibitions:

1968 Graham Gallery, New York
1969 Whitney Museum, New York
1970 National Gallery of Canada, Ottawa
1971 Gallery Reese Palley, New York
Gallery Reese Palley, San Francisco
National Gallery of Canada, Ottawa (and films)
Sculpture, Drawings, Films 1969–71, Neue Galerie der Stadt, Aachen, West Germany
Vassar College, Poughkeepsie, New York
Museum of Modern Art, New York (and films)
Wallraf-Richartz Museum, Cologne (and films)
University of California Art Museum, Berkeley (and films)
Walker Art Center, Minneapolis (and films)
Yale University School of Art and Architecture, New Haven, Connecticut
Pratt Institute, New York (and films)
1972 New Gallery of Contemporary Art, Cleveland
Janie C. Lee Gallery, Dallas
Institute of Contemporary Art, University of Pennsylvania, Philadelphia (and films)
Contemporary Arts Center, Cincinnati, Ohio (and films)
Whitney Museum, New York (and films)
1973 National Gallery of Canada, Ottawa
The Berkshire Museum, Pittsfield, Massachusetts
La Jolla Museum of Art, California
Janie C. Lee Gallery, Dallas

Nancy Graves with her sculpture *Bilanx.* AP/World Wide Photos. ©Nancy Graves Foundation/Licensed by VAGA, New York, NY.

Art Museum of South Texas, Corpus Christi
1974 André Emmerich Gallery, New York
Albright-Knox Art Gallery, Buffalo, New York
Janie C. Lee Gallery, Houston
Museum of Modern Art, New York (and films)
1975 Janie C. Lee Gallery, Houston
1977 André Emmerich Gallery, New York
Janie C. Lee Gallery, Houston
Galerie André Emmerich, Zurich
Galerie im Schloss, Munich
1978 Hammarskjold Plaza, New York
Knoedler & Co., New York
Gallery Diane Gilson, Seattle
Janie C. Lee Gallery, Houston
1979 Knoedler & Co., New York
1980 Knoedler & Co., New York
Albright-Knox Art Gallery, Buffalo, New York (toured the United States)
1981 Knoedler & Co., New York
Richard Gray Gallery, Chicago
1982 Knoedler & Co., New York
M. Knoedler AG, Zurich
1983 Santa Barbara Museum of Art, California
Gloria Luria Gallery, Bay Harbor Islands, Florida
Janie C. Lee Gallery, Houston
1984 Knoedler & Co., New York
Janie C. Lee Gallery, Houston
1985 Greenberg Gallery, St. Louis, Missouri
Knoedler & Co., New York
1986 Vassar College, Poughkeepsie, New York (travelled to Pittsfield, Massachusetts; Providence, Rhode Island)
Richard Gray Gallery, Chicago
Knoedler & Co., New York
1987 Hirshhorn Museum, Washington, D.C. (retrospective; travelled to Fort Worth, Texas; Santa Barbara, California; Brooklyn, New York, 1987–88)
Knoedler Gallery, London
1988 Associated American Artists, New York
Knoedler & Co., New York
Hedland Wetterling Gallery, Stockholm
Gallery Mukai, Tokyo
1989 Knoedler Kasmin Gallery, London
Knoedler & Co., New York
Linda Cathcart Gallery, Santa Monica, California
1990 Gerald Peters Gallery, Santa Fe, New Mexico (travelling to Dallas)
Heland Wetterling Gallery, Gothenburg, Sweden
1991 Locks Gallery, Philadelphia
Meredith Long & Co., Houston
Knoedler & Co., New York
1992 Irving Galleries, Palm Beach, Florida
Staff Tech Arts at Knoedler, New York
1993 Margulies Taplin Gallery, Boca Raton, Florida
Fine Arts Gallery, Baltimore, Maryland (travelling to Exeter, New Hampshire; Boston; Norfolk, Virginia; Jacksonville, Florida)
Knoedler & Co., New York
1994 Phillips Exeter Academy, New Hampshire
1995 National Gallery of Canada, Ottawa
1997 Locks Gallery, Philadelphia (catalog)
Nelson-Atkins Museum of Art, Kansas City (catalog)
Nancy Graves: Between Painting & Sculpture, Knoedler and Company, New York (catalog)
2001 *Nancy Graves: Paintings, Sculpture, and Works on Paper,* Lowe Gallery, Atlanta

Selected Group Exhibitions:

1970 *Information,* Museum of Modern Art, New York
1976 *American Bicentennial Exhibition,* Corcoran Gallery of Art, Washington, D.C. (toured the United States)
1977 *Documenta 6,* Kassel
1978 *American Painting of the 1970's,* Albright-Knox Art Gallery, Buffalo (toured the United States)
1979 *Supershow,* Hudson River Museum, Yonkers, New York (toured the United States)
1980 *Drawings: The Pluralist Decade,* United States Pavillion, *Biennale,* Venice
1982 *A Private Vision,* Museum of Fine Arts, Boston
1984 *Primitivism in 20th Century Art,* Museum of Modern Art, New York
1987 *Structure to Resemblance: 8 American Sculptors,* Albright-Knox Art Gallery, Buffalo, New York
1991 *IIIieme Biennale de sculpture Montecarlo 1991,* Montecarlo
1994 *Mapping,* Museum of Modern Art, New York
1996 *More than Minimal: Feminism and Abstraction in the '70s,* Rose Art Museum, Brandeis University, Waltham

Collections:

Whitney Museum, New York; Museum of Modern Art, New York; Metropolitan Museum of Art, New York; Albright-Knox Art Gallery, Buffalo, New York; Art Institute of Chicago; Des Moines Art Center, Iowa; Museum of Fine Arts, Houston; National Gallery of Canada, Ottawa; Wallraf-Richartz Museum, Cologne; Neue Galerie im Alten Kurhaus, Aachen, West Germany; Ludwig Museum, Cologne; La Jolla Museum of Contemporary Art; Art Museum of South Texas, Corpus Christi; Hirshhorn Museum and Sculpture Garden, Washington, D.C.; Akron Art Museum, Ohio; Allem Memorial Art Gallery, Oberlin, Ohio; Brooks Memorial Art Gallery, Memphis; Corcoran Gallery of Art, Washington, D.C.; Fort Worth Art Museum; Los Angeles County Museum of Art; Museum of Contemporary Art, Chicago; Museum of Fine Arts, Dallas; Museum of Modern Art, Vienna; Nelson-Atkins Museum of Art, Kansas City; Neuberger Museum, Purchase, New York; Academy of Fine Arts, Philadelphia; St. Louis Art Museum; Solomon R. Guggenheim Museum, New York; University Art Museum, Berkeley; Vassar Art Museum, Poughkeepsie; Walker Art Center, Minneapolis; Weatherspoon Art Gallery, Greensboro.

Publications:

By GRAVES: Articles—''A Conversation with Nancy Graves,'' with Emily Wasserman in *Artforum* (New York) October 1970; ''Remarks on Their Medium by 4 Painters: Pat Adams, Nancy Graves, Budd Hopkins and Irving Petlin,'' with Max Kozloff, in *Artforum* (New York), September 1975; statement in *American Painting: The 80's—A Critical Interpretation,* exhibition catalog by Barbara Rose, New York 1979; ''The Amazing Technicolour Dream Painter,'' interview in *Border Crossings,* Winter 1993; ''Mutual Implications: A Recent Conversation with Nancy Graves'' in *Art New England,* vol. 15, no. 1, December 1993/January 1994.

On GRAVES: Books—*Nancy Graves: Sculpture, Drawings, Films: 1969–71,* exhibition catalog with an introduction by Phyllis Tuchman, Aachen, West Germany 1971; *Neue Galerie Der Stadt Aachen Der Bestant 71: Kunst Um 1970—Sammlung Ludwig in Aachen,* exhibition catalog, Aachen 1972: *Nancy Graves,* exhibition catalog with an introduction by Martin Cassidy, Philadelphia 1972; *Bildwerke und Objekte* by Rainer Budde and Evelyn Weiss, Cologne 1973; *Nancy Graves,* exhibition catalog, La Jolla, California 1973; *Strata,* exhibition catalog, text by Lucy R. Lippard, Vancouver 1977; *Masks, Tents, Vessels, Talismans,* exhibition catalog by Janet Kardon, Philadelphia 1979; *Nancy Graves: A Survey 1969–1980,* exhibition catalog by Linda Cathcart, Buffalo, New York 1980; *Nancy Graves: Painting, Sculpture, Drawing, 1980–1985,* exhibition catalog by Debra Bricker Balken, Poughkeepsie, New York 1986; *The Sculpture of Nancy Graves: A Catalog Raisonne,* with texts by F. A. Carmean, Linda Cathcart, Robert Hughes and others, New York 1987; *Making Their Mark: Women Artists Move Into the Mainstream,* edited by Randy Rosen and Catherine Brouwer, New York 1989; *Nancy Graves: Icons of Language,* exhibition catalog by Pedro Cuperman, Sweden, 1990; *Nancy Graves: New Sculputre—Temptations of the Imagination—The Last Series,* exhibition catalog, New York 1996; *Nancy Graves: Excavations in Print: A Catalogue Raisonne* by Thomas Padon, New York 1996; *Nancy Graves (1940–1995): Points of Departure: Animal, Vegetable, Mineral,* exhibition catalog, New York 2000.

Articles—''The Moving Eye . . . Nancy Graves' Sculpture, Film and Painting'' by Robert Arn in *Arts-Canada* (Toronto), Spring 1974, ''Distancing: The Films of Nancy Graves'' by Lucy R. Lippard in *Art in America* (New York), November/December 1975; ''Out in Front: American Women Artists—Dorothea Rockburne and Nancy Graves'' by Barbara Rose in *Vogue* (New York), June 1977; ''Art: Nancy Graves'' by John Russell in the *New York Times,* 23 February 1979; ''Nancy Graves'' by Jeff Perrone in *Artforum* (New York), May 1979; ''Nancy Graves'' by Hilton Kramer in the *New York Times,* 21 March 1980; ''Nancy Graves at Knoedler'' by Elizabeth Frank in *Art in America* (New York), May 1980; ''Nancy Graves'' by Barbara Rose in *Vogue* (New York), June 1980; ''Nancy Graves: A Survey 1969—1980'' by Carolyn Kinder Carr in *Dialogue* (Akron, Ohio), July/August 1980; ''Nancy Graves'' by Cynthia Nadelman in *Artnews* (New York), September 1980; ''Nature into Sculpture'' by Michael Edward Shapiro in *Arts Magazine* (New York), November 1984; ''Nancy Graves' New Age of Bronze'' by Avis Berman in *Artnews* (New York), February 1986; ''The Sculpture of Nancy Graves'' by John Yau in *Sculpture* (New York), September/October 1987; ''Fossilization Evolves Into a Modern Metaphor'' by Michael Brenson in *The New York Times,* 31 January 1988; ''The Sum of the Parts'' by Amy Fine Collins and Bradly Collins Jr. in *Art in America* (New York), June 1988; ''Arts in Residence'' by Wendy Lyon Moonan in *Town & Country,* September 1988; ''Nancy Graves: Knoedler'' by G. Roger Denson in *Flash Art,* January/February, 1990; ''Nancy Graves'' by Peggy Cyphers in *Arts Magazine* (New York), January 1990; ''Nancy Graves'' by Frances DeVuono in *ARTnews* (New York), February 1990; ''Entering the Mainstream: Women Sculptors of the Twentieth Century (Part III: Jackie Winor & Nancy Graves)'' by Ann Sutherland Harris in *Gallerie Women Artists,* Number 8, Vol II, No. 4, 1990; ''Nancy Graves: Between Painting and Sculpture'' by Memory Halloway in *Art International,* Summer, 1990; ''Nancy Graves at Marian Locks'' by Judith Stein in *Art in America* (New York), December, 1991; ''Nancy Graves: Knoedler'' by Bonnie Barrett Stretch in *ARTnews* (New York), January 1992; obituary in *Sculpture* (Washington, D.C.), vol. 15, February 1996; ''Nancy Graves: The 'Missing Link''' by Cynthia Nadelman in *ARTnews,* vol. 95, no. 8, September 1996.

*

Without the aid of drawings I conceive a sculpture by selecting from an inventory of hundreds of directly cast organic forms. These are laid out on the floor and relationships are varied until the unexpected occurs. As parts are welded together changes in structure, balance, three-dimensional relationships come into play. What originally appeared to be a vertical element could become a base. Whereas the casting may take months, the assembly takes hours. Historical expectations for bronze are subverted by working against logic and without premeditation. In building I try to subvert what is logical—what the eye would expect—by transforming the function through size, placement, coloration of cast forms.

—Nancy Graves

* * *

It is no exaggeration to say that the career of Nancy Graves took off on the back of a camel. With the first sensational exhibitions of the large, life-size, enigmatic camel constructions in the late 1960s, Graves was placed at the forefront of the artists then involved in redefining sculpture. Made of polyurethane, burlap and paint, covered with animal skins and supported on wooden armature, the three-dimensional figures of the camels at rest or in grazing positions appeared at once shockingly real and strangely abstract. And like the sculptures which immediately followed, in most cases made of camel bones or hard forms— i.e. combinations of steel, latex, gauze, oil, marble dust, acrylic—fashioned to suggest bones, the camels were but part of Graves' ongoing investigations of perceptual issues. These issues concerned the relationship of illusionism, reality and motion. Then, there is the notion of art as magical object. And the introduction of new materials, previously used in industrial contexts, as well as the presentation to consider in the appreciation of the sculptures. These various concerns come together in ''Shaman'' (1970), one of the most suggestively ritualistic pieces; made of steel, latex, gauze, oil, marble dust and acrylic, the large-scale, multiple format hanging work is a confrontational presence.

Graves also made films about camels during the early 1970s; *Goulimine* (1970) and *Izy Boukir* (1971) are among the best known examples. After working on drawings in 1970–71 related to the shapes and patterns in the films, she stopped the sculpture and returned to painting in 1972. Patterns, also, dominate the ''Camouflage'' series paintings which followed. Based on sea animals that naturally camouflage themselves by blending into their surroundings, the paintings challenged the viewers to discern the creatures hiding within the colorful calligraphy of curves and straight lines. Another group of works executed at the same time used maps. The painting ''Antarctica'' (1972) in which pattern, again, was a primary concern, is an example. Satellite photographs of the moon and the other planets were the sources of the shaped, multiple and divided panels from 1973–74. And map-like information on place and atmosphere is evident in the monumental five panel work ''Painting U.S.A.'' (1975). A group of pastels from 1976, containing calligraphic imagery based on the kinds of tracking and tracing notations found in maps, serve as the transition to the autonomous spirited work she has executed since 1977.

She began to make sculptures again in 1976. The recent works, though abstract in imagery, are energetic, vibrant and suggestive structures. Some forms such as the sculpture ''Column'' (1979) hark back to the earlier examples based on camel bones. Others, such as ''Trace'' (1980), a brightly colored bronze, steel and oil standing piece, make more open-ended associations involving interplays of nature, art and archeology. A growing concern with the pictorial aspects is a strong direction in her recent work.

In the mid 1980s the more flamboyant appearance of the cast metal sculptures made stronger the associations with nature. ''Looping'' (1985), with its dynamic structure, brings to mind some fantastically exotic plan that has sprung to life in mysterious fashion.

Nature continues to be a major source of inspiration for the paintings as well. In a series of paintings from 1983–84, both the manifold perceptual aspects and the psychological implications of the shadow, one of nature's most fascinating of fleeting phenomena, are investigated.

—Ronny Cohen

In her later sculptures, Graves extended her interest in painted surfaces by experimenting with numerous innovative uses of color through manipulating chemical processes, to create complexly polychromed patinas. Her works of the nineties combine painted canvases with sculptural forms in anodized aluminum or laser-cut stainless steel. The earlier of these are characterized by bold and vibrant color contrasts while in her last works the colors are more muted, although rich and evocative.

When Graves returned to making sculpture after a six year hiatus in the late 1970s, she began to use the direct cast method, working with the Tallix Foundry, in which bronze castings were made directly from objects. During the latter part of her career she pushed this technique by constructing works that combined a wide variety of cast elements from disparate sources: pieces of rigatoni, a discarded snake skin, an old engine block. She also incorporated quotations from well-known works of art such as Venus de Milo, Adam on the Sistine Chapel ceiling, and fragments of other art historical elements.

Graves's early and later works are connected by her interest in making the inside of a work as important as the outside. When she moved from making images of camels to making their bones she was consciously trying to make visible and interesting their interior, the armature which had been previously covered up. This concern with interiors is seen in such later works as in her last work, ''Metaphore and Melanomy'' (1995), where there is a fluid, open movement between forms.

Graves's works are magical and totemic. The title of a 1990–92 wall sculpture, ''Mutual Implication,'' can be applied to Graves's intention in both her early and later works, in which she explores the interrelationship of multi-layered, diverse forms. Graves herself traced the merging of art and natural history in her work to her early experiences in the Berkshire Museum in Pittsfield, Massachusetts, where her father was the director. By combining so many different, seemingly disparate forms, she establishes a dialogue between these elements that invites the viewer to contemplate their mutual implications, to piece them together through an intuitive, archaeological process.

—Mara Witzling

GREEN, Alan

Nationality: British. **Born:** London, 22 December 1932. **Education:** Beckenham School of Art, Kent, 1949–53, and the Royal College of Art, London, 1955–58. **Family:** Married June Barnes in 1958; daughters: Paula and Julia. **Military Service:** Served as a corporal in the Royal Army Signal Corps, in Korea and Japan, 1953–55. **Career:** Visiting lecturer, Hornsey College of Art, London, 1959–61; senior lecturer in fine arts, Leeds College of Art, 1961–66; senior lecturer in painting, Ravensbourne College of Art and Design, Kent, 1966–74. **Awards:** Intaglio Print Prize 1974, and Giles Bequest Prize, 1976, *British International Print Biennale,* Bradford, Yorkshire; Third Prize, *Internationale de la Gravure,* Cracow, 1976; ''Writer's Award,'' *Listowel Graphic Art Open Exhibition,* Ireland, 1978; Grand Prix, *Norwegian International Print Biennale,* Fredikstad, 1978; National Museum of Art at Osaka Prize, *International Print Biennale,* Tokyo, 1979; Museum of Modern Art of Rijeka Prize, *International Biennale of Graphic Art,* Ljubljana, Yugoslavia, 1981; First Prize, *Graphica Creativa '81,* Luova Grafikka Alvar Aalto Museu, Jyvaskyla, Finland, 1981. **Agent:** Annely Juda Fine Art, 4th Floor, 23 Dering Street, London W1S 1AW England. **Address:** 291 Kent House Road, Beckenham, Kent BR31JQ, England.

Individual Exhibitions:

1963 A1A Gallery, London
1964 Wakefield City Art Gallery, Yorkshire
1967 London Press Exchange
1970 Annely Juda Fine Art, London
1972 Greenwich Theatre Gallery, London
1973 Annely Juda Fine Art, London
Galerie Liatowitsch, Basel
Editions Alecto, London
1974 Galerie Hervé Alexandre, Brussels
Galerie Art in Progress, Munich
1975 Annely Juda Fine Art, London
Galerie de Gestlo, Hamburg
Galleria Vinciana, Milan
Galerie Arnesen, Copenhagen
1976 Annely Juda Fine Art, London
Tate Gallery, London
Galerie Klaus Lupke, Frankfurt
Oliver Dowling Gallery, Dublin
Painting Box Galerie, Zurich
1977 Galerie Art in Progress, Dusseldorf
Mappin Art Gallery, Sheffield (travelled to the University of Newcastle upon Tyne)
1978 Annely Juda Fine Art, London
Oliver Dowling Gallery, Dublin
Nina Freudenheim Gallery, Buffalo, New York
Clark Gallery, Boston
Susan Caldwell Inc., New York
Roundhouse Gallery, London
Galerie Palluel, Paris
1979 Artline, The Hague
Galerie Loyse Oppenheim, Nyon, Switzerland
Paintings 1969–1979, Kunsthalle, Bielefeld, West Germany
Peterloo Gallery, Manchseter (with Nigel Hall)
1980 Museum of Modern Art, Oxford
St. Paul's Gallery, Leeds
Norwegian International Print Biennale, Fredrikstad
Galerie Heiner Hepper/Art in Progress, Dusseldorf
1981 Gallery Kasahara, Osaka
1982 Galerie Heiner Hepper/Art in Progress, Dusseldorf
Galerie Gimpel Hanover Emmerich, Zurich
Juda Rowan Gallery, London
Galerie Art in Progress, Dusseldorf
1984 Gallery Kasahara, Osaka, Japan
1985 Royal College of Art, London
Juda Rowan Gallery, London
1986 Gallery Kasahara, Osaka, Japan (catalog)
Paintings and Drawings, Donald Morris Gallery (catalog)
1994 *Small Paintings,* Annely Juda Fine Art, London (catalog)
1998 Annely Juda Fine Art, London

Selected Group Exhibitions:

1969 *British Movements,* Onnasch Galerie, Berlin
1973 *La Peinture Anglais Aujourdhui,* Musée d'Art Moderne de la Ville, Paris.
1974 *British Painting '74,* Hayward Gallery, London
1977 *British Painting 1952–1977,* Royal Academy of Art, London
1978 *Mechanized Image,* Walker Art Gallery, Liverpool (toured the U.K.)
1979 *Biennale of Graphic Art,* Ljubljana, Yugoslavia
1980 *Printed Art: A View of 2 Decades,* Museum of Modern Art, New York
1982 *Aspects of British Art Today,* Metropolitan Art Museum, Tokyo (toured Japan)
1984 *New Works on Paper,* British Council, London (toured Poland, Australia, New Zealand)
1986 *A Focus on British Art,* International Cultureel Centrum, Antwerp

Collections:

Tate Gallery, London; Victoria and Albert Museum, London; Kunstmuseum, Dusseldorf; Kunstmuseum, Zurich; Power Gallery of Contemporary Art, Sydney; Lousiana Museum of Modern Art, Humlebaek, Denmark; Musée d'Ixelles, Brussels; National Museum of Art, Osaka; Museum of Modern Art, New York; Guggenheim Museum, New York.

Publications:

By GREEN: Articles—''Alan Green on His Paintings'' in *Studio International* (London), October 1973; ''Every Artist Is a Con-man,'' a discussion with Roger Hilton, in *Studio International* (London), March 1974; ''Alan Green: A Dialogue,'' with Bernard Denvir, in *Art International* (Lugano, Switzerland), November 1974; statement in *Colour in Painting,* exhibition catalog, Rome 1976; interview, with Peter Rippon, in *Artscribe* (London), February 1977; interview, with Gerard Weber, in *Art Press,* (Paris), December 1978; statement in *Skira Annual,* Geneva 1979.

On GREEN: Books—*Alan Green: Paintings 1969–1979,* exhibition catalog, by Michael Pausenback and Martine Lignon, Bielefeld, West Germany, 1979; *Alan Green,* exhibition catalog by Waldermar Januszczak, Osaka 1981; *Alan Green,* exhibition catalog with text by Seiji Oshima, Osaka 1986. **Articles**—''The Annals of Juda'' in *Art Review,* vol. 46, December 1994-January 1995; ''Beyond Reason: Pre-reflexive Thought and Creativity in Art'' by John Haworth in *Leonardo,* vol. 30, no. 2, 1997.

*

I find it necessary to be very specific about the carrying out of quite minor activities connected with my work—starting from the beginning and taking nothing for granted.

Every event in the making of a work has its part to play in determining the final outcome. Initially, the nature of the support has to be considered. If stretchers are to be used, I make my own. This allows for a more physical awareness of the area and leaves more options open. For example, the number and precise width of the stretcher and cross-bar edges that actually come into contact with the canvas surface sets up a dialogue between the surface and the hidden structure of the stretchers. The nature of the support itself is another basic in determining the work. It may range from silk, paper laminates, cotton duck, linen, jute to board. I find it useful to think of paint primarily as a substance, then as a colour. This broadens the range of what can be included and of its function. (There can be no visible substance that does not have colour).

From this standpoint, it becomes a little more possible to actually move across a surface without recourse to gesture, calligraphy or any other devices. In the sequence in which one event determines another, parallels can exist between the on-going situation of a painting based on these premises and the interrelated and interdependent factors governing events in the external world. The neutrality of these premises allows a space for the natural inclusion of the human factor. Time spent, boredom, fatigue, excitement, impatience, can all be made visible. Again, the relation to the individual and the external world is evident. Thus a painting may be able to exist as a record of time lived. It is a form of action that has dispensed with heroics. Today, the most that can be reasonably hoped for is just to make an art statement.

—Alan Green

* * *

Alan Green's paintings require and deserve to have a great deal of time spent on them. At first walking into a room surrounded by seemingly sombre abstract paintings one feels bewildered—but when one stops and examines each work meticulously, one's feeling gradually change from distress to understanding and appreciation. Sometimes art which has to be worked hard at to be appreciated is the most rewarding.

In Green's 1982 exhibition there were ten paintings and five etchings. ''Three Rectangles/Square'' is similar to a piece of music—it begins with a bang in the left hand corner. A panel full of gauges and scratches becomes a smooth grey plane tinged with burgundy, as if the blood/excitement were still seeping through, and finally progresses to soft cloud-like formations, the calm after the storm. In ''Two Violets'' the highly textured and meticulous surface is almost obsessively created. ''Blue'' is more expansive, relaxed. Specks of red and black appear with occasional dots—they take you by surprise. Each time you look, new forms appear.

Most of Green's paintings are made up of various panels which interact. In ''Four Crimsons'' rigid lines become more fluid but never vanish totally. The artist seems to be playing hide and seek with shapes. The less successful paintings lack texture and movement. The preparatory drawings are also extremely disappointing. They prove that Green's vision needs large expanses to create a sense of grandeur and vitality. These elements are also missing in ''Blue Diagonal''; the use of colour is superb, but there is a total lack of thought. ''One to Four 3 Parts'' is almost completely uncoordinated although ''One'' is excellent—red glistens with mystery, peeping through the grey and blue. Green's etchings are not really resolved either. Texture is such an essential part of his work that without it the image cannot survive. Hence the etchings lack subtlety, mystery and surprise.

To look at Green's paintings is rather like looking at an Alain Resnais film. Something is constantly taking place from one panel to another. The mood is obsessive and melancholy and provokes an inexplicable affinity, especially when the blush of red seeps through.

—Carine Maurice

GREENBERG, Gloria

Nationality: American. **Born:** New York City, 4 March 1932. **Education:** High School of Music and Art, New York, 1946–52; studied at the Brooklyn Museum Art School, New York, 1952–53; influenced by instructors Nicholas Marsicano, Gabor Peterdi, John Ferren and Henrietta Schutz. **Family:** Married Martin Bressler in 1953; children: Rachel and Jonathan. **Career:** Worked as a clerk in the subscription department, *Esquire* magazine, Boulder, Colorado, 1953; now a full-time artist, based in New York; lived in La Rochelle, France, 1957–60; book designer and art consultant, Harper and Row publishers, New York, 1965–74. Instructor of drawing and design, Craft Students League, New York, 1965–66. **Awards:** Yale-Norfolk Summer Art Fellowship, 1952; MacDowell Colony Fellowship, 1965, 1973. **Agent:** 55 Mercer Gallery, 55 Mercer Street, New York, New York 11013. **Address:** 118 East 17th Street, New York, New York 10003, U.S.A.

Individual Exhibitions:

1965 Columbia University, New York
1970 55 Mercer Gallery, New York
1971 55 Mercer Gallery, New York
1972 55 Mercer Gallery, New York
1973 55 Mercer Gallery, New York
1974 55 Mercer Gallery, New York
1975 55 Mercer Gallery, New York
1976 55 Mercer Gallery, New York
1977 55 Mercer Gallery, New York
1978 55 Mercer Gallery, New York
1979 Looking Back/Looking Forward: The 60s and 70s, Marist College, Poughkeepsie, New York (retrospective)
1980 55 Mercer Gallery, New York
1981 55 Mercer Gallery, New York
1982 55 Mercer Gallery, New York
1984 55 Mercer Gallery, New York
1986 55 Mercer Gallery, New York
1988 55 Mercer Gallery, New York
1990 55 Mercer Gallery, New York
1992 55 Mercer Gallery, New York

Selected Group Exhibitions:

1953 *Regional Show,* Denver Art Museum
1964 *Waverly Gallery Group Show,* Waverly Gallery, New York
1967 *The Landscape,* Visual Arts Gallery, New York
1974 *New Drawings,* Women's Interart Center, New York
Group Show: 55 Mercer, 55 Mercer Gallery, New York (toured the United States)
1994 *Connections,* with Gloria Greenberg and Jonathan Bressler

Permanent Public Installations:

International Arrivals Building, Kennedy International Airport, New York; Bankers Trust, Los Angeles; IBM Building, Tarrytown, New York; Bank of America, Los Angeles.

Publications:

By GREENBERG: Books—*Strange Plants and Animals,* New York 1963; *Away We Go,* New York 1964.

On GREENBERG: Books—*Chimes of Change and Hours: Views of Older Women in 20th Century America* by Audrey Borenstein, 1983. **Articles—**by Jim Bishop in *Artnews* (New York), April 1971; by Jane Gollin in *Artnews,* (New York), April 1972; by Ellen Lubell in *Arts Magazine* (New York), May 1976.

*

The pieces are part of a larger piece.
The larger piece, in turn, is part of the wall.
The wall is part of a space.
The space makes the work.
The work makes the space.
The work grows *from* something, *Into* something.
When it has been realized,
It is real.

—Gloria Greenberg

GRIGELY, Joseph

Nationality: American. **Born:** Springfield, Massachusetts, 1956. **Education:** Studied at National Technical Institute for the Deaf, New England College, and Oxford University. **Career:** Teaches Art and Critical Theory at University of Michigan, Ann Arbor; lives and works in Jersey City, New Jersey. **Agent:** Cohan, Leslie and Browne Fine Arts, 138 Tenth Avenue, New York, New York 10011.

Selected Individual Exhibitions:

1994 *Conversations with the Hearing,* White Columns, New York
Body Signs: Deviance, Difference, and Eugenics, Washington Project for the Arts, Washington, D.C.
1995 *Figures of Speech,* AC Project Room, New York
1996 *The Pleasure of Conversing,* Anthony d'Offay Gallery, London
Migrateurs, Musée d'Art Moderne de la Ville de Paris/ ARC, Paris
Portraits, AC Project Room, New York
Ordinary Conversations, MIT List Center for the Visual Arts, Cambridge, Massachusetts
1997 *Little Piglet,* Air de Paris, Paris
Storytellers, Galerie Arndt & Partner, Berlin
1998 *Barbican Conversations,* Barbican Centre, London
Conversations and Portraits, Douglas Hyde Gallery, Trinity College, Dublin
Masataka Hayakawa Gallery, Tokyo
Pretty Paper, Center for Contemporary Art, Kitakyushu, Japan
1999 *The Pleasure of Conversing,* Wadsworth Atheneum Museum of Art, Hartford, Connecticut
Fireside Talk, Air de Paris, Paris
Addenda to Freud's Psychopathology of Everyday Life: Portraits of Conversations, Der Standard, Austria
2000 *Joseph Grigely: Something Say,* Cohan, Leslie and Browne, New York
Joseph Grigely: Index, Swedish Contemporary Art Foundation, Stockholm
Joseph Grigely, Jack Hanley Gallery, San Francisco
Matrix 140, Wadsworth Atheneum, Hartford, Connecticut

Selected Group Exhibitions:

1995 *La Belle et la Bête: Art contemporain américain,* Musée d'Art Moderne de la Ville de Paris/ARC, Paris (catalog)
TransCulture, Venice Biennale (traveled to Naoshima Museum of Contemporary Art, Japan)
Action Station, Santa Monica Museum of Art, California
Linking Worlds, Nicole Klagsbrun Gallery, New York
1996 *The Power of Suggestion: Narrative and Notation in Contemporary Drawing,* Museum of Contemporary Art, Los Angeles
De Rode Poort, Museum van Hedendaagse Kunst, Ghent, Belgium
NowHere, Louisiana Museum of Modern Art, Denmark
A Show for Pleasure, Air de Paris, Paris
1997 *Do It* (traveling exhibition) (catalog)
Uncovering Lost Fictions: Caravaggio's Musicians, MIT List Center for the Visual Arts, Cambridge, Massachusetts
Istanbul Biennial (catalog)
Transit, ENSBA, Paris (catalog)
1998 *The Manchester Storybooks: Art Transpennine 98,* Tate Gallery, Liverpool (catalog)
Printemps de Cahors, Cahors, France (catalog)
Sydney Biennial (catalog)
An Unrestricted View of the Mediterranean, Künsthaus, Zurich (catalog)
1999 *Retrace Your Steps: Remember Tomorrow,* Soane Museum, London
And. . . And. . . And. . . And, Het Consortium, Amsterdam
Events, Galerie Yvon, Lambert, Paris
2000 *Narcisse blessé: Autoportraits contemporains 1970–2000,* Passage de Retz, Paris
Voilà: le monde dans la tête, Musée d'art moderne de la Ville de Paris (catalog)
Whitney Biennial, New York
Etat des lieux #1: Contacts (relations, bricolage et travaux de consommation), FRIART, Centre d'art contemporain, Fribourg (catalog)

Publications:

By GRIGELY: Books—*Deaf and Dumb: A Tale,* New York 1994; *Textualterity: Art, Theory, and Textual Criticism,* Ann Arbor, Michigan, 1995; *Kitchen Conversations,* Frankfurt am Main 1996; *The Pleasure of Conversing,* London 1996. **Articles—**''Do It Now'' in *Do It,* New York 1997; ''Unrealized Turtles'' in *Unbuilt Roads,* Muenster 1997; ''Postcards to Sophie Calle'' in *Michigan Quarterly Review,* spring 1998.

On GRIGELY: Articles—"Joseph Grigely" by Jerome Sans in *Artforum* (New York), November 1996; "Visual Voices" by Raphael Rubinstein in *Art in America* (New York), April 1996; "Joseph Grigely: Ordinary Conversations" by Marcella Beccaria in *Artsmedia,* November 1996; "Joseph Grigely: Conversations and Portraits" by Maria Scott in *Circa: Irish and International Contemporary Visual Culture,* Summer 1998; "Writing Art" by Aaron Williamson in *Art Monthly,* 1999; "Playing Footsie on Top of the Table: A Conversation with Joseph Grigely" by Jan Estrep in *New Art Examiner,* June 2000; "Paula Hayes, Joseph Grigely: The Suburban, Chicago," by Karl Erickson in *New Art Examiner,* Summer 2000; "Whitney Biennial 2000" by Nancy Princenthal in *Artext* (Los Angeles), August-October 2000.

* * *

Joseph Grigely is the creator of a word-based art that addresses issues of communication, memory, sensuality, contact, and the document as form. He brings to this enterprise video and sketches, photographs of hands writing, printed pieces of paper, and complete, even room-sized, installations. A professor of literary theory and author of "Texualerity: Art, Theory and Textual Criticism" he had his first show in 1994, when he was already in his fifties. Although text-based installations have enjoyed a growing number of practitioners and presumably growing audiences, Grigely's work draws on unusually personal sources since the artist has been deaf/mute since the age of eleven. The scraps of paper that constitute the bulk of his work, including an on-going project called "Conversations with the Hearing," consist primarily of notes Grigely writes and receives in order to communicate with others.

Visual art and writing share some defining characteristics being often produced on paper and frequently meant as a communiqué. They borrow from each other's descriptive vocabulary that is to say one or the other uses "narrative" or is "linear." However Grigely's work does not presuppose the written word; it stands alone as an art object. In the 1998 "Barbican Conversations" the artist distributed scraps of paper on which he requested people (often strangers) to communicate with him. He then had the subsequent scribbles printed onto museum brochures. One effect of this is to grant universality to the material and another was to level the playing field, so to speak. Participants had to adhere to rules formulated by Grigely's condition. Yet more importantly, the transformative aspect of the process, from casual note to manipulation by the artist, exposes the dimensional aspect of words. The scraps are mysterious or even nonsensical because they lack context but, once "published" or printed they reach the viewer as a made object and they become a visual thing—a sign.

Intention, on the part of the artist and the material, is a theme that frequently reappears in Grigely's work. Often framed pieces of text accompany the scraps of paper that make up the artist's materials. The relationship between the narratives is emphatically visual. Grigely has said of his condition, "Deafness isn't 'visible' so we're not always aware there are deaf people near us even when they're standing right beside us." This quality of visibility equally applies to words that change in form when they become visible by being written down. An illustration of this concept is the 1995 "Untitled Conversation (Sex)." Here is a merchant's holiday card, with the word "sex" hand written, slightly aslant in one corner. Underneath, neatly framed and nearly square, Grigely has authored an account of the circumstances that led him to acquire the card. At first the pieces, one so casual and the other so mannered, seem entirely unrelated. It is necessary for the viewer to both read and see them together to gather the clever, poignant, and rather beautiful little story that it tells. Although the narrative is clearly important here, the piece gathers its force from the visual relationships of order (neat typing) and discordance (a scrawl on a business card). The effect would not be the same entirely written out or even simply spoken.

"The Study," a 1995 work that appeared in the Venice Biennial, is another facet of Grigely's work that also covers the terrain of memory, language, and contact, as well as formal challenges inherent in his work. This installation featured what appeared to be the artist's desk, books, and papers strewn everywhere, transferred whole to the exhibition. Although apparently chaotic and random, Grigely has repeatedly clarified that that he carefully controls the form of these pieces. Such installations have also featured table tops, replete with half-consumed drinks and cigarette butts and a deck set, also of table and chairs, with the detritus of recent, now silenced, human habitation. Unlike the framed text, with its grid of writing, here the surfaces appear anything but orderly. Yet further examination proves almost the reverse. It is in the writing, matted framed, pinned down which Grigely cannot control the content. These pieces are entirely dependent on the mechanisms of others. It is the table surfaces, on the other hand, with their look of utter disorder that constitute the artful arrangement of the of the writer.

—Merridawn Duckler

GRONK

Nationality: American. **Born:** Glugio Gronk Nicandro, Los Angeles, California, 1954. **Education:** East Los Angeles College. **Career:** Performance artist and painter, from 1972; member and founder of ASCO, conceptual performance art group, with Harry Gamboa, Patssi Valdez, and Willie Herron, East Los Angeles, 1972–87. **Awards:** Artist of the Year, Mexican American Fine Art Association, Los Angeles, 1977; Visual Artists Fellowship, National Endowment for the Arts, 1983. **Address:** Daniel Saxon Gallery, 552 Norwich Dr., Los Angeles, CA 90048, U.S.A.

Selected Individual Exhibitions:

1975 *Chicanismo en El Arte,* Vincent Price Gallery and Los Angeles County Museum of Art, Los Angeles
1984 *Gronk,* Molly Barnes Gallery, Los Angeles
1985 *The Titanic and Other Tragedies at Sea,* Galerie Ocaso, Los Angeles
1986 *The Rescue Party,* Saxon-Lee Gallery, Los Angeles
1987 *Bone of Contention,* Saxon-Lee Gallery, Los Angeles
1988 *She's Back,* Saxon-Lee Gallery, Los Angeles
1989 *Grand Hotel,* Saxon-Lee Gallery, Los Angeles (catalogue)
Grand Hotel, Ianneti-Lanzone Gallery, San Francisco
King Zombie, Deson-Sauders Gallery, Chicago
1990 *China is Near,* William Traver Gallery, Seattle
Coming Home Again, Vincent Price Gallery, East Los Angeles College
Hotel Senator, Saxon-lee Gallery, Los Angeles (catalogue)
1991 *50 Drawings,* Daniel Saxon Gallery, Los Angeles

1992 *Fascinating Slippers/Pantunflas Fascinantes,* Mexican Museum, San Francisco
Hotel Tormenta, Galerie Claude Samuel, Paris
1994 *Living Survey,* Mexican Museum, San Francisco
1996 *Café Cantata, The Art of Gronk,* Fine Art Gallery, California State University, Los Angeles

Selected Group Exhibitions:

1975 *Chicanismo en El Arte,* Los Angeles County Museum of Art (catalogue)
Chicano Art, Office of the Governor, State of California, Sacramento (catalogue)
1976 *New Works,* Galeria de Artes Nuevos, Buenos Aires, Argentina
1977 *Public Works,* Exploratorium Gallery, California State University at Los Angeles
1978 *Faces of Christ,* Malone Art Gallery, Loyola Marymount University, Los Angeles
Dreva/Gronk 1968–1978: Ten Years of Art/Life, Contemporary Exhibitions, New York
1979 *Gronk/Pattsi,* West Colorado Gallery, Pasadena
1980 *Gronk/ Herron:Illegal Landscapes,* Exploratorium Gallery, California State University, Los Angeles
1982 *Asco '82,* Galeria de la Raza, San Francisco
1983 *A Traves de la Frontera,* Centro de Estudis Economicos y Sociales Del Tercer Mundo, San Jeronimo, Mexico
1984 *Asco '84,* Armory for the Arts, Santa Fe, New Mexico
1986 *Crossing Borders/ Chicano Artists,* San Jose Museum of Art, San Jose
1987 *Hispanic Art in the United States: Thirty Contemporary Painter and Sculptors,* Museum of Fine Arts, Houston (toured)
1988 *Cultural Currents,* San Diego Museum of Art, San Diego
1989 *Hispanic Art on Paper,* Los Angeles County Museum of Art, Los Angeles
1990 *Chicano Art/Resistance and Affirmation, 1965–1985,* Wight Art Gallery, University of California, Los Angeles (toured)
1991 *Myth and Magic in the Americas: The Eighties,* Museum of Contemporary Art, Monterrey, Mexico
1992 *Chicano and Latino: Parallels and Divergence,* Kimberly Gallery, Washington, D.C.
1993 *Chicano/Chicana: Visceral Images,* The Works Gallery South, Costa Mesa, California
1995 *The Mythic Present: Gronk, Chagoya, and Valdez,* Fisher Gallery, University of Southern California
2001 *La Luz: Contemporary Latino Art in the United States,* National Hispanic Cultural Center, Albuquerque
Daniel Saxon Gallery, Los Angeles

Collections:

Philip Morris Companies; AT&T; Denver Art Museum; Museum of Contemporary Art, Los Angeles; El Paso Museum of Art; Corcoran Gallery; Mexican Museum, San Francisco; University of Texas.

* * *

GROOMS, Red

Nationality: American. **Born:** Nashville, Tennesse, 1 June 1937. **Education:** Attended Peabody College, Nashville, Tennesse; Art Institute of Chicago; New School for Social Research, New York; Hans Hofmann School, Provincetown, Massachusetts. **Family:** Married Mimi Gross in 1964; child: Saskia. **Career:** Settled in New York, 1957; first happenings and theatre events, New York, 1957; performed ''The Burning Building'' happening, New York, 1959; founded the multi-media environmental and performance company, Ruckus Production, New York, 1963. **Member:** Board of Directors, Filmmakers Co-Op, New York. **Awards:** Ingram Merrill Foundation Grant, 1968, 1974; American Academy of Arts and Letters Grant, 1969; Achievement in Art Award, *Who's Who in America,* 1970; Creative Artists' Program Service Grant in Filmmaking, New York, 1970; Recipient, President's Award, Rhode Island School of Design, 1985; Ten Best Illustrated Childrens' Books Award, New York Times, 1986; Governor's Award in Art, State of Tennessee, 1986; National Arts Club Award, 1986; New York City's Mayor's Award of Honor, 1988; Founders Medal, Pennsylvania Academy of Arts, 1990. **Agent:** Marlborough Gallery Inc., 40 West 57th Street, New York, New York 10019. **Address:** 85 Walker Street, New York, New York 10013–3523.

Individual Exhibitions:

1958 Sun Gallery, Provincetown, Massachusetts
City Gallery, New York
1959 City Gallery, New York
1960 Reuben Gallery, New York
1962 Nashville Artists' Guild
1963 Tibor de Nagy Gallery, New York
1965 Tibor de Nagy Gallery, New York
1966 Tibor de Nagy Gallery, New York
1967 Tibor de Nagy Gallery, New York
Allan Frumkin Gallery, Chicago
1968 Allan Frumkin Gallery, Chicago
1969 *Red and Mimi Hit the Road,* Tibor de Nagy Gallery, New York
1970 Tibor de Nagy Gallery, New York
1971 John Bernard Myers Gallery, New York
Institute of Contemporary Art, Boston
Harry N. Abrams Gallery, New York
1972 John Bernard Myers Gallery, New York
Allan Frumkin Gallery, Chicago
Barbara Fendick Gallery, Washington, D.C.
Cheekwood Museum of Art, Nashville
Graphics 1 and Graphics 2, Boston
1973 John Bernard Myers Gallery, New York
The Ruckus World of Red Grooms, Rutgers University Gallery of Art, New Brunswick, New Jersey (travelled to New York Cultural Center, and to the Museo de Arte Contemporaneo, Caracas, 1973–74)
1975 Brooke Alexander Gallery, New York
88 Pine Stret, New York
1976 *Red Grooms and the Ruckus Construction Company Present Ruckus Manhattan,* Marlborough Gallery, New York
1977 Galerie Roger d'Amecourt, Paris

New Gallery of Contemporary Art, Cleveland
1978 Galerie Roger d'Amecourt, Paris
Martin Wiley Gallery, Nashville
State University of New York at Purchase
1979 Hudson River Museum, Yonkers, New York
1980 Lowe Art Museum, University of Miami
Camp Gallery-Signet Fine Prints, St. Louis
Colorado State University, Fort Collins
1981 Aspen Center for the Visual Arts, Colorado
Montgomery Bell Academy, Nashville, Tennessee
Burlington House, New York
1982 Institute of Contemporary Art, Philadelphia
Benjamin Mangel Gallery, Philadelphia
New Gallery of Contemporary Art, Cleveland, Ohio
1983 Unicorn Gallery, Aspen, Colorado
Anderson Ranch, Aspen, Colorado
North Carolina Museum of Art, Raleigh
1984 Marlborough Gallery, New York
1985 Marlborough Fine Art, London
Hokin/Kaufman Gallery, Chicago
Benjamin Mangel Gallery, Philadelphia
Museum of Contemporary Art, Los Angeles
Tennessee State Museum, Nashville
1986 Cumberland Gallery, Nashville, Tennessee
Marlborough Gallery, New York
Marlborough Fine Art, Tokyo
1987 Carpenter Center for the Visual Arts, Harvard University, Cambridge, Massachusetts
Marlborough Gallery, New York
1994 *Target: Red Grooms,* Weisman Museum of Art, Pepperdine University, Malibu, California
1995 Wood Street Gallery, Pittsburgh
1996 *New York Stories,* Marlborough Gallery, New York
1997 *Works on Paper,* Marlborough Gallery, New York
1998 *Red Grooms and the Heroism of Modern Life,* Palmer Museum of Art, Pennsylvania State University, University Park
Red Grooms: Moby Dick Meets the New York Public Library, Norton Museum of Art, West Palm Beach, Florida
1999 *New Works,* Marlborough Gallery, New York

Selected Group Exhibitions:

1960 *New Media/New Forms,* Martha Jackson Gallery, New York
1966 *Still Life,* Museum of Modern Art, New York (toured the United States)
1974 *Poets of the Cities: New York and San Francisco 1950–1965,* Museum of Fine Arts and Southern Methodist University, Dallas (travelled to the San Francisco Museum of Art and the Wadsworth Atheneum, Hartford, Connecticut)
1975 *Realismus und Realität,* Kunsthalle, Darmstadt
1976 *The Great American Rodeo,* Fort Worth Art Museum (travelled to Witte Memorial Museum, San Antonio, and Colorado Springs Fine Art Center, 1976–77)
1978 *Art about Art,* Whitney Museum, New York
1982 *Homo Sapiens: The Many Images,* Aldrich Museum of Contemporary Art, Ridgefield, Connectictut
1984 *Metamanhattan,* Whitney Museum, New York
1986 *Hollywood: Legend and Reality,* Smithsonian Institution, Washington, D.C. (toured the United States)
1987 *Contemporary Cutouts,* Whitney Museum, New York
1995 *Fluxus and the New Realists,* Musée d'Art Contemporain, Marseilles, France
1997 *New Editions by Contemporary Artists,* Marlborough Gallery, New York
1999 *Champs de la Sculpture,* Champs-Elysees, Paris
2001 *Out of the Fifties—Into the Sixties: 6 Figurative Expressionists,* Michael Rosenfeld Gallery, New York

Collections:

Museum of Modern Art, New York; New School Art Center, New York; Brooklyn Museum of Art, New York; Hudson River Museum, Yonkers, New York; Hirshhorn Museum and Sculpture Gardern, Washington D.C.; Art Institute of Chicago; Denver Art Museum; Fort Worth Art Center, Texas; Northern Kentucky University, Highland Heights; Museo de Arte Contemporaneo, Caracas; Moderna Museet, Stockholm.

Public Installations:

Grand Central Station, 1993; The Tennessee Foxtrot Carousel, Nashville, 1999.

Publications:

By GROOMS: Book—*Drawing,* with Mimi Grooms, Florence 1961. **Article—**statement in *Art Now: New York,* July 1970; ''Who Hails from Hopper?'' by Ann Landi in *ARTnews,* vol. 97, no. 4, April 1998. **Films—***The Unwelcome Guests,* 1961; *Shoot the Moon,* with Rudy Burckhardt, 1962; *Ruckus Sports,* 1963–70; *Hippodrome Hardware,* 1972–73; *The Conquest of Libya by Italia 1912–13,* 1972–73; *Ruckus Manhattan,* 1975–76; *Little Red Riding Hood,* 1978; *Small Fry Gangster,* 1985.

On GROOMS: Books—*Happenings,* edited by Michael Kirby, New York 1965; *Assemblage, Environments and Happenings* by Allan Kaprow, New York 1966; *The Ruckus World of Red Grooms,* exhibition catalog by Dennis Cate, New Brunswick, New Jersey 1973; *Red Grooms,* exhibition catalog, Caracas 1974; *Ruckus Manhattan,* exhibition catalog, New York 1975; *Red Grooms and the Ruckus Construction Company Present Ruckus Manhattan,* exhibition catalog, New York 1976; *Red Grooms and Ruckus Manhattan* by Judd Tully, New York 1977; *Red Grooms: retrospective 1956–1984,* exhibition catalog with essays by Judith Stein, John Ashbery and Janet K. Cutler, Philadelphia 1985; *Western Art Masterpieces* by T.H. Watkins and Joan Watkins, New York 1996. **Articles—**''Red Grooms Has Artful Fun with High Culture—and Low'' in *Smithsonian,* vol. 16, June 1985; ''Red Grooms Builds a Tennessee Carousel'' in *American Artist,* vol. 62, no. 673, August 1998; ''Red Grooms: Tennessee Fox Trot Carousel, Nashville'' by Ariane Fehrenkamp in *Sculpture* (Washington, D.C.), vol. 18, no. 5, June 1999; ''Red Grooms: Grounds for Sculpture'' by Clare Henry in *Sculpture* (Washington, D.C.), vol. 19, no. 10, December 2000.

*

For months the piece is your real life, and then you're suddenly separated from it—it becomes an object.

There's a proletarian feeling about my work. That type of energy and subject matter excites me a lot. And I've always felt a kinship to commercial people.

It irritates me that people associate themselves with my sculpture, that they receive it so warmly. Maybe they perceive it too quickly, they don't make an effort.

—Red Grooms

* * *

For more than 40 years, Red Grooms has been chronicling the disparate surrealisms of urban America with humor, ingenuity, passion and anything else that's available. Closely allied with Happenings in their earliest stages, his own vision has not changed nearly as much as the context into which it fits. His cityscapes, though they retain their crazy meanderings, their stage presence and certainly an uncanny cross-breeding of diverse materials, now occupy a category all their own.

In the 1950s and 1960s environmental sculpture or sculptural painting was loaded with reference to the avant-garde. Grooms, whose background indicates that his interest in the Ringling Brothers was at least as acute as his interest in fine art, was ripe for animating his paintings on stage. He found, after producing and performing "The Burning Building" in 1959, that he so enjoyed enveloping his audience that even in the 1990s he continues to construct multimedia, all encompassing three-dimensional environments. You enter Grooms' sculptures, you don't simply view their caricatures of legendary figures, historical facts, and morsels of contemporary city life. Given Grooms' keen eye for detail, everyone and everything, no matter how minute, becomes material for his witty tales.

But Grooms is not merely entertainment. On closer examination, he strikes an edgy balance between simple documentation and an acerbic wit which encapsulates the ironies and inequities of life in New York City. His perceptions of the Big Apple, evidently fed by a rabid sense of devotion, shed light on life's harsher realities such as rats, prices, congestion, pollution, and graft.

In the mid-1970s Grooms, his wife, and the Ruckus Construction Company (a consortium of some thirty local artists, students, and various other enthusiasts) embarked on a monumental project to recreate all of Manhattan on Grooms's own scale and in his own vernacular. He called it "Ruckus Manhattan: A Sculptural Novel." One would be hard-pressed to find a more suitable title, for this work really is novelistic in its rambling satires. Using every available material from wood to paint to cardboard, Grooms distorted, "kitsched-up" and poked fun at much of New York City.

Red Grooms at Grand Central, a 21-piece installation from 1993, continues in the same vein of sweetly sardonic satire. Filling the main waiting room of the august terminal were Grooms's manic replicas of such New York City landmarks as the World Trade Center, Wall Street, and assorted newspaper kiosks. Viewers could climb aboard a creaking subway car or hail a cab complete with a stogie-smoking hack. In contrast to the darker, more didactic view of urban America prevalent in much recent art and popular culture, the unabashed humor and chaos of Grooms's sprawling theatrics manage to be socially incisive without being either naive or cynical. His populist art revels in our messy human scene, finding in it a source of perversely refreshing optimism.

—Essay by Janet Goleas; updated by Dorothy Valakos

GROSSMAN, Nancy

Nationality: American. **Born:** New York City, 28 April 1940. **Education:** Pratt Institute, New York, 1958–62 (Haskell Scholarship for Foreign Travel, 1962), B.F.A. 1962; artwork influenced by Richard Lindner and David Smith. **Career:** Independent artist since 1961; lives and works in New York. Member, sculpture jury, CAPS Fellowship, New York State Council on the Arts 1973; member, sculpture jury, Prix de Rome Fellowships, American Academy in Rome, 1974. **Awards:** Guggeheim Fellowship for Painting, 1965; Inaugural Contemporary Achievement Award, Pratt Institute, 1966; American Academy of Arts and Letters National Institute of Arts and Letters Award, 1974; Sculpture Fellowship, National Endowment for the Arts, 1984; Artist's Fellowship in Sculpture, The New York Foundation for the Arts, 1991; American Chapter of the International Art Critics Association, Best Art Exhibitions, 1991–92 art season. **Address:** c/o National Academy Museum, 1083 Fifth Avenue, New York, New York 10128, U.S.A.

Individual Exhibitions:

1964 Oscar Krasner Gallery Inc., New York
1965 Oscar Krasner Gallery Inc., New York (twice)
1967 Oscar Krasner Gallery Inc., New York
1969 Cordier and Ekstrom Inc., New York
1971 Cordier and Ekstrom Inc., New York
1973 Cordier and Ekstrom Inc., New York
1975 *Collage Paintings,* Cordier and Ekstrom Inc., New York
1976 Cordier and Ekstrom Inc., New York
1978 Church Fine Arts Gallery, University of Nevada, Reno
1980 Barbara Gladstone Gallery, New York
1981 Heath Gallery, Atlanta, Georgia
1982 Barbara Gladstone Gallery, New York
1984 Terry Dintenfass Gallery, New York
1986 Heath Gallery, Atlanta, Georgia
1988 The Gallery, Columbus College, Columbus, Georgia
1991 Hillwood Art Museum, Brookville, New York (travelling to Chicago; Little Rock, Arkansas; Honolulu)
1992 Binghamton University, New York
1993 Hooks-Epstein Galleries, Houston
1994 Ledis Flam, New York
Weatherspoon Art Gallery, Greensboro, North Carolina
2001 *Loud Whispers,* Greenville County Museum of Art, South Carolina

Selected Group Exhibitions:

1961 *Forty Painters,* City Center Gallery, New York
1969 *Contemporary American Sculpture,* Whitney Museum, New York
1972 *Recent Figure Sculpture,* Fogg Art Museum, Harvard University, Cambridge, Massachusetts

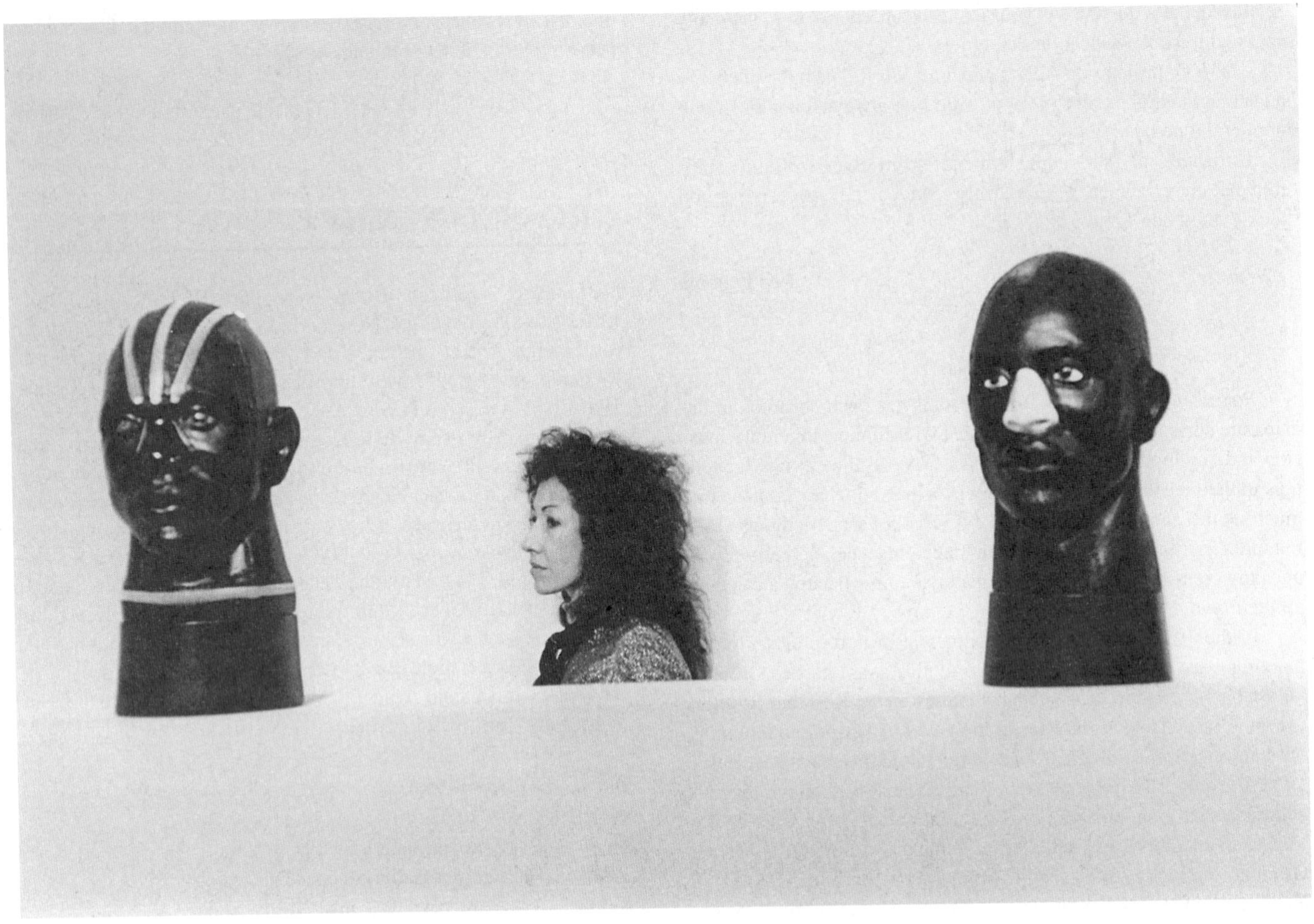

Nancy Grossman (flanked by two busts). Photo by Sylvia Plachy. ©Sylvia Plachy.

1977 *Contemporary Women: Consciousness Content,* Brooklyn Museum, New York
1980 *American Sculpture: Gifts of Howard and Jean Lipman,* Whitney Museum, New York
1982 *The Americans: The Collage,* Contemporary Arts Museum, Houston
1984 *Dreams and Nightmares,* Hirshhorn Museum, Washington, D.C.
1987 *Modern American Realism,* National Museum of American Art, Washington, D.C.
1989 *The Eloquent Object,* Orlando Museum of Art, Florida
1991 *The Hybrid State,* Exit Art, New York
1995 *Fetishism: Visualizing Power and Desire,* Brighton Museum and Art Gallery, Brighton (traveling exhibition) (catalog)
1996 *Large Drawings and Objects,* Arkansas Art Center, Little Rock (catalog)
Chips Off the Block: Carvers, Luise Ross Gallery, New York
1997 *Powerful Expressions: Drawing Today,* National Academy Museum, New York
The Artist's Eye, National Academy Museum, New York
1998 *Dangerous Cloth,* American Primitive Gallery, New York
2001 *The End: An Independent Vision of Contemporary Culture 1982–2000,* Exit Art/The First World, New York

Collections:

Whitney Museum, New York; Baltimore Museum of Art; Princeton University Art Museum, New Jersey; Museum of Fine Arts, Dallas; University of California Art Museum, Berkeley; Boymans Van Beuningen Museum, Rotterdam; National Museum of American Art/ Smithsonian Institution, Washington, D.C.; Phoenix Art Museum, Arizona; Rice Museum, Houston; Virginia of Fine Arts, Richmond; The Israel Museum, Jerusalem; The Metropolitan Museum of Art, New York.

Publications:

On GROSSMAN: Books—*Open Secrets* by Barbaralee Diamonstein, New York 1972; *Recent Figure Sculpture,* exhibition catalog with an introduction by J. L. Wasseman, Cambridge, Massachusetts 1972; *Nancy Grossman,* exhibition catalog, New York 1973; *Nancy Grossman: Collage Paintings,* exhibition catalog, New York 1975; *Nancy Grossman: Collages and Pastels,* exhibition catalog, New York 1976; *Art Talk,* conversations with 12 women artists, by Cindy Nemser, New York 1975; *Nancy Grossman,* exhibition catalog by Vals Osborne, Reno 1978; *Dreams and Nightmares,* exhibition catalog with essay by Valerie J. Fletcher, Washington, D.C. 1983; *Modern American Realism,* exhibition catalog with essays by Virginia M. Mecklenburg and William Kloss, Washington, D.C. 1987;

Exposures: Women and Their Art, by Arlene Raven and Betty Ann Brown, Pasadena, 1989; *American Women Sculptors* by Charlotte Streiffer Rubenstein, Boston, 1990; *Nancy Grossman,* exhibition catalog by Arlene Raven, 1991; *Nancy Grossman: Loud Whispers,* New York 2000. **Articles—**''Art Surprise from Nancy Grossman'' by John Canaday in the *New York Times,* May 1970; ''The Least Cruel Artist Alive'' by John Canaday in the *New York Times,* November 1971; ''Art and the Artist: Nancy Grossman'' by Emily Genauer in the *New York Post,* December 1971; ''New Realism in Sculpture: Look Alive!'' by R. Constable in *Saturday Review* (New York), April 1972; ''Art: Nancy Grossman'' by John Canaday in the *New York Times,* October 1973; ''Art and the Artist'' by Emily Genauer in the *New York Post,* December 1973; ''Man Is Anonymous: The Art of Nancy Grossman'' by Corrine Robins in *Art Spectrum* (Lugano, Switzerland), February 1975; ''Nancy Grossman'' by Douglas Blau in *Arts Magazine* (New York), February 1981; review by Stephen Westfall in *Arts Magazines* (New York), February 1981; ''Sculptors on Paper and a Gallery on the Move'' by Grace Glueck in *The New York Times,* 25 September, 1983; ''Nancy Grossman'' by Donald Kuspit in *Artforum* (New York), December 1984; ''American Women Artists, Part II'' by John Russell in *The New York Times,* 24 February, 1984; ''Smithsonian Gets Gift of Realist American Art'' by Michael Brenson in *The New York Times,* 11 June, 1984; ''Art: 'Modern Masks' and Assembly of Sculptures on Display'' by Michael Brenson in *The New York Times,* 28 December, 1984; ''Modern Masks'' by Kim Levin in *The Village Voice* (New York), 29 January, 1985; ''Not a Pretty Picture: Can Violent Art Heal?'' by Arlene Raven in *Village Voice* (New York), 17 June 1986; ''Depicting Society's Violence in Art'' by Karin Lipson in *Newsday* (New York), 19 April, 1986; ''Dark Images of Violence'' by Phyllis Braff in *The New York Times,* 15 June, 1986; ''The Modern Fetish'' by Donald Kuspit in *Artforum* (New York), October 1988; ''Shifting Power'' by Meg Campbell in *Women Artists Slide Library Journal,* May-June 1990; ''Going Beyond Leather Hooded Heads'' by Roberta Smith in *The New York Times,* 27 September, 1991; ''Doric Column'' by Robert C. Morgan in *Cover Magazine* (New York), November 1991; ''Figures Bound By Turmoil'' by Karin Lipson in *Newsday* (New York), 4 October, 1991; ''Life Sheathed in Leather'' by Natalia Kozlova in *Novoye Russkoye Slovo,* 4 October, 1991; ''Nancy Grossman's Heads and Other Symbols'' by Phyllis Braff in *The New York Times,* 27 October, 1991; ''Pain is Pleasurable'' by Josef Wood in *Spectrum Weekly,* 17 June, 1992; ''Nancy Grossman'' by Mitchell Stevens in *New Art Examiner,* June/Summer, 1992; ''Nancy Grossman—Exit Art, New York'' by Jude Schwendenwein in *Sculpture,* January-February, 1992; ''Art Out of Anger, Powerlessness and Conflict'' by Phyllis Rossiter in *New Directions for Women,* March-April 1992; ''Nancy Grossman'' by Robert C. Morgan in *Arts Magazine,* January 1992; ''Nancy Grossman—Exit Art'' by Pat McCoy in *Tema Celeste Art Magazine,* January-March 1991; ''Hesse's Robust Paintings at Miller Upend Expectations'' by Grace Glueck in *The New York Observer,* 2 November 1992; ''Covert Action'' by Elizabeth Hess in *The Village Voice* (New York) 9 March 1993; ''Nancy Grossman: Opus Volcanus'' by Robert C. Morgan in *Sculpture Magazine,* July-August 1998.

*

My work addresses both the philosophical and the physical. It is the Skeleton and Structure of my attempt to find my own meanings.

The Hebrew command not to make graven images reverberates, but to create art that did not exist in the physical world before is more compelling.

I have made things whole which were not whole. I have taken possession of, and mystified, the most common pedestrian objects of everyday life—a book of matches, a walnut, a pebble. By looking/looking/looking at the object—looking so carefully at the thing itself that nothing can remain beneath attention. Then there is no boredom.

My work is the only diary of my life. It is the physical revelation of my inner life and intellectual concerns of the moment.

Making art is magical in its imaging non-verbal, in its conjuring the non-visible into existence.

—Nancy Grossman

* * *

At the outset of her first wide renown, Nancy Grossman said of her work: ''It is the idea of making something and then hiding it again.'' And in the real sense, her entire mature career has been devoted to just that concept—both literally in the materiality of her work and, as well, metaphorically in the nature of her subject matter. Grossman, earlier in the mid-60s, had already used leather and metal (from her vast collection of objects) in planar and abstract collages with feminist subjects—Women Landscapes—and in paintings and prints has also surveyed sexual themes. Scarpitta's works, from earlier that decade, may have been an influence. Since the start of the 70s, her signature image has been three-dimensional, life-size heads which became clearly male after 1972—some few torsos—covered over by meticulously crafted leather. The carved wooden head forms within are apparently equally worked, and the airless fit of the at-first eyeless heads produced an exotic emblem of violence and a deviant sexuality. Yet with the focus entirely upon the head in the great majority of her work (a well-received exhibition in 1974 offered drawn and painted, collaged bodies), an oddly poignant and asexual mood of repression and struggle is also felt. The whole group of these works, to the present moment, is redolent of a 19th-century Maldoror-like abstracted, evil; moreover, the frozen eroticism of classicism may be suggested by her technical perfection aloofness. Perhaps her firmest success has been to bring the erotic emblem in high art up-to-date with her generalized Satanic and barbaric innuendo, so far removed from the urban and individualized decadence of Grosz, Lindner, and Bacon. This non-European quality—if that was her intention—was more clearly defined when Grossman added distinctly Negroid features to the nose and mouth parts of her sculptures; as well, large horns and other appendages have been added to the head form. After a perhaps telling three-year hiatus from exhibition activity (1977–80), Grossman returned with work that seemingly has not extended either the compass or the focus of her now-carefully cultivated image. Although the artist has always naturally disallowed any personal involvement in the innuendo of her subject matter, one might argue, considering its persistence, for the depth of its meaning for her. On the other hand, the obsessive craft-force of all these works may be her real focus—and the overtly scandalous subjects persist since they allow her continued access to her craft love. Until this recent exhibition Grossman usually has kept the entire head covered by leather, eyeless with nose and mouth alone visible. Now zippers, shells, buttons have begun to serve as eye and mouth form indicators and their bizarre aspect further increased by fine-filed gold and silver spikes. If these now manifold accessories were an expansion of her craft interests, it was not to continue into the later 1980s. As if bidding an end her long-held object-fascination, Grossman constructed *Succot,* a large columnar and totem-like collage tied with wire and labelled ''phallo-centric.'' Since 1983, the larger body of her work has been two-dimensional images which nonetheless continue with Grossman's signature rage and violence, albeit no longer implicit as in the earliest sculptures. These drawing and paintings, with allusions to Da Vinci and Mannerism, show dogs, men, women in hysterical confrontation—the women usually calm—with no narrative causation suggested. With the shift of medium there has been no easing of the grip of sexual unease upon her art.

An impressive 40 year retrospective—*Nancy Grossman: Loud Whispers*—which included assemblage and collage as well as her signature leather-covered heads, was offered by her New York dealer in 2000. It appears that she had been absent from New York solo exhibition activity for some time—small museums and college galleries were her prime venue.

This show did present one recent sculptural head ''Gunhead'' (1991) where a gun-form covered the eyes and mouth; it clearly was reference to her earlier black leather-covered heads of which two did as well appear here. Even though there were several wall-hung paper collages of torsos and heads, equally reminscent of her ''heads,'' the effort was to present Grossman as a collage and assemblage artist; and the majority of these works were quietly formal, even when not entirely abstract. Those with torn photographic imagery were homage to Bearden while those with more intense assemblage were painted a uniform black—a nod to Nevelson—and had an expressionist vigor in their debris. Other flat and cubist-grid assemblages were homage to a gentle modernist attitude with their worn, found object, carefully composed scenario. Since such current works also resemble some of her earliest work—the accompaniment to her 1960s heads—it is as if Grossman were attempting to reassemble her art and somehow put her unquenchable signature works behind her.

—Joshua Kind

GROSVENOR, Robert (Strawbridge)

Nationality: American. **Born:** New York City, 31 March 1937. **Education:** Ecole des Beaux-Arts, Dijon, France 1956; Ecole Supérieure des Arts Décoratifs, Paris, 1957–58; University of Perugia, Italy, 1958. **Family:** Married Jacqueline Gardner in 1966; children: Kali, Marina and Jeremy. **Career:** Sculptor: lives and works in New York. Formerly, instructor, School of Visual Arts, New York. **Awards:** National Council of the Arts Award, 1969; Guggenheim Fellowship, 1969; National Endowment for the Arts and Humanities Grant, 1970; American Academy of Arts and Letters Award, 1972. **Agent:** Paula Cooper Gallery, 534 West 21st Street, New York, New York 10011, U.S.A.

Individual Exhibitions:

1965 Park Gallery, New York
1966 Dwan Gallery, Los Angeles
1967 Park Place Gallery, New York
1970 Galerie Ricke, Cologne
Fischbach Gallery, New York
Paula Cooper Gallery, New York
1971 Paula Cooper Gallery, New York
La Jolla Museum of Contemporary Art, California
1974 Paul Cooper Gallery, New York
Galleria Francoise Lambert, Milan
1975 Galerie Stampa, Basel
Paul Cooper Gallery, New York
Galerie Eric Fabre, Paris
Pasquale Tridorio, Naples
1976 Institute for Art and Urban Resources, The Clocktower, New York
1977 Galerie Eric Fabre, Paris
1978 Cooper Gallery, New York
1979 Paula Cooper Gallery, New York
1980 Paula Cooper Gallery, New York
1981 Paula Cooper Gallery, New York
1984 P.S.I/Institute for Art and Urban Resources, New York
1986 Paula Cooper Gallery, New York
1992 Kunsthalle Bern, Switzerland (catalog)
1995 *Drawings, 1969–1994,* Lawrence Markey, New York
1996 *Drawings 1969–1994,* Lawrence Markey Gallery, New York
Sculpture, Paula Cooper Gallery, New York
1998 Paula Cooper Gallery, New York
2000 Paula Cooper Gallery, New York

Selected Group Exhibitions:

1966 *Primary Structures,* Jewish Museum, New York
1968 *Minimal Art,* Gemeentemuseum, The Hague (toured Europe)
1975 *Zeichnungen 3,* Städtisches Museum, Leverkusen, West Germany
1977 *Documenta 6,* Kassel, West Germany
1978 *Drawing for Outdoor Sculpture 1946–1977,* Amherst College, Massachusetts (travelled to the University of California at Santa Barbara, and the Massachusetts Institute of Technology, Cambridge)
1979 *The Minimal Tradition,* Aldrich Museum of Contemporary Art, Ridgefield, Connecticut
1981 *Amerikanische Zeichnungen der Siebriger Jahre,* Louisiana Museum, Humlebaek, Denmark (travelled to Basel, Munich and Ludwigshafen)
1983 *Objects, Structures, Artifice,* University of South Florida, Tampa
1985 *The Maximal Implications of the Minimal Line,* Bard College, Annandale-on-Hudson, New York
1987 *The Success of Failure,* Laumeier Sculpture Park and Gallery, St. Louis
1999 *Carnegie Museum of Art Presents Works by Robert Grosvenor, Andreas Gursky, and John Wesley,* Carnegie Museum of Art, Pittsburgh

Collections:

Museum of Modern Art, New York; Whitney Museum, New York; New York University; Storm King Art Center, Mountainville, New York; Aldridge Museum of Art, Ridgefield, Connecticut; Massachusetts Institute of Technology, Cambridge; Hirshhorn Museum and Sculpture Garden, Washington, D.C.; Walker Art Center, Minneapolis.

Publications:

On GROSVENOR: Books—*Constructivism* by George Rickey, New York 1967; *Minimal Art,* exhibition catalog with texts by Enno Develing, Lucy Lippard and Renata Sharp, Dusseldorf 1969; *Objects, Structures, Artifice: American Sculpture 1970–1983,* exhibition catalog by Michael Klein, Tampa 1983. **Articles—**''E=MC2 a GoGo'' by David Bourdon in *Art News* (New York), January 1966; ''Indoor-Outdoor: Space and Materials, 6 Sculptors'' by R. Mathias in *Arts Magazine* (New York), Summer 1972; ''Robert Grosvenor's Sculpture'' by Bruce Kurtz in *Arts Magazine* (New York), October 1975; ''Robert Grosvenor: Specific Clarity'' by Jeremy Gilbert-Rolfe in *Arts in America* (New York), March/April 1976; review by John Russell in the *New York Times* (New York), 21 April 1978; review by Deborah Perlberg in *Artforum* (New York), Summer 1978; ''Robert Grosvenor'' by Tiffany Bell in *Arts Magazine* (New York), January 1980; ''Robert Grosvenor'' by Donald Kuspit in *Artforum* (New York), Summer 1984; ''Robert Grosvenor'' by Ellen Hand in *Arts* (New York), Summer 1986; ''A Place in the World'' by Stephen Westfall in *Art in America* (New York), vol. 84, no. 9, September 1996; ''Robert Grosvenor'' by Barbara A. MacAdam in *Art News,* vol. 95, October 1996; ''Robert Grosvenor'' by Michael Klein in *Sculpture* (Washington, D.C.), vol. 17, no. 6, July/August 1998.

* * *

Robert Grosvenor's career, at least outwardly, has encompassed a distinct turnabout from his earlier sense of sculpture. He came to public prominence in the mid-60s with work both minimalist and aggressively techno-romantic in its clear engineering and drama; yet since the onset of the 70s, he has consistently used large, dressed, wooden beams as his prime material. He rejected both fabrication and industrial finish to achieve a heroic and mute primitivism.

His well-known works of the previous period depended upon both their hollowed and faceted columnar forms and a quality of forceful movement, given to them at times by cantilevering. The engineering of the latter type, which could not be discovered from their exterior, consisted of wiring systems and bolting to either ceiling (his still most well-known work ''Transoxiana,'' 1965), or to the floor (''Tapanga,'' 1965—this work often likened to the Kitt Peak Solar Telescope housing in Arizona). This same effect of involvement with the architecture was visible in a work of this same time at the Loeb Center at NYU in New York; there two sections of the sculpture on the roof of the building appear to be extensions and thus continuations of the sculpture penetrated to the roof from the gallery area below.

A life-long interest in sailing and several years spent as a student of nautical engineering might be offered as some reference for these effects—Grosvenor himself denies it. His art was always expressionist, and so his shift of material and attitude at the start of the 70s may find precedent in his previous Constructivist work; and the works of the 70s—baffling to many critics—may the more be truly Minimalist in their reductive form and manipulation. Many of these recent timber sculptures—the lumber as large as 12 inches square and telephone pole (which have also been used) in length—were subjected to great pressure which cracked them in either one or several places. (In this aspect, Grosvenor's works retain a ''technological'' aura, as we imagine the enormity of the pressure necessary to have fractured these beams.) The cracks were often carefully mended, or left partially visible—and these sculptures were usually displayed singly and on the floor itself.

In only the later 70s has Grosvenor returned to construction as a basis for his art. But his structures have remained as simple as their still beam-like parts and are composed of stacked beams, creosoted and dark; the obvious reference is the sea-coastal milieu. Perhaps these works might be understood as an eclectic blend of minimalism, the assemblage of abstract-expressionist sculpture, and earth art; or ironically, as sculpture really monumental and outdoor, yet seen only in traditional interior art gallery spaces. Their metaphorical poignance—their Promethean submission—may be but a guise for their more pointed reference to the currect artist's dilemma, akin perhaps to the anguish felt by the abstract-expressionist generation during the 1960s.

In a mid-80s piece, nest-like and metallic, an eclectic hovering of older motifs remains: large scale—the older giganticism is gone—industrial and blackened, yet carefully assembled and seemingly repaired. As his first public work in several years, the private pace (i.e., non-professional in its infrequency) of his art's appearance now is as if a reflection of its muteness and enigma.

Grosvenor's more recent works may recall Philip Guston's well-documented similar shift from a severe if tender formalism to an almost maudlin yet self-confident feeling for the every-day—and in Grosvenor's case with only a nuance of narrative.

While retaining an essential organizational simplicity, Grosvenor has as well continued to avoid a recognizable style, with present work making no reference to earlier works. It is as if the artist's over-arching satisfaction lies in his ongoing, carefully thought through, assembled, and constructed work—irrespective of style.

If not irony, then a continuance of Grosvenor's love of spatial control, was his use of wheels below the 15-foot-wide cemented brick and slate movable plane—with a patio-hint as well in a bench-like form at one side. Similarly alluding to some degree of the domestic was a gallery-housed 30-foot-long wall in stone and concrete,topped with both garden-like glass balls in color, and an antenna-like assembly of metal rods.

Other works were set apart from this immediate aura of the everyday, and evinced an almost futurist-Pop association: a brilliantly red-painted floor plane, on which were placed two silver plastic spheroids attached with poles; and piles of fossil rocks, partially painted with red spray.

—Joshua Kind

GRÜTZKE, Johannes

Nationality: German. **Born:** Berlin, 30 September 1937. **Education:** Studied with Peter Janssen, Hochschule für Bildende Künste, Berlin, 1957–64; with Oskar Kokoschka, Summer Academy, Salzburg, Austria, 1962. **Family:** Married Roswitha Steinke in 1964 (divorced, 1971); son: Julius; lives with the costume designer Barbara Naujok since 1979; son: Gustav. **Career:** Worked as a stagehand, Volksbühne Theatre, Theatre des Westens, and Renaissance Theatre, Berlin, 1958–64. Independent artist since 1964. Founder-member, Die Erlebnisgeiger music and performance group, Berlin, 1965 (from 1980 re-named Erlebnisgeigen und Klavier und Gesang); founder, with painters Manfred Bluth, Mattias Koeppel and Karlheinz Ziegler, Schule de Neuen Prächtigkeit artists' group, Berlin, 1973; founder with Barbara Naujok, *Die Schaukel* revue at the Metropol, Berlin, 1979; stage designer for director Peter Zadek and other, in Berlin, Stuttgart and Hamburg, from 1980; artistic adviser and designer,

Johannes Grützke: *Kerstiń am Fenster II,* 1990. ©Johannes Grützke.

Deutsche Schauspielhaus, Hamburg, since 1985. Guest instructor, Hochschule für Bildende Künste, Hamburg, 1976–77; instructor in painting, Summer Academy, Salzburg, 1987; Gewinner des Wettbewerbs um das Wandbild in der Paulskirche in Frankfurt/M, 1987, Fertigstellung, 1991; professor, Malerei an der Akademie der bildenden Künste in Nürnberg, 1992; Gründung des ''Goethe Verlages,'' Berlin, 1995. **Agents:** Ladengalerie Karoline Müller, Urbansraße 115, 10967 Berlin, Germany; Galerie Brockstedt, Magdalenenstraße 11, 20148 Hamburg, Germany. **Addresses:** Güntzelstraße 53, 10717 Berlin, Germany.

Individual Exhibitions:

1964 Galerie ''Pro,'' Bad Godesberg, West Germany
1965 Galerie Schütze, Bad Godesberg, West Germany
Artibus, Berlin (with Otmar Alt)
1967 Kleine Weltlaterne, Berlin (with Gonschorr and Romolla)
1968 Galerie Schütze, Bad Godesberg, West Germany
1969 Neue Münchner Galerie, Munich
Galleria La Bertesca, Genoa
1970 Galerie Tobies and Silex, Cologne
1971 Galerie Mikro, Berlin
Galerie Grafikmeyer, Karlsruhe
1972 Nurnberger Oper, Nuremberg
1973 Galerie Holeczek, Freiburg
Galerie Brusberg, Hannover
Galerie Kleber, Berlin
1974 Schloss Charlottenburg, West Berlin (retrospective travelled to the Kunsthalle, Nuremberg; Kunstverein, Freiburg; and the Kunstverein, Mannheim)
1975 Galerie Kleber, Berlin
University Museum, Marburg, West Germany
Galerie ''k,'' Darmstadt
1976 Galerie an der Farbmuhle, Wuppertal, West Germany
Galerie Schnecke, Hamburg
Galerie von Bartha, Basel
Galerie Buchholz, Munich
Galerie Heike Curtze, Vienna
1977 Galerie Heike Curtze, Dusseldorf
Galerie Kleber, Berlin
Gemälde 1964–1977, Kunstverein, Braunschweig, West Germany (retrospective)
Sydow Fine Art, Frankfurt
1978 Kunstverein, Wolfsburg, West Germany
Galerie Apex, Göttingen, West Germany
Editions le Cadre, Olten, Switzerland
1979 Kunstverein, Darmstadt
1980 Galerie Kunze, Berlin
Galerie Buchholz, Munich
1981 Galerie Etienne de Causan, Paris
Kunstverein, Unna, West Germany
Galerie Bäumler, Regensburg, West Germany
1982 Kunstverein, Neustadt/Weinstrasze, West Germany
Galerie Public Press, Dusseldorf
Luner Galerie, Lüneburg, West Germany
Galerie Kunze, West Berlin
1983 Galerie Brockstedt, Hamburg
Galerie Etienne de Causans, Paris
Kunstverein, Gifhorn, West Germany
Galerie Merlin Verlag, Gifkendorf bei Luneburg, West Germany
Staatstheater, Stuttgart
1984 Galerie Gunzenhauser, Munich
Ladengalerie, at *Art 84,* Basel
Kunstverein, Luneburg, West Germany
Galerie am Rathaus, Frankfurt
Galerie Mora, West Berlin
Kunstverein Artig, Velen, West Germany
Nationalgalerie, West Berlin
1985 Ladengalerie, at *Art 85,* Basel
Ladengalerie, at the Kunstmesse, Cologne
Galerie Mora, West Berlin
1986 Deutsches Schauspielhaus, Hamburg
Heitland Foundation, Schloss Celle, West Germany
Galerie Hilger, Vienna
Kramp und Graff, Hamburg
Asperger and Bischoff Gallery, Chicago
1987 Galerie in der Mühle, Oldenburg, West Germany
Galerie Schloss Rimsingen, Breisach-Oberrimsingen, West Germany
Galerie Niepel, Dusseldorf
Ladengalerie, at *Art 87,* Basel
Galerie Burgdorf, Hannover
Galerie Gunzenhauser, Munich
Hypotheken-Bank, Salzburg, Austria
Mittelrhein-Museum, Koblenz, West Germany
Ladengalerie, West Berlin
Große GildeART Galerie, Osnabrück
1988 Galerie Brockstedy, Hambury
Stadttheater Schweinfurt
Kornfeld Galerie, Reutlingen

Galerie KK, Essen
Galerie im Mora, Berlin
Kunstverein Gütersloh
1989 Galerie Nawrocki, Cologne
Burg Botzlar, Selm
A.C.R. Galerie, Eltville
Realismusgalerie Kassel
Galerie Rose, Hamburg
Samuelis Baumgarte Galerie, Bielefeld
1990 Museum für Kunst und Gewerbe, Hamburg
Kunsthalle zu Kiel
Kunststation Kleinsassen
Karl Marx Universität Leipzig, Krochhaus, Leipzig
1991 Ladengalerie, Berlin
Kunstverein Tauberbischofsheim
Galerie KK, Essen
Galerie Gres, Frankfurt
1992 Galerie Zuta, Wiesbaden
Ladengalerie, Berlin
Galerie Gunzenhauser, Munich
1993 Galerie Niepel, Düsseldorf
Kunstverein Bretten
1994 Berliner Ensemble, Berlin
Galerie KK, Essen
Landengalerie, Berlin
Galerie Gunzenhauser, Munich
1995 Galerie Gres, Frankfurt
Der Kunstkreis Hameln
Kulturspeicher Oldenburg
1996 Galerie im Theater der Stadt Gütersloh
Galerie M, Wilhelmshaven
Galerie Gunzenhauser, Munich
1997 Galerie Giesler & Nothelfer, Berlin
Kunstverein Stralsund
Galerie Bernsteinzimmer, Nürnberg
Schadow Haus, Berlin
1998 Galerie Weiß, Erlangen
Büchergilde Gutenberg, (toured Germany)
Ladengalerie, Berlin
1999 Büchergilde Gutenberg, (toured Germany)
Schering Kunstverein, Berlin
Kunstverein Aurich
2000 Museum Folkwang, Essen
Galerie KK, Essen
Trinkaus & Burkhardt, Berlin
Galerie Gunzenhauser, Munich

Selected Group Exhibitions:

1968 *Documenta 4,* Museum Fridericianum, Kassel, West Germany
1970 *Kunst und Politik,* Kunstverein, Karlsruhe (toured West Germany)
1972 *The Berlin Scene,* Gallery House, London (toured West Germany)
1974 *Schule der neuen Prächtigkeit,* Kunstverein, West Berlin (toured West Germany)
1976 *Méfiez-vous de l'art,* Kunstmuseum, Olten, Switzerland
1978 *13°E: 11 Artists Working in Berlin,* Whitechapel Art Gallery, London
1980 *Liebe—Dokumente aus unserer Zeit,* Kunsthalle, Darmstadt, West Germany (travelled to Hannover)
1982 *Spiegelbilder,* Kunstverein, Hannover (travelled to Duisburg and West Berlin)
1984 *Realisten in Berlin,* Berlinische Galerie, West Berlin
1986 *Die Maler und das Theater im 20. Jahrhundert,* Schirn Kunsthalle, Frankfurt
1987 *Die Nibelungen . . . ,* Haus der Kunst, Munich
1988 *Deutsche Kunst in den 50er und 60er Jahren,* Galerie Neher, Essen
1989 *Eberhard Roters zu Ehren,* Berlinische Galerie, Berlin
1990 *Berliner KUNSTstücke.* Museum der bildenden Künste, Leipzig
1991 *Künstlerpech,* Berlin
1993 *I. Realismustriennale,* Künstlersonderbund, Berlin
1996 *Die Kraft der Bilder,* Künstlersonderbund, Berlin

Collections:

Kunstmuseum, Basel; Kunsthalle, Hamburg; Kunsthalle, Kiel; Kunsthalle, Nuremberg; Staatsgalerie, Stuttgart; Kupferstichkabinett, Dresden; Museum Oberhausen, West Germany; Berlinische Galerie; Centre Georges Pompidou, Paris; Sprengel Museum, Hannover.

Publications:

By GRÜTZKE: Books—*Im Watt,* Hamburg 1978; *Pantalon Ouvert,* with Arno Waldschmidt and Jan Peter Tripp, Hamburg 1978; *Misch Du Dich nicht auch noch ein,* Frankfurt 1979; *Paarungen, Verwüstungen,* with Tilmann Lehnert, West Berlin 1983; *Aus den Leben Richard Wagners,* Gifkendorf 1983; *Der Kunstfreund, der Kunstler und die Kunst,* West Berlin 1984; *Kunzes Freunde,* 14 colour drawings, Gifkendorf 1985; *Kolophon,* with Tilmann Lehnert, West Berlin 1987; *Die Manuskripte von Belo Horizonte,* Hamburg 1987; *Die Paulskirche,* Frankfurt 1991; *Ein Parnasz,* Berlin 1996; *30 Jahre Bohren,* Berlin 1997; *Pauvre Bobo,* with Tilmann Lehnert, Berlin 2000; *7 Pamphlete Um den Begreff Kunst abzuschaffen,* Berlin 2000.

On GRÜTZKE: Books—*Johannes Grützke,* exhibition catalog, Cologne 1970; *Zu Johannes Grützke,* exhibition catalog by Lucy Schaner, Hannover 1973; *Johannes Grützke,* exhibition catalog by Tilman Lehnert, Berlin 1974; *Kunst nach 45* by Wieland Schmied, Berlin 1974; *Schule det Neuen Prächtigkeit,* exhibition catalog with text by M. Bluth, M. Koeppel and K. Zeigler, Berlin 1974; *Johannes Grützke: Gemälde 1964–1977,* exhibition catalog with texts by Ekkehard Schenk zu Schweinsberg, Tilmann Lehnert and Bernhard Holeczek, Braunschweig, West Germany 1977; *Grützke,* exhibition catalog, Paris 1981; *Johannes Grützke: Unser Fortschritt ist unaufhörlich,* exhibition catalog with text by Lucius Griesebach, West Berlin 1984; *Johannes Grützke—Klassisch, übertrieben,* exhibition catalog with text by Walter Schurian, Vienna 1986; *Johannes Grützke: Gedrucktes, Gemaltes, Gesagtes, Geschriebenes, Gespieltes* by Michael Perschke, West Berlin 1987; *Die Verbeugung,* Berlin 1987; *Einleitung zu Katalog* by Lucius Grisebach, Nürnberg 1989; *Rede auf J.G.* by Lucius Grisebach, Celle 1990; *Über die Bildwelt von J.G.* by Jens Christian Jensen, Kiel 1990; *Malerei der sechziger Jahre* by Horst Richter, Köln 1990; *Grützkes Sphinx* by Günter Kunert, Gifkendorf 1994; *J.G., selbstverständlich* by Jutta Bacher, Aachen,

Leipzig, Paris 1995; *G. oder die Freuden der Assoziation* by Joachim Bohnert, Berlin 1997; *Theater der Menschheit* exhibition catalog by Jutta Bacher, Aachen 1997; *Mysterium Kunst* by Carl Michael Hofbauer, Bucuresti 2000. **Film—***Johannes Grützke,* directed by Peter West, Contemporary Artists series, BBC Television, 1979.

* * *

Johannes Grützke was born in Berlin in 1937 and lived there until 1984. He belongs to the pioneers of a new realism which arose in the early 1960s in parallel with pop-art in a reaction to the informalism and abstraction. In 1973, together with Manfred Bluth, Mathias Koeppel and Karlheinz Zeigler, he founded ''The School of the New Magnificence,'' which he ironically celebrated several times in the following years with portraits of the members. The large format paintings have the effect of ordinary snapshots and show, in near life-size images, the trivial ritual of male group behavior as representations of alienated existence. Yet they are not really images of reality but rather arranged scenes in which the autonomous picture represses the image—actualized signs of a high degree of abstraction and level of artificiality.

Basically Grützke takes no position on realism as an artistic style but turns rather to reality which he spears both critically and satirically: ''I don't copy what I see at all; I make visible what I think and that as if it were everyday reality.'' His pictures appear photorealistic at first sight but quickly prove to be a skillful staging of quotations from reality. This also makes possible the playfully anachronistic inclusion of historical personages from other epochs in the ordinary context of today, so that they appear as contemporaries of the viewer. Typical examples of this are ''Sigmund Freud, Karl Marx, Herbert Marcuse and Julius Grützke'' (the small son of the painter), ''Bach Disturbed by His Children'' or ''Death of Socrates.'' Most frequently, however, Grützke quotes himself on the canvas—for example, even among ''The Composers of the 1972/73 Nuremberg Opera Season,'' together with Monteverdi, Johann Strauss and Bartok. Grützke appears in his pictures simply as the contemporary who normally stares at the viewer with the ironic smile and forced merriment comparable to the agitated attitudes in advertising photographs.

This looking out from the picture in the traditional romantic style of ''window pictures'' is significant in Grützke's works. Many of the pictures seem to invite the viewer into the picture by abolishing the boundaries between picture space and real space. Perspective extends into the viewer's plane of reality and thereby reverses itself, for the pictures themselves are painted peculiarly flat, without depth and without any relation of the people to their ground. They tend, in their technical precision of a quality equal to the old masters, towards baroque painting and are not always free from mannerist features.

Grützke's graphics, in which political expression is more strongly emphasized, although the painter categorically denies the political potential of art, are of a consistently individual quality.

From the beginning of the 1980s Grützke devoted himself increasingly to the theatre. In collaboration with the director Peter Zadek, he designed numerous stage sets often vast perspectives in the style of his pictures in the background of more or less empty playhouses. When Zadek took up the post as director of the Deutsche Schauspielhaus in Hamburg, Grützke followed him. In Hamburg Grützke not only designed stage decors but also took on acting roles.

—Werner Schulze-Reimpell

GURSKY, Andreas

Nationality: German. **Born:** Leipzig, Germany, 15 January 1955. **Education:** Folkwangschule, Essen, Germany, 1978–81; Kunstakademie, Dusseldorf, Germany, 1981–87; studied with Bernd Becher, 1985. **Awards:** Meisterschuler, Kunstakademie, Dusseldorf, Germany, 1987. **Agent:** Matthew Marks Gallery, 523 West 24th Street, New York, New York 10011–1104, U.S.A.

Selected Individual Exhibitions:

1987 Flughafen, Dusseldorf
1988 Galerie Johnen & Schottle, Cologne
1989 303 Gallery, New York
P.S.1 The Clocktower, New York
Centre Genevois de Gravure Contemporaine, Geneva
1991 303 Gallery, New York
Kunstlerhaus, Stuttgart
Galerie Johnen & Schottle, Cologne
Galerie Rudiger Schottle, Paris
1992 Hypobank, New York
Galleria Lia Rumma, Naples
Victoria Miro Gallery, London
Kunsthalle, Zurich
1993 Monika Spruth Galerie, Cologne
1994 Deichtorhallen, Hamburg
De Appel Foundation, Amsterdam
1995 Portikus, Frankfurt
Tate Gallery, London
Galerie Mai 36, Zurich
1996 Galerie Ghislaine Hussenot, Paris
1997 About Painting, Robert Miller Gallery, New York (catalog)
1998 Dissin' the Real, Lombard-Freid Fine Arts, New York (catalog)

Selected Group Exhibitions:

1985 Kunstlerwerkstatt Lothringer Strasse, Munich
1986 Galerie Rudiger Schottle, Munich
1987 Galerie Wittenbrink, Munich
1988 Galerie Mosel & Tschechow, Munich
1989 Galleria Lia Rumma, Naples
1990 National Museum of Modern Art, Tokyo
1992 Musee d'Art Moderne de la Ville de Paris, Paris
Hayward Gallery, London
1994 Galerie des Archives, Paris
1995 Matthew Marks Gallery, New York
1997 Andrea Rosen Gallery, New York
303 Gallery, New York
Berlinische Galerie, Berlin
1998 The Photographer's Gallery, London

Publications:

On GURSKY: Books—*Andreas Gursky: Photographs, 1984–1993* edited by Zdenek Felix, Munich 1994; *Andreas Gursky* by Peter Galassi, New York 2001; *Andreas Gursky: Photographs from 1984 to* *the Present* edited by Marie Luise Syring, Neues Publishing Company, 2001. **Articles—**''The Seeing Game'' in *Art in America* (New York), July 1998; ''New German Photography: The Look of the Modern Sublime'' in *The Economist* (New York), 13 February 1999; ''Andreas Gursky'' in *Artforum* (New York), March 2000; ''Seeing and Believing'' in *Architecture* (Washington, D.C.), March 2001; ''Seeing is Believing'' in *Newsweek* (Los Angeles, California), 19 March 2001.

* * *

The photography of Andreas Gursky has always delivered an arresting yet ambivalent statement on the central conditions and glaring contradictions of global, post-industrial modernity. But his perspective on contemporary culture is not solely that of a visual essayist using the transparency of the medium to convey, allegorically and thematically, the tenor of our age; it is a perspective also intimately intertwined with the history of photography and the medium's ubiquitous involvement with every aspect of social life. Turning his large-format camera on diverse scenes all over the world, Gursky has meticulously explored the broad themes of consumerism and trade, public spectacle, tourism, geopolitics, landscape, architecture, and the practice of art exhibition, while simultaneously opening his work to a reflexive consideration of the medium itself.

The physical attributes of Gursky's work are unmistakable. His richly colored, glossy chromogenic prints are often monumental in scale, spanning several meters in width and height. The pristine images they depict evoke a comparable sense of monumentality as they are almost always shot at a great distance with dense panoramic detail—often from an elevated or bird's-eye perspective. Although Gursky's work becomes inescapably saddled with the responsibility for preserving a particular time and place, they do so somewhere between prosaic documentation and hyperreal artifice. Suspended in the uncertain breach between objective certainty and withdrawn inaccessibility, Gursky's images deceptively appear as an index of the present moment while simultaneously challenging enduring assumptions about photographic authenticity.

In Gursky, there are always indications, references, and traces of the early history of photography, which inhabit his works like specters of the nineteenth century. His ouevre could be characterized as the late twentieth (and early twenty-first) century equivalent to the layered transformations of perception which developed throughout the industrial revolution, and to which photography was essential. But of all the early genres of photography that share kinship with Gursky, landscape photography is perhaps the most salient. While inheriting the detached quality of early land survey, Gursky inserts formal and compositional aestheticism into the instrumental documentation of vast exterior spaces. His photographs have a distinctively thematic quality: they not only illustrate but symbolize the subjects they depict. Somewhere between lyrical allegory and clinical authentication it becomes evident that Gursky studied with Bernd and Hilla Becher at the Staatliche Kunstakademie in Düsseldorf, whose serial documentations of water towers fuse the relentless scientific pursuit of land survey with fine art photography. While he shares the Becher's concern with the transformation of the specificity of place into a kind of atopia, he explores this question through decidedly different means. Departing from the serial and typological explorations of the Becher school, Gursky addresses the changing role of the human subject in increasingly domesticated and artificial landscapes.

The overwhelming size of Gursky's natural and artificial landscapes in relation to the tiny figures within them conveys, through scale, a sense of the diminished importance of the individual human subject. Although people are abundant in Gursky's images, their individuality is almost always subordinate to their function within a larger group or a system of relations. A soccer game, the floor of an international stock exchange, a rock concert: Gursky invariably selects those modern scenes where social relations between people are governed by—in fact necessitate—human anonymity and the interchangeability of the subject. In his 1992 photograph of Charles de Gaulle Airport, for example, one observes human beings shuttled around like tiny parcels through a maze of enclosed glass tubes. Although one might pause for a moment to envision the hundreds of individual narratives attributable to each figure, the composition of the picture suggests something else: an architectural study of a system of exchange, transportation, and flow. This reduced human significance also extends into the literalist space of exhibition as Gursky's mammoth photographs' relationship to the spectator is an analogue to the sense of human scale found within the images themselves. In an era where medium and world are becoming confusingly similar, the act of approaching a Gursky is itself reflexively transformed into a kind of artifice. What this ultimately suggests is that an apprehension of the world is today unthinkable without the intermediation of the photographic image, whose penetration of every aspect of social life has had a profound impact on the way we experience the real.

Given his interest in those social conventions that eclipse the human subject, it is unsurprising that his photographs often depict industrial sites and systems of exchange, trade, and commerce. From his photograph of an empty Prada display case to the grotesque rendering of a 99 cent store packed with aisle after aisle of brand-name products, much of the work involves an oblique critique of consumerism. Although this critique is undeniably penetrating and incisive, it is also contradictory, significantly undermined by Gursky's complicity with the very system he seeks to expose. The work's shameless populism and its slick inviting nature—part fashion, part commodity—are the inverse of its role as detached critical statement on modern life and place his works more akin to billboards and glossy magazines than to 'high' art. But far from being a compromise of Gursky's project, this ambivalence is a prime animating tension within the work, forcing us to reconcile our own contradictory relationship to art in the era of commodity culture.

—Ken Rogers

H

HAACKE, Hans

Nationality: German. **Born:** Cologne, August 1936. **Education:** Pädagogium Otto Kühne, Bonn-Bad Godesberg, 1948–52; Nocolaus-Cusanus-Gymnasium, Bonn-Bad Godesberg, 1952–56; Staatliche Hochschule für Bildende Künste, Kassel, 1956–60, M.F.A. 1960; Atelier 17, Paris, 1960–61; Tyler School of Art, Philadelphia, 1961–62. **Family:** Married Linda Snyder in 1965; sons: Carl and Paul. **Career:** Exhibited with the Zero Group, including Mack, Piene, Uecker, in Europe 1960–65. Assistant teacher, Pädagogische Hochschule, Ketswig, West Germany, 1963–64; instructor, Modeschule, Düsseldorf, 1964–65; visiting lecturer, University of Washington, Seattle, 1965; lecturer, Philadelphia College of Art, 1966–67; adjunct instructor, 1967–70, visiting professor, 1970–71, assistant professor, 1971–75, associate professor, 1975–79 and since 1979 professor, Cooper Union, New York. Guest professor, Hoschschule für Bildende Künste, Hamburg, 1973; guest professor, Gesamthochschule, Essen, 1979. **Awards:** Deutscher Akademischer Austauschdienst (D.A.A.D.), Paris, 1960–61; Fulbright Fellowship, Philadelphia, 1961–62; Guggenheim Fellowship, 1973–74; National Endowment for the Arts grant, 1978; College Art Association Distinguished Artist Award for Lifetime Achievement, 1991; Deutscher Kritikerpreis, 1991; Oberlin College, Ohio, Honorary Doctorate in Fine Arts, 1991; Golden Lion Venice Biennale, 1993; Honorary Doctorate, Bauhaus University, Weimar, 1998. **Agent:** John Weber Gallery, New York. **Address** The Cooper Union, Cooper Square, New York, New York, 10003.

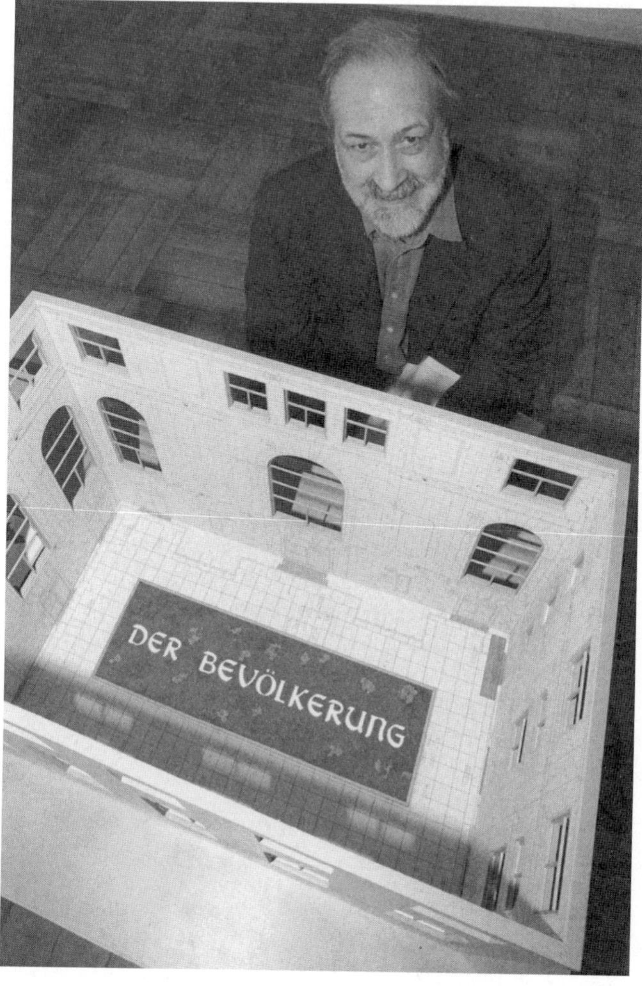

Hans Haacke with a model of his *Der Bevöelkerung* (*For the Population*), 2000. ©2001 Artists Rights Society (ARS), NY/VG Bild-Kunst, Bonn.

Individual Exhibitions:

1965 Galerie Schmela, Düsseldorf
1966 Howard Wise Gallery, New York
1967 Hayden Gallery, Massachusetts Institute of Technology, Cambridge
1968 Howard Wise Gallery, New York
1969 Howard Wise Gallery, New York
1971 Paul Maenz Galerie, Cologne
1972 Galerie Françoise Lambert, Milan
Museum Haus Lange, Krefeld, West Germany
1973 John Weber Gallery, New York
Paul Maenz Galerie, Brussels
1974 Paul Maenz Galerie, Cologne
1975 John Weber Gallery, New York
1976 Lisson Gallery, London
Max Protetch Gallery, Washington, D.C.
Kunstverein, Frankfurt
Galerie Francoise Lambert, Milan
1977 Galerie Durand-Dessert, Paris
John Weber Gallery, New York
Amherst College, Massachusetts
Badischer Kunstverein, Karlsruhe
Wadsworth Athenaeum, Hartford, Connecticut
University of California at Santa Cruz
1978 Galerie Durand-Dessert, Paris
California Institute of Technology, Pasadena
Museum of Modern Art, Oxford
1979 Stedelijk van Abbemuseum, Eindhoven, Netherlands
Recent Work, Renaissance Society, University of Chicago
John Weber Gallery, New York
1980 Museum of Contemporary Art, Zagreb
1981 John Weber Gallery, New York
Paul Maenz Galerie, Cologne
Banff Centre, Alberta
1982 *Bread and Roses,* District 1199 Cultural Center, New York
University of Alberta, Edmonton
1983 Galerie France Morin, Montreal
John Weber Gallery, New York
1984 Tate Gallery, London
Neue Gesellschaft für Bildende Kunst, Berlin
1985 Kunsthalle, Berne
John Weber Gallery, New York

1986 Le Consortium, Dijon, France
New Museum of Contemporary Art, New York (travelled to Saskatoon, Saskatchewan; La Jolla, California; Coral Gables, Florida; Charlotte, North Carolina)
1987 Victoria Miro Gallery, London
1988 John Weber Gallery, New York
1989 Musée Nationale d'Art Moderne, Centre Georges Pompidou, Paris
1990 John Weber Gallery, New York
1991 John Weber Gallery, New York
1993 German Pavilion, Venice Biennale
1994 John Weber Gallery, New York
1995 *Social Work,* Fundacio Antoni Tapies, Barcelona (catalog)
1996 Museum Boijmans Van Beuningen, Rotterdam

Selected Group Exhibitions:

1962 *nul,* Stedelijk Museum, Amsterdam (also 1965)
1968 *The Machine as Seen at the End of the Mechanical Age,* Museum of Modern Art, New York (toured the United States)
1969 *When Attitudes Become Form,* Kunsthalle, Berne (toured Europe)
1972 *Documenta 5,* Kassel (also 1982, 1987)
1976 *Biennale,* Venice (also 1978)
1987 *L'Epoque, la mode, la morale, la passion,* Centre Georges Pompidou, Paris
1989 *Les Magiciens de la Terre,* Centre Georges Pompidou, Paris
Image World: Art and Media Culture, Whitney Museum of American Art, New York
1992 *Territorium Artis* (inaugural exhibition), Bundeskunsthalle, Bonn
L'art conceptuel, une perspective, Musée de las Ville de Paris
1994 Kunsthalle Basel, Switzerland
The Institute of Cultural Anxiety, Institute of Contemporary Art, London (catalog)
1995 Museum of Contemporary Art, Los Angeles
Museum of Contemporary Art, Tokyo
1997 Skulptur Projekt Munster, Germany
Deutschlandbilder, Gropius-Bau, Berlin
Johannesburg Biennale
1998 Chicago Cultural Center
2000 *Biennial 2000,* Whitney Museum of American Art, New York

Collections:

Museum of Modern Art, New York; National Art Gallery of Canada, Ottawa; Art Gallery of Ontario, Toronto; Stedelijk van Abbemuseum, Eindhoven, Netherlands; Museum van Hedendaagse Kunst, Ghent, Belgium; Centre Georges Pompidou, Paris; Kaiser-Wilhelm-Museum, Krefeld; National Gallery of Australia, Canberra; New Museum of Contemporary Art, New York; Philadelphia Museum of Art; Tate Gallery, London.

Public Installations:

Reichstag Building, Berlin.

Publications:

By HAACKE: Books—*Hans Haacke—Werkmonographie,* with introduction by Edward Fry, Cologne 1972; *Art into Society—Society in Art,* exhibition catalog, London 1974; *Framing and Being Framed: 7 Works 1970–75,* Halifax and New York 1975; Seurat's ''Les Poseuses'' 1888–1975, small version, New York and Paris 1975; *A Breed Apart,* Oxford 1978; *Hans Haacke: 4 Works 1978–79,* New York 1979; *Der Pralinenmeister/The Chocolate Master,* Toronto 1982. **Articles—**''Questions to Hans Haacke,'' interview with Jack Burnham, in *Tri-Quarterly Supplement* (Evanston, Illinois), Spring 1967; ''An Interview with Hans Haacke,'' with Jeanne Siegel, in *Arts Magazine* (New York), May 1971; ''Editorial: Artists vs. Museums, Continued'' in *Artnews* (New York), September 1971; interview with Karin Thomas, in *Kunst-Praxis Heute: Eine Dokumentation der aktuellen Ästhetik,* Cologne 1972; interview with John Anthony Thwaites in *Art and Artists* (London), November 1972; ''Shapolsky et al Manhattan Immobilienbesita, ein gesellschaftliches Realzeitsystem, Stand 1.3.1972'' in *Interfunktionen* (Cologne), no.9, 1972; ''Rofil de l'habitat des visiteurs de al galerie'' in *Art Press* (Paris), December/January 1973; ''The Role of the Artist in Today's Society: A Symposium at Oberlin'' in *Supplement to Allen Memorial Art Museum Bulletin* (Oberlin, Ohio), vol. 30, no. 3, 1973; transcript of talk in *Selbstdarstellung: Kunstler über Sich,* edited by Wulf Herzogenrath, Dusseldorf 1973; ''Manet-Projekt '74'' in *EXTRA* (Cologne), July 1974; interview in *Art Journal* (New York), Summer 1975; ''Solomon R. Guggenheim Museum Board of Trustees'' in *Tri-Quarterly* (Evanston, Illinois), Winter 1975; ''Hans Haacke,'' interview with Margaret Sheffield, in *Studio International* (London), March/April 1976; ''The Good Will Umbrella'' in *Vision* (Oakland, California), no. 3, 1976; ''The Constituency'' in *Tracks* (New York), vol. 3, no. 3, 1977; ''The Agent/Der Agent'' in *What Do You Expect. . .* by Paul Maenz, Cologne 1977; ''Hans Haacke Interviewed by Michele Patterson'' in *Journal of Fine Arts* (Chapel Hill, North Carolina), Spring/Summer 1980; ''Radical Attitudes to the Gallery'' in *Studio International* (London), vol. 195, no. 990, 1980; ''Working Conditions'' in *Artforum* (New York), Summer 1981; ''Information Magic'' interview with Walter Grasskamp, 1984; ''On Social Grease'' in *Art Journal* (New York) Summer 1982; ''Leon Golub/Hans Haacke: What Makes Art Political?'' by Jeanne Seigel in *Arts Magazine* (New York), April 1984; ''A Conversation with Hans Haacke'' by Yves-Alain Bois *et al* in *October* (New York), Fall 1984; ''A Conversation with Hans Haacke'' by Robert D. Morgan in *Real Life Magazine* (New York), Fall 1984; ''Museums, Managers of Consciousness'' in *Art in America* (New York), February 1984; ''Sponsorship or Censorship?'' interview with Connie Samaras in *New Art Examiner* (Chicago), November 1985; ''Hans Haacke: Where the Consciousness Industry is Concentrated'' by Catherine Lord in *Cultures in Contention* edited by Kahn and Neumeier, Seattle, 1985; ''Interview with Hans Haacke'' by Paul Taylor in *Flash Art* (Milan), February-March 1986; ''Hans Haacke'' interview by Jos Van Den Berg in *Forum International* (Antwerp), March/April 1990; ''In the Vice'' in *Art Journal* (New York), Fall 1991; ''Beware of the Highjackers!'' in *Culture & Democracy: Social and Ethical Issues in Public Support for the Arts and Humanities* edited by A. Buchwalter, Boulder 1992; ''Gondola! Gondola!'' in *Bodenlos,* Stuttgart 1993;

''Free Exchange'' conversation between Pierre Bourdieu and Hans Haacke, Oxford 1995; ''Hans Haacke'' in *Art Press,* Special Issue, no. 17, 1996; ''Ein gluehender Verfassungspatriot'' in *Frankfurter Allgemeine Zeitung*, 16 February 2000; ''Haacke Provokes Reichstag'' by Peter Herbstreuth in *Flash Art (International Edition),* vol. 33, no. 213, Summer 2000; interview with Marius Babias in *Kunstforum International,* no. 151, July/September 2000.

On HAACKE: Books—*Hans Haacke: Wind and Water Sculpture* by Jack W. Burnham, Evanston, Illinois, 1967; *Hans Haacke: Werkmonographie* edited by Edward F. Fry, Cologne, 1972; *Framing and Being Framed: Seven Works 1970–75,* essays by Jack Burnham, Howard S. Becker and John Walton, Halifax, 1975; *Hans Haacke,* exhibition catalog with introduction by Georg Bussmann, Frankfurt, 1976; *Hans Haacke: Nach allen Regeln der Kunst,* exhibition catalog, Berlin, 1984; *Hans Haacke: Unfinished Business,* exhibition catalog, New York, 1987; *Artfairismes,* exhibition catalog, Paris, 1989; *Bodenlos,* Stuttgart, 1993; *Libre-Ecange* by Pierre Bourdieu and Hans Haacke, Paris, 1993. **Articles**—*Beyond Modern Sculpture* by Jack Burnham, New York 1968; ''Hans Haacke, the Guggenheim: The Issues'' by Edward Fry in *Arts Magazine* (New York) May, 1971; ''Hans Haacke's Cancelled Show at the Guggenheim'' by Jack Burnham in *Artforum* (New York), June 1971; ''Steps in the Formation of Real-Time Political Art'' by Jack Burnham in Hans Haacke's *Framing and Being Framed,* New York, 1975; *Hans Haacke,* exhibition catalog, with text by Nan Rosenthal, Pasadena, California 1978; *Hans Haacke: Recent Work,* exhibition catalog with text by Jack Burnham, Chicago 1979; *Hans Haacke's 'Cunning Involvement'* by David Craven in Peter D'Agostino and Antonia Muntadas *The UnNecessary Image,* New York, 1982; ''An Unpublished Text for an Unpainted Picture'' by Walter Grasskamp in *October* (New York), Fall 1984; ''Property Values: Hans Haacke, Real Estate and the Museum'' by Rosalyn Deutsch in *Hans Haacke: Unfinished Business,* New York, 1986; ''Hans Haacke and the Cultural Logic of Postmodernism'' by Fredrik Jameson *ibid.*; ''Some of Hans Haacke's Works Considered as Fine Art'' by Leo Steinberg *ibid.*; ''Institutions Trust Institutions'' by Brian Wallis *ibid.*; ''The Antidote'' by Yve-Alain Bois in *October* (New York), Winter 1986; ''Corporate Culture, Art, Inc., Artiste Provacateur'' by Mary Anne Staniszewiski in *Manhattan, Inc.* (New York), January 1987; ''A Polemicist Who Aims at Political and Corporate Targets'' by Grace Glueck in *The New York Times,* 25 January 1987; ''Hans Haacke: Unfinished Business'' by Arthur C. Danto in *The Nation* (New York), 14 February 1987; ''Hans Haacke: Memory and Instrumental Reason'' by Benjamin H.D. Buchloh in *Art in America* (New York), February 1988; ''Hans Haacke and the Era of Sponsorship'' by Mark Thomson in *Art Monthly* (London), September 1989; ''Touching the Rawest Nerve'' by Robert Atkins in *Contemporanea* (New York and Venice), April 1990; ''A Gigantic Artistic Gibe at Jesse Helms'' by Roberta Smith in *The New York Times,* 20 April 1990; ''Haacke's Helmsboro'' by Eleanor Heartney in *Art in America* (New York), May 1990; ''Conceptual Art 1962–1969: From the Aesthetic of Administration to the Critique of Institutions'' by Benjamin H.D. Bucholh in *October* (New York), Winter 1990; ''A Kind of Public Service'' by Grace Glueck in Hans Haacke, *Bodenlos,* Stuttgart, 1993; ''Project No-Man's Land'' by Walter Grasskamp, *ibid*; ''Hans Haacke'' by Jen Budney in *Flash Art (International Edition),* no. 178, October 1994; ''Hans Haacke on Museum Management'' by Derrick Chong in *Museum Management and Curatorship,* vol. 16, no. 3, September 1997; ''Das Volk und die Kruemel'' by Petra Kipphoff in *Die Zeit*, 23 March 2000; ''Ein Mischling für den Bundestag B Erd- und Steingemenge als Symbole politischer Einheit'' by Monika Wagner in *''Der Bevoelkerung'': Aufsaetze und Dokumente zur Debatte um das Reichstagsprojekt von Hans Haacke*, Cologne 2000; ''Lee Smith on Hans Haacke: Aye Raising'' by Lee Smith in *Artforum,* vol. 38, no. 9, May 2000.

*

If art contributes to, among other things, the way we view the world and shape social relations, then does it matter whose image of the world it promotes and whose interests it serves?

—Hans Haacke

* * *

Since the early 1960s, Hans Haacke has been making objects, events, prints and written works which use the forms, words and styles of various systems outside art to communicate the often hidden interdependencies and equivalencies between the various systems which surround us, from the physical and environmental to the social and political. By appropriating the means prevalent in these systems, selecting and organizing out of these sources and recontextualizing them into the art environment of the gallery or museum, Haacke offers possibilities for heightened consciousness of the ideas and implications underlying phenomena and events which we usually accept at face value as ordinary, everyday occurrences.

During the 1960s Haacke concentrated on natural systems. In 1963, in Germany, he began making ''weather boxes,'' including ''Condensation Cubes'' with water enclosed within transparent walls, the water either condensing or evaporating on the inside according to the specific conditions of air, light and temperature in the space where they were displayed. Characterizing his work as ''real time systems,'' Haacke continued his involvement with changes through time as effected by environmental conditions, producing a series of ice works and larger indoor and outdoor works about natural phenomena such as ''Wind In Water (Mist)'' (1968) and ''Moss Transparent—Maintained in Artificial Microclimate.'' He also did a number of works about actual biological growth in plants and animals such as ''Grass Cube'' (1967), ''Chickens Hatching'' (1969) and ''Grass Grows'' (1970, for the *Earth Art* exhibition at Cornell University). In the last one, Haacke constructed a cone-shaped mound of topsoil and peat moss and planted fast-growing rye seeds which grew and died, completing its life cycle during the course of the show. The role of the natural cycle of animals was explored in works such as ''Goat Feeding in the Woods, Thus Changing It'' (1970).

The 1970s launched Haacke into a new phase of systems art concerning socio-political systems and their connections with the art system. From 1969 to 1972 he did a series of ''Visitors' Profiles,'' in which questionnaires posed 10 demographic and 10 opinion queries on current socio-political issues to the audience/participants. Resulting information gathered by Haacke was correlated in various ways including bar graphs and charts and accompanied by comparisons, for instance, with other surveys or other Haacke questionnaire polls, casting new light on who and what are the people who view new art and even choose to be a part of making it. It was one of Haacke's ''Visitors' Profiles'' which became part of the 1971 controversy which resulted in the Guggenheim Museum's cancellation of a proposed Haacke exhibition and the firing of Edward Fry, the curator who fought for the artist's rights to show his work without censorship. Also at issue were Haacke's ''Real Estate'' works which consist of a series of photographs of the facades of Manhattan real estate holdings, some tenements, others commercial properties, accompanied by captions which contain business information about ownership, acquisition and money values which Haacke had gathered from the public records of the County Clerk's office. These works were determined to be too controversial (possibly making the museum legally liable) for the Guggenheim Museum, whose director, Thomas Messer, cancelled the exhibition. Ironically, the flurry of publicity and the events of the cancellation became part of Haacke's work, demonstrating the powers inherent in work which succeeds in being socially relevant and outside art-as-art-alone formalism.

In the late 1970s, Haacke produced a number of series of prints which deal with large corporations' pretensions to cultural ambassadorship and social commitment as a major thrust in their advertising and public relations campaigns. In a series of 4-color silkscreens titled ''The Good Will Umbrella'' (1976), Haacke reproduces facsimile pages from an address to the Eastern Annual Conference of the American Association of Advertising Agencies. The texts discuss in glowing terms the various ways in which the corporation is building up its public image, by supporting public television, holding contests, commissioning art and underwriting art exhibitions, for example. In each work, the familiar emblem ''MOBIL'' is printed in heavy lettering and followed by a subheading which encapsulated the two pages of textual information that appears below. The simple, direct use of advertising format and the concise choice of material directly convey the message which takes on new meanings simply by appearing as art in the gallery. In Haacke's 1979 work, ''Alcoa: We can't wait for tomorrow,'' Haacke's ability to hit the point with elegant directness is well exemplified. The work is a simple horizontal stretch of squared aluminum tubing on which mirror-polished aluminum letters spell out a quote from the president of Alcoa's address to the American Advertising Federation: ''Business could hold art exhibitions to tell its own story.'' It is one of many works by Haacke which appropriates exactly the most telling forms of extra-art communication to reveal how art is tacitly co-opted by the ideology of larger interests.

In recent years, Haacke has continued his complex investigations, taking on art-world complicity with corporate hypocrisy and government duplicity through topical installations that are consistently cogent and thoughtful. The artist has become somewhat of an elder statesman to a generation of younger artists whose art-making strategies underline the dialectics of cultural production and consumption.

The hostile climate in public funding for the arts since the late 1980s, the influence of politically mobilized right-wing religious fundamentalist groups on national politics, and the excesses of a spectacle-hungry news media have given new urgency and relevancy to Haacke's artistic enterprise of ''systems theory.'' *Helmsboro Country,* 1990, examines the connections between Phillip Morris, the manufacturer of Marlboro cigarettes, and the corporation's congressional mouthpiece, Senator Jesse Helms, the sponsor of a failed censorship bill directed at NEA-funded art. Haacke provokes us with such elements as a giant box of ''Helmsboro'' cigarettes, emblazoned with a portrait of Helms, complete with statements by the senator denouncing 'obscene' artwork and a tract called ''Phillip Morris and the Arts.'' Collage replicas of works from a Phillip Morris-sponsored Picasso and Braque exhibition consist of fragments of text from the company's promotional campaign for the show. Haacke includes portions from a ''Bill of Rights'' distributed by the corporation to promote ''the freedom to choose smoking.'' These elements allow Haacke to raise questions about patronage, censorship, freedom of speech, and First Amendment rights, leaving it up to the viewer to actively construct a response.

Haacke's work resists didacticism by its inventiveness and thoroughness—the sheer cumulative weight of its means, and its insistence on engaging the viewer in its conclusions. It is this ability to charge art institutions and their privileged audiences with responsibility for the hidden constructs of ethics and power that underlie them that gives Haacke's art its conviction and its staying power.

—Essay by Barbara Cavaliere; updated by Dorothy Valakos

During the 1990s, Hans Haacke has continued to create works taking up or provoking a socio-political debate. In this regard, his work *Der Bevoelkerung* may serve as a paradigmatic example for this aspect. Commissioned by the German Parliament in 1999, it led to a controversial debate but was finally carried out during the summer of 2000.

The artist had planned to build a huge trough carrying the words ''Der Bevoelkerung'' in fluorescent letters in one of the courtyards of the Reichstag. Additionally, every member of Parliament was asked to fill a certain amount of earth from their respective electoral districts into the trough. Haacke had intended the words ''Der Bevoelkerung'' (''To the Population'') to correct the inscription which read ''Dem Deutschen Volke,'' which can be translated as ''To the German People.'' Whereas the inscription on the building would limit its use to people of German nationality, Haacke's statement would propose that the German Parliament should represent everybody living in Germany, thus questioning the definitions of citizenship. This led to controversial reactions.

Another debate arose from the artist's choice of material. Some critics pointed out that ''earth-rituals'' had been a National Socialist practice. Consequently, the use of earth would imply an affinity of the German democracy with the blood-and-soil-ideology of the Third Reich.

Yet the discourse on historical questions connected with National Socialism had always been a part of Haacke's oeuvre. In his work *Germania* (shown at the Venice Biennale, 1993), the artist had destroyed the marble floor of the German Pavilion, which was erected during the National Socialist era. The open floor showing the earth lying beneath was intended to serve as a counterpoint to the architecture. In *Sanitation* (for the Whitney Biennial in 2000), the artist criticized right wing tendencies in American politics by displaying some politicians' statements in connection with the sound of marching feet. Although there is no direct display of National Socialist imagery, the topic is present in Haacke's essay for the exhibition catalogue. Due to the hostile public reaction, the exhibition was almost cancelled.

In general, Hans Haacke's recent works have concentrated on topics such as nationalism or the influence of National Socialist ideology on contemporary politics. Still defining public debates as a direct participation of the observer and therefore as an integral part of the artwork, the artist continues to create ''real-time-systems''.

—Vanessa Hirsch

HAINS, Raymond

Nationality: French. **Born:** Saint-Brieuc, 9 November 1926. **Education:** Académie des Beaux-Arts, Rennes, 1945. **Career:** Associated with Jacques de la Villeglé, 1946. Worked as photographer, *France Illustration* magazine, Paris 1947. Independent artist, working with photography, multiple objects, mirror-games and ''lettres eclatées,'' Paris, since 1947. **Agent:** Galerie Lara Vincy, 47 rue de Seine, 75006 Paris. **Address:** 20 rue Marbeau, 75016 Paris, France.

Individual Exhibitions:

1948 Galerie Colette Allendy, Paris
1949 Librairie des Norritures Terrestres, Rennes, France
1950 Falconnerie de Tytgat, Knokke-le-Zoute, Belgium
1957 Galerie Colette Allendy, Paris (with Jacques de la Villegle)
1961 Galerie J, Paris
1962 Galerie Handschin, Basel
Palais des Beaux-Arts, Brussels
Galerie du Cercle, Paris
1963 Galerie Henriette Legender, Paris
1964 Gallerie del Leone, Venice
1965 Galerie Iris Clert, Paris
Galleria Apollinaire, Milan
1966 Gallerie del Leone, Venice
1968 Gallerie Il Elefante, Venice
1970 Gallerie Sant'Andrea, Milan
1973 Gallerie della Trinita, Rome
1976 Centre National d'Art Contemporain, Paris
Galerie Verbeke, Paris
Galerie Lara Vincy, Paris
1983 Galerie Eric Fabre, Paris
1986 Fondation Cartier, Jouy-en-Josas, France
Galerie Lara Vincy, Paris
1987 Galerie Lara Vincy, Paris
1994 *Les 3 Cartier: du Grand Louvre aux 3 Cartier,* Fondation Cartier pour l'Art Contemporain, Paris (catalog)
1995 *Accents, 1949–1995,* Museum Moderner Kunst Stiftung Ludwig Wien (catalog)
1998 *Rendezvous,* Solomon R. Guggenheim Museum, New York
Lemot Passe a Travers, Nantes
Tours et Detours de R. Hains, Reims, France
1999 Museum of Contemporary Art, Barcelona
Castelli, les Jardineries du Sud, Galerie Daniel Templon, Paris
Congres Interprofessionnel de l'Art Contemporain, Tours, France
2000 Musées de Nice, Musée d'Art Moderne et d'Art Contemporain, France (catalog)

Selected Group Exhibitions:

1952 *Exposition Internationale de la Photographie,* Lucerne, Switzerland
1959 *1st Biennale de Paris,* Musée d'Art Moderne, Paris
1960 *Les Nouveaux Réalistes,* Galleria Apollinaire, Milan
1961 *The Art of Assemblage,* Museum of Modern Art, New York
1968 *Documenta IV,* Museum Fridericianum, Kassel, West Germany
1970 *Nouveau Réalisme 1960–70,* Rotonda della Besana, Milan
1971 *Plakatabrisse aus der Sammlung Cremer,* Staatsgalerie, Stuttgart
1978 *Les Nouveaux Réalistes,* Musee des Ponchettes, Nice
1982 *Westkunst,* Messehallen, Cologne
1986 *1960: Les Nouveaux Réalistes,* Musée d'Art Moderne de la Ville, Paris (travelled to the Kunsthalle, Mannheim; Kunstmuseum, Winterthur)
1994 *Murmures des Rues,* Centre d'Histoire de l'Art Contemporain, Rennes (catalog)
1997 *De Klein à Warhol,* Centre Georges Pompidou, Paris (catalog)
Skulptur Projekte in Munster, Munster, Germany
Documenta 10, Kassel, Germany
1999 *Le Peinture Aprés l'Abstraction, 1955–1975,* Musée d'Art Moderne de la Ville de Paris (catalog)
Printemps de Cahors, France (catalog)
2000 *Un Siecle d'Arpenteurs,* Musee Picasso, Chateau Grimaldi, Antibes, France (catalog)

Collections:

Musée National d'Art Moderne, Paris; Kunstmuseum, Winterthur; Stadtisches Museum, Monchengladbach; Westfalisches Landesmuseum, Munster; Kaiser Wilhelm Museum, Krefeld; Kunstmuseum, Dusseldorf; Museum Moderner Kunst, Vienna.

Publications:

By HAINS: Books—*Hepérile Eclaté,* with Jacques de la Villegle, poem by Camille Bryen, Paris 1953. **Films**—*Loi du 29 Juillet 1881,* 1949; *Saint-Germain-des-Pres-Colombien,* 1949; *Etude aux Allures,* 1950.

On HAINS: Books—*Lyrisme et Abstraction* by Pierre Restany, Milan 1960; *Le Revolution du Régard* by Alain Jouffroy, Paris 1965; *Nouveau Réalisme 1960–1970,* exhibition catalog with text by Pierre Restany, Milan 1970; *Raymond Hains,* exhibition catalog, Paris 1976. **Article**—''Kurzer Abriss der Geschichte der Affichistes'' by Dieter Schwarz in *1960: Les Nouveaux Réalistes,* exhibitions catalog, Mannheim and Winterthur 1986; ''Raymond Hains'' in *Artforum,* September 1999.

* * *

Raymond Hains was trained as a photographer and his first artistic works were photos, which he produced by means of special lenses in an attempt to develop his own style of abstract photography.

Hains and Villeglé took a special interest in the work of Camille Bryen, including his phonetic poems, since they saw in him the representative of an older generation with whom they felt a close affinity. In 1953 they used an optical screen of fluted glass to distort Bryen's text *Hepérile,* which had appeared three years earlier; a new work was thus created: *Hepérile éclaté. The ultra-letters,* which were created out of conventional letters by this optical method, differ from the contemporaneous letter constructions of the Lettristes in one important respect: they are not subjective deformations but distortions acquired through a technical process. The mechanics of the camera intervene between the authors of the *éclatements* and its object, and this distance is also a determining factor in the creation of the poster abstract. Hains' and Villeglé's work is not, therefore, simply an attack on art but, in the tradition of Futurism and Constructivism, an attack on artistic craft.

The real history of the poster abstract began in Paris in December 1949 when Hains produced his first abstract after photographing a number of other posters. The pre-history goes back, however, to the nineteenth century when the poster established itself alongside the newspaper as an industrially produced bearer of news to an anonymous city public. These media provide the basis for the invention of collage, photomontage and *décollage.* Like the reworking on Bryen's texts, the poster abstract is also a secondary artform which mirrors and comments upon primary aristic expressions. Hains selected numerous poster abstracts because their effect resembled the works of Abstract Expressionist paintings, without necessarily sharing the same aims. The technique of sticking loose poster sections on a board is still vaguely reminiscent of the art of collage. Hains appears to have been conscious of this problem from early on, for around 1950 he filmed his first *palissades,* or palings, which served the eager bill stickers as a welcome support. This conceptual extension of the art of the poster abstract clearly sufficed him, for it was not until 1959, under pressure from Dufrêne, that Hain exhibited at the first Biennale of Paris some twenty-seven lath frames entitled *Pallisade des emplacements réservés.* In 1960 Hains introduced *tôles,* or sheet zinc, into his work as an equally useful surface on which posters could be mounted.

There is the closest association in these works between the picture and its support, which is exposed to view, not concealed like an adjustable frame, particularly when only a few sections of poster are left over so that the base is clearly in evidence. By this radical formulation, the poster abstract ironically succeeds in overcoming the division, with which monochrome painters such as Yves Klein were concerned at the time, between background and application of colour.

On closer observation, poster abstracts are seen to be composed of scraps of paper whose industrial origins are indicated by fragments of text and image still visible on them. In this way they are reminiscent of Schwitters' Merz collages; though, in using a variety of everyday objects, Schwitters did in fact subordinate them to the formal laws of his composition. The poster abstracts do not render up their narrative content; on the contrary: certain statements on the posters are angrily denied by anonymous interventions and gain more weight thereby. Hains' 1961 one-man exhibition at Galerie J, entitled *La France déchirée,* showed abstracts whose principal theme was the Algerian war, and which as a result were unsaleable. Their titles read like a resume of internal conflicts in France, a socio-historical reportage: *Paix en Algérie, L'Humanite est la vérité, Cet homme est dangereux* (Poujade), *C'est ca le renouveau?, OAS—fusillez les plastiquers, La cinquiéme, fait naufrage, De Gaulle veut un bain de sang: il l'aura, De Gaulle compte sur vous, aidez-le,* etc. Unlike the autonomous work of modernism, these abstracts do not represent objects closed in upon themselves, but remain closely linked with a particular historical environment, that of France and more precisely that of Paris in the fifties and sixties.

Hains avoided the danger of self-repetition by weaving a sort of fictional web around his activity as a poster artist. From the *pallisade,* he progressed to *lapalissade,* named after the Village La Palice which lies halfway between Nice and Paris and which, according to Hains, constitute the turning point between the *Ecole de Nice* (Arman, Klein, Raysse) and the Parisian *Nouveaux Realistes;* and then to a 'sweet dish', the *entremets de la palissade,* which was the subject of an encyclopaedic exhibition at the Salon Comparaisons in 1960. Hains meanwhile became the ironic critic of his own work. "Le regardeur devient regardé," he said, calling himself—as the producer of *tôles—tôlard,* that is a prisoner of his own style.

In recent years Hains has turned his hand once more to photography. These latest photographs are not abstract works but arrangements of objects which playfully reflect the history of *Nouveau Réalisme.* In them, Hains demonstrates his theory of *abstractions personnifiées,* that is to say he discovers the trademarks of the artists of his generation in the things of everyday life.

—Dieter Schwarz

HAJDU, Etienne

Nationality: French. **Born:** Turda, Rumania, of Hungarian parents, 12 August 1907; emigrated to France, 1972: naturalized, 1930. **Education:** Ecole Technique d'Art Décoratif, Budapest, 1923; Kunstgewerbeschule, Vienna, 1926; Académie de la Grande Chaumière, under Antoine Bourdelle, Paris, 1927; Ecole des Arts Décoratifs, under Niclausse, Paris, 1928; Ecole Nationale des Beaux-Arts, under Boucher, Paris, 1928. **Military Service:** Served in French Army, 1931–32, 1939–40. **Career:** Worked as stone-mason in marble works, Bagneres de Bigorre, 1940–44; produced first marble sculptures and small reliefs, 1944. **Awards:** Sculpture Prize, Nordrhein-Westfalen, Germany 1965; Gold Medal, *International Exhibition of Ceramics,* Istanbul, 1967; Grand Prix National de Sculpture, Paris 1969. Officier, 1985, and Commandeur, 1993, Legion d'Honneur. **Agent:** Artcurial, 9 Avenue Matignon, 75008 Paris; Richard Norton Gallery, 612 Merchandise Mart, Chicago, Illinois 60654. **Address:** 24 rue Bertie-Albrecht, 92220 Bagneux, France.

Individual Exhibitions:

1939 Galerie Jeanne Bucher, Paris (with Vieira da Silva and Arpad Szenes)
1946 Galerie Jeanne Bucher, Paris
1948 Galerie Jeanne Bucher, Paris
1953 Galerie Jeanne Bucher, Paris
1956 Galerie Suzanne Feigle, Basel
Galerie Jeanne Bucher, Paris
1957 Kunsthalle, Bern (with Pierre Tal Coat)
Galerie Jeanne Bucher, Paris
1958 Galerie Jeanne Bucher, Paris
M. Knoedler and Company, New York
Guggenheim Museum, New York
1959 Museum Haus Lange, Krefeld, West Germany
M. Knoedler and Company, New York
1961 Kestner-Gessellschaft, Hannover
Galerie Jeanne Bucher, Paris
Museum am Ostwall, Dortmund
Städtisches Museum, Leverkusen, West Germany
Stedelijk Museum, Amsterdam
1962 M. Knoedler and Company, New York
Cincinnati Contemporary Arts Center, Ohio

Arts Club of Chicago
1964 Phillips Collection, Washington, D.C.
1965 *Sculptures: Encres de Chine,* M. Knoedler and Company, New York
1967 Centre Culturel, Bagneux, France
Centre Culturel, Thonon-les-Baines, France
1968 *Sculptures Récente,* Galerie Knoedler, Paris
1969 Nouveau Musée, Le Havre
Recent Sculptures, M. Knoedler and Company, New York
1970 Centre Culturel, Toulouse
1971 *Sculptures: Encres de Chine,* Galerie Regence, Brussels
Knoedler Galleries, New York
1972 *Werke der Sechziger Jahre 1964–1972,* Museum am Ostwall, Dortmund
Centre Rizzoli, Milan
1973 Musée National d'Art Moderne, Paris
Sculpteur, Estampilles, Dessins, Musée des Beaux-Arts, Nancy
1974 Galerie Regence, Brussels
Fundacao Calouste Gulbenkian, Lisbon (retrospective)
1975 Musée des Urselines, Mason
1977 Galerie La Cité, Luxembourg
1978 Musée des Beaux-Arts, Dijon (retrospective; toured France)
Mucsarnok Museum, Budapest (retrospective)
Musée des Beaux-Arts, Calais
Musée des Beaux-Arts, Dunkirk
Musée Galerie des Beaux-Arts, Bordeaux
1979 Musée des Beaux-Arts, Cannes
Musée Municipal, Limoges
Maison des Arts et des Loisirs, Montbeliard
Muzuel de Arta, Bucharest
Musée des Beaux-Arts, Cluj, Rumania
Oeuvres sur Papier, Centre Georges Pompidou, Paris
Terre Cuite et Porcelain, Musée de Arts Décoratifs, Bordeaux
Muzeul de Arta, Bucharest (retrospective; toured Rumania)
1980 Galerie Irtissen, Tunis
Galerie La Cité, Luxembourg
1981 Galerie ''M,'' Hannover
Palais des Arts et de la Culture, Brest
1982 Salle des Ecuries de St. Hugues, Cluny, France
Galerie Carré et Cie, Paris
1983 Galerie La Cité, Luxembourg
Musée St. Denis, Reims, France
1985 Galerie La Cité, Luxembourg
1986 Articurial, Paris
Centre Artistique de Poudeous, France
Galerie de Cluny, France
1993 Fondation de Coubertin, Saint-Rémy-lès-Chevreuse (catalog)
1995 *Hajdu,* Musée des Beaux-Arts de Dijon, France (catalog)
2001 *Sculptures and Drawings,* FundaçãArpad Szenes—Vieira da Silva, Lisbon

Selected Group Exhibitions:

1947 *Salon de Mai,* Paris
1951 *Biennale d'Anvers,* Antwerp
1958 *La Sculpture Contemporaine,* Musée Rodin, Paris
1976 *Un Siècle de Dessins des Sculpteurs,* Musée des Beaux-Arts, Lyon
1981 *Paris-Paris 1937–1957,* Centre Georges Pompidou, Paris
1983 *Sèvres de 1850 a nos jours,* Le Louvre des antiquaries, Pais
1985 *Fonds Régional d'Art Contemporain,* Musée du Luxembourg, Paris
1987 *Porcelaines de Sèvres au XXem Siècle,* Musée National de Céramiques, Sèvres, France
1989 Pavillion des Arts, Paris
1993 Fondation de Coubertin, St. Remy-les-Chevreuse

Collections:

Centre Georges Pompidou, Paris; Musée des Beaux-Arts, Dijon, France; Lehmbruck Museum, Duisburg, West Germany; Museum of Modern Art, New York; Guggenheim Museum, New York; Hirshhorn Museum and Sculpture Garden, Smithsonian Institution, Washington, D.C.; Arts Club of Chicago; Museum of Fine Arts, Montreal.

Publications:

By HAJDU: Articles—interview in *Chronique des Arts* (Paris), June 1973; text in *Christian Science Monitor* (Boston), 30 October 1977; ''La cellule et son espace'' in *Artcurial Journal* (Paris), May/June 1987.

On HAJDU: Books—*Hajdu,* exhibition catalog, with text by Michael Seuphor, New York 1958; *Etienne Hajdu,* exhibition catalog, with text by Werner Schmalenbach, Leverkusen, West Germany 1961; *Hajdu,* exhibition catalog with text by Dora Vallier, Paris 1961; *Hadju: Sculptures, Encres de Chine,* exhibition catalog, Paris 1965; *Hajdu: Recent Sculptures,* exhibition catalog with text by Dora Vallier, New York 1969; *Etienne Hajdu: Werke der Sechziger Jahre, 1964–1972,* exhibition catalog with text by Eugene Thiemann, Dortmund 1972; *Etienne Hajdu* by Jonel Jianou, Paris 1972; *Etienne Hajdu,* exhibition catalog with texts by Jean Leymarie, Dominique Bozo, Nicole Barbier and Dora Vallier, Paris 1973; *Etienne Hajdu* by Mircea Deac, Bucharest 1976; *Hajdu: Oeuvres sur Papier,* exhibition catalog with text by Pierre Georgel, Paris 1979; *Etienne Hajdu: Terre Cuite et Porcelaine,* exhibition catalog with text by Jacqueline du Pasquier, Bordeaux 1979; *Hajdu* by Alexandre Cebus, Bucharest 1984; *Etienne Hajdu: Dessins* by Pierre Descargues, Paris 1987. **Articles—**''Étienne Hajdu: Transparence et Reflets'' by Laure Meyer in *L'Oeil* (Lausanne), no. 455, October 1993; ''Studio of Etienne Hajdu: Or the Camera Lucida'' by Jacques-Louis Binet in *Cimaise,* vol. 43, November/December 1996.

*

As an adolescent I carved with a tool that has not changed its form since antiquity. In the mountains around me everyday objects—the cradle, the furniture, the door, even the facades of the house—were carved: art was everywhere.

The rare photographic reproductions of Greek or Egyptian statues which I received were statues of marble or granite, so at that time in my life carving meant releasing a preconceived image from a block, giving organic life to matter. Later when I was sent to a technical school in the town I learned the other method of producing sculpture, the art of modelling clay, a shapeless, soft and obedient material. I threw myself into this new experience with great pleasure: day after day I modelled flowers, fruit, animals, the bust of my parents. . .

Then in Paris life around me was different: machines were invading all the professions, cars and aircraft were changing customs, the new vision of the world was dawning, and the pulsations of the machines enticed the poets away towards a new sensibility. In the plastic arts, lines, colours, forms were adopting strange, geometric and breathtaking rhythms and combinations. One glorified the Machine which would give man liberty and unite the world.

If marble is fitting for the slow and sensitive passage of light and shadows, the new vision demanded a new medium. New sculpture could only be in metal.

In art, the medium and the tool are often determinant. Iron, aluminium, copper sheet or rod with multiple possibilities of machining, of assembly, of riveting and above all of welding. Little electric machines have given each of us personal possibilities, new hands have been multiplied by motors for shaping, milling, drilling, filling or polishing. Technology has profoundly changed our sensibility, our conception of space.

In 1945 I undertook the modelling of some large bas-reliefs; I orchestrated simple elements like the alphabet of a new language, a kind of totalisation of that which is living. I worked for eight years in clay, an intermediate material, and cast my reliefs in plaster; during that time I produced "The Aircraft Combat," "The Field of Force," "Homage to Bélà Bartok," "Poem of Fire," and numerous other works which are in various museums and collections. When my plastic language seemed to me conceivable, I carried them out in durable and definitive material; for that purpose I learnt to hammer large sheets of lead, copper and aluminium. In order to emboss copper one has to heat it. The fire gives to the metal an extraordinary coloration, the colour has a direct relationship with the depth of the forms, and is therefore organic to the expression. Aluminium can become silky, sensitive, luminous. Each material has its own personality; one has to understand, feel and respect this powerful alchemy charged with tellurial strength. The subtlety in the slow curves of forms brings to the density of the metal a suppleness, a sensuality, and unexpected tenderness; in addition the polish brings an incorporeal translucency: in this way common aluminium which in its lowliness was just good enough for kitchen utensils or industrial parts can become an astonishing medium. That is the series "Experiments with Metal."

Encouraged by the results, I multiplied forms in space, and on the undulating surface there are several high-reliefs and carvings. My elementary polished forms shimmering and intersecting, create luminous echoes of unusual volumes. By just manipulating the planes, one can achieve an expansion of volume, an accumulation which grows and diminishes according to the movement of our perception.

I draw a lot. On paper I do not feel the resistance of the material, and the ink allows me boldness of form and liberty of imagination. My engravings are white on white or black on black—like the reliefs, they exist only because of the light.

—Etienne Hajdu

* * *

Looking at the cool, exquisite, near-oriental gentleness of finish in the works of Etienne Hajdu, it is hard to believe that this sculptor born to Hungarian parents in Rumania once served an apprenticeship in the studio of the brawny Bourdelle. This only goes to prove that the best students learn something but stimultaneously preserve their own artistic personalities. One has only to check the list of the painters who passed through Léger's hands and survived his influence or, in the world of sculpture, those who were at one time or another students of or assistants to Henry Moore.

Hajdu's sculpture has featured in important museum exhibitions throughout the world. It is not that his imagery is out of step with contemporary styles so much as that the manner of presentation does not relate either to the passionate sturm-und-drang of much of modern sculpture or to the cold, often icy, anaemia of total non-figuration. In character, but not in appearance, his works have the same in-between flavour of the sculptures of Hans Arp, though there is no evidence of Arp's fat humour in them and certainly nothing of Arp's dadaistic disruption of visual platitudes.

Hajdu's pieces preserve hints of figuration but clothe them in his own kind of oriental sublimity. It seems to matter little whether he is carving marble or working in metal bas-relief (beaten sheets of aluminium or copper); the same impact of cultured peace is maintained. Even at war Hajdu is at peace. This paradox is beautifully emphasized in his sheet copper relief "Soldiers in Armour" in the Museum of Modern Art in New York.

—Sheldon Williams

HALL, Nigel

Nationality: British. **Born:** Bristol, 30 August 1943. **Education:** West of England College of Art, Bristol, 1960–64; Royal College of Art, London, 1964–67. **Family:** Married Elizabeth Claire in 1965 (divorced, 1972); married Lyn Plenderleith in 1976 (divorced, 1977); married Manijeh Yadegar in 1986. **Career:** Sculptor; lives and works in London. Lecturer, Royal College of Art, London, 1972–74; principal lecturer, Chelsea College of Art, London, 1974–84. **Awards:** Harkness Fellowship, 1967; Alecto Commission Prize, *Bradford Print Biennale, 1974.* **Agent:** Annely Juda Fine Art, 23 Dering Street, London W1R 9AA. **Address:** 11 Kensington Park Gardens, London W11 3HD, England.

Individual Exhibitions:

1967 Galerie Givaudan, Paris
1968 Nicholas Wilder Gallery, Los Angeles
1970 Galerie Neuendorf, Cologne
Serpentine Gallery, London
1971 Studio Show, London
1972 Nicholas Wilder Gallery, Los Angeles
Felicity Samuel Gallery, London
1974 Felicity Samuel Gallery, London
Primo Piano Galleria, Rome
Robert Elkon Gallery, New York
1975 Nicholas Wilder Gallery, Los Angeles
Galeri Galax, Gothenburg, Sweden
Galerie Jacomo-Sanitiveri, Paris
1976 Felicity Samuel Gallery, London
Arnolfini Gallery, Bristol
1977 Robert Elkon Gallery, New York
Tranegaarden Art Library, Copenhagen
1978 Annely Juda Gallery, London

Nigel Hall, *River,* 1998. ©Nigel Hall.

University of Melbourne (toured Australia, 1978–79)
Roundhouse Gallery, London
Aberdeen Art Gallery, Scotland
1979 Robert Elkon Gallery, New York
Primo Piano Galleria, Rome
University of Southampton
Galerie Reckermann, Cologne
Peterloo Gallery, Manchester (with Alan Green)
1980 Warwick Gallery, London
Ceolfrith Gallery, Sunderland, Country Durham
Nishimura Gallery, Tokyo
1981 Juda Rowan Gallery, London
Galerie Maeght, Paris
1982 Staatliche Kunsthalle, Baden-Baden, West Germany
Galerie Maeght, Zurich
Galerij S65, Aalst, Belgium
Kasahara Gallery, Osaka, Japan
1983 Robert Elkon Gallery, New York
Galerie Maeght-Lelong, Paris
Yuill/Crowley Gallery, Sydney
1984 Galerie Reckermann, Cologne
Nishimura Gallery, Tokyo
Galerie Lupke, Frankfurt
1985 Juda Rowan Gallery, London
Galerij S65, Aalst, Belgium
1986 Galerie Ziegler, Zurich
1987 Fondation Veranneman, Kruishoutem, Belgium
Garry Anderson Gallery, Sydney
Annely Juda Gallery, London
Hete Hunermann Gallery, Dusseldorf
1988 Nishimura Gallery, Tokyo
Galerie Ziegler, Zurich
1989 Galerie Blanche, Stockholm
Galerie Hans Mayer, Dusseldorf
1990 Garry Anderson Gallery, Sydney
Deutscher Gallery, Melbourne
1991 Annely Juda Fine Art, London
Galerie Terbuggen, Heigelberg
1994 Galerie Nova, Pontresina, Switzerland
1995 Galerie Renee Ziegler, Zurich
Veranneman Foundation, Belgium
1996 Annely Juda Fine Art, London
Shell Technology and Research Centre, Amsterdam
1997 Veranneman Foundation, Belgium

Economist Plaza, London
Park Ryu Sook Gallery, Seoul, South Korea
1998 New York Studio School Gallery, New York
1999 Galerie Hans Mayer, Dusseldorf
2000 Konstruktiv Tendens, Stockholm
Annely Juda Fine Art, London
Galerie C. Huärne, Helsingbor
Park Ryu Sook Gallery, Seoul, South Korea

Selected Group Exhibitions:

1967 *New British Painting and Sculpture,* University of California at Los Angeles (toured the United States and Canada)
1972 *British Sculpture 72,* Royal Academy of Arts, London
1973 *Young English Artists,* Gothenburg Art Museum, Sweden
1975 *9th Paris Biennale*
1976 *Arte Inglese Oggi,* Palazzo Reale, Milan
1977 *Documenta 6,* Kassel, West Germany
1979 *Contructivism and the Geometric Tradition,* Albright-Konx Art Gallery, Buffalo, New York (toured the United States)
1980 *Reliefs: Formprobleme Zwischen Malerei und Skulpturn im 20. Jahrhundert,* Westfälisches Landesmuseum, Münster, West Germany (travelled to the Kunsthaus, Zurich)
1982 *Aspects of British Art Today,* Metropolitan Art Museum, Tokyo (toured Japan)
1983 *The Sculpture Show '83,* Hayward Gallery, London
1984 *Drawings,* British Council Exhibition, Hyogo Prefectural Museum (toured Japan, Korea, and Far East)
1988 *Britannica, Trente Ans de Sculpture,* Musée des Beaux Arts, Le Havre (toured France and Belgium)
1993 *Drawings in Black and White,* Museum of Modern Art, New York
1994 *Prints of Darkness,* Fogg Art Museum, Harvard University, Massachusetts
British Drawings: A Selection from the Collection, Museum of Modern Art, New York
1997 *A Changed World,* British Council touring exhibition
1999 *Zum Kreis,* Museum zu Allerheiligen, Schaffhausen, Switzerland
45–99: A Personal View by Bryan Robertson, Kettle's Yard, Cambridge
2000 *Beyond the Circle,* Moran Museum, Seoul, South Korea
The Eye of the Storm, La Mandria Park, Turin

Collections:

Tate Gallery, London; Kunsthaus, Zurich, Louisiana Museum, Humlebaek, Denmark; National Museum of Art, Osaka, Japan; Australian National Gallery, Canberra; Museum of Modern Art, New York; Art Institute of Chicago; Nationalgalerie, West Berlin; Musée National d'Art Moderne, Paris; Metropolitan Museum of Art, Tokyo.

Publications:

By HALL: Article—''Introduction: Conversation with Bryan Robertson'' in *Nigel Hall,* exhibition catalog, London 1980.

On HALL: Books—*Arte Inglese Oggi,* exhibition catalog, by Norbert Lynton, Milan 1976; *Aspects of British Art Today,* exhibition catalog, by David Brown, Tokyo 1982; *Nigel Hall: Skulpturen und Zeichnugen,* exhibition catalog, Baden-Baden 1982; *Nigel Hall: Recent Sculpture and Drawings,* exhibition catalog, London 1985; *Nigel Hall: New Work,* exhibition catalog, London 1987; *Britannica Trent ans de Sculpture* exhibition catalog, Le Harvre, 1988; *Nigel Hall: Recent Sculpture and Drawing,* London, 1991, 1996, 2000; *Zum Kreis,* exhibition catalog, Schaffhausen, 1999; *Beyond the Circle,* exhibition catalog, Seoul, 2000. **Articles—**''Nigel Hall's Sculpture'' by Jane Livingston in *Art and Artists* (London), December 1970; ''London Letter'' by Bernard Denvir in *Art International* (Lugano, Switzerland), February 1974; ''Nigel Hall'' by R. C. Kenedy in *Art International* (Lugano, Switzerland), March/April 1976; ''Nigel Hall'' by Bryan Robertson in *Art Australia* (Sydney), Autumn 1985.

* * *

Nigel Hall is one of the most accomplished sculptors to emerge in England during the 70s. His sculptures are distinguished by the perfection of their finish and the degree of completion they reach in the technical sense. Aesthetically, they relate to Russian constructivism and have about them the quality of drawings suspended in space. This effect is due to several factors. The forms are made up of rods connected into geometric shapes like asymmetrical kites which are then cantilevered out from a supporting wall. Both the junctures where the rods meet and the sculpture attaches to the wall are superbly crafted so that we don't quite see how it is done. This sets up a mystery about technique which is not intrusive but thrilling. It is like the perfectionism of a jeweller taken to a larger scale. The big arcs and long lines move out from and double back to the anchoring wall and the viewer can see the structures from many angles simply by changing position. Depending on the lighting, there is the further element of the linear shadows cast by the rods onto the walls and floor. This, together with the fact that the rods may be painted different, close-valued colors—greys, dark greens, etc.—adds to the work's ambiguity. Color not only acts as a weight control, in the sense of how heavy or light any part looks, but plays havoc with our reading of light and shadows and perspective.

Hall's work has immense elegance while remaining strong, even bold. The scale is perfectly judged to achieve this blending. What we see is a daring balancing act, a kind of series of high-wire maneuvers, translated into sculptural terms and fashioned in such a way that we can zero in on the details to find the mechanics of the ''performance'' cunningly hidden. The combination is pretty irresistible.

—Ralph Pomeroy

HAMILTON, Richard

Nationality: British. **Born:** London, 24 February 1922. **Education:** Studied at Westminster Technical College, London, under Mark Gertler, 1936; attended evening classes at St. Martin's School of Art, London, under Bernard Meninsky, 1936; studied at Royal Academy Schools, London, 1938–40 and 1945–46; studied etching at the Slade School of Fine Art, London, under John Buckland Wright, 1948–51. Served in the Royal Engineers, Aldershot, Hampshire, 1946–47. **Family:** Married Terry O'Reilley in 1947 (died, 1962); children:

Dominy and Roderic; married Rita Donagh, 1991. **Career:** Worked as office boy in advertising department, Drake and Gouham, London, 1936–37; as display assistant, Reimann Studios, London, 1937–38; as engineering draftsman, EMI, London, 1941–45; organizer and designer, *Growth and Form* exhibitions, Institute of Contemporary Arts, London, 1951; member, Independent Group, London, 1952–53; worked on reconstruction of Marcel Duchamp's *Large Glass,* Newcastle-upon-Tyne, 1965–66; organized *The Almost Complete Works of Marcel Duchamp* exhibitions, London, 1966. Lecturer in Design, Central School of Arts and Crafts, London, 1952–53; lecturer in basic design, King's College, University of Durham, and created basic course ''Developing Process,'' with Victor Pasmore, Ian Stephenson, and others, 1956–58; lecturer in interior design, Royal College of Art, London, 1957–61. **Awards:** William and Norma Copley Award, 1960; First Prize, with Mary Martin, *John Moore's Exhibition,* Liverpool, 1969; Talens Prize, Amsterdam, 1970; World Print Award, 1983; Golden Lion, Venice Biennale, 1993. **Agent:** Tate Gallery, Millbank, SW1P 4RG, London, England; Petersburg Press, P.O. Box 2238, New York, New York 10101. **Address:** Northend Farm, Northend, Oxfordshire, RG9 6LQ, England.

Individual Exhibitions:

1950 Gimpel Fils, London
1955 Hannover Gallery, London
1957 Hatton Gallery, Newcastle-upon-Tyne (with Victor Pasmore)
1958 Hatton Gallery, Newcastle-upon-Tyne (with Victor Pasmore)
1964 Hannover Gallery, London
1966 Robert Fraser Gallery, London
1967 Robert Fraser Gallery, London
Galerie Ricke, Kassel, West Germany
Alexandre Iolas Gallery, New York
1968 Studio Marconi, Milan
1969 Studio Marconi, Milan
Robert Fraser Gallery, London
Galerie Neuedorf, Hamburg
1970 Galerie René Block, Berlin
Onnasch Galerie, Berlin
Tate Gallery, London (toured Europe)
National Gallery of Canada, Ottawa (toured Canada)
1971 Galerie René Block, Berlin
Studio Marconi, Milan
Stedelijk Museum, Amsterdam
Elvehjem Art Center, Madison, Wisconsin
Castelli Graphics, New York
1972 Studio Marconi, Milan
Whitworth Art Gallery, Manchester
Institute of Contemporary Arts, London
1973 Galerie René Block, Berlin
Neue Berliner Kunstverein, Berlin (with Dieter Roth and K. P. Brehmer)
Guggenheim Museum, New York (toured the United States and West Germany, 1973–74)
1974 Galerie Cadaques, Gerona, Spain
Studio Marconi, Milan
Scottish Arts Council Gallery, Edinburgh (toured Scotland and Wales)
1975 Serpentine Gallery, London
Kaiser Wilhelm Museum, Krefeld, West Germany
1976 Stedelijk Museum, Amsterdam (travelled to Bonnenfantemuseum,Maastricht, and the Gemeentemuseum, Arnhem)
1977 Le Musée, Grenoble, France (travelled to Musée des Beaux-Arts,Chambery, France)
Institute of Contemporary Arts, London (with Dieter Roth; toured the U. K. and Europe)
1978 *Studies 1937–1977,* Kunsthalle, Bielefeld, West Germany (travelled to the Kunsthalle, Göttingen and Kunsthalle, Tübingen)
Vancouver Art Gallery, British Columbia
1979 Stedelijk Museum, Amsterdam
1980 Anthony D'Offay Gallery, London
Waddington Graphics, London
Galerie Schellman + Kluser, Munich
Charles Cowles Gallery, New York
Severina Teucher AG, Zurich
1981 Galerie Maeght, Paris
1982 Provinciaal Museum, Hasselt, Belgium
Waddington Graphics, London
1983 Nishimura Gallery, Tokyo
Galerie Schellman + Kluser, Munich
Galeria Z, Zaragoza, Spain
Brooke Alexander Inc., New York
Tate Gallery, London
1984 Henie-Onstad Museum, Oslo
Nationalmuseum, Stockholm
Galerie Cadaques, Spain
Thorden and Wetterling, Stockholm
Wilheml-Hack-Museum, Ludwigshefen, West Germany
Waddington Graphics, London
1985 Fundació Joan Miró, Barcelona
Norton Gallery and School of Art, West Palm Beach, Florida
Fundació Caja de Pensiones, Madrid
DAAD-Galerie, West Berlin
Nishimura Gallery, Tokyo
Yale University Art Gallery, New Haven, Connecticut
1986 National Gallery of Canada, Ottawa
Nishimura Gallery, Tokyo
Philadelphia Museum of Art
Galeria Cadaques, Spain
Los Angeles County Museum of Art
Walker Art Center, Minneapolis
1988 Fruitmarket Gallery, Edinburgh
1989 Moderna Museet, Stockholm
1990 Kestner-Gesellschaft, Hannover
1991 Anthony D'Offay Gallery, London
1992 Tate Gallery, London (catalog)
1998 *New Technology and Printmaking,* Alan Cristea Gallery, London (catalog)
Subject to an Impression, Kunsthalle Bremen, Germany (retrospective) (catalog)

Selected Group Exhibitions:

1956 *This Is Tomorrow,* Whitechapel Art Gallery, London
1964 *Neuwe Realisten,* Gemeentemuseum, The Hague
1966 *European Drawings,* Guggenheim Museum, New York

1969 *Information,* Kunsthalle, Basel
1970 *Contemporary British Art,* Museum of Modern Art, Tokyo
1971 *Metamorphose de l'Objet,* Palais des Beaux-Arts, Brussels
1976 *Pop Art in England,* Kunstverein, Hamburg (travelled to the York Art Gallery, England)
1982 *Aspects of British Art Today,* Metropolitan Museum, Tokyo
1983 *Aspects of Postwar Painting in Europe,* Guggenheim Museum, New York
1986 *The Medium and the Media,* Los Angeles County Museum of Art
1987 *Berlinart 1961–87,* Museum of Modern Art, New York (travelled to San Francisco Museum of Modern Art)
1990 *The Independent Group: Postwar Britain and the Aesthetics of Plenty,* Institute of Contemporary Arts, London
1993 *XLV Biennale di Venezia,* British Pavilion, Venice, Italy (catalog)
1995 *Britain at the Venice Biennale 1895–1995,* Venice Biennale, Italy (catalog)
Our 100th Anniversary of Painting of People—Pictorial Worlds, Museum Ludwig, Cologne (catalog)
1996 *Language, Mapping and Power,* Galerie Nikki Diana Marquardt, Paris (traveled to Orchard Gallery, Londonderry, Northern Ireland) (catalog)
Art Against Apartheid, South African Parliament, Pretoria (catalog)
1997 *Documenta 10,* Kassel, Germany
Treasure Island, Centro de Arte Moderna Jose de Azeredo Perdiago, Lisbon
Hockney to Hodgkin: British Master Prints 1960–1980, New Orleans Museum of Art, Louisiana (catalog)
Artists' Books: The Invention of a Genre, 1960–1980, Galerie Mansart, Paris (catalog)
1998 *Head First: Portraits from the Arts Council Collection,* City Gallery, Leicester, England (traveling exhibition) (catalog)
1999 *The Museum as Muse: Artists Reflect,* Museum of Modern Art, New York (traveled to Museum of Contemporary Art, San Diego)
Nach-Bild, Kunsthalle Basel, Basel
2000 *Things: Assemblage, Collage and Photography Since 1935,* Norwich Gallery, Norwich, England
Retrace Your Steps: Remember Tomorrow, Sir John Soane's Museum, London

Collections:

Tate Gallery, London; Guggenheim Museum, New York; Museum of Modern Art, New York; Nationalgalerie, Berlin; Kunsthalle, Tubingen; Museum Ludwig, Cologne; Louisiana Museum, Copenhagen; Australian National Gallery, Canberra; Victoria and Albert Museum, London; National Gallery of Scotland, Edinburgh.

Publications:

By HAMILTON: Books—*The Bride Stripped Bare by Her Bachelors Even,* London 1960; *The Bride Stripped Bare by Her Bachelors Even Again,* Newcastle-upon-Tyne 1966; *Polaroid Portraits Vol. 2,* Stuttgart 1978; *Interiors 1964–79,* London 1980; *Polaroid Portraits Vol. 3,* Stuttgart 1982; *In Horne's House,* London 1982; *Collected Word,* Stuttgart 1982; *Prints 1939–83,* Stuttgart and London 1984; *The Transmogrifications of Bloom,* London 1986; *Interfaces* (with Dieter Roth), Basel 1988; *Talking Art 1,* with Adrian Searle, London 1993. **Articles—**''Hommage à Chrysler Corp'' in *Architectural Design* (London), March 1958; ''Diagrammer'' in *The Developing Process,* Newcastle-upon-Tyne, 1959; ''Persuading Image'' in *Design* (London), February 1960; ''An Exposition of She'' in *Architectural Design* (London), February 1961; ''Duchamp'' in *Art International* (Lugano, Switzerland), January 1964; ''Son of the Bride Stripped Bare,'' with Mario Amaya, in *Art and Artists* (London), July 1966; ''Roy Lichtenstein,'' in *Studio International* (London), March 1969; ''Motion: Perspective,'' in *Richard Hamilton: Studies 1973–1977,* exhibition catalog, Bielefeld, West Germany, 1978; ''Recollections of Joseph Beuys,'' in *Art Monthly* (London), March 1986; ''Richard Hamilton: Value and Judgement,'' with Marco Livingstone in *Art Press,* no. 190, April 1994; ''Anteckningar'' in *Paletten,* vol. 60, no. 4, 1999.

On HAMILTON: Books—*Pop Art* by Lucy Lippard, London 1966; *Richard Hamilton,* exhibition catalog, London 1970; *Richard Hamilton,* exhibition catalog, New York, 1973; *Richard Hamilton: Studies 1937–1977,* exhibition catalog, Bielefeld, West Germany 1978; *Die Entwicklung der Pop Art in England,* thesis by Peter Lang, Frankfurt 1986; *Teknologi, Ide, Konstverk: Richard Hamilton,* exhibition catalog, Stockholm, 1989; *Richard Hamilton: The Beginnings of His Art* by Dawn Leach, Frankfurt am Main 1993; *The Impact of Modern Paints* by Jo Crook and Tom Learner, New York 2000. **Articles—** ''Pop Art and After,'' by Jasia Reichardt in *Art International* (Lugano, Switzerland), February 1963; ''Hamilton's Guggenheim,'' by Gene Baro in *Art and Artists* (London), November 1966; ''Popular Culture and Pop Art,'' by Lawrence Alloway in *Studio International* (London), July/August 1969; ''Father of Pop Art,'' by Edwin Mullins in the *Daily Telegraph Magazine* (London), March 1970; ''Richard Hamilton: Towards a New Definitive Statement?'' by Gor Blok in *Museumjournaal* (Amsterdam), September 1970; ''Image and History in the Art of Richard Hamilton,'' by R. Martin in *Arts Magazine* (New York), October 1985; ''The Apollo Portrait: Richard Hamilton,'' by James Hall in *Apollo* (London), February 1990; ''Hamilton, IG, Mythmaking and Photography,'' in *Creative Camera* (London), April/May 1990; ''Snatched and Dabbed: Richard Hamilton at the Tate,'' by Mark Durden in *Creative Camera* (London), October/November 1992; ''Richard Hamilton: The Father of British Pop Art'' by Jonathan Jones in *The Guardian* (London), Saturday, 20 May 2000.

*

Although some of my pre-Pop pictures may seem to the casual observer to be 'abstract,'' I believe it is true to say that I have never made a painting which does not show an intense awareness of the human figure. In the case of earlier work it was the human configuration (two eyes situated at a certain distance from two mobile feet) confronting the picture that determined its composition.

Assumptions about the human figure were fundamental to the location of elements within the painting and the painting's relationship to the viewer was prescribed. That is to say, one justification for the picture was its value as a contribution to the total perspective of the spectator: a candid demonstration of the platitudinous concept that a work of art does not exist without its audience.

Later pictures of mine have absorbed into this external concern a recognition of the potency that representation of the human figure adds to this dialogue between image and witness. A fellow creature in the viewer's environment, either artificial (a semblance) or real, must be the strongest, most emotive factor in it; he will command attention for no other reason than his figurative identification with the ego. The force with which this *dramatis persona* can provoke displeasure is no less great than its capacity to provide companionship or to alter the construct of our lives. It, another self, real or semblance, revealed or implied, will always be a major factor in my art.

—Richard Hamilton

* * *

It should not be surprising that Richard Hamilton was already a mature artist at the time of *This Is Tomorrow,* the important exhibition held at the Whitechapel Art Gallery in London in August and September 1956, which launched him as a leading exponent of the Pop art movement it inaugurated. Hamilton's pre-Pop works included illustrations for James Joyce's *Ulysses* (1949), executed in various styles from realist to schematic, all intended as pictorial equivalents to the language of the scene from the book being interpreted; abstract drawings for paintings based on systematic notations of spirals and other linear markings (1950–51); and drawings and paintings that investigated different pictorial descriptions of movement: after the repetitive superimpositions of Muybridge, the Futurist emphasis on ''subject motion'' rendered by the devices of lines of force and centrifugal/centripetal planar structures, and the Cubist focus on ''spectator movement'' that involved the simultaneous rendering of an object or a scene from different perspectives (1952–54). His interests in such issues as the relationship of verbal and visual systems, the depiction of physical and perceptual sensations—i.e. weight and movement—found in the early art works are also developed in *Man, Machine & Motion,* the didactic exhibition he designed and organized in 1955.

In *This Is Tomorrow* the section that Hamilton designed offered sophisticated perceptual play with images borrowed from the popular culture of mass advertising. This is evident in his famous collage made specially for the exhibition, ''Just What Is It That Makes Today's Homes So Different, So Appealing?'' (1956). In it, he brought together in one interior an amalgam of images representative of popular commercial products and cosmetic fantasies—television, vacuum cleaner, pin-up girl, muscle man—and anticipated the major formal and thematic issues that would occupy the Pop art movements in Europe and America during the late 1950s and through the 1960s.

Hamilton's Pop subjects have ranged from cars and toasters to Marilyn Monroe, John F. Kennedy, and the Beatles. He has made paintings and reliefs, drawings and prints, and has used all sorts of popular, photographically based imagery as sources for his own creations. The impact, however, of his intellectual and ironical treatments depends on the right and precise rendering of the pictorial relationships involving scale, color, and elisions of forms. For example, in the painting ''Hers Is a Lush Situation'' (1958) a real automobile metamorphoses into a schematic image that not only suggest speed and power but the flashy, lustrous, and sexual qualities of the vehicle which are its main selling points. The sexual aspect is even more strongly evoked by the introduction of a woman rider. Sex is also at issue in ''She'' (1958–61), a humorous depiction of woman's intimate relationships with her kitchen appliances, and in ''Pin-Up'' (1961), a relief work that exaggerates the most popular parts of the female anatomy.

Interiors are a major theme in his works from the late 1970s and early 1980s. Using a mix of graphic techniques that mirror the high degree of sharp specificity of image that the public has come to expect from the media, Hamilton imbues the renderings of domestic, public, and pictorial interiors with sensual and emotive qualities. These aspects are evident in his paraphrases of ''Picasso's Meninas'' and Jan van Eyck's ''Arnolfini Wedding Portrait.'' In ''Putting On De Stijl'' (1979) the juxtaposition of two chairs by Gerrit Rietveld impresses as an ironic Pop statement.

Hamilton has also done actual interiors for exhibition installations. An example is the one he designed for *Rooms* (1984), the Arts Council touring exhibition. It was inspired, Hamilton said, by ''the bleak, disinterested, seedily clinical style of the establishment.'' In it, the impersonal and disquieting qualities of such spaces as a dentist's waiting room and a prison cell are chillingly captured. An installation of 1986–89, ''Swinging London,'' revisits his famous 1960s silkscreened variations on a *Daily Mail* photograph of Mick Jagger and Robert Fraser handcuffed together, building upon the theme of an authoritarian core within an outwardly permissive society.

Hamilton continued to experiment with multimedia manipulations (in this case, painting and photography) in a series of ''Self-Portraits'' made in 1990, which succeed in being both anonymous and autobiographical. The mass media remains central to both the form and content of Hamilton's work. ''War Games'' (1991–92), for example, addresses the (mis)representation of the Gulf War on television and in the newspapers.

Richard Hamilton is that rare artist who dares the audience to see and think about the perceptual and psychological implications of a forthright face-off between art and appearances, enlarging our conception of the former and encouraging us to question the latter.

—Essay by Ronny Cohen; updated by Britt Salvesen

HAMM, Gabi

Nationality: German. **Born:** Stuttgart, Germany, 3 January 1956. **Education:** Studied set design, Kunstakademie Stuttgart, 1976–77; studied painting, Staatliche Hochschule für Bildende Künste, Städelschule, Frankfurt, 1981–86. **Family:** One child. **Career:** Set designer, Schauspiel Frankfurt, 1978–80; painted murals, 1988–96; artist, 1997—. **Awards:** Ernst-Toepfer Prize, 1983; Preis der Bundeswettbewerbs ''Kunststudenten Stellen aus,'' Bonn, 1986; Reisestipendium des Hessischen Kulturstiftung, 1998. **Agents:** Galerie Hübner, Grüneburgweg Fr., 60323 Frankfurt/Main, Germany; Ausstellungsraum de Ligt, Oppenheimer Strasse 34a, 60594 Frankfurt/Main, Germany. **Address:** Vogelsbergstrasse 11, 60316 Frankfurt, Germany.

Individual Exhibitions:

1998 JG-Metall, Frankfurt (with W. Sachs; catalog)
1999 Galerie Malinowski de Ligt, Frankfurt
Galerie Hübner, Frankfurt (with M. Golla)

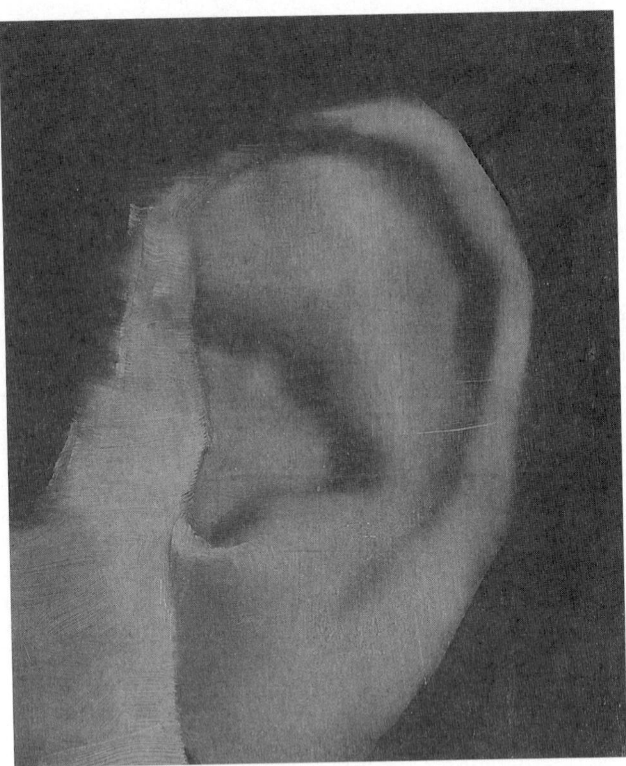

Painting by Gabi Hamm, 1998. ©Gabi Hamm.

2001 *Bilder,* Galerie Hübner, Frankfurt

Group Exhibitions:

1999 *Szenenwechsel XVI,* Museum für Moderne Kunst, Frankfurt
2000 *Gesichter,* Galerie Hübner, Berlin bei Manzini
August—die Hitze—Augustine, Ausstellungsraum de Ligt, Frankfurt
2001 *Szenenwechsel XX,* Museum für Moderne Kunst, Frankfurt
Galerie Mario Sequeira, Braga, Portugal

Collections:

Museum für Moderne Kunst, Frankfurt.

* * *

The artistic position of Gabi Hamm can be determined from her complex strategy of finding a picture. Her starting point is always an existing picture. This can be a photograph (possibly one taken by herself) or a picture from a magazine or book that she accidentally comes across. The choice is determined by a formal as well as an affective interest and both criteria have equal significance. The appeal of artistic problems and the affective reference to the selected pre-picture are the prerequisites for beginning the work. Against the background of painting tradition it is relatively easy for the observer to comprehend the formal challenges. Identifying the painter's affective interest is a much more difficult task. Gabi Hamm herself describes it as the sudden instance of attention that pre-pictures have to trigger within her. How can this be made clear? It is a common experience that specific situations take us out of our goal-oriented doings and completely turn us over to a state seeing. For short moments, a certain sight, a light reflex, or a small detail can capture us completely. Without being able to name sufficient reasons, this moment manifests itself in our minds. Through related situations, such an experience can be retrieved even after years. Often, however, it is impossible to reconstruct the past situation. What remains is a vague memory of a familiar ''mood.'' Gabi Hamm is only interested in pre-pictures that are capable of awakening such attention within her.

Starting out with such charged material, she selects a monochrome surface. The size and color of the board are carefully balanced to correspond with the as-yet-undecided picture idea. The picture emerges out of the selected primary color. It builds up from one color in variations and contrasts and, piece by piece, gains visibility. Every single step needs to be looked over to ensure its conformance with the primary color and the pre-picture. What is to be expressed in these two starting points will become visible when the artistic work has been completed. The pre-picture contains effective elements for her own work that allow the new picture to emerge. In order to make these elements visible, they need to be filtered out of the pre-picture's entirety. The painting process removes all disturbing and concealing elements until the intuitively realized parts come out clearly. Whatever has led the artist to work with the pre-picture has now been transformed and revealed. The result might best be described as an extract.

If the selection of the pre-picture is described as intuitive, then the result is an analysis with painterly means. It is necessary to point out, however, that the goal of Gabi Hamm's work is not only the analysis of the pre-picture, because that is left behind in the newly emerging picture. It is therefore not essential for the beholder to be familiar with the pre-picture. The new picture that has developed out of an artistic transformation stands for itself without pointing back to the original material. The affects that led to the selection of the pre-picture have now become a general experience for the beholder. This becomes clear when we look at the picture and encounter an exact correspondence with our own experiences.

It is essential for the picture's success that the ultimate result of its development remains unknown until it is completed. The fragile condition of a position open to whatever is to come has to be constantly prolonged in order not to become the victim of what the known and already done have to offer. This becomes all the more significant the more often the artist's working process produces and offers effective solutions. The work of Gabi Hamm is therefore accompanied by a second strategy: the strategy for the constant renewal of the process described above.

—Klaus Görner

HAMMONS, David

Nationality: American. **Born:** Springfield, Illinois, 24 July 1943. **Education:** Los Angeles Trade Technical City College, 1964–65; Chouinard Art Institute, Los Angeles, 1966–68; Otis Art Institute of the Parson's School of Design, Los Angeles, 1968–72. **Career:**

Painter, printmaker, and mixed-media artist; museum director. **Awards:** Guggenheim Memorial Foundation Award, 1983–84; National Endowment for the Arts Fellowship, 1983–84; New York State Council on the Arts Award, 1983–84; Art Matters Award, New York Foundation for the Arts, 1987; Rome Prize for Sculpture, American Academy of Rome, Italy, 1989; Tiffany grant, 1990; Brendan Gill Award, Municipal Art Society, 1991; MacArthur Foundation Fellowship, 1991; D.A.A.D. Award, Berlin 1992. **Agent:** Jack Tilton Gallery, 49 Greene Street, New York, New York 10013, U.S.A.; c/o AC Hudgins 94 Grand Ave, Englewood, New Jersey 07631, U.S.A.

Selected Individual Exhibitions:

1971 Brockman Gallery, Los Angeles
1974 Fine Arts Gallery, Los Angeles
1975 *Greasy Bags and Barbecue Bones,* Just above Midtown Gallery, New York
1976 Just above Midtown Gallery, New York
1977 Neighborhood Art Center, Atlanta, Georgia
1980 New Museum of Contemporary Art, New York
1986 Just above Midtown Gallery, New York
1989 Exit Art, New York
1990 P.S. 1 Museum, Long Island City, New York (traveling retrospective)
1991 Museum of Contemporary Art, La Jolla, California
1992 American Academy of Rome
1993 Williams College Art Center, Williamstown, Massachusetts (traveled)
Illinois State Museum, Springfield
1994 *VERAVITAGIOIA,* Milan, Italy
Sara Penn/Knobkerry, New York
1995 Salzberger Kunstverein, Austria

Selected Group Exhibitions:

1970 La Jolla Museum of Art, California
1976 *Printmaking New Forms,* Whitney Museum of American Art, New York
1985 Ronald Feldman Fine Arts, New York
1990 *The Decade Show,* Studio Museum in Harlem, New MOCA, New York
Dislocations, Museum of Modern Art, New York (catalog)
1992 Carnegie Institute, Pittsburgh, Pennsylvania
1994 Cleveland Contemporary Arts Center, Ohio
1995 *Ripple across the Water,* Watari Museum of Contemporary Art, Tokyo, Japan
1996 Tribes Gallery, New York
Art at the End of the 20th Century: Selections from the Whitney Museum of American Art (traveled)

Public Installations:

Higher Goals, Harlem, New York, 1982.

Publications:

On HAMMONS: Book—*David Hammons: Rousing the Rubble,* Cambridge, Massachusetts 1991. **Articles**—''Two Generations of Black Artists, California State College, Los Angeles; Brockman Gallery, Los Angeles; exhibits'' by J. E. Young in *Art International,* vol. 14, October 1970; ''Fine Arts Gallery, California State University, Los Angeles'' in *Art News,* vol. 73, November 1974; ''Statements Known and Statements New: Just Above Midtown Gallery, New York'' in *Arts Magazine,* vol. 51, January 1977; ''New Museum Window, New York'' in *Artforum,* vol. 19, October 1980; ''Chasing the Blue Train'' by Calvin Reid in *Art in America,* vol. 77, September 1989; ''Exit Art, New York; Installation'' by Joshua Decemberter in *Arts Magazine,* vol. 64, October 1989; ''Painting of White Jesse Jackson Attacked in D.C.'' in *New Art Examiner,* vol. 17, February 1990; ''Jesse Jackson Portrait Attacked'' by Brian Wallis in *Art in America,* vol. 78, February 1990; ''Issues and Commentary I: Are Art Museums Racist?'' by Maurice Berger in *Art in America,* vol. 78, September 1990; ''Issues and Commentary II—Speaking Out: Some Distance to Go'' by Maurice Berger in *Art in America,* vol. 78, September 1990; ''From the Avant-Garde'' by Kim Levin in *Connoisseur,* vol. 220, December 1990; ''Jack Tilton Gallery, New York'' by David Bussel in *Flash Art,* (International Edition) no. 156, January-February 1991; ''Jack Tilton Gallery; P.S. 1, Long Island City, New York'' by Frances De-Vuono in *Art News,* vol. 90, March 1991; ''Kinky Black Hair and Barbecue Bones: Street Life, Social History, and David Hammons'' by Calvin Reid in *Arts Magazine,* vol. 65, April 1991; ''Jack Tilton Gallery; P.S. 1, Long Island City, New York'' by Patricia C. Phillips in *Artforum International,* vol. 29, April 1991; ''Sculpture: A New Golden Age?'' by Steven-Henry Madoff in *Art News,* vol. 90, May 1991; ''No Place Like Home'' by Elizabeth Hess in *Artforum International,* vol. 30, October 1991; ''Man of the Street'' by Susan Wiggins in *Artweek,* vol. 22, 31 October 1991; ''San Diego Museum of Contemporary Art'' by David E. James in *New Art Examiner,* vol. 19, December 1991; ''The Art of the Topical'' by Nancy Princenthal in *Art in America,* vol. 79, December 1991; ''Dislocating the Modern'' by Holland Cotter in *Art in America,* vol. 80, January 1992; ''Documenta IX'' by Ilse Kuijken in *Kunst and Museumjournaal,* vol. 3, no. 6, 1992; ''The Documenta of the Dog'' by Peter Schjeldahl in *Art in America,* vol. 80, September 1992; ''David Hammons: Coming in from the Cold'' by Dan Cameron in *Flash Art,* (International Edition) no. 168, January-February 1993; ''Fri-Art: Centre d'Art Contemporain, Fribourg, Switzerland'' by Gabrielle Boller in *Artefactum,* vol. 11, December 1993-January 1994; ''David Hammons'' by Michel Ritter in *Du,* no. 1, January 1994; ''David Hammons'' by Laurie Palmer in *New Art Examiner,* vol. 21, February 1994; ''Williams College Museum of Art-Williamstown: David Hammons, new work'' by Leslie-Stewart Curtis in *Art New England,* vol. 15, February-March 1994; ''Public Art Woes in Williamstown'' by Leslie-Stewart Curtis in *Art in America,* vol. 82, February 1994; ''Malcolm X: The Artists' View'' by Ann-Wilson Lloyd in *Art in America,* vol. 82, May 1994; ''In the Spirit of Minkisi: The Art of David Hammons'' by Dawoud Bey in *Third Text,* no. 27, Summer 1994; ''Williams College Museum of Art, Williamstown, Mass'' by Patricia C. Phillips in *Artforum International,* vol. 33, September 1994; ''David Hammons'' by Peter Nesweda in *Kunstforum International,* no. 132, November 1995-January 1996; ''David Hammons'' by Christian Kravagna in *Artforum International,* vol. 34, January 1996; ''Make It Funky'' by Manthia Diawara in *Artforum International,* vol. 36, no. 9, May 1998; ''In the Thick of It: David Hammons and Hair Culture in the 1970s'' by Kellie Jones in *Third Text,* no. 44, Autumn 1998; ''American Costume, 1970'' by Raymond Hernandez-Duran in *Museum Studies,* vol. 25, no. 1, 1999.

* * *

What do snowballs, telephone poles, human hair, and jazz have in common? These disparate things have all appeared once or repeatedly in the sculpture and installations of the African-American artist David Hammons. Significant beyond superficial considerations of eclecticism, their presence testifies to the multi-faceted character of Hammons' overall practice. At times Hammons works solely with found objects in the tradition of the Duchampian ready-made. Take, for example, his use of the snowballs. Variously sized balls were simply laid out on the sidewalk and sold ''as is'' to interested passers-by. Nothing signaled their presence as art except Hammons designation. The snowballs are one instance of the impromptu street events Hammons carried out throughout the 1980s, and can be read as part of his general skepticism towards the market drive of the art establishment. The ephemerality of the ''objets d'ice'' versus lasting collectibles, their display on the sidewalk instead of a gallery or museum, and their sale by Hammons himself as opposed to a dealer or auction house all speak to his sporadic efforts to bypass the normative conduits to artistic success.

Since moving to New York from Los Angeles in the mid-1970s, Hammons has consciously engaged with the city at street level, particularly in the neighborhood of Harlem, thus imbuing his art with a strong sense of the local. Avoiding art supply stores, in part to save money and in part to make what he calls ''aesthetically correct'' art, Hammons scours thoroughfares and alleys drawing inspiration from the people, issues, and detritus he encounters there. Hammons' forte is his ability to reconfigure and amalgamate these found elements into a new visual lexicon. It is a language that bears a political and poetic force due to the priority Hammons gives to his role as an African-American artist, and his concern to illuminate issues of racial identity. Hammons usually collects individual items that resonate with particular fragments of African-American culture, and then pushes the associations further through calculated juxtaposition. The combinative aim being to enable black viewers to perceive a sense of themselves in the final work of art. Confronting racial stereotypes with an incisive wit that oscillates from playful to biting, Hammons produces works that disrupt the stereotypes' detrimental ability to simultaneously fix identities that in reality are more fluid and reduce issues that are in actuality more complex.

Part of this critical strategy is Hammons' penchant for word play. In the piece ''Higher Goals,'' originally installed in 1983 at 125th street in Harlem, Hammons used telephone poles to construct impossibly high basketball hoops. The poles sparkled with patterns of beer bottle caps. The work seems simultaneously to acknowledge the genuine allure of the game while suggesting that it may eclipse other ambitions in the minds of black children who dream of superstar status.

Perhaps the most tangible way that Hammons attempts to visualize black identity is through the use of hair. Culled from the floors of black barbershops, the hair is then delicately dispersed through Hammons' assemblages. ''Lady With Bones'' (1983) includes black hair as well as greasy barbecue bones and broken bits of jazz records, all things that have functioned variously in stereotypes about African-Americans. Through Hammons' re-contextualization, however, prejudicial symbolism can be considered in an alternate light. The provocative title, ''Lady With Bones,'' intertwines with the found objects to create the possibility for surfacing different historical narratives and meanings.

The figure that has perhaps most captivated Hammons' imagination is that of the jazzman. This is evident in his artwork as well as the role of the artist he constructs for himself—-simultaneously improvisational composer extraordinaire and man-about-town hipster. One of Hammons' most well-known works is an untitled mixed-medium installation that first appeared in a solo exhibition at the gallery Exit Art in 1989 and was redisplayed along with the work of other artists in Exit Art's 2000 retrospective of its eighteen-year existence. The main components of the installation were a toy train painted deep blue, recorded music, and the upended lids of baby grand pianos. As the train journeyed the makeshift track Hammons laid throughout the gallery, audio speakers played the music of John Coltrane, Thelonius Monk, and James Brown. The tiny blue train became a visual pun on Coltrane's album *Blue 'Trane* and Browns' song ''Night Train'' while metaphorically recalling the significance of the train in African-American history.

While all of Hammons' art can be said to have a political charge, some works are more electric than others. In 1990 he produced ''Cold Shoulders,'' an installation piece that addresses the social problem of homelessness. Returning to the ephemerality of frozen water, Hammons placed large blocks of ice inside a gallery space, draping winter coats over them as if over human shoulders. Evoking the precariousness of life on the streets, Hammons ensured that well before the close of the exhibition all that would remain were pools of water and disembodied crumples of wet fabric. At the close of 1991, Hammons had his most high-profile showing within Manhattan's art establishment. He was invited to be a part of the Museum of Modern Art's exhibition of installation art called ''Dislocations''. Not missing a beat, he used the opportunity to make a vociferous statement against racism in the United States. His contribution, ''Public Enemy,'' displayed life-size photographs of the statue of Theodore Roosevelt heroically astride a horse while a Native-American man and an African American man walk in servitude on either side. The photographs presented various perspectives of the statue and were illuminated to re-create the effect of sculpture-in-the-round. A barricade of sandbags, complete with toy and real guns poised atop and aimed inward, surrounded the monument. The real statue of Roosevelt, object of Hammons' appropriation, is a fixture outside of New York's Museum of Natural History, the significance of which is not likely contemplated by those who walk by or enter the institution. By bringing its facsimile into the Museum of Modern Art, historically a bastion of white, male, European culture, and making it the target of potential violence, Hammons uses art to engage the issue of white supremacy in both its historical and contemporary manifestations.

Over the course of the 1990s, Hammons attained the recognition in the established art world that he never expressly coveted. He did this while managing to keep his artistic sights focused on his related goals of visualizing issues of racial identity in general and creating positive images of black identity for black viewers in particular. Taken at face value these goals might seem easily understood. However, an important, yet often neglected, issue to keep in mind is the underlying assumption that we have unmediated access to what an ''authentic collective black identity'' is, and what ''positive images'' are. Within and across races, identity must always also be understood to intersect with issues of class, gender and sexuality. Hammons' artwork does not provide easy answers to these difficult problems of social identity, and at times become deeply embroiled in the debates. That the issues are woven into the very texture of his sculptures and installations, however, ensures that provocative questions are raised for the viewer's further pursuit.

—Mari Dumett

HANSON, Duane

Nationality: American. **Born:** Alexandria, Minnesota, 17 January 1925. **Education:** Parkers High School, Parkers Prairie, Minnesota 1943–44; Luther College, Decorah, Iowa, 1943–44, DFA, 1992; University of Washington, Seattle, 1944–45; Macalester College, St. Paul, Minnesota, 1945–46, B.A. 1946; Cranbrook Academy of Art, Bloomfield Hills, Michigan, 1950–51, B.F.A. 1951; Nova University, DHL, 1979, LHD, 1985. **Family:** Married Janice Roche in 1950; children Craig Curtis, Paul Duane, Karen Liane; married Welsa Host in 1968; children: Maja and Duane Jr. **Career:** Art Instructor, Twin Falls High School, Idaho, 1946–47; worked as a travelling salesman for Webb Publishing Company, St. Paul, serving western Minnesota and eastern South Dakota, 1949; Art Instructor, Decorah High School, Iowa, 1949–50; United States Army High School, Munich, 1953–57; United States Army High School, Bremerhaven, West Germany, 1957–60; United States Army High School, Atlanta, 1960–62; Oglethorpe University, Atlanta, 1962–65; Miami-Dade Junior College, Florida, 1965–69; Part-time Art Instructor, New York University, 1971–72. Full-time artist, since 1969; has lived and worked in Davie, Florida, since 1974. **Awards:** Grant for Sculpture, Ella Lyman Cabot Trust, 1963; Sculpture Award, *Florida State Fair Arts Exhibition,* 1968; Blair Award, Art Institute of Chicago, 1974; D.A.A.D. grant to work in Berlin, 1974; Moetti Award, Fort Lauderdale, Florida, 1984; *New York Times* Florida Artist Award, 1985. DHL: Nova University, Fort Lauderdale, Florida, 1979. **Agent:** Marisa del Rey Gallery, 41 E 5th St., New York, New York 10022. **Died:** Boca Raton, Florida, 6 January 1996, of lymphoma.

Duane Hanson, *Tourists,* 1970. Photo by Eric Pollitzer, courtesy of Mrs. Duane Hanson. ©Estate of Duane Hanson/Licensed by VAGA, New York, NY.

Individual Exhibitions:

1951 Museum of Art, Cranbrook Academy, Bloomfield Hills, Michigan
1952 Wilton Gallery, Wilton, Connecticut
1958 Galerie Netzel, Bremen, West Germany
1970 O.K. Harris Gallery, New York
1972 O.K. Harris Gallery, New York
Galerie Onnasch, Cologne
1974 Museum of Contemporary Art, Chicago
O.K. Harris Gallery, New York
Galerie de Gestlo, Hamburg
Württembergischer Kunstverein, Stuttgart (retrospective)
Neue Galerie, Aachen
1975 Louisiana Museum, Humlebaek, Denmark
Akademie der Kunste, Berlin
1976 O.K. Harris Gallery, New York
Edwin A. Ulrich Museum of Art, Wichita State University, Kansas
Sheldon Art Gallery, University of Nebraska, Lincoln
1977 Des Moines Art Center, Iowa
University of California Art Museum, Berkeley
Portland Art Museum, Oregon
William Rockhill Nelson and Atkins Museum of Fine Arts, Kansas City, Missouri
Colorado Springs Fine Arts Center
Virginia Museum of Fine Arts, Richmond
Corcoran Gallery, Washington, D.C.
1978 Whitney Museum, New York
1980 O.K. Harris Gallery, New York
Jacksonville Art Museum, Florida
1981 Lowe Art Museum, University of Miami
Norton Art Gallery, Palm Beach, Florida
Loch Haven Art Museum, Orlando, Florida
Jacksonville Art Museum, Florida (travelled to Coral Gables, Florida; Orlando, Florida; West Palm Beach, Florida)
1984 O.K. Harris Gallery, New York
Wichita State University, Kansas (travelled to Tokyo, Osaka and Nagoya, Japan)
1985 Cranbrook Academy of Art, Bloomfield Hills, Michigan
1986 Carl Milles Gärden, Lindingö, Sweden
1988 Auckland Art Gallery, 1988
1989 City Art Gallery, Wellington, New Zealand
McDougall Art Gallery, Christchurch, New Zealand
Dunedin Public Art Gallery, New Zealand
Waikato Museum of Art and History, Hamilton, New Zealand
World Design Exposition, Nagoya, Japan
Ft. Lauderdale Museum of Art, Florida
Tampa Museum of Art, Florida
Center for the Arts, Vero Beach, Florida
The Contemporary Museum, Honolulu, Hawaii
1990 Cranbrook Academy of Arts Museum, Bloomfield Hills, Michigan
Philbrook Art Center, Tulsa, Oklahoma

Pennsylvania Academy of Fine Arts, Philadelphia
Brown University Art Museum, Providence, Rhode Island
Kunsthalle, Tubingen, Germany
1991 Joseph Haubrich, Kunsthalle, Cologne, Germany
Kunstverein, Hamburg
Haus am Waldsee, Berlin
1992 Neue Gallery Wolfgang Gurlic Museum, Linz, Austria
Kunsthausverein, Vienna
1994 Montreal Museum of Fine Arts
Fort Worth Art Museum, Texas
1997 Saatchi Gallery, London
1998 Bienes Center Library, Ft. Lauderdale, Florida
Duane Hanson, A Survey of His Work from the '30s to the '90s, Museum of Art, Ft. Lauderdale, Florida
Flint Instiitute of Arts, Flint, Michigan
Duane Hanson: A Master Returns, Oglethorpe University Museum, Atlanta, Georgia
1998–99 Whitney Museum of American Art, New York
Duane Hanson, Ballroom, Royal Festival Hall, London
1999 Memphis Brooks Museum of Art, Mempis, Tennessee
2000 Palm Springs Desert Museum, California
2001 San Jose Museum, California
Nevada Museum of Art, Reno
Portland Art Museum, Oregon
2001–02 Schirn Kunsthalle, Frankfurt, Germany
2002 Galerie der Stadt, Stuttgart, Germany
Padiglione d'Arte Contemporanea, Milan
Kunsthal Rotterdam, Netherlands
2002–03 Ludwig Gallery, Schloss Oberhausen, Germany
2003 UNESCO World Cultural Heritage, European Centre for the Arts and Culture, Volkingen, Germany

Selected Group Exhibitions:

1968 *Human Concern/Personal Torment,* Whitney Museum, New York
1970 *Sculpture Annual,* Whitney Museum, New York (and 1973, 1978)
1972 *Documenta,* Kassel, West Germany
1974 *7 Realists,* Yale University Art Gallery, New Haven Connecticut
1975 *Super Realism,* Baltimore Museum of Art
1979 *Reality of Illusion,* Denver Art Museum, Colorado (toured the United States)
1981 *Contemporary American Realism Since 1960,* Pennsylvania Academy of Fine Arts, Philadelphia (toured the United States)
1983 *Contemporary Trompe l'Oeil Painting and Sculpture,* Boise Gallery of Art, Idaho (toured the United States)
1985 *Pop Art 1955–70,* Art Gallery of New South Wales,Sydney (toured Australia)
1987 *Independence Sites,* Independence Mall, Philadelphia
1996 *The Human Body in Contemporary American Sculpture,* Gagosian Gallery, New York
1998 *Selections from Fred R. Weisman Collection,* Pepperdine University
1999 *The American Century: Art and Culture 1900–2000,* Whitney Museum of American Art, New York
2000 *Cast of Characters Figurative Sculpture,* Albuquerque Museum, New Mexico
2000–01 *Let's Entertain,* Walker Art Center, Minneapolis, Minnesota (travelled to Portland Art Museum, Oregon; Centre Georges Pompidou, Paris; Museo Rufino Tamayo, Mexico City; Miami Art Museum, Florida)
A Century of the American Dream: The Sparkle of the ''American Way'' of Life, Aichi Prefectural Museum of Art, Nagoya, Japan (travelled to Hyogo Prefectural Museum of Modern Art, Kobe, Japan)
2001 *Hounds in Leash,* Albuquerque Museum, New Mexico

Collections:

Whitney Museum, New York; Wadsworth Atheneum, Hartford, Connecticut; Richmond Museum, Virginia; Milwaukee Art Museum; William Rockhill Nelson Art Gallery and Atkins Museum of Fine Arts, Kansas City, Missouri; Neue Galerie, Aachen; Wallraf-Richartz Museum, Cologne; Wilhelm Lehmbruck Museum, Duisburg; National Museum, Utrecht; Museum of South Australia, Adelaide; Stiftung Haus der Geschicte, Bonn; Orlando Airport, Florida; Ft. Lauderdale Airport, Florida; Hiroshima City Museum of Contemporary Art, Japan.

Publications:

By HANSON: Articles—''Presenting Duane Hanson'' in *Art in America* (New York), September/October 1970; ''Martin Bush Interviews Duane Hanson'' in *Art International* (Lugano, Switzerland), September 1977; ''Duane Hanson Confounded by Ivan Karp'' in *Interview* (New York), March 1978.

On HANSON: Books—*Radikaler Realismus* by Udo Kultermann, Tübingen, West Germany 1972; *Duane Hanson,* exhibition catalog, Cologne 1972; *The New Realism* by Udo Kultermann, New York 1972; *The Pop Image of Man* by Sam Hunter, New York 1972; *Neue Formen Des Realismus* by Peter Sager, Cologne 1973; *Duane Hanson* by Tilman Osterwold, Stuttgart 1974; *The New Humanism* by Barry Schwartz, New York and Washington, D.C. 1974; *American Art since 1900* by Barbara Rose, New York and Washington, D.C. 1975; *Duane Hanson,* exhibition catalog, by Martin Bush, Wichita, Kansas 1976; *Duane Hanson* by Kirk Varnedoe, New York 1985; *Duane Hanson* by Karl Ruhrberg, Stuttgart 1992; *Duane Hanson* by Marco Livingstone, Montreal 1994; *Armuts Zeugnisse,* exhibition catalog, Ostwall 1995; *Homeland of the Imagination,* exhibition catalog, Atlanta, Georgia 1996; *Scene of the Crime,* exhibition catalog, Los Angeles, California 1996; *Duane Hanson,* exhibition catalog, London 1997; *Duane Hanson: A Survey of His Work from the '30s to the '90s,* exhibition catalog, Fort Lauderdale, Florida 1998; *Let's Entertain: Life's Guilty Pleasures,* exhibition catalog, Minneapolis, Minnesota 2000; *Duane Hanson: Virtual Reality,* exhibition catalog, Palm Springs, California 2000; *Cast of Characters: Figurative Sculptures,* exhibition catalog, Albuquerque, New Mexico 2000; *Mennesket,* exhibition catalog, Copenhagen 2000.

*

In my sculpture, I attempt to detach myself from subject. Although my earlier works were rather expressionistic with outbursts against war, crime, and violence in general, I now find my most successful pieces are less topical and ideographic. They are naturalistic or illusionistic which results in an element of shock, surprise or psychological impact for the viewer. The subject matter that I like best deals with the familiar lower and middle class American types of today. To me, the resignation, emptiness and loneliness of their existence captures the true reality of life for these people. Consequently, as a realist I'm interested in the human form and especially faces and bodies which have suffered like some weather worn landscape the erosion of time. In portraying this aspect of life I want to achieve a certain tough realism which speaks of the fascinating idiosyncracies of our time.

Ultimately, making a successful sculpture is my major task, which involves manipulating forms to make them look convincing, I want my sculptures to convey a certain sense of stylelessness which will capture the contemporary feeling of reality.

The best way to get ahead is to make one!

—Duane Hanson

* * *

Duane Hanson has been making life-size, super-real, polyester, sculpted people since 1967 after he had decided to turn back (at 40-plus years old) on his previous abstract work which had always dissatisfied him anyway.

Hanson's earliest works in the realist mode were tableaux of topical situations loaded with issues of the social significance of violence. Groupings such as ''War,'' ''Race Riot'' and ''Gangland Victim'' capture a frozen moment of tense emotional/physical brutality and are more concerned with depicting the horror and waste within our contemporary society than with illusionism as such. Around 1970, with works such as ''Supermarket Shopper'' and ''Woman Eating,'' waste is seen on another plane, that of the ordinary classes of Americans who, steeped in overabundance, become careless in habits and appearances, lumpy, sloppy and filling themselves with junk to excess. Perhaps his most sardonically sarcastic work from this period is ''Tourists'' (1970) in which a 5-foot 2-inch little elderly man and his 5-foot-4-inch out-of-shape wife look up in the typical stance of the tourist who, from the look of their outfits of plaid and Hawaiian pattern and their carry-along equipment including camera and accessories and bag-full of stuff, can only be in Miami from New York, as most any American will easily notice. A more soulfully humane attitude appears in Hanson's work from these and following years, beginning with his marvelously expressive ''Hardhat'' (1970) who is seated in a more introspective mood in his well-used workclothes and hat flashing the American flag proudly. He is weary, resting from a hard day's work with beer can in hand, evoking a far more sympathetic response than Hanson's tourist types. Perhaps it is the relationship with the artist/worker which evoked such empathy from Hanson, a factor reinforced by his ''Seated Artist'' (1971) and ''Artist with Ladder'' (1972). Works since the early 70's tend to pare down on the accessories and build up the more contemplative approach as reaction to the regular, next door types closer to home and heart.

Although it is this human, communicative quality somewhere between alienation and repose which Hanson stresses, there is no escape from the element of deception which pops up on first view of his people who, life cast and dressed in real clothes, appear very near flesh-and-blood real. The illusionism of these works is carried as far as is seemingly possible with the aid of the newest plastic materials (fiberglass reinforced polyester resin), which are skillfully manipulated for the most intricate details from body hairs to boils to wrinkles and bulges. Such verisimilitude as this is strikingly effective at conveying tense feelings of ambiguity about the realness of artificiality and the artificiality of reality in our everyday world of small businessmen on vacation, repairmen, housewives, and even artists.

Could Hanson's art be somehow ''radical'' in the avant garde intellectualism which has been his context? This is entirely possible, especially if you consider the wide communicative effectiveness in evidence on observing the interactions between his people and the real folks who confront them in their gallery or museum settings with a mixture of amazement and disbelief that is both disarmingly humorous and a bit frightening to behold.

—Barbara Cavaliere

* * *

This eerie verisimilitude was broken in the early 1990s when Hanson switched from polyvinyl to painted bronze. The oddly life-in-death impression which his figures had projected—the seemingly alive yet not breathing person—now seems contradicted by the use of the new medium. The dull, dense underlayer of the metal contrasts in a surreal manner with the lifelike bloom of the painted flesh. The artist allows the shock of recognition: the ''person'' is replica. In life there is blood and breath. We are offered a newly vivid sense of life.

We are offered, also, in extension of the contemplative attitude presented in *Hardhat,* more quietly reflective pieces. As in Camus's essays about the courage of the ordinary working man in Algeria who sits in cafes and drinks his drink and knows that he will get on with things, so increasingly Hanson's ordinary people, typecast in their roles as tourist, cowboy, and security guard, look within themselves, accept their confinements, and go on.

—Barbara Cortright

HARE, David

Nationality: American. **Born:** New York City, 10 March 1917. **Education:** Attended schools in New York, Colorado, and California, studying in biology and chemistry, 1923–39. **Career:** Full-time artist since 1940. Collaborated with Dr. Clark Whistler of Museum of Natural History on portfolio of color photographs on the American Indian, 1940; editor, *VVV* surrealist magazine, in collaboration with Marcel Duchamp, André Breton, and Max Ernst, 1942–44; edited issue of *Temps Moderne* devoted to American writers, 1950. Artist-in-residence, Delgado Museum, New Orleans, 1964; visiting sculptor-instructor, Philadelphia College of Art, 1964–65; visiting artist, University of Oregon, Eugene, 1966; resident in Lithography, Tamarind Institute, University of New Mexico, Albuquerque, 1972. Honorary doctorate: Maryland Institute of Art, 1969. **Died:** Jackson Hole, Wyoming, 21 December 1992.

Individual Exhibitions:

1941 E. Weyhe Gallery, New York
1944 Peggy Guggenheim Gallery, New York
1946 Julien Levy Gallery, New York
Peggy Guggenheim Gallery, New York

Kootz Gallery, New York
1947 San Francisco Museum of Art
1948 Maeght Gallery, Paris
1949 Kootz Gallery, New York
Julien Levy Gallery, New York
1952 Kootz Gallery, New York
1955 Kootz Gallery, New York
1956 Kootz Gallery, New York
1958 Kootz Gallery, New York
1959 Kootz Gallery, New York
1960 Saidenberg Gallery, New York
Staempfli Gallery, New York
1961 Saidenberg Gallery, New York
1962 Saidenberg Gallery, New York
1963 Saidenberg Gallery, New York
1965 Philadelphia Museum College of Art
Delgado Museum of Art, New Orleans
1969 Staempfli Gallery, New York
Portland Museum of Art, Maine (retrospective)
1974 Watson/de Nagy Gallery, Houston
1976 *The Cronus Series,* Alessandra Gallery, New York
1977 *The Cronus Series,* Guggenheim Museum, New York
1978 *Landscapes,* Hamilton Gallery, New York
Major Works, Zolla Lieberman Gallery, Chicago
1979 *Drawings* Hamilton Gallery, New York
1980 *Elephants and Flying Heads,* Hamilton Gallery, New York
1981 Contemporary Arts Museum, Houston
1982 Museum of Fine Arts, Houston

Selected Group Exhibitions:

1946 *14 Americans,* Museum of Modern Art, New York
1951 *Bienal,* Sao Paulo
1954 *The New Decade,* Whitney Museum, New York
1956 *International Exhibition of Contemporary Sculpture,* Musée Rodin, Paris
1958 *World's Fair Exhibition,* Brussels
1962 *Contemporary Sculpture and Drawings,* Whitney Museum, New York
1968 *Dada, Surrealism and their Heritage,* Museum of Modern Art, New York
1969 *New American Painting and Sculpture: The First Generation,* Museum of Modern Art, New York
1976 *200 Years of American Sculpture,* Whitney Museum, New York
1978 *American Painting of the 1970's,* Albright-Knox Art Gallery, Buffalo, New York (travelled to 5 other museums)

Collections:

Metropolitan Museum, New York; Museum of Modern Art, New York; Guggenheim Museum, New York; Whitney Museum, New York; Wadsworth Atheneum, Hartford, Connecticut; Yale University Art Gallery, New Haven, Connecticut; Albright-Knox Art Gallery, Buffalo, New York; Museum of Art, Carnegie Institute, Pittsburgh; Washington University Gallery of Art, St. Louis; San Francisco Museum of Modern Art.

Publications:

By HARE: Articles—statement in *14 Americans,* exhibition catalog, New York 1946; ''The Work of the Artist'' in *Trojan Horse* (Ithaca, New York), December 1961; ''The Myth of Originality in Contemporary Art'' in *Art Journal* (New York), Winter 1964/65; ''On Robert Goldwater'' in *Art Journal* (New York), Fall 1973.

On HARE: Books—*14 Americans,* exhibition catalog, New York 1946; *Sculpture of the 20th Century,* exhibition catalog, New York 1952; *Dada, Surrealism and Their Heritage,* exhibition catalog, New York 1968; *The Artist Observed: 28 Interviews with Contemporary Artists* by John Gruen, Chicago, 1991. **Articles—**''L'Exceptionnel David Hare'' by Alain Jouffroy in *Opus International* (Paris), December 1971; ''Philosopher or Dog?'' by Dore Ashton in *Arts Magazine* (New York), May 1976; ''David Hare: A Painter of the Human Psyche'' in the *New York Times,* 30 September 1977; ''David Hare: American Surrealist'' by Katharine Kuh in *Saturday Review* (New York), 1 October 1977; ''An American Surrealist'' by Harold Rosenberg in *The New Yorker,* 24 October 1977; ''David Hare's Cronus Series'' by Deborah Perlberg in *Artforum* (New York), December 1977; ''David Hare: A Magician's Game in Context'' by Mona Hadler in *Art Journal* (New York), vol. 47, Fall 1988; ''Less Than Perfect: London Apartment'' by Mirabel Cecil in *World of Interiors,* vol. 18, no. 3, March 1998.

* * *

Photographer, editor (of surrealist Magazine *VVV* in the 1940s), painter, and sculptor, Hare is probably best known for surrealist-inclined, welded steel sculpture of the 1950's and for a prolonged series of works in several media based on the myth of Cronus which he did in the 1960's. Hare occupies an unusual position among American sculptors, for although many artists were influenced to some degree by the post war presence of Max Ernst, André Breton, and Marcel Duchamp, only Hare, and in a different direction Joseph Cornell, display a fully surrealist sensibility. As a sculptor Hare has experimented with many materials but prefers welded steel because the metal is flexible and easy to manipulate. The metal also gives the impression of strength, even when stretched out into the lace-fine webs which characterize his work. The attempt to render the workings of the subconscious in welded steel is clearly a hazardous undertaking, one which may be better suited to painting or tiny box assemblages, but Hare plunges right in, often starting directly with the metal, and by employing the constructivists convention of interior space, conveys a sense of ethereal figure, open mind, watcher and watched, and form in nature.

Following the period of surrealist sculpture, Hare immersed himself in one of the central concerns of abstract expressionism without ever assimilating the style. In the ''Cronus'' series, Hare has used the myth of the Titan who devours all his children (except one, Zeus, who escapes and murders his father) in an effort to maintain his power over the world. In its entirety, the tale of Cronus is a tale of creation and of the emergence of gods and man from the primordial ooze, a primary question of existence which inspired many abstract expressionists to refer to myths, totems, and rituals. Like the surrealists, Hare finds ideas through free associations, and like Picasso he carefully constructs composite images, always retaining a clearly defined sense of natural form.

It is not the intention of David Hare to create work with obscure, inaccessible meanings. A self-taught artist, Hare is also an articulate philosopher and theorist of art. His images often come from personal associations but unlike many surrealists and abstract expressionists he creates visual translations available to the careful viewer. ''In 'the water where the artist swims,' the spectator shall at least wade, and so be made to shiver with some of the 'chills and fever which stimulate the imagination.'''

—Mary Stofflet

HARRISON, Helen (Mayer)

Nationality: American. **Born**: New York City, 1 July 1929. **Education:** Studied psychology at Cornell University, Ithaca, New York; Queens College, Flushing, New York, B.A. in English Literature 1948; New York University, M.A. in philosophy of education 1953; did graduate and doctoral studies in philosophy of education at New York University, in psychology and human behavior at United States International University, San Diego, and in anthropology, literature and psychology at New School for Social Research in New York, University of Pennsylvania in Philadelphia, and at University of New Mexico in Albuquerque. **Family:** Married Newton Harrison, in 1953; children: Steven, Joshua, Gabriel and Joy. **Career:** Independent artist since 1972: now lives and works in California. **Awards:** DAAD Grant, to work in West Berlin, 1988. **Agents:** Ronald Feldman Fine Arts Inc., 31 Mercer Street, New York, New York 10013; The Wenger Gallery, 828 N. La Brea Avenue, Los Angeles, California 90038. **Address:** P.O. Box 446, Del Mar, California 92014, U.S.A.

Individual Exhibitions:

1974 Grandview Gallery, Los Angeles
Ronald Feldman Fine Arts, New York (with Newton Harrison)
1975 Ronald Feldman Fine Arts, New York (with Newton Harrison)
1976 Detroit Institute of Fine Arts, New York (with Newton Harrison)
1977 San Francisco Art Institute (with Newton Harrison)
San Francisco Museum of Modern Art (with Newton Harrison)
Floating Museum, San Francisco (with Newton Harrison)
1978 Portland Center for the Visual Arts, Oregon (with Newton Harrison)
Claremont Graduate School, California (with Newton Harrison)
Ronald Feldman Fine Arts, New York (with Newton Harrison)
1979 University of Idaho, Moscow (with Newton Harrison)
Williams College Museum of Art, Massachusetts (with Newton Harrison)
Brown University, Providence, Rhode Island (with Newton Harrison)
1980 Ronald Feldman Fine Arts, New York (with Newton Harrison)
Museum of Contemporary Art, Chicago (with Newton Harrison)
1981 Maryland Institute College of Art, Baltimore (with Newton Harrison)
1982 Washington Project for the Arts, Washington, D.C. (with Newton Harrison)
Ronald Feldman Fine Arts, New York (with Newton Harrison)
1983 Emory University, Atlanta, Georgia (with Newton Harrison)
San Jose Museum of Art, California (with Newton Harrison)
San Jose State University, California (with Newton Harrison)
Wenger Gallery, San Diego, California (with Newton Harrison)
1985 California Institute of Technology, Pasadena (with Newton Harrison)
University of California, Irvine (with Newton Harrison)
Cornell University, Ithaca, New York (with Newton Harrison)
Tortue Gallery, Santa Monica, California (with Newton Harrison)
Ronald Feldman Fine Arts, New York (with Newton Harrison)
Wenger Gallery, San Diego, California (with Newton Harrison)
1986 Palomar College, California (with Newton Harrison)
Culman Gouro, Los Angeles (with Newton Harrison
1987 Grey Gallery, New York University (with Newton Harrison)
Pasadena College of Art and Design, California (with Newton Harrison)
Los Angeles County Museum of Art (with Newton Harrison)
Wenger Gallery, San Diego, California (with Newton Harrison)
1988 Tel Aviv Museum, Israel
1990 Moderna Galerija, Ljubljana, Yugoslavia (with Newton Harrison)
1991 Ronald Feldman Fine Arts, New York
1993 *Helen Mayer Harrison and Newton Harrison: Recent Environmental Projects,* International Design Conference, Aspen (with Newton Harrison)
1996 *future Garden-Part 1,* Kunst-und Ausstellungshalle der Bundesrepublik Deutschland, Bonn (catalog) (with Newton Harrison)
1997 *Green Heart Vision,* Kunstmuseum Bonn, Bonn (catalog) (with Newton Harrison)

Reading/Performances and Events: Solo—*Portable Fish Feast: Survival Piece 3,* Hayward Gallery, London 1971; *Giveaway,* La Jolla Museum of Contemporary Art, California, 1971; *Catfish Feast,* Atelier Chapman Kelley, Dallas, 1972; *Citrus Feast,* California State University at Fullerton, 1972; *Fish Feast,* Palais des Beaux Arts, Brussels, 1972; *Making Strawberry Jam,* California State University at Fullerton, 1973, and at Grandview Gallery Women's Building, Los Angeles, 1974; *Visual Distortion: With My Glasses/ Without My Glasses,* Grandview Gallery, Women's Building, Los Angeles, 1975; *From the Lagoon Cycle* (and lecture), Center for Music Experimentation, University of California at San Diego, La Jolla, 1978; with Newton Harrison—*From the Centers of the World,* P.S. 1, New York,

1976; *From the Meditations,* Center for Music Experiment, University of California at San Diego, La Jolla, 1977; *From the Meditations* (and lecture), Center for 20th Century Studies, University of Wisconsin, Milwaukee, also San Francisco Art Institute, and United Artists Coalition of San Diego, 1977; *On the Lagoon Cycle,* Museum of Contemporary Art, Chicago, 1977; also Claremont Graduate School, California, 1978; *Street Graffiti,* San Francisco Art Institute, also streets of San Francisco, 1977; *San Diego as the Center of the World,* University of Wisconsin, Milwaukee, 1977; *From the Great Lakes Meditations* (and lecture), Center for 20th Century Studies, University of Wisconsin, Milwaukee, 1978; *From the Lagoon Cycle* and *From the Meditations,* Portland Center for Visual Arts, Oregon, and University of California at San Diego, La Jolla, 1978; *Readings,* Franklin Furnace, New York, 1979; *The Watershed Series,* Franklin Furnace, New York, 1979; *Talking Water, Ronald Feldman Fine Arts, New York, 1980; Reading and Rapping,* 424 F. Street, San Diego, 1980; *Baltimore Promenade,* Washington Project for the Arts, Washignton, D.C., 1982; *Fortress Atlanta,* Emory University, Atlanta, 1983; *San Jose,* San Jose Museum of Art, California, 1983; *The Urban Pieces,* San Jose State University, California, 1983; D.A.A.D. Gallery, Berlin, 1989; *Biodiversity and Landscapers: Human Challenges for Conservation in the Changing World,* Center for BioDiversity Research and Environmental Resources Institute, Penn State University, 1990; *TRILOGY-Art-Nature-Science,* Kunsthallen Brandts Klaedefabrik, Odense, Denmark, 1996.

Selected Group Exhibitions:

1972 *Vesuvio,* Henry Gallery, University of Wisconsin, Seattle
1973 *In a Bottle: Strawberry Jam,* California State University at Fullerton
1975 *A Response to the Environment,* Rutgers University, New Brunswick, New Jersey
1976 *Art in Landscape,* University of Montana, Missoula
1977 *A View of a Decade,* Museum of Contemporary Art, Chicago
1978 *Artists Investigate the Environment,* Barnsdall Park Municipal Gallery, Los Angeles
1980 *Drawing: The Pluralist Decade,* at the *Biennale,* Venice
1982 *Common Ground: Five Artists in the Florida Landscape,* Ringling Museum, Sarasota, Florida
1984 *Disarming Images,* Contemporary Arts Center, Cincinnati, Ohio
1987 *Documenta 8,* Museum Fridericianum, Kassel, West Germany
1990 *Terra Incognito,* Rhode Island School of Design Museum of Art, Providence (catalog)
Revered Earth, Contemporary Arts Museum, Houston (catalog)
1996 *Withdrawing,* Ronald Feldman Fine Arts, New York
1999 *As Far As the Eye Can See,* Atlanta (catalog)

Collections:

Brooklyn Museum, New York: Museum of Contemporary Art, Chicago; La Jolla Museum of Contemporary Art, California; Power Gallery of Contemporary Art, Sydney; Los Angeles County Museum of Art; Museum of Modern Art, New York; Georgia Museum of Art, Athens; Tel Aviv Museum, Israel.

Publications:

By HARRISON, with Newton HARRISON: Books—*The Book of the Crab,* 1980; *The Lagoon Cycle,* exhibition catalog, Ithaca, New York 1985. **Articles—**''Sea Grant and Related Projects'' in *Studio International* (London), May 1974; ''San Diego as the Center of the World'' in *Los Angeles Institute of Contemporary Art Journal,* February 1975; ''Notes on a Recent Project'' in *Los Angeles Institute of Contemporary Art Journal,* November 1977; ''Nobody Told Us When To Stop Thinking,'' interview, in *Grey Matters* (New York), Autumn 1987; ''Trummerflora: On the Topography of Terror'' in *CMP Bulletin,* vol. 9, no. 3, 1990; ''Trummerflora on the Topography of Terrors'' in *WhiteWalls,* no. 25, Spring 1990; ''Conversational Drift: Helen Mayer Harrison and Newton Harrison'' interview, in *Art Journal* (New York), vol. 51, no. 2, Summer 1992; ''A Conversation with Helen Mayer Harrison and Newton Harrison'' with M.A. Greenstein in *Artweek,* vol. 24, no. 17, 9 September 1993; ''Future Garden: The Endangered Meadows of Europe'' in *Art & Design,* vol. 12, November/December 1997.

On HARRISON: Books—*Common Ground: Five Artists in the Florida Landscape,* exhibition catalog, Sarasota, Florida 1982; *The Art of Performance: A Critical Anthology,* edited by Gregory Battcock and Robert Nickas, New York 1984; *Newton Harrison, Helen Mayer Harrison,* exhibition catalog, Ljubljana 1990; *Future Garden,* Bonn, 1996; *Green Heart Vision,* Bonn 1997; *As Far As the Eye Can See,* Atlanta, Georgia 1999. **Articles—**''Art and Technology'' by Maurice Tuchman in *Art in America* (New York), March/April 1970; ''Corporate Art'' by Jack Burham in *Artforum* (New York), October 1971; ''Off Shellfish Farms and Other Works of Art'' by David Bourdon in the *Village Voice* (New York), 16 December 1974; review by Paul Stinson in *Art in America* (New York), March/April 1976; ''Newton and Helen Harrison: Art as Ecology'' in *Artweek* (Oakland, California), 5 February 1977; ''Helen and Newton Harrison: New Grounds for Art'' by Kim Levin in *Arts Magazine* (New York), February 1978; ''The Earth as Their Palette'' by Grace Glueck in the *New York Times,* 4 April 1980; ''Helen Mayer Harrison and Newton Harrison'' by Ann Schoenfeld in *Arts Magazine* (New York), June 1980; ''Helen Mayer Harrison and Newton Harrison'' by Stephen Eiseman in *Arts* (New York), February 1983; ''Helen and Newton Harrison's Book of the Seven Lagoons'' by Kim Levin in *Village Voice* (New York), 16 December 1986; ''Improvising the Future: The Eco-aesthetics of Newton and Helen Harrison'' by Linda F. McGreevy in *Arts Magazine,* vol. 62, November 1987; ''Dynamic Duos: Artists Are Teaming Up In Growing Numbers'' by Glenn Zorpette in *ARTnews,* vol. 93, Summer 1994; ''Policing Paradise, Or Et In California Ego'' by Rebecca Solnit in *Art Issues,* no. 55, November-December 1998.

HARRISON, Newton

Nationality: American. **Born:** Brooklyn, New York, 20 October 1932. **Education:** Apprentice to sculptor Michael Lantz, New York, 1947–50; studied at Antioch College, Yellow Springs, Ohio, 1950–52; Pennsylvania Academy of Fine Arts, Philadelphia, 1952–53, 1955–57; Academia di Belle Arti, Florence, 1958; Yale University School of Art and Architecture, New Haven, Connecticut, 1963–65, B.F.A.

1964, M.F.A. 1965. Served in the United States Army, 1953–55. **Family:** Married the artist Helen Mayer (i.e., Helen Harrison) in 1953: children: Steven, Joshua, Gabriel, Joy. **Career:** Independent artist, since 1957: now lives and works in California. Lived in Florence, 1957–60; taught at Settlement House, New York, 1960–63; Assistant Professor, University of New Mexico, Albuquerque. 1965–67; Assistant Professor,1967–70, Associate Professor, 1970–73, and Professor and Chairman from 1973, Department of Visual Arts, University of California at San Diego. **Awards:** Research Grant, University of California at San Diego, 1969, 1972, 1973; Outstanding Educators of America Award, 1970; Ford Foundation Grant, 1974; Sea Grant, U.S. Department of Commerce, 1974; DAAD Grant, to work in West Berlin, 1988; Second Prize, Artec '91, second annual International Biennale, Nagoya, Japan, 1991. **Agents:** Ronald Feldman Fine Arts Inc., 31 Mercer Street, New York, New York 10013; The Wenger Gallery, 828 N. La Brea Avenue, Los Angeles, California 90038. **Addresses:** Department of Visual Arts B-027, University of California at San Diego, La Jolla, California 92093; P.O. Box 446, Del Mar, California 92014, U.S.A.

Individual Exhibitions:

1961 10/4 Group Gallery, New York
1963 Stryke Gallery, New York
Hudson River Museum, Yonkers, New York
1966 University of New Mexico, Albuquerque
1968 La Jolla Museum of Contemporary Art, California
1969 Washington State University, Pullman
University of Idaho, Moscow
1972 California State College at Fullerton
Atelier Chapman Kelley, Dallas
1974 Ronald Feldman Fine Arts, New York (with Helen Harrison)
1975 Ronald Feldman Fine Arts, New York (with Helen Harrison)
1976 Detroit Institute of Arts, Michigan (with Helen Harrison)
National Academy of Sciences, Washington D.C. (with Helen Harrison)
1977 San Francisco Art Institute (with Helen Harrison)
The Floating Museum, San Francisco (with Helen Harrison)
1978 Portland Center for Visual Arts, Oregon (with Helen Harrison)
Claremont Graduate School, California (with Helen Harrison)
Ronald Feldman Fine Arts, New York (with Helen Harrison)
1979 University of Idaho, Moscow (with Helen Harrison)
Williams College Museum of Art, Williamstown, Massachusetts (with Helen Harrison)
Brown University, Providence, Rhode Island (with Helen Harrison)
1980 Ronald Feldman Fine Arts, New York (with Helen Harrison)
Museum of Contemporary Art, Chicago (with Helen Harrison)
1981 Maryland Institute College of Art, Baltimore (with Helen Harrison)
1982 Washington Project for the Arts, Washington D.C. (with Helen Harrison)
Ronald Feldman Fine Arts, New York (with Helen Harrison)
1983 Emory University, Atlanta, Georgia (with Helen Harrison)
San Jose Museum of Art, California (with Helen Harrison)
San Jose State University, California (with Helen Harrison)
Wenger Gallery, San Diego, California (with Helen Harrison)
1985 California Institute of Technology, Pasadena (with Helen Harrison)
University of California, Irvine (with Helen Harrison)
Cornell University, Ithaca, New York (with Helen Harrison)
Tortue Gallery, Santa Monica, California (with Helen Harrison)
Ronald Feldman Fine Arts, New York (with Helen Harrison)
Wenger Gallery, San Diego, California (with Helen Harrison)
1986 Palomar College, California (with Helen Harrison)
Culman Gouro, Los Angeles (with Helen Harrison)
1987 Grey Gallery, New York University (with Helen Harrison)
Pasadena College of Art and Design, California (with Helen Harrison)
Los Angeles County Museum of Art (with Helen Harrison)
Wenger Gallery, San Diego, California (with Helen Harrison)
1988 Tel Aviv Museum, Israel
1991 Ronald Feldman Fine Arts, New York
1993 *Helen Mayer Harrison and Newton Harrison: Recent Environmental Projects,* International Design Conference, Aspen (with Helen Harrison)
1996 *future Garden-Part 1,* Kunst-und Ausstellungshalle der Bundesrepublik Deutschland, Bonn (catalog) (with Helen Harrison)
1997 *Green Heart Vision,* Kunstmuseum Bonn, Bonn (catalog) (with Helen Harrison)

Readings/Performances and Events: with Helen Harrison—*From the Centers of the World,* P.S. 1, New York, 1976; *From the Meditations,* Center for Music Experiment, University of California at San Diego, La Jolla, 1977; *From the Meditations* (and lecture), Center for 20th Century Studies, University of Wisconsin, Milwaukee, also San Francisco Art Institute, and the United Artists Coalition of San Diego, 1977; *On the Lagoon Cycle,* Museum of Contemporary Art, Chicago, 1977, also Claremont Graduate School, California, 1978; *Street Graffiti,* San Francisco Art Institute, also streets of San Francisco, 1977; *San Diego as the Center of the World,* University of Wisconsin, Milwaukee, 1977; *From the Great Lakes Meditations,* 1978; *From the Lagoon Cycle* and *From the Meditations,* Portland Center for Visual Arts, Oregon, and University of California at San Diego, La Jolla, 1978; *Readings,* Franklin Furnace, New York, 1979; *The Watershed Series,* Franklin Furnace, New York, 1979; *Talking Water,* Ronald Feldman Fine Arts, New York, 1980; *Reading and Rapping,* 424 F. Street, San Diego, 1980; *Baltimore Promenade,* Washington Project for the Arts, Washington, D.C., 1982; *Fortress Atlanta,* Emory University, Atlanta 1983; *San Jose Museum of Art, California, 1983; Three Urban Pieces,* San Jose State University, California, 1983; D.A.A.D. Gallery, Berlin, 1989; *Biodiversity and*

Landscapers: Human Challenges for Conservation in the Changing World, Center for BioDiversity Research and Environmental Resources Institute, Penn State University, 1990; *TRILOGY-Art-Nature-Science,* Kunsthallen Brandts Klaedefabrik, Odense, Denmark, 1996.

Selected Group Exhibitions:

1971 *Earth, Air, Fire Water: Elements of Art,* Museum of Fine Arts, Boston
1972 *10,* Museum of Contemporary Arts, Houston
1974 *Project 74,* Kunsthalle, Cologne
1975 *A Response to the Environment,* Rutgers University Art Gallery, New Brunswick, New Jersey (with Helen Harrison)
1976 *Art-World,* Whitney Museum, New York
1977 *A View of a Decade,* Museum of Contemporary Art, Chicago
1980 *Drawing: The Pluralist Decade,* at the *Biennale,* Venice
1982 *Common Ground: Five Artists in the Florida Landscape,* Ringling Museum, Sarasota, Florida
1984 *Disarming Images,* Contemporary Arts Center, Cincinnati, Ohio (toured the United States)
1987 *Documenta 8,* Museum Fridericianum, Kassel, West Germany
1990 *Terra Incognito,* Rhode Island School of Design Museum of Art, Providence (catalog)
Revered Earth, Contemporary Arts Museum, Houston (catalog)
1996 *Withdrawing,* Ronald Feldman Fine Arts, New York
1999 *As Far As the Eye Can See,* Atlanta (catalog)

Collections:

Everson Museum, Syracuse, New York; Museum of Contemporary Arts, Houston; Palais des Beaux-Arts, Brussels; Power Gallery of Contemporary Art, Sydney; Los Angeles County Museum of Art; Museum of Modern Art, New York; Brooklyn Museum, New York; Georgia Museum of Art, Athens: La Jolla Museum of Art, California; Tel Aviv Museum, Israel.

Publications:

By HARRISON: Books—*The Book of the Crab,* with Helen Harrison, 1980; *The Lagoon Cycle,* exhibition catalog, Ithaca, New York 1985. **Articles**—statement in *11 Los Angeles Artists,* exhibition catalog, London 1971; statement in *10,* exhibition catalog, Houston 1972; ''Sea Grant and Related Projects'' with Helen Harrison, in *Studio International* (London), May 1974; ''San Diego as the Center of the World,'' with Helen Harrison, in *Los Angeles Institute of Contemporary Art Journal,* February 1975; ''Forum: Should the Art School Curriculum Include Professional Job Training?'' with Judith Brodsky, in *American Artists* (New York), October 1977; ''Notes on a Recent Project,'' with Helen Harrison, in *Los Angeles Institute of Contemporary Art Journal,* November 1977; ''Nobody Told Us When To Stop Thinking,'' interview, in *Grey Matters* (New York), Autumn 1987; ''Trummerflora: On the Topography of Terror'' in *CMP Bulletin,* vol. 9, no. 3, 1990; ''Trummerflora on the Topography of Terrors'' in *WhiteWalls,* no. 25, Spring 1990; ''Conversational Drift: Helen Mayer Harrison and Newton Harrison'' interview, in *Art Journal* (New York), vol. 51, no. 2, Summer 1992; ''A Conversation with Helen Mayer Harrison and Newton Harrison'' with M.A. Greenstein in *Artweek,* vol. 24, no. 17, 9 September 1993; ''Future Garden: The Endangered Meadows of Europe'' in *Art & Design,* vol. 12, November/December 1997.

On HARRISON: Books—*Art and the Future* by Douglas Davis, New York and London 1973; *Art and Technology in the Future* by Jonathan Benthall, New York 1973; *Great Western Salt Works: Essays on the Meaning of Post-Formalist Art* by Jack Burnham, New York 1974; *Sunshine Muse* by Peter Plagens, New York 1974; *The Art of Performance: A Critical Anthology,* edited by Gregory Battcock and Robert Nickas, New York 1984; *Future Garden,* Bonn, 1996; *Green Heart Vision,* Bonn 1997; *As Far As the Eye Can See,* Atlanta, Georgia 1999. **Articles**—''Newton Harrison: Big Fish, Small Pool: by Jonathan Benthall in *Studio International* (London), December 1971; ''The Education of the Un-Artist-III'' by Allan Kaprow in *Art in America* (New York), January/February 1974; ''Newton Harrison's Fourth Lagoon: Strategy Against Entrophy'' by José Barrio-Gray in *Arts Magazine* (New York), November 1974; ''Newton and Helen Harrison: Art as Ecology'' in *Artweek* (Oakland, California), 5 February 1977; ''Helen and Newton Harrison: New Grounds for Art'' by Kim Levin in *Arts Magazine* (New York), February 1978; ''The Earth as Their Palette'' by Grace Glueck in the *New York Times,* 4 April 1980; ''Helen Mayer Harrison and Newton Harrison'' by Ann Schoenfeld in *Arts Magazine* (New York), June 1980; ''Helen and Newton Harrison's Book of the Seven Lagoons'' by Kim Levin in *Village Voice* (New York), 16 December 1986; ''Helen Mayer Harrison and Newton Harrison'' by Patricia C. Phillips in *Art-forum* (New York), September 1987; ''Improvising the Future: The Eco-aesthetics of Newton and Helen Harrison'' by Linda F. McGreevy in *Arts Magazine,* vol. 62, November 1987; ''Dynamic Duos: Artists Are Teaming Up In Growing Numbers'' by Glenn Zorpette in *Art News,* vol. 93, Summer 1994; ''Sculpting the Land'' by John Beardsley in *Sculpture,* no. 4, April 1996; ''Policing Paradise, Or Et In California Ego'' by Rebecca Solnit in *Art Issues,* no. 55, November-December 1998.

*

Our work begins when we perceive an anomaly in the environment that is the result of opposing beliefs or contradictory metaphors. It is the moment when reality no longer appears seamless and the cost of belief has become outrageous that offers opportunity to create new spaces, first for the mind and thereafter in everyday.

The works that we are doing now are narratives or stories of projects that we have been engaged in or are currently involved with. The locales are cities, such as Baltimore, Maryland; San José, Pasadena, Santa Barbara and San Diego, California. In these places, we developed promenades, argued for grand canals, or proposed, for example, to cover channelized rivers and turn the concrete areas into park lands or to make plant and animal refuges along their banks and under flight paths and freeways or to reclaim spoils-piles and dumps. We always compose with left-over spaces and invisible places. And there are many. We have worked in collaboration with ourselves, although lately, we have started to include other artists, ecologists, landscape architects, engineers, and alike in our dialogues.

—Helen and Newton Harrison

* * *

The Harrisons are working in a taboo area where art is dependent not on its own reflection but on the world at large. In their work art is given an aspect of both social comment and urgency, while social science is given a requisite amount of aesthetics, as well as the public relations which are necessary for any new system of observation. Here we have a case where the two disciplines assist each other, rather than vying, discipline-wise, for individual shares of "Progress." The projects they undertake have a sense of their own recognition, the type of cognizance cultures usually describe as some form of commonly-agreed upon knowledge, though usually remaining hidden as cultural visual activity. Because of the "real" nature of their work, the Harrisons are often subject to criticism from those who are more concerned with strictly visual advancement.

Helen Harrison's background was, specifically, the social sciences, while Newton Harrison has worked in both sculpture and painting, and with technological art. As they began collaborating, the disciplines began to mix, and the inadequacies and short sightedness of the contemporary specialized fields became more apparent. An early work, "Brine Shrimp Farm," at the Los Angeles County Museum of Art, consisted of several ponds, each 10 feet by 20 feet. The salt ponds, consisting of an ecological habitat of shrimp, algae, and water, netted a large number of shrimp. The ponds also had a look of painterly coloration from one pool to the next, as the salinity content changed in each habitat. "Brine Shrimp Farm" indicative, though, of the Harrisons' true interest in the earth as both material and medium, rather than as a purely aesthetic form, which many other earth artists were exploring at the time.

"The Lagoon Cycle" is a large work which has taken nearly 10 years to date, and which consists of meditations on the nature of human, animal and geologic ecology. For their exhibitions and presentations, the Harrisons used taped and live mantric-like readings, colored and detailed maps, and aerial and site photographs to examine several site-specific and terrain-specific problems. A recent work was titled "Thinking about the Mangrove and the Pine." The piece utilized an area in the Florida landscape for ecological observation. The text, which accompanied descriptive illustration, reads: "The pines colonize behind the mangroves/then gain the edge/and lose ground thereby." Much of the Harrisons' work emphasizes the problem of understanding the natural world through acute and simple perception. Certainly both the social sciences and the arts have defined themselves historically, in different periods, as being concerned with such perception. The Harrisons have realized the appropriateness of such vision, while living side-by-side with the specificity and grandiose nature of the technological vision. They see the importance of continuing personal observation in an era of machine-guided human vision.

—John Robinson

HARTIGAN, Grace

Nationality: American. **Born:** Newark, New Jersey, 28 March 1922. **Education:** Milburn, New Jersey schools, 1929–40; studied privately with Isaac Lane Muse, New York, 1942–46. **Family:** Married Robert Jachens in 1941 (divorced, 1947); son: Jeffrey; married Winston H. Price in 1960. **Career:** Worked as mechanical draftsman, in defense factory, 1943. Independent artist, since 1946: travelled in Europe; lived in San Miguel de Allende, Mexico, 1949; moved to Baltimore, 1960; director, Hoffberger Graduate School of Painting, Maryland Institute, Baltimore, since 1965; Avery Chair, Bard College, Annandale-on-Hudson, 1983. **Awards:** *Mademoiselle* magazine Merit Award for Art, 1957; Childe Hassam Purchase Award, National Institute of Arts and Letters, 1974. Honorary degrees: Moore College of Art, Philadelphia, 1969; Towson State University, Maryland; Goucher College, Towson; Maryland Institute College of Art, Baltimore; Lafayette College, Easton, Pennsylvania. **Agent:** C. Grimaldis Gallery, 523 N. Charles Street, Baltimore, Maryland 21201, U.S.A. **Address** 17011/2 Eastern Avenue, Baltimore, Maryland 21231, U.S.A.

Individual Exhibitions:

1951 Tibor de Nagy Gallery, New York
1952 Tibor de Nagy Gallery, New York
1953 Tibor de Nagy Gallery, New York
1954 Tibor de Nagy Gallery, New York
1955 Tibor de Nagy Gallery, New York
Vassar College Art Gallery, Poughkeepsie, New York
1957 Tibor de Nagy Gallery, New York
Robert Keene Gallery, Southampton, Long Island, New York
1959 Tibor de Nagy Gallery, New York
1960 Gres Gallery, Washington, D.C.
1962 Martha Jackson Gallery, New York
1963 University of Minnesota, Minneapolis
1964 Martha Jackson Gallery, New York
Franklin Siden Gallery, Detroit
1967 Martha Jackson Gallery, New York
Maryland Institute College of Art, Baltimore
University of Chicago
1969 Gertrude Kasle Gallery, Detroit
1970 Martha Jackson Gallery, New York
1972 Gertrude Kasle Gallery, Detroit
1974 Gertrude Kasle Gallery, Detroit
1975 William Zierler Gallery, New York
American University, Washington, D.C.
1976 Gertrude Kasle Gallery, Detroit
1977 Genesis Gallery, New York
1978 Genesis Gallery, New York
1979 University of Maryland, College Park
C. Grimaldis Gallery, Baltimore
1980 Baltimore Museum of Art, Baltimore, travelled to State University of New York, Plattsburgh, and University of Maryland Art Gallery, College Park
1981 Hamilton Gallery of Contemporary Art, New York
Georgia Museum of Art, Athens
Mint Museum of Art, Charlotte, North Carolina
Fort Wayne Museum of Art, Indiana
C. Grimaldis Gallery, Baltimore
1982 C. Grimaldis Gallery, Baltimore
1983 Van Wickle Gallery, Lafayette College, Easton, Pennsylvania
1984 Gruenebaum Gallery, New York
Dolly Fitterman Gallery, Minneapolis
C. Grimaldis Gallery, Baltimore

Grace Hartigan: *The-The #1,* 1962. ©State of New York/Corbis.

1986 Gruenebaum Gallery, New York
C. Grimaldis Gallery, Baltimore
1987 *Grace Hartigan: A Mini-Retrospective, 1954–1984,* Watkins Gallery, American University, Washington, D.C.
C. Grimaldis Gallery, Baltimore
1988 Gruenebaum Gallery, New York
1989 C. Grimaldis Gallery, Baltimore
Kouros Gallery, New York
1990 C. Grimaldis Gallery, Baltimore
1991 ACA Gallery, New York
1992 C. Grimaldis Gallery, Baltimore
ACA Gallery, New York
1993 C. Grimaldis Gallery, Baltimore
Grace Hartigan and the Poets, Skidmore College, Saratoga Springs, New York
1994 ACA Gallery, New York
1995 C. Grimaldis Gallery, Baltimore
1997 C. Grimaldis Gallery, Baltimore
ACA Gallery, New York
AB-EX Pointillism/1988–1993, Loyola College Art Gallery, Baltimore, and Lawrence Gallery, Rosemont College, Pennsylvania
Hartigan's Women, The Robeson Center Art Gallery, Rutgers University, Newark, New Jersey (travelled to New York and Wisconsin)
2000 *Aspects of the Far East,* C. Grimaldis Gallery, Baltimore
Grace Hartigan: Paintings from Popular Culture (retrospective), Susquehanna Art Museum, Harrisburg, Pennsylvania (catalog)

Selected Group Exhibitions:

1950 *Talent 1950,* Kootz Gallery, New York
1951 *9th Street Show,* New York
1956 *Twelve Americans,* Museum of Modern Art, New York
Third International Art Exhibition, India
1957 Fourth International Art Exhibition, Japan
1958–59 *The New American Painting,* International Council, Museum of Modern Art, New York (toured Europe)
1960 *Abstract Expressionists and Imagists,* Guggenheim Museum, New York
1964 *Figuration and Defiguration,* Art Museum, Ghent
1968 *Selections from Albright-Knox,* National Gallery, Washington, D.C.

Grace Hartigan: *Human Fragment,* 1986. ©Walker Art Center, Minneapolis.

1969 *20th Century Art from the Nelson Aldrich Rockefeller Collection,* Museum of Modern Art, New York
1973 *Art in Embassies,* American Embassy, San Jose, Costa Rica
1974 *1961,* Allan Frumkin Gallery, New York
1975 *Biennial,* Corcoran Gallery of Art, Washington, D.C.
1976 *Poets and Painters,* National Collection of Fine Arts, Washington, D.C.
1977 *Critic's Choice,* Lowe Art Gallery, Syracuse, New York
1980 *Art of the 50's,* Hirshorn Museum, Washington, D.C.
Modern American Painting, Baltimore Museum of Art
1982 *Hartigan/Louis/Still/Truitt,* Baltimore Museum of Art, Maryland
Contemporary American Prints and Drawings, 1940–1980, National Gallery of Art, Washington, D.C.
1983 *Tenth Anniversary Exhibition,* Gruenebaum Gallery, New York
1984–86 *Action-Precision: The New Direction in New York 1955–60,* Newport Harbor Art Museum, Newport Beach, California (toured the United States)
1987 *Color: Pure and Simple,* Stamford Museum and Nature Center, Stamford, Connecticut
1993 *Hand-Painted Pop: American Art in Transition, 1955–1962,* Museum of Contemporary Art, Los Angeles
1993–94 *Venues,* Museum of Contemporary Art, Los Angeles, Museum of Contemporary Art, Chicago, and Whitney Museum of American Art, New York
1995 *Artist's Choice—Modern Women,* Museum of Modern Art, New York
1996 *The Dialectic of Line* and *Summer '96 Part 2—The Painters,* C. Grimaldis Gallery, Baltimore
1997 *Forty Years of ULAE,* Corcoran Gallery, Washington, D.C., and Armand Hammer Museum, Los Angeles
1998 *Robert and Jane Meyerhoff Collection,* National Gallery of Art, Washington, D.C.
1999 *American Century, Part II,* Whitney Museum of American Art, New York
In Memory of My Feelings: Frank O'Hara and American Art, Museum of Contemporary Art, Los Angeles

Collections:

Whitney Museum, New York; Museum of Modern Art, New York; Metropolitan Museum of Art, New York; Solomon R. Guggenheim Museum, New York; Albright-Knox Gallery, Buffalo, New York; Wadsworth Atheneum, Hartford, Connecticut; Baltimore Museum of Art; Philadelphia Museum of Art; National Museum of American Art, Washington, D.C.; Corcoran Gallery of Art, Washington, D.C.; Carnegie Institute Museum of Art, Pittsburgh; Art Institute of Chicago; Walker Art Center, Minneapolis.

Publications:

By HARTIGAN: Article—''An Artist Speaks'' in *The Arrow* (Pittsburgh), December 1960.

On HARTIGAN: Books—*Modern American Painting and Sculpture* by Sam Hunter, New York 1959; *Art Since 1945* by Sam Hunter, New York 1959; *Art Autre* by Michel Tapie, Paris 1960; *Morphologie Autre* by Michel Tapie, Turin 1961; *The New York School* by Irving Sandler, New York 1978; *Action/Precision: The New Direction in New York 1955–60,* exhibition catalog by Paul Schimmel, B. H. Friedman and others, Newport Beach, California, 1984; *Grace Hartigan: A Painter's World* by Robert S. Mattison, Hudson Hills Press, 1990; *Hand-Painted Pop: American Art in Transition, 1955–1962,* exhibition catalog by Paul Schimmel, Los Angeles, 1992; *Grace Hartigan and the Poets: Paintings and Prints,* exhibition catalog by Terence Diggory, Saratoga Springs, New York, 1993; *Artist's Choice: Modern Women,* exhibition catalog by Elizabeth Murray, New York, 1995; *ART TALK: Conversations with 15 Women Artists* by Cindy Nemser, New York 1995; *AB-EX Pointillism/ 1988–1993,* exhibition catalog by Phyllis Rosenzweig, Loyola College, 1997; *Hartigan's Women,* exhibition catalog by Maria Rand Catalano, New York, 1997; *Robert and Jane Meyerhoff Collection,* exhibition catalog by Mark Rosenthal, Washington, D.C., 1998; *Originals: American Women Artists* by Eleanor Munro, New York 2000. **Articles—**''Grace Hartigan'' by Emily Dennis in *School of New York: Some Younger Artists,* edited by B. H. Friedman, New York 1959; ''Grace Hartigan'' in *Arts Magazine* (New York), May 1959; ''Miss Hartigan and Her Canvas'' in *Newsweek* (New York), May 1959; ''The Rawness and the Vast'' in *Newsweek* (New York), May 1959; articles by Klaus Jürgen-Fischer in *Das Kunstwerk* (Baden-Baden), August 1959; ''Woman in American Art'' in *Life* (New York), September 1960; articles by Barbara Gold in *Baltimore Morning Sun,* 12 February 1967; ''Women Artists'' by Michael and Arlene Batterberry in *Harper's Bazaar* (New York), July 1971; ''Hartigan'' by Allen Barber in *Art Magazine* (New York), June 1974; ''To See the World Mainly through Art: Grace Hartigan's Queen and Empresses'' by Lawrence Campbell in *Arts,* January 1984; ''Grace Hartigan at Gruenebaum'' by Gerrit Henry in *Art in America* (New York), May 1984; ''Grace Hartigan: Painting Her Own History'' by Robert Mattison in *Arts* (New York), January 1985; ''Second Generation: Mannerism or Momentum?'' by Kenneth Baker in *Art in America,* June 1985; ''Then and Now: Six of the New York School Look Back'' by Steven Westfall in *Art in America,* June 1985; ''Grace Hartigan'' by Peter Walsh in *ARTnews,* March 1994; ''100 Works by Women, Not Intended for Women Only'' by Holland Cotter in *New York Times,* 21 Jully 1995.

*

I feel that we are living a very fragmented life; the whole world—you too. So I perceive the world in fragments. It is somewhat like being on a very fast train and getting glimpses of things in strange scales as you pass by. A person can be very, very tiny. And a billboard can make a person very large. You see the corner of a house or you see a bird fly by, and it's all fragmented.

Somehow, in painting I try to make some logic out of the world that has been given to me in chaos. I have a very pretentions idea that I want to make life, I want to make sense out of it. The fact that I am doomed to failure—that doesn't deter me in the least.

—Grace Hartigan

* * *

Grace Hartigan was perhaps the only woman painter to come to the fore in the early 1950's in New York as a disciple of the Action Painters. De Kooning and Pollock had their influence particularly, and in 1950 Clement Greenberg selected her work for inclusion in a New York show. Until 1953 she signed her paintings as ''George Hartigan,'' but having made her point that there is sexual equality in the art, she subsequently dropped the forename.

Hartigan has expressed her viewpoint that she wishes her art to be resistant to entry, as a window in space, and her subject matter distilled until it evolves as its own essence. By the mid-1950s she had denied outright abstraction in favour of king-sized canvases on themes the contents of which could be recognized and bore relation to the given titles.

''Essex Market'' (1956) has the strong and evocative attack of expressionist handling, fruit and the busy atmosphere of the setting presenting their various equivalents in swiftly brushed areas of mixed and pure colour, in which the drawing of forms dictate their plastic urgency. ''City Life,'' another work of the same year, reflects the pace and the rhythms of street scenes in which the broad masses are hatched in a lateral diagonal progression. Life, one feels, is not frozen at a given moment of time but taken on the run—an impression that retains something of the movement inspiring it. The colour key tends to be aggressive and importunate, and the separation of the different masses is often defined by outline shadow as much as by differing colour contrasts.

Her commitment to the vulgarity and vitality of modern American life most usually in its urban environment gives a vivid monumentality to her canvases even when the physical references become fussed and ambiguously noted in the scheme of the composition. ''Interior 'The Creeks''' (1957) is a large canvas that teeters on the verge of the illusionistic yet relies on its abstract dynamic of freely written motives to set up the tensile push-pull of their arrangement in space. ''Shinnecock Canal'' (1957) is a large broadly handled reflection of reality paraphrased in plangent banners of colour. Celebrations of swatches of existence where people live in community: the chords are musically strong, distinguished by movements in which the brass and the woodwind predominate over the strings in moods recalling New Orleans saloon jazz more than tasteful Carnegie Hall concertos.

—G.S. Whittet

Poetry was an important source of inspiration to Hartigan. She was good friends with the poet Frank O'Hara (who dedicated at least one poem to her) and she collaborated with him on a series of twelve poem/paintings, *Oranges*, in the early 1950s. These works, like her other paintings of this period, combined abstract and figurative elements.

In her work of the last four decades Hartigan increasingly pushed the figurative tendency noted in her paintings from the Abstract Expressionist era until, by the late 1960s, she ''broke into imagery.'' Her images were drawn from the natural world, and sometimes focused on women, but most especially they were drawn from popular culture and included such diverse elements as dolls, movie stars, and toys. The importance of popular culture in Hartigan's work persists, as shown in a Spring 2000 retrospective of three decades of her work at the Susquehanna Art Museum, in Harrisburg, Pennsylvania, *Grace Hartigan: Paintings from Popular Culture.*

Since 1967, Hartigan has headed the Graduate School of Painting at Maryland Institute of Art in Baltimore. Her studio is in a downtown area that reminds her of New York's Lower East Side. She has gone from being an abstractionist to being a figurative artist with abstract tendencies. Nonetheless, abstract expressionist praxis still informs her working method: she often stains her canvases and uses a superimposed line to define form.

Masks are one other interest that has continued throughout her work, despite its stylistic variations. An exhibit of her new work at the Grimaldis Gallery in 2000, *Aspects of the Far East,* drew upon images of Japan's ''Floating World,'' especially geishas and the Kabuki theater. In the 1970s, Hartigan told Cindy Nemser: ''I am very interested in masks and charades . . . the face the world puts on to sell itself to the world.'' She was referring to her painting ''Grand Street Brides'' (1954), with its multiple images of women in bridal costume, perhaps as seen in a bridal shop window. Likewise, these recent works are also about costume and gesture.

—Mara Witzling

HASSAN, Kay

Nationality: South African. **Born:** Alexandra, Johannesburg, 1956. **Education:** Studied fine art, ELC Art Centre, Rorke's Drift, KwaZulu Natal, South Africa, 1977; studied printmaking with Stanley Hayter in Paris, 1986–88; guest student, Schule fur Gestaltung, Basel, 1988–89. **Career:** Taught fine art, Alliance Francaise, Soweto, South Africa, 1982–86; taught at F.U.B.A. Academy, Johannesburg, 1990–93; has a studio in Bag Factory, Johannesburg. **Awards:** Daimler Chrysler Award for South African Contemporary Art, 2000.

Selected Individual Exhibitions:

1999 Galerie Seippel, Cologne
2000 Durban Art Gallery
South African National Gallery
Pretoria Art Museum
Hans Huth, Berlin
Wurttembergischer Kunstvererin Stuttgart
2001 Soweto Exhibitions

Selected Group Exhibitions:

1992 *Two Decades of Fine Art,* FUNDA, Soweto
1994 *Place of Power,* Newtown Galleries, Johannesburg
1995 Kwangju Biennale, Korea
Deutsche Aerospace, Munich
1996 *Colours,* Haus de Kulturen der Welt, Berlin
Earth and Everything, Bristol, England
Hitchhiker, Generator Art Sapce, Johannesburg
Four Artists, Wright Gallery, New York
1997 *No Place Like Home,* Walker Art Centre, Minneapolis
Trade Routes and Geography, Second Johannesburg Biennale
1998 *Democracy's Images,* Bild Museet, Umea
La ville, le jardin, la memoire, Villa Medici, Rome
1999 *Disorder A3HB,* Camouflage, Brussels
2000 2000 Dak/Art 2000, Senegal

Memorias Intimas Marcas, Museum van Hedendaagse Kunst, Antwerp

2001 *The Short Century in Africa: Independence and Liberation Movements in Africa 1945–1994,* Villa Stuck, Munich (catalog)

Publications:

On HASSAN: Book—*No Place (Like Home)* by Zarina Bhimji, Minneapolis 1997. **Articles—**''Moving In: Eight Contemporary African Artists'' by Okwui Enwezor and Octavio Zaya in *Flash Art,* vol. 29, no. 186, January-February 1996; ''Johannesburg: A Fake Interview or What We Think They Said'' by Lorna Ferguson and Thomas Mulcaire in *Flash Art,* vol. 29, no. 189, Summer 1996; ''Four South African Artists'' by Robert Condon in *NKA: Journal of Contemporary African Art,* no. 5, Fall-Winter 1996; ''Insight: Four Artists from South Africa and Simunye/We Are One'' by John Peffer-Engels in *African Arts,* vol. 30, no. 1, Winter 1997; ''African Experiences'' by Rory Bester and Lauri Firstenberg in *Flash Art,* vol. 33, no. 210, January-February 2000.

* * *

The installations and large collages created by Johannesburg-based artist Kay Hassan depict scenes of everyday life in South Africa. While many of the artist's works focus on the constant displacement of families and workers, they demonstrate the resilience of a culture that is redefining itself in the aftermath of apartheid.

Hassan makes collages from materials taken from the urban landscape, specifically, scraps of billboard posters. Using this medium allows the artist to reconfigure the impersonal commercial space of modern life to reflect the intimate details of those who live in it. Voting lines, cab passengers, and bar scenes are only a few of the subjects that Hassan explores. Evidence of the original commercial imagery remains as the artist transforms, for example, beer ads into dress fabric and *Cosmopolitan* ads into cars.

Although the collages look like paintings from afar, the works nevertheless maintain some of their original billboard qualities in scale and in texture. The scraps' frayed edges suggest the constant layering of new posters in the urban setting. Similarly, the works' jagged outer edges are left unbounded by rectilinear framing. In the display space, Hassan loosely suspends the collages from walls using clips. Consequently, the works appear to have been ripped from a train platform or a building. Hassan's chosen medium, artistic process, and display techniques are particularly appropriate for depictions of a society characterized by impermanence and transformation, one in which lives are constantly put together and torn apart.

Although the social conditions in which the majority of South Africans live inspire Hassan's huge collages, the works themselves do not directly reference South African society. Instead, Hassan's compositions evoke universal settings with their spare backgrounds depicting landscapes that could be desert or ocean. Viewers identify with the human figures since the latter's features are general and undefined and their powerful gestures communicate emotion. The social situation in South Africa is not unique, and Hassan's collages remind viewers of shared situations, responses, and feelings.

Hassan's three-dimensional installations depict both public and private spaces. *Shebeen* (1997) is a meticulously detailed installation that replicates a type of bar commonly known as a juke joint in the southern United States. Visitors to the exhibit are encouraged to lounge around in a dark, smoky-smelling room while listening to South African pop music. The empty beer bottles and overflowing ashtrays that surround them add to the atmosphere and enhance their experience.

Shack (1996) is the makeshift living space of an imaginary family of transients. When visitors enter and explore the interior, they discover items including pots and pans, old suitcases, plastic tarps covering parts of the ceiling and the walls, and clothes hung on a clothesline. *Shack* encourages visitors to imagine living in a space made from less-than-adequate items.

The Flight (1995) confronts visitors with makeshift mattresses, packages, parcels, old suitcases, and a few bundles strewn across the floor. Looking more closely, visitors discover an open bible, a bottle, and some food on a suitcase. The scenarios presented in *The Flight* seem suspended in time, as if the owners of the objects abandoned them. Simultaneously, the items are provisional, and the visitor has the distinct impression that soon they will be quickly collected and packed.

Each of the objects in *The Flight* has a personal feeling, a private story to tell—a story of flight and dispossession. Walking through the installation is somewhat uncomfortable since visitors seem to invade the space of other people. Significantly, however, visitors begin to understand the lives of transient people. Like the human figures in Hassan's collages, the imaginary squatters whose abandoned possessions create *The Flight* have no faces. As a result, visitors may place themselves in the role of transient, making their experience first-hand rather than removed.

—Joyce Youmans

HATOUM, Mona

Nationality: Palestinian. **Born:** Beirut, Lebanon, 1952; moved to England, 1975. **Education:** Beirut University College, Beirut, 1970–72; Byam Shaw School of Art, London, 1975–79; Slade School of Art, London, 1979–81. **Career:** Performance artist until mid-1980s; artist, working in installations, video, sculpture, and photography. **Agent:** Alexander and Bonin, 132 Tenth Avenue, New York, New York 10011, U.S.A.

Selected Individual Exhibitions:

1983 *The Negotiating Table* (performance), SAW Gallery, Ottawa; N.A.C., St. Catherines; The Western Front, Vancouver

1984 *Variation on Discord and Divisions* (performance), ABC No Rio, New York; A.K.A., Saskatoon, Saskatchewan; The Western Front, Vancouver; Articule, Montreal

The Negotiating Table (performance), The Franklin Furnace, New York

Mona Hatoum: + *And* –, 1994. ©Christie's Images/Corbis.

1985 *Between the Lines* (performance), The Orchard Gallery, Derry
1989 *The Light at the End,* The Showroom, London
The Light at the End, Oboro Gallery, Montreal
1992 *Dissected Space,* Chapter, Cardiff (catalog)
Untitled, Mario Flecha Gallery, London
1993 *Positionings* (with Barbara Steinman), Art Gallery of Ontario, Toronto (catalog)
Le Socle du Monde, Galerie Crousel-Robelin Bama, Paris
Mona Hatoum (with Andrea Fisher), South London Gallery, London (catalog)
Recent Work, Arnolfini, Bristol (catalog)
1994 *Mona Hatoum,* C.R.G. Art Incorporated, New York
Mona Hatoum, Musee National d'Art Moderne, Centre Georges Pompidou, Paris (catalog)
Mona Hatoum, Galerie Rene Blouin, Montreal
1995 *Mona Hatoum,* British School at Rome
Short Space, Galerie Chantal Crousel, Paris
Inside the Visible, and *Begin the Beguine in Flanders,* Beguinage of Saint Elizabeth, Kortrijk, Belgium
Le Socle du Monde, White Cube/Jay Jopling, London
1996 *Mona Hatoum,* De Appel, Amsterdam (catalog)
Quarters, Via Farini, Milan
Current Disturbance, Capp Street Project, San Francisco
Mona Hatoum, Gallery Anadiel, Jerusalem
New Work, The Fabric Workshop and Museum, Philadelphia
1997 *Mona Hatoum,* Museum of Contemporary Art, Chicago; The New Museum of Contemporary Art, New York; Museum of Modern Art, Oxford; Scottish National Gallery of Modern Art, Edinburgh (catalog)
Mona Hatoum, Galerie Rene Blouin, Montréal
1998 *Mona Hatoum,* Kunsthalle Basel
1999 *Mona Hatoum,* Alexander and Bonin, New York
Mona Hatoum, Le Creux de l'Enfer/Centre d'Art Contemporain, Thiers; Le College, Frac Champagne-Ardenne, Reims; Museum van Hedendaagse Kunst Antwerpen-MUHKA, Antwerp (catalog)
Mona Hatoum, ArtPace, San Antonio, Texas
Mona Hatoum, The Box, Turin
Mona Hatoum, Castello di Rivoli, Museo d'Arte Contemporanea, Turin
2000 *Mona Hatoum,* SITE Santa Fe, Santa Fe, New Mexico
Images from Elsewhere, fig-1, London
The Entire World as a Foreign Land, Tate Britain, London (catalog)
2001 *Domestic Disturbance,* MASS MoCA, North Adams, Massachusetts (toured; catalog)

Selected Group Exhibitions:

1995 *Identity and Alterity,* Venice Biennale, Italian Pavilion, Venice

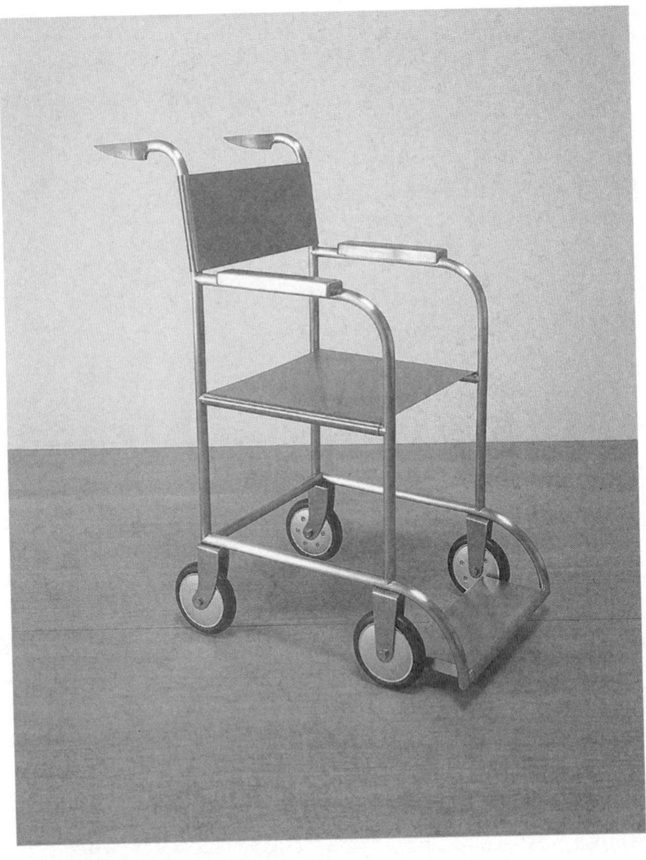

Mona Hatoum: *Untitled (Wheelchair),* 1998. ©Tate Gallery, London/Art Resource, NY; courtesy of Tate Gallery.

Masculin Feminin, Centre Georges Pompidou, Paris
Orient/ation: 4th Istanbul Biennale, Istanbul
Rites of Passage: Art for the End of the Century, Tate Gallery, London
The Turner Prize 1995, Tate Gallery, London
1996 *Distemper: Dissonant Themes in the Art of the 1990s,* The Hirshhorn Museum and Sculpture Garden, Washington, D.C.
Inside the Visible: An Elliptical Traverse of 20th Century Art, in, of, and from the Feminine, Institute for Contemporary Art, Boston; The National Museum of Women in the Arts, Washington; Whitechapel Art Gallery, London; Art Gallery of Western Australia, Perth
1998 *XXIV Bienal de Sao Paulo,* Fundaçao Bienal Sao Paulo, Sao Paulo, Brazil
Cairo Biennale, Cairo, Egypt
1999 *La Casa, Il Corpo, Il Cuore,* Museum Moderner Kunst Stiftung, Ludwig, Vienna
Looking for a Place: SITE Santa Fe's Third International Biennal, Santa Fe, New Mexico
2000 *Still,* Alexander and Bonin, New York
Through Melancholia and Charm, Galerie Nordenhake, Berlin
Sincerely Yours, Astrup Fearnley Museet for Moderne Kunst, Oslo

Collections:

The Museum of Modern Art, New York; Los Angeles County Museum of Art; Philadelphia Museum of Art; Dallas Museum of Art, Dallas; Arts Council of Great Britain, London; The British Council, London; Tate Gallery, London; Centre Georges Pompidou, Paris; FNAC, Paris; Louisiana Museum of Modern Art, Humlebaek, Denmark; The National Gallery of Canada, Ottawa; The Art Gallery of Ontario, Toronto.

Publications:

On HATOUM: Book—*Mona Hatoum* by Michael Archer et al., London 1997. **Articles—**''Mona Hatoum: The Witness Beside Herself'' by Desa Philippi in *Parachute* (Montréal), April-June 1990; ''Mona Hatoum'' by Dan Cameron in *Artforum,* April 1993; ''Mona Hatoums State of Emergency'' by Maria Lind in *Paletten* (Göteborg), no. 219, April 1994; ''Mona Hatoum: In Between, Outside and in the Margins'' by Laurel Berger in *Artnews,* September 1994; ''Mona Hatoum: Centre Georges Pompidou, Paris'' by Brian Holmes in *World Art,* November 1994; ''Mona Hatoum at CRG'' by Melanie Marino in *Art in America,* January 1995; ''Mona Hatoum, White Cube'' by Angela Kingston in *Flash Art,* March-April 1995; ''East Jerusalem: Mona Hatoum'' by Sarit Shapira in *Flash Art,* October 1996; ''Mona Hatoum's World-Wise Forms'' by Blake Gopnik in *The Globe and Mail* (Toronto), 23 August 1997; ''Gut Reaction'' by Peter Schjeldahl in *The Village Voice,* 3 December 1997; ''Mona Hatoum'' by Thomas Connors in *Sculpture,* vol. 16, no. 10, December 1997; ''Video Art so Intimate it Seems Alien'' by Edward J. Sozanski in *The Philadelphia Inquirer,* 18 January 1998; ''Mona Hatoum'' by Janine Antoni in *Bomb*, no. 63, Spring 1998; ''Blurred Visions Worthy of the Turner Prize'' by Tom Lubbock in *The Independent* (London), 7 April 1998; ''Mona Hatoum'' by Tamar Garb in *Art Monthly* (London), no. 216, May 1998; ''Visceral Geometry'' by Paula Harper in *Art in America*, September 1998; ''Mona Hatoum'' by Irene Small in *NY Arts*, vol. 4, no. 12, December 1999; ''Mona Hatoum'' by Frances Richard in *Artforum,* January 2000; ''The Appliance of Science'' by Rachel Halliburton in *The Independent* (London), 22 March 2000; ''Identity Parade'' by Sarah Kent in *Time Out* (London), 22–29 March 2000.

* * *

Mona Hatoum's work invokes the theme of displaced self through alienation of the physical body. Hatoum told *Art in America* contributor Paula Harper, ''There's always the feeling of in-betweenness that comes from not being able to identify with my own culture or the one in which I'm living.'' Born in Beirut to Palestinian emigrants, Hatoum herself was forced into exile in 1975 during a visit to England when civil war broke at home. At the age of 23, Hatoum attended art school in England where she took up permanent residency. During her education, she was intrigued by Minimalism and Conceptual Art after a fascination with Surrealism early in life. The contemporary movements, however, enforced the dichotomy between mind and body in Western thought. Through her work, Hatoum strives to undermine this split by engaging the viewer in uncomfortable or disorienting physical surroundings that effect the psyche and expose the mind/body relationship.

Hatoum frequently worked with performance art using her own body, a suitable medium to express the human experience of conflict and displacement. To these ends, the artist placed physical obstructions or barriers in communication to separate her from the spectator, as in ''Under Siege'' (1982). In this seven-hour performance, she attempts to stand within a clay-filled, transparent box the size of a shower stall. Nude, she repeatedly falls against the flexible polyethylene walls, the artist's struggle expressing the psychological aspects of oppression. In a solo performance for the Roadworks event in 1985, Hatoum walked barefoot with a pair of Doc Marten boots tied to her ankles. Some viewers felt she was being followed by an authority figure, while others viewed it as vacating power through the boots' emptiness. The work and local response to it were influenced by riots that took place the previous year protesting police violence in the neighborhood of Brixton, London, where the event was held.

Through the course of the 1980s, video-based work gradually replaced live performance. In ''So Much I Want to Say'' (1983), the artist's face is filmed close-up while her mouth is gagged and face partially covered by large hands. As Hatoum struggles to pull the hands away, she is physically prevented from speaking, which is emphasized by a voice over in which she repeats the work's title. Reflecting her literal silencing, she refers to many individuals who lack a voice: women, minorities, and oppressed people everywhere. In ''Measures of Distance'' (1988), Arabic letters fill the video monitor acting like a screen in front of scenes of Hatoum's mother showering. The soundtrack contains a joyful conversation between mother and daughter but is layered with a louder, sad voice of the artist reading letters from her mother translated into English. As the title eludes, the artist engages with issues of separation from her own family living in a war-torn region and simultaneously refers to the gap in communication as the viewer struggles to understand what is being spoken and depicted.

By the end of the 1980s, Hatoum took a more subtle approach to themes of oppression and displacement. Working mainly with sculpture and installation, the grid-like structures and geometric forms of Minimalism are transformed and imbued with new signification. In ''The Light at the End'' (1989), six vertical, red-hot heating elements block off a corner of the room imparting a sense of danger and recalling prison, captivity, and torture. The irony lies in the hopeful title, denied by what actually is at ''the end of the tunnel.'' Hatoum often uses well-known expressions for titles of her work, manipulating the meaning both literally and figuratively. The body's presence in these works is reduced to its palpably felt absence, while the viewer's body becomes an active force in providing meaning often with an imminent threat of danger. A similar experience is felt in ''Light Sentence'' (1992), an installation of empty wire metal lockers configured in a U-shape with a centrally placed light bulb rotating slowly up and down. The light's movement forces the shadow of the lockers projected on the walls to gradually move, disorienting the spectator as the room appears to shift. Typical of Hatoum's installation work she defines a space of confinement to simulate physical and psychological structures of power and control.

Another of Hatoum's tactics is to take normal objects and make them strange, as in ''Hair Necklace'' (1995). The artist also appropriates recognizable furniture forms and renders them unusable, even dangerous as in ''Marrow'' (1996), a crib constructed of rubber that has collapsed on itself. ''Pin Carpet'' (1995) lies on the ground as its name indicates yet remains completely dysfunctional. These examples of making the familiar strange are only surpassed in ''Corps étranger'' (1994). The viewer enters a dark, cylindrical structure with a circular video projection on the floor. The images are familiar yet unrecognizable. The audio element of a heart beating and stomach gurgling consumes the space. The video depicts the artist's body viewed both inside and out with the aid of an endoscopic camera. The excruciating detail of the body's surfaces, orifices, and inner passageways projected larger than life undermines a coherent understanding of the images and the body. The title—translated as ''foreign body''—appropriately describes the viewer's experience as well as the camera as foreign object penetrating the artist's body. Moreover, the piece reflects Hatoum's own foreign status both as woman in a patriarchal society and as living in a land not truly her own.

Hatoum's diverse artistic practice breaks and surpasses many boundaries, enriching our experience of the world. As she told Janine Antoni in *Bomb*: ''I want the work in the first instance to have a strong formal presence, and through the physical experience to activate a psychological and emotional response. In a very general sense I want to create a situation where reality itself becomes a questionable point. Where one has to reassess their assumptions and their relationship to things around them.''

—Kathleen Wentrack

HAUSER, Erich

Nationality: German. **Born:** Rietheim, Tuttlingen, 15 December 1930. **Education:** Volksschule, Rietheim, 1936–1940, and the Oberschule, Spaichingen, 1940–45; studied steel-engraving, Tuttlingen, and drawing, under Father Ansgar, Kloster Beuron, 1945–48; sculpture, Freien Kunstschule, Stuttgart 1949–51. **Family:** Married Gretl Kauwaletz in 1955; children: Andrea and Markus. **Career:** Sculptor and graphic artist, in Schramberg, 1952–58, in Rottweil, since 1959; first architectural sculpture commissions, 1959. Guest instructor, Hochschule für Bildende Künste, Hamburg, 1964–65; guest professor, Hochschule für bildende Künste, West Berlin, 1948–85. **Awards:** Kunstpreis der Jugend, Stuttgart, 1953, 1958; Kunstpreis Junger Westen, Recklinghausen, 1963; Kunstpreis der Stadt Wolfsburg, 1965; Sculpture Prize, *Bienal,* Sao Paulo, 1969; Verdienstkreuz, Bonn, 1972; Sculpture Prize, *Budapest Biennale,* 1975; Verdienstkreuz 1st class, Bonn, 1979; First Prize, Helmut-Kraft-Stiftung, Stuttgart, 1988; Oberschwäbischer Kuntspreis, Ehrenbürger der Stadt Rottweil, 1995. **Address:** 7210 Rottweil-Alstadt, 78628 Saline, Germany.

Individual Exhibitions:

1961 Galerie 62, Freiburg, West Germany
Studio F, Ulm, West Germany
1962 Kunstverein, Freiburg, West Germany
1963 Galerie Müller, Stuttgart
Galerie Nächst St. Stephan, Vienna
Galerie Brusberg, Hannover
1964 Museum der Stadt, Ulm, West Germany
Galerie Müller, Stuttgart
1965 Galerie Charles Lienhardt, Zurich
1966 Ausstellungsraum der Stadt, Hannover
Kunsthalle, Mannheim
Stadt Wolfsburg, West Germany
1967 Galerie Defet, Nuremberg
1968 Galerie der Stadt, Stuttgart
1969 Galerie Brusberg, Hannover

1970 *Werkverzeichnis Plastik 1962 bis 1969,* Galerie Defet, Nuremberg
Kuntsverein, Stuttgart
Kuntsverein, Mannheim
1971 Gimpel Hanover Galerie, Zurich
Gimpel Fils, London
1972 Studio F, Ulm, West Germany
Galerie KA, Mainz, West Germany
Kunsthaus, Aargau, Switzerland
1973 Kunsthalle, Kiel, West Germany
1974 Kuntsverein, Braunschweig, West Germany
1976 Galerie Hennemann, Bonn
Galerie Müller Stuttgart
1977 Städtische Galerie, Nordhorn, West Germany
1978 Forum Kunst, Rottweil, West Germany
Galerie der Spiegel, Cologne
Galerie St. Johann, Saarbrucken
Städtische Galerie Altes Theater, Ravensburg, West Germany
1980 Galerie Lauter, Mannheim
1981 Germanisches Nationalmuseum, Nuremberg, West Germany
1982 Forum Kunst, Rottweil, West Germany
1983 Galerie Domberger, at *Art 83,* Basel
Galerie Kunst und Design, Schloss Heutingsheim, Freiberg, West Germany
1984 Galerie Suzanne Fischer, Baden-Baden, West Germany
1985 Galerie am Winterberg, Vlotho, West Germany
1986 Landesgirokasse, Stuttgart
1987 Schlosshofgalerie Ewald Schrade, Schloss Mochental, West Germany
1992 *Erich Hauser: Recent Sculptures,* Rottweil, Germany
1999 Galerie für Gegenwarstkunst, Bonstetten
2000 Galerie Rössler, Munich

Selected Group Exhibitions:

1959 *Deutscher Kunstpreis der Jugend,* Kuntshalle, Baden-Baden, West Germany
1964 *Documents 3,* Kassel, West Germany (and *Documenta 4,* 1968; *Documenta 6,* 1977)
1969 *Bienal,* Sao Paulo
1973 *12th Biennale für Plastik,* Middleheim Park, Antwerp
1976 *Kunst Stuttgart,* Haus Baden-Würtemberg, Bonn
1979 *Im Namen des Volkes,* Wilhelm-Lehmbruck Museum, Duisburg, West Germany
1981 *Phoenix,* Alte Oper, Frankfurt
1983 *Deutsche Bildhauer der Gegenwart,* Kunstverein, Augsburg, West Germany
1985 *Kunst in der Bundersrepublik 1945–85,* Nationalgalerie, West Berlin
1987 *Mathematik in der Kunst der letzten 30 Jahre,* Wilhelm Hack Museum, Ludwigshafen, West Germany
1997 *''Taut'': The Diagonal as a Pictorial Structure—A Survey of 500 Years of Art on Paper,* Staatsgalerie Stuttgart

Collections:

Museum der Stadt, Ulm, West Germany; City of Hannover; Kuntshalle, Mannheim; Württembergischer Kunstverein, Stuttgart.

Publications:

On HAUSER: Books—*Erich Hauser,* exhibition catalog with text by Otto Mauer, Stuttgart 1963; *Erich Hauser,* exhibition catalog with text by Heinz Fuchs, Mannheim 1966; *Erich Hauser: Werkverzeichnis Plastic 1962 bis 1969,* exhibition catalog with text by Gerhard Bott, Nuremberg 1970; *Erich Hauser,* exhibition catalog with introduction by Robert Kudielka, Zurich 1971; *Deutsche Kunst der 60er Jahre: Plastik, Objekte, Aktionen* by Jürgen Morschel, Munich 1972; *Erich Hauser,* exhibition catalog with text by Rolf Lauter, Mannheim 1980; *Erich Hauser: Werkverzeichnis 1970–1980,* Zirndorf 1980; *Erich Hauser,* exhibition catalog with texts by Gerhard Bott, Manfred de la Motte and Jorn Merkert, Nuremberg 1981; *Erich Hauser: Werkverzeichnis III. Plastik 1980–1990* by Robert Kudielka, Neremberg 1990; *Erich Hauser,* exhibition catalog with text by Gerhard Bott, Cologne 1992; *Erich Hauser: Recent Sculptures,* exhibition catalog, Rottweil 1992.

HAYTER, Stanley William

Nationality: British. **Born:** London, 27 December 1901. **Education:** Croydon, Surrey; studied chemistry and geology at King's College, University of London, 1917–21, B.Sc.Hons. 1921; studied copper engraving with Joseph Hect, Paris, 1926. **Family:** Married Edith Fletcher in 1926 (divorced, 1929); married the sculptor Helen Phillips in 1940 (divorced, 1971); sons: William and Julian. **Career:** Etcher, engraver and painter: worked as a researcher for Mond Nickel Company, 1917, and worked for Anglo-Iranian Oil Company, Persia, 1922–25; made first prints, 1921; lived in Paris, 1926–39; founder member and director, Atelier, 17, Paris, 1927; close friendship with Paul Eluard from 1933; returned to London,1939, then lived in New York, 1940–46; founded Atelier 17, New York, 1941; returned to Paris: re-opened Atelier 17, 1950. Lecturer, California School of Fine Arts, San Francisco, 1940, 1948, 1960; lecturer in gravure, Brooklyn College, New York, 1949. **Awards:** Annual Prize, Philadelphia Print Club, 1943; Liturgic Prize, *Biennale,* Venice, 1958; First Prize, *International Exhibition of Prints,* Tokyo, 1960; Grand Prix des Arts de la Ville de Paris, 1972. Honorary Doctorates: Hamline University, St. Paul, Minnesota, 1983; New School for Social Research, New York, 1983. Chevalier, Legion d'Honneur, 1951; Chevalier, 1968, and Commandeur, 1986, Ordre des Arts et Letters; Honorary Royal Academician, London, 1982. C.B.E. (Commander, Order of the British Empire), 1967. **Died:** Of cardiac arrest, Paris, 4 May 1988.

Individual Exhibitions:

1927 Sacre du Printemps, Brussels
1929 Claridge Gallery, London
Palais des Beaux-Arts, Brussels
1932 Galerie Vignon, Paris
1938 Mayor Gallery, London
1940 San Francisco Museum of Fine Arts
1945 Mortimer Brandt Gallery, New York
1947 Durand-Ruel Gallery, New York
Esther Robles Gallery, Los Angeles
University of California at Los Angeles
1948 Gumps Gallery, San Francisco
1950 Perspectives, New York

1951 Galerie Louis Carré, Paris
1954 Kunsthalle, Bern
1955 Galerie Denise René, Paris
Galerie Otto Stangl, Munich
Galerie Betty Thommen, Basel
St. George's Gallery Prints, London
1957 Whitechapel Art Gallery, London (retrospective)
Museu de Arte Moderna, Rio de Janeiro
1959 Wallraf-Richartz Museum, Cologne (with William Scott and Kenneth Armitage)
1960 Esther Robles Gallery, Los Angeles
1961 Howard Wise Gallery, New York
Museum of Contemporary Art, Dallas
1966 Kunstnernes Kunsthandle Gallery, Copenhagen
Musée Rath, Geneva (toured Italy and the U.K.)
1967 City Art Gallery and Museum, Bradford, England (travelled to the University of Southampton, and Brighton College of Art, Sussex)
Victoria and Albert Museum, London
Grosvenor Gallery, London
Esther Robles Gallery, Los Angeles
University of Oregon Art Museum, Eugene
University of Texas Art Museum, Austin
Galerie Degée, Brussels
Galerie Madeleine Sothmann, Amsterdam
1968 Kunsthaus, Bielefeld, West Germany
Château-Musée, Dieppe, France
1969 Union Centrale des Arts Décoratifs, Paris
Musée du Louvre, Paris
1970 La Tortue Gallery, Santa Monica, California
1972 Musée d'Art Moderne de la Ville, Paris
1973 Christopher Drake Ltd., London
La Tortue Gallery, Santa Monica, California
1974 Galerie Madeleine Sothmann, Amsterdam
1976 Galerie de Seine, Paris
1977 University of Wisconsin, Madison (toured the United States, 1977–78)
1978 Kunsternes Hus, Oslo
Michael Parkin Gallery, London
1979 La Tortue Gallery, Santa Monica, California
1980 Galerie Madeleine Sothmann, Amsterdam
1981 Oxford Gallery (with former pupils)
Pier Arts Centre, Stromness, Scotland
Chichester District Museum, Sussex (toured the U.K., 1981–82)
1982 District Museum, Chichester, Sussex
1985 Gallery Santiza, Kobe, Japan
1986 Galerie J.C. Riedel, Paris
1987 Robert Douwma Gallery, London
1991 Day & Bird, London
1993 Musee du Dessin et de l'Estampe Originale, Gravelines

Selected Group Exhibitions:

1926 *Salon d'Automne,* Paris
1929 *Salon des Surindependants,* Paris
1934 *Atelier 17,* Galerie Pierre, Paris
1936 *Fantastic Art, Dada, Surrealism,* Museum of Modern Art, New York
1944 *Atelier 17,* Museum of Modern Art, New York
1947 *Salon de Mai,* Paris
1958 *Biennale,* Venice
1960 *International Exhibition of Prints,* Tokyo
1965 *Group Exhibition,* Howard Wise Gallery, New York
1989 *Modern American and European Prints: 55th Anniversary Exhibition,* Associated American Artists, New York
1991 *Print Europe,* Barbican Art Gallery, London
1997 *The Model Modern Art Gallery: Modern British Art in Miniature,* Pallant House Gallery, Chichester
1998 *Aspects of Modernism,* Elizabeth Harvey-Lee, North Aston

Collections:

Victoria and Albert Museum, London; Bibliothèque Nationale, Paris; Bibiothèque Royale, Brussels; Museum of Modern Art, New York; National Gallery, Washington, D.C.; National Gallery of Canada, Ottawa; National Gallery of Victoria, Melbourne.

Publications:

By HAYTER: Books—*New Ways of Gravure,* New York 1949, London 1966; *About Prints,* Oxford 1962. **Articles**—''The Development of Automatism'' in *Possibilities* (New York), 1943; ''The Lautrec Bite'' in *Artnews* (New York), November 1955; ''Execution d'un Tableau'' in *S.W. Hayter,* exhibition catalog, Paris 1976.

On HAYTER: Books—*S. W. Hayter,* exhibition catalog by Bryan Robertson, London 1957; *Stanley Hayter* by G. Limbour, Paris 1962; *The Engravings of S. W. Hayter* by Graham Reynolds, London 1867; *Modern English Painters* by John Rothenstein, London 1974; *S. W. Hayter,* exhibition catalog by Alexander Dunbar, Stromness, Scotland 1981; *For Stanley Hayter on His 80th Birthday,* Oxford 1981; S. W. Hayter, exhibition catalog with essay by Tokuhiro Nakajima, 1985; *Stanley William Hayter,* exhibition catalog with text by John Russell, Paris 1986; *Modern American and European Prints: 55th Anniversary Exhibition,* exhibition catalog, New York, 1989; *Print Europe,* exhibition catalog, with text by Irene Scheinman, Harland Walshaw and George Ball, London, 1991; *Stanley William Hayter 1901–88: Colour Engravings,* exhibition catalog, London, 1991; The *Prints of Stanley William Hayter: a Complete Catalogue,* by Peter Black, Desiree Moorhead and Jacob Kainen, London, 1992; *The Model Modern Art Gallery: Modern British Art in Miniature,* exhibition catalog, Chichester, 1997. **Articles**—''S.W. Hayter—Printmaker'' by Anne Stevens in *Antique Collector,* vol. 59, no. 10, October 1988; ''Ashmolean Museum, Oxford, England: Exhibit'' by Guy Burn in *Arts Review* (London), vol. 40, November 18, 1988; ''S.W. Hayter'' by David Cohen in *The Burlington Magazine,* vol. 131, February 1989; ''He Founded Atelier 17'' in *The Print Collector's Newsletter,* vol. 19, January/February 1989; ''The Expressive Qualities of Gravure: Calcongrafia; Accademia di San Luca, Rome; Exhibit'' by David Cohen in *Apollo* (London), ns. 132, July 1990; ''Stanley William Hayter: The Englishman from Montparnasse'' by Claude Bouyeure in *Cimaise,* vol. 37, June/August 1990; ''Relief Printing and the Development of Hayter's Colour Method'' by Peter Black in *Print Quarterly* (London), vol. 8, no. 4, December 1991; ''Hayter's Legacy in Paris'' by Duncan Scott in *Printmaking Today* (London), vol. 2, no. 2, Summer 1993.

* * *

From a family of artists—one of his ancestors was a miniaturist who published a treatise on perspective—Stanley William Hayter studied chemistry and geology and took a degree with honours at King's College, London. Until then he had played around with paints in his father's studio and made his first prints in his graduation year—1921. For three years he worked with an oil company on the Persian Gulf, then on completion of his contract he decided to exchange his scientific career for an artistic one. He went to Paris and took painting classes at the Académie Julian. He made friends with artists, among them Calder, Balthus and Joseph Hecht, who taught him how to use the burin. The last was the decisive step for Hayter.

In 1927 Hayter set up Atelier 17 (from the number of the street where he worked). It was to be a printmaking centre where masters and pupils would learn from each other. Since the 1930s the Academy has spread its repute across the world. During the 1939–1945 war, he was forced to move it to New York and re-established it in Paris in 1950.

While Hayter had for a long time a great reputation as an etcher and engraver (also as a teacher and educator having written a great deal on his subjects of printmaking) it was not until his large retrospective at the Whitechapel Gallery in 1957 that the public were made aware of his gifts as a painter. Yet in both media there are parallel histories of working that differ primarily only on questions of scale.

His early interest in Surrealism since 1929 brought him partly into the organization of the *International Surrealist Exhibition* in London in 1936, and he exhibited in it. His imagery was conditioned not so much by invention of new juxtapositions of objects from the world of reality as from a partial reliance on the unconscious in developing motives primarily abstract in nature. This automatism had its connection with the experiments of Miró and Masson in practising a drip technique, and in applying paint with string developed further by Jackson Pollock in later years. Hayter would perform an arabesque on the canvas over a ground of one pure colour, then elaborate in consecutive action, arriving at a complexity of pattern in the total of gestural signs.

Movement always preoccupied Hayter strongly in the work he performed, whether in paint or as prints. Movement in water, particularly, exerted a powerful pull born from firsthand experience, as he was an enthusiastic sailor. He has said: "The trajectory of movement is more clearly defined in water. I can follow the laws of space better in the substance of water which is dense and at the same time fluid." The concentric circles of ripples from a fallen stone, the curvilinear rhythms of waves and the contrasting colour and tone of convexities and concavities of the moving surface inspired Hayter in both paintings and prints to unique contemporary statements of abstract forms in tension and repose.

—G. S. Whittet

HEAD, Tim

Nationality: British. **Born:** London in 1946. **Education:** Studied fine art at the University of Newcastle, under Richard Hamilton, 1965–69, and sculpture at St. Martin's School of Art, London, 1969–70. **Career:** Lives and works in London. Worked on exhibition layout at Stedelijk Museum, Amsterdam, Summer 1967; assistant to Claes Oldenburg, New York, 1968, and to Robert Morris, Tate Gallery, London, 1971. Lecturer, Goldsmiths College, London, 1971–79. Since 1976, lecturer at the Slade School of Fine Art, London; Artistic Director, The Eurythmics Peacetour, 1999. **Awards:** Gulbenkian Visual Arts Award, 1976. Fellow, Clare Hall, Cambridge,1977–78. **Agent:** Anthony Reynolds Gallery, 37 Cowper Street, London EC2, England.

Individual Exhibitions:

1972 Museum of Modern Art, Oxford
1973 Gallery House, London
Studio Show, London
1974 Whitechapel Art Gallery, London
Gerage Gallery, London
1975 Rowan Gallery, London
Arnolfini Gallery, Bristol
1976 Rowan Gallery, London
1977 Anthony Strokes Gallery, London
1978 *Recent Work,* Kettle's Yard, Cambridge
Henie-Onstad Kunstcenter, Oslo
Rowan Gallery, London
1979 Institute of Modern Art, Philadelphia
Galleria Paola Betti, Milan
Serpentine Gallery, London (travelled to the Third Eye Centre, Glasgow, 1980)
1980 *Biennale,* Venice
Galerie Bama, Paris
1981 Vanilla Rehearsal Studios, London
1982 Tate Gallery, London
1983 Provinciaal Museum, Hasselt, Belgium
1985 Institute of Contemporary Arts, London
1988 Anthony Reynolds Gallery, London
Marlene Eleini Gallery, London
1992 *Return of the Body-Snatcher,* Whitechapel Gallery, London (retrospective) (catalog)
1995 Frith Street Gallery, London
Kunstverein, Freiburg, Germany (catalog)
Angelika Osterwalder Art Office, Hamburg
Kunstverein Braunschweig, Germany
Stadtgalerie Saarbrücken, Germany
Kunstverein Heilbronn, Germany
1997 *Blue Skies,* Chatham Historic Dockyard, City of Rochester Upon Medway, Kent, United Kingdom
Angelika Osterwalder Art Office, Hamburg, Germany

Selected Group Exhibitions:

1970 *New Sculpture,* Hayward Gallery, London (toured the U.K.)
1971 *Art Spectrum,* Alexandra Palace, London
1972 *Open Air Sculpture Exhibition,* Holland Park, London
1973 *Biennale,* Paris
1976 *Arte Inglese Oggi 1960–76,* Palazzo Reale, Milan
1977 *Documenta,* Kassel, West Germany
1979 *Un Certain Art Anglais,* Centre Georges Pompidou, Paris
1980 *British Art Now: A Modern Perspective,* Guggenheim Museum, New York
Beyond Surfaces, International Cultureel Centrum, Antwerp
1988 *The British Picture,* L.A. Louver Gallery, Venice, California

1994 *Red Ribbon Art Show 94,* Imagination Gallery, London
Endzeitstimmung, Gallery A, Stuttgart, Germany
1995 *Witness: Photoworks from the Collection,* Tate Gallery, Liverpool
From Picasso to Woodrow: Recently Acquired Prints and Portfolios, Tate Gallery, London
Open House, Kettle's Yard, Cambridge
Double-Click, Kingsgate Gallery, London
1996 *Paper Art 6,* Leopold-Hoesch Museum Der Stadt Düren
Geben und Nehmen, Schloss Plüschow, Mecklenburgischen Künstlerhaus
Happy End, Kunsthalle, Dusseldorf
Still But Not Silent, Tate Gallery, London
1997 *Threats and Containments,* Concourse Gallery, Byam Shaw School of Art, London
A Cloudburst of Material Possessions, South Bank National Touring Exhibition
1998 *Root,* Chisenhale Gallery, London
Family, Inverleigh House, Royal Botanical Gardens, Edinburgh
Thinking Aloud, Camden Arts Centre, London
1999 *Art to Z,* Zwemmer Gallery, London
2000 *Close Up,* Kunstverein Freiburg im Marienbad (also Kunsthaus Baselland and Kunstverein Hannover) (catalog)
Live in Your Head: Concept and Experiment in Britain 1965–75, Whitechapel Art Gallery, London

Collections:

Auckland City Art Gallery, Auckland, New Zealand; City Art Gallery, Southampton, UK; Fitzwilliam Museum, Cambridge, UK; John Creasey Museum, Salisbury, UK; Leeds City Art Gallery, UK; National Museums and Galleries on Merseyside, Walker Art Gallery, Liverpool, UK; The Arts Council of Great Britain; The British Council Collection; The Contemporary Arts Society; The Gulbenkian Foundation, London; The Solomon R Guggenheim Museum, New York; The Tate Gallery, London; The Victoria and Albert Museum, London.

Public Installations:

Light Rain, Artezium Arts and Media Centre, Luton, UK, 1998.

Publications:

By HEAD: Books—*Reconstruction,* London 1973; *Tim Head (1993),* London 1993. **Articles**—''Glossary: A Prelimination Sketch'' in *Flash Art* (Milan), October/November 1974; ''In Camera: A Projected Interview,'' with John Tagg, in *Studio International* (London), July/August 1975; statement in *Tim Head,* exhibition catalog, London 1981. **Film**—*Nelson Mandela 70th Birthday Tribute Concert,* 1988; Gavin *Bryars Concer Tour,* 1993–94.

On HEAD: Books—*Arte Inglese Oggi 1960–1976,* exhibition catalog Milan 1976; *Tim Head: Recent Work,* exhibition catalog by Fenella Crichton, Cambridge 1978; *Tim Head,* exhibition catalog by Norbert Lynton, Venice 1980; *Tim Head,* exhibition catalog with essay by Jean Fisher, Hasselt 1983; *The British Picture,* exhibition catalog with essays by Marina Vaizey, Catherine Lampert and William Feaver, Venice, California 1988. **Articles**—''Artist's Artist'' by Paul Overy in *The Times* (London), January 1975; ''Displacements'' by Caroline Tisdall in *The Guardian* (London), January 1975; ''The New Image of Culture'' in *Skira Annuel,* Geneva 1978; ''The Venice Biennale: The British Representatives'' by J. Bustard in *Art Monthly* (London), no. 38, 1980; ''Blasse Schatten Hinter Fahlen Feuern: Zu Den Arbeiten von Tim Head'' by Stephan Berg in *Kunstforum International,* no. 141, July/September 1998.

* * *

Tim Head is concerned, above all, with questions of illusion and reality as they manifest themselves in space, and thus he generally makes installation works expressly for the sites in which they are shown. But as titles such as ''Displacement,'' ''Dislocations'' and ''Present'' indicate, these are as much mental spaces as physical ones. Photographs, mirrors and slide projectors, which are normally verificatory devices, are used to demonstrate that the reality we perceive is far more complicated than we usually acknowledge. Outward appearances are not unassailable, and our perceptions of any space are transformed by numerous factors, not least illusion and allusion (imaginative engagement).

In ''Displacement'' (Tate Gallery 1975–76), for example, photographs were taken of part of a room in which certain mundane objects of the kind that might conceivably be present, like chairs, a ladder, a bucket and a cloak, had been placed. These photographs were then projected back into the same context though slightly moved aside from the originals. Since the spectator was free to wander through the space, he inevitably crossed the path of at least one of the four projectors, causing the image on the opposite wall to be momentarily blocked out and/or his own silhouette to be thrown there. Given that the carousels were the only source of illumination in the room, interrupting their paths emphasized the fact that light may simultaneously reveal both illusion and actuality; turn the projectors off and not only the illusions disappear but also the actual contents of the space.

Moreover, the viewer's silhouette thrown onto the wall reveals him to himself as mere shadow, without substance; he *knows* that he occupies the space physically yet the only means he has of verifying this is through illusion—an image in a mirror, a shape on a wall.

Such issues constantly inform Head's works, yet this is conceptual art only in the broadest sense of the term, for this installations must always be actively occupied in order to be completed. Head makes no attempt to disguise the mechanics of his *mise-en-scène,* for our recognition of what is going on is crucial to his challenging of our perceptions of the world we think we know. In a darkened space the objects in a colored photograph projected onto a wall can seem more convincing, and thus more authentic, than the dimly perceived objects actually present. Head does not want to fool the eye, for it is the ordinary world, not a fantasy one, which is the subject of his art. As he demonstrates, this world can be as elusive or mysteriously complicated as any we might invent.

—Lynne Cooke

In the 1990s, Head has come to rely less heavily on high-tech effects, his works more often examining cultural issues such as the visual and causal connections between the products of technology and what we as consumers are manipulated into believing about them. Head has also returned to painting, while remaining loyal to the Pop and minimalist movements that have influenced him all along.

Head frequently creates handmade reproductions of familiar items as ironic statements about the nature of the modern consumer-driven society. For his retrospective at London's Whitechapel Gallery, Head had the site transformed into a representation of the countryside in summer, the walls painted blue, the floor covered with artificial grass, creating a synthetic pastoral scene like those used by advertisers to appeal to the nostalgic, rural yearnings of consumers. Head's work explores the relationship of humanity to this new synthetic world in which the distinction between natural and artificial is disappearing. In his work, the imagery of advertising is transformed into a richly colored and textured—but ultimately disturbing—landscape.

—Joan Oleck

HEERICH, Erwin

Nationality: German. **Born:** Kessel, 29 November 1922. **Education:** Studied under Ewald Matare, Staatliche Kunstakademie, Dusseldorf, 1945–50. **Military Service:** Served in German Navy Artillery, in the North Sea, Atlantic and Adriatic, 1941–45; Lieutenant. **Family:** Married Hildegard Muller in 1950; children: Thomas, Stefan, Martin and Andrea. **Career:** Sculptor and graphic artist, Dusseldorf, since 1950. Lecturer, Seminar für Werktatige Erziehung, Dusseldorf, 1961–69. Professor, Staatliche Kunstakademie, Dusseldorf, since 1969. Honorary member, Akademie der Künste, West Berlin, 1974. **Awards:** Stankowski Foundation Award, 1995. **Agent:** Galerie Alfred Schmela, Mutter-Ey-Strasse 3,4000 Dusseldorf. **Addresses:** Schubertstrasse 6,4005 Meerbusch 2, Germany; and c/o Staatliche Kunstakademie, Eiskellerstrasse 1,4000 Dusseldorf, Germany.

Individual Exhibitions:

1964 Haus Grinten, Kranenburg, West Germany
1966 Galerie Alfred Schmela, Dusseldorf
1967 Galerie Müller, Stuttgart
Städtisches Museum, Mönchengladbach, West Gemany
1968 Stedelijk Van Abbemuseum, Eindhoven, Netherlands
Cardboard Sculptures 1956–1968. Dwan Gallery, New York
1969 Galerie Alfred Schmela, Dusseldorf
Galerie Borgmann, Cologne
1970 Galerie Appel und Fertsch, Frankfurt
Galerie Rénee Ziegler, Zurich
Galerie Borgmann, Cologne
1971 Galerie Droscher, Hamburg
Neue Galerie, Baden-Baden, West Gemany
Galerie Tangente, Heidelberg
1972 Kunstverein, Dusseldorf
Galerie Klein, Bonn
Galerie Szepan, Gelsenkirchen, West Gemany
Galerie René Block, West Berlin
1973 Landesmuseum, Darmstadt
1974 Landesmuseum, Bonn
Griffelkunst, Hamburg
Galerie Lauter, Mannheim
Galerie Hetzler und Keller, Stuttgart
1979 Städtische Kunsthalle, Dusseldorf
1982 *Raumliche und flachige Diagramme,* Museum Haus Esters, Krefeld, West Germany
1975 Galerie Schmela, Dusseldorf
1976 Kunstverein, Freiburg
Galerie Schmela, Dusseldorf
1979 Stadtische Kunsthalle, Dusseldorf
1980 Stadtisches Museum Schloss Morsbroich, Leverkusen
1981 Kunstverein, Mannheim
1982 Museum Haus Esters, Krefeld, West Germany
1994 *Plan and Process,* Muzeum Sztuki, Lodz (catalog)
1997 Musée Hombroich à Dusseldorf, Germany
1998 Museum Insel Hombroich, Neuss, Germany (catalog)
Skulptur und der Architektonische Raum, Cologne (catalog)
1999 *Making/Thinking: Artists Build #3,* The Matthew Architecture Gallery, The University of Edinburgh, Scotland

Selected Group Exhibitions:

1968 *Documenta 4,* Kassel, West Germany
1970 *Jetzt: Kunst in Deutschland,* Kunsthalle, Cologne
Strategy: Get Arts, Richard Demarco Gallery, Edinburg
1971 *Contemporary German Art,* National Museum of Modern Art, Tokyo
1972 *Szene Rhein-Ruhr,* Museum Folkwang, Essen
1973 *Bienal,* Sao Paulo
1974 *Projekt 74,* Kunstverein, Cologne
1979 *Matare und seine Schuler,* Akademie der Künste, West Berlin
1982 *Drawings for Sculpture Since 1945,* Kunstverein, Braunschweig
1998 *Hildegard und Erwin Heerich, Horst Keining: Stoffbilder, Gemälde,* Heidelberger Kunstverein (also Städtisches Museum Mühlheim, Ruhr (catalog)
1999 *The Space Here is Everywhere,* Bahnwärterhaus, Galerien der Stadt Esslingen, Germany (catalog)
Architektonische Skulptur in 20 Jahrhundert, Wilhelm Lehmbruck Museum, Duisburg, Germany
Von Beuys bis Cindy Sherman, Stadtische Galerie im Lenbachhaus, Munich

Collections:

Kunstmuseum, Dusseldorf; Städtisches Museum, Mönchengladbach, West Germany; Wilhelm-Lehmbruck Museum, Duisburg, West Germany; Stedelijk Van Abbemuseum, Eindhoven, Netherlands; Rheinisches Landesmuseum, Bonn; Museum Folkwang, Essen; Städtisches Museum, Hamburg; Kunstmuseum, Basel.

Public Installations:

Insel Hombroich Museum, Dusseldorf, Germany, 1994.

Publications:

By HEERICH: Books—*Kunst + Design: Erwin Heerich,* Dusseldorf 1995; *Erwin Heerich: Plastische Modelle für Architektur und Skulptur/Plastic Models for Architecture and Sculpture,* Dusseldorf 1995; *Erwin Heerich: Die Entwicklung Architektonischer Skulpturen,* Cologne 1999.

On HEERICH: Books—*Heerich* by Franz van der Griten, Kranenburg, West Germany 1964; *Erwin Heerich: Cardboard Sculptures 1956–1968,* exhibition catalog, New York 1968; *Heerich,* exhibition catalog with text by Johannes Cladders, Eindhoven, Netherlands 1968; *Deutsche Kunst: Eine neue Generation* by Rof-Günter by Jurgen Dienst, Cologne 1970; *Deutsche Kunst der 60er Jahre* Morschel, Munich 1971; *Kunstijahrbuch 2,* edited by Jürgen Harten, Horst Richter, Karl Ruhrberg and Wieland Schmied, Hannover 1972; *Projekt 74: Aspekte internationaler Kunst am Anfang der 70er Jahre,* exhibition catalog with texts by Dieter Ronte, Evelyn Weiss, Manfred Schneckenburger and others, Cologne 1974; *Erwin Heerich,* exhibition catalog with text by Walter Jürgen Hofmann, Dusseldorf 1979; *Erwin Heerich: Oeuvre-Catalog,* 4 vols., by Hans van der Grinten, Gerhard Storck and Johannes Cladders, Dusseldorf 1980–83; *Erwin Heerich: Raumliche und flachige Diagramme,* exhibition catalog with text by Julian Heynen, Krefeld, West Germany 1982. **Articles—** ''Museumsinsel Hombroich'' in *Werk, Bauen + Wohnen,* vol. 81/48, January/February 1994; ''Der Altar als Mitte: Eine Skulptur von Erwin Heerich als Ergebnis Eines Gemeindeprozesses in Münster/ Westfalen'' by Thomas Sternberg in *Kunst und Kirche,* no. 4, 1995; ''Form Entsteht aus dem Gefuhl'' by Gunder Clauss in *ART: Das Kunstmagazin,* no. 3, March 1999.

HEILIGER, Bernhard

Nationality: German. **Born:** Stettin, 11 November 1915. **Education:** Kunstgeweberschule, Stettin, 1935–37; Hochschule für Bildende Künste, Berlin, 1938–41. **Military Service:** Served in the German Army, 1941–45; prisoner of war, 1945. **Career:** Travelled to Paris, 1939; introduced to the modern art of Maillol, Despiau and Brancusi; began career as sculptor, Berlin, 1945; first portrait sculpture, 1951. Instructor, Hochschule für Angewandt Kunst, Berlin-Weissensee, 1947–49, and Hochschule für Bildende Kunst, Berlin, since 1950. Set designer, *Faust II,* Schiller Theatre, Berlin, 1966. **Awards:** First Prize, Max Planck Competition, Berlin 1949; Kunstpreis der Stadt Berlin, 1950; Kunstpreis der Stadt Köln, 1952; International Prize, Unknown Political Prisoner Competition, Institute of Contemporary Arts, London, 1953; Grosser des Landes, Nordrhein-Westfalen, Dusseldorf, 1956; First Prize, Sculpture Competition, Max Planck Institute für Physik und Astrophysik, Munich, 1959; Burda Prize for Sculpture, 1965; Lovis Corinth Prize, West Germany, 1975. Honorary member, Accademia Fiorentina, Florence, 1978. **Died:** 25 October 1995, Berlin. Bernhard Heiliger Foundation established 1996.

Individual Exhibitions:

1946 Galerie Buchholz, Berlin
Bernhard Heiliger/Mac Zimmerman, Galerie Rosen, Berlin
1948 Galerie Bremer, Berlin
1950 Haus am Waldsee, Berlin
1951 Museum am Ostwall, Dortmund (toured West Germany)
Galerie Bremer, Berlin
1954 Graphisches Kabinett Dr. Hanna Grisebach, Heidelberg
1955 Freiburger Kunstverein, Freburg
Städtisches Karl-Ernst-Osthaus Museum, Hagen, West Germany
Overbeck-Gesellschaft, Lübeck
Westfälischer Kunstverein, Münster
1956 *Kopfe,* Haus am Waldsee, Berlin (toured West Germany)
Kunstverein, Brunswick, West Germany
Kunsthalle, Bremen
Museum Folkwang, Essen
Kunstverein, Kassel, West Germany
Kunstverein, Cologne
Städtisches Museum, Mulheim an der Ruhr, West Germany
Plastik, Zeichnungen, Haus am Waldsee, Berlin
1958 Roland, Browse and Delbanco Gallery, London
Bernhard Heiliger/Alexander Camaro, Lindolinshof, Esslingen, West Germany
1959 Galerie Hella Nebelung, Dusseldorf
Stadthalle, Wolfsburg, West Germany (travelled to Kongresshalle, Berlin, the Städtischen Kunsthalle, Mannheim, and the Kunstmuseum, Lucerne, 1959–60)
1960 Galerie Guenther Franke, Munich
1961 Staempfli Gallery, New York
1962 Galerie der Edition Rothe, Heidelberg
1963 German Embassy, Paris
1964 Galerie Springer, Berlin
Galerie im Erker, St. Gallen, Switzerland
Galleria Il Canale, Venice
1965 Galerie Emmy Widmann, Bremen
Galerie der Edition Rothe, Heidelberg
Galerie Guenther Franke, Munich
1966 Staempfli Gallery, New York
1970 Galleria Il Canale, Venice
19 Neue Sculpturen, Galerie Guenther Franke, Munich
Staempfli Gallery, New York
1971 Galerie Wuensche, Bonn
Galerie Hella Nebelung, Dusseldorf
Galerie Commeter, Hamburg
1972 Kunstkabinett Hanna Bekker vom Rath, Dusseldorf
1973 Galerie Bremer, Berlin
1975 Akademie der Künste, Berlin (retrospective; travelled to the Saarland Museum, Saarbrucken)
1980 Erker-Galerie, St. Gallen, Switzerland (travelled to Grossplastic für der Noorwede, Hamburg)
1981 *8 Neue Sculpturen,* Galerie Dibbent, Berlin
1982 Galerie Pels-Leusden, Berlin
1984 Galerie Roswitha Haftmann, Zurich
1985 Wilhelm-Lehmbruck-Museum, Dusiburg, West Germany
Galerie Muhlenbusch, Dusseldorf
1986 Middelheim Open-Air Museum, Antwerp
Sculpture Park, Heilbronn, West Germany
1987 Galerie Pels-Leusden, West Berlin
Galerie Winkelmann, Dusseldorf
1991 *Bernhard Heiliger: Sculptures in the Lustgarten, Relief Objects and Collage Drawings in the Altes Museum,* Staatliche Museen
Nationalgalerie, Berlin
1992 Galerie Dube, Munich
1993 Galerie Breitling, Stuttgart
Stadtsmuseum, Frankfurt/Main
Galerie Roth, Frankfurt/Main
1995 Retrospective, Kunst-und Ausstellungshalle der Bundesrepublik Deutschland, Bonn
2000 *Bernhard of the Holy-The Headings,* Georg Kolbe Museum,

Selected Group Exhibitions:

1953 *Bienal,* Sao Paulo
1954 *Living Art in Germany,* National College of Art, Dublin
1956 *Biennale,* Venice
1958 *Pittsburgh International Exhibition,* Carnegie Institute
1959 *Berliner Festwoche,* Kongresshalle, Berlin
1960 *Arte Alema desde 1945,* Museo de Arte Moderna, Rio de Janeiro
1964 *Sculpture Allemande du 20e. Siècle,* Musée Rodlin, Paris
1967 *German Art in Berlin,* Musée des Beaux-Arts, Montreal

Collections:

Musée Royal des Beaux-Arts, Antwerp; Kunstmuseum, Winterthur, Switzerland; Nationalgalerie, Berlin; Museum am Ostwall, Dortmund; Kunsthalle, Hamburg; Tate Gallery, London; Israel Museum, Jerusalem; Museo de Arte Moderna, Sao Paulo; Museum of Modern Art, New York; Guggenheim Museum, New York.

Publications:

By HEILIGER: Books—text in *Bernhard Heiliger,* exhibition catalog, Wolfsburg 1959; reprinted in *Bernhard Heiliger,* exhibition catalog, Lucerne 1960; text in *Heiliger,* exhibition catalog, St. Gallen, Switzerland 1964.

On HEILIGER: Books—*Heiliger,* exhibition catalog, by Will Grohmann, Berlin 1950; *Heiliger*, exhibition catalog, by Will Grohmann, Dortmund 1951; *Bernhard Heiliger: Kopfe,* exhibition catalog with text by K. L. Skutsch, Berlin 1956; *Bernhard Heiliger: Plastik, Zeichnungen,* exhibition catalog with text by K. L. Skutsch, Berlin 1957; *Bernhard Heiliger,* exhibition catalog with text by Hanns Theodor Flemming and Will Grohmann, London 1958; *Heiliger,* exhibition catalog by Joachim Tiburitus, Kurt Martin, and Umbro Apollonio, Wolfsburg 1959, reprinted as *Heiliger,* Lucerne 1960; *Bernhard Heiliger,* exhibition catalog with introduction by Kurt Martin, New York 1961; *Bernhard Heiliger* by Hanns Theodor Flemming, Berlin 1962; *Heiliger,* exhibition catalog by George Schmidt and Martin Heidegger, St. Gallen, Switzerland 1964; *Bernhard Heiliger,* exhibition catalog with text by Piero Dorazio, Venice 1970; *Bernhard Heiliger: 19 Neue Sculpturen,* exhibition catalog, Munich 1970; *Bernhard Heiliger,* exhibition catalog by Wieland Schmied and Hanns Theodor Flemming, Berlin 1975; *Bernhard Heiliger* by A. M. Hammacher, St. Gallen, Switzerland 1978; *Bernhard Heiliger,* exhibition catalog with essay by Siegfied Salzmann, West Berlin 1987; *Bernhard Heiliger* by Siegfried Salzmann and Lothar Romain, Germany, 1989; *Weltkunst* by V. Bruckmann, Munich 1992.

* * *

After his studies at the Stettin School of Arts and at the Berlin Academy, Bernhard Heiliger visited Paris at a time when it was still possible to come under the influence of Despiau and Maillol, whom he met. For a young artist in his twenties, they were formative years, though the results were not seen until after 1946 when he began to work towards recognition and to teach.

He ranks as the most important figure in German sculpture reaching maturity in the 1960s. His direction could be classified as towards the symbolic in plastic terms, verging from the stylized figurative to the abstract in shape and concept. ''Recorded vitality'' is the phrase Heiliger has used to describe his work, and this is apparent through a considerable body of sculptures. It can be seen in 1950 with his ''Seraph I'' that harks back to the winged nike of the Parthenon, while at the same time reflecting something of Brancusi's electric vigour.

Tension and movement in a sculpture having no allusive properties are inherent factors in much of his monumental oeuvre. His entry for the Memorial to the Unknown Political Prisoner competition in 1953, despite its hackneyed motive—a caged-in figure—had elements such as the riven torso that wrought sculptural drama from the rupture of his material.

Vegetable growth possessed by the human form in a kind of Daphne paraphrase also took its place in his imagery about 1955, and this symbolization of regeneration occurs in much subsequent work accompanied by the broken and wounded aspects of man's vulnerability. The bronzes, ''Sebastian'' and ''Vogeltod,'' of 1961 are elegiac in treatment, yet retain in their diagonal emphasis a hint of man rising from his earthbound discomfiture.

Heiliger's capacity for giving plastic form to unmaterial idea is best known in ''Die Flamme'' (The Flame), standing more than six metres high in the Ernst Reuter Platz, Berlin, a bronze of colour and animation that is a remarkable example of public sculpture in the non-figurative canon.

Architecture as the setting for sculpture has interested Heiliger, but primarily as a contrasting environment where the image preserves its own identity. His figure groups in the open, though stylized in pared and bone-like silhouettes, preserve the upright dignity of Hellenic prototypes. This spare reduction of form is carried into the sphere of portraiture without compromise of artistic truth. The heads of Ernst Schroder and Comte Philippe d'Arscot might suggest a slightness of content were it not for the tautness and nervous energy they transmit.

In smaller-scale pieces, Heiliger invests his figures with the classic primitivism of Cycladic alabasters. This fusion of the present with the past is a significant contribution from Heiliger, marking his sculpture by its catalytic force.

—G. S. Whittet

HEIZER, Michael

Nationality: American. **Born:** Berkeley, California, 4 November 1944. **Education:** San Francisco Art Institute, 1963–64. **Career:** Lives and works in New York and Nevada. Began excavation projects, Nevada 1967–68; major earthworks, Central Eastern Nevada, 1969–71, 1972–76, 1980–88, 1980–1999. **Awards:** The National Endowment for the Arts Grant, 2000.

Individual Exhibitions:

1969 Heiner Friedrich Galerie, Munich
1970 Dwan Gallery, New York
1971 Detroit Institute of Arts
1974 Ace Gallery, Los Angeles
Fourcade Droll Inc., New York

1976 Xavier Fourcade Inc., New York
1977 Ace Gallery, Los Angeles
Xavier Fourcade Inc., New York
Ace Gallery, Venice California
Galerie am Promenadeplatz, Munich
1979 Folkwang Museum, Essen (travelled to the Kröller-Müller Museum, Otterlo, Netherlands)
Richard Hines Gallery, Seattle
1980 St. Louis Art Museum
Xavier Fourcade Inc., New York
1984 Museum of Contemporary Art, Los Angeles
1985 Rice University, Houston, Texas
1995 *Art Before Life: Michael Heizer 1994,* Ace Gallery, New York
1997 *Hard Edge Ejecta,* Knoedler & Company, New York
Fondazione Prada, Milan, Italy (catalog)
1998 David Zwirner Gallery, New York

Selected Group Exhibitions:

1968 *Sculpture Annual,* Whitney Museum, New York
1970 *When Attitude Becomes Form,* Kunsthalle, Berne (toured Europe)
1971 *Guggenheim International,* Guggenheim Museum, New York
1976 *200 Years of American Sculpture,* Whitney Museum, New York
1977 *Documenta,* Kassel, West Germany
Probing the Earth: Contemporary Land Projects, Hirshhorn Museum, Washington D.C. (toured the United States)
1978 *Painting and Sculpture Today: 1978,* Indianapolis Museum of Art
1980 *L'Amerique aux Independants,* Grand Palais, Paris
1982 *Twenty American Artists: Sculpture 82,* San Francisco Museum of Modern Art
1984 *Geometric Extraction,* Whitney Museum, New York
1995 *Different Sides: Drawings/Photographs/Prints/Paintings/ Sculpture,* Knoedler & Company, New York
Contemporary Masterworks, Knoedler & Company, New York
1997 *Land Marks,* John Weber Gallery, New York
47th Venice Biennale, Italy
1998 *Sculptors Draw,* Rosenberg + Kaufman Fine Art, New York

Collections:

Metropolitan Museum of Art, New York: Fogg Art Museum, Harvard University, Cambridge, Massachusetts; Kröller-Müller Museum, Otterlo, Netherlands; Kunstmuseum, Basel; Bayerische Staatsgemaldesammlungen, Munich; Museum Ludwig, Cologne.

Public Installations:

North, South, East, West, Bluffton College, Ohio, 1982; *45°, 90°, 180°,* Rice University, Houston, 1984; *Perforated Object,* Federal Courthouse, Reno, Nevada, 1997; *City,* Garden Valley, Nevada, 1972–99.

Publications:

By HEIZER: Book—*Michael Heizer: Double Negative—Sculpture in the Land,* with text by Mark C. Taylor, New York 1995. **Article—** "The Art of Michael Heizer" in *Artforum* (New York), December 1969.

On HEIZER: Books—*The New Avant-Garde: Issues for the Art of the 70's* by Gregoire Muller, New York 1972; *Michael Heizer,* exhibition catalog by Zdenek Felix and Ellen Joosten, Essen, Germany and Otterlo, Netherlands 1979; *Michael Heizer: Sculpture in Reverse,* exhibition catalog edited by Julia Brown, Los Angeles 1984; *Michael Heizer,* exhibition catalog with essay by William Camfield, Houston 1985. **Articles—**"Holes Without History" by Diane Waldman in *ARTnews* (New York), May 1971; "The Earth Mover" by Douglas Davis in *Newsweek* (New York), 18 November 1974; "Michael Heizer: Complex One" in *Domus* (Milan), February 1975; "Artworks on the Land" by Elizabeth C. Baker in *Art in America* (New York), January/February 1976; "Earth-Shaking News from the Art World: Sculpturing the Land" by Earl Gottschalk, Jr. in the *Wall Street Journal* (New York),10 September 1976; "Site Inspection" by Lawrence Alloway in *Artforum* (New York), October 1976; "New Landscapes in Art" by Kay Larson in the *New York Times Magazine,* 13 May 1979; "Sculpture on the Streets" by Hilton Kramer in the *New York Times,* 15 July 1979; "Sculpture in Public Places" in *Horizon* (New York), October 1979; "A New Stonehenge in Nevada" by Jed Horne in *Quest/80* (New York), September 1980; "Working with Earth, Michael Heizer Makes Art as Big as All Outdoors" in *Smithsonian,* April 1986; "Monuments to Making" by Virginia Rutledge in *Art in America* (New York), vol. 83, no. 7, July 1995; "Michael Heizer" by Loredana Parmesani in *Flash Art,* vol. 30, no. 193, March-April 1997; "A Sculptor's Colossus of the Desert" in *The New York Times,* 12 December 1999; "Michael Heizer: Das Nevada Projekt" by Michael Kimmelman in *ART: Das Kunstmagazin,* no. 3, March 2000.

* * *

Since the late 1960s, the artist Michael Heizer has made the surface of the earth the subject and site of numerous sculptural projects that address the confrontation between human (or material) presence and vast emptiness. Using the tools of modern industrial engineering and building technologies, Heizer has sought to invoke and maintain 'the venerable tradition of megalithic societies" from the Egyptian to the pre-Columbian.

Double Negative, 1969–70, one of the artist's earliest and best known earthworks, consists of two enormous vertical cuts of land in the remote Virgin River Mesa of Nevada. Whatever qualities of mass, volume, and space that the work conveys are paradoxically the result of absence: 240,000 tons of rhyolite and sandstone were removed to create the work. Its cut walls measure fifty feet high and thirty feet in length, but the piece is not visible until one has physically attained the site after a long, somewhat arduous approach. Heizer himself has stated that the two cuts are so large that there is an implication that they are joined as one single form. The title *Double Negative* is a literal description of two cuts but has metaphysical implications because a double negative is impossible. There is nothing there, yet it is still a sculpture.

Simultaneously monumental and transient, *Double Negative* has been subject to processes of erosion and siltation that have subtly altered its appearance over time. This intended interaction with wind and water has allowed the work to encompass geological time within itself, to be in a sense 'completed' by natural forces. But time has also shown the piece to be less resistant to assimilation by the art world. In keeping with the prevailing concerns of environmental sculptors of the late sixties and early seventies, *Double Negative* was conceived as being at a far remove—both psychologically and physically—from the urban context of the contemporary artworld, exempt from the relentless commodification of the art object. Ironically, the piece now forms part of the permanent collection of the Los Angeles County Museum of Art, acting a sort of far-flung satellite gallery. But true to Heizer's intent the full impact of the work can only be derived from a visit to its site amidst desert wind, sky, and scrub. "The earth itself was sculpted away. . . . The bottom was cooler though there were no shadows. Damp walls of earth surrounded and protected me from the relentless desert. Air from the valley moved up and through this space making those sounds usually called 'silence.' Absence was the prevailing sensation. . . . I was not apart, looking at it. I was in it. . . . Boulders stood like sentinels. A turkey buzzard lay on the sky." (Virginia Dwan, "*Double Negative:* A Recollection," 1983, as quoted in *Michael Heizer: Sculpture in Reverse,* The Museum of Contemporary Art, Los Angeles, 1984.) Subject to and part of the earth's own mass and energy, yet vast enough to render those forces inconsequential, *Double Negative* resounds with questions of human limitations in the face of nature and cosmos.

Heizer's *Complex One,* 1972–76, is the first completed phase of *City,* an ongoing, massive architectural project in the Nevada desert. Though not functional in any strict sense, *Complex One* uses the *mastaba* form of the original burial vault of the Pyramid of Zoser in Saqqara, Egypt, which Heizer, the son of a noted archeologist, calls "the first pyramid and the first big architecture." Nine thousand tons of concrete drawn directly from the site were poured to create the huge mound form. A concrete band inspired by the serpent motif from the pyramid of Chichen Itza in Mexico's Yucatan province runs round the periphery of the base. Heizer has employed a cantilever system, a modern engineering method, to suspend and project this horizontal band outward. This use of the most contemporary technologies to construct daunting megaliths, that in turn recall ancient, monumental engineering feats requiring vast expenditures of human energy, allows Heizer's work to commemorate both past and present. The gigantic scale of *Complex I,* with its mass of compacted earth held behind a frontal face of cement, reverses the excavation process of *Double Negative*. Here it is the desert—a low, ancient sea—that is elevated by Heizer's displacement of material, which rises all the more powerfully against the desert's stark, endless horizon.

While working on *Double Negative* and *City,* Heizer has been aware of the close proximity of nuclear testings sites in the Nevada desert. This perhaps accounts for *Complex One*'s artifactual quality and its impenetrable mass, which is conceived partially as a bulwark against destruction. In a more recent project, Heizer has been able to directly address and transform the threat of environmental devastation. *Buffalo Rock Effigy Tumuli,* from 1986, consists of five shaped-earth mounds in the form of water animals on the site of 60 once-barren acres of a toxic Illinois strip mine. Commissioned by the Ottawa Silica Company, with assistance from the Illinois Abandoned Mined Lands Reclamation Council, on land that had been abandoned since the 1940s, Heizer, with the help of environmental engineers, enlisted standard land-reclamation techniques such as earth moving, chemical treatment, and grass seeding to eliminate problems of erosion, sedimentation and acid run-off. Heizer's design of five mounds shaped like a water strider, frog, catfish, snake, and turtle, respectively, was inspired by the ancient burial mounds of early Native Americans, such as the famous serpentine mounds of southern Ohio. Here Heizer has adapted these antecedents and the reclamation process to his own vocabulary: the animal effigies are topographically married to their site, as are all of Heizer's outdoor works, requiring an aerial perspective to be instantly recognizable. Approached on foot, the animal mounds gain symbolic power, seen as they are in contrast to the devastated tracts of still unreclaimed land they adjoin. From either vantage point, the beauty, drama, and significance of *Effigy Tumuli* are readily accessible to a wide audience in a way that most public sculpture is not. Here Heizer's dialogue between modern technology and earth takes on expanded meaning.

—Dorothy Valakos

HELD, Al

Nationality: American. **Born:** Brooklyn, New York, 12 October 1928. **Education:** New York City public schools, 1933–45; Art Students League, New York, under Harry Sternberg, 1948–49; Grande Chaumière, Paris, under Zadkine, 1950–52. Served in the United States Navy, 1945–47. **Family:** Married to Sylvia Stone. **Career:** Associated with American painters Frank Lobdell, Bill Rivers, Ellsworth Kelly, Jack Youngerman, Sam Francis, Milton Resnick, George Sugarman, Jules Olitski, Shirley Jaffe, Ken Noland, Paris, 1950–52; returned to New York, 1953; worked as carpenter, truck-driver, and on road construction, San Francisco, 1954–55; started removal business, New York, 1955–60; founder, with others, Brata Gallery, New York, 1956; first black and white paintings, New York, 1967. Associate professor of Art, then professor, Yale University, New Haven, Connecticut, since 1962. **Awards:** Logan Medal, Art Institute of Chicago, 1964; Guggenheim Fellowship, 1966; Jack I. and Lillian L. Poses Brandeis University Creative Arts Award Painting Meday, 1983. **Address:** c/o Karen McCready Fine Art, 425 West 13th St., New York, New York 10014, U.S.A.; c/o Robert Miller Gallery, 524 West 26th Street, New York, New York 10001, U.S.A.

Individual Exhibitions:

1951 Galerie 8, Paris
1958 Poindexter Gallery, New York
1969 Poindexter Gallery, New York
1961 Poindexter Gallery, New York
Bonino Gallery, Buenos Aires
1962 Poindexter Gallery, New York
1964 Galerie René Ziegler, Zurich
Galerie Gunar, Dusseldorf
1965 André Emmerich Gallery, New York
1966 Stedelijk Museum, Amsterdam
Galerie Muller, Stuttgart
1967 André Emmerich Gallery, New York
1968 André Emmerich Gallery, New York
Museum of Art, San Francisco
Corcoran Gallery, Washington, D.C.
Recent Paintings, Institute of Contemporary Art, Philadelphia (travelled to the Contemporary Arts Association, Houston)
1970 Galerie René Ziegler, Zurich

André Emmerich Gallery, New York
1971 Donald Morris Gallery, Detroit
1972 *New Paintings,* André Emmerich Gallery, New York
1973 André Emmerich Gallery, New York
1974 Galerie André Emmerich, Zurich
Donald Morris Gallery, Detroit
Whitney Museum, New York (retrospective)
Galerie Muller, Cologne
1975 André Emmerich Gallery, New York
Jared Sable Gallery, Toronto
Adler Castillo Gallery, Caracas
1976 André Emmerich Gallery, New York
1977 Galerie Roger d'Amecourt, Paris
Galerie Marguerite Lamy, Paris
Galerie Renée Ziegler, Zurich
Annely Juda Fine Art, London
Donald Morris Gallery, Birmingham, Michigan
1978 *New Paintings,* André Emmerich Gallery, New York
Paintings and Drawings 1973–78, Institute of Contemporary Arts, Boston
Janus Gallery, Venice, California
Marianne Friedland Gallery, Toronto
1979 André Emmerich Gallery, New York
1980 *Al Held 1959–61,* Robert Miller Gallery, New York
Gimpel-Hanover, Zurich
Galerie André Emmerich, Zurich
Quadrat Bottrop-Modern Galerie, Zurich
1982 Robert Miller Gallery, New York
1984 André Emmerich Gallery, New York
1985 Robert Miller Gallery, New York
André Emmerich Gallery, New York
1987 André Emmerich Gallery, New York
Robert Miller Gallery, New York
1990 *Paintings After Paris 1953–55,* Robert Miller Gallery, New York (catalog)
1996 *Recent Work,* Andre Emmerich Gallery, New York
1998 *The Last Series,* Robert Miller Gallery, New York catalog (catalog)
2000 *Unfolding 2000,* Robert Miller Gallery, New York (catalog)

Selected Group Exhibitions:

1959 *Neue Amerikanische Malerie,* Kunstmuseum, St. Gallen, Switzerland
1964 *Post Painterly Abstraction,* Los Angeles County Museum of Art (toured the United States)
1967 *Documenta 4,* Museum Fridericianum, Kassel, West Germany
1970 *Contemporary American Painting and Sculpture from New York Galleries,* Wilmington Society of Fine Arts, Delaware Art Center
1973 *Whitney Biennial Exhibition,* Whitney Museum, New York
1976 *Drawing Today in New York,* Tulane University, New Orleans (toured the United States 1976–77)
1977 *A View of a Decade,* Museum of Contemporary Art, Chicago
1979 *Art Inc.: American Paintings from Corporate Collections,* Museum of Fine Arts, Montgomery, Alabama (toured the United States)
1982 *A Private Vision,* Museum of Fine Art, Boston
1986 *Action Precision,* Newport Harbor Art Museum, Newport Beach, California
1996 *New Visions,* Andre Emmerich Gallery, New York
1997 *The Quest for the Absolute: Geometric Abstraction to Minimalism,* Sheldon Memorial Art Gallery and Sculpture Gallery, University of Nebraska—Lincoln, Nebraska
1998 *Great Graphics,* Karen McCready Fine Art, New York
Abstracted Presence, Edward Thorp Gallery, New York
1999 *Jean Arp, Gianfredo Camesi, Gotthard Graubner, Al Held: Arbeiten auf Papier,* Galerie Renée Ziegler, Zurich

Collections:

Museum of Modern Art, New York; Whitney Museum, New York; Metropolitan Museum of Art, New York; Yale University Art Gallery, New Haven, Connecticut; Fogg Art Museum, Harvard University, Cambridge, Massachusetts; Delaware Art Museum, Wilmington; Hirshhorn Museum and Sculpture Garden, Washington, D.C.; San Francisco Museum of Modern Art; Staatsgalerie, Stuttgart; Kunsthaus, Zurich.

Public Installations:

Frieze, Ronald Reagan National Airport, Washington, D.C., 1997.

Publications:

By HELD: Articles—statement in *It Is* (New York), Autumn 1958; ''Jackson Pollock: An Artist's Symposium, Part 1'' in *ARTnews* (New York), April 1967; ''On Art and Architecture'' in *Perspecta: The Yale Architectural Journal* (New Haven, Connecticut), No. 11, 1967; interview with James Faure Walker, in *Artscribe* (London), July 1977.

On HELD: Books—*Al Held,* exhibition catalog, Amsterdam 1966; *Al Held,* exhibition catalog, San Francisco 1968; *Al Held: Recent Paintings,* exhibition catalog, Philadephia and Houston, 1969; *Al Held,* exhibition catalog, Zurich 1970; *La Pittura Americana del Dopoguerra* by Sam Hunter, Milan 1970; *Modern American Painting* by Dore Ashton, New York 1970; *The Visual Dialogue* by Nathan Knobler, New York 1971; *Icons and Images of the 60's* by Nicholas and Elena Calas, New York 1971; *Al Held: New Paintings,* exhibition catalog, New York 1972; *Al Held,* exhibition catalog by Marcia Tucker, New York 1974; *Al Held: New Paintings,* exhibition catalog with text by Andrew Forge, New York 1978; *Al Held: Paintings and Drawings 1973–78,* exhibition catalog, Boston 1978; *The New School: The Painters and Sculptors of the 50's* by Irving Sandler, New York 1978; *Dictionary of American Art* by Matthew Baigell, New York 1979; *Al Held 1959–1961,* exhibition catalog with essay by Irving Sandler, New York 1980; *Al Held,* exhibition catalog with introduction by Willy Rotzler, Zurich 1980; *Al Held,* exhibition catalog with essay by Irving Sandler, New York 1982; *Al Held,* exhibition catalog with essay by Donald Kuspit, New York 1987; *Al Held* by Irving Sandler, London 1987; *Ink, Paper, Metal, Wood: Painters and Sculptors at Crown Point Press* by Kathan Brown, San Francisco 1996. **Articles**—''Al Held: Reinventing Abstraction'' by Nancy Grimes in *Art News,* vol. 87, February 1988; ''Al Held'' by Kathan

Brown in *Crown Point Press Newsletter,* June 1994; ''Irrepressible Abstraction'' by Edward M. Gomez in *Art & Antiques,* vol. 23, no. 11, November 2000.

* * *

One wants to shout in Al Held's case, ''Boldness is all!'' Not in a negative sense but by way of recognition. For there is an exhilarating ambition in Held's work, a kind of manic confidence that compels our attention. When it doesn't work we get bombast or rhetoric or hysteria. But it works a good deal of the time, which is all one can expect from any artist.

Held likes to work to enormous scale—either literally on huge expanses of canvas or in intention within more modest dimensions. Either way the work is always expansive, big-voiced, almost Whitmanesque. By grasping only part of forms he shows us hugeness. Often his paintings are like fragments of some giant's world. The suggestion that there is much more of some form off the canvas is overwhelming, but the paintings don't fall apart. Strongly composed, strongly colored, they are held in by tensions within their asserted space that are the balancing act of a highly accomplished painter.

Essentially hard-edged, fairly minimal, Held's pictures play with space. There are suggestions of abstract-expressionism in the sense of gestural images in them as though, say, Kline had become neat. Diagonals thrust and cross, criss-cross in fact, setting up considerable activity. But this is not always true. There are also works with serene flat shapes that appear only skin deep except where the color reads as a field. And besides, even the thrust-and-parry works are checked by references to classical perspective so that our knowledge of ''where things should go'' serves to stabilize the rocketting, fast forms. Held's talent for depicting relationships enables him to go for the grandiose without ending up with the merely inflated.

—Ralph Pomeroy

HÉLION, Jean

Nationality: French. **Born:** Couterne, Normandy, 21 April 1904. **Education:** Ecole Auguste Janvier, Amiens, 1912–18; studied chemistry, Institut Industriel du Nord, Lille, 1920–21; architecture, Ecole des Arts Décoratifs, Paris. 1922; painting, Académie Adler, Paris, 1925–26. **Family:** Married Jacqueline Ventadour in 1963; children: Jean Jacques, Louis, Fabrice, David and Nicolas. **Military Service:** Served in the French Army, 1972; mobilized, 1940; prisoner-of-war, Pomerania, 1940–42; escaped, 1942. **Career:** Worked as pharmacist's assistant, Bagnoles-de-l'Orne, 1918–19; assistant, in architect's offices, Paris, 1921–24; private mathematics teacher, Paris, 1924–25. Produced first paintings, Paris, 1922; full-time painter, Paris, 1925–40, Rockbridge Baths, Virginia, and New York, 1942–46, Paris, 1946–73, and in Bigeonnette, near Chartes, 1973 until his death in 1987. Founder-member, with Theo Van Doesburg, Otto Carlsund and Leo Tutundjian, Art Concret group (renamed Abstraction-Creation group, 1930), Paris, 1929–34; contributor, *Pyrenees Review,* 1929, *L'Art Concret Review,* 1930, and *Abstraction-Creation,* review, 1932–34. Designed the sets and costumes for *King Lear,* French television production, Paris, 1964. **Awards:** Grand Prix de la Ville de Paris, 1979; Grand Prix National des Arts, France, 1983. Honorary member, American Academy and Institute of Arts and Letters, 1979; Chevalier de la Légion d'Honneur, France, 1984; Commandeur, Ordre des Arts et Lettres, France, 1985. **Agent:** Art of This Century, 3 rue Visconti, 75006 Paris. **Died:** Of pneumonia, Paris, 28 October 1987.

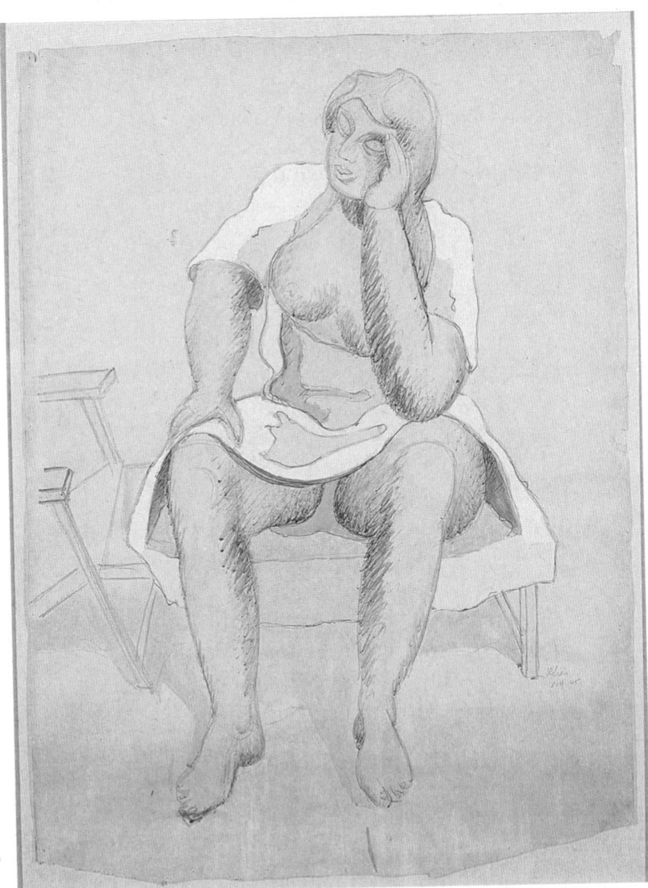

Jean Hélion: *Portrait of Peggy Guggenheim's Daughter.* Photo by Gérard Blot. ©2001 Artists Rights Society (ARS), NY/ADAGP, Paris.

Individual Exhibitions:

1932	Galerie Pierre, Paris
	Gallery John Becker, New York
1933	Gallery John Becker, New York
1936	Galerie Cashiers d'Art, Paris
	Valentine Gallery, New York
	Putzel Gallery, Hollywood, California
1937	San Francisco Museum of Art
1938	Arts Club of Chicago
	Galerie Pierre, Paris
	Grand Rapids Museum, Michigan
1939	Arts Club of Lynchburg, Virginia
	The Whyte Gallery, Washington
1940	Georgette Passedoit Gallery, New York
1942	Virginia Museum of Fine Arts, Richmond
1943	San Francisco Museum of Art
	Arts Club of Chicago
	Art of This Century, New York
	Bennington College, Vermont
	Stendahl Gallery, Los Angeles

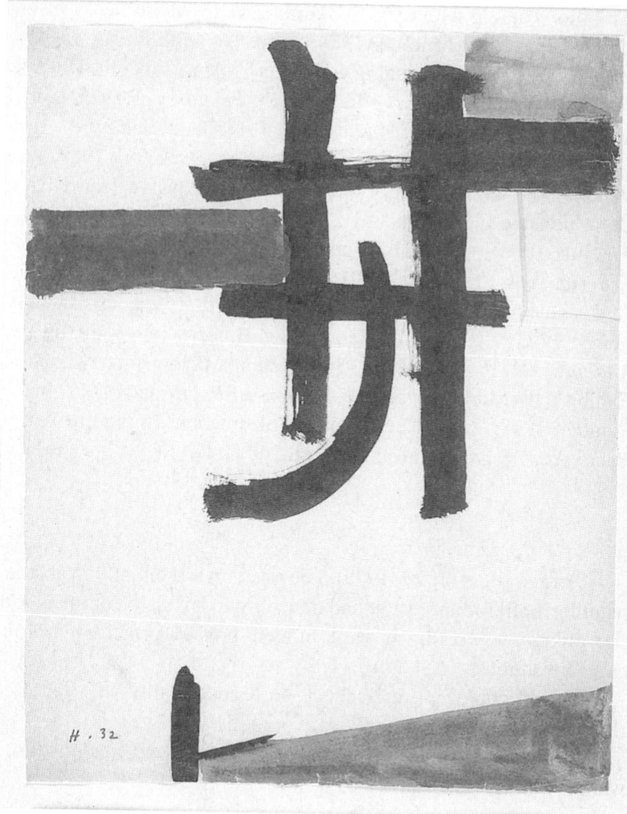

Jean Hélion: *Orthogonal Project,* 1932. Photo by Bertrand Prévost. ©2001 Artists Rights Society (ARS), NY/ADAGP, Paris.

1944 Paul Rosenberg Gallery, New York
Hollins College, Virginia
1945 Museum of Fine Arts, Baltimore
Caresse Crosby Gallery, Washington
Paul Rosenberg Gallery, New York
1947 Galerie Renou et Colle, Paris
1951 Hanover Gallery, London
Sala digli Specchi, Venice
Galleria del Milione, Milan
Feigl Gallery, New York
Galleria San Marco, Rome
1953 Chez Mayo, Paris
1956 Calerie Cahiers d'Art, Paris
1958 Galerie Cahiers d'Art, Paris
1961 Galerie Cahiers d'Art, Paris
1962 *Peintures 1929–1939,* Galerie Louis Carré, Paris
1964 *Paintings by Jean Hélion 1928–1964,* Gallery of Modern Art, New York
Galerie Yvon Lambert, Paris
1965 Leicester Galeries, London
Galerie René Andrieu, Toulouse
1966 Galerie du Dragon, Paris
1967 Willard Gallery, New York
Galerie Arcanes, Brussels
1968 Galleria Mutina, Modena
Galleria Il Fante di Spade, Rome
1969 Galerie Verriere, Lyon
Galleria Eunomia, Milan
1970 *Cent Tableaux 1928–1970,* Centre National d'Art Contemporain, Paris (toured France)
Maison des Jeunes et de la Culture, Paris
1971 Galerie Weiller, Paris
Galerie Henriette Gomes, Paris
1972 Galerie René Andrieu, Toulouse
1973 *Oeuvres Récentes,* Galerie Saint-Germain, Paris
1974 Musée Tavet, Pontoise, France
Galerie Chauvelin, Paris
1975 Galerie St. Germain, Paris
Galerie Flinker, Paris
Maison de la Culture, Saint-Etienne, France
Galerie der Spiegel, Cologne
1976 Spencer Samuels Gallery, New York
1977 Musée de l'Abbaye Sainte-Croix, Les Sables d'Olonne, France
Galerie du Centre, Paris
Musée d'Art Moderne de la Ville, Paris
1978 Galerie Karl Flinker, Paris
Galerie Sapone, Nice
Musée Ingres, Montaban, France
1979 *Bilder und Zeichnungen,* Galerie Thomas Borgmann, Cologne
Galerie Michael Hasenclever, Munich
Athens Gallery, Athens
Peintures et Dessins 1929–1979, Musée d'Art et d'Industrie, Saint-Etienne, France
Musée d'Art Moderne, Strasbourg
1980 Centre Georges Pompidou, Paris (toured France)
Bilder und Zeichnungen 1929–1980, Galerie Poll, West Berlin
Les Années 50, Galerie Karl Flinker, Paris
Museum of Art, Peking (travelled to Shanghai and Nanchang)
Musée des Beaux-Arts, Rennes
1981 Galleria Fonte d'Abisso, Modena
Paintings and Drawings from the Years 1939–60, Robert Miller Gallery, New York
Musée de Caen, France
Musée de la Bouére, Liège, Belgium
Kunstverein, Wolfsburg, West Germany
Galerie Academia, Salzburg, Austria
Galerie Karl Flinker, Paris
Galerie Bronda, Helsinki
1982 Musée d'Etat, Luxenbourg
1983 Galerie Karl Flinker, Paris
1984 Galerie Karl Flinker, Paris
Galerie Poll, West Berlin
Städtische Galerie im Lenbachhaus, Munich (retrospective; travelled to Musée d'Art Moderne de la Ville, Paris)
1985 Rachel Adler Gallery, New York
1986 Peggy Guggenheim Collection, Venice
1987 Louis Carré et Cie, Paris
Aarhus Kunstmuseum, Denmark
Albermarle Gallery, London
1988 Zentrum fur Kunstausstellungen der D.D.R., Berlin
Hotel Danadei, Campredon
Musee National d'Art Moderne, Paris
1989 Rachel Adler Gallery, New York
1990 Tate Gallery, London

Selected Group Exhibitions:

1971 *Mercedes-Benz Show,* Paris
1975 *European Painting in the 70's,* Los Angeles County Museum of Art (toured the United States)
1976 *Biennale,* Venice
Peinture Aujourd-hui, Maison de la Culture, Fontenay-sous-Bois, France
1980 *20th Century Art,* Centre Georges Pompidou, Paris (toured Japan)
1981 *A New Spirit in Painting,* Royal Academy of Arts, London
1982 *Panorama de l'Art Francais 1960–1980,* Vienna
1984 *Painting in France,* at the *Biennale,* Venice
1985 *Colour Since Matisse,* at the *Edinburgh Festival,* Scotland
1988 *Impressionist and Modern Masters,* Galerie Daniel Malingue, Paris
1996 *Anger,* Centre National d'Art et de Culture Georges Pompidou, Paris
1997 *The 1930s in Europe: the Menacing Times 1929–39,* Musee d'Art Moderne de la Ville de Paris, Paris
1999 *Drawing Exhibitions,* Drawing Center, New York (traveled to Armand Hammer Museum of Art, Los Angeles)

Collections:

Centre Georges Pompidou, Paris; Musée d'Art Moderne de la Ville de Paris; Musée d'Art et d'Industrie, Saint-Etienne, France; Pinacothek, Munich; Tate Gallery, London; Museum of Modern Art, New York; Guggenheim Museum, New York; Museum of Fine Arts, Philadelphia; Museum of Fine Arts, Boston; Art Institute of Chicago.

Publications:

By HÉLION: Books—*Book Upon Capitivity and Escape: They Shall Not Have Me,* New York 1943; *Kaleidoscope,* Paris, 1975; *Journal d'un Peintre: Carnets 1929–1984,* Marseilles 1984.

On HÉLION: Books—*Arp, Calder, Hélion, Miró, Seligman* by Anatole Jakovski, 1933; *Jean Hélion: A Coat of Many Colours,* edited by Herbert Read, London 1952; *Jean Héilon: Peintures 1929–1939,* exhibition catalog with text by Raymond Queneau, Paris 1962; *Paintings by Jean Hélion 1938–1964,* exhibition catalog with texts by Forrest Selvig, Pierre Bruguière and Christian Zervos, New York 1964; *Jean Hélion,* exhibition catalog with texts by Stephen Spender and Pierre Bruguière, London 1965; *Jean Hélion,* exhibition catalog with texts by Jean Pierre Burgant and others, Paris 1966; *Jean Hélion,* exhibition catalog with text by Katherine Kuh, New York 1967; *Jean Hélion,* exhibition catalog with text by René Micha, Rome 1968; *Hélion: Cent Tableaux 1928–1970,* exhibition catalog with texts by Francois Ponge, Roger Caillois, Daniel Abadie, Anatole Jakovsky, Pierre Mabille, Christian Zervos and Raymond Queneau, Paris 1970; *Hélion* by Pierre Bruguière, Paris, 1970; *Hélion: Oeuvres Récentes,* exhibition catalog with text by Daniel Abadie, Paris 1973; *Hélion,* exhibition catalog with text by Pierre G. Bruguière, Pontoise, France, 1974; *Jean Hélion* by René Micha, Paris 1979; *Hélion: Peintures et Dessins 1929–1979,* exhibition catalog, Cologne 1979; *Hélion: Les Années 50,* exhibition catalog with texts by Karl Flinker and Francois Ponge, Paris 1980; *Jean Hélion: Paintings and Drawings from the Years 1939–60,* exhibition catalog with text by Lawrence Alloway, New York 1981; *Jean Hélion: Abstraktion und Mythen des Alltags,* exhibition catalog with texts by Armin Zweite, Merle Schipper and Pierre Bruguière, Munich 1984; *Hélion: Peintures et Dessins 1925–1983,* exhibition catalog with texts by Anne Moeglin-Délcroix and Pierre Bruguière, Paris 1984; *Hélion: Peintures de 1929 a 1983,* exhibition catalog by Luc Lang, Paris 1987; *Jean Helion: Abstract Drawings from the 1930s,* exhibition catalog, New York 1989; *Jean Helion,* exhibition catalog, London 1990. **Articles—**''Jean Helion: Unfashionable Figuration'' by Luc Lang in *Art International,* no. 4, Autumn 1988; ''Helion's Optimism'' by Jed Perl in *The New Criterion,* vol. 10, October 1991; ''Jean Helion: les carnets ou l'entre-deux oeuvres'' by Martine Arnault in *Cimaise,* vol. 40, January/March 1993; ''Revisiting Helion'' by Hilton Kramer in *Art and Antiques,* vol. 19, June 1996; ''Jean Helion: Mayor Gallery, London; Exhibit'' by Mark Glazebrook in *Modern Painters,* vol. 11, no. 2, Summer 1998; ''Jean Helion: apres l'abstraction'' by Pierre Wat in *Beaux Arts Magazine,* no. 191, April 2000.

*

For ten years (1929–1939), I devoted myself entirely to abstract painting, until I found that it had transformed my vision of the world: the unknown world, so well hidden behind practical notions and conventions.

Then I could not resist trying to decode reality with renewed rhythms, sequences and qualities.

At the intersection of painting, experience and imagination, I wander and wonder.

—Jean Hélion (1983)

* * *

It is as if Jean Hélion has severed his roots and gone to another planet. For most people, if that happens, a period of reorientation must ensue. (Even a temporary visit to the moon is psychologically disturbing.) A new life, fresh vistas, different friends (although a few old faithfuls will still correspond and perhaps make occasional visits); but for some the break is crucial, the starting date for another existence.

Jean Hélion was/is a big name in the history of French modern art. His careful comments on bourgeois ambience, hard-edged and often like a dalliance with automata, helped launch him onto the Paris art scene, because such paintings, some of them of deft inventive charm, were exactly in tune with the tenor of art in the French capital of 1930. Nor did Hélion stay still. His chosen course and his increasing expertise won him natural admiration as the imagery became less and less figurative; matters reached a climax by 1934, by which time his canvases, some of them of commanding size, were completely non-figurative.

''Oh Hélion! Oh Headlights!'' exclaimed one critic of the day, and his comment was duly repeated in *Axis,* the abstract magazine produced by John Piper and Myfanwy Evans. Indeed, the colour areas in these new paintings were like great luminous lenses. They clubbed together on canvas to form compositions whose nearest visual complements were the bulky make-up of the fat upholstery of easy chairs and sofas. From some early flirting with abstract conceptions Hélion had gone on to really find himself and alert the world to an important newcomer—a different *peintre non-figuratif!* This was perhaps the particularly exceptional quality that he brought to the range of abstract in the 1930s, that his paintings were not only beautifully wrought (hard-edge in the original abstract painting manner, but not hard on the eye) but also intensely individual, independent and different, seeming to be subject to no outside influence other than the prevailing drift towards non-figurative art.

Then everything changed. Not immediately. The switch was not as sudden as that, but it was rapid. Hélion went back to naturalism. Many who had acclaimed his abstract work shrank away, but probably an equal proportion of his admirers stayed faithful to him.

And besides abandoning the non-figurative style, he also changed his approach to the canvas. Hard-edge, whether incorporated in his earlier style or carrying through into his style of the mid-1930s, disappeared to be replaced by rugged paint vigorously applied, a direct reflection of the countless drawings and water colours he was pouring out either through sheer enthusiasm, or as *croquis*, or as study sketches for some subsequent paintings. Only one element was constant: the keen appreciation he had always shown for logical composition remained intact.

Admittedly there were echoes of the subject matter from his earliest work which found their place in the paintings by the new Hélion—street scenes, shopping, bourgeois interiors, but to these were added ships and shipping and astonishing roofscapes. The new colours were wholly unrelated to what had gone before. Now there were plenty of cuprous pinks and cerulean blues, tints that had been scarcely ever evident previously.

The prevailing alteration in the pictures (qua pictures) was the atmosphere of crowded paint (and often crowded people—especially in butcher's shops). No more housefront compositions with perhaps a cast of one boy and one girl. No more cafe bars with one *serveuse* and maybe a couple of customers.

From the mid-1980s Hélion suffered from an increasing loss of sight. Until his death in 1987 he exercised his creative energy in writing—by dictation of course—lecture material and his theories on the realities of Art for the painter. He spent much of his time on a sort of memoir-journey based on notes kept about his entire artistic career. One of these notebooks was published in 1984. Rather more extraordinary was his dictation of instructions for imaginary pictorial compositions that he could, of course, never paint himself.

But before this loss of sight began to make itself felt, and particulary in the late 1970s and early 1980s, his pictures experienced a veritable Indian Summer. Compositions, especially those featuring a nude with the painter himself (as a young man) appeared on large canvases in glowing colours. The nude, mauve, natural or green, casually invaded the scene at ease or in painter's pose while the artist, soberly dressed in dark jacket, Breton-red trousers and open shirt, worked at a picture or lay back resting. In one such painting, three men on a visit are entertaining the painter with music from a trombone, to enhance the peace of the moment. This swansong is truly moving.

—Sheldon Williams

HENDRICKS, Geoffrey

Nationality: American. **Born:** Littleton, New Hampshire, 30 July 1931. **Education:** Studied at Amherst College, Massachsetts, 1949–53, B.A. (cum laude) 1953; studied sculpture at Smith College, Northampton, Massachusetts, under Peter Grippe, 1951–52, Cooper Union Art School New York, 1953–56, and Columbia University, New York, under Meyer Shapiro and Rudolf Wittkower, 1957–62, M.A. 1962. **Family:** Married Beatrice (Bici) Forbes in 1961 (divorced, 1974); children: Tyche and Bracken. **Career:** Lives and works in New York and Cape Breton Island, Nova Scotia, Canada; Fluxus artist group, since 1967; organized George Maciuna's *FluxMass/ Olympiad,* Douglas College, Rutgers University, New Brunswick, New Jersey, 1970; Organizer, Flux Festschrift Banquet for George Maciunas, New York 1976. Co-Founder, Black Thumb Press, New York, 1965–72; founder, with Brian Buczak, Money for Food Press, 1977. Member, Printed Editions, 1977–86. Teacher, St. Barnabas Hospital for Chronic Diseases, Bronx, New York, 1953–56; assistant instructor, 1956–58, art instructor, 1958–61, assistant professor, 1961–67, and associate professor, 1967–80, Art Department, Douglass College, Rutgers University; art instructor, Windham College, Putney, Vermont, Summer 1957. Professor of art since 1980, and graduate director for visual arts since 1981, Mason Gross School of the Arts, Rutgers University. **Awards:** Research Fellowship, MacDowell Colony, Peterborough, New Hampshire, 1955; National Endowment for the Arts Grant, 1976; DAAD Berlin Artists Program Fellowship, 1983, Canada Council Visiting Foreign Artist Grant, 1987; Künstlerstätte Schloss Bledecke, Bledecke/Elbe, Germany, 1993. **Address:** Office, Rutgers University Mason Gross School, Arts Department, Visual Art, 125 New Street, New Brunswick, New Jersey, 08901–1905.

Individual Exhibitions:

1950 Carpenter Art Gallery, Dartmouth College, Hanover, New Hampshire
1953 Meade Art Building, Amherst College, Massachusetts
1956 Putney School, Vermont
1957 Douglass College Art Gallery, Rutgers University, New Jersey
1958 Douglass College Art Gallery, Rutgers University, New Jersey
1962 Douglass College Art Gallery, Rutgers University, New Jersey
1965 Cafe au GoGo, New York (with Bici Forbes)
Cafe au GoGo, New York
Judson Memorial Church, New York
1966 Judson Memorial Church, New York (3 times)
Bianchini Gallery, New York
New York Public Library
1967 Judson Memorial Church, New York
Judson Gallery, New York
Trude Heller's Trik, New York (with Lawrence Kornfield, Bici Forbes)
Time-Life Auditorium, New York (with Flux Masters of the Rear Garde)
Fluxhouse, New York
1968 Barnard College, New York
Tokyo Gallery (twice)
1969 Fluxhouse, New York
Voorhees Chapel, Douglas College, Rutgers University, New Jersey
Loeb Center, New York University
1970 Loeb Center, New York University
Algol Theater, Brussels
1971 Higgins Hall, Pratt Institute, New York
California Institute of Arts, Burbank
Apple Gallery, New York (3 times)

331 West 20th Street, New York (with Bici Forbes, George Maciunas)
Neue Galerie der Stadt, Aachen, West Germany (with Dick Higgins, Stephen Varble)
1973 Art Center, Summit, New Jersey
La Mama Experimental Theatre Club, New York
1974 Byrkjefjellet, Kvamsskogen, Norway
Galerie Baecker, Bochum, West Germany
The Clocktower, New York
1975 Kunstverein, Munich
Incontri Internazionali d'Arte, Rome
Galleria Multhipla, Milan
Pari and Dispari Stand, *Art Fair,* Basel
1976 Studio Morra, Naples
Fine Arts Building, New York
113 Green Street, New York
The Clocktower, New York
Pari and Dispari Stand, *Art Fair,* Bologna
1977 Galleria d'Arte Moderna, Bologna (with Brian Buczak)
René Block Gallery, New York
1978 Aral Haus, Bochum, West Germany
Galerie Baecker, Bochum, West Germany
1979 *Ruhr Park Art Festival,* Bochum, West Germany
P.S. 1, New York (2 times)
1980 Studio Morra, Naples
1981 Studio Morra, Naples
1983 DAAD-Galerie, West Berlin
Galerie Donguy, Paris
Galerie Inge Baecker, Cologne
1984 Neue Galerie, Aachen, West Germany
Kunsthalle, Wilhelmshaven, West Germany
Badischer Kunstverein, Karlsruhe, West Germany
1986 Galerie Baecker, Cologne
1987 Art Center, Banff, Canada
1991 Galerie Hundertmark, Cologne, Germany
1992 *Himmels Aquarelle,* Rupertinum, Salzburg, Austria
1993 *Day into Night* (retrospective), Kunsthallen Brandts Klaedefabrik, Odense, Denmark
Sky Boots, Galleria 56, Budapest
1995 *Anatomia dei Cieli/Anatomy of the Sky,* Castelfranco, Italy
1997 *Rites of Passage,* Articule, Montreal, Canada
The Sky is Falling, Galleria Caterina Gualco, Genoa, Italy
1999 *Sky Notes 1–22,* Emily Harvey Gallery, New York
Sky Measures, Galerie Inge Baecker, Cologne
2000 *Constellations,* Galleria Caterina Gualco
Question: A Circle?, Galerie Pro Arte, Hallein, Austria

Selected Group Exhibitions:

1970 *Happening and Fluxus,* Kunstverein, Cologne
1974 *Multiples, Ein Versuch die Entwicklung des Auflagenobjektes darzustellen,* Neuer Berliner Kunstverein, Berlin
1976 *Personal Mythologies,* Fine Arts Building, New York
1978 *Artwords and Bookworks,* Los Angeles Institute of Contemporary Art, Los Angeles
1982 *Fluxus 1962–82,* Museum Wiesbäden, West Germany (and at Nassauischer Kunstverein, and Harlekin Art, Wiesbäden)
1983 *Fluxus etc.,* Neuberger Museum, Purchase, New York
1987 *Aspects of Conceptualism,* Avenue B. Gallery, New York
1988 *Fluxus,* Museum of Modern Art, New York
1990 *Fluxus,* Institute of Modern Art, Brisbane, Australia
Ubi Fluxus ibi motus 1962–1990, Venice Biennale, Venice, Italy
1993 *In the Spirit of Fluxus,* Walker Art Center, Minneapolis, and Whitney Museum of American Art, New York
1994 *Outside the Frame: Performance and the Object: A Survey History of Performance Art in the USA Since 1950,* Cleveland Center for Contemporary Art, Ohio (catalog)
1995 *25 Jahre Edition Hundertmark 1970–1995,* Stadtmuseum, Cologne (catalog)
1999 *Off Limits: Rutgers University and the Avant Garde, 1957–1963,* Newark Museum, Newark, New Jersey (catalog)

Collections:

Metropolitan Museum of Art, New York; Museum of Modern Art, New York; Springfield Art Museum, Massachusetts; Rose Art Museum, Waltham, Massachusetts; Franklin Furnace Archive, New York; New Jersey State Museum, Trenton; Hopkins Art Center, Dartmouth College, Hanover, New Hampshire; Witherspoon Gallery, University of North Carolina, Chapel Hill; Lehmbruck Museum, Duisburg, West Germany; Museum des 20. Jahrhunderts, Vienna.

Publications:

By HENDRICKS: Books—*Ring Piece,* Barton, Vermont 1973; *Between 2 points/Fra Due Poli,* Reggio Emilia, Italy 1974; *A Sheep's Skeleton and Rocks/Uno Scheletro di Pecaro e Sassi,* New York and Asolo, Italy 1977; *Flux Wedding: George and Billie,* with Brian Buczak, New York 1978; *The Wisdom of the Money for Food Lady,* with Brian Buczak, New York 1978; *100 Ways to Make Money,* with Brian Buczak, New York 1978; *Saved,* with Brian Buczak, New York 1979; *Le Capra,* New York and Naples, 1979; *5 Found Photos,* New York 1979; *A V TRE EXTRA,* New York 1979; *Vesuvius, Vesuvius in Eruption,* New York 1981; *A Short History of Fluxus,* New York 1981; *Sky Anatomy,* New York 1981; *100 Skies,* with text by Henry Martin, Worpswede, Germany 1987; *101 Skies,* Frankfurt am Main, Germany 1990; *Fertility of the Soil,* New York 1992. **Articles—**''A question, a letter to George Brecht,'' a statement in *10 from Rutgers,* exhibition catalog, New York 1965; data in *Film Culture—Expanded Arts Special Issue* (New York), Winter 1966; ''Sky/Why?'' in *Renewal* (Chicago) June 1967; ''Sky/Change'' documentation in *Manipulations,* New York 1968; ''Notations and Statement'' in *Notations* edited by John Cage, New York 1969; ''Fluxrelics'' in *Flux-Reliquary* New York 1970; ''101 Words'' in *Notebook,* edited by Dana Atchley, Victoria, British Columbia 1970; ''Skutterudite'' in *Space Atlas,* edited by Dana Atchley, Victoria, British Columbia 1971; ''When You Are Through . . .'' in *Arts and Artists Fluxus Issue* (London), October 1972; ''For Jackson'' in *Vort* (Silver Springs, Maryland), no. 2, 1975, ''Meetings, Beginnings, and Endings,'' in *Lund Art Press,* vol 2., no. 2, 1991; ''Springs, Nomads, the Eternal Network, and Francesco Conz,'' in *Under the Influence of Fluxus,* Winnipeg, Canada, 1993; ''On Coincidence, Collaboration, Psychic Phenomena, Brian Buczak, Ray Johnson, Fluxus, Artist Books, Life and Death'' in *New Observations,* no. 106, May-June 1995; ''Dissolving Categories: Statements by Gay Artists'' with Jonathan Weinberg and Flavia Rando in *Art Journal,* vol. 55, Winter 1996; ''4

Men Measuring Time and Space to the 21st Century from the Base of the Eiffel Tower & 21 Questions About Possibilities and Problems for the Arts (Approaching the Millennial Cross-Over)'' in *New Observations,* no. 116, Fall 1997; ''Flux Generations: Roundtable Discussion'' with Janet A. Kaplan in *Art Journal,* vol. 59, no. 2, Summer 2000.

On HENDRICKS: Books—*Experience Book* by Vlasta Cihakova-Noshiro, Tokyo 1978; *Fluxus: The Most Radical and Experimental Art Movement of the 60's* by Harry Ruhe, Amsterdam 1979; *Alternatives in Retrospect: An Historical Overview 1969–1975* by Jacki Apple, New York 1981; *Geoff Hendricks,* exhibition catalog with texts by Peter Frank and Lawrence Alloway, Aachen 1984; *Geoffrey Hendricks: Day into Night,* exhibition catalog with text by Robert Rosenblum, Denmark 1993. **Articles**—''Light Sculpture and a Sky'' by Michael Benedikt in *Art International* (Lugano, Switzerland), September 1966; The Art of Trompe-L'Oeil: Hendricks and Gilardi'' by Katsuo Nobuyki in *Bijutsu-Techo* (Tokyo), April 1968; ''Wolken und Gitarren'' by Gerd Winkler in *Kunstforum International* (Mainz), February 1974; ''Artists as Writers, Part II'' by Lawrence Alloway in *Artforum* (New York), April 1974; ''Geoffrey Hendricks'' in *Flash Art* (Milan), February 1976; New York Fluxus'' by Peter Frank in *Soho Downtown Manhattan,* Berlin 1976; ''American Performance'' by Szymon Bojko in *Projekt* (Warsaw), February 1981.

*

Following a recent performance, a woman came up to me and said that she was perplexed by what I had done. Would I explain my work to her? I instinctively felt that to try to put into words what I had been silently doing in activity for the previous hour would be wrong. Instead, I began to ask her questions.

She had found the work too much like nature . . . the randomness of nature. She could not connect it to her concepts of ''art.'' I liked her puzzlement and told her so. I spoke of how sometimes work which became most important for me on first encounter left me with a gnawing bewilderment. I suggested that she hold on to her feelings about my piece and that perhaps some answers would come to her. I felt the images she had experienced would be staying with her for some time.

One element in my performance was a chair with two brass plates on the back—French and German translations of the inscriptions: ''Sit carefully in this chair until you remember one important event from your past. Following this moment of recall get up immediately.'' I asked her if she had read what was on the chair. She said ''No.'' I proposed that she do so, and we parted.

From a distance I noticed that she spent some time looking at the chair, and finally sat in it for an extended period. When she got up she had a different expression on her face.

—Geoffrey Hendricks

* * *

Geoffrey Hendricks has been referred to as a ''cloud-smith,'' but the text in which we find this thumb-nail sketch (a text written in 1973 by Dick Higgins as a note for a small book by Hendricks, entitled *Ring Piece,* published by The Something Else Press) continues with a list of fourteen other activities (lettered from ''a'' to ''l'') in which Hendricks is likely to be discovered ''when not forming clouds.'' Higgins' duplex sense of symmetry seems quite right: painting clouds is only a fraction of Geoffrey Hendricks' creative activities, but it can also look like a unitary Ying that balances against and completes a Yang that scatters into manifold ritual expressions of itself.

Ever since the early 1960s, Geoffrey Hendricks has been one of the artists associated with the term ''Fluxus,'' and what he shares with most of these artists is an enormous lack of prejudice and preconception about what art can be, and where one does best to look for it. He has written: ''What is relevant for me in Art isn't objects, but what hovers in a meta-physical space between the artist and the object he is grappling with. I find art where I least expect it. What I see in galleries and museums often comes across to me as being about art, trying to be art, but isn't . . . . Art is about getting deep into your personal self, working, struggling (but all of this is not art), and then suddenly you have left yourself for something universal'' (In *Between Two Points,* Edizioni Pari & Dispari, Reggio Emilia, 1975). One might then suggest a slight emendation of this statement that has been made by Lawrence Alloway: ''Hendricks' development, as writers on art like myself like to call it, goes like this: from objects in the early 60s to the Sky paintings, 1965–68, to the present period [of performances] in which his concern is the experience and definition of self'' (New York, 1973). Even aside from how Hendricks' paintings and performance have subsequently come to present themselves as parallel or even intertwining activities, one might insist that ''the experience and definition of self'' is the central, exclusive concern of all of Geoffrey Hendricks' work. Making paintings and watercolors of the sky is as ritualistic as the rest of his activity. Self-exploration, moreover, can take any number of forms, and Hendricks' striving is less for the kind of self-knowledge emphasized by psychology analysis than rather for those moments of purifying intuition that grasp the certainty that the human mind, the human body, and the human artifacts through which they relate to one another are all continuous with nature, or rooted in nature, or motivated and energized by the very same forces that stand in control of nature. In pieces that are based on physically performed ritual (either in isolation or before an audience) Hendricks will bathe naked in frigid streams fed by mountain snows, pound rocks into colored pigments with which he covers his body, tie twigs and branches of flowering shrubs to his arms and legs and chest, cut off locks of his hair and weave it into locks of hair cut from goats, build cairns of stones or mounds of sea weed, cut chairs and ladders down the middle and lash the pieces back to back, perhaps decorating them with bones or flowers. Or at the opening of an exhibition he may put a bed in an art gallery and stay in it for two days, between blue sheets, making notes on thoughts and dreams in a journal, the floor around him scattered with leaves and twigs and pieces of rope. Or he will dig up soil from a hill in Canada and bury it many months later into a hill in Norway or Italy. Hendricks seeks out a direct, bodily interaction with nature, but he is also concerned with the ways in which our senses carry us out beyond our bodies. He makes paintings of the sky because it is the part of nature that he cannot touch.

These images of the sky, moreover, have had an evolution all their own. At first they were highly stylized, deliberately sterotypical, much as Magritte often rendered the sky, and they were painted on various real objects: over the entirety of an automobile, or an old pair of boots, or on pillow-cases, socks, pants, underwear and T-shirt, hung out on a clothes line as though to dry. We have an *idea* of the sky, superimposed upon things that are more local and terrestrial, and we feel free to complete these works with little poetic fantasies of our own: it can be rather as though the sky had suddenly appeared on your very own laundry in your very own backyard, most probably just as you had finished hanging it out and turned your back to re-enter the house. Or one might say that they have the presence of a visionary dream from which you run the risk of suddenly and sadly waking up. The more recent sky paintings are a much more direct and sensual engagement with the heavens, and a real attempt to catch momentary images of the sky as it constantly changes. They are acts of contemplation, if not of meditation, and they belong to a process of awareness that posits itself as a continuum. Grounded into the earth, it looks as well towards the sky, both implying and suspending our questions as to whether the mind might possibly reach our still further.

—Henry Martin

HENNING, Anton

Nationality: German. **Born:** Berlin, 23 February 1964. **Education:** Attended Staatliche Akademie für Bildende Künste, Karlsruhe, Germany; left school after two months; self-educated. **Career:** Lived in London, 1985, and New York, 1989–94; currently lives and works in Berlin and Manker. **Awards:** Förderpreis für Bildende Kunst, Akademie der Künste, Berlin, 2001. **Agent:** Wohnmaschine, Friedrich Loock, Tucholskystrasse 35, 10117 Berlin, Germany.

Individual Exhibitions:

1989 *Anton Henning: Neue Arbeiten 1989,* Galerie Hilger, Vienna (catalog)
1990 *Anton Henning,* University of Oklahoma Museum of Art, Norman, and Vrej Baghoomian Gallery, New York 1990 (catalog)
1991 Vrej Baghoomian Gallery, New York (catalog)
Galerie Brinkman, Amsterdam
1993 Wohnmaschine, Berlin
1994 Galerie Meile, Lucerne, Switzerland
1995 *Soup,* White Columns, New York (catalog)
1996 Galeria Ramis Barquet, Monterrey, Mexiko
1997 *Some Day My Prince Will Come,* Wohnmaschine, Berlin
1998 *Too Much of a Good Thing. . . ,* Espace des Arts, Chalon-sur-Saône, and Kasseler Kunstverein, Kassel
1999 Galerie Lindig in Paludetto, Nürnberg
Wohnmaschine, Berlin
Too Much of a Good Thing. . . , Kunstverein Heilbronn (catalog)
The Manker Melody Makers' Lounge, Galerie für Zeitgenössische Kunst, Leipzig
Tomorrow Is the Cool, Galerie Eugen Lendl, Graz
2000 *Nach Indien,* Galerie Andreas Schlüter, Hamburg
2001 *Interieur No. 97,* Kunstverein Ulm, Ulm
Interieur No. 112, Städtische Ausstellungshalle Am Hawerkamp, Münster
Interieurs 2001, Vous Etes Ici, Amsterdam
Interieurs 2001, Wohnmaschine, Berlin
Entwistle, London
OPQR, Kunstraum Neuruppin, Neuruppin

Group Exhibitions:

1990 *Korrespondenzen,* Berlinische Galerie und Art Museum Boras
1991 *Figuring Abstraction,* Vrej Baghoomian Gallery, New York
1992 *Erotiques,* AB Gallery, Paris
Works on Paper, Anina Nosei, New York
Surface Tension, The Art Museum, Florida International University, Miami
1994 *Galerie Wohnmaschine in the Russian Ethnographic Museum,* St. Petersburg
Trois Photographes Berlinois, Espace des Arts, Chalon-sur-Saône (catalog)
X 94, Akademie der Künste, Berlin
1995 *Room with a View,* Brandenburgischer Kunstverein, Potsdam
1996 *Neben den Linden ist die Mitte oder der Blick ins 21.,* Kunstverein Düsseldorf
Surfing Systems, Kasseler Kunstverein
1998 *The Promise of Photography,* Sammlung der DG Bank, Hara Museum, Tokyo
Art Club Berlin, Vienna/Barcelona
Transmission, Espace des Arts, Chalon-sur-Saône
Internationales Kunstforum Drewen
1999 *Fremdkörper-fremde körper,* Deutsches Hygiene Museum Dresden
Missing Link, Kunstmuseum Bern (catalog)
Szenenwechsel XVI, Museum für Moderne Kunst, Frankfurt am Main
Das Versprechen der Fotografie, Sammlung der DG Bank, Kestner Gesellschaft, Hannover
2000 Presselounge (Interieur No 67), Art Forum, Berlin
DIA/SLIDE/TRANSPARENCY, Kunstamt Kreuzberg/Bethanien und NGBK, Berlin
Malkunst, Fondazione Mudima, Milan
Colour Me Blind, Dundee Contemporary Arts, Dundee, and Städtische Ausstellungshalle Am Hawerkamp, Münster (catalog)
Szenenwechsel XVII, Museum für Moderne Kunst, Frankfurt am Main
2001 *Imagination-Romantik,* Stadtmuseum, Kunstverein, Romantikerhaus, Jena
Interieur No. 113, Art Unlimited, Basel
Playing Amongst the Ruins, Royal College of Art, London (catalog)
Offensive Malerei, Lothringer 13/halle, Munich

Collections:

Museum für Moderne Kunst, Frankfurt/Main; Sammlung der DG Bank.

Publications:

By HENNING: Article—Interview with Julian Scholl in *Körper & Betrug,* exhibition catalog, Berlin 1996. **Films**—*''Many Modern Films 97/98 Music: The Manker Melody Makers,''* 1998; *''Many Modern Films 97/98/99/2000 Music: The Manker Melody Makers,''* 2000.

On HENNING: Books—*Korrespondenzen,* exhibition catalog, Berlin 1990; *Dokumentation 1988–1993,* Berlin 1993; *Bild-malerei,* Berlin 1995; *Jahresgaben 1997,* Cologne 1997; *Jahresbericht 1996,*

Anton Henning: *Interieur No. 85.* ©Anton Henning.

Kassel 1997; *Copyright* by Ute Lindner and Patrik Huber, Berlin 1999; *Ich ist etwas Anderes: Kunst am Ende des 20. Jahrhunderts,* exhibition catalog, Düsseldorf, Köln 2000; *One of Those Days,* exhibition catalog, Mannheim 2000; *Offensive Malerei. Malerei im Spannungsfeld neuer Medien,* exhibition catalog, Munich 2001. **Articles—**''Echos of 60s and 70s. Among the Young and Little Known'' by Roberta Smith in *New York Times,* 30 November 1990; ''Anton Henning'' by Nancy Grimes in *ARTnews,* no. 4, 1991; ''Anton Henning'' by Donald Kuspit in *Artforum,* no. 2, 1992; essay by August Rezension in *Texte zur Kunst,* no. 12, 1993; ''Anton Henning'' by Stefan Raum in *Neue Bildende Kunst,* April 1994; ''Anton Henning'' by Wolf-Günter Thiel in *Flash Art International,* March-April 1996; ''Happening mit Henning'' by Peter Hauff in *Zeitung am Sonntag,* 13 June 1999; ''Missing Link: Menschenbilder in der Fotografie'' by Bernhard Bischoff in *Neue Bildende Kunst* (Berlin), October 1999; ''The Art of Design'' by Annette Tietenberg in *Form—Zeitschrift für Gestaltung* (Frankfurt/Main), November-December 1999; ''German Painting'' by Wolf-Günter Thiel in *Flash Art,* no. 210, January-February 2000; ''Berlin: Future Perfect?'' by Eleanor Heartney in *Art in America,* February 2000; ''Je est un autre'' by Necmi Sönmez in *Rredamento,* April 2000; ''*Ich ist etwas* in der Kunstsammlung NRW'' by Michael Krajewski in *Kunst-Bulletin* (Zurich), May 2000; ''Cool Soft and Crazy'' by Elke Trappschuh in *Architektur & Wohnen* (Hamburg), no. 5, October-November 2000; ''Anton Henning'' by Martin Coomer in *Time Out* (London), 31 January-7 February 2001.

* * *

Anton Henning is a painter, though his work crosses over into photography, video, performance and installation. His diverse, flamboyant practice is a very playful exploration of art and its attendant

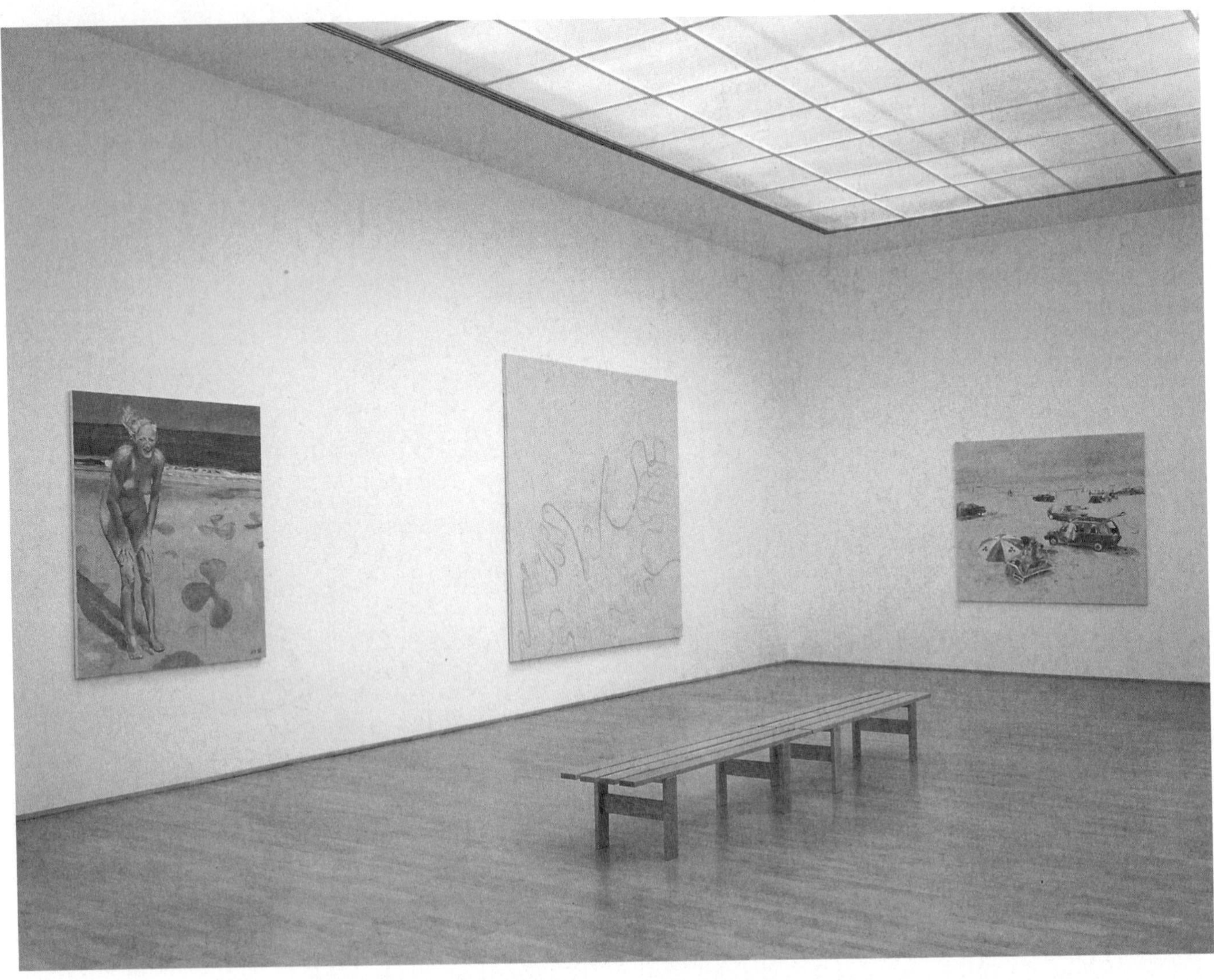

Anton Henning: *Interieur No. 85,* 2001. Photo by Jörg von Bruchhausen. ©Anton Henning.

histories, ideologies, and functions. He uses a number of recurring motifs and devices throughout his canvases—most notably the ''Hennling,'' a kind of phenomenological trademark—as well as an astute but cavalier approach to languages of representation, genre, and style. These strategies create complex visual dialogues between and across the works themselves, with art history and with the wider world.

In his installation at the Museum für Moderne Kunst in Frankfurt/Main in 1999, the viewer was presented with what appeared at first to be a small show of paintings by a number of different artists. Abstract canvases rubbed shoulders with loosely painted cityscapes and big, bold figurative works. As you looked at the paintings, though, conversations began to emerge. A symbol, present as a tattoo on the thigh of a naked sunbather, would reappear in another canvas as a piece of municipal sculpture or as a shadow cast on a beach.

In his most recent exhibitions, Henning has begun to create ''lounges.'' These colourful, funky, retro-styled spaces provide the environment in which the viewer encounters videos of his fictional band, ''The Manker Melody Makers,'' all of whose members are played by Henning himself. He fills these spaces, which he refers to as walk-in-paintings, with pop-ish canvases of pin-ups, rock stars, and home-made, 1970s style furniture. They are very slick, very sexy, and very funny.

A fundamentally performative quality underpins everything Henning does, the paintings as much as the videos or photographs. But, even when he is at his most light-hearted and witty, his sincerity and passion mean that these densely layered works never fall into cynical parody or empty posturing. Like the best jokes, they are deadly serious.

—Martin Clark

HEWARD, John

Nationality: Canadian. **Born:** Montréal, Quebec in 1934. **Awards:** Canada Council ''A'' grants, 1988–89 and 1995–96; Quebec ''A'' grant, 1994–95. **Address:** 301 Rue Murray, Montréal, Quebec, Canada HEC 2E1. **Web site:** http://www.ccca.ca.

Individual Exhibitions:

1971 Whitney Gallery, Montréal
1972 Galerie B. Montréal
1974 Centre Culturel Canadien, Paris
Canada House, London
Galerie B, Montréal
1975 Galerie B. Montréal
Galerie Gilles Gheerbrant, Montréal
1977 Musee d'Art Contemporain, Montréal
1978 Galerie Marielle Mailhot, Montréal
1979 Mercer Union, Toronto
1980 Nova Scotia College of Art and Design, Halifax
1981 Galerie Gilles Gheerbrant, Montréal
1982 Galerie Gilles Gheerbrant, Montréal
1984 Galerie Gilles Gheerbrant, Montréal
1985 Galerie John A. Schweitzer, Montréal
1987 Galerie Rene Blouin, Montréal
Costin and Klintworth Gallery, Toronto
1988 Costin and Klintworth Gallery, Toronto
1989 Paul Kuhn Fine Arts, Calgary
1990 Galerie Brenda Wallace, Montréal
Costin and Klintworth Gallery, Toronto
1992 Tribeca 148 Gallery, New York
Costin and Klintworth Gallery, Toronto
Paul Kuhn Fine Arts, Calgary
1993 Galerie Brenda Wallace, Montréal
John Heward, Centre International d'Art Contemporain, Montréal
1994 Costin and Klintworth Gallery, Toronto
Paul Kuhn Fine Arts, Calgary
The Ethics of Making: The Forming Rayons of John Heward, Agnes Etherington Art Center, Queen's University, Kingston, Ontario; Kerr Gallery, Alberta College of Art, Calgary; Centre Saidye Bronfman, Montréal
1995 Gallery 312, Chicago
1996 Galerie Yves Le Roux, Montréal
1997 Spruce Street Forum Gallery, San Diego, California
1998 Galerie Yves LeRoux, Montréal
2000 Centre culturel canadien, Paris
2001 Galerie Roger Bellemare, Montréal

Exhibitions with Sylvia Safdie:

1992 *Zakhor,* Centre D'Exposition St. Hyacinthe, St. Hyacinthe, Quebec
Zakhor, 115 Wooster Street, New York
1993 *Die Frie,* Copenhagen
1994 Paul Kuhn Fine Arts, Calgary
1995 Gallery 312, Chicago
1996 Wan Fung Gallery, Imperial Archives, Beijing, China
100 Yonge St. Paul Petro Gallery, Toronto

Selected Group Exhibitions:

1972 *Heward, Nolte, Vazan,* Vehicule Art, Montréal
1976 *17 Canadian Artists: A Protean View,* Vancouver Art Gallery
1979 *20 x 20,* Italia-Canada, Milan
1984 Sculpture International, Chicago
1986 *Adventures,* Centre Saidye Bronfman, Montréal (traveling exposition)
1987 *Stations,* Centre International d'Art Contemporain de Montréal
1988 *John Heward—Jean Poldaas,* Gallery 101, Ottawa
Contemporary Canadian Works on Paper, Concordia Art Gallery, Montréal
1989 *Montréal sur papier,* Centre Saidye Bronfman, Montréal
1993 *Presence,* Centre International d'Art Contemporain de Montréal
1994 *Within the Abstract,* B4A Projects, New York
1998 *Peinture, Peinture,* Montréal
La Biennale de Montréal, Montréal
1999–2000 *Les Bouches ouvertes,* Art Mûr, Montréal; Maison Hamel-Bruneau, Ste-Foy; and Salle Augustin-Chénier, Ville-Marie
2000 *Spilled Edge, Soft Corners,* Blackwood Gallery, University of Toronto, and Galerie Christiane Chassay, Montréal
Le son iconographe, Montréal Télégraphe, Montréal
2001 *Québec/New York,* Howard Scott Gallery, New York

Collections:

Conseil des Arts du Canada-Banque d'Oeuvres d'Art; Musee des Beaux-Arts de Montréal; Musee D'Art Contemporain de Montréal; Agnes Etherington Art Center, Kingston; Nickle Arts Museum, Calgary; Air Canada; Guarantee Trust; Westburne Collection; Art Gallery of Hamilton, Hamilton; University of Lethbridge, Lethbridge.

Publications:

By HEWARD: Article—''John Heward'' in *Parachute,* no. 1, 1975.

On HEWARD: Books—*17 Canadian Artists: A Protean View,* exhibition catalog with text by Alvin Balkind, Vancouver 1976; *John Heward,* exhibition catalog with text by Alain Parent, Montréal 1977; *John Heward* by James D. Campbell, Montréal 1986; *An Interpretive Paradigm: The Rayons and Sculptures of John Heward* by James D. Campbell, Montréal 1988; *Montréal sur papier,* exhibition catalog with text by Peter Krausz, Montréal 1989; *The Ethics of Making: The Forming Rayons of John Heward,* exhibition catalog, Kingston, Ontario; *John Heward* by David Clarkson, Montréal 1993; *The Thought from the Outside: The Art and Artefacts of John Heward* by James D. Campbell, Toronto 1996.

*

I make objects in order to see order in utter confusion. Rayon, paint, metal, ink, books are among the materials used in these utterances. The work may be placed on the floor, wall or hung in space inside or outside.

—John Heward

* * *

John Heward is an important Canadian Modernist painter who has pursued a resolutely abstract practice for almost three decades in Montréal. At an early stage in his career, Heward eschewed a traditional support—and traditional ways of making and thinking about painting. For many years, he used unstretched rayon exclusively. The work is simply tacked at the top corners to the wall plane. Decidedly minimal in its formal orientation, his work oscillates between drawn/painted forms and gestural collocations of marks (usually applied in his signature black acrylic paint).

Because his work is simply rolled up when not in visual use, it demonstrates an interesting and provocative ecological pragmatism too rare in today's—Western—art. The rayon itself is a found material—mostly seconds bought by the bale at a local manufacturer—and when painted on evinces a sense of flexibility, portability, malleability and acceptance which aligns them with a specifically Eastern tradition (Tibetan prayer flags readily come to mind).

In his *Forming* works of the 1980s, specific shapes seem a deliberate acknowledgement of the human element without overtly pictorializing it. All the *Forming* series works were executed on unused but irregular sheets of rayon (an important distinction, because Heward has often used old rayon sheets and even salvaged rayons from destroyed works when he feels they are useful) painted in declarative acrylic colours (such as yellow, red, blue, purple, ochre, orange and the ubiquitous black). In the *Forming* series, there is only one dominant colour and form per work. The form is ambiguous, occupying the centre of the otherwise untreated rayon sheet, and often resembles a head when seen in profile, perhaps reflecting Heward's longstanding interest in ethnographic art. Each rayon gives a sense of Heward's characteristic restraint and minimalist ethos, a remarkable quality of what we might term a Zen-like "isness."

In the most recent works from his *Events* series, executed over the last few years, Heward has convincingly transformed physically literal marks into nonphysical metaphorical things. Of course, he has always done so. But gesture has never been used so economically and well as in these recent rayons. Whether in long, lateral lengths on the wall plane, or in vertical form(ul)ation there, Heward's suggestively loaded signs have an uncanny ability to captivate the observer.

Indeed, the persuasive reduction of works from his classic *Mask, Sign* and *Forming* series of previous decades can be juxtaposed with these equally persuasive *Events,* with their Zen-like spirit of acceptance and endurance. Unframed and unstretched, as is the case with all Heward's paintings, these unfettered works allow the mark itself to achieve awesome primacy in space.

The recent paintings signal gesture as the event, the genesis of sense. The form, usually applied in black acrylic and/or ink—better yet, the collocation and conflux of black painted marks—traces gesture back to its source and beyond. The hegemony of the mark heralds a return to what is perhaps the most basic source of all painting: the primordial need to express what is in mind to say through the medium of the hand.

As a painter, John Heward has always been a stoic. The stark simplicity—and, yes, the selflessness—of his stoicism can be sensed in every painted gesture he makes on his unstretched lengths of canvas or rayon. Heward demonstrates just how much there is still to say about the act of painting, whether act of contrition or act of faith, and his manner of saying has never been more eloquent than now.

—James D. Campbell

HICKS, Sheila

Nationality: American. **Born:** Hastings, Nebraska, 24 July 1934. **Education:** Yale University, New Haven, Connecticut, under Josef Albers, 1954–59, B.F.A. 1957, M.F.A. 1959. **Family:** Married Henrik Schlubach in 1959 (divorced); married Enrique Zanartu in 1965; children: Itaka and Cristobal. **Career:** Creator of tapestries; has lived and worked in Paris since 1963. Instructor, University of Santiago, Chile, 1968, and University of Mexico, Mexico City, 1962; lecturer on Thread Exploration, Bath Academy of Art, England, 1964; established Taller-Huaquen Studio, Huaquen, Chile, 1968; worked on wall rugs with M. Nejjai, Rabat, Morocco, 1970; Founder, with Luis Barragan, Taller-Los Bravos, Valle de Bravo, Mexico, 1972; Chief Editor, *American Fabrics and Fashion* magazine, New York, 1980–83. **Awards:** Fullbright Scholarship, 1957; Fribourg Grant, 1959; Gold Medal, American Institute of Architects, 1974; Silver Medal, Academie d'Architecture, Paris, 1986. Fellow, American Crafts Council, 1983; Medal of Fine Arts, French Academy of Architecture, 1985; Officier des Arts et Lettres, French Government, 1996; Gold Medal, American Crafts Council, 1997. **Agents:** Carmen Martinez Gallery, 12 rue Roi de Sicile, 75001 Paris; Galerie Cora de Vries, Keizersgracht 516, 1017 Amsterdam. **Address:** 3 bis Coeur de Rohan, 75006 Paris, France.

Individual Exhibitions:

1958 Museum of Fine Arts, Santiago, Chile
1959 Galeria,Galiera, Buenos Aires
1961 Galeria Antonio Souza, Mexico City
1963 Art Institute of Chicago
Knoll Associates, Chicago
1964 Kunstgewerbemuseum, Stuttgart
Knoll International, Hamburg (toured Germany and Switzerland)
1965 Interiors International, London
1966 Artek Gallery, Helsinki
N.K. Inredning, Stockholm
Interiors International, Stuttgart
1968 Art Museum, Jinrichove Hradec, Czechoslovakia
American Cultural Center, Paris
1969 Benzon Gallery, Bridgehampton, Long Island, New York
Gallerie Art Mural, Paris
Crafts Alliance Gallery, St Louis
1970 American Library, Brussels
Galerie Suzy Langlois, Paris
Franco-American Institute, Rennes, France
1971 Bab Rouah National Gallery, Rabat, Morocco
Museum of Fine Arts, Brest, France
Benson Gallery, Bridgehampton, Long Island, New York
1972 Mobilier International, Lyons Art Center, Wichita, Kansas
Krannert Art Museum, University of Illinois, Urbana
American Cultural Center, Dakar
National Theatre, Abidjan, Dar es Salam
1974 Stedelijk Museum, Amsterdam (retrospective)
1977 Modern Master Tapestries, Inc., New York
1978 Galerie M. T. Douet, Montreuil, France
1980 Israel Museum, Jerusalem
1986 Konsthall, Lund, Sweden
Milwaukee Art Museum, Wisconsin
American Craft Museum, New York

1992 Walker's Point Center for the Arts, Milwaukee
1996 Museum of Nebraska Art, Nebraska
1997 Kiryu Municipal Arts Center, Japan

Selected Group Exhibitions:

1963 *Woven Forms,* Museum of Contemporary Crafts, New York
1964 *Gewebte Formen,* Kunstgewerbemuseum, Zurich
1967 *New Acquisitions Design,* Museum of Modern Art, New York
1969 *Perspectief in Textiel,* Stedelijk Museum, Amsterdam
1970 *Formen in Faden,* Galerie Buchholz, Munich
1971 *Contemporary Weaving,* Iowa State University Design Center, Ames
Experimental Textiles, Camden Arts Centre, London
Deliberate Entanglements, University of California Galleries, Los Angeles (toured the United States and Canada)
1972 *Objects USA,* Musée d'Art Moderne de la Ville, Paris
1973 *Biennale Internationale de la Tapisserie,* Musée Cantonal des Beaux-Arts, Lausanne, Switzerland (and 1975, 1977)
1995 *16th International Biennale of Tapestry,* Lausanne, Switzerland

Collections:

Museum of Modern Art, New York; Ford Foundation Headquarters, New York; Georg Jensen Center for Advanced Design, New York; Museum of Contemporary Crafts, New York; Art Institute of Chicago; Musée des Arts Décoratifs, Paris; Landesmuseum, Oldenburg, West Germany; Kunstgewerbemuseum, Zurich; Kunstgewerbemuseum, Stuttgart; Museo de Bellas Artes; Santiago.

Publications:

By HICKS: Book—*Tecnicas Textiles Andinas,* exhibition catalog, Santiago, Chile 1958. **Article—**In *Claire Zeisler: A Restrospective,* exhibition catalog, Chicago, 1980.

On HICKS: Books—*The American Tapestry* by Ruth Kaufmann, New York 1968; *La Nouvelle Tapisserie,* by André Kuenzi, Geneva 1973; *Beyond Craft: The Art Fabric* by Mildred Constantine and J. L. Larsen, New York 1973; *Sheila Hicks* by Monique Levi-Strauss, London 1974; *Handmade in America* by Barbaralee Diamonstein, New York 1983. **Articles—**review by Steve Hohenboken in *New Art Examiner,* vol. 19, May 1992; ''Collaboration: Sheila Hicks' Cross Cultural Trapeze'' by Debra Brehmer in *Fiberarts* (Asheville), vol. 19, September/October 1992; ''Sheila Hicks: With a Little Help From Her Friends'' by Betty Freudenheim in *Fiberarts* (Asheville), vol. 23, Summer 1996; ''Treasures and Secrets'' by Jenni Sorkin in *Fiberarts* (Asheville), vol. 27, no. 3, November/December 2000. **Television—** *Sheila Hicks-Soft World,* Nebraska Public Television.

*

Taken up during the 1950s with what Albers calls ''the lack of connection between physical facts and psychic effects,'' I painted, and I even wove. At that period, I undertook to study pre-Inca textiles in South America, to go back to the sources of American tapestry. A long stay in Mexico increased the interest in architecture I already had.

When I was settling in Paris in 1963, my ideas became more clearly defined, because I was able to compare them to those which inspired the Gobelin school. Going over all my experiments, I concluded that if a painter does paintings, an artist working in thread creates directly from the thread. A sketch, a drawing or a collage may be starting points; but nothing replaces the close relation of the artist with his chosen material. Today my judgement would be less categorical—but I still believe that most discoveries arise during work. A certain lack of authenticity is inherent in a reproduced or second-hand work—hence my preference for original work.

I like to work on a small scale—that of my miniatures, which require neither cumbersome tools nor costly immobilisation. They allow me to elaborate a mode of writing which is at once personal and legible.

I am often tempted to take part in an exhibition, a ''ritual,'' using only works to create an environment or a free space. This necessitates work on a larger scale and implies expenses and difficulties which may be considerable. These ephemeral manifestations arouse in me a sentiment of frustration, for which I try to compensate by making bas-reliefs of tapestry or voluminous hangings designed to integrate into contemporary architecture with some chance of lasting.

—Sheila Hicks

Sheila Hicks, since the early 1960s, has continued to explore the expressive potential in fiber forms. A strong fine arts background—she studied with Joseph Albers and Rico Lebrun at Yale University—has accounted no doubt for the emphasis on conceptual concerns and pictorial qualities in her work. Her studies of ancient Peruvian textiles and traditional Mexican weaving techniques were already evident in the first major series of artworks: the miniature woven pieces from the early 1960s. Made on a small weaving frame with heddles of her own design, they contained a wide variety of patterns and slits. ''White Letter'' (1962), a one color, single yard piece is revealing of her belief in the equivalents of threading/writing, fiber/culturally encoded communications.

By the middle 1960s, the scale of the works increased, and she began to experiment with industrial textile techniques. In Germany, she researched a special electric gun that allowed her to embroider dramatically sculptural wall hangings with heavily tufted sections in high relief. ''Red Prayer Rug'' (1964) is an example. In 1966 the experience of working in India as a consultant to a textile manufacturer led her to create a new kind of heavy woven fabric in which, using indigenous plain weave techniques, she embedded cotton inside the weaving to add sculptural mass and density. In 1967, working with interior designer Warren Platner and architect Kevin Roche, she executed a major commission for the Ford Foundation Building; a large-scale linen and silk wall piece in natural gray and gold featuring a series of round medallions in plied silks. By the late 1960s, her mastery of the techniques of wrapping is evident in the long cords in the hanging/suspended work ''Principal Wife'' (1969) and in the floor pieces.

Always sensitive to and even inspired by traditional textile techniques, she produced a striking group of rugs in 1970–71, based on her stay in Morocco, in which the colors as well as the imagery make references to Islamic architecture. Most of her recent work has been taken up with the execution of major public commissions. Stressing relief, bright colors, warmth and light, her fiber forms, whether shaped into a series of vertical cords, disks or horizontal tubes present a sensual visual experience.

''Free Fall,'' a collaborative project done in 1980 in conjunction with various elements of the Israeli textile community for the Israel Museum in Jerusalem attests to the deep-seated concerns she has for the many cultural implications that can be carried by contemporary fiber forms. In other exhibitions for which she has wrapped objects and even people, Sheila Hicks whilst taking textile art into the provocative arena between sculpture and performance is finding new expressive ground.

—Ronny H. Cohen

HIGGINS, Dick

Nationality: American. **Born:** Richard Carter Higgins in Cambridge, England, 15 March 1938. **Education:** St. Paul's School, Concord, New Hampshire, 1950–55; Yale University, New Haven, Connecticut, 1955–57; studied music at the New School for Social Research, New York, under John Cage, George Brecht, and Al Hansen, 1957–59; studied English and music, School of General Studies, Columbia University, New York, 1958–60; studied at Manhattan School of Printing, New York, 1960–61; studied English at New York University, 1975–79, M.A. **Family:** married Alison Knowles, in 1960 (divorced, 1970; remarried, 1984); daughters: Hannah and Jessica. **Career:** Founder, Something Else Press, Vermont, 1964–74; developed ''Intermedia'' concept, 1965; Founder, Something Else Gallery, New York, 1966–68; taught at California Institute of the Arts, Burbank, 1970–71; moved to West Glover, Vermont, 1971; Founder, with Nelleke Rosenthal, Unpublished Editions, 1972–85 (became Printed Editions, 1978); Fellow, Center for 20th Century Studies, University of Wisconsin at Milwaukee, 1977. Member, Literature Panel, New York State Council on the Arts, 1979–81; moved to Barrytown, New York, 1981; Visiting Clark Professor in Art, Williams College, Williamstown, Massachusetts, 1987; research associate, State University of New York at Purchase, 1983–89; Williams College, visiting Clark Professor in Art, 1987, research associate in history of art, 1989; Visiting teacher at Salzburger Sommerakademie, Salzburg, Austria, 1993. **Awards:** New York State Council on the Arts grant, 1968; D.A.A.D. Fellowship, Berlin, 1975, 1981–82; Research Support Grants, Purchase College Foundation, 1984–86; Bill C. Davis Drama Award, 1988; New York State Council on the Arts Collaboration Grant, 1989; Banff Centre, residency, 1990; Pollock-Krasner Grant, 1993. **Died:** Of a heart attack, Quebec City, Canada, 25 October 1998.

Individual Exhibitions:

1973 Galerie René Block, Berlin
1974 Centro de Arte y Comunicacion, Buenos Aires
Galerie S: T Petri, Lund, Sweden
Véhicule Art, Montreal
1976 Museu de Art Contemporânca, São Paulo
Galerie Ecart, Geneva
1977 Galerie Ecart, Geneva
La Mamelle, San Francisco
Studio Morra, Naples
1978 Galerie Inge Baecker, Bochum, West Germany
Micro Gallery, Sacramento, California
1979 Franklin Furnace, New York
C Space, New York
Galleri Sudurgata, Reykjavik, Iceland
1982 Galerie Inge Baecker, Bochum, West Germany
Galerie Ars Viva, Berlin
Gallery A, Amsterdam
1986 Emily Harvey Artworks, New York
1987 San Diego State University, Calexico, California
1988 Mid-Hudson Arts and Science Center, Poughkeepsie, New York
1989 Emily Harvey Artworks, New York
Galeria Potocka, Kraków, Poland
1990 Emily Harvey Gallery, New York
1991 Gallery of Fine Arts, Rome Georgia
Galerie Schüppenhauer, Cologne, BRD
Galerie Blau, Seeheim, BRD
1993 Galérie J.-et-J. Donguy, Paris
Emily Harvey Gallery, New York
1995 Sonja Heine-Niels Onstad Museum, Oslo (traveling to Finland, Denmark, Germany, Poland, France)
2001 *Betwixt and Between: The Life and Work of Fluxus Artist Dick Higgins,* Columbia College Chicago Center for Book and Paper Arts, Chicago (catalog)

Selected Group Exhibitions:

1961 *Hall of Issues,* Judson Gallery, New York
1969 *Telephone,* Museum of Contemporary Art, Chicago
1970 *Happening und Fluxus,* Kölnischer Kunstverein, Cologne
1972 *Data,* Museum of Modern Art, Copenhagen
Fluxshoe, School of Art, Falmounth (toured U.K.)
1977 *Bookworks,* Museum of Modern Art, New York
1981 *Ecouter par les yeux,* Musée d'Art Moderne, Paris
1982 *1962—Weisbaden Fluxus—1982,* Museum Weisbaden
1985 *Kunst in der Bundesrepublik 1945–85,* Nationalgalerie, West Berlin
1987 *Zauber der Medusa,* Kunstlerhaus Wien, Vienna
1993 *In the Spirit of Fluxus,* Walker Art Center, Minneapolis, Minnesota (traveled to New York, Chicago, Columbus, Ohio, San Francisco and Barcelona, Spain)
RolyholyOver, Los Angeles Museum of Contemporary Art, California (traveled to New York and Osaka, Japan)
1995 *L'Art du Tampon,* Musée de la Poste, Paris

Collections:

Museu de Arte Contemporânea, Sao Paulo; University Library, University of Exeter, England; Berlinische Galerie, Berlin; Gallery of Modern Art, Vienna; Sonja Henie-Nils Onstad Foundation, Oslo; Museum of Modern Art, Copenhagen; Neue Staatsgalerie, Stuttgart; Museo Vostell, Estremadura, Spain; Centre National des Arts

Plastiques, Paris; Fonds National d'Art Contemporain, Paris; Museum of Contemporary Art, Chicago.

Publications:

By HIGGINS: Books—*What Are Legends,* New York 1960; *Jefferson's Birthday/Postface,* New York 1964; *A Book about Love and War and Death, Canto One,* New York 1965; *Towards the 1970s,* Dunkirk, New York, 1969; *FOEW & OMBWHNW,* New York 1969; *A Book about Love and War and Death, Cantos Two and Three,* San Francisco 1969; *Pop Architektur,* with Wolf Vostell, Dusseldorf 1969; *Die Fabelhafte Geträme von Taifun-Willi,* Somerville, Massachusetts 1970; *Computers for the Arts,* Somerville, Massachusetts 1970; *Fantastic Architecture,* with Wolf Vostell, Millerton, New York 1971; *Eine Zweite Heutliche Deutliche Sprache,* Dusseldorf 1972; *Selected Early Works,* Berlin 1982; *1959/60,* Verona 1982; *Horizons: The Poetics and Theory of the Intermedia,* Carbondale, Illinois 1983; *Intermedia,* Warsaw 1985; *Fourteen Telephone Translations for Steve McCaffery,* edited by Piotr Rypson, Klodzko, Poland 1987; *Pattern Poems: Guide to an Unknown Literature,* Albany, New York 1987; *Fluxus: Theory and Reception,* Berkeley 1987; *Five Hear-Plays,* Berkeley 1988; *On the Composition of Images, Signs and Ideas,* New York, 1991; *The Journey,* Barrytown, New York, 1991; *The Autobiography of the Moon,* Mentor, Ohio, 1992; *Happytime the Medicine Man,* Genève, Switzerland, 1992; *Octette,* Providence, Rhode Island, 1993; *Buster Keaton Enters into Paradise,* Barrytown, New York, 1994; *Life Flowers, or Shadow of the Wind,* 1995; *Merle Armitage and the Modern Book,* Boston 1995; *Happenings and Other Acts,* edited by Mariellen R. Sandford, London 1995; *The Fluxus Reader,* edited by Ken Friedman, Chicester 1998. **Articles—**''Two Constellations'' in *An Anthology,* edited by Jackson Maclow and La Monte Young, New York 1961; text in *Happenings,* edited by Wolf Vostell and Jürgen Becker, Rheinbeck, West Germany 1966; ''3-Day Curry'' in *Anekdoten zu Einer Topographie des Zufalls von Daniel Spoerri mit Emmet Williams,* edited by Dieter Rot, Neuwied, West Germany 1969; ''Teacher'' in *Report to the President and Congress by the Commission on Instructional Technology,* Washington, D.C. 1970; text in *John Cage,* edited by Richard Kostelanetz, New York 1970; ''Something Else about Fluxus'' in *Art and Artists* (London), October 1972; ''Looking Back: Dick Higgins'' with Nicholas Zurbrugg in *PAJ,* vol. 21, no. 2, May 1999; ''Dick Higgins 1938–1998: Intermedia'' with Charles Dreyfus and Jacques Donguy in *INTER,* no. 73, Spring-Summer 1999; ''Dick Higgins: 1938–1998'' with multiple authors in *Umbrella,* vol. 21, no. 3–4, December 1998. **Films—***A Tiny Movie,* 1959; *The Flight of the Florence Bird,* 1960; *The Flaming City,* 1962; *Invocation of Canyons and Boulders for Stan Brakhage,* 1962; *Plunk,* 1964; *For the Dead,* 1965; *Scenario,* 1968; *Hank and Mary without Apologies,* 1969; *Mysteries,* 1969; *Men and Women and Bells,* 1970.

On HIGGINS: Books— *Kampen mod Borgermusikken* by Knud Pedersen, Copenhagen 1973; *Experimental Music: Cage and Beyond* by Michael Nyman, London 1974; *Metamorphosis in the Arts* by Richard Kostelanetz, New York 1980; *Something Else Press* by Peter Frank, New York 1983; *Dick Higgins: Catalogue* by Ina Bloom, 1995. **Articles—**''Dick Higgins: Jefferson's Birthday and Postface'' by Juliet Arning Siragusa in *Collage* (Palermo, Sicily), September 1964; ''Dick Higgins: Neo Dadaist'' by Hugh Fox in *Studies in the 20th Century,* Troy, New York 1970; ''An Analytical Checklist of Books from Something Else Press'' by Hugh Fox in *Small Press Review* (Paradise, California), March 1974; ''Dick Higgins and the Something Else Press'' by Hugh Fox in *Arts in Society* (Madison, Wisconsin), vol. 11, no. 1, 1974; ''Dick Higgins'' by Richard Kostelanetz in *Twenties in the Sixties,* New York 1979; ''Fluxus and Fluxism in Berlin'' by René Block in *1961-Berlinart 1987,* New York, 1987; *Down and In: Life in the Underground* by Ronald Sukenick in *Beech Tree,* New York, 1987; *L'Acte pour l'Art,* by Arnaud Labelle-Rojoux, Paris, 1988; ''Fluxus Redux'' by Bruce Alshuler in *Arts Magazine* (New York), 1989; ''Pattern Poetry: Guide to an Unknown Literature'' by Robert Peters in *Great American Poetry Bake-off,* Metuchen, New Jersey, 1991; ''One Among Many'' by Alan Jones in *Arts* (New York), December 1991; ''Something Else Press'' by Jean-Charles Masséra in *Arts et Métiers du Livre,* November-December, 1991; ''Dick Higgins: Avant-garde Publishing Venture'' by Christian Xatrec in *Art Press,* no. 188, February 1994; ''Critical Refluxtions: Recollections on Fluxus Performances'' by Hannah Higgins in *New Art Examiner,* vol. 21, March 1994; ''Tuhannen Sinfonian Runoilija'' by Kaisu Koivisto in *Taide,* vol. 35, no. 3, 1995; obituary in *Art in America* (New York), December 1998; ''Dick Higgins, 1938–1998'' by Jackson Low in *Afterimage,* vol. 26, no. 4, January-February 1999; ''Richard Carter Higgins, 1938–1998: Obituary'' by Simon Anderson in *New Art Examiner,* vol. 26, no. 6, March 1999; ''Dick Higgins (1938–1998): I Remember Dick Higgins'' by Richard Kostelanetz and Meredith Monk in *PAJ,* vol. 21, no. 2, May 1999.

*

I began as a composer, took to composing with words, and found that I had to involve myself with visual design—which involved visual art becoming a large part of what I do. For the last 25 years I have been interested in the interfacing of sounds, words and visual elements—and in the philosophical and social implications of this. For this reason what seems like a very heterogenous involvement is actually far more unified than it appears.

—Dick Higgins

* * *

Though Dick Higgin's work may be conventionally categorized as ''writing,'' ''theater,'' ''music,'' ''film'' and ''book publishing,'' it is best to regard him as not a specialized practitioner of one or another of these arts, but as a true polyartist—a master of several arts, a specialist in none. Indeed, he is as various as Moholy-Nagy or van Doesburg—to cite two exemplary precursors; and some of his works contribute to two arts at once. In less than 25 years, he has produced a wealth of materials, both large and small, permanent and ephemeral, resonant and trivial. All this diversity notwithstanding, Higgins reveals five fundamental ways of dealing with the materials of each art he explores. These procedures are collage, representation, permutation, aleatory, and expressionism. In nearly all works, one or another procedure (or two) is dominant. Collage, briefly, is the accurate portrayal of extrinsic reality; permutation is the systematic manipulation of limited materials; aleatory is chance; and expressionism reflects personality or personal experience.

It might help to describe a few of his pieces. ''7.7.73'' (1973) is a series of 899 unique prints of various visual imagery, both abstract and representational, mostly on paper (but also on other materials), with forms repeated from one print to the next; its organizing principles are collage and aleatory. *Amigo* (1972) is a book-length poetic memoir of Higgins' love for a young man. ''Danger Music No. 13 (May 1962)'' reads in its entirety: ''Scream! Scream! Scream! Scream! Scream! Scream!'' *Postface* (1962) is a percipient and prophetic critical essay about advanced arts in the early 60s. *St. Joan at Beaurevoir* (1959) is a complicated long scenario that includes such incongruities as Dr. Johnson and St. Joan appearing on the same stage. *Men & Women & Bells* (1959) is a film that incorporated footage made by both his father and his grandfather. I remember it as the best of his films. *FOEW & OMBWHNW* (1969) is a book with four vertical columns across every two-page horizontal spread—one column continuously reprinting critical essays, a second column with poetry, a third with theatrical scenarios (including *St. Joan at Beaurevoir),* a fourth with drawings. Though the experience of reading *FOEW* is that of collage, the book as a whole is, of course, a representation of a multifaceted man.

—Richard Kostelanetz

HILL, Anthony

Pseudonym: Achill Redo. **Nationality:** British. **Born:** London, 23 April 1930. **Education:** Studied at St. Martin's School of Art, London, 1947–49; at Central School of Art, London, 1949–51. **Career:** Worked on constructional reliefs, 1954; abandoned painting in 1956; organized *Construction: England, 1950–60* exhibition at Drian Galleries, London, 1960; worked on construction screen, commissioned for International Union of Architects Congress, 1961; began working as Achill Redo, 1980. Lecturer, Regent Street Polytechnic, London, 1955–63. Honorary Research Associate, 1971–72, and since 1972 visiting research associate, Department of Mathematics, University College, London. **Awards:** Leverhulme Fellowship, 1971. **Address:** 24 Charlotte Street, London W1, England.

Individual Exhibitions:

1958 Institute of Contemporary Arts, London
1963 Institute of Contemporary Arts, London
1966 Kasmin Gallery, London
1969 Kasmin Gallery, London
1980 Kasmin Gallery, London
1983 Hayward Gallery, London (retrospective)
Angela Flowers Gallery, London
1988 Angela Flowers Gallery, London
1994 Mayor Gallery, London

Selected Group Exhibitions:

1950 *Aspects of British Art,* Institute of Contemporary Arts, London
1956 *This is Tomorrow,* Whitechapel Art Gallery, London
1962 *Experiment in Construction,* Stedelijk Museum, Amsterdam
1968 *Relief: Construction: Relief,* Museum of Contemporary Art, Chicago
1974 *British Art from the Tate Gallery,* Palais des Beaux-Arts, Brussels
1977 *Constructive Concepts,* Musée National d'Art Moderne, Paris
1980 *Pier and Ocean,* Hayward Gallery, London (travelled to the Rijksmuseum Kröller-Müller, Otterlo, Netherlands
1981 *British Sculpture in the 20th century: Part II, 1950–1980,* Whitechapel Art Gallery, London
1984 *English Art 1950–1960,* Serpentine Gallery, London
1986 *Konstruktivisme,* Louisiana Museum, Humlebaek, Denmark

Collections:

Tate Gallery, London; Victoria and Albert Museum, London; Arts Council of Great Britain, London; British Museum, London; Southampton Art Gallery, Hampshire; University of East Anglia, Norwich; Scottish Gallery of Modern Art, Edinburgh; Louisiana Museum, Humlebaek, Denmark; Tel Aviv Museum, Israel; Musée de Grenoble, France.

Publications:

By HILL: Articles—''The Structural Syndrome'' in *Module: Proportion: Symmetry: Rhthym,* edited by Gyorgy Kepes, New York 1966; ''Constructivism: The European Phenomena'' in *Studio International* (London), April 1966; ''Structure: Program: Paragram'' in *Data: Directions in Art Theory and Aesthetics,* London 1968; ''Art and Mathesis: Mondrian's Structures'' in *Leonardo* (Oxford), vol. 4, no. 3, 1968; ''The Climate of Beiderman'' in *Studio International* (London), September 1969; ''On Construction, Nature and Structure'' in *Structure* (Amsterdam), 2nd series, no. 1, 1969, reprinted in *The Tradition of Constructivism* by Stephen Bann, New York 1974; ''The Spectacle of Duchamp'' in *Studio International* (London), January/February 1975.

On HILL: Books—*9 Abstract Artists: Their Work and Theory* by Lawrence Alloway, London 1954; *The Tradition of Constructivism* by George Rickey, London 1968; *Art Abstrait* by Michel Seuphor and Michel Ragon, Paris 1973; *The Tradition of Constructivism* by Stephen Bann, New York 1974; *Accretions, 1990–1994,* exhibition catalog with introduction by David Sylvester, London 1994. **Articles—** ''Anthony Hill'' by Kenneth Frampton in *Studio International* (London), September 1969; ''Anthony Hill'' by R.C. Kenedy in *Art International* (Lugano, Switzerland), October 1976; ''Towards an Art of Environment: Exhibitions and Publications by a Group of Avant-Garde Abstract Artists in London 1951–55'' by Alastair Grieve in *The Burlington Magazine* (London), vol. 132, November 1990; review by Clifford Myerson in *Art Monthly,* no. 177, June 1994.

*

An art which uses none of the expected elements—depiction, illusion and ''expression''—is in sharp contrast to all other forms of modern art which use the expected but in unexpected ways.

For artists working in this area there are extreme positions, but as yet not more so than in the heroic period, and, although there are marked differences, it is not clear if they are to be taken as advances or mutations in the evolution of a new tradition. The innovators tended to mount radical programs which sought to cover all the issues in propagating a new art, the rhetoric often pitched as if the main goal were an aesthetic revolution to be achieved on a world scale.

Reconvening the extreme innovations at a personal, rather than a collective, level has lead to a new polarising, viz, the over-projective (as in the capitalizing ''megalomania'' of minimalism) and attempts to find an alternate way, not for working, but for self-evaluation and object evaluation.

This, in turn, will involve the balance between the artist's innate subjectivity and the epistemic bias in a structure orientated art.

—Anthony Hill

* * *

Victor Pasmore's ''conversion'' to abstract art shortly after the end of the war is always quoted a signifying the emergence of a new movement of British abstract art. Anthony Hill was 20 in 1950, the year when he first came into contact not only with Pasmore but also with Kenneth and Mary Martin. The Martins and Hill have now for some time been recognized as the chief exponents of British Constructivism—a term which is widely disputed, as the aims and methods of all these artists have variously developed away from those of the great Russian pioneers.

But at the outset of his career Hill could not have been described as a Constructivist even in the loosest sense. At the time of his first exhibition, a group show at the I.C.A., he was a painter of abstract shapes, often delightfully wayward and dynamic. It was not until 1954 that he turned away from painting and began making constructions. From that moment, with the exception of a two-dimensional work made especially for the Hayward *British Painting 74,* he has worked exclusively in three dimensions. The experience which precipitated his development into an artist of exceptional formal rigour was Charles Biedermann's *The Evolution of Visual Knowledge.* Biedermann expanded an analysis of past art into the proposition that the relief was the only viable form of modern art, thereby implying that both painting and sculpture had become obsolete. Although Hill disagreed with Biedermann on certain significant points, most notably in that he did not accept that the structural process level of reality is the only starting point for non-mimetic art, Biedermann's ideas nevertheless exercised a profound and far-reaching effect on his work. He began to make reliefs, using planes which were either parallel or set at right angles to the wall. For a period Hill restricted himself entirely to orthogonals, but in 1962 he bagan using angles which were set on the diagonal in plan. As a result his work became more complex, making it imperative for the spectator to view each work laterally as well as frontally.

It was at about this time that Hill first became aware of the problem of symmetry, considered as a mathematical proposition. Since then he has become actively involved in mathematics and has contributed several important papers to international conferences. Meanwhile his art has developed parallel to but quite separate from his work as a mathematician. Perhaps the most striking example of the complexity of Hill's attitude towards life and art is his adoption of an alter-ego, whom he calls Rem Oxford, a contraction of Rembrandt's Dogdhsfoodt. This alter-ego first manifested itself in the *Studio International* issue devoted to Duchamp (Jan/Feb 75). This indulgence in a post-Dadaist fancy, coupled with his work as a graph theorist, illustrate the range of contradictions which make up Hill the artist.

Hill has become known as one of the most stringent and austere practitioners of British formal abstract art. This recognition is on an international level; Hill first visited Paris in the early 50s, where he met Kupka, Picabia, and Vantongerloo, with whom he remained in contact up until the time of his death. But while Hill's reputation is fully deserved, he is also capable of making works which destroy the notion that pure Constructivism is devoid of writ. Although they are always constructed to the most stringent principles, he possesses an aesthetic sense which ensures that they transcend the limitations implied by a mathematical basis. His most recent work is of such quality that it would seem that its value can only be increasingly recognized in the years to come.

—Fenella Crichton

HILL, Gary

Nationality: American. **Born:** Santa Monica, 1951; resides in Seattle, Washington. **Awards:** Merit Award, Experimental Video, Athens International Video Festival, Athens, Ohio, 1976, 1978; The Video Art Award, 3rd Annual Daniel Wadsworth Memorial Video Festival, Hartford, Connecticut, 1981; 2nd Prize, Video Art, United States Film/Video Festival, Salt Lake City, Utah, 1982; 1st Prize (shared), San Sebastian International Video Festival, San Sebastian, Spain, 1983; Merit Award, Chicago International Film/Video Festival, Chicago, Illinois, 1983; 1st Prize, 3/4 Inch Non-Narrative Art Video/New Media, Video Culture International, Montreal, Quebec, Canada, 1985; Sony Grand Prize, 3/4 Inch Video/New Media, Video Culture International, Montreal, Quebec, Canada, 1985; Grand Prix (shared), 1st Tokyo International Video Biennale, Tokyo, Japan, 1985; 1st Prize, Art Video/New Media, Video Culture International, Montreal, Quebec, Canada, 1985; James D. Phelan Art Award, San Francisco Foundation, San Francisco, California, 1986; 1st Prize, Structuralist Video, Athens International Video Festival, Athens, Ohio, 1987; Grand Prize, 6th Annual Daniel Wadsworth Video Festival, Real Art Ways, Hartford, Connecticut, 1987; Grand Prix, World Wide Video Festival, The Hague, Netherlands, 1988; Prix Alcan (video), 18th Annual Montreal Film and Video Festival, Montreal, Quebec, Canada, 1988; Prize Winner (Performance Video), 13th Atlanta Film/Video Festival, Atlanta, Georgia, 1989; Prize Winner, ''ARTEC 91'' International Biennale, Nagoya, Japan, 1991; Leone d'Oro, Prize for Sculpture, Venice Biennale, Venice, Italy, 1995; First Prize, 1994–1995 AICA (International Association of Art Critics) Best Show Awards, Best Video Show or Installation, Guggenheim SoHo, New York,

1995; CAA Artist Award for Distinguished Body of Work, College Art Association, New York, 1996; Second Prize, 1996 United States Chapter of the International Association of Art Critics Awards, Best Video or Installation, ''Gary Hill: *Withershins*'' at the Institute of Contemporary Art, Philadelphia, 1996; John D. and Catherine T. MacArthur Foundation Grant, 1998; Kurt Schwitters Award 2000, 2000; Joseph H. Hazen Rome Prize Fellowship at the American Academy in Rome, 2000–01.

Individual Exhibitions:

1968 El Jay Gallery, Los Angeles, California
1971 Polari Gallery, Woodstock, New York
1972 Polari Gallery, Woodstock, New York
1973 Woodstock Artists' Association, Woodstock, New York
1974 South Houston Gallery, New York
1977 Anthology Film Archives, New York
1978 Rochester Memorial Art Gallery, Rochester, New York
1979 The Kitchen Center for Music, Video and Dance, New York
1980 Museum of Modern Art, New York
1981 And/Or Gallery, Seattle, Washington
Museum of Modern Art, New York
1982 Long Beach Museum of Art, Long Beach, California
1983 Whitney Museum of American Art, New York
Center for Media Art, The American Center, Paris, France
1986 Whitney Museum of American Art, New York
1987 Museum of Contemporary Art, Los Angeles, California
1988 Espace lyonnais d'art contemporain (ELAC), Lyon, France
1989 Musée d'art moderne, Villeneuve d'Ascq, France
1990 Galerie des Archives, Paris, France
Video Galleriet, Huset, Denmark
Ny Carlsberg Glyptotek Museum, Copenhagen, Denmark
Museum of Modern Art, New York
1991 Galerie des Archives, Paris, France
OCO Espace d'art contemporain, Paris, France
1992 The Watari Museum of Contemporary Art, Tokyo, Japan
Le Creux de L'Enfer, Centre d'art contemporain, Thiers, France
Musée national d'art moderne, Centre Georges Pompidou, Paris, France
Stedelijk Museum, Amsterdam, The Netherlands
Künsthalle, Vienna, Austria
1993 Donald Young Gallery, Seattle, Washington
Museum of Modern Art, Oxford, England
Tate Gallery Liverpool, Liverpool, England
Long Beach Museum of Art, Long Beach, California
1994 Musée d'art contemporain, Lyon, France
Museum für Gegenwartskunst, Öffentliche Kunstsammlung, Basel, Switzerland
Hirshhorn Museum and Sculpture Garden, Washington, D.C.
Henry Art Gallery, Seattle, Washington
Museum of Contemporary Art, Chicago, Illinois
Museum of Contemporary Art, Los Angeles, California
Guggenheim Museum SoHo, New York
1995 Riksutställningar, Stockholm, Sweden
Moderna Museet, Stockholm, Sweden
Museet for Samtidskunst, Oslo, Norway;
Kunstforeningen, Copenhagen, Denmark
Bildmuseet, Urneå, Sweden;
Göteborgs Konstmuseum, Göteborg, Sweden
1996 Institute of Contemporary Art, Philadelphia, Pennsylvania
Galerie des Archives, Paris, France
Galleria Lia Rumma, Naples, Italy
Donald Young Gallery, Seattle, Washington
Barbara Gladstone Gallery, New York
White Cube, London, England
1997 Westfälischer Kunstverein, Münster, Germany
Centro Cultural Banco do Brasil, Rio de Janeiro, Brazil
Museu de Arte Moderna de São Paulo, Brazil
Center for Contemporary Art, Ujazdowski Castle, Warsaw, Poland
1998 Musée d'art contemporain de Montréal, Montreal, Quebec, Canada
Donald Young Gallery, Seattle, Washington
Capp Street Project, San Francisco, California
Museu d'Art Contemporani, Barcelona, Spain
Whitney Museum of American Art, New York
1999 Aarhus Kunstmuseum, Aarhus, Denmark
Barbara Gladstone Gallery, New York
2000 Donald Young Gallery, Chicago, Illinois
Centro Cultural Recoleta, Buenos Aires, Argentina
The Watari Museum of Contemporary Art, Tokyo, and Nagoya Art Station, Nagoya
Sprengel Museum, Hannover, Germany

Selected Group Exhibitions:

1982 Sydney Biennale, Sydney, Australia
1983 Whitney Biennial, Whitney Museum of American Art, New York
1984 Biennale di Venezia, Venice, Italy
1985 Whitney Biennial, Whitney Museum of American Art, New York
1987 Whitney Biennial, Whitney Museum of American Art, New York
Documenta VIII, Kassel, Germany
1989 Whitney Biennial, Whitney Museum of American Art, New York
1991 Whitney Biennial, Whitney Museum of American Art, New York
1992 Documenta IX, Kassel, Germany
1993 Whitney Biennial, Whitney Museum of American Art, New York
1994 Bienal Internacionale de São Paulo, São Paulo, Brazil
1995 ARS '95 Helsinki, Museum of Contemporary Art, Helsinki, Finland
Carnegie International, Carnegie Museum of Art, Pittsburgh, Pennsylvania
2000 12th Biennale of Sydney, Art Gallery of New South Wales, Sydney, Australia
Media City Seoul 2000, Seoul Historical Museum, Seoul, Korea

Video Installations:

Hole in the Wall, 1974; *Mesh,* 1978–79; *War Zone* 1980; *Around & About,* 1980 (destroyed); *Glass Onion,* 1981; *Primarily Speaking,* 1981–83; *Equal Time,* 1982; *CRUX,* 1983–87; *In Situ,* 1986–87; *Mediarite,* 1987; *DIG,* 1987–92; *DISTURBANCE (among the jars),* 1988; *And Sat Down Beside Her,* 1990;*BEACON (Two Versions of the Imaginary),* 1990; *Inasmuch As It is Always Already Taking Place,* 1990; *Between Cineam and a Hard Place,* 1991; *CORE SERIES* (two works: *Glasses* and *Leaves*), 1991, *Split Time Mystery,* 1991; *I Believe It Is an Image in Light of the Other,* 1991–92; *Suspension of Disbelief (for Marine),* 1991–92; *CORE SERIES (No Evil),* 1992 (destroyed); *Tall Ships,* 1992; *Cut Pipe,* 1992; *Some Times Things,* 1992; *If Two People,* 1993 (destroyed); *Between 1 & 0,* 1993; *House of Cards,* 1993; *Learning Curve,* 1993; *Learning Curve (still point),* 1993; *Searchlight,* 1986–94; *Circular Breathing,* 1994; *Clover,* 1994; *Remarks on Color,* 1994, and *Bemerkungen über die Farben,* 1994 (German version); *Red Technology,* 1994; *Dervish,* 1993–95; *Bind,* 1995;*Withershins,* 1995; *Placing Sense?Sens Placé,* 1995; *HanD HearD,* 1995–96; *Viewer,* 1996; *Standing Apart,* 1996; *Facing Faces,* 1996; *Standing Apart/Facing Faces,* 1996; *Reflex Chamber,* 1996; *Midnight Crossing,* 1997; *Conundrum,* 1995–98; *Liminal Objects #1-#8,* 1995–1998; *23:59:59:29—The Storyteller's Room,* 1998; *Switchblade,* 1998–99; *Crossbow,* 1999; *Namesake,* 1999; *Still Life,* 1999; *Cabin Fever,* 1999; *Rorrim Room Mirror,* 2000; *Remembering Paralinguay (with Paulina Wallenberg-Olsson),* 2000; *Wall Piece,* 2000.

Publications:

By HILL: Articles—''Processual Video'' in *Video Viewpoints* (New York), February 1980; ''War Zone'' in *Media Study/Buffalo,* January-May 1980; ''Gary Hill'' by John G. Hanhardt in *The New American Filmmakers Series 12,* New York 1983; ''Happenstance (Explaining It to Death)'' in *Video d'Artistes* (Geneva), 1986; ''URA ARU: The Acoustic Palindrome'' in *Video Guide,* vol. 7, no. 4, 1986; ''Primarily Speaking'' in *Video Communications,* no. 48, 1988; ''Eye for I: Video Self-Portraits'' by Raymond Bellour in *New American Film and Video Series 48,* New York 1989; ''And If the Right Hand Did Not Know What the Left Hand Is Doing'' in *Illuminating Video,* edited by Doug Hall and Sally Jo Fifer, New York 1990; ''Site Re:cite'' in *Camera Obscura,* no. 24, 1991; ''Gary Hill'' by Lori Zippay in *Video,* New York 1991; ''The Electronic Gallery'' in *New York Times Magazine,* 28 September 1997; ''Liminal Performance: Gary Hill in Conversation with George Quasha and Charles Stein'' in *Performing Arts Journal,* vol. 20, no. 1, January 1998; ''Charles Marclay/Gary Hill: Conversation'' in *Annandale,* vol. 139, no. 1, Spring 2000; ''Void Still Life'' in *Any Magazine,* no. 27, 2000.

On HILL: Books and Exhibition Catalogs—*Video and Language/Video as Language,* Los Angeles Contemporary Exhibitions 1986; *Video by Artists 2,* Toronto: Art Metropole 1986; *Video Transformations,* New York, Independent Curators Incorporated 1986; *Digital Visions: Computers and Art* by Cynthia Goodman, New York 1987; *Video Currents—Mediated Narratives,* Boston, Institute of Contemporary Art 1987; *Gary Hill: DISTURBANCE (among the jars),* Villeneuve d'Ascq, Musée d'Art Moderne 1988; *L'Oeuvre Video de Gary Hill* by Christine Devriendt, Rennes, France 1991; *Maurice Blanchot/Gary Hill: d'une Écriture l'Autre (et Son Double),* Paris 1992; *Chimaera Monographe No. 10 (Gary Hill)* by Stephen Sarrazin, Montbéliard, France 1992; *Gary Hill,* Paris, Galerie des Archives 1990; *Gary Hill, Video Installations,* Eindhoven, Stedelijk Van Abbemuseum 1992; *Gary Hill—I Believe It Is an Image,* Tokyo, Watari Museum of Contemporary Art 1992; *Gary Hill,* Paris, Centre Georges Pompidou 1992; *Gary Hill,* Amsterdam, Stedelijk Museum, and Vienna, Kunsthalle 1993; *Gary Hill: In Light of the Other,* Oxford, The Museum of Modern Art Oxford, and Liverpool, Tate Gallery Liverpool 1993; *Gary Hill: Imagining the Brain Closer than the Eyes,* edited by Theodora Vischer, Basel, Museum für Gegenwartskunst 1995; *Gary Hill: Hand Heard—Liminal Objects,* Paris, Galerie des Archives 1996; *Gary Hill: Midnight Crossing,* Münster, Westfälischer Kunstverein 1997; *Gary Hill* edited by Robert Morgan, Baltimore, Johns Hopkins University Press 2000; *Gary Hill en Argentina: textos, ensayos, dialogos,* Buenos Aires, Centro Cultural Recoleta, 2000; *Gary Hill: Instalaciones,* Córdoa, Ediciones Museo Caraffa 2000.

* * *

Gary Hill has been creating a wide variety of different experiences for the viewer of his works since he first started experimenting with video and sound in 1973. Starting out as a sculptor, he moved into the possibilities that video technology offered. One of his surprising early influences is surfing, which has prompted him to utilize wave imagery, as well as some of the popular notions about heightening one's sensibilities by ''becoming one with the wave.'' Hill regularly utilizes mystical imagery and invokes a meditative state in his work that resembles the solitude of surfing. His works are not always quiet, however, just as surfing involves the sound of the waves and the wind.

While many video artists critique technology and its problematic role in contemporary society and life, Hill is content instead to explore the more artistic implications of this time-based medium. He frequently examines the role of the viewer as spectator and active participant, perhaps seen most interestingly in the 1993 installation *Tall Ships,* in which hidden switches give the illusion of figures advancing as the viewer advances and receding as the viewer recedes. Another element permeating his art is the role of art in communicating and a broader examination of language. The viewer completes the work by experiencing it, often directly involved, sometimes more distantly engaged in the piece. He has collaborated extensively with poets George Quasha and Charles Stein in creating multimedia pieces in considering the metaphysics of expression and of existence.

In *Inasmuch as It Is Always Already Taking Place* of 1990, Hill exhibits a group of 16 black-and-white monitors varying in size from half an inch to twenty-one inches showing different close-ups of his naked body. He wants the viewer to consider the presence of the artist and the reality of the artist's (and, ultimately, the viewer's) body. Such a work as this one is a distant extreme from those involved in focusing on the alienating aspects of technology

Hill has created a body of work that is supremely inventive. He both explores the innovative elements video offers a time-based medium and creates a new syntax for others to follow. Although video art is often thought of as a new medium, Hill is really one of its ''old masters.''

—Anne Swartz

HILLIARD, John

Nationality: British. **Born:** Lancaster, 29 March 1945. **Education:** Lancaster College of Art, 1962–64; St. Martin's School of Art, London, 1964–67, Dip. A. D. 1967. **Career:** Artist and photographer since 1967. Part-time instructor, Somerset College of Art, Taunton, 1968–71; part-time lecturer, Brighton Polytechnic, 1969–76 and 1979–85; associate senior lecturer in painting, Camberwell School of Art, London, until 1991; visiting lecturer in painting, Slade School of Fine Art, London; presently teaches at Chelsea College of Art, London (since 1990), at the Rijksakademie van Beeldende Kunsten in Amsterdam (since 1989), and at the Slade School of Fine Art in London. **Awards:** Visual Arts Fellowship, Northern Arts Association, 1976–78; David Octavius Hill Medal, Gesellschaft Deutscher Lichtbildner, 1986. **Agents:** Lisson Gallery, 67 Lisson Street, London NW1, England; Galerie Durand-Dessert, 2 rue de Lappe, 75011 Paris, France. **Address:** The Vicarage, 49 Chatham Street, London SE17 1PA, England.

Individual Exhibitions:

1969 Camden Arts Centre, London
1970 Lisson Gallery, London
1971 Lisson Gallery, London
1972 Nova Scotia College of Art and Design, Halifax
1973 Lisson Gallery, London
1974 Museum of Modern Art, Oxford
Galleria Toselli, Milan
1975 Lisson Gallery, London
Galleria Banco, Brescia, Italy
1976 Galerie Hetzler + Keller, Stuttgart
Galerie Durand-Dessert, Paris
Robert Self Gallery, Newcastle upon Tyne
1977 Badischer Kunstverein, Karlsruhe
Galerie Durand-Dessert, Paris
Paul Maenz Gallery, Cologne
1978 Galerie Akumulatory 2, Poznan, Poland
Galleria Banco, Brescia, Italy
Studio Paola Betti, Milan
John Gibson Gallery, New York
Lisson Gallery, London
Laing Art Gallery, Newcastle upon Tyne
1979 Ikon Gallery, Birmingham
Galerie Foksal, Warsaw
Galerie Durand-Dessert, Paris
1980 Galerie Max Hetzler, Stuttgart
Lisson Gallery, London
1981 Galerie Durand-Dessert, Paris
Orchard Gallery, Londonderry
1982 Amano Gallery, Osaka, Japan
Ryo Gallery, Kyoto, Japan
1983 Galerie Durand-Dessert, Paris
Kunstverein, Cologne
Kunsthalle, Bremen, West Germany
1984 Kunstverein, Frankfurt
Kettle's Yard Gallery, Cambridge
Institute of Contemporary Arts, London
Galerie Media, Neuchatel, Switzerland
1985 Galerie Grita Insam, Vienna
1986 Provinciaal Museum, Hasselt, Belgium
1987 Sprengel Museum, Hannover
Galerie Durand-Dessert, Paris
1988 Bess Cutler Gallery, New York
1989 Renaissance Society, Chicago
Lisson Gallery, London
Galerie Grita Insam, Vienna
Galerie Le Réverbère, Lyon
1990 Art Affairs, Amsterdam
Kunstverein, Stuttgart
1992 Galerie Durand-Dessert, Paris
Art Affairs, Amsterdam
1993 Musée des Beaux Arts, La Chaux-de-Fonds
Galerie Gutsch, Berlin
1994 Galerie de l'Ancienne Poste, Calais
1995 Art Affairs, Amsterdam
1996 L A Galerie, Frankfurt
1997 Kunsthalle Krems, Germany
Ar/Ge Kunst, Galerie Museum, Bolzano, Italy
Kunstverein Hannover, Hannover
Galerie Durand-Dessert, Paris
1998 Arnolfini Gallery, Bristol
1999 Centro Internacional de Arte, Palacio de Revillagigedo, Gijón, Spain
Centro de Fotografia, Universidad de Salamanca, Spain
Art Affairs, Amsterdam
L A Galerie, Frankfurt
Kunst Haus Dresden
Württembergischer Kunstverein, Stuttgart
Stadtgalerie Saarbrücken, Germany
2000 Städtische Galerie Erlangen, Germany
Fig-1 Gallery, London
Galerie Seitz, Berlin
Senior and Shopmaker Gallery, New York
Galleria D'Arte Moderna, Bologna

Selected Group Exhibitions:

1971 *New English Enquiry,* at the *Bienal Sao Paulo Prospect '71,* Kunsthalle, Dusseldorf
1972 *The New Art,* Hayward Gallery, London
1976 *Arte Inglese Oggi,* Palazzo Reale, Milan
1977 *Malerei und Photographie im Dialog,* Kunsthaus, Zurich
1979 *Photographie als Kunst 1879–1979,* Tiroler Landes-museum Ferdinandeum, Innsbruck, Austria (travelled to Neue Galerie am Wolfgang Gurlitt Museum, Linz, Austria; Neue Galerie am Landes-museum Joanneum,

John Hilliard: *Second Screening,* 1998. ©John Hilliard.

Graz, Austria; and Museum des 20. Jahrhunderts, Vienna)
1981 *Facons de Peindre,* Maison de la Culture, Chalon sur Saone, France
1983 *Kunst mit Photographie,* Nationalgalerie, West Berlin
1985 *Alles Und Noch Viel Mehr,* Kunstmuseum, Berne
1987 *The Other Body,* University of Boston
1991 *Histoires d'Oeil,* Musée d'Art Contemporain
1992 *Whitechapel Open,* Whitechapel Art Gallery, London
1993 *Out of Sight, Out of Mind,* Lisson Gallery, London
1994 *Foundation Cartier: A Collection,* National Museum of Contemporary Art, Seoul
1995 *Contemporary British Art In Print,* Scottish National Gallery of Modern Art, Edinburgh

L'Effet Cinemá, Musée d'Art Contemporain, Montreal
1996 *Prospect 96,* Frankfurter Kunstverein, Frankfurt
1997 *The Impossible Document,* Camerawork Gallery, London
1998 *The Promise of Photography,* Hara Museum of Contemporary Art, Tokyo
1999 *Das Versprechen der Fotografie,* Kestner Gesellschaft, Hannover (travelled to Centre National de la Photographie, Paris and Akademie der Künste, Berlin)
2000 *Ten Times Over and More,* Art Affairs, Amsterdam
Into the Light, The Royal Photographic Society, Bath

Collections:

Tate Gallery, London; Victoria and Albert Museum, London; Leeds City Art Gallery; Centre Georges Pompidou, Paris; Musée d'Art Moderne, Grenoble; Musée d'Art Moderne, Toulon; Kunsthalle, Hamburg; Kunsthaus, Zurich; Museum of Fine Arts, Lodz, Poland; Art Gallery of South Australia, Adelaide.

Publications:

By HILLIARD: Books—*Elemental Conditioning,* Oxford 1974; *Black Depths, White Expanse,* London 1976; *From the Northern Counties,* London 1978; *Borderland,* Londonderry 1981. **Articles**—''Unpopulated Rural Black and White Exteriors, Populated Urban Colored Interiors'' in *Aspects* (London), Winter 1977; ''John Hilliard,'' interview with Ian Kirkwood in *Art Log* (London), Summer 1978; ''John Hilliard,'' interview with Colin Painter in *Aspects* (London), Autumn 1978; ''Drawings (in anticipation) of Photographs'' in *Aspects* (Newcastle-upon-Tyne), no. 16, 1981; ''Inverse Correspondences'' in *Furor* (Geneva), no. 10, 1983; ''Four Works by John Hilliard'' in *ZG* (New York), Summer 1984; ''John Hilliard,'' interview with Marlen Schnele Schneyder, in *European Photography* (Gottingen), July 1986; ''Backwards, Forwards and Sideways'' in *John Hilliard: Seven Monoprints,* London 1990; ''Notes on Recent Pictures'' and ''Being and Meaning'' in *John Hilliard: Scene* (exhibition catalog), Paris 1993; ''3 Statements'' in *Point* (London), no. 1, Winter 1995; ''The Pleasure of Erasure'' in *John Hilliard: Works 1990–96* (exhibition catalog), 1997; ''Notes on Working Procedures'' in *European Photography,* Fall/Winter 1997; ''Being and Meaning'' in *Innerscapes,* 1998; ''Les Vampires Sortent La Nuit'' interview with Patrick Bougelet, Denis-Laurent Bouyer and Richard Klein in *Un Mobile Home Dans Le Desert,* 1998; ''Recollections,'' ''The Pornography of Art (extracts),'' ''The Other Picture,'' ''A Camera Recording It's Own Condition (and Other Stories)'' and ''A Conflict of Anxieties'' in *John Hilliard,* Heidelberg 1999.

On HILLIARD: Books—*The New Art,* exhibition catalog, by Anne Seymour, London 1972; *Arte Inglese Oggi,* exhibition catalog by Luca Venturi and others, Milan 1976; *Analytical Photography* by Manfred Schmalreide, Karlsruhe 1977; *Fotografie als Kunst/Kunst als Fotographie* by Floris Neusüss, Cologne 1979; *Kunst als Photographie* by Peter Weiermair, Innsbruck 1979; *John Hilliard,* exhibition catalog with text by Paul Bonaventura, Hasselt 1986; *John Hilliard,* exhibition catalog, Chicago 1989; *Vanitas,* exhibition catalog, Stuttgart 1990; *John Hilliard: Scene,* exhibition catalog, La-Chaux-de-Fonds, France 1993; *John Hilliard: Works 1990–96,* exhibition catalog, Hannover 1997; *John Hilliard,* exhibition catalog, Gijón, Spain 1999; *John Hilliard,* exhibition catalog, Salamanca, Spain 1999. **Articles**—''3 Pieces by John Hilliard'' in *Studio International* (London), April 1972; ''Artist as Filmmaker'' by Annabel Nicolson in *Art and Artists* (London), December 1972; ''From Sculpture to Photography: John Hilliard and the Issue of Self-Awareness in Medium Use'' by Richard Cork in *Studio International* (London), July/August 1975; ''John Hilliard—Scènes Gelées par des Temps Différents'' by Regis Durand in *Art Press* (Paris), March 1984; ''Schiebung mit offenen Karten'' by Jörg-Uwe Albig in *Art* (Hamburg), no.9, 1986; ''Hilliard: Derrière le miroir'' by Mo Gourmelon in *Beaux-Arts,* No. 21, 1994; ''Linke Gegen Rechte Photographie'' by John Stathatos in *Kunstforum International,* No. 129, 1995; ''L'Effet Cinema'' by Karoline Georges in *Parcours,* Vol. 2, No. 1, 1995; ''Tracer'' by Libby Ansonin *Art Monthly,* No. 194, March 1996; ''Victor Burgin, Dan Graham, Rodney Graham, John Hilliard'' by Brian Hatton in *Art Monthly,* September 1996; ''The Riddles of Light'' by Marion Piffer Damiani in *John Hilliard: Works 1990–96,* exhibition catalog, 1997; ''Conceptualism and Conception'' by Marina Wallace in *John Hilliard: Works 1990–96,* exhibition catalog, 1997; ''John Hilliard'' by Marina Wallace in *Art Monthly,* March 1997; ''John Hilliard, Arbeiten der 90er Jahre'' by Martina Goldner in *Kunstverein Hannover,* No. 1, 1997; ''John Hilliard in der Kunsthalle Krems'' in *Kunstbulletin,* March 1997; ''The Beyond and the Ridiculous'' by Mark Durden in *Art Monthly,* June 1997; ''Les Ambiances Photocinématographiques de l'Anglais John Hilliard'' by Michel Guerrin in *Le Monde,* December 1997; ''John Hilliard—Arnolfini'' by Valerie Reardon in *Art Monthly,* December 1998; ''John Hilliard: A Retrospective'' by Mark Durdon in *Creative Camera,* January 1999; '''Full of Things Which Absorb the Light': Photography and Monochrome Painting'' by David Green in *Creative Camera,* June/July 1999; ''John Hilliard—Werke 1969–1999'' by Johannes Meinhardt in *Kunstforum International,* No. 148, 1999.

*

Using photography as a medium to discuss issues of representation, this practice seeks to be both critical and celebratory. In a body of work produced during the last five or six years, some conventions of picturing have been wilfully displaced, so that normally central components and strategies are quite literally sidelined, whereas those that are usually designated as merely peripheral are now brought centre-stage. To this end, and as a device to allow comparison, two ''versions'' of the same picture are presented together, usually with one largely obscuring the corresponding area of the other. What is normally ''transparent'' is rendered opaque; what is normally figurative is now an abstraction; what is normally sharply defined may have become blurred, unfocused, over-exposed, drained of colour or turned upside-down. These omissions or blockades, which defy pictorial access, are not merely negative, however. If they destroy photography's normative spatial illusion, they enliven a sense of the photograph's actual presence, and, however reductive they may appear, they are also calculated to be significant, to make a contribution to the overall reading of the image. There is both loss and gain.

—John Hilliard

HIRSCHHORN, Thomas

Nationality: Swiss. **Born:** Bern, Switzerland, 1957. **Education:** Studied at the Schule für Gestaltung, Zurich, 1978–1983 **Career:** Independent artist since 1986. **Awards:** Preis für Junge Schweizer Kunst der Zürcher Kunstgesellschaft; Prix Marcel Duchamp 2000, awarded by ADIAF (Association pour la diffusion internationale de l'art français). **Agents:** Arndt & Partner, Auguststrasse 35, 10119 Berlin, Germany; Galerie Chantal Crousel, 40 rue Quincampoix, 75004 Paris, France; Stephen Friedman Gallery, 25–28 Old Burlington Street, London W1X 1LB, United Kingdom; Barbara Gladstone Gallery, 515 West 24th Street, New York, New York 10011, U.S.A.; Galerie Susanna Kulli, Davidstr. 40, 9000 St. Gallen, Switzerland. **Address:** 56 rue du Moulin de la Pointe, 75013 Paris, France.

Individual Exhibitions:

1986 Bar Floréal, Paris
1987 Kaos-Galerie, Cologne
1991 Galerie Francesca Pia, Bern
1992 L'Hôpital Ephémère, Paris
1993 Galerie Francesca Pia, Bern
Raum für aktuelle Kunst, Luzern
Fondation Art et Société, Dijon (with Adrian Schiess)
Galerie Susanna Kulli, St. Gallen
1994 Filiale Basel, Bâle
APP Bruxelles, Brussels
1995 Künstlerhaus Bethanien, Berlin
Schauraum Dorothea Strauss und Konstantin Adamopoulos, Frankfurt am Main
Fri-Art, Centre d'Art, Fribourg
Centre Genevois de Gravure Contemporaine, Geneva
1996 *Virus—Ausstellung,* Galerie Arndt & Partner, Berlin
Galerie Susanna Kulli, St. Gallen
The Hal, Anvers
Institut Français de Bilbao, Salle Rekalde, Area 2, Bilbao
Merci-Bus II, Galerie Chantal Crousel, Paris
Vor Ort, Kunst in städtischen Situationen, Stadt Langenhagen
Kunstmuseum Luzern, Luzern (with Günter Förg)
1997 Galerie Chantal Crousel, Paris
7/7, 24/24, Blauer, schwebender Raum, Kunsthof Zürich, Zurich
Kunstverein Hannover, Hannover
Galerie im Künstlerhaus, Bremen
Lascaux III, FRAC Aquitaine, Bordeaux
1998 *World Corners,* Chisenhale Gallery, London
Ein Kunstwerk. Ein Problem, Portikus, Frankfurt am Main
Otto-Freundlich-Altar, im Rahmen des *Projektes Temporäres Strassendenkmal Wallisellenstrasse,* Bâle / Basel
Swiss Army Knife, Kunsthalle Bern, Bern
Rolex etc., Freundlichs ''Aufstieg'' und Skulptur-Sortier-Station-Dokumentation, Museum Ludwig, Cologne
Spin Off, Gramercy Art Fair, New York
Swiss Converter, Herzliya Museum of Art, Herzliya
1999 *Bernsteinzimmer,* Arndt & Partner, Berlin
World Corners, Musée d'art moderne de Saint-Etienne
Exchange Value Room, Project Room ARCO '99, Madrid
Robert Walser Kiosk, No. 1, Universität Zürich, Zurich
Sculpture Direct, Galerie Chantal Crousel, Paris
Ingeborg Bachmann Kiosk, No. 2, Universität Zürich, Zurich
Sculpture Direct II, III, IV, V, Galerie Erna Hécey, Luxembourg
Exergue 2, Musée d'Art et d'Histoire, Geneva
2000 *Focus,* The Art Insitute Chicago, Chicago
World Airport, The Renaissance Society, Chicago
Emmanuele Bove Kiosk, No. 3, Universität Zürich, Zurich
Raymond Carver Altar, The Galleries at Moore, Philadelphia
Meret Oppenheim Kiosk, No. 4, Universität Zürich, Zurich
2001 *Fernand Léger Kiosk, No. 5,* Universität Zürich, Zurich
POLE-SELF, Centre Georges Pompidou, Paris
Archeologie of Engagement, MACBA, Barcelona
Skulptur-Sortier-Station, Metro Station Stalingrad, Paris

Selected Group Exhibitions:

1988 Histoires d'hôtes, Ecole des Beaux-Arts, Poitiers
1989 *Babylone Bobigny,* Hôtel du conseil général, Bobigny
1990 *Salon d'Ephémère,* Fontenay-sous-Bois
1992 Shedhalle Zürich, Zurich
1994 *Invitations,* Galerie Nationale du Jeu de Paume, Paris
1995 *Africus: First Johannesburg Biennal,* Johannesburg
1996 *Actions urbaines,* FRAC Lorraine, Metz
1997 *Skulptur. Projekte in Münster,* Münster
1998 *Premises: Invested Spaces in Visual Arts & Architecture from France 1960s-1990s,* Solomon R. Guggenheim Museum Soho, New York
1999 *''d'APERTutto,''* Venice Biennale
Mirror's Edge, Bildmuseet, Umea (touring show)
2000 La Beauté, Mission 2000 en France, Avignon
2001 *Jheronimus Bosch,* Museum Boymans Van Beuningen, Rotterdam

Collections:

Fonds National d'Art Contemporain, Paris; Fonds Régional d'Art Contemporain, Provence-Alpes-Côtes-d'Azur; Fonds Régional d'Art Contemporain, Aquitaine; Stedelijk Museum Voor Actuele Kunst, Gent; Musée d'Art Moderne, Saint-Etienne; Bonnefanten Museum, Maastrich; Collections du Centre Pompidou, Musée National d'Art Moderne, Paris; Fonds Régional d'art Contemporain, Corse; The Art Institute of Chicago, Chicago (donation by Richard J. Stern); Fondation Musée d'Art Moderne Grand-Duc Jean, Luxembourg; Walker Art Center, Minneapolis; The Museum of Modern Art, New York; Fonds Municipal d'Art Contemporain, Genève; Kunsthaus Zürich; Kunstmuseum Bern; Kunstmuseum St. Gallen.

Publications:

By HIRSCHHORN: Books—*Les plaintifs, les bêtes, les politiques,* Centre Genevois de Gravure Contemporaine, Geneva 1992; *Thomas Hirschhorn, Katalog,* Berlin 1995; *Thomas Hirschhorn, 2. Auflage Katalog,* Fribourg 1995; *Thomas Hirschhorn 3. Auflage Katalog,* Luzern 1996; *Thomas Hirschhorn, 33 Ausstellungen im öffentlichen*

Raum, edited by Schweizerische Graphische Gesellschaft, Zürich 1998; *Thomas Hirschhorn: Deleuze Monument, les documents, La Beauté,* Avignon and Paris 2000.

On HIRSCHHORN: Books— *Sylvie Fleury, Daniele Buetti, Thomas Hirschhorn, Alex Hanimann,* exhibition catalog with text by Harm Lux, Zürich 1992; *Thomas Hirschhorn,* exhibition catalog with text by Manuel Joseph, École des Beaux-Arts de Rueil-Malmaison 1992; *Invitations,* exhibition catalog with text by Catherine David, Paris 1994; *Stiftung Kunst Heute,* exhibition catalog, Aargauer Kunsthaus, Aarau 1994; *Thomas Hirschhorn. Virus-Ausstellung,* exhibition catalog, Berlin 1996; *Thomas Hirschhorn. Im Rahmen der Ausstellung,* exhibition catalog, St. Gallen 1996; *Vor Ort. Kunst in städtischen Situationen (Georg Winter, Thomas Hirschhorn),* exhibition catalog with text by Peter Herbstreuth, Langenhagen 1996; *Fort! Da! Cooperations!,* exhibition catalog, Esslingen 1997; *Parisien(ne)s,* exhibition catalog, London 1997; *Skulptur. Projekte in Münster 1997,* exhibition catalog, Münster 1997; *Nonchalance,* exhibition catalog, Centre PasquART, Bienne 1997; *Delta,* exhibition catalog, Paris, 1997; *Swiss Army Knife,* exhibition catalog with text by Max Wechsler, Bern 1998; *Thomas Hirschhorn: Rolex etc., Freundlichs 'Aufstieg' und Skulpur-Sortier Station-Dokumentation,* exhibition catalog, Köln 1998; *Freie Sicht aufs Mittelmeer,* exhibition catalog, Zürich 1998; *Ein Kunstwerk. Ein Problem,* exhibition catalog with text by Angelika Nollert, Frankfurt am Main 1998; *Thomas Hirschhorn: London Catalog,* exhibition catalog with an interview and texts by Alison Gingeras, London 1998; *Premises: Invested Spaces in Visual Arts and Architecture from France, 1960s-1990's,* exhibition catalog, New York 1998; *Thomas Hirschhorn: Jumbo Spoons and Big Cake, World Airport,* exhibition catalog, Chicago 2000.

* * *

"The energy that fuels my work comes from being a critic of the state of the world, of the human condition." These words were used by Thomas Hirschhorn in an effort to programmatically formulate his artistic concern. The conscious lack of understanding in view of a world of contrasts, in which progress and under-development, wealth and poverty, violence and beauty are in close co-existence, is the most important incitement for the committed stance of resistance Hirschhorn expresses in his artwork. Hirschhorn's work emphatically resists the often bemoaned failure of contemporary art and seeks to reflect present social and political processes without drifting into polemic propaganda or didactic simplicity.

"More is more and less is less" expresses another principle of the artist and reflects not only the attempt to detach his artwork from the reduced aesthetics of modern art, but first of all refers to its obsessive wealth of material. Hirschhorn's sculptural works and often huge displays emerge out of cheap and many times used materials, e.g. timber, plastic foil, brown cardboard, aluminium foil, photocopied texts and pictures, posters and postcards, pictures and illustrations from newspapers worked into collages, videos, plastic objects and adhesive tape strips—namely "poor" and "dirty" material. All elements are created through manual craftsmanship and thus resist any form of modern industrial production.

As multi-facetted as the materials are the themes that the artist is concerned with in his works: globalization and minority problems, political trouble areas and environmental issues, societal utopias and philosophical world schemes, unemployment and status symbols as well as weight issues, disabilities, drug problems and animal protection. These and many more themes presented and discussed in the media find their way into Hirschhorn's artistic universe, which not only wants to reflect the political and social realities of our culture, but attempts to actively question them. Hirschhorn puts his own activism, namely the creation of a work that according to him needs to be done, into the center of his motivation as "artist-worker-soldier." Although the emphasis is not on the actual review of the artwork, the artist nevertheless asks for the thoughtful observer who is to be tempted to reflect on the condition of our world.

Already at the beginning of his artistic career, it was Thomas Hirschhorn's goal to create art politically rather than to create political art. During his studies of graphic design it was his attempt to eventually use his acquired skills in the service of political and social ideas. His time at Grapus, a French collective of communist graphic designers, however, left him disappointed in the pursuit of his goal. Hirschhorn's formal and textual interest in the works of Russian avant-garde artists such as El Lissitzky, Alexander Rodschenko, Kasimir Malewitsch and Ljubov Popova or the German dadaist Kurt Schwitter is led by the admiration for their artistic and political stance. Just like these and many other artists, writers, theorists, and philosophers that he refers to in his works, Hirschhorn strives towards an art for all that are concerned with generally known and applicable issues outside of the narrow boundaries of an elite art business. With the help of easily accessible means, this form of art is to be guided by a concerned content-based desire to create and less by questions of aesthetics.

The beginnings of Thomas Hirschhorn's works and the development of his formal vocabulary lie in the concern with his immediate surroundings. The emerging works, as invasions into the city landscape, are often given back to this environment by the artist: "I think my work comes from the street. It can go back to the street. But it doesn't have to." Hirschhorn used the materials typical for his work in early series such as "Fifty-Fifty" (1992), "Moins" (1993), "Virus" (1994), "Tränenzeichnungen" (since 1995), "Série nouvelle" (since 1995) and "Les plaintifs, les bêtes, les politiques" (1993–1995). He modifies the materials, adds pictures and adhesive tape strips as well as handwritten comments or questions, partly covers them with pen drawings, and wraps many into transparent plastic foil. The works that are created in this manner range from consistently acted out graphic experiments to textually charged collages that confront advertisements for luxury goods with human misery, war with technological progress, art history with his own artistic creations, often furnished with bitter-ironic comments that express the artist's criticism of the world around him. Just as his collages show similarities with ways of representation that are carried by a strong desire to express oneself—such as the signs of the beggars or the banners of political demonstrations—Hirschhorn also chooses forms of daily-life representations for the exhibitions of his works, which can take place in art institutions as well as in the public realm. Always on the search for a superordinate order, he displays his works on tables or on the floor, covers walls with them, builds simple show constructions that resemble market booths, tombola stands or buffets, exhibits them in his car or builds temporary exhibition chambers out of laths and plastic foil. The artist is interested in forms of presentations that came into existence based on their usefulness rather than developing against a background of art history discourse. By detaching his works from their initial correlation, he successfully manages to sensitize the observer for the main features of his artistic work: "to awaken senses, create sadness and ask questions concerning morals."

For some time Hirschhorn has dealt with art in the public realm and with forms of presentations that seek a bigger audience outside of an institutional framework. With his unusual materials, the author creates temporary ''monuments,'' ''direct sculptures,'' ''altars,'' and ''kiosks.'' All are dedicated to people whose stance Hirschhorn admires, among whom are Robert Walser, Ingeborg Bachmann, Otto Freundlich, Gilles Deleuze, or George Bataille. The ''monuments'' take on the form of the traditional monument that here loses its authoritarian claim through the use of short-lived materials. Part of them is always a temporary library that invites viewers to learn about the person whose lifework is being honored. While Hirschhorn's ''altars'' resemble the spontaneous street altars that are often erected in memory of murder or accident victims, ''kiosks'' are fixtures in public buildings made of cardboard in which books and videos are presented. With the ''direct sculptures,'' Hirschhorn develops a new model of monuments that first of all serve as carriers of their observers' messages.

A basic feature of Hirschhorn's works is the domination of the textual research of social and political issues that they are meant to present over their formal appearances. The question about the secret of artistic presentation is not meant to be asked and for that reason the works are not hiding their creation process behind what would generally be perceived as a beautiful form: ''Energy yes, quality no'' is therefore another one of the artist's guidelines. Behind all of Hirschhorn's works is the will to present, the will to connect contrasts and to ask questions, to express admiration or difficulties of understanding and to stimulate reflection on what has been seen. The big installations created in the last few years—such as ''Ein Kunstwerk. Ein Problem'' (1998), ''Flugplatz Welt/World Airport'' (1999), ''Jumbo Spoons and Big Cake'' (2000), or ''POLE-SELF'' (2001)—although on first sight appearing as mere confusing masses of materials, reflect the demands of confronting current global issues. Not only in his collages, which are essential elements of his so called ''displays'' and sculptural works, Hirschhorn abruptly presents contrasts right next to each other. He also ties his carriers into superordinate networks that take on form as long aluminium bulges and chains. The amount and the contradictions of the information offered is a necessary strategy that insistently and unequivocally confronts the observer with the disparities of his/her world.

—Petra Gördüren

HIRST, Damien

Nationality: British. **Born:** Bristol, England, 1965. **Education:** Goldsmiths School of Art, London, 1986–9. **Career:** Sculptor, painter, and designer; while still a student he won fame organizing the *Freeze* exhibition of student art, 1988. **Awards:** Turner Prize, 1995. **Agent:** Julia Royse, The White Cube Gallery, 44 duke Street, St. James's, London, SW1Y 6DD, England.

Selected Individual Exhibitions:

1991 *Internal Affairs,* ICA, London
When Logics Die, Emmanuel Perrotin, Paris
In and Out of Love, Woodstock Street, London
1992 *Pharmacy,* Cohen Gallery, New York
Where's God Now, Jay and Donatella Chiat, New York
Marianne, Hildegard, Unfair/Jay Jopling, Cologne
Damien Hirst: Third International Istanbul Biennial, British Council, Istanbul
1993 *Damien Hirst,* Galerie Jablonka, Cologne
Visual Candy, Regen Projects, Los Angeles
1994 *Pharmacy,* Dallas Museum of Art, Texas
A Bad Environment for White Monochrome Paintings, Mattress Factory, Pittsburgh (catalog)
A Good Environment for Coloured Monochrome Paintings, DAAD Gallery, Berlin
Currents 23, Milwaukee Art Museum, Wisconsin
Making Beautiful Drawings, Bruno Brunnet Fine Arts, Berlin
1995 *Still,* White Cube/Jay Jopling, London
Prix Eliette von Karajan '95, Max Gandolph-Bibliothek, Salzburg
Pharmacy, Kukje Gallery, Seoul
1996 *No Sense of Absolute Corruption,* Gagosian Gallery, New York

Selected Group Exhibitions:

1988 *Freeze,* Surrey Docks, London
1989 *New Contemporaries,* ICA, London
Third Eye Centre, Glasgow
1990 *Gambler,* Building One, London
Modern Medicine, Building One, London
1991 *Broken English,* Serpentine Gallery, London
Louder than Words, Cornerhouse, Manchester
1992 *Turner Prize Exhibition,* Tate Gallery, London
Strange Developments, Anthony d'Offay Gallery, London
British Art, Barbara Gladstone Gallery, New York
Avantgarde and Kampagne, Stadtische Kunsthalle, Dusseldorf
Posthuman, Fondation Asher Edelman, Lausanne
Contemporanea, Turin (catalog)
London Portfolio, Karsten Schubert, London
Young British Artists, Saatchi Collection, London
Moltiplici/Cultura, Rome (catalog)
1993 *A Wonderful Life,* Lisson Gallery, London
Displace, Cohen Gallery, New York
Venice Biennale, Aperto Section, Venice
Here and Now: Twenty-three Years of the Serpentine Gallery, Serpentine Gallery, London (catalog)
The Nightshade Family, Museum Fridericianum, Kassel
The 21st Century, Kunsthalle, Basel
1996 *Twentieth-century British Sculpture,* Jeu de Paume, Paris (catalog)
Private View, Bowes Museum, Barnard Castle, County Durham (catalog)
Faustrecht der Freiheit, Kunstammlung Gera, Berlin, Neues Museum Weserburg, Bremen (catalog)
Works on Paper, Irish Museum of Modern Art, Dublin (catalog)
Spellbound, Hayward Gallery, London (catalog)
Some Went Mad, Some Ran Away. . . , Serpentine Gallery (traveled) (catalog)

Virtual Reality, National Gallery of Australia, Canberra (catalog)

Publications:

By HIRST: Book—*I Want to Spend the Rest of My Life Everywhere, with Everyone, One to One, Always, Forever,* London 1997.

On HIRST: Books—*Damien Hirst* by Charles Hall et al, London 1991; *Ant Noises at The Saatchi Gallery* by Gemma De Cruz, London 2000. **Articles—**''London Calling: Intimacy and Chaos in Contemporary British Art'' by Eric Troncy in *Flash Art* (International Edition) no. 165, Summer 1992; ''Opinion: Strange Developments'' by Charles Hall in *Arts Review* (London, England) vol. 44, November 1992; ''Chiat Residence, New York'' by Christopher Phillips in *Art in America,* vol. 80, December 1992; ''Damien Hirst'' by Adrian Dannatt in *Flash Art* (International Edition) no. 169, March-April 1993; ''The Revolution Continues: British Art Now'' by James Hall in *Art News,* vol. 92, September 1993; ''Jablonka Gallery, Cologne'' by Jose Lebrero Stals in *Flash Art* (International Edition), no. 174, January-February 1994; ''Damien Hirst'' by Gordon Burn in *Parkett,* no. 40–41, 1994; ''Decadent Geometry'' by Boris Groys in *Parkett,* no. 40–41, 1994; ''Tod ist passiv, Denken an Tod ist aktiv: Damien Hirst im Gesprach'' by Noemi Smolik in *Kunstforum International,* no. 126, March-June 1994; ''Out of Control'' by Andrew Wilson in *Art Monthly,* no. 177, June 1994; ''Damien Hirst'' by Thomas Connors in *New Art Examiner,* vol. 21, Summer 1994; ''A Steady Iron-Hard Jet'' by Will Self in *Modern Painters,* vol. 7, Summer 1994; ''Cityscape: Berlin, Part 1'' by Peter Herbstreuth in *Flash Art,* (International Edition) no. 178, October 1994; ''Damien Hirst and the Sensibility of Shock'' by Loura Wixley Brooks in *Art and Design,* vol. 10, January-February 1995; ''Gory Boards'' by Louisa Buck in *Artforum International,* vol. 33, February 1995; ''Don't Run Away Mad'' by Jennifer Riddell in *New Art Examiner,* vol. 22, May 1995; ''More Life: The Work of Damien Hirst'' by Jerry Saltz in *Art in America,* vol. 83, June 1995; ''Damien Hirst'' by David Lee in *Art Review* (London, England), vol. 47, June 1995; ''Damien Hirst'' by David Barrett in *Art Monthly,* no. 188, July-August 1995; ''Damien Hirst'' by David Batchelor in *Artforum International,* vol. 34, September 1995; ''Critic's Diary'' by Edward Lucie Smith in *Art Review* (London, England), vol. 48, February 1996; ''Damien Hirst: The Exploded View of the Artist'' by Francesco Bonami in *Flash Art* (International Edition), no. 189, Summer 1996; ''Divide et impera'' by Juri Steiner in *Parkett,* no. 50–51, 1997; ''Meat for Thought'' by Helen Simpson in *Modern Painters,* vol. 10, Spring 1997; ''The Maverick Type'' by Rick Poynor in *ID* (New York), vol. 44, May 1997; ''Pop Star Divided: Damien Hirst and the Ends of British Art'' by Michael Corris in *Art Text,* no. 58, August-October 1997; ''I Mean to Say'' by Marchtin Gayford in *Modern Painters,* vol. 10, Autumn 1997; ''Damien Hirst'' by Yvonne Volkart in *Flash Art* (International Edition), no. 197, November-December 1997; ''Critic's Diary'' by Edward Lucie Smith in *Art Review* (London, England), vol. 49, November 1997; ''Graphic Art'' by Marchgaret Richardson in *U and LC,* vol. 24, no. 4, Spring 1998; ''A Saga Longer than Its Name'' by Hugh Aldersey Williams in *Graphis,* no. 315, May-June 1998; ''God, not Warhol'' by Andrew Wilson in *Art Monthly,* no. 217, June 1998; ''Pharmacy Restaurant in London'' in *Domus,* no. 806, July-August 1998; ''Back into the Pop Era: Pierre Restany Interviews Damien Hirst'' by Pierre Restany in *Domus,* no. 806, July-August 1998; ''Flash Art: XXXI Years, Three Decemberades Inside Art'' in *Flash Art,* (International Edition), vol. 21, no. 201, Summer 1998;''Shark Tactics'' by Jane Burton in *Art News,* vol. 97, no. 10, November 1998; ''Artistes Contemporains: Les Cotations Marchquantes'' by Judith Benhamou Huet in *Connaissance des Arts,* no. 559, March 1999; ''Artist Interview, New York: Damien Hirst: ''We All Feel Like a Died-Out Cigarette at Times"'' by Adrian Dannatt in *Art Newspaper,* vol. 11, no. 107, October 2000; ''Damien Hirst: Artist or Brand?'' by Nicholas Glass in *Art Review* (London, England), vol. 52, November 2000; ''Hirst Sales Soar'' by Colin Gleadell in *Art News,* vol. 99, no. 11, December 2000; ''Damien Hirst'' by Grady T. Turner in *Flash Art* (International Edition), vol. 34, no. 216, January-February 2001.

* * *

With Dead Head (1981–91) is a photograph of 16-year-old Damien Hirst cheek by jowl with the head of a corpse. Hirst grins wickedly and the bloated dead head seems to grimace, comically. The image is striking, playful, and disturbing and a concise portent of Hirst's mature work. Hirst's theme is death and his work is an extended *memento mori*; however, the work is not morbid, for it consistently betrays a wide-eyed and innocent sense of wonder at the mysteries of life and death. His best work is both aesthetically and viscerally challenging: it typically pushes at the limits of taste and acceptability, flirting with shock and disgust, but is leavened by a playful and cheeky bravado and is made compelling by simple but strong visual form and presence.

Hirst's work can, broadly, be classified into the following categories: the medicine cabinets, the paintings, the vitrines, and ''Natural History,'' the collective title for his notorious ''pickled animals.''

The medicine cabinets are amongst Hirst's earliest works, the first being produced while he was a student at Goldsmiths College, University of London. *God* (1989) is a glass fronted cabinet containing bottles and packages of drugs and proprietary medicines. The double life of drugs as both medicine and poison is revealed in these decaying, ageing packages. This potentially endless series reached its apotheosis in a gallery sized installation called *Pharmacy* (1992), a museum of the late 20th century pharmaceutical industry with its mission to keep people happy and alive and to make money.

The spot paintings, another potentially endless series, were begun around 1988. They consist of discs of colour in a grid pattern on a white background; the colours appear to be arbitrarily chosen and obey the rule that no colour should appear twice in the same painting. The paintings have a cool, minimalist, ''dumb'' character: they are entirely systematic and unexpressive (indeed production was assigned to assistants) and yet appear unremittingly cheerful. Hirst has called them, collectively, ''The Pharmaceutical Series,'' and individually, after drugs: *Acetaldehyde* (1991), *Arabinitol* (1994). These visual anti-depressants make reference to formal experiments in 20th century abstract painting and hint at our seduction by sweet-like pills of chemical happiness.

In 1995 Hirst embarked on a series of ''spin'' paintings, made by pouring paint onto a rotating, circular canvas. These large, spectacularly colourful and decorative paintings are hugely enjoyable but lack the conceptual edge of the spot paintings. The prolix titles reflect their excessiveness: *beautiful, vaginal, spiral, escalating, blood, space, escaping painting* (1995).

The vitrines are more austere and call to mind the museum's role of collecting, classifying, preserving, and displaying the artefacts of civilisations. *Still* (1994), for example, anatomises the technology of contemporary medicine through the cold, clinical display of surgical instruments: scalpels, saws, and steel bowls. *Sometimes I Avoid People* (1991), however, offers existential musings on the human condition: it consists of a steel framed glass case which is internally divided into six glass compartments designed to support, and confine, a human body: head, torso, arms and legs. The body's functioning would be sustained by a drip feed, oxygen mask connected to a bank of colour coded gas cylinders, and colostomy bag to remove bodily wastes. It is a life support system that denies life, an image of sensory deprivation and alienation: a robust structure which accentuates the fragility of life and deprives it of its vitality.

It is for the "Natural History" works, the creatures in formaldehyde, for which Hirst is most well known. The series was anticipated by two important works which did not merely offer the viewer an image of death, but presented an entire life cycle for contemplation. *A Thousand Years* (1990) comprises a pair of steel framed glass cubes containing maggots, a cow's head, and an "insectocutor": the maggots hatch into flies which mate, lay eggs in the cow's head, and eventually fly into the insectocutor and die. The viewer is presented with an uncompromising demonstration of the arbitrariness of existence which is both fascinating and repellent: a metaphor for human life as tragedy. *In & Out of Love* (1991) was an installation in two rooms. In the first, butterflies emerged from pupae attached to white monochrome paintings and fluttered through their brief existence in the alien space of the gallery, sustained by bowls of sugared water and banks of potted plants. In the second room, dead butterflies were trapped on the surface of a series of brightly coloured monochromes, their spectacular and fragile wings lapped by the lurid, viscous industrial gloss paint.

The "Natural History" series includes embalmed fish, pigs, sheep, cows and, most ambitiously, a fourteen foot Tiger Shark: *The Physical Impossibility of Death in the Mind of Someone Living* (1991). This is pure spectacle: the viewer is confronted with a killer monster in suspended animation. The work combines the thrill of the fairground with the fascination of the laboratory as well as an invitation to aesthetic contemplation. Like much of Hirst's work it is a "readymade" in the tradition of Marcel Duchamp: new meanings and perceptions are prompted by placing objects into new contexts. *Mother and Child Divided* (1993) offers the viewer a literal insight into animal physiology: a cow and her calf have been bisected and suspended in their tanks of formaldehyde so that the viewer is able to walk "through" the animals and confront the horror and beauty of the landscape of their internal organs.

The strength of Hirst's work lies in his preparedness to address the big questions of life and its meaning in a direct, accessible and unembarrassed manner and in his ability to create strong, unforgettable, and sometimes poetic images. Recent work has continued this theme: *Hymn* (2000) is a monumental 20-foot, 10-ton bronze enlargement of a child's anatomical toy in which the human internal organs are displayed as tidy components painted in friendly, glossy colours; *The History of Pain* (2000) consists of a plinth with a surface pierced by the upturned blades of knives, above which a pure white beach ball hovers, precariously, on a jet of air. An image of the fragility of life, and indeed of the artist's career.

—Richard Salkeld

HOBERMAN, Perry

Nationality: American **Born:** Cambridge, Massachusetts, 1954; lives in New York. **Education:** Attended the Pennsylvania Academy of Art, Phildelphia, 1972–73; Bennington College, Vermont, B.A. 1977; participated in the Whitney Museum Independent Study Program, New York, 1978. **Career:** Art director, assistant producer, and artistic director, with artist Laurie Anderson, on various recordings and performances, 1981–93; adjunct professor, Cooper Union, New York, 1992–1994; art director, Telepresence Research, Portola Valley, California, 1993–96; instructor of computer arts and photography, School of Visual Arts, New York, 1994, 1996—; artist in residence, Xerox PARC Pair Project, 1995. **Awards:** Engelhart Foundation Award, 1985; Archetype Award for Overall Excellence, Interactive Media Festival, 1995; Design Distinction Award, I.D. Interactive Media Design Review, New York, 1997; First Place, art's_edge Multimedia Competition, Western Australian Academy of Performing Arts, 1998; Award of Distinction in Interactive Art, Prix Ars Electronica, 1999; Grand Prix, ICC Biennale, 1999. **Web site:** http://www.hoberman.com/perry.

Individual Exhibitions

1983 Hallwalls, Buffalo, New York
Wake Forest University Fine Arts Gallery, North Carolina
1984 Galerie Pon, Zurich, Switzerland
1985 Capp Street Project, San Francisco
Postmasters Gallery, New York
1986 Postmasters Gallery, New York
1988 Postmasters Gallery, New York
1990 Postmasters Gallery, New York
1991 Museum of Contemporary Art, Dayton, Ohio
1992 Postmasters Gallery, New York
1994 Walter Phillips Gallery, Banff Centre for the Arts, Alberta, Canada
1995 Boston University, Massachusetts
1997 Otso Gallery, Espoo, Finland
Postmasters Gallery, New York
1998 Cornerhouse Gallery, Manchester, England
Fundació Joan Miro, Barcelona, Spain (with Galeria Virtual)
Ferens Gallery, Kingston-Upon-Hull, England
Mediamuseum, ZKM, Karlsruhe, Germany
1999 HTBA Time Base, Kingston-Upon-Hull, England
Postmasters Gallery, New York
2000 Postmasters Gallery, New York

Selected Group Exhibitions

1982 *Constructed Color,* Hayden Gallery, MIT, Boston, Massachusetts
1983 *Dark Rooms,* Artists Space, New York
1985 *Between Science & Fiction,* Sao Paulo Bienial, Brazil
Modern Machines, Whitney Museum at Philip Morris, New York
Biennial Exhibition, Whitney Museum, New York

Future Histories: The Impact of Changing Technology, Anderson Gallery, Richmond, Virginia

1986 *TV Generations,* Los Angeles Contemporary Exhibitions, Los Angeles, California

Film in the Cities, Minneapolis, Minnesota

1992 *In Praise of Folly,* Kohler Art Center, Sheboygan, Wisconsin

Art Show, Siggraph '92, Chicago, Illinois

1993 *Machine Culture,* Siggraph '93, Anaheim, California

Simply Made in America, Aldrich Museum of Contemporary Art, Ridgefield, Connecticut

Images du Futur 93, Montreal, Quebec, Canada

1994 *Cyber Art,* Ars Electronica, Linz, Austria

Simply Made in America, Contemporary Art Center, Cincinnati, Ohio

Resurrections: Objects with New Souls, William Benton Museum, Hartford, Connecticut

1995 *Arc Gallery,* International Media Festival, Los Angeles

DEAF 95 (Dutch Electronic Art Festival), Rotterdam

1998 *The Art of the Accident,* DEAF98, Rotterdam

1999 *Beyond Technology,* Brooklyn Museum of Art, New York

European Media Art Festival, Osnabruck, Germany

Cyberarts 99, Ars Electronica, Linz, Austria

2000 *Microwave Festival 2000,* Hong Kong

Alien Intelligence, Kiasma, Helsinki, Finland

Publications:

By HOBERMAN: Articles—''Excerpt from Smaller Than Life'' in *Tellus—The Audio Cassette Magazine* (New York), no. 5/6, 1984; ''Beyond Hope and Beyond Dreams: The Neo-Karaoke Story'' in *Publicsfear* (New York), no. 3, 1993; ''Bar Code Hotel'' and interview with Peter Weibel, *Art & Design Magazine* (London), no. 39, 1994; ''V-Art,'' interview with Pauline van Mourik Broekman in *Mute* (London), no. 3, Autumn 1995; ''Free Choice or Control'' in *Prix Ars Electronica 96,* edited by Hannes Leopoldseder and Christine Schöpf, Vienna and New York 1996; ''Meme and Variations'' in *Memesis: The Future of Evolution,* edited by Gerfried Stocker and Christine Schöpf, Vienna and New York 1996; ''The Sub-Division of the Electric Light'' (interactive artwork) in *artintact 3* (CD-ROM magazine), ZKM Zentrum für Kunst und Medientechnologie, Karlsruhe, Germany 1996; ''Mistakes and Misbehavior'' in *The Art of the Accident,* Rotterdam 1998.

On HOBERMAN: Books—*Postmodern Currents: Art and Artists in the Age of Electronic Media* by Margot Lovejoy, New York 1996; *Unexpected Obstacles: The Work of Perry Hoberman,* exhibition catalog edited by Paivi Talasmaa, Espoo, Finland 1997; *The Computer in the Visual Arts* by Anne Morgan Spalter, Reading, Massachusetts 1999. **Articles**—''Studio/Perry Hoberman'' by Regina Cornwell in *Sculpture* (Washington, D.C.), May/June 1991; ''State of the Art'' by Daniel Pinchbeck in *Wired,* December 1994; ''Checking into the Bar Code Hotel'' by Kris Malden in *The Independent Film & Video Monthly* (New York), vol. 18, no. 2, March 1995; ''Perverting Technological Correctness'' by Rafael Lozano-Hemmer in *Leonardo* (Cambridge), vol. 29, no. 1, 1996; ''Playing With Yourself: Pleasure and Interactive Art'' by Beryl Graham in *Fractal Dreams: New Media in Social Context,* edited by Jon Dovey, London 1996; ''Coping with Technofatigue'' by Robbin Murphy in *Intelligent Agent,* Fall 1997; ''Battery Included'' by K.D. Davis in *World Art,* no. 13, 1997; ''Beams of Light in a Virtual Void'' by Erkki Huhtamo in *Artbyte,* vol. 1 no. 1, April-May 1998; ''The Accidental Tourist'' by Lisa Haskel in *Mute* (London), no. 13, 1999.

* * *

The main issue in Perry Hoberman's art is interactivity between the spectator and technology. He has explored this concept by utilizing obsolete equipment, such as bar codes, as well as avant-garde, experimental technology, including virtual reality. His notion of interactivity is a purely postmodern sensibility, enabling the observer to participate in his artworks in a completely active way. In addition to interactivity, he also embraces the concept of immersion, which could easily be regarded as another method to prompt the viewer's participation. He deals most extensively with responsive surroundings and experiences to help focus the spectator on the possibilities of objects and images in relation to the audience.

Perhaps the most compelling aspect of Hoberman's art is his ability (and desire) to marry child-like play with complex, intellectual theory, evident in works such as *Cathartic User Interface* of 1995, in which the installation visitor throws balls at computer keyboards mounted on the wall as a method of prompting triggers and projections throughout the gallery environment. He has remarked that he likes to manipulate popular culture through technology filters so that the viewer experiences bizarre images, sensibilities, and content rather than staid, familiar simulations.

Until the mid-1980s Hoberman focused mostly on saturating environments, much in the way cinema dominates the viewer's experience. Then in the mid-1980s, Hoberman progressed more and more toward utilizing interactive and non-interactive devices to involve the spectator. In *Sorry, We're Open* of 1997, Hoberman plays with the office environment gone haywire as metaphors for the banality and monotony of such interior spaces. Computers are programmed to enact Rube Goldberg-like effects that grind pencils into nubs, among other mindless activities so common to the workplace. The aggravation and rancor of such spaces seem like inverted funhouses for the viewer to meditate on the alienating spaces provided by corporate life.

The idea of the interface is one that has additionally interested Hoberman. This kind of involvement is clearly in evidence in *Bar Code Hotel* of 1994. Each participant who checks into the hotel is issued a set of 3-D glasses and a bar code wand. The viewer uses the wand on the bar codes permeating the environment to stimulate a wide array of effects and projections. Technology is both a fun activity, stimulating, and involved, as well as a controlling feature that dominates the audience's surroundings and experience.

Hoberman has been a great communicator on the many aspects of art and science, and has spoken widely on technology, specifically the internet and virtual reality, and its implications in providing content for art. In addition to his visually related projects, he has worked extensively with sound and performance artist Laurie Anderson as an art director on her various projects.

—Anne Swartz

HOCKNEY, David

Nationality: British. **Born:** Bradford, Yorkshire, 9 July 1937. **Education:** Studied at Bradford College of Art, 1953–57, and the Royal College of Art, London, 1959–62. **Career:** Independent painter, graphic artist and photographer, from 1962, and stage designer, from 1966: worked in London, from 1962, in Paris, 1973–75 and 1979–80, and in Los Angeles, 1964, 1973, and since 1977. Instructor, Maidstone College of Art, Kent, 1962: University of Iowa, Ames, 1963–64; University of Colorado, Boulder, 1965; University of California, Los Angeles, 1966–67; Slade Professor of Fine Art, Cambridge University, England, 1990. **Awards:** Guinness Award, London, 1961; Painting Prize, *John Moores Exhibition,* Liverpool, 1961 and 1967; Gold Medal, Royal College of Art, London, 1962; Graphics Prize, *Biennale de Paris,* 1963; First Prize, *8th International Drawings and Engravings Biennale,* Lugano, Switzerland, 1964; Print Prize, *7th International Graphics Exhibition,* Liubliana, Yugoslavia, 1965; Graphics Prize, *First International Print Biennale,* Krakow, Poland, 1966; Gold Medal, *6th Norwegian International Print Biennale,* Oslo, 1982; Award of Excellence, Federal Republic of Germany, 1983; Skowhegan Graphics Award, Maine, 1983; Kodak Photography Book Award, Stuttgart, 1984; First Prize, International Center of Photography, New York, 1985. LL.D.: University of Bradford, Yorkshire, 1983; D.F.A.: San Francisco Art Institute, 1985; D.F.A.: Otis Parsons Institute, Los Angeles, 1985; Associate, Royal Academy of Art, London, 1985; Praemium Imperiale, Japan Art Association, 1989; Honorary Degree, Royal College of Art, London, 1992; 5th Annual Government of California Visual Arts award, 1994; named Companion of Honour by Her Majesty, the Queen of England, 1997. **Agent:** Cavan Butler, the Pantechnicon, 2 Heathfield Terrace, London W.4., England. **Address:** 7508 Santa Monica Boulevard, Los Angeles, California 90046–6407, U.S.A.

David Hockney, on the set he designed. ©Hulton-Deutsch Collection/Corbis.

Individual Exhibitions:

1963 *Paintings with People in,* Kasmin Gallery, London
The Rake's Progress and Other Etchings, The Print Centre/Editions Alecto, London
City Art Gallery, Bradford, Yorkshire
1964 Alan Gallery, New York
The Rake's Progress, Museum of Modern Art, New York
1965 *Pictures with Frames and Still Lifes,* Kasmin Gallery, London
1966 Stedelijk Museum, Amsterdam
Drawings for Ubu Roi and Cavafy Etchings, Kasmin Gallery, London
Palais des Beaux-Arts, Brussels
Studio Marconi, Milan
Gallerie dell'Ariete, Milan
1967 Landau-Alan Gallery, New York
1968 Kasmin Gallery, London
Galerie Mikro, West Berlin
Museum of Modern Art, New York
1969 *Paintings and Prints,* Whitworth Art Gallery, Manchester, England
Andre Emmerich Gallery, New York
Recent Etchings, Kasmin Gallery, London
1970 Lane Gallery, Bradford, Yorkshire
Paintings, Prints, Drawings 1960–70, Whitechapel Art Gallery, London (travelled to Hannover Rotterdam and Belgrade)
Kasmin Gallery, London
Andre Emmerich Gallery, New York
Galerie Springer, West Berlin
Kestner-Gesellschaff, Hannover, West Germany
1971 *Zeichnungen, Grafik, Gemalde,* Kunsthalle, Bielefeld, West Germany
1972 Victoria & Albert Museum, London
Kasmin Gallery, London
Andre Emmerich Gallery, New York
1973 Holburne Museum, Bath, Avon,
Andre Emmerich Downtown Gallery, New York
Knoedler Gallery, New York
1974 Kinsman Morrison Gallery, London
Garage Art, London
Musée des Arts Décoratifs, Paris
Dayton's Gallery 12, Minneapolis, Minnesota
Michael Walls Gallery, New York
Knoedler Contemporary Prints, New York

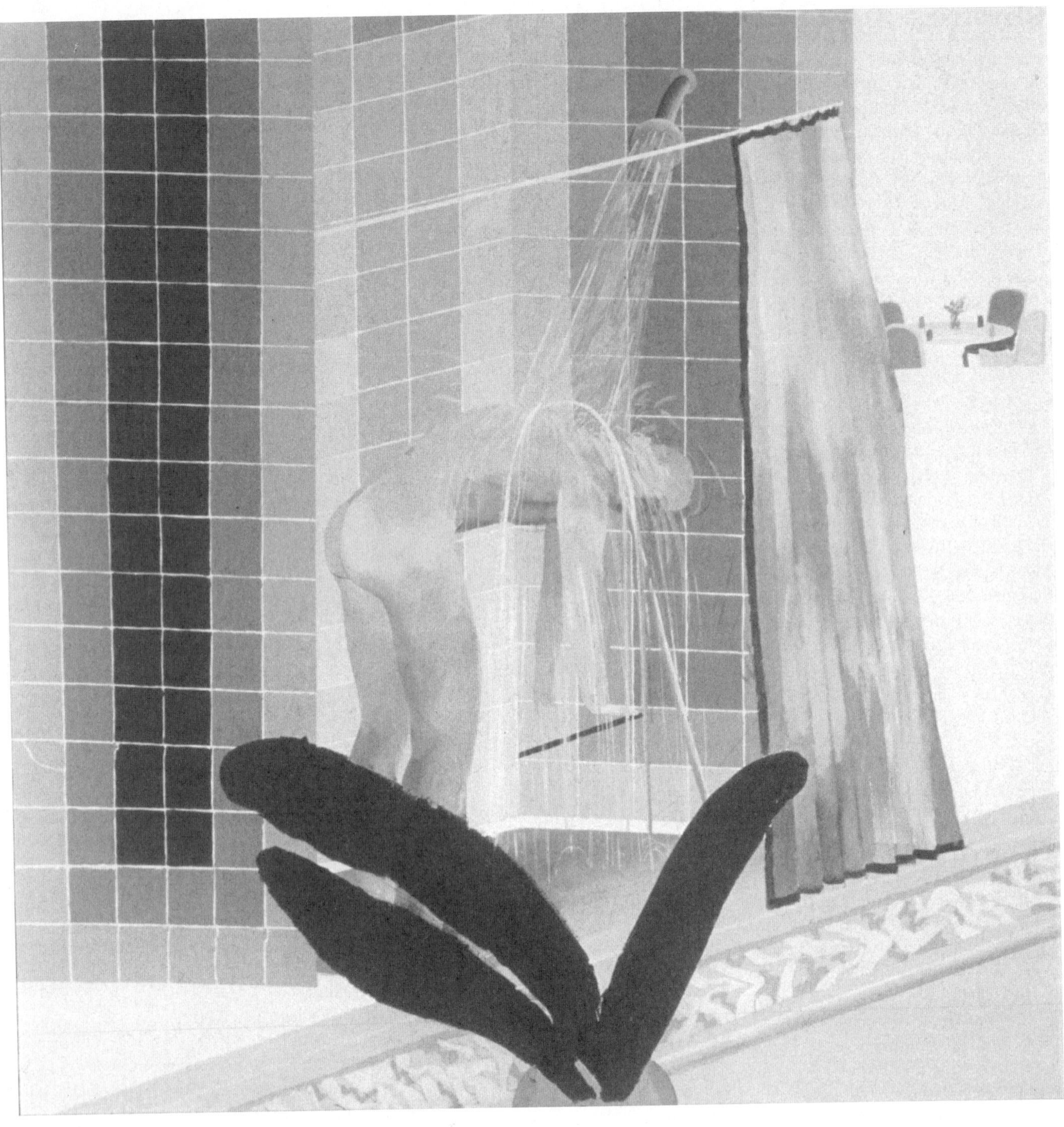

David Hockney: *Man in Shower in Beverly Hills*, 1964. ©Art Resource, NY/Tate Gallery, London.

La Medusa Graphica, Rome
1975 Dorothy Rosenthal Gallery, Chicago
Galerie Claude Bernard, Paris
European Gallery, San Francisco
City Art Gallery, Bristol, Gloucestershire
City Art Gallery, Manchester, England
Nishimura Gallery, Tokyo
1976 Nicholas Wilder Gallery, Los Angeles
Sonnabend Gallery, New York
Laing Art Gallery, Newcastle-upon-Tyne
Robert Self Gallery, London
Jordan Gallery, London
Festival Gallery, Bath, Avon
National Gallery of Victoria, Melbourne (toured Australia)
Henie-Onstad Kunstsenter, Oslo (travelled to the Kunstmuseum, Goteborg, Sweden)
Waddington Galleries, London
Galeria Juana Mordo, Madrid

1977 Andre Emmerich Gallery, New York
Dorothy Rosenthal Gallery, Chicago
Paintings and Drawings 1961–75, Galerie Neuendorf, Hamburg, West Germany
City Art Gallery, Wolverhampton, Staffordshire
1978 Gallery at 24, Miami, Florida
Drawings and Prints, Waddington Galleries, Toronto (travelled to the Albertina, Vienna; Tiroler Landesmuseum Ferdinandeum, Innsbruck; Galerie Bloch, Innsbruck; Kulturhaus, Graz; Kunstlerhaus, Salzburg; L. A. Louver Gallery, Venice, California
Travels with Pen, Pencil and Ink, Yale Center for British Art, New Haven, Connecticut (travelled to Minneapolis Institute of Arts, Minnesota; Cranbook Academy of Art, Bloomfield Hills, Michigan; Nelson Gallery and Atkins Museum, Kansas City)
Sudley Art Gallery, Liverpool, Merseyside
1979 Museum of Modern Art, New York
M. H. de Young Memorial Museum, San Francisco
Frances Aronson Gallery, Atlanta, Georgia
Bradford Art Gallery, Yorkshire
Gimpel & Hanover/Andre Emmerich Galleries, Zurich
Britten-Pears School, Aldeburgh, Suffolk
Warehouse Gallery, London
Knoedler Gallery, London
1980 Graves Art Gallery, Sheffield, Yorkshire
Ashmolean Museum, Oxford, England
Laguna Beach Museum of Art, California
Andre Emmerich Gallery, New York
Getler/Pall Gallery, New York
Petersburg Press, New York
Albert White Gallery, Toronto
Knoedler/Kasmin Gallery, London
Tate Gallery, London
Arun Art Centre, Arundel, Sussex
Art and Furniture, Manchester, England
Tyler Graphics, Bedford, New York
1981 Andre Emmerich Gallery, New York
Castelli Graphics, New York
Riverside Studios, London
Galerie Claude Bernard, Paris
Knoedler/Kasmin Gallery, London
Gallery at 24, Miami, Florida
Gallery at 24, Palm Beach, Florida
Galerie Meyer-Ellinger, Frankfurt, West Germany
Ashmolean Museum, Oxford, England
1982 Andre Emmerich Gallery, New York
Christie's Contemporary Art, New York
L. A. Louver Gallery, Venice, California
Photographies 1962–82, Centre Georges Pompidou, Paris
Knoedler/Kasmin Gallery, London
Rex Irwin Gallery, Sydney, New South Wales
Susan Gersh Gallery, Los Angeles
New York Public Library, New York
1983 Andre Emmerich Gallery, New York
Knoedler/Emmerich Gallery, Zurich
Richard Gray Gallery, Chicago
L. A. Louver Gallery, Venice, California
Knoedler/Kasmin Gallery, London
Nishimura Gallery, Tokyo
Bjorn Bengtsson Gallery, Stockholm
Hockney Paints the Stage, Walker Art Center, Minneapolis (travelled to Museo Tamayo, Mexico City; Art Gallery of Ontario, Toronto; Museum of Contemporary Art, Chicago; Fort Worth Art Museum, Texas; San Francisco Museum of Modern Art)
Thomas Babeor Gallery, La Jolla, California
William Beadleston Fine Art, New York
Fotografien 1962–82, Kunsthalle, Basel
Hockney's Photographs, Hayward Gallery, London (toured Britain)
1984 Milwaukee Art Museum, Wisconsin
Prints, Art and Sport Gallery, Brussels
Prints and Drawings, Bjorn Wetterling Gallery, Stockholm
Selected Prints, Knoedler Gallery, Zurich
New Paintings and Drawings, Andre Emmerich Gallery, New York
Photographic Collages, Fraenkel Gallery, San Francisco
Photographic Collages, Greenberg Gallery, St. Louis, Missouri
New Drawings, Richard Gray Gallery, Chicago
Prints and Photographic Collages, Galerie Esperanze, Montreal, Quebec
Photographic Collages, Carpenter/Hochman Gallery, Dallas, Texas
Works on Paper, Patricia Heesy Gallery, New York (with Jim Dine)
1985 *Hockney Paints the Stage,* Hayward Gallery, London
Prints and Photocollages, Greg Kucera Gallery, Seattle, Washington
Photocollages, Andre Emmerich Gallery, New York
Lithos, paintings and collages, Knoedler Gallery, London
Paintings from the 1960's, Andre Emmerich Gallery, New York
Photocollages, State University of New York, New Paltz
New Lithographs and Paintings, Andre Emmerich Gallery, New York
New Lithographs, Nishimura Gallery, Tokyo
New Lithographs, Richard Gray Gallery, Chicago
New Lithographs, L. A. Louver Gallery, Venice, California
New Lithos, Photocollages, Drawings and Paintings, Galerie Claude Bernard, Paris
Photocollages, State University of New York, Albany
Photocollages, College of Santa Fe, New Mexico
Photocollages, Elaine Horwitch Galleries, Scottsdale, Arizona (with Roland Reiss)
1986 *Theatre Sets, Models, Drawings and Etchings,* Contemporary Art Center, Honolulu, Hawaii
Photocollages, Paintings, Drawings, Honolulu Academy of Art, Hawaii
Photocollages, Cibachromes, Polaroids and Prints, Pasadena Art Center, California
Tyler Prints, Harvard University, Cambridge, Massachusetts
Tyler Prints, Tate Gallery, London
Photocollages and Theatre Drawings, Gallery One, Toronto
Photographs by David Hockney, Boca Raton Museum of Arts, Florida (travelled to Davenport Art Gallery, Iowa;

Spencer Museum of Art, Lawrence, Kansas; Elvehjem Museum of Art, Madison, Wisconsin; Santa Barbara Museum of Art, California;
Paintings and Photographic Collages, University of California, Berkeley
New Lithos and Mexican Hotel Painting, Andre Emmerich Gallery, Zurich
Self-Portraits, Blum Helman Gallery, New York (with Ellsworth Kelly and Francesco Clemente)
1987 Los Angeles County Museum of Art (travelled to the Metropolitan Museum of Art, New York; Tate Gallery, London, 1988)
Faces 1966–84, Loyola Marymount University, New York
1988 *Photocollages,* Santa Monica Community College, California
David Hockney's Images of His Model Celia: 1973–1986, Carl Schlosberg Fine Arts, Sherman Oaks (catalog)
David Hockney: A Retrospective, Los Angeles County Museum of Art (catalog)
1990 *David Hockney: Fax Pictures,* Rex Irwin Art Dealer, Woollahra (catalog)
1991 *Graphic Inventions: A Selection of Works on Paper by David Hockney in the 1960s,* Knoedler Gallery, London (catalog)
In View: David Hockney—Doll Boy, Kunsthalle, Hamburg (catalog)
1992 *David Hockney: Seven Paintings,* Tate Gallery, London (catalog)
David Hockney: Recent Pictures, Richard Gray Gallery, Chicago (catalog)
David Hockney: Prints, Museum Boymans-van Beuningen, Rotterdam (catalog)
1993 *David Hockney: Grimm's Fairy Tales,* South Bank Centre, London (catalog)
David Hockney, Tate Gallery Liverpool (catalog)
1995 *David Hockney: Drawings 1954–94,* Kunsthalle, Hamburg (catalog)
David Hockney: A Drawing Retrospective, Royal Academy of Arts, London (catalog)
David Hockney: Some Very Large New Paintings with Twenty-Five Dogs Upstairs and Some Drawings of Friends, L.A. Louver Gallery, Venice (catalog)
1996 *David Hockney: You Make the Picture—Paintings and Prints 1982–1995,* Manchester City Art Galleries, England (catalog)
1998 *David Hockney: Looking at Landscape/Being in Landscape,* L.A. Louver Gallery, Venice (catalog)
1999 *David Hockney: Space & Line—Grand Canyon Pastels on Paper 1998: Works on Paper 1966–1994,* Richard Gray Gallery, New York (catalog)
David Hockney: Space/Landscape, Centre National d'Art et de Culture Georges Pompidou, Paris (catalog)

Selected Group Exhibitions:

1960 *London Group,* RBA Galleries, London
1963 *British Painting of the 60s,* Whitechapel Art Gallery, London
1965 *London: The New Scene,* Walker Art Center, Minneapolis
1969 *Pop Art Redefined,* Hayward Gallery, London
1975 *European Painting in the 70s,* Los Angeles County Museum of Art
1977 *British Artists of the 60s,* Tate Gallery, London
1981 *Instant Fotografie,* Stedelijk Museum, Amsterdam
1983 *Painter as Photographer,* Camden Arts Centre, London (travelled to Windsor, Berkshire; Bradford, Yorkshire
1984 *Olympian Gestures,* Los Angeles County Museum of Art
1987 *Berlinart 1961–87,* Museum of Modern Art, New York (travelled to San Francisco)
1989 *Picturing People: British Figurative Art Since 1945,* National Art Gallery, Kuala Lumpur (traveling exhibition) (catalog)
1990 *Gifts of the Associates: 1975–1990,* Museum of Modern Art, New York (catalog)
1991 *Seven Master Printmakers: Innovations in the Eighties,* Museum of Modern Art, New York (catalog)
From Bacon to Now: The Outsider in British Figuration, Palazzo Vecchio, Florence (catalog)
1993 *The Painters' Art: Masterworks of Modernism,* Agnes Etherington Art Centre, Queens University, Kingston (catalog)
Seven British Painters: Selected Masters of Post-War British Art, Marlborough Fine Art, London (catalog)
The Portrait Now, National Portrait Gallery, London (catalog)
1994 *Donations 1989–94,* Musee d'Art Contemporain, Montreal (catalog)
1995 *Revolution: Art of the Sixties from Warhol to Beuys,* Hara Museum of Contemporary Art, Tokyo (catalog)
1996 *The Eye of the Collector,* Musee d'Art Contemporain, Montreal (catalog)
Picasso: A Contemporary Dialogue, Galerie Thaddaeus Ropac, Paris (catalog)
1997 *Networking: Art by Post and Fax,* Spacex Gallery, Exeter (catalog)
Drawing Distinctions: Twentieth-century Drawings and Watercolours from the British Council Collection, University Art Museum/Pacific Film Archive, University of California Berkeley (catalog)
Masterpieces of Modern Printmaking, Alan Cristea Gallery, London (catalog)
1998 *Head First: Portraits from the Arts Council Collection,* City Gallery, Leicester, Engalnd (traveling exhibition) (catalog)

Collections:

Albright-Knox Art Gallery, Buffalo; Art Institute of Chicago; Art Gallery of Ontario, Toronto; Arts Council of Great Britain; Arts Council of Northern Ireland; Astrup Fearnley Museum for Moderne Kunst, Oslo; Australian National Gallery, Canberra; Balliol College, Oxford; Baltimore Museum of Art; The Boston Museum of Fine Art; The British Council, London; The Brooklyn Museum, New York; Calouste Gulbenkian Foundation; Carnegie Museum of Art, Pittsburgh; Centre Georges Pompidou, Beaubourg, Paris; Centro Cultural Arte Contemporaneo, Mexico City; City Art Gallery, Bradford, England; City of Darmstadt Collection; Contemporary Art Society, London; Contemporary Museum, Honolulu; Detroit Institute, Michigan; Ferens Art Gallery, Hull; Graves Art Gallery, Sheffield, England; Hamburger Kunsthalle, Hamburg; Hirshhorn Museum and

Sculpture Garden, Washington, D.C.; J. Paul Getty Museum, Los Angeles; Kansas City Art Institute; Kunstmuseum, Basel; Kunstmuseum, Dusseldorf; Los Angeles County Museum of Art; London Borough of Camden; Louisiana Museum, Copenhagen, Denmark; Metropolitan Museum of Art, New York; Minneapolis Institute of Arts; Musee De Ghent, Belgium; Museum Ludwig, Budapest; Museum Ludwig, Cologne; Museum Moderner Kunst, Vienna; Museo Tamayo, Mexico City; Museum of Art, Rhode Island School of Design, Providence; Museum of Contemporary Art, Chicago; Museum of Contemporary Art, Los Angeles; Museum of Contemporary Art, Tokyo; Museum of Fine Arts, Boston; Museum of Modern Art, New York; Naoshima Contemporary Art Museum, Japan; National Gallery of Australia, Canberra; National Gallery of New South Wales; National Gallery of Victoria, Melbourne, Australia; National Museum of American Art, Washington, D.C.; New York Public Library—Spencer Collection; Olinda Museum, Sao Paulo, Brazil; Palais Lichtenstein, Vienna; Philadelpha Museum of Art; The Phillips Collection, Washington, D.C.; Preston Art Gallery, Bolton, England; Ringling Museum, Florida; Scottish National Gallery of Modern Art; Sioux City Art Center, Iowa; Solomon R. Guggenheim Museum; Stedelijk Museum, Amsterdam; Stuyvesant Foundation, London; Tate Gallery, London; Tokyo Metropolitan Art Museum; University of Colorado, Denver; University of Oregon, Eugene; Victoria and Albert Museum, London; Walker Art Center, Minneapolis; Walker Art Gallery, Liverpool, England; Whitworth Art Gallery, Manchester, England.

Stage Production Design:

Ubu Roi, Royal Court, London, 1966; *Rake's Progress,* Glyndebourne, England, 1975; *Magic Flute,* Glyndebourne, 1978; Parade Triple Bill, Stravinsky Triple Bill, Metropolitan Opera House, New York City, 1980–81; *Tristan and Isolde,* Los Angeles Music Center Opera, 1987; *Turandot,* Chicago Lyric Opera, 1992; *Die Frau ohne Schatten,* Covent Garden, 1992; Los Angeles Music Center Opera, 1993; San Francisco Opera, 1993.

Publications:

By HOCKNEY: Books—*72 Drawings by David Hockney,* New York and London 1971; *David Hockney by David Hockney,* edited by Nikos Stangos, London 1976; *Twenty Photographic Pictures,* portfolio, edited by Sonnabend Gallery, New York and Paris 1976; *Paper Pools,* edited by Nikos Stangos, New York 1980; *David Hockney: Photographs,* New York, London and Paris 1982; *Cameraworks,* with text by Lawrence Weschler, New York and London 1984; *David Hockney on Photography,* New York 1984, Bradford, Yorkshire 1985; *Martha's Vineyard and Other Places,* London 1985; *That's the Way I See It,* New York 1993; *David Hockney's Dog Days,* London 1998. **Articles**—"An Interview with David Hockney," with Peter Fuller, in *Art Monthly* (London), December 1978/January 1979; "A Conversation with David Hockney," with Mario Amaya, in *Architectural Digest* (Los Angeles), September 1980; "Paper Pools" in *Eastern Airlines Review* (New York), September 1980; "The Art World: True to Life," interview, with Lawrence Weschler, in the *New Yorker,* 9 July 1984; "Vogue par David Hockney" in *Vogue* (Paris), December 1985; interview with Susan Loppert in *Contemporary Art,* vol. 1, no. 2, Winter 1992–1993; interview with Peter Jenkins in *Modern Painters* (London), vol. 5, no. 1, Spring 1992; interview by Paul Melia in *Transcript,* vol. 1, no. 3, February-March 1996; "A Wider View" in *Modern Painters* (London), vol. 11, no. 1, Spring 1998.

On HOCKNEY: Books—*David Hockney: Paintings, Prints and Drawings 1960–70,* exhibition catalog with text by Mark Glazebrook, London 1970; *David Hockney: Zeichnungen, Grafik, Gemalde,* exhibition catalog with text by Gunther Gercken, Bielefeld, West Germany 1971; *David Hockney,* with an introduction by Henry Geldzahler, London 1976; *David Hockney: Prints and Drawings,* exhibition catalog with an introduction by Gene Baro, Washington, D.C. 1978; *David Hockney: Travels with Pen, Pencil and Ink,* with an introduction by Edmund Pillsbury, New York 1978; *David Hockney: Drawings and Prints,* exhibition catalog by Peter Weiemair, Vienna 1978; *Pictures by David Hockney* by Nikos Stangos, London 1979; *David Hockney by Marco Livingston, New York and London 1981; David Hockney: Paintings and Drawings for 'Parade,'* exhibition catalog, with text by Mark Glazebrook, London 1981; *Hockney Paints the Stage* by Martin Friedman and others, Minneapolis and New York 1983, London 1985; *Hockney's Photographs,* exhibition catalog with an introduction by Mark Haworth-Booth, London 1983; *David Hockney: Fotografien 1962–1982,* exhibition catalog with text by Alain Sayag, Basel and Paris 1983; *David Hockney: Paintings of the Early 1960s,* exhibition catalog with an introduction by Nicholas Wilder, New York 1985; *David Hockney: Faces 1966–1984,* exhibition catalog with essay by Marco Livingstone, New York 1987; *David Hockney: A Retrospective,* with multiple authors, London 1988; *Hockney on Photography* by Paul Joyce, London 1988; *Portrait of David Hockney* by Peter Webb, London 1988; *David Hockney* by Peter Webb, Paris 1991; *David Hockney: We Two Boys Together Clinging* by Paul Melia, London 1993; *David Hockney* by Peter Clothier, New York 1995; *David Hockney,* edited by Paul Melia, Manchester 1995; *David Hockney* by Marco Livingstone, London 1996. **Articles**—"Hockney Against the Stream of Modern Art?" by Bevis Hillier in *Modern Painters* (London), vol. 1, no. 3, Autumn 1988; "Hockney's Work in Perspective" by Richard Wollheim in *Modern Painters* (London), vol. 1, no. 4, Winter 1988–1989; "David Hockney: Printmaking and Technique I" by Craig Hartley in *Print Quarterly,* vol. 5, no. 3, September 1988; "David Hockney: Printmaking and Technique II" by Craig Hartley in *Print Quarterly,* vol. 5, no. 4, December 1988; "In Profile: David Hockney" by David Lee in *Art Review,* vol. 45, November 1993; "Drawing His Life" by Norbert Lynton in *Royal Academy Magazine,* no. 49, Winter 1995; "David Hockney: Figures in a Landscape" by Pierre Sterckx in *Art Press,* no. 242, January 1999; "The Looking Glass: How Did the Old Masters Draw so Well?" by Lawrence Weschler in *The New Yorker,* 31 January 2000. **Films**—*David Hockney's Diaries* by Michael and Christian Blackwood, 1971; *A Bigger Splash* by Jack Hazan, 1974; *Hockney at Work,* BBC television film, by Peter Adam, 1980; *South Bank Show: David Hockney,* London Weekend Television Film, by Don Featherstone, 1983.

* * *

David Hockney, born in England, has found a home in California. The work he paints is of his new home, as if the paintings were a way of creating that home. Hockney's imagination of Los Angeles has given a special quality to his paintings, most of which are lit with daylight.

The architecture and the people Hockney chooses to portray have a dry, controlled, slowly motive, though largely at rest, quality about them. As with the painting "My Parents," emotions are subjected to interrelated contexts. There is no need for extraneous emotion, though there is a need for factual representation. This factualness, separating Hockney from both representational and abstract painters, describes an imagined and constructed world, of which Los Angeles is an example.

The key to seeing Hockney's work is ignoring, as he does, the most obvious Hollywood movie symbolism of the area, and instead plunging into a newsworthiness, a *facility* of the image. The paintings, therefore, function as a form of reification of the L. A. imagination. Hockney is particularly a painter of a city, and a time in a city, so that we like his paintings as we observe L. A. The two are interchangeable. New York and San Francisco and Chicago and Des Moines and Washington, D.C. can see what they like of Los Angeles: the pools, art, boys, glass windows, low desert houses, irrigated and transported sprinkler and shower water.

The boys and men he paints contain the factuality, as discussed, which makes them both at home and, even while involved in appearances of homosexual relations, very approachable. So Hockney's paintings fight the Hollywood course of assumed romantic events. Life then appears before us before it passes. His ''Model with Unfinished Self-Portrait'' depicts an urban family life, Hockney and lover, as Hockney works throughout the night drawing. Flowers sit still, and only an approach of paint passes through the picture.

Hockney has worked with pulp paper of deep-hued watercolors. Recently he has worked on etchings, colored stage sets and now photographic arrangements of a three-dimensional nature. He went to art school in Bradford. His father was a pacifist, and he was a conscientious objector. In ''My Parents and Myself'' Hockney emerges as the artist in a mirror which is set in the room, a dressed young man, a mother looking out, the father quietly posed. ''A Bigger Splash,'' of a pool with only the splash observed, the body submerged, leaves the viewer to observe the house, the palm trees, an empty chair.

—John Robinson

The early 1990s brought changes in Hockney's work. Renewed attention, exemplified by major retrospectives in Los Angeles, New York and London in 1988, was followed by a period of production and innovation. Recent exhibitions have featured Hockney's first abstract pantings, and Jennifer Wolcott has remarked that ''the recent pieces are not only more vibrant and the mediums more varied (photography, stage design, and printmaking as well as drawing and and painting), but the artist's style also seems looser and less rigid about adhering to conventional rules of rendering, such as perspective.'' A series of works in which Hockney created collages from pieces of Polaroid photographs reflects his lifelong interest in the relation between representation and abstraction in art. In addition, Hockney has continued his activities in designing for the theater, incorporating computer technology into his design practices, as in the set he designed for the production Puccini's *Turandot* at the Chicago Lyric opera in 1992.

—Joann Cerrito

In 1997, David Hockney returned to Yorkshire, England—his place of birth—to visit his ailing friend Jonathan Silver. While there, he traveled throughout the lush countryside, photographing extensively. He returned to his Los Angeles studio and created a colorful series of landscape paintings as tribute to Silver. Also in 1997, he revisited the Grand Canyon (subject of a remarkable series of Polaroid collages form the early 1980s). He documented the canyon with new photographs and painting studies, then created a breathtaking new Grand Canyon painting which measures 8 X 24 feet.

A year later, Hockney noticed that the ''clean, fast [and] completely assured'' line of Ingres drawings resembled that created by Andy Warhol when he traced images projected with slides. Hockney began to explore the possible use of non-photographic refracting devices (like the camera obscura—first discussed by Aristotle and Euclid— and the camera lucida—created in 1807) as far back as the sixteenth century. Although scholars have little doubt that Vermeer and Canaletto, for example, used the camera obscura to block out their compositions, Hockney's claim that optical devices were used by Bellini and Holbein the Younger remains controversial. Hockney himself used the camera lucida in a remarkable series of small portraits drawn in pencil at the dawn of the new millennium.

—Betty Ann Brown

HODGKIN, Howard

Nationality: British. **Born:** London, 6 August 1932. **Education:** Attended primary schools in London, New York and Wales; studied at Camberwell School of Art, London, under Victor Pasmore, William Coldstream and Claude Rogers, 1949–50; at the Bath Academy of Art, Corsham, under Clifford Ellis, 1950–54. **Family:** Married Julia Lane in 1955; sons: Louis and Sam. **Career:** Painter: has visited India frequently since 1967; spent time at the Retreat in Ahmedabad, where he worked on a series of paintings, 1978. Lecturer, Charterhouse School, 1954–56, Bath Academy of Art, Corsham, 1956–66, and Chelsea School of Art, London, 1966–72; artist-in-residence, Brasenose College, Oxford, 1976–77. Trustee, Tate Gallery, London, 1973, and National Gallery, London, 1980. **Awards:** Turner Prize, Tate Gallery, London, 1985; D. Litt: London University, 1985; C. B. E. (Commander, Order of the British Empire), 1977: knighted 1992; D. Litt: Oxford University, 2000. **Agent:** M. Knoedler Gallery, 19 East 70th Street, New York, New York 10021, U.S.A. **Address:** 32 Coptic Street, London WC1A 1NP, England.

Individual Exhibitions:

1962 Arthur Tooth and Sons, London
1964 Arthur Tooth and Sons, London
1967 Arthur Tooth and Sons, London
1969 Kasmin Gallery, London
1970 Arnolfini Gallery, Bristol
Dartington Hall, Devon
1971 Kasmin Gallery, London
Galerie Muller, Cologne
1972 Arnolfini Gallery, Bristol
Galerie Staedler, Paris (with Patrick Caulfield and Michael Moon)
1973 Kornblee Gallery, New York
1976 Tate Gallery, London
Serpentine Gallery, London (toured the U.K.)
Museum of Modern Art, Oxford
Waddington Galleries II, London
1977 André Emmerich Gallery, Zurich (with David Hockney)
André Emmerich Gallery, New York

1980 Waddington Galleries II, London
Bernard Jacobson Gallery, New York
1981 M. Knoedler Gallery, New York
Bernard Jacobson Gallery, New York
Bernard Jacobson Gallery, Los Angeles
1982 Tate Gallery, London
Knoedler Gallery, New York
1984 Knoedler Gallery, New York
British Pavilion, *XLI Biennale,* Venice
Phillips Collection, Washington, D.C.
1985 Yale Center for British Art, New Haven, Connecticut
Kestner-Gesellschaft, Hannover
Whitechapel Art Gallery, London
1986 Knoedler Gallery, New York
1987 Museu Nacional de Belas Artes, Rio de Janeiro
Waddington Galleries, London
1988 Waddington Galleries, London
Knoedler & Co., New York
Solo Gallery, New York
Bjorn Olsson Gallery, Stockholm
1989 Joanne Chappell Gallery, Dan Francisco
1990 British Council of Arts, London (travelled to Nantes, Barcelona, Edinburgh, and Dublin)
Knoedler & Co., New York
Reynolds/Minor Gallery, Richmond, Virginia
Ganz Gallery, Cambridge, England
1991 University Art Museum, University of California at Berkley
1992 British School at Rome
1993 Anthony d'Offay Gallery, London (traveled to Knoedler & Co., New York)
1994 *Howard Hodgkin Prints: Vision and Collaboration*, The George Washington University, Dimock Gallery, Washington, D.C. (catalog)
1995 *Venetian Views 1995*, Alan Cristea Gallery, London (catalog)
Britain at the Venice Biennale 1895–1995, Italy (catalog)
1996 Hayward Gallery, London
Paintings 1975–1995, Modern Art Museum, Fort Worth (touring exhibition) (catalog)
Metropolitan Museum of Art, New York
Retrospektive 1975 bis 1996, Kunstverein für die Rheinlande und Westfalen, Dusseldorf (retrospective) (catalog)
1997 *Recent Work*, Galerie Lawrence Rubin, Zurich (catalog)
Hayward Gallery, London
1998 Galerie Haas & Fuchs, Berlin (catalog)
Arbeiten auf Papier von 1971 bis 1995, Schriftenreihe des Staatlichen Museums für Naturkunde und Vorgeschichte, Oldenberg (catalog)
Galerie Lutz & Thalmann, Zurich (catalog)
Gagosian Gallery, New York (catalog)
1999 *New Paintings*, Anthony d'Offay Gallery, London (catalog)

Selected Group Exhibitions:

1959 *London Group,* RBA Galleries, London
1964 *British Malerei der Gegenwart,* Kunsthalle, Dusseldorf (toured West Germany)
1970 *Contemporary British Art,* Museum of Modern Art, Moderne de la Ville, Paris
1973 *Le Peinture Anglaise d'Aujourdhui,* Musée d'Art Moderne de la Ville, Paris
1977 *British Painting 1952–1977,* Royal Academy of Arts, London
1981 *A New Spirit in Painting,* Royal Academy of Art, London
1982 *Aspects of British Art Today,* Metropolitan Art Museum, Tokyo (toured Japan)
1984 *Hard Won Image,* Tate Gallery, London
1987 *British Art in the 20th Century,* Royal Academy of Art, London
1994 *SOLO Impressions, Inc.,* College of Wooster Art Museum, Wooster, Ohio (catalog)
1995 *Peter Blake, Patrick Caulfield, Howard Hodgkin: Paintings from the 60s and 70s*, Waddington Galleries, London (catalog)
1997 *Treasure Island*, Fundacao Calouste Gulbenkian, Lisbon
British Art: A Collection from Waddington Galleries, Foire Internationale d'Art Contemporain, Paris (traveling exhibition) (catalog)
Hockney to Hodgkin: British Master Prints 1960–1980, New Orleans Museum of Art, Louisiana (catalog)
1999 *Portrait of a City: Seven Figurative Painters from London*, John Berggruen Gallery, San Francisco (catalog)

Collections:

Arts Council of Great Britain, London; Tate Gallery, London; British Museum, London; Victoria and Albert Museum, London; Louisiana Museum, Humlebaek, Denmark; Sao Paulo Museum; National Gallery of South Australia, Adelaide; Walker Art Center, Minneapolis; Museum of Modern Art, New York; Fogg Art Museum, Harvard University, Cambridge, Massachusetts.

Public Installations:

Highgate Ponds, London Underground Ltd., 1990; Painting, IMAX Cinema, Waterloo Building, 1999.

Publications:

By HODGKIN: Book—*Indian Drawing,* exhibition catalog, London 1983. **Articles—**"The Relevance of Matisse," discussion with Andrew Forge and Phillip King, in *Studio International* (London), July/August 1968; "An Artist in Residence" in *Oxford Art Journal,* October 1978; "Howard Hodgkin," interview with Timothy Hyman, in *Artscribe* (London), December 1978; "How to be an Artist" in *Burlington Magazine* (London), 1982; "The Subject in Question: A. M. Homes Talks with Howard Hodgkin" in *Artforum,* January 1996; interview with Elisabetta Planca in *Arte*, no. 289, September 1997.

On HODGKIN: Books—*Howard Hodgkin,* exhibition catalog by Edward Lucie Smith, London 1962; *Howard Hodgkin: Forty Five Paintings 1949–75,* exhibition catalog by Richard Morphet, London 1976; *Howard Hodgkin* by Lawrence Gowing, New York 1981; *Howard Hodgkin: Indian Leaves* by Bruce Chatwin, London 1982; *Howard Hodgkin: Forty Paintings 1973–84,* exhibition catalog with introduction by John McEwen, London 1984; *Howard Hodgkin Prints 1977 to 1983,* exhibition catalog by Richard Morphet, London

1985; *Howard Hodgkin,* exhibition catalog by Michael Werner, New York 1990; *Howard Hodgkin* by Andrew Graham-Dixon, London 1994, 2001. **Articles—**''Howard Hodgkin's Mandarin Pastimes'' by Lilly Wei in *Art in America* (New York), vol. 82, no. 4, April 1994; ''Hodgkin's Subtexts'' by Brooks Adams in *Art in America* (New York), vol. 84, May 1996; ''Abstract with Memories: The Paintings of Howard Hodgkin'' by William Boyd in *Modern Painters* (London), vol. 9, Spring 1996; ''The Secret World Concealed Inside the Paintings of Britain's Greatest Colorist'' in *New Statesman,* 29 November 1996; ''A Passion for Pachyderms'' by Michael Glover in *Art News*, vol. 99, no. 7, Summer 2000. **Video—***Howard Hodgkin* by Melvyn Bragg, Chicago 1998.

*

My pictures are finished when the subject comes back. I start out with the subject and naturally I have to remember first of all what it looked like, but it would also perhaps contain a great deal of feeling and sentiment. All of that has got to be somehow transmuted, transformed or made into a physical object and when that happens, when that's finally been done, when the last physical marks have been put on and the subject comes back—which, after all, is usually the moment when the painting is at long last a coherent physical object—well, then the picture's finished and there is no question of doing anything more to it. My pictures really finish themselves.

—Howard Hodgkin

* * *

A possible clue to Howard Hodgkin's strangely individual paintings is his love for Indian miniatures. His paintings are mixtures of reality, memory and abstracted shapes, making up elaborate asymmetrical patterns, in strong, decorative colours.

He is a far less sophisticated painter than Hockney or Allen Jones, the two English artists he most closely resembles. There are an easy, assured, satisfying flow of forms in their work and a knowing, worldly wit in the ironical, wry comments they make about modern life. Hodgkin, on the other hand, seems to be battling with the components of his pictures, wedging the shapes together, whilst the actual imagery and technique have a heavy, if not exactly naive, ponderousness.

He has explained that whilst he always paints from memory, his paintings have to relate to people and their relationships. It is only when working from a given theme that the free associations are able to function, and when completed he becomes aware that they concern intense, subjective recollections. This intensity is well conveyed in the solid, almost monumental, weightiness of the architectural divisions of the picture plane, and in the features of painstaking, enlarged pointillism. Strange stylistic juxtapositions relate to remembered details—wallpaper patterns, items of clothing, a particular colour, and especially the light or space connected with a given person.

He refuses to work self-consciously; it is rather on the basis of a stream of consciousness that he allows psychological and aesthetic preoccupations to intermingle and dictate the substance and style of his work. He never paints a ''scene,'' as does Hockney, a known landscape, an arranged still-life, a living being; nor, like Jones, will he bring known or recalled elements together in order to make a social painting, a genuine Expressionist, unfashionably concerned with the surface quality of paint, battling between the introverted nature of his imagination and the need to examine and display it in these ponderous, genuine statements. Although linked to a flow of memory, there is always a positive formality to Hodgkin's work, either based on a central, elementary, sexual feature, or space dramatically divided into lozenges of colour and ambiguous forms. Most recently, his work appears to be more relaxed and closer to landscapes with figures, similar to Keith Vaughan, or the lush rural scenery of Hitchens.

—Charles Spencer

HOFLEHNER, Rudolf

Nationality: Austrian. **Born:** Linz, 8 August 1916. **Education:** Staatsgewerbeschule für Maschinenbau, Linz, 1932–36; studied architecture at the Technische Hochschule, Graz, Austria, 1936–38; studied art at the Akademie der Bildenden Künste, Vienna, 1938–40. **Family:** Married Luise Schaffer in 1939; daughter: Hanna. **Military Service:** German Army, 1940–45. **Career:** Painter and sculptor, in Linz, 1945–51, Vienna, 1951–62 (in Fritz Wortruba's studio, 1951–54), Stuttgart, 1962–81, and in Sudstadt, Austria, since 1981. Professor, Kunstgewerbeschule, Linz, 1945–51, and Akademie der Bildenden Künste, Stuttgart, 1962–81. **Awards:** Kulturpreis des Landes Oberosterreich, 1949; Unknown Political Prisoner Prize, London, 1953; Unesco study-travel grant, to Greece, 1954; Preis der Stadt Wien, 1958; Adalbert-Stifter-Preise des Landes Oberosterreich, 1967; Preis der Stadt Berlin, 1967; Grosser Österreichischer Staatspreis, 1969; Jerg-Ratgebpreis, 1977; Kulturpreis des Landes Oberösterrich, 1986. **Member:** Akademie der Künste, West Berlin, 1968; Bayerische Akademie der Schonen Künste, 1970. **Died:** 3 September 1995.

Individual Exhibitions:

1951 Galerie der Stadt, Linz, Austria
Galerie d'Art Moderne, Basel
1952 Galerie Wurthle, Vienna
1960 Biennial Venezia, Italy
1963 Museum des 20. Jahrhunderts, Vienna
Kunsthalle, Basel
Museum Folkwang, Essen
Städtisches Museum, Wuppertal, West Germany
Württembergischer Kunstverein, Stuttgart
1964 Kunstverein, Hamburg
Stedelijk Museum, Amsterdam
1965 Odyssia Gallery, New York
1966 Galerie Valentien, Stuttgart
Galerie Schmucking, Braunschweig, West Germany
1967 *Skulpturen 1959–1966, Handzeichnungen, Druckgraphik,* Haus am Waldsee, West Berlin
Städtisches Museum Schloss Morsbroich, Leverkusen, West Germany
1968 Städtische Galerie, Stuttgart
Manus Presse, Stuttgart
1969 Galerie Marz, Linz
1970 Galerie Würthle, Vienna
1971 Galerie Mayer-Ellingen, Frankfurt
Galerie Die Treppe, Lahr, West Germany
1972 Graphische Sammlung Albertina, Vienna
Museum des 20. Jahrhunderts, Vienna

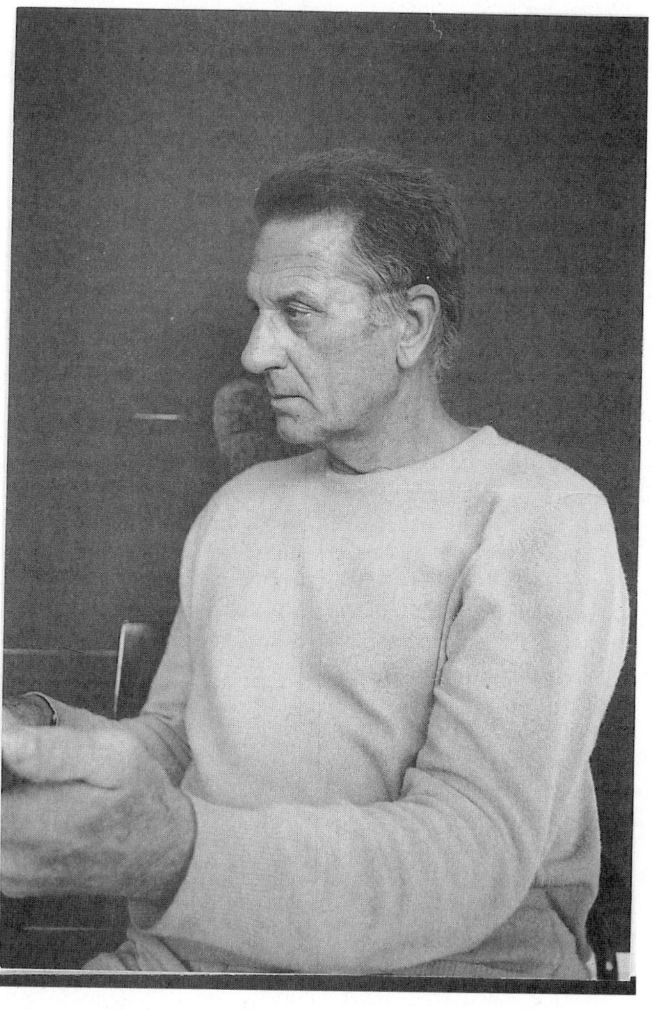

Rudolf Hoflehner.

Neue Galerie der Stadt, Linz, Austria
1975 Galerie Michael Hertz, Bremen, West Germany
1976 Austrian Pavilion, at the *Biennale,* Venice
1982 *Gemälde und Zeichnungen,* Württembergischer Kunstverein, Stuttgart
1983 Neue Galerie, Vienna
1987 Bawag Foundation, Vienna
1988 Galerie Valentien, Stuttgart
1997 Rupertinum, Salzburg, Austria
Landesgalerie Linz, Austria
1998 Kreissparkasse Esslingen, Germany

Selected Group Exhibitions:

1953 *Bienal,* Sao Paulo
1954 *Biennale,* Venice
1961 *2nd Exposition de la Sculpture Contemporaine,* Musée Rodin, Paris (and world tour)
1974 *20th Century German Graphics,* New School for Social Research, New York
1976 *5th International Exhibition of Drawings,* Rijeka, Yugoslavia
1977 *1st New York Drawing Biennal,* Bronx Museum of Art
1980 *Liebe-Dokumente unserer Zeit,* Kunsthalle, Darmstadt (travelled to the Kunstverein, Hannover)
1982 *Die Handzeichnung der Gegenwart,* Staatsgalerie, Stuttgart
1984 *Plastik seit 1945,* Museum Rupertinum, Salzburg
1987 *Neue Sezession,* Kunsthalle, Darmstadt, West Germany
1988 *Die Dritte Dimension,* Hamburger Kunsthalle, Hamburg
70 Jahre März, Linz, Austria
1990 *Kaleidoskop Farbe Blau,* Heidelberg, Germany
Österreichische Skulptur, Sezession, Vienna
1992 *Kunst seit 1945,* Rathaus Wien, Vienna
Kopfansichten, Kaiserslautern, traveled to Städtisches Museum, Hielbronn, Germany
1993 *Abstrakte Tendenzen,* Künzelsau, Germany
Kunst vor 25 Jahren, Stuttgart
1994 *Wotruba und die Folgen,* Rupertinum, Salzburg
3 aus 3 Generationen, Kulturhaus, Graz, Austria
Aufbrüche, 50 Jahre österreichische Malerei und Plastik, Oberes Belvederre, Vienna

Collections:

Museum des 20 Jahrhunderts, Vienna; Graphische Sammlung Albertina, Vienna; Nationalgalerie, West Berlin; Staatsgalerie, Stuttgart; Kunsthalle, Hamburg; Kunsthalle, Mannheim; Von der Heydt Museum, Wuppertal, West Germany; Niedersachsisches Landesmuseum, Hannover; Tate Gallery, London; Museum of Modern Art, New York.

Publications:

By HOFLEHNER: Book—*Krieauer Kreaturen,* with Werner Spies, Vienna 1971.

On HOFLEHNER: Books—*Plastik des 20. Jahrhunderts* by Werner Hofmann, Frankfurt 1958; *Contemporary Sculpture: An Evolution in Volume and Space* by Carola Giedion-Welcker, New York 1960; *Hoflehner,* exhibition catalog with text by Werner Hofmann, Vienna 1963; *Malerei und Plastik in Osterreich* by Kristian Sotriffer, Vienna 1963; *Rudolf Hoflehner,* exhibition catalog with text by Werner Hofmann, Hamburg 1964; *A Concise History of Modern Sculpture,* by Herbert Read, London 1964; *Rudolf Hoflehner,* exhibition catalog with text by Werner Hofmann, Amsterdam 1964; *Der nackte Mensch in der Kunst* by Frederich Bayl, Cologne 1964; *Hoflehner* by Werner Hofmann, Stuttgart, 1965; *Rudolf Hoflehner* by Werner Hofmann, Stuttgart 1966; *Österreichische Plastik seit 1945* by Johann Muschik, Baden bei Wien, Austria 1966; *Rudolf Hoflehner: Skulpturen 1959–1966; Handzeichnungen, Druckgraphik,* exhibition catalog with text by Kristian Sotriffer, West Berlin 1967; *A Concise History of Western Art* by Michael Levey, London 1970; *Hoflehner: Bilder und Skizzen 1967–71,* exhibition catalog, with texts by Alfred Schmeller and Walter Koschatzky, Vienna 1972; *Der Fall Rudolf Hoflehner* by Wieland Schmied, Bremen, West Germany 1976; *Rudolf Hoflehner: Gemälde und Zeichnungen,* exhibition catalog with texts by Tilman Osterwold, Andreas Vowinckel and Magdalena M. Moeller, Stuttgart 1982; *Hoflehner* by Wieland Schmied, Stuttgart, 1988; *Rudolf Hoflehner* by Werner Hofmann, Stuttgart, 1993.

*

Representation of mankind is the geometric place, the intersection point, of my decisions:

In sculpture in its existence as a plastic steely mass, impenetrable and capable of resistance. In painting as a rebellious and vulnerable, organic-sentient phenomenon.

The limit of my work is man, and the objective is form. Man is neither architecture nor machine. Man is a human being. But indifferent to architecture or flesh: art is artificial; that is the trouble.

Yet, in any event, art is an interpretation of the world.

—Rudolf Hoflehner

* * *

One of the features of post-war European sculpture (and to some extent painting) is the re-occurring symbols suggestive of human tragedy and suffering, of aggression, violence, destruction. In some cases, notably the sculpture of Germaine Richier, this takes the form of a complacent humanity, accepting, often with dignity, the woes which the gods have cast down. The Job-like stance also bears traces of the Greek sense of nemesis, in which man is both tested and made to reap his own human harvest.

Rudolf Hoflehner can be numbered among these humanist artists, who retain a basic interest in the human form and the human dilemma, but more than most others he has arrived at a symbolic style which enables him to express formal and emotional involvement with some degree of originality. Stylistically there is much in common with his compatriot, Wotruba, who also uses figures as reclining forms or tower-like totems, abstracted into featureless symbols. Wotruba, however, is much less complex than Hoflehner, building his forms in cubic blocks, or oblong volumes, arriving at a post-cubist formula. Hoflehner is altogether more passionate and aggressive, the violent forms and gestures increasing in intensity throughout his career. It was a visit to Greece, on a six-month Unesco scholarship, which helped him to consolidate his view of art. The great archaic figures of Greek sculpture, with the de-humanised realism, their dignified, formal manner, their ponderous symbolism, inspired Hoflehner to develop on similar lines. The early sculptures are altogether more heavy and solid, and the concentration on legs and feet, on the thrust of limbs, eventually resulted in the virtual elimination of body and head, their substitution being effected by limited symbols, often similar to hammer-heads. The figures have a curious sense of purpose, or even doom, as though striding blindly to their fate. Here one arrives at the post-war idiom of dignified suffering and tragedy.

The titles of these iron pieces range from ''Archaic Figure,'' concerned with frontality, ''The Strider,'' ''Split Figure,'' ''Doric Figure.'' The splitting of the form was Hoflehner's next development, literally cutting the figure in half, from head to feet, possibly a substitute token of the cruciform symbolism of the previous period. By the end of the 1950's a new curvilinear motif was introduced, not, as in some artists, to suggest a softness to the rigid uprights, but emphasizing their aggressive nature; these new head-like additions ended in huge pincers, rather like lobster limbs, or dangerous-looking rotary blades. The figures began to assume a science-fiction surrealism, followed by a more delicate period of dehumanized structures, seemingly standing on one leg, like slim dancers or oriental boxers, energetically forcing their second limb into wide-arched violence. It comes as no sunrise to find them entitled ''Aggressive Object''. The most recent figures have become more and more monumental, more and more dehumanized, into strange, fantasy structures, part human, part animal, part machine, attacking with their open nut-cracker limbs, or resembling mobile guns and tanks. Thrusting energy, defiance, defence, challenge, these are the strident features of Hoflehner's work, but not without an undeniable sense of proud dignity.

—Charles Spencer

HOLLAND, Tom

Nationality: American. **Born:** Seattle, Washington, 15 June 1936. **Education:** University of California, Santa Barbara and Berkeley, 1954–56; Williamette University, Salem, Oregon, 1956–58; Fulbright Fellow, Chile, 1959–60. **Family:** Married Judith Lyon in 1958; children: Randolph, Brendon, and Joel. **Career:** Independent artist, since 1960. Instructor, San Francisco Art Institute, 1963–68, 1971–75; Assistant Professor, University of California at Los Angeles, 1968–70. **Awards:** Fulbright Grant, 1975; National Endowment for the Arts Sculpture Grant, 1975–76; Guggenheim Fellowship, 1980–81. **Agents:** Charles Cowles Gallery, 420 West Broadway, New York, New York 10012; John Berggruen Gallery, 228 Grant Avenue, San Francisco, California 94108. **Address:** 8957 Norma Place, Los Angeles, CA 90069–4818.

Individual Exhibitions:

1961 Catholic University, Santiago, Chile
1962 Richmond Art Center, California
1963 Lanyon Gallery, Palo Alto, California
1964 Lanyon Gallery, Palo Alto, California
1965 Lanyon Gallery, Palo Alto, California
Nicholas Wilder Gallery, Los Angeles
1966 Hansen-Fuller Gallery, San Francisco
Richmond Art Center, California
1967 Nicholas Wilder Gallery, Los Angeles
1968 Hansen-Fuller Gallery, San Francisco
Nicholas Wilder Gallery, Los Angeles
Arizona State University, Tempe
1969 Nicholas Wilder Gallery, Los Angeles
1970 Helman Gallery, St. Louis
Neuendorf Gallery, Hamburg
Robert Elkon Gallery, New York
Hansen-Fuller Gallery, San Francisco
1971 Neuendorf Gallery, Hamburg
Robert Elkon Gallery, New York
1972 Hansen-Fuller Gallery, San Francisco
Nicholas Wilder Gallery, Los Angeles
Corcoran and Corcoran Gallery, Coral Gables, Florida
Multiples Gallery, Los Angeles
Rubin Gallery, New York
1973 Nicholas Wilder Gallery, Los Angeles
Knoedler Gallery, New York
Hansen-Fuller Gallery, San Francisco
Felicity Samuel Gallery, London
Current Editions, Seattle
1974 Hansen-Fuller Gallery, San Francisco
Corcoran and Greenberg, Inc., Coral Gables, Florida
1975 Knoedler Gallery, New York
Nicholas Wilder Gallery, Los Angeles
Dootson-Calderhead Gallery, Seattle

Seder-Creigh Gallery, Coronado, California
Richmond Art Center, California
Greenberg Gallery, St. Louis
1976 Nicholas Wilder Gallery, Los Angeles
Hansen-Fuller Gallery, San Francisco
1977 Hansen-Fuller Gallery, San Francisco
Nicholas Wilder Gallery, Los Angeles
Watson de Nagy and Company, Houston
1978 Smith Anderson Gallery, Palo Alto, California
Charles Casat Gallery, La Jolla, California
Droll Kolbert Gallery, New York
1979 Nicholas Wilder Gallery, Los Angeles
Watson de Nagy and Company, Houston
San Francisco Art Institute
Linda Farris Gallery, Seattle
Blum-Helman Gallery, New York
1980 Grossmonte College, San Diego, California
James Corcoran Gallery, Los Angeles
Hansen-Fuller-Goldeen Gallery, San Francisco
1981 Linda Farris Gallery, Seattle, Washington
Blum Helman Gallery, New York
Charles Cowles Gallery, New York
1982 Fuller Goldeen Gallery, San Francisco
James Corcoran Gallery, Los Angeles
Southern Alberta Art Gallery, Canada
1983 Smith Anderson Gallery, Palo Alto, California
James Corcoran Gallery, Los Angeles
Charles Cowles Gallery, New York
Bank of America Galleries, San Francisco
1984 Greenberg Gallery, St. Louis
Charles Cowles Gallery, New York
John Berggruen Gallery, San Francisco
1985 James Corcoran Gallery, Los Angeles
Charles Cowles Gallery, New York
John Berggruen Gallery, San Francisco
Arts Club, Chicago
1986 Linda Farris Gallery, Seattle, Washington
Charles Cowles Gallery, New York
John Berggruen Gallery, San Francisco
1987 John Berggruen Gallery, San Francisco
Crown Point Press, San Francisco
1988 Charles Cowles Gallery, New York
1989 John Berggruen Gallery, San Francisco
James Corcoran Gallery, Los Angeles
Persons Lindell Gallery, Helsinki
1990 Charles Cowles Gallery, New York
1991 James Corcoran Gallery, Los Angeles
1992 Allene Lapides Gallery, Santa Fe
John Berggruen Gallery, San Francisco (catalog)
1993 Frederick Spratt Gallery, San Jose
Charles Cowles Gallery, New York
John Berggruen Gallery, San Francisco
1994 *Tom Holland: New Works,* San Jose Museum of Art, San Jose
1995 John Berggruen Gallery, San Francisco
1996 Frederick Spratt Gallery, San Jose
1998 John Berggruen Gallery, San Francisco
Robert Mondavi Winery, Oakville
2000 Mills College Art Museum, Oakland
Charles Cowles Gallery, New York

Selected Group Exhibitions:

1964 *Bay Area Artists,* San Francisco Museum of Modern Art
1967 *Grotesque Images,* San Francisco Art Institute
1972 *New Options in Painting,* Walker Art Center, Minneapolis
1976 *California Painting and Sculpture: The Modern Era,* San Francisco Museum of Modern Art (travelled to the National Collection of Fine Arts, Washington, D.C.)
1979 *Artists Born Between 1935–1945: 20 Painters,* Nancy Caldwell Gallery, New York
1981 *New York on Paper,* Museum of Modern Art, New York
1983 *On and Off the Wall: Shaped and Colored,* Oakland Museum, California (travelled to Boise, Idaho; Salt Lake City: Miami, Florida: Jacksonville, Florida; Palm Springs, Florida: Laguna Beach, California)
1985 *Abstract Painting Redefined,* Louis K. Meisel Gallery, New York
1987 *Not So Plain Geometry,* Crown Point Press, New York
1994 *Here and Now: Bay Area Masterworks from the di Rosa Collections,* Oakland Museum, California (catalog)

Collections:

Art Institute of Chicago; The Solomon R. Guggenheim Museum, New York; Hirshhorn Museum and Sculpture Garden, Washington, D.C.; Honolulu Academy of Art; Aldrich Museum of Contemporary Art; Museum of Modern Art, New York; Oakland Museum, California; Phoenix Art Museum; San Francisco Museum of Modern Art; Seattle Art Museum; Sheldon Art Museum, Lincoln; Stanford University Museum, California; St. Louis Art Museum; University Art Museum, Berkeley; Walker Art Center, Minneapolis; Whitney Museum of American Art, New York; Brooklyn Museum, New York.

Publications:

On HOLLAND: Books—*14 Big Prints,* edited by Bernard Jacobsen, London 1972; *Tom Holland,* exhibition catalog, San Francisco 1972; *Yngre Amerikans Kunst,* exhibition catalog by S. Laursen and P. Aproaxine, Aarhus, Denmark 1973. **Articles—**''Tom Holland'' by Fidel Danieli in *Art International* (Lugano, Switzerland), January 1970; ''Tom Holland: Elkon Gallery'' by Robert Pincus-Witten in *Artforum* (New York), June 1970; ''New York: Tom Holland, Elkon Gallery'' by Carter Ratcliff in *Art International* (Lugano, Switzerland), Summer 1970; ''Peter Gutkin, Paul Harris, Tom Holland'' by J. Tarshis in *Artforum* (New York), October 1972; ''Tom Holland: 10 Years of Work'' by R. Losch in *Artweek* (Oakland, California), February 1974; ''Controlled Frenzy: Drunk with Love of Mediums and Materials, Tom Holland Creates Works of Daring Ambiguity'' by John Gruen in *Art News,* vol. 86, March 1987.

* * *

The Bay Area of California has cultivated a curious assortment of trends and traditions. The Beat generation had its heyday, funk art, what Hilton Kramer coined ''dude ranch'' Dada, a strong ceramics movement—and most of this was drenched with obscure humor and puns, eccentricity and individuality. But perhaps the most durable of all these movements, and one which still blankets much of the art being made there today, was expressionism. San Francisco developed its own brand of expressionism by interjecting figure and landscape into the bold, gestural canvases of post-war America.

Many would credit Clyfford Still with imparting his own sense of vehement individualism to the vicinity while living there and teaching in what is now the San Francisco Art Institute. Still may have laid the groundwork, but painters such as Elmer Bischoff, Richard Diebenkorn and David Park (to name only a few) are responsible for the sumptuous paintings which dominate this potent tradition of raw action painting. Though the northern California art scene has certainly transmulated in diverse paths since the 50's, second generation expressionists such as Tom Holland, Manuel Neri and Peter Voulkos continue their use of gushing gestures and strident slashes, splashes, and strokes.

Tom Holland rakes over his three-dimensional paintings with unabashed vehemence. He constructs some free-standing, some wall-hung assemblages made of aluminum sheets, fiberglass or paper which are drenched with vibrant epoxy paints. Though he insists that he is a painter, he really has developed a hybrid of both painting and sculpture. In the free-standing pieces, shards of aluminum or some such material writhe about and stab at larger forms all of which ooze glutinous drips of lusty color. Each splash or cascade of dribbles reveals the action and process of this painter, as they glide down sharp corners or around the protruding bolts by which the fragments are joined.

Holland has another side as well, one that is more mellowed, and introspective. Some of the wall pieces are laced with splashes of pale blues, ochres and whites which drip and roll over undulating strips floating on top or woven through sheets of paper or fiberglass. These paintings carry a similarly all-encompassing power, with a softer, more seductive vitality.

Though one can read each composition in structural terms, in all the paintings the overwhelming sense is an emotional one. Oddly figurative, the free-standing pieces seem almost to wander about their gallery rooms. One notices their ''gait,'' and inevitable comparisons to human scale arise, though many of Holland's pieces tower over one. Perhaps these impressions are unavoidable in any work which so underscores the rites of passion.

—Janet Goleas

HÖLLER, Carsten

Nationality: Belgian. **Born:** Brussels, Belgium, 1961. **Address:** Cologne, Germany.

Selected Individual Exhibitions:

1993 Lukas and Hoffmann, Berlin
Buchholz and Buchholz, Cologne
1994 Air de Paris, Paris
Schipper and Krome, Cologne
Ars Futura, Zurich
1995 Theoretical Events, Naples
1996 Kunstverein, Hamburg
Kunstverein, Cologne
Wiener Secession, Vienna
Espace Jules Verne, Bretigny-sur-Orge, France
Massimo de Carlo, Milan

Selected Group Exhibitions:

1992 *Tattoo Collection,* Air de Paris and Urbi et Orbi, Paris
240 Minuten, Esther Schipper, Cologne
1993 *Venice Biennale,* Venice
Sens et Sentiments, FRAC Languedoc-Roussillion, Montpellier
1994 *Please Don't Hurt Me,* Snoei, Rotterdam and Cabinet, London
L'Hiver de l'Amour, ARC, Paris
Winter of Love, PS1, New York
Cocktail II, Kunstverein, Hamburg
Rue des Marins, Air de Paris, Nice
Cloaca Maxima, Museum fur Stadtentwasserung, Zurich
Naked City, Massimo de Carlo, Milan
1995 *Toys,* Jousse Seguin, Paris
Take Me, I'm Yours, Serpentine Gallery, London
Vital Use, Museum in Progress, Vienna
Trust, Tramway, Glasgow
Moral Maze, le Consortium, Dijon
How Is Everything? Wiener Secession, Vienna
Kwang Biennale, Korea
Biennale de Lyon, Lyon
1996 *Traffic,* CAPC, Bordeaux
Drei Jahre, Ars Futura, Zurich
Berechenbarkeit der Welt, Kunstverein, Bonn
All of a Sudden, Aurel Scheibler, Cologne
Hermeneu tik und . . . , Sophia Ungers, Cologne
Manifesta, Rotterdam
Comme un Oiseau, Fondation Cartier, Paris

Publications:

By HÖLLER: Articles—''The Pealove Room'' in *Flash Art* (International Edition), no. 174, January/February 1994; ''A Thousand Words: Carsten Höller Talks About His Slides'' in *Artforum International,* vol. 37, no. 7, Mar 1999; *Synchro Systems* (exhibition catalog), with interview by Germano Celant Milan, 2000.

On HÖLLER: Articles—''Carsten Höller'' by Gregorio Magnani in *Flash Art* (International Edition), no. 171, Summer 1993; ''Context Kunstlers'' by Liam Gillick in *Art Monthly,* no. 177, June 1994; ''Carsten Höller: Getting Real'' by Michelle Nicol in *Parkett,* no. 43, 1995; ''Carsten Höller'' by Yvonne Volkart in *Flash Art* (International Edition), no. 180, January/February 1995; ''Dead Give-away'' by Sadie Murdoch in *Women's Art Magazine,* no. 64, May/June 1995; ''Rewind'' by Gilda Williams in *Art Monthly,* no. 191, November 1995; ''System-Surfing Cologne'' by Thiel Wolf-Gunter in *Flash Art* (International Edition), no. 186, January/February 1996; ''Carsten Höller, Philippe Parreno, Rirkrit Tiravanija'' by Jonathan Turner in *Art News,* vol. 95, Mar 1996; ''Carsten Höller: 'Maybe Because I Can Swim, I Decided to Learn to Fly''' by Wolf-Gunter Thiel in *Flash Art* (International Edition), no. 194, May/June 1997; 80–4"Rosemarie Trockel and Carsten Höller: Donald Young'' by Patricia Failing in *Art News,* vol. 97, no. 5, May 1998; ''Marie Jose Burki/Carsten Höller'' by Gilda Williams in *Art Monthly,* no. 216, May 1998; ''Rosemarie Trockel: Bardot and Brecht in the Chicken Coop'' by

Joan Simon in *Art Press,* no. 247, June 1999; ''Speed of Life'' by Ulf-Erdmann Ziegler in *Art in America,* vol. 87, no. 7, July 1999; ''Restless Anxiety'' by Giacinto Di-Pietrantonio in *Domus,* no. 833, January 2001; ''Mice and Man: The Art of Carsten Höller and Rosemarie Trockel'' by Daniel Birnbaum in *Artforum International,* vol. 39, no. 6, February 2001.

* * *

Carsten Höller's background in biology and natural sciences has influenced his artistic production in playful and often profound ways. Since the early 1990s the Belgian artist has created works which consider the viewer as both subject and conductor of quasi-scientific experiments. Positing the human as one among many animals, these ''experiments'' explore the necessity of human behaviors and cognitive functions for evolution.

Höller's *Upside Down Spectacles* of 1993 are a perfect example of this tendency. The eyeglasses consist of small prismatic lenses that cause one to see everything upside down, the way things really appear on the retina before the brain transposes it. An early twentieth century scientist wore such spectacles for over a week and his brain reputedly again adapted to turning the image around. In *The Pinocchio Effect* (1994) Höller places instructions for using electric stimulus pads to grow or shrink one's nose. When the pads are placed on biceps or triceps, respectively, the visitors/subjects touch their noses with their fingertips and their noses seem to extend or retract. Such hallucinatory effects, when the brain misreads or is tricked into process information incorrectly, remains part of Höller's work.

In a 1996 project for the Cologne Kunstverein, Höller created a series of obstacles or experiments which enticed viewer participation, but also made them the subject of sociological observation. In *New Worlds* (1998–1999) the artist created a number of fantastic racing vehicles that question the way a body traditionally moves through space and address the human desire for challenges and games. Accepting such strange vehicles and their movements would entail a shift in what humans perceive to be true about themselves and the physical world.

For the 1997 international exhibition Documenta X in Kassel, he collaborated with German artist Rosemarie Trockel to create *A House for Pigs and People.* This project placed animal and human worlds on even ground. In one half of the pavilion, the artists created a pigsty with a boar, two pigs, and a few piglets; in the other, a space for the exhibition visitors. Divided by a pane of one-way glass, the human viewers again take on the role of scientific observers. Watching the pigs in their natural habitat, viewers are prone to reflect on the evolutionary necessity of breeding and human-like qualities that have been preferred in the breeds we have domesticated in the course of time.

In most cases, Höller continues to posit the human being as the subject of these explorations. One of his most-loved works is a simple metal slide that has brought visitors in such places as Berlin, New York, and Milan (where versions are permanently installed) from one gallery level to another, or from inside to outside spaces. The inexplicable happiness that comes from the rush down the slide tube is an interesting effect. As the artist has remarked ''letting yourself go down the slide is an experience that is similar to hallucination because, when you get on it knowing precisely what's going to happen from the entrance to the exit, this is an experience that makes you happy,'' according to an interview with Germano Celant.

Höller continues to search for the physiological explanations behind hallucinatory experiences in new works. The most perceptory shift comes from his *Light Wall* (2000), a grand installation (at Fondazione Prada, Milan and Schipper & Krome, Berlin) of nearly 4,000 incandescent light bulbs that emit flashes of light at a specific frequency. The flashing of these lights challenges the brain to continuously change its reading of the light level in synchronization with the pulsing lights. It is impossible to avoid a physical involvement with this experiment: when the viewers close their eyes, the residual effects, colors, pulsing retinal images, and a feeling of disembodiment persist. The structure behind the machine—wires, dimmers, mixing boards—remains visible to demystify the experience, allowing the viewer ''in'' on the experiment.

Höller does not seek to gather any kind of objective scientific information by his works, but rather he makes possible a range of experiences that lie outside of our daily consideration. By stimulating unusual and surprising reactions, his experiments and objects encourage us to question the ''nature'' underlying our existence.

—Elizabeth Mangini

HOLT, Nancy

Nationality: American. **Born:** Worcester, Massachussets, 5 April 1938. **Education:** Jackson College, Tufts University, Medford, Massachusetts, 1956–60, B.S. 1960. **Family:** Married the artist Robert Smithson, in 1963. **Career:** Independent artist working in sculpture, film and video, and producing large-scale environmental and installation projects; lived and worked in New York, 1960–94, and Galisteo, New Mexico, 1995—. **Awards:** New York Creative Artists Public Service Grant (sculpture) 1975, (video) 1978; National Endowment for the Arts Fellowship, 1975, 1978, 1983, 1985; WNET-Channel 13 Artist-in-Residence Grant, 1977; Beard's Fund Grant, 1977; Guggenheim Fellowship, 1978; Design Honor Award, American Society of Landscape Architects, New Jersey Chapter, 1986; National Endowment for the Arts, Visual Arts Fellowship, 1988; Honorary Doctorate, Univeristy of South Florida, Tampa, 1996. **Agent:** John Weber Gallery, 142 Greene Street, New York, New York 10012.

Individual Exhibitions:

1972 University of Montana Art Gallery, Missoula
University of Rhode Island Art Center, Kingston
1973 Lo Guidice Gallery, New York
1974 Bykert Gallery, New York
Walter Kelly Gallery, Chicago
Clocktower, New York
1977 Franklin Furnace, New York
Whitney Museum, Young American Filmmakers Series, New York
1979 John Weber Gallery, New York
Miami University Art Museum, Oxford, Ohio
1981 Saginaw Art Museum, Michigan
1982 John Weber Gallery, New York
David Bellman Gallery, Toronto
1984 John Weber Gallery, New York
1985 Flow Ace Gallery, Los Angeles
1986 John Weber Gallery, New York
1987 Lakeside Gallery, Richland College, Dallas

Nancy Holt: *Sun Tunnels* interior detail, 1973–76. ©Nancy Holt/Licensed by VAGA, New York, NY.

1993 John Weber Gallery, New York

"Works in the Land": *Buried Poems,* Florida, New Jersey, 1969, and Utah, 1971; *Views Through a Sand Dune,* Narragansett Beach, Rhode Island, 1972; *Missoula Ranch Locators,* near Missoula, Montana, 1972; *Hydra's Head,* along the Niagara River, Lewiston, New York, 1972; *Sun Tunnels,* northwestern Utah desert, near Lucin, Utah, 1973–76; *Stone Enclosure: Rock Rings,* Bellingham, Washington, 1977–78; *Polar Circle,* Miami University, Oxford, Ohio, 1979; *Star Crossed,* Miami University, Oxford, Ohio, 1979–80; *30 Below,* Lake Placid, New York; 1979 *Wild Spot,* Wellesley College, Massachusetts, 1979–80; *Dark Star Park,* Rosslyn, Arlington, Virginia, 1979–84; *Annual Ring,* Saginaw, Michigan, 1980–81; *Time Span,* Laguna Gloria Museum, Austin, Texas, 1981; *Catch Basin,* St. James Park, Toronto, 1982; *Sole Source,* Marlay Park, Dublin, 1983; *Waterwork,* Gallaudel College, Washington, D.C., 1983–84; *Astral Grating,* IRT Subway Station, Fulton Street, New York, 1983–88; *End of the Line/ West Rock,* Southern Connecticut State University, New Haven, 1984–88; *Rain Drains,* Islip Museum of Art, Long Island, New York, 1985; *Pipeline,* Visual Arts Center of Alaska, Anchorage, 1986; *Starife,* Island in Sheepcreek River, Anchorage, 1986; *Spinwinder,* University of Southeastern Massachusetts, N. Darthmouth, Massachusetts, 1991; *Solar Rotary,* work in progress, University of South Florida, Tampa, 1996; *Up and Under,* Pinsio sand quarry, Nokia, Finland, 1998.

Selected Group Exhibitions:

1974 *Interventions in the Landscape,* Hayden Gallery, Massachusetts Institute of Technology, Cambridge
1977 *Probing the Earth: Contemporary Land Projects,* Hirshhorn Museum, Smithsonian Institution, Washington, D.C.
1980 *Architectural Sculpture,* Los Angeles Institute of Contemporary Art
1984 *Content: A Contemporary Focus 1974–84,* Hirshhorn Museum, Washington, D.C.
1987 *Women's Autobiographical Artists' Books,* University of Wisconsin, Milwaukee
1988 *Projects & Proposals: New York City's % for the Art Program,* Department of Cultural Affairs, New York
1991 *Consumer Tools: Personal Visions, Museum of Modern Art,* New York
1992 *Fragile Ecologies: Artists' Interpretations and Solutions,* Queens Museum, Flushing, New York
1993 *Differentes Natures, Art Defense,* (EPAD) Paris, Catalog

1994 *Mapping,* Museum of Modern Art, New York
A Natural Dialogue, International Sculpture Center, Washington, D.C. (travelling exhibition)
1996 *Present and Futures: Architecture in Cities,* Centre de Cultura Contemporania de Barcelona
1997 *Art About the Environment IV,* Center for Art and Earth, New York
1998 Wiener Kunstverein, Palmenhaus, Vienna
1999 *Primarily Structural,* P.S. 1, New York
Afterimage: Drawing through Process, Museum of Contemporary Art, Los Angeles, and Contemporary Arts Museum, Houston, Texas
The American Century: Art and Culture 1900–2000, Whitney Museum of Art, New York
2000 *Real to Reel: Land and Environmental Art on Screen,* OTA Fine Arts, Tokyo
Formations of Erasure: Earthworks and Entropy, Center for Land Use Interpretation, Culver City, California
2001 *Century City: Art and Culture in the Modern Metropolis,* Tate Modern, London

Collections:

Museum of Modern Art, New York; Hartwick College, Oneonta, New York; University of Massachusetts, Amherst; Wellesley College, Massachusetts; Miami University, Oxford, Ohio; Western Washington University, Bellingham, Washington; Vancouver Art Gallery.

Publications:

By HOLT: Books—Editor, *The Writings of Robert Smithson,* New York 1979; *Ransacked,* New York 1980; *Time Outs,* Rochester, New York 1985. **Articles**—''Hydra's Head'' in *Arts Magazine* (New York), January 1975; ''Views through a Sand Dune, Holes of Light'' in *TriQuarterly* (Evanston, Illinois), Winter 1975; article in *Artpack Catalog,* Lewiston, New York 1975; ''Some Notes on Video Works'' in *Video Art,* edited by Ira Schneider and Berly Korot, New York 1976; ''Sun Tunnels'' in *Artforum* (New York), April 1977; ''The Time Being (For Robert Smithson)'' in *Arts Magazine* (New York), May 1978; ''Massachusetts'' in *Born in Boston,* exhibition catalog, Lincoln, Massachusetts 1979; ''Stone Enclosure: Rock Rings'' in *Arts Magazine* (New York), June 1979; ''Situation Esthetics: Impermanent Art and the 70s Audience'' in *Artforum* (New York), January 1980; ''Notes on a Few Coincidences of Art and Life'' in *Chelsea* (New York), no. 39, 1981; ''Ecological Aspects of My Work,'' in *Creative Solutions to Ecological Issues* catalog, Gail Gelburd, New York, 1993 (photos); ''Site-Specific, Environmental Sculptures'' in *36th World Congress of the International Federation of Landscape Architects Abstract Book,* 1999. **Videotapes**—*East Coast—West Coast,* with Robert Smithson, 1969; *Locating #1 and #2,* 1972; *Zeroing in,* 1973; *Going Around in Circles,* 1973; *Points of View,* 1974; *Underscan,* 1974; *Revolve,* 1977; *Art in the Public Eye: The Making of Dark Star Park,* 1988. **Films**—*Swamp,* 1971; *Pine Barrens,* 1975; *Sun Tunnels,* 1978.

On HOLT: Books—*Probing the Earth: Contemporary Land Projects,* exhibition catalog by John Beardsley, Washington, D.C. 1977; *New Artists Video* by Gregory Battcock, New York 1978; *Originals: American Women Artists* by Eleanor Munro, New York 1979; *Nature/Sculpture,* exhibition catalog by Andres Vowinckel, Stuttgart 1981; *Art in the Land,* edited by Alan Sonfist, New York 1983; *The Desert Is no Lady: Southwestern Landscapes in Women's Writing and Art* by Vera Horwood and Janice Monk, New Haven, Connecticut 1987; *Refuge: An Unnatural History of Family and Place* by Terry Tempest Williams, New York 1992; *Contemporary Public Sculpture: Tradition, Transformation and Controversy* by Harriet F. Senie, New York 1992; *Land Art USA* by Patrick Werkner, Munich 1992; *Land Art* by Gilles A. Tiberghien, Paris 1993, and New York 1995; *Sculpting with the Environment: A Natural Dialogue,* edited by Baile Oakes, New York 1995; *En Chemin, Le Land Art* by Anne-Francoise Penders, Brussels 1999; *Space Site Intervention: Situating Installation Art,* edited by Erika Suderburg, Minneapolis 2000. **Articles**—''The Earth Is a Cruel Master'' by Robert Smithson and Gregoire Muller in *Arts Magazine* (New York), November 1971; ''Video Is Being Invented'' by Bruce Kurtz in *Arts Magazine* (New York), December 1972/January 1973; ''Camouflage: Films by Holt and Horn'' by Lucy Lippard in *Art Rite* (New York), Fall 1975; ''Art Outdoors: In and Out of the Public Domain'' by Lucy Lippard in *Studio International* (London), no. 2 1977; ''6 Women at Work in the Landscape'' by April Kingsley in *Arts Magazine* (New York), April 1978; ''Complexes: Architectural Sculpture in Nature'' by Lucy Lippard in *Art In America* (New York), January/February 1979; ''The Expulsion from the Garden: Environmental Sculpture at the Winter Olympics'' by Kay Larson in *Artforum* (New York), April 1980; ''Holt's Volts'' by John Perreault in the *Soho News* (New York), 2 February 1982; ''Nancy Holt, Siteseer'' by Ted Castle in *Art in America* (New York), March 1982; ''Dark Star Park'' by John Yau in *Artforum* (New York), April 1985; ''Earthwork Odyssey'' by Eleanor Munro in *Christian Science Monitor* (Boston), 25 March 1987; ''Touching the Sky: Conversations with Four Contemporary Artists'' by Janet Saad-Cook in *Archaeoastronomy,* April, 1987; ''Nancy Holt Brings the Heavens Down to Earth,'' by Carey Lovelace in *Arts: New Jersey,* Fall, 1987; ''Nancy Holt's ''Sky Mound'': Adaptive Technology Creates Celestial Perspectives,'' by Terry Ryan Leveque, in *Landscape Architecture,* April/May, 1988; ''Nancy Holt: Pipes and Tracks'' by Altti Kuusamo in *Strata* (catalog), 1992; ''Nancy Holt: Reconnecting to the Stars'' by Barbara C. Matilsky in *Fragile Ecologies,* New York 1992; ''A Park with Emptiness Below'' by Michael Leccese in *Landscape Architecture,* April 1993; ''Nancy Holt, Artiste Perceptuelle'' by Anne-Francoise Penders in *Pratiques* (Paris), no.3–4, Fall 1997; ''Gardens and the Death of Art'' by Stephanie Ross in *Landscape Architecture,* July 1998; ''Unbuilt Roads'' by Hans Ulrich Obrist in *Contemporary Visual Arts* (London), no. 20, 1998.

*

All of my work is involved with site, time, inside vs. outside space, orientation in space (often in some way astronimically designated), and aspects of perception—light, space, framing, focus.

Since 1969 my primary concern has been in making sculpture in the landscape or in open urban spaces using stone, concrete, brick, and steel. Although sometimes indoor spaces—entire rooms—are used as sites, the sites, both in and outdoors, are an integral part of the sculptures—the ideas for the works developing out of my involvement with the sites.

The sculptures of concrete, brick, stonemasonry, earth and steel evolve out of their sites and are concerned with, among other things, perception and space—changes in scale at various distances, perceptual disorientation between inside and outside space, and seeing in depth through layered openings and tunnels. Each work draws the viewer within its structure, creating a sense of transition from outside to inside, and often from light to dark. The works surround and enclose but at the same time frame and extend out to the horizon in the distance.

Natural elements—sunlight, stars, water, plants, earth, are part of the substance of the works. Patterns of sun and moonlight, astronomical alignments, and/or water reflections often bring the sky to earth, turning the landscape upside down, while astrally fixing each work in its site.

Some recent sculptures are functional, using systems of basic technology such as plumbing, electricity, drainage and heating to make often complex labyrinthian sculptures which can be walked through and turned on and off by the viewer.

The films, videotapes, and book, also conceived of in a perceptual framework, are usually evocations of landscapes or displacements of places. Indications of space (through tracking, pans, aerial, and walking shots) and aspects of nature—sunlight patterns, billowing dust, water reflections—are caught visually and transported elsewhere via film through time, while the psychology of the place is disclosed through the local voices, sounds, and/or music in the sound tracks or accompanying text.

—Nancy Holt

HOLZER, Jenny

Nationality: American. **Born:** Gallipolis, Ohio, 29 July 1950. **Education:** Ohio University, Athens, 1971–72, BFA 1972; Rhode Island School of Design, Providence, 1975–77, MFA 1977; independent study program fellowship, Whitney Museum, New York, 1977. **Family:** Married to Michael Glier, 1984; 1 child. **Career:** Independent artist, New York, since 1977. **Awards:** Blair Award, 79th Americans Show, Art Institute of Chicago, 1982; Golden Lion Award, best pavillion, 44th Venice Biennale, 1990; Planet of Europe, gold medal for title, gold medal for design Art Directors Club Europe, 1993; Skowhegan medal for installation Skowhegan School for Painting and Sculpture, 1994; Honorary Doctorate of Arts, Ohio University, 1994; Crystal award for outstanding contribution to cross-cultural understanding, World Economic Forum, Cologny-Geneva, Switzerland, 1996. **Agent:** Galerie Crousel-Robelin Bama, 40 rue Quincampoix, 75004 Paris, France.

Individual Exhibitions:

1978 Project Studio, New York
Franklin Furnace Window, New York
1979 Fashion Moda Window, Bronx, New York
Printed Matter Window, New York
1980 Galerie Rüdiger Schöttle, Munich
Onze Rue Clavel, Paris
1981 Le Nouveau Musée, Lyon, France
Museum für (Sub) Kultur, West Berlin
1982 Barbara Gladstone Gallery, New York
Galerie Chantel Crousel, Paris
American Graffiti Gallery, Amsterdam
Artists Space, New York
A Space, Toronto
1983 Barbara Gladstone Gallery, New York
Lisson Gallery, London
Institute of Contemporary Arts, London
Institute of Contemporary Arts, Philadelphia
1984 *Sign on a Truck,* Grand Army Plaza/Bowling Green Plaza, New York
Dallas Museum of Art, Texas
Kunsthalle, Basel
Cranbrook Museum, Bloomfield Hills, Michigan
Seattle Art Museum, Washington
1985 Barbara Gladstone Gallery, New York
Galerie Monika Spruth, Cologne
Contemporary Arts Center, Cincinnati (with Cindy Sherman)
Am Hof, Vienna (with Keith Haring)
Israel Museum, Jerusalem (with Barbara Kruger)
1986 Des Moines Art Center, Iowa (toured the United States, 1986–88)
1987 Rhona Hoffman Gallery, Chicago
1988 Institute of Contemporary Art, London
Interim Art Gallery, London
Brooklyn Museum, New York
Cleveland Center for Contemporary Arts, Cleveland
1989 Guggenheim Museum, New York
Dia Art Foundation, New York
Ydessa Hendeles Art Foundation, Toronto
1990 Biennale, Venice
Stadische Kunsthalle, Dusseldorf
1991 Laura Carpenter Fine Art, santa Fe
Louisiana Museum, Humlebaek, Denmark
Albright-Know Gallery, Buffalo, New York
Walker Art Gallery, Minneapolis
1992 Ydessa Hendeles Art Foundation, Toronto
Hammond Galleries, Lancaster, Ohio
Claremont Graduate School, California
North Dakota Museum of Art, Grand Forks
1993 St. Peters Church, Cologne
Haus der Kunst, Munich
Barry Whistler Gallery, Dallas
Dallas Museum of Art
1994 Barbara Gladstone Gallery, New York
Bergen Museum of Art, Norway
1997 *Jenny Holzer: Lustmord,* Contemporary Arts Museum, Houston (catalog)
1998 *En Vie,* Galerie Yvon Lambert, Paris

Selected Group Exhibitions:

1980 *Issue,* Institute of Contemporary Arts, London
1981 *Westkunst,* Messehallen, Cologne
1982 *Documenta 7,* Museum Fridericianum, Kassel, West Germany (and *Documenta 8,* 1987)
1984 *Biennale of Sydney,* Art Gallery of New South Wales, Sydney
1985 *Kunst mit Eigen-Sinn,* Museum moderner Kunst, Vienna
1986 *In Other Words,* Corcoran Gallery of Art, Washington, D.C.
1988 *Committed to Print,* Museum of Modern Art, New York
1990 *High and Low,* Museum of Modern Art, New York

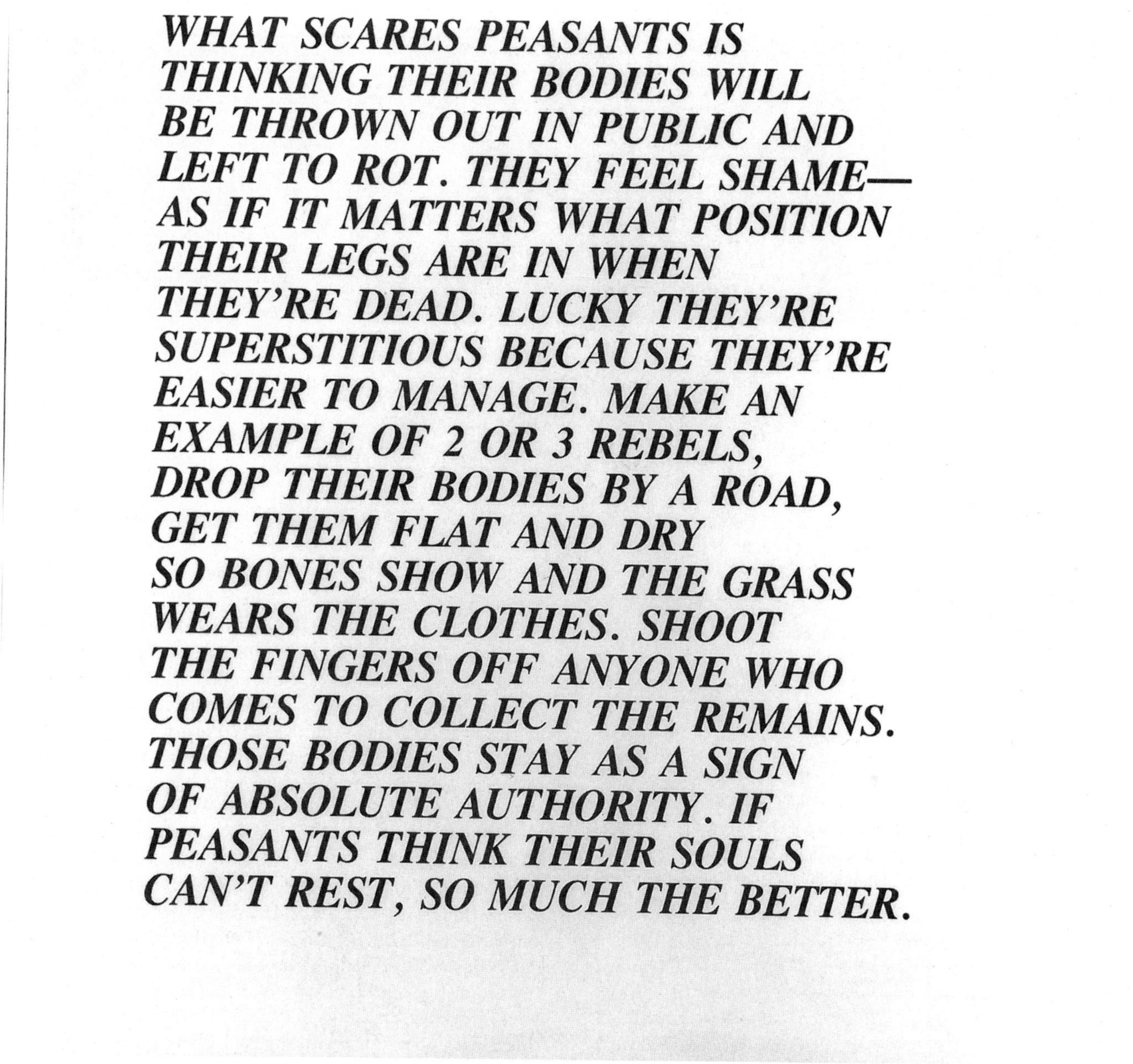

WHAT SCARES PEASANTS IS THINKING THEIR BODIES WILL BE THROWN OUT IN PUBLIC AND LEFT TO ROT. THEY FEEL SHAME— AS IF IT MATTERS WHAT POSITION THEIR LEGS ARE IN WHEN THEY'RE DEAD. LUCKY THEY'RE SUPERSTITIOUS BECAUSE THEY'RE EASIER TO MANAGE. MAKE AN EXAMPLE OF 2 OR 3 REBELS, DROP THEIR BODIES BY A ROAD, GET THEM FLAT AND DRY SO BONES SHOW AND THE GRASS WEARS THE CLOTHES. SHOOT THE FINGERS OFF ANYONE WHO COMES TO COLLECT THE REMAINS. THOSE BODIES STAY AS A SIGN OF ABSOLUTE AUTHORITY. IF PEASANTS THINK THEIR SOULS CAN'T REST, SO MUCH THE BETTER.

Jenny Holzer: *Inflammatory Essays ("What Scares Peasants Is...")*, 1979–82. ©2001 Jenny Holzer/Artists Rights Society (ARS), NY.

Culture and Commentary: An Eighties Perspective, Hirshhorn Museum and Sculpture Garden, Washington, D.C. (catalog)

1991 *Metropolis,* Walter Gropius Bau

1993 *Virtual Reality,* Guggenheim Museum, New York

1995 *Text and Art,* Logan Art Gallery, Australia (catalog)

Rosebud: Jenny Holzer, Matt Mullican, Lawrence Weiner, Kunstbau Lenbachhaus, Munich (catalog)

Articulations, Whitney Museum of American Art, New York (catalog)

In Five Words or Less: The Use of Language in Art, Museum of Modern Art at Heide, Bulleen, Australia (catalog)

1996 *The Art of the Body: The Body Exposed from Man Ray to Today,* MAC Galeries Contemporaines des Musees de Marseille, france (catalog)

1997 *Public Works,* Stedelijk Van Abbemuseum, Eindhoven, Netherlands (catalog)

Art/Fashion, Guggenheim Museum SoHo, New York (catalog)

Jenny Holzer: *Unex Sign #1: Selections from the Survival Series (Laugh Hard at the Absurdly Evil),* 1983. Photo by Geoffrey Clements. Collection of Whitney Museum of American Art, New York, Purchase, with funds from Louis and Bessie Adler Foundation, Inc., Seymour Klein, President. ©Jenny Holzer/Artists Rights Society (ARS), New York.

1998 National Gallery of Australia, Canberra
1999 *48th Venice Biennale,* Italy

Collections:

Museum of Modern Art, New York, Whitney Museum, New York; Centro Cultural Arte Contemporaneo, Polanco, Mexico City; Tate Gallery, London; Musée d'Art Moderne, Paris; Kunsthalle, Bern; Kunsthaus, Zurich; Museum of Contemporary Art, Chicago; Stedelijk Van Abbemuseum, Eindhoven; National Gallery of Canada, Ottawa.

Publications:

By HOLZER: Books—*A Little Knowledge,* New York 1978; *Black Book,* New York 1979; *Hotel,* with Peter Nadin, New York 1980; *Living,* with Peter Nadin, New York 1980; *Eating through Living,* with Peter Nadin, New York 1981; *Eating Friends,* with Peter Nadin, New York 1981; *Abuse of Power Comes As No Suprise: Truisms and Essays,* Halifax, Nova Scotia 1983; *Jenny Holzer: Writing,* with Noemi Smolik, Stuttgart, 1996; *Jenny Holzer,* with David Joselit, Renata Salecl and Joan Simon, London 1998. **Articles—**interview with Patrick JB Flynn in *The Progressive,* vol. 57, no. 4, April 1993; ''Jenny Holzer: *Wired* Interviews the Artist and Self-described Multi-disciplinary Dweeb,''interview by Burr Snider in *Wired,* February 1994; ''Jenny Holzer Live Chat Session Transcript,'' May 23, 1995, at *Club Hotwired,* http://adaweb.walkerart.org/context/artists/holzer/transcript.html; interview with Tamara Winikoff in *Artlink,* vol. 18, no. 2, June/August 1998; interview with Anne O'Hehir in *Artonview,* no. 14, Winter 1998.

On HOLZER: Books—*Jenny Holzer,* exhibition catalog, Basel and Lyon 1984; *New Art,* edited by Phyllis Freenan, Eric Himmel, Edith Pavese and Anne Yarrowsky, New York 1984; *Jenny Holzer/Keith Haring: Protect Me from What I Want,* exhibition catalog with texts by Hubert Klocker and Peter Pakesch, Vienna 1986; *Jenny Holzer/Cindy Sherman,* exhibition catalog with essay by Dennis Barrie, Cincinnati 1986; *Jenny Holzer: Signs,* exhibition catalog, Des Moines 1986; *Jenny Holzer,* with essay by Diane Waldman, New York 1989; *Jenny Holzer: The Venice Installation,* Buffalo 1990; *Jenny Holzer* by Michael Auping, 1992; *Leucht-Schrift-Kunst: Holzer, Kosuth, Merz, Nannucci, Nauman* by Andrea Domesle, Berlin 1998. **Articles—**''Jenny Holzer'' by Carter Ratcliff in *The Print Collector's Newsletter,* November/December 1982; ''Jenny Holzer'' by Elke Town in *Parachute,* Summer 1983; *Artwords 2,* Ann Arbor 1988; ''Jenny Holzer'' by Roy MacPherson in *Splash,* Summer 1988; ''Signs of the Times'' by Kay Larson in *New York,* 5 September 1988; ''Jenny Holzer Sees Aphorism as Art'' by Paul Taylor in *Vogue,* November 1988; ''The Only Immortal'' by Donald Kuspit in *Artforum,* February 1990; ''Jenny Holzer'' by Brigitte Granzen in *Kunstforum International,* no. 146, July-August 1999.

* * *

Since the end of the 1970s Jenny Holzer has distanced herself from those currents of contemporary New York art which place the highest premium on plasticity. Abandoning traditional techniques, she has elected to use language as her principal means of expression, so that we are obliged to locate her work in a no-man's-land between writing and the visual arts where the artist is, by her own definition, a communications specalist in the sense of a social mediator: ''It's strange; I don't even basically think of myself as an artist. Perhaps I'm half artist, half one of those odd individuals who stick up notices all over the place. Or perhaps just a universal voice'' (J. H.).

The words of Jenny Holzer's language do not form part of a conceptual discourse or of a semiological interpretation of the work of art, as they may do for Joseph Kosuth for example, nor do they concretise a political debate, as in the work of Hans Haacke. Presented in a mediatory form accessible to the public at large, they are, like the graffiti in the underground, above all subversive and interventionary, destabilising the imagery and depersonalised vocabulary of various information sectors.

Printed in capitals on plain paper, Holzer's first texts appeared in 1978 on the facades of public buildings in various quarters of New York, at the entrance to a bank, or a shop, or on already crowded hoardings. Taking possession of a collective space already saturated with symbols, the artist's placards, by their multiplication of messages, the studied neutrality of their format, and the shock quality of their content, could ''at the very least, suggest or demand a response, a stand on the part of the spectator'' (J. H.).

The first two series, *Truism* (1978) and *Inflammatory Essays (1979–1982),* are made up of short phrases which are written as affirmations or imperatives and sound like judgments or convey personal points of view with regard to the basic facts of daily life (sleep, food, money), or relate, in a more general way, to events and social situations which are sometimes cruel and violent, sometimes falsely trivial: ''PRIVATE PROPERTY CREATED CRIME,'' ''YOU MUST REMEMBER YOU HAVE FREEDOM OF CHOICE,'' ''INHERITANCE MUST BE ABOLISHED,'' etc. The artist does not intervene as critic, arbiter or denunciator, but takes a back seat behind a reality which is its own self-contradiction. Jenny Holzer's sentences pose as fragments of conversations or personal thoughts gleaned from a whole variety of socio-cultural milieus, from racial minorities, from men and from women, and whose sum total is no more than a web of contradictions denying supposed truths and revealing instead the fragmentation of society, its taboos and its crimes.

In a third series entitled *Living* (1981–1982) the texts are punctuated with paintings by the American artist Peter Nadin representing portraits of men and women, hands, an eye, faces and bodies trivialised by the simplicity of the lines and by the fact that they are attached to metal supports reminiscent of traffic signals. The discourse reflects on topics such as the family, work, religion and the relationships based on hate, fear, pain and power which they imply. This more personal and incisive quality is intensified in the work that followed in 1983, *Survival Series.* From there the artist went on to develop other frameworks capable of increasing the visual impact of her works: illuminated signs, particularly well-suited to conveying information in the New York environment, and self-adhesive notices placed at strategic points (telephone kiosks, fountains, traffic lights . . .). Holzer's works have also been on exhibition in art galleries and museums, where they form ''lecture tours'' studied in terms of a fixed visual unity.

In 1986 Holzer exhibited *Under a Rock,* an architectural construction in the form of a set of granite blocks engraved with various texts in gold lettering. These austere pieces, which inevitably make one think of funeral monuments, seem to be balancing the solemn immortality of the writing with the precariousness of human life. Other sculptural pieces—such as a marble bench onto the seat of which the artist has inscribed text—achieve a similar kind of false monumentality, with the civic permanence and sense of moral uplift implied by their materials undercut by the contradictory, ironic, and inconclusive nature of the aphorisms they bear.

Jenny Holzer's texts have also been made into books and video films. For one of these films, projected on to a giant screen outside the Centre Pompidou in Paris (1987), the artist presented an interrupted succession of anonymous faces, each seen close up and each spouting a sentence previously selected from *Truisms.* The spectator's preference for a certain type of message and his or her rejection of another points to one of the most fundamental aspects of this artist's work, the aim of which is to provoke reactions, thereby leading to an active participation on the part of the public.

In recent years Holzer has moved further away from the simplicity and formal sobriety with which she presented her early *Truisms. Lustmord* (German for ''sex murder''), 1993–94, takes as its subject rape and the ritualized, socially sanctioned perpetration of violence towards women. The main component of this multimedia installation consists of a large cave-like structure with two three-dimensional, red LED displays pulsing on its exterior; and a dim interior, upholstered in red-leather, with hand-tooled text in small letters. The texts and LEDs give voice to three perspectives on rape, that of victim, perpetrator, and onlooker. They narrate in clipped cadences phrases such as ''I am awake in the place where women die,'' or ''The color of her inside out is enough to make me want to kill her.'' In another part of the installation, viewers may handle an array of human bones, banded with engraved silver, laid out like specimens on a table. Color photographs of the same phrases appear again, handwritten in red on the Caucasian-colored flesh of a woman's stomach. With its aura of theatricality, of acute pain, and conversely, of impersonality and technological detachment, Holzer's meditation on fear, aggression, and injustice invites complex readings. Her use of language to explore extreme states of emotion and sensation here stretches the testimonial powers of language in the visual arts to new and acute ends.

—Essay by Dominique Liquois; updated by Dorothy Valakos

Jenny Holzer's use of text in public spaces shifted naturally into a more global realm in the mid-1990s, when she began using the Internet as an interactive gallery for her work. Sponsored by the Walker Art Center in Minneapolis, the web site features the piece *Please Change Beliefs.* Scores of Holzer's notable ''Truisms'' are listed here, and visitors to the site are encouraged to alter the statements or add their own truisms. These reworked texts become a part of the ever-growing list, ensuring particpatory thought on the type of social commentary Holzer creates. She has continued to explore the arena of the World Wide Web, with experiments in QuickTime movies and streaming audio and video. In 1994, the Guggenheim Museum SoHo featured *World War II,* a virtual reality piece sponsored by Intel and programmed by Sense8, a Sausalito based company. Visitors donned a virtual reality head-mount which enabled them to see and hear villagers describing atrocities they experienced. Said Holzer, ''it seemed that it would be much more immediate if the material was spoken by men and women rather than printed out.''

Holzer's *Black Garden* was created in Germany in 1995. An apparent extension of such works as *Lamentations,* done in the late 1980s, this work is another ''anti-memorial.'' Holzer describes the *Black Garden* as a space with many black or dark red plants and ''terrible texts on garden benches'' derived from the sentence, ''I am awake in the place where women die.'' Holzer continues to create interactive public works with a strong intention of social commentary on subjects as diverse as AIDS and human suffering in situations of war. A structurally similar piece is a permanent installation at the Castle's Square at the Centre for Contemporary Art in Warsaw, Poland. Ten stone benches are featured with commentaries carved into them from the ever-growing list of ''Trusims'' and from her ''Texts on Survival.'' In 1999, Holzer initiated a Sculpture Garden project in the neighborhood adjacent to the museum's Ujazdowski Castle.

Ohio University (where Holzer earned her B.F.A.) commissioned a piece in 1996 for Gordy Hall, the facility for the departments of linguistics and modern languages and the Ohio Program of Intensive English. Again text was used, streaming across an indoor LED panel, and dark green granite benches are featured both inside and outside the building. The text is written in various languages, a technique Holzer employed in her work at the Venice Biennale in 1990. It is obious that Holzer continues to push the boundaries of human expression, communication, and language in her installations and sculptural works.

—Tammy A. Kinsey

HONEGGER, Gottfried

Nationality: Swiss. **Born:** Zurich, 12 June 1917. **Education:** Kunstwerbeschule, Zurich, 1932; apprentice window-dresser, Zurich, 1933–36; studied graphic design, under Warja Lavater, Zurich, 1937–39. **Military Service:** Served in the Swiss Army, 1939–45: corporal. **Family:** Married Warja Lavater in 1940; daughters: Bettina and Cordelia. **Career:** Independent painter, sculptor and graphic artist, in Zurich from 1939, in New York 1957–60, and in Paris from 1961. Instructor, Kunstgewerbeschule, Zurich, 1937–39; visiting instructor, University of Dallas, 1969–70. **Member:** Swiss Werkbund, Zurich, 1944–45, and Association Internationale des Graphistes, 1952–56; Secretary, Swiss Graphic Artists Union, 1953–56. **Awards:** Guggenheim Award, 1964; Bovard Purchase Prize, *Carnegie International,* Pittsburgh, 1967; Medal of Honor, City of Rennes, 1992; medal, Akademie von Poitier, 1993. **Agents:** Gimpel-Hanover + Andre Emmerich Galerien, Todistrasse 40, 8002 Zurich; Galerie Muller-Roth, Blumenstrasse 25,7000 Stuttgart 1; Galerie Liliane et Michel Durand-Dessert, 3 rue des Haudriettes, 75003 Paris; and Annely Juda Fine Art, 4th Floor, 23 Dering Street, London W1S 1AW England. **Addresses:** 4 rude de Thorigny, 75003 Paris, France; Limmatstrasse 107,8005 Zurich, Switzerland. **Website:** http://www.ghonegger.ch.

Individual Exhibitions:

1950 Galerie Chichio Haller, Zurich
1951 George Wittenborn Gallery, New York
1952 Galerie 16, Zurich
1958 Galerie Laubli, Zurich
1960 Martha Jackson Gallery, New York
1961 Galerie Fillon, Paris
1962 Galerie Lawrence, Paris
1963 *Tableaux-Reliefs, Sculpture,* Gimpel und Hanover Galerie, Zurich
1964 Martha Jackson Gallery, New York
Gimpel Fils, London
1965 Galerie M. E. Thelen, Essen
Gimpel und Hanover Galerie, Zurich
1966 Württembergischer Kunstverein, Stuttgart
Gimpel und Hanover Galerie, Zurich
1967 Kunsthaus, Zurich
1968 Gimpel Fils, London
Museum am Ostwall, Dortmund, West Germany
Galerie Heseler, Munich
1969 Valley House Gallery, Dallas
1970 Galerie M. E. Thelen, Cologne
1971 Gimpel und Hanover Galerie, Zurich
Galerie Quader, Chur, Switzerland
1972 Valley House Gallery, Dallas
Galerie Swart, Amsterdam
Bilder, Plastiken, Graphik, Badischer Kunstverein, Karlsruhe, West Germany
Galerie Teufel, Cologne
White Gallery, Lutry-Lausanne, Switzerland
1974 *Tableaux-Reliefs 1971–1973,* Gimpel und Hanover Galerie, Zurich, Switzerland
Galerie d'Art Moderne, Basel
Galerie Denise René, Paris
1975 Galerie Muller, Stuttgart
Galerie Denise René, Paris
French Pavilion at the *Bienal,* Sao Paulo
1976 Gimpel und Hanover Galerie, Zurich
1977 Galerie Seestrasse, Rapperswill, Switzerland
Acht Rote Bilder/Acht blaue Bilder, Gimpel und Hanover Galerie, Zurich
1978 Musée d'Art Moderne de la Ville, Paris
Abbaye de Senanque, Gordes, France
Galerie Nouvelles Images, The Hague
1979 Trudelhaus Foundation, Baden, Switzerland
Annely Juda Fine Art, London
Gimpel und Hanover/André Emmerich Galleries, Zurich
1980 Galerie Muller-Roth, Stuttgart
Ulmer Museum, Ulm, West Germany
1981 Atelier Lafranca, Lugano, Switzerland
Le Coin du Miroir, Dijon, France
1982 Galerie Muller-Roth , Stuttgart
1983 Gimpel-Hanover-Emmerich Galerien, Zurich
Galerie Durand-Dessert, Paris
Juda/Rowan Gallery, London
Galerie Nouvelles Images, The Hague
1984 Galerie Konstruktiv Tendens, Stockholm
Galerie Convergence, Nantes, France
Kunsthaus, Zug, Switzerland
Sculpture Park, Lille, France
1985 Galeries de la Vieille-Charite, Marseille, France
Galerie Lupke, Frankfurt
1990 *Gottfried Honegger,* Gallery Georges Verney-Carron, Villeurbanne, France
1994 *Sculptures en Plein Air,* Stadthaus Uster, Uster
1995 Galerie Konstruktiv Tendens, Stockholm
1996 *10 Sculptures—Il Fallait une Vie,* Villa Aurélienne, Fréjus
Hyundai Gallery, Seoul

Galerie Jaques Girard, Toulouse
1997 *1983–1997,* Gallery Georges Verney-Carron, Villeurbanne, France
Tableaux-reliefs Petits Formats, Galerie Gilbert Brownstone, Paris
From Canvas to Space, Galerie Dorothea van der Koelen, Mainz (catalog)
1998 *Apprendre à Regarder,* Galerie G. Verney-Carron, Villeurbanne
Bilder und Skulpturen, Victor Hotz, Steinhausen
Centre Culturel Aragon, Oyonnax
1999 *Métamorphose,* Fondation Cartier pour l'Art Contemporain, Paris (catalog)
Corréard & Cie, Galerie Brownstone, Paris
Galerie ProArta, Zurich

Selected Group Exhibitions:

1958 *Kunst und Naturform,* Kunsthalle, Basel
1961 *Avant-Gard '61,* Städtisches Museum, Trier, West Germany
1962 *Carnegie International,* Carnegie Institute, Pittsburgh
1965 *Salon des Réalités Nouvelles,* Musée d'Art Moderne, Paris (and 1966, 1968)
1971 *The Swiss Avant-Garde,* New York Cultural Center
1972 *12 Ans d'Art Contemporian en France,* Grand Palais, Paris
1975 *Bienal,* Sao Paulo
1976 *Mouvement Peint Mouvement Agi,* Abbaye de Beaulieu-en-Rouerge, France
1980 *Art in Switzerland,* at the *Kunstmesse,* Basel
1988 *The Non-Objective World Revisited,* Annely Juda Fine Art, London
1994 *Quand je n'ai plus de Bleu, je Peins en Rouge,* Galerie Gisèle Linder, Basel
Nemours—Morellet—Honegger, Galerie Gisèle Linder, Basel
Art et Mathématiques, Goethe Institut, Nancy
1995 *Kleine Bilder,* Gesellschaft für Kunst und Gestaltung, Bonn
Reliefs et Découpes, Galerie Lahumière, Paris
Geométrisk Abstraktion XIV, Galerie Konstruktiv Tendens, Stockholm
1997 *Apprendre à Regarder: Gottfried Honegger, Sylvie Garraud,* Gallery Georges Verney-Carron, Villeurbanne, France
Gottfried Honegger, François Morellet, Bernar Venet: 1975–1997, Gallery Georges Verney-Carron, Villeurbanne, France
Art et Vêtement, Espace de l'Art Concret, Château de Mouans-Sartoux, France
1998 *Entre Métal et Végétal,* Académie de Nice, France
Règle et Déviance, Musée d'Art et d'Histoire, Neuchatel
Wand Bezogen, Galerie St. Johann, Saarbrücken
Konstruktive Kunst in der Schweiz, Frankfurter Kunstverein, Germany
1999 *Aurélie Nemours,* Réunion des Musées Nationaux, Paris (catalog)
2000 *Kunstkabinett am Goetheplatz,* Stadtmuseum Weimar, Weimar

Collections:

Kunsthaus, Zurich, Switzerland; Centre National d'Art Contemporain, Paris; Musée Cantini, Marseilles; Marie-Louise and Gunnar Didrichsen Art Foundation, Helsinki; Israel Museum, Jerusalem; Carnegie Institute, Pittsburgh; Dallas Museum of Fine Arts; Hirshhorn Museum, Washington, D.C.; Museum of Modern Art, New York; Princeton University Art Museum, New Jersey.

Publications:

By HONEGGER: Books—*Hommage à Cercle et Carre,* with Michel Seuphor, Zurich 1964; *Memoria,* with Jean-Yves Mock, Frankfurt 1985; *Gottfried Honegger: Art et Architecture,* with François Barré, Ambros Uchtenhagen and Udo Kultermann, Zurich 1993; *Le Vide est Plein,* Paris 1995. **Articles—**''Gottfried Honegger: The Art of Naivety, the Art of Truth,'' an interview with Thomas West in *Art International,* no. 4, Autumn 1988.

On HONEGGER: Books—*Gottfried Honegger,* exhibition catalog with text by Aleksis Rannit, New York 1960; *Honegger,* exhibition catalog with text by Herbert Read, Paris 1962; *Gottfried Honegger: Tableaux-Reliefs, Sculpture,* exhibition catalog with text by Herbert Read, Zurich 1963; *Gottfried Honegger,* exhibition catalog with text by Udo Kultermann, Essen 1965; *La vocation des mots* by Michel Seuphor, Lausanne, Switzerland 1966; *Gottfried Honegger,* exhibition catalog with texts by René Wehrli, Michel Seuphor, Udo Kultermann and others, Zurich 1967; *Neue Dimensionen der Plastik* by Udo Kultermann, Tübingen 1967; *The New Sculpture* by Udo Kultermann, London 1968; *Gottfried Honegger: Bilder, Plastiken, Graphik,* exhibition catalog with texts by Jorg Walter Koch, Willy Rotzler and Michel Seuphor, Karlsruhe, West Germany, 1972; *12 ans d'art contemporain en France,* exhibition catalog with texts by Francois Mathey, Daniel Cordier, Jean Clair and others, Paris 1972; *Gottfried Honegger: Works from 1939 to 1971* by Kurt W. Forster, Herbert Read, Willy Rotzler and others, Teufen, Switzerland, 1972; *Gottfried Honegger: Tableaux-Reliefs 1971–1973,* exhibition catalog with text by Max Frisch, Zurich 1974; *Gottfried Honegger: Acht rote Bilder/Act blaue Bilder,* exhibition catalog with texts by Willy Rotzler and Helmut Heissenbuttel, Zurich 1977; *Gottfried Honegger,* exhibition folder with text by Max Fritsch, Zurich 1979; *Peintres Suisses* by Marcel Joray, Zunich 1982; *Goffried Honegger: Tableaux/Relief/Skulpturen, 1971–83,* Zurich and Paris 1983. **Articles—**''To Love, Refuse Tragedy'' by Jean-Yves Mock in *Cimaise,* vol. 35, April/May 1988; ''Gottfried Honegger: Rêve d'Humanisme'' by Marielle Ernould-Gandouet in *L'Oeil* (Lausanne), no. 440, April 1992; ''Honegger, Radi Designers e Douglas: Colore, Forma e Musica a Parigi'' by Chiara Alpago-Novello in *Arte,* no. 308, April 1999; ''Artiste du Mois: Gottfried Honegger'' by Catherine Francblin in *Beaux Arts Magazine,* no. 180, May 1999.

*

If my work up to the year 1970 was based upon a definite programme, I have since been using—while still keeping up the idea of the programme—a calculation of probabilities; I submit myself to the aleatory game.

''Chance and necessity'' have become the terrain of my researches. This method gives me greater liberty and a link with the scientific thought of today. All my pictures and my sculptures, whether symmetrical or asymmetrical, are the result of this new conception.

The colour is monochrome, the treatment of the surface is subjective and completes the objectivity of forms. The sensual skin, the material of graphite and of colour are sustained by a geometry as simple as a spinal column. The relief of the pictures is obtained by a collage on canvas. Light, catching it, introduces the game of chance.

Fifteen years ago, I would have willingly explained the meaning of my work, its function, its goal. I knew exactly what I was doing and why.

Brought up in the spirit of the Bauhaus, I thought that art should improve the quality of life, of furnished and unfurnished rooms. I saw art as a means for reforming society.

Today, I have turned my back on the idealism which dominated part of my life. I produce a visual reality whose image is revealed in relation to the cultural landscape in which I am inscribed.

The meaning comes as much from what I show as from what I reject. Art can not be the maidservant of a morality without questioning the research into the unknown.

The mute and materialist language of my painting is above all an electrocardiogram of my existence.

—Gottfried Honegger

* * *

In all of his canvases Gottfried Honegger links a very simple geometric structure to a semi-monochrome—similar to ''color-field'' painting. Thus he links the constructivist thinking which is more common in Europe than American with the absolute predominance of color as in the paintings of Barnett Newman or Mark Rothko. Honegger spent three years in New York from 1957 to 1960. His first-hand experience of American art could explain the link in his work between the two artistic languages of opposite character.

Influenced by a first taste of modern painting at Picasso's exhibition in Zurich in 1933, Honegger has tended to make the shapes that inhabit his canvases strictly geometric. He discovered the problem of dialectic, that is to say the tension that arises in painting comprised of contradictions. His paintings of the 1950's and 60's are characterized by a dichotomy between structured and non-structured planes or by the opposition of irregular, open surfaces and those which are hidden, closed. When he created his first sculptures at the beginning of the 1960's, he created a synthesis of the rough and smooth, of the worked and unworked form. In 1963 he began to limit his formal language to elementary geometric forms: the circle, the square the triangle. It is a language that seems to him to be rigorous, objective and anonymous. It also possesses a certain vulnerability. He always adheres to a very restrained structure, without metaphor or symbolic meaning, regular to the point of monotony, but expressive of our desire for sensuality. He shows that pictorial material is not only to be ''thought'' but also to be ''felt.''

If geometry corresponds to the mathematical and scientific character of the modern world, then the emphasis of the manual intervention of the artist must satisfy our wish for a subjective and individual space for desire. He does not translate this wish through images or hallucinations but through his method of treating material. ''Concept'' and ''material"are the two essential elements of Honegger's work; its ''theme'' is their confrontation. The concept is defined through geometry in all of its solidity: its character is transparent and intelligible. Then the unforeseen element appears through the introduction of a calculated risk or the movement of the paint. Hence, the geometric forms run the risk of being disturbed or destroyed, and the perfection of the conceptual grid is smashed as if living had triumphed over the ideal.

In Honegger's work, contingency has many functions: it creates disorder within the world posited by science, an enclosed world subject to natural law; it represents the creative and innovative principle necessary for the evolution of life; it acts as the artist's advocate for the subjective, however disguised; finally, it has the task of confusing all meanings that might be imposed through geometry. Weary of the mass of images and messages that constitute our world, Honegger would like our art to be one in which contradictions destroy all assertions, an art that has nothing more to say other than through its materiality, beauty, form and substance. Behind this apparently brusque and anti-social attitude lies that ancient Platonic ideal, which influenced Bauhaus thinking and which therefore has strongly influenced Honegger, the conviction that beauty, goodness and usefulness are of necessity identical.

—Marie Luise Syring

HONERT, Martin

Nationality: German. **Born:** 26 May 1953 in Bottrop. **Education:** Staatliche Kunstakademie Dusseldorf, 1981; Meisterschüler Prof. Fritz Schwegler, 1985. **Career:** Professor, Hochschule für Bildende Künste, Dresden, since 1988. **Awards:** Peter-Mertes-Stipendium, Bonn; Renta-Preis, Neremberg; Kunstpreis der Böttcherstrasse, Bremen. **Agent:** Galerie Johnen & Schöttle; Kamekestrasse 21, D-50672, Cologne, Germany; 303 Gallery, 525 West 22nd Street, New York, New York 10011.

Individual Exhibitions:

1988 Galerie Johnen & Schöttle, Cologne
Galerie Rüdiger Schöttle, Munich (with Elke Denda)
1989 ''de Appel,'' Amsterdam (with Katharina Fritsch and Thomas Ruff)
1990 Galerie Johnen & Schöttle, Cologne
1991 Galerie Rüdiger Schöttle, Munich
1993 Galerie Rüdiger Schöttle, Munich
1994 Museum für Moderne Kunst, Frankfurt am Main (catalog)
1997 Museu d'Art Contemporani de Barcelona, Spain
1999 Matthew Marks Gallery, New York

Selected Group Exhibitions:

1990 *Carnet de Voyages,* Foundation Cartier, Jouy-en-Josas, France
1991 *Anni '90,* Galleria Comunale d'Arte Moderne, Bologna (travelled to Cattolica and Rimini, Italy)
1992 *Biennale,* Sydney
Post Human, Musée d'Art Contemporain, Pully/Lausanne (travelled to Turin, Athens, and Hamburg)

Qui, quoi, où?, Musée d'Art Moderne de la Ville, Paris
Museum für Moderne Kunst, Frankfurt
1993 *Biennale,* Venice (also 1995)
Menschenwelt (Interieur), Portikus Frankfurt (travelled to Turin; Norfolk, England; Stuttgart; and Munster) (catalog)
1994 Ecole Nationale des Beaux Arts, Bourges
Jahresmuseum 1994, Kunsthaus Mürzzuschlag, Austria (catalog)
1995 *Szenenwechsel,* Museum für Moderne Kunst, Frankfurt am Main
46th Venice Biennale, Venice Italy
Exposition Artistes/Architectes, Le Nouveau Musée/ Institut, Villeurbanne, France
Zwei und Zwanzig: Peter Mertes Stipendium 1985–1995, Bonner Kunstverein, Bonn (catalog)
1996 *Group Show,* 303 Gallery, New York
Private View, Bowes Museum, Barnard Castle, England (catalog)
1997 *Zuspiel,* Siemens Kulturprogramm, Cantz (catalog)
1998 *The House in the Woods,* Centre for Contemporary Art, Glasgow (catalog)
1999 *Vergiß den Ball und Spiel'weiter,* Kunsthalle Nürnberg
ZOOM—Ansichten zur Deutschen Gegenwartskunst, Sammlung Landesbank Baden-Württemberg, Kunsthalle zu Kiel
Unsichere Grenzen, Kunsthalle zu Kiel, Germany (catalog)
Mesto—Zeme—Reka, Institut für Auslandsbeziehungen Stuttgart, Goethe-Institut Praha, Brno (catalog)
Von Beuys bis Cindy Sherman: Die Sammlung Lothar Schirmer, Kunsthalle Bremen, Germany
2000 *Interventions: New Art in Unconventional Spaces,* Milwaukee Art Museum, Wisconsin (catalog)

Collections:

Museum für Moderne Kunst, Frankfurt; Kunsthalle, Bremen; Kunsthalle, Nuremberg; Musée des Beaux Arts, Montreal.

Permanent Public Installations:

Museum für Moderne Kunst, Frankfurt.

Publications:

By HONERT: Articles—''Mind's Eye Views,'' interview with Boris Groys in *Artforum International,* vol. 33, no. 6, February 1995; interview with Heinz-Norbert Jocks in *Kunstforum International,* no. 131, August/October 1995.

On HONERT: Exhibition catalogs—*Carnet de voyages 1,* Jouy-en-Josas 1990; *Anni Novanta,* Bologna 1991; *Martin Honert,* Bonn 1991; *Elisabeth-Schneider-Stiftung,* Freiburg 1992; *Post Human,* New York 1992; *Qui, quoi, où?,* Paris 1992; *The Boundary Rider,* Sydney 1992; *Martin Honert: The Model Child,* Bourges 1993; *Martin Honert* by Jean-Christophe Ammann, Frankfurt 1994. **Articles**—''Martin Honert'' by Julian Heynen in *Das Kunstwerk,* no. 4–5, 1988; ''Martin Honert. Pia Stadtbäumer'' by Andreas Denk in *Kunstforum International,* March/April 1991; ''Martin Honert: Out of the Deadpan'' by José Lebrero Stals in *Flash Art,* no. 171, 1993; ''Martin Honert: Out of the Deadpan'' by José Lebrero Stals in *Flash Art (International Edition),* no. 171, Summer 1993; ''Martin Honert'' by Julian Heynen in *Artist,* no. 20, 1994; ''Mind's Eye Views'' by Boris Groys in *Artforum,* February 1995; ''Zum Beispiel: Martin Honert—Arbeit an der Erinnerung'' by Jean-Christophe Ammann in *Kunst+Unterricht,* no. 192, May 1995; ''Look and Learn'' by James Roberts in *Frieze* (London), no. 27, March-April 1996.

HORN, Rebecca

Nationality: German. **Born:** Michelstadt, 24 March 1944. **Education:** Studied at the Hochschule für Bildende Künste, Hamburg, 1964–70. **Career:** Independent artist in film, video, and performance, Hamburg, 1968–71, London, 1971–72, in West Berlin, 1973–75, New York and West Berlin, 1976–80; since 1980, Berlin and Paris. Guest lecturer, California Art Institute, Los Angeles, and University of California at San Diego, 1974; professor at Hochschule der Künste, Berlin, since 1989. **Awards:** Deutsche Akademische Austendienst (D.A.A.D.), Fellowship to London and West Berlin, 1971–72; Kritikerpreis, West Berlin, 1975; Arnold Bode Prize, *Documenta 8,* Kassel, 1986; Pittsburger Carnegie International Grand Prize, 1988; Tragerin des Kaiserrings Goslar, 1992; Medienkunstpreis Karlsruhe, for achievement in technology and art, 1992. **Address:** Uhlandstrasse 144, 10719 Berlin, Germany.

Individual Exhibitions:

1973 Galerie René Block, West Berlin
1975 Galleria Saman, Genoa
1976 René Block Gallery, New York
Galleria Saman, Genoa
Galerie H, Graz, Austria
1977 *Zeichnungen, Objekte, Fotos, Video, Filme,* Kölnischer Kunstverein, Cologne (travelled to the Hausam Waldsee, West Berlin)
Galleria Ala, Milan
1978 *Der Eintanzer,* Kestner-Gesellschaft, Hannover
Galleria Saman, Genoa
1978 Van Abbemuseum, Eindhoven, Netherlands
Kunstverein, Münster, West Germany
Gallery Ala, New York
1982 *La Ferdinanda: Sonate für eine Medici-Villa,* Staatliche Kunsthalle, Baden-Baden, West Germany
Stedelijk Museum, Amsterdam
Galleria Saman, Genoa
1982 Galerie Gewad, Ghent, Belgium
1983 Galerie Eric Franck, Geneva
Centre d'Art Contemporain, Geneva
Kunsthaus, Zurich
Serpentine Gallery, London
John Hansard Gallery, Southampton, Hampshire
1984 Serpentine Gallery, London
Museum of Contemporary Art, Chicago
1985 Galerie Eric Franck, Geneva

1986 Marian Goodman Gallery, New York
Project Studio One, New York
ARC/Musee d'Art Moderne, Paris
Museum of Contemporary Art, Los Angeles
1987 Galerie Konrad Fischer, Dusseldorf
Galerie Elisabeth Kaufmann, Zurich
Marian Goodman Gallery, New York
1988 Marian Goodman Gallery, New York
Galerie de France, Paris
1989 *Missing Full Moon,* Bath International Festival, Bath
1990 *Diving through Buster's Bedroom,* Museum of Contemporary Art, Los Angeles
Marian Goodman Gallery, New York
1991 *Chorus of the Locus,* Galerie Franck & Schulte, Berlin
Galerie de France, Paris
Elisabeth Kaufmann Galerie, Basel
Marian Goodman Gallery, New York
1992 *El Rio de la Luna,* Fundacio Espai Poblenou, Barcelona
Mayor Gallery, London
Galerie de France, Paris
1993 Guggenheim Museum, New York (retrospective; travelled; catalog)
Van Abbemuseum, Eindhoven, Holland
1994 Nationalgalerie, Berlin
Kunsthalle, Vienna
Tate Gallery, London
Serpentine Gallery, London
1997 Kestner Gesellschaft, Das Neue Haus, Hannover
1998 Marian Goodman Gallery, New York
1999 Centre for Contemporary Art, Warsaw
Institute for Foreign Cultural Relations, Stuttgart

Selected Group Exhibitions:

1972 *Documenta 5,* Kassel, West Germany
1974 *Projekt '74,* Kunsthalle, Cologne
Video Artists, Museum of Modern Art, New York (travelled to the Institute of Contemporary Art, Philadelphia)
1975 *9th Biennale of Paris,* Musée d'Art Moderne de la Ville, Paris
1977 *Documenta 6,* Kassel, West Germany
1979 *Biennale of Drawing,* Nuremburg
1982 *Documenta 7,* Kassel, West Germany
1983 *Sculpture from Germany,* San Francisco Museum of Modern Art (toured the United States)
1985 *The European Iceberg,* Art Gallery of Ontario, Toronto
1987 *Wien Fluss,* Theater am Steinhof, Vienna
1994 *The Box from Duchamp to Horn,* Ubu Gallery, New York
1997 *Sequences: A Portfolio of Work by 29 Artists,* Edition Shellmann, New York (catalog)
Venice Biennale, Venice
1998 Premiere Biennale de Montréal

Collections:

Kunsthalle, Hamburg, Kestner-Gesellschaft, Hannover; Kölnischer Kunstverein, Cologne; Staatliche Kunsthalle, Baden-Baden, West Germany; Van Abbemuseum, Eindhoven, Netherlands; Stedelijk Museum, Amsterdam; Museum of Modern Art, New York; Anthology Film Archives, New York.

Publications:

By HORN: Books—*Dialogo della Vedova Paradisiaca,* Genoa 1976; *Die chinesische Verlobte,* exhibition catalog, Baden-Baden 1977; *Rebecca Horn: La Lune Rebelle,* 1993. **Films—***Der Eintanzer,* New York, 1978; *Die Chinesische Verlobte,* New York, 1978; *La Ferdinanda, Artemino,* 1981. **Videos—**numerous productions, including *Conversation I, New York,* 1972; *Transformation, New York, 1972–73; Exercises, New York,* 1973; *Bleistiftmaske, Hamburg,* 1973; *Performances, Hamburg,* 1973; *Mit beiden Handen gleichzeitig die Wande beruhren Blinzeln,* 1975; *Zwischen den Feuchten Zungenblattern,* 1974–75; *Mit zwei Scheren gleichzeitig Haare schreiden,* 1974–75; *Berlin—Unbungen in neun Stucken,* 1974–75; *Paradieswitwe 1/Paradieswitwe 2,* installation piece, 1975; *Die Chinesische Verlobte,* 1975; *Ubung zu: Der Eintanzer,* 1976.

On HORN: Books—*Il Carpo come Linguaggio* by Lea Vergine, Milan 1974; *Rebecca Book I* by Timothy Brann, West Berlin 1975; *Rebecca Horn,* exhibition catalog with text by Horst Gerhard Haberl, Graz, Austria 1976; *Rebecca Horn: Zeichnungen, Objekte, Fotos, Video, Filme,* exhibition catalog with texts by Wulf Herzogenrath, Marlis Gruterich, Timothy Baum, Lucy R. Lippard and Zdenek Felix, Cologne 1977; *Rebecca Horn: Der Eintanzer,* exhibition catalog edited by Carl-Albrecht Haenlein, texts by Marlis Gruterich and Roland H. Wiegenstein, Hannover 1978; *Rebecca Horn: La Ferdinanda: Sonate für eine Medici-Villa,* exhibition catalog with texts by Katherine Schmidt and Germano Celant, Baden-Baden, West Germany 1981; *Documenta 7 Katalog/Band 2,* with texts by R. H. Fuchs, Gerhard Storck, Germano Celant and Coosje van Bruggen, Kassel, West Germany 1982. **Articles—**''Rebecca Horn, Imminent Danger'' interview by Régis Durand in *Art Press,* no. 181, June 1993; ''Horn's Dilemma'' by Kim Levin in *The Village Voice,* vol. 38, no. 32, 10 August 1993; ''Rebecca Horn'' by Ann Wilson Lloyd in *Sculpture,* March/April 1993; ''Vanity and Gravity'' by Robert Mcgee in *Border Crossing,* Autumn 1993; ''Rebecca Horn: The Machinery of Longing'' by George Melrod in *Atelier,* no. 801, 1993; ''Rebecca Horn: Danger Imminent'' by Thomas Shannon in *Art Press,* no. 181, June 1993; ''Fountain of Mercury, a Piano Spitting Out Keys: Sculpture as Drama'' in *The New York Times,* 2 July 1993; ''Rebecca Horn, Solomon R. Guggenheim Museum'' by M.R. Rubenstein in *ARTnews,* vol. 92, no. 7, September 1993; ''Mechanics Illustrated'' by Robert Hughes in *Time,* vol. 142, no. 11, September 1993; ''The Mind-Body Problem'' by Kay Larson in *New York Magazine,* vol. 26, no. 37, September 20, 1993; ''Rebecca Horn'' by Dena Shottenkirk in by Roberta Smith in *Art and Antiques,* October 1993; ''Rebecca Horn at the Guggenheim'' by Karen Wilkin in *The New Criterion,* vol. 12, no. 2, October 1993; ''A Wily Dreamer's Poetic Gadgets'' by Amei Wallach in *New York Newsday,* vol. 53, no. 304, 4 July 1993; ''Art, the Guggenheim Museum'' in *The New Yorker,* 26 July 1993; ''Rebecca Horn: Delicacy and Danger'' by Holland Cotter in *Art in America,* vol. 81, no. 12, December 1993; ''Rebecca Horn'' by K. Marriott Jones in *Artforum,* February 1994; Essays by Gilbert Lascault and Werner Spies in special issue of *Parkett,* no. 40–41, 1994; ''Round the Horn'' interview by Stewart Morgan in *Frieze,* September/October 1994; ''Rebecca Horn'' by

Gregory Volk in *ARTnews,* March 1995; ''Rebecca Horn—Chorus of Locusts I and 11, 1991'' by Svetlana Alpers in *Artforum,* Summer 1996.

*

Entering this room for the very first moment—a room as a completely remote and isolated world of itself; enclosed in its own continuity, formed by the memory of those who have lived here before . . . .

The walls, mirrors, and windows—all living their own singular life and experience—breathing and changing continuously in harmony with the intensity of the ever-changing light.

You feel of these pasts alive in the objects which surround you, simultaneously evoking new associations and sensations—creating new and unoccupied space for your own fantasies. If you actually decide to inhabit this room, your daydreams will enlarge and become more intense; independence will re-arise as you become increasingly alive.

The only fact that will be unsure: Whether that story has already taken place or is now beginning to develop as an extension of the room itself . . . .

Until the new skin of events mingles so completely with the rest of the room that it finally becomes identical with the old skin.

—Rebecca Horn

In her work Rebecca Horn has inaugurated a new medium, which in its intensity and fascination explores dimensions of art previously unknown. By means of poetical imagination, mostly manifested in actions or processes, the artist has created a sensibility of great significance. In the center of all of her actions is the human being, specifically the body of woman, which is related to objects or instruments. The goal of Rebecca Horn is a ritual of initiation, which can not be achieved by means of rational argumentation; but which in its complexity provokes changes in the perceiving viewer or participant.

Born in 1944, the artist studied in Hamburg and in London and has taught in different countries. Through her actions in Italy, Netherlands, Austria and the USA she has become one of the most important protagonists of international performance art. Her actions date back to 1968 when she began using the human body as a vehicle to communicate an experience which transcends the former bordelines of painting, sculpture, dance and pantomine. Since 1970 most of her works have been documented in films and since 1972 in video.

Rebecca Horn's early works, such as *Arm-Extensions (Arms Extensionen)* of 1968, *Cornucopia-Seance for Two Breasts (Cornucopia-Seance fuer zwei Brueste* of 1970 and *Unicorn (Einhorn)* of 1971 use extensions of the body through which emotional and social forms of behavior are made transparent. The action *Pencil Mask (Bleistiftmaske)* of 1973 resembles magic ethnological rituals. In her work *Finger-Gloves (Handschuhfinger)* of 1972 fingers are extended through the use of light sticks of wood with which the artist touches certain objects but at the same time remains in a prescribed distance from them. In *Cockfeather Mask (Hahndefermaske)* of 1973 this principle is further extended into an interpersonal contact. In *Berlin Exercises in Nine Pieces (Berlin-uebungen in neun Stuecken)* of 1974/1975 these tendencies are fully explored and details of the human body by means of extension and magnets are manipulated into an orchestrated vocabulary. *Measure Box (Messkasten)* of 1975 brings the human body in contact with a container, the human form and the mechanical apparatus relate to each other in a newly imaginative manner.

One of the culminations of the work of Rebecca Horn is *Paradise Widow (Paradieswitwe)* of 1975, an installation which was documented on video and had a highly suggestive significance. In this work an imaginative manifestation of unconscious processes and projections is realized in a precise and carefully planned form. In the years since 1975 Rebecca Horn's vocabulary has extended into a wide range of thematic areas: *The Chinese Fiancee (Die Chinesische Verlobte)* of 1976 and especially *The Dancing Cavalier (Der Eintaenzer)* of 1978 explore new possibilities, the latter work for the first time as a film with actors and a continuous script. Earlier elements of Horn's art are here incorporated into a more comprehensive ensemble of human body, objects and processes. The sensibility of woman remains in the center, and dimensions of an art experience which in previous times was unexplored are made possible.

Later works by Rebecca Horn also incorporate space, and musical forms. *Dialogue Between Two Swings (Der Dialog der Zwillingsschaukeln)* of 1979 is with a musical composition by Hans Werner Henze. In *La Ferdinanda-Sonata for a Medici Villa (La Ferdinanda-Sonate fuer eine Medici Villa)* of 1981 several earlier tendencies are synchronized, and container, objects, feathers and human beings are elements of a larger ensemble which brings out mysterious and irrational realities. Works of recent years, such as *The Box of the Phoenix* of 1983, include alchemistic themes in a further extension of her earlier thematics and the theme of couples, such as *The Engaged Couple (Die Verlobten)* and *The Hybrid (Der Zwitter),* both of 1987. The essence of all her works are, as the artist in 1972 articulated it, attempts at ''creating new models of interaction rituals,'' a creative exploration of processes between human beings, their isolation and physical communication, their emotional and physical interrelatedness.

The creative development of Rebecca Horn since 1989 has radiated into several new areas, all encompassing, in a creative dialogue between the mechanics and the organics, energies manifesting emotional values in physical processes. More intensely than in her earlier works the focus is on symbols such as feathers, eggs, knifes, hammers, and elements of the alchemist such as lead, glass, coal, mercury, ink, and sulphur; in general it is movement, memories, the unpredictability of events and the frailties of human existence that dominate her art. In 1990 she created in collaboration with Jannis Kounellis and Heiner Mueller in Berlin the site-specific event *The Finitude of Freedom—A Moral Action Not an Exhibition.* Of major importance is her second feature film *Buster's Bedroom* of 1990 starring Donald Sutherland, Geraldine Chaplin, Valentia Cortese, and David Warrilov, as well as her mysterious constructions *The Kiss of the Rhinoceros* of 1990, *The Chorus of the Locust I and II* of 1991. The culmination of her recent work is the environment *El rio de la luna* in the Hotel Peninsular in Barcelona of 1992.

—Udo Kultermann

HORN, Roni

Nationality: American. **Born:** New York, New York, 1955. **Education:** Rhode Island School of Design, B.F.A. 1975, and Yale University School of Art, an M.F.A. 1978. **Career:** Installation artist;

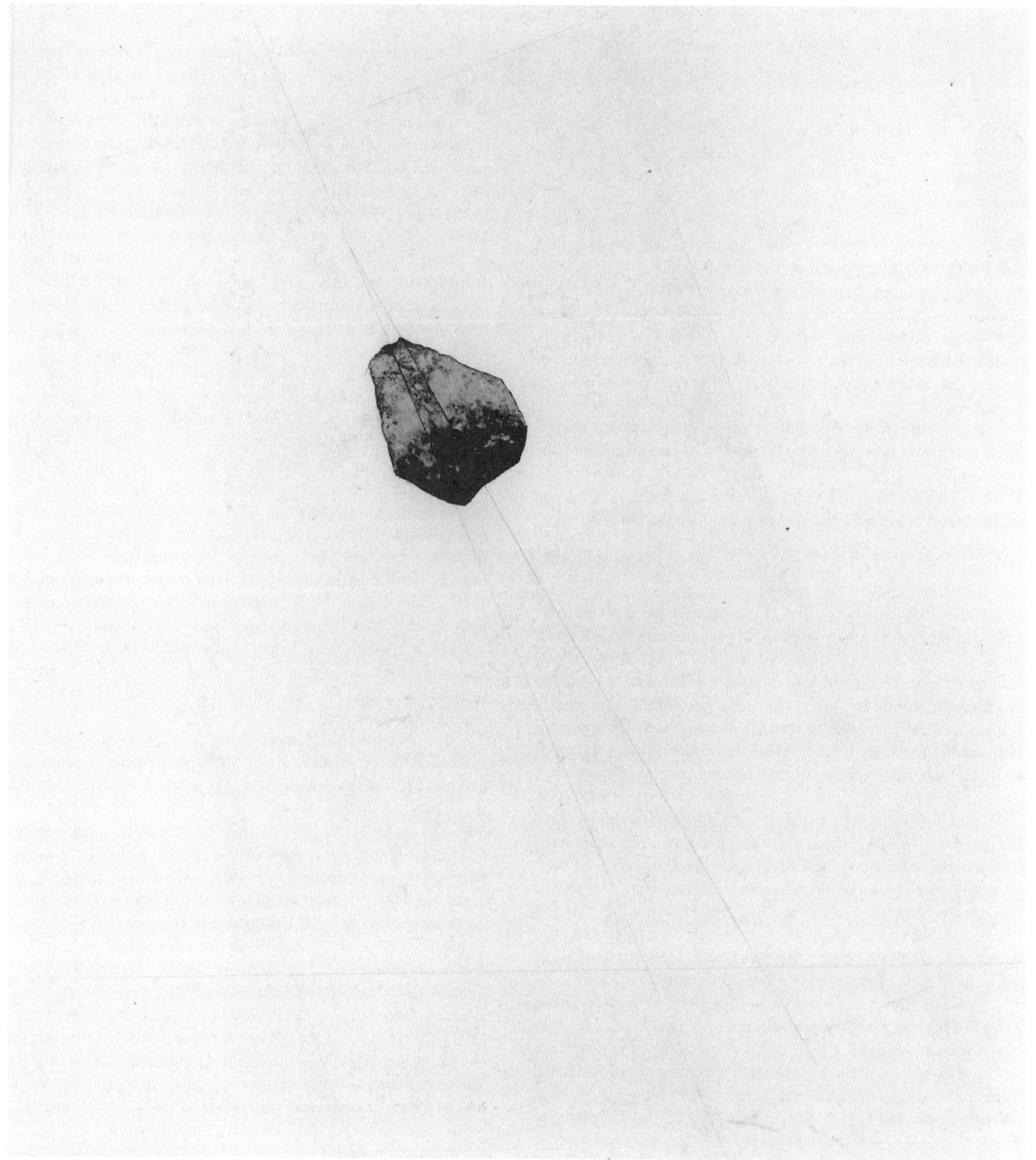

Roni Horn: *The XXXI,* 1989. Photo by Geoffrey Clements. ©Collection of the Whitney Museum of American Art, Purchase, with funds from the Norman and Rosita Winston Foundation, Inc.

photographer. **Awards:** Three, NEA Artists' Fellowships; Alpert Award in the Arts, 1998.

Selected Individual Exhibitions:

1995 Matthew Marks Gallery, New York, New York
St. Louis Museum of Art, St. Louis, Missouri
Jablonka Galerie, Cologne, Germany Sammlung Goetz, Munich, Germany
Making Being Here Enough, Kunsthalle, Basel, Switzerland (traveled)
1996 Earths Grow Thick, Wexner Center for the Arts, Columbus, Ohio (traveled)
You Are the Weather, German Meteorological Authority, Munich, Germany (permanent installation)
1997 You Are the Weather, Fotomuseum Winterthur, Winterthur, Switzerland
Jablonka Galerie, Cologne, Germany
Raffaella Cortese, Milan, Italy
Ingólfsstræti 8, Reykjavík, Iceland
Matthew Marks Gallery, New York, New York
Yous in You, Bahnhof Ost, Basel, Switzerland (permanent installation)
1998 You Are the Weather, De Pont Foundation for Contemporary Art, Tilburg, Holland Museum für Gegenwartskunst, Basel, Switzerland
Pooling (You), Jablonka Galerie, Cologne, Germany
Gallery Xavier Hufkens, Brussels, Belgium
Patrick Painter Gallery, Los Angeles, California
1999 Pi, Jablonka Galerie, Cologne, Germany
Pi, Matthew Marks Gallery, New York, New York
Events of Relation, Musée d'Art Moderne de la Ville de Paris, France
Still Water, CAPC Musée d'Art Contemporain, Bordeaux, France

Selected Group Exhibitions:

1976 Corning Museum of Glass, Elmira, New York
Seattle Museum of Art, Seattle
1980 The Material Object, Hayden Gallery, M.I.T., Cambridge
1983 Kunstraum, Munich
1995 Corners, Paula Cooper Gallery, New York, New York
Matthew Marks Gallery, New York, New York
Margo Leavin Gallery, Los Angeles, California
In a Different Light, University Art Museum, Berkeley, California
Word for Word, Beaver College Art Gallery, Glenside, Pennsylvania
1996 Thinking Print, Museum of Modern Art, New York
From Beuys to Trockel—Contemporary Drawings from the Kunstmuseum Basel, Centre Georges Pompidou, Paris, France
Artist's Books, Brooke-Alexander Gallery, New York, New York
Open Secrets, Matthew Marks Gallery, New York, New York and Fraenkel Gallery, San Francisco, California
Elsewhere, John Hansard Gallery, University of Southampton, England
Recent Acquisitions, Museum of Modern Art, New York
1997 Sleight of Mind/The Angle of a Landscape, (Roni Horn and Gabriel Orozco) Center for Curatorial Studies Museum, Bard College, Annandale-On-Hudson, New York Galerie Nächt St. Stephan, Vienna, Austria
Venice Biennale, Venice, Italy
Density of the Unimaginable Museum, Centre d'Art Contemporain du Domaine de Kerguehennec, Bignan, France
1998 Maverick, Matthew Marks Gallery, New York
View 2, Mary Boone Gallery, New York
Pi, Sydney Biennale, Sydney, Australia
Travel & Leisure, Paula Cooper Gallery, New York
Surrogate: The Figure in Contemporary Sculpture and Photography, Henry Art Gallery, University of Washington, Seattle

Publications:

By HORN: Books—*Bluff Life,* Book I of *To Place,* New York, 1990; *Folds,* Book II of *To Place,* New York, 1991; *Lava,* Book III of *To Place,* New York, 1992; *Pooling Waters,* Book IV of *To Place,* Cologne, Germany 1994; *Verne's Journey,* Book V of *To Place,* Cologne, Germany 1995; *Haraldsdottir,* Book VI of *To Place,* Denver, Colorado 1996; *Arctic Circles,* Book VII of *To Place,* Denver, Colorado 1998; *Another Water,* New York 2000.

On HORN: Books—*Pair Objects I, II, III,* with text by Jeremy Gilbert-Rolfe, Paris and New York 1988; *Roni Horn: Inner Geography* (exhibition catalog), Baltimore 1994; *Making Being Here Enough: Installations from 1980 to 1995* (exhibition catalog), Basel 1995; *Earth Grows Thick* (exhibition catalog), Ohio 1996; *Artists at Work: Inside the Studios of Today's Most Celebrated Artists* by David Seidner, New York 1999; *Roni Horn* by Louise Neri, London 2000.

* * *

Roni Horn employs a wide range of media in her work using sculpture, photography, text, drawings and the book form to explore the parameters of visual expression. There is a strong formal link to the language of minimalism particularly in her sculptural objects that duplicate geometric shapes and, at the outset, present a concise proposition of form. The clarity and idealism of the minimalist statement, however, is troubled by the artist, often through repetition, as in "Piece for Two Rooms," 1986–87 where a single object encountered by the viewer appears again in a separate room. The doubling calls into question the unique appearance of the first piece and opens up a field of comparison between the two identical objects, which in turn raises questions identity and difference. The significance of Horn's art thus lies at the edge of the visible—it is a phenomenological approach that privileges perception and being. In the site-specific commission "Yous in You," 1997–2000 a passageway of alternating hard and soft rubber tiles cast from an Icelandic basalt formation created for a railway station in Basel, Switzerland, Horn relies on sensory cues to signal the shifting density underfoot. The experience of Horn's work engages an individual's sense of being-in-the-world and relates that changing perspective to the flux of everyday life. For instance, the installation piece, "You are the

Weather,'' 1994–95, presents a set of 100 photographs of a young woman's face in linear succession around four walls. There is no beginning and no end, we are caught in her gaze, her head and shoulders always immersed in water, her countenance always the same and yet always different. Minute variations lap over one image to the next, and the usually imperceptible stirrings of individual identity are here captured in the association of different atmospheric light conditions. This piece was recorded in Iceland, a landscape the artist has made integral to her work. Horn revisits Iceland as place and inspiration the way other artists might return to a favourite material. The geological formations and lush green scenery framed in photographs rework the romantic tradition in art in a contemporary setting.

Water is also a recurrent theme in her work from the onomatopoeic utterances drawn on paper of ''Gurgles, Sucks, Echoes,'' 1993, to the photographs of the flowing current in ''Still Water (The River Thames, for Example),'' 1999, that give visual form to the philosophical statement of Heraclitean flux. Each image is littered with tiny numbers that refer to footnotes of text at the bottom of the print. The words literally insert a stream of consciousness into the river photographs with fact, observation and speculation mapped onto the visual field. *Another Water,* 2000, continues this text/image reflection in book format, one of several publications Horn has made that extends her artistic enquiry into the intimate realm of reading. Although her book projects bear a close relation to gallery works, with photographs often migrating between wall and page, it is important not to read the published editions as illustrations; they are independent investigations that deliberately eschew the public context of gallery display. Horn's art has strong literary ties. In works such as ''Key and Cues,'' 1994, the artist gives sculptural form to poetic fragments by Emily Dickinson and elsewhere she has evoked the writings of Kafka and Jules Verne. The ambiguity of poetic language finds resonance in the phenomenological complexity of Roni Horn's art, an art that is itself on the edge of visual and linguistic expression.

—Fiona Kearney

John Hoyland with Princess Margaret attending an exhibition at the Whitechapel Gallery, London, 1968. ©Hulton-Deutsch/Corbis.

HOYLAND, John

Nationality: British. **Born:** Sheffield, Yorkshire, 12 October 1934. **Education:** Sheffield College of Art, Yorkshire, 1951–56; Royal Academy Schools, London, 1956–60. **Career:** Independent painter, in Kingston-upon-Thames, Surrey, 1963–68, in Market Lavington, Wiltshire, 1968–73, and in London since 1970: visited New York, 1964, and associated with Helen Frankenthaler, Barnett Newmann, Robert Motherwell and other American painters, and subsequently spent long periods living and working in New York, 1967–79, and in Los Angeles, 1982. Lecturer, Croydon College of Art, Surrey, 1962; Lecturer, 1962, and Principal Lecturer, 1965, Chelsea School of Art, London; Charles A. Dana Professor of Fine Arts, Colgate University, Hamilton, New York, Spring/1972; Visiting Teacher, St. Martin's School of Art, Royal Academy Schools, and Slade School of Fine Art, all London, 1974–77; Artist-in-Residence, Studio School, New York, 1978, and Melbourne University, Australia, 1970; Teacher, Slade School of Fine Art, London, 1980, 1983. **Awards:** Gulbenkian Foundation Purchase Award, 1963; Peter Stuyvesant Bursary, 1964; International Young Artists Award, Tokyo, 1964; Prize, *John Moores Exhibition,* Liverpool, 1965; Prize, *Open Painting Exhibition,* Belfast, 1966; First Prize (with Robyn Denny), *Edinburgh Open 100* exhibition, 1969; First Prize, Chichester National Art Exhibition, 1975; First Prize, *John Moores Exhibition,* Liverpool, 1983; First Prize, Athena Art Awards, London, 1987. **Agent:** Waddington Galleries, 2 Cork Street, London W1. **Address:** 41 Charterhouse Square, London EC1, England.

Individual Exhibitions:

1964 Marlborough New London Gallery
1965 Chelsea School of Art, London
1967 Whitechapel Art Gallery, London
Waddington Galleries, London
Galerie Heiner Friedrich, Munich
Robert Elkon Gallery, New York
Nicholas Wilder Gallery, Los Angeles
Waddington Fine Art, Montreal

1968 Waddington Fine Art, Montreal
1969 Robert Elkon Gallery, New York
Waddington Galleries, London
Leslie Waddington Prints, London
Beinal, Sao Paulo (with Anthony Caro)
1970 Waddington Galleries, London
André Emmerich Gallery, New York
Galleria dell' Ariete, Milan
1971 Waddington Galleries, London
André Emmerich Gallery, New York
Waddington Fine Art, Montreal
1972 Leslie Waddington Prints, London
André Emmerich Gallery, New York
Harcus-Krakow Gallery, Boston
Picker Gallery, Colgate University, Hamilton, New York
1973 Waddington Galleries, London
Galleria I'Approdo, Turin
1974 Nicholas Wilder Gallery, Los Angeles
Waddington Galleries, London
Studio La Città, Verona
1975 Waddington Fine Art, Montreal
Galleria E, Bolzano, Italy
Waddington Galleries, London
1976 Galleria La Bertesca, Milan
Galerie Modulo, Porto Modula, Lisbon
Waddington Galleries, London
Studio La Città, Verona
1978 Waddington Fine Art, Montreal
Waddington Galleries, London
1979 André Emmerich Gallery, New York
Bernard Jacobson Ltd. New York
Waddington Fine Art, Toronto
Serpentine Gallery, London (travelled to the Birmingham City Art Gallery, and Mappin Art Gallery, Sheffield, Yorkshire)
Art Contact, Coconut Grove, Florida
1980 University of Melbourne
Galerie von Braunbehrens, Munich
Kammer Galerie, Hamburg
1981 Waddington Galleries, London
Gumps Gallery, San Francisco
1982 Jacobson/Hochman Gallery, New York
Bernard Jacobson Gallery, Los Angeles
Compass Gallery, Glasgow
1983 Waddington Galleries, London
Hokin/Kaufman Gallery, Chicago
1984 Castlefield Gallery, Manchester, Lancashire
1985 Waddington Galleries, London
1986 Waddington and Shiell, Toronto
1987 Waddington Galleries, London
Oxford Gallery, Oxford
Lever/Myerson Gallery, New York
1990 Waddington Galleries, London
1991 Eva Cohan Gallery, Chicago
1992 Graham Gallery, New York
Prints Josine Barhoven Gallery, Amsterdam
1994 CCA Galleries, London
Annandale Galleries, Sydney
1995 *John Holyand: Bali Paintings,* Theo Waddington Fine Art, London

Selected Group Exhibitions:

1959 *Young Contemporaries,* RI Galleries, London
1964 *The New Generation,* Whitechapel Art Gallery, London (toured the U.K.)
1965 *Biennale des Jeunes,* Musée d'Art Moderne de la Ville, Paris
1968 *New British Painting and Sculpture,* University of California at Los Angeles (toured the United States)
1973 *La Peinture Anglaise aujourd'hui,* Musée d'Art Moderne de la Ville, Paris
1976 *Arte Inglese Oggi,* Palazzo Reale, Milan
1978 *Critics' Choice,* Institute of Contemporary Arts, London
1982 *Aspects of British Art Today,* Metropolitan Art Museum, Tokyo (toured Japan)
1984 *English Expressionism,* Warwick Arts Trust, London
1987 *British Art in the 20th Century: The Modern Movement,* Royal Academy, London (travelled to the Staatsgalerie, Stuttgart)
1990 Peter Stuyvesant Foundation, Holland, Spain, France
1991 *Affinities in Paint,* Crane Gallery, London
1992 *The Poetic Trace: Aspects of British Abstraction Since 1945,* Adelson Galleries, New York
1993 *National Collection of Modern Art,* Tate Gallery, Liverpool
Royal Academy of Arts, Sackler Gallery, London
1994 *Here and Now,* Serpentine Gallery, London
The First Harlech Biennale 1994, Parc Tanycastell, Harlech, Wales
1997 *Lisbon: British Art 1960 to the Present,* Fundacao Calouste Gulbenkian, Lisbon
2001 *Five Masters of Imagination,* Graves Art Gallery, London

Collections:

Royal Academy of Arts, London; Tate Gallery, London; Victoria and Albert Museum, London; National Museum, Helsinki; Albright-Knox Art Gallery, Buffalo, New York; Colgate University, Hamilton, New York; Phoenix Museum, Arizona; Art Gallery of South Australia, Adelaide; University of Sydney.

Publications:

By HOYLAND: Articles—"John Hoyland Talking to Colin Painter," interview, in *Aspects* (Newcastle-on-Tyne), Autumn 1981; "Hoyland at Home," interview with Mike van Joel, in *Art Line* (London), February 1983; "Painting is the head, hand and the heart," interview with Liz Finch, in *Ritz* (London), June 1984; "On Colour," interview with Sally-Ann Schilling, in *The Artist* (London), September 1986.

On HOYLAND: Books—*The New Generation,* exhibition catalog by David Thompson, London 1964; *John Hoyland: Paintings 1960–67,* exhibition catalog by Bryan Robertson, London 1967; *Late Modern* by Edward Lucie Smith, New York 1969; *Anthony Caro/John Hoyland,* exhibition catalog, Sao Paulo 1969; *John Hoyland,* exhibition catalog by Bryan Robertson and others, London 1979; *John Hoyland,* exhibition catalog by John McEwen, London 1987; *John Hoyland* by Mel Gooding, New York, 1990; *John Hoyland* by Bryan Robertson, London, 1994; *John Holyland: Bali Paintings,* exhibition catalog, Theo Waddington Fine Art, London. **Articles—** "John Hoyland" by

Bryan Robertson in *Modern Painters,* vol. 7, Spring 1994; ''John Hoyland'' by William Feaver in *Art News,* vol. 95, January 1996; review by Richard Shone in *Burlington Magazine* (London), no. 1129, vol. 139, April 1997.

* * *

John Hoyland's painting is rich and subtle. It has evolved continually since 1960 from a linear, often symmetrical, abstraction to a free, painterly and complex arrangement of fields of intensely colored paint. His work may be considered as a celebration of the qualities of paint as an independent medium. His pictures are generally occupied by distinct shapes or forms, but the characteristic silhouettes and the relationships between these have changed over the years.

The pictures of 1963 contained forms that were isolated from the flatly painted background but adhered together in the illusory space by touching or intertwining with one another. A group in the mid-60s comprise roughly rectilinear forms, architecturally assembled on a ground that is stained so as to appear veil-like or transparent. Some of these are built up from the edges and so appear to lie in the plane of the canvas; others are not so strictly located. However, any certainty may be contradicted by the intrusion of diagonals and is more subtly subverted by the spatial effects of the combinations of colors chosen and of the varying densities of the paint. In some cases these forms completely fill the field and may suggest an extension into the real space around the painting.

The scale of these paintings was often very large; one might say architectural.

The occasional runs or drips of liquid paint that occur in these pictures became increasingly dominant in works of the late 60s and 70s in which Hoyland's own development had led him close to the concept of painting taught and exercised by Hans Hofmann. As before, the composition was dominated by a single colour or pair of colors and a specific division of the canvas. His paint became thicker as well as more vivid and often unexpected in hue. The painterly ''objects'' within the picture were organized and related to one another by a skillfully deployed range of devices harmonically related to the dominant division. Among them were conspicuous superimposition of forms, discontinuous surfaces which allow lower strata to show through, reinforced or frayed out edges, parallels and angular divergences, and juxtaposition of similar or of contrasting hues and shades.

One is always very much aware of the artist having worked on and built on the surface. In general the characteristics of the works of the early and mid 70s was rectilinearity, diagonals forming the necessary exception.

The most recent paintings, that is those since about 1977–78, have been increasingly dominated by the diagonal. At first, this figured as a structural division of the canvas. In the last two or three years the paint has become less luxuriant, pictures have often been smaller in scale, and the objects in them formed of diagonals, that is they are lozenges, like the diamonds of a pack of cards, which have broken free and float in the picture of space.

Hoyland shows no sign of repeating himself or abandoning his basic approach to painting, which has a vitality and range comparable to that of any artist who has more directly looked for refreshment to nature itself.

—Michael Compton

HRDLICKA, Alfred

Nationality: Austrian. **Born:** Vienna, 27 February 1928. **Education:** Studied art under Albert Gutersloh and Josef Dobrowsky, Vienna, 1946–53, and painting, under Fritz Wotruba, Vienna, 1953–57. **Career:** Painter, sculptor and graphic artist, Vienna, since 1958. Head of painting classes. Summer Academy, Salzburg 1963; Instructor, Akademie der Bildende Künste, Stuttgart, 1971–75, and Hochschule für Künste, Hamburg, 1973. **Awards:** Ehrenpreis, Vienna, 1961; First Prize, *Graphics Biennale,* Ljublijana 1963; Bianco e Nero Prize, Lugano, Switzerland 1964; First Prize, *Biella Internazionale,* Italy, 1965; Graphics Prize, *5th Print Biennale,* Tokyo 1966; Graphics Prize, *7th International Exhibition of Gravure,* Ljubljana, 1967; Golden Laurel Award, Künstlerhaus Association of Austrian Artists, 1999. **Member,** Akademie der Kunst der DDR, East Berlin, 1978. **Agent:** Galerie Rothe, Danneckerstrasse 39a, 60594 Frankfurt am Main, Germany; Galerie Mainetti, av. des Colléges 1, CH 1009 Pully, Lausanne, Switzerland. **Address:** Kirchengasse 48, 1010 Vienna, Austria.

Individual Exhibitions:

1960 Zedlitzhalle, Vienna
1962 Kunstlerhaus, Vienna
Wiener Sezession, Vienna
1963 *Druckgraphik und Steinskulpturen,* Galerie Welz, Salzburg
Tiroler Kunstpavillon, Innsbruck
1965 Galleria Penelope, Rome
Neue Münchner Galerie, Munich
Württembergischer Kunstverein, Stuttgart
1966 Galleria Torre, Turin
Badischer Kunstverein, Karlsruhe, West Germany
Galerie Peithner-Lichtenfels, Vienna
1967 Osterreichisches Konsulat, Baden-Baden, West Germany
1968 Marlborough Fine Art, London
Galerie Valentien, Stuttgart
Galerie André, West Berlin
Galerie Siemenshaus, Hamburg
1969 Osterreich-Haus, West Berlin
Randolectil, Graphische Sammlung Albertina, Vienna
Galerie im Taxispalais, Innsbruck
Graphik, Galerie Valentien, Stuttgart
Galerie Welz, Salzburg
1970 Galerie d'Eendt, Amsterdam
1971 *Skulpturen, Zeichnungen, Radierungen,* Galerie Rothe, Heidelberg
Galleria II Fante di Spade, Rome
Galerie Hartman, Munich
1972 Suermondt-Museum, Aachen, West Germany
1974 Kestner-Gesellschaft, Hannover
Konstakademie, Stockholm
1975 Nationalgalerie, West Berlin
Kunstverein, West Berlin
Wallraf-Richartz-Museum, Cologne
Skulpturen und Zeichnungen, Galerie Valentien Stuttgart
1976 Kunsthochshule, West Berlin
1978 *Wie ein Totentanz,* Kupferstichkabinette, Dresden
1981 Galerie Orangerie, Vienna
1982 Galerie Lietzow, West Berlin

1987 Galerie Hilger, Frankfurt
Galerie Hodl, Zurich
1994 *Zeichnungen,* Olaf Gulbransson Museum Tegernsee, Munich (catalog)
1995 *Radierungen: Eine Auswahl aus den Jahren 1959–1994,* Kulturspeicher Oldenburg, Germany (catalog)
1997 *Retrospektive—Skulpturen, Zeichnungen, Druckgrafik,* Frankfurter Kunstverein, Frankfurt am Main (catalog)
Sculptures et Oeuvres sur Papier, Musée-Galerie de la Seita, Paris (catalog)
2000 *Werke 1944–1997,* Magdeburger Museen, Magdeburg (catalog)
2001 *Die Kleist-Bilder von Alfred Hrdlicka,* Kleist Museum,

Selected Group Exhibitions:

1961 *The Object in Austrian Painting and Sculpture,* Wiener Sezession, Vienna
1964 *Biennale,* Venice
1966 *5th Biennale of Tokyo,* National Museum of Modern Art, Tokyo
1967 *Bienal,* Sao Paulo
1969 *6th Biennale Internazionale della Scultura,* Carrara, Italy
1973 *Biennale of Sculpture,* Middelheim Park, Antwerp
1994 *Vorbild Picasso,* Hochschule für Angewandte Kunst, Vienna (catalog)
1998 *Art Cologne,* Germany

Collections:

Staatsgalerie, Stuttgart; Staatliche Kunstsammlung, Dresden.

Publications:

By HRDLICKA: Books—*Alfred Hrdlicka,* edited by Heinz Moos, Munich 1969; *Stein des Anstosses: Gespräche mit Alfred Hrdlicka,* with Hans-Dieter Schütt, Berlin 1997.

On HRDLICKA: Books—*Alfred Hrdlicka: Druckgraphik und Steinskulpturen,* exhibition catalog with text by Ernst Koller, Johann Muschik and Josef Donnenberg, Salzburg 1963; *Alfred Hrdlicka,* exhibition catalog with text by Wolfgang Fischer, London 1968; *Alfred Hrdlicka: Randolectil,* with text by Kristian Sotriffer, Vienna 1969; *Alfred Hrdlicka, Alfred Hrdlicka,* by H. G. Dehr, G. Eisler and J. Muschik, Vienna 1969; *Alfred Hrdlicka: Drei Zyklen,* with text by Johann Muschik, Vienna 1969; *Alfred Hrdlicka,* exhibition catalog with text by Ina Stegen, Salzburg 1969; *Alfred Hrdlicka: Graphic,* exhibition catalog with text by Karl Diemer, Stuttgart 1969; *Alfred Hrdlicka: Skulpturen, Zeichnungen, Radierungen,* exhibition folder with text by Wolfgang Rothe, Heidelberg 1971; *Alfred Hrdlicka,* exhibition folder with text by Ernst Fischer, Rome 1971; *Alfred Hrdlicka,* exhibition catalog with texts by Wieland Schmied, Elias Canetti and Karl Diemer, Hannover 1974; *Malerei aus Bereichen des unbewussten* by R. P. Hartmann, Cologne 1974; *Alfred Hrdlicka: Skulpturen und Zeichnungen,* exhibition catalog with texts by Ernst Fischer, Wieland Schmied and Karl Diemer, Stuttgart 1975; *Alfred Hrdlicka: Wie ein Totentanz,* exhibition catalog with text by Werner Schmidt, Dresden 1978; *Alfred Hrdlicka,* exhibition catalog with essay by Gerhard Habarta, Vienna 1981; *Rodin—Breker—Hrdlicka* by Hermann Leber, New York 1998. **Articles—**''Frankfurt am Main: Alfred Hrdlicka—Mordopfer mit der Hand am Gemächt'' by Boris Hohmeyer in *ART: Das Kunstmagazin,* no. 4, April 1997; ''Der Vulgar Dargestellte Christus'' by Werner Roemer in *Munster,* vol. 52, no. 1, 1999; ''Gratwanderungen: Alfred Hrdlicka als Illustrator'' by Thomas Reche in *Illustration 63,* vol. 36, no. 2, August 1999.

* * *

To be a young boy in Vienna at the time of the Anschluss was a cathartic experience for anyone later to become an artist. Alfred Hrdlicka must early in his life have been cleansed of all the haunting doubts surrounding good and evil that run helter-skelter through the immature mind. As soon as he could think, he must have been aware of truth and lies and most of the gradations between the two. For him, truth spelt the ability to tell terrible stories that arose from a pervading atmosphere of cruelty, persecution, torture and blackmail. All these dark areas of existence are repeatedly present in both his graphic works and his sculpture. He allows himself a freedom of expression in manner and imagery that most times frightens the innocent or touches the passions and secret thoughts of the guilty.

Working in Wortruba's studio or casting wry looks at the paintings of Mondrian have done nothing to dull the spirit and inspiration of the uncensored commentator. The needle of his etchings is sharp with an acid hardly paralleled in the work of other graphic artists. However complex and tangled the ultimate print may appear, the storyline is lucid and devastating. As a painter he produced canvases that had all the venom of paintings by George Grosz but which, despite care and attention to detail, were bolder and more explicit than those of the German.

Hrdlicka's ''social comments,'' his horrifying anecdotes of life under the Nazis, the regurgitations of biblical classics like the story of Samson and Delilah, and the smut are all there in the graphics. Major opera.

But the monumental Hrdlicka is very different. Often using the most unyielding stone, he carves masculine figures whose nakedness—generally at odds with the social system, bound like slaves, caught in the central situation of a drama, even swinging head downwards with the feet lashed together—is over lifesize, if not always in fact, forever in the memory.

Hrdlicka is something of a titan. His mind, like his works, takes up grand themes. Yet this is the same man who plays games with the syndrome of the comic strip, fashioning its scenes and participants in his own fearless way, sometimes with an element of black humour, sometimes evoking a truer than life Grand-Guignol.

As Robert Graves pointed out, the White Goddess has many faces from the unspoilt countenance of a little girl to the raddled mask of a witch—and she has multiple personalities to match. Hrdlicka would say the same about SEX. In a series of outrageous photographs he shows a girl fondling the penis of one of his sculptures with the caption ''Why can't the sexually unfulfilled claim an art-orgasm?'' and goes on to title other photos ''Hrdlicka knows what women want,'' ''Women want Hrdlicka.''

—Sheldon Williams

HUEBLER, Douglas

Nationality: American. **Born:** Ann Arbor, Michigan, 27 October 1924. **Education:** University of Michigan, Ann Arbor, 1946–53, MFA 1953; Academie Julian, Paris, 1947–48; and Cleveland School of Art, Ohio, 1952. **Family:** Married Mary Brock (divorced 1973), son: Dorne Huebler, daughters: Darcy Huebler and Dana Hubler; married Stephani Weinschel, daughter: Kate Huebler. **Military Service:** Served in the United States Marine Corps, Air Combat Intelligence, South West Pacific, 1943–46. **Career:** Independent artist. Instructor, Miami University, Ohio, 1954–57; Instructor, Bradford College, Haverhill, Massachusetts, 1957–73; Instructor, Harvard University, Cambridge, Massachusetts, 1973–75; Dean of School of Art, California Institute of the Arts, Valencia, 1976–88. **Agent:** Leo Castelli Gallery, 59 East 79th Street, New York, New York 10021. **Died:** Of pancreatic cancer, Truro, Massachusetts, 12 July 1997.

Individual Exhibitions:

1953 Phillips Gallery, Detroit
1967 Obelisk Gallery, Boston
1968 Windham College, Putney, Vermont
Seth Siegelaub, New York
1969 Eugenia Butler Gallery, Los Angeles
1970 Galerie Konrad Fischer, Dusseldorf
Addison Gallery, Andover, Massachusetts
Galleria Sperone, Turin
Galerie Yvon Lambert, Paris
Art and Project, Amsterdam
1971 Leo Castelli Gallery, New York
Art and Project, Amsterdam
1972 California Institute of Arts, Valencia
Galerie Yvon Lambert, Paris
Galleria Toselli, Milan
Jack Wendler Gallery, London
Galerie Konrad Fischer, Dusseldorf
Leo Castelli Gallery, New York
Museum of Fine Arts, Boston
Westfälischer Kunstverein, Münster, West Germany
1973 Von der Heydt Museum, Wuppertal, West Germany
Städtische Kunsthalle, Kiel
Leo Castelli Gallery, New York
Galleria Fischer-Sperone, Rome
Museum of Modern Art, Oxford
Israel Museum, Tel-Aviv
1974 M.T.L. Gallery, Brussels
Galleria Lia Rumma, Naples
Galleria Sperone, Turin
Galerie Yvon Lambert, Paris
Galerie Konrad Fischer, Dusseldorf
Galerie Rolf Preisig, Basel
1975 Galerie Francoise Lambert, Milan
Cusack Gallery, Houston
1976 Galeria Akumulatory II, Poznan, Poland
Sperone Westwater Fischer, New York
Leo Castelli Gallery, New York
1977 Thomas Lewallen Gallery, Santa Monica, California
1978 Leo Castelli Gallery, New York
1979 Van Abbemuseum, Eindhoven, Netherlands
1981 Leo Castelli Gallery, New York
1983 Leo Castelli Gallery, New York
1984 Los Angeles Center for Photographic Studies (retrospective)
Museum of Contemporary Art, Los Angeles
1985 Albright-Knox Art Gallery, Buffalo, New York
Kuhlenschmidt/Simon Gallery, Los Angeles
1986 Leo Castelli Gallery, New York
1988 La Jolla Museum of Art, California
1990 Holly Solomon Gallery, New York (catalog)
1993 Fonds Régional d'Art Contemporain, Limousin (catalog)

Selected Group Exhibitions:

1966 *Primary Structures,* Jewish Museum, New York
1969 *When Attitudes Become Form,* Kunsthalle, Berne (toured Europe)
1970 *Software,* Jewish Museum, New York
1972 *Documenta, Kassel,* West Germany
1973 *Contemporanea,* Parcheggio Villa Borghese, Rome
1976 *72nd Annual Exhibition,* Art Institute of Chicago
1980 *Reasoned Space,* Center for Creative Photography, University of Arizona, Tucson
1984 *Content: A Contemporary Focus 1974–84,* Hirshhorn Museum, Washington D.C.
1987 *Avant Garde in the Eighties,* Los Angeles County Museum of Art
1996 *Reconsidering the Object of Art: 1965–1975,* Museum of Contemporary Art Temporary Contemporary, Los Angeles
1997 *Origin and Destination: Alighiero e Boetti, Douglas Huebler,* Société des Expositions du Palais des Beaux-Arts de Bruxells, Brussels (catalog)
1998 *Forty Years of Exploration and Innovation: The Artists of the Castelli Gallery 1957–1997,* Leo Castelli Gallery (SOHO), New York
Conceptual Photography from the 60s and 70s, David Zwirner Gallery, New York
1999 *Global Conceptualism: Points of Origin 1950s-1980s,* Queens Museum of Art, New York
The Museum as Muse: Artists Reflect, Museum of Modern Art, New York (catalog)
2000 *Voila: The World in Mind,* Musée Moderne de la Ville, Paris
2001 *American Minimalist and Conceptual Works from the 60s and 70s,* MAMCO, Geneva

Collections:

Museum of Modern Art, New York: Los Angeles County Museum of Art; Stedelijk Museum, Amsterdam; Boston Museum of Fine Art; Addison Gallery of American Art, Andover, Massachusetts; Tate Gallery, London; Israel Museum, Jerusalem; National Gallery of Canada, Ottawa; Australian National Gallery, Canberra; Van Abbemuseum, Eindhoven, Netherlands; Bayerische Staatsgemäldesammlungen, Munich, Germany.

Publications:

By HUEBLER: Books—*Untitled (Xerox-Book),* New York 1968; *Durata/Duration,* Turin 1970; *Selected Drawings 1968–1973,* Hong Kong 1975; *Contemporary Portraits,* St. Lucia, Queensland 1975; *Douglas Huebler,* exhibition catalog, Eindhoven 1979; *Crocodile Tears,* New York 1985, Los Angeles 1986. **Articles—**''Letter to the Editor'' in *Artnews* (New York), September 1966; ''Statements + Location Pieces 1, 2'' in *VH 101/3* (Paris), 1970; ''Trois Travaux'' in *VH101/6* (Paris), 1972; ''Concept vs. Art Object: A Conversation Between Douglas Huebler and Budd Hopkins'' in *Arts Magazine,* (New York), April 1972; ''Talking with Douglas Huebler,'' interview with Michael Auping, in *LAICA Journal* (Los Angeles), July/August 1977; ''Sabotage or Trophy? Advance or Retreat?'' in *Artforum* (New York), May 1982; ''Douglas Huebler'' in *Art Press Special Issue,* no. 17, 1996; interview with Robert C. Morgan in *Art into Ideas: Essays on Conceptual Art,* Cambridge 1996.

On HUEBLER: Books—*The Structure of Art* by Jack Burnham, New York 1971; *Concept Art* by Klaus Honnef, Cologne 1972; *Beyond Modern Art* by Carla Gottlieb, New York 1976; *Art Today, NYC* by Edward Lucie Smith, London 1977; *More Than You See* by Frederick Horowitz, New York 1985. **Articles—**''Huebler: Une Perception Nouvelle'' by Bernard Bourgeaud in *Pariscope* (Paris), March 1970; ''Douglas Huebler, Leo Castelli'' by W. Domingo in *Arts Magazine* (New York), September/October 1971; ''Douglas Huebler'' by April Kinsley in *Artforum* (New York), May 1972; ''Douglas Huebler: Everything about Everything'' by Lucy Lippard in *Artnews* (New York), December 1972; ''Douglas Huebler'' by Klaus Honnef in *Art and Artists* (London), January 1973; ''Douglas Huebler'' by Lynda Morris in *Studio International* (London), February 1973; ''Douglas Huebler'' by I. Lebeer in *Chroniques de l'Art Vivant* (Paris), April 1973; ''Douglas Huebler: Two Recent Works'' in Studio International (London), December 1974; ''Douglas Huebler's Strategies'' by James Welling in *Artweek* (Oakland, California), 3 December 1977; ''Fictional Escapades: Douglas Huebler'' by Paul Stimson in *Art in America* (New York), February 1982; ''The Crocodile Tears of Douglas Huebler'' by Hunter Drohojowska in *L.A. Weekly* (Los Angeles), 29 June 1984; ''Douglas Huebler'' by Colin Gardner in *Artforum* (New York), March 1986; ''Wo ist Douglas Huebler?'' by Robert C. Morgan in *Kunstforum International,* no. 125, January/February 1994; obituary in *New Art Examiner,* vol. 25, September 1997; ''Times of Our Lives: Remembering Doug Huebler,'' an obituary by Joseph Kosuth in *Artforum,* vol. 36, no. 3, November 1997.

HUNDERTWASSER, Friedensreich

Nationality: Austrian. **Born:** Friedrich Stowasser in Vienna, 15 December 1928; adopted the name Hundertwasser, 1949. **Education:** Montessori-School, Vienna, 1936–37; studied painting at the Academy of Fine Arts, Vienna, 1948. **Family:** Married Herta Leitner in 1958 (divorced, 1960); married Yuko Ikewada in 1960 (divorced, 1966). **Career:** Travelled in Tuscany with the painter René Brô, 1949; painted two murals with Brô at Saint Mandé, 1950; independent painter and graphic artist, Vienna, 1949–51, and in North Africa, France and Italy, 1951–68; has lived on his ship, *Regentag,* and travelled around the world, since 1968: concentrated on metal embossed graphics, Rome and Venice, 1967; worked with Peter Schamoni on the film *Hundertwasser's Rainy Day,* 1970–72; worked on architectural-ecological projects, 1972; collaborated with Japanese woodcutters for eleven years and produced first woodcut portfolio, *Nana Hiaku Mizu,* 1973; designed postage stamp, *Spiraltree,* for Austria, 1974; designed peace flag for the Middle East, 1978, environmental poster, ''Arche Noah 2000, 1980, anti-nuclear poster, *Plant Trees, Avert Nuclear Peril,* for Ralph Nader's Critical Mass Energy Project, Washington, D.C., 1980; worked on architectural projects at the Rosenthal Factory, Selb, West Germany, 1982; designs postage stamps for the United Nations, 193; redesigns buildings in Germany, 1987–88. Guest lecturer, Kunsthochschule, Hamburg, 1959. Lecturer, Master School, Academy of Fine Arts, Vienna, since 1981; Hundertwasser Museum opened in Vienna, 1991. **Awards:** Prix du Syndicat d'Initiative, *Biennale,* Bordeaux, 1957; Sanbra Prize, *Bienal,* Sao Paulo, 1959; Mainichi Prize, *International Art Exhibition,* Tokyo, 1961; Grosser Österreichischer Staatspreis für Kunst, Vienna, 1980; Austrian Naturschutzpreis, 1981; Environment Prize, Goslar, Germany, 1984; Gold Medal, Geneva, 1984; gold medal, City of Vienna, and gold medal, Federal Province of styria, both 1988; Officier dans l'Ordre des Arts et des Lettres, France, 1985. **Agent:** Joram Harel Management, Vienna, Post Office Box 28, A-1182 Vienna, Austria. **Died:** Of heart attack on board the Queen Elizabeth II en route from New Zealand to Austria, 19 February 2000.

Individual Exhibitions:

1952 Art Club, Vienna
1954 Studio Paul Facchetti, Paris
1955 Galleria del Naviglio, Milan
1956 Studio Paul Facchetti, Paris
1960 Galerie Raymond Cordier, Paris
1961 Tokyo Gallery
1962 Austrian Pavilion, *Biennale,* Venice
1963 *Hundertwasser ist ein Geschenk für Deutschland,* Galerie Anne Abels, Cologne
1964 Kestner-Gesellschaft, Hannover (toured Europe)
Stedelijk Museum, Amsterdam
Kunsthalle, Berne
1965 Moderna Museet, Stockholm
Museum des 20. Jahrhunderts, Vienna
Galerie Paul Facchetti, Paris
Hammerlunds Kunsthandel, Oslo
1967 Galerie Karl Flinker, Paris
Galerie Kugier/Galerie Georges Moos, Geneva
Galleria La Medusa, Rome
Galerie Welz, Salzburg
Hanover Gallery, London
1968 University of California, Berkeley (toured the United States)
1971 *Hundertwasser: Das Grafische Gesamtwerk Originale,* Galerie Hans Hoeppner, Hamburg
M. Fisher Gallery, London
1973 Auckland City Art Gallery (toured New Zealand and Australia)
Aberbach Fine Art, New York
1974 *Stowasser 1943—Hundertwasser 1974,* Graphische Sammlung Albertina, Vienna (and world tour from 1974)

Galerie Paul Facchetti, Paris
1975 Haus der Kunst, Munich (retrospective)
Austria Presents Hundertwasser, Musee d'Art Moderne de la Ville, Paris (and world tour from 1975)
1979 *Hundertwasser Is Painting,* Aberbach Fine Art, New York (and world tour)
1982 Artcurial, Paris
1985 Musée Gaugin, Tahiti
1989 Tokyo Metropolitan Teien Art Museum (toured Japan)
1992 *Creative Architecture: Eternal Longing* (toured Germany, then travelled to Vienna and Budapest)
1993 Ginza Pocket Park Gallery, Tokyo
1998 *Retrospektive 1948–1997,* Institut Mathildenhohe, Darmstadt, Germany

Selected Group Exhibitions:

1954 *Biennale,* Venice
1959 *Biennal,* Sao Paulo
Documenta, Kassel, West Germany
1972 *After Surrealism,* Ringling Museum of Art, Sarasota, Florida
1973 *Triennale,* Milan
1975 *Jewish Experience in the Art of the Twentieth Century,* The Jewish Museum, New York
1979 *Textilkunst aus Osterreich 1900–1979,* Schloss Halbturn, Austria
1982 *L'Art en Soie,* Musée des Arts Decoratifs, Paris
1985 *Osterreichische Avantgarde nach '45,* Milan (toured Italy)

Collections:

Kunsthalle, Hamburg; Kunsthalle, Mannheim; Bundesministerium, Vienna; Albertina Museum, Vienna; Stedelijk Museum, Amsterdam; Peggy Guggenheim Collection, Venice; Guggenheim Museum, New York; Museum of Modern Art, New York; St. Louis University; Hundertwasser Museum, KunsthausWien, Vienna.

Publications:

By HUNDERTWASSER: Books—*Der Transautomatismus: Eine allgemeine Mobilmachung des Auges,* Rome/Paris 1956; *Verschimmelungs Manifest gegen den Rationalismus in der Architektur,* Seckau, Austria 1958; *Architektur, Boykott Manifest,* Vienna 1968; *Scheisse-Manifest,* Munisch 1975; *Hundertwasser: Schöne Wege,* Munich 1983.

On HUNDERTWASSER: Books—*Handertwasser ist ein Geschenk für Deutschland,* exhibition catalog, Cologne 1963; *Hundertwasser,* exhibition catalog with text by Wieland Schmied, Amsterdam 1964; *Hundertwasser,* exhibition catalog with text by Wieland Schmied, Berne 1964; *Hundertwasser,* exhibition catalog edited by K. G. Hulten and Karin Bergquist Lindegren, Stockholm 1965; *Hundertwasser,* exhibition catalog with text by Wieland Schmied, Vienna 1965; *Hundertwasser,* exhibition catalog with text by Leif Ostby, Oslo 1965; *Hundertwasser,* by Chipp Herschel Richardson, New York 1968; *Hundertwasser: Das Grafische Gesamtwerk Originale,* exhibition catalog with text by Wieland Schmied, Hamburg 1971; *Hundertwasser 1973, New York,* with text by Joachim Jean Aberbach, Glarus, Switzerland 1973; *Zweihundert Jahre Phantastische Malerei* by Wieland Schmied, Berlin 1973; *Hundertwasser,* with text by F. Welz, S. Poppe and W. Koscharzky, Glarus, Switzerland 1975; *Hundertwasser 1975–1980: USA,* with text by Walter Koschatzky, Joachim Jean Aberbach and Wieland Schmied, Glarus, Switzerland 1975; *Hundertwasser 1981: Austria,* with texts by Bruno Kreisky, Leopold S. Senghor and Helmut Zilk, Glarus, Switzerland 1980; *Hundertwasser: peintures,* exhibition catalog with texts by Andre Pieyre de Mandiargues and Alain Jouffroy, Paris 1982; *Hundertwasser* by J. F. Mathey, Munich 1985; *Hundertwasser: Der Maler* by Harry Rand, Munich 1986; *Friedensreich Hundertwasser: The Complete Graphic* by Walter Koschatzky, New York 1986; *Hundertwasser,* exhibition catalog, Japan 1989; *Friedensreich Hundertwasser* by Harry Rand, Cologne 1991; *Hundertwasser,* Japan 1991, 1993. **Articles—**"Hundertwasser" by Annette Kuhn in *Artsmagazine* (New York), April 1969; "A Hundertwasser Retrospective" by B. A. Richardson in *Art Journal* (New York), September 1969; "Friedrich Hundertwasser" in *Mizue* (Tokyo), 1969; "Mr. Hundertwasser has Finally Built His Dream House" by Alfred Meyer in *Smithsonian,* vol. 16, January 1986; "Un Gaudí Viennese ha Dipinto il Palazzo dei Thonet" by Livia Fagetti in *Arte,* vol. 24, no. 255, October 1994; "Ein Putziges Phantom aus der Lego-Kiste" by Peter M. Bode in *ART: Das Kunstmagazin,* no. 11, November 1994; "I Maestri del Novecento: Friedensreich Hundertwasser" by Ermanno Krumm in *Arte,* no. 263, June 1995; "Hundertwasser: Night Train, 1978" by William T. Vollmann in *Artforum,* vol. 34, no. 6, February 1996; "Hundertwasser: L'Architecture Naturellement" by Hortense Lyon in *Beaux Arts Magazine,* no. 150, November 1996; "Friedensreich Hundertwasser: Maverick Architect Building Against the Grain" by Martin Pawley in *The Guardian* (London), Friday, 14 April 2000.

* * *

The faery world of Friedensreich Hundertwasser is brightly coloured and is often constructed like an onion, one skin within another within another. The figuration is not always immediately apparent, but it is there nonetheless, sometimes with actual figures woven into the pattern, at others in magical architecture, all coloured bricks and stained-glass windows.

Although the artist has travelled extensively across southern Europe, Morocco and Tunisia and was working in Japan during 1961, he has never shrugged off the Central European character of his style. If today he commutes between Normandy, Giudecca and Waldviertel (Austria), he never really strays far from the atmosphere of his native Vienna, the Imperial Vienna of bright lights and Hapsburg gaiety—no matter how plebean.

Hundertwasser is indifferent to reality or, if this is not so, he has a reality that has little to do with that of anyone else. The colour is for children, the images are for adults who have never truly grown up. It is the combination of the two that makes Hundertwasser really stand out. The danger, and it can be too close at times, is not that this Viennese will slop over into sentiment or sweetness but that he will allow his decorative talents too much free rein.

Too much silver, too much gold can be embarrassing even in a Hundertwasser painting, even worse in his graphics (which include: "Regenstag," the phosphorescent "gouache" series, using metal-leaf techniques and requiring no less than four stencils for each image.)

At his best, his strange vision lies somewhere between Marc Chagall and Ernst Fuchs. Chagall because of the colours and the *Märchen,* Fuchs because of the deft fashion in which Hundertwasser can build the framework of his pictures. Like both of them he has found a firm place in the public's favour.

—Sheldon Williams

HUNT, Bryan

Nationality: American. **Born:** Terre Haute, Indiana, in 1947. **Education:** University of South Florida, Tampa, 1966–68; Otis Art Institute, Los Angeles, 1969–71, B.F.A. 1971; member, Independent Study Program, Whitney Museum of American Art, New York, 1972. **Career:** Independent sculptor, since 1973. **Agent:** Blum Helman Gallery, 20 West 57th Street, New York, New York 10019. **Address:** 9 White Street, New York, New York 10013, U.S.A. **Web site:** http://www.bryanhunt.com.

Individual Exhibitions:

1974 Institute for Art and Urban Resources, at The Clocktower, New York
1975 Palais des Beaux-Arts, Brussels
1976 Daniel Weinberg Gallery, San Francisco
1977 Blum Helman Gallery, New York
1978 Blum Helman Gallery, New York
Daniel Weinberg Gallery, San Francisco
Greenberg Gallery, St Louis
1979 Blum Helman Gallery, New York
Bernard Jacobson Gallery, London
Blum Helman Gallery, New York
Galerie Bruno Bishofberger, Zurich
1980 Margo Leavin Gallery, Los Angeles
1981 Akron Art Institute, Ohio
Blum Helman Gallery, New York
Galerie Hans Strelow, Dusseldorf
1982 Daniel Weinberg Gallery, San Francisco
Bernier Gallery, Athens
1983 Blum Helman Gallery, New York
Margo Leavin Gallery, Los Angeles
Los Angeles County Museum of Art
Amerika Haus, West Berlin
California State University, Long Beach
1984 John C. Stoller and Company, Minneapolis
1985 Galerie Knoedler, Zurich
Blum Helman Gallery, New York
1986 Gillespie-Laage-Salomon, Paris
Akira Ikeda Gallery, Tokyo
1987 Barbara Mathes Gallery, New York
Blum Helman Warehouse, New York
1988 Wilhelm-Lehmbruck-Museum, Duisburg, West Germany
Bryan Hunt: Falls and Figures, Fort Worth Art Museum (traveling exhibition)
Bryan Hunt: Recent Sculpture, Cornell University, Herbert F. Johnson Museum of Art, Ithaca
1989 *Bryan Hunt: Recent Drawings,* Blum Helman Gallery, New York (catalog)
1990 *Sculpture: Bryan Hunt,* Blum Helman Gallery, New York (traveled to Galerie Daniel Templon, Paris)
1991 Tokyo Ginza Art Center Hall, Japan
Recent Works: 17 Sculptures, Kyoto Art Center Hall
1992 Aspen Art Museum, Aspen, Colorado
Blum Helman Gallery, New York
Locks Gallery, Philadelphia
1993 *Bryan Hunt: Paintings and Sculpture,* Tavelli Gallery, Aspen, Colorado
1994 *Bryan Hunt: Recent Works,* Laura Carpenter Fine Arts, Santa Fe
1995 *Bryan Hunt: Plunge, Crossing, Hoodoo,* Gagosian Gallery, New York
20 Years, Locks Gallery, Philadelphia (catalog)
1996 *Bryan Hunt: Drawings, Paintings, Sculpture,* Galerie Francoise e.s.f., Brooklandville, Maryland
Recent Work, Harley Baldwin Gallery, Aspen
1997 *Bryan Hunt: Sculptures,* Mary Boone Gallery, New York
1998 *Sculpture and Drawings,* Locks Gallery, Philadelphia (catalog)
1999 *Bryan Hunt: Recent Works,* Glenn Horowitz Bookseller, East Hampton, New York
Bryan Hunt: A Survey, Crown Point Press, San Francisco
2000 *Recent Sculpture,* Velge & Noirhomme, Brussels, Belgium
Paintings and Sculpture, Gallery Simonne Stern, New Orleans
Bryan Hunt, Indianapolis Museum of Art

Selected Group Exhibitions:

1978 *Young American Artists,* Guggenheim Museum, New York
Made by Sculptors, Stedelijk Museum, Amsterdam
1979 *Biennial Exhibition,* Whitney Museum, New York
Selections from the Collection: Contemporary Sculpture, Museum of Modern Art, New York
1980 *Biennale,* Venice
1982 *74th American Exhibition,* Art Institute of Chicago
1984 *Works in Bronze: A Modern Survey,* Sonoma State University, California (toured the United States)
1985 *Correspondences: New York Art Now,* Laforet Museum, Tokyo (travelled to Utsunomiya, Japan)
1987 *Cast in Bronze,* Kansas City Gallery of Art, Missouri
1989 *Sculptural Intimacies: Recent Small-Scale Work,* Security Pacific Gallery, Costa Mesa (catalog)
Figuratively Speaking: Drawings by Seven Artists, Roy R. Neuberger Museum, Purchase, New York (catalog)
1992 *Drawing Redux,* San Jose Museum of Art (catalog)
Four Friends, Aldrich Museum of Contemporary Art, Ridgefield (catalog)

Collections:

Akron Museum of Art, Ohio; Albright-Knox Art Gallery, Buffalo; Arkansas Art Center, Little Rock; Art Institute of Chicago; Dallas Museum of Art; Des Moines Art Center, Iowa; Chase Manhattan Bank Collection, New York; Fogg Art Museum, Cambridge; Frank Lloyd Wright Fallingwater Conservancy, Kaufman House, Bear Run, Pennsylvania; Herbert F. Johnson Museum of Art, Cornell University, Ithaca, New York; Indianapolis Museum of Fine Art; The High Museum, Atlanta; Hirschhorn Museum, Washington, D.C.; Kiasma Museum of Contemporary Art, Helsinki; Lannan Foundation, New

York; Lehmbruck Museum, Duisburg, West Germany; Leo Brunett Headquarters, Chicago; Los Angeles County Museum of Art; Louisiana Museum of Modern Art, Humlebaek, Denmark; Massachusetts Institute of Technology, Cambridge; The Metropolitan Museum of Art, New York; Mori Building Company, Tokyo; The Museum of Contemporary Art, Los Angeles; The Museum of Fine Arts, Houston; The Museum of Modern Art, New York; Museum of Twentieth Century Art, Vienna; National Museum of American Art, Washington, D.C.; The Newark Museum, New Jersey; Newport Harbor Museum, Newport Beach, California; Olympic Park, Seoul, Korea; National Museum of Art, Seoul, Korea; Orlando Museum of Art, Florida; Paine Webber Collection, New York; Parc del Clot, Barcelona; Rose Art Museum, Brandeis Unversity, Waltham; St. Louis Museum, Missouri; San Francisco Museum of Modern Art; Seattle Museum, Washington; Sheldon Memorial Art Gallery, University of Nebraska-Lincoln; The Solomon R. Guggenheim Museum, New York; Town of Vail Colorado, Vail Village; Stedelijk Museum, Amsterdam, Netherlands; Vassar College Art Gallery, Poughkeepsie, New York; Virginia Museum of Fine Arts, Richmond; Whitney Museum of American Art, New York; Yale University Art Gallery, New Haven, Connecticut.

Publications:

By HUNT: Books—*Conversations with Nature,* New York 1982; *Bryan Hunt: Unlocking Mainstream,* with David Bourdon, New York 1995. **Article—**''Bryan Hunt,'' with Robert Becker, in *Interview* (New York), January 1982.

On HUNT: Books—*Made by Sculptors,* exhibition catalog by Rini Dippel and Geert van Beijeren, Amsterdam 1978; *Bryan Hunt,* exhibition catalog with text by Carter Ratcliff, New York 1983; *Bryan Hunt: A Decade of Drawings,* exhibition catalog by Constance W. Glenn and Jane K. Bledsoe, Long Beach 1983; *Bryan Hunt,* exhibition catalog by Barbara Haskell, West Berlin 1983; *Bryan Hunt: Skulpturen und Zeichnungen,* exhibition catalog by Barbara Haskell, Zurich 1985. **Articles—**''A Pail of Water Without the Pail'' by James Poett in the *Village Voice* (New York), March 1977; ''Bryan Hunt: Blum Helman'' by Peter Frank in *Artnews* (New York), October 1978; ''Bryan Hunt: Blum Helman Gallery'' by Carrie Rickey in *Artforum* (New York), May 1979; ''Bryan Hunt: Blum Helman'' by Ellen Schwartz in *Artnews* (New York), Summer 1979; ''Art Boom'' by Calvin Tomkins in *New Yorker,* 22 December 1980; ''Sculptors Who Triumph in Bronze'' by Hilton Kramer in the *New York Times,* 24 May 1981; ''Reviews from New York, Las Vegas, Los Angeles, San Francisco, Cologne and Rome'' by Hal Foster in *Artforum* (New York), September 1981; ''Bryan Hunt'' by Dupuy Warrick Reed in *Flash Art* (Milan), October/November 1981; ''Forum: Bryan Hunt's Untitled (Rotation Drawing I)'' by David Bourdon in *Drawing,* vol. 14, no. 2, July-August 1992.

*

To me what sculpture is is creating, constructing, carving, modeling, pouring—a process or a conceptualization of mass. When you think in and translate mass, there is gravity to deal with. You want to release mass, and give it a life and a definition of its own, which I think good sculpture can do.

Motion is part of the equation of it, not that it has to seem like it's in motion, but that it has potential motion or that it has the potential of a life of its own.

—Bryan Hunt

* * *

Abstract sculptor Bryan Hunt made his first ''Airship'' in 1973, and since then he has produced a series of ''Airships'' along with ''Lakes'' and ''Waterfalls.'' In all three of these series Hunt shows his predilection for intimate scale, handmade surface tactility and summary form ultimately derived from either the natural landscape (water preferred) or the technology of the airship. Hunt's sculpture has become increasingly abstract, a prime concern being pinpointing the definition of pure from in its essence, but the hint of his ultimate relationship with seen sources persists as a positive element in the work's vocabulary of references.

The ''Airships'' are long, lean, sharp, sleek shapes which jut out horizontally from the wall, piercing it slightly as if about to penetrate the solid surface or perhaps as if just having emerged from the ''other side''. Over wooden frames, Hunt places silk and silk paper, metal leaf, or copper treated with acid, producing a handmade look, soft and luminous with painterly evanescence. Works are small in scale and are hung high on the wall, making the viewer's perspective that of looking upward, as if at some silent spaceship in the distant skies. The closest art historical connections are with the sleek verticals of Brancusi, but Hunt is obviously after a more scientific and late 20th century correspondence.

The ''Lakes'' are low-lying, horizontal, irregular ovoid shapes which rest on the floor to provoke sensations of aerial perspective as if seen from an Airship, perhaps. They are bronzes made through the lost wax process, and their tactile surfaces are indented in various patterns, linear configurations suggesting the rippling actions on water's surfaces caught in frozen suspension. Edges vary from sharp to fine to thick to dull, adding to the suggestion that Hunt's visual sources are in his studies of topographical maps and charts which show the different patterns which occur in various real bodies of water. The choice of either polished bronze or darker patinas for the surfaces of the ''Lakes'' evokes associations with various times of day or night. As in the ''Lakes,'' Hunt's ''Waterfalls,'' also reveal the more nature-oriented, even pantheistic, side of his personality which seems to regard water as a potent symbol of romantic ebb and flow.

Hunt himself credits such predecessors as Robert Smithson, Richard Serra, and Joel Shapiro, and the connections are surely in evidence in his development so far. Also involved is the Postminimalist combination of painting and sculpture in abstract forms which tend toward the idiosyncratic. Hunt's sculptures are less formally ambitious than these sources, and his work seems less involved with the grand or the art historically important. Whether you look up or down at Hunt's works, you get the feeling of a poetic, romanticizing humanist who sees both nature and technology with equally sympathetic eyes.

—Barbara Cavaliere

HUNT, Richard (Howard)

Nationality: American. **Born:** Chicago, Illinois, 12 September 1935. **Education:** School of the Art Institute of Chicago, 1953–57, B.A.E. **Military Service:** United States Army, 1958–60. **Career:** Sculptor; lives and works in Chicago. Instructor, School of the Art Institute of Chicago, 1960–61, and at University of Illinois at Chicago, 1960–62; visiting professor, Chouinard Art School, Los Angeles, 1964; visiting artist, Yale University, New Haven, Connecticut, 1964 and at Purdue University, Indiana, 1965; visiting professor, Northern Illinois University, De Kalb, summer 1968, and at Northwestern University, Evanston, Illinois, 1968–69; artist consultant, Hobart Welding School, Troy, Ohio, 1969; visiting artist, Wisconsin State University, Oshkosh, 1969, Southern Illinois University, Carbondale, 1969, and Washington University, 1977–78; The University of Arizona, Tucson, 1980; Utah State University, Logan, 1982; Cornell University, Ithaca, 1985; Eastern Michigan University, Yipsilanti, 1988; Harvard University, Cambridge, 1989–90; Kalamazoo College, Michigan, 1990; State University of New York, Binghamton, 1990; Michigan State University, East Lansing, 1997. **Member:** National Council on the Arts, 1968–74; Illinois Arts Council, 1970–75; Board of Directors, College Art Association, 1972–76; Board of Trustees, Museum of Contemporary Art, Chicago, 1975–79; Board of Directors, American Council for the Arts, since 1974; Board of Trustees, American Academy in Rome, 1980–82; Board of Trustees, The Institute for Psychoanalysis, Chicago, 1981–89; President & Founder, Chicago Sculpture Society, 1982–88; National Chairman, Alumni Council, School of the Art Institute, 1983–87; Advisory Committee, Getty Center for Education in Arts, 1984–88; Director, International Sculpture Center, 1984–96; Board of Governors, School of the Art Institute, 1985–91; National Board of Directors, Smithsonian Institute, 1994–97; American Academy of Arts & Letters, 1998. **Awards:** Logan Prize 1956, 1961, 1962, Palmer Prize 1957, James Nelson Raymond Travel Fellowship 1957, and Campana Prize 1962, Art Institute of Chicago; Guggenheim Fellowship, 1962; Tamarind Fellowship Artist, Ford Foundation, 1965; Cassandra Foundation Fellowship, 1970; Outstanding Chicagoan in the Arts Award, Chicago Junior Chamber of Commerce, 1971; Lincoln Academy of Illinois, 1993. D.F.A.: Lake Forest College, Lake Forest, Illinois, 1972; Dayton Art Institute School, 1973; University of Michigan, Ann Arbor, 1976; Illinois State University, Normal, Illinois, 1977; Colorado State University, Ft. Collins, Colorado, 1979; School of the Art Institute of Chicago, 1982; Northwest University, Evanston, 1984; Monmouth College, Monmough, Illinois, 1986; Roosevelt University, Chicago, 1987; Tufts University, Medford, Massachusetts, 1991; Columbia College, Chicago, 1996; Governors State University, Park Forest, Illinois, 1997. **Agent:** Terry Dintenfass Gallery, 50 West 57th Street, New York, New York 10019. **Address:** 1017 West Lill Avenue, Chicago, Illinois 60614, U.S.A. **Website:** http://www.h-net.msu.edu/~rhunt.

Individual Exhibitions:

1958 Alan Gallery, New York
1959 Stewart Rickard Gallery, San Antonio, Texas
1960 Alan Gallery, New York
1962 Alan Gallery, New York
1963 B. C. Holland Gallery, Chicago
Alan Gallery, New York
1964 Wesleyan College, Macon, Georgia
University of Tulsa, Oklahoma
1965 Felix Landau Gallery, Los Angeles
Occidental College, Los Angeles
1966 University of Notre Dame, Indiana
B. C. Holland Gallery, Chicago
Ohio State University, Columbus
1967 Cleveland Museum of Art
Milwaukee Art Center (retrospective)
1968 B. C. Holland Gallery, Chicago
Dorsky Gallery, New York
Fisk University, Nashville, Tennessee
1969 David Strawn Art Gallery, Jacksonville, Illinois
Dorsky Gallery, New York
Kendall College, Evanston, Illinois
Wisconsin State University, Oshkosh
1970 Southern Illinois University, Carbondale
Dorsky Gallery, New York
Living Art Center, Dayton, Ohio
Southern Illinois University, Carbondale
Macalester College, St. Paul, Minnesota
B. C. Holland Gallery, Chicago
Carleton College, Northfield, Minnesota
St. Olaf College, Northfield, Minnesota
1971 Museum of Modern Art, New York (retrospective)
Dorsky Gallery, New York
Art Institute of Chicago (retrospective)
1973 Dorsky Gallery, New York
1975 Dorsky Gallery, New York
University of Iowa
1976 Dorsky Gallery, New York
Sears Bank & Trust Co., Chicago
1977 Dorsky Gallery, New York
1979 Dorsky Gallery, New York
1980 *Prints by a Sculptor: Richard Hunt,* Baltimore Museum of Art
1981 Dorsky Gallery, New York
St. Joseph Art Association, Michigan
Springfield Art Museum, Missouri
Columbia University, New York
Westbeth Art Gallery, New York
Fordham University, New York
1982 Brooklyn Artists Cultural Association, New York
1983 Terry Dintenfass Gallery, New York
1984 Terry Dintenfass Gallery, New York
1985 Martin Gallery, Washington, D.C.
1986 Terry Dintenfass Gallery, New York
1994 Woodlot Gallery, Sheboygan, Wisconsin
1995 Worthington Gallery, Chicago
1996 Worthington Gallery, Chicago
Growing Forward, Snite Museum, Notre Dame University, Notre Dame, Indiana (catalog)
Addison/Ripley Fine Art, Washington, D.C.
1997 Studio Museum in Harlem, New York
Andre Zarre Gallery, New York
1998 Museum of African-American History, Detroit
Illinois State Museum, Chicago and Springfield, Illinois
George N'Namdi Gallery, Detroit

Worthington Gallery, Chicago
Affirmations, International Arts & Artists, Inc., Washington, D.C. (catalog)
1999 Laumeier Sculpture Park, St. Louis
Indiana State University Art Gallery, Terre Haute, Indiana

Selected Group Exhibitions:

1962 *World's Fair,* Seattle
1966 *World Festival of Negro Art,* Dakar, Senegal
1979 *100 Artists, 100 Years: Alumni of the School of the Art Institute of Chicago,* Art Institute of Chicago
1994 *Seventy-Fifth Annual Exhibition of Artist Members,* The Arts Club of Chicago, Illinois
Two Sculptors, Two Eras, Hunter Museum of Art, Chattanooga, Tennessee (catalog)
Anacostia Museum, Washington, D.C.
1996 *The Listening Sky,* Studio Museum, Harlem Sculpture Garden, New York
1997 *African-American Art: 20th Century Masterworks, IV,* Michael Rosenfeld Gallery, New York (catalog)
1998 *African-American Art: 20th Century Masterworks, V,* Michael Rosenfeld Gallery, New York (catalog)

Collections:

Albright-Knox Gallery, Buffalo, New York; The Art Institute of Chicago; Cincinnati Art Museum, Cincinnati; Cleveland Museum of Art, Cleveland; The Hirschhorn Museum and Sculpture Garden, Washington, D.C.; Los Angeles County Museum, Los Angeles; National Gallery, Washington, D.C.; National Museum of American Art, Washington, D.C.; National Museum of Israel, Jerusalem; Nelson Gallery—Atkins Museum, Kansas City, Missouri; New Jersey State Museum, Trenton; The Metropolitan Museum of Art, New York; Milwaukee Museum, Milwaukee; The Museum of Modern Art, New York; Museum of the Twentieth Century, Vienna; Storm King Art Center, Mountainville, New York; New York Whitney Museum of American Art, New York; The Wichita Art Museum, Wichita, Kansas.

Public Installations:

Growth Development Interaction, McHenry County College, Crystal Lake, Illinois, 1994; *Victory Reconstruction,* Jackson Community College, Jackson, Michigan, 1995; *Sculptural Enlightenment,* Roosevelt University, Chicago, 1995; *Shitown Totem,* McCormick Place, Chicago, 1997; *Bookends,* Evanston Public Library, Illinois, 1997; *Booktops,* Evanston Public Library, Illinois, 1997; *Wingways,* Belleville Area College, Granite, Illinois, 1997; *St. Procopius,* St. Procopius, Lisle, Illinois, 1997; *Ascension,* Western Illinois University, Macomb, 1997; *Active Hybrid,* Rudy Park, Dowagaic, Michigan, 1997; *Growing,* Civic Center of Leawood, Kansas, 1999; *Linked Forms,* Laumeier Sculpture Park, St. Louis, 1999.

Publications:

By HUNT: Article—interview with Paul Cummings in *Drawing* vol. 16, November-December 1994.

On HUNT: Books—*Modern American Sculpture* by Dore Ashton, New York 1968; *The Sculpture of Richard Hunt* by Lieberman, New York 1971; *The Afro-American Artist: A Search for Identity* by Elsa Honig Fine, New York 1982; *African-American Art* by Sharon F. Patton, Oxford 1998; *The Walter O. Evans Collection of African American Art* by Andrea D. Barnwell, Walter O. Evans, Kirsten Buick, Amy Mooney and Tritobia Hayes Benjamin, Detroit 2000. **Articles—**''Combining the Root with the Reach of Black Aspiration'' by Frank Getlein in *Smithsonian,* vol. 21, no. 4, July 1990; ''Sculptor Richard Hunt: Even His Trash is Art'' by Adrienne Drell in *Chicago Sun-Times,* 27 November 1994; ''The Life and Art of Richard Hunt'' by Les Payne in *Newsday,* 9 January 1997; ''Richard Hunt: Freeing the Human Soul'' by Jan Garden Castro in *Sculpture* (Washington, D.C.), vol. 17, no. 5, May/June 1998.

* * *

Richard Hunt has been described as a man both extremely reflective and as one unwilling to share his thoughts and feelings. Throughout his accomplished career since the 1950's, Hunt's work has been a response to his own introverted nature. His sculptures, charged with emotion yet without specific representational references, tend towards the sublime. As an abstract artist his statements are seldom direct, with the notable exception that he has always made explicit reference to the human figure. This technique of describing a clearly recognisable human form with abstraction illustrates Hunt's concern for understanding—and defining—the complex mechanisms of the human psyche.

In 1953 Hunt saw the work of the Spaniard Julio Gonzalez, who most influenced his development as a sculptor. Within two years of seeing Gonzalez's work, the young American had taught himself to be a master welder. Yet unlike the Spaniard, who forged and hammered the disparate metal parts which comprised his constructions, Hunt utilized the torch to maintain control over his medium.

More importantly than just being a member of the generation of ''junk'' sculptors, however, Hunt received critical acceptance as a result of a mid-century trend which valued the aesthetics of assemblage, a development which derived from Picasso and his innovative use of new materials. Hunt does not model or carve, and has consistently preferred to use metal, as opposed to plaster, stone, and wood. His favoured materials were discarded and broken machine parts, his scouring ground the metal junkyards of an industrial age. Not only were they an inexpensive source of material but the prefabricated shapes he found offered him immediate, direct, and conceptually clean forms which he could manipulate in space. He constructed and welded his first sculptures in copper and iron in the 1950's and gradually turned toward aluminum and steel in the subsequent decades.

In the 1960's Hunt constructed sculptures based on classical themes. In their conception and with their suggestion of velocity and energy, however, his works do credit more to the sculptures of Umberto Boccioni than to any Hellenistic examples. From classical experimentations he began a series somewhat more open and fused in space, out of which came his ''hybrid figures,'' which eloquently synthesised elements of the human trunk and limbs with botanical and organic references.

During the 1960's Hunt began to work less and less in a calligraphic way; his forms became monolithic and enclosed, more solid and dense, providing new weight for linear elements. Later on the physical scale of his sculptures increased dramatically, the size, height, and spacial positioning of each piece controlling the emotional representation.

Hunt's sculptures are much less spontaneously conceived than they initially appear. They are, however, examples of total contemplation. In the same vein, first impressions leave the viewer feeling somewhat disillusioned by what might be regarded as the leftovers of 1950's ''junk'' sculpture. Yet Richard Hunt's well-established ability to endow his work with the deepest levels of introspection is what ranks him as one of America's foremost living sculptors.

—Carrie Barker

HUYGHE, Pierre

Nationality: French. **Born:** Paris, France, 1962. **Education:** Studied at Ecole Supérieure des Arts Graphiques, Paris, 1981–82; studied at Ecole Nationale Supérieure des Arts Décoratifs, Paris, 1982–84; lives and works in Paris. **Award:** DAAD Artist in Residence, Berlin, Germany, 2000. **Agent:** Marian Goodman Gallery, 24 West 57th Street, New York, New York 10019.

Selected Individual Exhibitions:

1995 *L'usage de l'interprète,* Fonds Regional d'Art Contemporain Languedoc
Roussillon, Montpellier, France
1996 *Dubbing,* Galerie Roger Pailhas, Paris
1997 *Storytellers,* Le Consortium, Dijon, France
1998 ARC/Musée d'Art Moderne de la Ville de Paris
1999 *L'ellipse,* Aarhus Kunstmuseum, Denmark
Le procès de temps libre, Wiener Secession, Vienna, Austria (catalog)
The Serralves Museum of Contemporary Art, Oporto, Portugal
Index, Swedish Contemporary Art Foundation, Stockholm, Sweden
2000 *No ghost just a shell (Two minutes out of time),* Schipper und Krome, Berlin; Marian Goodman Gallery, Paris
Vivre sa vie: Pierre Huyghe and Philippe Parreno, Tramway, Glasgow
The Third Memory, Musée National d'Art Moderne-Centre Georges Pompidou, Paris (catalog)
Museum of Contemporary Art, Chicago, Illinois
2001 Marian Goodman Gallery, New York
Pierre Huyghe, Musée d'Art Contemporain, Montreal

Selected Group Exhibitions:

1994 *Economies,* Galerie Roger Pailhas, Marseilles
Surface de Réparation, Fonds Regional d'Art Contemporain Bourgogne, Dijon, France
1995 *Cosmos,* MAGASIN-Centre National d'Art Contemporain de Grenoble, France
Shift, De Appel, Amsterdam
Aperto, Le Nouveau Musée-Institut d'Art Contemporain, Villeurbanne, France
Biennale d'Art Contemporain de Lyon, France
1996 *Traffic,* CAPC Musée d'Art Contemporain de Bordeaux, France
Entre Deux and *Perfect,* Galerie Mot & Van Den Boogaard, Brussels
Joint Ventures, Stephano Basilico Fine Art, New York
Found Footage, Klemens Gasser & Tanja Grunert, Cologne
1997 *Moment Ginza,* MAGASIN-Centre National d'Art Contemporain de Grenoble, France; Färgfabriken, Stockholm
Coïncidences, Fondation Cartier, Paris
Venice Biennale, Venice
MUUten, Museum of Photography, Helsinki
1998 *Voices,* Le Fresnoy, France; Witte de With, Rotterdam, Netherlands; Miro Foundation, Barcelona (catalog)
Premises, Guggenheim Museum SoHo, New York
Musique en Scène, Oeuvres Sonores, Musée d'Art Contemporain, Lyons, France
When Worlds Collide, Center of Contemporary Art, Glasgow
1999 *Regarding Beauty: A View of The Late Twentieth Century,* Hirshhorn Museum and Sculpture Garden, Washington, D.C.; Haus der Kunst, Munich
d'APERTutto, Venice Biennale
Carnegie International, Carnegie Museum of Art, Pittsburgh
Notorious: Alfred Hitchcock and Contemporary Art, Museum of Modern Art, Oxford; Sydney Museum of Contemporary Art
2000 *Blanche-Neige,* Museum of Contemporary Art, Chicago
Pierre Huyghe and Philippe Parreno, Tramway, Glasgow
Let's Entertain, Walker Art Center, Minneapolis
Voilà, ARC/Musée d'Art Moderne de la Ville de Paris
2001 *Doublelife,* Generali Foundation, Wien, Austria

Publications:

On HUYGHE: Book—*The Third Memory: Pierre Huyghe* exhibition catalog, by Christine Van Assche, Paris 2000. **Articles—**''A Conversation with Pierre Huyghe'' by Pia Viewing in *Paletten,* no. 4, 1995; ''Pierre Huyghe'' by Olivier Zahm and Jeanine Herman in *Artforum International,* March 1997; ''Vertical Time'' by Holland Cotter in *New York Times,* 30 January 1998; ''Les 'remakes' de Pierre Huyghe'' by Muriel Caron in *Parachute,* January-March 1999; ''Action! An Interview with Pierre Huyghe'' by Jan Estep in *New Art Examiner,* July-August 2000; ''Stickup Artist: The Art of Pierre Huyghe'' by Daniel Birnbaum in *Artforum International,* November 2000.

* * *

At the forefront of contemporary art and thought, Pierre Huyghe uses video, television, and billboards to reinterpret the relationship between the work of art and lived experience. In innovative videos and remakes of classic films, he seeks to redefine narrative, exploring its connection to time and duration. Huyghe's manipulation of art and reality is more than playful speculation, however. On the contrary, his work often reveals subtle, almost tangential glimpses of economic, political, and social conditions. But most importantly, Huyghe forces viewers to examine their own mental processes and representations of reality.

Dubbing (1996) is an imageless film whose title is not revealed. Fifteen performers speaking in chorus interpret or ''dub'' the dialogue, which they read from a lip-sync band running along the bottom of the blank film, matching their words to those of the original actors. Following along silently, the viewer ''dubs'' the film with his own inner voice, confronting the artist's implicit query about the connections between speech and its utterances through time.

Other works are also provocative. The poignant video, *Blanche Neige Lucie* (1997), features the aging Lucie Dolène, who years ago provided the French voice for Disney's Snow White. In Huyghe's work, Dolène sings the movie's theme while spectators hear the story of her hiring and subsequent legal suit to keep the rights to her own recorded voice. The viewer thus contrasts reality with the filmic fantasy. *Remake* (1995) employs nonprofessionals to play the roles of Grace Kelly and Jimmy Stewart in Huyghe's version of Hitchcock's celebrated movie, *Rear Window*. Calling them ''stand-ins,'' he exploits the amateurs' hesitation and awkwardness as ''moments of reality.'' In *Chantier Barbès, Billboards, Paris 1994,* Huyghe teased the viewer by blurring the distinctions between actual experience and representations of it. At building sites, he set up billboards showing workmen engaged in their tasks. Was life imitating art, or was art mimicking life?

In some works, Huyghe's focus on social problems is more apparent. His trip to film the many unfinished houses between Rome and Naples is such a project. These uncompleted structures represent for him ''a transitory state, suspended time.''Often begun against the law without a building permit to avoid taxes, these abandoned houses also reflect harsh economic and political conditions. In a similar vein, *Light Conical Intersect* (1996) contrasts two periods, each with its own social perspective. Projecting Matta-Clark's 1975 documentary, *Conical Intersect,* onto the new building located on the site where Matta-Clark had worked, Huyghe thereby opposes two decades, the 1970s and the 1990s. Making a conical hole in townhouses facing the controversial Pompidou Center in Paris during its building, Matta-Clark had filmed curious spectators who stopped for a glance at the architecturally outrageous museum. Huyghe's projection in a contemporary setting of the earlier documentary revisits the former clash between tradition and innovation, always so passionate in France. Once a shocking—and proletarian—newcomer, the Pompidou is now an accepted landmark in the Marais.

In *The Third Memory* (2000), a reconstitution of the factual incident inspiring the 1974 film, *Dog Day Afternoon,* Huyghe continues his exploration of the creative process. Together with two companions, John Wojtowicz attempted to rob a branch of the Chase Manhattan bank in Brooklyn. One of the would-be bandits fled, but Wojtowicz and his companion took hostages and, during a nine-hour stand-off, negotiated with the police, appearing on television, and airing the crime's motive: a sex-change operation for Wojtowicz's male lover. This scenario inspired Sidney Lumet's well-constructed film starring Al Pacino. Later from prison, however, Wojtowicz wrote objecting to the movie's many deviations from actuality and misplaced emphases. In his ''reconstruction'' of the original incident, Huyghe invited Wojtowicz to discuss his actions, reclaiming, as it were, his own image from that of a derisory, pitiable stooge.

Huyghe's thoroughgoing exploration of the juncture between the real and its representation constitutes a radical departure from conceptual art's ascetic abnegation of living reality. It is rather an attempt to regain narrative's primordial dimension as the transmission of events, perception, and feelings—in short, of lived experience. ''It is the process,'' Huyghe says, ''that interests me.''

—Dorothy Joiner

I

IANNONE, Dorothy

Nationality: American. **Born:** Boston, Massachussets, 9 August 1933. **Education:** Boston University, 1953–57 (Phi Beta Kappa), B.A. 1957; graduate studies in English, Brandeis University, Waltham, Massachussets, 1958. **Military Service:** Employed as a Transportation Agent, Boston Army Base, 1951–53. **Married:** James Phineas Upham in 1958 (divorced, 1967); lived with the artist Dieter Roth, 1967–74. **Career:** Independent artist, since 1960: travelled extensively in Europe and the Far East, 1961–67; has lived in Europe since 1967, and in West Berlin since 1976; began study of Tibetan Buddhism, 1984. Instructor in open workshops, College of Arts, West Berlin, 1977, 1979; guest artist, Jan Van Eyck Academie, Maastricht, 1982, 1983, and Rijks Academie, Amsterdam, 1982, 1984. **Awards:** DAAD Grant, West Berlin, 1976; Art Foundation of Bonn Grant, 1988; Women Artists' Program Grant, Berlin Senate, 1994. **Agent:** Galerie Hundertmark, Bruesseler Strasse 29, D-05674 Cologne, Germany. **Address:** Leonhardt Strasse 2, D-14057 Berlin, Germany.

Individual Exhibitions:

1964 Stryke Gallery, New York
1965 Stryke Gallery, New York
1966 Stryke Gallery, New York
1967 Stryke Gallery, New York
Dieter Roth/Dorothy Iannone, Zwirner Galerie, Cologne
Galerie Hansjörg Mayer, Stuttgart
1969 Galerie Handschin, Basel
1971 Wilbrand Galerie, Cologne
Eat Art Galerie, Dusseldorf
Galerie Jule Hammer, Berlin
1973 Galerie Steinmetz, Bonn
Galerie Wahlandt, Schwabisch-Gmund, West Germany
1974 Sum Galerie, Reykjavik
1975 Galerie Ben Vautier, Nice, France
Galerie 38, Copenhagen
1976 Galerie Bama, Paris
1977 Studio Galerie Mike Steiner, West Berlin
Wiener und Würthle Galerie, West Berlin
Other Books and So, Amsterdam
1978 Haus am Lützow Platz, West Berlin
1979 Studio Galerie, at Art 79, Basel
1980 Neue Galerie, Ludwig Collection, Aachen, West Germany
1981 Galleri Wallner, Malmö, Sweden
1982 Nikolaj, Copenhagen
Galerie Ars Viva, West Berlin
1984 Galerie Rosenberg, Zurich
1986 Boekie Woekie, Amsterdam
1989 *Dorothy Iannone: Works from 1961–66,* Petersen Galerie, West Berlin
1990 Kunstfonds, Kunstraum, Bonn
Galerie Steinmetz, Bonn
1992 Kunst-Werke, Berlin
1993 Galerie Hundertmark, Cologne
1995 Galerie Roche, Bremen
Basel Art Fair Galerie Stahli, Zurich
1996 Galerie Holtmann, Cologne
1997 *Dorothy Iannone: Love is Forever, Isn't It?,* New Society Fine Arts, Berlin
1998 Museum of Modern Art, Arnhem
Boekie Woekie, Amsterdam

Selected Group Exhibitions:

1966 *La Cedille qui Sourit,* Villefranche-sur-Mer, France
1969 *Erotic Art Show: Collection of Drs. Phyllis and Eberhard* Kronhausen, Kunsthalle, Stockholm (toured Europe)
1970 *Edinburgh Festival of Arts*
1976 *Daily Bul Exposition,* Fondation Maeght, St. Paul de Vence, France (toured Europe)
1980 *Ecouter par les yeaux,* Musee d'Art Moderne, Paris
1985 *Livres d'Artistes,* Centre Georges Pompidou, Paris
1990 *Pianofortissimo,* curated by Gina DiMaggio, Fondazione Mudima, Milan, Italy
1991 *La Caravane Passe et. . . ,* Musee d'art Moderne et d'Art Contemporain, Nice, France
1993 *La Donation Vicky Remy,* Musee d'Art Moderne, Saint-Etienne, France
Berlin Americans, Dorothy Iannone and Emmett Williams and guest William Copley, Haus am Lützow Platz, Berlin

Collections:

Museum of Drawings and Prints (Kupferstich-kabinett), Berlin; National Museum of Women in the Arts, Washingon, D.C.; Neue Galerie, Aachen, West Germany; Museum of Modern Art, Saint-Etienne, France; Bibliotheque Nationale, Paris; Kunst Museum, Basel; Berlinische Galerie, Berlin.

Publications:

By IANNONE: Books—*Lists IV,* Cologne 1968; *Story of Bern,* Dusseldorf 1970; *Extase,* with Robert Filliou, Stuttgart 1970; *Uncomplimentary Cards,* and *75 Complimentary Cards,* Dusseldorf 1971; *Danger in Dusseldorf,* Stuttgart 1973; *Speaking to Each Other,* with Mary Harding, West Berlin 1977; *Follow Me,* West Berlin 1978; *The Berlin Beauties,* West Berlin 1978; *Dorothy Iannone and Her Mother Sarah Pucci,* Aachen 1980; *The Whip,* West Berlin 1980; *Censorship and the Irrepressible Drive Toward Love and Divinity,* West Berlin 1982; *How I Began to Paint,* West Berlin 1989; *Courting Ajaxander,* Berlin 1993.

On IANNONE: Book—*Dorothy Iannone,* exhibition catalog with text by Wolfgang Becker, Aachen 1980; *Dorothy Iannone: Works from 1961–66,* exhibition catalog, Berlin 1989; *There Was a Drawing in the Center of this Page* by Robert Filliou, Cologne 1993; *Dorothy Iannone: Love Is Forever, Isn't It?,* exhibition catalog, Berlin 1997. **Articles—**by Ed Sommer in *Kunstforum International* (Mainz),

Dorothy Iannone: *Penthesilea and Achilles,* 1980. ©Dorothy Iannone.

Spring 1973; by Francois Pluchart in *Artitudes* (St. Jeannet), January 1976; by Dieter Schwarz in *Sondern* (Zurich), no. 3, 1978; by Ernst Busche in *Der Tagespiegel* (West Berlin), 17 January 1978; by Barbara Schierle-Wien in *Kunstforum International* (Mainz), August 1982; by Liesbeth Brandt Corstius in *Ruimte* (Amsterdam), February 1986; by Barbara Wien in *TIP* (West Berlin), June 1989; by Heinz Ohff in *Der Tagespiegel* (West Berlin), 22 February 1989; by Andreas Kaps in *Tageszeitung* (West Berlin), 15 March 1989; by Ulrich Clewing in *ZITTY* (Berlin), August 1993.

* * *

COMPLIMENTARY CARD (1975)

I love you because from the outset you caught on to characteristics of the men I control.

UNCOMPLIMENTARY CARD (1975)

How revolting to torture me when I am tied to you.

All the 150 cards were exhibited at the MAGNAFEMININITY: ART & CREATIVITY Exhibition at the Galerie Nachst St. Stephan in Vienna, March/April 1975. Together with her pictures they offer some clues to the strange personality of this American-born artist.

Of all the Women's Liberation artists Dorothy Iannone is the most heterosexual in her approach to the visual interpretation of carnal knowledge and desires, and in order to make her messages abundantly clear she usually spells out her thoughts in capital letters upon her pictures. Cries like "Alas I still cherish Slavery," "What does it mean when we do it this way?," "I admit sometimes I revel in you as a father," and so on. Words are for her as magical as images.

All the pictures are linear, decorative and brightly coloured. Were it not for their style they might be compared with Egyptian hieroglyphic works at their most figurative—particularly those which are made up like comic strips.

Sound also plays its part. This is emitted from boxes whose every side presents opportunities for more pictures. Once in a while, the women in these paintings sport an elaborate head-dress, but for the most part they and their male paramours are naked save for jewellery.

—Sheldon Williams

IIMURA, Taka(hiko)

Nationality: Japanese. **Born:** Tokyo, 20 February 1937. **Education:** Keio High School, Hiyoshi, Kanagawa, graduated 1956: studied political science at Keio University, Tokyo, 1956–59, B.A. 1959. **Family:** Married Akiko Oguchi in 1966. **Career:** Independent artist and filmmaker, since 1960: worked as a film director for Nichei Elga Shin Sha, Iwanami Eiga Sha, TBS, etc., in Tokyo, 1960–66; formed Japan Film Independents, Tokyo, 1962. Has lived in New York, 1966–69, 1971–72, and since 1975. Visiting instructor, Department of Studio Arts, University of Minnesota, Minneapolis, 1975–76; visiting assistant professor, School of Art, Kent State University, Ohio, 1976–77; assistant professor, Department of Cinema, State University of New York, at Binghamton, 1978. **Awards:** Special Prize, *International Experimental Film Festival,* Knokke, Belgium, 1963; Asia Foundation, Fellowship Harvard University International Seminar, Cambridge, Massachusetts, 1966: Cultural Exchange Visitor's Grant, Japan Society, New York, 1966; D.A.A.D. Artist-in-Residence Grant, Berlin, 1973–74; Creative Artists Public Service Grant, New York, 1975; Canada Council Travel Grant, 1977; National Endowment for the Arts Fellowship, 1980; Canada Council Fellowship, 1981; Australia-Japan Foundation Fellowship, Melbourne, 1984; New York Foundation for the Arts Fellowship, 1986; First Prize, Thomas Edison Film and Video Festival, 1986; numerous fellowships and other awards. **Agents:** Filmmakers' Cooperative, 175 Lexington Avenue, New York, New York 10016; Stefanotty Gallery, 50 West 57th Street, New York, New York 10016; PAP Film Galerie, Fihrenstrasse 112, 8031 Grobenzell, West Germany. **Address:** 115 East 9th St., New York, New York 10003, U.S.A. **Web site:** www2.gol.com/users/iimura/home2.html.

Individual Exhibitions (mainly with performance):

1963 Naiqua Gallery, Tokyo (music by Yasunao Tone)
1966 Filmmakers' Cinematheque, New York
1968 Canyon Cinematheque, San Francisco
1969 Institute of Contemporary Arts, London Royal Film Archives, Brussels
1970 Scopio Theatre, Tokyo
1972 Millennium, New York
Kitchen, New York
1973 Galerie Becker, Bochum, West Germany
Stadtische Galerie Lenbachhaus, Munich
1974 Galerie Projection, Cologne
Cinematheque Francaise, Paris
Galerie 23, Paris
1975 Museum of Modern Art, New York
1976 University of California Art Museum, Berkeley
Anthology Film Archives, New York
1977 Millennium, New York
International Cultureel Centrum, Antwerp
Stedeliijk Museum, Amsterdam
1978 Art Gallery of Ontario, Toronto
Carnegie Institute, Pittsburgh
1979 *New Video: Taka Iimura and Shigeko Kubota,* Whitney Museum, New York
State University of New York at Buffalo
Centre Pompidou, Paris
Volksbank Museum, Essen
1980 Palais dex Beaux-Arts, Brussels
Galerie Malina Dinkler, Berlin
Seibu Museum, Tokyo
1981 Musée d'Art Contemporain, Montreal
Museum of Modern Art, New York
1982 Hara Museum of Contemporary Art, Tokyo
Contemporary Art Center, Osaka ,Japan
1983 Seibu Museum of Art, Tokyo
1984 Glass House Theatre, Melbourne
1985 Multi-Media Centre, Zagreb, Yugoslavia
1986 Museum Square, Osaka, Japan
1987 Ted Greenwald Gallery, New York
1991 Studio 200, Tokyo
Millennium, New York
1992 *Takahiko Iimura: Film and Video,* DAAD Galerie, Berlin
1995 Tokyo Metropolitan Museum of Photography
1996 Hiroshima Contemporary Art Museum, Japan
Landes Museum, Lindes, Austria
1997 Institute of Japanese Culture, Rome
1998 Lux Centre, London
Filmmuseum, Munich
1999 The Kitchen, New York

Selected Group Exhibitions:

1963 *International Experimental Film Festival,* Knokke, Belgium
1966 *Japanese Experimental Film,* Museum of Modern Art, New York
1971 *Tokyo Biennale,* Metropolitan Museum, Tokyo
1973 *Neue Medien/Neue Methoden,* Palais Thurna und Taxis, Bregenz, Austria
1974 *Projekt '74,* Kunsthalle, Cologne
1976 *Video Art,* Institute of Contemporary Art, Philadelphia
1978 *Recent Japanese Avantgarde Film,* Museum of Modern Art, New York
1983 *History of Video Art,* Museum of Modern Art, New York
1985 *Japan: Avantgarde of the Future,* City Hall, Genoa, Italy
1987 *Video From Japan,* San Francisco Museum of Modern Art
1991 *Millenium 25 Years,* Museum of Modern Art, New York
1993 *Art on Film/Film on Art,* Los Angeles County Museum of Art
1994 *Japanese Art After 1945: Scream Against the Sky,* Yokohama Museum of Art, Yokohama (traveled to Guggenheim Museum, New York)

Collections:

Anthology Film Archives, New York; Centre Pompidou, Paris; Neue Galerie Ludwig, Aachen, West Germany; Neue Berliner Kunstverein, Berlin; Royal Film Archives, Brussels; Metropolitan Museum, Tokyo; Hara Museum of Contemporary Art, Tokyo.

Publications:

By IIMURA: Books—*Geijutsu to Hi-Geijutsu no Aida* (Between Art and Non-Art), Tokyo 1970; *Paper Film-Love and Flowers' Orgy,* photos, Tokyo 1971; *Paris-Tokyo Cinema Journal,* Tokyo 1984; *Yoko Ono: Her Art and Life,* Tokyo 1985; *Eizo-Jikken no Tameni* (For Image Experimentation), Tokyo 1986; *Post Modern no Gensho* (New

York Art Diary), Tokyo 1987. **Articles**—"Cinema Experimental Japonaise" in *L'Art Vivant* (Paris), February 1975; "I Am (Not) Taka Iimura, I Am (Not) Akiko Iimura" in *The New Television,* Cambridge, Massachusetts 1977; "Cinéma Reflete" in *Cinéma Différent* (Paris), 1977; "Semiotics of Video" in *Art, Artist and the Media,* Graz, Austria 1977; "On Film Installation" in *Millennium Film Journal* (New York), 1978; "24 Frames Per Second" in *Ear Magazine* (New York), November 1978; "Visuality in the Structure of Japanese Art" in *Art and Cinema* (New York), December 1978; "The CD-ROM Eizo Jikken No Tameni (For Visual Experimentation)" in *Leonardo,* vol. 32, no. 1, 1999. **Films**—*Junk,* 1962; *Iro,* 1962; *Al/Love,* 1962–63; *Onan,* 1963; *A Dance Party in the Kingdom of Lilliput,* no. 1, 1964, no. 2, 1966; *I Saw the Shadow,* 1966; *White Calligraphy,* 1967; *Face,* 1968–69; *Film Strips I,* 1966–70; *Film Strips II,* 1966–70; *Filmmakers,* 1966–70; *Buddha Again,* 1969–70, later retitled *Cosmic Buddha: In the River,* 1969–70; *Shutter,* 1971; *Models* (2 reels), 1972; *Plus and Minus,* 1973; *1 to 60 Seconds,* 1973; *Parallel,* 1974; *24 Frames per Second,* 1975, revised 1978; *Sync Sound,* 1975, revised 1977; *Ma* (Intervals), 1975–77; *One Frame Duration,* 1977; *Repeated/Reversed Time,* 1980; *Talking in New York,* 1981; *Talking Pictures,* 1981; *MA—Space/Time in the Garden of Ryoan-Ji,* 1989. **Videos**—*A Chair,* 1970; *Blinking,* 1970; *Time, Time Trilogy 1,* 1971; *Moon Timed, Time Trilogy 2,* 1971; *Time Tunnel, Time Trilogy 3,* 1971; *Self Identity Series 1–5,* 1972–74; *Project Yourself,* Berlin tape 1973, Cologne tape 1974; *Register Yourself,* 1973; *Shifting,* 1974, revised 1975; *Field Works 1–3,* 1974; *Video Field 1–2,* 1975; *Observer/Observed,* 1975; *Observer/Observed/Observer,* 1976; *Camera, Monitor, Frame,* 1976; *Visual Logic (and Illogic),* 1977; *Talking to Myself: Phenomenological Operation,* 1978; *Double Identities (on Turning the Double Negative to the Positive),* 1979; *Self Introduction,* 1982; *Hit Your Own Back,* 1982; *Video Talking: Back to Back* (2 tapes), 1982; *Video Gesture* (2 tapes), 1982; *Video Self: I=You=He/She* (2 tapes), 1982; *A:I:U:E:O:N:* (2 tapes), 1982; *Eight Aspects of a Face* (8 tapes), 1982; *This Is A Camera Which Shoots This,* 1983; *A Conversation with Video,* 1983; *Robina Rese and Me,* 1983; *Talking to Myself at P.S.1,* 1984; *New York Hotspring,* 1984; *Ayers Rock,* 1985; *Moments at the Rock,* 1985; *John Cage Portrait,* 1985; *Nightsongs,* 1986; *Arakawa: Atmospheric Resemblance (A Life of Blank),* 1986; *Monet Garden Synthersized,* 1989; *Scared to Death,* 1989; *New York Day and Night,* 1989; *As I See You You See Me,* 1990; *To the Garden of Water Lilies,* 1990; *Excerpts from "Ayers Rock,"* 1990; *Fluxux Replayed,* 1991; *Sky and Ground,* 1991–93; *Aiueonn Six Features,* 1993; *Performance: Aiueonn Six Features,* 1995; *This Is a Camera Which Shoots This (No. 2),* 1996; *As I See You You See Me (No. 2),* 1997. **Film and video installations**—*Projection Piece #1,* 1968–72; *Projection Piece #2,* 1972; *A Loop Seen as a Line,* 1972; *Timing #1, #2, #3,* 1972; *Project Yourself,* 1972; *Minute and Second,* 1973; *A Loop Seen as a Line (Mobius),* 1973; *Register Yourself,* 1973; *Front and Back,* 1974; *Face/Ings,* 1974; *I=You=He/She,* 1974–79; *I Sec. And-,* 1975; *Identity Piece,* 1976; *Face to Face,* 1977; *Interviewer/Interviewed,* 1980; *Video Talking: Back to Back,* 1982; *The Structure of Seeing/Hearing,* 1983; *400 Frames,* 1984; *Ayers Rock,* 1985; *From Back to Back,* 1986; *Filmed Time,* 1991; *Film as a Line,* 1995; *Metamedia* (CD-ROM), 1997.

On IIMURA: Books—*Film and Videotapes of Taka Iimura,* Berlin 1972; *Taka Iimura: Videotapes 1970–73,* Berlin 1973; *Neue Medien/Neue Methoden,* exhibition catalog by Peter Weiermair, Bregenz, Austria 1973; *Aktionen der Avantgarde,* exhibition catalog, Berlin 1973; *Avantgardistischer Film 1951–71* by Gottfried Schlemmer, Munich 1973; *Taka Iimura: Video Plans,* Aalst, Belgium, 1974; *Taka Iimura: Film e Video,* Rome 1975; *Video Art,* exhibition catalog, Philadelphia, 1976; *Cinema Underground Oggi,* edited by Sergio Luginbuhl, Padua 1972; *Kunst als Lebens Ritual,* edited by Horst Gerhard Habel, Graz, Austria 1974; *Takahiko Iimura: Film and Video,* exhibition catalog, Berlin 1992; *Meta Media: Media Installation,* Tokyo 1995; *From "Time" to "See You,"* Rome 1997; *Eizo Jikken No Tameni* (CD-ROM of collected essays), Tokyo 1997. **Articles**—"Japanese Experimental Films" by Robert Steele in *Film Comment* (New York), Fall 1967; "On Taka Iimura" by Koichiro Ishizaki in *Bijutsu Techo* (Tokyo), June 1970; by Peter Gidal in *Ark* (London), October 1970; "Movie Journal" by Jonas Mekas in the *Village Voice* (New York), July 1972; "3X Avantgarde" by Gottfried Weimann in *Kino* (Berlin), no. 4, 1973; "Reflected Light" by Tony Rayns in *Sight and Sound* (London), Winter 1973; "Zeitablaufe, im Takt skandiert" by Wolfgang Kahlcke in *Die Welt* (Berlin), October 1973; "Vision" by Malcolm LeGrice in *Studio International* (London), November 1973; "Personal Cinema" by Paul Poggiali in the *Soho Weekly News* (New York), May 1974; "Taka Iimura" by Dominique Nogues in *Art Vivant* (Paris), February 1975; by Malcolm Le Grice in *Time Out* (London), April 1975; article by Scott Macdonald in *Afterimage* (Rochester, New York), April 1978; "Electronic Linguistics" by Dan Collins in *Artweek* (Oakland, California), 6 December 1980.

*

During the past few years I have studied the structural relationships of language and video, using English in this case. Video is a unique system for applying this study which is capable of recording image and sound simultaneously. In the closed circuit system, which is self-referential, a camera (observer) is fed back by the monitor (observed), so that the image not only refers to the object which is shot, but also refers back to the subject, who is shooting. This constitutes a sentence-like structure. In language, too, what I am concerned with is not the word as object, but the sentence and its structure.

What I have tried to do in video in the relation of image to language is to include the observer "I" (as the subject) as an integral part of system and sentence. It is the structure of "seeing" involved in both the observer and the observed which is set up by the closed circuit system of video. Unlike film, in closed circuit video one can see the observer and observed at the same time—a feedback in time/space. The relation of the observer and observed is taken at language level as "I" and "You," as a sentence "I see you." The very sentence is transferred to a closed circuit system in which a camera and a monitor are mediated between "I" and "You," and the one with the camera is not only "I" who observes but also "You" who is observed. This means that an image functions as the observer in relation to speech: these are double functions, and speech is equal in importance to the image, either working separately (de-synchronized) from, or identically (synchronized) with, the image. The words "I" and "You" switch roles between what is one and off the screen (monitor), and then assume each other's position.

For instance, if the picture says "I," the off-screen voice says "You," or the picture says "You" and the off-screen voice says "I," then the role of the observer and observed shift accordingly. It is the direction of observation that is affected: from subject to object and object to subject in an interrelated manner. Consequently, an identical image has different implications according to the description of the words, and, conversely, identical speech is also able to indicate different images. All of these are taped using feedback control of a closed circuit system which permits manipulation of image and sound simultaneously at different levels. The relation of the observer and observed, therefore, has the structure of a round trip. And the feedback in the system is used neither for technical nor for aesthetic aims but used for and within the conceptual framework.

The ''Observer/Observed'' series (1975–76) was developed out of the basic pattern of ''I see you'' with variations and more complicated sentences such as ''I see you (who is) shooting me'' and ''I see myself (who is) shooting you.'' These compound sentences are set up by two facing cameras and monitors which are fed back to each other, so that exact transfer of the sentence is possible, and are made switchable according to the image: who is shooting whom. The media employed in the tapes are three: image, voiced (and voiced over) sentence; and symbolic letters (superimposed). Each medium works independently, defining the others. The works are composed in advanced with diagrammed texts, and then taped.

—Taka Iimura

IMMENDORFF, Jörg

Nationality: German. **Born:** Bleckede bei Luneberg, 14 June 1945. **Education:** Volkschule and Gymnasium, Luneberg, until 1963; studied stage design, under Teo Otto, 1963–64, and art, under Joseph Beuys, 1964–66, Kunstakademie, Dusseldorf. **Career:** Independent artist, Dusseldorf, since 1966: performed first art actions at the Kunstakademie, Dusseldorf, 1965–66; organized ''Lidl'' activities in Dusseldorf and other locations, 1968–69; made joint painterly activities and exhibitions with the artist A. R. Penck (Ralf Winkler), 1977–78; first ''Cafe Deutschland'' works, Dusseldorf, 1978; opened Cafe La Paloma, Hamburg, 1984; created stage designs and costumes for the opera *Elektra* at the Bremen Stadttheater. Lived for three months in Auckland, New Zealand. Teacher, Dumont-Lindemann elementary school, Dusseldorf, 1968–80; guest professor, Konsthogskolan, Stockholm, 1981; guest instructor, Hamburg Kunstakademie and Trondheim Kunstakademie, 1982–83; head of course at the Werkschule, Cologne, 1984; professor, Städelschule, Frankfurt am Main, since 1989. **Agents:** Galerie Michael Werner, Gertrudenstrasse 24–28, 500 Cologne 1; Galerie Daniel Templon, 30 rue Beaubourg 75003 Paris; Michael Werner Gallery, 21 East 67th St., New York, New York 10021.

Individual Exhibitions:

1961 New Orleans Jazz Club, Bonn
1965 Galerie Schmela, Dusseldorf
1966 *Deutsch Deutsch Deutsch,* Galerie Fulda, Fulda West Germany
Vietnam Vietnam Vietnam, Galerie Aachen, Aachen, West Germany
1967 *Für alle Lieben in der Welt,* Galerie Art Intermedia, Cologne
1968 Galerie Patio, Frankfurt
Staatliche Ingenieurschule, Dusseldorf
1969 Galerie Lichter, Frakfurt
Lidl-Week, A 379089, Antwerp
Planungsübersicht einer Arbeitswoche, August 1968, Galerie Michael Werner, Cologne
1971 *Die Arbeit and einer Hauptschule,* Galerie Michael Werner, Cologne
Galerie Heiner Friedrich, Munich
1972 *Rechenschaftsbericht,* Galerie Michael Werner, Cologne
1973 *Hier und jetzt: Das tun was zu tun ist,* Westfälischer Kunstverein, Munster, West Germany
Galerie Michael Werner, Cologne
Galerie Loehr, Frankfurt
Galerie Cornels, Baden-Baden, West Germany
1974 Daner Galleriet, Copenhagen
Galerie Michael Werner, Cologne
Galerie am Savignyplatz, West Berlin
1975 Galerie Michael Werner, Cologne
Galerie Nächst St. Stephan, Vienna
1976 Galerie Seriaal/Helen van der Meij, Amsterdam
Galerie Michael Werner, Cologne
1977 Museum van Hedendaagse Kunst, Utrecht, Netherlands
Penck mal Immendorff, Immendorrff mal Penck, Galerie Michael Werner, Cologne (with A. R. Penck)
1978 Galerie Maier-Hahn, Dusseldorf
Café Deutschland, Galerie Michael Werner, Cologne
1979 *Café Deutschland,* Kunstmuseum, Basel
Galerie Helen van der Meij, Amsterdam
Positionen: Situation, Plastiken, Galerie Michael Werner, Cologne
Teilbau, Bleckede an der Elbe
1980 *Malermut rundum,* Kunsthalle, Bern
1981 *Pinselwiderstand (4x),* Van Abbemuseum, Eindhoven, Netherlands
Eisende, Van Abbemuseum, Eindhoven, Netherlands (with Jannis Kounellis)
Teilbau, Galerie Hans Neuendorf, Hamburg
Galeria Heinrich Ehrhardt, Madrid
1982 *Kein Licht für wen?,* Galerie Michael Werner, Cologne
Grüße von der Nordfront, Galerie Fred Jahn, Munich
Café Deutschland/Adlerhälfte, Kunsthalle, Dusseldorf
Galerie Strelow, Dusseldorf
Galerie Daniel Templon, Paris
Vereiniging Aktuele Kunst von Ghent, Gent, Belgium
Galerie Rudolf Springer, West Berlin
Sonnabend Gallery, New York
Edition Sabine Knust, Munich (with A. R. Penck)
1983 Kastrupgardsamlingen, Kastrup, Denmark
Café Deutschland gut, Galerie Rudolf Springer, West Berlin
Van Abbemuseum, Eindhoven, Netherlands
Kunsthalle, Dusseldorf
Ratinger Hof, Dusseldorf
Studio d'Arte Galleria Cannaviello, Milan
Edition Sabine Knust, Munich
Nigel Greenwood Gallery, London

Jörg Immendorff in his studio, ca. 1980–97. ©K.M. Westermann/Corbis.

38. Parteitag, Ratinger Hof, Dusseldorf
New 57 Gallery, Edinburgh
Kunsthaus, Zurich
Sonnabend Gallery, New York
Galerie Gillespie-Laage-Salomon, Paris
1983–84 *Sammler: Übermalte Linoldrucke,* Galerie Sabine Knust, Munich
Café Deutschland gut, Galerie Michael Werner, Cologne
1984 Museum of Modern Art, Oxford
Galerie Ascan Crone, Hamburg
Mary Boone Gallery, New York
Café Deutschland gut, Kunsthalle, Hamburg
Museo de Bellas Artes, Bilbao, Spain
Café Deutschland gut, Galerie Schurr, Stuttgart
Beben/beben, Galerie Michael Werner, Cologne
Galerie Gillespie-Laage-Salomon, Paris
Café Deutschland gut, Galerie Sabine Knust, Munich
Galerie Heinrich Erhardt, Madrid
Museo de Bilbao, Bilbao
Galerie Heinrich Erhardt, Frankfurt
Museum of Modern Art, Oxford
Galerie Rudolf Zwirner, Cologne
1985 Maison de la Culture de la Communication, St. Etienne, France
Kunstverein, Braunschweig
Jörg Immendorff: Bilder und die gesamte Grafik, W. Wittrock Kunsthandel, Dusseldorf
1986 Mary Boone Gallery, New York
Nigel Greenwood Gallery, London
Jörg Immendorff: 10 Bilder von 1978 aus Privatsammlungen, Galerie Michael Werner, Cologne
1987 *Jörg Immendorff: Neue Editionen,* Maximilianverlag/Sabine Knust, Munich
Jörg Immendorff: Neue Arbeiten, Galerie Michael Werner, Cologne
1988 *Jörg Immendorff in Auckland,* Auckland City Gallery, Auckland, New Zealand
Jörg Immendorff: Die Zauberflöte, Galerie Thaddaeus Ropac I, Salzburg
1989 *Jörg Immendorff—Zeichne!—Zeichnung 1959–1989,* Roemer-und Pelizaeus Museum Hildesheim, Hildesheim
Jörg Immendorff: Zeichnungen, Galerie Michael Werner, Cologne
Jörg Immendorff: Oeuvres récentes, Galerie Daniel Templon, Paris
1990 *Das großartige, ewige 1. Semester,* Portikus, Frankfurt am Main
Jörg Immendorff: Galeria Juana de Aizpuru, Madrid
Jörg Immendorff: Peintures 1981–1989, Galerie de l'Ecole d'Art, Marseille

Jörg Immendorff: Bilder und Arbeiten auf Papier, Galerie Raymond Bollag, Zurich
Jörg Immendorff: Pinturas, Galeria Juana de Aizpuru, Seville
Galerie Frank Hänel, Frankfurt am Main
1991 Villa Merkel, Esslingen
Museum für Moderne Kunst, Vienna
Galerie Krinzinger, Vienna
Michael Werner Gallery, New York
1992 Galerie Michael Werner, Cologne
Michael Werner Gallery, New York
Museum Boymans-van Beuningen, Rotterdam
Haags Gemeentemuseum, The Hague
Goethe Institute, Osaka
1993 Seoul Arts Center, Seoul
Hong Kong Arts Center, Hong Kong
Galerie Daniel Templon, Paris
Galerie Piece Unique, Paris
Is It About a Bicycle? Centre Georges Pompidou Musee National d'Art Moderne, Paris
Ace Contemporary exhibitions, Los Angeles
1994 *Jörg Immendorff: Café de Flore,* Museo Rufino Tamayo, Mexico City (catalog)
Malfiguren, Museum Moderner Kunst, Vienna
Jörg Immendorff: Reflective Painting, Abbaye Saint-Andre, Centre d'Art Contemporain, Meymac (catalog)
German Art 1964–1994, Galerie Thaddäus Ropac, Salzburg
1997 Michael Werner Gallery, New York
Jörg Immendorff: Rake's Progress—A Series Comprised of 8 Coloured Etchings, Stadtgalerie Sundern, Germany(catalog)
1998 *Malerdebatte,* Bonner Kunstmuseum, Bonn
1999 *Jörg Immendorff's Painter's Wood,* Museum Kuppersmuhle, Duisburg (catalog)
2001 *Lidl Work and Recent Paintings,* Anton Kern Gallery, New York
New Paintings, Michael Werner Gallery, New York

Selected Group Exhibitions:

1967 *Hommage a Lidice,* Galerie René Block, West Berlin
1972 *Documenta 5,* Museum Fridericianum, Kassel, West Germany
1973 *Medium Fotografie,* Stadtisches Museum, Leverkusen, West Germany
1976 *Attualita Internazionale,* at the *XXXVII Biennale,* Venice
1979 *Malerei auf Papier,* Badischer Kunstverein, Karlsruhe, West Germany
1981 *Art Allemagne Aujourd'hui,* Musée d'Art Moderne de la Ville, Paris
1982 *Documenta 7*
1983 *New Figuration,* University of California, Los Angeles
1985 *The European Iceberg,* Art Gallery of Ontario, Toronto
1987 *Avant-Garde in the Eighties,* Los Angeles County Museum of Art
1994 *Painter's Images,* Museum Moderner Kunst, Vienna (catalog)
1995 *West Choir East Portal: 12 Contemporary Artistic Positions in Germany,* Galerie im Marstall, Berlin (catalog)
1996 *Red Corona: Above the Volcano,* Centro Atlantico de Arte Moderno, Las Palmas, Spain (catalog)
Beuys and After: Contemporary German Drawings from the Collection, Museum of Modern Art, New York (catalog)
1997 *German Art in Singapore: Contemporary Art from the Collection of the Kunstmuseum Bonn,* Singapore Art Museum (catalog)
Violent Painting, Museum Wurth, Kunzelsau-Gaisbach, Germany (catalog)

Collections:

Kupferstichkabinett, Basel; Neue Galerie, Aachen; Museum voor Hedendaagse Kunst, Utrecht; Museum Boymans-van Beuningen, Rotterdam; Van Abbemuseum, Eidhoven.

Publications:

By IMMENDORFF: Books and leaflets—*Lidlstadt,* Dusseldorf 1968; *Den Eisbaren mal reinhalten,* Dusseldorf 1968; *Hier und jetzt: Das tun, was zu tun ist,* Cologne and New York 1973; *Deutschland mal Deutschland,* with A. R. Penck, Munich 1979; *Der Hund stosst im Laufe der Woche zu mir,* exhibition catalog with text by Siegfried Gohr, Stockholm 1981; *LIDL 1966–1970,* Eindhoven, Netherlands 1981; *Grusse von der Nordfront,* with poem by A. R. Penck, Munich 1982; *Kein Licht fur wen?,* Cologne 1982; *Brandenburger Tor,* with poems by A. R. Penck, New York 1982; *Cafe Deutschland-Gut,* Cologne 1983. **Articles**—interview with Heinz-Norbert Jocks in *Kunstforum International,* no. 125, January-February 1994.

On IMMENDORFF: Books—*Gedanken zu Jörg Immendorff's Babies und Aktionen,* leaflet by Chris Reinicke, Dusseldorf 1968; *Jörg Immendorff,* exhibition catalog with text by Wouter Kotte and Jurgen Kramer, Utrecht 1977; *Cafe Deutschland von Jörg Immendorff,* with text by Johannes Gachnang, Siegfried Gohr and Rudi H. Fuchs, Cologne 1978; *Jörg Immendorff: Cafe Deutschland,* exhibition catalog with text by Dieter Koepplin, Basel 1979; *Jörg Immendorff: Malermut rundum,* exhibition catalog by Johannes Gachnang, Bern 1981; *Jörg Immendorff: Cafe Deutschland/Adlerhalfte,* exhibition catalog by Jurgen Harten and Ulrich Kempel, Dusseldorf 1982; *Jörg Immendorff: Cafe Deutschland and Related Works,* exhibition catalog with text by David Elliott and Harald Szeemann, Oxford 1984; *Jörg Immendorff,* exhibition catalog by E. Daragon, St. Etienne 1985. **Articles**—"Jörg Immendorff: Tout Peindre" by Catherine Millet in *Art Press,* no. Hors-serie, no. 15, 1994; "Jörg Immendorff" by Francesco Bonami in *Flash Art,* vol. 30, no. 193, March-April 1997; "Jörg Immendorff" in *Sztuka,* vol. 21, no. 7–12, 1997.

* * *

Jörg Immendorf is one of those German artists who, having been pupils of Joseph Beuys in Dusseldorf, later on established themselves along a very different line to that of their teacher. Instead of exploring novel solutions to the problem of the relationship between thought and matter, Immendorff has always preferred the more traditional means of artistic expression—those of painting, sculpting and drawing.

From his teacher, though, Immendorff inherited a profound involvement with art at the level of ideas, which, in his case, is put into practice as political involvement. Immendorff studied stage design, and thus became involved with theatre and painting "on the road," which illustrates social issues by means of "agit prop" and the styles of popular culture (Ho Chi Min, 1974).

Immendorff's political engagement, however, does not merely identify itself with an ideology for the sake of opposition. His critical stance prevents him from identifying unconditionally with the policy of a traditional and institutionalized Marxist Left, that is to say, with "socialist realism."

The most renowned of Immendorff's works, the cycle *Cafe Deutschland,* was conceived after seeing Renato Guttuso's *Cafe Creco.* At the 1976 Venice Biennale, this work of the Italian artist was hung next to that of Immendorff. It was a chance for Immendorff to strengthen his attempts at deconstructing the language of realism—a realism that depended on imposing idealistic pretensions onto painting in order to re-present a reality, even in its "revolutionary" expression. To Immendorff, the "real" itself cannot be represented except by recurring as an excessive, overblown language. Instead of a Roman cafe (a meeting place for artists so minutely described in Guttuso's work in its realistic "truth"), in Immendorff we find a symbolic place, a locus of the mind bearing the marks of physical and spiritual degradation. *Cafe Deutschland* is a kind of bar-discotheque, crammed with mysterious and dark apparitions, full of private as well as collective symbols, all equally livid and unnerving. The atmosphere is vaguely anguished. The artist's intention, through the use of these symbolic images, is to make the viewer aware of the need to subvert political order.

Immendorff's concern with the political actualities of the two Germanies has been constantly at the core of his work, and just as deep is his determination to expose the recent past and its tragic implications for a contemporary Europe. Many of Immendorff's characters belong to German history: from Brecht to Schmidt and Honecker. Others represent the concept of despotic authority: the policeman, soldier or—as an allegory—the German Eagle or the Swastika. He includes portraits of himself, and of his friend and colleague Penck: their presence amounts to a declaration of the imperative need for the contemporary artist to be involved in social and political agitation.

Many of Immendorff's works are, in fact, the restatement of recurrent images with which he underlines this imperative. In his work, the Brandenburg Gate, a universal image of war and division, is often buttressed by Immendorff with extravagant totems of architectural detail or with common items of household furniture, so presenting it as an absurd and chaotic structure, deriding it as a mere piece of tinsel. Even more grotesquely rendered is the German Eagle or particular scenes of the urban landscape to be found in several of his drawings. In his drawings, Immendorff seems to reject the flat referentiality of realism as a parody or caricature of itself. He in fact adopts a degraded language, a kind of sketchiness borrowed, not so much from popular culture of an immediate readable quality, as from expressionism, especially from the contemporary "language" of juvenile urban culture.

It is not by chance that portraits of Punks appear often in Immendorff's paintings. From such a metropolitan culture or subculture, so rich in connotations as to render them near redundant, Immendorff adopts the degraded, derisive aspects, the expressive violence, and that anarchist spirit so difficult to label as "right" or "left." In no instance, though, does the parody of visual vocabulary and violence become the vehicle for an indifferent discourse in his work.

In some recent statements, Immendorff has affirmed that his painting transcends manifest meanings—in regard to German history—inasmuch as it touches only upon the question of the Subject's position in the World. The concept of "two Germanies," the clash between power and subversion, is to be understood as a metaphor for the universal principles of Good and Evil, either of which the Subject has to choose. His aim is to give historical identity to these two principles. Through the paintings, he demonstrates that the choice is unavoidable. In this sense, over and above any ideological certainty, Immendorff's art today represents one of the finest attempts to actualize the concept of Tragic Art.

—Giorgio Verzotti

INDIANA, Robert

Nationality: American. **Born:** Robert Clark in New Castle, Indiana, 13 September 1928. **Education:** John Herron School of Art, Indianapolis, 1946; Munson-Williams-Proctor Institute, Utica, New York, 1947–48; School of the Art Institute of Chicago, 1949–53, B.F.A. 1953; University of Edinburgh and Edinburgh College of Art, 1953–54. **Military Service:** Served in the United States Army, 1947–49. **Career:** Painter: has lived and worked in New York since 1954. Artist-in-residence, Center of Contemporary Art, Aspen, Colorado, summer 1968. Designed 8-cent U.S. postage stamp (400 million printed), 1973. **Awards:** George Brown Travelling Fellowship, 1953; Summer Scholarship, Skowhegan School of Painting and Sculpture, Maine, 1953; Indiana Arts Commission Award, 1973. D.F.A.: University of Indiana, Bloomington, 1977. **Agent:** Marisa del Re Gallery, 41 East 57th Street, New York, New York 10022; Jack Rutberg Fine Arts, 357 North La Brea Avenue, Los Angeles, California 90036. **Address:** c/o Vinalhanen Press, P.O. Box 464, Vinalhaven, Maine 04863–0464.

Individual Exhibitions:

1962 Stable Gallery, New York
1963 Walker Art Center, Minneapolis
Institute of Contemporary Art, Boston
1964 Stable Gallery, New York
1965 Rolf Nelson Gallery, Los Angeles
Dayton's Gallery 12, Minneapolis
1966 Stable Gallery, New York
Galerie Alfred Schmela, Dusseldorf
Stedelijk van Abbemuseum, Eindhoven, Netherlands
Museum Haus Lange, Krefeld, West Germany
Württembergischer Kunstverein, Stuttgart
1968 Institute of Contemporary Art, University of Pennsylvania, Philadelphia
Toledo Museum of Art, Ohio
Hunter Gallery, Aspen, Colorado
1969 Creighton University, Omaha, Nebraska
Graphics, St. Mary's College, Notre Dame, Indiana
Colby College Art Museum, Waterville, Maine
1970 Currier Gallery of Art, Manchester, New Hampshire
Bowdoin College Museum of Art, Brunswick, Maine

Brandeis University, Waltham, Massachusetts
1971 Galerie im Haus Behr, Hindenburgbau, Stuttgart
Galerie de Gestlo, Bremen, West Germany
Overbeck Gesellschaft, Lubeck
Galerie Christoph Durr, Munich
Galerie Droscher-Furneisen, Hamburg
Badischer Kunstverein, Karlsruhe
Amerika Haus, Berlin
1972 Denise René Gallery, New York
Louisiana Museum, Humblebaek, Denmark
Didrichsens Konstmuseum, Helsinki
1973 Summit Art Center, New Jersey
1975 Galerie Denise Rene, New York
1976 Galerie Denise Rene, New York
1977 University of Texas, Austin
Chrysler Museum, Norfolk, Virginia
1978 State University of New York at Purchase
South Bend Art Center, Indiana
1982 William A. Farnsworth Art Museum, Rockland, Maine
Colby College, Waterville, Maine
1983 Miami University, Oxford, Ohio
1984 National Museum of American Art, Washington, D.C.
1998 *Retrospective 1958–1998,* Musee d'Art Moderne et d'Art Contemporain, Nice, France (catalog)
1999 *Love and the American Dream: The Art of Robert Indiana,* Portland Museum of Art, Maine (catalog)

Selected Group Exhibitions:

1968 *Documenta,* Kassel, West Germany
1969 *Pop Art Redefined,* Hayward Gallery, London
1972 *The Modern Images,* High Museum of Art, Atlanta
1973 *The Zero Room,* Kunstmuseum, Dusseldorf
1974 *12 American Painters,* Virginia Museum, Richmond
Inaugural Exhibition, Hirshhorn Museum, Washington, D.C.
1975 *American Art since 1945,* Museum of Modern Art, New York
1977 *20th National Print Exhibition,* Brooklyn Museum, New York
1980 *100 Artists, 100 Years,* Art Institute of Chicago
American Sculpture: Gifts of Howard and Jean Lipman, Whitney Museum, New York
1997 *De Klein à Warhol: Face-à-Face,* Musée National d'Art Moderne et du Musée d'Art Contemporain de Nice (catalog)
1999 *In Company: Robert Creeley's Collaborations,* Castellani Art Museum of Niagara University, Niagara Falls, New York (catalog)
2000 *Crossroads of American Sculpture: David Smith, George Rickey, John Chamberlain, Robert Indiana, William T. Wiley, Bruce Nauman,* Indianapolis Museum of Art (catalog)

Collections:

Metropolitan Museum of Art, New York; Museum of Modern Art, New York; Whitney Museum, New York; Albright-Knox Art Gallery, Buffalo, New York; Baltimore Museum of Art; Indianapolis Museum of Art; Los Angles County Museum of Art; San Francisco Museum of Modern Art; Art Gallery of Ontario, Toronto; Stedelijk Museum, Amsterdam.

Publications:

By INDIANA: Book—*Robert Indiana: Figures of Speech,* with Susan Elizabeth Ryan, New Haven 2000. **Articles—**statement in *Art Now* (New York), 1969 ''Pop: Interview with Robert Indiana,'' with Phyllis Tuchman, in *Artnews* (New York), May 1974; statement, and interview with D. B. Goodal, in *Robert Indiana,* exhibition catalog, Austin, Texas 1977; ''American Pop Impressions: A Changing Perspective'' in *Printmaking Today,* vol. 5, no. 2, Summer 1996.

On INDIANA: Books—*Robert Indiana: Graphics,* exhibition catalog by Richard Raymond, Notre Dame, Indiana 1969; *Robert Indiana: Prints and Posters 1961–71* by William Katz, Stuttgart and New York 1971; *Icons and Images of the 60's* by Nicolas and Elena Calas, New York 1971; *Pop as Art: A Survey of the New Superrealism,* by Mario Amaya, London 1972; *Robert Indiana,* exhibition catalog with text by Marius B. Peladeau, Waterville 1982; *Wood Works: Constructions by Robert Indiana,* exhibition catalog with essay by Virginia M. Mecklenburg, Washington, D.C. 1984; *Pop Art: A Critical History,* edited by Steven Henry Madoff, Berkeley 1997. **Articles—**''The Top Bandanna'' by Polly Harrold in *Arts Indiana,* vol. 17, no. 6, September 1995. **CD—***Crossroads of American Sculpture,* Indianapolis 2000.

* * *

Like other Pop artists, Robert Indiana has developed his own characteristic recipe or formula—in his case the use of sign lettering combined with bold hard edge treatment. Esentially non-figurative, his simple geometric shapes are emblazoned with stenciled inscriptions in strong billboard colours. The work of other American pop artists, such as Lichtenstein and Rosenquist, also has an obvious affinity with the flat brilliance of a Hard Edge painter like Ellsworth Kelly, all having simple, uncompromising imagery and a common absence of any personality in the physical handling of the medium. Suzi Gablik has indeed tried to ''redefine'' Pop Art by limiting it to the particular variety with close affinities to Hard Edge abstraction—a redefinition which would exclude all the British pop artists, as well as such Americans as Jim Dine and Edward Kienholz.

At any rate the affinities of Indiana's work with Hard Edge abstraction are neither coincidental nor accidental, for in 1954 he settled in New York, living close to and becoming friendly with Ellsworth Kelly, who influenced his style. For several years Indiana painted Hard Edge pictures using the motif of the bilobed, fan-shaped Ginkgo leaf; for instance. ''The Sweet Mystery'' (1960–61), in which a double leaf is silhoutted on a dark rectangle, with the title stencilled below. The large ''Crucifix'' mural (1958–9) uses ginkgo and avocado as well as the circles which were to become so characteristic a motif in Indiana's work, and which seem to have been inspired by a circular stencil he had found in his sail loft. This also showed its influence on the geometric wood and metal constructions on which he stencilled insignia and slogans such as ''Cuba.''

American Pop art made its dramatic public debut in 1962 with exhibitions by Lichtenstein, Warhol, Rosenquist, Wesselman, and Indiana's first one-man show. And if his lettered signs and directional traffic symbols didn't have quite the same shock impact as the others' even more banal images, it was clear that he too had taken over crude commercial imagery and presentational technique. Indiana collaborated with Warhol on the film *EAT* in 1964, and for his first public commission he made a huge 20-foot *EAT* sign for the outside of the New York State Pavilion at the 1964 New York World's Fair.

Indiana's early water-colours reveal the influence of older American artists such as Hopper, Sheeler and Charles Demuth. The latter's ''poster-portraits'' incorporating the Cubist use of words, letters, and numerals as ready-made formal elements, have had a considerable influence on Pop Art, and his ''I Saw the Figure 5 in Gold'' (1928) inspired Indiana's use of numbers in such works as ''The Demuth American Dream No. 5'' (1963). The culmination of this use of numbers came with Indiana's vertical sequence of the numbers 1 to 10 hung in countdown to a height of over 50 feet for the American Pavilion at Montreal's Expo 67.

Indiana's LOVE paintings in 1966 were accompanied by LOVE sculptures made with Herbert Feuerlicht in carved aluminium. This and other typical Indiana slogans such as DIE, KILL, ERR, HUG, YIELD have been seen by some critics who long for a radical avant-garde as a satirical challenge to the naive optimism of the American dream, forcing an unwilling society to look at its underlying motivations, crude materialism, spritual vacuity and ludicrously sexualized environment. Certainly Indiana's stencilled legends in their concentric rings of bright colour refer to Americana in all its forms, including history and also literature in his poetic evocations of Melville and Whitman. But only rarely does he make any out-right social comment, as in his painting on the racial violence at Selma, Alabama, and his own comments on his EAT signs hardly suggest any satirical intent: ''The word 'eat' is reassuring, it means not only food, but life. When a mother feeds her children, the process makes her indulgent, a giver of life, of love, of kindness.'' Indiana in fact shares the ''cool'' disinvolved style common to American Pop Art, which makes it not so much subversive but a straightforward reflection of American society as it is, which thus made Pop Art so immediately acceptable.

—Konstantin Bazarov

INFANTE, Francisco

Nationality: Russian. **Born:** Francisco Infante-Arana, Vasilevka, Saratov Province, 1943, to a Spanish father and a Russian mother. **Education:** Studied art at the Surikov Art School and monumental sculpture at the Stroganoff Art School, 1956–62. **Family**: Married Nonna Goriunova, his frequent collaborator, 1964; children: two sons, Pakito and Patosha. **Career:** Independent artist, in Moscow, since 1965. Member of the group ''Dvizhenie'' (''Movement,'' 1964–1966) and founder of the group ''ARGO'' (''Authors' Working Group,'' 1970); began exhibiting kinetic sculptures in the mid-1960s; invented sculptural ''arkhitekturs,'' which he called ''autonomous artistic systems in cosmic space,'' in 1970; discovered his key artistic device, the ''artefact,'' in 1975. **Awards:** Russian State Prize for Literature and Art, 1996.

Individual Exhibitions

1974 Spanish Center, Moscow
1979 Palace of Culture, Moscow
Palace of Culture, Leningrad
1981 Center for Technological Aesthetics, Moscow
Exhibition Hall on Malaia Gruzinkaia Street, Moscow
Artefactions, Chernogolovka, Moscow Province
1982 The Central Institute for the Theory and History of Architecture, Moscow
Swallow Hills (performance), Moscow
The Polytechnic Institute, Moscow
Artists' House at Kuznetsky Bridge, Moscow
1984 Moscow Planetarium
House of Knowledge, Riga
Museum of Photography, Shyaulyai, Lithuania
Moscow Institute for the Study of Governance
Artists' House at Kuznetsky Bridge, Moscow
1985 SDRI, Moscow
1986 Scholars' House AN SSSR, Moscow
House of Cinema, Moscow
1987 Inter-Republic House of Independent Art, Moscow
The Journalists' Union, Moscow
Stara Radnitse Gallery, Brno, Czechoslovakia
1988 Cinematographers' House, Moscow
The State University House of Culture, Odessa
1989 EXPO, Chicago
Wilhelm Hack Museum, Ludwigshaffen, Germany
Gallery Rosa Esman, New York
1990 Galerie Alex Lachman, Cologne
1991 Galeria Fernando Duran, Madrid
Galerie Schoeller, Düsseldorf
Edition & Galerie Hoffmann, Fridberg
Gallery Regina, Moscow
1992 Tretiakovsky Gallery, Moscow
1993 La Base, Paris
Galeria Emilio Navarro, Madrid
1994 Tsaritsina Museum and Nature Preserve, Moscow
Hillside Gallery, Tokyo
Chateau de la Napoule, France
''In Your House'' Club, Moscow
1995 Sala de exposiciones Recalde, Bilbao, Spain
1996 Russian Education Academy, Moscow
Kino Gallery, Moscow
Zolgasse Gallery, Dornbern, Austria
Gallery Karenina, Vienna
1997 Shakespeare & Company, Moscow
Art Front Gallery, Tokyo
Instituto universitario orientale, Naples
An Evening with Francisco Infante, 83 Bodoni, Rome
Kurgan Province Museum, Russia
1998 Gallery Fenix, Moscow
Tabakman Gallery, New York
Tretiakovsky Gallery, Moscow

Selected Group Exhibitions:

1963 Central Home of Art Workers, Moscow
1965 *Alteernativa attuale 2,* Acuilla, Italy
1966 *Kunst-Light-Kunst,* Endhoven, Netherlands
Kinetika, Cologne
Documenta IV, Kassel, Germany
1968 *Documenta V,* Kassel, Germany
1969 *Nuova Scuola di Mosca,* Florence
La Bienalle-69, Nurenberg
1970 *Nuovi correnti a Mosca,* Lugano, Switzerland

1973 *Progressive Russiche Kunst,* Cologne
1976 *Exposition au Musée en Exil,* (Glezer Collection), Mongeron, France
1977 *La nuova arte Sovietica,* La Bienalle di Venezia
L'Art contemporain russe, Palais de Congrès, Paris
Unofficial Art from the Soviet Union, ICA, London
New Art from the Soviet Union, Washington, D.C., Ithaca, New York, and New York City
1978 *Contemporary Unofficial Art,* Municipal Museum, Tokyo
1981 *Nouvelles tendances de l'art russe non-officiel 1970–1980,* Paris
1984 *Photography and Art,* Tartu, Estonia
Tradition Gegenwart. Russiche und Sovietische Kunst, Hannover, Dusseldorf, Stuttgart
Foto-84, 28 Malaia Gruzinskaia, Moscow
1986 *Art of Today. 1st International Exhibition,* Club of Young Artists, Budapest
50 jahre moderne Farbfotografie, Cologne
1987 *Another Russia,* Museum of Modern Art, Oxford
1988 *Olympiad of Arts,* Museum of Contemporary Art, Seoul
Arco-88, Galerie de France, Madrid
1989 *The New Soviet Avant-Garde,* International House, New York
1990 *In de USSR Erbuiten—28 Kunstenaars1970–1980,* Stedelijk Museum, Amsterdam
The Quest of Self-Expression: Painting in Moscow and Leningrad 1965–1990, Wexner Museum of Arts, Columbus, Ohio
1991 *Seven Evenings,* State Literary Museum, Moscow
1994 *No and the Conformists,* Russian State Museum, Saint Petersburg
1995 *Exhibition of A. Glezer's Collection,* State Pushkin Museum, Moscow
1996 *Non-Conformists and the Second Russian Avant-Garde,* Moscow, Saint Petersburg, and Frankfurt
Contemporary Russian Art, Tretiakovsky Gallery, Moscow
1999 *Landshapes,* Southeast Museum of Photography, Daytona Beach, Florida

Collections:

Tretiakovsky Gallery, State Pushkin Museum, Moscow; Russian State Museum, Saint Petersburg; Museum of Contemporary Art, Moscow; Fine Arts Museum, Lodz, Poland; Brooklyn Museum, New York; Wilhelm Hack Museum, Kunstmuseum, Berne, Switzerland; Wexner Museum of Art, Columbus, Ohio; Museum of Contemporary Art, Seoul; Museum Art Gallery, Peterboro, England.

Publications:

On INFANTE: Book—*Monografiia* (includes theoretical statements by Infante). Moscow 2000. **Film—***Moscou—Première Vue* (for French TV), directed by Iusef Pasternak, 1992.

* * *

Francisco Infante has been a key figure in Russian art for the past thirty-five years. His earliest work, like that of many other Soviet artists of the 1960s, is marked—thanks to the Krushchev ''thaw''—by a turn away from the Socialist Realist canon, back toward the first Soviet avant-garde of the late 1910s and 1920s. Guided by two overriding sensations, ''infinity'' and ''the mystery of the world,'' Infante was naturally drawn to the geometrism and cosmic aspirations of Malevich's Suprematism; in his enthusiasm for an art that embraced engineering and the sciences of the cosmos, to Soviet Constructivism; in his interest in three-dimensionality, technology, and interactivity, to Naum Gabo.

Inspired by his optimistic faith in the harmony of art and technology, nature and mankind, Infante produced many series of geometric and kinetic art forms, his ''Spirals'' (1965), ''Project to Reconstruct the Starry Sky'' (1965–67), and ''Galactica'' (1967) being particularly successful. The ''Spirals'' series features tempera paintings of vertical and horizontal spirals soaring beyond the limits of the canvas, into infinity; in the ''Project to Reconstruct the Starry Sky'' Infante paints horizons of trees in fractal-like leafy patterns above which geometric arrangements of sparkling stars fill the heavens; in ''Galactica,'' the first kinetic object displayed (briefly) in Moscow, Infante combined sound (electronic music), motion (an elliptically-shaped motor at Gallactica's center), light (lamps), and material (netting attached to geometrically shaped metal poles) in a construction of ten by seven by five meters. However, unlike the more orthodox kinetic and cosmist artists of the time, Infante retained a Romantic faith in the human creator and the infinite power of nature itself which he strikingly demonstrated in his ''Suprematist Games'' (1968). Here, travelling to the outskirts of Moscow (just as the Conceptualists would later do to stage their installations), Infante placed Malevich's abstract, mathematical forms against a ''white background'' that was no longer a metaphysical abyss of white paint but the organic infinity of snow.

It was in the mid-1970s, with the ''discovery'' of the ''Artefact'' (or ''Artifact,'' as it has come to be translated), that Infante, undergoing a kind of Copernican revolution, found his personal postmodern style: instead of an exclusive emphasis on producing something akin to a metaphysically-mathematically ''exact'' picture of an external world or worlds, Infante made the interactive *process* of Technè-Nature-Man the very subject of his art. In his photographed Artifacts man encounters nature, finitude encounters the infinite, mind encounters soul, in the encounter between one of man's self-created objects (the Artifact) and nature's infinite ''otherness,'' an otherness that proves to be the foundation of objectness itself. Infante describes three levels of the Artifact. The Artifact is: 1) ''an artificial object, similar to technological devices''; 2) ''a cultural sign or symbol of a mystery''; and 3) ''an ART-fact, the finite product of my artistic activity, presented in the form of a photograph or slide.'' A single example, from the series ''Centers of Spatial Distortion,'' will have to do here. In 1979, with the help of his constant collaborator and wife, Nonna Goriunova, Infante traveled into the woods outside Moscow where he carefully placed geometrically-shaped mirrors amidst the trees, which he then photographed. The results are extraordinary: the mirrors, mirrored in the photograph, serve both to ''reflect'' the natural objects—and light—around them, and stand (hang) as separate ''objects'' in the field of nature. The photographing of these reflected and reflecting surfaces provides both an ''artifact'' for the viewer and and records the artist's own search for the moment of maximal interpenetration of art and technè. From the mid-1980s he began to incorporate color into these compositions.

While drawing on the avant-garde traditions of the 1920s, and the post-1960 Soviet-Russian and international postmodern movements, Infante's art fits easily into no reigning critical category. Although a self-proclaimed non-conformist, Infante is not a dissident, indeed he asserts that art is apolitical. As an artist who ''photographs installations in nature'' Infante is very much the postmodern meta-artist reflecting on the process and production of the art-fact; yet his work is neither impersonal (in fact it is profoundly autobiographical), hyper-intellectual (in particular it is neither verbal nor concerned with a critical reflection on art as a form of text, so central to the Moscow Conceptualists), nor aesthetically ''indifferent'': indeed the harmonious beauty and mathematical purity of many of his photographs has puzzled and even chagrined his postmodern critics, for whom beauty and balance are seen as outmoded concepts. This ''traditionalism'' points to the unusual way in which the ethic and aesthetics of 19th century plein-air painting also impact him. Finally, in spite of a lifetime of dogged non-conformism, this protean postmodern Romantic even managed, in 1996, to win the Russian State Prize for Art and Literature.

—Thomas Epstein

INSLEY, Will

Nationality: American. **Born:** Indianapolis, Indiana, 15 October 1929. **Education:** Amherst College, Massachusetts 1951–55, B.A. 1955; Graduate School of Design, Harvard University, Cambridge, Massachusetts, 1955–58, M. Arch. 1958. **Career:** Artist-in-residence, Oberlin College, Ohio, 1966; resident critic, University of North Carolina, Greensboro, 1967–68; visiting critic, Cornell University, Ithaca, New York, 1969; taught at School of Visual Arts, New York, 1969 to present; artist-in-residence, University of North Carolina, Chapel Hill, 1995. **Awards:** National Foundation for the Arts and Humanities grant, 1966; Guggenheim Fellowship, 1969; Gottlieb Foundation Grant, 1994. **Address:** 231-A Bowery, New York 10002, U.S.A.

Individual Exhibitions:

1951 Museum of Fine Arts, Amherst College, Massachusetts
1965 Stable Gallery, New York
1966 Stable Gallery, New York
1967 Stable Gallery, New York
Allen Art Museum, Oberlin College, Ohio
Wetherspoon Art Gallery, University of North Carolina, Greensboro
1968 Stable Gallery, New York
Walker Art Center, Minneapolis
Albright-Knox Gallery, Buffalo, New York
1969 *Space Diagrams,* Institute of Contemporary Art, University of Pennsylvania, Philadelphia
Insley/Mitchell/Poleskie, Andrew Dickson White Museum of Art, Cornell University, Ithaca, New York
John Gibson Gallery, New York
1971 *Ceremonial Space,* Museum of Modern Art, New York
1972 Galerie Paul Maenz, Cologne
Visual Arts Gallery, New York
1973 Fischbach Gallery, New York
Plane für Eine Andere Welt, Museum Haus Lange, Krefeld, West Germany
1974 Fischbach Gallery, New York
Württembergischer Kunstverein, Stuttgart
Galerie und Edition Annemarie Verna, Zurich
1975 Allen Priebe Art Gallery, Arts and Communications Center, University of Wisconsin at Oshkosh
College of the Arts, Ohio State University, Columbus
1976 Galerie und Edition Annemarie Verna, Zurich
Fischbach Gallery, New York
Museum of Contemporary Art, Chicago
1977 Max Protetch Gallery, New York
Protetch-McIntosh Gallery, Washington, D.C.
1978 Galerie Orny, Munich
1980 Max Protetch Gallery, New York
1982 Max Protetch Gallery, New York
1984 Guggenheim Museum, New York
1985 Max Protetch Gallery, New York
1988 Max Protetch Gallery, New York
Max Protetch Gallery, New York
Max Protetch Gallery, New York
1990 Max Protetch Gallery, New York
1992 Max Protetch Gallery, New York
1995 Hanes Art Center, University of North Carolina, Chapel Hill
1996 New Arts Program, Leigh Valley, Pennsylvania

Selected Group Exhibitions:

1965 *Shape and Structure,* Tibor de Nagy Gallery, New York
1970 *L'Art Vivant aux Etats-Unis,* Foundation Maeght, St. Paul de Vence, France
1972 *Documenta 5,* Museum Fridericianum, Kassel, West Germany (and *Documenta 6,* 1977)
1974 *Recent Acquisitions,* Museum of Modern Art, New York
1976 *20 Jahre Museum Haus Lange,* Museum Haus Lange, Krefeld, West Germany (travelled to Max Protetch Gallery, New York)
1978 *Dwellings,* Institute of Contemporary Art, University of Pennsylvania, Philadelphia
1979 *Art and Architecture, Space and Structure,* Protetch-McIntosh Gallery, Washington D.C.
1980 *Drawings-Structures,* Institute of Contemporary Arts, Boston
1981 *Amerikaanishe Zeichnungen der Siebziger Jahre,* Lousiana Museum, Humlebaek, Denmark
1984 *Dreams and Nightmares,* Hirshhorn Museum, Washington D.C.
1985 *Between Science and Fiction,* Fundacao Bienal de Sao Paulo, Brazil
1989 *Geometric Abstraction and the Modern Spirit,* Neuberger Museum, State University of New York, Purchase
1995 *American Sculptors in the 1960s, Selected Drawings from the Collection,* Museum of Modern Art, New York
1999 *Drawn from Artists' Collections,* The Drawing Center, New York

Publications:

By INSLEY: Articles—interview with Elayne H. Varian in *Schemata 7,* exhibition catalog, New York 1967; statement in ''Hexagonal Channel Space'' in *Art Now: New York* (New York), November 1969; ''Fragments from the Interior Building'' in *Will Insley: Space Diagrams,* exhibition catalog, Philadelphia 1969; notes in *Will Insley:*

Ceremonial Space, exhibition catalog, New York 1971;''Janet Kardon Interviews Some Modern Mazemakers'' in *Art International* (Lugano, Switzerland), April/May 1976; ''Seriocomic Sp(i)eleology: Robert Smithson's Architecture of Existence'' in *Arts Magazine* (New York), May 1978.

On INSLEY: Books—*Will Insley: Space Diagrams,* exhibition catalog by Stephen Prokopoff, Philadelphia 1969; *Insley/ Mitchell/ Poleskie,* exhibition catalog, Ithaca, New York 1969; *Will Insley: Ceremonial Space,* exhibition catalog with text by Arthur Drexler, New York 1971; *Will Insley: Plane für Eine Andere Welt,* exhibition catalog, Krefeld, West Germany 1973; *Will Insley,* exhibition catalog by Tilman Osterwold, Stuttgart 1974; *Unbuilt America* by Alison Sky and Michelle Stone, New York 1976; *Will Insley,* exhibition catalog, Chicago 1976; *Will Insley: THe Opaque Civilization,* exhibition catalog with texts by Diane Waldman and Linda Shearer, New York 1984.

IPOUSTÉGUY, Jean (Robert)

Nationality: French. **Born:** Dun-sur-Meuse, 6 January 1920. **Education:** Studied art at evening classes in the studio of Robert Lesbounit, Paris, 1938. **Career:** Independent artist in various media, Paris 1938–48; sculptor, in Choisy-le-Roi, Seine, since 1949: works in bronze, 1967–75, in Carrara marble, since 1968. **Awards:** Prize, *Biennale,* Venice, 1964; First Prize, *Kunstreferent,* Darmstadt, 1968; First Prize, *First International Exhibition of Original Drawings,* Rijeka, 1968; First Prize, *International Biennale of Sculpture,* Budapest, 1973; Grand Prix National des Arts, Ministère de la Culture, Paris, 1977; Légion d'Honneur, 1984; Heitland Foundation Prize, 1989. **Agent:** Claude Bernard Gallery, 900 Park Avenue, New York, New York 10021. **Address:** 35 rue Chevreul, 94600 Choisy-le-Roi, France.

Individual Exhibitions:

1962 Galerie Claude Bernard, Paris
1964 Albert Loeb Gallery, New York
Hanover Gallery, London
Galerie Claude Bernard, Paris
1965 Städtisches Museum, Leverkusen, West Germany
1966 Galerie Thomas, Munich
Galerie Claude Bernard, Paris
1967 Galleri Birch, Copenhagen
1968 Galleria Galatea, Turin
Galleria Odyssia, Rome
Pierre Matisse Gallery, New York
Galleria La Nuova Pesa, Rome
Galerie Claude Bernard, Paris
1969 Kunsthalle, Darmstadt
Galerie Claude Bernard, Paris
1970 Badischer Kunstverein, Kalsruhe, West Germany
Von-der-Heydt-Museum, Wuppertal, West Germany
Galerie Verannuman, Brussels
1971 Galerie Claude Bernard, Paris
Galleria Formi, Bologna
1972 Galerie Buchholz, Munich
Galerie Claude Bernard, Paris
1973 Galleria Gabbiano, Rome
Tolarno Galleries, Melbourne
1974 Galerie Claude Bernard, Paris
Nationalgalerie, West Berlin
Artel Galerie, Geneva
1975 Louisiana Museum, Humlebaek, Denmark
Suite Prussienne: Berlin 1973–1974, Galerie Claude Bernard, Paris
1976 Galeria Juana Mordo, Madrid
Galeria Trece, Barcelona
1978 Galleri Haaken, Oslo
Sculptures et Dessins de 1957 à 1958, Fondation Nationale des Arts Graphiques et Plastiques, Paris
1979 *Werke 1956–1978,* Städtische Kunsthalle, West Berlin
Galerie Alice Pauli, Lausanne
1981 *Dans le Noir et Sous la Lune: Fusains 1978–1979,* Galerie Claude Bernard, Paris
1982 Musée des Beaux-Arts, Lyons
1983 *Works on Paper,* Guggenheim Museum, New York
1985 *Natures Mortes,* Galerie Claude Bernard, Paris
1988 Galerie Sarver, Paris
1989 Heitland Foundation, Celle, Germany
Galerie Sarver, Paris
1990 Galerie Sarver, Paris
1991 Hotel du Départment, Bobigny, Maison de la Culture, Nevers (retrospective)
1992 Galerie Sarver et Galerie Jean Briance, Paris (Petit Jeu d'Adam et d'Eve, dessins)
Staadlische Galerie, Oberhausen; Kunsthalle, Berlin; Lehniner Institut, Lehnin, Germany (retrospective)
Galerie am Tiergarten 62, Hannover
1993 Galerie Municipale, Choisy-le-Roi, Maison de la Culture, Bourges (retrospective)
1994 Gerhard Marcks Haus, Bremen
Galerie Municipale, Vitry-sur-Seine

Selected Group Exhibitions:

1958 *Exposition Internationale de Sculpture,* Galerie Claude Bernard, Paris
1964 *Biennale,* Venice
1968 *The Obsessive Image,* Institute of Contemporary Arts, London
1970 *Zeitgenossen,* Stadtische Kunsthalle, Recklinghausen, West Germany
1976 *Boites,* Musée d'Art Moderne de la Ville, Paris (travelled to the Maison de le Culture, Rennes)
1981 *Anthropos,* at the *Festival of Vienna,* Australia
1987 *Rätsel Wirklichkeit,* Darmstadt, West Germany
1993 Chateau de Vascoeuil, Rouen
1994 *Collection d'un auteur, Jean Thuillier,* Musée de l'Evêché, Limoges
2000 *L'Automne des Transis,* Meuse, France

Collections:

Musée d'Art Moderne de la Ville, Paris; Fonds National d'Art Contemporain, Paris; Guggenheim Museum, New York; Museum of Modern Art, New York; National Gallery, London; Musée des

Beaux-Arts, Lyon; Arthotèque, Toulouse; Musée de Plein Air de la Ville de Paris; Metropolitan Museum of Art, New York.

Publications:

By IPOUSTÉGUY: Books—*Procès,* with poem by Henri Sylvester, Milan 1969; *Leaders et Enfants Nus,* book/object in aluminium, Paris 1970; *Un Nouvel Archiviste,* with text by Gilles Deleuze, Montpellier 1972; *Leonard ou la Fin de l'Humilité,* with text by Robert Lebel, Paris 1974; *Von Kleist-Ipoustéguy,* with text by Heinrich Von Kleist, Heidelberg 1974; *Michelangelo,* portfolio, Munich 1975; *Ronds dens l'O et le pessimisme,* Rome 1976; *Sauve qui Peut, Robin, or Don Heretique,* Paris 1978; *De Zero a treize (souvenirs d'enfance),* Paris 1982; *Ipoustéguy, Parlons,* with Evelyne Artaud, Paris 1993; *Bronze, Marbre, Ipoustéguy: Notes Sur la Sculpture,* with Alain Bosquet, Paris 1995; *Arcs et Traits,* Paris 1989; *Chronique des Jeunes Années,* Paris 1997.

On IPOUSTÉGUY: Books—*Ipoustéguy,* exhibition catalog with text by John Ashbery, London 1964; *Ipoustéguy,* exhibition catalog with text by Jürgen Claus and Dagobert Frey, Leverkusen, 1965; *Ipoustéguy,* exhibition catalog with text by Walter Lewino, Paris 1966; *Jean Ipoustéguy,* exhibition catalog with text by Luigi Carluccio, Turin 1968; *Ipoustéguy,* exhibition catalog with text by Bernd Krimmel, Darmstadt 1969; *Ipoustéguy,* exhibition catalog with text by Jean Paget and Werner Haftmann, Geneva 1974; *Ipoustéguy: Suite Prussienne, Berlin 1973–74,* exhibition catalog with text by Werner Haftmann, Paris 1975; *Jean Ipoustéguy,* exhibition catalog with text by Eduardo Chillida, Mandrid 1976; *Ipoustéguy: Sculptures et Dessins de 1957 à 1978,* exhibition catalog with text by Michel Troche, interview by Jean Paget, Paris 1978; *Ipoustéguy: Werke 1956–1978,* exhibition catalog with interview by Geneviéve Breerette, texts by Dieter Ruckhaberle, Walter Lewino and Bernd Krimmel, West Berlin 1979; *Ipoustéguy: Dans le Noir et Sous la Lune: Fusains 1978–1979,* exhibition catalog, Paris 1981; *Jean Ipoustéguy: Natures Mortes,* exhibition catalog with text by H. Sylvestre, Paris 1985; *Ratsel Wirklichkeit* by Elisabeth Krimmel, Darmstadt 1987; *Aquarelles,* exhibition catalog, Paris 1988; *Paysages,* exhibition catalog, Paris 1989; *Jeune Fille,* exhibition catalog, Paris 1990.

*

''What does the analysis of a vocation yield?'' Nothing very clear. The stronger the vocation, the more difficult it is to explain. Man, generally speaking, answers everything by questions. And the artist complicates the situation, moreover, by answering the questions that have not been asked. He is a relay of that which cannot be expressed verbally.

While the world grows more and more dependent on numbers, the artist expresses his efforts in their intervals. And these intervals are abysses. And you can see, palpitating at the bottom, writing that lets off a kind of perfume which defies analysis, as do the perfumes of color, of form and of sound. For the last twelve years or more, I have been preoccupied mainly with the theme of man accompanied by his first natural environment: his shadow.

—Jean Ipoustéguy

* * *

Originally a draughtsman and painter, Jean Ipoustéguy has devoted himself to sculpture since 1949. He belongs to the post-war humanist school, which in France includes Germaine Richier, and in England produced a series of artists who rejected abstraction to express the human condition through the human form.

Whilst Ipoustéguy has been largely concerned with the male torso, there are curious indications of fantasy and surrealism in some of his forms, objects which waver between reality and invention, symbolic suggestions of vague menace. Death has been a particular preoccupation, in which a faintly prehistoric, perhaps Etruscan, note appears in craggy, roughly hewn, hieratic monuments, on which rest primitively modelled heads. The upright male figures are powerfully created to suggest a rigid armature, in which the joints are openly displayed, areas of erosion frankly revealed. Whether this is a metaphor for skin, and therefore a symbol of inner erosion, or a covering of the body of precarious defence, is not made clear.

The Baroque mannerisms of these figures, and their universal pretensions, as faceless giants either blind or shielded, suggest god-like creatures, not human beings. There is no denying the audacity of these conceptions, the impressive handling of form, the powerful intellectual and spiritual questioning they propose. Even more perplexing is the famous ''L'homme,'' a standing nude with outspread arms, clearly based on the famous fifth century B.C. bronze figure of Poseidon in the Athens National Museum. Ipoustéguy shows the figure not only with the seared and pitted skin of armature, but with a third leg, suggesting that we are not meant to look and judge this replica of a man in realistic terms but as a metaphorical symbol of some aspect of the human condition. Certainly it provokes a sense of mystery, and concern. The squat female figures with their exaggerated proportions and flattened, depersonalised faces, are even further removed from naturalism.

As a manipulator and architect of form, Ipoustéguy is an acknowledged master, and as a sculptor in bronze he has few modern equals. The problem which seems to beset him is the difficulty of evolving from the long tradition of the human form a manner and a message still potent and relevant. One is forced to face the question whether this has been possible since Rodin, without radical, symbolic distortion. Picasso, Matisse, Henry Moore have succeeded; Ipoustéguy has tried to evolve a passionate, expressionistic manner, especially in the symbolic violence and brutality of the armature-skins, and the exaggerations of the human form, whilst at the same time attempting to retain the detached archaism of distant civilisations.

—Charles Spencer

IRELAND, David

Nationality: American. **Born:** Bellingham, Washington, 1930. **Education:** Attended Western Washington State University, Bellingham, 1948–50; studied industrial design, California College of Arts and Crafts, Oakland, B.A.A. 1953; studied plastics technology and printmaking, Laney College, Oakland, California, 1972–74; San Francisco Art Institute, California, M.F.A. 1974. **Career:** Artist. **Awards:** National Endowment for the Arts Fellowship grants, 1978, 1983; Artist of the Year Award, Contemporary Art Council, Oakland (California) Museum, 1982; Adaline Kent Award, San Francisco Art

Institute, 1987; Louis Comfort Tiffany Foundation Grant, 1987; Engelhard Award, Institute of Contemporary Art, Boston, 1988; Awards in the Visual Arts (AVA), 1988. **Agent:** Gallery Paule Anglim, 14 Geary St., San Francisco, California 94108.

Selected Individual Exhibitions:

1976 Whatcom Museum of Art and History, Bellingham, Washington
San Francisco Art Institute Annual (installation)
1978 Maintenance action at 500 Capp Street, San Francisco
1979 *South China Paintings* and *Mr. Gordon's Birthday Party* (action), 65 Capp Street, San Francisco
1980 White Columns Gallery, New York
1981 Leah Levy Gallery (off-site location), San Francisco
1982 Installation, Emily Carr College of Art, Vancouver, British Columbia
1983 American River College Gallery, Sacramento, California
1984 New Museum of Contemporary Art, New York
1986 Gray Gallery, East Carolina University, Greenville, North Carolina
1987 *Gallery as Place,* Emmanuel Walter and Atholl McBean Galleries, San Francisco Art Institute (catalog)
1988 Museum of Modern Art, New York
A Decade Documented, University Art Museum, University of California, Berkeley; traveled to other University of California campuses (catalog)
1989 Germans Van Eck, New York
Fabric Workshop, Philadelphia
1990 *A Clean Well-Lighted Place for Books,* Institute for Contemporary Art, Philadelphia
Hirshhorn Museum and Sculpture Garden, Washington, D.C.
Gallery Paule Anglim, San Francisco
1991 *You Can't Make Art by Making Art,* Helmhaus, Zürich
1992 Ruth Bloom Gallery, Santa Monica, California
David Ireland/Ann Hamilton, Walker Art Center, Minneapolis (catalog)
1993 Installation at Mattress Factory, Pittsburgh
Laura Carpenter Fine Art, Santa Fe, New Mexico
1994 Ansel Adams Center for Photography, San Francisco
1995 Jay Gorney Modern Art, New York
1996 Arts Club of Chicago
Center for the Arts at Yerba Buena Garden, San Francisco
1997 *David Ireland,* Institute of Contemporary Art at Maine College of Art, Portland (catalog)
The Gallery of the American Academy in Rome, Italy
1998 Gallery Paule Anglim, San Francisco
2000 *Reflections,* Jack Shainman Gallery, New York
Everyday Art, Freedman Gallery, Reading, Pennsylvania
2001 Gallery Paule Anglim, San Francisco
Christopher Grimes Gallery, Santa Monica, California

Selected Group Exhibitions:

1975 Museum of Modern Art Rental Gallery, New York
Oakland Museum, California
1976 *Eighteen Bay Area Artists,* Los Angeles Institute of Contemporary Art
1983 *Elegant Miniatures from San Francisco and Kyoto, Japan,* Kyoto, Japan, and the San Francisco Museum of Modern Art
1984 *Visions of Paradise: Installations by Vito Acconci, David Ireland, and James Surls,* Hayden Gallery, Massachusetts Institute of Technology, Cambridge (catalog)
1985 *New Furnishings,* Triton Museum of Art, Santa Clara, California
Inspired by Leonardo, San Francisco Art Institute
1987 *The Right Foot Show,* San Francisco Airport Commission, San Francisco
1988 The Home Show, Contemporary Arts Forum, Santa Barbara, California
Awards in the Visual Arts, Los Angeles County Museum of Art; Carnegie-Mellon Art Gallery, Pittsburgh, Pennsylvania; The Virginia Museum, Richmond, Virginia
1989 *Solid Concept,* Gallery Paule Anglim, San Francisco, California
40 Years of Assemblage, travelling exhibition organized by White Gallery, University of California at Los Angeles
1990 *Signs of Life, Process and Materials, 1960–1990,* Institute of Contemporary Art, University of Pennsylvania, Philadelphia
Paradox of Process: Collages and Assemblage in the Permanent Collection, Museum of Contemporary Art, Los Angeles
Constructing a History, Works from the Permanent Collection, Museum of Contemporary Art, Los Angeles
1991 *Selections from the Permanent Collection: 1975–1991,* Museum of Contemporary Art, Los Angeles, California
1994 *Solid Concept Three,* Gallery Paule Anglim, San Francisco, California
Duchamp's Leg, Walker Art Center, Minneapolis (toured)
Mapping, Museum of Modern Art, New York
David Ireland/Annette Messager/Bill Viola, Gallery Paule Anglim, San Francisco
1996 *Thinking Print,* Museum of Modern Art, New York
SFAI 125th Anniversary Tribute Show, Gallery Paule Anglim, San Francisco
1997 *The Art Orchestra: A Sculptors' Ensemble,* The Fine Arts Museums of San Francisco
1998 *Double Trouble: The Patchett Collection,* Museum of Contemporary Art San Diego, California
Affinities and Collections, California Center for the Arts, Escondido, California
pFORMative Acts, San Francisco Art Institute
1999 *Museum Pieces: Bay Area Artists Consider the de Young,* San Francisco, California
Ideas in Things, Irvine Fine Arts Center, Irvine, California
On the Ball: The Sphere in Contemporary Sculpture, DeCordova Museum and Sculpture Park, Lincoln, Massachusetts
2000 *Seascape,* Christopher Grimes Gallery, Santa Monica, California
Rapture, Massachusetts College of Art, Boston
Eccentric Forms and Structures, Microsoft Art Collection, Redmond, Washington
2001 *Making the Making,* Apex Art Curatorial Program, New York

Collections:

Museum of Modern Art, New York; San Francisco Museum of Modern Art, California; Whitney Museum of American Art, New York; Los Angeles Museum of Contemporary Art, California; Achenbach Foundation for the Graphic Arts, California Palace of the Legion of Honor, San Francisco, California; Oakland Museum, California; Berkeley Art Museum, California.

Publications:

On IRELAND: Books—*David Ireland Skellig* by Jane Levy Reed, with essay by Andy Grundberg, San Francisco 1994; *John Ashbery . . . by an Earthquake: A Visit in the House of David Ireland at 500 Capp Street* by John Ashbery, Poestenkill, New York 1994. **Articles—** ''David Ireland's Art Doesn't Just Hang on a Wall—It Is the Wall'' by Richard Lacayo in *People Weekly,* 10 April 1989; ''Artist Likes 'Invisible' Art; But David Ireland Does Show his Work in U.C. Irvine Exhibit'' by Cathy Curtis in *Los Angeles Times*, 23 April 1989; ''Images of Power'' by Mark Levy in *Art International*, Spring 1989; ''David Ireland's Accommodations'' by Bill Berkson in *Art in America,* September 1989; ''(Self-)Representation'' by Lois E. Nesbitt in *Arts Magazine,* Summer 1990; ''David Ireland'' by Mark Van de Walle in *Artforum,* Summer 1993; ''David Ireland, The Mattress Factory'' by Robert Raczka in *The New Art Examiner*, September 1993; ''David Ireland at Jay Gorney'' by Nancy Princenthal in *Art in America*, March 1996; ''David Ireland, The Arts Club of Chicago'' by Tim Porges in *New Art Examiner*, September 1996; ''Jubilant Heights; With a Bit of Inventiveness, a Cramped Attic is Converted into an Appealing Loft for Visiting Artists'' by Robert Campbell in *The Boston Globe*, 7 November 1996; ''Art in Residence'' by Jeff Weinstein in *Artforum*, March 1997. **Videos—***Repair of Sidewalk at 500 Capp Street,* directed by Tom Marioni, 1976; *Mr. Gordon at Lunch,* directed by Tony Labat, 1978.

* * *

''So much of what I do is living my life, and art simply occurs in the process,'' said David Ireland in 1984. Indeed, most of his oeuvre has been inextricably linked to his quotidian practice and projects. ''De-intellectualizing'' is the verb that Ireland uses for his early movement from painting and printmaking. He endeavored to strip the intelligence from things in order to save them from being subsumed by it.

Ridding himself of ''object seriousness,'' he created his 1974 ''94-pound series,'' carpeting his studio floor with a bag of cement powder, and created one drawing per day with it until no traces remained. Each drawing bore the title ''Repeating the Same Work Each Day.'' Then each was discarded at a rate of one per day until the ''work'' had disappeared. The artist has said, ''I got very excited by the notion that there was content in doing something so well it becomes (invisible).'' His profound conclusion at last was that the repeated gesture was of equal or greater value than the unique one.

In 1975, while commencing to strip down a dwelling at 500 Capp Street in San Francisco in which to live and work, Ireland paused. He sealed the bruised and marked surfaces of the house in clear polyurethane and moved his aesthetic enterprise into a new realm. The inside of the house, clad in polyurethane, was burnished looking and glassy, adding a saturation to the artifactual value of the Rothko-like wall pigmentation. The dilapidated Victorian house combined performance (the process of renovation), painting (by archeological reduction), and sculpture (the transformed house as a work of art), and dominated a number of years of the artist's works.

Abandoned objects from the home's past were carefully selected, revealing ''social systems,'' the activities that happened on a regular basis in this house. The house was not in ''real time,'' nor in any one time—it had appropriated the residue of a range of times and splayed them out as a sort of living diorama of impressions.

The house gave rise to commissions for similar projects: the Headlands Center for the Arts in Sausalito, for which he transformed bunk rooms in a barracks into meeting halls; an artist residency live and work space from an attic and planetarium at the Phillips Academy in New England, and other commissions.

At 65 Capp Street in San Francisco Ireland did a reverse adaptation of a dwelling, in that he demolished the existing house and created an enigmatic structure in its place that re-purposes light as a medium for the color and surface that he lovingly made his interest in his work. The consideration of how and when light would enter informed its structure entirely.

A public commission called ''Newgate'' at Candlestick Point on the San Francisco Bay (1986–1987) is a megalithic pair of walls made of concrete rubble that respond to their surroundings (a former refuse site being made into a public park). It was named to recall a stone age burial ground in Ireland called ''Newgrange.''

John Ashbery has called Ireland's work ''homegrown Art Povera,'' and there is an ancestry that Ireland makes no effort to disguise. He has displayed objects in museums that were removed from the contexts of former installations, allowing them to be ''purchased individually.'' Like Duchamp, Ireland defines art as he wishes, and questions what its composition is. His palette, though, relates to Duchamp's, whose ''Dust Breeding'' (1920) or ''50 cc of Paris Air'' (1919) have stylistic affinity with Ireland's work.

Mundane detritus, in the hands of David Ireland, can be reconfigured as ritualistic or pseudo-scientific work. ''Dumb Balls'' of 1983 are examples of his earthy, humorous appreciation of the mundane. Wet concrete passed from hand to hand until dry results in forms that resemble snow balls, and are a microcosm of Ireland's oeuvre. The balls require repetition and labor (15–20 hours each) to create and raise questions about dumbness and the worthiness of the enterprise. Yet they also contain an element of Zen practice, which was undoubtedly an inspiration.

Ireland's most recent project has added further ambiguity to his definition. *Skellig*, an installation and altered photos with sculptures and film all collectively depict the mood of a place; Skellig Michael, an uninhabited island off Ireland's coast that contains only the ruins of a graveyard and a monastery abandoned in the 13th century. Ireland altered the ruins, documented the approach by boat on 8mm film, created sculptures in response to the natural and artifactual forms on the island, and avoided any checklist or labels. Only the catalog offers clues about where the project fits into the artist's work.

''You Can't Make Art by Making Art'' read the poster for Ireland's 1980 exhibition at Claremont College in Southern California. Ireland does not make things for the marketplace, but holds up items that may inspire some deeper consideration about what we call art and what it has to do with our lives. A ''non-consumer'' artist, Ireland said he has never made work with the idea of selling it, and lives on a mix of grants, teaching, and public art commissions.

—Deirdre Donohue

IRWIN, Robert

Nationality: American. **Born:** Long Beach, California 12 September 1928. **Education:** Otis Art Institute, Los Angeles 1948–50; Jepson Art Institute, Los Angeles, 1951; and Chouinard Art Institute, Los Angeles, 1951–53. **Military Service:** United States Army, Heidelberg, Germany, 1946–48, California, 1951–53. **Career:** Independent painter, since 1953: lives and works in San Diego, California. Instructor, Chouinard Art Institute, Los Angeles, 1957–58; University of California at Los Angeles, 1962; and University of California at Irvine, 1968–69; John J. Hill Professor, University of Minnesota, Minneapolis, 1981; J. Paul Getty Lecturer, University of Southern California, Los Angeles, 1986; Cullinan Professor, Rice University, Houston, 1988. **Awards:** MacArthur Foundation Fellowship, Chicago, 1985–90. **Agent:** Pace Gallery, 32 East 57th Street, New York, New York 10022. **Address:** 1220 Rosecrans Street, Apt. 300, San Diego, California 92106, U.S.A.

Individual Exhibitions:

1957 Felix Landau Gallery, Los Angeles
1959 *Recent Paintings,* Ferus Gallery, Los Angeles
1960 Ferus Gallery, Los Angeles
Pasadena Art Museum, California
1962 Ferus Gallery, Los Angeles
1964 Ferus Gallery, Los Angeles
1966 Pace Gallery, New York
Robert Irwin/Kenneth Price, Los Angeles County Museum of Art
1968 Pasadena Art Museum, California
Jewish Museum, New York
1969 Pace Gallery, New York
72 Market Street, Venice, California
Robert Irwin/Doug Wheeler, Fort Worth Art Museum, Texas
1970 Museum of Modern Art, New York
Bell/Irwin/Wheeler, Tate Gallery, London
1971 Walker Art Center, Minneapolis
Pace Gallery, New York
Galerie Rudolf Zwirner, Cologne
1972 Sonnabend Gallery, Paris
Ace Gallery, Los Angeles
Fogg Art Museum, Harvard University, Cambridge, Massachusetts
Mizuno Gallery, Los Angeles
1973 Pace Gallery, New York
1974 Mizuno Gallery, Los Angeles
Pace Gallery, New York
Wright State University, Dayton, Ohio
University of California at Santa Barbara
1975 Fort Worth Art Museum, Texas
Museum of Contemporary Art, Chicago
Palomar College, San Marcos, California
1976 Walker Art Center, Minneapolis
Mizuno Gallery, Los Angeles
1977 Whitney Museum of Art, New York (retrospective)
1978 *Matrix,* University of California, Berkeley (installation)
Scrim Wall, Portland Center for the Visual Arts, Oregon (installation)
1979 University of California, Berkeley (installation)
Tumbling Glass Planes, Lake Placid, New York (installation)
University of Kansas, Lawrence
San Diego State University, California
Palazzo Reale, Milan
1980 *Portal Park Slice,* Dallas, Texas (installation)
Melinda Wyatt Gallery, Venice, California
Window Transformation, Oberlin College, Ohio (installation)
1981 *Security Stairwell,* Project Studio One, New York
1982 *Light to Solid,* Louisiana Museum, Humlebaek, Denmark (installation)
1983 University of California, San Diego
48 Shadow Planes, Old Post Office, Washington, D.C. (installation)
9 Spaces/9 Trees, Arts Commission Plaza, Seattle, Washington (installation)
Two Ceremonial Gates, San Francisco International Airport (installation)
University of California, San Diego
1985 Pace Gallery, New York
San Francisco Museum of Modern Art
1986 Museum of Contemporary Art, Los Angeles
1987 Wave Hill Gardens, Bronx, New York
1991 *Irwin,* Galerie Bleich-Rossi, Graz, Austria (catalog)
1992 Pace Gallery, New York
1993 *Robert Irwin,* Los Angeles Museum of Contemporary Art (traveling exhibition) (catalog)
1994 Musée d'Art Moderne de la Ville de Paris
1997 *1(degree)2(degree)3(degree)4(degree),* Museum of Contemporary Art, San Diego
1998 Dia Center for the Arts, New York
Robert Irwin: A Selection of Works 1958 to 1970, Pace Wildenstein, New York (catalog)

Selected Group Exhibitions:

1970 *Kompass IV,* Van Abbemuseum, Eindhoven, Netherlands
1971 *Transparency, Reflections, Light, Space,* University of California at Los Angeles
1973 *Five Artists/Five Spaces,* San Francisco Museum of Art
1975 *History of American Sculpture,* Whitney Museum, New York
1976 *Projects for PCA,* Philadelphia College of Art
1978 *20th Century American Drawings,* Whitney Museum, New York
1980 *Aspects of the '70s: Siteworks,* Wellesley College, Massachusetts
1981 *Seventeen Artists in the Sixties,* Los Angeles County Museum of Art
1982 *Form and Function,* Pennsylvania Academy of Fine Arts, Philadelphia
1997 *Sunshine & Noir: Art in L.A. 1960–1997,* Louisiana Museum of Modern Art, Humlebaek, Denmark (traveling exhibition) (catalog)

Collections:

Museum of Modern Art, New York; Whitney Museum, New York; Art Institute of Chicago; Walker Art Center, Minneapolis; Fort Worth Art Museum, Texas; Los Angeles County Museum of Art; Norton Simon Museum of Art, Pasadena, California; San Francisco Museum of Modern Art; Tate Gallery, London.

Publications:

By IRWIN: Books—*Being and Circumstances: Notes Toward a Conditional Art,* Lakspur, California 1985; *State of the Arts: California Artists Talk About Their Work* by Barbara Isenberg, New York 2000. **Articles—**statement in *Artforum* (New York), June 1965; letter to the editor in *Artforum* (New York), February 1968; interview with Frederick S. Wight, in *Transparencey, Reflection, Light, Space: 4 Artists,* exhibition catalog, Los Angeles 1971; ''Robert Irwin: An interview with Alistair Mackintosh'' in *Art and Artists* (London), March 1972; ''The State of the Real: Robert Irwin Discusses the Art of an Extendted Consciousness,'' with Jan Butterfield, in *Arts Magazine* (New York), June 1972; ''Reshaping the Shape of Things,'' with Jan Butterfield, in *Arts Magazine* (New York), September/ October 1972; interview with Lane Barden in *Artweek,* vol. 24, no. 15, 5 August 1993; interview with Vivian Sobchack in *Artforum,* vol. 32, no. 3, November 1993.

On IRWIN: Books—*Recent Paintings by Robert Irwin,* exhibition catalog, Los Angeles, 1959; *Robert Irwin/Kenneth Price,* exhibition catalog by Philip Leider, Los Angeles 1966; *Robert Irwin,* exhibition catalog with text by John Coplans, Pasadena, California 1968; *Robert Irwin/Doug Wheeler,* exhibition catalog by Jane Livingstone, Fort Worth, Texas 1969; *Kompass IV,* exhibition catalog by Jean Leering, Eindhoven, Netherlands 1970; *Larry Bell/ Robert Irwin/Doug Wheeler,* exhibition catalog by Norman Reid, London 1979; *Transparency, Reflection, Light, Space: 4 Artists,* exhibition catalog, Los Angeles 1971; *Robert Irwin,* exhibition catalog, Chicago 1975; *Robert Irwin,* exhibition catalog, New York 1977; *Robert Irwin: Mattrix,* exhibition catalog with essay by Lawrence Weschler, Berkeley 1978; *American Artists on Art: From 1940 to 1980,* edited by Ellen Johnson, New York 1982; *Robert Irwin's Garden at the Getty* by Lawrence Weschler, Los Angeles 2001. **Articles—**''Robert Irwin: The Artist's Premises'' by Peter Plagens in *Artforum* (New York), December 1970; ''The Searcher'' by Douglas Davis in *Newsweek* (New York), 29 December 1975; ''Robert Irwin: World Without Frame'' by Edward Levine in *Arts Magazine* (New York), February 1976; ''Robert Irwin: On the Periphery of Knowing'' by Jan Butterfield in *Arts Magazine* (New York), February 1976; ''Incredibly Beautiful Quandary'' by Gordon Hazlitt in *Artnews* (New York), May 1976; ''Robert Irwin's Line Paintings'' by Peter Plagens in *Artforum* (New York), Fall 1978; ''Taking Art to Point Zero'' by Lawrence Weschler in *New Yorker,* 8 March 1982; ''Like Water in a Glass'' by Calvin Tomkins in *New Yorker,* 21 March 1983; ''Robert Irwin: The Perceptive Conscience in Action'' by Adachiara Zevi in *L'Architettura,* vol. 39, June 1993; ''Robert Irwin: Vagaries of Perception'' by James Scarborough in *Flash Art,* vol. 27, no. 176, May-June 1994; ''Robert Irwin'' by Philippe Regnier in *Blocnotes,* no. 7, Autumn 1994; ''Robert Irwin'' by Christophe Domino in *Beaux Arts Magazine,* no. 125, July-August 1994; ''Robert Irwin'' by Rainald Schumacher in *Kunstforum International,* no. 142, October-December 1998; ''Robert Irwin'' by David Frankel in *Artforum,* vol. 37, no. 4, December 1998; ''Robert Irwin'' by Dean Kelly in *Art Criticism,* vol. 14, no. 1, 1999; ''Robert Irwin's Doors of Perception'' by Carol Diehl in *Art in America* (New York), vol. 87, no. 12, December 1999.

* * *

During the 1970s Robert Irwin joined the small group of Californians who have made a national reputation. Like that of other poetic, reductive artists, his work requires a slow and totally absorbed consideration by the viewer; and Irwin's own similar pace of conceptualization and realization has led to a small body of work. In his first museum retrospective, in 1977, the artist showed but 8 works—including his by-then well-known temporary installations where the space of the gallery itself was delineated only by taping, or by the boundaries and light effect created by large expanses of nylon scrim. The contents of that exhibition easily reflected Irwin's highly self-critical evolution—not so much production-oriented but rather philosophical in its intent. Further demonstrating the strongly idealist, if not ascetic, character of his art—its closeness to his life patterns—was Irwin's refusal to allow photographs of his work to be reproduced during the 1960s since he wished no misconceptions of his art to be promulgated.

Like other Californians of that moment, he had worked during the later 1950s in Rico LeBrun-like figuration, followed then by an abstract-expressionist period. Then at the onset of the next decade, Irwin committed himself to a still on-going search for an anonymous, non-tactile, and light-evoking art. His paintings then became extremely spare—monochromatic grounds with four horizontal bars in a different color, ca. 1962, were followed by a further reduction, Rothko-like, to but two bars, ca. 1963–64.

If Irwin's ''white style'' of spiritual purity might align him with the 1950s color-field artists, his desire for a non-sentimental clarity likewise aligns him with his California compatriots such as Valentine and Bell who similarly have sought an art of light—Orient-influenced perhaps—yet without electronic means. In the late 1960s Irwin produced a series, which became well-known, of aluminum and then cast acrylic discs; when hung away from a supporting wall, and carefully lit, their sprayed surfaces seemed to dissolve into light itself. These were followed by some cast plastic columns which attempted in their translucence to order reflected light in the surrounding space.

No doubt decisive in Irwin's development, and due to his heightened fascination with perception itself, were his experiences—at the turn of the decade—along with the artist James Turrell and the psycho-physicist Edward Wortz, in anechoic chambers and Ganzfelds designed for psychological sensory research. Irwin's installation which followed—both the temporary and more recently, several permanent outdoor works such as in Dallas and at Wellesley College, Massachusetts—are essentially ''dematerialized'' art objects where the spaces before the viewer, and their light, are the artist's goal. Those indoors have been accomplished by string, tape, and large expanses of scrim and light arrangements: demarcated areas, which the viewer was asked to observe, framed and intensified perception. Similarly, outdoors, natural plantings and topographic manipulation together with, for example, large planar sheets of steel, wire fencing and aluminum were placed in both urban and pastoral settings, to accomplish parallel ends. These public works continued through the 1980s to number almost twenty.

Irwin has suggested four terms—now in wide use—to define the relation of work to setting: site-dominant, site-adjusted, site-specific, and site-determined. In his desire for an art which, as unobtrusively as possible while still remaining a visible structure, offers the surrounding environment as the ''work of art,'' Irwin has reduced his art to space almost alone. The fourth of these relationships is the ideal—and not for his art alone, but perhaps for the future of art as a larger activity of mankind. In his own words—''Breaking the frame was easy . . . but then where is the frame of reference? Understanding through historical context is what most people do. What is the larger frame of reference? Being and circumstance.''

—Joshua Kind

J

JAAR, Alfredo

Nationality: Chilean. Born: Santiago de Chile, Chile, 1956. **Education:** Studied architecture and film direction. **Awards:** MacArthur Foundation ''Genius Grant,'' 2000.

Selected Individual Exhibitions:

1979 Galeria CAL, Santiago, Chile
1985 Grey Art Gallery, New York
1988 Institute of Contemporary Art, Philadelphia, Pennsylvania
1989 The Brooklyn Museum, New York
1990 *1+1+1,* La Jolla Museum of Contemporary Art, La Jolla, California
1991 Virginia Museum of Fine Arts, Richmond, Virginia
MVSEUM, Hirshhorn Museum and Sculpture Garden, Washington, D.C. (catalog)
1992 *The Aesthetics of Resistance,* The Pergamon Museum, Berlin, Germany (catalog)
The Museum of Contemporary Art, Chicago, Illinois
Whitechapel Art Gallery, London, England
The New Museum of Contemporary Art, New York
1993 Center for the Fine Arts, Miami, Florida
Gesellschaft fur Aktuelle Kunst, Bremen, Germany
1994 Galeria Oliva Arauna, Madrid, Spain
Frankfurter Kunstverein, Frankfurt, Germany
A Hundred Times Nguyen, Fotografiska Museet and Moderna Museet, Stockholm, Sweden
1995 Galerie Lelond, New York
Museum of Contemporary Photography, Chicago, Illinois
1996 City Gallery of Contemporary Art, Raleigh, North Carolina
1997 Galerie Franck + Schulte, Berlin, Germany
1997 Galeria Oliva Arauna, Madrid, Spain
Todd Hosfelt Gallery, San Francisco, California
Galeri Grita Insam, Vienna, Austria
1998 Galerie Lelond, New York
Stedelijk Museum Het Domein, Sittard, The Netherlands
Let There Be Light, Centre d'Art Santa Monica, Barcelona, Spain
1999 Museum of Art, Fort Lauderdale, Florida
Lament of the Images, MIT List Visual Arts Center, Cambridge, Massachusetts (catalog)

Selected Group Exhibitions:

1982 *12th Biennale de Paris,* Paris, France
1983 *In/Out: Four Projects by Chilean Artists,* Washington Project for the Arts, Washington, D.C.
1984 *Art & Ideology,* The New Museum of Contemporary Art, New York
1986 *Aperto,* Venice Biennale, Venice, Italy
1987 *Sao Paolo Biennale,* Sao Paolo, Brazil
Documenta 8, Kassel, Germany
1989 *Magiciens de la Terre,* Musee National d'Art Moderne, Centre Georges Pompidou, Paris, France
1990 *Latin American Artists for the XX Century,* Museum of Modern Art, New York
Sydney Biennale, Sydney, Australia
1995 *Istanbul Biennale,* Istanbul, Turkey
Kwangji Biennale, Kwangji, South Korea
The Spirit of Hiroshima and After, Museum of Contemporary Art, Hiroshima, Japan
1996 *Islands,* National Gallery of Australia, Canberra, Australia
Cuarta Pared, Museo del Oeste, Càracas, Venezuela
Thinking Print, Museum of Modern Art, New York
Happy End, Kunsthalle, Düsseldorf, Germany
1997 *Absolute Landscape,* Yokohama Museum of Art, Yokohama, Japan
American Stories, Setagaya Museum, Tokyo, Japan
The Eyes of Gutete Emerita, Johannesburg Biennale, Johannesburg, South Africa
1998 *Crossings,* National Gallery of Canada, Ottawa, Canada
Waterproof, Centro Cultural de Belém, Expo 98, Lisbon, Portugal
Photography as Concept, 4 International Foto-Triennale, Esslingen, Germany
Do All Oceans Have Walls? Gesellschaft fur Aktuelle Kunst, Bremen, Germany

Public Installations:

Public project for the University of Washington, Seattle, Washington, 1996; public project for Stockholm 98, Cultural Capital of Europe, Stockholm, Sweden, 1998; public project for Wereldwijd, Antwerp, Belgium, 1999; public project for Sant Boi, Barcelona, Spain, 1999; public project for Mois de la Photo, Montreal, Canada, 1999.

Publications:

By JAAR: Books—*A Hundred Times Nguyen,* Stockholm, Sweden, 1994; *The Eyes of Gutete Emerita,* Raleigh, North Carolina, 1996; *Studies on Happiness 1979–1981* by Alfredo Jaar and Adriana Valdes, Barcelona, Spain 1999; *Inferno and Paradiso: Essays* by Juan Goytisolo, Julia Kristeva, Alfredo Jaar, Jan-Erik Lundstrom and Magnus af Petersens, Stockholm, Sweden 2000.

On JAAR: Books—*An Open Work, A Non-Stop Record* by Adriana Valdes, Santiago, Chile 1981; *Gold in the Morning* by Dore Ashton, Patricia C. Phillips and Thomas Sokolowski, New York 1986; *Learning to Play* by Adriana Valdes, New York 1987; *1+1+1* by Tzvetan Todorov, New York 1987; *Alfredo Jaar* by Madeleine Grynsztejn, La Jolla, California 1990; *Investigations 88* by Judith Tannenbaum, Philadelphia, Pennsylvania 1990; *Alfredo Jaar* by Madeleine Grynsztejn, La Jolla, California 1990; *Alfredo Jaar: Geography = War* by W. Avon Draka, Steven S. High, H. Ashley Kistler and Adriana Valdés, Richmond, Virginia 1991; *Two or Three Things I Imagine About Them* by Patricia C. Phillips, London, England 1992; *1+1+1: Words by Alfredo Jaar* by Alice Yang, New York 1992; *Alfredo Jaar* by Louis Grachos, Miami, Florida 1993;

Alfredo Jaar by Eva Schmidt, Bremen, Germany 1993; *Alfredo Jaar* by Jan-Erik Lundstrom, Stockholm, Sweden 1994; *Europa* by Vicenc Altaio, Stuttgart, Germany 1994; *August 29, 1994,* Toronto, Canada 1997; *It Is Difficult, Ten Years* by Patricia C. Phillips and Rick Pirro, Barcelona, Spain 1998; *Let There Be Light: The Rwanda Project 1994–1998* by Ben Okri, David Levi Strauss and Vicenc Altaio, Barcelona, Spain 1998; *Alfredo Jaar: Lament of the Images* by Debra Bricker Balken, Boston 1999. **Web site—***MacArthur Fellows Program,* online at http://www.macfound.org/programs/fel/2000fellows/jaar.htm (accessed June 2001).

* * *

Alfredo Jaar is a social documentary photographer who is interested in the transformation of the conventions of photojournalism. He seeks to create work which shifts such imagery from the tendency toward objectification of the victims to an arena where viewer participation is encouraged in the construction and interpretation of the photographs. Jaar works in both installation and public space art.

His work in public art is confrontational and often politically charged. His 1980 billboard campaign in Santiago, Chile, *¿Es Usted Feliz? (Are You Happy?)*, posed the question to the viewers all over the city. Billboards displaying the seemingly simple question were placed alongside a major freeway interchange and at the international airport. Smaller placards presenting the text were placed below public clocks and at newspaper stands. Also notable is his 1987 work *A Logo for America,* a forty-five-second progression on a spectacolor lightboard in Times Square. The images displayed were large graphics interspersed with text. The cycle began with a United States map, followed by ''This is not America'' in text. Next the United States flag appears, followed by the words ''This is not America's flag.'' The final image displays a map with North, Central, and South America as connected countries, parts of a larger organism.

This theme is also apparent in Jaar's photographic installations. In 1985, he visited an Amazon rainforest in northeast Brazil, where he was moved by the situation at Serra Pelada (Naked Hill). That year the most massive discovery of gold in the twentieth century was found on the mountain. Poor local laborers were working long hours in the dangerous holes hauling sacks full of dirt and mud out to the prospectors for examination. Jaar felt a great need to tell the story of the plight of the workers in this highly lucrative endeavor. The owners of the mine were becoming extremely wealthy through the life-threatening, brutal labor of these men. *Gold in the Morning* (1986) features images culled from hundreds of photographs of these people struggling with the weight of the bags and the muddy slopes of the mine. This was Jaar's first major installation. It featured light boxes with large color transparencies placed below eye-level in a darkened room. These were presented in tandem with gilded metal boxes, some below the images on the floor, some on the wall beside the photograph. The images created mutated reflections in the gold boxes and required the active engagement of the viewer. The design of the presentation challenges the typical relationship between artist and audience. One must look down to see, and in doing so, the distance is destroyed. At the center of the room, a large bed of nails supported an ornate gold picture frame.

Jaar's concerns led him to many locations where the collision between the First and Third Worlds was most evident. A visit to Africa led to the 1991 exhibition *Geography = War*, an installation which explores the disparities between industrialized and non-industrialized nations. The exhibition catalog begins with a quotation from a 1988 interview with Jaar in which he expresses the impetus for his work. ''My dilemma as an artist is how to make art out of information that most of us would rather ignore. How do you actually make art when the world is in such a state?'' Jaar displays these images as large Cibachromes mounted on light boxes in various ways. Some simply hang on the wall in a darkened room, while others hang above 55-gallon metal barrels filled with water. The reflected images again demand the participation of the viewer. When one gazes into any of the fifty-one separate barrels, one cannot avoid the social commentary inherent in the work. Jaar actively explores the dichotomy between ''Us'' and ''Them'' as he addresses the power of place in social and political situations.

Roland Barthes wrote, ''Ultimately, photography is subversive not when it frightens, or even stigmatizes, but when it is pensive, when it thinks.'' Jaar seeks this level of interaction with his viewers. His travels in Rwanda just three weeks after the genocide ended in 1994 inspired the creation of more than twenty works. The Rwanda Project extended from 1994–1998. Jaar's 1996 piece, *The Eyes of Gutete Emerita*, is among his most potent work. Jaar was deeply affected by this Rwandan woman's story of seeing some men kill her husband and two young sons with machetes. The woman's eyes expressed her pain clearly to Jaar. The gallery installation of this piece featured a large light table on the floor covered with one million identical slides bearing an extreme close-up image of the woman's eyes. Loupes (photographic magnifiers) were placed around the pile of slides on the light table. The work functions as both individual components as well as a whole entity. The mound of slides in the darkened room is surely impressive, but the intensely personal experience of viewing a single slide a few inches from one's own face is something else indeed. Jaar succeeds again (perhaps beyond description) in breaking the barrier between subject and audience.

Alfredo Jaar's work has been displayed in both solo and group exhibitions all over the world. He was featured in the Venice Biennale in 1986 and received a Guggenheim Fellowship in 1985. Jaar's contributions to the art world and to the notion of humanism earned him the prestigious MacArthur Fellowship (''Genius Award'') in 2000. This is deserved recognition for an artist creating challenges to the traditions of photojournalism while issuing a loud global call to consciousness.

—Tammy A. Kinsey

JACCARD, Christian

Nationality: Swiss and French. **Born:** Fontenay-sous-Bois, France, 2 April 1939. **Education:** Ecole Nationale des Beaux-Arts, Bourges, France, 1956–60. **Family:** Married Daniele-Louise Jaccard in 1964; sons: Clarence and Philippe. **Career:** Independent painter, Paris, since 1964. **Awards:** Chevalier de L'Ordre des Arts et Lettres, France. **Address:** 40 rue Pascal, F 75013 Paris, France.

Individual Exhibitions:

1962 Cabinet des Estampes, Geneva
Galerie Cachet, Berne
1963 Cercle S.M.A., Geneva
Galerie Valentine Descombes, Paris
1966 Cercle S.M.A., Geneva

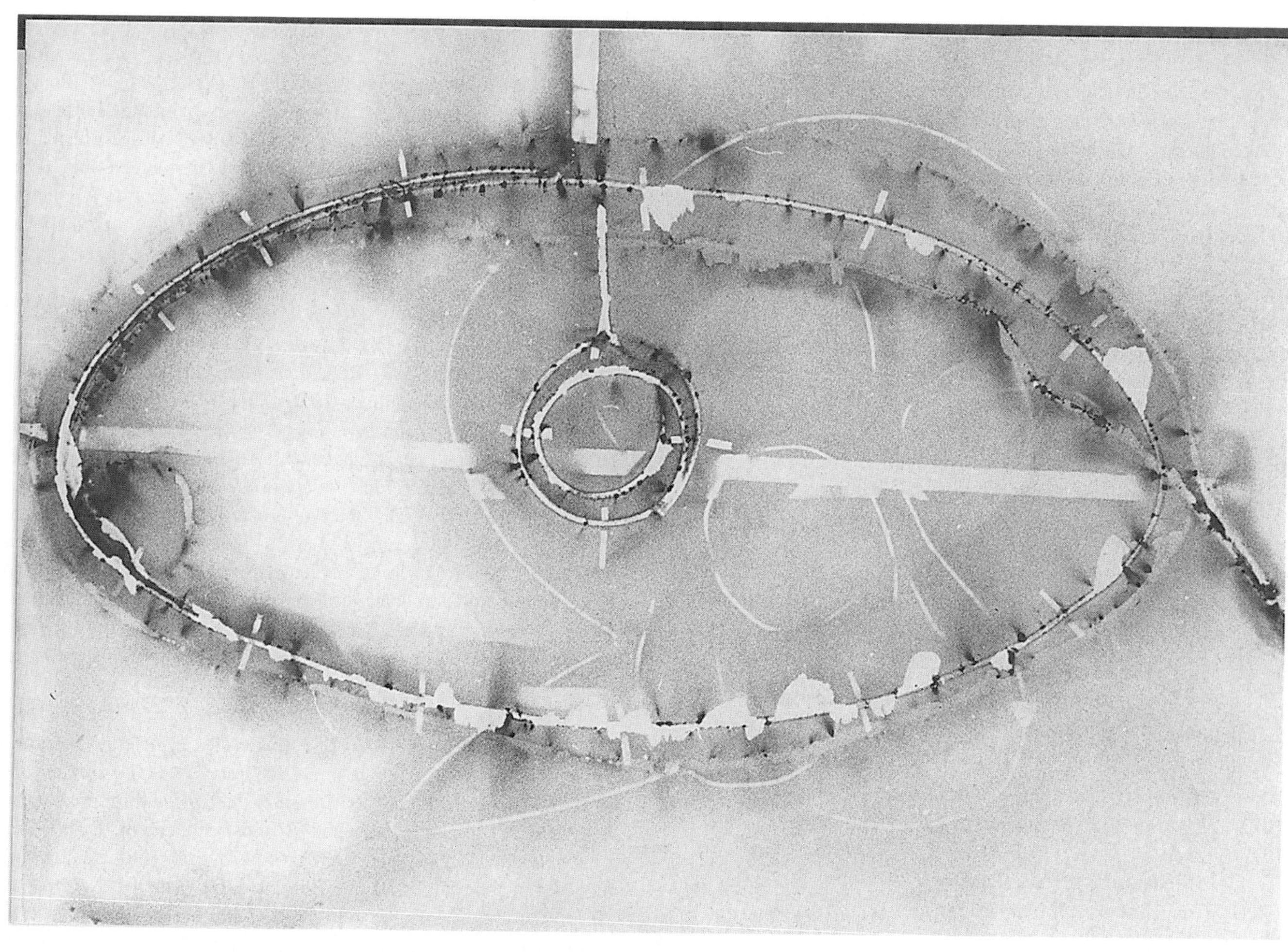

Lithograph by Christian Jaccard. ©2001 Artists Rights Society (ARS), NY/ADAGP, Paris.

1967 Maison de la Culture, Bourges
1972 Musée de l'Athenée, Geneva
1973 Institute of Contemporary Arts, London
1974 Galerie Lucien Durand, Paris
1975 Musée de l'Abbaye Sainte-Croix, Les Sables d'Olonne, France
Galerie d'Art T., Mulhouse, France
Centre Nationale d'Art Contemporain, Paris (toured France)
Musée des Arts Décoratifs, Nantes
Musée d'Art Moderne, Ceret, France
1976 Galerie Gerald Piltzer, Paris
Galerie Beaubourg, Paris
Galerie B, Paris
Musée d'Art et d'Industrie, Saint-Etienne, France
Institut Francais, Stockholm
1978 Galerie La Hune, Paris
Galerie Gerald Piltzer, Paris
Galerie Madoura, Vallaruis, France
Galerie Arta, Geneva
1979 *Suites Calcinées 1976–1978,* Musée d'Art Moderne de la Ville, Paris
Galerie Sapone, Nice
Brannserier 1976–1978, Henie-Onstad Kunstsenter, Oslo
1980 Galerie Athanor, Marseilles
Galerie Bornand, Geneva
1981 Center Culturel, Bretigny
1982 Galerie Jan Six, Paris
Musée Cantini, Marseille
1983 Galerie des Ponchettes, Nice
1984 Galerie Bornand, Marseille
Galerie Athanor, Marseille
L'Autre Musée, Brussels
Artothèque, Montpellier
Atelier Bordas, Paris
Galerie Gilbert Brownstone, Paris
1985 Centre d'Art Contemporain Pablo Neruda, Corbeil-Essonnes, France
Institut Francais, Naples
Pinacoteca, Foggia, Italy
Museo Campano, Capoue, Italy
Galleria Massimo Riposati, Rome
Centre Culturel Francais, Rome
Galerie Sapone, Nice
1986 Galerie Gilbert Brownstone, Paris
1987 Maison de la Culture, La Rochelle, France
Galerie Gilbert Brownstone, Paris
Galerie Athanor, Marseille

1988 Dernite Carole Art Project Inc., New York
Institut Français, Naples
1989 Galerie Municipale d'Art Contemporain, Montpellier
Galerie Municipale d'Art Contemporain, Saint-Priest
1990 Galerie Krief, Frankfurt
Musée Cantini, Marseille
Galerie Agora, Marseille
1991 Galerie Louis Carré et Cie, Paris
Galerie Municipale d'Art Contemporain, Vitry
1992 Galerie Louis Carré et Cie, Paris
1994 Musée des Collections Nationales, Bucharest
Institut Français, Sophia, Thessalonika, and Athens
Tada Gallery, Osaka
Itsutsuji Gallery, Tokyo
Recent Gallery, Sapporo
1996 Musée d'Art Moderne, Saint-Etienne
1997 Le 19 Centre Régional d'Art Contemporain, Montbéliard
Artothèque Antonin Artaud, Marseille
Galerie Cottard-Olsson, Stockholm
1998 Galerie Municipale Julio Gonzalez, Arcueil
Musée National, Osaka
Musée Municipal, Fukuoka
Musée Départemental, Ehimé

Selected Group Exhibitions:

1964 *La Jeune Gravure,* Cabinet des Estampes, Geneva
1972 *12 Ans d'Art Contemporain,* Grand Palais, Paris
1979 *Tendance de l'Art en France 1968–79,* Musée d'Art Moderne de la Ville, Paris
1981 *Fran frankrike: 37 aktuella konstnarer,* Liljevalchs Konsthall, Stockholm
1984 *Ecriture dans la peinture,* Centre National d'Art Contemporian, Nice
1989 *L'Art en Frank, un siècle d'in Variations,* Pushkin Museum, Moscow, and the Hermitage, Leningrad
4th International Biennal Print Exhibit 1989 Roc, Taipei Fine Arts Museum, Taiwan
1990 *Kunstregion Sutfran Kreiseh, (FRAC),* (toured Germany)
1992 *Manifeste, 30 ans de création 1960–1990,* Centre Georges Pompidou, Paris
1993 *Art Contemporain en France,* Galerie Enrico Navarra and Galerie Itsutsuji, Tokyo
Juxtapositions: 13 artistes dans le 13eme arrondissement, Gare d'Austerlitz, Paris
1995 *Duo: le dessin, la peinture, la sculpture,* Galerie Louis Carré & Cie, Paris
First International Triennal of Graphic Art, Old Town Hall, Prague
1996 *3rd Sapporo International Print Biennale,* Hokkaido Museum of Modern Art, Sapporo
La dimension du corps 1920–1980, Musée d'Art Moderne, Tokyo and Kyoto
1997 *Made in France, 1947–1997* and *L'Empreinte,* Musée National d'Art Moderne, Centre Georges Pompidou, Paris
1998–99 *Supports-Surfaces dans le collections des MNAM,* toured Europe
1999 *Weaving the World,* Yokohama Museum of Art

Collections:

Musée d'Art Moderne de la Ville, Paris; Bibliothèque Nationale, Paris; Musée National d'Art Moderne, Centre Georges Pompidou, Paris; Musée d'Art et Industries, Saint-Etienne; Musée des Sables d'Olonne, France; Musée des Beaux-Arts, Grenoble; Cabinet des Estampes, Geneva; Australian National Gallery, Canberra; University of Sydney, Sydney; Museum of Modern Art, New York; National Museum of Art, Osaka; and many others.

Publications:

By JACCARD: Articles—''Reflexions/Motivations/Connotations'' in *Art Press* (Paris), September 1976; ''Ecrire sur l'Art'' in *Opus International* (Paris), January 1979; ''Christian Jaccard ou l'eloge de feu,'' interview with Anne Dagbert, in *Art Press* (Paris), September 1982; ''Notion d'avant garde?'' in *Opus International* (Paris), Autumn 1983; ''Christian Jaccard,'' interview with Michel Giroud, in *Kanal* (Paris), January 1985; interview with M. L. Lamarque-Mouzon in *Arthèmes*, 1991; ''La vierge au chancelier Rolin'' in *C'est de l'Art,* Paris, 1993; ''Ici et maintenant'' in *Art dans la Ville,* Saint-Etienne, 1996; ''Quelles postures méthodologiques?'' in *Le discours critique dans le champ des art plastiques: champ référentiel et enseignement,* Paris, 1997.

On JACCARD: Books—*Art en France: Une Nouvelle Generation* by Jean Clair, Paris 1972; *Art Actuel en France* by Anne Tronche and Hervè Gloaguen, Paris 1973; *Christian Jaccard,* exhibition catalog with text by Claude Fornet and Alfred Pacquement, Paris 1975; *Christian Jaccard: Brannserier 1976–1978,* exhibition catalog with text by Suzanne Page and Ole Henrike Moe, Oslo 1979; *Christian Jaccard: Suites Calcinées 1976–1978,* exhibition catalog with text by Suzanne Page and Gerard-Georges Lemaire, Paris 1979; *Christian Jaccard l'Iconoclaste,* exhibition catalog by Achille Bonito Oliva and Gerard Georges Lemaire, Naples 1985; *1965–1990: Les Années Supports Surfaces* by Marie-Hélène Grinfeder, Paris, 1991; *Le Mou et ses Formes: essai sur quelques catégories de la sculpture du 20ème siècle* by Maurice Fréchuret, Paris, 1993; *L'Art en France 1960–1995* by Calude Minière, Paris, 1995; *La dimension du corps*, exhibition catalog by Calude Schweisguth, Tokyo, 1996; *La collection, acquisitions 1986–1996* by Didier Semin, Paris, 1997. **Articles**—review in *Connaissance des Arts* (Paris), January 1974; ''Christian Jaccard et le tissu de l'empreinte'' by Raoul Jean Moulin in *L'Humanité* (Paris), February 1974; ''Christian Jaccard'' in *L'Art Vivant* (Paris), May 1974; ''La Defense'' by Germain Viatte in *L'Oeil* (Paris), October 1974; ''Christian Jaccard ou l'Alphabetisation des Ficelles'' by G. Brerete in *Le Monde* (Paris), April 1975; ''L'Outil Fait le Peinture'' by Raoul Jean Moulin in *L'Humanité* (Paris), April 1975; ''L'Univers fetichiste de Christian Jaccard'' by Gerard-Georges Lemaire in *Quotidien de Paris,* 20 February 1978; ''Ecrire sur l'Art'' by G. Joppolo in *Opus* (Paris), January 1979; ''Christian Jaccard, inconolatre/iconoclaste'' by Alain Macaire in *Kanal* (Paris), June 1982; ''Les papiers brules de Christian Jaccard'' by France Borel in *Pourquoi pas* (Paris), 20 June 1984; ''Dossier Jaccard'' in *Opus International* (Paris), no. 129, September 1992. **Films**—*Christian Jaccard, Suite de suite* by Douglas Dunn, 1979; *Christian Jaccard, Chemin de cendre*, 1984; *Christian Jaccard, Anonymes calcinés à travers suite de suite,* 1985; *Christian Jaccard, Mille et un objets, 1971–1986,* 1987; *Christian Jaccard, un peintre, une ile* by Philippe Castanet et de Gérard Hoarau, 1989; *Christian Jaccard, les Blancs et les Rouges au*

Musée Cantini by Denis Caiozzi, 1990; *Le temps de voir. . . La vierge au chancelier Rolin—J. Van Eyck/C. Jaccard* by Pierre Coulibeuf, 1992; *L'Esprit du Feu* by William Mimoumi, 1994; *Le temps de voir. . . La mort de Caius Gracchus—Topino Lebrun,* 1997.

* * *

According to Nietzsche art carries the pleasure of destruction that then signifies the uneasiness of convention and the implicit need of linguistic regeneration perpetuated by the creative experience. This develops itself through the research of an image than doesn't already belong to the iconographical of the figurative culture but that for clarity and strength can always enter into the realm.

Christian Jaccard moves within a conception of art like the functions within a catastrophe, waiting like the intense unhinging of the tectonic equilibrium of language and like the unpredictable erosion of the imaginary. Until the 1970s avante-garde art was produced under the influence of a linear evolution and then connected to a rectilinear development; as a result, the evolution became softer and less linear.

In this sense Jaccard works outside the schemes and expectations of a culture and uses materials and techniques that produce ''an image of the regeneration of art'' which is directly linked to the Nietzschean idea of destruction and not only metaphorically.

In fact, the French artist uses fire as a technique to determine the final image of the work and materials that evidently and dutifully fold and change form according to the temperature. The burnings become scars of a memory absolutely emotionless but already taken to an obvious formulation.

Interesting, at the same time, in Jaccard's work is the special installation of a painting that tends toward a bi-dimensionality and di-dramatization of every effect of depth. The fire becomes an element that purifies every strict symbolic valence with its use and acquires a modern and laical force within itself like connecting material and structure between various signs and materials that bend and adapt under the heat. Cold construction or projects that supplant the flagrant theme of the works don't exist.

At this point enters the creative process that adapts the typical temperature of the fire, progressive and at the same time non-linear, able to rise above the rigidness of the formal organization of the works that supplant the unpredictable climate that accompanies contemporary art. For this reason, we have works that in the end create images of contortion and calm that tend toward a figure that develops into a system of abstract and ornamental signs.

Everything passes under the regenerative force of the fire, even the history of the art and the images passed over and reheated by Jaccard at high temperatures. A temperature adapted to substract at a distance ancient historic languages that in this way are actualized and humanized by the pyromanic passion of an artist that works in balance between the desire to carry history into a state of ruin and that of giving back vitality to the exhibit.

—Achille Bonito Oliva

JACQUET, Alain (Georges Frank)

Nationality: French. **Born:** Neuilly sur Seine, 22 February 1939. **Education:** University of Grenoble, B.A. 1959; studied achitecture at the Ecole Nationale des Beaux-Arts, Paris, 1960. **Career:** Independent painter and sculptor, Paris, since 1960. **Awards:** Premio Marzotto, 1967. **Agent:** Galerie de France, Paris. **Address:** c/o Galerie de France, 52 rue de la Verrière, 75004 Paris, France.

Individual Exhibitions:

1961 Galerie Breteau, Paris
1962 Galerie Breteau, Paris
1963 Galerie Aujourd'hui, Brussels
Robert Fraser Gallery, London
Galerie Breteau, Paris
1964 Alexander Iolas Gallery, New York
1965 Galerie J, Paris
Galerie Remy Audouin, Paris
Galerie Lawrence Rubin, Paris
Museo de Arte Moderno, Rio de Janeiro
Galerie Bischofberger, Zurich
1966 Galerie M. E. Thelen, Essen
Galerie 20, Amsterdam
1967 Galleria Apollinaire, Milan
Galerie de Boog, Curacao, Dutch Antilles
Galerie Heiner Friedrich, Munich
French Section, at the *9th Bienal,* Sao Paulo
1968 Museum of Contemporary Art, Chicago
Galerie Yvon Lambert, Paris
Waddell Gallery, New York
1969 Galerie Bonnier, Geneva
Museum Sztuki, Lodz, Poland
Galeria Foksal, Warsaw
Galerie Yvon Lambert, Paris
1970 Galleria Francoise Lambert, Milan
Galeria Foksal, Warsaw
1971 Galleria La Salita, Rome
Galerie Bonnier, Geneva
Galleria Francoise Lambert, Milan
Galerie René Block, West Berlin
1973 Galerie Bama, Paris
1974 Centre National d'Art Contemporain, Paris
1976 French Pavillion, at the *Biennale,* Venice
1977 Galleri Jacobson, Stockholm
1978 Musée d'Art et d'Histoire, Geneva
Galerie Bonnier, Geneva
Galerie Givaudan, Geneva
Musée d'Art Moderne de la Ville, Paris
1981 Galerie de France, Paris
1993 *L'Atelier de New York 1980–1993,* Centre Georges Pompidou, Galerie Beaubourg, Paris (catalog)
1994 *Terres/Peintures de Visions,* Centre Georges Pompidou, Galerie Beaubourg, Paris (catalog)
1998 *Oeuvres de 1951 à 1998,* Musée de Picardie, Amiens (catalog)
Musée de Picardie, Amiens, France

Selected Group Exhibitions:

1961 *2nd Biennale de Paris,* Musée d'Art Moderne, Paris
1962 *Salon des Réalités Nouvelles,* Musée d'Art Moderne, Paris (and 1965)

1964 *Guggenheim International,* Guggenheim Museum, New York
1965 *Biennale de San Marino* (and 1967)
1966 *Art in the Mirror,* Museum of Modern Art, New York (toured the United States)
1968 *The Obsessive Image,* Institute of Contemporary Arts, London
Documenta 4, Kassel, West Germany
1969 *When Attitudes Become Form,* Kunsthalle, Berne (toured Europe)
Art by Telephone, Museum of Contemporary Art, Chicago
1970 *3 to Infinity,* Whitechapel Art Gallery, London
1997 *Made in France 1947–1997,* Centre Georges Pompidou, Paris
De Klein à Warhol: Face-à-Face France, Centre Georges Pompidou, Paris (catalog)
2000 *Le Big Crunch 2,* Ecole Nationale des Beaux-arts, La Box, Bourges (catalog)

Collections:

Centre Georges Pompidou, Paris; Musée d'Art Moderne de la Ville, Paris; Moderna Museet, Stockholm; Stedelijk Van Abbemuseum, Eindhoven, Netherlands; Kaiser Wilhelm Museum, Krefeld, West Germany; Louisiana Museum, Humlebaek, Denmark; Galleria Nazionale d'Arte Moderne, Rome; Musée d'Art Moderne, Geneva; Muzeum Sztuki, Lodz, Poland; Arts Council of Great Britain, London.

Publications:

By JACQUET: Book—*Helen's Boomerang,* Geneva 1978. **Articles—** ''Alain Jacquet'' in *Art Press Special Issue,* no. 17, 1996.

On JACQUET: Books—*Alain Jacquet,* exhibition folder with text by John Ashbery, London 1963; *Alain Jacquet,* exhibition catalog with text by Otto Hahn, Zurich 1965; *Alain Jacquet,* exhibition catalog with text by Mario Barata, Rio de Janeiro 1965; *Alain Jacquet* by W. S. Childrens, Paris 1968; *Alain Jacquet,* exhibition catalog with texts by Ryszard Stanislawski and Gregoire Müller, Lodz 1969; *Alain Jacquet,* exhibition catalog with texts by Pierre Restany and Suzanne Page, Paris 1978; *Alain Jacquet,* exhibition catalog with texts by Pierre Restany and Renè Ricard, Paris 1981. **Articles—**''Alain Jacquet'' by Otto Hahn in *Art International* (Lugano, Switzerland), October 1967; ''Alain Jacquet'' by G. Pfeiffer in *Das Kunstwerk* (Baden-Baden, West Germany), October/November 1970; ''Lettre de Suisse Romande: Alain Jacquet'' by Jean-Luc Duval in *Art International* (Lugano, Switzerland), June 1971; ''Four Artists in France'' by D. Miller, in *Mundus Artium* (Athens, Ohio), vol. 7, no. 1, 1974; ''Alain Jacquet'' by Anne Dagbert in *Artforum,* vol. 32, no. 6, February 1994; ''Alain Jacquet: Vision et Visions'' by Catherine Millet in *Art Press,* no. Hors-serie no. 15, 1994.

* * *

Over something like a decade, Alain Jacquet (with a team of co-workers) set out to use the most sophisticated techniques employed by up-to-the-minute modern laboratories to bring into being what evolved as a kind of modern photographic silkscreen, greatly enlarged from the original. Sometimes these enormous productions stretched in extent of height or width to dimensions of 1 3/4 to 2 metres. Colours were bright and spectacular.

Those who remember these early works will recall that they were carried out in a most peculiar way (or most of them were). The huge enlargement included in its new magnification only too often in its transmogrification a ''blow-up'' of the actual printed *frame* (in process block-engraving terms) so that the horizontal breaks (unobservable in the smaller version of the original) sprang into evidence giving a curious new meaning and accent to whatever the subject happened to be.

Without a struggle, it was as if Jacquet's picture had transported the viewer into a printing world which had never heard of rotogravure, but on other occasions these silkscreens (usually applied on canvas laid down on Plexiglas) would go off on a variant like the haunting ''Gabrielle d'Estrée'' in which the familiar Ecole de Fontainbleau faces of the beauties in the bath were replaced by Jacquet with modern counterparts in full maquillage.

It almost goes without saying that such a creative artist would not continue in this vein forever. One swallow, however enormous (and these silkscreens could and did go into printed editions of 2000 and more), does not make a summer.

Today, Jacquet—the student who won his baccalaureat at Grenoble University and then went on to study architecture at the Ècole des Beaux-Arts in Paris—has, ever experimenting, set his sights still wider, toying first with esoteric subjects, but now exercising his talents as a sculptor (another of the offshoots of his expansive art training) in mysterious crypto-memorials like the one he put on exhibit at the Venice Biennale—a simplified monolith flanked left and right by two verticals at a respectful distance and each set on a flat round base. The large centre-piece, entitled ''Churn,'' on its right side has the pylon called ''Dough-Knot''; the one to the left is described by its author as ''Top.''

—Sheldon Williams

JANSSEN, Horst

Nationality: German. **Born:** Hamburg, 14 November 1929. **Education:** Oldenburg, 1937–40, and at the Napola Institute, Haselunne, 1941–45; studied art, under Alfred Mahlau, Staatliche Kunsthochschule, Hamburg, 1946–51. **Family:** Married Verena von Bethamann-Hollweg in 1960. **Career:** Painter and graphic artist, Hamburg, since 1952. **Awards:** German Government scholarship 1950; Lichtwark Grant, 1952; Art Price, City of Darmstadt, 1964; Edwin Scharff Award, Hamburg 1965; Grand Prize, *Biennale,* Venice, 1969; Schiller Award, Mannhein, 1975; Prize from ''Die oldenburgische Landschaft'' association, Oldenburg, 1990; named honorary citizen of the town of Oldenburg; opening of the Horst-Janssen-Museum, Oldenburg. **Agent:** Horst Janssen Nachlaß, Muhlenberger Weg 22, 22587 Hamburg, Germany. **Died:** Of a stroke, in Oldenburg, Germany, 31 August 1995.

Individual Exhibitions:

1964 Kestner-Gesellschaft, Hannover
1965 Konstmuseum Gothenburg, Sweden
1966 Kunsthalle, Basle

1970 Marlborough Fine Art, London
1971 *Etsningar,* Goteborgs Konstmuseum, Gothenburg, Sweden
Radierungen 1970–71, Galerie Kornfeld, Zurich
Dommuseum, Lübeck, West Germany (with Paul Gavarni)
1973 Lefebre Gallery, New York
Kestner-Gesellschaft, Hannover
Kunsthalle, Hamburg (travelled to the Kunsthalle, Bielefeld, West Germany)
1974 Lefebre Gallery, New York
1976 Kunstverein, Mannheim
Kunsthalle, Mannheim
1979 *Fruhe Arbeiter,* Kunstverein, Hamburg
1980 *Master Drawings,* International Exhibitions Foundation, Washington, D.C. (toured the United States)
1981 *Aquarelles, Dessins et Gravures,* Berggruen et Cie, Paris
1982 Albertina, Vienna
Kamakura Museum, Tokyo
Munch Museum, Oslo
1983 Lefebre Gallery, New York
1986 Berggruen et Cie, Paris
Novosibirsk and Moscow, U.S.S.R.
1991 Albertinum, Dresden
Odakyu Grand Gallery, Tokyo
Munch Museum, Oslo, Norway
1992 Museum der bildenden Künste, Leipzig
1994 Altonaer Museum, Hamburg (catalog)
1995 *Retrospektive,* Oldenburg, Germany
1997 Opening of Janssen-Cabinet, Gallery of Contemporary Art, Hamburger Kunsthalle (catalog)
1999 *Frühe Meisterschaft,* Galerie der Gegenwart, Hamburger Kunsthalle (catalog)
2000 Inaugural Exhibition, Horst Janssen Museum, Oldenburg

Selected Group Exhibitions:

1969 *Biennale,* Venice
1970 *Malerei nach Fotografie,* Münchner Stadtmuseum, Munich
1972 *4th Internationale Fruhjahrsmesse,* West Berlin
1973 *Kunst in Deutschland 1898–1973,* Kunsthalle, Hamburg (travelled to the Städtische Galerie im Lenbachhaus, Munich
1977 *Documenta 6,* Museum Fridericianum, Kassel, West Germany
1980 *Forms of Realism Today,* Musee d'Art Contemporain, Montreal (travelled to Ottawa and Toronto)

Collections:

Kestner-Gesellschaft, Hannover; Goteborgs Konstmusuem, Gothenburg, Sweden; Horst-Janssen-Museum, Oldenburg.

Publications:

By JANSSEN: Books—*Seid ihr alle da,* with poems by Rolf Italiaander, Hamburg 1948; *Plakate und Traktatchen,* Hamburg 1966; *Zehn Zeichnungen aus der Sammlung Poppe,* Hamburg 1966; *Zeichnungen von Horst Janssen und Fotos von Thomas Höpker,* Hamburg 1967; *Ballhaus Jahnke,* with text by Wieland Schmied, Frankfurt 1969; *Paul Wolf und die Sieben Zicklein,* Hamburg 1969; *Hensel und Gratel,* Hamburg 1969; *Horst Janssen Picture Book,* London 1970; *Zeichnungen,* West Berlin 1970; *Petty Fauer,* Hamburg 1970; *Radierungen 1970–1971,* West Berlin 1971; *Landschaftsradierungen 1970,* West Berlin 1971; *14 Biber,* Hamburg 1971; *Hokusai's Spaziergang,* Hamburg 1972; *Tessin,* Hamburg 1972; *Subversionen,* Hamburg 1972; *Fatter für Philip, Hamburg 1972; Norwegisches Skizzenbuch, September 1971,* West Berlin 1973; *Neue Zeichnungen 1970–1972,* West Berlin 1973; *Minusio,* West Berlin 1973; *Der Wettlauf zwischen Hase und Igel auf der Buxtehuder Heide,* Pfullingen 1973; *Carnevale di Venezia,* edited by Gerhard Schack, Hamburg 1973; *Missverstandnisse,* Hamburg 1973; *I. Gepferdie für Bettina,* Hamburg 1973; *Bettina,* Hamburg 1973; *Landschaft,* edited by Gerhard Schack, Hamburg, 1974; *Kleines Geste-Buch,* edited by Gerhard Schack, Hamburg 1974; *Selbstbildnisse zu "Hanno's Tod,"* edited by Gerhard Schack, Hamburg 1975; *November,* West Berlin 1975; *"Ich Komme weiter" agte Laotse; "Wie das?" frog dieser,* with Wieland Schmied and Gerhard Schack, Hamburg 1976; *Umsoonst,* Hamburg 1976; *Die Kopie,* edited by Gerhard Schack, Hamburg 1977; *Nocturno,* with Birgit Jacobsen, Hamburg 1977; *Janssenhof,* with Theodor Storm, Hamburg 1977.

On JANSSEN: Books—*Malerei nach Fotografie: von der Camera Obscura bis zur Pop Art, eine Dokumentation,* exhibition catalog, Munich 1970; *Horst Janssen: Etsningar,* exhibition catalog, with text by Jakob Brunn, Gothenburg. Sweden 1971; *Horst Janssen: Radierungen 1970–71,* exhibition catalog, Zurich 1971; *Deutche Kunst der 60er Jahre: Malerie, Collage, Op-Art, Graphik* by Juliane Rohe, Munich 1971; *Vierte Internationale Fruhjahrsmesse,* exhibition catalog, with introduction by René Block, West Berlin 1972; *Horst Janssen,* exhibition catalog, with text by Thomas Mann, New York 1973; *Kunst in Deutschland 1898–1973,* exhibition catalog, with text by Werner Hofmann, Hamburg 1973; *Zweihundert Jahre phantastische Malerei* by Wieland Schmied, West Berlin 1973; *Horst Janssen,* prints catalog, Munich 1975; *Bucherkatalog Horst Janssen,* edited by Ursula Neufedt and Wilfried Weber, Hamburg 1975; *Horst Janssen: Fruhe Arbeiter,* exhibition catalog, with texts by Carl Vogel and Wolf Stubble, Hamburg 1979; *Horst Janssen: Master Drawings,* exhibition catalog, with an introduction by Alfred Hentzen, Washington, D.C. 1980; *Horst Janssen: Aquarelles, Dessins et Gravures,* exhibition catalog, with a preface by Jean Clair, Paris 1981; *Horst Janssen: Retrospektiv auf Verdacht* by Heinz Spielmann, Hamburg 1982; *Frauenbildnisse 1947–1988,* edited by Dierk Lemcke, Hamburg 1988 (first of eight volume series, including *Landschaften 1942–1989,* 1989, *Eros Tod und Maske 1949–1992,* 1992, *Nature Morte 1946–1993,* 1993, *Selbstbildnisse 1945–1993,* 1994, *Das Tier 1946–1995,* 1995, and *Freunde und andere 1947–1994,* 1996, *Das Plakat 1957–1994,* edited by Helga and Erich Meyer-Schomann, 1999); *Radierungen 1957–1969,* Hamburg 1989; *der Foliant,* Hamburg 1992; *Radierzyklen,* Oldenburg/Hamburg 1995; *Ich sehe mich in allem anderen,* Oldenburg/Hamburg 2000.

* * *

Horst Janssen currently occupies, I suppose, the leading position among artists who methodically keep their distance from the avant garde. The antinomy between preoccupation with nature and with the art of the past troubles him as little as other contradictions in himself. In eccentric fashion Janssen takes the individual movements as much for a motive of his art as for an ego repressing contemplation of the objectivity of appearance. Supported by a stupendous visual fantasy, a brilliantly dexterous talent for drawing, an adequate command of language for the purpose, he stands opposed to an intellectual aesthetic in which direct observation is no longer regarded as a quality.

The continuing veneration of his teacher Alfred Mahlau, whose influence still has its effect on him, is based on an understanding of nature and art which refuses a reflective interpretation, although Janssen possesses all the qualifications necessary for an intellectual interpretation of his own work.

In his early work understanding of painters of the older generation is evident, above all of Kirchner in woodcuts, Picasso and Shan in lithography, of Klee and Dubuffet in etching, yet looking back we can see that his own hand was apparent even at an early stage. Janssen also turned to reality in abstract, satiric or paraphrastic drawing which, for him, remains an obligatory corrective. He uses his drawing ability in every medium, primarily in lithography and woodcuts, but also in tapestry and painting on glass, and later in his career in etchings which up to now in number and diversity can hardly be ignored. His work in posters and books has expanded since 1965. His style changes periodically and marks every area of his art. From the middle of the 1950s to the end of the 1960s planes, contours and hatching play a leading role, and later on bolder structures: since the late 1970s he has attached increasing importance to colour.

Janssen's development is reflected in countless self-portraits whose diversity is a demonstration of his creative fantasy and an interpretation of his own personality. There are cheerful sketches and poetic illustrations from his early years as a student, satiric and playfully erotic burlesques from "bachelor days," superbly drawn landscapes, paraphrases of European and Japanese drawing and large format graphic series in which the theme of death is ever more predominant. The etchings "Hanos death" and "Dance of death," in recent times the "Nigromontanus" series of drawings and etchings dedicated to Ernst Junger, number among his masterpieces, and not only within the suites representing death. Janssen shows death as a consequence of nature and Eros as the basis of his self knowledge.

Janssen comments, with pictorial and caricature-like references to the final catastrophe, on the danger to society in its own faults, its lack of judgment and foresight. He reveals, always in relation to a concrete event, the practices of the art world and places them in direct relation to the crisis in society.

—Heinz Spielmann

JAUDON, Valerie

Nationality: American. **Born:** Mississippi, 6 August 1945. **Education:** Mississippi State College for Women, Columbus, 1963–65; Memphis Academy of Art, 1965; University of the Americas, Mexico City, 1966–67; St. Martin's School of Art, London, 1968–69. **Career:** Independent artist, New York, since 1973. Visiting artist, Art Institute of Chicago, Philadelphia College of Art, 1985; Maryland Institute Colllege of Art, 1985; professor, Hunter College, New York, 1986-present. **Awards:** Creative Artists Public Service Grant for Graphics, New York, 1980; Art Award, Mississippi Institute of Arts and Letters, 1981; Special Commendation, Art Commission of the City of New York, 1987; National Endowment for the Arts Fellowship, Washington, D.C., 1988; New York Foundation for the Arts, Painting Grant, 1992. **Agent:** Lennon, Weinberg Gallery, 560 Broadway, New York, New York 10012, U.S.A. **Address:** 795A Accabonac Rd., East Hampton, NY, 11937–1807.

Individual Exhibitions:

1975 *Sonia Delaunay/Valerie Jaudon,* Livingston Learmonth Gallery, New York
1977 Holly Solomon Gallery, New York
Pennsylvania Academy of Fine Arts, Philadelphia
1978 Holly Solomon Gallery, New York
1979 Galerie Bischofberger, Zurich
Holly Solomon Gallery, New York
1980 Galerie Hans Strelow, Dusseldorf
1981 Corcoran Gallery, Los Angeles
Holly Solomon Gallery, New York
1983 Sidney Janis Gallery, New York
Museum Quadrat, Bottrop, West Germany
Amerika Haus, Chicago
Dart Gallery, Chicago
1985 Sidney Janis Gallery, New York
Fay Gold Gallery, Atlanta, Georgia
McIntosh/Drysdale Gallery, Washington, D.C.
1986 Sidney Janis Gallery, New York
1988 Sidney Janis Gallery, New York
1990 Sidney Janis Gallery, New York
1993 Sidney Janis Gallery, New York
1994 Barbara Scott Gallery, Bay Harbor Islands, Florida
1996 Mississippi Museum of Art, Jackson (retrospective)
Sidney Janis, New York
1998 Betsy Senior Gallery, New York
1999 Stadel Museum, Frankfurt
2000 *Abstraction at Work: Drawings by Valerie Jaudon, 1973–1999,* Mississippi Museum of Art, Jackson (catalog)

Selected Group Exhibitions:

1977 *Critic's Choice 1976–1977,* Joe and Emily Lowe Art Gallery, Syracuse, New York (travelled to the Munson-Williams-Proctor Institute, Utica, New York)
1978 *Dekor,* Mannheimer Kunstverein, Mannheim, Germany (travelled to Amerika Haus, Berlin, Germany; Museum of Modern Art, Oxford, England)
1980 *The Morton Neumann Family Collection,* The National Gallery of Art, Washington, D.C. (travelled to the Art Institute of Chicago)
1982 *A Private Vision: Contemporary Art from the Graham Gund Collection,* Museum of Fine Arts, Boston
1984 *Abstract Painting Redefined,* Munson-Williams-Proctor Institute, Utica, New York (travelled)
1985 *Geometric Abstractions: Selections from a Decade, 1975–1985,* Bronx Museum of Arts, New York
1987 *Generations of Geometry,* Whitney Museum of American Art at the Equitable Center, New York
1989 *Making Their Mark,* Cincinnati Art Museum (travelled to New Orleans Museum of Art, New Orleans; Denver Art

Valerie Jaudon: *The Best of Everything,* 1995. ©Valerie Jaudon/Licensed by VAGA, New York, NY.

Museum, Denver; Pennsylvania Academy of Fine Art, Philadelphia)

1991 *Conceptual Abstraction,* Sidney Janis Gallery, New York

1992 *American Figurations: A Directory—Works from the Lilja Collection,* Henie-Onstad Art Centre, Hovikodden, Norway

1993 *Italy-America, Abstraction Redefined,* The National Gallery of Modern Art, San Marino, Italy

Collections:

Museum of Modern Art, New York; Hirshhorn Museum and Sculpture Garden, Washington, D.C.; Aldrich Museum, Ridgefield, Connecticut; Indiana University Art Museum, Bloomington; Fogg Art Museum, Cambridge, Massachusetts; National Museum of Women in the Arts, Washington, D.C.; Dayton Art Institute, Dayton, Ohio; Sammlung-Ludwig Museum, Aachen, Germany; Albright-Knox Art Gallery, Buffalo; Birmingham Museum of Art, Birmingham, Alabama; St. Louis Art Museum; Ludwig Museum, Budapest; Mississippi Museum of Art, Jackson.

Publications:

By JAUDON: Articles—Interview with Shirley Kaneda, in *Bomb* (New York), Winter 1992.

On JAUDON Books—*The History of Modern Art,* by H.H. Arnason, 1986; *Valerie Jaudon: New Paintings,* exhibition catalog, with text by Carroll Janis, New York 1988; *Making Their Mark: Women Artists Move into the Mainstream, 1970–1985,* by Randy Rosen, 1989; *Valerie Jaudon,* exhibition catalog, New York 1990; *A History of Western Art,* by Laurie S. Adams, 1993; *Valerie Jaudon,* exhibition catalog, with introduction by Saul Ostrow, New York 1996. **Articles—** Review by Jeff Perrone, in *Artforum,* September 1977; ''Decoration, Ornament, Pattern, and Utility'' by Carrie Rickey, in *Flash Art,* June/July 1979; ''American Abstraction and Decorative Painting'' (catalog essay) by E. A. Carmean, Washington, D.C., 1980; review by Grace Glueck, in *The New York Times,* May 1981; ''Allusive Depths: Valerie Jaudon,'' by John Perreault, in *Art in America,* October 1983; ''Speakeasy: New Emphasis on Collaborative, Holistic Approach to Public Art'' by Malcolm Miles in *New Art Examiner,* vol. 16,

Summer 1989; ''Painting and Its Others: In the Realm of the Feminine'' by Shirley Kaneda in *Arts Magazine,* vol. 65, no. 10, Summer 1991; ''Valerie Jaudon at Sidney Janis'' by Reagan Upshaw in *Art in America* (New York), vol. 84, no. 9, September 1996; ''Degrees of Symmetry'' by Barry Schwabsky in *Art in America* (New York), vol. 84, no. 10, October 1996; ''Understanding Valerie Jaudon's Evolving Art'' by Stephen Young, in *The Southern Quarterly,* Spring 1999.

* * *

Decoration and ornamentation have always been looked on as something secondary and inessential in the history of western art. History is no more than the narration made from it, and if only what is past can be narrated, the historic temporality is made clear to man in the telling, verbally or with pictures. History is as old as man; ever since he began, he has told his own story by means of figures, tokens or words. But ornament does not have the quality of history because (in the great majority of cases) it is abstract; it does not reproduce man and his exploits iconographically. A narration in pictures tells of something more than itself: ornament tells only of itself. Decoration has no history, describes no deeds or enterprises; it just happens; it is inarticulate, it produces patterns. Thus the practice of decorative art (which has never had any great master, any subject, any author) falls outside the logocentric project of subsuming within the field of pictorial reproduction all the external reality that man ''controls,'' or thinks he can control. In the United States, pattern painting (regarded by most critics as part of a wider neo-decorative area) was considered objectively (even about the time it appeared, in 1975) as a reaction to mentalism and the formalism of minimal art, going back to the use of unusual materials and methods (cloth, textiles), the pleasures of pictorialism and the sensuality of colours. However, a typically minimal element is to be seen in the repetition of a plastic background shape (which is in any case part of the essence of decorative rhythm). And references are to be found also in the big United States abstractions of the 1950s and 60s (the recurrent use of a big format, the ''all-over'' employment of the surface of the picture), perhaps notably in the work of Newman, Agnes Martin and Frank Stella's shaped canvases and most recent metal reliefs. In this context Valerie Jaudon takes up again some decorative schemes using interlacing, typical of Arab and Middle Eastern culture and of the Celtic miniature.

Her compositions may be looked on as a number of grids applied to each other but never actually placed on top of each other. While the allusion to this progressive stratification is clear enough, there is still no suggestion of any depth of background. Or rather, the mental and psychological allusion to the third dimension that these networks might imply is firmly flattened on the surface by the distinct contraposition of dark and light making up the ribbons and by the flat versions of the knots and the background—though ''background'' is not the right term, for by ''thinking'' the canvas in negative it can be seen that the dark part is actually a dense, intricate juxtaposition of irregular triangles, lozenges and trapezoids. The flat, linear geometry of these works also arises from the fact that the brush always applies the paint (Valerie Jaudon uses metallic pigments and copper, to produce bright, reflecting surfaces) in the same direction as the edges of the ribbon (the ''band'' of colour), curved or straight according to the entire reticular composition.

—Massimo Carboni

JENKINS, Paul

Nationality: American. **Born:** Kansas City, Missouri, 12 July 1923. **Education:** Kansas City Art Institute, 1938–41; Art Students League, New York, 1948–52. **Military Service:** United States Naval Reserve Air Corps, 1943–45. **Career:** Lives in New York since 1948, and in Paris since 1952. Independent artist, since 1953. **Awards:** Film Prize, *Biennale,* Venice, 1964; Silver Medal, *Corcoran Biennial,* Washington, D.C., 1966; Golden Eagle Film Prize, New York, 1967. D.H.: Lindenwood College, St. Charles, Missouri, 1973; Humanitarian Award, National Committee of Arts for the Handicapped, U.S.A., 1982; Gold Medal, Art Directors Club of New York, 1983. Commander des Arts et Lettres, France, 1983; Life Achievement Award, Butler Institute of American Art, 1997; medal, City of Paris, 1997; Benjamin West Clinedinst Medal Artists' Fellowship, New York 2000. **Agents:** Meyerovich Gallery, 251 Post Street, San Francisco, California 94108; Joseph Rickards Gallery, 1045 Madison Avenue, New York, New York 10021; Galerie Iris Wazzau, Promenade 79, CH-7270 Davos. **Address:** Studio, Imago Terrae, PO Box 6833, Yorkville Station, New York, New York 10128.

Individual Exhibitions:

1954 Studio Paul Facchetti, Paris
Zimmergalerie Franck, Frankfurt
1955 Zoe Dusanne Gallery, Seattle
1956 Martha Jackson Gallery, New York
1957 Galerie Stadler, Paris
Martha Jackson Gallery, New York
1958 Martha Jackson Gallery, New York
Arthur Tooth and Sons, London
1959 Galerie Stadler, Paris
1960 Martha Jackson Gallery, New York
Esther Robles Gallery, Los Angeles
Gallery of Realities, Taos, New Mexico
Arthur Tooth and Sons, London
1961 Galerie Karl Flinker, Paris
Martha Jackson Gallery, New York
Esther Robles Gallery, Los Angeles
University of Minnesota, Minneapolis
1962 Galerie Karl Flinker, Paris
Galerie Charles Lienhard, Zurich
Esther Robles Gallery, Los Angeles
Galleria Toninelli Arte Moderna, Milan
Galleria Odyssia, Rome
Kunstverein, Cologne
1963 Arthur Tooth and Sons, London
Galerie Eva de Buren, Stockholm
Galerie Karl Flinker, Paris
Gallery Moos, Toronto
1964 Tokyo Gallery
Court Gallery, Copenhagen
Kumar Gallery, New Delhi
Martha Jackson Gallery, New York
Kestner-Gesellschaft, Hannover (retrospective; toured England, the United States, and Canada)
1965 Galerie Karl Flinker, Paris
Gertrude Kasle Gallery, Detroit
Court Gallery, Copenhagen

Gallery of Modern Art, Scottsdale, Arizona
American Embassy, Madrid
1966 Martha Jackson Gallery, New York
Galerie Agnes LeFort, Montreal
Hope Makter Gallery, Philadelphia
Galerie Europa, West Berlin
Savage Gallery, London
1968 Galerie D. Gervis, Paris
Galerie Moos, Toronto
Galerie Raber, Lucerne
Martha Jackson Gallery, New York
Seligmann Gallery, Seattle, Washington
1969 Martha Jackson Gallery, New York
1970 Martha Jackson Gallery, New York
Gertrude Kasle Gallery, Detroit
1971 Martha Jackson Gallery, New York
Richard Gray Gallery, Chicago
Suzanne Saxe Gallery, San Francisco
Museum of Fine Arts, Houston (retrospective)
Dryden Gallery, Charlotte, North Carolina
Gertrude Kasle Gallery, Detroit
1972 San Francisco Museum of Art (retrospective)
Gimpel Fils, London
Images Gallery, Toledo, Ohio
Abrams Original Editions, New York
Corcoran Gallery of Art, Washington, D.C. (toured the United States)
1973 Galerie Karl Flinker, Paris
University of Notre Dame Art Gallery, Indiana
Lindenwood College Art Gallery, St. Charles, Missouri
Oklahoma Art Center, Oklahoma City
Amarillo Art Center, Texas
Santa Barbara Museum of Art, California
Indianapolis Museum of Art
Brooks Memorial Art Gallery, Memphis, Tennessee
Martha Jackson Gallery, New York
Louisiana Gallery, Houston
1974 Musée des Beaux Arts, Charleroi, Belgium (retrospective)
Galerie Baukunst, Cologne
Gimpel and Weitzebhoffer, New York
Gimpel Fils Gallery, London
Comsky Gallery, Los Angeles
Kilcawley Centre Gallery, Youngstown State University, Ohio
Gimpel Fils Gallery, London
Comsky Gallery, Los Angeles
Youngstown State University, Ohio
North Texas State University, Denton
Abrams Original Editions, New York
Galerie Ulysses, Vienna
Canton Art Institute, Ohio
Zenesville Fine Arts Center, Ohio
St. Clair County Community College, Port Huron, Michigan
White Memorial Museum, San Antonio, Texas
Fort Lauderdale Museum of the Arts, Florida
Huntington Galleries, West Virginia
University of Florida, Gainesville
Hunter Museum of Art, Chattanooga, Tennessee
1975 Fort Lauderdale Museum of the Arts, Florida
Galerie Tanit, Munich
Galerie Farber, Brussels
Ohio University, Athens
Miami University, Oxford, Ohio
Carone Gallery, Fort Lauderdale, Florida
Closson Gallery, Cincinnati, Ohio
Lauren Rogers Library and Museum of Art, Laurel, Mississippi
Tampa Bay Art Center, Florida
Montgomery Museum of Fine Arts, Alabama
Columbia Gallery of Fine Arts, Columbus, Ohio
1976 Samuel Stein Gallery, Chicago
Basel Art Fair
Galerie Karl Flinker, Paris
Gimpel and Weitzenhoffer Gallery, New York
Jane Haslem Gallery, Washington, D.C.
The 24 Collection, Miami
Galerie Maillard, St. Paul de Vence, France
1977 Gimpel und Hanover Galerie, Zurich
La Galerie Cour St. Pierre, Geneva
Sears Bank and Trust Company, Chicago
Contemporary Gallery, Dallas
Philbrook Art Center, Tulsa, Oklahoma
Closson Gallery, Cincinnati, Ohio
Diane Gilson Gallery, Seattle
Martha Jackson Gallery, New York
Galerie d'Art de la MJC, Metz, France
1978 Galleria d'Arte Narciso, Turin
Gimpel and Weitzenhoffer Gallery, New York
1979 Gimpel and Weitzenhoffer Gallery, New York
Galerie Baukunst, Cologne
Galerie Charles Munchen, Luxembourg
Galerie Bronda, Helsinki
Elaine Horwitch Gallery, Scottsdale, Arizona
1980 Gimpel Fils Gallery, London
Elaine Horwitch Gallery, Scottsdale, Arizona
Contemporary Gallery, Dallas
Albert White Gallery, Toronto
Gallery Gwyn Hodges, Oxford
Galerie Karl Flinker, Paris
1981 Palm Springs Desert Museum, California (retrospective)
Irving Feldman Galleries, Sarasota, Florida
Western Carolina University, Cullowhee
Carone Gallery, Fort Lauderdale, Florida
Samuel Stein Gallery, Chicago
French Cultural Center, New York (and Theatre du Rond-Point, Paris)
Gimpel and Weitzenhoffer Gallery, New York
1982 Galerie Nicoline Pon, Zurich
Gimpel Fils, London
Irving Feldman Galleries, Detroit
Galerie Georges Fall, Paris
Contemporary Gallery, Dallas
1983 Mead Art Museum, Amherst, Massachusetts (retrospective)
Gimpel and Weitzenhoffer Gallery, New York
Galerie Georges Fall, Paris
Alex Rosenberg Gallery, New York
Contemporary Gallery, Dallas
1984 Carone Gallery, Fort Lauderdale, Florida
Musee d'Art Contemporain, Dunkerque, France

1985 Galerie Sapone, Nice
Gimpel and Weitzenhoffer Gallery, New York
Gallery Moos, Toronto
Galerie Georges Fall, Paris
Galleri Atrium, Stockholm
1986 Gimpel Fils, London
Gallery Art Point, Tokyo
Roswitha Haftmann Modern Art, Zurich
MR Galleria d'Arte Contemporanea, Rome
Galerie Michel Delorme, Paris
Butler Institute of American Art, Youngstown, Ohio
Focus Gallery, Lausanne
Elaine Horwitch Galleries, Santa Fe, New Mexico (and Scottsdale, Arizona)
Gimpel and Weitzenhoffer Gallery, New York
1987 Galerie 63, Klosters, Switzerland
Samuel Stein Gallery, Chicago
La Colomba Arte, Latina, Italy
Vismara Arte, Milan
Musee Picasso, Antibes, France
Galerie Regis Dorval, Paris
1993 Galerie Yoshii, Paris
1996 *Works on Canvas 1996–1997,* Joseph Rickards Gallery, New York
Spangler Cummings Gallery, Columbus, Ohio
Collage-Paintings, Associated American Artist, New York (catalog)
1997 *Paul Jenkins, 1923,* Galerie Proarta, Zurich (catalog)
1999 *Eyes of the Dove, Paintings from 1957–1959,* Joseph Rickards Gallery, New York
2000 *Microcosms,* Joseph Rickards Gallery, New York
Joseph Rickards, New York

Selected Group Exhibitions:

1956 *41 American Watercolorists of Today,* Museum of Modern Art, New York
1958 *Nature in Abstraction,* Whitney Museum, New York (toured the United States)
1964 *Painting and Sculpture of a Decade,* Tate Gallery, London
1965 *Abstract Watercolors by 14 Americans,* Museum of Modern Art, New York
1972 *Abstract Expressionists,* Albright-Knox Art Gallery, Buffalo, New York
1974 *Inaugural Exhibition,* Hirshhorn Museum, Washington, D.C.
1977 *American Postwar Painting,* Guggenheim Museum, New York
Quelques Americains a Paris, Centre Georges Pompidou, Paris
1997 *Three Americans,* Galerie Iris Wazzau, Davos

Collections:

Museum of Modern Art, New York; Guggenheim Museum, New York; Whitney Museum, New York; Corcoran Gallery of Art, Washington D.C.; Hirshhorn Museum and Sculpture Garden, Washington, D.C.; Tate Gallery, London; Stedelijk Museum, Amsterdam; Fondation Maeght, St. Paul de Vence, France; Musee Picasso, Antibes, France; Centre Georges Pompidou, Paris.

Publications:

By JENKINS: Books—*Observations of Michel Tapie,* with Esther Jenkins, New York 1956; lithographs for *Seeing Voice Welsh Heart* by Cyril Hodges, Paris 1965; *Strike the Puma,* play, Paris 1966; *The Sun in Scorpio,* with Joyce Wittenhorn, Venice 1959; *D. H. Lawrence and the Man Who Died,* lecture paper, Taos, New Mexico 1980; *Anatomy of a Cloud,* with Suzanne Donnelly Jenkins, New York and Paris 1985. **Articles—**''A Cahier Leaf'' in *It Is* (New York), Autumn 1958; ''An Abstract Phenomenist'' in *The Painter and Sculptor* (New York), Winter/Spring 1959; ''American Abstract Painting'' in *It Is* (New York), Winter/Spring 1959; ''Panel: Non-American Painting'' in *It Is* (New York), Winter/Spring 1959; ''A Reply to Purity'' in *It Is* (New York), Spring 1960; ''Gustave Moreau: Moot Grandfather of Abstraction'' in *Art News* (New York), December 1961; ''Beauford Delaney: A Quiet Legend'' in *Art International* (Lugano), 20 December 1962; ''Conversation in the Studio with Paul Jenkins,'' interview by Michel Butler, in *Cimaise* (Paris), July/August 1963; ''Jenkins Paints an Opinion'' in *Art News* (New York), November 1966; ''Jenkins on Matisse'' in *Art World* (New York), November/December 1978; ''Gustav Klimt Drawings'' in *Art World* (New York), December/January 1980; ''Tapies Paradox'' in *Art World* (New York), September/October 1981; ''Pour le Prisme du Chaman'' in *Opera de Paris* (Paris), April 1987.

On JENKINS: Books—*Dictionary of Abstract Painting* by Ferdinand Louis Berckelaers, New York 1957; *The Paintings of Paul Jenkins* by Kenneth B. Sawyer, Pierre Restany and James Fitzsimmons, Paris 1961; *Ein Halbes Jahrhundert abstrakte Malerie,* Munich and Zurich 1962; *Art U.S.A. Now,* edited by Lee Nordness and Allen S. Weller, New York 1962; *Paul Jenkins* by Jean Cassou, Paris 1963; *Lascaux and Jenkins: 14 Poems* by George P. Elliot, Lanthem, Maryland 1964; *A Dictionary of Contemporary American Artists* by Paul Cummins, New York 1966; *History of Modern Art* by H. H. Arnason, New York 1968; *The Joys and Sorrows of Recent American Art* by H. W. Janson, New York 1969; *Paul Jenkins Retrospective,* exhibition catalog by Gerald Nordland, Houston 1971; *Paul Jenkins* by Albert Elsen, New York 1973; *L'Art Abstrait* by Michel Seuphor, Paris 1974; *Paul Jenkins* by Alain Bosquet, Paris 1982; *Paul Jenkins: Viaggio in Italia,* with Beatrice Buscaroli Fabbri, Edisai 2000.

*

The world of phenomena for me is involved with the capture of ever-changing reality, both in the act of painting and in the perceiving of reality. I am drawn to ever-changing realities not because they seem to be the evidence of a hazardous world but because they draw me closer to the wonders. Marvels incite me not just to accept change but to *induce* it. A phenomenon which springs forth from the real, that which happens, is something we must continually strive to perceive.

There are two kinds of light in painting which I move toward that become and relate form. One is radiant, luminous light, that element which has its light from *within,* as in an orb. Luminous light comes from a central source or place and exists independently. The other is reflected light which appears as a mysterious substance on the surface. It is a light coming from the outside source which creates constant reflection. When these two kinds of light interpenetrate I discover unique forms which have a psychic substance, forms which build, hold on to one another, become alive and certain. Like psychic substances, they become caught in a state of abeyance. When this occurs, the color becomes what I call non-alternate color, color that cannot be any other color than what it is on the canvas. No other color can take its place. It becomes a constant not entirely dependent upon the color next to it.

Color is a fact of science: it is not an abstraction in itself. Color is the hidden fact of your psyche and you make it real or not. You make it your own or not. No two people have the same fingerprints. No two people have the same primary colors even if they should come out of the same Winsor Newton tube. Color becomes the factual evidence of the individual which is not discovered through theory or found through osmosis.

—Paul Jenkins

* * *

Aside from one brief aberration with black and white, Paul Jenkins was always a colourist obsessed by the accidental effects possible of achivement under the minimum of detailed control of the medium. His early experiences of working with glazes fired on clay in the ceramic factory where he worked for a short time undoubtedly left this feeling for the magical transformation that flow and heat can induce in colours. His travels from New York to Europe date from 1955 and took him away from the persuasive influences of the Abstract Expressionists that he felt too insistent. So much so that he destroyed all his work he had done prior to that year. Beginning afresh left him open none the less to ideas and impulses he could choose and deliberate on coolly. He took note of painters such as Moreau and Redon (Symbolists, it will be observed, who put colour high on their priorities), also Riopelle and Hokusai.

This was the date he began pouring paint and setting the course for the promised land he arrived at over the next few years. Another artist he found of common purpose was Wols, whose intuitional freedom struck sparks of sympathy. The ''veils'' that were developed from Wols by Frankenthaler, Louis and others in New York came to be of shared appeal though of subsequent individual evolution. Jenkins made his first works in acrylic around 1960, and the medium came to be employed along with oils and other synthetic paints to increase the limits to which he was committed. This activation of the vehicle by the gravity feed of colour involved manipulation of the canvas to direct the flow and direction of the pools of colours often in acts of physical complexity and resource. Large canvases would be laid on the floor and hooked up at one side to create valleys, and down them would flood full surges of red, ending on a verge like a tidal bore. The push-pull of linear white and luminous white left its mark. Indentations of ebb and flow were evident on the paintings that came to take a generic title of *Phenomenon.* Scale and variations of colours and strengths of tone conditioned the visual choreography.

Jenkins has made his charisma by his methods dictating their own form in colour to a large extent. But his colour is not invariably of negative purity. It gains and loses in its retinal impact through overprinting, mixing on surface level, opting for change by juxtaposition determined by gravitational flow rather than placing. Brushes are supplanted by an ivory blade in directing fluid paint on the support. Fusion without heat sets up optical stimulation of a subtle and delicate intensity. If many of the paintings and their prime choice of reds give a repeated suggestion of flower petals enlarged and isolated in their curving and elliptical outlines, in others the imagery is less determinate though allusions to other forms come through; butterfly wings in the iridescent glow and icebergs in the transparency of immense masses. Jenkins from the pure process of working the medium has come to distil an authentic spirit, staining instead of painting, colouring by flow rather than by application and in its potency having equal power to intoxicate the senses through the thirsty throat of the eye.

—G. S. Whittet

JENNEY, Neil

Nationality: American. **Born:** Torrington, Connecticut in 1945. **Career:** Painter and sculptor: lives in New York.

Individual Exhibitions:

1967 *Art to Artschwarger Annual,* Richard Bellamy Gallery/ Noah Goldowsky Gallery, New York
1968 Galerie Rudolf Zwirner, Cologne
1970 *Paintings,* Noah Goldowsky Gallery, New York
Sculpture, David Whitney Gallery, New York
1975 Blum Helman Gallery, New York
Wadsworth Atheneum, Hartford, Connecticut
1981 University of California Art Museum, Berkeley (retrospective; travelled to Corcoran Gallery of Art, Washington, D.C., and Contemporary Arts Museum, Houston; then a European tour organized by the Basel Kunsthalle)
2001 *The Bad Years, 1969–70,* Gagosian Gallery, New York (catalog)

Selected Group Exhibitions:

1969 *Anti-Illusion: Procedures/Materials,* Whitney Museum, New York
1978 *New Image Painting,* Whitney Museum, New York
1980 *Die Neue Wilden,* Neue Galerie-Sammlung Ludwig, Aachen, West Germany
American Art from the 70's, Nordjyllands Kunstmuseum, Aalborg, Denmark
1982 *Attitudes-Concepts-Images 1960–80,* Stedelijk Museum, Amsterdam
1983 *Paintings and Sculpture from 8 Collections,* Museum of Contemporary Art, Los Angeles
1987 *Avant-Garde in the Eighties,* Los Angeles County Museum of Art
1996 *Ornament and Sancscape: On the Nature of Artifice,* Apex Art Curatorial Program, New York (catalog)
2000 Holly Solomon Gallery, New York
Anne Plumb Gallery, New York

Publications:

On JENNEY: Book—*Neil Jenney: retrospective,* exhibition catalog with essay by Mark Rosenthal, Berkeley 1980. **Article—**''Neil Jenney: Elegance With a Political Twist'' by Hilton Kramer in the *New York Times,* 17 May 1981.

* * *

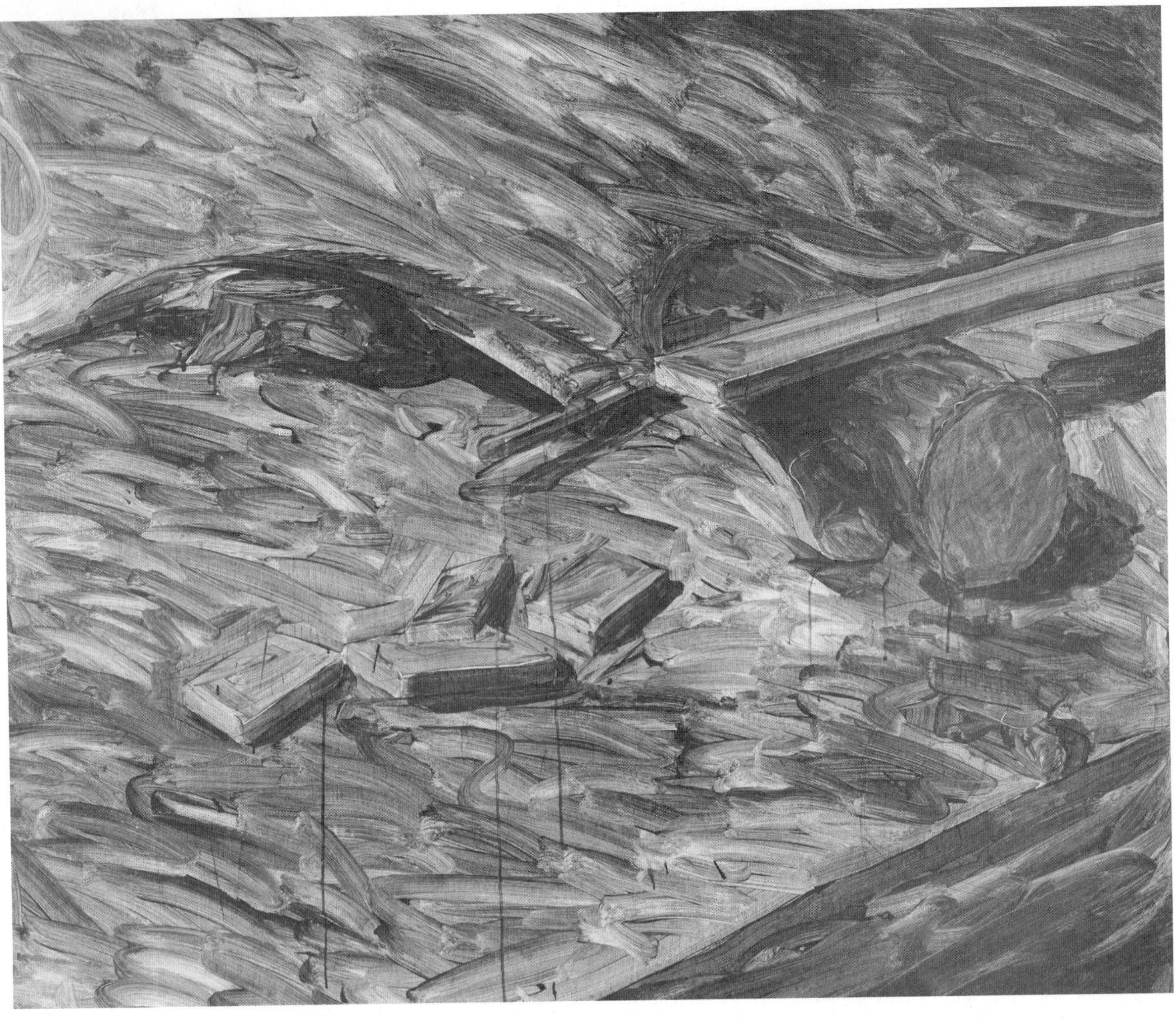

Neil Jenny: *Saw and Sawed,* 1969. ©Geoffrey Clements/Corbis.

Jenney has insisted on the ''mission'' of his current work, and presents his art as a ''social science.'' In such stance, he seemingly would align his production with the radical ethos of the 1960s; Jenney began his career in that decade, as a Minimalist, but left for a content-oriented, far more eclectic mode, the so-called Bad Paintings (1969–71). Long-known in New York for his maverick personality, Jenney appears to share—along with fellow New Englanders Winsor and Grosvenor—an almost fierce independence, both in commercial control and production of their work: Jenney served as his own dealer for a long period.

His works at the onset of the 1970s already evinced the clearly directed humane and environmental concerns which would become his signature content. Although distinct from his still-active approach in their loosely drawn and finger-painterly surface effects, these simple narratives, with their verbal play as given in printed titles, and severe framing, carried some feeling of a Conceptual mode. In the following years, his older Minimalist allegiance would come into focus with an austere yet theatrical format: paint was now applied precisely, images presented close-up and only in fragments, and frames expanded to become architraval-like, black and massive, onto which the titles appeared in large stencilled characters. Through the early 1980s, these images were presented in exaggeratedly horizontal format (often with a proportion of 1:11, as in *Meltdown Morning,* 1975), which of course had a strong viewer effect. This has been phrased by reviewers as a fortress-like slit, tomb-like, and producing a mock-panoramic view, but all working as if to force a sense of both viewer frustration and intense involvement. Given the insistence upon subject formed by the highly abbreviated views and information, it might seem that a mock-didactic mode is intended.

Although described as reportorial, these paintings—especially given the artist's own language about them—present themselves as a call to action on the issues shown, i.e. *Acid Story*—the destruction of nature. Yet, by their generality and aloof removal (in his 1985 exhibition, Jenney had the gallery entirely dark except for spotlight upon the slit-like pictures, with an armed guard present) the work acknowledges the only stifled message of any art that would be ''activist'' and speak of issues of profound complexity and magnitude—but all within the minute artworld itself.

In early 2001, Jenney ended his twelve-year-long absence from New York gallery activity—no surprise given the artist's long-established reputation for quirky behavior—with a show called *The Bad Paintings 1969–70.* These works were in his debut and break-through style as presented above, with several surprisingly having been never before seen.

However it was possible to grasp some career-continuity since three relatively recent works—from the mid-1990s—were included in this exhibition. Nature remained the constant thematic focus. These paintings appeared a continuation of the meticulous technique of Jenney's post-''bad-work'' period, and were almost ''Northern European in their perfection.'' But in the appearance of textural surface play, it was as if Jenney would retain some of his youthful perversity. His seemingly perennial pessimism also survives here with a focus on the Civil War and eco-destruction. The mordant power of the imagery is decisively reenforced, as in the past, by the titles emblazoned on the thick, black, and carefully contoured frames.

—Joshua Kind

JIMENEZ, Luis (Alfonso, Jr.)

Nationality: American. **Born:** El Paso, Texas, 30 July 1940. **Education:** Assistant to his father in El Paso, 1946–58; University of Texas at Austin, 1960–64, B.S. in art and architecture 1964, and Ciudad Universitaria, Mexico City, 1964. **Family:** Married Vicky Cardwell in 1961 (divorced, 1966); daughter: Elisa; married Mary Wynn in 1967 (divorced, 1970); married Susan Brockman in 1985; son: Luis Adan. **Career:** Sculptor: lived in New York City, 1966–73; assistant to Seymour Lipton, New York, 1965–67; program coordinator, New York City Youth Board, 1966–69; Named Goodwill Ambassador, City of Houston, 1993, 1998. **Awards:** National Endowment for the Arts Fellowship, 1977; Showhegan Sculpture Award, 1989; National Endowment for the Arts Residency Fellow, 1990; Governor's Award, State of New Mexico, 1993; Award of Distinction, National Council of Art Administrators, 1995; Texas Artist of the Year, Houston Art League, 1998. **Agent:** Hill's Gallery, 110 San Francisco, Santa Fe, New Mexico 87501. **Address:** P.O. Box 175, Hondo, New Mexico 88336, U.S.A.

Individual Exhibitions:

1969 Graham Gallery, New York
1972 O. K. Harris Gallery, New York
1973 Long Beach Museum, California
Bienville Gallery, New Orleans
1974 Contemporary Arts Museum, Houston
1975 Hills Gallery, Santa Fe, New Mexico
O. K. Harris Gallery, New York
Bienville Gallery, New Orleans
1977 University of North Dakota, Grand Forks
University of Santa Clara, California
1978 Yuma Fine Arts Association, Arizona
1979 Plains Art Museum, Moorehead, Minnesota
Landfall Press Gallery, Chicago
New Mexico Museum of Fine Arts, Santa Fe
Hills Gallery, Santa Fe, New Mexico
1980 Joslyn Art Museum, Omaha, Nebraska
1981 Franklin Struve Gallery, Chicago
Sebastian-Moore Gallery, Denver, Colorado
1982 Hydt-Blair Gallery, Santa Fe, New Mexico
1983 Candy Story Gallery, Folsom, California
Yares Gallery, Scottsdale, Arizona
Laguna Gloria Art Museum, Austin, Texas
1984 Phyllis Kind Gallery, New York
Alternative Museum, New York
Hammarskjold Plaza, New York
Sculpture Plaza, New York
Barnsdall Junior Arts Center, Los Angeles
Art Attack Gallery, Boise, Idaho
Roswell Museum and Art Center, New Mexico
1985 Dallas Museum of Art, Texas
Sette Gallery, Tempe, Arizona
Art Network, Tucson, Arizona
University of Arizona, Tucson
1986 University of Texas/El Paso Art Museum, Texas
Adair Margo Gallery, El Paso, Texas
1987 Moody Gallery, Houston
Marilyn Butler Fine Arts, Santa Fe, New Mexico
1991 Scottsdale Center for the Arts, Arizona
1992 SPARC Gallery, Spencer Museum of Art, Los Angeles
1994 Scottsdale Cultural Arts Center
National Museum of American Art, Washington, D.C.
Marsha Mateyka Gallery, Washington, D.C.
1995 Adair Margo Gallery, El Paso
Man on Fire, Albuquerque Museum of Art, New Mexico
1997 Dallas Museum of Art (retrospective)
1998 A.C.A. Galleries, New York
Working-Class Heroes: Images from the Popular Culture, Palm Springs Museum of Art

Selected Group Exhibitions:

1969 *Human Concern/Personal Torment,* Whitney Museum, New York
1973 *The Male Nude,* Hofstra University, Hempstead, New York
1975 *Richard Brown Collects,* Yale University, New Haven, Connecticut
1977 *Ancient Roots/New Visions,* Tucson Museum of Art, Arizona (toured the United States)
1978 *Figure in the Landscape,* Wave Hill Sculpture Garden, New York
1979 *First Western States Biennial,* Denver Arts Museum, Colorado (toured the United States)
1982 *Recent Trends in Collecting,* Smithsonian, Washington, D.C.
1983 *Myth of the Cowboy,* Library of Congress, Washington, D.C.
1985 *Power of Popular Image,* Queens College, Pennsylvania
1987 *Contemporary Hispanic Art in the United States,* Museum of Fine Arts, Houston (toured the United States)
1988 *Different Drummers,* Hirshhorn Museum and Sculpture Garden, Washington, D.C.
1989 *A Century of Sculpture in Texas, 1889–1989,* Archer M. Huntington Art Gallery, Austin

Luis Alfonso Jimenez, Jr.: drawing for *Southwest Pieta,* 1983. ©2001 Luis Jimenez/Artists Rights Society (ARS), NY.

Collections:

Witte Museum, San Antonio, Texas; Long Beach Museum, California; Roswell Museum and Art Center, New Mexico; Sheldon Memorial Art Gallery, University of Nebraska, Lincoln; Plains Art Museum, Moorehead, Minnesota; National Museum of American Art, Washington, D.C.; Art Institute of Chicago; Denver Art Museum, Colorado; Metropolitan Museum of Art, New York; Albuquerque Museum, New Mexico; Fine Arts Museum, Santa Fe; University of New Mexico, Albuquerque; Albright-Know Art Gallery, Buffalo, New York.

Publications:

On JIMENEZ: Books—*Human Concern/Personal Torment,* exhibition catalog by Robert Doty, New York 1969; *Humanist Art in the U.S.* by Barry Schwartz, New York 1971; *Plastic Sculpture* by Nick Roukes, Calgary, Alberta 1975; *Luis Jimenez,* exhibition catalog, Austin, Texas 1984; *Luis Jimenez for Children,* Austin, Texas 1984; *Luis Jimenez: Sodbuster,* Dallas 1985; *Latin American Art in the Twentieth Century,* edited by Edward J. Sullivan, London, 1996. **Articles—**''Luis Jiménez, Jr.: Southwest Pieta'' by William Peterson in *Artspace,* vol. 12, no. 3, Summer 1988; ''Profile: Luis Jiménez'' by Becky Duval Reese in *Texas Trends in Art Education,* Fall 1988; ''The Iconography of Chicano Self-determination: Race, Ethnicity and Class'' by Shifra M. Goldman in *Art Journal,* vol. 49, no. 2, Summer 1990; ''Luis Jiménez: Man of Fire'' by Victor Sorell in *Latin American Art,* vol. 5, no. 4, 1994; ''Luis Jiménez: View from La Frontera'' by Rudolfo Anaya in *Southwest Art,* vol. 23, March 1994; review by Kathleen Shields in *Art in America* (New York), vol. 82, November 1994; review by Rex Weil in *Art News,* vol. 93, December 1994; ''Man on Fire: Luis Jiménez—Communities, Cultures and Controversies'' by Kathleen Whitney in *Sculpture* (Washington,

Luis Alfonso Jimenez, Jr.: *Vaquero,* modeled 1980 (cast 1990). ©2001 Luis Jimenez/Artists Rights Society (ARS), NY.

D.C.), vol. 16, July/August 1997; ''A Baroque Populism'' by Charles Dee Mitchell in *Art in America* (New York), vol. 87, no. 3, March 1999.

*

My main concern is creating an ''American'' art: using symbols and icons. Sources for the work come out of popular art and esthetic (cowboys, western Indians, the Statue of Liberty, motorcycles), as does the material-plastic (surfboards, boats, cars). I feel I am a traditional artist working with images and materials that are of ''my'' time.

—Luis Jimenez

* * *

Luis Jimenez' sculptures are powerful, humorous, lusty and charged with explosive energy. They and the drawings communicate the artist's profoundly integrated understanding of classical form and inspired draughtsmanship. They also make visible his sources in the Mexican Renaissance expressions of J. C. Orozco which influenced some early murals which he painted as a student at the University of Texas. His subject-matter is folk art in the form of kitsch, involving border-town crafts: ''Progress I'' ultimately derives from this category of expression; ''Barfly'' is a politically charged reconstruction of the Statue of Liberty—a mythic ''non-art'' structure; ''Rodeo Queen,'' ''Rock Star'' and ''California Chick'' are personifications derived from popular culture.

These subjects affirm Jimenez' incisive concern with popular myth. The artist challenges or redefines each myth by penetrating its meaning in order to release its power.

The use of fibreglass, neon, electric lights, and strong color derived from sign technology invests the sculpture with the immediacy of contemporary experience. It also reflects the artist's experience working in all phases of sign construction in his father's company in El Paso, Texas.

The above references and those involving the demolition derby, television, comics, the saga of the West, and commercial sexuality, not only focus on their own reality but express an absurdly riotous humor, which is quintessentially a part of an indigenous tradition—one which has declined under the influence of European fashion and its false ideals of ''serious'' decoration as high art.

Jimenez' images of women relate to those used in product promotion and also to the symbolic role which emphasizes woman's sexuality as beauty queen or rodeo queen. Significant to this area of his art is the ''American Dream,'' the sexual confrontation between woman and Volkswagen, a new rendition of the theme ''Mechanical Bride.'' Jimenez makes such obvious imagery in his subject-matter but, unlike popular pornographic literature, he states it as a dramatic moral truth rather than exploits it for ulterior purposes.

''Progress'' involves a series of monumental sculptures depicting the history of the West. The first of the series is a full-sized buffalo being attacked and killed by an Indian on horseback. It represents both the end of an historical era and its consequences as myth.

It would be unfair to Jimenez to regard his work as social comment alone or simply as a form of documentary. The sculpture goes further—making visible the processes and images which are basic to contemporary experience. Advanced plastic values and traditional subject-matter merge in a unique perspective. While the artist's sculpture identifies ubiquitous American symbols and myths, it also communicates the energy and form which are basic to a mature, passionate, and more humane existence. Jimenez' work is a turning point in American art, as it evokes fresh insights from native sources, giving new life to the tradition. Jimenez ''tastelessness,'' frequently discussed and admired by New York critics, presents a dramatic break with high fashion attitudes. It is central to subject-matter which more explicitly belongs to the native culture.

As a Chicano, Jimenez reveals his own powerfully self-contained background in each work and expresses his cogently moralistic view of contemporary America. The sculpture ''Man of Fire'' and the drawing ''La Causa'' refer specifically to the political expressions of the Chicano struggle to come to grips with the complex social dilemma facing America.

Throughout all the work Jimenez deals with essential metaphors. For example, ''Birth Piece'' depicts a stylised woman giving birth to a soul-less astronaut/robot, fully equipped for space travel; and ''The End of the Trail'' presents a dying Indian chief in an electric sunset. These expose a cultural orientation in which electrical or mechanical substitutes for natural phenomena and processes are transformed into sentimental myth.

The concept of the sex-object and its implications as cultural symbol is a logical theme for Jimenez' art, for it is in this arena that American fantasy reaches as apex of symbolic absurdity. In nearly all social activities, the exaggeration of an innate physical drive is precipitated into mythic substitutes which in turn affect attitudes about race, ethnicity, nationality, as well as about art and metaphysics. Jimenez succeeds in making the viewer intensely aware of these issues through an art from which he probes reality without isolating it from contemporary experience.

—James Harithas

JOHNS, Jasper

Nationality: American. **Born:** Augusta, Georgia, 15 May 1930. **Education:** University of South Carolina, Columbia; attended art school in New York, 1949. **Military Service:** Served in the United States Army in Japan, 1949. **Career:** Worked as bookstore salesman, New York, 1952–59; also worked as a window display artist for various stores, including Tiffany's, New York. Director, Foundation for Contemporary Performance Arts Inc., New York, since 1963; set and costume designer and artistic adviser, Merce Cunningham Dance Company, New York, since 1970; collaborated on *Un Jour ou Deux* ballet, with Merce Cunningham and John Cage, 1973. **Awards:** First Prize, *Print Biennale,* Ljubljana, Yugoslavia, 1967; Prize, *Sao Paulo Bienal,* 1967; Skowhegan Award for Painting, 1972; Skowhegan Award for Graphics, 1977; Mayor's Award of Honor For Art and Culture, New York, 1978; Grand Prix, Venice Biennale, 1988. **Agent:** Brooke Alexander/Brooke Alexander Editions, 59 Wooster Street, New York, New York 10012; c/o Leo Castelli Gallery, 59 East 79th St., New York, New York 10021, U.S.A.; Knoedler & Company, 19 East 70th Street, New York, New York 10021. **Address:** PO Box 642, Sharon, Connecticut 06069–0642.

Individual Exhibitions:

1958 Leo Castelli Gallery, New York
1959 Galerie Rive Droite, Paris

Galleria d'Arte del Naviglio, Milan
1960 Tweed Gallery, Minneapolis
Columbia Museum of Art, South Carolina (retrospective)
Leo Castelli Gallery, New York
1961 Leo Castelli Gallery, New York
Galerie Rive Droite, Paris
1962 Everett Ellin Gallery, Los Angeles (retrospective)
Galerie Ileana Sonnabend,Paris
1963 Leo Castelli Gallery, New York
1964 Jewish Museum, New York (retrospective)
Whitechapel Art Gallery, London (retrospective)
1965 Pasadena Museum of Art, California (retrospective)
Minami Gallery, Tokyo
American Embassy, London
Ashmolean Museum, Oxford
1966 Leo Castelli Gallery, New York
The Drawings of Jasper Johns, Smithsonian Institution, Washington D.C.
1968 Galerie Ricke, Cologne
Galerie Buren, Stockholm
Museum of Modern Art, New York (circulating exhibit)
1969 Castelli Graphics, New York
Kunstmuseum, Basel
University of New Mexico, Albuquerque
Los Angeles County Museum of Art
Castelli-Whitney Gallery, New York
David Whitney Gallery, New York
1970 Leo Castelli Gallery, New York
New Gallery, Cleveland
Philadelphia Museum of Art
University of Iowa, Iowa City
Museum of Modern Art, New York
1971 Museum of Modern Art, New York
Castelli Graphics, New York
Kunsthalle, Bern
Minneapolis Institute of Arts
Dayton's Gallery 12, Minneapolis
Museum of the Sea, Hilton Head, South Carolina
Museum of Contemporary Art, Chicago
Marion Koogler McNay Art Institute, San Antonio, Texas
1972 Museum of Fine Arts, Houston
Museum of Modern Art, New York (circulating exhibition)
Galerie Buren, Stockholm
Heath Gallery, Atlanta
Johns/Stella/Warhol: Works in Series, South Texas Art Museum, Corpus Christi
Fendrick Gallery, Washington, D.C.
Jasper John's Decoy: The Print and the Painting, Emily Lowe Gallery, Hofstra University, Hempstead, New York
1973 Gertrude Kasle Gallery, Detroit
1974 Galerie de Gestlo, Hamburg
Knoedler Contemporary Prints, New York
Lo Spazil-Galleria d'Art, Rome
Lucio Amelio Modern Art Agency, Naples
Galerie Folker Skulima, Berlin
Museum of Modern Art, Oxford
Mappin Art Gallery, Sheffield
Herbert Art Gallery, Coventry
1975 Walker Art Gallery, Liverpool
City Art Gallery, Leeds
Serpentine Gallery, London
1976 Leo Castelli Gallery, New York
Janie C. Lee Gallery, Houston
Castelli Graphics, New York
1977 Castelli Graphics, New York (twice)
Brooke Alexander Inc., New York
Whitney Museum of American Art, Downtown Annex, New York
Whitney Museum of American Art, New York (retrospective)
1978 Museum Ludwig, Cologne (retrospective)
Georges Pompidou Center, Paris (retrospective)
Hayward Gallery, London (retrospective)
Seibu Museum of Art, Tokyo (retrospective)
San Francisco Museum of Modern Art (retrospective)
Margo Leavin Gallery, Los Angeles
Galerie Nancy Gillespie, Paris
Galerie Valeur, Nagoya
Prints 1970–77, Center for the Arts, Wesleyan University, Middletown, Connecticut (toured the United States)
John Berggruen Gallery, San Francisco
1979 Janie C. Lee Gallery, Houston
Galerie Valeur, Nagoya
Kunstmuseum, Basel
Staatliche Graphische, Munich
Stadtische Galerie, Stadelschen Kunstinstitut, Frankfurt
Kunstmuseum, Hannover
Tucson Museum of Art, Arizona
1980 Statens Museum for Kunst, Copenhagen
Moderna Museet, Stockholm
Castelli Graphics, New York
Tyler Museum of Art, Texas
1981 Tate Gallery, London
1982 Castelli Graphics, New York
L. A. Louver Gallery, Venice, California
1983 Akira Ikeda Gallery, Tokyo
Delahunty Gallery, Dallas
1984 Leo Castelli Gallery, New York
1985 Brooke Alexander Inc., New York
1986 Fondation Maeght, St. Paul de Vence, France
St. Louis Art Museum, Missouri
1987 Centro Reina Sofia, Madrid
1988 United States pavilion, *43rd Biennale,* Venice
1993 *Jasper Johns—35 Years—Leo Castelli,* Leo Castelli Gallery, New York (catalog)
1996 *Jasper Johns Flags: 1955–1994,* Anthony d'Offay Gallery, London (catalog)
Jasper Johns: A Retrospective, Museum of Modern Art, New York (retrospective) (catalog)
Jasper Johns: The Sculptures, Henry Moore Institute, Centre for the Study of Sculpture, Leeds (catalog)
The Prints of Jasper Johns, Leo Castelli Gallery, New York
1997 *Jasper Johns: The Seasons,* Exhibit A Gallery, Savannah College of Art and Design (catalog)
Jasper Johns, Prints 1968–1980, National Gallery of Australia, Canberra (catalog)

Jasper Johns: Retrospektiv, Museum Ludwig, Cologne (catalog)
1999 *Jasper Johns: Process and Printmaking,* Philadelphia Museum of Art, Philadelphia
2000 *Jasper Johns: New Paintings and Works on Paper Comp,* Dallas Museum of Art
Jasper Johns: New Paintings and Works on Paper, San Francisco Museum of Modern Art (catalog)

Selected Group Exhibitions:

1958 *39th Biennale,* Venice
1964 *Painting and Sculpture of a Decade,* Tate Gallery, London
1969 *New York Painting and Sculpture 1940–1970,* Metropolitan Museum of Art, New York
1974 *American Pop Art,* Whitney Museum, New York
1975 *Sculpture: American Directions 1945–1975,* National Collection of Fine Arts, Smithsonian Institution, Washington, D.C.
1978 *Retrospective of the Biennales of Paris 1959–1975,* Seibu Museum of Art, Tokyo
1980 *Printed Art: A View of 2 Decades,* Museum of Modern Art, New York
1985 *Transformations in Sculpture,* Guggenheim Museum, New York
1987 *American Painting: Abstract Expressionism and After,* San Francisco Museum of Modern Art
1994 *Old Glory: The American Flag in Contemporary Art,* Cleveland Center for Contemporary Art, Cleveland (catalog)
The Pop Image: Prints and Multiples, Marlborough Graphics, New York (catalog)
Gemini G.E.L: Recent Prints and Sculpture, National Gallery of Art, Washington, D.C. (catalog)
1995 *Contemporary Drawing: Exploring the Territory,* Aspen Art Museum, Colorado (catalog)
Sculpture, Anthony d'Offay Gallery, London (catalog)
Drawing the Line: Reappraising Drawing Past and Present, South Bank Center, London (catalog)
The Innocent Eye: Children's Art and the Modern Artist, Städtische Galerie in Leubachhaus, Munich (catalog)
1996 *The Robert and Jane Meyerhoff Collection: 1945 to 1995,* National Gallery of Art, Washington, D.C. (catalog)
Tanztheater und Bildende Kunst Nach 1945, Königshausen & Neumann, Würzburg (catalog)
1997 *Forty Years of Exploration and Innovation: The Artists of the Castelli Gallery 1957–1997,* Leo Castelli Gallery (SOHO), New York
De Klein à Warhol, Centre Georges Pompidou, Paris (catalog)
2001 *Jasper Johns to Jeff Koons: Four Decades of Art from the Broad Collections,* Los Angeles County Museum of Art (catalog)

Collections:

Museum of Modern Art, New York; Whitney Museum, New York; Guggenheim Museum, New York; Albright-Knox Art Gallery, Buffalo, New York; San Francisco Museum of Modern Art; Tate Gallery, London; Stedelijk Museum Amsterdam; Kunstmuseum, Basel; Moderna Museet, Stockholm; Seibu Museum, Tokyo.

Publications:

By JOHNS: Articles—statement in *16 Americans,* exhibition catalog, New York 1959; ''Whats Is Pop Art? Part II,'' interview with G. R. Swenson, in *ARTnews* (New York), February 1964; ''Sketchbook Notes'' in *Art and Literature* (Lausanne), Autumn 1965; ''Interview with Walter Hopps'' in *Artforum* (New York), March 1965, ''Marcel Duchamp (1887–1968): An Appreciation'' in *Artforum* (New York), November 1968; ''Sketchbook Notes'' in *Juilliard* (New York), Winter 1968/69; ''Sketchbook Notes'' in *Art Now: New York* (New York), April 1969; ''Thoughts on Duchamp'' in *Art in America* (New York), July/August 1969; ''Notes de Carnet'' in *VH 101* (Paris), Autumn 1970; ''Fragments According to Johns,'' interview with John Coplans, in *Print Collector's Newsletter* (New York), May/June 1972; interview with David Sylvester in *Jasper Johns' Drawings,* exhibition catalog, London 1974; *The Prints of Jasper Johns, 1960–1993: A Catalogue Raisonné,* with Richard S. Fields, West Islip 1994; interview with Marjorie Welish in *Bomb,* no. 57, Fall 1996. **Video**—*Jasper Johns: Ideas in Paint,* 1989, 2000.

On JOHNS: Books—*4 Amerikaner,* exhibition catalog, Bern 1962; *Jasper Johns,* exhibition catalog by Everett Ellin, Los Angeles 1962; *Amerikaner: Jasper Johns, Alfred Leslie, Robert Rauschenberg, Richard Stankiewicz,* exhibition catalog, Stockholm 1962; *Jasper Johns* by Leo Steinberg, New York 1963; *6 Painters and Their Object,* exhibition catalog by Lawrence Alloway, New York 1963; *Jasper Johns,* exhibition catalog with essays by Alan Solomon and John Cage, New York 1964; *Jasper Johns,* exhibition catalog, Japanese text by Yoshiaki Tono, Tokyo 1965; *The Drawings of Jasper Johns,* exhibition catalog with text by Stefan Munsing, Washington, D.C. 1966; *Die Graphik, Jasper Johns* by Carlo Huber, Bern 1970; *Jasper Johns* exhibition catalog, San Francisco 1970; *Jasper Johns: Lithographs,* exhibition catalog, with an essay by Riva Castleman, New York 1970; *Jasper Johns: Prints 1960–1970* by Richard S. Field, New York 1970; *Johns/Stella/Warhol: Works in Series,* exhibition catalog, Corpus Christi, Texas 1972; *Jasper Johns' Decoy: The Print and the Painting,* exhibition catalog with text by Roberta Bernstein and Robert Lottman, Hempstead, New York 1972; *Jasper Johns' Drawings* exhibition catalog, London 1974; *Jasper Johns* by Max Kozloff, New York 1974; *Foirades/Fizzles,* exhibition catalog with text by Samuel Beckett, introduction by Judith Goldman, New York 1977; *Jasper Johns* by Michael Crichton, New York 1977; *Jasper Johns: Prints 1970–77,* exhibition catalog, by Richard S. Field, Middletown, Connecticut 1978; *Jasper Johns: Drawings and Prints 1975–1979,* Houston 1979; *Jasper Johns,* exhibition catalog with essay by Judith Goldman, St. Paul de Vence 1986; *Jasper Johns: Obra Grafica 1960–1985,* exhibition catalog with text by Riva Castleman, Madrid 1987; *Jasper Johns* by Michael Crichton, London 1994. **Articles**—''The Parodic Strategies of Jasper Johns'' by Karen Trella in *Athanor,* no. 13, 1995; ''Split Decisions: Jasper Johns in Retrospect'' by Rosalind E. Krauss and Christopher Knight in *Artforum,* vol. 35, no. 1, September 1996; ''Jasper Johns: An American Iconoclast'' by Patrick Pacheco in *Art and Antiques,* vol. 19, no. 10, November 1996; ''Behind the Sacred Aura: Jasper Johns Gives Nothing Away, but His Cool, Lovely Mastery of Indirection Finally Becomes Claustrophobic'' by Robert Hughes in *Time,* vol. 148, no. 22, 11 November 1996; ''Flag Burning'' by Jed Pearl in *The New*

Republic, vol. 215, no. 23, 2 December 1996; "Jasper Johns and Ellsworth Kelly: The Dead End of Modernism" by Donald Kuspit in *Art New England,* vol. 18, February/March 1997; "Jasper Johns: The Examined Life" by Roni Feinstein in *Art in America* (New York), vol. 85, no. 4, April 1997; "Jasper Johns: Prints 1968–1980" by Christine Dixon in *Artonview,* no. 9, Autumn 1997; "Shots at a Moving Target: In a Series of 13 Short Meditations, the Author Reflects Upon the Elusive Qualities That Distinguish Jasper John's Art" by David Sylvester in *Art in America* (New York), vol. 85, no. 4, April 1997; "Jasper Johns: Diver, 1963" by John Elderfield in *Artforum,* vol. 36, no. 5, January 1998. **Video—***Ellsworth Kelly and Jasper Johns: Modern Masters?,* 1999.

* * *

Jasper Johns is with Rauschenberg the most influential of the American artists who followed Abstract Expressionism and reacted against it, raising some fundamental questions about art in the process. But in contrast to Rauschenberg's great variety, Johns has confined himself to much simpler means and a very small range of subjects. And unlike Rauschenberg he does not "act in the gap between art and life" or relate to life in any way, but instead his formal enigmas constantly question the nature of art. His images are not merely simple and banal, but very, very cool, and often ironic as well, so they weren't so easily dismissed as mere neo-Dada, as Rauschenberg's could be.

The era of Pop art is usually dated from Johns' first one-man show early in 1958, which included paintings of flags, of targets, of numerals and letters of the alphabet, all chosen as familiar images from everyday life, which are not only simple but also essentially two-dimensional. Numbers and letters by their very nature have no depth, and the flags are painted flatly on the surface, covering the whole canvas, or set off against a simple border. But the encaustic (wax-based) paint is richly and vibrantly handled, focusing attention on the act of painting and bringing out the profound ambiguity between image and object, and the constant interplay between painted illusion and real object. These ordinary, banal images thus become thought-provoking, and since such formal problems of pictorial reality as flatness and the two-dimensional nature of paintings were the sort of intellectual problem American critics of the 50's and 60's loved to discuss, "Johns provided everything the New York critical intelligence requires to requite its own narcissism," as Brian O'Doherty aptly observed. These were in fact seminal influences, though ambiguous ones which could lead to such different lines of develoment as Pop and Minimalism, and which prompted one of the great critical axioms of the period, Leo Steinberg's dictum that "Whatever else it may be, all great art is about art."

Johns focuses attention on the painting as an object, a thing in its own right, rather than as representation. And this is made even clearer in those paintings which incorporate such things as rulers, brooms and spoons. Thus his target with four boxes over it, each containing a plaster model of a face cut off below the eyes, creates a powerful interplay of thwarted alternatives, making the human association and the formal geometry equally impersonal, and contradicting the flatness of the target with spatial levels of the boxes. He breaks down and isolates the elements of painting itself and the ideas of illusion and literal fact in such paintings as "False Start" (1959), a series of visual puns in which patches of bright red, blue, orange or yellow are falsely identified by stencilling the names of other colours over them. Later paintings in which the public motifs such as flags and maps are replaced by more homely and domestic images such as coathangers and coffee cups are similarly relentless explorations of different ways of seeing.

The theme of illusion versus reality and the constant questioning of reality and identity is also basic to his sculptures. His bronze reproductions of beer cans, flashlights or cans with paint brushes in them are so carefully sculptured and painted that it is sometimes difficult to tell them from the originals, though they provide a highly ambiguous substitute. His irony directed towards art is seen in "The Critic Smiles," a toothbrush cast in sculptmetal, and "The Critic Sees," a pair of spectacles in the same material, with glass lenses reflecting opaquely back at the viewer.

Johns has regularly been compared with Duchamp, and certainly has the same sort of cool intelligence which has led him to challenge some cherished preconceptions about aesthetics and perception. But the limitations of an art so severely about art are seen all too clearly when carried to absurdity in the extreme reductivism of some of Johns' followers such as Frank Stella. Sir Karl Popper has mocked the reductive aridity of modern linguistic philosophy by comparing it to constantly polishing a pair of spectacles instead of ever looking through them at the world. Something similar might be said about the reductive path of much contemporary American art, and there may be greater irony in "The Critics Sees" than Johns himself ever intended.

—Konstantin Bazarov

JOHNSON, Lester

Nationality: American. **Born:** Minneapolis, Minnesota, 17 January 1919. **Education:** Minneapolis Institute School of Art, St. Paul Art School, Minnesota, and the School of the Art Institute of Chicago, 1942–47. **Family:** Married Josephine Valenti, 1949, children: Leslie Maria and Anthony Edwin. **Career:** Painter: moved to New York 1947; taught at St. Bernard School, New York, 1955–61, and at Ohio State University, Columbus, 1963; summer artist-in-residence, University of Wisconsin, Milwaukee, 1964; Yale University, New Haven, Connecticut: adjunct professor of painting, 1964–89, director of studies, graduate painting, School of Art and Architecture, 1969–74, and Fellow of Trumbull College; fire destroyed home in Milford, Connecticut, and many of his works, 1967; retired from Yale University, 1991. **Awards:** First Prize, Midwestern Artists Competition, 1942; Guggenheim Foundation Fellowship, 1973; Citation in Painting, Brandeis University Creative Arts Award, 1978; Elected Associate, National Academy of Design, 1987. **Agent:** Denise Cade Gallery, 1045 Madison Avenue, New York, New York 10021; Peter Findlay Gallery, 41 East 57th Street, New York, New York 10022; Joseph Rickards Gallery, 1045 Madison Avenue, New York, New York 10021; Michael Rosenfeld Gallery, 24 West 57th Street, New York, New York 10019. **Addresses:** PO Box 7582, Greenwich, Connecticut, 06836–7582.

Individual Exhibitions:

1951 Artists Gallery, New York
1953 Earl Pilgrim Gallery, Provincetown, Massachusetts
1954 Korman Gallery, New York
1955 Hansa Gallery, New York
Zabriskie Gallery, New York

1956 Sun Gallery, Provincetown, Massachusetts
1957 Sun Gallery, Provincetown, Massachusetts
Zabriskie Gallery, New York
1959 Sun Gallery, Provincetown, Massachusetts
Zabriskie Gallery, New York
1960 H. C. E. Gallery, Provincetown, Massachusetts
Sun Gallery, Provincetown, Massachusetts
1961 H. C. E. Gallery, Provincetown, Massachusetts
Minneapolis Institute of Arts
Zabriskie Gallery, New York
1962 B. C. Holland Gallery, Chicago
Orton Museum, Ohio State University, Columbus
Dayton Art Institute, Ohio
Fort Worth Art Center, Texas
Martha Jackson Gallery, New York
1963 Martha Jackson Gallery, New York
1964 Martha Jackson Gallery, New York
1965 Donald Morris Gallery, Detroit
Yale University Art Gallery, New Haven, Connecticut
Anderson-Mayer Gallery, Paris
1966 Martha Jackson Gallery, New York
1967 Martha Jackson Gallery, New York
University of Wisconsin-Milwaukee
Donald Morris Gallery, Detroit
1968 California College of Arts and Crafts, Oakland
1969 Martha Jackson Gallery, New York
B. C. Holland Gallery, Chicago
1971 Martha Jackson Gallery, New York
1972 Alpha Gallery, Boston
1973 Richard Gray Gallery, Chicago
Martha Jackson Gallery, New York
Ruth S. Schaffner Gallery, Los Angeles
Smith-Andersen Gallery, San Francisco
Gallery Moos, Toronto
1974 Procter Art Center, Bard College, Annandale-on-Hudson, New York
Donald Morris Gallery, Detroit
Tyler School of Art, Philadelphia
Ruth S. Schaffner Gallery, Los Angeles
1975 Livingstone-Learmouth Gallery, New York
Martha Jackson Gallery, New York
Jorgensen Gallery, University of Connecticut, Storrs
1976 Alpha Gallery, Boston
1977 Hurlbutt Gallery, Greenwich Library, Connecticut
Gimpel and Weitzenhoffer Gallery, New York
Gallery Moos, Toronto
1978 Ruth S. Schaffner Gallery, San Francisco
Donald Morris Gallery, Detroit
Peter M. David Gallery, Minneapolis
1979 Foster Gallery, Lousiana State University, Baton Rouge
Gimpel Fils, London
1980 Gimpel-Hanover and André Emmerich Galerien, Zurich
Gimpel and Weitzenhoffer Gallery, New York
1981 University of Virginia Art Museum, Charlottesville
London Arts, Detroit
Donald Morris Gallery, Detroit
1982 Alpha Gallery, Boston
Gimpel and Weitzenhoffer, New York
1983 Paperwork Gallery, Larchmont, New York
Zabriskie Gallery, New York
1984 Kansas City Arts Institute, Missouri
Munson Gallery, New Haven, Connecticut
1985 Zabriskie Gallery, New York
Donald Morris Gallery, Detroit
David Barnett Gallery, Milwaukee, Wisconsin
1986 Walter Moos Gallery, Toronto
Munson Gallery, New Haven, Connecticut
1987 Westmoreland Museum of Art, Greensburg, Pennsylvania (travelled)
Walter Moos Gallery, New York
1994 Edward Thorp Gallery, New York
1996 Peter Findlay Gallery, New York
Joseph Rickards Fine Art, New York (also Denise Cade Gallery, New York)
UFO Gallery, Provincetown, Massachusetts
1998 *The Sixties,* Peter Findlay Gallery, New York

Selected Group Exhibitions:

1957 *American Painting 1945–57,* Minneapolis Institute of Arts
1961 *Recent Painting U.S.A.: The Figure,* Museum of Modern Art, New York (toured the United States and Canada)
1962 *Recent Trends in Painting, U.S.A.,* Art Institute of Chicago
1964 *Contemporary American Drawings,* Guggenheim Museum, New York
1972 *70th American Exhibition,* Art Institute of Chicago
1976 *Painting & Sculpture Today 1976,* Indianapolis Museum of Art
1979 *100 Years-100 Artists,* Art Institute of Chicago
1983 *American Realism 1930s-80s,* Summit Art Center, New Jersey
1985 *The Artist Celebrates New York,* Metropolitan Museum of Art, New York (travelled)
1987 *State of the Arts,* Aldrich Museum of Contemporary Art, Ridgefield, Connecticut
1994 *American Art Today: Heads Only,* The Art Museum at Florida International University, Miami (catalog)
1995 *Editions,* Skoto Gallery, New York
Editions 1974–1991, Pharos Gallery, New York

Collections:

Univeristy of Michigan Museum of Art, Ann Arbor; Baltimore Museum of Art; Housatonic Museum of Art; Boca Raton Museum of Art; Albright-Knox Art Gallery, Buffalo; Art Institute of Chicago; Orton Museum, Ohio State University, Columbus; Dayton Art Institute; Detroit Institute of Arts; Guild Hall, East Hampton; Fort Lauderdale Museum of Art; Fort Worth Museum of Art; Westmoreland Museum of Art; The Bruce Museum, Greenwich; Wadsworth Atheneum, Hartford; Heckscher Museum, Huntington; Kalamazoo Institute of Arts; University of Nebraska Art Galleries, Lincoln; Museum of Contemporary Art, Los Angeles; University of Wisconsin-Milwaukee Fine Art Galleries, Milwaukee; Minneapolis Institute of Arts; Walker Art Center, Minneapolis; Yale University Art Gallery, New Haven; Museum of Modern Art, New York; Metropolitan Museum of Art, New York; New School for Social Research, New York; Solomon R. Guggenheim Museum of Art, New York; Chrysler Museum, Norfolk; Norwalk Community Technical College, Norwalk; Museum of Art, University of Oklahoma, Norman; Phoenix Art Museum; Museum of Art, Carnegie Institute, Pittsburgh; Museum of

Art, Rhode Island School of Design, Providence; Neuberger Museum, State University of New York, Purchase; Aldrich Museum of Contemporary Art, Ridgefield; Seattle Art Museum; University of Arizona Museum of Art, Tucson; Rose Art Museum, Brandeis University, Waltham; Hirshhorn Museum and Sculpture Garden, Washington, D.C.; National Museum of Art, Washington, D.C.

Publications:

By JOHNSON: Book—*Lester Johnson: Paintings 1970–74,* with an introduction by Burt Churnow, New York 1975.

On JOHNSON: Books—*Mother and Child in Modern Art,* edited by Bruce Hooten And Nina N. Kaiden, New York 1964; *Artwork and Packages* by Harold Rosenberg, New York 1969; *Art on the Edge* by Harold Rosenberg, New York 1975; *The New York School: The Painters and Sculptors of the Fifties* by Irving Sandler, New York 1978. **Articles—**''Lester Johnson Paints a Picture'' by Lawrence Campbell in *Arts Magazine* (New York), March 1961; ''Remarks of the Figure and Lester Johnson'' by Priscilla Colt in *Art International* (Lugano, Switzerland), January 1964; ''Lester Johnson, New Master'' by James Mellon in the *New York Times,* March 14, 1971; ''The Individual as a Crowd: Lester Johnson's Recent Paintings'' by Barbara Thompsen in *Art in America* (New York), November/December 1973; ''Lester Johnson'' by Burt Chernow in *Arts Magazine* (New York), November 1977; ''Lester Johnson at Gimpel and Weitzenhoffer'' by Robert Berlind in *Art in America* (New York), January/February 1978; ''Lester Johnson'' by Carter Ratcliff in *Art International* (Lugano, Switzerland), August/September 1981; ''Lester Johnson's Strolling Players'' by Dore Ashton in *Arts* (New York), April 1982; ''Lester Johnson'' by Ruth Bass in *Art News* (New York), December 1983; ''Lester Johnson'' in *Flash Art* (Milan), January 1984; ''Edward Thorp Gallery, New York'' by Vincent Katz in *Art in America* (New York), vol. 82, July 1994; ''Lester Johnson at Denise Cadé and Peter Findlay'' by Reagan Upshaw in *Art in America* (New York), vol. 85, April 1997.

* * *

Lester Johnson's pictures of the 1970s are composed of crowds of stylized figures enlivened by a broad range of vibrant colors and patternings and further energized by the bulbous limbs which variously motion in twisting diagonals of impossible gesture. Johnson's figuration is based on abstract principles, specifically on the ideas underlying the gestural wing of American Abstract Expressionism as developed and practised during the 1940s and 1950s by painters such as Franz Kline, Jackson Pollock and Willem de Kooning.

Johnson developed his mature paintings of the 1970's through a long and logical process which began with his works of the 1950's, when he was working in a more abstract, ''action painting'' vein closely akin with the sweeping black and white compositions of Franz Kline. In Johnson's dark, ominous, directly and heavily worked canvases of this period, thick, black brushstrokes often curved to form oval, headlike shapes, signalling his urge toward a figurative element very like that of Pollock in his paintings of the early 1950's. By around 1964, distinct changes were occuring. Johnson's ovals now forming into still life, table top configurations which show a deliberate move away from former flatness into more three-dimensional realms. During the mid to late 60's, in Johnson's ''Classical Figures'' and ''Street Scenes,'' dark and shadowy figures take over the scene, outlined in heavy black in near monochrome surroundings and frozen in agitated lateral movement. The dark, bowler-hatted men of this period are more fully modelled than ever before, but they remain crowded on frontal planes as they motion across and off the canvas surface. Compositions become more jampacked, like modern-day, primitivizing friezes of horror-vacuii whose all-over structure is bursting beyond the framing edges. In 1972 women appear, bringing with them a range of colors and flashy patterned dresses which completes Johnson's evolution from the 1950's from somberly toned gestural abstraction to exuberantly energetic schematized figuration.

During the 1970's images of contemporary urban youth recur persistently. They are dressed in look-alike jeans, T-shirts and patterned garb which both set them off from other times and places and blend them into a stereotypical amalgam of interpenetrating anonymity. Hairdos and facial expressions are nearly interchangeable in Johnson's chosen types who stare off into the distances with firmly set mouths. Even while their huge and stiffened arms and legs are thrusting and bending in intertwining motions of mechanized vigour, their deepset eyes never meet nor search in the same direction. The jostling, closepacked activity of the densely overlapping bodies coupled with their seeming indifference to one another creates a powerful sense of the alienation which characterizes present-day urban living. Johnson makes what is usually semi-conscious into a hyperconscious statement of the human state of crowded aloneness. The fullness of the scene, so heightened by colors, patterns and human bodies in transit, is utilized to convey a psychological reality, the vapid emptiness of all those rapidly-paced gestures which sweep outward into nowhere. Johnson is as much of the inheritor of Ernst Ludwig Kirchner or Fernand Léger as he is of gestural Abstract Expressionism. His pictures incorporate elements from each of these predecessors and turn them into an updated painterly vision of contemporary humanity mechanistically objectified.

—Barbara Cavaliere

JOHNSON, Ray

Nationality: American. **Born:** Detroit, Michigan, 16 October 1927. **Education:** Studied at the Art Students League, New York, 1944–45, and at Black Mountain College, Beria, North Carolina, under Josef Albers, Robert Motherwell, Mary Callery, and Ossip Zadkine, 1945–48. **Career:** Member, American Abstract artists, 1949–52; founder member, New York Correspondence School of Art, 1968–73. **Awards:** National Institute of Arts and Letters Award, 1966; National Endowment for the Arts Award, 1976. **Agent:** Gallery Schlesinger, 24 East 73rd St., New York, New York 10021, U.S.A. **Died:** Of apparent suicide, 13 January 1995, in Sag Harbor, New York.

Individual Exhibitions:

1965	Willard Gallery, New York
1966	Willard Gallery, New York
	Richard Feigen Gallery, Chicago
1967	Willard Gallery, New York
	Richard Feigen Gallery, Chicago
1968	Richard Feigen Gallery, New York (toured Germany)
	Wooster Community Art Center, Danbury, Connecticut

University of Virginia, Charlottesville
1969 Boylston Print Center, Cambridge, Massachusetts
1971 Angela Flowers Gallery, London
1972 Galleria Schwarz, Milan
1974 Rene Block Gallery, New York
1975 Galleria Massimo Valesecchi, Milan
Gertrude Kasle Gallery, Detroit
1976 North Carolina Museum of Art, Releigh (retrospective)
Sid Deutsch Gallery, New York
1977 Sid Deutsch Gallery, New York
1978 Brooks Jackson Iolas Gallery, New York
1984 Nassau County Museum of Fine Art, Roslyn Harbor, New York
1991 Goldie Paley Gallery, Philadelphia
1995 Richard L. Feigen (Memorial exhibition)
1996 University Gallery, University of Massachusetts

Selected Group Exhibitions:

1949 *Annual Exhibition,* American Abstract Artists, New York (and 1950, 1951, 1952)
1962 *Gang Bang,* Batman Gallery, San Francisco
1967 *Pictures to Be Read / Poetry to Be Seen,* Museum of Contemporary Art, Chicago
1969 *Pop Art Redefined,* Hayward Gallery, London
1970 *New York Correspondence School,* Whitney Museum, New York
1972 *Document Show,* David Gallery, Houston
1974 *Invitation Correspondence,* Western Illinois University, Macomb
1977 *Words at Liberty,* Museum of Contemporary Art, Chicago
1981 *New Wave,* Project Studio One, Long Island City, New York
1983 *Ma Como Fanno i Mamai,* Galleria Borgobello, Parma, Italy
1992 *Funny Dispatches: Mail Art—Art Postal,* Centre d'Animation Culturelle de Compiegne et du Valois, Compiegne
1995 *Beat Culture and the New America, 1950–1965,* Whitney Museum of American Art, New York (traveled to M.H. de Young Memorial Museum, San Francisco)
1997 *The Absolute Tone,* New York Studio School, New York
Networking: Art by Post and Fax, Spacex Gallery, Exeter

Collections:

Museum of Modern Art, New York; De Cordova Museum, Lincoln, Massachusetts; Art Institute of Chicago; Museum of Fine Arts, Houston; Dulin Gallery of Art, Knoxville, Tennessee.

Publications:

By JOHNSON: Book—*The Paper Snake,* anthology, New York 1965. **Articles—**''Follow Instructions'' in *Arts Magazine* (New York), November 1971; ''I Work Very Slowly'' in *Arte Milano* (Milan), May 1972; ''Abandoned Chickens'' in *Art in America* (New York), November/December 1974.

On JOHNSON: Books—*A Primer of Happenings and Time/Space Art* by Al Hansen, New York 1965; *Happenings, Fluxus, Pop, Nouveau Realisme* by Wolfgang Becker, Hamburg 1965; *Pop Art Redefined* by John Russel and Suzi Gablik, London 1969; *Mail Art* by Jean-Marc Poinsot, Paris 1972; *Ray Johnson,* exhibition catalog with essay by David Bourdon, New York 1984; *More Works by Ray Johnson, 1951–1991,* exhibition catalog, with text by Phyllis Stigliano and Janice Parente, Philadelphia 1991; *Ray Johnson 1927–1995; a Memorial Exhibition,* exhibition catalog, New York 1995; *Beat Culture and the New America, 1950–1965,* exhibition catalog with text by Lisa Philips and Maurice Berger, New York 1995; *The Ray Johnson Memorial Mail Art Show,* exhibition catalog, Amherst 1996; *Networking: Art by Post and Fax,* exhibition catalog, London 1997. **Articles—**''Inside Ray Johnson's House'' by Matthew Rose in *Lightworks,* no. 20–21, 1990; ''Obituary'' in *Art in America,* vol. 83, March 1995; ''Returned to Sender: Remembering Ray Johnson: Six Art Professionals Reflect on the Artist'' in *Artforum International,* vol. 33, April 1995; ''Obituary'' in *The Print Collector's Newsletter,* vol. 26, May/June 1995; ''Notes to the World (or bend, fold and spindle)'' by Holland Cotter in *Art in America* (New York), vol. 83, October 1995; ''Cosmic Ray: An Open Letter to the Founder of the New York Correspondence School'' by David Bourdon in *Art in America* (New York), vol. 83, October 1995; ''Ray Johnson, from The Paper Snake to Shelley Duvall'' by David Ebony in *New Observations,* no. 106, May-June 1995; ''Ray Johnson: Whitney Museum of American Art'' by Nayland Blake in *Artforum International,* vol. 37, no. 7, March 1999; ''Ray Johnson: Correspondences: Whitney Museum of American Art, New York'' by Paul Gardner, *Art on Paper,* vol. 3, no. 4, March/April 1999; ''Ray Johnson: Correspondences'' by Hilton Kramer in *Art and Antiques,* vol. 22, no. 4, April 1999; ''Male Art'' by Robin Laurence in *Border Crossing,* vol. 19, no. 1, 2000.

* * *

Ray Johnson, the most celebrated figure in the post–World War II international mailart movement, is also a talented collagist-painter who has interfaced life and art with provocative results in his lively and wondrously varied visual-verbal expression. He first developed a following for the letters, postcards, collages and small objects that he sent to friends and acquaintances in the New York art world soon after his arrival in the city in the early 1950s. By the late 1950s he was also making small collage paintings that ranged from abstract compositions with richly textured surfaces to pictures that featured rows of cut-up and painted letters and portraits of famous popular culture figures. ''Pink Circle'' (1959), ''Collage'' (1959) and ''Elvis Presley Collage'' (1957) are examples. At the same time, he continued the mailings, and filled with witty puns and drawings, his correspondence provided him with ample opportunity to display his hand as an orchestrator of art events. The receipt of a piece of mail from Ray Johnson was a special experience designed by him to turn the recipient into an active participant in a mailart piece. Instructions asked the recipient to do something further, whether it was to alter the original piece of mail and send it back to Johnson or to take part of the original piece of mail and send it on to a third party, often unknown to the original recipient. With his mail maneuvers, Johnson made the recipients and later the audiences who were able to read the mail in exhibitions concious of the function and the rituals of the postal institution, a major aspect of contemporary industrial life, while he tested the definition of art, taking the art-is-idea-whatever-is-designated approach of Marcel Duchamp to the fullest extension.

From about 1968 to the spring of 1973, when he announced its death with a letter to the obituary column of the *New York Times,* the New York Correspondence School under Johnson's leadership held a series of meetings in New York. It was succeeded by two other organizations, Buddha University and the Asparagus Club. What made other artists as well as the leading critics and curators of the day respond enthusiastically to Johnson's correspondence and participate in his planned activities were the twin elements of surprise and entertainment. At issue, also, in Johnson's work, both the correspondence and the collages, is an inquiring Pop attitude applied indiscriminately to life and art alike. This attitude animates the drawings and collage paintings of the late 1960s and early 1970s. Focusing on the "idols" of both the serious and popular culture, a group that included among others Virginia Woolf, Mondrian, Shirley Temple and actor Steve McQueen, Johnson made irreverent portraits of them, using photographs, intercut with drawn and painted motifs. He has also taken contemporary art events as subject: "The Ray Johnson History of the Betty Parsons Gallery" (1973).

—Ronny Cohen

JONAS, Joan

Nationality: American. **Born:** New York, 13 July 1936. **Education:** Mount Holyoke College Massachusetts; Boston Museum School; Columbia University, New York, M.F.A. **Career:** Visiting artist, Video School of Visual Arts, New York, 1972; guest lecturer, Princeton University, New Jersey, 1974; Yale University, New Haven, Connecticut, 1974; and Minneapolis College of Art, 1974; visiting artist, San Diego State University, California, 1975; Otis Art Institute, Los Angeles, 1975; and Kent State University, Ohio, 1977; Professor of Visual Arts, Massachusetts Institute of Technology, Department of Architecture, since 1997. **Awards:** CAPS (Creative Artists Public Service Program), 1972, 1973 and 1975; National Endowment for the Arts Grant, 1973 and 1975; DAAD Artist's Fellowship, West Berlin, 1982; AFI Maya Deren Award Recipient, 1989; Anonymous Was a Woman Program Grant, 1999. **Agent:** Rosamund Felsen Gallery, Bergamot Station B4, 2525 Michigan Avenue, Santa Monica, California 90404; Castelli-Sonnabend Videotapes and Films Inc., 142 Greene Street, New York, New York 10011; Pat Hearn Gallery, 530 West 22nd Street, New York, New York 10011. **Address:** 112 Mercer Street, New York, New York 10012–3873, U.S.A.

Individual Exhibitions:

1968 St. Peter's Church, New York
1970 Alan Saret's Loft, New York
University of California at San Diego
Jones Beach, Long Island, New York
14th Street YMCA, New York
1971 Loeb Student Center, New York
University of California at Irvine
Cape Breton Island, Nova Scotia
1972 LoGuidice Gallery, New York
Documenta, Kassel, West Germany
San Francisco Art Institute
empty lots, New York
The Tibur, Rome
L'Attico, Rome
Ace Gallery, Los Angeles
1973 Leo Castelli Gallery, New York
Toselli Gallery, Milan
Hofstra University, Hempstead, New York
Galerie Musée, Paris
1974 The Kitchen, New York
Contemporanea, Rome
Galleria Schema, Florence
Museum of Fine Arts, Boston
Texas Gallery, Houston
Walker Art Center, Minneapolis
Kunsthalle, Cologne
University of Massachusetts, Amherst
1975 Anthology Film Archives, New York
Leo Castelli Gallery, New York
San Diego State University, California
Institute of Contemporary Arts, Los Angeles
Womanspace, Los Angeles
And/Or Gallery, Seattle
1976 San Francisco Museum of Modern Art
Anthology Film Archives, New York
Institute of Contemporary Art, Philadelphia (twice)
1977 Institute of Contemporary Art, Philadelphia
Vanguard Theatre, Los Angeles
Documenta, Kassel, West Germany
The Kitchen, New York
St. Mark's Church, New York
Salle Patino, Geneva
Kunsthalle, Basel
Van Abbemuseum, Eindhoven, Netherlands
School of Visual Arts, New York
1978 Van Abbemuseum, Eindhoven, Netherlands
Vienna Performance Festival
1979 112 Mercer Street, New York
1980 Guggenheim Museum, New York
University of California Art Museum, Berkeley
University of California at Irvine
Los Angeles Institute of Contemporary Art
1982 Kino Arsenal, West Berlin
1983 Whitney Museum, New York
La Zattera de Babele, Genazzano, Italy
1984 DAAD-Galerie, West Berlin
1990 *Variations on a Scene,* Wave Hill, New York
1993 *Variations on a Scene,* Podvil Berlin (also Martin Gropius Bau, Berlin; Centre d'Art Contemporain de Vassiviere-en-Limousin, France)
1994 *Works 1968–1994,* Stedelijk Museum, Amsterdam (retrospective) (catalog)
Volcano Saga, Cleveland Center for Contemporary Arts
1996 *Mask, Decoy and Other Beasts,* Rosamund Felsen Gallery, Santa Monica
1997 *Props: Works 1994–1997,* Pat Hearn Gallery, New York
Songdelay (1973) and New Work, Pat Hearn Gallery, New York
2001 *Performance Video Installation: 1968–2000,* Neue Gesellschaft für Bildende Kunst, Berlin (also Galerie der Stadt Stuttgart) (catalog)

In the Shadows a Shadow, The Rosamund Felsen Gallery, Santa Monica

Selected Group Exhibitions:

1973 *Festival d'Automne,* Paris
Some Recent American Art, Australia (toured)
1974 *Xerox Corporation Show,* Rochester, New York
Bienal, Sao Paulo
Art Now '74, Washington
Project '74, Cologne
1975 *The Video Show,* Serpentine Gallery, London
Associated Students, University of California at Los Angeles
1982 *Documenta 7,* Museum Fridericianum, Kassel, West Germany
1995 *Lyons Biennial,* Lyons, France
1998 *Group Exhibition,* Pat Hearn Gallery, New York
1999 *Circa 1968,* Museu Serralves, Oporto, Portugal
2000 *Media_City Seoul 2000,* Various Venues, Seoul, Korea

Collections:

Museum of Modern Art, New York.

Publications:

By JONAS: Articles—''Paul Revere,'' with Richard Serra, in *Artforum* (New York), September 1971; ''Organic Honey's Visual Telepathy'' in *The Drama Review* (New York), vol. 16, no. 2, 1972; ''Show Me Your Dances. . .,'' with Simone Forti, interview with Carla Liss, in *Art and Artists* (London), October 1973; statement in *Dancescape,* New York 1973; documentation in *Castelli-Sonnabend Video Tape and Film Catalog,* New York 1974; statement in ''7 Years'' in the *Drama Review* (New York), March 1975; statement in *Joan Jonas,* exhibition catalog, West Berlin 1984; ''Scenes and Variations: An Interview with Joan Jonas,'' with Joan Simon in *Art in America* (New York), vol. 83, no. 7, July 1995; ''Artists as Teachers'' in *New Observations,* no. 118, Spring 1998. **Films**—*Wind,* 1968; *Paul Revere,* with Richard Serra, 1971; *Veil,* 1971; *Songdelay,* 1973. **Video tapes**—*Left Side, Right Side,* 1972; *Vertical Roll,* 1972; *Organic Honey's Visual Telepathy,* 1972; *2 Women,* 1973; *Barking,* 1973; *3 Returns,* 1973; *Glass Puzzle,* 1974; *Merlo,* 1974; *Disturbances,* 1974; *May Windows,* 1976; *Good Night, Good Morning,* 1976; *I Want to Live in the Country and Other Romances,* 1976; *Upside Down and Backwards,* 1981; *Double Lunar Dogs,* 1983; *He Saw Her Burning,* 1983; *Big Market,* 1984; *Brooklyn Bridge,* 1988; *Volcano Saga,* 1989.

On JONAS: Book—*Body Art and Performance: The Body of Language* by Lea Vergine, Milan 2000. **Articles**—''Joan Jonas'' by Laurie Anderson in *Art Press* (Paris), November/December 1973; ''Joan Jonas: Making the Image Visible'' by N. Carroll in *Artforum* (New York), April 1974; ''Notes on Performance and the Arts'' by A. Hayum in *Art Journal* (New York), Summer 1975; ''Joan Jonas's Performance Works'' by D. Crimp in *Studio International* (London), July 1976; ''Suspended in Shadow'' in *Art News* (New York), April 1977; ''View of Kassel'' by D. Shapiro in *Artforum* (New York), September 1977; ''Personal and Cultural Narratives'' by Mary Stofflet in *Artweek* (Oakland, California), 26 January 1980; ''Image of Silence'' by A. Rosenthal in *Artweek* (Oakland, California), 17 May 1980; ''Jonas's Futurism'' by Mary Stofflet in *Artweek* (Oakland, California), 5 July 1980; ''Wolf Calls and Frog Songs—Upside Down and Backwards'' in *Artnews* (New York), September 1980.

*

My thinking about the medium of performance began in the late 60s. In saying that, I am pointing to a particular conceptual context that was fully developed when I began to work—one that concerned itself with discovering new forms of movement and totally new ways of structuring the temporal shape of an event. Yet, when I survey my work against that background of performances in the 60s, I realize that those specific concerns with movement and temporality are not my concerns. My own thinking and production has focused on issues of space—ways of dislocating it, attenuating it, turning it inside out, always attempting to explore it without ever giving to myself or to others the permission to penetrate it. I have returned again and again to specific set of formal/material metaphors with which to shape this space. The two most important of these are the mirror—with its capacity to interrupt and therefore to fragment deep space and its property of disorientation through left-right reversal—and the transmission of signals through a dislocating medium, such as very deep landscape that creates delays and relays of the signal, or the video feedback, which both dislocates and fragments the signal.

—Joan Jonas

* * *

Joan Jonas is one of the pioneering performance artists in America; her work inaugurated the synchronization of disciplines which previously had been developing along separate lines. Although educated as a sculptor, she was strongly influenced by new forms of dance and subsequently environments. All orchestrated to evoke archetypal images as in fairy tales and legends, her work is nevertheless completely contemporary and reflects the spirit and ambivalence of our time.

Born in 1936 in New York, Joan Jonas studied art in Massachusetts and in New York, thereafter dance with Trisha Brown, and in 1968, in collaboration with Peter Campus, she made her first film ''Wind.'' In 1970, after a trip to Japan with Richard Serra and under the impact of the traditional Japanese theatre, she performed her ''Mirror Piece,'' first in New York and later in California. In this work the artist examines details of her own naked body using mirrors. For Joan Jonas this piece was the breakthrough into a new phase of her own development. In ''Organic Honey'' of 1972 she incorporated video, and the number of performers widened; her goal was again female identity, but the mirror here was destroyed, burning the bridges to her past. In the same year two other performances, ''Left

Side-Right Side,'' concentrate on the face of the artist and on her bodily movements and their meaningful contortions respectively. ''Funnel'' of 1974 extends the performance vocabulary, and video and participation of the audience are introduced. In ''Twilight'' of 1975, a haunting vision of woman, enclosed in a circular ring and confronted with a TV camera, is of archetypal significance.

After a tour to India she began performing with energies of previously unknown intensity, which can be seen in ''Mirage'' of 1975/1976. Her performances since 1976 have expanded into the area of fairy tales (''The Juniper Tree'' of 1976 and ''Upside Down and Backwards'' of 1979) and science fiction (''Double Lunar Dogs'' of 1978) and incorporated elements of music and dance as well as mirrors and light in order to create a new comprehensive universe of action. A culmination is reached in ''He Saw Her Burning'' of 1982/1983 in which Joan Jonas performs in combination with video, film and environmental ensembles. Based on a story about an American soldier in Germany and a woman in Chicago, two lines of narration are synchronized into a performance in which symptoms of our contemporary society are made transparent. In her 1987 performance ''Volcano Saga,'' based on her trip to Iceland, she includes multimedia, simultaneous integration of film, music, dance, props and spoken narrative in a brilliant performance.

Reality is mysterious in the work of Joan Jonas, and a new and complex language has been inaugurated by the artist in which she has found appropriate means of communication for a contemporary theme. The artist in this sense is conceived as a shaman who opens a world which otherwise would remain closed for most people; ''All the things I do seem to be signs or emblems against outside forces, like I was thinking of warding off the evil eye. They are ways of surviving, maintaining one's personality. . . not one's personality, one's existence.'' (Joan Jonas.)

—Udo Kultermann

JONES, Allen

Nationality: British. **Born:** Southampton, Hampshire, 1 September 1937. **Education:** Hornsey School of Art, London, 1955–59; N.D.D. 1959, A.T.D. 1961; and Royal College of Art, London, 1959–60. **Family:** Married Janet Bowen in 1964 (divorced, 1978); daughters: Thea and Sarah; married Deirdre Morrow in 1994. **Career:** Painter, sculptor and graphic artist, London, since 1961. Instructor in Lithography, Croydon School of Art, 1961; part-time teacher, Chelsea School of Art, London, 1965; visiting instructor, Hochschule für Bildenden Künste, Hamburg, 1968–70; guest instructor in painting, University of South Florida, Tampa, 1969, University of California at Irvine, 1973, and University of California at Los Angeles, 1977; visiting tutor in painting and drawing, Banff Centre School of Fine Arts, Alberta, 1977; guest professor, Hochschule der Kunste, West Berlin, 1982–83. **Awards:** Prix des Jeunes, *Biennale de Paris,* 1963; Tamarind Lithography Fellowship, Los Angeles, 1966. R.A., Royal Academy, London, 1981. **Address:** 41 Charterhouse Square, London EC1M 6EA, United Kingdom.

Individual Exhibitions:

1963 Arthur Tooth and Sons, London
1964 Richard Feigen Gallery, New York
Arthur Tooth and Sons, London
1965 Richard Feigen Gallery, Chicago
Feigen-Palmer Gallery, Los Angeles
Richard Feigen Gallery, New York
1966 Galerie Bischofberger, Zurich
Museum of Modern Art, New York
1967 Galerie der Spiegel, Cologne
Galerie Neuendorf, Hamburg
Arthur Tooth and Sons, London
1968 Alecto Gallery, London
1969 Galleria Milano, Milan
Museum Boymans-van Beuningen, Rotterdam (graphics retrospective; toured Netherlands)
Galerie Werigstatt, Bremen, West Germany
1970 Arthur Tooth and Sons, London
Richard Feigen Gallery, New York
Galerie Rudolf Zwirner, Cologne
Studio Condotti 85, Rome
Galerie Springer, West Berlin
Galleria Milano, Milan
1971 Galerie de Spiegel, Cologne
Galleria Il Fauno, Turin
Galerie Richard Foncke, Ghent
Galerie Delta, Rotterdam
Galerie Bischofberger, Zurich
Marlborough Graphics, London
1972 Studio Condotti 85, Rome
Galerie Multi-Art, Antwerp
Galleria Milano, Milan
New Paintings and Sculpture, Marlborough Fine Art, London
1973 Tolarno Galleries, Melbourne
Hogarth Galleries, Sydney
Galerie Von Loeper, Hamburg
1974 Seibu Gallery, Tokyo
Meitetsu Gallery, Nagoya, Japan
1975 Oriel Gallery, Cardiff (travelled to Glynn Vivian Gallery, Swansea; Arnolfini Gallery, Bristol; and Fruitmarket Gallery, Edinburgh)
Neue Galerie der Stadt, Linz, Austria
1976 Waddington Galleries II, London
Waddington and Tooth Graphics, London
Pander Kunstcentrum, The Hague
Galerie Wentzel, Hamburg
1977 James Corcoran Gallery, Los Angeles
Nova Gallery, Vancouver
University of California at Los Angeles
1978 Institute of Contemporary Arts, London
Kettles Yard, Cambridge
Waddington Galleries, Montreal (travelled to the Waddington Galleries, Toronto)
1979 Walker Art Gallery, Liverpool (toured Britain and West Germany)

Galerie Wentzel, Hamburg
1980 Waddington Galleries, London
1981 Galerie Engstrom, Stockholm
1982 Waddington Graphics, London
1983 Galerie Kammer, Hamburg
Waddington Galleries, London
Galeria Yerba, Murcia, Spain
1984 Galerie Wentzel, Cologne
Galerie Kammer, Hamburg
1985 Waddington Galleries, London
1986 Galerie Patrice Trigano, Paris
Zack-Shuster Gallery, Florida
1987 Galerie Hete Hünermann, Dusseldorf
1988 Galerie Joachim Becker, Basel
Charles Cowes Gallery, New York
1989 Galerie Patrice Trigano, Paris
Heland Wetterling Gallery, Stockholm
1991 Galerie Wentzel, Cologne
1992 Galerie Punto, Arco and Valencia
Galerie Levy, Madrid
Frank Pages Art Gallery, Baden-Baden
1992 Glynn Vivian Art Gallery, Wales
1994 Thomas Gibson, London
National Portrait Gallery, London
Galerie Eikelmann, Essen
1995 Barbican Art Gallery, London
Galerie Levy, Hamburg and Madrid
Victoria Art Gallery, Bath
1996 Kunsthalle, Darmstadt
Galerie Hilger, Vienna
Hauger Vestfold Kunstmuseum, Tønsberg, Norway
1998 Museo de Arte Moderno, Cuenca, Ecuado
Palácio das Artes, Belo Horizonte, Brazil
Centro Cultural, São Paulo
Museum of Modern Art, Rio de Janeiro
1999 Thomas Levy Galerie, Hamburg
Ars Nova Museum of Contemporary Art, Turku
Galleria d'Arte Maggiore, Bologna
Sho Gallery, London

Selected Group Exhibitions:

1963 *Biennale de Paris,* Musée d'Art Moderne, Paris (and 1965, 1971)
1965 *The New Generation,* Whitechapel Art Gallery, London
1974 *Hyperrealistes Americains / Realistes Europeens,* Centre National d'Art Contemporain, Paris
1977 *British Painting 1952–1977,* Royal Academy of Art, London
1983 *The Folding Image,* National Gallery of Art, Washington, D.C.
1985 *Pop Art 1955–70,* Museum of Modern Art, New York (and world tour)
1986 *Forty Years of Modern Art 1945–1985,* Tate Gallery, London
1987 *British Art in the Twentieth Century: The Modern Movement,* Royal Academy, London (travelled to Stuttgart and Staatsgalerie)
1992 *Pop Art,* Royal Academy, London (travelled to Museum Ludwig, Kunsthalle Cologne; Centro Arte Reina Sofia, Madrid; Musee des Beaux Arts, Montreal)
1993 *The Sixties Art Scene in London,* Barbican Art Gallery, London
The Portrait Now, National Portrait Gallery, London
1994 *Here and Now,* Serpentine Gallery, London; Centre Georges Pompidou, Paris
The Pop Image: Prints and Multiples, Marlborough Graphics, New York
1995 *1968,* National Gallery of Australia, Canberra
Fémininmasculin: Le Seze de l'art, Centre Georges Pompidou, Paris
1996 *The Sixties in France and Great Britain, 1960–1973,* Musée d'Histoire Contemporaine, Hôtel National des Invalides, Paris (travelled to the Royal Pavilion, Brighton)
The Spirit of the Staircase: 100 Years of Print Publishing at the Royal College of Art 1896–1996, Victoria and Albert Museum, London
1997 *The Power of Erotic Design,* The Design Museum, London
From Blast to Pop: Aspects of Modern British Art, 1915–1965, David and Alfred Smart Museum of Art, University of Chicago
1998 *Pop Art Spirits: Masterpieces from the Ludwig Collection,* Sezon Museum of Art, Tokyo
Augenlust: Erotische Kunst im 20.Jahrhundert, Kunsthaus Hannover
1999 *Europop,* Arken Museum of Modern Art, Denmark
Pop Impressions Europe/USA: Prints and Multiples from the Museum of Modern Art, Museum of Modern Art, New York
2000 *20 Jahre YHeitland Foundation,* Kunsthalle Darmstadt
L'Eroe Borghese: Temi Figure da Schiele a Warhol, Rocca di Vignola, Palazzina dei Giardini di Modena
2001 *Les années pop,* Centre Georges Pompidou, Paris

Collections:

Arts Council of Great Britain, London; Tate Gallery, London; National Portrait Gallery, London; Victoria and Albert Museum, London; Wallraf-Richartz Museum, Cologne; Kunstmuseum, Düsseldorf; Museum of 20th Century Art, Vienna; Stedelijk Museum, Amsterdam; Musée Royal des Beaux-Arts, Ghent; Moderna Museet, Stockholm; Konstmuseets Vanner, Gothenburg; Museum of Modern Art, New York; Whitney Museum of American Art, New York; Norton Simon Museum of Art, Pasadena, California; Chicago Museum of Art; Hirshhorn Museum and Sculpture Garden, Washington, D.C.; Vancouver Art Gallery; Power Art Gallery, Sydney.

Publications:

By JONES: Books—*Allen Jones: das graphische Werk,* with text by Hein Stunke, Cologne 1969; *Allen Jones: Figures,* West Berlin and

Milan 1969; *Allen Jones: Projects,* Boston, London 1971; *Waitress,* with Tim Street-Porter, London 1971. **Film—***Manner wir Kommen,* WDR television film, Cologne, 1970.

On JONES: Books—*Pop as Art: A Survey of the New Super-Realism* by Mario Amaya, London 1965, 1972; *Pop Art,* edited by Lucy R. Lippard, New York and London 1966; *Information: Tilson, Phillips, Jones, Paolozzi, Kitaj, Hamilton,* exhibition catalog, Basel 1969; *Image as Language: Aspects of British Art* by Christopher Finch, London 1969; *Allen Jones,* exhibition catalog, with text by Enrico Crispolti, Milan 1970; *British Painting and Sculpture 1960–1970,* exhibition catalog with text by Edward Lucie Smith, London 1970; *Erotic Art 2,* compiled by Phyllis and Eberhard Kronhausen, New York 1970; *Allen Jones: New Paintings and Sculpture,* exhibition catalog, London 1972; *Allen Jones,* exhibition catalog/book, Tokyo 1974; *Hyperrealistes Americains/Realistes Europeens,* exhibition catalog, with texts by Daniel Abadie, Jean Clair, Pierre Restany and others, Paris 1974; *Sheer Magic* by Marco Livingstone, New York 1979, London 1980; *Allen Jones,* exhibition catalog with text by Marco Livingstone, Liverpool 1979; *Allen Jones*, with essays by Victor Arwas, Charles Jencks, and Bryan Robertson, 1993; *Allen Jones Prints,* exhibition catalog with text by Marco Livingstone, Munich and New York 1995; *Allen Jones,* with text by Andrew Lambirth, London 1997.

* * *

Allen Jones has explored many different media: lithography, watercolour, sculpture, photography, video, poster art and painting. In my opinion he is at his best when painting. Jones's style is instinctive; the brush is used in a masterly fashion, achieving superb variations of colour, memorable imagery, all executed with a tremendous clarity of thought and panache. ''Thinking'' painters are few and far between these days—in 1962 Jones entitled one of his paintings ''The Artist Thinks.'' A symbol representing the artist appears regularly throughout his work, especially in the ''Stage'' series. A performance is taking place, and at the forefront of the canvas a figure almost always watches, encouraging the viewer to do the same and participate. In fact the viewer can identify with the seated figure, use it as a point of reference. Jones mixes abstract with figurative. Once I saw a painting before the figures had been added: it could have stood on its own without any additions, and John Hoyland wanted Jones to leave it as it was, but he instinctively added the figurative element.

Jones works from meticulous small sketches, with signs for ideas rather than completed images. He lets his feelings take over when he is painting. Unlike Kitaj, who feels that a painting is never finished, Jones considers a canvas completed if it tells a story with the traditional beginning, middle and end. Jones wants the points of reference to be contained only within the canvas. At one stage in his career he depicted a scene by using his own vocabulary made up of symbols—women were represented by the appearance of a bra, stocking tops or girdles. Jones admits that he did this owing to a lack of practice in modeling. In fact, later on he proved to be excellent at it, especially in painting such as ''Leopard Lady'' or ''Bare me.''

Female imagery has always played a major role in Jones's career. Those who know his work superficially always associate him with the Pirelli Calendar or else the woman on all fours with a sheet of glass on her back representing a table. It is sad that Jones is best known for this type of work. He defends it by saying that it is unreal, the proportions could never be attributed to *real* women. That may be, but one cannot help but find them offensive, particularly the fetishistic accoutrements. It is best to concentrate on Jones' paintings, because here he excels.

—Carine Maurice

JOURNIAC, Michel

Nationality: French. **Born:** Paris, 7 October 1943. **Education:** Lycée Voltaire, Paris; studied philosophy at St. Sulpice Seminary, Paris, and theology at the University of Paris; self-taught in art. **Career:** Independent artist, Paris, since 1968. Professor, faculty of plastic arts and sciences, University of Paris, Sorbonne. **Agent:** Galerie Stadler, Paris. **Died:** In Paris, 1995.

Individual Exhibitions:

1968 Cloitre des Billettes, Paris
1969 Galerie Daniel Templon, Paris
Galerie Martin-Malburet, Paris
Bonino Gallery, New York
1970 Galerie Daniel Templon, Paris
Galerie Martin-Malburet, Paris
1971 America-Center, Paris
1972 Galerie Stadler, Paris
U. E. R. des Arts Plastiques et Sciences de l'Art, Paris
Galerie Arges 2, Brussels
1973 Galerie Stadler, Paris
Espace 640, St. Jeannet, France
1974 Galerie Stadler, Paris
1975 Forum für Aktuelle Kunst, Innsbruck
Galerie Stadler, Paris
1976 Galleria Diagramma, Milan
Galleria Unimedia, Genoa
Galerie Stadler, Paris 1977
Galerie Artcurial, Paris
FIAC 77, Paris
1978 Galerie Sylvia Bourdon, Paris
Galerie Stadler, Paris
Galerie N.R.A., Paris
1979 Galerie Sylvia Bourdon, Paris
Galerie 32, Lyons
1980 International Cultureel Centrum, Antwerp
1981 *Rituel de Corps Interdit II* (action), Centre Georges Pompidou, Paris
Rituel de Corps Interdit III (action), Museum of Modern Art, Stockholm
Rituel de Corps Interdit IV (action), L'Autre Musée, Brussels, Belgium

1983 Galerie M. Ozenne, Paris
Action de Corps Exclu, Centre Georges Pompidou
1985 *Auto-Portraits,* Palais Drumine, Lausanne
Meutre et Sacre, Galerie Donguy, Paris
1986 *Rituel Initiatique,* Galerie Marcel Vidal, Paris
1988 *Icones du Temps Present,* Galerie Donguy, Paris
1993 *Rituel de Transmutation,* Collège Marcel Duchamp, Cateauroux
Itineraire d'Aujourdhui et d'Hier, Galerie Donguy, Paris
1994 *Rituel de Transmutation,* Museum of Bilbao, Spain

Selected Group Exhibitions:

1968 *Occupation des Lieux,* America-Center, Paris
1969 *Stand de tir,* Musée Galliera, Paris (toured Japan)
1970 *Manifeste du Cheque,* Maison Francois Pluchart, Paris
1972 *Autopsie de la Venus de Milo,* Palais des Beaux-Arts, Brussels
1975 *Teyssedre: Art Sociologique,* Galerie Rencontres, Paris
1976 *Mythologies Quotidiennes 2,* Musée d'Art Moderne de la ville, Paris
1977 *Le Corps,* Galerie Isy Brachot, Brussels
1978 *Lecon de Mots/Lecon de Maux,* Université de Nancy, France
1979 *Exposition Artitudes,* Galerie d'Art Contemporain, Nice
1994 *Hors Limite,* Centre Georges Pompidou
1996 *Une Aventure Contemporaine, la photographie 1955–1995,* Maison Européenne de la Photographie, Paris

Publications:

By JOURNIAC: Books—*Le sang nu: recueil des poèmes,* Paris 1968; *24 heures de la vie d'un femme ordinaire,* 1974; *Delit du corps,* 1978; *Actes du colloque,* Paris 1987. **Articles—**''De la Censure à la Revolution Culturale'' in *Artitudes* (St. Jeannet, France), March 1972; ''Entretien avec Michel Journiac'' in *Artitudes* (St. Jeannet, France), July 1972; ''Body of Evidence: Michel Journiac'' interview with Vincent Labaume in *Blocnotes,* no. 6, Summer 1994.

On JOURNIAC: Books and Pamphlets—*Journiac: piège pour une execution capitale,* exhibition leaflet, Paris 1971; *Journiac: contract pour un corps,* exhibition leaflet, Paris 1972; *Il corpo come linguaggio* by Lea Vergine, Milan 1974; *Art, Action, Participation* by Frank Popper, Paris 1975; *Michel Journiac; L'Ossuaire de l'Egypte* by Marcel Pacquet, Paris 1977; *Michel Journiac,* exhibition catalog, Antwerp 1980. **Articles—**''Michel Journiac'' by Catherine Millet, in *Flash Art* (Milan), November/December 1970; ''Attitudes Critiques de Journiac'' by Francois Pluchart in *Combat* (Paris), February 1971; ''Le Peiges de Michel Jouniac'' in *Opus International* (Paris), March 1973; ''Les Pièges de Michel Journiac'' in *Artitudes* (St. Jeannet, France), December 1973; ''Dix Questions sur l'Art Corporel et l'Art Sociologique'' in *Artitudes* (St. Jeannet, France), December 1973; ''Adam ou Eve: Michel Journiac'' by René Rozan in *Vie des Arts* (Paris), no. 80, 1975; review by Clio Mitchell in *Art International,* no. 6, Spring 1989; review by Vincent Labaume in *Art Press,* no. 187, January 1994; ''Michel Journiac'' by Juan Vicente Aliaga in *Artforum International,* vol. 33, May 1995.

*

Six interrogative propositions

1. Ideologies, games which are no longer being played outside the pulsions of the word, have torn away the masks of promised liberties standing in the form of a scaffold of bodies.

2. Words which have become dead from the links in a chain of reasoning which erects the verbal trial of desire.

3. The inverted structure of a falsified language traps the naked body as a reified support to an economic production, chaining up of the gesture.

4. The bound body, tortured, reduced to being nothing but an instrument of work, object of production and end of a reified activity, is at the point of death.

5. The social rituals, work, family, fatherland, liberty, equality, fraternity are becoming alibis for oppressions, marking out of bodies.

6. From dead rationalism are born a hidden fascism, out of which springs the pseudo-liberalism of a society which, conscious of not being unanimous, veils its lacerations and tries to restructure Man and his desire by subjugating him.

In the form of interrogative conclusion.

—Michel Journiac

JUDD, Donald

Nationality: American. **Born:** Excelsior Springs, Missouri, 3 June 1928. **Education:** Tutored privately in Omaha, 1939–40, then at Westwood High School, New Jersey, 1943–46; studied at the Art Student's League, New York, 1948, 1949–53; College of William and Mary, Williamsburg, Virginia, 1948–49; Columbia University, New York, 1949–53, 1957–62, B.Sc. 1953, M.A. 1962. **Military Service:** United States Army, in Korea, 1946–47. **Family:** Married Margaret Hughan (Julie) Finch in 1964; children: Flavin Starbuck, Rainer Yingling. **Career:** Settled in New York; taught art part-time, Christadora Home and Police Athletic League, 1953; reviewer, *ARTnews,* New York, 1959; contributing editor, *Arts Magazine,* New York, 1959–65; reviewer, *Art International,* Lugano, 1965. Instructor, Brooklyn Institute of Arts and Sciences, New York, 1962–64; visiting artist, Dartmouth College, Hanover, New Hampshire, 1966; taught sculpture at Yale University, New Haven, Connecticut, 1967; conducted Emma Lake Artists' Workshop, Lac La Ronge, Saskatchewan, 1968; Baldwin Professor, Oberlin College, Ohio, 1976. **Awards:** Travel Grant, Swedish Institute, Stockholm, 1965; National Endowment for the Arts grant, 1967 and 1976; Guggenheim Fellowship, 1968; Skowhegan Medal for Sculpture, Skowhegan School of Painting and Sculpture, 1987, Poses Brandeis Univeristy Creative Arts Medal for Sculpture, 1987; Stankowski Prize, Stankowski Foundation, 1992, 1993; Sikkens award, Sikkens Foundation, 1993. **Address:** c/o Leo Castelli Gallery, 59 East 79th

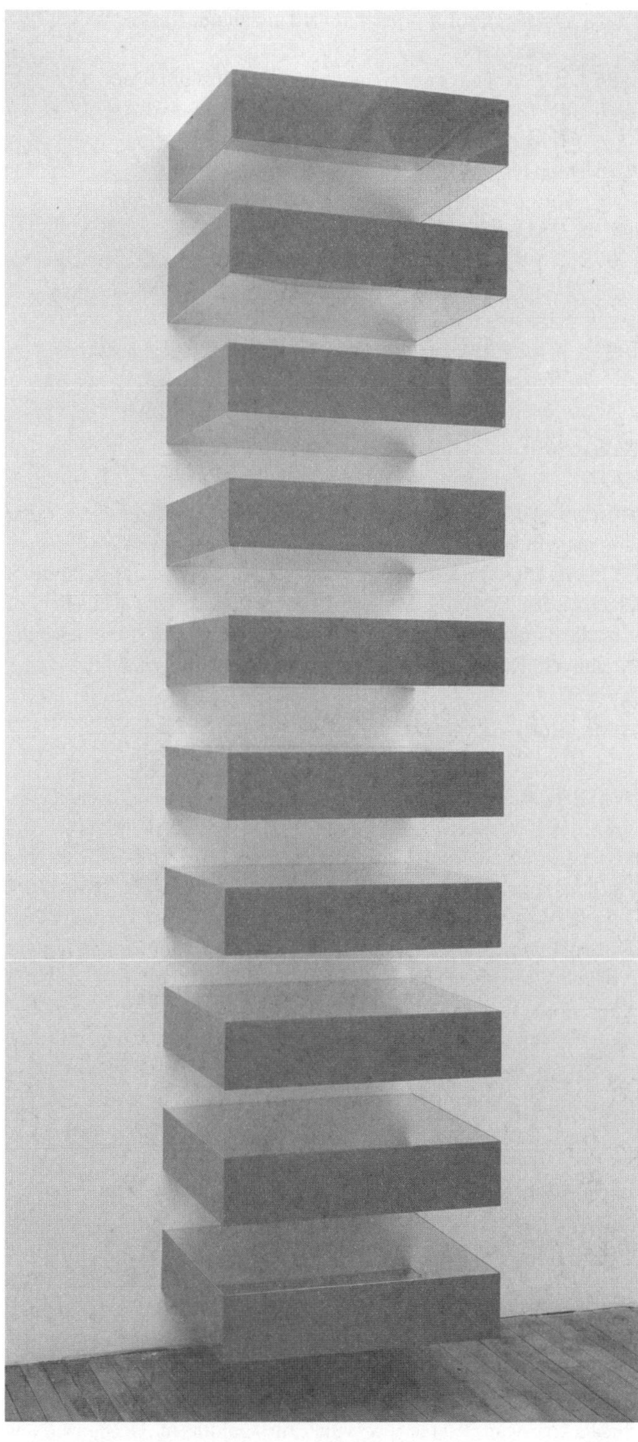

Donald Judd: *Untitled,* 20th century. ©Donald Judd Foundation/Licensed by VAGA, New York, NY.

St., New York, New York 10021, U.S.A. **Died:** Of lymphoma, in New York, 12 February 1994.

Individual Exhibitions:

1956 *Don Judd and Nathan Raisen,* Panoras Gallery, New York
1957 Panoras Gallery, New York
1963 Leo Castelli Gallery, New York
1968 Whitney Museum, New York (retrospective)
Irving Blum Gallery, Los Angeles
1969 Irving Blum Gallery, Los Angeles
Leo Castelli Gallery, New York
Galerie Ileana Sonnabend, Paris
Galerie Rudolf Zwirner, Cologne
1970 Stedelijk van Abbemuseum, Eindhoven, Netherlands (toured Germany and the U.K.)
Helman Gallery, St. Louis
Leo Castelli Gallery, New York
Galerie Konrad Fischer, Dusseldorf
Janie C. Lee Gallery, Dallas
Locksley Shea Gallery, Minneapolis
1971 Locksley Shea Gallery, Minneapolis
Pasadena Art Museum, California (retrospective)
1972 Greenberg Gallery, St. Louis
Richard Serra/Don Judd, Leo Castelli Gallery downtown, New York
Galerie Ricke, Cologne
Galerie Daniel Templon, Paris
1973 Leo Castelli Gallery, New York
Galleria Gian Enzo Sperone, Rome
Konrad Fischer Galleria, Rome
Locksley Shea Gallery, Minneapolis
Galleria Gian Enzo Sperone, Turin
1974 Lisson Gallery, London
Don Flavin/Don Judd/Sol LeWitt, Galleria La Bertesca, Milan
Ace Gallery, Venice, California
Galerie Aronowitsch, Stockholm
1975 Lisson Gallery, London
Galerie Aronowitsch, Stockholm
National Gallery of Canada, Ottawa (retrospective)
Galerie Templon, Paris
1976 Heiner Friedrich Galerie, Munich
Drawings 1956–1975, Kunstmuseum, Basel (travelled to Tübingen and Oxford)
Skulpturen, Kunsthalle, Bern
Janie C. Lee Gallery, Houston
Galerie Annemarie Verna, Zurich
Sable Gallery, Toronto
Leo Castelli Gallery, New York
1977 Museum of South Texas, Corpus Christi
Heiner Friedrich Gallery, New York
Max Protetch Gallery, Washington, D.C.
Contemporary Arts Center, Cincinnati, Ohio
Moderne Galerie, Bottrop, West Germany
Heiner Friedrich Galerie, Cologne
Ace Gallery, Venice, California
1978 Heiner Friedrich Gallery, New York
Galerie Watari, Tokyo
Leo Castelli Gallery, New York
Vancouver Art Gallery
Young Hoffman Gallery, Chicago
1979 Stedelijk van Abbemmuseum, Eindhoven, Netherlands
Leo Castelli Gallery, New York
Akron Art Institute, Ohio
Galerie Annemarie Verna, Zurich

Lisson Gallery, London
Thomas Segal Gallery, Boston
Heiner Friedrich Galerie, Cologne
1980 Galerie Annemarie Verna, Zurich
1981 Leo Castelli Gallery, New York
Newport Harbor Art Museum, California
1982 Larry Gagosian Gallery, Los Angeles
1983 Leo Castelli Gallery, New York
Galerie Annemarie Verna, Zurich (twice)
Carol Taylor Gallery, Dallas
Spirit Square Art Center, Charlotte, North Carolina
Blum Helman Gallery, New York
1984 Leo Castelli Gallery, New York
Max Protetch Gallery, New York
101 Spring Street, New York
Margo Leavin Gallery, Los Angeles
Neuberger Museum, Purchase, New York
1985 Galerie Annemarie Verna, Zurich
Texas Gallery, Houston
Galleria Lia Rumma, Naples
Rhona Hoffman Gallery, Chicago
Galerie Barbel Grasslin, Frankfurt
1986 Waddington Galleries, London
Paula Cooper Gallery, New York
1987 Lawrence Oliver Gallery, Philadelphia
1988 Galerie Nachst St. Stephan, Vienna
Castello di Rivoli, Italy
Vivian Horan Fine Art, New York
1990 Barbara Krakow and Thomas Segal Galleries, Boston
Persons & Lindell Gallery, Helsinki
1991 Inkong Gallery, Seoul
1992 Shizuoka Prefectural Museum of Art, Japan
1993 *Donald Judd: Large-Scale Works,* Pace Gallery, New York (catalog)
1994 PaceWildenstein Gallery, New York
1995 PaceWildenstein Gallery, Los Angeles
Susan Inglett Gallery, New York
1996 PaceWiildenstein Gallery, Los Angeles
Brooke Alexander/Brooke Alexander Editions, New York
1998 *Donald Judd: Early Fabricated Work,* PaceWildenstein Gallery, New York
1999 Museum of Modern Art, Saitama, Japan
2000 Sprengel Museum, Hannover
Dia Center for the Arts, New York

Selected Group Exhibitions:

1965 *Flavin/Judd/Morris/William,* Green Gallery, New York
1967 *American Sculpture of the 60s,* Los Angeles County Museum of Art
1970 *Discovery of Harmony,* Expo Museum of Fine Arts, at the *World's Fair,* Osaka
1973 *Art 4,* at the *Basel Art Fair*
1974 *Choice Dealers—Dealers' Choice,* New York Cultural Center
1978 *American Art 1950 to the Present,* Whitney Museum, New York
1980 *Minimal Skulpturen: Sammlung Panza,* Kunstmuseum, Dusseldorf
1982 *Documenta VII,* Museum Fridericianum, Kassel, West Germany
1984 *The Languages of Geometry,* Kunstmuseum, Bern
1986 *Qu'est-ce que la sculpture moderne,* Musee d'Art Moderne, Paris
1995 Leo Castelli Gallery, New York
1996 *A Century of Sculpture,* Solomon R. Guggenheim Museum, New York
1997 *Forty Years of Exploration and Innovation: The Artists of the Castelli Gallery, 1957–1997,* Leo Castelli Gallery, New York
1999 *White Fire—Flying Man,* Museum für Gegenwartskunst, Basel, Switzerland

Collections:

Museum of Modern Art, New York; Whitney Museum, New York; Guggenheim Museum, New York; Hirshhorn Museum, Washington, D.C.; Art Museum of South Texas, Corpus Christi; Art Institute of Chicago; San Francisco Museum of Modern Art; National Gallery of Canada, Ottawa; Kunsthaus, Zurich; Stedelijk van Abbemuseum, Eindhoven, Netherlands; The Cincinnati Art Museum, Ohio.

Publications:

By JUDD: Books—*Complete Writings 1959–1975,* Halifax and New York, 1975; *Complete Writings 1975–1986,* Eindhoven 1987. **Articles—**reviews for *ARTnews* (New York), September-November 1959; reviews for *Arts Magazine* (New York), 1959–65; ''New York City: A World Art Center'' in *Envoy* (New York), Winter 1962; ''Chamberlain: Another View'' in *Art International* (Lugano, Switzerland), Christmas/New Year 1963/1964; ''At the Fair'' in *Art in America* (New York), August 1964; ''Local History'' in *Arts Yearbook 7,* New York 1964; ''To Encourage Sculpture and Specific Objects'' in *Arts Yearbook 8,* New York 1965; ''John Chamberlain'' in *7 Sculptors,* exhibition catalog, Philadelphia 1965; reviews for *Art International* (Lugano Switzerland), April/May 1965; statement in *Primary Structure: Younger American and British Sculptors,* exhibition catalog, New York 1966; ''Questions to Stella and Judd,'' interview with Bruce Glaser, in *ARTnews* (New York), September 1966; response to question by Lawrence Alloway in *Arts Yearbook 9,* New York 1967; statement in ''Sensibilities of the 60s'' by Barbara Rose and Irving Sandler in *Art in America* (New York), January/February 1967; letter to the editor in *Arts Magazine* (New York), April 1967; statement in ''Homage to the Square'' by Lucy Lippard in *Arts in America* (New York), July/August 1967; ''The Anti-Hierarchical American,'' interview with Amy Goldin, in *ARTnews* (New York), September 1967; statement in ''Portfolio: 4 Sculptors'' in *Perspecta* (New Haven, Connecticut), March-May 1968; statement in ''La Sfida del Sistema'' in *Metro* (Milan), June 1968; statement in *Art Now: New York* (New York), January 1969; ''Complaints: Part I'' in *Studio International* (London), April 1969; ''Aspects of Flavin'' in *Art and Artists* (London), March 1970; ''Don Judd: An Interview with John Coplans'' in *Don Judd,* exhibition catalog, Pasadena, California 1971; statement in *Newspaper-Lower Manhattan Township* (New York), January 1971; ''WOHO'' in *Newspaper-Lower Manhattan Township* (New York), April 1971; ''Greater Westbeth'' in *Newspaper-Greater Manhattan Township* (New York), May 1971;

article in *George Segal,* exhibition catalog, Paris 1972; ''Complaints: Part II'' in *Arts Magazine* (New York), March 1973; ''Malevich: Independent Form, Color, Surface'' in *Art in America* (New York), March/April 1974; interview with Jean Claude Lebensztejn in *Art in America* (New York), July/August 1975; ''A Long Discussion Not About Masterpieces But Why There Are So Few of Them'' in *Art in America* (New York), September and October 1984; *Art Monthly* (London), February and March 1985; ''Interview with Donald Judd,'' with Paul Taylor, in *Flash Art* (Milan), May 1987; ''Donald Judd'' in *Flash Art (International Edition),* no. 177, Summer 1994; ''Some Aspects of Color in General and Red and Black in Particular'' in *Artforum* (New York), vol. 32, no. 10, Summer 1994.

On JUDD: Books—*Minimal Art,* edited by Gregory Battcock, New York 1968; *Don Judd,* exhibition catalog, by William Agee, New York 1968; *Beyond Modern Sculpture* by Jack Burnham, New York 1968; *The New Sculpture: Environments and Assemblages* by Udo Kultermann, London 1968; *Don Judd,* exhibition catalog, Pasadena, California 1971; *The Structure of Art* by Jack Burnham, New York 1971; *The Definition of Art: Action Art to Pop to Earthworks* by Harold Rosenberg, London 1972; *Donald Judd,* exhibition catalog, edited by Brydon Smith, Ottawa 1975; *Donald Judd: Zeichrungen/drawings 1956–1975,* exhibition catalog, Basel 1976; *Profiles in American Art* by Barbara Rose, New York, 1981; *Artists Observed,* edited by Harvey Stein, New York 1986; *Donald Judd,* exhibition catalog with essay by Ronald Jones, Philadelphia 1987; *Donald Judd, Colorist,* edited by Dietmar Elger, New York 2000. **Articles—** ''Donald Judd'' by Barbara Rose in *Artforum* (New York), June 1965; ''Allusion and Illusion in Donald Judd'' by Rosalind Krauss in *Artforum* (New York), May 1966; ''The Nart-Art of Donald Judd'' by Martin Friedman in *Art and Artists* (London), February 1967; ''The Serial Attitude'' by Mel Bochner in *Artforum* (New York), December 1967; ''Don Judd: The complexities of Minimal Art'' by Barbara Rose in *Vogue* (New York), March 1969; ''Don Judd'' by Louwrien Wijers in *Museumjournaal* (Amsterdam), April 1969; ''Judd and After'' by Roelof Louw in *Studio International* (London), November 1972; ''Donald Judd: 10 Years'' by Gregoire Muller in *Arts Magazine* (New York), February 1973; ''Ply Me with Judd'' by Roberta Smith in *Village Voice* (New York), 23/29 September 1981; ''Donald Judd: The End of Sculpture'' by Eric Gibson in *The New Criterion,* vol. 7, April 1989; ''Renovation of Fort Russel, Texas'' by Aldo Rossi in *Lotus International,* no. 66, 1990; ''Judd and Panza Squre Off'' by Patricia Failing in *ARTnews,* vol. 89, November 1990; ''Donald Judd's Swiss Retreat: The Artist Transforms a Provincial Inn on the Shores of Lake Lucerne'' by Nicholas Fox Weber in *Architectural Digest,* vol. 48, September 1991; ''Cold Metal: Donald Judd's Hidden Historicity'' by Charles Reeve in *Art History,* vol. 15, December 1992; ''Donald Judd: Early Work'' by John Russell in the *New York Times,* 18 November 1983; ''After Judd: Notes at Season's End'' by Jed Perl in *The New Criterion,* vol. 12, June 1994; ''Donald Judd'' in *Architectural Design* (London), vol. 64, July/August 1994; ''Donald Judd'' by Owen Drolet in *Flash Art (International Edition),* no. 179, November/December 1994; ''My Own Private Marfa'' in *Texas Monthly,* vol. 22, no. 7, July 1994; ''Donald Judd at Pace Wildenstein'' by Lilly Wei in *Art in America* (New York), vol. 82, no. 12, December 1994; ''Just Judd'' by Michael Archer in *Art Monthly,* no. 184, March 1995; ''Multiples: Donald Judd Furniture'' by Erika Lederman in *Art Monthly,* no. 184, March 1995; ''Donald Judd'' by William Feaver in *ARTnews,* vol. 94, April 1995; ''Donald Judd'' by Tony Godfrey in *The Burlington Magazine* (London), vol. 137, April 1995; ''Sequential Geometry: Prints by Judd, Kelly, Levine & Schuyff'' by Charles Wylie in *The Print Collector's Newsletter,* vol. 26, January/February 1996; ''The Judds: Donald Judd's Spare Aesthetic and Store Design'' by David Rimanelli in *Interior Design* (New York), vol. 67, December 1996; ''Art in Residence: Environments in the Homes of Eight Artists'' by Jeff Weinstein in *Artforum International,* vol. 35, March 1997; ''Fixing the House(s) That Judd Built'' by Janet Tyson in *Art Newspaper,* vol. 10, no. 84, September 1998; ''The Century's 25 Most Influential Artists: 25 Article Special Section'' in *ARTnews,* vol. 98, no. 5, May 1999; ''Perfect Unlikeness'' by Philip Leider in *Artforum International,* vol. 38, no. 6, February 2000; ''Finishing the Fort'' by Elizabeth McBride in *ARTnews,* vol. 99, no. 7, Summer 2000; ''Donald Judd (Art Reproduction)'' by Annabelle d'Huart in *Art Press,* no. 262, November 2000.

*

Somewhat new work is usually described with the words that have been used to describe old work. These words have to be discarded as too particular to the earlier work or they have to be given new definitions. Occationally new terms have to be invented. I discarded ''order'' and ''structure.'' Both words imply that something is formed. Material, area, volume, space or color are ordered or structured. The separation of means and structure—the world and order—is one of the main aspects of European or Western art and also of most older, reputedly civilized art. It's the sense of order of Thomist Christianity and of rationalistic philosophy which developed from it. Order underlies, overlies, is within, above, below or beyond everything.

I wanted work that didn't involve incredible assumptions about everything. I couldn't begin to think about the order of the universe or the nature of American society. I didn't want work that was general or universal in the usual sense. I didn't want it to claim too much. Obviously, the means and the structure couldn't be separate and couldn't even be thought of as two things joined. Neither word meant anything.

A shape, a volume, a color, a surface is something itself. It shouldn't be concealed as part of a fairly different whole. The shapes and materials shouldn't be altered by their context. One or four boxes in a row, any single thing or such a series, is local order, just an arrangement, barely order at all. The series is mine, someone's, and clearly not some larger order. It has nothing to do with either order or disorder in general. Both are matters of fact. The series of four or six doesn't change the galvanized iron or steel or whatever the boxes are made of.

—Don Judd

* * *

Donald Judd's mature art arose—like that of other major American artists in the mid-60s, and larger and continuing drives in literature and music even earlier—from the need to produce a muted and reductive art still clearly based upon a notion of the aesthetic and thus removed from life. All this reflected the exhaustion, as felt then, with art forms of high personal expression and complex internal construction, an uneasiness that extended easily into the nature of traditional materials, format, means of conception and construction. And so the real fascination of Judd's art, along with that of the others to be titled Minimalists in their geometric impulse, is that to satisfy itself, his work had to touch upon the boundary of anonymous object where whatever spiritual energy survived in the color field and geometric pictorial traditions was decisively nullified.

Yet now, in retrospect, Judd's first large body of mature work, that in metal (ca. 1965–73) and now ensconced in the textbooks, seemingly present quite traditional visual conceits in their measured precision, material and textural distinctions, reliance upon color, light, and even, in some, a rhythm, for their aura. And, as such, even when felt as a part of the longer Western anti-Romantic stance of elitist elegance, this formal manipulation may well be Judd's own Beckett-like device of play to keep the ultimate condition within the logic of his art—void—constantly at bay. When the entirety of the work is seen together, as in catalog reproduction, the artist's extensive use of ''theme and variation'' is clear, but not in any one single work. He has had fabricated extended series of variants of all of his well-known basic form-types: for instance, after arriving at the format of a signature work in 1967, the vertical stack of wall-hung, frame-like boxes, at least 32 versions of such units, each usually numbering 10 elements, were made through 1973. Outwardly similar, the works differed in their use of many colors for the Plexiglas sheets inserted into the metallic frames while the latter were produced in brass, copper, galvanized iron, copper, aluminum, with stainless steel the most frequently used.

After working as a painter in the later 1950s and into the first year of the 60s—to support himself at the time, Judd wrote art criticism—he then turned to free-standing sculptural forms which at first included both mixed media and found objects. He then executed a series of painted wooden objects—''harps,'' ''bleachers,'' and slotted boxes—before, at mid-decade, his creative concept came to include industrial fabrication and a relatively small family of form types all centered about a box form, mostly open, and in metals. Constantly re-thought and reworked with no major external changes, the most characteristic types of this period centered upon this box-like-frame, horizontal, or vertical, singular or composed of multiple units, tied together with a bar form and wall-hung, or detached and floor-placed. (Judd has never titled his works, no doubt to further their anonymity and specificity—he himself uses the phrase ''specific objects'' to designate his work; ironically, this may have all the more personalized them, since by necessity they are referred to by the name of the collection in which they appear.)

Within the most recent decade of his career, from 1972 on, Judd has used untreated plywood for interior works—outdoor pieces have been executed in concrete and in steel. Both in larger ensembles, whole gallery wall-length, and in smaller individual works exhibited together, as in 1981, the box form dominates and there are no color or material shifts; but the rhythmic changes available earlier only in the wall-hung horizontal bar form with its oft mathematically based size and interval variance, can be easily seen in the plywood pieces. Especially in the smaller plywood works, where the external box-frame is visible, the work appears as a search for internal variety, softened by the wood-grain though still distinctly non-hierarchal. Recent work of the mid-'80s has played variant upon earlier metal and tinted Plexiglas rectangular construction. Critical complaint has spoken of their ''old-fashioned'' reliance upon craftsmanship and chaste material; whereas more pointed views see the work as ''archetype of corporate avant gardism'' (J. Dechter) in its preciosity—use of copper, corten steel, brass, and mellifluous hues—and thus jewel-like seductiveness, and a ''commodification'' of Minimalist style. Others of course still admire without reservation such ''stubborn orthodox Minimalism.'' And so Judd's art has continued as symbols representative of non-symbolic statement, which in their austerity and order can present thought if not feeling as well. But, as in any evolved creative idiom, there is a time when its emblem-value becomes more significant than its inventive flexibility. With such lessened contemporary adaptiveness, it is then a collector's art rather than the artist's; apparently for Judd, the minimalist mode is still under his control and operates without dilemma.

—Joshua Kind

JULIEN, Isaac

Nationality: British. **Born:** Bow, east London, England, 1960. **Education:** Central St. Martin's School of Art, B. A. in Fine Art Film (1st Class Honors), 1984. **Career:** Founded Sankofa Film and Video Collective, 1984; drama-documentary *Looking for Langston* gains cult following, 1989; founding member of Normal Films, 1990; Art Pace, International Artist in Residence, San Antonio, 1999. Visiting lecturer at Harvard University, Cambridge, Massachusetts; visiting lecturer for Whitney Museum of American Art's Independent Study Program, New York; trustee of Serpentine Gallery, London; currently Research Fellow of Fine Arts, Oxford Brookes University. **Awards:** Semaine de la Critique Prize for best film, Cannes Film Festival, 1991; John McKnight International Artist Award, Minneapolis, 1993; Rockefeller Humanities Fellowship Award, New York University, Centre for Media, Culture and History, 1995; Wexner Center for the Arts International Artist Award, Columbus, Ohio, 1996; Pratt and Whitney Canada Grand Prize, 15th International Festival of Films on Art, 1997; Andy Warhol Foundation Award, U.S.A., 1998.

Selected Individual Exhibitions:

1999 *The Long Road to Mazatlan,* Art Pace, San Antonio (traveled to Grand Arts, Kansas City, Missouri)
Three, Victoria Miro Gallery, London
The Arena, Oxford
2000 *Cinerama,* Corner House Museum, Manchester (traveled to South London Gallery)
After Mazatlan, Victoria Miro Gallery, London
2001 *Vagabondia,* Studio Museum, Harlem, New York
The Long Road to Mazatlan, Museum of Contemporary Art, Chicago
The Film Art of Isaac Julien, Bard Curatorial College, Annandale on Hudson, New York (traveling to Museum of Contemporary Art, Sydney; Bildmuseet Umeå, Sweden, Henie Onstad Museum, Norway) (catalog)

Selected Group Exhibitions:

1990 *Edge 90,* various sites in London and Newcastle-upon-Tyne (catalog)
1991 Walker Art Center, Minneapolis

1993 *Abject Art: Repulsion and Desire in American Art,* Whitney Museum of American Art, New York (catalog)

1995 *Mirage: Enigma of Race, Difference and Desire,* Institute of Contemporary Arts, London (catalog)

1996 *Hotter Than July,* the Margo Leavin Gallery, Los Angeles
Scream and Scream Again, Museum of Modern Art, Oxford (traveled to Irish Museum of Modern Art; Helsinki Museum of Contemporary Art (catalog)
New Histories, Institute of Contemporary Art, Boston (catalog)
AIDS World, Centre d'Art Contemporain Geneve, Geneva; Centro d'Arte Contemporanea Ticino, Italy (catalog)

1997 2nd Johannesburg Biennale (catalog)
The Look of Love, The Approach, London; Southampton City Art Gallery
Beauty and the Beast, Banff Centre for the Arts, Vancouver

1998 *Rhapsodies in Black,* Corcoran Gallery of Art, Washington, D. C.; California Palace of the Legion of Honour; Fine Arts Museum of San Francisco; Hayward Gallery, London

1999 *Retrace Your Steps,* Saint John Sir Museum, London
Rhapsodies In Black, Museum of Fine Arts, Houston

2000 *Strength and Diversity: African American Artists,* Harvard University, Cambridge, Massachusetts
Raw, Victoria Miro Gallery, Wharf Road, London

Publications:

By JULIEN: Book—*Diary of a Young Soul Rebel,* by Isaac Julien and Colin MacCabe, London 1991. **Articles—**''The Passion of Remembrance: An Interview with Isaac Julien'' by L. Jackson and J. Rasenberger in *Cineaste,* 1988; ''Interview with Isaac Julien'' by Bruce Morrow in *Callaloo,* Spring 1995.

On JULIEN: Books—*Black Popular Culture,* by Michele Wallace and Gina Dent, Seattle 1992; *Black Male: Representations of Masculinity in Contemporary American Art,* by Thelma Golden, New York 1994; *Welcome to the Jungle: New Positions in Black Cultural Studies,* by Kobena Mercer, New York and London 1994; *The British Avant-Garde Film, 1926–1995, An Anthology of Writings,* edited by Michael O'Pray, London 1996; *British Cinema in the 1980s: Issues and Themes,* by John Hill, Oxford 1999. **Articles—**''Isaac Julien: Filmmaker'' by Ruby B. Rich in *OUT-LOOK: National Lesbian & Gay Quarterly,* Fall 1988; ''Visualizing Theory: An Interview with Isaac Julien'' by Coco Fusco in *Nka: Journal of Contemporary African Art,* Summer-Fall 1997.

* * *

Isaac Julien is a British filmmaker whose work navigates the often rocky terrain of race, gender, and sexuality. As a black and openly gay artist working in the white, heterosexually dominated world of film, Julien makes films that interrogate mainstream filmmaking and what it means to be black and gay in post-colonial England. In 1983 Isaac Julien, along with Martina Attile, Maureen Blackwood, Robert Crusz, and Nadine Marsh-Edwards, founded Sankofa, a cutting-edge film collective located in London (Sankofa is an Akan word that means ''to go back and retrieve''). Sankofa's mission was to create politically-committed films that touch on the lives of black people in modern Europe and to develop themes and stories that are at once beautiful and pleasurable while still provocative in their queries about class, race, gender, and sexuality. Sankofa, and Julien, are careful to distinguish between their making films that speak *from* the experience of being black, gay, and English, rather than films that speak *for* black Britain. Additionally, although Julien's films explore serious and difficult issues—-AIDS, repressed desire, racism—-they never deny the sensuality and beauty that can be cultivated in medium of film.

In 1989, Julien made *Looking for Langston.* This film is perhaps his best-known work and was included (along with the 1987 film *This is Not an AIDS Advertisement*) in the Whitney Museum of American Art's 1995 exhibition *Black Male: Representations of Masculinity in Contemporary American Art. Looking for Langston* is a dreamy and beautifully rendered short film which explores the sexuality of Harlem Renaissance poet Langston Hughes. The work is credited with being the forerunner of the New Queer Cinema movement. Critic Kobena Mercer has called the film ''an archaeological inquiry,'' which is fitting since in the film Julien archives vintage photographs and documentary footage to compile a meditation about the life of the famous poet. The film attempts to recreate Hughes's historical moment and the difficulties the poet must have faced in a world where racism was inescapable and different sexualities were demonized. By juxtaposing house music and contemporary photography with the historical and documentary images in the film, Julien is able to make a timeless statement about the still present forces that work against free expression of sexuality and love.

Films such as *Looking for Langston* and *Franz Fanon: Black Skin, White Mask* are typical of one type of film that Julien makes—filmic biographies that explore the importance and identity of well-known black or African American figures. Often, these biographies pose questions about the significance of the figure—-the famous poet or the Caribbean psychoanalyst—-to the black diaspora. Julien has also made feature length films, the best known of which is *Young Soul Rebels* which won the Critic's Week Prize at the Cannes International Film Festival in 1991. The making of *Young Soul Rebels* was documented in Julien's book *Diary of a Young Soul Rebel,* published the same year.

Young Soul Rebels is a film about the year 1977 in England. Julien was keen to construct a story about the hip, black disco and soul movement that swept through London that year. Oppositional pop culture at the time is most typically considered to be the punk movement, a white male dominated culture. However, in this film Julien brings to light the alternate and politically left culture of the club/disco scene that allowed for interracial desire and a slackening of mainstream gender mores. The film ultimately questions what it means for the main characters to be young, black, and gay in a culture that on one hand represses them and on the other hand considers them to be cutting edge purveyors of style.

Young Soul Rebels interrogates the creation of national identity, and how young people come of age in post-colonial England. Julien's films are critical and political as well as consciously artistic. His sensual use of film and poetic direction highlight the important issues of race and sexuality. In addition to making films about these issues, Julien is also a writer and critic who has lectured widely on his theories about de-essentializing blackness. His critical stance allows for difference—-interracial partnering, homosexuality—within the black diaspora. It is a stance that he promotes in his films as well.

—Jennifer S. Zarro

JUNG, Dieter

Nationality: German. **Born:** Bad Wildungen, Germany, 9 October 1941. **Education:** Studied theology, Kirchliche Hochschule, Berlin, 1962–63; studied art, Hochschule der Künste, Berlin, 1962–67, and École Nationale des Beaux Arts, Paris; studied film, German Film and Television Academy, Berlin, 1971–73; studied holography, New York School of Holography, 1977. **Family:** Married Annette Jung, 1994; children: Luca. **Career:** Independent artist, Berlin, 1967—; created first experimental documentary films, 1970–74; guest professor, Universidade Federal da Bahia, Brazil, 1975; created first holograms, 1977; Rockefeller Fellow, Center for Advanced Visual Studies, Massachusetts Institute of Technology, Cambridge, 1985–86; professor of media arts, Academy of Media Arts, Cologne, 1990—; member of board of trustees, Center for Art and Media, ZKM, Karlsruhe, 1992–96; board member, Center for the Holographic Arts, Long Island City, New York, 2000. **Awards:** Paris grant, Institut Français de Berlin, 1965; Studienstiftung des Deutschen Volkes, Bonn, 1967; USA Fellowship, German Academic Exchange Service (DAAD), 1968–69; artist-in-residence at MacDowell Colony, Petersborough, New Hampshire, 1977, Yaddo, Saratoga Springs, New York, 1978, and Museum of Holography, New York, 1983; Holography Award, Shearwater Foundation, New York, 1988. **Agent:** Galerie Schoeller, Poststrasse 2, 40213 Düsseldorf, Germany. **Address:** Vionvillestrasse 11, 12167 Berlin, Germany; Academy of Media Arts Cologne, Peter-Welter-Platz 2, 50676 Köln, Germany.

Individual Exhibitions:

1968 Galerie Defet, Nuremberg (catalog)
1970 Staedt Kunstsammlung, Gelsenkirchen (catalog)
1973 Galerie Haus Seel, Siegen (catalog)
1974 Galeria Arte Moderna, Bogota
Museu de Arte Moderna, Rio de Janeiro (catalog)
Museu de Arte de Sao Paulo
1975 Haus am Waldsee, Berlin (catalog)
1976 Galeria Michaud, Florence
Goethe Institut, Rome
1979 Pointdexter Gallery, New York (catalog)
1980 Musée Français de l'Holographie, Paris
1981 *Écriture Holographique,* Revue parlée de Blaise Gautier, Centre Georges Pompidou, Paris
1982 Poindexter Gallery, New York (catalog)
AM Sachs Gallery, New York
Goethe House, New York (travelled to San Francisco, Ottawa, Toronto, Montreal, Boston, Atlanta, Houston)
1983 Hara Museum of Contemporary Art, Tokyo (catalog)
Osaka Contemporary Art Center, Osaka
1984 Hong Kong Arts Center, Hong Kong (catalog)
Hologram Gallery, Stockholm
1985 Musée de Québec, Québec
Museum of Holography, New York (catalog)
1986 Center for Advanced Visual Studies, M.I.T., Cambridge
1988 Paris Art Center, Paris (book)
1990 Zamalek Art Center, Ekhnaton Gallery, Cairo (catalog)
1991 Staatliche Kunsthalle, Berlin (book)
Karl Ernst Osthaus-Museum, Hagen
1992 Ulmer Museum, Ulm
Goethe Institut, Madrid
Galerie Schoeller, Düsseldorf
Nouvelle Abstraction (with Unger/Agaggio), Palais du Luxembourg, Paris
1993 Escola das Belas Artes, Salvador, Brazil
1994 Artcapi, École Nationale Supérieure de Physique de Strasbourg, Illkirch
1995 *Räume im Raum,* Skulpturengarten am Klostersee, Lehnin
1996 Galerie Redmann, Berlin
1997 *Bewegte Räume,* Galerie der Jenoptik, Jena
1998 Galerie Schoeller, Düsseldorf
1999 *das Licht—der Raum—die Farbe,* Landesvertretung NRW, Bonn
Stone of Light, Trinitatiskirche, Cologne
2001 Museo Carlos Cruz-Diez, Caracas

Group Exhibitions:

1966 Galerie Paul Facchetti, Paris
1968 *Nouvelle École de Berlin,* Galerie Motte, Genf, Milano, Paris
1969 New York Studio School, New York
1971 Kunsthalle, Baden Baden
1976 Musée National de Monaco, Monte Carlo
1977 *Berlin Now,* Gallery Denise René, New York (catalog)
New York Avant Garde Festival, World Trade Center, New York
Museum of Holography, New York
1979 Museum of Holography, New York
Holographie, Neuer Berliner Kunstverein, Berlin (catalog)
1980 Kunstmuseum, Düsseldorf
1981 Museum of Natural History, Beijing
1983 *Light Dimensions,* The Octagon Gallery, Bath, and Science Museum, London (catalog)
Holographie, Kunstmuseum Hannover mit Sammlung Sprengel, Hannover (catalog)
1984 Museum of Holography, New York
1985 *East-West,* National Center for the Performing Arts, Bombay
National Geographic Society's Explorers Hall, Washington, D.C. (book)
Mehr Licht—More Light, Kunsthalle, Hamburg (catalog)
1986 *Lumiére, Perception—Projection,* Centre International d'Art Contemporaine, Montreal (catalog)
Installation, The International Conference on Holography, Beijing
1987 *Immagini Per Il Futuro,* Museo de Historia della Fotographia, Florence
Image in Time and Space, National Museum of Science, Ottawa and Montreal

Dieter Jung: *HoloMobile—Constallation,* 2001. ©Dieter Jung.

1989 *150 Ans de Photographie,* Musée de la Photographie, Charleroi, Belgium
Flash-Back, Paris Art Center, Paris
1992 *Moving Image,* Fundaciô Joan Mirô, Barcelona (catalog)
1993 *Virtual Real Image,* Daimaru Museum, Tokyo (catalog)
1994 *Light—Space—Time,* Center for Advanced Visual Studies, MIT Museum, Cambridge
Fundus, Mittelrhein Museum, Koblenz
1996 *Holographic Network,* Akademie der Künste Berlin, Bauhaus-Archiv Berlin, and Parochialkirche, Berlin
1997 *Les Sciences dans l'Art,* UNESCO, Paris
Kunst der Gegenwart, Museum für Neue Kunst ZKM, Karlsruhe
1998 *KunstRaum Stadt,* Museum Ettlingen
1999 *Natura della Luce,* Galleria d'Arte Contemporaneo, Venice (catalog)
Lumia, International Lyskunst, Charlottenborg Museum, Copenhagen (catalog)
2000 *Media Art Fest,* Manege, St. Petersburg, Russia
Kajaanin Taidemuseo, Kajaani, Finland (catalog)
2001 *Maschine Times,* V2, Amsterdam (catalog)
Palais du Luxembourg, Paris

Collections:

Metropolitan Museum of Art, New York; Brooklyn Museum, New York; Musée de Québec, Canada; Museu de Arte Moderna, Rio de Janeiro; Hara Museum of Contemporary Art, Tokyo; Landesmuseum-Berlinische Galerie, Berlin; Kunsthalle Hamburg, Hamburg; Museum für Neue Kunst, Karlsruhe; Museu de Arte de São Paulo, São Paulo, Brazil.

Permanent Public Installations:

The Holographic Prismchanger, European Patent Office, Munich; *HoloMobile,* European Patent Office, Den Haag; *Sehwege,* Treptowers, Berlin; *Ten no Kakehashi,* Deutsch Japanisches Zentrum, Hamburg.

Publications:

By JUNG: Book—Editor, *Holographic Network,* Köln 2001. **Articles—**''Holographic Space'' in *Leonardo,* vol. 22, no. 3/4, 1989; ''Bildräume der Holographie'' in *Kultur und Technik im 21 Jahrhundert,* edited by G. Kaiser, Frankfurt and New York 1993; ''Luz na Arte/Arte da Luz'' in *Dieter Jung* (exhibition catalog),

Salvador, Brazil 1995; ''Ein Kubikmeter Licht'' in *Otto Piene: Kunst die fliegt,* Köln 1998; ''L'Espace Holographique'' in *La Science et la Métamorphose des Arts,* edited by R. Daudel, Paris 1998.

On JUNG: Books—*Experiment Design* by Igildo Biesele, Zürich 1986; *Holographie* by Peter Zec, Köln 1987; *Dieter Jung, Bilder-Zeichnungen-Hologramme,* Köln 1991; *Art in the Electronic Age* by Frank Popper, London and Paris, 1993. **Article—**''Verse im Raum'' in *Der Spiegel,* no. 11, 1979.

* * *

Dieter Jung is one of the pioneers of holographic art. This art, apart from being a form of optical illusion, constitutes a specific phase in the history of Light Art. Illusionist tendencies existed in art since the earliest times and were at certain periods even considered as forming an integral part of Western art. As to the luminous phenomenon, with its curious ambiguity between presence and absence, it is at the heart of all holographic art and can be compared to our perception of the stars whose physical presence has been superseded by the luminous wave which reaches our eye long after having been emitted. The aesthetics of absence has been the privilege of the mystics of all times, but its metaphysical side is counterbalanced by its scientific connotation in the area of holographic art.

Dieter Jung has played a prominent role in both of these aspects, both the religious and the artistic-scientific. He in fact studied theology at Berlin's Kirchliche Hochschule in the 1960s while frequenting the city's Art School. The blend of plastic arts and theology played an important role in the work of this artist when the hologram was introduced. Already in 1972 he was highly impressed by the discovery of religious tapestries held at the Florence Cathedral Museum, which depicted scenes from the life of Saint John the Baptist based on drawings by Antonio Pollaiuolo. The system underpinning the fabrication of these tapestries, composed of thousands of interwoven threads, would be adopted by Dieter Jung for his future pictorial research.

Once he had definitely renounced theology in favor of the plastic arts (not without reminding us of Van Gogh and Mondrian), Jung painted a series of portraits on canvas, composed of crossing vertical and horizontal lines, the resulting ''grid'' of which revealed the warp and woof of the canvas.

There followed a series of collage paintings made of bird feathers, the structure, texture, and color-range of which refract and reflect light especially well by creating iridescent optical illusions. One could mention in passing that iridescence is an aesthetic theme introduced in 1912 by Giacomo Balla in a series of abstract paintings, some of the genre's first, made of interlinked rainbow-colored circles. These paintings are one of the sources of what in the 1960s and 1970s was called Optical Art. Balla talked about the ''iridescent beauty'' of his compositions, while Dieter Jung speaks of ''fractal beauty'' to qualify his holographic production.

One of the first projects using this technique and carried out with the help of a scientist, Donald White, consists of transposing a poem by Hans Magnus Enzensberger, called ''Hologram,'' specially composed for Dieter Jung. The poem begins with the words, ''It is easy to build a poem in the air. All you need are a few well-lit words, light-footed, light-fingered, light-minded words. . . . '' There follow thoughts on the fragility and transience of human existence.

Jung is particularly fascinated by the rainbow and uses Benton's rainbow holographic techniques to produce several holographic cycles: the multi-slit full-color holograms ''Butterfly'' (1982), ''Feather Shadows'' and ''Into the Rainbow'' (1983), and the multi-exposure holograms ''Present Space'' (1984) and ''Different Space'' (1985). These project their color fields in wide vertical bands in front of, and behind, the image plane. They can be experienced as a spatially indefinable artistic effect of changing colorful shadows of light which melt into the air.

In his most recent works, ''Holomobiles'' and ''Transoptical Mobiles,'' Dieter Jung manages to establish with the aid of unforeseeable constellations an harmonical canon of lyrical light paintings in space. The regular circulation of self-creative image developments is here modified by the physical position and individual perception of the spectator, who becomes part of a playful cosmology of light.

In all these holographic works Dieter Jung seeks to combine the visual knowledge acquired in his work as a traditional painter with his more recent experience of the hologram so as to explore the aesthetic potential. His goal is to stimulate spatial imagination, generate new mental images, and visualize spatial fusion. For him, holography is both an exploration of the space and the illusion of light's aesthetic qualities. In his works the holograph is not only a product or a tool, but its manifestations are based on the structure of its medium, light. Dieter Jung is aware that holographic space cannot copy reality, and that the effect of holographic space as well as its substantial existence derive solely from the self-creating energy of light to which holography gives absolute reality. As light is not only a generative principle but a subject and the basic substance of the holographic image as well, the self-reference of light represents an essential form for the articulation of the holographic message.

It is on this level that Dieter Jung's theological studies combine his former plastic work and his technologically advanced recent artistic statements in a well thought-out synthesis.

—Frank Popper

K

KABAKOV, Ilya

Nationality: Russian. **Born:** Soviet Union, 1933. **Education:** Surikov Institute of Art, 1951–57. **Career:** Worked as an illustrator of children's books in Moscow; moved to New York in 1988; lives and works in Moscow, New York, and Paris. **Awards:** Ludwig Prize, Friends of the Museum of Ludwig, Aachen, Germany, 1989; DAAD Fellowship, Berlin, 1989; Arthur Koptcke Award, Koptcke Foundation, Copenhagen, 1992; Joseph Beuys Prize, Beuys Foundation, Basel, 1993; Max Beckmann Prize, Frankfurt, 1993; Honorary Diploma, Venice *Biennale,* 1993. **Agent:** Ronald Feldman Fine Arts, Inc. **Address:** c/o Ronald Feldman Fine Arts, Inc., 31 Mercer St., New York, New York, 10013, U.S.A.

Individual Exhibitions:

1985 Dina Vierny Galerie, Paris
Kunsthalle, Bern (travelled to Marseill and Dusseldorf)
1986 Neue Galerie, Dierikon, Switzerland
Kunstverein, Graz, Austria
1987 Museum of Modern Art, Basel
Centre National des Artes Plastiques, Paris
1988 Portikus-Austellung 9, Frankfurt
Ronald Feldman Fine Arts, New York
Kunstverein, Graz, Austria
Neue Galerie Dierikon, Switzerland (with V. Pivovarov)
Kunstverein, Bonn (with Erik Bulatov)
1989 Institute of Contemporary Art, Philadelphia
Daadgalerie, Berlin
De Appel, Amsterdam
Genia Schreiber University Art Gallery, Tel Aviv (with Micahel Grobman)
Kunsthalle, Zurich
Institute of Contemporary Art, London (with Erik Bulatov)
Riverside Studios, London
University of Saarbrucken, Germany
Galerie de France, Paris
1990 Museum Ludwig, Aachen, Germany
Orchard Gallery, Derry, Ireland
Kunstverein, Kassel, Germany
Hirshhorn Museum, Washington, D.C.
Fred Hoffman Gallery, Santa Monica, California
Ronald Feldman Fine Arts, New York
Peter Pakesh Galerie, Vienna
1991 Ateliers Municipaux d'Artistes, Marseille (travelled to Rennes, France)
The Power Plant, Toronto
FIAC International Art Fair, Paris
Peter Pakesch Gallery, Vienna
Wewerka and Weiss Galerie, Berlin
Dresdener Bank, Frankfurt
1992 Ludwig Museum, Cologne
Koninklijke Academie voor Schone Kunsten, Kortrijk, Belgium
Deweer Art Gallery, Otegem, Belgium
Galleria Sprovieri, Rome
Ronald Feldman Fine Arts, New York
Galerie Dina Vierny, Paris
University of Illinois at Urbana-Champaign
Kölnischer Kunstverein, Cologne
1993 Musée Maillol, Paris
Kunsthalle, Hamburg
Chinati Foundation, Marfa, Texas
Kunstverein, Salzburg
Museum of Contemporary Art, Chicago
Biennale, Venice
Chateau d'Oiron, France
Ikon Gallery, Birmingham, England (travelled to Glasgow)
Staatliche Hochschule für Bildende Künste, Frankfurt
Stedelijk Museum, Amsterdam
1994 Kulturhuset, Stockholm
Kunstverein, Ludwigsburg, Germany
National Museum of Contemporary Art, Oslo
Exhibition Space, Reykjavik, Iceland
Jablonka Galerie, Cologne
Center for Contemporary Art, Warsaw
Centre National d'Art Contemporain, Grenoble, France
Hessisches Landesmuseum, Darmstadt, Germany
Galerie Barbara Weiss, Berlin
Museum of Contemporary Art, Helsinki, Finland
47th Venice Biennale, Italy
1995 Centre Georges Pompidou, Paris
Thaddeus Ropac Gallery, Paris
1996 *This is Where We Live,* Beaubourg Center, Paris
1998 *Ilya Kabakov: 16 Installations,* Museum van Hendendaagse Kunst, Antwerp (catalog)
Treatment With Memories, Hamburger Bahnhof, Museum of Contemporary Art, Berlin
Ilya & Emilia Kabakov, The Roundhouse, London
Ilya Kabakov: Drawings, Sprengel Museum Hannover (catalog)
1999 *Memorial to a Lost Civilization,* Cantieri Culturali Alla Zisa, Palermo, Italy (with Emilia Kabakov)
Ten Characters, Hessisches Landesmuseum Darmstadt
2000 *The Boat of My Life,* David Winter Bell Gallery, Brown University, Providence (catalog)

Selected Group Exhibitions:

1977 *Biennale,* Venice
1988 *Ich Lebe, Ich Sehe,* Kunstmuseum, Bern
1989 *The Green Show,* Exit Art, New York (travelled to Regina and Saskatoon, Canada)
Magiciens de la Terre, Musée National d'Art Moderne, Paris
1990 *At Last, Freedom,* Daadgalerie, Berlin

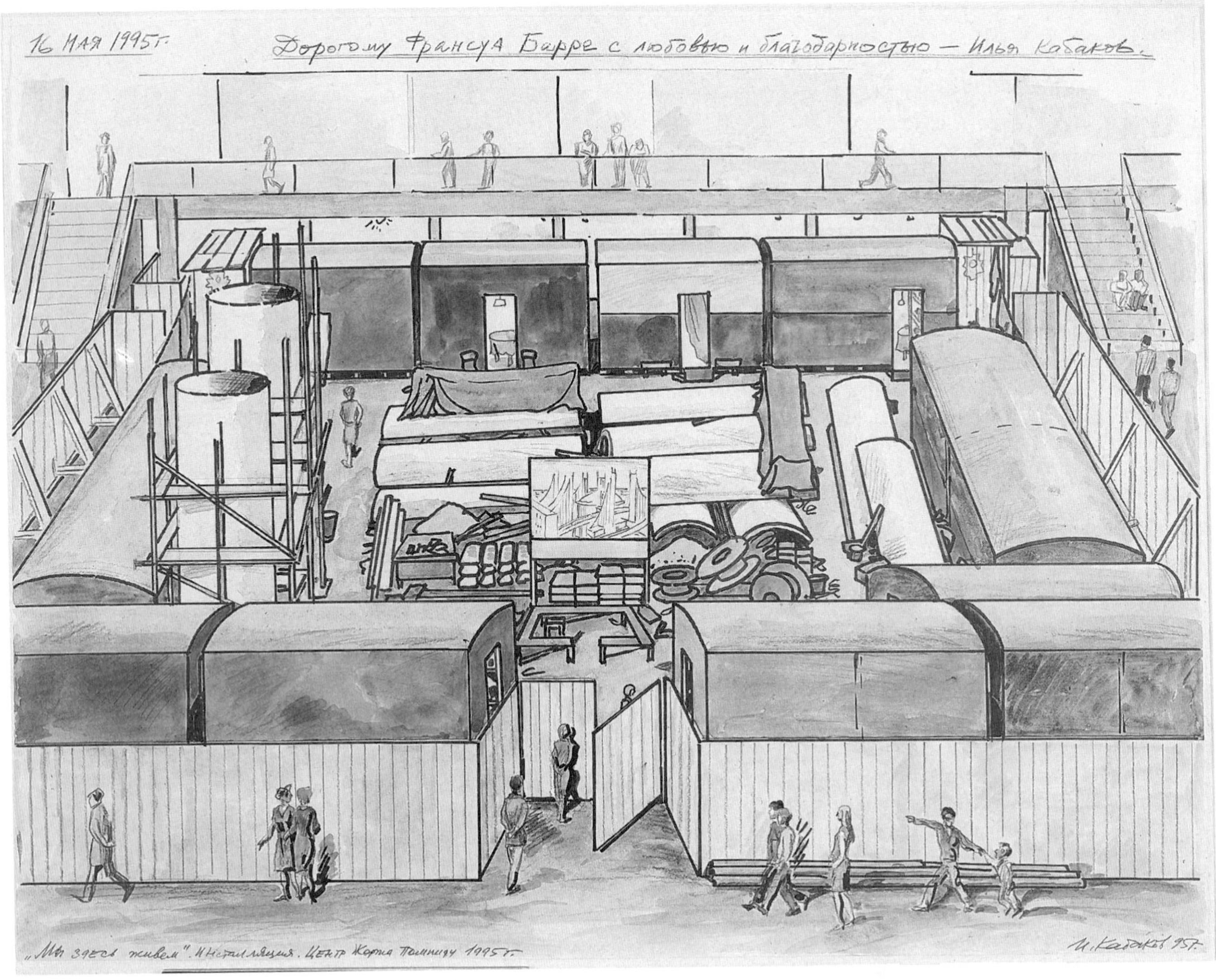

16 мая 1995 г.
Дорогому Франсуа Барре с любовью и благодарностью — Илья Кабаков.

Ilya Jossifovich Kabakov: Preparatory drawing for *This is where we live* (detail), 1995. Photo © Jean-Claude Planchet. ©2001 Artists Rights Society (ARS), NY/VG Bild-Kunst, Bonn.

Biennale, Sydney

1991 *Dislocations,* Museum of Modern Art, New York

1992 *Documenta IX,* Kassel, Germany

Ex USSR: Contemporary Artists from the CIS, Groninger Museum, Netherlands (catalog)

1993 *Biennale,* Venice

1994 *Europa-Europa,* Kunst un Ausstellungshalle der Bundesrepublik Deutschland, Bonn

Refuge Moscow: Work from the Ludwig Collection and Work for Aachen, Ludwing Forum for Internationale Kunst, Aachen (catalog)

Virtual Reality, National Gallery of Australia, Canberra (catalog)

1995 *Hisa v Casa/House in Time,* Moderna Galerija, Ljubljana (catalog)

Abstraction, Pure and Impure, Museum of Modern Art, New York (catalog)

1996 *Urban Evidence: Contemporary Artists Reveal Cleveland,* Cleveland Center for Contemporary Art (catalog)

1997 *1997 Whitney Biennial,* Whitney Museum of American Art, New York

1998 *The Edge of Awareness,* World Health Organization Headquarters, Geneva (traveling exhibition) (catalog)

Artranspennine98, Tate Gallery Liverpool (traveling exhibition) (catalog)

Crossings/Traversees, National Gallery of Canada, Ottawa (catalog)

A Meeting: Jan Fabre & Ilya Kabakov, Deweer Art Gallery, Otegem, Belgium (catalog)

Permanent Public Installations:

The Blue Dish, Seville, Spain; *Whose Wings Are These?* Utrecht, Netherlands; *Normandy-Neman,* Orly, France.

Publications:

By KABAKOV: Books—*The Art of One Who Flees* with Boris Groys, Munich 1991; *Life of Flies,* Cologne 1992; *Ilya Kabakov:*

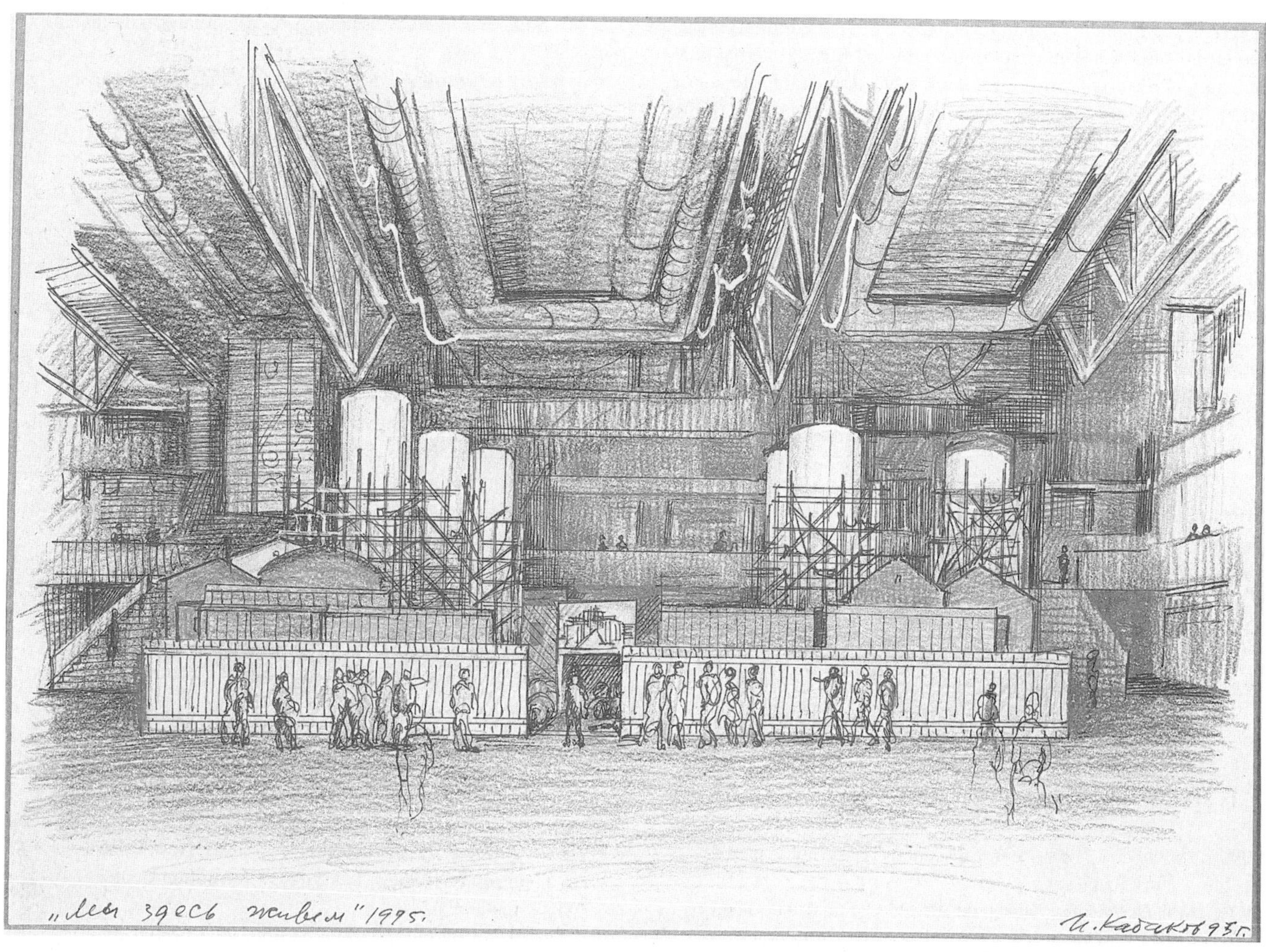

Ilya Jossifovich Kabakov: Preparatory drawing for *This is where we live* (detail), 1995. Photo © Jean-Claude Planchet. ©2001 Artists Rights Society (ARS), NY/VG Bild-Kunst, Bonn.

Installations 1983–1995, Paris 1995; *On the Roof,* with foreword by Piet Coessens, Dusseldorf 1996; *Ilya Kabakov: The Man Who Never Threw Anything Away,* with Amei Wallach and Robert Storr, New York 1996. **Articles**—''An Interview with Ilya Kabakov'' with Robert Storr in *Art in America,* Janaury 1995; ''Ilya Kabakov: A Story About a Culturally Relocated Person'' in *Transcript,* vol. 2, no. 1, June 1996; interview with Amei Wallach in *Contemporary Visual Arts,* no. 14, 1997; interview with Christine Breyhan in *Kunstforum International,* no. 146, July-August 1999.

On KABAKOV: Books—*Ilya Kabakov's Everyday Art* by H. Huttel, Billefeld 1985; *Ordinary Spaces, Ordinary Voices* by H. Gunther, Billefeld 1985; *The Theme of Rubbish in Kabakov's Art* by Boris Groys, Billefeld 1985; *Kabakov,* exhibition catalog with essay by Bertrand Lorquin, Paris 1991; *Kabakov,* exhibition catalog, Rome 1992; *Ilya Kabakov,* exhibition catalog, Paris 1992; *Culture or Trash* by James Gardner, New York 1993; *Ilya Kabakov: Five Albums,* exhibition catalog, Helsinki 1994; ; *Ilya Kabakov: Soppelmannen—The Garbage Man* by Boris Groys, Oslo 1996; *Ilya Kabakov* by Boris Groys, David A. Ross and Iwona Blazwick, London 1998. **Articles**—interview with Robert Storr in *Art in America* (New York), vol. 83, no. 1, January 1995; ''A Psychodrome of Misreading: Ilya Kabakov and Harold Bloom'' by Viktor Tupitsyn in *Third Text,* no. 33, Winter 1995–1996; ''Ilya Kabakov'' by Gerhard Mack in *Kunstler,* no. 33, 1996; ''Ilya Kabakov: The Secret Anthropologist'' by Robert Storr in *Tate: The Art Magazine,* no. 10, Winter 1996; ''Ilya Kabakov: Zwei Folgen aus 'Ten Characters''' by Johannes Meinhardt in *Kunstforum International,* no. 147, September-November 1999; ''Ilya Kabakov Flies into His Pictures'' by Amei Wallach in *Art in America* (New York), vol. 88, no. 11, November 2000.

KAC, Eduardo

Nationality: Brazilian. **Born:** Rio de Janeiro, Brazil, 1962. **Education:** School of Communications, Pontifícia Universidade Católica, Rio de Janeiro, B.A., 1985; School of the Art Institute of Chicago, M.F.A., 1990; Center for Advanced Inquiry in the Interactive Arts, University of Wales College, Newport, United Kingdom, Ph.D. candidate, since 1998. **Career:** Involved with linguistic forms in holography since 1983; involved with computers and telecommunications art events since 1985; artist-in-residence, Museum of Holography, New York, 1986; involved with the Ornitorrinco project of telepresence installations since 1989; member of the Editorial Board, *Leonardo,* 1995–2000; member of the Editorial Board, International Directory of Electronic Art, Kaos, Paris, 1997. Assistant Professor of Art and Technology, Art and Technology Department, School of the Art Institute of Chicago. **Awards:** Acquisition Prize, VII Salão Nacional de Artes Plásticas, Museu de Arte Moderna, Rio de Janeiro, 1985; New Forms Grant, Randolph Street Gallery, Chicago/National Endowment for the Arts, 1991; First Place, Siggraph's Education Committee Animation Competition, 1992; City of Chicago Department of Cultural Affairs CAAP Grant, Chicago, 1993 and 1994; Shearwater Holography Award, Shearwater Foundation, Fort Lauderdale, Florida, 1995, 1997, and 1998; ArtsLink Award, CEC International Partners, New York, 1998; Leonardo Award for Excellence, International Society for the Arts, Sciences and Technology, 1998; ICC Biennale Award, InterCommunication Center, Tokyo, 1999. **Web site:** http://www.ekac.org.

Selected Individual Exhibitions:

1982 Biblioteca Central, Pontifícia Universidade Católica, Rio de Janeiro
1984 *Eletropoesia,* Centro Cultural Cândido Mendes, Rio de Janeiro
1985 *Holopoesia,* Museu da Imagem e do Som, São Paulo; Escola de Artes Visuais do Parque Lage, Rio de Janeiro
1986 *Holopoesia-2,* Fundação Nacional de Arte, Rio de Janeiro (catalog)
1988 *Holofractal,* Fundação Nacional de Arte, Rio de Janeiro (catalog)
1990 *Holopoetry 1983–1990,* Museum of Holography, New York (catalog)
1991 *New Holopoems,* Museu de Arte Moderna, Rio de Janeiro
1994 Center for Contemporary Art, University of Kentucky, Lexington
1997 West Gallery, California State University, Fullerton
1998 *Language Works,* Aldo Castillo Gallery, Chicago
Teleporting an Unknown State, Kibla Art Gallery, Maribor, Slovenia (catalog)

Selected Group Exhibitions:

1982 *Mostra de Arte Postal,* Galeria de Arte Cândido Mendes, Rio de Janeiro
14 Noites de Performance, Sesc Pompéia, São Paulo
1983 *Salão Nacional,* Museu de Arte Moderna, Rio de Janeiro (catalog)
Telegraphy and Mail Art Projects, Hasselt Museum, Belgium (catalog)
Mostra Internacionale di Arte Postale, Sala Pace, Rome
1984 *Arte na Rua-2,* Museu de Arte Contemporânea, São Paulo (catalog)
Como vai você, Geração 80?, Escola de Artes Visuais do Parque Lage, Rio de Janeiro (catalog)
Intervenções no Espaço Urbano, Fundação Nacional de Arte, Rio de Janeiro
Arte Xerox Brasil, Pinacoteca do Estado de São Paulo (catalog)
1985 *Exhibition of Holography,* School of The Art Institute of Chicago
Salão Nacional, Museu de Arte Moderna, Rio de Janeiro (catalog)
Arte e Tecnologia, Museu de Arte Contemporânea, São Paulo
Arte Novos Meios/Multimeios 70/80, Fundação A. Álvares Penteado, São Paulo (catalog)
1986 *Brasil High Tech,* Galeria de Arte Centro Empresarial Rio, Rio de Janeiro (catalog)
Polaroid, Fundação Nacional de Arte, Rio de Janeiro (catalog)
Território Ocupado, Escola de Artes Visuais do Parque Lage, Rio de Janeiro (catalog)
Salão Nacional-Sudeste, Palácio das Artes, Belo Horizonte, Brazil
1987 *I Festival Internacional de Poesia Viva,* Museu Municipal, Figueira da Foz, Portugal (catalog)
Salão Paulista, Pinacoteca do Estado de São Paulo
Arte e Palavra, Forum de Ciência e Cultura, Universidade Federal, Rio de Janeiro (catalog)
Arte Holográfica, Universidade Federal de Goiás, Goiânia, Brazil
1988 *Arte High Tech,* Galeria Diferença, Lisbon
1990 *Cyberthon: A 24-hour Adventure in Virtual Reality,* Colossal Pictures, San Francisco
City Portrait, Gallerie Donguy, Paris
Laser Exhibit, Holos Gallery, San Francisco
1991 *Beyond Photography,* Laguna Gloria Art Museum, Austin, Texas (traveled through 1993) (catalog)
Emerging Expressions Biennial: The Third Dimension and Beyond, Bronx Museum of the Arts, New York
Siggraph Art Show, Las Vegas Convention Center (catalog)
The Fourth International Exhibition of Holography, Durand Art Institute, Lake Forest College, Lake Forest, Illinois (catalog)
1992 *Avanguardia dell'Arte Olografica,* Centro Espositivo Rocca Paolina, Perugia, Italy (catalog)
Artistic States of Light, Museum of Holography, Chicago
Third International Symposium on Electronic Art, Black Gallery, Sydney; Institute of Modern Art, Brisbane, Queensland, Australia (catalog)
The Earth and the Frequencies of Life Art, Science and Technology Institute, Washington, D.C.
1993 *Entgrenzte Grenzen II,* Künstlerhaus, Graz, Austria (catalog)
Montage '93, Strong Museum, Rochester, New York
Third International Conference on Word and Image Studies, Carleton University Art Gallery, Ottawa, Canada
Fourth International Symposium on Electronic Art, Minneapolis College of Art and Design Gallery (catalog)
1994 *Elastic Visions,* Zoller Gallery, College of Arts and Architecture, Pennsylvania State University, University Park (traveled through 1997) (catalog)
Computer Graphics in the Fine Arts I, Medium Gallery, Academy of Fine Arts and Design, Bratislava, Slovakia (catalog)
Seriality/Randomness, Kalisher Five Gallery, Tel Aviv, Israel

Mostra de Realidade Virtual, Centro Cultural Cândido Mendes, Rio de Janeiro (catalog)

1995 *Electronic Art 95,* Rauma Art Museum, Finland; Kuopio Art Museum, Finland (catalog)

Emerging Images, Susquehanna Art Museum, Harrisburg, Pennsylvania (catalog)

Arte no Século XXI, Museu de Arte Contemporânea-USP, São Paulo, Brazil (catalog)

1996 *Out of Bounds: New Work by Eight Southeast Artists,* Nexus Contemporary Art, Atlanta; Archer M. Huntington Art Gallery, University of Texas, Austin (catalog and CD-rom)

The Bridge, Contemporary Art Center, New Orleans (catalog)

Holographic Network, Akademie der Künste, Berlin (catalog)

KYSC/ny, National Arts Club, New York (catalog)

1997 *Diffraction and Interference: The Holographic Image,* Hopkins Hall Gallery, Ohio State University, Columbus

CyberForum, Centro Cultural de Belém, Lisbon (catalog)

I Bienal do Mercosul, Porto Alegre, Rio Grande do Sul, Brazil (catalog)

International Symposium on Electronic Art-ISEA, School of The Art Institute of Chicago

1998 IMMEDIA98, University of Michigan, Ann Arbor

3° VideoSoundPoetry Festival, Link Bologna—Galleria d'Arte Moderna, Bologna

Ars Interruptus, Festival de Vídeo de Navarra, Pamplona, Spain

1999 Ars Electronica, OK Center for Contemporary Art, Linz, Austria (catalog)

ICC Biennale, Tokyo, Japan (catalog)

Holographic Art, Rauma Art Museum, Finland (traveled to: Kajaani Art Museum, Finland; Kuopio Art Museum, Finland; Kemi Art Museum, Finland; Salo Art Museum, Finland; Norrtälje konsthall, Sweden) (catalog)

Paranoiquear: Monitoring Cyber Art in Latinamerica, Museum of Modern Art Juan Astorga Anta, Merida, Venezuela

Collections:

Museum of Modern Art, New York; Museum of Holography, Chicago; Museu de Arte Moderna, Rio de Janeiro; Museum of Holography, New York; Museu Nacional de Belas Artes, Rio de Janeiro; Harvard University, Houghton Library, Department of Printing and Graphic Arts, Cambridge, Massachusetts; Museo Internacional de Electrografia, Cuenca, Spain; Joan Flasch Artists' Books Collection, Chicago; University of New Mexico, General Library, Albuquerque; Karas Studios, Madrid, Spain; Light-Wave Galleries, Chicago; Light-Wave Galleries, Detroit; Light-Wave Galleries, San Francisco; Ruth and Marvin Sackner Archive of Concrete and Visual Poetry, Miami; Academy of Fine Arts and Design, Bratislava, Slovakia.

Publications:

By KAC: Articles—''Poesia holográfica: A ruptura fotônica'' in *Módulo,* July 1985; ''Holopoetry and perceptual syntax'' in *Holosphere,* 1986; ''Holopoésie et dimension fractale'' in *Colóquio Artes,* 1987; ''Holopoetry and Fractal Holopoetry: Digital Holography as an Art Medium'' in *Leonardo,* 1990; ''Holopoem Blends Pulsed and Computer Holography'' with Hans Bjelkhagen in *Laser News,* 1991; ''Towards Telepresence Art'' in *Interface,* November 1992; ''Holopoetry Explores Metamorphosis and Particle Animation'' in *Laser News,* 1993; ''Storms, a Hyperpoem'' in *Leonardo Electronic Almanac,* June 1994; ''Beyond the Spatial Paradigm: Time and Cinematic Form in Holographic Art'' in *BLIMP Film Magazine,* fall 1995; ''Holopoetry'' in *Visible Language,* 1996; ''Foundation and Development of Robotic Art'' in *Art Journal,* 1997; ''L'art de la Téléprésence sur l'Internet'' in *Alliage,* 1998; ''New Directions in Interactive Art'' in *Blimp,* 1999; ''Telepresence Art and Net Ecology'' in *The Robot in the Garden: Telerobotics and Telepistemology on the Internet,* Cambridge, Massachusetts, 2000.

On KAC: Books—*Eduardo Kac: Teleporting an Unkown State* edited by Peter Tomaz Dobrila and Aleksandra Kostic, Maribor, Slovenia, 1998; *Eduardo Kac: Telepresence, Biotelematics, Transgenic Art* edited by Peter Tomaz Dobrila and Aleksandra Kostic, Maribor, Slovenia, 2000. **Articles**—''Data Bank: Eduardo Kac'' by Maria Victoria Infantes in *Revistita Karas,* July 1993; ''Telepresence and Holography: The New Media of Eduardo Kac'' by Joyce Probus in *Kultur,* 1994; ''Eduardo Kac: Language Works'' by Pablo Helguera in *Art Nexus,* February-April 1999; ''Eduardo Kac défricheur et visionnaire'' by Annick Bureaud in *Artpress,* May 1999; ''Eduardo Kac: Interview'' by Daniele Perra in *Tema Celeste,* July-September 2000; ''Kacs Zeitkapsel: Selbsteinkapselung'' by Steve Tomasula in *Kunstforum,* July-September 2000. **Films**—*Eduardo Kac: Eight Dialogues* by Bruno Vianna, 2000.

* * *

Eduardo Kac is an artist whose works deal with issues that range from the Mythopoetics of Online Experience to the cultural impact of biotechnology, from the changing condition of memory in the digital age to distributed collective agency, from the problematic notion of the ''exotic'' to the creation of life and evolution. This great variety in the intellectual and artistic pursuits of Eduardo Kac is accompagnied by an exceptional courage in the choice and accomplishment of his daring projects.

After creating in 1980 a performance group focused on public interventions and undertaking regular performances on beaches, squares, in theatres, and on television he made experiments with multiple media and processes, including graffiti, photography, and visual poetry. This led in 1983 to his inventing Holopoetry. His holographic poems are essentially holograms that address language both as material and subject matter. These holograms do not rest quietly on the surface. When the viewer starts to look for words and their links, the texts will transform themselves, change in colour and meaning, coalesce and disappear.

In 1986, several years before the full advent of the Internet, Kac first proposed the term of ''telepresent art'' and pioneered this art which can be defined as the coupling of telecommunications and telerobotics, i.e. the projection of one's sense of presence to a remote space. It can also be defined as a remote agency, i.e. the ability to affect a remote physical space through the network.

Among Kac's telepresence art works ''Ornitorrinco'' was constantly developed between 1989 and 1996. ''Ornitorrinco,'' which means platypus in Portuguese, is the name of both a series of telepresence art installations and the telerobot used to realize them. This noun was chosen as the robot's name because of the unique nature of the platypus, which is popularly thought of as a hybrid of bird and mammal. The objective was to imply kinship between the organic (animal) and the inorganic (telerobot).

Ornitorrinco events always involve at least two locations geographically remote from each other and implicate one or more members of the public, who navigate at a remote location by pressing keys on a telephone keypad and receive visual feedback in the form of still or moving images on a computer or video monitor. The first international Ornitorrinco event linked Chicago and Rio de Janeiro in 1990; another, ''Ornitorrinco in Eden,'' spanned the placeless space of the Internet with physical spaces like Seattle, Chicago, and Lexington, Kentucky, linking these three nodes of active participation with the multiple nods of observation world-wide. Other important telepresence artworks by Kac included ''Rara Avis'' (1996) and ''Uirapuru'' (1999) which received a reward at the ICC Biennale that year.

From 1994 onwards, Kac expanded telematic art into a biological domain, thus creating an art form which he called ''Biotelematics.'' His first biotelematic work was named ''Essay Concerning Human Understanding.'' This was followed by ''Teleporting an Unknown State'' (1994–1996), a classic of telematic art, and by ''Time Capsule'' (1997). This latter work required considerable courage since the artist had a microchip with a programmed identification number subcutaneously inserted into his left leg at an event that took place in Sao Paulo, Brazil. Kac placed his leg into a scanning apparatus, and his ankle was then webscanned from Chicago. Kac subsequently registered himself in a Web-based animal identification database, originally designed for the recovery of lost animals. It was the first time a human being was added to the database—Kac registered himself both as animal and owner. The event was shown live on television in Brazil and on the Web.

In 1997, Kac proposed the term ''Biorobotics'' in the context of the artwork ''A-positive.'' Biorobotics proposes that in the future robots will have biological elements inside their bodies performing specific functions. This was followed, one year later, by the coining of the notion of ''Transgenic Art'' for a project that envisaged the creation of a green, fluorescent dog and its social integration. In 1999, Kac first presented his transgenic artwork ''Genesis'' at Ars Electronica in Linz, Austria, and again a year later, he created the revolutionary artwork ''GFP Bunny.'' This transgenic work comprises the creation of a green fluorescent (protein) rabbit named ''Alba,'' its social integration and also the ensuing debate. ''GFP Bunny'' was actually realized that year and was first presented publicly in Avignon, France.

''Transgenic Art'' is an art form based on the use of genetic engineering to transfer natural or synthetic genes to an organism to create unique living beings. Kac is conscious of the fact that this must be done with great care, with acknowledgment of the complex issues thus raised and, above all, with a commitment to respect, nurture, and love the life thus created. However, Kac insists that the formal and genetic uniqueness of the animal is not the only component of the ''GFP Bunny'' artwork, but that it includes at its core an ongoing dialogue between professionals of several disciplines and the public on the cultural and ethical implications of genetic engineering.

The impact of Eduardo Kac's ''Transgenic Art'' and in particular the daring animal experiments on the contemporary art scene has been considerable, but one can see the whole of the artist's audacious inventions and achievements as a decisive contribution in the realm of biotechnological and telecommunication art.

—Frank Popper

KALINOWSKI, Horst Egon

Nationality: German. **Born:** Dusseldorf, 2 January 1924. **Education:** Staatliche Kunstakademie, Dusseldorf, 1945–48; Académie de la Grande Chaumiére, under Jean Dewasne, Paris, 1950–52. **Career:** Travelled in Rome and Venice, 1949–50. Independent artist, since 1952: first collages and assemblages, 1956; first stage designs, 1959; first caisson sculptures, 1960; first lithographs, 1963. Professor, Kunstakademie, Karlsruhe, 1968–89. **Member:** Preussische Akademie der Bildenden Künste, Berlin. **Awards:** Carl Einstein Prize, Essen, West Germany, 1966; First Prize in Sculpture, Haus der kunst, Munich, 1967; Burda Prize, 1967; Heitland Foundation Prize, Celle, 1992; Preis des Freundeskreises des Künstlerbundes Baden-Württemberg, 1994. **Agent:** Galerie Rothe, Werderplatz 17, Heidelberg. **Address:** c/o Staatliche Akademie der Bildende Künste, Reinhold Frankstrasse 81, 7500 Karlsruhe, West Germany.

Individual Exhibitions:

1953 Galerie Arnaud, Paris
1954 Galerie Arnaud, Paris
1955 Galerie Arnaud, Paris
Galerie Franck, Frankfurt
1956 Galerie St. Laurent, Brussels
Galerie Creuze, Paris
1957 Galerie Franck, Frankfurt
Galerie Accent, Antwerp
Galerie St. Laurent, Brussels
Galerie Creuze, Paris
1958 Galerie Daniel Cordier, Paris
1959 Galerie 22, Dusseldorf
1961 Gallery Krzywe Kolo, Warsaw
1962 Robert Fraser Gallery, London (twice)
Galerie Chave, Vence, France
Galerie Daniel Cordier, Paris
1963 Galerie Daniel Cordier, Paris
1964 Robert Fraser Gallery, London
Galerie Rothe, Heidelberg
Galerie Miniature, Berlin
Cordier-Ekstrom Gallery, New York
1966 Galerie Rothe, Heidelberg
Cordier-Ekstrom Gallery, New York
1967 Städtische Kunsthalle, Mannheim (toured West Germany)
1969 *Caissons et Stèles 1961–1969,* Centre National d'Art Contemporain, Paris
Galerie Rothe, Heidelberg
Kestner-Gesellschaft, Hannover
Kunst und Kunstgewerberverein, Pforzheim
Lefebre Gallery, New York
1970 Makler Gallery, Philadelphia
1971 Galerie Charles Lienhard, Basle
Caissons Ensachements 1970–71. Galerie Rothe, Heidelberg
1972 Kunstverein, Kassel
Kunstverein, Cologne
1973 Chateau d'Ancy-Le-Franc, France
Galerie Defet, Nuremberg
1974 Kunstverein, Trier, West Germany
Goethe-Institut, Marseilles

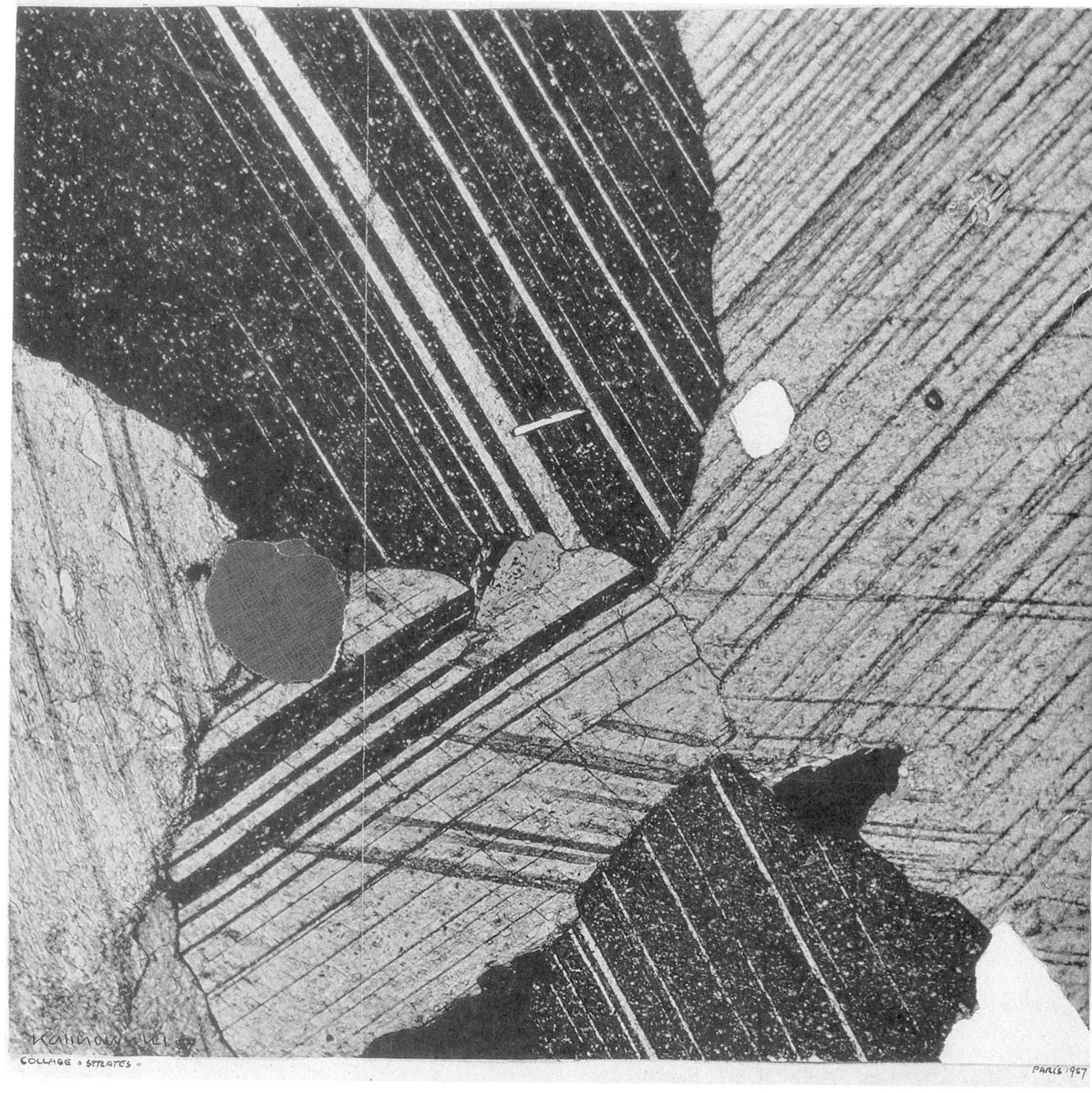

Horst Egon Kalinowski: *Strates,* 1957. ©CNAC/MNAM/Dist. Réunion des Musées Nationaux/Art Resource, NY; courtesy of Musee National d'Art Moderne, Centre Georges Pompidou, Paris, France.

Galerie Athanor, Marseilles
Goethe-Institut, Paris
Galerie Marcel Billiot, Paris
Galerie Rothe, Heidelberg
1975 Kunstforum, Bensheim, West Germany
1976 Galerie Rothe, Heidelberg
1977 Kunstmuseum, Dusseldorf
Galerie Rothe, Heidelberg
1978 Neue Galerie, Aachen
Kunsthalle, Mannheim
1979 Kunsthalle, Bremen
Galerie Hilbur, Karlsruhe
1980 Galerie von Laar, Munich
1981 Galerie Rehklau, Augsburg
Objekte 1975–80, Galerie Rothe, Heidelberg
1982 *Objekte, Reliefs, Ensachements, Termes,* Kunsthalle, Darmstadt
Kleine Grafikgalerie, Bremen
Kunstverein, Freiburg im Breisgau, West Germany
1983 Galerie Rothe, Heidelberg
1985 Galerie von Laar, Munich
Deutsches Ledermuseum, Offenbach, West Germany

Markuskirche, Frankfurt-Nied, West Germany
1986 Kunstverein, Kirchzarten, West Germany
1987 Arbeitskreis Galerie im Ganserhaus, Wasserburg, West Germany
Galerie Rothe, at *FIAC 87,* Grand Palais, Paris
1988 Kunstverein, Albstadt, West Germany
1989 *Horst Egon Kalinowski: Examples of Works 1956–1988,* Badischer Kunstverein, Karlsruhe, Germany
1990 Galerie Albert Loeb, Paris
1991 L'hillodrome, Centre d'Action Culturelle de Douai
1995 Galerie Boisserée, Köln
Galerie Rothe, Frankfurt am Main
1996 Galerie Fritz Winterhaus, Ahlen
Dommuseum, Frankfurt am Main
1998 Kunstverein Niebüll

Selected Group Exhibitions:

1956 *Divergences,* Stedelijk Museum, Amsterdam
1958 *Exposition Phases,* Galerie St. Laurent, Brussels
1959 *Phases,* Galerie Krzysztofory, Cracow
1963 *Art of Assemblage,* Museum of Modern Art, New York
1965 *Carnegie International,* Carnegie Institute, Pittsburgh
1968 *Art Vivant 1965–1968,* Fondation Maeght, St. Paul de Vence, France
1978 *Idee, Konzept und Werk,* Akademie der Bildenden Künste, Berlin
1981 *Dimensions des Plastischen,* Bildhauertechniken Neuer Berliner Kunsteverein in der Staat Kunsthalle, Berlin
1986 *Internationale Bildhauer Triennale,* Fellbach, West Germany
1987 *Europaischer Manierismus,* Kunsthaus, Vienna

Collections:

Neue Nationalgalerie, Berlin; Kunstmuseum, Dusseldorf; Galerie Rothe, Heidelberg; Städtische Kunstsammlungen, Bonn; Rheinisches Landesmuseum, Bonn; Wallraf-Richartz Museum, Cologne; Centre Georges Pompidou, Paris; Moderna Museet, Stockholm; Victoria and Albert Museum, London; Museum of Modern Art, New York.

Publications:

On KALINOWSKI: Books—*Kalinowski,* exhibition catalog, with text by Wieland Schmied and Frantisek Smejkal, Hannover 1969; *Kalinowski: Caissons et Stèles 1961–1969,* exhibition catalog with text by Frantisek Smejkal, Alain Bosquet, Heinz Fuchs and Gerard Gassiot-Talabot, Paris 1969; *Horst Egon Kalinowski,* exhibition catalog with text by Alain Bosquet, New York 1969; *Kalinowski: Caissons Ensachements 1970–71,* exhibition catalog with text by Franz Josef van der Grinten, Heidelberg 1971; *Kalinowski,* with texts by Jean Dewasne, Pierre Bettencourt, and Pol Bury, Stuttgart 1975; *Kalinowski: Zeichnungen/Dessins, Bilder, Tableaux, Caissons,* exhibition catalog with texts by Wolfgang Becker and Andreas Franzke, Aachen 1978; *Kalinowski: Objekte 1975–80,* exhibition catalog, Heidelberg 1981; *Kalinowski: Objekte, Reliefs, Ensachements, Termes,* exhibition catalog with text by Heusinger von Waldegg and Dr. Sperlich, Darmstadt 1982; *Kalinowski: Collagen und Bildschreine,* with text by Hans Hoffstätter and Dr. Ludwig, Heidelberg 1982; *Kalinowski:Papiers collés,* exhibition catalog with text by Rainer Malkowski, Heidelberg 1983; *Kalinowski: Bandreliefs,* exhibition catalog with text by Heusinger von Waldegg, Heidelberg 1985; *Horst Egon Kalinowski: Examples of Works 1956–1988,* exhibition catalog with text by Andreas Vowinckel, Karlsruhe 1989. **Article—**''Horst Egon Kalinowsky: A Mysticism of the Skin'' by Gilles Lipovetsky in *Cimaise,* vol. 36, September/October 1989.

*

My caissons have always been containers as far as I was concerned. Their architecture enclosed a 'content', and their leather covering was intended to signify defence and protection. Leather has always possessed that function. Human beings used to protect themselves against the weather with animal hides; then came the loin cloth and the leather apron, the helmet, cuirass and glove. Water hose and bottle were made of leather; even tents were rooms made of leather. It is according to these particular qualities of leather that I have developed my caissons. The dimensions of the old bits of leather used in these designs determine the final form. The overall shape is simple and geometrical in order to accommodate flat surfaces and partitions on which the grained material is stuck and nailed. The spectator is thus presented with an empirical object to which he relates physically. The question I am frequently asked—what kind of leather do I use, or where do I find it?—is of no importance to me. I am primarily concerned with 'skin'. The experience and observation of the skin is my starting point.

The diverse forms of my objects, be they more geometric-static or more soft-organic, 'contain' within them IMAGINATION. They may be regarded as sexual, cryptic, repellent, sinister or magical, but such descriptions merely serve the spectator's need for associations, since only once he can name it does he banish the threat of an alien object. I do my best to achieve a direct, literally skin-tight relationship between the spectator and my objects so that they appear to him as part of an additional reality, They are meant to affect him physically, to disturb him. His hand should feel compelled to touch, but in the moment of advancing to hesitate, out of fear that the object, at present immobile, might suddenly move. The anatomy as the expression of symmetry and the forms of vegetative life support the conception on which my works are based. Awareness of form determines the first, while a fluent softness defines the second. Both obey the aim of assimilating the notion of life and death with that of untearable skin.

—Horst Egon Kalinowski

* * *

In one's mind it is hard to divorce Horst Egon Kalinowski from his leathern *caissons* and *steles*. It is for these works that he is best known and, in personal terms, they are the outward forms of his thought and being. Nevertheless, they represent a stage in his career that was reached after that sundry and perhaps routine struggling through which the artist must pass before he finds his natural style.

By the time he was 26 Kalinowski had already become a non-figurative painter, but by 1956 he was at work upon collages and ''objects.'' The cases and the sepulchral tablets and portways first appeared in 1965, although evidence presaging their imminent arrival was seen in London in 1962 and 1964.

These caissons and steles are hermetic in character and in gestation. Kalinowski is not reticent about what they signify. These objects clad in leather are for him outside the debris of material existence. They are magical in the antique sense that emanates from the sacred paraphernalia of primitive societies. Messages from the unknown. As the artist puts it: "I want to get from this same magic presence that which flows from ritual objects." His work is his expression of his inner experiences. Intensely *human* (they frequently relate to torsos, backbone vertebrae, shoulders, eyes, tailbone, ears and sexual organs), they have, besides their mystery, a poetic resonance, and, well aware of this characteristic, Kalinowski gives to them poetic titles.

Those who seek here for a geometry will in many cases find it, but it is a geometry softened by its leather skin and invaded by the occult gravity of ancient secrets, all of which, in Kalinowski's work, take palpable form. The unity of monumentality, awesomeness, mystery and emotional contact makes these caissons and steles exceptionally tactile.

They have undoubtedly added their own (and new) vocabulary to the language of modern art.

—Sheldon Williams

KALMBACH, Michael

Nationality: German. **Born:** Landau, Pfalz, Germany, 7 May 1962. **Education:** Studied under Michael Croissant, Städelschule, Staatliche Schule für Bildende Künste, Frankfurt am Main, 1983–1989. **Awards:** Rhineland Palatinate State Scholarship (to attend the Künstlerhaus Edenkoben), 1987–88; German National Merit Scholarship to Study Abroad (New York), 1989–90; Support Prize, Frankfurter Künstlerhilfe e.V., 1996; Hessen Ministry of Science and Art, work stipend, 1997; Hessen Cultural Foundation, Wiesbaden, travel stipend, 1999; Karl Ströher Prize, Museum für Moderne Kunst, Frankfurt/Main, 1999; Kunstfond e.V., work stipend, Bonn, 2000. **Agents:** Thomas Rehbein Galerie, Maria-Hilf-Strasse 17, 50677 Köln, Germany; Ausstellungsraum de Ligt, Oppenheimer Strasse 34a, 60594 Frankfurt, Germany. **Address:** Kaiser-Friedrichstrasse 35, 10627 Berlin, Germany.

Selected Individual Exhibitions:

1988 Forum der Stadtsparkasse, Frankfurt am Main
1992 Galerie Ute Parduhn, Düsseldorf (with Peter Schubert)
1995 *Jürgen und Michael am Brunnen,* Florian Haas and Martin Schmidle, Frankfurt am Main (with Jürgen Kisch)
1998 Förderkoje Thomas Rehbein Galerie, Art Cologne, Köln
1999 *Untersuchungshäftlinge,* Galerie Malinowski de Ligt, Frankfurt am Main, Germany
2000 *Diverse Hintergründe,* Ausstellungsraum de Ligt, Frankfurt am Main, Germany

Selected Group Exhibitions:

1985 *Kunst in Frankfurt,* Kunstverein Frankfurt am Main, Germany
1988 Künstlerhaus Edenkoben, Germany
1995 *Auf die Straße Gesetzt,* Neuer Kunstverein Aschaffenburg, Germany (catalog)
1999 *Szenenwechsel XVI,* Museum für Moderne Kunst, Frankfurt am Main, Germany
2000 *One of Those Days,* Mannheimer Kunstverein, Germany
2000–01 *Kabinett der Zeichnung,* Kunstverein für die Rheinlande und Westfalen, Düsseldorf (traveled to Kunstverein Lingen; Kunstsammlung Chemnitz; Kunstverein Stuttgart)

Collections:

Museum für Moderne Kunst, Frankfurt am Main, Germany; Diözesanmuseum Köln, Germany; Kupferstichkabinett, Öffentliche Kunstsammlung Basel, Switzerland.

Publications:

By KALMBACH: Book—*Jürgen und Michael am Brunnen,* with Jürgen Kisch, Frankfurt 1996.

On KALMBACH: Book—*Michael Kalmbach* by Jean-Christophe Ammann, Natalie de Ligt, Kerstin Thomas, and Claus Zittel, Frankfurt am Main, Germany 2000. **Article**—Janneke de Vries in *Artist,* no. 40, vol. 3, 1999; Janneke de Vries in *Art Kaleidoscope,* No. 1–01.

* * *

Facts and dates are the essence of today's life. We are to stick to the real and the actual everywhere we go and hardly anyone dares to enter the slippery road of magical and metaphysical imaginations. Fantasy and creative doubts are, at best, merely supporting acts on the positivistic world stage.

Michael Kalmbach, however, has certainly acquired a taste for fairy tales and myths. And he is still completely grounded in the present. His strange creatures made from plaster or on paper tell of the realms beyond our sober perception of the world. But perhaps the fairy tale is not as far away from reality as it appears on first sight. It also tells fantastically encrypted and exaggerated stories about real conditions. Those stories speak of love and violence, betrayal and power, longing and feelings of loss. In short: of issues that shake us in our down-to-earth reality. They speak of this in their own language. And this brings us back to Michael Kalmbach.

But Kalmbach hints at things rather than putting them into a scene unmistakably, and he rather creates a basis for association than presents clear-cut statements. This openness is especially dominant in his plaster sculptures. Puckish figures appear in abstract landscapes, the limbs of fragment-like creatures stretch over a wall like the arms of octopi and entangle in the most different formations. Strange head mutations spout water into plastic buckets and mollusk-like shapes lie on the floor and stretch their plump fingers into the room. Kalmbach's white creations are often connected with the wall, as if they were its weird offspring.

Typical for Kalmbach's plaster creatures is their oscillation between narrative and formal aspects, between the representational and the abstract. The Pinocchio-like doll can, for example, be taken apart into different form modules and the small head with the round cheeks and the grotesquely protruding ears consists of circular forms of various sizes. Going back and forth between abstract and representational aspects stands for openness between the known and the unknown, between reality and a dream world.

Kalmbach's method of casting organ-like forms in plaster and combining them in ever-new creations defines his plasterwork as an infinite process, in which finality does not exist. Using a module as an

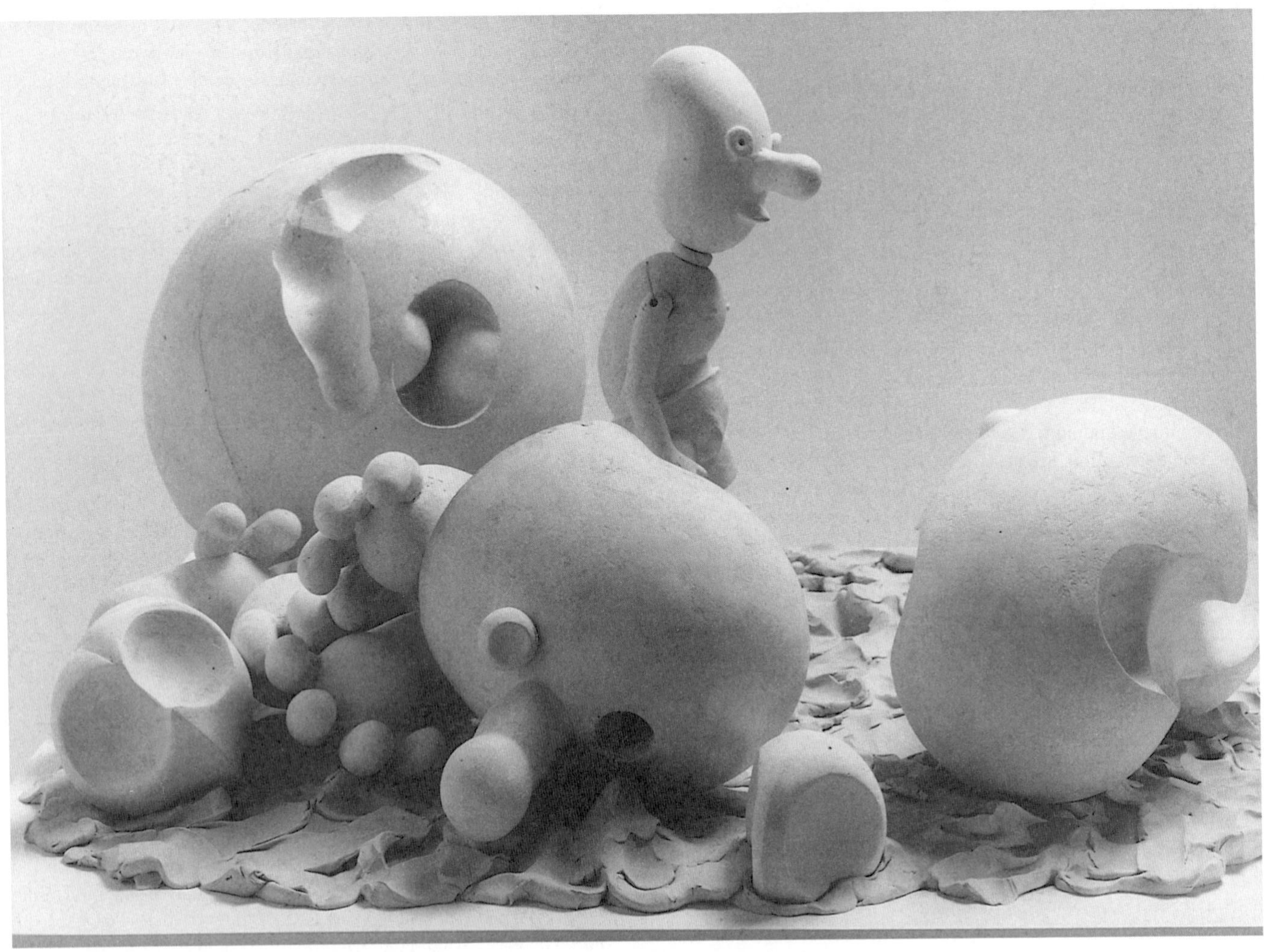

Michael Kalmbach: *Ohne Titel,* 1997. Photo by Axel Schneider, courtesy of Museum Für Moderne Kunst. ©Michael Kalmbach.

arm does not prevent it from ending up as a head or as a means to sit on in a different context. Thus the artist's studio resembles an accumulation of spare parts, in which plaster models of all sizes and shapes wait to be turned into noses, torsi, or parts of a landscape.

Kalmbach's drawings and paintings demand as much space in his artistic work as his sculptures. They are neither sketches for the plaster scenarios nor their post processing, but rather they explore the same themes on a different terrain. The human figure is again at the center—often alone and moving through the picture realm as if on the search, but also questioning its relationship with others where the artist places more than one into the picture. Formally the paper works for the most part detach themselves from the sculptural works' variation of abstract forms and are more grounded in the representational. Kalmbach often uses a subtly graded, warm color palette that clearly distinguishes itself from the clear white of his plaster creations. But explicit and clear-cut statements are again not part of his work. The sheets are ambivalent and can be read in many different ways.

On first sight, the works tempt the beholder to enter a path of playfully naive cuteness. Kalmbach, however, does not present peaceful harmony, but poses the question of his figures' position in the world. He is thereby often pitiless and sometimes even aggressive, always loving and never moralizing. He asks questions of their being at a loss and their longing for security and comfort, of dependencies in their relationships with each other—and always asks about the body, its various needs and the joys and difficulties caused by it.

One work that formally and technically differs significantly from Kalmbach's other creations is named ''Untersuchungshäftlinge'' (Prisoners on Remand): 65 small figures created from glazed and baked clay are standing placidly in an upright position. All are wearing blue prisoner garments, the arms are hanging beside the body. But what seems to be the representation of an anonymous mass turns out to be the assembly of individuals and single portraits. The artist has carefully created differences in clothing, figures, facial features, and hair. A white shirt stretches over a beer belly on one figure while his neighbor has carefully buttoned a jacket up to under his chin. One is wearing a mustache and hackle, the next has a neat short haircut, and another a pony tail and glasses. The ''Untersuchungshäftlinge'' plead for the individual and for the respect and dignity of each person, especially where it seems impossible to detect the special within the general. They do not address the issue of an individual's guilt or innocence, and they do not mean to be a memorial or social critique. It is rather their factual existence, their this-is-what-we-are-and-nothing-else and their normality that is captured.

The awareness that the world undergoes constant changes is far from new. Only those that adapt to this phenomenon and are capable of taking on new viewpoints can deal with these changes. The one who remains static and propagates a single valid point of view cannot cope. In view of a flowing reality, we need everything that can open up different positions towards the real. This is what Michael Kalmbach does.

—Janneke de Vries

KANOVITZ, Howard

Nationality: American. **Born:** Fall River, Massachusetts, 9 February 1929. **Education:** Providence College, Rhode Island, 1945–49, B.S. 1949. Studied at Rhode Island School of Design, Providence, 1949–51; New School for Social Research, New York, 1951; and privately, with Franz Kline, New York, 1951–52. **Family:** Married Mary Rattray in 1961 (divorced 1990); daughter: Cleo. **Career:** Travelled as jazz musician in the United States, 1943–50; moved to New York, 1951; worked as window display artist, B. Altman, and freelance, New York, 1951–56; independent artist, since 1952; travelled extensively in France, Italy, Spain and Morocco, 1956–58; returned to New York, 1958; taught painting and design, Brooklyn College, New York, 1961–64; taught foundation design, Pratt Institute, New York, 1964–66; lived in Cologne, 1971–72, and in London, 1927–73; returned to New York, 1974; produced, directed and narrated film *Hampton's Drive-In,* New York, 1974; taught painting, Southhampton College, Southhampton, New York, 1977–78; lived and worked in Berlin, 1979; taught painting, School of Visual Arts, New York, 1981–85. **Awards:** DAAD Fellowship, to West Berlin, 1979. **Agent:** Galerie Inge Baecker, Zeughausstrasse 13, 50667 Cologne, Germany. **Address:** 361 No. Sea Mecox Rd., Southampton, New York 11968, U.S.A.

Individual Exhibitions:

1962 Stable Gallery, New York
1964 Fall River Art Association, Massachusetts
1966 Jewish Museum, New York
1969 Waddell Gallery, New York (twice)
1970 Galerie M. E. Thelen, Cologne
Benson Gallery, Bridgehampton, Long Island, New York
1971 Benson Gallery, Bridgehampton, Long Island, New York
Waddell Gallery, New York
Galerie Ostergren, Malmo, Sweden
Everyman Gallery, New York
1973 Galerie M. E. Thelen, Cologne
Hedendaagse Kunst, Utrecht
1974 Hedendaagse Kunst, Utrecht (retrospective)
Wilhelm Lehmbruck Museum, Duisburg, West Germany
1975 Stefanotty Gallery, New York
1977 Galerie Jollenbeck, Cologne
Benson Gallery, Bridgehampton, Long Island, New York
1978 Alex Rosenberg Gallery, New York
1979 Akademie der Künste, Berlin (retrospective)
Kestner-Gesellschaft, Hannover (retrospective)
Kunstverein, Freiburg (retrospective)
Forum Künste, Rottweil (retrospective)
1982 Alex Rosenberg Gallery, New York
1986 Benson Gallery, Southhampton, Long Island, New York
1987 Galerie Inge Baecker, Cologne
1988 Marlborough Gallery, New York
1988 Galerie Inge Baecker, Cologne
1989 Hokin Kaufman Gallery, Chicago
Galerie Gering-Kulenkampff, Frankfurt
1990 Marlborough Gallery, New York
A.J. Lederman Fine Art, Hoboken
Gana Art Gallery, Seoul, Korea
1991 Galerie Inge Baecker, Cologne
1995 Galerie Inge Baecker, Cologne
1997 Galerie Ulrich Gering, Cologne Kunstmarkt
1998 Nabi Gallery, Sag Harbor
1999 Galerie Inge Baecker, Cologne
2000 Clark Fine Art, Southampton, New York

Selected Group Exhibitions:

1971 *Radical Realism,* Museum of Contemporary Art, Chicago
1972 *Sharp Focus Realism,* Sidney Janis Gallery, New York
1973 *Photo-Realism,* Serpentine Gallery, London
1974 *American Hyperrealists, European Realists,* Kestner-Gessellschaft, Hannover (toured Europe)
1978 *Aspects of Realism,* Guild Hall, East Hampton, New York
1980 *Portraits Real and Imaginary,* Guild Hall, East Hampton, New York
1982 *Spiegel-Bilder,* Whilhelm-Lehmbruck Museum, Duisburg, West Germany (travelled to West Berlin)
1984 *Automobile and Culture,* Los Angeles Museum of Contemporary Art
1990 *20th Century Long Island Landscape Painting,* The Museum at Stony Brook, Brookhaven
1991 *Sammlung Onnasch,* Museum Weserberg, Bremen, Germany
1993 *Reflet-Restitution, Pop and Hyperrealist Sculpture,* Abbage St. André, Meymac, France
1995 Benson Gallery, Bridgehampton, New York
1997 *Creatures,* Benson Gallery, Bridgehampton, New York
1999 Nabi Gallery, Sag Harbor
2000 *Times Are Changing,* Kunsthalle Bremen, Germany

Collections:

Whitney Museum, New York; Museum of Art, Indianapolis; Ludwig Museum, Cologne; Wilhelm Lehmbruck Museum, Duisburg, West Germany; Museum Moderner Kunst, Vienna; Boymans van Beuningen Museum, Rotterdam; Museum of Contemporary Art, Utrecht; Sara Hilden Collection, Museum Atheneum, Helsinki; Hirschhorn Museum, Washington, D.C.; Metropolitan Museum of Art, New York; Tate Gallery, London; Kunsthalle Bremen, Germany.

Publications:

On KANOVITZ: Books—*Howard Kanovitz,* exhibition catalog by Sam Hunter, New York 1966; *Neue Formen des Bildes* by Udo Kultermann, Tubingen, West Germany 1969; *Howard Kanovitz,* exhibition catalog by Sam Hunter, New York 1969; *Howard Kanovitz,* exhibition catalog by Udo Kultermann, Cologne 1970; *Radikaler Realismus* by Udo Kultermann, Tübingen, West Germany 1972; *The Painter and the Photograph, from Delacroix to Warhol* by Van Deren Coke, Albuquerque, New Mexico 1972; *Sign and Image* by Ichiro Haryu, Tokyo 1973; *Man-Made Nature* by Yusuke Nakahara, Tokyo 1973; *American Art of the 20th Century* by Sam Hunter, New York 1973; *Kanovitz,* exhibition catalog by Udo Kultermann, Duisburg, West Germany 1974; *Howard Kanovitz,* exhibition catalog by Wouter Kotte, Utrecht 1974; *Howard Kanovitz,* exhibition catalog by Deiter Wellershoff, Cologne 1977; *Super Realism* by Edward Lucie Smith, London 1979; *Between Worlds: Howard Kanovitz,* exhibition catalog by Jorn Merkert, Berlin and Hannover 1979; *Howard Kanovitz: Works of the 1980s,* exhibition catalog with text by Peter Frank, New York 1988.

*

In the summer of 1965 I painted *Second Avenue Still Life* in tones of gray—a mess of art materials on a table in front of a window. The view, however, was set in place by a jet black grid of window pane dividers. This geometry presented an interesting format for observing the scene, a row of tenement buildings across Second Avenue. Later that year, when I was to paint *New Yorkers I* and *II*, I used this window view as a counterpoint to a group of friends circled around the poet, Frank O'Hara. It was not until 1968, when I began to isolate figures and objects as sculptural cut outs, that I introduced the Window as a theme.

The Studio Window (1968), painted on a shaped stretched canvas, was the first work in which I arrived at the illusion of a 3D object. It then seemed to me inevitable that I should move from window to wall, from wall to door. That year I painted *The Painting Wall and Waterbucket Stool* (1968), finding in these works a new hybrid which excited me because the depiction of the object and the object itself appeared as one.

In 1970 I exhibited in Germany for the first time at Galerie Joellenbeck, Koeln. My principal theme was the window and door as a sculptural cutout. Works such as *Cloud Window* (1970), *Open Studio Window* (1969) and *42 Britannia Walk* (1969) were the centerpieces of this exhibition.

I used elements of trompe l'oeil in 1971 in the painting *Projected Street Scene*. In it, I depicted a slide projection on a wall in a darkened room, and six photographs pinned to the wall. *Composition* and *One By Threes* of the same year, explored other facets of illusion and the image/object relationship. These three paintings were exhibited in Dokumenta 4.

In the London paintings of 1972–1973, the seemingly real and imagined share the same spotlight. *Chair Shadow* (1973) is a piece of wall in which a broken window dissolves along its edges. Below, a projection of a burning red sky is interrupted by the cool interior shadow of a chair. This shadow play, useful in its willingness to simplify, still identified the object. It also hinted at a source of light, which in many instances was artificial as that of a slide projector. Alongside this kind of illumination, a ''natural'' light was to be felt in the landscape of *Projected Man* 1977.

Light, then, became a principle player in *Moonlit Wall* (1984) and *Grand Piano (For the Dance)* (1987). There is an urge in these paintings to become objects, to partake of real space, but they are reluctant to fully enter. It is left to the painted wood and polymer constructions, *Gardiner's Bay* (1987), *River Edge* (1989) and *Night Harbor* (1989) to express relief in the third dimension.

—Howard Kanovitz

* * *

The work of Howard Kanovitz is one of the pioneering achievements toward the reintegration of the realist tradition into contemporary art. Along with parallel, but different, approaches by artists such as Philip Pearlstein, Alfred Leslie, Richard Estes, and Malcolm Morley, Kanovitz created a basis for a complex realism and the various facets that followed. His realism is a fresh reappraisal of the urban environment of New York in the 1960's and 70's and thus different from all the earlier types of realist painting. Among the several innovations of his artistic approach is the democratization of subject matter, which includes portraits of his friends, major figures of the New York art scene, banal objects taken from the daily environment of the artist, popular media imagery and objects from the world of advertising—all themes reflecting a specific and unique iconography and a real-life approach to the perception of a real environment.

Like the Florentine painters Masaccio, Andrea del Castagno and Uccello in their time, Kanovitz established methods by which it was possible to visually understand and represent the complex and sophisticated cultural milieu in his time. He developed a specific technique, including photography, opaque projection, and silk screen methods, and with these achieved an appropriate documentation of the multi-layered reality of the New York urban scene (*New Yorkers* of 1965; *The Opening* of 1967). In several of his works the process of the development of the painting remains visible to the viewer, while in other works, by means of human scale cut-out figures standing on the floor in front of the painting, the viewing itself becomes the theme (*The People* of 1968). In still other works he inaugurates a new and ambivalent approach of revitalizing the tradition of trompe l'oeil painting (*Projected Man* of 1977).

Since 1971–1972 Kanovitz's use of sophisticated forms of illusion has played an especially important role in his work, which becomes a philosophical challenge that questions the traditional vision of realism. The awareness of this dimension was articulated by Kanovitz himself: ''Fidelity to the subject as seen begins to shift as elements not usually associated with subjects take on symbolic importance.'' The complex formal and iconographic range of Kanovitz's works since 1980 has furthermore increased and encompasses images of memory, literary analogies and details of the cultural environment of Amagansett, in the State of New York, where Kanovitz lives after extensive travels in Europe during the late 'seventies. His works in recent years include landscapes, still-lifes and scenes with figures—not in the tradition of these categories, but often in a combination, thus constituting new pictorial forms. Consistently through all the various phases of his work Howard Kanovitz is concerned with the reality of seeing. Seeing and knowing, the problematic and human dimension of perception, are the main concern of the artist. The art of Howard Kanovitz reflects on the process and essence of painting, on the continuity of an art form which opens new perspectives not only for the eye but also for the mind and thus is in line with the general reflected consciousness of our time. The eternal question of how reality can be perceived has been transcended into a creative and visual articulation of the unsolvable question of what reality is.

—Udo Kultermann

KANTOR, Tadeusz

Nationality: Polish. **Born:** Wielopole, 16 March 1915. **Education:** Academy of Fine Arts, Krakow, 1936–39: influenced by Stanislaw Ignacy Witkiewicz and Bruno Schulz. **Military Service:** Served in the Polish Resistance, directing underground theatre, Krakow, 1942–44. **Family:** Married the painter and actress Maria Stangret in 1962. **Career:** Worked as a stage designer in theatres in Krakow, Warsaw, and throughout Poland, 1944–45. Independent painter and graphic artist, Krakow and Warsaw, since 1948: organized first postwar exhibition of contemporary art, Krakow, 1948; founder-director, Cricot 2 theatre group, Krakow, 1956. Nominated professor, Academy of Fine Arts, Krakow, 1949, 1968; visiting professor, Academy of Fine Arts, Hamburg, 1961. **Awards:** Painting Prize, *Bienal de Sao Paulo,* Brazil, 1969; Premio Roma Medal, Galleria Nazionale d'Arte Moderna, Rome, 1969; Tadeusz Boy-Zelenski Theatre Critics' Prize, Warsaw, 1977; Comune di Roma Mayor's Medal, Rome, 1978; Cyprian Norwid Art Critics' Prize, Warsaw, 1978; Rembrandt Prize, Goethe Foundation, 1978; Comune di Milano Mayor's Prize, Milan, 1979; OBIE prize, 1979, 1982; Comune di Firenze Mayor's Gold Medal, Florence, 1980; Gold Medal, City of Gdansk, 1980; Diploma of Minister of Foreign Affairs, 1982; Chevalier, Ordre de la Legion d' Honneur, 1986. **Agent:** Galeria Foksal, U1. Foksal 1/4, Box 256, Warsaw 1, Germany. **Died:** In Cracow, 8 December 1990.

Individual Exhibitions:

1956 Galeria Po Prostu, Warsaw
1957 Galeria Krzysztofory, Cracow
1958 Muzeum Miejskie, Lublin, Poland
Galleri Samklaren, Stockholm
1959 Galerie Legendre, Paris
Kunsthalle, Dusseldorf
1960 Sandberg Gallery, New York
Galerie 54, Gothenberg, Sweden
1961 Galerie Legendre, Paris
1963 Galeria Krzysztofory, Cracow
1964 Galerie Alice Pauli, Lausanne, Switzerland
1965 Galeria Foksal, Warsaw (with Cricot 2)
1966 Galeria S. H. S., Cracow
Galerie Handschin, Basle
Galerie de l'Université, Paris
Galleri Pierre, Stockholm
Kunsthalle, Baden-Baden, West Germany
1967 Galeria Foksal, Warsaw
Osieke, Baltic shore, Poland (happening)
Galeria Krzysztofory, Cracow
1968 Kunsthalle, Nuremberg (2 performance-exhibitions)
Galeria Foksal, Warsaw
Kunsthalle, Nuremberg (tableau vivant)
Galeria Krzysztofory, Cracow
1970 Galeria Foksal, Warsaw
1971 Musée des Arts Décoratifs, Lausanne, Switzerland
Henie-Onstad Kunstsenter, Oslo
Atelier des Recherches Théatrales, Dourdan, France
1972 Galeria Foksal, Warsaw
Galeria Desa, Cracow
1973 Galeria Foksal, Warsaw
1975 *Emballages,* Museum Sztuki, Lodz, Poland
Kulturhuset, Stockholm
1976 Henie-Onstad Kunstsenter, Oslo
Galeria Zapiecek, Warsaw
Emballages 1960–1976, Whitechapel Art Gallery, London
Riverside Studios, Hammersmith, London (with Cricot 2)
1977 Galerie Ricard, Nuremberg, West Germany
1982 Galerie de France, Paris
Riverside Studios, Hammersmith, London
1986 Galerie Eva Poll, West Berlin
1991 Muzeum Narodowe, Cracow
Musee d'Art Contemporain de Nimes, Nimes

Selected Group Exhibitions:

1948 *Modern Art in Poland Since World War II,* Krakow
1957 *Grupa Krakowska,* Krakow
1958 *Documenta II,* Museum Fridericianum, Kassel, West Germany (and *Documenta 6,* 1977)
1960 *30th Biennale,* Venice
1963 *Polish Painting,* Museum Folkwang, Essen, West Germany
1965 *Kunst und Theater,* Kunsthalle, Baden-Baden, West Germany
1967 *Bienal de Sao Paulo,* Brazil
1970 *Happening und Fluxus,* Kunstverein, Cologne
1978 *Painters from the Cricot 2 Theatre,* Rome
1991 *The Interrupted Life,* New Museum of Contemporary Art, New York
1994 *Contemporary Classics: Exhibitions from the Collections of the National Museum of Warsaw,* Muzeum Narodowe, Warsaw

Collections:

Muzeum Sztuki, Lodz, Poland.

Publications:

By KANTOR: Books—*Emballages,* Warsaw 1976; *Le theatre de la mort,* Paris 1978; *La classa morta,* with photos by Maurizio Buscarina, Milan 1981; *Wielopole Wielopole,* Milan 1981; *Metamorphosis,* Paris 1982; *Le theatre cricot 2,* Paris 1983.

On KANTOR: Books—*Happening und Fluxus,* exhibition catalog compiled by Hanns Sohm, Cologne 1976; *Tadeusz Kantor: Emballages,* exhibition catalog with texts by Wieslaw Borowski and Ryszard Stanisklawski, Lodz 1975; *Tadeusz Kantor: Emballages 1960–76,* exhibition catalog with essay by Ryszard Stanislawski, London 1976; *Tadeusz Kantor* by Wieslaw Borowski, Warsaw 1982; *The Interrupted Life,* exhibition catalog, with text by France Morin, Sylvere

Lotringer and Bell Hooks, New York 1991. **Articles—**"Tadeusz Kantor: a Theatre of Visual Confrontation" by Michael Gibson in *Art International,* no. 7, Summer 1989; "Window on Performance: The Poetics of Space" by David Hughes in *Performance,* no. 59, Winter 1989–1990; "Kantor's Last Production" by Andrzej Matynia in *Projekt,* no. 3, 1991; "Kantor: An Anniversary" by Anka Ptaszkowska in *Art Press,* no. 212, April 1996.

*

In artistic development there are frequent moments when the vital creative act degenerates into a pursuit of a convention, when a work of art no longer involves any risk, adventure, revolt or uncertainty and becomes respectable and well established in its seriousness, dignity and prestige.

When this happens, the wisest thing to do is to leave the recognized stage and to shift to disinterested activities, on the verge of the ridiculous and shameful, deserving scorn and doomed to neglect.

Instinctively, I gave all my attention, and very soon all my passion, to objects of the "lower rank" that normally pass unnoticed, are skipped over, forgotten, and then simply dumped off. I started to collect my own notes, sketches, scraps of paper, hasty records of the "urgent" matters, those early discoveries when nothing is known for certain yet, when the "arrangements" are still under way and it doesn't even occur to make things that are "ready" for consumption, varnished, openly demonstrating the perfection of the work and its maker. . .

The imagination was suddenly no longer a store of materials for constructing and executing pictures, but a space into which objects from my own past were falling, in shape of wrecks or shams, but also not my own, strange, trite, schematic, accidental, mixed with important ones, valuable and negligible, facts, persons, letters, prescriptions, addresses, traces, dates, appointments. It was an inventory without any timing, hierarchy or location. Personally, I was in the midst of all this, without any definite role.

Such an adjustment of my own ambition to "create" near the zero point automatically brought about an essential shift in my attitude towards the past, with its relics and claims, as well as towards the object. For the aim was not repeat it, but to recapture!

—Tadeusz Kantor

* * *

Tadeusz Kantor was one of the central figures of modern Polish art and one of those whose activities are born from the continual polemics which inspire many artists. His creativity raised problems for debate, not only in the fields of painting and the theatre, but also in the new relationship created between author and audience in many other areas of activity.

Kantor developed artistically under the influence of two great Polish visionaries from the period between the wars: Stanislaw Ignacy Witkiewicz, painter, writer, philosopher and playwright, and Bruno Schulz, draughtsman and writer. Their work can be related very loosely to Surrealism.

Kantor's early artistic formation was completed by the experiences of the occupation of Poland and the terror of the Second World War. His independent theatrical activity began after the war with performances by his underground theatre, at which the audience was amazed by the non-conformity of the stage design and the anti-psychological interpretation of the hero's character. A similar non-conformity was the characteristic feature of his postwar paintings: they were dramatic but not literary compositions, revealing his deep knowledge of the Surrealist theory of painting. Through the work of Kantor and other Cracow painters, Surrealist theory became well known in Polish artistic circles. These same circles had faced moral defeat after the war and were searching for dramatic forms to express their personal nightmare memories. Kantor's independent attitude resulted from the fact that he always considered creativity to be a constantly regenerating phenomenon—that is, an inner pressure to consider one new problem after another.

In the years following 1955 Kantor was the first in Poland to suggest the existence of the unintentional, or spontaneous, gesture in painting: in other words that same improvisation which found its expressive meaning in Informal Art. Later he also realized that a similar shapeless structure could become the characteristic feature of theatrical performances. From 1956 he became, in many ways, a theatre reformer. In his successive productions of S. I. Witkiewicz's plays after 1961, this intentional shapelessness emphasized even more those elements in which we can recognize the origins of Theatre of the Absurd.

In the theatre this fascination with an object translated itself into the creation of wretched junk which disturbed both the course of action and the verbal contacts between the actors. In the Happenings of 1965, it produced a confusion of themes and simultaneous actions with accessories collected from various sources. The origins of this deliberate incoherence in Kantor's happenings can be traced to his earlier productions of Witkiewicz's plays, which contributed such elements as a lack of phychological contact between the actors, and a fragmentation of the script.

A similar incoherence appears in paintings executed at the same time and to some extent in Kantor's later works. His technique consists of mixing fragments of objects fixed to the canvas (for instance an umbrella) with traces of themes belonging to the former abstract Informal method.

In all his artistic manifestations, the presence of a letter or an envelope, a pocket, or a wretched traveling bag, plays a significant role. These symbols or keys represent the essence of the fate of a perpetual wanderer, the secrecy and the freedom which Kantor violated by tearing up envelopes and ripping out the inner linings of clothes. In other words, in his paintings and happenings, Kantor violated everyone's fundamental right to intimate secrecy. Moreover, Kantor often expected the audience to participate in this violation of privacy. During the course of a happening in 1967 *(A Letter),* the enthusiastic audience listened carefully to the reading of informal letters from unknown people and then destroyed a huge symbolic writing case. Similarly in *Multipart* the spectators had to complete an unfinished painting (using any free and unrestricted actions) by damaging or destroying it.

Is the *emballage* theme more significant than others and therefore sufficiently representative of Kantor's work? I think so, for several reasons. The most important is that the *emballage* theme is the starting-point for many of Kantor's artistic manifestations and therefore an exhibition with *emballage* as a *leit-motif* documents the work not only of the artist as a painter, but also as an author of happenings, theatrical productions, and events.

Kantor was particularly significant not only for his outstanding vision, but also because he managed to bring together the disciplines of painting, theatre design, theatre direction, poetry, and theory of art, which are usually separated into rigid categories. The extraordinary result was in keeping with the power of his personality.

—Ryszard Stanislawski

KAPOOR, Anish

Nationality: Indian. **Born:** Bombay, 12 March 1954. **Education:** Studied at Hornsey College of Art, London, 1973–77; Chelsea School of Art, London, 1977–78. **Career:** Independent sculptor, London, since 1979. Instructor in sculpture, Wolverhampton Polytechnic, Staffordshire, 1979–82. Artist-in-residence, Walker Art Gallery, Liverpool, 1982. **Awards:** Premio Duemila, Venice Biennale, 1990; Turner Prize, 1991; Honorary Fellowship, London Institute, 1997. **Agents:** Barbara Gladstone Gallery, 515 West 24th Street, New York, New York 10011, U.S.A.; Lisson Gallery, 67 Lisson Street, London NW1 5DA. **Address:** 33 Coherne Road, London SW10, England.

Individual Exhibitions:

1980 Studio Patrice Alexandre, Paris
1981 Coracle Press, London
1982 Lisson Gallery, London
Walker Art Gallery, Liverpool
1983 Galerie 't Venster, Rotterdam
Walker Art Gallery, Liverpool (travelled to Lyon, France)
Lisson Gallery, London
1984 Barbara Gladstone Gallery, New York
Galerie Paul Maenz, Cologne (with Bill Woodrow)
1985 Lisson Gallery, London
Kunsthalle, Basel (travelled to Eindhoven, Netherlands)
Donald Young Gallery, Chicago (with Bill Woodrow)
1986 Kunstnernes Hus, Oslo
Barbara Gladstone Gallery, New York
Albright-Knox Art Gallery, Buffalo, New York
University of Massachusetts, Amherst
1987 Ray Hughes Gallery, Sydney (travelled to Brisbane)
1988 Lisson Gallery, London
1989 Barbara Gladstone Gallery, New York
Kohji Ogura Gallery, Nagoya, Japan
Void Field, Lisson Gallery, London
1990 *Biennale*, Venice
Barbara Gladstone Gallery, New York
Tate Gallery, London
1991 Palacio de Velazquez, Madrid
Kunstverein Hannover, Germany
Ushimado International Art Festival, Ushimado, Japan
1992 Galeria Soledad Lorenzo, Madrid
Stuart Regen Gallery, Los Angeles
San Diego Museum of Contemporary Art (travelled to Des Moines, Iowa; Ottawa; and Toronto)
1993 Lisson Gallery, London
Tel Aviv Museum of Art
Barbara Gladstone Gallery, New York
1994 Moderna Galerija, Ljubljana, Slovenia
Stuart Regen Gallery, Los Angeles
1995 Fondazione Prada, Milano, Italy (catalog)
Lisson Gallery, London
De Pont, Tilburg, Netherlands
Nishimura Gallery, Tokyo
1996 Angles Gallery, Santa Monica, California
Um Fontana, Schirn Kunsthalle, Frankfurt, Germany
Massimo Minini, Brescia, Italy
Lisson Gallery, London
Kunst-Station St. Peter, Cologne
1998 Centro Galego de Arte Contemporanea, Santiago de Compostela
Massimo Minini, Brescia, Italy
1000 Names, Lisson Gallery, London (catalog)
Anish Kapoor, Hayward Gallery, London (catalog)
CAPC, Musee d'art contemporain de Bordeaux (catalog)
Her Blood, La Chapelle de la Salpetiere, Paris
1999 Galeria Andre Viana, Porto, Portugal
Scai The Bathhouse, Tokyo, Japan
Installation by Anish Kapoor, Baltic Center for Contemporary Art, Gateshead, United Kingdom
2000 Regen Projects, Los Angeles
Lisson Gallery, London
The Edge of the World (permanent installation), Axel Vervoordt Kanal, Wijnegem, Belgium
2001 Barbara Gladstone Gallery

Selected Group Exhibitions:

1974 *Art Into Landscape I,* Serpentine Gallery, London
1975 *Young Contemporaries,* Royal Academy of Art, London
1978 *Northern Young Contemporaries,* Whitworth Art Gallery Manchester
1981 *Objects and Sculpture,* Institute of Contemporary Art, London
1983 *New Art,* Tate Gallery, London
1984 *International Survey of Recent Painting and Sculpture,* Museum of Modern Art, New York
1987 *A Quiet Revolution: British Sculpture Since 1965,* San Francisco Museum of Modern Art (travelled to Newport Beach, California; Washington, D.C.; Buffalo, New York)
1988 *Carnegie International,* Carnegie Museum of Art, Pittsburg
1991 *The 1991 Turner Prize,* Tate Gallery, London
1993 *Art against AIDS,* Venice Biennale
1995 *Ripple Across the Water,* Watari Museum of Contemporary Art, Tokyo
ARS' 95, Museum of Contemporary Art, Finland (catalog)
1996 *Cut, Cast, Assemble: Contemporary Sculpture from the Permanent Collection,* San Francisco Museum of Modern Art, California
23rd International Biennial of Sao Paolo, Brazil
1997 *Meditations,* Madrasa Ibn Youssef, Marrakech
Belladonna, Institute of Contemporary Arts, London
1998 *Spatiotemporal: Works from the Collection,* Magasin 3 Stockholm, Konsthall (catalog)
Wounds Between Democracy and Redemption in Contemporary Art, Moderna Museet Stockholm (catalog)

2000 *Around 1984: A Look at the Eighties,* P.S. 1 Contemporary Art Center, New York

Collections:

Museum of Modern Art, New York; Albright Knox Art Gallery, Buffalo; Walker Art Center, Minneapolis; Stedelijk Museum, Amsterdam; Stedelijk Van Abbemuseum, Eindhoven; Rijkmuseum Kroller-Muller, Otterlo; Walker Art Gallery, Liverpool; Fukuoka Art Museum, Fukuoka; Hara Museum of Contemporary Art, Tokyo; Hirshhorn Museum and Sculpture Garden, Washington, D.C.; Moderna Museet, Stockholm; Museo National Centro de Arte Reina Sofia, Madrid; National Gallery of Canada, Ottawa; Stedelijk Museum, Amsterdam; Tate Gallery, London.

Publications:

By KAPOOR: Article—''Mother as a Mountain,'' with Sylvie Primard and Pier Luigi Tazzi, in *Artforum,* September 1989.

On KAPOOR: Books—*Anish Kapoor: Feeling into Form,* exhibition catalog with essay by Marco Livingstone, Liverpool 1983; *The Sculpture Show,* exhibition catalog with texts by Fenella Crichton, Stuart Morgan, Bryan Robertson and others, London 1983; *Anish Kapoor,* exhibition catalog with texts by Jean-Christophe Ammann and Alexander von Graevenstein, Basel 1985; *Currents: Anish Kapoor,* exhibition catalog with essay by David Joselit, Boston 1985; *The British Show,* exhibition catalog with text by Stuart Morgan, Perth 1985; *Anish Kapoor,* exhibition catalog with texts by Lynne Cooke and Arne Malmedal, Oslo 1986; *Anish Kapoor: Recent Sculpture and Drawings,* exhibition catalog with essay by Helaine Posner, Amherst 1986; *Anish Kapoor,* exhibition catalog with essay by Helen Raye, Buffalo 1986; *Anish Kapoor: Works on Paper 1975–1987,* exhibition catalog with interview by Richard Cork, Brisbane 1987; *Anish Kapoor,* exhibition catalog with text by Pier Luigi Tazzi, London 1989; *Anish Kapoor: Drawings,* exhibition catalog with text by Jeremy Lewison, London 1990; *Anish Kapoor,* exhibition catalog with essays by Lynda Forsha and Pier Luigi Tazzi, San Diego 1992. **Articles—**''An Air of Light Relief'' by William Feaver in *The Observer,* 26 June 1981; ''Anish Kapoor's Shades of Meaning'' by Patrick Kinmouth in *Vogue,* August 1983; ''Forms a Hole Can Take. . .'' by Caroline Collier in *Studio International,* vol. 198, no. 1010, 1985; ''Original Sites: The Sculpture of Anish Kapoor'' by Marjorie Allthorpe-Guyton in *Artscribe,* May 1990; ''Anish Kapoor Interviewed by Douglas Maxwell'' in *Art Monthly,* May 1990; ''Anish Kapoor'' by Donald Kuspit in *Artforum,* March 1994; ''Into the Wild Blue Yonder'' by Isabel Carlisle in *New Statesman,* 1 May 1998.

* * *

Within the group of new British sculptors brought to international prominence at the beginning of the 1980s, Anish Kapoor represents the most hermetic artist, a characterization that can also be applied to Shirazeh Houshiary.

Kapoor, of Indian origin, does not employ commonly used materials or contemporary images. On the contrary, he filters out any form of mundane connotation and suspends it in a lyrical dimension. Since his first works from about 1970, Kapoor has concentrated on assemblages and the installation of multiple elements in space, in the name of a certain stylistic and cultural electicism.

In his sculptures he expresses allegiance to two different cultural traditions—Western and Eastern. In so doing, he permeates his works with ideas gathered during frequent trips to India. These ideas stem from the rediscovery of art, philosophy, mythology, and even everyday life in India, transformed into mysterious plastic and visual equivalents, the origins of which are to be found in his prolific activity as a draughtsman. The precise correspondence between form and content, myth or achitectural detail, is often completely accidental. It is the tendency of much Indian culture to express philosophical and spiritual concepts through sensual imagery. Kapoor's forms inherit that tendency: they almost invariably assume a biomorphic or phytomorphic aspect or, at any rate, allude to living organisms. In certain cases they suggest, by means of metaphor, a discourse on the imagery of the human body. Their form is the result of an interpenetration of different forms; it is a complexity of structures seeming to represent the idea of organic accretion, of endogenous proliferation—in a word, of vital rhythm.

In *Hole and Vessel* (1984), for instance, Kapoor accomplishes what can be termed a semantic displacement in the form of a vessel, one that can illustrate at the same time both the idea of a vessel and that of a hole as a container. Both such elements, as well as designating items of common use, are treated as symbols of the maternal womb, of the vagina—and therefore of fecundation and birth. The vessel, moreover, alludes to the food that is preserved therein, and enlarges that micro-universe of the 'maternal' by indicating the nutrition and preservation of the species.

Kapoor's sculptures are not easily decoded: symbols are not employed in order to reveal a whole range of meanings, least of all those pertaining to a new definition of sculpture. The use of ensembles of sculptures rather than the single work (which takes on the character of a totem) is aimed at transfiguring the ordinary space of the exhibition into a sacred space. This aspect is then accentuated by the complexity—at times by the extravagance—of forms and of saturated colours covering the surfaces of the work. His use of colour is particular and suggestive, since pigments are treated as highly significant elements.

The artist does not confine himself to painting his sculptures, very often made out of wood, cement or gypsum, but onto them he drops pigment in powder form. In such a way, the work is encompassed by colour, even seeming to emerge from the sculpture as its own aggregation. Alternatively, the work appears to sink into the colour: the pigment indeed forms thick haloes of richly hued matter all around the work.

This method of treating the work induces a dialectic between rigid complex structures and impalpable fluid matter—heavily loaded with meaning. The act of allowing pure pigment to fall around the forms recalls ritual gestures, and so accentuates the mysterious allusiveness of the sculpture. Dense pigmentation applied without evidence of the artist's hand serves to dematerialize the sculpture, to nullify it, so that absence and presence are simultaneously signified.

Kapoor's work from the late eighties continues this dialogue between presence and absence with the introduction of holes drilled into sandstone blocks which are heavily pigmented in deep black or blue so as to appear limitless. Another work consists of a beveled frame covered in red pigment suspended in air to literally 'frame' the void.

The artist's newest works lack pigmentation, and while they initially appear less seductive, their ability to evoke issues of solidity and penetration, sound and silence, fear and sublimation, is no less profound. *Untitled*, 1993, has a single central hole drilled horizontally to the grain of the stone, which flares out into the interior walls of the rock at one end and dissolves into darkness at the other, drawing the viewer inward. With its lingering associations of cave and vagina, Kapoor's void transcends duality and opposition; creation and destruction are here two aspects of the same reality. The void here is a consummate absence, defying physical apprehension or rational understanding, which are of course the fundamental conditions of spirituality. This noetic quality speaks to what is simultaneously elusive and familiar, and reflects Kapoor's interest in erasing boundaries between culture, self, and other, "the moment of contact between the thing and the world." (AK)

Elegant, complex, mysterious, Kapoor's work is offered to the viewer not as a unique and absolute object, but is given rather as a dissemination of elements in relationship with space—and ultimately as a moment in a process of creation, which is potentially infinite.

—Essay by Giorgio Verzotti; updated by Dorothy Valakos

KAPROW, Allan

Nationality: American. **Born:** Atlantic City, New Jersey, 23 August 1927; spent childhood in Tucson, Arizona. **Education:** High School of Music and Art, Tucson, 1943–45, New York University, 1945–49, B.A. 1949, Hans Hofmann School of Fine Arts, New York, 1947–48, and New York University, 1949–50; studied art history at Columbia University, New York, under Meyer Schapiro, 1950–52, M.A. 1952, and studied at the New School for Social Research, New York, under John Cage, 1956–58. **Family:** Married Vaughan Peters in 1955; children: Anton, Amy and Marisa. **Career:** Performance Artist, lives in Encinitas, California. Co-founder, Hansa Gallery, New York, 1952, and Reuben Gallery, New York, 1960; co-director, Judson Gallery, New York, 1961. Instructor, 1952–56, and assistant professor, 1956–61, Fine Arts Department, Rutgers University, New Brunswick, New Jersey; lecturer in Aesthetics, Pratt Institute, Brooklyn, New York, 1960–61; associate professor of Fine Arts, 1961–66, and Professor, 1966–69, Department of Fine Arts, State University of New York at Stony Brook; Director of Experimental Education, Institute of Contemporary Art, Boston 1965–66; co-director, Project Other Ways, Berkeley, California Public Schools, 1968–69; associate dean, 1969–73, and member of the faculty, 1973–74, California Institute of the Arts, Valencia. Professor, Visual Arts Department, University of California at San Diego, since 1974. Founding member, Advanced Placement Committee on Art and Art History, Educational Testing Service and College entrance Examination Board, Princeton, New Jersey, 1969–72; member, Board of Trustees, and Chairman of the Education Committee, Museum of Modern Art, Pasadena, California, 1973; consultant panelist, Visual Arts Program, National Endowment for the Arts, Washington, D.C., 1975. **Awards:** Katherine White Award, New York, 1952; William and Norma Copley Foundation Award, 1963; Guggenheim Fellowship, 1967; Gold Medal, City of Milan, 1971; National Endowment for the Arts Award, 1974; Video Grant, University of California at San Diego, 1975; Annual Award and Gold medal, Skowhegan School of Painting and Sculpture, Maine, 1975; D.A.A.D. Grant, West Berlin, 1975; National Endowment for the Arts Award, 1979; Guggenheim Fellowship, 1979. **Address:** 1225 Linda Rosa Avenue, Los Angeles, California 90041, U.S.A.

Individual Shows/Environments/Happenings:

1953 Hansa Gallery, New York
Rutgers Art House, New Brunswick, New Jersey
Earle Pilgrim Gallery, Provincetown, Massachusetts (with L. Johnson)
1954 Hansa Gallery, New York
1955 Urban Gallery, New York
1956 Bernard-Ganymede Gallery, New York
Z & Z Delicatessen, New Brunswick, New Jersey (with George Segal)
The Jewish Community Center, Highland Park, New Jersey
Rutgers Art House, Rutgers University, New Brunswick, New Jersey
1957 Hansa Gallery, New York
Sun Gallery, Provincetown, Massachusetts
1958 Hansa Gallery, New York
Centaur Restaurant, New York
Untitled, Douglass College, New Brunswick, New Jersey
Untitled, Hansa Gallery, New York
1959 *Intermission Piece,* Reuben Gallery, New York
18 Happenings in 6 Parts, Reuben Gallery, New York
1960 *An Apple Shrine,* Judson Gallery, New York
1961 *A Spring Happening,* Reuben Gallery, New York
1962 *A Service for the Dead,* Maidman Playhouse, New York
Words, Smolin Gallery, New York
Chicken, YMHA, Philadelphia
Courtyard, Mills Hotel, New York
1963 *Bon Marché,* Bon Marché Department Store, Paris
1964 *Eat,* Old Ebling Brewery, Bronx, New York
Birds, Southern Illinois University, Carbondale
Orange, unused citrus warehouse, Coral Gables, Florida
Paper, parking lot, University of California, Berkeley
1965 *Soap,* city and beach, Sarasota, Florida
Calling, New York and George Segal's woods, New Brunswick, New Jersey
1966 *Self-Service,* Boston, New York and Los Angeles areas
Gas, Hamptons area of Long Island (with Charles Frazier)
1967 *Interruption,* State University of New York at Stony Brook
Fluids, Los Angeles area
Moving, Chicago area
Art Museum, Pasadena, California (retrospective; toured the United States)
Museum of Contemporary Art, Chicago (twice, once with Wolf Vostell)
1968 *Runner,* Washington University, St. Louis
Transfer, Wesleyan University, Middletown, Connecticut
Record I, University of Texas, Austin
Record II, University of Texas, Austin
Round Trip, State University of New York, Albany
Arrivals, Nassau Community College, Hempstead, New York

Population, Colby Junior College, New London, New Hamsphire
Overtime, University of California, San Diego
Travelog, Fairleigh Dickinson University, Madison, New Jersey
Refills, Hofstra University, New York
1969 John Gibson Gallery, New York
Charity, Project Other Ways, Berkeley, California
Pose, Project Other Ways, Berkeley, California
Fine!, Project Other Ways, Berkeley, California
Shape, Project Other Ways, Berkeley, California
Hello, WGBH-TV, Boston
Giveaway, Project Other Ways, Berkeley, California
Purpose, Project Other Ways, Berkeley, California
Transplant, University of Southern Nevada, Las Vegas
Dial, San Francisco Art Institute
Takeoff, U.S. International University, La Jolla, California
Takeoff II, Sacramento State University, California
Course, University of Iowa, Iowa City
Homemovies, C. & D. Schmidt wedding, New Jersey and New York
1970 *Moon Sounds,* H. & R. Blau wedding, El Mirage Dry Lake, California
Graft, Kent State University, Ohio
Level, Aspen Institute of Contemporary Art, Colorado
Don't, Los Angeles County Parks
Publicity, California Institute of the Arts, Burbank
Car Spaces, California Institute of the Arts, Burbank
Tracts, California Institute of the Arts, Burbank
Sweet Wall, Galerie René Block, Berlin
1971 Galerie Baecker, Bochum, West Germany
Dial II, California Institute of the Arts, Valencia
Good Morning!, San Francisco State University
Print Out, Cultural Affairs Commission, Milan
City Works, Galerie Baecker, Bochum, West Germany
Calendar, California Institute of the Arts, Valencia
Scales, California Institute of the Arts, Valencia
1972 *Message Units,* California Institute of the Arts, Valencia
Baggage, Rice University, Houston
Meters, California Institute of the Arts, Valencia
Meteorology, Galerie Baecker, Bochum, West Germany
Easy, California Institute of the Arts, Valencia
Idea, Portland Center for the Visual Arts, Oregon
Entr'acte, California Institute of the Arts, Valencia
1973 *Loss,* New York
Highs, University of Kansas, Lawrence
Basic Thermal Units, Folkwang Museum, Essen
Clockwork, California Institute of the Arts, Valencia
Wink, California Institute of the Arts, Valencia
Art Condition, California Institute of the Arts, Valencia
Routine, Portland Center for the Visual Arts, Oregon
1974 *2nd Routine,* Stefanotty Gallery, New York
Galleria La Bertesca, Milan
Galerie Baecker, Bochum, West Germany
Galleria Martano, Turin
Galleria Martini & Ronchetti, Genoa
On Time, Galerie Gerald Piltzer, Paris
1975 *Rates of Exchange,* Stefanotty Gallery, New York
Echo-logy, Merrieworld West Gallery, Far Hills, New Jersey
Comfort Zones, Galerie Vandres, Madrid
Match, von der Heydt Museum, Wuppertal, West Germany
Warm-Ups, Center for Advanced Visual Studies, Massachusetts Institute of Technology, Cambridge
Likely Stories, Galleria Luciano Anselmino, Milan
Useful Fictions, Galleria Schema, Florence
1979 University of Northern Iowa, Cedar Falls
Ullrich Museum, Wichita, Kansas
1980 Pasadena Film Forum, California
1981 Provincetown Art Center, Massachusetts
1986 Museum am Ostwall, Dortmund, West Germany
1991 Fondazione Mudima, Milan (retrospective)
1992 Galerie Donguy, Paris (retrospective)
1995 John Gibson Gallery, New York (retrospective)
1996 *Allan Kaprow: Reinventions: Course, Recourse,* University of Iowa Museum of Art, Iowa City (catalog)

Selected Group Exhibitions:

1957 *The New York School—Second Generation,* Jewish Museum, New York
1961 *Environments, Situations, Spaces,* Martha Jackson Gallery, New York
1965 *11 from the Reuben Gallery,* Guggenheim Museum, New York
1969 *Software,* Jewish Museum, New York
1970 *Happening und Fluxus,* Kölnischer Kunstverein, Cologne
1973 *Aktionen der Avant-garde,* Neue Berliner Kunstverein, Berlin
1974 *Poets of the Cities, New York and San Francisco, 1950–1965,* Museum of Fine Arts, Dallas (toured the United States, 1974–75)
1975 *Activity Dokumente 1968–76,* Kunsthalle, Bremen
1981 *California Performance: Now and Then,* Museum of Contemporary Art, Chicago
1987 *Berlinart 1961–87,* Museum of Modern Art, New York (travelled to San Francisco)
1994 *Medienbiennale Leipzig,* Leipzig, Germany
inSITE94, Stephen Birch Aquarium, University of California, San Diego (also Centro Escolar Agua Caliente, Tijuana, Mexico) (with Nina Karavasiles)
1994 *Neo-Dada: Redefining Art 1958–1960,* Scottsdale Center for the Arts, Scottsdale, Arizona (catalog)
1995 *Hors Limites: L'Art et la Vie 1952–1994,* Centre Georges Pompidou, Paris
1997 *The Hansa Gallery—1952–1959—Revisited,* Zabriskie Gallery, New York
1999 *Off Limints: Rutgers University and the Avant-Garde, 1957–1963,* Newark Museum, New Brunswick, New Jersey (catalog)
1998 *Out of Actions: Between Performance and the Object 1949–1979,* Museum of Contemporary Art, Los Angeles
2000 *Made in California Now,* Boone Children's Gallery, Los Angeles County Museum of Art
Experiments in the Everyday: Allan Kaprow and Robert Watts, Events, Objects, Documents, Wallach Art Gallery, Columbia University, New York (catalog)
Castelli in Aria, Castel Sant'Elmo, Naples, Italy

Collections:

Museum of Modern Art, New York.

Publications:

By KAPROW: Books—*Assemblage, Environments and Happenings,* New York 1966; *Some Recent Happenings,* New York 1966; *Untitled Essay and Other Works,* New York 1967; *Echo-logy,* New York 1975; *Rates of Exchange,* New York 1975; *Warm-Ups,* Cambridge, Massachusetts 1975; *Sweet Wall Testimonials,* Berlin 1976; *Essays on the Blurring of Art and Life,* edited by Jeff Kelley, Berkeley 1993; *Allan Kaprow,* Milan 1998. **Articles—**''Rub-a-Dub, Rub-a-Dub'' in *Anthologist* (New Brunswick, New Jersey), Spring 1957; ''The Legacy of Jackson Pollock'' in *Artnews* (New York), October 1958; ''The Demiurge'' in *Anthologist* (New Brunswick, New Jersey), Spring 1959; ''One Chapter from 'The Principles of Modern Art''' in *It Is* (New York). Autumn 1959; ''Happenings in the New York Scene'' in *Artnews* (New York), May 1961, reprinted in *Design Annual* (Bombay), July 1962, and as ''Happenings in New York'' in *Randstad* (Amsterdam), 1966; ''About Words'' in *Randstad* (Amsterdam), 1966; ''Impurity'' in *Artnews* (New York), January 1963; ''A Service for the Dead'' in *Art International* (Zurich), 25 January 1963; ''An Artist's Story of a Happening'' in the *New York Times,* 6 October 1963; ''The World View of Alfred Jensen'' in *Artnews* (New York), December 1963; ''Effect of Recent Art upon the Teaching of Art'' in the *Art Journal* (New York), Winter 1963–64; ''Nature in the Art of Irving Kriesberg'' in *Art International* (Lugano, Switzerland), 16 January 1964; ''Segal's Vital Mummies'' in *Artnews* (New York), February 1964; ''What Is an 'Environment''' in *Vogue* (New York), April 1964; ''The Happening'' in the *Ithaca Journal* (Ithaca, New York), 9 May 1964; ''Should the Artist Be a Man of the World'' in *Artnews* (New York), October 1964; ''Eating'' in *Second Coming Magazine* (New York), January 1965; ''Eat'' in *Tulane Drama Review* (New Orleans), Winter 1965; ''Possibility of Contemporary Art'' in *Mizue* (Tokyo), January 1966; ''Hans Hofmann'' in *Village Voice* (New York), 24 February 1966; ''The Happenings Are Dead, Long Live the Happenings'' in *Artforum* (New York), March 1966, reprinted in *Aujourd'hui: Art et Architecture* (Paris), January 1967; ''Experimental Art'' in *Artnews* (New York), March 1966; ''Female Art: No Games'' in the *Village Voice* (New York), 28 April 1966; ''Untitled Manifesto'' in *Manifestos,* edited by Dick Higgins, New York 1966; ''Self-Service'' in *Soundings* (Long Island), Spring 1966; ''Letter to the Editor'' in *Tulane Drama Review* (New Orleans), Summer 1966; ''Happenings: Interview mit Allan Kaprow'' in *Magazin Kunst* (Mainz), 3rd quarter 1966; ''Total Theatre'' in *World Theatre 2,* Paris 1966; ''The Sensibility of the 60s'' in *Art in America* (New York), January/February 1967; ''Death in the Museum'' in *Arts Magazine* (New York), February 1967; ''Jackson Pollock: An Artists' Symposium, Part 1'' in *Artnews* (New York), April 1967; ''The End of the Concert Hall'' in the *Statesman* (Long Island), 3 May 1967; ''An Interview with Allan Kaprow,'' with Martin Fishgold, in *Cacophony* (Sea Cliff, New York), Spring 1967; ''Pop Art: Past, Present and Future'' in the *Malahat Review* (Victoria, British Columbia), July 1967; ''What Is a Museum,'' with Robert Smithson, in the *Museum World Arts Yearbook,* New York 1967; ''Gas'' in *Theatre Experiment* by Michael Benedikt, New York 1967; ''Pinpointing Happenings'' in *Artnews* (New York), October 1967; ''Happenings in the New York Scene'' in the *Modern American Theatre: A Collection of Critical Essays,* edited by Alvin Kerman, New Jersey 1967; ''The Happenings Are Dead, Long Live the Happenings'' in *Arts in Society* (Madison, Wisconsin), 1968; interview, with Richard Kostelanatz, in *The Theatre of Mixed Means* by Kostelanatz, New York 1968; ''Art and Education,'' with Jim Hinton and Herbert Kohl, in *Cultural Affairs* (New York), March 1968; ''Extensions in Time and Space,'' interview, with Richard Schechner, in the *Drama Review* (New York), Spring 1968; ''A Conversation with Allan Kaprow,'' with Donald J. Cyr, in *Arts and Activities* (New York), April 1969; ''6 Ordinary Happenings'' in *Aktionen* by Wolf Vostell, Hamburg 1970; ''Home Movies'' and ''Moon Sounds'' in *Arts in Society* (Madison, Wisconsin), Fall/Winter 1970, ''Days Off'' in *Sipario* (Milan), March 1970; ''Mid 20th Century Environments and Happenings'' in *The Changing World and Man,* edited by Chandler M. Brooks, Stony Brook, New York 1970; ''The Education of the Un-Artist, Part 1'' in *Artnews* (New York), February 1971; ''Publicity'' in *Box* (Burbank, California), March 1971; interview with Robert Filliou, in *Teaching and Learning as Performing Arts* by Filliou, Cologne and New York 1970; ''The Education of the Un-Artist, Part 2'' in *Artnews* (New York), May 1972; ''The Education of the Un-Artist, Part 3'' in *Art in America* (New York), January/February 1974; ''L'Utilité d'un Passee Determinée'' in *Opus International* (Paris), March 1974; ''Easy'' in *Art in America* (New York), July/August 1974; ''Baggage'' in *Source* (Sacramento, California), Spring 1974; ''Old Wine, New Bottles'' in *Artforum* (New York), June 1974; ''Formalism: Flogging a Dead Horse'' in *Quadrille* (Bennington, Vermont), Fall 1974; ''Hello—Plan and Execution'' in *Art Rite* (New York), Autumn 1974; ''Routine'' in *Journal of the Los Angeles Institute of Contemporary Art,* February 1974; ''Animation: Stephan von Huene's Sound Sculptures'' in *Sound Sculptures,* edited by John Grayson, Vancouver 1975; ''Air Condition'' in *Journal of the Los Angeles Institute of Contemporary Art,* June/July 1975; ''Easy Activity'' in *Art Studies for an Art Editor: 25 Essays in Memory of Milton S. Fox,* New York 1975; interview with Helena Kontová and Giancarlo Politi in *Flash Art (International Edition),* no. 162, January/February 1992; ''Allan Kaprow in Conversation with Beatrice von Bismarck'' in *Be Magazin,* no. 2, October 1994.

On KAPROW: Books—*Happenings* by Jürgen Becker and Wolf Vostell, Hamburg 1965; *A Primer of Happenings and Time/Space Art,* New York 1965; *Happening* by Michael Kirby, New York 1965; *Le Happenings* by Jean-Jacques Lebel, Paris 1966; *Happenings and Other Acts* by Mariellen R. Sandford, London 1995. **Articles—**''Mr. Kaprow's 18 Happenings'' by J.H. Livingston in the *Village Voice* (New York), 7 October 1959; ''Allan Kaprow'' by Toshi Ichiyanagi in *Bijutsu Techo* (Tokyo), Fall 1965; ''Allan Kaprow'' by Dick Higgins in *Arts in Society* (Madison, Wisconsin), Spring/Summer 1968; ''Allan Kaprow'' by Kuniharu Akiyama and ''Allan Kaprow'' by Yusuke Narahara in *Bijutsu Techo* (Tokyo), August 1968; ''Allan Kaprow'' by Mirella Bandini in *Data* (Milan), June/August 1975; article by Jonathan Gray in *Arts Magazine* (New York), September 1976; ''Reinventing the Past'' by Jeff Kelley in *Art in America* (New York), vol. 82, no. 6, June 1994; ''Reinventing His Past: Allan Kaprow's Series of Remakes of His Own Early Environments'' by Jeff Kelley in *Art in America* (New York), vol. 82, June 1994; ''A Funny Thing Formed on the Way to the Happening: A Conversation with Allan Kaprow'' by Robert Enright in *Border Crossings,* vol. 17, no. 2, May 1998.

* * *

Allan Kaprow's stature as practitioner and theoretician in the field of performance art is well earned by his over 25-year-long creation and evolution from the late 1950s until the present. This respected pioneer in the field has a reputation and influence which covers New York, California and Europe.

Beginning around 1956, Kaprow began making large assemblages incorporating a variety of found objects from the surrounding environment and also created environments and happenings. From these beginnings, he was expressing his intentions to delimit the boundaries between the arts, between art and life, and between the art maker and the viewer. Kaprow's view is expansionist, one which sees art in the streets and in the everyday environments of life, urban and country. It is not an anti-art Dada approach, but rather is geared toward separating art from the artificiality of the art world context, blurring categories to make art more an organic part of living experience. The happenings were mostly ''spectaculars'' in which clusters of groups of people took part in situations which were not art-derived and were carried out in varying time and place units. Many were ritualistic in theme such as the 1962 ''Chicken'' and ''A Service for the Dead.'' Always interested in the audience getting more involved in the doing and seeing of the event, Kaprow moved away from the theatrical concept, omitting the audience as viewer and creating ''non-theatrical, participation'' performance during the 1960s. By 1967 Kaprow was using the term happening less and less, and after his 1967 piece ''Fluids,'' the work became increasingly quieter, more intimate and more intimately involved with ordinary everyday routines. From 1967 to 1971 Kaprow did a series of ''Work Pieces'' in which physical labor became a kind of play, leisure situation. In ''Sweet Wall'' (1970), for example, participants built and subsequently destroyed a wall made with bricks held together by a ''mortar'' of bread and jam. The activity took place just a few steps away from the Berlin Wall, and like other works, called attention to the underlying symbolism of the task by removing the element of practical usefulness.

Around 1971 the works began to center on smaller groups, usually one, two or three, who performed routines which involve personal and interpersonal relationships. Kaprow named these works ''Activities,'' a nomer meant to help convey the honing down of theatrics and centering in on the regular actions of everyday life which we often ignore and relegate to the semi-conscious of the ''routine''. As in all Kaprow's work, there is the interplay of choice and chance. The artist as director/participant remains in control but allows for and even welcomes chance and change by leaving choices open for the execution particulars which develop in the activity's duration. The Activities follow this basic format: first, there is a preliminary gathering of the preselected participants during which Kaprow (always a participant) distributes and explains the ''script'' he has written. This script is an outline of the procedures to be followed; it tends to be spare and leave openings as to particulars in between designated actions. Second, participants split up into groups (2 or 3) and carry out the script's directions simultaneously and separately, with points of overlap along the route. Third, they regroup to discuss (Kaprow included, perhaps taping the talks) what has happened and put it in some perspective. There is no specific documentation of the work, but Kaprow produces what he calls ''instruction manuals'' which include the script and simulated photographs of the activity in process.

Actions and interactions which would normally be considered ordinary are brought into heightened consciousness, more powerfully so because they are gone through directly in real-life time and places by participants who are going through the motions in a tense state of choice between refusing or complying with each step along the way. The regular becomes strange and capable of fostering real anxieties and new insights alike. Beginning out of what Lawrence Alloway has called ''a fertile misreading of Pollock,'' Kaprow has develop a body of work with potent psychological and social implications which can often affect people quite dramatically. They give apt pertinence to the active participation element in a time dominated more and more by the passivity induced by television. In recent works Kaprow is becoming less distanced personally, more introspectively meditative and willing to incorporate his personal experiences. As always, however, there is the persistently intellectual element of the creator at the controls, never to dominate answers but rather to bring to the fore possibilities of a unique nature. The Happening has become a term widely co-opted in popular culture, but Kaprow has reached far beyond the implications of his earlier work and is still searching for further penetration into his very fertile ideas and realizations.

—Barbara Cavaliere

KARAVAN, Dani

Nationality: Israeli. **Born:** Tel Aviv, 7 December 1930. **Education:** Studied art with the painters Avni, Stematsky, Streichmann, and Marcel Janco in Tel Aviv, and at the Bezalel Academy of Arts in Jerusalem with the painter Ardon; studied fresco techniques with the painter Colacicchi at the Accademia delle Belle Arti in Florence, 1956–57; studied drawing at the Academie de la Grande Chaumiere, Paris. **Family:** Married to Eva; daughters: Noa, Tamar, and Yael. **Career:** Painter and sculptor. Created first paintings 1950; created stage sets 1960–73; created monumental sculptures and installations beginning in 1960. Created stage sets for the Batsheba Dance Company Israel, the Martha Graham Dance Company New York, and for Giancarlo Menotti for the festivals of Florence and Spoletto, Italy. Lives and works in Tel Aviv, Florence, and Paris. **Awards:** Israeli Prize for Art, Culture, and Sciences, 1977; Picasso Medal, 1994; Medal for Plastic Arts, Academy of Architecture, Paris, 1994; Crystal Award, World Economic Forum, Davos, Switzerland, 1995. Commander, Order of Arts and Letters, Italy, 1973; officer, 1984, and commander, 1993, Ordre des Arts et des Lettres, France; Goslar Kaiser Ring, Germany, 1996; UNESCO nomination as first ''artist for peace,'' 1996; Doctor Honoris Causa—Doctor of Philosophy Haifa University, Israel, 1997; appointed member, Order pour le mérite, Germany, 1997; Praemium Imperiale, Japan, 1998; Goethe Medal, Germany, 1999; Doctor Honoris Causa, Doctor of Philosphy Hebrew University Jerusalem, Israel, 1999; appointed member, Academy of Arte e Disegno, Florence, Italy, 2000. **Address:** Leteris Str. 7, Tel Aviv 64166, Israel; 8 rue de Ridder, 75014 Paris, France.

Individual Exhibitions:

1954 Kiboutz Harel, Israel
1971 Galeria Bellini, Florence
1973 Gordon Gallery, Tel Aviv
1978 Forte di Belvedera, Florence; Castello del Imperatore, Prato, Israel
1982 Kunsthalle, Baden Baden, Germany
Tel Aviv Museum

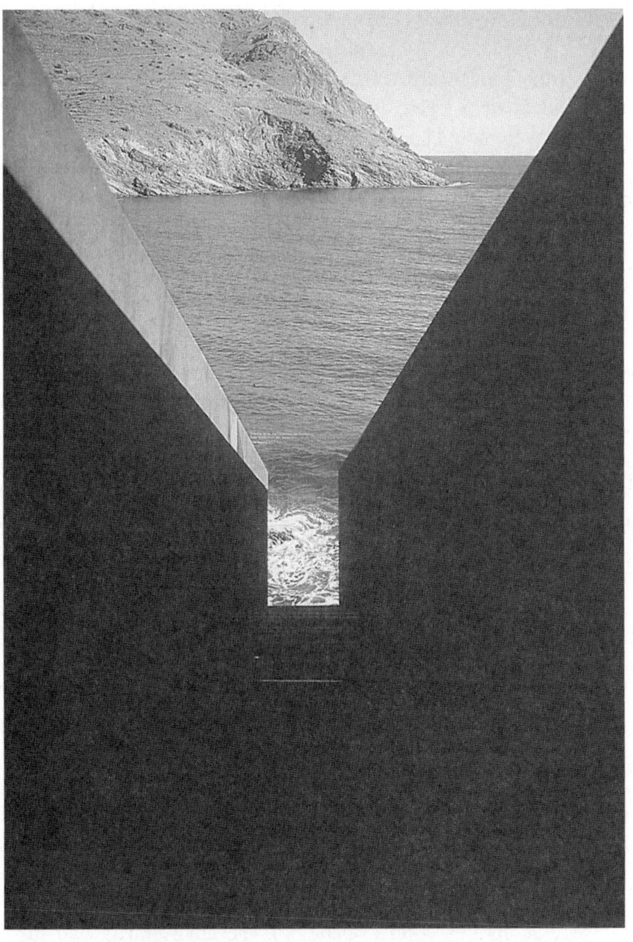

Dani Karavan: *Passage.* Photo by Jaume Blassi. ©Dani Karavan.

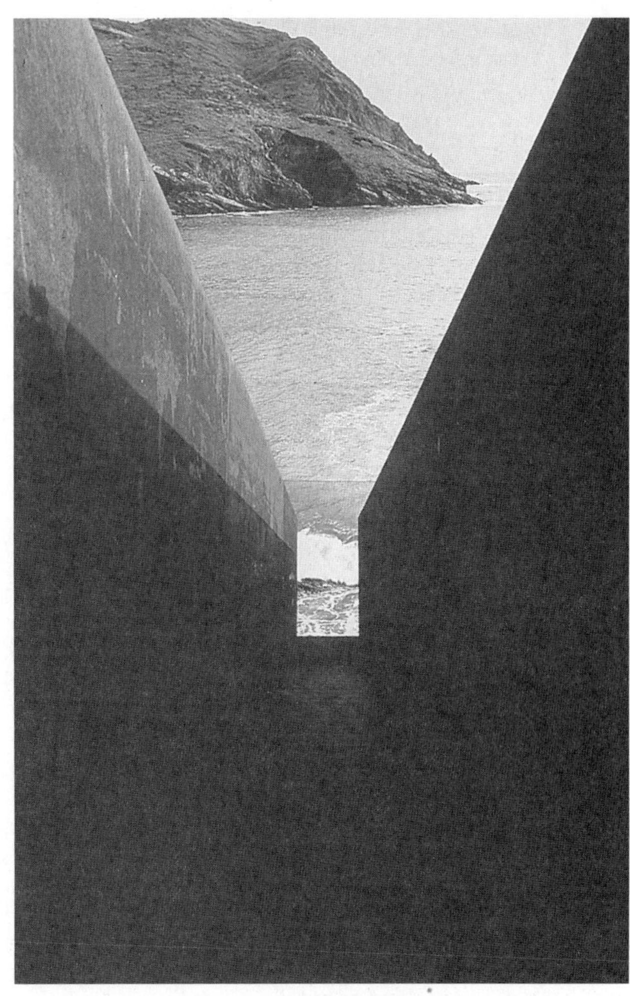

Dani Karavan: *Passage.* Photo by Jaume Blassi. ©Dani Karavan.

1983 Musée d'Art Moderne de la Ville, Paris
1984 Museum de Beyerd, Breda, Netherlands
1989 Nordrhein-Westfalen Museum, Dusseldorf
1992 Ludwig Museum, Cologne
1993 Stedelijk Museum, Amsterdam
Germanisches Nationalmuseum, Nuremberg
1994 Kunstmuseum, Bonn
1994–95 *Time Space Meditation—Dani Karavan,* temporary installations in different museums in Japan (Kamakura Museum of Modern Art; Ohara Museum, Kurashiki; The Miyagi Museum of Art, Sendai; Tsukuba Museum of Art, Ibaraki; Mie Prefectural Art Museum, Tsu; Museum of Contemporary Art, Sapporo; Yamanashi Prefectural Museum of Art, Kofu)
1996 *Retrospective,* Goslar, Germany
Shamaim, Sagacho Exhibit Space, Tokyo, Japan
1997 *Mimaamakim,* environment in two former coal factories (BUGA 97), Gelsenkirshen, Germany
Winter 97: Dani Karavan, The Museum of Israeli Art, Ramat Gan, Israel
Dani Karavan: Passages Homage to Walter Benjamin, Tel Aviv Museum of Art, Israel
1998 Retrospective exhibition, Galerie Jeanne Bucher, Paris
1999 *20 Years Later,* four exhibitons related to the exhibitions in Firenze and Prato in 78: *Homage to Arnolfo di Cambio,* Palazo Vechio Piaza Segnoria Florence; *Homage to Frederic II,* Prato Museum Pecci; *Nursery Garden for Peace,* Pistoia Piaza della catedrale; *The Tea Ceremony,* Celle (became a permanent project)

Selected Group Exhibitions:

1976 *Biennale,* Venice
1977 *Documenta VI,* Kassel, Germany
1980 Grand Palais, Paris
1984 *Electra,* Musée d'Art Moderne de la Ville, Paris
1987 *Documenta VIII,* Kassel, Germany
1988 *40 Sculptures for Israel,* Brooklyn Museum, New York
1990 *From Chagall to Kitaj,* Barbican Art Gallery, London
1991 *First Venice Biennale of Architecture,* Venice
1993 *Differentes Natures,* La Defense, Paris
1994 *La Ville,* Centre National d'Art et de Culture, Paris
1998 *The Axe Majeur of Cergy Pontoise,* IX Biennale International, Carrara, Italy
1999 *Soukat Shalom,* Champs de la Sculpture 2000, Paris
The Garden a Metaphor, Botanic Garden, Hebrew University, Jerusalem
Kadima, Museum Israel, Jerusalem

2000 Global Art Rheinland 2000, Wilhelm Lehmbruck Museum Duisburg, Germany
Yotam Fable, Tel Aviv Museum of Art

Collections:

Museum of Tel Aviv; Uffizi Gallery; Prado, Madrid; Pavillion de l'Arsenal, Paris; Musée d'Art Moderne de la Ville, Paris; Wilhelm-Lehmbruck-Museum, Duisburg; Jewish Museum, New York; Museum of Israel, Jerusalem, Israel; Ein Harod Museum, Israel; Park of Sculptures, Celle, Italy; Uffizi Gallery, Firenze, Italy; Prato Museum, Italy; Centre National d'Art et de Culture Georges Pompidou, Paris; Musée Ludwig, Cologne, Germany; Moka, Antwerpen, Holland; Louisiana Museum Humleback; Miyagi Museum of Art-Sendai, Japan; Kitakiushu Municipal Museum of Art, Japan; Kamakura Museum, Kamakura, Japan; Sagacho Exhibit Space, Tokyo.

Permanent Public Installations:

Weizmann Institute of Science, Rehovot, Israel; Court of Justice, Tel Aviv; Negev Monument, Beersheba, Israel; Knesset assembly hall, Jerusalem; Diener & Diener offices, Basel; Hilton Hotel, Jerusalem; El Al Terminal, Kennedy Airport, New York; *White Square,* Tel Aviv; Wallraf Richartz Museum and Ludwig Museum, Cologne; Cergy Pontoise, France; Joint Distribution Committee Building, Jerusalem; Lyn House, Tel Aviv; Pistoia, Italy; Louisiana Museum, Humlebaeck, Denmark; Bank Leumi, New York; Center West Building, Los Angeles; Germanisches Nationalmuseum, Nuremberg; Portbou, Spain; Shiba Hospital, Tel Aviv; Camp de Gurs, France; Zurich, Switzerland; UNESCO Headquarters, Paris; *Homage to Mercure,* environment for Clermont Ferrand, France; Courtyard Roquette Street, Paris, France; *Maala,* environmental sculpture, Osaka stadium, Japan; environmental sculpture, Tong Young, Korea; *Homage to Tadashi Tonoshiki,* Kitakyushu Municipal Museum of Art, Kityakushu, Japan; *Carré Urbain,* environment for the park Sources de la Bièvre, Saint Quentin en Yvelines, France; *Way to the Hidden Garden,* environmental sculpture, Sapporo Open Air Sculpture Park, Japan; *Migdal ha hadmaot,* Memorial Space for the armoured division, Latrun, Israel; *Garden of Memories,* environment, Altstadtpark, Duisburg architect Norman Forster, Germany; *Yad Lebanim ve Gan ha Meyasdim,* Hedera, Israel; *Way of Peace,* three kilometer environmental sculpture, Nitzana, near Egyptian border; *Bereshit,* sculpture for the Kagoshima Sculpture Park, Japan; *Bridges,* environment, Goslar, Germany; *Esplanade Charles de Gaulle,* La Défense, France.

Publications:

By KARAVAN: Book—*Way of Human Rights,* Nurnberg, 1995.

On KARAVAN: Books—*Makom,* exhibition catalog, Tel Aviv, 1982; *Dani Karavan: Ma'alot* by Christophe Brockhaus, Cologne, 1986; *Dani Karavan: Dialog Düsseldorf-Duisburg* with text by Bernd Finkeldey and Gottlieb Leinz, Düsseldorf and Duisburg, 1989; *Dani Karavan* by Pierre Restany, trans. by Jan Marie Clarke and Caroline Beamish, New York, 1992; *Kulturraume: Skulptur seit 1970,* exhibition catalog with text by Christophe Brockhaus, Cologne, 1999.

*

In the early sixties I had been creating environments from natural materials: wind, sunlight, water, sand, earth, vegetation, concrete, stone, iron. Later I created environments from glass, laser beams, neon, video, etc. I created site-specific sculptures. At the time, these concepts were not yet part of the language of art criticism.

My work is mainly commissioned. Commissioner + place + aim + budget + time = a sculpture. That is the formula that constitutes the stimulus and the process of creation.

I do not have objects that I produce in order that they might seek a buyer, or a home, or a place. If I am not offered a commission I will not propose any ideas for any place.

My sculptures are always made for a particular, specific site. My work considers the form and the levels of the ground, the sunrise, the sunset, the water, the trees, and the views from the site, whether the site is a natural landscape or an urban one, and all these qualities are connected with memory. My process of creation begins when all the data are available to me, and then the dialogue with the immediate environment begins. I learn it, try to understand it, listen to it, try to be guided by it, try to serve it and the people for whom I am building the sculpture or environment.

I employ the language I have built and am continuing to build and, with the experience that I have accumulated, I build my models to a precise scale along with everything that exists at the site. I sculpt and build the forms in three dimensions and connect them with what exists at the site. All this is still in the model stage, while taking the human scale into consideration.

My sculptures exist only in their relations to the human scale, to the point of view and the senses of people. I address all the senses, including sight, hearing, smell, touch—contact with all parts of the body and the motion of people. This is a total address, a total dialogue with the environment, with people constituting a part of it.

My sculptures connect people to the environment and invite them to be a part of it, while they themselves constitute an inseparable part of the urban or natural environment. The distance between the forms, the spaces, the void, is part of the whole, and the whole constitutes part of the void. Both are equal. The time, the passage through and within, is itself the outcome, the sum of it all, which are the measurement, the digit. The aspiration is harmony, and I will never know if I have attained it.

—Dani Karavan

* * *

Dani Karavan is an environmental artist who creates on-site sculptures and installations with various traditional but also such modern means as the laser beam.

To have a better picture of the personality and aims of this Israeli sculptor one must know that he was born in Tel-Aviv in 1930 where his father was a town engineer and planner. Dani Karavan therefore spent his entire childhood on a constantly evolving site. The conquest by the town of the desert is a phenomenon that marked this artist's imagination and sensibilities forever.

After his art training in Tel-Aviv and Jerusalem, Dani Karavan went to Florence in 1956 to study fresco techniques. Back in Israel in 1957, he tended towards integrating bi-dimensional murals into architecture. In 1963 he opened a new era in his work with a minimalist and conceptualist sculpture of monumental and symbolic bent, entitled *Monument of Life.* It was done near Beersheba in the Negev desert.

Karavan's environmental installations are generally constructed with the aid of such more traditional sculptural materials as wood, stone or white concrete, but also with natural elements such as grass, olive and cypress trees, water, wind organs and sun lines.

The laser was introduced to Dani Karavan's artistic repertoire towards the end of the 70's, but he had already become familiar with the technique and its aesthetic possibilities when he collaborated with the Czech scenographist Josef Svoboda, and also during his research at the Massachusetts Institute of Technology in the United States and the Weizmann Institute in Israel. The laser became a prominent part of his work in 1978 at a spectacular demonstration entitled *Environment for Peace* and *A Tribute to Galileo.* In this work a highly powerful laser symbolically joins Sangallo's Belvedere Fort in Florence's suburbs to the cupola of Brunelleschi's Duomo. In 1983 Karavan executed another environmental work entitled *The Bridge,* which linked the left and right banks of the Neckar River with a laser beam extending between the castle standing over the town of Heidelberg and the trail on the other side known as the "Philosopher's Walk." That same year at the *Electra* exhibition in Paris, he used two vivid-green laser beams to join the city's Museum of Modern Art, where the exhibition was being held, with the nearby Eiffel Tower and the district known as La Défense to try to make a relationship between historical and modern events tangible, as well as between architectural and technological creations and especially to illustrate the mutation of the mechanical era into that of electronics.

More recently, Karavan, ever faithful to the introduction of the laser in combination with more traditional sculptural and environmental materials, has been developing an urban project in the new town of Cergy-Pontoise near Paris. A laser beam follows the town's main street to serve as both a directional signpost and as a decorative element. But it is meant to be projected much further in order to symbolically link Cergy-Pontoise with one of the leading districts of Paris, the Etoile, without forgetting the historic monuments, like Versailles, along the way.

To better understand not only Karavan's artistic commitments, but also those concerned with his socio-psychological intentions, we can refer to Theodor Adorno and his aesthetic theories. For Adorno (and up to a certain point also for Karavan) art is neither a reflection of reality nor an aspect of ideology as various dogmatists would have it. It is a witness to history, i.e. accumulated experiences and suffering as well as a place of desire. It is therefore the ferment and promise of a free world. Dani Karavan's urban environment in Nuremberg, *Way of Human Rights* (1993), bears witness to this.

From the beginning of his artistic career Karavan's socio-aesthetic position has never wavered. His attempts to conquer space are linked to a veritable solidarity with his fellow citizens. His research has always leaned towards socially oriented urban planning. This has enabled him to be accepted as both an artist and individual without ever distancing himself from his immediate entourage or from those he frequents when carrying out a work in other countries.

Dani Karavan is an artist who combines an exceptional awareness of the physical and psychological implications related to the history and geography of a site. The introduction of advanced technology in his work not only represents a possible transcending of human limits, but testifies to a firm determination on his part to be of his time by assuming the implications of cultural and political circumstances.

Karavan is a good example of an artist whose penchant for utopian issues is compensated for by a social and aesthetical commitment *hic et nunc.*

—Frank Popper

KASAHARA, Emiko

Born: Tokyo, Japan, 1963. **Education:** Tama Art University, M.A., 1988. **Career:** Conceptual painter. **Address:** Lives in Brooklyn, New York.

Selected Solo Exhibitions:

1988 Gallery Yamaguchi, Tokyo
1990 Kobayashi Gallery, Tokyo
1992 Kobayashi Gallery, Tokyo
1993 Kobayashi Gallery, Tokyo
1997 Deitch Projects, New York
1998 Dieu Donne Papermill, New York

Selected Group Exhibitions:

1990 *A Cabinet of Signs—Contemporary Art from Postmodern Japan,* Tate Gallery, Liverpool (toured Whitechapel Art Gallery, London, and Malmo Kunsthall, Sweden)
Emiko Kasahara and Monika Brandmeier joint exhibition—Floating Scale, Spiral/Wacol Art Center, Tokyo
Woman Artists of the Day, imp Hall, Osaka
1991 *Zones of Love,* Tuoko Museum of Contemporary Art, Tokyo (toured Australia and New Zealand)
1995 *Age of Anxiety,* Power Plant, Toronto

Publications

On KASAHARA: Books—*The Age of Anxiety* (exhibition catalog), Toronto 1995; *Art in Japan Today,* Tokyo 1995; *Photography and Beyond in Japan: Space, Time and Memory,* Tokyo 1995. **Article—** "Japanese Art: Young Crowd, Wide Horizons" by Carol Lufty in *ARTnews,* vol. 94, no. 9, November 1994.

* * *

Emiko Kasahara's enigmatic sculptural installations are simultaneously alluring and off-putting. Their materials evoke the antiseptic and clinical, as well as the fleshy and succulent. Coolly preying on the semiotic instability of signs and the elusiveness of metaphors, Kasahara sets up situations to confound and confuse her viewer, teasing with the promise of a narrative or meaning that is perpetually withheld. Each of her works is a visual puzzle or conundrum that the viewer tries in vain to solve. Interpretation is frustratingly elusive, a slippery eel. Rejecting metaphor and allegory, Kasahara focuses on the complexity of meaning and the impossibility of its expression. It is in this rich realm of indeterminacy, which she calls a "magnetic force," that Kasahara's passive-aggressive works operate.

Kasahara has long been intrigued by the tension between oppositional states or forces, and it is the strategy of incorporating this tension in the formal make-up of her works that ties them together. *LAMB* (1994), a billboard-sized poster of a grazing flock of sheep, explores the delicate balance between the private and the public, and the individual and the collective, in the group-oriented society of Japan. The bland and inexpressive image takes on an eerie, disturbing quality when suspended above an intersection swarming with people in downtown Tokyo.

The most memorable of Kasahara's works are those which appropriate and subvert sexual symbols and their associations. With a knowing reference to Duchamp and the Surrealists, she created *Untitled—Double Urinal* (1994), a pair of urinals in the shape of breasts hand-carved from pink marble. Although at first the work seems to playfully evoke gender ambiguity, the disturbing scent of the bleach that fills the urinals sterilizes and sanitizes humorous associations and renders the work paradoxically taciturn. Similar dynamics are at work in *Untitled—A Flower of Stone* (1991), an installation of white marble roses displayed like precious specimens in glass cases on white and gray-tiled pedestals. The multiple contrasts Kasahara sets up between her sculptural interpretation of the cliché rose metaphor and what one typically expects from its representation, render the experience of the work at once titillating and disappointing. Unable to smell, touch, or enjoy the lush hues of natural roses or revel in their feminine associations, the viewer is left pondering the cold, death-like permanence of heavy, colorless stone. *Untitled—Three Types* (1993) is an unlikely pairing of three immaculately undisturbed twin-sized beds with an equal number of smooth, stainless steel tubes lined with pink silicone rubber. The tubes, which the viewer peers into at close range, evoke bodily orifices and sexual penetration, yet the rigid, sanitized beds contradict this sense of a private sensual experience.

Although Kasahara derives her imagery from the iconography of female sexuality, she does not consider her project a feminist one. Her works exploit the constructed nature of gender and its images, but in doing so, they bear witness to the evasiveness and indeterminacy of interpretation.

—Alicia Volk

KASSEBÖHMER, Axel

Nationality: German. **Born:** Herne, Germany, 21 April 1952. **Education:** Kunstakademie Düsseldorf, 1976. **Career:** Independent artist in Düsseldorf, since 1976; guest professor, Hochschule der Künste, Berlin, 1990–91; professor for painting and graphics, Akademie der Bildenden Künste, Munich, 1995 to present. **Agent:** Monika Sprüth Galerie, Wormser Strasse 23, D-50677 Köln, Germany. **Address:** Akademie der Bildenden Künste, Akademie Strasse 2, 80799 München, Germany.

Selected Individual Exhibitions:

1982 Galerie Rüdiger Schöttle, Munich
1984 Monika Sprüth Galerie, Köln
1985 Galerie Rüdiger Schöttle, Munich
1988 Galerie Grässlin-Ehrhardt, Frankfurt/Main
1989 *Bilder 1979–89,* Westfälischer Kunstverein Münster (traveled to Kunstverein München) (catalog)
1990 Galerie Philip Nelson, Paris
1991 Galerie Grässlin-Ehrhardt, Frankfurt/Main
1993 Monika Sprüth Galerie, Köln
1994 Galerie Philip Nelson, Paris
1997 Monika Sprüth Galerie, Köln
1999 Monika Sprüth Galerie, Köln

Selected Group Exhibitions:

1982 *Ausstellung B,* Lothringer Straße, Munich (catalog)
1983 Castello di Portofino, Portofino (catalog)
Standort Düsseldorf, Kunsthalle Düsseldorf (catalog)
1984 *Tiefe Blicke: Kunst der Achtziger Jahre,* Hessisches Landesmuseum, Darmstadt, Germany (catalog)
Kunstlandschaft Bundesrepublik: Junge Kunst in Deutschen Kunstverein, Kunstverein Karlsruhe (catalog)
1986 *Der Andere Blick,* Wissenschaftszentrum Bonn (traveled to Kunstverein München) (catalog)
1987 *Reason and Emotion in Contemporary Art,* Royal Scottish Academy, Edinburgh (catalog)
1988 *BiNationale: Deutsche Kunst der Späten 80er Jahre/ Germany Art of the Late 80s,* Kunsthalle Düsseldorf (traveled to The Institute of Contemporary Art/Museum of Fine Arts, Boston, Massachusetts) (catalog)
1989 *Refigured Painting: The German Image 1960–1988,* Toledo Museum of Art, Toledo, Ohio (traveled to Williams College Museum of Art, Williamstown; Solomon R. Guggenheim Museum, New York)
1992 *Ars pro Domo: Zeitgenössische Kunst aus Kölner Privatbesitz,* Museum Ludwig, Köln (catalog)
1994 *Still-Life Painting in the Museum of Fine Arts, Boston,* Museum of Fine Arts, Boston, Massachusetts (catalog)
1995 *Optical Consciousness,* Stelling Gallery, Leiden, Netherlands (traveled to H. Spaeti Gallery, Verduno, Italy) (catalog)
1999 *Zoom: Ansichten zur Deutschen Gegenwartskunst, Sammlung Landesbank Baden-Württemberg,* Württembergischer Kunstverein Stuttgart (catalog)

Collections:

Museum für Moderne Kunst, Frankfurt/Main; Museum of Fine Arts, Boston, Massachusetts; Victoria Versicherung, Düsseldorf; Landesbank Baden-Württemberg, Stuttgart.

Publications:

By KASSEBÖHMER: Book—*8 Landschaften,* Achenbach 1992. **Articles—**''Lieber M.'' in *Code,* May 1984; ''Vom Allgemeinen'' in *Catalogue Münster,* Munich 1990; ''Diese Suche Nach dem Besonderen. . .'' in *Catalogue Blau: Kaleidoskop einer Farbe,* Heidelberg 1990; ''A Short Text for a Small Picture'' in *Still-Life Painting in the Museum of Fine Art,* Boston, Massachusetts 1994.

On KASSEBÖHMER: Book—*Axel Kasseböhmer: Gemälde/Paintings* edited by Walter Grasskamp and Friedrich Meschede, 2002. **Articles—**''Abdankung des Hier und Jetzt: Ausstellung B in der Lothringerstraße München'' by Jörg Johnen in *Kunstforum International,* vol. 56, December 1982; ''Axel Kasseböhmer'' by Gepke

Axel Kasseböhmer: *Landschaft mit Stier-schödel,* 1985. ©Axel Kasseböhmer.

Bouma in *Metropolis M,* no. 2, May 1985; ''Axel Kasseböhmer'' by Stephan Schmidt-Wulffen in *Flash Art,* no. 137, 1987; ''Respekt vor den Alten Meistern'' by Karlheinz Schmid in *Kunstmagazin,* December 1989; ''Axel Kasseböhmer'' by Norbert Messler in *Artforum,* March 1990; ''Axel Kasseböhmer at Monika Sprüth'' by Janet Koplos in *Art in America,* December 1997.

KATZ, Alex

Nationality: American. **Born:** New York City, 24 July 1927. **Education:** Cooper Union, New York, 1946–49; Skowhegan School of Painting and Sculpture, Maine, 1949–50. **Military Service:** United States Navy, 1945–46. **Career:** Independent artist, since 1950. Visiting artist, Skowhegan School of Painting and Sculpture, Maine, 1960; visiting lecturer, Brooklyn Museum, New York, 1960; visiting lecturer, Yale University, New Haven, Connecticut, 1960–63; instructor, Pratt Institute, New York, 1962–65; visiting critic, New York Studio School, 1967, and University of Pennsylvania, Philadelphia, 1973–74; artist in residence, American Academy, Rome, 1983. Lives in New York. **Awards:** Guggenheim Painting Grant, 1972; Cooper Union Professional Achievement Citation, 1973; NEA grant for *Polaris* sets, 1976; St. Gauden's Medal in Art, Cooper Union, 1980; Skowhegan Award for Painting, 1980; *Art Direction Magazine Award,* New York, 1982; Graphic Design USA Award, New York, 1983; Art in Public Places Award, Chicago Bar Association, 1985. D.F.A.: Colby College, Waterville, Maine, 1984. Inducted by American Academy and Institute of Arts and Letters 1988; Opening of Paul J. Schupf wing for the Alex Katz collection, Colby College Museum, Waterville, 1996. **Agents:** Galerie Marguerite Lamy, 4 rue Beaubourg, 75004 Paris, France; Marlborough Gallery Inc., New York. **Address:** 435 W. Broadway, New York, New York, 10012–5902.

Alex Katz: *Jennifer and Mathieu,* 1986. ©Alex Katz/Licensed by VAGA, New York, NY.

Individual Exhibitions:

1954 Roko Gallery, New York
1957 Roko Gallery, New York
University of Pennsylvania, Philadelphia
1958 Sun Gallery, Provincetown, Massachusetts
1959 Sun Gallery, Provincetown, Massachusetts
Tanager Gallery, New York
1960 Stable Gallery, New York
1961 Stable Gallery, New York
Mili-Jay Gallery, Woodstock, New York
1962 Tanager Gallery, New York
Martha Jackson Gallery, New York
1963 Thibaut Gallery, New York
1964 Fischbach Gallery, New York (twice)
Grinnel Gallery, Detroit
1965 Fischbach Gallery, New York
1966 David Stuart Gallery, Los Angeles
1967 Fischbach Gallery, New York (twice)
1968 Fischbach Gallery, New York
Bertha Eccles Art Center, Ogden, Utah
Towson State College, Baltimore
Gotham Book Mart and Gallery, New York
1969 Mont Chateau Lodge, Morgantown, West Virginia
Phyllis Kind Gallery
1970 Fischbach Gallery, New York
1971 Fischbach Gallery, New York
Museum of Fine Arts, University of Utah, Salt Lake City (retrospective; toured the United States)
University of California at San Diego
Minnesota Museum of Art, St. Paul
Wadsworth Atheneum, Hartford, Connecticut
Galerie Dieter Brusberg, Hannover
Phyllis Kind Gallery, Chicago
Galerie Thelen, Cologne
1972 Reed College, Portland, Oregon
Sloan-O'Sickey Gallery, Cleveland
1973 Carlton Gallery, New York
Assa Galerie, Helsinki
Marlborough Gallery, New York
1974 Picker Gallery, Colgate University, Hamilton, New York
Davison Art Center, Wesleyan University, Middletown, Connecticut
Marlborough Goddard Gallery, Toronto
Marlborough Goddard Gallery, Montreal
Alex Katz: Prints, Whitney Museum, New York (toured the United States)
1975 Marlborough Fine Art, London
Galerie Marguerite Lamy, Paris
Galerie Arnesen, Copenhagen
Marlborough Graphics, New York
Marlborough Goddard Gallery, Toronto
American Foundation for the Arts, Miami
1976 Marlborough Gallery, New York
Marlborough Goddard Gallery, Toronto
1977 Galerie Roger d'Amecourt, Paris
Marlborough Galerie AG, Zurich
Fresno Arts Center, California (toured western United States and Canada)
1978 Marlborough Gallery, New York
Rose Art Museum, Brandeis University, Waltham, Massachusetts
1979 Brooke Alexander Gallery, New York
Suzanne Hilberry Gallery, New York
Robert Miller Gallery, New York
1980 *Scale and Gesture,* Queens Museum, Flushing, New York
Marlborough Gallery, New York
Hokin Gallery, Miami
1981 Portland Center for the Visual Arts, Oregon
Robert Miller Gallery, New York

Alex Katz: *View,* 1962. ©Alex Katz/Licensed by VAGA, New York, NY.

Mira Godard Gallery, Toronto
Contemporary Arts Center, Cincinnati
University of California, Santa Barbara
1982 Hokin Gallery, Chicago
Mira Godard Gallery, Chicago
Brooke Alexander Gallery, New York
Marlborough Gallery, New York
John Stoller Gallery, Minneapolis
Suzanne Hilberry Gallery, Birmingham, Michigan
Marlborough Fine Art, London
1983 Suzanne Hilberry Gallery, Birmingham, Michigan
Grace Hokin Gallery, Palm Beach, Florida
Texas Gallery, Houston
Marlborough Gallery, New York
McIntosh/Drysdale Gallery, Houston
1984 Michael Lord Gallery, Milwaukee, Wisconsin
Mira Godard Gallery, Toronto
Colgate University, Hamilton, New York
Suzanne Hilberry Gallery, Birmingham, Michigan
Robert Miller Gallery, New York
Asher-Faure Gallery, Los Angeles
Benjamin Mangle Gallery, Philadelphia
1985 Robert Miller Gallery, New York
Cooper Union, New York
Marlborough Gallery, Tokyo
Cleveland Center for Contemporary Art, Ohio (travelled to Colby College, Maine)
Wichita State University, Kansas
Farnsworth Museum, Maine
O'Farrell Gallery, Brunswick, Maine
Mario Diacono Gallery, Boston
1986 Whitney Museum, New York (retrospective)
McIntosh/Drysdale Gallery, Washington, D.C.
Marlborough Gallery, New York
Texas Gallery, Houston
1987 Grace Hokin Gallery, Palm Beach, Florida
Mira Godard Gallery, Toronto
Suzanne Hilberry Gallery, Birmingham, Michigan

Robert Miller Gallery, New York
Galerie Inge Baecker, Cologne
1988 *A Print Retrospective,* Brooklyn Museum, New York
Galerie Daniel Templon, Paris
Marlborough Gallery, New York
Seibu Museum of Art, Tokyo
Noctural Paintings, Cleveland Museum of Art, Ohio
1989 Galerie Bernd Klüser, Munich
1990 *Pinturas y Dibujos,* Fandos Galeria de Arte Moderno, Valencia, Spain
Galerie Ascan Crone, Hamburg
Paintings, Drawings and Cutouts, Orlando Museum of Art, Florida
Making Faces: Self-Portraits by Alex Katz, North Carolina Museum of Art, Raleigh (travelled to New Jersey and Kentucky)
Institute of Contemporary Arts, London
Marlborough Fine Arts, Tokyo
1991 Marlborough Gallery, New York
Munson-Williams-Proctor Institute, Utica, New York (retrospective, travelled to Maine and Arkansas)
1992 Colby College Museum of Art, Waterville, Maine (twice: *Drawings 1946–1989,* and *Alex Katz at Colby College*)
1993 Robert Miller Gallery, New York
Allene Lapides Gallery, Sante Fe, New Mexico
Marlborough Gallery, New York
1994 *Landscapes 1954–1956,* Robert Miller Gallery, New York
1995 *The Herbert W. Plimpton Collection of Realist Art,* Rose Art Museum, Brandeis University, Waltham (catalog)
Alex Katz: American Landscape, Staatliche Kunsthalle, Baden-Baden, Germany (catalog)
1996 *Alex Katz at Colby College,* Colby College Museum of Art, Waterville, Maine (catalog)
Alex Katz, IVAM Centre Julio Gonzalez, Valencia, Spain (catalog)
Alex Katz Under the Stars: American Landscapes 1951–1995, Baltimore Museum of Art, Maryland (traveling exhibition) (catalog)
1998 *Alex Katz,* Galerie Thaddaeus Ropac, Paris (catalog)
Saatchi Gallery, London
1999 Marlborough Gallery, New York
2000 *Alex Katz: Smile Again: Paintings of the Sixties,* Jablonka Galerie, Cologne (catalog)

Selected Group Exhibitions:

1960 *Young America 1960,* Whitney Museum, New York (toured the United States)
1967 *Large Scale American Paintings,* Jewish Museum, New York
1969 *Aspects of a New Realism,* Milwaukee Art Center (toured the United States)
1971 *Contemporary Realism,* Pennsylvania Academy of Fine Arts, Philadelphia
1973 *American Drawings 1963–1973,* Whitney Museum, New York
1975 *Portrait Painting 1970–75,* Allan Frumkin Gallery, New York
1979 *Printed Art: A View of Two Decades,* Museum of Modern Art, New York
1982 *The Human Figure,* Contemporary Arts Center, New Orleans
1984 *Visions of Childhood,* Whitney Museum Downtown, New York
1986 *The Painter-Sculptor in the 20th Century,* Whitechapel Art Gallery, London
1995 *Face Value: American Portraits,* Parrish Art Museum, Southampton, New York (traveling exhibition) (catalog)
1997 *Birth of the Cool: American Painting from Georgia O'Keeffe to Christoper Wool,* Deichtorhallen, Hamburg (traveled to Kunsthaus Zurich) (catalog)
2000 *1999 Carnegie International,* Carnegie Museum of Art, Pittsburgh

Collections:

Museum of Modern Art, New York; Metropolitan Museum of Art, New York; Whitney Museum, New York; Fogg Art Museum, Harvard University, Cambridge, Massachusetts; Hirshhorn Museum, Washington, D.C.; Art Institute of Chicago; Art Gallery of Ontario, Toronto; Atenium Taidemuso, Helsinki; Tate Gallery, London; Metropolitan Museum of Art, Tokyo, Japan; Brandeis University, Waltham; Detroit Museum; Allentown Art Museum; Weatherspoon Gallery of Art, Greensboro, North Carolina; Tokyo Gallery, Japan; Allen Memorial Art Museum, Oberlin; Houston Museum; The Israel Museum, Jerusalem; Iwaki City Museum, Japan; Hiroshima Museum; Museo Rufino Tamayo, Mexico; Honolulu Academy of Art.

Publications:

By KATZ: Books—*Fragment,* with John Ashbery, New York 1968; *Interlocking Lives,* with Kenneth Koch, New York 1970; *Selected Declarations of Dependence,* with Harry Mathews, Calais, Vermont 1977; *Face of the Poet,* New York 1978; *Give Me Tomorrow,* with Carter Ratcliff, New York 1985. **Articles**—''Is There a New Academy?'' in *Art News* (New York), September 1959; statement in *Art in America* (New York), January/February 1967; statement in *Art Now: New York* (New York), September 1970; ''10 Portraitists,'' interview with Gerrit Henry, in *Art in America* (New York), January/February 1975; interview with Merlin James in *Modern Painters* (London), vol. 9, no. 2, Summer 1996.

On KATZ: Books—*Minimal Art: A Critical Anthology,* edited by Gregory Battcock, New York 1968; *Alex Katz,* edited by Irving Sandler and William Berkson, New York 1971; *Alex Katz,* exhibition catalog, New York 1973; *Alex Katz,* exhibition catalog, Hamilton, New York 1974; *Alex Katz: Prints,* exhibition catalog with text by Richard S. Field and Elke M. Solomon, New York 1974; *Art Chronicles 1954–1966* by Frank O'Hara, New York 1975; *Alex Katz,* exhibition catalog, London 1975; *Alex Katz,* exhibition catalog, New York 1976; *Alex Katz,* exhibition catalog with an essay by Robert Rosenblum, Fresno, California 1977; *Alex Katz: Recent Paintings,* exhibition catalog, New York 1978; *Alex Katz: Cutouts,* exhibition catalog, New York 1979; *Alex Katz* by Irving Sandler, New York 1979; *Alex Katz: Scale and Gesture,* exhibition catalog, Flushing, New York 1980; *Alex Katz,* exhibition catalog, New York 1980; *Alex Katz,* exhibition catalog by Takahiko Okada, Tokyo, Japan 1990; *Alex Katz: Night Paintings,* by Donald Kuspit, Abrams, New York 1991; *Alex Katz,* by Sam Hunter, Rizzoli, New York 1992; *Alex Katz*

Under the Stars: American Landscapes 1951–1995, exhibition catalog, by Alanna Heiss, with and essays by Simon Schama and Dave Hickey, New York 1998; *Alex Katz: A Retrospective* by Irving Sandler, New York 1998; *Alex Katz,* exhibition catalog, by Martin Maloney, New York 1999. **Articles**—''Hipster'' in *Newsweek* (New York), December 1965; ''Art as Likeness'' by Lawrence Alloway in *Arts Magazine* (New York), May 1967; ''Alex Katz: Faces and Flowers'' by Nicolas Calas in *Art International* (Lugano, Switzerland), December 1967; ''Alex Katz'' by Scott Burton in *Art Scene* (New York), March 1969; ''Alex Katz and the Tactics of Representation'' by David Antin in *Art News* (New York), April 1971; ''The World of Alex Katz: Big Numbers . . . Fast Moves'' by Hilton Kramer in the *New York Times,* January 1973; ''Alex Katz at the Marlborough Gallery'' by Sarah Kent in *Studio International* (London) March/April 1975; ''Katz Advertises His Family'' by David Bourdon in the *Village Voice* (New York), 7 September 1979; ''Cool Katz'' by John Perreault in *Soho News* (New York), 14 April 1980; ''The Rockwell of the Intelligentsia'' by Robert Hughes in *Time,* 14 April 1986; ''Emptiness as a Form of content: Alex Katz's Self-Portraits at NCMA'' by Max Halperen in *The Arts Journal,* June 1990; ''Interview with Paul D. Schweizer. Alex Katz: A Drawing Retrospective'' by Carter Ratcliff in exhibition catalog, Utica, New York, 1991; ''Artist's Dialogue: Alex Katz'' by Carter Ratcliff in *Architectural Digest,* September 1992; ''Alex Katz, Interview'' by Vincent Katz in *Flash Art,* vol. no. 198, January/February 1998; ''Katz Appeal'' by David Cohen in *Royal Academy Magazine,* no. 58, Spring 1998; ''Alex Katz at Marlborough and Brent Sikkema'' by Richard Kalina in *Art in America,* March 2000. **Video**—*Alex Katz Five Hours* by Vivien Bittencourt and Vincent Katz, 1996.

*

I work with gestures for one thing. It's in tight motion, and you can't do it with a camera. People accept the camera without thinking: the camera makes a nice sign of a dancer, for example, but it isn't a good symbol. So, a camera doesn't really help me with gestures.

How people stand . . . the paintings look like photographs because it looks like a specific instant, but the paintings are very carefully worked out and often they are part of that instant and made to appear like one instant. I work empirically in the beginning and then it gets enlarged, the lines get larger and the scale gets broader. Sometimes it will take 3 or 4 days to make one line of a large drawing. I'll take one line and make it stretch.

—Alex Katz

* * *

Early in his career Alex Katz began to swim upstream by painting portraits when no one was painting portraits. While abstract expressionism was still the leading style, Katz painted members of his family and his friends, and he made a further break with conventionality, by making large rather than small-to-medium-sized realist paintings. The results were unusual. Katz responded to some of the same sources that influenced the abstract expressionists—Matisse (especially ''The Red Studio'') and the large flat color areas of Milton Avery—and devised a portrait style that resembles a precisionist landscape.

Katz often cuts off the figure or even a group of figures just below the shoulders, establishing an immediate association with antique portrait busts. Then he proceeds to assign qualities of monumentality to his subjects which in previous eras would have been apparent through dress, or by the mere existence of a portrait bust. Katz paints his figures on a grand scale, the sort reserved in earlier cultures for pharaohs and emperors. But, so far as we know, his subjects are not pharaohs and emperors, nor are they modern equivalents. Katz seldom provides a setting, and sometimes not even a costume, to help us understand why these people are bigger than life. Their features are reduced to simplified areas, so stylized that each reads as a separate element rather than as components of a physiognomy.

Certain art world individuals can be recognized among these subjects, but the anonymous faces take on a cinematic aura; their features are reduced to movie-poster bluntness, and they are larger than life. It is impossible to determine if Katz intended this movie star quality to envelop his subjects, but the associations with gigantic portrait busts these days have nothing to do with pomp and circumstance and everything to do with images found on the silver screen.

Alex Katz's work achieved enormous visibility in the 1980s, as a result of a retrospective exhibition at the Whitney Museum of American Art in 1986 and the 1987 published book on the artist by novelist Ann Beattie, for which Beattie made her own selections of work since 1980 on which to construct her essays. The essays appear in chapters with such titles as ''A Reading of Alex Katz,'' ''Ada,'' ''Narratives,'' ''Inanimate Portraits,'' and ''Couples,'' and include references to films, literature, rock stars, other artists and the contemporary scene that Beattie and Katz both capture in their work. She concludes that ''Like Beckett, Katz had always been more interested in raising questions about what is meaningful and, by implication, how to live, than he is in attempting to offer interpretations of reality.''

—Mary Stofflet

When examining the impressive body of art of Alex Katz, it is intriguing to note that he is of the same generation as Robert Rauschenberg, Jasper Johns, and Andy Warhol. All of these artists who emerged in the aftermath of Abstract Expressionism's ''Sturm and Drang.'' Each sought an alternative path for art making, were inspired by the large scale of the New York School, and asserted their ideas unburdened by trendy ideological interference.

The art career of Alex Katz spans nearly five decades. Throughout this period he has produced a convincing body of work and has expanded the definition of modernist representation. Katz's art has evolved to a state of substantiality—his paintings have become classics within the discourse of modern and contemporary figuration. Although once he was a cutting-edge photo realist, whose reputation became identified with figurative portraiture, his work continues to grow and change, being neither in nor out of fashion. However, it remains a distinctive brand of American realism. Despite his roots in Modernism, his current mammoth canvases depict an enlivened youthful freshness as well as an effortless mastery of the medium of painting.

In recent years the focus of his compositions has switched over from blank face portraits to landscapes that signify a synthesis of abstraction and representation. However, Katz's avid transfer to painting landscapes in the 1990s is not new. This subject has held his attention and has been ongoing concern from the start of his career. Evidence of this predilection is found in such early works such *Lake Time,* 1960, as well as *Walk,* 1970, in which the landscape is a significant component of the work of art. His paintings of landscapes, buildings, and people tend to resemble advertising posters, with simplified motifs and flat applications of color. Through his flat expanses of color and monumental scale he captures the fragile character of nature and organic plant matter. As Turner was not interested in imitating nature but found a metaphor for the sublime through light, atmosphere, and organic elements, Alex Katz appears to exploit the malleability of his symbols and intensifies complementary color.

Unlike many post-modern artists who make art for illuminating or emancipating a commodity driven society, Katz presents mostly an external appearance of things, concealing the inner state behind the façade. The bold approach in his unhesitating works of art is derived from the ordinary, and the mural scale of his recent landscape imagery functions as a type of window into a real life view of nature. *Autumn,* 1999, an expansive piece exhibited in the 53rd Carnegie International exerts a curious pull, beckoning the viewer to step closer despite its imperturbable indifference. Its vast scale, close-up vantage point and radically cropped image engulf the viewer in an imaginary space located somewhere between physical existence and intrigue. In *West 2,* 1998, a distinctive power of the urban nocturnal landscape is seized in this image that evinces a kindred sensibility with Edward Ruscha flattened space, as well as the empty void of Barnett Newman's color fields. Rows of fluorescent-lit windows against a dark background capture the sense of isolation and emptiness of an office building late at night. Despite the cool detachment of this series of paintings, they nevertheless exert a quiet romantic perceptiveness.

In his review for *ARTFORUM* of Katz's exhibition at the Marlborough Gallery in the fall of 1999, Barry Schwabsky wrote, ''Katz brings to the countryside neither the native eye of someone intimate with its every detail, the inhabitant for whom woods like those in *Green Dusk,* 1996, may be ones 'have been loved in and wept in,' as they were for Robert Frost, nor the romantic idealization of the city newcomer who thereby betrays his essential alienness to the scene.''

—updated by Elaine A. King

KAUFFMAN, (Robert) Craig

Nationality: American. **Born:** Eagle Rock California, 31 March 1932. **Education:** School of Architecture, University of Southern California, Los Angeles, 1950–52; University of California at Los Angeles, 1952–56, B.A. 1959, M.A. 1956. **Career:** Independent painter and sculptor, living in Paris, 1960–62, in California and New York since 1962. Instructor, University of California at Irvine, 1967–77; University of California, Berkeley, 1969; School of Visual Arts, New York, 1970–71; Professor Emeritus of Studio Art, University of California at Irvine. **Awards:** United States Government Fellowship for the Arts, 1967; First Prize, *69th American Exhibition,* Art Institute of Chicago, 1970. **Agents:** Patricia Faure Gallery, Bergamot Station, 2525 Michigan Avenue, Santa Monica, California 90404–4014.

Individual Exhibitions:

1953 Felix Landau Gallery, Los Angeles
1958 Dilexi Gallery, Los Angeles
Ferus Gallery, Los Angeles
1963 Ferus Gallery, Los Angeles
1965 Ferus Gallery, Los Angeles
1967 Ferus Gallery, Los Angeles
Pace Gallery, New York
1969 Pace Gallery, New York
Irving Blum Gallery, Los Angeles
1970 Pace Gallery, New York
Pasadena Art Museum, California
University of California at Irvine
1972 Irving Blum Gallery, Los Angeles
1973 Pace Gallery, New York
Galerie Dorothea Speyer, Paris
1975 Riko Mizuno Gallery, Los Angeles
1976 Galerie Dorothea Speyer, Paris
Robert Elkon Gallery, New York
Comsky Gallery, Los Angeles
1977 *Moses, Delap, Kauffman,* Cassat Gallery, La Jolla, California
1978 Arco Center, Los Angeles
1979 Blum-Helman Gallery, New York
Grapestake Gallery, San Francisco
1996 Patricia Faure Gallery, Santa Monica

Selected Group Exhibitions:

1965 *5 at Pace,* Pace Gallery, New York
1971 *Transparency, Reflection, Light, Space: 4 Artists,* University of California at Los Angeles (with Larry Bell, Peter Alexander, and Robert Irwin)
1975 *60 and 70: Trends of 6 California Artists,* Ruth Schaffner Gallery, Los Angles
1976 *75 Years of California Art,* San Francisco Museum of Modern Art
Recent Los Angeles Work, Museum of Modern Art, New York
1977 *Painting and Sculpture in California: The Modern Era,* Smithsonian Institution, Washington, D.C. (travelled to San Francisco Museum of Modern Art)
1978 *Works on Paper,* Margo Leavin Gallery, Los Angeles
1979 *Whitney Biennial,* Whitney Museum, New York
1986 *California Sculpture 1959–80,* San Francisco Museum of Modern Art
1990 *Billy Al Bengston, Peter Alexander, Larry Bell, Laddie John Dill, Craig Kauffman, Ed Moses, Eric Orr, Ed Ruscha in Barcelona: Etchings and Lithographs 1988–1989,* Ediciones Polígrafa, Barcelona (catalog)
1991 *Finish Fetish: LA's Cool School,* University of Southern California Fisher Gallery, University Park Campus, Los Angeles
1995 *Selections from the Robert A. Rowan Collection,* Alyce de Roulet Williamson Gallery, Pasadena, California
1997 *Sunshine & Noir: L.A. Art 1960–1997,* Louisiana Museum of Modern Art, Danemark, Humlebaeck
2001 *Perfect 10: Ten Years in Soho,* Sandra Gering Gallery, New York

Collections:

Museum of Modern Art, New York; Whitney Musuem, New York; Aldrich Museum, Ridgefield, Connecticut; Fort Worth Art Center

Museum, Texas; Pasadena Art Museum, California; Los Angeles County Museum of Art; Santa Barbara Museum of Art, California; San Francisco Museum of Modern Art; Tate Gallery, London.

Publications:

By KAUFFMAN: Articles—interview in *Transparency, Reflection, Light, Space: 4 Artists,* exhibition catalog, Los Angeles 1971; interview with Jan Butterfield in *Art in America* (New York), July 1976; interview with Josef Woodard in *Artweek,* vol. 22, 4 April 1991.

On KAUFFMAN: Books—*5 At Pace,* exhibition catalog with an introduction by John Coplans, New York 1965; *Craig Kauffman,* exhibition catalog, New York 1970; *Transparency, Reflection, Light, Space: 4 Artists,* exhibition catalog by Frederick Wight, Los Angeles 1971; *Painting and Sculpture in California: The Modern Era,* exhibition catalog, San Francisco 1977; *Craig Kauffman,* exhibition catalog by Melinda Wortz, Los Angeles 1978. **Articles—**''Notes on the Absorption of the Avant-Garde into the Culture'' by Paul Stitleman in *Arts Magazine* (New York), May/June 1973; ''New Paintings by Craig Kauffman'' by Melinda Wortz in *Artweek* (Oakland, California), March 1975; ''Kauffman's Subtle Joke'' by Melinda Wortz in *ARTnews* (New York), June 1975; ''The Trip from Abstract Expressionism'' by Pamela J. King in the *Los Angeles Herald Examiner,* 16 April 1978; ''Artists in the 70s—Free to See and Be Seen'' by William Wilson in the *Los Angeles Times,* 30 April 1978; ''Craig Kauffman's Interiors'' by Melinda Wortz in *Artweek* (Oakland, California), 13 May 1978; ''Unslick in L. A.'' by Peter Frank in *Art in America* (New York), September/October 1978; ''A Passel of Patterners'' by Peter Frank in the *Village Voice* (New York), 19 February 1979; ''Painterly Surface, Architectonic Structure'' by R. McDonald in *Artweek* (Oakland, California), 24 November 1979.

* * *

A native Californian, Craig Kauffman contributed at least as much as any other artist to the rise of the characteristic style which in the 1960s established Los Angeles as a major creative center. Kauffman's sophisticated works, and personal cosmopolitanism, are credited with having inspired in a generation of Southern California artists a level of professionalism that made possible the creation of an aesthetic expression no longer dependent upon New York and European examples. An exhibition of early abstract paintings at the avant-garde Ferus Gallery in 1958 was particularly critical in its influence, pointing the direction for other prominent artist such as Billy Al Bengston, Ken Price, and Robert Irwin. Laden with sexual imagery akin to that of still another colleague, John Altoon, these highly original works displayed a sophisticated union of the mechanical and biomorphic that invokes Duchamp and Picabia.

Kauffman began as a typical, albeit precocious, art-school Abstract Expressionist; by 1957 his paintings became more simplified, delineated, and hard-edged, incorporating the typical bulb and the tube shapes that provide the illusion of relief in the acrylic on Plexiglas paintings of the early 1960s. These in turn led to the low-relief vacuum-formed wall paintings for which Kauffman is justifiably famous. Paradigmatic exemplars of the high-finish, reflective transparency, and sensual colorism of the L.A. look, these simple Plexiglas shapes established the stylistic basis for an innovative group of Southern California artists.

In this respect, Kauffman's most important contribution began in 1964 with his experimentation with plastic. In works like ''Yellow-Orange'' (Los Angeles County Museum of Art), he distinguised himself as probably the first artist to ''paint'' in plastic using industrial techniques. This lesson was not lost on those fellow artists who turned to new materials, acquiring the technological skills necessary to manipulate them. Pursuing these interests, Kauffman produced into the early 1970s a series of plastic works in high-key transparent acrylic pigments. Maintaining a basic repertory of simple minimalist forms, he evolved by 1968 his large vacuum-formed half-bubbles in which light and color are magically suspended like yolks in translucent eggs. In these pieces the ovals and lozenges appear to be dematerialized by color; the viewer looks through the surface, into the painting itself. These perceptual interests were shared concurrently by several Los Angeles area artists, notably DeWain Valentine, who were also preoccupied with light and space. These concerns spawned another important regional phenomenon, the large-scale light and color installations of the ''environmentalists,'' among them Irwin and James Turrell.

Although Kauffman's own process pieces of 1970 were clearly moving in the same direction, he opted for return to the object. From about 1972 to the present, Kauffman has created a series of closely related works, the content of which is the basic elements of a painting; an interpretation of structure, surface, color. The earlier pressed formed Plexiglas versions resemble stained glass windows in which banded color has been applied to the ''leading'' rather than the glass. This linear architectural geometry reasserted itself further after 1974 (when Kauffman abandoned Plexiglas) in paintings which bring to mind building construction framing or, most notably in works of 1976–77 such as ''L'Atelier #1'' and ''Interior #2,'' the backs of canvases with unconventionally arranged stretcher bars.

Over the past years Kauffman has divided his time between studios in New York City and Laguna Beach, California. The recent acrylic paintings on paper and silk continue his interest in abstracted interiors, reintroducing the biomorphic shapes of his earlier work along with a more painterly and expressionistic technique. ''Tell Tale Heart, 3rd Version'' of 1980 (Blum Helman Gallery, New York) shares more than the title with its predecessor from 1958. Kauffman's continuity of vision and development lies not in the stylistic similarities between his early and most recent work but in his ability to apply the important lessons learned during the intervening years.

—Paul J. Karlstrom

KAWAGUCHI, Tatsuo

Nationality: Japanese. **Born**: Kobe, 15 February 1940. **Education:** Tama University of Fine Art, Tokyo, 1958–62, B.F.A. 1962. **Family:** Married Chikako Kawaguchi in 1970; children: Yuki and Makiko. Lives and works in Kobe. **Career:** Member, Group ''i.'' Taught art in Yamada Junior High School, Kobe, 1962–64, and Komagabayashi Junior High School, Kobe, 1964–66; assistant professor, Akashi Junior College, Akashi, 1968–78. Since 1978, professor of art, Kansai Art College, Osaka. **Awards:** First Prize and Collectors' Prize, *New Faces Exhibition,* Tokyo, 1965; Mainichi/French Government Scholarship Competition Prize, 1966; Prize for Excellent Work, *Japanese Art Festival,* Tokyo, 1968, 1973; Grand Prize, *Contemporary Space '68: Light and Environment,* Kobe, 1968; Prize for Excellence, First

Hakone Open-Air Exhibition, 1973; Iue Cultural Prize, Kobe, 1974; Grand Prize, Osaka Citizens Gallery Opening Competition, 1974; Purchase Prize, *Biennale,* Sydney, 1976; Prize of the Museum of Modern Art, Hokkaido, at *International Biennale Exhibition of Prints,* Tokyo, 1979; Appointed Professor of Fine Arts, The University of Tsukuba, 1991. **Agents:** Toa-Gallery, Miyaboshi Building, 3–12-16 Kitanagase-Dori, Chuo-ku, Kobe 650; Gallery 16, Sakuranocho, Sanjo-Teramachi, Nakagyo-ku, Kyoto 604; Sakura Gallery, Fushimi Building 5F, 1–20-12 Nishiki, Naka-ku, Nagoya 460; and Art Front Gallery, 29–5 Sakuraoka, Shibuya-ku, Tokyo 150, Japan.

Individual Exhibitions:

1965 Gallery Anneau, Osaka
1966 Gallery 16, Kyoto
1967 Gallery 16, Kyoto
1968 *Dark,* Muramastu Gallery, Tokyo
1971 *172800 Seconds,* Gallery 16, Kyoto
1972 *Relation-Energy,* Gallery Piner, Tokyo
1975 *Tatsuo Kawaguchi's Recent Works,* Minami Gallery, Tokyo
2 Artists: Tatsuo Kawaguchi and Keiji Uematsu, City Museum of Namban Art, Kobe
1977 Gallery Kitano Circus, Kobe
1978 *Works: Made of Parts,* Gallery 16, Kyoto
Gallery U, Nagoya
1968–1979: Tatsuo Kawaguchi, Art Center M, Obama
Iron of Iron, Toa-Road Gallery, Kobe
1979 Toa-Road Gallery, Kobe
1980 *Relation-Quality,* Kobayashi Gallery, Tokyo
Sakura Gallery, Nagoya
Toa-Road Gallery, Kobe
1981 Toa-Road Gallery, Osaka
Gallery Le Coin, Osaka
Relation-Friction/Relation-Temperature, Art Front Gallery,Tokyo
1982 *Relation-Quality,* Sakura Gallery, Nagoya
1989 Hillside Gallery, Tokyo
1998 *Kawaguchi Tatsuo 1990–1998,* Contemporary Art Gallery, Art Tower Mito, Mito City, Japan
1999 *The Work of Tatsuo Kawaguchi,* Kyoto Municipal Museum of Art, Japan

Selected Group Exhibitions:

1968 *Fluorescent Chrysanthemum: Contemporary Japanese Art,* Institute of Contemporary Arts, London
1971 *Man and Nature,* Metropolitan Art Gallery, Tokyo
1973 *20 Years of Contemporary Art in Restrospective,* Metropolitan Art Gallery, Tokyo
Bienal, Sao Paulo
1974 *Japan, Past and Present,* Kunsthalle, Dusseldorf
Contemporary Japanese Art, Louisiana Museum, Humelbaek, Denmark (toured Denmark, Sweden, and Norway)
1977 *The Structure of Seeing,* Seibu Museum of Art, Tokyo
1981 *Art Now 1970–1980,* Hyogo Museum of Modern Art, Kobe
Trends in Japanese Art in the 1970s, Institute of Culture and Arts, Seoul
1982 *Fifth Triennale: India 1982,* New Delhi
1996 *Six Artists: Interactive—Individual,* Ibaraki-ken Kindai Bijutsukan, Mito-shi (catalog)
1997 *Group Exhibition in Summer 97 Part 2,* Gallery Yamaguchi, Osaka

Collections:

National Museum of Modern Art, Tokyo; Ministry of Culture, Tokyo; Japan Foundation, Tokyo; Museum of Contemporary Art, Ngaoka, Japan; Okayama Cultural Center, Japan; Open-Air Museum, Ube, Japan; Osaka Prefectural Contemporary Art Center, Okayama, Japan; Museum of Modern Art, Hokkaido, Japan; Louisiana Museum, Humlebaek, Denmark; Art Gallery of New South Wales, Sydney.

Publications:

By KAWAGUCHI: Books—*Tokyo Biennale '70,* exhibition catalog, Tokyo 1970; *Aspects of New Japanese Art,* exhibition catalog, Tokyo 1970; *Sonzai,* editor, Kobe 1974; *Trends in Contemporary Art,* Tokyo 1977; *Tatsuo Kawaguchi,* with Fusako Araki and Kazuko Yamaguchi, 1996. **Articles—**''The Starting Point of Creation'' in *Mizue* (Tokyo), February 1972; ''To Make a Photo an Object: The Distance Between Reality and the Photograph'' in *Bijutsu-Techo* (Tokyo), June 1972; preface to *Part,* exhibition catalog, Osaka 1972; interview with Yoshiaki Tono in *Mizue* (Tokyo), August 1974; ''Sounding Out Conceptual Artists on Their Concepts,'' interview with Shuji Terayama, in *Geijutsu-Club* (Tokyo), vol. 8, 1974; ''Fragments of a Journey'' in *Bijutsu-Techo* (Tokyo), February 1977; ''Hand-Made Paper'' in *Misho* (Osaka), May 1980.

On KAWAGUCHI: Books—*172800,* exhibition catalog with preface by Yusuke Nakahara, Kyoto 1971; *Relation-Energy,* exhibition catalog with preface by Ichiro Haryu, Tokyo 1972; *Thoughts on Photography* by Koen Shigemori, Tokyo 1972; *Tatsuo Kawaguchi's Recent Works,* exhibition catalog with an essay by Yoshiaki Tono, Tokyo 1975; *Japanese Contemporary Art 18: Art of Tomorrow,* Tokyo 1980. **Articles—**''From Here to Here'' by Toshiaki Minemura in *Bijutsu-Techo* (Tokyo), May 1972; ''The Apocalypse of the Death of Art'' by Jean Clair in *Bijutsu-Techo* (Tokyo), December 1973; ''Tatsuo Kawaguchi'' by Akio Fujieda in *Art in Japan Today,* edited by Suji Takashina, Yoshiaki Tono and Yusuke Nakahara, Tokyo 1984; ''Tatsuo Kawaguchi'' by Katuo Akane in *Way* (Osaka), April 1976; ''Today, What is Technique in Art?'' by Shigemitsu Hirano in *Mizue* (Tokyo), August 1977; ''Tatsuo Kawaguchi's Relation-Quality'' by Toru Matsumoto in *Bulletin of the National Museum of Modern Art* (Tokyo), May 1982.

*

I have been lying on the beach for a long time, gazing at the sea and the sky.

On a fine day, in between the sea and the sky, we can see the mountains on the far shore. Today, however, they are obscured, as if scratched out, in the total grayness of clouds and mist.

The sea and the sky are the same color and have the same brightness. The horizon is nowhere in sight. These drifts in the grayness have some quality that makes the sea the sea and some quality that makes the sky the sky. And where they meet, the sea and the sky blur indistinguishibly, floating in the distant haze.

I stand up, looking at the distant vagueness. I drop my eyes to where I have been lying, and find that the weight of my body has left a slight depression in the sand.

—Tatsuo Kawaguchi

* * *

Suppose Tatsuo Kawaguchi, stopping over a large photocopy of the constellations spread out in front of him, checking each star carefully, keeps jotting down on it every figure of the light-hours that separate a star from the earth. Then, the photocopy of the starry heavens, when he is done with the job, becomes a figurative ruin that contains heaps of manifold times. Thus, however profound the thoughts you may entertain, or sweet the dreams you may be enraptured in, while looking wistfully at the starlit sky, what you think is that the light of each star is in fact the debris of the light that, having left the star several years, or even several centuries, ago, had just come down to meet your eyes, and the source of the light, that is, the star, might have perished ages ago. This is exactly why Buckminster Fuller had to define the universe as the ''aggregate of nonsimultaneous . . . energy events.'' How interesting that the collection of lights observable from the earth simultaneously should involve such different lengths of time! Thus, Kawaguchi, having replaced the act of seeing with function of time, has virtually become a modern astrologist. (Professional astronomers don't usually bother to measure the light-hours of the stars that have no value for their research.)

Another time Kawaguchi will attempt to be a ''carrier of darkness.'' For nothing but darkness is contained in the cast iron box which he closed up tight with bolts. Not even a little clatter, such as Duchamp's ''Hidden Sounds,'' can be heard there, ''but, certainly the air . . .'' you might suggest—but then I would have to call you an old-fashioned materialist. Because the thing sealed up in it is surely just ''darkness.''

It is the kind of ''darkness'' that, even if the box were opened, you wouldn't be able to see at all. This is a gracious contempt for the fact that the act of ''seeing'' is impossible without light. Furthermore, this box was crated in Kobe and carried to Tokyo by Shinkansen, the Bullet Train. Kawaguchi, with mischievous twinkles in his eyes, would ask you: ''Is this Kobe darkness carried to Tokyo, or is it just Tokyo darkness?'' This unanswerable question exists by itself as a pure conception of ''darkness.''

There is another cast metal box, cylindrical in shape and also closed up tight, inside which are blended two beams of light in different primary colors radiating from each end of the cylinder. But nobody can see exactly how the two colors blend there. The only thing you can be sure about is that there is no ''hope'' sealed in this Pandora's box. So, this time Kawaguchi becomes a Proteus who has sealed up his own eyes with a special kind of imagination.

The most distinctive feature of these works is that they are more or less severed from any circumstantial conditions; concepts are condensed and embodied in actual things that are sustained by themselves. As is clear in his works of stars, darkness and light—what the artist has been doing is to recapture the meaning of time, space and the act of seeing. But by working in this direction, he has been taking advantage of the given conditions in terms of time and place, producing in some respects a predominant effect that might be described as ''environmental.'' When Kawaguchi participated, nearly 20 years ago, in a show called *Group i* at Gifu, Japan, what he did was symbolic, for it was to dig up a huge hole on the river-bed of the Nagara and then fill it up again. The hole, like his starlights, existed for a certain length of time and then disappeared. At the show called *172800 Seconds* (Gallery 16, Kyoto), placing an 8mm movie camera and a tape recorder in the showroom, the artist captured all the scenes and activities and sounds that occurred there during the show, and when the show was over, he sealed up in a box both films and tapes, just as he did with the ''darkness'' in those metal boxes, never showing anybody the results of the recording. The idea was to produce a canned time. In his work entitled *Relation-Energy* shown in 1972 Kawaguchi displayed all kinds of electrical gadgets to show how electric energy transforms itself into varied forms, sometimes just electric current running through inside the wire creeping on the floor, sometimes the heat in a nichrome wire, sometimes the light in a fluorescent lamp, sometimes the wind coming forth through a fan, and so forth. In doing this, however, the artist's purpose was to weigh the balance between things seen and things unseen, showing how, in terms of energy, all those things, i.e. lights you can see, electric current you cannot see, an iron rod that doesn't move, are all identical after all.

Kawaguchi's more recent works, while still retaining a bit of environmental tendency, have added a new aspect, the emphasis on presenting *objects.* However, the degree of this new tendency in his works depends mainly upon how directly the specific concepts in his creative ideas can be expressed in the material on hand, after having gone through the process of condensation in the ''thingness'' of the given material. The movements of the conceptual world must come through the ''thingness'' of the material, as if they were dull, almost inaudible hums in the bottom of a deep sea, accompanied by tiny waves of a certain feeling—a feeling I might describe as something like the lyricism of slight flush concealed in the cool, distant expression of a face.

Conceptual art which had long seemed to refuse the world of things and objects so obstinately had reached, so to speak, the extreme of simply linguistically manipulating concepts. Is it too presumptuous to feel conceptual art has now arrived at the phase where it begins to reconsider the actual presentation of objects?

—Yoshiaki Tono

KAWAMATA, Takashi

Nationality: Japanese. **Born:** Hokkaido, Japan, 1953. **Web site:** http://www5a.biglobe.ne.jp/~onthetab/.

Selected Projects:

1979 *By Land,* Tama Riverside, Tachikawa
1980 *Project Work in Takayama,* Takayama Architecture School, Takayama
1982 *Takara House Room 205,* Apartment project, Tokyo
1983 *Otemon, Wada-So,* Apartment project, Materials and Spaces Exhibition, Fukuoka
Project Work in Saitama, Shape and Spirit in Wood Work Exhibition, The Museum of Modern Art, Saitama, Urawa
Slip in Tokorozawa, Apartment project, Tokorozawa
Tetra House N3 W26, Apartment project, Mr. and Mrs. Endo's House, Sapporo

1984 *Ginza Network,* Gallery Kobayashi, Jewelry Shop Olphe, Kaneko Art Gallery and Tokyo Gallery, Tokyo
Okaido Installation, collaborated with PH Studio, Matsuyama
Under Construction, collaborated with PH Studio, Hillside Terrace, Tokyo
1985 *Limelight Project,* Limelight, New York
P. S. 1 Project, P. S. 1, Long Island City
1986 *Spui Project,* Construction site project, The Hague
1987 *La Maison des Squatters,* Construction site project, Japon Art Vivant '87, Grenoble
Destroyed Church, Documenta 8, Kassel
Nove de Julho Cacapava, Construction site project, The 19th Sao Paulo International Biannual Exhibition, Sao Paulo
1988 *Fukuroi,* Construction site project, Aka-Renga Final, Suruga Bank, Fukuroi
Hien-So, Kyoto
1989 *Toronto Project: Colonial Tavern Park,* Toronto
1990 *Sidewalk,* New Works for New Spaces: Into the Nineties, Columbus
1991 *Favela in Houston,* Landscape, Bayou Riverside, Houston
Favela in Ottawa, A Primal Spirit, National Gallery of Canada, Ottawa
Favela in Ushimado, The 4th Biannual/Japan Ushimado Art Festival, Ushimado
1992 *People's Garden,* Documenta 9, Kassel
Project on Roosevelt Island, Small Pox Hospital, Roosevelt Island, New York
1993 *Passaggio,* Museo Citta Eventi: Inside Out, Prato
Frauenbad, Limmat River and Helmhaus, Zurich
1994 *Prefabrication in Hiroshima,* Asian Art Now, Hiroshima
Transfert, Centre de Creation Contemporain, Tours and Atelier Calder, Sache
1995 *Tram Passage,* Verein StadtRaum Remise, Vienna
Bunker, Kunsthalle, Recklinghausen
1996 *Work in Progress,* Zug
Sidewalk, Wiener Neustadt
Working Progress, Alkmaar
1997 *Working Progress: Boat Travelling,* Alkmaar, traveled to Munster
Relocation, Annely Juda Fine Art and Serpentine Gallery, London
Le passage de chaises, Chapelle Saint-Louis de la Salpetriere, Paris
1998 *Working Progress: Boat Traveling,* Alkmaar, Zaandam, Purmerend, Haalem and Beverwijk
Les Chaises de Traverse, Hotel Saint-Livier, Metz and Sinagogue de Delme, Delme
Haus der Kunst, Staatsgalerie Moderner Kunst, Munchen
Garden Sheds, every day/11th Biennale of Sydney, Royal Botanic Garden, Sydney
Tokyo Project: New Housing Plan, Tokyo
1999 *Matsunoyama Project,* Matsunoyama, Niigata
Tokyo Project B New Housing Plan, Galerie Deux, Tokyo
2000 *Sue la voie,* Evreux
Trench and Bridge, Middelheimopenluchtmuseum, Middelheim
Matsunoyama Project, Matsunoyama, Niigata (from 1996)
Work in Progress: Project in Toyota City, Toyota
Kawamata Coal Mine Project: Tagawa 2000, Project Site in Jodoji Park, Tagawa (from 1996)
Lodging London, London
2001 *Lodging Tokyo,* Haneda, Tokyo
Kawamata Coal Mine Project: Boat Project, Tagawa-Wakamatsu Bay
Tadashi Kawamata: Boston Project, Plan in Progress, Sert Gallery, Harvard University, Boston

Publications:

By KAWAMATA: Books—*Kawamata 80's Document,* Tokyo 1980; *Takara House Room 205 Project,* Tokyo 1986; *Tetra House N-3 W-26 Project,* Tokyo 1986; *Tadashi Kawamata: Project 1982- 1990,* London 1990; *Kawamata: Field Work,* Tokyo 1991; *Field Work,* with Karin Orchard, 1998; *Kawamata Coal Mine Project, Tokyo 2000; Artless,* Tokyo 2001.

On KAWAMATA: Books—*Tetra House 326 Project, No. 1,* with text by Kazuhiro Endo, Iori Manabe, Tomoya Sato and Tomoo Shibahashi, Sapporo 1983; *Tetra House 326 Project, No. 2,* with text by Shigeo Anzai, Hajime Masaki, Makoto Murata and Masashi Sato, Sapporo 1984; *Slip in Tokorozawa,* with text by Ryuji Miyamoto and Naoyuki Takashima, Sapporo 1984; *Kawamata Project,* with text by Tom Finkelpearl and Claudia Gould, Tokyo 1986; *Kawamata: Under Construction,* interview by the editors of Gendaikikakushitsu, Tokyo 1987; *Kawamata Project in Roosevelt Island 1990,* by Claudia Gould, Osaka 1989; *Kawamata Begijnhof Kortrijk,* with text by Geert Bekaert, Cathy de Zegher, and Michael Tarantino, Tokyo and Kortrijk 1991; *Kawamata* (exhibition catalog), Tokyo 1991; *Kawamata: Toronto Project 1989,* by Rosemary Donegan, with interview by Linda Genereux, Detlef Mertins and Steven Pozel, Toronto 1991; *Kawamata: Temporary Structures, Artrandom No. 97* (exhibition catalog), Kyoto 1991; *Tower Cranes, Paris: Urban Project with Temporary Structures* (exhibition catalog), Tokyo 1991; *Kawamata: maquettes 1992,* by Akio Obigane, Osaka 1992; *Kawamata: prefabrication* (exhibition catalog), Tokyo 1993; *Kawamata in Zurich,* by Marie-Louise Lienhard, Zurich 1993; *Kawamata Project on Roosevelt Island,* with text by Yve-Alain Bois, Elizabeth A. Frosch, Claudia Gould and Kostas Gounis, Tokyo and New York 1993; *Kawamata Project on Roosevelt Island* edited by Claudia Gould, New York 1993; *Tadashi Kawamata,* interview by Motoi Masaki, Tokyo 1993; *Kawamata: construction site projects 1984–1994,* by Kikuo Okouchi, Itami 1994; *Kawamata,* with text by Marie-Ange Brayer, Alain Julien-Laferriere, Kyong Park and an interview by Frederic Migayrou, Tours and Sache 1994; *Kawamata: Tram Passage,* by Gabriele Koller, W. Valentin Jurjevec, Rudiger Wischenbart, interview by Eva Rotter to Claus Hanl and Hans Janusz and Rudolf Wottawa, Vienna 1995; *Kawamata: Recklinghausen 1995,* by Olaf Arndt, Claudia Herstatt, Philip Peters, Hans-Jurgen Schwalm and Ferdinand Ullrich, Cologne 1995; *Kawamata: Sidewalk Wiener Neustadt,* by Katharina Blaas-Pratsche, Eberhard Jordan and Andreas Lehner, Norbert Koppensteiner and Knechtl oder Eichinger, and Angelica Baumer, Wiener Neustadt 1996; *Tadashi Kawamata: Work in Progress in Zug; Proposals,* by Matthias Haldemann and Ronald Schenkel, Zug 1996; *Tadashi Kawamata: Relocation,* London 1997; *Tadashi Kawamata: Field Work,* by Karin Orchard, Ostfildern-Ruit 1997; *Tadashi Kawamata: Haus der Kunst,* by Joachim Kaak and Andreas

Strobl, Bayerische, Munich 1998; *Tadashi Kawamata (Les Chaises de Traverse),* with text by Beatrice Josse, Olivier Kamoun, interview by Olivier Reneau, Metz and Delme 1999; *Work in Progress: Project in Toyota City; Proposals,* with text by Yoko Nose and interview by Masahiro Aoki, Toyota 1999; *Tadashi Kawamata/Working Progress in Alkmaar,* by Lucien van Ruth, Suzanne Oxenaar and others, Alkmaar + Amsterdam 1999; *Tadashi Kawamata: Tokyo Project 1998; New Housing Plan,* by Junko Ii, discussion with Kengo Kuma and Yasuo Kobayashi, Tokyo 1999; *Tadashi Kawamata: Work in Progress in Zug, 1996–1999,* by Adolf Muschg, Matthias Haldemann, Oskar Batschmann, and Carl Fingerhuth, Ostfildern-Ruit 2000; *Kawamata 190500 Evreux,* Catherine Grout, Olivier Reneau, Evreux 2000; *Tadashi Kawamata,* by Eric Antonis, Geert Bekaert, Antwerp 2000; *Work in Progress: Project in Toyota City 2000; Document,* by Yoko Nose, Toyota 2000.

* * *

Kawamata has been active as a site-specific installation artist in Japan, Europe, and the Americas since the early 1980s. His temporary interventions into pre-existing physical and social spaces—primarily assemblages of standard milled lumber—have been concerned with activating the poetic nature of urban capitalist space and exposing its cycle of growth and decay. Kawamata's relationship to the sites and audiences of his works has varied over the course of his career, yet his art has consistently evidenced a social commitment that speaks to his belief in the social responsibility of the artist and the imperative of art to act in the public realm.

Kawamata's oeuvre comprises a trajectory that has moved from art objects in the museum space to phenomenological processes in the non-art domain, while consistently bringing to bear the critical and practical relationships between the two spheres. As a student of painting in the 1970s, Kawamata found that he was interested more in the frame of a painting than its canvas and began creating gallery installations with pieces of wood, which he used to partition and modify interior space. In this respect, he was clearly working in the wake of the 1970s Japanese Mono-ha (School of Things) movement. Mono-ha stressed the primacy of unmediated material, humbly presented so as to allow it to interact meaningfully with the surrounding space, but without the expressive trace of the artist's hand. Kawamata broke from Mono-ha, however, when he moved his installations out of the gallery and into "real time." He did this for the first time in 1979 in Tokyo, but he also continued to experiment within museums and galleries, penetrating walls and challenging the boundaries that demarcate various types of physical space. In this way, he began to question institutional space and the social and symbolic presence of architecture, which has remained a focus of his projects to the present day.

In the 1980s, Kawamata went around the world setting up temporary installations constructed in a relationship to buildings and urban space that he has characterized as "parasitic," "cancerous," and "symbiotic." A self-proclaimed "guerrilla," Kawamata sought to expose the structure of social practice and systems inscribed in public spaces by attacking and destabilizing these sites.

Attaching his unruly wooden conglomerations to the solid walls of public buildings, the very archetype of permanence, he hoped to shock his audience out of the illusion of stability and order. An important aspect of Kawamata's work has been its emphasis on process and collaboration. The form and content of his works include their entire life cycle, from the collaborative process of their creation to their subsequent dismantling. With "no beginning and no end," Kawamata's projects are metaphors for the cycles of time and metabolic growth the city and its structures—both physical and social—undergo.

Kawamata has extended his exploration of temporal processes by engaging with the historical and metaphorical resonance of certain sites and their place within the collective memory. The most successful of these projects have involved ruins, those highly symbolic yet forgotten monuments to time and history. For Documenta 8 in Kassel (1987) Kawamata presented *Destroyed Church,* an installation at the site of a ruined church closed since the end of World War II, which was intended to reawaken the inhabitants of the city to a forgotten and tragic aspect of its history. Between 1987 and 1993 Kawamata worked on *Roosevelt Island* in New York at the decayed ruins of the former smallpox hospital, which is separated from Manhattan by a body of water. The temporary structure he built at this isolated site was a reminder of the maintenance of social order through the banishment of the sick and diseased.

Critics have commented on the expressive, almost calligraphic, nature of his creations, an aesthetic quality Kawamata has wished to avoid. Perhaps this, as well as an evolving sense of social activism, led him to add "Field Works" and *favelas* (shanty-like slum structures) to his repertoire of projects from the mid-1980s. Built from materials found in-situ, such as cardboard boxes, discarded furniture and scrap metal, these haphazardly constructed and colorless shacks, like those used by the homeless and dispossessed the world over, refuse aesthetic appreciation. Assimilated into the margins, gaps and interstices of the city, they are literal and metaphorical objects of transience and displacement. Unlike his large-scale architectural projects, which are dismantled under the artist's direction as an integral component of the work, the "Field Works" are left to their own uncertain fates in the streets of the city.

Kawamata has long been interested in the transitions between realms and the in-between nature of passages, which he has constructed since the early 1990s. *Sidewalk* (Lyon, 1993) led viewers through the various spaces of the museum, through storage and exhibition areas, without actually allowing them to view any artworks. *Transfer* (Sache, 1994) incorporated the space between the artist's atelier and the exhibition gallery, questioning the nature of the studio/gallery and private/public divides. *Bridge Walkway* (Barcelona, 1996) led from the museum across a wall meant to hide a view of neighboring lower-class apartment buildings.

In recent projects, Kawamata has moved from his earlier militant stance towards one of healing and dialogue. *Work in Progress, Alkmaar* (1996) extended the idea of passage to an institutional setting, where rehab patients collaborated in the building of a real and symbolic path from sickness back to normal society. Other projects have abandoned the artist's previous insistence on transitoriness and continue over long periods. In *Work in Progress in Zug* (1996–1999), Kawamata sought to make a more lasting impact on the site by enlisting the input of community members. Using this format, which involves a series of dialogic exchanges with the town's inhabitants over time, Kawamata listens to the voice of the community and shapes his works with their concerns in mind. With this give and take, Kawamata is sustaining a prolonged and productive dialogue with the public about the role of art and artist in society.

—Alicia Volk

KAWARA, On

Nationality: Japanese. **Born:** Kariya, Aichi Prefecture, 2 January 1933. **Education:** Kariya High School, until 1951; self-taught in art from 1951. **Career:** First environmental sculptures, Tokyo, 1953; first date paintings, New York, 1966; travelled in the United States, Mexico and Europe, 1969–65; settled in New York City, 1965; travelled in South America and Mexico, 1968. **Awards:** Carnegie Prize, 1991; Kunstpreis Aachen, 1992. **Agent:** Sperone Westwater Fischer, 142 Greene Street, New York, New York 10012. **Address:** 140 Greene Street, New York, New York 10012, U.S.A.

Individual Exhibitions:

1971 Galleria Toselli, Milan
1972 Galerie Konrad Fischer, Dusseldorf
Situation Gallery, London
1974 Kunsthalle, Berne
1976 Sperone Westwater Fischer, New York
1977 *Date Paintings,* Lisson Gallery, London
Centre Georges Pompidou, Paris
1979 Yvon Lambert Gallery, Paris
1980 *Continuity/Dicontinuity 1963–79,* Moderna Museet, Stockholm (retrospective; travelled to Essen, Eindhoven and Osaka)
1982 Sperone Westwater Fischer, New York
1983 Akira Ikeda Gallery, Tokyo
1984 Akira Ikeda Gallery, Tokyo
1985 Lisson Gallery, London
1987 DAAD-Galerie, West Berlin
1991 *Again and Against,* Portikus, Frankfurt am Main (catalog)
Date Paintings in 89 Cities, Museum Boymans-van Beuningen, Rotterdam (catalog)
On Kawara, Museum für Moderne Kunst, Frankfurt am Main (catalog)
1993 *One Thousand Days One Million Years,* Dia Center for the Arts, New York (catalog)
1994 *Pictures of the Real World (In Real Time),* Paula Cooper Gallery, New York (traveling exhibition) (catalog)
On Kawara: 1952–1956 Tokyo, Museum für Moderne Kunst, Frankfurt am Main (catalog)
On Kawara: Date Paintings for the Years 1973–1993, Musée d'Art Contemporain de Bordeaux (catalog)
Date Paintings in 89 Cities, Museum Boymans-van Beuningen, Rotterdam
On Kawara: The 80s, Art & Public, Geneva (catalog)
1995 *To Appear—To Disappear,* Kölnischer Kunstverein, Cologne
Pictures of the Real World (In Real Time), Hara Museum, Tokyo (traveling exhibition)
1996 *Whole and Parts 1964–1995,* Nouveau Musée/Institut d'Art Contemporain, Villeurbanne, France
1997 *Paris—New York Drawings,* Kunstverein Kunstmuseum, St. Gallen (catalog)
Codes, Yvon Lambert, Paris
1998 *Whole and Parts 1964–1995,* Tokyo Museum of Contemporary Art (catalog)
Selection from the Elaine and Werner Dannheisser Collection, Museum of Modern Art, New York
1999 *One Million Years (Future),* Dia Center for the Arts, New York (catalog)
2001 *Date Paintings,* Zwirner & Wirth, New York
One Million Years (Past and Future), David Zwirner Gallery, New York
Horizontality/Verticality, Städtischen Galerie im Lenbachhaus (also Kunstbau München) (catalog)

Selected Group Exhibitions:

1967 *Language I,* Dwan Gallery, New York
1968 *Language II,* Dwan Gallery, New York
1969 *Language III,* Dwan Gallery, New York
557087, Seattle Art Museum
Konception, Städtisches Museum, Leverkusen, West Germany
1970 *An Opening Project,* Socrates Perakis Gallery, Philadelphia
Conceptual Art and Conceptual Aspects, New York Cultural Center
Information, Museum of Modern Art, New York
1974 *Andre/Broodthaers/Buren/Burgin/Gilbert & George/Kawara/Long/Richter,* Palais des Beaux-Arts, Brussels
1980 *Printed Art: A View of Two Decades,* Museum of Modern Art, New York
1994 *Bildumak/Colecciones,* Diputación Foral de Guipuzkoa, San Sebastián (catalog)
1995 *Call it Sleep,* Witte de With, Rotterdam
1996 *The Froehlich Foundation: German and American Art from Beuys and Warhol,* Tate Gallery, London (traveling exhibition) (catalog)
Selection from the Collection, Van Abbemuseum, Eindhoven
1997 *Deep Storage—Arsenals of Memory,* Haus der Kunst, Munich
1998 *11th Biennale,* Sydney (catalog)
Inviter/7, Casino/Forum d'Art Contemporain, Luxembourg
1999 *Chronos & Kairos: Die Zeit in der Zeitgenössischen Kunst,* Museum Fridericianum, Kassel, Germany
White Fire—Flying Man, Museum für Gegenwartskunst, Basel
Global Conceptualism: Points of Origin, 1950s-1980s, Queens Museum of Art, New York (traveled to Walker Art Center, Minneapolis and Miami Art Museum)
2000 *Orbis Terrarum: Ways of Worldmaking,* Plantin-Moretus Museum, Antwerp
Diary, Cornerhouse, Manchester
The Office of Misplaced Events, Lotta Hammer, London
Rendezvous, Hotel de Caumont, Avignon, France
Zeitwenden: Ausblick, Kunstmuseum Bonn, Bonn

Collections:

Kaisier Wilhelm Museum, Krefeld, Germany; Yvon Lambert Collection, Hotel de Caumont, Avignon; Nagoya City Art Museum, Japan; Tokyo Museum of Contemporary Art; Museum für Moderne Kunst, Frankfurt am Main; Van Abbemuseum, Eindhoven; Museum of Modern Art, New York; CAPC Musee d'Art Contemporain, Bordeaux; Moderna Museet, Stockholm.

Publications:

By KAWARA: Book—*On Kawara,* with Henning Weidemann, Ostfildern 1994. **Article—**''On Kawara'' in *Art Press Special Issue,* no. 17, 1996. **CD—***One Million Years (Future),* 1999.

On KAWARA: Books—*557087,* exhibition catalog, Seattle 1969; *Concept Art* by Klaus Honnef, Cologne 1971; *6 Years: The Dematerialization of the Art Object* by Lucy Lippard, New York 1973; *Art on the Edge and Over: Searching for Art's Meaning in Contemporary Society 1970s-1990s* by Linda Weintraub, Arthur Coleman Danto and Thomas McEvilley, Litchfield 1996. **Articles—**''On Kawara Since Then'' by Masayoshi Homma in *Bijutsu-techo* (Tokyo), December 1965; ''The Dematerialization of Art'' by Lucy R. Lippard and John Chandler in *Art International* (Lugano, Switzerland), February 1968; ''Kawara'' by Friedrichs in *Kunstwerk* (Baden-Baden, West Germany), May 1972; ''U.K. Commentary'' by Richard Cork in *Studio International* (London), March 1972; ''Borderlines in Art and Experience'' by J. Bodolai in *Artscanada* (Toronto), Spring 1974; ''Facteur chevals posttasche, die bild postkarte in der kunst'' by S. Methen in *Kunstwerk* (Baden-Baden, West Germany), January 1974; ''Carl Andre/Marcel Broodthaers/Daniel Burne/Victor Burgin/Gilbert and George/On Kawara/Richard Long/Gerhard Richter'' by B. M. Reise in *Art in America* (New York), January 1975; ''On Kawara's Databank'' by Rutger Pontzen in *Jong Holland,* vol. 10, no. 1, 1994; ''Was von Tage Übrig Blieb: On Kawara im Kölnischen Kunstverein'' by Holger Liebs in *Texte zur Kunst,* vol. 5, no. 20, November 1995; ''On Kawara: The Recording Angel'' by Stuart Morgan in *Frieze,* no. 33, March-April 1997; ''On Kawara: Vanities Numeriques'' by Denis Gielen in *Art et Culture,* vol. 12, no. 2, October 1997; ''On Kawara'' by Magnus Bartas in *Index,* no. 2, 1998; ''Kawara On Kawara'' by Kathryn Chiong in *October* (Cambridge), no. 90, Fall 1999.

* * *

It is a paradox, but an intriguing paradox, that On Kawara, an extraordinary artist in such a seclusive, self-obliterative, impassive and undiversified style, has been drawing considerable attention in America and Europe as well as in Japan since the middle of the 1960s. He has been rarely visible as an artist in the traditional sense, but because of that, his art became literally universal. He reduced a myriad of unsettled discussions about the relationships between art and life to the simplest, the most explicit art form, namely, the ''date paintings,'' excluding every polysemous equivocation from both form and content.

Individuality and universality became unified in his art through obliterating every semantic trace that lay between the two opposites. Kawara has been regarded as one of the most taciturn but thought-provoking Conceptual artists up to the present.

Born in 1933 at Kariya in Aichi Prefecture, Japan, he moved to Tokyo after he graduated from a local high school in 1951. His *Bathroom* series in 1953, the pencil drawings depicting odd, dismembered human bodies, brought the artist into public notice, though, later in life, he repudiated all his early representative styles. He went to America in 1959, travelled around Mexico and Europe, settled down in New York in 1965, and has been a permanent resident of the city since then.

Kawara has been engaged in the ''date paintings'' since 1966, simply recording the dates when he was at work with white letters on monochrome canvases. The *I Read* series, a collection of clippings from the daily newspapers assembled in loose-leaf binders, was started in 1966, followed by other two series, *I Went* and *I Met,* both started in 1968 in Mexico City. In the former series, he recorded his movements of each day, tracing his route of the day on a photocopied map with a red ball point pen. In the latter, the names of the people he met in a day were typewritten on a sheet of paper with the date.

In 1968, he also started his famous ''post-cards'' series. He continued mailing the cityscape post-cards of the places he stayed to his friends every day until September 1979 with the simple information of what time he got up that day. There was a similar series by telegraph sent to his friends, saying only ''I am Still Alive.'' The minimum information about the date, time, and place carries no idiosyncrasy, making the artist On Kawara anybody as well as somebody. The artist become a liminous and anonymous body that flickers with the factual messages emitting to the world, so that the people who receive the messages question the meanings of the existence of the world, recalling what the ''date'' really means.

Kawara's persistent concern about the continuity and momentariness of time led him to produce *One Million Years,* a pair of 10-volume sets, each of which is filled with the record of one-million-years' dates; in the first 10 volumes, completed in 1971, were registered every date of one million years up to 1969, and the second, brought out in 1980, was the future version, starting from 1981.

His major retrospective, *On Kawara: Continuity/Discontinuity 1963–1979,* was held in Stockholm, Essen, Eindhoven, and Osaka between 1980 and 1981.

—Tazmi Shinoda

KAZUHIKO, Hachiya

Nationality: Japanese. **Born:** Saga, Japan, 1966. **Education:** Kyushu Institute of Design, graduated 1989. **Career:** Planned and directed life attached mail software, *Post Pet,* 1996. **Awards:** 1993 Multimedia Grand Prix, 1993; 4th Japan Art Scholarship, Grandprix ARTEC 95, Nagoya, 1995; The Prix Ars Electronica 96 Interactive Art Category, 1996; 1997 Multimedia Grand Prix, Minister of International Trade and Industry's Award, 1997; The Prix Ars Electronica 97 Interactive Art Category, 1997.

Selected Individual Exhibitions:

1993 *Inter Dis-Communication* (one night exhibition), Rentgen Kunst Institut, Tokyo
1994 *Over the Rainbow,* P3 Art and Environment, Tokyo
1995 *World System,* SPIRAL Garden, Tokyo
1996 *Seeing is Believing,* Hiroshima City Museum of Contemporary Art, Hiroshima
Love Doubler, ARTIUM, Fukuoka

Selected Group Exhibitions:

1992 *Video Art after Video Art,* Machida International Print Museum, Tokyo
1994 *Shinjyuku Juvenile Art,* Kabukicho, Tokyo
1994 Museum City Tenjin, Fukuoka

1996 *Art is Fun 7 IN/OUT,* Hara Museum ARC, Shibukawa, Gunma, Japan
1997 *De-Genderlism,* Setagaya Art Museum, Tokyo
1997 *EXIT,* Maison des'Arts, France
1997 *Fukui Biennale: Media and Body,* Fukui Art Museum, Japan
1999 *Zeitwenden,* Kunst Museum, Bonn, Germany
2000 *Milk: Experiment for Aichi—EXPO 2005,* Aoyama, Tokyo

Publications:

By HACHIYA: Videos—*Inter Dis-Communication Machine*; *Post Pet*; *Seeing is Believing*.

* * *

Hachiya Kazuhiko is an artist who uses new media and consumer trends deftly turn what most consider the source of contemporary alienation into a means of subverting, interrupting, and overcoming it. In a country that laments the gradual demise of interpersonal relationships, Hachiya has made it his project to use technology to enable a more meaningful form of communication in society.

His rise to success began in 1993 with the work *Inter Dis-Communication Machine*, an interactive project in which two participants are outfitted with devices that blind and deafen them to their own immediate environment, and replace their own senses of sight and hearing with those of their partner. This project, in which video and audio feeds from headpieces worn by each participant are fed into the headpiece of the other participant, is a deeply disorienting experience designed to alter the viewers' experience of their own subject position. By blurring the distinction between the perceptual I/You, a situation is created where each participant can literally see the world through the other's eyes. Ideally, the work is experienced between close friends or lovers, and reveals both the inherent inadequacy of human communication, and new possibilities for enriching it.

After the *Inter Dis-Communication Machine*, Hachiya began to expand his notion of community beyond that of intimates to that of a larger public. In particular with the works *Light/Depth* (1993–1995), and *Over the Rainbow* (1994), Hachiya created interactive works of public art that encouraged participants to physically participate in the creation of community. *Over the Rainbow* was, for example, a giant swing set created for adults. Each swing was programmed to emit a different colored light depending on the angle of the participant's body with the ground, and participants were challenged to coordinate their movements in order to create a perfect rainbow.

Hachiya further enlarged his idea of the public to include the digital community with works such as *Mega Diary* (1995–2000) and the extremely successful *Post Pet* (1996–2001). The fundamental concept of community is redefined in both cases to include individuals linked through the internet rather than through physical or geographic ties. In the case of the *Post Pet,* Hachiya collaborated with Sony to create a product that became one of the most widely diffused internet programs in Asia. By creating an interface program which uses virtual ''pets'' with artificial intelligence that ''deliver'' e-mail to other users and ''write'' letters back to their owners, Hachiya gave the internet a more accessible entry point, as well as a model for communication through the pre-programmed interactive pets. By creating a mass-market product, Hachiya blurred the boundaries between art and life, using the power of consumerism to diffuse his work beyond the conventional borders of the art world, and encouraged scores of first-time users to take advantage of the internet for personal communication. In so doing, Hachiya also raises the question, ''What is art?''

Recently, there has been a return to the body in Hachiya's work, which attempts to recover that one remaining element of interpersonal communication that telecommunications have yet to embody—physicality. As with *Mega Diary*, in which individuals were encouraged to post their diaries on-line, *Vanishing Body* (1997) questions the role of the spectator, forcing them to perform, should they wish to view the work. In this case, however, the viewers are forced to make themselves physically vulnerable within the piece by removing their clothes inside the space of the work. It is only then that they are given special viewing glasses that allow them to see the silhouette of the person on the other side of the screen. The two viewers—now performers—can touch each other through the flexible screen, creating a moment of anonymous intimacy, much like encounters on the internet.

Hachiya's most recent work-in-progress returns to the idea of lovers, intimates, or the community of two that began his oeuvre. In his effort to enable a more complete form of communication between individuals, Hachiya is attempting to create a technology that would allow people, especially long-distance lovers, to physically feel each others' presence during a conversation. Outfitted with a small ring on each end of the telephone connection, the apparatus would digitally transmit movement sensed in one ring to the other. In so doing, each lover could feel the other's tug—much like a pinkie promise, which fills in the silent gaps where nothing is said, but everything is understood.

Endlessly experimenting, Hachiya could move in any number of directions from this point forward. With a belief in technology that's almost utopian, Hachiya blurs the boundaries between art, design, and life to create work that aims to make a difference within the art world and beyond.

—Miang Tiampo

KELLEY, Mike

Nationality: American. **Born:** Detroit, Michigan, 1954. **Education:** University of Michigan, Ann Arbor, B.F.A., 1976; California Institute of the Arts, Valencia, California, M.F.A., 1978. **Career:** Artist. **Awards:** Louis Comfort Tiffany Foundation Grant, 1984; National Endowment for the Arts Visual Artists Fellowship Grant, 1985; Artists Space Interarts Grant, 1986; Awards in the Visual Arts Grant, 1987; National Endowment for the Arts Museum Program Exhibition Grant, 1990; Skowhegan Medal in Mixed Media, 1997; The University of Michigan School of Art and Design Distinguished Alumni Award, 1998. **Address:** Lives in Los Angeles.

Selected Individual Exhibitions:

1979 *The Poltergeist: A Work Between David Askevold and Mike Kelley,* Foundation for Art Resources, Los Angeles
1981 *Meditation On a Can of Vernors,* Riko Mizuno Gallery, Los Angeles
1982 *Monkey Island* and *Confusion,* Metro Pictures, New York
1983 *Monkey Island,* Rosamund Felsen Gallery, Los Angeles

The Sublime, Hallwalls, Buffalo, New York
1984 *The Sublime,* Metro Pictures, New York, and Rosamund Felsen Gallery, Los Angeles
1985 *Plato's Cave, Rothko's Chapel, Lincoln's Profile,* Rosamund Felsen Gallery, Los Angeles, and Metro Pictures, New York
1987 *Vintage Works: 1979–1986,* Rosamund Felsen Gallery, Los Angeles (with Chris Burden)
Half a Man, Rosamund Felsen Gallery, Los Angeles
1988 *Three Projects: Half a Man, From My Institution to Yours, Pay for Your Pleasure,* The Renaissance Society at the University of Chicago, Chicago (catalog)
1989 Rosamund Felsen Gallery, Los Angeles
Mike Kelley, Jablonka Galerie, Cologne, Germany (catalog)
Pansy Metal/Clovered Hoof, Metro Pictures, New York, and Robbin Lockett Gallery, Chicago
1990 Metro Pictures, New York
Galerie Ghislaine Hussenot, Paris
1991 *Mike Kelley: Half a Man,* Hirshhorn Museum and Sculpture Garden, Smithsonian Institution, Washington, D.C. (catalog)
1992 *Mike Kelley,* Kunsthalle, Basel, Switzerland; Institute of Contemporary Art, London; CAPC, Musee d'art contemporain, Bordeaux, France (catalog)
Alma Pater (Wolverine Den), Portikus, Frankfurt, Germany; Metro Pictures, New York
1993 *Mike Kelley: Catholic Tastes,* Whitney Museum of American Art, New York; Los Angeles County Museum of Art, Los Angeles (1994); Haus der Kunst, Munich, Germany (1995) (catalog)
Mike Kelley and Tony Oursler: White Trash Et Phobic (Installation-Video), Centre d'Art Contemporain, Geneva, Switzerland
1994 Rosamund Felsen Gallery, Los Angeles
New Photographs, Metro Pictures, New York
1995 *The Thirteen Seasons (Heavy on the Winter),* Jablonka Galerie, Cologne (catalog)
Missing Time: Works on Paper 1974–1976 Reconsidered, Kestner-Gesellschaft, Hannover, Germany (catalog)
Towards a Utopian Arts Complex, Metro Pictures, New York
1996 *Land O'Lakes,* Wako Works of Art, Tokyo (catalog)
1997 *Plato's Cave, Rothko's Chapel, Lincoln's Profile,* Wako Works of Art, Tokyo
Mike Kelley, Museu d'Art Contemporani de Barcelona; Rooseum, Malmo, Sweden; Stedelijk Van Abbemuseum, Eindhoven, The Netherlands (catalog)
The Poetics Project: 1977–1997 (Barcelona Version), Patrick Painter, Inc., Santa Monica, and Lehmann Maupin Gallery, New York California (with Tony Oursler)
The Poetics Project: 1977–1997 (Documenta version), Documenta 10, Kassel, Germany, The Watari Museum of Contemporary Art, Tokyo, and Metro Pictures, New York (catalog) (with Tony Oursler)
1998 *Mike Kelley and Paul McCarthy,* Vienna Secession, Vienna, Austria (catalog)
1999 *Mike Kelley: Two Projects,* Kunstverein Braunschweig, Germany (catalog)
Mike Kelley: Framed and Framed, Test Room, Sublevel, MAGASIN: Centre National d'Art Contemporain de Grenoble Grenoble, France (catalog)
Mike Kelley (Franz West)?, Hotel Empain, Brussels, Belgium; traveled to FRAC Poitou-Charentes Angouleme, France (catalog)
2000 *The Poetics Project: 1977–1997,* Centre Georges Pompidou, Paris
Consolation Prize: Mike Kelley and John Miller, Belkin Art Gallery, Vancouver, B.C. (catalog)
Mike Kelley and Paul McCarthy: Collaborative Works, Power Plant Contemporary Art Gallery, Toronto, Canada (catalog)
Mike Kelley & Peter Fischli and David Weiss, Sammlung Goetz and Lenbachhaus, Munich, Germany (catalog)

Selected Group Exhibitions:

1979 *Sound,* Los Angeles Institute of Contemporary Art, Los Angeles; P.S. 1, Institute for Art and Urban Resources, Long Island City, New York (catalog)
1980 *Los Angeles Contemporary Exhibitions,* Los Angeles
Annina Nosei Gallery, New York
1981 *Exhibition: Tenth Anniversary,* California Institute of the Arts, Valencia (catalog)
1983 *The First Show: Painting and Sculpture from Eight Collections 1940–1980,* Museum of Contemporary Art, Los Angeles (catalog)
Summer Show, Rosamund Felsen Gallery, Los Angeles
1984 *The First Newport Biennial: Los Angeles Today,* Newport Harbor Art Museum, Newport Beach, California (catalog)
Metro Pictures, New York
1985 *Currents—7: Words in Action,* Milwaukee Art Museum, Wisconsin (catalog)
1985 Biennial Exhibition, Whitney Museum of American Art, New York (catalog)
1986 *Individuals: A Selected History of Contemporary Art,* 1945–1986, Museum of Contemporary Art, Los Angeles (catalog)
Metro Pictures, New York
1987 *Avant-Garde in the Eighties,* Los Angeles County Museum of Art, Los Angeles (catalog)
Art Against Aids, Metro Pictures, New York
1988 Venice Biennale, Italy (catalog)
The BiNational: American Art at the Late Eighties/German Art in the Late Eighties, Museum of Fine Arts and The Institute of Contemporary Art, Boston; Stadtische Kunsthalle, Kunstsammlung Nordrhein-Westfalen, Kunstverein fur die Rheinlande und Westfalen, Dusseldorf, Germany; Kunsthalle, Bremen, Germany; Wurttembergischer Kunstverein, Stuttgart, Germany (catalog)
1989 *A Forest of Signs: Art in the Crisis of Representation,* Museum of Contemporary Art, Los Angeles (catalog)
1989 Biennial Exhibition, Whitney Museum of American Art, New York (catalog)
What is Contemporary Art?,'' Rooseum, Malmo, Sweden (catalog)

They See God, Pat Hearn Gallery, New York; Metro Pictures, New York
1990 *Figuring the Body,* Museum of Fine Arts, Boston
1992 *Helter Skelter: L.A. Art in the 1990s,* The Museum of Contemporary Art, Los Angeles (catalog)
Allegories of Modernism: Contemporary Drawings, The Museum of Modern Art, New York (catalog)
1993 *Oh! Cet Echo!,* Centre Culturel Suisse, Paris (catalog)
1993 Biennial Exhibition, Whitney Museum of American Art, New York (catalog)
Abject Art: Repulsion and Desire in American Art, Whitney Museum of American Art, New York (catalog)
American Art of this Century, Martin-Gropius-Bau, Berlin; Royal Academy of Art, London
1994 *Radical Scavenger(s): The Conceptual Vernacular in Recent American Art,* Museum of Contemporary Art, Chicago (catalog)
Transformers: The Art of Multiphrenia, Bard Center for Cultural Studies, Annandale-on-Hudson, New York (catalog)
Hors limites: L'art et la vie, Centre national d'art et de culture Georges Pompidou, Paris (catalog)
Uber Leben, Kunstverein, Bonn, Germany (catalog)
1995 *1995 Biennial Exhibition,* Whitney Museum of American Art, New York (catalog)
Everything That's Interesting Is New, Museum of Modern Art, Copenhagen (catalog)
1996 *Thinking Print: Books To Billboards, 1980–95,* Museum of Modern Art, New York (catalog)
L'informe: Le modernisme a rebours, Centre Georges Pompidou, Paris (catalog)
Distemper: Dissonant Themes in the Art of the 1990s, Hirshhorn Museum and Sculpture Garden, Smithsonian Institution, Washington, D.C. (catalog)
It's Only Rock and Roll: Rock and Roll Currents in Contemporary Art, Contemporary Arts Center, Cinncinnati, Ohio, and toured in United States (catalog)
Feminimasculin: Le sexe de l'art, Centre national d'art et de culture Georges Pompidou, Paris (catalog)
1997 *Sunshine & Noir,* Lousiana Museum of Modern Art, Humlebaek, Denmark (toured; catalog)
Scene of the Crime, UCLA at the Armand Hammer Museum of Art and Cultural Center, Los Angeles (catalog)
Gothic, Institute of Contemporary Art, Boston (catalog)
Documenta X, Kassel, Germany (with Tony Oursler) (catalog)
Art at the End of the 20th Century, Whitney Museum of American Art, New York (catalog)
In De Collectie Peter Stuyvesant, Peter Stuyvesant Foundation, Amsterdam (catalog)
1998 *Out of Actions: Between Performance and the Object, 1949–1979,* The Museum of Contemporary Art, Los Angeles; MAK-Austrian Museum of Applied Arts, Vienna; Museu d'art Contemporani de Barcelona, Spain; Museum of Contemporary Art, Tokyo (catalog)
Wounds: Between Democracy and Redemption in Contemporary Art, Moderna Museet, Stockholm, Sweden (catalog)
10 Years: Portikus Frankfurt, P.S.1, Institute for Art and Urban Resources Long Island City, New York
1999 *Zeitwenden,* Kunstmuseum Bonn, Bonn, Germany; Museum Moderner Kunst Siftung Ludwig, Vienna, and Kunstlherhaus, Vienna (catalog)
Vergiss den Ball und speil'weiter: Das Bild des Kindes in zeitgenossischer Kunst und Wissenschaft, Kunsthalle Nuremberg, Germany (catalog)
On the Sublime, Center for Contemporary Art Rooseum, Malmo, Sweden (catalog)
Making It Real, Independent Curator's International, New York (toured)
The American Century: Art and Culture 1950–2000, Whitney Museum of American Art, New York (catalog)
2000 *Open Ends: 11 Exhibitions of Contemporary Art from 1960 to Now,* Museum of Modern Art, New York, New York
Au-dela du spectacle, Centre Georges Pompidou, Paris, France
Apocolypse: Beauty and Horror in Contemporary Art, Royal Academy of Arts, London, United Kingdom (catalog)
Let's Entertain, Walker Art Center, Minneapolis (toured) (catalog)
Made in California, Los Angeles County Museum of Art (catalog)
2001 *Homes for the Soul: Micro-Architecture in Medieval and Contemporary Art,* Gallery 4, Henry Moore Institute, Leeds, United Kingdom

Selected Video Screenings:

Head Hunters, Los Angeles Contemporary Exhibitions, Los Angeles, 1983; *Performance On/And Video,* Hallwalls, Buffalo, New York, 1984; *Signal Approach,* The Funnel, Toronto, 1985; *Kappa* (with Bruce and Norman Yonemoto), Saxon-Lee Gallery, Los Angeles, 1987; *An Evening with Ericka Beckman and Mike Kelley,* Museum of Contemporary Art, Los Angeles, 1989; *New Works, First Runs* (with Ericka Beckman), The Kitchen, New York, 1990; *My Life and Media,* Broadway Cinema, Cologne, Germany, 1991; *American Videos,* Stadelschule, Frankfurt, Germany, 1992; *Videos by and with Mike Kelley,* Institute of Contemporary Art, London (toured), 1992; *Mike Kelley et Tony Oursler,* Centre d'Art Contemporain, Geneva, Switzerland, 1993; *World Wide Video Festival,* The Hague, Netherlands, 1995; *Re-Read,* AC Project Room, New York, 1996; *Cross Gender/ Cross Genre,* Palais Attems, Graz, Austria, 1999; *Videos by Mike Kelley,* Filmuseum, Munich, 2000.

Publications:

By KELLEY: Books—*Plato's Cave, Rothko's Chapel, Lincoln's Profile,* Venice, California, and New York 1986; *Reconstructed History,* Cologne, Germany and New York 1990; *The Uncanny,* Arnhem, Netherlands 1993. **Articles**—"The Runaway Wheel" in *Journal: Los Angeles Institute of Contemporary Art,* March 1979; "The Parasite Lily" in *High Performance,* no. 11–12, Fall-Winter 1980; "Meditation on a Can of Vernors" in *High Performance,* no. 17–18, Spring-Summer 1982; "Slow Boat to Lesbos" in *Barney,*

1984; ''Ajax'' in *Journal: Los Angeles Institute of Contemporary Art,* Spring 1984; ''Urban Gothic'' in *Spectacle,* no. 3, 1985; ''Foul Perfection: Thoughts on Caricature'' in *Artforum,* January 1989; ''Theory, Garbage, Stuffed Animals, Christ (Dinner Conversation Overheard at a Romantic French Restaurant)'' in *Forehead 2,* 1989; ''Ahh. . . .Youth!'' in *21st Century,* Winter 1991–1992; ''Larry Clark. In Youth Is Pleasure'' in *Flash Art,* May-June 1992; ''Monster Manse'' in *Grand Street,* no. 49, 1994; ''Jutta Koether'' in *Journal of Contemporary Art,* Cologne: Summer 1994; ''Mike Kelley on the Aliens Among Us'' in *World Art,* 14 November 1997; ''We Communicate Only Through Our Shared Dismissal of the Prelinguistic'' in *New Observations,* no. 118, Spring 1998; ''Cross Gender/Cross Genre'' in *Performing Arts Journal,* January 2000.

On KELLEY: Books—*Powers of Horror: An Essay on Abjection* by Julia Kristeva, translated by Leon S. Rondiez, New York 1982; *Helter Skelter: Los Angeles Art in the 1990s,* edited by Paul Schimmel, Los Angeles 1992; *Mike Kelley,* New York 1992; *Abject Art: Repulsion and Desire in American Art,* New York 1993; *Mike Kelley/Thomas Kellein: A Conversation,* Stuttgart, Germany Verlag, 1994; *Formless: A User's Guide,* edited by Yve-Alain Bois and Rosalind E. Krauss, New York 1997; *Bad Girls and Sick Boys,* edited by Linda Kauffman, Berkeley, California 1998; *Art of the 20th Century,* vol. 2, edited by Ingo F. Walther, New York 1998. **Articles—**''Art Attack'' by Carrie Rickey in *Art in America,* May 1981; ''Artists the Critics are Watching'' in *Art News,* November 1984; ''Mike Kelley's Art of Violation'' by Dan Cameron in *Arts Magazine,* June 1986; ''Under Western Eyes'' by Peter Plagens in *Art in America,* January 1989; ''The Price of Goodness'' by Jeremy Gilbert-Rolfe in *Artscribe,* November-December 1989; ''Mike Kelley: Toying with Second-Hand Souvenirs'' by Paul Taylor in *Flash Art,* no. 23, October 1990; ''Pathetic Aesthetic (Does the Low Frontier of Pathetic Art Signal the End of Irony?)'' by Tom McKusik and Mike Tronnes in *Utne Reader,* November-December 1992; ''Mike Fucking Kelley'' by Trevor Fairbrother in *Parkett,* no. 31, 1992; ''Yet Another Discovery: Mike Kelley in Video'' by Diedrich Diederichsen in *Parkett,* no. 31, 1992; ''Kelley's Junk-shop Pop'' by Michael Duncan in *Art in America,* June 1993; ''Mike Kelley: Operaio Anarchico del Midwest'' by Elizabeth Sussman in *Flash Art,* no. 186, 1994; ''The Mike Kelley Problem'' by Terry R. Myers in *New Art Examiner,* Summer 1994; ''Kelley's Junk Shop Pop'' by Michael Duncan in *Art in America,* June 1994; ''Stupidity as Destiny: American Idiot Culture'' by Joshua Decter in *Flash Art,* vol. 27, no. 178, October 1994; ''Mike Kelley'' by Von Jorg-Uwe Albig in *Art,* April 1995; ''Obscene, Abject, Traumatic'' by Hal Foster in *October,* no. 78, Fall 1996; ''Special Feature: Mike Kelley and the L.A. Art Scene'' in *BT,* February 1997; ''Mike Kelley, A Minor Art'' by Vincent Pecoil in *Documents sur l'art,* Autumn 1997; ''Monster Men'' by Ashley Crawford in *World Art,* Winter 1998; ''Mike Kelley: Le Magasin'' by Yves Aupetitallot in *Artpress,* October 1999; ''I Rip You, You Rip Me'' by Vincent Pecoil in *Documents Sur L'Art,* no. 12, 2000; ''Mike Kelley: Non Aprite Quella Porta'' by Barbara Casavecchia and Helena Kontova, in *Flash Art,* no. 223, 2000.

* * *

An early student at the California Institute of the Arts, Mike Kelley studied with conceptual artists John Baldessari, Douglas Huebler, and David Askevold. Although Kelley began to exhibit at New York's Metro Pictures gallery in 1979, he distanced himself from the painting and photographic practices that were most prominent in the 1980s. Instead, his work draws on an astonishing eclecticism of materials and genres. Throughout his career Kelley has made use of sewing, drawing, cartooning, carpentry, painting, video, live performance, and rock music. In Kelley's hands, these wide-ranging elements contribute to a critique of traditional fine art media, and a challenge to the autonomous modernist art object. Kelley exploits strategies pioneered by feminist artists to challenge identity, particularly sexual identity, as a fixed category. Merging the personal and the political, Kelley's work probes the American social condition, frequently using his own persona as a case study. Again and again, his work asks what it means to be an artist, particularly a white, working-class, lapsed-Catholic male artist from the suburbs of Detroit.

Many of Kelley's best-known works in the 1980s appropriate handmade stuffed animals. These pathetic, dirty castoffs serve as sentimentally charged counterparts to the hard-edged commodity sculptures then being exhibited by Jeff Koons and Heim Steinbach. A work such as ''More Love Hours Than Can Ever Be Repaid'' (1987), an unruly accretion of stuffed animals sewn onto a homemade crochet afghan, challenges ideas about the kinds of objects it is appropriate for men to make, and highlights the difference between the traditionally masculine, elevated field of sculpture, and the low cultural vernacular modes of craft, more often associated with women and their hobbies. ''More Love Hours'' was the centerpiece of a small but influential 1993 group exhibition at the Whitney Museum in New York entitled, *Abject Art: Repulsion and Desire in American Art.* The exhibition followed the writings of Julia Kristeva who defines the abject as ''what disturbs identity, system, order. What does not respect borders, positions, rules. The in-between, the ambiguous, the composite.'' The role of ''Abject Art,'' as theorized in the catalogue, is to confront taboos, examine and undermine constructed identities, to reintroduce the body, to expose elements repressed within modernist aesthetics and to recover the sadistic impulses of childhood. While insufficient to explain Kelley's project as a whole, the concept of abjection provides valuable insights on the subversive power of Kelley's degraded materials and recurring references to social deviance.

Kelley's fascination with domestic themes and materials is matched by his fascination with the social dynamics of the workplace. This is perhaps most evident in his 1992 installation for the exhibition *Helter Skelter: Los Angeles Art in the 1990s,* ''Proposal for the Decoration of an Island of Conference Rooms (with Copy Room) for an Advertising Agency Designed by Frank Gehry.'' Working within a framework of rooms designed by architect Gehry, Kelley brings layers of kitsch office humor to the surface, silkscreening the walls of the space with appropriated jokes and cartoons. Blowing up the clichéd images and texts to monumental scale, Kelley pays homage to the experience of the office worker, while using humor to highlight the undercurrents of aggression, sexuality, and frustration in the workplace.

In Kelley's recent production, large-scale installations are increasingly infused with memory, both his own, and artificial memories constructed from traces. In Cologne in 1998, Kelley produced an elaborate installation entitled ''Sublevel: Dim Recollection Illuminated by Multicolored Swamp Gas.'' The catalogue for the exhibition frames the work as a composite reconstruction of the artist's childhood home and every school he ever attended. The room-size labyrinthine plywood structure includes sections lined with sparkling pink crystals. The construction features a dark basement (modeled on the sublevel of the California Institute of the Arts), into which the viewer must crawl in order to discover a display of colored lights.

Nostalgic, while at the same time evoking repressed childhood trauma, the piece offers a dark, complex model of memory as artistic inspiration.

Kelley's contribution to the *Apocalypse* exhibition, at London's Royal Academy in 2000, was a video and installation entitled ''Extracurricular Activity Projective Reconstruction #1 (A Domestic Scene).'' The first of what Kelley claims will be a 365-part series, the piece reconstructs an experience—a high school drama production that Kelley never attended—on the basis of an old yearbook photograph. The installation recreates the set from what little can be seen in the photograph, while the video depicts a version of the play, developed out of Kelley's imaginings and projections of what it might or ought to have been like. As in the ''Sublevel'' installation, the logic of this piece is paranoid; Kelley makes it seem as if illogical connections are not only sensible but inevitable.

Kelley has never hesitated to engage with potentially upsetting subject matter. He has worked with serial killing, masturbation, and Nazism as readily as with religion, philosophy, or science. Some of the most transgressive imagery has emerged in Kelley's collaborations with fellow Los Angeles artist Paul McCarthy. Their 1992 video *Heidi* blended perky images of Aryan childhood with deeply disturbing sexual and scatalogical play. In 2000 the artists worked together on a larger-scale video collaboration, exhibited alongside production stills and props at the Power Plant Gallery in Toronto. In this work, transgender sexuality in the U.S. military joins the themes of family violence and defecation to pose an unprecedented challenge to good taste and propriety.

An artist of prodigious originality and creative force, Kelley has been tremendously influential on contemporary art, both in America and internationally. He has contributed to the break-down of distinctions between art media, has brought charged everyday materials and objects into mainstream art, and has plumbed aspects of human experience previously unimagined within the walls of galleries or museums.

—Lucy Soutter

KELLY, Ellsworth

Nationality: American. **Born:** Newburgh, New York, 31 May 1923. **Education:** Pratt Institute, Brooklyn, New York, 1941–42; Boston Museum School, 1946–48; Academie des Beaux-Arts, Paris, 1948. **Military Service:** Served in the United States Army, 1943–46. **Career:** Independent artist, since 1947. Taught evening classes, Roxbury, Massachusetts, 1947–48; travelled in France, 1948–54; taught at the American School, Paris, 1950–51; lived in New York, 1954–70; Gemini, G.E.L., Los Angeles, 1970; collaborated with Tyler Graphics, Katonah, New York, 1976. Friends of Park Sculpture Commission, Lincoln Park, Chicago, 1979. **Awards:** Painting Prize, *Carnegie International,* Pittsburgh, 1961, 1964; Flora Mayer Witowsky Prize, Art Institute of Chicago, 1962; Brandeis University Creative Arts Award, Waltham, Massachusetts, 1963; Education Minister's Award, *International Art Exhibition,* Tokyo, 1963; Painting Prize, Art Institute of Chicago, 1974; President's Fellow Award, Rhode Island School of Design, Providence, 1980; Medal, Pratt Institute, Brooklyn 1993; Friend of Barcelona Medal Recipient, 1993; Medal for Outstanding Achievement, Sch. Museum of Fine Arts, Boston, 1996; Annual Tribute Award, Friends of Art and Preservation in Embassies, U.S. Department of State, 1996; New York State Governor's Arts Award, 1998. D.F.A.: Pratt Institute, 1993; Bard College, 1996; Royal College of Art, London, 1997; Praemium Imperiale, Japan Art Association, 2000. **Member:** National Institute of Arts and Letters, 1974. **Agent:** Leo Castelli Gallery, 59 East 79th Street, New York, New York 10021. **Address:** P.O. Box 151, Spencertown, New York 12165, U.S.A.

Individual Exhibitions:

1951 Galerie Arnaud, Paris
1956 Betty Parsons Gallery, New York
1957 Betty Parsons Gallery, New York
1958 Galerie Maeght, Paris
1959 Betty Parsons Gallery, New York
1961 Betty Parsons Gallery, New York
1962 Arthur Tooth Gallery, London
1963 Betty Parsons Gallery, New York
Paintings, Sculptures and Drawings, Washington Gallery of Modern Art, Washington, D.C.
1964 Institute of Contemporary Art, Boston
Galerie Maeght, Paris
1965 *27 Lithographies,* Galerie Maeght, Paris
An Exhibition of Recent Paintings, Sidney Janis Gallery, New York
Ferus Gallery, Los Angeles
Galerie Ricke, Kassel, West Germany
1966 Ferus Gallery, Los Angeles
Knoll International, Dusseldorf
1967 Irving Blum Gallery, Los Angeles
New Works, Sidney Janis Gallery, New York
1968 Irving Blum Gallery, Los Angeles
An Exhibition of Paintings and Sculptures, Sidney Janis Gallery, New York
1971 Dayton's Gallery 12, Minneapolis
Recent Paintings, Sidney Janis Gallery, New York
1972 *Paintings,* Galerie Denise René-Hans Mayer, Dusseldorf
Albright-Knox Gallery, Buffalo, New York
Galerie Ziegler, Geneva
1973 Museum of Modern Art, New York (United States touring retrospective)
Leo Castelli Gallery, New York
Irving Blum Gallery, Los Angeles
Greenberg Gallery, St. Louis
1975 Ace Gallery, Venice, California
Blum-Helman Gallery, New York
Leo Castelli Gallery, New York (twice)
1976 Janie C. Lee Curtis Gallery, Houston
1977 Blum-Helman Gallery, New York
Margo Leavin Gallery, Los Angeles
Leo Castelli Gallery, New York
Castelli Uptown Gallery, New York
1978 Museum of Modern Art, New York
1979 Metropolitan Museum of Art, New York
Blum-Helman Gallery, New York
Galerie Maeght, Zurich
Paintings and Sculptures 1963–79, Stedelijk Museum, Amsterdam (toured Europe)
1980 Leo Castelli, New York
Castelli Graphics, New York

Albright-Knox Art Gallery, Buffalo, New York
1981 Leo Castelli Gallery, New York
Leo Castelli Uptown, New York
Larry Gagosian Gallery, Los Angeles
Blum-Helman Gallery, New York
1982 Margo Leavin Gallery, Los Angeles
John Berggruen Gallery, San Francisco
Thomas Segal Gallery, Boston
Castelli Graphics, New York
Whitney Museum, New York (travelled to St. Louis)
Blum-Helman Gallery, New York
1984 Margo Leavin Gallery, Los Angeles
Leo Castelli Gallery, New York
Blum-Helman Gallery, New York
Castelli Graphics, New York
1985 Blum-Helman Gallery, New York
Leo Castelli Gallery, New York
Katonah Gallery, New York
Ann Weber Gallery, Georgetown, Maine
1986 Blum-Helman Gallery, New York
1987 Fort Worth Art Museum, Texas (travelled to Boston; Toronto; Baltimore; San Francisco; Kansas City)
American Federation of Arts, New York (print retrospective; toured the United States, 1987–90)
Museum of Fine Arts, Boston
List Visual Arts Center, Massachusetts Institute of Technology, Cambridge
1988 Blum-Helman Gallery, New York
Blum-Helman Gallery, Santa Monica
Castelli Graphics, New York
1989 Galerie Daniel Templon, Paris
Greenberg Gallery, St. Louis, Missouri
Museum Overholland, Amsterdam
Art Institute of Chicago
Blum-Helman Gallery, New York
1990 Castelli Graphics, New York
Susan Sheehan Gallery, New York
Gallery Kasahara, Osaka, Japan
Portikus, Frankfurt, Germany
65 Thompson Street, New York
Museum of Modern Art, New York
1991 Jack Glenn Gallery, Los Angeles
Margo Leavin, Los Angeles, (travelled to San Francisco and New York)
1992 StellaR, Paris
Galerie Daniel Templon, Paris
BenedicteSaxe Gallery, Beverly Hills, California
Anthony d'Offay Gallery, London
Galerie Nationale du Jeu de Paume, Paris (travelled to Münster, Germany, and Washington, D.C.)
Laura Carpenter Gallery, Santa Fe
Susan Sheehan Gallery, New York
Matthew Marks Gallery, New York
Blum-Helman Gallery, New York
Leo Castelli, New York
1993 Greenberg Gallery, St. Louis, Missouri
Hirschl & Adler Modern, New York
1994 The Eli Broad Family Foundation, Santa Monica
New Van Straaten Gallery, Chicago
Anthony d'Offay Gallery, London (travelled to New York)
Milwaukee Art Museum, Wisconsin
Walker Art Center, Minneapolis
1995 Matthew Marks Gallery, New York
Die Frühen Zeichnungen 1948–1955, Kunstmuseum Winterthur
The Process of Seeing, Walker Art Center, Minneapolis (catalog)
Colored Paper Images 1976–77: The Creative Process, Susan Sheehan Gallery, New York (catalog)
1996 *Ellsworth Kelly: A Retrospective,* Guggenheim Museum, New York (traveled to London and Munich) (retrospective) (catalog)
1997 *An Installation: Seven New Paintings,* Matthew Marks Gallery, New York
Plant Lithographs 1973–1997, Susan Sheehan Gallery, New York (catalog)
Tate Gallery, London (retrospective)
1998 *In Black and White,* Susan Sheehan Gallery, New York
Ellsworth Kelly Masterworks: Two-panel Paintings, Joseph Helman Gallery, New York (catalog)
1999 *The Early Drawings: 1948–1955,* The High Museum, Atlanta (also Fogg Art Museum, Cambridge) (catalog)
Drawings 1960–62, Matthew Marks Gallery, New York
Sculpture for A Large Wall and Other Recent Acquisitions, Museum of Modern Art, New York
Spectrums 1953–1972, Mitchell-Innes & Nash, New York (catalog)

Selected Group Exhibitions:

1949 *Premier Salon des Jeunes,* Galerie des Beaux Arts, Paris
1959 *Sixteen Americans,* Museum of Modern Art, New York
1964 *Post Painterly Abstraction,* Los Angeles County Museum of Art (toured the United States and Canada)
1970 *New York Painting and Sculpture: 1940–1970,* Metropolitan Museum of Art, New York
1977 *Exposition Paris-New York,* Musée National d'Art Moderne, Paris
1979 *36th Biennial of American Painting,* Corcoran Gallery of Art, Washington, D.C.
1984 *La Grande Parade: Paintings after 1940,* Stedelijk Museum, Amsterdam
1988 *La Couleur Seule, L'Experience du Monochrome,* Musée St. Pierre, Lyon, France
1993 *American Art in the Twentieth Century,* Martin-Gropius-Bau, Berlin (travelled to Royal Academy of Arts, London)
1994 *To Brancusi,* Malmo Konsthall, Sweden
Western Artists/African Art, Museum of Modern Art, New York
Gemini G.E.L., National Gallery of Art, Washington, D.C.
Line + Movement, Annely Juda Fine Art, London (catalog)
1995 *Inside/Outside,* Laurence Miller Gallery, New York
Flavin, Judd, Kelly, Serra, Leo Castelli Gallery, New York
1996 *Contemporary Prints: Judd, Kelly, Levine, Schuyff,* Saint Louis Art Museum

1997 *Forty Years of Exploration and Innovation: The Artists of the Castelli Gallery 1957–1997,* Leo Castelli Gallery (SOHO), New York
2000 *Pasted Pictures: Collage and Abstraction in the 20th Century,* Knoedler & Company, New York (catalog)

Collections:

Museum of Modern Art, New York; Whitney Museum, New York; Metropolitan Museum of Art, New York; Guggenheim Museum, New York; National Gallery of Art, Washington, D.C.; Albright-Knox Art Gallery, Buffalo, New York; Art Institute of Chicago; Carnegie Insitute of Art, Pittsburgh; Los Angeles County Museum of Art; Stedelijk Museum, Amsterdam; Tate Gallery, London.

Publications:

By KELLY: Books—*Ellsworth Kelly,* exhibition catalog, Los Angeles and New York 1984; *Ellsworth Kelly: Recent Prints,* with Mary Drach McInnes, Seattle 1998. **Articles**—Interview with Henry Geldzahler in *Art International* (Lugano, Switzerland), February 1964; ''Notes from 1969'' in *Ellsworth Kelly: Paintings and Sculptures 1963–1979,* exhibition catalog, Amsterdam 1979; *Fragmentation and the Single Form,* exhibition catalog, 1990; ''Where the Eye Leads: Interview with Ellsworth Kelly,'' with Martin Gayford in *Modern Painters* (London), vol. 10, Summer 1997.

On KELLY: Books—*Ellsworth Kelly,* exhibition catalog by Lawrence Alloway, London 1962; *Abstract Painting: 50 Years of Accomplishment from Kandinsky to the Present* by Michel Seuphor, New York 1962; *Paintings, Sculptures, and Drawings by Ellsworth Kelly,* exhibition catalog with foreword by Adelyn D. Breeskin, Washington D.C. 1963; *An Exhibition of Recent Paintings by Ellsworth Kelly,* exhibition catalog, New York 1965; *Kelly: 26 Lithographies,* exhibition catalog by Dale McConathy, Paris 1965; *American Painting in the 20th Century* by Henry Geldzahler, New York 1965; *New York by Ellsworth Kelly,* exhibition catalog, New York 1967; *Constructivism: Origins and Evolutions* by George Rickey, New York 1967; *American Art since 1900* by Barbara Rose, New York 1967; *Minimal Art: A Critical Anthology,* edited by Gregory Battcock, New York 1968; *An Exhibition of Paintings and Sculpture by Ellsworth Kelly,* exhibition catalog, New York 1968; *Ellsworth Kelly: Drawings, Collages and Prints* by Diane Waldman, Greenwich, Connecticut 1971; *Recent Paintings by Ellsworth Kelly,* exhibition catalog, New York 1971; *Ellsworth Kelly: Paintings,* exhibition catalog, Dusseldorf 1972; *Ellsworth Kelly,* edited by E. C. Goossen, New York 1973; *Ellworth Kelly* by John Coplans, New York 1973; *The Age of Avant-Garde* by Hilton Kramer, New York 1973; *Ellsworth Kelly: Recent Paintings and Sculptures,* exhibition catalog, with an introduction by Elizabeth C. Baker, New York 1979; *Ellsworth Kelly: Paintings and Sculpture 1963–1979,* exhibition catalog with an introduction by Barbara Rose, Amsterdam 1979; *Ellsworth Kelly: Sculpture,* exhibition catalog by Patterson Sims and Emily Pulitzer, New York 1982; *Ellsworth Kelly: Works on Paper,* exhibition catalog by Diane Upright, Fort Worth 1987; *Ellsworth Kelly: A Print Restropective 1949–1986,* exhibition catalog by Rick Axom, New York 1987; *Ellsworth Kelly: Seven Paintings (1952–55/1987),* exhibition catalog by Trevor J. Fairbrother, Boston 1987; *Ellsworth Kelly: Small Sculpture 1958–87,* exhibition catalog by Katy Kline, Cambridge 1987; *Ellsworth Kelly: Yellow Curve,* exhibition catalog by Gottfried Boehm, Germany, 1990; *Ellsworth Kelly: At Right Angles, 1964–1966,* exhibition catalog by Roberta Bernstein, New York 1991; *Spencertown,* exhibition catalog by Yves-Alain Bois with photographic essay by Jack Shear, London 1994. **Articles**—''Ellsworth Kelly: Portrait by Armin Linke'' by Ann-Sargent Wooster in *Du,* no. 1, January 1994; ''Kelly et Matisse: Une Filiation Inavouée'' by Eric de Chassey in *Cahiers du Musée National d'Art Moderne,* no. 49, Autumn 1994; '''Things to Cover Walls': Ellsworth Kelly's Paris Paintings and the Tradition of Mural Decoration'' by Michael Plante in *American Art,* vol. 9, Spring 1995; ''Ellsworth Kelly: Towards Another Laocoön'' by Owen Drolet in *Flash Art (International Edition),* no. 186, January/February 1996; ''Kelly Read on Ellsworth Kelly: 6 Article Special Section'' in *Artforum International,* vol. 35, October 1996; ''Mass Appeal'' by Dore Ashton in *Artforum,* vol. 35, no. 2, October 1996; ''Ellsworth Kelly: An Iconoclast Looks at the Shape of Things'' by Patrick Pacheco in *Art & Antiques,* vol. 19, October 1996; ''Jasper Johns and Ellsworth Kelly: The Dead End of Modernism'' by Donald Kuspit in *Art New England,* vol. 18, February/March 1997; ''How to be Tangential: Ellsworth Kelly and American Art'' by Jeremy Gilbert-Rolfe in *Art/Text,* no. 57, May/July 1997; ''Kelly: Making Abstraction New'' by Linda Nochlin in *Art in America* (New York), vol. 85, no. 3, March 1997; ''Never Judge a Picture by its Title, Especially When It's Called 'Untitled' or 'Red Yellow Blue White and Black''' by Stuart Jeffries in *New Statesman,* vol. 126, no. 4351, 12 September 1997; *Ellsworth Kelly and the Legacy of Linear Drawing* by Clare Bell in *On Paper,* vol. 2, September/October 1997; ''Ellsworth Kelly: 4 Article Special Section'' in *Parkett,* no. 56, 1999. **Video**—*Ellsworth Kelly and Jasper Johns: Modern Masters?,* 1999.

*

I have wanted to free shape from its ground, and then to work the shape so that it has a definite relationship to the space around it; so that it has a clarity and a measure within itself of its parts (angles, curves, edges, amount of mass); and so that, with color and tonality, the shape finds its own space and always demands its freedom and separateness.

In sculpture, the work itself is the form and the ground is the space around it. In painting, the form and the ground have always shared the same surface.

It was in the period from 1949 to 1954, when I lived in Paris, that I first achieved the separation of form and ground in a series of joined-panel paintings. The canvas panels were painted solid colors with no incident, lines, marks, brushstrokes or depicted shapes; the joined panels became a form, and thereby, transferred the ground from the surface of the canvas to the wall. The result was a painting whose interest was not only in itself, but also in its relation to things outside it.

From the time I returned to New York in 1954 and until 1965, I made few joined-panel works. The salient feature of my painting during that period was a large curved form that squeezed the ground to the edge of the canvas. Later, it was through the making of sculpture and cutting form out of metal, that I returned to making joined-panel works on canvas in which the ground was eliminated.

Since 1965, most of the painting and sculpture has been single or multiple monochrome panel works where the ground has moved to the wall or to the space around the free-standing pieces.

—Ellsworth Kelly

* * *

Ellsworth Kelly has been discussed in regard to Constructivist geometric abstraction, Abstract Expressionist scale, and 1960s Minimalism, and he has been termed a ''hard-edge,'' ''systemic'' and ''post-painterly abstraction'' painter. As is usually the case with such art-historical relationships and labels, each seems to miss the overall intentions and effects of the work by stressing one or another element too strenuously. Kelly might be compared even more fruitfully with the American precisionists such as Georgia O'Keeffe or Charles Sheeler, whose basically hard-edge distillations from the contemporary landscape relate quite closely with Kelly's approach. He also equates with the elements of the color-field painters, expecially Barnett Newman who, like Kelly, found inspiration in elements of Mondrian's contributions. The point is that, although all of these sources and overlaps may have credence in varying degrees, it is Kelly's early and unique synthesis and transformation of them which is the overriding feature in the body of work he has created beginning from about 1949.

It was in that year that Kelly painted a small oil on wood called ''Kilometer Marker'' in France. In this picture he visually realized the general characteristics which would continue to develop in his work over the following three decades. The generalized curved and rectangular shapes originate out of phenomena experienced personally. Along with the two-color combination of pale yellow and white, the crisply outlined shapes in juxtaposition work toward achieving a taut balance between positive and negative space which questions the nature of perception. Also in 1949, Kelly made a low relief construction titled ''Window, Museum of Modern Art, Paris,'' anticipating his uses of relief and sculpture in subsequent years to express his intentions in more literal terms.

In 1951–1952, Kelly made a group of pictures which used the grid as a basic structure to convey patterns of light and shadow, form and reflection, employing either rows of singly colored rectangles or combinations of curved wedges of one color together with a second color sharing the grid sections. By 1952, Kelly was juxtaposing squares or rectangular panels of one color each, distilling color and shape in drastically reduced terms which conveyed implications of perceived nature very different from the strictly purist readings of Malevich, and also from the energies of Mondrian's late works which seem the closest to Kelly's pictures of this period.

With his formal means and his visual intentions firmly in pace, Kelly proceeded to systematically analyze his possibilities, working to deduce the essential character of seen phenomena, using shape, color and proportion to visualize these essences more directly and simply. During the 1950s, curved and straight-edged shapes reach for the canvas edges, resting on the periphery, jutting in from the outside, butting or overlapping in various pictures. They seem to be both encroaching on the smoothly painted unitary surface and extending outward into the surrounding environment. In their elegant combinations of the sensuous and the pristine, they never lapse into either the decorative or the purely conceptual and always maintain hints at things seen, calling new attention to the ways solid objects and their shadows or reflections interact, examining the nature of physical phenomena and the effects of colored light. It is the perceived qualities of weight, perspective, fracturing which pervade the black-and-white works and the brightly colored ones as well.

Seen in the context of Minimalism, Kelly's works from the late 1960s to the present are often misinterpreted as fitting in with the formally based line of reductivism. It should not be forgotten that both his paintings and his sculptures of the 1950s had reached a level of distillation which was then radical in the context of the overriding expressionistic bent of the period and which had already achieved a statement of perceived essentials involving content outside the boundaries of the purely formal, both geometrically based and color based. Kelly's recent large, monochromatic shaped canvases and reliefs reiterate his intuitive capacities and his longtime practice, both of which combine to infuse his extremely distilled works with a distinctively individual understanding which never denies its roots in the memories of things seen.

—Barbara Cavaliere

KENNY, Michael

Nationality: British. **Born:** Liverpool, 10 June 1941. **Education:** Liverpool College of Art, 1959–61; Slade School of Fine Art, London, under Reg Butler, 1961–64, **Family:** Married 1) Rosemary Flood in 1968 (divorced); children: Dominic and Camilla; 2) Angela Fraser in 1978 (divorced); 3) Susan Rousland, 1993. **Career:** Independent full-time sculptor, since 1965; lives and works in London. Part-time lecturer, Canterbury College of Art, Kent, 1964–65; Bristol College of Art, 1964–65; Goldsmiths College, London, 1968–72. Visiting lecturer, Slade School of Fine Art, London, 1971–82; external assessor for the Council for National Academic Awards since 1972; director of fine art studies, University of London, Goldsmiths' College, 1983–88; external assessor, Kent Institute of Art & Design, since 1994; artist-in-residence, Dulwich Picture Gallery, London. Sculpture faculty, British School, Rome, 1974–87, chairman 1980–87; board of governors, St. Martin's School of Art, 1982–86; Fine Art Board, Council for National Academic Awards, 1976–79; Court of Governors, The London Institute, since 1986; Cathedrals Commission, since 1987; advisor and member of selection panel, Royal Academy Schools, London, since 1989. **Awards:** Prize, Littlewoods' Sculptural Design Competition, 1964; Postgraduateship in fine art, University of London, 1964–65; Sainsbury Award, 1965; Major Award, Arts Council of Great Britain, 1975, 1977 and 1980. Associate, 1976, and Royal Academician, 1986, Royal Academy of Arts, London. **Agent:** Juda Rowan Gallery, 11 Tottenham Mews, London WIP 9PJ. **Address:** 71 Stepney Green, London EL 3LE, England.

Individual Exhibitions:

1961 Walker Art Gallery, Liverpool
Hope Hall Gallery, Liverpool
1964 Bear Lane Gallery, Oxford
1965 University of Southampton
1966 Hamilton Galleries, London
1969 Hanover Gallery, London
1977 Peterloo Gallery, Manchester
Sculpture and Drawings, Serpentine Gallery, London
1978 Annely Juda Fine Art, London
1979 Roundhouse Gallery, London
1981 Annely Juda Fine Art, London
Bluecoat Gallery, Liverpool (toured the U.K.)
1983 Tokyo Gallery, Tokyo
Murdoch Lothian Fine Art, Liverpool
1984 Galerie Site, Paris

Juda Rowan Gallery, London
Arcade Gallery, Harrogate, Yorkshire
Wilhelm Lehmbruck Museum, Duisberg, West Germany
1985 Galerie Lupke, Frankfurt
Tokyo Gallery, Tokyo
1986 Royal Academy of Arts, London
1987 Galleria del Naviglio, Milan
1988 Galerie Kremer-Tengellman, Cologne
Koplin Gallery, Tokyo
1989 Tokyo Gallery
Annely Juda Fine Art, London
1990 *Michael Kenny: Sculptures, Reliefs and Drawings, 1982–1990,* John Hansard Gallery, Southampton
1993 Galerie Dorfman, Paris
Alesford Gallery, London
1994 Dulwich Picture Gallery, London
Michael Kenny R.A.: New Work, The Gallery at John Jones, London

Selected Group Exhibitions:

1966 *International Sculpture Exhibition,* Battersea Park, London
1968 *English Landscape Tradition in the 20th Century,* Candem Arts Centre, London
1976 *Arts Council Collection 1975–1976,* Hayward Gallery, London
1977 *Silver Jubilee Exhibition of Contemporary British Sculpture,* Battersea Park, London
1978 *Certain Traditions,* travelling exhibition (toured Canada and the U.K., 1978–80)
1979 *European Dialogue,* at the *Biennale,* Sydney (toured Australia and Tasmania, 1979–80)
1981 *British Sculpture in the 20th Century: Part II,* Whitechapel Art Gallery, London
1983 *Drawing in Air,* Sunderland Arts Centre, Cumbria (travelled to Swansea and Leeds)
1985 *Human Interest,* Cornerhouse Gallery, Manchester, Lancashire
1987 *The London Group,* Royal College of Art, London

Collections:

Arts Council of Great Britain, London; Tate Gallery, London; Jesus College, Oxford; Wilhelm Lehmbruck Museum, Duisberg, West Germany; Staatsgalerie, Stuttgart; British Council, London; British Museum, London; Victoria and Albert Museum, London; Leeds City Art Gallery, Yorkshire; Hara Museum of Contemporary Art, Tokyo.

Publications:

By KENNY: Illustrated book—*I Know the Place,* poems by Harold Pinter, Warwick 1979. **Articles**—statements in *Contemporary British Sculpture,* exhibition catalog, London 1966; *Tate Gallery Acquisitions 1969,* London 1969; ''Theory for Art'' in *11 Sculptors: One Decade,* exhibition catalog, London 1972; statements in *Art into Landscape,* exhibition catalog, London 1974; *Directory of Artists: Space Open Studios,* London 1975; ''The Crisis of Skill in Contemporary Painting and Sculpture'' in *Fine Art Letter* (London), February 1982; ''Michael Kenny interviewed by Adrian Lewis'' in *Aspects* (Newcastle-upon-Tyne), Summer 1982.

On KENNY: Books—*Michael Kenny,* exhibition catalog by Andrew Forge, Oxford 1964; *Battersea Open-Air Exhibition,* exhibition catalog by Alan Bowness, London 1966; *English Landscape Tradition in the 20th Century,* exhibition catalog by Charles Spencer, London 1968; *Slade Centenary,* exhibition catalog, London 1971; *11 Sculptors: One Decade,* exhibition catalog, London 1972; *Directory of Artists,* London 1975; *Michael Kenny: Sculpture and Drawings,* exhibition catalog by William Packer, London 1977; *Contemporary British Artists,* edited by Charlotte Parry-Crooke, London 1979; *The Sculpture of Michael Kenny,* exhibition catalog with introduction by David Brett, Liverpool 1981; *The Sculpture of Barry Flanagan, Michael Kenny and Hubert Dalwood* by Graham Stacey, Gotheborg, Sweden, 1981; *The Sculpture Show,* exhibition catalog with introduction by Nicholas Wadley, London 1983; *Michael Kenny: Sculptures, Reliefs and Drawings, 1982–1990,* exhibition catalog with text by Mary Rose Beaumont, Southampton 1990; *Liverpool Seen Post-War Artists on Merseyside* by Peter Davies, Bristol 1992; *Flesh and Blood,* exhibition catalog, Lancaster 1993; *Michael Kenny R.A.: New Work,* exhibition catalog, London 1994; *Michael Kenny* with essay by Peter Davies, Aldershot, Hants 1997. **Articles**—reviews: by Oswell Blakeston in *Arts Review,* 17 March 1978; by Ben Jones in *Artscribe,* April 1978; by Elisabeth Falconbridge in *Arts Review,* 27 April 1979; by William Packer in *Financial Times,* 3 April 1979; ''Sculpture as Picturing,'' by Jon Thompson, *Art Monthly* No. 44, 1981; ''On the Floor,'' by William Packer, *Financial Times,* 10 February 1981; ''Modern British Sculpture,'' by Mary Rose Beaumont, *Art & Artists,* January 1982; ''Two of a Kind,'' by William Packer, *Financial Times,* 20 March 1994; ''Symbols of Ancient Faith,'' by William Packer, *Royal Academy Magazine,* September 1986; ''Michael Kenny: Sculptor'' by Peter Davies in *Contemporary Art,* vol. 3, no. 3, Late Spring 1996; ''Michael Kenny'' by Rosemary Simmons in *Printmaking Today* (London), vol. 6, no. 3, Autumn 1997.

*

> A carpenter, using a metal ruler, draws a pencil line across a board to use as a guide in cutting. The line he has drawn is a physical thing; it is a deposit of graphite on the surface of a board. It has width and thickness of varying amounts, and in following the edge of the ruler, the tip of the pencil reacts to the inequalities in the surface of the board and produces a line which has warp and corrugation. Alongside this real, concrete instance of a straight line, there exists the mental idea of the mathematical abstraction of an ideal straight line. In the idealised version, all the accidentals and imperfections of the concrete instance have been miraculously eliminated. There exists an idealised, cosmeticised, verbal description of a straight line—Davis & Hersh (*The Mathematical Experience*)

I use drawing as a means of symbolic understanding; it is the unifying thread in all the work that I do, whether sculpture, drawing, or painting. In both the drawing and the sculpture there is an overt and covert geometry, it is the conceptual framework which holds things together. Drawing exists beyond medium, it is not simply the making of more-or-less academic marks on paper, but a way of seeing and symbolising the world. Sometimes drawing is descriptive of the natural world whether in the contour lines of a figure drawing or in the way that the form of a Yorkshire hillside is described by the drystone walls that crisscross it. Sometimes it is totally symbolic, a method of drawing a structure onto the night sky. Drawing is a means of understanding, of searching for order out of chaos through images.

I cannot separate my thoughts, and the rest of my life, from the activity of sculpture or drawing; creativity for me has to be a synthesis of the material, emotional and the spiritual—the integrity of a personality in making art. Making love and making art bring the closest integration of thought and action (soul and body)—for isn't the sexual act a unification of the spiritual and the physical? The recent sculpture and drawings have developed a sexual ambience, a kind of archetypal and symbolic sexuality. Most recently this has included the large sculptures in the studio.

I have long been interested in the poetry of Saint John of the Cross, and the manner in which spiritual ecstasy is expressed by him in terms of the sexual love between a man and a woman:

Oh, night that guided me,
Oh, night more lovely than the dawn,
Oh, night that joined Beloved with lover,
Lover transformed in the Beloved!

The metaphysical poet John Donne described how in his poetry he learnt to feel his thoughts; he was able to integrate intellectual thought and intuitive feeling into a creative whole. For the rest of us the one remains the servant of the other. This integration—or psychocracy—exists in memorable art of both past and present. It is part of the private mind of the artist, that which probes the space between reality and appearance.

I believe that what Wollheim once called the ''institution of art'' works against the unity of those who have knowledge (in the know) and those who do not, between those who think and those who do and make. Thus the idealisation of squalor and the celebration of egocentrism becomes a function of art (and psychology). When belief is lost, what remains is irony and wit—thus art breeds mistrust.

To acknowledge gravity is absolutely essential for me in terms of my sculpture. Because sculpture is unique of all the art forms in that it is a part of the world that it describes—it is the art form that has to obey the laws of physics. A painting does not. A painting may contain something hanging in the air. Magritte for example painted clouds made of rock, but sculpture is made out of rock and sits on the ground—it obeys the laws of gravity, and I think that coming to terms with this in a formal and conceptual way is crucial. A lot of my concern with the diagonal and the vertical is in a way an answer to this question.

There is in the sculpture, a tension between symmetry and asymmetry: the symmetry of the concentric circles and the clusters of three stones within the circles, and the asymmetrical and intuitive placement of the stones.

Symmetry principles are at the core of modern avant-garde physics, particularly at the interface between cosmology and quantum mechanics; so much so that the physicist Stephen Weinberg wrote: ''Matter . . . thus loses its central role in physics, all that is left is the principle of symmetry.'' In some ways I suppose that my concern with ''drawing and ordering'' is analogous to this. Order occupies a conceptual and unifying domain—it is the common denominator no matter what material is used.

—Michael Kenny

* * *

Outside the post-Caro school of English sculpture, Michael Kenny (a student of the Slade School, not St. Martin's, where Caro exerted so great an influence), shows none of the predilection for metal engineering forms or for the abstract Constructivist style. His works have a positive sense of realism to them, without being specifically tied to objects.

They are usually groups of separated forms, in mixtures of aluminum, marble, perspex and plastics, resembling, in some curious manner, the still-life paintings of Morandi. They seem to be searching for the same sense of interrelated balance as the great Italian artist sought in his rows of bottles or fruit. And like Morandi, Kenny infuses a disturbing sense of drama, almost of theatre, in formal confrontations. One is clearly invited to ''read'' these static groups, which may not necessarily be pieces of sculpture, but serializations to be assessed as sequences of time and space, not single objects. They are meticulously arranged with elegance and positive directions to the viewer, all mounted on platforms which make the presentation all the more formal. Like the Morandi still-lifes, they combine uprights, symbols of the human figure perhaps, with diverse quasi-geometrical shapes—square slabs of marble, pieces of aluminum arranged as pyramids, rows of metal rods bearing slabs of stone, variously suggesting tables, trestles, even gardens.

There is something speculative about these visual conundrums, as though the artist is challenging the preoccupations. The deceptive informality of Kenny's group of forms does not hide their premeditated planning and the sense of public occasion they suggest. The recent development from ''still-life'' to figure sculpture opens up interesting possibilities in Kenny's work; the new reclining figures retain the same sense of anonymity and enigma, with the body equating architectural linearity. This turn to overt reality is the result of the artist's fear of becoming too involved in an introverted, rarefied world, the search for a direct human expression. It would be interesting and beneficial if the artist were afforded the opportunity to enlarge his scale and site them in a public place, where, whilst they might arouse doubt or hostility, it is unlikely they would be met with indifference.

—Charles Spencer

KENTRIDGE, William

Nationality: South African. **Born:** Johannesburg, South Africa, 1955. **Education:** University of the Witwatersrand, Johannesburg, B.A. in Politics and African Studies, 1976; studied under Bill Ainslie at Johannesburg Art Foundation, 1976–78; studied mime and theater at École Jacques LeCoq, Paris, 1981–82. **Family:** Married physician Anne Stanwix, 1982; daughter Alice Irene born, 1984; daughter Isabella May born, 1988; son Samuel Woolf born, 1992. **Career:**

Founding member of the Junction Avenue Theatre Company, based in Johannesburg and Soweto, 1975–91; taught etching at Johannesburg Art Foundation, 1978–80; worked in Johannesburg as Art Director on television series and feature films, 1982–84; founding member of Free Filmmakers Cooperative, based in Johannesburg, 1988; created first animated film, 1989; staged first theater project, 1992; residency as Master Artist, Civitella Ranieri Center, Italy, 2000. Worked extensively in theater as an actor, designer, and director; lives and works in Johannesburg. **Awards:** First Prize, National Graphics competition Bellville, Cape Town, South Africa, 1981; Blue Ribbon Award, American Film Festival, New York, 1982; Olive Schreiner Prize for Drama, Cape Town, South Africa, 1984; Blue Ribbon Award, American Film Festival, New York, 1985; Merit Award, Cape Town Triennial Exhibition, 1985; Standard Bank Young Artist Award, Grahamstown, South Africa, 1987; Weekly Mail Short Film Competition Award, Johannesburg, 1990 and 1991; Rembrandt Gold Medal, Cape Town Triennial, 1991; Hugo Boss Prize (nomination), SoHo Guggenheim, New York, 1998; Carnegie Prize, Carnegie International, Carnegie Museum of Art, Pittsburgh, 2000. **Agent:** Marian Goodman Gallery, 24 West 57th Street, New York, New York 10019.

Selected Individual Exhibitions:

1979 *William Kentridge,* Market Gallery, Johannesburg
1981 *Domestic Scenes,* Market Gallery, Johannesburg; Association of Arts, Cape Town, South Africa
1985 *William Kentridge,* Cassirer Fine Art, Johannesburg
1986 *William Kentridge,* Cassirer Fine Art, Johannesburg; Association of Art Gallery, Pretoria, South Africa
1987 *In the Heart of the Beast,* Vanessa Devereux Gallery, London
Standard Bank Young Artist Award, Grahamstown Festival, Grahamstown, South Africa; Tatham Art Gallery, Pietermaritzburg, South Africa; University Art Galleries, University of the Witwatersrand, Johannesburg; University Art Gallery Unisa, Pretoria, South Africa; Durban Art Gallery, Durban, South Africa
1988 *William Kentridge,* Cassirer Fine Art, Johannesburg
1989 *Responsible Hedonism,* Vanessa Devereux Gallery, London
1990 *William Kentridge: Drawings and Graphics,* Cassirer Fine Art and Gallery on the Market, Johannesburg
1991 *William Kentridge: Drawings,* Gallery International, Cape Town, South Africa
1992 *Drawings for Projection,* Goodman Gallery, Johannesburg; Vanessa Devereux Gallery, London (catalog)
1993 *William Kentridge,* Ruth Bloom Gallery, Los Angeles
1994 *Felix in Exile,* Goodman Gallery, Johannesburg
1996 *Eidophusikon,* Annandale Gallery, Sydney
1997 *Applied Drawings,* Goodman Gallery, Johannesburg
1998 *WEIGHING . . . and WANTING,* Museum of Contemporary Art, San Diego; North Dakota Museum of Art, Grand Forks; MIT List Visual Arts Center, Cambridge, Massachusetts; Forum for Contemporary Art, St. Louis, Missouri; Salina Art Center, Salina, Kansas; Art Gallery of Ontario, Toronto; University of Michigan Museum of Art, Ann Arbor; Bowdoin College Museum of Art, Brunswick, Maine (catalog)
William Kentridge, Palais des Beaux-Arts, Brussels; Kunstverein München, Munich; Neue Galerie Graz, Austria; Museu d'Art Contemporani de Barcelona; Serpentine Gallery, London; Centre de la Vieille Charité (Musées de Marseille), Marseilles (catalog)
William Kentridge, Drawing Center, New York
William Kentridge, Stephen Friedman Gallery, London; A22 Gallery, London
1999 *Stereoscope, Projects 68,* Museum of Modern Art, New York
Sleeping on Glass, Galerie Marian Goodman, Paris
2000 *Procession: Sculpture by William Kentridge,* Goodman Gallery, Johannesburg
Marian Goodman Gallery, New York
Annandale Galleries, Sydney
Stephen Friedman Gallery, London
2001 *William Kentridge,* Hirshhorn Museum and Sculpture Garden, Washington, D. C.; New Museum of Contemporary Art, New York; Museum of Contemporary Art, Chicago; Contemporary Arts Museum, Houston; Los Angeles County Museum of Art (catalog)

Selected Group Exhibitions:

1978 *Exhibition,* Akis 101 Gallery, Johannesburg
1981 *National Graphic Show,* South African Association of Art, Bellville, Cape Town, South Africa
1982 *American Film Festival,* New York
1985 *Cape Town Triennial,* South African National Gallery, Cape Town, South Africa
American Film Festival, New York
London Film Festival, London
Eleven Figurative Artists, Market Gallery, Johannesburg
1986 *Visions,* Market Gallery, Johannesburg
Claes Eklundh, William Kentridge, Thomas Lawson, Simon/Neuman Galleries, New York
But This is the Reality, Market Gallery, Johannesburg
Cape Town Film Festival, Cape Town, South Africa
1987 *Three Hogarth Satires,* University Art Galleries, University Witwatersrand, Johannesburg
1988 *William Kentridge and Simon Stone,* Gallery International, Cape Town, South Africa
1989 *South African Landscapes,* Everard Read Gallery, Johannesburg
African Encounters, Dome Gallery, Brooklyn
Weekly Mail Film Festival, Johannesburg
1990 *Art from South Africa,* Museum of Modern Art, Oxford (catalog)
Zabalaza Festival, Institute for Contemporary Art, London
Weekly Mail Short Film Festival, Johannesburg
1991 *Little Morals,* Taking Liberties Gallery, Durban, South Africa
Newton Art Gallery, Johannesburg
Gala, Arts Association of Bellville, Cape Town, South Africa
Weekly Mail Short Film Festival, Johannesburg
1992 *The Art Fair,* Waterfront, Cape Town, South Africa
1993 *Easing of the Passing (of the Hours): William Kentridge, Robert Hodgins, Deborah Bell,* Goodman Gallery, Johannesburg

45th Venice Biennale, *Incroci del Sud: Affinities- Contemporary South African Art,* Fondazione Levi Palazzo Giustinian Lolin, Venice; Stedelijk Museum, Amsterdam
Best of Annecy, Museum of Modern Art, New York
Musée National d'Art Moderne-Centre Georges Pompidou, Paris

1994 *Trackings: History as Memory, Document & Object, New Works by four South African Artists,* Art First, London
Goodman in Grahamstown, Victoria Primary School, Grahamstown, South Africa (catalog)
Displacements, Block Gallery, Northwestern University, Chicago
David Krut Editions, Spacex Gallery, Exeter, England

1995 *Memory and Geography,* 1st Johannesburg Biennial, Africus Institute for Contemporary Art, Johannesburg; Stefania Miscetti Gallery, Rome (catalog)
Panoramas of Passage: Changing Landscapes of South Africa, Albany Museum, Grahamstown, South Africa; Meridian International Center, Washington, D.C. (catalog)
On the Road: Works by 10 South African Artists, Delfina Studio Trust, London (catalog)
Mayibuye I Africa: 8 South African Artists, Bernard Jacobson Gallery, London

1996 *Colours: Art from South Africa,* Haus der Kulturen der Welt, Berlin
Simunye: We are one, Ten South African Artists, Adelson Galleries, New York (catalog)
Don't Mess with Mr. In-between: 15 South African Artists, Culturgest, Lisbon (catalog)
Campo 6, The Spiral Village, Galleria Civica d'Arte Moderna e Contemporanea, Turin, Italy; Bonnefanten Museum, Maastricht, Netherlands

1997 Documenta 10, Museum Fridericianum, Kassel, Germany
Ubu: Å 101, Observatory Museum, Standard Bank National Festival for the Arts, Grahamstown, South Africa; Gertrude Posel Gallery, Senate House, South Africa; University Art Galleries, University Witwatersrand, Johannesburg (catalog)
Trade Routes: History and Geography, 2nd Johannesburg Biennial, AICA-Africus Institute for Contemporary Art, Newtown, Johannesburg (catalog)
Delta, ARC/Musée d'Art Moderne de la Ville de Paris

1998 *Breaking Ground,* Marian Goodman Gallery, New York
Vertical Time, Barbara Gladstone Gallery, New York
Hugo Boss Prize, SoHo Guggenheim, New York
Unfinished History, Walker Art Center, Minneapolis; Museum of Contemporary Art, Chicago (catalog)

1999 Carnegie International, Carnegie Museum of Art, Pittsburgh, Pennsylvania
La Ville, le Jardin, la Memoire, Villa Medici, Rome
Kunstwelten im dialog, Museum Ludwig Koln, Cologne
dAPERTutto, Venice Biennale

2000 *Illuminations: Contemporary Film and Video Art,* Ackland Art Museum, University of North Carolina at Chapel Hill
Outbound: Passages from the 90's, Contemporary Arts Museum, Houston (catalog)
Das Lied von der Erde, Museum Fridericianum Kassel, Germany
A Double View: Three Exhibitions, Tel Aviv Museum of Art, Israel

2001 Havana Biennial, Cuba
Beyond Borders, Coninx Museum, Zurich
Das Gedächtnis der Kunst: Geschichte und Errinerung in der Kunst der Gegenwart, Historisches Museum in collaboration with Schirn Kunsthalle, Frankfurt

Publications:

On KENTRIDGE: Books—*William Kentridge 1987* by Elza Miles, Grahamstown, South Africa, 1987; *William Kentridge* by Dan Cameron, London 1999; *William Kentridge* by Neal Benzara, New York 2001. **Articles—**''William Kentridge'' by Amanda Jephson and others in *ADA: Art, Design, Architecture,* 1987; ''William Kentridge'' by Michael Godby in *Revue Noire,* December 1993-February 1994; ''William Kentridge'' by Rose Korber in *ADA: Art, Design, Architecture,* 1995; ''Memento Mori'' by Roger Taylor in *World Art: The Magazine of Contemporary Visual Art,* 1996; ''William Kentridge: Retrospective'' by Michael Godby in *Art Journal,* fall 1999; ''William Kentridge: l'écran et le trace'' by Stephen Wright in *Parachute,* April-June 2000; '''The Rock': William Kentridge's Drawings for Projection'' by Rosalind Krauss in *October,* spring 2000; Michael O'Sullivan, ''Kentidge's Troubling Shades of Truth,'' *Washington Post,* 9 March 2001. **Videos—***William Kentridge, Artist: 'The End of the Beginning'''* by Beata Lipman and Catherine Meyburgh, 1994; *William Kentridge: Drawing the Passing* by Maria Anna Tappeiner, 1999. **CD-rom—***William Kentridge,* Johannesburg 2000.

* * *

Emerging from post-apartheid South Africa, William Kentridge has come to be recognized as one of his country's most eloquent depicters of its painful history. Working in the unique medium of drawing and film, Kentridge creates short handmade animations engaging themes of loss, memory, guilt, and uncertainty central to the recent experience of white South Africa.

Capturing a few frames at a time, Kentridge's practice of film-making is centered on the *process* of drawing as integral to the creation of meaning. As he politicizes memory—forgetting and remembering, truth and fiction—Kentridge uses drawing as part of the film's development; a process of layering, erasing and re-drawing that uses visual history as a reminder of the uncertainty and contradictions inherent in his narratives. Making literally thousands of changes to a small number of drawings, his films record this evidence of the artist's hand. Working in charcoal and pastel, Kentridge's drawing has a traditional 19th century quality that, though expressionist, reminds us of the likes of Honoré Daumier and Francisco Goya as it echoes as their commitment to realistic, and often traumatic social commentary.

Deftly weaving cultural paradox, Kentridge has described the present situation in South Africa as ''a struggle between paper shredders and photocopying machines,'' according to art critic Michael O'Sullivan, as evidence of apartheid is simultaneously documented and destroyed. Though embedded in politics, Kentridge's work is contextualized and made human through the deeply personal, and often self-indicting. Identifying with the moral perspective presented while also exploring its limitations, Kentridge noted in his exhibition catalog in 1999 that "there needs to be a strong understanding of fallibility and how the very act of certainty or authoritativeness can bring disasters." The contradictory nature of identity, as un-fixed and often multiple, is used by Kentridge as a way of approaching the very nature of South African history; a divided nation whose past, like its identity, is in need of recovery, remembrance and recognition.

Representing this process, Kentridge has created a cast of characters who recur throughout his films: oppressors and the oppressed, witnesses and victims, who form an intimate, yet often horrific portrait of South Africa, while attempting to bring us closer to truth. Soho Eckstein, a powerful and (self) destructive white real estate developer, and Felix Teitlebaum, an ineffectual artist and Soho's alter-ego, are two characters who appear together in a series of Kentridge's films. Set against the South African landscape, Kentridge rejects nostalgic colonial interpretations of his country and portrays the earth as a separate character—a wasteland being exploited and plundered, often circled red in a surveyor's crosshairs. The cultural and social construction of the land thus parallels the characters of Soho and Felix: contradictions of wealth and abandonment, pride and sorrow, rapaciousness and loneliness.

In 1997 William Kentridge made "Ubu Tells the Truth," a video installation in response to the Truth and Reconciliation Commission in South Africa B, a national forum of public hearings on human rights violations under apartheid that granted amnesty in exchange for testimony. With a long-standing involvement in theatre, this film grew out of a multi-media stage play written and directed by Kentridge. Incorporating disturbingly violent documentary footage, "Ubu Tells the Truth" directly confronts apartheid and its atrocities. Using the image of a camera as protagonist, Kentridge comments on the editing of history and truth, the guilt of witness and compliance.

As moving commentaries on his time, William Kentridge has created a complex and intimate visual language that is unique in both process and imagery. Rejecting simplistic historical readings of apartheid, Kentridge's work reflects on the honesty of ambiguity, while also acknowledging responsibility. As an on-going series, Kentridge speaks of his work as part of a "single project"—a project for which the greatest danger, like that of his country's history, is of "a completed narrative"—the end of understanding and dialogue.

—Carly Butler

KIEFER, Anselm

Nationality: German. **Born:** Donaueschingen in 1945. **Education:** Studied art under Joseph Beuys at the Staatliche Kunstakademie, Dusseldorf. **Family:** Married to Julia Kiefer. **Career:** Independent painter, in Dusseldorf, subsequently in Hornbach/Odenwald; now works in Barjac, France. **Awards:** Hans Thoma Memorial Prize, 1983; Carnegie Prize, Carnegie Museum of Art, 1988; Kaiserring Prize of Goslar, Germany, 1990; International Center of Photography Infinity Award, 1993. **Agent:** Gagosian Gallery (Chelsea), 555 West 24th Street, New York, New York 10011; Richard Gray Gallery, 875 North Michigan Avenue, Chicago, Illinois 60611; Galerie Paul Maenz, Bismarckstrasse 50, 5000 Cologne 1. **Address:** La Ribaute, 30430 Barjac, France.

Individual Exhibitions:

1969 Galerie am Kaiserplatz, Karlsruhe
1973 *Nothing,* Galerie Michael Werner, Cologne
Der Niebelungen Leid, Goethe-Institut, Amsterdam
1974 *Alarichs Grab,* Galerie Felix Handschin, Basle
Heliogabal, Galerie t'Venster, Rotterdam
Malerei der verdrannten Erde, Galerie Michael Werner, Cologne
1975 *Unternehmen Seelowe,* Galerie Michael Werner, Cologne
1976 *Siegfried vergisst Brunhilde,* Galerie Michael Werner, Cologne
1977 Kunstverein, Bonn
Galerie Helen van der Meij, Amsterdam
Ritt an die Weichsel, Galerie Werner, Cologne
1978 *Wege der Weltweisheit-Hermannsschlacht,* Galerie Maier-Hahn, Dusseldorf
Bilder und Bucher, Kunsthalle, Berne
1979 Stedelijk Van Abbemuseum, Eindhoven, Netherlands
Bucher, Galerie Helen van der Meij, Amsterdam
1980 *Verbrennen-Verholzen-Versenken-Versanden,* West German Pavilion, at the *Biennale,* Venice (with Georg Baselitz)
Bilderstreit, Kunstverein, Stuttgart
Württembergischer Kunstverein, Stuttgart
Galerie Helen van der Meij, Amsterdam
Bilder und Zeichnungen, Galerie Sigrid Friedrich-Sabine Kunst, Munich
Holzchnitte und Bucher, Groninger Museum, Groningen, Netherlands
1981 *Und, Werdandi, Skuld,* Galerie Paul Maenz, Cologne
Marian Goldman Gallery, New York
Galleria Salvatore Ala, Milan
Bucher, Galerie Sigrid Friedrich-Sabine Kunst, Munich
Aquarelle 1970–1980, Kunstverein, Freiburg
Margarete/Sulamith, Museum Folkwang, Essen (travelled to the Whitechapel Art Gallery, London)
1982 Galerie Paul Maenz, Cologne
Whitechapel Art Gallery, London
1983 Musée d'Art Contemporain, Bordeaux, France
Anthony d'Offay Gallery, London
1984 Stadtische Kunsthalle, Dusseldorf
Musée d'Art Moderne de la Ville, Paris
Israel Museum, Jerusalem
Galerie Paul Maenz, Cologne
1985 Marian Goodman Gallery, New York
1986 Kunsthalle, Basle
1987 Galerie Foksal, Warsaw
Philadelphia Museum of Art, Pennsylvania (retrospective; toured the United States, 1987–88)
1989 *The High Priestess,* Anthony d'Offay Gallery, London
Der Engel der Geschichte, Galerie Paul Maenz, Cologne
Mohn und Gedächtnis, Galeria Foksal, Warsaw
1990 *Lilit,* Marian Goodman Gallery, New York
Jason, Douglas Hyde Gallery, Dublin
Bücher 1969–1989, Kunsthalle Tübingen
Kaiserring Goslar 1990: Anselm Kiefer, Mönchehaus Museum, Goslar, Germany
1991 *Bücher 1989–1990,* Kunstverein Munich and Kunsthaus Zürich

Neue Nationalgalerie, Berlin
Nachtschattengewächse, Galery Yvon Lambert, Paris
1992 Fuji Television Gallery, Tokyo
The Women of the Revolution, Anthony d'Offay Gallery, London
Lia Rumma Gallery, Naples
1993 *Melancholia,* Sezon Museum of Art, Tokyo (travelled to Kyoto National Museum of Art and Hiroshima Museum of Contemporary Art)
1996 *I Hold All Indias in my Hand,* South London Gallery, London (catalog)
Del Paisaje A La Metáfora: Pinturas Y Libros Del Artista Aleman, Centro Cultural Arte Contemporáneo, A.C., Mexico City
1997 *Anselm Kiefer Woodcuts,* Museo di Capodimonte, Naples
Himmel Erde, La Biennale di Venezia (47th), Museo Correr, Venice
Guggenheim Museum, Bilbao, Inaugural Exhibition
1998 *Dein und mein Alter und Das Alter der Welt/Your Age and Mine at the Age of the World,* Gagosian Gallery (Uptown), New York
Anselm Kiefer: Works on Paper 1969–1993, The Metropolitan Museum of Art, New York
1999 *Stelle Cadenti/Shooting Stars,* Galleria d'Arte Moderna di Bologna, Italy (catalog)
Che Cento Fiori Fioriscano, Lia Rumma, Milan
2000 *Select Works,* Eaton Fine Art, Inc., West Palm Beach, Florida
Let a Thousand Flowers Bloom, Anthony d'Offay Gallery, London (also Gagosian Gallery Chelsea, New York)
2001 *Painting, Sculpture, Woodcuts, Books,* Smart Museum of Art, Chicago
Lichtfalle, Goethe-Institut, Chicago

Selected Group Exhibitions:

1973 *14 mal 14,* Kunsthalle, Baden-Baden, West Germany
1976 *Beuys und seine Schuler,* Kunstverein, Frankfurt
1977 *Documenta 6,* Museum Fridericianum, Kassel, West Germany (and *Documenta 7,* 1982; *Documenta 8,* 1987)
1981 *A New Spirit in Painting,* Royal Academy of Art, London
1982 *60–80: Attitudes, Concepts, Images,* Stedelijk Museum, Amsterdam
1987 *Avant-Garde in the Eighties,* Los Angeles County Museum of Art
1989 *Magiciens de la terre,* Centre Georges Pompidou and Grande Halle La Villette, Paris
Modern Masters '89, Helsingfors Konsthall, Helsinki
1990 *Life Size,* Israel Museum, Jerusalem
1990—Energieen, Stedelijk Museum, Amsterdam
1995 *Recaptured Nature,* Marian Goodman Gallery, New York
1996 *19th & 20th Century European and American Works of Art,* Edward Tyler Nahem Fine Art, New York
1997 *On the Edge: Contemporary Art from the Werner and Elaine Dannheisser Collection,* Museum of Modern Art, New York
Veronica's Revenge, Centre d'Art Contemporain, Geneva

Collections:

Neue Galerie/Sammlung Ludwig, Aachen, West Germany; Stedelijk Van Abbemuseum, Eindhoven, Netherlands; San Francisco Museum of Modern Art; Metropolitan Museum of Art, New York; Seattle Art Museum.

Publications:

By KIEFER: Books—*Die Donauquelle,* Cologne 1978; *Bildersprache: Celan-Motive bei László Lakner und Anselm Kiefer,* with Theo Buck and Anselm Kiefer, Aachen 1993; *Anslem Kiefer: After the Catastrophe,* London 1997. **Articles**—''Besetzungen 1969'' in *Interfunktionen* (Cologne), no. 12, 1975; ''Gilgamesch und Enkidu im Zederwald'' in *Artforum* (New York), June 1981; ''Martin Heidegger'' in *Tumult,* Munich 1987; ''Nachts fahre ich mit dem Fahrrad von Bild zu Bild'' in *Süddetusche Zeitung Magazin,* November 1990; ''Anselm Kiefer: 'This Dark Light That Falls from the Stars''' in *Art Press,* no. 216, September 1996.

On KIEFER: Books—*Anselm Kiefer,* exhibition catalog with texts by Dorothea von Stetten and Evelyn Weiss, Bonn 1977; *Anselm Kiefer: Bilder und Bucher,* exhibition catalog with texts by Johannes Gachnang and Theo Kneubuhler, Berne 1978; *Malerei auf Papier,* exhibition catalog by Michael Schwarz and others, Karlsruhe 1979; *Anselm Kiefer,* exhibition catalog with text by Rudi H. Fuchs, Eindhoven, Netherlands 1980; *Biennale Venedig 1980: Deutscher Pavillon,* exhibition catalog with texts by Klaus Gallwitz and Rudi H. Fuchs, Stuttgart 1980; *Anselm Kiefer,* exhibition catalog with text by Rudi H. Fuchs, Mannheim 1980; *Anselm Kiefer,* exhibition catalog with text by Tilman Osterwold, Stuttgart 1980; *Anselm Kiefer,* exhibition catalog with texts by Carel Blotkamp and Gunter Gercken, Groningen, Netherlands 1980; *Anselm Kiefer: Aquarelle 1970–1980,* exhibition catalog with text by Rudi H. Fuchs, Freiburg 1981; *Anselm Kiefer,* exhibition catalog with texts by Zdenek Felix and Nick Serota, Essen and London 1981; *Anselm Kiefer: Watercolours 1970–82,* with text by Anne Seymour, London 1983; *Anselm Kiefer,* exhibition catalog with texts by Rudi Fuchs, Suzanne Page and Jurgen Harten, Dusseldorf and Paris 1984; *The High Priestess,* with texts by Armin Zweite and Anne Seymour, New York 1989; *Anselm Kiefer: Jason,* exhibition catalog with text by John Hutchinson, Stuttgart 1990; *Anselm Kiefer: Bücher 1969–1990,* with text by Götz Adriani, Zdenek Felix, Toni Stoss, and Peter Schjeldahl, Stuttgart 1990; *Anselm Kiefer: Lilith,* exhibition catalog with text by Doreet LeVitté-Harten, New York 1990; *Fire on the Earth: Anselm Kiefer and the Postmodern World,* by John C. Gilmour, Philadelphia 1990; *Anselm Kiefer,* exhibition catalog with texts by Dieter Honisch and others, Berlin 1991; *Anselm Kiefer: The Winged Zeitgeist,* exhibition catalog with text by Tatsumi Shinoda, Tokyo 1992; *Anselm Kiefer: Melancholia,* exhibition catalog with text by Mark Rosenthal, Tokyo 1993; *Anselm Kiefer: The Psychology of 'After the Catastrophe'* by Rafael López-Pedraza, London 1996; *Anselm Kiefer and the Philosophy of Martin Heidegger* by Matthew Biro, Cambridge 1998; *Anselm Kiefer and Art After Auschwitz* by Lisa Saltzman, Cambridge 1999. **Articles**—''Theory of Flight'' by Ida Panicelli in *Artforum,* January 1990; ''German Memory: The Art of Anselm Kiefer'' by Allan M. Jalon in *South-West Review,* Spring 1990; ''Anselm Kiefer'' by Bernd Skupin in *Vogue,* July 1990; ''Anselm Kiefer'' by Bill Jones in *Arts Magazine,* September 1990; ''Kiefer's Approaches'' by Andrew Benjamin in *Thinking Art: Beyond Traditional Aesthetics,* London 1991; ''Anselm

Kiefer'' by Thomas Wulffen in *Flash Art,* Summer 1991; ''The World, the Book, and Anselm Kiefer'' by Charles W. Haxthausen in *Burlington Magazine,* 1991; ''The Alchemist'' by Jack Flam in *New York Review of Books,* 13 February 1992; ''Keith Patrick on Anselm Kiefer's Elizabeth'' in *Contemporary Art,* vol. 2, no. 3, Summer 1994; ''Anselm Kiefer'' by Tim Martin in *Third Text,* no. 38, Spring 1997; ''Anselm Kiefer as Printmaker: 1—A Catalogue, 1973–1993'' by James Hyman in *Print Quarterly,* vol. 14, no. 1, March 1997; ''Anselm Kiefer's Identity Crisis'' by Laurie Attias in *ARTnews,* vol. 96, no. 6, June 1997; ''Anselm Kiefer: Nurnberg, 1982'' by Ted Mooney in *Artforum,* vol. 36, no. 8, April 1998; ''Anselm Kiefer'' by Donald B. Kuspit in *Artforum,* vol. 37, no. 8, April 1999.

* * *

Germans and non-Germans alike blanched when Anselm Kiefer kicked off his career by exploring his national identity in the mock-Nazi self-portrait photographic series, *From Summer to Fall of 1969, I Occupied Switzerland, France, and Italy.* Subsequent paintings that utilized Nazi and Aryan iconography sparked political and art-world controversy and prompted many critics to dismiss his work as sensationalism. Kiefer's apparent refusal to maintain the solemnity required when addressing the Holocaust further infuriated the public. Such investigations, however, conducted with an intelligent if irreverent sensibility, now seem like the start of a process of self-analysis that was inevitable for both the artist and his country.

In *Germany's Spiritual Heroes,* Kiefer confronts his German heritage in a cavernous interior thick with the sediment of cultural arrogance and human shame. His confining landscapes offer no chance to escape, as written reminders of the interconnections between German myth and history seem to spring up from the soil. In Operation ''Seelöwe,'' the terrain comprises row upon row of soldiers standing at attention but metaphorically, at least, interred. In the foreground of the painting, Kiefer depicts three battleships, the middle one sporting a plumage of fire and smoke. In preparing the work, he spent many hours arranging toy ships that he used as models, thereby eliciting comparisons between the roles of the artist and the admiral.

Although the paintings for the most part derive from a monumental narrative-historical genre that was perfected by Nicolas Poussin and effectively superseded by a hundred years of modernism's economical aesthetic, Kiefer swerves away from generic exercise by acknowledging postwar innovations in form. Many of the surfaces recall the gestural attack and spatial ambiguity of abstract expressionism. From Joseph Beuys, who taught him in the late 1960s not to shrink from his heritage, Kiefer borrowed the use of nontraditional materials and has had an especially rewarding experience with the harsh physicality and signifying potential of lead. This adventurousness with material has resulted in a fragility and sometimes a breakdown of highly collectible works—a situation that adds other layers of aesthetic interest: the durability of personal expression, the commodification of industrial dross, the sticky issue of restoration.

In subsequent years, Kiefer and Beuys have had differences of opinion regarding the aims and ideals of artistic activity, with Kiefer emphasizing process and denying the likelihood or desirability of closure, and Beuys taking a Utopian approach. In order to fulfill his ideal, Beuys gradually developed a career in which conceptual and theatrical endeavors play at least as great a role as painting, whereas Kiefer has generally concentrated on following a chain of questions about painters and paintings in an age where the art is often thought to have exhausted itself. Kiefer does not pose the modernist questions of how pure or flat a painting can be. Instead, he inquires how much philosophical and intellectual content can be imported before a work of art loses its humanity.

Kiefer incorporates into the paintings and includes in their titles names and places that refer to Richard Wagner, Friedrich Nietzsche, and Martin Heidegger, three thinkers who are considered to be the great apologists for German fascism, though, as the painter realizes, these perceptions have at least somewhat arisen from misinterpretation. Kiefer's *Parsifal,* titled after Wagner's opera, displays a bowl filled with blood atop a table in an otherwise empty room. Spare and austere where Wagner was multifarious and ornate, the work refuses to comment one way or the other on the composer's politics or aesthetics. Heidegger, whom Kiefer portrays, along with Immanuel Kant and others, in *The Battle of Teutoborg Forest,* has inspired the painter with his advocacy of a return to an ontology composed of the basic elements of earth, sky, divinities, and mortals. Though Kiefer has not spoken explicitly about Nietzsche, the philosopher's bifurcation of Greek drama into Dionysian and Apollinian has had an obvious effect on his thought. The twin forces of destruction and dream are played out in such works as *The Order of Angels,* the upper left corner of which is inscribed with the name of Dionysus, and many others in which peaceful scenes have been wrecked by dark and horrendous forces. Kiefer's engagement with such controversial figures reveals the purposeful encouragement of those critics who would condemn him for probing subject matter that is considered too harsh to acknowledge but also seemingly relevant in light of reunification.

Kiefer's intellectual baggage is somewhat lightened by his approach to the material at hand, impressionistic rather than analytical; he says, ''I read. But it's not really reading. I immediately see everything I read in images.'' His scholarship may in fact come from a desire to find interesting *looking* words. Unlike René Magritte, who utilized an impersonal calligraphy, or Jasper Johns, who utilizes even more impersonal stencils, Kiefer scrawls across his canvases in a hand shaking with delight and/or passion. His script represents another stage in the tension between image and word that has gone unresolved ever since the seventeenth-century modernist Poussin wrote, ''Et en Arcadia ego.''

——Mark Swartz

KIENHOLZ, Edward

Nationality: American. **Born:** Fairfield, Washington, 1927. **Education:** Washington State College, Pullman; Eastern Washington College of Education, Cheney; Whitworth College, Spokane, 1945–52; self-taught in art. **Family:** Married Nancy Reddin; children: Noah, Jenny and Chrisi. **Career:** Independent artist known for life-sized sculptural tableaux: lived in Los Angeles, 1953–73; director, Now Gallery, Los Angeles, 1956–57; director, with Walter Hopps, Ferus Gallery, Los Angeles, 1957–63; moved to Berlin, 1973; now spends six months each year in Berlin and six months in Hope, Idaho; opened the Faith and Charity in Hope Gallery, Hope, Idaho, 1977; acknowledged collaboration of his wife in his work, 1981; buried in the passenger seat of 1940 Packard coupe with the ashes of his dog in back seat and bottle of vintage wine in glovebox. **Awards:** DAAD grant for residence in Berlin, 1973; Guggenheim grant, 1975. **Agent:** Whitney Museum of American Art, 945 Madison Avenue at 75th,

New York, New York 10021; Jack Ruthberg Fine Arts, 357 North La Brea Avenue, Los Angeles, California 90036. **Died:** Of heart attack, Hope, Idaho, 10 June 1994.

Individual Exhibitions:

1955 Cafe Galleria, Los Angeles
1956 Syndell Studios, Los Angeles
1958 Ferus Gallery, Los Angeles
Exodus Gallery, San Pedro, California
1959 Ferus Gallery, Los Angeles
1960 Ferus Gallery, Los Angeles
1961 Ferus Gallery, Los Angeles
Pasadena Art Museum, California
1962 Ferus Gallery, Los Angeles
1963 Ferus Gallery, Los Angeles
Iolas Gallery, New York
Dwan Gallery, Los Angeles
1964 Dwan Gallery, Los Angeles
1965 Los Angeles County Museum of Art
1966 Institute of Contemporary Art, Boston
University of Saskatchewan, Regina
1967 Dwan Gallery, New York
Washington (D.C.) Gallery of Modern Art
1968 Boise Art Museum, Idaho
Vancouver Art Gallery
1970 *11 Tableaux,* Moderna Museet, Stockholm (toured Europe)
1971 Onnasch Galerie, Cologne
1972 Gemini G. E. L., Los Angeles
Onnasch Galerie, Cologne
1974 Galerie Christel, Helsinki
Galleria Bocci, Milan
Galeria LPS, Turin
1975 *Roxys,* Ville de Strasbourg, France
1977 *The Art Show,* Galerie Folker Skulima, Berlin (travelled to the Centre Georges Pompidou, Paris, Städtische Kunsthalle, Dusseldorf, and Apollon Galerie Die Insel, Munich)
The Volksempfangers, Nationalgalerie, Berlin (travelled to Galerie Maeght, Zurich, Städtischen Galerie im Lenbachhaus, Munich, and Galleria Il Gabbiano, Rome)
1979 Louisiana Museum, Humlebaek, Denmark
University of Idaho, Moscow
University of Washington, Seattle
1981 Douglas Hyde Gallery, University of Dublin
Galerie Maeght, Zurich
Middendorf/Lane Gallery, Washington, D.C.
L.A. Louver Gallery, Los Angeles
1982 GAK-Gesellschaft für Aktuelle Kunst, Bremen, West Germany
Dibbert Gallery, Berlin
1983 Galerie Maeght, Paris
1984 San Francisco Museum of Modern Art
Contemporary Arts Museum, Houston
Walker Art Center, Minneapolis
1994 Galerie Lelong, Paris
The Hoerengracht, Museum of Contemporary Art, San Diego
1995 *Edward Kienholz 1954–1962,* Menil Foundation, Houston (catalog)
L.A. Louvre Gallery, Venice, California
1996 *Kienholz: A Retrospective,* Whitney Museum of American Art, New York (also Museum of Contemporary Art, Los Angeles and Berlinische Galerie, Berlin) (catalog)
1997 *De Klein à Warhol: Face-à-Face France,* Centre Georges Pompidou, Paris (catalog)
Good-bye Edward Kienholz?, Martin-Gropius-Bau, Berlin
1999 *The Hoerengracht,* Nevada Museum of Art, Reno

Selected Group Exhibitions:

1961 *Art of Assemblage,* Museum of Modern Art, New York
1962 *50 California Artists,* Whitney Museum, New York
1968 *Dada, Surrealism and Their Heritage,* Museum of Modern Art, New York
1972 *Documenta 5,* Kassel, West Germany
1974 *ARS '74,* The Ateneum, Helsinki
1977 *Biennale,* Venice
1981 *Biennial,* Whitney Museum, New York
1982 *One Hundred Years of California Sculpture,* Oakland Museum, California
1984 *Salvaged: Altered Everyday Objects,* Project Studio One, Long Island City, New York
1987 *Berlinart 1961–87,* Museum of Modern Art, New York (travelled to San Francisco)
1994 *Love in the Ruins: Art and the Inspiration of L.A.,* Long Beach Museum of Art, California (catalog)
1997 *Die Epoche der Moderne-Kunst im 20. Jahrhundert,* Martin-Gropius-Bau, Berlin

Collections:

Whitney Museum, New York; Los Angeles County Museum of Art; Stedelijk Museum, Amsterdam; Centre National d'Art Contemporain, Paris; Moderna Museet Stockholm; Louisiana Museum, Humlebaek, Denmark; Staatsgalerie, Stuttgart; Nationalgalerie, Berlin; Museum of Modern Art, Tokyo

Publications:

On KIENHOLZ: Books—*Pop Art Redefined* by John Russell and Suzi Gablik, London 1969; *Edward Kienholz,* exhibition catalog with texts by Lawrence Weschler and Ron Glowen, San Francisco 1984; *The Madonna of the Future: Essays in a Pluralistic Art World* by Arthur Coleman Danto, New York 2000. **Articles—**"A Portfolio of California Sculptors" by Donald Factor in *Artforum* (New York), August 1963; "The Savage Eye of Edward Kienholz" by John Coplans in *Studio International* (London), September 1965; "Crossing the Bar" by Suzi Gablik in *Artnews* (New York), October 1965; "Edward Kienholz" by Henry Hopkins in *Art in America* (New York), October/November 1965; "Edward Kienholz" in *Time* (New York), December 1965; "The Beanery" in *Newsweek* (New York), December 1965; "Beanery Built for Art" in *Life* (New York), January 1966; "The Underground Pre-Raphaelitism of Edward Kienholz En Vastkustrealist" by Beate Sydhoff in *Konstrevy* (Stockholm), January 1967; "68 High Art and Low Art" by Philip Leider in *Look* (New York), January 1968; "Edward Kienholz, A Remembrance" by Walter Hopps in *American Art,* vol. 8, Summer/Fall 1994; obituary in *The New York Times,* 13 June 1994; obituary in *Art in America* (New York), vol. 82, September 1994; obituary in *Flash Art*

(International Edition), no. 178, October 1994; ''All-American Barbaric Yawp'' by Robert Hughes in *Time,* 6 May 1996; ''Ed and Nancy: The Kienholzes' Art of Collaboration'' by Kay Larson in *The Village Voice,* 12 March 1996; ''Scavenger's Parade'' by Reagan Upshaw in *Art in America* (New York), vol. 84, no. 10, October 1996. **Video—***The Age of Anxiety,* 1997.

* * *

Edward Kienholz's assemblages and *tableaux vivants* possess at their core a moralist's critical assessment of contemporary society's conditions, institutions and values as they impact the life of the individual. Little escapes his scrutinizing gaze: sexual repression, social and political violence, racism, agism, the manipulation of social and sexual mores. His works are steeped in allegory and archetype, focused on the individual (either as figuration within the *tableau* or the viewer-as-participant) and commonplace objects and surroundings. A narrative often ensues as a direct means of quotation, but the implications of that narrative speak of a larger and more pervasive social phenomenon that conditions the story.

As an assemblagist, Kienholz has a remarkable eye for selective and suggestive detail, and an ability to imbue discarded common objects and consumer goods with metaphorical and allegorial significance. His ''Volksempfangers'' and ''Tin TV'' series of the 1970s invoke radios and television sets as a kind of human cipher (in the former) and as the vehicle for overt or covert propaganda purpose. A flophouse room, saved from the wrecking ball and re-assembled in all its sordid detail, becomes in ''Sollie 17'' a humanistic monument to loneliness and despair.

Kienholz's works agitate, but they are not agitational. They attack the repressiveness of complacency, particularly with respect to social and moral issues of our time. Thus a work like ''Still Live'' (1974), with its notorious randomly activated and timed firing mechanism facing a chair in which the viewer is invited to sit, places the viewer in a life-and-death situation not for the sake of risk but as comment on the randomness and violence of terrorism and the inhumaness of para-military means of political control.

Kienholz's art presents a dichotomy of familiarity and reproachment, often in direct extremes (the seat in ''Still Live'' is placed in comfortable and homey surroundings) to forcefully extract the symptomatic social cancer at the base of his commentary. Yet his art has also a poetic sensitivity: a respect for once-meaningful objects (such as old photographs and furniture), the *bricoleur's* facility of mechanical skills, the dramatist's eye for observation. At face value, Kienholz's works have the power to disturb and alienate. At a deeper level of meaning and intent, they force a confrontation with contemporary and universal aspects of society that manifest or conceal the foibles and imperfections of human nature. But, most importantly, they confront hypocrisy.

—Ron Glowen

KING, Phillip

Nationality: British. **Born:** Kheredine, Tunisia, 1 May 1934; moved with his family to London, 1946. **Education:** Attended primary schools in London; studied modern languages at Cambridge University, 1954–57, and sculpture at St. Martin's School of Art, London, 1957–58. **Military Service:** Royal Signal Corps, 1952–54. **Family:** Married Lillian Odelle in 1957; son: Anthony. **Career:** Sculptor, living and working in London and Dunstable, Hertfordshire, since 1958. Worked as an assistant to Henry Moore, 1959–60; first fiberglass structures with colour, 1962; began working in steel, 1969. Lecturer, St. Martin's School of Art, 1959–80; Bennington College, Vermont, 1964; Slade School of Fine Art, London, 1967–70; Trustee, Tate Gallery, London, 1967–69; Hochschule für Kunst, Berlin, 1979–80; artist-in-residence, Alexander Mackie College, Sydney, 1980; Professor of sculpture, Royal College of Art, London, 1980–1990; Professor Emeritus, Royal College of Art, London, 1990; Professor of Sculpture, Royal Academy Schools, London, 1990; elected President, Royal Academy of Arts, London, 1999. **Awards:** Boise Scholarship, Slade of School of Fine Art, 1960; Peter Stuyvesant Travel Bursary, 1965; First Prize, Socha Pietanskych Parkov, Piestany, Czechoslovakia, 1969. Associate, Royal Academy of Arts, London, 1977. C. B. E. (Commander, Order of the British Empire), 1975; elected Royal Academician, Royal Academy of Arts, London, 1990. **Agent:** New Rowan Gallery, 25 Dover Street, London, W1X 3PA, England.

Individual Exhibitions:

1957 Heffer's Gallery, Cambridge
1964 Rowan Gallery, London
1966 Richard Feigen Gallery, New York (travelled to Richard Feigen Gallery, Chicago)
Isaac Delgado Museum of Art, New Orleans
1968 Galerie Yvon Lambert, Paris *Biennale,* Venice (with Bridget Riley; travelled to the Stadtgalerie, Bochum, West Germany, and Museum Boymans van Beuningen, Rotterdam)
Whitechapel Art Gallery, London
1970 Rowan Gallery, London
1972 Rowan Gallery, London
1973 Rowan Gallery, London
1974 Rijksmuseum Kröller Müller, Otterlo, Netherlands (toured Europe, 1974–75)
1975 *Sculptures by Phillip King,* Rowan Gallery, London
Mappin Art Gallery, Sheffield (toured the U.K., 1975–76)
1976 Third Eye Centre, Glasgow
Oriel Gallery, Cardiff
1977 Rowan Gallery, London
1979 Rowan Gallery, London
1981 Hayward Gallery, London (travelled to the Fruit Market Gallery, Edinburgh)
1983 Juda Rowan Gallery, London
1987 Nishimura Gallery, Tokyo
1992 *Skulpturen,* Städtische Kunsthalle Mannheim (catalog)
1993 Musée des Beaux-Arts André Malraux, Le Havre (catalog)
1997 *Ceramic Vessels,* Yorkshire Sculpture Park, Wakefield, West Yorkshire (retrospective) (catalog)
Forte de Belvedere, Florence (retrospective) (catalog)
1999 Bernard Jacobson, London

Selected Group Exhibitions:

1961 *British Sculpture,* Jewish Museum, New York
1963 *International Biennale des Jeunes Artistes,* Paris

1965 *The New Generation,* Whitechapel Art Gallery, London
1969 *Contemporary Art: Between the East and the West,* National Museum of Modern Art, Tokyo
1977 *Silver Jubilee Exhibition of Contemporary British Sculpture,* Battersea Park, London
1980 *British Art 1940–1980,* Hayward Gallery, London
1982 *British Sculpture in the 20th Century,* Whitechapel Art Gallery, London
1985 *Sculpture,* Fondation Cartier, Jouv-en-Josas, France
1987 *British Art in the 20th Century,* Royal Academy, London

Collections:

Arts Council of Great Britain, London; Tate Gallery, London; Ulster Museum, Belfast; National Gallery of Modern Art, Edinburgh; Rijksmuseum Kröller-Müller, Otterlo, Netherlands; Musée Royaux des Beaux-Arts, Brussels; Centre Georges Pompidou, Paris; Galleria d'Arte Moderna, Turin; Museum of Modern Art, New York; National Gallery of Victoria, Melbourne.

Publications:

By KING: Book—*Phillip King,* with Peter Murray, Milan 1997. **Articles—**statement in *King,* exhibition catalog, London 1964; ''Phillip King, Young British Sculptor Working Mainly in Plastics, Answers Some Questions by John Coplans'' in *Studio International* (London), December 1965; statement in *Primary Structures,* exhibition catalog, New York 1966; ''British Artists at Venice: Phillip King Talks about His Sculpture'' in *Studio International* (London), June 1968; ''The Relevance of Matisse: A Discussion between Andrew Forge, Howard Hodgkin and Phillip King'' in *Studio International* (London), July/August 1968; ''Colour in Sculpture: Statements by Phillip King, Tim Scott, David Annesley and William Turnbull'' in *Studio International* (London), January 1969; statements in *Phillip King,* exhibition catalog, Otterlo, Netherlands 1974; ''An Interview with Courturier'' in *Art Press* (Paris), July/August 1975; ''Phillip King,'' interview with Francis Spalding, in *Arts Review* (London), 10 April 1981; interview with Richard Demarco in *Studio International* (London), September 1982; interview with Andrew Lambirth in *Royal Academy Magazine,* no. 47, Summer 1995; interview with Gareth Fisher and Arthur Watson in *Transcript,* vol. 2, no. 2, November 1996.

On KING: Books—*Movements in Art since 1945* by Edward Lucie-Smith, London 1969; *Phillip King,* exhibition catalog by David Thompson, Otterlo, Netherlands 1974; *Sculptures by Phillip King,* exhibition catalog by Norbert Lynton, London 1975; *Phillip King,* exhibition catalog by Rudolf Oxenaar and others, London 1981 (includes bibliography); *Open Air Sculpture in Britain* by W. J. Strachan, London 1984. **Articles—**''Phillip King'' by William Feaver in the *Financial Times* (London), 12 March 1975; ''Phillip King'' by Norbert Lynton in *Art International* (Lugano, Switzerland), September 1977; ''The Tree Within'' by William Feaver in the *Observer* (London), 1 April 1979; ''Phillip King in a Challenging Phase of Development'' by John Russell in the *New York Times,* 28 June 1981; ''Phillip King and Gottfried Honegger'' in *Arts Review* (London), 10 June 1983; ''Vessel as Vessel'' by Richard Cork in *Ceramic Review,* no. 163, January-February 1997; ''Phillip King in Florence'' by Bryan Robertson in *Modern Painters* (London), vol. 10, Autumn 1997; ''Phillip King'' by Daniela Lancioni in *Sculpture* (Washington, D.C.), vol. 16, December 1997; ''Phillip King: Bernard Jacobson'' by William Feaver in *Art News,* vol. 98, no. 1, January 1999.

*

I would like my work to be essentially something *of nature,* not parallel to it, nor evocation of nature but appearing as nature itself, by growing within its own laws, determined by our mutual reaction—for instance, our mutual near-ness and far-ness during the working process, my physical make-up equals its physical make-up. Not a metaphor for something else but an identity being revealed.

—Phillip King

* * *

Although Phillip King emerged among that group of young artists working with Anthony Caro at St. Martin's School of Art in London in the early 1960s, his art has always had a singularly individual flavour. A guiding concern of this group, the returning of sculpture to first principles after the excesses of 1950s expressionism, produced a kind of minimal definition of sculpture as a self-sufficient three-dimensional object inhabiting space. They regarded abstraction as crucial for emphasizing these fundamental qualities, as was the positioning of the sculpture directly on the ground, without the intermediary of a pedestal. Only thus would the spectator be forced to confront and examine this ''intruder'' into his world. In a series of cone-based works, often vividly colored like the startling pink and green ''Rosebud,'' King explored certain ways in which the viewer apprehends the object in front of him; how, by discerning its mass, volume, stability, structure and other such qualities, he constructs its ''character.''

Towards the end of the decade, in a series of multi-partite works, like ''Call,'' in which the emphasis has shifted from the sculptural object per se to the space it inhabits, King sought to define a sense of place, and invest it with a character. Although the various components articulate an area, such works are not installations, for they do not simply orchestrate a pre-existing space; rather, they segregate, then shape, a particular zone from within a larger arena: a sculpture is still a self-sufficient entity.

In the 1970s King began using materials like slate, elm, steel and wire mesh in their raw states, exploiting their surface and textures for expressive effect. He reverted to the notion of a sculpture as a single entity, but continued to seek to define and characterize space and place, as titles like ''Sure Place,'' ''Open Bound,'' ''Within,'' and ''Ring Rock'' indicate. Although the scale at times increased considerably, as in ''Shogun,'' the sculptures were never removed from the realm of human dimensions. A confrontation between spectator and object remains central to his work, a confrontation in which the spectator learns something not only about the piece in front of him but about himself as well. This potential for increasing self-awareness is one of the essential justifications of sculpture for King. One of the constants in his art, it unifies a body of work which is very diverse in appearance.

—Lynne Cooke

KING, William (Dickey)

Nationality: American. **Born:** Jacksonville, Florida, 25 February 1925. **Education:** University of Florida, Gainesville, 1942–44; studied at Cooper Union Art School, New York, with John Hovannes and Milton Hebald, 1945–48 (Sculpture Prize, 1948); Skowhegan School of Painting and Sculpture, Maine, 1948; Brooklyn Museum Art School, New York, with Milton Hebald, 1949; Accademia di Belle Arti, Rome, 1949–50; Central School of Arts and Crafts, London, 1952. **Family:** Married Lois Dodd in 1948; married Shirley Bowman in 1955; married Ann Kovin in 1965. **Career:** Independent sculptor, since 1952. Instructor, Brooklyn Museum School of Art, New York, 1952–55; lecturer in sculpture, University of California, Berkeley, 1965–66; sculpture instructor, Art Students League, New York, 1968–69; instructor, University of Pennsylvania, Philadelphia, 1972–73; artist in residence in State University of New York system. **Awards:** Fulbright Travel Fellowship to Italy, 1949–50; Brooklyn Museum Prize, 1949; First Prize, Margaret Tiffany Blake Competition, 1951; Moorehead Patterson Sculpture Award, 1961; Augustus Saint Gaudens Medal, Cooper Union, 1964; New York State Creative Artists Public Service Award and Grant, 1974; Distinction Prize, Hakone Open-Air Museum, Japan, 1980; Gold Medal, National Academy of Design, New York, 1986; Louise Nevelson Award, American Academy of Arts and Letters, New York, 1995; Lifetime Achievement in the Arts Visual Arts Award, Guild Hall of East Hampton, New York, 1997. **Agent:** Kraushaar Galleries, 724 Fifth Avenue, New York, New York, 10019. **Address:** c/o Terry Dintenfass, 50 West 57th Street, New York, New York 10019, U.S.A.

Individual Exhibitions:

1954 The Alan Gallery, New York
1955 The Alan Gallery, New York
1958 The Alan Gallery, New York
1960 The Alan Gallery, New York
1961 The Alan Gallery, New York
1962 Terry Dintenfass, New York
1963 The Gallery, Norwalk, Ohio
1964 Donald F. Morris Gallery, Detroit
Terry Dintenfass, New York
Washington Federal Savings and Loan, Miami Beach
1965 Terry Dintenfass, New York
1966 Feliz Landau Gallery, Los Angeles
Berkeley Gallery, San Francisco
Feigen-Palmer Gallery, Los Angeles
Terry Dintenfass, New York
1967 Terry Dintenfass, New York
William King: A Comprehensive Look, Lowe Art Gallery, University of Miami
1968 Terry Dintenfass, New York
1969 Terry Dintenfass, New York
Guild Hall, East Hampton, New York
1970 Terry Dintenfass, New York
Galerie Ann, Houston
Berenson Gallery, Bay Harbor Island, Florida
San Francisco Museum of Art
Art Gallery, University of California at Los Angeles
Santa Barbara Museum of Art, California
University of New Mexico, Albuquerque
Arkansas Art Center, Little Rock
1971 Terry Dintenfass, New York
Alpha Gallery, Boston
Dag Hammarskjold Plaza, New York
Oklahoma Art Center, Oklahoma City
University of Iowa, Iowa City
Indianapolis Museum of Art
Contemporary Arts Center, Cincinnati, Ohio
Colby College, Waterville, Maine
Syracuse University, New York
Broward Community College, Ft. Lauderdale, Florida
Ringling Museum, Sarasota, Florida
1972 Jacksonville Art Museum, Florida
Hopkins Art Center, Dartmouth College, Hanover, New Hampshire
Worcester Art Museum, Massachusetts
Wadsworth Atheneum, Harford, Connecticut
Montgomery Museum of Fine Arts, Alabama
Tennessee Fine Center, Nashville
Borough Hall, Brooklyn, New York
Terry Dintenfass-Steel Gallery, Bridgehampton, Connecticut
1973 Terry Dintenfass, New York
William Benton Museum, Storrs, Connecticut
Aronson Gallery, Atlanta
University of Georgia, Athens
Elvehjem Art Center, University of Wisconsin
Marion Koogler Mcnay Art Institute, San Antonio, Texas (travelled to Colorado Springs Fine Arts Center; Littleton Area Historical Museum, Colorado; Sangre de Cristo Arts and Conference Center, Pueblo, Colorado)
State University of New York at Potsdam
State University of New York at Fredonia
State University of New York at New Paltz
Terry Dintenfass, New York
Moravian College, Bethlehem, Pennsylvania
David Stuart Galleries, Los Angeles
1975 Amagansett Square, New York
1976 Terry Dintenfass, New York
1977 Terry Dintenfass, New York
Zabriskie Gallery, New York
1979 University of Connecticut Library, Storrs
1980 Terry Dintenfass, New York
1981 Terry Dintenfass, New York
Houshour Gallery, Albuquerque, New Mexico
Wingspread Gallery, Northeast Harbor, Maine
1982 Terry Dintenfass Gallery, New York
Alpha Gallery, Boston
1983 Terry Dintenfass Gallery, New York
1984 Terry Dintenfass Gallery, New York
1985 Gallery Paule Anglim, San Francisco
1986 Hooks-Epstein Gallery, Houston
Terry Dintenfass Gallery, New York
1987 Houshour Gallery, Albuerque, New Mexico
Gallery Paule Anglim, San Francisco
David Heath Gallery, Atlanta, Georgia
Montgomery Museum, Alabama
Hunter Museum, Chatanooga, Tennessee
1988 Marilyn Pearly Gallery, New York
1989 Polk Museum of Art, Lakeland, Florida

The Atrium at Maison Aican, Quebec, Canada
Terry Dintenfass Gallery, New York
1990 Brunnier Gallery and Museum, Iowa
Terry Dintenfass Gallery, New York
1992 Simmons Visual Art Center, Gainesville, Georgia
Terry Dintenfass Gallery, New York
1994 Terry Dintenfass Gallery, New York
1995 Pitt Program Council, University of Pittsburgh, Pennsylvania
1996 Seacon Square, Bangkok, Thailand
1997 Miami Dade Junior College, Miami, Florida
Terry Dintenfass Gallery, New York
1998 Lisan Tops Gallery, East Hampton, New York
Dorothy Blau Gallery, Miami
1999 Brenda Taylor Gallery, New York
Lisan Tops Gallery, East Hampton, New York
2000 Kraushaar Galleries, New York

Selected Group Exhibitions:

1948 *Third International Sculpture Exhibition,* Philadelphia Museum of Art, Pennsylvania
1955 *Recent Sculpture U.S.A.,* Museum of Modern Art, New York
1962 *American Sculpture,* University of Tennessee, Knoxville (travelled to Conway, Arkansas; Tuscaloosa, Alabama)
1972 *Recent Figure Sculpture,* Fogg Art Museum, Harvard University, Cambridge, Massachusetts (toured the northeastern United States)
1973 *Sculpture in the Streets,* San Diego Fine Arts Gallery, California
1974 *WAVES: An Artist Selects,* Cranbrook Academy of Arts, Bloomfield Hills, Michigan (travelled to Grand Rapids Art Museum, Michigan)
1976 *Skowhegan Retrospective,* Institute of Contemporary Art, Boston (travelled to Colby College, Waterville, Maine)
1978 *Human Figure in Contemporary Painting and Sculpture,* Genesis Gallery, New York
1980 *Sculpture in the 70s: The Figure,* Pratt Manhattan Center Gallery, New York (toured the United States)
1982 *Directions in Metal,* State University of New York at Potsdam
1988 *Drawings on East End,* Parrish Art Museum, Southampton, New York
1995 *Invitational Exhibition of Painting and Sculpture,* American Academy of Arts and Letters, New York
Face Value: American Portraits, Parrish Art Museum, Southampton, New York
Twentieth Century American Sculpture, The White House, Washington, D.C.
1998 *Group Exhibition,* Pratt Institute, Brooklyn, New York
1999 *Fall/Winter,* Grounds for Sculpture, Princeton, New Jersey

Collections:

Cornell University, Ithaca, New York; Syracuse University, New York; State University of New York at Potsdam; Addison Gallery of American Art, Andover, Massachusetts; Allentown Art Museum, Pennsylvania; Hopkins Art Center, Dartmouth College, Hannover, New Hampshire; First National Bank of Chicago; Fine Arts Center, Cheekwood, Tennessee; Weatherspoon Art Gallery, University of North Carolina, Greensboro; University of California, Berkeley; Hirshhorn Museum and Sculpture Garden, Smithsonian Institution, Washington, D.C.; Los Angeles County Museum of Art; Metropolitan Museum of Art, New York; Whitney Museum of American Art, New York.

Publications:

On KING: Books—*Sculpture: William King,* exhibition catalog, New York 1954; *William King,* exhibition catalog, Detroit 1964; *William King: A Comprehensive Look,* exhibition catalog with text by August L. Reundlich, Miami 1967; *Recent Figure Sculpture,* exhibition catalog by J. L. Wasserman, Cambridge 1972; *Photography Year Book 1973* by John Sanders, London 1972; *An Artist in Residence: William King,* exhibition catalog with texts by Hilton Kramer and others, New York 1974; *The Age of the Avant-Garde* by Hilton Kramer, London 1974. **Articles—**''San Francisco: William King'' by P. D. French in *Artforum* (New York), May 1970; ''The Witty Sculpture of William King'' by John Canaday in the *New York Times,* 5 September 1971; ''Something Funny's Going On'' by Peter Scheldjhahl in the *New York Times,* 7 January 1973; ''Many Small Grotesques in Sculpture by King'' by Hilton Kramer in the *New York Times,* 1 December 1973; review by Jane Bell in *Arts Magazine* (New York), April 1976; ''King's Woods'' by S. Schwartz in *Art in America* (New York), September 1976; ''King's Personalities'' by W. Peterson in *Artweek* (Oakland, California), 13 January 1979; ''William King'' by Ruth Bass in *ARTnews,* February 1989; ''William King at Marilyn Pearl and Terry Dintenfass'' by Walter Thompson in *Art in America,* April 1989; ''William King'' by Gerrit Henry in *ARTnews,* November 1990; ''William King at Terry Dintenfass'' by Brooks Adams in *Art in America,* March 1991; ''William King'' by Laurel Berger in *ARTnews,* January 1995; ''William King at Terry Dintenfass'' by Reagan Upshaw in *Art in America,* January 1995; ''William King and Connie Fox'' by Laurel Berger in *ARTnews,* November 1998.

* * *

A man of many parts—an experimenter with many materials. Rumour has it that William King was an unwilling pioneer, curiously unaware of the inherent value of his artifacts. Not surprisingly, when he first seriously considered becoming a sculptor, forgetting his previous ambitions in the field of architecture, he was quite prepared to sell his sculptures for $40–50 apiece. Budding artists of any sort have endured that sort of grind too often.

That was back in the late 1940s when he had abandoned his home State of Florida and was moving on to New York and the Brooklyn Museum of Art School preparatory to spending a year at Rome's Accademia di Belle Arti and another with the Central School in London; a respectable and extended period of varied tuition which did nothing to deflate his prying talents or their reflections on the recognizable quirks and behavioral performances of human types. So, what has transpired?

The thing about William King is that he has essentially found a quizzical (without a hint of malice) vision of the OK well-heeled USA. The sculptural version of this keenly observed North American has been a telling factor in almost all of King's oeuvres over the past

40 years regardless of his adventures with different media and into their unexpected potentialities.

Here is a remarkably fluid interpreter of at least one stand of Americana from a local boy if one includes all the states of the union as a locality. For those living outside the confines of the Monroe Doctrine William King mirrors a world only seen by courtesy of Hollywood and the New Yorker. This means that psychological portrayal of *types* is not a cardinal message that his sculptures relate to most non-Americans. In the main they will not appreciate gentle nuances of gentlemen wearing the "right" suits or of ladies carefully—and sometimes uncarefully—posing in eternal *autre-jour* modish garb (except of course when they are naked, and even then they have a way of making their nudity privately stylish).

These remarks help underline the longlasting enthusiasm King has aroused amongst so many collectors in the United States and how this confirms continuous success. Fortunately, there is more than one William King. He is a sculptor who, with increasing viability, is able to make his presence felt in the realms of novelty, ideas and inspirations. This is the *social* artist who, not content with the foibles of Mr. and Ms. America, yearns for another definition of the word *social;* maybe not the configuration of world problems, but certainly an imagery (often on a large scale) which spells out personal decisions. Taken together, these two aspects of William King emphasize why a captious dismissal of his work as humorous is unacceptable. Whatever whims may appear, and unquestionably it does sometimes percolate through some of his ideas, the real approach to the output of this artist should be to size up ability culturally, in order to pursue sculptural solutions which are visually appetizing without any psychological kickbacks or indulging in any mental parlour games.

Globally speaking, William King should be regarded as an artist rich in invention and with the insinuation of his personal style into a scarcely influenced number of subjects of humanity and their variants in widely differing raw materials.

Chipping away for hours with a blunt instrument at coral fragments when he was a child, he developed a love of creation that has never deserted him. Early application of carving craft to wood increased his understanding of the value of perfecting techniques (and time and again he has come back to timber as a sculptor's faithful ally), before he turned his attentions to exploring bronze (another material offering continuous promise). The next step was to investigate ways and means of operating with steel and aluminum, and here the very nature of the metals led him to concentrate on the assembly of shaped flat sheeting bolted and welded into constructions, tall in structure and frequently wide in extent. All these involvements with different raw elements, even if one seemed to succeed another, actually, once discovered, continued as part of his repertoire and co-existed with his astonishing control of fashioning terracotta (the example of "Marilyn"—now unfortunately stolen—is supremely beautiful both in expression and execution).

In the 1960s—and thereafter—King has also been vividly expanding sculptural developments in the uses of fabrics (including various examples of tailors' cloth and burlap) and metallics (naughahide, vinyl on linden wood and mylar), almost as if upon a quest to discover the philosopher's stone. Exotically alterego collages and monotypes have followed.

Thus the tangled web of King's processes and the ingredients he has involved to achieve a happy out-come from those processes need to be examined before coming to descriptions of his actual completed works. "Forest Folk" (1978), seven inches high in wood, for instance, shows how he can fit together a wood jigsaw of boughs, while the 49-inch-high "Coat" of 1981 is a carefully carved work in wood, upright as the preferred majority of his single figures are. The bronze sculpture of the couple "Max and Peggy" of 1986 is adeptly worked and highly figurative except in the fashioning of the pair's faces. Sheet metal (cast aluminum) in a piece like "Magic" is in the form of a subtle chevron but betraying no sharpened angles in order to bring into being a female figure bent so that one extended hand almost touches the ground. The three striding figures of "Collegium" (1984) are a monument at Houston University, at least six times the height of a man and wrought in cast and plate aluminum. Even the trees are dwarfed by this towering eminence. As for the vinyl-covered figures, as opposed to all of King's other "people," they are richly endowed with glossy colour-shining blacks and reds and gleaming opalescent whites.

In virtually every case where the carving or modelling is not scrupulously worked, limbs, outlines and features of men and women tend to be simplified or merely indicated—everything depends on stance. In such a manner William King, through his sculptures, stands astride the regionalisms of figuration and near-nonfiguration.

—Sheldon Williams

KIRILI, Alain

Nationality: French. **Born:** Paris, 1946. **Career:** Sculptor, associated with artist Philippe Sollers and "Tel Quel" literary group, Paris. Independent artist, Paris, since 1970, and New York, since 1975. **Agent:** Galerie Sonnabend, 12 rue Mazarine, 75006 Paris. **Address:** 13 rue Herold, 75001 Paris, France.

Individual Exhibitions:

1972 Galerie Sonnabend, Paris
1974 *Peintures, designs, sculptures, gravures,* Galerie Sonnabend, Paris
1976 Galerie Sonnabend, Paris
Galerie Rencontres, Paris
1977 P. S. 1, Institute for Art & Urban Resources, Long Island City, New York
1978 *Sculpture: A Record of Past Work 1972–78,* Dartmouth College, Hanover, New Hampshire
Geschmeidese Eisenskulpturen, Museum Haus Lange, Krefeld, West Germany
Sonnabend Gallery, New York
Galerie im Taxispalais, Innsbruck
1979 Galerie Schellmann & Kluser, Munich
Galerie Sonnabend, Paris
E. & O. Friedrich, Berne
Sonnabend Gallery, New York
1980 Ernst Beyeler Galerie, at the *Art Fair '80,* Basel
1981 Sonnabend Gallery, New York
Diane Brown Gallery, Washington, D. C.
Recent Sculptures, Dallas Museum of Fine Arts
1982 Sonnabend Gallery, New York
Storm King Art Center, Mountainville, New York
1983 French Embassy, New York

Kunstverein, Frankfurt
Bonnier Gallery, New York
1984 Galerie Adrien Maeght, Paris
Centre d'Art Contemporain, Chateauroux, France
Musée Saint-Pierre, Lyon, France
Musée des Beaux Arts, Besancon, France
1985 Musée Rodin, Paris
1990 Holly Solomon Gallery, New York
1992 Brooklyn Museum
1994 Stux Gallery, New York
Open Form Sculpture, Sainsbury Center for Visual Arts, University of East Anglia, Norwich (catalog)
Alain Kirili: Atelier-Residence, Centre d'Art Contemporain de Vassiviere, Limousin (catalog)
French Institute, London
1995 *Improvisations,* Galerie Daniel Templon, Paris
1996 *Workshop,* Centre d'Art Contemporain, Castres (catalog)
1997 Galerie Philippe et Hélène Leloup, Paris
1998 *Sculptures,* Marlborough Gallery, New York (catalog)
1999 *A Dialogue with Rodin,* Fine Arts Museums of San Francisco, California Palace of the Legion of Honor (catalog)
Musée de Grenoble (also Réunion des Musées Nationaux, Paris) (catalog)
2000 Université de Bourgogne, le Consortium, Dijon (catalog)
Recent Sculptures, Marlborough Chelsea, New York (catalog)

Selected Group Exhibitions:

1975 *John Weber Invitational,* John Weber Gallery, New York
1976 *Soho Downtown Manhattan,* Akademie der Künste, West Berlin
1977 *Documenta,* Kassel, West Germany
1978 *Pour la Gravure,* Musée de l'Abbaye Sainte-Croix, Les Sables-d'Olonne, France
1979 *Contemporary Sculpture,* Museum of Modern Art, New York
1980 *Zeitgenossische Plastik,* Kulurhistorische Museum, Bielefeld, West Germany
1981 *Directions 1981,* Hirshhorn Museum, Washington, D. C.
1982 *Post Minimalism,* Aldrich Museum of Contemporary Art, Ridgefield, Connecticut
1985 *Maximal Implications of the Minimal Line,* Bard College, Annandale-on-Hudson, New York
1996 *Drawing From Life,* Stark Gallery, New York
1999 *Champs de la Sculpture,* Champs-Elysees, Paris
2001 *Connecting Worlds: Alain Kirili and Brigitte Nahon,* Kennedy Center for the Performing Arts, Washington, D.C.

Publications:

By KIRILI: Books—*Die Yoni/Linga Plastiken,* Munich 1979; *Wer Hat Angst vor der Vertikalitat?,* Berne 1979; *Sculpture et Jazz: Autoportrait,* Paris 1996; *Alain Kirili,* with Ariane Lopez-Huici, Olivier Kaeppelin and Raphael Rubinstein, Paris 1997; *Rodin: Eros and Creativity,* with Auguste Rodin and Rainer Crone, New York 1997; *Jardin des Tuileries: Sculptures Modernes et Contemporaines: Installation conçue par Alain Kirili, 1997–2000,* with Julia Kristeva and Robert Storr, Paris 2001. **Articles—**''Philippe Sollers et Alain Kirili: texte aporistique'' in *VH 101* (Paris), Spring 1971; ''Thoughts on Samuel Yellin and Blacksmithing'' in *Artforum* (New York), May 1978; ''La Sculpture par l'Espirit,'' in *Art Press* (Paris), March 1980; ''Sexual Atheism,'' conversation with Philippe Sollers in *Arts Magazine,* October 1990.

On KIRILI: Books—*Mail Art, Communication à Distance, Concept* by Jean-Marc Poinsot, Paris 1971; *Conceptual Art* by Ursula Meyer, New York 1972; *Alain Kirili: peintures/ dessins/sculptures/gravures,* exhibition catalog with text by Marcelin Pleynet, Paris 1974; *Alain Kirili: Sculpture—A Record of Past Work 1972–78,* exhibition catalog with text by Jan Van der Marck, Hanover, New Hampshire 1978; *Alain Kirili: Geschmiedete Eisenkulpturen,* exhibition catalog with text by Gerhard Storck, Krefeld, West Germany 1978; *Alain Kirili,* exhibition catalog with text by Peter Weiermair, Innsbruck 1978; *Pour la Gravure,* exhibition catalog with texts by Marcelin Pleynet and Christian Prigent, Les Sables-d'Olonne, France 1978; *Alain Kirili: Recent Sculptures,* exhibition catalog with text by Steven A. Nash, Dallas 1981; *Alain Kirili: Iron Sculptures,* exhibition catalog with text by Monique Laurent, Paris 1985. **Articles—**''The Imaginary Sense of Forms: with Alain Kirili'' by Julia Kristeva in *Arts Magazine,* vol. 66, September 1991; ''Alain Kirili: Open Form Sculpture'' by Julian Stallabrass in *Art Monthly,* no. 174, March 1994; ''In Concert'' by Raphael Rubinstein in *Art in America* (New York), vol. 84, no. 12, December 1996; ''New Sculpture in the Jardin des Tuileries in Paris'' by Dana Mouton Cibulski in *Sculpture* (Washington, D.C.), vol. 18, no. 8, October 1999. **Video—***Kirili* by Chrystel Egal, Phillippe Monpontet and Jack Kerouac, 1995.

* * *

Sculptor Alain Kirili began his career on a theoretical note. In the late 1960s and early 1970s, he wrote texts on both the theory and practice of art influenced by his associations with the Tel Quel group in Paris. During this period he painted and drew; in 1972 he made his first sculptures in zinc, iron and terra cotta, and he often employed various mixed-medium combinations. By 1975 his interests had narrowed to iron and the forge. Kirili's fascination with the rich, tradition-bound process of the forge, his deep-seated awareness of the importance of craft, as well as his recognition of the metaphorical associations implicit in the artist's manipulation of iron, are issues evident in his writings as well as in his sculptures.

The early iron sculptures were the product of a formally manipulated method, recalling the ''drawing in space'' approach of Julio Gonzalez. They consisted of metal rods hammered into tall, thin elements which Kirili joined by ''threading'' them through small loops and holes; whether standing or leaning against the wall, the inter-locking compositions appeared to shape the surrounding space, and they drew attention to the description of volumes among the parts. In certain examples—such as the ones in which a vertically disposed element can bring to mind an extended hand holding a triangle—figurative associations are tentative.

In the early 1980s, he turned to investigating simple geometric forms that have been encoded for centuries with religious significance. In the seventeen variations of the cross it contains, the floor piece *Commandment V* (1981) is revealing of the sacred power of the Christian cross. *Commandment* (1991), another floor piece in the ''Commandment'' series, also suggests the power of the symbol in language. Its forty-five forged iron pieces are spread over the surface of a low, white platform. Taken individually, the pieces are abstract sculptures; considered as a whole, they suggest a symbolism of language beyond the expected alphabetic iconography. Iconic traditions of statuary are wrestled with in a number of the abstract sculptures, in particular the examples of upright forged iron with curved, indented or scooped out tops. In the ''Kings'' series, the reflective surfaces of these forged aluminum pieces, tall uprights with columnar shafts and crown-like capitals, are used to intensify the aura of majesty Kirili is seeking to convey.

In *Grande Nudité* (1985) and other bronzes, Kirili is making clear his enormous admiration for the powerful torsos of Rodin and their dynamically heaving surfaces. Among his most recent works, a grouping of three pieces cast in black, rust red, and white resin (1994) recall the powerful and energetic sculptures of de Kooning.

—Essay by Ronny H. Cohen; updated by Beth Duncan

KIRKEBY, Per

Nationality: Danish. **Born:** Copenhagen, 1 September 1938. **Education:** Studied geology at the University of Copenhagen, 1957–64, Ph.D. 1964. **Family:** Married Elisabeth Therkeisen in 1965 (separated, 1976); daughter: Rebecca; married Vibeke Windelow in 1979; son: Sophus. Worked as a geologist in Greenland, 1958–72. **Career:** Independent artist, Copenhagen, also working in New York, Greenland, and Central America, since 1965; member, Fluxus group of artists, New York, 1966–67. Instructor, Staatliche Akademie der Bildenden Künste, Karlsruhe, 1978; Professor, Staatliche Hochschule für Bildende Künste, Städelschule, Frankfurt am Main, since 1988. **Awards:** Painting Scholarship, 1965, and Writing Scholarship, 1973, Statens Kunstfond, Copenhagen; Gold Medal, Royal Danish Academy of Art, Copenhagen, 1968; D.A.A.D. Fellowship, West Berlin, 1982; Coutts Contemporary Art Award, 1996. **Member:** Det Danske Akademi, Copenhagen, 1982. **Agent:** Knoedler & Company, 19 East 70th Street, New York, New York 10021; Michael Werner Gallery, 4 East 77th Street, New York, New York 10021.

Individual Exhibitions:

1964 Hoved-Bibliotek, Copenhagen
1965 Den Frie, Copenhagen
Galerie Jensen, Copenhagen
1966 Galerie 101, Copenhagen (with Joseph Beuys, Bengt af Klintberg and Traakvogn 13)
1967 Galerie 101, Copenhagen
St. Mark's, New York (with Nam June Paik, Takehisa Kosugi and Allen Kaprow)
Neue Galerie, Aachen, West Germany (with Bjorn Norgard)
Arkitektskolen, Aarhus, Denmark (with Bjorn Norgard)
1968 Studentersamfundet, Aarhus, Denmark (with Norgard and Nielsen)
Jysk Kunstgalerie, Copenhagen
Fyns Stifmuseum, Odense, Denmark
1969 Jysk Kunstgaleri, Copenhagen
1970 Jysk Kunstgaleri, Copenhagen
1972 Daner Galleriet, Copenhagen
Gentofte Kunstbibliotek, Copenhagen
1973 Galerie St. Petri, Lund, Sweden
1974 Hadersley Museum, Denmark
Galerie Michael Werner, Cologne
1975 Statens Museum for Konst, Copenhagen
Henie-Onstad Kunstsenter, Oslo
Daner Galleriet, Copenhagen
Kunstbygningen, Aarhus, Denmark
1976 Gallery Cheap Thrills, Helsinki
Ribe Museum, Ribe, Denmark
1977 Museum Folkwang, Essen
1978 Galerie Michael Werner, Cologne
Kunstraum München, Munich
1979 Kunsthalle, Berne
1980 Galerie Fred Jahn, Munich
Galerie Helen van der Meij, Amsterdam
Galerie Michael Werner, Cologne
1981 Museum Ordrupsgaardsamlingen, Copenhagen
Galerie Fred Jahn, Munich
1982 Galerie Michael Werner, Cologne
Galerie Springer, West Berlin
Galerie Crone, Hamburg
Nigel Greenwood Gallery, London
Van Abbemuseum, Eindhoven, Netherlands
Galerie Fred Jahn, Munich
1983 Galerie Zwirner, Cologne
Galerie Sabine Knust, Munich
DAAD-Galerie, West Berlin
1984 Van Abbemuseum, Eindhoven, Netherlands
Strasbourg Museum, France
Galerie Thaddaeus Ropac, Salzburg, Austria
Kunstverein, Braunschweig, West Germany
Galerie Ulysses, Vienna
1985 Fruitmarket Gallery, Edinburgh
Douglas Hyde Gallery, Dublin
Galerie Knoedler, Zurich
Whitechapel Art Gallery, London
1986 Michael Werner Gallery, New York
Projekt fur Munster, West Germany
1987 Museum Boymans-van Beuningen, Rotterdam
Galerie Maeght Lelong, Zurich
1994 Galerie Susanne Ottese, Copenhagen
Kunstausstellung der Ruhrfestspiele Recklinghausen (catalog)
Per Kirkeby: Malerei, Neue Galerie, Staatliche Museen Kassel (also Kunstkabinett am Goetheplatz, Stadtmuseum Weimar) (catalog)
Early Works, Michael Werner Gallery, New York (catalog)
1995 Musée des Beaux-Arts de Nantes, France (catalog)

1996 *New Shadows,* Michael Werner Gallery, New York (catalog)
Peintures 1992–1996, Maison des Arts Georges Pompidou, Paris (catalog)
Museum for Modern Kunst, Arken, Denmark (catalog)
Michael Werner Gallery, Cologne (catalog)
1997 *Bronze Models and Works on Paper,* Michael Werner Gallery, New York
Dallas Museum of Art (catalog)
Cluster's Field, The Aarhuus Stiftsbogtrykkerie Group, Demark (catalog)
L.A. Louver Gallery, Venice, California (catalog)
1998 *Per Kirkeby: Arbejder på Papir,* Vejle Kunstmuseum, Denmark (catalog)
Bild Zeichnung Skulptur, Kunstsammlung Nordrhein-Westfalen, Köln (catalog)
Skulpturen und Zeichnungen, Terrakotten, Gerhard Marcks-Haus, Bremen (also Oldenburger Kunstverein, Oldenburg) (catalog)
Manuel: Per Kirkeby, Musee d'Art Moderne de la Ville de Paris (catalog)
Tate Gallery, London (catalog)
1999 *Recent Paintings,* Knoedler & Company, New York (catalog)
Per Kirkeby: Holzschnitte von 1980 bis 1999, Staatliche Kunstsammlungen Dresden (catalog)
Bild Zeichnung Skulptur, Kunstsammlung NRW, Dusseldorf
2000 *Per Kirkeby: Die Karlsruher Jahre,* Städtische Galerie Karlsruhe, Germany (catalog)
Per Kirkeby: Tafeln, Zeichnungen, Monotypien, Michael Werner Gallery, Köln (catalog)
2001 *Zeichnungen des Bildhauers,* Neuer Berliner Kunstverein, Berlin
Grafik, Skulptur, Galerie Holm & Wirth, Zurich
Museum für Kunst und Kulturgeschichte, Goch

Selected Group Exhibitions:

1962 *Den Eksperimenterende Kunstskole,* Galerie Gammel Strand, Copenhagen
1966 *Nordisk Ungdomsbienale,* Louisiana Museum, Humlebaek, Denmark
1968 *Anonymiteter,* Konsthall, Lund, Sweden
1970 *Happening und Fluxus,* Kunstverein, Cologne
1973 *Fluxshoe,* Midland Group Gallery, Nottingham (toured the U.K.)
1976 *Biennale,* Venice (and 1980)
1980 *A New Spirit in Painting,* Royal Academy of Arts, London
1982 *Documenta,* Kassel, West Germany
1983 *Erste Konzentration,* Galerie Boibrino, Stockholm
1985 *Promenades,* Parc Lullin, Genthod, Geneva
1992 *Documenta IX,* Kassel
1994 *Figur, Natur,* Sprengel Museum Hannover, Hannover (catalog)
Malfiguren, Museum Moderner Kunst Stiftung Ludwig, Wien (catalog)
1996 *Editions from Maximilian Verlag—Sabine Kunst, Munich,* Brooke Alexander/Brooke Alexander Editions, New York
Group Show, Avanti Galleries, New York
Group Show of Prints and Multiples, Gotham Editions, New York
1997 *Skulptur. Projekte in Munster,* Germany
1999 *Summertime,* Knoedler & Company, New York
2000 *Europa,* Galerie Academia, Salzburg (catalog)

Collections:

Statens Museum for Konst, Copenhagen; Aarhus Kunstforeningen, Denmark; Silkeborgs Konstmuseum, Denmark; Odense Stiftsmuseum, Denmark; Louisiana Museum, Humlebaek, Denmark; Silkeborg Museum, Denmark; Moderna Museet, Stockholm; Van Abbemuseum, Eindhoven, Netherlands; Bavarian State Galleries, Munich; Henie-Onstad Kunstsenter, Oslo.

Publications:

By KIRKEBY: Books—*Per Kirkeby Litt,* Morso, Denmark 1965; *Bla 5,* Copenhagen 1965; *Copyright,* Copenhagen 1965; *2.15,* Copenhagen 1967; *I Orkennen Moder Maigret Entropien,* Copenhagen 1968; *Bla, Tid,* Copenhagen 1968; *Billedforkafinger,* Copenhagen 1968; *Landskaberne,* Copenhagen 1969; *Bla, Ornament,* Copenhagen 1969; *Ornamentet er. . . . ,* Copenhagen 1969; *Personerne,* Copenhagen 1970; *Jungling auf der Wanderschaft,* Copenhagen 1970; *Handlingen,* Copenhagen 1971; *Haandelser pa Rejsen,* Copenhagen 1971; *Vejret,* Copenhagen 1972; *Indianeriüv i regnskoven,* with Teit Jorgensen, Copenhagen 1973; *Mayalandet,* with Teit Jorgensen and Ib Michael, Copenhagen 1973; *Foyvende Blade,* Copenhagen 1974; *Gron Ornament,* Copenhagen 1974; *Under Duebla Himmel,* Copenhagen 1975; *Et Billedudvalg,* Copenhagen 1975; *Perspektivet,* Copenhagen 1975; *Naturens Blyant,* Copenhagen 1978; *Rejser,* Copenhagen 1978; *Serie,* Copenhagen 1978; *Naturstudiet,* Copenhagen 1979; *Billeder of Haderslev,* Copenhagen 1979; *Hus + Billede + Dekorations, 20'erne in Danmark* with Troels Andersen and Allan de Waal, Copenhagen 1978; *Bravura,* Copenhagen 1980; *Den Fortsatte Tekst,* Copenhagen 1982; *Tegninger II,* Copenhagen 1982; *Selected Essays from Bravura,* Eindhoven 1982. **Articles**—interview in *Arti,* no. 20, May-July 1994; interview with Heinz-Norbert Jocks in *Kunstforum International,* no. 135, October 1996-January 1997. **Films**—*Brigitte Bardot,* 1968; *Stevns Klin og Mons Kling,* 1969; *Gronlandsfilm I,* 1969; *Gronlandsfilm II,* 1970; *Fraendelos,* 1970; *Dyrehaven—den romantiske skov,* 1970; *Tre piger og en gris,* 1971; *Wilhelm Freddie,* 1972; *Og myndighederne sagde stop,* 1972; *En erindring omet besog hos en lacandon-familie i regnskoven i Mexico,* 1975; *Normannerne,* 1975; *Asger Jorn,* 1977; *Carl Brumer,* 1980; *Thorvaldsen I,* 1980; *Geologi—er det egentlig videnskab?,* 1980.

On KIRKEBY: Books—*Per Kirkeby: Danmark, Norge, Sverige* by Troels Andersen, Allan de Waal and Per Hovdenakk, Copenhagen 1975; *Fliegende Biatter,* exhibition catalog with text by Zdenek Felix and Treols Andersen, Essen 1977; *Kunstraum,* exhibition catalog with text by Hermann Kern, Munich 1978; *Per Kirkeby,* exhibition catalog with texts by Johannes Gachnang and Theo Kneubuhler, Berne 1979; *Per Kirkeby,* exhibition catalog with texts by Rudi H. Fuchs and Johannes Gachnang, Cologne 1980; *Per Kirkeby,* exhibition catalog with texts by Hanne Finsen and Rudi H. Fuchs, Copenhagen 1981; *Per Kirkeby,* exhibition catalog with text by Johannes Gachnang, Eindhoven 1982; *Per Kirkeby: Projekt fur Munster,* exhibition catalog with essay by Freidrich Meschedem, Munster 1986; *Per Kirkeby,* exhibition catalog with text by Peter Schampers, Rotterdam 1987; *Coutts Contemporary Art Award 1996: Per Kirkeby, Boris Michajlov, Andrea Zittel,* Zurich 1996. **Articles—**''Paintings by Per Kirkeby'' by Erik Steffensen in *Siksi,* no. 4, 1995; ''Per Kirkeby: The Clouds of Despair'' by Valère Bertrand in *Cimaise,* vol. 42, no. 236, June-August 1995; ''Espaces Anachroniques: Reflexions sur l'Oeuvre en Brique de Per Kirkeby'' by Angela Lampe in *Cahiers du Musee National d'Art Moderne,* no. 65, Autumn 1998; ''Per Kirkeby: 'Bild Zeichnung Skulptur''' by Heinz-Norbert Jocks in *Kunstforum International,* no. 144, March-April 1999.

*

The world is outside language and outside writing. The world is material. Material thinks in material. Material you can handle is better material than that which you cannot handle. Writing is better material than language. Language is material too, and when that material thinks in that material we call it thoughts. The rest of the world cannot be translated into thoughts because thoughts are not thought in the rest of the world's material. That, for example, is the great problem of geology, that geologists do not express themselves on the material's material but in thoughts. The old ones were more at one with their material because at that time everything was unified even though they also said (even though they said it too)—yet Stensen became so aware of the problem by saying the geology that he stopped and became a Catholic bishop. All, all rocks from the oldest to the youngest were formed on the water, said Stensen, and later on the Neptunists, and from fire comes everything, all rocks have a volcanic origin, Moro said, and along with him the Plutonists. And in that way there was still something in the craft. Language has become arrogant because the world has been transformed into thoughts. But there is material writing that is pure because there is more material than in thoughts. *De solido intra solidum naturaliter contento dissertationis prodomus,* as Stensen said, even though in Latin and in that way it became more material and because of that just a little bit better geology too.

—Per Kirkeby

* * *

The work of the Norwegian artist Per Kirkeby resists easy categorization due to its wide range of materials and subjects. Perhaps best known for his brooding abstract landscapes, the artist also creates large architectural sculptures from brick and abstract figurative bronzes, as well as literary essays, poems, films, and numerous drawings. Kirkeby began his career as a geologist and he also continues to make frequent expeditions to observe and record remote locales. Running through these seemingly disparate activities is an ongoing dialogue between order and chaos that allows Kirkeby to maintain his ideas in a state of flux, where the free and fertile interchange of knowledge and sensation may occur.

Kirkeby's gestural landscapes are generally dark in tonality. Brushy passages of black and murky olive greens are overlaid with swatches of evanescent color, broad strokings of nuanced blue, white, red, or ocher, thin scratches and scribbled lines. Some of the colored markings have the character of hastily scrawled scientific diagrams, others allude to natural forms such as trees, fungus, earth, fog, or pools of water. The effect is like that of moving through deep woods or murky bogs with all the senses alert, the painted elements like moments of sensation that never coalesce into stasis. This is landscape in motion, in flux, what Robert Fleck has called a ''liquid, molecular state of perception,'' forever pulled by cyclical processes of growth and decay. As such, Kirkeby's landscape is also the landscape of death and of memory, the emblem of a Northern Romantic desire for sublimation, and yet finally only an emblem. Areas of chalky flatness, of sgraffito, of artful geometry interrupt the painterly evocation of a natural eden, hinting at a kind of distancing and artificiality that suggests that painting as an organic process might not be wholly analogous to the experience of nature. Kirkeby himself prefers to call his landscapes ''pornographic'' rather than ''romantic,'' for painting here hints at simulation, the enactment of desire for a nature that has lost its power to subsume us, a damaged nature, perhaps, or an indifferent one.

The suggestion of unease, the enigmatic, raw, yet intensely lyrical beauty of Kirkeby's landscapes finds an unlikely counterpart in his large brick sculptures, which at first glance seem to display an almost classical sense of order and harmony. Kirkeby has asserted, ''I think my brick sculptures are very explicit demonstrations of the structures in my paintings.'' These large architectural edifices read variously as pedestals, chimneys, towers, gates, the housing for heating and cooling systems, even mausoleums. Though they are based on classical motifs they feature aberrations—such as jutting bricks, off-kilter proportions, and idiosyncratic combinations of brick patterns—that lend them a simultaneous geometric and organic plasticity. Recalling common vernacular built structures as much as ancient monuments patinaed with layers of history and association, Kirkeby's architectural structures are comfortingly familiar and strangely inaccessible, a disarming concurrence of past and present, logic and irrationality, permanence and transience. These functionless buildings, with their odd dispositions of weight and mass, still relate nonetheless to human scale. Kirkeby here calls attention to the problematic nature of classicism in its attempt to wrest order and stability out of chaos, and its positioning of man as the measure of all things: ''I see classicism as a big traffic accident with a lot of people lying around dead.'' The proportions of any attempted classicism are bound to be distorted in order to enfold human experience, much as the viewer entering one of Kirkeby's brick pieces must ''stoop slightly and measure [him]self against the structure.''

This sense of truncated physicality is found in Kirkeby's black-patinaed bronze sculptures, whose highly worked surfaces reveal a sense of touch strongly reminiscent of the artist's paintings. Influenced by the Danish neoclassical sculptor Bertel Thorwaldsen, and, significantly, Auguste Rodin, Kirkeby's ''painterly lumps'' suggest, in the words of Leo Steinberg, ''not a part *for* the whole, but a part *as* the whole.'' Just as Kirkeby's landscapes record a generalized sense of the organic, so must the viewer search to identify those nameable parts of the figure contained within the dark surface encrustations of a sculpture like *Large Head with Arm,* 1983. The deep folds that enclose space in *Large Head with Arm* are achieved by Kirkeby's process of draping layers of plaster over an armature to make the casts for his bronzes, endowing them with a pictorial, figure-ground spatial quality in addition to their sculptural presences as concrete physical masses. Formless yet figurative, Kirkeby's fragmented and clumsy bronzes suggest the loss of classical harmony and self-containment, subverting the tradition-laden, monumentalizing tendencies of their medium in favor of an organic distortion, a sensuous mutability bordering on dissolution, like the more transient landscapes, into *prima materia.*

For Kirkeby, then, the choice of medium represents not just certain technical possibilities, but the opportunity to situate himself in relation to particular historical tendencies in order to focus on what may be experienced through them. This tension between felt personal experience and larger historical constructs points to the processes of transformation through which man, nature and history themselves must continually pass.

—Dorothy Valakos

KITAJ, R(onald) B(rooks)

Nationality: American. **Born:** Ronald Brooks in Cleveland, Ohio, 29 October 1932; adopted name of stepfather, 1941; moved with his family to Troy, New York, 1943. **Education:** Cleveland and New York primary schools; attended children's art classes, Cleveland Museum of Art, 1937–42; studied briefly at the Cooper Union, New York, under Sydney Delevante, R. B. Dowden, Paul Zucker and John Ferren, 1950–51; at Akademie der Bildenden Künste, Vienna, under Albert von Gutersloh and Fritz Wotruba, 1951–53; at Ruskin School of Drawing and Fine Art, Oxford, under Edgar Wind, 1957–59; at Royal College of Art, London, 1960–62. **Military Service:** Served in the United States Army, 1955–57. **Family:** Married Elsi Roessler in 1953 (died, 1969); children: Lem, Dominie Lee, Max. **Career:** Painter; worked on a Norwegian cargo ship, and travelled to Havana and Mexico, 1950; travelled as American seaman to Carribbean and Venezuela; visited Europe, 1951–53; lived in Vienna; joined the U.S. National Maritime Union, and worked on ships travelling to South America; returned to Europe, 1953; travelled extensively in Europe and North Africa, then settled in England; formed close friendship with David Hockney and collaborated briefly with Eduardo Paolozzi; worked with Chris Prater on collage-prints, 1962–72; has spent summers in Sant Feliu de Guixols, Spain, since 1962; visited the United States, 1965–66; worked on drawings for *Sports Illustrated,* 1966; lived in California, 1967–68; formed close friendship with poet Robert Creeley, with whom he collaborated on two books, and painter Jess Collins; returned to England, 1968; lived in Hollywood, 1970–71; produced first life drawings, 1975; organized the *Human Clay* exhibition, London, 1976; lived in the United States, 1978–79. Lecturer, Ealing Technical College, 1961–63, and Camberwell School of Art and Crafts, London, 1961–63; visiting professor, University of California, Berkeley, 1967, and University of California at Los Angeles, 1970; artist-in-residence, Dartmouth College, Hanover, New Hampshire, 1978. **Awards:** Arts Council Prize, London, 1960; Honorary Doctorate, University of London, 1982; Honorary Doctorate, Royal College of Art, London, 1991; Honorary Doctorate, California College of Arts & Crafts, 1995; Recipient 1st Prize in Painting for Golden Lion at Venice Bienalle, 1995; Honorary Doctorate, University of Durham, 1996. **Agent:** Marlborough Fine Art Ltd, 6 Albemarle St., London, 41X 4BY England. **Address:** c/o Marlborough Fine Art, 6 Albemarle Street, London W1X 4BY, England.

Individual Exhibitions:

1963 Marlborough New London Gallery, London
1965 Marlborough-Gerson Gallery, New York
Los Angeles County Museum of Art
1967 Cleveland Museum of Art
Stedelijk Museum, Amsterdam
1969 *Complete Graphics 1963–1969,* Galerie Mikro, Berlin (toured Weest Germany)
1970 Kestner-Gesellschaft, Hannover (travelled to the Museum Boymans-van Beuningen, Rotterdam)
1971 Graphics Gallery, San Francisco
1973 Amerika Haus, Berlin
Cincinnati Art Museum, Ohio (with Jim Dine)
1974 Marlborough Gallery, New York
1975 New 57 Gallery, Edinburgh
Petersburg Press, New York
1976 Petersburg Press, New York
Mala Galerija, Ljublijana, Yugoslavia
1977 Ikon Gallery, Birmingham, England
Marlborough Fine Art, London (travelled to Marlborough Galerie, Zurich)
1978 Beaumont-May Gallery, Hopkins Center, Hanover, New Hampshire
1979 Marlborough Gallery, New York
1980 Marlborough Fine Art, London
1981 Hirshhorn Museum and Sculpture Garden, Washington, D.C. (travelled to Cleveland Museum and the Kunsthalle, Dusseldorf, 1981–82)
1985 Marlborough Fine Art, London
1986 Marlborough Gallery, New York
1991 *R. B. Kitaj: Mahler Becomes Politics,* Kunsthalle, Hamburg (catalog)
1994 *R. B. Kitaj: A Retrospective,* Tate Gallery, London (traveled to Los Angeles County Museum of Art, Metropolitan Museum of Art, New York) (catalog)
R. B. Kitaj: Graphics 1974–1994, Marlborough Graphics, London (catalog)
1995 Metroplitan Museum of Art, New York
1997 Robert Brown Gallery, Washington, D.C.
1998 *R. B. Kitaj: An American in Europe,* Astrup Fearnley Museet for Moderne Kunst, Oslo (traveled to Museo Nacional Centro de Arte Reina Sofia, Madrid; Judisches Museum der Stadt Wien, Vienna; Sprengel Museum Hannover, Germany) (catalog)
2001 *How to Reach 67 in Jewish Art: 100 Pictures,* Marlborough Gallery, New York (catalog)

Selected Group Exhibitions:

1963 *Towards Art?,* Graves Art Gallery, Sheffield (travelled to Laing Art Gallery, Newcastle upon Tyne, and the Municipal College of Art, Bournemouth)
1965 *Pop Art: Nieuwe Figuratie: Nouveau Realisme,* Palais des Beaux-Arts, Brussels

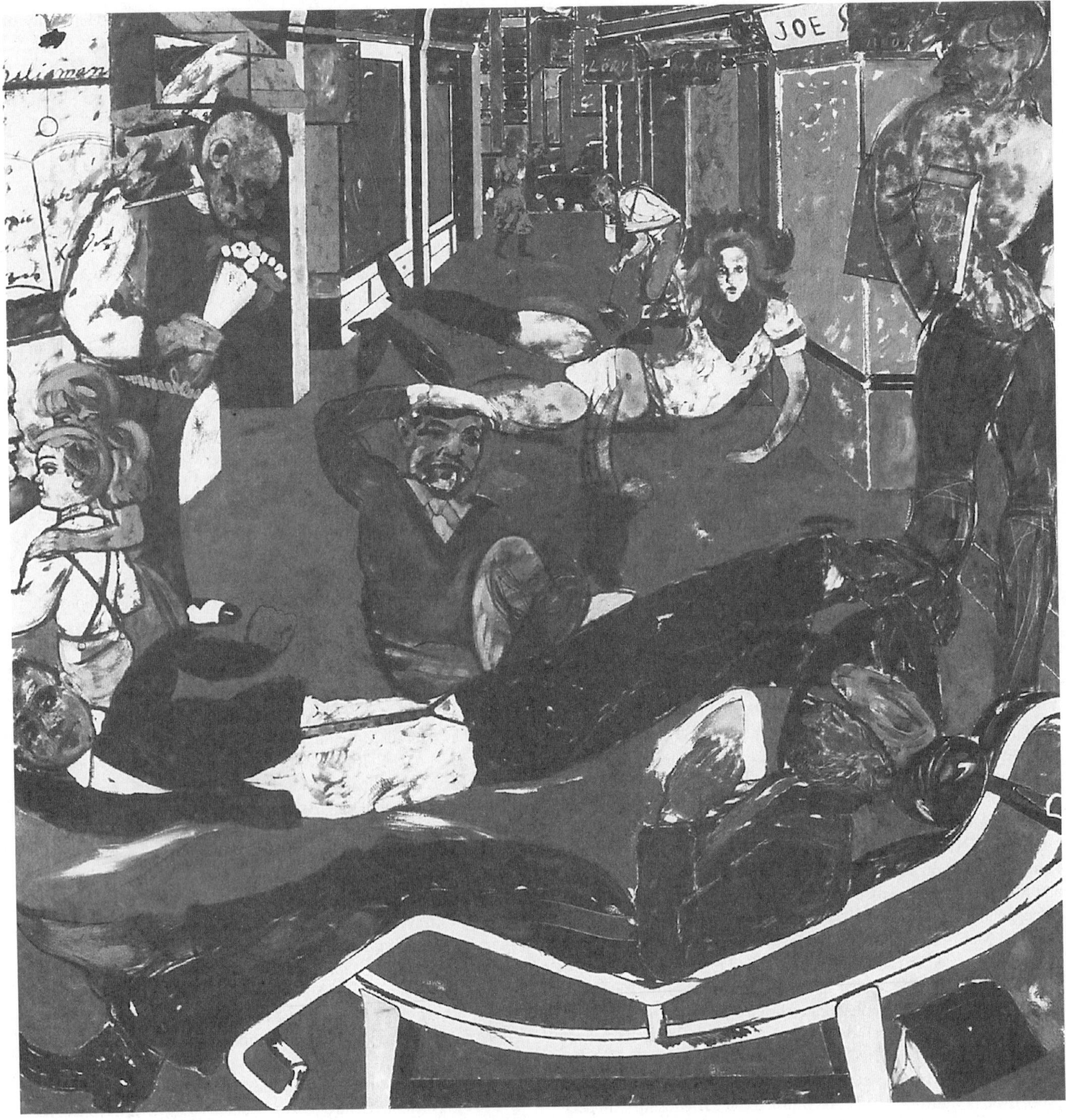

R. B. Kitaj: *The Refugees 1983–84.* ©Tate Gallery, London/Art Resource, NY.

1967 *Visage de l'Homme dans l'Art Contemporain,* Musée Ruth, Geneva

1969 *Information,* Kunsthalle, Basle (travelled to the Badischer Kunstverein, Karlsruhe)

1973 *Hommage à Picasso,* Nationalgalerie, Berlin (toured Europe)

1976 *The Human Clay,* Hayward Gallery, London (toured the U.K. and Belgium)

1981 *A New Spirit in Painting,* Royal Academy of Arts, London

1982 *Aspects of British Art Today,* Metropolitan Art Museum, Tokyo (toured Japan)

1984 *The British Art Show,* City Art Gallery, Birmingham (and Ikon Gallery, Birmingham; travelled to Edinburgh, Sheffield and Southampton)

1987 *A London School,* Louisiana Museum, Humlebaek, Denmark (travelled to Venice and Dusseldorf)

1988 *Exhibition Road: Painters at the Royal College of Art,* Royal College of Art, London (catalog)

1990 *British Prints of the 1960s and 1970s from the Collection of Tony Reichardt,* Art Gallery of New South Wales, Sydney (catalog)
1991 *The Marlborough Gallery Re-Opening Exhibition,* Marlborough Fine Art, London (catalog)
1992 *From Bacon to Now: The Outsider in British Figuration,* Palazzo Vecchio, Florence (catalog)
1993 *Seven British Painters: Selected Masters of Post-War British Art,* Marlborough Fine Art, London (catalog)
Arikha, Auerbach, Kitaj: Recent Works, Galeria Marlborough, Madrid (catalog)
1994 *Split Personalities: Portraiture and the Imagination,* Norman Mackenzie Art Gallery, Regina (catalog)
1997 *Contemporary Prints,* Yvonne Andrews Gallery, London (catalog)
British Art: A Selection from Waddington Galleries, Foire Internationale d'Art Contemporain, Paris (traveling exhibition) (catalog)
Hockney to Hodgkin: British Master Prints 1960–1980, New Orleans Museum of Art (catalog)
1998 *Forty Years at Curwen Studio 1958–1998,* Curwen Gallery, London (catalog)
The School of London from Bacon to Bevan, Fondation Dina Vierny-Musee Maillol, Paris (catalog)
1999 *Portrait of a City: Seven Figurative Painters from London,* John Berggruen Gallery, San Francisco (catalog)

Collections:

Tate Gallery, London; Victoria and Albert Museum, London; Walker Art Gallery, Liverpool; Nationalgalerie, Berlin; Wallraf-Richartz Museum, Cologne; Kunsthalle, Hamburg; Stedelijk Museum, Amsterdam; Museu de Arte Moderna, Sao Paulo; Museum of Modern Art, New York; Art Institute of Chicago.

Publications:

By KITAJ: Books—*Wings: A Collection of Works Produced at the Facilities of Lockheed, California,* Los Angeles 1971; *Open Photography 1978,* exhibition catalog with John Szarkowski, Nottingham 1978; *First Diasporist Manifesto,* London 1989; *The Prints of R.J. Kitaj,* with Jane Kinsman, Aldershot 1994. **Articles—**''Two Paintings with Notes'' in *London Gazette,* no. 3, 1961; ''Round the Art Galleries,'' letter to the editor, in *The Listener* (London), February 1963; ''On Associating Texts with Paintings'' in *Cambridge Opinion,* January 1964; ''Why Do Artists Make Prints?'' answers to questions from Mark Glazebrook, in *Studio International* (London), June 1967; ''Mainly about Using Photos'' in *Art and Artists* (London), November 1969; ''Letters from 31 Artists to the Albright-Knox Art Gallery'' in *Gallery Notes* (Buffalo, New York), Spring 1970; ''R. B. Kitaj: An Interview with Michael McNay'' in *The Guardian* (London), 8 May 1970; ''Painter's Reply'' in *Artforum* (New York), September 1975; ''R. B. Kitaj and David Hockney Discuss the Case for a Return to the Figurative'' in *New Review* (London), February 1977; ''Censorship of Erotic Art,'' letter to the editor, with Richard Hamilton and David Hockney, in the *Sunday Times* (London), 20 February 1977; ''Commentary: World and Image'' in the *Times Literary Supplement* (London), March 1977; ''Dine . . . Some Historical Notes Apropos'' in *Jim Dine: Works on Paper 1975–1976,* exhibition catalog, London 1977; ''A Love for Pictures and an Enthusiasm for Life,'' interview with Roger Berthoud, in *The Times* (London), 7 May 1977; ''Chris . . . A Note Aproppos'' in *Arts Review* (London), August 1977; ''The Horror! The Horror! . . . Conrad'' in *Irving Petlin: Rubbings: The Large Paintings and the Small Pastels,* exhibition catalog, Purchase, New York 1978; ''The Autumn of Central Paris'' in *Art International* (Lugano, Switzerland), March 1979; ''A Return to London: R. B. Kitaj Replies to Some Questions Put to Him by Timothy Hyman'' in *London Magazine,* February 1980; introduction to *The Artist's Eye,* exhibition catalog, London 1980; ''Glasgow Sale of Whistles,'' letter to the editor, with John Golding and others, in *The Times* (London), 12 July 1980; introduction to *Leland Bell: Paintings,* exhibition catalog, London, 1980; interview with Krzysztof Z. Cieskowski in *Art Libraries Journal,* vol. 14, no. 2, 1989; interview with Frederic Tuten in *Interview,* vol. 24, no. 7, July 1994; interview with Martin Gayford in *Modern Painters* (London), vol 7, no. 2, Summer 1994. **Film—***R. B. Kitaj,* with Christopher Finch, directed by James Scott, London 1967.

On KITAJ: Books—*R. B. Kitaj: Complete Graphics 1963–1969,* exhibition catalog by Werner Haftmann, Berlin 1969; *R. B. Kitaj,* exhibition catalog with texts by John Ashbery, Joe Shannon and Jane Livingston, Washington, D.C. 1981; *R. B. Kitaj* by Marco Livingstone, Oxford 1985; *Kitaj* by Marco Livingstone, London 1994. **Articles—**''An Eagerly Awaited First Exhibition'' in *The Times* (London), 7 February 1963; ''Kitaj's Drawings from Life'' by Jasia Reichardt in *Connoisseur* (London), October 1963; ''R. B. Kitaj and the Scene'' by Dore Ashton in *Arts and Architecture* (Los Angeles), April 1965; ''Silkscreening—Any Number Can Play'' by James R. Mellow in the *New York Times,* 30 January 1972; ''Didactic and Dramatic'' by Marina Vaizey in *Art News* (London), December 1974; ''Kitaj Observed'' by Michael Shepherd in *Arts Review* (London), April 1977; ''R. B. Kitaj: Avatar of Ezra'' by Timothy Hyman in *London Magazine,* August/September 1977; ''Some Notes on Kitaj'' by Michael Podro in *Art International* (Lugano, Switzerland), March 1979; ''The Last History Painter: Expatriate, R. B. Kitaj Brings Home the Bacon'' by Robert Hughes in *Time* (New York), April 1979; ''Iconology as Theme in the Early Work of R. B. Kitaj'' by Marco Livingstone in *Burlington Magazine* (London), July 1980; ''The Kitaj Retrospective: Too Late or Too Early?'' by Franz Schulze in *Artnews* (New York), January 1982; ''Photomontage in the Early Work of R. B. Kitaj'' by Catherine Klaus Schear in *Arts Magazine* (New York), September 1984; ''Conversations with R. B. Kitaj'' by Andrew Brighton in *Art in America* (New York), June 1986; ''R. B. Kitaj: The Sensualist 1973–84'' by Timothy Hyman in *For Art,* vol. 1, no. 1, 1991; ''R. B. Kitaj and Chris Prater'' by Pat Gilmour in *Print Quarterly,* vol. 11, no. 2, June 1994; ''In Profile: R. B. Kitaj'' by David Lee in *Art Review,* vol. 46, June 1994; ''Kitaj in Retrospect'' by Michael Podro in *The Burlington Magazine* (London), vol. 137, April 1995; ''R. B. Kitaj's 'Good Bad' Diasporism: The Body in Jewish Art'' by Sander L. Gilman in *New Art Examiner,* vol. 24, April 1997; ''In Search of Kitaj'' by David Cohen in *Art Criticism,* vol. 12, no. 2, 1997; ''Welcome to the Hotel California'' by Peter Plagens in *Newsweek,* vol. 131, no. 17, 27 April 1998.

* * *

R. B. Kitaj has produced such a diverse oeuvre that the best way to create an impression of his work is to select and describe specific paintings:

In *Where the Railroad Meets the Sea,* Kitaj expresses how difficult love can be in a hostile world. The painting is inhabited by only two people: a woman who bears a striking resemblance to Eva Braun, and a man whose face seems to be disintegrating a la Frances Bacon. Their goodbye kiss seems particularly painful for the man, whose gestures indicate his strong affection for the woman. The figures are rendered with fluid lines, yet the scenery is harsh and unbending.

Erie Shore illustrates human isolation in the face of suffering. Fires blaze, naked torsos emit screams of terror and two bodies fall from a great height, while a prisoner gazes pleadingly into a nurse's eyes, and a walrus looks on unperturbed. Similarly, in *Juan de La Cruz,* the ''hero'' remains passive as a woman is sodomized in the background by a blob-like creature, then forced to walk a gangplank by a gangster and a pirate.

The artist's well-known work *The Autumn of Central Paris* depicts an enigmatic cast of characters arranged in a disjunctive manner. Four people sit in the Tuilleries, engaged in discussion. The woman bears an uncanny resemblance to Virginia Woolf and one man is sight-impaired while another wears a hearing aid. In the foreground a revolutionary brandishes a sickle, and in the background, a soldier savours a pristine blue sky. Hidden behind a tree is a building with shattered windows. This painting speaks to the condition of modernity, simultaneously vibrant, complex, fractured and alienated. In this work, symbols of both hope and despair intermingle.

If Not, Not is a masterpiece that testifies to the artist's mastery of line, color, and above all, unsettling iconography. Here the landscape is populated by suffering people, and only nature remains unscathed. The blue lagoon and giant palm trees appear resplendent, in contrast with a wounded fighter, a fleeing man, a still corpse, and the looming presence of the gates of Auschwitz.

Though his canvases can be visually stunning—the figures flow beautifully, and the Fauve-like color schemes are both pleasing and jarring—Kitaj is, above all, a literary and philosophical painter. In his later years, the artist has become deeply affected by his Jewish heritage, hence the persistence of moral, political and historical content in his work. That he can only depict, not solve, the problem of human suffering and isolation contributes to the sense of tragic unresolve one gets from his imagery.

Perhaps in order to find refuge from these weighty issues, Kitaj has recently begun to focus on more personal content. An example of this trend can be seen in the series of his self-described ''little hypochonds,'' executed between 1990 and 1992, in which his various ailments are depicted with expressive angst and a touch of humor. These works, with titles such as *Bad Back, Bad Sinus, Bad Thoughts,* and *Bad Character,* reveal the artist's conflict with aging and his compulsively self-critical disposition.

—Essay by Carine Maurice; updated by Audrey Mandelbaum

KLAPHECK, Konrad

Nationality: German. **Born:** Dusseldorf, 10 February 1938. **Education:** Humboldt Gymnasium, Dusseldorf, 1946–54; Staatliche Kunstakademie, Dusseldorf, 1954–58. **Family:** Married Lilo Lang in 1960 (died, 1987); children: Elisa and David. **Career:** Independent painter, Dusseldorf, since 1958. **Agents:** Galerie Beyeler, Baumleingasse 9, 401 Basle, Switzerland; and Galerie Maeght, 13 rue de Teheran, 75008 Paris, France.

Individual Exhibitions:

1959 Galerie Schemela, Dusseldorf
1960 Galleria Schwarz, Milan
1962 Galerie Zwirner, Essen
1963 Galleria Schwarz, Milan
1964 Robert Fraser Gallery, London
1965 Galerie Ileana Sonnabend, Paris
Palais des Beaux-Arts, Brussels
Kestner-Gesellshaft, Hannover
1966 Kestner-Gesellshaft, Hannover
1968 Galleria Schwarz, Milan
1969 Sidney Janis Gallery, New York
1971 Galerie Rudolf Zwirner, Cologne
1972 Galleria Schwarz, Milan
Galleria la Medusa, Rome
1974 Museum Boymans van Beuningen, Rotterdam (travelled to the Palais des Beaux-Arts, Brussels and the Städtische Kunsthalle, Dusseldorf)
1976 *Objekte Zwischen Fetisch und Libido,* Galerie Beyeler, Basle
1977 Galerie Rudolf Zwirner, Cologne
1980 *Derriere le Miroir,* Galerie Maeght, Paris
Druckgraphik und Zeichunungen 1977–80, Kunsthandel Wolfgang Wittrock, Dusseldorf
1982 Galerie Maeght, Paris
1983 Kunstverein für die Rheinlande und Westfalen, Dusseldorf
1985 Galerie Maeght Lelong, Paris
Kunsthalle, Hamburg (retrospective)
1986 Kunsthalle, Tubingen (retrospective)
Haus der Kunst, Munich (retrospective)
1990 Galerie Lelong, Paris (catalog)
1994 Edward Thorp Gallery, New York
1995 *Great Opening: Konrad Klapheck,* Galerie Brusberg, Berlin
1997 *Klapheck,* Galerie Lelong, Paris; Galerie Lelong, Zurich (catalog)

Selected Group Exhibitions:

1962 *Phases,* Galerie de Université, Paris
1965 *Biennale de Paris*
1968 *European Painters Today,* Jewish Museum New York
1971 *Contemporary German Art,* National Museum of Modern Art, Tokyo
1972 *Amsterdam/Paris/Dusseldorf,* Guggenheim Museum, New York
1974 *Réalism Européen, Hyperréalisme Americain,* CNAC, Paris
1977 *Documenta,* Kassel, West Germany
1980 *Dessins de la Fondation,* Fondation Maeght, St. Paul de Vence, France
1983 *Samlung Wormland,* Haus der Kunst, Munich
1985 *Rheingold,* Plazzo Promotrice delle Belle Arti, Turin
1986 *Taking Stock: Two Diametrically Opposed Surveys of 20th Century German Art,* Royal Academy, London; Nationalgalerie, Berlin

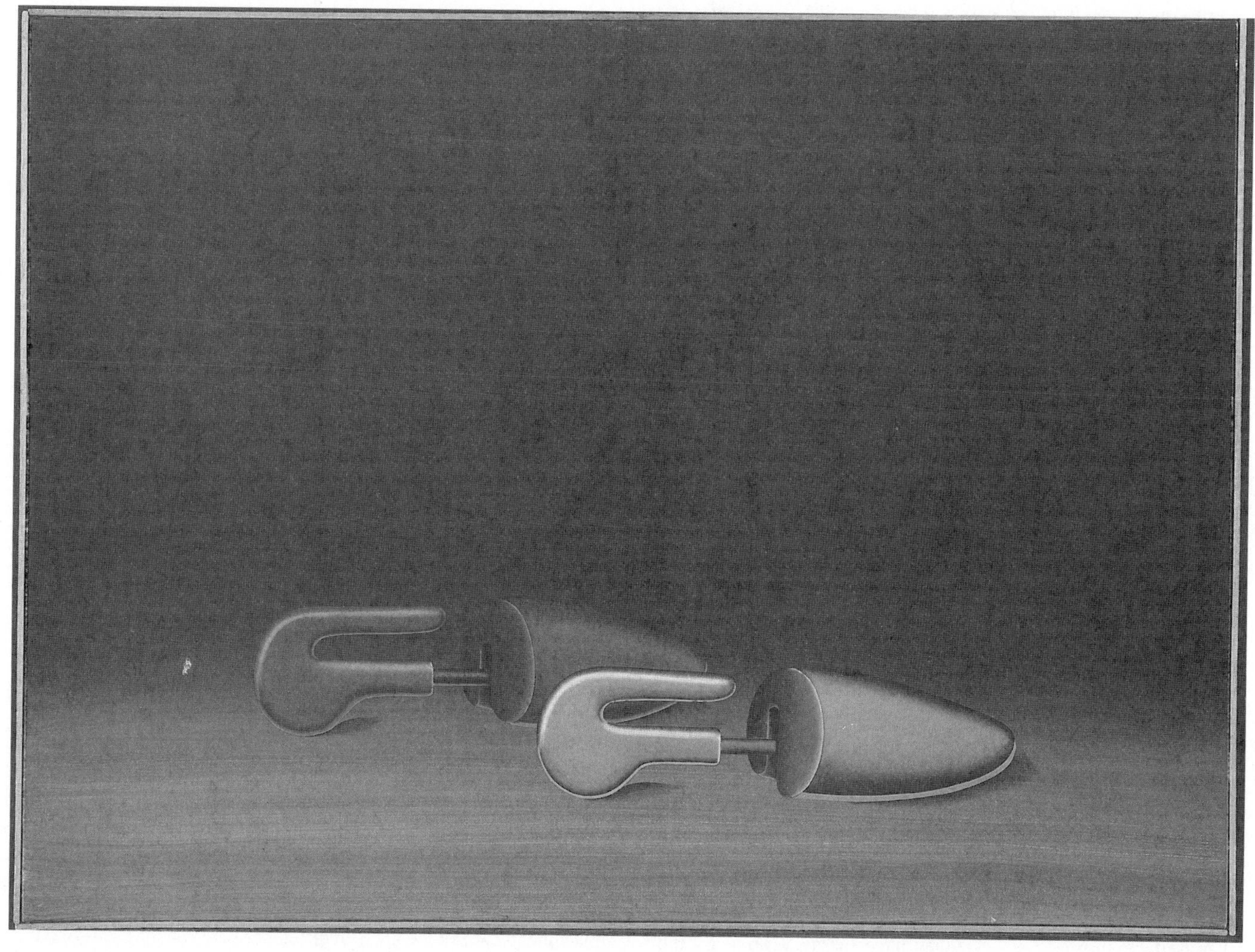

Konrad Klapheck: *The Ambitious Ones (Die Ehrgeizigen),* 1959. Photo by Christiane Bahier & Philippe Migeat. ©2001 Artists Rights Society (ARS), NY/VG Bild-Kunst, Bonn.

1990 *Trusting the Picture: 20 Years of the Studio Jaeschke,* Museum Bochum, Germany

1995 *Our 100th Anniversary of Paintings of People—Pictorial Worlds,* Museum Ludwig, Cologne

Collections:

Musée Royaux de l'Etat Belge, Brussels; Neue Galerie, Aachen, West Germany; Kunstmuseum, Dusseldorf; Karl-Ernst-Osthaus Museum, Hagen, West Germany; Kunsthalle, Hamburg; Städtisches Museum, Leverkusen, West Germany; Museum von der Heydt, Wuppertal, West Germany; Centre National d'Art Contemporain, Paris; Museum Ludwig, Cologne; Staatsgalerie, Stuttgart.

Publications:

By KLAPHECK: Articles—''La Machine et Moi'' in *Opus International* (Paris), October 1970; statement in *Konrad Klopheck,* exhibition catalog, Milan 1972; ''Uber meine Zeichnungen'' in *Konrad Klapheck,* exhibition catalog, Dusseldorf 1983; ''Pourquoi je peint'' in *Konrad Klapheck,* exhibition catalog, Paris 1985; ''Entretien avec Konrad Klapheck'' with Alain Jouffroy in *Opus International,* no. 118, March-April 1990.

On KLAPHECK: Books—*Konrad Klapheck,* exhibition catalog with text by José Pierre, Milan 1960; *Konrad Klapheck,* exhibition catalog by André Breton, Paris 1965; *Konrad Klapheck,* exhibition catalog with text by Wieland Schmied, Hannover 1966; *Konrad Klapheck,* exhibition catalog with text by José Pierre, New York 1969; *Konrad Klapheck* by José Pierre, Cologne 1970; *Konrad Klapheck,* exhibition catalog with texts by Wieland Schmied, Edouard Jager, José Pierre and others, Rotterdam 1974; *Konrad Klapheck: Objekte Zwischen Fetisch und Libido,* exhibition catalog by Werner Schmalenbach, Basle 1976; *Konrad Klapheck: Werkverzeichnis der Druckgraphik 1977–1980,* exhibition catalog edited by Wolfgang Wittrock, text by Hans Kinkel, Dusseldorf 1980; *Konrad Klapheck: ''Derriere le Miroir,''* exhibition catalog with text by Bernard Noel, Paris 1980; *Konrad Klapheck* by Rolf-Gunter Dienst, Bonn 1992; *Great Opening: Konrad Klapheck,* exhibition catalog, Berlin 1995; *Klapheck,* exhibition catalog, Paris 1997. **Articles**—review by J. A. Thwaites in *Art in America* (New York), fall 1962; ''El Mundo Mechanico de Konrad Klapheck'' by Robert Altmann in *Islas 2*

(Cuba), 1964; ''Pop Art and Surrealism'' by D. Irvin in *Studio International,* (London), May 1966; ''Germany: The New Generation'' by J. A. Thwaites in *Studio International* (London), October 1966; ''The Machine and the Psyche: Klapheck's Exploration at Janis'' by Gregory Battock in *Arts Magazine* (New York), February 1969; ''Shift in Perspective'' by F. Bowling in *Arts Magazine* (New York), Summer 1969; ''Konrad Klapheck: Quotes and Comments'' by Henry Martin in *Art International* (Lugano, Switzerland), December 1972; ''Les Machines de Konrad Klapheck'' by Georges Raillad in *La Quizaine Litteraire* (Paris), 1981; ''Konrad Klapheck'' by Peter Sager in *Zeit-Magazin* (Hamburg), November 1985; ''Konrad Klapheck'' by Heinz Peter Schwerfel in *Beaux Arts Magazine* (Paris), no. 111, April 1993; ''Konrad Klapheck at Edward Thorpe'' by Ken Johnson in *Art in America* (New York), vol. 82, no. 2, February 1994; ''Kondrad Klapheck'' by Barry Swabsky in *Artforum* (New York), vol. 32, no. 6, February 1994; review by Terry R. Myers in *Flash Art (International Edition),* no. 17, May/June 1994. **Film—***Konrad Klapheck* by Elila Hershon and Roberto Guerra, premiered on German Television ARD, November 1980.

*

My pictures are to be seen as a whole, as an epic whose protagonists are embodied not in man but in his most important everyday objects. Perhaps the latter are more fitted than a portrait of their inventors to represent today's human comedy.

However clear and logical my pictures may look, it is chance I must thank for half their success. If at one point I can literally take over an image, at another I am forced by the unpredictable consequences of the size of the canvas to paint a picture that I did not have in mind to paint. Chance is the matter of inspiration.

I do not use things as symbols. I simply paint them as I can and let myself be surprised at what they have to say. Eventually the paintings must be cleverer than their creator and go beyond his intentions.

My chief weapons are humour and precision. It is only through the coldness of precision that you gain entry to the fires of the soul and only under cover of a joke that you can say outright what you have seen.

My subjectivity must be unrestrained for my pictures to become objective. It is in oneself that one finds the riddles of the world and their solution.

—Konrad Klapheck

* * *

Objects Between Fetishes and Libido was the title of the introduction that Werner Schmalenbach wrote to describe the art of Konrad Klapheck for the catalog of his exhibition at the Galerie Beyeler, Basel, in 1976. Although the 46 exhibits were all new, they showed no shrinkage from the essential Klapheck, which goes back to his first painting of the typewriter in 1955.

Klapheck, the son of two art historians, went to two art schools in Dusseldorf (though at the first of these he entered as a scholarship student in social studies). But everything that matters about Klapheck-as-artist began with that first painting of the typewriter.

The machine came late into the world of art, and at first it served merely to provide a variation in subject matter. Turner may have been fascinated by the locomotive rushing down the track through a fuzzy atmosphere, part mist, part steam, and the Impressionists may have been intrigued by the crowded scene at a mainline station with the big train playing a central *rôle,* but for the most part any pictorial imagery of the machine age cropped up in drawings and steel engravings produced by illustrators for magazines before the camera took over.

When the machine came into its own as art, it was ushered in with fanfares from iconoclastic trumpets blown by Malevich and his contemporaries in Russia or by the Futurists in Italy. Touches of witty sophitication were added to the ''machine image'' by the Dadaists, by Picabia, by Marcel Duchamp and in the early works by Max Ernst. But even these ''modern art'' interpretations had their pretensions. They were still the products of entrancement rather than understanding. Artists like Léger even took mechanics and altered their true appearance to the point where they become unrecognizable. Epstein might flirt with a conception like his ''Rock-Drill,'' but it was a dalliance that did not turn into a love affair.

Against such a background Klapheck would not claim to be a father-figure of machine art, and he certainly has no connection with mec-artists like Bertini, but he did bring to fruition actual portraits of machines and machine parts, and did this in such a way that they became—for all their hyperreality—personalized, rather as the late Gnoli gave added personality to his perfected realism of subjects like the stretched bottom of a pair of skintight trousers (whose owner plainly had thick-fleshed buttocks.)

Of all the artists of contemporary times, Gnoli comes closest to Klapheck in presentation. Thereafter, the relationship is not so close; Klapheck confines his paintings to machines. Unlike Gnoli, he is quite capable of suffusing areas in his paintings with luscious colour as background, if not in some manner introduced as part of the machine itself. But the greatest difference between the two—and it is difference which has played a large part in giving Klapheck his exceptional reputation—is there in the titles of so many of his pictures, titles that immediately bestow upon the machine portraits an extra dimension of drama or irony. The name of a picture ought to mean so little, but in Klapheck's case it is the key to the safe. The titles, he says, have to come from inspiration and, judging from their potency, this is probably an accurate statement.

For Klapheck, all machines are masculine or feminine, or both (never neuter!). The buzzer on the chair with its playful flex against a candy pink wall is called ''The Pasha''; the row of rearing metal punches is called ''Law and Order''; a flat iron is called ''The House-Dragon''; the sewing-machine is called ''Inquisition;'' the bathroom spray is called ''The Diva''; the schoolboy's all-purpose penknife is called ''The Misanthrope''; and so on.

Just as the pictures without their titles are ''nameless,'' so the titles without their pictures are without body. It is therefore difficult to underpin in cold print Schmalenbach's assertion that the subjects of this artist's pictures are fetishes or outright demands by libido. Klapheck injects ''Life'' into these inanimate objects, and it is a particularly exciting and unexpectedly alchemic performance. He really does change base metals into *gold.* Near to Surrealism, suggest Schmalenbach, but even closer to the psychologist's practice.

—Sheldon Williams

KLUNDER, Harold

Nationality: Canadian. **Born:** Deventer, Netherlands, 14 October 1943; immigrated to Canada, 1952. **Education:** Central Technical High School, Toronto, 1960–64; largely self-taught in art. **Career:** Painter, printmaker, musician. **Awards:** Elected to the Royal Canadian Academy, 1983. **Agent:** Sable-Castelli Gallery, 33 Hazelton Avenue, Toronto, Ontario, Canada M5R 2E3; Trépanier Baer Gallery, Calgary. **Address:** c/o Sable-Castelli Gallery, 33 Hazleton Avenue, Toronto, Ontario, Canada M5R 2E3.

Individual Exhibitions:

1974 Hart House, University of Toronto
1976 Sable-Castelli Gallery, Toronto
1977 The Gallery, Stratford, Ontario
Sable-Castelli Gallery, Toronto
1978 Art Gallery of Cambridge Central Library
Sable-Castelli Gallery, Toronto
1979 Sable-Castelli Gallery, Toronto
1980 Equinox Gallery, Vancouver (with David Craven)
Winnipeg Art Gallery (with David Craven)
Sable-Castelli Gallery, Toronto
1981 Sable-Castelli Gallery, Toronto
1982 Mercer Union, Toronto
Sable-Castelli Gallery, Toronto
1984 Kamloops Public Art Gallery, Kamloops, British Columbia
Art Gallery of Ontario, Toronto
McPherson Library Art Gallery, University of Victoria, British Columbia
1985 Memorial University of Newfoundland Art Gallery, St. John's
Concordia University Art Gallery, Montreal
Sable-Castelli Gallery, Toronto
1986 Galerie Don Stewart, Montreal
1987 Rodman Hall Arts Centre, St. Catherines, Ontario
Sable-Castelli Gallery, Toronto
1988 Noosa Regional Gallery, Tewantin, Australia
Art Gallery of Hamilton, Ontario
Sable-Castelli Gallery, Toronto
Forest City Gallery, London, Ontario
Agnes Etherington Art Centre, Queens University, Kingston, Ontario
1989 Tom Thomson Memorial Art Gallery, Owen Sound, Ontario
Sable-Castelli Gallery, Toronto
1990 49th Parallel Gallery, New York
1991 Sable-Castelli Gallery, Toronto
1992 Memorial University of Newfoundland Art Gallery, St. John's
1993 Sable-Castelli Gallery, Toronto
Windsor Printmaker's Forum, Windsor, Ontario
1995 Sable-Castelli Gallery, Toronto
James Baird Gallery, St. John's, Newfoundland
1996–98 Tom Thomson Memorial Art Galley, Owen Sound, Ontario
Sir Wilfred Grenfell College Gallery, Corner Brook, Newfoundland
MacLaren Art Centre, Barrie, Ontario
University of Waterloo Art Gallery, Waterloo, Ontario
Rodman Hall Arts Centre, St. Catharines, Ontario
Frederick Horsman Varley Memorial Art Gallery, Markham, Ontario
1997 Sable-Castelli Gallery, Toronto, Ontario
1998 Trépanier Baer Gallery, Calgary, Alberta
1999 London Regional Art and Historical Museums, London, Ontario
Sable-Castelli Gallery, Toronto, Ontario
Art Gallery of Newfoundland and Labrador, St John's, Newfoundland
2000 Southern Alberta Art Gallery, Lethbridge, Alberta
Trépanier Baer Gallery, Calgary, Alberta
Trianon Gallery, Lethbridge, Alberta
James Baird Gallery, St-John's, Newfoundland
Durham Art Gallery, Durham, Ontario
Gallery One, One, One, Winnipeg, Manitoba
2001 Open Studio, Toronto, Ontario
Winchester Gallery, Victoria, B.C.

Selected Group Exhibitions:

1973 *Pacific Vibrations,* Vancouver Art Gallery
1976 *Abstractions,* Montreal XXI Olympiad (travelled to Stratford, Ontario; Paris; and London)
1982 *Canadian Contemporary Printmakers,* Bronx Museum of the Arts, New York
1984 *Art Today,* Hokaido Museum of Modern Art, Sapporo, Japan
1984 *Toronto Painting '84,* Art Gallery of Ontario (travelled throughout Canada)
1988 *Art under Fire,* Royal Academy of Arts Gallery, Toronto
1989 *Living Impressions,* Art Gallery of Hamilton, Ontario
1989 *Graafika Triennaal,* Tallinn, Estonia
1992 *The Public Room,* Canadian Cultural Centre, Rome
1993 *Abstraction: Which Way from Here?,* The Glenbow Museum, Calgary, Alberta
1994 *Selected Works from the Collection of Daniel Donovan,* Art Gallery of Hamilton, Ontario
1996 *The Third Kochi International Triennial Exhibition of Prints,* Kochi, Honmaki, Japan
1998 *Wood: An Aesthetic and Social Ecology,* Tom Thomson Memorial Art Gallery, Owen Sound, Ontario
1999 *Abstract Art,* McMaster Museum of Art, Hamilton, Ontario
2000 *10 X 10 (Ten Decades),* Kitchener Waterloo Art Gallery, Kitchener, Ontario

Collections:

National Gallery of Canada, Ottawa; Art Gallery of Ontario, Toronto; Art Gallery of Hamilton, Ontario; Agnes Etherington Art Centre,

Harold Klunder: *DNA,* 1997–98. Photo by Cheryl O'Brien. ©National Gallery of Canada.

Queens University, Kingston, Ontario; Nickle Arts Museum, University of Calgary, Alberta; Winnipeg Art Gallery, Manitoba; Noosa Regional Art Gallery, Tewantin, Australia.

Publications:

On KLUNDER: Books—*Harold Klunder* by Peter White, Stratford 1977; *David Craven/Harold Klunder,* exhibition catalog with text by Karyn Allen, Winnipeg 1980; *David Craven, Harold Klunder,* exhibition catalog with text by Elizabeth Nichols, Vancouver 1980; *Provincial Essays, Vol. 2* by Barrie Hale, 1985; *Harold Klunder: Painting Tableaux,* exhibition catalog with essay by Sandra Paikowski, Montreal, Quebec 1985; *The Best Contemporary Canadian Art* by Joan Murray, Edmonton 1987; *Harold Klunder: Twelve Paintings,* exhibition catalog, St. Catherines 1987; *Harold Klunder: Love Comes and Goes Again,* exhibition catalog with essay by Ihor Holubizky, Owen Sound, Ontario 1997; *Harold Klunder: In the Forest of*

Symbols, exhibition catalog with essay by Ted Fraser, London, Ontario 1999; *Harold Klunder: Prints and Paintings,* exhibition catalog with essay by Cliff Eyland, St-John's, Newfoundland 1999. **Articles—**''Harold Klunder'' by James Purdie in *Artmagazine,* vol. 9, no. 36, 1978; ''Toronto's Assimilation Consolidation and Search'' by James Purdie in *ArtNews,* vol. 77, no. 1, 1978; ''Hamilton, Harold Klunder, Schoenberg Drawings'' by Linda Genereux in *Art Post #30,* fall 1988; ''Klunder Emotes in Oils'' by Deirdre Hanna in *Now Magazine,* 14 December 1989; ''Focus on Harold Klunder'' by Linda Genereux in *Canadian Art,* fall 1990; ''Focus on Harold Klunder: Slow Hand'' by Gary Michael Dault in *Canadian Art Magazine,* Winter 1999; ''The End of the Earth'' by Gary Michael Dault in *Canadian Art,* Fall 2000; ''The Quest for Certainty, Harold Klunder at Sable-Castelli'' by Steve Rockwell in *d'Art International,* 19 January 2000; ''Beauty by the Back Door, Gallery Going, Harold Klunder at Open Studio'' by Gary Michael Dault in *Globe and Mail,* 13 January 2001.

* * *

For Harold Klunder, painting is a no-holds-barred contact with materials and is unyielding in its declaration of visceral presence. His work has touched on many diverse sources—the music of Arnold Schoenberg, for one—and as some have noted, stylistic connections to a broad range of precursors: De Kooning, the COBRA group and Soutine. To this list we may also add British modernists, from Bomberg to Auerbach. Such declarations of association, however self-evident, have their short-comings in determining what constitutes style, signature, or the signature of anti-style. Klunder's search for a vocabulary is not for the new—to displace other vocabularies—but the manner in which he, as all modernist artists, is cut from the past, genre, and tradition, to be a free agent, to move forward or backwards. A key body of work, the Schoenberg series (1979 to 1988), were titled after the fact—of Schoenberg and ''the series.'' Works were assigned to this grouping as deemed appropriate by Klunder.

Death Angel, 1978, can be seen as a defining moment and prime Klunder (as a cut of beef). It is an allover, mural-sized painting without the mannerism of the overall—an epic of small events by trial and error which has been described in terms of geometric and constructivist influences. Whether such determinations can be proven, the topology of paint amply describes its condition—pushed, pulled, splattered and layered (but never reduced), and whipped into a finale. Like opera, *Death Angel* is rescued from wooden staging by a glorious lament—the death scene. Other grand gestures are in evidence, as with the temporary wall painting *Schoenberg XVIII* (Mercer Union Gallery, Toronto, 1982). This endeavour took the relative security of easel/studio painting into another realm. The hall has been rented, the audience arrives, and the show must go on. The pressure may be too much for painters schooled in the careful performance, irrespective of how they behave or rehearse in private. A prime example of this mythology is Nick Nolte's character in Martin Scorsese's short film, *Life Lessons in New York Stories* (1989): a full tilt rock and roll painter playing out his hypomania in exuberant, gorging movements. The myth of modern style also extends to lifestyle.

Study for Schoenberg IV, 1982, is further evidence of Klunder's approach and playing freely with the rules. *Schoenberg IV,* 1980–1, predates the study and reverses the normal order—the ''study'' on canvas, and the ''completed work'' on paper. *Schoenberg IV* has the eloquence of a loping orchestrated movement—Kandinsky flirting with Cab Calloway—but the ''study,'' in contrast, is so humble in origin as to defy pompous claims for modernism or painting. These are the not-so-accidental markings of consequence—those of Tapies or Schoenberg—but equally, a moment of brutal honesty. Here is the drop cloth underneath the painting—''the same thing as the painting,'' as another artist once remarked of his own work—only organized in a different fashion and pulled off the floor. The Emperor's new clothes are real.

Klunder's paintings at the end of the 1980s coalesced in a grotesquery and continues in this fashion, as another brute honesty. Faces are painted as if seen in fun house mirrors—paint in the act of forming and deforming as some primordial matter. Klunder's excursion cannot be for shock value because we have already been shocked. Dubuffet, Lucebert, Saura, Bacon and others have shown us the tortured face of the moderns. *The Poet's Garden IV (Self Portrait),* 1986, a multi-faced gridlock, is unmistakably a personal event and difficult to unravel to any singular truth. The viscid, resistive gestures and poses can be regarded as the abandonment of conventional wisdom and practice, a Spruce Goose. At the same time, this painting is ''strangely organic,'' never ''strangely scientific'' (William Burroughs-isms). The science of painting or making such images may rest in 19th century liberalism—Ralph Waldo Emerson, *The Method of Nature,* 1841—nature having control over its own destiny and in this instance, the nature of paint determining a form, waiting for humankind to decode and measure. All the time, nature moves on.

In part, this may explain the notational quality of Klunder's paintings. They are akin to manuscript pages with edit notes, compelling words, syntax and a narration with characters and events inscribed on separate pages at the same time. Klunder often works on several paintings at the same time, completed over a period of time. Like *My Dinner with Andre,* the conversation weaves and bobs. Patience is a virtue. At this moment, Klunder has discovered a secret: that painting not only has a life in an information driven world, but is meaningful because it is neither simulation nor demonstration.

Klunder's work has come to maturity in the second half of the century, a lost generation distanced from abstract expressionism in its heyday, and arriving too soon for the smart weaponry of painting irony: that endgame to sweep away the last vestige of painting genre. His approach may lead to an appreciation and understanding of the modernist condition rather than painting as an endangered species. Painting can, as Klunder shows, appear without an agenda of post-structural strategy and subtext, and the late modernist can rehabilitate pictorial and formal devices without sentiment or overstaying its welcome. As Lucebert stated in 1964, the concrete and the abstract are conceptions originated in a conceptual world, ''in which I am and want to remain a xenophobic stranger.''

—Ihor Holubizky

KNÍŽÁK, Milan

Nationality: Czechoslovakian. **Born:** Pilsen, 19 April 1940. **Education:** Marienbad Primary School, 1946–54, Pianá High School, 1954–57, and the Pedagogic School, Prague, 1957–58; studied at the Art School, Prague, 1958–59, and the Art Academy, Prague, 1963–64; also studied mathematics, Prague, 1976–77. **Military Service:** Czech

Milan Knížák: *New Paradise,* 1990–91. ©Milan Knizak.

Army, 1959–61. **Family:** Married 1) Sonia Svecová in 1967 (divorced, 1968); 2) Jarka Charvátová in 1970 (divorced, 1974); and 3) Maria Saudková in 1975. **Career:** Worked as a road digger, carpenter, electrician, and stonemason's assistant, Prague, 1969–66; now a full-time artist; involved in musical activities, 1952–54, 1963–68, 1968–76, and 1978; in painting, objects, sculpture and environments, 1954–64; in fashion, 1962–70; in architecture, 1973–76. Founder, with Sonia Svecová, Jan Maria Mach, Vit Mach, Jan Trticek, and Robert Wittmann, Aktual group, Prague, 1964; associated initially with the Fluxus artists, Dick Higgins, Alison Knowles, and Ben Vautier, Prague, 1966. Imprisoned in Prague, 1966, 1974–5, and many short term takings; travelled in Austria, Germany, Luxembourg, Iceland, 1968–70, in New York and throughout the United States, 1968–70. Guest professor, summer academy, Salzburg, 1987; professor and president of Academy of Fine Arts in Prague, since 1990; general director of National Gallery in Prague, since 1999. **Awards:** DAAD Scholarship, Berlin, 1974 (took up scholarship in Berlin, 1979–80); Kolar Prize, Czechoslovakia, 1977; Worpswede-Barkenhoff Award, West Germany, 1982; Schloss Bleckade Prize, West Germany, 1985; Czech Republic Prize, *5th International Trienale of Drawing,* Wroclaw, Poland 1992; 1st Rate Medal of Minister of Education, Czech Republic. **Agent:** Wewerka Gallery, Potsdamerstrasse 55, D-10785 Berlin, Germany. **Address:** Rašínovo nábřeží 70 Praha 2, 120 00, Czech Republic.

Individual Exhibitions:

1958 KASS, Marienbad, Czechoslovakia
1964 Galerie Viola, Prague
1968 Fluxus West, San Diego, California
1970 Galerie Art Intermedia, Cologne
1972 Museum am Ostwall, Dortmund
1976 Galerie A, Amsterdam
1980 Galerie Ars Viva, Berlin
Galerie A, Amsterdam
Galerie Baecker, Bochum, West Germany
Museum Helmstedt, West Germany
Kunstverein, Oldenburg, West Germany

1981 Private Apartment, Prague
1983 Galerie Ars Viva, West Berlin
Galerie Gruppe Grun 1, Bremen
Rank Xerox, Hannover
1984 Galerie Inge Baecker, Cologne
Licht + Raumdesign, Cologne
1985 Galerie Camomille, Brussels
1986 Galleria UXA, Novara, Italy
Kunsthalle, Hamburg
Museo Alchimia, Milan
Galerie OEKBZ, Cologne
1987 Galerie Potocka, Krakow, Poland
Liget Galeria, Budapest
Museum Sprengel, Hannover
Galerie Wewerka, Hannover
Ustav makromolekularni chemie CSAV, Prague
Kunstmuseum, Bochum, West Germany
1988 *Proposals for Rebuilding the Old Town Hall,* VHMP Prague
A Bit of Architecture, Opatov, Prague
Design MK, Gallery DAAD, Berlin
1989 ZSSV, Kosice, Czech Republic
Dům umění měnsta Brna, Brno, Czech Republic
First Exhibition in Preunschen, Preunschen, Germany
Milan Knížák Works 63–89, Editions Hundertmark, Köln, Germany
Gallery La Coupolle, Neu Isenburg, Germany
1990 Gallery of the City of Prague
Gallery Benedikta Rejta, Louny, Czech Republic
Gallery 4, Cheb, Czech Republic
Powder Tower, Prague
Holesovice market hall, Prague
Prodomo, Vienna, Austria
Gallery of the City of Bratislava, Mirbachüv Palace, Czech Republic
1991 *Neo-Knížák,* Museo Mudima-Foundation, Italy
Gallery of Art, Nové Zámky, Slovak Republic
Gallery Ghislave, Paris
Gallery Inge Baecker, Cologne
Try to Fly, Schloß Solitude, Stuttgart
1992 *Něco,* Gallery U Bílého jednorožce, Klatovy (travelled to Slovak Republic)
New Paradise, School of Art Gallery, North Adelaide, Australia
Das geküste Haus, Ruine der Künste Berlin
UFO-OFU, Gallery MxM, Prague
North School of Art, Adelaide Festival International, Australia
Double Compositions, Gallery Gelbe Music, Berlin
Erotic drawings, Poland Kultur Center, Prague
Museum Olomouc, Czech Republic
1993 Micro Hall Art Center Literaturium, Edewecht-Klein Scharrel, Germany
Milan Knížák-Objeckte, Skulturen, Gallery Traklhaus, Salzburg, Austria
Castle in the Castle, Sovinec, Czech Republic
BMC, Galerie MxM, Czech Republic
1994 *Dialogue ''Liebliche Trauma,''* Reichstag Berlin, Germany
Confused Pictures, AVU, Prague
Bigger Size Pictures, Třinec, Czech Republic (travelled to Česky Těšín, Czech Republic)
Foyer of Theater, Kolín, Czech Republic
1995 *Table as a Picture, Picture as a Table,* Gallery Genia Loci, Prague
1996 *New Paradise,* Gallery Mánes, Decorative Arts Museum, Prague (travelled to TV Hall, Prague; Gallery Ranný Arch, Prague; Gallery of Modern Art, Hradec Králové, Czech Republic; Castle Bítov, Czech Republic)
Without a Reason, Centre of Culture and Education, Ostrava, Czech Republic
Ruins of New Paradise, Gallery Genia Loci, Prague
1997 *Unsure Look,* Gallery Caesar, Olomouc, Czech Republic
Attempt at Convention, Gallery Malovaný dům, Třebíč, Czech Republic
Hidden Originality, Gallery Kramář, Prague
1998 *Concrete Statues for Outside,* CONCON '98, Veletržní Palác, Prague
Van Gogh's Dream and a Few Sculptures, Trade Fair, Damascus, Syria
Vacation with an Alien, Gallery V. Špály, Prague
1999 *Pictures—Objects,* Gallery Prostejov, Czech Republic
2000 *Memories on Memories,* Gallery 761, Ostrava, Czech Republic
Weiche Schatten, Tschechisches Zentrum, Berlin
Hommage a Wolf Vostell, Wewerka Galerie, Berlin
Gallery of the Town, Blansko, Czech Republic
Happily to Nowhere, Exhibition Hall Mánes, Prague

Selected Group Exhibitions:

1967 *Aktual Art International,* San Francisco Museum of Art
1970 *Sammlung Feelisch,* Museum am Ostwell, Dortmund
1972 *Multiples: The First Decade,* Philadelphia Museum of Art
1974 *Biennale,* Musée d'Art Moderne, Paris
1976 *Monumente durch Medirn Resetzen,* Kunstmuseum and Kunstverein, Wuppertal, West Germany
1982 *Art Book Fair,* Akademie der Kunste, West Berlin
1987 *Berlinart,* Museum of Modern Art, New York (travelled to San Francisco Museum of Modern Art)
1988 *Fluxus,* Museum of Modern Art, New York
1990 *Ready Made Boomerang,* 8th Bienale of Sydney, Australia
1993 *In the Spirit of Fluxus,* Walker Art Center, Minneapolis, Minnesota (toured eastern U.S.)
1995 *L'Esprit FLUXUS,* Musées de Marseille, Paris
1996 *23rd Bienal Internacional,* Sao Paulo, Brazil
1998 *''Out of Actions,'' Between Performance and the Object,* Moca, Los Angeles, California
1999 *Aspekte/Positionen 50 Jahre Kunst aus Mitteleuropa 1949-1999,* Palais Liechtenstein un 20er Haus, Museum Moderner Kunst Stiftung Ludwig, Vienna
2000 *2000 Nains a Bagatelle (2000 Sculptures de l'Antiquité a nos Jours),* Route de Sevres a Neuilly, Bois de Boulougne, Paris

Collections:

Cranbrook Museum, Bloomfield Hills, Michigan; Kunstmuseum, Stuttgart; Museo Mudima, Milan; Museo Vostell, Malpartida, Spain;

Sammlung Feelisch, Remscheid, Germany; Muzeum Sztuki, Lodz, Poland; Moravian Gallery, Brno, Czech Republic; Museum Narodowe, Warsaw, Poland; Tate Gallery, London; Kunsthalle Hamburg, Germany.

Publications:

By KNÍŽÁK: Books—*Flux White Meditation,* New York 1968; *Flux Dreams,* New York 1968; *Flux Snacks,* New York 1968; *Flux Papers,* New York 1968; *Zeremonien,* Remscheid, Germany 1971; *4 Objektes,* Berlin 1971; *Kurton,* Berlin 1971; *Aktual Schmuck,* editor, Cullompton, England 1973; *Flussiges Schweigen,* West Berlin 1983; *Mode/Fashion,* Worpswede, West Germany 1983; *Probable Poems,* Remscheid, West Germany 1983; *Die Korper-Prozesse 1982–85, 85,* Luneburg, West Germany, 1985; *Travel Books,* Prague 1990; *Selected Poems,* Olomouc, Czech Republic 1991; *Mudima Fondation,* Milan 1991; *Názory 1995–1964 (Views 1995–1964),* Brno 1996; *Dharmasputnik,* Brno 1997; *Possible Ways How to Be With Art,* Olomouc 1998; *The Fact I Was Born I Take as an Appeal,* Prague 1999; *Here in Scotland,* with John Lancaster, Brno 2000; *Akce/ Actions,* Prague 2000. **Articles**—in *Aktual Art* (Prague), nos. 1, 2 and 3, 1964–66; in *Actual Newspaper* (Prague), nos. 1, 2 and 3, 1966–67; ''Aktual in Czechoslovakia'' in *Arts and Artists* (London), October 1972.

On KNÍŽÁK: Books—*Assemblage, Environments and Happenings* by Allan Kaprow, New York 1966; *Uměni dnes* by J. Chalupecky, 1966; *Notations* by John Cage, New York 1969; *Fluxfest Kit 2,* edited by George Maciunas, New York 1969; *Fantastic Architecture* by Wolf Vostell and Dick Higgens, New York 1969; *Sammlung Feelisch,* exhibition catalog, Dortmund 1970; *Leben und Kunst* by Udo Kultermann, Tübingen 1970; *Multiples: The First Decade,* exhibition catalog, Philadelphia 1972; *Milan Knížák* by Albrecht, Feelisch and Sohm, Stuttgart 1973; *Source No. 11,* edited by Kenneth S. Friedman, Sacramento, California 1973; *Environments and Happenings* by Adrian Henri, London 1974; *Documenta 6,* exhibition catalog, Kassel, West Germany 1977; *Aktionskunst* by J. Schilling, Lucerne and Frankfurt 1978; *L'Art Aujourd'hui en Tchescoslovaquie* by Genevieve Benamon, Paris 1969; *Fluxus: The Most Radical and Experimental Art Movement,* edited by H. Ruhe, Amsterdam 1979; *Knížák,* exhibition catalog, Berlin 1980; *Für Augen und Ohren,* exhibition catalog, Berlin 1980; *Ecouter par les yeux,* exhibition catalog, Paris 1980; *Milan Knížák,* exhibition catalog, Oldenburg, West Germany 1980; *The Art of Performance* by Gregory Battcock and Robert Nickas, New York 1984; *Milan Knížák: Action as a Life Style,* exhibition catalog, Hamburg 1986; *Milan Knížák: Kleider auf den Korper Gemalt,* exhibition catalog, Hannover 1987; *M. Knížák: Arbeiten 63/79,* Cologne 1989; *Milan Knížák,* exhibition catalog, Vienna 1990; *Milan Knížák,* Prague 1990; *Tradition und Avantgarde in Prag,* exhibition catalog, Germany 1991; *Prague-Batislava d'une génération l'autre,* exhibition catalog, Paris 1992; *Zeitkunst: Wolfgang Feelisch,* exhibition catalog, Remscheid, Germany 1992; *Zweiter Ausgang, Second exit,* exhibition catalog, Aachen 1992; *Ludwig Forum für Internationale Kunst,* exhibition catalog, Aachen Germany 1992; *In the Spirit of Fluxus,* exhibition catalog, Minneapolis 1993; *Action Art* by John Gray, Westport, Connecticut 1993; *Europe without Walls, Art-Posters and Revolution,* edited by J. Aulich and Tim Wilcox, Manchester City, England 1993; *L'Art au Corb,* exhibition catalog, Marseille 1996; *Mezi Tradicí a Experimentem,* exhibition catalog, Olomouc 1997; *Out of Actions: Between Performance and the Object, 1949–1979,* exhibition catalog, Los Angeles, California 1998; *Van Gogh's Dream and a Few Sculptures,* exhibition catalog, Prague 1998; *Crossings,* exhibition catalog, Vienna 1998; *Stop the Violence!!! Stop Nasilju!!! Ndal Dhunes!!!,* exhibition catalog, Vienna 1999.

*

It is feeling and experience which shape my work, not any commitment to an aesthetic theory with its rules and regulations. In such theories there is always the seed of dogmatism, which can be dangerous to both art and life.

I do not believe, for example, that we can regard a statue as simply the result of the sculptor's efforts; or that we can regard a painting, novel, conceptual system, or indeed any human action, as a ''product.'' Products are things which have an immediate usefulness, like shoes and pots and nails—although to look at them in this way will also raise some problems. If we think of human products as something different from and perhaps superior to natural things, then we should see such products as concrete stimuli which evoke or create the conditions for a response which will be different in kind and intensity for each individual (these matters can be demonstrated, although I will not stop to do so here). The result of artistic effort, then, is to cause a change in the inner life of the individual: it begins when we experience the work of art and is invisible; it cannot be measured or controlled.

It follows, then, that the work of art is not a fixed, static product, but a process which to some extent can make our lives richer and more intelligible, a process whose function, therefore, is didactic and ritualistic. Art is a kind of aid, like a vitamin, to the process of living. At its best it can enhance our individual lives and perhaps the quality of life in general. Once this ideal goal has been reached, the work itself simply disappears. It is no longer a necessary presence.

I emphasize this way of looking at art because it also defines the responsibility of the creative artist—his personal, moral obligations to the world he lives in and to the moral codes which govern it. Furthermore, I believe there is a close, causal connection between the artist's life and his work. Honor, responsibility, and all the other words which are losing their meaning in the modern world can regain their vitality in the work of the true artist. There is no difference between him and his work, and this is something which it is especially important for him to realize.

Thus the artist has a kind of duty to educate himself and this is not, of course, a question of attending schools and winning degrees. I mean self-education in the matters of ordinary everyday experience, the strengthening of a complete humility in the presence of even the most basic and primitive manifestations of life around us. This humility does not deify the things of the world; but it gives them a new significance, and in such a way that we can enjoy their presence and enter into their very being. If we can achieve this, the process of ordinary living becomes an absorbing, self-sufficient good.

For me art is not something I merely hear or see or touch. Art closes the gap between us and our dreams; it fills the space which separates us from a god who does not really exist except as the embodiment of our own ideals. The degree to which we can possess these ideals depends on our own abilities and efforts.

—Milan Knížák

* * *

Milan Knížák, the best-known representative of Happenings and Fluxus in Eastern Europe, began his first "actions" in the streets of Prague in 1964, completely unaware of what was going on in western art. The first action, called "Demonstration of All the Senses," also performed in the street together with his friends in the Aktual group and a number of anonymous participants, was a follow-up to his earlier works, the paintings with piles of *objéts trouvés* left out in the street for the casual, or not so casual, viewer.

Knížák's interest in the common people, in ordinary everyday things and doings, was in line with his idea of changing life, not merely art. Knížák intended his activities "as a kind of primary illumination, or as hygiene, as the manifestation of a Messianism of a thousand heads."

His criticism was directed mainly at the sphere of the sentiments, which are fully realized in human life but suffocated and repressed by habits and platitudes. To unblock the fixed patterns he thought it important to acquire as wide and varied knowledge as possible, concentrating on the study not only of such sciences as mathematics, sociology and psychology, but also of architecture and of contemporary ideologies—and so also of the forms of entertainment.

His therapies are based at the same time on sacrifice and on hedonism, on asceticism and on free love—a synthesis, that is, of anti-materialism and a primitive paganism.

The performers in his actions had to learn how "to love the fusion of two gases, to determine the qualities of a restaurant by its smell, to know how to stroke a cat's fur."

At the same time as his actions Knížák was also producing objects, or else suits of clothes and jewelry or even drawings and collages. All these came from his accumulation and collection of found images and images produced by his actions.

The actions in the street, open to everyone, and the life lived in common with his young followers were changed in the 1970s into private activities, and the only disciples that remained were his friends and relatives. The noise demonstrations gave way to silent acts based on more inward experiments, on imagination and evocation.

—Helena Kontova

KNOWLES, Alison

Nationality: American. **Born:** New York City, 29 April 1933. **Education:** Attended high school in Scarsdale, New York, 1948–52; French school, Middlebury College, Vermont, 1952–54 (scholarship, 1952); studied illustration, Pratt Institute, Brooklyn, New York, 1954–57 (scholarship, 1954), B.F.A. 1957; painting, under Richard Lindner, Adolph Gottlieb, and Josef Albers, Syracuse University, New York, 1957–59; graphics, Manhattan School of Printing, New York, 1962. **Family:** Married 1) James Ericson in 1957 (divorced, 1959); 2) Dick Higgins in 1963 (divorced, 1970; remarried, 1984); daughters: Hannah and Jessica. **Career:** First involvement with the Fluxus artists, 1962. Independent artist, establishing Something Else Gallery, with Dick Higgins, New York, 1966; director, Graphics Laboratory, California Institute of Arts, Valencia, 1970–72; teacher, Douglass College, New Brunswick, New Jersey, 1977; founder, with Dick Higgins, Printed Editions publishing co-operative, New York, 1978–85; established shop/studio, Barrytown, New York, 1984. **Awards:** Guggenheim Fellowship, 1968; National Endowment for the Arts Grant, Washington, D.C., 1981, 1985; Karl Sczuka Award, West-deutscher Rundfunk, 1982; DAAD Grant, West Berlin 1984. **Agents:** René Block Gallery, 409 West Broadway, New York, New York, 10012; Galerie René Block, Schaperstrasse 11,1000 West Berlin 15, Germany; Galerie Inge Baecker, Berggate 69, 4630 Bochum, Germany. **Address:** 122 Spring Street, New York, New York 10012–3815, U.S.A.; P.O. Box 27, Station Hill Road, Barrytown, New York, 12507–0027.

Individual Exhibitions:

1958 Nonagon Gallery, New York
1962 Judson Gallery, New York
1972 *Artesian Festival of Art,* California Institute of Arts, Valencia
Shoes for Ken Dewey, New York
Proposition IV, Mercer Art Center, New York (travelled to Goddard College, Plainfield, Vermont)
1973 *Identical Lunch,* Galerie Inge Baecker, Bochum, West Germany
1974 *Collections from the Full Moon,* Galerie René Block, Berlin (travelled to De Appel, Amsterdam)
1976 *Objects in Hand,* De Appel, Amsterdam (travelled to Gallerie 38, Copenhagen)
The Bean Garden, Vehicule Gallery, Montreal (travelled to New School, New York; and Studio Morra, Naples)
1977 *Japanese Bean Garden,* St. Mark's Church, New York
Take a New Name, Whitney Museum, New York
Sound and Image, Aarhus Kunstmuseum, Denmark
1978 *Leone D'Oro,* C-Space Gallery, New York
I Am Festival, Remont Gallery, Warsaw (performance)
3 Songs, Franklin Furnace, New York (perfomance)
Bean Bag, 3 Mercer Street, New York
1979 *Jacob's Cattle,* Micro Gallery, University of California at Sacramento
Inge Baecker Galerie, Bochum, West Germany
Natural Assemblage and the True Crow Kitchen, New York (travelled to the School of Visual Arts, Rochester, New York)
Natural Assemblages and the True Crow, Japanese Bean Garden, Fishes of the Philippine Seas, University of California at Sacramento (travelled to the University of California at San Diego and San Francisco State College)
1980 *The Bean Garden,* Walker Art Center, Minneapolis (travelled to School of Visual Arts, Rochester, New York)
Coffin Gallery, University of Minnesota, Minneapolis
House of Dust, Galerie A, Amsterdam
20 Years of Performance Art: Dick Higgins and Alison Knowles, University of Massachusetts, Amherst
1983 *Leone d'Oro,* Moon Gallery, Mount Berry, Georgia
1984 *Bohnenweg,* Peter Schiller Galerie, West Berlin
1985 Galerie Inge Baecker, Cologne
1987 Nordyllands Kunstmuseum, Aalborg, Denmark
1995 *Indigo Island: Art Works,* Stadtgalerie Saarbrucken (catalog)
1998 *Vintage Themes,* Gracie Mansion Gallery, New York
2000 *Footnotes,* Emily Harvey Gallery, New York (catalog)

Selected Group Exhibitions:

1963 *Street Object Cologne,* Vostell Studio, Cologne
1967 *Artypo Exhibition,* Stedelijk Museum, Amsterdam
1970 *Happennings and Fluxus,* Kunstverein, Cologne
1974 *Fluxus Group,* Galerie Rene Block, West Berlin
1977 *03 23 03 Exhibition,* Museum of Fine Arts, Montreal (travelled to National Gallery, Ottawa)
1978 *Fluxus Exhibition,* Ecart Gallery, Switzerland
1980 *Fluxus Group Show on Food Art,* Maison de la Culture, Chalon-Sur-Saône, France
1982 *Fluxus 1962–82,* Kunstverein, Wiesbaden, West Germany
1984 *II Fascino della Carta,* Museo Civico, Reggio Emilia, Italy
1986 *Breath River Route,* 537 Artworks, New York
1994 *Outside the Frame: Performance and the Object,* Cleveland Center for Contemporary Art, Cleveland (catalog)
In the Spirit of Fluxus, Walker Art Center, Minneapolis
1998 *Do It at Surrey Art Gallery,* Surrey, British Columbia
2000 *Zirkulierende Arten: Edition, Distribution, Interaktion Heute,* Bonner Kunstverein, Bonn, Germany

Collections:

Nordyllands Kunstmuseum, Aalborg, Denmark; Aarhus Museum, Denmark; Bibliothèque Nationale, Paris; Galerie De Appel, Amsterdam; Hans Sohm Archives, Markgroeningen, West Germany; Kunstbibliotek, Hellerup, Denmark.

Publications:

By KNOWLES: Books—*Bean Rolls: A Canned Book,* New York 1963; *The T Dictionary in 4 Suits,* New York 1965; *By Alison Knowles,* pamphlet of performance scores, New York 1965; *The House of Dust,* computer score, programmed by James Tenney, Cologne 1969; *Journal of the Identical Lunch,* San Francisco 1970; *Proposition VI,* computer score, programmed by Mike Plesset, Los Angeles 1970; *Proposition IV,* computer score, programmed by Andrew Schloss, Benington, Vermont 1973; *Women's Work,* edited with Anna Lockwood, 1975; *More,* New York 1976; *Gem Duck,* Italy 1977; *Days Running,* Denmark, 1978; *Natural Assemblages and the True Crow,* Rochester, New York 1980; *The Red, the Green, the Yellow, the Black and the White,* with George Brecht, Brussels 1983; *A Bean Concordance, Vol 1,* Barrytown, New York 1983; *Spoken Text,* Barrytown 1993; *Footnotes: Collage Journal 30 Years,* with preface by Jerome Rothenberg, New York 2000. **Articles—**''Road Shows, Street Events, and Fluxus People: A Conversation with Alison Knowles,'' with Estera Milman in *Visual Language,* vol. 26, Winter/Spring 1992; ''Flux Generations: Roundtable Discussion'' with Janet A. Kaplan in *Art Journal,* vol. 59, no. 2, Summer 2000. **Audiotapes—***3 Songs,* Copenhagen 1979; *Audiographics,* New York 1980. **CD—***Fluxus Anthology: A Collection of Music and Sound Events,* 1995.

On KNOWLES: Books—*Musical America* by Tom Johnson and others, New York 1976; *The Amazing Decade,* edited by Moira Roth, New York 1983. **Articles—**''Alison in Wonderland'' by Emmett Williams in *Books* (New York), September 1966; ''Follow Alice But . . .'' by B. Hale in *The Telegram* (Toronto), September 1967; ''Pandora's Book'' in *Newsweek* (New York), April 1968; ''Your Guernica Is Very Good Looking'' by Jill Johnston in the *Village Voice* (New York), February 1972; ''Lunch ohne Mayonaise'' in *Ruhr Nachrichten-Bochumer Zeitung* (Bochum, West Germany), May 1973; ''New Music'' by Tom Johnson in *High Fidelity* (New York), June 1975; ''The House of Dust'' in *New Wilderness Letter* (San Francisco), no. 8, 1980; ''The Book of Bean'' in *Aperture* (Rochester, New York), Winter 1984; ''Alison Knowles'' by Franziska Brand in *Schattengrenze,* exhibition catalog, Bremen, 1985; ''Alison Knowles at Emily Harvey'' by Sarah Valdez in *Art in America* (New York), vol. 89, no. 1, January 2001.

*

The events I perform, the prints I have made and the environments I build are designed to put the spectator/performer in touch with him/herself and the real world. Natural sound, found objects and small familiar things are collected and investigated. Those things undergo considerable research to make a piece. It is useful to examine a button at great length. My personal investigations concern beans and shoes.

—Alison Knowles

* * *

Alison Knowles is sometimes known as ''the woman in Fluxus,'' which, although Fluxus quite consciously included many women's work, is quite true in the sense that she was the only woman among the actual founders of Fluxus, the only woman who actually took part in all the original Fluxus Festivals in 1962–63.

Her earliest works were Abstract Expressionist, but by 1960 she began to include figurative elements usually based on found or everyday objects in her paintings, using radiator screens as stencils, blowing up objects found in the street with an opaque projector, etc. Since that time her work has remained, above all, as concrete as possible with daily living. The ongoing imagery in her work, which clarified in the early 1960s, is based on beans, books, fishes, shoes. Not only has she written a dozen or so visual books (or collected them), but she has also done several ''editions'' (that is, different versions) of a concept called *The Big Book,* collage environments with pages, usually about 2.5 meters high and 1.7 meters wide, the most recent of which uses bean folklore, imagery, science, stories and traditions as well as, for example, paper made by crushing beans into the pulp. Fishes, too, have featured prominently, from a series called *The Identical Lunch* (1966–81) in which a number of people ate tunafish sandwiches and buttermilk and described their experiences, or *Fishes of the Philippine Seas,* a series of graphic works and performance works based on texts by the early- twentieth-century naturalist Barton Appler Bean.

The shoe series has been an ongoing one since the early days of Fluxus, when she did ''Shoes of Your Choice'' (1962) in which members of the audience came forward and described what the shoes they were wearing meant to them. It includes graphics made from photographs of found shoes and parts of shoes and several objects made from such parts.

Her major work in progress is *A Bean Concordance,* a book which contains as much as possible of the materials she has collected over 20 years concerning beans of all kinds. It was published in early 1983.

—Dean Higgins

KOCMAN, J(iři) H(ynek)

Nationality: Czech. **Born:** Nové Mésto na Moravě, 6 August 1947. **Education:** University of Veterinary Medicine, Brno, Czechoslovakia, 1965–71; private studies in aesthetics with Jiří Valoch, since 1965; medium of paper and fine book binding with Jindřich Svoboda, since 1976; paper and books restoration with Tomáš Vyskočil, since 1979; Habilitation in Art Academy in Prague, 1976. **Career:** Has practiced as a doctor of veterinary medicine, working in clinical pharmacology, Brno, 1971–1998. Also an artist: has worked with graphics, poems, texts, since 1965; book-objects, reports, stamps, project/concepts, ecology, entomology, and studies of communication, since 1970; hand-made papers, paper re-making, and studies about paper and bookbinding, since 1979; teacher of fine arts, University of Technology, Brno, 1993 to present; founder and head of Studio of Paper and Book, University of Technology, Brno, 1998 to present. **Address:** Vackova 64, 612 00 Brno, Czech Republic.

Individual Exhibitions:

1966 Vysokoskolsky Klub, Brno
1968 *Tinktury,* Galerie Klubu A. Tryba, Brno
1970 *Collyrie,* Galerie Mladych, Brno
1973 Stedelijk Museum, Amsterdam
1978 *Bücher und Stempel,* Galerie Leaman, Dusseldorf
17 Butterflies, Mala Galerie Cs. Spisovatale, Brno
Rubber Stamp Works, Stempelplaats, Amsterdam
1983 Galerie für visuele Erlebnisse, Weddel, Germany
1989 *Original Books,* Archive Space, Antwerp
1991 *Handmade papers and artists' books,* Dumumnení, Brno
1992 *Pure Experiences,* University of Reading, England
1993 Galerie Palisády, Bratislava
1997 *Artists' Books and Papers,* Galery Rudolfinum, Prague
2000 *Kunstobjekt Buch,* Tsch. Zentrum, Berlin

Selected Group Exhibitions:

1974 *Tampons d'Artistes,* Institut de l'Environment, Paris
1975 *Visual Poetry International,* Galerie de Doelen, Rotterdam
1979 *Sprachen Jenseits von Dichtung,* Westfälischer Kunstverein, Munster
1980 *Von Aussehen der Wörter,* Kunstmuseum, Hannover
1982 *Young Fluxus,* Artists Space, New York
1986 *Turning Over the Pages,* Kettle's Yard Gallery, Cambridge
International Biennal of Paper Art, L. Hoesch Museum, Duren
1990 *40 Artistes: tcheques + slovaques 1960–90,* Coupole Haussmann, Paris
1992 *Zufall als Prinzip,* Wilhelm Hack Museum, Ludwigshafen
1993 *Concept Books,* Galerie Henn, Maastricht
1994 *Das Jahrhundert des Multiple,* Deichtorhallen, Hamburg
1995 *České Umění 1960–1995,* Veletržní Palác NG, Prague
1996 *1. Nový Zlínský Salon,* Státní Galerie, Zlín
1997 *Mezi Tradicí a Experimentem,* Muzeum Umĕni, Olomouc
1998 *9. Trienále Umĕlecké Knižní Vazby,* Muzeum Kromĕřížska, Kromĕříž, Czech Republic
1999 *Současná Tvorba Favu Vut,* Dum Umení, Brno, Czech Republic
2000 *Papír a Kniha,* Moravská Galerie, Brno, Czech Republic

Collections:

Moravska Galerie, Brno; Schubladenmuseum für Moderne Kunst im 20. Jahrhundert, Berne; Kunsthaus, Zurich; Collection Hundertmark, Berlin; Fluxus West Archive, San Diego, California; Archiv Sohm, Stadtgalerie, Stuttgart; DAAD-Archiv, Berlin; Sackner Archive, Miami Beach, Florida; National Galery, Prague.

Publications:

By KOCMAN: Books—*Europe-America: The Different Avant-Gardes,* edited by A. B. Oliva, Milan 1976; *Rubber No. 10,* edited by A. de Varbeneld, Amsterdam 1978; *Médium Papír,* Brno 2000. **Articles—**visual poetry in *Lotta Poetica,* Brescia 1971; ''Touch Activity'' in *Aktuelle Kunst in Ost Europa,* edited by Klaus Groh, Cologne 1972; rubber stamp facsimiles in *Art et Communication Marginale,* edited by Hervé Fischer, Paris 1974; ''The Magazine Network'' by Géza Pernecky, Köln, 1993; ''Josef Váchal—ein tsch. Buchkünstler'' in *Bindetechnik,* no. 3, 1986.

On KOCMAN: Books—*Tinktury,* exhibition catalog by Jiri Valoch, Brno 1968; *Collyrie,* exhibition catalog by Jiri Valoch, Brno 1970; *JHK: My Activity 1965–73,* with text by Jiri Valoch, Brno 1973; *JHK: 17 Motylku,* exhibition catalog with text by Jiri Valoch, Brno 1978; *JHK 1976–80,* with text by Jiri Valoch, Brno 1980; *JHK: Handmade Papers and Artists' Books,* exhibition catalog with text by Jiri Valoch, Brno 1991; *JHK: Artists' Books and Papers,* exhibition catalog with text by Jiří Valoch, Prague 1997. **Articles—**''Künstlerstempel'' by G. F. Schwarzbauer in *Magazin Kunst* (Mainz), no. 3, 1974; ''The Stamp and Stamp Art'' by Kenneth S. Friedman and G. M. Gugelberger in *Front* (San Francisco), no. 4, 1976; ''Buchobjekte—das Buch als Kunstwerk'' by A. Heibe in *Kunstnachrichten* (Zurich), no. 3, 1983; ''The Contemporary Renaissance of Fine Bookbinding in Czechoslovakia'' by E. Minar in *Fine Art* (New York), no. 1, 1987; ''Reflections of a Book Artist'' by Jan Sobota in *New Bookbinder,* vol. 10, 1990; ''Contigency and the Ontic Book'' by Ted Purves in *Journal of Artists' Books,* 1998.

*

I started to take an interest in paper at the time of my ''graphic activities'' (1965–70) when I got my first real experience with the material. In the first half of the 1970s I was engaged in Concept Art, Project Art, Stamp Art, Mail Art, etc. In 1976 I met the art-bookbinder master Professor Jindrich Svoboda and had the opportunity to watch and learn the bookbinding processes. I feel that paper is a fantastic material and I am fascinated by paper's sensibilities.

In my book-objects made between 1970 and 1972 I placed different visual (especially colored) aspects in the foreground. From 1977 on, I made ''HandSewn Books,'' book-concepts without text or illustration, books as material objects in themselves. In my bookbinding activity I like best to be able to work with various kinds of paper and to make something out of them: to be together with the paper. My first

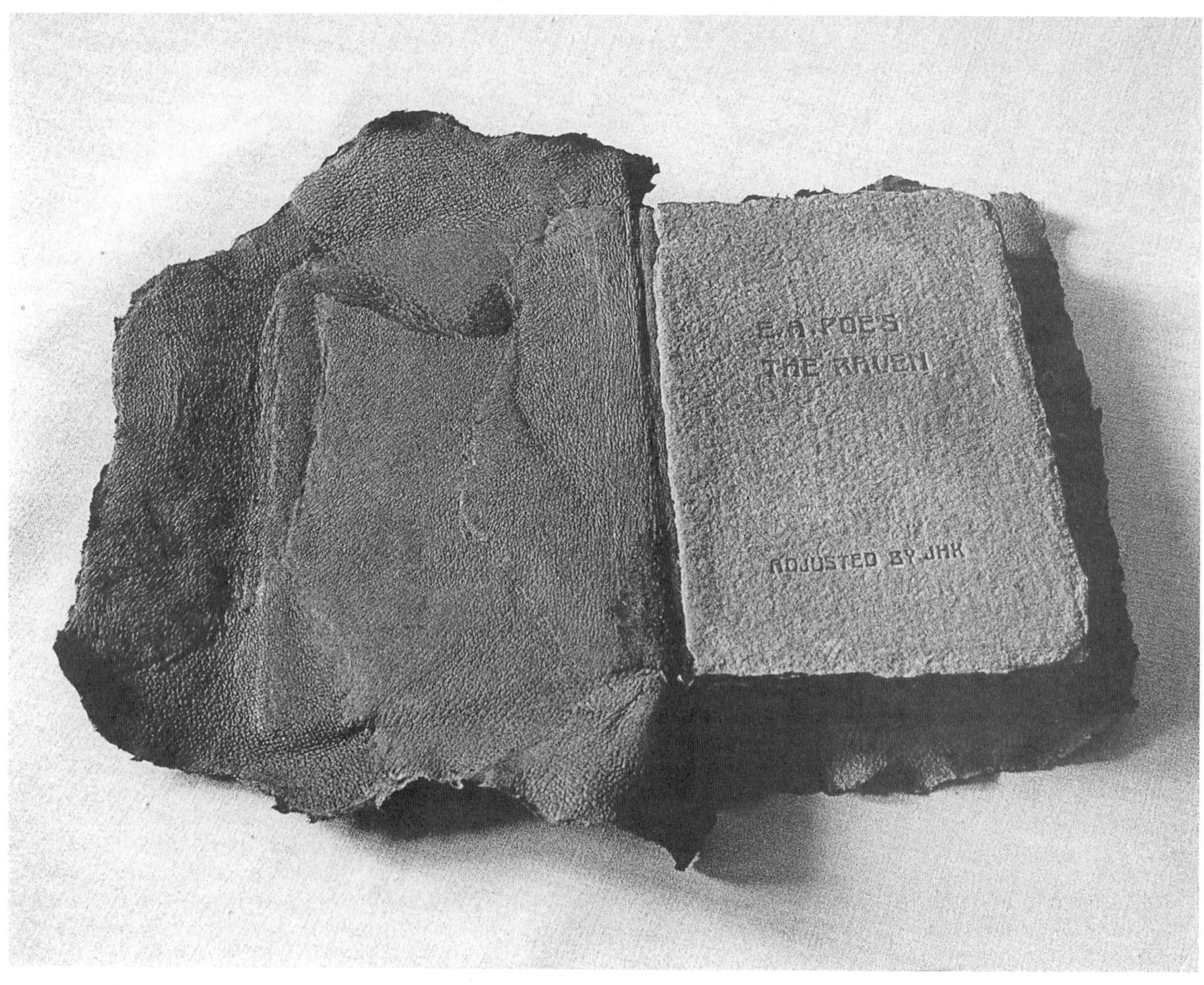

Jiří Kocman: *E. A. Poe's The Raven adjusted by JHK,* 1986. ©J. H. Kocman.

''Hand-Made Papers'' were produced in January 1979. I employed a technique I called Paper-Re-Making. The papers I make are not for ordinary use: they are intended as pieces of work in themselves. I find it always exciting to make new paper, being especially interested in the fineness of its structure, transparency, the appearance of both sides of each sheet, the nature of its construction and individual character. As important as its visual appearance are the tactile aspects: touching, feeling, tracing. Paper is made for the hands. All these notions are too ''intimate'' to talk much about.

—J. H. Kocman

* * *

The Czech artist, J.H. Kocman—best known as JHK—is concerned with systems. Kocman is not concerned with the cold, impersonal precision of systems, but rather with their poetry, with their musicality, with their suggestive valences.

Kocman is best known internationally for the seminal role he has had as a major developer of rubber stamp art. He organized some of the first international rubber stamp activities by contemporary artists, and edited the first true anthology of rubber stamp art. He is also known for his contributions to mail art and communications art, and to visual poetry.

The vast majority of his works walk the borderline between intimate art experience and science. Unlike many artists who organize data related to biological or astronomical processes, presenting them in good formats on large scale, Kocman presents his material in small, almost, tender fragments. He takes one idea or process at a time, and uses its poetic, human potential to map lyrical aesthetic structures. In one regard, he removes from the idea of a system its rigid, systemic nature. In another, he heightens our consciousness of the fragile relationships which obtain in most systems which a scientist or an artist can investigate.

Many artists today employ scientific notions or the idea of systemic structures in their work. They often appear to do so simply to keep abreast of recent tendencies in the art world, despite the fact that the work itself is incapable of yielding interesting results. All too often, even the data, as science, and as systems, are invalid. As it is, therefore, the practitioners of these art forms take their art too seriously, and joke poorly with the science involved. Kocman takes an opposite and exemplary tack: his works frequently embody sly jokes on the history and practice of art, but his science is always accurate and serious, even though it may be presented in an intimate atmosphere of personalized poetics. This might perhaps be expected: after all, Kocman was trained as a scientist, and is a doctor of veterinary medicine. As a scientist, biological processes hold a fascination for him; as a practitioner of the healing arts, he holds life in high esteem. While he makes a playful or delightful art from the processes of science and life, therefore, it would be impossible for him to abuse them.

The key to Kocman's work is the intersection between the content of his systems and the delights which lie hidden within them. He is not concerned with the difference or similarity between art and life. The art/life battle has been well fought out by previous artists, and while it has some points left to be made, most of the art/life problems pursued by artists today are in reality retrograde tactics useful only in claiming career status. Even at that, the tactics are only useful in a provincial atmosphere where the arty world is not aware of the nature and discourse of art as it has played out over the recent decades of this century. Kocman's strategy is an appropriate international strategy: he accepts his position as a member of this generation of artists just come to prominence, a generation which accepts the results of the discourse between art and life, using those results as a platform from which new investigations may be launched.

Because he accepts his place in history, he is free to contribute to the next stages in art history. He is not trapped in any past doctrine, and will not be dismissed as an artist who spent his career re-stating the issues of the past for the benefit of tenure in an art school or academy. Instead, he takes the risk of his own search: the search for a personal style in a freshly discovered world which accepts itself as having a dual nature, rooted equally in art and life. In a peculiar regard, he is the most free among artists. As a full professional in another discipline than art, he is able to make his living without any concern for the ups and downs of the art world. As an artist who draws on the disciplines of his profession, he is freed by the knowledge of his science to do work which does not demean itself by presenting its scientific content poorly.

Kocman's presentation is perhaps the most interesting phenomenon of his interaction with the art world. JHK does not prepare, as mentioned earlier, large format explorations for exhibition and museum appreciation. Instead, he makes his works lovingly, individually, too personally, in fact, to be appreciated truly in the Byzantine atmosphere of most art situations. His works reach their audience in small, hand-made books, experiments, and individually bound monographs. They include maps, plates, injected dye-samples, hand-cut pages, photographs, diagrams. They capture the pleasant spirit of correspondence art during its personalist phases of the 1960s, and join it to the environmental and structuralist sensibilities of the 1970s. When one acquires a Kocman piece, one does not have the feeling that one has outbid another collector of impersonally acquisitioned a new work. One feels that one is sharing part of an experiment which might have taken place recently in a friend's laboratory. Kocman's presentations summon up the image of a Royal Society as it might have been some centuries ago, a Society in which we are all colleague-scientists, working together to advance the frontiers of knowledge. We are content in this work together, and leave it to another group to bally-hoo the knowledge into fame and fortune. Kocman's work approaches the framework of the pure research end of research art in its tone, even though its content is warm and conversational.

Some artists succeed very well in the use of environmental and biological science for large-format presentations. Most notable, of course, are the Harrisons and Hans Haacke. In another way—particularly in the preparatory phases of his projects—we find Christo. The wonder and artful delight of the work of these artists is the fact that their use of science is not distorted in order to make it art, but that the science is managed properly as the art.

Kocman is unique in presenting scientific systems and their spinoff in intimate and poetic forms. His beautiful monograph, *Micro-Macro,* in fact, echoes in its title his role in the art world. Where others—some successfully, most badly—strive to fill out roles and careers on the macrocosmic scale, Kocman stands out as an artist whose work emerges beneath the microscope. Because of the intimacy of its presentation, in fact, even his non-microscopic work has a sensibly small scale, even when the ideas it presents are large, important ideas.

Success as an artist requires several facilities. One must be aware of that which has gone before, and play off it without repeating it. One must discover for one's work an authority of scale, tone and diction that is suitable to its content. One must develop a personal style of engagement and presentation which balances aesthetic concerns of content and the direct form of the work in a manner which is both unique to a great enough degree to be remarkable and which is congenial enough to enter into the dialogue of the art world. Kocman grapples well with these problems, and his growing success as an artist on the international scene bears witness to his talent and skill as a potentially major figure in contemporary art.

In some regards, Kocman's career is just freshly begun. He is considered by many to be the fourth major contemporary figure to emerge from Czechoslovakia, following the pioneers Kolar and Knizak, and following his better-known friend, Valoch. He is widely esteemed and has claimed a major place for himself in one field of art, rubber stamp art. Because his career rests more on poetic environmental concerns, however, his image is not as clearly defined as the other three—who are best-known for their major works, rather than for one or another career sidelight. In this regard, Kocman's stamp work is both a help and a hindrance to his total career. Because he is an intimist, as well, he is in some circles less well-known than Czech artists who have emerged more recently, but whose work is better given to wide exhibition and publication. In this regard, one thinks of the talented young Czechs such as Zorka Saglova, Olaf Hanel, Eugen Brikcius, Peter Stembera, and others. With Valoch, Kocman is seen as one of the first generation of Czechs of the post-Fluxus, post-Aktual period, and like Valoch, his work overlaps the activity of those movements in Czech contemporary art. As an intimist, he is also logically placed in context with Endre Tot and Jaroslav Kozlowsky—of Hungary and Poland respectively. It is to his credit, but a problem in publishing his work, that Kocman's work requires special printing techniques, many of which can only be done by hand, while many of the works of Tot and Kozlowsky can simply be reprinted photographically. It is, of course, for this reason that his rubber stamp work is so much better than his biological or systematic works and process pieces.

In terms of his career, the greatest problem facing Kocman is the problem of scale. Can he retain his intimate tone and personalized qualities which so distinguish and enliven his use of systems, while translating them into a scale which will render them more visible to the world at large? This may well be a useless question, of course, since we have noted that Kocman is an extraordinary artist in relation to career concerns and art-world politics. Nevertheless, in viewing—or better put, in handling and contacting Kocman's work, it is a question which is frequently asked.

That he, himself, is not overly concerned with such questions is part of the nature and character which makes him and his work so refreshing. The vitality and delight in Kocman's work arises from this spirit as much as from the way in which it handles important art issues in surprising and unique ways.

J. H. Kocman is a surprising and unique artist. A scientist who presents his work as a visual and intellectual poetics. A systematist who demonstrates the humanistic uses of systems, rather than using systems toward dehumanizing ends. A fresh voice out of the increasingly important art world of Eastern Europe which offers to engage and revitalize the often moribund West. J. H. Kocman is an artist who, through his intimates and personalized style, engages others in his work as colleagues, and as human beings.

—Kenneth Friedman

KOGLER, Peter

Nationality: Austrian. **Born:** Innsbruck, 1959. **Career:** Professor, Academy for Applied Art, Vienna, 1997—. **Agent:** Galerie Krinzinger, Seilerstätte 16, 1010 Wien, Austria.

Selected Individual Exhibitions:

1983 Gallery Krinzinger, Innsbruck and Vienna
1986 Gallery Krinzinger, Innsbruck and Vienna (catalog)
1988 Gallery Krinzinger, Innsbruck and Vienna (catalog)
1995 Viennese Secession
1996 Art Association, Bonn (catalog)
1997 Association for Recent Art, Bremen
2000 Kunsthaus Bregenz, Köln (catalog)

Selected Group Exhibitions:

1986 *Aperto,* Venice Biennial
1992 Documenta IX, Kassel
1997 Documenta X, Kassel
1993 *Ars Electronica,* Linz
1995 Austrian Pavilion, Venice Biennial
1998 *Threshold,* Power Plant, Toronto, Ontario
Anticipation—Version 4, Centre pour l'Image Contemporaine, Geneva

Publications:

On KOGLER: Articles—''Peter Kogler'' by Helmut Draxler in *Kunstforum International,* no. 89, 1987; ''Peter Kogler'' by Sabine Schütz in *Noema,* no. 11, 1987; ''Peter Kogler, Galerie Krinzinger, Wien 1988'' by Fe Rakuschan in *Nike,* no. 23, 1988; ''Peter Kogler: 'Ants,' wo gruene Ameisen traeumen'' by Gerhard Bachleitner in *Nike,* no. 39, 1991; ''Peter Kogler'' by Peter Fleck in *Jetztzeit,* exhibition catalog, Kunsthalle Wien, Ostfildern-Ruit 1994; ''Impuls—kein Impuls. Zwischen Verführung und Beobachtung'' by Amelie Pohlen in *Peter Kogler,* exhibition catalog, Bonn 1996; ''Struktur und Ornament, Symbol und Zufall'' by Martin Prinzhorn in *Parnass,* no. 3, 1999.

* * *

Upon entering the room at the Documenta IX, visitors were confronted with a maze-like structure of giant ants covering the walls. In Peter Kogler's wall-piece, the black image of the same ant recurred again and again. Thus a multitude of the insects seemed to have conquered every single inch of the walls—wandering about in orderly, linear paths and thereby forming an elaborate system of roads and crossroads. The puzzling impression of crawling animals filled the room with an intense, dramatic atmosphere. Everyone in the room immediately became part of the work of art as a participant. Demonstrating paradigmatically Kogler's major thematic issues as well as his technical standard during the 1990s, this installation is to be considered a representative example of his *oeuvre.*

Peter Kogler refers to the computer as his basic tool. After scanning the image of an ant out of a book, the artist retouches it on the computer. After that, he uses enlarged laser print-outs of the retouched images to produce silk-screens for re-printing them, this time on large rolls of paper which are then used like wallpaper to cover the surfaces of entire rooms. Sometimes, Kogler prints on cloth which is made into curtains or screens blocking the visitors' passage through the room.

The Austrian-born artist uses standard hardware as well as standard software—technically perfect images are not an issue for him. Kogler relies on them for scanning, and even more so, for reproducing his images. Yet he strictly refuses to have his work labelled as ''computer art.'' The computer serves as a tool, not as an end in itself. Although the artist's sources are changed on the computer, this is only one stage among others: the final product is a silk-screen-print. Nevertheless, Kogler changes the role of the artist as there is no personal touch of an artist's hands on his final product. The making of this type of art has not been a unique act: it could be redone anytime.

Kogler's sources undergo a technical process reducing them to some pixels, and, consequently, to binary structures. Reality and its images are analyzed and pressed into an electronic pattern. In a second step, the single motif is repeated and arranged into a visual pattern that will finally be silk-screened, and therefore can be reproduced without limit. This use of a serial imagery which arranges the reiterations of its motif into a system of lines and their junctions is a major characteristic of the artist's works.

Finally, being used like wallpaper, the multiplied images turn into mere ornaments. These ornaments are created by an analytical gaze picking out details and exalting them by repetition and arrangement. Thus, they are reflections of Kogler's work with the computer on another level—analyzing and therefore demystifying the visible.

During the 1990s, Kogler repeatedly used a small set of motifs: pictures of ants, of the human brain and other organs, or of tubes. They offer connotations such as individuality versus heteronomy, the process of thought versus mere corporeality, nature versus technology. Through the intensity of their arrangement, these motifs question the state of human consciousness.

Upon entering the Kogler-designed room, the observer is spontaneously drawn into a dialogue. Visitors are surrounded by Kogler's vibrant ants or brains along the walls as they are moving in a space marked entirely as ''art.'' Their entire bodies are involved. They are confronted with the installation in an individual way as every observer's moves and perceptions are unique and not comparable to anyone else's. Hence, possible answers can be found only in the visitors' own bodies and in their individual minds.

Corporeality has been a major issue in Kogler's oeuvre from the beginning. His early drawings dealt with the human figure. In 1983 he showed three-dimensional sculptures made of cardboard applied with a "net" of drawn or cut human bodies. During the mid-eighties, he started to work with the computer, producing distorted portraits based on electronically retouched drawings. These portraits, however, were painted by hand copying the grid of a computer-print-out. Since 1990, Peter Kogler's wallpaper-rooms combine both issues: computer-generated, they still deal with corporeality, firstly by including their observers' entire bodies into the work of art, and secondly by using images of organs as their sources. Taking up questions of corporeality and human consciousness, Kogler's works challenge the possibility of individual experience in a technically standardized world.

—Vanessa Hirsch

KOLÁŘ, Jiří

Nationality: French. **Born:** Protivin, Southern Bohemia (Czechoslovakia), 24 September 1914; emigrated to France, 1980: naturalized, 1984. **Education:** Trained as apprentice carpenter, Protivin, 1928–34; mainly self-educated in art; influenced by writings of Marinetti and Surrealist artists. **Family:** Married Bela Helclova in 1949. **Career:** Worked as carpenter, laborer and waiter, Protivin, 1928–42; as independent artist/writer, as children's book author and translator, Kladno and Prague, 1942–80, in Paris, since 1980. Founder-member, Group 42, Prague, 1942–48; editor, Dilo Publishers, Prague, 1945–48. **Awards:** International Art Biennale Prize, Lignano, Italy, 1968; Central Committee Prize, 50th Anniversary of the Czech Socialist Republic, Prague, 1968; International Joan Miro Drawing Prize, Barcelona, 1968; Czechoslovakia Prize, *Bienal,* Sao Paulo, 1969; Gottfried-von-Herder Prize, Vienna 1971; DAAD Fellowship, West Berlin, 1979. **Agents:** Galeria Schwarz, Via Gesu 17, 20121 Milan, Italy; Leonard Hutton Galleries, 41 East 57th Street, New York, New York 10022; New Museum of Contemporary Art, 583 Broadway, New York, New York 10012; Joseph Rickards Gallery, 1045 Madison Avenue, New York, New York 10021; and Galerie R., Bismarckstrasse 45, Nuremberg, Germany. **Address:** 61 rue Olivier-Métra, 75020 Paris, France.

Individual Exhibitions:

1937 Mozarteum, Theatre 37, Prague
1962 Club VU Manes, Prague
1963 Arthur Jeffers Gallery, London
Museum of Modern Art, Miami
Europaisches Forum, Alpbach, Austria
Oblastni Galerie, Liberec, Czechoslovakia
1964 Galerie Gravura, Lisbon
Metska Galerie, Louny, Czechoslovakia
Schwitters/Kolář/Mesens, Grosvenor Gallery, London
1965 Die Kleine Galerie, Vienna
Club VU Manes, Prague
La Carabaga Club, Genoa
1966 Galerie Riquelme, Paris
Galerie M. E. Thelen, Essen
Galerie H., Hannover
Centro Proposte, Florence
Studio d'Informazione Estetica, Turin
1967 Klus Pratel Vytarneho Umeni, Prague
Galerie Seyfried und Alten G. Z. Neuhaus, Munich
1968 Galerie V. Spala, Prague
Kunstlerhaus am Konigster, Nuremberg
1969 Kestner-Gesellschaft, Hannover
Overbeck Gesellschaft, Lübeck, West Germany
Junge Galerie, Kassel, West Germany
Ulmer Museum, Ulm, West Germany
Kunstverein, Munich
Kleine Grafik Galerie, Bremen, West Germany
Galerie am Klosterstern, Hamburg
Galerie Hansjorg Mayer, Stuttgart
Willard Gallery, New York
1970 Museum P. Bezruc, Opava, Czechoslovakia
Galerie Wentdorf und Swetec, Dusseldorf
Galerie Gmurzynska, Aachen, West Germany
1971 Librairie-Galerie La Hune, Paris
ARC/Musée d'Art Moderne de la Ville, Paris
Hofer Galerie H, Weinelt/Hof, West Germany
Galerie K, Mainz, West Germany
1972 Galleria Schwarz, Milan
Galerie M. Goebels, Kaiserslautern, West Germany
Kleine Grafik Galerie, Bremen, West Germany
Aktionsgalerie, Berne
1973 La Boetie Gallery, New York
Collagen, Rollagen, Chiasmagen, Crumblagen, Museum Haus Lange, Krefeld, West Germany
Museum Boymans-van Beuningen, Rotterdam
Galerie Gunter Sachs, Hamburg
1974 Union des Arts Plastiques, St. Etienne-du-Rouvray, France
Galerie R, Nuremberg
Galerie Suzanne Bollag, Zurich
Städtische Galerie, Siegen, West Germany
1975 Guggenheim Museum, New York
Willard Gallery, New York
Harriette Griffin Gallery, New York
Jacques Caplan Gallery, New York
1976 Jasa Fine Art, Munich
Galerie Wentdorf und Swetec, Dusseldorf
Cheap Thrills Gallery, Helsinki
Halvat Hulit, Helsinki
Galerie Lowenadler, Stockholm
1977 Fairweather-Hardin Gallery, Chicago
Université de Genéve, Geneva
Galerie Yves Lambert, Paris
Galerie Schreiner, Basle
1978 Guggenheim Museum, New York
Albright-Knox Art Gallery, Buffalo, New York
Galerie Schoeller, Dusseldorf
Art Gallery of Ontario, Toronto
1979 Institut für Moderne Kunst, Nuremberg
1980 *Collagen, Rollagen, Chiasmagen, Materialbilder, Objekte,* Städtische Kunsthalle, Recklinghausen, West Germany
Unterwegs ins Paradies, Gutenberg Museum, Mainz, West Germany

Kunstverein, Wolfsburg, West Germany
Kunstmuseum, Dusseldorf
Neue Berliner Kunstverein, Berlin
Galerie Zellermayer-Lorenzen, Berlin
Galerie Inge Baeker, Bochum, West Germany
1981 Kassler Kunstverein, Kassel, West Germany
Genevieve and Serge Mathier, Besancon, France
Collagen und Objekte aus Berlin und Paris, Museum Folkwang, Essen
Galerie Maeght, Paris
Froissages, Galeria Metronom, Barcelona
1982 *Colleges, Objectes,* Galeria Maeght, Barcelona
Galleria Primo Piano, Rome
Galleria Pecollo, Livorno
Die Welle Galerie, Iserlohn, West Germany
Galerie Schiessel, Munich
Centre Georges Pompidou, Paris
Southern Methodist University, Dallas
Padiglione d'Arte Contemporanea, Milan
Hokin Gallery, Palm Beach, Florida
1983 Stadtische Galerie, Bergisch Gladbach, West Germany
Galerie Maeght Lelong, Paris
Galerie Slavia, Bremen, West Germany
Galleria Zarathustra, Milan
Galerie Kraus, Pfaffikon, Switzerland
1984 Galerie Praxis, Essen, West Germany
Stamparte Galleria, Bologna, Italy
Kunsthalle, Nuremberg, West Germany
Vancouver Art Gallery, British Columbia
Museum of Modern Art, Oxford
Galerie Schoeller, Dusseldorf
1985 Leopold-Hoesch-Museum, Duren, West Germany
Kunstverein, Heilbronn, West Germany
Galerie Rafay, Kronberg, West Germany
Galerie Svetlana, Munich
Centro d'Arte Contemporanea, Syracuse, Italy
Museum Rupertinum, Salzburg, Austria
Guggenheim Museum, New York
1986 Galerie Maeght Lelong, Paris
Galerie Grita Insam, Vienna
1987 *Collages, 1952–1982,* Albemarle Gallery, London
Haus am Checkpoint Charlie, Berlin
Zellermayer Galerie, Berlin
1988 Kulturgeschichtliches Museum, Osnabrück, Germany
Poèmes du silence, Galerie Lelong, Paris
Galerie Schoeller, Düsseldorf
1989 *Question de collage 1979–1989,* Galerie municipale, Vitry-sur-Seine, France
Galleria Tega, Milan
Kulturgeschichtliches Museum, Osnabrück, Germany
1991 Galleria d'Arte Elleni, Bergamo, Italy
Historiska Museet, Stockholm
Galerie Gerulata, Bratislava, Slovakia
Galerie Le Pont Neuf, Paris
1992 Galerie Lelong, Paris
Dictionnaire des méthodes, Comenius Museum, Naarden, Netherlands; Galerie Isy Brachot, Paris
1993 *Dictionnaire des méthodes,* National Gallery, Prague (travelled to Malmö Konsthall, Malmö, Sweden; L'Espace des Arts, Colomiers, France)
Villa Manzoni, Lecco, Italy
Studio Pino Casagrande, Rome
1993 *Dictionnaire des méthodes,* Miró Foundatió Joan Miró, Barcelona
1994 *Objects and Collages,* Visconti Fine Art, Ljublana, Slovenia Galleria
That is not Mondrian: Collages by Jiří Kolár, Stedelijk Museum Schiedam, Netherlands (also Van Reekum Museum, Apeldoorn, Netherlands; De Beyerd Centrum voor Beeldende Kunst, Netherlands) (catalog)
Colusa, Udine, Italy
Galerie Paul Sties, Kronenberg
Museo Reina Sofia, Madrid
1998 *ART! MAGIC!: The Magic of Kolar,* Deutsche Bank, Lobby Gallery, New York

Selected Group Exhibitions:

1963 *9 Europaische Kunstler,* Haus am Waldsee, Berlin
1965 *Between Poetry and Painting,* Institute of Contemporary Arts, London
1968 *Documenta 4,* Museum Fridericianum, Kassel, West Germany
1969 *Bienal,* Sao Paulo
1970 *Expo '70,* Osaka, Japan
1971 *Konkrete Poezie,* Stedelijk Museum, Amsterdam (toured Europe)
1973 *Hommage à Picasso,* Nationalgalerie, West Berlin (toured Germany)
1976 *20 Jahre Museum Haus Lange,* Museum Haus Lange, Krefeld, West Germany
1982 *Internatonal Air Fair* (Galerie Maeght display), Chicago
1994 *Zwischen Prag und Paris,* Galerie Schüppenhauer, Cologne (catalog)
Ceské Muzeum Výtvarných Umení (catalog)
1995 *Temporarily Possessed,* New Museum of Contemporary Art, New York
Objetos y Collages, Museo Nacional Centro de Arte Reina Sofía, Madrid (catalog)
Auto Collages 1994–1995, Francis Graham-Dixon Gallery, London
1999 *Jiří Kolář, Bela Kolárová,* Galerie Práchenského Muzea v Pisku (catalog)
L'Oro di Praga, Poesie Visive, Palazzo dei Sette, Orvieto, Italy (catalog)

Collections:

Narodni Galerie, Prague; Kunsthalle, Nuremberg; Institut für Moderne Kunst, Nuremberg; Museum Haus Lange, Krefeld, West Germany; Museum der Kunst, Vienna; Museum Boymans-van Beuningen, Rotterdam; Muzeum Szuki, Lodz, Poland; Musée National d'Art Moderne, Paris; Guggenheim Museum, New York; Museum of Modern Art, New York.

Publications:

BY KOLÁŘ: Books—*Birth Certificate,* Prague 1941; *Night,* Prague 1943; *Limb and Other Poems,* Prague 1945; *7 Cantatas,* Prague 1945;

Odes and Variations, Prague 1946; *Days of the Year,* Prague 1948; *One Day of Vacation,* Prague 1949; *Mister Sun on the Art of Poetry* Prague 1957; *The Chance Witness,* Prague 1964; *In 7th Heaven,* Prague 1964; *Poems of Silence,* Prague 1965; *Poems R,* Copenhagen 1965; *The Plague in Athens, The Light of the World,* playtext, Prague 1965; *Aesop of Varsovice,* Prague 1966; *Signboard of Gersaint,* 1966; *Unser Taeglich Brot (Die Grube),* Vienna 1966; *New Epictetus,* Prague 1968; *Hinauf und Hinunter,* Hannover 1969; *Und 2: 10 Blatter aus Gersaints Auschaengeschild,* Kassel, West Germany 1969; *Poems of Silence,* Prague 1970; *The Liver of Prometheus,* Prague 1970; *Das Sprechende Bild,* Frankfurt 1971; *Hommage à Baudelaire,* Nuremberg 1972; *Wahlverwandschaften,* portfolio, Nuremberg 1972; *Dny v roce, Roky v dnech,* Prague 1975; *Suite* (poems), West Berlin 1980; *20 Gedichten* (poems), Rotterdam 1981; *Ocity Svedek,* Munich 1983; *Temoin oculaire,* Paris 1983; *Prometheova jatra,* Toronto 1985; *Jours de l'anne—Annees des jours,* Paris 1986; *Vrsovicky Ezop,* Munich 1986. **Film—***Attention, Mr. Veronese,* with Bohumil Musil, 1968.

ON KOLÁŘ: Books—*Neue Dimension der Plastik* by Udo Kultermann, Tübingen 1967; *Concrete Poetry: A World View* by Mary Ellen Bolt, London 1968; *Jiří Kolář* by Dietrich Mahlo and Miroslav Lamac, Cologne 1968; *Verso la Poesia Totale* by Adriano Spatola, Salerno 1969; *Jiří Kolář,* exhibition catalog with text by Wieland Schmied and Dietrich Mahlow, Hannover 1969; *Jiří Kolář* exhibition catalog with text by Jindrich Chalupecky, New York 1969; *Jiří Kolář* by Miroslav Lamac, Prague 1970; *Sign and Image* by Ichiro Haryu, Tokyo 1971; *Man-Made Nature* by Yusuke Narahara, Tokyo 1971; *Jiří Kolář: Collages,* exhibition catalog with text by Raoul-Jean Moulin, Paris 1971; *Jiří Kolář: L'Arte come forma della liberta,* edited by Arturo Schwarz, Milan 1972; *Jiří Kolář: Collagen Rollagen, Chiasmagen, Crumblagen,* exhibition catalog, with text by Paul Wember, Krefeld West Germany 1973; *Jiří Kolář: An Exhibition of Chiasmages, Rollages, Objects, Collages,* exhibition catalog, New York 1975; *Jiří Kolář,* exhibition catalog, with text by Thomas Messer and Jindrich Chalupecky, New York 1975; *Jiří Kolář: Collages* by Angelo Ripellino, Turin 1976; *Jiří Kolář: Transformations,* exhibition catalog, with text by Charlotte Kotik, New York 1978; *Jiří Kolář,* exhibition catalog, with texts by Wieland Schmied, Eberhard Roters and Lucie Schauer, Berlin 1980; *Kolář: Collagen, Rollagen, Chiasmagen, Materialbilder, Objekte,* exhibition catalog, with texts by Thomas Grochowiak and Dietrich Mahlow, Recklinghausen, West Germany 1980; *Jiří Kolář: Untewegs ins Paradies,* exhibition catalog, with texts by Siglinde Hohenstein, Friedrich W. Heckmanns, Hans-Pieter Riese and Claus Groger, Mainz 1980; *Jiří Kolář: Froissages,* exhibition catalog, with text by Gloria Picazo, Barcelona 1981; *Jiří Kolář: Collagen und Objekte aus Berlin und Paris,* exhibition catalog, with texts by Helmut Heissenbuttel and Zdenek Felix, Essen 1981; *Jiří Kolář: Collages, Objectes,* exhibition catalog, with text by Antonio Saura, Barcelona 1982; *Jiří Kolář: Poetry of Vision/Poetry of Silence,* exhibition catalog with preface by Luke Romboudt, Vancouver 1984; *Jiří Kolář: Diary 1968,* exhibition catalog with preface by David Elliott, Oxford 1984; *Jiří Kolář,* exhibition catalog with introduction by Ronald Alley, London 1987; *Jiří Kolář* by Jindrich Chalupecky, Paris 1987; *Dictionnaire des méthodes,* exhibition catalog with introduction by Suzanne Borova, Colomiers, 1993. **Articles—**''Der Mut Eines Denkenden Entdeckers'' by Hans-Peter Riese in *ART: Das Kunstmagazin,* no. 10, October 1994; ''Jiří Kolářr: Dictionnaire des Méthodes: Collage Work of the Czech Artist'' by Vivian Constantinopoulos in *Art & Design,* vol. 9, March/April 1994; ''Jirí Kolář: Auto Collages 1994–1995'' by Tom Lubbock in *Modern Painters* (London), vol. 8, Summer 1995; ''Cutting Edge: Autocollages of Jiří Kolář'' by Ian Hunt in *Art Monthly,* no. 187, June 1995.

*

Art is still capable of making its everyday discoveries of the world as a part of the general effort to achieve universality of knowledge, regardless of what field it takes place—in science, for example. For this reason, the arbitrary has no place in art: there is no room for alien beginnings and processes, but only beginnings and processes which already belong, by their very nature, to the realm of art. It's the same as in science, where nothing can begin in isolation, but only when it's already inherent in the thing itself, as in mathematics. Of course, what matters is always a shift in things. Without this, no creative act has any meaning. Basically, it's impossible to think up anything entirely new.

Every new discovery in art, just as in science, expands the field of human perception and knowledge. This noetic aspect is for me the primary one. The same holds true for all the notions of so-called beauty with which some esthetics operate. If the idea of beauty is continually perfected, then the field of esthetic cognition in general is widened. If art produces a new view of the world, then the whole field of human perception is expanded. Of course, even today it's still possible to paint a beautiful portrait—but Leonardo's portraits were perfect. Van Dyck consummated this perfection such that subsequently it became necessary to begin a new way. Rembrandt had already abandoned all forms of idealization. Picasso enriched his painting with impulses inspired by Negro art, children's drawings, etc.

If art is the art of expanding human consciousness, then no form of this effort can be alien to it. One-sidedness is a great obstacle to such expansion, and may even retard it no matter what direction it may be going, even if it's heading forward. One-sidedness may be possible in times of crisis, but because crisis, it would seem, is something lasting, all the art of our time is somehow crisis-ridden, if not retrogressive, in spite of all the courage and the discoveries it has produced. I would say that one might even distrust it. It genuinely seems more against man than for him.

These questions perhaps aren't relevant to the artist, who needn't concern himself with them in the least, but it's a fact which I personally find essential to any further thinking. Even if art in itself is not something meaningless. Quite the contrary, it's surprising how necessary and useful it can be precisely for showing where modern man is. And this is immensely important. Art, and poetry in particular, is not the consequence of already expanded consciousness, but rather an outcome of the process of expansion. The aim of a picture, a poem, etc., is always to enthrall, and that is ultimately where the significance of all artistic enthusiasm lies. Such enthusiasm will bear fruit in relation to its strength and scope. There's an unwritten law—and it applies to poetry as well—that if one kind of art is no longer capable of expressing something, or if someone thinks a different kind might take him further, it can never be claimed that the new art is redundant. Because, on the contrary, precisely at that point in time, it may be indispensable for expressing the new idea, the new discovery. Today, it's unthinkable that a single approach to creation would be enough to insure development. Each way is no more than necessary, and this very necessity is a proof of its insufficiency. A certain type of art is capable of producing discoveries only as long as it doesn't claim a monopoly on development.

—Jiří Kolář

* * *

The pronunciation of Jiří Kolář's Czech name comes very close to *Collage,* the artist's predominant medium, but the similarity is altogether accidental. (In Czech, *Kolo* means wheel and *Kolář,* therefore, would be something like *Wheeler.*) It is a fact, however, that the collage and various variants have occupied Jiří Kolář intensively since the beginning of the 1960s and to some extent long before.

He got to this art form by indirection, since his first creative metier was not painting, or for that matter any of the plastic arts, but poetry. In a broader sense, Kolář remained, and thinks of himself even now, as a poet but one who has largely departed from reliance upon words in favor of forms, thus having in the main tranferred communicative emphasis from verbal to plastic means.

This gradual transfer takes off from the printed page which Kolář initially covered with his own, compelling Czech poems. These derived partly from Kolář's interest in traditional and modern poetry written in his native tongue and partly from an intense preoccupation with symbolist, futurist and surrealist texts that have become accessible to him in translation. The latter shaped the artist's modern sensibility and awareness.

In any case his verse already in the 1950s showed a tendency towards letterism and developed from there toward concrete and ''evident'' poetry as his formally explicit verbal meanings receded in favor of a new plastic and visual presence. This process completed itself in the 1960s when screws and razor blades, nuts and bolts took the place of words, thereby creating a poetry of things. Such transformations confirmed Kolář's aspirations according to which in his own words, ''The time may come when we shall be making poetry out of anything whatsoever . . . . ''

Given Kolář's interest in placing objects on a flat surface it is not surprising that the collage medium (with which he had exprimented early in the 1930s) would particularly recommend itself. He therefore not only accepted this cubist and surrealist device as his principal plastic expression but developed it toward highly original and personal ends. By controlled crumpling of reproduced images borrowed mostly from art history he created the *crumplage;* by introducing into the collage composition movable parts that could be lifted, the *ventilage;* and through the fragmentation and reconstitution of written and printed texts (which often used occult and arcane alphabets) he created his plastic style through the Greek lettered *chiasmage.* It is these alphabetic surfaces in black and white, sometimes interspersed with pictorial images, used two dimensionally or bulging into relief and sculpture, that have established Kolář's uniqueness and that have recommended him to a world-wide public, first at the 1968 *Documenta* and subsequently in 1969 in Sao Paulo where he carried away the first prize for Czechoslovakia.

His so-called *rollage* is Kolář's alternate, most prominent development. It is based on pictorial rather than lettered content. Here, superimpositions of thin stripes that carry one particular image are carefully spaced to make their impact felt over a ground projecting another. The result is a synthetic double or triple view that is not only witty and humorous but that also has the capacity to vitalize the reproduced material and raise it to the level of an original work of art.

The almost exclusive dependence upon secondary material, printed and reproduced, is characteristic for Kolář's work and sets the artist apart from his Dada and surrealist collage precursors. Disinterested in the cubist use of collage as a means to engage in a dialogue between formal and palpable reality and equally unconcerned with Dada and surrealist anti-art attitudes, Kolář seeks to recreate a ''white humor'' universe that combines a maximum of apparent irreconcilables and that casts its net widely across categoric limitations. His glue and scissors, therefore, assemble fragments from art together with those from life so that the newly created sequences contain (alternatively or occasionally even in a single work) quotations from the cultural heritage and from urban folkart. Art history spoofs thus intermingle with trivia drawn from our quotidian existence and both find a malleable common denominator in the printed matter that constitutes the material, pre-esthetic essence of Kolář's medium. One hardly needs to stress that such consistent reliance upon our printed universe also carries obvious symbolic overtones which, whether deliberately sought or not, sharpen the artist's profile as a witness of his time.

—Thomas Messer

KOMAR and MELAMID

Nationality: American. **Born:** Vitaly Komar born in Moscow, 11 September 11 1943; Alex Melamid born in Moscow, 14 July 1945; became United States citizens, 1978. **Education:** Komar and Melamid attended Moscow Art School, 1958–60; Stroganov Institute of Art and Design, Moscow, 1962–67. **Career:** Began working together in 1965; began the SOTS Art movement (the Soviet version of Western Pop Art), 1967. **Awards:** National Endowment for the Arts grant, 1981. **Agent:** Ronald Feldman Fine Arts, 31 Mercer St., New York, New York 10013.

Selected Joint Exhibitions:

1965 Academy of Art, Vilnius, Lithuania
Stroganov Institute of Art and Design, Moscow
1967 Blue Bird Cafe, Moscow
1968 Scientists Club, Gorodok Academy, Pushino
1972 *Sotsart,* exhibit in private apartment, Moscow
Paradise, installation in private apartment, Moscow
1974 *Art Belongs to the People,* performance in private apartment, Moscow
1976 *Color Is a Mighty Power!,* Ronald Feldman Fine Arts, New York
1977 *TRANSSTATE,* Ronald Feldman Fine Arts, New York
Ohio University Gallery of Fine Arts, Columbus
Berry College, Rome, Georgia
A Space, Toronto
1978 White Gallery, Tel Aviv
MATRIX 43, Wadsworth Atheneum, Hartford, Connecticut
The Temple, Ronald Feldman Fine Arts, New York
1979 *We Buy and Sell Souls* (auction performance), Ronald Feldman Fine Arts, New York
The Hirshhorn Museum and Sculpture Garden, Smithsonian Institution, Washington, D.C.
1980 Ronald Feldman Fine Arts, New York

Edwin A. Ulrich Museum of Art, Wichita State University, Wichita, Kansas (catalog)
1981 Massachusetts College of Art, Boston (lecture-performance)
Museum of Contemporary Art, Chicago (lecture-performance)
1982 *Sots Art,* Ronald Feldman Fine Arts, New York
1983 Portland Center for Visual Arts, Portland, Oregon
Anderson Gallery, Virginia Commonwealth University, Richmond, Virginia
1984 *Business as Usual,* Ronald Feldman Fine Arts, New York
Saidye Bronfman Center, Montreal
Palace Theater of the Arts, Stamford, Connecticut
University of Iowa Museum of Art, Iowa City
1985 Swen Parson Gallery, Northern Illinois University, DeKalb
New Paintings, Ronald Feldman Fine Arts, New York
Fruitmarket Gallery, Edinburgh, travelled to Museum of Modern Art, Oxford; Musée des Arts Decoratifs, Paris; and Arts Council Gallery, Belfast (catalog)
1986 Tyler School of Art, Temple University, Philadelphia
Anarchistic Synthesism, Ronald Feldman Fine Arts, New York
Sable-Castelli Gallery, Toronto
1987 Artspace, Sydney, Australia, travelled to Institute for Modern Art, Brisbane; School of Art Gallery, University of Tasmania, Hobart; Australian Centre of Contemporary Art, Melbourne; Praxis, Perth; Experimental Art Foundation, Adelaide
Ronald Feldman Fine Arts, New York
1988 Kicken Pauseback, Cologne, West Germany
Gallery Paule Anglim, San Francisco
Van Straaten Gallery, Chicago and New Work
Death Poems, Moriarty Gallery, Madrid (catalog)
Galerie Barbara Farber, Amsterdam
Death Poems, Neue Gesellschaft fur Bildende Kunst, West Berlin
1989 Bowdoin College Museum of Art, Brunswick, Maine
Ronald Feldman Fine Arts, New York
Russians in America, University of North Texas, Denton (toured)
Galerie Montenay, FIAC, Paris
1990 *Painting: 1980 to 1986,* Gallery 210, University of Missouri, St. Louis, Missouri
Brooklyn Museum, New York
Forty Monotypes, South Campus Art Gallery, Miami Dade Community College, Miami, Florida
In America, Fuller Elwood Gallery, Seattle
1991 *Paintings for the Holy Rosary Church,* Ronald Feldman Fine Arts, New York
Ljubljana Congress Center, Cankarjev Dom, Yugoslavia
Komar and Melamid: Art/History, The University Gallery, Memphis State, Memphis, Tennessee
1992 *Komar & Melamid: Searstyle with Psalms,* Ronald Feldman Fine Arts, New York
1993 *Death & Immortality,* Ronald Feldman Fine Arts, New York
Proposal for the Lenin Tomb, Contemporary Art Centre, Guelman Gallery, Moscow
1994 *People's Choice,* Contemporary Arts Center/Guelman Gallery, Moscow
People's Choice, Alternative Museum, New York, travelled to Washington Project for the Arts, Washington, D.C., and Herbert F. Johnson Museum of Art, Cornell University, Ithaca, New York
1995 *Between War and Peace: 50 Years After World War II,* Storefront for Art and Architecture, New York
1996 *Made to Order: America's Most Wanted Paintings,* Alternative Museum, New York
1997 *Jukebox: Sound Works,* Copenhagen Contemporary Art Center, Denmark
The Most Wanted—The Most Unwanted Painting, Kunst Museum Ludwig, Köln, Germany
American Dreams, Ronald Feldman Fine Arts, New York
1998 *The People's Choice,* Akron Art Museum, Akron, Ohio (toured United States)
Offbeat: Humor in Life and Art, Eyewash, New York

Selected Group Exhibitions:

1968 Eighth Show of Young Artists, Moscow Artists Union
1974 Outdoor exhibition, Beljaevo, Moscow (show bulldozed by authorities)
Outdoor exhibition, Izmailovsky Park, Moscow, September 29.
1977 *New Art from the Soviet Union,* Arts Club of Washington, D.C., and the Herbert F. Johnson Museum of Art, Cornell University, Ithaca, New York (catalog)
Venice Biennale
1978 *Artist and Society, 1948–1978,* Tel Aviv Museum
1981 *Russian New Wave,* Contemporary Russian Art Center of America, New York
1982 *Counterparts and Affinities,* Metropolitan Museum of Art, New York (catalog)
1984 *Artistic Collaboration in the 20th Century,* Hirshhorn Museum and Sculpture Garden, Smithsonian Institution, Washington, D.C.
An International Survey of Recent Painting and Sculpture, Museum of Modern Art, New York (catalog)
1985 *Correspondences: New York Art Now,* Laforet Museum, Harajuka, Tokyo, travelled to Tochigi Prefectural Museum of Fine Arts, Tochigi, and Tazaki Hall Espace Media, Kobe (catalog)
1986 *Recent Acquisitions,* Museum of Modern Art, New York
Sots Art, New Museum of Contemporary Art, New York (toured; catalog)
Avant Garde in the Eighties, Los Angeles County Museum of Art, Los Angeles (catalog)
Biennale of Sydney, Sydney, Australia
Prospect 86, Frankfurter Kunstverein, Frankfurt, West Germany
1987 *Documenta 8,* Kassel, West Germany (catalog)
Metropolitan Museum of Art, New York
Fifty Years of Collecting: An Anniversary Selection, Solomon R. Guggenheim Museum, New York (catalog)
1988 *Committed to Print,* Museum of Modern Art, New York (catalog)
Hommage/Demontage, Neue Gallery, Museum Ludwig, Aachen, West Germany (toured Europe; catalog)
1989 *Image World: Art and Media Culture,* Whitney Museum of American Art, New York

1991 *Black Lights,* Stedelijk Museum, Amsterdam (catalog)
Soviet Contemporary Art: From Thaw to Perestroika, Setagaya Museum, Tokyo (catalog)
1992 *Parallel Visions: Modern Artists and Outsider Art,* Los Angeles County Museum of Art, Los Angeles
Not For Sale, Tel Aviv Museum of Art, Israel (catalog)
1993 *Monumental Propaganda,* World Financial Center, New York, and Institute of Contemporary Art, Moscow
After Perestroika: Kitchenmaids or Stateswomen, Le Centre International d'art de Montreal, Montreal, Quebec (toured; catalog)
Stalin's Choice: Soviet Socialist Realism 1932–1956, The Institute for Contemporary Art, P.S.1 Museum, Long Island City, New York
1995 *Our Century,* Museum of Modern Art, Cologne, Germany
Monumental Propaganda, Smithsonian Institute, International Gallery, Washington D.C.
1996 *Heroic Painting,* Southeastern Center for Contemporary Art, Winston-Salem, North Carolina (toured; catalog)
Zeitgenossische Kunst im Museum Ludwig, Kunst Museum Ludwig, Cologne, Germany
1999 *The Museum as Muse: Artists Reflect,* Museum of Modern Art, New York (catalog)

Public Installations:

Design for boy and girl scouts' summer camp, Institute of Aviation, Moscow, 1972; Den Haag Municipal Museum, Den Haag, Netherlands, 1986; *Unity,* First Interstate World Center, Los Angeles, 1992–93; murals, Bronx Housing Court Lobby, 1992–95; *Naked Revolution,* The Kitchen, New York, 1997.

Collections:

Australian National Gallery, Canberra Australia; Israel Museum, Jerusalem; Pushkin Museum, Moscow, Russia; Victoria and Albert Museum, London; Russian Museum, St. Petersburg, Russia; Whitney Museum of American Art, New York; Metropolitan Museum of Art, New York; Museum of Modern Art, New York; Solomon R. Guggenheim Museum, New York; Stedelijk Museum, Netherlands.

Publications:

By KOMAR and MELAMID: Books—*Gedichte uber den Tod/ Poem About Death,* NGBK Nishen 1988; *Painting by Numbers: Komar and Melamid's Scientific Guide to Art,* edited by JoAnn Qypijewski, New York 1997; (with Mia Fineman) *When Elephants Paint: The Quest of Two Russian Artists to Save the Elephants of Thailand,* New York 2000. **Articles—**''Ziablov'' in *The Unmuzzled Ox, Poets' Encyclopedia,* vol. 5, no. 4, 1979; ''The Barren Flowers of Evil'' in *Artforum,* March 1980; ''In Search of Religion'' in *Artforum,* May 1980; ''On Constructivism'' in *Print Collector's Newsletter,* no. 11, May-June 1980; ''The Role of the War Ministry in Soviet Art'' in *A-Ya,* no. 2, 1981; ''On the Experiment of Artistic Association in Soviet Russia'' in *Journal of Arts Management and Law,* no. 13, Spring 1983; ''Bayonne, New Jersey, U.S.A'' in *Artforum,* April 1989; ''Beyond Manhattan: Bayonne Manifesto'' in *Glass Art Society Journal,* 1990; ''Extracts from Poem About Death'' in *Lovely Jobly,* vol. 1, no. 1, March 1990; ''Komar & Melamid Kunstlermannerpaare'' in *Kunstforum,* April-May 1990; ''What Is To Be Done?'' in *Spark,* March-April-May 1992; ''What Is to Be Done with Monumental Propaganda'' in *Artforum,* May 1992; ''PostMonument Propaganda: A Proposal'' in *Art & Text,* no. 42, May 1992; ''Painting by Numbers: The Search for a People's Art'' (with others) in *The Nation,* vol. 258, no. 10 14 March 1994.

On KOMAR and MELAMID: Books—*Russian Art 1875–1975,* Austin, Texas 1976; *Komar/Melamid: Two Soviet Dissident Artists,* edited by Melvyn B. Nathanson, Carbondale and Edwardsville, Illinois 1979; *Komar & Melamid,* Edinburgh 1985; *Sots Art,* New York 1986; *Komar & Melamid* by Carter Ratcliff, New York 1988; *Russians in America: Collaborations by Komar and Melamid,* New York 1990; *Sots Art: Soviet Artists of the 1970s and 1980s* by Ekaterina Andreeva, Roseville East, New South Wales, Australia 1995. **Articles—**''Komar & Melamid—Post-USSR—Get Religion'' by Jack Burnham in *Art in America,* no. 67, February 1979; ''Komar & Melamid and the Luxury of Style'' by Marc Fields in *Artforum,* no. 16, April 1982; ''Komar & Melamid Confidential'' by Gary Indiana in *Art in America,* no. 73, June 1985; ''Komar & Melamid'' by Peter Schjeldahl in *Flash Art,* no. 125, December 1985-January 1986; ''Le pop a la mode sovietique'' by Margarita Tupitsyn in *Cahiers du Musee National d'Art Moderne,* Winter 1988; ''A la recherche du pouvoir artistique perdu'' by Boris Groys in *Cahiers-du-Musee-National-d'Art-Moderne,* Winter 1988; ''Vers le realisme capitaliste: Komar et Melamid'' in *Connaissance des Arts,* October 1989; ''Some Uses of Politics: Soviet Art in the West, Before and After Gorbachev'' by Jamey Gambrell in *Kunst and Museumjournaal,* vol. 2 no. 3, 1990; ''Monumental propaganda: solution for Russia's outdated monuments'' by Andrea M. Couture in *Graphis,* July-August 1994; ''Numbers Racket'' by Richard Vine in *Art in America,* October 1994; ''The Art of Democracy'' by Luis Camnitzer in *Art Nexus,* October-December 1994; ''Poll Stars: Komar and Melamid's The People's Choice'' by Andrew Ross in *Artforum International,* January 1995; ''Sond'art: An Exhibition which Reflects the French Taste in Art'' by Denis Picard in *Connaissance des Arts,* October 1995; ''Web-Specific Works: The Internet as a Space for Public Art'' by Miriam Rosen in *Art and Design,* January-February 1996; ''Pavilion politics: Komar and Melamid lose their slot at the Venice Biennale'' by Konstantin Akinsha in *Art News,* June 1997; ''Entretien avec Komar et Melamid'' by Camille Labro in *Beaux Arts Magazine,* April 1998; ''The People's Painting—Only What We Deserve'' by Tom Flynn in *Art Newspaper,* November 1998; ''Komar and Melamid's Dialogue with (Art) History'' by Valerie L. Hillings in *Art Journal,* Winter 1999; ''Wanted: Komar and Melamid'' by Zinovy Zinik in *Modern Painters,* Spring 1999; ''Russland'' by Michael Hubl in *Kunstforum International,* September-November 1999; ''The March of the G.O.P. Elephants'' by David D'Arcy in *Art Newspaper,* September 2000.

* * *

Painters and conceptualists who deploy subversive humor with equal force at the extremes of capitalism and communism, the New York-based Komar and Melamid are media darlings in the West. They have collaborated—often indistinguishably—on social realist pictures, socially critical experiments, and conceptual actions. Chiefly ironic and often political and literary, they tend to elude categorization.

Initially the artists teamed up at Moscow's Stroganov Institute for Art and Design in 1965, when they held the first of their ''one-men'' shows, *Joint Works on the Theory of Art.* They strived to supplant their individual styles with a non-individual version of reality. Inspired by the Pop-Art movement, in 1972 Komar and Melamid coined ''Sots Art,'' a term they derived from ''sotsialisty,'' the Russian word for socialist realism. Their artistic objective, though, was precisely the reverse of Pop-Art, which monumentalized the banal consumer product. They strove to make the exaggeratedly heroic art of the Soviet regime insignificant. To that end, they embraced the establishment artistic style, but tampered with the content, increasing their subversions over time.

When they ventured into whimsical installation, as in the privately shown ''Paradise'' (1973), with its bizarre images of Stalin dripping blood and a lice-covered Buddha, it attracted considerable renown outside the Soviet Union. The team was among the artists whose works were bull-dozed by authorities in the notorious unsanctioned outdoor exhibition in Belijaevo, a suburb of Moscow, in 1974.

Because of the publicity surrounding that incident, as well as the efforts of Melamid's cousin Aleksandr Goldfarb, the pair became well-known in the West beginning in 1974, resulting in feature articles in the *New York Times* and the *Los Angeles Times.* Their series ''Scenes from the Future'' (1974) depicts such capitalist monuments as the Solomon R. Guggenheim Museum and the Kennedy Airport in ruins. The first U.S. show of their work at New York's Ronald Feldman Gallery in 1976 precipitated their dismissal from their jobs as book designers and night-school teachers in Moscow.

In 1977 Komar and Melamid were permitted to emigrate to Israel, and they moved to the United States the following year. Since they were forced to relinquish their Soviet passports, they were temporarily stateless persons. To dramatize that, they created *TransState,* a condition in which each became his own state, and was empowered to enter into alliances, issue his own currency and passports, and so on. They made their own portable border posts to mark the boundaries of their *TransStates.* Their motto was the statement attributed to Louis XIV: ''L'etat, c'est moi.''

Words have long been a part of their work because of the portability of concepts compared to monumental canvases. For ''Color Writing: Ideological Abstraction #1'' (1974) they assigned a color to each letter of the Cyrillic alphabet, then encoded a ''secret'' article in the Soviet constitution that guarantees freedom of speech, assembly, and religion. Quite deliberately, the artists made it impossible to crack the code. In ''Music Writing: Passport,'' Komar and Melamid created an atonal composition by assigning a musical value to each Cyrillic character and then transcribing articles from a Soviet internal passport in that ''alphabet.''

A gleeful period of post-Soviet recycling occurred in the period around 1990, when the artists returned to the familiar terrain of their artistic origins to contemplate possible solutions for disposing of the ''devotional'' images of Soviet leaders being retired. Lenin's tomb in Moscow was a drawing board for their imaginations: they proposed mounting an electronic message board above the entrance displaying the word ''Leninism,'' but only on days associated with his name; on the other days there would be a never-ending series of changing texts, including poetry, weather reports, and news. They suggested that pink flamingoes might wander about on the roof of the mausoleum where the party leaders once stood.

Komar and Melamid placed a call to artists in *Artforum* seeking proposals for transforming thousands of paintings, statues, and busts of former Soviet leaders into objects of practical or philosophical worth. They subsequently displayed the proposals in 26 wooden cases supported on upturned plaster busts of Stalin.

''The People's Choice,'' a multi-layered project, commenced with hiring polling agencies to query audiences in 17 nations about their specific visual art preferences. Komar and Melamid converted the questionnaire results ''scientifically'' into two paintings per country: the most desired and the least wanted. Questioning the relationship between artist and client, the results included the obvious and the unexpected, with ''America's Most Beautiful'' featuring George Washington and a deer in an autumnal landscape.

The project tended to confirm Komar and Melamid's ideas about the ''universality'' of art, since the paintings from the 17 countries all bear striking resemblances to one another. The artists, however, avoided any conclusions, and presented the whole as the traveling exhibition *People's Choice: The Polling of America,* which included photocopies of the full poll results beside the resulting canvases. A book with reproductions of all of the research and responses, and a web site seeking data on the ''Internet's Most Wanted Painting'' followed.

Building upon an abiding interest in empowering animals to paint, the pair responded to an article about hungry and jobless Thai elephants in 1995 by establishing an academy of art there to teach elephants to produce abstract expressionist paintings. The relationship between the storybook humanitarian idea of training endangered elephants to paint on easels and the fantasy quality of Bangkok, the city where the works produced were auctioned at the Hilton International, appealed to them. The artists' satire always has an underlying intelligence. The project, more than about elephants, is about Asia's economic crisis and the need to adapt to change, with the beneficiaries being the children who care for and train the elephants.

Komar in Hebrew means ''priest'' (in Russian it means ''gadfly'') and Melamid means ''teacher.'' Always erudite and attentive to the spirit, impish Komar and Melamid take Duchampian pleasure in whimsy while plumbing the very philosophical quandaries of our times.

—Deirdre Donohue

KOONS, Jeff

Nationality: American. **Born:** York, Pennsylvania, 1955. **Education:** Maryland Institute College of Art, Baltimore, 1972; School of the Art Institute of Chicago, 1975; Contemporary Art Mecca, New York, 1976. **Career:** Worked at the Cotton Stock Exchange to finance his artistic production, 1979; leading exponent of Neo Geo, a movement that also included Ashley Bickerton, Peter Halley, Haim Steinbach, and Meyer Vaismann, 1986.

Selected Individual Exhibitions:

1980 *The New (window installation),* New Museum of Contemporary Art, New York

1985 *Equilibrium,* Feature Gallery, Chicago, Illinois (traveled to International With Monument Gallery, New York)

Jeff Koons in front of his sculpture *Puppy,* 1977. ©Archive Photos, Inc.

1986 *Luxury and Degradation,* Daniel Weinberg Gallery, Los Angeles, California (traveled to International With Monument Gallery, New York)
1987 *The New: Encased Works 1981–1986,* Daniel Weinberg Gallery, Los Angeles, California
1988 *Banality,* Donald Young Gallery, Chicago, Illinois (traveled to Sonnabend Gallery, New York; Galerie Max Hetzler, Cologne, Germany)
Museum of Contemporary Art, Chicago, Illinois
1989 *Jeff Koons—Nieuw Werk,* Galerie 'T Venster, Rotterdamse Kunststichting, Rotterdam, Netherlands
1991 *Made In Heaven,* Galerie Max Hetzler, Cologne, Germany (toured)
1992 Stedelijk Museum, Amsterdam (traveled to Staatsgalerie Stuttgart, Germany; San Francisco Museum of Modern Art, California; Walker Art Center, Minneapolis, Minnesota)
1994 Anthony d'Offay Gallery, London
1997 Galerie Jérôme de Noirmont, Paris (catalog)
Guggenheim Museum, Bilbao, Spain
1998 *Encased,* Anthony d'Offay Gallery, London
1999 Sonnabend Gallery, New York
2000 *Puppy,* Rockefeller Center, New York,
Easyfun, Sonnabend Gallery, New York

Selected Group Exhibitions:

1982 *Energie New York,* Espace Lyonnais D'Art Contemporain, Lyon, France
1985 *Signs II,* Michael Klein Inc., New York (traveled to Galerie Crousel-Hussenot, Paris)
1986 *Damaged Goods,* New Museum of Contemporary Art, New York (traveled to Otis Parsons Exhibition Center, Los Angeles, California)
1987 *Collection Sonnabend,* Centro de Arte Reina Sofia, Madrid (traveled to CAPC, Bordeaux, France)
Les Courtiers du Desir, Galeries Contemporaines, Centre Georges Pompidou, Paris
1988 *The Bi-National,* Kunsthalle, Dusseldorf, Germany (traveled to Boston Museum of Fine Arts, Massachusetts)
Artschwager: His Peers and Persuasion, 1963–1988, Leo Castelli Gallery, New York
1989 *Image World,* Whitney Museum of American Art, New York
1990 *1990-Energies,* Stedelijk Museum, Amsterdam
1990–91 *High & Low: Modern Art and Popular Culture,* Museum of Modern Art, New York (traveled to Art Institute of Chicago, Illinois; Museum of Contemporary Art, Los Angeles, California) (catalog)
1991 *Power: Its Myths, Icons, and Structures in American Culture, 1961–1991,* Indianapolis Museum of Art, Indiana (traveled to Akron Art Museum, Ohio; Virginia Museum of Fine Arts, Richmond)
1992 *Strange Developments,* Anthony d'Offay Gallery, London
Post Human, Musee D'Art Contemporain Pully, Lausanne, Switzerland
1997–98 *On the Edge: Contemporary Art from the Werner and Elaine Dannheisser Collection,* Museum of Modern Art, New York
1999–2000 *The American Century: Art & Culture 1900–2000 Part II, 1950–2000,* Whitney Museum of American Art, New York (catalog)
2000 *Apocalypse,* Royal Academy of Arts, London

Publications:

By KOONS: Articles—''Luxury and Desire: An Interview with Jeff Koons'' by Giancarlo Politi in *Flash Art,* no. 132, February-March 1987; ''Collaborations'' by Jeff Koons and Martin Kippenberger in *Parkett,* no. 19, 1989; ''Gym-Dandy: An Interview with Jeff Koons'' by Robert Storr in *Art Press,* no. 151, October 1990.

On KOONS: Books—*Post- to Neo-: The Art World of the Eighties* by Calvin Tompkins, New York 1988; *Jeff Koons* by I. Michael Danoff, Chicago 1988; *The Jeff Koons Handbook,* edited by Anthony d'Offay, New York 1992; *Jeff Koons* by John Caldwell, San Francisco 1992; *Art on the Edge and Over: Searching for Art's Meaning in Contemporary Society 1970s-1990s* by Linda Weintraub, Litchfield, Connecticut 1996. **Articles—**''Pretty as a Product'' by Dan Cameron in *Arts Magazine,* no. 60, May 1986; ''Jeff Koons: Case Study'' by Jean-Christophe Amman in *Parkett,* no. 19, 1989; ''Big Fun: Four Reactions to Jeff Koons'' by Stuart Morgan, et al in *Artscribe,* no. 74, March-April 1990; ''L'Industria dell'Arte'' by Jeffrey Deitch in *Flash Art,* June 1991; ''Beyond Redemption'' by Jim Lewis in

Artforum, Summer 1991; ''Not for Repro'' by Carter Ratcliff in *Artforum,* February 1992; ''Appropriation Under the Gun'' by Martha Buskirk in *Art in America,* June 1992; ''The Real Cliché'' by Pamela Haskin in *New Art Examiner,* December 1993.

* * *

A quintessential postmodern artist, Jeff Koons uses consumer products that saturate the world around us and exhibits them as high art objects. Koons has created works that address issues of consumerism and class distinction through his choice of subject matter and materials. As an appropriation artist, Koons takes manufactured products such as basketballs, inflatable toy rabbits, and advertisements and exhibits them as art. While similar to the Dada artist Marcel Duchamp who used everyday objects to question the status of the art object, Koons targets consumer culture. As such, Koons's work is equally indebted to the works of 1960s Pop artists, such as Andy Warhol's series of Campbell soup cans, Tom Wesselman's interiors filled with consumer products, and Roy Lichtenstein's Ben Day dots replicating mechanical reproduction, which all target the growing presence of mass-produced items in contemporary culture.

In his earliest works from 1979, Koons focused on the aesthetics of display and introduced his interest in consumerism in his arrangements of inflatable flowers and rabbits. His next series, *The New* (1980–82), which consisted of vacuum cleaners displayed in neon-lit cases and advertising posters, attempted to replicate the newness of manufactured objects. In 1985, Koons continued this interest, but redirected it towards issues of class. Composed of basketballs floating in tanks and advertisements featuring African-American basketball players, his *Equilibrium* (1985) series makes reference to the possibilities for social mobility that basketball offers to inner-city African-American youth. Accompanied with heavy, bronze sculptures of lifesaving devices, this series serves as a metaphor for the struggle that accompanies the possibility of social mobility.

In his next two series, Koons focused on items cast in stainless steel. His *Luxury and Degradation* series (1986) uses objects that refer to the consumption of alcohol. For example, *Jim Beam—J.B. Turner Train* is a toy train cast in stainless steel and filled with bourbon. Koons's choice of this odd juxtaposition of a child's toy and an adult beverage highlights the oddities that appeal to consumers. Koons's next series, *Statuary* (1986), is characterized by an inflatable toy rabbit cast in stainless steel. Accompanied by other objects, such as a stainless steel bust of Louis XIV, the reflective surfaces of these works are intended to comment on the reflective nature of art—that art reflects those who produce or collect it. Koons's frequent use of stainless steel also alludes to consumers' desire for luxury items, or at least objects that resemble luxury items.

Koons's interest in non-utilitarian kitsch objects became the exclusive focus of his *Banality* series (1988). This series includes his popular work, *Michael Jackson and Bubbles,* which depicts the well-known musician with his pet monkey in a bright white ceramic with gold details. In exhibiting banal objects, Koons hoped to reach a popular audience through his juxtapositions and transformations of the original objects into the realm of high art. While ultimately elevating kitsch to high art, he retains their kitsch quality by emulating traditionally low culture aesthetics.

In his *Made in Heaven* series (1989–1992), Koons turns to the subject of sex. Here, glossy, airbrushed photographic images set in a technicolor fantasyland and the ''Kama Sutra'' series of colored glass figurines depict Koons and his wife at the time, Ilona Stalla, a former porn star and member of Italian Parliament, engaging in explicit sexual acts. In response to arguments that these works constitute pornography, Koons insists that he is more concerned with love and spirituality. He argues that these depictions of graphic sexual acts between a husband and wife, which were exhibited alongside representations of flowers and dogs, are not pornographic if they eliminate the shame and the resulting arousal associated with viewing such material.

Throughout Koons's career, the reception of his work has varied considerably. Many scholars and critics have praised him as a postmodern genius, but just as many have responded with hostility and disgust claiming that he is an opportunistic, market-driven egomaniac. Often referred to as the most publicized American artist after Warhol, Koons candidly admits that he actively sought to become an art world celebrity. Koons exploited 1980s consumerism and used skillfully devised marketing strategies learned as a Wall Street commodities broker and as a salesperson selling Museum of Modern Art memberships to market both his image and his art. In line with his business mentality, Koons creates his works like a businessman; he oversees the production while other artists do the hands-on labor. In his aim to achieve fame, he targeted his art to the masses, using common, banal subjects, and used his inflated prices to attract collectors who wanted to display their own wealth and power. In this way, Koons simultaneously catered to the elitist nature of art through high prices and the masses through popular subjects.

In order to fashion himself as art world celebrity, Koons creatively manipulated the media. For instance, when he was not invited to participate in the 1992 Documenta International Art Fair in Kassel, Germany, Koons constructed a forty-foot high puppy covered with living flowers to make his presence known and successfully dominated the press for the fair. Similarly, although probably unintentionally, Koons has been involved in several copyright lawsuits. The most publicized case, *Art Rogers v. Jeff Koons/Sonnabend Gallery* from 1990, involved Koons's sculpture *String of Puppies* (1988), which quoted Rogers's greeting-card photograph of a couple holding a litter of German Shephard puppies. Koons argued that his use of the image was fair use and sought to establish legal precedent for appropriation as parody, but the court ruled that this sculpture constituted unauthorized use of a copyrighted work because the parody was not obvious. While Koons did not orchestrate these court cases, he benefited from the free publicity.

In the spring of 2000, Koons returned to Sonnabend Gallery for a solo exhibition, his first in New York since his controversial 1991 show. *Easyfun* included large monochromatic mirrors shaped to suggest cartoon characters as well as a few oil paintings and sculptures. This exhibition revealed Koons's return to banal subjects from popular culture.

—Sharon Matt Atkins

KOPYSTIANSKY, Igor and Svetlana

Nationality: Russian. **Born:** Igor: Lvov, Ukraine, 1954; Svetlana: Voronez, Russia, 1950. **Career:** Worked as unofficial artists in Moscow in 1970s and 1980s and made many unofficial underground exhibitions and performances; after Russia's political climate made it possible, their work was exhibited internationally; moved to the United States in 1988; artists-in-residence, Artist Program of DAAD,

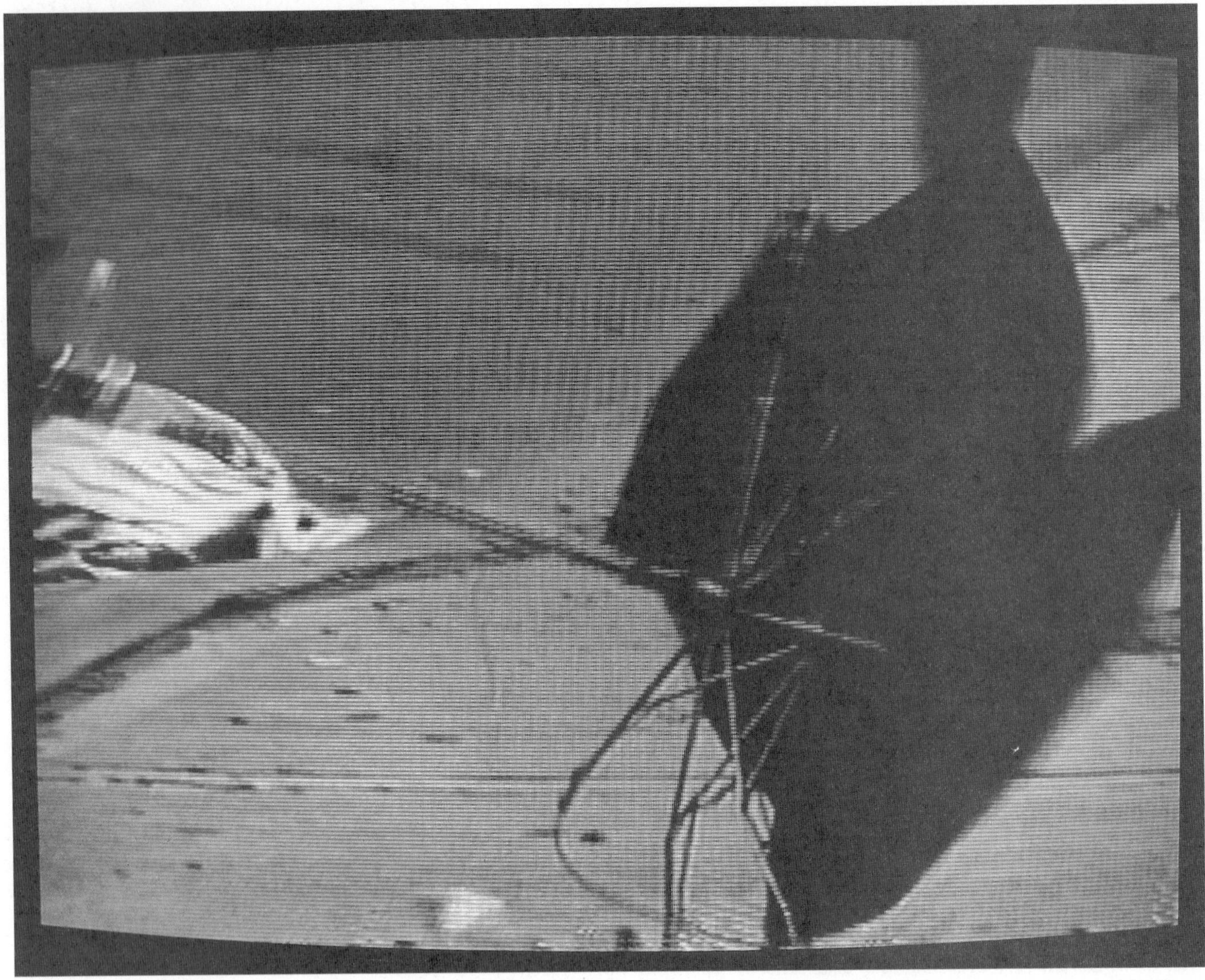

Igor and Svetlana Kopystiansky: *Incidents,* 1998. ©Igor and Svetlana Kopystiansky.

Berlin, 1990. **Awards:** Both: DAAD grant, 1990; Svetlana: Käthe-Kollwitz-Preis, Academy of Art, Berlin, 2000. **Agent:** Lisson Gallery, 52–54 Bell Street, London NW1 5DA, England. **Address:** 526 West 26th Street, #608, New York, New York 10001, U.S.A.

Selected Individual Exhibitions:

2000 Muzeum Sztuki, Lodz

Selected Group Exhibitions:

1992 Sydney Biennial
1994 Sao Paulo Biennial
1995 Istanbul Biennial (catalog)
1997 2nd Johannesburg Biennale (catalog)
1997 Lyon Biennale (catalog)
1999 *Trace,* First British Biennial of Contemporary Art, Tate Gallery, Liverpool (catalog)
Cocido y Crudo, Reina Sofia, Madrid
Szenewechsel, Museum of Moderne Kunst, Frankfurt
Chronos and Kairos, Museum Fridericianum (catalog)
Wait, Kunst-Werke, Berlin
2000 *Children of Berlin,* Folkwang Museum, Essen
Moment, Dundee Contemporary Arts (catalog)
Incidents, Kunstmuseum, Düsseldorf
2001 *Armory Show,* Lisson Gallery, New York

Publications:

On KOPYSTIANSKY: Books—*Igor and Svetlana Kopystiansky,* Berlin and München, 1991; *Shadow of Gravitation,* Orange Siemens, 1996; *Dialog,* exhibition catalog, with text by Barbara Barsch, Hannes Bohringer, and Heinz Schutz, Berlin 1998.

* * *

When art from what was then still the Soviet Union began appearing in Western galleries in the late 1980s, it was like something out of a science fiction tale—the kind in which a sort of tunnel suddenly opens up between a parallel universe and our own, making the latter, too, seem unexpectedly strange. While most of the formal moves in the repertoire of the ''unofficial'' or ''nonconformist'' artists from Russia would have been familiar to anyone conversant with European and American Pop and Conceptual Art, underlying them was a distinctive ethos that was quite unlike anything we'd encountered before.

Igor and Svetlana Kopystiansky were among the most notable of those artists, perhaps the outstanding exponents of what might be called the ''second generation'' of the new Soviet avant-garde. Its pioneers, like Ilya Kabakov and Erik Bulatov, had been born in the 1930s, and their art was essentially a product of the 1960s. By the time the Kopystianskys began making their work in the late 1970s, much had changed, and the difference between the two generations can perhaps be summed up by saying that, whereas the earlier artists seemed to address a nearly hermetically sealed-off Soviet reality, the work of artists like the Kopystianskys implied horizons that had already somehow been broadened. By the time the Soviet Union actually broke up in 1991, most of the significant Russian artists had relocated to one or another of the Western capitals—Berlin, Paris, New York—but it is significant that, while an artist like Kabakov has never ceased to reflect on the experience of Soviet Russia even as the memory of it seems to fade into oblivion, the Kopystianskys have been able to make work that reflects their experiences in New York, Berlin, and elsewhere without rejecting anything of their origins: their work today is still consistent with what they first sent West more than a decade ago.

The Kopystianskys seem to have an unusually flexible and equilibrated relationship as artists who are also a couple. They work (in the same studio) mostly separately, sometimes together; they exhibit mostly together, sometimes separately. Each one has a clearly marked artistic persona, yet their work moves easily between parallelism and complementarity.

But the paradigm for Igor's work is essentially that of painting, while for Svetlana's, language is the underlying model. And yet for neither of them is the paradigm closed; it is incomplete or even, one might say, broken or wounded. Some of Igor's works have taken the form of academic-style paintings (painted by himself) which were then torn or lacerated, then patched up with approximate copies of the same paintings. In other words, these paintings display their own vulnerability; also the possibility that painting might ''heal'' its own damage; and finally the inadequacy of that same reparation. In the process, furthermore, the paintings tended to lose their purely pictorial status to become manifest as objects. In Svetlana's works made from texts that have been broken into parts and then systematically interwoven, our ability to infer meaning from even the most disjointed linguistic sequences comes into a sort of competition with the fragility of communication.

In both cases, there is a sort of double perspective. Something—whether painting or language—fails and succeeds at the same time. Moreover, it is possible that painting and language succeed just insofar as they fail, and vice-versa. A clear example of this may be found in the work Svetlana made for the Skulptur Projeckte Münster in 1997: two sets of photograph, one of objects used by other artists in the exhibition as means to produce their artworks, photographed in situ outdoors, and one of objects used by construction workers during the restoration of the Westfälisches Landesmuseum there. Her intention, forcefully fulfilled by the images themselves, was to present those objects as already in themselves sculpture. The irony and melancholy of the work emerge from the fact that these sculptures could only be brought into being—or into consciousness, which may well be the same thing—by means of photography, while the objects themselves had already disappeared. One could only see them as sculptures insofar as it was too late to see them as sculptures. That same year, at the Johannesburg Biennale, Igor showed, amidst the classical European paintings at the Johannesburg Art Gallery, cut-up fragments of paintings which had been rolled up on dowels—again, parts of destroyed paintings, yet communicating the sense of preserving some essence of painting, though precisely because they could no longer be viewed as such (in contrast to what might seem to be the almost brutally or heartlessly whole pictures that surrounded these poor objects).

The Kopystianskys' slide projection piece *The Day Before Tomorrow* (1998–99) gives one very clear and touching metaphor for the way their togetherness/separateness as artists articulates the quandary at the heart of their distinct bodies of work: its two screens show two different versions of the same everyday events on the streets of New York, one shot by Svetlana and one by Igor. With each screen reflecting a slightly different angle (and not necessarily at the same moment), it is as though each artist were but a single eye, but where then is the brain in which these two inputs can be synthesized into a single three-dimensional, perspectival image? That of God? Or maybe just the ideally imaginative and sympathetic viewer?

—Barry Schwabsky

KOSICE, Gyula

Nationality: Argentinian. **Born:** Kosice, Czechoslovakia, 26 April 1924. Emigrated to Argentina, 1928: subsequently naturalized. **Education:** Academia de Bellas Artes, Buenos Aires, 1938–42. **Family:** Married Diyi Laan in 1947; daughters: Vivian Luz and Irina Sol. **Career:** Independent artist, Buenos Aires, from 1944: founder, *Arturo* magazine, 1944, and *Concrete Invention Art* magazine, 1945; works with neon gas being used for the first time in the world; father of the Hydrospatial City as announced in *Arturo* (1944) and ''Manifesto Madí'' (1946); founder-director, Madi art movement, Buenos Aires, 1946–58. Argentine commissioner for the *Bienal de Sao Paulo,* 1961; Venice *Biennale,* 1962; *Biennale de Paris,* 1963. **Awards:** National Sculpture Prize, Instituto Di Tella, Buenos Aires, 1962; Acquisition Prize, Museo Nacional de Bellas Artes, Buenos Aires, 1966; Casa Argentina in Israel Prize, Museo de Arte Moderno, Buenos Aires, 1967; Award of Honour, Sociedad Argentina de Escritores, 1968; Fondo Nacional de Las Artes Prize, Buenos Aires, 1971; Hidronor Prize, Buenos Aires, 1972; Konex Prize, Buenos Aires, 1982; Book Prize, Associacion Argentina de Criticos de Arte, 1982; Literature Prize, Municipality of Buenos Aires, 1986; Sculpture Prize, Museo Sivori, 1987; *Chevalier des Arts et Lettres,* France 1989. **Addresses:** (studio) Humahuaca 4662, Buenos Aires 1192, Argentina; (home) Republica de la India 3135–6A, 1425 Buenos Aires, Argentina. **Web site:** www.kosice.com.ar.

Individual Exhibitions:

1947 Galerias Pacifico, Buenos Aires
1953 Galeria Bonino, Buenos Aires
1960 Galerie Denise Rene, Paris
Drian Gallery, London
1963 Galerie L'Oeil, Paris

1964 Galerie La Hune, Paris
1965 Terry Dintenfass Gallery, New York
1966 Galeria de Arte Moderno, Cordoba, Argentina
1967 Bonino Gallery, New York
1968 Instituto Di Tella/Galeria Bonino, Buenos Aires
1969 Galerie Lacloche, Paris
1970 Estudio Actual, Caracas
1971 Galeria Bonino, Buenos Aires
1972 Galeria de Arte del Banco Continental, Lima
1972 Museo Teatro San Martin, Buenos Aires
1973 Biblioteca Luis Angle Arango, Bogota, Colombia
1974 Israel Museum, Jerusalem
Espace Cardin, Paris
1975 Galeria Pozzi, Buenos Aires
Espace Cardin, Paris
1977 Galeria La Ciudad, Buenos Aires (retrospective)
International Water Conference, Mar del Plata, Argentina
Galeria Birger, Buenos Aires
1979 Galeria Unika, Punta del Este, Uruguay
City Planetarium, Buenos Aires
1982 Hakone Open-Air Museum, Tokyo
Plaza de la Ingenieria, La Plata, Argentina
Secretaria de Cultura, Quilmes, Buenos Aires
1983 Casa de la Cultura, Cordoba, Argentina
1985 Centro Cultural Recoleta, Buenos Aires
1988 Olympic Stadium, Seoul, Korea
1991 Museo Nacional de Bellas Artes, Buenos Aires (retrospective)

Selected Group Exhibitions:

1948 *Salon des Realites Nouvelles,* Paris (and 1963)
1956 *38th Biennale,* Venice
1964 *New Art from Argentina,* Walker Art Center, Minneapolis
1968 *Documenta 4,* Museum Fridericianum, Kassel, West Germany
1970 *Kinetics,* Hayward Gallery, London
1976 *2nd Triennale of Photography,* Israel Museum, Jerusalem
1981 *Operation Equinoxe 80,* Centre Georges Pompidou, Paris
1988 *International Sculpture Exhibition,* Garden of Sculpture, Seoul, Korea
1989 *Art in Latin America,* Art Council, London (travelled to Stockholm and Madrid)
1993 *Latin American Artists,* Museum of Modern Art, New York

Collections:

Museo Nacional de Bellas Artes, Buenos Aires; Museo de Arte Moderno, Buenos Aires; Musée d'Art Moderne, Grenoble, France; Museo Nacional de Bellas Artes, Montevideo; Centre Georges Pompidou/Musée National d'Art Moderne, Paris; Moderna Museet, Stockholm; Israel Museum, Jerusalem; Museum of Fine Arts, Houston.

Publications:

By KOSICE: Books—*Invencion,* Buenos Aires 1945; *Manifesto Madí,* Buenos Aires 1946; *Golse-Se,* Buenos Aires 1952; *Peso y medida de Alberto Hidalgo,* Buenos Aires 1953; *Antologia Madi,* Buenos Aires 1955; *Geocultura de la Europa de hoy,* Buenos Aires and Paris 1959; *Poème hydraulique,* Paris 1960; *Arte hidrocinetico,* Buenos Aires 1968; *La ciudad hidroespacial,* Buenos Aires 1972; *Arte y arquitectura del agua,* Caracas 1974; *Arte Madi,* Buenos Aires 1982; *Obra poetica,* Buenos Aires 1984; *Entrevisiones,* Buenos Aires 1985; *Teoria sobre el arte,* Buenos Aires 1987; *A partir de Arte Madí,* Buenos Aires 1993. **Articles**—''Arte y realidad virtual,'' *La Nacion,* 19 December 1993.

On KOSICE: Books—*Non-figurative Art Trends in Latin America,* edited by George Wittenborn, New York 1957; *Las esculturas hidraulicas de Kosice* by Guy Habasque, Santa Fe 1960; *Art in Latin America Today: Argentina* by Manuel Mujica Lainz, Washington, D.C. 1961; *Kosice entre Calder et Tinguely* by Otto Hahn, Paris 1964; *Kosice* by Guy Habasque, Paris 1965; *Naissance de l'art cinetique* by Frank Popper, Paris 1967; *Escultura Argentina de vanguardia* by Romualdo Brughetti, Buenos Aires 1970; *Madi y la vanguardia argentina* by Jorge B. Rivera, Buenos Aires 1976; *Science and Technology in Art* by Stewart Kranz, New York 1980; *Science + Art* by Ans van Berkum, Utrecht 1986; *Lenguaje y entropia,* by José García Mayoraz, Buenos Aires 1989; *L'art abstrait* by Michel Ragon, Switzerland 1992; *Latin American Art of the 20th Century,* by Edward Lucie Smith, New York & London 1993. **Articles**—''The Madis'' in *Time,* 16 December 1946; ''Gyula Kosice: The Water Tamer'' by Bonnie Tucker in *Comments on Argentine Trade,* June-July 1994; ''Kosice Homenajeado en el Mam'' in *Mensual,* 15 June 1994; ''Variaciones espaciales'' by Marina Gambier in *La Nacion,* 15 October 2000.

* * *

The work of Gyula Kosice, one of the forerunners in the renewal of abstract forms in the post-war years, enlarges the field of kinetic research by its original use of an element virtually unexplored in plastic terms: water.

The wide range of the artist's interests, including sculpture and painting, poetry and theoretical essays, the monumental or architectural quality of some of his works, and the cosmic implications he draws from the dynamics of the creative process all make of Kosice a multi-faceted artist for whom the liberating function of the imagination finds its expression in the elaboration of a rational system.

Born in Czechoslovakia, Kosice was taken to Argentina at the age of four and received Argentinian citizenship. He studied at the Academy of Fine Arts in Buenos Aires and stayed on in Buenos Aires to pursue his artistic career. From 1944 he became involved with a group of young artists who were rebelling against establishment trends in Argentina—still dominated by the epigones of the Paris School—and drawing their inspiration from the Bauhaus, Constructivism and Max Bill in an attempt to develop an abstract language that was ''pure and hard.'' With them Kosice founded the Madi movement, becoming its leading theoretican and organiser. Bypassing the over-rigorous system of ''concrete'' art, he developed what was to become the theoretical basis for his own researches: ''to invent objects for a classless society which liberates energy and dominates space and time in all its fullness, and matter as far as its ultimate consequences'' (*The Madi Manifesto,* 1946). It was around this time too that he met the Italo-Argentinian sculptor Lucio Fontana and witnessed the publication of the first spatialist manifesto.

Open to all manner of technical experimentation, Kosice first exhibited a collection of paintings with irregular mounts, worked in blocks of colour, but it was to sculpture that he was to turn definitively, forcing dynamic effects from matter in order to create an impression of movement. His preference was for non-traditional materials, frequently of industrial origin, such as aluminum, Plexiglas, glass and iron wire, and he executed two particularly innovative works at this time: one, in wood, mobile, jointed and transformable; the other a ''luminary structure'' of geometrical shape modelled out of a neon tube.

In 1948 he exhibited with the Madi artists at the *Salon des realites nouvelles* in Paris. This exhibition marked for him the beginning of an international career which would lead him, a few years later, to show his first hydrokinetic works at the Denise Rene gallery. One particular quality can help us to define the aesthetic of these sculptures: transparency, proceeding from a desire to appropriate the space without disturbing its visual unity. From now on, Kosice was to work principally with translucent materials (Plexiglas, glass fibres) which asserted or effaced themselves under the spectator's gaze in a seductive play of appearances and reflections. The sculptures were composed in a subtle balance of fixed and mobile pieces. But it was through the use of water that the artist perfected the dynamisation of his sculptural system. The element of chance deriving from the displacement of liquid masses and from the very nature of water, which is intrinsically mobile and transformable, disrupted the traditional relationships of fullness—emptiness, depth—leading Kosice to exercise scientific control over his materials. His formal language appropriated, by metaphorical transcriptions, the diverse forms which water can take: the bubbles, drops, jets, fountains, splashes, waves, pools of the liquid part of the works became spheres, cylinders or planes in their solid representations.

Gradually, the works were to expand in extent and complexity to become veritable polysensorial environments, bringing together over large surfaces, from the ground to the walls, luminous and sonorous elements which completed the hydraulic effects.

Naturally, Kosice also came to consider the architectural implications of his work, and its capacity to intervene directly in the transformation of the social environment. He realised a number of fountains and urban sculptures in various Latin American cities, as for example his impressive *Water Tower* (Buenos Aires, 1972), a hydraulic composition of monumental proportions which has as its base a long cylinder reaching up towards the sky.

Kosice's *Hydrospatial City,* shown in France in 1974, provided the synthesis of his architectural ideas. It consisted of the futurist projection in space of a revolutionary and liberating social structure so that ''imprecise science becomes superhuman.'' Presented in the form of plans and models, the transparent cosmic city suppresses current divisions in living spaces, insisting on a necessary improvement in human relations. Its realisation is scientifically plausible thanks to the energy potential contained in the hydraulic power of clouds. Through this work the Argentinian artist developed ''an invitation to take part in the supreme journey of technological humanism, an appeal to feel more acutely, to see higher and further, to live better'' (Pierre Restany, Kosice exhibition catalog at Espace Cardin, 1974).

—Dominique Liquois

KOSSOFF, Leon

Nationality: British. **Born:** London, 7 December 1926. **Education:** St. Martin's School of Art, London, 1949–53; also attended evening classes at the Borough Polytechnic, London, under David Bomberg, 1949–53; Royal College of Art, London, 1953–56. **Military Service:** Jewish Brigade and Royal Fusiliers, in France, Belgium, Holland and Germany, 1945–48. **Family:** Married Rosalind Pearl in 1954; son: David. **Career:** Independent painter, London, since 1956; member, London Group, 1962. Lecturer, Regent Street Polytechnic, London, 1959–64, Chelsea School of Art, London, 1959–64, and St. Martin's School of Art, London, 1966–69. **Agent:** Anthony d'Offay Gallery, 9 Dering Street, London, W1. **Address:** 147 Chatsworth Road, London NW2, England.

Individual Exhibitions:

1957 Beaux Arts Gallery, London
Bruton Place Gallery, London
1959 Beaux Arts Gallery, London
1961 Beaux Arts Gallery, London
1963 Beaux Arts Gallery, London
1964 Beaux Arts Gallery, London
1968 Marlborough Fine Art, London
1972 *Recent Paintings,* Whitechapel Art Gallery, London
1973 Fischer Fine Art, London
1974 *Recent Drawings and Paintings,* Fischer Fine Art, London
1975 Fischer Fine Art, London
1979 Fischer Fine Art, London
1980 Riverside Studios, London
1981 *Paintings from a Decade 1970–1980,* Museum of Modern Art, Oxford (travelled to the Graves Art Gallery, Sheffield, Yorkshire)
1982 L.A. Louver Gallery, Los Angeles
1983 Hirschl and Adler Modern Gallery, New York
1984 Fischer Fine Art, London
L.A. Louver Gallery, Los Angeles
1988 *Leon Kossoff: Recent Paintings,* Anthony d'Offay Gallery (also Robert Miller Gallery), London
1993 *Leon Kossoff: Drawings 1985–1992,* Anthony d'Offay Gallery, London (also LA Louver Gallery, Los Angeles)
Leon Kossoff, Rex Irwin Art Dealer, Woollahra (catalog)
1995 *Leon Kossoff: Recent Paintings,* British Pavilion, Venice (traveled to Stedelijk Museum, Amsterdam) (catalog)
1996 *Leon Kossoff,* Tate Gallery, London
2000 *Leon Kossoff,* Mitchell-Innes & Nash Gallery, New York
2001 Annandale Galleries, Sydney
J. Paul Getty Museum, Malibu, California

Selected Group Exhibitions:

1963 *British Painting in the 60s,* Tate Gallery, London
1964 *Painting and Sculpture of a Decade 1954–64,* Tate Gallery, London
1967 *Recent British Painting,* Tate Gallery, London
1974 *Body and Soul,* Walker Art Gallery, Liverpool
1977 *British Painting 1952–1977,* Royal Academy of Arts, London

Leon Kossoff: *Booking Hall, Kilburn Underground,* 1987. ©Tate Gallery, London/Art Resource, NY; courtesy of Tate Gallery.

1979 *The British Art Show,* Mappin Art Gallery, Sheffield (toured Britain)

1981 *13 Britische Kunstler,* Neue Galerie, Aachen, West Germany

1985 *The British Show,* Art Gallery of Western Australia, Perth (travelled)

1987 *A School of London,* Kunstnernes Hus, Oslo (travelled)

1988 *The British Picture,* L.A. Louver Gallery, Venice, California

1991 *Freud, Kossoff,* Tate Gallery, London
1993 *Drawing on these Shores: A View of British Drawing and Its Affinities,* Harris Museum and Art Gallery, Presont, Ipswich
1994 *Double Reality,* Astrup Fearnley Museet for Modrene Kunst, Oslo, Norway
1995 *Identity and Alterity: Figures of the Body 1895–1995,* XLVI Venice Biennale, Italy
From London, Scottish National Gallery, Edinburgh (traveling exhibition) (catalog)
1998 *L'Ecole des Londres de Bacon à Bevan,* Foundation Dina Vierny, Paris (catalog)
1999 *Portrait of a City: Seven Figurative Painters from London,* John Berggruen Gallery, San Francisco (catalog)
Sublime: The Darkness and the Light, John Hansard Gallery, Southampton (traveling exhibition) (catalog)
2000 *La Mirada Fuerte: Pintura Figurativa de Londres,* British Council London

Collections:

Tate Gallery, London; British Museum, London; Fitzwilliam Museum, Cambridge; Whitworth Art Gallery, Manchester; Thyssen-Bornemisza Collection, Lugano, Switzerland; Chrysler Museum, Provincetown, Massachusetts; National Gallery of Victoria, Melbourne.

Publications:

By KOSSOFF: Articles—statement in *Leon Kossoff: Recent Drawings and Paintings,* exhibition catalog, London 1974; ''An Extract from a Letter'' in *Leon Kossoff: Paintings from a Decade 1970–1980,* exhibition catalog, by David Elliott, Oxford 1981.

On KOSSOFF: Books—*Leon Kossoff: Recent Paintings,* exhibition catalog by David Mercer, London 1972; *Leon Kossoff: Paintings from a Decade 1970–1980,* exhibition catalog by David Elliott, Oxford 1981; *The British Picture,* exhibition catalog with text by Marina Vaizey, Catherine Lampert and William Feaver, Venice, California 1988; *Leon Kossoff,* edited by Paul Moorhouse, London 1996; *Drawn to Painting: Leon Kossoff's Drawings and Paintings after Nicolas Poussin* by Richard Kendall, London 1999. **Articles—** ''Kossoff's Doubt'' by David Cohen in *Art in America* (New York), vol. 83, no. 12, December 1995; ''Hats Off to Kossoff'' by Martin Gayford in *Modern Painters* (London), vol. 9, no. 2, Summer 1996; ''Kossoff's London'' by James Hyman in *Tate: The Art Magazine,* no. 9, Summer 1996; ''Living with a Kossoff'' by Al Alvarez in *Tate: The Art Magazine,* no. 9, Summer 1996.

* * *

Although Leon Kossoff was born in England and a student at some of the country's best-known art schools, there is virtually nothing English about his art. His subjects are himself and his family and friends, or views from his home and studio in North London. This narrow field of vision reflects an intensely personal, almost autobiographical artform, its emotional quality rendered in an equally intense, mud-like impasto.

Kossoff is of Jewish origin, as is his friend and colleague Frank Auerbach, who shares his technical manner and also the narrow personal range of subject matter. Both of them were deeply influenced by another Anglo-Jewish painter, David Bomberg, who, from analytical, cubist drawings and paintings, later developed a rich, Rembrandtesque style. Indeed, in considering this interesting group of painters, one must retrace artistic steps to artists like Rembrandt and Goya, to a concern for the human condition and the idea of the artist as an isolated representative of that universal situation.

Kossoff's work is of special interest since, whilst the medium and the subject always remain based in expressionism, by the use of cool, pleasant colour, and a refusal to be explicit as a portraitist or a painter of urban landscape, he refrains from over-dramatisation or sentimentality. The result is a dignified monumentality, which persuades the viewer that, whilst the painter starts from the particular, namely himself and his milieu, his aim is the general, even the universal. Equally surprising is that from the thick morass of churned-up pigment, Kossoff extracts forms and compositions of elegance, even charm, and has proved his ability to constantly extend and develop his range of technique and expression, without, in fact, adopting gimmicks or moving away from what is of personal significance.

—Charles Spencer

KOSUTH, Joseph

Nationality: American. **Born:** Toledo, Ohio, 31 January 1945. **Education:** Studied at Toledo Museum School of Design, 1955–62 (also studied privately, under Belgian painter Line Bloom Draper, Toledo, 1956–62); studied painting, Cleveland Art Institute, 1963–64; C.A.S.A. Program, under Roger Barr, Paris, 1964–65; School of Visual Arts, New York, 1965–67; anthropology and philosophy, New School for Social Research, New York, 1971–72. **Career:** Lives and works in New York City and Rome, Italy. Organized visiting artists program (including Don Judd, Sol Le Witt and Ad Reinhardt), School of Visual Arts, New York, 1966–67; founder-director, Museum of Normal Art (formerly Lannis Gallery), New York, 1967; reviewer, *Arts Magazine,* New York, 1967; instructor, School of Visual Arts, New York, 1968; editor, Art and Language Press, Coventry, England, and New York, 1969–73; lecturer, University of Chile, Santiago, 1971; co-editor, the *Fox* magazine, New York, 1975–76; professor, Hochschule Bildende Kunst, Hamburg, Germany, 1987–89; professor, Staatliche Akademic Der Bildende Kunst, Stuttgart, Germany, 1991. **Awards:** Cassandra Foundation Grant, New York, 1968; Brandeis Award, 1990; Frederick Wiseman Award, 1991; Chevalier de l'Ordre des Arts et des Lettres, Government of France, 1993; Menzione d'Onore, Venice Biennale, 1993. **Agent:** Leo Castelli Gallery, 420 West Broadway, New York, New York 10012, U.S.A. **Address:** 591 Broadway, New York, New York 10012, U.S.A.

Individual Exhibitions:

1967 Museum of Normal Art, New York
1968 Gallery 669, Los Angeles
Bradford Junior College, Massachusetts (with Robert Morris)
1969 Douglass Gallery, Vancouver
Instituto Torquato di Tella, Buenos Aires

Nova Scotia College of Art, Halifax
St. Martin's School of Art, London
Museum of Contemporary Art, Chicago (in association with *Art by Telephone)*
Art and Project, Amsterdam
Coventry College of Art, England (in association with *Oxford Project)*
Galleria Sperone, Turin
A 37 90 89 Gallery, Antwerp
Kunsthalle, Berne
Pinacotheca, St. Kilda, Victoria
Leo Castelli Gallery, New York
Art Gallery of Ontario, Toronto

1970 Pasadena Art Museum, California
Jysk Kunstgalerie, Copenhagen
Aarhus Kunstmuseum, Denmark
Kunstbiblioteket i Lyngby, Denmark
Galerie Daniel Templon, Paris
Galleria Sperone, Turin

1971 Galerie Paul Maenz, Cologne
Protetch-Rivkin Gallery, Washington, D.C.
Galerie Bruno Bischofberger, Zurich
Centro de Arte y Comunicacion, Buenos Aires
Lia Rumma Studio d'Arte, Naples
Carmen Lamanna Gallery, Toronto
Leo Castelli Gallery, New York
Galleria Toselli, Milan
Protetch-Rivkin Gallery, Convention Hall, Atlantic City, New Jersey (in association with *Boardwalk Show*)

1972 New Gallery, Cleveland
Leo Castelli Gallery, New York (2 shows)
Sperone-Fischer Gallery, Rome

1973 Galerie Gunter Sachs, Hamburg
Galerie Paul Maenz, Brussels

1974 Carmen Lamanna Gallery, Toronto
Sperone-Fischer Gallery, Rome
Claire S. Copley Gallery, Los Angeles
Galerie La Bertesca, Dusseldorf

1975 Leo Castelli Gallery, New York
Galleria Peccolo, Livorno, Italy
Galerie MTL, Brussels
Lia Rumma Studio d'Arte, Naples
Galerie Liliane and Michel Durand-Desert, Paris (with Sara Charlesworth)

1976 Rennaissance Society, University of Chicago
International Cultureel Centrum, Antwerp

1977 Kunstmuseum Van Hedeendagse, Ghent

1978 Van Abbemuseum, Eindhoven, Netherlands
Museum of Modern Art, Oxford
Carmen Lamanna Gallery, Toronto

1979 New 57 Gallery, Edinburgh
Galerie Eric Fabre, Paris
Galerie Paul Maenz, Cologne
Galerie Rudiger Schottle, Munich
Leo Castelli Gallery, New York
Saman Gallery, Genoa
Musée de Chartres, France

1980 P.S. 1, Institute for Art and Urban Resources Inc., Long Island City, New York

1981 Staatsgalerie, Stuttgart
Saman Gallery, Genoa, Italy

1982 Kunsthalle, Bielfeld, West Germany

1985 Centre d'Art Contemporain, Geneva

1993 Wurttembergischer Kunstverein, Stuttgart
Galerie Anselm Dreher, Berlin

1994 *The Thing-in-Itself is Found in Its Truth Through the Loss of Its Immediacy,* Leo Castelli Gallery, New York

1995 *Joseph Kosuth og Amerikansk Konseptualisme,* Kunstnernes Hus, Oslo, Norway (catalog)

1996 Galerie Yvon Lambert, Paris
Barbara Krakow Gallery, Boston

1997 *Re-defining the Context of Art: 1968–1997: The Second Investigation and Public Media,* List Visual Arts Center, Cambridge, Massachusetts

1999 *Les Rencontres Rossiniennes di Joseph Kosuth,* Galleria di Franca Mancini, Ravenna (catalog)

2001 *Essays,* Sean Kelly Gallery, New York

Selected Group Exhibitions:

1967 *Non-Anthropomorphic Art,* Lannis Gallery, New York

1969 *When Attitudes Become Form,* Kunsthalle, Berne (toured Europe)

1970 *Idea Structures,* Camden Arts Centre, London

1972 *Das Konzept ist die Form,* Westfalischer Kunstverein, Munster, West Germany

1973 *Art Investigations and Problematics since 1965,* Kunstmuseum, Lucerne, Switzerland

1974 *Painting and Sculpture Today,* Indianapolis Museum of Art (travelled)

1977 *Illusion and Reality,* Australian National Gallery, Canberra (toured Australia)

1979 *Concept/Narrative/Document: Recent Photographic Works from the Morton Neumann Family Collection,* Museum of Contemporary Art, Chicago (travelled to the Contemporary Art Center, Cincinnati, and Joslyn Art Museum, Omaha, Nebraska)

1980 *Printed Art: A View of Two Decades,* Museum of Modern Art, New York

1981 *Westkunst,* Rheinhallen, Cologne

1993 *Venice Biennale,* Italy

1994 Camden Arts Centre, London
Translucent Writings, Neuberger Museum, State University of New York at Purchase (catalog)

1996 *René Magritte: Die Kunst der Konversation,* Kunstsammlung Nordrhein-Westfalen, Dusseldorf (catalog)
Urban Evidence: Contemporary Artists Reveal Cleveland, Cleveland Museum of Art (catalog)
Devant et Derrière la Lumière, Espace de l'Art Concret, Mouans-Sartoux (catalog)
Public Works, Van Abbemuseum, Eindhoven, Holland (catalog)

1997 *Sarajevo,* Fondazione Querini Stampalia, Venice (catalog)

1999 *Wände/Wall Works,* Museum Villa Stuck, Munich
Art-Cologne 1999, Germany (catalog)

1999 *Gäste und Fremde: Goethes Italienische Reise,* Schirn Kunsthalle, Frankfurt (catalog)

Collections:

Museum of Modern Art, New York; Guggenheim Museum, New York; Whitney Museum, New York; National Gallery of Canada, Ottawa; Tate Gallery, London; Van Abbemuseum, Eindhoven, Netherlands; Stedelijk Museum, Amsterdam; Kunstmuseum Van Hedendaagse, Ghent; Centre Pompidou, Paris; Australian National Gallery, Canberra.

Publications:

By KOSUTH: Books—*January 5–31, 1969,* New York 1969; *Notebook on Water, 1965–66/Joseph Kosuth,* New York 1970; *Art and Language,* with Atkinson, Baingridge and others, Cologne 1972; *Joseph Kosuth,* exhibition catalog, Stuttgart 1981; *Art After Philosophy and After: Collected Writings, 1966–1990,* edited by Gabriele Guercio, Cambridge 1991; *Two Oxford Reading Rooms: The (Ethical) Space of Cabinets 7 & 8,* London 1994; *Intervenciones en el Espacio: Diálogos en el MBA,* with María Elena Ramos, Caracas 1998. **Articles—**''Four Interviews with Barry, Huebler, Kosuth, Weiner,'' with Arthur R. Rose in *Arts Magazine* (New York), February 1969; ''Art after Philosophy'' in *Studio International* (London), October-December 1969; ''Picasso: A Symposium,'' with others, in *Art in America* (New York), December 1980; ''Les Limites du Regard: Voir et Lire Ad Reinhardt'' in *Art Press,* Special Issue no. 17, 1996; ''Joseph Kostuth'' in *Art Press,* Special Issue no. 17, 1996; *A Range of Critical Perspectives: Writing (and) the History of Art,* with Paul Barolsky, David Carrier, Ivan Gaskell in *Art Bulletin* (New York), vol. 78, no. 3, September 1996; ''Joseph Kosuth: The Production of Consciousness,'' an interview with Eleanor Heartney in *Art Press,* no. 222, April 1997; ''Times of Our Lives: Remembering Doug Huebler'' in *Artforum International,* vol. 36, November 1997.

On KOSUTH: Books—*Idea Structures,* exhibition catalog, London 1970; *Joseph Kosuth,* Buenos Aires 1971; *Concept Art* by Klaus Honnef, Cologne 1971; *6 Years: The Dematerialization of the Art Objects* by Lucy Lippard, New York 1973; *Joseph Kosuth: Investigationen über Kunst und ''Problemkreise'' seit 1965m,* exhibition catalog with texts by M. Ramsden and others, Lucerne 1973. **Articles—**''Joseph Kosuth: 2 Shows'' by Bruce Boice in *Artforum* (New York), March 1973; ''Art Theory and Practice; Art Theory and the Decline of the Art Object'' by Ian Jeffrey in *Studio International (London),* December 1973; ''10th Investigation: Proposition 5'' by S. Buettner in *Arts Magazine* (New York), October 1975; ''Long Night at the Movies'' in *Art in America* (New York), March 1979; ''Park Avenue Palazzo: Interior Design'' by M. Filler in *Progressive Architecture* (New York), May 1979; ''Joseph Kosuth'' in *Flash Art* (Milan), June 1979; ''Kosuth in Europa'' in *Domus* (Milan), August 1979; ''A. Reinhardt, J. Kosuth, F. Gonzalez-Torres: Symptoms of Interference, Conditions of Possibilities'' in *Art and Design,* vol. 9, January/February 1994; ''Joseph Kosuth: Portrait by Armin Linke'' by Richard Kostelanetz in *Du,* no. 1, January 1994; ''Joseph Kosuth'' by Suzanne Ramljak in *Sculpture* (Washington, D.C.), vol. 14, May/June 1995; ''A Conceptualist's Self-conceptions: Joseph Kosuth Explains a Movement'' by Barbara Macadam in *Art News,* vol. 94, December 1995; ''Joseph Kosuth in Belgium: Conceptual Play Animates His Ghent House'' by Elizabeth Helman Minchilli in *Architectural Digest,* vol. 54, April 1997; ''Words, Index Fingers, Gaps: The Critique of Language in the Late Poetry of William Carlos Williams and the Conceptual Art of Joseph Kosuth'' by Zsofia Ban in *Word and Image,* vol. 15, no. 2, April/June 1999; ''Joseph Kosuth: The Context is the Stuff of Art'' by Adachiara Zevi in *L'Architettura,* vol. 45, no. 524, June 1999.

* * *

In 1965, Kosuth executed a work titled *Any Five Foot Sheet of Glass to Lean Against Any Wall,* a gesture that alluded at once to Marcel Duchamp's *Large Glass* and to the glass industry in the artist's hometown of Toledo, Ohio. Characteristically, the work seemed simple but actually addressed complex artistic and cultural issues. Though he is known as a difficult artist, his works can often be described in a few short sentences.

In a series of installations executed during 1985–86, titled *Zero & Not,* he completely covered the walls with text from Freud, marking the fiftieth anniversary of Freud's death, then crossed it all out, at once affirming and negating the dominance of language. In the 1990s, he has transcribed quotations from such diverse people as James Joyce, Samuel Goldwyn, and Garry Trudeau and balanced these against newspaper articles on such pop-controversy figures as Lorena Bobbitt and Jack Kevorkian. Such works undeniably appear didactic, a charge Kosuth finds no reason to deny, the separation of art and politics being a modernist tenet that has resulted in what he perceives to be a homogenous and irrelevant artistic tradition.

In broad terms Kosuth's career has followed a pattern similar to that of Barbara Kruger, another artist who started out using some text and who has moved into a modus operandi (to use one of Kosuth's favorite phrases) that is mainly textual. Both continue to be known as artists even as they publish essay after essay, and neither feels any qualms about teaching an occasional civics lesson as they proceed with their theoretical observations. The differences between Kruger and Kosuth come mainly when Kruger is termed a ''feminist'' artist and Kosuth an ''avant-garde'' artist. Kosuth's version of avant-garde art, like many avant gardes, insists on rebuilding the foundation of art, sometimes in a locale altogether different from where it had previously been.

In his essay ''Art after Philosophy,'' published in 1969, Kosuth justified the conceptual art then emerging nationwide and set it against the history of Western art. Dismissing virtually all the art ever made and registering special disdain for the formalist aesthetics outlined by Clement Greenberg, he divided art into that which uncritically accepts the conventional definitions of art and that which proposes new definitions. In articulating his vision of the latter, he noted the relevance of Donald Judd, Ad Reinhardt, and, above all, Duchamp. The death of philosophy implicit in the essay's title notwithstanding, Kosuth continues to write essays of a philosophical nature, invoking Ludwig Wittgenstein and other philosophers who examine the relationships between language and the world. His artistic output, too, in many ways takes ''after philosophy.''

Wittgenstein had an unwitting influence on other significant artists of the 1960s, most notably Jasper Johns and Robert Morris, whose investigations into textual and visual forms take cues from his *Philosophical Investigations,* but Kosuth has made perhaps the most rigorous study of the philosopher and has reenacted most compellingly his ''language games.'' Kosuth recognized that Wittgenstein's overall contention that philosophy is ultimately ''about'' language might be better illuminated in a medium other than language. Kosuth started out exploring particular words, *chair, water,* and *nothing,* in such a manner as to expose the discontinuity between the dictionary definitions, the items they signify, and photographic images of these terms.

As his career has developed, he has softened the focus; instead of one word he presents entire sentences and more. ''Kosuth's work is a meditation on writing,'' Jean-François Lyotard has stated.

Unwilling to meditate on the subject only within the confines of the gallery and the museum, Kosuth has left sentences on the sides of buildings, on billboards, and in the classified section of periodicals. Such tactics are meant to avoid the conventional trappings of the art world, most notably the buying and selling of paintings. Though he works with dealers, he usually refuses to sell his work to collectors, preferring to work, as he says, like a scientist to whom grants are awarded.

Kosuth is a prolific and rhetorically sophisticated writer, and his essays have accomplished as much as his art the goal he sets forth for all art: the inspiration of still more art. Furthermore, like Joseph Beuys, another titan of conceptual art, Kosuth has always returned to teaching art students, sending them back to Wittgenstein and Duchamp in the hopes that they will draw on them to form the art of the future.

——Mark Swartz

KOUNELLIS, Jannis

Nationality: Greek. **Born:** Piraeus, 1936. **Career:** Independent artist, Rome, since 1956; first stencilled number paintings, Rome, 1959; first tableaux vivants, Rome, 1966; held floating retrospective on boat called *Ionian* docked in his home port of Piraeus, 1994; professor, Kunstakademie Düsseldorf. **Agents:** Sonnabend Gallery, 420 West Broadway, New York, New York 10012, U.S.A.; Ace Gallery New York, 275 Hudson Street, New York, New York 10013; Marian Goodman Gallery, 24 West 57th Street, New York, New York 10019; Galerie Lelong, 20 West 57th Street, New York, New York 10019; Anthony Meier Fine Arts, 3007 Jackson Street, San Francisco, California 94115; Sonnabend Gallery, 536 West 22nd Street, New York, New York 10011. **Address:** Via del Banco de Santo Spirito 21, 00186 Rome, Italy.

Individual Exhibitions:

1960 Galleria la Tartaruga, Rome
1961 Galleria la Tartaruga, Rome (with Schifano and Twombly)
1964 Galleria la Tartaruga, Rome
1966 Galleria Arco d'Alibert, Rome
1967 Galleria l'Attico, Rome
1968 Galleria Iolas, Milan
1969 Galleria Enzo Superone, Turin
Galleria l'Attico, Rome
Galerie Alexandre Iolas, Paris
1970 Modern Art Agency, Naples
1971 Galleria Enzo Sperone, Turin
Galleria l'Attico, Rome
Galerie Folker Skulima, West Berlin
1972 Modern Art Agency, Naples
Sonnabend Downtown Gallery, New York
1973 Galerie Sonnabend, Paris
Galleria l'Attico, Rome
Modern Art Agency, Naples
1974 Sonnabend, Gallery, New York
Galleria Stein, Turin, Italy
Galleria l'Attico, Rome
Galerie Folker Skulima, West Berlin
1975 Modern Art Agency, Naples
Galerie Rudolf Zwirner, Cologne
Galleria Mario Pieroni, Pescara, Italy
1976 Galleria l'Attico (Hotel Luneta), Rome
Galleria Salvatore Ala, Milan
Galerie Art-in-Progress, Dusseldorf
1977 Museum Boymans-van Beuningen, Rotterdam
Kunstmuseum, Lucerne
Galleria Tucci Russo, Turin
Galerie Jean & Karen Bernier, Athens
Villa Pignatelli, Naples
1978 Städtisches Museum, Möchengladbach, Germany
Galleria Mario Diacono, Bologna (with Calzolari and Merz)
1979 Galerie Konrad Fischer, Dusseldorf
Galerie Jean & Karen Bernier, Athens
Salvatore Ala Gallery, New York
Pinacoteca di Bari, Bari, Italy
Museum Folkwand, Essen
1980 Galleria Lucio Amelio, Naples
Galleria Mario Diacono, Rome
Sonnabend Gallery, New York
1981 Galerie Durand-Dessert, Paris
Galerie Karsten Greve, Cologne
1982 Galeria Obra Social, Madrid
Whitechapel Art Gallery, London
Staatliche Kunsthalle, Baden-Baden, Germany
1983 Sonnabend Gallery, New York
Galerie Konrad Fischer, Dusseldorf
Galerie Durand-Dessert, Paris
1984 Galerie Schellmann und Kluser, Munich
Sonnabend Gallery, New York
Galleria Ugo Ferranti, Rome
Galleria Lucio Amelio, Naples
1985 Galleria Christian Stein, Milan
Stadtische Galerie im Lenbachhaus, Munich
CAPC/Musée d'Art Comtemporain, Bordeaux, France
1986 Kunstnernes Hus, Oslo
Anthony d'Offay Gallery, London
Kunsthalle, Basel
1988 Galleria Christian Stein, Milan
Mary Boone Gallery, New York
1990. Margo Leavin Gallery, New York
1992 Lelong Gallery, Paris
1994 Marian Goodman Gallery, New York
Cargo Vessel *Ionion,* Piraeus, Greece (traveling retrospective)
1995 *Die Eiserne Runde,* Die Kunsthalle, Hamburg (catalog)
1996 Gallery of Contemporary Art, Hamburg Kunsthalle
Museo Nacional Reina Sofía, Madrid (catalog)
Christian Stein Gallery, Milan
1997 *Die Front/Das Denken/Der Sturm,* Museum Ludwig Köln, Cologne (also Halle Kalk, Cologne) (catalog)
Galleria del Gruppo Credito Valtellinese, Milan (catalog)
1998 *Sculptural Installaton,* Ace Gallery, New York
Galerie Lelong, Paris
1999 *Il Sarcofago degli Sposi,* Osterreichisches Museum fur Angewandte Kunst, Vienna (catalog)

En México, Universidad Nacional Autónoma de México, Museo Universidario de Ciencias y Arte, Mexico (catalog)

Selected Group Exhibitions:

1967 *6th Biennale de Paris,* Musée d'Art Moderne, Paris (and *7th Biennale,* 1971)
1968 *Recent Italian Painting and Sculpture,* Jewish Museum, New York
1969 *When Attitudes Become Form,* Kunsthalle, Berne (toured Europe)
1971 *Arte Povera,* Kunstverein, Munich
1976 *Ambiente/Arte,* at the *Biennale,* Venice
1977 *Documenta 6,* Kassel, Germany (and *Documenta 7,* 1982)
1981 *Italians and American Italians,* Crown Point Gallery, Oakland, California
1982 *Vergangenheit-Gegenwart-Zukunft,* Wurttembergischer Kunstverein, Stuttgart
1985 *Promenades,* Parc Lullin, Genthod, Geneva
1987 *Avant-Garde in the Eighties,* Los Angeles County Museum of Art
1995 *Recaptured Nature,* Marian Goodman Gallery, New York
Metàfores del Real, Museu d'Art Contemporani, Barcelona (catalog)
XVI Biennale Internazionale del Bronzetto, Piccola Scultura, Padova 95, Padova (catalog)
Where is Abel, Thy Brother?, Galeria Zacheta, Warsaw (catalog)
1997 *New Editions,* Galerie Lelong, New York
1999 *Atelier del Bosco di Villa Medici,* Villa Medici, Rome (catalog)
2000 *Arte Povera in Collection,* Castello di Rivoli, Museo d'Arte Contemporanea, Rivoli-Torino (catalog)
Europa, Galerie Academia, Salzburg (catalog)

Collections:

Galeria Nazionale d'Arte Moderna, Rome; Art Gallery of Ontario, Toronto; Solomon R. Guggenheim Museum, New York; Museo Nacional Reina Sofía, Madrid.

Publications:

By KOUNELLIS: Books—*Kounellis,* edited by Gloria Moure, New York 1990; *Jannis Kounellis im Gespräch mit Heinz Peter Schwerfel,* Cologne 1995; *Kounellis: Mistral,* with Bruno Corà, Aurelio Amendola and Chiara D'Afflitto, Bergamo 1996; *Jannis Kounellis,* with preface by Peter Noever, Ostfildern 2000. **Articles—**''Discorsi, Carla Lonzi e Jannis Kounellis,'' interview in *Marcatre* (Milan), December 1966; ''4 Domands (semiseries) a Jannis Kounellis'' in *Flash Art* (Milan), November/December 1967; ''Ponente, Volpi, Kounellis, una conversazione'' in *Flash Art* (Milan) January/February 1968; ''Technique e Materiali,'' with M. Volpi in *Marcatre* (Milan), May 1968; ''Jannis Kounellis: Pensierie osservazione,'' edited by G. Bartolucci, in *Marcatre* (Milan), July/September 1968; ''Per Pascali'' in *Qui Arte Contemporanea* (Rome), March 1969; ''Non per il teatro, ma con il teatro,'' edited by Italo Moscati, in *Sipario* (Milan), April 1969; ''Structure and Sensibility: An Interview with Jannis Kounellis,'' with Willoughby Sharp, in *Avalanche* (New York), Summer 1972; ''On the Teaching of Art: Interview with Jannis Kounellis'' in *Domus,* no. 778, January 1996; interview with Doris von Drathen in *Kunstforum International,* no. 146, July-August 1999.

On KOUNELLIS: Books—*Jannis Kounellis,* exhibition catalog with text by Cesare Vivaldi, Rome 1964; *When Attitudes Become Form,* exhibition catalog edited by Harald Szeemann, Berne 1969; *7th Paris Biennale; Italy,* exhibition catalog, edited by Achille Bonito Oliva, Paris 1971; *Jannis Kounellis,* exhibition catalog with texts by Jean-Christophe Ammann and Marlis Gruterich, Lucerne 1977; *Avanguardia di Massa* by Maurizio Calvesi, Milan 1978; *Jannis Kounellis,* exhibition catalog with texts by Zdenek Felix and Bruno Cora, Essen 1979; *Italians and American Italians,* exhibition catalog with introduction by Kathen Brown, Oakland, California 1981; *Vergangenheit-Gegenwart-Zukunft,* exhibition catalog with an introduction by Tilma Osterwold, Stuttgart 1982; *Urban Configurations* by Gloria Moure, Barcelona 1994. **Articles—**''Kounellis Unbound: Dialogue of the Old World and the New'' by Alan Jones in *Arts Magazine* (New York), vol. 64, no. 6, February 1990; ''Jannis Kounellis: Peintre sans Pinceau'' by Heinz Peter Schwerfel in *Beaux Arts Magazine,* no. 124, June 1994; ''When the Boat Comes In'' by Mark Durden in *Art Monthly,* no. 182, December 1994/January 1995; ''Jannis Kounellis'' by Bruno Corà in *Artforum,* vol. 33, no. 5, January 1995; ''Jannis Kounellis at Ace'' by Janet Koplos in *Art in America* (New York), vol. 86, no. 10, October 1998; ''Kounellis e la Sostenibile Pesantezza dell'Arte'' by Elisabetta Planca in *Arte,* no. 303, November 1998.

* * *

At Rome's Attico Gallery in 1969 Jannis Kounellis displayed his best-known work—a group of eleven live horses. In doing so Kounellis marked an important stage in his development as an artist and his concern for the relationship between the ''natural'' and the ''artificial,'' for the relationship, that is, between elements which exist in nature and those things which the artist makes. For Kounellis, ''nature'' means not only earth, fire, water, minerals and the realms of animal and vegetable life, but coal and wool as well, which seem closer to the world of nature than to the world of man-made things. The ''artificial,'' on the other hand, refers to things made by man's interventions: art can subvert nature; it is an organized cultural gesture. Two works from 1967, ''Parrot'' and ''Daisy of Fire,'' clearly illustrate this interplay between art and nature. In the first piece, a live parrot sits on a perch which projects from a gray, monochrome canvas; in the second we have a large black metal daisy with a tube at its center, from which a live flame issues.

But in fact Kounellis began his artistic experiments several years earlier. In one of his first works, for example (dating from 1958), we have a long, narrow table from which the word ''oil'' stands out in bold relief, while the words ''wine'' and ''vinegar'' shine through the varnished surface of the table. A few years later there were large canvases in which numbers and letters played an important role. In 1966 we have works like ''Yellow,'' ''Come,'' and ''Night,'' which serve as a kind of conclusion to Kounellis' experiments with removing objects from their natural surroundings and subjecting them to new pressures. The word ''yellow,'' for example, is actually painted in red; the red roses are black, and so on. In such works Kounellis seems to express, in generalized terms, the relationship between artistic expression and formal qualities.

''Horses,'' referred to earlier, comes as the climax to Kounellis' first period of artistic development. In the mature works which follow, his aesthetic becomes complex, personal, and rich in tensions. In his 1971 exhibition at the La Tartaruga Gallery there were works from the 1960s and new works which built upon them but went beyond them as well. And at a group show in Bologna in 1978, we have a work which can stand as a summary statement of his art to date: in front of a yellow canvas, a small ship rests on sacks of coal. Kounellis brings together elements that become parts of an intriguing whole and give ample evidence of his enduring vitality as an artist.

—Roberto G. Lambarelli

In his work of the 1980s and 1990s, Kounellis uses industrial materials—coal, steel, burlap—to suggest both the passing of time and the need to mark history. For the 1990 opening of a nonprofit gallery in Barcelona, Kounellis hung freshly killed carcasses from iron sheets and lit the installation with oil lamps. The lamps and the carcasses themselves, which had to be changed every few days, served as constant reminders of the passing of time; the site-specific exhibition (the gallery is located in a working-class neighborhood) was reminiscent of the area's industrial past. Various works from the early 1990s feature coal-filled burlap bags attached to sheets of steel or lumps of coal attached to burlap with wire; these works hang from gallery walls, oddly defying the labels of ''painting,'' ''sculpture'' or ''installation.'' A fence of steel erected in the Marian Goodman Gallery for a 1993 exhibition divides time as well as space. On one side of the partition, the space feels cramped and time seems compressed. On the other side, the expansiveness of the room echoes the nostalgic, even mournful, tone set by the rectangular, gray steel panels hung on the walls.

—Beth Duncan

KOWALSKI, Piotr

Nationality: French. **Born:** Lvov, Poland, 2 March 1927; immigrated to Paris, 1953; naturalized, 1971. **Education:** Attended schools in Poland and the United States; studied architecture, physics and mathematics, Massachusetts Institute of Technology, Cambridge, 1947–52, Dip. Arch. 1952. **Career:** Worked as a mechanic in Poland, 1940–44; travelled in Europe and South America, 1946–47; architect in the office of I.M. Pei, New York, 1952–53, and with the Marcel Breuer team, Unesco Building Project, Paris, 1953–55; established own architectural practice, Paris, 1955; also, painter and sculptor, Paris, from 1954, subsequently in Montrouge, France: first paintings, 1954; first polyester sculptures, 1960. Founder, Atelier for Experimental Architecture, Paris, 1958; member, Visiting Arts Committee, Massachusetts Institute of Technology, 1980–85; professor, l'Ecole Nationale Supérieure des Beaux Arts à Paris, 1987–92; member, Advisory Council on Art and Technology, Massachusetts Institute of Technology, since 1994. **Awards:** First Prize, Rail Station Competition, Tunis, 1961; International Baumuseum Prize, Paris, 1962; Graham Foundation Award, Chicago, 1963; Chatelet Square Prize, Paris, 1969; DAAD Fellowship, West Berlin, 1972; Massachusetts Institute of Technology Fellowship, 1978–85; Rockefeller Grant, New York, 1979; Fulbright Fellowship, New York, 1979; French Ministry of Culture Scholarship (to the United States), 1982; Plaza at La Defense Prize, Paris, 1982; City Entry Prize, St. Quentin, France, 1983. Chevalier des Arts et Lettres, France, 1985. **Agent:** Gallery Sonia Zannettacci, 16 rue des Granges, 1204, Geneva, Switzerland. **Address:** 77 Avenue de la Republique, 92120 Montrouge, France.

Individual Exhibitions:

1961 Galerie des Beaux-Arts, Paris
1963 Kunsthalle, Bern
1966 Museu de Arte Moderna, Sao Paulo
Museu de Arte Moderna, Rio de Janeiro
1967 Galerie Claude Givaudan, Paris
1969 Musée d'Art Moderne, Paris
Galerie Claude Givaudan, Paris
Galerie X-One, Antwerp
1970 Stedelijk Museum, Amsterdam
Moderna Museet, Stockholm
Galerie Claude Givaudan, Paris
Amos Andersonin Taidemuseo, Helsinki
1971 Musée Picasso, Antibes, France (with Jean Dewasne)
1973 Galerie René Block, West Berlin
Galerie Edouard Loeb, Paris
1974 Museé Galliera, Paris
Galerie Eric Fabre, Paris
1975 Galerie Eric Fabre, Paris
1978 Galerie Eric Fabre, Paris
1979 Ronald Feldman Fine Arts, New York
Galerie Eric Fabre, Paris
Galerie Claude Givaudan, Geneva
1981 Galerie Eric Fabre, Paris
Centre Georges Pompidou, Paris
1983 Galerie Acapa, Angouleme, France
Hara Museum of Contemporary Art, Tokyo
1986 Seoul Gallery, Korea
2000 *Sculpture, Drawing, Objects and Architectural Designs,* Center for Contemporary Art, Ujazdowski Castle, Warsaw
Atelier Brouillard Precis, La Galerie de la Friche Belle de Mai, Marseille

Selected Group Exhibitions:

1965 *Light and Movement,* Kunsthalle, Bern (travelled to Brussels, Baden-Baden, Dusseldorf and Paris)
1967 *Science Fiction,* Kunsthalle, Bern (travelled to Paris and Dusseldorf)
1969 *10th Middelheim Biennale,* Kunsthistorisches Museum, Antwerp
1970 *Kinetics,* Hayward Gallery, London
1972 *Documenta 5,* Museum Fridericianum, Kassel, West Germany
1975 *Les Machines Celibataires,* Kunsthalle, Bern (travelled to Venice, Brussels, Dusseldorf, Paris, Malmo, Amsterdam, Rennes and Vienna)
1976 *Museum of Drawers,* Museum Solothurn, Switzerland (travelled to Antwerp, Dusseldorf, Jerusalem, Washington, Los Angeles and Bern)

1983 *Electra,* Musee d'Art Moderne, Paris
1986 *XLII Biennale,* Venice
1995 *3rd Biennale d'Art Contemporain,* Lyon, France

Collections:

Stedelijk Museum, Amsterdam; Centre Georges Pompidou, Paris; Bibliotheque Nationale, Paris; Moderna Museet, Stockholm; Kunstmuseum, Bern; Guggenheim Museum, New York; University of Southern California, Long Beach; Museum of Modern Art, Jerusalem; Hara Museum of Contemporary Art, Tokyo; Seoul Gallery, Korea.

Publications:

By KOWALSKI: Articles—''The Explosive Form of Piotr Kowalski,'' interview, in *Architectural Forum* (New York), December 1965; ''Sculpture a la dynamite'' in *Le Nouvel Observateur* (Paris), 5 January 1966; ''L'Art et la Technologie'' in *Protee* (Quebec), no. 1, 1981; ''Un point de vue peut-etre aussi representé par une matrice'' in *Alea* (Paris), March 1982; ''Brief Encounters: A Physicist Meets Contemporary Art'' by Jean-Marc Lévy-Leblond in *Leonardo,* vol. 27, no. 3, 1994; ''Piotr Kowalski: Intervention/ Conversation'' in *Transcript,* vol. 2, no. 3, 1997.

On KOWALSKI: Books—*Piotr Kowalski,* exhibition catalog with text by Harald Szeemann, Bern 1963; *A Concise History of Modern Scuplture* by Herbert Read, New York 1964; *Kowalski,* exhibition catalog with text by Harald Szeemann, Rio de Janeiro 1966; *Kowalski,* exhibition card folder, Paris 1967; *Kowalski,* exhibition catalog with text by Frank Popper, interviews by Gilbert Brownstone and Pierre Gaudibert, Paris 1969; *Piotr Kowalski,* exhibition catalog edited by Coosje Kapteyn and Ad Petersen, with an interview by Harald Szeemann, Amsterdam 1970; *Piotr Kowalski,* exhibition catalog, with an interview by Harald Szeemann, Stockholm 1970; *Documenta 5: Befragung der Realität,* exhibition catalog edited by Harald Szeemann and others, Kassel, West Germany 1972; *12 Ans d'Art Contemporain en France,* exhibition catalog with texts by Francois Mathey, Daniel Cordier and Jean Clair, Paris 1972; *Piotr Kowalski: Time Machine + Projets,* exhibition catalog with texts by Pontus Hulten, Dominique Bozo and Jean-Christophe Bailly, Paris 1981; *Kowalski,* exhibition catalog with text by Alain Jouffroy, Tokyo 1983.

*

I do not find it comfortable to voice ideas underlining my work otherwise than in front of it or its illustration. So I chose the following text of a friend and critic, Jean-Christophe Bailly, which sums up my thoughts best now:

''How is space apprehended. How do we master data, mountains of scientific data, and how do we put them to use to shape our material world? How do we articulate experience within the given reference frames, frames that have to be made manifest in order to be changes? How sculpture is but an instant made evident of such an articulation.

It is all this that Kowalski seeks to render by linking again art with science as the notion of 'cosa mentale' once proved, and seeks to render with no trace of nostalgia, with the elements of our time in all scales and variations, ordered with a demontrative logic as a tool.

Pioneer of an encyclopedic issue in art, Kowalski appears today to be one of those rare artists that are conscious of the world they live in. World no more of frontal contemplation, not that of linear times, but of infinite and aleatory production, where it became vital to place landmarks. Art becoming markings of portative knowledge and a vehicle for immediate poetics of experience such as Kowalski's 'sculpture.'''

—Piotr Kowalski

* * *

Piotr Kowalski throughout his career has aimed to achieve a wide scientific and artistic awareness through acting on the psychology of the spectator, who is invited to experience the elements of the technological universe and exploit certain of its meanings. In his *Grand Manipulateur* (1967), the spectator was impelled to act upon volumes of rare coloured gas within an overall electronic field, which caused it to light up and then become transparent once again in relation to the movements of the manipulator. Kowalski's *Mesures á prendre,* exhibited at the 1972 *Documenta,* involved both a subtle use of neon light and the integral participation of the public, which illuminates the neon tubes through placing them next to electrically active screens. Kowalski's spatial preoccupations can be observed in a series of laconic pseudo-scientific statements that lend themselves to realization on a range of different scales: ''ici'' (The Point/Time/ Sound on the threshold of perception), ''La-bas'' (a vector indicated by a red arrow), ''XYZ'' (three axes of coordinates defined by the three primary colours of light in a corner) and ''Distance'' (wire at red heat, stretched between two points in space and varying its length according to the degree of heating).

The time factor dominates in Kowalski's most recent constructions. *Time Machine I,* a computer used as an art tool, transmits the immediate materiality of time, and its reversal manipulations. It treats time not as a trace or a memory but as a phenomenon in a real-time world accessible directly to the senses. *Time Machine II* is conceived as an open-ended system, capable of progressive upgradings. It adds to the sound treatment of the earlier work a video treatment. Both *Time Machines* are public-oriented and are interactive pieces which capture both the existing sound and the public's image and actions, and restitute them backward in real-time on television screens and through a sound system. The artist thus proposes to the spectator's enhanced attention, time events which move forward and backward.

Kowalski's interest in scientific phenomena, town planning and spectator participation has recently evolved into such environmental statements as *Field of Interaction,* a work in which the physical interactions of the spectators modify the structure of luminous elements in a simulation of urban space. Among other realisations on the environmental and the architectural scale, *L'axe de la terre,* at the Technical College of Marne-la-Vallée, consists of a giant steel needle of 32 metres in length which is placed at a traffic roundabout in front of the college. It forms an angle of 48° 51′ with the horizon and, parallel with the earth's axis, it points into the sky in the direction of the pole star. Kowalski, by placing this sculpture at such an angle in and on the earth, wants to stress the fact that our planet is after all only an object depending on its position in the universe. *Porte de Paris* is an arch in glass and stainless steel thrown intrepidly over a stretch of water at Saint-Quentin-en-Yvelines (1991), and a second architectural installation after *La Place des degrés* (1982–1988), at La Défense in Paris, has been realized in 1995 and consists of a monumental staircase placed at the centre of a totally remodelled square in strong denivellation. Light plays a decisive part in the scenographic rearrangement of this environmental sculpture-architecture. In fact, at the foot of the staircase, an architectural axial element is painted in blue, whereas at the top of it a steel mast is painted in red. The dramatic presentation of the site is completed by a luminous band placed at the bottom of the staircase and by some lamp-posts specially designed to illuminate the steps according to an orthogonal rhythm.

Kowalski's more political, 'demographic,' research culminated in his *Population Cube 3* which saw the light in 1992 on the occasion of the opening of the National Kunsthalle at Bonn, Germany. This was the development of an idea that had been in the artist's mind since 1975. Tiny, almost microscopic glass balls circulate throughout this 'Cube,' each one of them representing the birth or the death of a human being. The Cube's computer management programme follows the world demographic statistical data published every year. Kowalski considers that abstract population numbers do not speak directly to the people, whereas the glass balls which one can touch and which are visually modified in real time give the spectator a better insight into this vital problem.

Kowalski's research into the light phenomenon has lately also been concretized in works putting special emphasis on daylight as well as on nocturnal illumination such as *Lumière I,* elaborated for the Pavilion of Discoveries at the World Exhibition at Sevilla in 1992. His interest in this area is now moving towards the use of holography and he produced an installation in 1989 in which a holographic spherical mirror encapsuled in sheet of glass serves as an 'information transcript' of two identical light objects. Two vases with artificial flowers form a superimposed image which a mirror projects and transforms into a third identical but totally dematerialized flower vase. *Information Transcript* is now in its fourth version. Among other holographic works, the vertical *Holographic Totem* (1993) for the Lycée Polyvalent at Cergy-Pontoise functions day and night and produces a kind of colourful diffraction grating as the spectator views it from different angles. In fact, most of Kowalski's holographic works must be seen less as physical objects than as optical instruments which change the usual aspect of the world.

Kowalski's recent activities are also linked to high-tech advances in computer art. *La Flèche du temps* (1990–1992) is an interactive video-computer installation where each one of the 18 monitors is controlled individually by the computer. This is a new version of Kowalski's preoccupation with time which allows him more than ever to play directly with this 'dimension' without having to resort to data other than those stored on a disk or on a magnetophone. *La Flèche du temps* is designed to allow the perception of the nature of information and of television, or rather of what the media try to hide from the observer. Real time presented as 'real' in these media is in fact always manipulated.

For Kowalski, technological procedures are essentially linked to an acceptance of the present, while genuine scientific advance is always open to the future and cannot be technocratic. Although he dismisses any too-facile notion of the inclusion of the public in the creative process, he holds that scientific and technological progress is basically mental in character and thus indissolubly linked with an aesthetic factor. And if art and science are connected as a result of the abolition of any hard and fast distinction, it is in man that all scientific and artistic preoccupations must reside.

—Frank Popper

KOZLOFF, Joyce

Nationality: American. **Born:** Joyce Blumberg, in Somerville, New Jersey, 14 December 1942. **Education:** Art Students League, New York, 1959; Carnegie Institute of Technology, Pittsburgh, 1960–64, B.F.A. 1964; Rutgers University, New Brunswick, New Jersey, 1962; University of Florence, Italy, 1963; under Stephen Greene and Theodoros Stamos, Columbia University, New York, 1965–67, M.F.A. 1967. **Family:** Married Max Kozloff in 1967; son: Nikolas. **Career:** Instructor, elementary and secondary schools, Pittsburgh, 1964; junior high school, Cranford, New Jersey, 1964–65; Ox-Bow Summer School of Painting, Saugatuck, Michigan, 1972; Queens College, New York, 1972–73; and School of Visual Arts, New York, 1973–74; visiting artist, School of the Art Institute of Chicago, 1975; San Francisco Art Institute, 1975; instructor, Syracuse University, New York, 1977; University of New Mexico, Albuquerque, 1978; Brooklyn Museum Art School, New York, 1978–79; Washington University, St. Louis, 1986; Cooper Union, New York, 1990; International Art Workshop, Teschemakers, New Zealand, 1991; Rutgers University, New Brunswick, New Jersey, 1992; Vermont College of Norwich University, Montpelier, Vermont, 1994; Anderson Ranch Arts Center, Snowmass, Colorado, 1996; Rhode Island School of Design, Providence, 1997; Skowhegan School of Art, Maine, 1998. **Awards:** Tamarind Lithography Institute Grant, Albuquerque, New Mexico, 1972; Creative Artists Program Service Grant, New York, 1972–73 (printmaking), and 1975–76 (painting); American Association of University Women Grant in Painting, 1975; National Endowment for the Arts Grant, 1977, 1985; Yaddo Fellowship, Saratoga Springs, New York, 1984; Arts/Industry Program Award, John Michael Kohler Art Center, Sheboygan, Wisconsin, 1986–87; Rockefeller Foundation Grant, Bellagio, Italy 1992; Djersassi Resident Artists Program, Woodside, California 1995; Diane Wood Middlebrook Fellowship, 1996; Jules Guerein Fellowship, Rome Prize, American Academy in Rome, Italy, 1999–2000. **Member:** Advisory Board Member, Public Art Fund, New York, 1984–86; Board of Directors Member, College of Art Association, 1985–89; Department of Art Advisory Board, Carnegie Mellon University, Pittsburgh, 1992–98; Board of Governors, Skowhegan School of Painting and Sculpture, Maine, 1998 to present. **Agent:** DC Moore Gallery, 724 Fifth Avenue, New York, New York 10019. **Address:** 152 Wooster Street, New York, New York 10012, U.S.A.

Individual Exhibitions:

1970 Tibor de Nagy Gallery, New York
1971 Tibor de Nagy Gallery, New York
1973 Mabel Smith Douglass Library, New Brunswick, New Jersey
Tibor de Nagy Gallery, New York
1974 University of Rhode Island Fine Arts Center, Kingston
Tibor de Nagy Gallery, New York
1975 Kingpitcher Gallery, Pittsburgh (with Howardena Pindell)
San Francisco Art Institute
1976 Tibor de Nagy Gallery, New York
Women's Building, Los Angeles
Queens College, New York
1977 Watson/de Nagy Gallery, Houston
Jasper Gallery, Denver
Tibor de Nagy Gallery, New York

Joyce Kozloff: *La Conquista,* 1999. Photo by Mimmo Capone. ©Joyce Kozloff.

Wilcox Gallery, Swathmore College, Pennsylvania
Ross Graphics, Minneapolis (with Herb Jackson and Adja Yunkers)
1978 University of New Mexico, Albuquerque (with Max Kozloff)
1979 *An Interior Decorated,* Tibor de Nagy Gallery, New York (travelled to Everson Museum, Syracuse, New York; Mint Museum, Charlotte, North Carolina; Renwick Gallery, Smithsonian Institute, Washington, D.C.)
1980 Mint Museum, Charlotte, North Carolina
The Renwick, Washington, D.C.
1981 Tibor de Nagy Gallery, New York (with Betty Woodman)
1982 *Etchings and Other Works on Paper,* Crown Point Gallery, Oakland, California
Projects and Proposals, Barbara Gladstone Gallery, New York
I-80 Series, Joslyn Art Museum, Omaha, Nebraska
1983 Berkshire Community College, Pittsfield, Massachusetts
Barbara Gilman Gallery, Miami (with Miriam Schapiro)
Architectural Fantasies/Urban Sites, McIntosh/Drysdale Gallery, Houston (with Richard Haas and Ned Smyth)
Investigations 4, Institute of Contemporary Art, Philadelphia
Lincoln Center for Performing Arts, New York (with Elizabeth Murray and Judith Murray)
1984 *Three Train Stations,* Delaware Art Museum, Wilmington
Project Studio One, New York
San Antonio Art Institute, Texas
1985 *Architectural Caprices,* Barbara Gladstone Gallery, New York
1986 San Antonio Art Institute, Texas
Visionary Ornament, Boston University, Massachusetts (toured the United States, 1986–87)
1990 *Patterns of Desire,* Lorence-Monk Gallery, New York (toured U.S. and Germany, 1990–93)
1991 *The Movies: Fantasies,* 152 Wooster Street Space, New York
1992 *Informed Sources,* State University of New York at Old Westbury (with Jeff Perrone and Kim MacConnel)
1995 *Mapping Public and Private,* Midtown Payson Galleries, New York
Around the World on the 44th Parallel, Tile Guild, Los Angeles
1997 *Other People's Fantasies: Maps, Movies, and Menus,* D.C. Moore Gallery, New York
1998 *Crossed Purposes* (with Max Kozloff), List Gallery, Swarthmore College, Pennsylvania (toured United States)
1999 *Knowledge: An Ongoing Fresco Project by Joyce Kozloff,* DC Moore Gallery, New York
2000 *Targets,* DC Moore Gallery, New York
2001 *Joyce Kozloff: Mapping Worlds,* National Museum of Women in the Arts, Washington D.C.

Selected Group Exhibitions:

1972 *Painting Annual,* Whitney Museum, New York
1975 *Color, Light and Image,* Women's Inter-Art-Center, New York
1978 *Arabesque,* Contemporary Arts Center, Cincinnati
1979 *The Decorative Impulse,* Institute of Contemporary Art, Philadelphia
1980 *Printed Art: A View of Two Decades,* Museum of Modern Art, New York
1982 *Polychrome Sculpture,* Lever House, New York
1983 *Back to the U.S.A.,* Kunstmuseum, Lucerne, Switzerland
1985 *Working on the Railroad,* Whitney Museum, Stamford, Connecticut
1987 *Prints in Parts,* Crown Point Press, New York
1990 *Hassam and Speicher Fund Purchase Exhibition,* American Academy of Arts and Letters, New York
1993 *Architectural Clay,* The Clay Studio, Philadelphia, Pennsylvania
1995 *Division of Labor: Women's Work in Contemporary Art,* Bronx Museum of Art, New York
1996 *Graphics from Solo Impressions, Inc.,* Member's Gallery, Albright-Knox Art Gallery, Buffalo, New York
1997 *Patchworks: Contemporary Interpretations of the Quilt Form,* Islip Art Museum, East Islip, New York
1998 *Food for Thought: A Visual Banquet,* D.C. Moore Gallery, New York
1999 *World Views: Maps and Art,* Frederick R. Weisman Art Museum, University of Minnesota, Minneapolis
1999–2000 *The American Century: Art and Culture, 1900–2000,* Whitney Museum of American Art, New York
2000 *Home Abroad,* Sala Uno, Rome

2001 *Fresh/Fresco,* Educational Alliance Art Gallery, New York

Collections:

Museum of Modern Art, New York; Metropolitan Museum of Art, New York; Brooklyn Museum, New York; Vassar College, Poughkeepsie, New York; Albright-Knox Art Gallery, Buffalo, New York; Massachusetts Institute of Technology, Cambridge; Municipal Gallery and Museum of Modern Art, Udine, Italy; Allen Memorial Art Museum, Oberlin, Ohio; Norton Gallery of Art, West Palm Beach, Florida; Neue Galerie Sammlung Ludwig, Aachen, Germany; Library of Congress, Washington, D.C.; National Gallery of Art, Washington D.C.; National Museum of American Art, Smithsonian Institution, Washington, D.C.; Whitney Museum of American Art, New York.

Permanent Public Installations:

Harvard Square Subway Station, Cambridge, Massachusetts; Wilmington Train Station, Delaware; Humboldt-Hospital Subway Station, Buffalo, New York; International Terminal, San Francisco Airport; 1 Penn Center Suburban Station, Philadelphia; Detroit Transportation Corporation Financial Station, Detroit; 7th and Flower Metro Rail Station, Los Angeles; Washington National Airport.

Publications:

By KOZLOFF: Books—*Interviews with Women Artists,* editor, New York 1975; *Patterns of Desire,* with introduction by Linda Nochlin, New York 1990. **Articles**—''Letter to the Editor'' in *Anonymous Was a Woman,* Valencia, California 1974; ''Women Artists Speak on Women Artist,'' edited with May Stevens, in *Women's Studies* (New York), Fall 1976; ''The Women's Movement: Still a Source of Strength or One Big Bore?'' with Barbara Zucker, in *Artnews* (New York), April 1976; ''Frida Kahlo'' in *Women's Studies* (New York), vol. 6, no. 1, 1978; essay in *An Interior Decorated,* exhibition catalog, New York 1979; ''Frida Kahlo at the Neuberger Museum'' in *Art in America* (New York), May/June 1979; ''An Ornamented Joke'' in *Artforum* (New York), December 1986; ''Like a Dense Curry with Coconut Milk,'' in *American Ceramics,* summer 1987.

On KOZLOFF: Books—*From the Center* by Lucy Lippard, New York 1977; *Arabesque,* exhibition catalog by Ruth K. Meyer, Cincinnati, Ohio 1978; *Joyce Kozlof: An Interior Decorated,* exhibition catalog, New York 1979; *I-80 Series: Joyce Kozloff,* catalog with essay by Holliday T. Day, Omaha 1982; *Investigations 4: Joyce Kozloff,* with essay by Janet Kardon, Philadelphia 1984; *Working on the Railroad,* exhibition catalog with text by Pamela Gruninger Perkins, New York 1985; *Joyce Kozloff: Visionary Ornaments* by Patricia Johnston, Boston 1986; *American Ceramics 1876 to present,* by Garth Clark, New York 1987; *Women Artists: An Illustrated History,* by Nancy G. Heller, New York 1987; *Hands in Clay* by Charlotte F. Speight, Mountain View, California 1989; *Women, Art and Society* by Whitney Chadwick, London 1990; *Contemporary Art* by Klaus Honnef, Cologne, Germany 1990; *Mutiny and the Mainstream: Talk that Changed Art 1975–1990* by Judy Siegel, New York 1992; *Race, Sex and Gender in Contemporary Art* by Edward Lucie-Smith, New York 1994. **Articles**—''New York Letter'' by Carter Ratcliff in *Art International* (Lugano), January 1978; ''Atelierbeschuche'' by Madeleine Stricler and Dominik Keller in *Du* (Zurich), June 1979; ''Zurück and Hinzur 'Wurde des Dekorativen''' by Harald Szeemann in *Du* (Zurich), June 1979; ''Decoration, Ornament, Pattern and Utility'' by Carrie Rickey in *Flash Art* (Milan) June/July 1979; ''The New Decorativeness'' by John Perreault in *Portfolio* (New York), June/July 1979; ''A Room with a Coup'' by John Perreault in the *Soho Weekly News* (New York), 13 September 1979; ''Joyce Kozloff'' and ''The Decorative Impulse'' both by Jeff Perrone in *Artforum* (New York), November 1979; ''Joyce Kozloff'' by Nancy Stapen in *Artforum* (New York), Summer 1986; ''Pattern and Decoration in the Public Eye'' by Sally Webster in *Art in America,* (New York), February 1987; ''Angels in the Architecture,'' by Robert Jensen in *Metropolitan Home,* May 1988; ''American Craft Museum Design in Art,'' by Peter Carlsen in *Art News,* May 1988; ''A Sense of Time, a Sense of Place,'' by Mason Riddle in *American Ceramics,* Summer 1988; ''Her Infinite Variety,'' by Sue Allison in *Life,* June 1989; ''Crimes of Passion,'' by Peggy Phelan in *Artforum,* May 1990; ''Patterns of Desire,'' by Rafael Meyer Rubinstein in *Arts,* May 1991; ''Monsters on the Blue Line,'' by Peter Clothier in *Art News,* Feb 1992; ''Glossy Journey to the Center of the Earth,'' by Christopher Knight in *Los Angeles Times,* 14 February 1993; ''Underground Movies in L.A.'' by Robert Kushner in *Art in America,* December 1994; ''Accessories of Destination: The Recent Work of Joyce Kozloff'' by Akiko Busch in *American Ceramics,* vol. 21, no. 1, 1995; ''One Square at a Time: Joyce Kozloff's Tile Murals'' by Charlene Roth in *Artweek,* April 1995; ''Joyce Kozloff'' in *New Yorker,* 15 May 1995; ''Joyce Kozloff: Public Art Works'' by Joyce Lyon in *Public Art Review,* Fall/Winter 1996; ''Husband and Wife Team Up for an Exhibition'' by Edward J. Sozanski in *Philadelphia Inquirer,* 27 March 1998; ''Joyce and Max Kozloff: Crossed Purposes'' by Robert Bambic in *Art Papers,* September/October 1998; ''Joyce Kozloff'' by David Frankel in *Artforum,* September 1999; ''The Likeness of Being'' by Joyce B. Korotkin in *New York Art World,* February 2000; ''L'America dei Nuovi Talenti'' by Furio Colombo in *Republica,* 24 July 2000; ''An Interview with Joyce and Max Kozloff'' by Vicki Goldberg in *Art Journal,* Fall 2000. **Films—** *Tape No. 15—New Public Art (Joyce Kozloff, Keith Haring, John Ahearn),* 1983; *Joyce Kozloff: Public Art Works,* 1996; *Pattern and Decoration: The Great Untold Story* by Anne Swartz.

*

My art of the last seven years or so has been for urban transportation systems. We city dwellers experience those systems daily. For me, the challenge has been to enchance and clarify their architecture without obstructing function, and to celebrate each city's visual and cultural history without alienating or pandering to a self-defined public.

—Joyce Kozloff

KRIEG, Dieter

Nationality: German. **Born:** Lindau, Bodensee, 21 May 1937. **Education:** Studied art, under H. A. P. Grieshaber and Herbert Kitzel, at the Kunstakademie, Karlsruhe, 1958–62. **Family:** Married Irene

Kehne in 1970. **Career:** Independent painter, in Karlsruhe and Baden-Baden, 1963–78, in Cologne from 1978. Guest instructor, Kunstakademie, Karlsruhe, 1971–72; Stadelschule, Frankfurt, 1975–76; professor, Kunstakademie, Dusseldorf, 1978. **Awards:** Deutscher Kunstpreis der Jugend, Baden-Baden, 1966; Preis der Veranstalter, *Biennale Danuvius '68,* Bratislava, 1968; Kunstpreis der Bottscherstrasse, Bremen, 1969; Kunstpreis, City of Darmstadt, 1970. **Agent:** Galerie Heinz Herzer, Gabelsbergerstraße 17, 80333 Munich, Germany.

Individual Exhibitions:

1966 Badischer Kunstverein, Karlsruhe
1967 Galerie der Spiegel, Cologne
1968 Galerie der Spiegel, Cologne
1969 Galerie Thomas, Munich
Gegenverkehr, Zentrum für Aktuelle Kunst, Aachen, Germany
Staatliche Kunsthalle, Baden-Baden, Germany
1970 Galerie im Zimmertheater, Tübingen (with Hans Baschang)
Württembergischer Kunstverein, Stuttgart
Galerie Lauter, Mannheim
Galerie Regio, Lorrach, Germany
Galerie der Spiegel, Cologne
1971 Neue Galerie, Baden-Baden, Germany
Galerie Stangl, Munich
1972 Kunsthalle, Darmstadt
Westfalischer Kunstverein, Münster, Germany
Kunsthalle, Bielefeld, Germany
Städtischer Kunstpavillon, Soest, Germany
Frankfurter Kunstverein, Frankfurt
Galerie Centro, Oldenburg, Germany
1973 Galerie der Spiegel, Cologne
Galerie Regio, Basel
Galerie Schneider, Karlsruhe
Städtische Galerie, Nordhorn, Germany
1974 Bottcherstrasse, Bremen
Galerie der Spiegel, Cologne
1976 Galerie Centro, Oldenburg, Germany
Galerie der Spiegel, Cologne
Galerie am Promenadeplatz, Munich
1977 Galerie am Promenadeplatz, Munich
1978 Galerie am Promenedeplatz, Weissadlergasse, Frankfurt
Studio F, Ulm, Germany
German Pavilon at the *Biennale,* Venice
Galerie am Promenadeplatz, Munich
Krutzraedthuis, Sittard, Netherlands
1979 Galerie am Promenadeplatz, Munich
1980 Galerie der Spiegel, Cologne
1981 Galerie Dibbert, Berlin
Galerie am Promenadeplatz, Munich
1982 Galerie Ha Jo Muller, Cologne
1983 Galerie Heinz Herzer, Munich
Artothek, Cologne
1984 Badischer Kunstverein, Karlsruhe
1985 Galerie Heinz Herzer, Munich
1991 *Dieter Krieg: Bilder, 1986–1990,* Kunstmuseum Düsseldorf im Ehrenhof (catalog)
1993 *Dieter Krieg,* Hans-Thoma-Museum, Bernau (catalog)
1999 *Band 2,* Galerie der Stadt Stuttgart (also Staatliche Kunsthalle Baden-Baden) (catalog)
Radierungen, Museum Waldhof, Bielefelder Kunstverein, Stuttgart (catalog)
"In der Leere ist Nichts," Von der Heydt-Museum, Wuppertal, Germany (catalog)
2000 *Foto,* Galerie Der Spiegel, Cologne

Selected Group Exhibitions:

1967 *Wege 67,* Museum am Ostwall, Dortmund
5th Biennale de Paris, Musée d'Art Moderne de la Ville, Paris
1968 *Krieg/Kriwet/Mavignier/Vostell,* Kunst und Museumverein, Wuppertal, Germany
1970 *3rd Internationale der Zeichnung,* Mathildenhohe, Darmstadt
1971 *Aktiva '71,* Munich
1977 *Documenta 6,* Museum Fridericianum, Kassel, Germany
1979 *Schlaglichter,* Rheinisches Landesmuseum, Bonn
1981 *Hartmann/Krieg/Kristiansen/Vogt,* Von der Heydt-Museum, Wuppertal, Germany
1982 *Ansichten-Struckturen-Horizonte: Landschaften,* Bundeskanzleramt, Bonn
1983 *8 in Koln,* Kunstverein, Cologne
1995 *26th Art Basel,* Switzerland
Staatliche Kunsthalle Karlsruhe: Impuls Südwest—Kunst der 60er Jahre in Baden-Württemburg, Staatliche Kunsthalle Karlsruhe, Germany (catalog)
1996 *On Object Things in Contemporary Art,* Museum zu Allerheiligen, Schaffhausen, Germany (also Stadtische Galerie Rahnitzgasse, Dresden, Germany) (catalog)
1997 Schloss Randegg, Gottmadingen, Germany

Collections:

Kunsthalle, Bielefeld, Germany; Sammiung Schulza-Vellinghausen, Ruhr-Universitat, Bochum, Germany; Städtisches Kunstmuseum, Bonn; Museum am Ostwall, Dortmund; Kunsthalle, Hamburg; Städtische Kunsthalle, Mannheim; Staatsgalerie Moderner Kunst, Munich; Staatsgalerie, Stuttgart; Von der Heydt Museum, Wuppertal, Germany; Museum des 20. Jahrhunderts, Vienna.

Publications:

By KRIEG: Books—*Dieter Krieg: Arbeiten,* Stuttgart 1993; *Dieter Krieg: Vorhänge,* Ostfildern 1996.

On KRIEG: Books—*Tage, Tage, Jahre* by Marie Luise Kaschnitz, Frankfurt 1968; *Dieter Krieg,* exhibition catalog with text by Klaus Honnef, Aachen Germany 1969; *Deutsche Kunst—eine neue Generation* by Rolf-Günter Dienst, Cologne 1970; *Deutsche Kunst der 60er Jahre* by Juiane Roh, Munich 1971; *Neue Formen des Realismus* by Peter Sager, Cologne 1973; *Deutsche Malerie nach 1945* by Weiland Schmied, Frankfurt 1974; *Biennale di Venezia 1978: Dieter Krieg,* exhibition catalog with texts by Klaus Gallwitz, Jürgen Morschel, and Volker Klinnius, Cologne 1978; *Hartmann/Kreig/Kristiansen/Vogt: 4 beitrage zur neuen malerei,* exhibition catalog with text by

Günter Aust, Wuppertal, West Germany 1981; *Dieter Krieg,* exhibition catalog with essays by Hans Gunter Wachtmann and Andreas Vowinckel, Karlsruhe 1984. **Articles—**''Aus Matschiger Masse Erheben Sick Hähnchenkeule und Cognac-Schwenker'' by Ruth Händler in *ART: Das Kunstmagazin,* no. 2, February 1995; ''Krieg: Tazze King-size sul Mondo la Potenza del Banale'' by Andrea Petricca in *Arte,* no. 268, December 1995; ''Mit Gewalt den Dingen auf den Leib Gerückt'' by Angelika Kindermann in *ART: Das Kunstmagazin,* no. 3, March 1996; ''Dieter Krieg: 'In der Leere ist Nichts': Von der Heydt-Museum, Wuppertal'' by Claudia Posca in *Kunstforum International,* no. 149, January/March 2000.

* * *

An enormous meat-hook looms in a large-format (256 x 180 cm.) untitled 1986 painting by Dieter Krieg. A note with the inscription ''Idiot'' pierces the canvas. The work's yellow-ocher palette consists of paint laid on in compact swirls of color, a work with its surface space solely built up with relief-type mountaintop crusts of color, and the downward-thrusting meat-hook—which bends up from the lower left plane of the painting and points away—stands out against this surface. The meat-hook pierces the dirty-white note behind the letter ''D'', a mark of distinction in much the same way as the meat-hook itself. Such is a typical painting from a series of similar painted works created by Krieg in a seemingly expressive manner during the 1980s. The quick application of painting typical of the neo-Expressionist painters simultaneously denotes possibly a reflex and at the same time an unmistakable attitude. Such a work likewise hearkens back to an unmistakable uttering of the words of Paul Cezanne almost a century before: ''The painter is not an idiot.'' Perception and thought were to him one, for Cezanne held that the subconscious should always be visible in painting. Most painters run aground at this pretentious task, giving way to the assertion of the only mediocre-gifted painter Marcel Duchamp, an utterance met without great opposition: ''Stupid as a painter.'' Dieter Krieg is aware of such provocations. He is not a painter of passion, but rather of necessity. In his work he has not established any influential trend in modern painting nor does he belong to the brilliant exalted prolificness typical of the breed of artists like Gerhard Richter and Sigmar Polke. He is a little younger than the one, and a little older than the other. He has certainly executed his artistic work in a tension-rich relation to the artistic sketches—and in this regard he is at a similar place as the both of them—before the font of an all-devouring world of images stemming from electronic observation. Where many attempt to drive out the devil by means of Lucifer, Krieg offers a delayed resistance. He tests the instrumentation of painting under aggravated conditions. His attitude has been characterized by Klaus Gallwitz, considered an expert on Krieg's work, as one of a ''sarcastic'' reality. The banal topics that Krieg assembles in his paintings, the cutlets and walking sticks, the drumsticks and buckets, the tree branches and phonograph records, the heads of fish and lettuce, the chromosomes, all frequently blown up to superhuman dimensions, deal in their decimated, penetrated present reality of losses—and offer a remarkable yet disturbed beauty and nevertheless a learning experience in spite of their notorious and often thought-provoking unpleasantness by virtue of aesthetic transformation. With such a crude object, whose evident hulking materiality differs in materialistic hindsight just as sometimes it also differs in the artistic treatment scarcely conveyed through other maelstroms, is a lightning of the spirit. ''I demand that the painter interpret (the thing),'' said Cezanne; in a such a deed, perception and thought are inseparable. Dieter Krieg continually undertakes the risk of interpretation, again and again from the new. And he constantly exposes the danger of the wreckage. With this the gruesome banality of the painted objects has not disappeared, but instead the painting gains a tenuous authenticity, or in more common terms, a truth. The painting ''turns out the face of truth,'' according to Gallwitz. While Duchamp, through the removal of the banal circumstance of the everyday, lent to the art a halo of singularity, Krieg destroys this ''beautiful appearance'' through simple empiricism: through the artistic practice of the painter. He goes up to the border of painting, he even steps over it, not freely in the direction of some kind of quality separate from it, but rather the other way around: in the determined reflex toward the possible impossibility of the earlier discipline of art, but now in the time of mass media.

Externally his paintings burst out of their traditional frames: 4 to 5 meters in height, 7 to 8 meters in width are not the rule, but also not an exception. Although megalomania does not propel the artist, much more important is the question of the general weight of the painting as means of communication. The writing is also for Krieg an applied way of considering the object. ''Loss'' stands in strong dark letters, letters that throw singular raw intimated shadows on a three-part untitled canvas (1992) almost ten meters in length. ''A year of sorrow'' appear on another canvas, one that is scarcely smaller. The provocation that the painter overcomes becomes the shape by which the observer is also challenged.

—Klaus Honnef

KRIESCHE, Richard

Nationality: Austrian. **Born:** Vienna, 28 October 1940. **Education:** Fine Arts Academy, Vienna, 1958–63. **Military Service:** Austrian Army, 1965–66. **Family:** Married Gerlinde Well in 1969; daughters: Sarah and Rosa. **Career:** Artist, working with videotapes and performances, Graz, since 1971. Instructor, Technical School, Graz, since 1963; art director, Audio-Visual Centre, Graz, 1977–79; founder, Kulturdata centre, Graz, 1984; Professor for electronic imaging at ''Hochschule feur Gestaltung'' Offenbach, Germany; guest professor, École Supérieure des Beaux Arts, Paris, 1995–96; assistant director of science and research with local government, Styria, 1996; ember of the committee ''Cultural Capital Graz 2003.'' since 1999. **Awards:** DAAD Fellowship, West Berlin, 1983; Research Grant, Massachusetts Institute of Technology, Cambridge, 1985–86. **Address:** Trautmansdorffgasse 1, 8010 Graz, Austria.

Individual Exhibitions:

1968 Forum Stadpark, Graz
1970 Galerie im Griechenbeisl, Graz
1971 Sigi Krauss Gallery, London
1972 Galerie im Taxispalais, Innsbruck
1973 Neue Galerie, Graz
1975 Kölnischer Kunstverein, Cologne
Galerie Stampa, Basle
1976 Galerie Nächst St. Stephan, Vienna

1977 Archivio Storico delle Arti Contemporaneo, Venice
1980 Modern Art Galerie, Vienna
Galerie Dr. Schurr, Stuttgart
1981 Hartmannsdorf, Austria
Bob Adrian/Peter Hoffman/Richard Kriesche, Galerija Suvremene Umjetnosti, Zagreb
1982 Kunsthaus, Zurich
Forum Stadpark, Graz
1983 Gedachtniskirche, West Berlin
1985 Massachusetts Institute of Technology, Cambridge
1987 Opera-Graz, Graz
Art Radio, Museum of Contemporary Art, Los Angeles
1989 *Radioman,* Manchester Cornerhouse
1990 Wien Galerie, Krinzinger
1991 *Artsat,* Russian Space Station Mir
1993 *Teleskuptur 3,* Graz Kunstlerhaus
Virtuelles Innsbruck, Hörraum Innsbruck, Innsbruck
Kunsthistory Museum, Diskurse der Bilder, Vienna
1994 *Poiesis,* Institut für Botanik, Hamburg
1995 *Am anfang war. . . ,* kunsthalle tirol, Hall
Telematische Skulptur 4, 46th Biennale di Venezia, Venice
1996 *The Butterfly Effect,* Museum Mucsarnok, Budapest
Sphären der Kunst, Neue Galerie, Graz
Espaces interactifs europe, Pavillon de Percy, Paris
1997 *The E-mail Show,* Chicago Art Institute
Deutschlandbilder, Neuer Berliner Kunstverein, Martin-Gropius-Bau, Berlin
Guggenheim Museum, New York
1998 *World Wide Networkart 98,,* Asahi Beer Squea-A, Tokyo
Transformation3, Theatro Trieste, Trieste
Electronically Yours, Tokyo Metropolitan Museum of Photography
1999 *Transformation3,* Biennale di Venezia, Venice
2000 *Dynamik im Datenraum,* Industriemesse, Hannover
Re-play, Generali Foundation, Vienna
Art, Science and Communication, Vienna
Recodierung-decodierung, Kunsthalle Wien, Vienna
Postbiological Consciousness, Gaiia Institute, Newport, United Kingdom

Selected Group Exhibitions:

1977 *Documenta 6,* Museum Fridericianum, Kassel, Germany
Massachusetts Institute of Technology, Cambridge
1983 *Kunst und Photographie,* Nationalgalerie, Berlin
1984 *Arte Austriacca 1960–84,* Galleria d'Arte Moderna, Bologna, Italy
1985 *Brainwork,* Municipal Art Gallery, Los Angeles
1986 *42nd Biennale,* Venice
1987 *Documenta 8,* Museum Fridericianum, Kassel, Germany
1988 *Sitting Technology,* Danff
1989 *Weltmodell II,* Ars Electronica, Linz
1993 Kunsthistorisches Museum, Vienna
1994 Ars Electronica, Linz

Collections:

Neue Galerie, Graz; Museum des 20. Jahrhunderts, Vienna; Kunsthalle, Hamburg.

Publications:

By KRIESCHE: Books—*Life-video-sound-polaroid installation,* Graz 1973; *Video End, Konzepte Theorien und Dokumente Osterreichischer Videoproduktionen,* Graz 1977; *Wirklichkeit gegen Wirklichkeit,* Kassel, Germany 1977; *Kulturinitiative Weiz I,* Weiz 1977; *Kulturinitiative Weiz II,* Weiz 1978; *Kulturinitiative Bruck,* Bruck 1978; *Art, Artist and the Media,* Graz 1978; *Kinderfreundliches Kranzenzimmer,* Graz 1979; *Kunst Mikrokunst Makrokunst,* Graz and Zagreb 1981; *Humane Skulpturen,* Graz 1981; *Artsat,* Graz 1991; *Teleskulpur III,* Graz 1993; *Space,* Graz 1993; *The Electronic Academy,* Offenbach 1991; *Telesculpture: Debounded Boundaries II,* Graz 1993; *Informationmachine,* Venice 1995; *Am anfang war. . .* (with CD), Tyrol 1995; *Spheres of Art* (with CD-ROM), Graz 1996; *Journey to the Moon* (with CD-ROM), Graz/Poitiers 1998; *Art, Science and Communication* (with CD-ROM), Graz 2000.

On KRIESCHE: Books—*Situation Concepts,* exhibition catalog, Vienna 1971; *Bob Adrian/Peter Hoffmann/Richard Kriesche,* exhibition catalog, Zagreb 1981; *Brainwork: Artificial Intelligence in the Arts,* exhibition catalog, Los Angeles 1985; *Videokunst,* Vienna 1991; *Diskurse der Bilder,* Vienna 1993; *Radio Rethink,* Banff Canada 1994.

*

The determining question for me is the question for the signification of an artist. If there are besides the important global issues (e.g, Peace) any others—the way of survival—then art is nothing else but a strategy for survival. The question remains: How does ''survival strategy'' look at any given moment? What is the task of the artist? What is the task of art? To me, it is solely a question of society needing new forms and languages to get through, over, under its barriers to solve its ''home-made'' contradictions. Specifically, in relation to the artist, it means that he himself has to overcome these barriers, has to get through the contradictions, and find an authentic formulation. It means that the artist has to abandon the secure and ritualized conditions of art-dialogue and involve himself in the risk of life-dialogue—to become again a *real* artist.

I am interested in farmers (project: humane skulturen), prisoners (project: Karlau prison), small towns with a heavy provincialism (project: Weiz and Bruck), children in hospitals (project: Kinderfreundliches krankenzimmer), strikes (project: Dustmen's strike, London), etc., with a view to finding or developing a social language for learning forms for social living in and with the given reality, and for overcoming that reality. The penetration of the second—the media reality—counts in this as well. And so I am interested in 1 + 1 = 3, which I demonstrated electronically at the *Basle Art Fair,* or in ''Technology as a Moral of the Ruling Class,'' which I have again demonstrated in Basle, at Galerie Stampa.

From the dialectics of both realities my concern is to develop media-relevant references out of life, and life-relevance out of the media. I guess that's what ''artworking'' is about.

The visionary video installation at the end of the 1970s on the art fair in Basle—''Technology is the Moral of the Ruling Class''—has come true in reality. The myth of avant garde has been taken over in realtime and realspace by e-based capital, industry and commerce. (Call it techno-based neo-liberalism.) If art will ever become human capital, then art's function in contrary is to strengthen the e-based structure given in our archaic bodies and minds. ''Retrogarde'' is at stake now.

—Richard Kriesche

KRUGER, Barbara

Nationality: American. **Born:** Newark, New Jersey, 26 January 1945. **Education:** Studied at Syracuse University, New York; Parsons School of Design, New York; School of Visual Arts, New York. **Career:** Independent artist/photographer, New York, since 1972. Visiting artist, California Institute of Art, Valencia; Art Institute of Chicago; University of California, Berkeley. **Awards:** Creative Artists Public Service Grant, New York, 1976; National Endowment for the Arts Grant, Washington, D.C., 1983. **Agents:** Rhona Hoffman Gallery, 215 West Superior Street, Chicago, Illinois 60610; Larry Gagosian Gallery, 510 North Robertson Boulevard, Los Angeles, California 90048; Galerie Crousel-Robelin, 40 rue Quincampoix, 75004 Paris, France. **Address:** c/o Mary Boone Gallery, 745 Fifth Avenue, New York, New York 10151, U.S.A.

Barbara Kruger: *Untitled (No),* 1985. ©Smithsonian American Art Museum, Washington, DC/Art Resources, NY; courtesy of Smithsonian American Art Museum.

Individual Exhibitions:

1974 Artists' Space, New York
1975 Fischbach Gallery, New York
1976 John Doyle Gallery, Chicago
1979 Franklin Furnace, New York
Printed Matter Window, New York
1980 Project Studio One, Long Island City, New York
1982 Larry Gagosian Gallery, Los Angeles
Hallwalls Gallery, Buffalo, New York
1983 Annina Nosei Gallery, New York
Galerie Chantal Crousel, Paris
Institute of Contemporary Arts, London
1984 Le Nouveau Musee, Lyon-Villeurbanne, France
Galerie Crousel-Hussenot, Paris
Kunsthalle, Basel (with Jenny Holzer)
1985 Los Angeles County Museum of Art
1987 Galerie Monika Spruth, Cologne
Crousel/Hussenot Galerie, Paris
Galerie Monika Spruth, Cologne, Germany
1988 National Art Gallery, Wellington, New Zealand
1989 Mary Boone Gallery, New York
Galerie Bebert, Rotterdam
Fred Hoffman Gallery, Santa Monica, California
1990 Duke University Museum of Art, Durham, North Carolina
Monika Spruth Galerie, Cologne, Germany
Rhona Hoffman Gallery, Chicago, Illinois
Kolnischer Kunstverein, Cologne, Germany
1991 Mary Boone Gallery, New York
1992 Magasin, Centre National d'Art Contemporain, Grenoble, France
1994 Mary Boone Gallery, New York
1996 Museum of Modern Art at Heide, Melbourne, Australia
1997 Mary Boone Gallery, New York
18 Wooster Street/Deitch Projects, New York
1998 Parrish Art Museum, Southampton, New York
1999 Galerie Yvon Lambert, Paris
Retrospective, Museum of Contemporary Art, Los Angeles, California
2000 Retrospective, Whitney Museum of American Art, New York

Selected Group Exhibitions:

1973 *Whitney Biennial,* Museum, New York (and 1983)
1978 *False Face,* Name Gallery, Chicago
1980 *Four Different Photographers,* Padiglione d'Arte Contemporanea, Milan
1981 *19 Emergent Americans,* Guggenheim Museum, New York
1982 *Documenta 7,* Museum Fridericianum, Kassel, Germany
1983 *The Revolutionary Power of Women's Laughter,* Protetch McNeill Gallery, New York
1984 *Content: A Contemporary Focus,* Hirshhorn Museum, Washington, D.C.
1985 *New York: Ailleurs et Autrement,* ARC, Museé d'Art Moderne, Paris
1986 *Ein Anderes Klima: Kunsterinnen Gebrauchen Neue Medien,* Kunsthalle Dusseldorf
1987 *El Arte y Su Doble,* Centro Cultural de la Fundacio Caixa de Pensions, Barcelona
1988 *L'Epoque, La Mode, La Morale, La Passion,* Centre Georges Pompidou, Paris
1989 *Image World: Art and Media Culture,* Whitney Museum of American Art, New York
1990 *Opening Exhibition, 20th Century Pavilion,* The Israel Museum, Jerusalem

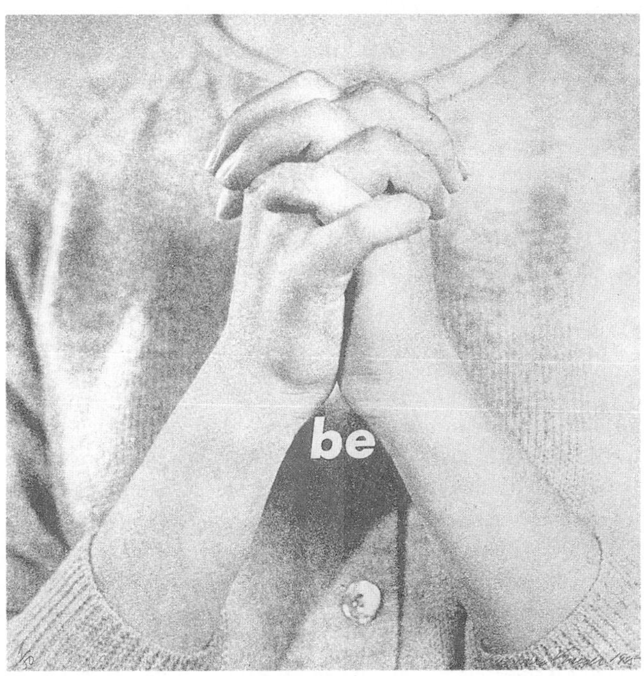

Barbara Kruger: *Untitled (be),* 1985. ©Smithsonian American Art Museum, Washington, DC/Art Resource, NY; courtesy of Smithsonian American Art Museum.

1991 *Beyond the Frame: American Art, 1960–1990,* Setagaya Art Museum, Tokyo (travelled to National Museum of Art, Osaka; Fukuoka Art Museum, Fukuoka, Japan)
1992 *More Than One Photography: Works Since 1980 from the Collection,* Museum of Modern Art, New York
1993 *Inside Out,* Centro per l'Arte Contemporanea Luigi Pecci, Prato, Italy
1994 *An American Century of Photography: From Dry-Point to Digital,* Nelson-Atkins Museum of Art, Kansas City, Missouri (toured United States, Australia and New Zealand)
1995 *Passions Privees,* Museé d'Art Moderne de la Ville de Paris
1996 *Thinking Print: Books to Billboards, 1980–95,* Museum of Modern Art, New York
1997 *Word to Word,* Linda Kirkland Gallery, New York
1998 *Read My Lips: Jenny Holzer, Barbara Kruger, Cindy Sherman,* National Gallery of Australia, Canberra
1999 *The American Century: Art and Culture 1950–2000,* Whitney Museum of American Art, New York
2000 *Sentimental,* Galerie Yvon Lambert, Paris

Publications:

By KRUGER: Books—*Picture/Readings,* New York 1978; *No Progress in Pleasure,* New York 1982; *Beauty and Critique,* New York 1983; *Remote Control*, Cambridge, Massachusetts 1993. **Film—** *Next to Nothing,* with Jane Weinstock, 1983.

On KRUGER: Books—*Four Different Photographers,* exhibition catalog with essay by Carol Squiers, Milan 1980; *19 Emergent Americans,* exhibition catalog with text by Peter Frank, New York 1981; *Inespressionismo Americano,* exhibition catalog with essay by Ingrid Sischy, Genoa 1981; *The Revolutionary Power of Women's Laughter,* exhibition catalog with essay by Joanna Isaak, New York 1983; *We Won't Play Nature to Your Culture: Works by Barbara Kruger*, exhibition catalog, London 1983; *Love For Sale: The Words and Pictures of Barbara Kruger* by Kate Linker, New York: Harry N. Abrams, 1990; *Voicing Today's Visions: Works by Contemporary Women Artists* by Mara Witzling, New York and London 1994, 1995; *Thinking of You: Barbara Kruger,* exhibition catalog, Los Angeles and Cambridge, Massachusetts, 1999. **Articles—**''Barbara Kruger'' by Catherine Liu in *Flash Art,* November 1987; ''Barbara Kruger'' by Margaret Sundell and Thomas Beller in *Splash,* October 1988; ''Diversionary (Syn)tactics/Barbara Kruger Has a Way with Words'' by Carol Squiers in *Bijutsu Techo,* April 1989; ''Barbara Kruger's After-Effects: The Politics of Mourning'' by Therese Lichtenstein in *Art and Text,* July 1989; ''When Worlds Collide'' by David Deitcher in *Art in America,* February 1990; ''Text. Tid. Truismer.'' by Karl Holmqvist in *Clic,* October 1990; ''Barbara Kruger: Resisting Arrest'' by David Deitcher in *Artforum,* February 1991; ''You Thrive on Mistaken Identity'' by Mignon Nixon in *October,* April 1992; ''Shock of the Nasty: Art's Bad Girls'' by Lois Nesbitt in *Elle,* December 1992; ''Barbara Kruger'' by Carol Squiers in *Aperture,* February 1995; ''Barbara Kruger'' by Nick Dent in *Black + White,* October 1996; ''The Art of Public Address'' by Thyrza Nichols Goodeve in *Art in America,* November 1997; ''Histoire de l'Art Feminin'' by Vanina Costa in *Beaux Arts Magazine,* March 1999; ''Barbara Kruger: Un Giorno di Ordinaria Violenza'' by Roberta Franceschetti in *Arte* (Milan), January 2000; ''Familiar Icons with a Bold Face'' by Michael Kimmelman in *New York Times,* 14 July 2000.

* * *

Barbara Kruger is among those artists who seek filiation with other forms of expression for art. She employs written texts and images which are already functioning in public consciousness. She creates large tabloids with black and white women's, sometimes children's, faces and clashes them with short inscriptions running across the whole plate. Photographs are appropriated from posters, advertisements and various media images, that is representations which have been already elaborated upon and many a time reproduced, so that it is impossible to detect the ''original.'' What is more, in this procedure a traditional division into the original and a replica becomes immaterial; just as futile is the search for authorship of individual motifs. Instead, we have here a popular lexicon of images of contemporary American culture, loaded with images multiplicated by the media.

The same goes for the texts used by Kruger: they are fragments of various sentences, opinions, convictions and truisms functioning in public opinion, which are shaped not by different people in an individual intellectual effort but—like images—by the media (press, television,advertisements as well as film). Therefore, the texts also have no authors; they are replicas of replicas.

Therefore, Barbara Kruger's art refers to public space, but it draws its energy from subversion applied by the authoress towards this space. The tabloids make us realize that for a long time we have been surrounded with images and phrases that are used by ''all.'' And we have grown accustomed to using them because we could no longer live and communicate otherwise. The inscription on one of the works, ''We are obliged to steal language'' (1980), tells us something about our condition in the world and about coercion we undergo while constructing our sentences, which we consider to be our own. We appropriate both sentences and images. In this world the identity of our ''ego'' is dispersed; it is everywhere and nowhere. Kruger's works tell us that we are not free in our thinking and perception, that it is not us at all; we live and express ourselves in a world staged by others and we do not know who the authors of this staging are.

However, Kruger not only undermines our consciousness of self; she also makes a subversion as regards the codes she appropriates. She does not use whole images but their fragments and combines them in such a way that they lose their original context. She does the same to the fragments of texts. She emulates the methods applied by the media themselves, which feed us only with fragments of unknown wholes. Therefore, she uses towards them the rule of mimesis in order to disclose their manipulations all the more effectively.

Image-and-text clashes created by Kruger have a strong feminist aspect; they refer to the situation of women in the men's world. In this world an individual appearance of a woman becomes obliterated in favour of ''ideal'' looks, in favour of a convention recorded by the media and served by advertisements. The authoress shows how all of us fall victim to a double falsification. Since we not only accept artificiality of the convention as the image of nature, but we fail to notice that the staging of a women's image is a doing of the men's world, which managed to impose this image on women as a binding one, what's more—as the one they desire. Kruger uses the tempting force of the advertisement image to disclose the fallacy of our identification with it. She refers to the trait so strongly functioning in the American culture to undermine its apparent rationality and hit the essence of power with which these images grasp public imagination.

Kruger's art is a plot against plots: against manipulations of the media and against the world subject to patriarchal oraganization. The authoress's plotting includes also visual forcefulness of her art, emulating graphic aggressiveness of American popular culture. This is an additional blow at the mechanisms of power exercised by this culture.

The destructive perception reaches even deeper. Destroying the primary context of appropriated images and texts, shifting their motifs in space and time, she pushes the viewer into a state of frustrating uncertainty. The viewer is not able to detect the original meaning of these motifs, although they are known to him in a way; he does not know what is the order of thinking behind it. The tension between what is known and what is unclear is a great force in Kruger's works. These works tell us that no image and no text have a permanent place in culture any longer, that points of view have become dispersed, that we have to live among contradicting categories and discrete choices, that motifs of the world become more and more illegible. Finally, that we can no longer expect either an ultimate code or an ultimate explanation. We gradually become—as Roland Barthes' ''author''—nomads among images and meanings, none of which is privileged. And this is our new place in culture, the only one we can be sure of.

Barbara Kruger's art (both tabloids and books) strikes with the gravity of problems tackled by the authoress and the vastness of reflections aroused by these problems. This made her one of the most important artists of the 1980s.

—Alicja Kepinska

In the 1990s, Kruger has emphasized the textual basis of her attack, creating museum installations where floor, walls, and ceiling are covered with politically and artistically challenging pronouncements in the bold typeface that has become her trademark. She has also published essays in the *New York Times,* the *Village Voice*, and *Artforum*, where she frequently appears as a columnist and movie reviewer. Kruger scours popular culture, praising such unlikely figures as Howard Stern and analyzing little-known films and videos from her unique feminist, unsentimental perspective.

—Mark Swartz

Barbara Kruger once said: ''I want to welcome a female spectator into the world of men.'' She achieves this goal through visual/textual strategies that collaborate to disrupt the power imbalance associated with the gaze in western culture. In her earlier works from the 1980s, Kruger began to use ''pronomial shifters''—e.g. ''you,'' ''we,'' ''I,'' ''they''—that formed the basis of the majority of her images. Most often, ''you'' is presumed to be male and ''me,'' ''I,'' and ''we'' are presumed female. Thus it is the male gaze that ''hits the side of my [female] face,'' (*Untitled*, 1982) and it is male ''manias [that] become science'' (*Untitled*, 1982). By inserting a female presence as the speaking and seeing subject, Kruger disrupts the dominant point of view.

These early works were comprised of black and white images obtained from sources in popular culture superimposed with similarly appropriated textual elements executed in bold white letters against a red ground. Although in her subsequent works Kruger varied the scale, format, and sometimes medium of her images, her work continues to challenge the power imbalances in western culture, not only of gender, but also of wealth and class.

Since the 1980s, Kruger has effectively resituated her works in the popular media, in billboards, advertising posters, on matchbooks, and on tee-shirts. A phrase such as ''I shop therefore I am'' has a particularly double-edged resonance when emblazoned on a laden shopping bag.

Kruger has pushed the public aspect of her endeavor in her later work in gallery installations, billboards, and other popular media. For example, she designed a series of bus-shelter images that each show a man emblazoned with the word ''HELP,'' and containing a narrative that included the words ''I just found out I was pregnant. What should I do?'' (1991). In 1994 she was commissioned to do a permanent installation in the train station in Strasbourg, France, in which she emblazoned the architectural elements with a series of questions such as ''Who is silent?'' ''Who speaks?'' ''Who dies first?'' ''Who laughs last?'' in German and French.

Recently she has worked with sculptural groupings in such works as *Family* (1997) that shows Jack and Bobby Kennedy holding aloft an image of Marilyn Monroe, skirts rippling to reveal her genitals. She has also used projected images, as in *Power, Pleasure, Desire, Disgust* (London, 2001), in which there is a constant barrage of projected slogans covering every inch of the gallery's surfaces. A major retrospective of her work was held in 1999–2000 at the Museum of Contemporary Art, Los Angeles, and the Whitney Museum of American Art, New York.

—Mara Witzling

KRUSHENICK, Nicholas

Nationality: American. **Born:** New York City, 31 May 1929. **Education:** Dewitt Clinton High School, Bronx, New York, 1945–47; studied at Art Students League, New York, 1948–50, Hans Hofmann School of Fine Arts, New York, 1950–51. **Military Service:** United States Army, 1947–48. **Family:** Married Julia Greenfield in 1951, son: Shawn. **Career:** Painter. Co-founder of Brata Gallery, New York, 1958–61. Visiting artist/critic: School of Visual Arts, New York, 1965; Minneapolis School of Art, 1967; Cooper Union, New York, 1967–69; University of Wisconsin, 1968; Yale University, 1969, 1970; Cornell University, New York, 1970; Ball State University, Indiana, 1971; Lehmann College, New York, 1972; California State University, Long Beach, 1973; University of Alabama, 1973; St. Cloud State University, Minnesota, 1973; University of California, Berkeley, 1973, 1974; Ohio State University, 1974; University of Washington, 1974; California State College, San Bernardino, 1975; University of North Carolina, 1975; University of Kentucky, 1976; University of Delaware, 1976–77; Memphis Art Academy, 1978; Corcoran School of Art, Washington, D.C., 1978; Virginia Commonwealth University, 1982; Syracuse University, New York, 1982; Wilkes College, Pennsylvania, 1984; Visiting Critic, Virginia Commonwealth University, 1982; Visiting Critic, Syracuse University, 1982; Assistant professor, University of Maryland, College Park, 1977–91. **Awards:** Longview Foundation Award, 1962; Tamarind Fellowship, Los Angeles, 1965; Guggenheim Fellowship, 1967. **Agent:** Mitchell Algus Gallery, 25 Thompson Street, New York, New York 10013. **Died:** Of liver cancer in Manhattan, 29 January 1999.

Individual Exhibitions:

1957 Camino Gallery New York
1958 Brata Gallery, New York
1960 Brata Gallery, New York
1962 Graham Gallery, New York
1964 Graham Gallery, New York
1965 Fischbach Gallery, New York
1966 Galerie Muller, Stuttgart
1967 Galerie Sonnabend, Paris
Pace Gallery, New York
Franklin Siden Gallery, Detroit
Galerie Nächst St. Stephan, Vienna
1968 Walker Art Center, Minneapolis (retrospective)
Galerie Der Spiegel, Cologne
1969 Pace Gallery, New York
Dartmouth College, Hanover, New Hampshire
Harcus-Krakow Gallery, Boston
Galerie René Ziegler, Zurich
1970 University of South Florida, Tampa
Galerie René Ziegler, Zurich
1971 Galerie Beyeler, Basel
1972 Lehman College, New York
Galerie Kestner-Gesellschaft, Hannover
Pace Gallery, New York
1973 Galerie Denise René-Hans Mayer, Dusseldorf
University of Alabama, Birmingham
Jack Glenn Gallery, Corona del Mar, California
California State College, Long Beach
1974 ADI Gallery, San Francisco
Portland Center for the Visual Arts, Oregon
Henry Gallery, University of Washington, Seattle
Reed College, Portland Oregon
1975 Foster-White Gallery, Seattle
California State University, San Bernardino
1976 Alfred University, New York
University of Kentucky, Lexington
1977 Bucknell University, Lewisburg, Pennsylvania
Newport Art Association, Rhode Island
1978 Pyramid Gallery, Washington
Hokin Gallery, Chicago
Elizabeth Weiner Gallery, New York
1979 Metropolitan Museum of Miami, Florida
1981 Aldrich Museum, Ridgefield, Connecticut
Gallery K, Washington, D.C.
Carnegie Mellon University, Pittsburgh
1982 Kaber Gallery, New York
River Gallery, Westport, Connecticut
Medici-Berenson Gallery, Miami, Florida
1984 18th Street Gallery, Santa Monica, California
1991 Fernando Alcolea Gallery, Barcelona
1997 The Mattatuck Museum, Waterbury, Connecticut
1999 Mitchell Algus Gallery, New York

Selected Group Exhibitions:

1963 *Drawing Exhibition,* Museum of Modern Art, New York
1964 *Post-Painterly Abstraction,* Los Angeles County Museum of Art (toured the United States and Canada)
1966 *Systemic Painting,* Guggenheim Museum, New York
1968 *Documenta 4,* Kassel, Germany
1973 *Biennial,* Whitney Museum, New York
1978 *Homage to Hans Hofmann,* Metropolitan Museum of Art, New York
1983 *Art and Dance,* New York State University, Purchase
1985 *Exuberant Abstraction,* 100 Church Street, New York
1986 *Embellishment of the Statue of Liberty,* Cooper-Hewitt Museum, New York
1987 *Color Pure and Simple,* Stamford Museum, Connecticut

Collections:

Metropolitan Museum of Art, New York; Museum of Modern Art, New York; Whitney Museum, New York; Albright-Knox Art Gallery, Buffalo, New York; Walker Art Center, Minneapolis; Museum of Fine Arts, Dallas; Los Angeles County Museum of Art; Stedelijk Museum, Amsterdam; Folkwang Museum, Essen; Staatsgalerie, Stuttgart.

Publications:

By KRUSHENICK: Article—statement in *Art Now* (New York), June 1970.

On KRUSHENICK: Articles—''New York Letter'' by Barbara Rose in *Art International* (Lugano, Switzerland), Summer 1964; review by Vivien Raynor in *Arts* (New York), May 1965; review by Sue Greene in *Art Voices* (New York), Spring 1965; ''New York Letter'' by Lucy Lippard in *Art International* (Lugano, Switzerland) September 1965; ''Krushenick's Blazing Blazons'' by John Perreault in *Artnews* (New York), March 1967; review by T. Mussman in *Arts* (New York), April 1967; review by J. Mellow in *Art International* (Lugano, Switzerland), May 1967; ''Krushenick'' by Dean Swanson, in *Art International* (Lugano, Switzerland) April 1968; ''Krushenick's Cultural Revelations'' by Gregory Battcock, in *Arts* (New York), April 1969; ''The Artist Speaks'' by Connie Robbins, in *Art in America* (New York), May 1969; ''Nicholas Krushenick: New Paintings'' by Connie Robbins in *Arts* (New York), December 1975; ''A Two-Fisted Vocabulary in Two Time Zones'' by William Zimmer in *The New York Times,* 26 January 1997; ''Nicholas Krushenick at Mitchell Algus'' by David Ebony in *Art in America* (New York), vol. 86, no. 2, February 1998; obituary in *The New York Times,* 7 February 1999; ''Pop Secret'' by Peter Halley in *Artforum International,* vol. 37, no. 9, May 1999.

* * *

The impact of Nicholas Krushenick's works is bold, brassy and belligerent. The imagery, very much his own invention, a kind of illegitimate offspring of pop and non-figuration, is a kind of rich pattern well defined by thick black outline, generally—but not always—against a plain primary background of scarlet, or yellow or ultramarine, There is nothing fussy about shapes or composition. The paint lies flat and unvaried. Some of the pictures have the flash reaction of op art upon the retina, but this is rendered by colour contrast, not by any mixed media tricks.

The paintings have names. Their titles usually relate to sociological phenomena—''Drop Out,'' ''Moon Maid,'' ''King Kong,'' ''Malibu'' and the like, but they are not without undertones that suggest an industrial world, an ambiance of technology. In a sense they are crude symbols, albeit expertly painted, of subliminal gossip. The pictures mean much more than their titles.

These are the paintings of Krushenick—a voice of contemporary times—but he also brings the same system of updated heraldry to his papier-collés and his graphics.

As one of the New York invaders, he has been able to exhibit in most of the European art centres and, of course, Tokyo. Unlike some of his compatriots of this genre, he has been able to relegate geometry to a back seat. The immediate impression is one of ineluctable flow in which the curvilinear takes precedence over the straight line. His shapes are fat, female and gaudy, but this first reaction—given time to mellow, as it should be—grows into an awareness that Krushenick has found a new and exciting way of turning random pattern into well organized programme.

—Sheldon Williams

KUDO, Tetsumi

Nationality: Japanese. **Born:** Osaka, 23 February 1935. **Education:** Tokyo University, 1954–58, diploma in art 1958. **Family:** Married Hiroko Kurihara in 1959. **Career:** Taught in private art school for children, Tokyo, 1955–58. Independent artist, producing objects and performances, since 1958; has lived and worked in Paris since 1962. **Awards:** Grand Prix, *International Young Artists Exhibition,* Tokyo, 1962; Grand Prix, *Festival International de la Peinture,* Cagnes, 1976; Special Citation, *Bienal,* Sao Paulo, 1977. **Died:** 1990.

Individual Exhibitions:

1965 *Rien n'est laissé au hasard,* Galerie J, Paris
1966 Galerie 20, Amsterdam
Galerie Thelen, Essen
1967 Galerie Mathias Fels, Paris
1968 Galerie Mickery, Amsterdam
1970 *Document 70,* Kunsthalle, Dusseldorf
1972 Stedelijk Museum, Amsterdam
1973 Galerie Beaubourg, Paris
Galerie Mathias Fels, Paris
1975 Galleria Valsecchi, Milan
1977 Galerie Beaubourg, Paris
Galerie Vallois, Paris
1978 Galerie Wunderland, Berlin
Galerie Bellechasse, Paris
1979 Galerie Bellechasse, Paris
1981 Galerie Jöllenbeck, Cologne
Sogetsu Museum, Tokyo
1982 UNAC, Tokyo
Gallery 16, Tokyo
Takagi Gallery, Nagoya, Japan
1983 Tenmaya Hall, Okayama, Japan
Tamako Gallery, Tokyo
1984 Space Niki, Tokyo
Shibuya Parco, Tokyo
Espace Japon, Paris
1985 M. Gallery, Tokyo
Galerie Brownstone, Paris
1986 Hirosaki City Museum, Japan
Galerie Brownstone, Paris
Galerie Claude Samuel, Paris
1991 *Tetsumi Kudo,* Gemeentelijke van Reekummuseum, Apeldoorn, Netherlands; Stedelijk Museum, Amsterdam
1994 *Tetsumi Kudo: Contestation/Creation,* National Museum of Art, Osaka

Selected performances: *Harakiri of Humanism* and *Bottled Humanism,* at the *Biennale,* Paris, 1963; *Instant Sperm,* Centre American d'Artistes, Paris, 1964; *For Nostalgic Purposes* and *For Young Living Room,* Musée d'Art Moderne, Paris, 1966; *Quiet Event,* Kassel, West Germany 1968; *Your Portrait,* Kunsthalle, Cologne, 1970; *Your Portrait in the Pollution,* at the *Bienal,* São Paulo, 1977; *Meditation-Buddha,* Theatre Diogenes and Galerie Wunderland, Berlin, 1978; *La Lumière non Perdue,* Centre Georges Pompidou, Paris, 1980; *Le Trou noir sacré,* Escape Japon, Paris, 1984.

Selected Group Exhibitions:

1963 *Biennale,* Paris
1965 *Les Objecteurs,* Paris
1970 *Happening & Fluxus,* Kunstverein, Cologne
1974 *Japan: Past and Present,* Kunsthalle, Dusseldorf
1976 *Boítes,* Musée d'Art Moderne, Paris
1979 *Tendances de l'Art en France 1968–1979,* Musée d'Art Moderne, Paris
1981 *Contemporary Art of Japan—Year 1960,* National Museum of Modern Art, Tokyo
1984 *Electra,* Musée d'Art Moderne de la Ville, Paris

1985 *Reconstruction: Avant-Garde Art in Japan 1945–65,* Museum of Modern Art, Oxford
1986 *Japon des Avant-Gardes,* Centre Georges Pompidou, Paris
1997 *Made in France, 1947–1997: 50 ans de création en France,* Centre George Pompidou, Paris

Collections:

Stedelijk Museum, Amsterdam; Centre Georges Pompidou Paris; Musée d'Art Contemporain, Ghent, Belgium; Louisiana Museum, Humlebaek, Denmark; Museum des 20 Jahrhunderts, Vienna; Hara Museum, Tokyo; Sogetsu Museum, Tokyo; Musée d'Art Moderne de la Ville de Paris; Musée Cantini, Marseille; Tokyo Metropolitan Art Museum.

Publications:

By KUDO: Books—*Pollution-cultivation-nouvelle ecologie,* exhibition catalog, Amsterdam 1971; *La Lumière non perdue,* Paris 1980; *Satori,* exhibition catalog, Tokyo 1981. **Articles—**''Kudo: Dialogue et monologue,'' interview with Ichiro Haryu in *Opus International* (Paris), no. 47, 1973; ''Boite'' and ''Mythologies quotidiennes'' in *Info Artitudes* (Paris), no. 15, 1977; ''Meditation-Buddha in Berlin'' in DAAD catalog, Berlin 1978. **Films—***Votre Portrait,* with Van Zylen, 1967; *Monument of Metamorphosis,* 1969/70; *La Vase* by Ionesco, 1970; *Cérémonie de Kudo,* Berlin 1978.

On KUDO: Books—*Tetsumi Kudo: Rien n'est laissé au hasard,* exhibition catalog by Pierre Restany, Paris 1965; *Tetsumi Kudo,* exhibition catalog by Udo Kultermann, Essen 1966; *Assemblage, Environments and Happenings* by Allan Kaprow, New York 1966; *Kudo/Document 70,* exhibition catalog by Beeren, Nakahira, Jouffroy, and Gassiot-Talabot, Dusseldorf 1970; *Pop Art & Cie* by Francois Pluchart, Paris 1971; *Art en France une nouvelle generation* by Jean Clair, Paris 1973; *Art Actuel en France* by Anne Tronche and Hervé Gloaguen, Paris 1973; *Contemporary Art in Japan* by Ichiro Haryu, Tokyo 1977; *Kudo,* exhibition catalog, by Yusuke Nakahara, Tokyo 1981; *Tetsumi Kudo,* exhibition catalog, Apeldoorn 1991; *Tetsumi Kudo: Contestation/Creation,* exhibition catalog, Osaka 1994. **Articles—**''Art de détachment'' by Shuji Takashina in *Art et Architecture* (Paris), January 1964; ''Lettre de Paris'' by Otto Hahn in *Art International* (Lugano, Switzerland), May 1965; ''Objecteur avec conscience'' by Otto Hahn in *L'Express* (Paris), December 1965; ''Lettre de Paris—la nouvelle glaciation'' by Gérald Gassiot-Talabot in *Art International* (Lugano, Switzerland), February 1966; ''Miner la terrain'' by Jean-Luc Godard and Alain Jouffroy in *L'Oeil* (Paris), May 1966; ''Ils frappent au visage'' by Pierre Cabanne in *Arts et Loisirs* (Paris), no. 85, 1967; ''We Have Nothing to Lose But Our Brains'' by John Lyle in *Art and Artists* (London), August 1969; ''Kudo: Monument of Metamorphosis'' by Ad Peterson in *Museumjournaal* (Amsterdam), June 1970; ''Le monument de Kudo'' by Gérald Gassiot-Talabot in *Opus International* (Paris), June 1971; ''Guérillero du monde artistique'' by Jacques Michel in *Le Monde des Arts* (Paris), October 1971; ''Kudo: Ionesco et la décomposition de l'homme'' by Jean-Clarence Lambert in *Opus International* (Paris), November 1971; ''Kudo, ou fragments d'un paradis perdu'' by Alain Jouffroy in *Sogetsu* (Tokyo), no. 128, 1980; ''Kudo'' by Anne Tronche in *25 Ans d'Art en France 1960–1985,* Paris 1985.

* * *

What characterizes Tetsumi Kudo's art is his intense concern for dismantling and dissolving away the human body and its parts. But it is also characteristic that there is a strong provocativeness inherent in Kudo's work. The year Kudo graduated from Tokyo University of Fine Art, 1958, he put on a performance in which he dumped raw eggs and tomatoes on a cloth spread upon the floor, and ran about over the mixture. This early work was as lucid as it was provocative. After that, Kudo, by making a series of works consisting of so many knots strung out so as to appear to extend into infinity, emphasized anti-human space; at the same time he took up the ''philosophy of impotence'' and emphasized both man's sexual relationships and collapse. In 1962 he gained the grand prize in the *Young Asian Artists Exhibition,* for one of his knotted string works, and used the prize money to go to France, where he has continued to live.

Kudo's activities after settling in Paris gradually became more radical. His series of happenings starting with ''Philosophy of Impotence'' in 1962 and ''Harakiri of Humanism'' in 1963 served to demonstrate by deed Kudo's thoughts, while the ''Your Portrait'' series depicted human bodies and parts of bodies which had been, it would seem, wrenched asunder, corroded by acid, and enlarged to greater than life size, to become grotesque fragments, barely held together by ragged skin and contraposed with ordinary articles used in daily life.

Provocative as Kudo is, he is not a sculptor. By his persistent orientation to the human body and his concern through his philosphy of impotence for Eros, Kudo's ultimate, underlying concern is for a New Man. The preoccupation with death is in fact a step toward a new life, and the philosophy of impotence is a sign of concern for the whole human being. Kudo cannot but be provocative, considering all this. Such works as ''You Are Metamorphosing'' and ''Souvenir La Mue'' or ''Hommage à Jeune Génération'' show clearly his concern for the twin principles of Life and Death. In 1971 Kudo cooperated in a production of a Eugéne Ionesco film *La Boue,* during which he made a plaster replica of Ionesco, which he then cut to pieces to create a series of works.

How might man survive this age of electronics? Through his recent works on the theme ''Electrocircuit,'' Kudo faces this very question. The art and death of man at the same time bespeak a concern for the life and death of art. It must be said that in his grotesque works there is this character.

—Tamon Miki

KUEHN, Gary

Nationality: American. **Born:** Plainfield, New Jersey, in 1939. **Education:** Studied art history at Drew University, Madison, New Jersey, 1958–62, B.A. 1962, and Rutgers University, New Brunswick, New Jersey, 1962–64. **Career:** Sculptor: lives and works in New Jersey. Instructor, Fairleigh Dickinson University, New Jersey, 1965, Drew University, 1965–68, School of Visual Arts, New York, 1968, Hochschule für Bildende Kunst, Braunschweig, Germany, 1970, and Douglass College, Rutgers University, 1971–73; visiting lecturer, Princeton University, New Jersey, 1973. Since 1974, professor and chairman of the Art Deparment, The Mason Gross School of the Arts at Rutgers University Graduate School. **Awards:** National Council on the Arts grant, 1967; Governor's Purchase Award, New Jersey State Museum, Trenton, 1972; National Endowment for the Arts grant, 1977; Louis Comfort Tiffany Foundation grant, 1977; DAAD Artist's Fellowship, Berlin, 1979. **Agent:** Margarete Roeder Gallery, 545 Broadway, Fourth Floor, New York, New York 10012.

Individual Exhibitions:

1966 *One Man/One Piece,* Douglass College, Rutgers University, New Brunswick, New Jersey
Bianchini Gallery, New York
1967 Bianchini Gallery, New York
Kunstverein, Cologne
Galerie Ricke, at the *Kunstmarkt,* Cologne
Galerie Ricke, Kassel, Germany
1968 Galerie Ricke, Kassel, Germany
Milwaukee Art Center
Galleria von Stein, Turin
1969 Fischbach Gallery, New York
Galerie Ricke, Cologne
1970 Galerie Ernst, Hannover
Galerie Thomas Borgmann, Cologne
1971 Fischbach Gallery, New York
1972 Galerie Ricke, Cologne
Paley and Lowe Gallery, New York
1974 Stefanotty Gallery, New York
Douglas Drake Gallery, Kansas City
Galerie Carlsson I, Gothenburg, Sweden
1975 Galerie Arnesen, Copenhagen
1976 Landau Gallery, Los Angeles
Douglas Drake Gallery, Kansas City
Marion Locks Gallery, Philadelphia
112 Greene Street Gallery, New York
1977 Galerie Ricke, Cologne
Galerie Nothelfer, Berlin
Eugenia Cucalón Gallery, New York
1978 Eugenia Cucalón Gallery, New York
Drew University, Madison, New Jersey
1979 Eugenia Cucalón Gallery, New York
Galerie Ricke, Cologne
Galerie Zellermayer-Lorenzen, Berlin
1980 Wurttembergischer Kunstverein, Stuttgart
Amerika Haus, Berlin
Douglas Drake Gallery, Kansas City, Kansas
1981 Sergio Tosi Gallery, New York
1982 Sergio Tosi Gallery, New York
1985 *Gary Kuehn: Sculpture 1963–1985,* Galerie Rudolf Zwirner, Cologne (catalog)
1988 Galerie Jule Kewenig, Frechen-Bachem, Germany
Galerie Jule Kewenig, Frechen-Bachem, Germany (catalog)
1996 Margarete Roeder Gallery, New York
1998 *New Sculpture,* Margarete Roeder Gallery, New York
2001 *The Black Paintings, 1972–73,* Margarete Roeder Gallery,

Selected Group Exhibitions:

1967 *Painting and Sculpture Today,* Herron Museum, Indianapolis
1968 *Cool Art Today,* Larry Aldrich Museum, Ridgefield Connecticut
1969 *Programm I,* Galerie Ricke, Cologne
When Attitudes Become Form, Kunsthalle, Berne
1970 *Programm II,* Galerie Ricke, Cologne
1973 *Sculptors' Drawings,* Margo Leavin Gallery, Los Angeles
1977 *Documenta,* Kassel, Germany
1980 *From Reinhardt to Christo,* Allen Memorial Art Museum, Oberlin College, Ohio
1985 *Clearly Stated,* Margarete Roeder Fine Arts, New York
1996 *Paintings & Sculptures,* Margarete Roeder Gallery, New York
Six Artists: The 1990s, New Jersey State Museum, Trenton
1998 *A Space Between,* Margarete Roeder Gallery, New York
Drawing into Sculpture, Rutgers University, New Brunswick, New Jersey (traveling exhibition)
1999 *Versteigerung von Aktuellen Werken der Kunst,* Neuer Aachener Kunstverein, Aachen

Collections:

New Jersey State Museum, Trenton.

Publications:

By KUEHN: Article—''Gary Kuehn'' in *Art Press,* Special Issue, no. 17, 1996.

On KUEHN: Books—*Gary Kuehn,* exhibition catalog with text by Andreas Vowinckel, Stuttgart 1980; *From Reinhardt to Christo,* exhibition catalog, Oberlin, Ohio 1980. **Articles—**''Gary Kuehn's Pressure Principle'' by Harris Rosenstein in *Artnews* (New York), December 1969; ''Gary Kuehn'' by Robert Pincus-Witten in *Artforum* (New York), January 1970; ''Gary Kuehn, Fischbach Gallery'' by Carter Ratcliff in *Art International* (Lugano, Switzerland), January 1970; ''New York Letter'' by April Kingsley in *Art International* (Lugano, Switzerland), January 1973; ''Gary Kuehn, Stefanotty Gallery'' by J. Gilbert-Rolfe in *Artforum* (New York), May 1974; ''Gary Kuehn at Margarete Roeder'' by Nancy Princenthal in *Art in America* (New York), vol. 84, no. 1, January 1996.

* * *

A feeling of impending doom and implosive psychological compression permeates the 20 years of work, first sculpture and now painting, of Gary Kuehn. What gives his work power is a sense of edgy uncertainty. Will the apocalyptical burdens portended in Kuehn's work actually dominate and terror reign? Or, will the warrior, implied or figuratively represented (the artist and/or the viewer), fend them off? Regardless of unacceptability in the art world, Kuehn has tenaciously persisted in a psychological exploration of the dark and light realms of psyche which has given him both feelings of exuberance and fear. He grapples with large metaphysical questions, taking the risk of being considered trite or being superficially understood. The compellingly primary tasks in his life/work have been working toward an integration of his soul, understanding/exploring the archetypes within him, and attempting to comprehend humanity's place in the universe. Formal concerns have always been secondary to the intentions and messages expressed.

The sculptures and paintings are wrought with struggles. His early work (sculptures) emotes this in more abstract and almost muddlingly but intriguingly unspecific way. Made of wood and steel with foam, the materials are very heavy and pliable. They transmute the pressures of living into formal metaphors, their internal tensions and squeezings conveying a free-floating sense of humanity's impassivity and conformity to Fate. After working abstractly for a number of years, a particular sculpture, ''Mythic Responsibility,'' was a shocking move into figuration and pivotal in his work. It is of three decapitated deer, joined in a triad by large hooks placed in the center of their necks. Considering Kuehn's lifelong examination of the psychological, an interest in the history and evolution of mythology is relevant. Historically, the symbol of a doe was known as a sacred moon animal; the lithe movement of deer correlated to moon dances, acts of ritual devotion. But this sculpture brings isolation and misfortune. Regarding Fate, Kuehn's pessimistic belief at the time—''Nothing good comes from the sky''—is embodied in this piece.

After making ''Mythic Responsibility,'' Kuehn felt at that time he had gone the limit (psychologically and artistically) with sculpture. Expanding the intensity of his art, he moved into painting. He has continued to be concerned with various animal images since.

Bird imagery is a recurring theme in his work—traditional symbols of spirituality and freedom. It is difficult to discern whether these birds are flying or static. Throughout Kuehn's career circles have been ever-present. Sometimes perfectly round and at others manipulated. Even, fluid, or constricted, this symbol could hold many meanings: the sun, the moon, and the earth (or other planets); of creativity and the artist's anima; or the mythological and complex Great Goddess. Most likely, they are any mixture of these things at different times. They seem to serve as spiritual guardians and enemies, images of birth and destruction. This would be fitting, considering that Kuehn has long been intrigued by the relationships between things which are only seemingly opposite.

Soon thereafter (c. 1979), he began to incorporate simply rendered stocky male figures. Then he began to add similar female figures. Sometimes they coexist in the same space and at others they are alone on a canvas. But, they never really seem to be together. The black and white figures represent the artist as well as humanity. Exuding silent but primitive power, they inhabit places without time in abandoned mindscapes of icy blues, greens and reds (with some highlights of yellow).

One could describe the way Gary Kuehn works as mediumistic; unconsciously it flows through him. The ancient goddess, Mnemosyne, was the mother of the muses and guide of memory and journeys to oracular caves. The travels do not aid in memorization but in recalling entire stories and remembering all details of the narrative of one's life. It is Mnemosyne who partners with and protects Gary Kuehn. The process of moving beyond the apocalypse foreshadowed in his work becomes a process of individuation.

—Elise LaRose

KURYLUK, Ewa

Nationality: Polish. **Born:** Cracow; moved to New York in 1982. **Education:** Academy of Fine Arts, Warsaw; Jagiellonian University, Cracow. **Career:** Artist, art historian, and writer. Co-founder and co-editor of *Zeszyty Literackie;* contributing editor to *Formations* and *Private Arts.* Instructor: Film Academy, Lodz, Poland; Catholic University, Lublin, Poland; New School for Social Research, New

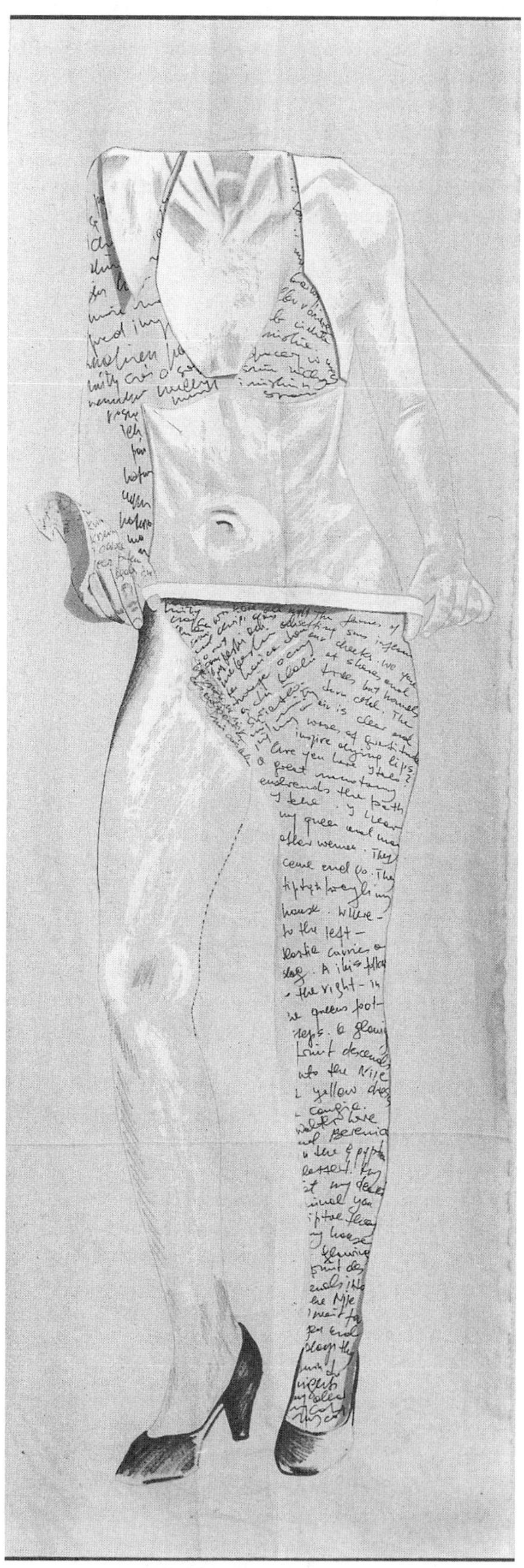

Ewa Kuryluk: *Drawriting,* 1990. ©Ewa Kuryluk.

York; Justus-Liebig University, Giessen, Germany; University of California, San Diego. **Awards:** Award of the Fund for Free Expression, New York 1985; General Electric Award, 1986; fellowships: Italian Institute, Vienna, 1964; European Exchange Program, New York University, 1982; Institute for the Humanities, New York University, 1983–85; Rockefeller Fellowship, 1988–89; Asian Cultural Council, Japan, 1991; Foundatin of Culture, Warsaw, 1995. **Address:** 23 rue Campagne Premiere, 75014 Paris, France.

Individual Exhibitions:

1969 PWSM Gallery, Warsaw
1970 Woodstock Gallery, London
1972 Richard Bradley Atelier, Billingford, England
1973 Christian M. Nebehay Galerie, Vienna
Gallery Współczesna, Warsaw
1974 Galerie Lambert, Paris
1975 Pryzmat Gallery, Cracow
1976 Zapiecek Gallery, Warsaw
Galerie Länderbank, Graz, Austria
1977 Nowa Gallery, Poznan, Poland
National Museum, Wroclaw, Poland
Sciana Wschodnia, Warsaw
1979 Sciana Wschodnia, Warsaw
1980 Critic's Gallery, Warsaw
Art Gallery of Middlesborough, England
1982 Helen Shlien Gallery, Boston
1984 Art in General, New York
Carnegie Lake, Princeton, New Jersey
Princeton Woods, Princeton, New Jersey
1985 Princeton University, New Jersey
1986 Centro de Arte y Communicacion, Buenos Aires
Justus-Leibig University, Geissen, Germany
Kunsthalle, Kleinsassen, Germany
1987 Mobius, Boston
1988 Catholic University, Lublin, Poland
National Humanities Center, Research Triangle Park, North Carolina
1989 Studio TM, Warsaw
National Humanities Center, Research Triangle Park, North Carolina
1990 Art in General, New York
1992 University of California, San Diego
1994 Polish Artists Union, Warsaw (retrospective)
1997 *Installations, 1977–1997,* National Museum and Centre for Japanese Art and Technology, Cracow
Drawings, 1974–78, Artemis Gallery, Cracow
1998 *The Secret Life of Cloth,* Artium Gallery, Fukuoka, Japan
2000 *Trio for the Hidden,* Artemis Gallery, Cracow

Selected Group Exhibitions:

1972 *Fourth Internationa Print Biennale,* Cracow
1975 *Kontraste,* Österreichsches Museum für Angewandte Kunst, Vienna (travelled to Linz and Graz)
1977 *Contemporary Polish Art,* Nevers and Reims, France
1979 *Documents of Reality,* National Museum, Warsaw
1980 *International Art Fair,* Basel
1981 *Bienale de Arte,* Medellin, Colombia
1983 *International 2,* Kunststation, Kleinsassen, Germany
1985 *International Biennale of Tapestry,* Musée des Beaux Arts, Lausanne
1992 *Voices of Freedom,* National Women's Museum, Washington, D.C.
1994 *Ars Erotica,* National Museum, Warsaw
1997 *Small Drawings,* National Museum, Gdausk, Poland

Collections:

National Museum, Warsaw; National Museum, Cracow; National Museum, Wroclaw; National Museum, Poznan; Museum of Modern Art, Lodz; Muzeum Okregowe, Radom; Bibliotheque Nationale, Paris; Graphische Sammlung Albertina, Vienna; Kettle's Yard Museum, Cambridge, England; Bass Museum of Art, Miami Beach, Florida.

Public Installations:

Rooms for Memories, Nieborow Palace, Poland 1994; *Who's This Mysterious Boy?,* 8th International Textile Triennale, Lodz, Poland 1995; *Three Chairs and a Shroud,* Gerlesborgsskolan, Hamburgsund, Sweden 1996.

Publications:

By KURYLUK: Books—*Wiedenska Apokalipsa,* Cracow 1974; *Salome albo o Rozkoszy,* Cracow 1976; *Hyperrealizm-Nowy Realizm,* Warsaw 1979; *Kontur,* Cracow 1979; *Podróż do Granic Sztuki,* Cracow 1982; *Pani Anima,* Cracow 1984; *Salome and Judas in the Cave of Sex,* Evanston 1987; *The Fabric of Memory,* Wilmette 1987; *Veronica and Her Cloth,* Oxford 1991; *Century 21,* Normal, Illinois 1992; *Grand Hotel Oriental,* Warsaw 1997; *Trio dla Ukrytych,* Cracow 2000. **Article—**''On My Artistic Development Leading to Drawing on Fabrics'' in *Leonardo,* vol. 14, no. 4, 1981.

On KURYLUK: Books—*Ewa Kuryluk: Human Landscapes,* exhibition catalog, Middlesborough, England, 1979; *The American Experience: Contemporary Americam Immigrants,* exhibition catalog, New York 1985; *Polish Women Artists,* exhibition catalog, Washington, D.C., 1991; *Ars Erotica,* exhibition catalog, Warsaw 1994; *Drawings and Installations 1974–1996,* exhibition catalog, Cracow 1997; *The Secret Life of Clothes,* exhibition catalog, Fukuoka, Japan 1998. **Articles—**''Ewa Kuryluk'' by Margaret Hoggarth in *Arts Review,* 27 April 1979; ''Metaphor for Caring'' by Eileen Roche in *Sojourner,* February 1982; ''From Poland: A New Breed of Emigre'' by Eva Hoffman in the *New York Times Magazine,* 20 May 1984; ''Ewa Kuryluk and Bart Uchida'' by Thomas Frick in *Art in America,* October 1987; ''World Wide Webs'' by Janes Koplos in *Art in America,* February 1996.

*

I draw what I cannot write, I write what I cannot draw.

—Ewa Kuryluk

KUSAMA, Yayoi

Nationality: American. **Born:** Matsumoto City, Nagano, Japan, 22 March 1929; immigrated to the United States, 1960; naturalized, 1966. **Education:** Arigasaki High School, Matsumoto, 1943–47; studied at the Arts and Crafts School, Kyoto, 1948–51; Art Students League, Brooklyn Arts School, and Washington Irving School, all in New York, 1957–58. **Career:** Independent painter, sculptor and environmental artist, in Kyoto, 1951–57, in New York, 1957–74, in Tokyo since 1974; first monochrome pattern paintings, 1957; soft sculptures, 1961; infinity mirror works, 1964; happenings and kinetic works, 1965; films, 1966; ceramics and pastel collages, from 1974. Founder-director, Kusama Enterprises, Kusama Polka Dot Church, Kusama Musical Productions, Kusama Fashion Company Ltd., Kusama International Film Company Ltd., Body Paint Studio Company model agency, and KOK Homo Social Club, all in New York, 1968; Japan Edition Art Company publishing house, Tokyo, 1977. Founder-editor, *Kusama Orgy* weekly newspaper, New York, 1968; editorial board member, *Kindai Foudo (Modern Climate)* magazine, Tokyo, 1978. **Awards:** Rockefeller Foundation Scholarship, New York, 1965; Film Prize, Belgian International Short Film Festival, Knokke-le-Zoute, 1968; Gold Award, Accademia di Belle Arti, Rome, 1982; Kadokawa Shoten Novelist Prize, Tokyo, 1983. **Agent:** Robert Miller Gallery, 524 West 26th Street, New York, New York 10001; Victoria Miro Gallery, 16 Wharf Road, London N1 7RW. **Address:** 1008 Ushigome Heim, Shinjuku-ku 30–2 chome, Haramachi, Tokyo, Japan.

Individual Exhibitions:

1952 Matsumoto Civic Hall, Japan
1954 Shirokiya Department Store, Tokyo
Mimatsu Shobo Gallery, Tokyo
1955 Takemiya Gallery, Tokyo
Kyuryudo Gallery, Tokyo
1957 Zoe Dusanne Gallery, Seattle, Washington
1959 Brata Gallery, New York
Nova Gallery, Boston
1960 Gres Gallery, Washington, D.C.
Stephen Radich Gallery, New York
1961 Detroit Gallery, Michigan
Stephen Radich Gallery, New York
1962 Gertrude Stein Gallery, New York
1963 Castellane Gallery, New York (twice)
1964 Stedelijk Museum, Schiedam, Netherlands
1965 Orez Gallery, The Hague
Stedelijk Museum, Schiedam, Netherlands
1966 Galleria del Naviglio, Milan
Galerie M. E. Thelen, Essen, Germany
1971 Orez Gallery, The Hague
1975 Nishimura Gallery, Tokyo
1976 Osaka Form Gallery, Tokyo
1977 Galerie Nikko, Tokyo
1978 Chamber of Commerce and Industry, Matsumoto, Japan
1979 Chugeki Art Salon, Matsumoto, Japan
Inoue Department Store, Matsumoto, Japan
1980 Toho Gallery, Osaka, Japan
American Center, Tokyo
Tokyu Department Store, Nagano, Japan
Yurakudo Gallery, Matsumoto, Japan
Gallery Toshin, Tokyo (twice)
1981 Shibuya Seibu Department Store, Tokyo
Gallery Kodosha, Ichinoseki, Japan
Gallery Kumo, Tokyo
1982 Box Gallery, Nagoya, Japan
Fuji Television Gallery, Tokyo
Galleria del Naviglio, Milan
1983 Jardin de Luseine, Harajuku, Tokyo
Supplement Gallery, Tokyo
Video Gallery Scan, Tokyo
Galerie Ornis, The Hague
1984 Fuji Television Gallery, Tokyo
Video Gallery Scan, Tokyo
1985 Missoni Boutique, Yurakucho-Marion, Tokyo
1986 Tamagawa-Takashimaya, Tokyo
Fuji Television Gallery, Tokyo
Galerie Christian Cheneau, Paris
1987 Municipal Museum of Art, Kitakyushu, Japan
1994 *Kusama Yayoi Ten: Yayoi Kusama,* Nagano-Ken Shinano Bijutsukan (catalog)
Japanese Art After 1945: Scream Against the Sky, Yokohama Museum of Art, Yokohama (traveling exhibition)
When the Body Becomes Art, Itabashi Art Museum, Tokyo (traveling exhibition)
1995 *Division of Labor: ''Women's Work'' in Contemporary Art,* Bronx Museum of Arts, Bronx
View of Contemporary Prints, Part II, Niigata City Art Museum, Niigata
Revolution: Art of the Sixites From Warhol to Beuys, Museum of Contemporary Art, Tokyo
1996 *The 1950s and 1960s,* Paula Cooper Gallery, New York (catalog)
With Drawing, Robert Miller Gallery, New York (catalog)
1964: A Turning Point in Japanese Art, Museum of Contemporary Art, Tokyo
Now Here, Louisiana Museum of Modern Art, Humlebaek, Denmark
1997 *A Snake,* D'Amelio Terras, New York
Recent Work and Paintings from the New York Years, Baumgertner Galleries, Inc., Washington, D.C. (catalog)
Mattress Factory, Pittsburgh, Pennsylvania
Obsessional Vision, The Arts Club of Chicago (catalog)
1998 *Works from the 1950s,* Peter Blum Gallery, New York
Tension, Robert Miller Gallery, New York (catalog)
Essence of the Orb, Michael Rosenfeld Gallery, New York
Painting: Now and Forever Part 1, Pat Hearn Gallery, New York
1999 *Love Forever: Yayoi Kusama, 1958–1968,* Los Angeles County Museum of Art, (also Walker Art Center, Minneapolis; Museum of Modern Art, New York and Museum of Contemporary Art, Tokyo) (catalog)
In Full Bloom: Yayoi Kusama, Years in Japan, Museum of Contemporary Art, Tokyo (catalog)
2000 *Yayoi Kusama: Early Drawings from the Collection of Richard Castellane, Class of 1955,* Birmingham Museum of Art (traveled to The Art Museum, Princeton University, Princeton, New Jersey; Art Gallery of York University, Toronto; Indianapolis Museum of Art,

Indiana; and Munson-Williams-Proctor Arts Institute, Utica, New York) (catalog)
From Zero to Infinity: Yayoi Kusama in Context, Jack S. Blanton Museum of Art, University of Texas at Austin, Texas (catalog)
Yayoi Kusama, Serpentine Gallery, London
2001 *Death of an Illusion,* Galerie Pièce Unique, Paris

Major Happenings and Performances: *Mirror Ball Sale Happening,* Giardini della Biennale, Venice 1966; *Self-Obliteration,* Black Gate Theater, New York, 1967; *Horse Play,* Washington Square, New York, 1967; *Body Festival,* Washington Square, New York, 1967; *Phallics Festival,* St. Patrick's Cathedral, New York, 1968; *Weekend Body Festival,* Central Park, New York, 1968; *Naked Demonstration,* Wall Street, New York, 1968; *Anti-War Happening,* United Nations Building, New York, 1968; *Nixon Orgy,* New School for Social Research, New York, 1968; *Polka Dot Happening,* Kusama Studio, New York, 1968; *Alice in Wonderland,* Central Park, New York, 1968; *Bust Out,* Sheepsmeadow, Central Park, New York, 1969; *Naked Orgy Performance,* Museum of Modern Art Garden, New York, 1969; *Happening for Venice,* Giardini Della Biennale, Venice, 1970; *Polka Dot Obliteration,* Video Gallery Scan, Tokyo, 1983; *Infinity Nets,* Video Gallery Scan, Tokyo, 1984; *The Flower of Basara,* Joshin Temple, Tokyo, 1985.

Selected Group Exhibitions:

1955 *International Biennial of Watercolor,* Brooklyn Museum, New York (and 1959)
1960 *Monochrome Malerei,* Stadtische Museum, Leverkusen, Germany
1962 *Tentoonstelling Nul,* Stedelijk Museum, Amsterdam
1966 *The Object Transformed,* Museum of Modern Art, New York
1973 *American Art,* Civic Center, Philadelphia
1977 *Improbable Furniture,* Institute of Contemporary Art, Philadelphia
1979 *Soft-Art,* Kunsthaus, Zurich
1982 *Art Today—November Steps,* Yokohama City Hall, Japan
1985 *Reconstructions: Avant-Garde Art in Japan 1945–65,* Museum of Modern Art, Oxford
1986 *Le Japon des Avantgardes,* Centre Georges Pompidou, Paris
1993 *XLV Biennale di Venezia* (catalog)
1998 *Bienal de São Paulo 98,* Brazil
1998 Taipei Biennial, Taipei Fine Arts Museum, Taipei
2000 *Repetitive-vision, Phallus-boat,* Galerie Pièce Unique, Paris
12th Biennale of Sydney, Australia

Collections:

Stedelijk Museum, Amsterdam; Chrysler Museum, Provincetown, Massachusetts; Oberlin College, Ohio; Jack S. Blanton Museum of Art, The University of Texas at Austin.

Publications:

By KUSAMA: Books—*Seven,* with Masataka Sekou and Masatoshi Tamaoki, Tokyo 1977; *Manhattan Suicide Addict,* Tokyo 1978; *Christopher Homosexual Brothel,* Tokyo 1983; *Fired St. Mark's Church,* Tokyo 1985; *Yayoi Kusama (Contemporary Artists),* with Akira Tatehata, Laura Hoptman and Udo Kultermann, London 2000. **Articles**—interview with Grady Turner in *Bomb,* no. 66, Winter 1999. **CD**—*EVE: An Interactive Music and Art Adventure* by Peter Gabriel, 1996.

On KUSAMA: Book—*Yayoi Kusama,* exhibition catalog with essay by Toshiaki Minemura, Tokyo 1986. **Articles**—''Yayoi Kusama: Love Forever'' by Michael Cohen in *Flash Art,* vol. 27, no. 175, March-April 1994; ''Yayoi Kusama: In Between the Outside and Inside'' by Pamela Wye in *M/E/A/N/I/N/G,* no. 15, May 1994; ''Yayoi Kusama's Feminism'' by Dana Friis-Hansen in *Art and Text,* no. 49, September 1994; ''Yayoi Kusama'' by Tone O. Nielsen in *Louisiana Revy,* vol. 35, no. 3, June 1995; ''Lucid Logic'' by Udo Kultermann in *Sculpture* (Washington, D.C.), vol. 16, no. 1, January 1997; ''Dot Dot Dot: Yayoi Kusama'' by Andrew Solomon in *Artforum,* vol. 35, no. 6, February 1997; ''Love Forever: Yoyoi Kusama 1958–1968'' by Renate Puvogel in *Kunstforum International,* no. 141, July-September 1998; ''Yayoi Kusama'' by Mimi Thompson in *Bomb,* no. 64, Summer 1998; ''Is She Famous Yet?'' by Pamela Wye in *Art Journal,* vol. 57, no. 4, Winter 1998; ''Yayoi Kusama'' by Libby Lumpkin in *Artforum,* vol. 37, no. 1, September 1998; ''The Phoenix Returns'' by Janet Koplos in *Art in America* (New York), vol. 87, no. 2, February 1999; ''La Creacion de Una Vision Femenina del Mundo: El Arte de Yayoi Kusama'' by Udo Kultermann in *Goya,* no. 271–272, July-October 1999; ''Obsession'' by Maria Walsh in *Art Monthly,* no. 234, March 2000; ''Yayoi Kusama: 3 Article Special Section'' in *Parkett,* no. 59, 2000.

* * *

What makes Yayoi Kusama's art notable is a kind of cosmological obsession integrated into art as forms of proliferating repetition and endless accumulation. She is a painter, sculptor, performing artist, film maker and novelist.

In her childhood in Matsumoto city in Nagano, Japan, where she was born in 1929 and graduated from a local high school, Kusama was a great visionary; it was reported that she frequently saw aurora-fringed objects and heard animals and plants uttering human languages. She studied art at Kyoto Arts and Crafts School, and her extraordinary visions in paintings caught the interest of a psychopathologist, who reported her case at academic meetings.

She held her first one-person show with 240 paintings at Matsumoto city in 1952, and became known to the avant-garde art circles in Tokyo.

It was after 1957 when she went to New York and studied at the Art Students League that her idiosyncratic vision and idea began to bloom as comprehensive art forms. Her repetitive pattern painting in monochrome starting in 1957 was one of the earliest examples of Systematic Painting which was to come out of New York in the 1960s, though Kusama's obsession for microbiological multiplication was quite different from the ideas of the Systemic painters.

She gradually aroused interest in New York by the end of the 1950s, creating paintings with multiplicative net patterns or polka-dotted overall surfaces. In 1961, she took up making soft sculptures which developed into perhaps one of her best known works in 1962, *1,000 boats,* boats made of thousands of phallic sacks with stuffing in each of them.

Kusama's activities in the 1960s depict the worldwide explosion and expansion of ideas in art of the decade, ranging over kinetic art, environmental art, Happenings, Pop art, filmmaking, fashion, publication and private enterprise.

In the early 1960s, she began to create works with mirrors and electricity which led the artist into making moving sculptures. Her shows were apt to be accompanied with Happenings around the middle of sixties, and she received the Rockefeller Foundation Scholarship in 1965. She staged an enterprising *Mirror Ball Sale Happening* at the premiere of the Venice Biennial, 1966, and made a film, *Kusama's Polka Dot Obliteration,* written and played by herself in 1967. The film was honored at the Belgian International Short Film Festival in 1968. In this period, she repeatedly performed artistic, anti-establishment and immoral Happenings in New York. She established her private enterprises for purposes of producing and selling her dresses and films.

After coming back to Japan in 1974, she began to make ceramic works and pastel collages. Her first novel came out in 1978; the second, *Christopher Homosexual Brothel,* won a new novelist prize from Kadokawa publishing company. A golden prize was awarded to the artist in 1982 from Art Academy of Italy. She never lost her energy throughout the 1980s, showing her works in lot of exhibitions in and out of Japan.

Kusama's obsessive idea for self-obliteration (frequently the titles of her Happening shows), seems to have been derived from an inner desire to be emancipated from the psychopathic anguish which has been her old complaint. But it is obvious to anyone's eyes that the nightmarish beauty in Kusama's art claims a high reputation as one of the wondrous achievements created by an avant-garde artist regardless of her continuous endeavoring to conquer sufferings.

—Tazmi Shinoda

KUSHNER, Robert

Nationality: American. **Born:** Pasadena, California, 19 August 1949. **Education:** University of California at San Diego, 1967–71, B.A. (honors) 1971. **Family:** Married Ellen Saltonstall, 1978; children: Max Saltonstall, Lila Saltonstall, Josef Nathaniel. **Career:** Independent artist, since 1971. Created dance costumes for *The Masque of the Red Death,* WGBH, Boston, 1971; costumes, with Jim Burton, for *Ballet Electronique,* 1973; costumes and set, with Sara Rudner, for *Dancing on View,* 1975; costumes, with Wendy Rogers, for *Gull's Meadow,* New York, 1976; costumes and set design for *November Duets* by Sara Rudner, 1977; costumes for *Oriental Dance* by Ellen Saltonstall, 1977; costumes and set for *Tropical Chenille* by Wendy Rogers, Berkeley and New York, 1978; sets for *Living Rooms* for Wendy Rogers, Berkeley, 1980; costumes and sets for *As Is* by Sara Rudner, 1980; costumes and sets for *The White Snake* by Ed Friedman, New York, 1982. **Awards:** American Institute of Architect's Award for Excellence in Design, Rockefeller Center, New York 1991; Benjamin Franklin Award, Publishers Marketing Association 1994. **Address:** DC Moore Gallery, 724 5th Avenue, New York, New York, 10019–4106, U.S.A.

Individual Exhibitions:

1975 *Recent Works,* Rasdall Gallery, University of Kentucky, Lexington
1976 *Persian Line Part II,* Holly Solomon Gallery, New York
1977 Thorpe Intermedia Gallery, Sparkhill, New York
Philadephia College of Art
Holly Solomon Gallery, New York
1978 Lunn Gallery, Washington, D.C.
Mayor Gallery, London
1979 Daniel Templon Gallery, Paris
Holly Solomon Gallery, New York (twice)
1980 Dart Gallery, Chicago
1981 *New Works,* Mayor Gallery, London
The Question, the Answer, Another Question, Barbara Gladstone Gallery, New York
Galerie Bischofberger, Zurich
Paintings of Some Recent Acquaintances, Holly Solomon Gallery, New York
Dreams and Visions, Holly Solomon Gallery, New York
Asher/Faure Gallery, Los Angeles
Akira Ikeda Gallery, Nagoya, Japan
1982 Galerie Rudolf Zwirner, Cologne
University of Colorado Art Galleries, Boulder
Holly Solomon Gallery, New York
American Graffiti Gallery, Amsterdam
Studio Marconi, Milan
University of Southern California, Los Angeles
Castelli-Goodman-Solomon, East Hampton, New York
1983 Dart Gallery, Chicago
Holly Solomon Gallery, New York
1984 McIntosh/Drysdale Gallery, Houston
Brentwood Gallery, St. Louis
Galleria Giulia, Rome
Brooklyn Museum, New York
1985 Holly Solomon Gallery, New York
Galleria Capricorni, Venice
Mayor Gallery, London
Crown Point Press, New York
1986 Rugg Road, Boston
Galerie Rudolf Zwirner, Cologne
1987 Holly Solomon Gallery, New York
Fay Gold Gallery, Atlanta, Georgia
Institute of Contemporary Art, Philadelphia
1988 Iannetti-Lanzone Gallery, San Francisco
Michael Lord Gallery, Milwaukee, Wisconsin
D & J Bittker Gallery, Birmingham, Michigan
J.B. Speed Art Museum, Louisville, Kentucky
1989 The Aspen Art Museum, Colorado
Holly Solomon Gallery, New York
Silent Operas, Staller Center for the Arts, SUNY, Stony Brook, New York
1990 Gloria Luria Gallery, Bay Harbor Island, Florida
Michael Lord Gallery, Milwaukee, Wisconsin
Opulent Subversions, Holly Solomon Gallery, New York
Gallery Basque, Fukuoka, Japan (toured Japan)
Black and White Prints, Crown Point Press, New York

Painting of faces by Robert Kushner, ca. 1970–85. ©Geoffrey Clements/Corbis.

1991 *Perennial Diary,* Holly Solomon Gallery, New York (catalog)
Seasonal Furbelos: A One Year Installation, American Craft Museum, New York
Leaves, First Gallery, Moscow, Russia
1992 Timothy Brown Fine Art, Apsen, Colorado
Kunsthallen Brandts Klaedefabrik, Odense, Denmark
Yoshiaki Inoue Gallery, Osaka, Japan
Four Seasons, Midtown Payson Galleries, New York
1993 *Robert Kushner, Japanese Ceramics,* Yoshiaki Inoue Gallery, Osaka, Japan
Holly Solomon Gallery, New York
Forcing the Spring, Floria/Brown Gallery, Woody Creek, Colorado
Seasons, Montclair Art Museum, Montclair, New Jersey
1994 *Works on Paper,* Nina Freudenheim Gallery, Buffalo, New York
Works on Paper, Gallery APA, Nagoya, Japan
New Etchings, Crown Point Press, San Francisco, California
Neo Rimpa: Robert Kushner & Hiroshi Senju, Gallery Inoue & Yoshiaki Inoue Gallery, Osaka, Japan
Pele's Garden: Recent Monoprints, Quartet Editions, New York
Gallery OZ, Paris
Blacpain/Stepczynski Gallerie, Geneva, Switerland
1995 *Mille Fleurs: A Cornucopia of New Paintings,* Midtown Payson Galleries, New York
1996 *Celestial Banquet,* The Fabric Workshop and Museum, Philadelphia
1999 *Robert Kushner: The Language of Flowers,* DC Moore Gallery, New York (catalog)

Performances: *Costumes for Moving Bodies,* University of California at San Diego, 1971; *An Evening of Theatre and Dance,* Parker 470 Gallery, Boston, 1972; *Costumes Constructed and Eaten,* Jack Glenn Gallery, Corona del Mar, California, and University of California at San Diego, 1972; *Robert Kushner and Friends Eat Their Clothes,* Acme Productions, New York, 1972; *The Orange County Book,* with Ed Friedman, Acme Productions, New York, 1973; *Hors d'Oeuvres Costumes,* Fairleigh Dickinson University, Teaneck, New Jersey 1973; *Demonstrations from the Wonderful World of Food,* St. Mark's Church, New York, 1973; *Masque of Clouds,* The Kitchen, New York, 1973; *The Masque of Monuments: Rocks and Water,* 98 Greene Street Loft, New York, 1973; *Food Fashion Show,* Art-Rite, New York, 1974; *The Persian Line,* The Kitchen, New York, 1975; *The New York Hat Line,* The Clocktower, New York, 1975; *Masque of Clouds: An Opera in Three Acts and 132 Variations,* with Tom Johnson, The Kitchen, New York, 1975; *Persian Line Part II,* Holly Solomon Gallery, New York, 1976; *That Kushner Look: One Size Fits All,* University of California at San Diego, California Institute of the Arts, Valencia, 541 Broadway, New York, Galleria Communale di Arte Moderna, Bologna, Fourmiere III, Zurich, and Philadelphia College of Art, 1977; *The New York Hat Line,* Thorpe Intermedia Center, Sparkill, New York, 1977; *Layers,* Galerie Alexandra Monett, Brussels, Holly Solomon Gallery, New York, Kunstverein, Vienna, Forum Stadpark, Graz, Austria, University of California at San Diego, University of California at Irvine, and IDEA, Santa Monica, California, 1978; *The New York Hat Line,* Museum of Modern Art, New York, 1978; *That Kushner Look: One Size Fits All,* Soho TV, New York, 1978; *Hat Party,* Holly Solomon Gallery, New York, 1979; *Sentimental Fables,* Los Angeles Institute of Contemporary Art, 1979; *Sentimental Fables,* IMAC, Bayville, New York, and 87 Leonard Street, New York, 1980; *Hats for Tea,* Institute of Contemporary Art, Philadelphia, 1980; *Sentimental Fables,* Associate Council of the Museum of Modern Art, New York, 1981; *Travelling,* Institute of Contemporary Art, Boston 1983; *Imprimatur,* Greenville County Museum of Art, South Carolina (traveled to North Carolina Museum of Art, Raleigh)

Selected Group Exhibitions:

1975 *Biennial,* Whitney Museum, New York
1978 *Patterning Painting,* Palais des Beaux-Arts, Brussels
1980 *Drawings: The Pluralist Decade, at the Biennale,* Venice (travelled to the Kunstforeningen, Copenhagen; Henie-Onstad Museum, Oslo; Biblioteca Nationale, Madrid; and the Gulbenkian Museum, Lisbon)
1981 *Alternatives in Retrospect: An Historical Overview 1969–75,* New Museum, New York
1982 *New American Graphics,* Madison Art Center, Wisconsin (toured the United States, 1982–84)
1983 *Minimalism to Expressionism,* Whitney Museum, New York
1985 *Illuminating Color,* Pratt Institute, New York
1987 *Americana,* Groninger Museum, Groningen, Nertherlands
1991 *Les annees 80: Mouvrements et individualities,* Musee d'Art Moderne et d'Art Contemporain, Nice, France
1992 *American Figurations: A Directory—Works from the Lilja Collection,* Henie-Onstad Art Centre, Hovikodden, Norway (catalog)
1994 *Osaka Triennale,* 5th International Contemporary Art Competition, Osaka, Japan
1996 *Flora: Contemporary Artists and the World of Flowers,* Leigh Yawkey Woodson Art Museum, Wausau, Wisconsin (traveling exhibition) (catalog)

Collections:

Museum of Modern Art, New York; Australian National Gallery, Canberra, Australia; Ufizzi Gallery, Florence; Library of Congress, Washington, D.C.; Metropolitan Museum of Art, New York; Museum Ludwig, Cologne, Germany; Tate Gallery, London; Peter Stuyesant Foundation, Amsterdam, Holland; J. Paul Getty Trust, Los Angeles; Denver Art Museum, Colorado; San Francisco Museum of Modern Art; Oakland Museum, California; Cleveland Center for Contemporary Art, Ohio; Boston Museum of Fine Arts; Albright-Knox Art Gallery, Buffalo; Whitney Museum of American Art; Brooklyn Museum; Philadelphia Museum of Art; Los Angeles County Museum of Art; Baltimore Museum of Art; Milwaukee Art Museum.

Publications:

By KUSHNER: Books—*Robert Kushner: New Bronze Sculpture,* exhibition catalog, New York 1987; illustrations for *Kathy Goes to Haiti* by Kathy Acker, New York 1977; *The Wonderful World of Food,* with Amy Goldin, New York 1978; *The New York Hat Line,* with Ed Friedman and Katherine Landman, New York 1979; book cover and drawings for *The Telephone Book* by Ed Friedman, New York 1979; illustrations for *The Persian Poems by Janey Smith* by Kathy Acker, New York 1980. **Articles**—''Conceptual Art as Opera'' in *Artnews* (New York), May 1970; ''Aida'' in the *Paris Review* (New York and Paris), Fall 1979; ''Letters to the Editor,'' with Kim MacConnel, in *Arts Magazine* (New York), January 1982; ''Io, Kushner,'' interview with Francesca Alinovi in *Bolaffiarte* (Turin), January 1981; ''Things I Think about My Work'' in *Flash Art* (Milan), Summer 1981; ''Books: Man as Art'' in *Artforum* (New York), March 1982; ''Life in the Produce Aisle'' in *Art Journal,* Spring 1995; ''Defiant Decoration: A Short History of Decoration'' in *Studio Potter,* vol. 24, no. 2, June 1996. **Video**—*Video Evening,* Interart Center, New York 1993.

On KUSHNER: Books—*Art in the Seventies* by Edward Lucie-Smith, London and New York 1980; *Ornamentalism: The New Decorativeness in Architecture and Design* by Robert Jensen and Patricia Conway, New York 1982; *Trans Avant Garde International* by Achille Bonito Oliva, Milan 1983; *The New Image: Painting in the 1980s* by Tony Godfrey, New York 1986; *50 New York Artists* by Richard Marshall and Robert Mapplethorpe, New York 1986; *Art Against Aids,* exhibition catalog, New York 1987; *Un Balo in Maschera,* New York 1989; *A Guide to Contemporary Ideas, Movements, and Buzzwords,* by Robert Atkins, Abbeville Press, New York 1990; *Under the Spell of Orpheus: The Persistence of Myth in Twentieth Century Art* by Judith E. Bernstock, Carbondale, Illinois 1991; *The Power of Feminist Art: The American Art Movement in the 1970s,* edited by Norma Broude and Mary G. Garrad, Abrams, New York 1994; *Flora: Contemporary Artists and the World of Flowers,* exhibition catalog, Wausau, Wisconsin 1995; *Robert-Kushner: Gardens of Earthly Delight* by Alexandra Anderson-Spivy and Holland Cotter, New York 1997. **Articles**—''Decoration Days'' by John Ashbery in *New York Magazine,* 2 July 1979; ''Art of the Whole Cloth'' by Carrie Rickey in *Art in America* (New York), November 1979; ''Robert Kushner'' by Douglas Blau in *Flash Art* (Milan), January/ February 1980; ''Art: Kushner Exalts a Study in Goofiness'' by Alan G. Artner in the *Chicago Tribune,* 14 March 1980; ''The Joy of Ornament: The Prints of Robert Kushner'' by Roberta Bernstein in the *Print Collector's Newsletter,* January/February 1981; ''Artist and Printer: A Coincidence of Sympathies'' by Deborah C. Phillips in *Artnews* (New York), March 1981; ''Kim MacConnel and Robert Kushner at Mayor'' by Stuart Morgan in *Artscribe* (London), March 1981; ''Post-Modernist Painting'' by Sam Hunter in *Portfolio* (New York), January/February 1982; ''Robert Kushner'' by Theodore F. Wolff in *Christian Science Monitor* (Boston), 10 June 1986; ''Robert Kushner: New Bronze Scultpure,'' by Michael Brenson in the *New York Times,* 17 April 1987; ''Robert Kushner at Holly Solomon'' by Donald Kuspit in *Artforum,* September 1987; ''Blurring the Line that Separates Art from Decorating'' by Edward J. Sozanski in the *Philadelphia Inquirer,* 18 October 1989; ''The Pleasure of His Painting'' by Theodore F. Wolff in the *Christian Science Monitor,* 12 March 1989; ''Soho Eye'' by Jonathan Phillips in *Art/World,* 23 February 1989; ''Robert Kushner at Holly Solomon'' by Brooks Adams in *Art in America,* December 1990; ''Art in Review: Robert Kushner'' in *The New Yorker,* 16 November 1992; ''Literary Aspirations'' by Angela Choon in *Art and Antiques,* October 1993; ''From Painted Textiles, Poetic Images'' by Betty Freudenheim in the *New York Times,* 12 November 1993; ''Robert Kushner at Midtown Payson'' by Janet Koplos in *Art in America,* June 1995; ''Robert Kushner: Boldly Elegant Silk Paintings'' by Kathleen McCloud in *Fiberarts,* vol. 26, no. 5, March/April 2000.

* * *

Since his debut in the early 1970s, Robert Kushner has challeged the conventional notions of aesthetic suitability by creating fabric wall-hangings and costumes filled with ecstatically moody colours, unusual subject matter, old-fashioned motifs, and commercial designs. Seeking an alternative to the impersonal aspects of the minimalism and formalism then dominating the art world, he explored the neglected area of decorative art. His main disagreement with these traditions stemmed from his refusal to regard art—or any of its components—as an isolated element. Kushner is concerned with how art adapts to and enhances an already established decor without demanding its refinement and the elimination of conflicting decorative detail (a special problem of minimalist sculpture.)

Since 1971 Kushner has succeeded in erasing the distinction between decoration and art. His emulation of the decorative is manifested in his ability to make art that is expansive and additive, embellished and exuberant. The images, colours, and patterns expand beyond the physical edge of the support, carrying the eye across the surface and implying an infinite continuation of the fluid and energetic line. He is unconcerned with illusionist spatial effects; instead, he fashions broad, flat outlines of the basic motif of each piece, applying colour to add tonal surrogates for modelled mass. It is a relatively fast method of working and one that discourages intricate brushwork. Except for the decorative appliques, there is no topology to his work. Content is of minimal importance; as a result, the formal aspects of his imagery are highlighted. He subjugates his forms and figures to decorative principles through cropping, non-naturalistic colours, and repetitive patterns.

Kushner's taste in colour has been central to his work, arresting, tropical hues freely positioned against flat, interior tones; mauves, gilts, oxblood, dark blues and reds, tertiary browns. The flat, inscribed nature of the drawing style and the physical flatness of the painting shift the considerable sensuality of the work onto its colour. The reflective ornamentation—glitter and metallic thread, for instance—and the varieties of translucent fabrics that Kushner favours heighten this sensuality.

Kushner first produced fabric wall hangings in 1971. His early large-scale ink drawings emerged from a technique of copying intricate pattern motifs from historical fabrics and rugs onto paper. Consequently, he developed a vocabulary of forms, including the leaf, vine seed pod, and floral images which recur in his work. A trip to the Middle East in 1974 left Kushner resolute to promote a continuity between his art and daily existence. The costumes which occupied him prior to his trip became, on his return, more than just props for performances. They became functionally androgynous—equally at home as shelter and as non-functional decoration—in a way that paralleled their deliberate sexual androgyny. Whithin a short time the paintings adopted the qualities of these costumes.

By 1975 he increased his scale and enlarged his repertory of images by selecting a wider range of subject matter—from books on European fabric and wallpaper design to advertising images and collections of Chinese commercial designs. *Bunnies Eating Bok Choy* (1977), *Empty Pagoda* (1977), and *Fishes and Lilies* (1977) were inspired by Chinese line-drawings. During the late 1970s Kushner exhibited a series of multi-panel vertical works influenced by Matisse, among them: *Gisela* (1979), *Henrietta* (1979), and *Henri* (1978). In this series he achieved a continuation of the fluid line by carrying the viewer's eye across the zig-zag positioning of the faces in the paintings.

At the same time Kushner produced figural pieces which derived from newspaper and magazine photographs, images already composed and flattened. Not until 1982 did he begin drawing from a live model in the studio, a technique which prompted a series of ink drawings executed on oriental and handmade papers embedded with fibres, leaves, and sequins. Kushner fully integrated the figure into his decorative style with the use of commercially produced wallpaper. The flattened components of the figure served to emphasize the ornamentation. The wallpaper pieces, such as *Wrapped* (1984) and *Contemplative* (1984), utilized the same technique as his large fabric paintings—the drawn image of the figure is viewed through cuts in the applied papers.

In his new works, Kushner has returned to floral motifs. His blossoms, painted in rich, saturated hues, careen over large canvases, playing off grid-like panels of variously colored patterns and textures. This tension with the grid locates the paintings within the idiom of 1990s painting, as does Kushner's occasional use of crude paint-handling or 'ugly' color. Elsewhere, Kushner employs metallic leaf, iridescent paint, glitter, and even lamé, materials that push the boundaries of acceptable taste but lend his pictures a dense and at times mysterious opulence.

Kushner's unabashed lushness sets him apart from the main thrust of post-modernist painting, which tends to be self-conscious and ironical; nor does it relate to modernist notions of transcendence and purity. His paintings beg several questions: Can we still *enjoy* painting? Is that enough? Does a harmonious conception of beauty still have validity as a subject for art? Kushner's origins in body art suggest a notion of the world as eroticized, hinting at a kind of nirvana. Kushner places himself in an Eastern tradition that emphasizes ornament, sensuality, and the joy of creation; moreover his newest works, with their close cropping and large scale, recall Symbolist ideals of the physical and intellectual self as merged, subsumed by the earthly senses. Whether or not one agrees that this kind of painting, which by Kushner's own admission does not attempt to acknowledge the existence of evil in the world, can be relevant, Kushner's virtuosity with color and texture is undeniable, and achieves it own kind of rigor.

—Essay by Carrie Barker; updated by Dorothy Valakos

Continuing to embrace the idiom of beauty, Kushner has sustained his interest in ornament, decoration, and splendor. His works remain large, sometimes reaching the scale of murals. He persists in utilizing flowers and other decorative images in glorious colors with equally magnificent materials, such as gold leaf and beautiful handmade papers. Kushner also continues to display his care in painting, sustaining the carefully worked surfaces and technical virtuosity that has underscored much of his body of work, except in the most informal kinds of costume/painting-related pieces. This emphasis on beauty has its origins in a shared desire to find a way out of the cool, bland cerebral severity of Minimalism. By embracing non-western, and craft sensibilities, abundant ornament typified by the ''horror vacuui'' of Indian art, as well as the plentiful images of quilts and textiles, Kushner's visually playful sense has prompted him to expand and extend his treatment of beauty even as other painters disdain its attributes. His balanced treatment of beauty also stems from the equalizing aspect of conceptually-oriented modernist art in that all areas are treated uniformly. His compositions embrace the ubiquity of much ornament in art, in that the subjects are profuse and copious, occupying the entire space of the surface. His focus on the still life in recent years is fresh and inviting, showing that he has an entirely inventive approach to this conventional subject. His dramatic treatment of the object has shown the way to a future in painting with constructive possibilities; his art ultimately has social value in its provision for stimulating the viewer with images and surfaces of immense beauty.

—Anne Swartz

KUWAYAMA, Tadaaki

Nationality: Japanese. **Born:** Nagoya City, 4 March 1932. **Education:** Tokyo National University of Art, 1952–56, B.F.A. 1956. **Family:** Married Rakuko Naito in 1958; children: Maki, Sono. **Career:** Moved to New York in 1958; independent painter, since 1960. **Awards:** *Art in America* New Talent Prize, New York 1964; National Endowment for the Arts Grant, Washington, D.C., 1969; Adolph and Esther Gottlieb Foundation Grant, New York, 1986. **Agents:** Folin/Riva, 529 West 20th Street, New York, New York 10011; Satani Gallery, Tokyo, Japan; Gallery Yamaguchi, Osaka, Japan; Galerie Rechermann, Albertusstrasse 16, 5000 Cologne 1, Germany; Galerie Renate Bender, Hohenzollernstrasse 122, D-80796 München, Germany. **Address:** 136 West 24th Street, New York, New York 10011, U.S.A.

Individual Exhibitions:

1961 Green Gallery, New York
1962 Swetzoff Gallery, Boston
Green Gallery, New York
1964 Kornblee Gallery, New York
1965 Daniels Gallery, New York
1966 Red Carpet Gallery, Minneapolis
1967 Tokyo Gallery, Japan
Gallery Bischofberger, Zurich
Galerie Mutzenbach, Dortmund, Germany
Richard Gray Gallery, Chicago
Franklin Siden Gallery, Detroit
1968 Gallery Del Leone, Venice
Galerie Bischofberger, Zurich
Galerie D'Aujuord'hui, Brussels
1969 Galerie Reckermann, Cologne
Henri Gallery, Washington, D.C.
1972 Henri Gallery, Washington, D.C.
1973 Galerie Kowallek, Frankfurt
Henri Gallery, Washington, D.C.
1974 Museum Folkwang, Essen
Kaneko Art, Tokyo
1975 Denise René Gallery, New York
Galerie Muller, Stuttgart
1977 Denise René Gallery, New York
1978 Koh Gallery, Tokyo
1979 Sakura Gallery, Nagoya, Japan
Protetch-McIntosh Gallery, Washington, D.C.
1980 Akira Ikeda Gallery, Nagoya, Japan
1981 Akira Ikeda Gallery, Nagoya, Japan
1982 Galerie Reckermann, Cologne
Gimpel-Hanover and Andre Emmerich Galleries, Zurich
1983 Akira Ikeda Gallery, Tokyo
Sakura Gallery, Nagoya, Japan
1984 Akira Ikeda Gallery, Tokyo (and Nagoya)
1985 Kitakyushu Municipal Museum of Art, Japan
Yamaguchi Gallery, Osaka, Japan
Kasahara Gallery, Osaka, Japan
1989 O.K. Harris, New York
Michael Walls Gallery, New York
Nagoya City Art Museum, Japan
1990 Satani Gallery, Tokyo
1991 Gilbert Brownstone, Paris
Yamaguchi Gallery, Osaka, Japan
1992 Satani Gallery, Tokyo
Yamaguchi Gallery, Osaka, Japan
1993 Yamaguchi Gallery, Osaka, Japan
1994 Yamaguchi Gallery, Osaka, Japan
1995 Stiftun fur Konkrete Kunst, Reutlingen, Germany
Yamaguchi Gallery, Osaka, Japan
1996 Kawamura Memorial Museum, Sakura, Japan
Chiba City Museum, Chiba, Japan
1997 Museum fur Konkrete Kunst, Ingolstadt, Germany
Galerie Renate Bender, Munich, Germany
Yamaguchi Gallery, Osaka, Japan
1998 *The Zurich Intervention,* Stiftung fur Konstruktive und Konkrete Kunst, Zurich
1999 Kitakyushu Municipal Museum of Art, Japan
2000 Rupertinum Museum, Salzburg, Austria
Contemporary Art Space Osaka, Japan

Selected Group Exhibitions:

1961 *Carnegie International,* Pittsburgh (and 1967)
1963 *Formalist Show,* Washington Gallery of Modern Art, Washington, D.C.
1964 *Motion and Movement,* Contemporary Art Center, Cincinnati, Ohio
1968 *First Indian Triennale of Contemporary World Art,* New Delhi
1973 *Art of Surface,* Art Gallery of New South Wales, Sydney
1974 *Japan: Tradition and Gegenwart,* Stadtische Kunsthalle, Dusseldorf
1979 *Constructivism and the Geometric Tradition,* Albright-Knox Art Gallery, New York
1982 *Kunst wird Material,* Nationalgalerie, Berlin
1985 *Contemporary Japanese Painting,* National Gallery of Modern Art, New Delhi
1987 *Painting 1977–87,* National Museum of Art, Osaka, Japan
1990 *Gengenwart Ewigkeit,* Martin Gropius Bau, Berlin
1994–95 *Japanese Art After 1945: Scream Against the Sky,* Yokohama Museum of Art, Japan, Solomon R. Guggenheim Museum, New York, and San Francisco Museum of Art
1997 Japanisches Kulturinstitut, Cologne, Germany
1999 *5th Kitakyushu Biennale: The Aesthetics of Repetition and Continuity,* Kitakyushu Municipal Museum of Art, Japan

Collections:

Albright-Knox Art Gallery, Buffalo, New York; Larry Aldrich Museum, Ridgefield, Connecticut; Wadsworth Atheneum, Hartford, Connecticut; Worcester Art Museum, Massachusetts; Akron Art Institute, Ohio; Indianapolis Museum of Art; Texas University Art Museum, Austin; Museum Folkwang, Essen; Museum of Modern Art, New York; Seattle Art Museum, Seattle, Washington;

Tadaaki Kuwayama: *Positionenreihe 17,* at the Rupertinum in Salzburg, 2000. ©Tadaaki Kuwayama.

Nationalgalerie Berlin, Germany; Chiba City Museum, Japan; Hara Museum of Contemporary Art, Tokyo; The Metropolitan Museum of Contemporary Art, Tokyo; The National Museum of Modern Art, Tokyo; The National Museum of Art, Osaka; and many others.

Publications:

By KUWAYAMA: Articles—statement in *Art Now* (New York), September 1970; statement in *Flash Art* (Milan), June 1973; text in *Kunst wird Material,* catalog, Berlin 1982; statement in *Contemporary Painting,* catalog, Tokyo 1987.

On KUWAYAMA: Books—*Japan: Tradition und Gegenwart,* exhibition catalog by Jurgen Harten, Joseph Love and others, Dusseldorf 1974; *Tadaaki Kuwayama,* exhibition catalog with text by Willy Rotzler, Kitakyushu, Japan 1985. **Articles**—''Tadaaki Kuwayama: Green-White Green'' in *Art Now* (New York), no. 2, 1970; ''Washington Letter'' by David Bourdon in *Art International* (Lugano, Switzerland), December 1972; ''Japan pa Louisiana'' by Y. Tono and J. Love in *Louisiana Revy* (Humlebaek, Denmark), September 1974; ''Tadaaki Kuwayama and Rikuro Okamoto'' by Mary Anne Staniszewski in *ARTnews,* January 1981; ''Tadaaki Kuwayama'' by Holland Cotter in *Art in America,* November 1989; ''The Reversal of Form as 'Pure Space''' by Robert C. Morgan in *Sculpture,* July/August 2000.

* * *

Born in Nagoya in 1932, Tadaaki Kuwayama is a 1956 graduate of the Nihon-ga-department of Tokyo University of Fine Art. In 1958 he moved to the United States, and settled in New York. He had his first one-man show at New York's Green Gallery in 1961, and has shown his works elsewhere in the United States, as well as in Europe and Japan. He has participated in group shows including the Guggenheim Museum's *Systematic Painting* (1966), Amersterdam's Stedelijk Museum's *New Forms and Shapes of Color* (1966), and Buffalo's Albright-Knox Gallery exhibition *Plus by Minus: Today's Half-Century* (1968).

Kuwayama's paintings, at the outset, were based on a technique which permitted no variation; but since his monochrome paintings of the latter half of the 1950s, he has divided his paintings into symmetrical parts and made paintings by bringing together panels of the same form. (The absence of the thin, chrome dividers that strictly delineated panels in his earlier works gives his recent paintings a softer symmetry.) It may be said that the paintings appear to be pure abstracts, but they have no relationship to the traditional category of so-called abstract art. The framework of the paintings resists any formative positioning or arrangement and presents a superficiality devoid of intervention by the spirit of the work. Although the paintings are beyond doubt the work of an artist, they have an existence quite remote from the artist. In other words, the works principally exist as objects and are one manifestation of the subjects with which contemporary art is concerned.

Kuwayama has always been associated with the Minimalist painters in the United States, but his recent approach to the subtlety of the surface with exquisitely applied overall brushstrokes, as exemplified in his works of the 1980s and early 1990s, suggests his transcendental contemplation on the spiritual element that makes his paintings something more than deadpan art-objects.

—Essay by Yoshiaki Tono; updated by Beth Duncan